WITHDRAWN

AMERICAN NATIONAL BIOGRAPHY

AMERICAN
NATIONAL BIOGRAPHY

Published under the auspices of the
AMERICAN COUNCIL OF LEARNED SOCIETIES

General Editors

John A. Garraty

Mark C. Carnes

VOLUME 5

OXFORD UNIVERSITY PRESS
New York   1999   Oxford

OXFORD UNIVERSITY PRESS

Oxford New York
Athens Auckland Bangkok Bogotá
Buenos Aires Calcutta Cape Town Chennai
Dar es Salaam Delhi Florence Hong Kong Istanbul
Karachi Kuala Lumpur Madrid Melbourne Mexico City
Mumbai Nairobi Paris São Paulo Singapore
Taipei Tokyo Toronto Warsaw
and associated companies in
Berlin Ibadan

Published by Oxford University Press, Inc.,
198 Madison Avenue, New York, New York 10016
http://www.oup-usa.org

Funding for this publication was provided in part by
the Andrew W. Mellon Foundation, the Rockefeller Foundation,
and the National Endowment for the Humanities,
a federal agency.

Library of Congress Cataloging-in-Publication Data

American national biography / general editors, John A. Garraty, Mark C. Carnes
p.   cm.
"Published under the auspices of the American Council of Learned Societies."
Includes bibliographical references and index.
1. United States—Biography—Dictionaries.   I. Garraty, John Arthur,
1920– .   II. Carnes, Mark C. (Mark Christopher), 1950– .
III. American Council of Learned Societies.
CT213.A68   1998   98-20826   920.073—dc21   CIP
ISBN 0-19-520635-5 (set)
ISBN 0-19-512784-6 (vol. 5)

Printing (last digit): 9 8 7 6 5 4 3 2 1

Printed in the United States of America
on acid-free paper

C

CONTINUED

CLARKE, Mary Bayard Devereux (13 May 1827–30 Mar. 1886), poet and editor, was born in Raleigh, North Carolina, the daughter of Thomas Pollock Devereux—Yale graduate, lawyer, and owner of several large plantations—and Catherine Anne Johnson, great-granddaughter of Samuel Johnson (1696–1772), first president of King's College (now Columbia University) in New York. Among her other ancestors were five colonial governors. Her brother, John, was educated at Yale; and after her mother's death in 1836, Mary and her sisters were taught at home by an English governess who closely followed the Yale course of study.

Having inherited a susceptibility to tuberculosis, Mary spent the year 1847 with her aunt, the wife of Leonidas Polk, in Lafourche, Louisiana, where, it was thought, her condition would be improved by breathing fumes from sugar mills. Here she was married by her Uncle Leonidas, the Episcopal bishop of Louisiana, to Major William J. Clarke of Raleigh, just released from the Mexican War, whom she had known at home. The Clarkes returned to North Carolina, where William resumed the law practice he had left at the beginning of the war.

In 1854, under the pseudonym Tenella, Mary Bayard Clarke compiled and published a two-volume anthology of poems, *Wood-Notes; or, Carolina Carols: A Collection of North Carolina Poetry.* It included poems by a number of men and women of the state, among whom were four former governors, a chief justice and other judges, a congressman, lawyers, teachers, newspaper editors, the author of a novel, and some contributors who left no other evidence of a literary bent. A few of the authors had been published heretofore, but Clarke persuaded others to write specifically for this collection, assuring the men that writing poetry was not an unmanly pursuit. Several of her own poems appeared, as did four by her husband. Her poem "The Triumph of Spring" was cited by an anonymous reviewer as evidence that finally "there is a poet in North Carolina." This seemed to justify the purpose of the anthology—to demonstrate that the state possessed people with literary talent.

Wood-Notes drew attention to the compiler, and soon both poetry and prose by Mary Bayard Clarke began to appear in newspapers and magazines. Some, however, continued to appear over the name Tenella or La Tenella, and she also sometimes used the pseudonyms Stuart Leigh and "A Busy Woman." The pseudonym Tenella derived from her stay in Louisiana when she and several other young women began to write poetry in which they referred to each other by the names of flowers. Mary was called Tenella, the name of a jasmine. During Reconstruction, using the pseudonym Betsey Bittersweet, she wrote for magazines and newspapers satirizing political personalities.

Because of Mary's persistent poor health, she and William spent the winter of 1854–1855 in Cuba, where Mary's "easy and graceful manners" as well as her "delicate and fragile beauty" made her popular. She was the toast of the international community and perfected her knowledge of French, German, Spanish, and Italian. A product of this stay was a series of articles, "Reminiscences of Cuba," which was published in the *Southern Literary Messenger* in 1855. This experience perhaps also contributed to her ability to translate the works of European poets such as Victor Hugo, Dante, Alphonse de Lamartine, Antoine Arnauld, Charles H. Millevoye, Pietro Metastasio, and Pietro Bembo.

Because of Mary's chronic lung condition, after returning from Cuba the Clarkes settled in San Antonio, Texas, where they remained until the beginning of the Civil War. William practiced law and was president of a railroad until he joined the Confederate army. Mary returned to Raleigh with her four children in June 1861 to become involved in volunteer war work and to compose patriotic poems for the Confederacy. For a Confederate publication she translated from the French "Marguerite; or, Two Loves," which had been written by Felicia D. Hemans, a favorite of Mary Clarke. After Colonel Clarke's capture and imprisonment in 1865, Mary supported the family by her writings. For a brief time she was assistant editor of the magazine *Southern Field and Fireside*, published in Augusta, Georgia, which proclaimed itself to be "entirely devoted to Polite Literature, [a] gem for the fireside, an ornament for the parlor, and an indispensable companion to the housewife and agriculturist."

Soon after Colonel Clarke returned to North Carolina, the family went to live at Boon Hill near Smithfield, where he operated a sawmill. After a short time, however, they moved again and settled in New Bern. From there in 1868 Mary wrote that she was "busy editing my paper, the *Literary Pastime*; corresponding with two others; [and] contributing to two magazines."

Continuing her literary career, she wrote prose articles for a variety of magazines, including *The Old Guard* (New York), *Demorest's Monthly* (New York), *Peterson's Magazine* (Philadelphia), *The Land We Love* (Charlotte), and *Literary Magazine* (Richmond). She also reviewed books for the publishing firms of Harper, Appleton, Scribner, Sheldon, and Hale. In 1866 she published a volume of poems, *Mosses from a Rolling Stone: or, Idle Moments of a Busy Woman,* consisting largely of verses that she had recently written for newspapers. Income from the book aided women in

1

Winchester, Virginia, to establish the Stonewall Jackson Cemetery. Clarke was also the author of *Miskodeed*, an operatic libretto, and of another opera intended for publication, and she wrote Sunday school hymns, reputedly for five dollars each. In 1871, after the publication of *Clytie and Zenobia or the Lily and the Palm*, a long narrative poem, a contemporary commended her "on the happy & charming rendering of the classic legend. You have succeeded in making a pretty & graceful Poem of smooth and polished verse."

Her poems focused on a wide variety of subjects, from the seasons to religion to love, as well as on prominent persons of her day and scenes and events from her home state. Both her poetry and her novelettes appeared in national as well as regional journals. She developed a lively following during her lifetime, and her work continued to be reprinted into the next century. She died of a stroke in New Bern one month after the death of her husband.

• Clarke family papers are in the North Carolina State Archives, Raleigh, and in the Southern Historical Collection at the University of North Carolina in Chapel Hill. The manuscript of Mary's unpublished novel, "Chalmette: A Tale of Creole Life in Louisiana," is the Bayard Wootten Collection in the Southern Historical Collection. For a detailed account of the family in the context of the Civil War, see Beth G. Crabtree and James W. Patton, eds., *"Journal of a Secesh Lady": The Diary of Catherine Ann Devereux Edmondston, 1860–1866* (1979). The best account of the life of Mary Bayard Clarke and an appraisal of her work was written by her friend Winchester Hall as an introduction to her edition of *Poems of Mrs. Mary Bayard Clarke* (1905). Another contemporary, Edwin G. Reade, wrote of Clarke in Mary T. Tardy, ed., *Living Female Writers of the South* (1872). Richard Walser, *North Carolina Poetry* (1951), presents a brief appraisal of her work. An obituary is in the Raleigh *News and Observer*, 1 Apr. 1886.

WILLIAM S. POWELL

CLARKE, Mary Frances (2 Mar. 1803?–4 Dec. 1887), founder of the Sisters of Charity of the Blessed Virgin Mary, was born in Dublin, Ireland, the daughter of Cornelius Clarke, a leather merchant, and Catherine Quartermas. Clarke received her education at a "penny school," the local neighborhood school for poor children in Dublin, and from private tutors. She then worked as a bookkeeper in her father's leather and harness shop. Following a disastrous fire in the shop that disabled her father, Clarke, as the eldest child, assumed the management of the business.

After England lifted the penal laws in Ireland in the late eighteenth century, Clarke and four of her friends, Margaret Mann, Eliza Kelly, Rose O'Toole, and Catherine Byrne, were caught up in the movement, sponsored by the Roman Catholic church, to provide education, health care, and social welfare for the country's neglected population. Inspired by the example of St. Francis of Assisi and his concern for the poor, the five young women banded together, making promises as secular Franciscans. They moved into a vacant building on the corner of North Ann Street and Cuckoo Lane, Dublin, that provided space for both living quarters and schoolrooms. There in 1832 they opened Miss Clarke's Seminary, a school for young girls who could not afford the tuition at the convent schools. The school soon became overcrowded, and the young women considered ways of expanding.

A Roman Catholic missionary from Philadelphia visited Miss Clarke's Seminary and described the poverty of the Irish immigrants living in the United States. In 1833 the five young women agreed to move to Philadelphia in order to teach the children of the Irish living there. They sailed from Liverpool aboard the *Cassandra* on 18 July 1833 and arrived in New York harbor on 2 September. While disembarking from the boat, Eliza Kelly dropped the purse containing all the women's money into the ocean. A fellow passenger who witnessed this tragic loss gave them sufficient funds to continue the trip. They journeyed by ferry, stagecoach, and train to Philadelphia, arriving five days later.

The women met the Reverend Terence Donaghoe, a Roman Catholic priest and also a native of Ireland, at St. Joseph Church, Willings Alley, Philadelphia. Through his encouragement and support they organized as a Roman Catholic religious congregation, which became known as the Sisters of Charity of the Blessed Virgin Mary, commonly referred to as BVMs. The small group designated Clarke as the mother superior, and Donaghoe served as the spiritual director. The sisters supported themselves by doing piecework for a dressmaking shop while they established their school for girls, Sacred Heart Academy, in a small building at 520 North Second Street, Philadelphia. After other women joined the first five in the congregation, the sisters also began teaching at St. Michael Parish School.

In 1842 the Reverend Pierre J. DeSmet, a Jesuit missionary to the Native Americans of the Northwest, visited the sisters and described the need for education among the Native Americans. When Mathias Loras, the bishop of the Dubuque diocese, encompassing Iowa, Minnesota, and Wisconsin territories, wrote to Donaghoe seeking a religious congregation of women to assist him in educating Native Americans, Clarke and her companions enthusiastically responded. She sent five sisters to open a school in Dubuque, an early harbor village located on the banks of the Mississippi River in the Iowa Territory.

At the same time, the animosity of the Nativist party of Philadelphia toward Catholics was becoming more threatening. This movement endangered the lives of the teachers and the children in the Catholic schools. To protect the sisters from Nativist threats, the father of one of the sisters accompanied them each day as they walked from the convent to the schools.

The Sisters of Charity, BVM, who now numbered nineteen, and Donaghoe accepted Bishop Loras's invitation to relocate the entire congregation in Dubuque. The BVMs closed their Philadelphia schools and packed all their possessions, including a piano. On 12 September 1843 they began the cross-country trip to Pittsburgh and then traveled by steamboat down the

Ohio River to St. Louis and up the Mississippi, arriving in Dubuque on 8 October 1843.

Clarke and the sisters taught in a log cabin behind the rustic St. Raphael's Church on Bluff Street. However, instead of Native American pupils, the children of Irish and German immigrant lead miners and pioneer farmers filled the school. The educational demands of these inhabitants of the Dubuque area required all the resources of the sisters, preventing them from moving on to the Native Americans.

This small group of women religious led by Clarke attracted other young pioneer women. During her lifetime 440 women joined the congregation. This growth caused her to purchase land from the federal government with funds Donaghoe received from a Philadelphia court settlement against the Nativist party, which had burned St. Michael's Church and convent after the sisters vacated them. On this site, ten miles west of Dubuque, the women built their first motherhouse, St. Joseph's on the Prairie. The building housed those being trained as novices, and it also served as a boarding academy for other young women. The sisters supported themselves by farming and bartering their produce.

Clarke also sent sisters from the motherhouse to teach in schools opened for children of settlers along the Mississippi River and along the westward trails of the American frontier. These schools were small buildings attached to the Catholic churches founded by the settlers as well as boarding academies the congregation built for the daughters of the pioneers. Clarke maintained close contact with her sisters through letter writing. Her letters encouraged and supported the women, who often experienced great hardship and poverty living in primitive conditions along the frontier. The congregation began as a circle of friends, and Clarke's letters nourished that relationship as a friend to all the women who joined her. Her letters also revealed a collaborative and compassionate leadership style.

During Clarke's fifty-four years as mother superior she established forty parochial schools and nine boarding academies. She sent sisters from Dubuque to conduct schools as far east as Chicago and as far west as San Francisco. After Iowa became a state, she incorporated the congregation under its laws in 1869. In 1877 she obtained approbation from the pope in Rome, which enabled the congregation to function globally within the Roman Catholic church structure.

After Clarke's death at St. Joseph's on the Prairie, the congregation moved the motherhouse into the city of Dubuque. Since 1833 over 4,800 women have entered the BVMs, and they continue to serve in educational fields in twenty-six states as well as in Africa and Central and South America. On 27 August 1984 Mary Frances Clarke was inducted into the Iowa Women's Hall of Fame for her role in the education and religious formation of the American frontier.

• The original letters of Mary Frances Clarke are preserved in the Mount Carmel Archives in Dubuque, Iowa. These letters have been published by the Sisters of Charity of the Blessed Virgin Mary as *My Dear Sister*, ed. Laura Smith-Noggle (1987). In the Mount Carmel Archives is the first published copy of the rules of the congregation written by Clarke, *Constitutiones Sororum Charitatis Beatae Marie Virginis* (1877). Clarke's philosophy of education is contained in chap. 9 of *Common Observances* (1882), also in the Mount Carmel Archives. The original articles of incorporation of the Sisters of Charity of the Blessed Virgin Mary of Dubuque County, Iowa, 1869, and the first bylaws, 1869, formulated by Clarke, are also in the Mount Carmel Archives. Other sources of information are Lambertina Doran, *In the Early Days* (1912); Pulcharia McGuire, "Annals" (unpublished manuscript, 1900?); and Jane Coogan, *The Price of Our Heritage*, vol. 1 (1975) and vol. 2 (1978). Obituaries are in the (Dubuque) *Mount Saint Joseph Messenger* 6 (Dec. 1887); the (Dubuque) *Telegraph Herald*, 5 Dec. 1887; and the (Dubuque) *Catholic News*, 8 Dec. 1887. A reprint of the obituary from the *Milwaukee Sentinel* is included in the (Chicago) *Sacred Heart Messenger* 21 (Feb. 1888), and a reprint of the obituary from the *Monitor* (San Francisco, Calif.) is included in the *Mount Saint Joseph Messenger* cited above.

KATHRYN LAWLOR

CLARKE, McDonald (18 June 1798–5 Mar. 1842), poet, was born in Bath, Maine, the son of John Clarke, Jr., a sea captain, and Ann McDonald. Little is known about Clarke's childhood except what is occasionally revealed in his volumes of poetry. Early in his life, Clarke's family moved to New London, Connecticut, where he became a playmate of the poet John Brainard. The family lived in comfortable, yet modest, circumstances, and Clarke expressed an early and abiding interest in religion, especially church music. His mother was very protective of her son, who describes himself in the preface to one of his books as "a sad sickly looking boy" who was mocked and abused by most of his boyhood friends "'cause I try to get their sweethearts from 'em."

Clarke's mother died of consumption while on a sea journey in 1810, and his father was lost when his ship sank in the Atlantic in 1813. Their untimely deaths are mentioned in a number of his unusual, yet moving, early poems and generally contributed to the melancholic tone of his work. No record remains of Clarke's whereabouts after his father's death, but the dates and locations of his first two poems suggest that he most likely lived for a while in Jamaica, where his father had often traded. There is some indication that he may also have spent time in Philadelphia.

On 13 August 1819 Clarke appeared in New York and rapidly became well known as an eccentric public figure. He initially wrote for the newspapers, but in the way that he dressed and behaved during his rambles along Broadway and around the city, he quickly became famous enough to sell his poetry. References to him as the "mad poet of Broadway" began to appear in newspapers and magazines, and visitors to the city were advised to look out for him. Typically appearing in a dark coat with a brightly colored neckerchief that made his thick head of blond hair stand out, he cultivated his public reputation. The initial extent to which

Clarke actually suffered from mental illness, and the ultimate causes of his condition, are unknown.

Clarke's daily routine, which was well noted by contemporaries, began in St. Paul's churchyard in the morning, where he sometimes wept and soliloquized over forgotten and broken graves. By the afternoon, he could be seen walking pensively along Broadway as he composed his verse. His evenings were usually spent at the theater or opera when he could afford it, or in Windust's restaurant and tavern (a central gathering place for actors and writers). He was a familiar figure to most involved in the theatrical and literary world such as the poet Fitz-Greene Halleck, who depicted Clarke in his comic poem, "The Discarded." Clarke was also a regular attender of Grace Church, a fashionable Episcopal parish, where he came into contact with some of the city's most prominent and wealthy families.

Within a year of his arrival in New York, Clarke married a young actress, Mary Brundage, over the strenuous objections of her mother. Buoyed by a small inheritance that he collected in the summer of 1820, the couple eloped. Once their money ran out, Mary returned to her mother and Clarke never saw her again. The dissolution of his marriage haunted Clarke and led to increasingly eccentric behavior. His tendency to become obsessively interested in fashionable young ladies he barely knew (especially those named Mary) made him the butt of jokes among his literary friends. He served as a fool of sorts, bearing their practical jokes and jibes, but he was also known for his quick wit and sharp rejoinders.

Clarke's verse has often been called grotesque or irregular because of his erratic shifts in tone—ranging from uncontained exuberance to profound melancholy. His poetry reflects an intimate (and unfiltered) response to all that he saw and felt, and it anticipates in significant ways the poetic method of Walt Whitman. Although his volumes contain some devotional verse, patriotic poems, and parody, the majority of his work can be classified as social observation and satire. For instance, he often wrote with violent indignation about the aristocratic pretensions and prejudices of the wealthy. Feelings such as these typically appear within the context of his many longing poems written about the women (the "belles of Broadway") that he saw and met every day. In some pieces, he idealizes the beauty and character of his subjects, while in others he becomes bitter about women who are described as, ultimately, shallow and faithless. The scandalous and usually unwanted attention expressed in these poems sometimes got Clarke into trouble and served to confirm his reputation for madness.

Clarke made little money from the sale of his poetry, and he quickly spent or gave away what little he did earn. He relied on the generosity of friends, publishers, and curiosity seekers for his meals and lodgings. However, by the late 1830s, and especially after the depression of 1837, Clarke found it difficult to sell his verse or to get assistance. Moreover, his mental condition worsened, and contemporaries report that he increasingly withdrew from normal associations and into his own delusions. Given working space in the studio of the painter Asher Durand, Clarke appeared to those around him to become more childlike and to lose his ability to engage in conversation. Although generally considered harmless, in March 1842 he was taken by a city watchman to the insane asylum on Blackwells Island (now called Roosevelt Island). Several days later he drowned in his cell beneath an open faucet. It is impossible to determine whether he died accidentally while getting a drink of water or whether it was suicide. He was eulogized several days later in the *Aurora* newspaper by a young Walt Whitman, who praised Clarke as "not polished, perhaps, but yet one in whose faculties that all important vital spirit of poetry burnt with a fierce brightness."

• Clarke's principal volumes of poetry include *A Review of the Eve of Eternity and Other Poems* (1820), *The Elixir of Moonshine* (1822), *The Gossip* (1823), *Poetic Sketches* (1826), *Afara; or, The Belles of Broadway* (1829), *Death in Disguise: A Temperance Poem* (1833), *Poems of McDonald Clarke* (1836), and *A Cross and a Coronet* (1841). A comprehensive source of biographical information on Clarke is C. Carroll Hollis, "The 'Mad Poet' McDonald Clarke," in *Essays and Studies in Language and Literature*, ed. Herbert H. Petit (1964). For additional biographical and genealogical research, see Joseph V. Medeiros, *McDonald Clarke, "The Mad Poet of Broadway": His Life and Works* (master's thesis, Brown Univ., 1944). For earlier material on Clarke, see William Sidney Hillyer, "McDonald Clarke, 'The Mad Poet,'" *Monthly Illustrator* 12 (May 1896): 357–67; Charles Hemstreet, *Literary New York, Its Landmarks and Associations* (1903); Jason Grant Wilson, *Bryant and His Friends* (1886); Clark Jillson, *Sketch of M'Donald Clarke* (1878); and William L. Stone, "Reminiscences of McDonald Clarke, the Mad Poet," Appendix 5, *History of New York City* (1872).

ROBERT D. STURR

CLARKE, Parker (3 Apr. 1748–25 Mar. 1823), surgeon and soldier, was born in Ipswich, Massachusetts, the son of Parker Clarke and Lydia Phillips. In 1769 he married Judith Lunt; they had three sons. After obtaining some medical training in New England, Clarke immigrated to Cumberland Township on the Isthmus of Chignecto in Nova Scotia. By 1770 he was living in Fort Lawrence, where he farmed and practiced medicine as a prominent member of the New England planter community, which by then formed the majority of the population on the isthmus and throughout Nova Scotia.

At the beginning of the American Revolution, Nova Scotia remained loyal, as was demonstrated by its prompt and sustained support of the British garrison besieged in Boston. In late 1775 the royal governor enacted ill-considered militia legislation that provoked widespread political opposition. This legislation gave local revolutionaries the support they hoped for and needed to attempt an indigenous rebellion. In Cumberland, where a spirit of political dissent had long thrived, a patriot party emerged, led by Jonathan Eddy and John Allan. Clarke joined this radical group and took his place on the local committee of safety. After the government abruptly withdrew the militia legislation, the majority of Nova Scotians proved quiescent, and patriots now saw little chance of mounting an indigenous rebellion without the stimulus of an American invasion.

In late October 1776 Eddy who had been sent to seek American help, returned from Massachusetts with a small band of Americans from the Machias region of Maine and Nova Scotians from the St. John River valley and Passamaquoddy district. Clarke and other locals joined him, with the bold intent of capturing Fort Cumberland, which a contingent of provincial troops had recently garrisoned. They planned to ultimately win the entire province for the American cause. Unable to surprise the defenders of the fort, Eddy besieged it for a month, during which Clarke joined in a patriot patrol that plundered loyal residents of the district. The siege was lifted on 29 November 1776 when Eddy was defeated by the reinforced garrison in a skirmish at his headquarters. Many leading patriots, including Eddy, managed to escape and flee to Maine, but others were not as lucky. Clarke was one of the five "principal prisoners" captured on the day the siege was lifted. He was taken to Halifax and indicted on a charge of high treason.

Other patriots were captured or surrendered in the days following the siege, and as many as forty were indicted for high treason, yet only two were ever tried. These were Thomas Faulkner, one of Eddy's officers, and Clarke, whose trial was held in the supreme court at Halifax on 18 April 1777. Clarke had made himself notorious during the siege by using armed patrols to collect old and previously settled accounts for medical expenses. When one of his victims protested that he had already paid his bill, Clarke "demanded in a threatening manner" that if he did not pay immediately he would be taken as a prisoner to Eddy's headquarters. The Crown prosecutors called three witnesses to attest to Clarke's activities, to the fact that he had made derogatory comments about the government, and to the circumstances of his capture. According to the evidence, Clarke "had gun and bayonet fixed at the time the forte was invested" and with others was seen "once before in arms." Leading Halifax criminal lawyer Daniel Wood defended Clarke but appears not to have examined the prosecution witnesses or to have called any witnesses on behalf of the defense. The jury had no trouble finding Clarke guilty of high treason, a verdict presumably based principally on his being in arms against the Crown. The next day Faulkner was tried, and a similar verdict was reached.

Sentencing for both Clarke and Faulkner was postponed until the following term of the court. In the interim, believing himself to be "a fit object of compassion," Clarke petitioned the court for a pardon from the death sentence that would inevitably follow a conviction on a charge of high treason. Halifax authorities could only reprieve; pardons for murder and treason had to be granted in London. A few weeks after conviction, on 11 May 1777, Clarke and Faulkner, with some "regular" criminals, escaped custody in a dramatic mass jail break. Faulkner fled quickly to the United States, but Clarke was sufficiently courageous or foolhardy to linger in Nova Scotia and to assist the patriot leader Allan in the St. John River valley. Allan had appeared there at the vanguard of a second, much larger invasion of Nova Scotia, sponsored by the Continental Congress. This time a reinforcement arrived promptly from Halifax and other provincial centers and defeated the patriots in a skirmish at Manawogonish Cove on 1 July 1777. Allan, Clarke, and other patriots barely escaped by fleeing overland to Maine.

Clarke remained in exile in Machias, Maine, where he served with Allan and other Nova Scotia refugees in the local patriot militia. At the end of the war he and other refugees were rewarded for their revolutionary service. In 1785 Massachusetts granted him 500 acres of land in Eddington, Maine, and in 1801 Congress granted him 1,000 acres in Ohio. He died in Machias.

Clarke and Faulkner were the only patriots convicted of high treason in the British American colonies that remained loyal during the American Revolution. That other patriots indicted on the same charge were not also tried can be explained by the response of the Nova Scotia government to rebellion, which was characterized more by leniency than by vengeance. The trials of Clarke and Faulkner, the most notorious patriots, illustrated the government's strength and were no doubt applauded by the loyalists at Cumberland; yet even in these cases sentencing was postponed. The government, which could afford to respond with leniency because of the improving political situation in the months and years following the siege, was careful not to overreact. The emerging evidence of loyalty in the population ultimately enabled the government to mark the legal process with moderation rather than retribution.

• Sources for Clarke's trial are at the Public Archives of Nova Scotia, RG 39, Supreme Court, ser. J, vol. 1, and the Benchbook of Isaac Deschamps, ser. C, box A, no. 3. Clarke's petition and other documents related to his trial are in J. T. Bulmer, "Trials for Treason in 1776–1777," *Collections of the Nova Scotia Historical Society*, vol. 1 (1876).

The most complete modern critical assessments are Ernest Clarke, *The Siege of Fort Cumberland, 1776: An Episode in the American Revolution* (1995), and E. Clarke and J. Phillips, "Rebellion and Repression in Nova Scotia in the Era of the American Revolution," in *Canadian State Trials*, vol. 1, 1670–1837, ed. Barry Wright and Murray Greenwood (1996); both contain a list of sources. Other critical assessments include G. W. Rawlyk, *Nova Scotia's Massachusetts: A Study of Massachusetts–Nova Scotia Relations, 1630–1784* (1973), and W. B. Kerr, *The Maritime Provinces of British North America and the American Revolution* (1941).

ERNEST A. CLARKE

CLARKE, Rebecca Sophia (22 Feb. 1833–16 Aug. 1906), author, also known by the pseudonym Sophie May, was born in Norridgewock, Maine, the daughter of Asa Clarke and Sophia Bates. Her grandfather John Clark was an early settler of Norridgewock; her father was register of deeds and town clerk and helped organize Norridgewock's first Unitarian church. Moderately wealthy, the family was able to provide Rebecca with a very good education for the time. Her first school was held in the home of Miss O'Dee; next she attended the Female Academy of Norridgewock, a private school; at home she was tutored in Greek and Latin. Already determined to be a teacher at age fifteen, Rebecca, with her older sister Harriet and a friend, began teaching summer sessions, first in a school at Palmyra, Maine, and then at nearby Corinna. At eighteen she took a teaching position in Evansville, Indiana, where she lived with Harriet, now married to a schoolmaster. But after a few years a serious hearing loss caused her to resign and return to her home in Maine.

As a child, she had kept a diary and had written stories that she sewed into paper books. As she grew up, she continued to write stories for her own pleasure. In 1861, at the suggestion of a friend, she wrote a story that he published in his newspaper, the *Memphis (Tenn.) Daily Appeal*. She signed it with her pen name, "Sophie" for her middle name and "May," telling her younger sister, "I may write again and may not." She did write again and became known to a multitude of children and adults as "Sophie May."

During the next years she contributed stories to a children's magazine, *The Little Pilgrim*, edited by "Grace Greenwood" (Sara Jane Lippincott), and to the *Boston Congregationalist*. The stories featuring Prudy Parlin, a mischievous, charming, true-to-life three-year-old girl, were collected into a book, *Little Prudy* (1864), soon followed by five more volumes to become Clarke's first series, the "Little Prudy" series. Next came the "Dotty Dimple" series (1867–1869) about Prudy's little sister. Clarke's stories were eagerly awaited, and Lee and Shepard published three more series of six volumes each: the "Flyaway" series (1870–1873), the "Flaxie Frizzle" series (1876–1884), and the "Little Prudy's Children" series (1894–1901). Clarke also wrote a series for teenage girls, the "Quinbassett" or "Maidenhood" series (1871–1891). However, this series and the novels she wrote for adults, *Drone's Honey* (1878), *The Campion Diamonds* (1887), and *Pauline Wyman* (1898), never reached the popularity of her stories for children.

Drawing her settings and stories from the village life around her, Clarke created her characters from the children she saw, especially her nieces and nephews, who often spent summers in Norridgewock. Miss O'Dee of Clarke's earliest school, a funny Irish woman, was the model for Miss O'Neill, Prudy Parlin's first school teacher. Some names were local names; Frizzle and Parlin can be found in the town records. The stories told of ordinary, everyday happenings, and Clarke put in the mouths of her little characters the speech of children, making her books quite different from the usual children's stories of the time that were written mainly to teach moral lessons. Clarke taught her lessons much more subtly. Of her books, the *Catholic World* (June 1869) said that they "teach important lessons without making the children feel that they are taught them." But some reviewers found fault with the ungrammatical baby-talk: *Atlantic*

Monthly (Jan. 1879) called it "ungrammatical nonsense," and Caroline Hewins in *Library Journal* (Aug. 1901) protested the use of "Dottie Dimple" and "Flaxie Frizzle" books for third graders, saying that it "would demoralize their English."

Clarke was known for her kindliness, unselfishness, and love of children. Her niece, Elizabeth Morse, thought to be the model for Little Prudy, said, "We all adored Aunt Becca, who told us the most delightful stories." For a time she and her sister Sarah, who also wrote children's stories using the name "Penn Shirley," lived in a house along the Kennebec River and were active in the Village Improvement Society; together they gave a handsome brick building to the town to be used as a public library. Maine was always her home, but in later years she traveled abroad and sometimes spent winters in Maryland, Florida, or California. She died in Norridgewock in the same house in which she was born.

Clarke wrote more than forty books for children, which were described by one reviewer as the most popular juvenile books at the time. Contemporary reviewers praised Clarke's books for their realistic portrayal of children. The *North American Review* (Jan. 1866) said that in Little Prudy were embodied "all the quaintness of childhood, its originality, its teasing,—its infinite, unconscious drollery." The *American Literary Gazette and Publishers' Circular* (15 July 1871) called Clarke's stories the "brightest, sprightliest child-literature in print, . . . books that grown people as well as children enjoy." *A Critical History of Children's Literature* (1953) praises Clarke's sense of humor and her portrayal of "children who are natural and engaging."

The stories of Sophie May helped to move children's literature toward a more pleasurable experience for children, as well as a useful tool for teachers. Though her books have long been relegated to rare book shelves, one of the stories from *Little Prudy's Fairy Book*, a story based on the Scottish ballad "Tamlane," was given new life when it was retold and illustrated by Susan Jeffers as *Wild Robin* (1976).

• Information on Rebecca Clarke's life and the importance of her work is to be found in Elizabeth Miller, *Sophie May* (1983), and in Robert Cohen, "Rebecca Sophia Clarke (1833–1906)," in *19th Century Maine Authors* (1981). An earlier source is Florence Waugh Danforth, "Sophie May (Rebecca S. Clarke)," in *Just Maine Folks* (1924), a book written to be used in the schools to acquaint young people with the "distinguished men and women of Maine." Also of interest are the entries in Frances E. Willard and Mary A. Livermore's *A Woman of the Century* (1893).

BLANCHE COX CLEGG

CLARKE, Thomas Benedict (11 Dec. 1848–18 Jan. 1931), art collector, was born in New York City, the son of George Washington Clarke, an educator, and Mary Jane McKie. Clarke attended the Mount Washington Collegiate Institute, in New York City, a school founded and run by his father. In 1871 he married Fannie Eugenia Morris, the daughter of grocer-alderman John J. Morris; the couple had five children, a son and four daughters. By 1872 Clarke was dealing in laces, collars, and linens in partnership in New York City with one John Carmichael. Four years later he was manufacturing linen collars in partnership with Thomas King of Troy, New York. He retired from Clarke & King in 1892 to devote his full attention to collecting and selling art. Clarke held several semi-public positions, including trustee of the Brooklyn Bridge (1880), and became practically a professional clubman, joining, among other clubs, the Brook, Metropolitan, Century, Union League, Manhattan, New York Athletic, and New York Yacht Club.

Clarke began collecting art around 1872. Like most collectors, he first purchased European narrative pictures. By 1879, however, approximately 170 of his 185 pictures were American. Clarke obtained the best new paintings by haunting artists' studios, arriving early at opening receptions for exhibitions, and consulting endlessly with artist friends. He battled collectors' preferences for European art and between 1872 and 1900, acting as an unpaid agent, bought 400 paintings for friends and the Union League Club.

In 1883 Clarke exhibited his collection at the American Art Galleries in New York. The 25 cents admission paid by each visitor—supplemented by public subscription—funded the Clarke Prize at the National Academy of Design. The prize awarded $300 annually thereafter to the best figure painting by a nonacademician exhibited in the academy's spring annual. Between 1879 and 1898 Clarke regularly lent paintings and other works of art to the most important exhibitions held around the country. In so doing he both helped popularize the subjects and styles of Winslow Homer, George Inness, and others and made his paintings the most familiar examples of their work. Clarke actively added to and weeded his collection, and by 1891, when he exhibited it at the Pennsylvania Academy of the Fine Arts in Philadelphia, it contained works by many fewer artists and stressed his favorite painters, most notably Inness and Homer. In 1889 Clarke had become Inness's primary dealer. After retiring from the lace business Clarke opened the Art House at 4 East 34th Street, a gallery selling Greek antiquities, Asian porcelain, and miscellaneous objets d'art. Clarke's gallery did not sell paintings, except those of Inness. He privately represented painters Louis Moeller and Homer D. Martin and sought, unsuccessfully, to become Winslow Homer's exclusive dealer. Clarke helped to launch William Macbeth's gallery, which soon became the preeminent dealer in contemporary American paintings.

Clarke served as treasurer of the National Society of Arts (1885), as an officer of the Barye Monument Association (1889), as president of the New York School of Applied Design for Women (1898), and was elected that same year as the leader, the Shepherd, of the Lambs, America's premier club for actors and theater lovers. He helped to found the National Sculpture Society (1893) and the National Arts Club (1899) and was an honorary life fellow of the National Academy of De-

sign. Clarke strongly influenced tastes among New York's wealthy collectors through his role as chair of the Art Committee of the Union League Club, at which he staged regular exhibitions of American paintings. According to Charles de Kay, art editor of the *New York Times*, "It was Mr. Clarke's initiative that broke down the popular idea of the costliness of paintings, and more especially of the worthlessness of native works as a form of investment" (p. 39).

In 1899 Clarke auctioned off his paintings, thus ending the first half of his career. This auction generated enormous press coverage around the country and grossed $306,930; writers took this as proof that collectors had finally realized the worthiness of American art. Editors lauded Clarke as the greatest champion of American art. Historians disagree. Because his collection fetched approximately 40 percent more than it cost Clarke and he stopped collecting contemporary art, scholars have concluded that Clarke collected mostly for profit. This conclusion is simplistic and probably spurious. His 40 percent return over twenty-five years was no return at all. He would have done better buying most anything but art. Many of Clarke's pictures, including several by Homer, sold for much less than they cost Clarke. Despite the high prices paid for a few of his pictures, such as $10,150 for Inness's *Grey Lowery Day*, collecting American art remained largely unprofitable until the 1960s. Clarke's collecting should be seen as his way of playing a prominent role in New York's cultural scene. Through his efforts Clarke gained the friendship of important artists and writers and won both recognition as a generous and cultivated patron of the arts and membership in prestigious clubs and societies.

After 1900 Clarke turned his attention to historical American portraits. Details about this period in his career are sketchy and somewhat mysterious. In 1919 he sold one collection at auction, and in 1928 he lent a second, larger collection to the Philadelphia Museum of Art, where it hung for more than three years. During the 1920s Clarke was a central figure in the embryonic trade in old American portraits. Apparently, Clarke "manipulated the portrait market and flooded it with overrestored and overattributed pictures, as well as outright frauds" (Saunders, p. 144). Years after Clarke's death in New York City, financier Andrew Mellon bought the collection shown in Philadelphia to obtain several important portraits, including Gilbert Stuart's *Mrs. Richard Yates* and Edward Savage's *Washington Family*, for the National Gallery of Art.

Clarke occupied an influential position in American art for fifty years. Artists as diverse as Inness, Thomas Moran, and Childe Hassam proclaimed him the foremost benefactor of American painters during the late nineteenth century. Clarke was Homer and Inness's most devoted patron, and more than any other individual he encouraged nouveau-riche collectors to patronize native artists and stimulated widespread interest in American historical portraiture.

• The collection memorandum book Clarke used during the 1870s is in the Winterthur Library in Wilmington, Del. Two extensive scrapbooks kept during the 1890s, and a third assembled on Inness (1889–1918), are in the Archives of American Art, Washington, D.C. One of Clarke's few personal statements on art is in the *New York Times*, 25 Feb. 1900. The earliest inventory of Clarke's collection appears in Edward Strahan, *Art Treasures of America*, vol. 3 (c. 1880), p. 126, which names fifty paintings he owned. Three catalogs trace the evolution of his collection: *Private Collection of Paintings by Exclusively American Artists, Owned by Thomas B. Clarke* (1883), *Catalogue of Thomas B. Clarke's Collection of American Pictures* (1891), and American Art Association, *Catalogue of the Private Collection of Thomas B. Clarke* (1899). The most illuminating contemporary discussions of Clarke are Clarence Cook, "Thomas B. Clarke's Pictures," *Art Amateur* 10 (1884): 61–62; Montezuma, "My Notebook," *Art Amateur* 15 (1886): 69; and Charles de Kay, "Movements in American Painting: The Clark Collection in New York," *Magazine of Art* 10 (1887): 37–42. The most useful treatments of Clarke's 1899 auction are "Art World," *Art Collector* 5 (1899): 113, 125, 129–30; "The Prices at the Clarke Sale," *Art Collector* 5 (1899): 139–43; and "Great American Paintings," *New York Times*, 5 Feb. 1899. Between 1902 and 1931, the American Art Association issued nine important auction catalogs of his various collections; those related to his work with American portraits included *Deluxe Illustrated Catalogue of Early American Portraits, etc.* (1919) and *Private Collection of Mr. Thomas B. Clarke* (1925). The main document of his late career remains Philadelphia Museum of Art, *Portraits by Early American Artists* (1928). Clarke's career is also treated in Linda Skalet, "Thomas B. Clarke, American Collector," *Archives of American Art Journal* 15 (1975): 2–7; H. Barbara Weinberg, "Thomas B. Clarke: Foremost Patron of American Art from 1872 to 1899," *American Art Journal* 8 (May 1976): 52–83; and Frederick Baekeland, "Collectors of American Paintings, 1813–1913," *American Art Review* 3 (Nov.-Dec. 1976): 120–66. The one study of the second phase of Clarke's career is Richard Saunders, "The Eighteenth-Century Portrait in American Culture of the Nineteenth and Twentieth Centuries," in *The Portrait in Eighteenth-Century America*, ed. Ellen G. Miles (1993). An obituary is in the *New York Times*, 19 Jan. 1931.

SAUL E. ZALESCH

CLARKE, William Newton (2 Dec. 1841–14 Jan. 1912), Baptist theologian, was born in Cazenovia, New York, the son of William Clarke, a Baptist minister who served many pulpits in northern New York, and Urania Miner. Clarke was educated at Madison College (now Colgate University), where he earned a B.A. in 1861, and at Hamilton Seminary (1861–1863). Following seminary, he served several Baptist congregations: Keene, New Hampshire, 1863–1869; Newton Centre, Massachusetts, 1869–1880; Montreal, Canada, 1880–1883; and Hamilton, New York, 1887–1890. Clarke married Emily A. Smith in 1869. Increasing problems with an injury sustained to his knee and elbow in an 1883 fall on the ice led him to seek more academic employment. He taught the New Testament briefly at Toronto Baptist College from 1883 to 1887, but his major academic post was as professor of theology at Colgate Seminary, where he served from 1890 to 1908. Clarke lectured thereafter in Christian ethics until 1912.

Even as a pastor, Clarke was withdrawn and scholarly. While his sermons were adequate, his deeper vocation was to scholarship. From his first days in the ministry, Clarke avidly followed developments in biblical studies. He was an excellent Greek student who believed that the new directions in textual and higher criticism made the ancient book more understandable. His *Commentary on Mark* (1881) reflected the best contemporary scholarship, and Clarke's biblical studies always informed his theology. Partly because of his study of Scripture, he came to realize that the church and its doctrines evolved in history; each age needed to formulate its own theology. Clarke found the works of the Congregational theologian Horace Bushnell useful. In particular, Bushnell's *The Vicarious Sacrifice* (1866) helped Clarke escape the strict Calvinism of his youth. Yet, Clarke never became a disciple of the Connecticut divine. He also read Adolf von Harnack and other German theologians, who sharpened his awareness of the place of the Kingdom of God in Jesus's teachings.

Clarke's most important work was *An Outline of Christian Theology* (1898), which he wrote after his appointment at Colgate. In preparing for his systematic theology class, he found no theological text that summarized the more modern type of theology. He put together an outline of the conclusions that he and other progressive theologians had reached. The book must have met a common need. Many seminaries in the United States and Asia adopted Clarke's *Outline*, and it was the most influential Protestant theological text at the turn of the century. The book had three noteworthy features. First, Clarke emphasized the presence of God within nature, suggesting that God was creating the world through evolutionary processes and guiding the world's development through natural law. Even the Bible, Clarke insisted, evolved from primitive religious forms. Second, he argued, the character of God is learned through the human Jesus who teaches humans to revere God as our parent and to serve our neighbor sacrificially. Third, according to Clarke, the most human response to God is to live in imitation of Christ. Jesus's life was one of service and sacrifice in which the moral always predominated.

Similar views marked Clarke's other important theological publications: *What Shall We Think of Christianity* (1899) and *The Christian Doctrine of God* (1909). Clarke often approached classical Christian doctrines from a moral perspective. For example, he believed that one reason evil exists in the world is that human beings could not attain true moral excellency without struggle. True faithfulness, he said, is robust. People grow through overcoming the obstacles before them and developing a deeper moral character.

Clarke's evangelical liberalism was an eclectic response to the problems of modern faith rather than an academic approach to the study of religion. In his *Sixty Years with the Bible* (1912), his intellectual biography, Clarke describes the gradual way in which his views changed. As Clarke remembered his pilgrimage, his most seminal thinking occurred while he was preparing to preach. Clarke's habit was to read widely, take notes, think about the material, and then to find ways to make what he had learned clear to his congregation. Harry Emerson Fosdick, Clarke's best-known student, followed a similar method throughout his long career as a preacher and theologian.

Clarke was critical of Protestant missions, which he believed were overly directed toward individual conversion. In the place of such missions, Clarke believed that churches should export the best of western culture, including science and technology. The presence of Christ within western culture would naturally attract the best and the brightest minds. This interpretation of Christian missions met a ready response in China and Japan, where many young intellectuals embraced westernization as a solution to Asia's social problems. These same ideas often made Clarke's works controversial with mission boards at home. Clarke died in Deland, Florida.

Clarke was widely recognized as one of the United States' most important theologians. In many ways, his theology was transitional. When Clarke began his theological reflections, the thought of Horace Bushnell was just beginning to be popular. At the time of his death, many younger and better trained theologians were ready to take up the liberal cause. His emphasis on religious experience was an important inspiration for many people who had lost faith in the old doctrines but who had not formulated newer teachings, more adequate to the present.

• Clarke's *Sixty Years with the Bible* is an excellent source for his life, although the work is somewhat idealized. His wife Emily A. Clarke wrote an account of her husband, *William Newton Clarke: A Biography* (1916), that is often insightful about his thought. Augusta M. Stoehr, "Mission Cooperation in Japan: The Meiji Gakuin Textbook Controversy," *Journal of Presbyterian History* 54 (Fall 1976): 336–54, is particularly useful for the reception of Clarke's works abroad. Robert T. Handy, "The Ecumenical Vision of William Newton Clarke," *Journal of Ecumenical Studies* 17 (Spring 1980): 84–93, provides an excellent summary of Clarke's theology. An obituary is in the *New York Times*, 16 Jan. 1912.

GLENN T. MILLER

CLARKSON, John Gibson (1 July 1861–4 Feb. 1909), major league baseball player, was born in Cambridge, Massachusetts, the son of Thomas G. Clarkson, a Scottish immigrant and well-to-do jewelry manufacturer, and Helen W. Hackett. As a boy, Clarkson attended Webster Grammar School and Comer's Business School in Cambridge. A versatile athlete, he played baseball for his grammar school team and later became a star pitcher for the amateur Beacon club of Boston.

In 1882 the 20-year-old, 5'10", 160-pound right-hander became a major league player when he signed with the Worcester team of the National League. Hampered by a shoulder injury, he was released, having compiled a 1–2 won-lost record. Later that year he was signed by manager Arthur Whitney of the Saginaw, Michigan, team of the Northwestern League. In

1884 his 35–8 record marked him as the league's best pitcher. When the Saginaw team disbanded in August 1884, Clarkson again became a major leaguer when he joined the Chicago White Stockings. Over the last weeks of that season, pitching overhand as permitted by the new rules, he posted a 10–3 record.

During the next three seasons, in the judgment of Chicago manager Adrian "Cap" Anson, Clarkson became the best pitcher in the National League. In 1885, by augmenting his intimidating fastball with curve balls and a change of pace, he won 53 games, second only to Charles "Hoss" Radbourn's 59 victories for a single season in 1884. In leading Chicago to the league championship, Clarkson enjoyed his greatest season; he lost only 16 games while leading National League pitchers in games started (70), games completed (68), innings pitched (623), and strikeouts (308). He also pitched a no-hit game against Providence. The following season, while recording a 36–17 mark, he again pitched a no-hitter, was league runner-up in strikeouts, and helped Chicago win another pennant.

Clarkson married Ella Barr in 1886. They had no children.

In 1887, despite rule changes that effectively increased the pitching distance from 50' to 55½' and that gave batters four strikes, Clarkson's 38 victories led the league. He also led pitchers in games played (60), games started (56), innings pitched (523), and strikeouts (237).

Clarkson's four seasons with Chicago ended after 1887. A sensitive player who thrived on praise, he had clashed with teammates, and early in 1888 he angered fans by publicly announcing that he would not play for Chicago again and that he wanted to pitch for Boston, where he could assist his father in business. His defiant stand ended when his contract was sold to the Boston club for $10,000; it was a record sale price for a pitcher at the time.

By winning 141 games for Boston over the next four years, Clarkson became the idol of local fans. He won 33 games in 1888, and his league-leading 49–19 record almost carried Boston to a pennant in 1889. During that four-year span he led National League pitchers at least one time in earned run average, innings pitched, games, complete games, strikeouts, and shutouts. But his yeoman efforts, which saw him pitching more than half his team's games, took a toll on his arm.

So did the strain of the 1890 Players League War. As a member of the players' brotherhood organization, he was asked to join the rival Boston club of the Players League. When he remained loyal to the National League owners in Boston, he was denounced as a traitor to the players' cause. He turned down an offer of $6,000 per season to pitch in the new league and accepted a three-year contract at a higher seasonal salary to remain with the National League team. During the 1890 season he was hit hard by opposing batters, and he admitted that his arm was weak; that year he fell off to a 26–18 record.

Rebounding somewhat in 1891, Clarkson's 33–19 won-lost record helped Boston win its first pennant since 1883. But recurring arm soreness plagued him the following year, and after posting an 8–6 record early on, he was asked to take a pay cut. When he refused, his contract was sold to Cleveland, where his 17–10 pitching helped the Spiders win the second half of the National League's split-season format. Pitching despite being barely able to lift his right arm above his head after finishing a game, his gritty performance won the admiration of his teammates, including pitcher Cy Young, who credited him for improving his own pitching techniques.

The 1893 rule changes that increased the pitching distance to 60′6″ and replaced the pitcher's box with a narrow slab atop a mound hastened the end of Clarkson's career. After he went 16–17 in 1893, his 8–10 effort in early 1894 prompted Cleveland to trade him to Baltimore. Instead of continuing, he chose to retire, ending his major league career with 328 victories, 178 losses, and a 2.81 ERA.

After retiring in 1894, Clarkson and his wife operated a tobacco store in Bay City, Michigan. In 1895 he organized and managed a local team in the Michigan State League. After suffering a nervous breakdown in 1905 that confined him to a Michigan sanatorium for several months, and now incapacitated, he moved to Winthrop, Massachusetts; he died at McLean Hospital, in nearby Waverly, Massachusetts, of lobar pneumonia. Two of his younger brothers, Walter Clarkson and Arthur "Dad" Clarkson, pitched in the major leagues. In 1963 Clarkson was voted into the National Baseball Hall of Fame.

• The National Baseball Library at Cooperstown, N.Y., has a file of newspaper clippings on Clarkson's career. No biography has been published. Contemporary sources touching on his career include A. G. Spalding, *America's National Game* (1911), and A. C. Anson, *A Ball Player's Career* (1900). Clarkson's years with Boston are covered in Harold Kaese, *The Boston Braves* (1948). His pitching feats are included in John Thorn and John Holway, *The Pitcher* (1988), Kevin Kerrane, *The Hurlers* (1989), and John Thorn and Pete Palmer, eds., *Total Baseball*, 3d ed. (1993). Clarkson's place in nineteenth-century baseball is covered in David Q. Voigt, *American Baseball*, vol. 1 (1983). An obituary is in the *Boston Globe*, 4 Feb. 1909.

DAVID Q. VOIGT

CLARKSON, Matthew (17 Oct. 1758–25 Apr. 1825), revolutionary war soldier and businessman, was born in New York City, the son of David Clarkson and Elizabeth French. After attending boarding school in Kingsbridge, New York, he enlisted at age seventeen in a corps of fusiliers under the command of Richard Ritzema and Henry Livingston. In February 1776 he joined as a volunteer the Tenth Company of Colonel Joseph Smith's regiment, where his older brother David was a captain, and thus became part of one of the first groups to cross the East River during Washington's retreat from Long Island.

Joining his family in New Brunswick, New Jersey, Clarkson used the good offices of General Nathanael Greene to obtain an appointment as aide-de-camp to Benedict Arnold, with whom he remained for nearly two years. Under Arnold, he participated in the successful campaign against the British general John Burgoyne at Saratoga, where he was commended for his heroism, having been severely wounded in the neck while carrying a message from his commanding officer across the lines of battle. He was seconded to Philadelphia with Arnold. In Philadelphia Clarkson's alleged authorship of a newspaper article relating to the Silas Deane affair led to a bitter dispute with Thomas Paine. Clarkson then incurred the enmity of the executive council of the state of Pennsylvania by failing to appear as a witness against Arnold when summoned to testify about an illegal pass Arnold had reportedly issued to a female civilian. Inflexible about what seemed to him a matter of military honor, Clarkson was forbidden by Congress to leave the city.

Over the protest of Joseph Reed, the president of the council of state of Pennsylvania, Clarkson was allowed to join Major General Benjamin Lincoln in South Carolina at his own request after a Congressional reprimand. As aide-de-camp to Lincoln, Clarkson was once again able to participate in major battles of the war, where he performed with great distinction. Following the fall of Charleston in January 1780 he was, with Lincoln, taken prisoner and remained in Philadelphia until, having been exchanged for a British officer, he was able to rejoin his commander in Boston and eventually to fight with him in the successful siege of Yorktown. Commissioned as major and then as lieutenant colonel and formally commended by Washington for his service, Clarkson retired from military duty soon after the conclusion of peace.

Clarkson married Mary Rutherfurd in 1784; she died in childbirth, leaving one child, a daughter. Clarkson and his second wife, Sara Cornell, whom he married in 1792, had seven children before her death in 1803.

During the winter of 1784–1785, Clarkson entered into partnership in New York with John Vanderbilt to carry on trade with Holland. After the dissolution of this arrangement, Clarkson continued independently for a short time, then joined his brother in the mercantile firm S. & L. Clarkson & Company. A member of the Federalist party, Clarkson was elected to the New York state assembly in 1789 and served one term. He was appointed U.S. marshal in 1791 and in 1794 was elected to the state senate, where he served two terms. His last two attempts at elected office, as a candidate for the U.S. Senate in 1802 and for the assembly in 1807, were unsuccessful. From 1804 until shortly before his death in New York City, General Clarkson, as he was always known, was president of the Bank of New York, the city's oldest banking institution.

In addition to his many business and political activities, Clarkson took on numerous military, voluntary, and philanthropic roles. Made brigadier general of the militia of Kings and Queens Counties in 1786, he was appointed major general of the Southern District of New York in 1801, a position he held for three years. From 1784 until 1825 he served as regent of the State

University of New York; he was also a member of the commission to build a new prison in 1796–1797, the president of New York Hospital in 1799, an officer of the American Bible Society, and a trustee of the Free School Society. An active member of the Protestant Episcopal church, he was also a supporter of the Humane Society, the African Free School, and the New York City Dispensary. In later life he became widely known for his strong antislavery sentiments and his public opposition to the Missouri Compromise.

Because of his prominence in charitable circles, Clarkson's death elicited tributes and testimonials from a myriad of men prominent in New York commerce and culture. Typical of these are the words of James Kent, chancellor of the New York Court of Chancery, who said of the general, "It was his business and his delight to afford consolation to the distressed, to relieve the wants of the needy, to instruct the ignorant, to reclaim the vicious, to visit the fatherless and the widow in their affliction and to keep himself unspotted from the world."

• An extensive biography of Clarkson is *The Clarksons of New York: A Sketch*, vol. 2 (1876), a memoir privately printed for the Clarkson family, which contains a contemporary portrait of the subject and genealogical material in addition to a lengthy sketch of Clarkson's life. Further information may be found in Henry W. Domett, *A History of the Bank of New York, 1784–1884* (1884), and Allan Nevins, *History of the Bank of New York and Trust Company, 1784–1934* (1934). Other brief descriptions of Clarkson may be found in W. W. Spooner, ed., *Historic Families of America* (1907), and Martha J. Lamb, *History of the City of New York* (1877). *Journals of the Continental Congress* 13 (Feb. 1779), reports the congressional censure.

JEAN W. ASHTON

CLAUDE, Albert (24 Aug. 1899–22 May 1983), cell biologist, was born in Longlier, Belgium, the son of Florentin Joseph Claude, a baker, and Marie-Glaudicine Watriquant. Claude's mother died after a long battle with cancer when he was seven. He attended the village school for a few years, but before World War I his family moved to the German-speaking village of Athus. At age twelve Claude went to work in a steel mill, first as an apprentice and then as a draftsman. When World War I broke out, he volunteered for the British Intelligence Service; he was cited for bravery in 1918, receiving the British War Medal, the Interallied Medal, and a personal citation from Winston Churchill. These activities, however, did not prevent him from pursuing a course of self-education. All his life he had desired to study medicine, but his lack of a high school degree prevented him from entering medical school. In 1921 Claude reluctantly took and passed the entrance examination to the School of Mining Engineering in Liège. He was accepted but never attended, because in 1922 the government removed the high school diploma requirement, and he was allowed to enter the medical school at the University of Liège. He received his M.D. in 1928, writing a thesis on sarcoma in mice.

Claude's thesis won him a government scholarship, which he used for postdoctoral study in Berlin at the Institut für Krebsforschung. Soon after he began working at the institute, however, his ideas conflicted with those of the director, Ferdinand Blumenthal. Claude demonstrated that rats injected with the blood of other rats with mammary tumors themselves developed cancer. This refutation of Blumenthal's hypothesis that cancer was caused by bacteria resulted in Claude's transfer to the Kaiser Wilhelm Institute in Dahlem-Berlin, where he completed his fellowship working with the tissue-culture pioneer Albert Fischer. Claude decided to concentrate on isolating and characterizing the agent for Rous sarcoma. He knew that he could pursue this work effectively at the Rockefeller Institute in New York. Without an invitation, he submitted a research proposal to Simon Flexner, outlining his studies on Rous sarcoma cells. Flexner accepted the unsolicited proposal, but he disappointed Claude by informing him that Peyton Rous and Alexis Carrel, established Rockefeller scientists, had no position for him in their laboratories. However, Claude was invited to work in the laboratory of James B. Murphy, who was interested in viruses and cancer. Claude sailed from Antwerp on 13 September 1929 and spent the next twenty years at the Rockefeller Institute. He married Joy Gilder in 1938. They had one daughter, Phillipa Claude, who became a neurobiologist. The marriage ended in divorce. He became a U.S. citizen in 1941.

When Claude began working in Murphy's laboratory, he set out to isolate the tumor agent through cell fractionation, first disintegrating the cell and then separating the suspended fragments by centrifugation at increasing speeds. This separated the cell particles of different density into distinct layers containing sufficient material for characterization. In this way Claude was able to isolate a fraction that had a high capacity for producing tumors in chickens. Further work on this tumor-producing fraction revealed that it was rich in ribonucleic acid (RNA). Later, after Claude had worked out procedures for obtaining electron micrographs, he demonstrated the presence of chicken sarcoma 1 virus (Rous sarcoma) in these particles. Claude's demonstration of the Rous sarcoma virus did a great deal to dispel doubts that a virus could cause a sarcoma.

From these early studies, Claude realized that his cell fractionation method yielded rich material for biochemical studies, and he shifted his interest to work on liver cells, which are easier to fractionate. Through continually improving the cell fractionation techniques, he began to identify different particles in the cytoplasm. Two biochemists, George Hogeboom and Rollin Hotchkiss, joined Claude in the 1940s; using the techniques previously worked out, they went on to identify some of the basic constituents of the cell and to demonstrate their functions. They determined that certain large granules were mitochondria, and by 1945 they had reported that these were the respiratory sites in which oxygen was consumed in the production of energy. In 1943 Claude also separated out a fraction rich in RNA that was shown to consist of the smallest particles; he named this fraction "microsomes." George Palade later demonstrated that these particles, now called ribosomes, are the site of protein synthesis in the cell.

To understand better the relationship between the functions of the various granules of the cell and their anatomy, Claude sought help from the Interchemical Corporation, which then had the only electron microscope in New York City. With Ernest Fullham and Keith R. Porter, Claude developed methods that allowed study of the various fractions obtained from cell fractionation; in time they also developed methods to obtain electron micrographs of the whole cell. The first successful micrographs of the whole cell, of cultured fibroblasts, revealed a lacework pattern in the cell, now called the endoplasmic reticulum. Claude's pioneering work on developing cell fractionation techniques and electron microscopy, combined with that of his collaborators Palade and Christian deDuve on the function of cellular components, allowed scientists to examine for the first time the inside of the cell and launched the modern era of cell biology.

At the end of World War II Claude accepted an urgent call from the Free University of Belgium to become the director of the Institute Jules Bordet in Brussels, where administrative duties diverted him from research. He did not return to laboratory work until he resigned in 1971 and joined the faculty of the Catholic University of Louvain. In 1972 he was named director of the university's Laboratory of Cellular Biology and Oncology. Claude was awarded the Nobel Prize in 1974 for his work in cell physiology, sharing it with Palade and deDuve. He died in Belgium.

Claude approached science, the arts, and other facets of life unprejudiced and eager to analyze them. He had the stubborn independence of the Ardennes peasant, derived from his love of life and the rugged beauty of the countryside where he was raised.

• Short biographies of Claude are in Frank N. Magil, ed., *The Nobel Prize Winners: Physiology and Medicine* (1991), pp. 1168–76; and Christian R. deDuve and George E. Palade, "Albert Claude, 1899–1983," *Nature* 304 (1983): 588. Descriptions of Claude's work include Keith R. Porter, "The 1974 Nobel Prize for Physiology or Medicine," *Science* 186 (1974): 516–17; "Three Cell Biologists Get Nobel Prize," *New York Times*, 11 Oct. 1974, p. 22; Albert Claude, "The Coming of Age of the Cell," in *Nobel Lectures: Physiology of Medicine*, ed. Jan Lindsten (1970–1980); Palade, "Albert Claude and the Beginnings of Biological Electron Microscopy," *Journal of Cell Biology* 50 (1971): 5–19; deDuve, "Tissue Fractionation, Past and Present," *Journal of Cell Biology* 50 (1971): 20–55; and Marcel Florkin, "Pour saluer Albert Claude," *Archives Internationales de Physiologie et de Biochimie* 80 (1972): 633–47. An obituary is in the *New York Times*, 24 May 1983.

DAVID Y. COOPER

CLAUSEN, Jens Christen (11 Mar. 1891–22 Nov. 1969), botanist, geneticist, and ecologist, was born in Eskilstrup, Denmark, the son of Christen Augustinus

Clausen and Christine Christensen, farmers and house builders. Clausen was educated at home until he was eight years old, when he enrolled in a country school and then a private secondary school. When he was ten, his younger brother died, leaving Clausen an only child. At the age of fourteen he took on the responsibility of managing the family farm and also began to read widely in the sciences, showing a special interest in the new field of genetics. Over the next eight years he continued to educate himself in the basic sciences, and with the aid of a supportive schoolteacher, he studied Mendelian genetics and Darwinian evolutionary theory. He also gained linguistic proficiency in German and English.

Although he had intended to enroll at the Royal Agricultural College in Copenhagen to improve his knowledge of farming, he changed his mind and in 1913 entered the University of Copenhagen, where he studied botany, genetics, and ecology. While there he worked with noted scientists Chresten Raunkier (his major professor) in botany, P. Boysen Jensen in plant physiology, Wilhelm Johannsen in plant genetics, and August Krogh in animal physiology. Clausen studied physics with Niels Bohr and H. M. Hansen, chemistry with Einar Biilmann and Christian Winther, and he met retired ecologist Eugenius Warming, one of his boyhood heroes. Largely at the suggestion of Raunkier, Clausen chose to study the genetics and ecology of the Violaceae (the pansy family) because they were known to contain hybrid forms. Performing a detailed study of hybridization patterns in wild forms of *Viola arvensis* and *Viola tricolor* over a range of ecological environments, Clausen noted that hybrids between the species formed at certain zones of contact and that genes in these forms could travel between the initial point of contact back to the original species, a phenomenon described as introgression. Shortly after publishing his results in 1921 and 1922, he became aware of similar research done by pioneer Swedish genecologist Göte Turesson, with whom he had numerous subsequent exchanges. Having completed his master of science degree in genetics in 1920, Clausen was appointed assistant professor to the noted geneticist Øvjvind Winge at the Royal Agricultural College in Copenhagen. The 1926 publication of Clausen's research on the Violaceae, which earned him a Ph.D. in genetics, was one of the first monographs to combine knowledge of systematics, ecology, and genetics for any plant group.

In 1927–1928 Clausen was granted a Rockefeller fellowship to study at the University of California, Berkeley, where he collaborated with E. B. Babcock on the genetics of the genus *Crepis* and met noted California botanist Harvey Monroe Hall. Shortly after returning to Denmark Clausen was visited by Hall, who invited him to join the new interdisciplinary team that Hall was organizing at Stanford University for the Carnegie Institution of Washington to study the ecological genetics of plants native to California. Clausen arrived in California in the autumn of 1931 to join Hall, taxonomist David Keck, and physiologist William Hiesey but suddenly found himself the leader of the team when Hall died in March 1932. The group of Clausen, Keck, and Hiesey led the first interdisciplinary effort to combine the recent advances of genetics, ecology, and systematics in order to understand the ecological genetics of the evolutionary process in California plants. Over the next twenty years, the team performed what are now regarded as classic experiments involving transplants of plants grown at three different locations across altitudinal gradients of the California terrain. Their experiments were performed at Stanford (near sea level), at Mather (at about 4,600 feet), and at Timberline in the Sierra Nevada (at about 10,000 feet).

In a first set of experimental studies, the team demonstrated that adaptation to different environments was accompanied by the formation of well-defined, genetically different races, or ecotypes. In some of the families they studied, eight to eleven different ecologic races were observed. In a second set of experiments on *Potentilla glandulosa*, the team hybridized lowland and timberline races and analyzed progeny to observe the relationship between genetic and ecological differentiation. They found that character differences between these ecological races were in fact determined by several gene pairs and that genetic recombination as a result of such crosses conferred on the progeny new adaptive properties not seen in either parent. In yet another set of experiments using members of the Madiinae (the hayfield tarweeds) in hybridization crosses, the team investigated the genetic basis of the stages of evolution involving adaptive differences between races, species, and genera. Although their experiments were extensive and elaborate, much of the rich and interesting data they generated were never published, in part because Clausen's sense of thoroughness called for an exactness and perfection that was difficult to reach. What did appear was published largely as monograph-length studies in the Carnegie Institution publications. Although Clausen could have reworked the results of these experiments into a synthetic project on genetic mechanisms involving the origin of plant species that took ecological parameters into account, he chose not to do so. Instead, he produced only an introductory summary of his work, derived from the Messenger Lectures he gave at Cornell and published in 1951 as *Stages in the Evolution of Plant Species*. Clausen's synthetic and interdisciplinary attempts to understand the totality of processes involved in the origin of new plant species were themselves so significant that they alone guaranteed him recognition as a pioneer in the history of plant evolution.

Clausen's honors included election to the National Academy of Sciences in 1959 and a certificate of merit from the Botanical Society of America in 1956; also in 1956 he served as president of the Society for the Study of Evolution. He was a fellow of the California Academy of Sciences and of the American Association for the Advancement of Science and was an honorary fellow of the Botanical Society of Edinburgh. In 1961 he became a member of the American Academy of Arts and Sciences and of the Royal Swedish Academy of Science and was knighted as knight of Danneborg by King Frederick IX of Denmark.

A somewhat quiet person, Clausen was a devoted researcher and demonstrated both innovation and great meticulousness in experimental design. He generally was well regarded by his colleagues, though there appears to have been some friction between the team members. In later years the team expanded to include Malcolm Nobs. Because Clausen held a research appointment at the Carnegie Institution, he did not teach extensively but did supervise some graduate research. In 1951 Stanford University appointed him professor of biology, and he retired formally in 1956. Though strongly committed to the scientific method, he also held strong religious beliefs, as was demonstrated by his extensive involvement in the First Baptist Church of Palo Alto and in the Berkeley Baptist Divinity School, where he served as trustee. He and his wife, the former Anna Hansen, whom he married in 1921, did not have any children. Citizens of Denmark, the couple became naturalized U.S. citizens in 1943. He died in Palo Alto, California. Clausen is still regarded as one of the pioneers in ecological and evolutionary genetics of plants and one of the foremost California botanists of the twentieth century. The experiments of Clausen, Keck, and Hiesey continue to be included in textbooks of evolution, ecology, and genetics.

• A biographical file on Clausen is located at the Stanford University Archives. Some of Clausen's papers are still with the Carnegie Institution of Washington at Stanford University. Among the Carnegie Institution publications generated as a result of experiments conducted by Clausen, Keck, and Hiesey are *Experimental Studies on the Nature of Species. I. Effect of Varied Environment on Western North American Plants* (1940) and *Experimental Studies on the Nature of Species. II. Plant Evolution through Amphiploidy and Autoploidy, with Examples from the Madiinae* (1945). The most complete biographical essay is C. Stacy French, "Jens Christian Clausen," National Academy of Sciences, *Biographical Memoirs* 58 (1989): 75–107. For a historical assessment of the work of Clausen, Keck, and Hiesey see Joel Hagen, "Experimentalists and Naturalists in Twentieth-century Botany, 1920–1950," *Journal of the History of Biology* 17 (1984): 249–70. Obituaries are in the *Carnegie Institution of Washington Year Book*, vol. 69 (1969–1970); in *Genetics* 68 supp., no. 1, pt. 2 (1971): 97, written by his student Robert K. Vickery, Jr.; and in the *Palo Alto Times*, 24 Nov. 1969.

VASSILIKI BETTY SMOCOVITIS

CLAUSEN, Roy Elwood (21 Aug. 1891–21 Aug. 1956), geneticist, was born in Randall, Iowa, the son of Jens Clausen and Mathilda Christianson, farmers. In 1900 his family moved to Newkirk, Oklahoma, where he completed his secondary education. He studied animal husbandry at the Oklahoma Agricultural and Mechanical College and received a B.S. in agriculture in 1910. After graduation, he turned down the opportunity to run the family farm and instead entered the

University of California at Berkeley, where he studied plant pathology. He received a second B.S. in agriculture in 1912 and a Ph.D. in biochemistry in 1914.

As both an undergraduate and graduate student at Berkeley, Clausen was profoundly influenced by William A. Setchell, the chairman of the botany department. Setchell was involved in a project that had begun as an effort to reclassify the hundreds of cultivated varieties of *Nicotiana tabacum*, or common tobacco, and then evolved into an ambitious study of the ancestry of its many varieties in an effort to identify one parent species. He was motivated to expand the scope of the project by the ongoing debate over evolution; specifically, he wanted to test the saltation theory of William Bateson and Hugo de Vries, who declared that mutations appear suddenly rather than slowly as Charles Darwin's theory of evolution claimed. In 1912 Clausen joined Setchell and Thomas Harper Goodspeed, who had earned his Ph.D. under Setchell, as an assistant, and the hunt for *tabacum*'s ancestors became the research interest of his career.

Although Clausen had received no formal training in genetics, his involvement in Setchell's tobacco project attracted the attention of Ernest Brown Babcock, head of the Department of Agriculture's Division of Genetics at Berkeley, who hired Clausen as an instructor of genetics in 1914. In 1916 Clausen was promoted to assistant professor and married Mae Winifred Falls, with whom he had one child. He continued his involvement in the tobacco project by collaborating more closely with Goodspeed after Setchell began to rely increasingly on his assistants. At the same time, he and Babcock began writing a textbook on genetics. Thomas Hunt Morgan, winner of the 1933 Nobel Prize for medicine or physiology, had recently developed strong evidence linking the factors controlling Mendelian characteristics to chromosomes in fruit flies, and Clausen and Babcock realized that his work had important implications for animal and plant breeders. In *Genetics in Relation to Agriculture* (1918) Clausen and Babcock commit unequivocally to the chromosome theory of heredity and offer "an adequate presentation in a single text of the facts and principles of genetics and their practical applications" (foreword) in plant and animal husbandry. The book was so widely adopted as a textbook for teaching genetics that Clausen and Babcock put out a second, greatly expanded edition in 1927.

From 1917 to 1919 Clausen served in the U.S. Army as a supply officer at Camp Lewis, Washington. After being discharged he returned to Berkeley, where he continued to investigate the origins of *tabacum*. By 1923 he had concluded that *tabacum*'s numerous varieties had not originated in the wild via interbreeding between different strains of *tabacum* and other species of *Nicotiana* because the hybrids that resulted from such interbreeding were sterile and that, therefore, the *tabacum* varieties must have resulted from intrabreeding after its domestication a few thousand years ago. In addition to suggesting the correctness of Darwin's views regarding the nature of evolutionary change, this conclusion led Clausen to concentrate on those hybrid varieties of *Nicotiana* with either haploidy (twelve chromosomes), monosomy (lacking a chromosome), or trisomy (having an extra chromosome) in his search for the ancestor of *tabacum*. By this time his international reputation as a geneticist had grown to the point that in 1926 he was invited to conduct cytogenetic research under the auspices of the International Education Board in Stockholm, Sweden, and to inspect genetics institutions throughout Europe.

In 1928, the same year he was promoted to full professor, Clausen began to suspect that *tabacum*, an amphidiploid (forty-eight chromosomes) species, might have originated from a cross between two diploid (twenty-four chromosomes) species of *Nicotiana*. By looking at *tabacum*'s forty-eight chromosomes as two sets of twenty-four, he realized that one set was an exact duplication of *N. sylvestris*'s twenty-four chromosomes while the other set was an exact duplication of *N. tomentosa*'s twenty-four chromosomes. Reasoning that *tabacum* must therefore contain twenty-four duplicate genes, he set out to produce twenty-four monosomic *tabacum* specimens, each missing a different one of the twenty-four "duplicate" chromosomes, by transferring individual chromosomes from *sylvestris* and *tomentosa* to *tabacum*. His theory regarding *tabacum*'s evolution from two diploid parents received a great deal of credibility in 1938 when Walter H. Greenleaf, one of his students, succeeded in producing a *sylvestris* X *tomentosa* hybrid that closely resembled *tabacum*; moreover, because it had forty-eight chromosomes instead of twenty-four, it appeared to be fully fertile. Clausen continued his work with monosomic *tabacum* specimens, working closely with Donald R. Cameron after 1934, and by 1944 he had successfully isolated all twenty-four of the possible monosomic varieties.

Although *Nicotiana* was the primary research interest in Clausen's 42-year career, he occasionally experimented with other plants. He spent part of 1941 in Hawaii as a special consultant in genetics for the Hawaiian Agricultural Experiment Station as well as the experiment stations of the Hawaiian Sugar Planters Association and the Pineapple Producers Cooperative Association. From 1944 to 1945 he performed "special duties" for the Los Alamos Scientific Laboratory. In 1947 he succeeded Babcock as chairman of the Department of Genetics, a position he held until his death in Berkeley, California. He also played an active role in professional societies and served as secretary general of the Sixth Pacific Science Congress in 1939, president of the Pacific Division of the American Association for the Advancement of Science from 1947 to 1948, vice president of the genetics section at the Seventh International Botanical Congress in Stockholm, Sweden, in 1950, and president of the Genetics Society of America in 1953. He was elected to the National Academy of Sciences in 1951.

Clausen contributed to the advance of genetics in two ways. His textbooks served as an introduction to the field for many future geneticists, and, as a result of his work with *Nicotiana*, he helped to perfect the techniques of monosomic analysis, thereby making it possible to study the genetic differences between species at the level of individual chromosomes.

• Clausen's papers are located in the Thomas Harper Goodspeed Collection in the Bancroft Library of the University of California at Berkeley. A biography of Clausen and a complete bibliography of his scholarly work appear in James A. Jenkins, "Roy Elwood Clausen," National Academy of Sciences, *Biographical Memoirs* 39 (1967): 37–54. Obituaries are in the *New York Times*, 23 Aug. 1956, and in *Science*, 28 Dec. 1956.

CHARLES W. CAREY, JR.

CLAVELL, James (10 Oct. 1925–6 Sept. 1994), screenwriter and novelist, was born James du Maresq Clavell in Sydney, Australia, the son of Sir Richard Charles Clavell, a captain in the British Royal Navy, and Lady Eileen Ross. As a child, Clavell listened to the "swashbuckling" stories told by his father and grandfather, also a career military man; these tall tales of the sea and far-flung ports prepared Clavell for his career. Clavell proudly described himself as an "old-fashioned storyteller," not a novelist; yet it is for his novels, which typically focus on the clash between the West and the Far East, that he is best known.

Like his fiction, Clavell's life spanned several continents. He was taken to England while still an infant; after public schooling, he followed in his father's military footsteps and joined the Royal Artillery in 1940. He was trained for desert warfare, but when Japan began to wage war on British colonies, he was sent to Singapore in 1941. Wounded by machine gun fire in Malaysia, he hid for several months in Malay villages until he was captured by the Japanese in 1942. He spent the next three and a half years in the notorious Changi prison near Singapore, where only 10,000 of the 150,000 prisoners of war incarcerated there survived. In a 4 October 1975 interview for the *Guardian*, Clavell considered prison life to be his real education:

Changi was a school for survivors. It gave me a strength most people don't have. I have an awareness of life others lack. Changi became my university instead of my prison. Among the inmates there were experts in all walks of life—the high and the low roads. I studied and absorbed everything I could from physics to counterfeiting, but most of all I learned the art of surviving.

With his release at the end of the war and his promotion to the rank of captain, Clavell returned to England planning to continue his military career, but he was discharged in 1946 because of injuries suffered in a motorcycle accident. From 1946 to 1947 he attended Birmingham University, where he considered careers in law or engineering, and held a series of odd jobs, including carpentry. During this time he met April Stride, an aspiring actress and dancer, whom he married in 1951; the couple had two daughters. When visiting movie sets with her, he was drawn to writing and directing films. He started as a film distributor, then moved into production, and by 1953 he and his wife

had immigrated to the United States, where he saw more opportunities for work in the movie industry.

In New York Clavell worked briefly in television production. He moved to Los Angeles in 1954 and then bluffed his way into screenwriting for Hollywood. His first success was a 1958 screenplay for *The Fly*, a science fiction thriller about a crazed "atomic" scientist. Other successful screenplays followed, including *Watusi* (1959); *Five Gates to Hell* (1959); *Walk Like a Dragon* (1960); *The Great Escape* (1963), for which he won a Writers Guild Best Screenplay Award; *633 Squadron* (1964); *The Satan Bug* (1965); and *Where's Jack?* (1968). In 1969 he wrote, produced, and directed *To Sir with Love*, the acclaimed film, starring Sidney Poitier, about a black teacher and his class of juvenile delinquents, and *The Last Valley*.

In 1960 a screenwriters' strike in Hollywood prompted Clavell to begin a novel based on the memories of Changi prison that continued to haunt him. He completed the draft of *King Rat* (1962) in twelve weeks. The novel established the pattern of Clavell's fiction: larger-than-life heroes, gripping narrative, and a setting so vivid and powerful that it became a character in its own right. *King Rat*, a bestseller adapted for film in 1965, describes the friendship between two prisoners of war, an Englishman and an American, as they struggle to survive the cruelties of Changi. But it is the prison—"the impersonal, soul-disintegrating evil of Changi itself," as Martin Levin noted in a *New York Times Book Review* essay—that is the novel's true subject.

In 1963 Clavell and his wife became naturalized citizens of the United States, and in that same year they moved to Hong Kong, where Clavell did the research for his next novel, *Tai-Pan: A Novel of Hong Kong* (1966). Set in 1841, the novel traces the empire-building of Dirk Struan, founder of the Noble House trading company. Although critics deplored its inaccuracies and its style, they grudgingly acknowledged its mesmerizing power. Orville Prescott noted in the *New York Times* that although *Tai-Pan* is "crude" and "grossly exaggerated," "seldom does a novel appear so stuffed with imaginative invention, so packed with melodramatic action, so gaudy and flamboyant with blood and sin, treachery and conspiracy, sex and murder."

Clavell's most successful novel was *Shogun: A Novel of Japan* (1975), inspired by a brief note in his daughter's history textbook about an Englishman who traveled to Japan and became a samurai. Clavell's research resulted in the story of John Blackthorne and ultimately enabled him to understand the treatment he had received in the Changi prison. Critics disparaged the novel's historical inaccuracies but praised Clavell's depiction of feudal Japan as "riveting" by virtue of its nonstop plot and its ability to capture the "peculiar flavor of life" in medieval Japan. In 1980 the novel was made into an immensely successful television miniseries, drawing more than 120 million viewers, the largest audience for a miniseries since Alex Haley's *Roots* (1977).

Clavell's next novel, *Noble House: A Novel of Contemporary Hong Kong* (1981), was a sequel of sorts to *Tai-Pan* as it traced the fortunes of the trading company in the twentieth century. Christopher Lehmann-Haupt, writing in the *New York Times*, described the 1,200-page novel as "long as life" and "rich with possibilities," despite its "comic-book" dialogue. It, too, was developed into a television miniseries, in 1988.

Clavell's ability to draw millions of readers and viewers made him a highly sought-after commodity for publishers; his next novel, *Whirlwind* (1986), netted him a record-breaking $5 million advance. Even though this novel about the 1979 overthrow of Mohammad Reza Pahlavi, the shah of Iran, got mixed reviews, it was an immediate bestseller, remaining on the bestseller list for twenty weeks and reinforcing the publisher's faith that any book with Clavell's name on it would be successful. In what would be his final novel, *Gai-Jin: A Novel of Japan* (1993), Clavell returned to the Far East in this tale of 1860s Japan and the conflict of cultures between the East and the West.

Although he wrote two other books, *The Children's Story* (1981), described as a political fable, and *Thrump-O-Moto* (1896), a children's book, in addition to his numerous screenplays, Clavell's fame rests on his novels about Japan and Hong Kong. Clavell always denied any literary artistry, claiming to the *Los Angeles Times* that "I watch a story happen, and I describe what I see." He had a unique ability to give readers what they wanted: adventure, violence, sex, obsession—all graphically situated in exotic settings. Clavell died in his Vevey, Switzerland, home.

• In addition to the screenplays and novels noted above, Clavell wrote and published poetry as well as a play, *Countdown to Armageddon: E=mc²*, which was first produced in Vancouver, British Columbia (1966). He also wrote the introduction to *The Making of James Clavell's "Shogun"* (1980) and in 1983 edited *The Art of War* by Sun Tzu. The best biographical information can be found in the *Los Angeles Times* interviews, 7 Nov. and 11 Dec. 1986; Paul Berstein, "The Making of a Literary Shogun," *New York Times Magazine*, 13 Sept. 1981; and the obituary by William Grimes in the *New York Times*, 8 Sept. 1994.

JUDITH E. FUNSTON

CLAXTON, Kate (24 Aug. 1848–5 May 1924), actress and manager, was born Catherine Elizabeth Cone in Somerville, New Jersey, the daughter of Spencer Wallace Cone, a lawyer and writer, and Josephine Martinez. Educated in private schools in New York, including Miss Rostand's Institute, and married "ill-advisedly" at seventeen to Isadore Lyon, whom she later divorced (they had no children), Claxton claimed she went on the stage seeking "the independence of self-support." Although in his literary pursuits her father had written several produced plays and her grandfather acted before he joined the clergy, Claxton's family was not supportive of her chosen profession. But Claxton saw acting as one of the few professions that enabled women to match the earning power of men. Aware of the familial opposition she would face in New York, she opted to begin her theatrical career in Chicago.

She debuted as Mary Blake in *Andy Blake* at the Dearborn Street Theatre on 21 December 1869. The next week she performed with Lotta Crabtree's company at McVicker's, and she played three weeks at the National Theatre in Washington, D.C. Within three months of leaving New York to begin her career, Claxton returned with an engagement at Augustin Daly's Fifth Avenue Theatre. She made her first appearance with the company in Wilkie Collins's *Man and Wife* on 13 September 1870. Claxton played small roles in Daly's company for two and a half years under the tutelage of leading actresses such as Clara Morris, Agnes Ethel, and Fanny Davenport.

In 1873, after asking A. M. Palmer to give her an audition, Claxton left Daly's company to join Palmer's company at the Union Square Theatre. In her first role with the company Claxton played Georgette in *Fernande*. Her success led Palmer to engage her for the next three seasons. After her accomplishment as Mathilde in *Led Astray* in 1873 she played a series of leading roles. The most important of her new roles became the blind girl Louise in *The Two Orphans*, a melodrama that opened on 26 December 1874. For the part she bought the ragged clothing of an applewoman on the street. She played the role her entire career, her name becoming synonymous with Louise. *The Two Orphans* became the greatest financial success ever at the Union Square Theatre to that time and was also a hit on subsequent tours.

In her move from minor roles to leading lady, Claxton next played in *Ferréol* and *Conscience*. In 1876 she formed her own company and produced a tour of *Conscience*. The public, however, clamored for Louise, so Claxton wisely bought the rights to the play from Palmer and made a fortune playing the role all over the country. The play retained its popularity, and even after Claxton retired she was still able to support herself from the royalties. Admittedly, she never found another play with the "continuous drawing power" of *The Two Orphans*, although *The World against Her* (1888) became another long-term vehicle for the actress.

From the mid-1870s on Claxton produced her own plays. She married the leading man of Palmer's company, Charles A. Stevenson, in 1878. Until their separation in 1901 the couple produced a number of shows together, including *The Double Marriage* (1878), *Pauvrette* (1880), *The World against Her* (1888), and *Lady Reckless* (1894). They managed the Third Avenue Theatre in New York for a brief time but preferred production to management. The couple had six children, all of whom died young. The only child to survive to adulthood committed suicide at the age of twenty-one.

In 1904 Claxton retired from the stage after a final tour of *The Two Orphans*, concluding a successful and lucrative career as an actress. It is estimated that she played the role of Louise more than 4,000 times in her career. After her divorce from Stevenson (a judge ruled the 1901 divorce invalid, and Claxton sued for annulment in 1911), Claxton continued to produce and manage her company. Claxton died in New York City.

Recognizing her success in melodramatic roles such as Louise, Claxton built her career on playing this kind of character. Although a popular actress, Claxton developed a reputation for a limited range of characterization and a highly studied style. One critic wrote of her performance in *Conscience* that "the whole performance is so full of artifices, deliberation, and calculation, and is consequently so unspontaneous and unnatural, that it gives little pleasure." On the other hand, as an astute businesswoman, she understood well what would appeal to audiences and played to those tastes. While perhaps capable of a wider range of parts, her repertoire suggests that she rarely diverged from the highly emotional roles of the melodrama. This is supported as well by critics who made comments like "Miss Claxton acts the part of Helen in her accustomed manner" or "Miss Claxton impersonates in her familiar, but always pleasing and sympathetic manner." Claxton acted with pathos and intensity. One critic said Claxton acted Louise with "an earnestness and realism almost painful to watch too closely." Despite her supposed limitations as an actress, Claxton was well liked by the public and was one of the first American female producers to be financially successful.

• A brief autobiographical manuscript written by Claxton is in the Walter Hampden Memorial Library at the Players in New York City. An interview with Claxton appears in the *New York Dramatic Mirror*, 8 Dec. 1894. Her family's history, *Some Account of the Cone Family* (1903), was written by William Cone. Mention of Claxton appears in A. M. Palmer, "The History of the Union Square Theatre," in the Harvard Theatre Collection; John B. Clapp and Edwin F. Edgett, *Players of the Present, Part I* (1899); T. Allston Brown, *History of the New York Stage* (1903); Arthur Hornblow, *History of the Theatre in America* (1919); and George C. D. Odell, *Annals of the New York Stage* (1937–1942). Obituaries are in the *New York Times*, *New York Herald-Tribune*, and *New York Sun*, all 6 May 1924, and in *Variety*, 10 May 1924.

MELISSA VICKERY-BAREFORD

CLAY, Albert Tobias (4 Dec. 1866–14 Sept. 1925), Assyriologist, was born in Hanover, Pennsylvania, the son of John Martin Clay, a machinist, and Mary Barbara Sharpe. He graduated from Franklin and Marshall College in 1889 and from the Lutheran Theological Seminary, Mount Airy, Pennsylvania, in 1892, with ordination in 1893. He then went to the University of Pennsylvania as the first fellow there in Assyriology to study with Herman Hilprecht. He received his Ph.D. in Assyriology in 1894 for a study of a group of business documents from Nippur of the Achaemenid period. From 1892 to 1895 he taught Hebrew at the University of Pennsylvania and then taught Old Testament theology for three years at Chicago Lutheran Seminary. Clay was married in 1895 to Elizabeth Sommerville McCafferty; they had two children.

Hilprecht was eager to have him back at the University of Pennsylvania, and so Clay was appointed lecturer in Hebrew (until 1903), assistant curator of Babylonian and Semitic antiquities (1899–1910), assistant professor (1903–1909), and then professor (1909–1910) of Semitic philology and archaeology. He served for five years as instructor of Hebrew at Mount Airy Lutheran Seminary and as pastor of St. Mark's Church at South Bethlehem, Pennsylvania, for a year.

While working on J. Pierpont Morgan's collection of Babylonian tablets, Clay became on cordial terms with the great financier, and it was largely because of his enthusiasm that Morgan endowed a professorship of Assyriology at Yale, which the Yale trustees offered to Clay in 1910. For the publication of Morgan's tablets, a series called *Babylonian Records in the Library of J. Pierpont Morgan* was inaugurated. Clay contributed three of the four volumes that appeared (1912, 1913, 1923). In 1911 the Yale Babylonian Collection was organized, with Clay as the first curator, and he set out to create a major research collection of tablets and other antiquities, primarily from Mesopotamia. By World War I he had amassed over 14,000 specimens. He helped finance his purchases by buying large quantities of tablets, then reselling those of less interest to him. Clay founded other text series: *Babylonian Inscriptions in the Collection of James B. Nies* (one volume by Clay published posthumously, 1927), *Yale Oriental Series of Babylonian Texts* (two volumes by Clay, 1915, 1919), and a series of researches (five volumes by Clay, 1912, 1919, 1920 [two], 1922). His energies made Yale the most active center of Assyriology in America at the time.

An expert epigrapher, Clay was one of the most versatile and productive copyists of cuneiform documents in the history of Assyriology. He published three volumes of business documents of the Achaemenid period from the Pennsylvania expedition to Nippur (1898, 1904, 1912), three volumes of Kassite period documents, also from Nippur (1906, 1912), three volumes of Neo-Babylonian documents and letters (1908, 1912, 1919), a volume of documents from Hellenistic Uruk (1913), a volume of literary and scholarly texts (1923), another of Old Assyrian documents (1927), and another of miscellaneous inscriptions (1915). These works were distinguished by the beauty and accuracy of their copies. Clay also published an important early manuscript of the Babylonian Gilgamesh Epic at Yale, together with a reexamination of a companion manuscript at the University of Pennsylvania, in collaboration with Morris Jastrow, Jr. (1920), and what he called *A Hebrew Deluge Story in Cuneiform* (1922), a Babylonian story of the flood. He was author of several other monographs and numerous articles and reviews in the field of Assyriology and Old Testament studies.

Besides epigraphy, Clay's main intellectual interests were the relations between the Hebrew Bible and ancient Mesopotamian texts and traditions. A scholarly view referred to as "Pan-Babylonianism" maintained that significant elements in Israelite culture and religion were of Mesopotamian origin, and so were derived from paganism rather than from a unique religious experience. Extremists asserted that even Christianity and Islam could be traced to Babylonian roots. Shock waves from this controversy were felt widely in European and American society and religious circles. Clay's religious convictions impelled him to bring his Assyriological interests to bear on this controversy in *Amurru, the Home of the Northern Semites: A Study Showing That the Religion and Culture of Israel Were Not of Babylonian Origin* (1909) and in *The Empire of the Amorites* (1919). For him, northwest Mesopotamia and north Syria were the home of a common Semitic culture already in the third millennium, and especially in the second. The people living in this region, known as the Amorites, formed a cultural commonality in which both Mesopotamia and Israel were to develop as local forms, and from which both derived aspects of their traditions, such as the story of the deluge. Thus to him the Mesopotamian legends in common with those of the Bible were actually derivative from the land of the Israelites, rather than the opposite. Clay's thesis was rejected by most of his Assyriological contemporaries. Yet it stemmed the tide of Pan-Babylonianism in America, as Clay's work was warmly welcomed in conservative religious circles.

In 1913 Clay joined the Mesopotamian Committee of the Archaeological Institute of America, which sought to promote American archaeological research in the Near East. This initiative led to the expansion of the American School of Oriental Research in Jerusalem, for which Clay served as a manager beginning in 1916 and as incorporating trustee after 1921. He served as annual professor in Jerusalem in 1919–1920 and again in 1923–1924. In the spring of 1920 he journeyed to Baghdad for the purpose of creating a center there for research, scientific archaeology, and epigraphic training and as a residence for foreign scholars. This was formally inaugurated as the Baghdad School in 1923.

A further example of Clay's organizational skills was his service to the American Oriental Society. He served as librarian from 1913 to 1924 and treasurer from 1915 to 1923. He established an Oriental Texts and Translation Project, of which only one volume was published (1929). He was also a contributing editor to two other series, *Records of the Past* and *Art and Archaeology*, and organized a cuneiform syllabary project.

Clay's commitment to basic epigraphy was strongly inculcated in his students, many of whom prepared volumes of texts in the Yale collections along the lines laid down by Clay's work. Clay's philological abilities were inferior to his copying skills; likewise most of his students' publications were primarily of an epigraphic character.

Clay had a strong practical and business sense. He drew detailed architectural plans for his home in New Haven and contributed his engineering skills to the design of the American School building in Jerusalem. He was one of the most influential American scholars of the Near East of his generation. He died in New Haven, Connecticut.

• Clay's professional correspondence is in the files of the Yale Babylonian Collection, Sterling Memorial Library, New Haven, Conn., with additional materials in the Yale University archives concerning the establishment of the Laffan professorship. His account of his journey to Mesopotamia appeared in *Bulletin of the American Schools of Oriental Research* 13 (1924): 5–10, and his annual reports appearing in that journal give detailed accounts of his work in Palestine. A bibliography of his publications, compiled by Ettalene Grice, is in the *Journal of the American Oriental Society* 45, no. 4 (1925): 295–300. Clay's work in establishing the Yale Babylonian Collection is discussed in F. J. Stephens, "History of the Babylonian Collection," *Yale University Library Gazette* 36, no. 3 (1962): 126–32, which also contains an account of the syllabary project and remarks on Clay's students. An authoritative reassessment of Clay's Amorite hypothesis is A. Goetze, "Professor Clay and the Amurrite Problem," *Yale University Library Gazette* 36, no. 3 (1962): 133–37. Obituaries include those by W. F. Albright in *Journal of the Palestine Oriental Society* 6 (1926): 173–77; P. Dhorme in *Journal of the Palestine Oriental Society* 6 (1926): 169–72; J. A. Montgomery in *Journal of the American Oriental Society* 45, no. 4 (1925): 289–94; and the *New Haven Register*, 15 Sept. 1925.

BENJAMIN R. FOSTER

CLAY, Cassius Marcellus (19 Oct. 1810–22 July 1903), antislavery politician and diplomat, was born in White Hall, Kentucky, the son of Green Clay, a land speculator, and Sally Lewis. Green Clay was one of the wealthiest landowners and slaveholders in Kentucky, and young Cassius was raised in comfort and affluence. He attended Transylvania University (1829–1831) and Yale College (1831–1832), where he received his bachelor's degree. After returning to Transylvania to study law in 1832–1833, Clay married Mary Jane Warfield in 1833. The marriage produced ten children.

From earliest adulthood Clay coveted political office. He eventually served three terms in the Kentucky House of Representatives, in 1835, 1837, and 1840. Like his distant cousin Henry Clay, he was an ardent Whig who championed a program of government-sponsored development of commerce and manufacturing.

During the depression that followed the panic of 1837, Clay's economic views prompted him to join the antislavery movement, which soon became his life's major work. Seeking to understand the ongoing depression, Clay developed an economic critique of slavery that some historians consider to be the most penetrating analysis of slavery produced by a southerner. Clay blamed slavery for the South's economic malaise, arguing that the inefficiency of slave labor prohibited the growth of industry and commerce in the South. Industrious free workers fled from the South, where manual labor was held in contempt. Artisans had difficulty selling their products to a population made up largely of penniless slaves. Clay gained national attention for his economic analysis of slavery, which he presented in a series of speeches, editorials, and pamphlets, the most famous of which was *Slavery: The Evil—The Remedy* (1843). Acting on these arguments, Clay led a campaign during the late 1830s and 1840s to retain a legislative ban against the importation of slaves into Kentucky.

Clay's efforts brought him into contact with northern abolitionists, who admired Clay for boldly challenging slavery from a position within the South. Clay's reputation was sufficiently good among antislavery types that he was sent north in 1844 to court the abolitionist vote for Henry Clay's presidential campaign. In 1845–1846 Clay published an antislavery newspaper, the *True American*, in the slaveholding town of Lexington, Kentucky. The temporary suppression of the newspaper by a mob in August 1845 made Clay into a hero and martyr of the antislavery crusade.

Clay's reformist career was marked by a reckless willingness to use violent tactics to defend himself and his beliefs. He fought a duel in 1841 and engaged in several public brawls on the campaign trail. During one brawl, on 15 June 1849, Clay killed a political opponent with a bowie knife. Threatened with a mob attack against his newspaper in 1845, he armed the newspaper building with cannons and filled it with gunpowder so that he could explode the building around an encroaching mob. In the 1850s Clay openly carried arms to protect abolitionist co-workers.

Clay had a lifelong fascination with military matters, and in 1846 he raised a volunteer cavalry unit for the Mexican War. Captured during a scouting expedition at Encarnación, Mexico, he was a prisoner of war from January to September 1847. His enlistment stunned northern abolitionists, who viewed the war as an aggressive war to gain new lands for the expansion of slavery. Many northerners canceled their subscriptions to Clay's paper, forcing the Clay family to transfer ownership of the *True American* to other reformers.

After the war Clay resumed his antislavery work in Kentucky. He helped to establish the Emancipation party of Kentucky in 1849. He campaigned unsuccessfully to place an antislavery clause in the Kentucky state constitution. In 1851 he was defeated in an effort to become governor on the Emancipationist ticket. In the 1850s Clay helped finance an antislavery newspaper published by William S. Bailey in Newport, Kentucky. He also gave financial support and armed protection to John G. Fee, who was building a network of abolitionist communities and churches in the mountains of Kentucky.

By these actions Clay restored his antislavery reputation among the conservative and moderate reformers who created the Republican party. Seeing Clay as an inspiration for building a southern branch of the party, early Republican leaders welcomed him into their highest national councils. Clay served on the first Republican National Committee in 1856 and was widely mentioned in the national press as a potential presidential or vice presidential candidate in 1856 and 1860. Clay finished second in the balloting for the Republican vice presidential nomination in 1860.

Upon the election of the first Republican president, Abraham Lincoln, in 1860, Clay was appointed to serve as the U.S. minister to Russia, a position he held during 1861–1862 and 1863–1869. His years in Russia were the beginning of his decline as a public figure. Though relations between the United States and Russia were good during Clay's tenure, he personally did little to improve Russo-American relations. Absent for seven years from the United States, hamstrung by bureaucratic infighting, and plagued by charges of financial corruption, Clay's political influence declined. Rumors regarding his extramarital affairs in Russia especially injured his career. One affair produced an embarrassing blackmail scheme, and another produced a son, whom Clay later adopted and brought to the United States. The charges of sexual misconduct resulted in Clay's divorce from Mary Jane Clay in 1878.

After returning to the United States in 1869, Clay became disenchanted with federal intervention in the South during Reconstruction. He was an early champion of the Liberal Republican movement, which sought to abandon the more radical aspects of Reconstruction and to eliminate corruption in government. Clay eventually drifted into the Democratic party and campaigned in several states for Democratic candidates during the late 1870s and early 1880s. Yet he was never happy as a Democrat and became a Republican again by 1884.

In old age Clay's behavior became especially erratic. In 1894, at the age of eighty-four, Clay scandalized his neighbors by marrying his fifteen-year-old servant, Dora Richardson. The marriage ended in divorce four years later. The man who had once fearlessly championed unpopular causes became obsessed with the delusion that someone was trying to kill him. Clay greeted visitors to his estate with his weapons drawn. He once fired a cannon at the sheriff who had come to collect a past-due property tax bill, and in 1877 he killed a former employee who trespassed on the Clay estate. Such actions colored the public's memory of Clay. He has often been remembered as a colorful eccentric rather than as a brilliant and courageous reformer who had challenged moral injustice. He died at White Hall, Kentucky.

• Significant collections of Clay's papers are located at Lincoln Memorial University, Harrogate, Tenn., the University of Kentucky, the Library of Congress, and the Filson Club in Louisville. Letters from Clay in the Salmon P. Chase Papers at the Historical Society of Pennsylvania, Philadelphia, and in the John G. Fee Papers at Berea College, Berea, Ky., are especially significant. Cassius M. Clay, ed., "Cassius M. Clay, 'Lion' of White Hall: Some Unpublished Letters Of and About," *Filson Club History Quarterly* 31 (1957): 3–22, 122–46, reprints many important Clay letters from the private collections of the Clay family. *The Writings of Cassius Marcellus Clay*, ed. Horace Greeley (1848), contains the most important of Clay's writings from the 1830s and early 1840s, including his speeches, pamphlets, and editorials from the *True American*. Clay's autobiography, *The Life of Cassius Marcellus Clay* (1886), is riddled to an unusual degree with distortions, errors, and self-justification.

David L. Smiley, *The Lion of White Hall: The Life of Cassius M. Clay* (1962), is the standard biography, but it must be supplemented with H. Edward Richardson, *Cassius Marcellus Clay: Firebrand of Freedom* (1976), a work that is especially helpful in understanding Clay's personality, family life, and later career. A dated but still useful work on Clay's diplomacy is James Rood Robertson, *A Kentuckian at the Court of the Tsars: The Ministry of Cassius Marcellus Clay to Russia, 1861–1862 and 1863–1869* (1935).

HAROLD D. TALLANT

CLAY, Clement Claiborne (13 Dec. 1816–3 Jan. 1882), U.S. and Confederate senator, was born near Huntsville, Alabama, the son of Clement Comer Clay, a lawyer and later governor and U.S. senator, and Susanna Claiborne Withers. He used the designation C. C. Clay, Jr., to distinguish himself from his father. He graduated from the University of Alabama in 1834 and studied law under John B. Minor at the University of Virginia, receiving his degree in 1839. During his father's tenure as governor of Alabama, 1835–1837, Clay was his father's secretary. He practiced law with him from 1839 to 1846, after which he became Madison County judge. He resigned in 1848 for financial reasons. Debt was a lifelong problem, along with chronic bad health, particularly asthma. Clay was associated with the *Huntsville Democrat*, a family organ, most closely in the 1840s, when he was an assistant editor during important campaigns. He was elected to the lower house of the Alabama legislature in 1842 and 1844–1845, then to the U.S. Senate in 1853 and again in 1857. A Jacksonian Democrat, and a strong opponent of Henry Clay (a distant relation) and the Whigs, he moved closer to states' rights and John C. Calhoun over a proposal for the gradual abolition of slavery in the District of Columbia and was active in the Nashville convention of 1850. Yet he was never one of the fire-eaters. He strongly supported President Franklin Pierce and, with less enthusiasm, President James Buchanan in the political disputes of the 1850s.

Clay's marriage in 1843 to Virginia Caroline Tunstall was in most respects a good match. Her social skills were unsurpassed in antebellum Washington, and she assisted him materially in his career. She lived until 1915 and is perhaps better known than her husband because of her memoir, *A Belle of the Fifties* (1904). They had no children.

Clay believed the national government was "a confederation, not a consolidation, a union, not a nation" (Nuermberger, p. 168). As senator he opposed most public expenditures, including homesteads and college land grants, but favored aid to southern railroads. A close friend of Jefferson Davis, Clay helped him avert a duel with Judah P. Benjamin, a Louisiana senator. He was a bitter foe of Democrat Stephen A. Douglas but also of abolitionists and Republicans like Charles A. Sumner and John P. Hale.

Clay resigned his Senate seat after Alabama's secession (11 Jan. 1861) and went to Minnesota because of violent asthma attacks in late winter. Though invited to Montgomery by Davis's wife, his health prevented it. He was instrumental in the selection of Leroy Pope Walker, a North Alabama rival, as the first Confederate secretary of war after Clay had declined the post. Walker was a bad choice yet one that eased Clay's election to the Confederate Senate in November 1861. He took his seat in Richmond in February 1862. Clay was a moderate in Congress, sometimes supporting the states' rights group, at other times the conservative faction, but he generally backed President Davis. He mediated between Davis and his fellow Alabama senator, William Lowndes Yancey, a bitter critic of the administration. Clay also headed a committee that exonerated the Navy Department for the loss of New Orleans. His loyalty to Davis and his vote against a pay increase for Confederate soldiers helped defeat him for reelection. His term expired in February 1864.

Clay was one of three Confederates sent by Davis on a mission to Canada. In May he ran the blockade out of Wilmington, North Carolina, to Halifax, Nova Scotia. He headed a War Department espionage team charged with rescuing Confederate prisoners and fomenting discontent against Lincoln's government among copperheads and the Knights of the Golden Circle. In July 1864 Clay was involved in the Niagara Falls "peace conference" with publisher Horace Greeley, an attempt to embarrass Abraham Lincoln and influence the 1864 presidential election. He recruited Bennett H. Young and directed his raid on St. Albans, Vermont, on 19 October 1864. The raiders robbed all three banks in the town and escaped across the border with a quarter million dollars. It was the only successful action carried out by Confederates from Canada and caused international repercussions between Great Britain and the United States.

Clay left Canada in January and reported to Secretary of State Benjamin and President Davis in Richmond on 2 April 1865, as the Confederate government was evacuating its capital. He traveled as far as Danville with the presidential party and headed for Mexico after learning of Lincoln's death. As he moved west across Georgia he heard of President Andrew Johnson's proclamation for his arrest and that of other Confederates as conspirators in the assassination. Clay rode 150 miles from La Grange to Macon, Georgia, to surrender himself to General James H. Wilson. With Davis and other officials, he was taken to Augusta and then by steamship to Fort Monroe, Virginia, where he was held as a prisoner from May 1865 to April 1866.

Virginia Clay eventually won her husband's freedom with the help of Ulysses S. Grant and northern politicians who had known Clay before the war. He was pardoned by Congress in 1880. Upon his release, the couple returned to Huntsville, which had endured early Union occupation. Though they suffered little during the conflict, they faced near poverty in Reconstruction. Yet Virginia managed to socialize in various cities, while Clay struggled to pay his own debts and those of his late father. He experimented unsuccessfully with freedmen as laborers, tried a variety of crops on his "Wildwood" plantation, practiced law, and sold insurance. He died near Huntsville without recovering his family's social or political importance or achieving solvency.

Clay "did nothing in his public life to ease sectional tension, and much to exacerbate it" (Nuermberger, p. 321) and was second only to Yancey in Alabama's secession movement. While it has not been proved that Clay met John Wilkes Booth in Canada, a charge that he always denied, he probably knew of a plot aimed at Lincoln. Clay was among the "officers . . . who seem to have played important roles in intelligence activities" and was "an aggressive man . . . not averse to a fight" (Tidwell, *Come Retribution*, pp. 49, 189, 250). He seemed willing to take direct action for the cause he believed in.

• Clay's papers are at Duke University. The best available study is Ruth Ketring Nuermberger, *The Clays of Alabama: A Planter-Lawyer-Politician Family* (1958), a carefully researched and fascinating collective biography, more than two-thirds of which is primarily devoted to Clay and his wife. The first part of the volume deals with his father's career and early life on the frontier in Alabama's Tennessee River valley. The bibliography is a guide to works on local and family history and genealogy. Walter L. Fleming, *Civil War and Reconstruction in Alabama* (1905), is supplemented by J. Mills Thornton, *Politics and Power in a Slave Society: Alabama, 1800–1860* (1978). Wilfred Buck Yearns, *The Confederate Congress* (1960), and Thomas B. Alexander and Richard E. Beringer, *The Anatomy of the Confederate Congress* (1972), analyze Clay's performance in the Confederate Senate. William A. Tidwell et al., *Come Retribution: The Confederate Secret Service and the Assassination of Lincoln* (1988) and *April '65: Confederate Covert Action in the American Civil War* (1995), document Clay's involvement in espionage while in Canada. Extensive discussion of his imprisonment and the possible charges against him as well as correspondence from the Clays is in *The War of the Rebellion: A Compilation of the Official Records of the Union and Confederate Armies*, ser. 2, vol. 8 (1899), and Douglas Southall Freeman, *A Calendar of Confederate Papers* (1908).

MICHAEL B. CHESSON

CLAY, Clement Comer (17 Dec. 1789–6 Sept. 1866), governor of Alabama and U.S. senator, was born in Halifax County, Virginia, the son of William Clay, a planter, and Rebecca Comer. The family moved to Grainger County, in northeastern Tennessee, about 1795. Clement was graduated from Blount College in Knoxville (the future University of Tennessee) in 1807. He then read law in Knoxville under Hugh Lawson White, for whom he would name one of his sons. He was admitted to the bar in December 1809 and moved to Huntsville, Alabama, in November 1811. He served under Andrew Jackson in the Creek War of 1813–1814. In 1815 he married Susanna Claiborne Withers. They would have three children.

Clay purchased a plantation near Huntsville and became a stockholder in and director of the Huntsville Bank. After the creation of the Alabama Territory in 1817, Clay represented Madison County in the territorial assembly. In 1819, when Alabama framed a constitution preparatory to admission to the Union, Clay became a delegate to the constitutional convention and chaired the Committee of Fifteen that drafted the document. He fought for life terms for judges and supported the pro-bank forces in their unsuccessful effort to permit the legislature to charter banks by a majority, rather than a two-thirds, vote.

At its first meeting, the legislature unanimously chose Clay as one of the state's five circuit judges, who together also constituted the state supreme court. The other judges selected Clay as chief justice. However, he resigned from the bench in 1823 in order to become an attorney for the creditors in the first of the "big interest" cases, suits that arose from the territorial assembly's repeal of any usury limitations.

In 1825 Clay ran for Congress, but because of his association with banking and creditor elements he received only 29 percent of the vote against the demagogic Gabriel Moore. Undeterred, in 1826 he became a candidate for the U.S. Senate. His opponent on this occasion was John McKinley. Both Clay and McKinley claimed to be followers of Andrew Jackson. But Clay committed the strategic blunder of reaching out to the handful of legislators who admired John Quincy Adams, by saying that he would offer no factious opposition to the Adams administration; and McKinley was elected, 41 to 38. At the same time that Clay and McKinley were opposing each other for the Senate, they were serving together as the attorneys for the creditors in the second of the "big interest" cases, in which the creditors were triumphant.

In 1828 Madison County elected Clay a state representative, and his legislative colleagues unanimously chose him Speaker of the house. He continued to embrace the attitudes that had identified him as an elitist, seeking maximum prices for the sale of public lands, opposing an exemption of non-slaveholders from patrol duty, opposing a constitutional amendment to limit the life terms of judges, and favoring the repeal of the law forbidding participants in duels to hold office. He also opposed efforts to secure women their separate estates and voted to extend Alabama's jurisdiction over the Creek Indians.

In 1829 Clay again was a candidate for Congress, and against an opponent who made him seem the more popular figure, he won with about 52 percent of the vote. In Congress Clay at last managed to establish egalitarian credentials. He embraced the cause of squatters and public land debtors, quite ironic crusades for him given his past positions. But his actions finally freed him in the eyes of his constituents from an identification with aristocracy. He did vote to override Andrew Jackson's veto of the Maysville Road bill, but in later years he publicly recanted this heterodoxy.

Clay was returned to two more house terms without opposition. He served as chairman of the Committee on Public Lands during his final term and throughout this period vigorously sought preemption rights for squatters and the reduction of public land prices. He denounced the Bank of the United States as a threat to liberty and hailed Jackson's withdrawal of the government's deposits from it. He opposed nullification but equally opposed protective tariffs.

In 1835 Clay received the Democratic nomination for governor and was easily elected. He devoted his first annual message largely to condemning the mass mailing of abolitionist pamphlets to the South. He urged strong provisions against slave insurrection and warned against the building unrest among the Creek Indians.

In the spring of 1836 some 3,000 Creeks under Neamathla rose in open revolt. Clay called out the state militia and took personal charge of the mobilization. But most Creeks, led by Opothle-yoholo, actively assisted Clay's efforts. With the arrival of U.S. forces, the rebellion collapsed. At Clay's urging, the United States then compelled all Creeks to leave for Oklahoma immediately.

A year later the state was caught up in the panic of 1837. In June Clay summoned the legislature into special session and proposed two of the disastrous measures that were in great part responsible for bankrupting the state-owned Bank of Alabama. These acts ordered all banks to suspend the collection of their debts and authorized lending millions of dollars in bonds to debtors. At this session, the legislature unanimously elected Clay to the U.S. Senate.

In the Senate Clay resumed his crusade for preemption rights for squatters and for low public land prices. He pressed for the immediate removal of the Cherokees and the defeat of the Seminoles. He voted for the independent subtreasury and fought both the bill to distribute surplus revenue among the states and the bankruptcy act.

The deepening depression created a crisis in Clay's own finances, compelling his resignation from the Senate in 1841. In 1830 Clay had owned fifty-two slaves, and shortly thereafter he had acquired a second large plantation in neighboring Jackson County. But by 1840 he had already begun selling off his slaves to meet his debts, and throughout most of the coming decade Clay continued these reductions.

At the beginning of 1842, desperate for cash, Clay accepted Governor Benjamin Fitzpatrick's appointment to compile a new digest of the state's laws. However, though the legislature eventually accepted his digest, it did so only after a lengthy and painful floor fight. In June 1843 state supreme court justice Henry B. Goldthwaite resigned his seat to run for Congress, and Governor Fitzpatrick appointed Clay to the vacancy. Clay sat on cases during the summer and fall, and in December he became a candidate for a full term. But by this time Goldthwaite had been defeated for Congress and wanted to return to the court. The Whigs and Calhounite Democrats joined to vote for Goldthwaite, and Clay was defeated, 71 to 55. In 1848 the legislature dealt Clay yet another blow, abolishing the position that he had held since 1846 on the commission to oversee the liquidation of the Bank of Alabama.

After these successive humiliations, Clay retired from public life. Thereafter he devoted himself to his law practice in Huntsville, in partnership with his sons, and resumed his business speculations. With the return of prosperity in the 1850s, his economic situation improved. By 1860 he owned eighty-four slaves; his real estate was valued at $60,000 and his personal property at $85,000. During the early 1850s Clay took a leading part in the organization of the Memphis and Charleston Railroad and became a large stockholder in it. He went as a delegate to the Southern Commercial Conventions in Memphis in 1845 and in Charleston in 1854.

During the crisis of 1850 Clay served as president of the Madison County Southern Rights Association, and a decade later he strongly supported secession. Federal forces occupying Huntsville detained him briefly in August 1862. When they withdrew at the end of the month, Clay refused to flee to a safer location. With the return of Federal forces, Clay was again seized in December 1864. The close of the war left him an invalid. He died in Huntsville.

• Clay's personal papers are in the Perkins Library of Duke University, Durham, N.C. His gubernatorial correspondence is in the Alabama Department of Archives and History, Montgomery. Ruth Ketring Nuermberger, *The Clays of Alabama: A Planter-Lawyer-Politician Family* (1958), is a thorough biography of Clay and his sons, though one rather partial to its subjects.

J. MILLS THORNTON III

CLAY, Edward Williams (19 Apr. 1799–31 Dec. 1857), artist and political cartoonist, was born in Philadelphia, Pennsylvania, the son of Robert Clay, a sea captain, and Eliza Williams. Clay, whose father died when he was five, was reared in the house of his grandfather, Curtis Clay, a Philadelphia merchant. Members of the Clay and Curtis families were educated, prosperous, and prominent as merchants and ministers during the eighteenth century and as bankers, lawyers, and politicians during the early nineteenth century. Clay received a liberal education, read law, and was admitted to the Philadelphia bar in 1825. His interest and training in art probably began after his mother's brief marriage in 1814 to Joseph Anthony, a goldsmith and jeweler. Goldsmiths and silversmiths often engraved their work and engraved metal plates for printing. Although he served no known formal apprenticeship, Clay had learned the basics of engraving before he went to Europe to study art in 1825.

Some of Clay's earliest engravings were illustrations in *Analectic Magazine* (1819) and *American Monthly Magazine* (1824), a frontispiece for James Fenimore Cooper's *The Spy* (1822), and four etchings for Mason L. Weems's pamphlet *God's Revenge against Duelling* (1821).

After Clay returned to Philadelphia in 1828, he etched social cartoons as well as *Life in Philadelphia*, a series of fourteen single-sheet etchings of the pretensions of upwardly mobile Philadelphians, both black and white. This series, issued from 1828 to 1830, contains some of the earliest published images of African Americans. Although some modern viewers see these pictures as racist stereotypes, Clay intended them as comic, theatrical sketches, peopled with character types similar to the black servants and dandies found in contemporary plays. *Life in Philadelphia* was popular in England as well as the United States. In 1830 abolitionist rallies were held in Philadelphia, followed by anti-Negro riots that summer. Clay discontinued the series in the face of rising racial tensions, but he continued to depict African-Americans in the street scenes that form the stage sets for some of his political cartoons. The innocent, comic character of *Life in Philadelphia* is evident when the series is compared to Clay's "Amalgamation" lithographs of 1839. These political cartoons depict blacks as repulsive and overbearing and their white abolitionist friends as simpleminded and ineffectual. Taken together, the two series graphically illustrate changing racial attitudes in the United States before the Civil War.

In 1831 Clay drew his first widely circulated single-sheet political cartoon, "The Rats Leaving a Falling House," satirizing the dissolution of President Andrew Jackson's first cabinet. Printed by the new process of lithography, "Rats" depicts President Jackson slumped in the collapsing president's chair, his foot firmly clamped on the tail of the rat with Secretary of State Martin Van Buren's head. Rats with the heads of the rest of the Cabinet members scurry off in all directions. Mrs. Trollope noted in her *Domestic Manners of the Americans* (1832) that it was the "only tolerable" political cartoon she had seen in the United States.

Clay continued to design illustrations for books, magazines, and sheet music, as well as views, theatrical portraits, and social cartoons that reflected the changing cultural life around him throughout his career. However, inspired by the coalescence of political parties for and against Andrew Jackson and his policies, Clay increasingly concentrated on political caricature during the 1830s. In 1833–1834 he moved to New York. There, in the growing financial and cultural center of the United States, he drew inspiration from the political machinations of the Albany Regency and Tammany Hall as well as the doings of the Whigs and the Democrats. His personal politics varied with the times. He drew Henry Clay as a sideshow huckster in "The Monkey System or Every One for Himself at the Expense of His Neighbor! ! ! ! ! ! ! !" in 1831 and as the rising sun in "Impure Spirits Disappearing before the Rising Sun" for the presidential campaign of 1844.

Clay was the first American artist to specialize in political caricature. A key figure in the establishment of political caricature as an integral part of American life before the Civil War, he worked with lithography, a new and efficient method of reproducing pictures for an expanding audience. Of the more than 200 images he published, 120 are political cartoons, a significant fraction of the 650 published in the United States during Clay's working life. Printed in the single-sheet format, independent of newspapers or magazines, Clay's pictorial satires of Andrew Jackson's political battles, the Panic of 1837, and the Log Cabin Campaign of 1840 show a simplicity of design and a directness of idea that are unusual for the period. Well drawn and often very funny, Clay's cartoons directly document contemporary political opinions, relevant current events, and details of everyday life. Although his work is generally found only in libraries and museums, Clay is a frequent, if often uncredited, illustrator of modern books on American politics and culture.

He was most productive between 1836 and 1840, but he was active until his eyes failed in 1852. He served the state of Delaware as the clerk of the Court of Chancery and clerk of the Orphan's Court from 1854 to 1856. Clay, who never married, died of "pulmonary consumption" in New York City. His unusually long but inaccurate obituary (*Philadelphia Press*, 5 Jan. 1858) is the often unacknowledged primary or secondary source for the many garbled accounts of Clay's life. It may also be a final satire written by Clay himself during his long terminal illness.

• The best collections of Clay's work are in the American Antiquarian Society, the New-York Historical Society, and the Library of Congress. There are no known portraits of Clay or collections of his papers. The major secondary source of information about Clay is Nancy R. Davison, *E. W. Clay: American Political Caricaturist of the Jacksonian Era* (Ph.D. diss., Univ. of Michigan, 1980). Davison's "E. W. Clay and the American Political Caricature Business" in *Prints and Printmakers of New York State, 1825–1940*, ed. David Tatham (1986), focuses on the printing, publishing, and selling of the single-sheet lithographic political cartoon.

NANCY R. DAVISON

CLAY, Green (14 Aug. 1757–31 Oct. 1828), pioneer and soldier, was born in Powhatan County, Virginia, the son of Charles Clay and Martha Green, farmers. Green Clay had little formal education but at an early age mastered the techniques of surveying. Born poor, he realized that a fortune could be made by acquiring land and accompanied a surveying party to Kentucky in 1777. He was with Daniel Boone at the siege of Boonesborough in September 1778, and in 1780 Clay returned to Kentucky to stay. In 1781 he was appointed deputy surveyor for Lincoln County, Kentucky, by the Virginia government. As a surveyor he was in much demand by veterans holding revolutionary war land warrants in Kentucky, and as was customary, he received as fees one-half of the property he surveyed that cleared titles. Clay specialized in lands in southwestern Kentucky. Residing for a short while at Boonesborough and Fort Estill, he then established himself on his lifelong estate a few miles west of Boonesborough on the Kentucky River.

In 1782 Clay served as a militia lieutenant on the George Rogers Clark expedition against the Shawnee Indians in Ohio. Clay was a trustee for Boonesborough in 1787, and after the creation of Madison County in 1785, he was a justice of the peace and commander of the local militia. He represented Madison County in the Virginia House of Delegates from 1788 to 1789. As a delegate to the Virginia convention to ratify the U.S. Constitution in June 1788, he voted with the majority of the Kentucky members against approval, largely in fear of eastern domination of the new government and continued acquiescence to the Spanish closure of the Mississippi River to American trade.

In 1792 Clay was commissioned to operate a toll road from the falls of the Great Kanawha River to Lexington. He also owned the ferry at the Kentucky River crossing of that highway. He represented Madison County in the Kentucky House of Representatives, 1793–1794, and in the state senate, 1795–1798 and 1802–1808, serving as the Speaker of the senate from 28 December 1807 to 12 December 1808. As a legislator he worked for reform in law administration, promoted education, and wrote Kentucky's first banking law.

Clay became the richest man in Kentucky and the state's largest landowner. His son, Cassius Marcellus Clay, wrote that Green Clay's "life was one rather of business than anything else; and here he passed all his contemporaries in the West." Besides farming and livestock raising, Clay engaged in extensive commercial and industrial activity. He owned two distilleries, warehouses, a resort at Estill Springs, and taverns, which he built and rented as outlets for his bourbon whiskey. He refused to raise tobacco because he considered the use of it harmful and addictive.

In 1795 Clay married Sally Lewis; six of their seven children survived infancy. The youngest of their children was Cassius Marcellus Clay, an antislavery leader and minister to Russia. Clay brought his wife to his home, a log cabin with a dirt floor. During 1798–1799 he built a Grecian-style brick mansion with rangework of marble and limestone. The edifice was called "Clermont" and later renamed "White Hall."

At the second Kentucky constitutional convention in 1799, Clay served on the committee that drafted a new state constitution. He ran for governor in 1808 against General Charles Scott of revolutionary war fame and lawyer John Allen. His political base was poor squatters in southwestern Kentucky, many of whom had been unable to prove their military land warrants and could not afford to meet payments on preemption grants of state lands. Favoring debtor relief, Clay gained the support of settlers south of the Green River, but the regional division in Kentucky politics gave the balance of power to the older, conservative farmers north of the river who favored Scott or Allen. The election returns yielded 5,516 votes for Clay, 8,430 for Allen, and 22,050 for Scott.

With the outbreak of the War of 1812, Kentucky troops suffered a disastrous defeat at the battle of the River Raisin on 22 January 1813. General William Henry Harrison called for another contingent of Kentucky militia to join his army in northern Ohio. Clay, a major general, led 3,000 Kentucky volunteers northward. With 1,200 men from this force he sought to relieve the siege of Fort Meigs, just below the rapids of the Maumee River, that British general Henry Proctor and American Indians led by Tecumseh began on 28 April. Following orders from Harrison, Clay descended the river on 5 May, dividing his force. Clay and 400 men landed on the south bank and, while fighting Indians, made their way to the fort. The enemy lifted the siege on 9 May, and Clay was left in command of Fort Meigs. The British and Indians returned on 25 July. Tecumseh failed to lure Clay and his troops out of the fort, and the enemy departed on 28 July. Because their enlistments expired, Clay and his troops returned to Kentucky and did not accompany Harrison's army into Canada.

Although many frontier Kentuckians resented Clay for being so wealthy, he earned his success by hard work and astute business practices. He seldom sold on credit. A health enthusiast, he was one of the first in his region to drill artesian wells to obtain pure water. Clay was a Deist, but his wife was a Calvinist Baptist. He died at his residence near Boonesborough. Clay County, Kentucky, was named for him in 1806.

• Substantial holdings at the Filson Club, Louisville, Ky., include the Green Clay Papers, the Green Clay Land Papers, and the Sidney Payne Clay Papers. The University of Kentucky Library has Clay papers, which include letters and legal and business transactions. A short biographical sketch by Cassius Marcellus Clay is at the Filson Club. Cassius Marcellus Clay, *The Life of Cassius Marcellus Clay: Memoirs, Writings, and Speeches*, vol. 1 (1886), evaluates Green Clay's character and contains family anecdotes. Two biographies of Cassius Marcellus Clay comment on Green Clay, David L. Smiley, *Lion of White Hall* (1962), and H. Edward Richardson, *Cassius Marcellus Clay: Firebrand of Freedom* (1976). For a brief discussion of sidelights of Green Clay's dealings in a neighboring county see C. Frank Dunn, "Gen. Green Clay in Fayette County Records," *Register of the Kentucky State Historical Society* 44 (1946): 146–47. For Clay and politics see Charles G. Talbert, *Benjamin Logan: Kentucky Frontiersman* (1962), and Harry M. Ward, *Charles Scott and the "Spirit of '76"* (1988). Lewis Collins, *History of Kentucky*, rev. Richard H. Collins (2 vols., 1874; repr. 1966), puts Clay in the context of Ky. history and includes a sketch on him. For Clay's residence in Madison County see William Chenault, "The Early History of Madison County," ed. J. T. Dorris, *Register of the Kentucky State Historical Society* 30 (1932): 119–61; Dorris, *A Glimpse at Historic Madison County and Richmond, Kentucky* (1934); and David C. Greene, *White Hall State Shrine: Home of General Green Clay and His Son General Cassius Marcellus Clay* (1972). A death notice is in the (Lexington) *Kentucky Reporter*, 19 Nov. 1828.

HARRY M. WARD

CLAY, Henry (12 Apr. 1777–29 June 1852), statesman, was born in Hanover County, Virginia, the son of John Clay, a Baptist minister, and Elizabeth Hudson. John Clay died during the American Revolution when Henry was four years old. The following year Henry's mother married Captain Henry Watkins, a planter and militia officer, and later they moved to Kentucky. Henry received his early schooling at the Old Field School and the St. Paul's School in Virginia. Although he had a gifted mind, his formal education was extremely limited. Nor did he apply himself to his studies. As he later put it, he "relied too much upon the resources of my genius." But growing up in Hanover County, he heard Patrick Henry and several other noted orators of the era speak before juries and on the stump. Their powers of persuasion made an enormous impression on him, and he trained himself to become verbally fluent.

When he was fifteen Clay gained a position in the state chancery office in Richmond through his stepfather's influence. His intelligence was quickly noticed, particularly by Chancellor George Wythe, who had Clay assigned to him as a secretary. Wythe, a professor of law and classics at the College of William and Mary and the teacher of Thomas Jefferson, John Marshall, and others, was the most learned jurist in Virginia. Under Wythe's direction Clay studied law and history and tackled translations of Homer, Plutarch, and other classics. He completed his law training in the office of the state's attorney general, Robert Brooke, and was admitted to the bar on 6 November 1797. Clay then decided to follow his mother to Kentucky. He eventually settled in Lexington, opened a law office, and won immediate success pleading both civil and criminal cases.

In April 1799 Clay married Lucretia Hart; the marriage allied him to one of the most eminent Kentucky families, the so-called Blue Grass gentry. Although Clay started as a Jeffersonian Republican, which was understandable given his Virginia birth and training, once he married into the Hart family he began to develop political and economic ideas more in keeping with the mercantile and banking interests of his Blue Grass friends. These ideas struck some as more Hamiltonian than Jeffersonian, but Clay always insisted that he remained fundamentally faithful to republicanism, states' rights, and Jefferson's Republican party.

Because of his extraordinary speaking skills, his amiable disposition and personality, and his intelligence, Clay was immediately pegged for a political career by his wealthy constituents. In 1803 he was elected to the lower house of the Kentucky legislature and quickly assumed an influential role in the assembly. Consequently, he was chosen a U.S. Senator on 19 November 1806 to serve out the unexpired term of John Adair. No one noticed that he was ineligible because he had not yet reached the constitutionally mandated age of thirty.

Aaron Burr, the former vice president of the United States, engaged Clay to represent him against charges that his recent activities threatened the Union. Convinced of Burr's innocence, Clay won an acquittal. When President Jefferson issued a proclamation warning the nation of the existence of a military conspiracy and calling for the apprehension of those involved, Clay realized that he had been deceived. His involvement in the case was later used against him when he ran for the presidency.

Clay returned to the Kentucky legislature in 1807 and the following year was elevated to the position of Speaker. He was also elected a professor of law and politics at Transylvania University. By this time he had become the most promising young politician in Kentucky, someone expected to achieve national prominence in the very near future. Many called him "Harry of the West" and "Star of the West."

In 1810 Clay was again elected to the U.S. Senate, this time to complete the term of Buckner Thruston. He gave several notable speeches in the Senate that emphasized his vision of an expanding nation directed by a dynamic central government. A staunch nationalist, he railed against Britain's seizure of American ships, impressment of American sailors, and failure to leave its American forts along the northern border of Canada in compliance with the peace treaty of 1783. These speeches drew the attention of his colleagues; John Quincy Adams called him a "republican of the first fire." But Clay preferred the excitement and turbulence of the lower house. The Senate was too quiet, too dignified. He preferred action over discourse, movement over contemplation, passion and impulsiveness over caution and circumspection. So he decided to seek a seat in the House of Representatives, and in August 1810 Clay was elected overwhelmingly. He took his House seat in November 1811.

Clay was chosen Speaker of the House on the first day of the session by a huge majority. His speeches had attracted the support of a group of new, young congressmen, known as "War Hawks," whose intense nationalism matched Clay's. They believed he could provide the leadership to force the government into declaring war on Great Britain, and so they elected him Speaker.

As Speaker, the Kentuckian assigned War Hawks to all the important committees so that the business of the House rested in the hands of the most rabid advocates of war. When President James Madison in 1812 finally asked Congress for a declaration of war against Great Britain, many wrongly gave Clay the credit for bringing it about.

Clay rejected the role of traffic director of the House intended by the Founding Fathers. Instead he established the concept of the Speaker as its political leader. Exercising his many political skills, Clay infused his office with so much authority that the Speaker became the second most powerful man in the government after the president. He assumed the right to refer all bills to standing committees whose members he had chosen. In the past the House itself had appointed the standing committees and controlled the flow of legislation. He strictly enforced House rules and blocked filibusters by directing floor managers to move the previous question, which, when approved, ended debate. He also retained his right to engage in debate by directing the House into a committee of the whole and thereby retained his right to speak and vote. Because of the fairness with which Clay controlled House business and the respect and affection the other representatives had for him, he was Speaker for a total of ten years, longer than any other man in the nineteenth century.

His service in the House was interrupted when President Madison appointed him in 1815 as one of five commissioners to treat with the British about ending the war. After many months of negotiations in Ghent, Belgium, the commissioners signed a treaty on 24 December 1814 ending the war on the basis of status quo antebellum. Although the treaty failed to settle any of the issues that had precipitated the war, the nation had not suffered any loss of honor. British demands over trade and an Indian buffer zone had been turned back and the way prepared for the nation's continued expansion.

Following the conclusion of the negotiations Clay was directed to join John Quincy Adams and Albert Gallatin in London to seek a treaty of commerce with Great Britain. What resulted was the Convention of 1815 (so called because of the limited extent of its provisions) that provided a most-favored-nation treatment of each other's products, a feature that became a model for similar conventions with other nations.

Clay returned from Europe with a reinforced sense of nationalism that found responses throughout the country and within Congress. Returned to his House seat and the Speakership, he regularly argued that the government should actively participate in strengthening the nation at home and abroad as it moved into an increasingly industrial age. He advocated a protective tariff to encourage domestic manufactures, a strong central bank to provide stable currency and credit, and government-sponsored public works, such as the building of roads, bridges, canals, and other means of transportation. Home markets, he said, "can only be created and cherished by the PROTECTION of our own legislation against the inevitable prostration of our industry, which must ensue from the action of FOREIGN policy and legislation."

This so-called American System constituted the centerpiece of Clay's legislative agenda for several decades, and it represented his basic philosophical thinking about the role of government in national affairs. Accordingly, he supported the chartering of the Second National Bank of the United States in 1816; the protective tariffs of 1816, 1824, and 1828; the extensions of the National Road westward from its starting point in Cumberland, Maryland; and the passage of bills requiring that the money from land sales be used for education and internal improvements. He believed his American System would promote economic development and diversification, reduce dependence on imports, and benefit Americans in all sections and among all classes and endeavors. It was intended to strengthen the bonds that tied the nation together to ensure the perpetuity of a united country.

In addition Clay became the leading spokesman in the nation favoring the independence of Latin America. Indeed, his many speeches on the subject were translated into Spanish and read to the armies rebelling against Spain. Later he also spoke eloquently in favor of the independence of Greece from Turkish rule. Abraham Lincoln rightly maintained that Clay's "predominant sentiment, from first to last, was a deep devotion to the cause of human liberty." He also favored the abolition of slavery and tried repeatedly to induce Kentucky into accepting his position on the question.

When Missouri applied for admission into the Union as a slave state, a series of crises resulted that nearly precipitated southern secession and possible civil war. The problem centered on the question of the right of Congress to restrict slavery in the territories. Largely through Clay's efforts the crises were resolved. To maintain the existing balance between slave and free states, both Missouri and Maine were admitted into the Union. Clay believed that compromise was essential to the political process and that moderation and harmony should be the guiding principles in sectional disputes. As he later said, "I go for honorable compromise whenever it can be made. Life itself is but a compromise between death and life, the struggle continuing throughout our whole existence. . . . All legislation, all government, all society, is formed upon the principle of mutual concession, politeness, comity, courtesy; upon these, every thing is based." The American people acknowledged his achievement in resolving the crises and dubbed him the "Great Pacificator" and the "Great Compromiser."

Clay retired from Congress in 1821 to recoup financial losses he suffered following the panic of 1819. He rebuilt his law practice, served as legal counsel for the Second National Bank in Ohio and Kentucky, and pleaded several important cases before the U.S. Supreme Court, such as *Osborne v. Bank of the United States*. Over a two-year period he reestablished his financial solvency, including the repayment of loans he had received from John Jacob Astor. Clay returned to the House and Speakership in 1823 and started campaigning for the presidency. He was nominated by his state and in 1824 ran against Secretary of State John Quincy Adams, Secretary of the Treasury William H. Crawford, and the newly elected senator from Tennessee, General Andrew Jackson, the hero of the battle of New Orleans.

No one received a majority of electoral votes in the contest, and the choice therefore fell to the House of Representatives. According to the Twelfth Amendment to the Constitution, Clay was excluded from consideration because his electoral count was the lowest among the four candidates. Yet, as Speaker, he exercised enormous influence in the final decision. Unquestionably, he would have been elected president had he been among the top three candidates. Instead, he threw his support to Adams, who was elected on the first ballot. It was undoubtedly understood but unspoken that Adams would appoint Clay his secretary of state, a position the Kentuckian desperately wanted because it traditionally led directly to the presidency. Jackson and his friends condemned the appointment, calling it a "corrupt bargain," and whenever Clay later ran for the presidency the charge was leveled against him. He fought a duel on 8 April 1826 with John Randolph over remarks by Randolph in Congress about the appointment, but neither man was injured.

As secretary of state Clay continued his efforts to assist the liberated South American republics. He promoted what he called a "good neighborhood" policy, but the Jacksonians in Congress defeated his efforts to participate in a congress in Panama, suggested by Simón Bolívar, to discuss problems of mutual concern. He signed most-favored-nation agreements with numerous South American and European nations, but he failed in his attempt to purchase Texas from Mexico.

Jackson defeated Adams in the presidential election of 1828, and Clay once again retired to "Ashland," his Lexington home that he had built in 1811. He resumed his law practice and started preparing to run again for the presidency in 1832. In 1831 the Kentucky legislature elected Clay to the U.S. Senate where, except for the years from 1842 to 1849, he served until six months before his death.

After his return to Congress, Clay assumed control of the National Republican party, which had formed in opposition to Jackson's Democratic party. He was officially nominated for the presidency by his party in December 1831 and expected to defeat Jackson on the issue of the recharter of the Second National Bank. He talked Nicholas Biddle, president of the bank, into applying to Congress for the recharter four years before the current charter was due to expire. Jackson vetoed the recharter bill, and Clay was unable to win an override in Congress.

The presidential election of 1832 centered on the bank issue, and Clay suffered a crushing defeat largely because the American people loved and trusted Jackson. Clay received forty-nine electoral votes, mostly from New England, a few middle Atlantic states, and Kentucky. Jackson took virtually everything west and south of the Potomac River for a total of 219 electoral votes.

Following the election Jackson ordered the removal of the government's deposits from the bank and placed the funds in state "pet" banks, an action that prompted Clay to introduce resolutions into the Senate censuring the president and the secretary of the treasury. An unprecedented action that has not yet reoccurred, the resolutions passed but were later expunged after the Democrats gained control of the upper house.

Clay also guided the passage of the Tariff of 1832, which South Carolina nullified. To help resolve the confrontation when South Carolina threatened secession if the government used force to win compliance, Clay worked out the Compromise Tariff of 1833. South Carolina then repealed its ordinance of nullification.

By 1834 the opponents of Jackson's Democratic party called themselves the Whig party. Clay was recognized as its leader, and he, Daniel Webster, and John C. Calhoun constituted the "Great Triumvirate" in the Senate. Clay exercised such control of the party and Congress that during the presidency of John Tyler he was denounced as a dictator. His efforts to legislate his American System into law, especially the rechartering of a national bank, triggered a series of presidential vetoes. Clay resigned from the Senate on 16 February 1842 to prepare for the presidential election of 1844.

Nominated by the Whigs in 1844 against Democratic candidate James K. Polk, Clay wrote a letter, the "Raleigh letter," opposing the annexation of Texas because of the possibility of war with Mexico. Then he wrote two more "Alabama letters," in which he seemed to reverse himself. His apparent straddling of this important issue cost him the election in a close contest. Polk won a mere 1.4 percent more of the popular vote than did Clay.

The Kentuckian's opposition to the Mexican War as well as his reputation as a loser prevented his nomination for president in 1848. Instead, the Kentucky legislature again elected him to the Senate on 5 February 1849. Two months later he celebrated his golden wedding anniversary.

Clay's home life was described by Harriet Martineau, the celebrated British writer, as "desolate." His wife hated the social life of Washington and refused to travel with him, preferring her domestic duties at home. Nor did she write to him. In his vast correspondence there are no letters from her, and he himself mentions receiving only one letter from her. Of the couple's eleven children, all six daughters died at an early age. The eldest son was committed to a "lunatic asylum," another suffered several mental breakdowns, and a third was an alcoholic. His favorite son, Henry Clay, Jr., was killed in the Mexican War. Following his son's death, Clay joined the Episcopal church.

Because the treaty ending the Mexican War brought a vast geographic expansion of the United States, including California and the New Mexico territory, and provoked a heated controversy over slavery, specifically the right of Congress to exclude slavery in these new territories, the nation faced the breakup of the Union when Clay returned to the Senate. The difficulties were compounded by the convention that was underway in Nashville to demand southern rights under threat of secession. Although Clay owned slaves all his life he abominated the "peculiar institution" and sought to bring about gradual emancipation through compensation. But he also favored returning blacks to Africa when they gained their freedom. He was a founding member of the American Colonization Society in 1816 and its president from 1836 until his death.

In his last great effort to produce a compromise by which secession and civil war could be prevented, Clay brought to the Senate a series of eight resolutions that dealt with California, New Mexico, Utah, the Texas boundary and debt, slavery in the District of Columbia, and fugitive slaves. These resolutions sought to provide both the North and the South with enough incentives to agree to a settlement. Packaged as an "omnibus" bill, it went down to defeat on 31 July 1850, but each resolution was then reintroduced as a separate bill, and Senator Stephen A. Douglas successfully shepherded all through Congress in the late summer. The Compromise of 1850 undoubtedly prevented secession.

Clay's extraordinary vision of an economically powerful and united nation was largely realized after his death. He succumbed to tuberculosis while living in a Washington hotel. Clay was the first man to lie in state in the Capitol rotunda.

• The largest single collection of Clay's papers is in the Library of Congress, but copies of virtually all known Clay documents have been collected at the University of Kentucky, and many of them are published in *The Papers of Henry Clay* (1959–1992). See also Calvin Colton, ed., *The Works of Henry Clay* (1857) and *The Private Correspondence of Henry Clay* (1856). A scholarly biography is Robert V. Remini, *Henry Clay: Statesman for the Union* (1991). Earlier biographies include Glyndon G. Van Deusen, *The Life of Henry Clay* (1937), and Clement Eaton, *Henry Clay and the Art of American Politics* (1957). Bernard Mayo, *Henry Clay: Spokesman of the New West* (1937), ends with the outbreak of the War of 1812. See also Daniel Walker Howe, *The Political Culture of the American Whigs* (1979); Thomas Brown, *Politics and Statesmanship: Essays on the American Whig Party* (1985); and Van Deusen, "Some Aspects of Whig Thought and Theory in the Jacksonian Period," *American Historical Review* 63 (1958): 305–22, for Clay's political and economic thinking.

ROBERT V. REMINI

CLAY, Laura (9 Feb. 1849–29 June 1941), farm manager and women's rights leader, was born at "White Hall," her family's estate, located between Lexington and Richmond, Kentucky, the daughter of Cassius M. Clay, a notable politician, emancipationist, and diplomat, and Mary Jane Warfield. Clay's formal education was interrupted by the outbreak of the Civil War, when the family accompanied her father to Russia, where he had been appointed U.S. minister. Returning to Kentucky in 1862, she attended Sayre School in Lexington, graduating in 1865. Aside from a year at a finishing school in New York City and brief stints of study at the Universities of Michigan and Kentucky, this completed her formal education. In 1873 she leased a 300-acre farm from her father and became its owner upon his death in 1903. Describing herself as a "practical farmer," she skillfully managed this rich Bluegrass land, deriving from it her own livelihood and most of the finances for her long public career.

Clay's commitment to women's rights arose from her parents' bitter divorce in 1878, which made her aware that the property and legal rights of Kentucky women, especially those who were married, were woefully inadequate. After considering careers in teaching, law, and the missionary field, Clay, who never married, decided to devote herself to the women's movement. In 1888 she took the leading role in organizing the Kentucky Equal Rights Association (KERA), which she served as president until 1912. Although the growth of the association was slow, by the mid-1890s its lobbying had won a number of legislative and educational victories, including protection of married women's property and wages, a requirement that there be women physicians in state female insane asylums, and the admission of women to a number of all-male colleges.

As an officer in both the Women's Christian Temperance Union and the Kentucky Federation of Women's Clubs, Clay persuaded those groups to join the KERA in advocating additional benefits for women and children. By the turn of the century their efforts had secured legislation that provided for a women's dormitory at the University of Kentucky, established juvenile courts and detention homes, and raised the age of sexual consent from twelve to sixteen years. Clay and other women activists saw the vote as the capstone of their movement. With the state legislature's grant of school suffrage in 1912, they won a partial victory in their long quest for full enfranchisement.

During the 1890s Clay became the best-known southern suffragist and the South's leading voice in the councils of the National American Woman Suffrage Association (NAWSA). Her efforts were largely responsible for the establishment of suffrage societies in nine of the former Confederate states. Clay addressed constitutional conventions in Mississippi and Louisiana and managed an unsuccessful NAWSA effort to add woman suffrage to the South Carolina constitution of 1895. In 1896 Clay was elected auditor of the NAWSA, a post she held for fifteen years. She maintained a position of moderation and conciliation on the NAWSA board in conflicts over both race and personality. As an unpaid NAWSA field worker, she also directed suffrage campaigns in Oregon, Oklahoma, and Arizona. While chair of the association's membership committee, she introduced recruiting innovations that almost tripled the number of members, from 17,000 in 1905 to 45,501 in 1907. In 1911 Clay lost her bid for reelection as auditor, following a dispute between the southern and western suffragists and those from the East over administrative and organizational matters. Contrary to some accounts, neither the race question nor the issue of the federal amendment versus the state route to enfranchisement figured in this dispute. Despite her removal from the board of the NAWSA, Clay continued to chair association committees, contributed to fund drives, and worked in numerous state suffrage campaigns.

In 1913 Clay was elected vice president at large of a new organization, the Southern States Woman Suffrage Conference, founded to win the vote through state enactment. Clay saw this organization as an auxiliary, not a rival, of the NAWSA, whose activities she continued to support. It was not until 1919, when the U.S. Congress passed the Nineteenth Amendment, that Clay withdrew from the NAWSA, turned her energies to securing a state suffrage bill in Kentucky, and began openly to oppose the federal bill. She based her opposition to it on states' rights, asserting that the Nineteenth Amendment was a vast and unneeded extension of federal power. A product of her time, Clay was a believer in Anglo-Saxon superiority but was paternalistic, rather than Negrophobic, in her attitudes.

After the ratification of the suffrage amendment, Clay continued to work for women's rights and the involvement of women in civic life. She helped organize the Democratic Women's Club of Kentucky, served as a delegate to the Democratic National Convention in 1920, and ran unsuccessfully for the state senate in 1923. A firm believer in women's church rights, she was instrumental in winning vestry and synod eligibility for women in the Lexington diocese of the Episcopal church. In the 1928 presidential campaign, she made a number of speeches for the Democratic nominee, Alfred E. Smith, and vigorously condemned national prohibition. She remained active in women's causes throughout the 1930s, especially championing equal pay for equal work. She died in Lexington, Kentucky, where she is buried.

From the time of her eleventh-hour opposition to the Nineteenth Amendment, Clay became a controversial and misunderstood figure, both to contemporaries and to later historians. This brief apostasy—occasioned by her belief in states' rights—has overshadowed Clay's important contributions to the struggle for women's rights at the state, regional, and national levels. Founder and longtime president of the Kentucky Equal Rights Association, leader of the national effort to organize the South for suffrage, and campaign organizer and officer of the National American Woman Suffrage Association for many years, Clay unselfishly and unstintingly devoted more than fifty years of her life to the cause of women's equality in America.

• The Laura Clay Papers, comprising the bulk of her letters from the 1880s to the 1930s, are located in the Margaret I. King Library of the University of Kentucky. Marjorie Spruill Wheeler's excellent study, *New Women of the New South* (1993), places Clay in the overall context of the suffrage movement in the South, and Paul E. Fuller, *Laura Clay and the Woman's Rights Movement* (1975; repr. 1992), attempts a broader coverage of her reform activities. An obituary is in the *New York Times*, 30 June 1941.

PAUL E. FULLER

CLAY, Lucius DuBignon (23 Apr. 1898–16 Apr. 1978), army general, was born in Marietta, Georgia, the son of Alexander Stephens Clay, a lawyer and three-term U.S. senator, and Sarah Frances White. Clay received his primary education in Marietta public schools and attended the University of Georgia for one year. He entered the U.S. Military Academy at West Point, New York, in 1915. Because of U.S. entry into World War I, the curriculum was curtailed, and Clay graduated near the top of his class in 1918 with a bachelor of science and a commission in the Engineer Corps. In 1918 he married Marjorie McKeown; they had two children. His early career included a number of military schools and engineering assignments at Camp Humphreys, Virginia, the Panama Canal Zone, and Pittsburgh, Pennsylvania. He was also an instructor at both Alabama Polytechnical Institute (now Auburn University) and West Point.

Clay was promoted to the permanent grade of captain in June 1933 and transferred to the River and Harbor Section of the Office of the Chief of Engineers in Washington, D.C. During the major work projects that began in 1933, he was responsible for the preparation of reports and estimates to Congress for river, harbor, and flood control projects throughout the United States. For the next four years, he was the Corps of Engineers spokesman to Congress, and he assisted presidential aide Harry Hopkins in establishing the Works Project Administration (WPA). In 1934 he was a delegate to the Permanent International Congress of Navigation at Brussels. During this period, Clay demonstrated uncommon administrative talents in highly visible positions within the Franklin D. Roosevelt administration.

From 1937 to 1938 Clay served on the staff of General Douglas MacArthur in the Philippines, acting as an adviser to the Philippine government on hydroelectric development. Upon returning to the United States in 1938, he served for two years as the district engineer at Denison, Texas, where he was responsible for the design and construction of the Red River dam project, which included a hydroelectric plant, a flood control reservoir, and Denison Dam, which is still one of the largest earth-filled dams in the United States.

Clay was promoted to major on 1 March 1940, and in October of that year he was appointed assistant to the administrator of the Civil Aeronautics Authority and secretary of the Airport Approval Board. In this capacity, he organized and directed the nationwide defense airport improvement program, improving or enlarging 277 airports and building 197 new airports in the United States, Alaska, and several Pacific Islands. This project, completed in less than two years, resulted in a national system of airports that proved invaluable to the U.S. war effort in World War II.

Clay was promoted to lieutenant colonel on 12 June 1941 and to colonel on 23 September 1941. His first wartime assignment was a mission to Brazil to ensure air bases to support the Allied war effort. Clay was promoted to brigadier general on 12 March 1942 and was assigned to General Staff duty in Washington as the deputy chief of staff for requirements and resources, Services of Supply. In July 1942 he was promoted to assistant chief of staff for materiel (later changed to director of materiel), Army Service Forces. His primary responsibilities in these assignments included supervising and directing the vast production and procurement programs to obtain army supplies and equipment. He worked closely with both administration officials on the War Production Board and civilian manufacturers. He wrote in *Fortune* magazine in February 1943, "Production must be controlled by the necessities of war; it should never dictate requirements." Clay believed that industry should respond to the needs of the armed services during war and not the other way around; he was instrumental in providing a framework that ensured American industry was responsive to America's war needs.

Having made a name for himself as the army's "prize troubleshooter," Clay was ordered to Europe in November 1944 to take command of the snarled supply bases in Normandy. He directed adjustments that resulted in an immediate doubling and then tripling of thru-put capacity (the capacity to receive, process, and disseminate supplies) of the port at Cherbourg, which provided the materiel and supplies for the Allied thrust into Germany.

In December 1944 Clay was recalled to Washington, where he became an aide to James F. Byrnes in the position of deputy director of war programs and general administration in the Office of War Mobilization and Reconversion. He took a leave of absence from the army while in that post and became what one reporter described as the "third most powerful" man in the United States, after the president and Byrnes. He was responsible for the coordination of all governmental agencies in the exercise of their war production responsibilities. Criticized for his direct manner and "military first" perspective, Clay nevertheless made sure that those at the fighting fronts had everything they needed.

In March 1945 Clay returned to the army as General Dwight Eisenhower's deputy for military government, directing civil-military affairs in the U.S. zone of occupation in southern Germany. He was promoted to lieutenant general in April 1945 and named the deputy military governor of the American zone of occupied Germany under theater commander General Joseph T. McNarney. Clay was responsible for establishing all aspects of military government in the U.S. zone, including food, housing, health, currency, industry, refugees, denazification, and restoration of German self-rule.

In March 1947 Clay was promoted to general and succeeded McNarney as military governor and theater commander of all U.S. forces in occupied Germany and Europe. As deputy and then military governor, Clay operated with little or no guidance from Washington. He and his political adviser, Robert Murphy of the State Department, often broke new ground but fostered an environment that would eventually lead to the establishment of a viable German state. In 1948 Clay instituted West German currency reform and took steps to draw up a West German constitution.

As commander in chief of U.S. forces in occupied Germany, Clay sat on the Allied Kommandatura, the body responsible for overall Allied occupation policy. He ran into difficulties with the French and Soviets, who resisted Clay's efforts to reestablish centralized functions within Germany. They were slower to allow the Germans to return to the beginning of self-rule, and both opposed the reunification of Germany. By early 1948 Soviet attitudes had become bellicose, and Clay warned Washington that the Soviets might try something. His premonition proved prescient in June, when the Soviets first restricted and then blocked ground access to West Berlin. Acting on his own initiative as commander in chief of U.S. forces in Europe, Clay ordered the initiation of Operation Vittles, a massive airlift of food, fuel, and other supplies that kept the city functioning. The around-the-clock airlift lasted until May 1949 and took in over two million tons of food, supplies, and military reinforcements. Hailed as the savior of Berlin, Clay departed Germany on 15 May 1949 with a hero's farewell from the German people and a ticker-tape parade in New York City.

Upon his return to the United States in 1950, Clay retired from the army and became the chairman of the board and chief executive officer of the Continental Can Company. Holding that position until 1962, he built the company into a billion-dollar multinational business. From 1963 to 1973 he was a senior partner in the investment banking firm of Lehman Brothers.

During the years after his retirement from the military, Clay was a frequent adviser at the highest government levels. In 1952 he helped convince Eisenhower to run for president and subsequently assisted in organizing his campaign. After the election, he played a major role in helping Eisenhower put together his cabinet. He frequently advised the Eisenhower administration on matters concerning Berlin. In 1961, when the Soviets built a wall around East Berlin to stem the flow of East Berliners to the West, President John F. Kennedy named Clay as his presidential representative with the rank of ambassador for a mission to West Berlin. While there, Clay dealt with a number of crises that demonstrated the U.S. intention to maintain its occupation rights in Berlin while continuing to support the West Berliners. He returned to the United States in May 1962, continuing as a governmental adviser and remaining active in a number of civic groups, including the Red Cross and the Public Development Corporation of New York City, until his death in Chatham, Massachusetts.

Clay was an outstanding engineer, administrator, businessman, diplomat, and army leader who, according to former secretary of state Byrnes, "could run either General Motors or General Eisenhower's armies." According to the *Washington Post*, "Lucius D. Clay played a pivotal role in three epochal events of the twentieth century: the rescue of America from Depression, the mobilization for World War II, and—his crowning achievement—the rehabilitation of West Germany." His sixty years of dedicated and selfless public service left an indelible mark on post–World War II America as well as on America's European allies.

• Lucius D. Clay Papers are in the National Archives, Washington, D.C., and at the Marshall Foundation, Lexington, Va. Selected papers are published as *The Papers of General Lucius D. Clay: Germany, 1945–1949*, ed. Jean Edward Smith (2 vols., 1974). Clay wrote of his experiences as military governor in *Decision in Germany* (1950). The most comprehensive biography of Clay is Jean Edward Smith, *Lucius D. Clay: An American Life* (1990). A detailed account of the rebuilding of West Germany is in John Gimbel, *The American Occupation of Germany: Politics and the Military, 1945–1949* (1968). An obituary is in the *New York Times*, 17 Apr. 1978.

JAMES H. WILLBANKS

CLAY, Lucius DuBignon, Jr. (6 July 1919–7 Feb. 1994), U.S. Air Force general, was born in Alexandria, Virginia, the son of Lucius D. Clay, Sr., an army general, and Marjorie McKeown. Clay, Jr., lived the life of an army "brat," but, as the son of an engineer officer, he spent more time in nonmilitary environments than most peers whose fathers served in other branches. He attended Western High School in Washington, D.C., and finished his secondary education at Valley Forge Military Academy in Pennsylvania. Clay first entered the U.S. Military Academy at West Point,

New York, in 1937 as a member of the class of 1941, but he was turned back his plebe (freshman) year and finished with the class of 1942.

After graduation from West Point in June, Clay opted for the army air corps and received his pilot wings at Lubbock, Texas, in December 1942. After additional flight training in bombers, he was assigned in June 1943 to the 616th Bombardment Squadron at McDill Field, Florida. While there he married Betty Rose Commander of Tampa. They had four children. He moved with his squadron to Lakeland, Florida; Hunter Field, Georgia; and then to the European Theater of Operations of World War II. From early 1944 until February 1946 Clay served with the 344th Bombardment Group, successively as operations officer, squadron commander, and group commander. During this period Clay flew more than sixty combat missions in support of the D-Day invasion, the breakout at St. Lo, and the Battle of the Bulge. Following the end of the war, Clay remained in Germany and served as deputy commander and deputy for base services with the European Air Depot in Erding.

Upon his return to the United States, Clay served in a variety of increasingly important command and staff positions in the newly established U.S. Air Force. In February 1947 he served on the staff of the deputy chief of staff, Operations for Atomic Energy, Headquarters, U.S. Air Force. In June 1952, after three years at the Air War College in Alabama, he went to the Pentagon as a member of the Joint Strategic Plans Group of the Joint Chiefs of Staff. He later was assigned as chief of the Joint Plans Division, Deputy Chief of Staff Operations Headquarters U.S. Air Force. From the Pentagon he was transferred to Ramey Air Force Base in Puerto Rico, where he served as deputy commander of the Seventy-second Bombardment Wing (B-36s). Upon departing Puerto Rico in 1958, he was assigned as chief of Plans Division at Headquarters Strategic Air Command at Offut Air Force Base, Nebraska. From 1961 through 1964 he served once more with the Joint Chiefs of Staff, where he became the deputy director of operations.

On 1 August 1964 Clay became the first member of his West Point class to win a brigadier general's star. He was subsequently reassigned to Waco, Texas, as vice commander of the Twelfth Air Force; in January 1966 he moved up to assume command of the Twelfth Air Force. In July of the same year Clay returned to the Pentagon for duty with the air force staff, becoming in 1969 the deputy chief of staff for plans and operations.

Subsequently, after a short stint as vice commander in chief, Pacific Air Forces, Clay assumed command in September 1970 of the Seventh Air Force at Tan Son Nhut Airfield, Republic of Vietnam, serving also as deputy commander for operations, U.S. Military Assistance Command Vietnam. On 1 August 1971 he became commander in chief, Pacific Air Forces. His last assignment was for two years as commander in chief, North American Defense Command, in Colora-do Springs, Colorado; Clay and his wife settled there. He retired from active duty on 1 September 1975.

In 1990 they moved to Alexandria, Virginia, on account of Clay's deteriorating lung condition. Shortly after arriving in Virginia, his wife died. Clay died in Alexandria.

Clay was a gifted combat leader who commanded a bomb squadron at the age of twenty-three and rose to the rank of general. During the postwar years, he played a pivotal role in the establishment of the U.S. Air Force and the development of American airpower.

• Although Clay did not write of his experiences, his early years are covered in the biography of his father, Jean Edward Smith, *Lucius D. Clay—An American Life* (1990). The development of the air force, in which Clay played a significant role, is discussed in Carroll V. Glines, *The Compact History of the United States Air Force* (1963).

JAMES H. WILLBANKS

CLAY, Matthew (25 Mar. 1754–27 May 1815), U.S. congressman, was born in western Halifax County (later Pittsylvania County) near Danville, Virginia, the son of Charles Clay and Martha Green, planters. His grandfather, Henry Clay, participated with Nathaniel Bacon in the 1676 rebellion against Governor William Berkeley; his father's brother was the grandfather of the famous statesman Henry Clay of Kentucky.

Like most inhabitants of the eighteenth-century Virginia frontier, Clay had limited opportunities for formal schooling. He acquired a basic education but did not attend college. A young man when the American Revolution began, he enlisted in the Continental army in October 1776 as an ensign in the Ninth Virginia Regiment. He was transferred to the First Virginia Line in 1778 as regimental quartermaster and ended his service with the Fifth Virginia, which he joined in 1781. When he was mustered out in 1783 he retired at a first lieutenant's half-pay for life and was awarded 3,680.66 acres of bounty land in the Virginia military district of Ohio.

During his military service Clay witnessed firsthand the difficulty of fighting a war with a poorly trained militia. Although he was a founding member of the Society of the Cincinnati and believed strongly in the citizen-soldier concept, he did not believe that the militia, as it was then constituted, could adequately defend the nation against its enemies.

After the Revolution Clay resided for a time in Richmond, Virginia, where he read law while clerking in the state auditor's office. After gaining admission to the bar he returned home to Pittsylvania County to practice law and farm. In 1788 he married Mary "Polly" Williams, the niece and ward of Colonel Robert Williams, one of the county's wealthiest planters; they had three children. Mary died in childbirth in 1798, and Clay subsequently married Ann Saunders (date unknown); they had one child. After his second wife died in 1806 at the age of twenty-two, Clay was grief stricken and did not marry again.

From 1788 to 1790 Clay stayed busy managing his tobacco plantation and practicing law. But he was drawn to politics. With support from Williams, his wife's influential guardian, he won a seat in 1790 in the Virginia House of Delegates, where he served two terms (1790–1794). His most notable activity there was authoring a bill disposing of all unused glebe lands of the pre-Revolution established church. Thus he had a hand in completing the separation of church and state, which Thomas Jefferson had begun in 1779. He also played a major role in obtaining legislative authorization in 1793 to establish the tobacco inspection depot that became the town of Danville.

In 1796 Clay won election to Congress from the Sixth Congressional District of Virginia, which consisted of the southside counties of Halifax, Pittsylvania, and Campbell. He was reelected to the seven succeeding Congresses, sitting without interruption from 1797 to 1813.

A Republican, Clay entered the House of Representatives just as the United States's quasi war with France strengthened the political hand of the Federalist party. In 1798 Federalists passed the repressive alien and sedition laws along with a series of war preparedness measures, which included establishing a larger military and a direct tax to pay for the anticipated war. Clay opposed these measures, but before they came to a vote he was called home because his wife had died. By the time he resumed his seat in early 1799, the Federalists had passed their program, leaving nothing for Clay and his party to do except work for Republican victory in the upcoming election of 1800.

Jefferson carried Clay's district overwhelmingly. Clay took his seat in the newly elected, Republican-controlled Sixth Congress as a political conservative who strongly endorsed the "Principles of '98"—strict construction of the Constitution and economy of government. On most issues he stood solidly with the Republican majority. He voted for repeal of the Judiciary Act of 1801, applauded Jefferson's reduction of the public debt, favored the Louisiana Purchase, supported the Embargo of 1807, and voted against rechartering the national bank in 1811. He frequently sided with John Randolph and the "Quids," opposing, for example, Jefferson's compromise proposal to compensate claimants in the Yazoo land fraud and favoring James Monroe over James Madison for president in 1808. But he never allied himself permanently with the Old Republican faction.

Only in his oft-expressed views regarding the military did Clay consistently differ with the Republican majority. He repeatedly called for a complete reorganization of the militia. Training, discipline, organization, and leadership were all deficient. As chairman of the House Committee on the Militia he worked to achieve the desired changes. His pleas for reform fell on deaf ears. Not until the War of 1812 had almost disastrously revealed the weakness of the militia system and the error of Republican faith in the citizen army did Congress finally institute reforms.

Although he is not thought of as a war hawk, Clay was in fact a strong supporter of the war. He voted for most of the military preparedness measures that Congress passed in 1811–1812, including the tax increase needed to finance the war. He revealed the extent of his hawkish, expansionist sentiments when he told his congressional colleagues: "I am not for stopping at Quebec or anywhere else; but I would take the whole continent from them [Britain] and ask no favors. . . . If we get the continent, she must allow us the freedom of the sea."

Inexplicably, Clay abstained from the 4 June vote declaring war. Apparently he thought the country required more time to prepare for the conflict. Whatever the reason, he heartily supported the war once it began. "It is a righteous war into which I go with hand and heart," he told his House colleagues in January 1813. But Clay's constituents were unhappy with his abstention and did not return him to Congress in 1813. They reelected him to the postwar Fourteenth Congress, which convened in December 1815, but before he could take his seat he died suddenly while traveling to Halifax Courthouse to make a political speech.

• The principal collection of Clay's papers is the Matthew Clay Papers, 1758–1834, which consists of twenty-seven items and is located in the Mississippi Department of Archives and History in Jackson. The collection contains political announcements and broadsides, speeches, and Clay's correspondence with friends and political constituents. The Stuart Family Papers, 1758–1881, at the Virginia Historical Society in Richmond, and the James Monroe Papers at the Library of Congress, contain some Clay correspondence. Lawrence W. Williamson, "Matthew Clay: Old School Republican" (master's thesis, Virginia Polytechnic Institute and State Univ., 1984), offers a full account of his life and work. Some useful information about Clay can be gleaned from Maud Carter Clement, *The History of Pittsylvania County, Virginia* (1929), Daniel P. Jordan, *Political Leadership in Jefferson's Virginia* (1983), and Norman K. Risjord, *The Old Republicans: Southern Conservatism in the Age of Jefferson* (1965). An obituary is in the *Richmond Enquirer*, 10 June 1815.

CHARLES D. LOWERY

CLAY-CLOPTON, Virginia Tunstall (16 Jan. 1825–23 June 1915), society leader, author, and suffragist, was born Virginia Caroline Tunstall in Nash County, North Carolina, the daughter of Peyton Randolph Tunstall, a physician, and Ann Arrington. She lost her mother before the age of three, and her father left her upbringing to her maternal relatives in Tuscaloosa, Alabama. Initially she lived with her aunt, the wife of Henry Collier, who became chief justice of Alabama's supreme court and later its governor. Later she moved to the home of her uncle Alfred Battle, a planter. She graduated in 1840 from the Female Academy in Nashville, Tennessee.

In 1842 Virginia met Clement Claiborne Clay of Huntsville, Alabama. After a brief courtship, the Clays were married in 1843. For the next ten years the couple lived in Huntsville; Clement Clay served one term in the state legislature and subsequently practiced law. After his 1853 election to the U.S. Senate, the Clays moved to Washington, D.C. Shortly after the long trip Virginia Clay delivered a stillborn daughter, the couple's only child.

Washington provided Virginia Clay with diversions, and her social accomplishments quickly propelled her into a leading role in society. In her memoirs she described her "rich and exclusive" social circle, which included Senator and Mrs. Jefferson Davis, President and Mrs. Franklin Pierce, Senator and Mrs. James Chesnut, and Mr. and Mrs. Roger A. Pryor. Like her contemporary and friend Mary Boykin Chesnut, Clay's childlessness and lack of a home to manage gave her ample time to play the belle despite her married status. Vain and elitist, Clay relished her position and the social bustle of the capital. Her company was widely sought by both men and women who enjoyed her wit, intelligence, and brilliant conversation.

As sectional tensions mounted in Washington in 1860, Clement Clay was forced to take a year off to recuperate from asthmatic seizures and chronic poor health. In 1861 Clay, a strong supporter of slavery and states' rights, resigned from the Senate after Alabama seceded from the Union. Later that year he was elected to the newly formed Confederate Senate in Richmond, Virginia. Following the 1862 Union occupation of Huntsville, Virginia Clay spent the remainder of the war living with friends and relatives in Georgia and South Carolina. A comfortable refugee given to extravagance, she periodically joined her husband in Richmond, where she entered the social circle surrounding Confederate first lady Varina Howell Davis and recaptured her social radiance. She eschewed the charitable wartime activities to which many women of her class devoted their time.

As the war progressed the Clays' financial problems intensified, and Clement Clay's political career declined. His bid for reelection was unsuccessful, and when his term ended in 1864, Jefferson Davis appointed him a member of a delegation to Canada charged with fomenting Copperhead opposition to Abraham Lincoln in the Old Northwest. In 1865 Clement Clay returned and surrendered to federal authorities in Georgia after hearing of a proclamation calling for the arrest of himself, other delegation members, and Davis. He and Davis were incarcerated in Fort Monroe, Virginia, in 1865, accused of participating in the plot to assassinate President Lincoln. Virginia Clay helped to secure her husband's release eleven months later, having tirelessly written letters to important figures and former friends and making numerous personal appeals to President Andrew Johnson.

The couple returned to Huntsville, where they faced a loss of position, staggering debts, and Clement Clay's defunct political career. Clement's health and spirits deteriorated, but the bond between the couple flourished. Virginia Clay became the stronger party in the marriage, maintaining her vivacity and optimism, accommodating to postwar changes in her cherished way of life, and to some extent assuming her husband's political mantle. Potential candidates sought her endorsement. Discontented on the farm where Clement Clay spent most of his time, she often traveled to visit friends, both before and after Clement's

death in 1882, touring Europe in 1884. In 1887 she married twice-widowed David Clopton, a friend and former political colleague of her first husband. She resided in Montgomery until Clopton died suddenly in 1892.

Virginia Clay-Clopton (the surname she now adopted) returned to the Huntsville plantation cottage she called "Wildwood" and maintained an active life there. She traveled when she could, delighting in the reunions held by Confederate organizations. However, she was no longer simply a socialite; convinced that women had an unrecognized aptitude for politics, she joined the woman suffrage crusade. Clay-Clopton, then in her seventies, was president of the Alabama Woman Suffrage Association from 1896 to 1900. Although she was not publicly active in the movement, her name held tremendous clout and bolstered the cause. In 1890, with the assistance of journalist Ada Sterling, she began working on her memoirs, published in 1904 as *A Belle of the Fifties*; it focuses on the years 1853 to 1866. She died at Wildwood.

Virginia and Clement Clay, like many southerners of their class, had a difficult adjustment to make in the postwar years. Virginia successfully adapted to the changing South, while her husband retired to his plantation discouraged and disillusioned. She represents a group of southern women who emerged from the war with an expanded sense of self-worth, political consciousness, and increased power in their marriages, a departure from their circumscribed antebellum lives. She not only demonstrated resilience in adversity but despite her background came to believe in political equality for women. Her talents impressed even Jefferson Davis, who wrote to her in 1870, "When woman's rights become the law of the land, you will become an available southern candidate for the Presidency."

• The Clay Family Papers are at the Duke University Library. Ruth Ketring Nuermberger, *The Clays of Alabama: A Planter-Lawyer-Politician Family* (1958), and Bell Irvin Wiley, *Confederate Women* (1975), are important sources. Sara Agnes Rice Pryor, *Reminiscences of Peace and War* (1905), describes Washington and Richmond social life and mentions Clay-Clopton's role in both capitals. See Carol K. Bleser and Frederick M. Heath, "The Impact of the Civil War on a Southern Marriage: Clement and Virginia Tunstall Clay of Alabama," *Civil War History* 30 (Sept. 1984): 197–220, for an assessment of the Clays' marriage. For her suffrage activities see Lee N. Allen, "The Woman Suffrage Movement in Alabama, 1910–1920," *Alabama Review* 2 (Apr. 1958): 83–84; and Elizabeth Cady Stanton et al., *History of Woman Suffrage*, vol. 4 (1902), pp. 465–69, 926, and vol. 6 (1922), pp. 1–3. An obituary is in the *Mobile Daily Register*, 25 June 1915.

LIBRA HILDE

CLAYTON, Augustin Smith (27 Nov. 1783–21 June 1839), lawyer and politician, was born in Fredericksburg, Virginia, the son of Philip Clayton and Mildred Dixon. The family soon moved to Richmond County, Georgia, and in 1804 Clayton was in the first graduating class at that state's university. He read law and was admitted to the bar in 1806. After marrying Julia

Carnes in 1807, he moved to Athens, where he remained active in civic affairs and raised nine children. From 1809 until his death he was associated with the University of Georgia, first as treasurer and land agent to the Board of Trustees and after 1815 as a trustee.

Clayton was chosen by the legislature in December 1809 to compile a digest of Georgia laws adopted since 1800. (The digest was published in 1812.) From 1810 to 1812 he represented Clarke County in the Georgia House of Representatives, in which he introduced in 1811 a bill giving state courts jurisdiction over criminal offenses committed within Indian territory. He served as clerk of the House from 1813 to 1815.

In 1819 Clayton published a manual for Georgia justices of the peace and other local officials, and the legislature elected him a judge of the Superior Courts of the Western Circuit. Reelected in 1822, he served until November 1825.

Active in the Georgia political party led by George M. Troup, Clayton was elected as a Troupite to the state senate in 1826 and 1827. He chaired the Judiciary Committee, introduced legislation on legal matters and education, and favored an expanded suffrage and lower taxes. He supported Governor Troup's resistance to federal authority in Indian affairs both in the legislature and in a series of newspaper essays written under the pseudonym "Atticus." Although as a state senator Clayton had voted twice against resolutions recommending Andrew Jackson for president, he was on the Troupite ticket of presidential electors pledged to Jackson in 1828.

The legislature returned Clayton to the bench in November 1828. He presided over the courts in the frontier counties bordering Cherokee territory as Georgia extended state jurisdiction over Indian territory in an effort to force the tribe to move west of the Mississippi River with aid from the United States. In 1830 Clayton ruled that Georgia's extension of jurisdiction over the Cherokee was constitutional because the state had the right "to territory, jurisdiction or sovereignty, over the people, red, black, or white, citizen or alien, found within its acknowledged limits." He accordingly sentenced the Cherokee George Tassels to death for a murder committed in Indian territory and sentenced to prison Samuel A. Worcester and several other missionaries for remaining in Cherokee territory without the required license from the governor of Georgia. In 1831, however, Clayton released the Cherokee Canatoo, who had been arrested for digging gold on his property, concluding that the state law protecting Indians in the peaceable possession of their homes superseded that prohibiting their digging of gold. The decision cost him reelection in November 1831.

On 12 December Clayton was sent to Congress in a special election. He took his seat in the House of Representatives on 21 January 1832, serving until 3 March 1835. A slaveholder, he was an outspoken advocate of southern interests, strict construction, and states' rights. Clayton vigorously attacked the Second Bank of the United States and the protective tariff on constitutional and sectional grounds. While joining with the Jacksonians in 1832 to block recharter of the bank, he soon broke with the Democrats. He opposed Jackson's Nullification Proclamation and the Force Bill, feared that Jackson was becoming a tyrant, and criticized the president's abuse of patronage. He insisted that the federal government lacked the power to deposit its funds in either the Bank of the United States or state banks; the only constitutional course was a complete separation of the United States from all banks. He also attacked government waste, corruption, and special privilege for government officials.

From 1829 Clayton was part owner of a cotton mill in Athens. He helped bring the Georgia Railroad to his hometown, was a delegate to the Georgia state rights convention in 1832, and was active in the reorganization of the Troup party into a states' rights party (which evolved into the Georgia Whig Party). As one of the few prominent advocates of nullification in Georgia, the unpopularity of his extremist views convinced him to withdraw his candidacy for governor in 1835. There is some evidence that he was the ghost writer for David Crockett's 1835 polemic, *The Life of Martin Van Buren, Heir-Apparent to the "Government," and the Appointed Successor of General Andrew Jackson*. He suffered a paralytic stroke in 1838 and died in Athens the next year.

• Clayton letters are in the Henry Jackson papers, University of Georgia; the Robert Watkins Lovett papers and Georgia Political Leaders Autographs, Emory University; the Tazewell family papers, Virginia State Library; the Mellen Chamberlain Collection, Boston Public Library; and File II, Names, Georgia Department of Archives and History. His judicial opinions appear in the *Athenian*, 23 March and 22 June 1830; 11 and 18 Oct. 1831; in the *Niles' Weekly Register*, 2 Oct. 1830 and 4 June 1831; and in the Macon *Georgia Messenger*, 20 Nov. 1830. Several of Clayton's lengthy congressional speeches appeared as pamphlets. He wrote *The Mysterious Picture* (1825), a fictional work appearing under the pseudonym Wrangham Fitz-Ramble. His "Atticus" essays were published with a prefatory address to the people of Georgia as *A Vindication of the Recent and Prevailing Policy of the State of Georgia, Both in Reference to Its Internal Affairs, and Its Relations with the General Government* (1827). In 1830 he issued a *Review of the Report of the Committee of Ways and Means, to Whom Was Referred So Much of the Message of the President, as Related to the Bank*. . . . A biographical sketch of Clayton is in Stephen F. Miller, *The Bench and Bar of Georgia* . . . (1858). See also Paul Murray, *The Whig Party in Georgia, 1825–1853* (1948), and the editorial by John O. Eidson, *Georgia Review* 9 (1955): 247–49.

CHARLES H. SCHOENLEBER

CLAYTON, Buck (12 Nov. 1911–8 Dec. 1991), jazz trumpeter and arranger, was born Wilbur Dorsey Clayton in Parsons, Kansas, the son of Simeon Oliver Clayton, a musician, and Aritha Anne Dorsey, a schoolteacher, pianist, and singer. His father's church orchestra rehearsed at their home, and in his youth Clayton experimented with different instruments, learning their basic scales. He took piano lessons from ages six to eighteen. At about age sixteen he was deeply impressed by a trumpeter in George E. Lee's big band, and he decided to take up that instrument.

Before graduating from high school, Clayton hoboed by train to Los Angeles. Failing in his attempt to secure work as a musician, he returned home, resumed his schooling, and graduated, probably in about 1932. On his second attempt at Los Angeles, Clayton succeeded as a trumpeter, holding a long engagement in a dime-a-dance hall, the Red Mill, until it burned down. He then became a member of Charlie Echols's big band for over a year, during which time he began to learn to orchestrate for big bands. As work diminished for Echols, Clayton began performing on Hollywood movie soundtracks and at local clubs with Earl Dancer's band, until Dancer's habitual gambling problems forced all his employees to mutiny and disband in 1934.

Shortly thereafter Clayton secured a job as a bandleader in Shanghai, China. Just before leaving, he and a dancer named Gladys Henderson (known as "Derb") obtained a marriage license, but they were unsure about marrying. Duke Ellington forced the issue by staging the marriage as a grand publicity event at Paramount Studios, without Clayton's prior knowledge.

Clayton's band held residencies in Shanghai from 1934 into 1936. Returning once again to Los Angeles, he led bands but soon decided to seek the more challenging musical scene in New York City. En route in midsummer 1936, he stopped in Kansas City, Missouri, and met pianist Count Basie and his band. They had heard Clayton on radio broadcasts from California, and since trumpeter Hot Lips Page had recently left the group, Basie asked Clayton if he would join. Clayton went to Parsons to visit his family and then returned to Kansas City to join Basie at the Reno Club, thus becoming a featured soloist in what was about to become one of jazz's greatest ensembles.

A few months later Basie left on a tour designed to get the band in shape for New York. In Chicago the group had a disastrous experience trying to serve as the pit orchestra for a show at the Grand Terrace Ballroom, owing to the poor musical reading skills of some members of the ensemble, newly expanded to suit New York demands for a big band. Clayton, one of the best readers, wore his lip out trying to cover for others and hence was unable to appear on Basie's legendary small-group recording, made in Chicago in October 1936 under the name of Jones-Smith Inc., with trumpeter Carl "Tatti" Smith taking Clayton's place.

On 24 December 1936 Basie made his debut in New York, where Clayton's wife was then working. Soon afterward she left him permanently. Over the next six years Clayton's career followed Basie's energetic routine of extensive national touring. During this time Clayton contributed memorable solos on "Swingin' at the Daisy Chain," "One O'Clock Jump," "Topsy" (all 1937), "Sent for You Yesterday," "Jumpin' at the Woodside" (both 1938), "Dickie's Dream" (1939), and "Goin' to Chicago Blues" (1941; arranged by Clayton). He may be seen with the band in the film *Reveille with Beverly* (1943). Clayton also recorded apart from Basie, but not extensively. The most notable sessions were as a sideman accompanying singer Billie Holiday in Teddy Wilson's groups and her own, including versions of "Why Was I Born?" "Getting Some Fun out of Life," "He's Funny That Way" (all 1937), "My First Impression of You," and "If Dreams Come True" (both 1938). Clayton became one of Holiday's closest friends; in her autobiography she called him "the prettiest man I'd ever seen."

Drafted into the army in November 1943, Clayton was stationed in New Jersey until the end of the war, playing in army bands. Early in 1946, soon after his discharge, he finally obtained his divorce from Derb and immediately married Patricia Roberta DeVigne; they had two children. In October 1946 he made the first of several tours with Jazz at the Philharmonic. The following year he established a sextet at Cafe Society in New York. From September 1949 to April 1950 Clayton toured Europe with his group.

After returning home, Clayton continued his work as a leader while also playing in clarinetist Tony Parenti's Dixieland band and holding a residency at the Embers Club as a member of pianist Joey Bushkin's quartet. In February 1953 he embarked on a lengthy European tour, working first with clarinetist Mezz Mezzrow, continuing with singer Frank Sinatra, and visiting Sweden with singer Babs Gonzales.

Back in New York at year's end, Clayton was asked by promoter John Hammond to head a series of long-playing jam sessions recorded for the Columbia label, including *The Huckle-buck and Robbins' Nest* (1953). Extending to 1956, these sessions, together with contemporary ones recorded by fellow ex-Basie trombonist Vic Dickenson for the Vanguard label, became the central documents of "mainstream jazz," amalgamating swing and Dixieland styles. During this period Clayton held further residencies in New York and made regional tours, including one with Bushkin. He appeared in the movie *The Benny Goodman Story* (1955) and toured with Goodman to South America.

Clayton performed in April 1958 on the television series "The Subject Is Jazz," early in July at the Newport Jazz Festival (preserved on the film *Jazz on a Summer's Day* [1958]), and again on television in mid-July on "Art Ford's Jazz Party," with Holiday's group. Late that same month he traveled with promoter and pianist George Wein's band to the Brussels World's Fair, where they worked with reed player Sidney Bechet. Clayton performed in London in September 1959. Later that year he joined guitarist Eddie Condon's band in New York. He worked with pianist Marian McPartland's trio, with Dickenson, and with tenor saxophonist Bud Freeman. Sometimes he played in all-star swing and Dixieland bands at the Central Plaza and Stuyvesant Casino in New York.

During the first of his annual European tours during the 1960s, Clayton made the film *Buck Clayton and His All Stars* (1961) in Belgium. He toured with singer Jimmy Rushing in the summer of 1962. That November he went with Condon to Toronto, where he subsequently led his own band. From 1963 he often worked with English trumpeter Humphrey Lyttelton during his European tours, moments of which were captured on the British television series "Jazz 625" (1965) and "Jazz Goes to College" (1966 and 1967). Clayton also toured Japan and Australia with Condon in 1964, and he participated in American jazz festivals.

From 1967 Clayton suffered various illnesses, including hernias, severe lip troubles, and later, a near-fatal ulcer. He virtually abandoned the trumpet and instead held day jobs of little interest to him. He managed to play trumpet for the film *L'Adventure* [*sic*] *du jazz* (1970), and he was interviewed for the film *Born to Swing* (1973). After undergoing major dental work in 1974, Clayton began to focus on writing arrangements. He resumed playing for a State Department sponsored tour to Africa in 1977 but finally gave up playing after performing at the Grande Parade du Jazz in Nice in 1979.

From 1978 to 1982 Clayton taught at the Hunter College campus of the City University of New York. In 1983 he joined the Countsmen for a European tour, for which he served as leader, arranger, and conductor. After writing further arrangements for a small group, Clayton established his own big band in 1987. Writing many new scores for it, he remained active up to the weekend of his death in New York City.

Clayton was a controlled, tasteful, nearly perfect trumpeter who adopted moderated elements of Louis Armstrong's style. He never achieved the mind-boggling originality and audacity of Armstrong in his melodies, but in his ever-present tunefulness he had the good taste to avoid Armstrong's propensity for gaudy technical displays.

Clayton complained that he came to hate the cup mute, because Basie always wanted him to record with it (although Basie did not mind if Clayton played unmuted in public performance). Perhaps the truth is somewhat more complicated, since he used the device routinely in Basie's absence, on the sessions with Holiday. The several aforementioned Holiday titles encapsulate his style, ranging from simple renderings of pop song melodies to tricky improvised lines, and from delicate muted embroideries barely heard beneath Holiday's voice to forceful, unmuted leadership of collectively improvised passages.

• Clayton's oral history, taken by interviewer Stanley Dance (c. 1975), is at the Institute of Jazz Studies, Newark, N.J. His autobiography is coauthored by Nancy Miller Elliott, *Buck Clayton's Jazz World* (1986); Elliott is donating Clayton's papers to the institute. Clayton recalls his relationship with Holiday in the foreword to John Chilton, *The Billie Holiday Story* (1975). Numerous brief surveys and interviews complement these sources: George Hoefer, "A Brief Biography of Buck Clayton," *Down Beat*, 19 Jan. 1961, pp. 16–17; Albert J. McCarthy, "Buck Clayton: The Post-Basie Period," *Jazz Monthly*, Apr. 1961, pp. 4–8; Helen McNamara, "Travelin' Man," *Down Beat*, 4 June 1964, pp. 13–15; Valerie Wilmer, *Jazz People* (1970), pp. 123–30; Bob Rusch, "Buck Clayton: Interview," *Cadence*, June 1977, pp. 11–14; "Buck Clayton: The Good Road Back," *Crescendo International*, Sept. 1979, p. 8; Stanley Dance, *The World of Count Basie* (1980), pp. 37–46; Chris Sheridan, *Count Basie: A Bio-Discography* (1986); Chip Deffaa, "Buck and Basie," *Mississippi Rag*, Oct. 1986, pp. 1–2; Deffaa, "Clayton Bucks the Tide," *Crescendo*

International, Sept. 1989, pp. 4–6; Deffaa, "Buck Clayton Is Back," *Coda*, June–July 1990, pp. 26–27; and Dan Morgenstern, album pamphlet notes to *The Complete CBS Buck Clayton Jam Sessions*. For musical analysis, see Gunther Schuller, *The Swing Era: The Development of Jazz, 1930–1945* (1989). A catalog of his recordings is Bob Weir, *Buck Clayton: A Discography* (1989). An obituary is in the *New York Times*, 12 Dec. 1991.

BARRY KERNFELD

CLAYTON, Henry De Lamar (10 Feb. 1857–21 Dec. 1929), congressman and judge, was born in Barbour County, Alabama, the son of Henry De Lamar Clayton and Victoria Virginia Hunter. His father was a lawyer, a major general in the Confederate army, and president of the University of Alabama from 1886 to 1889. His mother was also devoted to the Confederate cause and was the author of *White and Black under the Old Regime* (1899), a defense of the Old South and the paternalistic race relations under the slave system. In 1875 young Henry entered the University of Alabama, earning his A.B. in 1877 and a law degree one year later. He then began the practice of law in the Barbour County seat of Clayton. From 1880 to 1884 he held the office of county registrar in chancery. In 1882 he married Virginia Ball Allen, who died one year later. A second marriage to Bettie Davis followed in 1910. There is no record of children in either marriage.

In 1888 Clayton became Democratic national committeeman from Alabama and from 1890 to 1891 served a term in the state house of representatives. When Grover Cleveland resumed the presidency in 1893, he appointed Clayton U.S. attorney for the middle district of Alabama. Clayton held this post for three years, but in 1896 he split with the Cleveland wing of the Democratic party and became a devoted convert to the free-silver crusade led by William Jennings Bryan. In the following years he was an unquestioning believer in Bryan's various causes. He shared Bryan's anti-imperialism and opposed entry into the Spanish-American War and the annexation of the Philippines. In 1914 a national journal reported, "Mr. Clayton has made all the Bryan policies his own" (Hendrick, p. 502).

From 1897 to 1914 Clayton served in the U.S. House of Representatives. Moreover, he continued to build his reputation within the Democratic ranks, serving as permanent chairman of the national party convention of 1908. At that convention he helped to secure the presidential nomination for his hero Bryan. When the Democrats assumed control of the lower branch of Congress in 1911, Clayton's seniority ensured him the chairmanship of the House Judiciary Committee. For the next three years he held this post and ranked among the nation's leading lawmakers. In 1913 Alabama's governor chose Clayton to fill the U.S. Senate seat left vacant by the death of Joseph F. Johnston. When some senators challenged the validity of the appointment under the newly ratified Seventeenth Amendment, which provided for the popular election of senators, Clayton asked that his name be withdrawn.

Clayton's most notable contribution as chair of the Judiciary Committee was his work on the Clayton Antitrust Act. From December 1913 through the early months of 1914, the Alabama congressman worked closely with President Woodrow Wilson on legislation to clarify the rather broad and vague Sherman Antitrust Law of 1890. Clayton himself had not previously shown much interest in the antitrust question. "Strange to say," noted one observer, "the one important question upon which Mr. Clayton has not gone conspicuously on record is the particular one with which he is now called upon to deal" (Hendrick, p. 502). Yet in 1914 the Wilson administration's antitrust bill came before Congress bearing Clayton's name, and Clayton was responsible for guiding it through the House. After considerable revision in both the House and Senate, it became law in October 1914.

By this time Clayton himself was no longer a member of Congress, having resigned in May 1914 to accept an appointment as U.S. District Court judge for the middle district of Alabama. Worn down by patronage battles in his congressional district, he seems to have relinquished his seat in the House of Representatives with little reluctance.

For the remainder of his life, Clayton served as federal district court judge, a position of considerably less political and legal significance than the chairmanship of the House Judiciary Committee. With the passage of the Clayton Antitrust Act, his name was immortalized, but that triumph also ended his short stay in the national limelight. After fifteen years on the bench, he died in Montgomery, Alabama.

Clayton was a loyal southern Democrat who parlayed his long service to the party into a place in history. A portly, tobacco-chewing politician known to all the people in his congressional district as Henry, he differed little from many of his colleagues south of the Mason-Dixon line. He was at the helm of the House Judiciary Committee when President Wilson launched his reform of the antitrust law, and consequently Clayton's name survives in the history books.

• Clayton's papers are in the University of Alabama Library. A contemporary account of Clayton is Burton J. Hendrick, "A New Leader and a New Trust Policy," *World's Work*, Mar. 1914, pp. 499–504. Other articles on Clayton and his career are David E. Alsobrook, "'Remember the Maine!' Congressman Henry D. Clayton Comments on the Impending Conflict with Spain, April 1898," *Alabama Review* 30 (1977): 227–31; Jack E. Kendrick, "Alabama Congressmen in the Wilson Administration," *Alabama Review* 24 (1971): 243–60; Karl Rodabaugh, "Congressman Henry D. Clayton and the Dothan Post Office Fight: Patronage and Politics in the Progressive Era," *Alabama Review* 33 (1980): 125–49; and Rodabaugh, "Congressman Henry D. Clayton, Patriarch in Politics: A Southern Congressman during the Progressive Era," *Alabama Review* 31 (1978): 110–20. An obituary is in the *New York Times*, 22 Dec. 1929.

JON C. TEAFORD

CLAYTON, John (1694–15 Dec. 1773), botanist, was born in Fulham, England, the son of John Clayton, a lawyer and civil servant, and Lucy (maiden name unknown). Little is known of Clayton's early life; he was educated in England before immigrating to Virginia to join his father, who was attorney general of the colony. His biographers speculate that he attended Eton and Cambridge, but there is no clear evidence of his enrollment at either. Clayton served as clerk of Gloucester County, Virginia, with responsibility for the county's court records, wills, land surveys, and other official documents, subsisting through this position for fifty-three years. He also had a 450-acre plantation, which he farmed and on which he is reputed to have had a botanical garden. In 1723 he married Elizabeth Whiting, with whom he had eight children.

Clayton's grandfather, also named John Clayton, was a member of the Royal Society and is thought to have inspired the younger Clayton's interest in botany. Young Clayton began collecting specimens and corresponding with European authorities shortly after his arrival in the colonies. Although most of his correspondence and specimen exchange was with the Natural History Circle, a semiformal group of American and British naturalists, his most significant correspondence was with the Dutch botanist Johann Friedrich Gronovius, to whom Clayton sent specimens of New World flora with descriptions. The result was Gronovius's *Flora Virginica* (1739–1743), the first work to reflect Carolus Linnaeus's revolution in systematics, the identification and classification of organisms. Many improvements in nomenclature and classification later found in Linnaeus's *Species Plantarum* (1753) first appeared in Gronovius's work. The 1762 edition of *Flora Virginica* included further improvements and marked the onset of botany's modern era in North America. Clayton played a small role in the preparation of the work, a bone of some contention between him and Gronovius. Two additional volumes of manuscripts and instructions for plates were lost in a fire.

Clayton also sent specimens and observations to Linnaeus and to the American naturalists Alexander Garden and John Bartram, among others. He traveled and collected extensively in eastern Virginia but rarely ventured farther afield. He was a devout man who found evidence of God's hand in the plant world and felt that it was "impossible for a botanist to be an atheist." He was well regarded by his fellow Virginians, who elected him the first president of the Virginia Society for the Promotion of Useful Knowledge in 1773. His reputation among American naturalists won him membership in the American Philosophical Society. He died in Gloucester County.

For his contributions to knowledge of the flora of the New World, Clayton was elected to membership in the Swedish Royal Society of Science, one of a handful of Americans so honored, in 1747 on the recommendation of Linnaeus. Jefferson is reputed to have called him "America's first botanist." He is remembered through several plants that bear his name, most notably the genus *Claytonia*, or spring beauty.

• There is no collection of Clayton papers, most of which were destroyed by fire. The major biographical source is Edmund Berkeley and Dorothy Smith Berkeley, *John Clayton: Pioneer of American Botany* (1963), with footnotes that are the best guide to other materials. Considerable confusion over significant dates in Clayton's life has arisen, in part because there was another colonial Virginian of the same name with botanical interests.

LIZ KEENEY

CLAYTON, John Middleton (24 July 1796–9 Nov. 1856), U.S. senator and secretary of state, was born in Dagsborough, Delaware, the son of James Clayton, a tanner and farmer, and Sarah Middleton. Clayton attended boarding school before spending four years at Yale University under the tutelage of arch-Federalist Timothy Dwight (1752–1817). Upon graduation in 1815, he refined his Federalist deals by apprenticing in law with his cousin Thomas Clayton in Dover and also by studying at the prominent Litchfield Law School in Connecticut. Admitted to the bar in 1819, Clayton spent the next decade in a variety of Delaware government posts, including clerk of the state senate (1820) and house of representatives (1820–1821), auditor of accounts (1821–1824), member of the House (1824), and secretary of state (1826–1828).

Clayton married Sarah Ann Fisher in 1822; they had two children. In 1825 Sarah died after childbirth, and Clayton never remarried.

A divided Federalist party remained a force in Delaware politics throughout the 1820s. Clayton battled Louis McLane for political prominence, a rivalry based upon power and spoils as much as issues. In 1829 Delaware sent Clayton, who had supported John Quincy Adams (1767–1848) in the recent presidential contest, to the U.S. Senate, and the victorious Andrew Jackson named McLane as U.S. minister to England.

Clayton, the youngest member of the Senate, promptly made a positive impression. Standing a burly six feet, he delighted listeners with his mellifluous voice and oratorical skills. Henry Clay soon became his mentor and friend. Tending toward the Whig positions supporting an activist role for the federal government in the economy (for example, by creating a national bank, by funding internal improvements, and by instituting a protective tariff) and a strong navy to protect American commercial interests abroad, Clayton, a lifelong moderate, sought to maintain balance and order in society and politics. He consequently denounced in 1832 the arrogance of state sovereignty reflected in the nullification ordinance of South Carolina and the executive tyranny of Jackson's veto of the recharter of the Second Bank of the United States.

Reelected in 1835, Clayton chaired the Judiciary Committee but focused his attention on foreign affairs. He advocated treaties, a strong national defense, and commercial expansion as ways to achieve world stability. Frustrated by Democratic domination of the national government, Clayton resigned his seat in 1836 and became the chief justice of Delaware (1837–1839). Although Clayton was against slavery in principle, his views reflected the values and racial tenets of white society—he opposed civil rights for free blacks and abolition, believed in white supremacy, and supported colonization.

In 1840 Clayton, a loyal Clay supporter, refused to consider serving as vice president under William Henry Harrison, an unfortunate decision since Harrison died only one month after taking the oath of office. Clayton then suffered the dual indignities of the denial of a cabinet post under Harrison and rejection for the second spot on the unsuccessful Whig ticket with Clay in 1844.

Clayton maintained his power base in Delaware, however, by practicing law and advising the governor until his return to the Senate in 1845. Fearing a Democratically provoked conflict with Great Britain, he approved the Convention of 1846, whereby Great Britain relinquished its claims on Oregon. Clayton denounced the U.S. annexation of Texas as immoral. Although he believed that James K. Polk incited a war with Mexico in 1846, Clayton supported war measures. However, he opposed the movement to annex all of Mexico, claiming that the addition of Mexican labor would jeopardize American slavery. Domestically, Clayton rejected the president's reduction of the Walker tariff and establishment of the independent treasury. A centrist on territorial issues, Clayton opposed popular sovereignty. He favored an extension of the Missouri Compromise line to the Pacific Ocean, and he chaired a bipartisan committee that recommended a compromise on California and New Mexico in July 1848. The measure, passed by the Senate but tabled by a fearful House of Representatives, would have provided for a judicial solution to the constitutional question of slavery in the territories.

In 1848 Clayton, briefly considered for the Whig nomination, deserted the thrice-defeated Clay and endorsed the triumphant Zachary Taylor. Although the general had never met Clayton, he appointed him secretary of state on the recommendation of Governor John J. Crittenden of Kentucky, Clayton's longtime friend and Senate colleague. The new secretary rapidly emerged as an influential leader in the cabinet. Spurning the Omnibus Bill of 1850, Clayton preferred the drawing up of separate measures for granting statehood in the new lands in the West.

In foreign affairs, Clayton's focus remained on commercial rather than territorial expansion. He dispatched representatives to Cochin China, Siam, and Brunei, advocated contacts with Japan, and urged recognition of Louis Kossuth's ill-fated Hungarian revolution. Clayton supported trade with Santo Domingo and Peru and opposed Cuban annexation. In Europe, tensions mounted when Clayton assumed a strident posture over American reparations claims against Portugal and with France over a series of French claims against the United States. The latter, a "tempest in a teapot," produced extensive name-calling between Clayton and the French minister to the United States, Guillaume Poussin, and embroiled the two nations in diplomatic confrontation before calmer heads prevailed.

A committed Republican, Clayton contended that the United States should promote political and commercial stability to foster a new era of global progress. Anglo-American cooperation was a key element in this strategy, which could be applied most directly in Central America. A cornerstone of this policy was the treaty negotiated with Sir Henry Bulwer and signed by the president on 5 July 1850, whereby the United States and Great Britain agreed to cooperate on construction of the Panama Canal and to forswear future colonization in the region.

After Taylor died in July 1850, Clayton swiftly resigned. During his year on the cabinet, the press and Congress had severely criticized the cabinet for their mediocre talent and inefficiency and, most particularly, for the unfair distribution of patronage. The embittered secretary to state refused to serve further, particularly under Millard Fillmore, a man he considered of "small timber."

Prompted by Democratic attacks on the Clayton-Bulwer Treaty, Clayton returned to the Senate in 1853 to defend his policies. Recognizing that the Whig party was doomed, he hoped to build a unionist coalition that would rally the nation around foreign policy issues. However, the passage of the Kansas-Nebraska Act of 1854, which provided that the new territories could decide for themselves whether to allow slavery, crushed Clayton's hopes for the triumph of the politics of moderation and drove him into cooperation with the Know-Nothing party. Politically homeless and anachronistic in a milieu of growing extremism, he continued to plead unsuccessfully for compromise and accommodation in "Bleeding Kansas" during the conflict in the state between slave and free interests.

Clayton experienced declining health from kidney disease in 1855. He died at Dover.

• The major collection of Clayton's papers and those of his primary correspondents, such as John J. Crittenden and Zachary Taylor, are in the Library of Congress. No published biography of Clayton exists. The most comprehensive work is Richard A. Wire, "John M. Clayton and the Search for Order: A Study in Whig Politics and Diplomacy" (Ph.D. diss., Univ. of Maryland, 1971), which corrects the older and weaker study by Joseph Comegys, *Memoir of John Middleton Clayton* (1882). Most other works on Clayton focus on his return to the Senate in 1845 and his limited tenure as secretary of state. See Mary W. Williams's article on Clayton in *American Secretaries of State and Their Diplomacy*, ed. Samuel Flagg Bemis, vol. 6 (1928); Brainerd Dyer, *Zachary Taylor* (1946); Holman Hamilton, *Zachary Taylor*, vol. 2 (1951); K. Jack Bauer, *Zachary Taylor: Soldier, Planter, Statesman of the Old West* (1985); and E. B. Smith, *The Presidencies of Taylor and Fillmore* (1988).

JOHN M. BELOHLAVEK

CLAYTON, Powell (7 Aug. 1833–25 Aug. 1914), governor of Arkansas, U.S. senator, and diplomat, was born in Bethel County, Pennsylvania, the son of John Clayton and Ann Clarke. His father was an orchard keeper and carpenter and was prominent locally in Whig politics. Clayton attended local public schools and the Partridge Military Academy at Bristol, Pennsylvania, and he studied civil engineering in Wilmington, Delaware. In 1855 he moved to Leavenworth, Kansas, where he was a land speculator and surveyor.

Clayton's political career began in 1860 when he was elected city engineer at Leavenworth, but his term was cut short because of the Civil War. In 1861 Clayton joined the Union army as a captain of Company E, First Kansas Infantry. In August 1861 his unit was engaged at Wilson's Creek, where it lost forty-nine of seventy-four men. Clayton was cited for his service in the action. In February 1862 he was named lieutenant colonel of the Fifth Kansas Cavalry; the next month he was promoted to colonel. Clayton's command moved to Helena, Arkansas, in the spring of 1862 and engaged in foraging and cotton-seizing expeditions in that state and Mississippi. Clayton again demonstrated bravery in the battle of Helena on 4 July 1863. The following September he participated in General Frederick Steele's occupation of Little Rock, Arkansas, and was named post commander at Pine Bluff, Arkansas, a city he successfully defended from an attack in October 1863 by Confederate general John S. Marmaduke. In 1864 he was promoted to brigadier general.

While commander at Pine Bluff, Clayton leased abandoned plantations and grew cotton employing freedmen as laborers. With his profits he purchased a plantation near Pine Bluff, where he settled after the war. In December 1865 he married Adaline McGraw of Helena, daughter of a steamboat captain and major in the Confederate army; the couple had five children.

Clayton became involved in local politics in 1867 when he participated in the formation of the state Republican party, which revolutionized politics in Arkansas with its acceptance of black suffrage. At the state convention on 2 April 1867 he served on the committee on resolutions and was named to the state committee for the Second Congressional District. As a hero of the Union cause and a wealthy planter, Clayton quickly emerged as a major figure in the party. The Republican state nominating convention chose him to run for governor under the new constitution of 1868. The Democrats ran no candidate and Clayton was elected.

Inaugurated on 2 July 1868, Clayton faced widespread violence and lawlessness, products of social upheaval generated by the war, the end of slavery, and political conflict that accompanied the beginning of congressional Reconstruction in 1867. Attacks on Republican officials by opponents organized in the Ku Klux Klan particularly threatened the viability of his party and the new government. Clayton responded decisively, with actions that earned him the unending hatred of many white Arkansans but pacified the state. Clayton organized the integrated state militia, imposed martial law in areas where Klan violence was the greatest, and effectively ended the Klan's activities within the state.

In addition to suppression of violence, Clayton's term as governor was marked by legislation encouraging internal improvements—construction of levees, reclamation of swamplands, and building of railroads. The Republican legislature created the state's first system of free (although segregated) public schools and established a school for the physically handicapped. The Republican party under Clayton also pushed progressive legislation that prohibited racial discrimination of public facilities. Although the legislation passed, in practice little was changed.

A skilled politician, Clayton used his party organization and extensive patronage to enforce party discipline in the state. The measures that he took, however, won him enemies, including many within his own party. As early as April 1869 Republican moderates, led by lieutenant governor James M. Johnson, bolted from the party charging Clayton with mismanagement of railroad interests, extravagant appropriations for state government, and criminal misuse of power in his use of the militia. Known as Liberal Republicans or Brindletails and led by Joseph Brooks, this faction remained a permanent problem for the regular Republican organization (called the Minstrels) and in 1871 even succeeded in having Clayton impeached. Despite their claims, Clayton was never tried or convicted of any charges.

In January 1871 the state legislature elected Clayton to the U.S. Senate. Clayton's career in the Senate was undistinguished, although he served on at least two important committees—military affairs and territories and levees on the Mississippi River. He was not re-elected by the Democratic majority that had regained power by the time his term expired in 1877.

After he stepped down from the Senate, Clayton remained active in Republican politics. He was on the state central executive committee and the national committee through most of the rest of his life. He was the arbiter of federal patronage in the state as well, still being consulted on appointments during the administration of President William Howard Taft.

In addition to his political career, Clayton was a successful businessman. In 1882 he moved from Little Rock to Eureka Springs, Arkansas, where he helped build and was president and manager of the Eureka Springs Railway and also was president of the Eureka Springs Improvement Company, formed to develop the town. He retired from both of these positions in 1897. Clayton also maintained his 40,000-acre plantation on the Arkansas River below the city of Pine Bluff.

In 1896 Clayton actively campaigned for William McKinley. As a reward, Clayton was appointed U.S. ambassador to Mexico. He held that position from 1897 to 1905. At the time of his resignation, he moved to Washington, D.C., rather than returning to Arkansas, although he continued to play an important role in Arkansas Republican politics. He spent his remaining life in Washington, where he died and was buried in Arlington National Cemetery.

• There is no known collection of Clayton's papers. A short scholarly study of Clayton is William H. Burnside, "Powell Clayton," in *Governors of Arkansas* (1981), pp. 43–54, which provides an abbreviated version of Burnside's later *The Honorable Powell Clayton* (1991). Clayton's own story of his Reconstruction career is presented in *The Aftermath of the Civil War in Arkansas* (1915); it is a fairly accurate portrayal of events, although the interpretation favors Clayton.

CARL H. MONEYHON

CLAYTON, William (17 July 1814–4 Dec. 1879), chronicler of early Mormonism, pioneer, and musician, was born in Penwortham, England, the son of Thomas Clayton, a schoolteacher, and Ann Critchley. He was schooled by his father and learned to play both the piano and the violin. While employed as a clerk in a Preston textile factory, he listened to the preaching of Heber Kimball, then an apostle in the Mormon church, and converted to the newly organized religion. After his baptism in 1837, Clayton served as second counselor in the British mission presidency (1838–1840)—a post that included acting as a full-time proselytizing missionary and as president of the Manchester congregation—before migrating with his family to the United States in 1840 to join the main body of Latter-day Saints, who were then settled in Nauvoo, Illinois. He became a U.S. citizen in 1853.

Clayton was given numerous clerking duties in the church. These assignments began in England, with his participation in the publication of the church's *Millennial Star* and in the compilation of a hymnal; they continued after his migration, beginning in 1841, when he was appointed clerk of the Zarahemla (Iowa) stake. The following year he was assigned to record all activities associated with the rising Nauvoo temple, including the contributions made for its construction; he also became the personal secretary to founder-prophet Joseph Smith, Jr., a position he maintained until Smith's assassination in 1844. Clayton enjoyed the close association with Smith; competent and loyal, he became part of Smith's private prayer circle and was named to the important Council of Fifty (both 1844). In 1843 Clayton recorded a revelation, dictated by Smith, which introduced the doctrines of eternal families and of "plural" marriages. Clayton was at the time already married, having wedded Ruth Moon in 1836, but he accepted the teaching when he was invited to do so and ultimately married nine additional women, fathering forty-seven children in all. In 1845 he was commissioned by the church's Twelve Apostles to write a short history of the Nauvoo temple, to be sealed within the cornerstone of the edifice. This he did, but Brigham Young, who succeeded Smith as president, did not approve the hastily written manuscript, and so it was not included. The work was published posthumously, however.

Heavy persecution prevailed against the Mormons in Nauvoo. In 1846 Clayton was forced to flee westward with three of his four wives, his four living children, and hundreds of his fellow church members, crossing Iowa that year and finally establishing the encampment they named Winter Quarters on the western side of the Missouri River. In February, as the exodus commenced, Clayton was named "general clerk of the Camp of Israel"; as such he frequently wrote official and personal correspondence for Young and other church leaders. Along the way he also became president of the camp's band. It was during this arduous trek that he penned the words to the now traditional Mormon hymn "Come, Come Ye Saints," offering words of hope and encouragement to the pioneers as they trudged across the plains of Iowa. Many sang the hymn during the journey.

After wintering at Winter Quarters, Clayton was personally selected by Young to join the exploring team that would precede the other "saints" on the continuing migration west. This advance company, composed of 143 men, three women, and two children, was assigned to travel to the Great Basin in search of a permanent place to settle and arrived in the valley of the Great Salt Lake in July 1847. He calculated the distances the group traveled by counting the revolutions of a wagon wheel, and he occasionally posted signs that were intended to communicate these distances to subsequent travelers. Because of the tediousness of the wheel-revolution counting, Clayton was influential in the design and development of the "roadometer," a mechanical counter with wooden cogwheels that permitted the travelers to measure distances with greater ease and precision than any method previously available. He used a working roadometer during the return journey from the Salt Lake Valley to Winter Quarters (also in 1847) to complete his cataloging of the location of all major landmarks along the way. He compiled this information into a guidebook, which he had published that winter in St. Louis, Missouri. The book, *The Latter-day Saints' Emigrants' Guide* (1848), became an essential item for Mormon pioneers, followers of the Oregon trail, and many other travelers west.

Clayton returned to the Salt Lake Valley with this family to establish their permanent residence in 1848. There he spent the rest of his life, except for a visit in 1852 to several Utah settlements (where once again he served as camp historian) and a brief proselytizing mission to England (1852–1853). He served in several capacities as a public official, including public auditor of the provisional State of Deseret (1849), territorial auditor of Utah and recorder of marks and brands (both 1852–1879), two-term Salt Lake City alderman (1862 and 1864), secretary of Utah's 1862 constitutional convention, and chief clerk of the territorial House of Representatives (also 1862). In addition, in 1867 Clayton was made treasurer of Deseret Telegraph Company, and from 1869 through 1871 he was employed first as secretary and later as treasurer of Zion's Cooperative Mercantile Institution. He died in Salt Lake City.

From the time Clayton converted to Mormonism, he remained loyal to the religion and to Smith—the man he revered as a prophet of God. This loyalty honed and shaped the rest of his life. In addition, much of what is known about early Mormonism and the pioneering journeys comes through the detailed records Clayton kept along the way. Not only did he maintain careful journals and record many official church proceedings; he also was the ghostwriter of the pioneer journal of Heber Kimball and of other important writings, all of which combine to render important historical insight into the lives of these people.

• Clayton's original journals are kept in the historical archives of the Church of Jesus Christ of Latter-day Saints and in the Harold B. Lee Library at Brigham Young University, Provo, Utah. Selected journals are also available in excerpted form; the best of these is George D. Smith, ed., *An Intimate Chronicle: The Journals of William Clayton* (1995). In addition, James B. Allen, *Trials of Discipleship: The Story of William Clayton, a Mormon* (1987), is an important source.

BRUCE GELDER

CLAYTON, William Lockhart (7 Feb. 1880–8 Feb. 1966), businessman and statesman, was born near Tupelo, Mississippi, the son of James Clayton and Martha Fletcher Burdine, cotton farmers. Raised in modest circumstances in Jackson, Tennessee, Clayton left school at thirteen to work as a court stenographer and typist. Offered work in St. Louis as a secretary by a visiting businessman impressed with his diligence, Clayton followed his employer to New York City in 1896 to join the American Cotton Company. Clayton entered the cotton business at a time when the rapid improvement of communications was cutting costs and prices, creating a highly concentrated marketing system. Clayton learned the ropes of the new system and won promotion. He married Susan Vaughan in 1902; the couple had four daughters. By 1902 he had become manager of the sales department and had been appointed secretary-treasurer of a subsidiary, the Texas Cotton Products Company. Worried that the American Cotton Company would founder from mismanagement, in 1904 Clayton joined his brother-in-law Frank Anderson in establishing a cotton brokerage, Anderson, Clayton & Company, in Oklahoma City.

Within twenty years the partnership had emerged as the world's largest cotton brokerage thanks to a combination of hard work, good luck, and a shrewd strategy. Great opportunities for growth existed in the newly opened Oklahoma Territory, and the company welcomed technological innovation by employing round-bale cotton presses that were more efficient than traditional square presses. However, Clayton's determination to bypass the intermediaries who normally stood between American cotton factors and the foreign cotton mills best explains the rise of the firm. Clayton built up personal contacts with European buyers in trips during 1905 and 1907, bought warehouses and presses in southern port cities, shifted the firm's headquarters to Houston in 1916, and opened offices in Europe and Asia during and immediately after the First World War. Thus well positioned, Anderson, Clayton garnered a huge share of the booming wartime sales. Clayton's appointment to the War Industries Board in 1918, his successful campaign to force the New York Cotton Exchange to accept delivery of cotton futures at southern ports, and Senate hearings on the company's alleged manipulation of the cotton market all registered the company's dominant position in the cotton trade.

A concern with world markets continued to dominate Clayton's thinking between the wars. Clayton fervently denounced Republican policies of raising tariffs and collecting war debts on the grounds that they prevented Europeans from earning the dollars they needed to buy American goods. Only by opening American markets to foreign producers, he insisted, could Americans themselves export enough to earn high incomes. Clayton further opposed government intervention in free markets when he criticized measures such as the New Deal's Agricultural Adjustment Act, which attempted to support low agricultural prices by limiting production. Higher American prices, Clayton correctly argued, would surrender export markets—the major target of American cotton production—to foreign producers drawn to expand production without improving the lot of farmers. Clayton briefly joined the American Liberty League, but he supported Franklin D. Roosevelt in the 1936 election when Republicans attacked Secretary of State Cordell Hull's efforts to negotiate international tariff reductions. Meanwhile, Clayton expanded cotton production in Egypt and Latin America in order to escape the baleful impact of New Deal legislation.

The mounting threat from the European dictatorships turned Clayton's energies from business to government. In June 1940 Clayton joined the Century Group, a committee organized to support intervention on behalf of Britain. He then served as adviser to Coordinator of Inter-American Affairs Nelson Rockefeller (Aug.–Oct. 1940), as deputy federal loan administrator (Oct. 1940–Feb. 1942), and as assistant secretary of commerce (Feb. 1942–Jan. 1944). In all these posts Clayton organized the purchase of strategic materials from around the world to fuel the American war effort or to prevent them from falling into enemy hands. Clayton then became surplus war property administrator as planning for the eventual reconversion of industry to a peacetime basis began. By the time he became assistant secretary of state for economic affairs in December 1944, Clayton had become an expert on wartime trade and production at home and abroad.

As assistant secretary, then under secretary (Aug. 1946–Oct. 1947), and finally special adviser to the secretary (Oct. 1947–Nov. 1948), Clayton pursued a dual policy. Over the long run, he sought to build an open world-trading system. Thus Clayton guided the negotiations in 1947 and 1948 of both an International Trade Organization, which Congress failed to approve, and of the General Agreement on Trade and Tariffs (GATT), which framed the progressive liberalization of world trade for over forty years. In the short run, Clayton lobbied for financial assistance to war-ravaged countries in order to revive trade. He negotiated a $3.75 billion loan to Britain in December 1945, channeled Export-Import Bank loans toward Europe, and settled lend-lease obligations on generous terms. His discussions with European officials at the GATT negotiations in Geneva during the spring of 1947 persuaded him that Europe was approaching an economic crisis. His vigorous, lucid presentations to Secretary of State George Marshall helped galvanize the State Department to propose the European Recovery Program in June 1947. Clayton then took a leading role in helping to guide the European nations toward a recovery plan which the Congress would accept. Until March 1948 Clayton headed the U.S. delegation to the United Nations Conference on Trade and Employment in Havana.

In retirement Clayton advocated an "Atlantic Union" of Western Europe, Canada, and the United States and engaged in philanthropy. Intelligent, able, and energetic, Clayton exemplified the twentieth-century transformation of American political economy. One left-wing publication judged him "as articulate and intelligent a spokesman for capitalist conservatism as Henry [A.] Wallace is of capitalist liberalism." The self-disciplined Clayton did not smoke, drink, or swear, a remarkable attainment for anyone intimately informed about the problems facing American business and government in the first half of the twentieth century. He died in Houston, Texas.

• Clayton's papers are scattered among Rice University, Houston, Tex.; the Truman Library, Independence, Mo.; and the National Archives, Washington, D.C. See Ellen Clayton Garwood, *Will Clayton: A Short Biography* (1958); Frederick J. Dobney, ed., *Selected Papers of Will Clayton* (1971); Harold D. Woodman, *King Cotton and His Retainers* (1968); Michael Hogan, *The Marshall Plan* (1987); and Jesse Jones, *Fifty Billion Dollars* (1951).

J. S. HILL

CLEAVELAND, Parker (15 Jan. 1780–15 Oct. 1858), educator and author of the first American textbook on mineralogy, was born in Byfield Parish, Massachusetts, the son of Parker Cleaveland, Sr., a medical doctor who served in the American Revolution, and Elizabeth Jackman. Cleaveland attended the Dummer Academy near his home and went to Harvard College for his undergraduate education. An honors graduate in the class of 1799, he took teaching jobs at secondary schools in Haverhill, Massachusetts, and York, Maine, until returning to Harvard to earn a master's degree in 1802 and work as a tutor in 1803. Just two years later he accepted a position as professor of mathematics and natural philosophy at Bowdoin College in Brunswick, Maine, where he remained on the faculty until his death. In September 1806 he married Martha Bush; they raised eight children.

Early in his carreer Cleaveland held appointments in mathematics, natural philosophy, chemistry, and mineralogy. He soon concentrated on mineralogy and geology, but beginning in 1820 he also served as a faculty member and then dean of the Maine Medical School in Brunswick.

Cleaveland's long-standing interest in mineralogy and chemistry intensified as he tried to communicate to his students about the workings of the mineral kingdom. In 1807 local workmen brought him some samples of "gold and diamonds," but he realized that the specimens were really pyrite and quartz; nonetheless, he was embarrassed by his lack of depth in mineral science. His solution was to read all he could in the European literature, attend lectures on natural history, and correspond with American and European naturalists. Cleaveland's correspondents included many amateur collectors of minerals, as well as a "who's who" of early nineteenth-century geoscientists, including Alexandre Brongniart, Amos Eaton, Ebenezer Emmons, Edward Hitchcock, William Maclure, the Sillimans of Yale, Gerard Troost, and Benjamin Vaughan.

Within a decade of joining the Bowdoin faculty, Cleaveland produced the first American textbook on mineralogy, *An Elementary Treatise on Mineralogy and Geology* (1816). The book profited from his rigorous pursuit of French and German writings about minerals, crystallography, and classification concepts. He concluded that the optimal approach was the French system of using chemistry as the foundation of classification, but he also appreciated the German reliance on external form as an important attribute of minerals. One of the merits of the text is Cleaveland's judicious explanation of the various European methodologies. Another positive feature was the distinctly American flavor of the text, including information gleaned from his many correspondents, and his incorporation of data about American mineral-collecting localities. As the title hinted, the broader discipline of geology also received attention. Cleaveland discussed the origins of rocks such as basalt and provided readers with commentary on William Maclure's striking geologic map, included as a plate in the book.

Reviews of the *Treatise* were almost uniformly laudatory. Benjamin Silliman's reaction in the *American Journal of Science* (1819, p. 52) set the tone by stating, "This work does honour to our country. . . . The manner of execution is masterly." Silliman particularly applauded Cleaveland's extraction of the best elements of French classification theory, with its debts to Brochant, Haüy, and Brongniart, and the German descriptive rigor of the Wernerian school. "A happier model could not, in our opinion, be chosen," Silliman concluded (1819, p. 41). In Europe, the prime players in mineralogy also reacted favorably. Greene and Burke (1978) report that Brongniart, Haüy, Alexander von Humboldt, and Abraham Werner all praised the book. The Geological Society of London elected Cleaveland as its first American honorary member. Brongniart and Cleaveland became correspondents and sent each other samples of minerals and their writings.

The two-volume second edition of the *Treatise* (1822) retained much of the same basic information but expanded the treatment of mineral localities in North America and incorporated a discussion about meteorites, one of the few omissions in the original work that Silliman had criticized. Reaction continued to be positive, and the book became the standard American textbook in mineralogy.

Cleaveland's hope of producing a third edition never came to fruition. An extensive manuscript exists in the Bowdoin College archives, but the final stages of production did not occur. Part of the problem was Cleaveland's very heavy teaching and administrative load. He enjoyed Bowdoin and refused offers to join other faculties, including Harvard, but his obligations at Bowdoin and at the Maine Medical School were heavy. It is also true that the appearance of Charles Shepard's work on systematic mineralogy (1832) and James Dwight Dana's *A System of Mineralogy* (1837) may have limited the marketability of a third edition. Finally, failing eyesight, along with concern about geoscience's collision with his conservative Christian world view (Greene and Burke, 1978), may also have played a role in Cleaveland's inability to see the third edition through to completion.

Cleaveland retained the conservative character of his Puritan forebears in religion, politics, and pedagogy. In curricular matters, he argued against suggested innovations, including the addition of new courses in natural history. As a newspaper put it at the time of his death, with Harvard as his standard, he "effectually resisted the spirit of innovation to which other colleges have yielded, to their harm" (*Boston Daily Advertiser*, 23 Oct. 1858). Even in his scientific writings he continued to embrace Wernerian concepts of aqueous origin for basalts, while his contemporaries moved toward a volcanic source. Agreeing with Cuvier and Brongniart, Cleaveland rebelled against the overtheorizing that they felt detracted from older-style natural history. They celebrated the value of fieldwork and the collection of facts prior to any attempts at generalization. "Commence in the cabinet, pursue in the field," Cleaveland admonished, going on to state that if we "patiently continue to collect facts, and impartially compare and arrange them, we shall undoubtedly obtain the true theory" (lecture notes, Bowdoin Archives).

Along with conservatism, punctuality, dry wit, and a few idiosyncrasies that entertained his students, Cleaveland displayed a real gift for teaching. Nathaniel Hawthorne, Henry Wadsworth Longfellow, and Franklin Pierce were among the Bowdoin students who relished his rigorous preparation, clarity in lecturing, and disciplined classroom style. His fears of lightning, high winds, dogs, lockjaw, and travel, especially involving bridges, were well known in Brunswick, but so was his bravery as commander of the fire department. Loyal to his students, bound to duty, and unwilling to admit the ravages of time, Cleaveland asked to be carried to his last classes and went horseback riding the day before he died, at home in Brunswick. As Bowdoin President Woods noted at Cleaveland's funeral, "He died with the harness on, with his armor burnished bright, and his lamp trimmed and burning" (*Portland Argus*, 22 Oct. 1858).

The legacy of Parker Cleaveland includes the tangible mineral cleavelandite, a feldspar, but the intangibles are more substantial. His life, correspondence, and works represent a window on American and European intellectual currents in the early nineteenth century, as well as offering insight on the maturing of American science and education during that formative period.

• A rich collection of papers concerning Cleaveland's life, correspondence, and professional interests is in the Archives of the Hawthorne-Longfellow Library at Bowdoin College; it includes a handwritten booklet, "Biographical Notes on Parker Cleaveland" (1858), by his cousin, Nehemiah Cleaveland. Benjamin Silliman, Sr., a friend and colleague, wrote a brief account of Cleaveland's life in the *American Journal of Science and the Arts* 26 (Nov. 1858): 448–49; see also Silliman's review of Cleaveland's *Treatise, American Journal of Science and the Arts*, 1818–1819: 35–52. Nehemiah Cleaveland and A. S. Packard, *History of Bowdoin College, with Biographical Sketches* (1882) features Cleaveland in the context of liberal arts education in nineteenth-century America. More recent accounts include John C. Greene and John G. Burke, "The Science of Minerals in the Age of Jefferson," *Transactions of the American Philosophical Society* 68, pt. 4 (1978), including a section, "Cleaveland and the Unification of American Mineralogy." Vandall King, *History of Maine Mining and Minerals, Pt. II* (1990) contains numerous details about Cleaveland, particularly his ties to Benjamin Vaughan. See also Julie R. Newell, "The Formation of the American Geological Community, 1780–1865" (Ph.D. diss., Univ. of Wisconsin, 1993); and Arthur M. Hussey III, *The Legacy of James Bowdoin III* (1994), pp. 127–39, which illustrates Cleaveland's role in the evolution of American mineralogy and science education.

KENNARD B. BORK

CLEAVES, Margaret Abigail (25 Nov. 1848–13 Nov. 1917), physician, was born in Columbus City, Iowa, the daughter of John Trow Cleaves, a physician, and Elizabeth Stronach. As a child, Margaret often accompanied her father on his rounds. She attended the University of Iowa in Iowa City but was unable to complete her baccalaureate degree for financial reasons. Alternately, she taught school and attended classes until she began reading medicine and entered the medical department of the University of Iowa in 1870. She received her medical degree in 1873, graduating at the head of her class.

From 1873 to 1876, Cleaves, one of the first women to serve on the medical staff of an insane asylum, was an assistant physician at the Iowa state hospital in Mount Pleasant. In 1876 she moved to Davenport, Iowa, to set up a private practice in general medicine. She pursued her interest in the plight of the insane by serving as a trustee of the state hospital and in the condition of other dependent peoples by becoming actively involved in the National Conference of Charities and Corrections. Her paper at the 1879 national meeting of the conference, entitled "The Medical and Moral Care of Female Patients in Hospitals for the Insane," was well received.

In 1880 Cleaves's growing professional reputation brought her an opportunity to become one of the first women doctors to manage the care of mentally ill female patients. Pennsylvania had passed legislation intended to require women doctors on the staffs of all public institutions with women patients. Although the legislation ultimately encouraged rather than required women doctors, the trustees of the state hospitals in Norristown and Harrisburg decided to place women doctors in charge of the care of women patients. The Harrisburg trustees recruited Cleaves as physician in chief of the hospital's Female Department, and in August 1880 she set out to test her theories about insanity in women.

Cleaves had entered the professional debate about the cause of mental illness in women on the side of those who believed that insanity in women was directly related to the female reproductive system. Cleaves instituted regular gynecological examinations and treatment at the Harrisburg asylum. She quickly observed that local treatment brought only limited, and probably coincidental, relief, and the evidence led her to reject the idea that utero-ovarian disease was related to insanity. More compelling in the lives of the majority of working-class patients she treated, Cleaves thought, was the "endless monotony" of their lives, their "never ceasing routine of work," and their "too frequent child bearing" (Harrisburg State Lunatic Hospital, *Annual Reports* [1880–1883]).

Unable to change the lives of her patients and debilitated by her own health problems, Cleaves resigned in 1883, traveled in Europe for two years, and then returned to Des Moines, Iowa, where she opened a practice. During the next five years, she operated a private retreat for women patients with nervous afflictions and actively participated in county and state medical societies. Her continuing devotion to civic concerns and women's issues led her to organize the Des Moines Women's Club, becoming its first president in 1885. She became increasingly interested in the use of electricity in medicine, delivering a paper to the Polk County Medical Society on the treatment of uterine fibers by electrolysis in 1888.

In 1890 Cleaves moved to New York City, where for the next twenty-five years she operated the New York Electro-Therapeutic Clinic Laboratory and Dispensary on Madison Avenue. She remained an active member of the American Medical Association and the local and county medical societies in New York City as well as the more short-lived electrotherapeutic groups. She was a contributor to the *Journal of Nervous and Mental Disease* in the 1890s and served on the editorial staff of the *Women's Medical Journal* in 1909. In 1904 she published her professional magnum opus, *Light Energy: Its Physics, Physiological Action, and Therapeutic Applications*, and in 1910 her personal saga, *The Autobiography of a Neurasthene, As Told by One of Them and Recorded by Margaret A. Cleaves, M.D.* In the late nineteenth and early twentieth centuries, neurasthenia had become the medical label for a syndrome whose causes doctors could not clearly identify. Symptoms attributed to neurasthenia included a limited capacity to deal with stress and an oversensitized nervous system; thus, women were diagnosed as neurasthenics more often than men. Cleaves believed that she suffered from the illness, and, indeed, her autobiography is an account of her lifelong struggle with the affliction.

Margaret Cleaves was part of that pioneering generation of women who broke the barriers of gender in the medical profession. When she joined medical societies, she was always either the first or second woman to gain membership. She encouraged other women to confront the established mores of professional organizations, and she never stopped challenging traditional modes of treatment in psychiatry and neurology. She died in a Mobile, Alabama, hospital and was buried in Davenport, Iowa.

• There is no manuscript collection for Cleaves. The biographical sketch in Frances Willard and Mary Livermore, *A Woman of the Century* (1893), offers considerable detail. Constance M. McGovern, "Doctors or Ladies?: Women Physicians in Psychiatric Institutions, 1872–1900," *Bulletin of the History of Medicine* 55 (1981): 88–107, and F. G. Gosling, *Before Freud: Neurasthenia and the American Medical Community, 1870–1910* (1987), provide helpful medical and social background. A death notice is in the *New York Times*, 15 Nov. 1917.

CONSTANCE M. McGOVERN

CLEBSCH, William Anthony (19 July 1923–12 June 1984), church historian, developer of religious studies, and university professor, was born in Clarksville, Tennessee, the son of Alfred Clebsch, an owner of tobacco warehouses, and Julia Wilee. In 1944 he married Betsy Birchfield, a horticulturalist; they had two children.

Clebsch received a B.A. in history and philosophy from the University of Tennessee at Knoxville in 1946 and a B.D. the same year from Virginia Theological Seminary. He studied English and American literature at Michigan State from 1946 to 1949, and he earned an S.T.M. from Virginia Theological Seminary in 1951 and a Th.D. from Union Theological Seminary in 1957. His dissertation *Baptism of Blood: Christian Contributions to the Civil War* was published in revised form in 1961. As the grandson of a German businessman who had been detained by the U.S. government during World War I, a southerner, and a conscientious objector during World War II, Clebsch was sensitive to the negative aspects of sanctifying bloodshed and patriotism. *Baptism of Blood* is a pioneering study of religion's important role in American political and civic life and one of the first scholarly efforts to analyze what later came to be called American "civil religion."

After studying at Clare College, Cambridge University, in 1959–1960 and teaching at Michigan State, Virginia Theological Seminary, and the Theological Seminary of the Southwest in Austin, Texas, Clebsch joined the faculty at Stanford University in 1964. There he received a dean's Distinguished Teaching award and became the first George Edwin Burnell Professor of Religious Studies and Humanities. A major figure in university governance, Clebsch helped define the intellectual climate at Stanford and led the way in articulating a rationale for the university's expansion of minority recruitment and financial aid. He

presided over the university senate during years of student unrest precipitated by the war in Vietnam and aggravated by Stanford's role as a think tank for American foreign policy. He played a leading role in curricular development at Stanford and in founding interdisciplinary programs in American Studies and in Values, Technology, and Society. Both of these programs enabled students to combine traditional methods of inquiry in new ways and to reflect creatively on tensions and problems within modern society. Clebsch also played a leading role in conceptualizing and raising money for a program of library expansion that secured the Stanford University Libraries a world-class ranking. Through all these activities Clebsch expressed his commitment to the importance of university life as a defining subculture within modern society.

A humanist outlook guided Clebsch's scholarly work as well as his commitment to university life. He was adamantly interested in the human nature of religion, and he focused on the intellectual, experiential, and behavioral aspects of religion throughout his career. This approach to religion distanced him from theologians of the 1960s and 1970s who concerned themselves with God and who, in many cases, wanted a more prominent role in the developing field of religious studies than Clebsch believed they should have. Clebsch's interest in religion also led him to chafe at the focus on institutions and doctrines that characterized traditional church history, and his work contributed to the expansion of that field.

Clebsch's book *England's Earliest Protestants, 1520–1535* (1964) established him as a church historian of the first rank. Focusing on the emergence of Protestant thought in England, which he saw as an important but poorly understood episode in modern intellectual history, Clebsch pointed to the development of a distinctly English concern for the effect of grace in moral action. In this work he explored an antecedent of his own humanistic interest in the behavioral effects of religious experience.

In *From Sacred to Profane America: The Role of Religion in American History* (1968) Clebsch explored the relationship between religion and culture in U.S. history. He developed a provocative thesis about religion's success, arguing that Protestant ideas about equality, education, welfare, and individual freedom have considerably influenced social policy and cultural expectation in the United States. But this influence was a paradoxical achievement for religion: the price of success for public acceptance of mandates based in Protestant religion was their removal from religion's domain and control. As Clebsch wrote, "The unintended but nevertheless salutary effect of religion on American history has been to make a nation profaned—a society standing *pro-fanum*, outside of religion's temple."

In the most affirmative work of his career, *American Religious Thought: A History* (1973), Clebsch focused on Jonathan Edwards, Ralph Waldo Emerson, and William James as pivotal figures in the development of a distinctively American tradition of religious thought characterized by the aesthetic experience of "being at home in the universe." This tradition of religious thought involved concepts of moral responsibility but was distinct from theology, which focused on God rather than humanity, as well as from forms of psychological analysis that reduced religious experience to something else.

Clebsch's most ambitious work, *Christianity in European History* (1979), comprehended its subject in fewer than 300 pages by means of an innovative scheme of paired religious "types"—martyrs and monks, mystics and theologians, pietists and moralists, activists and apologists—with each pair exemplifying a stage in the history of European Christianity. Challenging both social historians who overlooked the influence of Christianity in European history and church historians who ignored the diversity of Christian experience and behavior and focused instead on the unfolding of Christian doctrine, Clebsch situated the study of Christianity squarely in the context of the study of religion, defined as an expression of human nature and its inherent diversity.

Clebsch's colleagues recognized his erudition, strength of mind, and foundational role in establishing religious studies as a full partner in the humanities by electing him president of the American Society of Church History in 1972–1973, chair of the Council on the Study of Religion in 1974–1975, and president of the American Academy of Religion in 1979–1980. This succession of national offices reflected both the direction of his own development as a scholar and the connection between his prominence and the development of religious studies. He died in his office at Stanford University.

Clebsch might be seen as a transitional figure who helped establish a bridge between church history and religious studies. But it might also be said that he was a pathfinder whose ideas were not immediately followed or fully implemented. During his lifetime, Clebsch's ideas about how religion should be studied were often overshadowed by the work of scholars more concerned than he with theology and less concerned about religious experience and its behavioral consequences. In the years following Clebsch's death, religious studies scholars turned emphatically toward the diversities of religious expression, thus partly following his path; but most eschewed bold efforts to compare particular religious episodes in the kind of large interpretive frameworks that he proposed.

• Clebsch's papers are held by Stanford University and by Betsy Clebsch. These papers include unfinished manuscripts on the comparative study of religions and on the intellectual history of academic disciplines in the humanities and social sciences. Also see his *Contemporary Perspectives on Word, World, and Sacrament* (1963); *Pastoral Care in Historical Perspective* (1964; repr. 1983 and 1994); and "A New Historiography of American Religion," *Historical Magazine of the Protestant Episcopal Church* 32: 3. The last publication of Clebsch's life was an edition of John Donne's *Suicide* (1983), which defended the taking of one's own life against the decision of the Roman Catholic Church that it was unforgivable. Clebsch highlighted Donne's seventeenth-century argument that suicide could be a moral act, understood in the context of Christ's willing acceptance of death.

AMANDA PORTERFIELD

CLEBURNE, Patrick Ronayne (17 Mar. 1828–30 Nov. 1864), Confederate officer, was born in Ireland, the son of Joseph Cleburne, a physician, and Mary Ann Ronayne. In 1846, failing to gain admission to medical school in Dublin, he enlisted in the British Forty-first Regiment of Foot. In 1849, receiving a small legacy, he purchased his discharge from the British army and, with other family members, emigrated to the United States. In 1850 he took over a pharmacy in Helena, Arkansas; later he became a lawyer.

In the summer of 1860 Cleburne joined the Yell Rifles, a local infantry company; his previous military experience later led to his election to the captaincy. Arkansas seceded on 6 May 1861, after the firing on Fort Sumter and the outbreak of the Civil War. When the Yell Rifles became part of the Fifteenth Arkansas Regiment, Cleburne was elected colonel of the regiment, and when the regiment became part of a brigade, Cleburne was appointed its commander. Cleburne's brigade served under Albert Sidney Johnston, P. G. T. Beauregard, and Braxton Bragg in what became the Army of Tennessee. At Shiloh, Cleburne's brigade fought in the front lines on the extreme left of the Confederate army; Cleburne's commander, William J. Hardee, praised his gallantry.

In December 1862 Jefferson Davis promoted Cleburne to division commander, with the rank of major general, in part because of his performance at the battle of Shiloh. Cleburne's division fought at Murfreesboro and Chickamauga, and they served as rear guard to the Confederate retreat after the battle of Missionary Ridge. Cleburne gained the reputation of being the best division commander in the Army of Tennessee, owing to his coolness and courage and to his division's discipline and morale. The Confederate Congress twice voted him thanks.

Cleburne, however, is best remembered as the first prominent Confederate officer to advocate enlisting blacks in the army and rewarding them with emancipation. During the winter of 1863–1864 Cleburne circulated through the Army of Tennessee a proposal to use slaves as soldiers. It did not garner much support, but a copy was sent to Jefferson Davis.

What made Pat Cleburne willing to promote black freedom? Most likely, his Irish birth gave him a perspective different from that of his fellow Confederates. On the one hand, he believed that Confederate defeat would put the South in the same relationship to the North that Ireland had to Britain, and he was willing to sacrifice slavery to prevent that. He believed that the Confederate patriot should "give up the negro slave rather than be a slave himself." On the other hand, he had no doubts that an agrarian labor force could be exploited without the institution of slavery.

Finally, despite more than a decade's residence in the southern United States, Cleburne had never owned a slave.

Cleburne's vision brought him little applause. Davis ordered his proposal suppressed. Cleburne received no preferment after filing his proposal—a case where a man's ideological unreliability overshadowed his undeniable competence. Instead of earning promotion, he continued to serve under inferior commanders. By the end of the war the Confederacy reluctantly undertook the experiment of arming blacks. At that time, Pat Cleburne was dead. He was one of six Confederate generals killed at the battle of Franklin, Tennessee. Before the hopeless charge that led him to his death, he told fellow commander D. C. Govan, "Well, Govan, if we are to die, let us die like men."

• The standard biography is Howell Purdue and Elizabeth Purdue, *Pat Cleburne, Confederate General* (1973). See also Irving A. Buck, *Cleburne and His Command* (1908).

REID MITCHELL

CLEMENS, Jeremiah (28 Dec. 1814–21 May 1865), politician and novelist, was born in Huntsville, Alabama, the son of James Clemens, a merchant. His mother's maiden name was Mills, but her first name is unknown. Clemens spent the formative years of his life in the northern Alabama upcountry town of Huntsville with his affluent family. He entered La Grange College in 1830, but in 1831 he moved to the newly opened University of Alabama, graduating in 1833. He also spent a year studying law at Transylvania University in Lexington, Kentucky. In 1834 he married Mary Read; they had one child.

After practicing law in Huntsville for several years, Clemens entered the Alabama House of Representatives in 1839. Capitalizing on the anxieties of his upcountry constituents about the machinations of commercial interests, he began a crusade against fraud and irregularities in the Bank of the State of Alabama. He charged several senior legislators with financial misconduct for receiving money from the state bank. Clemens launched a high-profile investigation of corrupt activities among the banks and legislators, but he soon abandoned the issue.

In 1842 Clemens left the house to form a company of volunteers to help Texas in its war with Mexico. After five months of fighting, Clemens and Texas leader Sam Houston had a falling out over the volunteers' usefulness. Houston felt the Alabamians were undisciplined and that scarce resources should be reserved for more disciplined Texas militia. Clemens and his men went home, and the Alabama troops were not paid until 1851. After a brief return to the legislature, Clemens in 1846 joined the army for the Mexican War. He rose to the rank of colonel under the command of Winfield Scott and was discharged in 1848.

In 1848 Clemens was chosen for the U.S. Senate in a controversial legislative session that produced charges that Clemens, a Democrat, had given assurances he would back Whig president Zachary Taylor. Clemens received virtually unanimous Whig support and entered the Senate as a "Taylor Democrat" pledged to support the president, who lacked the backing of either of the political parties. Despite his denials that he had made a secret pledge to the Whigs, a cloud of suspicion remained in Alabama over the so-called "Clemens sellout." He entered the Senate at the age of thirty-five, the youngest man to do so to that time.

During the early part of 1850, Clemens devoted himself to slavery and southern rights. He vocally opposed the admission of California to the Union as a free state, arguing that such a move would be tantamount to adopting the Wilmot Proviso, a measure restricting slavery in the land acquired by the United States after the Mexican War. Early in 1850 he denounced both abolitionists and southern "submissionists" while opposing the Compromise of 1850. Yet he was absent for many key votes, and when proslavery extremists in Alabama talked of secession in 1851 and 1852, Clemens kept his distance. He reversed his position, moving to an openly pro-Union stance. His shift from southern radical to cautious Unionist left him virtually without allies, and he became certain the legislature would not reelect him to his seat. In 1851 and 1852 he devoted himself to convincing the people of Alabama to accept the compromise and to reject the doctrine of the right of secession. He was a rare southern politician in denying the right to secede, but he argued that the South should not disguise threats of revolution with the language of constitutional legality.

By 1852 Clemens was seen as more Whig than Democrat in Alabama, in spite of his formal party affiliation, and Democrats refused to elect him to another term in the Senate. C. C. Clay, Sr., a leading Democrat, expressed the sentiment of many when he charged Clemens with inconsistency, calling him "a man who had betrayed his party." In 1856 Clemens formally broke with the Democrats, joining the short-lived Know Nothing party, a nativist organization that had limited appeal in a state with few immigrants.

Following the collapse of the Know Nothings, Clemens temporarily left politics and began publishing historical fiction. He wrote *Bernard Lile* (1856) and *Mustang Gray* (1858), both of which were dramatic stories that drew on his experience of the Southwest in the Texas Revolution and Mexican War. He spent 1858 in Tennessee editing a newspaper, the *Eagle and Enquirer*. In 1859 he published *The Rivals*, a tale of the American Revolution that depicted the young Aaron Burr as a heroic figure victimized by the plotting of a malevolent Alexander Hamilton. Although Clemens showed some facility with action scenes, the dialogue in the novels is wooden and pretentious, and the characters are not well developed. The novels have never been reprinted and have received little critical attention.

Clemens reentered politics in the secession crisis. He led the Unionist forces in North Alabama and was elected to the state's secession convention. In a dramatic speech he declared disunion to be "wrong" and "treason." He nevertheless signed the ordinance of secession and wrote a crucial letter declaring "every [convention] member from North Alabama stands pledged to abide by the action of the Convention." His endorsement dampened opposition to the Confederacy in North Alabama in 1861. That same year he was appointed major general of Alabama.

Failing to receive a powerful Confederate military commission that he believed was due him because of his military experience, Clemens led Alabama Unionists in opposition to the Confederacy by 1862, earning the title of "archtraitor" among Confederates in his home state. He traveled between Huntsville and Philadelphia until his death, producing anti-Confederate political documents and writing a Unionist novel, *Tobias Wilson: A Tale of the Great Rebellion* (1865). He died in Huntsville.

Clemens had a deep distrust of centralized authority that was characteristic of Alabama's political culture in the mid-nineteenth century. Hostility to central power linked his opposition to the bank and his resistance to supposed abolitionist attempts to control the government in 1850. Distaste for strong central power also lay behind his anger at both northern Republicans and the planter class and served as the consistent thread linking his actions throughout the war. His fiction reveals a theme consistent with his political career, a dislike for the conspiratorial machinations of authority. Nevertheless, while Clemens justified each move in his inconsistent public career within the framework of his republican political principles, the vast majority of his contemporaries ascribed his actions to opportunism.

• A small file of Clemens's papers is at the Alabama Department of Archives and History. Vergil Bedsole, "The Life of Jeremiah Clemens" (master's thesis, Univ. of Alabama, 1934), focuses on politics. J. Mills Thornton III, *Politics and Power in a Slave Society: Alabama, 1800–1860* (1978), is the best guide to Clemens's Ala. William R. Smith, *History and Debates of the People of Alabama* (1861), documents Clemens's role in the secession crisis; and William R. Garrett, *Reminiscences of Public Men in Alabama for Thirty Years* (1872), provides a useful sketch. Walter Fleming, *Civil War and Reconstruction in Alabama* (1905), remains an excellent source on the war years.

WALLACE HETTLE

CLEMENS, Samuel Langhorne. *See* Twain, Mark.

CLEMENT, Frank Goad (2 June 1920–4 Nov. 1969), politician and 3-term governor of Tennessee, was born in Dickson, Tennessee, the son of Robert Samuel Clement and Maybelle Goad. During the 1920s and 1930s the Clement family moved frequently (briefly to Vt., to Ky., and back to Tenn.) and experienced difficult times. The elder Clement held a variety of positions and lost an investment after the crash of 1929 before earning a one-year law degree at Cumberland University and resettling his family in Dickson.

Frank Clement attended Cumberland University (1937–39) then the law school of Vanderbilt University, from which he graduated three years later. Mean-while, he had married Lucille Christianson in 1940; they had three sons. Clement easily passed the state bar examination in 1941, before he was old enough to practice law. Upon graduation, he joined the Federal Bureau of Investigation after securing a waiver of the bureau's minimum age requirement. Entering the army as a private in 1943, Clement served in the military police and attained a first lieutenancy before his discharge in 1946.

Already ambitious for a political career, Clement quickly won election as president of the Young Democratic Clubs of Tennessee and appointment as the youngest general counsel of the state railroad and public utilities commission (1946). He gained further exposure by becoming prominent in activities of the American Red Cross, the March of Dimes, and the American Legion. He was a member of the state's delegation to the Democratic National Convention of 1948. In 1949 the Tennessee Junior Chamber of Commerce named Clement as the state's "Outstanding Young Man of the Year." The following year Clement resigned his state position to join his father's law practice and to launch a campaign for the governorship. The Korean War, which led to Clement's recall to active military duty, delayed his gubernatorial bid until 1952.

Clement entered Tennessee elective politics during a period in which Democratic victories in state elections could still be taken for granted. Democratic factionalism was fading. Clement accepted the endorsement of "Boss" Edward H. Crump of Memphis, but his primary campaign owed more to personal allies than to party workers. His public appeal was largely personal: he spoke in generalities, criticizing Governor Gordon Browning and endorsing the expansion of favored government programs, but not the levying of new taxes. Clement toppled Browning in a four-way race for the Democratic gubernatorial nomination, polling 47 percent of the vote, then trounced a hapless Republican in the general election, 79 percent to 21 percent, even as the Democratic national ticket narrowly lost the Volunteer State. Two years later, Clement won a second term, this one (thanks to a constitutional change) for four years, again defeating Browning, this time in a 3-way primary (with 68 percent of the vote), and a sacrificial Republican in the general election (with 87 percent).

During his first gubernatorial term, Clement sought laws to give cities a fixed share of the state's gasoline and vehicle fuel taxes to fund urban road work (levies in which counties already shared) and to provide for free public school textbooks, both of which passed the legislature, and to modify the state's open shop policy, which failed. A state department of mental health was created; teachers were to receive pay for a minimum of ten months; and funding for programs serving the aged, the blind, the disabled, and dependent children was increased. Costs, however, were shifted to the future by borrowing rather than by increasing taxes, which Clement had pledged not to raise. During his subsequent term, the governor with difficulty won approval of an increase in the state sales tax, with the addition earmarked by the legislature for education and a salary hike for teachers. Clement made an appearance on the national political stage, delivering a heralded but ultimately disappointing keynote address at the Democratic National Convention of 1956: his stump oratorical style (extended speeches, expansive gestures, religious allusions), which had earned him fame in Tennessee and beyond, was ill-suited to the cool medium of network television.

Following the *Brown v. Board of Education* decision and implementation order (1954, 1955), the school desegregation struggle quickly came to dominate Tennessee politics. Governor Clement, no desegregationist, nevertheless was able to have a statewide pupil assignment bill bottled up in the legislature and vetoed local bills to achieve the same segregationist purpose in specified counties (1955). The following year he sent state police and national guardsmen to restore order in Clinton, where mob violence threatened the sole desegregation of a public school system then being undertaken in Tennessee. Early in 1957 Clement, addressing the general assembly (and state), spoke eloquently of blacks' right to equality in public education but then, he responded to the growing fears of whites by proposing bills to permit families (freedom of choice) and local school boards (pupil placement) to preserve, for the time being, school segregation. The measures passed, but the time for such a "compromise" was passing.

Ineligible to succeed himself in 1958, Clement practiced law and languished until he recaptured the governorship at the first opportunity, in 1962, by defeating two rivals to win nomination (with 43 percent of the vote) and an independent and a Republican to win election (with 51 percent). During this term, additional state spending was financed by broadening coverage of the sales tax and increasing other regressive taxes and fees. The governor created a human relations commission but balked at signing a fair practices code drafted by that very body. The code forbade racial discrimination by state government and private companies doing business with the state; it "urged" nondiscrimination by owners and operators of public accommodations. Having failed to secure legislative repeal of the state's death penalty law, about which he had long anguished, Governor Clement commuted five death sentences during his final term.

The death of U.S. senator Estes Kefauver in 1963 set the stage for Clement's political demise. The following year Clement (36 percent) lost the Democratic nomination to complete Kefauver's term to Ross Bass (51 percent), who then defeated Howard Baker, Jr., in the general election. In 1966 Clement edged out Bass, 51 percent to 49 percent, but lost to Baker, 44 percent to 56 percent, who became the state's first popularly elected Republican senator. A growing disaffection toward the Democratic party among white voters, together with the Republicans' traditional support in East Tennessee, was breaking the Democrats' long grip on senatorial and state elections.

Clement likely would have sought to return to the political arena, but he died in an automobile crash in Nashville. A sister, Anna Belle Clement O'Brien, and one son, Bob Clement, also followed political careers.

• The Tennessee State Library and Archives, Nashville, holds the body of Clement's papers; a smaller collection is housed in the Clement Foundation, Dickson. Lee Seifert Greene, *Lead Me On: Frank Goad Clement and Tennessee Politics* (1982), is basic, but also see James B. Gardner, "Political Leadership in a Period of Transition: Frank G. Clement, Albert Gore, Estes Kefauver, and Tennessee Politics, 1948–1956" (Ph.D. diss., Vanderbilt Univ., 1978). Two important works place Clement's career in historical perspective: Numan V. Bartley and Hugh D. Graham, *Southern Politics and the Second Reconstruction* (1975), and Dewey W. Grantham, *The Life and Death of the Solid South: A Political History* (1988). Bartley and Graham, *Southern Elections: County and Precinct Data, 1950–1972* (1978), provides election returns and leads to other sources. Obituaries are in the *Nashville Tennessean* and the *New York Times*, 5, 7 Nov. 1969.

SAMUEL T. McSEVENEY

CLEMENT, Martin Withington (5 Dec. 1881–30 Aug. 1966), railroad executive, was born in Sunbury, Pennsylvania, the son of Charles M. Clement, an attorney and commander of the National Guard's famous Twenty-eighth Division, and Alice Withington. He graduated from Trinity College in Hartford, Connecticut, in 1901. Clement was first employed by a Pennsylvania Railroad (PRR) subsidiary—the United New Jersey Railroad and Canal Company—in various civil engineering tasks related to the construction of the Hudson River tunnels. Beginning in 1910 he served for seven years as track supervisor and chief civil engineer for various eastern divisions of the parent PRR. Early in 1917 he was named superintendent of another subsidiary—the New York, Philadelphia and Norfolk Railroad—thus beginning his career as an operating officer.

When the federal government assumed ownership of the railroads as a wartime measure in 1917, the U.S. Railroad Administration named Clement superintendent of freight transportation for all PRR lines east of Pittsburgh. The following year he assumed direction of passenger traffic in that territory as well. Clement continued his rapid rise after Congress returned the railroads to their private owners in 1920. That year he became superintendent of the Lake division, headquartered in Cleveland. In 1923 he was promoted to general manager of the Central Region, which included all operating divisions between Altoona, Pennsylvania, and Crestline, Ohio.

When William Wallace Atterbury was named the Pennsylvania's president in 1925, he brought Clement to corporate headquarters in Philadelphia as assistant vice president in charge of operations. Clement was promoted to vice president in charge of operations, the PRR's third-ranking post, a year later. During the next four years, his primary task was to oversee the conversion of the 245-mile main line between New York and Washington from steam to electric traction. Including related terminal improvements, this was the largest single capital-improvement project yet undertaken by an American railroad and cost more than $250 million. Clement also took charge of reducing operating costs systemwide as the PRR struggled to combat a loss of traffic brought on by the Great Depression. In the nadir of the depression, the Pennsylvania remained at least marginally profitable.

Clement had married Irene Harrison Higbee in 1910; they had three children. She died in 1929, and in 1931 he married Elizabeth Wallace.

Clement was named acting president of the railroad in 1934, and when Atterbury retired in 1935, Clement succeeded him.

In 1938 Clement completed the extension of electrification west to Harrisburg, Pennsylvania, but World War II intervened before additional improvements could be effected. The railroad easily handled an enormously swollen wartime traffic—a reflection of the increased efficiency achieved in the 1930s—but in the postwar era systemwide modernization of rolling stock, motive power, and physical plant was imperative. Consequently, the last four years of Clement's presidency were devoted largely to containing rapidly rising operating costs and finding means of capital renewal. The task was not easy, since the PRR was hit by rising labor costs and an erosion of heavy industry in the Northeast. High terminal costs and a plethora of money-losing passenger trains compounded the railroad's problems. In its centennial year of 1946, the company reported its first-ever annual net loss. Clement's most far-reaching decision, announced in 1947, was to replace all steam engines with diesel-electric traction, an essential $400 million investment that left little capital for other improvements. He also became a prominent industry spokesman for relaxation of government regulation and for equal treatment of all transportation modes by the federal government.

Clement retired from the presidency in 1949 but was named to the newly created post of chairman of the board, in which he served until 1951. He remained a PRR director until 1957. Clement died at his home in the Rosemont suburb of Philadelphia.

With his extensive background in engineering and operations, Martin Clement typified the kind of up-from-the-ranks executive that ruled the PRR for more than a century. His gruff manner and forthright speech set him apart from more patrician executives. He was a widely respected operating man, but his disdain for modern managerial techniques and for new approaches to such fields as accounting and statistics handicapped the Pennsylvania as it sought to compete with other modes of transportation. His abilities were perhaps better suited to an earlier era than to the changing demands of midtwentieth-century railroading.

• At least some of Clement's presidential papers and an abundance of corporate documents relating to his administration are in the Pennsylvania Railroad collection of the Pennsylvania Historical and Museum Commission. The best insights into Clement as manager are in "Pennsylvania Railroad," *Fortune*, May 1936, pp. 67–77; June 1936, pp. 89–98; and "Pennsy's Predicament," *Fortune*, Mar. 1948, pp. 84–93. Clement was the author of a booklet, *A Railroad President Looks at His Job* (1936), that is more useful in a general managerial sense than for specific references to the PRR. George H. Burgess and Miles C. Kennedy, *Centennial History of the Pennsylvania Railroad* (1949), is a good company history, but since it was commissioned by the Clement administration, it is of limited use in studying his tenure. Obituaries are in the *New York Times* and *Philadelphia Inquirer*, both 31 Aug. 1966.

MICHAEL BEZILLA

CLEMENT, Rufus Early (26 June 1900–7 Nov. 1967), university president, was born in Salisbury, North Carolina, the son of George C. Clement, a bishop in the African Methodist Episcopal (AME) Zion church, and Emma Clarissa Williams, who in 1946 was the first black woman in the United States to be chosen as American Mother of the Year. As a precocious youngster, Clement attended public schools in Charlotte, North Carolina, and Louisville, Kentucky, and graduated from Livingstone College with a B.A. at the early age of nineteen. Three years later, in 1922, he received a B.D. from Garrett Biblical Institute in Evanston, Illinois. During that same year he received an M.A. from Northwestern and married Pearl Ann Johnson of Summer, Mississippi, with whom he had one child. In 1930 he also received a Ph.D. from Northwestern.

During his years of graduate study, he worked as instructor, professor, and dean (in 1925) at Livingstone College, where he was instrumental in the college's obtaining accreditation. He also served as the pastor of an AME Zion church in Landis, North Carolina. He was a baseball coach at Livingstone and a football official of the Colored Intercollegiate Athletic Association. From 1931 to 1937, as dean of the Louisville Municipal College for Negroes, he helped the school to obtain full accreditation. These accomplishments brought him to the attention of the board of trustees of Atlanta University, who selected him to be the university's sixth president. Clement held this position for the rest of his life (almost exactly thirty years). He eventually also became a trustee and forged a significant path for the university and the surrounding community.

Having been recently restructured as a black graduate school in close proximity to several black undergraduate institutions (particularly Morehouse and Spelman), the university joined the Georgia state university system in 1937 with the goal of enhancing the educational and cultural status of blacks. This allowed the university to serve as the hub of a complex of contiguous institutions that under Clement's administration later became known officially as the Atlanta Center of Colleges (composed of Atlanta University, Morehouse College, Spelman College, Clark College, Morris Brown College, and the Gammon Theological Seminary). Clement served as the chief administrator and leader of the initial nucleus and the ultimate six-institution center that provided educational, cultural, and civic background for the historic national civil rights movement that was engendered and nurtured in Atlanta during the 1950s and 1960s. Furthermore, Clement's astute coordination and emphasis on cross-fertilization enabled the center to provide an extensive array of educational options, and it became nationally known for its autonomy and highly productive exchange of curricula and resources among its institutions.

During the 1940s the Clement administration expanded the accredited graduate schools and programs at Atlanta University to include library science, education, business administration, social work, and the People's College for adult education. One daunting task that Clement implemented in 1944 involved his forcibly retiring 75-year-old W. E. B. Du Bois, who had maintained an extremely impressive career at Atlanta University and had a strong national and local reputation as a brilliant scholar and advocate for civil rights. In spite of strong opposition to the contrary, Clement persisted in his contention that Du Bois had reached retirement age and was not eligible for special considerations. This action further established Clement in the enviable position of a national role model of a principle-governed university president.

Throughout his career Clement held a belief that indirect action through professional and civic involvement could help ease racial tension. His life was a testament to that conviction, for he was active in numerous educational and professional associations. Principal among them are his memberships on the Council on Inter-Racial Cooperation, the Southern Regional Council, an advisory committee to the U.S. Office of Education, the Commission on Citizenship of the Association of American Colleges, the American Council on Education (second vice president), the Commission on International Affairs, the World Confederation of the Teaching Profession (a National Education Association delegate), the Institute of International Education (trustee), the National Science Board, and the National Commission on Accrediting. He was the first black to be elected to public office in Atlanta since Reconstruction (he was elected to the school board for four consecutive terms). He was also a charter member of the Georgia Science and Technology Commission, trustee of at least four colleges, trustee of the Phelps-Stokes Fund, and president of the Conference of Presidents of Negro Land Grant Colleges.

An active writer and scholar, Clement served on the editorial board of *Phylon*; he was also a contributing editor to the *Journal of Negro Education* and author of articles on black education in a number of reference journals. He was involved extensively in civic affairs ranging from the Urban League, Planned Parenthood, and the National YMCA to being a member of the U.S. Department of State's Advisory Council on African Affairs. His numerous awards included recognition from *Time* in 1966 as one of the fourteen most influential university presidents in America as well as local recognition of his service.

Clement's major contribution was his devotion to the role of higher education in enhancing the status of blacks and in the maintenance of democracy and world peace. He felt that educators and university administrators must fulfill the requirements of two roles simultaneously: one inside academia—guided by professional ethics and institutional policies—and the other outside—guided by humanitarian goals of service. Until his death in New York City, Clement showed that the two roles could be fulfilled effectively without contradiction.

• The Clement papers are in the Woodroofe Library and in the Presidential Archives of Atlanta University. Clement's correspondence is in the General Education Board Papers, Rockefeller Archive Center, North Tarrytown, N.Y. A useful source is Clarence A. Bacote, *The Story of Atlanta University* (1969). See also *Time*, 11 Feb. 1966. Obituaries are in the *New York Times* and the *Atlanta Constitution*, both 8 Nov. 1967, and the *Atlanta Daily World*, 8 and 12 Nov. 1967.

CLYDE O. MCDANIEL, JR.

CLEMENTE, Roberto Walker (18 Aug. 1934–31 Dec. 1972), baseball player, was born in Carolina, Puerto Rico, the son of Melchor Clemente, a sugar mill foreman, and Luisa Walker. When he was fourteen, Clemente was playing in exhibition games in Puerto Rico alongside Negro League and major league players. During his first season (1952) with the Santurce Cangrejeros, he impressed Brooklyn Dodgers' scout Al Campanis. On his high school graduation in 1954 he signed with the Dodgers for $10,000 and was sent to their highest-level farm team, the Montreal Royals.

The Dodgers took a risk by giving Clemente a year's seasoning at Montreal because of baseball's rules at the time, which stated that players receiving bonuses above $4,000 had to be kept on a team's major league roster during their initial summers or else become eligible for selection by other teams in the minor league draft at season's end. Clemente batted .257 with two home runs and 12 runs batted in in 87 games for the Royals, statistics that seemed hardly good enough to attract outside attention. Nevertheless, the Dodgers' gamble backfired. Former Dodgers' president Branch Rickey, then general manager of the Pittsburgh Pirates and a shrewd finder of talented young players, chose Clemente as the draft's first selection.

Before joining the Pirates in 1955, Clemente played another winter season for Pedrin Zorrilla's Santurce team. In the outfield with future Hall of Fame player Willie Mays and former Homestead Grays' slugger Bob Thurman, he continued to develop his knowledge and skills. These former Negro Leaguers, along with James "Buster" Clarkson, made the young Puerto Rican their special project. After helping his team win the Caribbean championships in Venezuela, Clemente joined the Pirates in Florida for spring training.

Forced into segregated sleeping quarters and denied the opportunity to travel and eat with his teammates, Clemente encountered more virulent prejudice than he had experienced before. His refusal to submit meekly to such arrangements probably led to his reputation as a hothead.

Clemente's 1955 rookie season was unremarkable, but in his second year the graceful, 5′11″, 185-pound outfielder realized some of the potential that the Dodgers, Rickey, and others had predicted for him by batting .311 while driving in 60 runs. Marked by injuries, his next three years with Pittsburgh saw him tail off from his sophomore season. Although his batting average improved each year, it remained under .300; as a right fielder, however, he displayed confidence, daring, a thorough knowledge of National League ballparks, and a virtually matchless throwing arm.

In 1960 he had his best year yet in the major leagues. He played superlatively in the field, batted .314 (with 179 hits and 16 home runs), scored 89 runs, drove in 94 runs, and was named to his first National League All-Star team. Sportswriters began comparing him with Mays, whom many considered the best National League player of the time. But Clemente finished eighth in the Most Valuable Player award voting that autumn. According to teammate Bill Mazeroski, the snub left him bitter and hurt.

In 1961 Clemente improved again, coming into his own as a hitter. That season he led the league in batting at .351, had more than 200 hits for the first time, scored 100 runs and batted in 89, and posted an outstanding .559 slugging average. Still, much of his bitterness remained.

"Latin American Negro ballplayers," he said, "are treated today much like all Negroes were treated in baseball in the early days of the broken color barrier. They are subjected to prejudices and stamped with generalizations. Because they speak Spanish among themselves, they are set off as a minority within a minority. And they bear the brunt of the sport's remaining racial prejudices."

Voicing a sentiment widely held by African-American and Hispanic athletes of his day, Clemente argued that "the Latin player doesn't get the recognition he deserves. Neither does the Negro unless he does something really spectacular." He would fight that stereotyping the rest of his life, both on and off the field.

An intense, driven man, Clemente channeled much of his passion into his playing. His body paid for his reckless style. He suffered from a curved spine, hematomas, a paratyphoid infection, bone chips, and tension headaches as well as everyday bruises, strains, and injuries. The contrast between his grace on the field and his frequent inability to play stirred a frequently heard complaint that Latinos, and especially Clemente, "couldn't take it."

Gradually, Clemente overcame these racial and cultural obstacles. Already a sports hero in Puerto Rico and the Caribbean basin where he starred in winter ball, he won the respect and admiration of Pittsburgh fans and others wherever he competed. Throughout the 1960s, along with Mays and Henry Aaron, he became the standard of excellence for National League outfielders. He led the league in batting three times, recording averages of .339 in 1964, .329 in 1965, and

.357 in 1967. He twice topped the league in hits with 211 in 1964 and 209 in 1967. He became a standout clutch hitter, a legitimate extra-base slugger, and a skilled batter at getting on base. In 1966 and 1967 he both scored and batted in more than 100 runs. And in every season but one during the sixties he was named to the league's All-Star team.

In 1964 Clemente married Vera Cristina Zabala. They had three children.

Finally, in 1971 Clemente achieved the greater recognition he felt he deserved after leading the Pirates to a World Series championship. He collected 12 hits and a .414 batting average, with two home runs, two doubles, and a triple over seven games. Voted the Series' most valuable player, he made several exceptional fielding plays. Moreover, with the Pirates trailing the Baltimore Orioles two games to none, his hustle on a routine groundball caused Orioles' pitcher Mike Cuellar to throw wildly to first base and allow the Pirates to break the third game open, reversing the Series momentum. Afterward he told the press that, at first, sportswriters "thought Latins were inferior to the American people. Now they know they can't be sarcastic about Latins, which is something I have fought for all my life." In two World Series Clemente hit safely in all games in which he played, ending with a .362 average.

On 30 September 1972 Clemente hit a double off New York Mets' pitcher Jon Matlack for his 3,000th hit in regular season play, making him only the eleventh major league player to reach that plateau at the time. The hit marked his last regular season at bat.

During his eighteen seasons with Pittsburgh, Clemente was one of baseball's premier hitters with four batting titles, 240 home runs, 1,305 runs batted in, 1,416 runs scored, and a career .317 average. A fixture in the National League's All-Star lineup and the league's 1966 Most Valuable Player, he also won twelve Gold Gloves for his fielding. Among all outfielders in modern baseball, his throwing arm is known as one of the best.

Clemente was a U.S. citizen, but his sense of himself as Puerto Rican was paramount. Like other ballplayers from the islands, he felt an obligation, despite his many injuries, to play winter ball for his countrymen. After playing during fifteen winters, he sat out 1972–1973 to manage Puerto Rico's team in the Mundiales, the world amateur baseball championships. He spent November and December with the team in Nicaragua. "When we went to Nicaragua that November," Vera Clemente recalled, "Roberto saw himself in the boys in the streets—without shoes, living in a one-room house with ten people—much like it had been when his father worked for the sugar mill in Carolina" (unpublished interview with Rob Ruck, 1989).

After the Clementes returned to Puerto Rico, an earthquake rocked Managua. He and his wife spearheaded relief efforts organized on the island. When reports surfaced of the Nicaraguan National Guard pilfering aid shipments, Clemente decided to fly there himself to be sure that the relief reached those in need.

But his plane, which took off on New Year's Eve 1972, plunged into the waters off San Juan. Clemente's body was never recovered.

As early as 1964, Clemente had conceived of building a sports city for the children of Puerto Rico. His death was the catalyst for the creation of Ciudad Deportiva, a sporting complex financed by government donations of land and corporate and private financial contributions.

In 1971 the Baseball Writers Association of America waived its five-year waiting period and overwhelmingly elected Clemente to the National Baseball Hall of Fame. Lou Gehrig was the only other player for whom the waiting period was dismissed. Clemente was the first Latin ballplayer enshrined in Cooperstown. As time passed, Clemente has become a legendary figure wherever baseball is played throughout the Caribbean basin and in Hispanic communities in the United States. If Babe Ruth is the classic hero for baseball's preintegration era, and Jackie Robinson the modern game's pioneer, Clemente was the paladin for Latin Americans in the "American" pastime.

• The best biography is *Clemente!* by Kal Wagenheim (1973). Another good source is *Roberto Clemente: Aun Escucha Las Ovaciónes* by Luís Rodríguez-Mayoral (1987). See also *Who Was Roberto? A Biography of Roberto Clemente* by Phil Musick (1974) and *Roberto* by Bill Christine (1973). There are several juvenile biographies but no other social or career history of the man and his impact. His obituary is in the *New York Times*, 2 Jan. 1973.

ROB RUCK

CLEMENTS, Frederic Edward (16 Sept. 1874–26 July 1945), botanist and ecologist, was born in Lincoln, Nebraska, the son of Ephraim George Clements, a photographer, and Mary Angeline Scoggin. At the age of sixteen Clements entered the University of Nebraska, where he studied under the influential botanist Charles Bessey and earned a B.Sc. in 1894, an M.A. in 1896, and a Ph.D. in 1898. During his student years he was an active member of the "Botanical Seminar," an informal group of Bessey's students who carried out an ambitious survey of the vegetation of Nebraska. Together with classmate Roscoe Pound, who would later become a famous jurist, Clements wrote *The Phytogeography of Nebraska* (1898), a work that brought the authors international recognition among botanists.

Clements began teaching at the University of Nebraska as an instructor in 1897, and after the publication of his first major book, *Research Methods in Ecology* (1905), he was promoted to full professor of plant physiology. Although Clements continued to conduct taxonomic and phytogeographical research, this book marked a shift in his interests toward the new science of ecology. *Research Methods in Ecology* was a manifesto for the emerging field. Describing ecology as a synthetic approach to the study of plants, Clements wrote, "Ecology is therefore considered the dominant theme in the study of plants, indeed, as the central and vital part of botany." According to Clements, ecology was closely related to physiology in that both involved studying the relationship between organic structure and function, but while physiologists studied plants in the laboratory, ecologists studied plants in their natural environments. Plant communities were "complex organisms" each with a characteristic life cycle (succession) determined by the physical conditions of the environment. Like laboratory physiologists, ecologists would need to use rigorous quantitative and experimental methods to study these developmental processes. These ideas were controversial because many botanists denied that the theories and laboratory methods used by plant physiologists could be directly applied to ecology. Nonetheless, Clements's physiological claims struck a responsive chord among some plant ecologists, and *Research Methods in Ecology* propelled him to the forefront of the new discipline.

In 1907 Clements was appointed chairman of the botany department at the University of Minnesota, a position that he held for the next ten years. During these years he wrote his most important book, *Plant Succession* (1916), in which Clements restated his ideas of the plant community as an organism and succession as a developmental process: "The unit of vegetation, the climax formation, is an organic entity. As a complex organism the formation arises, grows, matures, and dies." To support these views, Clements synthesized an impressive body of observations, and he created an elaborate terminology to describe the various stages of plant succession. Like his earlier book, *Plant Succession* was controversial, for many prominent ecologists denied that succession was as progressive as the development of a mature plant from a seed. Even critics, however, admitted that Clements's massive treatise provided an important foundation for ecology. In a critique written two decades later (*Journal of Ecology* [1935]), Arthur Tansley, the leading British plant ecologist, prefaced his critical comments with the statement, "Dr. Clements has given us a theory of vegetation which has formed an indispensable foundation for the most fruitful modern work [in ecology]. . . . Clements is by far the greatest individual creator of the modern science of vegetation."

In 1917 Clements was appointed research associate of the Carnegie Institution of Washington. He devoted the rest of his career completely to research, working summers at his Alpine Laboratory near Pikes Peak, Colorado, and winters at Santa Barbara, California. During the 1920s he and his co-workers published several monographs on diverse topics in plant ecology, physiology, taxonomy, and evolution. None of these books proved to be as influential as *Plant Succession*, but they solidified Clements's reputation as the leading plant ecologist of the day. During this period he also began to collaborate with Victor Shelford on *Bio-Ecology* (1939), which attempted to synthesize plant and animal ecology.

During the 1930s Clements became increasingly preoccupied with attempts to demonstrate the inheritance of acquired traits. He claimed that he was able to convert lowland species into related alpine species by transplanting them to a higher elevation. These claims were never substantiated. Coming during the period of the modern synthesis of Mendelism and Darwinian natural selection, Clements's neo-Lamarckian views were considered idiosyncratic by his contemporaries. He continued his evolutionary studies after he retired in 1941, but the Carnegie Institution refused to publish the results after his death at Santa Barbara.

The careers of Clements and his wife, Edith Schwartz, whom he had married in 1899, were virtually inseparable. A skilled illustrator and professionally trained botanist, Edith Clements helped her husband prepare several taxonomic manuals. Because of her husband's delicate health, she also assisted his research in many other ways, acting as his secretary, field assistant, driver, and nurse. The couple had no children.

Later in his career Clements chose to work in his private laboratories at Pikes Peak and Santa Barbara, even after other botanists with the Carnegie Institution had moved to a new laboratory building at Stanford University. This further isolated him from his colleagues. Some of his contemporaries considered him to be aloof, dogmatic, and arrogant. Nonetheless, Clements was widely admired, and he was among the leading ecologists before World War II. Although many of the details of his work have not stood the test of time, the broad outline of his view of ecological succession as a dynamic process has continued to be influential.

• A large collection of Clements's correspondence, field notebooks, and photographs is housed in the American Heritage Center at the University of Wyoming. Included in this collection is a revealing, unpublished biographical sketch by Edith Clements. The archives of the Carnegie Institution of Washington contain many records dealing with his years there as a research associate. Short biographical sketches by former colleagues include those by Raymond Pool, *Ecology* 35 (1954): 109–12, and Roscoe Pound, *Ecology* 35 (1954): 112–13. Some important insights into Clements's life and career are also provided by Edith Clements's informal biography, *Adventures in Ecology: Half a Million Miles . . . from Mud to Macadam* (1960). Malcolm Nicolson, "National Styles, Divergent Classifications: A Comparative Case Study from the History of French and American Plant Ecology," *Knowledge in Society* 8 (1989): 139–86, discusses Clements's work in some detail. For other scholarly analyses of particular aspects of Clements's work and his role in the history of ecology see Donald Worster, *Nature's Economy: The Roots of Ecology* (1977); Ronald C. Tobey, *Saving the Prairies: The Life Cycle of the Founding School of American Plant Ecology, 1895–1955* (1981); and Joel B. Hagen, "Clementsian Ecologists: The Dynamics of a Research Group," *Osiris* 8 (1993): 178–95. Obituaries include those by former colleagues H. L. Shantz, *Ecology* 26 (1945): 317–19, and Arthur Tansley, *Journal of Ecology* 34 (1947): 194–96.

JOEL B. HAGEN

CLEMENTS, Gabrielle DeVaux (11 Sept. 1858–23 Mar. 1948), oil and mural painter and etcher, was born in Philadelphia, Pennsylvania, the daughter of Richard Clements, a physician, and Gabrielle DeVaux. When she was seventeen, Clements studied lithography with Charles Page, an ornamental designer and printmaker, at the Philadelphia School of Design for Women. She made scientific drawings and lithographs for Cornell University, from which she received a B.S. in 1880. Although her coursework specialized in science, she wrote her senior thesis on "A Study of Two German Masters in Medieval Art, Dürer and Holbein." Clements studied with painter Thomas Eakins from 1880 to 1883 at the Pennsylvania Academy of the Fine Arts. In 1883 she won the academy's Toppan Prize for the second-best painting by a student.

In 1883 Clements studied etching from Stephen Parrish in Philadelphia. Clements immediately began to make her name known as a professional etcher, exhibiting a variety of subjects early the next year with the New York Etching Club, including *A Tramp*, which art reviewer Ripley W. Hitchcock included in his 1884 portfolio *Some Modern Etchings*. Clements's etchings were also published by L. Prang & Co. and Christian Klackner.

Clements traveled with her mother to Paris in 1884 to study at the Académie Julian with prominent painters Tony Robert-Fleury and William A. Bouguereau. She was joined in 1885 by her friend Ellen Day Hale, a painter and printmaker who was to become Clements's lifelong companion. During the summer they visited Chartres, where Clements taught Hale to etch. Later that year Clements returned to her studio in Philadelphia, where she taught etching to other artists, including Margaret White Lesley (later, Margaret Lesley Bush-Brown), a painter who championed feminism. Clements had begun exhibiting at the Pennsylvania Academy in 1882. Over the years she also exhibited at the National Academy of Design, the Museum of Fine Arts in Boston, the Philadelphia Society of Artists, the New York Etching Club, the Boston Art Club, the Association of Canadian Etchers, the Boston Art Students' Association, the Boston Water Color Club, and the Massachusetts Charitable Mechanic Association. She entered twenty-one etchings in the Museum of Fine Art's *Women Etchers of America* in 1887, the first museum exhibition of women artists' work.

Clements moved to Baltimore in 1895 to teach art at the Bryn Mawr School, a school for girls established in the early 1890s. She taught at the school until 1908. Between 1896 and 1931 Clements was commissioned by the Bendann Galleries to etch a series of nine views of Baltimore, for which she became well known in the city. Between 1895 and 1908 Clements painted murals in five churches in the Washington, D.C.–Maryland area and one in Detroit. She was also commissioned to paint a mural, *Harvest*, for the Ladies' Reception Room of the Pennsylvania State Building at the 1893 World's Columbian Exposition in Chicago, and a mural for the New Century Club building in Philadelphia.

For years Clements and Hale, who moved to Washington, D.C., in 1904, spent summers on Cape Ann near Gloucester, Massachusetts, where Hale had purchased a house at Rockport's Folly Cove in 1884. Clements designed her studio to accommodate mural painting and printed all of her etchings and aquatints there. She exhibited, painted, and etched scenes of the working aspects of ships and harbors with the Rockport Art Association, the Folly Cove Etchers, and the North Shore Arts Association. Clements and Hale traveled frequently and produced scenes of France, Italy, Egypt, Syria, and Palestine. During World War I they remained in the United States, spending the winters in Charleston, South Carolina. There Clements, with Hale, trained a new generation of women etchers. In the 1920s she and Hale were in the forefront of color printmaking, experimenting with soft-ground etching and aquatint in color *à la poupée* (dabbing colored ink onto the plate with a small rag bag for each run through the press) in their Rockport studio with several younger Cape Ann artists. They documented their processes with careful notes, which have been preserved in the National Museum of American History, Smithsonian Institution.

Clements exhibited in major expositions, including the 1888 Ohio Valley Centennial, the 1893 World's Columbian Exposition in Chicago, the 1895 Cotton States and International Exposition in Atlanta, the 1901 Inter-State and West Indian Exposition in Charleston, the 1904 Louisiana Purchase Exposition in St. Louis, and Philadelphia's 1926 Sesqui-Centennial International Exposition. She also exhibited with the Society of American Etchers, the Chicago Society of Etchers, the Baltimore Charcoal Club, the Society of Washington Artists, the National Art Club, the Library of Congress, and at Goodspeed's in Boston. The J. B. Speed Art Museum in Louisville, Kentucky, and the U.S. National Museum, Smithsonian Institution in Washington, D.C., held special exhibitions of experimental color etchings made by Clements and her colleagues.

Clements died in Rockport, Massachusetts. While clearly a professional artist highly regarded by her peers, she, like most of her female colleagues, received only occasional attention from critics, who singled her out as one of a group of "lady amateurs" who were "'somebody' in society" (*Art Amateur* 20 [Jan. 1889]: 28). Clements, who remained single all her life, was active, energetic, and forceful. Her friend and fellow artist Cecilia Beaux wrote in a letter from Paris to her aunt Eliza Drinker (14 Feb. 1889) that neither a bout with poor health nor disappointments would ever cause Clements the "supreme wretchedness of thinking herself a failure." Clements's long professional career, filled with variety and experimentation, was an inspiration to the many young women she taught and to the many artists with whom she associated and shared her skills.

• Clements's papers are in the Archives of American Art, Smithsonian Institution, and in the Department of Manuscripts and University Archives, Cornell University. See also the Cecilia Beaux Papers in the Archives of American Art, and the Hale Family Papers in the Sophia Smith Collection, Smith College. The Graphic Arts Division of the National Museum of American History, Smithsonian Institution, holds Clements's descriptions of her experiments in color printing, as well as a collection of her rare prints. See also

Goodspeed's Bookshop, *Exhibition and Sale of Etchings and Soft-ground Aquatints in Color of French, Italian and American Subjects by Ellen Day Hale and Gabrielle DeV. Clements* (1924); and J. B. Speed Memorial Museum, *Exhibition of Etchings in Color by Ellen Day Hale, Gabrielle DeVeaux Clements, Lesley Jackson, Margaret Yeaton Joyt, Theresa F. Bernstein, and William Meyerowitz, November 30 to December 30, 1935* (1935). An obituary is in the *New York Times*, 28 Mar. 1948.

PHYLLIS PEET

CLEMMER, Mary. *See* Ames, Mary Clemmer.

CLENDENING, Logan (25 May 1884–31 Jan. 1945), physician, was born in Kansas City, Missouri, the son of Edwin McKaig Clendening, a businessman, and Lide Logan. Clendening attended the University of Michigan in 1903–1904 and received an M.D. from the University of Kansas in 1907. Clendening then spent a year of internship at Chicago's Augustana Hospital, after which he pursued postgraduate medical work in England and at the University of Edinburgh. In 1912 Clendening returned to his alma mater, the University of Kansas, as an instructor of internal medicine. In 1914 he married Dorothy Scott Hixon; they had no children. Called into active duty in 1917, Clendening served two years as a major in the U.S. Army Medical Corps, in which he held command of the medical practice of Fort Sam Houston's base hospital in San Antonio, Texas. He returned to the University of Kansas School of Medicine in 1919 as assistant professor, and later became associate professor (1924) and professor (1928) of clinical medicine, a position he held until his death. Before a class of medical students, Clendening typically assumed the disabilities manifested by a particular disease and performed a series of apparently well-rehearsed one-act skits. These skits—occasionally intermixed with ribald anecdotes—were his forte, and they supported his claim that "it isn't enough to throw facts at medical students . . . [you have to] cover your facts with mud to make them stick."

Clendening pursued both an academic and a media-based medical career. Following the publication of his academic *Modern Methods of Treatment* in 1924, one reader, Baltimore author H. L. Mencken, urged the publisher Alfred P. Knopf to engage Clendening in writing a popular work about human physiology. Clendening's *The Human Body* first appeared in 1927. Clendening specifically desired to "make intelligible some of the intricacies of the human body for the adult and otherwise sophisticated reader" (p. v). His work was an attempt to fill the gap between the plethora of writings that offered "rules for the sudden acquisition of health," publications "designed to prolong . . . life" (p. v), and high school physiology texts, which, he claimed, tended to be "filled with a pious pedantry designed to instil a horror of alcohol, adultery, houseflies, and school desks" (p. 6). Critics compared the stature of this work written for the lay audience to H. G. Wells's *The Outline of History* (1920) and Will

Durant's *The Story of Philosophy* (1926). Durant, himself, added Clendening's bestseller to his "Hundred Best Books for an Education." *The Human Body* was translated into Italian and Spanish, and it also appeared in a "Pocket-Book" edition.

Clendening's success and apparent ease at writing for the public soon led to a daily newspaper column, "Diet and Health," which was eventually syndicated in 382 newspapers with a combined readership of 25 million. Running daily from 1928 through 1943, the column addressed such issues as vitamins, diabetes, prickly heat, poison ivy, hay fever, body odor, bowel function, overeating, and heart failure. Clendening's written advice varied from the cynical to the optimistic, but, as medical historian Robert Hudson noted, even when Clendening was "imparting knowledge," he was "entertaining—purely and simply entertaining." His cynical side is expressed in the closing line of *The Human Body*: "When death comes, you may be certain you will disappear like all the rest and that you will not be missed nearly as much as in your sanguine moments you have been inclined to suppose." Elsewhere, he more cheerfully advised laughter as the best medicine. "If you've got the high blood pressure, laugh! If you've got the low blood pressure, laugh! The more you laugh, the longer you'll live."

In addition to Clendening's extensive efforts to create new daily columns, he maintained an active teaching schedule and published ten more books as well as popular articles in the *Saturday Evening Post, Atlantic Monthly,* and *American Mercury.* Through the financial assistance of his wife as well as his own lucrative publishing career, Clendening became an avid collector and reader of rare medical books. For many years, he kept these books in a "retreat, a hideout, for literary research," in an office building in downtown Kansas City. He later moved this working library into his already "bookish" Kansas City home. He incorporated extensive historical insight into his classroom teaching and writing.

At a time when medical history became a special field of scholarly study in the United States, Clendening contributed two choice works to the field. The first, *The Romance of Medicine* (later titled *Behind the Doctor*) was published in 1933 as a layman's guide to medicine and the treatment of disease throughout human history. In it, he incorporated tales of "all those men and women, from private herb-gatherers, to skilled modern scientists, whose shadows stand 'behind the doctor' whenever he treats" patients. The other, *Source Book of Medical History* (1942), is a collection of original writings in the field of medicine from ancient Egypt through the late nineteenth-century discovery of X-rays. Clendening promoted the founding of a Department of the History of Medicine at the University of Kansas and became its first professor in 1940. He was also an active member of the American Association for the History of Medicine, serving as this organization's vice president in 1942 and ascending to the presidency upon the death of Jabez Elliott later that year.

Active in many professional societies, Clendening was a fellow of the American College of Physicians and served on its board of governors from 1926 to 1930 and its board of regents in 1931, as well as of the American Therapeutic Society and the American Clinical and Climatological Society. He held memberships in the Kansas City Country Club, the Grolier Club (N.Y.), and the Santa Barbara Country Club (Calif.). He presided over the weekly meetings of a Kansas City "version of the Algonquin round-table which its members [including psychiatrist Karl Menninger] called 'the vicious Circle'" (*Kansas City Daily Journal*, 28 July 1982). Clendening died in Kansas City.

• Clendening's rare book collection forms the nucleus of the Logan Clendening Library for the History of Medicine at the University of Kansas School of Medicine in Kansas City, Kans. Clendening's writings for a lay audience include *The Care and Feeding of Adults* (1931), *The Balanced Diet* (1936), *Handbook to "Pickwick Papers"* (1936), and *Common Sense Health Chats* (1936). His Sherlockiana essay, *The Case of the Missing Patriarchs Translated from the Thyroid* (1934), is well known amongst Sherlock Holmes enthusiasts. For practitioners, Clendening composed his *Work Book in Elementary Diagnosis* (1938), and his *Methods of Diagnosis* was posthumously published in 1947. Robert P. Hudson collected anecdotes about Clendening's teaching style and overall character in "Logan Clendening: The Anatomy of A Teacher," *Journal of the Kansas Medical Society* 69 (1968): 154–56, 160; and in "A Clendening Sampler," *Journal of the Kansas Medical Society* 70 (1969): 151–55. Ralph Major, Clendening's successor to the chair of medical history, offered an illuminating account in *Logan Clendening* (1958). An obituary is in the *New York Times*, 1 Feb. 1945.

PHILIP K. WILSON

CLEVELAND, Benjamin (26 May 1738–Oct. 1806), frontiersman and militia officer in the revolutionary war, was born in Prince William County, Virginia, the son of John Cleveland, a house-joiner, and Martha Coffee. Cleveland had a limited education and hated the drudgery of farm life. He spent his early years hunting, gambling, drinking, fighting, and "frolicking." Marriage to Mary Graves in 1761 did little to reform his ways. They had two children, but Cleveland also fathered a child by another woman in Virginia.

In 1769 Cleveland convinced his father-in-law to move to North Carolina. The Cleveland-Graves family settled in the upper Yadkin River valley. Cleveland still showed little interest in farming, however, and while his father-in-law's slaves cleared land for a new plantation, Cleveland continued to hunt. Later Cleveland moved to a tract he called "the Round About" on the north side of the Yadkin River.

From a neighbor, Daniel Boone, Cleveland learned in the early 1770s of the bountiful hunting grounds of Kentucky. In 1772 Cleveland and four companions set out to explore and hunt in Kentucky. Cherokee Indians, however, intercepted them and seized all their horses, guns, skins, and valuables. Cleveland's hunting party barely made it back to the settlements. With typical audacity, Cleveland returned to the Cherokee nation to recover his stolen property, boldly moving from village to village.

When the Revolution began, Cleveland quickly assumed a leading military role. A "most zealous patriot," Cleveland earned a fearsome reputation as a scourge of Loyalists. Declining an appointment as ensign in the Second Regiment of North Carolina Continental troops in 1775, he remained in the militia with the rank of captain and took part in the Moores Creek campaign against Scottish Loyalists in February 1776 and the campaign against the Cherokee in the summer of 1776. In 1777 he patrolled the Watauga settlements to protect them from Cherokee attacks while a peace treaty was negotiated at Long Island on the Holston River. In 1778 he was appointed colonel of the Wilkes County militia.

Probably the most powerful figure in the county, Cleveland also held many civil posts. When the county court, of which he was a justice, transformed itself into the safety committee in 1775, Cleveland was elected chairman. He also served as commissioner of confiscated estates of Tories, superintendent of elections, and county ranger or stray master. He represented Wilkes County in the North Carolina House of Commons in 1778 and 1779 and the North Carolina Senate in 1780. As a member of the General Assembly and a slave owner, he voted against bills to raise taxes and ascertain taxable property but voted for a bill to apprehend and sell slaves set free contrary to law.

Cleveland's merciless treatment of the Loyalists spawned many stories about his cruel behavior. Cleveland summarily hanged Tories whom he regarded as "obnoxious." Others he allowed to take an oath of allegiance to the state on a pledge of future good conduct. Still others received severe whippings. Indicted in the superior court of Salisbury for murdering two Loyalists in 1779, he received a pardon from the governor after the General Assembly passed a resolution requesting it. Cleveland himself was captured by Tories in 1781, but his brother Bob rescued him.

The pinnacle of Cleveland's military career was the battle of Kings Mountain on 7 October 1780. As Lord Cornwallis advanced north from South Carolina into North Carolina, he sent Major Patrick Ferguson deep into the backcountry to protect his left flank, rouse the Tories, and crush any Whig resistance. Approximately 900 "overmountain men" responded to Ferguson's challenge at Kings Mountain on the North Carolina–South Carolina border. Cleveland led one of the four columns of militiamen, who utterly defeated Ferguson's force of approximately 125 British regulars and 1,000 Tories in a battle regarded as the turning point of the war in the South. In the aftermath of the battle nine Tory prisoners were hanged, and Cleveland was said to be the most insistent of the Whig leaders in carrying out the executions.

"Much addicted to plunder," Cleveland did not always distinguish between Whig and Tory property. The pacifist Moravians around Salem complained bitterly about the militiamen under Cleveland who went into stores and workshops, took what they wanted,

and charged it to the "public account." A land speculator, Cleveland amassed considerable holdings during the Revolution. Although he lost his Round About plantation to a better claim, he recorded 7,432 acres, and 4,000 acres, respectively, in the Wilkes County tax lists of 1784 and 1785. In the latter year Cleveland moved to South Carolina and took up land along the Tugaloo River.

In his final years he served as an associate judge on the Pendleton County court with partisan leader Andrew Pickens. Always a large man, Cleveland ballooned to 450 pounds. Unable to mount a horse any longer, he traveled by wagon and wore only a shift or blouse in warm weather. He died at his plantation on the Tugaloo River, in what is now Oconee County, South Carolina.

Cleveland represented a crude class of backcountry gentry who led the Revolution on the frontier. Experienced in American Indian warfare, acquisitive for land, and already in control of local government, they eagerly opposed Great Britain and ruthlessly quashed any Loyalist dissent, real and imagined. Despite his reputation for brutality, Cleveland's exploits passed into local legend. In 1841 the state of North Carolina named a county in his honor.

• The Lyman C. Draper Collection, State Historical Society of Wisconsin, comprises by far the richest source of materials on Cleveland. Information on Cleveland is also found in the Lenoir Family Papers, Southern Historical Collection, University of North Carolina at Chapel Hill. The best account of his life remains Lyman C. Draper, *King's Mountain and Its Heroes* (1881). Scattered references to him appear in William L. Saunders and Walter Clark, eds., *Colonial and State Records of North Carolina* (30 vols., 1890–1914); Adelaide L. Fries et al., eds., *Records of the Moravians in North Carolina* (11 vols., 1922–1969); and J. G. de Roulhac Hamilton, ed., "Revolutionary Diary of William Lenoir," *Journal of Southern History* 6 (1940): 247–59. Betty Linney Waugh offers a modern assessment of Cleveland in "The Upper Yadkin River in the American Revolution: Benjamin Cleveland, Symbol of Continuity" (Ph.D. diss., Univ. of New Mexico, 1971). Jeffrey J. Crow places Cleveland's activities in the context of an internal war in "Liberty Men and Loyalists: Disorder and Disaffection in the North Carolina Backcountry," in *An Uncivil War: The Southern Backcountry during the American Revolution*, ed. Ronald Hoffman et al. (1985).

JEFFREY J. CROW

CLEVELAND, Emeline Horton (22 Sept. 1829–8 Dec. 1878), surgeon, medical professor, and dean at the Woman's Medical College of Pennsylvania, was born in Ashford, Connecticut, the daughter of Chauncey Horton and Amanda Chaffee, farmers. In 1831 her family settled in a remote farming area in Madison County, New York. Cleveland received her initial education from private tutors engaged by her father at a school he fashioned on the Horton property.

By the time Cleveland had attained education sufficient to allow her to attend college, her father had died, eliminating any financial assistance she might have had from her family. Like many of her female contemporaries who would seek medical degrees,

Cleveland taught school to secure the necessary funds for her college education. During the fall term of 1850, she matriculated at Oberlin College in Ohio, a flourishing coeducational and liberal institution. She graduated with a Bachelor of Arts degree in August 1853.

Infused with a missionary zeal and the desire to be a physician, Cleveland was drawn to the Female Medical College of Pennsylvania (renamed in 1867 the Woman's Medical College of Pennsylvania), whose reputation for training medical missionaries promised spiritual fulfillment. Typically, a mid-nineteenth-century medical education did not require a college degree and consisted of a four-month course of lectures that was repeated the second year. Cleveland began her medical preparation in October 1853. After the first year's course, she returned to her home and married the Reverend Giles Butler Cleveland in March 1854. Her husband, with whom she had grown to adulthood in New York State, was a Presbyterian minister and graduate of the Oberlin College Theological Seminary. Cleveland returned to Philadelphia, graduating in March 1855 from the Female Medical College with a medical degree, then opened a practice near her New York home. Although the couple had hoped to pursue missionary work, her husband's poor health closed that career avenue.

In 1856 the Female Medical College beckoned her to demonstrate anatomy, and the couple moved to Philadelphia, where Cleveland opened a private practice to augment income from her teaching duties. An appointment as chair of anatomy and physiology followed in 1857. During the winter months of 1857–1858, her husband became seriously ill, resulting in partial paralysis. Cleveland became the sole support of the family.

At the urging of Dr. Ann Preston, the first woman dean of the Female Medical College, and with financial aid, Cleveland entered in 1860 the School of Obstetrics at the Maternité of Paris, from which she received a diploma and five awards in 1861. Subsequently, she visited hospitals and medical schools in Paris and London to enrich her understanding of hospital management.

In September 1861 Cleveland began her duties as chief resident of the Woman's Hospital of Philadelphia, a joint venture with the medical college, which opened 16 December. In addition to her appointment at Woman's Hospital, she was professor of obstetrics and gynecology and diseases of women and children at the medical college.

Cleveland and Preston shared a common vision for training women physicians. Their simultaneous presence on the boards of the medical college and the hospital linked medical instruction in the classroom with clinical instruction in the hospital. Still, they realized that the best clinical instruction was available at the nearby male-only medical institutions. Both believed that attendance at lectures would place women medical students on an equal footing with their male counterparts. To that end they gained admission to lectures for their students at the Philadelphia Hospital at Blockley in January 1869. The women attended classes without rancor from the male students there, but on 6 November 1869, when the women students attended their first lectures at the University of Pennsylvania, they were met with hostile resistance by the male medical students. On that occasion, male students staged an uproar, prompting local physicians to protest against coeducational clinical instruction. Cleveland and Preston penned a reply pointing out that the women students were to attend lectures on alternate days from the male students, forestalling any embarrassment that might flow from exhibitions of body parts in mixed company. By May 1871 the furor had subsided.

Elsewhere, the Philadelphia County Medical Society and the Pennsylvania State Medical Society refused to admit women. Cleveland and Preston appealed to the Pennsylvania State Medical Society to rescind its resolution rejecting women members. Both women were dead, however, before the Pennsylvania State Medical Society relented in 1881 and the Philadelphia County Medical Society followed in 1888.

In 1872 Cleveland was selected dean of the Woman's Medical College of Pennsylvania to succeed Ann Preston, a position she held until 1874, when she resigned because of poor health. During her tenure as dean, the school's enrollment grew by 5 percent, attracting women who desired to be surgeons. Cleveland had the distinction of being one of the first female surgeons in the United States to successfully remove ovarian tumors. Despite her skill as a surgeon, she was denied admission to the Philadelphia Obstetrical Society, yet, the society published one of her papers in its journal ("A Complicated Case of Vesico-Vaginal Fistula," *Transactions* [1877]). At the time of her death in Philadelphia from tuberculosis, she held the position of gynecologist for the Department of the Insane at Philadelphia Hospital.

Reared in an environment of religious fervor, it was not coincidental that Cleveland subscribed wholeheartedly to the notion of scientific motherhood. Education, she believed, enhanced a woman's knowledge and made her a superior mother. Her only child, a son, was born in 1865. Unlike the prevailing attitude, Cleveland conceived of motherhood and medicine as complementary rather than as antithetical. She taught by example, successfully combining feminine attributes and surgical skill. An astute critic, Mary Putnam Jacobi, wrote in *Woman's Work in America* (p. 158), "Dr. Cleveland was a woman of real ability, and would have done justice to a much larger sphere than that to which fate condemned her."

• The largest body of information about Cleveland, housed at the Allegheny University of the Health Sciences Archives and Special Collections on Women in Medicine in Philadelphia, includes Eliza Mosher, "The History of American Medical Women," *Medical Woman's Journal* 29 (Nov. 1922): 292–96; Bertha L. Selmon, "Woman's Medical College of Pennsylvania," *Medical Woman's Journal* 52 (Oct. 1945): 41–43; and Martha Tracy, "A Retrospect," reprinted from the *Seventy-fifth Anniversary Volume of the Woman's Medical College of Pennsylvania* (1926), pp. 1–6. At that same location is Gulielma Fell Alsop, *History of the Woman's Medical College Philadelphia, Pennsylvania 1850–1950* (1950), and Clara Marshall, *The Woman's Medical College of Pennsylvania: An Historical Outline* (1897). Contextual understanding of Cleveland's time is provided in Regina Markell Morantz-Sanchez, *Sympathy and Science: Women Physicians in American Medicine* (1985). A valuable unpublished source that illustrates the congenial relationship between Cleveland and Ann Preston is Pauline Poole Foster, "Ann Preston, M.D. (1813–1872): A Biography: The Struggle to Obtain Training and Acceptance for Women Physicians in Mid-Nineteenth Century America" (Ph.D. diss., Univ. of Pennsylvania, 1984). Genealogical records are published in Edmund J. and Horace G. Cleveland, *Genealogy of the Cleveland and Cleaveland Families* (1899). Mary Putnam Jacobi offered her contemporary view of women in medicine in *Woman's Work in America*, ed. Annie Nathan Meyer (1891; repr. 1972). An in-depth obituary is in *Papers Read at the Memorial Hour Commemorative of the Late Prof. Emeline H. Cleveland, M.D.* (1879), a pamphlet housed at the Allegheny University of the Health Sciences Archives and Special Collections on Women in Medicine.

JAYNE CRUMPLER DEFIORE

CLEVELAND, Frances Folsom (21 July 1864–29 Oct. 1947), wife of Grover Cleveland, was born in Buffalo, New York, the daughter of Oscar Folsom, an attorney, and Emma Harmon. Frances Folsom knew Grover Cleveland as her father's law partner. When Oscar Folsom died in an accident in 1875, his law partner took over management of his estate and became in effect, although not in fact, Frances Folsom's guardian. Twenty-seven years her senior, he played the part of doting uncle to "Frankie" while piling up remarkable political victories, rising from mayor of Buffalo to governor of the state.

Frances Folsom enrolled at Wells College in 1882 and graduated three years later, celebrating her accomplishment with a tour of Europe from September 1885 to May 1886. Before setting off on that journey with her mother, she had visited the White House, then occupied by bachelor president Grover Cleveland, and had accepted his marriage proposal. Wedding plans remained secret, however, and journalists continued to speculate on various romantic interests of the president. Reports linked him with the widow Emma Folsom and with other women.

On 2 June 1886, in the only White House wedding of an incumbent chief executive, Frances Folsom and Grover Cleveland were married. The bride's grandfather, whose home might have served for the nuptials, had recently died, and the Folsoms did not have access to another home offering adequate security and space. The ceremony occurred in the Blue Room in the presence of about thirty relatives and cabinet members. The president had penned the invitations himself.

Just short of her twenty-second birthday at the time of the wedding, Frances Cleveland was the youngest woman to become first lady, at least as wife of the president (female relatives had sometimes substituted for ailing wives of presidents at a younger age). In addition to her youth, she brought a remarkably attractive personality to her position, and she became enormously popular. American women copied her hairstyle,

adopted her nickname, and emulated her in various other ways. Advertisers seized on her fame by linking her with their products until one irate congressman introduced legislation (never passed) that would have made it illegal to use images of female relatives of political leaders in advertisements.

His young, popular bride helped improve the reputation of the president, who had, at the time of the 1882 election, been linked publicly with a Buffalo woman whose child he admitted supporting. Rumors of his boorishness continued, however, and in the 1888 election Frances Cleveland made public a letter she had sent in reply to one asserting that the president mistreated her: "I can wish the women of our country no greater blessing than that their homes and lives may be as happy and their husbands may be as kind, attentive, considerate and affectionate as mine." Notwithstanding that disclaimer, Grover Cleveland failed to win reelection (he captured the popular vote but did not win in the electoral college). As Frances Cleveland prepared to vacate the White House, she predicted correctly that she would return four years later.

During the interim between the two terms, the Clevelands lived in New York City, where their first daughter was born in October 1891. Soon after they returned to the White House in 1893, a second daughter was born, the only child of a president to be born in the mansion.

During the summer of 1893, when her husband was operated on for cancer of the jaw, Frances Cleveland participated in the ruse that kept the surgery a secret from the public. Because of an already bad economic climate, the president and his advisers feared that news of his illness might adversely affect business, so he arranged for the operation to be performed in secrecy on a private yacht near New York City. When he did not arrive, as scheduled, at the Clevelands' summer home in Massachusetts, reporters approached his wife for some news of his whereabouts and threatened to write articles calling attention to his disappearance. She reassured them that no mystery was involved and requested that they write nothing. As a result, the details of the surgery were not generally known until 1917, long after the president had died of other causes.

At the end of Cleveland's second term in 1897, the family (now including three daughters) moved to Princeton, New Jersey, where two sons were later born. After her husband died in 1908, Frances Cleveland continued to live in Princeton with her children. In February 1913 she married Thomas Jex Preston, an archaeology professor who had quit the business world at age forty to enroll at Princeton where he earned first a bachelor's degree and then a doctorate. She thus became the first widow of a president to remarry.

Until her death, Frances Folsom Cleveland Preston retained much of the attention afforded presidents' widows. She was granted the franking privilege in 1909 and continued to use it after her second marriage, when she amended her name to read Frances F. Cleveland Preston. In 1936 Congress authorized an annual pension of $5,000 for her.

Active in many charitable organizations, Frances Cleveland Preston did volunteer work with several patriotic groups during World War I, served on the board of managers of the Woman's University Club, participated in the Needlework Guild of America (which collected clothing for distribution to the poor), and worked for the endowment fund of Wells College. After she died in Baltimore, where she had gone to help celebrate her son's fiftieth birthday, she was buried beside her first husband in Princeton, New Jersey.

• No biography of Frances Cleveland exists, but several of her husband's biographers cover her White House years. See Allan Nevins, *Grover Cleveland* (1932), and Robert McElroy, *Grover Cleveland* (2 vols., 1923). Several books on first ladies devote considerable space to her success in that role. See Betty Boyd Caroli, *First Ladies* (1987), and Carl Sferrazza Anthony, *First Ladies*, vol. 1 (1990). An obituary is in the *New York Times*, 30 Oct. 1947.

BETTY BOYD CAROLI

CLEVELAND, Grover (18 Mar. 1837–24 June 1908), twenty-second and twenty-fourth president of the United States, was born Stephen Grover Cleveland in Caldwell, New Jersey, the son of Richard Falley Cleveland, a Presbyterian minister, and Ann Neal. The fifth of nine children, Grover Cleveland grew up in the household of an itinerant clergyman whose profession called him to Fayetteville, New York, in 1841 and to Clinton, New York, in 1850. He attended the local academy in both communities until the death of his father in 1853 impelled him to abandon schooling in order to help support his mother and his younger sisters, who then resided in Holland Patent, New York. After spending a year as assistant teacher at the New York Institution for the Blind, young Cleveland set out for the West in 1855 but got no farther than Buffalo, where an uncle persuaded him to remain as his assistant registering the pedigrees of Shorthorn cattle. By the end of the year Cleveland had begun reading law in the Buffalo firm of Rogers, Bowen, and Rogers in preparation for a legal career.

Cleveland was admitted to the bar in 1859 and practiced law with his mentors' firm until he accepted a position as an assistant district attorney in 1863. That year, two years into the Civil War, his name was called in the military draft, but he hired a substitute as the law permitted. By 1869, when he formed a law firm with two partners, Cleveland had acquired a reputation as a hard-working attorney who possessed abundant common sense and boundless energy. He also entered politics, representing the Second Ward in Buffalo's Democratic City Convention in 1862. He was elected a ward supervisor of the party in 1863 and was selected as a delegate to the state Democratic convention in 1868. Two years later he won a close race for sheriff of Erie County, a position whose fees doubled his income. Cleveland returned to private practice at the end of the three-year term, forming a partnership with Lyman K. Bass and Wilson S. Bissell, and advanced to the front ranks of Buffalo's legal establishment.

Cleveland's legal reputation and his standing with Buffalo Democrats led to his nomination for mayor in 1881, a race he won handily. The victory presented him with the problems of a growing industrial city when public health arose as a civic concern. His willingness to put "engineering skill" and "the principle of economy" ahead of cronyism and partisan politics in handling sewerage and other municipal operations earned him praise throughout the state and boosted his appeal among feuding factions of Democrats, who nominated him for governor. Without campaigning directly, Cleveland won election in 1882 to a three-year term.

Cleveland's budding reputation rested considerably on his battle against excessive partisanship. He reiterated this commitment in his first annual message as governor, in which he recommended that appointments be based on "fitness and efficiency." Lawmakers complied by passing the nation's first state civil service law. Cleveland quickly staffed the new commission, which established merit procedures for hiring state governmental employees. The reform annoyed politicos in Tammany Hall, the Democratic party stronghold in New York City. Cleveland's refusal to knuckle under to their demands for patronage caused a running feud during his administration. The governor rubbed salt in these wounds in 1884 by approving legislation that enlarged the power of New York City's mayor over appointments and reformed other aspects of local government, measures championed by Theodore Roosevelt, then a young state legislator. Cleveland also signed legislation that created a bureau of labor statistics, formed a commission to plan a state preserve at Niagara Falls, reorganized the militia, abolished the hiring-out of state prisoners, established milk standards, and placed a discriminatory tax on oleomargarine. The governor's proclivity to reject measures of dubious merit or shoddy drafting, however, won him the most notoriety. His 1883 veto of the Five Cent Bill, which mandated a fare reduction for users of Jay Gould's elevated railroad in New York City, captured the most attention. Cleveland argued that the legislation violated the terms of the company's contract with the state and unwisely undermined private investment in public services.

New York's large bloc of electoral votes automatically assured governors of the state consideration as potential presidential nominees. Cleveland's second asset in his quest for the presidency was his well-publicized opposition to blatant partisanship and political corruption. This reputation won him the support of Mugwumps, who supported civil service reform. In 1884 careful planning by Daniel Manning, chairman of New York's state party, brought Cleveland the nomination at the Democratic convention in Chicago on the second ballot. Building on the party monopoly in the South, the Democracy's strategy targeted key northern states, where the close division between Democrats and Republicans held prospects for picking up enough electoral votes to carry the election. Indiana was one of these states, so the Democrats chose

Thomas A. Hendricks as the nominee for vice president.

The Republicans ran James G. Blaine of Maine, hero to many party faithful but morally suspect to Mugwumps. Cleveland took little part in the campaign, which party activists managed within each of the states. Although his 48.5 percent of the vote was less than a popular majority, Cleveland carried New York, Indiana, New Jersey, and Connecticut and with them the election. A moderate downturn in the economy probably helped Democrats in some states and perhaps offset negative reaction to the charge that Cleveland had fathered a child out of wedlock in 1874. Several years later Cleveland had accepted responsibility for the child without admitting paternity. In New York, Blaine's failure to repudiate a prejudiced characterization of Democrats as the party of "Rum, Romanism, and Rebellion" (referring to liquor, Catholics, and the former Confederacy); rain in upstate New York, which depressed voter turnout; and Republican defections to the Prohibition party helped tip the scales toward Cleveland.

Cleveland was the first Democrat to occupy the White House since James Buchanan left office in 1861. With the executive transition came a crush of requests for positions. Assisted by his private secretary, Daniel Lamont, Cleveland gave careful attention to appointments. The mainstays of his cabinet were Thomas Bayard as secretary of state, Manning as head of the Treasury, and William C. Whitney as secretary of the navy. A priority in his administration was correction of the mismanagement in the Navy Department, to which Congress had assigned the task of building a modern, steel-plated navy during the preceding Chester A. Arthur administration. Cleveland's support of this goal in his first and second administrations was critical to the American naval victory in the Spanish-American War. In 1888 he appointed Melville W. Fuller as chief justice of the Supreme Court, a position Fuller held for twenty-two years.

At home, Cleveland sought to prevent fraudulent acquisition of the nation's public lands, prohibited unlawful fencing of grazing areas, and forced railroads to return unused land grants. The Supreme Court's rejection (1886) of the Illinois law that regulated railroad charges convinced Cleveland that national controls for carriers engaged in interstate commerce were necessary. Congress agreed and in 1887 created the Interstate Commerce Commission, which represented the federal government's first significant regulation of an industrial business. Cleveland also approved the Hatch Act (1887), which authorized national subsidies of state agricultural experiment stations. He signed a measure that elevated the Department of Agriculture to departmental status (1889) and supported agricultural science. While he demonstrated less concern for industrial workers, Cleveland did urge Congress to consider an arbitration board in the wake of a major railroad strike. On several occasions, moreover, he echoed the unease that many citizens expressed about the growing power of business. But neither Cleveland

nor any other president during the Gilded Age recommended a labor program.

As chief executive, Cleveland continued to scrutinize legislation closely and reject measures he regarded as indefensible. Congress's habit of passing pension bills for individual Civil War veterans, many of whose applications had been turned down by pension officials, particularly incurred his hostility. He also rejected a general pension bill that would have assisted veterans whose disabilities were acquired after their service. The president turned down river and harbor appropriations and, in one of his most famous vetoes, an appropriation of $10,000 to buy seed grain for Texas farmers devastated by a drought. Cleveland called these spending measures unsupportable public "paternalism" that exceeded the proper functions of the national government. His 414 vetoes during his first administration set a record for a single term.

The president's personal life changed dramatically during his first administration. He arrived in Washington a bachelor, and on 2 June 1886, after a secret engagement, he married Frances Folsom in the Blue Room of the White House. Cleveland had acted as her guardian since the death of her father, Oscar Folsom, with whom Cleveland had practiced law. The couple honeymooned in western Maryland, hounded by a "carload of reporters." The following year the Clevelands purchased a home just north of Georgetown, which neighbored Washington. Frances Cleveland became a capable and admired first lady, taking over responsibilities that Cleveland's sister Rose Cleveland had performed. Grover and Frances Cleveland had five children, one of whom, Esther Cleveland, was the first child of a president to be born in the White House in 1893, during Cleveland's second term.

Cleveland surprised the country midway in his first term by launching a frontal attack on the tariff. He devoted his entire message of 1887 to the issue, an unprecedented use of the State of the Union Address. Cleveland warned that "unnecessary taxation" imposed by existing customs duties were a "peril" to the nation. Reflecting classical American political thinking, he regarded taxation as potentially hazardous to individual liberty. Amassing revenue in excess of "the just obligation of the Government," he wrote in his 1886 message, "becomes ruthless extortion and a violation of principles of free government." He also argued that tariff duties formulated to shield certain industries from foreign competition conveyed unjustifiable "favoritism." Furthermore, "unnecessary taxation" generated surplus revenue, which tempted the national government to stray from its proper mission and raised the cost of living.

The House Committee on Ways and Means drafted legislation that embodied Cleveland's recommendation to reduce tariff duties. Named after the chair of the committee, Roger Q. Mills, the bill became lawmakers' primary preoccupation in the Fiftieth Congress (1888). Exhorted by the president, Democrats marshaled virtually their entire delegation to pass their proposal over united Republican opposition. Arguing that the tariff stimulated economic growth and prosperity, the GOP killed the Mills Bill in the Senate, where Republicans held a slender majority. It was a bitter defeat for the president, but he had given his party a clear issue on which to campaign for his reelection.

The presidential contest of 1888 pitted Cleveland against Benjamin Harrison of Indiana, a former U.S. senator and supporter of the Republicans' high tariff position. In the absence of Vice President Hendricks, who had died in 1885, Cleveland picked as his running mate 75-year-old Allen G. Thurman, a moderate on tariff reform and the volatile currency issue. Cleveland hoped the Ohioan would help him win one or two of the crucial midwestern states, and Thurman was willing to campaign for the ticket while Cleveland tended to presidential business. Once again neither party commanded a majority of the popular vote, although Cleveland won the plurality, raising his percentage slightly over 1884. But the distribution of the returns favored Harrison, who took Ohio, Indiana, and New York and thus the election. Cleveland's cool relations with New York governor David Hill, whom Mugwumps disdained; veterans' denunciation of Cleveland's pension vetoes; and Republicans' success in raising campaign contributions from businessmen, many of whom feared tariff revision, handicapped the president.

Returning to private life, Cleveland accepted an offer to join Bangs, Stetson, Tracy, and MacVeagh, a New York City law firm, where he served primarily as a court-appointed referee. He argued one case before the Supreme Court, becoming the first former president to do so. With profits earned from the sale of his Georgetown home, Cleveland purchased "Gray Gables" near Bourne, Massachusetts, on Cape Cod, where he relished slow-paced summer days, relaxing with his family, socializing with his well-to-do neighbors, and fishing in Buzzards Bay. But the ex-president had not abandoned politics. The sweeping Democratic victory in the congressional elections of 1890 whet his appetite for another try for the presidency.

Under the management of Whitney, Cleveland forces outmaneuvered Hill, the ambitious governor of New York, and then coasted to the Democratic party nomination in 1892. Turning a third time to the Midwest for a running mate, Cleveland approved Adlai E. Stevenson of Illinois, a former Greenbacker with appeal among the growing silver wing of the party. With the South solidly Democratic and upper New England and much of the West loyal to Republicans, the race centered on the competitive counties that lay between Hartford and Chicago. Cleveland scored a solid victory over President Harrison, regaining New York, holding reliable Connecticut, and capturing Illinois, four other northern states, and California. Aggressive Republican support for prohibition and other social issues that alarmed the members of some ethnic groups, the dissatisfaction of some voters with the high rates of the McKinley Tariff of 1890, and several strikes by workingmen contributed to the Democratic victory.

Populist candidate James B. Weaver, who won four western states, helped to depress Cleveland's popular vote to 46.1 percent.

Besieged once again by office seekers, Cleveland's key appointments put Walter Gresham in charge of the State Department, former Speaker of the House John Carlisle in the Treasury, his old law partner Bissell in the post office, and his former secretary Lamont in the War Department. Richard Olney of Massachusetts became attorney general. Shortly after these appointees took office, the panic of 1893 inaugurated the worst economic depression of the century. Depositors withdrew their savings and hoarded gold, hundreds of banks failed and the remainder restricted their loans, joblessness reached a third of the workforce in some cities, and agricultural prices plummeted, pushing some farmers into foreclosure. These hard times threw a pall over Cleveland's second administration and colored most aspects of governance between 1893 and 1897. Given his constitutional views, Cleveland felt that the national government could do little to relieve the distress. The president retained a stoic faith in the economy's natural capacity to correct itself.

Cleveland's most emphatic response to the depression was defense of the gold standard as the basis for the nation's currency. The money question had simmered since the late 1860s, fed by an inflexible currency, a cumbersome banking structure that restricted credit available to westerners and southerners, and persistent price deflation throughout the late nineteenth century. Many individuals, debtors especially, saw the purchase of silver by the U.S. Treasury as a monetary solution for raising prices and regenerating the economy. The idea was particularly appealing to western and southern farmers, most of whom had been debtors at some point in their lives. The emergent urban middle class, most large merchants and industrialists, and eastern bankers, on the other hand, saw currency inflation as economically harmful and morally repugnant. Cleveland counted himself among the latter group. During his first administration he had warned against the abandonment of the gold standard, which he saw as crucial to maintaining business confidence, and had taken steps to prevent the Treasury from adopting a bimetallic standard for the nation's currency.

By 1893 the Treasury's supply of gold dwindled rapidly. The primary cause of the outflow, the president reckoned, was the Sherman Silver Purchase Act of 1890, which obligated the government to purchase a fixed amount of silver each month. Cleveland called a special session of Congress to repeal the statute. At this critical moment in the nation's monetary history, Cleveland left the capital ostensibly because of illness but in actuality to have a cancerous growth removed from the roof of his mouth. After surgeons conducted the secret operation aboard a borrowed yacht anchored in New York's East River, the president recuperated at Gray Gables, where he was fitted with a vulcanized prosthesis to replace the removed portion of his jaw. Five weeks later Cleveland was back at work in Washington, but he lived with discomfort the remainder of his life.

With cooperation from Republicans, Congress repealed the Silver Purchase Act. When this action failed to halt the drainage of gold, the president decided that the government must replenish the reserve through borrowing. Rebuffed in the effort by Congress, the president floated four bond issues between 1894 and 1896 to finance the acquisitions, claiming executive authority to carry out the transactions. The third bond sale, placed in the care of the financier J. P. Morgan, earned Cleveland the enmity of western Democrats, who denounced his collusion with eastern money kings. Still, the president observed in his annual message, whose domestic sections concentrated on the currency issue, the "perplexing and delicate predicament" of the nation's finances persisted through the end of 1895. By then Cleveland faced a full-scale revolt within his party.

The depression presented Cleveland with additional challenges. George Pullman, the Chicago manufacturer of railroad sleeping cars, cut wages but not dividends or the cost of housing for his employees. The affront provoked a walkout of Pullman workers in 1894 that escalated into a nationwide railroad strike under the leadership of Eugene Debs. With transportation in Chicago paralyzed, Attorney General Olney, a railroad lawyer and foe of labor unions, backed a consortium of railroad managers who were intent on breaking the strike. His key weapon was a federal court injunction that commanded workers to cease their disruption of rail service on grounds that they impeded the delivery of the U.S. mails. To emphasize the point, Olney had Debs arrested and gained Cleveland's permission to position federal troops in Chicago, setting the stage for violence and fatalities. Cleveland rebuffed a protest from Governor John Altgeld of Illinois, who charged that the president had exceeded his power in authorizing the federal intervention into local affairs without a request for assistance from state officials. Cleveland replied that he had ample authority to act unilaterally "in the emergency" and asserted, "If it takes the entire army and navy . . . to deliver a postal card in Chicago, that card will be delivered." Perceiving civic order at stake, Cleveland did his duty as he saw it.

Whereas the Pullman strike earned Cleveland a reputation as a union buster, his handling of tariff reform in 1894 incurred criticism from other quarters. Cleveland had reiterated his opposition to the "burden of federal taxation" at the onset of his second administration and encouraged Congress to reduce tariff rates. But he handled the matter clumsily, and the resulting Wilson-Gorman Bill, laden with special interest provisions, became law without his signature. One innovative section of the legislation that Cleveland supported was a 2 percent tax on incomes over $4,000, a levy judged unconstitutional by the Supreme Court in *Pollock v. Farmers' Loan and Trust Co.* (1895). Cleveland's interest in tariff reduction was predicated both on a desire to reduce customs rates and on disdain for special interest favoritism. But the president was a foe neither of business nor its uncritical mouthpiece. He accepted the premises of private enterprise and watched over his personal investments. Yet on several occasions he expressed alarm at the widening gulf between the wealthy and wage earners and at the growth of corporate power. When Olney's antimonopoly case against the Sugar Trust was rebuffed by the Supreme Court in 1895, Cleveland asked Congress to reexamine the nation's antitrust statute. He also believed that some of the responsibility to regulate business lay with state government, but the political climate did not favor new regulation in 1895. The depression decimated the Democrats in the 1894 elections and installed a Republican majority in the House and a plurality in the Senate.

Cleveland devoted little time to external affairs during his first administration, but events in Hawaii, Venezuela, and Cuba forced greater attention to diplomacy during his second term. Hawaii had been drawn closer to the orbit of the United States during the Gilded Age, as the American minority on the island gained commercial influence and the navy's interest in the island grew. Prodded by fear of a native challenge to their position and the loss of favorable status for sugar under the tariff of 1890, Americans led by Sanford Dole overthrew the native Hawaiian regime of Queen Liliuokalani in 1893. The intervention of a small contingent of U.S. marines materially assisted the coup. The Harrison administration acquiesced in the American islanders' request for annexation, but Cleveland recalled the proposed treaty from the Senate days after assuming office. He objected to the collusion of the U.S. military with the conspiracy to overthrow the queen, which he termed "an abuse of power." Annexation, to his mind, was contrary to American traditions. With public opinion split over the issue, he placed the matter with Congress, which recommended recognition of the provisional government controlled by local Americans. The matter lingered in this limbo for the remainder of his administration.

Cleveland took a more decisive posture regarding the Caribbean. When a dispute over the boundary of British Guiana threatened war between Venezuela and Great Britain, Cleveland in 1895 sent a stern warning to the British, asserting that "the United States is practically sovereign" in the Western Hemisphere. Britain noted the bellicose tone and opted for a negotiated settlement. Cleveland's position toward Spain was only slightly less assertive. Following the outbreak of a revolt against Spanish rule in Cuba in 1895, the president declared American neutrality and attempted to restrain assistance to Cuba from the United States. Responding to an aroused public, Congress became adamant that Spain grant home rule to the island, a position the president implied in his annual message of 1896. Thirteen months after Cleveland left office, Congress declared war against Spain.

By then Cleveland was watching events from his retirement home in Princeton, New Jersey. He had expressed disgust as silverites captured the Democratic party in 1896 and denounced the administration's sound currency policy, which Cleveland refused to abandon. Although he took no active part in the campaign of the Gold Democrats, Cleveland voted for this rump faction of his party. He preferred William McKinley over William Jennings Bryan for the presidency, but he did not embrace McKinley's imperialism following the defeat of the Spanish. A few years into retirement Cleveland became a trustee of Princeton University, a role he took seriously. He helped block a plan by Woodrow Wilson, Princeton's president, that would have reorganized undergraduate residences along the British model. Cleveland died in Princeton.

An outpouring of tributes at his death indicates a recovery of Cleveland's reputation since the Democratic debacle of 1896. These eulogies probably sprang as much from admiration of Cleveland's personal integrity as from agreement with his political philosophy, which was rooted in Jacksonian principles. Cleveland favored a strict reading of the Constitution and the traditional homily that the activities of the federal government should be limited. Deviation from these principles threatened to convey special interest favoritism and upset the balance of power between the states and the nation. Economy should temper public spending, excessive taxation was morally unpalatable, and the gold standard was the only acceptable basis for the currency. He thought government should be run according to business methods and civil service principles, although he recognized that parties were a fact of political life.

Cleveland argued that the president's role lay in executing the will of Congress, not in fashioning legislative programs. While he made recommendations to Congress, he seldom pressed for their adoption, and his style was clumsy and often unsuccessful when he did. His cold relationship with the press, to which he rarely granted interviews, hindered his legislative leadership. Despite his general philosophy about the presidency, Cleveland asserted his independence of Congress from time to time. His refusal to comply with a demand from the Senate for documentation of his removals from office constitutes his most aggressive defense of executive prerogative during his first term. Congress relented in 1886 by repealing the Tenure of Office Act, on which the Senate had justified its requests. Cleveland's action to break the Pullman strike and to maintain the gold standard represent his most forceful use of presidential authority during his second term. Coupled with his unprecedented number of vetoes, these actions prepared the foundation for the rise of autonomous presidential leadership later.

Cleveland's personal style contributed to these assertions of presidential authority. All of his biographers have noted the president's distinctive temperament. "He possessed honesty, courage, firmness, independence, and common sense," wrote Allan Nevins (*Grover Cleveland*, p. 4) who subtitled his classic biography *A Study in Courage*. Nevins also notes that Cleveland's conscientious devotion to detail outran his

capacity to articulate a vision of the future. More critical, Horace Merrill argues that Cleveland failed "to supply effective leadership" (*Merrill*, p. 183). Richard Welch's conclusion that Cleveland embodied "a tangle of contradictions" (*Welch*, p. 17) gets closer to the man. Despite describing him as a person of "little charisma" and "less eloquence," more admired than beloved, Welch saw Cleveland as "the dominant figure in United States politics for more than a decade" (Welch, p. 213). Welch believed that Cleveland's willingness to temper his ideology with political practicality and his forthright moralism helps to explain this achievement. Richard Hofstadter observes that Cleveland was "the ideal bourgeois statesman for his time" (*Hofstadter*, p. 185). The president's public persona epitomized middle-class steadiness and Victorian manhood.

Such attributes offered reassurance to a public apprehensive of the rapid changes in society. Cleveland's moderate course radiated a sense of stability and caution at a time when government began to confront these new circumstances. During his administrations the municipal, state, and federal governments adopted numerous new laws, anticipating the reforms of the Progressive Era. By and large Cleveland viewed this legislation as practical responses to contemporary problems. In his willingness to accept most incremental reforms, Cleveland exhibited an eminently American approach to statecraft.

• The major collection of Cleveland's papers is in the Library of Congress. These manuscripts have been microfilmed and are listed in *Index to the Papers of Grover Cleveland* (1965). Allan Nevins, ed., *Letters of Grover Cleveland, 1850–1908* (1933), is the most important publication of his private correspondence. Nevins's magisterial *Grover Cleveland: A Study in Courage* (1932) is the classic biography. Richard Welch, *The Presidencies of Grover Cleveland* (1988), offers a short, balanced analysis. More critical is Horace Samuel Merrill, *Bourbon Leader: Grover Cleveland and the Democratic Party* (1957). Robert McElroy, *Grover Cleveland: The Man and the Statesman* (1923), has limited utility. Cleveland's formative years are reviewed in Geoffrey Blodgett, "The Emergence of Grover Cleveland: A Fresh Appraisal," *New York History* 73 (1992): 132–68. Robert Kelley, *The Transatlantic Persuasion* (1969), appraises Cleveland's Presbyterian background and his personality. Aspects of Cleveland's presidencies are discussed in Blodgett, "The Political Leadership of Grover Cleveland," *South Atlantic Quarterly* 82 (1983): 288–99; Louis Fisher, "Grover Cleveland against the Senate," *Capitol Studies* 7 (1979): 11–25; and Gerald G. Eggert, *Richard Olney: Evolution of a Statesman* (1974). Richard Hofstadter, *The American Political Tradition*, chap. 7 (1948), and R. Hal Williams, *Years of Decision: American Politics in the 1890s* (1978), comment on Gilded Age politics. Ballard C. Campbell, *The Growth of American Government: Governance from the Cleveland Era to the Present* (1995), locates Cleveland within the evolution of American government. An obituary is in the *New York Times*, 25 June 1908.

BALLARD C. CAMPBELL

CLEVENGER, Shobal Vail (22 Oct. 1812–30 Sept. 1843), sculptor, was born near Middletown, Ohio, the son of Samuel Clevenger, a weaver who migrated in 1808 from New Jersey to take up farming in Ohio; although his mother's first name is unknown, her maiden name was Bunnell. Young Clevenger was sent at the age of fifteen to do masonry work on the Centerville Canal. Contracting malaria, or perhaps tuberculosis, he returned to his family to recuperate, sought work in Louisville, Kentucky, and then in Cincinnati, where he was enthralled by the sight of a female figure carved in wood for the market house. Determined then to become a sculptor, he apprenticed himself from 1829 to 1833 to David Guion, a stonecutter.

Though virtually illiterate, Clevenger did well as an apprentice from the start. He was soon carving angels' heads and other ornaments in Guion's shop. Clevenger married Elizabeth Wright of Cincinnati in 1833; the couple had three children. He unsuccessfully sought commissions in Xenia, Ohio, but quickly returned to Cincinnati to resume working with Guion. A little later he went into partnership with a stonecutter named Bassett and also took lessons from Frederick Eckstein, a skilled sculptor from Germany, who also taught Hiram Powers and Henry Kirke Brown. In 1835 Clevenger chiseled a delightfully realistic bust in freestone of Ebenezer Smith Thomas, editor of the *Cincinnati Daily Evening Post*. The resulting praise led not only to several commissions but also to a patron, the wealthy Nicholas Longworth, whose generosity enabled Clevenger to study anatomy at the Ohio Medical College (1836–1837).

After executing more busts, including one of Henry Clay, the powerful senator, and another of William Henry Harrison, the future president, Clevenger made plans to follow his friend Powers to Italy; Powers had lived and worked in Florence since 1837. Clevenger first traveled to Boston and Salem, Massachusetts, New York City, Philadelphia, and Washington, D.C., and modeled in plaster numerous busts of highly placed Americans, including John Quincy Adams, Washington Allston (Boston painter), Nicholas Biddle (Philadelphia financier), Edward Everett (governor of Mass.), Philip Hone (New York politician and diarist), Harrison Gray Otis (Mass. politician), Lemuel Shaw (Mass. Supreme Court justice and later Herman Melville's father-in-law), Julia Ward (poet, later Julia Ward Howe), and Daniel Webster. With commissions to sculpt several of these models in marble, and assisted by a loan from Longworth, Clevenger and his family set sail for Europe in October 1840.

They stopped for a few days in Paris, so that Clevenger could visit the Louvre, and then continued on to Florence, where Powers helped them find a house they could afford to rent on their already strained budget. Brown, by then also an expatriate sculptor in Florence, also assisted. Clevenger was intensely busy for the next two years. He modeled bust drapery, visited the Vatican sculpture gallery, was inspired by Sir Walter Scott to do an ideal head titled *The Lady of the Lake* (1842), and modeled a life-size *Indian Chief* (also 1842). He also hired Italian copyists to put twenty of his bust models into marble—a regular practice of sculptors. He shipped the finished work to the United States on commission—for pay that was sometimes

slow in coming. Clevenger socialized only a little with Horatio Greenough, the first and premier American sculptor in Florence; but Clevenger's wife and children occasionally met with Greenough family members.

Then came tragedy. Already plagued by money problems, the somewhat spendthrift Clevenger was diagnosed as having tuberculosis. He rapidly grew worse and was ordered by his Italian physician to return to the United States. Money was collected from fellow American artists in Florence to help the Clevengers. Everett, at that time American minister to England, sent a sizable sum. Powers and Brown had to carry Clevenger aboard ship at Leghorn. When he and his family were two days west of Gibraltar, Clevenger died and was buried at sea. His widow was obliged to accept gifts and temporary housing from well-wishing professional friends in the East, but in less than two years she and her children began to make their home with relatives in Missouri and then Louisiana.

Clevenger completed about forty busts, an ideal head, and a model of the first Native American ever sculpted. His busts, and many plaster copies, are widely placed in museums and elsewhere in Massachusetts, New York, Ohio, Pennsylvania, Rhode Island, and Washington, D.C. Although Powers agreed to complete Clevenger's *Indian Chief*, financial plans fell through and Clevenger's model disappeared. An engraving of it was published in the *United States Magazine and Democratic Review* in 1844. Several of Clevenger's realistic and expressive busts were, like those of Powers and Brown, in advance of their times aesthetically. Until long after his death, most American sculptors, especially those working in Italy, continued the popular neoclassical tradition, especially when their subjects were biblical and mythological. Clevenger, on the other hand, surprised many sitters by not only his swift but more importantly his realistic busts. His *Otis* (1840) includes a believably wrinkled, downturned mouth and a tensed neck. His *Allston* (also 1840) inspired the painter to write, almost in surprise, that his friends called it an exact likeness. And his *Webster* (modeled in plaster in 1838), probably Clevenger's best bust, was often reproduced in marble and widely praised for avoiding idealism and presenting the mighty senator's head as it really looked. Clevenger's professional example, which was only made better by a unique combination of self-confidence and humility, assisted—as did the portrait bust work of Powers and Brown, among others—in clearing the path for realists and naturalists to follow.

• Only four letters by Clevenger seem to have survived. They are at the Essex Institute Museum, Salem, the Boston Athenaeum, the Historical Society of Pennsylvania, Philadelphia, and in private hands. Early general treatments of Clevenger are in "Shobal Vail Clevenger, the Sculptor," *Southern Literary Messenger* 5 (Apr. 1839): 262–64; "Clevenger," *United States Magazine and Democratic Review* 14 (Feb. 1844): 202–6; Henry T. Tuckerman, *Book of the Artists: American Artist Life . . .* (1867); Lorado Taft, *The History of American Sculpture* (1903); and Edna M. Clark, *Ohio Art and Artists* (1932).

More discriminating, though brief, comments are in Margaret Farrand Thorp, *The Literary Sculptors* (1965), Wayne Craven, *Sculpture in America* (1968; rev. ed. 1984); and Sylvia E. Crane, *White Silence: Greenough, Powers, and Crawford: American Sculptors in Nineteenth-Century Italy* (1972). The finest discussion is Thomas B. Brumbaugh, "Shoval Vail Clevenger: An Ohio Stonecutter in Search of Fame," *Art Quarterly* 29 (1966): 29–45. Informative also is Brumbaugh's "Letters of an American Sculptor, Shobal Clevenger," *Art Quarterly* 24 (1961): 370–77. Both of Brumbaugh's articles are well illustrated.

ROBERT L. GALE

CLEWELL, John Henry (19 Sept. 1855–20 Feb. 1922), Moravian clergyman and educator, was born in Salem, North Carolina, the son of John David Clewell and Dorothea Schultz. Following his primary education in Salem, Clewell entered Moravian College and Theological Seminary in Bethlehem, Pennsylvania, where he earned an A.B. in 1875 and a B.D. two years later. He pursued postgraduate study at Union Theological Seminary in New York City between 1878 and 1879. Moravian College awarded him a Ph.D. in 1900. In 1882 Clewell married Alice Cornelia Wolle, daughter of a prominent Moravian family in Bethlehem, Pennsylvania; they had five children. Alice Clewell took an active role in her husband's professional life, particularly during his tenure at Salem Female Academy in Winston-Salem, North Carolina. The institution recognized her contributions through its construction of the Alice Clewell Memorial Dormitory.

After his ordination as a Moravian deacon in 1879, Clewell accepted his first pastorate in Uhrichsville, Ohio, where he served until 1884. Two year after his arrival in the Midwest, Clewell was ordained a presbyter. An energetic individual, he founded a Moravian church in nearby Port Washington and between 1880 and 1884 served both congregations. While leading these churches, Clewell developed his fundraising abilities, which later served him well in the cause of women's education.

Despite his theological training, Clewell devoted only five years of his over forty-year career exclusively to the ministry. In 1884 he accepted a position as assistant principal at Salem Female Academy, a Moravian institution for women in Winston-Salem, North Carolina. Founded in 1802 as Salem Female Academy, the school was one of the earliest institutions in the South devoted to higher education for women. Throughout the region, however, although the number of academies and colleges for women increased, few met the rigorous standards of their counterparts in the Northeast. As assistant principal, Clewell grew increasingly sensitive to the quality of women's education in the South. In 1888 he became the eleventh president of Salem Academy and devoted the subsequent twenty-five years to enhancing the facilities, academic standards, and reputation of the institution. Clewell first used his fundraising skills to establish a building program. He traveled throughout the country soliciting contributions to Salem. During his presidency the institution not only renovated its facilities, but also added a gymnasium and classroom buildings.

Clewell recognized, however, that neither new facilities nor the designation "college" was of particular significance if the institution did not maintain rigorous academic standards. Although he added a collegiate department, offering a liberal arts curriculum, to Salem Female Academy, Clewell closely supervised the quality of both the faculty and the courses they taught. Not content with an ornamental curriculum, which emphasized social skills and little else, he included practical courses in business, nursing, and home economics. Anxious that women's college presidents throughout the region cooperate in raising standards, Clewell also founded the Association of Presidents of Women's Colleges in the South. As a consequence of his achievements at Salem, Moravian Seminary in Bethlehem, Pennsylvania, invited him in 1909 to assume its presidency. Founded in 1742, the school achieved collegiate status in 1907 and changed its name to Moravian Seminary and College for Women. For the remaining eleven years of his life, Clewell continued his efforts to enhance the quality of higher education for women.

At Moravian, Clewell faced immediate problems of finances and faculty. Though anxious to function as a reputable college, the institution, because of its modest endowment and low tuition, was unable to attract the necessary faculty members. Cognizant of innovations in women's higher education throughout the country, Clewell utilized the resources of nearby Lehigh University to supplement the offerings at Moravian. Employing the coordinate method, he persuaded a number of faculty members at Lehigh to devote a portion of their energies to teaching women at Moravian.

Clewell, in addition to his advocacy of higher education, never forgot his mission as a Moravian clergyman. He traveled to Europe in 1899 to attend the General Synod of the Moravian Church. Despite his myriad responsibilities at Salem, in 1902 Clewell published *History of Wachovia in North Carolina*, a narrative of the work of the Moravian church in his home state between 1752 and 1902. As both a minister and a college president, Clewell demonstrated the ability to raise and to manage money prudently. Fortunately for college women at Salem and Moravian, he chose to use those considerable skills in the service of higher education for women.

Clewell died in Philadelphia, Pennsylvania, where he had sought medical treatment for pulmonary tuberculosis. He is buried at Niesky Hill Cemetery in Bethlehem, Pennsylvania.

• Although no biography of John Henry Clewell is available, there are several sources, in addition to his *History*, from which one can construct the chronology of his life and career. These include Reinhold Riemer, "The Moravian Seminary and College for Women," *The Moravian*, 16 Aug. 1922, and John R. Weinlick, *Twentieth Century Moravian College Challenge and Response* (1977), p. 92. An obituary is in *The Moravian*, 1 Mar. 1922.

CAROLYN TERRY BASHAW

CLIFFORD, James Lowry (24 Feb. 1901–7 Apr. 1978), biographer, literary critic, and professor of literature, was born in Evansville, Indiana, the son of George Clifford, a businessman and amateur astronomer, and Emily Orr. In 1918 he attended Wabash College in nearby Crawfordsville, where he studied science, graduating in 1923 with an A.B. and Phi Beta Kappa honors. Two years later he received a B.S. in chemical engineering from the Massachusetts Institute of Technology. After several years in business back in Evansville, managing the manufacture of railroad coal cars, he relocated to Tucson, Arizona, where he taught mathematics, polo, and English at a preparatory school. Discovering in his teaching a love of literature, he entered the graduate program in English at Columbia University in 1931 and gained his M.A. the next year.

In 1935 Clifford was awarded the prestigious Cutting Fellowship, went to England, and began researching his first biography, that of Hester Lynch Salusbury Thrale Piozzi, the great friend and confidant of Samuel Johnson and one of his first biographers. Clifford and his traveling companion, his cousin Bob Orr (later governor of Indiana), made important finds of Piozzi papers in a vicarage in Flintshire and in an old Welsh farmhouse.

Clifford returned and married Virginia Iglehart, also from Indiana, in 1940; they had three children. In the same year he began the *Johnsonian News Letter*, the first literary newsletter, which he wrote and edited for three decades. It provided a centralized forum for the exchange of useful information and debatable ideas, helping create and promote the contemporary swell of interest in Johnson and his age. It also established Clifford's reputation in the field. With the publication in 1941 of *Hester Lynch Piozzi (Mrs. Thrale)*, Clifford received his Ph.D., as well as a good review from Virginia Woolf in the *New Statesman*.

From 1937 to 1944 Clifford taught at Lehigh University, where he attained the rank of associate professor. Then he accepted a post at Barnard College and was soon recruited as a full professor in the graduate faculty at Columbia University. His pedagogy, famous among generations of students, was to invite, encourage, and inspire them to share his enthusiasm for literature and scholarship. He was commonly seen carrying a suitcase or two to class, full of first and variant editions of the semester's texts for his students to peruse, so they could see the evidence of scholars at work and feel something of the excitement he felt in following first hand the history of literature.

Clifford's next important work, *Johnsonian Studies, 1887–1950: A Survey and Bibliography* (1951), was a comprehensive list of all texts from the late Victorian era to the present that offered new knowledge, original interpretation, or valuable critical insight concerning Johnson and his works. The bibliography, and in particular the "Survey of Johnsonian Studies" that prefaced it, readjusted the focus of centuries of Johnson scholarship, which, beginning with James Boswell, had placed Johnson's personality, wit, and eccentrici-

ties in the foreground, at the expense of the literature he created. The critical perspective emergent in the work of Clifford and his generation clarified Johnson's image, voice, and values, as discovered in his writing, not that of his famous biographer.

Clifford was awarded a Guggenheim Fellowship in 1951 and returned to England, to London and Lichfield, to research a second biography, *Young Sam Johnson* (1955), characteristically retitled *Young Samuel Johnson* by its British publisher. A close study of a major portion of Johnson's life to which Boswell gives short shrift, the book brings its subject up to his fortieth year and the publication of his important poem "The Vanity of Human Wishes." By that time, Clifford insisted, Johnson's "convictions and tastes were well formed" and "he was essentially the man so graphically described" in Boswell's *Life*. Clifford's portrait of Johnson as a boy, an adolescent, and a maturing man, full of contradictions and disabilities, utterly changed the image Boswell had created and his readers had perpetuated. The critical community accepted the biography immediately, not simply as a supplement to Boswell's but as an exhaustive source of little-noted but significant scholarship and as a compelling portrait in and of itself.

Biography as an Art: Selected Criticism from 1560–1960, published in 1962, is a collection of writings with editorial commentary by Clifford that chart the history of Western biography and biographical study and address the theoretical and technical issues of lifewriting, providing the critical groundwork, the source material, and the critical questions for the study and appreciation of biography as a literary genre. Clifford's 1970 edition of *Twentieth-Century Interpretations of Boswell's Life of Johnson* demonstrates the extraordinary range of his scholarship, including material not usually found in such collections, from the contemporary to the antiquarian: a transcript of a radio roundtable of eighteenth-century scholars, and a reprint of the "Caldwell Minute," Johnson's record of his conversation with King George. The next book he authored, *From Puzzles to Portraits: Problems of a Literary Biographer* (1970), is partly a memoir of his adventures doing what he called "outside research," hunting down evidence in the field, and partly categorical criticism, defining the discipline in new terms, distinguishing among the formal approaches to biography from the dual perspective of a practitioner and an analyst. This book-length academic study of literary biography by one of the most respected figures in the discipline opened the field for future critics and theorists, many of whom were Clifford's students and protégés.

Clifford retired in 1971 from the faculty at Columbia, where he held the William Peterfield Trent chair of English, having been honored as a fellow of the Royal Society of Literature and the Royal Society of the Arts. He spent his retirement writing the rest of Johnson's life up to the point when he met Boswell. *Dictionary Johnson* (1979) covers the bulk of Johnson's life as a professional writer. It focuses on its subject's middle years and the works that made him famous: the

Rambler, Adventurer and *Idler* essays, *Rasselas*, and *The Dictionary of the English Language*. Clifford also provided the introduction to a facsimile edition (1978) of Johnson's *Dictionary*. On 7 April 1978 Clifford dropped the typescript of *Dictionary Johnson* off at his publisher, fulfilling the goal he had set for himself when he began his biography of the middle age of Johnson, to "hand him over to Boswell." Later that day, at his home in New York City, he suffered a fatal heart attack. In eulogies and reviews of the new biography, Clifford was memorialized by literary critics and Johnson scholars as among "the most eminent of American Johnsonians" and "one of the four major Johnsonians of this century," and his work as "one of the most important reasons for revived popular interest in the eighteenth century."

Clifford was a significant figure in the development of eighteenth-century studies in general and the study of the life of Samuel Johnson in particular. He also helped establish biography as a literary genre that not only complements criticism but is worthy of criticism itself, and in that effort he was instrumental in relocating biography in the mainstream of Western literature.

• Clifford's collected papers are in the Rare Book Room of Butler Library at Columbia University and in the Clifford Collection at the University of Evansville. The most complete bibliography and most thorough appreciation of Clifford is Dennis Paoli's article in the *Dictionary of Literary Biography*, vol. 103 (1991), which includes interview material and quotes from unpublished memorials by Clifford's former students and colleagues.

DENNIS PAOLI

CLIFFORD, Nathan (18 Aug. 1803–25 July 1881), jurist, was born in Rumney, New Hampshire, the son of Deacon Nathanial Clifford and Lydia Simpson, farmers. He received his early education at the Haverhill Academy, but the death of his father prevented him from attending college. He studied law with a local attorney, Josiah Quincy (1772–1864), and in 1827 was admitted to the bar. He eventually settled in Newfield, Maine, where he not only began his legal practice but also met and married Hannah Ayer, daughter of a prominent townsman; they had six children.

In 1830 Clifford embarked on a political career under the banner of the recently created Democratic party. He served four one-year terms in the lower house of the Maine legislature, including two terms as its Speaker (1833–1834). In 1834 he was appointed attorney general for the state, ran unsuccessfully for U.S. senator in 1837, and a year later was elected to the House of Representatives, serving for two terms. Redistricted out of his House seat by his own party in 1843, he returned to Washington in 1846 when Democratic president James K. Polk appointed him attorney general. His principal achievement as attorney general was his political service as a liaison between the president and Secretary of War James Buchanan. At the end of the Mexican War in 1848, Clifford was sent to Mexico to help negotiate the final treaty and to reestablish peaceful relations between Mexico and the United States.

The defeat of the Democrats by the Whigs in 1848 brought an end to Clifford's political career. He moved to Portland, Maine, where he practiced law for the next eight years. In 1858 U.S. Supreme Court Justice Benjamin Curtis resigned suddenly. Buchanan, Clifford's old ally, was now president and, needing to replace the New Englander, nominated Clifford. According to one account, Clifford was chosen less because of his intellectual or legal abilities than because he was "politically orthodox, constitutionally conservative, and temperamentally safe." Moreover, Clifford's nomination produced a storm of protest from northern Whigs and Republicans already angered over the Court's recent decision in the *Dred Scott* (1857) case. For these men Clifford was another "doughface," a northerner who sympathized with the proslavery, states' rights philosophy of the South. His confirmation vote was one of the closest in Supreme Court history (26 to 23, with 13 senators absent).

Given the turbulence of the times, Clifford's position on the Court was precarious from the start. Although no supporter of slavery, in one of his first decisions on the Court he voted to uphold the constitutionality of the Fugitive Slave Law in *Ableman v. Booth* (1859). He also opposed southern secession, calling it a "wicked heresy." Yet, like his hero Chief Justice Roger Taney, Clifford was a Democrat in a Republican administration during wartime. He admitted that supporting the government's policies in prosecuting the war "was a task to try the nerves and tax the strength of a very giant." And in general he did so, while opposing the use of arbitrary power. He concurred in dissenting in the 1863 *Prize Cases* in which the Court upheld the constitutionality of Union seizure of Confederate ships attempting to run the blockade of southern ports. He also sided with the Court's majority in overturning the conviction of the prosouthern Ohio Democrat Clement Vallandigham and in declaring arbitrary arrests and martial law invalid in *Ex parte Milligan* (1867).

During Reconstruction, Clifford's distrust of federal authority became most apparent, especially in light of the fact that by 1870 a majority of the Court were Republican appointees and presumably supportive of Republican efforts to pass legislation expanding the role of federal authority. He voted with the majority in the *Test Oath Cases* (1867) to ban the use of loyalty oaths for voters and public officials, and he supported the majority in cases such as *U.S. v. Reese* (1876) and the *Slaughterhouse Cases* (1873), in which the Court limited the effectiveness of the Fourteenth and Fifteenth Amendments in protecting the rights of freedmen in the South. At the same time, he opposed such protection when the Court upheld federal authority in *Ex parte Siebold* (1880) and *Strauder v. West Virginia* (1880).

Clifford's commitment to the Jeffersonian ideals of state sovereignty and strict constitutional construction also was evident in the increasing number of cases dealing with economic issues after 1877. In *Knox v. Lee* (1871), he dissented when the Court upheld Congress's Legal Tender Act. He argued that the measure was invalid because the Constitution did not expressly allow Congress to authorize payments of debt in paper currency if it was worth less than the coin money had been before passage of the measure. He did, however, support state economic regulation, concurring with the Court in upholding the Granger Laws in *Munn v. Illinois* (1877). In *Collector v. Day* (1871), the Court supported Clifford in striking down a federal tax on state employees; in a notable dissent, in *Loan Association v. Topeka* (1875), he argued that, unless specifically prohibited by the Constitution, state legislative powers were "practically absolute."

During his 23-year tenure on the Court, Clifford wrote the Court's opinion in almost 400 cases. The fact that he dissented in almost 100 cases is perhaps a better testament to both his fidelity to his principles and his minimal impact on the constitutional developments of the times. Although he developed into an expert in specialty areas, such as patent and admiralty law, his opinions tended to be long and obtuse. Even his admirers admitted that his rise to prominence had been in the "absence of extraordinary gifts." His service on the special Electoral Commission to settle the disputed presidential vote in 1877 only deepened his political frustrations with the Republican party. Despite illness and increasing mental incapacity, he refused to step down from the Court, presumably until the Democrats again came to power. He died in Cornish, Maine.

• Clifford's papers can be found in the Maine Historical Society; his Supreme Court opinions, in *U.S. Reports*. The only full-length study is Phillip G. Clifford, *Nathan Clifford, Democrat, 1803–1881* (1922); its primary usefulness is its collection of Clifford's letters. For an uncritical and laudatory view see Walter Chandler, "Nathan Clifford: A Triumph of Untiring Effort," *American Bar Association Journal* 11 (Jan. 1925): 57–60. An opposite interpretation can be found in William Gillette, "Nathan Clifford," in *The Justices of the United States Supreme Court, 1789–1978*, vol. 2, ed. Leon Friedman and Fred L. Israel (1969), pp. 963–85. The most complete accounts of the Supreme Court during Clifford's tenure are the relevant volumes in the Oliver Wendell Holmes Devise, *History of the Supreme Court of the United States*; Carl B. Swisher, *The Taney Period, 1836–64*, vol. 5 (1985); and Charles Fairman, *Reconstruction and Reunion, 1864–88*, pts. 1 and 2 (1987). For Clifford's role on the Electoral Commission in 1877 see Fairman's supp. to vol. 7, *Five Justices and the Electoral Commission* (1987). Clifford's work on the Court during the Civil War is analyzed in David M. Silver, *Lincoln's Supreme Court* (1957). The best description of Clifford's final years on the Supreme Court is C. Peter Magrath, *Morrison R. Waite: The Triumph of Character* (1963). An obituary is in the *New York Times*, 26 July 1881.

ROBERT M. GOLDMAN

CLIFFTON, William (4 July 1771–25 Nov. 1799), poet, was born in the Southwark district of Philadelphia, Pennsylvania, the son of William Cliffton, a prosperous blacksmith, and Catherine Hallowell. The family was Quaker. William, who never married, was consumptive and suffered severe hemorrhaging when he was nineteen. Ill health restricted his activities, and he spent his entire life in and near Philadelphia.

Poor health did not prevent Cliffton from developing his talents for music, art, and poetry, as well as enjoying the pastimes of shooting and swordsmanship. He was a member of the Anchor Club, a short-lived social and political club for which he wrote several political satires. A portrait of him, first published in *Poems, Chiefly Occasional, by the late Mr. Cliffton* (1800), shows a handsome face and a gentlemanly demeanor. His editor Leo A. Bressler comments, "Nowhere in his writings is there a hint of complaint or a suggestion of obsession with disease or death" (p. xxv). Bressler sees Cliffton as optimistic and buoyant in lyric poetry, vigorously masculine in his satires.

In his own day Cliffton was known primarily for his political satires *The Group; or, An Elegant Representation*, published in 1796, and *Talleyrand's Descent into Hell* (c. 1797). Most of his lyric poetry was left in manuscript or published anonymously. His friend John Ward Fenno published sixteen of Cliffton's poems in *Poems, Chiefly Occasional*. In a contemporary review of this edition Charles Brockden Brown cites "originality of ideas, combined with precision, strength, and elegance of expression" (Bressler, p. liv). Thereafter Cliffton's reputation declined to the point where Bressler found in 1952 that his work was "known to a few specialists."

Cliffton was politically conservative, siding with the Federalists and the British during the turmoil of the French Revolution. The Jay Treaty, a commercial agreement negotiated with Great Britain by Chief Justice and Ambassador-at-Large John Jay in 1794 (ratified in February 1796), resulted in a furor of opposition from French sympathizers in America. Cliffton was bitter in his denunciation of Jacobins in America who "Blaspheme their country's dearest name, and life," a reference in *The Group* to attacks on President George Washington. This lengthy satire attacks some eleven French sympathizers under fictitious names, concluding with hope for the eventual defeat of the Jacobins:

> The hour is hastening, when on equal feet,
> Exalted Virtue, and low Vice shall meet;
> When Envy, Faction, Indolence shall rage,
> In one wild tempest, thro' the troubled age:
> . . . .
> And true Equality shall bless mankind.

Another political poem, "The Chimeraid," satirizes the philosophies of the French Revolution in a characterization of the Greek mythological monster Chimera:

Full of herself she soar'd aloft to prove
The joys which float in endless change above;
And saw obedient to her mad command,
Incongruous nothings into chaos plann'd.

Ellis Oberholtzer comments that Cliffton was "wasting his poetical energies in political satire of no lasting value to his fame" (p. 155).

Cliffton's lyric gift is seen in his short poems and songs such as "Il Penseroso," "To Fancy," "To a Robin," "To Sleep," and a song celebrating Horatio Nelson's victory of the Nile. "Il Penseroso," with its Miltonic title, exhibits a pensive romanticism:

Why should I mingle in the mazy ring
Of drunken folly at the shrine of chance?
Where insect pleasure flits on burnished wing?
Eludes our wishes, and keeps up the dance?

When in the quiet of an humble home,
Beside the fountain, or upon the hill,
Where strife and care and sorrow never come,
I may be free and happy, if I will.

A few of Cliffton's songs were set to music. His tribute to Lord Nelson, with its refrain "hearts of oak," was sung at a Philadelphia festival. "Mary Will Smile" was written for a popular actress, Miss Broadhurst, to sing at the New Theatre in Philadelphia. The music was composed by Benjamin Carr, "the greatest American composer of the time" (Bressler, p. xxiii). First published in the Fenno edition of 1800, it presents Mary's lament for her lover William's departure "to camp and war":

Yet go, brave youth! to arms away!
My maiden hands for fight shall dress thee,
And when the drum beats far away,
I'll drop a silent tear and bless thee.

Return'd with honor, from the hostile plain,
Mary will smile, and all be fair again.

A neoclassical poet, influenced by John Dryden, Alexander Pope, and John Gay, Cliffton was adept at using the iambic pentameter couplet, as in most of the satires, but also exhibited a true musical quality in the quatrains and refrains of his songs. "Cliffton had perhaps more feeling, more quality, than any other American writer of his day save Freneau," Thomas O. Mabbott states in the *Dictionary of American Biography*. "And, finally, he is worth remembering," concludes Leo Bressler (p. civ), "as one of the cultured few who realized the poverty of the arts in eighteenth century America and spoke for a cultured nationalism." There is regret that an early death prevented William Cliffton from developing into a major poetic voice in early American literature.

• "Notices of the Late Mr. Cliffton," the unsigned introduction to *Poems, Chiefly Occasional*, is presumed to have been written by John Ward Fenno and gives Cliffton's year of birth as 1772. Leo A. Bressler, in "William Cliffton: Philadelphia Poet 1771–1799, A Critical and Biographical Essay and a Collection of His Writings" (Ph.D. diss., Univ. of Pennsylvania, 1952), cites the birthdate as 4 July 1771. Bressler adds to Fenno's collection of sixteen poems another thirty-one complete poems, six fragmentary poems, and four incomplete prose essays. These works were discovered by Bressler in a manuscript in the possession of the Historical Society of Pennsylvania titled "The Works of William Cliffton, 1791–1798." Many are in Cliffton's own handwriting. Ellis Paxson Oberholtzer, in *The Literary History of Philadelphia* (1906; repr. 1969), pp. 154–56, comments on Cliffton and prints parts of three poems. Lengthy quotations from the poems are included in Evert A. Duyckinck and George L. Duyckinck, *Cyclopedia of American Literature*, vol. 1 (1856), pp. 604–8. Most histories of early American literature make brief mention of Cliffton.

DORA JEAN ASHE

CLIFT, Montgomery (17 Oct. 1920–23 July 1966), actor, was born Edward Montgomery Clift in Omaha, Nebraska, the son of William Brooks Clift, a banker and investment broker, and Ethel Anderson. When Clift was four, his father became sales manager of a Chicago brokerage firm and moved the family to suburban Highland Park, which served as home base while Mrs. Clift traveled extensively with the children. In 1925 she took Monty, as he was called, his twin sister, and his older brother on the first of several European sojourns to experience Old World culture. To this end, she imposed an unwavering educational and cultural regimen. A private tutor in St. Moritz, visits to the Louvre, concerts at Salzburg, and frequent attendance at opera, theater, and ballet gave Clift a liberal education in the arts and proficiency in French and German; yet his childhood was lonely and not fondly remembered. As an adult, he refused to discuss his early years, noting in an interview: "My childhood was hobgoblin—my parents traveled a lot. That's all I can remember."

Clift was only thirteen when he embarked on his acting career. At the suggestion of the children's tutor, Mrs. Clift took him to audition for a small part in *As Husbands Go* in Sarasota, Florida, where she moved with the children following her husband's losses in the stock market collapse. Clift not only won the part but gave an impressive performance. He had developed into an exceptionally handsome youth, and, on stage, according to his brother Brooks, "his physical presence and intensity were hypnotic." His success in this first role provided incentive for additional theater work, and, following a series of modeling jobs, he got a role in a summer stock production of *Fly Away Home* (1935) at Stockbridge, Massachusetts. When the play moved to Broadway with Thomas G. Mitchell in the starring role, Clift advanced from amateur status to that of salaried actor at $50 a week. At the close of the two-season run, he played a small part in the Cole Porter–Moss Hart musical *Jubilee* (1935–1936), and, a month before his eighteenth birthday, he won his first leading role in the critically acclaimed *Dame Nature* (1938), in which he gave a moving portrayal of a fifteen-year-old French schoolboy struggling to understand his impending fatherhood.

In 1940 Clift appeared with Alfred Lunt and Lynn Fontanne, both of whom he admired, in the propaganda drama *There Shall Be No Night*. The depth and sensitivity he brought to his depiction of an idealistic young soldier who fights not for glory, but for lasting peace led to similar portrayals in *The Searching Wind* (1944) and *You Touched Me!* (1945). Although Clift's considerable talent was evident from the start, he credited Lunt with contributing to the excellence of these and other performances. "Alfred taught me how to select. Acting is an accumulation of subtle details," he said, and accordingly he mastered something new for each of his roles. For instance, he memorized the entire Latin Mass for his part as a priest in the film *I Confess* (1953) and learned to play the bugle for the movie of *From Here to Eternity* (1953).

Clift was a charter member of the Actors Studio, considered by many to be the ultimate means of preparation for the theater; he did not, however, subscribe to the philosophy that actors should respond in similar ways to imaginary events in the script as they would to situations in their own lives. Instead, he preferred to use imagination to create a mental image of a fictional character and then determine that character's behavior in various situations. He thus was able to enrich his portrayals, often those of intense loners, with a diversity of individual personality traits. His performances further benefited from his ability to convey emotion through just a glance, a pause, or a gesture.

On completing his thirteenth Broadway play, Clift made an extraordinary entry into motion pictures, appearing opposite John Wayne in *Red River* (1948), a classic western. He received an Academy Award nomination as best actor for his work in a second 1948 film, *The Search*, in which he portrayed a lonely GI who befriends an equally forlorn war orphan. His work in two later films, *A Place in the Sun* (1951) and *From Here to Eternity*, also earned him nominations for best actor awards. Although he never won an Oscar, his portrayals of sensitive, moody protagonists established his screen identity, influenced numerous actors to follow, and secured his position in Hollywood.

In spite of his status as a "hot property," Clift steadfastly refused to conform to Hollywood standards of stardom, insisting that he was simply "trying to be an actor—not a movie star." He asserted his individuality by shunning glamorous social affairs, dressing casually in old chinos and frayed shirts, and favoring his inexpensive New York apartment over a Hollywood mansion. "I like living in New York . . . where I can still be around so-called ordinary people," he said. His nonconformist behavior intrigued the viewing public and resulted in diligent reporting on all aspects of his private life, including his numerous romantic involvements.

After completing *From Here to Eternity*, Clift returned to New York to star in Chekhov's *The Sea Gull* (1954). When the play, which received mixed reviews, closed in July after a two-month run, Clift remained in the East, for his physical condition, always precarious, took a downward turn. Plagued for many years by a metabolic disorder characterized by muscle spasms, imbalance, cramps, and premature cataracts, he had gradually become addicted to barbiturates and alcohol, and for almost two years he did not work. Then, in 1955, at the urging of his longtime friend Elizabeth Taylor, he agreed to star with her in *Raintree County* (1957). Before completion of the film, however, he ran his car into a telephone pole and suffered a badly scarred and partially paralyzed face. Although his changed appearance caused severe psychological suffering, he completed *Raintree County* after his recuperation and, shortly thereafter, accepted several additional offers. In *The Young Lions* (1958) he did an inspired characterization of Noah Ackerman, a vulnerable young Jew, undaunted by profound suffering. The following year, Clift's increasing health problems and erratic behavior on the set endangered completion of the filming of *Suddenly, Last Summer* (1959); in *The Misfits* (1961), however, as Perce Howland, a punch-drunk cowhand, he won acclaim from his fellow actors in the film when he rode a bucking horse and barehandedly roped an angry mare. Clift's next performance as the title figure in *Freud* (1962), described by one critic as "eerily illuminating," proved to be a frustrating experience, for the production was marred by conflicts over the script, shooting delays, over expenditures, and eventual litigation between Clift and Universal Studio. Although the Universal suit claimed that surgery to remove cataracts from both of Clift's eyes during filming caused much of the over expenditure, Clift eventually won the case and collected $131,000 back salary. The resultant publicity, however, had a damaging effect on his career.

Whereas none of these films received the glowing reviews of Clift's earlier performances, a cameo role in *Judgment at Nuremberg* (1961) resulted in his fourth Oscar nomination, this time for best supporting actor. Interestingly, though offered $100,000 for the part, he performed without salary, explaining that he "strongly disapproved of taking an astronomical salary" for a single scene. His last picture *The Defector*, a low-cost spy thriller, filmed in the early part of 1966 in Munich, was released posthumously. Ironically, Clift had accepted this role and had personally executed numerous stunts in spite of his physical ills in order to qualify for a part opposite Elizabeth Taylor in John Huston's forthcoming film, *Reflections in a Golden Eye*.

Clift, who never married, spent his final months in semiseclusion in his New York brownstone under the care of a male nurse-companion, who found the actor in bed near death one morning. According to the medical examiner's autopsy, Clift died of occlusive heart failure.

• Clippings on Clift are in the Theater Collection of the New York Public Library at Lincoln Center. Two excellent biographies are Robert LaGuardia, *Monty* (1977), and Patricia Bosworth, *Montgomery Clift* (1978). See also Robert Lewis, *Slings and Arrows* (1984), and Judith M. Kass, *The Films of Montgomery Clift* (1979). An obituary is in the *New York Times*, 24 July 1966.

DOROTHY KISH

CLIFTON, Josephine (1813?–21 Nov. 1847), was the first American actress to star in England. The details of Clifton's birth date, birthplace, parentage, and childhood are inconclusive and contradictory. Most sources say she was born in 1813. An 1832 press release in *The American* stated that Clifton had "not yet attained . . . her nineteenth year," which is consistent with a birth date of 1813 or 1814. Most sources, including the *American* press release, relate that Clifton was born in New York City. Other sources, however, including Charles Durang, *The Philadelphia Stage*, and the *Enciclopedia dello spettacolo*, give her birthplace as Philadelphia. No official records have been recovered to confirm these details. Although her parents are unknown, a scandal sheet, *Polyanthis*, printed a story that her mother was a brothel-keeper, and other contemporary sources accepted the story. Joseph Ireland in his *Records of the New York Stage* said that Clifton had the best education the "ill-gotten wealth of an indulgent mother could procure," and H. P. Phelps in *Players of a Century* called her the child of "a mother whom it is better not to mention."

Despite the sketchiness of her beginnings, it is known that Clifton made her debut on 21 September 1831 at the Bowery Theatre as Belvidera in *Venice Preserved* after studying with the manager, Thomas Hamblin. An expert promoter, Hamblin helped Clifton's star rise quickly. Regarding her first performance, Ireland said that "her surpassing beauty of face and person, her youth and aptitude, her fine voice and expressive action (for she had been drilled by an experienced stager) commanded a success almost unprecedented for a debutante, and she soon became an acknowledged star of the first attraction" (vol. 2, p. 17). During her first season Clifton was performing an impressive list of leading roles, including Elvira in *Pizarro*, Imogen in *Bertram*, Constance in *King John*, and Shakespeare's Lady Macbeth and Juliet. She also appeared successfully in Philadelphia as Belvidera at the Chestnut Street Theatre and as Lady Macbeth at the Walnut Street Theatre.

In 1834 Clifton extended her popularity with a brief tour of the United States, after which she became the first American actress to perform in England. She made her London debut as Belvidera on 4 October at the Covent Garden Theatre. For the next year in England she regularly played leading roles both at the Covent Garden and the Drury Lane Theatres, the two leading London theaters. The English critics seemed to agree that for an actress of her age and inexperience—she had been on the stage for only three years—Clifton had great potential if she continued her studies. While in England she also toured the provincial theaters and gained popular success with the audiences.

Clifton returned to the United States in March 1836 to great acclaim. The reports of her engagements in England, doubtless exaggerated, preceded her return and the American public welcomed her home in triumph. She began to tour immediately after her return and became a popular star playing in both comedy and

tragedy throughout the country. She played the Park Theatre on 25 August 1837 in the title role of *Bianca Visconti*, written expressly for her by Nathaniel Parker Willis as the result of a contest she had sponsored; the playwright was awarded $1,000. Bianca became Clifton's most celebrated role. She had obviously improved as an actress during her time abroad and on the road because reviewers of *Bianca Visconti* seemed surprised at her portrayal. "We scarce know which of the five grades of feeling, in the five acts, Miss Clifton best represented," the reviewer for the *New York Mirror* wrote on 9 September. "Miss Clifton was all that the author could desire—all that it was profecied [*sic*] she would not be. She played in a new style, and on new principles. It was a performance full of mind."

In 1838 the scandal concerning Clifton's mother's brothel-keeping erupted in conjunction with reports of Clifton trying to stop her half sister Louisa Missouri Miller from becoming an actress. While Clifton insisted that her concern was only that her sister not associate with her former manager, Hamblin, the newspapers made much of her supposed jealousy. Miller made her debut at the age of sixteen, but the scandal concerning their mother reportedly caused her death shortly after her debut. All this scandal also had its effect on Clifton and may have contributed to her ill health. During the 1842–1843 season Clifton toured successfully with Edwin Forrest. (Later, during Forrest's famous divorce hearing in 1851, Clifton's name arose posthumously as one actress with whom Forrest had committed adultery.) By 1844 Clifton seems to have stopped performing regularly. Why she retired at the height of her career is unknown, but in July 1846 she married Robert Place, the manager of the American Theatre in New Orleans, and never performed again. She died childless a year later in New Orleans.

The two features most associated with Clifton were her beauty and her physical stature. At almost six feet tall, this imposing "amazon" certainly attracted attention. Ireland claimed that her "tall and elegantly moulded person gradually expanded into Brobdingnagian proportions." He concluded that her success as an actress came from a combination of her "imposing personal presence" with training and talent. Despite her success in her brief career, Clifton's full potential as an actress was perhaps unreached. Ireland concluded his discussion of Clifton by saying, "at the time of her death, no other American actress, with the exception of Miss [Charlotte] Cushman, had created so wide (we do not add deep) a sensation, and had she combined the latter's commanding intellect and unwearied application with her own early personal requisites, she would have reigned the legitimate empress of our National Stage" (vol. 2, p. 18). Whatever her potential, Clifton was a major star and cleared the way for Cushman and other American actresses to command an audience outside their native country.

• Because Clifton left no personal papers, an account of her life must be garnered from various sources. The most helpful of these are Joseph Ireland, *Records of the New York Stage from 1750 to 1860* (1866–1867; repr. 1968); George C. Odell, *Annals of the New York Stage*, vols. 3 and 4 (1927–1949); Charles Durang, *The Philadelphia Stage, from the Year 1749 to the Year 1855* (1868); H. P. Phelps, *Players of a Century* (1880); and F. C. Wemyss, *Chronology of the American Stage* (1852). See also Theodore Shank, "The Bowery Theatre, 1826–1836" (Ph.D. diss., Stanford Univ., 1956), and Ernest Frederick Meinken, "American Actors in London, 1825–1861: Reception by London Professional Critics" (Ph.D. diss., Univ. of California at Los Angeles, 1972). Obituaries are in the *New Orleans Daily Picayune*, 22 Nov. 1847, and *New York Spirit of the Times*, 11 Dec. 1847.

MELISSA VICKERY-BAREFORD

CLINCH, Charles Powell (20 Oct. 1797–16 Dec. 1880), writer and government official, was born in New York City, the son of James Clinch, a wealthy ship chandler; his mother's name is unknown. After a public school education he became confidential secretary to Henry Eckford, a New York shipbuilder and marine architect through whom he met Fitz-Greene Halleck and other New York writers. Clinch admired the poetry of Halleck and William Cullen Bryant and was eventually included in the company of the Knickerbockers, a group of writers in and around New York during the first half of the nineteenth century that established the city as a major literary and cultural center. Its other major luminaries were James Fenimore Cooper and Washington Irving.

In 1819, at age twenty-two, Clinch became one of five men who knew the true identity of "The Croakers" (Joseph Rodman Drake and Halleck), anonymous contributors to the *New York Evening Post* who published satiric verses on the political and social life of New York City. "There was no circumstance in the career of this worthy Knickerbocker [Clinch] of which he was so proud as of having been the intimate and confidential friend of the literary partners Halleck and Drake" (J. G. Wilson, *Bryant and His Friends*, p. 396).

Although a Democratic member of the state legislature in Albany from 1835 to 1836, Clinch's prime financial support came from his 38-year career as an inspector (appointed in 1838) and later assistant collector (appointed in 1863) in the U.S. Custom House in New York. But he was also an editorial writer and literary and drama critic for the New York press during these years. He himself ventured into creative writing by successfully adapting Cooper's *The Spy* for the stage, opening at the Park Theatre on 1 March 1822, less than ten weeks after the novel was published. *The Spy* toured the eastern seaboard for the next thirty years and proved as popular as Cooper's book. Subtitled *A Tale of the Neutral Ground*, the play dramatizes the conflicts faced by a man of no identifiable loyalty. Clinch altered the plot so that the death of Harvey Birch and the revelation of his true identity occur at the time of the present action, rather than thirty-two years later. Clinch's version of *The Spy* retains Cooper's insights into revolutionary war patriotism as well as his focus on the tension between justice and the law on the one hand and personal principles on the

other. But the play's melodramatic qualities, stiffness of dialog, and formal soliloquies detract from the fairly durable modern themes of honor and commitment to a cause. Nor would most current audiences approve of Cooper's condescending treatment toward women and blacks, which Clinch incorporated into his adaptation.

Clinch excelled in oration, delivering a speech, later published, at the New York Fire Department's Fourth of July celebration in 1823. By 1830 he had written a crime melodrama, *The Avenger's Vow* (1824), and two farces, *The Expelled Collegians* (1822), also produced at the Park and reviewed favorably in Odell's *Annals of the New York Stage*, and *The First of May in New York* (1830) produced at the Bowery Theatre.

As a great admirer of Bryant, Clinch wrote a poem in the writer's honor that appeared posthumously in J. G. Wilson's *Bryant and His Friends* in 1886. This poetic tribute to Bryant's character and genius contained twenty-five quatrains with classical references to the muses, nature, and the poet's power. The last stanza illustrates Clinch's effort to immortalize Bryant in a flowery style that borders on doggerel:

> His civic crown was gemmed so oft,
> So early—on the scroll of fame,
> Each coming age will "look aloft,"
> To woo and worship Bryant's name.

According to his obituary in the *New York Times*, Clinch knew Shakespeare's works by heart and "there were not many better Shakespearean scholars in the United States than he." Despite his considerable literary efforts, however, Clinch will be noted more for his connections to famous literary figures than for his own work. He was twice married and at his death had an adopted daughter. His first wife Abby M. died in 1870; his second wife Anna A. died in 1890. Clinch died in New York City.

• A copy of Clinch's 4 July 1823 oration is in the New-York Historical Society. The original 1823 oration and the original manuscript prompt book of *The Spy* are held at the New York Public Library. See George Odell, *Annals of the New York Stage*, vol. 3, *1821–1834*, for a favorable assessment of this play. Editor Eugene Richard Page provides a brief but effective prefatory note on the publication of *The Spy* in "Metamora and Other Plays" in his *America's Lost Plays*, vol. 14 (1941). For contemporary references to Clinch, see J. G. Wilson, *Life and Letters of Fitz-Greene Halleck* (1869) and *Bryant and His Friends: Some Reminiscences of the Knickerbocker Writers* (1886). See also Hamilton W. Mabie, *The Writers of Knickerbocker New York* (1912). Brief references showing Clinch as a lesser-known Knickerbocker are in Nelson Adkins, *Fitz-Greene Halleck: An Early Knickerbocker Wit and Poet* (1930). For more modern assessments of *The Spy*, see James Wallace, *Early Cooper and His Audience* (1986), and C. H. Adams, *The Guardian of the Law: Authority and Identity in James Fenimore Cooper* (1990). For a detailed account of Clinch's years in the New York Custom House and an assessment of his professional and literary abilities, see the *New York Times* obituary, 17 Dec. 1880. Other obituaries appear in New York's *Evening Post*, 16 Dec. 1880, and the city's *Herald, Tribune, World*, and *Sun* newspapers, 17 Dec. 1880.

BARBARA KRALEY YOUEL

CLINE, Genevieve Rose (27 July 1877–25 Oct. 1959), federal judge, was born in Warren, Ohio, the daughter of Edward B. Cline, a Hungarian immigrant who operated a lunchroom, and Mary Fee. Cline attended the public schools in Warren until the family moved to Cleveland, where she lived her adult life. She attended the Cleveland Spencerian School, where she studied stenographic skills and found her first job with the Osborn Manufacturing Company for five dollars a week.

In 1904 Cline returned to Warren, studying for a year at Oberlin College. By 1905 she was back in Cleveland, filling a position as clerk for her attorney brother, John A. Cline, later county prosecutor and a Court of Appeals judge in Cleveland. Following her brother's advice, Cline studied law at the Old Cleveland Law School and graduated from Baldwin Wallace College. Cline passed the bar exam in 1921 when it was rare for women to become attorneys. For eight years she practiced law with her brother in Cleveland.

During this period Cline was introduced to politics and the law as well as to women's club work on the city and state levels, which became a lifelong interest of hers. She became very involved in Republican politics and worked to increase women's participation in the activities of the party even before the Nineteenth Amendment giving women the right to vote became law. She scored a victory in the party before she had the right to vote for it. "At the first GOP women's organization meeting in Cleveland, she objected to a ruling, then formed a rival club," her obituary states. When her group received official recognition by the Republican party, Cline was named Cuyahoga County chair for women.

In 1922 President Warren G. Harding appointed Cline the first woman to serve as the U.S. appraiser of merchandise in the Cleveland customs office. In this position, she was accountable for the inspection and appraisal of international goods shipped through customs to Ohio and northwestern Pennsylvania. Cline possessed a keen knowledge of tariff law that provided her with the expertise required to accurately determine the value of such merchandise. She remained as appraiser for six years until 1928 when President Calvin Coolidge appointed her to the U.S. Customs Court in New York City. With this appointment, Cline became the first woman ever appointed to a federal judgeship.

Although Cline's appointment to the federal court had the support of Maurice Maschke, longtime head of the Cleveland Republican party, her appointment to the judgeship drew heated opposition from several U.S. senators who were shocked at the idea of a woman in such a specialized position. Judges on the U.S. Customs Court had jurisdiction over appeals from custom collectors and appraisers. They usually related to the value or classification of imported merchandise. After a favorable report from the Senate judiciary committee, however, Cline received unanimous confirmation and subsequently presided in cities throughout the country.

During the years 1916–1927 Cline also served as the president of the Cleveland Federation of Women's Clubs, chair of the Ohio Federation of Women's clubs, vice chair of the legislation department of the General Federation of Women's Clubs, and Ohio vice president of the National Republican Women's Association. Her involvement with these groups brought her to the attention of Republican party leaders in Washington, D.C., and contributed significantly to her appointment to the federal judgeship. In 1940 she helped organize the Women Lawyer's Association of Cleveland, a group committed to encouraging women's active participation in the state and local bar associations and to promoting a spirit of friendship and cooperation among all women attorneys.

Less than five feet tall and weighing only eighty-seven pounds, Cline's appearance was often a surprise to court officials. Nevertheless, she served on the U.S. Customs Court for twenty-five years, returning to Cleveland upon her retirement at age seventy-six in March 1953. Cline never married. She served tirelessly on the court and brought extensive knowledge of tariff law and trade policy to her work. She also worked for child labor laws, care for the mentally retarded, and civil service reform. She died in Cleveland.

• Cline's activities in the Republican party are mentioned in the Frank Willis Papers at the Ohio Historical Society, Columbus. The *Women Lawyer's Journal* (Aug. 1940): 24, briefly discusses her involvement with the Women's Lawyer's Association of Cleveland. Obituaries are in the *Warren (Ohio) Tribune Chronicle* and the *Cleveland Plain Dealer*, 27 Oct. 1959.

KAREN L. VOSHALL

CLINE, Maggie (1 Jan. 1857–11 June 1934), entertainer, was born Margaret Cline in Haverhill, Massachusetts, the daughter of Patrick B. Cline and Ann Degman. Educated in Haverhill's public schools, Maggie worked in a show factory before running away from home with a traveling theatrical company at the age of fifteen.

In 1880 Cline joined Col. T. C. Snellbaker's *Majestics*, a burlesque company. Her early songs were mostly sentimental until she introduced "Mary Ann Kehoe" at the Academy of Music in Pittsburgh. Success was swift, and Cline became a favorite of the working-class patrons at Tony Pastor's variety theater on Fourteenth Street in New York City. She was identified with a number of songs, including "Drill Ye Tarriers, Drill," first introduced by a trio in the musical *A Brass Monkey* in 1888, and "Down Went McGinty to the Bottom of the Sea," about an accident-prone Irishman, written in 1889.

Cline married John F. Ryan, a Brooklyn café proprietor, in 1888 but kept the marriage secret for the sake of her career. (She was once photographed with one John Sweeney, identified as her adopted son.) Cline was a large woman, weighing over 200 pounds with a voice reputedly as loud as 100 choristers.

Among her many fans on New York's Bowery, Cline was known as "The Irish Queen."

Cline's most famous song, "Throw Him Down Mc-Closkey," was written by John W. Kelly, vaudeville's famous "Rolling Mill Man," in 1890. Epitomizing the Irishwoman "with hot blood coursing through her veins and fire in her eyes," she strode across the stage, swinging her arms and hips and hitching her belt while telling how McCloskey and Pete McCracken "covered themselves with glory" in a fight that left both men disfigured. Stagehands provided sound effects during the chorus, and Cline was obliged to sing it at almost every performance for the rest of her career. She claimed to have "thrown McCloskey" no less than 6,000 times from 1891 until her retirement in 1917, and managers often hired her to sing the song between the acts of melodramas in order to placate and draw the rough gallery element. The only complaint about "McCloskey" came from her own father: "Maggie, it ain't ladylike."

Cline sang between the acts of both *Garry Owen*, an Irish theme play by Murphy O'Hea at the Grand Opera House in New York in 1895, and a revival of Dion Boucicault's *After Dark* at the New York Academy of Music in the spring of 1896. In October of that year she played Mary Brady, heroine of a four-act comedy-melodrama by Clay Greene and Ben Teal titled *On Broadway* at New York's Bowdoin Square Theatre. Cline also starred in *Fun aboard the Pacific Mail* and sang between the acts of *The Man in the Moon, Jr.* at the New York Theatre in the fall of 1899.

Cline was one of the first vaudeville favorites lauded in the press. James Huneker of the *Musical Courier* dubbed her "The Brunhilde of the Bowery" due to her ample proportions and powerful voice, and the attention given brought the carriage trade to Pastor's. She was also known as a past master of repartee with the gallery. One night, as she finished singing "Don't Let Me Die till I See Ireland," a gallery patron called out, "Well why don't you go there?" "Nit," Cline replied, "it's too far from the Bowery."

Cline's other songs included "The Hat Me Father Wore," "The Pitcher of Beer," "Choke Him, Casey, Choke Him," "When Hogan Pays the Rent," and "None of Them's Got Anything on Me."

Cline retired in 1917 but returned for the dedication of the Hammerstein Theatre at Fifty-third Street and Broadway in new York in 1927. She made her last public appearance two years later at the Savoy Theatre in Asbury Park, New Jersey, where she was called to the stage during a benefit performance given by the Holy Spirit Roman Catholic Church. The orchestra struck up "McCloskey," and Cline sang it as the spotlight was turned on her.

Cline lived in Red Bank, New Jersey, from 1917 to 1927 when she moved to Fair Haven, New Jersey, where she suffered a severe cold through the winter of 1933–1934 and was cared for by her sister, Elizabeth Hudson, until her death, from a stroke the following June.

Maggie Cline epitomized the boisterous, rebellious spirit of the late nineteenth-century Irish working class and was one of the leading variety stars immediately prior to the formation of the theater chains that would make vaudeville big business in the first three decades of the twentieth century.

• *Stage Deaths: A Biographical Guide to International Theatrical Obituaries, 1850 to 1990*, comp. George B. Bryan (1991), lists the names of Maggie Cline's parents and husband on p. 256. John F. Ryan is given a listing of his own on p. 1094, but Bryan has confused him with the John F. Ryan who died on 6 Apr. 1913 and was married to actress Mabel Leonard. The John F. Ryan married to Maggie Cline died on 30 Sept. 1937.

The lengthy obituary on Maggie Cline in the *New York Herald Tribune* of 12 June 1934 remains a prime source of biographical information. The *New York Times* reviewed her appearances in *Garry Owen, After Dark, On Broadway*, and *The Man in the Moon, Jr.*

HERBERT G. GOLDMAN

CLINE, Patsy (8 Sept. 1932–5 Mar. 1963), singer, was born Virginia Patterson Hensley in Gore, Virginia, the daughter of Samuel Lawrence Hensley, a laborer and farmer, and Hilda Patterson. The family settled in Winchester, Virginia, in 1945. After a childhood fantasy of a Hollywood career, Cline discovered the radio broadcasts of the Grand Ole Opry and became obsessed with becoming a member. With her mother, she sang in the choir of the Gore Baptist Church. At fourteen she began singing on WINC Radio, Winchester, making her stage debut at sixteen on Wally Fowler's Gospel Caravan. Fowler arranged a Grand Ole Opry audition in Nashville, but owing to financial constraints, Cline returned home. She quit school after the tenth grade, when her father deserted the family, to work at a series of odd jobs, all the while singing at socials, benefits, carnivals, and finally area clubs.

In September 1952 she auditioned for disc jockey and regional country bandleader Bill Peer, who made her his lead vocalist. Peer changed her name to Patsy and groomed her for stardom. They began an intense romance, but in March 1953 she married Gerald Cline, a truck driver from an affluent Frederick, Maryland, family. In spite of their marriages, however, Patsy Cline and Bill Peer continued their affair.

In September 1954 Peer secured a recording contract for Cline with California-based Four-Star Records, which was also a music publisher. Cline recorded her first songs in January 1955 at Nashville's Decca Records, and Four-Star leased them to the label. Cline's recordings were produced by pop bandleader Owen Bradley, later to head Decca's Nashville operations. The early songs forced on Cline by Four-Star were wrong for her smooth and elegant voice, a natural four-octave instrument. Four-Star was determined to make her a pop star, but Cline only wanted to sing country songs. Her first release in July 1955 was a remarkably telling ballad, "A Church, a Courtroom, and Then Goodbye." This first single appeared on Coral, a division of Decca. All of her remaining releases would be on Decca.

After breaking with Peer in October 1955, Cline developed a following opposite Jimmy Dean on the first live country television variety program, "The Town & Country Jamboree," a telecast on a regional network from Washington, D.C. In January 1957 she skyrocketed to fame singing, much against her will, a pop song, "Walkin' after Midnight," on CBS-TV's "Arthur Godfrey's Talent Scouts" and worked briefly for Godfrey. The song became a country and pop hit—the first for a female country singer. In April it reached the number two position on *Billboard*'s country chart and, ultimately, the number twelve spot on the magazine's pop music chart. Two days after her Arthur Godfrey debut, Gerald Cline filed for divorce, which was granted in March 1957. Patsy and Gerald Cline had no children. In September Patsy Cline married Charles Dick, a Linotype operator. They had two children.

Cline was the first challenger to Kitty Wells, who had emerged from her husband's act to be known as "the queen of country music," and Cline's sales surpassed those of her idol Patsy Montana. Cline was well known and toured with country stars such as Faron Young and Ferlin Huskey, and she became a member of the Grand Ole Opry in 1960. Her initial recording success, however, was not repeated for four years. In 1961 she signed a recording contract with Decca. Bradley believed Cline had great potential but in a different direction, and influenced by him, she broke with tradition to sing the material of radical songwriters.

The first of these recordings was "I Fall to Pieces," by Hank Cochran and Harlan Howard. Cline despised the song, but within six months it was a massive country and pop success, becoming *Billboard*'s number one country song and breaking above Elvis Presley on the pop charts. The turning point of her recording career was "Crazy," written by Willie Nelson, another song she hated but which Bradley coerced her to sing in August. In its innovative arrangement (which included strings) "Crazy" was a departure from standard country, and her career subsequently changed direction.

In June 1961, with "I Fall to Pieces" climbing the charts, Cline was critically injured in an automobile collision. It was not thought that she would live, but three months later she was singing. She returned to touring sooner than her doctor recommended, however, and suffered a nervous breakdown. Two days after being ordered to rest for two weeks, she returned to the studio to cut "She's Got You," written by Hank Cochran. It proved to be another top seller.

Although not always willing, Cline was an innovator. As a female country music vocalist, she achieved a number of firsts: she was first to have sustained crossover pop appeal, to challenge numerous taboos in male-dominated country music, to record in stereo, to have a solo album, to be on network television variety shows (even "American Bandstand"), to have a teen following, and to tour as a solo act. She changed the perception of the female country singer by gradually opting for cocktail dresses and gowns instead of western outfits. She opened the door for artists such as Loretta Lynn, Dottie West, and Jean Shepard to emerge as stars in their own right and not as part of a husband-wife duo or group.

In November 1961 Cline appeared at Carnegie Hall; in June 1962 she performed at the Hollywood Bowl. In November 1962, at the height of her stardom, she opened a record-breaking 35-night engagement in Las Vegas. Cline recorded over 100 songs, many of which—"I've Loved and Lost Again," "Lovin' in Vain," "That's How a Heartache Begins," and "Faded Love"—reflect her own life experience. Cline could not read music, but she composed the music to two of the songs she recorded.

Cline was killed in a plane crash near Camden, Tennessee, en route from a benefit. Also killed were Opry stars Hawkshaw Hawkins and Cowboy Copas and Cline's manager/guitarist Randy Hughes, who was piloting the plane.

The hallmark of Patsy Cline's legacy is a voice that mesmerized a new breed of devotees at a time when rock and roll put a stranglehold on country music. If Cline cannot be given credit for birthing the "Nashville Sound" (Eddy Arnold and Jim Reeves did), she was the first country female singer to bring it out of diapers. Her recordings from 1961 until her death redefined country music and brought it wide appeal.

• Ellis Nassour, *Honkey Tonk Angel: The Intimate Story of Patsy Cline* (1993), an updated and revised edition of his *Patsy Cline* (1981; rev. ed., 1985), is the definitive biography. Margaret Jones, *Patsy: The Life and Times of Patsy Cline* (1994), further explores her life. Joli Jensen, "Patsy Cline's Recording Career: The Search for a Sound," *Journal of Country Music* 9, no. 2 (1982): 34, discusses Cline's recording career. Diane Cynthia Pansen, "Filming Her Life: Patsy Cline, Dian Fowwery and Ruth First" (M.A. thesis, Univ. of Texas, Austin, 1989), discusses the representation of fact in the biographical film *Sweet Dreams* (1985). Cline was also portrayed in the film adaptation of Loretta Lynn's autobiography, *Coal Miner's Daughter*, but the depictions of events involving Cline are mostly fictitious. *The Patsy Cline Collection* (MCA Records), featuring 104 tracks, is the definitive anthology of her recordings.

ELLIS NASSOUR

CLINGMAN, Thomas Lanier (27 July 1812–3 Nov. 1897), politician and businessman, was born in Huntsville, North Carolina, the son of Jacob Clingman, a merchant, and Jane Poindexter. After graduating from the University of North Carolina at Chapel Hill in 1832, he studied law at the office of William A. Graham. He represented Surry County as a Whig in the house of commons in 1835 but was defeated for reelection. He moved to Asheville in 1836 and was elected to the state senate in 1840. In an era of intense East-West sectionalism, he advocated state-financed railroads and other measures of internal development favored by westerners, resisting efforts by the wealthy plantation counties to limit government services in order to keep taxes low.

In 1843 Clingman won election as a Whig to the U.S. House of Representatives by defeating James Graham, the veteran Whig incumbent. Except for one term he served continuously until his appointment to the U.S. Senate in May 1858, remaining there until 28 March 1861. An able debater and an effective parliamentarian, Clingman did not distinguish himself in the House as a policymaker. He attracted widespread attention during his first term through several highly partisan speeches in which he characterized the Democrats as "a spoils party, held together by the cohesive attraction of public plunder." He also gained notoriety by supporting the repeal of the "gag rule," under which Congress had refused to receive abolitionist petitions. His controversial vote led to a bloodless duel with William L. Yancey of Alabama in 1845.

Intensely ambitious and arrogantly self-confident, Clingman grew frustrated by the failure of the Whigs to elevate him to the U.S. Senate. In 1848 he burned his bridges with his party by soliciting Democratic votes in an unsuccessful bid to unseat Senator George E. Badger. To cultivate Democratic support for his senatorial ambitions, Clingman adopted that party's militant position on southern rights. Like most residents of the North Carolina mountain region, Clingman was not a slave owner himself. But mountain voters accepted the legitimacy of slavery and resented northern efforts to interfere with southern social relations. Although his strident rhetoric led enemies to brand him as a disunionist, he did not publicly endorse secession until after the failure of the Crittenden Compromise in 1861.

Clingman continued to win elections in his heavily Whig congressional district during the early 1850s by avoiding too close an identification with Democrats, designating himself first as a Southern Rights Whig and, later, as an independent. Even after formally joining the Democrats in 1856, he maintained an independent stance by opposing efforts of southern Democrats to impose a slave code on the territories and by supporting Stephen A. Douglas for president.

A man of wide-ranging interests, Clingman explored and measured the mountains of western North Carolina and gave his name to Clingman's Dome in the Great Smoky Mountains. During the 1850s he engaged in a debate with Elisha Mitchell of the University of North Carolina over who had been the first to identify, ascend, and measure present-day Mount Mitchell, the highest point in the eastern United States. The controversy eventually led to Mitchell's accidental death.

After the outbreak of the Civil War, Clingman became North Carolina's commissioner to the Confederacy. In August 1861 he was elected colonel of the Twenty-fifth North Carolina Regiment and was promoted to brigadier general the following May. He performed creditably at the battle of Goldsboro in 1862, during the siege of Charleston in 1863, and in the campaigns in 1864 around Richmond and Petersburg, where he was severely wounded.

Clingman's hopes for returning to the U.S. Senate after the war were frustrated by the former Whigs who controlled the dominant Conservative party. However, he regularly attended the sessions of Congress and served as a delegate to the Democratic National Convention in 1868, 1872, and 1876. As a member of the North Carolina Constitutional Convention of 1875, he fended off efforts to repudiate the Reconstruction debt. A rival of Thomas A. Edison, Clingman received two patents for electric lighting. Although not significant in itself, his work called the attention of other inventors, including Edison (to whom Clingman tried to sell zircon from his mines), to the use of zirconia as an incandescing substance. He also practiced law, established a company to promote the medicinal properties of tobacco, engaged extensively in mining ventures and land speculation, and published and lectured widely on scientific and religious topics.

Highly regarded for his intellectual attainments, Clingman was noted as well for his irascible temperament and his eccentric mannerisms, particularly his habit of talking to himself. He enjoyed the company of women and courted several, but he never married. His financial resources, along with his physical and mental health, deteriorated steadily during the 1890s, and he spent his final years under the care of relatives. He died at the state hospital in Morganton, North Carolina.

• Letters to and from Clingman are in the Clingman and Puryear Family Papers and the Thomas Lanier Clingman Papers in the Southern Historical Collection, University of North Carolina at Chapel Hill; in the Jarratt-Puryear Family Papers and the Thomas L. Clingman Papers in the Duke University Library; and in the archives of the Edison National Historic Site, West Orange, N.J. His major speeches, along with autobiographical comments, are in his *Selections from the Speeches and Writings of Hon. Thomas L. Clingman of North Carolina* (1877). For his antebellum political career, see Thomas E. Jeffrey, "'A Whole Torrent of Mean and Malevolent Abuse': Party Politics and the Clingman-Mitchell Controversy," *North Carolina Historical Review* 70 (1993): 241–65, 401–29, and "'Thunder from the Mountains': Thomas Lanier Clingman and the End of Whig Supremacy in North Carolina," *North Carolina Historical Review* 56 (1979): 366–95. See also Marc W. Kruman, "Thomas L. Clingman and the Whig Party: A Reconsideration," *North Carolina Historical Review* 64 (1987): 1–18, and John C. Inscoe, "Thomas Clingman, Mountain Whiggery, and the Southern Cause," *Civil War History* 33 (1987): 42–62. For his postwar activities, see Jeffrey, "Thomas Lanier Clingman and the Invention of the Electric Light: A Forgotten Episode," *Carolina Comments* 32 (1984): 71–82, and Billy Arthur, "The Cure-All of General Clingman," *State* 50, no. 2 (1982): 9–10. An excellent obituary is in the *New York Times*, 5 Nov. 1897.

THOMAS E. JEFFREY

CLINTON, De Witt (2 Mar. 1769–11 Feb. 1828), New York City mayor and New York State governor, was born in Little Britain, New York, the son of James Clinton, a career military man who became a brigadier general in the American army, and Mary De Witt. He was educated by a neighboring Presbyterian minister until he reached age thirteen and then spent two years at the Kingston Academy. After the revolutionary war came to an end, and the city of New York was liberated, Clinton was among the first to enroll at the newly named Columbia College, formerly known as King's

College, which reopened in 1784. On graduating, with honors, in April 1786, he read law in the Manhattan office of Samuel Jones and was admitted to the bar in 1790. By then, he had succeeded his recently deceased older brother, Alexander, as secretary to his uncle, George Clinton, who had been the only governor of the former colony of New York since it established its constitution in 1777. Sharing his uncle's opposition to the proposed federal Constitution, he entered the newspaper war over the issue of ratification in the guise of "A Countryman," author of a series of essays that cleverly laid bare a number of the Constitution's peculiarities, such as the euphemisms applied to slavery. Clinton's precociously developed rhetorical skills, accented by classical allusions and historical analogies, complemented his noble bearing and considerable physical stature, which earned him the sobriquet "Magnus Apollo." His unequaled political connections suggested a limitless future.

In 1795, when his uncle chose not to seek reelection as governor, Clinton entered into a full-time law practice with partner John McKesson; he also had the leisure to engage in scientific study with Professors Samiel L. Mitchell and David Hosack at Columbia. In 1796 Clinton married Maria Franklin, daughter of a wealthy Quaker merchant, Walter Franklin. They had ten children. While the marriage brought Clinton into close contact with the philanthropic Quaker community, it also made him independently wealthy, although the vast Franklin landholdings became subject to considerable litigation.

Clinton was elected to the assembly in 1797, after an unsuccessful try the previous year, and in 1798 won a seat in the state senate. By being designated one of the four senators who joined the governor in forming the Council of Appointment, he came into direct confrontation with his uncle's successor, the Federalist John Jay. The council, an anomaly of the state constitution of 1777, was empowered to dispense New York's extensive patronage (several thousand positions); in the absence of constitutional strictures on the respective roles of the council members, governors had recommended appointments, and senators had approved or disapproved. Clinton's insistence that senators could also make recommendations, subject to approval of the full council, amounted to tacit recognition of political parties. In effect, the party that controlled the Council of Appointment—in this instance, the Jeffersonian-Republicans—would control the state's patronage. The ensuing deadlock with Governor Jay, accompanied by much public debate, was only resolved when a special constitutional convention, with a Republican majority, was held in the summer of 1801 and determined that Clinton's view was correct. Named again to the council, Clinton and his close ally Ambrose Spencer purged Federalist jobholders, replacing them with Republicans. Hence Clinton has been blamed for originating the spoils system in the United States.

Appointed in February 1802 to the U.S. Senate, Clinton was not long in Washington. In October 1803 he resigned to take the appointment of mayor of New York City. His brief tenure in the U.S. Senate has raised persistent questions concerning the appointment process, including speculation as to whether the shift to the mayoralty was a deliberate attempt to remove him from the national scene, deflecting his ambition for gaining the presidency. However, Clinton was, he said, delighted to accept the post both to secure the city for the Republicans and to avoid the cost of maintaining homes both in New York and Washington, D.C. He served as mayor for approximately ten years: from 1803 to 1815, except during 1807–1808 and 1810–1811, when the Council of Appointment was in unfriendly hands, and was simultaneously a state senator, from 1806 to 1811, and lieutenant governor, from 1811 to 1813. His longevity as mayor had a profound effect on Clinton's career. As the city's population more than doubled—from 60,000 inhabitants at the start of the nineteenth century—the accelerating commercial growth made New York the nation's largest port. The ills resulting from urban overcrowding—such as fire-prone buildings, epidemics, and mass unrest—challenged Clinton's administrative skills and heightened his humanitarian instincts. He was highly visible and seemingly indefatigable, whether attending fires, inspecting markets, organizing the Public School Society (1805), or supervising the harbor's defense. The last to hold the so-called mayor's court, Clinton supported Columbia College's administrators and faculty in strongly reprimanding "rioters" who disrupted the commencement in 1811; that marked him as an advocate of law and order. His concern for commercial interests caused him to equivocate on the embargo policy so cardinal to the Republican administrations of Thomas Jefferson and James Madison, who felt that the best way to block England and France from interfering in American shipping was to suspend trade with those countries; Clinton was thereby drawn away from his own Republican roots. His concern for the welfare of Irish immigrants earned him their continuing support, but in the eyes of the politicos of the Tammany Society, an organization that was later to become synonymous with collusion and graft, Clinton was vulnerable to accusations of personal self-aggrandizement.

In 1812, perhaps because of deep differences with the Madison administration, along with his highest aspirations having been frustrated, Clinton ran for president. When he received the New York legislature's nomination, the War of 1812 had not yet started, but it became the central issue of the campaign. Supported by antiwar Federalists, Clinton was said to be, not without plausibility, the candidate who would either end the war or fight it more effectively than President Madison. With his voting strength centered in the Northeast, where he was second to Madison only in Vermont, Clinton captured 89 electoral votes, while the incumbent, aided by decisive ballots from Pennsylvania, retained his office with 128.

The failed run for the presidency and Clinton's advocacy of the Federalist-connected Merchant's Bank prompted New York Republican leaders, including Ambrose Spencer, his brother-in-law and former ally, to cast Clinton into political exile. He was denied renomination for lieutenant governor in 1813; and when his opponents wrested control of the Council of Appointment, he was ousted as mayor in 1815. Two events enabled him to return from apparent oblivion: New York governor Daniel D. Tompkins's election as vice president in 1816 and the growing movement to build the Erie Canal. Originally elected in 1807, Tompkins was the creature of Clinton and Spencer and had been returned to the governor's office successively in 1810, 1813, and 1816. Tompkins had become so popular that he rivaled Clinton as New York's leading aspirant for the presidency, and his unsuccessful quest for the presidential nomination in 1816 brought him the sop of the vice presidency. Under the state constitution, a special election had to be held to fill the vacancy left by Tompkins, and a law was enacted to provide for a new three-year term, beginning in 1817. By that time, the idea of creating a waterway connecting the Hudson River to Lake Erie had become enormously popular and was essentially identified with Clinton, who had been designated a canal commissioner in 1810. Early canal boosters had been largely Federalists, and Clinton stood in marked contrast to his fellow Republicans in the degree to which he believed that government should foster economic development. When opposition to his candidacy evaporated, he secured the governorship. During the first year of his initial term, the legislature passed his canal bill, and the $7 million project was immediately underway.

When Clinton's wife Maria died in 1818, seven of their children were still alive. The following year he married Catharine Jones, who assumed care of his household and survived him.

Clinton was reelected in 1820, defeating the popular Tompkins by a margin of fewer than 1,500 votes. Two years later (the term of governor having been shortened by a year), he chose not to run, in large part because his opponents had seized control of the legislature. Ironically, Clinton was instrumental, albeit indirectly, in the emergence of the second American party system, which pitted the Whigs against the Democrats. Anti-Clintonism had been a factor in New York politics since his mayoralty, and during his governorship it assumed statewide dimensions, thanks to the rise of Martin Van Buren, who appropriated the Tammany symbol of the Bucktail. Clinton's persona lent itself to party division: the epithet "Magnus Apollo" was applied derisively to mock his aristocratic affinities with the Federalists; yet his "high-minded" Federalist opponents were antagonistic to his democratic principles. His not being a consistent party man, however, was the main point of contention.

The Bucktails, who were the progenitors of the Democratic party in the state, rode to power on the issue of holding a convention to remedy serious flaws in the state constitution of 1777. Clinton's ambivalence toward a constitutional convention arose from his fear that his opponents would shape it to their ends, but it cost him significant support. The victorious and immediately powerful "Albany Regency" was under the direction of Senator Van Buren in Washington. In 1824, however, the Bucktails in Albany acted without Van Buren's knowledge to remove Clinton from his long-held position as canal commissioner, thus making him a political martyr. As anti-Regency sentiment spread throughout the state, Clinton became the obvious gubernatorial candidate of the recently formed People's party, and he won the 1824 election. Clinton's early support of Andrew Jackson, which predated that of the Bucktails, made the picture of political alliances all the more complicated. When Van Buren and his followers became Jacksonians, there existed the basis for a modest accommodation with the governor, and the senator did not work at trying to defeat Clinton in the gubernatorial race of 1826. Although he never stopped aspiring to the presidency himself, Clinton—who said he admired Jackson's abilities and firm integrity—backed Jackson in part because the Tennesseean then supported internal improvements, as symbolized by the Erie Canal.

The completion of "Clinton's Ditch" in 1825 was marked by the governor's ceremonial journey from Buffalo to New York City. To underscore how the new link from Lake Erie to the Hudson River dramatically connected the far end of the state to rest of the world—and further enhanced the commercial importance of the port of New York—Clinton poured water from Lake Erie into the Atlantic Ocean. Three years later, the governor died at his home in Albany.

The achievement of the Erie Canal tends to overshadow Clinton's other accomplishments. He was a man of parts, whose personal attainments were of a magnitude not necessarily to be expected of someone so engaged in public life. As a naturalist, he could claim the discovery of a species of wheat and a species of fish; he wrote scientific papers on numerous subjects and published in 1814 his *Introductory Discourse*, which was considered a lucid account of the current state of American scientific research. He also had keen antiquarian interests, reflected in his role in founding the New-York Historical Society, which he served as president in 1817, and his efforts, while governor, to have Dutch archival documents translated. In his manner and tastes Clinton evinced the habits of an aristocrat. He was, however, relatively open-minded, as evidenced by his having brought about the end, in 1806, of the restrictions on Catholic participation in New York City politics. His life-long support of public education and his advocacy of normal schools for the training of teachers were important gestures toward involving government in the welfare of the populace. As a patrician democrat, Clinton differed significantly from his famous Virginia contemporaries, whose republicanism militated against the kind of activist role that the governor of New York wished to promote for the state. In that sense, he was more of the twentieth century than of his own.

• Clinton's correspondence is located at Columbia University, and his diary at the New-York Historical Society. His gubernatorial messages are to be found in volumes 2 and 3 of C. Z. Lincoln, ed., *Messages from the Governor* (1909). A neglected aspect of Clinton's career is his jurisprudence, a deficiency that can be corrected by reading his opinions on the Court of Errors, on which he served by virtue of being a state senator. These are found in 2 *Johnson's Cases* at 457, 2 *Caine's Cases in Error* at 283, 2 *Johnson's Reports* at 543 and 565, 3 *Johnson's Reports* at 560, 7 *Johnson's Reports* at 617, 5 *Johnson's Reports* at 434 and 528, and 6 *Johnson's Reports* at 362 and 453. Clinton's early biographies are useful primarily as sources: David Hosack, *Memoir of De Witt Clinton* (1829); James Renwick, *Life of De Witt Clinton* (1840); and W. W. Campbell, *Life and Writings of De Witt Clinton* (1849). A collection of contemporary editorials is available in Cuyler Staats, *Tribute to the Memory of De Witt Clinton* (1828). While not a biography, Jabez D. Hammond's *The History of Political Parties in the State of New York* (2 vols., 1842) framed consideration and understanding of Clinton. Howard L. McBain examines Clinton's role in developing patronage in *DeWitt* [sic] *Clinton and the Origin of the Spoils System in New York* (1907). For much of the twentieth century, the only available biography was Dorothie Bobbé, *De Witt Clinton* (1933). Renewed interest in Clinton's role in helping to shape the politics of the early Republic has led to more attention to his life: Craig Hanyan, *De Witt Clinton: Years of Molding, 1769–1807* (1988); Stephen Siry, *De Witt Clinton and the American Political Economy: Sectionalism, Politics, and Republican Ideology, 1787–1828* (1990); and Craig Hanyan (with Mary L. Hanyan), *De Witt Clinton and the Rise of the People's Men* (1996).

DONALD M. ROPER

CLINTON, George (1686–10 July 1761), colonial governor of New York, was the son of Sir Francis Clinton, the sixth earl of Lincoln, and Susan Penniston. His place of birth is not known. Born into a noble family as a second son, George Clinton had all the advantages of that status. As his older brother, the seventh earl of Lincoln, had male issue, Clinton had to pursue a career and joined the Royal Navy during 1707. His naval career illustrates the British patronage system at its worst. The Lincoln family had marital ties with the powerful officeholder Thomas Pelham-Holles, the duke of Newcastle, and Clinton used Newcastle's influence to acquire naval rank.

In 1716 Clinton was promoted to captain and served for some time in the Baltic fleet. From 1726 on, he saw duty in the Mediterranean Sea, but his superiors found work for him that kept him out of the way when there was trouble with Spain. Primarily, he escorted ships to destinations such as Portugal and the Ottoman Empire. He fired on the Spanish only in what the *Biographia Navalis* calls "trivial" actions. In 1731 he became Newfoundland's governor, which only meant he was responsible for protecting the yearly influx of fishermen there. During 1737 Clinton was placed in command of the Mediterranean fleet. Yet when relations with Spain worsened, a higher-ranking officer was sent to take over the command. After the War of Jenkins' Ear with Spain finally erupted, Clinton's ship in 1740 became part of the British armada directed against Spanish Cartagena. Clinton, however, was ordered to stay behind.

Clinton had wed Anne Carle (d. 5 Aug. 1767), an heiress. The date of their marriage is not known. (One of their six offspring, Sir Henry Clinton, gained prominence during the American Revolution.) Despite this advantageous marriage, he owed some £3,000, which he could not repay. The only way out, he believed, was to become a colonial governor. After pestering Newcastle for help, Clinton obtained a commission dated 3 July 1741 as New York's governor.

Without any experience in colonial government, Clinton soon made a shambles of the royal prerogative in New York after his arrival on 20 September 1743. Needing an experienced adviser, Clinton rejected Lieutenant Governor George Clarke as his helper, suspecting that Clarke would merely ensnare him in old disputes stemming from the administration of William Cosby, former royal governor of New York and New Jersey. Instead, Clinton picked Chief Justice James De Lancey (1703–1760) as his adviser, and the crafty De Lancey, who controlled a powerful political faction, made short work of the neophyte governor. De Lancey, already influential in the New York Assembly, convinced Clinton to have pre–De Lancey men appointed to the governor's council, which gave the chief justice control of it. Furthermore, Clinton, following De Lancey's advice, agreed to accept a yearly salary from the assembly instead of the customary longer period. In 1744 Clinton even gave De Lancey a new commission as chief justice "during his good behaviour" (*Documents Relative to . . . New York*, vol. 6, p. 356), which made his removal difficult.

Nevertheless, Clinton began to understand his office and the colonials. On 13 December 1744 he warned Newcastle that a parliamentary stamp tax would cause much trouble in the colonies. By November 1745 he had also discovered that the Dutch fur traders in Albany were unreliable in imperial disputes with French Canada. The traders preferred to stay neutral and keep receiving lucrative profits.

King George's War (1743–1748) led to the split between Clinton and De Lancey, who favored neutrality. Governor Clinton supplied many cannons that were used in the English victory at Louisbourg (1745). But during 1746 De Lancey opposed the governor on a proposal about army deserters and allowed a drunken quarrel to end their alliance. Clinton, now deserted by his erstwhile allies, turned to a surprised Cadwallader Colden (1688–1776), who was not part of De Lancey's Faction, for help.

In August 1746 Governor Clinton, assisted by Colden and Sir William Johnson, conferred with the Six Nations of the Iroquois. The British had planned an assault upon Canada, and Iroquois assistance was essential. In 1744 the Iroquois had vowed to support the British cause but wanted to wait until the French attacked the colonists. On 19 August 1746 Clinton explained that the French had murdered colonists and asked the Iroquois to fulfill their promise. Four days later the Iroquois agreed to war against the French and their allied Indians. Clinton then placed Johnson in charge of Indian relations, an act that would be his most lasting achievement. The Iroquois admired Johnson as much as they distrusted the Indian commissioners they had previously dealt with.

While the colonists waited for British assistance, Clinton had to provide for the colonial troops that had been raised to attack the French. The New York Assembly refused to support the troops, and the governor personally accepted some £93,000 of debt, all for an expedition that the British canceled in 1747. His enemies falsely charged that he had embezzled much of that sum. Colden vouched for the governor and in 1749 pointed out that the pro–De Lancey faction never provided any specifics to prove the assertion. Clinton went through much grief before the British government finally settled these debts in 1751.

In the meantime, the Six Nations—especially the Mohawks—had become exasperated at the colonists' failure to attack the French. The Iroquois had already attacked the enemy and had suffered casualties. In July 1748 the Mohawks expressed concern for their own security. Clinton moved to protect them and assured them of his support so "that we may live and Dye together" (*William Johnson Papers*, vol. 1, p. 177).

While the war waged, Clinton could not seriously try to battle the assembly. However, in August 1748 Massachusetts governor William Shirley urged Clinton to attempt to regain the ground he had lost to the assemblymen. Beginning in October of that year, Clinton refused to accept a yearly salary and demanded a multiyear grant. The only result was that he received no salary until 1750, when he abandoned the effort. But the governor did succeed in regaining control of the council. In 1747 he suspended pro–De Lancey councilor Daniel Horsmanden. As other vacancies appeared, Clinton secured the appointment of his own followers, such as James Alexander and William Smith (1697–1769).

De Lancey had another weapon. In 1747 a deceived Newcastle had accepted De Lancey's appointment as lieutenant governor. Clinton, who had been trying to sell his commission and return to naval duty, now had to stay or else surrender New York to his foe.

The factional fight heated up again in June 1750. H. M. S. *Greyhound*, after a private vessel did not salute it, fired two warning shots at the craft, accidentally killing a woman on board. Because the *Greyhound*'s captain was the governor's son-in-law, this incident became a political crisis. The lieutenant who had given the order was shipped back to England for a friendly trial that cleared him. But the sailor who had fired the gun was seized in New York City and jailed by Chief Justice De Lancey. After a trial and a guilty verdict, the governor obtained the sailor's release.

Governor Clinton's downfall followed a dispute between New York and New Jersey over their border. Although in 1748 rioting occurred along the border, Clinton refused to intervene. The situation attracted the attention of the Privy Council, which in 1749 ordered an investigation into the two colonies. On 2 April 1751 the Board of Trade declared that the problems in New York could be better dealt with by a new governor not involved in their creation.

Clinton confronted multiple border disputes with New Hampshire and Massachusetts. In 1749 New Hampshire's governor, Benning Wentworth, granted land west of the Connecticut River, which New York claimed as its border with that colony. These New Hampshire grants, Clinton observed in 1750, involved land already distributed by New York. During 1751 Wentworth appealed to the Board of Trade, claiming that his province extended as far west as Massachusetts. This dispute continued for decades.

Moreover, Massachusetts claimed some of Livingston Manor, which was between its territory and the Hudson River. In March 1753 Clinton complained to Massachusetts about its actions. Yet in July violence erupted on the manor. On 28 July 1753 Clinton ordered New York constables to act against rioting caused by adherents of New Hampshire and Massachusetts. Livingston Manor quieted, but the crisis reappeared after Clinton's departure.

In October 1753 Clinton's successor, Sir Danvers Osborne, arrived, took over the government, and promptly killed himself—putting De Lancey in charge. As Clinton left only in early November, he witnessed his foe's triumph.

In England, the Royal Navy refused to give the former governor any command. Clinton sought a place in Parliament in the 1754 election. For £500 he purchased a seat for Saltash, a Cornish borough dominated by the admiralty. He was presumably consulted about colonial affairs as, for example, when gossipy members of Parliament asked him how many Indian mistresses William Johnson kept. Clinton did claim credit for Johnson's royal appointment as Indian agent. Nonetheless, Newcastle was not impressed by Clinton's record in Parliament, and the member for Saltash surrendered his seat in 1761. Upon his death (exact site unknown), Clinton had debts of £1,500.

Despite his various promotions, which culminated with his being named admiral of the fleet in 1757, Clinton was ill suited for every position he held.

• The William L. Clements Library, Ann Arbor, Mich., has an extensive collection of George Clinton Papers. Others are at the New Jersey Historical Society, Newark, and the New-York Historical Society, New York City. The Ayer collection at the Newberry Library, Chicago, has a Clinton item plus council minutes from his administration. In London, the Public Record Office has Clinton material in the Treasury 1 and Admiralty 1 series. The British Library has the Newcastle papers, a valuable source for Clinton. At the Essex Record Office, County Hall, Chelmsford, the Audley End Papers has a Clinton report. Two collections edited by E. B. O'Callaghan, *The Documentary History of the State of New York* (4 vols., 1849–1851) and *Documents Relative to the Colonial History of the State of New York* (15 vols., 1853–1887), reprint much official correspondence. Other items are printed in *The Letters and Papers of Cadwallader Colden*, New-York Historical Society, *Collections*, vols. 50–56 (1917–1923) and vols. 67–68 (1934–1935); James Sullivan et al., eds., *The Papers of Sir William Johnson* (14 vols., 1921–1965); Charles H. Lincoln, ed., *Correspondence of William Shirley*, vol. 1

(1912); and Peter Wraxall, *An Abridgment of the Indian Affairs* (1915). William Smith, Jr., *The History of the Province of New-York* (2 vols., 1757–1826; rev. ed., 1972), still has value. There is no biography. Genealogical data is in *Collin's Peerage of England*, vol. 2 (1812), pp. 211–13, and *Burke's Genealogical and Heraldic History of the Peerage* (1963), p. 1792. For his naval career see John Charnock, *Biographia Navalis*, vol. 4 (1796), pp. 59–62, and Daniel A. Baugh, *British Naval Administration in the Age of Walpole* (1965). The best political account is Stanley N. Katz, *Newcastle's New York* (1968). Different perspectives are displayed in William B. Willcox, *Portrait of a General* (1964); Lawrence H. Gipson, *The British Empire before the American Revolution*, vol. 3 (1936); Douglas E. Leach, *Roots of Conflict* (1986); Sung Bok Kim, *Landlord and Tenant in Colonial New York* (1978); Sir Lewis Namier and John Brooke, *The History of Parliament: The House of Commons, 1754–1790* (3 vols., 1964). A death notice is in the *Gentleman's Magazine* 31 (July 1761): 334.

PHILIP RANLET

CLINTON, George (26 July 1739–20 Apr. 1812), soldier, governor of New York, and vice president of the United States, was born in Little Britain, New York, the son of Charles Clinton, a farmer and surveyor, and Elizabeth Denniston. After schooling with a private tutor, George left home in 1757 to serve as a steward's mate on the *Defiance*, a sixteen-gun privateer. Following service in the Caribbean, he returned to New York in the spring of 1760 and enlisted as a subaltern in a militia company commanded by his brother.

Following his participation in the September 1760 capture of Montreal, Clinton went to New York City to study law under the direction of William Smith, Jr., one of the most prominent attorneys in the colony. On 12 September 1764 he was admitted to the bar. In 1768 he was elected to represent Ulster County in the colonial assembly; there he aligned himself with the Livingston faction, which formed the nucleus of the anti-British party. In February 1770 he married Cornelia Tappen, with whom he had six children. This marriage solidified his political base by linking him with one of the preeminent families in Ulster County.

By the time of his marriage Clinton had established himself as one of the leading members of the patriot faction in the assembly. On 22 April 1775 he was appointed to represent New York at the Second Continental Congress, where he was a strong supporter of George Washington's elevation to commander in chief. After returning to New York, he was appointed a brigadier general of militia; his responsibilities in this area prevented him from attending the Continental Congress at the time it passed the Declaration of Independence. For two years he was responsible for fortifying the Highlands of the Hudson River and obstructing British use of the river. Most of his time and energy, however, was devoted to the task of raising troops.

In June 1777 Clinton was nominated for both governor and lieutenant governor. To the surprise of many, he won election to both offices comfortably, thanks to strong support from the yeomanry. His ascension to the governor's office marked a shift away from the traditional dominance of the aristocracy represented by the man who had been his leading rival, Philip Schuyler. On 30 June 1777 the former militia general began the first of six successive terms as governor.

In October 1777 Clinton directed the futile defense of Fort Montgomery against a large contingent of British forces under the command of Sir Henry Clinton. Although Governor Clinton's troops were eventually forced to surrender, the stubbornness of American resistance at Fort Montgomery played a significant role in the British commander's decision not to continue north to join an army under John Burgoyne then marching south from Canada, which enabled the Americans to win a crucial victory at Saratoga.

Despite a less-than-auspicious start, Clinton established himself as an effective governor during the war. One of his principal tools was his control of patronage, through which he forged a formidable political organization around his leadership that pushed the state in a moderate direction. His successful management of the state's finances, his skillful handling of the western Indians, his ability to inspire and sustain popular morale, his efforts to prevent the secession of Vermont, and his hard line toward Tories endeared him to the people of New York during the war and its immediate aftermath.

The postwar period was a difficult one for the new republic, however. In 1787 a convention convened to consider revision of the Articles of Confederation instead produced a new federal Constitution that dramatically strengthened the power of the federal government. When it was submitted to the states for ratification, Clinton immediately emerged as one of its most vigorous opponents.

His opposition was driven by two factors. First, because of its fine harbor, New York had natural advantages in trade over other states in the union. Clinton feared that a federal government with the power to regulate commerce provided in the Constitution could be used to negate New York's commercial hegemony over neighboring states. Second, Clinton had built his political machine through the great patronage power provided by the 1777 New York constitution, which he feared might be threatened by a federal charter that diminished the sovereignty of the states in any way.

When the federal Constitution was submitted to the states for ratification in September 1787, Clinton mobilized his supporters in opposition. In addition, he wrote seven letters under the pseudonym "Cato," in which he attacked the new Constitution. In these letters, Clinton made frequent reference to the theory advanced by Montesquieu that republics could only survive in small territories and warned New Yorkers that the Constitution would replace the system of sovereign states essential to the preservation of liberty with a consolidated national government headed by a chief executive whose powers were too vaguely defined. He made specific objections to the Constitution's provisions for biennial elections for the national legislature rather than annual ones, the election of senators by the state legislatures rather than the people, the continuation of the slave trade, and the maintenance of standing armies. The publication of these letters in the *New York Journal* prompted Alexander Hamilton, the leader of the Federalist cause in New York, to write letters under the name "Caesar" to the *Daily Advertiser* to rebut "Cato." Not until June 1788, with Clinton presiding, did the convention finally convene in Poughkeepsie, New York. Only after the ratification of the Constitution by the required nine states, thus threatening to shut New York out of the new government, did the Federalists prevail.

Clinton's opposition to ratification cost him much support, however. In the 1789 gubernatorial contest, he was only able to secure a slim majority for his reelection. Three years later, it took the partisan machinations of the state election canvassers, who threw out the ballots of three counties that had provided the margin of victory for his opponent, to keep Clinton in office. Nonetheless, a Federalist majority in the assembly curtailed much of the governor's power. In 1795, facing certain defeat at the polls, Clinton decided to retire from the post.

Four years later Aaron Burr persuaded Clinton to come out of retirement and again seek the governorship as the Republican candidate. In 1800 the ouster of the Federalists from power in Washington was duplicated in New York, as Clinton was elected governor. In 1804 he became the Republican vice presidential candidate, taking Burr's place, and won election. In 1808 he sought the presidency, but his effort to establish a coalition with disgruntled Republicans and Federalists that could defeat James Madison failed, and Clinton instead served another term as vice president. Age, poor health, and the nature of the office made both of Clinton's terms as vice president uneventful ones. His only significant deed as vice president occurred in February 1811, when he voted against rechartering the Bank of the United States, thus breaking the deadlock in the senate. After a four-week bout with illness, Clinton died at his home in Washington, D.C., the first vice president to die in office.

Clinton served the people of New York for more than twenty years, and no man played a more important role in New York's successful transition from colony to state. The most prevalent image of Clinton, however, is of a man who opposed the Constitution of 1787 out of a desire to preserve his own personal power. Yet, Clinton was among the first politicians to base his power on the support of the people, rather than the traditional ideal of deference to an aristocratic elite. His opposition to the Constitution no doubt reflected the sentiment of the majority of the people, not only in New York, but in the rest of the Union as well. Nor would he be the last to express fear of an overly powerful federal government that could undermine or subvert the sovereignty of the states.

• *Public Papers of George Clinton*, ed. Harold Hastings (10 vols., 1899–1914), contains hundreds of texts related to Clinton's career, since destroyed by a fire at the New York State Library in 1911. A recent biography of Clinton is John P. Kaminski, *George Clinton: Yeoman Politician of the New Republic* (1993). See also E. Wilder Spaulding, *His Excellency George Clinton, Critic of the Constitution* (1938), and Major B. Jenks, "George Clinton and New York State Politics, 1775 to 1801" (Ph.D. diss., Cornell Univ., 1939). Valuable works on the events that shaped Clinton's career include Edward Countryman, *A People in Revolution: The American Revolution and Political Society in New York, 1760–1790* (1981); Stephen L. Schechter and Richard B. Bernstein, eds., *New York and the Union: Contributions to the American Constitutional Experience* (1990); Schechter, ed., *The Reluctant Pillar: New York and the Adoption of the Federal Constitution* (1985); and Alfred F. Young, *The Democratic Republicans of New York: The Origins, 1763–1797* (1967).

ETHAN S. RAFUSE

CLINTON, James (9 Aug. 1736–22 Dec. 1812), revolutionary war officer, was born in Little Britain (six miles west of Newburgh), New York, the son of Charles Clinton, a farmer and army officer, and Elizabeth Denniston. The father was English and the mother Irish (or Scotch-Irish). The Clintons had immigrated from Longford, Ireland, in 1730 and settled in Ulster County (that part which is now Orange County), New York. James Clinton was the older brother of George Clinton, governor of New York and vice president. He received his early education from tutors.

In 1756 James Clinton was appointed an ensign by Governor Charles Hardy in an Ulster County militia company commanded by his father. As a captain in August 1758, Clinton served in the expedition of Colonel John Bradstreet that captured the French-held Fort Frontenac (now Kingston, Ontario). He remained in the provincial army until 1763, at which time he ended his service as a commander of four companies of frontier guards from Ulster and Orange counties and turned to farming. From 1765 to 1773 Clinton lived at New Windsor and then moved back to Little Britain. He married Mary DeWitt in 1765. There were seven children, one of whom was DeWitt Clinton, Federalist candidate for President in 1812.

In 1774 Clinton was lieutenant colonel of a militia regiment from Ulster County, and in June 1775 he entered the Continental army as colonel of the Third New York Regiment. In May 1775 he was a delegate to the New York Provincial Congress. Clinton participated in the Canadian expedition under General Richard Montgomery and fought in the ill-fated assault on Quebec, 31 December 1775–1 January 1776. On 8 March 1776 he became colonel of the Second New York Regiment, and on 9 August 1776 Congress elected him brigadier general in the Continental army. In May 1776 Clinton was given responsibility for erecting fortifications for defense of the Highlands along the Hudson River.

During 1777 Clinton served under his brother, George, in keeping charge of Forts Montgomery and Clinton. On 6 October 1777 the British commander in chief, Sir Henry Clinton, intending to remove pressure on General John Burgoyne's army as it faced General Horatio Gates's troops at Saratoga, attacked both posts. The Americans surrendered both forts, with 250 of the 600 defenders either killed, wounded, or missing. James Clinton, severely wounded by a bayonet thrust in the thigh, escaped by dropping down a 100-foot precipice, clinging to shrubs and bushes.

For most of 1778 Clinton served at West Point, and at the year's end he was given command of the army's northern department at Albany. In April 1779 he led troops into Tryon County, unsuccessfully searching out hostile Indians and Tories. However, with western New York and Pennsylvania settlements becoming more vulnerable to the enemy, George Washington authorized a dual expedition against the offending Iroquois tribes. Major General John Sullivan led a force of 2,500 troops, and Clinton, 1,500. Clinton was to move along the Mohawk Valley and then southward to link up with Sullivan at the Pennsylvania–New York border. On 2 July Clinton reached the south end of Lake Otsego, having destroyed three Indian villages along the way. Here he built a dam, and eventually had his men break it, allowing his troops to float down the east branch of the Susquehanna. The Clinton and Sullivan forces joined at Tioga on 22 August. Seven days later the combined army fought the only battle of the campaign—an attack on an Indian town at Newton (near Elmira). After six hours of fighting, the Indians were routed and fled toward Fort Niagara. Sullivan and Clinton then led their troops through a sweep of the Indian country, covering the 150 miles to the Genessee River. The expedition destroyed 160,000 bushels of corn and burned forty villages of the Senecas, Cayugas, and Onondagas. The troops returned to Tioga on 30 September, and Clinton headed homeward by way of the Mohawk Valley. Though temporarily driving the Indians from central and western New York, the Sullivan-Clinton expedition did not strike the Indians a crushing blow.

In 1780 Clinton assumed command of the Northern Department of the army, with headquarters at Albany. Clinton remained in this capacity, attempting to further secure the New York frontier, until linking his brigade with Washington's army as it made its way to Virginia in August 1781. Clinton's brigade was attached to Benjamin Lincoln's division at the siege of Yorktown.

Returning northward, Clinton was stationed for a while at Pompton, New Jersey. Congress refused to promote him on grounds that New York state was entitled to only one major general. But after termination of Clinton's military service, Congress, as was customary, awarded him a brevet major generalship on 30 September 1783.

After the war, Clinton resided at Little Britain and engaged in farming and real estate dealings. He often surveyed his own lands. In 1784 he acted as a commissioner for running the boundary between New York and Pennsylvania and was chosen one of the regents of the newly established "University of the State of New York" (actually Columbia College, renamed from King's College). At the New York ratifying convention of July 1788 he voted against acceptance of the Constitution because the inclusion of a bill of rights was not made a condition of ratification. Clinton was a delegate to the New York assembly in 1788, and from 1789 to 1792 a state senator for the middle district. After the death of his first wife in 1795, Clinton married Mary Little Gray in 1797. They had six children. In October 1801 he served in the New York constitutional convention. Clinton died at Little Britain.

• James Clinton correspondence may be found in the Philip Schuyler Papers at the New York State Library and in the Washington papers at the Library of Congress. *The Public Papers of George Clinton: War of the Revolution Series* (10 vols., 1899–1914) contains letters of Clinton, many of which in the originals were destroyed by fire along with most of the George Clinton Papers at the New York State Library. Journals for the Sullivan-Clinton expedition of 1779 abound; see especially Frederick Cook, ed., *Journals of the Military Expedition of Major General John Sullivan against the Six Nations of Indians in 1779* (1887) and *The Order Book of Capt. Leonard Bleeker, Major of the Brigade in the Early Part of the Expedition under Gen. James Clinton . . . in the Campaign of 1779* (1865). For biographical information, see Charles B. Moore, "Introductory Sketch of the Clinton Family," *New York Genealogical and Biographical Record* 13 (1882): 5–10, 139, and 173–80; William W. Campbell, *Lecture on the Life and Military Services of Gen. Jas. Clinton* (1839); David Hosack, *Memoir of DeWitt Clinton* (1829); William W. Campbell, *Life of DeWitt Clinton* (1849), James Clinton biographical note, pp. xv–xxiv; and E. Wilder Spaulding, *His Excellency George Clinton: Critic of the Constitution* (1938). For Clinton's role along the New York frontier, see Robert B. Roberts, *New York's Forts in the Revolution* (1980). A brief obituary is in *New-York Gazette & General Advertiser*, 28 Dec. 1812.

HARRY M. WARD

CLOPTON, John (7 Feb. 1756–11 Sept. 1816), congressman, was born near Tunstall, New Kent County, Virginia, the son of William Clopton, a well-to-do planter, and Elizabeth Dorrall Ford. John graduated in 1776 from the College of Philadelphia (now the University of Pennsylvania), read law immediately afterward, and entered the bar probably in the late 1770s. His law practice quickly gave way, however, to service in the American Revolution as a first lieutenant in the Virginia militia. Surviving wounds at the battle of Brandywine Creek in September 1777, Clopton rose eventually to the rank of captain. After the war, in the early 1780s, he married Sarah Bacon. They raised several children, but the exact number is not known. Through the 1780s Clopton practiced law in New Kent County. A member of the Virginia House of Delegates from 1789 to 1791, he gained an introduction to legislative politics.

Clopton's identity in politics developed in the late 1790s, a time of turmoil between the Federalist government and their Jeffersonian rivals for national power. Ardently following the latter, Clopton saw himself as a vigorous defender of republicanism. In his mind, this meant a narrow construction of the Constitution, resistance to federal encroachment on state and individual rights, and a healthy contempt for monied "aristocrats." Records show Clopton with 450 acres and twenty-nine slaves in 1810, and his social ranking among the lesser Virginia gentry helps to explain his distrust of the wealthy elite. Voters in the Richmond District, which included New Kent, sent him to the Fourth and Fifth Congresses, where he served from 4 March 1795 until 3 March 1799. During this time of mounting partisanship at home and threat of war abroad, Clopton scorned Federalist leaders in 1796 for refusing the House of Representatives access to presidential papers on the Jay Treaty negotiations with the British. In 1798 he vehemently opposed the Alien and Sedition Acts, the highhanded Federalist moves to limit growth of the Jeffersonian Republican party and to muzzle them politically. Outraged at such an affront to civil liberties and discouraged by mounting public fever for a war against France in early 1799, Clopton and three other Virginians gave up and went home before the House adjourned.

Clopton's narrow defeat for reelection that spring was owed in part to the climate of suspicion in national politics. As of 1798 Republicans had dominated the state, holding all but four of nineteen congressional seats and controlling the legislature. With publication of the XYZ dispatches in April 1798, however, Federalist fortunes began to soar. This correspondence, released to an astonished Congress by President John Adams, announced a French ploy to choke monetary concessions from American negotiators in return for a promise not to declare war on the United States. The Federalist candidate picked to unseat Clopton in the Richmond District was John Marshall, one of the three XYZ envoys to France, whose campaign received the prestigious endorsement of George Washington. Amid mounting Francophobia and the suppression of dissent, Clopton tried to defend the Virginia Resolutions, passed by the legislature in 1798 to protest the Alien and Sedition measures. He also battled an unfounded charge that he had libeled President Adams in a private letter, supposedly accusing Adams of offering bribes to members of Congress. Upon hearing this rumor, Adams's secretary of state Timothy Pickering threatened to prosecute Clopton under the Sedition Act until calmer heads in the Marshall camp dissuaded him. Whiskey flowed liberally on election day in April, courtesy of the two candidates and in keeping with Virginia campaign tradition. Undaunted by hooting partisan crowds on both sides, voters registered their preferences publicly, while Clopton and Marshall sat at the judge's table and thanked each supporter in person. The final tally revealed an advantage of 108 votes for future chief justice Marshall, part of an anomalous Federalist gain of four congressional seats in Virginia. During his brief retirement from national politics, from 1799 to 1801, Clopton served on the state's privy council.

On the crest of Thomas Jefferson's "Revolution of 1800," the election victory that put Republicans in firm control of the executive and legislative branches, Clopton returned to the House on 4 March 1801 and entrenched himself there until his death. He was a model of ideological consistency and, for the most part, a loyal party man. Though a "naturally feeble" voice limited his efforts from the floor, he spoke on matters close to his role as a guardian of liberty in the face of coercive power. Condemning the transparency of Federalist warnings against violating the judicial branch, which Adams had packed before leaving office, he gave vocal support to the revised Judiciary Act of 1801. Enthusiatic for westward expansion, he favored the admission of Ohio to the Union in 1803 and the Louisiana Purchase that year. Believing the selection of public officials "ought ever to be a complete expression of the public will," Clopton proposed constitutional amendments to change the selection of presidential electors and to enable state legislatures to recall U.S. senators who violated instructions from home. The controversy that inflamed Clopton most during his time in public service was the fight over congressional recharter of the Bank of the United States, based on power not explicitly mentioned in the Constitution. He warned against "the strong propensity existing in human nature to grasp at unwarrantable power." Gratified to see the first bank allowed to expire in 1811, Clopton strenuously opposed creation of the Second Bank of the United States in 1816.

In matters of foreign policy Clopton stood indignantly anti-British. With the "honor of the nation" at stake, he endorsed Jefferson's Embargo of 1807 and the following year reversed his 1798 stand against military preparedness on grounds that "more than a speck of war now appears in our horizon." Though privately reluctant to embrace war against Britain in 1812, he thought it necessary as a last resort.

Debilitated by a "tedious illness" during his last few years, Clopton died near Tunstall. A week later the *National Intelligencer* praised him as a man of "unostentatious" virtue, "esteemed for his private worth, as well as for his undeviating firmness and sincerity as a politician." His son, John B. Clopton, also professing a "firm and inflexible" brand of republicanism, tried unsuccessfully to gain election to his father's vacated House seat.

• The John Clopton Papers are preserved in the Duke University Library, Durham, N.C. His career in Congress is most easily traced in Joseph Gales and William W. Seaton, comps., *Annals of Congress, 1789–1824* (42 vols., 1834–1856). The story of the Va. election campaign of 1799 is told in Charles T. Cullen, ed., *The Papers of John Marshall*, vol. 3 (1979). On Clopton's involvement in the early Jeffersonian Republican party, see Noble E. Cunningham, Jr., *The Jeffersonian Republicans: The Formation of Party Organization, 1789–1801* (1957). Also of value are the sections representing Clopton in Cunningham, ed., *Circular Letters of Congressmen to Their Constituents, 1789–1829* (1978). His obituary is in the *(Washington, D.C.) National Intelligencer*, 17 Sept. 1816.

JOHN R. VAN ATTA

CLOUD, Henry Roe (28 Dec. 1884–9 Feb. 1950), Native American educator and leader, was born on the Winnebago reservation in Nebraska, the son of Chayskagah (White Buffalo) and Aboogenewingah (Hummingbird), who lived by trapping and gathering. He was called Wohnaxilayhungah, or Chief of the Place of Fear (the battleground). He was named Henry Cloud by a reservation school administrator and as a boy was the tribe's first convert to Christianity. After his parents died in 1898 and further Indian school education, he went to the Mount Hermon School, a workstudy school in Massachusetts, and thence to Yale, becoming that university's first Native American graduate, in 1910. As a college sophomore he worked successfully for the release of Apache prisoners who were incarcerated at Fort Sill, Oklahoma, because their leader, Geronimo, had made war on the United States. The survivors of the band were allowed to settle on the Mescalero reservation in New Mexico. While an undergraduate he met Dr. and Mrs. Walter C. Roe, a missionary couple who informally adopted him and from whom he took his middle name. He received his bachelor of divinity degree from Auburn Theological Seminary in 1913 and in 1914 his master's degree in anthropology from Yale.

Cloud was active in the 1911 founding and the early years of the Society of American Indians and on several occasions addressed the annual conference at Lake Mohonk of the Friends of the Indian. In 1915 he founded the first college preparatory school for Indian boys, the Roe Indian Institute, at Wichita, Kansas. In 1916 he married Elizabeth Georgian Bender of Fosston, Minnesota. They had five children, one of whom died at age three. Cloud spent much of his time for the next dozen years traveling to raise money, while his wife served as de facto principal of the school, which was now called the American Indian Institute.

Cloud was active as well in lobbying for passage of the Indian Citizenship Act of 1924, and that year he was appointed to Secretary of the Interior Hubert Work's Committee of 100, which made recommendations to President Calvin Coolidge regarding federal Indian policy. This led to his appointment as Indian adviser on the Brookings Institution's survey team that under Lewis Meriam investigated the situation of Native Americans. The team's 1928 report, *The Problem of Indian Administration*, disclosed miserable conditions on reservations caused in large part by government neglect and the inefficiency of the Indian Service. In 1927 Cloud had arranged for a three-year transitional takeover of his school by the Board of the National Missions of the Presbyterian church. He aspired then and later to be commissioner of Indian affairs but was not appointed. His friend Meriam commented to another survey member that the job would bring Cloud only "bitterness and disappointment." Instead, Cloud in 1931 became a field representative for the Indian Service.

In 1933 John Collier became commissioner of Indian affairs, and Cloud was named superintendent of Haskell Institute, the government's largest Indian boarding school. He was also working on the document that resulted from the Meriam survey's findings and accusations, to be passed by Congress as the Indian Reorganization Act of 1934. The measure provided for tribal governments and courts, funds for education and Indian chartered corporations, elimination of the land allotment policy and provision for purchase of surplus land for the tribe, and regulations for management and protection of reservation forest and range land. Cloud spent considerable time going from reservation to reservation explaining the proposed measure to sometimes unreceptive audiences. Ultimately almost three-quarters of the tribes accepted the act. Cloud's tenure at Haskell was only two years. He wanted tribal traditions preserved while assimilation progressed, and he saw the school's vocational curriculum as hobbling to students. Changes he instituted and sought were unpopular with the old guard there and in the Indian Service, although Collier called him the "most important living Indian."

Cloud became assistant supervisor of Indian education and moved to Minneapolis in 1936. He continued to annoy the Indian Affairs bureaucracy and in 1939 was offered, at reduced pay, the post of superintendent of the Umatilla reservation at Pendleton. He told his family he thought the Indian Service was trying to make him quit, but he took the job, which he said in a later interview made him the "great red father" to the Cayuse, Umatillas, and Walla Wallas. He worked to reform both the local white view of the Indians and the Indians' use of their land, on a reservation that had voted down the Indian Reorganization Act. He sought to have the Indians farm their own land rather than rent it to whites at low rates and then demand "side money" when they needed more cash. Cloud was at odds with Collier's hopes of restoring traditional ways, because Indian religions and cultures were based on hunting and gathering of resources that were now insufficient. Instead, "opportunity for greatness is again knocking at the door for the Indian race, but only through a dynamic and mobile society." Ultimately he became frustrated in his Pendleton job. He unsuccessfully sought appointment to the Indian Claims Commission created in 1946. The land use issue remained contentious, and in 1948, after a group from the reservation complained to Congress, Cloud accepted transfer to the superintendency of the Grande Ronde-Siletz agency on the Oregon coast. Cloud died in Siletz, Oregon.

• Cloud's published articles and personal papers, including letters to Mary Wickham Roe, are at the Sterling Memorial Library, Yale University, in the Roe Family Papers. Many articles written by Cloud are in the *Indian Outlook*, collected at Yale's Beineke Library. The Presbyterian Historical Society in Philadelphia houses documents related to the American Indian Institute. Regional archives of the federal government in Kansas City, St. Louis, and Seattle include correspondence while Cloud worked at Haskell, Umatilla, and Grande Ronde-Siletz. Hazel Hertzberg, *The Search for an American Indian Identity* (1971), examines his life as an important transitional figure and major contributor to Indian reform. Steven Crum, "Henry Roe Cloud, a Winnebago Reformer: His Quest for American Indian Higher Education," *Kansas History, Journal of the Kansas State Historical Society* 11, no. 3 (Autumn 1988): 171–84, is an excellent treatment of Cloud's contributions to Indian education. For general biography, see Thomas Sorci, "Latter Day Father of the Indian Nations," the *News, Northfield Mount Hermon School Magazine*, Summer 1988, pp. 17–19.

SHERIDAN ZACHER FAHNESTOCK
THOMAS CHARLES SORCI

CLUBB, Oliver Edmund (16 Feb. 1901–9 May 1989), Foreign Service officer, was born in South Park, Minnesota, the son of Oliver E. Clubb, a cattle rancher, and Lillian May Nichols. He attended the University of Washington (1922–1923), graduated with a B.A. from the University of Minnesota (1923–1927), and earned an M.A. at the California College in China (1940). In 1928 he married Mariann E. H. Smith; they had two children.

Clubb qualified for the Foreign Service in 1928, having become interested in China at the University of Minnesota, and began his career in Peking (Beijing) in 1929 through 1931 in language training. Clubb's China postings before Pearl Harbor included Hankow (Hankou) as vice consul from 1931 to 1934, Peking from 1934 to 1938, Nanking (Nanjing) in 1939, administering the embassy, and in 1941, and Shanghai in 1939–1940. He also served for a few days in Hanoi (1941) where he was almost immediately interned by the Japanese and exchanged for Japanese nationals eight months later. During the United States's Pacific war he completed a brief four-month stint in Chungking as second secretary (1942), then two months at Lanchow (Lanzhou), after which he opened a consulate at Urumchi where he remained until December 1943. His next assignment at the Department of State was curtailed when the post of consul general opened at Vladivostok (1944–1945) for which his skills in Chinese and Russian made him the logical choice. After the war he served as consul general successively at Mukden (Shenyang) in 1946, Changchun in 1946–1947, and Peking in 1947–1950. His final months in Peking proved difficult as the Chinese Communists put increasing pressure on the United States to open diplomatic relations. Clubb had to deal with confiscation of a portion of the consulate's physical plant, former military barracks provided to the United States after the Boxer Rebellion (1900–1901), and ultimately presided over the closing of the consulate in April 1950. In July 1950 he took up a new position as director of the Office of Chinese Affairs in the department.

Clubb will be best remembered for the ordeal that he suffered at the hands of Whittaker Chambers and Senator Joseph R. McCarthy during the early 1950s. Chambers and McCarthy targeted him as one of several supposedly disloyal State Department officials responsible for the "loss of China." The charges grew out of his China reporting which, beginning in the 1930s, they believed to have had "pink" tendencies, because Clubb warned the U.S. government of the growing popularity of the Chinese Communists and the bankruptcy of the Nationalist regime under Chiang Kai-shek. Clubb received his first interrogatory from the State Department's Loyalty Security Board on 28 December 1950.

Clubb did, in fact, take a moderate line toward the Chinese Communists. He emphasized their nationalism and unwillingness slavishly to follow policies dictated by Moscow. He based this judgment in part upon two decades of careful observation of and solid reporting on the Communist movement. Contacts with Chinese Communist officials, who on several occasions in 1949 and 1950 discussed with him opportunities for commercial intercourse between the United States and China, weighed heavily in his assessments. Clubb also aligned himself with those who thought Mao Zedong would follow an independent Titoist path in China. He argued that Mao's violent anti-American rhetoric served primarily to deflect Stalin's suspicions regarding his loyalty. During 1949 Clubb recommended that the United States extend diplomatic recognition to the People's Republic of China, reasoning that trade and relations could be used to elicit better behavior from the Chinese. In 1950, when Peking's decision to requisition embassy property from governments which did not open diplomatic relations with China led to the withdrawal of remaining American Foreign Service personnel, he stalwartly pursued negotiations with Chinese officials until the eve of his departure, attempting to avoid the severing of all contacts. Ultimately his efforts fell short of Chinese Communist requirements that the United States recognize the new regime and abandon Chiang Kai-shek. Clubb similarly failed in his efforts later that year to convince American officials that the Chinese would enter the Korean War if U.S. forces crossed the thirty-eighth parallel.

Whereas in retrospect Clubb's assessments seem to have reflected developments in China accurately, Chambers in 1950 and McCarthy in 1952 capitalized on contemporary hysteria about the spread of communism to undermine Clubb's credibility and patriotism. They utilized an imprudent 1932 visit by Clubb to the offices of the *New Masses* to demonstrate his association with undesirable elements. Returning from China on home leave, Clubb had used a letter of introduction from left-wing journalist Agnes Smedley to present himself to an editor of that communist-leaning magazine in New York City. The hapless young officer instead met Whittaker Chambers, who years later, as a reformed communist and accuser of State Department official Alger Hiss, precipitated the condemnation of Clubb as well. In 1951 the State Department's Loyalty Board declared Clubb a security risk, removing him from his position as director of the Office of Chinese Affairs. Among those who wrote statements in his behalf, Colonel David Barrett commented, "I always thought you were secure to the point of being boring." Although Clubb was exonerated in February 1952, his new assignment in the department's historical division suggested little future use of his experience and prompted his resignation within a week.

In the 1950s Clubb spent his time writing and occasionally addressing university audiences. The university connections became more formal at the end of the decade as he began to lecture regularly at Columbia. During his university career Clubb lectured at Columbia University (1959–1962, 1964–1970), Brooklyn College (1959–1961), New York University (1960–1963), and the New School for Social Research (1962–1965). He wrote two much-used studies of modern China, *Twentieth Century China* (1964) and *China and Russia: The 'Great Game'* (1971). He also published *Communism in China: As Reported from Hankow in 1932* (1968) and contributed to a variety of journals and volumes of collected essays. From 1960 to 1966 he served as staff editor for the Columbia University Research Project on Men and Politics in Modern China. Based on his experience with the Chinese Revolution and the Nationalist Chinese government, he became an early opponent of the American war in Vietnam. Between 1970 and his death, Clubb lived in retirement in New York City. He continued lecturing and writing and in 1974 published an account of his Foreign Service career and its ugly demise, *The Witness and I*. He died in New York.

• Clubb's cables, reports, and memoranda are scattered throughout the General Records of the Department of State and the files of the Office of Chinese Affairs at the National Archives in Washington, D.C., and at the presidential libraries. An oral history that Clubb recorded on 26 June 1974 can be read at the Harry S. Truman Library in Independence, Missouri. He is among the China hands whose careers were examined by E. J. Kahn, Jr., in *The China Hands: America's Foreign Service Officers and What Befell Them* (1972). Obituaries appear in the *New York Times*, 11 May 1989, and the *Washington Post*, 12 May 1989.

NANCY BERNKOPF TUCKER

CLURMAN, Harold Edgar (18 Sept. 1901–9 Sept. 1980), founder of the Group Theatre, director, and critic, was born on the Lower East Side of Manhattan, New York, the son of Samuel Michael Clurman, a physician, and Bertha Saphir. When asked late in life who had been most influential in shaping his character, Clurman "answered without hesitation, 'My father.'" Clurman's formal education included matriculation at Columbia University from 1919 to 1921 and at the Faculty of Letters of the University of Paris-Sorbonne from September 1921 through 1923. He received the *doctorat de l'université* with a thesis on contemporary French drama. In Paris he roomed and became lifelong friends with American classical music composer Aaron Copland.

Clurman's theatrical career commenced in New York City in 1924 when he was cast as an extra in Stark Young's *The Saint* at the Greenwich Village Theatre. That assignment led to several small roles for the Theatre Guild, followed by the position of stage manager for the guild's production of Richard Rodgers and Lorenz Hart's earliest Broadway success, *The Garrick Gaieties* (1925). In 1926 he enrolled in a course for directors given by Richard Boleslavsky at the Laboratory Theatre. There he developed "a sense of the theatre in relation to society" and met his future wife Stella

Adler, a member of the Laboratory acting company and the youngest daughter of his childhood stage hero Jacob Adler. In January 1929 Clurman was appointed the guild's play reader, and from there he deepened his association with guild executive Cheryl Crawford, with whom in 1931, along with actor and director Lee Strasberg, he cofounded the Group Theatre.

Conceived as an alternative to Broadway's commercial fare, the Group Theatre was posthumously heralded by critic John Gassner as having achieved the best ensemble acting Broadway had ever known. Originally a managing director or producer of the Group, on 19 February 1935 Clurman initiated his directorial career with the Group's production of member Clifford Odets's *Awake and Sing!* featuring Stella Adler. Clurman continued to foster the work of Odets, directing his *Paradise Lost* (1935), *Golden Boy* (1937), *Rocket to the Moon* (1938), and *Night Music* (1940). For the humorous, dignified, flirtatious, quasi-aristocratic character of Mr. Prince in *Rocket to the Moon* Odets ostensibly drew on Clurman's own personality. Following the resignations of Strasberg and Crawford in 1937, Clurman, as sole executive, held the Group together and directed, in addition to the later Odets plays, Irwin Shaw's *The Gentle People* (1939) and the Group's final production, Shaw's *Retreat to Pleasure* (1940). In an article in the *New York Times* (May 1941) Clurman announced his unwillingness to continue the compromise of "running the Group on an unsound [financial] basis," and so permitted its dissolution. He had been, according to playwright Arthur Miller, "the leader of its [American theater's] only renovative movement."

With the end of his decade-long struggle to keep the Group alive, Clurman journeyed to Hollywood, California, sometimes working as an associate producer and once as a director of Odets's screenplay *Deadline at Dawn* (1946) for RKO. The movie studios were not his métier, however. In 1934 in Paris with Stella Adler, on Jacques Copeau's recommendation, he had met the Russian master of acting Konstantin Stanislavsky, whose system radically influenced the Group and, under Strasberg, developed into the "method." In 1934 and 1935 in Moscow Clurman had found his own mode of directing when the variety of Soviet theater styles showed him "concretely how many possibilities there were."

In 1943 the long-standing, tempestuous romantic affair between Clurman and Adler was seemingly resolved in a marriage that survived for at least seven years. The couple had no children of their own, but Clurman essentially became father to Adler's daughter born of a former marriage. Divorced from Adler by 1960, in that year Clurman married actress Juleen Compton. They had no children and were eventually divorced.

During the 1940s Clurman directed six productions in New York, none acclaimed (although in 1945 he gave Marlon Brando his first adult role in Maxwell Anderson's *Truckline Café*), and one production in Tel Aviv in 1949, the same year he and Elia Kazan coproduced Arthur Miller's *All My Sons* on Broadway. In

1950 the blight on Clurman's directorial ventures was lifted when his production of Carson McCullers's *Member of the Wedding* (for which he received the Donaldson Award in directing) enjoyed artistic and popular success. Among other plays that Clurman went on to direct for the New York stage were memorable productions of Lillian Hellman's *The Autumn Garden* (1950); a revival of Eugene O'Neill's *Desire under the Elms* (1951); Jean Anouilh's *Mademoiselle Colombe* (1953), with Julie Harris; William Inge's *Bus Stop* (1954), a smash success; Jean Giraudoux's *Tiger at the Gates* (1955), produced in both London and New York with Michael Redgrave as Hector; Anouilh's *The Waltz of the Toreadors* (1957), with Ralph Richardson; O'Neill's *A Touch of the Poet* (1958); and a revival of George Bernard Shaw's *Heartbreak House* (1959). In Tel Aviv earlier in 1959 he directed Shaw's *Caesar and Cleopatra*. Overall, in the judgment of critic Walter Kerr, Clurman was "Broadway's best invisible director because he permitted the author's work to absorb his powers and his personality so entirely." With the exception of Arthur Miller's *Incident at Vichy* (1965) and Inge's *Where's Daddy?* (1966) during the 1960s Clurman directed exclusively outside New York. During this decade, "the years of his prime," according to author Irving Howe, "when [Clurman] should have been doing Ibsen and Shaw, Chekhov and Pirandello, there was apparently no room in America for the classic modern theatre which was his deepest love."

In addition to his success as a director, Clurman became a first-rate critic. According to Arthur Miller, "He had no peer among the theatre commentators in this country." His writing career took shape as critic of the arts for *Tomorrow* magazine (1946–1952), theater critic for the *New Republic* (1949–1952), and guest theater critic for the *London Observer* (1955–1963). His criticism reached an apotheosis of insight with his role as theater critic for *The Nation* (1953 until his death in 1980). In the audience, always impeccably suited with the addition of a jaunty fedora and boulevardier's cane, he was considered by his critic colleagues something of a dandy as well as a deeply serious person. According to Jack Kroll of *Newsweek*, "He [approached] the work in question with a humane gallantry and the clear senses of a man, not a glibly clicking judgment machine." In the words of his obituary in the *New York Times*, "He did not so much judge a play as put it into context." Besides *The Fervent Years: The Story of the Group Theatre and the Thirties* (1945), Clurman's books include three anthologies of his own theater criticism, one of which, *Lies Like Truth* (1958), received the George Jean Nathan award. At the time of his death he was working on a study of O'Neill.

As a teacher Clurman conducted scene-study classes for professional actors at various times from 1954 into the 1970s. He served as the Andrew Mellon lecturer on "The World of the Theatre" at Carnegie Institute of Technology during 1962–1963. He was appointed professor of theater at Hunter College from 1964 and guest professor of theater at the Graduate Center of the City University of New York from 1968 until his death. As director, teacher, and friend he was conspicuous, as noted by writer Irwin Shaw, for "his wild harangues on acting, politics, drama, sex, theatre, which he delivered . . . with . . . unflagging zest and wisdom." In 1958 he was made Chevalier of the French Legion of Honor, the red-thread croix insignia of which he had sewn into the lapel of his tailored suits. In 1976 Brandeis University, where he served as chair of the arts commission, awarded him the Medal for Creative Arts. He also served as executive consultant of the Repertory Theatre of Lincoln Center from 1964 to 1965.

Sixteen months after attending the May 1979 inauguration of the Harold Clurman Theatre on West Forty-second Street, Clurman died in New York City. In the words of critic/artistic director Robert Brustein, Clurman was "shrewd but kindly, penetrating but humane; . . . he could speak his opinions without leaving blood on the floor . . . [having] the same combination of warmheartedness and toughmindedness as Chekhov," whom he took for his soul brother. Indeed, a spiritual and not religious person, Clurman wrote that "art for me is the bearer of an essence . . . [and] whatever that essence may be, . . . it is surely a holy spirit . . . far more profound even than religion."

• Collections of Clurman's correspondence are at the Billy Rose Theatre Collection at the New York Public Library for the Performing Arts, Lincoln Center; the John Gassner Collection at the University of Texas, Austin; and the Wisconsin Center for Theatre Research, Madison. Helen Krich Chinoy, ed., "Reunion," *Educational Theatre Journal*, Dec. 1976, is a chronology and account of the Group Theatre, with statements from Clurman and other Group alumni along with documents and photographs. In addition to *The Fervent Years* and *Lies Like Truth*, Clurman published two more collections of drama criticism and essays: *The Naked Image* (1966) and *The Divine Pastime: Theatre Essays* (1974). He also authored an account of his artistic approaches, *On Directing* (1972), and a memoir, *All People Are Famous: Instead of an Autobiography* (1974). His last book was *Ibsen* (1977). He served as editor for *Famous American Plays of the 1930s* (1959), *Seven Plays of the Modern Theatre* (1962), and *Famous American Plays of the 1960s* (1972). His collected works, *Six Decades of Commentary on Theatre, Dance, Music, Film, Arts and Letters*, were issued by Applause Books in 1994. He is the subject of a video, *Harold Clurman: A Life of Theatre* (1987), part of the American Masters Series produced by the National Endowment for the Arts. Another video from the American Masters Series, *A Tribute to the Group Theatre* (1987), features Clurman. A detailed obituary and a remembrance are in the *New York Times*, 10 Sept. 1980. Remembrances are also in *The Nation*, 11 Oct. 1980, and the *New Republic*, 18 Oct. 1980.

JOANNA ROTTÉ

CLUSKEY, Charles Blaney (1806–? Jan. 1871), architect, surveyor and building contractor, was born in Tulloware, King's County, Ireland. His dates of birth and death, family background, and education are obscure, though the sophistication of his architecture suggests that his training went beyond the study of contemporary Irish neoclassical design. One of several

Irish immigrant architects, including the more talented and productive James Gallier, Sr., Cluskey arrived in New York City on 3 October 1827. By 1829 he had moved to Georgia. He took U.S. citizenship the following June and in August 1831 married Johanna Elizabeth Walsh, whom he may have met in New York. Their first child, Michael Cluskey, the Democratic political writer, was born in April 1832, to be followed by five daughters, the last born only months before Johanna's death in September 1842. Cluskey apparently worked as a carpenter and builder, as indicated by his advertising in 1838 for carpentry apprentices and by his membership in the Savannah Mechanics Benevolent Association. His architectural practice began in 1832 when he designed the Screven County Courthouse and peaked over the ensuing decade. Outstanding is the Medical College of Georgia in Augusta (1834–1837), the two-and-a-half-story rectangular fabric having neatly proportioned neoclassical articulation fronted by a six-column Greek Doric portico. The revivalist idiom, influenced by the neo-Greek architecture he had seen in New York and in architectural pattern books, was synthesized with Palladian conventions in his other major commissions. The main building of Oglethorpe University, Atlanta (1836–1840), has been demolished, but the elegant governor's mansion at Millidgeville, Georgia (1837–1839), remains, distinguished by a fine Greek Ionic portico and unusual placing of the staircase to one side of the through hall.

Thereafter, his work was mainly domestic and in Savannah, apart from Lockerly, built in 1840 in Millidgeville for Judge Daniel Tucker. Notable are the Hermitage, which is usually attributed to him as having been constructed in 1840–1841, just prior to the Sorrel, Eastman, and Champion houses (the last involved a major addition to an existing structure). For these he might also have served as contractor, as he did in the enlargement of the Savannah Exchange, 1840–1843. Despite having had several lawsuits filed against him and declaring bankruptcy in 1843, he was appointed city surveyor in 1845 (he was replaced the next year). Reputedly popular, if irascible and inefficient, Cluskey supported local Irish and Democratic associations, through whom he was promoted in 1845 as architect for the Federal Customs House at Savannah. In this project, however, he lost out to John S. Norris, who then became the leading architect in the city.

In January 1848 he was invited to Washington, D.C., by Congressman John W. Houston as a "professional and practical architect of established reputation" to report on the design and structural condition of the federal buildings in the district. His report is a valuable historical resource. Cluskey generally praised the new federal buildings designed by Robert Mills and by Ithiel Town, Andrew J. Davis and William Elliot, Jr., acknowledging that their deficiencies resulted more from budgetary than professional inadequacy, and he presciently proposed extending the Capitol with north and south wings. However, his entry in the 1850 Capitol extension competition was rejected, although he claimed that Thomas Ustick Walter had imitated his proposal for a cast-iron columned rotunda. Equally unsuccessful was Cluskey's endeavor to secure the 1856–1857 commission and contract (in partnership with Edwin W. Moore) for the Galveston, Texas, Custom House. During this period he is believed to have completed some houses in New Orleans. He returned permanently to Washington, D.C., in 1858 to undertake government contracting work, including the laying out of streets adjacent to the U.S. Patent Office. In 1869 he undertook the building of the St. Simon's Island lighthouse at Brunswick, Georgia. It was begun shortly before his death in Washington. Intelligent in the adaptation of ancient motifs to contemporary American architectural conventions, Cluskey's main contribution was the development of the Greek Revival in the South.

• The main documentary sources are in the Savannah City Council Minutes, Deed Records, Tax Digest, and Superior Court Judgments; the Department of Treasury, Senate, District of Columbia, and U.S. Court of Claims Records at the National Archives (record groups 21, 46, and 123); and the Texas State Archives (record group 60). Notes on these and references in contemporary newspapers collected by Walter C. Hartridge and Mary J. Morrison are held at the Georgia Historical Society, Savannah. The most detailed studies of his architecture in Georgia are Florence F. Corley, "The Old Medical College and The Old Governor's Mansion," *Journal of the Richmond County Historical Society* 8, no. 2 (Summer 1976); Frederick D. Nichols, *The Architecture of Georgia* (1976); John Linley, *The Georgia Catalog: Historic American Buildings Surveys* (1982); and Mills Lane, *Architecture of the Old South: Georgia* (1986). The later phase of his career, and especially his part in the Galveston Custom House commission, are reviewed by Donald J. Lehman, *Lucky Landmark: A Study of a Design and Its Survival* (1973). Also see Walter C. Hartridge, "Charles B. Cluskey," *Savannah Morning News Magazine*, 27 Jan. 1965.

R. WINDSOR LISCOMBE

CLYMER, George (16 Mar. 1739–23 Jan. 1813), merchant, was born in Philadelphia, Pennsylvania, the son of Christopher Clymer, a sea captain and an Episcopalian, and Deborah Fitzwater, a disowned Quaker. Clymer's parents died by 1746, and he was raised by his maternal aunt Hannah Coleman and her husband William, a wealthy Quaker merchant and Proprietary party leader. The Proprietary party was aligned with the Penn family (proprietors of Pennsylvania) against the Quaker party, which sought to turn Pennsylvania into a royal colony. By the late 1750s Clymer himself had become a merchant. In 1765 Clymer, an Episcopalian, married Elizabeth Meredith, the daughter of the Quaker merchant Reese Meredith; like Clymer's mother, she was disowned for marrying a non-Quaker. Five of their eight children attained maturity. Following his uncle William Coleman's death in 1769, Clymer inherited £6,000. Three years later Clymer entered into partnership with his father-in-law and his brother-in-law Samuel Meredith. By 1774 Clymer had the second highest residential tax assessment in Philadelphia and ranked third in gross income from property.

Clymer's wealth permitted him to indulge his passion for politics. A Proprietary party member, he began to sit regularly on Philadelphia's city council in 1769, remaining there until elevated to alderman in 1774. Clymer was appointed a justice of the peace for the city and county courts in 1772. He opposed British imperial policy and became an early advocate of independence. From 1770 to 1776 he sat on six of the seven Philadelphia resistance committees and served as one of the rotating chairmen of the first Committee of Observation and Inspection. In July 1775 the Second Continental Congress appointed Clymer and Michael Hillegas "joint Treasurers of the United Colonies"; he held office until August 1776. Clymer sat regularly on Pennsylvania's committee of safety from October 1775 to July 1776, acting as one of its rotating chairmen. His committee work drove his political career, and he was elected to the state constitutional convention (July–Sept. 1776). Clymer opposed the unicameral legislature created by the convention's new constitution. He refused to sign the constitution and became a leader of the Republican party, which worked to overturn it. Clymer was elected to the first assembly under the constitution in November 1776 and was reelected the next fall.

Clymer also moved into national politics. In July 1776 the state constitutional convention elected him to the Second Continental Congress, where he signed the Declaration of Independence. Reelected to Congress in February 1777, he attended until September. As a congressman, Clymer sat on the boards of treasury and war and on the three-man executive committee that remained in Philadelphia after Congress fled to Baltimore, and he worked to improve the army's medical and commissary departments. In December 1777 Congress appointed Clymer to a commission to investigate conditions on the frontier. He spent four months at Fort Pitt, where he developed a low opinion of westerners that never left him. Clymer and Samuel Meredith engaged in a lucrative trade with St. Eustatius in 1779 and 1780; in the latter year, he was codirector of the Pennsylvania Bank, an institution established to obtain army supplies. The state assembly elected him to Congress in November 1780 and again in November 1781. Attending Congress until November 1782, he served on the Finance Committee and on a committee deputized to visit the southern states to request that they comply with the requisitions of Congress.

Clymer retired as a merchant in 1782, and with Samuel Meredith he speculated in western lands, first in Kentucky then in northeastern Pennsylvania. In the fall of 1782 Clymer moved his family to Princeton, New Jersey, where they lived until they returned to Philadelphia in 1784. Philadelphia placed Clymer in the assembly in the fall of 1785 and reelected him in 1786, 1787, and 1788. A Republican party leader, he was an effective committeeman, advocating the recharter of the Bank of North America, the reform of

the penal and criminal laws, and the call of a state convention to revise the constitution. He opposed state-issued paper money and the permanent assumption by Pennsylvania of the interest on Continental securities.

Most importantly, Clymer supported an independent revenue for the Confederation Congress, believing that "revenue confers power." He also wanted to increase the Congress's powers over commerce. Consequently, he favored the calling of a convention to meet in Philadelphia in May 1787 to revise and amend the Articles of Confederation. In December 1786 the assembly appointed him a delegate to the convention. Immediately after the Constitutional Convention adopted the new Constitution on 17 September 1787, Clymer took his assembly seat and introduced resolutions calling for a state convention to ratify the Constitution and for offering Philadelphia as the site of the new federal capital. He argued in debate that America's future existence as a nation depended upon ratification.

In early November 1788 the Federalist Lancaster Conference nominated Clymer for the U.S. House of Representatives, and later that month he was elected one of the state's eight representatives, receiving the fourth highest vote total. Clymer served only one term (1789–1791) and, once again, made his mark as a committeeman. He was a leading advocate of Alexander Hamilton's financial program, a lukewarm supporter of amendments to the Constitution, and a strong proponent of locating the federal capital in Philadelphia.

After leaving Congress in 1791, Clymer was appointed by President George Washington to be supervisor of revenue for Pennsylvania, responsible for collecting the federal excise on spirits. The tax's unpopularity and Clymer's distrust of westerners ensured his devastating failure as collector, and he resigned in July 1794. Shortly after, the Whiskey Rebellion broke out. The next year Washington placed him on a commission that negotiated the Treaty of Coleraine with the Creeks of Georgia in 1796.

Clymer spent the remainder of his life engaged largely in philanthropy. From 1791 to 1813 he was an active trustee of the University of Pennsylvania. He was president of the Pennsylvania Academy of Fine Arts and vice president of the Philadelphia Society for Promoting Agriculture from 1805 to 1813. Lastly, he was president of the Philadelphia Bank from 1803 until his death at his son Henry's Morrisville home, across the Delaware River from Trenton. He was buried in Trenton's Quaker cemetery.

• No large collection of Clymer's papers exists. Indispensable on Clymer's life is Jerry Grundfest, *George Clymer: Philadelphia Revolutionary, 1739–1813* (1983), which includes a description of the widely scattered Clymer manuscripts. On Pa. politics, see Richard Alan Ryerson, *The Revolution Is Now Begun: The Radical Committees of Philadelphia, 1765–1776* (1978); Robert L. Brunhouse, *The Counter-Revolution in Pennsylvania, 1776–1790* (1942); Douglas M. Arnold, *A Republican Revolution: Ideology and Politics in Pennsylvania, 1776–1790* (1989); and Harry Marlin Tinkcom, *The Republicans and Federalists in Pennsylvania, 1790–1801* (1950). For

Clymer in the Second Continental Congress, see Paul H. Smith et al., eds., *Letters of Delegates to Congress, 1774–1789* (1976–). For his role in the adoption and ratification of the Constitution, the first federal elections, and the first federal Congress, see Merrill Jensen et al., eds., *The Documentary History of the Ratification of the Constitution*, vol. 2 (1976–); Merrill Jensen et al., eds., *The Documentary History of the First Federal Elections, 1788–1790*, vol. 2 (4 vols., 1976–1989); and Linda Grant De Pauw et al., eds., *Documentary History of the First Federal Congress, 1789–1791*, vols. 3, 9–14 (1972–). For his service as supervisor of revenue for Pa., see Harold C. Syrett et al., eds., *The Papers of Alexander Hamilton*, vol. 12 (27 vols., 1961–1987); and Thomas P. Slaughter, *The Whiskey Rebellion: Frontier Epilogue to the American Revolution* (1986).

GASPARE J. SALADINO

COACOOCHEE (1809?–Jan. 1857), Seminole leader, whose name in English means "Wildcat," was born in the region of Lake Apopka, Florida, the son of Philip, evidently a Mikasuki headman, and his wife, sister of Micanopy, the principal civil chief (*micco*) of the Alachua Seminole. Linked to influential clan kin in the two most important Seminole groups, Coacoochee possessed strong hereditary claims to leadership, but he also proved himself as a war leader (*tastanagi*) and during the Second Seminole War was recognized by Americans as "by far the most dangerous chieftain in the field." Individually gifted, Coacoochee was also a fluent orator, strong leader, and a politician of vision, but his career throughout also reflects powerful personal ambition.

In 1834 the United States attempted to remove the Seminoles from Florida to present-day Oklahoma on the basis of agreement made with some of the Indians at Payne's Landing, Florida (9 May 1832) and Fort Gibson, Indian Territory (28 Mar. 1833). When armed resistance began, Philip and Coacoochee were among the first Indians in action, leading raids upon rich American sugar plantations east of the St. Johns River near St. Augustine in December 1835. Coacoochee was only one of several enterprising Seminole war leaders during the struggle, but American officers learned to respect his skill and determination.

On 8–9 September 1837 troops under Brigadier General Joseph M. Hernandez captured Philip and members of his family and band near the Tomoka River, and Coacoochee shortly came into St. Augustine, where his father was being held, under a flag of truce. He was induced by Hernandez and Major General Thomas S. Jesup to set up talks between the Americans and hostile Seminoles under Osceola and Coa Hadjo. The treacherous seizure of Osceola's party (21 Oct.) and the incarceration of Coacoochee, too, in Fort Marion, St. Augustine, two violations of the white flag, probably convinced Coacoochee that the United States could not be dealt with honestly. On the night of 29–30 November 1837 he led a party of followers in a daring breakout from Fort Marion and carried his opinions back to the Seminoles still at large.

Coacoochee's information probably strengthened the Seminole will to resist, and at Lake Okeechobee on 25 December 1837 several hundred Indians and blacks under Sam Jones (?–1867), Alligator, and Coacoochee inflicted 138 casualties on Colonel Zachary Taylor's 1,000-man army and checked its advance south. Thereafter there were no pitched battles, but a war of attrition continued for several years in which groups of Seminoles were captured or surrendered and shipped west. Coacoochee generally harried American communications in the area of the St. Johns, but on 5 March 1841 the chief, flamboyantly dressed as Shakespeare's Hamlet, one of a number of theatrical costumes captured the previous year, appeared at Fort Cummings to discuss terms. In further negotiations at Fort Brooke he agreed to assemble his band for emigration, but the Americans grew suspicious of his intentions, had him seized at Fort Pierce on 4 June, and rounded up his following. Coacoochee and 200 others left Tampa Bay for the West on 12 October. "It was my home," Coacoochee said of Florida. "I loved it and to leave it now is like burying my wife and child."

Indian Territory (Okla.) proved as unsatisfactory as Coacoochee had supposed. Afraid that they would sacrifice some of their independence if they moved onto the Creek lands assigned them between the Canadian River and its north fork, Coacoochee and many Seminoles remained for some years on Cherokee land near Fort Gibson. But attempts to cultivate the soil were hindered by floods and droughts, and the condition of the Indians remained pitiable.

After 1845, when a new treaty promised the Seminoles greater autonomy within the Creek nation, Coacoochee moved on to Little River, but his dissatisfaction remained. One problem concerned the blacks, of whom there were many among the Seminoles, some intermarried with Indians, some Maroons (free black runaways), and some slaves or prisoners. Generally, blacks had more freedom and standing with the Seminoles and had been strong opponents of removal, fearing seizure by Americans or other Indians. Despite the U.S. attorney general's upholding of Seminole rights in the matter of the blacks in 1848, they continued to be threatened by white and Indian slavers. Then, too, Coacoochee's private ambitions were frustrated when he was passed over as Seminole head chief upon the death of Micanopy in 1849. Quarreling also with the Creeks, Coacoochee began searching for a haven in which he could satisfy his appetite for leadership and protect the Seminoles and blacks from molestation.

In December 1845 Coacoochee had accompanied American officials to Texas to help the United States establish peace with the Comanches, and the next year he tried opening a regular trade between these people and the Seminoles. His interest in the Southwest deepened, and by 1848 he nursed a plan to head a confederacy of Seminoles, blacks, Comanches, Kickapoos, Kiowas, Tonkawas, Lipans, Apaches, Wacoes, Caddoes, and Kichai and to form a colony on the Rio Grande beyond the interference of the United States. In 1849 he left Indian Territory with some blacks and Seminoles, circulated among the Texas Indians (recruiting some Kickapoos), and in July 1850 arrived at present

Zaragoza to petition the Mexican government for land, arms, and economic assistance. The Mexicans saw advantages in an Indian colony as a buffer against hostile tribes to the north. Encouraged, Coacoochee returned to Indian Territory to offer asylum to Indians and blacks. In the "sensation" that followed, American officials accused Coacoochee of disaffecting Indians from the United States, while white, Creek, and Cherokee slaveowners believed he was inciting blacks to flee. Armed conflict with Coacoochee's party was avoided, but the chief made a few recruits, and some black emigrants were dispersed en route by Creek pursuers and raiding Comanches.

The president of Mexico ratified Coacoochee's grant to land near Piedras Negras on 16 October 1850, and the chief swore an oath of fidelity on 4 February following. He was appointed a justice and received a colonel's commission in the Mexican army. After the defection of Kickapoo allies, Coacoochee's fighting force stabilized at over 100 Seminole and black warriors, and for several years they patrolled border areas and assisted Mexican forces. Where appropriate, they received the pay of national soldiers and the thanks of the Mexican government. The colony did experience difficulties. Piedras Negras proved an unsuitable location, and after Coacoochee visited Mexico City in 1852 the Seminoles and blacks were awarded an alternative tract at Nacimiento, near Muzquiz, but they never secured full title. However, it was only after Coacoochee's death that civil war in Mexico and improved Seminole conditions in Indian Territory induced the chief's Indian followers, including his son (Gato Chiquito, the Little Cat) to return to the United States.

Coacoochee was active to the end of his life. Returning from an expedition, he camped at Alto, Muzquiz, where he contracted smallpox and died. In his prime Coacoochee was lightly built and of middle height, but impressive. An American who served against the Seminoles in Florida, John T. Sprague, remembered his "extremely youthful and pleasing" countenance, his "clear and soft" voice, and limbs of "the most perfect symmetry." The greatest of the Seminoles, he strengthened resistance to removal from Florida and imaginatively confronted the problems of adjustment in the West.

• No full biography of Coacoochee exists. In lieu, Kenneth W. Porter's rigorous articles, giving full reference to American and Mexican sources, provide the best account: "Wild Cat's Death and Burial," *Chronicles of Oklahoma* 21 (1943): 41–43; "Seminole Flight from Fort Marion," *Florida Historical Quarterly* 22 (1944): 113–33; "The Hawkins Negroes Go to Mexico," *Chronicles of Oklahoma* 24 (1946): 55–58; "The Seminole in Mexico, 1850–1861," *Chronicles of Oklahoma* 29 (1951): 153–68; "The Seminole in Mexico, 1850–1861," *Hispanic American Historical Review* 31 (1951): 1–36; and "Origins of the St. Johns River Seminoles: Were They Mikasuki?" *Florida Anthropologist* 4 (1951): 39–45. Contemporary comment can conveniently be sampled in John T. Sprague, *Origin, Progress and Conclusion of the Florida War* (1848), which uses a fragment of Coacoochee autobiography printed in the *Savannah Georgian* of Feb. 1842;

"Letters of Samuel Forry, Surgeon U.S. Army, 1837–1838," *Florida Historical Quarterly* 7 (1928): 88–105; and Nathan S. Jarvis, "An Army Surgeon's Notes on Frontier Service, 1833–1848," *Journal of the Military Service Institution of the United States* 39 (1906): 272–86. Of secondary works the most useful are Charles H. Coe, *Red Patriots* (1898); Edwin C. McReynolds, *The Seminoles* (1957); and John K. Mahon, *History of the Second Seminole War* (1967).

JOHN SUGDEN

COATES, Robert Myron (6 Apr. 1897–8 Feb. 1973), writer, was born in New Haven, Connecticut, the son of Frederick Coates, an inventor of special tools and machinery, and Harriet Davidson. Coates's father was a restless man, and the family rarely remained in one place for long. Their stay in any given town depended, Coates explained in his memoirs, *The View from Here* (1960), on his father's "mood and his commitments." The family crisscrossed the country, residing in such various cities as New York City; Springfield, Massachusetts; Seattle, Washington; Portland, Oregon; and Salt Lake City, Utah. The strong sense of detachment and displacement Coates admits in his memoirs to having felt growing up provided an important theme to much of his fiction. "That was just the way life *was*, I thought, and while it did make for stretches of loneliness and uncertainty, it had its excitements, too. . . . No, I don't want to give the impression that our home life, ever or anywhere, was bleak or depressing. Yet I can see now that underneath it all there was a certain loneliness" (pp. 4–5).

Coates graduated from Yale University in 1919 after having interrupted his undergraduate career with an eight-month stint as a naval aviation cadet in 1918. He wrote poetry and fiction with little success in New York City until 1921, when his father agreed to give him enough money to sail steerage class to Paris and begin his career anew as a serious writer.

Once in France, Coates took up residence in the village of Giverny, fifty miles from the commotion of Paris, and then set about making the acquaintance of French literary figures and members of the American expatriate community. (It was Coates who introduced Ernest Hemingway to Gertrude Stein.)

Coates supported himself in France by selling his short stories to the various fiction journals that had sprung up everywhere in Europe in the 1920s. With Stein's help his first novel, *The Eater of Darkness*, appeared in a small French edition in 1926 and was published in New York three years later. Its surreal blend of fantasy and reality revealed the unmistakable influence of dadaism, and it is considered the first dada novel to be published in the United States. At this early stage in his career, Coates seems to have been attracted by the dadaists' sense of playfulness. He wrote nostalgically that this "was predominantly a gay time, and it's no accident, I think, that it was the Dada period—the one artistic movement I know of whose main purpose was having fun" (*The View from Here*, p. 209).

Coates returned in 1926 to New York, where, with the help of his friend James Thurber, he found work reviewing books and contributing to the "Talk of the Town" column for a new magazine, the *New Yorker*. It was at this time that he also began his long tenure as the magazine's art critic, a position he held until his retirement from the *New Yorker* in 1967. During most of these years Coates lived and worked in rural Connecticut, continuing to write fiction. Coates married Elsa Kirpal, a sculptor, in 1927; they had one child.

Coates was a prolific writer of short stories, contributing more than 100 pieces to the *New Yorker* and many more to other well-regarded magazines such as *Esquire*. Two of these works, "The Fury" and "The Net," were selected as O. Henry Memorial Prize stories in 1937 and 1940, respectively, and are often anthologized. Collections of his stories include *All the Year Round* (1943), *The Hour after Westerly* (1957), and *The Man Just Ahead of You* (1964). In 1930 Coates wrote his best-known piece of longer nonfiction, a historical study titled *The Outlaw Years: The History of the Land Pirates of the Natchez Trace*.

Coates's second novel was the semiautobiographical *Yesterday's Burdens* (1933), which has become his most highly regarded work. *The Bitter Season* (1946), his third novel, is also autobiographical, a treatment of his life on the home front during the Second World War. In 1946 Coates and his wife divorced; the same year he married Astrid Peters. In 1948 Coates finally achieved the popular success that had been eluding him with the publication of *Wisteria Cottage*, a work that nearly became a bestseller. Coates's last novel, *The Farther Shore*, was published in 1955, and he was elected to the National Institute of Arts and Letters the same year. Coates died in New York City.

Despite the esteem in which his works were held by friends such as Malcolm Cowley, Coates remains in the eyes of most literary critics an interesting, though minor, writer. His carefully crafted and intensely subjective fiction is, however, suffused with a stylistic elegance that was enormously influential in its heyday. His short stories in particular, along with the prose he wrote as resident art critic, helped shape what came to be called the "*New Yorker* style." Though his vivid depictions of the loneliness of everyday life in the twentieth century are powerful, it is primarily as a stylist that Coates will be remembered.

• For Malcolm Cowley's contention that Coates's works deserve wider recognition, see his comments in the Lost American Fiction Series edition of *Yesterday's Burdens* (1975), and "Reconsideration," *New Republic*, 30 Nov. 1974, pp. 40–42. Constance Pierce offers a scholarly examination of Coates's best-known work in "Divinest Sense: Narrative Technique in Robert Coates's *Yesterday's Burdens*," *Critique: Studies in Modern Fiction* 19 (1977): 44–52. Obituaries are in the *New York Times*, 10 Feb. 1973, and the *Washington Post*, 11 Feb. 1973.

KEVIN R. RAHIMZADEH

COBB, Andrew Jackson (12 Apr. 1857–27 Mar. 1925), jurist and legal educator, was born in Athens, Georgia, the son of Howell Cobb, a statesman, and Mary Ann Lamar. Howell Cobb was secretary of the treasury at his son's birth and previously had served as Speaker of the U.S. House of Representatives. The elder Cobb later served as governor of Georgia and president of the Provisional Congress of the Confederate States of America.

Andrew Cobb earned both his A.B. (Phi Beta Kappa) and LL.B. from the University of Georgia in Athens in 1876 and 1877, respectively. He immediately became a member of the bar in Athens, where he began the practice of law. In 1880 he married Starkie Campbell. The marriage, which produced five children, lasted until her death in 1901. He did not remarry.

At various times during his career, Cobb was a practicing attorney, both in Athens and Atlanta, a judge, both at the trial and appellate levels, and a legal educator, both at the Atlanta Law School and the University of Georgia. From 1877 until 1893, when he left for Atlanta, he practiced law in Athens, alternately alone and with others. He also began a career in legal education during this time, serving as a professor of law at his alma mater beginning in 1884. He continued his academic career in Atlanta, assuming the deanship of the Atlanta Law School on his arrival there in 1897. The simultaneous practice of law and service on a law school faculty was not unusual during this era.

Former students prevailed on Cobb to stand for election to the Georgia Supreme Court in 1896, when the court's membership expanded from three to six justices. At the time of his election, he was the second-youngest man ever elected to that court. He began ten years of service in 1897. After retiring from the court, he returned to his hometown and resumed the private practice of law in 1908. Called on again for judicial service in 1917, however, he accepted appointment as a trial court judge, riding circuit in the Western Circuit of Georgia, which was based in Athens. Sixty years old at the time of his election, he found the work very burdensome. In 1921 he stepped down from the bench again. At that point he resumed his legal academic career by rejoining the University of Georgia law faculty, where he remained until his death in Athens.

Cobb's major contribution to his state and nation was made during his service on the Georgia Supreme Court. While he was known primarily as an expert in constitutional and procedural law, his most significant opinion concerned a question in the private law field of torts. In *Pavesich v. New England Life Insurance Co.* (1905), on behalf of a unanimous court, Cobb wrote the first appellate court opinion in the United States recognizing the common law tort of invasion of privacy.

Paolo Pavesich, an Atlanta artist, sued New England Life for invasion of privacy, asserting it had used a photograph of him in an advertisement without permission, along with a fictitious endorsement. Acknowledging that a right of privacy had never before been recognized in Georgia or elsewhere, Cobb wrote:

The right of privacy has its foundation in the instincts of nature. It is recognized intuitively, consciousness being the witness that can be called to establish its existence. Any person whose intellect is in a normal condition recognizes at once that as to each individual member of society there are matters private and there are matters public so far as the individual is concerned. Each individual as instinctively resents any encroachment by the public upon his rights which are of a private nature as he does the withdrawal of those of his rights which are of a public nature. A right of privacy in matters purely private is therefore derived from natural law.

Cobb's opinion in *Pavesich*, which drew support from probably the most famous law review article ever written, Charles Warren and Louis Brandeis, "The Right to Privacy," published by the *Harvard Law Review* in 1890, remains a landmark in the field of privacy law generations later. In *Martin Luther King, Jr., Center for Social Change v. American Heritage Products, Inc.* (1982), a member of the Georgia Supreme Court described *Pavesich* as "perhaps the most noted product of our court in terms of nationally recognized precedent." One of the most influential torts scholar in the United States, William Prosser, called it the "leading case" in the field ("Privacy," *California Law Review* 48 [1948]: 386). According to Harold R. Gordon, *Pavesich* "remains a landmark and is universally cited as one of the most comprehensive and well-reasoned decisions in the field" ("Right of Property in Name, Likeness, Personality and History," *Northwestern University Law Review* 55 [1960]: 559). Most importantly, virtually every state in the country now recognizes, either through statue or judicial decision, the existence of the right of privacy as a protectible interest in tort.

Cobb's contributions to the public life of his state and country were not limited to his service on the trial and appellate bench. He was, at various times in his career, city attorney in Athens, a member and president of the Athens Board of Education, an active member of the American Bar Association and the Georgia Bar Association and president of the latter, a presidential elector and president of the Georgia electoral college in the election of 1912, president of the Georgia Historical Society, and a trustee of the University of Georgia. He was also active in the Baptist church.

A staunch Democrat, Cobb vigorously defended the policies of the national administration during World War I. A memorial prepared by a distinguished group of attorneys and presented to the Georgia Supreme Court recalled that during that war Cobb's "clarion voice range over the state in support of the National Administration, and he had no patience with those who hesitated or criticized." As a legal educator he taught a wide range of subjects, including constitutional law, Roman law, international law, practice and procedure, damages, and conflict of laws.

As quoted in the memorial, Judge Blanton Fortson said of Cobb:

He was a learned lawyer. He was an excellent teacher. But his outstanding quality was character. I knew him for more than a score of years; and if during all that time there was ever voiced the slightest criticism of his conduct, either public or private, whether as a teacher, practitioner, a judge, a citizen or a man, I did not hear it. Indeed, there was none, for he was above reproach. . . . But he was not austere, cold or forbidding . . . but he was one of the most lovable and companionable of men.

• The lengthiest and most comprehensive single source of information is the memorial prepared by a committee of Georgia attorneys and friends of Cobb that was presented to the Georgia Supreme Court on 17 May 1926; it appears in vol. 162 of the *Georgia Reports*, p. 842. Along with the memorial itself is a response by a fellow member of the court, Presiding Justice Marcus W. Beck. Profiles of Cobb appear in numerous multivolume histories of Georgia, including Allen Dan Candler and Clement A. Evans, *Cyclopedia of Georgia*, vol. 1 (1906), p. 409; Lucian L. Knight, *A Standard History of Georgia and Georgians*, vol. 5 (1917), p. 2385; and *Memoirs of Georgia*, vol. 1 (1895), p. 749. In addition to the Prosser and Gordon articles cited in the text, a number of other law review articles discuss the right of privacy, including Edward J. Bloustein, "Privacy as an Agent of Human Dignity: An Answer to Dean Prosser," *New York University Law Review* 39 (1964): 962. These articles, while focusing on the law and not on Cobb, provide a context in which to judge his work. An obituary is in the *Atlanta Constitution*, 28 Mar. 1925.

PAUL M. KURTZ

COBB, Cully Alton (25 Feb. 1884–7 May 1975), agricultural educator, editor, and publisher, was born in a log cabin on the farm of his paternal grandfather near Prospect, Tennessee, the son of Napoleon Bonaparte Cobb, a farmer and rural minister, and Mary Agnes Woodward. Cobb attended public school in Giles County, Tennessee, and Decatur, Alabama. He entered Mississippi Agricultural and Mechanical College (now Mississippi State University) in 1904 and graduated in 1908 with a bachelor of science degree in agriculture. From 1908 to 1910 he served as principal of Chickasaw County Agricultural High School at Buena Vista, Mississippi. The first of fifty such institutions established in the state between 1908 and 1920, the school afforded rural youths a college-preparatory education as well as practical training in farming. In 1910 he married Ora May "Byrdie" Ball, with whom he had two children.

Also in 1910 Cobb returned to Mississippi Agricultural and Mechanical College to serve as the second director of the state's corn club movement, a precursor of the modern 4-H program. Part of the agricultural extension movement of the early twentieth century, the corn clubs constituted a cooperative effort between the United States Department of Agriculture, which directed the clubs, and land-grant colleges, where the state agents who supervised the clubs were headquartered. The clubs were designed to instruct rural youths in scientific methods of soil improvement and the cultivation of corn and other crops. Under Cobb's leadership, membership in the corn clubs grew to more than 23,000 in 1918. One of his major contributions to club work, not only in Mississippi but also nationally, was sending state club winners in livestock judging to visit the International Livestock Show in Chicago, an idea that would evolve into the National 4-H Club Congress.

In 1919 Cobb was promoted to the position of assistant director of cooperative agricultural extension in Mississippi, but in that same year he resigned the post and left Mississippi to become editor in chief of the *Southern Ruralist*, a farm journal published in Atlanta. In his editorials, Cobb particularly stressed the need for diversification in southern agriculture, more scientific methods of farming in order to reach higher crop yields, and the value of agricultural extension work and the land-grant colleges as means to achieve those ends. He also advocated a federal farm program to deal with the problem of overproduction in agriculture and was a supporter of the McNary-Haugen bill, the Agricultural Marketing Act, and the domestic allotment concept later enacted under Franklin D. Roosevelt's New Deal. As president of the American Agricultural Editors' Association, a trade group for rural journalists, Cobb conducted from 1924 to 1930 a series of agricultural study tours to Europe, Canada, and Mexico.

Although the circulation of the *Southern Ruralist* increased to 513,000 in 1930, the periodical ranked only third in readership among the five regional farm journals published in the South during the 1920s. Because advertising revenue, as well as the overall size of the issues, was declining, Cobb and the other executives of the *Southern Ruralist* agreed to merge with the *Progressive Farmer* in 1930. After the merger, Cobb served as vice president and managing editor of the Progressive Farmer–Southern Ruralist Company and editor of the Georgia-Alabama edition of the *Progressive Farmer*. This affiliation with the South's premier farm journal, which now enjoyed a combined readership in excess of one million, enhanced Cobb's reputation in agricultural circles. As a result, he became a leading contender for the position of secretary of agriculture under Roosevelt. During this period, in 1932, his first wife died. Two years later, in 1934, he married Lois P. Dowdle; they had no children.

Cobb did not win the secretaryship, but in 1933 he was named chief of the Cotton Production Section of the Agricultural Adjustment Administration (AAA) in the Department of Agriculture. There, his main duty was to oversee the AAA's cotton acreage reduction program. While the program succeeded in reducing cotton production and raising cotton prices, its tendency to displace sharecroppers in the South led to a bitter landlord-tenant controversy within the AAA. The opposing factions were the "agrarians," such as Cobb, who feared that a disruption of the traditional landlord-tenant relationship might jeopardize economic recovery, and the "urban liberals," who viewed the AAA as an instrument of social reform. There also was division within the AAA over the manner in which AAA programs should be administered, with one group advocating decentralized administration at the local level, including citizen participation and a wider role for such entities as the land-grant colleges, while an opposing group supported centralized administration with authority and control over the implementation of agricultural policy remaining at the federal level. On the losing end of these controversies, Cobb resigned from the Department of Agriculture in 1937.

Cobb returned to Atlanta to become president of the Ruralist Press, Inc., a commercial printing corporation that previously had printed the *Southern Ruralist*. During Cobb's thirty-four years as owner and president of the firm, it became a leading printer of telephone directories, with the Southern Bell system one of its major customers. In 1971 Cobb sold the company to the New York textile firm J. P. Stevens and Company.

In retirement, Cobb purchased an antebellum home on an 85-acre farm near Decatur, Georgia, where he put his ideas about agriculture into practice by growing grain crops and raising turkeys. A dedicated Baptist, he contributed to educational and religious organizations such as Emory University and the Southern Baptist Theological Seminary at Louisville, Kentucky. The chief recipient of Cobb's philanthropy was Mississippi State University, to which he gave nearly $1.5 million, including a donation of more than $1 million to finance the Cobb Institute of Archaeology. He died in Atlanta.

Cobb's greatest contributions were as an agricultural leader. He was a pioneer in agricultural extension work, a staunch advocate of agricultural education, a capable administrator, and a spokesman for improved farming techniques in southern agriculture and a more equitable standard of living for the American farmer.

• Cobb's papers are located in the Mississippi State University Library. A favorable account of Cobb's life, including his role in the struggle in the AAA between the agrarians and the liberals, can be found in Roy V. Scott and J. G. Shoalmire, *The Public Career of Cully A. Cobb: A Study in Agricultural Leadership* (1973). An interpretation of the controversy in the AAA that is highly critical of Cobb is David Eugene Conrad, *The Forgotten Farmers: The Story of Sharecroppers in the New Deal* (1965). Theodore Saloutos gives a balanced account of the conflict in his *The American Farmer and the New Deal* (1982). See also Edward L. Schapsmeier and Frederick H. Schapsmeier, *Henry A. Wallace of Iowa: The Agrarian Years, 1910–1940* (1968). Obituaries are in the *Atlanta Constitution* and the Starkville (Miss.) *Daily News*, both 8 May 1975.
SANDRA S. VANCE

COBB, Frank (6 Aug. 1869–21 Dec. 1923), editor and editorial writer, was born Francis Irving Cobb in Shawnee County, Kansas, the son of Minor H. Cobb and Mathilda Clark, farmers. He spent his early life in small towns and the countryside and experienced the hardships of rural life. After the collapse of the Kansas farm, the family moved to Michigan, where from 1887 to 1890 Cobb attended Michigan State Normal College in Ypsilanti. In 1890, at the age of twenty-one, he was appointed superintendent of the high school at Martin, Michigan. A year later he left teaching and joined the *Grand Rapids Herald*, first as a reporter, and later as correspondent and city editor. He worked for the *Grand Rapids Daily Eagle* in 1893 and the *Detroit Evening News* from 1894 to 1900. In 1897 he married Delia S. Bailey. In 1900 he became chief editorial writer for the *Detroit Free Press*.

By then Joseph Pulitzer had made the *New York World* one of the country's preeminent newspapers. But when blindness and emotional problems forced him to give up direct supervision, the paper began to decline. In 1904 he began a search for a new editor who could revive the paper's editorial stature. He wanted a young man who knew history and politics, who had a keen perception and forceful writing style, and who could provide dynamic leadership for the liberal causes Pulitzer supported. After a nationwide search, Pulitzer's envoy came across Cobb's editorials, which seemed to reflect a writing style and a political mind very similar to Pulitzer's. But Pulitzer wanted details. "What," he asked, "has Cobb read in American history, Rhodes, McMaster, Trevelyan, Parkman? What works on the Constitution and constitutional law? Has he read Buckle's *History of Civilization*? . . . Search his brain for everything there is in it" (quoted in Allen Churchill, *Park Row* (1958), pp. 268–69). In fact, besides his broad political and historical knowledge, Cobb knew a great deal about science, philosophy, music, and literature. He eventually was convinced to travel to New York to be interviewed by Pulitzer. Afterward Pulitzer proclaimed: "Cobb will do. He knows American history better than anyone I have ever found. . . . In time, we can make a real editor of him."

Cobb reported to the *World* as one of its several editorial writers, not knowing that he had been picked as Pulitzer's eventual replacement. Like Pulitzer, Cobb believed that a newspaper's prime purpose was to be a public servant, a fighter for liberal causes in aid of the mass of the people rather than a profit-motivated corporation. In 1905 Pulitzer made Cobb chief editorial writer, which gave Cobb virtually complete control over the *World*'s news and editorial operations. Pulitzer, however, retained the title of "editor" until his death in 1911. In 1913 Cobb married his second wife, Margaret Hubbard Ayer, a writer for the *World*; they had two children.

Cobb had a clean and forceful writing style that combined lightness of touch with brilliant sarcasm and biting irony. It was said that "No one could hit harder than he. . . . Yet for all the vigor of his blows, he could write with a light touch when he wished" (*New Republic*, 2 Jan. 1924). Henry Watterson, editor of the *Louisville Courier-Journal* and a brilliant editorial writer himself, called Cobb "the strongest writer of the New York press since Horace Greeley." In many respects, Cobb was the first outstanding modern editorial writer, his style marked by conciseness, economy, simplicity, and clarity. Ralph Pulitzer, who replaced his father as publisher of the *World*, said of his writing: "Everything he handled became simple in his han-

dling of it. Sometimes he would simplify a bewildering situation or a tangled thought with one easy touch of intuitive analysis. Sometimes he would labor with his might on some cunningly elusive subtlety, and in the end his directness would simplify it into surrender."

Many contemporaries considered the *World*'s editorial page the most influential in the nation and credited it for a renaissance of the newspaper editorial function. Under Cobb the *World* crusaded vigorously against political corruption and what it considered to be social injustices. Cobb's editorial leadership was recognized in a number of causes. The *World*'s campaign against abuses by the Equitable Insurance Company and New York State's two other major insurance companies, New York Life and Mutual Life, from 1905 to 1907 encouraged government investigation and reform legislation in New York that served as a model for laws in other states. Its investigation of the construction of the Panama Canal focused public attention on the corrupt financial dealings of government officials involved. Contemporaries credited Cobb's editorials with securing the Democratic presidential nomination for Woodrow Wilson during the party's deadlocked convention of 1912. Cobb was the leading editorial writer cautioning restraint toward U.S. entrance into World War I. He was American journalism's strongest supporter of the League of Nations. He was recognized also for his insight into the problems of the U.S. form of government in the twentieth century, believing that the Constitution was not flexible enough for contemporary life and that the parliamentary system would be a more workable system, and for his strong advocacy of human freedom.

Fellow journalists admired Cobb not only for his editorial ability, but also for his personal characteristics. He was unassuming, honest, and generous. He enjoyed the company of other, less important staff members of the *World* and was a favorite among the staffers in the newsroom. While he was a dynamic, engaging, and knowledgeable conversationalist, he did not condescend toward anyone of lesser knowledge or station. He was known as a man who had received no special favors but had earned every benefit he had gotten out of life.

By the time Cobb died after an extended illness, he had become recognized, although writing anonymously in a corporate newspaper, as the leading editorial writer of his time. Ralph Pulitzer eulogized him as a man who "became a power and a personality in the United States, writing editorials he did not sign in a paper he did not own." The *World* itself expired only eight years after Cobb's death, in a merger with the *New York Telegram* in 1931.

• Although a prolific writer, Cobb devoted most of his efforts to his daily newspaper material and published only one book, *Woodrow Wilson—An Interpretation* (1921), along with a few nonfiction magazine articles. Some of his best editorials are collected in John L. Heaton, ed., *Cobb of the World: A Leader in Liberalism* (1924). He left no collected personal papers, and most biographical details are contained in reminiscences of fellow journalists and in obituaries written shortly after his death. See John L. Heaton, *The Story of a Page* (1913); J. Schermerhorn, "Editorial Writer," *American Magazine*, Jan. 1913, pp. 29–30; "Sketch," *Everybody's*, Mar. 1916, p. 356; "Appreciation," *New Republic*, 2 Jan. 1924, p. 137; "Frank I. Cobb," *Nation*, 2 Jan. 1924, p. 3; "Great Editor," *Outlook*, 2 Jan. 1924, pp. 8–9; "An Editor of the 'World' and the World," *Literary Digest*, 12 Jan. 1924, pp. 40–42; "Cobb, a Leader in Liberalism: An Editor Who Made the Nation His Debtor," *Current Opinion*, Aug. 1924, pp. 163–64; and Lindsay Denison, "Cobb, the Man," in *Cobb of the World: A Leader in Liberalism*, ed. John L. Heaton (1924).

WILLIAM DAVID SLOAN

COBB, George Linus (31 Aug. 1886–26 Dec. 1942), composer, was born in Mexico, New York, the son of Linus Cobb and Jeanette Maine. Virtually nothing is known about his parents or about his younger years, except that Cobb attended Syracuse University, where he studied music. After college he lived in Buffalo, New York, for several years before moving to New York City. The length of time he stayed in New York City and his activities there also are unknown.

Around 1909 Cobb moved to Boston, where he began working as a clerk for popular music publisher Walter Jacobs. Cobb's first ragtime piano composition, "Rubber Plant Rag," was published by Walter Jacobs Publishers that same year and marked the beginning of a long-standing professional relationship between composer and publisher. Later, in 1913, Cobb's "Bunny Hug Rag," published by Jacobs, became a hit during the animal dance craze of the early 1910s. Also in 1913 Cobb teamed up with lyricist Jack Yellen of Buffalo and composed "All Aboard for Dixie Land," a song that was popularized after Elizabeth Murray sang it in Rudolf Friml's operetta *High Jinks* in December of that year. "Alabama Jubilee," also a product of Cobb and Yellen and sung by Murray, was released in 1915 and sold nearly one million copies of sheet music. (The song was later revived in the 1950s.)

By the mid-1910s Cobb had joined the Walter Jacobs permanent staff as a composer and arranger. Cobb wrote hundreds of compositions for Jacobs's four monthly publications, *Jacobs' Band Monthly*, *Jacobs' Orchestra Monthly*, *Tuneful Yankee* (after 1918 called *Melody*), and *Cadenza*, each of which contained at least two full arrangements or original compositions by staff composers. Nearly half of the compositions that appeared in these publications for a period of nearly two decades were written by Cobb.

Cobb's compositions contained in *Jacobs' Band Monthly* and *Jacobs' Orchestra Monthly* allowed for interchangeable parts and/or doubling of parts and were orchestrated primarily for small dance bands that were the fashion of the time period. These syncopated compositions included most of the standard dance band formats of the day: the one-step, two-step, fox trot, waltz, march, and so on. His most popular arrangement was a parody of the "Peer Gynt Suite" entitled "Peter Gink—One-Step," a 1918 composition published separately as sheet music as well as in *Jacobs' Band Monthly*.

The compositions in *Tuneful Yankee/Melody* were primarily popular Tin Pan Alley type songs or piano rags. Many of Cobb's compositions appeared only in these two magazines and were not copyrighted or published separately. Most of Cobb's original compositions that appeared in these magazines were copyrighted by Walter Jacobs, but in individual magazines Cobb was credited as the composer of each of his songs contained therein. The record thus suggests that Cobb worked as a salaried employee and/or agreed to give up royalty money. Cobb's somewhat lackadaisical attitude about copyrighting popular songs is affirmed by his own words. Around 1918 he began to write a monthly column for *Melody* called "Just between You and Me" in which he answered readers' questions about composing and marketing popular songs. In his February 1918 column Cobb advised a reader that it was not necessary to copyright a popular song before submitting it to a publisher. This advice was possibly elicited by the viewpoint he expressed in his September 1918 column, that "Writing popular music is not really composing."

In addition to the band arrangements and popular songs published in the Walter Jacobs magazines, Cobb also wrote band arrangements for several of the *Jacobs' Dance Folios* and many musical pieces for silent movies published in *Musical Mosaics*, a Walter Jacobs series. Not necessarily composed for a particular film, these compositions were short (often only several lines), and each piece had a title and a description of what types of scenes it was to be used for.

Cobb is also remembered for his novelty ragtime piano compositions, several of the best known of which were published under different auspices. Among them was his 1918 arrangement of Rachmaninoff's Prelude in C-sharp Minor entitled "That Russian Rag," published by Will Rossiter. This particular composition, which sold well over one million copies, was recorded both as an instrumental version by James Reese Europe's Hellfighter's Band in the 1920s and later, in the 1950s, as an original piano solo by Joe "Fingers" Carr. Cobb's ragtime compositional style was marked by complex harmonic patterns and difficult technical demands, both of which lead one to surmise that he was an excellent pianist, though there is no record of his ever having performed.

Cobb's compositions have yet to be totaled, but roughly one thousand pieces were published in Jacobs's monthly magazines, and that alone makes him one of the most prolific composers/arrangers of his time. His versatility as a composer/arranger and the quality of his work no doubt guaranteed him a long, successful career in the music industry. His compositions were published by Walter Jacobs Publishers well into the 1930s, but it is unclear when he retired as a staff composer.

Few details are known about Cobb's life outside of music, but he appears to have been well known and liked in the community around Boston. He was married to Claire Bailey but had no children and later was divorced. He was an active Mason and held the position of secretary of the Chamber of Commerce of Brookline and Newton, Massachusetts. He was a securities salesman at the time of his death, of coronary thrombosis and duodenal ulcer, in a convalescent home in Brookline.

• A partial list of Cobb's piano ragtime compositions appears in David Jasen and Trebor Tichenor, *Rags and Ragtime: A Musical History* (1978). Walter Jacobs's magazines *Cadenzo, Jacobs' Orchestra Monthly,* and *Tuneful Yankee/Melody* are available on microfilm at the Library of Congress. For a short biography see Jasen, *Tin Pan Alley: The Composers, the Songs, the Performers, and Their Times: The Golden Age of American Popular Music from 1886 to 1956* (1988). An obituary is in the *Brookline Chronicle,* 31 Dec. 1942.

KAREN HARROD REGE

COBB, Howell (7 Sept. 1815–9 Oct. 1868), lawyer and politician, was born at Cherry Hill in Jefferson County, Georgia, the son of John Addison Cobb, a planter, and Sarah Robinson (Rootes). Enrolling in Franklin College (now the University of Georgia) in Athens, Georgia, in 1829, he graduated in 1834. His college years were marked by his expulsion from school after participating in a riot to protest disciplinary action by the faculty for a minor infraction of leaving campus without permission; he was later readmitted. At the same time, they saw him first show signs of his strong Unionism, for he opposed the nullification movement in South Carolina. On 26 May 1835 he married Mary Ann Lamar; the couple had six children. With marriage Cobb acquired his wife's sizable estate, including several cotton plantations and some 200 slaves.

Cobb studied law and was admitted to the bar in February 1836. That year also saw him commence his political career in earnest when he served as a Democratic presidential elector pledged to Martin Van Buren's candidacy. The following year, as a reward for his support, he became solicitor general for the state's western judicial circuit, covering northeast Georgia; he served in this position until 1841. In 1843 he won election to Congress, serving four consecutive terms in the House of Representatives (1843–1851), the last two as Speaker of the House (although it took sixty-three ballots to secure his election). In 1844 he reluctantly abandoned his support for Van Buren and endorsed the candidacy of James K. Polk; at the same time he gradually came to support the annexation of Texas. In the wake of the Mexican War he opposed efforts to unify white southerners regardless of party to promote the section's interests, preferring to work within the constraints of party politics. As Speaker during the debates on the Compromise of 1850, he mustered support first for Henry Clay's compromise package and later for Stephen Douglas's resubmission of its elements as separate bills.

Cobb's commitment to the Union and to the Democratic party placed him increasingly at odds with those white southerners who advocated the realignment of political allegiances along sectional lines and were willing to exercise the prerogative of secession to protect southern interests. In Georgia these differences were reflected in the replacement of the old Democratic-Whig rivalry with a contest between states' rights adherents and Unionists. Cobb joined the latter group, working alongside former Whig opponents, including Alexander H. Stephens and Robert Toombs. The Unionists triumphed in elections for a state convention in 1850; in turn that convention endorsed Cobb's role in the passage of the Compromise of 1850 by passing the Georgia Platform, which pledged Georgia's adherence to the compromise so long as northerners complied with the Fugitive Slave Act of 1850.

In 1851 Cobb ran for governor on the Unionist ticket, defeating Southern Rights candidate Charles J. McDonald. In office he supported educational reform; health care for blind, deaf, and mute Georgians; improvements in the care of mental illness; property tax reform; railroad construction; and the virtual closure of the state bank. However, his party's problematic relationship to the still-dominant Democratic-Whig system on the national level caused him endless difficulty; while Cobb had been willing to use the patronage directed his way by President Millard Fillmore, he did not want to enter into formal association with the Whigs. When the Southern Rights faction dissolved, its adherents claimed that they would reconstitute the state's Democratic party, thus leaving Cobb out in the cold. Eventually Cobb maintained his ties with the national Democratic organization, although he remained on uneasy terms with the state party.

After failing to secure Georgia's Democratic nomination for U.S. senator in 1853, Cobb retired to his law practice but maintained an avid interest in politics. Although he originally supported the Kansas-Nebraska Act, he had second thoughts when he observed its impact on Democratic unity. Declining an appointment as minister to Spain in 1854, he stayed clear of Benjamin Pierce's administration and moved to support the presidential ambitions of James Buchanan. In 1855 he returned to the U.S. House of Representatives, chairing the Ways and Means Committee; he also served on the committee formed to determine the punishment for Representative Preston Brooks for beating Senator Charles Sumner with a cane while Sumner sat at his desk in the Senate chamber. Pointing out that no rule existed to discipline Brooks, Cobb argued that the House could take no action. Such a position suggested his willingness to appease southern rights advocates in an effort to advance his political career within the Democratic party.

Cobb campaigned for Buchanan during the 1856 presidential contest. Speaking to northern audiences, he left them with the belief that he supported the right of a territory's residents to exclude slavery long before applying for statehood, although in fact he preferred to postpone that decision as long as possible to enhance slaveholders' chances of winning. With a Democratic victory, Cobb secured his reward when Buchanan named him Secretary of the Treasury, although Cobb had set his sights on the State Department. In the cabinet Cobb supported the president's course in Kansas, including Buchanan's decision to publicly endorse and politically endure Robert J. Walker's adverse comments about the future of slavery there as well as the administration's advocacy of the proslavery Lecompton Constitution. This effort to quell sectional discord by bringing matters in Kansas to a quick conclusion backfired, promoting continued divisive debate through 1858, when at last the question of Kansas statehood was postponed. Meanwhile, as treasury secretary Cobb proved unable to offer relief to the nation's economy in the wake of the Panic of 1857; his decision to sell off the government's specie surplus eroded that reserve at a time when the federal government ran a deficit due to declining revenues. Efforts to borrow money through bond sales and through a higher tariff also fell short.

Divisions in the Democratic party, the growing unpopularity of the Buchanan administration, and the rise of the Republicans dampened Cobb's ambitions for the presidency in 1860. In March of that year the state party convention, meeting at Milledgeville, failed to name a slate of delegates solidly committed to his candidacy. At the first national party nominating convention at Charleston, South Carolina, in April, Cobb did not emerge as a serious contender; when, in the wake of that deadlocked meeting, a second convention assembled at Baltimore in June, Stephen Douglas refused to withdraw his candidacy in favor of a Cobb nomination, and Cobb refused to seek a compromise alternative. Cobb's own chances dissolved when bolters from the main Baltimore meeting turned instead to Vice President John C. Breckinridge as their choice. Although Cobb supported Breckinridge, Republican Abraham Lincoln won the election.

Cobb's commitment to the preservation of the Union had eroded during the 1850s, in part because the course of politics rendered his original stance unfeasible if he was to pursue a political career. By 1860 his desire for advancement led him to advocate measures that contributed to the disruption of his once-beloved Democratic party. In the aftermath of Lincoln's victory, Cobb went back on his Unionist principles and supported secession. He resigned his cabinet post on 10 December 1860; on his return to Georgia, he spoke on behalf of immediate secession. Although he was not a delegate to the January 1861 secession convention, he attended its discussions; the next month he served as one of Georgia's representatives to the Montgomery Convention, which established the Confederate States of America. Although he won election as chair of the convention, his ambitions to be named the new slaveholding republic's first president were doomed to disappointment; it was little consolation that he also chaired the provisional congress.

Cobb joined the Confederate army in 1861 as colonel of the 16th Georgia Infantry, and he rose to the rank of brigadier general (1862) and major general (1863). He participated in the campaigns of the Army of Northern Virginia through the battle of Antietam in September 1862, and Robert E. Lee employed him to negotiate prisoner exchanges. While in military service Cobb retained his seat in the Confederate Provisional Congress. In late 1862 he secured a transfer southward to head the military district of Middle Florida; the following September he took command of the Georgia State Guard. When that unit dissolved in early 1864, he took command of the Georgia Reserve Force, but had minimal impact on that year's campaigns in the state. In April 1865 he surrendered to Federal forces at Macon, Georgia.

Following the war, Cobb cultivated the favor of President Andrew Johnson, although he failed to secure a presidential pardon until 4 July 1868. He advocated resistance to congressional reconstruction measures and eventually became an active Democrat, setting forth the unusual proposal that the party should nominate Millard Fillmore for president in 1868. Accompanying his wife to New York City for yet another in her series of efforts to secure medical treatment, he suffered a massive heart attack in the lobby of the Fifth Avenue Hotel, dying instantly.

• Three major collections of Cobb's papers are at Emory University, the University of Georgia, and the Library of Congress. John Eddins Simpson, *Howell Cobb: The Politics of Ambition* (1973), remains the primary scholarly biography, despite its lack of source notes; see also Horace Montgomery, *Howell Cobb's Confederate Career* (1959).

BROOKS D. SIMPSON

COBB, Irvin Shrewsbury (23 June 1876–10 Mar. 1944), newspaperman, author, and humorist, was born in Paducah, Kentucky, the son of Joshua Clark Cobb, a Confederate army soldier and later a tobacco trader, steamboat businessman, and manager of a river-supply store, and Manie Saunders. Cobb attended Paducah schools until 1892 and then became a reporter for the *Paducah Daily News* at $1.75 a week. His father died of alcoholism in 1895, and Cobb had to support the family. He edited the *Daily News* at $12 a week (1895–1897) and was a political reporter and writer of humorous "Kentucky Sourmash" columns for the *Louisville Evening Post* (1898–1901), for which he covered the murder of William Goebel, governor of Kentucky, whose bleeding body he helped carry away (1900). In 1900 Cobb married Laura Spencer Baker of Savannah, Georgia. The couple had one child.

Cobb became managing editor of the *Paducah Daily Democrat*, a new newspaper, and then of what was called the *Paducah News Democrat* when the *Daily Democrat* merged with the *Daily News* (1901–1904). He went to New York City, on money borrowed from his father-in-law, to improve his professional position; joined the staff of the *New York Evening Sun* at $15 a week in 1904; and was sent to cover the Russo-Japanese Peace Conference, held at Portsmouth, New Hampshire, in 1905. Joseph Pulitzer hired him, at $65 a week, for his *New York Evening* and *Sunday World* (1905–1911). He trusted key assignments to Cobb, who also contributed humorous columns called "New York through Funny Glasses," "The Hotel Clerk Says," and "Live Talks with Dead Ones." His salary rose to $150 a week, probably the highest for any American reporter at the time. In 1906 he covered the first trial of Harry Kendall Thaw, the railroad mogul who had murdered the architect Stanford White. Capitalizing on his own system of shorthand, Cobb filed 600,000 words and gained international renown for his seriocomic accounts. He scripted a musical comedy, *Funabashi* (1907), in five days. He sold "The Escape of Mr. Trimm," his first short story, for $500 to the *Saturday Evening Post* in 1909; it is a grim tale of a bank embezzler who fails in an escape bid. Cobb wrote many more Poesque stories in the same vein. "Words and Music" (*Post*, 28 Oct. 1911) is the first of his more than forty stories featuring Judge Priest, a clever, loquacious old jurist. Quitting regular newspaper work, Cobb joined the *Post* as staff contributor, writing fiction, articles, and essays (1912–1922). Meanwhile, George H. Doran, Cobb's main book publisher, issued his first two collections, both in 1912: *Cobb's Anatomy* and *Back Home: Being the Narrative of Judge Priest and His People.*

During World War I the *Post* dispatched Cobb to Europe twice as a frontline war correspondent. In 1914 he went to Belgium, France, and Germany, was often in extreme danger, observed horrific scenes, was held captive by German soldiers for three weeks, and filed neutral dispatches. In 1918, after the United States entered the war, he went again, this time to file pro-Allied reports on American military action in France. Betweentimes, he published a collection of his early *Post* dispatches titled *Paths of Glory: Impressions of War Written at and near the Front* (1915), lectured widely on the war (1915), was critical of Germany in *Speaking of Prussians* (1917), and interviewed President Woodrow Wilson (1917). He also published his most popular book, *Speaking of Operations* (1915), which is a comic response to his hernia surgery and satirizes cold medical specialists and modern technology, as well as *The Glory of the Coming: What Mine Eyes Have Seen of Americans in Action in This Year of Grace and Allied Endeavor* (1918), which is a collection of his final *Post* reports. Cobb's cleverest postwar coup was "Oh, Well, You Know How Women Are!" (*American Magazine*, Oct. 1919). This was a response—all planned beforehand—to Mary Roberts Rinehart's bestselling anti-male whimsy, "Isn't that Just Like a Man?" Listing women's self-effacing activities, Cobb closed his soft jibe by agreeing that we do indeed know how women are. Cobb was also active in the movie and radio industries. He wrote his first movie script in 1919. He and his close friend Will Rogers combined talents in *Boys Will Be Boys*, based on a Cobb story and starring Will Rogers, in 1921. Two years later, Cobb not only took a film role in *The Great White Way* but was also featured on radio in the pioneering "Eveready Hour" as a southern comic.

Signing on as staff contributor of the *Cosmopolitan* (1922–1932), Cobb continued writing at an incredible pace. Twenty-eight of his sixty-one books were issued in his heyday decade of the 1920s. *The Abandoned Farmers* (1920) is about life in a barn while the Cobbs built a country house near Ossining, in Westchester County, New York. The centerpiece of *Snake Doctor and Other Stories* (1923) is the prizewinning "Snake Doctor," his most hypnotic horror story—about ophidian superstitions, white-trash swamp life, jealousy, murder, and grisly retribution. *A Laugh a Day Keeps the Doctor Away* (1923) and *Many Laughs for Many Days* (1925) collect many of Cobb's short jokes. *Alias Ben Alibi* (1925) neatly links episodes about several newspapermen and a complex editor. *Here Comes the Bride—and So Forth* (1925) gathers Cobb's essays on miscellaneous subjects, including marriage, manners, bores, zoo animals, holidays, the insanity plea, and after-dinner speakers. *Some United States* (1926) is one of Cobb's "Guyed Books" and contains squibs about several states. *Red Likker* (1929) is a sentimental novel of sociohistorical interest about the rise and fall of Kentucky's so-called "Bourbon Aristocracy."

After the crash of 1929, which cost him dearly, Cobb turned restless and was often ill. In addition to a steady, though diminished, stream of publications, he debuted on a national radio network in 1933 and reappeared three years later in his own show. Meanwhile, he had moved to Santa Monica, California, to act in several movies, most notably *Steamboat round the Bend*, with Will Rogers (1935), and *Pepper*, with Slim Summerville and Jane Withers (1936). In 1943 the Cobbs moved back to New York City. Already weakened by chronic ulcers and diabetes, Cobb took to his bed with dropsy, relished and entertained many old friends who visited him, and died in a coma.

Irvin S. Cobb is now remembered only as a humorist. But he should also be celebrated as the most famous newspaperman of his times, as a popular radio, movie, and lecture-circuit personality, and as a spellbinding short-story writer. Critics during his lifetime compared him to Bret Harte, O. Henry, Jack London, Edgar Allan Poe, and Mark Twain. Recently, however, he has been too exclusively defined as a cracker-barrel sage satirizing little but familiar targets. In truth, however, Cobb was one of the most talented and versatile Americans who ever lived.

• Cobb's papers are scattered in more than fifty repositories. Most of them, however, are in the Crabbe Library, Eastern Kentucky University, Richmond; in the King Library, University of Kentucky, Lexington; and in the Butler Library, Columbia University, New York City. *Exit Laughing* (1941) is Cobb's delightful, rambling autobiography. His daughter Elisabeth Cobb's *My Wayward Parent: A Book about Irvin S. Cobb* (1945) is understandably loving and biased. Anita Lawson's *Irvin S. Cobb* (1984) is a thorough, objective biography. George H. Doran, Cobb's main publisher, reminisces in *Chronicles of Barabbas* (1952). Wayne Chatterton, *Irvin S. Cobb* (1986), is the best critical evaluation and includes a thorough primary and secondary bibliography. H. L. Mencken has a chapter, titled "The Heir of Mark Twain," in *Prejudices: First Series* (1919), in which he downgrades Cobb's humor. More positive is Norris Wilson Yates, who in *The American Humorist: Conscience of the Twentieth Century* (1964) compares and contrasts Cobb and Will Rogers. John Tebbel, *The American Magazine: A Compact History* (1969), discusses Cobb as a contributor to *McClure's Magazine* and the *Saturday Evening Post*. Evaluations of Cobb as a war correspondent are contained in Joseph J. Mathews, *Reporting the*

Wars (1957); Frank Luther Mott, *American Journalism: A History, 1690–1960* (3d ed., 1962); and John Hohenberg, *Foreign Correspondence: The Great Reporters and Their Times* (1964). Edward J. O'Brien, in "The Best Sixty-three American Short Stories of 1917," *Bookman* 46 (Feb. 1918): 696–706, explains why three of Cobb's short stories, "Boys Will Be Boys," "The Family Tree," and "Quality Folks," are among the best short stories published in 1917. An obituary is in the *New York Times*, 11 Mar. 1944.

ROBERT L. GALE

COBB, Lee J. (9 Dec. 1911–11 Feb. 1976), stage, film, and television actor, was born Leo Jacob Cobb on New York City's Lower East Side, the son of Benjamin Jacob Cobb, a compositor for the Yiddish newspaper *Daily Forward*, and Kate Neilecht. As a child, Leo was a gifted musician, but his study of violin and harmonica ended when he broke his wrist. At age seventeen he left New York for California and premiered as an actor with the Pasadena Playhouse in 1929. He returned to New York in 1929 and, until 1931, attended the City College of New York in the evening while he also acted on the radio. He then performed and directed with the Pasadena Playhouse from 1931 through 1933. He made his Broadway debut on 22 January 1934 as Koch and the Saloon Keeper in *Crime and Punishment*.

Cobb worked often in the 1930s with the renowned Group Theatre in New York. The Group was known for its highly realistic performances that emphasized ensemble work and for its left-wing point of view. Among its most notable members were Lee Strasberg, Harold Clurman, Cheryl Crawford, Morris Carnovsky, Stella Adler, Luther Adler, Phoebe Brand, Jules (lated changed to John) Garfield, Elia Kazan, Sanford Meisner, Robert Lewis, and Clifford Odets.

A permanent member since 1936, Cobb appeared in numerous Group Theatre productions, including *Waiting for Lefty* (1935), by Clifford Odets; *Johnny Johnson* (in New York in 1936 and in London in 1938), by Paul Green; and *Golden Boy* (in New York in 1937 and in London in 1938), by Odets. Cobb, who was then in his twenties, was known for playing character roles for the group, such as the sixty-year-old father in the touring production of *Golden Boy*. He also displayed a talent for comedy in the group's production of Irwin Shaw's *The Gentle People* (1939). Cobb appeared in a number of other New York productions in the 1930s and 1940s, including *Mother* (1935), at the leftist Theatre Union; *The Fifth Column* (1940); *Clash by Night* (1941), directed by Lee Strasberg; and *Jason* (1942), as a replacement for Alexander Knox, the star of the comedy.

During the late 1930s and early 1940s Cobb also began to establish his film career, going to Hollywood in 1937 under an agreement between the Group Theatre and independent producer Walter Wanger. Cobb was immediately successful as a character actor and among his best-known early films were *Golden Boy* (1939) and *The Song of Bernadette* (1943). World War II disrupted Cobb's career. In 1943 the actor joined the Army Air Corps and was assigned to a radio unit and also per-

formed in Moss Hart's *Winged Victory*. After his discharge he continued his film career, appearing, for example, in the suspense film *Northside 777* (1948).

However, Cobb was drawn back to the New York stage by a script that was given to him by Elia Kazan. Arthur Miller's classic *Death of a Salesman* provided Cobb with his most acclaimed role, that of Willy Loman, the salesman destroyed by his pursuit of the American dream. *Death of a Salesman* premiered in New York on 10 February 1949; it was Cobb's first stage performance after his military service and time in Hollywood. All subsequent portrayals of Willy Loman have been compared to his seminal performance, which is often described as Shakespearean in stature. As Brooks Atkinson noted in his review in the *New York Times*, "Lee J. Cobb gives a heroic performance. . . . Mr. Cobb's tragic performance of the defeated salesman is acting of the first rank. Although it is familiar and folksy in the details, it has something of the grand manner in the big size and deep tone." In his longer 20 February 1949 review, Atkinson went on to say: "Lee J. Cobb brings a touch of human grandeur to the acting. He keeps it on the high plane of tragic acting—larger than the specific life it is describing. Willy is not a great man, but his tragedy is pure, partly because of the power and range of Mr. Cobb's acting. . . . Mr. Cobb fills the play with so much solid humanity. . . . Mr. Cobb knows what Willy is worth, and so do all of us." For his performance the actor received the Donaldson Award and won *Variety*'s New York Drama Critics' Poll. Cobb's internal reality coupled with his hulking, stooped physical representation brought Willy to life. Almost thirty-five years later, when Dustin Hoffman played the role, critics still expressed concern about the physical disparity between Hoffman and Cobb. Ironically, Fredric March, not Cobb, was cast as Willy in the film version.

Early in the 1950s Cobb appeared on stage in a revival of *Golden Boy* (1952), in which he again played Mr. Bonaparte, and in *The Emperor's New Clothes* (1953). However, the hunt for Communists among theater and film personalities by the House Un-American Activities Committee (HUAC) cast a shadow over Cobb's career. For two years, according to Cobb, he refused to cooperate with the committee and testify about his and other colleagues' political activities in the 1930s, but he relented in 1953 when it became apparent that his refusal was keeping him from getting work in Hollywood. Cobb cooperated with HUAC, admitting that he had joined the Communist party briefly during his tenure with the Group Theatre. He defended his affiliation with the party by noting that he left quickly when he discovered the totalitarian control it exerted over members. However, in his testimony Cobb named twenty other people as having had Communist affiliation, including his Group Theatre colleagues Morris Carnovsky, Phoebe Brand, and J. Edward Bromberg. Not long after testifying, Cobb had a major, life-threatening heart attack. Cobb married Helen Beverly in 1940; they had a son and a daughter and were divorced in 1952. Cobb claimed that his first wife was institutionalized for alcoholism because of the pressures exerted by the investigations of the House Un-American Activities Committee.

In the years following his testimony, Cobb's Hollywood career improved. Among his best known films of the 1950s and 1960s were *On the Waterfront* (1954), directed by Elia Kazan, who had also turned informant when he testified before HUAC; *The Man in the Gray Flannel Suit* (1956); *Twelve Angry Men* (1957); *Three Faces of Eve* (1957); *Exodus* (1960); *How the West Was Won* (1962); and *Come Blow Your Horn* (1963). Cobb was twice nominated for Academy Awards for best supporting actor, first in 1954 for the role of Johnny Friendly, the vulgar and corrupt labor boss in *On the Waterfront*, and again in 1958 for his role of the father in *The Brothers Karamazov*.

During this same time period, Cobb also frequently appeared on television, often in live dramatic series. He performed in teleplays for "Ford Theatre," "Producers Showcase," "Playhouse 90," "Dupont Show of the Month," and "Studio One." In 1955 he starred in a live TV adaptation of Arthur Koestler's anti-Stalinist *Darkness at Noon*, the theme of which mirrored Cobb's own experiences with the House Un-American Activities Committee. His best known television performance was as Willy Loman in the 1966 adaptation of *Death of a Salesman*. He married Mary Hirsch in 1957, with whom he had two sons.

By the late 1960s Cobb's career had deteriorated, and he was reduced to doing second-rate films and television series, in which he was often miscast, though highly paid. Among the movies he appeared in during the last decade of his life were *In Like Flint* (1967), *Coogan's Bluff* (1968), *The Liberation of L. B. Jones* (1970), and *The Exorcist* (1973). He also had a continuing, supporting role in the TV series "The Virginian." The one highpoint during this period in his career was the 1968 production of *King Lear* at the Vivian Beaumont Theatre at New York's Lincoln Center, in which he played the title role, unfortunately to mixed reviews. Cobb died at his home in Woodland Hills, California.

Cobb was an actor of great versatility and stature. His performance career and style was greatly shaped by his work in the 1930s with the Group Theatre. His powerful physical presence, combined with his representation of honest humanity, often imbued his theater and film characters with a stature that made them memorable. While recognized by the public for his numerous roles in popular movies, Cobb told interviewers that he had never done any acting in a film that was as rewarding as his work in the theater. Possibly he was publicly recognizing that his later film work was not of the quality and stature of his earlier stage performances. Still, in his *New York Times* obituary, Arthur Miller was quoted as saying: "Lee is the greatest dramatic actor I ever saw."

• A filmography of Cobb's roles can be found in Ephraim Katz, *The Film Encyclopedia*, 2d ed. (1994). Articles on Cobb that detail his theater career can be found in Walter Rigdon,

ed., *The Biographical Encyclopedia and Who's Who of the American Theatre* (1966); William C. Young, ed., *Famous Actors and Actresses on the American Stage: Documents of American Theatre History* (1975); Gerald Bordman, ed., *The Oxford Companion to American Theatre* (1992); and Don B. Wilmeth and Tice L. Miller, eds., *The Cambridge Guide to American Theatre* (1993). There are also extended references to Cobb's career in Victor S. Navasky, *Naming Names* (1980), and Wendy Smith, *Real Life Drama: The Group Theatre and America, 1931–1940* (1990). Atkinson's original reviews of *Death of a Salesman* can be found in the *New York Times*, 11 and 20 Feb. 1949. Popular articles that provide useful information include "Higher Call," *New Yorker*, 26 Mar. 1949, p. 21; "He Wears Well," *Newsweek*, 26 Jan. 1959, pp. 98–99; and M. Nichols, "Lee J. Cobb: Man of the Ages," *Coronet*, Nov. 1960, p. 16. Obituaries are in *Variety Obituaries* (1988) and the *New York Times*, 12 Feb. 1976.

ALVIN GOLDFARB

COBB, Lyman (18 Sept. 1800–26 Oct. 1864), educator and author, was born in Lenox, Massachusetts, the son of Elijah William Cobb and Sally Whitney. His early years are shrouded in obscurity, but he most likely obtained an education in local country schools before entering the teaching profession at the age of sixteen. Cobb made his greatest contribution to the field of primary education as the author of numerous school textbooks, the first of which—*Cobb's Spelling Book*—appeared sometime between 1819 and 1821. Having at some point relocated to upstate New York, he married Hannah Chambers of Tompkins County, New York, in April 1822; the couple had eight children.

Cobb entered the field of primary education just as a great reform movement was beginning to take shape. Widespread dissatisfaction with the quality of instruction in so-called district schools extended to the poor-quality textbooks then in use. Following the publication of his first book (which was well received and went through numerous revisions and updates between 1821 and 1849), Cobb continued to produce school textbooks at a steady pace. These included *Just Standard for Pronouncing the English Language* (1825), *Spelling Book* (1826), *Expositor* (1835), and a series of *Juvenile Readers* (nos. 1, 2, and 3; 1831) that marked a real innovation in textbook instruction. Before 1825 most children's primary texts had been written with the assumption that the child was merely a small adult and, consequently, promoted instruction by memorization and rote recitation. Cobb, heavily influenced by educational reformers such as J. H. Pestalozzi (who thought that schooling should stimulate personal growth in mind and spirit and that instruction should be geared to the child's stage of development), tried to make his books not only interesting but educational as well, hoping in the process to avoid students "becom[ing] disgusted or fatigued" by the type of textbook then available in American schools.

Concerns about the quality of textbooks were related to issues regarding the "American-ness" of the available books, including the use of "American" spellings and a focus on "American" culture. Driven by feelings of patriotism as well as a desire for profits, several strongwilled authors competed during this period for recognition of their efforts. Noah Webster, author of the famous *American Dictionary of the English Language* (1828), engaged in a dispute (soon labeled the "War of the Dictionaries") with Joseph Emerson Worchester concerning the authorship and accuracy of each other's work. The dispute, fueled in part by nebulous copyright standards, soon expanded to spelling books. Cobb launched a campaign to support his own writings while denigrating the efforts of other authors. He wrote letters to newspapers, spoke with teachers, and even offered a prize in the *Albany Argus* for the best essay on American school spelling books. Failing to receive an entry, Cobb himself published a review of all available spelling books (*A Critical Review of Noah Webster's Spelling Book* [1828]), focusing his attack on Webster's efforts in the field. In the book he urged "that correct systems of education be adopted," and that spelling books were "the first elementary work placed in the hands of the scholar. From this he derives his earliest impressions of the nature and utility of the language in which he is to speak and write."

The controversy simmered until 1831, when Webster successfully engineered an extension of existing copyright laws (from fourteen to twenty-eight years) through Congress. While in Washington, Webster collected a large number of testimonials regarding his work, which he then published across the nation. Cobb, enraged by this new provocation (as well as by Webster's publisher's description of Cobb as "a schoolmaster in one of our western villages, who had the misfortune to compile a Spelling-Book and small Dictionary"), was moved to action. He produced *A Critical Review of the Orthography of Dr. Webster's Series of Books for Systematick [sic] Instruction in the English Language . . .* (1831), in which he alleged that Aaron Ely, Webster's assistant, had actually completed the spelling book. Webster's equally harsh retort (*To the Friends of American Literature* [1831]) stated that "the tenor of [Cobb's] remarks discovers indeed a degree of persevering malevolence rarely exhibited even in this world of evil; but the weakness of the man must be equal to his malevolence, if he supposes that twenty wagon loads of such pamphlets distributed by mail would do me any harm or himself any good." Webster was only partly correct, for while his own superiority in the field was never challenged, the controversy helped Cobb sell several million copies of his books.

Cobb continued to produce school texts, most notably the *North American Reader* (1835), which contributed to the conscious effort to nationalize instructional literature by textbook writers who were loyal and nationalistic Americans, wanted to get rich by establishing one book or methodology as dominant, and were motivated partly by egotism. His primary contribution to pedagogical theory was *The Evil Tendencies of Corporal Punishment* (1847), in which Cobb listed thirty "objections" to the practice, along with forty "substitutes for and preventives of, the use of the rod." The book was well received and earned commendations from such educational leaders as Thomas Hopkins Gallaudet and Horace Mann.

Cobb relocated around 1860 to Westchester County, New York, where he spent the last years of his life with his son Lyman, Jr., a noted local Episcopal clergyman who in earlier years had assisted in his father's work. Cobb died at Colesburg, Potter County, Pennsylvania.

Cobb's career took place during the first great push towards reform in American education. His efforts in the field of textbook production, although superseded by others, provide insight into the actions and motives of the men involved in the effort to improve American public schools.

• A small collection of Cobb correspondence is in the Benson J. Lossing Papers at the Rutherford B. Hayes Library, Fremont, Ohio. Secondary literature on Cobb is scarce, but his controversy with Webster receives coverage in Harry R. Warfel, *Noah Webster: Schoolmaster to America* (1936). He also receives mention in Ervin C. Shoemaker, *Noah Webster: Pioneer of Learning* (1936), and in J. T. Scharf, *History of Westchester County* (1886). An obituary is in the *Ithaca (N.Y.) Journal*, 1 Mar. 1865.

EDWARD L. LACH, JR.

COBB, Stanley (10 Dec. 1887–25 Feb. 1968), physician, neurologist, and psychiatrist, was born in Brookline, Massachusetts, the son of John Candler Cobb, a developer of Boston's South Bay, and Leonore Smith of New York. A solitary child, handicapped by stammering, Cobb was tutored at home during his early years. He enjoyed observing birds and animals and developed a lifelong interest in natural history. His interest during his teenage years in pursuing a medical career received impetus from the comment of a distinguished surgeon, who on observing Cobb's deftness in skinning a shrew, remarked, "With that ability you should go into medicine!" (White, p. 13).

After entering Harvard College in 1906, Cobb developed socially, but his stammering persisted. His interest in medical research received encouragement from publication as coauthor with Professor W. E. Castle of *Studies of Inheritance in Rabbits* (publication no. 114 of the Carnegie Institution in Washington). After graduation from college in 1910, Cobb entered Harvard Medical School. During one summer spent studying pathology at the Boston Floating Hospital, he was apprehensive about presenting his autopsy specimens to a group of distinguished visiting doctors. Their hearty applause greatly enhanced his self-esteem.

In spring 1914, before his medical school graduation that June, Cobb undertook a surgical internship at the Peter Bent Brigham Hospital in Boston. Having already planned to concentrate on the nervous system as his medical career, he heeded the recommendation of Harvey Cushing, the neurosurgeon and chief of surgery at the Brigham, that he complete an internship in surgery, to be followed by European study and then a suitable residency. After the internship and Cobb's marriage in July 1915 to Elizabeth Mason Almy, the couple moved to Baltimore, Maryland, for a stay of four years, during which their three children were born. In Baltimore, Cobb worked for several months on the sympathetic nervous system in cats under William Henry Howell, professor of physiology at Johns Hopkins University, and published a brief note as sole author in the *American Journal of Physiology* (46 [1918]: 478–82). In 1916 Cobb's primary mentor, Adolf Meyer, director of the Henry Phipps Psychiatric Clinic, established for Cobb a laboratory, where he used a modified string galvanometer to study muscle-fiber contractions in various nervous-system disorders, including chorea (*Johns Hopkins Hospital Bulletin* 30 [1919]: 336–41) and hysteria (*Archives of Neurology and Psychiatry* 4 [1920]: 8–15). In 1917 entry of the United States into World War I was imminent, and to avoid immediate draft Cobb was advised to stop his laboratory research and take an internship on Meyer's psychiatric service to prepare himself for useful military duty. He was inducted as a first lieutenant in September 1918 and, after two preliminary assignments, wound up on the head-injury service of Philadelphia's prominent neurosurgeon, Lieutenant Colonel Charles Frazier, at U.S. Army General Hospital No. Eleven in Cape May, New Jersey.

After the war Meyer tried to persuade Cobb to remain in Baltimore, but despite his appreciation of Meyer as a person and of Meyer's psychobiological approach to psychiatry, Cobb chose to follow his own roots to Boston. David L. Edsall, dean of Harvard Medical School, with no position to offer Cobb, gave constructive suggestions about how he might fit into the Boston academic and hospital scene and support his family. Cobb occupied a private office at the Massachusetts General Hospital in 1919–1920. Then in 1920, after the unexpected death of Elmer E. Southard, Bullard Professor of Neuropathology at Harvard Medical School, Cobb inherited Southard's laboratory there and later his professorship.

From 1923 to 1925 Cobb traveled in England, France, the Netherlands, and Germany as a fellow of the General Education Board of the Rockefeller Foundation, which was active in funding progressive teaching and research programs in medicine. At the Deutsche Forschungsanstalt für Psychiatrie (German Psychiatric Research Institute) in Berlin, Cobb learned Oskar Vogt's meticulous technique for studying the microscopic architecture of the brain. Then he and Max Bielschowsky, whose laboratory was in the same building, devised a special intravital stain that, when injected intravenously into an experimental animal, would selectively stain the desired tissues for post-mortem microscopic examination. This stain is described in the *Journal für Psychologie und Neurologie* (31 [1925]: 301–4). Cobb intended to use it in his own studies of cerebral blood vessels with the thought that localized oxygen depletion might play a role in epileptic seizures. After his return to Boston, Cobb taught John H. Talbott, who later became the editor of the *Journal of the American Medical Association*, to master Vogt's technique for studying the microanatomy of the

brain, with particular reference to the cerebral circulation that Cobb was investigating in relation to the seizures in epilepsy. Further information was obtained in Cobb's laboratory from the method developed by Henry Stone Forbes for examining the circulation in the superficial blood vessels of the cat's brain as viewed through an artificial opening in the skull. Then in 1929, as a part of the epilepsy work, Cobb and his colleagues Forbes and Harold Wolff, using the skull-window approach in cats, made fine photomicrographs showing dilation of the meningeal arteries after injections of histamine (*American Journal of Physiology* 89 [1929]: 266–72).

Cobb's plans for his neurological unit at the Boston City Hospital awaited space in a medical building that was completed in 1930. During the interval Cobb conducted the neurological service from his laboratory at the Harvard Medical School. In addition, he taught a neuropathology course for second-year medical students. His ambidextrous drawing of cross sections of the spinal cord on the blackboard, simultaneously with both hands, was viewed by his students with amazement. After the new building was finished, Cobb's personal work continued to be primarily investigational in an environment enriched by excellent clinical neurology, neurosurgery, and psychiatry.

Cobb's growing interest in psychiatry was stimulated by the improvement in his stammering that followed three months of analytic psychotherapy in 1928 with Leonard Seif of Munich, Germany, who was visiting in the United States. Seif was a disciple of Alfred Adler, an early Freudian, who had questioned Freud's emphasis on sex as excessive, stressed man's inherent lust for power, and attributed to inferiority of the affected organs such psychosomatic symptoms as stammering. Cobb's interest in psychiatry was also stimulated by William Herman, a consultant on the Boston City Hospital neurological unit and a personal friend, who in lectures often emphasized physiologic responses to nervous tension. Cobb later undertook a partial analysis under Hanns Sachs, the successor after 1931 to Franz Alexander as the official training analyst of the by-that-time exclusively Freudian Boston Psychoanalytic Society. Cobb promoted psychoanalysis at Harvard by his medical school appointments and through its laboratory of experimental psychology in Cambridge. Yet he regretted not having seen controlled studies adequate to support psychoanalysis as an academic science. Although, with his laboratory background, Cobb was unable to classify psychoanalysis as a science, he was intrigued by Freud's work because he was convinced that psychoanalysis did in reality bring about change.

Cobb's new psychiatric department at the Massachusetts General Hospital opened in the summer of 1934. Cobb was not only a proficient investigator, a good manager, and an authority on neuropathology and clinical neurology; he was also well oriented in psychiatry. His Harvard and Old Boston background helped him deal with a number of practical problems. Some conservative surgeons believed that psychiatry belonged in isolated institutions outside medicine's mainstream. Some of the resident psychiatrists in answering consultation requests from other departments used psychoanalytic language that confused non-psychiatrists. Other conservative staff members were uncomfortable with the increasing number of Jewish psychiatrists. Cobb handled these problems with both tact and persistence.

Cobb refused to differentiate sharply between functional and organic disorders. By pointing out clinical situations brought about or aggravated by emotional causes, as well as those with potential psychiatric complications, he eloquently demonstrated the connection between psychiatry and mainstream medicine. For teaching about psychosomatic relationships, Cobb looked to Herman. After Herman's sudden death in January 1935, Cobb sought out Felix Deutsch of Vienna, Freud's former personal physician. Originally an internist, Deutsch, after a didactic analysis under Siegfried Bernfeld, was the first to introduce the new term, "psychosomatic," at the 1927 General Medical Congress for Psychotherapy at Bad Nauheim, Germany. Deutsch arrived in Boston in the fall of 1936. His sensitivity and skill in conducting his psychiatric interviews were widely appreciated.

There was widespread collaboration between psychiatry and other departments in caring for the 1942 Coconut Grove fire victims as well as their grieving relatives and friends. Other topics studied on an interdepartmental basis were anxiety related to tonsillectomy in childhood; anorexia nervosa; various forms of colitis; arthritis; neurocirculatory asthenia; studies of pain threshold; and psychological as well as endocrine aspects of thyroid and ovarian disorders. A confidential staff conference took place each week. While the psychiatric resident was presenting the patient's story, Cobb made notes on a blackboard chart, modified from Adolf Meyer's prototype, showing in columns the severity of symptoms, supposedly traumatic events, and relevant medical history. The staff members then, in reverse order of their seniority, would express their views. Cobb, as the senior staff member, would conclude by summarizing what had taken place, without heavy reliance on the traditional textbook diagnosis, and round out the clinical picture.

Popular interest in Freudian psychoanalysis, new and effective medications for combat fatigue, therapeutic contributions from psychoanalysis, and the availability of publicly funded residencies led many returning World War II veterans to seek specialty training in psychiatry. A demanding teacher, Cobb cared about the quality of his students' work and promoted their future personal and professional plans. In publications and in other ways he insisted that they receive full recognition for their work. He attracted foreign students from the United Kingdom and elsewhere. He was on the editorial boards of several neurological and psychiatric journals, and he published an annual review of neuropsychiatric literature for the *Archives of Internal Medicine*. He wrote many review articles for *Psychosomatic Medicine*.

After his retirement in 1954, Cobb studied functional and anatomical aspects of the avian brain in a variety of species, collected avian brains for studies of comparative anatomy at the Peabody Museum, and continued his own laboratory work. A representative article is "On the Angle of the Cerebral Axis in the American Woodcock" (*Auk* 67 [1959]: 55–59). When the state employed DDT for mosquito control in 1962, Cobb noted in his own salt pond the extermination of arthropod fiddler crabs along with the insects. A letter to the Barnstable *Patriot* that appeared as "Death of a Salt Pond" in *Audubon Magazine* (65 [1963]: 70–72) and in Audubon publications throughout the United States was widely quoted and influential in a nationwide environmental struggle. Between his retirement and his death in Cambridge, Massachusetts, Cobb spent three half-days a week at Massachusetts Institute of Technology as a psychiatrist to students. He had a close relationship with the institute's Walle Nauta, a foremost neuroanatomist and head of neurophysiology, to whose laboratory Cobb left the slides from his lectures on neuropsychiatry and ornithology.

Presentation of three Salmon Lectures before the New York Academy of Medicine in 1949 (*Emotions and Clinical Medicine* [1950]) was probably a significant factor in Cobb's being awarded the Salmon Medal later that year. In those lectures Cobb proposed that the rhinencephalon, or primitive nose brain, might not have been just cortex specialized for smell but, through connections in the hypothalamus to the pituitary body, might affect the visceral organs and give rise to various powerful emotions. Cobb also mentioned the work of his research fellow, Paul MacLean, who in 1946 had visited J. W. Papez at Cornell University in Ithaca, New York. Papez had recognized the importance of several coordinated brain structures on the border (limbus) of the fluid-containing lateral ventricles in "A Proposed Mechanism for Emotion" (*Archives of Neurology and Psychiatry* 38 [1937]). In the preface to *Emotions and Clinical Medicine*, Cobb wrote that MacLean "worked out many of the ideas put forward in these and earlier lectures, which we gave as trial runs" in the laboratory. MacLean coined the term "Limbic system" to tie together the coordinated structures that, particularly in stress situations, generate feelings and make decisions independently of the neocortex, or thinking brain.

Bernard Bandler, who transferred from Cobb's staff to Boston University as chief of psychiatry in 1946, recorded in a taped interview (19 Feb. 1978) that he saw Cobb's effectiveness in teaching as coming not so much from his outstanding presentations as from his role as a facilitator who helped students grow in their own way: "As soon as I began to think that way and see Stanley that way, I began to think about great teachers, like Socrates. Stanley, I think, was of that order."

Cobb's comprehensive knowledge of the nervous system, both structurally and functionally, complemented by his openness to change, his knowledge of human nature, his awareness of the feelings of others, his tact in administrative matters, and his strong sense of purpose, came to fruition at the Massachusetts General Hospital. At this in many ways traditional institution, he was able to overcome attitudinal resistance and achieve the first psychiatric service fully integrated into an American general hospital. Cobb derived deep satisfaction from the professional careers of his psychiatric residents and fellows, a number of whom worked in general hospital settings.

• Cobb's papers are in the Francis A. Countway Library of Medicine in Boston, along with the directory, *Stanley Cobb, An Inventory of his Correspondence and Related Materials* (1991). A biography by Benjamin V. White, *Stanley Cobb, a Builder of the Modern Neurosciences* (1984), contains biographical sketches of essentially all Cobb's post–World War II residents and assistant residents, as well as listings of all the residents and research fellows from 1934 to Cobb's retirement in 1954. Cobb's guiding interest in relating psychiatry to general medicine and surgery led to his *Borderlands of Psychiatry* (1943), which cites interdisciplinary studies such as anorexia nervosa, neurocirculatory asthenia, and anxiety states. A graphic isosceles triangle in Cobb's *Foundations of Neuropsychiatry*, 3d ed. (1944), reflects his evolving concepts about neuroscience and psychiatry. The theoretical and observational fields, philosophy, psychoanalysis, sociology, and clinical psychiatry are at the triangle's apex. At the triangle's base are the most exact sciences, physics, anatomy, and chemistry, and just above them are pathology, physiology, neurology, and experimental psychology. Cobb describes the gray middle area in between top and bottom as the locus for future investigations, the cutting edge.

BENJAMIN V. WHITE

COBB, Sylvanus, Jr. (5 June 1823–20 July 1887), writer, was born in Waterville, Maine, the son of Sylvanus Cobb, Sr., a Universalist clergyman, and Eunice Hale Waite. Cobb attended high school in Waltham, Massachusetts. Young Cobb's expulsion over a point of English grammar that he argued with his teacher, Master Smith, displayed his tenacious dedication to the written word, which he maintained throughout his prolific writing life. Cobb was reinstated in school through the influence of his father, who was a member of the school board. Rather than pursue a tutorial preparation for college and legal study, however, he chose to work on his father's newspaper, the *Christian Freeman*, as a proofreader, editor, and printer.

In 1841, at the age of seventeen, and without his parent's knowledge, Cobb enlisted in the U.S. Navy as a ship's guard. A relic from his days working on the *Freeman* brought Cobb good luck and promoted his literary career. One day when Cobb was on watch, his captain noticed him scraping his fingernails with a printer's rule. Learning that Cobb had experience with printing, the captain made him his personal clerk and charged Cobb with editing his naval manuscripts. In addition to pulling light and congenial "literary" duty, Cobb's navy experience gave him material for his many romantic tales. The young writer acquired nautical lore, enriched his imagination serving in the Mediterranean, and had the opportunity to observe an exotic Muslim culture. Algiers, Gibraltar, Mahón,

Marseille, Naples, Palermo, Trieste, Tunis, Tripoli, and Venice were among the ports Cobb visited.

After returning from naval service, Cobb married his Waltham High School sweetheart, Mary Jane Head, on 29 June 1845 and set up domestic life in East Boston. The couple had at least one child. About a year later he began, with his brother Samuel Tucker, a weekly temperance paper entitled the *Rechabite*, in which appeared Cobb's first published story, "The Deserter." Cobb served as editor and literary contributor to the *New England Washingtonian* (which had purchased the *Rechabite* in 1848) and the *Waverly Magazine*. Cobb also contributed many short stories and novels to Frederick Gleason's two magazines, *Flag of Our Union* and *Pictorial Drawing Room Companion*. Writing under both his own name and a number of pen names, Cobb was greatly responsible for the commercial successes of the magazines and gained a reputation as a prolific and entertaining author. In the *Flag*, Cobb published his first serial, the literary form that became most closely associated with him. The serial's title, *The Prophet of the Bohmer Wald; or, The Venetian Buccaneer—A Tale of the Time of Joseph II, Emperor of Germany* (1850), reflected Cobb's characteristic romantic subject matter. Another romantic serial that he published at this time was *Fernando; or, The Moor of Castile—A Romance of Old Spain* (1853). In the weekly publications to which Cobb contributed, his novels in serial form typically consisted of about ten installments, each made up of about three chapters.

Cobb advanced his writing career when, in 1856, he signed an exclusive contract with Robert Bonner, the tireless promoter and publisher of the *New York Ledger*. Cobb's first, and perhaps most famous, contribution to the *Ledger* was the commercially successful serial *The Gunmaker of Moscow; or, Vladimir the Monk*.

In 1857 Cobb moved to Norway, Maine, a longed for vacation home of his boyhood, where he became a prominent citizen and public speaker. He served as captain of the Light Infantry, Maine Volunteer Militia, but saw no active service in the Civil War. While living in Maine, Cobb continued to write for the *Ledger*, publishing serials under his own name and contributing travel and adventure sketches under the pseudonym of Colonel Walter B. Dunlap.

In 1869 Cobb and his family moved into a spacious house in Hyde Park, Massachusetts, built especially for the successful author and patriarch. Cobb continued as a civic leader and pursued his involvement with Freemasonry, a commitment he had enthusiastically begun in 1854. An active member of the Masonic fraternity, Cobb held many of its offices over his lifetime and attained the highest Masonic degrees. The Masonic principles of brotherhood and spiritual truth became Cobb's "religion" and also influenced his fiction, most notably in *The Mystic Tie of the Temple* (1868).

A tireless author, Cobb continued to write for the *Ledger* virtually until his death from pneumonia at his Hyde Park home. Although modern critics have found his fiction too sensationalistic, sentimental, and naive,

Cobb was esteemed in his own day for his sympathetic, patriotic character and suspenseful and imaginative fiction, and he was widely and warmly eulogized.

• A sizable collection of miscellaneous Cobb family papers is held at the George Arents Research Library, Syracuse University. Cobb published about 150 serial novels and over 1,000 short stories. The following list of serial novels not cited in the biography indicates the scope of his historical-romantic subject matter, which includes fiction set in the United States, Europe, the Near East, and the Mediterranean world: *The Pioneer Patriot* (1857), *The Scourge of Damascus* (1862), *The Foundling of Milan* (1867), *Florian, the Bandit of Syracuse* (1868), *The Royal Outlaw* (1868), *Blanche of Burgundy* (1876), *Eleanor, the Jewess of Heidelberg* (1865), *The Granadan Duel* (1872), *Rinaldo, the Paladin* (1883), and *The Knight's Motto* (1887). All of these works appeared originally in the *New York Ledger*. A biography of Cobb has been written by his daughter Ella Waite Cobb, *A Memoir of Sylvanus Cobb, Jr.* (1891). Stanwood Cobb, *The Magnificent Partnership* (1954), is a concise dual biography of Sylvanus Cobb and his editor Robert Bonner.

CHARLES ZAROBILA

COBB, Thomas Reade Rootes (10 Apr. 1823–13 Dec. 1862), lawyer and Confederate congressman and military officer, was born in Jefferson County, Georgia, the son of John Addison Cobb, a planter, and Sarah Robinson Rootes. His older brother, Howell Cobb—congressman, governor, and secretary of the treasury under James Buchanan—would be very influential in his life. After graduation from Franklin College (the University of Georgia) in 1841, he studied for the law and was admitted to the bar in 1842. Two years later he married Marion Lumpkin, the daughter of Joseph Henry Lumpkin, a Whig, who became the chief justice of Georgia when a supreme court was created in 1845. Marion and Thomas had six children, but three died in childhood. As a tribute to one of these he founded the Lucy Cobb Institute for the education of young women, which lasted into the early years of the twentieth century. Cobb's interest in educational reform was deep, and he was particularly concerned that southern youth receive a southern education steeped in the values of a hierarchical society based on human bondage.

Cobb's greatest significance lay in his work in the law. He worked, from 1849 to 1857, as the reporter for the Georgia Supreme Court. He also argued cases in that court as well as in other southern courts. He was a driving force in the creation of a law school at the University of Georgia in 1859. An often overlooked part of his legal work concerned the codification of the law of Georgia. Codification was a highly controversial legal movement resisted vigorously by those steeped in the common law. It reduced basic but flexible common law principles to the more rigid language of statutes. Most of the successful codification efforts before the Civil War concerned procedural law, but when Cobb went to work on the law of Georgia he included the substantive principles and rules of common law. This inclusion was very progressive, but because it did not

appear until 1863 the significance of his achievement was lost in the defeat of the Confederacy.

His work on the law of slavery was especially significant. *An Inquiry into the Law of Negro Slavery* (1858), to which he affixed *A Historical Sketch of Slavery from the Earliest Periods* (1859), amounted to a leading apologia for slavery. Southern slavery, for Cobb, was a divinely inspired institution based on racial inferiority. He claimed, for instance, that the "natural affection" of the black "is not strong, and consequently he is cruel to his own offspring, and suffers little by separation from them." Cobb's work on the law of slavery was the preeminent effort by a southerner to lay out that law. His work, however, covered the slave as person but not as property. Cobb promised to treat the latter subject in another volume, and although he had collected some material a second volume never appeared. His attention shifted to the secession movement and to the war.

Despite his legal work Cobb is perhaps remembered more for his role in the secession of Georgia and for his contributions to the Confederacy. Cobb had been a moderate Unionist most of his life and had sought to promote the presidential aspirations of his brother Howell. By the late 1850s he had switched dramatically to become one of the most fiery supporters of secession in order to preserve the society he deemed sacred. He gave a widely circulated and influential speech to the Georgia Assembly in November 1860 in which he argued for and defended the right of secession. Separation was not only constitutional, he claimed, it was necessary because each section was made up of "a distinct people, having different social organizations, different pursuits, different memories, different hopes, different destinies." He spent the next few months speaking around Georgia, urging withdrawal from the Union. Privately he deprecated the timidity of those who wanted Georgia to secede only with other southern states, and when Georgia finally withdrew Cobb worked on the new state constitution. After he and his brother Howell were selected to serve in the provisional Confederate congress, he worked on the Confederate constitution as well.

Despite his efforts he never emerged as a major figure in Confederate politics, and he spent his political energy snarling at those who did. He despised most of them, especially Judah Benjamin, the secretary of war, whom he believed to be inept, and he once referred to Benjamin in a private letter as a "Jew dog" and a "sycophantic dodging Jew." Cobb's desire to protect the society he loved found expression, however, in military service. He studied manuals to learn the art of war, and he organized "Cobb's Legion" in Georgia and took it to Virginia. He worked vigorously to protect the interests of the army in the Confederate congress as well as in the field, and he retained his position in the congress despite his military position, going back and forth between the two. He finally was promoted to the rank of brigadier general in November 1862.

Whether as a southern legalist, proslavery apologist, or Confederate officer, Cobb was at heart an evangelical Presbyterian. His religiosity was sometimes so self-righteous that it exasperated others. After a visit to New Orleans before the war he wrote that he was appalled to see the youth violating the sabbath by flying kites. He also expressed his unbending religion during the war with complaints against a superior officer who insisted on drilling troops on Sunday. Thomas Cobb was very impressed with the puritanical general Thomas J. "Stonewall" Jackson, and his profound commitment to the evangelical religion he practiced colored almost everything he did. To celebrate the secession of South Carolina he had these words spread across the front of his house: "Resistance to Abolition is Obedience to God." He died for that belief at the Battle of Fredericksburg, one month after his promotion to brigadier general and shortly before the Georgia code appeared.

• The most important collection of Cobb's letters is in the University of Georgia Library. Other significant material is in the Georgia Department of Archives and History, Atlanta, and the Perkins Library, Duke University. A full-length biography with a very useful bibliography is William B. McCash, *Thomas R. R. Cobb, 1823–1862: The Making of a Southern Nationalist* (1983). See also George M. Frederickson, *The Black Image in the White Mind: The Debate on Afro-American Character and Destiny, 1817–1914* (1971), and Michael P. Johnson, *Toward a Patriarchal Republic: The Secession of Georgia* (1977). On the role of religion in Cobb's life and thought see Eugene D. Genovese, *"Slavery Ordained of God": The Southern Slaveholders' View of Biblical History and Modern Politics* (1985), and Jack Maddex, Jr., "Proslavery Millennialism: Social Eschatology in Antebellum Southern Calvinism," *American Quarterly* 31 (1979): 46–62.

THOMAS D. MORRIS

COBB, Ty (18 Dec. 1886–17 July 1961), baseball player and manager, was born Tyrus Raymond Cobb in Banks County in northeastern Georgia, the son of William Herschel Cobb and Amanda Chitwood. When Cobb was about six years old, his father, an itinerant schoolmaster, moved the family to Royston in Franklin County. There, William Herschel Cobb served not only as school principal but as editor of the town newspaper, county school superintendent, and, for one term, state senator. Meanwhile, young Tyrus grew up under the demands of being "Professor Cobb's boy," with little enthusiasm for schoolwork but a developing passion for baseball.

In the spring of 1904, much against the wishes of his stern and demanding father, seventeen-year-old Cobb left home to make a career as a professional ballplayer. Initially cut from the roster of the Augusta team in the newly organized South Atlantic League, Cobb returned later that season but performed unimpressively. In 1905, however, he became the league's outstanding player. An outfielder who hit lefthanded and threw righthanded, he led the league in batting average and other offensive categories. In August, the Detroit Tigers of the American League (AL) purchased his contract for $700. He was preparing to leave for Detroit when he received news of his father's death. Hurrying home, he learned that William Herschel Cobb had died from shotgun blasts fired by his wife, who said she had mistaken him for a nighttime prowler.

As local gossips buzzed that her husband had actually been trying to catch her with a lover, Amanda Chitwood Cobb was indicted for voluntary manslaughter and bound over for trial the following spring. Meanwhile, Tyrus (quickly dubbed "Ty" by baseball writers covering the Tigers) finally reached Detroit. In his first major league game on 30 August 1905 at Bennett Park, Detroit, he rapped a double off New York's Jack Chesbro, one of the majors' top pitchers. After this promising beginning, however, he batted only .240 in the forty-one games he played that season, fielded erratically, and failed to solidify his standing with his teammates.

"The most miserable and humiliating experience I've ever been through" was the way, long afterward, that Cobb described spring training in 1906 at Augusta. Besides worrying about the outcome of his mother's trial (she was acquitted late in March), he underwent the kind of hazing by veteran teammates to which baseball rookies were routinely subjected in that period. Naturally sensitive and high-strung, Cobb, a native southerner and a Baptist, found himself in intimate contact with players who were nearly all northern-born, with a large proportion of them Roman Catholics. Unlike other rookies, he could not and would not abide such petty cruelties as having his favorite bats sawed in half, being shouldered away from the plate when he tried to take batting practice, or getting locked out of the bathroom at the team's hotel.

Cobb fought back, both verbally and physically, becoming increasingly an estranged, ostracized figure on the team. He remained alienated from the other players, so much so that he slept with a pistol in his Pullman berth on road trips. When he joined the Detroit club, Cobb later said, "I was just a mild-mannered Sunday School boy. But those old-timers turned me into a snarling wildcat." The aloof, suspicious Cobb went his own way, never really a friend to any of the hundreds of men who would be his teammates during his long career.

Once the 1906 season started, Cobb roomed alone, usually ate alone, and occupied himself—alone. On the ball field, he was a fierce, ruthless competitor, determined to prove his worth as a player and vindicate his family's reputation to people back home in Georgia. Despite missing much of the season because of physical and emotional exhaustion, Cobb established himself as a big-leaguer. He batted .320 in ninety-six games, twenty-five points higher than his nearest teammate. At the end of the season he was "sick at heart and disillusioned. I'd dreamed of becoming part of the Detroit organization, and all I'd known, so far, was jealousy and persecution." His wounds never fully healed.

Cobb battled his teammates again the following spring, when the Tigers again trained at Augusta, and ended up taking a bad beating from a brawny catcher. Hugh Jennings, the Tigers' new manager, even tried to trade his troublesome young star to another AL club. It was Jennings's great good fortune that his efforts were unsuccessful, because that 1907 season Cobb became the league's most spectacular performer. In sparking the Detroit club to its first pennant, he led the league in batting average, base hits, runs batted in, and stolen bases.

Detroit won three consecutive pennants, but lost all three World Series (to the Chicago Cubs in 1907 and 1908 and to the Pittsburgh Pirates in 1909). The franchise, hitherto one of the weakest financially in the league, became one of its most profitable. The single biggest reason for the Tigers' success on the field and at the ticket windows was the "Georgia Peach" (as one Detroit sportswriter nicknamed Cobb). Cobb's hellbent playing style and frequent brawls—with opposing players and fans in other cities, sometimes even with fans in his home ballpark—made him the top gate attraction in baseball.

Cobb won the AL batting title every year from 1907 through 1919, except for 1916 when Cleveland's Tris Speaker beat him out, .386 to .371. Cobb batted .420 in 1911 and .410 in 1912, and in 1915 he stole ninety-six bases—a record that would stand for forty-six years. By then the Georgian's salary had climbed to $20,000 per season, the highest in the sport.

"I have observed," Cobb said in 1914, "that baseball is not unlike war." A decade later, he added, "it is just as sportsmanlike to make the other fellow tremble as to let him make me tremble." Frequently criticized in the press for inflicting injury on opposing infielders, he replied that "The base runner has the right of way and the man who blocks it does it at his own peril." Sooner or later, opponents learned that it was in their best interest not to rile Cobb unnecessarily. "The one thing we didn't want to do was get him mad," recalled Ray Schalk, longtime Chicago White Sox catcher.

Cobb never played on a championship ball club after 1909, although in 1915 and 1916 the Tigers made strong pennant bids. Regardless of his team's fortunes, he remained its dominating presence and the country's most famous baseball player at a time when the sport truly was the "National Pastime."

Beginning in 1919, though, Cobb was overshadowed by the home run-hitting exploits of Babe Ruth. Cobb's "scientific" playing style—based on place-hitting the ball to all parts of the field, dropping unexpected bunts, and derring-do on the base paths—gave way to the Ruth-inspired "big inning" baseball that dominated the game in the twenties. Cobb openly voiced his contempt for Ruth and the other "musclemen" who had taken over "my game." At the same time, he remained puzzled by how Ruth could manage such heroic ballplaying feats in tandem with such heroic feats of dissipation off the field. Cobb had always taken good care of himself, watching his weight and getting plenty of off-season exercise, while Ruth violated every precept Cobb believed vital to success as a professional athlete.

In 1921, following the Tigers' poorest season since Cobb's arrival, the Georgian succeeded Hugh Jennings as Detroit manager. His additional duties did not hurt his ballplaying, as he continued to be among the AL's most dangerous hitters; in 1922 he topped .400 for the third time (.401). After a sixth-place showing in his first season as manager, the Tigers finished third in 1922, second the next year, and third again in 1924. Cobb's Tigers played with plenty of spirit and were loaded with potent hitters; his 1922 outfit batted .316, highest team average in AL history. But his pitching staffs were chronically weak; consequently, none of his teams came closer than six games to winning a pennant.

Demanding, overbearing, often intimidating, Cobb inspired respect but never affection in his players. After the Tigers finished a poor fourth in 1925 and fell to sixth the next season, dissatisfaction with his leadership spread, and he probably would have been forced out anyway. In November 1926, however, American League president Ban Johnson privately confronted Cobb and Tris Speaker (now player-manager at Cleveland) with accusations made by Hubert "Dutch" Leonard, a former Detroit pitcher. Leonard maintained that seven years earlier, he, Cobb, Speaker, and another player had plotted for Cleveland deliberately to lose to Detroit in a game on which the four had placed bets. At Johnson's behest, both Cobb and Speaker resigned their jobs as managers. Both were also released by their teams as players.

Subsequently, Kenesaw Mountain Landis, baseball's all-powerful commissioner, made public Leonard's charges and undertook to determine the truth. After an agonizing month in which the two beleaguered baseball stars vehemently protested their innocence and national press opinion generally rallied around them, Landis pronounced their complete exoneration. Early the following February, Cobb agreed to terms with the venerable Connie Mack, president and manager of the Philadelphia Athletics, for about $70,000 in salary and bonuses for the coming season.

For Cobb, the 1927 season marked a time for vindication. Playing in 133 of his team's 154 games, the forty-year-old Georgian batted .357 (fifth best in the AL) and was a major factor in his new team's best winning percentage since 1914. Cobb always said that he enjoyed playing for the soft-spoken Mack more than anything else he did in baseball. Cobb's feeling for Mack—and lack of any real post-baseball plans—brought him back for one final season in 1928, in which he batted .323 in ninety-five games. He played only sparingly after July. He finally retired, ending a career that produced an overall .367 batting average on 4,191 base hits, plus 893 stolen bases and about forty other offensive marks that were major league or AL records at the time.

When Cobb retired, he was among the first men to have become a millionaire principally from his earnings as a professional athlete—and his prudent use of those earnings. While still in his early twenties, he made the acquaintance of many of Detroit's business elite and invested profitably in the city's burgeoning automobile industry. Other investments, including real estate, cotton, aluminum, and especially Coca-Cola, built a personal fortune close to $10 million.

In the early 1930s, Cobb purchased a small estate near Atherton, California. He moved his family from Augusta, his home since his marriage in 1908 to Charlie Marion Lombard, member of a well-to-do Augusta family. Between 1910 and 1921 the Cobbs had five children—three sons and two daughters. The eldest, Tyrus Raymond Cobb, Jr., hated baseball, flunked out of various colleges, and became estranged from his famous father, as eventually did Cobb's other offspring. More and more, Cobb was a restless, discontented, ill-tempered man who spent much of his time on golf courses and on hunting and fishing trips. The brightest spot in his thirty-three-year retirement was being the first man elected to the National Baseball Hall of Fame, which opened at Cooperstown, New York, in 1939.

In 1947, after Charlie Marion Cobb had filed and withdrawn several actions, the Cobbs' marriage ended in a divorce decree in Nevada, where Cobb lived part-time at Lake Tahoe. Two years later, Cobb married Frances Fairburn Cass, a widow, but that marriage lasted only until 1956. Various philanthropies, such as a college scholarship fund for needy Georgia youths and a new hospital for Royston, his hometown, could not keep Cobb from increasingly withdrawing into himself. When he died at Emory University Hospital in Atlanta, few people left had remained truly his friends. Whereas many thousands had passed by Babe Ruth's casket in 1948 in New York City, at Cobb's funeral at Cornelia, and burial at Royston, Georgia, only two hundred people, including only four with baseball connections, attended.

• The National Baseball Library, Cooperstown, N.Y., has a sizable Ty Cobb collection. His complete professional record can be found in Craig Carter, ed., *Daguerreotypes* (8th ed., 1990), pp. 57–58. Cobb's posthumously published autobiography, *My Life in Baseball: The True Record* (1961), is extraordinarily valuable. Biographical treatments include Charles C. Alexander, *Ty Cobb* (1984), and John D. McCallum, *Ty Cobb* (1973); also useful is Fred Lieb, *The Detroit Tigers* (1946).

CHARLES C. ALEXANDER

COBB, William Montague (12 Oct. 1904–20 Nov. 1990), physical anthropologist and anatomist, was born in Washington, D.C., the son of William Elmer Cobb, a printer, and Alexzine Montague. Experiencing racial segregation in education, he graduated in 1921 from Dunbar High School, an elite college-preparatory school for African Americans. Cobb attended Amherst College, where he pursued a classical education in arts and sciences, graduating in 1925. After graduation he received a Blodgett Scholarship to study biology at Woods Hole Marine Biology Laboratory in Massachusetts. There he met Howard University biologist Ernest Everett Just and decided to attend Howard University's College of Medicine. At the time, Howard

was undergoing a transformation as its first African-American president, Mordecai Johnson, attempted to place the university under greater African-American control. Showing great academic promise, Cobb was groomed to become a new member of the faculty. After receiving his medical degree in 1929, he was sent to Cleveland for postgraduate study at Western Reserve University.

Even before he could read, Cobb had been intrigued by pictures of human biological variation, or "race." At Western Reserve he pursued this interest by studying anatomy and the emerging discipline of physical anthropology under T. Wingate Todd, who amassed one of the two most extensive research collections of human skeletons in the United States, the Hamman-Todd Collection. Cobb spent two years at Western Reserve, earning a doctoral degree in 1932 on the basis of a thesis that inventoried skeletal material available for anthropological study in the United States. He was the first and, until the early 1950s, the only African American to earn a Ph.D. in physical anthropology.

In 1932 Cobb returned to Howard University as professor of anatomy, intent on establishing a skeletal collection for the use of African-American scientists. He prepared more than 700 skeletons from cadavers and compiled documentation on 300 more. Through his efforts, the Cobb Collection at Howard grew to become comparable to the Hamman-Todd Collection and the Terry Collection at the Smithsonian Institution—an irreplaceable resource for studying the remains of Washington's poor from the Great Depression. Such skulls were particularly valuable because they provided a unique record of past states of sickness and health.

During his early years on the Howard faculty, Cobb continued to work on skeletal collections. His work resulted in important publications on the cranio-facial union, showing how the cranial portion of the skull grows relatively fast and remains stable after birth, while the facial portion grows relatively slowly and can be modified by the environment. He also undertook a massive study of cranial suture closure, showing that it is an unreliable estimator of skeletal age. In the 1930s many Americans believed that the emerging preeminence of African-American sprinters and broad-jumpers in Olympic competition was due to racial anatomy. Cobb refuted this view by carefully measuring African-American Olympic athletes and comparing their measurements to European-American and African-American skeletal averages. Jesse Owens's measurements, for example, turned out to be more "typical" of European-Americans than of African-Americans, showing that racial biology and behavior are not fixed. This important finding had broad application outside athletics.

Cobb believed that African Americans represented a population whose physical and intellectual vigor had been enhanced by the evolutionary bottleneck of slavery. Slave-traders had selected superior physical specimens to transport to the Americas, and of these, only the strongest had survived the new diseases and brutal labor they encountered there. Considering the social barriers, their achievements were extraordinary. Furthermore, he believed that African Americans were highly adaptable and would become more genetically varied as social barriers to racial mixing crumbled. These views were intended to counteract prevailing views that African Americans were inferior because they had been insufficiently exposed to European-American culture.

Cobb also undertook to show how racism and segregation were exacting a biological toll on African Americans and, through the added cost of separate and unequal health care, a financial toll on all Americans. He worked diligently for the racial integration of American hospitals and medical schools. To this end, he created the Imhotep National Conference on Hospital Integration, which met annually from 1957 through 1963, ending with the passage of the 1964 Civil Rights Act. Cobb was invited to attend the formal signing of the 1965 Medicare Bill, which the Conference had promoted. On the subject of race, he published many articles in both popular and scientific journals, especially the *Journal of the National Medical Association*, which he edited for twenty-eight years. Among his associates in the integration effort were Ralph Bunche and W. E. B. DuBois. He was among the first physical anthropologists to direct the resources of that discipline toward social problems.

Cobb graduated from Howard in the same year that the American Association of Physical Anthropologists was founded; he contributed actively to the association in its formative years and was its president (1957–1959). As Cobb matured professionally, he rose to prominence in other anthropological and medical organizations, serving as president of the National Medical Association (1964–1965) and the National Association for the Advancement of Colored People (1976–1982). He chaired the department of anatomy at Howard University College of Medicine from 1949 until 1969, when he became distinguished professor, then distinguished professor emeritus in 1973.

Cobb was accomplished in the arts as well as science, playing violin and reciting literature and poetry, often in class. He was remembered by associates as a well-rounded Renaissance man. Later in life, his humanistic side flourished as he philosophized about the duality of human nature. Cobb presented his last professional paper in 1987. In his lifetime he received more than 100 awards, published more than 1,000 articles, and taught several thousand students. He died in Washington, D.C.

• Documents relating to Cobb, including transcripts of interviews, are in the Moorland-Spingarn Research Center at Howard University. His publications include "Race and Runners," *Journal of Health and Physical Education* 7 (1936): 1–9; "The Negro as a Biological Element in the American Population," *Journal of Negro Education* 8 (1939): 336–48; "The Cranio-Facial Union in Man," *American Journal of Physical Anthropology* 26 (1940): 87–111; "Suture Closure as a Biological Phenomenon," in *Estratto dal Volume degli Atti,*

Fourth Congress of the International Association of Gerontology, ed. Tito Mattioli (1957); and "The Imhotep National Conference on Hospital Integration," *Journal of the National Medical Association* 49 (1957): 54–61. For an assessment of Cobb's contributions to anthropology, see Lesley M. Rankin-Hill and Michael L. Blakey, "W. Montague Cobb (1904–1990): Physical Anthropologist, Anatomist and Activist," *American Anthropologist* 96, no. 1 (1996): 74–96. An obituary by Rankin-Hill and Blakey is in *American Journal of Physical Anthropology* 92 (1993): 545–48.

PAUL A. ERICKSON

COBBS, Nicholas Hamner (5 Feb. 1796–11 Jan. 1861), Episcopal bishop, was born in Bedford County, Virginia, the son of John Lewis Cobbs and Susan Hamner, farmers. His father, who was hostile to religion, has been described as "an infidel of the Jeffersonian type" (White, p. 18), but his mother was a devout Episcopalian and carried her infant son on horseback for sixty or seventy miles from Bedford to Albemarle so that he could be baptized by an Episcopal priest. Because there was no parish in the vicinity of his home, young Cobbs participated only once in the public worship of the Episcopal church before the day of his ordination to the diaconate. The school of Bedford County, known as the Old Field School, provided Cobbs with his only formal education, and he began teaching there in 1813. In 1821 he married his fifteen-year-old first cousin, Lucy Landonia Cobbs; they had ten children, two of whom became priests in the Episcopal church.

While teaching, Cobbs decided to take holy orders and studied on his own to be ordained. He was confirmed and ordained deacon by Richard Channing Moore, the second bishop of Virginia, at Trinity Church in Staunton on 23 May 1824. That same day he received Holy Communion for the first time. After his ordination to the diaconate he continued teaching at the Old Field School and served churches on Sundays in Bedford County. On 22 May 1825 Bishop Moore ordained him priest at Monumental Church in Richmond. When a University of Virginia professor requested that an Episcopal chaplain be assigned to Mr. Jefferson's School, the diocesan convention selected Cobbs for the post. He assumed his duties at Charlottesville in September 1834 but devoted only about a year to the chaplaincy before returning to his ministry in Bedford. At this time he also had charge of the Edgeworth Female Seminary in Liberty, Virginia.

In October 1839 Cobbs became rector of St. Paul's Church in Petersburg. He was there four years when he was called to be rector of St. Paul's Church in Cincinnati, Ohio. While in Virginia he was a clerical deputy to all the triennial General Conventions of the Episcopal Church, 1829–1841. In 1842 Geneva College (now Hobart College) conferred upon him the degree of doctor of sacred theology *honoris causa*.

On 4 May 1844 Cobbs was elected the first bishop of Alabama and was consecrated on 20 October 1844 at Christ Church in Philadelphia by Presiding Bishop Philander Chase, assisted by Bishop William Meade of Virginia and Bishop Charles P. McIlvaine of Ohio.

The Diocese of Alabama had been organized on 25 January 1830 but did not have a bishop until 1844. When Cobbs arrived as bishop the Episcopal church had 450 communicant members out of a total population of over 600,000. His work would be largely that of an evangelist and pioneer.

Bishop Cobbs recognized the need for educational institutions and the obligation to evangelize among the slaves. On 1 January 1851 the Diocesan Female School opened in Tuscaloosa but ceased operation in 1854. The most significant educational institution with which Cobbs was associated was the University of the South, the foundation of which was proposed to the southern bishops by Bishop Leonidas Polk of Louisiana in a letter dated 1 July 1856. At the second meeting of the board of trustees, on 28 November 1857, on the seventeenth ballot, Sewanee, Tennessee, was selected as the site of the proposed university. Bishop Cobbs thought that the university should be located near a cultural center and so opposed the Sewanee location. Once he was defeated, though, Cobbs told his colleagues, "Since you will not come down from the mountain, I will climb the mountain and join you there."

Cobbs freed his slaves while in Virginia, but there is no evidence that he ever denounced slavery as an institution. He was committed to the religious instruction of slaves, and by 1860 more than 1,600 had been baptized and 214 had become communicants.

Bishop Cobbs was not sympathetic to the advocates of states' rights and as a strong supporter of the Union opposed the secession of the southern states. He died in Montgomery just minutes before Alabama seceded from the Union.

The primary issue in the Episcopal church during Cobbs's episcopate was churchmanship. He was a high churchman in the tradition of Bishop John Henry Hobart of New York, whose slogan was Evangelical Truth and Apostolic Order. Cobbs believed in evangelical truth in that he taught the doctrine of justification solely by the merits of Jesus Christ, and his favorite hymn was "Rock of Ages." He stressed apostolic order by insisting on the apostolic succession of bishops, believing that this gave the ministry a divine commission and made the Episcopal church a church and not a sect. He stressed the doctrine and worship of the Book of Common Prayer and insisted that baptismal regeneration was the distinct dogma of the church. On his deathbed he stated his position: "Tell them I dislike party names and loathe party lines in the church of Christ: but next to Christ, who is the head, I love the church, which is His Body, with my whole heart" (quoted in White, p. 173).

• Cobbs published only a few sermons and left very few papers, which have since been lost. The *Virginia Convention Journals, 1824–1844*, the *Alabama Convention Journals, 1844–1861*, and the *Journals of General Convention, 1826–1859* are primary diocesan sources of information. Greenough White, *A Saint of the Southern Church: Memoir of the Right Reverend Nicholas Hamner Cobbs* (1897), is the only biography of Cobbs. Henry C. Lay, "Nicholas Hamner Cobbs, Late Bishop of Alabama," *The American Quarterly Church Review* 20 (Jan. 1869): 543–71, is an essay of appreciation for Cobbs's life and piety. Walter C. Whitaker, *History of the Protestant Episcopal Church in Alabama, 1763–1891* (1898), treats Cobbs's episcopate.

DONALD S. ARMENTROUT

COBLE, Arthur Byron (3 Nov. 1878–8 Dec. 1966), mathematician, was born in Williamstown, Pennsylvania, the son of Reuben Coble, a general store owner and, later, a bank president, and Emma I. Haegy, a teacher. Coble grew up in Lykens, Pennsylvania, where his parents raised him in the Evangelical Lutheran church, an affiliation he would abandon as an adult. Coble earned an A.B. in 1897 from Pennsylvania College (renamed Gettysburg College in 1921) and taught in the public schools for a year before enrolling in the graduate program in mathematics at the Johns Hopkins University in 1898. He took a Ph.D. in mathematics there under the Cambridge-trained Englishman Frank Morley in 1902, with a dissertation in algebraic geometry, before becoming an instructor at the University of Missouri.

Coble returned to Baltimore in the fall of 1903 as a research assistant under his adviser, Morley. Their work was supported by the recently founded Carnegie Institution of Washington, and Coble used part of his stipend to make what, for a mathematician, was then an almost obligatory study trip abroad. Coble spent part of 1904 in Germany, where, first at Greifswald University and then at Bonn, he undoubtedly heard the lectures of the noted German geometer and invariant theorist Eduard Study, whose mathematical interests closely paralleled his own. Coble returned to the United States in the fall of 1904 to take up an instructorship in mathematics at Johns Hopkins. In 1905 he married Abby Walker Adams Whitney; they had four children. Coble served on the Johns Hopkins faculty until 1918, when he left the associate professorship he had been promoted to in 1909 for a professorship at the University of Illinois in Urbana-Champaign.

While at Johns Hopkins, Coble worked on several related topics in algebraic geometry. In particular, he analyzed certain aspects of finite geometries and finite groups and did important work in the Galois theory of higher degree equations. His growing stature within the American mathematical community was recognized in 1911 with his election to the governing council of the American Mathematical Society (AMS), a post he held until 1914. He followed this from 1915 to 1919 with an associate editorship of the society's *Transactions* and, in 1917, was elected AMS vice president.

Except for a visiting position at the University of Chicago in 1919 and a one-year return to Johns Hopkins (1927–1928), Coble spent the rest of his active career at Illinois. There, he not only continued his researches in the Galois theory of equations but also took up intensive studies of hyperelliptic and Abelian theta functions as well as related topics in invariant theory. These and related research contributions to the field of algebraic geometry won him election to the National Academy of Sciences in 1924 and the high honor of presenting a series of AMS Colloquium lectures on his work in 1928.

Coble's Illinois years also found him maintaining a high profile in the broader affairs of American mathematics. From 1918 to 1926 he served as an associate editor of the *American Journal of Mathematics*, the oldest continuing research-level publication in mathematics in the country (founded in 1878), and took on an editorship from 1927 to 1933. From 1920 to 1925 he also held an editorship of the *Transactions of the American Mathematical Society*. His peers recognized his untiring efforts in 1932 when the AMS elected him to its presidency (1933–1934).

At the University of Illinois, Coble served as the head of the Department of Mathematics from 1934 until his retirement in 1947. During World War II, he also managed the university's navy V12 program, an accelerated degree program for naval personnel, as his contribution to the war effort. Following his retirement from Illinois, Coble accepted a year-long appointment at Haverford College but resigned after only one semester, most likely as a result of complications brought on by Parkinson's disease. After an automobile accident in 1956 that left him unable to walk without assistance, he lived in his hometown of Lykens, Pennsylvania. He died in a Harrisburg hospital.

As a mathematician, Coble pursued lines of research in algebraic geometry that had deep nineteenth-century roots, and he trained at least twenty-two doctoral students in this classical area. Most of his active career (1900 through the 1930s) fell within the period of consolidation and growth for research-level work in mathematics in the United States and exemplified the defining characteristics of that period: Coble trained a relatively large number of new researchers, who took their research credentials and ideals to mathematics departments in colleges and universities throughout the United States, and through his dedicated editorial work, he helped to set and maintain America's new research-level standards of mathematical scholarship.

• The Arthur B. Coble Papers in the archives at the University of Illinois at Urbana-Champaign contain correspondence and mathematical manuscripts dating from the years 1903–1953 and 1964. Among Coble's most important works are his dissertation, "The Quartic Curve as Related to Conics," *Transactions of the American Mathematical Society* 4 (1903): 65–85; "An Application of Finite Geometry to the Characteristic Theory of the Odd and Even Theta Functions," *Transactions of the American Mathematical Society* 14 (1913): 241–76; and *Algebraic Geometry and Theta Functions* (1929). On Coble's life and works through 1938, consult Raymond C. Archibald, *A Semicentennial History of the American Mathematical Society, 1888–1938* (1938), pp. 233–36, which includes a photograph of Coble and a list of his doctoral students through 1938. For a historical sketch of the period of consolidation and growth in American mathematics in which Coble played a role, see Karen Hunger Parshall and David E.

Rowe, *The Emergence of the American Mathematical Research Community 1876–1900: J. J. Sylvester, Felix Klein, and E. H. Moore* (1994), pp. 427–53.

KAREN HUNGER PARSHALL

COBLENTZ, William Weber (20 Nov. 1873–15 Sept. 1962), physicist, was born near North Lima, Ohio, the son of David Coblentz and Catherine M. Good, farmers. Between 1891 and 1896 he prepared for college at the Poland (Ohio) Union Seminary and Rayen High School in Youngstown, Ohio, while working at a variety of odd jobs. After receiving his B.S. from the Case School of Applied Science in 1900, he enrolled at Cornell University to study physics. He was fascinated by the fact that the molecules of every substance absorb and emit infrared radiant energy in a unique pattern so that the composition of an unknown molecule can be determined by observing these absorption and emission characteristics. However, in 1900 infrared spectroscopy was still in its infancy and only those wavelengths of less than five microns could be observed. He partially solved this problem in 1901 when he built a radiometric device that permitted the detection of infrared wavelengths between five and fifteen microns. He received his M.S. that same year and his Ph.D. in physics in 1903.

Coblentz remained at Cornell for an additional two years both as an honorary fellow of the school and as a research associate of the Carnegie Institution of Washington. These positions enabled him to identify the infrared absorption and emission spectra of thousands of organic molecular substances, thereby creating an invaluable database for future infrared spectroscopic investigations. In 1905 he joined the staff of the newly organized National Bureau of Standards as a laboratory assistant and continued his groundbreaking investigations in infrared spectroscopy by observing the spectra of many inorganic substances, especially metals. That same year he founded and became chief of the bureau's Radiometry Section, a position he held for forty years. In this capacity he developed methods and equipment to establish standards for measuring infrared and other forms of radiant energy in scientific applications.

In 1909 Coblentz contributed to the development of quantum physics when he made the first accurate determination of the radiation constants of a blackbody, a hypothetical substance that absorbs and emits electromagnetic radiation of all frequencies fully and equally. A close approximation of a blackbody, such as a piece of charcoal, emits different colors as it is heated to progressively higher temperatures, a phenomenon that cannot be explained sufficiently by the laws of classical thermodynamics. In 1900 Max Planck, the German physicist, had hypothesized that radiant energy is emitted in discrete packets or quanta, each of which exists in a different state of equilibrium, and that the optical wavelength (and therefore the color) of the energy radiated by a blackbody is a function of its temperature. The mathematical formula for this function is known as Planck's Law. By using data obtained from experiments with a fluorite prism, Coblentz recalculated the value of the two constants in the formula, thereby lending veracity to Planck's Law and furthering the new field of quantum physics.

In 1914 Coblentz made a major contribution to astrophysics by conducting the first systematic infrared astronomical observations. Cosmic dust does not block infrared wavelengths as it does optical wavelengths, and so stars and nebulae at considerable distances from the Earth can be studied by observing their infrared spectra. By observing celestial bodies through a telescope and then comparing their infrared spectra to those of molecular substances for which the temperatures were known, he was able to measure the heat emitted by Venus, Mars, and Jupiter as well as 110 stars. Between 1921 and 1938 he conducted similar studies and one involving solar ultraviolet radiation. In 1924 he married Catherine Emma Cate, and they had two children. As a member of the Harvard University eclipse expedition, he studied the electromagnetic radiation of the Sun's corona during solar eclipses in 1925 and 1926.

Between 1928 and 1945 Coblentz gradually shifted his focus away from infrared spectroscopy and began studying the ultraviolet spectrum. He was particularly interested in measuring ultraviolet radiation and establishing dosage units for medical treatment. In 1945 he retired from the Bureau of Standards but continued to work there as a consultant while devoting most of his attention to the scientific investigation of extrasensory perception. He had become interested in psychic phenomena as a boy and studied telekinesis, mental telepathy, materializations, and clairvoyance in his spare time in the hope that they could somehow be used to detect crime and prevent aggression. Because the spectrum of electromagnetic radiant energy ranges in wavelength from 10^{-15} to 10^9 centimeters and yet the human eye can perceive only those wavelengths between 4×10^{-5} and 7.5×10^{-5} centimeters, he believed in the existence of a human organic receptor of cerebral radiant energy that makes clairvoyance possible, thereby allowing human perception to transcend time and space, and he spent his retirement trying to find such a receptor. In *Man's Place in a Superphysical World* (1954) he summarizes over forty years of scientific investigations into the realm of extrasensory perception and argues in favor of "the possibility of consciousness surviving death and of using the same means of communication as are employed between minds in the living" (p. x).

Coblentz received a number of awards for his contributions to physics, including the Franklin Institute's Howard N. Potts Gold Medal in 1910, the Institute of France's Janssen Medal in 1920, the City of Philadelphia's John Scott Medal in 1924, a gold key from the American Congress of Physical Therapy in 1934, the American Academy of Arts and Sciences' Rumford Gold Medal in 1937, the Optical Society of America's Frederick Ives Medal in 1945, a silver med-

al from the Society of Applied Spectroscopy in 1953, and the International Congress of Photobiology's Niels Finsen Medal in 1954. He was elected to the National Academy of Sciences in 1930. In 1954 the Coblentz Society was organized to promote the application of infrared spectra data; after his death in Washington, D.C., it established the Coblentz Memorial Prize.

Coblentz contributed to the development of American science by overseeing the establishment of radiometric standards for both the ultraviolet and the infrared spectra. His pioneering work in the field of infrared astronomy dramatically increased scientific knowledge of the universe. His investigations into psychic phenomena opened new avenues of research into the so-called "sixth sense."

• Coblentz's papers are in the Manuscript Division of the Library of Congress. An autobiography is *From the Life of a Researcher* (1951). A biography, including a complete bibliography, is William F. Meggers, National Academy of Sciences, *Biographical Memoirs* 39 (1967): 55–102. He was commemorated in *Applied Optics*, Nov. 1963. Obituaries are in the *New York Times*, 19 Sept. 1962, and *Physics Today*, Dec. 1962.

CHARLES W. CAREY, JR.

COBURN, Charles Douville (19 June 1877–30 Aug. 1961), theatrical actor, manager, and director and film character actor, was born in Macon, Georgia, the son of Moses Douville Coburn and Emma Louise Sprigman. The family moved to Savannah, Georgia, when Charles was nine months old. An avid playgoer at the age of fourteen, Coburn was mistaken by the manager for a program boy as he stood in front of the Savannah Theatre, and he was ordered back to work inside; by the time he was seventeen he was managing the theater. Two years later he moved to New York City to pursue an acting career, surviving by wrapping bundles, ushering, and once by working as a six-day bicycle racer. His first acting job, in the 1898–1899 season, was with a Chicago company of *Quo Vadis* at $12 a week plus room and board. During the next two years Coburn acted with touring repertory companies and developed his skills by playing more than 400 roles, including some in Shakespearean plays and other classics. His first New York appearance was at the Fourteenth Street Theatre in 1901 in *Up York State*. His first New York leading role was in *The Christian* in 1903.

In 1905 Coburn organized the Coburn Shakespearean Players. While touring with the company he fell in love with Ivah Wills, his leading lady in *As You Like It*. They married in Baltimore in 1906 and had no children. Throughout their 31-year marriage, this famously loving theater couple addressed each other as "Orlando" and "Rosalind" and refused to be separated professionally. They toured the country with their company of young actors for twelve years. In 1910, at the request of President and Mrs. William Howard Taft, the Coburn Players performed for two days on the White House lawn in *Twelfth Night* and *As You Like It*.

The Coburns produced and played together in *The Yellow Jacket* at New York's Cort Theatre in 1916, in what was called "the most imaginative and significant production ever given of the famous Chinese play." Made part of the company's repertoire, the production was presented in New York again in 1921 and 1928 and on their road tour in 1933–1934. In February 1917 the troupe appeared in Moliere's *Imaginary Invalid* at the Harris Theatre. In 1918 Coburn's company produced a dramatization of a British wartime cartoon, *The Better 'Ole*, with Coburn in the role of Old Bill, the cartoon's famous cockney soldier. This was the Coburns' greatest box office success; they had four road companies touring while it played on Broadway for two years. Among other productions, the Coburns also appeared together in *So This Is London* (1922–1924), *The Farmer's Wife* (1924), and *Lysistrata* (Sept. 1930). One of Coburn's other notable successes was as Colonel Ibbetson in the 1931 New York production of *Peter Ibbetson*.

In the summer of 1934, concerned by the disappearance of the touring stock companies that had been the training schools for themselves and generations of American actors, the Coburns founded the Mohawk Drama Festival at Union College in Schenectady, New York. During an eight-week season of four plays the Coburns taught, directed, and acted with student casts. Though profoundly shocked by the death of his wife in 1936, Coburn continued to guide the festival that summer and every summer until World War II brought an end to the venture.

The title role in *Boss Tweed* (1933) had been Coburn's first film appearance, and shortly after his wife's death he moved to Hollywood to pursue a film acting career. He continued to appear onstage in summer stock and on tour, most notably in 1946, when he toured the nation as Sir John Falstaff in an all-star Theatre Guild production of *The Merry Wives of Windsor*.

Coburn's role in MGM's *Of Human Hearts* (1938) firmly established him in the film industry. He was an Academy Award nominee for *The Devil and Miss Jones* (1941) and *The Green Years* (1946), and he won the best supporting actor award for his role in *The More the Merrier* (1943), a satire of crowded housing in wartime Washington in which Coburn's "crafty impersonation of an elderly cupid" stole many scenes from the stars.

A versatile and highly paid character actor, Coburn appeared in seventy-one films. Among the better known are *Idiot's Delight*, *The Story of Alexander Graham Bell*, and *Stanley and Livingstone* (all 1939); *The Road to Singapore* (1940); *The Lady Eve* and *King's Row* (both 1941); *In This Our Life* and *George Washington Slept Here* (both 1942); *Heaven Can Wait* and *Princess O'Rourke* (both 1943); *The Paradine Case* (1947); *B. F.'s Daughter* (1948); *Monkey Business* (1952); *Gentlemen Prefer Blondes* (1953); and *Around the World in Eighty Days* (1956). In June 1955 the National Theatre Arts Council presented a scroll to Coburn to honor his seventy-eighth birthday and his "unexcelled contributions to the theatre, films, radio and television as actor, director and producer over a span of sixty years."

Coburn enjoyed life both in and out of his profession. In his touring days the Coburn Players fielded a baseball team that played local college and semipro teams. While in Hollywood Coburn continued his boyish enthusiasms, placing small wagers and cheering loudly at Hollywood athletic events and even keeping a small stable of race horses for a time. In the 1940s he was reported to be a popular dancing partner among Hollywood's young women. In 1959 Coburn was married a second time, to Winifred Jean Clements Natzka. They had no children.

Coburn continued to act on the stage all his life: he was appearing as the eccentric Grandpa Vanderhoff—long a favorite role—in an Indianapolis summer stock production of *You Can't Take It with You* only one week before his death in New York City.

• Extended but dated summaries of Coburn's career are in *Who Was Who in the Theatre*, *Who's Who in America*, and *Current Biography* (1944). The *International Dictionary of Films and Filmmakers*: vol. 3, *Actors and Actresses* (5 vols., 1984–1987), offers a complete listing of Coburn's films. A retrospective article by Jimmie Hicks, "Charles Coburn," is in *Films in Review*, May 1987, pp. 258–79. An obituary is in the *New York Times*, 31 Aug. 1961.

DANIEL KREMPEL

COCHISE, (1810?–8 June 1874), Chiricahua Apache chief, was probably born in southeastern Arizona, the son of either Relles or Pisago Cabezon, prominent leaders of the Chokonen band. Cochise matured in a relatively tranquil period during which relations between his people and Mexico were generally peaceful. In 1831, however, war broke out. Cochise likely participated in a major three-day battle that ended on 23 May 1832, when a Mexican force of 138 men defeated some 300 Chiricahuas near the Gila River.

By 1835 Cochise had become a successful warrior and organized a raid against the Mexicans in the state of Sonora. In late October 1836, the Chokonens, weary of war, agreed to a treaty at Fronteras, Sonora, but in March 1837 they resumed raiding. In the late 1830s Cochise married Dos-teh-seh, a daughter of Chihenne chief Mangas Coloradas, the dominant Chiricahua leader of the time. They had two sons, Taza and Naiche, both Chokonen leaders after Cochise's death. With a second wife, he had two daughters.

In July 1842 the Chokonen band made peace with the Mexicans at Janos, Chihuahua, and lived there until February 1844, when they left because of smallpox. In June 1846 several hundred Chokonens encamped near Galeana, Chihuahua, after agreeing to an armistice. On 7 July scalp-hunter James Kirker clandestinely attacked the band at night, slaughtering 130 of them. Cochise's father was probably among the slain.

On 21 June 1848 Cochise was captured by the Mexicans during a Chokonen raid on Fronteras. The Chokonens surrounded Fronteras, captured eleven Mexicans, and traded them for Cochise on 11 August. War with Mexico continued for most of the next decade. After Miguel Narbona's death in 1856, Cochise replaced him as the principal chief of the Chokonen band.

Wary of the Americans settling in Arizona in the mid-1850s following the end of the Mexican War, Cochise resumed relations with Mexico, agreeing to armistices at Janos in the summer of 1857 and at Fronteras that fall. However, after thirty Chokonens were massacred by Mexican soldiers at Fronteras on 14 July 1858, Cochise left Mexico for Arizona and met with U.S. Apache agent Michael Steck on 30 December 1858 at Apache Pass. The band's dealings with Americans remained friendly until late 1859, when the Chokonens became dissatisfied with the paucity of rations allotted to them and began sporadic raiding against American ranches and travelers.

Cochise's relations with Americans broke down in February 1861, when Lieutenant George Bascom's command arrived at Apache Pass seeking a boy who had been kidnapped by western Apaches. Bascom invited Cochise to parley and arrested him despite his innocence. Cochise escaped by cutting his way out of a tent, but five members of his family among other Apaches who were also imprisoned were unable to escape. Within days, Cochise captured four Americans and offered to exchange them for his relatives. Bascom, however, refused to release them until the boy was returned. Cochise next tried unsuccessfully to free his relations, and a few days later he tortured his prisoners to death. Bascom retaliated by hanging Cochise's brother Coyuntura, two nephews, and three other men. His wife and son were later released.

Thus the Cochise War (1861–1872) began, and Cochise emerged as the dominant Chiricahua tribal chief. His antipathy toward Americans became legendary. Initially he fought for revenge, which led to a bloody cycle of raids, American campaigns, and further Chiricahua retaliation. Cochise was the aggressor for the first five years of the war, during which time he was able to enlist the aid of other Chiricahua bands, notably the Bedonkohes and Mangas Coloradas's Chihennes. They attacked Americans at Cook's Canyon, New Mexico, in July and August 1861; at Pinos Altos, New Mexico, in September 1861; and at Apache Pass in July 1862. In these clashes, both sides fought hard and lost many men. Cochise's passionate hatred of Americans was aroused again when Americans duped Mangas Coloradas into parleying and executed him on 18 January 1863.

After the Civil War, the American military increasingly made its presence felt in Arizona. In 1865, however, Cochise refused to consider a truce, vowing to never make peace with Americans. From 1866 until 1868, he divided his time between Arizona and Mexico, carrying on guerrilla warfare against his enemies in both regions. In late 1868 Sonorans forced him north. U.S. troops from Fort Bowie doggedly pursued him in the Chiricahua Mountains in October and November 1869 in two major battles and several skirmishes.

By 1870 Cochise was willing to consider peace, conferring with Americans in New Mexico at Camp Mogollon in August and the Apache agency at Cañada Alamosa in October. His profound distrust of Americans and disdain for reservation life, however, led him to leave the reservation. Troops hunted his people during 1871 and compelled them to return to Cañada Alamosa that September. The following spring, after the agency was relocated to Tularosa, New Mexico, Cochise returned to his beloved Dragoon Mountains in Arizona, dispatching his men to "make a living," which meant more raiding during the summer of 1872. The Americans sent General Oliver Otis Howard to make peace with the Apaches, particularly Cochise. Enlisting the help of Thomas Jeffords, an American trusted by Cochise, Howard, with five other Americans and two Chiricahuas, left New Mexico to find Cochise. On 1 October 1872, they met him in the Dragoon Mountains and made peace, setting aside a reservation in his ancestral country. Cochise faithfully kept the agreement. He died in the Dragoon Mountains.

Cochise was a man of dignity with strong principles, a keen intellect, natural talents, and impressive physique. Renowned for his skill with bow and lance, Cochise led his men into battle, bringing his own audacious and warlike presence to a fight. His survival skills were legendary, his camps almost impossible to surprise. Perhaps his most remarkable characteristic was his autocratic sway among his people, a rare phenomenon in Apache culture and tradition.

• The most notable sources on Cochise are Edwin R. Sweeney, *Cochise: Chiricahua Apache Chief* (1991); Dan L. Thrapp, *The Conquest of Apacheria* (1967); and Frank C. Lockwood, *The Apache Indians* (1938).

EDWIN R. SWEENEY

COCHRAN, Jacqueline (1910?–9 Aug. 1980), pioneer aviator and business executive, was born in Muscogee, Florida, near Pensacola. Her parents both died during her infancy, and she was raised by foster families with whom she worked in the lumber mills of the Florida panhandle. By the age of fifteen she had also worked in a Columbus, Georgia, cotton mill and learned how to cut hair in a beauty shop. Cochran took nursing training at a hospital in Montgomery, Alabama, from 1925 to 1928, but by 1930 she had returned to Pensacola to work in a beauty salon. In 1932 she traveled to Philadelphia to work in a beauty shop and then moved in the same year to New York City, where her skill earned her a job at Antoine's, a well-known Saks Fifth Avenue beauty shop. For the next four years she worked for this business, spending every winter working in Antoine's branch in Miami Beach, Florida. She met Floyd Bostwick Odlum, a banker and industrialist, in the winter of 1932 and married him in 1936. They settled on a 1,000-acre ranch near Indio in southern California.

In the summer of 1932, Cochran's future husband introduced her to the idea of flying. She spent three weeks at Roosevelt Field, Long Island, learning to pilot an airplane. Her pilot's license followed immediately. She began entering air races and seeking sponsors to finance her racing ventures. In 1934 she entered the McRobertson London-to-Melbourne air race but dropped out after engine trouble developed in her Gee Bee aircraft near Bucharest. Cochran next entered the prestigious Bendix air race from California to Cleveland, Ohio. She was the only woman to compete in 1935 and was required to gain the permission of all the other pilots in the race before the judges would agree to let her compete. After a difficult takeoff in California, engine trouble near the Grand Canyon again forced her out of the race.

In 1935 Cochran started her own cosmetics business, Jacqueline Cochran Cosmetics. She used her abilities as a pilot to establish a chain of beauty shops, a research laboratory in New Jersey, and product outlets in the United States, often flying 90,000 miles per year. Her cosmetics business was at its height in the fifteen years after World War II. She was voted Woman of the Year in Business in 1953 and 1954. In March 1961 she relinquished direct supervision of the business.

Cochran's marriage in 1936 enabled her to spend much of her time flying. She set three speed records in 1937 and was awarded the Harmon trophy as the outstanding woman aviator of the year. In 1938 she again entered the Bendix air race and this time won, setting another speed record. In 1939 she set an altitude record of 33,000 feet and won the New-York-to-Miami air race.

In 1941 Cochran became the first woman to ferry a B-17 bomber to Britain. At the request of the U.S. military, she recruited twenty-five other female pilots to ferry bombers across the Atlantic Ocean, freeing male pilots to fly front-line missions. She overcame attempted sabotage of the program by unknown persons, and the success of the group and Cochran's administration of it led to her appointment in the summer of 1943 as head of the Woman's Airforce Service Pilots (WASP). One thousand women worked to fly aircraft across the Atlantic for service in Europe as well as fly training missions in the United States. The WASPs continued their efforts until December 1944. She received the army's Distinguished Service Medal in 1945 for the work she accomplished as head of the WASPs. At the end of World War II Cochran served as a reporter for *Liberty Magazine*. She interviewed and published reports on Chinese leaders Chiang Kai-shek and Mao Tse-tung and observed and sent articles to *Liberty* on the Nürnburg war crimes trials in 1946. Finally, in 1954, she published her autobiography, *The Stars at Noon*.

Cochran returned to record-setting flights in May and June 1953 when she arranged with a Canadian manufacturer of U.S. Air Force F-86 Sabrejets to become a test pilot for them. Working at Edwards Air Force Base in California with Chuck Yeager, the first pilot to break the sound barrier in 1947, she became the first woman to do so. Cochran also set an altitude record of 55,253 feet that year. For these accomplishments she received the Gold Medal of the Fédération Aéronautique Internationale. She later went on to become the first woman to fly at twice the speed of sound (6 June 1960), and the first woman to take off and land a jet from an aircraft carrier at sea. In 1962 she set the final two speed records of her career. In 1971 Cochran was elected to the Aviation Hall of Fame. She died in Indio.

Jacqueline Cochran held more aviation records at the time of her death than any other pilot in the United States. Her stated interest in aviation was the advancement of knowledge about flying and she certainly contributed in a major way to acquiring that knowledge.

• K. Leish's 1960 interview with Jacqueline Cochran is stored in microfilmed, transcript form in the Columbia University Oral History Collection, pt. 2, no. 39. Marquita O. Fisher, *Jacqueline Cochran: First Lady of Flight* (1973), supplements Cochran's own 1954 autobiography. A later autobiography is *Jackie Cochran: An Autobiography*, with Maryann Bucknum Brinley (1987). Two volumes of Florida history that provide focused treatment of Cochran are Rodney F. Allen, *Fifty-five Famous Floridians* (1985), and Gene M. Burnett, *Florida's Past: People and Events That Shaped the State* (1986). Robert A. Searles, "The Leading Lady of Aviation," *Business and Commercial Aviation*, May 1988, p. 94, examines her effect on the development of aviation.

ERIK THOMAS ROBINSON

COCHRAN, Jerome (4 Dec. 1831–17 Aug. 1896), physician and sanitarian, was born in Moscow, Tennessee, the son of Augustine Cochran and Frances Bailey, farmers. Cochran worked on the family farm and attended local schools when he could. He supplemented this scant formal education with private study of biology, philosophy, and foreign languages. After teaching school from the age of nineteen until he was twenty-four, he attended lectures for two years at the sectarian Botanico-Medical College in Memphis, where he earned an M.D. in 1857. The two years of medical practice that followed in rural Mississippi convinced Cochran that he needed a more thorough and orthodox education, which he received at the University of Nashville from 1859 to 1861. He was then appointed resident physician in Nashville by his mentor, W. K. Bowling, and received a second M.D. in 1861. This hospital-based residency took the place of an apprenticeship, a style of medical learning that was becoming less and less common. In 1856 Cochran married Sarah Jane Collins; they had three children.

After serving the Confederacy first as a contract surgeon at a hospital in rural Mississippi (1861–1862) and then as head of the conscript board (1862–1865), Cochran moved his family to Mobile, Alabama, where he set up a private practice. In 1868 he became a professor of public hygiene and medical jurisprudence at the Medical College of Alabama, where he remained until his death.

In Mobile Cochran published on the local endemic and epidemic diseases, making recommendations for their amelioration. With the support of the local medical society, he helped to create a local board of health and became its main officer. During the 1870s he emerged as the leading voice for public health in the state. In 1875 he shepherded through the state legislature the bill establishing the first state board of health in Alabama and was the obvious choice for its head. In this position, which he retained for the remainder of his career, Cochran fought to ensure that the board was established within the state's medical society so that physicians would have the predominant role in its function. Although he succeeded in this, it took four years, the restoration of a Democratic government, and a yellow fever epidemic before the state legislature voted to fund the board. His efforts as state health officer included lobbying for public health legislation on such topics as vital statistics and quarantine, investigating outbreaks of disease, and urging local medical societies to form city and county boards of health to promote sanitary reform. Cochran was also instrumental in passing legislation to improve physician licensing standards in 1877. This reform was part of a national movement, spearheaded by the American Medical Association, that aimed to elevate the quality of medical practice. In addition it promoted the prosperity of licensed physicians by limiting competition, leading some contemporaries and, later, historians to charge that its main motivation was economic.

Cochran's principal interest was in the major public health menaces of his place and time—yellow fever, smallpox, and cholera. He served on the first federal yellow fever commission, which examined the major southern epidemic of 1878. His investigations of this and later epidemics were recorded in thoughtful publications that reflected the most sophisticated contemporary understanding of the disease. Cochran became one of his region's best-known authorities on yellow fever's etiology, diagnosis, and control.

Cochran's main genius was as an institution builder. He almost single-handedly created and nurtured the Alabama State Board of Health for its first twenty years. Realizing the limits of what one state could do, he rallied fellow southern board chiefs to regional cooperation. Cochran lobbied in Washington for stronger federal public health action as well, seeing in federal quarantine the best hope for protecting the Alabama coast from imported yellow fever.

During Cochran's active career as a sanitarian (1870–1896), the federal government went from almost no involvement in public health and quarantine to the administration of a full-scale public health service. Cochran consistently supported this growth but advocated a national body composed of state public health representatives that could act on the federal level as a sort of sanitarian's congress, while at the same time being sensitive to individual states' rights. Instead, a federal agency, the U.S. Public Health Service (then called the Marine Hospital Service), grew independently of state overview and frequently clashed with Cochran and other state health officers over particular epidemic control practices. The differences generally were not over etiological theory or public

health techniques but centered instead around different interpretations of events or data, which were fueled by local fears of federal tyranny. Cochran frequently tried to reverse this trend by drafting national department of health bills along his model, but he was unable to win sufficient congressional support for them. The national board of health bills came up frequently in Congress from 1880 until Cochran's death in 1896, and he was active in most of the discussions. Other state board of health officials shared his views on state control of the federal agency, but the supporters of the U.S. Public Health Service prevailed.

Cochran's work in Alabama set a high standard for other southern sanitarians to follow. His expert opinion settled disputed cases, and he supplied the driving force for consensus on regional quarantine regulations. His intelligence and analytic skills are evident in the many publications of the Alabama board during his tenure and in his abundant articles on yellow fever and other public health problems of his time. While Cochran did no research that generated a new understanding of these diseases, he quickly assimilated the best epidemiology of his age and promulgated it in his teaching, articles, and public health administration. He died in Montgomery, Alabama.

• Letters from and to Cochran are in the National Archives (National Board of Health Papers and Marine Hospital Service Papers) and the State of Alabama Department of Archives (William Henry Sanders Papers). His reports as state officer of health were published in the *Transactions of the Medical Association of the State of Alabama*, where his articles also frequently appeared. Cochran's work is discussed in Carey V. Stabler, "The History of Alabama's Public Health System" (Ph.D. diss., Duke Univ., 1944), and in Howard Holley, *History of Medicine in Alabama* (1982). The role of southern health officials in congressional discussions around a federal public health service is outlined in Margaret Humphreys, *Yellow Fever and the South* (1992). Obituaries are in the *Journal of the American Medical Association* 27 (1896): 448–49, and *Transactions of the Medical Association of the State of Alabama* 50 (1897): 90–107.

MARGARET HUMPHREYS

COCHRAN, John (1 Sept. 1730–16 Apr. 1807), physician and hospital director, was born in the area of Sadsbury (now Cochranville), Chester County, Pennsylvania, the son of Ulster emigrants James Cochran and Isabella Cochran. Cochran grew up in the rough community surrounding his father's tavern, which was the center of all local activities. At age thirteen he attended the school in nearby New London opened recently by the Reverend Francis Alison, a famous educator, who infused students with his passion for freedom. Cochran had as fellows such future revolutionaries as Thomas McKean, George Reed, and Charles Thomson. Apparently he did well in school; his father apprenticed him to Robert Thompson, an eminent physician in Lancaster, Pennsylvania, in whose busy office Cochran learned to treat wounds, set bones, bleed and cup, and prepare drugs.

When Cochran completed his apprenticeship in 1755, the French and Indian War was gaining momentum, and an army enlistment seemed attractive for the aspiring young surgeon. The next year, at the battle of Fort Oswego, he nearly died when a cannonball from a French vessel blasted through the room where he was preparing to operate. Cochran benefited greatly from his long connection with Dr. George Monro, a member of the famous Scottish family of anatomists, who as head of medical services in the British army in America brought advanced knowledge of military medicine. While stationed at Fort William Henry, Cochran became increasingly knowledgeable about inoculation against smallpox, acquiring an expertise that would play an important role later in his medical career. In 1758 he was at Fort Ticonderoga when the British suffered a crushing defeat. To care for the numerous wounded a hospital was opened at "The Flatts," the ancestral home of the Schuyler family in Albany. Cochran later served under General Jeffrey Amherst in the recapture of Ticonderoga and Crown Point, where he spent his last year of war service.

While working at The Flatts, Cochran met Gertrude Schuyler, the recently widowed sister of Philip Schuyler, the grand seigneur of the region. They married in 1760. After two years in Albany, finding the town too quiet and possibly to escape the omnipresent influence of his in-laws, Cochran moved south to the bustling community of New Brunswick in East Jersey. There he soon rose to public attention as physician and citizen. He was a prime leader in the establishment in 1766 of the New Jersey Medical Society, the first such organization in the colonies. He was its first treasurer, served on the committee that drafted its fee bill, and served as president from 1768 to 1770. Now a specialist in inoculation, in 1771 he opened a small hospital outside the limits of town, where patients remained during their treatment and convalescence.

As resentment against British government policies increased, Cochran took his place firmly in the American camp, sent his wife and three sons to safety, and joined the army as a volunteer. He was with George Washington on the fateful crossing of the Delaware on Christmas Eve 1776, assisted in the attack on Princeton, and became a member of Washington's "family" at Morristown, where he spent the winter and spring of 1777 inoculating soldiers arriving from the South. Congress ordered the dismissal of John Morgan as director general of the medical department of the Continental army on 9 January, and shortly thereafter Washington advised Dr. William Shippen, Jr., to consult with Cochran on a plan for reorganizing the medical service. Shippen was named director general on 11 April, and Cochran was formally appointed physician and surgeon general of the army in the middle department.

At the battle of Brandywine in 1777 Cochran treated the wound of the young Lafayette; both men narrowly escaped capture. By the beginning of January 1778 Cochran was at Valley Forge, where the threat of smallpox prompted the building of an isolation hospital at Yellow Springs under Cochran's supervision. Among his patients was Benedict Arnold, who suf-

fered a severe thigh fracture incurred at the battles of Saratoga. In late 1778 Lafayette received permission from Congress to return to France but fell ill with pneumonia. Washington, greatly concerned, ordered Cochran to devote his efforts to Lafayette's recovery and to accompany him to his ship in Boston Harbor. When Cochran returned to camp in January 1779 he rented a house in Morristown for his now reunited family and granted James Tilton permission to erect at Basking Ridge a hospital hut of Tilton's original design. From March to June, during the court-martial of Shippen, which had been instigated by the second director, Morgan, and Benjamin Rush, Cochran was ordered to take over the administrative duties of the medical department. In the bitter rivalries that surfaced in the trial, he maintained a neutral position. Although Shippen was technically cleared of serious misdoings and reappointed to his former post, he found his position untenable and soon resigned. On 17 January 1781 Congress appointed Cochran director general of the Hospital of the United States.

Cochran avoided controversy during his term of office, tried to maintain friendly relations between the line and the medical service, and made every effort to obtain for the military physicians and surgeons recognition, hitherto denied, of their status as fellow officers. On 11 August 1783 Washington sent his old friend a formal testimony of his "Attention, Skill and Fidelity" in all his activities. Several years earlier Washington had named Cochran and chief army physician James Craik as "the two men who had the greatest claim to their country's notice." Upon leaving Newburgh, Washington purportedly gave Cochran all the furniture in his headquarters.

After the war Cochran decided to move to New York City, where he acquired twin houses with his stepson-in-law, Walter Livingston. He soon gained a notable reputation in his profession; formed a friendship with John Bard and Samuel Bard, leaders in the medical community; and became a member of Alexander Hamilton's party. He served as a trustee of the recently revived Columbia (formerly King's) College. In May 1786 he was selected receiver of continental taxes for the state of New York, and two years later he became a figure in the disturbing episode known as "the Doctors' mob," when a crowd, incited by a report of grave robbing, attacked the houses of physicians who were thought to have encouraged the practice. The day after Washington's presidential inauguration, Cochran was appointed commissioner of loans of the United States for the state of New York. The position eventually proved too onerous for the easygoing Cochran. A series of mild strokes forced him to retire in 1795 to an estate in Palatine, New York, granted to him by a grateful nation, where he built a palatial home, entertained travelers, and lived peacefully until his death there.

• Some materials relating to Cochran are in the Continental Congress Papers at the Library of Congress. For a biography of Cochran, see Morris H. Saffron, *Surgeon to Washington: Dr. John Cochran (1730–1807)* (1977). See also Mary C. Gillett, *The Army Medical Department (1775–1818)* (1981).

MORRIS H. SAFFRON

COCHRAN, William Gemmell (15 July 1909–29 Mar. 1980), statistician, was born in Rutherglen, Scotland, the son of Thomas Cochran, a railroad employee, and Jeannie (maiden name unknown). After residing at several locations, the family settled in Glasgow when Willie ("Wully") was sixteen years old. In 1927 Cochran won a competitive scholarship enabling him to attend Glasgow University, where he received an M.A. in 1931. Cochran was then awarded another scholarship to attend St. John's College, Cambridge. There he studied mathematics and statistics with John Wishart. The Great Depression both interested Cochran in a rigorous analysis of economic problems and led him to leave the university before completing requirements for a Ph.D. A position opened at Rothamsted Experimental Station, so Cochran took the post as an assistant to Frank Yates. He worked at Rothamsted for five years, compiling *Fifty Years of Field Experiments at Woburn Experimental Station* (with E. J. Russell and J. A. Voelcker [1936]), continuing the work of analyzing crop and meteorological data begun by Ronald A. Fisher and writing two dozen articles. Cambridge subsequently awarded him an M.A. in 1938. The previous year he had married Betty I. M. Mitchell, an entomologist. The couple had three children.

During his years at Rothamsted, Cochran became interested in experimental design, the analysis of count data, sampling distributions, and agricultural experiments. This wide range developed in part because of Cochran's eagerness to help any interested researcher with a statistical problem. In 1938 Cochran visited Ames, Iowa, and returned to the United States in the following year as an assistant professor at Iowa State College (now University). The college placed great emphasis on applied statistics, which appealed to Cochran. There he began long-standing collaborative relationships with George Snedecor and Gertrude Cox and helped develop the graduate program in statistics.

In 1946 Cochran left Iowa State to head the graduate program in Experimental Statistics at North Carolina State College (now University) in Raleigh and to join Cox's newly established statewide Institute of Statistics, which served the major public universities in North Carolina. His efforts to create a curriculum emphasizing applied statistics at North Carolina State complemented the more theoretical program in mathematical statistics at the University of North Carolina at Chapel Hill.

Cochran helped organize the Biometric Society in 1947. The focus of his research shifted from experimental research to medical and other observational studies as he moved to Johns Hopkins University in 1949 to chair the Department of Biostatistics in the School of Hygiene and Public Health. Cochran continued research with Gertrude M. Cox on issues related to the theory and the practice of experimental

design. Their classic handbook, *Experimental Designs* (1950; rev. ed., 1957), presented applied statistics in a fashion accessible to practitioners and received an enthusiastic response. In addition to authoring a series of papers on design of experiments, Cochran turned his attention to survey sampling. Cochran had often emphasized that the type of data to be analyzed determined the choice of appropriate statistical procedures. Observational studies and human populations often required different methods of analysis than agricultural or other controlled experiments. Cochran knew the importance of randomization in surveys, and his *Sampling Techniques* (1953, 1963, 1977) presented statistical applications for research workers in public health and in the social sciences.

In 1957 the newly created Department of Statistics at Harvard University offered Cochran a position as its first tenured appointment, and he accepted. Cochran joined Frederick Mosteller in organizing the undergraduate and graduate curricula. He maintained an active research agenda. One of the most influential texts in the field of statistics and one of the most widely cited is *Statistical Methods*; George W. Snedecor prepared the original manuscript (1937), though he consulted Cochran regarding sampling in later editions. Cochran rewrote one chapter in the fifth edition and shared authorship for the sixth (1967) and subsequent editions (1980, 1989). Cochran retired from Harvard in 1976, though he maintained a high level of professional activity. He was working on the seventh edition of *Statistical Methods* shortly before his death.

Statistical applications to real world problems fascinated Cochran. During World War II, he participated in the Statistical Research Group, led by Samuel S. Wilks at Princeton University, which made assessments of military effectiveness. The Kinsey Report on human sexual behavior sponsored by the National Research Council was widely criticized on methodological grounds, and the American Statistical Association established a committee of Cochran, Frederick Mosteller, and John W. Tukey to evaluate its findings. Their criticisms of the statistical design and analysis were presented in *Statistical Problems of the Kinsey Report* (1954). He served for many years on the Advisory Committee to the Surgeon General and contributed to the reports on smoking and health. He chaired the ASA's advisory committee on the U.S. Census. Other studies analyzed the Salk polio vaccine trials, Hiroshima radiation effects, equal employment opportunity, and battery additives. He developed creative statistical techniques for revealing relationships in dirty data. Cochran's final monograph, *The Planning and Analysis of Observational Studies* (1983), edited by Lincoln E. Moses and Frederick Mosteller, was published posthumously.

Cochran edited the *Journal of the American Statistics Association* (1945–1950). He was president of the Institute of Mathematical Statistics (1946), the American Statistical Association (1953), the Biometric Society (1954–1955), and the International Statistical Institute (1967–1971). Among the numerous awards Cochran received were the Guy Medal of the Royal Statistical Society (1936), a Guggenheim Fellowship (1964), and the Wilks Medal of the American Statistical Association (1967). Cochran was elected to the Academy of Arts and Sciences (1971) and the National Academy of Sciences (1974). He died at Hyannis, Massachusetts, near his Cape Cod home in Orleans, following an extended illness.

Cochran's work bridged statistical theory and practice; his life was devoted to improvements in applied statistics. Though his theoretical work was strong, Cochran had a unique ability to communicate and to apply statistical methods to practical problems. He was frequently called in as a consultant on experimental studies and as an evaluator of scientific and public policy research. Cochran was a gifted and patient teacher, a clear and thoughtful writer. Whether the subject was higher agricultural yields, efficient sampling of demographic characteristics, or improved medical treatments, William G. Cochran sought to improve methods of statistical analysis and discovery. His students and colleagues remembered Cochran as the ideal scholar: an important researcher, a caring teacher and a dedicated, professional statistician.

• Cochran's papers are collected in the archives of Harvard University. In addition to his six books, Cochran wrote more than 100 papers on statistics and the history of statistics. Most of these articles were compiled by his wife and published as *Contributions to Statistics* (1982). A valuable and comprehensive evaluation of Cochran's work is provided in Poduri S. R. S. Rao and Joseph Sedransk, eds., *W. G. Cochran's Impact on Statistics* (1984). See also R. L. Anderson, "William Gemmell Cochran, A Personal Tribute," *Biometrics* 36 (1980): 574–78; Arthur P. Dempster and Frederick Mosteller, "In Memoriam," *American Statistician* 35 (1981): 38; Theodore Colton, "Bill Cochran: His Contributions to Medicine and Public Health and Some Personal Recollections," *American Statistician* 35 (1981): 167–70; chapters by Rao and H. O. Hartley in D. Krewski et al., *Current Topics in Survey Sampling* (1981); G. S. Watson, "William Gemmell Cochran," *Annals of Statistics* 10 (1982): 1–10; and Mosteller's informative foreword to *Contributions to Statistics*.

JAMES W. ENDERSBY

COCHRANE, Mickey (6 Apr. 1903–28 June 1962), baseball player and manager, was born Gordon Stanley Cochrane in Bridgewater, Massachusetts, the son of Scots-Irish immigrants John Cochrane, a caretaker, coachman, and movie theater owner, and Sarah Campbell. Known as "Kid" at Boston University (1921–1924), "Mike," or "Black Mike" (for his thick raven hair and black mood when his team lost a game), Cochrane endures as "Mickey," a name pinned on him when scout Tom Turner sent word that he was signing a "Mick" from Boston.

Cochrane was a fleet-footed halfback and expert dropkicker at BU; while there, he won ten varsity letters in various sports. He also was an infielder on a local semipro baseball team. In 1923 he heard of an opening at Dover, Delaware, in the Class D Eastern Shore League. When he discovered the team was looking for a catcher only, he reluctantly agreed to try that

position. Playing under the name Frank King, he was an awkward receiver who reputedly could not catch a pop foul with a basket. But he ran fast, and he could hit. At 5'10½" and 180 pounds, he had good size for the position. He batted left-handed and threw right-handed. To establish and sharpen his skills behind the plate, he practiced for hours every day, and he eventually became one of the best-fielding (as well as best-hitting) catchers in baseball history. Veteran umpire and Detroit manager George Moriarity later summed up the widely held assessment of his abilities: "For aggressive headwork, footwork, throwing skill and batting ability, I have never seen anyone like him."

In 1924 Cochrane married Mary G. Bohr; they had three children. That same year Cochrane's .333 batting average at Portland in the Pacific Coast League placed his contract in the high-price range to possible major league buyers. After obtaining a controlling interest in the Portland team, the Philadelphia Athletics under owner-manager Connie Mack acquired Cochrane for $50,000 and put on their roster their star catcher of the next nine years. Cochrane became the leader of one of baseball's greatest teams, the 1929–1930–1931 pennant winners and twice World Series champions. He caught more than 100 games for 11 straight years and batted above .300 in nine of them. His lifetime batting average of .320 is the highest for any catcher. When he was elected the American League's Most Valuable Player in 1928, however, it was for his leadership, defensive ability, and handling of pitchers, not his .293 batting average. That subpar hitting mark was an aberration. Throughout his career he showed a remarkable batting eye. Overall, he struck out fewer than 17 times per season (about once every seven games), and he averaged almost 70 bases on balls each year. His career On Base Percentage of .419 ranks among the highest on the all-time list, surpassing those of players such as Stan Musial, Mel Ott, Hank Greenberg, and Joe DiMaggio.

In 1934 Cochrane became player-manager of the Detroit Tigers. That season he led the team to its first pennant in twenty-five years and received his second Most Valuable Player honor. When the Tigers won their first world championship in 1935, he scored the run that clinched the title, calling it his "greatest day in baseball." Detroiters celebrated for days, and Cochrane was the city's most popular star since Ty Cobb.

Cochrane was named vice president as well as player-manager of Detroit in 1936, but that season he was slowed by illnesses and injuries and caught in only 42 games. On 25 May 1937 he was struck on the right temple by a fastball thrown by Bump Hadley of the New York Yankees. He suffered a triple skull fracture, was unconscious for ten days, and nearly died. He never played again, and in August 1938 he was fired as Detroit's manager.

Cochrane served in the U.S. Navy during World War II. He was elected to the National Baseball Hall of Fame in 1947. In 1950 he returned to the Philadelphia Athletics as a coach in Connie Mack's final season of managing. Cochrane also served as general manager of the Athletics from 28 May until the end of the 1950 season, and in 1961–1962 he was vice president of the Detroit Tigers. He owned a ranch in Nye, Montana, and an automobile dealership in Billings, Montana. After a lengthy illness and frequent hospitalizations, he died in Lake Forest, Illinois.

• Cochrane wrote an autobiography of sorts, *Baseball: The Fan's Game* (1939; repr. 1992). Another source of information is the Cochrane file in the National Baseball Library, Cooperstown, N.Y. A lengthy profile is in *Baseball Magazine*, Aug. 1929. An obituary is in the *New York Times*, 29 June 1962. The *Sporting News* obituary appeared 14 July 1962.

NORMAN L. MACHT

COCKE, William (1748–22 Aug. 1828), legislator, soldier, and Indian agent, was born in Amelia County, Virginia, the son of Abraham Cocke, a member of the tobacco gentry. As a young man, Cocke studied law and soon became prominent in public affairs. After moving in the early 1770s with his wife, Sarah Maclin (whom he married in 1773 or earlier), and the first of their nine children to a settlement in the Holston Valley near the present Virginia-Tennessee boundary, he served in the Virginia House of Delegates and was an officer in the Virginia militia. Sometime later, he married Keziah (or Kissiah) Sims; they had no children. While in the Holston Valley, he participated in the formation of Sullivan and Washington counties and held several minor positions. In 1776 he raised a company of troops, was commissioned captain, and established "Cocke's Fort" in the nearby wilderness. He took part in several military encounters with the British and Indians and in 1780 led his troops—along with Isaac Shelby and John Sevier—to victory over the British at Kings Mountain.

When the Revolution ended, Cocke joined Sevier and others from three western North Carolina counties in a movement for separate statehood. He played a significant role in the organization and brief operation of the state of Franklin (1784–1788), serving as a brigadier general, a member of the legislature, and a writer of the state's constitution. He was active in the affairs of the Southwest Territory during Tennessee's territorial period (1790–1796) and represented Hawkins County in the territorial house of representatives. An eloquent orator, he sponsored many bills, including one that established Blount College, the forerunner of the present University of Tennessee in Knoxville. When Tennessee became a state in 1796, Cocke became one of its two U.S. senators, and in the following year the state legislature named a county in his honor.

Cocke is best remembered for his service in the Senate; many years after he had retired and moved from the state, Thomas Jefferson pointed to him as one who had made a truly significant contribution toward establishing the new government on a firm and lasting footing. The U.S. Constitution, when adopted in 1789, divided senators into three groups. Each group was assigned a term of two, four, or six years. Cocke was in the two-year group, to serve from 1789 to 1791.

He thought that he would then be chosen perfunctorily for a full six-year term, but the powerful William Blount faction, which controlled the state legislature, decided not to reelect him, in retaliation for his having voted to expel Blount from the Senate. Andrew Jackson, then serving in the House, had maintained unwavering loyalty to the Blount group and was chosen to succeed Cocke. This maneuver brought enmity between Jackson and Cocke and resulted in talk of a duel. Although friends of both were able to calm ruffled tempers, more than a decade elapsed before their friendship was renewed. Blount, in the meantime, holding Tennessee's other Senate seat, was expelled from the Senate for having engaged in a conspiracy with the British, and Cocke was named to replace him for a full six-year term in 1799.

Cocke did not seek reelection in 1805 and returned to Hawkins County, where he became active in state politics and business affairs. He was defeated in 1807 when he challenged John Sevier for governor and lost again in a close race two years later to Willie Blount, a half brother of William Blount. In 1809 he was appointed state circuit judge but was impeached and removed from office in 1812 for alleged failure to dispense justice impartially. Within the same year, apparently smarting from his impeachment, he enlisted as a 65-year-old private in the army and fought in the War of 1812 under the command of Jackson. His services impressed the general, who prepared a special commendation for his bravery and patriotism.

Near the end of the war, President James Madison appointed Cocke, on Jackson's recommendation, agent to the Chickasaw Indians. This significant position required him to move to Columbus, Mississippi. He soon resigned as agent and became active in state and local politics, including service in the Mississippi legislature in 1822. He died in Columbus. The state of Mississippi erected a monument to his memory, citing his patriotism, bravery, and lengthy public service.

• Very little has been written about Cocke, although all of the standard histories of Tennessee include information about his service in the U.S. Senate. Samuel C. Williams includes a brief sketch of his life in *History of the Lost State of Franklin* (1924), and Kenneth D. McKellar writes of Cocke's Senate career in his *Tennessee Senators, as Seen by One of Their Successors* (1942). Robert H. White gives details of his impeachment as circuit judge in his *Messages of the Governors*, vol. 1 (1952), and John Spencer Bassett includes in his *Correspondence of Andrew Jackson* (1926–1935) several letters exchanged between Jackson and Cocke regarding Jackson's election to the Senate in 1799 and prospects of a duel between the two. William Goodrich published a brief scholarly article, "William Cocke; Born 1748, Died 1828," in the *American Historical Magazine* 1 (1896): 224–29. See also Robert M. McBride and Daniel Robison, *Biographical Directory of the Tennessee General Assembly*, vol. 1 (1975).

ROBERT E. CORLEW

COCKERELL, Theodore Dru Alison (22 Aug. 1866–26 Jan. 1948), entomologist and systematic biologist, was born in Norwood, England, the son of Sydney J. Cockerell, a gentleman, and Alice Bennett. After the death of his father in 1878, the family moved to Margate, England. Cockerell attended various schools, including the Middlesex Hospital School, but he did not earn a degree.

"My own interest in natural history began as early as I can remember anything," Cockerell stated in the first installment of "Recollections of a Naturalist," in *Bios* (6, no. 4 [Dec. 1935]). In that essay he recalled being encouraged as a child by his father and a beloved teacher, Miss Sarah Marshall, who took great care to foster in him a love for science. Cockerell also cited as influential the availability of good, inexpensive natural history books when he was a child, as well as visits to his grandfather's farm and museums. As a result of these factors, when he was a teen he developed an interest in invertebrates, including mollusks, snails, and slugs.

He began to publish papers by the age of twenty, though tuberculosis interrupted his studies. Believing that a mountain climate would be therapeutic, he moved to Westcliffe, Colorado, in 1887 and worked as a biologist. Cockerell entrenched himself immediately in the academic community there and helped to establish the Colorado Biological Association in 1888. His health improved in Colorado, but he returned in 1890 to England, where he worked at the British Museum of Natural History.

There Cockerell met the renowned naturalist Alfred Russel Wallace, with whom he maintained a close personal and professional relationship until Wallace's death in 1913. Their lengthy correspondence included discussions of evolution, natural history, and personal matters.

In 1891 Cockerell married Annie S. Fenn; they had two children, both of whom died before the age of ten. That same year Cockerell left the British Museum and moved to Jamaica, where he secured a position as curator at the Public Museum of Kingston. There he began to describe and name scale insects of the family Coccidae, an interest that he retained throughout his life.

By the age of only twenty-six, in 1892, Cockerell had successfully established himself as an entomologist and was elected a member of the Entomological Society of Washington.

After the untimely death of his wife and a recurrence of his health problems, Cockerell moved to New Mexico in 1893. He exchanged places with C. H. T. Townsend of New Mexico Agricultural College, Las Cruces, where he was appointed professor of entomology and zoology while Townsend took over Cockerell's duties at the museum in Jamaica. In New Mexico Cockerell began to study insects of the order Hymenoptera, including bees, which henceforth comprised the bulk of his work. As with the scale insects, he set about describing and naming bee species and genera.

Cockerell became a U.S. citizen in October 1898, in Doña Ana County, New Mexico. He married Wilmatte Porter, an American biology teacher and naturalist, in June 1900. Over the years they published several papers together on various topics in biology.

From 1900 through 1903 Cockerell taught biology at New Mexico Normal University, Las Vegas. He was then appointed curator at the Museum at Colorado College, Colorado Springs, a post that he held from 1903 to 1904. At Colorado College, Cockerell completed some important studies on the flowering plant *Hymenoxys*.

In 1906 Cockerell was appointed to the position of professor of systematic zoology at the University of Colorado. Six years later he was appointed professor of zoology, a position that he held until his retirement in 1934. At Colorado Cockerell conducted research on fossils and fish scales that, like many of his other studies, were primarily taxonomic in nature. In 1923 he was elected president of the Entomological Society of America.

Over the course of his career, Cockerell published nearly 4,000 papers, some of them only a few lines long. Though criticized for his haste in publishing, he persisted in publishing brief papers, appearing to use publication as a method of communication rather than one of recording dicta. Cockerell was also criticized for incompletely consulting, and casually referring to, the literature on any given topic in his papers.

Cockerell's special interest in bees led him to describe and name specimens from the United States, the West Indies, Honduras, the Philippines, Africa, and Asia. He published at least 5,500 names for species and varieties of bees and almost 150 names for genera and subgenera. It has been estimated that this represented over a quarter of all known species of bees during his lifetime.

Above all, however, Cockerell was a general systematist. In addition to extensive studies of bees and scale insects, he published papers on slugs, moths, fish scales, fungi, roses and other flowers, mollusks, and a wide variety of other plants and animals. His publications on nontaxonomic topics in biology included papers on insect coloration, plant and animal distribution, and evolution. He was also a naturalist, composing works, for example, on the general entomology of Colorado and a list of reptiles in part of New Mexico, among many others.

Cockerell was also interested in religion, politics, and poetry and published several works in those fields, many as a book reviewer for *Dial* (Chicago). He wrote poems and contributed to the debate regarding education in New Mexico around the turn of the century. He wintered yearly in California after his retirement and died in San Diego.

• A collection of Cockerell's papers is in the Western Historical Collection at the University of Colorado, Boulder. William A. Weber, *University of Colorado Studies, Series in Bibliography*, no. 1 (1965), includes a comprehensive listing of Cockerell's publications and offers insights into his motivations for publishing so prolifically and often such brief works. For Cockerell's autobiographical writings, "Recollections of a Naturalist," see *Bios*, vols. 6–11 (1935–1940). Obituaries are in *Science*, 17 Sept. 1948, and the *Proceedings of the Entomological Society of Washington* 50, no. 4 (Apr. 1948).

SUE ANN LEWANDOWSKI

COCKERHAM, Fred (3 Nov. 1905–8 July 1980), banjo player, fiddler, and singer, was born in Round Peak, North Carolina, near the Virginia border, the son of Elias Cockerham and Betty Jane (maiden name unknown), subsistence farmers. One of seven children, Fred grew up among a musical family; many of his brothers played music, and his father played harmonica and buckdanced. His uncle Troy was a fiddler, as was his older brother Pate. Given such a musical background, Fred began playing music when he was about eight years old. On the banjo he was influenced by local players Mal Smith and Charlie Lowe, who both played in the traditional frailing style, although Lowe "dropped his thumb" from the fifth (drone) string to play melody notes, a method that also influenced Cockerham's melodic playing. Cockerham's interest in the fiddle was spurred by hearing Fiddling Arthur Smith on WSM's "Grand Ole Opry" broadcasts; Smith played in a modern, jazz-influenced style. Cockerham competed against Smith in a local fiddlers' contest in the late 1930s, coming in second to the professional fiddler.

Still a teenager, Cockerham married Eva Gaylean, whose grandfather, Houston Gaylean, was a well-known local fiddle player. The family (eventually growing to include four children) settled in and around Galax, Virginia, although they moved sporadically as Cockerham found jobs working as a musician, primarily as a fiddler. He performed semiprofessionally with a group of local entertainers, including Lowe, Lowe's son Laurence, Kyle Creed, Earnest East and his two brothers, and Paul Sutphin, at various times and in various combinations, picking up radio work and playing for local dances and events. Cockerham also earned prizes in several fiddlers' contests, most notably taking second place at the 1934 Galax Fiddlers' Convention. For a brief period, he played with the Ruby Tonic Entertainers, a group that was sponsored by the South Atlantic Chemical Company, makers of a rhubarb-based medicinal product of dubious efficacy. With this group Cockerham played for approximately six months on Charlotte's WBT radio station on an early morning show. He landed another brief stint as a radio entertainer in the early 1940s, working a similar early morning program on WFMR in High Point, North Carolina.

During World War II Cockerham began working as a laborer. Employed by a local contractor and banjo player named Kyle Creed, who was hired by the navy to build temporary shelters in the area, Cockerham continued in this line of work through the late 1950s. The family then relocated in 1959 to Lowgap, North Carolina, close to his original home of Round Peak. That year a devastating snowstorm hit the area; Cockerham, stranded in his car, was nearly paralyzed for a brief time and lost his high singing voice. A year later he also lost most of his sight during a botched cataract operation. Unable to work Cockerham was encouraged to take up full-time music making again, this time playing with a local group called the Camp Creek Boys, featuring Creed, East, Sutphin, and Verlin Clif-

ton. Creed made Cockerham a fretless banjo, and this became his instrument of choice.

In the mid-1960s the group was "discovered" by northern folklorists and record producers Richard Nevins and Charles Faurot, who recorded material for the County Record label. They partnered Cockerham with fiddler Tommy Jarrell, an excellent player in the traditional style from the region, and the two recorded together on several albums. Another folklorist and record producer named Ray Alden also championed Cockerham's music and helped introduce him to a new generation of listeners. Cockerham became popular among urban revivalists, traveling throughout the North in the early 1970s with North Carolina–based musicians Barry and Sharon Poss on a short concert tour. The couple also arranged for an operation that helped restore Cockerham's sight. He continued to perform and record through the remaining years of his life. He died at his home.

• Ray Alden has documented Cockerham's life story in several places. See his liner notes to the excellent CD collection, *Tommy and Fred* (County 2702), which preserves the best recordings Cockerham made with Tommy Jarrell.

RICHARD CARLIN

COCKERILL, John Albert (5 Dec. 1845–10 Apr. 1896), journalist, was born in Locust Grove, Adams County, Ohio, the son of Joseph Randolph Cockerill and Ruth Eylar. His father served in Congress and was a colonel in the Civil War. Cockerill was christened Joseph Daniel Albert, after his father and grandfather, but to avoid confusion the family called him John. He attended public schools in West Union, Ohio, and was a printer's devil for the weekly *Scion of Temperance* until he enlisted in the army as a drummer boy in 1861 at age fifteen. He carried a musket at Shiloh in 1862 but was discharged soon afterward. He reenlisted as a bugler and served until the end of 1862.

On returning home, Cockerill became editor and co-owner of the weekly *Democratic Union*. After two years he sold his interest and went to work for the weekly *True Telegraph* in Hamilton, Ohio. He and his brother Armstead purchased the newspaper in October 1865 and then Cockerill bought out his brother in April 1867. It was during this time that Cockerill's lively writing style and innovative news display caught the attention of J. B. McCullagh of the *Cincinnati Enquirer*, who hired Cockerill as his Hamilton correspondent. Cockerill left Hamilton in 1868 and spent four months as editor and part owner of Clement Laird Vallandigham's *Dayton Daily Ledger*.

He became a reporter for the *Cincinnati Enquirer* in 1869, but he quickly rose to city editor and then managing editor by the end of 1870. Cockerill believed reporters were central to a newspaper's success. He could be abrasive to individual reporters or nurturing, as he was with young Lafcadio Hearn. Under Cockerill the newspaper's circulation quadrupled. In 1876 he became the *Enquirer*'s correspondent in the Russo-Turkish War, but when he returned in 1877 his old position was no longer open.

Instead, Cockerill became editor and part owner of the new *Washington Post*, but after about a year he sold his interest and left to become managing editor of the *Baltimore Gazette*. Once again, Cockerill's keen news sense and innovative style of display caught the attention of a publisher looking for talent. Joseph Pulitzer asked Cockerill to come to St. Louis as managing editor of the *Post-Dispatch*, only a year old but already the city's leading paper. Cockerill arrived in 1880 and put Pulitzer's idea for a "new journalism" into practice. He used eye-catching graphics, lively writing, and solid news judgment to create a fresh, exciting, and very marketable style of journalism that combined sensationalism with a strong democratic spirit.

Cockerill's tenure with the newspaper was brief but fiery. In the fall of 1882 the *Post-Dispatch*, a Democratic paper, broke with the party and opposed the congressional candidacy of the city's most prominent attorney, James O. Broadhead, calling him unfit for office. Also Cockerill editorially criticized the law firm of Broadhead, Slayback & Haeussler for accepting a $10,000 retainer from the city in a suit against the gas company, then dumping the city and defending the company. On 13 October 1882, after a series of heated exchanges in print, Broadhead's partner, Alonzo W. Slayback, stormed into Cockerill's office vowing to avenge his and Broadhead's honor. What exactly happened is unclear, but in the end Slayback lay dying after being shot by Cockerill, who claimed self-defense.

The shooting outraged St. Louis, and threats were made against Cockerill, Pulitzer, and the newspaper. The backlash continued for weeks and resulted in canceled subscriptions and withdrawn advertising. Pulitzer defended Cockerill, but it was clear that Cockerill's continuation with the paper hurt it. Early in 1883 he either resigned or was dismissed; the record is unclear.

However, in May 1883 Pulitzer called on Cockerill again when he purchased the struggling *New York World* from Jay Gould. As the *World*'s managing editor, Cockerill made liberal use of woodcut illustrations, urged his reporters to write the news "as you would tell it to a friend," and encouraged promising young reporters such as Elizabeth Cochrane ("Nellie Bly") to experiment with story ideas. When he began, the paper's daily circulation was 20,000. It rose to 100,000 by September 1884 and to more than 250,000 by the time he left in 1891. His departure was instigated by Pulitzer's decision to place Cockerill and two others in charge of the *World* without clear delineations of authority. Pulitzer liked to pit his staff against one another, but Cockerill found the situation intolerable, and he walked out. Cockerill had married Leonora Barner, a young actress, in 1884; they had no children.

After leaving the *World*, Cockerill became a critic of journalistic practices such as sensationalism, in articles for *Harper's* and the *Review of Reviews*. Between 1891 and 1894 Cockerill tried to revive two ailing New York dailies, the *Commercial Advertiser* and the *Continent* (later the *Morning Advertiser*), but to no avail. He became the Far East correspondent of the *New York Herald* in early 1895, covering Japan and China, a position in which he distinguished himself. Homeward bound by way of Cairo, Egypt, Cockerill suffered a cerebral hemorrhage and died there.

• Cockerill's papers are in Butler Library, Columbia University. Homer W. King, *Pulitzer's Prize Editor: A Biography of John A. Cockerill* (1965), is well documented but uncritical. Also helpful are Don Carlos Seitz, *Joseph Pulitzer: His Life and Letters* (1924), Julian S. Rammelkamp, *Pulitzer's Post Dispatch, 1878–1883* (1967), and W. A. Swanberg, *Pulitzer* (1967). Obituaries are in the *New York Herald* and the *New York World*, both 11 and 12 Apr. 1896.

JOSEPH P. MCKERNS

COCKRAN, William Bourke (28 Feb. 1854–1 Mar. 1923), orator and U.S. congressman, was born in Carrowkeel, Ireland, the son of Martin Cockran and Harriet Knight, prominent farmers. He attended school in France and college in Ireland. At the age of seventeen he emigrated to the United States. In 1876 he was admitted to the bar and two years later set up practice in New York City. Cockran amassed a substantial fortune through his civil practice. His expertise in public utilities brought clients from the major gas and electric companies in the New York City area. Cockran married three times but remained childless. In 1876 he married Mary Jackson, who died in childbirth in 1877; in 1885 he married Rhoda Mack, who died in 1895; and in 1906 he married Anne L. Ide. In 1887 he bought an estate, "The Cedars," at Sands Point, Long Island, which remained his chief residence.

Cockran's public speaking on behalf of the Democratic party brought him to political prominence. As an orator who rivaled William Jennings Bryan, his one- and two-hour speeches attracted large and enthusiastic audiences. "People had rather hear him than eat," the *New York Times* eulogized (2 Mar. 1923). Usually speaking without a written text, Cockran embroidered his erudite passages with numerous classical and historical allusions, expansive logical arguments, and a rich vocabulary. His presence on a platform commanded attention, and his facial expressions and gesticulations added drama to the proceeding. Most important in an age without electronic amplification, the "indescribable charm" of Cockran's rich and musical Irish brogue could be appreciated in the farthest reaches of the largest amphitheaters.

Cockran was a popular speaker at Democratic party functions, and he joined the Tammany Hall organization in 1884. Over the next forty years his relationship with Tammany waxed and waned. Although consulted by Tammany leaders and sometimes identified as one himself, Cockran was not involved in the business of running the organization. He took a prominent part in state and national conventions, rallies, and other party functions, especially in drafting platforms and resolutions.

Cockran was elected to Congress from New York City's Twelfth Congressional District in 1886 and was in and out of Congress over the next thirty-five years

(1887–1889, 1891–1895, 1904–1909, 1921–1923). When he was out of favor with Tammany, Cockran was out of office. As a minority member during most of his career, his opportunities to influence important legislation were few. He did, however, serve on the Ways and Means Committee beginning in 1891 and took a leading role in the repeal of the Silver Purchase Act in 1893.

Whether in or out of office, Cockran made his views known on most of the major controversies of his day. In 1896 he split with his party over the "free silver" plank. Cockran traveled through nineteen states, denouncing the proposal to monetize silver as a scheme by western and southern farmers to raise prices for their commodities while lowering the wages of working people. In 1900 Cockran returned to the Democratic fold to make impassioned speeches against the annexation of the Philippines. "Imperialism is not the diffusion of American constitutionalism over new lands, but the establishment in conquered territory by this government of another government, radically irreconcilable to the spirit of our Constitution and essentially hostile to it" (McGurrin, p. 194).

On most economic issues Cockran preached the gospel of laissez-faire and envisioned only a very limited role for government. Since the state created nothing, any effort to assist one group necessarily and unjustly robbed from another. He denounced the income tax, municipal ownership of public utilities, and most especially the protective tariff as "class" or "socialistic" legislation. When he returned to Congress in 1904, however, Cockran was carried along by the tide of progressive reform. He backed the Pure Food and Drug Act and supported greater regulation of the railroads as embodied in the Hepburn Act. Theodore Roosevelt's Oyster Bay residence was not far from Cockran's Long Island estate, and Cockran often visited the president. Conversations with Cockran, Roosevelt recalled, "always open up new avenues of thought for me" (McGurrin, p. 279). In 1912 Cockran deserted the Democrats again to join the Progressive party.

Cockran returned to the Democratic party as World War I churned up new issues at home and abroad. Pacifist sympathies drew him to President Woodrow Wilson's neutrality in the early stages of the war. He endorsed American entry into the war in 1917 as well as the Fourteen Points, which embraced some of Cockran's cherished causes: free trade, international disarmament, and national self-determination. The British government's ruthless suppression of Irish nationalists during the war revived Cockran's longstanding support for Irish independence. As a devout Roman Catholic who took pride in his Irish heritage, Cockran deplored the nativist spirit stirred up by the Great War and the consequent demands for cultural conformity. A proponent of personal liberty, he castigated Prohibition in a lengthy debate with Bryan at the 1920 Democratic convention. He consistently opposed immigration restriction, most notably after returning to Congress in 1921.

Cockran built his political career around controversial causes and public speaking, activities that organization-minded Tammany politicos privately scorned. George Washington Plunkitt, the celebrated Tammany exponent of practical politics, lauded Cockran as "the greatest orator in the land" but ultimately branded him an undependable politician. "He calls himself a Democrat but his heart was never in Tammany Hall. One look at him will tell you that he's as much of an aristocrat as old Lord Salisbury himself. He wouldn't lower his dignity to mix with the boys who work late and early to keep the organization going; and while he was in Congress he never darkened the door of a Tammany clubhouse" (McGurrin, p. 52). Aloof and independent-minded, Cockran violated some of the cardinal political precepts of the Gilded Age. His recurrent partisan apostasy brought forth charges of opportunism and inconstancy. The truth, he insisted, was quite otherwise: "I was forced to change candidates to avoid changing principles. Gentlemen on the other side have always cheerfully changed principles to avoid changing candidates" (McGurrin, p. 256). Cockran owed his enduring political success to his eloquence and to a political culture that revered oratory and its practitioners. He died in Washington, D.C.

• A sizable body of Cockran's papers is in the New York Public Library. Robert McElroy has edited a selection of Cockran's speeches under the title *In the Name of Liberty: Selected Addresses* (1925). Cockran has been the subject of two biographies. James McGurrin, *Bourke Cockran, A Free Lance in American Politics* (1948), provides the fuller account of his life, especially outside of politics. Florence T. Bloom, "The Political Career of William Bourke Cockran" (Ph.D. diss., CUNY 1970), is a richer and more focused account. Cockran's public speaking style is dissected in Mother Mary Margaret Crowley, "Bourke Cockran, Orator" (Ph.D. diss., Univ. of Wisconsin, 1941). An obituary is in the *New York Times*, 2 Mar. 1923.

JOHN F. REYNOLDS

COCKRELL, Francis Marion (1 Oct. 1834–13 Dec. 1915), Confederate general and U.S. senator, was born in Johnson County, Missouri, the son of Joseph Cockrell, a sheriff, and Nancy Ellis. He attended local schools and then Chapel Hill College in adjoining Lafayette County, from which he graduated in 1853. That same year he married Arethusa Dorcas Stapp. He taught at the college the following year while studying law. Admitted to the bar in October 1855, Cockrell returned to Johnson County to establish his practice in Warrensburg. He had inherited considerable land holdings from his father and, by special act of the Missouri legislature in 1852, had been granted his legal majority to manage these. His wife died in 1859, leaving him with two small children. He actively participated in Democratic politics and in 1860 received appointment to the Board of Curators of the University of Missouri.

At the outbreak of the Civil War, Cockrell, a slaveowner, organized a company of pro-southern Home Guards and was elected its captain. The group joined the army raised by Sterling Price to resist the Union occupation of Missouri and fought with him at Wilson's Creek (10 Aug. 1861) and Lexington (14–20 Sept. 1861). In December the Missouri Home Guard became officially part of the Provisional Army of the Confederate States, and Cockrell received a Confederate commission as captain. His company participated in the battle of Pea Ridge (7–8 Mar. 1862) and then was transferred with other Missouri troops to Mississippi. Cockrell gained promotion to lieutenant colonel on 12 May and to colonel on 20 June and was given regimental command. His regiment engaged that fall in the battles of Iuka (19 Sept.) and Corinth (3–4 Oct.) before retiring to the Vicksburg area, where they were involved in all of the major battles of that campaign.

Cockrell was promoted to brigadier general in the aftermath of Vicksburg's surrender. Following his parole and exchange, he received the command of the reorganized First Missouri Brigade, which he led throughout the remainder of the war. His brigade served in Mississippi and Alabama during the latter half of 1863 and early 1864. In May 1864 Cockrell's brigade joined General Joseph E. Johnston's forces opposite Union general William T. Sherman in the defense of northern Georgia and Atlanta, during which Cockrell was wounded at the battle of Kennesaw Mountain (27 June). Following the fall of Atlanta, the First Missouri went with General John Bell Hood's army into Tennessee, where Cockrell was wounded again at the battle of Franklin (30 Nov.). He was given a division command in February 1865 and ordered to Mobile, where he surrendered on 9 April. He was imprisoned at Fort Gaines on Dauphin Island but was released on 14 May.

Cockrell remained in Alabama until November 1865, when he returned to Missouri to find himself under indictment, along with others, for the wartime crimes of aiding and abetting the Confederacy. He went to Washington, where, with the help of former congressman and Union general Frank Blair, he secured a pardon from President Andrew Johnson in March 1866. Cockrell reestablished his law practice in Warrensburg with Thomas T. Crittenden, former Union colonel and future Missouri governor. In 1866 he married Anna Eliza Mann, who died childless five years later. He married Anna Ewing in 1873, and they had seven children.

Cockrell entered actively into Democratic politics following the war. He was named a presidential elector for the Democratic–Liberal Republican ticket in 1872 and two years later actively sought the Democratic nomination for governor, narrowly losing in the state convention to Charles H. Hardin, a member of the Conservative Union faction of the party. In January 1875 the Missouri legislature elected Cockrell to succeed Carl Schurz in the U.S. Senate, where he would remain for the next thirty years, being reelected unopposed four times. Taking a special interest in monetary and tariff legislation, Cockrell was a staunch advocate of the monetization of silver and lowering of the tariff. A delegate to the 1896 Democratic National Convention, he strongly supported the party's silver plank that year.

Cockrell also championed greater managerial efficiency in government. During the years that the Democrats controlled the Senate, he chaired the Appropriations Committee and championed the adoption of modern labor-saving devices, such as typewriters and copying machines, in the executive departments. In 1893 he cochaired with Congressman Alexander M. Dockery a commission that secured the modernization of the Treasury Department's accounting and auditing systems. In the aftermath of the Spanish-American War, Cockrell actively promoted legislation to reorganize the army command structure on a more efficient basis and then worked closely with Secretary of War Elihu Root to facilitate the legislation. His reputation for honesty and bipartisanship led President William McKinley to send him to Cuba in 1899 to investigate a scandal in the postal service, resulting in the indictment and conviction of the postal inspector there on charges of embezzlement. He was nominated as a favorite son for the presidency at the Democratic National Convention in 1904 but received only a scattering of votes beyond the Missouri delegation.

Cockrell retired from the Senate in 1905 and was appointed by President Theodore Roosevelt (1858–1919) to the Interstate Commerce Commission, where he served until 1910. His interest in railroad regulation had begun because of the experiences of rural Missouri with railroad bond fraud during the post–Civil War era. As commissioner, Cockrell played an active role in curbing the power of the Standard Oil Company and in seeking more uniform railroad rates. In 1911 President William Howard Taft appointed him a commissioner to help determine the Texas–New Mexico border, and in 1913 President Woodrow Wilson made him a civilian member of the Board of Ordnance and Fortifications of the War Department. He died in Washington, D.C.

Throughout his Senate career and service on the Interstate Commerce Commission, Cockrell gained a reputation as a champion for reform and efficiency. He was widely respected by leaders of both political parties and received particular praise from Roosevelt on several occasions.

• No body of Cockrell papers is known to exist. The only biography was written by a grandson, Francis M. Cockrell II, *The Senator from Missouri: The Life and Times of Francis Marion Cockrell* (1962), and contains some personal correspondence. Obituaries are in the *St. Louis Globe-Democrat*, 14 Dec. 1915, and the *Kansas City Star*, 13 Dec. 1915.

WILLIAM E. PARRISH

CODDINGTON, William (c. Oct. 1603–1 Nov. 1678), founder of Newport and governor of Rhode Island, was born in rural Lincolnshire, England, the son of Robert Coddington, a prosperous yeoman, and Margaret (maiden name unknown). As a result of his mother's advantageous remarriages, William Coddington entered the uppermost commercial circles of the nearby city of Boston and learned some law. Steadily, his ambition and prosperity boosted his estimate of his importance, ultimately to gentry level. In 1625 or earlier, he married Mary (probably Burt), who bore two sons, both of whom died in infancy. He also heard the preaching of John Cotton and became acquainted with some of the leading Puritans of the county. He began a long spiritual quest.

Coddington was one of the men in his neighborhood who refused to give forced loans to Charles I. The others went to prison; he went to Massachusetts in 1630. Shortly after the crossing, Mary died. Although Coddington held the office of assistant (member of the governor's council), he went back to England in 1631, where he married Mary Mosely, and took her to the new Boston two years later. She lived until 1647 and bore two sons who died young and a daughter who lived at least until 1649.

In the Massachusetts capital he became a leading merchant and served as assistant and colonial treasurer. He built an imposing brick house in town and began another on his land in Braintree. The direction of his life changed when John Cotton arrived in 1633, followed shortly by Anne Hutchinson, who gained a wide following, called Antinomians by their enemies, by interpreting Cotton's sermons. Cotton taught the doctrine of predestination in terms that left the individual unable to do more than welcome grace when God preferred it and cautiously endorsed the possibility of direct divine inspiration in the modern age. Hutchinson went beyond him in both lines and proceeded to a rather mystical reliance on Christ. Coddington was among those who thrilled to her new light and stayed with her when Cotton turned against her. In 1637 the government of Massachusetts decided to banish her.

Well before she obeyed the sentence in March 1638, Coddington chose to join the exodus of Antinomians during that spring. He took the lead in organizing the move to Aquidneck, the Indian name of the island of Rhode Island. There he served as judge, the highest official in a professedly theocratic government. When disagreements broke out among Hutchinson's followers over new doctrines that sprang up among the Antinomians and possibly also over the theocratic concept of government, Coddington led several others who left the original settlement at Portsmouth and founded Newport in 1639. There he was judge for a year until the government was secularized and rejoined Portsmouth to form a small commonwealth with Coddington as governor. He held the office until 1647.

He was allotted the largest land grant in Newport, over a square mile, and put servants and tenants to work on it, raising a variety of products, including sheep, for export. He built another large house near the harbor and carried on commerce with considerable success. He and at least three other leading men left the town church in 1640 when it was deciding not to draw up a church covenant or to ordain a minister and was turning against infant baptism. Coddington saw social disruption as the consequence and sought reconciliation with the First Church in Boston. He turned

his back on Antinomian excitements for the time being.

After Roger Williams had procured a charter in 1644 to put Aquidneck into a colony with the mainland towns of Providence and Warwick, Coddington thwarted the plan for three years by holding the island independent. He opposed the union, probably because it threatened his preeminence, though he mentioned only his abhorrence of being joined with the followers of Samuel Gorton in Warwick. In 1639 Gorton had defied Coddington's authority in Portsmouth by preaching a form of Christian anarchism, far worse than the heterodoxy spreading in Newport. Nevertheless, Coddington briefly pretended to accept the union and accepted the office of assistant when a government finally was organized in 1647. By then he was deep into secret negotiations with Massachusetts and Plymouth to detach Aquidneck and achieve a combination short of merger with one of those colonies or an independent membership in the United Colonies of New England (which excluded Rhode Island). These efforts failing, he refused to serve as president of his colony in 1648 and went back to England the next year to get a charter for Aquidneck with himself as governor, to rule with a small elected council. While there he married Anne Brinley and returned to Newport with her in 1651.

His success in obtaining the patent threw Rhode Island into turmoil. The mainland towns thought he had taken the island out of the union and sent Williams back to England to get confirmation of his charter at least as it referred to them. Coddington's opponents on Aquidneck thought government should go on under the charter of 1644, with jurisdiction over the entire territory, and sent John Clarke to ask an annulment of the grant to Coddington. Small-scale fighting broke out in Newport. Even when Coddington obeyed orders from England to give up his government, the two trying to continue government under the first charter (one for the mainland only, the other trying to embrace all four towns) quarreled over the terms of reunion until 1654. Coddington remained disaffected for two more years and was excluded from office until 1663. He served a few times in secondary positions in the early years of the successor government organized under the royal charter granted in 1663.

About that time he became a Quaker. This religion slaked his spiritual thirst at last and, oddly, gave him a new way to assert what he believed was his innate superiority over others in New England. He wrote letters to John Winthrop, Jr. (1606–1676), in Connecticut and Richard Bellingham in Massachusetts proclaiming his new faith in a blend of showy humility and spiritual arrogance. He welcomed the leading Friend, George Fox, to Newport in 1672 and entertained him at a lavish wedding. Just before Fox's arrival the Rhode Island Quakers had decided on concerted action in politics, had gained vital positions in the annual election, and tried to settle a boundary with Connecticut by compromising some major disputes over land. Coddington backed these measures and soon rose to high office again, becoming deputy governor in 1673 and governor for two years after.

Ironically, as a Quaker governor he faced two wars, England's Third Dutch War in 1673 and King Philip's War in 1675. Probably not a pacifist himself, he enthusiastically did what he could to back the English side in both conflicts. Knowing that most Friends and some Baptists in Rhode Island were pacifists, he officially maintained Rhode Island's neutrality in regard to the Indians, while giving his government's help to the neighboring colonies as they waged the war, sometimes on Rhode Island's territory. He left office as the war was ending but served again briefly just before his death in Newport. His third wife outlived him by thirty years. Of their eight children, four sons and two daughters lived to maturity and prominence.

Coddington's years as a Quaker governor, strange to say, brought his life to a fitting summation. He regained political direction of his colony and for a short time achieved the alliance with the neighboring colonies that had been beyond his reach earlier. No longer fearful that radical religion would bring social chaos, he could enjoy leadership in church and state in the undifferentiated superiority he had long regarded as his due. His earlier life revealed some of the ways in which the original Puritan migration could succumb to centrifugal impulses when spiritual yearnings escaped restraint. It also revealed the struggle of the gentleman—even if, as in his case, the rank was self-asserted rather than recognized by English society—to gain and hold a suitable position in seventeenth-century America. Coddington's strivings both built and bedeviled Rhode Island.

• A substantial number of Coddington letters can be found in the Massachusetts Historical Society, especially in the Winthrop papers. His only publication was *A Demonstration of True Love unto You the Rulers of the Colony of the Massachusetts in New-England . . .* (1674), a short remonstrance against Massachusetts's persecution of Quakers. An amateur biography exists in Emily Coddington Williams, *William Coddington of Rhode Island, a Sketch* (1941). Scattered through Dennis A. O'Toole, "Exiles, Refugees, and Rogues: The Quest for Civil Order in the Towns and Colony of Providence Plantations, 1636–1654" (Ph.D. diss., Brown Univ., 1973) are much fuller and less sympathetic explanations of Coddington's life in Rhode Island before 1654. Scattered references to Coddington may also be found in Sydney V. James, *Colonial Rhode Island: A History* (1975), and in Carl Bridenbaugh, *Fat Mutton and Liberty of Conscience: Society in Rhode Island, 1636–1690* (1974).

SYDNEY V. JAMES

CODMAN, William Christmas (25 Dec. 1839–7 Dec. 1921), designer, was born in Norfolk, England. Information about Codman's parents and his years in England remain elusive. A member of the Masonic fraternity, Codman married Emma Rolle in 1865; they had six children. After studying painting and drawing in Norwich, Codman's first significant employment took place at Ely Cathedral, on the Isle of Ely, in Cambridgeshire. He assisted T. Gambier Parry, the artist in charge of painting the nave ceiling, during the ca-

thedral's restoration between 1858 and 1862. Sometime afterward Codman worked as a designer, especially of ecclesiastical ware. In that capacity, he is believed to have worked for Sir Gilbert Scott, one of the most important architects in nineteenth-century England. Codman's work included communion plate for the See of Liverpool and the Memorial Chapel in Delhi, India; candelabra for St. Paul's in London; lighting fixtures for the Luxembourg Cathedral; and, likely, ecclesiastical ware for Westminster Abbey. Later, Codman worked for Elkington and Company, the well-known Birmingham firm that introduced the technique of electroplating silver. He served as chief designer for the prestigious London silversmithing company Cox and Son. Besides his success with silver, Codman also became involved in furniture making. Between 1884 and 1887 he supervised the construction of furniture designed by the English painter Sir Lawrence Alma-Tadema for the company of Messrs. Johnstone, Norman & Company of London.

By 1890 the Gorham Manufacturing Company in Providence, Rhode Island, was searching for a new head designer. Since the company had previously hired Europeans, it was not unusual for them to seek someone overseas. Codman's son William had joined the company as the head of its ecclesiastical department in 1887. In 1891 Codman and his wife moved to Rhode Island. He began as the chief designer at Gorham on 16 November 1891.

Initially, Codman produced designs for Gorham's display at the 1893 World's Columbian Exposition in Chicago, Illinois. Objects like Codman's elaborate Nautilus centerpiece, which incorporated shell, pearls, and semiprecious stones with silver, helped establish Gorham as the premier silver company in the world. However, Codman's work for Gorham was not limited to showpiece objects for world's fairs. He created at least fifty-five flatware designs, which represent one-sixth of Gorham's total inventory of flatware patterns. The most significant design was "Chantilly," for which he received a patent on 30 July 1895. Named after an eighteenth-century chateau outside of Paris, the pattern incorporates rococo elements: overlapping scrolls surround plain surfaces. The design is topped by a fleur-de-lis. Neither too decorative nor too plain, "Chantilly" found immediate success and became the most popular flatware design of the twentieth century.

In 1896, Codman and Gorham's president, Edward Holbrook, introduced a new line of silver that was far different from anything being sold. In seeming contradiction to the modern mechanical processes Gorham used, Codman and Holbrook created a line of handmade silver. Commercial silversmiths at Gorham were retrained to master traditional smithing techniques. They hand-hammered flat pieces of silver into forms. Then, chasers shaped the objects by using a blunt tool to work out the sculptural visions prepared by Codman. Silversmiths were encouraged to interpret Codman's plans rather than reproduce them exactly. This process blurred the lines between designer and silversmith. Hammer marks were left visible to highlight craftsmanship. Ironically, visible hammer marks once signified incompetence. Leaving evidence of hand-work reflected a great shift in the perception of quality wares.

Such hand-wrought products fit the tenets of the flourishing Arts and Crafts movement. English in origin, it promoted the creation of beautiful and functional objects that also celebrated the skills of the artisan. Codman was well aware of these principles and incorporated them into the making of the new line. However, rather than looking to the past for design inspiration, he focused on a modern aesthetic: art nouveau. In striking contrast to academic or traditional designs, this new art emphasized natural lines. Codman incorporated undulating curves, women's long flowing hair, and floral motifs creating sensuous shapes. First displayed in 1897, the wares were officially named Martelé, French for "hand-hammered," at their debut at the 1900 Paris Exposition. Likely, the decision to use a French name was calculated. Martelé was to be an exclusive, quality, modern product; associations with the French and their stylish capital city were likely perceived to enhance that image.

Perhaps the most complex and technically difficult of all of Codman's Martelé creations was displayed at the exposition. A dressing table, mirror, bench, and dressing set made on speculation was designed primarily in the French rococo style. However, the table and bench showed design elements of English furniture evident in the crook of the front legs and the use of both pad and claw-and-ball feet. The elaborate design symbolically referenced the times it would be used through an image of Aurora (day) and an owl (night). At the exposition, Gorham won the grand prix and gold medal for its silverwares.

Four years later, at the St. Louis Exposition, the Gorham display directed by Codman dominated the prizes and medals. Again, an elaborate table contributed to the firm's success. More academic in style, with elements of art nouveau, the ebony writing table and chair included ornamental silver mounts and inlay in silver, ivory, redwood, boxwood, and mother-of-pearl.

By 1909 Martelé's popularity began to wane. Regular production ceased in 1912, although some objects were made as late as 1930. Codman retired from Gorham in 1914 and returned to England.

As chief designer for nearly twenty-three years, Codman helped establish the Gorham Manufacturing Company at the top of its field. His Martelé line became one of the most significant examples of art nouveau in the United States, producing a lasting contribution to American decorative arts. Considered proud and ambitious, Codman was also devoted outside of work. A lover of animals, he was an original member of the Bulldog Club of America and served as its president from 1909 to 1913. He died at his home in Woking, Surrey.

• Objects made from Codman's designs can be found in numerous museum collections, including the Metropolitan Mu-

seum of Art; the Museum of Art at the Rhode Island School of Design; the Dallas Museum of Art; the Newark Museum; the Art Institute of Chicago; and the Chrysler Museum in Norfolk, Va. More details about his life may be found in England. Within the United States, most information is located in the Gorham Company Records at Brown University Library. Especially of note is an unpublished typescript, "History of the Gorham Company since 1878" (c. 1935), by his son William Codman. Additional information can be located in the archives of the Bulldog Club of America. Codman's work for Gorham is discussed in detail in Charles H. Carpenter, Jr., *Gorham Silver 1831–1981* (1982). Additional sources include Charles L. Venable, *Silver in America 1840–1940* (1994), and Samuel J. Hough, "Service de Toilette, Martelé," *Silver* 23 (1990): 24–26. An obituary is in the *Providence Journal*, 8 Dec. 1921.

KRISTIN HERRON

CODRINGTON, Christopher, Jr. (1668–7 Apr. 1710), scholar, soldier, and governor general of the Leeward Islands, was born in St. John's parish, Barbados, the son of Christopher Codrington, a plantation owner and governor general of the Leeward Islands, and Gertrude (maiden name unknown). Codrington's grandfather was one of the first English settlers of Barbados. Codrington spent his early years studying with a tutor, but his early education was also influenced by the unique social environment in which he lived, surrounded by and in regular contact with a substantial slave majority, not only on his father's plantation, but across the island. At age twelve Codrington was sent to England to continue his education, entering a private school near London. In 1685 he began his studies as a gentleman-commoner of Christ Church in the University of Oxford. By 1690 Codrington was formally elected as a Fellow at All Souls College, and he earned his master of arts degree in 1694. While at Oxford, Codrington earned a reputation as a scholar and as a wit.

In 1693 Codrington took a leave from his Oxford fellowship to join a military expedition to the West Indies, part of King William's plans to challenge the French in America by capturing their holdings in the Caribbean and Canada. The expedition was unsuccessful in the West Indies, and Codrington returned to England in late 1693. From 1694 to 1697 Codrington served King William's campaign in Flanders, advancing to the rank of lieutenant colonel. After the treaty of Ryswick in 1697, Codrington returned to London as "one of most courted men in the literary society of the capital" (Harlow, p. 91). His return to the peaceful and privileged life of gentleman-scholar was short-lived. In 1698 he received news that his father had died, and soon thereafter King William appointed the son to succeed the father as governor general of the Leeward Islands. Codrington did not travel to his new post until 1700, spending the intervening year settling his father's affairs in England and recovering from a serious illness.

When Codrington arrived in the Leeward Islands, he found a political situation that threatened trade and social stability. Not only did he find conflict among the several island communities in the region, but he found that planters and merchants alike were openly flaunting established judicial procedures and administrative regulations formulated in London. Complicating these internal problems, poor relations with the French colonies in the region threatened regularly to erupt into local military conflicts. During his tenure as governor general, Codrington attempted a number of different reforms. He argued that administrators sent from England (such as himself) needed to be independent of the local assemblies, on whom colonial administrators relied for funding. He worked to reorganize and reform the local judicial systems. As a way to attract more settlers, Codrington recommended that new settlers be given ten-acre grants of land as a beginning stake. Perhaps one of his most important—and most difficult—projects was his attempt to change the ways slaves were treated. Though he supported slavery as an institution, Codrington advocated more humane treatment of slaves, arguing that they should be educated and that they should receive instruction in Christianity.

Shortly after King William died in 1702, war with the French was declared, and Codrington led the English forces in the Leeward Islands, first taking control of the French half of St. Christopher and then planning to join with forces from England to take Guadeloupe and Martinique. The initial phases of Codrington's attack at Guadeloupe were successful; however, the expected reinforcements from England did not arrive, and Codrington was incapacitated by a fever. Without his leadership and without the support of forces from England, the attack faltered, and Codrington's forces had to withdraw from Guadeloupe and sure victory. Weakened by his illness and faced with growing resistance to his attempts at reform, Codrington asked the Lords of Trade for a leave; instead, they replaced him in July 1704.

Codrington never returned to England. Instead, he moved back to his birthplace, Barbados, and after recovering from his illness he devoted his remaining years to managing his extensive holdings—the entire island of Barbuda and substantial plantations on Barbados, Antigua, and St. Christopher—and to immersing himself again in intellectual pursuits. He died on Barbados.

Having never married and having no children to carry on his name, Codrington is perhaps best remembered not so much for his life, as diverse and as meaningful as it might have been, but for his death, or more specifically for the will he wrote shortly after he had arrived in the Leeward Islands. In addition to distributing his landholdings and his wealth among family and friends, Codrington made two significant bequests. He stipulated that All Souls at Oxford receive ten thousand pounds, "six thousand pounds thereof [to] be Expended in Building of a Library for the use of said Colledge and . . . the remaining four thousand pounds be Laid out in Books to furnish the Same" (Harlow, p. 217). In addition, he bequeathed his own substantial collection to this library. Codrington Library continues to serve Oxford scholars, and a statue of Codrington dominates the center of the library.

Perhaps Codrington's greater legacy was the bequest of his two Barbados plantations and one-half of the island of Barbuda to the Society for the Propagation of the Gospel, the missionary arm of the Anglican church. With this bequest, Codrington "set in motion a revolutionary idea," initiating an experiment in which the church attempted to make slaves into Christians (Klingberg, p. 10). Though the conservative church was slow to condemn slavery, its experiences with the Codrington plantations contributed to the church's eventual support of emancipation in 1834. Further, Codrington College, which first opened to students in 1745, was a pioneer in establishing a model of education that would serve the unique needs of the colonies, before and after emancipation. The college helped fulfill the ideals that Codrington promoted— more humane treatment of the slave population and educational opportunities for colonists, encouraging them to remain in the colonies and, perhaps more important, providing them with the kinds of education that would enable them to "meet the [unique] problems of their environments" (Klingberg, p. 18).

By the early decades of the eighteenth century, colonies such as Barbados and those of the Leeward Islands were integral parts of colonial British America. Like all colonies south of New England, the Caribbean colonies were a vital part of the complex web of cultural, political, and economic forces that were shaping colonial identity. During Codrington's lifetime, Barbados was nearer the "center" of colonial British America than was New England, and Codrington was a central and influential figure in Barbados, during his lifetime and after.

• Vincent Harlow's exhaustive biography, *Christopher Codrington, 1668–1710*, first published in 1928 and reissued in 1990, includes the most extensive bibliography of available primary materials. Harlow also reprinted in his appendices a full copy of Codrington's will and a thorough selection of "Literary Remains and References." Codrington's correspondence as a governor general is available in the *Calendar of State Papers, Colonial Series: America and West Indies* (44 vols., 1860–1969). Jerome S. Handler, *A Guide to Source Materials for the Study of Barbados History, 1627–1834* (1971), and Handler, *Supplement to A Guide to Source Materials for the Study of Barbados History, 1627–1834* (1991), lead to a wide range of primary materials.

The Codrington family's links to the West Indies are explored in the numerous histories of the region. Richard Dunn's *Sugar and Slaves* (1972) and Richard Sheridan's *Sugar and Slavery* (1974) both situate the Codrington legacy in the larger social, political, and economic contexts of the seventeenth- and eighteenth-century Caribbean and colonial British America. Two important studies of the Codrington plantations and Codrington College after Codrington's death include useful accounts of Codrington's life and the consequences of his legacy: Frank J. Klingberg, ed., *Codrington Chronicle: An Experiment in Anglican Altruism on a Barbados Plantation, 1710–1834* (1949); and J. Harry Bennett, Jr., *Bondsmen and Bishops: Slavery and Apprenticeship on the Codrington Plantations of Barbados, 1710–1838* (1958).

GLENN BLALOCK

CODY, John Patrick (24 Dec. 1907–25 Apr. 1982), Roman Catholic archbishop and cardinal, was born in St. Louis, Missouri, the son of Thomas Joseph Cody and Mary Begley, Irish immigrants. His father was a fireman who rose to the rank of district fire chief. Cody was a seminarian at the North American College in Rome. He then studied philosophy and theology at the Pontifical Urbanian College of the Congregation de Propaganda Fide, receiving a Ph.D. in 1928 and an S.T.D. in 1932. He was ordained a priest on 8 December 1931. Returning to the North American College as an assistant rector (1932–1938), he earned a doctorate in canon law from the Pontifical Institute Utriusque Iuris of the Lateranum and worked for the secretariat of state under Giovanni Battista Montini (the future Pope Paul VI).

After returning to St. Louis in 1938, Cody worked as the secretary to Archbishop John J. Glennon, the chancellor, the vice officialis, and a pastor in Richmond Heights. During World War II he was in charge of three National Catholic Community Service Clubs for members of the armed forces and directed Vatican relief work for Italian and German prisoners of war in the area. On 2 July 1947 he was consecrated a bishop as auxiliary to the archbishop of St. Louis, Joseph E. Ritter. In 1954 he was appointed coadjutor to the bishop of St. Joseph, Missouri, Charles H. Leblond, and the next year became apostolic administrator of the diocese. In 1956 he was transferred to the newly created diocese of Kansas City–St. Joseph as the coadjutor to Archbishop Edwin Vincent O'Hara and later the same year was installed as bishop when O'Hara died. He launched an extensive building program and a diocesan newspaper, the *Reporter* (1959). In 1961 he was named coadjutor to the archbishop of New Orleans, Joseph F. Rummel. The next year he became the apostolic administrator of the archdiocese, firmly executing the decision previously adopted by the archbishop to racially integrate the Catholic schools. Cody thus set an example of racial justice for Catholics in the South. At the same time he vigorously promoted the construction of elementary and high schools, thereby incurring a sizable debt, and planned even more expansion. He also founded a diocesan weekly, the *Clarion Herald* (1962).

Cody became the archbishop of New Orleans late in 1964. Meanwhile, from mid-1962 to mid-1965, he was the president of the National Catholic Educational Association; he was also the chairman of the Youth Department of the National Catholic Welfare Conference from 1964 to 1965. During the preparation and course of the Second Vatican Council, he was a member of the Commission for Seminaries, Studies, and Catholic Education; he addressed the full assembly of bishops only once, recommending the proposed Declaration of Christian Education.

In 1965 Cody was transferred to the Metropolitan See of Chicago, consisting of Cook and Lake Counties (the largest archdiocese in the United States). He also became the ex officio chancellor of the Catholic Church Extension Society. In 1967 he was elevated to the cardinalate (with the titular church of Santa Cecilia in Rome) and was attached to the Congregations for the Clergy and for the Evangelization of the Peoples and later to other Vatican bodies. In his archdiocese he introduced many innovations. He reorganized the seminary system, provided medical and hospital insurance coverage for the clergy, established the Priests' Retirement and Mutual Aid Association in 1967, and instituted the Diocesan Clergy Personnel Board in 1966. In 1966 Cody also allowed the organization of an independent Association of Chicago Priests, which became increasingly radical and hostile toward his leadership; in 1971 he established the long-awaited Presbyteral Senate. He divided the archdiocese into seven vicariates under vicars delegate with administrative functions, and in 1976 he redivided it into twelve vicariates under urban vicars (nominated by the clergy) with more pastoral responsibilities.

In 1967 Cody inaugurated a plan called "Project: Renewal," which in spite of the resistance of some of the clergy and laity raised $32 million for the modernization and expansion of parishes and schools and the renovation of the cathedral. He also founded new parishes, mainly in the suburbs. The system of "twinning," pairing a more affluent (white) parish in the city or suburbs with a poorer (black or Hispanic) parish in the inner city for reciprocal visits as well as financial support, had existed unofficially among some parishes since 1969. Cody expanded the practice by setting up in 1976 the Archdiocesan Sharing Program for all parishes to foster not only financial but also social and cultural exchanges. In 1975 he founded the Catholic Television Network of Chicago, the largest diocesan enterprise of its kind in the country. The network featured full production facilities and a professional staff, and offered service to 420 parishes, 396 schools, and other institutions. Numerous new pastoral and social service agencies, such as the Center for Pastoral Ministry and the Office of Conciliation and Arbitration, were also initiated by Cody, as well as new organizations specifically for the laity.

Under Cody's direction, too, the liturgical and other changes mandated by the Second Vatican Council or ordered by the Holy See in execution of its decrees were carried out. The first candidates for the permanent diaconate were admitted in 1970, and the program became the largest among American dioceses. Financial statements of the central archdiocesan administration were issued for the first time, and a uniform bookkeeping system was imposed. Beyond the archdiocesan boundaries, Cody was active as a treasurer of the old National Catholic Welfare Conference in 1966–1967 and of the new National Conference of Catholic Bishops and United States Catholic Conference in 1968–1969. Not limiting his interests to the Catholic church, he established the Archdiocesan Commission on Human Relations and Ecumenism in 1967, and he successfully advocated open-housing legislation in Illinois. Through the Chicago Conference on Religion and Race he cooperated with Protestant and Jewish leaders in Chicago to secure better housing, handgun control, and other social benefits. Cody participated in the two conclaves (papal elections) of 1978 and welcomed Pope John Paul II to Chicago in 1979.

During the socially turbulent era of the 1960s and 1970s, Cody was not spared public criticism and denigration. In 1971 he inaugurated a subsidy program for needy parishes and their schools; but later, when deficits in diocesan budgets necessitated reductions in the subsidies and consolidation of institutions, those affected and their sympathizers protested in the newspapers and to the apostolic delegate in Washington, D.C., as well as to the pope. When Cody closed four inner-city schools in 1975 because of declining enrollment and insufficient support, he was chastised for having acted unilaterally. An advertisement signed by 224 priests appeared in two Chicago newspapers on the church's mission to the inner city and the need for long-range planning. He came into conflict with both the Presbyteral Senate and the Archdiocesan School Board, and in 1978 the Association of Chicago Priests complained to the Congregation of the Clergy about his governance of the archdiocese, requesting an official visitation; a year later the association appealed directly to the pope.

Cody was beset by unprecedented difficulties: numerous defections of priests, loss of many sisters and brothers in Catholic institutions, fewer vocations to the priesthood, shifts of Catholic population, declining church attendance and support, an influx of Spanish-speaking Catholics, and diminishing respect for episcopal authority. In 1981 the *Chicago Sun-Times*, informed by two of Cody's disgruntled associates, revealed that a federal grand jury was investigating allegations made to the U.S. attorney for the Northern District of Illinois that Cody had illegally diverted as much as $1 million in tax-exempt church funds. The money was allegedly given to an elderly woman whom Cody called his "stepcousin" (the stepdaughter of his maternal aunt and an openly acknowledged lifelong friend) or to her children, and subpoenas for records and documents had supposedly been issued. The cardinal steadfastly denied the charges and maintained that he had been falsely accused, but the newspaper waged a vicious campaign against him. After he died in Chicago, the investigation was closed without any indictments ever having been sought. After conducting a study, an accounting firm engaged by his successor concluded that Cody's personal expenditures did not exceed his total estimated personal receipts. His personal estate was valued at $85,000, all of which he bequeathed to the archdiocese for the care and support of aged and infirm priests.

Cody's character defects—some believed him to be overly self-confident, somewhat autocratic, reluctant to share his authority, and too sensitive to insults or offenses—did not outweigh his positive qualities, including his high intelligence, diligence, devotion to the church, personal warmth, and graciousness. He was clearly unable to contend with the unfounded expectations aroused by a misunderstanding of the Sec-

ond Vatican Council or with popular demands for greater consultation, delegation, and permissiveness inspired by the times. At the same time, he lost popularity among others by forthrightly defending civil rights and integration within the church and its schools. He was admired by black Catholics. Of all the Catholic ecclesiastical careers in the United States in the twentieth century, Cody's most dramatically reflected the tumultuous period.

• Cody's personal papers are in the Archives of the Archdiocese of Chicago. Published sources include the strongly biased Charles W. Dahm, *Power and Authority in the Catholic Church: Cardinal Cody in Chicago* (1981), and Harry C. Koenig, ed., *Caritas Christi Urget Nos: A History of the Offices, Agencies, and Institutions of the Archdiocese of Chicago* (2 vols., 1981).

ROBERT TRISCO

CODY, William Frederick (26 Feb. 1846–10 Jan. 1917), frontiersman and entertainer better known as "Buffalo Bill," was born in Scott County, Iowa, the son of Isaac Cody and Mary Ann Bonsell Laycock. Cody's father managed several farms and operated a state business in Iowa. In 1854 the family moved to the Salt Creek Valley in Kansas, where Cody's father received a government contract to provide hay to Fort Leavenworth. After his father died in 1857, Cody went to work as an ox-team driver for fifty cents a day. Shortly thereafter, the firm of Majors and Russell hired him as an express boy. Cody attended school periodically, although his formal education ended in 1859 when he joined a party heading to Denver to search for gold. He prospected for two months without any luck. He arrived back in Kansas in March 1860 after a trapping expedition. He rode for a time for the Pony Express during its short lifetime (Apr. 1860–Nov. 1861). After the start of the Civil War he joined a group of antislavery guerrillas based in Kansas. Later the Ninth Kansas Volunteers hired him as a scout and guide. On 16 February 1864 Cody enlisted into Company F of the Seventh Kansas Volunteer Cavalry. He saw quite a bit of action in Tennessee, Missouri, Arkansas, and Kansas during his one year and seven months of duty. He was mustered out of the army as a private on 29 September 1865.

Cody married Louisa Frederici in St. Louis in 1866; they had four children. The couple moved back to Kansas, where Cody briefly ran a hotel in the Salt Creek Valley. For a short time in 1866 and 1867 he worked as a scout at Fort Ellsworth, but then he formed a partnership with William Rose, a grading contractor for the Kansas Pacific Railroad. The two partners established the town of Rome, Kansas, opening a saloon and store. However, once the railroad bypassed the town, it did not survive long. Soon after, the company hired to board the railroad workers contracted with Cody to provide meat for the workers, which he did by killing twelve buffalo a day. Because of these exploits, he first became known as "Buffalo Bill." The army then hired him as a scout, a position he held for several years. He participated in a number of expeditions against Indians, including General

Philip Sheridan's campaign against the Plains Indians in 1868–1869.

Cody began to attain some national fame by 1869. In July he met dime novelist Ned Buntline, who interviewed him and wrote a serial story for the *New York Weekly*, "Buffalo Bill, the King of Border Men." Even though Buntline advertised the story as "the wildest and truest story he ever wrote," it did not relate any of Buffalo Bill's actual adventures and more closely followed the life of Wild Bill Hickok.

While Cody scouted for the army, he also guided hunting parties of notables who traveled west. In January 1872 he guided the party of Grand Duke Alexis, a son of the czar of Russia. He also entertained other dignitaries and put on his first Wild West show for the grand duke, which was reported in newspapers across the country. In February 1872 Cody traveled to Chicago and New York, where he saw the play based on Buntline's Buffalo Bill serial. After Cody returned to the West, Buntline wrote his second Buffalo Bill dime novel. For heroic actions during an engagement with Indians during April 1872, Cody was awarded the Medal of Honor. However, an act of Congress on 16 June 1916 struck his name from the rolls because he was a civilian at the time of the battle. Also in 1872 Cody was elected to Nebraska's legislature representing the Twenty-sixth District, but he never claimed his seat. Later that year Buntline encouraged Cody to return east and appear on the stage, which Cody did, starring with another frontiersman, Texas Jack, in *The Scouts of the Prairie*. Following the success of the play, Cody's life changed. During the next several years he scouted for the army, guided hunting parties during the summer months, and toured in plays from fall to spring. Some of the experiences on the frontier, such as the killing of Cheyenne chief Yellow Hand during the Sioux War of 1876, provided material for plays or his later Wild West shows. Cody last served as a scout during August 1876, when he participated in General George Crook's Big Horn and Yellowstone expedition.

Beside the plays, Cody and a number of ghostwriters added to his growing reputation through dime novels and serials about Cody's western experiences. These did not document his actual adventures, however, but only served to publicize his shows. His press agents produced many more dime novels about the wonders of the western frontier and Cody's many adventures. Cody's final season of acting in plays was 1882–1883. The plays by that time incorporated events such as Indian dances and shooting exhibitions, which became staples of Cody's later Wild West shows. Before his last year on stage, Cody produced the "Old Glory Blow Out" on 4 July 1882 in North Platte, Nebraska, where Cody owned a ranch. One thousand cowboys entered this forerunner of the rodeo, competing for prizes in broncobusting, shooting, and riding. There began Cody's Wild West show.

Cody launched his touring Buffalo Bill Wild West show at the fairgrounds of Omaha, Nebraska, on 17 May 1883. An outdoor show, it included re-creations of the Pony Express, Indian attacks on the Cheyenne-to-Deadwood stage, horse races, roping events, and wild horses. Cody was the main attraction, however, sitting on his horse and directing the action wearing a buckskin jacket, shiny black boots, and a white Stetson over his long, flowing hair. Nate Salsbury joined the show as a partner the following year, a business arrangement that lasted many years. The show lost money at first, but by 1886 it was a profitable operation.

Annie Oakley, a trick shooter also known as "Little Sure Shot," had joined the tour in 1884. Sitting Bull, the famed Sioux chief, toured with the show during the 1886 season. The following year Cody took his entourage to Europe, where the Wild West show was a tremendous success. The show returned to Europe in 1889 and again in 1891. Buffalo Bill and his western show attained their greatest success in 1893 at the World's Fair held in Chicago. Six million people saw the show that year. Cody continued to tour with the show until 1912, when he retired. Continuing debts, however, forced him to join the Sells-Floto Circus for the 1914 and 1915 seasons. For his last season of shows in 1916, Cody joined the Miller Brothers and Arlington 101 Ranch Wild West.

Cody attempted to capture the West in another way during 1913 when he started his own film company. With the assistance of the Essanay Film Company of Chicago, Cody started the Colonel W. F. Cody (Buffalo Bill) Historical Pictures Company. His intention was to depict events in his life and of the Old West as accurately as possible, using many of the original participants. Cody starred in and produced the eight one-reel subjects, which included his killing of Yellow Hand, the battle of Summit Springs, and the battle of Wounded Knee. Only a short portion of the films survives.

Even though the Wild West show was generally a profitable undertaking, Cody was a poor businessman. Most of his ventures ended in failure. Investments in Arizona mines failed to provide for his retirement, in fact costing him approximately $500,000. The most interesting venture, however, was Cody's attempt at the turn of the century to develop Wyoming's Big Horn Basin, one of the last areas in the country to be settled. He joined George Beck and others in trying to construct the Cody Canal, a project of the Shoshone Land and Irrigation Company. They also founded a town that became known as Cody. Their efforts to irrigate Wyoming's arid landscape failed, however. It took the federal government, by means of the 1902 Newlands Act, to complete the project with the construction of the Shoshone Dam, finished in 1910 and, in 1946, renamed the Buffalo Bill Dam. In 1902 Cody built the Irma Hotel in Cody, named for his youngest daughter. Although the hotel is still operating, it was a money-losing venture for Cody when it first opened.

Cody died in Denver, Colorado, outliving two of his four children. Colorado's legislature passed a special resolution that authorized that his body lie in state in the capitol for one day, during which time 25,000 people paid their respects. Five months later, on 3 June, Cody was buried in a steel vault on the top of Lookout Mountain near Denver.

Although an authentic frontier hero, Cody through most of his career was a showman who helped perpetuate the mythic image of the West. His internationally popular Wild West shows entertained millions, and some 550 dime novels relating to fictional exploits attributed to him added to the legend that persists.

• The Buffalo Bill Historical Center in Cody, Wyo., houses many Cody-related artifacts, an extensive permanent exhibit on his life and significance, and many of the frontiersman's papers. Materials concerning Cody's attempt to develop Wyoming's Big Horn Basin can be found in the George Beck and Buffalo Bill collections, American Heritage Center, University of Wyoming, Laramie. Cody's autobiography, *Life and Adventures of "Buffalo Bill"*, has gone through numerous editions and was first published as *Buffalo Bill's Own Story of His Life and Deeds* (1917). The most comprehensive biography of Buffalo Bill Cody is Don Russell, *The Lives and Legends of Buffalo Bill* (1960). For an examination of Cody's Wild West show, see Sarah J. Blackstone, *Buckskins, Bullets, and Business: A History of Buffalo Bill's Wild West* (1986). See also Joseph G. Rosa, *Buffalo Bill and His Wild West: A Pictorial Biography* (1989); Helen (Cody) Wetmore, *Last of the Great Scouts: The Life Story of Colonel William F. Cody, "Buffalo Bill," as Told by His Sister, Helen Cody Wetmore* (1899); and Dixon Wecter, *The Hero in America: A Chronicle of Hero Worship* (1941). For an explanation of Cody's filmmaking endeavors, see Kevin Brownlow, *The War, the West, and the Wilderness* (1978). An obituary is in the *Denver Post*, 10–12, 15 Jan. 1917.

RICK EWIG

COE, Fred Hayden (23 Dec. 1914–29 Apr. 1979), television, film, and theater producer and director, was born in Alligator, Mississippi, the son of Frederick Hayden Coe and Annette Harroll. Coe was raised in Buckhorn, Kentucky, and Nashville, Tennessee, where he attended Peabody Demonstration School, writing the class play when he was twelve years old. He later studied at Peabody College for Teachers in Nashville. In 1938 he attended Yale Drama School, taking graduate studies until 1940, when he returned to Nashville to accept a job at radio station WSM. He also directed plays at a local Nashville community theater. He served in the U.S. Army from 1942 to 1945. In the postwar period Coe became a pivotal figure in the early development of television, particularly the realm of live drama. In 1945 Coe was hired as a production manager at NBC and in 1948 produced and directed the acclaimed live dramatic series "Philco Television Playhouse," which later became "Goodyear Playhouse." These productions were intended to bring Broadway to American households, which they did admirably. From 1952 to 1956 Coe produced a variety of programs for NBC, including the situation comedy "Mr. Peepers," with Wally Cox, for which he won a Peabody Award; "Producers' Showcase"; and the enormously popular musical version of *Peter Pan* star-

ring Mary Martin. In 1957 Coe left NBC to produce and direct "Playhouse 90," another landmark television anthology series, for CBS.

In the late 1950s Coe turned his attention to Broadway, where he produced many notable plays, including *A Trip to Bountiful* in 1953; *Two for the Seesaw* in 1958; *The Miracle Worker* in 1959, which he would make into a film in 1962; *All the Way Home* in 1960; *A Thousand Clowns* in 1962; *Fiddler on the Roof* in 1964; and *Wait until Dark* in 1966. He also produced *The Left Handed Gun* (1958), the first film directed by Arthur Penn, a friend from his army days, and directed the film versions of *A Thousand Clowns* (1965) and *Me Natalie* (1969). In 1978 Coe became the first person to receive the Evelyn Burkey Award from the Writers Guild of America, awarded to television executives who advance the work of writers. Coe had two children with his first wife, Alice Griggs, and two children from a second marriage to Joyce Beeler. He died in Los Angeles shortly after completing production on a made-for-television film of *The Miracle Worker*, starring Patty Duke.

Fred Coe was a potent and prolific force in the American entertainment industry, producing and directing some of the most influential television programs, motion pictures, and Broadway plays of the 1950s, 1960s, and 1970s. Rising to prominence during what became known as the "golden age of television," Coe produced more than 500 live dramatic presentations. A remarkable judge of talent, Coe discovered or encouraged many young writers, actors, and directors, including Paddy Chayefsky (whose acclaimed *Marty* was written for Coe's "Philco Playhouse"), Horton Foote, Tad Mosel, Gore Vidal, Arthur Penn, Delbert Mann, Francis Ford Coppola, Rod Steiger, Paul Newman, Grace Kelly, and Walter Matthau.

• Some discussion of Coe's work on several projects with Delbert Mann is in the Delbert Mann Papers at the Jean and Alexander Heard Library, Vanderbilt University. No single source details Coe's career; however, several books provide excellent information on Coe's impact on television, among them Frank Sturken, *Live Television: The Golden Age of 1946–1958 in New York* (1990); Sally Berke, *When TV Began: The First TV Shows* (1978); Robert Campbell, *The Golden Years of Broadcasting: A Celebration of the First 50 Years of Radio and TV on NBC* (1976); and Gorham Kindem, *The Live Television Generation of Hollywood Film Directors: Interviews with Seven Directors* (1994). An obituary is in the *New York Times*, 1 May 1979.

MICHAEL ABBOTT

COE, George Albert (26 Mar. 1862–9 Nov. 1951), psychologist of religion, religious educator, and political activist, was born in Mendon, New York, the son of the Reverend George W. Coe, a Methodist minister, and Harriet Van Voorhis. He completed the A.B. at the University of Rochester in 1884 and then enrolled in the Boston University School of Theology, where he received the S.T.B. in 1887 and the A.M. in philosophy and world religions in 1888. In 1891, after a year of study at the University of Berlin, he completed a Ph.D. at the Boston University School of All Sciences.

Reared in an atmosphere of evangelical piety and drawn to church life and its problems through his father's work, Coe had expected to become a minister himself. His theological studies convinced him, however, that theology was incompatible with historical criticism and scientific method. He turned instead to philosophy, which then still included psychology. In 1888 he married Sadie E. Knowland, a musician; they had no children. That same year Coe took a teaching position in philosophy at the University of Southern California. Five years later, in 1893, he was appointed to the faculty of Northwestern University as the John Evans Professor of Moral and Intellectual Philosophy. In his position of responsibility in the philosophy department, Coe laid the foundations for a department of psychology by establishing a course on "physiological psychology" and recruiting an experimentalist to run a psychology laboratory.

Convinced from his study of Charles Darwin that scientific method may be used to address spiritual as well as intellectual questions, Coe undertook empirical studies of conversion and mystical experience. As a youth he had been distressed by his inability to undergo the experience of conversion, which Methodist piety took to be a sign of God's acceptance. As a follower of the new psychology, he used hypnotic experiments to demonstrate that certain temperaments, along with a tendency toward automatisms, predispose individuals to having religious experiences. Rejecting what he was as the Christian tradition's one-sided emphasis on feeling, he argued that religion "ought to rest upon and call into exercise all the faculties of the mind." Coe's early applications of scientific method to religious experience are summed up in his first book, *The Spiritual Life* (1900).

The functional view of religion that Coe gradually worked out was deeply influenced by the writings of Walter Rauschenbusch and others prominent in the Social Gospel movement as well as by Coe's participation in settlement work and local political reform. The heart of religion, he concluded, lies not in exceptional experience but in the heightening and fostering of personal and social values. The problem of religion, he wrote, "is the problem of the nature, history, outlook, and final significance of persons-realizing-themselves-as-such-in-society." Coe explored religion's significance for both personal and social realization in *The Psychology of Religion* (1916).

Increasingly interested in education, Coe joined with others in 1903 to·found the Religious Education Association. Described by later historians as the association's "most significant intellectual mentor" and the leading figure in religious education, Coe was elected president of the organization in 1909, the same year he was appointed as the Skinner and McAlpin Professor of Practical Theology at Union Theological Seminary in New York City. At Union, where the Social Gospel was long in ascendance, Coe established a department of Religious Education and Psychology. He was soon joined by Hugh Hartshorne, who also served as principal of the Union School of Religion, an experimental Sunday school sponsored by the new department. Through his popular courses and major writings such as *Social Theory of Religious Education* (1917), Coe exerted a profound influence on liberal Protestant educators. Outspoken and forceful, he also found himself at odds with Union's president and other colleagues for minimizing traditional biblical themes in religious education and emphasizing instead the development of personality in the context of relations with others. When Hartshorne was denied tenure in 1922, Coe resigned in protest and took a position in religious education at Teachers College, Columbia University. He retired five years later.

While at Teachers College and for some time afterward, Coe was known for leading protests against the presence of the military in high schools and colleges. In 1928, as chair of the Committee on Militarism in Education, he pressed presidential candidates for their views on compulsory military training while informing them of the opposition to such training by numerous national organizations. He likewise chaired a Citizens Committee of One Hundred, which was organized to oppose discrimination against three teachers who had been identified with left-wing politics.

In his last book, *What Is Religion Doing to Our Consciences?* (1943), Coe directed his liberal social conscience to the pernicious effects of the American economic system. He concluded that capitalistic society, by rewarding selfishness and measuring success in terms of possessions, seriously deforms personality. The churches, as class institutions themselves, perpetuate a class economy, he said, and thus they fail to address the social injustices that ought to be the concern of religion. In objecting to capitalism and championing the Marxist ideal of a classless society, Coe in his last years won a place on the infamous list of subversives compiled by the House Committee on Un-American Activities.

Through his research, writings, and collegial support of other scholars, Coe was a major contributor to two early twentieth-century movements, the psychology of religion and the religious education movement. Like Coe's own thinking, both movements were products of the liberal religious impulse, including the Social Gospel movement. When that impulse faltered under the weight of the disillusionment that followed World War I, Coe's influence gradually declined. He died in Claremont, California.

• Collections of Coe's correspondence and other papers are in the libraries of Northwestern University and Yale Divinity School. An account of the development of Coe's religious thinking is presented in his semiautobiographical essay, "My Own Little Theater," in *Religion in Transition*, ed. Vergilius Ferm (1937). A complete bibliography of his writings can be found in the Mar.–Apr. 1952 issue of *Religious Education*, the entirety of which is devoted to Coe. More recent works on Coe include Eldrich C. Campbell, *George Albert Coe and Religious Education* (1974), Helen Allen Archibald, "George Albert Coe: Theorist for Religious Education in the Twentieth Century" (Ph.D. diss., Univ. of Illinois, 1975); Carol Jane Allen, "George Albert Coe: A Social Theory of Religious Education" (M.T.S. thesis, Garrett-Evangelical Theological Seminary, 1991); and Ian Nicholson, "Academic Professionalization and Protestant Reconstruction, 1890–1902: George Albert Coe's Psychology of Religion," *Journal of the History of the Behavioral Sciences* (1994): 30, 348–68. On Coe's role in the Religious Education Association, see Stephen A. Schmidt, *A History of the Religious Education Association* (1983). On his situation at Union Theological Seminary, see Robert T. Handy, *A History of Union Theological Seminary in New York* (1987). An obituary is in the *New York Times*, 10 Nov. 1951.

DAVID M. WULFF

COERNE, Louis Adolphe (27 Feb. 1870–11 Sept. 1922), composer and college professor of music, was born in Newark, New Jersey, the son of Adolphe M. Coerne and Elizabeth Homan. After an early education in Germany and France, Coerne moved with his family to Boston. Following Coerne's graduation from the Boston Latin School in 1888, he studied composition, harmony, and counterpoint with John Knowles Paine at Harvard University and studied violin privately with Franz Kneisel. From 1890 to 1893 Coerne studied organ and composition with Joseph Rheinberger at the Royal Academy of Music in Munich, Germany, and graduated with highest honors. After his return to the United States, Coerne held various positions as musical director of vocal societies and churches in Buffalo, New York, and Columbus, Ohio. In 1897 he married Adele Turton.

Following another period of residence in Germany from 1899 to 1902, during which he composed various works and completed Rheinberger's unfinished Mass in A Minor, Coerne served as associate professor at Smith College in Northampton, Massachusetts (1903–1904). After further research at Harvard and in New York (1904–1905), Coerne earned a Ph.D. in 1905 from Harvard University; according to Henry E. Krehbiel (introductory note to Coerne's *Evolution of Modern Orchestration* [1908]), it was the "first time that the university bestowed the degree for special work in music." Coerne's degree was awarded on the basis of two notable achievements: the score of *Zenobia. Oper in drei Akten*, op. 66, considered the first opera by an American-born composer to be performed in Germany (1902; premiere Bremen, 1 Dec. 1905) as well as the only one of Coerne's stage works to be produced; and a dissertation entitled *The Evolution of Modern Orchestration* (1908).

Zenobia, set to Oskar Stein's libretto about a proud queen's victory in war followed by defeat and death, reveals Coerne's capability for creating fluent dramatic exchange between vocal and instrumental lines in continuous music within each of its three acts. Because of the small number of set arias and the effective choral scenes, *Zenobia* provides opportunity for pageantry and dance.

The Evolution of Modern Orchestration comprises pedagogical analysis, musical examples, and a historical review of the evolution of the orchestra as well as principles of orchestration. After consulting the available standard orchestration treatises, including the one by Hector Berlioz as revised by Richard Strauss, Coerne recognized that the field lacked a comprehensive work in English on the history of orchestration. In his own treatise, Coerne explores modern orchestrational practice, referring not only to the innovations of Berlioz, Liszt, and Wagner but also including analysis of lesser known scores by Brahms, Saint-Saëns, Tchaikovsky, and Dvořák. In a section on American orchestrational practices, Coerne praises compositions by Paine, George Whitefield Chadwick, and Amy Beach and urges the American public to support its composers. With characteristic seriousness of purpose and assured professional competence based on careful score study as well as his own compositional experience, Coerne produced an ambitious and valuable work.

After another period abroad from 1905 to 1907, Coerne returned to the United States to fill posts as director of the conservatory at Olivet College in Michigan (1909–1910), director of the school of music at the University of Wisconsin (1910–1915), and professor at the Connecticut College for Women in New London (1915–1922). In the three years before his death in Boston, he was also editor of the school and college department of the Oliver Ditson Company.

Coerne composed more than 500 works, of which some 300 were published. They comprise a wide range of genres and include cantatas, operas and other stage works (such as *A Woman of Marblehead*, op. 40; *Sakuntala*, a melodrama after Kalidasa, op. 67; and *The Maiden Queen*, op. 69), incidental music, orchestral overtures, symphonic poems, a concerto for violin and orchestra, a sonata for violin and piano, chamber music for various instrumental combinations, solo and part songs, and piano and organ pieces.

One of Coerne's major instrumental works is the symphonic poem *Excalibur*, op. 180 (1921; pub. 1931), a poetic evocation of King Arthur's heroism. The work earned Coerne a prize offered by the Ohio Federation of Music Clubs and was first performed by the San Francisco Symphony Orchestra 23 June 1931 under Walter Damrosch's direction. *Excalibur* shows Coerne's impressive control of large orchestral forces, including elaborate percussion parts, varied instrumental timbres, rhythmic and thematic transformation of initial melodic material, and the impassioned gestures of a late Romantic style.

A Cycle of Love-Lyrics, op. 73 (1915), set to words by William Ellery Leonard, reveals an interest in harmonic, rhythmic, and thematic transformation similar to that displayed in *Excalibur* but on the smaller scale of a song cycle. Each of the five songs adheres to traditional structural conventions (ternary, modified strophic, binary) but the device uniting the whole is a post-Wagnerian application of what Coerne referred to in his score as "thematic correlations" of melodic kernels, eighteen in all, each of which is associated with a specified emotion.

Coerne's predilection for the violin is evident in his idiomatic treatment of the instrument, even in a pedagogical work such as the attractive *Concertino in D für Violine und Piano,* op. 63. In sum, Coerne's musical gifts and excellent education assured his distinguished contribution to his era.

• Coerne's manuscripts are in the Boston Public Library. There is an entry by Richard Aldrich on Coerne in *The New Grove Dictionary of American music,* vol. 1 (1986); the American Supplement of *Grove's Dictionary of Music and Musicians,* vol. 6 (1939), includes a list of Coerne's works. An obituary is in the *Boston Transcript,* 12 Sept. 1922.

ORA FRISHBERG SALOMAN

COFFIN, Charles Albert (30 Dec. 1844–14 July 1926), first president of the General Electric Company, was born in Somerset County, Maine, the son of Albert Coffin and Anstrus Varney. He graduated from the Bloomfield Academy in Maine and then went to Boston to work in the shoe and leather business. He went to Lynn, Massachusetts, in 1862 to establish with his uncle Charles F. Coffin and an investor, Micajah P. Clough, the company of Coffin and Clough, a manufacturer of shoes and boots. The company was quite profitable, for Charles A. Coffin developed an aggressive sales staff for the distribution of its products. In 1872 he married Caroline Russel of Holbrook, Massachusetts. They had no children.

Coffin became involved during the early 1880s in the blossoming electrical industry. In 1883 he entered the Lynn Syndicate; in that same year members of this group purchased Elihu Thomson's American Electric Company of New Britain, Connecticut. They moved the firm to Lynn and renamed it the Thomson-Houston Electric Company. Coffin knew little about the technical facets of the electrical industry; however, he recognized the talents of Elihu Thomson and Edwin Houston, who had patents for arc-lighting systems and for alternating-current dynamos. Between 1884 and 1886 Coffin, with help from Edwin W. Rice, established the most effective sales force in the electrical business; Coffin's product managers were responsible for the manufacturing and distribution of arc lights and lamps, of dynamos and generators, and of electric railway motors. The company expanded and became profitable, because Coffin also insisted that his salesmen accept payment from their customers both in cash and in securities from the purchaser.

Coffin helped to establish and direct the nation's largest electrical company. To avoid patent conflicts over the lamp and other electrical products and to increase markets in the quickly expanding electrical industry, he succeeded in 1892 in merging the Thomson-Houston company with the Edison General Electric Company of New York. Coffin that year was named as president of the newly established General Electric Company, for J. P. Morgan, who was on its board of directors, thought highly of his business skills. Coffin brought administrative efficiency to General Electric during the middle and last years of the 1890s. As president, he appointed vice presidents of finance, of engineering and manufacturing, and of products and sales, who were responsible directly to him in the corporation's centralized structure.

Coffin in other ways promoted the development of General Electric. Under his capable management between 1894 and 1899 the company manufactured and effectively marketed products such as Thomas Edison's incandescent lamp, electric motors and meters, and electrical power equipment. To widen the company's assortment of electrical products and to increase its profits, Coffin in 1901 approved the creation of General Electric's research laboratory; that year he also appointed Willis R. Whitney as the first director of this institution. Between 1901 and 1913, under Coffin's watchful eye, the company's laboratory in Schenectady, New York, the first of its kind in the nation, discovered and perfected the Curtis steam turbine for power stations (1901), the electric stove (1906), the refrigerator (1911), and Irving Langmuir's gas-filled light bulb (1913). Coffin in 1913 relinquished his position as president of General Electric, serving between 1913 and 1922 as chair of its board of directors. As an indication of Coffin's successful leadership, two years before his departure from the board of General Electric, the company grossed approximately $1 million a day, as compared to the $12 million that the company took in during its entire second year of business.

Coffin was also associated with many worthy projects. In 1915 he established the War Relief Clearing House. He also was quite active in the Red Cross, which had been merged with this clearing house. As a result of his contributions to the war effort, he was appointed as an officer in the French Legion of Honor, as a commander of the Order of Leopold II of Belgium, and as a member of the Order of St. Sava of Serbia. Coffin also assisted in creating American scholarships for students from Europe and the United States. Endowed by the board of the General Electric Company at the time of his retirement in 1922, the Charles A. Coffin Foundation awarded fellowships to graduate students in the field of electrical engineering. Coffin was known for "his tireless energy" and for "his encouragement of invention along useful lines" (Martin and Coles, p. 82). He was a shy, modest man who avoided publicity. He enjoyed reading and gardening.

Coffin contributed greatly to American industrial and business history by recognizing the enormous potential of electrical technology and marketing a vast assortment of electrical products. To bring about the rapid expansion of General Electric, he acquired financial backing from Morgan, effectively centralized the diverse departments within the company, and promoted electrical research. Coffin's career attests to the success of the managerial revolution in American capitalism and to the effectiveness of vertical integration within a large corporation. These management principles became the foundations upon which General Electric would build, developing into a leading multinational corporation. Coffin died in Locust Valley, Long Island, New York.

• Select letters and memoranda of Coffin are in the files of the General Electric Company and in the archives of its research laboratory in Schenectady, N.Y. Terse biographical accounts appear in T. C. Martin and S. M. Coles, *The Story of Electricity*, vol. 1 (1919); John W. Hammond, *Men and Volts: The Story of General Electric* (1941); and Bernard Gorowitz, *A Century of Progress: The General Electric Story, 1876–1978*, vol. 2 (1981). Harold C. Passer, *The Electrical Manufacturers, 1875–1900* (1953), describes Coffin's involvement in the Thomson-Houston company. His managerial and marketing contributions to General Electric are assessed in Matthew Josephson, *Edison: A Biography* (1959); Alfred D. Chandler, Jr., *The Visible Hand: The Managerial Revolution in American Business* (1977); Vincent P. Carosso, *The Morgans: Private International Bankers, 1854–1913* (1987); and Lisa Mirabile, ed., *International Directory of Company Histories*, vol. 2 (1990). Coffin's role in supporting the research laboratory of General Electric is explained in Kendall Birr, *Pioneering in Industrial Research: The Story of the General Electric Laboratory* (1957), and George Wise, *Willis R. Whitney, General Electric and the Origins of U.S. Industrial Research* (1985). Obituaries are in the *Engineering News-Record*, 22 July 1926, the *Electrical Record*, Aug. 1926, and the *Link* of the General Electric Company, Aug. 1926.

WILLIAM WEISBERGER

COFFIN, Charles Carleton (26 July 1823–2 Mar. 1896), novelist, journalist, and lecturer, was born in Boscawen, New Hampshire, the son of Thomas Coffin and Hannah Kilburn, farmers. He grew up on the family farm, attended the village school, and studied for a year at the local academy. Coffin, after his marriage to Sallie Russell Farmer in 1846, earned his living by farming and surveying, a skill he had taught himself. The couple had no children. In 1852, with his brother-in-law Moses Gerrish Farmer, he installed Boston's first electric fire-alarm system. During this period he began writing for newspapers in New Hampshire.

By 1853 Coffin was a journalist, as well as the assistant editor of the *Boston Atlas*. From there he moved to the *Boston Journal*, where he served as a correspondent from 1854; however, he spent most of his time sending back news from the Midwest. With the outbreak of the Civil War, Coffin attempted to enlist, but he was turned down because of a bad foot. Determined to be part of the war effort, he covered the battles of Manassas on his own, and he became the *Journal's* official war correspondent after the paper received his precise but graphic reports. Coffin was the only reporter who covered the entire Civil War from beginning to end. He soon became noted as a stickler for accuracy who would venture onto the battlefield in order to obtain the facts.

According to his biographer, William Elliot Griffis, Coffin's reputation as an accurate, honest reporter combined with his assumption that leaders, such as Ulysses S. Grant, would want to talk to him led to his success. Coffin was known for describing the progress of the war in positive terms, as in a July 1864 report when he wrote that "prospects of crushing the rebellion never have been so bright as at the present" (Weisberger, p. 246). He was not afraid to criticize when he thought it appropriate either; he censured General Don Carlos Buell for returning runaway slaves to their owners by noting "'every secessionist' spoke well of Buell" (Weisberger, p. 235). Coffin's reports in 1863 that generals with apathetic views of the Emancipation Proclamation were to be replaced inferred that these men were responsible for the defeats suffered by the Union army. The implication was that once these men had been replaced, the position of the North should improve. Coffin was also known for using florid language, as he did in his 1 July 1864 report, when he wrote that a dying soldier said, "*I have tried to do my duty to my country and to God. . . . Tell them [his regiment] to stand by the dear old flag!*" (Weisberger, p. 294).

Coffin's eyewitness accounts of events such as the battles at Manassas, the capture of Fort Donelson, and the fall of Richmond were the first real reports received by those waiting at home. Coffin's moving reports in the *Journal* about George E. Pickett's charge at Gettysburg, Grant's Wilderness campaign, and the retaking of Fort Sumter were the first to inform President Abraham Lincoln and his cabinet of the outcome of these events. When the president traveled to Richmond, Coffin was there to meet him and was part of Lincoln's official escort through the former capital of the Confederacy. His description of the president inspired Thomas Nast's portrait of Lincoln in Richmond.

Coffin had begun writing about his wartime experiences in 1864 with the first of his thirteen books, *My Days and Nights on the Battlefield*. Numerous other first-person reminiscences followed, such as *Four Years of Fighting: A Volume of Personal Observation with the Army and Navy from the First Battle of Bull Run to the Fall of Richmond* (1866). In this volume Coffin pointed out that the book was mainly his views of what occurred and that more time had to pass before an impartial history of the Civil War was possible. His style was flowery and somewhat melodramatic and gives an idea of how the 2,000 lectures he gave over his lifetime must have sounded.

The Boys of '76: A History of the Battles of the Revolution (1877) was one of Coffin's most popular and readable books aimed at young people. In this book he attempted to provide his readers with eyewitness accounts of the battles. *The Story of Liberty*, which traces the history of the search for liberty from the Magna Carta to early Americans, followed in 1898. Coffin also wrote complimentary biographies of James A. Garfield (1880) and Abraham Lincoln (1893). The Lincoln biography is especially interesting as it discusses the conspiracy theory of the president's assassination from the viewpoint of a contemporary. The book also contains reactions to the assassination and Lincoln from newspapers around the world.

Coffin was elected to the Massachusetts state assembly in 1884 and to the state senate in 1890. He died in Brookline, Massachusetts.

• Additional books by Coffin include *The Boys of '61* (1866), *My Days and Nights on the Battlefield* (1866), *Winning His*

Way (1866), *Our New Way round the World* (1869), *The Seat of Empire* (1870), *Caleb Krinkle* (1875), *Old Times in the Colonies* (1881), *Following the Flag* (1882), *Building of the Nation* (1882–1883), and *The Drum-Beat of the Nation* (1887). William Elliot Griffis, *Charles Carleton Coffin: War Correspondent, Traveller, Author, and Statesman* (1898), is a complete biography. A thorough bibliography of Coffin's works can be found in *Literary Writings in America: A Bibliography*, vol. 2 (1977). Also informative are F. Lauriston Bullard, *Famous War Correspondents* (1914), and Bernard A. Weisberger, *Reporters for the Union* (1953). An obituary is in the *New York Times*, 3 Mar. 1896.

DIANE LOOMS WEBER

COFFIN, Charles Fisher (3 Apr. 1823–9 Sept. 1916), banker, Quaker minister, and philanthropist, was born at New Garden, Guilford County, North Carolina, the son of Elijah Coffin, a teacher and banker, and Naomi Hiatt, a Quaker minister. In 1824 his family moved to Milton, Indiana, and in 1833 they went to Cincinnati for a year before moving to Richmond, Indiana, where Charles would live for the next half-century.

Both Elijah Coffin and Naomi Hiatt came from large and prominent Quaker families, and Quaker influences were critical in Charles Coffin's early life. Elijah Coffin served as clerk, or presiding officer, of both North Carolina and Indiana yearly meetings of Friends, the latter from 1827 to 1857. As American Quakers divided into Orthodox and Hicksite factions in the 1820s, Elijah Coffin played a crucial role in making Indiana an Orthodox stronghold. Orthodox Friends were closer to other evangelical Protestants in emphasizing the authority of the Bible and the divinity of Christ. Hicksite Friends, while not rejecting these doctrines, emphasized the doctrine of the Inward Light. In the 1840s, when Orthodox Friends split into Gurneyite and Wilburite groups, Elijah Coffin led Indiana Quakers as a body into the Gurneyite camp. Gurneyite Friends were open to forming ties in reform movements and good works with other Protestants. Wilburites were unyielding conservatives opposed to such innovations. His position and abilities made Elijah Coffin one of the most influential Quakers in the United States, and Charles Coffin thus formed acquaintances and friendships with prominent Friends from England and the United States.

Coffin received his education in Quaker primary schools before entering his father's bank in Richmond in 1835. In the 1840s he received his first appointments in Indiana Yearly Meeting. In 1847 he married Rhoda Moorman Johnson; they were the parents of six children. After his marriage, he continued to work in his father's bank.

In 1857 Coffin succeeded his father as clerk of Indiana Yearly Meeting, which by that time was the largest yearly meeting of Friends in the world. In the 1850s Gurneyite Friends, who made up about 70 percent of all American Quakers, had moved closer to the dominant evangelical religious culture of the United States, and Charles and Rhoda Coffin were enthusiastic supporters of such tendencies. They took the lead in a re-

form movement of young Gurneyite Friends in the 1860s that tried to preserve Quaker distinctiveness while paring away anachronisms, such as peculiarities of speech and dress and suspicion of other denominations. In 1866 Coffin was recorded a Quaker minister. Late in the 1860s, however, the reform movement was pushed aside by a group of young Quaker ministers committed to second-experience sanctification doctrines, the belief that perfect holiness, or freedom from sin, could be obtained instantaneously after conversion. They led a wave of revivals that transformed the society, sweeping away most of the old ways of plainness and silent worship and bringing music and pastors to Gurneyite Friends meetings. Initially caught up in this enthusiasm, Coffin later became skeptical about it. He played a critical role in holding Indiana Yearly Meeting to a more moderate course, accepting many innovations while trying to preserve a sense of Quaker distinctiveness. Indiana thus remained the most influential Gurneyite yearly meeting in the United States well into the twentieth century.

Meanwhile, Charles and Rhoda Coffin were acquiring national reputations as philanthropists. They were active in both home and foreign mission work and in support of education. Both played an important role in transforming the Friends Boarding School in Richmond into Earlham College in 1859. They were also central figures in founding the Indiana women's prison and the boy's reformatory. In 1871 and 1872 they traveled in Europe to study prison conditions and visit prison reformers. A contemporary commented that they showed little interest in museums or cathedrals but never passed by a jail or madhouse.

Coffin also became influential in Republican politics in Indiana. During the Civil War, although remaining a committed pacifist, he was on intimate terms with leading Indiana Republicans like Governor Oliver P. Morton and Congressman George W. Julian. He used his connections to protect Quaker exemptions from military service while enthusiastically supporting the Union in other ways. In 1869 Coffin declined appointment by President Ulysses S. Grant as superintendent of the Bureau of Indian Affairs.

In 1859 Coffin became president of the Richmond National Bank. Based on his reputation for honesty, and that of other Quakers involved, it became the favored bank for the small savings of Richmond's working people. As his sons Charles H. and Francis reached maturity, they too joined the bank. In June 1884 the bank failed, and all three were caught up in its ruin. The causes remain murky; some thought that Francis and Charles H. Coffin were to blame for using bank money for speculation, but there was considerable evidence that Charles F. Coffin himself had watered the bank's stock, misrepresented its assets, and looted estates and trusts in his care. Numerous civil lawsuits followed, and although none of the Coffins was ever convicted of criminal wrongdoing, many in Richmond held them responsible for the suffering the bank's failure brought to its depositors. In 1886, after a year of painful debate, Richmond Friends publicly disowned (excommunicated) Coffin for deceptive and illegal business practices.

Their property gone, Charles F. and Rhoda Coffin moved to Chicago. There they regained a modest prosperity on his earnings as an insurance agent and broker. Coffin was immediately admitted into membership in the Chicago Friends Meeting. After 1900 he became a regular contributor of historical and reminiscent pieces to various newspapers and periodicals, especially Quaker ones. Beginning in 1905 he quietly lent his support to liberal Quakers like Elbert Russell and Rufus Jones, who emphasized the introduction of modernist methods of critical Bible study, were skeptical of revivalism, and were fervent proponents of the Social Gospel. Many Friends feared these innovations and attacked liberals for their alleged ties with Hicksite Friends. Coffin encouraged the liberals to be forthright in their views, and he helped to blunt some attacks on them. By the time of his death in Chicago, Coffin had become a respected elder figure in American Quakerism.

Coffin was a paradoxical figure. His most enduring legacies are in his leadership of American Friends from the 1850s to the 1880s. He was a critical figure in the transformation of most of American Quakerism from sect to denomination, a vital moderating influence in a time of rapid change. He and Rhoda Coffin also played a vital role in reforming Indiana's prison system, becoming nationally known among prison reformers. Simultaneously, however, Coffin apparently was guilty of questionable business practices that brought ruin to himself and hardship to many. Had he not lived another thirty years after the bank failure to rebuild his reputation, it probably would have been ruined beyond redemption.

• There are large collections of Charles F. and Rhoda M. Coffin's papers in the Friends Collection at Earlham College and in the Friends Historical Library of Swarthmore College. The former includes his autobiography. Charles F. Coffin's published works consist of a number of pamphlets on religious and reform subjects. The only biography is Mary Coffin Johnson and Percival Brooks Coffin, comps., *Charles F. Coffin: A Quaker Pioneer* (1923). It should be supplemented by Mary Coffin Johnson, comp., *Rhoda M. Coffin: Her Reminiscences, Addresses, Papers, and Ancestry* (1910). For Coffin's role in nineteenth-century American Quakerism, see Thomas D. Hamm, *The Transformation of American Quakerism: Orthodox Friends, 1800–1907* (1988).

THOMAS D. HAMM

COFFIN, Henry Sloane (5 Jan. 1877–25 Nov. 1954), Presbyterian minister and educator, was born in New York City, the son of Edmund Coffin, an attorney, and Euphemia Sloane, daughter of the founder of the furniture company W. and J. Sloane. Although his father never joined the church, Coffin's mother was a devout Presbyterian and, along with his maternal grandmother, instilled in Coffin a deep appreciation for the church. After graduating from the Cutler School, a private school for boys in New York City, Coffin received his B.A. from Yale in 1897, winning

election to Phi Beta Kappa and the prestigious Skull and Bones. While at Yale he served as president of the Yale Christian Association and participated in the Northfield summer conferences of the renowned evangelist Dwight Moody.

Feeling the call to ministry, Coffin matriculated in 1897 at New College, Edinburgh, Scotland, where he absorbed the biblical higher criticism of the faculty. In the spring of 1899 he traveled to Marburg, Germany, where he studied with the renowned liberal theologian Wilhelm Herrmann and then returned home to finish his B.D. at Union Theological Seminary (N.Y.) and an M.A. at Yale. Coffin was ordained by the Presbytery of New York in 1900 and called to serve the Bedford Park Presbyterian Church in the Bronx. In 1904 he began serving as part-time faculty at Union and in 1905 accepted a call to Madison Avenue Presbyterian Church. Under his leadership the program, Sunday school, and physical plant of the church grew, and Coffin expanded the staff of the church to keep pace. A dedicated proponent of the Social Gospel, Coffin worked to break down economic and social barriers in the church.

In 1906 Coffin married Dorothy Eells, the daughter of family friends; they raised two children. Coffin lectured widely at colleges and universities and published a number of works, mostly collections of sermons, such as *The Creed of Jesus* (1907), *Social Aspects of the Cross* (1911), and *University Sermons* (1914). Although Coffin opposed growing militarism in the United States with the outbreak of World War I, he ultimately supported American entrance into the war and went to Europe, under the auspices of the YMCA, to minister to the troops.

In 1921 Coffin was a leading contender for the presidency of Yale and the following year was named to the Yale Corporation. A devoted alumnus with a passion for preserving religious influence in the college, Coffin served on the corporation until 1945. Indeed, when recent Yale alumnus William F. Buckley, Jr., charged, in *God and Man at Yale* (1951), that Yale was promoting atheism, Coffin chaired a special committee of Yale alumni to review and respond to these allegations.

A convinced theological liberal or modernist, Coffin was the most prominent spokesman for the liberal cause during heated battles between fundamentalists and modernists in the Presbyterian Church in the U.S.A. in the 1920s. Christian theology, he insisted, needed to accommodate the dominant ideas of the era or suffer from irrelevance. As such, he was a leading force behind the promulgation of the "Auburn Affirmation" in 1924, a document defending theological liberty in the church against conservative efforts to maintain strict doctrinal uniformity. In 1927 his efforts bore fruit, and the church opened itself to greater theological diversity.

In 1926 Coffin was elected president of Union Theological Seminary. His inaugural address stressed the need for the school to concentrate on scholarship, worship, and service to the church and the Kingdom of

Christ. Under his leadership Union admitted women to all rights and privileges of the seminary, increased the number of African-American students, and developed close ties to Columbia University. He attracted Reinhold Niebuhr and Paul Tillich to the faculty and was instrumental in founding the School of Sacred Music at the seminary. His interest in liturgy was reflected in his work *The Public Worship of God* (1946), which sought to serve as a guide for leaders of worship.

Influenced by world events in the 1930s and 1940s and by the theological movement of Neo-orthodoxy, Coffin modified, but never explicitly abandoned, his theological liberalism. His theological position led him throughout his career to work to break down what he considered to be anachronistic denominational divisions. In 1929 he represented the Presbyterian church at the reunion of the Church of Scotland and the United Free Church of Scotland. Throughout the 1930s and 1940s he worked for the union of the Presbyterian and Episcopal churches and, after his election as moderator of the General Assembly in 1943, labored unsuccessfully for reunion between the southern and northern branches of the Presbyterian church. After retiring from the presidency of Union and from the Yale Corporation in 1945, Coffin lectured widely in the United States and abroad. He died in his home in Lakeville, Connecticut.

In many respects Coffin embodied the Protestant mainline establishment when that establishment still dominated the American religious landscape. A prominent speaker at universities and colleges, he influenced students not only at Yale but also at elite institutions across the country. In the midst of the fundamentalist/modernist controversy in the 1920s he was instrumental in convincing the Presbyterian church to broaden its doctrinal boundaries to maintain its influence on the culture. Under his presidency Union Seminary strengthened its position as one of the preeminent theological institutions in the nation and trained many of those who would lead the church in the next generation.

• Coffin's papers are housed in the Burke Library of Union Theological Seminary in New York City. Other important works by Coffin include *Some Christian Convictions: A Practical Restatement in Terms of Present-Day Thinking* (1915), *In a Day of Social Rebuilding: Lectures on the Ministry of the Church* (1918), and *God Confronts Man in History* (1947). G. K. Chesterton et al., eds., *Twelve Modern Apostles and Their Creeds* (1926), contains an autobiographical article by Coffin, "Why I Am a Presbyterian." The most complete biographical study of Coffin is Morgan Phelps Noyes, *Henry Sloane Coffin: The Man and His Ministry* (1964). Reinhold Niebuhr, ed., *This Ministry: The Contribution of Henry Sloane Coffin* (1946), contains reflections on Coffin's life by his contemporaries; Bradley J. Longfield, *The Presbyterian Controversy: Fundamentalists, Modernists, and Moderates* (1991), assesses Coffin's role in the fundamentalist/modernist controversy; and Robert T. Handy, *A History of Union Theological Seminary in the City of New York* (1987), contains a chapter on Coffin's leadership of Union.

BRADLEY J. LONGFIELD

COFFIN, Howard Earle (6 Sept. 1873–21 Nov. 1937), automotive engineer and airline pioneer, was born near West Milton, Ohio, the son of Julius Vestal Coffin and Sarah Elma Jones, farmers. In 1893 Coffin enrolled at the University of Michigan in Ann Arbor, where his mother ran a boardinghouse, but dropped out in 1896 to take a job with the Ann Arbor post office. He was allowed to conduct experiments at the university's engineering shops, however, and built a one-cylinder gasoline engine and a steam-powered car, which he drove on his mail route.

In 1900 Coffin resumed study at the university but withdrew in 1902 to head the Olds Motor Works' experimental engineering operation in Detroit. (In 1911 the university took the unusual step of granting Coffin a mechanical engineering degree in the class of 1903.) In 1905 he was promoted to chief engineer. The following year, with sales manager Roy D. Chapin and two other Olds employees, Frederick O. Bezner and James J. Brady, Coffin joined the Buffalo automaker Edwin R. Thomas to form E. R. Thomas-Detroit. The company produced a runabout model that Coffin had designed but that the Olds Motor Works had decided not to build. Coffin became vice president and chief engineer. In 1907 he married Matilda Vary Allen; they had no children.

In 1908 Thomas sold half of his interest in Thomas-Detroit to Hugh Chalmers, who took over as president of what now became the Chalmers-Detroit Company. The next year Chalmers, Coffin, Chapin, Bezner, and Brady became stockholders in the Hudson Motor Car Company, which was formed to produce a lower-priced car for Chalmers's dealers. However, at the end of the year Chalmers sold his Hudson stock to Chapin, Coffin, and Bezner and bought their holdings in Chalmers-Detroit. Brady stayed with Chalmers and sold his Hudson stock to his former partners.

Chapin, as president, and Coffin, as vice president and chief engineer, developed the Hudson Company into one of the most innovative in the automobile industry. In 1912 Coffin replaced Hudson's initial four-cylinder models with a highly successful six-cylinder car. Unlike many engineers, he recognized that the car's appearance would have to be emphasized in promoting new models. The approach was evident in ads for the 1916 Hudson that singled out its "Yacht-like Body" and "Ever-Lustre Finish" as its distinguishing features.

Coffin's most important contribution to the auto industry, as chairman of the committee on tests of the Association of Licensed Automobile Manufacturers and then as a founder of the Society of Automobile (later changed to Automotive) Engineers, was in promoting standardization of basic auto parts and materials. He was one of two men credited with pushing through the Patent Cross-License Agreement in 1915, which ended the costly litigation that had plagued the industry in its earlier years by making patents awarded to individual companies available to all other member firms.

Although Coffin held the title of vice president of Hudson until 1930, by 1915 he was withdrawing from an active role in the company's affairs and taking advantage of the wealth he had acquired to develop other interests. With the onset of World War I he became a member of the Naval Consulting Board. In 1916 President Woodrow Wilson named him to the advisory commission of the Council of National Defense. Coffin gave special attention to mobilizing the aircraft industry for war production, and when the United States entered the war in 1917, he became chairman of the aircraft production board, a position he held until April 1918. The principles of standardization that he had applied in the auto industry he now applied to the design and production of military aircraft.

In 1922, concerned about the slow progress of aeronautical development, Coffin led in organizing the National Aeronautical Association and was elected its first president. In 1925 he was a founder and the first president of National Air Transport, a venture that evolved into United Air Lines.

Coffin also developed large real estate interests in the 1920s in the Grosse Pointe suburbs of Detroit, on Long Island, and especially in the Sea Island region of Georgia, to which he had been attracted as early as 1911 when he bought 20,000 acres on Sapeloe Island. There he built a mansion with over sixty rooms. He sought to rebuild the economy of the area and, as chairman of the Sea Island Company, oversaw the development of the Sea Island Resort and Golf Club, a luxurious vacation site.

The Great Depression had a severe impact on Coffin's income. To finance Southeastern Cottons, Inc., a textile marketing company that he headed until his death, Coffin sold his Sapeloe Island land holdings. He urged President Herbert Hoover to employ emergency powers to fight the depression, but like most of his business associates he regarded Franklin D. Roosevelt's New Deal policies as dangerously radical.

In 1932, Coffin's wife died after a long illness. In 1937 he married Gladys Baker. Six months later, while at his nephew's home on Sea Island getting ready to go hunting, Coffin died from an apparently accidental gunshot wound.

• Although there is no collection of Coffin's papers, a good deal of material on his career can be found in the papers of Roy D. Chapin in the Michigan Historical Collections of the Bentley Historical Library, University of Michigan, Ann Arbor. There is no complete biography of Coffin. Additional details of his career are in Robert J. Kothe's article on Coffin in the *Encyclopedia of American Business History and Biography: The Automobile Industry, 1896–1920* (1990) and in an uncritical sketch in the *National Cyclopedia of American Biography* (1943). References to Coffin's automotive work may be found in such histories as John B. Rae, *American Automobile Manufacturers: The First Forty Years* (1959), and George S. May, *A Most Unique Machine: The Michigan Origins of the American Automobile Industry* (1975).

GEORGE S. MAY

COFFIN, Sir Isaac (16 May 1759–23 July 1839), Loyalist and British admiral, was born in Boston, Massachusetts, the son of Nathaniel Coffin, the last receiver general and cashier of His Majesty's Customs at Boston, and Elizabeth Barnes. Born into a family of wealth and social prominence, Isaac Coffin attended the Boston Latin School and then entered the British Royal Navy in May 1773. Assigned to the brig *Gaspee*, he might have passed an unremarkable service in the king's navy had not the American Revolution begun in 1775. Loyal to King George III, Coffin stayed in the Royal Navy and served on the Halifax, Nova Scotia, station.

Coffin demonstrated both skill and a knack for finding problems during his early service. In 1779 he was court-martialed for the wreck of an armed ship under his command, *Le Pinson*, on the coast of Labrador. Acquitted of all blame, Coffin proceeded to London and then to the Caribbean, where he was promoted to captain of the 74-gun *Shrewsbury* in June 1782. One month later Coffin was court-martialed on a charge of contempt and disobedience; he had refused to accept three young men as lieutenants on board his ship. Acquitted at the trial, Coffin soon left the Caribbean for England, where he invested his prize money wisely. For three years he lived in both England and France before he was recalled to active duty. In 1786 Coffin transported Lord Dorchester (formerly Sir Guy Carleton) to Quebec. He then returned to England, after which he was suspended from the service for his failure to comply with naval regulations (his listing of four nonexistent "captain's servants" may have been aimed at getting a larger allowance based on the size of the crew). While judgment of Coffin's appeal of the ruling was pending, he went to the Continent where he became involved in the Brabant insurgency against Austria. His rank restored in 1790, he became the commander of the 28-gun *Alligator*. In the same year he was injured in the rescue of one of his men who had fallen overboard; the injury worsened in 1794 and active duty soon became impossible. Thereafter, Coffin held a succession of positions as resident naval commissioner at Corsica, Lisbon, Minorca, Halifax (where Coffin again overstepped his bounds and conflicted with naval regulations), and Sheerness.

Despite his early difficulties, Coffin rose slowly but surely in the navy. Less than a month after he was made a rear admiral in April 1804, he was named a baronet. Upon his promotion to vice admiral in April 1808, he retired from the navy. In March 1811 he married Elizabeth Browne, whose father was William Greenly of Titley Court. For a time, with the permission of King George III, Coffin was allowed to display the arms of the Greenly family. If he thereby intended to improve either his social standing or his fortune, he was to be disappointed. Coffin found no common ground with his father-in-law, and his new wife drove him to distraction with her eccentric habits, such as staying up nights writing sermons. The couple soon separated, amicably but with finality; they had no children.

Coffin's activities between 1808 and 1814 are in other respects unknown. In June 1814 he was promoted to full admiral, perhaps merely by virtue of his seniority. Soon he decided to enter politics, and in 1818 he won a parliamentary seat representing the borough of Ilchester. During his tenure in the House of Commons (1818–1826), Coffin was noted for his use of Latin quotations, knowledge of naval matters, and a coarse sailor-type humor. He was on excellent terms with the duke of Clarence, who would later become King William IV, the "Sailor King." Indeed, during the constitutional crisis that preceded the vote on the Reform Bill of 1832, it appears that King William placed Coffin's name on the list of men who might be made peers of the realm (in order to persuade the House of Lords to pass the legislation). Although he did not become a peer, Coffin rose to as high a position in British society as any ex-colonial American could hope to achieve.

Despite his devotion to England, Coffin did not neglect the land of his birth. In his lifetime he made at least thirty voyages across the Atlantic Ocean. He brought English racehorses to breed in North America, and he introduced a fish of commercial value, the European turbot, to American waters. Most notable among his works in the United States was his creation of a school on Nantucket Island for the descendants of Tristram Coffin. Concerned for the future education of his many relatives on the island, Coffin gave £2,500 sterling for the creation of "Sir Isaac Coffin's Lancastrian School," chartered by Massachusetts in February 1827. The school opened in May 1827 with some 230 Coffin children enrolled. In 1829 Coffin made a voyage to Nantucket; following the celebrations that attended his arrival he purchased a brig to serve as a training ship for young sailors from the school. From what is known of Coffin's character it can be surmised that the development of the school was his proudest accomplishment. Coffin died at Cheltenham, Gloucestershire, England, without an heir to his baronetcy.

Coffin's transatlantic life and career were rather unusual during the early nineteenth century. The days of the late colonial period—when Americans had been welcomed in Britain—had passed, and the American infatuation with British customs and society had not yet appeared. During the trying period in British-American relations that led to the War of 1812, Sir Isaac Coffin was one of the most visible ex-Americans in British society. Had he not been injured in 1790, Coffin might well have been called on to serve against his native country in 1812. It is a testimonial to his charm that Coffin was apparently resented by neither side during this period. In his ability to bridge the gap between the venerable British kingdom and the young American republic, Coffin was quite remarkable. As a result of his creation of the Nantucket school and his friendship with British notables such as King William IV, Coffin was remembered favorably on both sides of the Atlantic Ocean.

• Documents pertaining to Coffin's naval career are in the British Public Record Office. Most of the writing about Coffin has been laudatory and sentimental. Thomas C. Amory wrote *Life of Sir Isaac Coffin, Bart* (1886), and chroniclers of Nantucket have fastened on his story: notable among these are William O. Stevens, *Nantucket: The Far-Away Island* (1936), and Will Gardner, *The Coffin Saga: Nantucket's Story, from Settlement to Summer Visitors* (1949). One of the few critical sources is James E. Candow, "Sir Isaac Coffin and the Halifax Dockyard 'Scandal,'" *Nova Scotia Historical Review* 1, no. 2 (1981): 50–63, which suggests that Coffin was far from exemplary as a naval administrator. The meager documentary record of Coffin's life and career is supplemented by an obituary in *Gentleman's Magazine*, Feb. 1804, p. 205.

SAMUEL WILLARD CROMPTON

COFFIN, James Henry (6 Sept. 1806–6 Feb. 1873), meteorologist and mathematician, was born in Williamsburg, Massachusetts, the son of Matthew Coffin, a bank broker, and Betsy Allen. Several bank failures and his father's death in 1820 left his family destitute. At the urging of his cousin William Hallock, Coffin abandoned his intention of learning a trade and in 1821 went to live on the farm of his uncle, Rev. Moses Hallock of Plainfield, Massachusetts, where he finished his college preparatory studies. Coffin entered Amherst College in 1823 with some financial aid and worked as a teacher and tutor to make ends meet. Sickly as a child, Coffin contracted measles in the first term, which confined him to bed for three weeks and impaired his vision for several years. In 1824 the separation of an internal adhesion made him "dangerously sick" and delayed his graduation until 1828. While at Amherst, he joined the Baptist church.

In 1829 Coffin opened a school for boys in Greenfield that attracted widespread attention among educators. Later incorporated as the Fellenberg Manual Labor Institution, Coffin's school included a boarding house, farm, and shops that allowed students to work their way through school. Coffin taught, among other things, science, mathematics, and surveying. He also published a system of practical bookkeeping. In 1833 he married Aurelia Medici Jennings, a pupil whom he had met six years earlier while conducting a select school at Dalton. The couple had three children.

Coffin became principal of the Ogdensburg Academy in New York in 1837 and began his lifelong study of meteorology. He conducted evaporation studies for the Genesee Valley Canal, supervised student weather observations for the state system, erected a self-registering wind vane, and prepared reports on winds for the *Annual Reports* of the Regents of the State of New York. He also attempted to publish the *Meteorological Register and Scientific Journal*, but the journal failed for want of patronage. In 1839 Coffin established a meteorological observatory on Mount Greylock near Williamstown, Massachusetts, and traveled to Washington at the invitation of the Topographical Bureau to examine the growing amount of meteorological data being collected by the federal government. The following year he became a tutor in Williams College, where he revitalized the college's meteorological association. In addition to taking his own observations, Coffin began a systematic search for wind observations covering the northern hemisphere. He gathered data from libraries, military posts, missionaries, ship owners, polar explorers, telegraph operators, scientists, and other sources. After his observatory was vandalized in 1842, he abandoned his observations there. Coffin left Williams for financial reasons and became the principal of Norwalk Academy in Connecticut from 1843 to 1846. In 1845 he became the chairman of a committee of the American Association of Geologists and Naturalists, which investigated wind systems of the globe. He nevertheless yearned for an academic position that would allow him time for research and access to scientific journals and instruments. In October 1846 Coffin was appointed professor of mathematics and natural philosophy at Lafayette College in Easton, Pennsylvania, where he remained for the rest of his life. He wrote textbooks on solar and lunar eclipses (1843), analytic geometry (1849), and conic sections (1852). After the death of his first wife, Coffin married Abby Elizabeth Young in 1851; they had one child.

In 1853 the Smithsonian Institution published Coffin's monograph, "On the Winds of the Northern Hemisphere." In this work Coffin presented a series of wind charts using data from 579 stations in the Northern Hemisphere. He demonstrated the existence of three latitudinal surface wind belts and three vertical circulation cells. This result proved that George Hadley's hypothesis of a single circulation cell between the equator and the pole was inadequate. William Ferrel used Coffin's wind data to confirm his theory of the general circulation of the atmosphere. Ferrel's theory was based on mechanical principles and assumed only that the rotation of the earth generated certain forces and that the surface of the globe was heated at the equator and cooled at the poles. The wind and circulation patterns predicted by Ferrel's theory agreed closely with those observed by Coffin. Joseph Henry, the secretary of the Smithsonian Institution, asked Coffin to take charge of tabulating and reducing the data collected by the Smithsonian meteorological project. Between 1856 and 1860 he spent approximately half of his time on the project and employed as many as fifteen people as calculators. Coffin and his employees logged an average of 8,276 hours of work per year on the project. One product of this effort was a massive two-volume report published by the government, *Results of Meteorological Observations Made under the Direction of the United States Patent Office and the Smithsonian Institution from the Year 1854 to 1859, Inclusive* (1861 and 1864).

An extremely methodical man, Coffin kept an accurate account of his activities from 1827 to 1860. According to his biographer, Coffin spent his time as follows: sabbaths and religious engagements, 4 years 322.7 days; teaching and business, 16 years 119 days; scientific and literary pursuits, 5 years 328 days; visiting literary institutes, 136.7 days; traveling, 1 year 288.4 days; visiting friends, 166.8 days; accounts, records, journals, 341.5 days; various business, 1 year 217 days; sick, 194.1 days; lost or unrecorded, 82.9 days—for a total of 33 years. Coffin's final publication,

"The Winds of the Globe: or the Laws of Atmospheric Circulation over the Surface of the Earth," appeared posthumously in 1875 in the Smithsonian *Contributions to Knowledge.* This publication, edited by his son Seldon J. Coffin and the Russian climatologist Alexander Woeikof, incorporated wind data from 3,223 stations worldwide and results from all available historical sources. Coffin died in Easton, Pennsylvania.

• The Smithsonian Institution Archives holds a small collection of Coffin's papers, which date from 1848 to 1884. These papers consist of correspondence concerning temperature, wind, and weather reports of the Hudson Bay region from 1848; resolutions of condolence to Coffin's son Seldon J. Coffin from students and alumni of Lafayette College after Coffin's death; newspaper articles; a photograph of Coffin; and the original manuscript of "Winds of the Northern Hemisphere." The Joseph Henry Collection also contains a group of letters exchanged by Henry and Coffin between 1842 and 1873, primarily regarding his meteorological work for the Smithsonian. Other related materials are found in the Smithsonian Meteorological Project Records and in the Meteorological Correspondence of the Smithsonian Institution in the National Archives. There are letters on meteorology from Coffin in the papers of Elias Loomis and William Redfield (both prominent meteorologists) at the Beinecke Rare Book and Manuscript Library, Yale University.

The standard biography of Coffin is John C. Clyde, *Life of James H. Coffin, LL.D.* (1881). This book reproduces the text of Arnold Guyot, "Memoir of James H. Coffin," U.S. National Academy of Sciences, *Biographical Memoirs* 1 (1877): 257–64. It also contains the "Autobiography of Professor Coffin" covering the years to 1846, the text of a number of letters to and from Coffin, and Coffin's diary entries, which chronicle his use of time from 1827 to 1860. The location of the unpublished documents cited by Clyde is unknown. James Rodger Fleming, *Meteorology in America, 1800–1870* (1990), contains an extended discussion of Coffin's role in meteorology and a comprehensive bibliography.

JAMES RODGER FLEMING

COFFIN, John (1756–12 June 1838), Loyalist and British general, was born in Boston, Massachusetts, the son of Nathaniel Coffin, the last receiver general and cashier of His Majesty's Customs at Boston, and Elizabeth Barnes. Coffin attended the Boston Latin School and went to sea at an early age. He rose to command of a ship by the age of eighteen, and in 1775 he was engaged to bring a regiment of British troops from England to Boston, which at that time had just broken out in armed rebellion against King George III. Coffin appears to have had no conflict in his loyalties; he brought the troops on his ship to Boston and soon engaged in the war on the side of the king.

Coffin fought as a volunteer at the battle of Bunker Hill. He demonstrated leadership qualities in the fighting, was promoted to ensign during the battle, and was soon promoted to lieutenant by General Thomas Gage. Later in his life Coffin would declare that Bunker Hill had been the crucial engagement of the revolutionary war: that the solidarity shown by the patriot fighters that day had inspired the other colonies to join Massachusetts in the general rebellion.

Coffin went to New York City in March 1776 and recruited 400 Loyalists from Orange County, New York, to form the King's Orange Rangers. He fought as a captain in the battles of Long Island (1776) and Germantown (1777), and then he transferred into the New York Volunteers (1778). Coffin went to the southern colonies in 1778 and raised a troop of cavalry in Georgia. He fought with distinction at Savannah, at Hobkirk's Hill, and at the battle of Eutaw Springs (8 Sept. 1781), one of the fiercest engagements of the entire war.

Coffin's cavalrymen began the action at Eutaw Springs and suffered heavy casualties in the early part of the battle. Later in the day, Coffin rallied his men and captured the cavalry commander of the patriots, Colonel William Washington. Notwithstanding Coffin's determination, Eutaw Springs was officially a drawn battle, which actually led to a further decline of British strength in the American south. Coffin soon left to join General Charles Cornwallis at Yorktown. Following the surrender of the British troops there on 19 October 1781, Coffin escaped through the American lines and made his way to Charles Town (now Charleston), South Carolina, where he soon married Ann Mathews of nearby St. John's Island. Coffin then traveled northward by land to New York City, where General Guy Carleton made him a major in the British army.

When the revolutionary war ended, Coffin and his wife emigrated to British-held New Brunswick, Canada, where they were among the first settlers of King's County. There they carved out a large estate, which they named Alwington Manor in honor of the Coffin ancestral homestead in England. The couple eventually had eight children who grew to adulthood; of those, one became a general in the British army and two became admirals in the Royal Navy.

Remaining in the British army as an officer on half pay, Coffin was promoted to lieutenant colonel in 1793 and to major general in 1803. He visited England in 1805 and was presented to King George III by the commander in chief of the British army. A decade after rising to the penultimate British rank of lieutenant general in 1809, he was made a full general (12 Aug. 1819). Coffin raised a regiment of 600 men, known as the New Brunswick Fencibles, during the War of 1812, but they did not see any action.

Coffin was also prominent in civil affairs. He was a member of the assembly of New Brunswick, chief magistrate of King's County and a member of the king's council for the province. In his later years, Coffin alternated between living in New Brunswick and living in England. He died at the home of his son, Admiral John-Townsend Coffin, in King's County. At the time of his death he was the oldest general in the British army.

Coffin was a firm Loyalist, a vigorous soldier for the king's cause, and an important early settler of New Brunswick. His decision to fight on the British side during the Revolution was probably an easy one; his early years in Boston and his service at sea both dis-

posed him to favor the British cause. Just as he had identified the battle of Bunker Hill as a determining factor in the revolutionary war, so too was 17 June 1775 a crucial day in his life and career. Serving in the British forces on that day reemphasized and perhaps revivified Coffin's belief in the glory of being a member of the British Empire. He went on to fight with verve and skill in the Tory ranks. Seeing the failure of the British cause in the original thirteen colonies, Coffin perhaps meant to make a good start in the founding and the furthering of another province—New Brunswick—that would remain loyal to the king and the British Empire. To a large extent he succeeded in his aim; the service of three of his sons in the British armed forces provides a testimony to his vision and the ideas that he bequeathed to his children.

• Few sources on Coffin exist. Basic information can be found in James H. Stark, *The Loyalists of Massachusetts and the Other Side of the American Revolution* (1910), which cites as a source Captain Henry Coffin, *Memoir of General John Coffin* (1880). Greater depth is available in Lorenzo Sabine, *Biographical Sketches of Loyalists of the American Revolution* (1864; repr. 1966). Coffin's military activities in the American south during the Revolution are mentioned in several books, notably Elswyth Thane, *The Fighting Quaker: Nathanael Greene* (1972). An obituary is in *Gentleman's Magazine* (Sept. 1838).

SAMUEL WILLARD CROMPTON

COFFIN, John Huntington Crane (14 Sept. 1815–8 Jan. 1890), astronomer, was born in Wiscasset, Maine, the son of Nathanael Coffin and Mary Porter. He received an A.B. in mathematics from Bowdoin College in 1834. After graduating, he assisted his maternal uncle King Porter, a ship's captain, who for the next two years tutored Coffin in the finer points of celestial navigation and the ways of the sea. In 1836 he joined the U.S. Navy as a professor of mathematics, a position that had been created five years earlier as a means of instructing midshipmen while at sea and that was discontinued in 1851 with the establishment of the U.S. Naval Academy. For eight years he was attached to the West Indies Squadron and sailed aboard the USS *Constitution* and the USS *Vandalia*. He also served occasionally as navigation officer, took part in surveys of the Florida coast, and was stationed at the Norfolk (Va.) Navy Yard while on shore duty.

In 1845 Coffin was assigned to the newly opened U.S. Naval Observatory in Washington, D.C., the first facility of its kind in the New World. The same year he married Louisa Harrison, with whom he had five children. Because of its geographical location, the new observatory permitted astronomers to observe the sun, moon, planets, and brighter stars at latitudes a full 15° further south than the observatories of Europe. In 1846 Coffin and other navy astronomers began fixing their gaze on the southernmost part of the night sky in an effort to catalog the visible stars more completely and correctly than had been done by German astronomer Friedrich Wilhelm Bessel or Russian astronomer Friedrich Georg Wilhelm von Struve, the principal European catalogers of stars in the early nineteenth century. The difficulty of this task was compounded by the fact that Lieutenant Matthew Fontaine Maury, the head of the observatory by virtue of his position as superintendent of the Depot of Charts and Instruments, was a hydrographer and meteorologist instead of an astronomer. Maury was more interested in charting the global movements of wind and ocean currents in an effort to discover the swiftest courses by which to traverse the world's oceans, and much of the observatory's resources were devoted to compiling the necessary data from the ship's logs of men-of-war and merchantmen and converting these data into charts. Consequently, little attention was paid to the work being done by the observatory's astronomers.

Despite this official neglect, Coffin was able to contribute to the accumulation of astronomical knowledge through his skillful use of the mural circle, a wall-mounted instrument used to measure the altitudes of celestial bodies as they pass over the meridian on which the wall is aligned. Most of his work involving the mural circle was published anonymously in the first five volumes of the observatory's *Washington Observations* in the form of ephemerides, or tables showing the positions of a heavenly body on a number of dates in a regular sequence. One of his contemporaries noted that "to [Coffin] more than any other man is due the credit . . . of saving the Government observatory from destructive ignorance" (Comstock, p. 5).

In 1849 Coffin contracted an eye disease that prevented him from observing the heavens. In 1855 he became the head of the Department of Mathematics at the U.S. Naval Academy, where in 1860 he was appointed head of the Department of Astronomy and Navigation as well. During the Civil War the academy was moved to Newport, Rhode Island, and many of its professors were called into active duty. Consequently, Coffin became the de facto dean of instruction until the war ended and taught several courses outside of his fields of expertise. While at the academy he wrote *Navigation and Nautical Astronomy* (1863), a textbook based on manuscripts written by William Chauvenet, whom he succeeded as head of the astronomy and navigation department, that in time was pressed into service as the basic textbook on the subject for midshipmen. In 1865 he was appointed superintendent of the Nautical Almanac Office and became responsible for publishing the *American Ephemeris and Nautical Almanac*, a publication designed to provide navigational aid to ships at sea. In 1867 he oversaw the movement of the office from Cambridge, Massachusetts, to Washington, D.C. He retired in 1877 from his position as superintendent and from the navy, and remained in Washington, D.C., where he died.

Although Coffin's contributions to the advance of science in the United States were for the most part made anonymously, his achievements were well known to his colleagues and peers, who elected him to fellowship in the American Philosophical Society and the American Academy of Sciences. He became one of the charter members of the National Academy of Sciences when it was created in 1863. In addition to his scientific contributions, Coffin played important roles in helping to ensure the vitality of the Naval Observatory and the Naval Academy when these venerable institutions were in their infancy.

• Coffin's papers have not been located. A biography appears in George C. Comstock, "John Huntington Crane Coffin," National Academy of Sciences, *Biographical Memoirs* 8 (1913): 1–7.

CHARLES W. CAREY, JR.

COFFIN, Levi (28 Oct. 1789–16 Sept. 1877), abolitionist and merchant, was born in New Garden, North Carolina, the son of Levi Coffin and Prudence Williams, farmers. The only son in a family of seven children, Levi was needed to work on the family farm. He was educated at home by his father until at age twenty-one when he enrolled in school to obtain a formal education. A superior student, he taught school himself from time to time.

The Coffins were a Quaker family with antislavery views, and Levi was shocked when he witnessed, at the age of seven, a coffle of slaves being moved to a new plantation. When he was fifteen he helped free a black man who had been kidnapped into slavery. In 1821 he and a cousin established a school for blacks, but local slaveholders pressured them to close it. Coffin also helped organize a manumission society; however, he and some others later withdrew over their opposition to colonization.

In 1824 Coffin married Catherine White, and two years later they moved to Newport (now Fountain City) in Wayne County, Indiana. They had at least four children, although the exact number is unclear. In Newport Coffin opened a highly successful mercantile business, later adding an oil mill. He soon became involved in helping fugitive slaves, work that previously had been conducted mostly by neighboring black families. Fugitives were provided with food, clothing, and temporary housing before the Coffins arranged for their transportation north. Levi Coffin's leadership and more than twenty years of service eventually earned him the sobriquet "President of the Underground Railroad" among abolitionists in the region.

The Coffins aided an average of 100 fugitive slaves a year passing through on their way to Canada. One of the fugitives they helped is said to have inspired the Eliza Harris character in Harriet Beecher Stowe's *Uncle Tom's Cabin*. Coffin himself was the model for the book's Simeon Halliday. Although Coffin was well known for his clandestine work, his house was never searched for fugitives. The well-knit organization that he created in Newport and later in Cincinnati contributed to the legendary status of the Underground Railroad.

Coffin was a founding member of the Indiana State Anti-Slavery Society established some time around 1838. Differences over antislavery tactics—some

Quakers favored colonization and opposed agitation against slavery—led Coffin and other Quakers, to split from the Indiana Yearly Meeting of Friends and to found their own Yearly Meeting of Anti-Slavery Friends in 1842. A leader in the movement to boycott products of slave labor and to popularize the use of free-labor goods and cotton, Coffin moved to Cincinnati in 1847 to open a free-labor wholesale center and a commission business. After a decade he sold the store but continued to operate the commission trade.

Coffin viewed the Civil War as divine punishment for slavery. As a nonresistant, he gave no personal support to the Union military effort, but he did care for the wounded and provided supplies to those who were prepared to defend Cincinnati against possible Confederate raids. He also visited former slaves—then called contraband—behind Union lines and collected money to provide them with warm clothing and bedding. He helped organize the Western Freedmen's Aid Commission and traveled to the British Isles to raise money for its support. While in England he organized the London Freedmen's Aid Society. In 1867 he attended the International Anti-Slavery Conference in Paris.

In addition to his antislavery work, he was active in the temperance movement and in efforts to improve the condition of free blacks and former slaves. In 1844 he traveled to Canada to investigate the condition of former slaves there, and after the Civil War he worked for passage of the Fifteenth Amendment and other civil rights measures.

Although he contributed greatly to the reform cause, Levi Coffin was a shy person who seldom spoke at public gatherings. Most of his work was done quietly, though he made no effort to hide his underground activity. He was mild-mannered and nonconfrontational in encounters with opponents, including slaveholders he met on several trips to the South. His position as a successful businessperson offered him some protection from criticism. During his retirement, Coffin wrote his autobiography, which was published a year before his death in Cincinnati.

• No known collection of Levi Coffin's papers exists, and very few of his letters appear in the major antislavery manuscript collections. Much information on his life comes from his *Reminiscences of Levi Coffin, Reputed President of the Underground Railroad* (1876). His work is discussed in Wilbur H. Siebert, *The Underground Railroad from Slavery to Freedom* (1898); Stephen B. Weeks, *Southern Quakers and Slavery* (1896); Carleton Mabee, *Black Freedom: The Nonviolent Abolitionists from 1830 through the Civil War* (1970); and Laura S. Haviland, *A Woman's Life-work: Labors and Experiences of Laura S. Haviland* (1882). Obituaries are in the *Cincinnati Enquirer*, 18 Sept. 1877, and the *Christian Worker*, 4 Oct. 1877.

LARRY GARA

COFFIN, Nathaniel, Jr. (3 May 1744–18 Oct. 1826), physician, was born in Portland, Maine, the son of Nathaniel Coffin, also a physician and surgeon, and Patience Hale. He was educated in local schools in Portland and studied the rudiments of medicine with his father. Coffin, Sr., would frequently invite surgeons from ships docking in Portland to his home to learn of developments in the medical profession, as many were recent graduates of London hospitals. Coffin, Jr., ambidextrous from birth, had early demonstrated surgical abilities that his father sought to develop. In 1764 he was sent to study in London medical institutions, where he worked under the tutelage of luminaries such as the surgeon John Hunter.

In 1766 Coffin returned to Portland and assumed the extensive practice of his father, who had died that January. Educated well beyond the norm for his times, Coffin frequently was a consultant in the cases of fellow physicians. He traveled extensively for such consultations and gained a widespread reputation as a physician and surgeon. Jeremiah Barker, himself a noted surgeon, regarded Coffin "as the most skillful surgeon east of the Massachusetts Bay Colony." Coffin was considered especially skilled in performing trephining operations and amputations necessitated by frostbite, gangrene, or injury. In 1770 Coffin married a daughter (name unknown) of Isaac Foster of Charlestown, Massachusetts; they had eleven children.

During the American Revolution Coffin was locally active. He was one of those commissioned in October 1775 to visit the British sloop-of-war commander, Lieutenant Henry Mowatt, to plead that Portland be spared bombardment. The effort was unsuccessful, and when the British landed and began torching the city, Coffin and many other inhabitants fled to the countryside, where he cared for their medical needs. He eventually returned to Portland to care for the sick and wounded brought in on men-of-war or privateers. He also worked as a common laborer in the rebuilding and repairing of homes destroyed or damaged in the attack, raised money for the indigent, and recruited for the war effort. There is some indication that he was especially interested in the medical problems of sailors, for he served for years after the war as a hospital surgeon for all marine patients in the Portland area, set up a private hospital for sailors with other doctors on Bramhall's Hill in Portland, and with Dr. John Merrill worked to create a system of marine hospital service.

Coffin was active in professional organizations, including the Massachusetts Medical Society. In 1804 he, with others, petitioned successfully for the formation of a district society for Maine, and that same year he served as the first president of the Maine Medical Society. In his later years he suffered from gout and asthma, which precipitated his death in Portland.

Coffin's contributions as a trained surgeon were significantly appreciated not only by those he treated but by fellow doctors who drew on his expertise to improve themselves and thereby the medical profession. While few specifics have survived regarding his life and practice, it seems clear that Coffin was held in high esteem by colleagues and community alike.

• No manuscript records by or about Coffin, other than obituaries, exist. Among secondary sources are Howard Kelly, *Cyclopedia of American Medical Biography*, vol. 1 (1920), pp. 191–92; Maine Historical Society Collection 1606, Spalding papers, "Old Doctors of Portland"; and James Spalding, *Maine Physicians of 1820* (1928).

BRIAN C. LISTER

COFFIN, Robert Peter Tristram (18 Mar. 1892–20 Jan. 1955), poet and teacher, was born in Brunswick, Maine, the son of James William Coffin, a farmer, and Alice Mary Coombs. Robert spent his early years living on various islands off the coast of Maine, where often the nearest neighbor was two or more miles away. While his father created working farms out of this wilderness, the ten Coffin children learned far more than a formal education under the tutelage of their mother; they were taught to adapt the rugged surroundings to their needs, whether in collecting berries and fish for preserves or steaming oak strips over a boiling kettle to bend boat ribs. These early lessons instilled in Coffin a love of Maine and its wilderness that would later reemerge, meshed with a strong New England Puritanism, as the foundation of much of his literary work.

When he reached the seventh grade, Coffin was sent to Brunswick to attend school and to prepare him eventually to enter Bowdoin College, to which he matriculated in 1911 following the expectations of his father, already three years dead. He excelled at his studies, graduating not only summa cum laude in 1915 but "with the highest marks in his class" (Swain, p. 19). Yet throughout his college years, Coffin pursued his writing craft. He had long since begun to write poetry and stories alike and while at Bowdoin, both edited the college's literary magazine and received the college's coveted Hawthorne Prize for promising short stories. Although born Robert Peter, with the publication of his first poem he had already chosen to commemorate his roots, adopting the "Tristram" in honor of an ancestor who was conscripted by the British, fought in the War of 1812, and then worked his way home to his family from London following the war.

After his graduation from college, he spent a year at Princeton University, receiving an M.A. in English in 1916, during which time he was funded through Bowdoin's Henry W. Longfellow Scholarship. He continued his studies in Trinity College, Oxford University, Oxford, England as a Rhodes scholar, but like many of his countrymen, Coffin interrupted his career in 1917 to enlist in the U.S. army in which he underwent officers' training in Oxford, Plattsburgh, New York, and Fort Monroe, Virginia. He was eventually commissioned a second lieutenant and sent abroad as an adjunct with the 72nd artillery, but not before he was wed in Boston to Ruth Neal Phillip, the daughter of a Jamaica Plains, Massachusetts, merchant in 1918; they had four children. He served in the Camouflage Corps in France, where he was wounded and subsequently discharged. Coffin spent ten years fighting the Veterans Administration to finally receive a 10 percent disability rating, conceding that "being that I was a stubborn Maine Yankee . . . I stuck to my guns. And I won, too. But the cost of postage alone was more than the rating was ever worth" (Swain, p. 19).

Coffin returned to Oxford University where he was awarded a B.A. in 1920 and a B.Litt. in 1921. Following his Oxford degrees, he joined the faculty of Wells College in Aurora, New York, as an instructor, rising with meteoric speed to the rank of professor in seven brief years. During these years, he published his first two books of poetry, *Christchurch* (1924), and *Dew and Bronze* (1927). Although the first volume, as its name suggests, found its roots more in religious fervor, the latter collection begins to explore Coffin's lifelong fascination with the fixation on his native Maine. During this period, he also published a collection of essays, *A Book of Crowns and Cottages* (1925), chronicling his European experiences.

Coffin arrived at Wells, however, with far more than his penchant for writing poetry, his love of literature, and his desire to educate; he brought with him the belief that since the "independent type of education tended to set my own independence at an early age" (Swain, p. 14), he should create the same atmosphere among his own students. Adapting the Oxford University system of tutorials and independent motivation, Coffin instituted a similar system at Wells College. In 1929 he took a leave of absence to return to Oxford University for the purpose of studying the honors program, anticipating instituting a somewhat reconfigured version of it at his own college. He returned to Wells to assume the role of departmental chairman following this Oxford sabbatical and was presented with an honorary Doctor of Letters degree from Bowdoin from Bowdoin in 1930.

Coffin's next five years at Wells College were especially prolific. He continued his volumes of poetry, with *Golden Falcon* (1929), *The Yoke of Thunder* (1932), and *Ballads of Square-Toed Americans* (1933). He also published four historical volumes, two chronicling British history (*Laud: Storm Center of Stuart England* in 1930 and *The Dukes of Buckingham* in 1931), before moving toward a much more personal historical approach with a biography commemorating his father, *Portrait of an American* (1931), and an autobiographical account of his own Maine childhood, *Lost Paradise* (1934). He also put together a second volume of essays, *An Attic Room* (1929), focusing upon his Maine upbringing.

In 1934 Coffin returned to his beloved Maine as Bowdoin College's Franklin Pierce Professor of English, where he remained despite numerous sabbaticals for twenty years. In 1935 Coffin published *Strange Holiness*, a collection of poems that was destined to win the Pulitzer Prize for poetry the following year. Throughout his later life, Coffin lectured frequently to a wide audience. He delivered the Percy Turnbull Memorial Lectures at Johns Hopkins University in 1938, commemorating and commenting on the poetry of his good friend Robert Frost. Additionally, he lectured or taught at the University of New Hampshire, the Fine

Arts Colony in Corpus Christi, Columbia University, the University of Florida, and the University of Athens, where he was a Fulbright special lecturer on American literature and civilization. Coffin died in Portland, Maine.

Coffin was one of the most prolific poets of his generation, publishing at least one poem each month between 1930 and his death in such widely circulated magazines as *Saturday Evening Post* and *Cosmopolitan*. Although he lectured often and was beloved by his students, Coffin never received a faithful critical following despite winning numerous awards, most notably the Pulitzer Prize. His place in modern poetry has faded somewhat since the front-page commemoration given him following his death by the *New York Times*, but he remains one of Maine's favorite sons.

• For the entire bibliography of Robert Peter Tristram Coffin's forty some works, see the 1965–1966 issue of the *Colby Library Quarterly* commemorating the tenth anniversary of his death. For the life of Coffin, see both Raymond Charles Swain, *A Breath of Maine: Portrait of Robert P. Tristram Coffin* (1967), written by an eighteen year friend of the poet, and Annie Coffin Sanborn, *The Life of Robert Peter Tristram Coffin and Family* (1963). An obituary is in the *New York Times*, 21 Jan. 1955.

CHRISTOPHER J. NEUMANN

COFFMAN, Lotus Delta (7 Jan. 1875–22 Sept. 1938), educator, was born near Salem, Indiana, the son of Mansford E. Coffman and Laura Ellen Davis, farmers. Following his father's early death, Coffman assisted his mother with farmwork and also attended local schools. After graduating from the local high school, he taught in a country school before entering Indiana State Normal School (now Indiana State University) in Terre Haute. After graduating in 1896, he again taught school for a year before returning to his hometown as a school principal. Later he assumed the duties of superintendent of schools in both Salem and Connersville, Indiana, and at the same time continued his academic studies. He married Mary Emma Farrell of Paoli, Indiana, in 1899; they had two children. By combining summer school and correspondence study and commuting once a week to Indiana University, he graduated from that institution in 1905 with an A.B. degree in education.

In 1907 Coffman became director of teacher training at Illinois State College at Charleston. He remained in that position until 1909 when he moved to New York City for two years to pursue graduate studies at Columbia University, where he also served as an instructor. He received an A.M. degree in education from Indiana University in 1910 and in the following year, after receiving his Ph.D. from Columbia, returned to his former post at Charleston. The peripatetic Coffman remained in Charleston for a year before becoming professor of education at the University of Illinois at Champaign-Urbana in 1912. He remained at Illinois for three academic years before assuming the post of dean of the College of Education at the University of Minnesota, following repeated requests on the part of university president George E. Vincent. Coffman remained at Minnesota for the remainder of his life, and it was there that he made his greatest contributions to the field of education.

After serving as dean of the College of Education for five years, Coffman assumed the duties of university president on 1 July 1920. His tenure as president, which lasted eighteen years, was one of unparalleled growth for the university. Fundraising, always a critical component of university administration, became increasingly important as the demand for higher education grew in the years following World War I. Coffman excelled at this task; not only did he benefit from a 30 percent increase in state educational funding during his first year in office, but after conducting a vigorous campaign to increase the level of private gifts, he raised more than $12 million, a huge sum for that time. Much of the money went into badly needed construction projects. The list of new campus buildings that had their genesis under the Coffman administration is impressive: a new library and new administration, music, and electrical engineering buildings appeared, as did new facilities for the law school, the medical school (greatly helped by a gift of more than $2 million from William J. and Charles H. Mayo, leading to the establishment of the Mayo Foundation for graduate medical studies and research), and the physics and botany departments. Student needs were not neglected; three dormitories (two for men and one for student nurses) and a student health services building were erected. Even intercollegiate sports benefited, with a new football field, Memorial Stadium, and the indoor Northrup Auditorium, which also facilitated on-campus concerts by the Minneapolis Symphony Orchestra, adding to the recreational possibilities at the university.

The Coffman administration was marked by a tremendous growth in the number and scope of academic offerings. Coffman oversaw the addition of a fine arts department and a school of journalism, as well as the beginnings of a graduate curriculum in business administration. Instruction in the medical sciences benefited from the addition of a department of preventative medicine and public health. Psychiatric work began at the university hospital, which then became Minnesota General Hospital. A unique course of instruction in hospital librarianship, the first of its kind in the country, was also added to the curriculum.

Coffman oversaw many innovative changes in the University of Minnesota's academic structuring, many influential beyond the state's borders. He began a university college for academically gifted students, as well as the Center for Continuation Study, which enabled college graduates in a variety of fields to receive instruction in so-called short courses. He also pioneered in the development of an orientation program for incoming freshmen and initiated a two-year collegiate course for students who were either unable or unwilling to undertake a four-year course of study. Student population virtually doubled during his tenure, and in

1923 Frederick J. Kelly was hired as the first dean of administration to coordinate that growth.

The development of the university did not pass unnoticed in the world of academia. As a consequence of his many achievements at Minnesota, Coffman served as president of a number of professional organizations, including the National Society for Study of Education (1917–1918), the National Society of College Teachers of Education (1917–1918), the North Central Association of Colleges and Secondary Schools (1921–1922), and the National Association of State Universities (1930). He was secretary of the board of trustees of the Carnegie Foundation for the Advancement of Teaching and served the Carnegie Corporation of New York as a trustee. In addition, he was a member of the Minnesota Education Association, the National Education Association, and the American Council on Education, which he led on several occasions.

A more than full schedule of administrative duties did not deter Coffman from pursuing his research interests. He undertook pedagogical surveys in several states. His doctoral dissertation, *The Social Composition of the Teaching Population*, was published in 1911, and he also wrote *Teacher Training Departments in Minnesota High Schools* (1920) and *The State University: Its Work and Problems* (1934). Besides his own writings, he served as coeditor of the *Journal of Educational Administration and Supervision*.

Coffman remained active until his death in Minneapolis. The growth and development of the University of Minnesota remains his greatest legacy, but he will also be remembered for his general influence on the development of modern American universities.

• The papers of Lotus Delta Coffman are held at the University of Minnesota Archives, Minneapolis-St. Paul. A bibliography of his writings can be found in his own *Freedom through Education* (1939). The best single secondary source of information on his life and career remains James Gray, *The University of Minnesota, 1851–1951* (1951). An obituary is in the *New York Times*, 23 Sept. 1938.

EDWARD L. LACH, JR.

COGAN, Edward (5 Jan. 1803–7 Apr. 1884), coin dealer, was born at "Higham Hill" in Walthamstow, Essex, England, the son of Reverend Eliezer Cogan, a schoolmaster, and Mary Atchison, both originally from Northamptonshire, England. Cogan was educated at his father's school. He married Louise Webb at Hoxton, near London; they had eight children. Cogan immigrated to Philadelphia in 1853, and after a brief career selling books and paintings he devoted all his time to dealing in coins. The beginning of Cogan's coin dealings was quite modest. A friend persuaded him to buy an electrotype of a 1792 Washington cent for twenty-five cents. "Upon showing it as a curiosity to a gentleman," Cogan reported, "he offered me fifty cents." Other friends informed him that an 1815 cent (none exists) would fetch $5 and that demand for U.S. cents was "springing up." "I collected the whole set

[U.S. cents] from 1793," Cogan stated, "and then started selling duplicates" (*American Journal of Numismatics*, Mar. 1867, p. 87).

Cogan developed a clientele interested in coin collecting and opened a coin store in Philadelphia in late 1855. He was the first coin dealer in the United States to hold auction sales exclusively of coins, with accompanying catalogs. Between 1858 and 1879 he held seventy auction sales. In his first auction, held 1 November 1858, he sold his seven best U.S. cents through private bidding for the "extraordinary" amount of $128.63. Cogan credited the 1856–1857 change in the size of the cent coinage (from a weight of 10.89 grams and a diameter of about 29 mm to a weight of 4.67 grams and a 19 mm diameter) with generally increasing interest in coins and the widespread newspaper publicity of his first sale with launching his full-time coin-selling career. In 1867 he reported that newspaper accounts of his sale generated from ten to fifteen out-of-town letters daily, offering to sell and requesting to buy coins. Before his first sale and its accompanying publicity, he had but one or two clients outside of Philadelphia. The risk inherent in handling valuable coins came dramatically to realization for Cogan. After his auction purchase of the W. C. Tripler Collection, his store was burglarized on 25 October 1859 and a "very large number of duplicates" were taken. This loss disheartened him, but business was so brisk that he persevered.

Cogan issued tokens advertising his coin business in 1859 and 1860. These tokens were struck in various metals with a number of reverses so that many varieties exist. In the early twentieth century the copper pieces were considered common, but the exact number issued is unknown. About 1860 Cogan also issued similar tokens for the Mount Holly Paper Company in copper, brass, nickel, and white metal. For Cogan's first four sales, a single manuscript was posted in his shop, listing available coins. Patrons could peruse the list and make sealed bids, which were opened at an appointed time. During the 1861 to 1862 period, these listings were reprinted. John W. Adams classified Cogan's coin grading as falling in the conservative end of the spectrum, along with that of Henry Chapman and Lyman Low, and Cogan's reputation of offering only authentic pieces was seldom challenged. After his initial sales, Cogan produced auction sale catalogs, which he distributed by mail.

In late 1863 or early 1864 Cogan moved to Brooklyn, New York. His first sale there was the Francis S. Edwards Collection. Cogan produced the first American auction catalog with photographic plates for the Mortimer McKenzie sale of 23 June 1869. He also issued many auction catalogs without plates, and although he used photographic plates in six other sale catalogs, the quality of the photography never matched that of the McKenzie sale. In 1871 Cogan published a six-page pamphlet in New York titled *Table of Gold, Silver and Copper Coins NOT issued by the U.S. Mint*. He also issued a widely margined list of

American store cards so that readers could make notations about rarity and condition.

Cogan worked closely with the *American Journal of Numismatics*, serving as a subscription agent from its inception until his retirement from coin dealing in 1879. He also frequently wrote columns for it. In the March 1867 issue of that journal, Cogan made a Mark Twainesque retort to a critic writing in the journal (1, no. 10 [Feb. 1867], p. 76) who apparently thought he had died. "I am at all events sufficiently alive to be able to give a more correct account, than he has done—in betraying the great secret he alluded to—of the Nickel cents of 1856." Cogan went on to say that he believed these coins came from someone in the employ of the director of the mint and that he himself had obtained 135 of them. Cogan was also among the first to attempt to compile listings of coin sales during the early nineteenth century.

Cogan proved that numismatics could provide a respectable livelihood for someone willing to focus time and energy on fostering its development and coordinating the existing market for collectible coins. Bringing marketing skills and knowledge to the largely disorganized collecting fraternity, he established a new career, which has been followed by many illustrious dealers. Two of Cogan's sons went into the coin business; Richard Cogan used Bangs & Co. of New York as his auctioneers and George W. Cogan took over his father's business when he retired. Edward Cogan died at his home in Brooklyn.

• Cogan's colorful personality is revealed in his two-part "Concerning the Coin Trade in America," *American Journal of Numismatics* 1, no. 11 (Mar. 1867): 86–87, and 1, no. 12 (Apr. 1867): 95–96. Cogan's achievements are most clearly presented in John W. Adams, *United States Numismatic Literature*, vol. 1 (1992), pp. 17–24; Pete Smith, *American Numismatic Biographies* (1992), p. 58; and a staff-written piece, "Father of the Coin Trade in America," in *The Numismatist* 29, no. 6 (June 1916): 267–68. For Cogan's venture in token manufacture, see A. R. Frey, "Tokens and Medals Relating to Numismatists and Coin Dealers," *The Numismatist* 16, no. 10 (Oct. 1903): 301–3. The most complete obituary was printed in *American Journal of Numismatics* 19, no. 1 (July 1884): 23.

ERIC P. NEWMAN

COGGESHALL, George (2 Nov. 1784–6 Aug. 1861), sea captain and author, was born in Milford, Connecticut, the son of William Coggeshall, a shipmaster, and Eunice Mallett. A Revolutionary War veteran, William Coggeshall was financially ruined when one of his vessels was seized by a British cruiser for trading at a French island, and another was captured by France for trading with English colonies. As a result, George Coggeshall and his six siblings were left destitute. Thus, he was denied a formal education and was forced to teach himself by reading every book available. A devoted son, Coggeshall determined that he would go to sea as soon as possible, thereby reducing the family's expenses and affording him a chance to recoup his father's losses.

He soon had an opportunity. His uncle by marriage, Captain Henry Turner, needed a cabin boy for his schooner, the *Charlotte*. Just fifteen, Coggeshall left for Cadiz, Spain, with a cargo of flour and tobacco and with the news of General Washington's death. In 1809, having sailed as an able seaman on numerous voyages, he received his first command, the *Henry and Isabella*. During the War of 1812, he served as captain of the privateer schooners *David Porter* and *Leo*. Early in 1815, the *Leo* was captured off Lisbon by the British frigate *Granicus*. Coggeshall and his crew were delivered as prisoners to the authorities at Gibraltar. Two days later, through a clever ruse, Coggeshall escaped and, aided by some smugglers, reached Algeciras. There, the American consul helped him get passage to Cadiz and then, via Lisbon, to New York. He arrived safely on 9 May 1815.

In his "Sketch of the Author's Early Life and Parentage," Coggeshall states that he had "severely felt [his] father's misfortunes" and "mentally resolved" to improve the family's economic situation. Ever the devoted son and sibling, Coggeshall made good on his promise to recoup the family fortunes. As he achieved financial success in his own career, he employed many of his brothers as mates or captains under him and frequently visited his mother, who had been left a widow. In 1816 he married Sarah Brent Pierpont; they had two children, both of whom died in infancy. She died in 1822. In 1831 he married Elizabeth Cottrill of New York; they had five children. Elizabeth died in 1851.

Captain Coggeshall's sea career was long and exciting, spanning nearly six decades. On every voyage, he read assiduously and kept a detailed journal. Having visited ports in nearly every part of the world, he incorporated his travel experiences that he wrote into various books following his retirement in 1841. In rapid succession he published *Voyages to Various Parts of the World* (1851), *Second Series of Voyages to Various Parts of the World* (1852), *Thirty-Six Voyages to Various Parts of the World* (1855), *History of the American Privateers and Letters-of-Marque* (1856), and *An Historical Sketch of Commerce and Navigation from the Birth of the Saviour down to the Present Date* (1860). Also attributed to him is a volume of *Religious and Miscellaneous Poetry*.

In his *Thirty-Six Voyages*, Coggeshall observed:

As a general principle, if shipmasters are not intelligent and well-informed men on most subjects, it is their own fault for not improving their precious privileges. In the first place, what can exalt and elevate the human mind more than the boundless ocean, and where can be found a scene better adapted to deep thought and silent contemplation?

Coggeshall's months at sea, facing high adventures and sobering solitude, forged a strong, vigorous writing style, tempered with a smooth elegance. His voyage books, respectively covering the years 1799–1844, 1802–1841, and 1799–1841, are pleasantly entertaining, as the captain relates his rise through the maritime ranks and describes the people and cultures he encounters. Coggeshall's writings reveal him to be a man of piety, patriotism, and great strength of character.

Coggeshall's best-known work, *History of the American Privateers*, an account of the naval battles of the War of 1812, generally lacks the grace and vigor of his earlier works. Although valuable to naval historians, it is marred by reams of tedious detail. Clearly he put a great deal of work into its composition, including sundry letters, charts, and newspaper extracts concerning military actions. Unfortunately, however, what should prove the strength of the historical compilation is instead its weakness. The narrative flow is compromised by the dizzying wealth of catalogues listing "Prizes Captured by Privateers." One important detail saves the *History* from total tedium. Well into his work, Coggeshall inserts two lively chapters describing his own daring exploits. He relates how, following his capture in Gibraltar, he disguised himself as an English naval officer, nonchalantly boarded a Norwegian vessel, and, with the commander's help, escaped his captors.

Coggeshall concluded his writing career with *An Historical Sketch of Commerce and Navigation from the Birth of the Saviour down to the Present Date*. As the unwieldy title suggests, he had an enormous undertaking in mind. However, the book is haphazardly arranged, reflecting Coggeshall's deteriorating health. "Although a seaman's life is one of hardship and privation, and often beset with extreme danger," Coggeshall wrote in *Thirty-Six Voyages*, "still there is much to alleviate and recompense him for his personal sufferings. . . . In short, it is a bold, daring life." The world has changed dramatically since the days of Captain Coggeshall. The barnacles of time have encrusted his sea books with quaint dignity. For anyone wishing to examine the life and times of a brave nineteenth-century seafarer, Coggeshall's writings afford an excellent opportunity. Having served the sea faithfully for over half a century, George Coggeshall died in Milford, Connecticut.

• Coggeshall's works are virtually the only source of information about him. However, they provide a great deal of insight into his family, actions, and character. The scholar should, therefore, read his writings in their entirety. Coggeshall's "Sketch of the Author's Early Life and Parentage," in *Thirty-Six Voyages*, describes his early years. He traces his career through his final voyage on the brig *Brilliant*. His other works further illuminate his life and provide a wealth of information about the kind, quantity, and destination of cargoes shipped in the nineteenth century. Coggeshall's exploits during the War of 1812 are related in detail in the *History of the American Privateers* (1856; 3d ed., 1861), and have been retold in E. S. Maclay, *A History of American Privateers* (1899). The reader may wish also to consult Walter Magnes Teller, ed., *Five Sea Captains* (1960), which includes the works of captains Delano Amasa, Edmund Fanning, Richard Cleveland, Joshua Slocum, and George Coggeshall.

KAREN N. SCHRAMM

COGGESHALL, William Turner (6 Sept. 1824–2 Aug. 1867), journalist, state librarian, and diplomat, was born in Lewistown, Pennsylvania, the son of Wil-

liam C. Coggeshall, a coachsmith, and Eliza Grotz. At the age of eighteen he headed west and settled in Akron, Ohio. There he launched his career by starting the *Cascade Roarer*, a temperance periodical published from 1844 to 1845. He married Mary Maria Carpenter in 1845; they had one child. In 1847 Coggeshall moved to Cincinnati and edited the *Western Fountain*, one of the city's many transitory newspapers. According to one account, his journalistic experience around this time also included work on the staffs of the *Cincinnati Times* and the *Cincinnati Gazette*.

Coggeshall's career followed a circuitous course over the next decade. From 1851 to 1852 he served as guide, secretary, and reported for Hungarian revolutionary Louis Kossuth, who was touring the United States. Afterward Coggeshall returned to Cincinnati, wrote an unpublished biography of Kossuth, and entered the newspaper business again. In the autumn of 1852 he established the *Commercial Advertiser*, which folded soon after. Coggeshall then became assistant editor for the *Daily Columbian*, but in August 1854 he resigned to help publish the *Genius of the West*, a fledgling literary journal. He stayed there for the next year and a half, eventually becoming editor and chief proprietor. In May 1856 the paper's bleak financial prospects encouraged him to accept an offer from Salmon P. Chase, the newly elected antislavery governor of Ohio, to become state librarian.

By then Coggeshall had already become known as an author of books; his volumes included *Signs of the Times* (1851), a study of spirit rappings in the Cincinnati area; two popular novels directed at young readers, *Easy Warren and His Contemporaries* (1854) and *Oakshaw; or, The Victims of Avarice* (1855); and *Cash and Character* (1855), a volume of moralistic instruction. While state librarian in Columbus, a position he held from 1856 to 1862, Coggeshall authored another moralistic work, *Home Hits and Hints* (1859), edited the *Ohio Educational Quarterly* (1858–1859), and wrote or edited several books more directly related to his official duties. Among these were the *Need and Availability of the Writing and Spelling Reform* (1857), *Index to Ohio Laws* (1858), *Frontier Life and Character in the South and West* (1860), and *The Protective Policy in Literature* (1859), a booklet that promoted regionalism as a value in literature, particularly in the upper Mississippi Valley. In *Poets and Poetry of the West* (1860), his most famous work, Coggeshall put these sentiments into practice with an anthology of 159 authors active between 1789 and 1860. His intent was to chronicle the accomplishments of native writers and thus demonstrate the injustice of eastern critics. "In poetry breathing an earnest spirit of moral and political reform," he boasted in this first volume of a planned series, "expressing just appreciation of material beauty; revealing domestic affections; representing noble aspirations for intrinsic work and force, the West is rich" (p. vi).

In the 1860s Coggeshall's involvement with the antislavery movement increasingly drew him into politics and government service. In *The Issue of the November*

Election (1860) he urged voters to support the Republican presidential ticket. In 1861 he accepted an appointment as colonel on the staff of William Dennison, Ohio's Republican governor at the outset of the Civil War. For much of the next year Coggeshall served as a secret agent for the United States, but he resigned in 1862 after contracting tuberculosis. He then set out in search of work more compatible with his weakened condition. From 1862 to 1865 he owned and edited the *Springfield Republic*, worked for the *Ohio State Journal* in Columbus, and authored two patriotic books: *Ohio's Prosperity, Social and Material* (1863) and *The Journeys of Abraham Lincoln as President-elect, and as President Martyred* (1865), an account of Lincoln's trip to Washington, D.C., and the return of his body to Illinois after his assassination.

In 1866 political associates secured Coggeshall an appointment as U.S. minister to Ecuador. He arrived at his post in August 1866 after a brief term as personal secretary to Jacob Dolson Cox, Ohio's new Republican governor. Coggeshall died in Quito from the effects of high altitude and cold. His fifteen-year-old daughter died in Quayaquill, Ecuador, four months later. In 1869 congressional legislation funded the return of both bodies to Columbus, where in October 1870 they were interred in the Green Lawn Cemetery.

As an author, Coggeshall did not attain the highest levels of fame known to American writers of his era. Others proved far more successful at producing literature of enduring quality. Coggeshall's importance rests instead on his role in promoting and preserving the work of better-known writers such as Sarah T. Bolton, Alice and Phoebe Cary, and William Dean Howells and on the vision of a unique middle western literature that he shared with contemporaries like Timothy Flint, William Davis Gallagher, and James Hall.

• Most of Coggeshall's surviving papers are at the Ohio Historical Society, either in his own collection or in those of Friedrich Hassaurek, the Janney family, John Hancock Klippart, and Louis Kossuth. Additional documents are also kept in the papers of Salmon P. Chase at Dartmouth College. Coggeshall's government service is partly covered in the *Congressional Globe*, 40th Cong., 2d sess., 1868–1869, pt. 1: 232–35, 321; and U.S. House, "Message of the President and Accompanying Documents . . . ," 39th Cong., 2d sess., 1867, H. Exec. Doc. 1, 477. Major secondary sources include William D. Andrews, "William T. Coggeshall: 'Booster' of Western Literature" *Ohio History* 81 (1972): 210–20; "Ohio State Library Centennial," *Ohio Archaeological and Historical Society Publications* 28 (Jan. 1919): 103–5, which includes a copy of Coggeshall's portrait; and W. H. Venable, *Beginnings of Literary Culture in the Ohio Valley: Historical and Biographical Sketches* (1891), pp. 109–18. His obituary is in the *Ohio State Journal*, 6 Sept. 1867, repr. in the *New York Times*, 9 Sept. 1867; for information about his burial see the *Ohio State Journal*, 19 Oct. 1870.

LEIGH JOHNSEN

COGHLAN, Rose (18 Mar. 1851–2 Apr. 1932), actress, was born in Peterborough, England, the daughter of Francis Coghlan, a well-known author and journalist who founded *Coghlan's Continental Dispatch* and published "Coghlan's Continental Guides," and Anna Maria Kirby. Rose's older brother Charles married an actress who convinced him to abandon his law career to become an actor. Rose Coghlan followed her brother, making her stage debut as a witch in *Macbeth* at the Theatre Royal in Greenock (Greenwich), Scotland, where she had gone to live with her sister-in-law after her father's death. Coghlan's London debut took place at the Old Gaiety Theatre in 1869 as Pippo in *Linda of Chamouni*. She later appeared at the Gaiety as Bianca in *The Life Chase*, Marguerite in *Uncle Dick's Darling*, and Richard II in *Wat Tyler, M.P.* At the Royalty Theatre in 1871 she appeared in the breeches roles of Charles II in *Nell Gwynne*, and at the Court the same year she played Tilda Price in *Dotheboy's Hall*, her first substantial success. In London she also appeared as Gretchen in *Rip Van Winkle* with Joseph Jefferson III.

Also in 1871 Coghlan made the first of many trips to the United States, intending to support Katherine Rogers in *The Woman in White*, but the management failed to open the show, so Coghlan signed on with Lydia Thompson and her burlesque troupe at Wallack's Theatre in New York City. Coghlan therefore made her American debut in September 1872, at Wallack's as Mrs. Honeystone in *A Happy Pair* and Jupiter in *Ixion*, so successfully that Wallack offered her an engagement for $75 a week for the rest of the season. At the same time E. A. Sothern engaged her for his season at the same theater, where she appeared as Mary Meredith in *Our American Cousin* and Alice in *Brother Sam*.

Coghlan returned to London in 1873 for appearances with Charles J. Mathews and Barry Sullivan. For a time she starred in the English provinces as Lady Teazle in *The School for Scandal*, as well as appearing in *Twelfth Night* (as Viola) and *East Lynne*. Her successes led her to successive engagements as leading lady at the Princess's Theater in Manchester and Adelphi Theater in London.

Wallack lured her back to the United States in 1876, where she appeared with her brother Charles in Wallack's company. She remained with Wallack through the 1887–1888 season, successfully appearing as Lady Teazle, Lady Gay Spanker, Peg Woffington, Rosalind, and other substantial roles, elevating herself to stardom within the confines of a stock company. Between engagements with Wallack she appeared in San Francisco (where, she said, "they made a great deal of me") and at Booth's Theatre. In 1885 she appeared in the title role of *Our Joan* and thereafter produced *Jocelyn* and *Lady Barter*, written by her brother. She continued to appear in her old comedy roles successfully. Coghlan became a naturalized American citizen in 1902. In 1893 she appeared as Mrs. Arbuthnot in Oscar Wilde's *A Woman of No Importance*, a controversial script in which she scored an immense box-office success. For the next several years she repeated her more successful roles, producing undistinguished scripts that contained starring vehicles for her.

In 1907 Coghlan toured the United States as Mrs. Warren in Shaw's *Mrs. Warren's Profession*. She continued to perform roles of little distinction (e.g., Zicka in *Diplomacy* and Stephanie in *Forget-Me-Not*), making her last appearance in 1921 as Madame Rabouin in *Deburau*, staged by David Belasco at his theater. While playing the role she celebrated her seventieth birthday. In 1922 Coghlan was overcome by illness and poverty. Learning of this, the Producing Managers' Association staged a benefit, raising $10,000 for her relief. Coghlan was too ill to attend the benefit, at which actors, authors, and managers combined to salute an actress who had stood for so long for the highest artistic ideals of the theater.

Coghlan's acting career included several motion pictures, beginning with a silent film of *As You Like It* in 1912. A decade later she made two more silents, *Secrets of Paris* and *Beyond the Rainbow*. In 1932 she appeared in her first talky, *Hot Saturday*. There followed *Jennie Gerhardt* in 1933, *Finishing School* in 1934, and *The Bride Walks Out* in 1936.

Coghlan married twice: first in 1885 to Clinton J. Edgerly, a Boston lawyer who gave up his practice to manage her company. They divorced in 1890. She next married John Taylor Sullivan in 1893, they divorced in 1904.

Coghlan was a longtime favorite of American audiences. As F. E. McKay said, "The United States has never loved . . . another English actress as it has Rose Coghlan, the wide-eyed, velvet-voiced, caressing, fascinating, divinely-smiling." McKay likened Coghlan's voice to an aeolian harp. She wisely never attempted tragedy, but in comedy and melodrama she proved herself one of the best of her generation, especially as Lady Teazle in *The School for Scandal*, Rosalind in *As You Like It*, and Lady Gay Spanker in Boucicault's *London Assurance*. The critic Charles Wingate applauded Coghlan's "noble-toned voice, her crystal enunciation, and her dashing bearing," which gave her Rosalind "a robust style and an incessant animation." Lewis C. Strang opined that although she lacked their individuality and personal magnetism, Coghlan surpassed such idols as Maude Adams and Julia Marlowe in tragic power.

Coghlan died in New York City at St. Vincent's Retreat for Nervous and Mental Disorders, where she had resided for four and a half years.

• Some archival material on Coghlan may be found in the Harry Ransom Humanities Research Center, University of Texas, Austin. The Theatre Collection at Harvard University contains a clipping file, and a scrapbook of Coghlan materials is held by the New York Public Library for the Performing Arts, Lincoln Center. Coghlan reportedly worked on an autobiography, to be combined with a biography of her brother Charles, but they never reached print, although a four-part autobiographical series appeared in the *Boston Sunday Herald*, beginning 21 Sept. 1919. Ada Patterson, "The Stage Honors Rose Coghlan," *Theatre*, July 1922, describes the $10,000 benefit held for Coghlan. See also the interview in the *New York Dramatic Mirror*, 15 Dec. 1894. Other sources include Lewis C. Strang, *Famous Actresses of the Day in America* (1899); John Clapp and Edwin Francis Edgett, *Players of the Present* (3 vols., 1899–1901); Alan Dale (pseud.), *Familiar Chats with the Queens of the Stage* (1890); and Frederic E. McKay and Charles E. L. Wingate, eds., *Famous American Actors of To-Day* (1896). J. Ranken Towse described the actress in his autobiographical *Sixty Years of the Theater* (1916), and William C. Young included her in his *Famous Actors and Actresses on the American Stage* (1975). Obituaries are in the *New York Herald Tribune*, 5 Apr. 1932, and the *New York Times*, 5 and 6 Apr. 1932.

STEPHEN M. ARCHER

COGLEY, John (16 Mar. 1916–29 Mar. 1976), religious journalist, was born in Chicago, Illinois, the son of John F. Cogley, a city employee, and Anne Geenty, who died giving birth to him. Cogley was educated at Catholic elementary and secondary schools. He lived with his grandmother after his father remarried, and he remained quite distant from his father for the rest of his life. After high school, Cogley held a series of odd jobs and took some part-time classes at Loyola University; then in 1937 he joined the Catholic Worker movement founded by Dorothy Day and Peter Maurin. He operated a Catholic Worker "house of hospitality" for homeless men on the Near West Side of Chicago from 1938 to 1941. He also edited a Chicago Catholic Worker newspaper.

He married another Catholic Worker volunteer, Theodora Schmidt, in 1942 shortly before being drafted into military service. They eventually had six children. He served in the Army Air Force in a series of stateside posts during the Second World War, then reentered Loyola University on the G. I. Bill, receiving his B.A. in philosophy in 1948. Taking his family to Switzerland for a year, he was the first Catholic layman to enroll in a theology course of studies at the University of Fribourg.

In 1949 he became an editor of the *Commonweal*, which had been founded twenty-five years earlier as a journal of opinion, modeled loosely on the *New Republic* and the *Nation*. In the words of its founding editor, Michael Williams, the magazine attempted to present "the Catholic outlook" rather than "the Catholic inlook," that is, to give a religious slant on current affairs rather than write about parochial denominational matters. Over the years, it gathered a small but devoted readership among what came to be called "Commonweal Catholics." These were well-educated Catholic laypeople who were socially assimilated, politically liberal, and religiously tolerant. Cogley was part of a younger generation of Catholic writers, from immigrant working-class backgrounds, who joined the *Commonweal* about the same time. Rodger Van Allen, the historian of the *Commonweal*, characterized the staff as "an Irish-Catholic intellectual mafia, unabashed both in their liberalism and their Catholicism."

As features editor and executive editor from 1949 to 1954, then as a regular columnist until 1963, Cogley wrote frequently on church-state relations. He denounced Senator Joseph R. McCarthy's anti-Communism crusade and ghost-wrote an anti-McCarthy speech delivered by Chicago auxiliary bishop Bernard

J. Sheil in 1954. He analyzed the role of intellectuals in the Catholic church, questioned the morality of nuclear deterrence, and discussed the prospect of a Catholic running for president of the United States.

Cogley was so closely identified with the *Commonweal* that he was sometimes referred to as the "Pope of Commonweal Catholics," that is, the leading voice for liberal lay Catholics. Yet, he only worked for the magazine full-time for five years. In 1954 he accepted a commission from Robert Maynard Hutchins's think tank, the Fund for the Republic, to investigate anti-Communist blacklisting in the motion picture industry. His two-volume report on blacklisting appeared in 1956 and resulted in a summons to appear before the House Un-American Activities Committee. Cogley then joined the Fund for the Republic staff as director of research on religious institutions in a free society, remaining with the organization when it moved to Santa Barbara, California, and was renamed the Center for the Study of Democratic Institutions.

Cogley served briefly on the campaign staff of John F. Kennedy in 1960, helping to rehearse the presidential candidate for his pivotal speech to the Houston Ministerial Conference that largely defused the religious issue in that election. He also spent a year as a freelance journalist covering the Second Vatican Council in Rome, in 1963 and 1964. Then he became religious affairs editor for the *New York Times* and covered the last session of the council in 1965. After suffering a heart attack in 1966, he returned to Santa Barbara as founding editor of the *Center Magazine*, remaining in that position until he suffered a stroke in 1974. Two years later he died in Santa Barbara of a heart attack.

In September 1973 Cogley shocked American Catholics by leaving the Catholic church and becoming an Episcopalian. He wrote his autobiography, *A Canterbury Tale* (1976), in part to justify this decision. Although he had long been attracted to the liturgy of the Episcopal church, he had first told himself that this was simply an "aesthetic idiosyncracy." Fundamentally, however, his argument with Catholicism was based on the issue of papal and clerical authority. His years in Rome at the Second Vatican Council stimulated what he called his "Anglican interpretation of Christianity"; that is, it deepened his doubts about papal authority. Then, Pope Paul VI's 1968 encyclical, *Humanae Vitae*, affirming the Catholic ban on the use of artificial birth control, astounded him as it did many liberal Catholics. Finally, he decided he could no longer stay in a church that exercised authority without evidence. As he explained in his autobiography, his new faith "enjoyed antiquity, it claimed apostolic succession, it avoided nonbiblical superstitions, it admitted historic errors, it did not propose outmoded explanations . . . for the mysteries of the faith, and it allowed for real weight in the authority possessed by all its members, lay or clerical" (p. 101).

Cogley's career typified the lives of many liberal Catholics during the twentieth century. He identified himself with the embattled minority within the church, helping the outcasts of society at the Catholic Worker, trying to form a politically liberal Catholic intelligentsia at the *Commonweal*, and endeavoring to show that Christianity was relevant to modern life in his work at the Center for the Study of Democratic Institutions. Although the Second Vatican Council gave him hope that the divisions in Christianity would soon be healed, he was disillusioned by the postconciliar assertions of papal authority and finally left his ancestral church. His religious attitudes can best be summed up in his own words: "It seems to me that the churches must be united or disappear from the modern world" (*Canterbury Tale*, p. 124). He was widely considered the outstanding religious journalist of his time.

• The University of Notre Dame archives contain a small file of Cogley material, mainly copies of articles and speeches; they also hold a large collection of documents from the *Commonweal*. Extensive documents from the Center for the Study of Democratic Institutions are located in the special collections department of the library at the University of California, Santa Barbara. This collection contains numerous audio tapes of seminars and conferences that Cogley chaired but not much printed material about him. Cogley's published works include *Religion in America: Original Essays on Religion in a Free Society* (1958), the published edition of a conference he chaired; *Religion in a Secular Age: The Search for Final Meaning* (1968), published first as a lengthy *Encyclopaedia Britannica* article; and *Catholic America* (1973), a readable brief history of the Catholic church in the United States written for the nation's bicentennial. The best source for Cogley's life and career, in addition to his autobiography, *A Canterbury Tale*, is Rodger Van Allen's monograph, *The Commonweal and American Catholicism: The Magazine, the Movement, the Meaning* (1974). Obituaries are in the *New York Times*, 30 Mar. 1976, and the *Commonweal*, 23 Apr. 1976. *Commonweal* also published a tribute to Cogley and a sampling of his columns for that magazine on 7 May 1976.

EDWARD R. KANTOWICZ

COHAN, George M. (3 or 4 July 1878–5 Nov. 1942), performer, writer of songs, musicals, and plays, and producer, was born in Providence, Rhode Island, the son of Jeremiah "Jerry" John Cohan and Helen "Nellie" Frances Costigan. (Cohan's middle initial stands for Michael.) At the age of seven, Cohan was sent to the E Street School in Providence. His formal schooling lasted six weeks, after which the school sent him to rejoin his parents and sister, Josie, in their theatrical travels. He took violin lessons and played the instrument both in the theater orchestra and in a trick violin act he devised. The Cohans went on their first road show as a family in 1889; when the show failed they went back to B. F. Keith's vaudeville (Keith had started continuous vaudeville), establishing a pattern—independence, failure, vaudeville—that lasted during much of Cohan's youth. He got a lead role in *Peck's Bad Boy* at thirteen, after which the family played country fairs. Their initial appearance as "The Four Cohans" came in 1893, but Keith broke them up into separate acts for his three-a-day shows.

Cohan published his first song, "Why Did Nelly Leave Her Home," when he was sixteen. Within the next few months, six of his manuscripts had been accepted for publication (he claimed he could play only four chords on the piano, all in F sharp, and never got any further—"I've used them ever since"). His phenomenal energy began to show itself at this point: he wrote one or two songs each week, plus parodies and patter for comedians, afterpieces for burlesque shows, and sketches for variety teams.

The family toured the Midwest in the Moore Circuit of Museums and then honky-tonks. (Since the eighteenth century, American museums had featured variety acts; on the Moore circuit the Cohans gave five shows a day). Cohan later said he was always happiest on stage; he claimed that he was a dyed-in-the-wool "song-and-dance man." "I still am," he wrote in his autobiography, "for that matter—always will be, I dare say."

Gus Williams, a Dutch comedian, hired the family in 1895 for character roles in his play *April Fool*, and they toured with him for thirty-five weeks; all the while, Cohan was writing eight to ten hours each day. The Cohans performed at the prestigious Hyde and Behman's Adam Street Theatre in Brooklyn, in a skit called "Goggles Doll House," and it was here that Cohan first used the curtain line, "Ladies and Gentlemen, my mother thanks you, my father thanks you, my sister thanks you, and I thank you," a phrase he used for twenty years. At this time, too, Cohan became business manager for the family and also began to write short skits. By the end of 1897 he claimed that he and his family were the most successful four-act in the United States.

In 1899 he married Ethel Levey (born Ethelia Fowler); they had one child. His wife joined the Cohan company and was evidently a delightful performer. On 11 February 1901, the Four Cohans and "Their Company of Comedians" opened in Hartford, Connecticut, in *The Governor's Son*, an expansion of a skit Cohan had written; the show was composed, directed, and coproduced by him. His instructions to the cast might have served for all of his subsequent shows: "don't wait for laughs. Side-step encores. Crash right through this show tonight. Speed! Speed! and lots of it; that's my idea of the thing. Perpetual motion. Laugh your heads off; have a good time; keep happy. Remember now, happy, happy, happy. . . . And don't forget the secret of it all. . . . Speed! a whole lot of speed!"

While *The Governor's Son* did not receive favorable notices in New York, it was quite popular on the road, as was his next conversion of a vaudeville skit into a three-act musical play, *Running for Office*. During this time Josie married Fred Niblo, a comedian, and joined her husband, leaving Cohan's wife to fill Josie's place in the act. In 1904 Cohan and Sam H. Harris formed a producing partnership that lasted until 1920, resuming for a short time in 1937. Their first production was *Little Johnny Jones* in 1904; the story of an American jockey in England featured the hit songs "Give My Regards to Broadway," "The Yankee Doo-

dle Boy," and "Life's a Funny Proposition After All"; a film version was produced in 1930.

Cohan published a four-page illustrated newspaper, the *Spotlight*, which publicized himself and attacked his critics. His next show, *Forty-Five Minutes from Broadway*, first produced in Columbus, Ohio, featured three hit songs: "Mary's a Grand Old Name," "So Long, Mary," and the title song. Cohan now had three road companies touring: *Forty-Five Minutes from Broadway*, *Little Johnny Jones*, and *Running for Office*. He wrote a star part for himself in *George Washington, Jr.* (1906); the show's big hit was "You're a Grand Old Flag" (written before the show and originally titled "You're a Grand Old Rag"). His shows followed one another at a furious pace: *Popularity* (a flop), then *Fifty Miles from Boston* (featuring the song "Harrigan"), *The Honeymooners*, *The Talk of New York*, and *The Yankee Prince* (1908).

While blackface singers still appeared in vaudeville, the minstrel show was almost dead, as Cohan discovered when he organized, wrote, and produced the Cohan and Harris Minstrels in 1908; the project lost more than $100,000. He continued to churn out works for the theater: *The American Idea*, *The Man Who Owns Broadway* (a "musicalized" version of his failed *Popularity*), and *Get Rich Quick Wallingford* (a straight play). He wrote both book and music for *The Little Millionaire* in 1911.

During this period the team of Cohan and Harris was producing many plays, some starring the biggest names of the day—John Barrymore, Laurette Taylor, and Douglas Fairbanks, for example. They produced forty-six plays together. After they separated, Cohan produced thirty-three shows on his own. The partners owned several theaters, including the George M. Cohan Theatre in Times Square. All the while he was producing and writing and composing, Cohan was trouping as well.

He and his first wife divorced in 1907, and later that year he married Agnes Mary Nolan. They had three children.

Cohan wrote a "Frolic" for the Friars Club in 1911, a comedy titled *Broadway Jones* in 1912, and the following year one of his best plays, *Seven Keys to Baldpate*. In 1914, the year his parents retired from the stage, he wrote *The Miracle Man*. His writing now included play-doctoring, farces, and revues (he wrote one with Irving Berlin in 1918). He also extended his acting to films. In 1917 he wrote his most famous song, "Over There," a significant contribution to the country's wartime fighting spirit; in 1936 he was awarded a special Congressional Medal of Honor for "Over There" and "It's a Grand Old Flag."

The Actors' Strike of 1919, in which the Actors' Equity Association fought the Producing Managers' Association, was difficult for Cohan, since he was both performer and manager. When the strike was over he retired from the firm of Cohan and Harris and started George M. Cohan Productions. Although the strike had lasted only four weeks, he remained bitter to the end of his life over what he felt was a personal betrayal by the actors who had been friends and who had appeared in many of his productions. When Actors' Equity declared a closed shop on all independent managers, he closed all twelve shows he had in operation; he planned to try his luck in England, but friends convinced him to continue to produce plays in the United States. Those plays he later produced in England he pronounced a "huge success."

Cohan soon began to write for the stage again, with new musicals, *Little Nellie Kelly* and *The Rise of Rosie O'Reilly*, and a straight comedy, *The Song and Dance Man*. In his autobiography (1925) he said that in the past twenty years he had written thirty-one of his own plays and collaborated with other authors on fourteen plays to which his name was never attached; so, he was responsible for forty-five plays in twenty years, plus about five hundred songs and musical numbers. He produced, owned, controlled, and was involved in 128 theatrical productions. He bought and sold various theaters. He appeared, over that period of time, in his own plays for 428 weeks, in 3,471 performances. He also claimed to have given more than two hundred testimonial and benefit performances. And yet an important part of his career was still to come.

He followed his autobiography with a comedy, *American Born*, and continued to produce plays. In 1927 he wrote a farce, *The Baby Cyclone*, and appeared in *The Merry Malones*; the following year found him presenting four plays (two of which he wrote himself), and in 1929 he acted in his own *Gambling* and in revivals of *The Tavern* and *The Song and Dance Man*. He was still writing and starring in his own productions when he was offered the lead, Nat Miller, in Eugene O'Neill's *Ah, Wilderness!* in October 1933; he played the part in New York and on tour in 1934. He continued to write and play in his own works (notably *Dear Old Darling* in 1936) until his next major role—as President Franklin D. Roosevelt in the musical *I'd Rather Be Right* (book by George S. Kaufman and Moss Hart, music by Richard Rodgers, lyrics by Lorenz Hart); he stayed with the show in New York and on tour from 1937 to 1939. He starred in his last work, a melodramatic satire, *The Return of the Vagabond*, in 1940. He died in New York City.

Cohan had an extraordinary range of talents—as actor (for stage and film), composer, lyricist, play doctor, librettist, playwright, director, and producer. His musicals corresponded with the nation's emergence as a world power, and the resulting chauvinism was clearly reflected in his work. He has been called the personification of the American spirit at the beginning of the twentieth century—brash, superpatriotic, cocky, quick-witted, with supreme self-assurance. And these are the characteristics he brought to the musical, forming it into the sharpest possible contrast to the reigning operetta with its exotic locales, speech, and characters. He drew on a long tradition in the United States of portraying real-life settings and characters; he leaned heavily, for example, on Edward Harrigan's comic portrayals of Irish and blacks and such immigrant groups as Jews, Italians, and Germans. (Harrigan's Mulligan Guard musicals, satirizing the quasimilitary organizations so popular with newly arrived aliens, were the immediate predecessors of Cohan's musical plays.) Cohan added a freshness and immediacy in all of his productions. His leading character, frequently modeled on himself, was brash, fast-talking, breezy, and flag-waving. "Think you can write a play without a flag?" he was asked. "I could write without anything but a pencil," he answered, with the typical tone he helped set in the musical.

Cohan's memory has been kept alive through some delightful songs, a movie (*Yankee Doodle Dandy*, 1942, starring James Cagney), and a musical (*George M.*, 1968)—plus the changes he brought to American drama. Musical comedy is perhaps a misnomer for Cohan's works, as none had more than four or five songs. Perhaps "musical play" or "musical melodrama" is more descriptive. In plot and tone he reached for the gallery, and even his excessive use of slang seemed designed for blue-collar workers. Cohan tended to be moralistic when the music stopped, but when it started the audience could count on exciting song and dance (his own peculiar dance style became almost a trademark).

Throughout much of his career, critics were unhappy with his shows; they objected to his songs (tinkly), libretti (trite), language (slangy), and themes (chauvinistic), although audiences never seemed to agree. His straight plays are frequently revived, although his musicals no longer stand up on the modern stage. Still, the enormous popularity of his musical plays in the first decade of the twentieth century, using the best of the past, laid the foundation for American musical comedies to come.

• Cohan's plays are in the George M. Cohan Collection of the Museum of the City of New York. His autobiography is *Twenty Years on Broadway, and the Years It Took to Get There* (1925). There are two biographies: John McCabe, *George M. Cohan, The Man Who Owned Broadway* (1973), and Ward Morehouse, *George M. Cohan, Prince of the American Theatre* (1943). Excellent criticism of Cohan's works may be found in Gerald Bordman, *American Musical Comedy* (1982), Stanley Green, *The World of Musical Comedy* (1980), and David Ewen, *All the Years of American Popular Music* (1977). An obituary is in the *New York Times*, 6 Nov. 1942.

JULIAN MATES

COHEN, Alfred J. *See* Dale, Alan.

COHEN, Benjamin Victor (23 Sept. 1894–15 Aug. 1983), lawyer, was born in Muncie, Indiana, the son of Moses Cohen and Sarah Ringold. His Polish-born father was a well-to-do ore dealer who provided a comfortable living for his family. Cohen received a Ph.B. from the University of Chicago in 1914, a J.D. from the University of Chicago Law School in 1915, and an S.J.D. from the Harvard Law School in 1916.

At Harvard, Cohen, a brilliant student, attracted the attention of Professor Felix Frankfurter. Frankfurter's mentor was Louis D. Brandeis, the famed "People's Attorney," who had been appointed by

Woodrow Wilson to the Supreme Court in 1916 and who worked with Frankfurter to recruit promising students into government service. Working as a legal secretary in 1916–1917 for Julian Mack, a friend of Frankfurter's and a federal circuit court judge, Cohen learned to master the legal complexities of corporate reorganization. He then became an attorney for the U.S. Shipping Board from 1917 to 1919. With the encouragement of Brandeis, who was a leader in the American Zionist movement, Cohen worked as a counsel for the American Zionists from 1919 to 1921, and he helped negotiate the Palestine Mandate at the Paris Peace Conference.

In 1922 Cohen entered private legal practice, using his considerable economic acumen to profit significantly in the stock market. At the same time, however, he continued his public service career by working as an unpaid counsel for the National Consumers' League and by helping Frankfurter draft a model minimum-wage bill for women.

Franklin D. Roosevelt's New Deal provided Cohen with an opportunity to exert his influence at the national level. Brought to Washington, D.C., in 1933 by Brandeis and Frankfurter, the latter having become an influential though unofficial presidential adviser, Cohen initially worked on Roosevelt's securities legislation. In conjunction with James Landis and Thomas G. Corcoran (two other Frankfurter protégés), Cohen refined the Securities Act of 1933, which sought to prevent manipulation by stock-market insiders by placing trading practices under governmental supervision; it was approved unanimously by the House of Representatives.

For a year Cohen served as associate general counsel for the Public Works Administration, and then in 1934 he became counsel for the National Power Policy Committee. Both agencies were under the supervision of Harold Ickes, who was secretary of the Department of the Interior. A superb legislative craftsman, Cohen was far more important to the New Deal than his job titles would indicate. Working in an increasingly productive and highly visible partnership with Corcoran, Cohen helped draft the Securities Exchange Act of 1934, which established the Securities Exchange Commission, and the Public Utility Holding Company Act of 1935, which attempted to regulate the giant utility corporations. The Cohen-Corcoran legislative team drafted numerous significant New Deal measures, such as the Rural Electrification Act of 1935 and the Fair Labor Standards Act of 1938, one of the last important New Deal reforms.

As the New Deal lost its momentum and foreign-policy issues came to dominate Roosevelt's attention, Cohen's importance as a domestic adviser inevitably declined. Yet his varied talents enabled him to continue in effective public service. Deeply concerned over the Nazi threat, Cohen gave Roosevelt legal advice on the 1940 destroyers-for-bases deal with Great Britain and also helped draft the Lend-Lease Act. In 1941 he left the Department of the Interior to become counsel for John G. Winant, American ambassador to the

Court of St. James's. From 1943 to 1945 he served as general counsel to the Office of War Mobilization and helped to draft the Dumbarton Oaks agreement, which established the basic provisions of the United Nations Charter.

Although Cohen served capably in a variety of positions, he suffered from persistent job dissatisfaction, which puzzled even his closest associates. He resigned from government service after Roosevelt, fearing political complications harkening back to the "Court-packing" bill of 1937, did not support him as general counsel to the State Department. President Harry S. Truman, however, appointed him to the position in July 1945, and Cohen became one of Secretary of State James F. Byrnes's closest aides. He devoted himself for the most part to the United Nations and served as a member of the U.S. delegation to the United Nations General Assembly from 1948 to 1952 and to the United Nations Disarmament Commission in 1952. Cohen continued to speak and write about the United Nations after he left public service in 1952; see, particularly, his *The United Nations: Constitutional Developments, Growth, and Possibilities* (1961).

A lifelong bachelor, Cohen lived most of his life in Washington, D.C. He remained vitally interested in the issues of the day, staying in contact with a number of Washington insiders. He occasionally served as an ad hoc adviser to the passing administrations. In 1977 civil-rights activist Joseph Rauh characterized him as the "best informed man in Washington."

Cohen was a self-effacing public servant best known for his legal acumen. He was a dedicated New Dealer in the Brandeis/Frankfurter circle with a zeal for reform, a distrust of concentrated economic power, and high standards for public service. Cohen, whose career spanned several decades, has earned a solid reputation in the history of the New Deal as an innovative legislative craftsman. His career extended beyond the New Deal, however, and he was unusual in making significant contributions to both domestic and foreign-policy issues in the period from the New Deal to the Cold War. He died in Washington, D.C.

• In the absence of a biography, it is necessary to turn to a number of sources to obtain a complete account of Cohen's many contributions. *Current Biography* for 1941 provides a helpful account of his early life and New Deal activities. Michael Parrish discussed his role in securities legislation in *Securities Regulation and the New Deal* (1970). See John M. Blum, *Roosevelt and Morganthau* (1970), for a discussion of his contributions during World War II. Harold Ickes commented frequently on Cohen's activities in *The Secret Diary of Harold Ickes* (1953). Cohen's career in the 1930s is discussed in a number of books on the New Deal. See particularly Katie Louchheim, *The Making of the New Deal* (1983), and Joseph P. Lash, *Dealers and Dreamers: A New Look at the New Deal* (1988). A front-page obituary is in the *Washington Post*, 16 Aug. 1983.

NELSON L. DAWSON

COHEN, Felix Solomon (3 July 1907–19 Oct. 1953), lawyer, was born in New York City, the son of Morris Cohen, an academic and philosopher, and Mary Ryshpan, a former teacher. Cohen attended Townsend Harris High School, which conducted a joint program with City College. After graduating magna cum laude from City College, he earned his M.A. in philosophy from Harvard in 1927. Cohen entered Columbia Law School in 1928, completed his Ph.D. comprehensive exams at Harvard and received his doctorate in 1929, and received his LL.B. from Columbia in 1931. That year he accepted a position as research assistant for a judge on the New York Supreme Court and married Lucy M. Kramer. They had two children.

Cohen entered private legal practice in New York in 1932. The following year he accepted an offer for a one-year position as an assistant solicitor in the Department of the Interior in the Franklin D. Roosevelt administration. Solicitor Nathan Margold had requested that Cohen be hired for the purpose of drafting legislation known as the Indian Reorganization Act or the Wheeler-Howard bill.

Despite several flaws, the Indian Reorganization Act represented a major change in federal policy toward Native Americans. The bill ended the practice of allotment, which was intended to destroy the tribal ownership of land through the assignment of individual plots to Indians. Because it fostered the creation of tribal governments, it permitted a limited degree of Indian self-determination. The legislation reflected Cohen's belief that Indians possessed fundamental rights as U.S. citizens and deserved specific special treatment from the government because of treaty obligations. In 1934 Cohen accompanied Bureau of Indian Affairs commissioner John Collier on a tour of ten Indian congresses in order to garner Indian support for the bill. In addition, he drafted a model tribal constitution for tribes to use in designing their governments. Although Congress extensively revised the legislation before passing it, the bill Cohen drafted marked the start of a new era in Native American history.

Cohen remained with the Interior Department long after the one-year appointment expired. He refused a transfer to the Justice Department in 1938 but agreed to spend one year as a special assistant to the attorney general and to head the Indian Law Survey. Cohen was assigned the task of compiling laws and statutes regarding Indians and then creating a guide to Indian law. Despite staffing problems, Cohen and his assistants eventually compiled forty-six volumes of Indian law. As work on the guide began, conflicts developed over the purpose of the project. Cohen insisted that the guide would not serve as a litigation manual for attorneys; rather, he envisioned a document that would "safeguard our national resources and the rights and property of our nation's wards" (Martin, p. 42). The dispute over the guide's purpose led the Justice Department to terminate the project. Cohen successfully lobbied the Interior Department to resume work on the guide, and the *Handbook of Federal Indian Law* was published in 1941.

Cohen also participated in a number of lawsuits regarding Indians. In 1941 he successfully argued in *United States ex re. Hualapai Indians v. Santa Fe Railroad*, a landmark case, that Indian title to land had to be formally and not merely implicitly extinguished, a position that strengthened Indians' control of their lands. In 1947 he represented the All-Pueblo Council in an attempt to force the states of New Mexico and Arizona to offer public assistance to aged and disabled Indians.

In addition to Indian affairs, Cohen worked on several other projects during his career, including the creation of the Fair Employment Practices Commission, the economic development of U.S. territories, and the conservation of natural resources. He was also interested in legal theory and published articles on various legal topics throughout his career. Like many other New Deal attorneys, he adhered to a school of thought known as "legal realism." The realists maintained that the legal process was not merely the rational application of understood laws; rather, emotions and value judgments played important roles in the interpretation of law. The debate between the legal realists and the defenders of a more traditional understanding of the law continued through the 1930s, with Cohen contributing frequently.

In 1948, dissatisfied with what he perceived as a growing conservatism in the Interior Department following the 1946 retirement of Secretary Harold Ickes, Cohen retired from public service and returned to private practice. He maintained a busy schedule, teaching law at Yale University and philosophy at City College, writing, and doing legal work. He was affiliated with a number of organizations, including the American Jewish Committee, the Institute of Ethnic Affairs, and the New York Association for New Americans. His interest in Indian affairs continued, and he acted as general counsel for several Indian tribes. In 1948 his oral argument convinced a panel of federal judges that Arizona and New Mexico could no longer deny Indians the right to vote. He was a vigorous opponent of termination, a policy that would end the special obligations of the federal government to Native Americans. In 1952 Cohen became head of the Washington office of Riegelman, Strasser, Schwarz & Spiegelberg, a New York law firm. He died of cancer in Washington, D.C.

Cohen's formidable skills as a lawyer, his concern for minority groups, and his capacity for hard work led to a distinguished career in both the public and private sectors. His *Handbook of Federal Indian Law* remains an important reference work. As an attorney drafting legislation for the Interior Department and later as an advocate for Indian concerns, Cohen contributed to an enlightened understanding of Native American culture and federal responsibilities toward the first inhabitants of the continent.

• The papers of Felix S. Cohen are located at the Beinecke Rare Book and Manuscript Library at Yale University. Cohen was a prolific writer; a number of his published and previously unpublished articles are available in *The Legal Conscience: Selected Papers of Felix S. Cohen* (1960). His doctoral thesis was published as *Ethical Systems and Legal Ideals*

(1933). A brief biographical sketch and a bibliography of Cohen's publications appear in the *Rutgers Law Review* 9 (Winter 1954): 345–53. Stephen Haycox, "Felix Cohen and the Legacy of the Indian New Deal," *Yale University Library Gazette* 64 (Apr. 1994): 135–56, is useful. Stephen M. Feldman, "Felix S. Cohen and His Jurisprudence: Reflections on Federal Indian Law," *Buffalo Law Review* 35 (Spring 1986): 479–525, examines the impact of legal realism on Indian law. Jill E. Martin, "A Year and a Spring of My Existence: Felix Cohen and the *Handbook of Federal Indian Law*," *Western Legal History* 8 (Winter–Spring 1995): 35–60, is a detailed account of Cohen's involvement in writing the *Handbook*. Kenneth R. Philp, *Indian Self-Rule: First-hand Accounts of Indian-White Relations from Roosevelt to Reagan* (1986), contains a panel discussion regarding Cohen's contributions to the Indian Reorganization Act that includes comments from Lucy Kramer Cohen. An obituary is in the *New York Times*, 20 Oct. 1953.

THOMAS CLARKIN

COHEN, Mickey (4 Sept. 1913–29 July 1976), criminal and celebrity, was born Meyer Harris Cohen in Brooklyn, New York, the son of Max Cohen, whom Cohen remembered as having been in the "import business with Jewish fishes," and Fanny (maiden name unknown). Both parents were Jewish immigrants. His father died shortly after Cohen's birth, and Cohen's mother moved the family to the Boyle Heights Jewish district of Los Angeles, where she opened a grocery store. According to his own account, he attended school rarely, if at all, rejected religious education, and was incorrigible from his earliest days selling newspapers, using his natural pugnacity to secure the best locations. He committed minor crimes and took up amateur boxing. Cohen ran away from Los Angeles around age fifteen to avoid having to attend school further.

The next several years Cohen spent as a professional prizefighter, chiefly in Cleveland and Chicago. He insisted he had been encouraged by some of the outstanding boxers of that era and later told a Senate committee that he had appeared in thirty-two main events in which he was chiefly victorious. His career was probably less than what he liked to recall, and he was described by a reporter as "a second-rater with a glass chin" who was "knocked out in most of his fights."

His boxing career over, Cohen drifted into petty crime. Later, he liked to boast himself an acquaintance of mob leader Al Capone. It is more likely he made a connection to Capone's accountant, Jack "Greasy Thumb" Guzik, for whom he conducted bookmaking and an occasional pistol-whipping. It was after one such event in 1939 that he left Chicago and returned home to Los Angeles.

In Los Angeles Cohen operated a portable craps table, which he trucked to wherever he could get a game. He later was associated with Benjamin "Bugsy" Siegel, a more formidable gangster, who operated gambling and bookmaking on the West Coast. Cohen asserted that in 1945 he had been put in charge of local southern California gambling operations when Siegel turned his interest to Las Vegas. Others insisted Cohen was never more than an errand boy.

Los Angeles in the post–World War II era underwent rapid growth, and disorganization and disruption rippled through political life and law enforcement. Cohen, loving notoriety and enamored of Hollywood's café society, thrived in the unsettled postwar city. He associated with newspaper editors and reporters, the most famous of whom was the *Los Angeles Herald*'s James Richardson, who had a reputation for recasting mundane events in headline-sized stories. In exchange for headlines, Cohen passed along information and offered his opinions, and in general whenever some outrage to public order occurred, "the Mick" seemed inevitably somewhere in the vicinity.

Cohen was the perfect front-page gangster. He spent lavishly in the city's nightclubs and was always accompanied by well-endowed striptease artists and Hollywood celebrities—Cohen seemed to know them all. At the drop of a hat he would show visitors closets stocked with 500 hundred pairs of socks and 60 pairs of shoes. In his heyday he refused to wear his custom-made suits after they had been dry-cleaned. At one time Cohen opened a haberdashery, Michael's, but it was not successful.

In 1945 Cohen shot and killed gambler Maxie Shaman but was cleared on grounds of self-defense. On several occasions there were attempts on Cohen's life. In 1948 gunmen entered Cohen's place of business and opened fire. Cohen evaded death, having moments before gone to the bathroom, but one of his bodyguards was killed. A year later, outside a Sunset Strip nightclub, Cohen was again the target of gunshots, which missed him but killed another of his attendants. That same year a bomb exploded outside Cohen's fashionable West Los Angeles home; Cohen was not injured, but his neighbors complained.

Cohen was married in 1940 to LaVonne (maiden name unknown). They were divorced in 1956. There is no record of his having had children. He was linked romantically to a number of members of the gangster demimonde, including strippers Liz Renay and Candy Bar.

In the early 1950s the federal government took an interest in Cohen's finances. In 1952 he was convicted of tax evasion and spent three and one-half years at McNeil Island Federal Prison. When released, he returned to Los Angeles and his "wise guy" role. Cohen's fame was boosted by unseemly incidents, such as when one of his henchmen, Johnny Stampanato, became romantically involved with movie star Lana Turner and was stabbed to death by Turner's daughter.

In 1962 Cohen was again convicted of tax evasion and was sent to the federal prison at Atlanta. He was clubbed by a fellow prisoner for unknown reasons and suffered brain damage and paralysis as a result of the attack. Cohen sued the federal government and eventually won a judgment of $110,000, which was promptly seized by the Internal Revenue Service.

Cohen was released in January 1972. He lived the balance of his years in West Los Angeles, never reluctant to give an interview or inject himself into the criminal events of the day. Near the end of his life he offered to use his underworld connections to locate kidnapped heiress Patty Hearst. At the time of his death in Los Angeles, the *Los Angeles Times* noted that Cohen "seemed to be striving for the title of 'Public Enemy no. 1'" but that local lawmen rated him "no higher than the leading public nuisance."

• There are, of course, innumerable newspaper stories from 1945 to the early 1960s in which Mickey Cohen's name appears. Few are illuminating beyond the immediate events of the day. One of the few lengthy contemporary pieces on Cohen is Dean Jennings, "Mickey Cohen: The Private Life of a Hood," *Saturday Evening Post*, 20 Sept. 1958. At the end of his life Cohen published an autobiography, *Mickey Cohen: In My Own Words*, with John Peer Nugent (1976). The book is not more than a series of transcribed interviews. What it lacks in background regarding the period it makes up for in the authenticity of Cohen's language. Obituaries are in the *Los Angeles Times*, the *Los Angeles Examiner*, and the *New York Times*, all 30 July 1976.

BRUCE HENSTELL

COHEN, Morris Raphael (25 July 1880?–28 Jan. 1947), philosopher and educator, was born in Minsk, Russia, the son of Abraham Mordecai Cohen, a handyman and tailor, and Bessie Farfel, a seamstress. He lived his first twelve years in the traditional society and culture of a Jewish shtetl in imperial Russia. His father and elder brothers resided in the United States during most of these years, while Cohen was reared in impoverished circumstances by his mother and maternal grandfather. Mother and son joined the rest of the family in New York City in 1892. When obliged to indicate his date of birth, Cohen chose 25 July because it was the approximate date of his arrival in his new country. His parents were unable to specify even the year of his birth, but agreed upon 1880 in order to justify Cohen's bar mitzvah in 1893, which was to take place at the end of his thirteenth year.

Cohen responded passionately to the intellectual worlds opened to him in the United States, especially at the Educational Alliance, a settlement house on the Lower East Side of Manhattan. In the public schools he proved to be an exceptionally able and energetic student. Cohen's account of these years in his autobiography, *A Dreamer's Journey* (1949), is one of the most revealing and sensitive memoirs of the accommodation of Eastern European Jewish culture to the America presented by settlement workers, philanthropists, and schoolteachers of the 1890s. Cohen completed an undergraduate degree at the City College of New York in 1900 and, after teaching high school for several years, began graduate work at Harvard University under the direction of William James and Josiah Royce. At Harvard Cohen roomed with law student Felix Frankfurter, later an associate justice of the U.S. Supreme Court and Cohen's lifelong friend. In 1906 Cohen became the first Jew to earn a Ph.D. in philosophy at Harvard.

Discrimination against Jews at first prevented Cohen from obtaining employment as a teacher of philos-

ophy. He taught mathematics at the City College of New York from 1906 to 1912 and was then transferred to the department of philosophy where he remained until his retirement in 1938. Cohen's ferocious wit and great erudition made him a legendary teacher, appreciated as a cultural hero by many of his approximately fifteen thousand students at City College, some of whom dubbed him "the Paul Bunyan of the Jewish intellectuals." Although students inspired by Cohen went on to distinguished careers in business, law, and medicine, his pedagogic progeny among scholars and writers was sufficient to win him recognition as one of the most influential undergraduate teachers in the United States in the twentieth century. Among his pupils prominent in American letters or scholarship were Kenneth J. Arrow, William Barrett, Lewis S. Feuer, Louis Finklestein, Paul Goodman, Sidney Hook, Joseph P. Lash, Richard B. Morris, Ernest Nagel, Benjamin Nelson, Samuel Thorne, Paul Weiss, Morton White, Philip P. Wiener, and Bertram D. Wolfe.

During his teaching career, Cohen held a number of visiting appointments, including in departments of philosophy or schools of law at the Johns Hopkins University, Cornell University, the New School for Social Research, Columbia University, and Harvard University. Upon his retirement from the City College of New York, he taught philosophy briefly at the University of Chicago. At professional meetings of philosophers, Cohen was for three decades an animating presence and a formidable, if sometimes feared, antagonist. The most able of his contemporaries, including C. I. Lewis and Arthur O. Lovejoy, held his critical powers in high regard. The American Philosophical Association elected Cohen president of its Eastern Division for 1929 and in 1940 elected him its sixth Paul Carus lecturer. He was among the first to appreciate the significance of the philosophical contributions of Charles S. Peirce and edited an influential collection of Peirce's essays, *Chance, Love, and Logic* (1923). Cohen was also a regular contributor to the *New Republic*, especially during its first decade (1914–1924), and he wrote critical essays on a wide range of topics in literature, history, and politics, as well as philosophy. Many of these diverse essays were collected in *Faith of a Liberal* (1946) and *American Thought* (1954). Cohen was the first Eastern European Jew to become a prominent public moralist in the United States.

Cohen reacted strongly against two movements prominent in the philosophical milieu of the early twentieth century: the religious idealism that presented philosophy as a form of Christian apologetics and the irrationalism of Nietzsche and Bergson that condemned the classical philosophical tradition for its emphasis on reason. Against the religious idealists, Cohen denied the reality of disembodied spirits and thus joined George Santayana, John Dewey, and Roy Wood Sellars as a leader in the naturalist movement in American philosophy. A volume designed to advance this movement, *Naturalism and the Human Spirit* (1944), edited by Yervant H. Krekorian, was dedicated to Cohen. Against the irrationalism of Nietzsche and Bergson, Cohen defended reason as a vital element in the universe and as a precious human capacity. He was the most rationalistic of the American naturalists and a resolute champion of scientific method as an agent of culture. Cohen pioneered the development of philosophy of science as an academic field in the United States, especially in the essays collected in *Studies in Philosophy and Science* (1949). In *The Meaning of Human History* (1947) he defended the reality of historical knowledge against extreme relativists.

Cohen believed the necessary truths of formal logic to be invariant in all areas of the universe accessible to human thought but resisted the idea that specific knowledge in any branch of science could be absolutely true. There were elements of genuine change and of genuine permanence in the universe, Cohen insisted, in a characteristic application of the metaphysical principle of polarity with which he became the most identified. In this view, "opposites such as immediacy and mediation, unity and plurality, the fixed and the flux . . . all involve each other when applied to any significant entity." *Reason and Nature* (1931) contained Cohen's most sustained discussion of polarity, but nowhere in his writings did Cohen develop a full-scale metaphysical system. The principle of polarity rendered in formal terms Cohen's most persistent philosophical disposition, which was the balancing of oppositions and the mediating of extreme doctrines. Although he often identified himself as a logician, his work was less a contribution to the technical development of logic than it was a vindication of logic itself. This is evident, for example, in his essays in *Preface to Logic* (1944) and in his most enduring book, *An Introduction to Logic and Scientific Method* (1934), a college text written with his student Ernest Nagel. Cohen saw himself as a "cleaner of stables," committed to the Herculean tasks of sweeping away intellectual rubbish and disinfecting the instruments of human thought.

One discourse especially in need of such cleansing, Cohen believed, was the law. He was broadly allied with his friend Supreme Court Associate Justice Oliver Wendell Holmes (1841–1935) in attacking a formalist jurisprudence prone to develop law as a series of logical deductions from principles. Yet Cohen's most widely discussed contributions to philosophy of law were attacks on the more radical followers of Holmes who came to be known around 1930 as "legal realists." These thinkers went too far in denigrating the role of reason in the law, Cohen insisted in *Law and the Social Order* (1933), the most sustained and influential work of legal philosophy written by a professional philosopher of Cohen's generation in the United States. This book also included Cohen's most analytically powerful and historically learned critiques of laissez-faire individualism, which he had opposed since his adolescent involvement in socialist politics on New York's Lower East Side. Cohen's subsequent legal essays were collected in *Reason and Law* (1950).

Late in life Cohen intensified his previously intermittent interest in Jewish history and in contemporary Jewish affairs. He was the chief organizer in 1933 of the Conference on Jewish Relations, a response to rising anti-Semitism. Cohen's perspective on Jewish experience was secular: he had drifted away from Judaism shortly after his bar mitzvah and throughout his adulthood did not attend religious services. He was skeptical of the idea of a Jewish state and was often embroiled in controversy with Zionists. His essays on Jewish themes were collected in *Reflections of a Wondering Jew* (1950).

Cohen suffered a stroke in January 1942 that effectively terminated his career. The works he published during the five years until his death in Washington, D.C., were put together with the assistance of his son, Felix S. Cohen, who also supervised the publication of Cohen's many posthumous books. Felix Cohen was the first of three children born to Morris Cohen and his wife, Mary (Ryshpan) Cohen, who were married in 1906.

Cohen was a critical rather than a systematic philosopher, whose work responded more vividly to the enthusiasms and peculiarities of his contemporaries than to the perennial questions of metaphysics, epistemology, and ethics. His reputation among philosophers declined rapidly during the 1940s and 1950s with the ascendancy of the more technical styles of philosophy associated with the Vienna Circle and linguistic analysis. Yet in his own generation of American intellectuals he was a giant, at once a philosopher's philosopher and a broadly ranging cultural critic, inferior in range and stature only to John Dewey among his contemporary philosophers. As an Eastern European Jew in an academy overwhelmingly Anglo-Protestant, Cohen was a highly distinctive social being who challenged the prejudices of his native-born, Gentile colleagues and inspired within many of them mixed feelings of respect and ambivalence. To many young Jews from the mid-1910s through the early 1940s, Cohen was the chief exemplar of what it meant to be a successful intellectual in U.S. society. His career was a pivotal episode in the emergence of a secular, ethnically diverse intelligentsia in the United States.

• Cohen's papers, including extensive correspondence with family members and with several leading philosophers of his generation, are in the Regenstein Library at the University of Chicago. A substantial selection of this correspondence is available in a book edited by his daughter, Leonora Cohen Rosenfield, *Portrait of a Philosopher: Morris R. Cohen in Life and Letters* (1962). The only book-length biographical study is David A. Hollinger, *Morris R. Cohen and the Scientific Ideal* (1975). A helpful study of Cohen's career in relation to that of other Jewish academic intellectuals of his generation can be found within Susanne Klingenstein, *Jews in the American Academy, 1900–1940: The Dynamics of Intellectual Assimilation* (1991). A sympathetic and discerning assessment of Cohen's contributions to philosophy is Abraham Edel, "The Unity of Morris Raphael Cohen's Thought," *Transactions of the Charles S. Peirce Society* 17 (1981): 107–27. An evocative memoir by a former student is Sidney Hook, "Morris Cohen—Fifty Years Later," *American Scholar* 45 (Summer 1976): 426–36. A document revealing the depth and character of the hero-worship Cohen inspired during his greatest years as a teacher at the City College of New York is *A Tribute to Professor Morris Raphael Cohen, Teacher & Philosopher*, a book published by "The Youth Who Sat at His Feet" (1928).

DAVID A. HOLLINGER

COHEN, Octavus Roy (26 June 1891–6 Jan. 1959), fiction writer, playwright, and screenwriter, was born in Charleston, South Carolina, the son of Octavus Cohen, a lawyer and editor, and Rebecca Ottolengui. He graduated from the Porter Military Academy, Charleston, in 1908, worked as a civil engineer for a Tennessee railroad company from 1909 to 1910, earned his B.S. in engineering at Clemson College in 1911, and worked for newspapers in Alabama, South Carolina, and New Jersey from 1910 to 1912. He returned to Charleston to study law in his father's office, passed the bar in 1913, and practiced law for two years. He married Inez Lopez in 1914. The couple lived in Birmingham, Alabama, and had one son. Upon selling his first short story in 1915, Cohen determined to become a full-time professional writer. The Cohens moved to New York in 1935 and to Los Angeles in 1948. Inez Cohen died in 1953.

The versatile and prolific Cohen wrote about 1,100 short stories, sixty or so books, six plays, reams of radio material—including items for the "Amos 'n' Andy" show (1945–1946)—and thirty movie scripts for Paramount Pictures, Columbia, Universal, and RKO-Pathé. Some of his plots were also adapted for television.

Success came swiftly to Cohen. "False Alarm," his first story, appeared in *Collier's* (17 Apr. 1915). He was soon publishing regularly in the *Saturday Evening Post, Argosy, Black Cat, McCall's,* and *Munsey's.* Meanwhile, his mystery stories appeared in *Mystery Magazine, Illustrated Detective Magazine, Best Detective Magazine, New Mystery Adventure, Triple Detective, Malcolm's,* and *Mystery Digest.* Cohen's *Cameos* (1931) contains fifty-three tricky little 1,000-word stories. Much of his book-length fiction grew out of his short stories. His first mystery novel was *The Other Woman* (1917, coauthored by John Ulrich Giesey). Cohen's first series novel featuring a detective was *The Crimson Alibi* (1919); its protagonist is David Carroll, who meets later challenges in *Gray Dusk* (1920), *Six Seconds of Darkness* (1921), and *Midnight* (1922). Cohen's first play was *The Crimson Alibi*, adapted from the novel, coauthored by George Broadhurst, and produced on Broadway in 1919. Cohen also adapted *Come Seven*, his collection of stories about African Americans, for Broadway (1920). He introduced his next series detective in *Jim Hanvey, Detective* in 1923. Hanvey surfaced again in *The May Day Mystery* (1929), *The Backstage Mystery* (1930), *Star of Earth* (1932), *The Townsend Murder Mystery* (1933, based on Cohen's radio play), and the cleverly titled *Scrambled Yeggs* (1934). Police detectives Max Gold (in New York City) and Marty Walsh (in Los Angeles) were still later detectives in Cohen mystery series. His last mystery novel was *Love Can Be Dangerous* (1955), depicting Hollywood hotel life.

Each of Cohen's detectives is singularly characterized. David Carroll and James H. Hanvey are the most notable. The thin and boyish Carroll must help justice, law, and order triumph despite influential and corrupt citizens, slightly sadistic policemen, and tainted attorneys. Carroll's work in *The Crimson Alibi* is complicated because the suspects all feel that the victim is better off dead. The reading public of the 1920s and 1930s found Cohen's second detective, Hanvey, the most delightful. He is crude, multi-chinned, grotesquely fat, semi-illiterate, and seemingly brainless and half-asleep. But he solves every case. He does not employ incandescent brilliance, the hallmark of nineteenth-century sleuths C. Auguste Dupin and Sherlock Holmes and their descendants. Instead, he uses country-bred common sense, a memory for details, and experience gained through friendships with criminals of many stripes. One of the most successful movies based on any Cohen character was *Jim Hanvey, Detective*, starring Guy Kibbee, in 1937.

Cohen's most popular fictional character was Florian Slappey. This tall, well-dressed African-American resident of "Bummin'ham," Alabama, is limned with amiable condescension as "a sepia gentleman." Cohen collected scores of Slappey stories in many books, beginning with *Come Seven*; the character is later featured in *Florian Slappey Goes Abroad* (1928), in which he represents his Midnight Pictures Corporation, and in *Florian Slappey* (1938), in which he visits Harlem briefly. Slappey's two closest African-American cohorts are Evans Chew, a lawyer, and Epic Peters, a philosophical Pullman porter; other, rather caricatured blacks include Marshmallow Jeepers and Acey Upshaw. In these works, Cohen drew heavily on his southern childhood and early youth. He always insisted that he portrayed southern blacks with affection, knowledgeably, and without bias; furthermore, he insisted that northern blacks, whom he never depicted, may have been more cultured but were never happier than his southern friends. A side effect of the civil rights movement is critical disapproval of seemingly patronizing but well-intentioned presentations in various media of blacks in the early twentieth century. The following Cohen titles, to be sure, may give offense to some modern readers: *Polished Ebony* (1919), *Highly Colored* (1921), *Assorted Chocolates* (1922), and *Carbon Copies* (1932).

From 1920 through 1950 Cohen published one or two—and occasionally even three—books a year. An interesting experiment, *Lady in Armor* (1941), features a female sheriff. *Borrasca* (1953), his one historical novel, is about gold and silver mining in the Comstock Lode from 1868 through the 1870s; over-researched but precisely crafted, it tells about a San Franciscan who joins a medicine show to investigate a Nevada mine that proves "borrasca" (that is, worthless). Dozens of Cohen's short stories have punning titles, including "The Birth of a Notion," "Here Comes the Bribe," "Poppy Passes," and "The Wild and Woolly Vest." Adverse reviewers of Cohen's bewilderingly frequent publications called them smooth, slick, smart, breezy, gaudy, farcical, trivial, obvious, superficial, and even synthetic and "metallic." More discerning reviewers, however, praised Cohen for his delightfully entertaining style, accurate dialogue, meticulous handling of details, precise craftsmanship, and logical plot structures. His day may be past, but his immense popularity reveals much about the tastes, values, and cultural standards of America between World War I and World War II.

Life was not all writing for the energetic Octavus Roy Cohen. He was a lieutenant in the U.S. Naval Reserve (1930–1940), was a member of several associations and clubs, enjoyed golf and table tennis, was a philatelist, and—rare among notable Americans in any walk of life—played jai alai. He died in Los Angeles.

• A collection of Cohen's letters is in the University of Oregon Library. His one autobiographical piece, "The Woman Who Changed My Life," *American Magazine*, July 1954, pp. 36–37, 101–3, sentimentally portrays a woman in Birmingham who told a white lie to help him regain his faith in people. Cohen receives brief mention in Chris Steinbrunner and Otto Penzler, eds., *Encyclopedia of Mystery and Detection* (1976), pp. 92–93. In Michael L. Cook, ed., *Mystery, Detective, and Espionage Magazines* (1983), Cohen's work is frequently noted. Bill Pronzini and Marcia Muller, eds., *1001 Midnights: The Aficionado's Guide to Mystery and Detective Fiction* (1986), pp. 150–51, singles out Cohen's 1946 thriller *Don't Ever Love Me* for laudatory analysis. The best general discussion of Cohen's work is "Octavus Roy Cohen," in *Critical Survey of Mystery and Detective Fiction*, ed. Frank N. Magill (1988). A detailed obituary is in the *New York Times*, 7 Jan. 1959.

ROBERT L. GALE

COHEN, Rose Gollup (4 Apr. 1880–1925?), author, was the daughter of Abraham (Avrom) Gollup, a tailor, and Annie (maiden name unknown). Rose, the oldest child in her family, grew up in a small village in western Russia, probably what is today Belarus. The onset in the early 1880s of attacks on Jewish communities—known as pogroms—and the expulsion of Jews from numerous Russian towns and cities made life increasingly intolerable for the Jewish minority. These attacks, coupled with increasingly systematic discrimination against Jews in higher education and economic life, contributed to the growth of the large-scale exodus of Russian Jews. About two million emigrated between 1880 and 1914, with the vast majority going to the United States.

The Gollup (sometimes spelled Gallup) family was part of this massive immigrant flow, and Rose Gollup Cohen's autobiography, *Out of the Shadow* (1918), is among the richest and most detailed accounts of the immigration process and work and acculturation of Russian Jews on New York's Lower East Side. As was common in Russian Jewish families, Rose Gollup's father emigrated first, leaving his family behind. Lacking proper papers, he was arrested and had to escape from custody before crossing into Germany and securing steamship passage to the United States in 1890. There he worked and got a foothold for himself in

New York City, and after a year and a half he sent two prepaid steamship tickets to his family. In 1892 rose and her unmarried aunt, Masha, joined him in a trip that is described in Rose's autobiography. A year later, her mother, two brothers, and two sisters joined the rest of the family.

The autobiography provides the main source for our knowledge of Cohen's life, describing in particular detail sweatshop garment work in the Lower East Side. She began in the shop where her father worked but soon graduated to work on her own, stitching sleeve linings for men's coats. She recounts union organizing among the men of her shop, her own attendance at a mass union meeting, and finally joining the union herself. This was probably the United Hebrew Trades, though it remains unnamed, and Rose's participation in union activities appears to have been quite limited. After the arrival of her mother and other siblings, her story continues with accounts of a brief stint as a domestic servant, her rejection of a prospective suitor, and increasing health problems. During one illness, she was visited by the noted settlement worker Lillian Wald, who may have introduced her to the world of the Nurses' Settlement on Henry Street. Through the settlement she was referred to the uptown Presbyterian Hospital, and there she met wealthy non-Jews who sponsored summer outings for children of the Lower East Side. She worked successive summers at a Connecticut retreat established for immigrant children and, like others, found herself torn between the world of her family in the immigrant ghetto and the broader American culture beyond its bounds.

Lillian Wald helped Rose Gollup in yet another way, by referring her in 1897 to a cooperative shirtwaist shop under the direction of Leonora O'Reilly, later a board member of the National Women's Trade Union League. That work proved short-lived, but when O'Reilly began teaching machine sewing in 1902 at the Manhattan Trade School for Girls, she recruited Rose Gollup to be her assistant.

Little is known about Cohen's later life. She married Joseph Cohen and stopped working following the birth of her daughter, Evelyn. She continued her education after her marriage and slowly overcame her self-consciousness about the English language. She attended classes at Breadwinners' College at the Educational Alliance (also known as the Thomas Davidson School) and the Rand School, there coming under the influence of Joseph Gollomb, a Russian Jewish immigrant who later wrote his own autobiographical novel, *Unquiet* (1935). In a 1922 article she expressed gratitude toward those who had helped her on her journey to becoming a writer: "I owe much of what I know of writing to all my teachers, from the blue-eyed girl in the Thomas Davidson School long ago, who explained a sentence to me, to my present teachers."

In addition to her autobiography, she wrote at least five short pieces published in New York City literary magazines between 1918 and 1922. In an autobiographical piece addressed "To the Friends of 'Out of the Shadow,'" she summed up her motivation for writing. She sought to communicate her origins "among the Russian peasants," her recent past "among the Jews of Cherry Street," and her present life "among the Americans" (*Bookman*, Mar. 1922, pp. 36–40). Her autobiography captures that cultural journey in rich and vivid tones.

Her writing was received enthusiastically by contemporaries. Reviews in *The Outlook* and the *New York Times* were glowing. Wald and O'Reilly both praised the work as well. *Out of the Shadow* appeared in two European editions, translated into French and Russian. Cohen's short story, "Natalka's Portion," was reprinted six times, including in the prestigious *Best Short Stories of 1922*. In addition, in the summers of 1923 and 1924 Cohen was invited to the MacDowell Colony in Peterborough, New Hampshire. There she met and enjoyed the company of American impressionist painter Lilla Cabot Perry and poet Edwin Arlington Robinson, both of whom she kept in touch with after her time at the colony. She probably also met philosopher Morris Raphael Cohen and playwright Thornton Wilson, both residents at the colony in 1924. MacDowell Colony notes Cohen's death in 1925, but no obituary or death record remain to tell us anything about the circumstances of her death. She may have committed suicide, an outcome suggested by a short story written by her friend and fellow writer Anzia Yezierska and also confirmed by family stories passed down to a surviving niece. Such may account for Cohen's sudden disappearance from the literary and historical stage. Her autobiography survives as Rose Gollup Cohen's legacy, a moving account of a cultural journey shared with many other Russian and Eastern European Jewish immigrants at the turn of the twentieth century.

• There are no known papers for Rose Cohen. Her published writings, reviews of her autobiography, and a possible family listing in the 1900 federal manuscript census of population for the Lower East Side are the main sources for reconstructing her life. The census listing included a father Abraham Gulob, tailor, and a daughter Rosie, "tailoress," on Cherry Street as well as other family members consistent with information provided in *Out of the Shadow*; see T623, reel 1084, e.d. 82, sheet 9, line 10. The most important source is her autobiography, Rose Cohen, *Out of the Shadow* (1918; repr. 1995). Also see her article "My Childhood Days in Russia," *Bookman*, Aug. 1918, pp. 591–608. See also Leonora O'Reilly, "Rahel and 'Out of the Shadow,'" *Life and Labor*, May 1919, pp. 103–5.

THOMAS DUBLIN

COHEN, Walter L. (22 Jan. 1860–29 Dec. 1930), businessman and politician, was born a free person of color in New Orleans, Louisiana, the son of Bernard Cohen and Amelia Bingaman, a free woman of color. Although Cohen's father was Jewish, he was raised as and remained throughout his life a Roman Catholic. His parents died when he was in the fourth grade, whereupon he had to quit school, though he later attended Straight University in New Orleans for several years. As a boy Cohen became a cigar maker and later

worked in a saloon. His entrée into the world of politics came during the post–Civil War period of Reconstruction, when he worked as a page in the state legislature, then meeting in New Orleans. In the legislature, Cohen became acquainted with several influential black Republicans, among them, Oscar J. Dunn, C. C. Antoine, and P. B. S. Pinchback. Pinchback, founder of and dominant figure in the city's Fourth Ward Republican organization, in particular helped steer Cohen into the patronage system that has always been the bread and butter of Louisiana politics.

Cohen joined Pinchback's organization and, around 1885, received his first political appointment, as a night inspector on the river front. Although the end of Reconstruction forced many older black Republicans into retirement, Cohen's star continued to rise. Appointed as secretary of the Republican State Central Committee, he rose to become its most powerful member until President Herbert Hoover removed him in the late 1920s. Cohen was made a U.S. inspector in New Orleans in 1889 and later was promoted to lieutenant of inspectors, serving until 1893. His most important federal position came in 1898, when he was named register of the United States Land Office in New Orleans. In 1904, however, when the time came for Cohen to be reappointed, he was opposed by F. B. Williams, Republican State Central Committee chairman and leader of the "lily white" faction. Cohen, who was head of the state's "black and tan" Republicans (Cohen himself was very light skinned), asked his friend and mentor, Booker T. Washington, then the most influential spokesman for black Americans, to intercede on his behalf. Washington appealed directly to President Theodore Roosevelt and, with additional pressure from Pinchback, secured Cohen's reappointment to the post, which President William Howard Taft later abolished, in 1910.

Finding himself without a political position but not without influence, in 1910 Cohen, along with a few partners, organized the People's Benevolent Life Insurance Company and became president of the firm, a position he held until his death. The company remained profitable for decades. By 1942, when it had become People's Industrial Life Insurance, the firm had more than $300,000 in assets and total insurance in force of about $6 million.

Cohen had other business ventures as well. In 1914 he established the People's Drug Store on South Rampart Street, in an area where many black residents lived. Putting his political networking skills to good business use, Cohen contacted local benevolent and fraternal organizations and asked them to include his store on their lists of druggists. He also installed a soda fountain and an ice cream parlor—both very popular with his customers—and he hired a physician to be present from 9 A.M. until 7 P.M. in case someone in the store needed medical attention. Cohen's efforts to make People's Drug Store the best drugstore for blacks in the city were so successful that eventually he expanded into a second location. In addition, from 1910 to 1912 Cohen was a partner in a roof garden business at the Pythian Temple, ultimately leaving because of differences with one of his partners. In many of these endeavors Cohen secured the endorsement of Washington, who engaged Cohen as his primary contact and representative in Louisiana, particularly in relation to the activities of Washington's National Negro Business League.

In 1920 Cohen's first wife, the former Wilhelmina Selden, whom he had married in 1882 and with whom he had had at least two children, died. Soon thereafter he married Antonia Manade from nearby Lutcher, Louisiana. Then, in 1924, he received his final political appointment—but not without a struggle. President Warren G. Harding's choice of Cohen for the post of controller of the Port of New Orleans was vehemently opposed by white southerners, and the U.S. Senate rejected Cohen three times before Harding's successor, Calvin Coolidge, finally pushed the appointment through. Political opposition to Cohen came in other forms as well. His opponents—primarily white southerners who simply could not abide the inclusion of blacks in the social and political realm—often accused Cohen of wrongdoing, but it is impossible to determine, given the bias of his detractors, if any of the various charges was warranted. In 1925, in the midst of Prohibition, Cohen and fifty-two white officials were indicted for accepting bribes to allow liquor to be smuggled through the Port of New Orleans. At his trial, Cohen was found not guilty.

An active party member throughout his life and a confidant of many top party leaders, Cohen attended every Republican National Convention from 1896 through 1928. He was a member (and for many years president) of the Iroquois Literary and Social Club, an elite Republican organization founded in 1899, and from the late 1890s on, he served as president of the prestigious Société d'Economique, arguably the most exclusive black organization in the United States at that time. Cohen was also a member of the National Association for the Advancement of Colored People, the Knights of Pythias, Odd Fellows, and Elks. He died in New Orleans.

Cohen's political and business careers bridged the years from Reconstruction to the Great Depression, a period that witnessed a stunning rise followed by a precipitous fall in political power for African Americans. His life is representative also of the emergence of independent businesses and organizations as championed by Booker T. Washington. Cohen was indeed, as his obituary in the *Louisiana Weekly* described him, the last of the city's "Old Guard."

• Cohen's private papers are not available to the public, but correspondence with Booker T. Washington and Emmett J. Scott can be found in the Washington papers at the Library of Congress and at Tuskegee University. Letters between P. B. S. Pinchback and Blanche Kelso Bruce that make important references to Cohen can be found in the Pinchback papers and the Bruce papers, both at the Moorland-Spingarn Research Center at Howard University. The most complete biographical sketch on Cohen is in John N. Ingham and Lynne B. Feldman, *African-American Business Leaders* (1994); also see Clement Richardson, *The National Cyclopedia of the Colored Race* (1919); Charles B. Rousseve, *The Negro in Louisiana: Aspects of His History and His Literature* (1937), pp. 130–31; *Who's Who in Colored Louisiana* (1930), pp. 112–13; and *Sepia Socialite*, Apr. 1942. Obituaries are in the New Orleans *Times-Picayune*, 30 Dec. 1930, and *Louisiana Weekly*, 3 Jan. 1931.

JOHN N. INGHAM

COHEN, Wilbur Joseph (10 June 1913–18 May 1987), secretary of the Department of Health, Education, and Welfare (HEW), was born in Milwaukee, Wisconsin, the son of Aaron Cohen and Bessie Rubenstein, managers of a small grocery store. In 1930 he entered the University of Wisconsin as a student in Alexander Meiklejohn's Experimental College. He chose economics as his upperclass major and studied with John R. Commons and Selig Perlman, leaders of the institutional school of economics. After graduating in 1934, Cohen secured a job as a research assistant to Edwin Witte, another of his professors, who had been asked to serve as executive director of the Committee on Economic Security, appointed that year by President Franklin Roosevelt. This committee laid the intellectual basis for the Social Security Act of 1935.

Remaining in Washington, D.C., after the August 1935 passage of the act, Cohen took a job as a research analyst for the Social Security Board. He also assisted state governors and legislators in the passage of unemployment compensation laws. He became the technical adviser to the chair of the board when Arthur Altmeyer assumed that post late in 1936. Between 1936 and 1953 Cohen aided Altmeyer in the preparation of legislative proposals to expand social security coverage and benefits, and he served as congressional liaison for the Social Security Administration, created in 1946. In these capacities, Cohen assisted Senator Robert F. Wagner in the preparation of a health insurance bill in 1943 and helped to write President Harry S. Truman's November 1945 message on health policy. Beginning in 1939 Cohen attended nearly all of the executive sessions of the congressional tax committees as they considered proposed legislation to expand and refine the social security system. In 1947 Cohen also served as research director of the President's Advisory Committee on Universal Training (which considered the enactment of a permanent military conscription system) and between 1950 and 1952 chaired the Wage Stabilization Board Committee on Health, Pensions, and Welfare.

In 1938 Cohen had married Eloise Bittel, whose background as a Baptist raised in the Texas hill country contrasted sharply with Cohen's urban, Jewish upbringing. The couple had three children.

In 1953 the Dwight D. Eisenhower administration fired Altmeyer and changed Cohen's job classification so that his position became a presidential appointment. Cohen accepted a transfer to become director of the Social Security Administration's research bureau and remained there until the end of 1955. He helped to convince HEW secretary Oveta Culp Hobby of the importance of contributory social insurance. His urging led President Eisenhower to support social security expansion in 1954.

In 1956 Cohen left government service to become professor of public welfare administration at the University of Michigan's School of Social Work. Outside of government, Cohen remained an aggressive advocate of social security expansion. In 1956 he wrote speeches for Senator Walter George that proved successful in convincing the Senate to pass disability insurance. In 1958 he prepared a comprehensive social security bill for Senator John F. Kennedy, and in 1960 he advised Senator Robert Kerr on a program of medical assistance to the elderly, a forerunner of the Medicaid program.

Cohen's *Retirement Policies in Social Security*, published in 1957, combined legislative history with economic analysis and solidified Cohen's credentials as one of the nation's leading experts in social security. This book complemented *Readings in Social Security*, which he had edited with William Haber and published in 1948.

Cohen served as an adviser to the Kennedy presidential campaign in 1960, and after the election he chaired a transition task force on health and social security. This assignment led to his appointment in January 1961 as the assistant secretary of HEW in charge of legislation. Cohen played an active role in the preparation of the 1962 Public Welfare Amendments that added rehabilitative services to the federal assistance available to the states. Cohen's main assignment was to prepare and lobby for a health insurance program for the elderly, later known as Medicare.

Under President Lyndon B. Johnson, Cohen successfully headed a lobbying effort to pass Medicare, which the president signed on 30 July 1965. He also assisted in the passage of the Economic Opportunity Act of 1964 and the Elementary Education Act of 1965. Johnson rewarded Cohen by promoting him to undersecretary of HEW, a post that Cohen assumed on 1 June 1965. His work centered on the implementation of Medicare and Medicaid and the passage of additional Great Society legislation. Early in 1968 Secretary John Gardner left his post, and Cohen became the acting secretary. After announcing his decision not to run for president at the end of March, Johnson appointed Cohen secretary of HEW, and Cohen served until 20 January 1969. As secretary, he advocated, but failed to convince Congress to pass, the expansion of Medicare to cover infants and young children and continued to press for the passage of other Great Society legislative measures.

Cohen returned to academe, and between 1 July 1969 and 30 June 1978 he served as dean of the University of Michigan's School of Education. He continued to advocate plans for social security expansion, national health insurance, and welfare reform, using the presidency of the American Public Welfare Association and other such vehicles to advance his views. In 1978 he became a professor of education and public welfare at Michigan but left in 1980 to serve as Sid

Richardson Professor at the Lyndon Baines Johnson School of Public Affairs at the University of Texas. In 1979 he helped to found the Save Our Security coalition, funded mainly by labor unions, which lobbied against proposed cuts in disability insurance and in old-age insurance advocated by the Jimmy Carter and Ronald Reagan administrations.

Until his death Cohen defended America's social welfare programs and called for their improvement. "Every single major social reform that is now on the law books was once vigorously opposed as being unwise, unnecessary, too expensive, impractical, socialistic, or un-American," he wrote in a posthumously published essay.

Cohen died in Seoul, South Korea, where he was attending a gerontological conference. After Cohen's death Congressman Claude Pepper stated that Wilbur Cohen was the "most knowledgeable man in the field of social welfare that we have in our nation." Pepper echoed a remark made in 1961 by Senator Paul Douglas, who claimed that an expert in social security was anyone with Cohen's telephone number.

• A very complete set of Cohen's personal papers is in the Wisconsin State Historical Society. The Lyndon Baines Johnson Library and the Bentley Historical Library at the University of Michigan also have collections of his personal papers. An obituary is in the *New York Times*, 19 May 1987.

EDWARD D. BERKOWITZ

COHN, Al (24 Nov. 1925–15 Feb. 1988), jazz tenor saxophonist and arranger, was born Alvin Gilbert Cohn in New York City, the son of David Emanuel Cohn, a textile worker, and Gertrude (maiden name unknown). Gertrude Cohn played piano, and Al began taking piano lessons at age six. He switched to clarinet at age twelve and then to tenor saxophone after hearing Count Basie's star soloist, Lester Young.

At about age fifteen Cohn began writing for a neighborhood dance band formed with fellow students from Erasmus Hall High School who were trying to emulate Basie's big band. At age seventeen he joined clarinetist Joe Marsala's band. From 1943 to 1946 Cohn worked intermittently with tenor saxophonist Georgie Auld while doubling in bands led by trumpeter Henry Jerome (1944) and Boyd Raeburn (1946).

Cohn joined guitarist Alvino Rey's big band at the beginning of 1947. Three months later he transferred into the big band of drummer Buddy Rich, for whom he arranged "The Goof and I." Reed player Woody Herman's Second Herd recorded that arrangement on Christmas Eve, and in mid-January Cohn joined Herman in Salt Lake City as a replacement for Herbie Steward. He thus sat with tenor saxophonists Stan Getz and Zoot Sims and baritone saxophonist Serge Chaloff, known collectively as the four brothers. Although Steward, not Cohn, is on Herman's famous recording of "Four Brothers," Cohn joined before the record was released, and most people associate him rather than Steward with the "brothers." Cohn is among the soloists in the film short *Woody Herman and*

His Orchestra, made in February and released later that same year.

During this period Cohn became a heroin addict, one of eight in Herman's sixteen-piece band. He told writer Gene Lees, "I got an infection from a dirty needle. It settled in my eye, and it had to be removed. That's enough to make you quit." As a consequence of this catastrophe, Cohn had a glass eye. He became a heavy drinker after giving up narcotics.

Details of Cohn's family life are quite confusing. By several accounts he married Herman's singer, Mary Ann McCall, but Cohn told interviewer Bob Rusch that actually they were not married. Evidently during the 1940s and 1950s he had five children; jazz guitarist Joseph Cohn was born around 1956, and he is named last (and therefore was presumably the youngest) in Cohn's entry in *Who's Who in America, 1984–1985*. But obituaries, published only a few years later, list only two of the five children, for reasons unknown.

Early in 1949 Cohn left Herman's band. He worked with saxophonist Charlie Ventura's band, spent a brief period in clarinetist Artie Shaw's band in 1949, and rejoined Herman for an engagement at Bop City in New York in April 1950. After making his first recordings as a leader in July 1950, including the blues "Groovin' with Gus," Cohn set music aside for two years under pressure to participate in his father's textile business. This proved a futile endeavor, and in 1952 Cohn joined Elliot Lawrence's band.

Upon returning to jazz, Cohn made numerous recordings, including four buoyantly swinging tracks from a sextet session under Sims's leadership in September 1952. For his own quintet session of June 1953 Cohn composed "That's What You Think," presenting trumpet and tenor saxophone interlocked in a cleverly helter-skelter manner. He provided understated solos in the context of trumpeter Buck Clayton's extroverted jam session of 31 March 1954. Another of his own albums, *The Natural Seven* (1955), afforded a chance to feature his small-group arrangements, together with those of Manny Albam and Ernie Wilkins, and he was a featured soloist with trumpeter Bernie Privin's band on *Dancing and Dreaming* (1956).

Cohn and Sims co-led sessions for two albums, *From A to Z* (1956) and *Al and Zoot* (1957), and they toured together for about four months in 1957. The two tenor saxophonists kept this group going, recording further albums, including *You 'an Me* (1960), and appearing mainly at the Half Note in New York annually for about a dozen years from 1959 on. They also held residencies at Ronnie Scott's club in London (1962 and 1967) and toured Europe in 1965. In 1963 Cohn married Flora Ann Morse; details of the ending of his relationship with McCall are unknown.

Cohn's bread and butter over these decades came from his work as a studio arranger. This work extended into the 1980s, as he wrote for televised award shows, beauty pageants, and assorted show business specials. He also contributed scores to the Broadway shows *Raisin* (1973), *Music, Music, Music* (1974), and *Sophisticated Ladies* (1981).

As a jazz performer, Cohn dubbed solos for the movie *Lenny* (1974), and he toured Scandinavia with Sims (also 1974). From 1976 to Herman's death in 1987 he participated in occasional Herman reunions, both in performance and on record. A series of albums on Xanadu, including the duo *Heavy Love* with pianist Jimmy Rowles (1977), brought Cohn some renewed fame. He toured Japan with Sims in 1978, made annual trips to Europe in the late 1970s and early 1980s, and recorded regularly. Performances with Sims continued occasionally into the early 1980s. Cohn also worked with his son Joe, but he mainly led a quartet with piano, bass, and drums during this last part of his career. He also was the featured soloist on an album of his arrangements recorded in Munich with a European big band under the direction of the expatriate American trumpeter Al Porcino in 1987. He was incapacitated by liver cancer after playing on 31 December 1987 in Chicago. He died in East Stroudsburg, Pennsylvania.

As demonstrated by numerous recorded moments of playing in unison, the closely matched sounds of Sims and Cohn are not something that the casual listener will easily discern. Splitting hairs, one may find Cohn's sound to be edgy, and Sims's, darker, breathier, prettier. Both were among the leading jazz tenor saxophonists who took the airy and soft tone, delicate vibrato, and swinging improvisations of Lester Young as a model, amended by the more angular and less tuneful sounds of bebop lines. Pianist Lou Levy told writer William D. Clancy, "Al . . . was a totally melodic player. . . . He just composed as he went along. . . . Stan Getz once told me, jokingly, but maybe it was true, 'The perfect tenor player would be Zoot Sims' time, Al Cohn's ideas, and my technique.'"

• Cohn's papers are held at the Al Cohn Memorial Foundation in Stroudsburg, Pa. Published surveys and interviews include those by Les Tomkins, "Al Cohn and Zoot Sims: Duet," *Crescendo* 3 (June 1965): 2–4; Larry Birnbaum, "Al Cohn Arranges to Make Longevity Count," *Down Beat* 47 (Apr. 1980): 27–29; Stan Woolley, "Al Cohn Now and Then," *Jazz Journal International* 33 (June 1980): 21; Tomkins, "Al Cohn Today: Back to That Applause," *Crescendo International* 20 (Apr. 1982): 20–22, continued as "Al Cohn and the Broadening World of a Player/Writer" (May 1982): 16–17; Martin Isherwood, "Al Cohn," *Jazz Journal International* 36 (Oct. 1983): 8–9; and Bob Rusch, "Al Cohn: Interview," *Cadence* 12 (1986): 5–16, 92. For details of his association with Herman, see James A. Treichel, *Keeper of the Flame: Woody Herman and the Second Herd, 1947–1949* (1978); William D. Clancy with Audrey Coke Kenton, *Woody Herman: Chronicle of the Herds* (1995); and Gene Lees, *Leader of the Band: The Life of Woody Herman* (1995). An obituary is in the *New York Times*, 17 Feb. 1988.

BARRY KERNFELD

COHN, Alfred A. (26 Mar. 1880–3 Feb. 1951), screenwriter, was born in Freeport, Illinois. Nothing is known of his parents or education. At the age of fifteen Cohn (who was also known as Al Cohn) went to work for a Chicago newspaper, working his way up to the position of reporter. Eventually, he became a newspaper and magazine editor, a columnist, and a publicist.

Cohn began his screenwriting career at the height of the silent film era in 1918. He is credited with working on more than 100 screenplays. For various pictures he wrote scenarios, stories, titles, or original screenplays. Some of his earliest assignments included writing the script and titles for *Legend of Hollywood* (1924) and the script and story for *His People*, which he cowrote (1925), *Flames* (1926), *The Cohens and the Kellys* (1926), and *Frisco Sally Levy* (1927). Both *The Cohens and the Kellys* and *Frisco Sally Levy* featured Jewish characters and themes, as did *His People*, which is the story of a rabbi who disowns his too-worldly son. These projects supplied the perfect background for the screenwriting job that would be the high point of Cohn's Hollywood career, *The Jazz Singer* (1927).

Despite the fact that there had been several novelty experiments with sound movies for a number of years, the Warner Bros. partial talkie *The Jazz Singer*, starring the legendary stage entertainer Al Jolson, made sound film commercially viable. Cohn, who began work on the movie on 14 March 1927, contributed the scenario to the film. This historic motion picture was based on Samson Raphaelson's hit 1925 play of the same name, which, in turn, was based on Raphaelson's 1922 short story, "The Day of Atonement." When George Jessel, the play's star, made exorbitant salary demands, Warner Bros. offered the role of Jakie Rabinowitz to Jolson, then the most popular American performer of stage and recordings. As the son of a poor Jewish cantor who upsets his family with plans of a singing career instead of following in his father's footsteps, Jolson found his defining role. Editor Robert Carringer writes in notes accompanying the published screenplay of *The Jazz Singer* that "Cohn's script for *The Jazz Singer* is a skillful job of converting the scene structure of a play into the more episodic sequence continuity needed for a film. He also added new opening sequences (scenes 1–138) showing Jakie Rabinowitz's boyhood on the Lower East Side and his early efforts to launch a career as Jack Robin." However, one of the movie's most memorable sequences, the final scene in which Jolson sings "My Mammy" on the stage of New York's Winter Garden, is not found in Cohn's scenario. Cohn's adaptation received an Academy Award nomination at the first awards ceremony in May 1929, but the award went to Benjamin Glazer for *Seventh Heaven* (1928), while *The Jazz Singer* received a special award as a pioneering effort in talking pictures.

Few of Cohn's subsequent films in the era of the dawn of sound, including *The Carnation Kid* (1929), *Divorce Made Easy* (1929), and *The Last Warning* (1929), for which Cohn also supplied the story, are much remembered today. Although his script for *The Cisco Kid* (1931) provided the source for a popular and long-running serial on film, television, and radio, other films like *Feet First* (1930) and *A Holy Terror* (1931) had little public impact. A better effort was *Me and My Gal* (1932), low-budget Fox film on which Cohn was a contributing writer. It gave screen legend Spencer Tracy one of his best early roles in a broad comedy about the rocky romance of a cop and a wisecracking waitress, played by Joan Bennett. With the exception of 1939's *The Return of the Cisco Kid*, a follow-up to his 1931 movie, Cohn's last screen credits are for *The Defense Rests*, *Ever Since Eve*, *Harold Teen*, and *Here Comes the Navy*, all forgettable films released in 1934. Cohn also wrote several books, including *Gun Notches*. In collaboration with Joe Chisholm, Cohn wrote *Take the Witness*, a biography of Earl Rogers, a noted criminal lawyer of the era. During his screenwriting days, Cohn also wrote a column for the *Los Angeles Examiner* for a time.

After 1934 Cohn turned his attention to a career in public service. In 1935 he was named collector of customs for the city of Los Angeles, a post he held for four years. Subsequently, he served as a member of the Board of Public Utilities and Transportation and as president of the police commission, introducing several reforms in police procedures. Cohn, who never married, died in Los Angeles, his screenwriting career having long since faded into oblivion.

• For information on Cohn, see Robert Carringer, ed., *The Jazz Singer* (1979); and James Fisher, *Spencer Tracy: A Bio-Bibliography* (1994). Obituaries are in the *New York Times*, 5 Feb. 1951, and *Variety*, 7 Feb. 1951.

JAMES FISHER

COHN, Alfred Einstein (16 Apr. 1879–20 July 1957), physician and scientist, was born in New York City, the son of Abraham Cohn, a tobacco merchant, and Maimie Einstein. He received an A.B. (1900) and an M.D. (1904) from Columbia and did his internship at Mount Sinai Hospital in New York City. From 1907 to 1909 he studied abroad. He first went to Freiburg, where he studied pathological anatomy with Ludwig Aschoff. He then traveled to London, where he was one of the first Americans to study heart disease with Thomas Lewis, an early pioneer in the use of the electrocardiogram. Cohn also worked with and became a close friend of the noted British physician and expert on heart diseases, James Mackenzie, by whom he was much influenced. From 1909 to 1911 Cohn was on the staff of the Mount Sinai Hospital in New York. In 1911 he joined the staff of the Rockefeller Institute for Medical Research, where he stayed until 1944, becoming a member in 1920. During World War I he went to France, where he studied the poorly characterized disorder known as "soldier's heart." Cohn married Ruth Walker Price in 1911; they had no children.

In the summer of 1909, Cohn installed the first electrocardiograph machine in the United States in the Mount Sinai Hospital; he later brought the same machine to the Rockefeller Hospital. Invented around the turn of the century, the electrocardiograph machine provided physicians and scientists with a graphic registration of the electrical activity of the heart. Although the first systematic use of this instrument was to examine abnormalities of the rhythm of the heart, by around the second decade of the twentieth century Cohn and others had turned their attention to abnormalities in the morphology of the electrocardiogram tracing. Cohn examined the effects of digitalis (a drug commonly used to treat heart disease) on the shape of the tracing. He did important work on bundle-branch block, a cardiac disorder in which the electrical stimulus to the lower cardiac chambers is partially blocked and which produces a characteristic electrocardiogram tracing. Cohn also published what may have been the first recorded case of the abnormal activation complex, later known as Wolff-Parkinson-White syndrome, in which part of the heart is activated prematurely, also producing characteristic changes in the electrocardiogram tracing. In 1920 Cohn introduced a new way of recording electrocardiograms. Previously, the patient's limbs were immersed in buckets of saline; this requirement made it difficult to take recordings from seriously ill patients and limited the tool's transportability. Cohn simplified the process by inventing an electrode that one could simply strap onto the person to be examined.

Cohn, like most early twentieth-century American physicians interested in cardiovascular disease, actually saw public health, not machines, as the basis for the study of heart disease. He was one of the first members of the New York–based Association for the Prevention of Heart Disease (later the New York Heart Association), founded in 1916, which became a model for the American Heart Association (1924). The American Heart Association emphasized social approaches to heart disease, such as improving economic conditions and educating the public about the importance of practicing better health habits. Cohn thought that record keeping at cardiac clinics should ascertain the economic impact of chronic heart disease. He emphasized the increasing importance of chronic disease as a cause of illness and death in his 1924 introductory essay for the new *Journal of Clinical Investigation*, the journal of the American Society for Clinical Investigation. In a two-part article (*American Heart Journal* 2 [1927]: 275–301, 386–407), Cohn pointed out that the decrease in number of deaths from acute infectious diseases, at the time the major cause of human disease, would lead to an increase in deaths from cardiac disease. Furthermore, he realized that cardiac disease could have many causes, only some of which were infectious, particularly in people over the age of forty. His studies of the diseases important for public health, carried on with Claire Lingg, culminated in the 1950 publication of *The Burden of Diseases in the United States*.

Cohn belonged to a new generation of investigators who rejected the physiology laboratory as the primary source of new knowledge about human disease, turning instead to the clinical study of human beings. Many of those investigators joined Cohn in the American Society for Clinical Investigation. Rockefeller Hospital, where Cohn spent most of his career, was a key location for the early pursuit of clinical studies. In

that setting Cohn encouraged quantitative studies of the heart. At the same time he viewed clinical investigation as a broad-based process and opposed specialization. In a 1926 letter to Canby Robinson, editor of the *Journal of Clinical Investigation* and professor of medicine at Vanderbilt University, Cohn complained bitterly about the formation of the *American Heart Journal*: "I am quite frankly opposed to the founding of journals devoted to the study of specific viscera. . . . [T]he tendency is created for fellows who work on heart disease to study no other journals and for the fellows who do not work on heart disease not to study the heart journals."

For almost twenty-five years Cohn presided over the bimonthly dinner meetings of the Rockefeller Institute Journal Club with urbane charm and gentle wit. Despite his emphasis that research, not patient care, belonged at the center of academic medicine, Cohn was a highly cultured individual who cared deeply about events outside the laboratory. By the 1930s, after he had ceased most of his active scientific investigation, Cohn turned to the history and philosophy of science and medicine. He was active in the New York Academy of Medicine, helping to publish books on diverse topics, such as *The Role of Scientific Societies in the Seventeenth Century* by Martha Ornstein (1938). At home and in his office Cohn was almost completely surrounded by books, and his far-flung interests and philosophical bent were reflected in his extensive library, some 6,000 volumes of which were presented upon his death to the Rockefeller University Library. He wrote several volumes of wide-ranging essays. From 1933 to 1945 Cohn helped refugees as a member of the Executive Committee for Displaced Foreign Scholars, and from 1945 to 1947 he was a member and treasurer of the American Committee for Emigré Scholars, Writers, and Artists. He was a close friend of Justice Felix Frankfurter for almost forty years. Cohn died at his home, Iron Hill Farm, in New Milford, Connecticut.

• Approximately 60 cubic feet of Alfred Cohn's papers are preserved in the Rockefeller Archive Center in North Tarrytown, New York. What remains of his library is preserved in the Cohn Library of the Rockefeller University in New York City. In addition to those mentioned above, his major publications include *Medicine, Science, and Art: Studies in Interrelations* (1931); *Minerva's Progress: Tradition and Dissent in American Culture* (1946); "Recollections Concerning Early Electrocardiography in the United States," *Bulletin of the History of Medicine* 29 (1955): 93–96. *No Retreat from Reason, and Other Essays* (1948) includes an autobiographical essay. Discussions of his library are in the *Rockefeller Institute Quarterly* 1, no. 4 (1957): 1–3, and 3, no. 5 (1960): 5–6. See also George E. Burch and Nicholas P. DePasquale, *A History of Electrocardiography* (1964, 1990); Clarence E. de la Chapelle, *The New York Heart Association: Origins and Development 1915–1965* (1966); George W. Corner, *History of the Rockefeller Institute: 1901–1953, Origins and Growth* (1964); Joel D. Howell, "Hearts and Minds: The Invention and Transformation of American Cardiology," in *Grand Rounds, One Hundred Years of Internal Medicine*, ed. Russell C. Maulitz and Diana E. Long (1988); Dennis M. Krikler, "Wolff-Parkinson-White Syndrome: Long Follow-Up and an Anglo-American Historical Note," *Journal of the American College of Cardiology* 2 (1983): 1216–18.

Obituaries are in the *New York Times*, 23 July 1957; the *Journal of the American Medical Association* 165 (1957): 380; and the *Rockefeller Institute Quarterly* 1, no. 3 (1957): 3–4.

JOEL D. HOWELL

COHN, Edwin Joseph (17 Dec. 1892–1 Oct. 1953), biological chemist, was born in New York City, the son of Abraham Cohn, a successful tobacco merchant, and Maimie Einstein. He was educated at Amherst College and the University of Chicago, from which he received a B.S. in 1914 and a Ph.D. in zoology and chemistry in 1917. Having decided to devote his career to the study of proteins, he won a National Research Council Fellowship and studied under the protein chemists Søren S. P. Sørensen in Copenhagen, Svante August Arrhenius in Sweden, William B. Hardy and Sir Joseph Barcroft in Cambridge, England, and Thomas Burr Osborne at Yale. In 1920 he was invited to join Lawrence J. Henderson at the Harvard Medical School in a new laboratory being formed to study proteins. In 1917 Cohn had married Marianne Brettauer; they had two sons.

At this time, scientific knowledge about proteins was in a rudimentary state. Proteins were known to be too large to pass through the pores of membranes that are permeable to salts and to migrate in an electric field. It had been proposed that amino acids are the building blocks of proteins, but the amino acids were still being discovered into the 1930s. There was a debate about whether proteins were amenable to study by the established principles of physical chemistry or were merely ill-defined aggregates, termed colloids. No protein's molecular weight was known with certainty, although measurements were being attempted. In 1925 Cohn and James B. Conant published the results of an important experiment that was instrumental in establishing that proteins are discrete molecular entities with high molecular weights and that they obey the classic laws of chemistry.

After the 1926 discovery by George R. Minot at Harvard that a diet of liver was effective in curing pernicious anemia, an intractable, invariably fatal disease, Cohn undertook to isolate the active principle in liver. Working with Thomas L. McMeekin, John F. Fulton, William T. Salter and John H. Weare, Cohn succeeded in preparing a purified extract that was effective in treating pernicious anemia patients. Once Cohn's liver extract was made available in 1928 for general use, pernicious anemia was almost completely eradicated.

Cohn's scientific investigations on proteins were greatly influenced by the 1923 finding of the Danish chemist Niels J. Bjerrum that the amino acids exist in solution as electrically charged dipolar ions ("Zwitterionen") rather than as neutral substances as previously thought. Cohn became interested in the possibility that Bjerrum's finding could explain the origin of the electrical charges on proteins and set to work to obtain scientific evidence concerning the chemical nature of the electrical charges and their effect on the behavior of proteins. In 1930, concluding that protein molecules were too large and their chemical behavior too complex to interpret by methods then available, Cohn together with John T. Edsall, John D. Ferry, Jesse P. Greenstein, McMeekin, and Jeffries Wyman initiated an elaborate series of studies on the physical chemical properties of the amino acids and some simple synthetic peptides as prototypes of proteins. The importance of the findings from these studies was augmented by George Scatchard and John Kirkwood at the Massachusetts Institute of Technology, who modified and adapted the interionic attraction theory of Peter Debye and Erich Hückel (1923) to form a theoretical framework for the findings. Taken together, the studies on the amino acids and peptides by Cohn and his collaborators comprised a landmark advance and were later gathered into a monograph, which Cohn coedited with Edsall, *Proteins, Amino Acids and Peptides* (1943). This work provided a sound theoretical basis for much of the subsequent development of knowledge about proteins.

In 1940, with the prospect of U.S. involvement in the war in Europe increasing, Cohn was asked by the National Research Council to investigate the possibility of developing a therapeutic agent from animal blood for use in the treatment of battlefield shock. Based largely on knowledge gained from their study of the amino acids and peptides, Cohn and a group of associates under his direction developed a process termed plasma fractionation for isolating protein fractions from plasma. When applied to bovine plasma, a fraction known as bovine serum albumin was obtained. During clinical trials, however, bovine serum albumin proved to be unsafe for use in humans. The work on bovine plasma was therefore abandoned. Anticipating that possibility, the Harvard group had applied the same method to obtain human serum albumin from human plasma separated from blood collected by the American Red Cross. Human serum albumin prepared in a pilot plant at the Harvard Medical School proved safe and efficacious in clinical trials and was first used in the field to treat armed services personnel wounded during the 1941 Japanese attack on Pearl Harbor. When the risk of transmission of viral diseases by blood products began to be recognized, Cohn and his collaborators developed a process for inactivating viral contaminants in serum albumin by heating the albumin solution for ten hours at 60 degrees Centigrade.

In 1942 the fractionation process was transferred to U.S. pharmaceutical laboratories, beginning with the training of industrial managers at the Harvard Medical School. Production of human serum albumin under government contracts began late in 1942. More than half a million units of albumin were produced during World War II. Among the other clinically important plasma products Cohn and his colleagues developed during the war are immune serum globulin, more familiarly known as gamma globulin, for the treatment of infectious disease; fibrinogen; antihemophilic factor; and fibrin films and foams. All of these products continue to be produced, using the basic Cohn methods. To accomplish these achievements, Cohn relied upon the collaborations of more than forty scientific and clinical associates both at Harvard and at other universities. Their names are cited on the collective publications that came out of their work.

Having maintained strict standards of quality control over all the products that he and his associates prepared for use by the armed services, Cohn received Harvard's approval, as the end of the war approached, to patent the processes for plasma fractionation. Royalty-free nonexclusive licenses to use the Cohn procedures were then granted to qualified producer organizations with the condition that the safety and efficacy of the products so produced meet strict standards. To set standards and control the quality of the products produced during the life of the patents, Cohn established in 1944 a nonprofit Commission on Plasma Fractionation. Human albumin has since been produced by a worldwide pharmaceutical industry that uses the Cohn methods, which make it safe from risk of transmission of diseases, including human immunodeficiency virus, the virus responsible for acquired immune deficiency syndrome. Human albumin and gamma globulin prepared by the Cohn methods have achieved a remarkable record of safety and efficacy in use around the world.

In 1948 Cohn was awarded the U.S. Medal for Merit by President Harry S. Truman in recognition of his services to the country during the war. He was also the recipient of numerous honorary degrees. W. Kitchener Jordan, the late historian and president of Radcliffe College, described Cohn as "a complex human being, a man at once a gifted and most exacting scientist, and an imaginative and searching philosopher. He was a remarkable amalgam of the qualities of his own age and those which were more characteristic of the eighteenth century. His manners, his great elegance, his concern for first principles, his scorn for the immediate—all these attributes are those of a century now too little remembered for its contributions to the graces as well as to the wisdom of mankind." Cohn died in Boston.

• Some of Cohn's personal and scientific papers are in the archives of Harvard University, in the Countway Medical Library. For additional biographical information, see John T. Edsall, "A Historical Sketch of the Department of Physical Chemistry, Harvard Medical School: 1920–1950," *American Scientist* 34 (1950): 580–93, and "Edwin Joseph Cohen, 1892–1953," National Academy of Sciences, *Biographical Memoirs* 35 (1961): 46–84, which includes a complete bibliography of Cohn's publications. Edsall also wrote about Cohn in the German publication *Ergebnisse Der Physiologie Biologischen Chemie und Experimentellen Pharmakologie* 48 (1955): 22–48. An obituary is in *Nature* 173 (16 Jan. 1954): 104.

DOUGLAS MacN. SURGENOR

COHN, Fannia (5 Apr. 1885?–24 Dec. 1962), labor educator and leader, was born Fannia Mary Cohn in Kletzk, Minsk, Russia, the daughter of Hyman Cohn, a manager of a family-owned flour mill, and Anna Rosofsky. Fannia received her formal education at a private school and her radical political views from her middle-class Jewish parents. She joined the outlawed Socialist Revolutionary party in 1901 and arrived in New York City three years later filled with the romantic idealism of socialism.

Following a brief job as a representative of the American Jewish Women's Committee on Ellis Island, Cohn intended to complete pharmacy school and work in a drug supply company owned by relatives. But a year after her arrival, invigorated with the idea of understanding and sharing the worker's life, she dropped out of school to work as a sleevemaker at a garment factory. In 1909 she joined the International Ladies' Garment Workers' Union (ILGWU) and shortly afterward was elected to the executive board of the newly organized Wrapper, Kimono, and House Dress Makers, ILGWU Local 41. She chaired the board in 1913–1914.

In 1914 the National Women's Trade Union League (WTUL) opened a training school for women organizers in Chicago, and Cohn became one of the first three students to attend. At the time she felt that the courses did not meet labor movement needs and that the middle-class women running the WTUL were ineffective because they had no experience as workers. Although she found the school experience unrewarding, its limitations left an indelible mark. Cohn saw the need for a "real school" not merely for organizers but for members of the union, run not by middle-class reformers but by union personnel.

Cohn stayed on in Chicago after completing the program and worked for the ILGWU as a general organizer in 1915–1916. During the Herzog Garment Company strike, she helped to organize striking workers and served as an interpreter, translating proposals into Yiddish. In writing about the strike, Amy Walker Field said that Cohn was of "inestimable value in the holding and steadying of the people." Following the strike, ILGWU Local 59 was established, and Cohn was elected president.

In 1916 Cohn returned to New York having already gained prestige in union circles as an efficient worker and aggressive leader. In the same year she won election to the General Executive Board of the ILGWU becoming the first woman vice president of a major international, and she served in this position until 1928. In 1917 the groundwork for an educational committee was laid, and Cohn was named organizing secretary. A contribution of $5,000 established an Education Department of which Cohn was appointed educational director in 1918, and she performed her work with "missionary zeal." Seeking to provide education to the worker, she wrote numerous articles, assembled reports, attended meetings on education, organized and taught classes, and delivered her message about education's importance. Responsible for opening neighborhood Unity Centers where courses and lectures were offered in public school buildings, she also helped in the founding of Unity House, a recreational retreat for ILGWU workers in the Pocono Mountains in Pennsylvania. Through her unending work the ILGWU's educational facilities expanded and became the largest union program in the United States.

An ardent fighter for women's right to hold union offices, Cohn was well aware of the discrimination women faced in male-dominated unions. She supported intellectual and cultural education to decrease women's feelings of dependency and inferiority. She believed that once women had confidence they had the potential to become responsible and loyal union workers. Even though she felt that women's education was important, she did not advocate sex-segregated classes. She stated that "men and women working together . . . or in the classroom have much to gain from each other."

In 1921 Cohn helped to found Brookwood Labor College, the first residential college for workers. She argued that education would give workers the capacity to establish a "new social order." Designed to train both men and women workers for positions in labor organizations, the school taught a two-year course in social sciences. Cohn remained a member on its board of directors until a lack of union support brought the college to a close in 1937. She also helped institute the Workers' Education Bureau that oversaw union educational programs and the founding of the Labor Publication Society, which produced *Labor Age*, a monthly periodical. Until 1961 she held the position of executive secretary at the Workers' Education Bureau. In 1924 she became one of the organizers for the Manumit School for Workers' Children and the Pioneer Youth of America, which provided recreational activities for working-class children. She directed Manumit until 1933.

Cohn remained neutral during the 1920s when communists sought to take over leadership of the ILGWU. Her main concerns were to maintain workers' education programs and to keep them separated from political maneuvering. In 1925 she lost her bid for a fifth term as the ILGWU vice president but continued in her role as head of the Education Department.

The depression brought hard times as ILGWU membership and funds diminished. When the union could no longer provide Cohn with a salary, she continued her work through financial support from her family. When the Education Department underwent reorganization in 1935, Cohn lost her position as educational director because her ideas were representative of an earlier immigrant culture tied to socialism. Her replacement, Mark Starr, had a stronger identity with young American workers. Cohn remained in a lesser capacity as executive secretary. Over the decades her activities were reduced, and in the 1950s her only function was overseeing the book division. Though reduced in power, Cohn remained undaunted in her

mission to educate. Her refusal to retire prompted a forced retirement in 1962. A few months later she died in New York City.

Opinions on Cohn varied widely. Some saw her as "the movement itself"; others, such as unyielding unionists of the International, never felt that her approach to education was effective. At times called "irritable" and "demanding," Cohn aggressively pursued the goals of education for all union workers and for the rights of women in labor unions. She wrote reams of correspondence attempting to bring together people who believed both in labor education and reform. She also wrote articles for *Labor Age, American Federationist, Justice,* and *Workers' Education Bureau of the American Quarterly.* Her energetic capacity to work astonished others. Although frustrated by the union's lack of interest in giving women equal treatment, she kept her early idealism and revolutionary spirit. To her, education provided the tools for a worker's fight and for success in the "social revolution."

• The Fannia Cohn Papers are located in the Manuscript Division of the New York Public Library. Her articles on workers' education are listed in Richard E. Dwyer, *Labor Education in the U.S.: An Annotated Bibliography* (1977). A biographical account of Cohn is Ricki Carole Myers Cohen, "Fannia Cohn and the International Ladies' Garment Workers' Union" (Ph.D. diss., Univ. of Southern California, 1976). Other sources relating to her life and work are Amy Walker Field, "More about the Herzog Strike," *Life and Labor* 5 (Oct. 1915): 157–58; Wilfred Carsel, *A History of the Chicago Ladies' Garment Workers' Union* (1940); Lewis Levitzki Lorwin, *The Women's Garment Workers: A History of the International Ladies' Garment Workers' Union* (1924); Benjamin Stolberg, *Tailor's Progress: The Story of a Famous Union and the Men Who Made It* (1944); Robert Schaefer, "Educational Activities of the Garment Unions" (Ph.D. diss., Columbia Univ. Teachers Coll., 1951); James O. Morris, *Conflict within the AFL* (1958); Alice Kessler-Harris, "Where Are the Organized Women Workers?" *Feminist Studies* 3 (1975): 92–110; Kessler-Harris, "Organizing the Unorganizable: Three Jewish Women and Their Union," *Labor History* 17 (1976): 5–23; Nancy Schrom Dye, *As Equals and As Sisters* (1980); Meredith Tax, *The Rising of the Women: Feminist Solidarity and Class Conflict, 1880–1917* (1980); Nancy MacLean, *The Culture of Resistance: Female Institution Building in the International Ladies' Garment Workers' Union 1905–1925,* Michigan Occasional Paper No. 21 (1982); and Gus Tyler, *Look for the Union Label: A History of the International Ladies' Garment Workers' Union* (1995).

MARILYN ELIZABETH PERRY

COHN, Harry (23 July 1891–27 Feb. 1958), studio executive, was born in New York City, the son of German and Russian immigrants Joseph Cohn and Bella Hudesman. His father was a tailor, and with his parents, four siblings, and two grandmothers, he shared four rooms on Eighty-eighth Street in abject poverty. At the age of fourteen, in 1905, Cohn quit school to appear in the chorus of a popular play, *The Fatal Wedding,* produced by Al Woods. He also worked as a song plugger in vaudeville, a shipping clerk for a music publishing firm, a fur salesman, a trolley conductor, and a pool hustler. In 1913 in partnership with Harry Ruby (who later achieved great success as a composer), Cohn appeared in an unsuccessful vaudeville act. That same year, with his brother Jack, Cohn made a low-budget film called *Traffic in Souls*, which was modestly successful. Drafted into the army in 1917, Cohn discovered that he hated the regimentation of life at Fort Slocum (he never left the country during World War I). His father died about this time, so upon leaving the army it became imperative for Cohn and his brothers to support their mother. In 1918 Cohn became personal secretary to pioneer moviemaker Carl Laemmle at IMP Studios, which later evolved into Universal Studios. Cohn learned much from Laemmle, one of Hollywood's most experienced filmmakers. After some time, Cohn aggressively pursued opportunities for more responsibility with Laemmle. He served as executive producer for the first time in 1918 on *My Four Years in Germany* while still working as Laemmle's secretary. Ever ambitious, Cohn left Laemmle and, in partnership with his brother Jack Cohn and with Joseph Brandt, in 1920 formed CBC ("Corned Beef and Cabbage") Film Sales Company, which subsequently became known as Columbia Pictures. The studio successfully produced its first feature length film in 1924, and Harry Cohn assumed the presidency of Columbia in 1929. In 1932 his brother Jack's unsuccessful attempt to oust him helped to consolidate his power as the unchallenged head of Columbia Pictures.

Cohn's golden era spanned from the early days of sound films through the mid-1950s. Although many considered Cohn the most ruthless and vulgar of Hollywood's all-powerful moguls, he was similarly known to be sentimental and often took risks with improbable, off-beat, and controversial projects. Under Cohn, Columbia stressed economy and speed in the filmmaking process, often to the intense frustration of writers, directors, and actors, and Columbia was often referred to derisively in Hollywood as "Poverty Row" among the larger film studios. But it is also true that a significant number of the screen's finest directors and greatest stars worked for Cohn at one time or another. His battles with his creative talents have become the stuff of movieland legend. Cohn allegedly used studio employees as informants and also bugged offices to keep complete control over his underlings. Among Columbia employees, the writers were paradoxically the most respected and the most abused. Writers who could be bullied found working with Cohn very unpleasant, while those who stood up to the studio head often won his grudging admiration and, more important, his cooperation. Cohn seemed to enjoy his reputation as a tyrant, but his eye for talent and good writing, along with his confident business sense, made him one of Hollywood's longest reigning studio heads.

Cohn's era as head of Columbia Pictures ultimately reaped the studio forty-five Academy Awards, including five for *It Happened One Night* (1934), directed by Frank Capra and starring Clark Gable and Claudette Colbert; eight for *From Here to Eternity* (1953), direct-

ed by Fred Zinnemann and starring Burt Lancaster, Deborah Kerr, Montgomery Clift, and Frank Sinatra; eight for *On the Waterfront* (1954), directed by Elia Kazan and starring Marlon Brando and Eva Marie Saint; and seven for *The Bridge on the River Kwai* (1957), directed by David Lean and starring Alec Guinness, Sessue Hayakawa, and William Holden.

Among directors, Frank Capra was the first truly outstanding director at Columbia. Capra directed important Columbia movies such as *Platinum Blonde* (1931), *American Madness* (1932), *The Bitter Tea of General Yen* (1933), *Mr. Deeds Goes to Town* (1936), *Lost Horizon* (1937), *You Can't Take It with You* (1938), and *Mr. Smith Goes to Washington* (1939), most of which are regarded as classic films. Other classics produced at Columbia during the Cohn era were *Love Affair* (1932), directed by Leo McCarey; *Man's Castle* (1933), directed by Frank Borzage; *Twentieth Century* (1934), directed by Howard Hawks; *The Whole Town's Talking* (1935), directed by John Ford; *Crime and Punishment* (1935), directed by Josef von Sternberg; *The Awful Truth* (1937), directed by McCarey; *Holiday* (1938), directed by George Cukor; *Golden Boy* (1939), directed by Rouben Mamoulian; *His Girl Friday* (1939), directed by Hawks; and *Here Comes Mr. Jordan* (1941), directed by Alexander Hall. The studio turned much of its attention to musical entertainments in the early 1940s and had particular success with *You Were Never Lovelier* (1942), directed by William A. Seiter; *Cover Girl* (1944), directed by Charles Vidor; *The Jolson Story* (1946), directed by Alfred E. Green; and *Gilda* (1946), directed by Vidor. A return to more serious films after World War II produced classics like *The Lady from Shanghai* (1948), directed by and starring Orson Welles; *All the King's Men* (1949), directed by Robert Rossen; *Born Yesterday* (1950), directed by Cukor; *The Big Heat* (1953), directed by Fritz Lang; *The Long Gray Line* (1955), directed by John Ford; *Picnic* (1956), directed by Joshua Logan; and, in a rare return to musicals, *Pal Joey* (1957), directed by George Sidney. Along with feature films, Columbia made more than sixty sound serials, and among the short subjects emerging from the studio, the Three Stooges series gained lasting popularity when the shorts were shown frequently in the early days of television.

The leading stars most associated with the Columbia emblem during Cohn's long reign include Barbara Stanwyck, Cary Grant, James Stewart, Gary Cooper, Rita Hayworth, William Holden, Glenn Ford, Jack Lemmon, and Kim Novak. Most fought bitterly with Cohn, who was dubbed "Harry the Horror" until Ben Hecht nicknamed him "White Fang." The forgettable 1968 film *The Legend of Lylah Clare* is alleged to depict Cohn's development of the unknown Kim Novak for movie stardom.

Cohn was married twice. His first marriage in 1923 to Rose Barker ended in divorce in 1941 and produced no children. The same year as his divorce he married a much younger actress, Joan Perry (whose visage became the face on the statue of Columbia that serves as the studio's logo on pictures), with whom he had two sons and a daughter. Cohn died suddenly of a heart attack in Phoenix, Arizona. At Cohn's funeral, Danny Kaye eulogized the mogul by noting that "Harry Cohn's breadth and size were of an older day that we shall not see again. I am glad that I knew Harry Cohn and his brawny vigor—he was an unforgettable man."

• For information on Cohn, see Bernard F. Dick, *The Merchant Prince of Poverty Row: Harry Cohn of Columbia Pictures* (1993); Neil Gabler, *An Empire of Their Own* (1988); Rochelle Larkin, *Hail Columbia* (1975); and Bob Thomas, *King Cohn: The Life and Time of Harry Cohn* (1967). An obituary appears in the *New York Times*, 28 Feb. 1958.

JAMES FISHER

COHN, Jack (27 Oct. 1889–8 Dec. 1956), motion picture executive, was born Jacob Cohn in New York City, the son of Joseph Cohn, a tailor, and Bella Hudesman. Jacob (always called Jack) was the product of immigrant parents—the father from Germany, the mother from Russia—who met and married in the United States. The family lived on Manhattan's Upper East Side, home of assimilated Jews who spoke German at home, not Yiddish.

Family life was a struggle. Cohn was educated in New York's public schools, but he left at age fourteen to work at the Hampton Advertising Agency. A devoted movie fan, he joined Carl Laemmle's Independent Motion Picture Company as a laboratory assistant in 1908. IMP was amalgamated with several other companies four years later to become Universal, and as the new company grew, Cohn took on more responsibility, first as an editor and producer of *Universal Weekly*, a popular newsreel. During the late 1910s he rose to become an invaluable Laemmle aide, helping set up Universal's animation department and producing *Traffic in Souls* (1913), an early Universal hit.

By the early 1920s his brother Harry Cohn also had gained experience in the film business, and so the brothers formed their own company, Columbia Pictures. Harry Cohn journeyed to Hollywood and made the movies. But the great Hollywood studios always had someone who was able to get the films distributed and exhibited. Making sure that Columbia films got into theaters was Jack Cohn's lifelong duty. Harry Cohn became a legendary Hollywood producer, the whispered subject of hate, scorn, and envy. Jack Cohn stayed in New York City and handled distribution of films, dealing with theater owners around the world.

This fraternal pair needed all of their skills to survive first the coming of sound and then the economic calamity of the Great Depression. The dark days of the depression narrowed Hollywood's nontheater-owning companies to three: Laemmle's Universal Pictures; the United Artists of Charlie Chaplin, Mary Pickford, and Sam Goldwyn; and the Cohns' Columbia. Warner Bros., Paramount, RKO, Twentieth Century-Fox, and Loew's/MGM had far more famous stars and owned all of the highest-grossing movie theaters in the United States. With Columbia's pictures all but shut out of the large, centrally located movie palaces of the

"Big Five," Jack Cohn excelled at placing films in smaller, neighborhood theaters. Operating at tight margins, the Cohn brothers built Columbia into a movie industry powerhouse.

The Cohns took advantage of any opportunity they came across. For example, Columbia Pictures won fame and fortune with the 1934 release of director Frank Capra's *It Happened One Night,* starring Clark Gable and Claudette Colbert. Harry Cohn was able to sign these two stars only because MGM and Paramount wanted to "punish" the pair for refusing certain parts. Jack Cohn was able to exploit these marquee names to sell normally reluctant exhibitors. *It Happened One Night* swept the 1934 Academy Awards and during the midst of hard times made Columbia millions.

But such a coup was not business as usual for Columbia. Typically, during the 1930s it had to rely on its low-budget B-westerns and low-cost shorts, serials, and cartoons for the bulk of its profits. Columbia too often is remembered only for only its few high-cost productions, principally the work of Capra (*Mr. Deeds Goes to Town*) and George Stevens (*Penny Serenade*), but far more typical were the efforts of western stars Buck Jones and Gene Autry.

Columbia Pictures' low-budget fare included more than men on horses. Popular characters such as Blondie (based on the favorite comic strip character), Boston Blackie (from a radio show), and the Lone Wolf (from detective fiction) drew in millions of fans. Serials with continuing stories became a Columbia Pictures staple; *Batman* and *Terry and the Pirates* proved to be particular favorites.

Columbia Pictures' comic short subjects offered a mainstay for neighborhood theaters. Starting in 1934 the Three Stooges launched their experiments in madness for Columbia. With scripts that could be filmed in no more than a week, and edited and readied for theaters in only seven more days, Stooges' shorts quickly created cash for Columbia. And they always made money, even though fewer than half the theaters in the United States regularly booked them. Small-town America never seemed to get enough of Curly, Larry, and Moe.

His considerable skill as a businessman made Jack Cohn a rich man. He and his wife, the former Jeanette Lesser, lived on a Connecticut farm with their three children and enjoyed horseback riding on the rolling hills.

During the 1950s Columbia Pictures, not burdened with "white elephant" movie palaces, signed up independent movie producers and rose to the ranks of a major studio. Its share of hits included *From Here to Eternity* (1953), *On the Waterfront* (1954), and *The Caine Mutiny* (1954). More important, the Cohn brothers embraced television and started a successful production unit, Screen Gems. This vaulted them to the top of the Hollywood TV industry.

Jack Cohn died in New York City. Harry Cohn survived until 1958. Thereafter, the Cohn-created movie and television empire passed into the hands of others.

• There are no papers or published writings on Jack Cohn, but there is a growing literature on the remarkable enterprise that the Cohn brothers created, Columbia Pictures. Bob Thomas, *King Cohn* (1967), and Bernard F. Dick, *Columbia Pictures* (1992), offer a basic guide to the studio's rise. For the position of Columbia within the Hollywood studio system, see Douglas Gomery, *The Hollywood Studio System* (1986). Clive Hirschhorn, *The Columbia Story* (1989), lists Columbia releases. An obituary is in *Variety*, 12 Dec. 1956.

DOUGLAS GOMERY

COHN, Roy (20 Feb. 1927–2 Aug. 1986), anti-Communist crusader, powerbroker, and attorney, was born Roy Marcus Cohn in New York City, the son of Al Cohn, a state judge and Democratic party figure, and Dora Marcus. Dora's father, Sam Marcus, had founded the Bank of United States, which served a largely Jewish, immigrant clientele. The bank failed during the Great Depression, and the trial of Dora's brother Bernie Marcus for fraud was one of the formative influences of Roy's childhood. Al Cohn was the son of a pushcart peddler, had attended law school at night, and used his political influence in the Bronx, as well as Dora's money, to gain a position as a state trial court judge and later a seat on the intermediate state appellate court. Roy was educated at the Horace Mann School. He had an undistinguished career as an undergraduate at Columbia College and was only admitted to Columbia Law School because of the dearth of students caused by World War II and his father's political influence. Roy did, however, finish both college and law school in three and a half years and, at age twenty, was too young to enter the bar. He spent a year as a clerk/typist for the U.S. attorney for New York and was promoted to assistant U.S. attorney after his twenty-first birthday.

Cohn gained public notoriety prosecuting suspected Communists in Manhattan. He achieved his first national publicity in 1951 as one of the attorneys prosecuting Julius and Ethel Rosenberg for atomic espionage for the Soviet Union. Cohn was soon promoted to special assistant to the attorney general, where he prosecuted Americans working for the United Nations who were suspected of Communist affiliations. At age twenty-six Cohn was appointed counsel to Senator Joseph McCarthy's Government Operations Committee. He beat out Robert F. Kennedy for the position, and Kennedy treated Cohn as an enemy until his death.

Cohn, with an unpaid staffer named G. David Schine, quickly undertook an inspection tour of U.S. State Department libraries in Europe to detect Communist influences. Their identification of books by Dashiell Hammett and Langston Hughes as Communist propaganda earned Cohn and Schine criticism abroad and at home. While Cohn had developed anti-Communist credentials, Schine was a wealthy socialite whose entire expertise on communism was encapsulated in an eight-page pamphlet he had written. They became close friends, and Cohn provided Schine with an entry into the exciting work of exposing Communists, while Schine introduced Cohn to New York society.

In 1953, when Schine was drafted by the army, Cohn began a campaign to reverse his enlistment or, failing that to find him easy duty near Washington. The Army-McCarthy hearings, held in 1954 before the Special Subcommittee on Investigations of the Senate Committee on Government Operations, which involved many of Cohn's allegations of Communist influence in the military, backfired as Cohn's attempts to gain preferential treatment for Schine were revealed. Army counsel Joseph Welch outmaneuvered the young Cohn and brought about the censure of Senator McCarthy. Cohn subsequently resigned his position and returned to New York to private practice.

In New York, Cohn earned a reputation as powerbroker with connections to many of the city's judges. He was known for his links to the media, which he had cultivated during his anti-Communist days by frequently leaking stories to commentators such as Walter Winchell and George Sokolsky. Also, Si Newhouse, who controlled the newspaper chain by that name, was a childhood friend and lifetime confidant. In 1963 Cohn was indicted by U.S. Attorney Robert Morgenthau for tampering with a grand jury in a case involving a stock swindle. In his successful defense, Cohn claimed that Morgenthau, whose father had been investigated by McCarthy and Cohn, and Attorney General Kennedy were pursuing a vendetta against him. In 1969 Morgenthau again indicted and failed to convict Cohn for bribery. Later Cohn's contempt for the Internal Revenue Service resulted in a continuous series of liens against him by the IRS for his refusal to pay income tax. Cohn did not report income because he received almost no salary from his law firm, which picked up most of his living expenses, and when he died it was estimated he owed the government several million dollars. He also owed large sums to vendors, whom he often refused to pay until they brought suit against him. Cohn's tendency to live outside of the law was evident in his clientele, which included reputed Mafia bosses Carmine Galante, Anthony "Fat Tony" Salerno, and Joseph Gambino. In 1986, just before his death, Cohn was disbarred for violating clients' trust.

Cohn was a homosexual, a contradiction with his public persona with which he often struggled. He had threatened several suspected Communists with the revelation of their homosexuality in the 1950s, and his frequent appearances with designer Carol Horn and broadcaster Barbara Walters did not dispel the persistent rumors of Cohn's own homosexuality. Toward the end of his life, he appeared in public with his boyfriends, taking one to meet Ronald and Nancy Reagan at the White House, but he continued to deny his sexual orientation in public. Even as he was visibly dying, Cohn denied that he was infected with the AIDS virus, claiming on the nationally broadcast news program "60 Minutes" that he suffered from liver cancer. After Cohn's death in New York City, many in the gay community were further scandalized when it was revealed that he had used his connections to gain access to the then experimental drug AZT. In a posthumous characterization, Cohn's struggle with both his homosexuality and AIDS was used by Tony Kushner in his Pulitzer Prize–winning drama *Angels in America* (1993) as a symbol of homosexual denial and self-hatred. Cohn is as much remembered for his tough guy persona and connections as a powerbroker as for his earlier work fighting communism with Senator McCarthy.

• Cohn wrote two books about his life, *A Fool for a Client: My Struggle against the Power of a Public Prosecutor* (1971), about Robert Morgenthau's repeated attempts to convict him, and *McCarthy* (1968), a biography of his mentor. Cohn's *How to Stand Up for Your Rights—and Win* (1981) is part legal advice and part motivational exhortation. Sidney Zion, *The Autobiography of Roy Cohn* (1988), is a collection of entertaining stories told to the author. The best biography of Cohn is Nicholas von Hoffman, *Citizen Cohn* (1988).

DANIEL LEVIN

COHON, Samuel Solomon (22 Mar. 1888–22 Aug. 1959), Reform rabbi and scholar, was born in Lohi, Minsk, Russia, the son of Solomon Cohon, a shoemaker, and Rachael Leah Starobinetz Kushner. As a young boy in Russia, Cohon was exposed to both classical Jewish learning and, as a reflection of the changing era, a modicum of secular studies. However, Cohon interrupted his childhood education following the Kishniev pogroms of 1903 and, like thousands of other Russian Jews, immigrated to the United States, arriving in 1904. After graduating from Barrington High School in Newark, New Jersey, in 1908, Cohon entered the Hebrew Union College in Cincinnati, where he was ordained a rabbi in 1912. In that same year he married A. Irma Reinhart; they had one child.

Cohon began his career in the pulpit rabbinate in 1912, serving in Springfield, Ohio, for a year. The following year Cohon was called to Chicago, where he ministered to Zion Temple until 1918, and then he officiated at a newly organized congregation, Temple Mizpah. During this period, Cohon achieved prominence in the Reform Central Conference of American Rabbis for his distinguished scholarly work as chair of a committee charged with the task of revising the Reform Haggadah for Passover use. In addition, he published numerous academic articles and reviews in a variety of journals. As a result, in 1923 Cohon was appointed to the Chair in Jewish Theology at the Hebrew Union College, a post that allowed him to play a seminal role in the development of Reform Jewish thought in the United States. Cohon held this position until 1956, when he moved to Los Angeles. There, until his death in Los Angeles, he played a formative role in the development of Hebrew Union College's Los Angeles campus.

Cohon's writings were voluminous. His erudition and mastery of Jewish and non-Jewish sources and scholarship, as well as his catholicity of interests, found expression in almost three hundred published sermons, popular articles, and scholarly historical essays. His expository work on Jewish religious history and law justly earned him great fame as a scholar, and he lectured often at institutions such as Columbia, Un-

ion Theological Seminary, and Vanderbilt during the 1930s and 1940s, and he carried on correspondence with scholarly colleagues in the Conservative and Orthodox seminaries during those same years. His theological oeuvre comprised the central core of his teachings. Cohon, in his era, was the preeminent Reform Jewish theologian in the United States.

In two principal works, *What We Jews Believe* (1931) and the three-volume *Theology Lectures: Theology and Religion* (1933–1935), Cohon expressed his own theological position. In these works, Cohon validated "intuition as a ground of faith," and though he did not abandon a commitment to reason and ethics as a vital element in religion, he did assert that Judaism goes beyond ethics to affirm the holy. As he wrote, "To the three dimensions of man's higher life: the true, the good, and the beautiful—corresponding to science, ethics, and aesthetics—religion adds a fourth: the *holy*." Religion therefore seeks to unify "*the diverse activities and aspirations of man in the single aim of the sanctification of life*." In expressing these themes, Cohon obviously reflected the romantic influence of a non-Jewish theologian such as Friedrich Schleiermacher and a religious phenomenologist such as Rudolf Otto. Moreover, he also placed himself squarely within the rationalist-ethical tradition of contemporary Reform Jewish thought as represented by spokesmen such as Hermann Cohen and Leo Baeck in Germany and Kaufmann Kohler in the United States. The ethical, universalistic dimensions of Judaism always remained prominent in his teachings.

Cohon's theology, for all its openness to the modern world, was nevertheless more traditionally Jewish and openly nationalistic than was that of his Reform forebears and colleagues. For example, Cohon, in keeping with the views of the prominent medieval Spanish Jewish philosopher Judah Halevi, emphasized the historical experience of the Jewish people as the foundation for the faith of Israel. As Cohon wrote in his posthumously published volume, *Jewish Theology: A Historical and Systematic Interpretation of Judaism and Its Foundations* (1971), "Judaism is not a theistic philosophy, derived by speculative reflection, but the millenial response of the Jewish people to the holy." In arriving at this position, Cohon laid the theoretical foundations for the practical work he accomplished as a leader of the Reform Movement's Central Conference of American Rabbis (CCAR).

While classical American Reform Judaism had been hostile to the use of modern Hebrew as a spoken language, as well as to the Zionist impulse that promoted it, Cohon was not. Nor was he, like many of his Reform colleagues, hostile to Jewish ritual tradition. At a time when modern Hebrew literature was not included in the curriculum of the Hebrew Union College, Cohon contributed often to American Hebrew periodicals and held informal seminars on modern Hebrew literature in his home. It was in this spirit of a "turn to tradition" that Cohon in 1923 guided the revision of the Reform movement's *The Union Haggadah: Home Service for the Passover*, turning it "into a more recognizably Jewish text" by adding more traditional Hebrew passages and classical themes. Cohon was similarly responsible for introducing more Hebrew and a more traditional liturgical structure into the revised edition of the Reform *Union Prayerbook* in 1940. His efforts to provide practical guidance for his colleagues in the Reform rabbinate resulted in his composition and editing of the *Rabbi's Manual* for the CCAR in 1928. Most significantly, Cohon drafted the "Guiding Principles of Reform Judaism," which were incorporated into the "Columbus Platform." This platform, adopted by the CCAR in 1937, superseded the anti-Zionist "Pittsburgh Platform" of 1885 and asserted that ritual ought to play a vital role in Reform religious life. It further affirmed the importance of Hebrew, the centrality of Zion, and the rebuilding of the land of Israel in contemporary Jewish life. Cohon, as the architect of this statement, charted the course of Reform Judaism in the United States for years to come and came to be a central figure in the transition of American Reform Judaism from its earlier period of opposition to ritual practice and Zionism to a contemporary stance that integrates these very elements into Reform religiosity and practice.

• During his lifetime Cohon was best known for his concise, popular *What We Jews Believe* (1931) and his more elaborate *Judaism: A Way of Life* (1948). These works articulate for lay audiences Judaism's teachings on the three great themes of God, Torah, and Israel, and they present the relevance of Judaism for persons seeking guidance and order in the modern world. The latter book is a revision, intended for a popular audience, of *Judaism as a Way of Living* (1935), volume 3 of Cohon's sophisticated academic collection *Theology Lectures*, of which volume 1 is *Theology and Religion* (1933) and volume 2 is *Man and His Destiny* (1934). His most important theological essays have been collected and published under the title *Essays in Jewish Theology* (1987). In addition, an autobiographical, posthumously published account of Cohon's life, *Day Book of Service at the Altar*, appeared in 1978. More than a source of insight and detail into his life, it also reveals a great deal about twentieth-century American Jewish history. A Hebrew volume, *Mekorot ha-Yahadut* (*Sources of Judaism*), drawn from Cohon's manuscripts, was published in 1988. The work contains a detailed collection of Jewish sources on a wide range of theological, liturgical, and ethical topics. The most complete listing of Cohon's publications remains Theodore Wiener, "The Writings of Samuel S. Cohon," *Studies in Bibliography and Booklore* 2 (1956): 160–78. A complete assessment of Cohon's significance has yet to be published.

DAVID ELLENSON

COHOON, Hannah Harrison (1 Feb. 1788–7 Jan. 1864), Shaker artist, was born in Williamstown, Massachusetts, the daughter of Noah B. Harrison, a revolutionary war veteran who died a year after her birth, and Huldah Bacon. She was raised in Williamstown and apparently was married there, to a man named Cohoon, but nothing is known of her husband, though she probably was widowed or abandoned. In 1817, with her five-year-old son, Harrison, and three-year-old daughter, Mariah, she entered the Hancock (Mass.) Shaker Village established twenty-six years earlier by members of the communitarian sect known formally as the United Society of Believers in Christ's Second Appearing and more commonly as the Shakers. Cohoon remained at Hancock (just west of Pittsfield) until her death. Her son and daughter left around 1838, but the daughter, having married and presumably become widowed, returned later in life.

Little is known about the daily work performed by Cohoon, who was called Sister Hannah. Her fame rests on four extant drawings, which she signed and which Patterson refers to as "The Tree of Light or Blazing Tree" (1845), "The Tree of Life" (1854), "A Bower of Mulberry Trees" (1854), and "A Little Basket Full of Beautiful Apples for the Ministry" (1856). Cohoon's "tree of life" image has since become recognized as the symbol of the American Shakers. Shaker "spirit drawings," such as the four composed by Cohoon, date to the Shaker Era of Manifestations, a time beginning in 1837 and extending for up to two decades, when the Shakers claimed to be visited by spirits of former Shakers and other personages already in heaven. Each of Cohoon's drawings, which contain strong, centered images of trees or fruit, is embellished by a paragraph either placed under the drawing or integrated into the central figure describing the visionary circumstances that elicited the drawing. In those passages she claimed that the drawings had been shown to her by Shaker spirits and that Mother Ann Lee herself, through a spirit medium, had identified her 1854 tree as the biblical Tree of Life. In interpreting the tree images, Shakers relied on biblical references and also recalled the words of an early leader, Father James Whittaker, who believed that his vision of a shining tree represented a new church to be established in the United States. The centralized tree image appeared, as well, in the work of Polly Collins, a younger Shaker artist who also lived at the Hancock community. Other Shaker artists, most of them women, worked with ink or watercolor, but Cohoon used a heavy paint; sometimes she scratched the painted surface of the tree trunks to add texture, and sometimes she varnished over the paint, making her simple centered images appear strong and unified.

The dramatic, yet balanced images of order and religious dedication evident in Cohoon's work have been incorporated into the logos and stationery that designate Shaker museums and historical sites. The Hancock Shaker community closed in the 1960s and became a nonprofit educational museum. A small community of Shaker believers has continued to live at Sabbathday Lake, Maine.

• Cohoon's four drawings can be seen by special request and arrangement at the Hancock Shaker Community museum in Pittsfield, Mass. For biographical and critical assessments, see Edward D. Andrews and Faith Andrews, *Visions of the Heavenly Sphere: A Study in Shaker Religious Art* (1969); Jane F. Crosthwaite, "The Spirit Drawings of Hannah Cohoon: Window on the Shakers and Their Folk Art," *Communal Studies*, Vol. 7 (1987), pp. 1–15; Daniel W. Patterson, *Gift Drawing and Gift Song: A Study of Two Forms of Shaker Inspiration* (1983); June Sprigg, *The Gift of Inspiration* (1979); and

Ruth Wolfe, "Hannah Cohoon," in *American Folk Painters of Three Centuries*, ed. Jean Lipman and Tom Armstrong (1980).

JANE F. CROSTHWAITE

COIT, Eleanor Gwinnell (6 May 1894–7 June 1976), labor educator and leader in adult education, was born in Newark, New Jersey, the daughter of Henry Leber Coit, a pediatrician and pure-milk reformer, and Emma Gwinnell. She grew up in Newark, attended public schools, and followed an older sister to Smith College, from which she was graduated with an A.B. in history and English in 1916.

Like many women's college graduates of her day, Coit tried the more traditional women's role before finding her life's work. "The first year out of college I was a perfect lady and studied the violin and sat on committees," she recalled. Following the death of her father in 1917, Coit went to work as the work and industrial secretary of the Young Women's Christian Association (YWCA) of the Oranges in New Jersey. She left the YWCA to study sociology, economics, and education at Columbia University and completed her M.A. thesis, "Some Primary Effects of the Organization on Women in Industry," in 1920. By then Coit had caught the eye of Florence Simms, who headed the YWCA National Board's programs for working women. Simms found her "a person of great power" who worked as if "consumed by a burning social fire." Coit returned to work for the YWCA in 1920, and when Simms died in 1923 Coit was one of the sturdy band poised to pick up the torch.

In 1920, when the YWCA dispatched Coit to a troubled branch, naming her as the director and executive of industrial work in Bayonne, New Jersey, she quickly succeeded in reuniting the staff and strengthening the branch's operations. In 1922 she transferred to the YWCA in Buffalo, New York, to head its business and industry department. Her supervisor there was Amy Gordon Bruce, a woman a few years her senior who was to become her closest friend and lifetime companion.

Coit left the YWCA briefly to conduct research for the Children's Bureau of the U.S. Department of Labor and the National Conference on the Christian Way of Life, but she was lured back in 1926 to take over the post of industrial secretary for the national YWCA in New York. In 1929 Hilda W. Smith picked Coit as educational secretary for the newly formed Affiliated Schools for Workers, a Manhattan-based agency designed to coordinate fundraising and recruitment for summer schools established by Bryn Mawr and other colleges earlier in the decade. The schools trained thousands of hosiery toppers, garment stitchers, and cigarette packagers in such leadership skills as public speaking, critical reading and thinking, and group dynamics. They enabled labor leaders Mary Anderson, Rose Pesotta, and a host of other working-class women to rise through the ranks of labor and politics and contribute to a more equitable economic order.

Coit was thirty-nine years old when she took the helm of Affiliated Schools, following Smith's resignation to head the New Deal's program of workers' education. She directed the organization, later renamed the American Labor Education Service (ALES), from 1934 until it closed its doors in 1962. Under Coit's leadership, a small, predominantly female staff organized conferences, experimented with teaching techniques, developed innovative curricular materials, and published workers' narratives and scholarly studies. As the women's movement faltered and labor unions grew powerful in the 1930s, the ALES widened its focus to include men and white-collar workers and farmers in addition to factory workers.

In the 1930s and 1940s Coit obtained grants to visit Scandinavia and Germany, where workers' education was more advanced. Following World War II, she secured Ford Foundation funding to permit the ALES to conduct United Nations workshops and worker exchanges that aimed to teach workers to broaden their thinking beyond the narrow interests of their own unions and industries. While she claimed that she did not like to write, she and her staff prepared the grant proposals that ensured the survival of the ALES. A number of Coit's reports, articles, and speeches were published, among them *Government Support of Workers' Education* (1940) and *Labor Education in Germany* (1950). Although Coit was past retirement age in 1962 when the ALES was forced to disband, she was saddened by its failure to survive. Its continuance through three economically volatile decades owed much to Coit's agility in winning the cooperation of both labor and management.

The granddaughter of a Methodist minister, Coit was inspired by the Social Gospel movement and the example of her father's crusading efforts to get laws passed to regulate the dairy industry to secure a safe supply of milk for infants. She was also influenced by Eduard Lindeman, a social philosopher and innovator in adult education whose teaching and writing championed the use of democratic means in the classroom to achieve a more democratic society.

Coit remained active in a large number of organizations in labor, adult education, church work, and social work well into her retirement. She tried to increase the participation of working-class women in the New York League of Women Voters, chaired a committee of the New York YWCA that attempted to secure jobs for African-American women, and was active locally in the so-called War on Poverty in the 1960s. In her old age, she ignored arthritic pain that required the use of a cane to pour her still considerable idealism and energy into the work of the Committee of Correspondence, an effort of prominent U.S. women to build bridges to their counterparts in the developing world nations.

Coit devoted her life to the belief that an informed citizenry, including its women, strengthened the democratic process. "We want the kind of world in which the best in each of us is encouraged to grow and where each individual is free to do his best for the common welfare," she wrote in a speech given during World War II. She never lost her idealism or her fiercely independent spirit, but by the 1970s her days were spent with responsibilities relating to the care of her companion and her younger sister, both invalids. Coit died in Hanover, New Hampshire.

• The largest collection of Coit's papers is in the Sophia Smith Collection at Smith College. A smaller body of her papers is housed in the Schlesinger Library at Radcliffe College. Her work for the ALES is fully documented in the organization's records in the Labor-Management Documentation Center of Catherwood Library, Cornell University. ALES material is also available at the State Historical Society of Wisconsin, Madison. Additional writings by Coit are "Why Do Married Women Work?" *Survey* 64 (15 Apr. 1930): 79–80; "Workers' Education in the United States," *Monthly Labor Review* 49 (July 1939): 1–21; and "Progressive Education at Work," in *Workers' Education in the United States: Fifth Yearbook of the John Dewey Society*, ed. Theodore Brameld (1941). Brief biographical entries appear in Judith O'Sullivan and Rosemary Gallick, *Workers and Allies: Female Participation in the American Trade Union Movement, 1824–1976* (1975), and Lois Decker O'Neill, ed., *The Women's Book of World Records and Achievements* (1979). See also "Pioneer of Labor Leaves U.S. Scene," *New York Times*, 29 Apr. 1962; and "Worker Schools Found Big Aid," *New York Times*, 27 Aug. 1939, a review of a book by Coit and Mark Starr titled *Workers' Education in the United States*. Joyce L. Kornbluh, *A New Deal for Workers' Education: The Workers' Service Program, 1933–1942* (1987), places Coit's work in context. Doris Cohen Brody, "American Labor Education Service, 1927–1962: An Organization in Workers' Education" (Ph.D. diss., Cornell Univ. 1973), contains a brief biography and analysis of Coit's contributions to the ALES. An obituary is in the *New York Times*, 9 June 1976.

SHERRILL REDMON

COIT, Elisabeth (7 Sept. 1892–2 Apr. 1987), architect and urban planner, was born in Winchester, Massachusetts, the daughter of Robert Coit, an architect, and Eliza Richmond Atwood. Her mother died when she was a young girl. After attending Radcliffe College (1910–1911) and the Museum School of the Boston Museum of Fine Art (1911–1913), Coit graduated in 1919 from the Massachusetts Institute of Technology with a degree in architecture.

Upon graduation Coit joined her father's architecture firm, Grosvenor Atterbury, in New York City. At the firm Coit worked first as a draftsperson and later as an assistant to the chief designer. In the mid-1920s she opened her own architectural office, and in 1929 she became a member of the American Institute of Architects. For the next ten years she designed private homes for a primarily female clientele in Westchester County, New York; New Hampshire; and Virginia. Her design for the home of Anna Van Nort in Croton Heights, New York, was awarded an honorable mention in the 1931 "Better Homes in America" competition. Other works of domestic architecture by Coit include her home for Mary Burnham (1927, Croton Heights, N.Y.), featured in the May 1936 issue of *Architecture*. In spite of her success, Coit stated in a *New York Sun* article that the biggest hurdle she faced as a

female architect was "getting people to trust her" (19 Nov. 1935).

In the late 1930s Coit became interested in aeronautics and with a friend, Wolfgang Langewiesche, made numerous flights up and down the East Coast. In a résumé dating from 1940 Coit describes her hobbies as including "light plane flying, which takes one further for less money than does automobiling, and is far more fun" (Coit papers). Her visits to the numerous small airports scattered along the Atlantic seaboard fostered an interest in this form of municipal architecture and led to her study of airports and the article "The Smaller Airport," which appeared in the architectural journal *Pencil Points* 18, no. 11 (Nov. 1937).

Coit's professional career reached a turning point in 1937, when she was awarded the prestigious Langley Fellowship by the American Institute of Architects. Choosing as her topic the economical design of single-family homes and low-income apartments, Coit's investigation of the topic proved so fruitful that the scholarship was renewed for the 1938–1939 year. The end result of almost three years of study was her report, "Notes on the Design and Construction of the Dwelling Unit for the Low-Income Family." A condensed version of this prescient report, in two parts, appeared in November and December 1941 issues of *The Octagon*.

Focusing on how low-income families actually used their residences, Coit offered suggestions on how better to design homes for them. She documented the use of public housing by low-income residents and contended that their use patterns should be integrated into public housing design. The report made Coit a well-known figure in urban planning and led to her appointment in 1942 to the Technical Division of the Federal Public Housing Authority's Office of Development. During her tenure in Washington, D.C., Coit oversaw the publication of the *Manual of Instruction for Erecting Temporary Dwellings* (1942) and *Public Housing Design: A Review of Experiences in Low Rent Housing* (1946).

Coit returned to New York City in 1947 and worked as a design assistant for the architectural firm of Mayer and Whittlesey, where she worked primarily on domestic design projects. The next year she went to work for the New York City Housing Authority, where she was the principal project planner for the design division. Under Coit's leadership, the New York City Housing Authority implemented many of the ideas she had explored during her Langley scholarship years.

Coit retired from the New York City Housing Authority after fourteen years in 1962. Remaining active in her field, she continued to work as a consultant for government and private organizations. During her career as a consultant she published her *Report on Family Living in High Apartment Buildings* (1965). In her later years Coit received numerous honors, including the 1969 New York City chapter of the American Institute of Architects award for pioneering work in architecture. The next year New York mayor John V. Lindsay appointed Coit to the city's Landmarks Preservation Commission.

Coit was a frequent contributor to architectural journals and served as the book review editor of the *Architectural Record* from 1940 to 1943. Her effervescent personality and playfulness were reflected in the light verse she contributed to various architectural publications and scattered throughout her correspondence. *Stone Cutter*, a collection of plays for children illustrated with her own watercolors, was submitted to publishers in 1942 but was not published.

In her last years, Coit divided her time between her Manhattan apartment and a Rockport, Massachusetts, home she shared with her brother; she never married. She died in Amherst, Massachusetts.

• Coit's papers, both personal and professional, are located at the Schlesinger Library of Radcliffe College. Nancy Jane Olive, "Elisabeth Coit: Pioneer in Architecture" (master's thesis, Michigan State Univ., 1989), is a source of biographical information and an analysis of Coit's public housing reports. Jean Lyon, "Women Architects Are Proving Successful Home Builders," *New York Sun*, 19 Nov. 1935, includes information on Coit. A home by Coit is featured in *Architecture* (May 1936): 271. An obituary is in the *New York Times*, 8 Apr. 1987.

MARTIN R. KALFATOVIC

COIT, Henry Augustus (20 Jan. 1830–5 Feb. 1895), clergyman and educator, was born in Wilmington, Delaware, the son of Joseph Howland Coit, a priest of the Episcopal church, and Harriet Jane Hard. He spent most of his childhood in Plattsburgh, New York, where his father was rector of Trinity Church. He attended William A. Muhlenberg's Flushing Institute, Long Island, and studied for one year (1847–1848) at the University of Pennsylvania before illness forced him to leave. To recuperate he spent a winter in the South, where he served as tutor to the family of the bishop of Georgia, Stephen Elliott (1806–1866). Coit then went to the College of St. James, a boarding school near Hagerstown, Maryland, that was run by a Muhlenberg protégé, John Barrett Kerfoot. There Coit taught Greek and Latin and continued his own studies, earning a B.A.

In the early 1850s Coit moved to Lancaster, Pennsylvania, where, under the direction of the Episcopal rector, Dr. Samuel Bowman, he took charge of a parish school for boys. After his ordination to the priesthood in 1854, he undertook missionary work in the diocese of Albany, New York, and established several new congregations in Clinton County.

In 1855 the Boston physician George Cheyne Shattuck, Jr. (1813–1893), decided to convert his summer estate at Millville, two miles west of Concord, New Hampshire, into an Episcopalian boarding school, which became St. Paul's School. The trustees of the new school, having been turned down by their first choice for rector, voted in January 1856 to offer the post to Coit, who accepted. Coit arrived at the school on 3 April 1856 with his bride, Mary Bowman Wheeler, whom he had married only a week before. (They

had four children.) St. Paul's School began with three boys (including the founder's two sons); by the time of Coit's death, the school comprised 345 boys and thirty-six masters.

Both the founder and the rector of St. Paul's were high churchmen, and the school reflected their theological commitments. A believer in baptismal regeneration and the doctrine of the Real Presence of Christ in the elements of bread and wine, Coit stressed gradual growth in holiness through participation in the rites of the Episcopal church. He made the chapel the center of school life, and his own influence was felt most powerfully there. Like Muhlenberg and Kerfoot, he provided chapel services—three on Sunday and one each weekday—that were aesthetically rich and appealing. President James A. Garfield mistook his man when he said, "I see, Dr. Coit, that you have the faculty of impressing yourself upon the boys." The rector replied, "I have another Image in mind which I hope to impress."

Coit was austere, autocratic, even unworldly. The writer Owen Wister, a graduate of St. Paul's, observed that Coit's "marble effigy, recumbent in the School Chapel, is rightly clothed in a monastic gown"; Wister thought the rector was born "seven hundred years later than the days of his spiritual kin." Some of his contemporaries believed that Coit became aware of the life of the nation only on those occasions when the Prayer Book obliged him to pray for the president of the United States. But Coit saw enough of his era to convince him of the need to preach against riches, fame, and pleasure as sources of lasting happiness and to praise personal virtue instead. "The training of conscience," he affirmed, "is the highest part of education."

Under Coit's leadership St. Paul's remained committed to a traditional curriculum based on the classics. However, as universities raised their own admission and intellectual standards in the late nineteenth century, the school found itself more and more preparing its boys for college rather than business. Athletic interests changed from such informal pursuits as nature walks, skating, and sledding to cricket, rowing, and, finally, football and ice hockey. As the school grew to over 300 students, the old, nurturing, familial atmosphere gave way to a regimen that could seem impersonal and repressive. Coit ventured to instill his own taste for severe simplicity and self-sacrifice in the sons of rich city dwellers—Morgans, Mellons, and Vanderbilts. In 1866 he established the Orphans' Home on a hill overlooking the school to care for the children of those who had died in the Civil War; the home gave St. Paul's students the opportunity to practice Christian charity.

Mrs. Coit died in 1888, and in his final, lonely years the rector turned for friendship and spiritual counsel to the Cowley Fathers, an Anglican religious community for men. He died at the school. His brother, Joseph Howland Coit, Jr., succeeded him as rector. The school was highly successful; it became the most influential model for the dozens of boarding schools founded in the decades following the Civil War. The image of Henry Coit, the tall priest in a long black coat, remained as a kind of abiding presence at the school long after his death.

• Coit's papers are in Ohrstrom Library, St. Paul's School, Concord, N.H. In the Owen Wister Papers, Manuscript Division, Library of Congress, there are twelve pieces of correspondence from Coit to Wister. Coit's reflections, "An American Boys' School—What It Should Be," were published in the *Forum*, Sept. 1891, pp. 1–11, and reprinted in James P. Conover, *Memories of a Great Schoolmaster (Dr. Henry A. Coit)* (1906). Coit's *School Sermons* appeared in 1909. Other worthwhile depictions of Coit and life at St. Paul's are provided in Joseph H. Coit, *Memorials of St. Paul's School* (1891); James Carter Knox, *Henry Augustus Coit* (1915); Frederick Joseph Kinsman, *Salve Mater* (1920); Owen Wister, "Dr. Coit of St. Paul's," *Atlantic Monthly*, Dec. 1928, pp. 756–68; and Arthur Stanwood Pier, *St. Paul's School, 1855–1934* (1934). The definitive history of Shattuck and Coit's enterprise is August Heckscher, *St. Paul's: The Life of a New England School* (1980).

DAVID HEIN

COIT, Henry Leber (16 Mar. 1854–12 Mar. 1917), pediatrician, was born in Peapack, New Jersey, the son of John Summerfield Coit, a Methodist minister, and Ellen Neafie. He received his early education in Newark public schools. In 1876 he graduated class valedictorian from the College of Pharmacy in New York and then went to work as a chemist for Tarrant & Company in New York City. He worked as a chemist and taught at the College of Pharmacy while he attended the College of Physicians and Surgeons of Columbia University, from which he graduated with a degree in medicine in 1883.

Coit interned in a Newark hospital for one year before opening his practice in that city in 1884. In 1886 he married Emma Gwinnell of Newark; they would have five children. He began his medical practice as a general practitioner, but his concern for the well being of children and the death of his infant son strengthened his resolve to practice pediatrics, a relatively recent medical specialty that provided him with both a good income and the opportunity to participate in the campaign for pure milk and other public health initiatives.

Coit's quest for pure milk began in 1888 during a milk-borne diphtheria epidemic. In his search for noncontaminated milk to nourish his sick son he canvassed dairy farms in Essex County and saw the filthy conditions that existed there as well as unsanitary methods of collection and distribution of milk and undernourished and sick cows. For the next five years Coit visited dairy farms in the Newark area to study and critique their operation. Through this contact with the milk industry he developed a set of standards necessary to ensure the production of pure milk. An active participant in public health affairs, Coit believed that the state had enacted sufficient protective legislation; what was lacking were the funds and personnel necessary to enforce the existing laws. Because dairy farmers had considerable political influence in

the state capital, he bypassed the state legislature and instead organized a voluntary program of compliance that enlisted physicians and veterinarians to establish clinical standards of purity for cow's milk. The standards were inclusive, from cleanliness at the point of milk production to the milk's handling and transportation, good and uniform nutritional qualities, reliable keeping qualities, and freedom from foreign matter and pathogenic bacteria. In addition the dairies were subject to periodic inspections as well as bimonthly examinations of the dairy stock to prevent the spread of cow-borne diseases.

On 5 December 1892 Coit presented his proposal to the members of the Practitioners Club of Newark, an influential medical organization. His plan outlined every production detail and established the concept of a volunteer medical milk commission to administer the program. In order to ensure conformity with the policies of the commission, Coit prepared a contract to be signed by the participating dairy farmers. The Practitioners Club approved his proposals, and the Essex County Milk Commission, the first of its kind in the world, was elected with Coit as president. The commission held its first meeting on 13 April 1893, whereupon Coit's plan to provide a source of pure (certified) milk was put into operation. "Certified milk" was defined by Coit as the product of a dairy that met the established standards of quality, purity, and safety and operated under the supervision of a medical milk commission.

On 19 May 1893 Stephen Francisco, owner of the Fairfield Dairy of Essex County, and the Essex County Medical Milk Commission signed an agreement for Francisco to provide bottled certified milk. That same day Emma Coit received, tied with a blue ribbon, the first bottle of certified milk, from which she gave her two-year-old daughter her first glass of pure milk. To avoid the unauthorized and illegal use of the term "certified milk," Francisco had it copyrighted and held it in trust for the Essex County Medical Milk Commission and any other authorized commission. A medical milk commission was organized in New York City in 1896 and in Philadelphia in 1897; by 1917 more than sixty such commissions were operating in the United States, two were operating in Canada, and several were operating in Europe and Asia. In 1907 the American Association of Medical Milk Commissions and the Certified Milk Producers' Association of America were organized, and in 1909 the New Jersey legislature enacted a law defining the term "certified milk." The infant mortality rate declined in areas where certified milk was used almost exclusively. In time the addition of vitamin D increased the nutritional value of milk, and pasteurization provided an additional safety factor.

Coit's interest in children did not end with his successful campaign for pure milk. Assisted by prominent Newark citizens, in 1896 he founded the Babies Hospital of Newark, now called Coit Memorial. It was the third such hospital in the nation, the Child's Hospital and Nursery in New York City (1854) and the

Children's Hospital of Philadelphia (1855) being the first two. In addition to the hospital, several "Baby Keep Well Stations" were opened in various parts of Newark. It was Coit's fundamental belief that every child had a natural right to grow into healthy maturity.

In 1910 Coit became the founder and first president of the New Jersey Pediatric Society. He was a member and served as an officer of numerous national and international medical societies and public health organizations, such as the American College of Physicians, the American Pediatric Society, the American Association of Medical Milk Commissions, the American Medical Association, the International Congress for the Protection of Children, and the English Speaking Congress of Infant Mortality. He was a consulting pediatrician for the St. Vincent's Foundling Hospital of Montclair and the Home for Crippled Children in Newark. He also was author of more than twenty-five books and articles dealing with children and the subject of milk.

Coit was a deeply religious man and a tireless worker in behalf of childrens' health and welfare. He was deeply involved in the poliomyelitis epidemic of 1916. During the crisis he organized the Citizen's Relief Committee, which raised funds to pay for the high cost of caring for the stricken children. As a result of his untiring efforts he succumbed to pneumonia and died at his home in Newark forty-eight hours later. In 1953, in a vote taken by the American Public Health Association among experts in milk sanitation, Coit was designated as the person who had made the greatest contribution in their field of public health.

• The Henry L. Coit Papers are in the National Library of Medicine. Among Coit's many publications are *The Feeding of Infants* (1890), *The Care of the Baby* (1894), *Causation of Disease by Milk* (1894), *Rational Infant Feeding* (1902), *The Public School as a Factor in Preventing Infant and Child Mortality* (1912), and *The Relation of the Physician in Philanthropic and Sociologic Work of the Community in Child Life* (1912). For more biographical information see Mildred V. Naylor, "Henry Leber Coit: A Biographical Sketch," *Bulletin of the History of Medicine* 12 (Aug. 1942): 367. Coit and his public health work are featured in Fred B. Rogers and A. Reasoner Sayre, *The Healing Art: A History of the Medical Society of New Jersey* (1966); Rogers, *The Help-Bringers: Versatile Physicians of New Jersey* (1959); Wilson G. Smillie, *Public Health: Its Promise for the Future* (1955); and Manfred J. Wasserman, "Henry L. Coit and the Certified Milk Movement in the Development of Modern Pediatrics," *Bulletin of the History of Medicine* 46 (July–Aug. 1972): 359–90. Obituaries include Rowland G. Freeman, "Henry Leber Coit," in *Archives of Pediatrics*, vol. 34 (1917), p. 212; the *Journal of the American Medical Association* 68 (13 Mar. 1917): 925; the *New York Times*, 14 Mar. 1917; and the *Newark Evening News*, 13–15 Mar. 1917.

SAM ALEWITZ

COIT, Stanton (11 Aug. 1857–15 Feb. 1944), settlement house worker and Ethical Culture Society minister, was born in Columbus, Ohio, the son of Harvey Coit, a dry goods merchant, and Elizabeth Greer. He grew up in a prosperous, Episcopalian family. One of the

major early influences on Coit was his mother's belief in spiritualism, or communication with the dead, a belief Coit did not abandon until his second year in college. At the age of fifteen, Coit, who had a strongly philosophical bent, became interested in Ralph Waldo Emerson's thought, especially his idea of a religion of "pure ethics." Coit remained influenced by Emerson throughout his life.

When Coit graduated Phi Beta Kappa from Amherst in 1879, he placed first in philosophy. He then became an English literature tutor at Amherst. Two years later, having met Felix Adler, founder of the Ethical Culture movement, a religious approach to the useful application of ethics, he moved to New York City, where he attended Columbia University (1882–1883) and prepared to become an Ethical Culture lecturer. With Adler's encouragement and financial support, Coit then enrolled at the University of Berlin in 1883, studying the philosophy of Kant and earning a Ph.D. in 1885.

On his way home from Germany, Coit spent three months at Toynbee Hall in London. Established the year before and named for British sociologist Arnold Toynbee (1852–1883), Toynbee Hall was the first settlement house in the world. Located in a slum, its purpose was to give well-educated men the opportunity to live among the poor, help their less-fortunate neighbors in a secular fashion, and bring about fundamental reforms. Coit took this idea back to the United States, where he established the first American settlement house, Neighborhood Guild, on New York City's Lower East Side in 1886. Rather than merely copying the British model, Coit developed the concept of organizing the settlement's neighbors into guilds. Ideally, each guild would consist of around 100 families. These families not only would help each other, but also would determine which social reforms they wanted and then join with other guilds to work for their enactment. Although this idea never came close to working as Coit envisioned it, several other settlements were begun on the guild model, of which New York's Hudson Guild was the most successful. Coit deserves credit for recognizing the paternalism in the basic settlement house idea and for trying to devise an alternative to give poor people a direct policymaking role in bringing about social change. However, at Neighborhood Guild Coit was more successful at starting half a dozen social clubs and a kindergarten than in grass-roots organizing.

Coit's major commitment was to the Ethical Culture movement. In 1887 London's South Place Chapel, which had earlier shifted from a Unitarian position to one similar to Ethical Culture, invited Coit to become its minister. Coit accepted and, as a result, became the exporter of the American ethical culture movement to England. Neighborhood Guild almost collapsed after his departure, but his assistants there were able to reconstitute it as University Settlement, thus making it the oldest settlement house still operating in the United States. Coit briefly returned to University Settlement as director for sixteen months between 1892 and

1894. When the depression began in 1893, he advocated public works projects for the unemployed. Criticized as an agitator, he left for England, where he became a British citizen and spent the remainder of his life.

Coit was an energetic leader of the British Ethical Culture movement, though not always successful. One way to usefully apply ethics was through the settlement house. In 1892 he published *Neighborhood Guilds*, his conception of what settlement houses should be. His Kentish Town Neighborhood Guild soon developed a full range of educational and recreational activities in a north London working-class community. South Place Chapel doubled its membership during his three years there. Coit's efforts resulted in the formation of other British Ethical Culture societies and the Moral Instruction League, which advocated the teaching of ethics in tax-supported schools. He also became a woman suffrage advocate, which led to his meeting and marrying a German émigré suffragist, Fanny Adela Wetzler, in 1898; they had three children. Coit also became interested in Fabian socialism. In 1906 he ran unsuccessfully as a Labour party candidate for Parliament.

After 1909 Coit's major base of operations was the Ethical Church he established in the prosperous middle-class Bayswater neighborhood of London. There he promulgated ideas synthesized mainly from Emerson, Kant, and socialist thinkers. He departed from the American Ethical Culture movement when he tried to develop a churchlike ritual for ethical culture in England. This effort failed mainly because part of the appeal of Ethical Culture for many of its followers was the absence of religious ritual. To Adler and other American adherents of ethical culture, Coit's emphasis on symbols and ritual was alien and came close to a betrayal of the movement. Coit's writings include *National Idealism and a State Church* (1907), *National Idealism and the Book of Common Prayer* (1908), *Two Responsive Services: In the Form and Spirit of the Litany and Ten Commandments for Use in Families, Schools, and Churches* (1911), and *The Soul of America* (1914). After 1914, when interest in Ethical Culture subsided, Coit capped his long career by publishing a translation in 1932 of *Ethik* by German philosopher Nicolai Hartmann. He died in England, near Eastbourne, Sussex.

Although Stanton Coit devoted his life mainly to promoting Ethical Culture, he is best remembered as the founder of the first settlement house in the United States.

• No collection of Coit's papers exists, but material relevant to Coit may be found in the University Settlement Records and the Henry Demarest Lloyd Papers, both at the State Historical Society of Wisconsin, and in the National Federation of Settlement Records at the Social Welfare History Archives Center, University of Minnesota. In addition to the books mentioned in the text above, Coit published "Necessity of State Aid to the Unemployed," *Forum* 17 (May 1894): 275–86. For a collection of Coit's writings and a detailed biographical sketch, see Harold J. Blackham, ed., *Stanton Coit, 1857–1944: Selections from His Writings with a Prefatory Memoir* (1944). Other biographical sketches are contained in Walter I. Trattner, ed., *Biographical Dictionary of Social Welfare in America* (1986), and Patricia Mooney Melvin, ed., *American Community Organizations: A Historical Dictionary* (1986). Obituaries are in the London *Times*, 16 Feb. 1944, and the *New York Times*, 17 Feb. 1944.

JUDITH ANN TROLANDER

COKE, Richard (13 Mar. 1829–14 May 1897), governor of Texas and U.S. senator, was born in Williamsburg, Virginia, the son of John Coke and Mary Eliza Hawkins, wealthy farmers. He attended schools at Williamsburg, including the College of William and Mary, where he graduated with honors in 1849. He studied law in Virginia and passed the bar in 1850.

Coke moved to Waco, McLennan County, Texas, in 1850. He practiced law and became active in Democratic party politics in his new home. He married Mary Elizabeth Horne in 1852; they had four children. In 1859 he served as a commissioner appointed by Governor Hardin Runnels to negotiate the removal of American Indians on the upper Brazos River to the Indian Territory.

Coke favored secession in the sectional crisis of 1860–1861, and he served in the Texas secession convention. He went to Virginia after the outbreak of war but in 1862 returned to Texas, where he helped to raise Company K of Colonel Joseph W. Speight's Fifteenth Texas Infantry. As captain of Company K, Coke served primarily in Arkansas, Louisiana, and Texas and was engaged in the battle of Sabine Crossroads, 8 April 1864, as a part of Polignac's Brigade.

At the end of the war Coke returned to Waco. In June 1865 Provisional Governor Andrew Jackson Hamilton appointed him district judge despite his secessionist stance in 1860. He ran as a Conservative for the state supreme court in 1866 and was elected an associate justice. He served for one year, but like other state officials, he was removed in 1867 as "an impediment to Reconstruction" by General Philip H. Sheridan.

Returning to private life in Waco, Coke was active in Democratic party politics. He ran for governor of Texas in 1873 against the Republican incumbent, Edmund J. Davis. The election was marred by fraud and violence, but Coke clearly won. Despite a state supreme court ruling that the election was unconstitutional, the state legislature inaugurated him governor in January 1874.

Coke had campaigned promising fiscal conservatism, urging a reduction in the size of state government and a subsequent decrease in taxes. He attracted broad support with such policies, particularly among the agrarian elements of his party. The newly formed state Grange became the core of his political constituency. Coke was frustrated in his efforts to reduce government costs, however, by pressing demands for state services. He presided over the dismantling of the expensive state public school system in favor of county-based schools. The governor was also instrumental in the calling of the state constitutional convention in

1875, which produced a new constitution that reduced salaries for public officials and severely restricted the powers of the state government to tax. At the same time, other demands presented obstacles to his efforts at cutting costs. Coke's own economic philosophy plus pressure from railroads led the governor to resist all efforts to repudiate the state's bonds issued by his Republican predecessor to promote railroad construction. New expenses also were incurred when he used Texas Rangers and state militia against American Indians and bandits. As a result, his administration actually increased state expenditures.

Coke stood for reelection in February 1876 in an election called by the constitutional convention to ratify the proposed constitution and elect officers under it. Despite complaints about the state debt and the continuing problem of lawlessness on the frontier, plus allegations that he had given the state printing to a favored newspaper in violation of state law, Coke was renominated by his party without serious opposition. He easily defeated his Republican opponent, William M. Chambers, and was inaugurated in April 1876. The next month the legislature elected him to the U.S. Senate. He continued to serve as governor, however, until December 1876 and did not assume his seat in the Senate until March 1877.

In the spring of 1877 Coke began a career in the U.S. Senate that lasted until 1895. During those years he served on the Committee on Commerce, the Judiciary Committee, and the Fisheries Committee. As a senator he aggressively supported internal improvements favorable to Texas, particularly deepening harbors of Texas ports and protection of the Rio Grande frontier. At the same time, many of his stands on national issues reflected agrarian ideas, in particular his support for repeal of the Specie Resumption Act of 1875, advocacy of free coinage of silver in 1878, opposition to the protective tariff, and backing of federal regulation of interstate railroads. As a white southerner concerned with any federal intervention in civil or political affairs within his state, he opposed efforts in the 1880s to provide federal aid to education and the 1890 federal election bill known as the Force Bill. Reelected in 1882 and 1888 without opposition, he left office in March 1895, declining to run for a fourth term. He returned to his family plantation and died two years later in Waco, Texas.

• There is no full-length biography of Coke. An examination of his early career may be found in B. J. Fett, "Early Life of Richard Coke," *Texana* 4 (1972): 310–20. His later political career is followed extensively in Alwyn Barr, *Reconstruction to Reform: Texas Politics, 1876–1906* (1971). His obituary is in the *Dallas News*, 14, 15, 16 May 1897.

CARL H. MONEYHON

COKE, Thomas (28 Sept. 1747–3 May 1814), Anglican priest and Methodist bishop, was born in Brecon, South Wales, the son of Bartholomew Coke, an apothecary, and Anne Phillips. In April 1764 he entered Jesus College, Oxford, as a gentleman commoner. He graduated with a B.A. in 1768 and an M.A. in 1770. In 1775 he obtained a doctorate in Civil Law.

Coke was ordained deacon in 1770 and priest in 1772. Failing to obtain preferment through influential friends, he became in 1771 curate to the vicar of South Petherton, Somerset. His youthful energy, increasingly tinged with Methodist "enthusiasm," alienated many of the parishioners. On 13 August 1776 he rode to Kingston St. Mary, north of Taunton, to meet John Wesley. After lengthy conversations, Wesley encouraged him to return to his parish work, "omitting no part of his clerical duties" but avoiding "every reasonable ground of offense." Less than a year later, however, following a change of vicar, Coke was driven ignominiously out of the parish, and he threw in his lot with the Methodists.

Coke became an increasingly useful aide to the elderly Wesley, accompanying him on many journeys and traveling as his lieutenant throughout the British Isles. At this period British Methodism was troubled by contentions and divided loyalties. Coke was actively involved both in the attempt to hold it together and in new ventures and developments. Socially and culturally isolated from the majority of Wesley's itinerant preachers and resented as a youthful upstart who had Wesley's ear, he nevertheless was seen as their champion against Charles Wesley, who was deeply suspicious of their motives and aspirations. Coke's own churchmanship vacillated between loyalty to the established church and advocacy of separation from it.

In 1784, following the revolutionary war, John Wesley ordained two of his lay preachers and sent them, accompanied by Coke as "superintendent," to minister to the spiritual needs of his American followers. Coke was already in holy orders, but Wesley administered a form of presbyteral consecration to give him authority among the American Methodists. Charles Wesley strongly condemned this irregularity on his brother's part, attributing it to the influence of an ambitious and self-seeking Coke.

Arriving in the United States, Coke in turn ordained and consecrated Francis Asbury, the acknowledged leader of the American Methodists, at the Christmas Conference in Baltimore in December 1784. Coke and Asbury thus became the first bishops of the newly constituted Methodist Episcopal church. Coke traveled extensively between New York and North Carolina, taking a public stand against slavery. The visit made him liberal in both his political and his ecclesiastical sentiments. In June 1785 he returned home to report to Wesley but was back in the United States in 1787. He made a total of nine visits to the United States between 1784 and 1804.

Although Asbury never allowed him any effective authority in the American church, Coke played a part in its early development, especially in drawing up *The Doctrines and Discipline of the Methodist Episcopal Church in America* (8th ed., 1792), by which it was governed. His influence was decisive in defeating Asbury's plans to govern the church by means of a council in the intervals between conferences. Through his repeated visits and his correspondence with the American preachers, Coke was virtually the only link with British Methodism.

After Wesley's death in 1791, Coke was a key figure in the troubled years during which the Methodist connection groped its way toward a separate identity. Though disappointed in any aspirations he may have had to inherit Wesley's unique position and authority, he was twice elected president of the conference, in 1797 and in 1805.

In Britain Coke is remembered particularly as the pioneer of overseas missions. His first proposal, in 1784, for a missionary society financed by private subscriptions foundered because it lacked Wesley's backing. In 1786 his next attempt, endorsed by Wesley, successfully sponsored Methodist missionaries to the Caribbean, Nova Scotia, the Channel Islands, and remote parts of Scotland. Coke was designated by the conference as superintendent of these missions, and he paid four visits to the West Indies. Under his enthusiastic supervision, the extent of the missions increased steadily, often taxing the resources available. He spent much time soliciting subscriptions and advocating the cause from the pulpit, and he often made up the deficit from his own resources. Beginning in 1805 Coke instigated the first home missionary appointments in rural areas so far untouched by Methodism, along with native-speaking missions in Scotland, Ireland, and his native Wales. By 1814 missions had also been established in West Africa and were about to be launched in Ceylon and India.

Despite his busy and peripatetic life, Coke published over sixty works, ranging from sermons and tracts to *Commentary on the Bible* (1801–1803) and *History of the West Indies* (1808–1811). These more substantial works and his revision of Samuel Wesley's poem, *The Life of Christ* (1809), were heavily derivative. He also collaborated with Henry Moore on the official life of Wesley, *The Life of the Rev. John Wesley, A. M.* (1792). Of this considerable output, only the extracts from the journals he kept during visits to the United States and the Caribbean are still legible.

Coke remained a bachelor until 1805, when he married Penelope Goulding Smith; they had no children. This brought his transatlantic voyages to an end but not his travels in England, on which his wife joined him until her death in 1811. Coke was devastated by his bereavement, but within a year he married again, to Ann Loxdale, one of Wesley's confidantes; they had no children. Her delicate health broke down within a year, and Coke was again plunged into grief, from which he was roused only by a call to go to the East. Accompanied by six young missionaries, he sailed from Portsmouth, England, at the end of 1813. He died at sea and was buried in the Indian Ocean. Sometimes naive and unpredictable but energetically devoted to the Methodist cause, Coke was a key figure on both sides of the Atlantic during a climactic period in Methodism's history.

• Major collections of manuscript sources, chiefly letters, are in the John Rylands University Library, Manchester, England, and the archives of the Methodist Missionary Society at the School of Oriental and African Studies, London, England. Smaller collections are at Wesley College, Bristol, England; Wesley's Chapel, London; the Public Record Office, London; Drew, Duke, Emory, and Southern Methodist Universities; and Garrett-Evangelical Seminary, Evanston, Ill. A collected edition of his *Extracts of the Journals of the Late Rev. Thomas Coke, L.L.D.* was published in 1816 with a prefatory memoir by Joseph Sutcliffe. A list of other manuscript sources and details of Coke's writings are in the documented study by John A. Vickers, *Thomas Coke, Apostle of Methodism* (1969). Early biographies are Jonathan Crowther, *Life of the Rev. Thomas Coke, LL.D., a Clergyman of the Church of England* (1815); Samuel Drew, *Life of the Rev. Thomas Coke, LL.D.* (1817); J. W. Etheridge, *The Life of the Rev. Thomas Coke, D.C.L.* (1860); and W. A. Candler, *Life of Thomas Coke* (1923). A number of articles on aspects of Coke's life and ministry are in *Methodist History* and the *Wesley Historical Society Proceedings*.

JOHN A. VICKERS

COKER, Daniel (1780?–1835?), a founder of the African Methodist Episcopal Church, author, and educator, was born a slave in Frederick County, Maryland, the son of Susan Coker, a white indentured servant, and Edward Wright, a black slave belonging to the same plantation owner whose name is unknown. Daniel Coker was educated with his master's son, who refused to go to school without his slave. When Coker was in his early teens he escaped to New York City where he joined the Methodist Church and was ordained as a lay minister.

Empowered by his education and ordination, Coker returned to Maryland in 1801 to become the first African-American teacher at the African Academy, a school founded by the Baltimore Abolition Society for the education of free blacks. He was the first black licensed minister in Baltimore, and the spiritual leader of an independent prayer meeting formed by black Methodists dissatisfied with their position within the white Methodist church. But because the twenty-one-year-old Coker was still legally a slave, he was forced to remain in hiding until a Quaker abolitionist purchased and freed him. In 1806, Coker founded the Daniel Coker School, which by 1810 had an enrollment of one hundred fifty African-American students.

In 1810, Coker wrote *A Dialogue Between A Virginian and An African Minister*, generally considered the first published antislavery tract written by an African American. In this pamphlet, Coker exposed the failure of white Methodists to address the evils of slavery and refuted the notion that the Bible defended the institution. "But the question," Coker argued, "is concerning the liberty of a man. The man himself claims it as his own property. He pleads (and I think in truth) that it was originally his own; and he has never forfeited, nor alienated it; and therefore, by the common laws of justice and humanity, it is still his own."

In 1814, responding to the continued failure of Baltimore's white Methodists to grant ministries or autonomy to African-American Methodists, Coker led the trustees of the black Methodist congregation in withdrawing entirely from the white Methodist Church and in buying their own church.

During this time, Coker frequently communicated with the Reverend Richard Allen, another African-American Methodist minister, whose struggles to form a separate black church in Philadelphia paralleled Coker's efforts in Baltimore. Coker's "Sermon Delivered Extempore in the African Bethel Church in the City of Baltimore," delivered on 21 January 1816, was a response to Allen's labors on behalf of black Methodism in Philadelphia.

In 1816, Baltimore's black Methodists met with their brethren from Pennsylvania, New Jersey, and Delaware and combined their separate churches into a single denomination, the African Methodist Episcopal Church. Richard Allen was elected chairman of the convention with Coker as vice-chairman. Because Coker was one of the few participants who could read and write, the task of drafting the convention's resolutions fell to him.

After Coker and Allen were both elected bishops, Allen insisted the new denomination needed only one and, according to many accounts, offered to resign. In a second election on 11 April 1816, Allen was chosen sole bishop. Coker was made pastor of Bethel, Baltimore's AME Church, but for unknown reasons he was expelled from the AME within two years and reduced to a life of itinerant preaching.

Inspired by an earlier meeting with Paul Cuffe, a pathbreaking black businessman and ship builder who had come to Baltimore in 1812 seeking support for his plan to transport free blacks to Sierra Leone, Coker allied himself with the American Colonization Society. In 1820, Coker set out for Sierra Leone in the company of Samuel Bacon and John P. Bankson representing the federal government and Samuel Crozer, an agent for the colonization society and eighty-three black emigrés. Envisioning himself as a Christian pilgrim, Coker kept a detailed record of the voyage, later published in Baltimore as the *Journal of Daniel Coker, A Descendant of Africa, From the Time of Leaving New York in the Ship Elizabeth, Capt. Sebor, On a Voyage for Sherbro, in Africa, in Company With Three Agents and about Ninety Persons of Colour* (1820). In the new settlement's early days, Coker served as a justice of the peace, held church services, and acted as a mediator between the white agents and black emigrants. The initial optimism of the voyagers was soon eroded by torrential rains, malaria, and polluted water. Within months, the U.S. government and ACS agents had died, leaving Coker in charge of the struggling settlement. But Coker's close ties with the white agents before their deaths undermined his authority with the surviving black settlers, and when they moved to their permanent settlement in Liberia in 1821 they left him behind. In 1821, Coker's wife, Maria (d. 1824), and his three sons sailed from Baltimore and joined him in Sierra Leone.

In 1822 the governor of Sierra Leone made Coker the superintendent of Hastings, a village that func-tioned as a repatriation center for West Africans retrieved from coastal slave traders after the abolition of the slave trade. In Hastings, Coker continued to preach, eventually seceding from the AME Church and founding the West African Methodist denomination. He died in Sierra Leone.

The trajectory of Coker's life is salient, in part, because it intersected with a number of important institutions—slavery, the AME, and the American Colonization Society. But it is the power of his voice as one of a small number of literate African Americans in the early national period that remains his most potent legacy. "May the time speedily come," Coker wrote in his Baltimore sermon, arguing for the formation of a separate black church, "when we shall see our brethren come flocking to us like doves to us their windows. And we as a band of brethren, shall sit down under our own vine to worship, and none to make us afraid."

• Because there is no biography of Daniel Coker, his own writings remain the richest source of information about his life and thought. The *Journal of Daniel Coker* is available on microfilm at the New York Public Library. Coker's second *Journal* written in Africa and covering the period from April 1821 to September 1821 is in the Library of Congress, Manuscripts Division. Coker's "Sermon" of 1816 is reprinted in Herbert Aptheker, *A Documentary History of the Negro People in the United States*, vol. 1 (1973). His *Dialogue* of 1810 can be found in *Early American Imprints*, 2d series, Clifford K. Shipton, ed., index 19794.

The most detailed biographical sketch of Coker is Josephus R. Coan's "Daniel Coker: Nineteenth-Century Black Church Organizer, Educator, and Missionary," *Journal of the Interdenominational Theological Seminary* 1 (1975): 17–31. The most exhaustive work concerning Coker and the AME in Baltimore is Glen A. McAnich, "We'll Pray For You: Methodist Ethnocentrism in The Origins of the African Methodist Episcopal Church in Baltimore" (M.A. thesis, Univ. of North Carolina, 1973).

MARY F. COREY

COKER, James Lide (3 Jan. 1837–25 June 1918), entrepreneur and philanthropist, was born on a plantation near Hartsville, South Carolina, the son of Caleb Coker, a planter and merchant, and Hannah Lide. Coker's father also served as a director of the Chersaw and Darlington (S.C.) Railroad. His wealth afforded Coker considerable advantages that he used and built upon. His education was similar to that of other sons of South Carolina's planter elite. Schooled in a local, privately supported academy, he then attended The Citadel. However, in 1857 he took the unusual step of going to Harvard to take courses in chemistry and botany, working under Louis Agassiz and Asa Gray, to gain knowledge that he could apply to the plantation near Hartsville his father had given him that year. He married Susan Stout, daughter of a Baptist minister, in Alabama in 1860. They had seven children, several of whom entered business with their father.

The Civil War profoundly changed the lives of the Cokers. When the war started, James volunteered to the service of South Carolina the Hartsville Light Infantry, which he had organized in 1859. Captained by

Coker, Company G of the Ninth South Carolina Infantry Regiment, later renamed Company E of the Sixth South Carolina Regiment, fought throughout the war and in some of the bloodiest battles in Virginia and Tennessee. Twice wounded, the second time gravely at the battle of Lookout Mountain, Coker had to retire to rear quarters, where he was later captured. After a long convalescence, he was paroled in July 1864. He walked with a cane most of the remainder of his life and sometimes used a wheelchair in his later years.

Coker was elected to the state house of representatives in 1864 and served until 1865, when the defeat of the Confederacy ended the legislature. During his brief legislative career he proposed creating a state-wide system of public education under a superintendent. The first measure of its kind to be introduced in the South Carolina legislature, it passed the house of representatives but died in the senate. Coker never held elective office again. He disliked being a public official and declined further invitations to run for office.

Returning from the war, Coker resumed farming with depleted work livestock and freedmen as laborers. When hostilities ceased, he was ready to profit from the high cotton prices of the immediate postwar years. Obviously an able planter and probably in better financial circumstances than most, Coker enjoyed success in agriculture for years. In 1894, one of the worst years for southern farmers, he claimed to have made 7 percent net profit on the $100,000 he had invested in farming at the time.

As early as 1866 Coker opened a mercantile business with his father. He and a friend, George Norwood, opened Norwood and Coker, a firm that traded in naval stores and cotton, in Charleston in 1874; it became one of the largest department stores in the state. Coker moved to Charleston in 1877 to run the company but returned to Hartsville in 1881, the year Norwood and Coker ceased operations. Thereafter he centered most of his activities at Hartsville, though in the early 1880s he had a hand in a bank, a cotton mill, and a wholesale grocery business in Darlington.

On his return to Hartsville Coker founded the Bank of Hartsville and served as its president. Eight years later he built a ten-mile-long railroad from Hartsville to Darlington in order to establish rail connections between Hartsville and the Atlantic Coast Line, which bought the Coker railroad in 1892. By that time, another project was laying the groundwork for the most important product of Coker's entrepreneurial efforts. With Coker's backing, his son James, a graduate of Stevens Institute of Technology in New Jersey, had started Carolina Fiber Company, the first commercially successful effort to produce paper from southern pine. In 1899 Coker's Southern Novelties Company began turning the paper into products used by the textile industry. The company evolved into Sonoco Products Company, a major international manufacturer of packaging products for industrial and consumer markets. Coker's interest grew with Hartsville, the population of which increased from 300 in 1890 to 2,900 in 1910. His other interests included the Hartsville Electric and Water Company, a cotton mill, a cotton gin, a cotton seed oil mill, a fertilizer factory, a lumber company, and a furniture factory. His son David founded the well-known firm, Coker's Pedigree Seed Company.

Education was the principal beneficiary of Coker's philanthropic and community efforts. In the 1860s he helped establish a Sunday school in Hartsville, the main purpose of which was to teach illiterate children to read. Later he supported the introduction of graded elementary schools in the town and helped start the privately funded Welsh Neck High School in the 1890s. One of the first high schools in the state, Welsh Neck had 200 students at its peak and dorms for those who needed to board at the school. In 1908, when the state instituted public high schools, Welsh Neck became Coker College. It was named for its main benefactor, whose gifts to the new college totaled more than $200,000.

Coker had serious reservations about traditional religious beliefs and ideas. He claimed that nondenominational institutions like Coker College "helped the cause of education in the State, and that the teachings of the colleges tended to get people away from narrow and irrational religious opinions" (Norwood, p. 436). Charles Darwin obviously influenced Coker, who read widely, especially in the sciences.

Coker died in Hartsville. Success in his many agricultural and business activities made him one of the richest men in South Carolina, possibly the richest in his lifetime. He embodied Henry W. Grady's aspirations for the postbellum New South: diversification of economic activities, urban boosterism, application of modern science and technology, and investment of time and money in the community. Coker's life and career, which spanned the Old South and the New, belie the notions that there was a sharp dichotomy between the two, that the Old South lacked an entrepreneurial spirit, and that the economy of the postbellum South experienced little change or growth.

• Coker's papers are in the South Caroliniana Library at the University of South Carolina. He recorded the history of his Civil War company in *History of Company G, Ninth S.C. Regiment, Infantry, S.C. Army and of Company E, Sixth S.C. Regiment, Infantry, S.C. Army* (1899). The best sources available on Coker are James Lide Coker, *Memorial Exercises, Founder's Day, Coker College* (1919), and George Lee Simpson, Jr., *The Cokers of Carolina: A Social Biography of a Family* (1956). Also useful are J. W. Norwood, "Major James Lide Coker," in *Rambles in the Pee Dee Basin*, ed. H. T. Cook (1926), and Edwin Mims, "The South Realizing Itself," *World's Work* 22 (1911): 14972–87.

THOMAS E. TERRILL

COLBERT, Levi (1759–3 June 1834), Chickasaw political leader, was born at Oldtown, near present-day Tupelo, Mississippi, in the old Chickasaw nation, the son of James Logan Colbert, a Scots trader, and the second of his three Chickasaw wives (name unknown). Over five decades the elder Colbert became a dominant figure among the Chickasaws. Through his two daughters and sons William, George, Levi, Samuel, Joseph, and James he founded a Chickasaw dynasty prominent for more than 150 years. Levi Colbert emerged as the most influential Chickasaw leader in the critical period during which his people were pressured to emigrate west of the Mississippi River.

Levi Colbert and his brothers exemplified the biracial, bicultural elite that assumed leadership among the Five Civilized Tribes at the turn of the nineteenth century. In matrilineal Chickasaw society, they were fully accepted as clan and tribe members. Although illiterate, they were bilingual. From their father they learned to function in the developing market economy and political system of the Anglo-American frontier. These factors, combined with shrewdness and ambition, allowed the Colberts to manipulate Chickasaw government and diplomacy.

Levi Colbert differed from his brothers in that he entered Chickasaw politics relatively late. While his brothers aided and emulated their father, Colbert remained quietly at home, probably near Oldtown, living a comfortable life with his wives Te-mush-sharhoc-tay and Mintahoyo and their children. In 1795, when a war party of 1,000 Creeks swept down on Oldtown, from which nearly all the warriors were absent, Colbert rallied 200 old men and boys and decisively repelled the invaders. In recognition of his success, the Chickasaw council named him "Itawambo-mingo" (Bench Chief).

During the next decade Colbert pursued his own interests while gradually involving himself in Chickasaw politics. By 1805 he had moved his trading and agricultural operations to Buzzard's Roost Creek just south of the Tennessee River. Near present-day Margerum, Alabama, Levi, George, and James Colbert operated a ferry. Meanwhile, in the Spanish-American rivalry to control their common frontier, the Colberts usually sided with Piomingo, head of the pro-American faction, and inherited his power at his death. As Anglo-American settlers flooded neighboring public lands, Levi and his brothers steered diplomacy. In 1805 they helped negotiate the cession of all Chickasaw lands north of the Tennessee River.

The Colberts assumed de facto leadership of the Chickasaw nation that same year. The death of their main rival left a power vacuum not filled by the ineffective king, Chinubby. With changing times, traditional Chickasaws, comprising three-fourths of the nation, yielded control to men such as the more acculturated Colberts, who better understood the new conditions. The Colberts responded by managing the economic and political systems of the Chickasaw nation with "imagination, ingenuity, initiative, and unmitigated brass" (Gibson, p. 134). In 1818 Levi moved to Cotton Gin Port at the head of navigation on the Tombigbee River to exploit trade between the Tennessee Valley and New Orleans. With their political power, Levi and his brothers influenced the Chickasaw council. They saw to it that the 1816 treaty with the United States excluded Anglo-American traders from Chickasaw lands. In 1819 their insistence that the federal trading post be moved out of their country eliminated the last obstacle to their commercial monopoly. By the 1820s their trading, shipping, planting, and stock raising enterprises placed the Colberts among the wealthiest Chickasaws.

However, federal pressure to vacate more land disturbed the Chickasaw nation. Although Levi Colbert led those who opposed any further cessions, he was persuaded to sign the 1818 Jackson Purchase agreement ceding western Kentucky and Tennessee, for which he received $8,500 and considerations. Even this failed to satisfy public demand that all eastern tribes be removed west of the Mississippi River. Removal demands escalated during the late 1820s; at the same time Levi succeeded his older brother William as the leader of the Colbert faction. Thomas McKenney, sent in 1827 to negotiate with Chickasaws, noted that Levi was the soul of the nation: "They move at his bidding. . . . As to the King, he is without power. . . . He is but the subject of some more able and intelligent minds—Levi Colbert is that mind" (Braden, p. 231). Still opposed to removal, Colbert was persuaded by McKenney at least to explore the southwest frontier in search of a new Chickasaw homeland. His agreement caused a split among the people, but his 1828 expedition failed to find an acceptable location.

President Andrew Jackson's support of the Indian Removal Act of 1830 increased the seriousness of the problem. Concurrent actions of Alabama and Mississippi to extend their jurisdiction over Chickasaw lands allowed depredations against the Chickasaws to go unpunished. Eventually Chickasaws saw no alternative except removal to the West. At Franklin, Tennessee, in 1830 Colbert agreed that the Chickasaws would remove if acceptable lands in the West were found, but this treaty was not ratified by the U.S. Congress. In October he led a reconnaissance of present-day Oklahoma and Texas, again failing to find a suitable place. Unremitting pressure on the Chickasaws ended in new negotiations in 1832. Colbert's illness during the writing of the resulting Treaty of Pontotoc meant the Chickasaws were poorly represented as they finally agreed to remove. However, it did contain a Colbert provision that their lands be surveyed, allotted, and sold on the open market, thus increasing their compensation substantially. Fit again, Colbert won treaty revisions, including creation of the Chickasaw Incompetent Commission charged with protecting the rights of Chickasaws ignorant of land laws. Colbert was still struggling to repair unfavorable elements of the treaty, find a Chickasaw homeland, and prevent their incorporation with the Choctaws in the West when he died at his daughter's home near Buzzard's Roost Creek.

Astute, acquisitive, and self-interested, sometimes at the expense of his people, Levi Colbert was also hospitable and accessible to fellow Chickasaws, who held him in great respect. He aided Christian missionaries and supported English education, particularly for his twelve sons, eight daughters, and adopted children. Thereby he assured continuing Colbert leadership and helped preserve Chickasaw nationhood in the new homeland in the Indian Territory.

• Levi Colbert was illiterate, so the few surviving documents bearing his mark were probably dictated. They may be located in federal records such as those relating to the Chickasaw Agency. A useful article is Guy B. Braden, "The Colberts and the Chickasaw Nation," *Tennessee Historical Quarterly* 17 (Sept. 1958): 222–49 and 17 (Dec. 1958): 318–35. A self-published genealogical work by Don Martini, *Chickasaw Empire: The Story of the Colbert Family* (1986), is fairly comprehensive. Colbert's career may best be understood in context from Arrell M. Gibson, *The Chickasaws*, vol. 109 of *The Civilization of the American Indian* (1971).

MARY JANE WARDE

COLBERT, William (fl. 1794–1834), Chickasaw tribal leader, was born probably near the Chickasaw tribal center of present-day Tupelo, Mississippi, the son of James Logan Colbert, a Scottish trader, and his second wife, a Chickasaw woman whose name is not recorded. James Logan Colbert had entered Chickasaw country soon after arriving in the United States in 1736 and was soon accepted by the Chickasaw tribe. Through effective trading and by demonstrating prowess in battle against the French and later the Spanish, the elder Colbert acquired great wealth (including slaves) and became a political force within the tribe as well. Fathering a total of eight children by three wives, his six sons all achieved social and political leadership within the Chickasaws at a time when the tribe was undergoing profound changes. The advent of the first white traders, several of whom were readily accepted into the Chickasaw ranks, created a mixed-blooded elite within the tribe that, although it did not exceed a quarter of the tribe in membership, soon came to dominate tribal proceedings.

William Colbert (whose Native American name was Chooshemataha) may have assisted his father in his early military campaigns during which the Chickasaws (allied with the British) clashed with both the French and later the Spanish. He definitely participated in the Battle of Fallen Timbers on 20 August 1794, where he led Chickasaw warriors in support of General "Mad" Anthony Wayne's campaign against the hostile Native American tribes of the Northwest. In the following year Colbert, as a tribal leader, led a delegation of Chickasaws to Washington, D.C., where they met with President George Washington in an attempt to gain support against Spanish encroachment on their territory, as the Spanish had established a post at Chickasaw Bluff (modern-day Memphis, Tenn.).

In later years Colbert, like his brothers, turned his interests toward commerce. The treaty signed by the Chickasaws on 24 October 1801 (Colbert was apparently present on that occasion, as he frequently was when such matters were under consideration) gave the United States the right-of-way through Chickasaw land that soon became the Natchez Trace, while the Chickasaws received the exclusive right to maintain ferryboats and inns along the pathway. The Colbert brothers seized this opportunity, with William taking

over the operation of a ferry on the Duck River in Tennessee. His verbal agreement with John Gordon regarding the operation of the ferry (with Colbert serving as silent partner and Gordon conducting the actual operations) soon fell apart. Their contract was placed in writing on 4 February 1804, at which time it was witnessed by James Robertson and Andrew Jackson, among others.

William Colbert's martial habits proved hard to break, however; he returned to military campaigning in the service of the United States during the War of 1812, serving for nine months in the Third Infantry Regiment of the army. He later fought (late 1814) against the Creeks, engaging in combat with that tribe in the vicinity of the Escambia River. After encountering a Creek fort, Colbert and his men destroyed the structure and returned to camp with eighty-five prisoners who had escaped death in the battle. Several sources indicate that he was a personal favorite of Andrew Jackson, who rewarded him for his services with a fine military uniform coat, which Colbert wore only on special occasions.

While it is likely that Colbert married at least once and had several children, their names have been lost to history. At some point in his life Colbert joined the Presbyterian church, later becoming an elder. He also donated land for a church of that denomination in present-day Pontotoc County, Mississippi, and his last recorded appearance occurred in 1834, when he appeared before a church meeting and was forced to repent of an episode of drunkenness.

The Colbert brothers played a significant role in the affairs of the Chickasaws during what was, in all probability, the most tumultuous period in their history. Faced with changes in their location as well as their very way of life, the Colberts managed to profit handsomely from their business opportunities yet also strove to defend their tribe against all aggressors, both military and economic.

• Material relating to the Colberts and their activities is in the Draper collection, Frontier Wars Manuscripts, Western History Collections, University of Oklahoma Library, Norman, and in the Records of the Office of Indian Affairs, National Archives, Washington, D.C. The best secondary sources regarding the family are Don Martini, *Chickasaw Empire: The Story of the Colbert Family* (1986); Arrell M. Gibson, *The Chickasaws* (1971); and Guy B. Braden, "The Colberts and the Chickasaw Nation," *Tennessee Historical Quarterly* 17 (Sept. 1958): 222–49 and (Dec. 1958): 318–35. Dated but still useful are Grant Foreman, *Indian Removal* (1932), and H. B. Cushman, *History of the Choctaw, Chickasaw and Natchez Indians* (1899).

EDWARD L. LACH, JR.

COLBY, Bainbridge (22 Dec. 1869–11 Apr. 1950), lawyer and U.S. secretary of state, was born in St. Louis, Missouri, the son of John Peck Colby, a lawyer, and Frances Bainbridge. He received an A.B. from Williams College in 1890; he then entered Columbia University Law School but transferred to the New York Law School after a year. Upon receiving an LL.B. in

1892 he began law practice in New York, soon winning recognition as a litigation lawyer. Among his many well-known clients was Mark Twain. He was a counsel in cases involving the Equitable Life Assurance Society and the Northern Securities Corporation. He married Nathalie Sedgwick Washburn of Stockbridge, Massachusetts in 1895. They had three children.

Colby entered politics as a Republican but was elected to the New York Assembly on a fusion ticket in 1901. Declining a second term, he nonetheless remained active in politics. He supported Theodore Roosevelt (1858–1919) for president in 1912 and helped organize the Progressive National Convention of that year. He wrote "The Stolen Nomination," a widely circulated Progressive manifesto claiming that William Howard Taft's followers had stolen the Republican nomination from Roosevelt.

Colby devoted much effort to keeping the Progressive party alive after the 1912 defeat. He accepted the party's nomination for senator from New York in 1914 but was not elected. When the Republicans nominated Charles Evans Hughes for president in 1916, he called upon the Progressive convention to nominate Roosevelt. The convention did so, unanimously, but Roosevelt declined and advised Progressives to support Hughes. Angered, Colby transferred his support to President Woodrow Wilson, praising the president's support for progressive legislation. Colby became a member of the Democratic party but declined to serve on its campaign committee, instead forming a committee of Progressives to support Wilson. He toured the country, speaking in the president's behalf.

After the United States entered World War I Colby accepted appointment as a commissioner of the Shipping Board and its Emergency Fleet Corporation. As a member of a mission headed by Colonel Edward M. House he took part in negotiations in London and Paris establishing the Allied Maritime Transport Council.

In February 1920, after Wilson forced Secretary of State Robert Lansing to resign, telling him he wanted "some one whose mind would more willingly go along with mine," the president asked Colby to succeed Lansing. Most observers had believed Wilson would choose either Undersecretary of State Frank Polk or Secretary of War Newton D. Baker, but the president believed that, despite Colby's lack of diplomatic experience, he was the best person to express in writing his ideas about international relations—something he himself could do only with difficulty because of his stroke. Warning that the president's illness and the vice president's fragile health meant that the new secretary would be their possible successor, Senator Henry Cabot Lodge (1850–1924) insisted that the Foreign Relations Committee, of which he was chairman, give the nomination a prolonged investigation. Irritation over Colby's changes of party allegiance and political animosities were other reasons for delay. Four days before Colby took the oath of office on 23 March, the Senate voted on the Versailles Treaty, only to repeat its failure of November 19. Wilson and Colby continued the struggle for Senate consent and membership in the League of Nations. Believing he could run for the presidency again and garner new support for the treaty, Wilson asked Colby to attend the Democratic National Convention to further his plans. But other Democratic leaders, aware that for Wilson another presidential race was impossible, persuaded Colby not to present the president's name.

The League issue notwithstanding, Colby's record as secretary of state was of considerable importance. In a note of 20 November 1920, usually called the "Mesopotamia note" because it dealt with American rights in Iraq, he refuted a British contention that only the League and its members could settle the terms of mandates. He sent a similar note to the League concerning the former German islands in the Pacific. His stand contributed to Secretary of State Charles Evans Hughes's successful diplomacy at the Washington Conference of 1921–1922 concerning a cable station on the island of Yap. Colby's statements in regard to the Bolshevik government of Russia were even stronger and became the basis of the U.S. policy of nonrecognition that lasted until 1933. In regard to Latin America, his actions were more positive. His negotiations with Mexico over American-owned oil and land interests facilitated Hughes's later agreements with the Mexican revolutionary government and the restoration of normal diplomatic relations. Marking the administration's retreat from interventionist policies, Colby announced that American marines would in due course leave Haiti and the Dominican Republic, and in December 1920 he visited Brazil, Uruguay, and Argentina, explaining the president's hemispheric policies and disavowing imperialistic intentions on the part of the United States.

When the Wilson administration ended, the former president and Colby formed a law partnership, but this was dissolved after a year. Colby's stature as a lawyer increased as years passed. When Franklin D. Roosevelt ran for president in 1932, Colby supported him, but his enthusiasm for Roosevelt soon waned. The Hearst Press retained him as counsel in its struggle with the National Recovery Administration, which sought to impose regulations on the press. Colby had discovered another cause. He published articles on freedom of the press, one of them an editorial for the Hearst Press that received honorable mention for the Pulitzer Prize. He supported the Republican presidential candidates in 1936 and 1940.

Colby's marriage ended in 1929 after Nathalie Sedgwick Colby had won acclaim for novels describing the shallow lives of wealthy Americans. Believing she had satirized him, Colby insisted upon divorce. That same year he married Anne Ahlstrand Ely, a widow. He died at his home in Bemus Point, New York.

• Colby's papers are in the Library of Congress. His official papers as secretary of state are in the State Department files in the National Archives. Colby wrote *The Close of Woodrow Wilson's Administration and the Final Years* (1930). John Spargo, "Bainbridge Colby, Secretary of State March 23, 1920, to March 3, 1921," in *American Secretaries of State and Their Diplomacy,* vol. 10, ed. Samuel Flagg Bemis et al. (1928), is a brief sketch by a well-known writer who knew Colby. Daniel M. Smith, *Aftermath of War: Bainbridge Colby and Wilsonian Diplomacy, 1920–1921* (1970), is the most comprehensive study of its topic. It includes much of the material in Smith's "Bainbridge Colby and the Good Neighbor Policy, 1920–1921," *Mississippi Valley Historical Review* 50 (June 1963): 56–78. Colby's role in 1920 presidential politics appears in Wesley M. Bagby, *The Road to Normalcy: The Presidential Campaign and Election of 1920* (1962), and in Arthur C. Walworth, *Woodrow Wilson* (2 vols., 1965). An obituary is in the *New York Times,* 12 Apr. 1950.

CALVIN D. DAVIS

COLBY, Clara Dorothy Bewick (5 Aug. 1846–7 Sept. 1916), woman's rights activist and publisher, was born in Gloucester, England, the daughter of Thomas Bewick and Clara Willingham. The Bewicks immigrated to the United States in 1849, settling on a farm in Windsor, Wisconsin; Clara and her maternal grandparents joined them in 1854. She entered the University of Wisconsin in 1865, initially enrolling in the "normal department" set up for women. However, with faculty assistance, she pursued the "classical course" designed for men. In 1869 she graduated as valedictorian of Wisconsin's first class of women to be awarded the bachelor of philosophy degree. She remained at the university until 1871, teaching Latin and history and taking graduate classes in French, Greek, and chemistry.

Clara married Leonard Wright Colby in June 1871. They moved to Beatrice, Nebraska, where they lived until 1889. For the next four years, owing to Leonard's government appointment, they alternated between Beatrice and Washington, D.C. The couple adopted three children, two of whom survived to adulthood. Their third child was a daughter, an infant Sioux taken from the battlefield of Wounded Knee when Leonard directed the burial detail there as commander of the Nebraska National Guard. The preferred Sioux spelling of her name is Zintkala Nuni, but she was called Zintka her whole life. After 1893 Clara Bewick Colby (as she was known throughout her life) established Washington as her permanent residence. Leonard eventually returned to Nebraska where the Colbys finalized a divorce in 1906 after a separation of ten years. Bewick Colby's daughter and divorce were frequent points of attack from her detractors inside and outside the woman's rights movement. The divorce also contributed to Bewick Colby's longstanding financial difficulties.

Bewick Colby began her public life through community service. She was instrumental in initiating a library, community theater, and Chautauqua Park for Beatrice. Her woman's rights activity began with the editing of a local newspaper column called "Woman's Work." Her specific involvement with woman suffrage began in 1881 with her election as vice president at large for the newly organized Nebraska Woman

Suffrage Association. In 1885 she became the group's president, a position she held until 1898.

In 1883 Bewick Colby began her life's central undertaking, the publication of the *Woman's Tribune,* a suffrage newspaper. For its first year, it was the official publication of the Nebraska Woman Suffrage Association; thereafter, it was maintained solely by Bewick Colby, who performed all tasks from editing to typesetting. Although Susan B. Anthony represented it as the organ of the National Woman Suffrage Association, the paper was never formally affiliated with any national group. However, as the second-longest-running woman suffrage newspaper, it was significant for several reasons. First, Bewick Colby designed the *Tribune* as a general circulation newspaper, an approach unique among suffrage publishers. For example, in 1898 she received the first war correspondent's pass issued to a woman publisher of a woman's paper. Second, the *Tribune* was probably the first woman's paper published daily by a woman. From 27 March to 5 April 1888, while reporting the activities of the International Council of Women, the *Tribune* achieved a daily circulation of 12,500 copies. Finally, the *Tribune* was highly regarded by movement leaders. Elizabeth Cady Stanton considered it "the best suffrage paper ever published" and allowed it to serialize two of her most important works, her autobiography and *The Woman's Bible.* In 1904 Bewick Colby moved publication of the *Tribune* to Portland, Oregon, where she lived until the paper ceased in 1909.

From 1887 to 1896 Bewick Colby also published, on an irregular schedule, the *National Bulletin,* an offshoot pamphlet. Whereas the *Tribune* was circulated largely to supporters of woman's rights, the *Bulletin* was overtly designed as "propaganda." It was smaller and cheaper than its parent publication so that suffrage societies could circulate it more easily to nonsupporters. In spite of the fact that these publications were serious financial drains for Bewick Colby, she maintained her commitment to publishing. She had enunciated her commitment in the March 1885 edition of the *Woman's Tribune*: "The spoken word has its power for the day, but for building up a new line of thought in the popular heart there must be the written word, which shall be quietly digested and made part of the reader's own thought. Then the change in belief comes irresistibly."

Bewick Colby was also an activist and speaker. She served as an officer of reform organizations such as the National Woman's Press Association, the International Women's Union, the Association for the Advancement of Women, the Federal Suffrage Association, and the International New Thought Alliance. As a member of the National (later National American) Woman Suffrage Association, she chaired the Federal Suffrage Committee and the Committee on Industrial Problems Relating to Women and Children, and she spoke regularly at conventions between 1886 and 1914. She worked in several state suffrage campaigns and testified before congressional committees. Ultimately she became one of the chief spokespersons for federal suffrage, arguing that woman suffrage was granted in preexisting constitutional provisions, thereby negating the need for state action or a constitutional amendment. She also worked for women abroad, serving as a delegate to the International Congress of Women (1899), the first International Moral Education Congress (1908), the first International Races Congress (1911), the International Woman Suffrage Alliance (1913), and the International Peace Congress (1913).

Bewick Colby spent the years 1909 to 1916 lecturing throughout the United States and Europe. This period saw the culmination of her interest in spirituality. She had served on the revising committee of Stanton's *The Woman's Bible* (1895), writing several of the commentaries. She was Stanton's staunchest defender when the work came under attack by suffragists. By the end of her life, Bewick Colby identified herself as a New Thought follower and supported herself by giving lecture courses on spirituality. She maintained a link between religion and reform, as in her address "The Spiritual Significance of Woman Suffrage." She died in Palo Alto, California.

Bewick Colby is representative of what Anthony called suffragist "lieutenants," women who, while not themselves national officers, influenced movement leaders and members. Anthony said that no one wrote, edited, or spoke better than Bewick Colby. What separated her from her more successful and visible counterparts was her commitment to marginal positions, fringe philosophies, and her own newspaper. She preferred to be a "free lance" rather than compromise her principles or her positions, ultimately sacrificing her family and her financial well-being to her cause.

• Bewick Colby's papers are in two primary collections. The larger is the Clara Bewick Colby Collection in the State Historical Society of Wisconsin Library, Madison. This library also holds a complete set of the *Woman's Tribune* and most available issues of the *National Bulletin*. The Henry E. Huntington Library, San Marino, Calif., has a substantial collection of Bewick Colby materials, primarily correspondence. The *Tribune* is available on microfilm from the Library of Congress. The *Bulletin* is available on microfiche in the Gerritsen collection of the University of Kansas. Important materials relevant to her work in Nebraska are in the Nebraska State Historical Society Library, Lincoln. The six-volume work, *History of Woman Suffrage*, ed. Elizabeth Cady Stanton et al. (1881–1922), contains many excerpts from Bewick Colby speeches.

An important contemporary biography of Bewick Colby is by her associate Olympia Brown, *Democratic Ideals: A Memorial Sketch of Clara B. Colby* (1917). The sole comprehensive modern assessment is E. Claire Jerry, "Clara Bewick Colby and the *Woman's Tribune*: Strategies of a Free Lance Movement Leader" (Ph.D. diss., Univ. of Kansas, 1986). The most inclusive list of her works is Jerry, "Clara Bewick Colby," in *Women Public Speakers in the United States, 1800–1925*, ed. Karlyn Kohrs Campbell (1993).

E. CLAIRE JERRY

COLBY, Gertrude Kline (1875?–1 Feb. 1960), dance educator, was born in Minneapolis, Minnesota. Her parents' names and occupations are unknown. While little is known of her childhood, Colby was reportedly interested in physical activities from an early age. She began her higher education with a brief stint at the University of Minnesota School of Medicine (dates unknown). In 1910 she attended Harvard University for the first of four summer sessions led by Dudley A. Sargent, a leader in American physical education. The program exposed future teachers to current theory and practice, including an educational dance form developed by Melvin Ballou Gilbert, which consisted of ballet technique in soft shoes with adapted arm and torso movements. Gilbert's approach was specifically designed to provide female students with training in physical fitness and grace. Colby studied ballet teacher training with Louis Chalif, American Delsartism and pantomime with Eva Allen Alberti, and Dalcroze eurythmics with an unknown instructor. American Delsartism was an approach to physical culture and expression founded on the theories of the French teacher and theorist François Delsarte and developed by his followers in the United States in the late nineteenth century. Eurythmics was a method of music training through physical exercises created by the French music teacher Emile Jaques-Dalcroze in the late nineteenth and early twentieth centuries. Both approaches were appropriated by dance educators and adapted to dance education. Colby received a B.S. in physical education from Teachers College, Columbia University probably in 1913.

From 1913 to 1916 Colby was engaged at the Speyer School, a progressive laboratory school connected with Teachers College. She was asked to develop a rhythmic movement program based on children's "natural" movements that would encourage their individual expression and relate to other elements in the curriculum. This assignment reflected the progressive educators' emphasis on creative activities as a necessary aspect of education for the "whole child." Colby's supervisors at Speyer insisted that she abandon the traditional dance genres that she had learned and find a new approach that would encourage the children's own creativity. She proved so successful that, after the Speyer School was dismantled in 1916, she was appointed instructor at Teachers College with the charge of developing a teacher training program in dance. Colby offered the resulting course, "Natural Dance," from 1918 until her retirement in 1931. She also taught at the University of California at Berkeley in 1922 and at the University of California at Los Angeles in 1923. She trained hundreds of prospective physical education teachers, several of whom, including Ruth L. Murray, Mary P. O'Donnell, and Martha Hill, became the next generation of leaders in educational dance.

When Colby began teaching in 1913, none of the approaches she had studied seemed appropriate to the new educational ideas that were being explored at Teachers College. She sought "something less formal and more in harmony with the interests and activities of everyday life" (*Natural Rhythms and Dances*, p. 7). While she experimented with elements from her varied training, Colby reported that her ideas did not fully crystallize until she saw a performance (probably in 1917) by Isadora Duncan, whose dance art was based on ideals of naturalness and expressivity and a close relationship between music and movement.

In 1921 Colby published *The Conflict: A Health Masque in Pantomime*. In this guide for teachers, she describes her 1920 revised version of a physical education masque that had first been presented at Teachers College in 1913. The 1920 production—performed at the annual American Physical Education Association convention—combined pantomime, dance, and music in a statement promoting health.

Colby's second book, *Natural Rhythms and Dances* (1922), is a collection of the studies and dances she developed for college women's physical education classes. She based these dances on familiar actions such as walking, skipping, running, leaping, playing ball, rolling hoops, and flying kites. She considered such movements "natural" in contrast with formalized dance vocabularies such as those that had been adapted from ballet and folk dance for educational purposes. The rationale of her work, as set forth in the introduction, reflects the typical 1920s progressive educator's faith in the child as the source of art, beauty, and spontaneity. Her program was not designed to teach difficult dance techniques but rather to help the students develop the kinds of movements they had known from childhood "to a higher form of the art of dancing" (p. 3). Her goal was to preserve "the natural spontaneity of the child while developing depth and maturity of expression and experience" (p. 8). Colby apparently never married or had children. She died in New York City.

Colby synthesized various trends in education and dance that had developed in the late nineteenth and early twentieth centuries. She created an educational dance form that fulfilled the early twentieth-century goals of progressive education, particularly women's physical education. Her technique not only provided physical exercise but also offered opportunities for creativity and exploration of the ways the body could reflect and express ideas and feelings. Through Colby's work, dance in American higher education was launched in a direction that it has continued to follow, in many respects, to the present day.

• There is a clipping file on Colby in the Dance Collection of the New York Library for the Performing Arts at Lincoln Center. Information on Colby is in Mary P. O'Donnell, "Gertrude Colby," *Dance Observer*, Jan. 1936, pp. 1, 8; and in Mildred C. Spiesman, "Creative Dance in American Life and Education" (D.Ed. diss., Teachers College, Columbia Univ., 1949). See also Spiesman's series titled "American Pioneers in Educational Creative Dance," especially chap. 3, "The Natural Dance Program," *Dance Magazine*, June 1951, pp. 16, 42–45; and Nancy Lee Chalfa Ruyter, *Reformers and Visionaries; The Americanization of the Art of Dance* (1979).

NANCY LEE CHALFA RUYTER

COLBY, Luther (12 Oct. 1814–7 Oct. 1894), Spiritualist editor, was born in Amesbury, Massachusetts, the son of Captain William Colby and Mary (maiden name unknown). After a common school education, Colby learned the printing trade as a youth. In 1836 he moved to Boston to work for the *Boston Daily Post*, where he rose from journeyman to night editor. In 1856, together with fellow printer William Berry, Colby attended séances with the Boston medium Frances (Mrs. J. H.) Conant. Deeply impressed by Conant's mediumship, he became convinced of the reality of communication with the spirits of the dead and an advocate of the new religious movement of Spiritualism. Later that year a spirit speaking through Conant told William Berry that he and Luther Colby would start a paper titled the *Banner of Light* to spread word of the new revelation. Within a few months Luther Colby & Co. issued a prospectus for the new paper, stating that "the spiritual manifestations now being developed demand a vehicle of communication which all will respect." He devoted the rest of his life to the *Banner of Light*, which served as the foremost organ of American Spiritualism from 1857 to 1907.

Between the inception of Spiritualism as a popular movement in 1848 and the debut of the *Banner of Light* in 1857, a few dozen editors attempted to provide a newspaper for the movement, and dozens more would join them before the century was out. But Luther Colby succeeded where almost all of his colleagues failed. The vast majority of Spiritualist publications folded within five years. Of the 200 or so Spiritualist periodicals published in the nineteenth century, the *Banner* was the longest lived and the most widely circulated. It was a truly national organ, uniting advocates of a popular but controversial faith in every state and territory. Unlike many editors in the special-interest press of his day, Colby kept himself in the background, devoting his efforts to the production of a first-rate vehicle for the propagation of Spiritualism.

Colby's recipe for success placed spirit communication at the center of an attractive, readable, and meticulously edited publication. One page of the eight-page weekly was devoted solely to spirit messages received at the "*Banner* Free Circle," at which Conant was employed by the paper to give séances open to the public. Subtitled "A Journal of Romance, Literature, and General Intelligence," the *Banner* also published serial fiction as well as philosophical articles about Spiritualism and reports of Spiritualist meetings and conventions. The editors took a moderate position in favor of women's rights, antislavery, and other reforms that demanded the attention of religious liberals. This moderation helped avoid the controversies that plagued many more radical Spiritualist editors. An unflagging critic of what he believed to be a brutal and unjust government policy toward Native Americans, Colby never tired of editorializing on Indian affairs.

William Berry died at the battle of Antietam, and the financial upheaval caused by the Civil War forced the paper into bankruptcy. Colby lost ownership temporarily to William White but remained editor. At White's death, Colby again became proprietor together with Isaac Rich. In addition to their newspaper, Colby & Rich published a great deal of Spiritualist literature in book form, including the thirty-volume uniform edition of the works of Andrew Jackson Davis. Colby never married, devoting himself entirely to the *Banner of Light* for thirty-seven years, until his death at the hotel in Boston at which he had lived for twelve years.

• The *Banner of Light* reveals little about Colby's life but much about his beliefs and intellectual outlook. Biographical information is available in John W. Day, *A Biographic Memorial of Luther Colby* (1895), and in memorial articles in the *Banner of Light*, 13 and 20 Oct. 1894. On the Spiritualist press, see Ann Braude, "News from the Spirit World: A Checklist of American Spiritualist Periodicals, 1847–1900," *Proceedings of the American Antiquarian Society* 99 (1989): 339–462. On the movement to which Colby devoted his life, see R. Laurence Moore, *In Search of White Crows: Spiritualism, Parapsychology, and American Culture* (1977), and Braude, *Radical Spirits: Spiritualism and Women's Rights in Nineteenth-Century America* (1989).

ANN D. BRAUDE

COLCORD, Joanna Carver (18 Mar. 1882–8 Apr. 1960), social work administrator and leader, was born at sea—delivered by her ship-captain father—to Jane Sweetser and Lincoln Alden Colcord. Both her parents were seagoing people from Maine; her father often brought his family, which included a younger son, on his voyages, so that Joanna Colcord spent many years at sea and abroad. Later, as a middle-aged social worker, she wrote two books on sea chanties and one on the language of sailors.

Joanna completed high school through correspondence courses and attended the University of Maine (1902–1909). After earning a B.S. and M.S. in chemistry, she held several applied chemistry jobs in which she was disappointed. Had universities been more open to women as Ph.D. students and faculty, Colcord might had have a career as an academic scientist, for she always liked research and endeavored to make social work a scientific discipline.

Colcord studied at the New York School of Philanthropy, where she was influenced and mentored primarily by Mary Richmond. She began her social work career in 1911 with the New York Charity Organization Society. Except for a stint with the Red Cross in the Virgin Islands from 1920 to 1921, she held this position until 1925, when she became general secretary of the Family Welfare Association of Minneapolis. In 1929 she returned to New York City to head the Charity Organization Division of the influential Russell Sage Foundation; from this position, which she held until 1945, she became one of a handful of national social work leaders.

Throughout her career Colcord worked to raise the standards of professional training required of social workers and to promote what she considered scientific research and administration in social work. Her influence was at its greatest during the depression, when she was a leading voice in encouraging the private social work establishment to support federal relief and economic security provisions. She argued that it was part of social work's appropriate function to agitate for better social provision. Above all she was quick to understand that casework methods, which during the Progressive Era had come to form the essence of social work's claim to professionalism, were no longer adequate in this period of mass deprivation. For example, in 1930 she called a national conference of private social work executives to plan for relief for the hard winter that she correctly anticipated.

During the New Deal she became an important liaison between private social work and the federal government's welfare and relief administrators. She supported federal responsibility not only for relief, but also for a comprehensive economic security program—including not only programs that were passed, but other vital ones, such as health insurance, that were not—and she organized private social work support for such a program. By 1936 she was among those social workers who were critical of the Roosevelt administration for not doing enough to relieve poverty and redistribute wealth and for retaining poor-law traditions in public provision, such as the scrutinizing of public-assistance applicants to make sure they were deserving. Yet she also defended her profession. In 1943 she responded critically to an influential book (Josephine Brown's *Public Relief 1929–1939*) that took private social work to task for its late and reluctant support of mass public relief.

Colcord's private life ended as unconventionally as it had begun. She retired in 1945 and returned to the sea she loved so much, to live with her brother's family in Searsport, Maine. She had always been single, in this respect typical of a generation of white professional and activist women who had accepted the necessity of choosing between marriage and career. In 1950, at age sixty-eight, she married her friend and co-worker of forty years, Frank Bruno. She died of a stroke in Lebanon, Indiana, where she had been living with a stepson.

• There are slightly longer biographies of Colcord in Clarke Chambers, *Notable American Women*, and in Beverly Stadum, *Biographical Dictionary of Social Welfare in America*. Materials by and about Colcord can be found in several collections at the Social Welfare History Archives at the University of Minnesota. Her own works include *Broken Homes: A Study of Family Desertion and Its Social Treatment* (1919); *The Long View: Papers and Addresses by Mary E. Richmond* (1930), which she edited; *Community Planning in Unemployment Emergencies* (1930); *Setting Up a Program of Work Relief* (1931); *Community Programs for Subsistence Gardens* (1933), with Mary Johnston; *Cash Relief* (1936); and *Your Community, Its Provisions for Health, Education, Safety, and Welfare* (1939). She also wrote two books on sea culture: *Roll and Go, Songs of American Sailormen* (1924; republished as *Songs of American Sailormen* 1938) and *Sea Language Comes Ashore*

(1945). She wrote a regular column in *Survey* from 1932 to 1935, published many articles, and several of her speeches can be found in the *Proceedings* of the National Conference of Social Work.

LINDA GORDON

COLDEN, Cadwallader (7 Feb. 1689–20 Sept. 1776), physician, natural scientist, and lieutenant governor of New York, was born of Scottish parents in Ireland, where his mother (name unknown) was visiting. His father was the Reverend Alexander Colden of Duns, Scotland. Colden graduated in 1705 from the University of Edinburgh. He then studied medicine in London but, lacking the money to establish a medical practice in Great Britain, migrated to Philadelphia in 1710. Welcomed by his mother's sister Elizabeth Hill, Colden established himself as a merchant and physician. He returned to Scotland briefly in 1715, where in November of that year he married Alice Chrystie of Kelso, Scotland. After their marriage they returned to Philadelphia; the couple had eleven children. During a 1717 visit to New York, Colden was persuaded by Governor Robert Hunter to move to that colony. In 1720 Colden was appointed surveyor general of New York.

The assured income of his surveyor post gave Colden the leisure to pursue other interests. A multifaceted man, he became a leading scientist of his era. He was a cartographer, compiled astronomical tables, invented stereotyping, and wrote extensively on history, botany, physics, and medicine. Although Colden gave up the active practice of medicine after he moved to New York, he retained his interest in the profession and corresponded with other physicians throughout his life. He also maintained a lifelong correspondence with the leading American and European scientists and thinkers of the day, including Benjamin Franklin, John Rutherfurd, John Bartram, John Friedrich Gronovius, Carl von Linné (Linnaeus), and Robert Whytt.

In science, Colden was most successful with his work in botany, which won the attention of Gronovius and Linnaeus, who named a plant, *Coldenia*, for him. Colden next turned his attention to physics, where he attempted to clarify the work of Sir Isaac Newton by explaining the source of gravity. The work, *Principles of Action in Matter*, was published in London in 1751 and was widely criticized by Newtonian scientists. In philosophy Colden's thinking was a synthesis of and a reaction to the work of leading thinkers of his day, but he did not formulate any new ideas. As a historian, Colden published in 1727 *The History of the Five Indian Nations*, an imperialist tract designed to illustrate the importance of Iroquois allegiance to the English.

Colden was active in New York politics until his death. His political career began in 1720, when Governor William Burnet recommended Colden to serve on the province's council. Although Colden enjoyed the confidence of several of New York's provincial governors, he was a strong opponent of others. As a member of the opposition during the administrations of governors John Montgomerie and William Cosby, Colden instituted a press campaign to attack them. A staunch Whig in his youth, he believed that authority for government came from the people and that rulers who did not protect the best interests of the people should be removed. He appealed to the masses to stir popular discontent that could lead to the recall of both governors.

Colden's commitment to Whig principles later faded when he was allied with royal governors or when he himself was lieutenant governor. As chief adviser to Governor George Clinton (1746–1753), Colden assisted the governor in his ongoing struggle with the opposition, headed by New York's chief justice, James DeLancey. When DeLancey became lieutenant governor in 1753, Colden found it practicable to retire from active participation in politics. He returned to the political scene after DeLancey's death in 1760, when Colden, as senior councillor, became acting governor. He received a commission from the Crown as lieutenant governor and was head of New York's government during 1760–1761, 1763–1765, 1769–1770, and 1774–1775.

Colden's terms as lieutenant governor were difficult because he had alienated New York's two leading families, the DeLanceys and the Livingstons. On taking office Colden was determined to reduce the political and judicial influence of the large merchants and manor lords whose interests were represented by the DeLanceys and the Livingstons. To shake the elite's control of the courts, Colden refused to grant commissions for life for the province's judges. The colony's lawyers protested vigorously. Colden, who detested most of New York's attorneys, countered by saying he would be willing to negotiate the tenure issue if the assembly, also dominated by the elite, would guarantee permanent salaries for judges. His point was that judges should be free of control by the legislature as they were from control by the executive.

The next major test of the elite's control of the judicial system came with the *Forsey v. Cunningham* case. Cunningham, the defendant, was found guilty of assault and was ordered to pay damages to Forsey of £1,500. Cunningham appealed the verdict and Colden, as chief judge of the appellate, heard the appeal, contrary to English and New York practice. His decision was later overruled by the London government.

Turmoil raised over the *Forsey v. Cunningham* appeal turned many New Yorkers against Colden and against the royal rule he represented. In 1765 agitation over the case blended with indignation over the Stamp Act. Colden blamed the rising discontent on the attorneys, who urged the public to oppose unpopular parliamentary measures and imperial programs. As discontent over the Stamp Act escalated, fearing for his life Colden fled the city to seek refuge on a British man-of-war. He was burnt in effigy by mobs, who resented his arming Fort George and having the fort's guns turned from the harbor to face the city. Under pressure from an irate citizenry, Colden turned stamped paper over to city officials, and on his return to the city he locked himself in Fort George.

Colden remained on the periphery of New York politics from the 1765 arrival of Governor Henry Moore until the governor's death in 1769. He then returned to the office of lieutenant governor and allied with the DeLanceys, much to the outrage of the Livingstons. In return for Colden's approval of a much-needed currency bill, the assembly, now controlled by the DeLanceys, agreed to raise £2,000 to supply British troops stationed in New York. This measure was bitterly opposed by the Livingstons and by New York's urban mobs, who saw the assembly's actions as a capitulation to the British ministry. The leader of the egalitarian Sons of Liberty organization, Alexander McDougall, published a pamphlet tirade, *To the Betrayed Inhabitants of New York* (1769), in which he criticized both the lieutenant governor and the assembly. The assembly demanded, and Colden agreed, that the author be arrested and charged with seditious libel. McDougall was freed only because the principal witness against him died before he could testify. By permitting the prosecution, Colden further alienated New Yorkers and raised animosity toward the royal prerogative he represented.

Colden was again in retirement during the administrations of John Murray, earl of Dunmore (1770–1771), and William Tryon (1771–1780). Opposition mounted to British rule during Tryon's administration, forcing Tryon to return in 1774 to England to consult with British ministers. During Tryon's absence, Colden again assumed the governorship. Only a few weeks after Tryon's departure, New Yorkers staged a tea party to protest parliamentary taxation and to prevent East India Company tea from being landed in the province. Colden was still head of government when news of the Intolerable Acts was received in New York. By the time Tryon returned on 15 June 1775, royal authority had collapsed in New York and a revolutionary government was being formed. A distraught Colden, powerless to stop the drift of events, returned to his country estate in Flushing. Tryon soon sought refuge on a British man-of-war in the harbor, where he remained until the British retook New York on 24 September 1776.

The British reoccupation of New York came just four days after the 87-year-old Colden died at Flushing. Colden's public career in New York spanned the rise and fall of British influence in that colony. He was a study in contrasts, as was true of most royal officials. A Whig by birth and inclination, Colden was an outspoken critic of colonial policy when in opposition but defended imperial rule when he allied with royal governors or when he himself represented the royal prerogative. Ignoring his own youthful efforts to use the press to harass royal officials, he prosecuted opponents who criticized him in print. While Colden abhorred democracy, which he equated with mob rule, he distrusted more the motives of the elite and tried to curb their influence. He supported the royal prerogative and scorned excessive wealth, but as governor he ignored royal directives and approved extravagant land claims for his allies. His own personal wealth was substantially increased by collecting exorbitant fees for his approval of these illegal land grants.

Despite his efforts to govern effectively, Colden was vilified during his terms of office. In part, this was because unlike most royal governors whose stay in the province was limited, Colden was a permanent resident. His presence was a constant reminder to his enemies of long-held grudges. He was also vilified because he failed to comprehend that colonial society had changed and matured between his 1710 arrival in North America and his death in 1776. Assemblies had grown more politically astute, the elite more entrenched in power, and the lower classes more politically active. Colden also was vilified because of his rigid and unbending personality. By his own analysis, the governors who were most effective were those who appealed to a broad range of the people, both voters and nonvoters. Cadwallader Colden sought but never achieved wide popular support. He recognized and loathed the growing Whig republican tendencies that he had himself once helped to propagate. In the end he could not understand how these principles could be used to subvert the very system that he hoped to preserve.

• Much of Cadwallader Colden's personal and official correspondence has been published. See publications of the New-York Historical Society, including "The Letters and Papers of Cadwallader Colden," *Collections* (10 vols., 1917–1923, 1931–1935), "Colden Letter Books," *Collections* (2 vols., 1877, 1878), "The Colden Letters on Smith's History," *Collections* 1 (1868), "History of Gov. William Cosby's Administration and of Lt. Gov. George Clarke's Administration through 1737," *Collections* 68 (1935), and "Correspondence between Lieutenant Governor Cadwallader Colden and William Smith, Jr.," *Collections: 1848* (1849). See also Edmund B. O'Callaghan, ed., *Documents Relative to the Colonial History of New York* (15 vols., 1856–1887) and *Documentary History of the State of New York* (4 vols., 1849–1851).

For unpublished correspondence see Additional MSS, British Library, London; Colonial Office Papers, Public Record Office, London; and Colden Scientific Papers, New-York Historical Society. A full-length biography is Alice M. Keys, *Cadwallader Colden: A Representative Eighteenth Century Official* (1906); for a modern biography and a study of Colden as a scientist, see Stephen Charles Steacy, "Cadwallader Colden: Statesman and Savant of Colonial New York" (Ph.D. diss., Univ. of Kansas, 2 vols., 1987).

For a contemporary historian's view of Colden, see William Smith, Jr., *The History of the Province of New York*, ed. Michael Kammen (2 vols., 1972), and William H. W. Sabin, ed., *Historical Memoirs of William Smith* (2 vols., 1956, 1958). For a modern analysis of Colden's influence during George Clinton's administration, see Stanley Nider Katz, *Newcastle's New York, Anglo-American Politics, 1732–1753* (1968). See also Patricia U. Bonomi, *A Factious People, Politics and Society in Colonial New York* (1971), and Kammen, *Colonial New York* (1975).

MARY LOU LUSTIG

COLDEN, Cadwallader David (4 Apr. 1769–7 Feb. 1834), lawyer and politician, was born at "Spring Hill," the family estate, near Flushing, Long Island, New York, the son of David Colden, a scholar, and Ann Willett. He was the grandson of Cadwallader Colden, who was lieutenant governor and often acting governor of the province in the years before the Revolution. As a member of the famous Colden family, he grew up in privileged circumstances, receiving his education in Flushing, then spending a year (1784) at a school in London, England. Following the death of his father, he returned to the United States and took up the study of law, pursuing the subject by moving to St. John, New Brunswick, and working under the guidance of William Wylly, the Crown counsel. Imbibing Wylly's vast learning and his love of British law, Colden became thoroughly knowledgeable in, and respectful toward, English jurisprudence. In 1791, having completed his legal studies under Wylly, he returned to New York City and opened his own law office. Two years later he married Maria Provoost, a daughter of Samuel Provoost, the first Episcopal bishop of the diocese of New York; the number of their children, if any, is unknown. He then moved his practice to Poughkeepsie. Returning again to New York City in 1796, Colden continued to establish himself as an able lawyer and a prominent member of society. He also became a strong advocate of Federalist party principles. In 1798, and again in 1810, he held the office of district attorney for New York City and by the latter date had become the leading practitioner of commercial law in his state.

During the War of 1812, which he actively supported (despite his Federalist party inclinations) because of patriotism and martial interests, Colden was colonel of a volunteer regiment in New York and served in defense of the city. One day in 1814 Captain Samuel Swartwout complained to Colden that his troopers' muskets were too heavy, whereupon Colden sagely replied, "Put two men to a gun, Sam" (Gilder, p. 138). Seven years later Colden achieved the rank of major general in the state militia.

In 1817 Colden published his *Life of Robert Fulton.* He competently outlined the career of his intimate friend and gave him the lion's share of credit for inventing the steamboat. Two years later he wrote *Vindication of the Steamboat Right Granted by the State of New York* to bolster Fulton's patent claims.

In 1818 Colden was elected to the legislature with the support of the Tammany political machine, which incorrectly thought he was an ally. Quickly repudiating his erstwhile associates, he declared himself a friend of Governor DeWitt Clinton, who was fighting Tammany Hall, and was rewarded with appointment to the mayoralty of New York, an office that he held until 1820. That year, on the basis of his solid and trustworthy record as mayor, he was elected to Congress, serving for one term without significant accomplishment, except to oppose a national fugitive slave law that did not dovetail with a program of emancipation in his own state. From 1824 to 1827 he was a member of the state senate, working with Clinton on the promotion of internal improvements (particularly the development of New York port facilities), public school education, and the reform of young criminals. Concerned about the quality of medical care in his city, he continued to serve, as he had for many years, as one of the governors of the New York hospital. He was also interested in canal building. In 1825 he wrote *Memoir of the Celebration of the Completion of the New York Canals*; in it he asserted that the Erie Canal would be the making of New York City as a commercial center.

As a state senator, Colden continued to cultivate his lifelong fascination with the law by serving on the senate judiciary committee. In 1825 he abandoned his earlier veneration of English jurisprudence and urgently advocated a codification and procedural simplification of New York's legal system. He had a strong hand in formulating a committee report that was later instrumental in bringing those changes to the state's system of jurisprudence. He died in Jersey City, New Jersey.

• A number of Colden letters are in the New-York Historical Society. Some information on Colden is in the "Colden Letter Books," New-York Historical Society, *Collections, 1876–1877* (2 vols., 1877–1878). Short sketches of his life are found in Edwin R. Purple, "Notes Biographical and Genealogical of the Colden Family," *New York Genealogical and Biographical Record* 9 (1873): 161–83, and Lorenzo Sabine, *Biographical Sketches of the Loyalists of the American Revolution*, vol. 1 (1864). His legal education is discussed in Edward Alfred Jones, *American Members of the Inns of Court* (1924). Hugh Hastings, ed., *Military Minutes of the Council of Appointment of the State of New York, 1783–1821* (1901), gives information on his law practice, and Jabez D. Hammond, *The History of Political Parties in the State of New York*, vol. 1 (1852), provides background on his political career. Rodman Gilder, *The Battery* (1936), is useful for his military career. See also Wallace Brown, *The Good Americans: The Loyalists in the American Revolution* (1969), and Philip Ranlet, *The New York Loyalists* (1986).

PAUL DAVID NELSON

COLDEN, Cadwallader, II (26 May 1722–18 Feb. 1797), farmer, public official, and Loyalist, was born in New York City, the son of Cadwallader Colden, a physician, scientist, and colonial official, and Alice Christie. In 1727 the family moved to the Ulster County, New York, estate of "Coldengham," where Colden received an informal education from his mother. He also learned surveying, which enabled him to serve later as deputy to his father, the surveyor general of the colony. But Cadwallader neither showed the intellectual brilliance that distinguished his father and younger siblings David and Jane nor received the strong political support that advanced his older brother Alexander. Instead, he received 525 acres from his family and married Elizabeth Ellison, a member of a prominent local family, in 1745. The couple eventually had twelve children, eight of whom survived childhood. Colden also speculated in land (although on a small scale compared to the colony's great magnates), ran various smaller enterprises on his estate, and, after 1753, practiced law.

Colden took over Coldengham's 3,000 acres in 1761, when his father, as the colony's newly appointed lieutenant governor, moved to New York City with Alexander. Six years later Colden began constructing an elegant stone mansion, a sign of his growing prominence. An active and devout Anglican, Colden not only supported local congregations but corresponded with churchmen and the Society for the Propagation of the Gospel. Colden's influence also extended into local politics. He served as a justice of the peace and a precinct supervisor, helping to determine county taxation and spending. He failed, however, to achieve wider office. In both 1768 and 1769 he lost elections to the assembly. One of the successful candidates was George Clinton, later the state's governor. Having passed the bar in 1753 and practicing a little in the following decade, Colden became a justice of the Ulster County Court of Common Pleas in 1769. Colden also served in the military. After acting as commissary for the militia at Albany during King George's War in 1747, Colden used his father's influence to become captain of the local militia. He had advanced to major by the time of the French and Indian War and was promoted to colonel in 1774.

The growing ambitions of the local squire, however, would be thwarted by the Revolution. Colden opposed independence from the start, protesting that elections to the Provincial Convention in April 1775 could lead to "a Republican Government with its Horrid concomitants, Faction, Anarchy and finally Tyranny" (*Calendar of Historical Manuscripts, Relating to the War of the Revolution, in the Office of the Secretary of State, Albany, N.Y.*, vol. 1 [1868], p. 23). Under pressure from "our Tarring & feathering Gentry," he signed the Articles of Association the following month (Fingerhut, p. 45). The Newburgh–New Windsor committee, disgusted at the failure of the local Hanover committee to punish Colden, raided his estate on 24 June 1776. Although the soldiers failed to find the expected cache of arms, they arrested him. A hearing on 4 July 1776 provoked Colden's personal declaration against independence, something he stated that "he should ever oppose with all his might" (Fingerhut, p. 55). The arrest began two years of intermittent harassment that included periods of imprisonment in a courthouse and on a prison ship, a sentence of banishment to Boston that was never carried out, and periods of parole at Coldengham and elsewhere. This period of uncertainty was extended by wartime inefficiency and Colden's repeated personal appeals to revolutionary leaders such as Clinton and John Jay.

Although Colden maintained a forthright verbal opposition to independence and was less scrupulously neutral than he claimed, revolutionaries actually had little to fear from his activities. His Loyalist actions were limited—primarily receiving his British officer son at Coldengham (two other sons later served in the revolutionary militia) and aiding a party of fleeing Loyalists that included a deserting American soldier. Colden's threat to the revolutionary cause, if any, ultimately rested less on his actions or leadership than on his standing as the eldest surviving son of an acting governor who had actively resisted the growing opposition to Britain (Colden's older brother died before the Revolution; his father died at its start). As Jay explained to Colden, "He Did not know of any Gentlemen of Distinction who had avowed these Sentiments as I had Done, that was left at Liberty" (Morris, ed., p. 358).

The revolutionary government finally acted decisively in July 1778, bringing Colden before the Commission of Conspiracies to demand his loyalty to the new government. Colden refused, carefully stating that he would obey the new government but not grant its legitimacy. The commission decided to banish him to New York City, where he lived for the remainder of the war at his late father's "Springhill" estate with his younger brother David, supported by a British subsidy. Exile fed Colden's ambition. He actively pursued office, even asking to be made a council member and the colony's secretary when the British won the war. In August 1779 he served as president of a group of "Loyal Refugees" from a number of states who similarly sought aid and office. Colden received appointment the following month as "commissary to the british prisoners in the possession of the enemy."

Despite his opposition to the revolutionary cause, Colden made a relatively easy transition to peace. A personal petitioning campaign induced the state legislature to include him in a May 1784 law that reversed the banishment of twenty-seven Loyalists. His brother David, however, was not permitted back; he died that year in England. As the surviving head of the family, Colden took in David's family at Coldengham and assumed the complex task of settling both David's and their father's estate. Although his own properties failed to prosper, Colden sold land and sought recovery of prewar debts to resume his earlier living standard—and to settle his eight surviving children around him at Coldengham, where he died.

• Colden's papers are at the New-York Historical Society. An autobiographical letter written by Colden in 1796 from this collection is printed in Samuel W. Eager, *An Outline History of Orange County* (1846–1847). Colden's 1776–1779 letterbook, which also includes journal entries and memoranda, is at the Henry Huntington Library, San Marino, Calif. Selections appear in *John Jay: The Making of a Revolutionary. Unpublished Papers 1745–1780*, ed. Richard B. Morris (1975). Joseph Bragdon, "Cadwallader Colden, Second: An Ulster County Tory," *New York History* 14 (1933): 411–21, was superseded by Eugene R. Fingerhut, *Survivor: Cadwallader Colden II in Revolutionary America* (1983). For Colden's stand against independence, see Michael Kammen, "The American Revolution as a *Crise de Conscience*: The Case of New York," in *Society, Freedom, and Conscience: The American Revolution in Virginia, Massachusetts, and New York*, ed. Richard M. Jellison (1976).

STEVEN C. BULLOCK

COLDEN, Jane (27 Mar. 1724–10 Mar. 1766), botanist, was born in New York City, the daughter of Cadwallader Colden, a physician, scientist, and politician, and Alice Christie. Her father was lieutenant governor of New York and had attained many distinctions in science. Trained in medicine at the University of Edinburgh, he practiced in Philadelphia before accepting a position as surveyor general in New York. Her mother is reported to have been exceptionally lively, with many interests. Jane was educated at home by her parents. Noting her interest in reading and natural philosophy, her dependability, and her intense interest in the garden, her father provided her with botanical training early in her life, including knowledge of the system of taxonomy being developed by Carolus Linnaeus, with whom he corresponded. Jane herself later corresponded with the Swedish naturalist, and Linnaeus named a plant *Coldenia* after her father.

Working from the family home at Coldenham, New York, near Newburgh, by 1757 Jane Colden had assisted her father in the study of New York's flora, compiling a catalog of more than 300 species of plants from the lower Hudson River Valley. She is best known, however, for her work on the gardenia; she published her observations on the plant in Edinburgh's *Essays and Observations*. Her father encouraged her work and introduced her to many of the leading scientists of the time; she was regarded as something of a phenomenon among American women of her day.

Colden's skills in describing plants included developing a technique for making ink impressions of leaves, and she was known for her beautiful paintings of plants and flowers. She was also interested in the culinary and medicinal uses of plants. As she helped her father with his large botanical correspondence and eventually took over much of his botanical work, she became part of the famous international natural history circle of the eighteenth century. Her botanical activities appear to have ended, however, when she married.

Colden's only clearly attributed publication is two pages in Alexander Garden's *Description of a New Plant* (Edinburgh Philosophical Society, *Essays and Observations, Physical and Literary*, vol. 2 [2d ed., 1770]: 5–7). Her manuscript "Flora Nov-Eboracensis," with 341 plant descriptions, is in the British Museum (Natural History, Catalog No. 26.e.19). Records of her personal and professional life are scanty, and she is best known through her father's correspondence, containing loving praise of her botanical accomplishments.

In 1759 Colden married William Farquhar, a medical doctor many years her senior. They had one child, who died in 1766. That same year Colden died, probably in New York City.

• A portion of Colden's manuscript flora in the British Museum is reproduced in H. W. Rickett and Elizabeth Hall, eds., *Botanic Manuscript of Jane Colden, 1724–1766* (1963). Biographical sketches include James Britten, "Jane Colden and the Flora of New York," *Journal of Botany, British and Foreign* 33 (1895): 12–15; Anna Murray Vail, "Jane Colden, an Early New York Botanist," *Contributions from the New York Botanical Garden* 4 (1966–1967): 21–34; and Marilyn Bailey Ogilvie, "Jane Colden," in her *Women in Science: Antiquity through the Nineteenth Century* (1986). See also Raymond Phineas Stearns, *Science in the British Colonies of America* (1970); and Margaret W. Rossiter, *Women Scientists in America before 1920* (1982).

BONNIE SHAPIRO

COLE, Anna Virginia Russell (16 Jan. 1846–6 June 1926), philanthropist, was born in Augusta, Georgia, the daughter of Henry F. Russell, a cotton merchant and commodities speculator, and Martha Danforth. Henry Russell was a civic leader, restoring local control of the municipal government while serving as mayor of Augusta in 1868 and 1869. The Russells were devout Methodists. The great tragedy in Anna's life was the death of her brother, Whitefoord, the only male of nine children, killed fighting for the Confederacy in 1864.

Anna Russell briefly attended Wesleyan College in Macon, Georgia, during 1862. Her only other formal education came from auditing classes at the University of Berlin, where she spent 1866 to 1871 tutoring the children of her uncle, a professor at the university, and boarding at the home of Leopold von Ranke, widely regarded as a progenitor of the modern history profession. On returning to Augusta, Russell taught French and German at a local girls' school.

On Christmas Eve 1872 Anna Russell married Edmund W. Cole, who was president of the Nashville & Chattanooga Railroad but also served as an officer of the Georgia Banking & Railroad Company of Augusta. They had met just over one year before. On moving to Nashville, Anna Cole oversaw her new husband's unfinished house and took care of three of his five children from a previous marriage, the two oldest having already married. Together the couple had two children. Cole spent the first ten years of her married life attending carefully to her children and alternately consoling and encouraging her husband through his business reverses and successes. The only noteworthy exception came in 1877 when she entertained Rutherford B. Hayes.

Cole consistently emphasized home and family life, philanthropy and charity, first through her husband and later of her own initiative. After her stepson Randal Cole died in an accident in 1884, Cole persuaded her husband to endow a school for wayward and orphaned boys, initially named for the son but later called the Tennessee Industrial School. By the time of his death in 1899, E. W. Cole had given $100,000 to the school. The Coles also donated to temperance societies and Methodist missions.

Perhaps the single most frequent object of the Coles' beneficence was Vanderbilt University. E. W. Cole served on the university's Board of Trust from 1886 to 1899, and son Whitefoord Russell Cole, a graduate, served from 1899 to 1934, as chairperson from 1915 to 1934. In 1894 the Coles gave the first half of a $10,000 endowment for an annual lecture devoted "to the defense and advocacy of the Christian religion." Being less concerned than her husband with denominational distinctions, Cole was probably responsible for the breadth of the charge. The lectureship has attracted such leading religious figures as Harry Emerson Fosdick, S. Parkes Cadman, and John R. Mott. The couple also gave $2,500 as a scholarship fund. Between 1905 and 1918 Cole's $5,000 gift was the library's sole endowment. Shortly before her death Cole gave another $10,000 to endow the office of dean of women. Perhaps most importantly for the university's development, in 1914 Cole and her son Whitefoord firmly supported Chancellor James H. Kirkland's battle to assert Vanderbilt's independence from the Methodist church hierarchy. During the crucial endowment campaign of the following year, Cole donated $10,000.

In the years after her husband's death Anna Cole spent her summers in Wequetonsing, Michigan, and her winters in Washington, D.C., where she was "the centre of a large circle of literary, artistic and social personages." She entertained lavishly both in Washington and in Nashville at "Colemere," her house just outside the city. Her guests in Nashville included Presidents Theodore Roosevelt and William Howard Taft. On the grounds of Colemere there was a huge number of rose bushes, from which Cole would distribute roses liberally to friends, neighbors, and anyone who she happened to hear was ill. She also left freezers full of ice cream on the back porch of her Methodist minister's house.

In 1912 the report from the first meeting of the Southern Sociological Conference carried a picture of Cole, with the caption "Founder." Cole endowed the conference with $7,500; with Whitefoord among its leaders, the conference addressed issues of child welfare, prison reform, public health, education, and "Negro Problems" during its existence from 1912 to 1919. Long a supporter of Woodrow Wilson, Cole became increasingly involved in international peace efforts, attending a conference in Vienna in 1916, writing an editorial in the *Nashville Tennessean* on Wilson's behalf that year, and donating $2,000 to the Democratic National Committee to support congressional candidates in 1920, while debate over the League of Nations raged in the Senate. In addition to politics Cole had a keen interest in poetry; she donated a memorial in Augusta honoring four southern poets whom she had known: Sidney Lanier, Father Abram Joseph Ryan, James R. Randall, and Paul Hamilton Hayne. She offered encouragement to John Crowe Ransom and Merrill Moore in their early efforts.

Cole frequently elicited comments about her beauty or her striking appearance, although according to *Harper's Bazar*, "It is, however, her manner and conversation that most impress one." She consistently impressed those who knew her with her unfailing generosity and compassion. Cole's charity and philanthropy exemplify the trends toward social involvement in theology and the concerns of southern progressivism; she was hardly shy about enjoying her money, but she put much of it to good use as well. She died at Colemere.

• Cole's correspondence and family papers are in the possession of the family; her will is in Will Book #43, Davidson County Courthouse, Nashville. The fullest biographical treatment is Jesse C. Burt, Jr., "Anna Russell Cole: A Study of a Grande Dame," *Tennessee Historical Quarterly*, June 1954, pp. 127–55. For a brief description of her later life, see Mable Ward Cameron, *Biographical Cyclopaedia of American Women*, vol. 1 (1924), p. 105. Other short sketches and interviews are in the *Nashville Christian Advocate*, 1 June 1899; the *St. Louis Globe-Democrat*, 8 Mar. 1914; and *Harper's Bazar*, 7 Aug. 1897, p. 663. Obituaries are in the *Nashville Tennessean* and the *Nashville Banner*, 7 June 1926, and the *Vanderbilt Alumnus* 11, no. 5 (1926): 145.

WILLIAM B. TURNER

COLE, Bob (1 July 1868–2 Aug. 1911), actor, director, and composer, was born Robert Allen Cole, Jr., in Athens, Georgia, the son of Robert Allen Cole, Sr., a successful carpenter and political activist in the black community. Cole received musical training in Athens and finished elementary school after his family moved to Atlanta. He made his first stage appearance in Chicago, performing in Sam T. Jack's *The Creole Show* in 1891; later he became the show's stage manager. He and his partner, Stella Wiley, moved around 1893 to New York, where they performed in vaudeville. Cole and Wiley may have married, but there is no evidence; by the end of the 1890s they had parted company. Returning to Jack's *Creole Show*, Cole soon emerged as the headliner, developing his popular stage character, the tramp Willy Wayside. During the mid-1890s, he formed the first school for black performers in New York City, the All-Star Stock Company. This group, working out of Worth's Museum, became a center for many future productions.

Cole joined Black Patti's Troubadours as a performer and songwriter in 1895. His music gained rapid popularity; he soon found himself writing songs for groups such as the Georgia Jubilee Singers (c. 1895), the show *Black America* (c. 1896), and the popular singer May Irwin. By 1896 his music and performance in Black Patti's Troubadours' production of *At Jolly Cooney-Island* had become popular, prompting him to ask the producers for a raise. Denied the increase, Cole bolted from the show, taking with him a number of talented artists. He then created *A Trip to Coontown* (1897–1901) with Bill Johnson.

A Trip to Coontown proved to be significant for two reasons: it was the first show on Broadway to be written, produced and managed by African Americans, and it was the first black-produced show to break with minstrel tradition. Although he was "labeled a disturber and was blackballed" by white producers (Riis, *Just before Jazz*, p. 28), Cole enjoyed a successful tour of *A Trip to Coontown* throughout the United States. In establishing the production company, Cole enunciated his goals: "We are going to have our own shows. We are going to write them ourselves, we are going to have our own stage managers, our own orchestra leader and our own manager out front to count up. No divided houses—our race must be seated from the boxes back" (Foster, p. 48).

Around 1902 Cole dissolved his relationship with Billy Johnson and began working with J. Rosamond Johnson, the brother of writer and poet James Weldon Johnson. For the next decade Cole abandoned the tramp figure Willy Wayside in his vaudeville shows, opting instead for performances in black tie and coattails. Cole and Johnson were credited with initiating a few trends in music, such as the use of eye, moon, and tree images in songs. They emerged as one of the most popular black musical comedy duos, appearing in New York and London, circa 1903–1905. Their act, wrote James Weldon Johnson, "started a vogue of acts consisting of two men in dress suits and a piano" (*Along This Way*, p. 188).

Cole was one of the most versatile performers in early black theater. A good singer and an excellent dancer, he was, according to James Weldon Johnson, "able to play several musical instruments" (*Black Manhattan*, p. 98). He wrote more than 150 songs for over a dozen shows. While many of these might be regarded as "coon songs," others were romantic ballads devoid of references to race. He authored such popular hits as "Under the Bamboo Tree," "Congo-Love Song," "The Conjure Man," "Gimme de Leavin's," and "The Maid with the Dreamy Eyes."

Cole also wrote songs for his own shows, *The Shoo Fly Regiment* (1905–1907) and *The Red Moon* (1908–1909). *The Shoo Fly Regiment* depicted African American university students and teachers who enlist in the military during the Spanish-American War and, during the second act, display acts of bravery and patriotism. Cole portrayed the janitor, Hunter Wilson, providing comic relief. *The Red Moon*, which co-starred Abbie Mitchell and later Aida Overton Walker, dealt with a scheme to recover a kidnapped African–Native-American princess. Cole also wrote an unpublished libretto, *The Czar of Czam*.

In 1911 Cole collapsed from what was probably syphilis, although the disease would not be the cause of his death. While recuperating near Catskill, New York, he drowned in an apparent suicide.

• Clippings related to Cole are found in the Billy Rose Theatre Collection, New York Public Library for the Performing Arts, Lincoln Center; the Harvard Theatre Collection; the Moorland-Spingarn Research Center, Howard University; and the Music Division of the Library of Congress. Thomas L. Riis, *More than Just Minstrel Shows: The Rise of Black Musical Theatre at the Turn of the Century* (1992), *Just before Jazz: Black Musical Theatre in New York, 1890 to 1915* (1989), and "'Bob' Cole: His Life and His Legacy to Black Musical Theatre," *The Black Perspective in Music* 13 (Fall 1985): 135–50, are the most complete portraits of Cole. Thomas L. Morgan and William Barlow, *From Cakewalk to Concert Halls: An Illustrated History of African American Popular Music from 1895 to 1930* (1992), James Weldon Johnson, *Black Manhattan* (1930) and *Along This Way* (1933), are also useful. Cole wrote "The Negro and the Stage," *Colored American Magazine*, Jan.–Feb. 1902, pp. 301–6. See also Will Foster, "Pioneers of the Stage: Memoirs of William Foster," in the *1928 Edition of the Official World of Colored Artists*, ed. Theophilus Lewis (1928); and Bernard L. Peterson, *A Century of Musicals in Black and White* (1993). Obituaries are in the *Chicago Defender* and the *Indianapolis Freeman*, both 12 Aug. 1911.

DAVID KRASNER

COLE, Charles Woolsey (8 Feb. 1906–7 Feb. 1978), twelfth president of Amherst College, was born in Montclair, New Jersey, the son of Charles Buckingham Cole, a lawyer, and Bertha Woolsey Dwight. As a student at Amherst, Cole impressed both faculty and fellow students with the brilliance and range of his mind, won prizes in Latin, mathematics, and public speaking, served as editor in chief of the student newspaper, and graduated summa cum laude in 1927. The next summer he married Katherine Bush Salmon; they had two children.

By 1931 Cole had earned his Ph.D. in economics at Columbia University and had published his dissertation, *French Mercantilist Doctrines before Colbert*. He was also an instructor in history at Columbia, where, he later wrote, "I taught everything from the cave man to modern art, but gradually settled down into the history of Europe from 1560 to 1789 with special emphasis on French economic history in the 17th century." His intellectual versatility led the Columbia physics department to ask him to write a 100-page text on physics and the modern world to ensure its intelligibility for nonscientists. In 1932–1933 a fellowship from the Social Science Research Council enabled him to do nine months of research in the French archives, resulting in the publication six years later of his definitive two-volume study, *Colbert and a Century of French Mercantilism*. (Jean-Baptiste Colbert was a powerful politician and financial policy maker during the reign of Louis XIV in France.) The *London Times Literary Supplement* said of it, "This formidable work of Professor Cole must be accounted a masterpiece."

From 1935 to 1940 Cole taught at Amherst College, where he soon became the George D. Olds Professor of Economics and where a colleague described him as "a master teacher [who] introduced his students to the joy of knowing." The publication in 1939 of his major work on Colbert led Columbia University to call him back to a professorship on its graduate faculty in history in 1940. The coming of World War II, however, took him to Washington as chief of the Service Trades Branch of the Office of Price Administration and then back as regional price executive for the New York region. After that he joined the staff of the Navy School of Military Government and Administration at Columbia for two years and also was a lecturer at the Army School of Military Government in Charlottesville, Virginia.

Cole's most important wartime contribution proved to be his writing of a major report in 1945 as chairman of an alumni committee on "Amherst Tomorrow." Together with an even more extensive report at the same time from a faculty committee it embodied a bold new vision for the postwar college. The vision for a new Amherst called first for a much wider, more democratic, more selective recruitment of students. It also required a set of innovative general education courses in the first two years, followed by more independent honors work in a major field during the final two years, and elimination as far as possible of the undemocratic, anti-intellectual aspects of the fraternities. In 1946 Cole, at age thirty-nine, was selected by the trustees to become Amherst's youngest president and to put this vision into effect. President Victor Butterfield of Wesleyan, a college of comparable ranking, observed, "Professor Cole is one of the top-ranking scholars in the country, and one of its most gifted teachers. . . . He has, in addition, a brilliance of mind, a common sense, an affability, and a sense of humor that will draw the loyalty and support of the college community."

Under Cole's leadership the faculty plunged into the task of creating six core courses: humanities (readings from great works), English composition, history of Western civilization, problems in American civilization, physics and mathematics, and evolution of Earth and man. He persuaded the trustees to require that each fraternity "formally advise the Board of Trustees that there is no prohibition or restriction by reason of race, color, or creed affecting the selection of the members of such chapter."

Meanwhile Cole's first appointment at the college had made Eugene S. Wilson the new dean of admissions. By the end of Cole's presidency Wilson had raised the ratio of applications to Amherst versus openings in the freshman class from 2–1 to 7–1 and had reversed the proportion of preparatory school acceptances from two-thirds to one-third. He also had reduced the proportion of alumni sons or relatives from 39 percent (sometimes even 51 percent) to 15 percent, had widened the sources of Amherst students from sixteen (mostly northeastern) states to a national market, and had raised the average Scholastic Aptitude Test scores of entering students from 498 to 595 for verbal skills and from 519 to 645 in math.

During his fourteen years as president of Amherst, Cole made a number of distinguished senior faculty appointments along with "an array of exciting younger teachers." Where before the war only 20 percent of graduates had gone on to graduate school, 85 percent were doing so by 1960. Where Amherst had produced only one Rhodes scholar in the twenty years before 1946, it produced eight during the Cole years. Cole also increased Amherst's endowment from $16 million to $42 million. A contemporary account in the *Amherst Alumni News* characterized Cole as seeming to possess "an intangible quality . . . that makes him personify Amherst. . . . The amusing thing about the President's frequent references and definitions concerning the educated man, usually made in chapel talks, are that they seem invariably to be definitions of Cole, the man who collects old French coins, writes about Colbert, monogamous youth, and fly fishing, and who chooses the wines for the Davis dinner because he is an authority" (July 1959).

Cole had helped Amherst to ride the wave of postwar confidence in higher education unleashed by the G.I. Bill and spurred by the Sputnik scare. The two Amherst wartime reports gave the college a head start in leading the way toward a new model for a highly selective liberal arts college drawing on a national market for both students and faculty, priding itself on its academic excellence and its teaching faculty, and sending almost all its graduates on to graduate schools. Although by 1970 Amherst abandoned the core courses on which its early success had been built to return to an elective system, which Cole had scorned, it nevertheless maintained much of its national leadership role attained under Cole's presidency.

After Cole resigned from Amherst at age fifty-four, having held his position as long as any of his predecessors (and longer than most), he served briefly as a vice president of the Rockefeller Foundation. In 1961 he accepted President John F. Kennedy's appointment as ambassador to Chile. Accredited to the government of Jorge Alessandri, Cole and his wife helped promote an era of good feelings with the United States during the development of the Alliance for Progress. At the end of his term in 1964 he became only the second foreign citizen ever to be granted the Order of Merit Bernardo O'Higgins.

Returning to a home on a hill above Amherst, Cole served from 1966 to 1968 as a director of the Federal Reserve Bank of Boston (deputy chairman in 1967), revised his several textbooks, and did much fly-fishing. After the death of his first wife in 1972, he married in 1974 the woman who had been her roommate at Smith College, Marie Donohue, and moved to Seattle, Washington. Cole died of a heart attack on a cruise ship off Los Angeles.

• Most of Cole's surviving papers are located in the archives of the Robert Frost Library, Amherst College; his papers from his ambassadorship to Chile are at the John F. Kennedy Library in Boston. Cole published an article on his college presidency, "A Decade of Development at Amherst," *School and Society*, Summer 1957; see also Peter Schrag, "The Cole Era," *Amherst Alumni News*, Summer 1959, pp. 2–7. Concerning his experiences in Chile, see Cole, "The Role of the Ambassador," *Amherst Alumni News*, Winter 1965, pp. 8–11. "The Relativity of History," *Political Science Quarterly*, June 1933, is a scholarly article from early in his career. He also collaborated on three college textbooks: Shepard B. Clough and Charles W. Cole, *Economic History of Europe* (1941; rev. 1946, 1952); Carlton J. H. Hayes et al., *History of Europe* (1949), revised and republished as *History of Western Civilization* (1962; rev. 1967); Henry Bragdon et al., *A Free People: The United States in the Formative Years*, 2 vols. (1970). In addition to the major scholarly books cited in the text above, Cole published *French Mercantilism, 1683–1700* (1943). Gail Kennedy, *Education at Amherst* (1955), provides an excellent account of Amherst's post-war reforms. An obituary is in the *New York Times*, 8 Feb. 1978.

THEODORE P. GREENE

COLE, Cozy (17 Oct. 1909–29 Jan. 1981), jazz percussionist, was born William Randolph Cole in East Orange, New Jersey. He was led into a musical career by his three brothers, all of whom were jazz musicians. Cole took up the drums while a young boy and continued to study the instrument in high school. He began playing professionally as a teenager before attending Wilberforce College in Ohio for two years.

In 1926 Cole moved to New York City, where he continued his study of jazz percussion with Billy Gladstone and Charlie Brooks, two noted drummers in the New York jazz scene of the 1920s. In 1928 he was hired by clarinetist and bandleader Wilbur Sweatman and then led his own group before joining several prominent jazz bands in the 1930s. During that decade Cole performed and recorded with bands led by Jelly Roll Morton, Blanche Calloway, Benny Carter, Willie Bryant, Jonah Jones, and Stuff Smith. Cole made his first records at age twenty with Jelly Roll Morton's Red Hot Peppers.

In 1939 Cole gained national recognition as a performer with Cab Calloway's famed band. Cole stayed with Calloway for four years and was featured on many of Calloway's recordings, including "Crescendo in Drums," "Paradiddle," and "Ratamacue." In 1943 he joined the CBS Orchestra, becoming one of the first African Americans on a radio network musical staff. In the same year Cole was featured in the Broadway musical *Carmen Jones*, an adaptation of Bizet's *Carmen*. His volcanic drum solo on "Beat Out Dat Rhythm on a Drum" in the show brought him recognition in the theater world. "I think I'm the only drummer to have been featured in a big Broadway show with his name on the program," he later said (*New York Times*, 31 Jan. 1981).

Although an unusual step for a professional musician, in 1943 Cole entered the Juilliard School of Music, where he studied musical theory, harmony, piano, timpani, and drums. In 1944 he appeared with Benny Goodman's band in the stage production of *Seven Lively Arts* and recorded "Thru for the Night" and "Concerto for Cozy" as a leader, and "St. Louis Blues" with Roy Eldridge.

In 1945 Cole left Juilliard and the CBS Orchestra and began a four-year period of freelancing with various bands in New York City. In 1949 he joined Earl Hines, Jack Teagarden, and Barney Bigard in Louis Armstrong's All Stars and toured with the group for over four years. During that period he was featured in *The Glenn Miller Story* (1954) and other films with Armstrong; he toured with the band in Europe in 1949 and 1952.

Following his tenure with the Armstrong band, Cole opened a drum school in New York City with Gene Krupa in 1953 and recorded several pieces as a leader, including "Drum Fantasy" in 1954. From 1955 to 1958 he appeared regularly at the Metropole, a New York City nightclub, and on Arthur Godfrey's radio show. During that period Cole also toured Europe with an all-star band led by Jack Teagarden and Earl Hines. In 1958 Cole made a solo record, "Topsy," that became an unexpected hit and gave his name considerable commercial value. More than one million copies of the record were sold, enabling him to tour with his

own group in the late 1950s and 1960s. In 1962 he was sent by the State Department on a tour of Africa. Through the 1960s Cole's band was one of the most popular regular performers in New York City's nightclubs.

In 1969 Cole rejoined the trumpeter Jonah Jones in a quintet with which he played through the end of his career. He retired from performing in 1976, when he became an artist in residence and student lecturer at Capital University in Columbus, Ohio. At Capital, Cole continued his lifelong study of music, expanding his knowledge to include arranging, piano, and harmony. He died in Columbus.

Cole was one of the most versatile drummers in jazz history. He mastered virtually every style in jazz, including swing, bebop, and the popular form featured in Broadway musicals and on radio. Cole was also known for his deep knowledge of music and percussion and for his ability to deliver precise yet explosive drum solos.

• Stanley Dance, *The World of Swing* (1974), explains Cole's importance in the swing and bebop eras. Useful guides to Cole's career and recordings can be found in Leonard Feather, *The Encyclopedia of Jazz* (1960), and in Jack Salzman et al., eds., *The Encyclopedia of African American Culture and History* (1996). An obituary is in the *New York Times*, 31 Jan. 1981.

THADDEUS RUSSELL

COLE, Edward Nicholas (17 Sept. 1909–2 May 1977), automobile manufacturing executive, was born in Marne, Michigan, the son of Franklin Benjamin Cole and Lucy C. Blasen, farmers. Growing up in rural Michigan, Cole exhibited a mechanical bent, building radios and rebuilding cars. After two years of prelaw at Grand Rapids Junior College, he transferred to the General Motors Institute in 1930, graduating with an engineering degree in 1933. At the depths of the depression, Cadillac—a division of General Motors—hired the young engineer as a lab assistant. Cole celebrated by marrying his childhood sweetheart, Esther Engman; they had two children. As General Motors earned a profit every year of the depression, Cole advanced within the Cadillac division to lab technician, technician and designer, engineer, and, eventually chief design engineer. He earned a reputation as an enthusiastic engineer, fascinated by engines, intent on reducing engine noise and improving cooling. Friends remember Cole leaving parties during those years to tinker under the hood.

In 1941 Cole was picked to design a new rear-mounted engine for the U.S. Army's M-5 tank; he finished in ninety days, a very fast turnaround but altogether typical of the pace of wartime projects. He continued to design ordnance equipment throughout the war and was promoted to chief design engineer in 1943 and assistant chief engineer of the Cadillac division in 1944. The rear-engine concept stuck with Cole, and by war's end he had built a rear-engine Cadillac. The engine of this ungainly car filled the back seat and required dual rear tires, but the car handled well in the snow. Cole was intrigued with this idea despite many technical obstacles.

In 1946 Cole became chief engineer at Cadillac and led the effort to develop a short-stroke, high-compression V-8 engine. Generating 170 horsepower, it was 221 pounds lighter and more economical than the engine it replaced. This power plant was essential to the introduction of larger, heavier automobiles in the early 1950s. In his spare time, Cole designed a tank powered by an air-cooled, horizontally opposed engine, and the army accepted the design when war broke out in Korea. Cadillac built this T-41 tank in Cleveland, and Cole moved to Cleveland as works manager in 1950. At night he filled pages with drawings of a small rear-engine car.

Cole's engineering ability attracted the attention of General Motors's top management. In 1952, Thomas Keating, head of Chevrolet, arranged for Cole to move as chief engineer to Chevrolet, where conservative management was to blame for a sales drop of 40 percent during the period 1950–1952. As expected, Cole shook things up at Chevrolet. Beginning in 1952, he tripled the engineering staff and set it to work designing a lighter, more powerful V-8 engine (Cole himself led this effort) and totally revamping the 1955 Chevy. Advertised as "The Hot One," the car sold 1.14 million units. More important, the engine permitted the steady increase in the size and weight of Chevrolets during the 1950s. To further reduce the stodgy image of Chevrolet, Cole agreed to develop the Corvette.

Cole had not forgotten his small rear-engine car. Secretly he began to work with a dozen top engineers, exploring numerous options before settling on a rear-engine, rear-wheel drive design. Promoted to general manager of Chevrolet in 1956, Cole continued designing parts himself and soon tested a suspension and horizontally opposed "pancake" engine mounted in a Porsche shell. In September 1957 he sold the concept to GM president Harlow Curtice, bypassing the normal review committees. In December 1957 the GM Board of Directors approved the still-secret Corvair. The car debuted in 1959 as one of the first American compact cars. It had some problems at first: the carburetor iced up in winter, leading one writer to quip that this was "the perfect economy car. It won't even start." But the 1959 steel strike closed GM for a month, giving Cole time to solve those problems. In its first year, GM sold 230,000 Corvairs. But all was not well with the car. In his book *Unsafe at Any Speed* (1965), consumer advocate Ralph Nader claimed that the Corvair had a faulty rear suspension that caused poor handling. More damning was Nader's indictment of General Motors for knowingly selling an unsafe automobile. GM launched personal attacks against Nader, seeking to harass and discredit a man who became a persistent critic of the auto industry. Caught in the act, GM was deeply embarrassed. Cole, meanwhile, quickly remedied the car's technical problems, and GM won the court suits prompted by Nader's accusations. Cole also became the only auto executive willing to debate Nader—and won his respect. But the Corvair, never regaining its reputation, was canceled.

Despite this episode, Chevrolet increased its sales under Cole from 22 percent of the American market in 1952 to 30 percent in 1961. That year, Cole became group executive in charge of car and truck sales and a GM vice president. In 1964 he was divorced and shortly thereafter married Dollie Ann McVey, a clothing designer twenty years his junior; they had three children. Within the strait-laced GM hierarchy such a step normally ended an executive's chances of becoming president. But in July 1965 Cole became head of the operations staff, and in 1967 he was elected president and chief operating officer of General Motors.

Cole faced several problems, including threats of an antitrust suit, declining sales, escalating wage demands by labor, and rising prices for steel. Cole responded by centralizing authority in an effort to make it harder to break up the corporation and easier to buy steel at lower prices. Cole was not a vocal critic of governmental regulations and in fact argued publicly that the auto industry should take aggressive action to meet federal mandates or expect criticism. He endorsed the development of less-polluting automobiles and urged the petroleum industry to develop fuels without lead. He also pushed automotive safety, an ironic move for the Corvair's designer. Not surprisingly, Cole was the key figure in GM's decision to offer optional air bags on 1974–1976 Oldsmobiles, Buicks, and Cadillacs, although only 10,000 were sold.

In 1971 Cole added the duties of chairman to his other responsibilities at GM. He once commented, "I am dedicated to General Motors and its success." But Cole was an unconventional company man who consistently advised subordinates, "Kick hell out of the status quo." His career was filled with paradoxes. While designing engines that made possible the finned behemoths of the 1950s, he championed a small car. While climbing to the top of the GM bureaucracy, he launched his Corvair by means of an end run around a bureaucracy. Then, as president, he strengthened that bureaucracy. Most auto executives damned governmental pressure on safety and environmental issues, while Cole sought engineering solutions to these challenges. Not surprisingly, he was the only member of the GM board who favored exploring cooperative quality programs with the auto workers union in the mid-1970s.

Above all, Cole was a car man at a time when accountants and the bottom line had assumed primacy at General Motors. In 1963 he told one reporter, "I love engines," and *U.S. News* wrote in 1967, "he is one of the few auto executives who can repair their own cars." *Automotive* business analyst Maryann Keller labeled him "a car nut," while automotive writer Brock Yates labeled Cole "the ultimate engineer." The title was earned, for his Cadillac and Chevy V-8 engines were still in production in 1977, at a time when another idea he championed, the all-aluminum engine, was introduced in the Chevy Vega. The only real engineering fiasco with which he was associated was GM's pursuit of the Wankel rotary engine, a design crippled by its poor fuel economy after the Arab oil embargo.

Cole retired from General Motors in 1974 but did not slow down. He became chairman and CEO of Checker Motors, where he planned to redesign a stodgy line of taxicabs; he even considered introducing lengthened Volkswagen Rabbits to create very fuel-efficient taxis. He also joined Husky International to develop a huge commercial airliner three times the size of the Boeing 747. Finally, Cole worked on a project with an Arab country to develop hydrazene fuel and converted an Opel to run on it.

Obviously a superb engineer, Cole was active in the Society of Automotive Engineers, the National Industrial Pollution Control Council, the American Society for Metals (of which he was a distinguished life member), and the Motor Vehicle Manufacturer's Association. He was elected to the National Academy of Engineering and several engineering honor fraternities. Cole was a director of several corporations and helped numerous Detroit area service organizations, including the Detroit Area Council of the Boy Scouts, the Detroit United Fund, and the Environmental Research Foundation of Michigan.

Like most hard-driving auto executives, Cole's life was his work. He gardened a bit and raised orchids; he even created a Japanese garden in his living room. Cole occasionally did some bird hunting and trap shooting, played a little golf, and loved gin rummy. He also flew his own small plane on business until GM ordered him to stop. Cole died when his small plane crashed near Kalamazoo, Michigan.

• The most thorough biographical sketch of Edward Cole's life can be found in an essay in *Current Biography* (1972). Because of his prominence within General Motors, he was frequently mentioned in articles about the corporation and its products. The most important of these are "Chevy's Man Cole," *Newsweek*, 20 Aug. 1956, pp. 79–80; "Autos—The New Generation," *Time*, 5 Oct. 1959, pp. 90–94, 96; "Ed Cole—The Man Who Hits on All Cylinders," *Newsweek*, 25 Feb. 1963, p. 69; "Executives," *Time*, 10 Nov. 1967, p. 93; and "People of the Week," *U.S. News and World Report*, 13 Nov. 1967, p. 19. Among the books examining the woes of the American auto industry in the 1980s are several accounts that mention Cole in passing, including Brock Yates, *The Decline and Fall of the American Automobile Industry* (1983); Robert Sobel, *Car Wars* (1984); and Maryann Keller, *Rude Awakening* (1989). An obituary is in the *New York Times*, 3 May 1977; see also Jim Norris, "Measuring Ed Cole's Life," *Motor Trend*, Aug. 1977, pp. 105–6.

BRUCE E. SEELY

COLE, Frank Nelson (20 Sept. 1861–26 May 1926), mathematician, was born in Ashland, Massachusetts, the son of Otis Cole, a farmer and entrepreneur in lumber and manufacturing, and Frances Maria Pond. The Cole family had settled in Rehoboth, Massachusetts, before 1690. Cole finished high school in Marlboro, Massachusetts, before enrolling at Harvard College in 1878. He received his A.B. *summa cum laude* (ranking second in a class of 189) in 1882. He was awarded a Parker Travelling Fellowship for 1883–1885, which he spent in Leipzig and Göttingen, Germany. Upon returning to Harvard, Cole received his A.M. and his Ph.D. in 1886. His doctoral dissertation, "A Contribution to the Theory of the General Equation of the Sixth Degree," was suggested and supervised by Felix Klein, the premier German educator of research-level mathematicians.

Cole remained at Harvard for three more years, as a lecturer (1885–1887) and then a tutor (1887–1888). On 26 July 1888 he married Martha Marie Streiff of Göttingen; they had one daughter and three sons. Cole proceeded to the University of Michigan, where he was an instructor (1888–1889) and then an assistant professor (1889–1895). In 1895 he became a professor at Columbia University, and he remained there for the rest of his life. While at Columbia he was notably one of the three professors involved in giving lectures at Barnard College. He was also a member of the Commission of Admissions to Barnard (1901–1914) and secretary of the Faculty of Pure Sciences at Columbia (1908–1923).

Cole's mathematical reputation essentially rests on three accomplishments. One of the first Americans to study mathematics in Germany, during the nineteenth-century wave of study abroad, he worked under Klein when the latter was near the peak of his creative powers. Cole mastered Klein's geometric function theory (complex variables), and his algebraic-geometric theory of the icosahedron (i.e. group theory), and introduced these ideas to the United States. Second, Cole was an enthusiastic and gifted lecturer, who played the dual role of expositor and interpreter of Klein's theories. His early lectures at Harvard were well received and attended by the faculty—James Mills Peirce, Benjamin Osgood Peirce, and William E. Byerly—as well as by students such as future Harvard stars Maxime Bôcher and William F. Osgood. These lectures were credited with breathing new life into the Harvard program, and some forty years later Osgood—who was not inclined to be easily influenced—remembered them as being "truly inspiring." While Cole initially employed Klein's methods, he later advocated a more abstract "pure group theory" approach, which was a forerunner of later methodology.

The third accomplishment, no less important than Cole's advocacy of pure group theory, was his translation into English of Eugen Netto's book, *Substitutionstheorie* (1882). Done with Netto's active cooperation, the resulting *Theory of Substitutions* (1892) was the first textbook in English on group theory (it preceded the famous treatise of the Englishman William S. Burnside by some five years). Cole's translation helped to stimulate the growth of both the American and British schools of group theorists, and one of his students at Michigan was the noted group theorist George A. Miller.

Notwithstanding these contributions, Cole's production of original research papers was surprisingly modest, amounting to only some two dozen papers.

These publications covered work related to his dissertation (1886); a discussion of the icosahedron (1887); linear functions of complex variables (1890); group theory, including an enumeration of simple groups of order 200 to 600 (1891–1893) and substitution groups (1893–1894); the factoring of large numbers (1903); and the theory of triple (triad) systems (1913–1919), prepared in collaboration with Louise D. Cummings and Henry S. White. This latter work was significant in that it led to a final solution of the so-called "fifteen school girls" problem, a combinatorial question posed by Thomas P. Kirkman in 1850. Cole's solution (1922) was also independently anticipated by the Dutch mathematician Pieter Mulder (1917), but the entire problem allowed for numerous generalizations and variations. In 1903, in a poll of the leading scientists in America conducted by *American Men of Science*, Cole was ranked sixteenth out of eighty in mathematics.

Cole was heavily involved in the early work of the American Mathematical Society. He served as secretary of the organization (1895–1920) and editor-in-chief of the *Bulletin of the American Mathematical Society* (1897–1920). By all accounts his service was exemplary; one of his contemporaries observed that one could not think of the American Mathematical Society without recalling his dedication and personality. Cole also served as the society's vice president in 1921, and he reportedly declined to accept a nomination as its president. On the occasion of the relinquishment of his secretarial and editorial duties, several hundred members of the society raised a purse as a token of their recognition of his quarter-century of distinguished service. Cole returned this cash award to the society with the recommendation that it be used to establish a mathematical prize. This led to the founding of the Cole Prize in Algebra, which was first awarded in 1928. In an unusual tribute, volume 27 of the *Bulletin of the American Mathematical Society* (1921) was dedicated to Cole.

In 1926 Cole announced his intention to retire from Columbia in September of that year. However, in late May, following surgery for an infected tooth, he died of heart failure at his home in New York City. Subsequently, it became known that he had been estranged from his family since 1908, and for his last two years he had lived in the Bronx under the assumed name of Edward Mitchell and pretended to be an "ordinary bookkeeper." The reasons for Cole's unusual behavior, which generated much comment and speculation, were only partially explained after his death.

• W. W. Rouse Ball, *Mathematical Recreations and Essays*, 11th ed. (1939), includes a chapter on the Kirkman Problem and its generalizations and solutions. On Cole's education under Klein and his influence in the American mathematical community, see Karen Hunger Parshall and David E. Rowe, *The Emergence of the American Mathematical Research Community, 1875–1900* (1994). Obituaries are in the *Bulletin of the American Mathematical Society* 33 (Nov./Dec. 1927); the *American Mathematical Society Semicentennial Publications* 1 (1938); and the *New York Times*, 27 May 1926. Additional details and tributes are in the *New York Times*, 28, 29, and 31 May 1926, and 3 and 7 June 1926.

JOSEPH D. ZUND

COLE, George Watson (6 Sept. 1850–10 Oct. 1939), librarian and bibliographer, was born in Warren, Litchfield County, Connecticut, the son of Munson Cole, a businessman and inventor, and Antoinette Fidelia Taylor. Cole studied at both Phillips and Exeter Academies and had some interest in literature. In 1865 his father died, and two years later his mother married Levi W. Thrall, a widower with nine children, of Guilford, Connecticut. In 1872 he married one of his stepsisters, Martha A. Thrall, and then taught at a small country school in Litchfield County. Within one year of his marriage, his wife died. While continuing to teach, he took up the study of law, and in 1876 he was admitted to the bar and practiced at Plymouth, Litchfield County. At this time he also mastered takigraphy, or shorthand, Lindsley's System, which he would use for the rest of his life. In 1877 he married Louise E. Warner of New Haven, Connecticut; they had no children. He continued his private law practice in Plymouth, taking on the politically unpopular job of prosecuting liquor violations. In addition to his law duties, to supplement his income, he wrote articles for a small paper in a neighboring county. He noted later in his unpublished autobiography that these early endeavors were unfulfilling.

When he was thirty-five Cole started a career in the library field, which was becoming increasingly professionalized. He had already been serving on the board of the local library, where he improved the new size rules the American Library Association used for measuring books. His innovation put this information on cards, which became known as Cole Size Cards.

In 1885 Cole gave up his law work, went to New York City, and met with Melvil Dewey, head of the Columbia College Library. Dewey, impressed by Cole's library work, found an opening for him in Fitchburg, Massachusetts. Taking the job, Cole met with Dewey again and copied the as yet incomplete cataloging rules that Dewey was formulating. Cole returned to Fitchburg and commenced the process of putting the collection in order based on these rules, making the Fitchburg library a model for small libraries throughout the country. That same year he attended the conference of the American Library Association, formally joining the association.

In 1886 Cole, with Dewey's assistance, began to work for Charles Pratt of Astral Oil, who planned to open the Pratt Institute and Free Library. His new responsibilities allowed him to attend Dewey's newly founded School of Library Economy at Columbia College. In 1888, after graduating with his certificate, Cole moved to Chicago, Illinois, to work with William F. Poole, who was organizing the Newberry Library. His wife, who had always been in poor health, stayed in New Haven. In Chicago, Cole immersed himself in cataloging the treasures of the Probasco collection, a private collection of 2,500 highly valued books gathered by a merchant in Cincinnati named Probasco and sold to the university. In 1891 his wife died. After her death, he became the head librarian of the public library in Jersey City, New Jersey.

In 1894 Cole married Laura Ward Roys of Lyons, New York; they had no children. They traveled to England, the first of many trips abroad. Upon their return, Cole, who was suffering from the effects of typhoid fever, gave up the Jersey City job. That same year, he and his wife traveled to Bermuda for an extended stay. After the trip he began work on his first major bibliography, *Bermuda in Periodical Literature* (1907).

In 1901 Cole was hired by E. Dwight Church of Brooklyn to catalog his private library. This considerable labor consumed Cole's attention from 1902 until 1909, resulting in a seven-volume catalog, which was a milestone in bibliographical study. In 1914, prior to leaving for a home he had set up in California, he met with another noted book collector, Henry E. Huntington. Huntington was in the process of buying several famous libraries, including that of E. Dwight Church. The following year in Los Angeles, Huntington asked Cole to become his librarian. Cole accepted and began his duties at Huntington's home in New York, where the priceless book collection was stored.

Cole's background made him invaluable to Huntington. He set to work cataloging the immense corpus with the help of a handpicked staff. Cole and his assistants published the *Checklist of English Literature to 1640 in the Library of Henry E. Huntington* (1919), which was followed by *Additions and Corrections* (1920). Meanwhile, Huntington, often on the advice of Cole continued to add individual works and entire libraries to his collection. When Huntington relocated his sizable library to San Marino, California, in 1920, Cole helped facilitate the move. In 1924 Cole retired and was named the Huntington Library's Librarian Emeritus.

In his later years Cole continued to lecture and work in the library field. As a result of his interest in postcards, he published *Postcards—The World in Miniature* (1935), which provided a model for organizing postcard collections. He died in Pasadena, California.

Cole is best remembered for his work as a bibliographer and librarian. A member of the American Library Association and the American Antiquarian Society, he was instrumental in creating the profession of library science. In 1904 he helped found and was an early president of the Bibliographical Society of America.

• Cole's personal papers are in the American Antiquarian Society as well as the Huntington Library. His bibliographical library was given to Yale University. Cole's works are cited in *A List of the Printed Productions of George Watson Cole* (1936). His bibliographies for the library of E. Dwight Church, *Books Relative to the Discovery and Early History of North and South America* (1907) and *Books of English Literature and Miscellanea* (1909), are notable examples of his bibli-

ographical skill. The most comprehensive biographical sketch of Cole is Donald C. Dickinson, "George Watson Cole, 1850–1939," in *The Great Bibliographers Series*, no. 8. (1990), pp. 3–20. Obituaries are in *The Papers of the Bibliographical Society of America* 33 (1939): 22–24, and in the *Proceedings of the American Antiquarian Society*, n.s., 49 (1939): 215–23.

DENNIS H. CREMIN

COLE, Jack (27 Apr. 1911–17 Feb. 1974), dancer, choreographer, and director, was born John Ewing Richter in New Brunswick, New Jersey, the son of Charles F. Richter, a druggist, and Mae Ewing. Charles and Mae Richter separated, but his mother told the young Jack (falsely), that his father had died sometime before she married Cole, whose first name and occupation are unknown. In later years, Jack Cole, who took his stepfather's name when he became a dancer, regaled colleagues with tales of his mother's "rowdy Irish" family. Sent away to boarding schools such as the Academy of the Sisters of St. Dominic and Newton Academy in New Jersey, Cole remembered his childhood as unhappy. For a man who was to become an outstanding dancer and choreographer, apparent childhood injuries to his knee, which would trouble him all his career, and to his eyes, which were slightly crossed and caused him continual embarrassment, were handicaps to be overcome by sheer willpower. Graduating from Columbia High School in South Orange, New Jersey, Cole's goal was college, but Dartmouth, which he claimed to have attended, has no record of him. He did briefly enroll at Columbia University, though only in the extension division. Coming to Manhattan, where he soon joined the Denishawn dance ensemble, proved the turning point in his life. Not trained as a dancer, he soon made up for his physical deficiencies by developing intensive training exercises—some derived from his new mentors, some devised by himself—in which he would, to the close of his career, drill his dancers.

Cole essentially had three related careers, beginning as a dancer but also almost immediately becoming a choreographer, both of show dances, for which he was to achieve critical acclaim, and of more serious works, suggesting what he might have achieved with the modern dance ensemble he planned to create but never did. He also became a theater director late in his career, though none of his works achieved success. His professional activities were divided into three arenas of performance: cabarets and nightclubs, Hollywood motion pictures, and the Broadway musical theater. He also occasionally choreographed and taught in college dance programs, and when he died, he was teaching young dancers at the University of California at Los Angeles (UCLA).

Cole is important in the history of American dance and American theater for evolving what has been called jazz dance or theater dance, although others who copied Cole have claimed that honor. As Anna Kisselgoff noted in the *New York Times* obituary (20 Feb. 1974), "It was as a teacher as well as on the Columbia Pictures lot in the nineteen-forties that he trained an entire generation of dancers in a jazz-influenced style that came to represent American show dancing throughout the world and that was widely copied on television." Agnes de Mille insisted that "Jack Cole was the first commercial choreographer to put a lasting stamp on the national style. . . . From him stems the idiom of Broadway ballet, a vernacular style that requires enormous technique, in that it requires considerable classic training, plus acrobatic falls and many kinds of knee slides. This dance idiom is called ballet-jazz" (*American Dances*, 1980). Trained by and performing with Ted Shawn and Ruth St. Denis and then with Doris Humphrey and Charles Weidman, Cole rapidly mastered the fundamentals of the Cecchetti classical training as well as various modern modes. From St. Denis—whose "Oriental" choreographies he thought were phoney—he acquired a deep interest in dance forms of India. His initial choreographic breakthrough was to combine Hindu dance movements with American swing and jazz accompaniment. To this dance vocabulary Cole soon added distinctive movements from Latin American and African dance, especially as derived through the Caribbean and Harlem.

Because Cole's choreographies were so difficult to perform, requiring that dancers be not only in top physical form but also thoroughly grounded in his distinctive vocabulary, he was extremely selective about those with whom he would work. The intensive daily training, coupled with Cole's often cutting comments, ensured that only the most hardy and dedicated would survive. For that reason, he preferred to work with a core of Cole-trained dancers who appeared with him or for him in cabaret, film, and stage engagements. Among dancers who worked closely with Cole were Gwen Verdon (who often assisted him), Carole Haney, Buzz Miller, Matt Mattox, Marc Platt, Florence Lessing, Eleanor King, Rod Alexander, George Martin, Ethel Martin, Anna Austin, Bob Hamilton, Alex Romero, and Ruth Godfrey. Fundamental to the Cole choreographies is mastery of the techniques of "isolation" and "placement." Isolation requires precise control over individual muscles so that different parts of the body—in movement and gesture—can perform in opposition to each other: so that, for example, each finger can achieve a different conformation, as in some Asian dances. Placement refers to the precision required of parts of the body or the whole in sustaining a particular pose or gesture, often in a sequence of movements, so that there is nothing inexact or sloppy in the movements.

Working in cabarets, which in the 1930s were often controlled by underworld figures, Cole learned how to astonish his employers and audiences with strikingly dramatic dance conceptions as well as how to protect himself and his dancers from threats and criticism. Even when working in Hollywood or on Broadway, Cole, with partners or an ensemble, would also appear at clubs such as the Chez Paree, Palais Royale, and Ciro's. He was a favorite in the Rainbow Room at Rockefeller Center, where one breath-stopping entrance involved Cole's rushing down the steps into the room, dropping abruptly to his knees, and sliding swiftly across the floor in that position, to stop short at the edge of a startled patron's table. Both of New York's premier dance critics, John Martin and Walter Terry, recognized Cole's brilliance as a dancer and choreographer, at a time when many serious dance experts disdained show dancing. Terry recalled not only Cole's Rainbow Room "oriental dances to jazz" but also "Harlem dances, in brown chinos, with bare feet and bare torso." Terry noted that Cole was the first to use "Harlem rhythms that weren't done in terms of taps."

While Cole created the cabaret choreographies for himself, partners, or ensembles, on Broadway he initially danced in numbers devised by others. Cole made his Broadway debut with the Humphrey-Weidman dancers in Molière's *The School for Husbands* (Empire Theatre, 1933). Some of the more than thirty musicals in which Cole appeared or that he choreographed did not reach Broadway, but among the more notable were *Thumbs Up* (1934), *May Wine* (1935), *Keep 'Em Laughing* (1942), *Something for the Boys* (1943), *Ziegfeld Follies* (1943), *Allah Be Praised!* (1944), *Magdalena* (1948), *Alive and Kicking* (1950), *Kismet* (1953), *Jamaica* (1957), *A Funny Thing Happened on the Way to the Forum* (1962), and *Foxy* (1964). *Magdalena*, with a score by Villa-Lobos, was not a commercial success, but Cole's unusual choreographic concepts were critically saluted and much admired by fellow choreographers such as Agnes de Mille. At a time when few choreographers also directed Broadway musicals, in 1961 Cole tried to combine the tasks twice in the same year with *Donnybrook!* and *Kean*. He did a lot of research on Irish customs and dance for the first, a musicalization of the film *The Quiet Man*. Co-workers suggested Cole was overwhelmed, especially with *Kean*, which was perceived as too long. Both were commercial failures, and Cole was not again asked to direct. He had a penchant for shock and violence in some of his choreographies such as the mass ravaging of women in *Carnival in Flanders* (1953) and the dance-rape of Aldonza in *Man of La Mancha* (1965). By the late 1960s, however, he seemed blocked, unable to complete choreographies. Broadway producer-director Harold Prince noted, "On the street, the word was you'd be lucky to get one good dance-number from Cole. But it would be terrific!"

Four-time Tony-winner Gwen Verdon, who said she passed Cole's techniques on to her choreographer-director husband Bob Fosse, worked closely with Cole in his cabaret acts, some musicals, and films. His experience with Mafioso club owners, she noted, gave him the courage to stand up to Harry Cohn, head of Columbia Pictures, when Cole insisted on having a core ensemble of dancers for movie musicals, a hand-picked ensemble that would train daily whether it was being used in a film or not. This was unheard of in Hollywood, and after Cole's heyday it was not repeated. Not only did Cole create some ingenious cinema choreographies, incorporating the most demanding of his techniques, but he was also able to make major stars, some of whom were not dancers at all, look talented in musical numbers. Among them were Betty Grable, Jane Russell, Mitzi Gaynor, Rita Hayworth—a trained dancer who insisted Cole made her look "even better"—and Marilyn Monroe. Although Cole was not credited, Monroe insisted on having him help her with movement and interpretation in some major nonmusical roles. When Russell decided to appear in a one-woman show, it was Cole who helped her create it.

Among the more than twenty-five films in or on which Cole worked are *Cover Girl* (1944), *Gilda* (1946), *The Jolson Story* (1947), *Down to Earth* (1947), *On the Riviera* (1951), *Gentlemen Prefer Blondes* (1953), *There's No Business like Show Business* (1954), *Kismet* (1955), *Les Girls* (1957), and *Some Like It Hot* (1959). Not only was Cole able to devise unusual visual effects in his film choreographies, but he was also gifted in making them seem appropriate for the particular song or plot event they helped illustrate.

Cole was proud of most of the work he created for Broadway and Hollywood, but he longed for critical plaudits in the world of serious modern dance. A memorable moment was the choreography he set for Alberto Ginastera's opera *Bomzarzo* (New York City Opera, 1967), which was highly praised. Early in his career, he had created some stark, simple choreographies in Manhattan dance studios, some of which were produced at Carnegie Hall. He was commissioned by the Harkness Ballet to create a work for the company, but his *Requiem for Jimmy Dean* (1967) was never finished. He planned it in six parts, but, after extended and exhausting rehearsals in which Cole drilled the Harkness dancers endlessly, choreographer-director Donald Saddler, then with the Harkness troupe, decided to present what had been mastered as *A Work in Progress*. Cole tried to prevent the performances, but critics were excited even with these fragments. Saddler recalled that the Harkness dancers who mastered the Cole techniques later became among the company's best but that in rehearsal Cole seemed to jump from section to section of the projected work, finally achieving only about seven minutes of choreography. As with his Broadway choreographies, Cole had become blocked and frustrated by the late 1960s, despite the success of *Bomzarzo*. His dances for *Mata Hari* in 1967 did not reach Broadway nor did those for the 1971 *Lolita, My Love*. Cole never got beyond the casting of *Escadrille* in 1973. His teaching at UCLA kept him going until he was incapacitated by the cancer that killed him. He died in Woodland Hills, California.

From private correspondence, it is clear that "Papa" Ted Shawn took a special interest in the difficult and disobedient young Jack Cole as he prepared to found his new male dance ensemble, having broken with St. Denis, his longtime partner and wife. Cole married briefly and had two children, but he never discussed his marriage for the record nor was he permitted contact with the children. In Los Angeles, his companion of many years was David Gray. Cole was intensely secretive about his family and early life. From many reports of former Cole dancers, he was not only a driven man but also a tormented one, often working off his anger by attacking his dancers verbally with his wounding sarcasm and his unrelentingly demanding training sessions. His cabaret and Broadway dancing and choreographies are only memories, but his cinema dance spectaculars survive, at least in archives. As Agnes de Mille has noted, his techniques are now taught in many dance schools and have "gone into the vocabulary of later choreographers—Robbins, first, then Bob Fosse, Michael Kidd, Herbert Ross, Gower Champion, Donald McKayle, and Peter Gennaro."

• In 1978 most of Cole's personal papers, production books, musical scores, professional photographs, and memorabilia were sent for auction to Sotheby's in London by his companion and heir, David Gray. Unfortunately, some of the documents did not find buyers, and their whereabouts are unknown. After the sale, a set of Cole's large scrapbooks was bought from Sotheby's for the Theatre Collection, then in the Victoria & Albert Museum, for possible use in mounting clippings. These contain a number of important documents, mounted and decorated by Cole, as well as loose pictures, letters, and clippings. There are films, videotapes, and other materials in the Dance Collection of the New York Public Library for the Performing Arts relating to Cole and his dancers. The Theatre Collection of the UCLA library contains all of the research materials gathered for the thirteen-part Cole series in *Dance Magazine* (1983–1984); additional documents and interviews for the subsequent book, *Unsung Genius: The Passion of Dancer-Choreographer Jack Cole* (1984); the complete manuscript of the Loney biography, only half of which was published; and a valuable cache of Cole materials bought at the Sotheby's sale. Because Cole worked in theater and cinema, relevant materials may also be found in the Billy Rose Theatre Collection of the New York Public Library for the Performing Arts. During Cole's long career, articles by and about him and reviews of his work appeared occasionally in *Dance Magazine*. Walter Terry and John Martin, among other critics, analyzed his work in newspapers such as the *New York Herald-Tribune* and the *New York Times*. See also Kimberly Susan Kaufman, "A Biographical-Bibliographical Study of Jack Cole" (master's thesis, Univ. of California at Los Angeles, 1976). Cole and/or his work has been discussed in Agnes de Mille, *America Dances* (1980); Eleanor King, *Transformations* (1978); Jane Sherman, *Denishawn* (1983); Marcia B. Siegel, *At the Vanishing Point* (1972); Marshall and Jean Stearns, *Jazz Dance* (1979); and Walter Terry, *The Dance in America* (1956) and *I Was There* (1973).

As previously noted, most of Cole's cinema choreographies survive in archives, and there is some footage of television dance routines. There are photographs and reviews of his performances and choreographies for nightclubs, Radio City Music Hall, and Broadway, and Lee Theodore reconstructed some of his Broadway show dances, where possible with the assistance of those who originally danced them. A grant in 1976 from the National Endowment for the Arts enabled Theodore and the American Dance Machine (ADM) to create the *Jack Cole Interface*, documenting his technique, training, and dances. *Recollections*, a 25-minute film of Cole clips and some ADM reconstructions, is now on deposit at the Library of Congress.

GLENN LONEY

COLE, Kenneth Stewart (10 July 1900–18 Apr. 1984), biophysicist, was born in Ithaca, New York, the son of Charles Nelson Cole, an educator, and Mabel Stewart. Known in later years by colleagues and friends as Kacy, Cole described his childhood as lonely. He grew up in the intellectually challenging environment of college towns, and his mother encouraged his scientific curiosity. In 1917 Cole entered Oberlin College, where his father was a dean. His sophomore year was interrupted for a brief period of army service at the end of 1918. During the summer months of 1920 and 1921 and a year's leave of absence (1921–1922), Cole worked at the General Electric Research Laboratory in Schenectady, New York. After receiving his A.B. in physics in 1922, Cole chose to pursue graduate studies in physics at Cornell, where he studied with F. K. Richtmyer. He spent the summer of 1923 at the Cleveland Clinic as a biophysicist, working with Hugo Fricke.

The following summer Cole began a lifelong association with the Marine Biology Laboratory at Woods Hole, Massachusetts, where the young physicist first became interested in biological phenomena and taught himself how to sail. After receiving his Ph.D. in 1926, Cole began postgraduate training at Harvard and Woods Hole, inaugurating his research in experimental and theoretical studies of the electrical properties of living cell membranes. In Cambridge Cole roomed in a boardinghouse run by the widow of the anatomist L. W. Williams, who had investigated the nervous system of the squid; Cole would eventually be recognized for his own work on the squid axon. Cole concluded his training at the University of Leipzig (1928–1929), working under Peter Debye, the 1936 Nobel laureate in chemistry.

In 1929 Cole was appointed assistant professor of physiology at Columbia University's College of Physicians and Surgeons. He was also the consulting physicist to Presbyterian Hospital, where he performed self-described "odd jobs" in radiology, anesthesiology, and surgery. In 1932 Cole married Elizabeth Evans Roberts, an attorney from Chicago whom he had known since childhood; they had two children. During this period at Columbia Cole also began a research program to measure impedance in biological samples as a means of studying membrane properties. Some of his samples were taken from marine organisms such as sea urchins and starfish, which he obtained on his many trips to Woods Hole, Long Island, and Bermuda. In 1936 he began working on the squid giant axon and became the first to record intracellular nerve impulses. Cole was promoted to associate professor in 1937 and remained at Columbia until 1946. Two years as a Guggenheim Fellow at the Institute for Advanced Study (Princeton) in 1941 and 1942 were followed by war service (1942–1946) as the principal biophysicist of the Metallurgical Laboratory at the University of Chicago, where Cole investigated the biological effects of radiation. This was followed by a brief period (1946–1949) as professor of biophysics and physiology at the University of Chicago, when much of the curriculum and

direction of graduate training in this field was first conceived.

In 1949 Cole became technical director of the Naval Medical Research Institute in Bethesda, Maryland. He was discouraged both by the large amount of administrative work this position demanded and by the recent award of the Nobel Prize to Alan Hodgkin and Andrew Huxley for the sodium theory of nerve transmission, which was based on Cole's previous research. In a 1979 memoir Cole reported, "I was feeling sorry for myself because Hodgkin and Huxley had done all that I had ever hoped to do. Consolingly, Hodgkin said they had just followed my lead" (p. 18).

In 1954 Cole began a longstanding association with the National Institutes of Health (NIH) when he was recruited to become founding chief of the Laboratory of Biophysics at the National Institute of Neurological Diseases and Blindness. This allowed him the opportunity to design a new facility in which he enjoyed his most productive scientific period. During this time he continued development of the "voltage clamp" (a term Cole was not entirely happy with) for the measurement of membrane electrical activity. This technique was reproduced in hundreds of laboratories and resulted in thousands of publications. In addition, Cole continued his research on the squid axon at NIH, including work reported in the newly created *Biophysical Journal* (1, no. 1 [1960]: 1–14). Although Cole's affiliation with NIH continued until his retirement in 1978 (he left the job as lab chief in 1966 to become senior research biophysicist), he also began a second career on the West Coast. He was Regents Professor at the University of California, Berkeley, during a leave of absence from the NIH (1963–1964) and continued as a part-time professor of biophysics until his move to southern California in 1978.

Cole played an active role in the development and establishment of biophysics as an independent scientific discipline. Before World War II biophysics was a loose organization of scientists who used physical methods to study biological phenomena. In fact, Cole recounted that his graduate advisor Richtmyer said to him early in his career, "Darned if I know what a biophysicist is." Once the field became established, Cole favored affiliation with the Institute of Physics; however, in 1956 he was a member of the Committee of Four that organized the Biophysical Society, and Cole and his wife Elizabeth wrote the society's constitution and bylaws. He was also a member of its executive board, council, and editorial board, and served as president in 1963. Cole also held numerous memberships and leadership roles in international scientific organizations, including Cold Spring Harbor Laboratory, the Foundation for Advanced Education in the Sciences Board, National Academy of Sciences, American Academy of Arts and Sciences, American Physiological Society, Société Philomatique de Paris, General Physiologists, Sociedade Brasileira de Biologia, Sigma Xi, Alpha Epsilon Delta, and Epsilon Chi.

Cole was a fellow of the American Physical Society, American Academy of Arts and Sciences, and New

York Academy of Science. His greatest honor came in 1967 when he was awarded the National Medal of Science, the nation's highest award for distinguished achievement in science, mathematics, and engineering. President Lyndon Johnson, in presenting the award, stated that "As a result [of Cole's work], we know far more about how the nervous system functions." In 1972 he was given the rare honor of being inducted as a foreign member of the Royal Society of London.

Cole died in La Jolla, California, where since 1980 he had been adjunct professor in the department of neurosciences at the Scripps Institute of Oceanography. His numerous innovations and technical developments for the measurement of membrane electrical properties and the analysis of nerve impulse transmission were among the earliest work to apply the theory and methods of physics to the study of biological phenomena. Through this work, combined with his leadership roles in the establishment of biophysics as an independent scientific discipline, he justifiably earned the title "father of biophysics."

• Five years before his death Cole published an autobiographical essay in *Annual Review of Physiology* 41 (1979): 1–24. He published more than 100 articles on his research in the scientific literature, including a paper he called his "pride and joy": "Electric Impedance of *Nitella* during Activity," *Journal of General Physiology* 22 (1938): 37–64. Much of his work is described in his book *Membranes, Ions, and Impulses* (1968, repr. 1972), as well as in symposia proceedings dedicated to him: *Perspectives in Membrane Biophysics—A Tribute to Kenneth S. Cole* (1972), and *The Biophysical Approach to Excitable Systems* (1981). Obituaries are in the *New York Times*, 20 Apr. 1984, *Boston Globe*, 22 Apr. 1984, and *Washington Post*, 19 Apr. 1984.

DAVID S. GOTTFRIED

COLE, Nat King (17 Mar. 1919–15 Feb. 1965), pianist and singer, was born Nathaniel Adams Coles in Montgomery, Alabama, the son of the Reverend Edward James Coles, Sr., and Perlina Adams, a musician. Cole's family moved to Chicago when he was four. He first studied piano with his mother, then with bassist Milt Hinton's mother, and at the age of twelve, classical piano with a Professor Thomas. The family home was located near the Grand Terrace Ballroom, where Cole often heard his first and most important influence, pianist Earl Hines. In high school Cole played a variety of instruments in a band that included future jazz stars Hinton, Lionel Hampton, and Ray Nance. His father eventually agreed to allow the teenager to play jazz on weeknights if he continued to play organ for Sunday services. At about the age of sixteen Cole organized a big band known as the Rogues of Rhythm and a quintet known as Nat Coles and His Royal Dukes. The groups played for a quarter each, or for hot dogs, hamburgers, and soda.

Cole already had a deft style at the keyboard and a genius for arranging; his band even won a cutting contest against the Hines group at the Savoy Ballroom, which then hired the group to play occasional dances.

By 1935 he had also become friends with Louis Armstrong.

Cole left high school that same year. He made his first recording in 1936 with his brother Eddie's quintet, the Solid Swingers. He worked as pianist in the musical "Shuffle Along," where he met his first wife, Nadine Robinson, a dancer in the show. They married while the show was on tour in Michigan, and when "Shuffle Along" closed in Long Beach, California, they decided to remain in the area. The couple had no children.

In late 1937 Cole met guitarist Oscar Moore. Together with bassist Wesley Prince, they formed a trio called King Cole and His Swingsters. They soon became the King Cole Trio (Cole had dropped the *s* from his name; he legally changed it in 1948). By 1938 they were making $110 a night and had established a solid reputation in the Los Angeles area; by the end of that year they had become one of the first black groups to broadcast live nationally, on the NBC Blue network. They began recording in 1938 and in 1940 and 1941 cut several sides for Decca's Sepia series. They made their first trip to New York City in 1939, where they occasionally backed Billie Holiday at Kelly's Stables on West Fifty-second Street.

During the late winter of 1941 the trio went on tour, including a four-week gig at Nick's in Greenwich Village, followed by eight months, off and on, at Kelly's. They returned to Los Angeles at the end of 1941, then were back in Chicago and New York City in 1942. Though still struggling financially, the trio had begun to establish a national reputation.

In July 1942 Cole made a series of recordings with tenor saxophonist Lester Young, including superb renditions of "Body and Soul" and "I Can't Get Started." That summer the 331 Club in Los Angeles hired the Cole trio as its house group, with bassist Johnny Miller replacing Prince. The classic Cole trio was now in place. Cole and Moore in particular complemented each other perfectly; though rooted in swing, they often played unusual harmonies that partially foreshadowed the bop revolution.

The trio signed with the fledgling Capitol Records in 1943, and their new manager, Carlos Gastel, booked them at the Orpheum Theater in Los Angeles at $1,000 a week. The group immediately made a series of outstanding recordings, beginning in November with "Straighten Up and Fly Right," the humorous homily that sold a half-million records at a time when 200,000 was a major hit. They toured nationally with the Benny Carter Orchestra and other groups in 1944 and 1945; appeared in movies; played often on Bing Crosby's radio show, "The Kraft Music Hall"; and were regulars on the "Wildroot Cream Oil Show" from 1946 to 1949. The trio won the 1946 Metronome small group award. All the while the hits continued to flow: "The Man I Love" (1944); "Route 66" (1946); the phenomenally popular "Christmas Song" (1946); and "Too Marvelous for Words (1947). The haunting "Nature Boy" sold over a million copies by the fall of 1948 and over two million eventually.

By now, Cole's style was immediately identifiable. His singing had matured; he was a marvelous story-teller with a warm baritone voice, perfect pitch, precise enunciation, and an intimate, easy delivery. His playing was endlessly melodic, Hines's intricate right-hand style—clearly articulated single-note lines—leavened with the lyricism of Teddy Wilson. At the same time, Cole's harmonic approach was ahead of most of his contemporaries, as he anticipated future bop innovations in his choice of unusual chords and harmonies; the sparse but powerful rhythmic pulse in his left retained the ability to propel a group of any size. The Cole–Moore interaction was almost ideal, the latter playing beautifully shaped solos and providing sensitive accompaniment. The two often reversed the roles of soloist and accompanist, as in 1943's "It's Only a Paper Moon."

Cole divorced his wife in 1948 and that same year married Maria Ellington, who took increasing responsibility for his career and professional image. They had five children, two of whom were adopted. Perhaps in reaction to her growing influence, and openly over a salary disagreement, Moore left the trio in 1947, and Miller left in 1948. The Coles also confronted racism when they purchased a luxurious home in the Hancock Park section of Los Angeles. The neighbors tried (in vain) to enforce a restrictive covenant to force the Coles out. As a lawyer for the neighbors explained to Nat, "Mr. Cole, I want you to understand our position. We don't want any undesirable people coming into the neighborhood, you know." Cole agreed. "If I see anybody undesirable coming in," he responded, "I'll be the first to complain" (Gourse, p. 104). Cole often faced such racism in his national tours, and in 1956 members of the White Citizens Council stormed the stage at a performance in Birmingham, Alabama, and physically assaulted the singer.

Cole's new trio included Irving Ashby on guitar and Joe Comfort on bass. In 1949 Cole added conga and bongo player Jack Costanzo to provide greater textural contrast and rhythmic variety. Ashby and Comfort were unhappy with Costanzo's presence, believing that he thickened the traditional light sound of the trio and made it too choppy. But Cole proved more perceptive, and the group continued to enjoy success and popularity. They made their first English tour in 1950, and in 1951 they traveled with the Big Show, an all-star cast that included singers, clowns, dancers, and musicians like Duke Ellington and Sarah Vaughan. However, at the end of 1951 Ashby and Comfort both left the group. Costanzo was only one cause of their discontent. Cole was increasingly separating himself from the group. In March 1949 he recorded "Lush Life," orchestrated by Pete Rugolo, with strings and Latin percussion; the recording's success convinced both Cole and Capitol that his future lay as a star act, backed by various groups. The shift paid off with the enormous success in 1950 of "Mona Lisa" (orchestrated by Nelson Riddle).

The hits continued to come, highlighted by "Unforgettable" (1951) and "Lover Come Back to Me"

(1953), with the Billy May Orchestra. Even an attack of bleeding ulcers in April 1953 failed to slow Cole down for long. The group enjoyed great success on a seven-week European tour, and Cole appeared in several films, including the 1955 *Nat King Cole Story*. In 1956 he signed a three-year, half-million-dollar contract to appear at the Sands in Las Vegas for three weeks each year. During 1955–1965 he recorded a string of successful albums with Nelson Riddle, including *Songs for Two in Love* (1953); *To Whom It May Concern* (1958); *St. Louis Blues* (1958); and, with the Count Basie Orchestra, *Welcome to the Club* (1958). After a brief interlude, Cole also hit the charts again with the singles "I Just Found Out about Love" (1957); "Can't Help It" (1958); the countryish "Ramblin' Rose" (1962); and the more frivolous "Those Lazy-Hazy-Crazy Days of Summer" (1963). He appeared on television shows hosted by Perry Como, Milton Berle, Ed Sullivan, Dinah Shore, and Pat Boone. Finally, in October 1956 he signed a contract for his own show. But the show suffered from a lack of sponsors throughout its existence, due partly to fears of a southern backlash.

By the mid-fifties Cole's billing featured only himself and various band leaders and arrangers; the trio was no longer mentioned. He toured Latin America before huge crowds, enjoyed another successful European tour, and performed at the White House. He also achieved a lifelong ambition when he starred in a Broadway show, *I'm with You*. Though the show's music was excellent, the plot was weak, and audiences seemed uncomfortable at the sight of white women and black men mixing on stage. Cole never achieved his dreamed-for success on Broadway. In late 1964 he was diagnosed with lung cancer. He died a few months later in Santa Monica, California.

Cole recorded more than a thousand songs and sold more than nine million albums. Much of his later popularity stemmed from his singing. His voice had less than a two-octave range, but it deepened as he got older, heightening the unique sense of intimacy it always conveyed. Cole also recorded several creative versions of classical pieces, including MacDowell's "To a Wild Rose"; "In the Cool of the Evening," inspired by Debussy; and a swinging rendition of Rachmaninoff's "Prelude in C-sharp Minor" (1944). He was almost certainly the most versatile of all those who have graced the stage of American popular music.

• There is a wealth of critical literature on Cole's life and music. The best and most recent biography is by Leslie Gourse, *Unforgettable: The Life and Mystique of Nat King Cole* (1991), but the reader should also consult James Haskins, with Kathleen Brown, *Nat King Cole: The Man and His Music* (1986), and Maria Cole with Louie Robinson, *Nat King Cole: An Intimate Biography* (1971). Will Friedwald's assessments of Cole should be the starting point for all critical discussion. See his *Jazz Singing: America's Great Voices from Bessie Smith to Bebop and Beyond* (1990), and his essay, "The Nat King Cole Trio," together with session notes, in Mosaic Records' Grammy-winning compilation, "The Complete Capitol Recordings of the Nat King Cole Trio" (1991). Jazz pianist Dick

Katz offers an analysis of Cole's piano style in "Nat Cole—The Pianist," also in the Mosaic collection. Finally, Gunther Schuller, *The Swing Era: The Development of Jazz, 1930–1945* (1989), provides a perceptive analysis of Cole's and the trio's place in jazz history. An obituary is in the *New York Times*, 16 Feb. 1965.

RONALD P. DUFOUR

COLE, Richard Beverly (12 Aug. 1829–15 Jan. 1901), physician, was born in Manchester, Virginia, the son of John Cole, a mine owner, and Pamela Wooldrich. Physically fragile as a child, Cole was the youngest and only son of three children. His mother, unskilled and left without a steady income after her husband died while Cole was only an infant, operated a boarding-house, which enabled her to support and educate her children. Cole entered school late, at age thirteen, and was apprenticed to Dr. Benjamin Dudley of Lexington, Kentucky. He later enrolled at Transylvania University and transferred to Jefferson Medical College, where he acquired his medical degree in 1849. Cole supported himself through school by serving as a prosector, preparing and selling anatomical sections and small dissections to students and professors. These activities resulted in a mediocre scholastic record, but the experience proved advantageous later when Cole was called on to perform emergency surgery in near darkness. In 1848 Cole married Eugenie Irene Bonaffon, with whom he would have three children.

Between 1849 and 1852, while establishing a private practice in Philadelphia, serving as obstetrician at three dispensaries, and continuing as prosector and assistant demonstrator at Jefferson Medical College, Cole contracted tuberculosis. This condition probably influenced his decision to move to San Francisco, though his wife remained in Philadelphia.

Cole traveled by way of Panama, where he battled dysentery and a cholera epidemic. In 1854, after arriving in San Francisco, a revolver that he had loosely packed in his coat pocket accidentally fell to the floor and discharged into Cole's stomach. Two weeks later, five doctors removed the ball from Cole's back near his twelfth rib, enabling him to recover.

Cole's early mishaps, though physically debilitating, may have strengthened his involvement in municipal activities. In 1856 when the editor for the *San Francisco Evening Bulletin*, "James King of William," was shot by James Casey, a politician and editor of the *Sunday Times*, Cole was summoned. Over Cole's objections, Dr. William M. Hammond, King's personal physician, decided to insert a sponge to plug up the wound; King died six days later. His death occasioned political and social unrest, the formation of a vigilante force, and the indictment of Edward McGowan, a police judge who was accused of conspiring with Casey to assassinate King. Cole testified at the subsequent trial that it was the medical treatment King had received that had caused his death and exhibited a corpse of an executed prisoner to demonstrate the wound and its treatment. Cole was unable to persuade the jury, however, and although McGowan was acquitted the jury

declared that Casey had fired the fatal shot. A short time later, further political unrest resulted in the stabbing of the marshall of the vigilante committee, Sterling Hopkins. Because Hopkins's carotid artery was severed, Cole was called in at dusk to perform emergency surgery by candlelight. Owing in large measure to Cole's experience and training as an anatomist, Hopkins recovered.

During the same year, Cole sent for his wife and began to specialize in the practice of obstetrics. In 1858 Cole became chairman of the Committee on Obstetrics and Diseases of Women of the California Medical Society. In addition, he was appointed dean of faculty as well as professor of obstetrics, diseases of women, and physiology by its founder, Elias Samuel Cooper of the newly opened medical school at the University of the Pacific in San Francisco, where Cole served from 1859 to 1864.

After the death of Cooper in 1862 and the opening of the rival Toland Medical College in 1864, Cole decided to seek more professional training abroad. While traveling in Europe and studying in Paris, Berlin, and Heidelberg, Cole joined several organizations, including the Royal College of Surgeons, the British Gynecological Society, and the Obstetrical Society of London. On his return to San Francisco in 1865, he expanded his practice and dabbled in politics. After the death in 1861 of his son from toxic poisoning arising from improperly disposed sewage beneath his house, Cole rallied for better public health measures in San Francisco. In 1868 a smallpox epidemic struck the city. Cole was appointed to a hospital committee created by the board of supervisors and after inspecting the pesthouse, demanded strict quarantine, compulsory vaccination, and reorganization of the clinical accommodations. His advocacy of strong public health measures prompted the governor to appoint Cole surgeon general of the state of California. Cole's chief accomplishments as surgeon general were to draw public awareness to the dark, cramped conditions of the San Francisco Lying-In Hospital and Foundling Asylum, a temporary refuge for unmarried mothers and unwanted children, and to the health repercussions of garbage dumps at the edge of the city on the shore of the bay.

Cole's ability to motivate others, as well as his own considerable teaching talents, prompted Hugh Toland, with whom he had tangled in the past, to recruit him as dean of the faculty and professor of obstetrics and clinical diseases of women for the Toland Medical College. Cole accepted the position and persuaded Toland to affiliate the college with the new University of California. In 1873 Toland Medical College, with Cole as dean, became the medical department of the University of California.

Ambitious and influential, Cole attempted to bolster the reputation of California, and particularly its university, by making another trip to Europe in 1874. He also lobbied the state legislature for funds to construct new buildings to house the colleges of medicine, dentistry, pharmacy, and law. In 1897 the cornerstone of the medical building was laid, and Cole was hailed as "Father of the Affiliated Colleges." In 1895 and 1896 he served as president of the American Medical Association.

In 1899 Cole sustained a stroke. Instead of completely retiring, he became coroner of the city of San Francisco, the office in which he served until the day of his death. A colorful participant in the medical, public health, and political life of San Francisco, Cole made a lasting contribution in his successful transfer of Toland Medical College to the University of California system. He was instrumental in bringing attention to the need for better public health policies and for his medical activities, particularly during the smallpox crisis of 1868. Active until the end of his life in the medical and political affairs of his adopted city, Cole dominated the medical scene in California for almost half a century.

• Writings by Cole include "Alum in the Treatment of Uterine Hemorrhage," *San Francisco Medical Press* 1 (1860): 15–19, and an article on pestilence in the *Occidental Medical Times* 14 (1900): 221. A thorough assessment for the events of Cole's life are in F. T. Gardner, "King Cole of California," *Annals of Medical History*, 3d ser., 2, no. 3 (1940): 245–58; 2, no. 4 (1940): 319–47; 2, no. 5 (1940): 432–42. See also Henry Harris, *California Medical Story* (1932). A short biographical sketch of Cole's medical career is in *Journal of the American Medical Association* 32 (1899): 1212. A bibliographical notice by William Henry Mays is in *A Cyclopedia of American Medical Biography*, ed. Howard A. Kelly, vol. 1 (1912), p. 194.

YNEZ VIOLÉ O'NEILL

COLE, Rufus (30 Apr. 1872–20 Apr. 1966), physician, was born in Rowsburg, Ohio, the son of Ivory Snethen Cole, a physician, and Ruth Smith. Raised in a medical family, Cole was influenced in his early life to become a physician. His mother urged her son to continue beyond high school, although Cole had to earn money to pay for continuing his education. In 1892 Cole entered the University of Michigan and received his undergraduate degree in 1896. Originally he planned to study medicine at the University of Michigan but, impressed with the new Johns Hopkins Medical School exhibit that he saw at the World's Columbian Exposition of 1893 in Chicago, he changed his plan and applied and was accepted at Johns Hopkins. Cole was influenced in his medical education by the excellent teaching and integrity of William Henry Welch, William Osler, Lewellys Barker, and other medical greats of the Hopkins faculty. After receiving his M.D. in 1899, Cole was appointed to the resident staff, where he served under William Osler, for whom he retained a lasting regard. As this was Osler's last year before departing for Oxford as the Regius Professor, Cole spent his second resident year studying under Lewellys Barker. Barker at that time was an ardent advocate of the full-time system for academic medicine; he felt strongly that academic medical professors should abandon the private practice of medicine and devote full time to research. To encourage his system,

Barker established laboratories adjacent to the patient wards and urged his staff to apply scientific methods to study the diseases of their patients.

Cole was the first resident appointed to direct one of the laboratories, the one called the biological laboratory. Since there was an epidemic of typhoid in Baltimore at that time, he initiated a study of typhoid fever. Cole cultured the blood from typhoid patients and demonstrated that typhoid bacilli were present in the bloodstream at an early stage of the disease. Since Cole's novel discovery was made in a small clinical laboratory, it attracted the attention of the Johns Hopkins medical staff and stimulated their support for Barker's research program.

Cole remained at Johns Hopkins until 1909. The years 1903–1904 were spent in Berlin working in the Robert Koch Institut für Infektionskrankheiten (infectious diseases). Under Professor August Paul von Wasserman, Cole worked out a method for distinguishing the strains of typhoid bacilli, which was published in 1904. This work was important for the development of a vaccine to prevent typhoid.

In 1908 Cole married Annie Hegeler; they had three daughters. That same year he was appointed the first director of the hospital of the Rockefeller Institute for Medical Research. Although the hospital was not to be opened for another two years, Cole immediately set to work forming plans for the new project. In 1909, for the new hospital to benefit from the advances being made in Europe in the clinical study of diseases, Cole and his family went abroad to observe the medical work being carried out in Great Britain and on the Continent.

The hospital at the Rockefeller Institute was to be a small unit with fifty beds designed for the intensive study of a few patients. Influenced by Barker, Cole pursuaded the trustees to adopt a full-time system with no attending physicians; the hospital physicians would be paid by the institute and would have no private practices. The staff was to be clinically competent and also able to carry out the laboratory investigation of the diseases presented for study. Although the Rockefeller Institute owned laboratories engaged in studies of related problems, Cole insisted that the hospital operate its own laboratories so as to permit the staff to carry out their investigations near the wards where their patients were, as Barker had introduced at Hopkins. Cole's ideas in this regard conflicted with those of Simon Flexner, director of the Rockefeller Institute, who wanted to use the hospital to test theories that evolved from experimental work in the laboratories of the institute. Cole would have none of this, for he wanted a clinical research unit that was to be free to investigate disease independently. After some arguments Cole gained the support of the trustees, and they authorized the construction of laboratories equipped with the latest instrumentation, as well as modern experimental animal quarters. To facilitate research on patients, the trustees agreed that patients were never to be charged for their care in the Rockefeller Hospital. This unique research hospital opened in 1910.

Initially five diseases were selected for study: poliomyelitis, pneumonia, syphilis, heart disease, and intestinal infantilism (celiac disease). Three were infectious diseases about which there were different levels of knowledge. Poliomyelitis was of interest because its causative agent was unknown. Pneumonia was included because pneumococci could be cultivated to study the biology of the disease-producing organism as well as the patient's defense reaction. Syphilis was added because a chemical, salvasan ("606"), had been discovered as a cure for the disease. This offered an opportunity to study the mechanism by which chemicals killed bacteria *in vivo* in humans. The two noninfectious diseases were heart disease, included because it gave a chance to compare the physiology of the failing heart with a normal one, and intestinal infantilism, because of Christian Herter's interest in this condition.

Cole took on the study of pneumonia because of its prevalence at that time. Using type I pneumococci, Cole immunized horses and produced the first effective serum for the treatment of pneumonia caused by that pneumococcus type. This study resulting in the serum was eventually published as *Acute Lobar Pneumonia. Prevention and Serum Treatment*, which appeared in Monographs of the Rockefeller Institute for Medical Research. Although this was mainly Cole's work, through modesty he placed the names of the collaborators—Oswald Theodore Avery, Henry T. Chickering, and Alphonse R. Dochez—in alphabetical order, not with his name first.

Probably Cole's greatest contribution to science was bringing Avery, then a young Canadian bacteriologist, to the Rockefeller Institute. Avery devoted his entire career to the study of pneumonia and eventually made the important discovery, using pneumococci, that genetic information could be transferred by nucleic acids. When the United States entered World War I, Cole studied pneumonia on the wards of military hospitals and gathered data from military records. Based on this research, he pointed out to the surgeon general the severity of pneumonia in armies, that those individuals who had escaped previous exposure to the organism were at much greater risk, and that most pneumonia was caused by pneumococcus types I and II. Cole and two assistants, Dochez and Avery, were sent by the surgeon general to Fort Sam Houston in Texas to study pneumonia. Here they found that although a few cases were caused by pneumococcus, most of the pneumonia resulted from infection with hemolytic streptococci as a complication of measles.

In the 1920s and 1930s Cole's interest turned to finding ways to improve medical education and stimulate clinical investigation. In this interval he continued his interest in the epidemiology of pneumonia and methods for improving the ventilation of public schools. Another of Cole's great contributions was the example he set that stimulated his students to become distinguished medical scientists. In addition to Avery, Dochez, and Herter, these included George Draper, Francis Weld Peabody, George Canby Robinson, and Homer Fordyce Swift. Among his trainees were twenty-two members of the National Academy of Sciences and forty-six members of the Association of American Physicians; five were awarded the association's highest award, the Kober Medal.

Cole was also instrumental in establishing clinical investigation as a discipline in the United States. He argued for organizing a medical school in which all members of the faculty including the clinicians would be on staff full time. Cole chose the University of Chicago as the site for the school because all its basic science departments were strong and gave medical students good preclinical instruction before they entered their clinical training at the Rush Medical College, which was affiliated with the university.

In 1937 Cole retired from the staff of the Rockefeller Institute, at which time he and his wife moved from New York City to their home in Mount Kisco, New York, which they had owned for many years and had used as a weekend retreat. Cole's wife died in 1951 but, in spite of this loss, Cole continued serving on boards and dedicated considerable time to improving nursing care of the sick in hospitals in the vicinity of Mount Kisco. Cole also published a book on English gardening, painted in watercolors and oils, and wrote poetry. His most scholarly work was his book, *Human History: The 17th Century and the Stuart Family* (1959). Another main interest of Cole's was maintaining the welfare of the library of the New York Academy of Medicine. Cole died in Washington, D.C.

• Cole's personal papers are in the library of the American Philosophical Society. The Rockefeller University archives maintain no collection of Cole's papers, but correspondence of his colleagues there contain many references to him, as do documents relating to the university's administration while Cole was there. A good account of Cole's life is Phillip Miller, National Academy of Sciences, *Biographical Memoirs* 50 (1979): 117–39. Information about Cole's activities at the Rockefeller Institute are in George W. Corner, *A History of the Rockefeller Institute: 1901–1953, Origins and Growth* (1964); Thomas Rivers, "Reflections on a Life in Medicine and Science," an oral history prepared by Saul Benison (1967); Rene J. Dubos, *The Professor, the Institute, and DNA* (1976); and A. McGehee Harvey, *Science at the Bedside: Clinical Research in American Medicine, 1905–1945* (1981).

DAVID Y. COOPER

COLE, Thomas (1 Feb. 1801–11 Feb. 1848), landscape painter, was born in Bolton-le-Moor, Lancashire, England, the son of James Cole, a muslin manufacturer, and Mary (maiden name unknown). His parents encouraged his artistic tendencies but were incapable of providing him with an artistic education. For a short time he attended a boarding school in Chester and at about age fourteen went to work as an engraver at a calico printworks in Chorley. James Cole's business failed in the depression following the end of the Napoleonic wars, and in 1818 the Cole family immigrated to the United States. Cole spent his first year in the New World working as an engraver in Philadelphia. Joining his family in Steubenville, Ohio, he began a career as an itinerant portraitist and artistic jack-of-all-trades. In 1823 he moved back to Philadelphia, where he studied the paintings on view at the Pennsylvania Academy of the Fine Arts, including landscapes by Thomas Birch and Thomas Doughty, and drew from the academy's cast collection.

Although fascinated by landscape painting and already a passionate student of nature, Cole was also attracted to history painting, which ranked higher in the academic hierarchy of artistic genres. However, history painting required expensive, time-consuming training in figure drawing and perspective; landscape was thus a practical choice for an impecunious young artist. At this point Cole's knowledge of landscape painting was at best rudimentary. In an effort to remedy his deficiencies, in the spring of 1825 he turned to William Oram's *Precepts and Observations on the Art of Colouring in Landscape Painting* (1810), a how-to manual that offered precise formulae for rendering tonal gradations and aerial perspective and for choosing colors for different types of landscape situations. This book exerted a lasting influence on his technique.

By then Cole had moved to New York, where he began to exhibit his work. In October 1825 three paintings representing scenes in the vicinity of the newly opened Catskill Mountain House came to the attention of Colonel John Trumbull, celebrated painter of the revolutionary war scenes in the Capitol rotunda, president of the American Academy of Fine Arts, and an enormously influential figure in the small world of American art. In an encounter that soon became legendary, the aged Trumbull is said to have praised Cole for having accomplished in landscape painting what he himself had for years attempted in vain (Trumbull's surviving landscapes look leaden by comparison with Cole's). More importantly, Trumbull arranged for the exhibition of Cole's work in the rooms of the American Academy and also put him in touch with an extensive network of aristocratic patrons and collectors that included Philip Hone, a politician and leader of New York's social elite; Stephen Van Rensselaer III, proprietor of a vast quasi-feudal estate near Albany, New York, and holder of the ancient title "Patroon"; Daniel Wadsworth, heir of a great Hartford financier and an amateur landscapist; and Robert Gilmor of Baltimore, the knowledgeable owner of a large collection of European and American painting.

Cole appeared at precisely the right historical moment. With landscape tourism growing by leaps and bounds and with nature now identified with American nationality and religious sentiment, the demand for landscape painting had never been greater. From the beginning of his career in New York, Cole demonstrated a unique ability to infuse his portrayals of American scenery with an urgency, a sense of sublime drama lacking in the work of such contemporaries as Birch and Doughty. His depictions of American nature appealed to a wide audience, and he rapidly gained a reputation as the nation's foremost landscape painter.

Cole painted Catskill Mountain scenery throughout his career (he settled permanently in the town of Catskill after his marriage in 1836 to Maria Bartow, a Catskill resident, with whom he had three children who survived infancy), but he began almost immediately to enlarge his range of landscape subjects, traveling to Lake George in 1826, the White Mountains in 1827, 1828, and 1839, the northern Adirondacks in 1837, and Mount Desert Island in Maine in 1845. He visited Niagara Falls twice and also traveled extensively in southern New England. His spectacular rendition of the view from Mount Holyoke, Massachusetts, popularly known as *The Oxbow* (1836), is with reason considered his masterpiece. In this portrayal of a vast landscape, Cole deliberately juxtaposed contradictory perspectives and modes of seeing along with other sets of visual and symbolic oppositions—storm and sunshine, wilderness and pastoral landscape—to produce a species of optical excitement, a cacophony of vision that can be taken as a pictorial equivalent of the exhilaration associated with actual landscape panoramas.

Although often taking liberties with foreground details, in his landscapes Cole generally worked in a naturalistic vein, relying heavily on conventional compositional devices derived from the work of the seventeenth-century landscapists Salvator Rosa (known for his depictions of wild and sublime nature) and Claude Lorrain (a specialist in pastoral scenes) as well as more recent English landscape painting. Adapting European artistic forms and aesthetic theories to American scenery, Cole depicted a pristine American wilderness, often omitting the accoutrements of modern-day tourism while adding figures of Native Americans, as in his well-known *Kaaterskill Falls* (1827). He also painted pastoral scenes in the manner of Claude Lorrain—for example, *View on the Catskill, Early Autumn* (1837), a vision of a peaceful valley as yet undisturbed by the inroads of industry. Traveling to Europe in 1829–1832 and again in 1841–1842, Cole added subjects from the grand tour to his repertory: the Alps, the Colosseum, ruined aqueducts in the Roman Campagna, Tivoli, Mount Etna seen from Taormina, and so forth. His European trips afforded him opportunities to study the works of the Old Masters as well as those of such contemporary landscapists as J. M. W. Turner, John Constable, and John Martin. (He met all three artists in London and on at least one occasion went sketching with Constable.)

European art and the ruins he saw in Italy intensified Cole's interest in history painting. Yet even before his first European tour, he had begun producing "historical landscapes"—landscape compositions with subjects taken from the Bible, John Milton's *Paradise Lost*, and contemporary literature, including James Fenimore Cooper's *Last of the Mohicans*. In 1828 Cole exhibited *The Garden of Eden* and *The Expulsion from the Garden of Eden*, the first of several attempts to produce narrative sequences consisting of two or more paintings. An able poet and talented essayist—his "Essay on American Scenery" of 1836 is a classic statement of American landscape aesthetics—he employed texts of his own devising for most of these narrative works.

Cole assumed that pairs and series executed in what he called "a higher style of landscape" would secure his lasting fame as an artist, but convincing patrons to purchase such works became a recurrent source of frustration. In 1833 he managed to persuade Luman Reed, a nouveau riche dry-goods merchant who was adding a large gallery to his Greenwich Street mansion, to commission *The Course of Empire*. Completed in 1836, this five-painting allegory—the artist's most ambitious series—depicted in vivid detail the rise and fall of an unnamed ancient empire. Based on the cyclical theory of history, which held that republics rise from savagery to an ideal pastoral or arcadian state, only to be corrupted by "luxury" and undermined by demagogues and tyrants, *The Course of Empire* could be interpreted as a thinly veiled attack on Jacksonian democracy, which Cole and his aristocratic patrons, many of them diehard Federalists, believed was destroying the virtuous republic of the founding fathers. *The Course of Empire* led to commissions for two smaller allegories set in the Middle Ages—*The Departure* and *The Return* (1837) for William P. Van Rensselaer (the Patroon's son) and *Past* and *Present* (1838) for P. G. Stuyvesant—which in effect allegorized aristocracy in decline, idealizing aristocratic strength and authority while at the same time mourning its passing.

Highly critical of democracy, fearful of the effects of industrialization, and believing that American society was irrevocably headed for disaster, Cole turned increasingly to religious subjects. For his earlier pairs and series Cole had employed imagery derived from the European tradition of high art; however, for *The Voyage of Life*—a set of four paintings executed for the banker Samuel Ward—he drew upon the literature and imagery of English religious Dissent, the popular religious and cultural tradition in which he had been raised in Lancashire. Inspired by works such as John Bunyan's *Pilgrim's Progress*, Cole conceived of *The Voyage of Life* as a series of painted emblems—arbitrary and unrealistic compilations of traditional images and symbols that depended for their meaning on such familiar cultural conceits as life as a river journey. Thus the series showed the nameless voyager emerging from the "cave of birth" in *Childhood*, imagining castles in the air in *Youth*, praying for Christian salvation as his rudderless boat braves the shoals and rapids of *Manhood*, and arriving in *Old Age* at the placid "ocean of eternity."

Despite the popular success he achieved with *The Voyage of Life*, Cole found it impossible to secure patronage for a second large-scale Bunyanesque series, this one involving five large paintings and entitled *The Cross and the World*. Embittered by what he considered the low level of American taste and now deeply involved in religion—in Catskill he attended St. Luke's Episcopal Church, and in 1844 he and his wife were baptized by the Reverend Louis Legrand Noble,

his future biographer—he spent the last two years of his life in Catskill working without commission on *The Cross and the World*. (The series remained unfinished at his death and was eventually lost.) Cole died in Catskill, probably of pleurisy.

Cole's religious allegories enjoyed a tremendous vogue during the years immediately following his death. *The Voyage of Life* served as the centerpiece of a large memorial exhibition held in New York City in the spring of 1848. The series helped to attract perhaps as many as 500,000 people (then the equivalent of half the population of New York City) to the exhibition. Later in 1848, when the American Art-Union selected *The Voyage of Life* as a prize in its annual lottery, its membership nearly doubled. And during the 1850s and 1860s, an engraved version of the series by James A. Smillie was a common feature of middle-class American homes. Yet by the mid-1850s American critics, taking a cue from John Ruskin's aesthetic theories, were condemning Cole's allegories as untrue to nature, and his series quickly went out of fashion among professional artists and elite collectors. The vogue for romantic landscape painting waned more slowly, but by the turn of the century Cole's landscapes too were all but forgotten.

During the 1930s a renewed interest in the history of American culture led to a revival of Cole's art. By the mid-1950s such works as *The Oxbow*, *The Course of Empire*, and *The Voyage of Life* had become fixtures in a canonical history of American art. In the 1960s, as the market for nineteenth-century American art began to boom, museums and private collectors increasingly sought examples of the artist's work. Scholars celebrated Cole as the founder of the Hudson River school of landscape painting and quite rightly saw such artists as Frederic Church, his pupil, along with Asher B. Durand, Jasper F. Cropsey, Albert Bierstadt, and Thomas Moran, as building on Cole's achievements as a landscapist. These artists dominated American painting in the 1850s, 1860s, and 1870s, creating large-scale works that extolled the doctrine of Manifest Destiny. Yet by the 1980s it had become evident that Cole differed substantially in outlook from later members of the Hudson River school. If they were romantic optimists, he was, by contrast, a romantic pessimist, prone to dark prophecies for the future of the United States and finding in the Christian promise of salvation an antidote to the disappointments and crises of secular history. In crucial respects he shared the outlook of his aristocratic patrons. Like them, he longed for an unchanging, hierarchical world based on deference and noblesse oblige. This deeply conservative viewpoint may be unfamiliar or unexpected, but it was profoundly of its period, and it furnished Cole's art with an underlying unity.

• Major collections of Cole's letters, journals, sketchbooks, and drawings can be found at the New York State Library in Albany and the Detroit Institute of Arts and are available on microfilm at the Archives of American Art at the Smithsonian

Institution. For transcriptions of Cole's writings, see Marshall B. Tymn, ed., *Thomas Cole's Poetry* (1972), and Thomas Cole, *The Collected Essays and Prose Sketches*, ed. Marshall Tymn (1980). For early accounts of Cole's life see William Dunlap, *History of the Rise and Progress of the Arts of Design in the United States*, vol. 2 (1834; repr. 1969), pp. 350–67, which includes a revealing autobiographical statement; William Cullen Bryant, *A Funeral Oration Occasioned by the Death of Thomas Cole* (1848); and Louis Legrand Noble, *The Life and Works of Thomas Cole*, ed. Elliot S. Vesell (1853; repr. 1964), which traces the artist's life and reprints excerpts, often highly edited, from the artist's letters and journals. For an extended treatment of Cole's life and art, see Ellwood C. Parry III, *The Art of Thomas Cole* (1988). For a revisionist view, see William C. Truettner and Alan Wallach, eds., *Thomas Cole: Landscape into History* (1994).

ALAN WALLACH

COLEMAN, Alice Blanchard Merriam (7 May 1858–22 Oct. 1936), lay church leader, was born in Boston, Massachusetts, the daughter of James Whyte Merriam, a city missionary, and Ellen Maria Blanchard. After she graduated from Bradford (Mass.) Academy in 1878, an eye condition kept her from learning a language, which was necessary for foreign mission service, so she joined the Woman's Home Missionary Association (Congregational), was elected to its board of managers, and in 1884 toured mission stations as far west as Salt Lake City. Two years later, however, influenced in part by the pastor of Boston's Clarendon Street Church, Adoniram Judson Gordon, an American (northern) Baptist, she changed denominations by joining that church. She then became active in the Woman's American Baptist Home Mission Society (WABHMS) and served as its president from 1890 to 1909. The society's headquarters was in Boston; it was primarily an eastern organization.

In 1891 she married George William Coleman, nine years her junior, who then was business manager of the reformist *New England Magazine* and later became president of the Babson Institute, a business school. A lay leader in Baptist affairs, he became president of the Northern Baptist Convention in 1917 for the regular term of one year. The couple had no children. George Coleman warmly supported his wife's activities in the home mission and other church and humanitarian movements.

Under Alice Coleman's leadership the WABHMS extended its outreach in Alaska, managed an orphanage for Indians, and conducted educational efforts among African Americans in the South, causes she earnestly supported. Her interest in improved educational and vocational opportunities for black Americans never flagged; she was a trustee at various times of Spelman Seminary in Atlanta, Georgia, Hartshorn Memorial College in Richmond, Virginia, and Atlanta University. In 1909, when the WABHMS united with another Baptist regional home mission society that had a similar name but served a midwestern clientele, Coleman became the merged society's first vice president. Beginning in 1920, when the enlarged organization moved its headquarters from Boston to New York City, she served with distinction as its president and chair of its board of managers for eight years.

Coleman's leadership extended beyond her own denomination. In 1908, for example, she helped found the interdenominational Council of Women for Home Missions and served as its first president for eight years, putting this cooperative agency of some twenty women's boards on a secure foundation. Under her guidance the council placed special emphasis on publishing missionary literature in order to encourage interest in and support for missions in cooperating denominations as well as on developing summer conferences based on missionary themes. She took the lead in securing professional paid leadership to guide the growing activities of the council. Coleman wrote numerous articles and pamphlets in support of home missions. Recognizing her growing prominence in interdenominational work, the Northern Baptist Convention later named her as a delegate to the Federal Council of Churches.

From 1907 through 1917 the Colemans hosted the Sagamore Sociological Conferences at their summer home on Cape Cod, Massachusetts, where church, business, and social leaders met for discussion and study. Coleman also helped her husband guide Boston's famous Ford Hall Forum, which he had founded in 1908 for public discussions of community affairs and which became the model for many other such enterprises in the Progressive Era. Active in Boston civic affairs, Coleman served as a founder and second president of the Women's City Club, president of the School Voters League, and trustee of Gordon College. For many years she also was a nonresident worker at Denison House, a social settlement in Boston's South End.

Troubled by poor eyesight all of her life—it even forced her in 1905 to give up teaching a Sunday school class, a task very important to her—Coleman fulfilled her leadership role by depending on her winning personality and her skill in presiding over gatherings. When she retired as president of the WABHMS in 1928, she was praised for her "fervent piety and lofty idealism" and for the "grace and dignity, considerateness and tact" that she had exhibited throughout her forty years of leadership. Along with many other church leaders of her time, Coleman believed that the social causes that were dear to her were also religious causes and that they contributed to the building of the kingdom of God on earth. At her death, a colleague with whom she had worked closely over the decades spoke of "the extraordinary quality of her intellectual grasp and her keen discernment." Survived by her husband, she died at their home on the Fenway in Boston.

• A good deal of information about Alice Coleman and the organizations she served is at the American Baptist Historical Society Library in Rochester, N.Y. For articles about her, see *Watchman-Examiner* 9 (21 July 1921): 919; 16 (19 July

1928): 921; and 24 (24 Dec. 1936): 1430. Her work is discussed by Bertha G. Judd, *Fifty Golden Years: The First Half Century of the Woman's American Baptist Home Mission Society, 1877–1927* (1927). An obituary is in the *New York Times*, 24 Oct. 1936.

ROBERT T. HANDY

COLEMAN, Bessie (26 Jan. 1892–30 Apr. 1926), aviator, was born Elizabeth Coleman in Atlanta, Texas, the daughter of George Coleman, a day laborer of predominately Indian descent, and Susan (maiden name unknown), an African-American domestic and farmworker. While Bessie was still very young, the family moved to Waxahachie, Texas, where they built a three-room house on a quarter-acre of land. She was seven when her father left his family to return to the Indian Territory (Oklahoma). The Coleman household was Baptist, and Bessie was an avid reader who became particularly interested in Booker T. Washington, Harriet Tubman, and Paul Lawrence Dunbar. After finishing high school, she studied for one semester at Langston Industrial College, in Langston, Oklahoma.

Between 1912 and 1917 Coleman joined her two brothers in Chicago, where she studied manicuring at Burnham's School of Beauty Culture and worked at the White Sox Barber Shop. She supplemented her income by running a chili parlor on the corner of Twenty-fifth and Indiana avenues. In 1917 she married Claude Glenn. It was during this time that her brother Johnny related World War I stories to her about women flying planes in France. She decided that this would be her ambition.

Coleman was rejected by a number of American aviation schools because of her race and sex. Robert Abbott, the founder of the *Chicago Defender*, a newspaper dedicated to black interests, suggested that she study aviation in France; she left the United States in November 1920. With Abbott and banker Jesse Binga's financial assistance, she studied at the School of Aviation run by the Caudron Aircraft Manufacturing Company in Le Crotoy. She later trained in Paris under a French pilot who reportedly shot down thirty-one German planes in World War I. Coleman's plane of choice was the 130-horsepower Nieuport de Chasse.

On 15 June 1921 Coleman received her pilot's license, number 18310, the first awarded to an American woman by the French Federation Aeronautique Internationale, and she became the only licensed African-American woman pilot in the world. She returned to the United States in September 1921 but went back to Europe to study in Germany, where she received the first flying license granted to an American woman. She returned to the United States in August 1922.

With her goal of obtaining a pilot's license fulfilled, Coleman then sought to become an accomplished stunt and exhibition pilot. Barnstorming was the aviation fashion of the day, and Coleman decided to become part of these aerial acrobatics. United States air shows were attended by thousands of people. Sponsored by Abbott and Binga, Coleman made her first air show appearance at Curtiss Field in Garden City, Long Island, New York, during Labor Day weekend 1922 flying a Curtiss Aeroplane. She then appeared at an air show at Checkerboard Airdrome in Chicago on 15 October. By this time Coleman had purchased three army surplus Curtiss biplanes.

Coleman's third exhibition was held in Gary, Indiana, where she met David Behncke, the founder and president of the International Airline Pilots Association, who became her manager. The Gary exhibition was supervised by Reynolds McKenzie, an African-American real estate dealer. There Coleman made a parachute jump after a white woman changed her mind.

On 4 February 1923, while Coleman was flying from municipal flying field in Santa Monica, California, to Los Angeles on her first exhibition flight on the Pacific Coast, her Curtiss JN-4 "Jenny" biplane engine failed, and she plunged 300 feet to the ground. The airplane was completely demolished, and Coleman had to be cut from the wreckage. During her recuperation she went on the lecture circuit and resumed flying as soon as she was able. Newspapers reported that she planned to establish a commercial passenger flight service.

Using Houston as her base, Coleman performed at air shows in Columbus, Ohio; Waxahachie and Austin, Texas; Memphis, Tennessee; and Wharton and Cambridge, Massachusetts. She thrilled crowds and became widely known for her flying outfit, which consisted of a pilot's cap, helmet, and goggles, a Sam Browne belt, long jacket and pants, white shirt and tie, and high boots. In 1924 Coast Firestone Rubber Company of California hired Coleman to do aerial advertising.

While recuperating from another airplane accident, which occurred during a race from San Diego to Long Beach, Coleman reflected on her third goal, opening the field to African Americans by establishing an aviation school in Los Angeles. She lectured to church and school groups and attended private dinners, speaking on the opportunities for blacks in aviation. She appeared in a number of documentary news films, and Coleman reportedly was scheduled to appear in *The Flying Ace*, billed as the "greatest airplane mystery thriller ever made"; it was produced in 1926 and featured an all-black cast.

In late April 1926 Coleman was in Florida at the invitation of the Negro Welfare League of Jacksonville to perform in an air show in Orlando for the annual First of May celebration. When the Orlando Chamber of Commerce informed her that African Americans would not be allowed to view her performance, she refused to participate in the show until "the Jim Crow order had been revoked and aviators had been sent up to drop placards letting the members of our race know they could come into the field" (Marjorie Kritz, "Bessie Coleman, Aviator Pioneer," undated leaflet, U.S. Department of Transportation). William D. Wills, Coleman's publicity agent and mechanic, flew her Jenny plane from Texas because local agencies would not rent a plane to a black person. Mechanical problems had occurred during the flight from Texas, and on the morning of Friday, 30 April, at Paxon Field, during a practice run, after the plane had been in the air only twelve minutes and had reached 3,000 feet, Wills, who was at the instruments, attempted to complete a nose-dive, but the plane did not right itself. Though safety conscious, Coleman apparently had failed to secure her seat belt or wear a parachute. "Brave Bessie" was catapulted out of the plane and fell to her death. The plane continued in a downward spiral and crashed; Wills was also killed. Members of the Eighth Regiment of the Illinois National Guard served as pallbearers at Coleman's funeral in Chicago.

Coleman's place in aviation history is secure. In 1929 William J. Powell, author of *Black Wings* (1934), organized the Bessie Coleman School in Los Angeles. Bessie Coleman Aero Clubs, which promoted interest in aviation within the African-American community, soon sprang up all across the United States, and the *Bessie Coleman Aero News*, a monthly periodical edited by Powell, first appeared in May 1930. On Labor Day 1931 the Bessie Coleman Aero Club sponsored the first all-black air show in the United States. Every Memorial Day African-American aviators fly over her gravesite at Lincoln Cemetery in Chicago in single-file nose low to allow women passengers to drop flowers on her grave. Chicago mayor Harold Washington proclaimed 26 April 1986 Bessie Coleman Day. Also in 1986 the Federal Aviation Administration created the Bessie Intersection, located forty miles west of Chicago's O'Hare Airport, in her honor. She is included in a monument to African-American aviators, *Black Americans in Flight*, at Lambert–St. Louis International Airport. On 27 April 1994 a U.S. Postal Service Bessie Coleman commemorative stamp was issued. She continues to be an inspiration to young African-American women.

• Doris L. Rich, *Queen Bess: Daredevil Aviator* (1993), and Elizabeth Freydberg, *Bessie Coleman: The Brownskin Lady Bird* (1994), are modern biographies. Elois Patterson, *Memoirs of the Late Bessie Coleman, Aviatrix; Pioneer of the Negro People in Aviation* (1969), is an account of Coleman by her sister. *The Negro in Chicago, 1779 to 1929* (1929) contains a photograph of Coleman's tombstone showing her date of birth. See also articles on Coleman in the *Chicago Defender*, 8 Oct. 1921 and 14 Oct. 1922, and the *New York Times*, 14 and 27 Aug. 1922; *Bessie Coleman Aero News* 1 (1930); James Goodrich, "Salute to Bessie Coleman," *Negro Digest* 8 (1950): 82–83, which includes a photo; Philip St. Laurent, "Bessie Coleman, Aviator," *Tuesday Magazine*, Jan. 1973, pp. 10–12; Anita King's two-part "Brave Bessie: First Black Pilot," *Essence*, May 1976, p. 36, and June 1976, p. 48; and Michelle Bergen, "They Take to the Sky: Group of Midwest Women Follow Path Blazed by Pioneer Bessie Coleman," *Ebony*, May 1977, pp. 88–90. An account of her fatal accident is in the *Chicago Defender*, 8 May 1926.

CONSTANCE PORTER UZELAC

COLEMAN, Bill (4 Aug. 1904–24 Aug. 1981), jazz musician, was born William Johnson Coleman in Centerville, Kentucky, the son of Robert Henry Coleman, a cook, and Roberta Johnson, a seamstress. Coleman's parents had separated by the time he was five, and he grew up with his mother and an aunt in Crawfordville, Indiana. When he was seven, he moved with his mother to Cincinnati, a popular stop on the Theater Owners' Booking Association circuit and a city that hosted traveling circuses, riverboats, jug bands, and medicine shows. He saw blues singers Mamie Smith, Ma Rainey, and Bessie Smith at local vaudeville houses. When he was fourteen, he joined a band organized to teach young boys music, and he began playing alto saxophone. At seventeen he took piano lessons and did some singing. A year later, he bought a cornet he saw in a pawnshop window. While earning money in a variety of odd jobs, he taught himself the instrument and began to perform at social gatherings. He also started to play with trombonist J. C. Higginbotham, pianist Edgar Hayes, and others at area roadhouses. He led his own group (as Professor Johnson Coleman and His Band) for an engagement in Richmond, Indiana, and he played weekends at a vacation camp in Kalamazoo, Michigan.

In 1923 Coleman joined the Clarence Paige orchestra and traveled more widely. He heard players such as Louis Armstrong with Fletcher Henderson on a 1925 recording of "Money Blues," and Rex Stewart, with the Henderson band in 1926. (He had married his first wife, Madelyn Grant, in 1925.) In early 1927 he joined the Lloyd Scott orchestra for six months, first on tour and then playing at New York's Savoy Ballroom. In New York he heard the Duke Ellington band and Armstrong play in person for the first time. The Scott group toured extensively. Coleman struggled to earn a living over the next five years, playing for theater shows, at black dances in places like the Renaissance Ballroom, and occasionally as an accompanist at dancing schools. But he also played in groups led by Cecil Scott (1929–1930), Horace Henderson (1930), Charlie Johnson (1930), and Luis Russell (1929, 1931–1932). In 1933 he went overseas for the first time, with Lucky Millinder's group. When he returned, he joined Benny Carter's orchestra and played at the Apollo, the Harlem Club, and the Empire Ballroom. He joined the Teddy Hill group in January 1934, and he recorded with Hill and with Fats Waller.

In September 1935 Coleman became one of the first American jazz musicians to seek escape from American racism by moving to Paris, where he found "a mellow, cultural city where you were accepted for what you were!" (Carr et al., p. 99). He worked with the dancer and bandleader Freddy Taylor in 1935 and 1936, and he recorded with Willie Lewis's band in 1936. In January 1936 he made his first recordings under his own name. He traveled to India with Leon Abbey's band (1936–1937), returning to Paris to record in July 1937 with guitarist Django Reinhardt and trombonist Dickie Wells and in November 1937 with violinist Stéphane Grappelli. He traveled to Egypt with the Harlem Rhythm Makers (1938–1940); in March 1939 he played at the wedding of Muhammed Reza Pahlevi, the future shah of Iran, in Cairo. On jazz standards like "I Got Rhythm," recorded with Reinhardt, Coleman played with "light phrasing and almost translucent tone" (Liam Keating, liner notes to Charly Records' 1993 CD issue of Wells and Coleman, *Swingin' in Paris*); he also exhibited an "irrepressible vivacity" and the elegant sensitivity that made him increasingly popular throughout Europe.

Coleman returned to New York City in March 1940. He continued to tour widely and record often, playing with Carter and Fats Waller (1940), Teddy Wilson (1940–1941), Andy Kirk (1941–1942), Ellis Larkins (1943), Mary Lou Williams (trio and orchestra, 1944), John Kirby (1945), Sy Oliver (1946–1947), and Billy Kyle (1947–1948). He made recordings with most of these groups, highlighted by a series of excellent solos with Carter's group on "Embraceable You," "But Not for Me," and "Lady Be Good," among others. He also recorded with Lester Young for Commodore Records in 1942 and 1944. In March 1945 he recorded in Los Angeles with the Capitol International Jazzmen, a group that included Carter, Coleman Hawkins, Nat "King" Cole, and drummer Max Roach. He also continued to perform abroad, touring the Philippines and Japan with a USO group during 1945.

Invited to play at the opening of a new club in Paris, Coleman returned to Europe in December 1948. He remained in France for the rest of his life. His lyrical playing, lively singing, and open personality made him enormously popular throughout France and Europe. He played often in Belgium, Germany, and especially Switzerland at festivals, in concerts, and on television programs, and he recorded extensively with both European and American jazz artists. By now he had divorced his first wife, and in Paris in October 1953 he married his second wife, Lily Renee Yersin, who took over managing his career. He had no children from either marriage. He returned for brief visits to the United States in 1954 and 1958, only to be reminded in several ugly incidents of the pervasive racial prejudice that had driven him away.

Despite mounting health problems, Coleman toured and recorded in the 1960s and 1970s, playing in England in 1966 and 1967 and recording with tenor saxophonist Ben Webster. In 1968 he was elected to the French Academy of Jazz; in 1969 he realized a lifelong ambition by playing in the band accompanying Duke Ellington during Ellington's appearance on French television. In 1971 the U.S. Cultural Center's African programming office engaged him to go to West Africa to familiarize the National Orchestra of the Ivory Coast with jazz. In 1972 the French celebrated his jubilee (fifty years of playing the trumpet) with articles in jazz magazines, appearances on TV, and recognition throughout the country, and in 1974 the government made him a knight of the Order of Merit, the second-highest official distinction in France. He lived his last few years in the village of Cadeillan and died in Toulouse.

Like all trumpet players of his generation, Coleman was greatly influenced by Armstrong. But he gradually developed his own style and voice and became noted for his elegant, fluid phrasing, lovely melodic ideas, ease in the upper register, and relaxed approach. Essentially a swing player, he remained musically adventurous, even adopting some bop ideas during the 1940s and 1950s. Perhaps his greatest contribution to jazz, though, lies in his work as "a modern-time minstrel," an ambassador of jazz to the rest of the world.

• Coleman's autobiography, *Trumpet Story* (1981), a detailed overview of his career, is the best available source. Max Harrison et al., *The Essential Jazz Recordings*, vol. 1, *Ragtime to Swing* (1984), perceptively analyzes several of Coleman's recording sessions. Dan Morgenstern provides knowledgeable commentary in his notes for the 1944 session with Lester Young in Mosaic Records' *The Complete Commodore Jazz Recordings*, vol. 2 (1988). A succinct overview appears in Ian Carr et al., *Jazz: The Essential Companion* (1987). The most comprehensive obituary was published in *Jazz Journal International*, Nov. 1981.

RONALD P. DUFOUR

COLEMAN, Warren Clay (25 Mar. 1849–31 Mar. 1904), businessman, was born a slave in Cabarrus County, North Carolina, the son of Rufus C. Barringer, a white lawyer and politician, and Roxanna Coleman. Little is known about his parents, but as a youngster he learned the shoemaker's trade and also barbering. After the Civil War he briefly attended Howard University in Washington, D.C., paying for his board and room by hawking jewelry. He also worked as an itinerant salesman in North Carolina; he saved his earnings, and in 1869 he purchased a 130-acre farm in Cabarrus County, paying $600 for the well-timbered land. In 1870 he was listed in the census as the proprietor of a small grocery store in the town of Concord, North Carolina, with a total estate of $800 in real and personal property. During the same period he also began purchasing low-priced rental houses in and around Concord, paying between $125 and $300, and renting them for between $.50 and $1.25 per week. He continued this real estate activity for many years, and according to one estimate he eventually owned nearly 100 rental houses. In 1873 he married Jane E. Jones, a native of Alabama, in a church wedding; the couple had no children. He later became a trustee of the African Methodist Episcopal Zion Church.

During the late 1870s and early 1880s Coleman engaged in a variety of business enterprises, including a barber shop, a bakery shop, and a grocery store. He advertised in the *Concord Times* in 1880 that he specialized in selling teas, coffee, sugar, syrups, home and imported molasses, cakes, and candies. In 1881 he purchased a lot on Main Street in Concord and later opened a mercantile store, but only four years later he was temporarily put out of business by a disastrous fire. He rebuilt, and in 1890 the business was worth $5,000, a large enterprise when compared with other black-owned businesses of the time. Coleman had become one of the most prosperous African Americans in North Carolina.

In 1896, near the end of a depression, Coleman decided to construct a cotton mill in Concord, to be operated by blacks. Toward that end he wrote Booker T. Washington to solicit funds. "The books have been open for subscriptions only a very short time," he wrote, "and shows upwards of the amount of $10,000, already subscribed, with a steady increase and a bright future" (*Booker T. Washington Papers*, ed. Louis Harlan, vol. 4 [14 vols., 1972–], p. 117). In 1898 Coleman opened the Coleman Manufacturing Company, beginning not only with subscriptions from blacks, but also with a loan in 1899 from the wealthy white tobacco magnate Benjamin Duke for the purchase of new machinery. The company manufactured cotton goods and yarn. In 1900, according to a report issued by the National Negro Business League, Coleman employed 230 black workers, possessed a 270-horsepower Corliss engine and a three-story brick building, and boasted assets worth $100,000. "Our business grows more and more," he said in 1902, and the next year he was employing about 350 black workers. Coleman billed his company as a cooperative venture, one that would help the race. In the entire South in this period there was only a small number of black manufacturers (including brick maker Richard Fitzgerald of Durham and doll maker Richard Henry Boyd of Nashville). Black textile companies were especially rare and typically short-lived.

Coleman's enterprise began experiencing difficulties even as it reached its zenith. Inefficient machinery, insufficient materials, inexperienced management, and untrained workers, compounded by marketing problems and the belief in the southern Piedmont that cotton mill management and labor should be controlled by whites, caused the company to become unstable. Coleman's untimely death in Concord brought the experiment to an end, and the Coleman Manufacturing Company was sold to whites, who subsequently employed white operatives.

While establishing an all-black enterprise, Coleman had sought the support of whites, especially Washington Duke, who purchased stock in the company. He believed, as did his acquaintance Booker T. Washington, that a successful business enterprise would reveal to those of the "white race who are our friends" that blacks were on the rise. "Coleman was a colored man of great energy and great force of character," the *Concord Times* said the day after his death. "He was always respectful to white people and maintained pleasant relations with the white population generally."

• For Coleman correspondence, see the Washington Duke Papers, Duke University. Also see Allen Edward Burgess, "Tar Heel Blacks and the New South Dream: The Coleman Manufacturing Company, 1896–1940" (Ph.D. diss., Duke Univ., 1977), J. E. Rouse, *The Noble Experiment of Warren C. Coleman* (1972), and Holland Thompson, *From the Cotton Field to the Cotton Mill* (1906). An obituary is in the *Concord Times*, 1 Apr. 1904.

LOREN SCHWENINGER

COLEMAN, William Tell (29 Feb. 1824–22 Nov. 1893), merchant and vigilante, was born near Cynthiana, Kentucky, the son of Napoleon Bonaparte Coleman, a civil engineer and lawyer (mother's name unknown). Both his parents had died by the time the boy was nine, and an aunt mothered him and his three siblings on their maternal grandfather John Chinn's plantation in Kentucky. At fifteen Coleman was given a job on a railroad survey in Illinois by his uncle Marcus Chinn, but when the state's program for railroads collapsed the next year, he went to St. Louis where he worked in an insurance and later a lumber company. At the age of eighteen, he entered St. Louis University and completed the four-year legal course in two, but overstudy had brought on the symptoms of tuberculosis. After regaining his health in Florida, he became the overseer of a plantation at West Baton Rouge, Louisiana, for his uncle, Whig ex-congressman Thomas W. Chinn. He soon left Louisiana, however, for St. Louis, and his former employers in the lumber company sent him to Wisconsin to look after their timber tracts and sawmills.

With his brother DeWitt, Coleman went overland to California, arriving at Sutter's Fort on 14 August 1849. The two young men became builders and speculators in real estate in Sacramento but soon moved on to Hangtown (Placerville) to establish a mercantile business. Their activity in this field was short-lived; DeWitt went to Oregon and William to San Francisco, where he started the merchandising firm of William T. Coleman & Company, first locating on Sansome Street and then moving to Montgomery Street. The fire of 4 May, 1851, the fifth and greatest in a series of fires, burned him out, but he quickly rebuilt and soon had the largest commission business in San Francisco.

Coleman came to prominence as a member of the executive committee of the 1851 Committee of Vigilance for the suppression of crime. Founded in June and dominated by commission merchants and sea captains, it came to have a membership of approximately 500. Coleman usually favored a more moderate and deliberate course than the quick decision and execution advocated by the leader, Sam Brannan. Before its extrajudicial activities ended in September, the Committee of Vigilance had arrested nearly ninety-one people, of which four were hanged and twenty-eight sentenced to deportation.

In 1852 Coleman went east by way of the Isthmus of Panama to Boston, where in August he married Carrie M. Page, the daughter of Daniel D. Page, one of the founders of the banking firm of Page & Bacon in St. Louis. Coleman and his wife were to have at least two children. Without his bride, he made a hurried trip to California in 1853 and on returning to the East established a branch of his firm in New York City.

In 1856 he again went to San Francisco alone and in his words "found a state of affairs not at all encouraging for the prospect of a comfortable residence, or the prosperity of the country, or security; social, political, or otherwise" (quoted by Scherer, p. 147). The city had been governed mainly by Democrats under David C. Broderick. Improvements had been made in the booming, cosmopolitan city, but merchants—concerned about the rampant graft, the soaring municipal debt, and skyrocketing taxes—were not averse to taking control of the government. But the immediate cause of the revival of the vigilance movement was the 14 May shooting of James King of William, the anti-Catholic editor of the *Daily Evening Bulletin*, by the politician James P. Casey. King had denounced the Tammany-style political machine of Broderick and accused him of having imported Casey, an Irish Catholic, from New York City as an expert ballot-box stuffer. He also revealed that Casey had served a term in the penitentiary at Sing Sing.

The shooting of King became interrelated in the public mind with the earlier killing of a U.S. marshal by an Italian-Catholic gambler named Charles Cora. Cora's first trial ended in a hung jury, which had brought scathing editorials from King. Cora was in jail awaiting a second trial on the day King was shot, and the Committee of Vigilance, with Coleman as chairman of its powerful committee, was organized. The vigilantes seized Casey and Cora from the jail, tried them, and on the day of King's funeral, hanged them with great public ceremony.

The vigilance committee made further arrests, strengthened the defenses of its headquarters building known as Fort Gunnybags, scuffled with the Law and Order party, and defied the governor. Approximately 6,000 joined the movement before it was disbanded in August 1856. It hanged four accused murderers, including Cora and Casey, sentenced twenty-eight others to deportation, and possibly frightened several hundred other bad characters into leaving the city. During the 1851 movement, the expatriated had largely been ex-convicts from Sydney, Australia; in 1856 they were primarily Americans, either by birth or adoption, and more tainted by political corruption than the others. As a result of the movement, former vigilantes won control of city offices and slashed taxes.

After completing his vigilante work, Coleman left almost immediately for New York, which became his base of operations for the next fourteen years, although he frequently traveled to and from California. In developing a fleet of clipper ships (Coleman's California Line) and a steamship line for sailing around Cape Horn, he was more often the charterer than the owner of the vessels. As a Union Democrat, he helped subdue the New York City draft riots during the Civil War.

He took his family to San Francisco in the early 1870s and erected a white Roman villa on Nob Hill and a spacious country home in San Mateo county. In the anti-Chinese agitation of July 1877, during which a mob wrecked Chinese laundries and tried to burn the docks of the Pacific Mail Steamship Company, thought to be the largest importer of Chinese laborers, business owners organized a Committee of Public Safety with Coleman as president. The U.S. Army put rifles and ammunition at his disposal, but Coleman armed the 5,000 or so men who enlisted in the "merchants' militia" with hickory pick handles. Within a few days, order was restored and the committee was disbanded.

In addition to its normal wholesale mercantile trade, Coleman's company acted as commission agents for numerous manufacturers and put money into the salmon, fruit, and sugar industries. His last venture, a heavy investment in borax property in Death Valley, proved ruinous. His economic kingdom, which had an estimated business of $14 million a year, collapsed in 1886. He finally paid off his creditors a year before his death in San Francisco.

Among the honors conferred on Coleman were the presidencies of the Society of California Pioneers and the San Francisco Chamber of Commerce. Various newspapers and officials sought his candidacy as a Democrat for the presidency, but he was never nominated. Hubert Howe Bancroft, a historian of early California, praised Coleman in the highest terms, noting that physically he was "tall, large, symmetrical in form." General William T. Sherman described him as "a man of fine impulses, manners, character, and intelligence. . . . He has not much education and not the least doubt of himself, his motives or intentions." That Coleman was able to maintain his prestigious status in San Francisco over three decades is a tribute to his ability to adapt to the ever-shifting economic and social structure of the city.

• Coleman's short pamphlet, *The Chinese Question Considered by a Calm and Dispassionate Merchant* (1882), was an argument against further "Mongolian" immigration. James A. B. Scherer, *"The Lion of the Vigilantes," William T. Coleman and the Life of Old San Francisco* (1939), is a laudatory biography. A more critical treatment is Richard Maxwell Brown, *Strain of Violence: Historical Studies of American Violence and Vigilantes* (1975). Peter R. Decker, *Fortunes and Failures: White-Collar Mobility in Nineteenth Century San Francisco* (1978), characterizes the vigilantes as businessmen seeking to bolster their economic position. Doyce B. Nunis, Jr., ed., *The San Francisco Vigilance Committee of 1856: Three Views* (1971), has a fine bibliography and shows how writers' assessments of the work and value of the 1856 vigilance committee has changed over time. Nunis reprints from *Century Magazine* (Nov. and Dec. 1891) Coleman's reflections on the 1851, 1856, and 1877 movements, William T. Sherman's 1856 letters articulating the attitude of the "Law and Order" faction, and the little pamphlet of James O'Meara, a trained journalist who was in San Francisco at the time but did not participate on either side. The second volume of Hubert Howe Bancroft's massive two-volume *Popular Tribunals* (1887) is devoted entirely to the vigilance committee of 1856. Mary Floyd Williams edited the *Papers of the San Francisco Committee of Vigilance of 1851* (1919); her *History of the San Francisco Committee of Vigilance of 1851* (1921) is generally very admiring. An obituary is in the San Francisco Chronicle, 23 Nov. 1893.

MARY LEE SPENCE

COLES, Edward (15 Dec. 1786–7 July 1868), slavery opponent and second governor of Illinois, was born in Albemarle County, Virginia, the son of Colonel John Coles and Rebecca Tucker, wealthy, slaveholding planters. The eighth of twelve children, almost from the day of his birth Edward was associated with the great and near-great in revolutionary American society. One of the first families of Virginia, the Coles moved in a social circle that included national figures such as Thomas Jefferson, James Madison, James Monroe, and Patrick Henry.

Coles studied first at Hampden-Sydney College and then at the College of William and Mary, but a severe leg injury prevented him from graduating. His father's death in 1808 left him the owner of a 782-acre plantation and twenty slaves. Already the young planter had severe misgivings over the propriety of holding fellow human beings in bondage and had begun to make plans to move his property to free territory in the West. He served for six years (1809–1815) as private secretary to President Madison before making his first exploratory visit to Illinois in 1815. On that trip he purchased 6,000 acres of land in Madison and St. Clair counties near Edwardsville in the Illinois Territory.

At President Madison's request, in 1816 Coles undertook a delicate diplomatic mission to Russia. Completed successfully, he traveled leisurely across Europe and the British Isles before returning home in the spring of 1817. A second trip west in 1818 confirmed Coles's decision to move to Illinois, then becoming the twenty-first state in the Union. He was able to attend the constitutional convention meeting in Kaskaskia. Slavery had existed in Illinois since the days of French settlement and had continued to flourish in spite of the Ordinance of 1787, but Coles was satisfied when the delegates approved an admittedly weak antislavery provision.

After settling his affairs in Virginia, Coles moved to Illinois in the spring of 1819, taking his slave property with him. While on a boat floating down the Ohio River on what Coles described as "a mild, calm and lovely April day," he announced to his dumbfounded chattels that they were free. In addition to formal deeds of emancipation, Coles gave each head of family 160 acres of land and assisted his former slaves in making a new start in life.

Moving to Illinois with the appointment from President Monroe as registrar of the Edwardsville land office enabled Coles to extend his acquaintance widely among the people of his adopted state. The discussion of slavery, which had been soft-pedaled in the constitutional convention, suddenly came to the fore. It became clear that the advocates of slavery in Illinois hoped to call a new convention among whose goals could be the legalization of black slave labor.

Coles, bitterly opposed to slavery, announced his candidacy for governor in 1822, even though he had been a resident of the state for only three years. Exaggerated individualism with its attendant factionalism dominated Illinois politics in the early years. Coles's candidacy was taken seriously, but when Joseph B. Phillips, chief justice of the Illinois Supreme Court, resigned to seek the governorship the judge's election seemed certain. Phillips was known to be sympathetic to slavery and a supporter of the proposed constitutional convention. Two additional candidates entered the race late in the contest, greatly affecting the outcome. The proslavery position captured nearly 60 percent of the ballots cast, but their total was divided between two candidates. With 33 percent of the vote, Coles was elected governor, having received 167 more votes than Phillips.

Coles was the only antislavery figure among the state's elected leaders, and the general assembly was heavily proslavery. In his inaugural message the governor appealed to the assembly to remove the final vestiges of slavery remaining in Illinois. The general assembly responded that only a constitutional convention could address the governor's concerns. Though the legislative report did not call specifically for the legalization of slavery, lawmakers obviously expected that any such convention would do so.

The proslavery forces prevailed in the general assembly, and the convention referendum was placed on the August 1824 ballot, eighteen months away. Approval seemed almost inevitable at the outset of the bitter campaign. Convention supporters, reflecting on the 1822 election, believed the weight of numbers was on their side, but the governor developed an impressive network to oppose the convention resolution. Coles devoted his entire salary ($4,000) to the contest, purchased the *Illinois Intelligencer* published in Vandalia, and with others contributed weekly articles to the newspapers opposing the convention call. The convention forces mounted a similar operation, making for what one observer called a "long, excited, angry, bitter and indignant contest" (Ford, vol. 1, pp. 62–63).

In heavy balloting on 2 August 1824 the antislavery cause turned back the convention forces by a convincing margin of 57 percent to 43 percent. The interest and excitement generated by the constitutional convention issue is evidenced by the 3,000 more votes recorded in 1824 than had been cast during the spirited four-way race for governor in 1822 and more than double the state's vote for president in 1824. In spite of the prolonged and memorable struggle that convulsed the state, peace and quiet soon returned and the matter of making Illinois a slave state was put to rest forever. Unfortunately, the ambivalent situation of slaves already in Illinois remained. Long-term indenture contracts still prevailed, and the state renewed its harsh Black Laws as late as 1853.

Ironically, state leaders who opposed the convention referendum fared poorly at the polls in subsequent elections, while those who favored it went on to political success and high office. Coles's term as governor was clearly dominated by the convention issue, but his administration revealed a genuine concern for a wide range of other interests. Coles recognized the weaknesses in the state banking system and attempted to remedy its abuses. A vigorous advocate of state-supported internal improvements, he was especially active in pushing the Illinois and Michigan Canal idea. The state's first "free school act" (and one of the first in the nation) was passed in 1825, and the governor was an effective watchdog over the public lands held for educational purposes. Earlier he had taken the initiative in organizing the first Illinois agricultural society, and after he left office he participated in the formation of the state's first historical society.

The anticonvention triumph of 1824 was not only Coles's finest hour, it was virtually his only hour. In spite of his extraordinary and memorable services to the prairie state, he was never able to live down the impression that as a wealthy eastern aristocrat he was completely out of place in the fluid society of the frontier. A polished gentleman, erect and handsome with impeccable manners, to the public he often appeared cold and lacking in personal magnetism. When a U.S. Senate seat became vacant during his administration, Coles received only four votes on the first ballot and one on the final ballot; six years later, in 1830, as a candidate for Congress he ran third in a three-man field.

At the conclusion of his term as governor (Illinois governors could not then succeed themselves) Coles retired to a quiet bachelor life on his Edwardsville farm. He traveled extensively, made money from his St. Louis real estate investments, and maintained a lively interest in politics and public affairs. When it became clear that he would not again win high office in Illinois, he moved in 1832 to Philadelphia. The next year, at age forty-seven, he married Sally Logan Roberts, a member of a prominent Quaker family; they had three children.

Edward Coles lived in Illinois only thirteen of his eighty-two years, yet in those years he did more to shape the course of Illinois history than any other of the state's early governors. Surviving the Civil War, he lived to see the legal extinction of slavery in the United States. He died at his home in Philadelphia.

• The sources for Edward Coles's life and public career are sufficiently broad and well preserved. These include manuscripts, official papers, published sources, and newspapers. The bulk of Coles's private papers are at the Historical Society of Pennsylvania and the Princeton University Library. The most important published sources are Clarence W. Alvord, ed., *Governor Edward Coles*, Collections of the Illinois State Historical Library, vol. 15 (1920), and Evarts B. Greene and Alvord, eds., *The Governors' Letter Books, 1818–1834*, Collections of the Illinois State Historical Library, vol. 4 (1909). Early state histories, all produced in the nineteenth century, cover Coles's campaign and administration in depth; see Alexander Davidson and Bernard Stuvé, *A Complete History of Illinois from 1673 to 1873* (1874); Thomas Ford, *A History of Illinois from Its Commencement as a State in 1818 to 1847* (1854); and John Reynolds, *The Pioneer History of Illinois* (1852) and *My Own Times, Embracing Also the History of My Life* (1855). A more recent scholarly treatment of Coles is Kurt E. Leichtle, "Edward Coles: An Agrarian on the Frontier" (Ph.D. diss., Univ. of Illinois-Chicago, 1982). Indispensable as a study of Illinois governors is Robert P. Howard, *Mostly Good and Competent Men: Illinois Governors, 1818–1988* (1988).

ROBERT M. SUTTON

COLES, Honi (2 Apr. 1911–12 Nov. 1992), tap dancer, raconteur, and stage, vaudeville, and television performer, was born Charles Coles in Philadelphia, Pennsylvania, the son of George Coles and Isabel (maiden name unknown). He learned to tap dance on the streets of Philadelphia, where dancers challenged each other in time step "cutting" contests, and made his New York debut at the Lafayette Theater in 1931 as one of the Three Millers, a group that performed over-the-tops, barrel turns, and wings on six-foot-high pedestals. After discovering that his partners had hired another dancer to replace him, Coles retreated to Philadelphia, determined to perfect his technique. He returned to New York City in 1934, confident and skilled in his ability to cram several steps into a bar of music. Performing at the Harlem Opera House and Apollo Theatre, he was reputed to have the fastest feet in show business. And at the Hoofer's Club, where only the most serious tap dancers gathered to compete, he was hailed as one of the most graceful dancers ever seen.

From 1936 to 1939 Coles performed with the Lucky Seven Trio, who tapped on large cubes that looked like dice; the group went through ten costume changes in the course of their act. Touring with the big swing bands of Count Basie and Duke Ellington, the 6'2" Coles polished his style, melding high-speed tapping with an elegant yet close-to-the-floor style where the legs and feet did the work. In 1940, as a soloist with Cab Calloway's orchestra, Coles met Charles "Cholly" Atkins, a jazz tap dancer who would later choreograph for the best rhythm-and-blues singing groups of the 1960s. Atkins was an expert wing dancer, while Coles's specialty was precision. They combined their talents after the war by forming the class act of Coles & Atkins. Wearing handsomely tailored suits, the duo opened with a fast-paced song-and-tap number, then moved into a precision swing dance and soft-shoe, finishing with a tap challenge in which each showcased his specialty. Their classic soft-shoe, danced to "Taking a Chance on Love" played at an extremely slow tempo, was a nonchalant tossing off of smooth slides and gliding turns in crystal-cut precision. Coles performed speedy, swinging, and rhythmically complex combinations in his solos, which anticipated the prolonged cadences of bebop that extended the duration of steps past the usual eight-bar phrase. In 1944 Coles married Marion Evelyn Edwards, a dancer in the Number One chorus at the Apollo Theatre; they had two children.

Through the 1940s Coles & Atkins appeared with the big bands of Calloway, Louis Armstrong, Lionel Hampton, Charlie Barnet, Billy Eckstine, and Count Basie. In 1949, at the Ziegfeld Theater in the Broadway musical *Gentlemen Prefer Blondes*, they stopped the show with the Jule Styne number "Mamie Is Mimi," to which choreographer Agnes de Mille had added a ballet dancer. By the time the show closed in 1952 the big-band era was drawing to a close and a new style of balletic Broadway dance that integrated choreography into the musical plot became the popular form over tap dance. Though Coles opened the Dancecraft studio on Fifty-second Street in New York City in 1954 or 1955 with tap dancer Pete Nugent, there was a steady decrease in the interest of tap dance in the

1950s. "No work, no money. Tap had dropped dead," Coles remembered of that decade.

Coles and Atkins broke up in 1960; for the next sixteen years Coles worked as production stage manager for the Apollo Theatre with duties that included introducing other acts. He served as president of the Negro Actors Guild and continued his association with the Copasetics, a tapping fraternity named in honor of Bill "Bojangles" Robinson, which he had helped to found in 1949. At the Newport Jazz Festival in 1962 Coles was in the forefront of the tap revival that brought veteran members of the Copasetics back to the stage. He joined the touring company of *Bubblin' Brown Sugar* in 1976 and regained his stride as a soloist, performing at Carnegie Hall and Town Hall. After receiving a standing ovation for his performance in the Joffrey Ballet production of Agnes de Mille's "Conversations on the Dance" in 1978, Coles firmly placed tap dance in the world of concert dance. In 1983, at age seventy-two, he received both the Tony and Drama Desk awards for best featured actor and dancer in a musical for the Broadway hit, *My One and Only.* Jack Kroll in *Newsweek* called Coles "Brilliant!" in that musical, adding that his feet had "the delicacy and power of a master pianist's hands."

Coles was a tap dancer of extraordinary elegance whose personal style and technical precision epitomized the class-act dancer. "Honi makes butterflies look clumsy. He was my Fred Astaire," the singer Lena Horne said of Coles. The historian Sally Sommer wrote that Coles was "a supreme illusionist . . . he appeared to float and do nothing at all while his feet chattered complex rhythms below." He was also a master teacher who preached, "If you can walk, you can tap." As an untiring advocate of tap dance, Coles often claimed that tap dance was the only dance art form that America could claim as its own. He was awarded the *Dance* magazine Award in 1985, the Capezio Award for lifetime achievement in dance in 1988, and the National Medal of the Arts in 1991. Coles last appeared as master of ceremonies at the Colorado Tap Festival with former partner Atkins, performing up to the end of a long and rhythmically brilliant career. He died in New York City.

• Coles has appeared in the films *The Cotton Club* (1984) and *Dirty Dancing* (1987) and the documentaries *Great Feats of Feet, Charles Honi Coles: The Class Act of Tap,* and *Milt and Honi.* His television credits include "The Tap Dance Kid," "Mr. Griffin and Me," "Conversations in Dance," "Charleston," "Archives of a Master," and Dance in America's "Tap Dance in America" for PBS. Coles & Atkins's classic softshoe can be seen in the 1963 *Camera Three* television program, "Over the Top with Bebop," narrated by jazz historian Marshall Stearns. The most descriptive material on Coles & Atkins is Marshall Stearns and Jean Stearns, *Jazz Dance: The Story of American Vernacular Dance* (1968); and "Let the Punishment Fit the Crime: The Vocal Choreography of Cholly Atkins" in Jaqui Malone, *Steppin' on the Blues* (1996). The most comprehensive articles on Coles include Sally Sommer, "Smooth and Mellow," *International Tap Association Journal* (Spring 1990): 3–7); David Hinckley, "A Honey of a Hoofer," *New York Daily News Magazine,* 7 Aug. 1983, pp. 2–5;

Tom Russell, "Bippidy-Boom-Shaga-Daga," *Connoisseur,* Nov. 1983, pp. 56–57; Claude Reed, Jr., "A Conversation with Charles 'Honi' Coles," *National Scene Magazine Supplement,* Aug. 1983, pp. 14–15. An obituary is in the *New York Times,* 13 Nov. 1992.

CONSTANCE VALIS HILL

COLEY, William Bradley (12 Jan. 1862–16 Apr. 1936), surgeon, was born in Westport, Connecticut, the son of Horace Bradley Coley and Clarine Bradley Wakeman, farmers. After completing his undergraduate studies at Yale University in 1884, Coley taught Latin and Greek at Bishop Scott Government School in Portland, Oregon. In 1886 he entered Harvard Medical School, where he completed the three-year program early, graduating in 1888. Coley interned at the New York Hospital until 1890 and remained in New York City for his entire career. In 1891 he married Alice Lancaster of Newton, Massachusetts; they had three children, the eldest of whom was the surgeon Bradley Lancaster Coley.

In 1890 Coley began a 41-year tenure on the surgical staff of the Hospital for the Ruptured and Crippled, an orthopedic hospital established in 1863 by the New York Society for the Relief of the Ruptured and Crippled. In 1924 he was made its surgeon in chief, a post that he held until 1931. From 1890 to 1897 Coley also served as instructor in surgery at the New York Post-Graduate Medical School and Hospital. In 1898 he was appointed clinical lecturer in surgery at the College of Physicians and Surgeons (Columbia University), where in 1908 he was made associate professor. The following year Coley moved to the Cornell University Medical College, where he was professor of clinical surgery and later, in 1915, joined the clinical cancer research faculty. Coley held the post of chief of surgery from 1918 to 1936 at the Mary McClellan Hospital in Cambridge, New York, and from 1908 to 1932 was surgeon to the New York Central Railroad.

In addition, Coley was consulting surgeon to the Fifth Avenue Hospital, the Sharon Hospital of Sharon, Connecticut, the Physicians' Hospital in Plattsburgh, New York, and the New York Cancer Hospital (later the Memorial Hospital for the Treatment of Cancer and Allied Diseases). In 1902 he established the nation's first endowed fund for cancer research at this last institution through the generosity of one of his patients, Arabella Huntington, wife of railroad magnate Collis P. Huntington.

Coley's most notable surgical contributions include his adoption of the Bassini method of operating for the radical cure of hernia and his development of "Coley's toxin" for the treatment of particular malignant tumors. In 1887 Edoardo Bassini, professor of surgery at the University of Padua, first published the description of his method for the radical cure of hernia, a condition that was considered impossible to treat without its recurrence. The success of Bassini's method was based on his novel understanding of the anatomy of that part of the abdomen surrounding the inguinal canal and a procedure for reconstructing the inguinal canal so that its normal oblique direction was restored, thus diminishing the chances of the condition recurring.

Bassini's technique became known outside of Italy only with its translation into German for publication in the surgical journal *Archiv für klinische Chirurgie* (1890), which is probably where Coley first learned of it. Coley performed the operation for the first time at the Hospital for the Ruptured and Crippled in December 1891. Six years later he was able to report only three recurrences in 361 operations that employed Bassini's technique. In an editorial published in the *American Journal of Surgery* the year of his death, Coley could still claim a permanent cure in 95 percent of adult cases using the Bassini method.

Coley is perhaps better known for his treatment of cancer with bacterial toxins. While still an intern at the New York Hospital, Coley became intrigued by the case of a patient who had undergone five unsuccessful operations for the extirpation of a recurring sarcoma of the neck but was inexplicably still alive after seven years. The patient's hospital chart showed that during his last illness he had contracted erysipelas, a streptococcal infection not uncommon among surgical patients before the advent of sulfa drugs and antibiotics. What surprised Coley was that this patient had recuperated not only from the infection, which was seldom fatal, but from the sarcoma for which he had been admitted. Tracking the patient to a tenement in Manhattan's Lower East Side, Coley verified the total remission of the cancer.

Coley was not the first to note the regression of tumors under acute bacterial infections. Half a century earlier Karl Rokitansky in Vienna had noted that cancers subsided when their hosts contracted tuberculosis. Sir James Paget in London noted this same phenomenon in the instance of erysipelas. In April 1891 Coley began experiments in which he attempted to produce erysipelas in patients with inoperable malignant tumors. In October of the same year he induced erysipelas in a patient whose cancer disappeared within two weeks of the onset of the infection. His initial success was not easily repeated, however. In successive experiments Coley found that cancer-ravaged patients were often unable to survive the added illness and perished before the possible benefits of streptococcal infection could become manifest.

To hasten the effectiveness of the treatment, Coley intensified the virulence of the erysipelas streptococcus by growing it with the bacillus prodigiosus, work suggested to him by experiments being done at the Institut Pasteur in Paris. Coley injected his first patient in December 1892 with what was to become known as "Coley's toxin," a suspension of streptococci and the bacillus prodigiosus. Four months of repeated injections caused his patient's inoperable abdominal tumor to entirely disappear.

Coley's results remained uncertain, however, because he was unable to produce consistently effective batches of the toxin and could not explain why his material worked. In spite of reservations expressed by many of his colleagues, it was evident that Coley's toxin was more effective in the treatment of malignant tumors than could be attributed to spontaneous regression alone. Patient reaction to the injections, however, was often so severe and the results so unpredictable that the treatment lost favor. Even so, Coley continued to advocate his toxin for inoperable sarcomas and as a prophylactic measure after operation for bone sarcoma. Eventually the research of Coley and others in cancer immunotherapy was overshadowed by the more predictable results of radiation therapy.

Coley died in New York.

• Two indispensable sources for understanding Coley's contributions to medical science are his article "Review of Radical Cure of Hernia during the Last Half Century," *American Journal of Surgery*, n.s., 31 (1936): 397–402; and H. C. Nauts et al., "The Treatment of Malignant Tumors by Bacterial Toxins as Developed by the Late William B. Coley, M.D. Reviewed in the Light of Modern Research," *Cancer Research* 6 (1946): 205–16. An obituary is in the *New York Times*, 17 Apr. 1936.

CHRISTOPHER HOOLIHAN

COLFAX, Schuyler (23 Mar. 1823–13 Jan. 1885), congressman and vice president of the United States, was born in New York City, the posthumous son of Schuyler Colfax, a bank clerk, and Hannah Stryker. He and his mother lived with his widowed grandmother while he attended public schools. At age ten he entered the workforce as a store clerk. In 1834 his mother married George W. Matthews, who removed the family to New Carlisle, Indiana, in 1836. Matthews ran a store (in which Colfax clerked) and held the patronage position of village postmaster. In 1841 Matthews was elected county auditor on the Whig ticket and moved to the county seat, South Bend. Colfax served as his deputy until 1849. Following his parents' wishes, Colfax read law, but his real love was politics. He corresponded with prominent Whigs, contributed to Horace Greeley's *New York Tribune*, reported on the state senate for the *Indiana State Journal* in 1842–1843, and campaigned for his hero, Henry Clay, in 1844.

In 1844 Colfax married Evelyn Clark; they had no children. Shortly thereafter he bought a half interest in a local paper, which he renamed the *St. Joseph Valley Register*. He edited it for nearly two decades, developing it into the major Whig (later Republican) newspaper of northern Indiana. Since the Democrats were strong in Indiana, Colfax preferred issues, such as internal improvements (he was the secretary for the Chicago Rivers and Harbors Convention of 1847) and slavery expansion, that divided local Democrats. He only reluctantly supported the Compromise of 1850, which resolved temporarily the slavery issue. As a delegate to Indiana's constitutional convention of 1850, he favored election of judges and opposed exclusion of African Americans from the state. He opposed African-American voting because of widespread public opposition to it and insisted the electorate approve state borrowing.

In 1851 he was defeated for Congress, but when the local Democratic congressman supported the Kansas-Nebraska Act repealing the Missouri Compromise on slavery, in 1854, he recognized a golden opportunity to destroy the Democrats. Colfax not only took an anti-Nebraska position but, as a dedicated Protestant and teetotaler, joined the anti-foreign and anti-Catholic Know Nothing party as well, and he ran successfully for Congress as a representative of the People's party, a forerunner of the Republicans. With many German and Irish immigrants in northern Indiana, Colfax's views were very divisive. As a delegate to the Know Nothing National Convention in 1855, he tried to pass off his listing among the delegates as an error and ascribe his presence to being a reporter. Running for reelection as a Republican in 1856, he was attacked physically by Irish railroad workers, and the nativist charge followed him in every subsequent campaign.

Colfax served seven consecutive terms (1855–1869) in Congress, the last three as Speaker. Despite a lengthy period in office by mid-nineteenth-century standards, no major legislation is associated with him. As chair of the Post Offices and Post Roads Committee, he did try to improve overland service to California, but primarily Colfax defined his role as serving his constituents. He faithfully answered letters directed to him and ran constituents' errands. As patronage opportunities increased with the expansion of government during the Civil War, he was able to reward many supporters.

Colfax promoted his political party as well. As an editor, he was sensitive to public opinion. A speech he gave on Kansas prior to the war was a major campaign document in 1856. In 1859 Colfax stumped Minnesota for the Republicans. While not an early supporter of Abraham Lincoln in 1860, he campaigned hard for the party. Lincoln considered him briefly for postmaster general but gave the position to Montgomery Blair. Although never a Lincoln intimate, Colfax advised the administration on Indiana politics, recommending against closing the Plymouth *Democrat* for disloyalty, because the negative publicity would be worse than any damage the small paper could do. Colfax maintained good relationships with reporters, holding weekly receptions for as many as a thousand at his Washington, D.C., home.

As Speaker, Colfax was a figurehead, conservative in his use of power. Thaddeus Stevens, not Colfax, galvanized Republicans on issues. Yet Colfax did serve to smooth matters for his party by selecting committee chairs and members who were acceptable to the cabinet officials with whom they worked most closely. On most issues he followed the party majority, favoring Congressional Reconstruction and the impeachment of Andrew Johnson.

Colfax's actions made him few enemies. At worst he was regarded as a "happy mediocrity" (Smith, pp. 290–91n). Safe, competent, and loyal, Colfax made an ideal running mate for Ulysses S. Grant in 1868. Shortly after their victory, the widowed Colfax married Ellen Wade, with whom he had his only child.

Colfax made a late start in seeking renomination in 1872 and lost out to Henry Wilson.

Ethical issues dominated the latter stages of Colfax's career. In 1868 he accepted a large contribution from a government contractor. He was a frequent requester of railroad passes, and he told Jay Cooke he saw no problem representing a railroad in Congress while he was vice president. Overshadowing all this, however, was his involvement in the Crédit Mobilier scandal. Oakes Ames, a Massachusetts representative, offered Colfax and other congressmen shares of this company at below market prices, to be paid for from company dividends (sure to be high since the company's chief customer was the Union Pacific Railroad being supported by Congress). Ames held the stock in his own name so that recipients could honestly claim they did not "own" the stock. Colfax did not regard this as a bribe, since he had always supported the railroad. To him such financial opportunities (although he wished to keep them secret) were normal, compensation for the aid he gave others. His congressional salary had never covered his expenses. Colfax's decision to leave politics in 1873 after a congressional investigation that neither cleared his name nor took action against him was dictated not by shame but by anger at the ingratitude shown him for his years of service.

Many of his constituents seemingly agreed that Colfax had been treated unfairly. He remained popular, and even Indiana Democrats defended him. Colfax became one of the highest paid orators in the country, giving talks on the American West, Lincoln, temperance, and the Odd Fellows (of which he was a longtime member). On one of his lecture tours, he collapsed and died in Mankato, Minnesota. Exceptional neither in his abilities nor his transgressions, Colfax marked the average for politicians of his era.

• Colfax's papers are located in the Library of Congress, University of Rochester Library, Chicago Historical Society, Hayes Memorial Library, Indiana State Library, Indiana University Library, and Northern Indiana Historical Society. Willard H. Smith, *Schuyler Colfax: The Changing Fortunes of a Political Idol* (1952), is the best biography, surpassing O. J. Hollister, *Life of Schuyler Colfax* (1886), which was written by a relative, and A. Y. Moore, *The Life of Schuyler Colfax* (1868), a campaign biography. On Crédit Mobilier see Mark W. Summers, *The Era of Good Stealings* (1993). See also Patrick J. Furlong and Gerald E. Hartdagen, "Schuyler Colfax: A Reputation Tarnished," in *Gentlemen from Indiana: National Party Candidates, 1836–1940*, ed. Ralph Gray (1977). An obituary is in the *New York Times*, 14 Jan. 1885.

PHYLLIS F. FIELD

COLGATE, James Boorman (4 Mar. 1818–7 Feb. 1904), capitalist and philanthropist, was born in New York City, the son of William Colgate, a prominent manufacturer, and Mary Gilbert. Educated at local schools and in Connecticut, he abandoned formal schooling at the age of sixteen to enter the commission house of Boorman, Johnson & Company. For a number of years he remained with the firm, which was headed by a relative, James Boorman. After returning from an extended trip to Europe in 1841–1842, he entered the employment of a wholesale dry-goods firm, where he worked for nine years. In 1844 he married Sarah Ellen Hoyt of Utica, New York; the marriage produced one son before his wife's death in 1846.

In 1851 Colgate married Susan Farnham Colby, with whom he had two children. In the following year he formed a partnership with John B. Trevor and entered what would prove to be his life's work, the field of finance. The firm of Trevor & Colgate, initially involved in both stock brokerage and banking, added a bullion (gold trading) department in 1857. The firm, located at 47 Wall Street in New York City, soon became the leading bullion house in the United States. Colgate devoted most of his time to the firm's newest endeavor and also took a leading role in the establishment of the New York Gold Exchange during the Civil War. After the U.S. government suspended specie payments at the end of 1861, the exchange became the scene of wild speculative activities as investors struggled to determine the respective values of gold and newly issued "greenbacks." Colgate served as president of the exchange—which came under the control of the New York Stock Exchange in 1877—and in his later years served as both vice president and director of the Bank of the State of New York.

In addition to running his firm, which was renamed James B. Colgate & Company in 1873, Colgate drew upon his daily experiences in the bullion trade to become a firm advocate of the remonetization of silver. In doing so he stood nearly alone among his peers in the Eastern financial establishment, most of whom favored a retention of the gold standard. Colgate spoke out often and fearlessly on the subject. In a notable exchange of letters in the New York press, he debated the issue with Congressmen Levi P. Morton and S. B. Chittenden in the summer of 1879. Colgate summed up his position by stating "Silver and gold have gone side by side like twin sisters for forty centuries and it is not in the power of legislation to divorce them. I would not depreciate the importance of gold, which is a banker's currency, yet silver, which is the people's currency, has some advantages which gold does not possess" (*New York World*, 9 June 1879).

Having achieved notable success in the business world, Colgate made his greatest mark in the area of educational philanthropy. Following the example of his father, who labored tirelessly on behalf of Madison University and other Baptist institutions for years, he served on the Board of Trustees at the Hamilton, New York, institution from 1864 until his death. Although he built (with the assistance of Trevor) the Warburton Avenue Baptist Church in his adopted hometown of Yonkers, New York, and also gave generously to institutions such as the University of Rochester, Columbian (later George Washington) University, and the Colby (New Hampshire) Academy (his second wife's alma mater), Madison remained the focus of his efforts. Along with his brother Samuel, Colgate in 1873 founded an academy in Hamilton that bore his name. Upon the merger of Madison University and Colgate

Academy in 1890, the university was renamed Colgate University in honor of the many contributions of the Colgate family, which included at least one million dollars given by James Colgate.

In addition to his business and philanthropic activities, Colgate was a member of the New York Stock Exchange and the New England Society, as well as a patron of the Metropolitan Museum of Art and the American Museum of Natural History. He died at his home in Yonkers following a long period of declining health. The firm of James B. Colgate & Company continued to operate under his son James's direction until its dissolution at the end of 1941.

James B. Colgate is noteworthy for his part in the establishment of the New York Gold Exchange, as well as for his various philanthropic efforts. Although his business no longer exists, his financial generosity played a large part in the creation of today's Colgate University.

• Colgate's papers are in the Colgate University archives in Hamilton, N.Y. Although his activities receive some attention in Allen Weinstein, *Prelude to Populism: Origins of the Silver Issue, 1867–1878* (1970), the best sources of information on his life and career remain his obituaries in the *New York Times*, the *New York Herald*, and the *New York Tribune*, all 8 Feb. 1904.

EDWARD L. LACH, JR.

COLGATE, William (25 Jan. 1783–25 Mar. 1857), manufacturer and philanthropist, was born in Hollingbourne parish, Kent, England, the son of Robert Colgate, a gentleman farmer, and Sarah Bowles. In 1795 he emigrated with his family to the United States because his father, an outspoken critic of King George III, was forced to flee England to avoid prosecution for treason. The family disembarked in Baltimore, Maryland, and purchased a modest estate in nearby Harford County, which was lost two years later when it was discovered that they did not possess a clear title. They then moved to present-day Randolph County, West Virginia, where his father attempted unsuccessfully to farm and mine coal. In 1800 they returned to Baltimore, where he and his father went into business with Robert Mather, a soap and candle maker. After the partnership dissolved two years later and his family relocated to Ossining, New York, he remained in Baltimore and opened his own soap and candle works.

During this era most American households made their own soap by combining potash with tallow or animal fat from the kitchen dripping-pan and boiling the mixture in a tub in the back yard. Although homemade soap cleaned tolerably well, it abraded the skin and offended the nostrils. Soap made commercially was a little easier on the palms because some of the tallow was replaced with low-grade oil and all of the ashes were replaced with slaked lime. Otherwise, it was almost as crude as the homemade variety because the chemistry of saponification was understood poorly outside England and France. Nevertheless, Colgate quickly realized that a sizable market existed in a large, crowded city for a manufactured soap that was easy on the hands and purse. In 1803 he closed his business and moved to New York City, where he entered the employ of John Slidell & Company, a manufacturer of soap and candles. He quickly rose to the position of business manager, and in 1806 he resigned to form William Colgate & Company.

Colgate catered to busy housewives by offering free delivery, and he did all of the buying, manufacturing, selling, delivery, and bookkeeping himself. In 1807 he sold part of the company to Francis Smith; the two partners benefited greatly from the passage of the Embargo and Non-Intercourse Acts in 1807 and 1809, respectively, because these laws virtually eliminated their European competitors from the New York market. By the latter year Colgate had made enough money to buy a farm for his parents in Delaware County, New York, and in 1811 he married Mary Gilbert, with whom he had nine children. In 1813 he bought Smith's share of the company.

By 1817 Colgate was producing a soap of sufficiently good quality and low price that it dominated the market in New York and competed successfully in Europe. Three years later he expanded his production facilities in order to manufacture starch, which was frequently used as a filler in low-grade soap. At one time he operated one of the largest starch factories in the United States. In 1829 he began producing scented soap by introducing small amounts of perfume into the lime-and-tallow mix, an innovation that proved to be extremely popular and drove sales higher. In 1845, in order to keep up with the demand for this and other products, he oversaw the construction of "Colgate's Folly," a soap-boiling pan with a capacity of 43,000 pounds, reckoned by many to be the largest pan of its kind in the world and one that many critics predicted would drive the company into bankruptcy. Two years later he expanded his production facilities again, this time by relocating them to a larger, more modern plant in Jersey City, New Jersey, and in 1850 he introduced a line of high-quality hand soap. Colgate & Company ("William" was dropped from the company's name when his son Samuel joined the business in 1838) apparently never suffered a serious business setback during his lifetime, continuing to grow after his death under the management of his sons. In 1928 it merged with Palmolive-Peet Company to form Colgate-Palmolive Company, which eventually became one of the world's largest manufacturers of household and personal products.

In addition to being a capable businessman, Colgate was also a man of powerful philanthropic instincts. He became a devout Baptist in 1808, and each year thereafter he donated at least a tenth of his net earnings to support missionary work and education. In 1816 he helped to organize the nonsectarian American Bible Society (ABS) for the purpose of providing twenty-eight regional societies with enough Bibles and money so that every household in the United States, particularly those of immigrants, possessed a copy of the Old and New Testaments. In 1832 he helped to found the American Baptist Home Mission Society so that the

Gospel might be preached throughout North America. Five years later he withdrew from ABS because it refused to print sectarian versions of the Bible; he then helped to found the American and Foreign Bible Society, a predominantly Baptist organization, which he served as treasurer for thirteen years. In 1850 he helped to found the American Bible Union and underwrote to a considerable degree its Revised Version of 1850. This first major English translation of the Bible since the King James Version emphasized the Baptist belief that baptism involves immersion. He also gave generously to Hamilton (N.Y.) Literary and Theological Seminary. By 1846, when it was renamed Madison University, over half of its property had been donated by Colgate and his company. He continued to support the school until his death in New York City. In 1890, when Madison merged with nearby Colgate Academy (which was supported financially by his sons), it was renamed Colgate University in his honor.

Colgate contributed to the advance of American society in two ways. As a businessman he developed new techniques for making and selling soap and contributed significantly to the development of the household products industry. As a philanthropist he supported the work of Bible and missionary societies and contributed to the development of an important institution of higher learning.

• Biographies of Colgate include Shields T. Hardin, *The Colgate Story* (1959); Saxon Rowe Carver, *William Colgate: Yeoman of Kent* (1957); and W. W. Everts, *William Colgate, the Christian Layman* (1881). His role as a businessman is discussed in David R. Foster, *The Story of Colgate-Palmolive: One Hundred and Sixty-Nine Years of Progress* (1975), and William Lee Sims, *150 Years . . . and the Future! Colgate-Palmolive (1806–1956)* (1956). His role in various Bible and Baptist organizations is discussed in William Henry Brackney, ed., *The Baptists* (1988). An obituary is in the *New York Tribune*, 26 Mar. 1857.

CHARLES W. CAREY, JR.

COLLENS, Thomas Wharton (23 June 1812–3 Nov. 1879), Creole jurist and writer, was born in New Orleans, Louisiana, the son of John Wharton Collens and Marie Louise de Tabiteau. Collens's father was descended from an English officer who had settled in Louisiana in the eighteenth century. His mother was a member of one of the city's French-speaking, Creole families. Raised in a bilingual, Catholic household of modest means, Collens overcame a limited education during an apprenticeship in the print shop to which he was sent as a youth. By the age of twenty-one he had advanced to the position of associate editor of the *True American*. He married Amenaide Milbrou, and they had eight children. In 1833 he was admitted to the bar, and the following year he embarked upon a highly successful law career by serving as clerk and reporter of the Louisiana Senate. Between 1836 and 1838 he occupied the post of deputy clerk for the U.S. Circuit Court, and two years later voters elected him district attorney for Orleans Parish (1840–1842). From 1842 to 1846 he served as judge of the City Court of New

Orleans, and he later participated in the Louisiana Constitutional Convention of 1852. In 1856 he won the judgeship of the First District Court of New Orleans.

Of Creole descent in the nation's nineteenth-century "Creole Capital," Collens imbibed the religious Gallicanism, Romantic idealism, and republican militancy of the city's Franco-American community. He developed close ties to the proscribed republicans, journalists, and other political dissidents who, fleeing revolutionary upheaval in France and the French Caribbean, reinforced the city's resident cluster of French-speaking free thinkers and political liberals. Caught up in the excitement of the Romantic literary movement, he even drafted an ambitious, pro-republican play in 1833, *The Martyr Patriots; or, Louisiana in 1769*, a historical drama based on the Gallic population's revolt against Spanish rule, which was performed before an enthusiastic audience in 1836 at the St. Charles Theater. Another literary work, a well-received poem titled "Lines to the Memory of Father Turgis," appeared in a number of publications, including the *Living Writers of the South* in 1869.

As Collens commenced his legal career in the early 1830s, he immersed himself in the utopian doctrines of Scottish industrialist Robert Dale Owen and French socialist Charles Fourier, thereby developing a lifelong commitment to the reorganization of society on the basis of cooperative, communitarian ideals. In articles published during the 1830s in the city newspapers and the *True American*, he discussed social problems and even drew up his own utopia in an unfinished manuscript, "The Code of Collenia." In utopian "Collenia," the community owned all land, and each man would receive a share of the collective's profits commensurate with "his proportion of labour & talents."

A freemason, Collens nurtured his radical views in the city's French lodges. Like many other urban professionals, businessmen, and workers, he resented the slaveholding elite's increasing dominance of Louisiana's political economy. Under the cover of freemasonry, he and other French-speaking leaders refined their political agenda, preserved their republican idealism, and studied the works of European socialists.

In 1841, undoubtedly angered by an extremely bitter dispute between freemasons and the city's Catholic church leadership—a leadership that had aligned itself with the region's planter autocracy—Collens announced the organization of a discussion group, the Atheneum. In the society's constitution he condemned "Religion and her companions Superstition, Bigotry, Intolerance and Persecution" and urged those "who desire the welfare of the human race" to unite. When the short-lived Atheneum dissolved, Collens helped organize an important circle of New Orleans Fourierists who communicated with Albert Brisbane, Horace Greeley, and other prominent leaders of the American Union of Associationists.

With the 1848 French revolution, Collens rallied to the support of the Second Republic. Together with French emigré and fellow freemason Pierre Soulé,

Collens appeared at the head of the movement. Paying tribute to the new republic's radical labor policies at a large public assembly in April 1848, Collens toasted Fourier:

To the great genius who as early as 1808 proclaimed the idea of industrial association which the triumph of republican France today assures;—to the one whose sublime reason and philanthropic soul has known how to resolve the problem of harmonizing the interests of the capitalist with the rights of the laborer, . . . to the founder of the eternal bases of well-being for the worker, to the apostle of social harmony, to the immortal Charles Fourier!

Influenced as much by Catholicism and French freemasonry's religious-political doctrines as by Fourierism, Collens theorized a Christian socialist philosophy in *Humanics*, his first major book. Published in 1860, *Humanics* revealed a Christ-centered ethic in which the "welfare of society is the paramount law."

During the 1850s Collens supported the wing of the Democratic party led by Senator Stephen A. Douglas of Illinois, and though, like Douglas, he opposed secession, he nonetheless refused to take an oath of allegiance when Federal forces occupied the city in 1862. Instead he fled to Pass Christian, Mississippi, where he suffered great hardship for the remainder of the war. Upon his return to the city in 1865, he practiced law and, having relented in his anticlericalism, assumed an activist role in Catholic church affairs.

At Reconstruction's outset in 1867, Collens broke with French freemasonry when the white leadership proclaimed the ideal of *fraternité* and ordered the lodges to open their membership to all "without distinction as to race or color." Elected Democratic judge of the Seventh District Court of New Orleans (1867–1873) at about the same time, he fought the Republican regime. In retaliation, they withheld his salary for three years. Collens apparently viewed Reconstruction as a ploy by northern businessmen to unleash a system of unfettered, predatory capitalism.

In his second book, the *Eden of Labor; or, The Christian Utopia*, published in 1876, Collens depicted a fictional Eden of labor in which the "brotherhood of humanity" and the "legal equality of persons" prevailed. Eden's economy rested upon the principle that the worker's labor was the real measure of value of all goods and services—a principle rooted in the "law of *neighborly love* propounded by our Lord Jesus Christ." Eventually, however, the "idle non-producer" appropriated all of the land and created a social hierarchy based on wealth—a system that reduced all workers to a condition of serfdom. While the *Catholic World*'s reviewer applauded *Eden of Labor*'s Christian spirit, he concluded that the "danger besetting works of this kind, where the author is dissatisfied with the existing order of things and feels a strong sympathy with oppressed labor, is that they insensibly verge toward the vindication of the theories of communism and the revolutionary rights of man."

During the postwar years Collens advocated labor reforms including full employment, unionization, an eight-hour day, and a "just principle of economic distribution" in articles in the *Communist*, a St. Louis utopian socialist periodical; the *Workingman's Advocate*, the official journal of the National Labor Union; the *Catholic World*; the New Orleans *Morning Star and Catholic Messenger*; and *Equity* and *Labor-Balance*, two Christian socialist journals in Massachusetts that he helped to found. In *Labor-Balance*, a quarterly declaring in its premier issue in October 1877 that capitalism was the "embodied Anti-Christ of our times," Collens likewise deplored entrepreneurs who made their "monstrous fortunes off the substance of the bodies and souls of their God-made equals" and declared that work at "living wages" was a right. A working man denied an equitable wage, he insisted, must "summon society to provide it." At the time of his death in New Orleans, Collens was a director of St. Mary's Catholic Orphan Asylum.

• Collens's "The Era of Guarantism," *The Harbinger* 7 (12 Aug. 1848), offers insight into his Fourierist affiliation. The most important source for Collens's life and philosophy is Robert C. Reinders, "T. Wharton Collens: Catholic and Christian Socialist," *Catholic Historical Review* 52 (July 1966). Brief sketches of Collens's career and a number of his works appear in James W. Davidson, *The Living Writers of the South* (1869); and *The Louisiana Book: Selections from the Literature of the State*, ed. Thomas McCaleb (1894). Carl J. Guarneri, "Two Utopian Socialist Plans for Emancipation in Antebellum Louisiana," *Louisiana History* 24 (Winter 1983); Joseph G. Tregle, Jr., "Thomas J. Durant, Utopian Socialism, and the Failure of Presidential Reconstruction in Louisiana," *Journal of Southern History* 45 (Nov. 1979); and Caryn Cossé Bell, *Revolution, Romanticism, and the Afro-Creole Protest Tradition in Louisiana, 1718–1868* (1997), offer important insights into his political/intellectual milieu though the Tregle article makes no mention of Collens himself.

CARYN COSSÉ BELL

COLLETT, Glenna (20 June 1903–3 Feb. 1989), champion golfer, was born in New Haven, Connecticut, the daughter of George H. Collett, a life insurance agent, and Ada Wilkinson. Collett, the leading woman golfer in the United States in the 1920s and early 1930s, became interested in golf as a teenager accompanying her father on a course in Providence, Rhode Island. At fourteen she took her first lessons from John Anderson of the Metacomel Club in Providence; he helped her develop the rhythmic swing that was her hallmark. Later, she received instruction from Alex Smith, the Scotsman who won the U.S. Open in 1906 and 1910.

Collett entered her first U.S. Women's Amateur tournament, then the leading women's open in the nation, in 1919; she won the championship in 1922. She went on to claim that title five more times, the last in 1935. She also won the Canadian Women's Amateur twice, the French Amateur once, and the North and South Women's championship six times. But she could not win the world's most prestigious tournament, the British Ladies' Amateur; she lost twice in the final match, once to the great British player Joyce

Wethered. From 1932 to 1948, she played in the Curtis Cup, the biennial series between U.S. and British women golfers that she was instrumental in reinstituting. After her sixth triumph in the national amateur, she played in fewer competitive events, entering her last tournament in 1962, a seniors'. Thereafter she retired from the game and lived in Gulfstream, Florida, where she died.

When Collett played golf, the game and the way women played it were changing substantially. Golf was then assuming a public character; once the sport of the upper "Four Hundred," it was becoming the sport of thousands of Americans, an upper "Four Million," who helped to swell the galleries at amateur and professional tournaments. The number of U.S. courses increased from about 500 in 1915 to more than 5,000 by 1930. More women than ever were playing. Only about a dozen had entered the national amateur in the 1890s; by the 1920s, more than 100 played the qualifying rounds.

Just as American women were throwing off old social, political, and sumptuary restraints in the 1920s, American women golfers, with Collett as an important leader, were breaking with orthodox golf practices among their sex. They gave up tight-fitting "proper" attire for loose-fitting clothes that allowed freer movement; they adopted the interlocking or overlapping grip, rejecting the notion that they had to use the palm grip because they were less muscular than men; they employed a more vigorous, aggressive swing.

Collett embodied all of these changes. Sportswriters often used the adjective "mannish" to describe her swing. Standing 5'6" and weighing about 125 pounds, she had, said Grantland Rice, a "free-slashing swing." Rice, a prominent sports journalist, pointed out that she used an "unusual amount of pivot, coming well up on her left toe through the back swing." Influenced by J. Douglas Edgar, the innovative golf analyst, she used a long backswing and full shoulder turn but restricted her hip turn. Rice called her "Alice in Wallopland" and cited instances of her hitting drives of more than 250 yards, a result largely of her rhythmically accelerated swing.

For all her success and power, Collett never commanded the adulation that Americans gave to the men who were creating a "Golden Age" of sports in the nation. She acted tomboyish and vibrant but did not exude power or flash the colorful personality of a Babe Ruth in baseball, a Jack Dempsey in boxing, or a Bill Tilden in tennis. Even the description of her as the "women's Bobby Jones" implied a secondary status for women athletes. However, President Calvin Coolidge, who disliked golf, did receive her at the White House after one of her national amateur victories.

Collett reached out to an audience after 1925 when she wrote many articles for popular American magazines on golf and other subjects. She instructed readers of *Ladies' Home Journal* on the proper use of every club in the bag. For *Collier's*, she offered advice on the correct attire for golf, noting especially the need for comfortable clothing. She wanted to control her own fate and urged readers of *Collier's* to set aside superstitions and notions of jinxes in golf and everyday life. In the *Saturday Evening Post* she chronicled the progress of women in golf since the 1890s, emphasizing that qualifying scores for the national amateur had improved from about 150 to around 93 and that she had been the first player to break 80 in a qualifying round. She examined these subjects in detail as coauthor of *Ladies in the Rough*, published in 1928.

In her articles, Collett often hinted at a problem troubling many American women: reconciling a career with femininity and domesticity. She feared that women who were serious about golf had to enlarge their "shapely arms" with muscles and otherwise remove their "softly alluring curves," thus destroying the qualities holding a man to a woman. In another article, she concluded that women could never develop the physical abilities to match men in golf, and she accepted such limitations as natural and good: "to make our bodies hard as nails by muscular training . . . is far beyond our desires." She added that "brooms and mixing spoons [were] more likely to hold their attention yet awhile." Collett also praised other women golfers for their interests beyond golf—for their "other halves." She particularly seemed to admire Helen Hicks because her "one thought" after finishing a tournament was to go home for chocolate cake, and she applauded Wethered for romping in her garden with her dog. Nonetheless, she asserted that her marriage to Edwin Vare in 1931, despite its demands for domesticity, gave her a steadiness in golf that she had not known before. She denied that her game had deteriorated because of the routines of marriage, noting that she had won the national amateur title in 1935, a year after the birth of a son. (She later had a second child.)

Women golfers have given Collett a special place in their history. In 1950 the newly organized Ladies' Professional Golf Association selected her as a charter member of the Ladies' Golf Hall of Fame. Two years later, Betty Jameson, a professional golfer, gave a trophy to the association to be awarded annually to players with the lowest scoring average in official tournaments; she requested that it be named the Vare Trophy in Collett's honor.

• Collett's golf career is discussed in Peter Alliss, *The Who's Who of Golf* (1983); Will Grimsley, *Golf: Its History, People & Events* (1966); and John M. Ross, ed., *Golf Magazine's Encyclopedia of Golf* (1979). Articles by Collett include "For Wearing on the Green," *Collier's*, 25 Oct. 1930; "From Tee to Fairway," *Ladies' Home Journal*, June 1931; "Golf We Women Play," *Saturday Evening Post*, 9 July 1927; "If I Were Starting to Play Golf," *Ladies' Home Journal*, May 1931; "In Defense of Us Sportspeople," *Publishers' Weekly* 23 Aug. 1930; "Junk that Jinx," *Collier's* 22 Feb. 1930; "On and Off the Fairway," *Pictorial Review*, Aug. 1930; "Smooth and Better Golf," *Woman's Home Companion*, Aug. 1931; "Why Golf Widows?" *Outlook*, 27 Aug. 1930. Contemporary articles on Collett include Nancy Dorris, "The Amazing Glenna Collett," *Woman Citizen*, May 1926; Grantland Rice, "Alice in Wallopland," *Collier's*, 7 Feb. 1925, "Lady of the Links," *Collier's* 6 Dec. 1930, "The Old Familiar Faces," *Collier's*, 2 Jan. 1926, and "A Pair of Queens," *Collier's*, 23 April 1927; William D. Richardson, "The Woman on the Links," *Country Life*, July 1925. Collett probably gave her last views on golf in an interview with Carl Becker, 8 Nov. 1985. An obituary is in the *New York Times*, 6 Feb. 1989.

CARL M. BECKER

COLLIER, Barron Gift (23 Mar. 1873–13 Mar. 1939), advertising entrepreneur and capitalist, was born in Memphis, Tennessee, the son of Cowles Miles Collier, a naval officer and artist, and Hannah Celeste Shackelford. Collier attended the Memphis public schools until age sixteen, when he dropped out to solicit business for the Illinois Central Railroad, to contract with the city of Memphis to improve the street lighting, and to learn advertising and selling for his uncle, owner of the *Memphis Appeal-Avalanche*.

Collier acquired half interest in the G. S. Standish print shop, which printed advertising placards for horsedrawn streetcars, soon replaced by enclosed electric streetcars. He recognized the potential for cheap advertising to get increased exposure on the new mass transit and obtained city advertising contracts in Memphis, Little Rock, Chattanooga, Birmingham, and New Orleans. Unaffected by the panic of 1893, Collier moved to New York City and began the Consolidated Street Railways Advertising Company, reputed to be one of the biggest financial successes in the advertising industry, under which he purchased franchises for streetcar and subway advertising in more than a thousand U.S. cities. One of these cities, St. Petersburg, took Collier to Florida.

Florida real estate agent Walter P. Fuller recalled that Collier always did his homework before a business deal, worked out the details favorable to both parties, and then made his offer. Another man who had early business dealings with Collier in Florida observed that "Barron was always generous, polite and considerate. But if you stood in his way, he'd run you over. He'd still be polite and considerate, you understand, but he did what he thought was right."

At the invitation of John M. Roach, president of the Chicago Street Railway Company, Collier visited him on Useppa Island off Fort Myers in 1911. As part of a deal to obtain the advertising franchise on Roach's company, Collier agreed to purchase Roach's Florida property. Collier's son, Barron, Jr., recalled that "the implication was he would obtain the ad contract if he bought the land. He bought the land—but he didn't get the ad franchise." Nevertheless, Collier saw the potential in Florida real estate development and began purchasing vast acreages in the southwest area of the state.

Between 1911 and 1926 Collier spent winters on Useppa Island, finally making it his permanent residence in 1926. Collier then focused the drive and determination he exhibited in building his successful advertising business on developing Florida. When Fuller offered to sell him land ready for development, Collier replied, "What I want is wild country that no one else wants and that I can make into a place where people can live." He then amassed 1.25 million acres, becoming the largest landowner in the state.

Collier acquired all the holdings of the land companies in southern Lee and Hendry counties in six transactions between 1921 and 1928. In a deal with the state legislature to create Collier County from Lee County in 1923, Collier agreed to finance the building of the Tamiami Trail from Naples to Miami, an achievement at the time compared to the opening of the Panama Canal. Collier's workers blasted through granite-like limerock for three years to create the 100-mile road, opening the way for settlers from the East Coast to populate Collier's county.

Collier established dozens of companies in southwest Florida to transform the area into thriving farms, groves, and resorts: Bank of Everglades, *Collier County News*, Florida Railroad and Navigation Corporation, Florida Inter-Island Steamship Company, Ltd., Inter-County Telephone and Telegraph Company, Tamiami Trail Tours bus passenger service, Florida Gulf Coast Hotels, Inc., and the Manhattan Mercantile Corporation (operating nine retail businesses). Collier also owned the *Fort Myers Press*, Immokalee and Deep Lake Railroad, all the mills and shops at DuPont, and most of the county seat, Everglades. As he saw a need for a particular service such as lighting, ice, and power, Collier established a company.

As with the panic of 1893 and stock market crash of 1929, Collier believed the depression of the 1930s would not affect his business. He continued to invest millions in developing Florida while his advertising business declined; the transit systems and advertisers could not pay their contracted bills. By 1933 Collier's liabilities nearly eclipsed his assets and the federal courts and creditors granted him a moratorium on paying his debts. Before settling his affairs, Collier died in New York City. Married in 1907 to Juliet Gordon Carnes, Collier had three sons; the eldest, Barron, Jr., continued his father's Florida land development after the accountants and lawyers took ten years to determine that he left a large fortune rather than debt.

Collier also served as a special deputy police commissioner in charge of the Public Safety Bureau from 1922 to 1925 in New York City, where he developed the use of white or yellow lines down the center of roads. He was commissioner in charge of foreign relations of the International Association of Chiefs of Police, and he was a founder of Interpol, the International World Police, for which nine foreign governments decorated him. Collier was acting president of the Boy Scout Foundation of Greater New York, director of Boy Scouts of America, and founder and director of the Museum of the City of New York. Oglethorpe University bestowed upon Collier an honorary doctorate of commercial science. He wrote two books, *Stopping Street Accidents* (1925) and *How Is Business in the United States* (1927). He belonged to the Union League Club of New York and Chicago, New York Yacht Club, Metropolitan Club of New York, and

Sons of Confederate Veterans, among many other groups.

Barron Collier invested millions of his advertising fortune in Florida's future by creating a new county, developing the infrastructure, and using his advertising skills to attract settlers. Before environmentalists recognized the damage to the freshwater aquifer, Collier drained part of the Everglades to create dry land. But he also left a legacy of scenic primitive wetlands—Everglades National Park, Big Cypress Swamp, Corkscrew Cypress Rookery, and Collier Seminole State Park.

• There is no known repository of Collier's papers. The most expansive biographical information about Collier can be found in Charles E. Harner, *Florida's Promoters: The Men Who Made It Big* (1973) and *Florida from Indian Trail to Space Age*, vol. 3 (1965). Additional illuminating articles appear in the *Floridian*, 10 Mar. 1974, and the *Sarasota News*, 22 Mar. 1959. An obituary is in the *New York Times*, 14 Mar. 1939.

SUSAN HAMBURGER

COLLIER, Henry Watkins (17 Jan. 1801–28 Aug. 1855), chief justice of the Alabama Supreme Court and governor of Alabama, was born on a plantation in Lunenburg County, Virginia, the son of James Collier and Elizabeth Bouldin, planters. When he was one year old, his family moved to the Abbeville District of South Carolina. Collier received a classical education at Moses Waddel's well-known academy. In 1818 he moved with his parents to Madison County, Alabama, a booming cotton-producing area of the Tennessee Valley. Over the next few years he read law in Nashville, Tennessee, with Judge John Haywood of the Tennessee Supreme Court. Collier began practicing law in Huntsville in 1822 and the next year was admitted to the bar of the Supreme Court of Alabama. He moved in 1823 to Tuscaloosa, Alabama, and soon established a law practice with Simon L. Perry. In 1826 Collier married Mary Ann Battle. The Colliers had four children and were devout Methodists who took a leadership role in the church and often entertained visiting Methodist dignitaries in their home.

In 1826 Collier stood for the Alabama legislature. He was elected to the house on a platform of constructing a new capitol in Tuscaloosa, where the legislature had recently relocated the state capital. His dignified demeanor, keen knowledge of the law, generous nature, judicious temperament, and reputation for fairness so impressed the legislature that in 1828 it elected him a circuit judge (and thus a member of the supreme court). In 1836, when the Alabama Supreme Court was constituted separately, the legislature elevated him to associate justice. The next year he became chief justice and held the office for twelve years. On the bench, Collier wrote more than 1,165 opinions, more than any other justice to that time, and he was frequently cited in appellate court decisions. His opinions varied from brief, one-paragraph summations to many pages. He was always mindful of constitutional principles and tried to apply them with fairness. He was known as an attentive listener with a reflective and impartial nature and as a judicial scholar with a gift for analysis. Of the legal profession, Collier wrote in 1838 that the lawyer "explores the abstruse and obscured learning of other ages, that he may more successfully protect the weak, vindicate the innocent, and punish the oppressor—looking to the consciousness of having performed his duty for his chief reward." Collier maintained his home in Tuscaloosa, although after the Alabama capital was moved to Montgomery in 1846, he spent much time there.

With sectional issues causing divisive politics in Washington, D.C., and the state Whig party increasing its influence, the Alabama Democratic Convention refused to renominate Governor Reuben Chapman and in 1849 selected Collier as its nominee instead. Collier faced no opposition candidate since his views were decidedly Whiggish, especially on the dominant political question of the day—the issue of the state bank. He received all but 704 of the 37,925 votes cast. Collier favored a state public education system, private banking, a state insane asylum, and prison and judicial reforms. He believed in the importance of an educated citizenry, advocated more equitable funding and centralized oversight of education through a state superintendent, and called the attitude in Alabama of neglecting to fund schools a "blighting apathy that pervades the community." Because of the economic importance of agriculture to the state, he advocated establishing a professorship of geology and agriculture at the University of Alabama.

Although Collier supported southern rights in his inaugural address on 17 December 1849, he remained a moderate, not disturbed by sectional conflict, which he viewed as a natural consequence of democratic politics. Collier agreed that Alabama should send delegates to the Nashville convention to discuss the deteriorating relationship between the southern states and the federal government, but when they returned he refused to call a state convention as the radicals wished. Judicious and conservative, he supported Henry Clay's Compromise of 1850, and he did not believe that the people of Alabama were ready to make secession an issue.

Collier accepted renomination in 1851 but refused to campaign across the state, standing instead on his record. He was reelected decisively with only token opposition coming from both extremes—staunch Unionist Benjamin G. Shields and disgruntled southern rights fire-eaters.

Collier believed that the problems of the nation could be solved by voters, who had the opportunity to repudiate "political hucksters for high places and the supplicants for federal favors." He supported the prison reform work of Dorothea Dix, and she consulted with him during her visits to Alabama. He frequently toured the state penitentiary and followed its administration closely. He also advocated economic diversification, especially increasing the number of textile mills in Alabama, which would locate the manufacturing process close to raw-material production and de-

crease shipping and commission costs for the planter. As his second gubernatorial term drew to a close in 1853, Collier declined to be considered for a legislative appointment to the U.S. Senate and retired to his plantation near Tuscaloosa. Suffering poor health in the summer of 1855, he visited Bailey Springs in Lauderdale County in hopes that the waters might restore his strength, but he died there of cholera morbus, an early term for gastroenteritis.

Collier's experience on the Alabama bench and his twelve years as chief justice came in the formative period of Alabama statehood, and his extensive judicial decisions form the basis of numerous citations and case comments. His gubernatorial leadership paved the way for the enactment of an Alabama public education system in 1854, moved the state toward diversification and investment in manufacturing, and strengthened the Alabama Democratic party at a pivotal time in its history. His successor, Governor John A. Winston, called him "a man of ability, integrity, and sterling worth." Collier's guidance and example were calming influences in Alabama during the growing emotionalism and extremism of the sectional conflict, and his death left a vacuum in the moderate political leadership of the state at a critical time.

• Collier's gubernatorial papers are preserved in the Alabama Department of Archives and History in Montgomery. His judicial opinions are in the Alabama Court Reports. Biographical sketches are in Thomas M. Owen, *History of Alabama* (4 vols., 1921); William Garrett, *Reminiscences of Public Men in Alabama* (1872); Willis Brewer, *Alabama* (1872); Benjamin F. Riley, *Makers and Romance of Alabama* (n.d., 1915?); and John Craig Stewart, *The Governors of Alabama* (1975). Alabama politics and Collier's role are explored in J. Mills Thornton III, *Politics and Power in a Slave Society: Alabama, 1800–1860* (1978); and William W. Rogers et al., *Alabama: The History of a Deep South State* (1994). An obituary is in the *Mobile Daily Register*, 9 Sept. 1855.

LEAH RAWLS ATKINS

COLLIER, John (4 May 1884–8 May 1968), reformer best known for his role in federal Indian policy, was born in Atlanta, Georgia, the son of Charles A. Collier, a prominent banker and mayor, and Susie Rawson. Following his mother's death in 1897, Collier was sent to a Roman Catholic convent in rural Georgia for one year. He returned home to finish his education at an Atlanta high school, where he graduated valedictorian. In 1900 his father died. Collier spent the summer of 1901 camping in the wilderness of the southern Appalachian Mountains to help recover from his parents' deaths. During this period, convinced that his father had committed suicide, he rejected all desire for worldly success.

In 1902 Collier moved to New York City to attend Columbia University as a special student. Sponsored by a family friend, he enrolled in noncredit graduate literature and French drama courses. Collier also studied under Lucy Graham Crozier, a freelance teacher, who directed his interest from literature to philosophy, sociology, natural science, and broad social concerns. By this time he had come to question the philosophy of social Darwinism with its free-market and laissez-faire doctrines as well as many other values of his social class.

Crozier persuaded Collier to return to Georgia in order to convince railroads and chambers of commerce that their resettlement of unemployed northern immigrants on vacant land would enrich the ethnic diversity of the New South. When this endeavor failed to receive financial support, Collier accepted an invitation in March 1905 to become executive director of the newly established Associated Charities of Atlanta. He resigned a few months later when the board of directors disapproved of his costly proposal to create jobs for poor people rather than provide them with commodities and cash handouts.

Collier traveled to Paris in 1906 to study psychology at the Collège de France under Pierre M. F. Janet. On the voyage he met Lucy Wood, whom he married in 1906; they had three children. They divorced in 1943.

In 1908 Collier became civic secretary of the People's Institute in New York City, where he worked as a community organizer among immigrants on the Lower East Side. He investigated safety standards at New York cinemas and served on the institute's National Board of Censorship. In 1914 he organized a pageant that used art, drama, and dance in hopes of preserving Old World immigrant customs.

At the institute Collier edited the *Civic Journal,* a magazine that endorsed progressive urban reform. He also studied the causes of juvenile delinquency and participated in the school community center movement where public schools coordinated immigrant educational and leisure activities. Apart from his duties at the institute, Collier was personally involved with bohemian and intellectual concerns at Greenwich Village.

In March 1914 he resigned from the People's Institute. He then camped with his family in the Appalachians of North Carolina where he composed poetry that romanticized nature and wrote essays that discussed how drama could give people a sense of common purpose. After his return to New York a few months later, he established the Home School, a utopian educational experiment based on the theories of John Dewey. In 1915, resuming his work at the People's Institute, he founded a training school for community workers that staffed public school community centers, settlement houses, and neighborhood associations. Collier also helped organize, and in 1916 he was appointed president of, the National Community Center Conference. He edited its journal, the *Community Center.*

In 1919 Collier again resigned from the People's Institute, having found it impossible to secure financial and political support for his reforms in New York City. He moved to California, where he served as director of Americanization for the California State Housing and Immigration Commission. In 1920, inspired by watching tribal dances at the Taos, New Mexico, Pueblo, he made a lifelong commitment to preserve tribal community life because it offered a cultural alternative to modernity. After teaching sociology at San Francisco State College in 1921–1922, he was appointed research agent for the Indian Welfare Committee of the General Federation of Women's Clubs. He gained national recognition as an Indian reformer by blocking the U.S. Senate Bursum Bill, which would have ended Pueblo land and water rights without adequate compensation.

Collier organized and became executive secretary of the American Indian Defense Association in 1923. For a decade he worked as a lobbyist in Washington, D.C. There, he set the agenda of the AIDA, advocating a reorganization of the Indian Bureau, the conservation of tribal resources, federal credit and improved social services for reservation communities, recognition of Indian cultural freedom, and an end to the land allotment system. During the 1920s he also assisted in organizing the All Pueblo Council, which fought for tribal independence and the right of Indian self-rule. He wrote for *American Indian Life* and other AIDA publications that criticized the Indian Bureau because of its failure to provide adequate services to tribal communities. He defended Indian religious freedom and water rights, publicized the mismanagement of Indian property and tribal funds, and lobbied for the Indian Oil Act of 1927, which guaranteed Indian royalties from subsurface minerals on executive order reservations.

In response to Collier's criticism, the Interior Department requested an outside examination of the Indian Bureau. In 1928 the Brookings Institution published the results of this review in *The Problem of Indian Administration,* which advocated increased federal appropriations for Indians, limited tribal self-rule, and the end of land allotment. Between 1929 and 1932 Collier constantly criticized federal officials for not following the Brookings recommendations; he also joined members of the Senate Indian Investigating Committee who traveled the country to publicize substandard living conditions on western reservations.

In April 1933 President Franklin D. Roosevelt appointed him as commissioner of Indian affairs. In that capacity Collier supported legislation that provided additional compensation for Pueblo Indians who had lost land to settlers, and he canceled reimbursable debts charged against tribal funds. He also endorsed abolition of the Board of Indian Commissioners, which had encouraged land allotment and assimilation. Furthermore, he stopped the sale of Indian trust land, upheld religious freedom by curtailing missionary activity at Indian schools, supported legislation that provided states with special funds for Indian education, and worked to repeal twelve law codes that restricted Indian civil liberties.

In 1934 Congress passed the Indian Reorganization Act. This legislation authorized tribal self-rule under federal supervision, discontinued land allotment, and permitted the consolidation, restoration, and purchase of tribal land for Indian reservations. The act set up a federal revolving credit fund to stimulate reservation economic development, and it provided tuition and scholarships to encourage Indian education.

Collier's Indian New Deal included other reforms. In 1935 the Interior Department created an Indian Arts and Crafts Board to market and improve the production of Indian-made goods. Collier contracted with federal agencies to bring Indians into New Deal relief programs, and he organized a separate Indian Civilian Conservation Corps and publicized its activities in a journal, *Indians at Work*.

In 1940, at the First Inter-American Conference on Indian Life, held at Patzcûaro, Mexico, Collier and other delegates recommended that governments throughout the Western Hemisphere provide Indians with land, credit, and technological assistance to maintain their separate group identities. The conference endorsed a treaty that established a permanent Inter-American Indian Institute that was required to meet every four years to discuss issues of common concern.

Collier encountered many problems as a federal administrator. His romantic stereotyping of Indians often did not fit the reality of contemporary tribal life. He suffered a major setback when the Navajo resisted his stock reduction programs and voted against the IRA. He was unable to persuade Congress to appropriate adequate funds for the political and economic development of reservation communities. The Senate Indian Affairs Committee on several occasions publicly criticized him for advocating racial segregation; it also recommended repealing the IRA and dismantling the Indian Bureau.

Collier found it difficult to promote cultural pluralism and tribal sovereignty during World War II. In 1940 Secretary of War Henry Stimson rejected his suggestion that the government form separate Indian military units. Instead, Stimson endorsed compulsory integrated military service, which rapidly accelerated the process of tribal assimilation.

In January 1945 Collier resigned as commissioner. In July he became president of the Institute of Ethnic Affairs in Washington, D.C., where he edited the institute's newsletter, which criticized the Cold War and defended the civil liberties of native peoples in Guam, Samoa, and Micronesia. In 1946, at the first session of the United Nations General Assembly in London, he worked to create an international trusteeship system for people under colonial rule.

In 1947 he accepted a faculty position in sociology and anthropology at the City College of New York. For the next six years he taught classes, published research on Indian life in the New World, and worked at the Institute of Ethnic Affairs. After his retirement in 1954, he taught classes for one semester at Columbia University and a summer seminar at the Merrill-Palmer School for social workers in Detroit.

In 1955 Collier was divorced from Laura Thompson, whom he had married in 1943. He then fulfilled a one-year appointment as visiting professor of anthropology at Knox College before returning to Taos to live near the Pueblo Indians. In 1957 he married Grace Volk. He wrote newspaper columns and book reviews, and he finished a memoir of his life. In 1964 he received a distinguished service award from the Interior Department. He died in Taos.

• Major manuscript collections of Collier's papers are the People's Institute Papers, Manuscript and Archives Division, New York Public Library; the John Collier Papers, Yale University Library; and the Office Files of Commissioner John Collier at the National Archives. For his important published works, see *Indians of the Americas* (1947), *Patterns and Ceremonials of the Indians of the Southwest* (1949), *On the Gleaming Way* (1962), and *From Every Zenith* (1963). Biographical accounts are Lawrence C. Kelly, *The Assault on Assimilation* (1983), and Kenneth R. Philp, *John Collier's Crusade for Indian Reform* (1977). For books on Collier's career, consult Lawrence C. Kelly, *The Navajo Indians and Federal Indian Policy* (1968); Donald Parman, *The Navajos and the New Deal* (1976); Graham D. Taylor, *The New Deal and American Indian Tribalism* (1980); Laurence M. Hauptman, *The Iroquois and the New Deal* (1981); Robert F. Schrader, *The Indian Arts and Crafts Board* (1983); Paul Prucha, *The Great Father* (1984); Vine Deloria and Clifford Lytle, *The Nations Within* (1984); Harry A. Kersey, *The Florida Seminoles and the New Deal* (1989); and Alison R. Bernstein, *American Indians and World War II* (1991). An obituary is in the *New York Times*, 9 May 1968.

KENNETH R. PHILP

COLLIER, Peter Fenelon (12 Dec. 1849–24 Apr. 1909), publisher, was born in Myshall, County Carlow, Ireland, the son of Robert C. Collier and Catherine Fenelon. With his family he immigrated to the United States at the age of seventeen. He began his education in the Irish countryside and continued at St. Mary's Seminary in Cincinnati, Ohio. His parents had often urged him to join the priesthood, but at the age of twenty Collier left the seminary and settled in New York City, where he found work as a salesman with a publishing firm specializing in Catholic books.

Distressed by the economic impediments that prevented the urban poor from purchasing religious literature, Collier devised a system of selling on installment payments. Collier's employers, however, would not be persuaded to accept the installment plan. Determined to see his plan through, he began publishing and selling Catholic books independently. The moderate success he attained through this first independent venture provided him with the capital to begin publication of a small series of literary classics, priced affordably and available through installment payments. In 1873 he married Katherine Dunn. They had one son. In 1877 the first series, compilations of Charles Dickens and William Shakespeare, was published in collaboration with a New York printer and binder. Within three years Collier had expanded his list of titles and begun construction on his own printing factory. In the true entrepreneurial spirit, he directed every detail of the press's rapid expansion, and before long he was the owner of one of the most prolific and technologically advanced book publishing firms in the country. His New York offices expanded to include thirty-two cities, which directed a large bureaucratic network of ninety-six sub-branches. During his lifetime Collier's firm printed and sold more than 50 million books.

Furthermore, Collier remained true to his original intention of bringing literary classics to the masses through affordable monthly payment plans. Even after his press achieved prominence, he refused to print more expensive additions for a limited audience, maintaining an average price between fifty and sixty cents per volume. Collier himself was a man of refined literary taste, and he remained diligent in ensuring the literary integrity of his publications. In addition to Dickens and Shakespeare, Collier published works by Honoré de Balzac, Lord Byron, and James Fenimore Cooper, among others, as well as an exclusive printing of the Sherlock Holmes stories by Sir Arthur Conan Doyle. Historical books were also added to the Collier list, eventually comprising more than 17 percent of the press's total sales.

In 1888 Collier renewed his commitment to informing the public through the creation of the periodical *Once a Week*, which was replaced in 1896 by *Collier's Weekly*. The second journal enjoyed rapid success and quickly became one of the premier national weekly news magazines. It retained his initial literary bent, focusing the public eye on aspiring young writers, while also taking an independent political stance that attracted a devoted national readership. In his privately published *In Memoriam* (1910), Collier's son Robert recalled that his father had "wanted the *Weekly* to be a force of good in the community, rather than a commercial success if the choice had to be made." In adherence to these principles the journal refused advertisements for alcoholic beverages and patent medicines staking dubious claims. Despite his social and political connections (to Mark Twain and Theodore Roosevelt, among many others), Collier maintained an editorial stance that included a pronounced distaste for New York "society" publications, one of which brought a libel suit against the journal that was decided in favor of the defendants.

Oddly enough, Collier himself was, in the latter half of his life, a fixture in New York society. His free time was devoted almost entirely to the exclusive Meadowbrook and Rockaway Hunting and Riding Clubs and the Rumson Polo Club, where his love of sports and the outdoors became renowned. Despite leading the sporting life of an aristocratic nobleman, Collier's values and ideals were firmly rooted in the experience of an immigrant's struggle. Throughout his life he maintained a philanthropic ethos, in both business and personal endeavors, that aimed to empower the American underclass. Having endured the struggle to succeed, Collier grew averse to complacency even in his later years. Robert Collier's *In Memoriam* cites the "remarkable will power that enabled [Collier] to drive alternately the two dynamos of mind and body at top speed." He died of a stroke at a riding club in New York City. His son, Robert, editor of the *Weekly* from its inception, succeeded his father as publisher of the magazine.

Collier's undertakings heralded both the democratization of print and the growth of a national news media that was trying to keep pace with the expanding corporate and government sectors. As the *Weekly* eulogized upon his death, "His business was personal." Collier entered the arenas of sport and politics with equal vigor. He furnished information and education to a public who did not receive them through the existing publishers.

• Robert Collier's *In Memoriam* was published independently in 1910. Other sources include an editorial from *Collier's Weekly*, 8 May 1909, and obituaries in the *New York Herald*, 25 Apr. 1909, and the *New York Tribune*, 24 Apr. 1909.

PATRICK JOHN GRIZZARD

COLLIER, Price (25 May 1860–3 Nov. 1913), writer and minister, was born Hiram Price Collier in Davenport, Iowa, the son of Robert Laird Collier, a Unitarian clergyman who collected European labor statistics for the U.S. government, and Mary Price, whose father, Hiram Price, was a U.S. congressman. After his mother's death in 1872 Collier spent five years in Europe with his father and became fluent in French and German. In 1882 Collier finished Harvard Divinity School, where he was the youngest student to graduate up to that time. He first occupied the pulpit of the First Parish Church in Hingham, Massachusetts, and in 1888 arrived at the First Unitarian Church of Brooklyn, New York, where he almost instantly became both a sought-after preacher and a man about town. Early in 1890 the New York *World* stated that Collier "has been in Brooklyn only a short time, but has already gained a reputation as one of the cleverest men among us. He is . . . of marked intellectual force and is very popular in society" (15 Jan. 1890). Not only did Collier, whose sermons were noted for their eloquence and fire, fill his church each Sunday, but he was also in great demand as a public speaker. His every move was reported by the local press, and his sermons were published weekly in the Boston *Saturday Evening Gazette* (as was his unsigned column "Modern Society").

Finding that his church—whose leading member was Alfred T. White, the housing reformer—had already started a settlement house, Collier shaped it to emphasize recreation more than religion and self-direction by youths more than discipline imposed by adults. Ahead of his time, in 1889 he started a Boys' Club at the settlement house, which was a forerunner of the Boys' Clubs of America. "Just as far as possible the boys run the club themselves," he explained. Regularly dedicating two evenings a week to the club, Collier admitted, "It requires a casing of rubber for one's nerves not to be seriously disturbed by the subdued roar that goes on for two hours in the room" (*Brooklyn Daily Eagle*, 21 Nov. 1889). In 1891—as an ongoing experiment in practical sociology—Collier, who was athletic and vigorous, took twenty-five members of his Boys' Club, mostly bootblacks and newsboys, to a camp on Huntington Bay, Long Island, where for ten days they participated in arduous outdoor activities. A lover of military drill who would later serve in the Spanish-American War, Collier was also the chaplain of the Twenty-third Regiment of the New York State National Guard.

In September 1892 Collier's triumphs in Brooklyn abruptly ended with his resignation from his pastorate. Rumors had been rife that Collier, who had been married since 1886 to Gertrude A. Dame, with whom he had one child, was having an affair with Katharine Delano "Kassie" Robbins, a recently widowed parishioner who was the aunt of Franklin D. Roosevelt. The situation had come to a head in the spring of 1892 when Gertrude Collier departed for Massachusetts after finding her husband seated with Robbins in Delmonico's Restaurant. In August 1893 Collier married Robbins after spending ninety days on a Sioux Indian reservation while getting a divorce in South Dakota. Almost immediately the newlyweds went to England, where Collier became the European editor of *Forum*, at that time one of the most influential and entertaining monthlies in the United States. After two years abroad, they settled in Tuxedo Park, New York, where, when not traveling, they brought up Kassie's children from her former marriage and their own two daughters. Their younger daughter, Katharine Price Collier St. George, served eighteen years in the U.S. Congress, where she opposed the programs of her cousin Franklin D. Roosevelt.

Writing "sprightly books about manners and politics in foreign lands," Collier was as popular a writer as he was a minister (*New York Times*, 9 Nov. 1913). Besides Europe, he and his wife visited numerous countries in South America and Asia, gathering material for his books and magazine articles. Credited with a "taking manner and a large stock of information," Collier claimed to get more enjoyment out of reading a census report than a novel (*New York Times*, 9 Nov. 1913).

Beginning with *Mr. Picket-Pin and His Friends* (1894), which he wrote while waiting for his divorce, readers of Collier's books stepped with him inside another culture. Admiring Indians for their strenuous outdoor life, Collier wrote about them during a decade when their population was at its lowest level, a time when many Americans were romanticizing them as a disappearing race. Accompanying Collier on hunting expeditions with Picket-Pin and other Sioux Indians made readers realize that, even though "the real Indian has been bayoneted out of the red man," there was more of him left than appeared in the "loafing, soup-kitchen-fed Redskin of the Indian Reservations." Through Collier, readers glimpsed the "wild, fearless, roaming savage" with "an unconquering love of a nomadic existence" and with him lamented that, having no more "future than . . . the American bison," the "descendants of red warriors, statesmen, and orators will be found here and there weaving baskets, making harmless bows and arrows, peddling pseudo-Indian work."

In *America and the Americans from the French Point of View* (1897), at first published anonymously, Collier viewed his own land through the critical eyes of a Frenchman. Jews were excluded from the various New York clubs, and Collier recorded that "on all hands one hears sneers, innuendoes, and dislike expressed," although "no one criticizes or attacks them openly." Collier had his Frenchman encounter a young American woman with "bright eyes, a tireless tongue, and a frank independence of manner, which would have been suspicious in a Frenchwoman." In twenty-four hours "she knew every unattached man on board the ship, and had walked and chatted with most of them," including him. Collier gained a wide audience with *England and the English from an American Point of View* (1909). In that book, first published in serial form, he claimed that "the Germans since 1870 have taken the place of the English as the boors of Europe" and predicted that "should England go to war now with Germany she would probably win." Taken aback by these comments, some German newspapers complained when the kaiser and his family hobnobbed with Collier and his family while Collier was researching *Germany and the Germans from an American Point of View* (1913). Calling himself a friendly critic, Collier maintained that Germany was "quite able to name her boors and take her hard knocks" (*New York Times*, 4 Nov. 1913). Between his books on England and Germany and after ten years of wanderings in Burma, China, India, Japan, and Korea, Collier wrote *The West in the East from an American Point of View* (1911). In it, he noted that instinct, rather than training or prejudice, seemed to account for his "racial likes and dislikes," and he called the Chinese "the most agreeable people in the East." He detected "something virile and independent about them; some quality of playing the game the way we play it, that is lacking in the others."

In the summer of 1913 Collier with his wife and daughters toured Scandinavia, where he wrote articles for *Scribner's Magazine* and collected material for yet another book, "Scandinavia and the Scandinavians from an American Point of View," which was never published. Collier died in Denmark following a heart attack while on a hunting expedition on the Baltic island of Fyn. In summing up Collier's career, the *New York Times* predicted, "Historians of the future may not altogether disregard books which created so much dispute when they were new" (9 Nov. 1913).

• For Collier's years in Brooklyn and his successful ministry there, see his *Sermons* (1892); the First Unitarian Church Collection, Brooklyn Historical Society; and Olive Hoogenboom, *The First Unitarian Church of Brooklyn: One Hundred Fifty Years* (1987), which also gives an overview of Collier's two careers. Biographical information can also be found in his other writings. Collier collaborated on two books, *A Parish of Two* (1903), a story told in letters, written with Henry G. McVickar, and *Riding and Driving* (1905), part of Macmillan's Sportsman's Library, for which he wrote the chapters on driving and handling the horse. Collier's literary career is summed up in his obituary and a later editorial in the *New York Times*, 4 and 9 Nov. 1913.

OLIVE HOOGENBOOM

COLLINGE, Patricia (20 Sept. 1894–10 Apr. 1974), actress and writer, was born in Dublin, Ireland, the daughter of Frederick Channon Collinge, a musical director and conductor, and Emmie Russell. She was privately educated in Dublin. It was there, admitted free to plays as a professional courtesy to her father, that she first saw and loved theater. At the age of ten she made her first professional appearance at London's Garrick Theatre, playing Ching-a-Ling in a 1904 Christmas pantomime, *Little Black Sambo and Little White Barbara*. In 1908 Collinge joined her father in New York City and played the Flower girl in *The Queen of the Moulin Rouge*. She then appeared in *The Girl and the Wizard* at the Casino Theatre, at which her father conducted. Collinge also understudied the Girl, which she subsequently played on tour.

Leaving the musical comedy stage in 1910, Collinge acted with the prestigious and artistically ambitious New Theatre company in *The Blue Bird* and *The Thunderbolt*. She was then cast in the modern morality play *Everywoman* (Feb. 1911), playing the part of Youth for three years in New York and London. She then returned late in 1913 to the United States, and by age twenty-one Collinge had established herself as a Broadway leading lady after performing in four plays and the subsequent tours opposite the popular and athletic actor Douglas Fairbanks between December 1913 and the summer of 1915.

In August 1915 Collinge opened at the Blackstone Theatre in Chicago in the title role of *Pollyanna*, and she played there for a year before opening in New York the next September. Though critics complained about the play's structural faults and cloying sentimentality, they correctly predicted its great popular success. Collinge toured *Pollyanna* throughout the country in 1917–1918. To her own occasional chagrin, Collinge was remembered and headlined as "the original 'glad' girl" throughout most of her later career.

Collinge's first "star" part, advertised to cash in on her *Pollyanna* success, came in January 1919: the title role in another dramatization of a novel, *Tillie, the Mennonite Maid*, set in Pennsylvania Dutch country. This was followed in 1920 by two short runs, *Golden Days* at Chicago's Blackstone and *Just Suppose* in New York. In 1921 Collinge married James Nichols Smith; they had no children.

From 1922 to 1935 Collinge appeared in some forgettable new plays and a number of revivals. Among the roles indicating her growing versatility were Lucy in *The Rivals* (1922), Mrs. Elvsted in *Hedda Gabler* and Cecily Cardew in *The Importance of Being Earnest* (both with the Actor's Theatre in 1926), the title role in *Candida* and Maggie Wylie in *What Every Woman Knows* (both Baltimore, Md., 1927), Constance Neville in an all-star revival of *She Stoops to Conquer* (1928), Amelia Selby in an all-star *Becky Sharp* (1929), and Gabrielle in *Anatol* (1931).

After performing in *To See Ourselves* (1935), Collinge left acting to focus on writing. Her witty satiric pieces and short stories appeared in newspapers and magazines, notably *Vanity Fair* and the *New Yorker*.

In 1938, at the request of the Theatre Guild, Collinge adapted a French play, André Birabeau's *Dame Nature*, for production by the guild. She wrote two books. The first, written with actress Margalo Gilmore, is *The B. O. W. S.* (1945), which tells the story of the American Theatre Wing unit that toured *The Barretts of Wimpole Street*, starring Katherine Cornell, to the troops in Italy and France during World War II. Collinge's second book is *The Small Mosaics of Mr. and Mrs. Engel* (1959), a collection of stories of an American couple's travels in Italy. The latter received Italy's Premio Enit Gold Medal for furthering good relations between Americans and Italians.

Collinge returned to the stage as a character actress in the short but impressive role of Birdie Hubbard in Lillian Hellman's *The Little Foxes* (1939). In October 1941 Collinge succeeded Josephine Hull as one of the wine-poisoning Brewster sisters in the farce *Arsenic and Old Lace*. She later appeared in *The Heiress* (New York, 1947; on tour 1948–1949), *The Curious Savage* (Playhouse, Wilmington, Del., 1950), and *Mary Rose* (American National Theater & Academy Playhouse revival, New York, 1951). Her last stage appearance was in *I've Got Sixpence* at the Ethel Barrymore Theatre in New York (Dec. 1952).

As her first film role, Collinge repeated Birdie in *The Little Foxes* (1941), for which she was nominated for an Academy Award. Other films include Alfred Hitchcock's *Shadow of a Doubt* (1943), *Tender Comrade* (1943), *Casanova Brown* (1944), *Teresa* (1951), *Washington Story* (1952), and *The Nun's Story* (1959). She appeared frequently on television, mostly for CBS, on "Golden Age of TV" drama programs such as "Studio One," the "US Steel Hour," "Omnibus," "Alfred Hitchcock Presents," and "Armstrong Circle Theatre." Collinge also received a citation for her war work in hospitals during World War II as a member of the Stage Women's Relief Committee. She died at her home in New York City.

When Collinge appeared in *Autumn Crocus* (1932), *New York Times* critic Brooks Atkinson praised "the soft, pliant sincerity that makes her one of the most endearing actresses." Endearing qualities were also present in her writing. *The Small Mosaics of Mr. and Mrs. Engel* was praised for "an exactness of observation and rightness of touch that would be breathtaking if they were not so unobtrusive," words that might also have been used to describe her acting.

• Files of clippings and photographs of Collinge at the New York Public Library for the Performing Arts at Lincoln Center also contain copies of some of her newspaper articles and magazine stories. An obituary is in the *New York Times*, 11 Apr. 1974.

DANIEL S. KREMPEL

COLLINGWOOD, Charles Cummings (4 June 1917–3 Oct. 1985), broadcast journalist and foreign correspondent, was born in Three Rivers, Michigan, the son of George Harris Collingwood, a professor and forester, and Jean Grinnell Cummings. In 1935 Collingwood spent two years at Deep Springs College in Death Valley, California, an experimental school modeled on the Oxford system. In 1937 Collingwood transferred to Cornell, where he graduated cum laude in 1939. The same year he was awarded a Rhodes scholarship. In 1940, while attending Oxford University, he worked for the United Press wire service. In March 1941 he was invited by Edward R. Murrow to join CBS radio. At their first meeting Murrow was reportedly put off by Collingwood's seeming dandyism. However, when they began talking about lumberjacking (Murrow spent his adolescence working in lumber camps) Murrow warmed to him.

Collingwood was one of the first of a number of foreign correspondents hired by Murrow and subsequently referred to as "Murrow's boys." They included William L. Shirer, Eric Sevareid, and Howard K. Smith. They were primarily distinguished by having some press service or other journalistic experience and being very knowledgeable about the countries and events they covered. Collingwood distinguished himself among them by winning a 1943 George Foster Peabody Award, radio's highest honor, for his reporting of the North African campaign in World War II, and especially for his scoop on the assassination of the Vichy commander Admiral Jean-Louis-Xavier-François Darlan.

On D-Day Collingwood landed with American troops on Utah Beach. He was present for the liberation of Paris and took part in the coverage of the German surrender. Not only did Collingwood distinguish himself for his heroic reporting during the war, he was also noted for his sybaritic lifestyle, which earned him the nickname among Murrow's team as "Bonnie Prince Charlie," and later on as the "Duke of Collingwood."

After the war Collingwood served as the first CBS United Nations correspondent during the organization's founding meetings in San Francisco in 1946–1947. While he was CBS's Los Angeles correspondent, he met and married actress Louise Albritton in 1946. She died in 1979. They had no children. He was married again in 1984 to Swedish singer Tatiana Angelina Jolim, and they also had no children.

In 1952 Collingwood took a leave of absence from CBS to become the assistant to former ambassador Averell Harriman, who had become the director of the Mutual Security Administration. Upon his return to CBS in 1953, he plunged into work in early television. One of his first duties before his 1952 leave was hosting the series "The Big Question," which dealt with major domestic and foreign issues.

In 1954 Collingwood was named chief of CBS's London bureau and served there until 1959. In 1959 he succeeded Murrow as the host of the extremely popular "Person to Person" television program. The program usually featured interviews with celebrities in their homes. However, Collingwood's most famous hearthside interview took place outside the confines of "Person to Person," when he accompanied Jacqueline Kennedy on her famous televised tour of the White House on 14 February 1962.

During the 1950s, like his mentor Murrow, Collingwood was conspicuous in the fight against McCarthyism. In 1955 he was elected president of the American Federation of Television and Radio Artists (AFTRA), on a ticket of those who opposed the blacklist and loyalty oaths of the period. One of Collingwood's supporters, John Henry Faulk, host of a CBS variety and talk show, was also elected a vice president of the union, but he soon found himself blacklisted and out of work in broadcasting as a result of his being labeled a communist by the anticommunist group Aware, Inc. In 1956 Faulk sued Aware, Inc., for libel. The case, however, did not come to trial until 1962, and Faulk was supported financially by Collingwood and others during this period. Based on the testimony of Collingwood and others, Faulk won a judgment of $3 million (later reduced to $550,000 on appeal).

In 1953 Collingwood hosted CBS's "Adventure," a science series that won many Peabody awards; the documentary series "Eyewitness" in 1962; and the cultural series "Chronicle" in 1963–1964. From 1964 through 1975 he was CBS's chief foreign correspondent, and in that capacity he covered the Arab-Israeli war in 1967. During the Vietnam War he made more than eighteen trips to Vietnam and hosted the series of news specials "Vietnam Perspective." His most significant achievement during the Vietnam War was, however, to be the first American correspondent to report from inside North Vietnam. In 1968 in two programs, "Charles Collingwood's Report from Hanoi" and "Hanoi: A Report by Charles Collingwood," he gave Americans their first glimpses into the communist capital. In 1972 he was also on hand for President Richard Nixon's visit to mainland China.

As a result of his work as a foreign correspondent and his years as head of the CBS London Bureau, Collingwood was awarded the Order of British Empire in 1975 and was also made a chevelier of the French Legion of Honor. In the years before his retirement in 1982, Collingwood was used sparingly by CBS News, which caused resentment among many of the older reporters and some of the younger foreign correspondents who had been trained by Collingwood.

Collingwood was one of the first of a new generation of broadcast foreign correspondents who could combine the wire services credo of "get it first and get it fast" with the broadcast medium's need to provide intelligent and informed reporting of the events and personalities in foreign affairs. He was also versatile enough to move easily between the role of tough reporter and that of host of more entertainment-oriented programs. In addition, he was one of the heirs to the Murrow tradition at CBS News and often served as a mentor to a newer generation of CBS correspondents such as Dan Rather. Collingwood died in New York City.

• The Mass Communications History Center of the State Historical Society of Wisconsin holds the papers of Charles

Collingwood. The National Archives contains many of his World War II broadcasts. The Museum of Television and Radio in New York City has many of his most important television programs. Collingwood's life is sketched in some detail in Stanley Cloud and Lynne Olson, *The Murrow Boys: Pioneers on the Front Lines of Broadcast Journalism* (1996). His career with CBS News is dealt with in Gary Paul Gates, *Airtime: The Inside Story of CBS News* (1978). His relationship with Edward R. Murrow is discussed in Anne M. Sperber, *Murrow: His Life and Times* (1986).

ALBERT AUSTER

COLLINS, Eddie (2 May 1887–25 Mar. 1951), baseball player, coach, and executive, was born Edward Trowbridge Collins in Millerton, New York, the son of John Rossman Collins, a railroad freight agent, and Mary Meade Trowbridge. Collins spent his first years in Millerton before the family moved to Tarrytown, New York, where he attended school. He enrolled at Columbia University in 1903.

A football and baseball star in college, Collins in 1906 was scouted by Connie Mack, manager and part-owner of the Philadelphia Athletics, who was among the first in organized baseball to recruit college players. Without the university's knowledge, Mack signed Collins and played him that summer in six games at infield positions under the name Edward Sullivan. However, Columbia learned that Collins earlier had played semiprofessional ball in Vermont and Connecticut. Although Collins deservedly lost his amateur status, Columbia appointed him its baseball captain and coach during his senior year.

After graduating with a bachelor's degree in 1907, Collins rejoined the Athletics and within two years became the team's regular second baseman. From 1911 through 1914 he was part of the star-studded "$100,000" infield consisting of John "Stuffy" McInnis at first base, Jack Barry at shortstop, and Frank "Home Run" Baker at third. By then, Mack regarded Collins as a son, and Collins developed a lasting devotion to his manager.

Small, strong, and wiry, Collins was a well-coordinated left-handed batter with a discerning eye at the plate; he also was unusually fast. Almost 80 percent of his career hits were singles, supplemented by 1,499 bases on balls. All of his base hits and walks—he had a remarkable .424 career on-base percentage—contributed to his eventual 744 stolen bases. Collins had large hands, which helped him become an outstanding fielder. He led American League second basemen in fielding nine times, a major league record that remained standing more than sixty years later.

In his first stint with Philadelphia, Collins played on four pennant winners and three world champions. From 1906 through 1914 he batted .337 and stole 370 bases, a club record. He won the 1914 American League Chalmers Award, equivalent to the later Most Valuable Player award. In 1910 he established a club single-season record with 81 stolen bases. That year he married Mabel Harriet Doane. They had two sons, one of whom, Edward, Jr., played three seasons for

Mack's Athletics and later worked in the Philadelphia Phillies' front office.

In late 1914 Charles Comiskey, the Chicago White Sox owner, paid Mack $50,000 for Collins's contract (then a record price) after being assured by American League president Ban Johnson that the league would pay for a $4,000 raise in Collins's salary. At Chicago, Collins enjoyed a dozen fine seasons (1915–1926); he also managed the 1925 and 1926 teams to fifth-place finishes with a two-year .521 winning percentage. He batted .331 during his years with Chicago and stole 368 bases, also a club record. His fielding average led American League second basemen in six seasons, and he played on two pennant winners. He scored the winning run in the 1917 Series against the New York Giants, and he was that Series' batting leader. The 1919 pennant lived in infamy because eight teammates conspired, unknown to Collins, to throw the World Series to Cincinnati and were banned from baseball for life.

After Collins was released by Chicago in November 1926, Mack signed him as third base coach and part-time player, keeping him in mind as a managerial successor. In 1927 Collins led the league in pinch hits and raised his club record by six stolen bases. He declined a New York Yankees' managerial offer in the winter of 1929. During his twenty-five years as an active player, he batted .333. Collins ranks exceptionally high among the all-time major leaguers in numerous batting and fielding categories, most prominently in batting average for second basemen, stolen bases, hits, games played, runs, on-base percentage, walks, and at bats. As a second baseman in the field, he stands at or near the top in total chances (14,591), assists (7,630), and put outs (6,526). He also was a leader in sacrifice hits.

In 1933 the Boston Red Sox, last-place finishers in nine of their most recent eleven seasons and financially strapped following the 1932 season, were about to be bought by the wealthy, young Thomas A. Yawkey, a great admirer of Collins. Yawkey insisted on having Collins as his professional associate and adviser. With Mack's blessing, Philadelphia released Collins to become Yawkey's vice president, general manager, and treasurer.

Boston's renaissance began with a new Fenway Park (the old one had opened in 1912) and a new roster. For a little more than $600,000 famous names were acquired. From the A's came Jimmie Foxx, Doc Cramer, and Lou Finney; from the Washington Senators came player-manager Joe Cronin. In 1936 Collins made his only scouting trip, signing stars Ted Williams and Bob Doerr. Collins was elected to the National Baseball Hall of Fame in 1939.

In 1945, two years after the death of his wife, Collins married Emily Jane Mann Hall. Steadily declining health in 1950 forced Collins to resign from the Boston organization. He died in Boston.

Jean Yawkey, majority owner and general partner of the Red Sox, observed, "Tom and I really loved and respected Eddie. He was devoted to baseball. He was one of the best businessmen we knew in baseball."

• Collins's statistical records are based on Macmillan's *Baseball Encyclopedia*, 9th ed. (1993), and John Thorn and Pete Palmer, *Total Baseball*, 3d ed. (1993). His role with the Red Sox is discussed in valuable interviews with Jean Yawkey, Dom DiMaggio, Dave Ferriss, Ted Williams, Bobby Doerr, Johnny Pesky, and Red Sox vice president Dick Bresciani. An informative series of articles by Jim Leonard, "From Sullivan to Collins," appeared in the *Sporting News* during Oct.–Nov. 1950. See also Ellery H. Clark, Jr., *Boston Red Sox: 75th Anniversary History* (1975), *Red Sox Fever* (1979), and *Red Sox Forever* (1977).

ELLERY H. CLARK, JR.

COLLINS, Edward Knight (5 Aug. 1802–22 Jan. 1878), merchant and shipping operator, was born in Truro, Cape Cod, Massachusetts, the son of Israel Gross Collins, a sea captain, merchant trader, and ship owner, and Mary Ann Knight, an Englishwoman who died soon after Edward's birth. After his mother's death, his father moved to New York City, leaving Edward to be raised by the Collins family. Edward's uncle (and later business associate), John Collins, was an important influence.

At age thirteen Edward left Truro for a brief period of schooling in New Jersey before going to New York City, where his father arranged for him to work as apprentice clerk in the mercantile counting house of McCrea and Slidell. Within a few years Edward moved to a well-established mercantile firm, Delaplaine & Co., located on South Street near the East River docks of New York Port and next door to Israel Collins's trading and general commission business. In 1821 Edward joined his father's company, which by this time had shifted from European trade to the Gulf Coast and Caribbean waters.

Edward made a few voyages for his father's firm, but he soon took over managing the business from the New York office. Early in January 1824 he became partner of I. G. Collins & Son, which three years later started the first regularly scheduled packet service between New York and Veracruz, Mexico. In 1826 Edward Collins had married Mary Ann Woodruff, daughter of the wealthy and politically active New York City building contractor, Thomas T. Woodruff. After his father's death in 1831, Edward shifted his business to the booming coastal cotton trade between New Orleans and New York. He was appointed manager of a line of large, well-appointed sailing vessels that soon dominated the Gulf Coast–New York trade. Edward owned shares in several of the vessels and also operated as a wholesale merchant.

Rapidly increasing his fortune and his reputation as a maritime entrepreneur, Collins then challenged the well-established transatlantic sailing packet lines between New York and Liverpool, England. Late in 1836 he initiated a liner service to Liverpool that was a remarkable success from the outset. Collins's "Dramatic Line" of unusually large and swift sailing ships was highly profitable and was remarkably well publicized, especially by James Gordon Bennett's *New York Herald*. Collins and his sailing ships became synonymous with quality, luxury, elegance, speed, daring, and style during America's "Go Ahead" age.

By the 1840s Collins's fortune was estimated as even larger than his father-in-law's; and Collins, a conservative Democrat like Thomas Woodruff, became generally recognized as one of the prominent gentlemen of New York City. He had a large estate, "Larchmont," outside of New York City, membership in the New York Yacht Club, and selective involvement in local charities and benefits.

With the surprisingly successful crossing of the Atlantic in April 1838 by the British steamships *Sirius* and *Great Western*, Collins was among those Americans who saw that U.S. domination of the transatlantic sealanes by sailing packets was soon to end. Within a few years premium passenger and cargo transportation across the Atlantic Ocean was largely controlled by the British-owned and operated Cunard Line, which had begun regularly scheduled service in 1840 with heavy financial support from both private investors and the British government. Such public support of private enterprise was justified at the time by the extraordinary expense of building and operating steamships. Use of such steam-powered vessels as naval auxiliaries in wartime, or even possibly as warships, resulted in private steamship companies receiving contracts that produced large subsidy payments for carrying the mails overseas.

Faced with the British domination of transatlantic mail service and looking to create greater American naval capability without having to build and maintain more steam warships, the U.S. Congress in 1845 sought to encourage private American shipping operators to venture into the risky and largely untried business of ocean steam transportation. Edward Collins was among the first of those to propose a transatlantic liner service; unlike others, he sought to compete directly with Cunard for the most lucrative and heavily traveled route: Liverpool to the United States.

With a large federal government contract in hand and with major financial backing from the internationally powerful banking firm of the Brown Brothers, Collins supervised the construction in New York City of four essentially identical wooden-hulled, sidewheel steamships that would be the largest, fastest, and most luxurious in the world. The challenge of building machinery of unprecedented size and weight, along with numerous naval requirements adding to the difficulties of design and construction, created frequent delays. Expenses mounted far beyond expectation, but late in April 1850 the first Collins Line steamer, *Atlantic*, departed New York on its maiden voyage to Liverpool. By the end of the year the *Baltic*, *Pacific*, and *Arctic* were in service; and soon the New York and Liverpool United States Mail Steamship Company, or "Collins Line," was making serious inroads on the Cunard Line's transatlantic trade while continually setting transatlantic speed records.

In an attempt to stabilize and control the transatlantic steam transportation of premium cargoes and first-class passengers, the Cunard Line and Collins Line, with the direct involvement of the Brown Brothers firm, entered into a secret agreement to fix freight rates and also to pool and then apportion their earnings from this trade. This contract continued in force for several years, but even with all the advantages from this cartel—and a doubling of its annual government subsidy to $858,000 in 1852—the Collins Line failed to make a profit or pay any dividends on the corporation's stock. The loss of the Collins liner *Arctic* in a September 1854 collision off Newfoundland was a serious blow to the firm and a personal tragedy for Edward Collins, whose wife and two of their three children were drowned. Collins hoped to restore his company's fortunes with the addition of an even larger and swifter steamship, the *Adriatic* (designed by George Steers), but well before that long-delayed vessel went into service in late 1857 another Collins liner, the *Pacific*, was lost with all hands early in 1856.

Unable to maintain scheduled sailings satisfactorily, the Collins Line suffered from increasingly hostile treatment by Congress, so that when the subsidy was cut back late in 1857 at a time when a severe financial panic already had disrupted business, the Collins Line was unable to continue operations. By early 1858 the firm declared bankruptcy, the three remaining steamships were sold, and Collins ended his maritime career.

Moving to his summer home, "Collinwood," near Wellsville, Ohio, Collins tried to restore his fortune through iron manufacturing, coal mining, and drilling for oil, but all his efforts soon failed. Collins remarried, to Mrs. Sarah Browne, and by 1862 moved back to the New York City area, where he lived in declining comfort and increasing obscurity. After several decades of remarkable success as a maritime entrepreneur, his business failure with the collapse of the heavily subsidized Collins Line would tarnish his reputation, as well as the principle of government subsidy, for many years afterwards. Collins died in New York City.

• Warren Armstrong, *The Collins Story* (1957), is a highly fictionalized effort to write a historical romance about Collins's life. Most authoritative accounts are limited to the steamship phase of Collins's career, especially the pertinent chapters in David B. Tyler, *Steam Conquers the Atlantic* (1939); John Malcolm Brinnin, *The Sway of the Grand Saloon* (1971); and Cedric Ridgely-Nevitt, *American Steamships on the Atlantic* (1981). Brief accounts of Collins's maritime career are in Ralph Whitney, "The Unlucky Collins Line," *American Heritage* 8 (1957): 48–53, 100–102; Edward Sloan, "Edward Knight Collins: Maritime Entrepreneur and Impresario," *The Log of Mystic Seaport* 40 (1988): 3–17; and Sloan, "Private Enterprise and Mixed Enterprise: The Changing Fortunes of Edward Knight Collins, American Maritime Entrepreneur," in *Frontiers of Entrepreneurship Research, 1990*, ed. Neil Churchill et al. (1991): 603–17. More specialized accounts of Collins by Sloan include "The Roots of a Maritime Career: E. K. Collins and the New York–Gulf Coast Trade, 1821–1848," *Gulf Coast Historical Review* 5 (1990): 104–13; "The Nightingale and the Steamship: Jenny Lind and the Collins Liner *Atlantic*," *American Neptune* 51 (1991): 149–55; "Collins versus Cunard: The Realities of a North Atlantic Steamship Rivalry, 1850–1858," *International Journal of Maritime History* 4 (June 1992): 83–100; and "The *Baltic* Goes to Washington: Lobbying for a Congressional Steamship Subsidy, 1852," *Northern Mariner/Le Marin du Nord* 5 (1995): 19–32. An obituary is in the *New York Herald*, 23 Jan. 1878.

EDWARD W. SLOAN

COLLINS, Isaac (16 Feb. 1746–21 Mar. 1817), printer, was born near Centerville, Delaware, the son of Charles Collins and Sarah Hammond, farmers. The family were members of the Society of Friends. When his father died in 1760, Isaac was indentured as a printer's apprentice to James Adams, whose recent arrival in Wilmington marked the beginning of printing in Delaware. Collins stayed with Adams about five years, during which time he probably met Shepard Kollock, another Adams apprentice, who, like Collins, later worked for William Goddard in Philadelphia, Pennsylvania. Similarly, both Collins and Kollock eventually became printers and newspaper publishers in New Jersey.

A slowdown in business in 1766 forced Adams to release Collins, then twenty years old, to complete the last year of his apprenticeship elsewhere. Collins secured another apprenticeship in Williamsburg, Virginia, with William Rind, who had recently moved from Annapolis to start the second *Virginia Gazette*, a Whig-oriented newspaper. Shortly after the official end of Collins's apprenticeship in 1767, he found his first journeyman position in Philadelphia with William Goddard, who had left Providence, Rhode Island, in 1766 to create a folio-size, four-column newspaper on a grand scale, the *Pennsylvania Chronicle*, first issued on 26 January 1767.

The years Collins lived in Philadelphia—from the spring of 1767 to the summer of 1770—were decisive ones for the colonies. With the passage of the Townshend Act in 1767, opposition to British control and taxation flared up as it had in the days following the Stamp Act, the first direct tax levied by Parliament on the American colonies in 1764. Goddard's *Chronicle* was the first colonial newspaper to carry John Dickinson's *Letters from a Pennsylvania Farmer*, a series of essays against the right of Parliament to tax the colonies. During his Philadelphia years Collins also met Joseph Crukshank (or Cru/kshank), probably through the Philadelphia Monthly Meeting of Friends, which Collins joined in January 1770. During a partnership that lasted less than a year, Collins and Crukshank issued seven imprints.

The death of New Jersey's official government printer, James Parker, presented Collins with a new opportunity. In 1770 the young Quaker tradesman moved to Burlington, New Jersey, where he advertised that he had "met with Encouragement, from a number of the most *respectable* Gentlemen in New Jersey." The printer said he had stocked a supply of books and stationery at his one-room shop on High Street, which had been formerly used by Benjamin Franklin for printing currency for New Jersey. Almost immediately Collins issued the *Burlington Almanack*, the first of its kind in the colony; it became the *New-Jersey Almanack* in 1778. In September Collins petitioned the assembly for the post of official government printer, which he won over James Parker's son, Samuel. On 8 May 1771 Collins married Rachel Budd, a member of a ranking Philadelphia Quaker family.

Collins, who early freed his own slave, was closely associated with the antislavery movement and published tracts by such prominent Quaker writers as John Woolman, Anthony Benezet, and Granville Sharp. Benezet, whom Collins had known in Philadelphia, had written three important books on slavery before he contracted with Collins to print his fourth, *Brief Consideration on Slavery, and the Expediency of Its Abolition* (1773). Not all colonial printers accepted manuscripts from Quaker reformers, who were frequently controversial. Collins also issued works by other denominational writers, including Richard Baxter's Puritan masterpiece, *The Saints Everlasting Rest*, and William Mason's *Methodism Displayed*.

Political and military events, many of which reached a climax in New Jersey, helped create the need for a newspaper in the newly independent state. Collins, who had been close to newspaper publishing in Williamsburg and Philadelphia, lifted the first edition of the *New-Jersey Gazette* from his press on 5 December 1777. In the first issue, Collins carried a "call to arms" from General George Washington and a message from Governor William Livingston exhorting the militia to "turn out with alacrity, at a time when Providence seems to have presented you with a glorious opportunity for defeating the common enemy." Likewise, the *Gazette* of 29 April 1778 carried the "Articles of Confederation and Perpetual Union," in effect the nation's first constitution, on its front page. A supplement to the 8 July 1778 issue was also devoted entirely to Washington's description of the Battle of Monmouth.

Only thirteen issues of the *Gazette* were published in Burlington. Collins soon moved into larger quarters in Trenton, New Jersey, where, on two occasions in 1779 and in 1783, he had to suspend publication for lack of money and supplies. Ultimately, with the issue of 27 November 1786, the printer dropped the publication permanently. Nevertheless, Collins's career flourished with respect to his other printing and publishing enterprises and his involvement in community affairs. For example, in 1781 he helped establish the Trenton School Company, attended over time by nine of his fourteen children.

By 1789 Collins had gained a wide reputation and sufficient experience to undertake his most ambitious project: the publication of a King James Bible, the second quarto edition to be printed in America. Biblical scholars have long referred to the Collins Bible as one of the most correct editions. In the late summer or early fall of 1796, Collins moved his business and family to New York City, where he set up shop and residence at 189 Pearl Street. His wife died in 1805 during a yellow fever epidemic. Collins, with his business in the hands of sons, returned to Burlington in early 1808 and on 9 October 1809 married Deborah Smith, a widow. He died in Burlington.

• For more details on Collins's life and career, see *Reminiscences of Isaac and Rachel (Budd) Collins* (1893), a series of family recollections; Charles R. Hildeburn, *A Century of Printing: The Issues of the Press in Pennsylvania, 1685–1784* (1885–1886); and Richard F. Hixson, *Isaac Collins: A Quaker Printer in 18th Century America* (1968), the standard scholarly biography of Collins and a general history of printing in the Middle Colonies. Also useful are William Nelson, *Check-List of the Issues of the Press of New Jersey, 1723, 1728, 1754–1800* (1899); Isaiah Thomas, *The History of Printing in America*, 2d ed. (1874); and Frederick B. Tolles, *Meeting House and Counting House: The Quaker Merchants of Colonial Philadelphia, 1682–1763* (1948). Tolles, *Quakers and the Atlantic Culture* (1960), likewise provides helpful information.

RICHARD F. HIXSON

COLLINS, James Daniel (12 July 1917–19 Feb. 1985), historian of philosophy, was born in Holyoke, Massachusetts, the son of Michael Joseph Collins, a salesman, and Mary Magdalen Rooney. Stricken with polio at the age of fourteen, Collins was largely confined to a wheelchair his entire life. After graduating from the Catholic University of America in Washington, D.C., in 1941, Collins won a Knights of Columbus fellowship and was admitted to the School of Philosophy of the same institution. There he completed his doctoral studies in 1944 with a dissertation published in 1947 as *The Thomistic Philosophy of the Angels*. At Catholic University Collins's principal mentors were two priests: historian John Tracy Ellis and philosopher Charles Aloysius Hart. With the help of another fellowship, Collins pursued postgraduate research on the thought of Boethius and Immanuel Kant at Harvard University's Widener Library. In 1945 he married Yvonne Marie Stafford, a librarian at Catholic University, and three months later the young couple found themselves in Missouri, where Collins had accepted a position in the department of philosophy of St. Louis University. They would spend the next forty years in St. Louis, eventually taking up lifelong residence in Normandy, Missouri, a suburb of St. Louis. They had one child.

Collins's teaching career at St. Louis University began fittingly with a graduate course on Descartes. He became known as a very demanding but fair-minded teacher and as a scholar of uncommon erudition with a contagious enthusiasm for the thinkers he studied. He strove to instill in his students his own penchant for pursuing the history of philosophy according to the highest standards of both the historian and the philosopher. His graduate seminars were regularly conducted in a two-year cycle of four semesters on some particular theme in modern European philosophy, for example, "cognitive models" or "theory and practice," developing the treatment of that theme by one of the rationalists (Descartes, Spinoza, Leibniz) in the first semester, its treatment by one of the empiricists (Locke, Berkeley, Hume) in the second semester, and then by Kant and Hegel in the third and fourth semesters, respectively. This intersection of thematic and historical perspectives is characteristic of Collins's own philosophy of the history of philosophy. As he later put the matter,

The historian's proper concern is neither with an archaicized past nor with a detemporalized present but with seeking the significance of past philosophizing, as being brought in relation to the present existence and problems of men. Such a relationship supposes that we are not in possession of complete lucidity about either pole: whether ourselves or the great philosophers of the modern centuries.

Given Collins's statements, it is perhaps not surprising that his first major publication was *The Existentialists: A Critical Study* (1952). Collins had already published several articles on existentialists in the previous decade, a time when American philosophers largely viewed the work of their Continental contemporaries (or at least what little they knew of it) with apprehension and mistrust. Despite or perhaps due to the fact that it was undertaken from the critical standpoint of "a philosophical theism and realism," Collins's careful examination of the thought of Sartre, Jaspers, Marcel, and Heidegger helped change this attitude. The work first won him some degree of acclaim and was reissued in a revised, briefly expanded version in 1959. Collins had gravitated to an examination of the existentialists as an extension, as he put it, of his studies of Kierkegaard and phenomenology. *The Existentialists* was followed a year later by *The Mind of Kierkegaard*, a book that remains an often-cited, standard work on Kierkegaard's thought.

In 1954 Collins (then president of the American Catholic Philosophical Association) published his monumental study, *A History of Modern European Philosophy*, containing extensive chapters on every major philosopher from the Renaissance to Nietzsche and Bergson. (Several chapters of the book reappeared in the two volumes *The British Empiricists: Locke, Berkeley, Hume* and *The Continental Rationalists: Descartes, Spinoza, Leibniz* in 1967.) A textbook written from an antihistoricist point of view and designed primarily for students who have some acquaintance with Scholastic philosophy, *A History of Modern European Philosophy* sets out to explain the method and guiding principles of each philosopher covered and, in the process, to describe and appraise critically the respective philosopher's stance on perennial philosophical problems. In 1959 in *God in Modern Philosophy*, Collins completed his most prolific decade as a scholar by attempting "to determine the main kinds of philosophical approaches taken toward God during the modern period."

In the early 1960s Collins edited two books, *Readings in Ancient and Medieval Philosophy* (1960) and *Philosophical Readings in Cardinal Newman* (1961) and published three others. In the first of these books, *The Lure of Wisdom*, based on the Aquinas Lecture of 1962, which he delivered at Marquette University, Collins turns in typical fashion to the work of Descartes and even a few contemporary authors in order to show that the topic of wisdom is not confined to the ancient and medieval worlds. Also in 1962 Collins served as president of the Metaphysical Society of America and published his *Three Paths in Philosophy*, a compilation of articles that appeared previously in journals such as the *Commonweal*, the *Journal of Religion*, *Thought*, the *New Scholasticism*, the *Review of Metaphysics*, *International Philosophical Quarterly*, and *America*, as well as various anthologies. Existentialism, naturalism, and theistic realism make up the three paths to which Collins refers in the title of the book, which was successful enough to be reissued as *Crossroads in Philosophy* in 1969. Complementing his earlier work on the existentialists with studies of the thought of Karl Jaspers, Edith Stein, and Max Scheler, he also examines the naturalism of John Dewey and (to a lesser extent) Karl Marx. The final portion of the book, the account of theistic realism, ranges over territory from Étienne Gilson and Jacques Maritain to various analytic philosophers and Edmund Husserl.

In 1963 Collins received a Guggenheim fellowship to study Hume's, Kant's, and Hegel's treatments of religion. This research led to the St. Thomas More Lectures at Yale University that same year and, ultimately, to the publication of *The Emergence of Philosophy of Religion* in 1967. Whereas his 1959 work examined the modern philosophical conceptions of God, *The Emergence of Philosophy of Religion* is based on modern philosophers' insistence that, as Collins put it, "their inquiry into our knowledge of God was only part of a larger inquiry into the religious relationship between man and God." In 1964, with Thomas P. Neill, Collins published *Communism: Why It Is and How It Works*.

Collins published *Descartes' Philosophy of Nature* in 1971 and, a year later (again an outgrowth of lectures, this time delivered at Notre Dame University in 1968), he published his last book, *Interpreting Modern Philosophy*, an attempt "to illuminate the methodology and epistemology of the history of modern philosophy, by reflecting upon the concrete ways of historians in this field." During a distinguished career Collins served on the editorial boards of several major philosophical journals, including *American Philosophical Quarterly* and *Modern Schoolman*. Among his more than eighty articles he was perhaps best known for his "Annual Review of Philosophy," published in *Cross Currents* every year from 1957 to 1980. He died in Normandy, Missouri.

Collins was one of the foremost historians of modern European philosophy in the United States between the 1950s and the 1980s. In addition, he made singular contributions to American Catholic intellectual life during this period. While steeped in the Thomistic schools of thought prevailing in so many departments of philosophy of Catholic universities (especially during the early decades of his career), he insisted on the necessity of both confronting the challenges and acknowledging the fresh insights that European philosophy after the Renaissance presents to traditional Catholic thought. He taught this lesson chiefly by example, making European thinkers from Bacon and Descartes to Nietzsche and Heidegger the focus of his life work. In an address to the American Catholic Philosophical Association in 1965 (upon being awarded its Aquinas Medal) he outlined his own conception of the relation between the autonomous activities of religious reflection and philosophical investigation. "The primary responsibility," he asserted,

lies with the Christian philosopher himself to see to it that the strength of his religious reflection is matched by the radical depth and rigor of his philosophical investigation. Any watering down of either component would result only in a fraudulently harmonious union, one which would lose the values of tension and challenge marking every human effort at synthesis in our nonvisional, historical condition.

• For more information, see Linus J. Thro, ed., *History of Philosophy in the Making: A Symposium of Essays to Honor Professor James D. Collins on His 65th Birthday by His Colleagues and Friends* (1982).

DANIEL O. DAHLSTROM

COLLINS, James Lawton (10 Dec. 1882–30 June 1963), army officer, was born in New Orleans, Louisiana, the son of Jeremiah Bernard Collins, a grocery store owner in Algiers, Louisiana, and Catherine Lawton. Collins attended Tulane University from 1901 to 1903. He then entered the U.S. Military Academy at West Point, New York, in 1903, from which he graduated in 1907, ranking ninety-four in a class of 111. Commissioned a second lieutenant in the cavalry, he served with the Eighth Cavalry Regiment at Fort Robinson, Nebraska, until December 1910, when the regiment was sent to the Philippines. In the Philippines, Collins was initially stationed at Camp McGrath at Batangas on the island of Luzon, and in 1912 he led his regiment's first detachment in operations against insurgent Moros on the island of Jolo. He then was appointed aide-de-camp to Brigadier General John J. Pershing, commanding general of the Department of Mindanao, and in July 1913 he was acting chief of staff for Pershing's field forces in the Bud Bagsak campaign against Moros on Jolo, personally commanding the American forces for the last two days of the Bud Bagsak battle.

In December 1913 Collins returned to the United States, where he again became aide-de-camp to Pershing, who was serving as commander of the Eighth Brigade at the Presidio of San Francisco and later at El Paso, Texas. In 1915 Collins married Virginia Caroline Stewart; they had four children. Following service with the Eleventh Cavalry Regiment at Fort Oglethorpe, Georgia, from December 1915 to March 1916, Collins was aide-de-camp to Pershing during the punitive expedition into Mexico in pursuit of Pancho Villa in 1916–1917, an assignment in which he sometimes carried out special scouting missions for Pershing.

After the United States entered World War I in April 1917, Collins, now a captain, went to France,

again as aide-de-camp for Pershing, who commanded the American Expeditionary Forces (AEF). Through the early summer of 1917 Collins was an observer with the First French Army at Verdun, gathering data for Pershing on trench warfare and the French organization for combat. In July 1917 Collins transferred from the cavalry to the field artillery, and in the fall, with the temporary rank of major, he attended the AEF Field Artillery School at Saumur. Following the completion of the course in December 1917, Collins once more served as Pershing's aide-de-camp until May 1918, assisting him in particular on promotion matters and the awarding of decorations. He then was appointed secretary of the AEF General Staff, a post he held until October 1918. During the last weeks of the war, Collins, who had been promoted to the temporary rank of lieutenant colonel in June, commanded an artillery battalion in the First Division during the final stages of the Meuse-Argonne offensive. After the armistice in November 1918, Collins was reappointed secretary of the AEF General Staff and participated in the preparation of a report on the AEF General Staff organization that helped shape the postwar reorganization of the War Department General Staff.

Following his return to the United States in August 1919, Collins attended the Army War College from 1919 to 1920. During the next two decades he rose in permanent rank from major to brigadier general while holding a variety of assignments. From 1920 to 1924 he was assigned to the War Department General Staff, first as executive officer of the Military Intelligence Division and then in the War Plans Division. While in the latter assignment, Collins was sent to India during the first half of 1922 to study the organization of the Indian army and the operation of the British colonial system. Between 1924 and 1926 he attended the Field Artillery School at Fort Sill, Oklahoma, and the Command and General Staff School at Fort Leavenworth, Kansas. After duty with the Second Field Artillery Regiment, Collins was military attaché in Rome, Italy, from 1928 to 1932. Thereafter, he served at Fort Sill from 1932 to 1934 as commander of the First Field Artillery Regiment and the troops at the Field Artillery School; at Governors Island, New York, from 1934 to 1938 as a staff officer with the II Corps Area Headquarters; and successively from 1938 to 1940 at Fort Hoyle, Maryland, and at Fort Sam Houston, Texas, as commander of the Sixth Field Artillery Regiment, the First Field Artillery Brigade, the Second Field Artillery Brigade, and the Artillery Section of the Second Division.

In October 1940 Collins, with the temporary rank of major general, was appointed commander of the Second Division at Fort Sam Houston, and in April 1941 he was named commander of the Puerto Rico Department. Completing that assignment in April 1943, he was director of administration in the Army Service Forces, the War Department command charged with the supply and administration of the army, from May to November 1943. Collins then was appointed commander of the Fifth Service Command, headquartered in Columbus, Ohio, a position he occupied until February 1946 and which made him responsible for the supervision of the army posts and installations in that region. Collins retired in August 1946 with the permanent rank of major general. A soldier who is best known as an aide to Pershing, Collins died in Washington, D.C.

• Collins's papers are in the U.S. Army Center of Military History, Washington, D.C. James L. Collins, "The Battle of Bud Bagsak and the Part Played by the Mountain Guns Therein," *Field Artillery Journal*, Nov.–Dec. 1925, pp. 559–70, describes Collins's role in the Bud Bagsak campaign. For his military career see *Biographical Register of the Officers and Graduates of the U.S. Military Academy*, vols. 5–9 (1910, 1921, 1931, 1941, 1951). References to Collins's service as aide to Pershing are in Donald Smythe, *Guerrilla Warrior: The Early Life of John J. Pershing* (1973), and *Pershing: General of the Armies* (1986); and Frank E. Vandiver, *Black Jack: The Life and Times of John J. Pershing* (2 vols., 1977). An obituary is in the *New York Times*, 1 July 1963.

JOHN KENNEDY OHL

COLLINS, Jennie (1828–20 July 1887), labor reformer and woman suffragist, was born in Amoskeag, New Hampshire, to humble circumstances. Orphaned by the age of fourteen and largely self-taught, Collins joined the ranks of New England women employed in the textile mills of Lawrence and Lowell, Massachusetts. In the 1840s she moved to Boston, where she worked briefly as a domestic servant and then became a tailor in the city's prospering garment industry.

Protest against the fugitive slave law brought Collins into the local abolitionist movement. During the Civil War she organized the seamstresses in her shop into an after-hours team to make small items for soldiers' personal use. She also helped to raise money for the new hospitals built for soldiers returning to the Boston area and started a school for their children.

Like many New England reformers, Collins turned her attention after the Civil War from chattel slavery to wage slavery. In April 1869 a committee affiliated with the New England Labor Reform League staged a working women's convention in Boston. The participants discussed proposals ranging from demands for greater occupational opportunities, higher wages, and better housing to vocational training programs in the city's public schools. Collins became an officer in the short-lived Working-Women's League organized at this meeting, and throughout the year she lectured to groups of women laborers in Massachusetts and New Hampshire. She delivered spellbinding orations to striking textile operatives in Dover, New Hampshire, during the late fall of 1869.

Collins's participation in the abolitionist movement and her advocacy of woman suffrage allied her with those leaders of the Boston women's movement who shared her concern for the plight of wage-earning women. Collins worked closely with several members of the newly formed New England Women's Club, and she wrote occasionally for the *Woman's Journal*, published in Boston and edited by Mary Rice Livermore, as well as for the *Revolution*, published by Elizabeth Cady Stanton and Susan B. Anthony in New York City. Collins valued her association with these activists and depended on them to assist her financially in what became her life's work.

During the spring of 1870 Collins formulated plans for a downtown headquarters for Boston's working women. She raised sufficient funds from local clothing manufacturers, including her own employer, to rent rooms in the center of Boston's business district. In October 1870, Collins opened Boffin's Bower, a name invented by Charles Dickens in *Our Mutual Friend*. She chose this title, rather than a name such as "Headquarters for Working Women," in order to distance her project from the growing number of philanthropies for destitute women. She believed in reform, not charity, and designed Boffin's Bower as a "rustic and unpretending" social center for working women rather than as a charitable institution. For the next seventeen years, until her death, Collins served as its sole proprietor.

Her plan, Collins wrote, was "to collect in the warm, well-lighted bower all the over-taxed, weary working girls, and with entertainments of music, lectures, and readings . . . to advance them morally and intellectually by giving them opportunity for improvement." Collins designed Boffin's Bower to serve as a place where working women might learn and relax in comfort. With donations from local merchants she provided a piano, newspapers, magazines, and over 400 volumes of "well-selected reading matter." Collins served large numbers of newcomers searching for employment and kept a guest chamber for their use until they found their own lodgings.

Collins maintained a job registry, which assisted between 1,100 and 2,000 women annually. She also set up a workroom to train women for the dressmaking and tailoring trades. Although she dissociated her enterprise from charity, Collins nevertheless provided assistance in times of crisis. From January to April of each year, the slow season in the garment industry, she served free lunches to hundreds of unemployed seamstresses. During the great fire of 1872, which destroyed a large section of the city's commercial district, and again during the 1877–1878 recession, Collins provided meals, clothing, and shelter to large numbers of unemployed working women. She also procured free passes from the rail lines to let the most destitute women return to their homes.

Collins was an avid believer in the dignity of labor. Her treatise, *Nature's Aristocracy; or, Battles and Wounds in a Time of Peace, a Plea for the Oppressed* (1871), argued that labor was the source of all wealth and one of God's greatest blessings. Throughout her life she urged working women, as well as their employers, to honor their craft. "I have seen women exult over triumphs in the drama, literature, music, on the rostrum, and in the drawing-room," she wrote in 1877, "but—NEVER MORE PROUDLY THAN IN THE WORKSHOP OR THE HOUSEHOLD."

Many Boston reformers revered Collins for her perseverance. Following her death from consumption, her friend Mary Livermore wrote: "That a poor working woman, without position or training, should be able to accomplish so large and beneficent a work among the most unfortunate and hopeless classes was simply a marvel." For a short time, the work of Boffin's Bower was taken up by the Helping Hand Society, a local philanthropy.

• Annual reports of Boffin's Bower are located at the Massachusetts Historical Society, Boston. Articles about or by Jennie Collins appear in scattered issues of *American Workman* (Boston), *Banner of Light* (Boston), the *Revolution* (New York), and the *Woman's Journal* (Boston). Eulogies were written by Mary A. Livermore, *Woman's Journal*, 6 Aug. 1887, reprinted in *Faith and Works*, Sept. 1887; and by Lilian Whiting, *Chautauquan*, Dec. 1887. Margaret Andrews Allen located Boffin's Bower within the settlement house movement in "Jennie Collins and Her Boffin's Bower," *Charities Review* 2 (Dec. 1892): 105–15. A biographical sketch by Elizabeth F. Hoxie appears in *Notable American Women*, vol. 1, pp. 362–63. Obituaries are in the Boston *Daily Globe*, the *Evening Transcript*, and the Boston *Herald*, 21 July 1887.

MARI JO BUHLE

COLLINS, Jimmy (16 Jan. 1870–6 Mar. 1943), baseball player, was born James Joseph Collins in Niagara Falls, New York, the son of Anthony Collins, a policeman, and Alice O'Hara. When Jimmy was two years of age, the family moved to Buffalo, New York, where he grew up. He attended St. Joseph's Collegiate Institute and also worked briefly for the Lackawanna Railroad. But he permanently dropped out of school and began his baseball career when he was signed by Buffalo of the Eastern League to play shortstop.

In 1893, his first season, Collins hit a credible .286, but his sorry fielding—a preposterous 67 errors in 76 games—made his future in baseball uncertain. But the next year he was moved to the outfield, and his fielding greatly improved. He led all outfielders in the league with 34 assists, led the league in total hits with 198, and displayed a rewarding .352 batting average. Collins's hitting impressed the Boston Beaneaters (later called the Braves) of the National League, and he became a major leaguer in 1895. He played only 11 games for Boston that year; however, as was permitted by one of the peculiar rules of early baseball, he was sent to Louisville, Kentucky, of the same league on a sort of loan arrangement. As a Louisville outfielder he batted .279 and gave promise of respectability in that position.

About two weeks after Collins joined Louisville, a strange event occurred that changed his career. The team played a series against the league champion Baltimore Orioles, who were renowned for their trickery as much as for their unquestioned skills. The Orioles' lineup included four men ultimately to be in the National Baseball Hall of Fame—Huey Jennings, Joe Kelley, Willie Keeler, and John McGraw. On this occasion the Orioles demonstrated their mastery of the bunt, rarely used by most teams in the 1890s. Reportedly seven consecutive bunts were successfully laid down, most being badly misplayed by the Louisville third baseman, who charged in from his rather stable stance alongside the base, then, in great haste, threw wildly to first. The Louisville manager replaced him with Collins, who by a drastic change in tactics threw out four Orioles in a row. Collins thus appears to have been the first third baseman to play away from the base, move in toward the batter when he anticipated a bunt, pick up the ball barehanded, and throw it to first in the same motion. In short, a fixture at third base was replaced by a more mobile person who could cover far more territory. Soon every team copied Collins's practice. No other strategy would have worked during the "dead ball" era before 1920. The livelier ball employed later in the twentieth century made the technique dangerous, but it has remained the prescribed method of playing third base.

In 1896 Boston recalled Collins, and he played there through the 1900 season. In 1897 he hit .346, his best ever, and in 1898 he led the league in home runs with 15. The next year he set a record by fielding 601 chances, and he broke another record in 1900 with 252 putouts. In 1901 he signed with a new crosstown franchise, the Boston Red Sox (known also as the Pilgrims) of the upstart American League. Many Bostonians were greatly distressed by his move, but Collins could not pass up the increased salary and the managerial duties offered by the new club. The change did not affect his playing. In seven years with the Red Sox Collins's batting average ranged from .271 to .332, and twice he led league third basemen in fielding percentage. He proved to be a successful manager as well. In his first season the team finished in second place largely through the efforts of pitcher Cy Young, who won 33 games. In 1902 Boston came in third place, and in 1903 the Red Sox won the American League pennant handily and then defeated the Pittsburgh Pirates in the first modern World Series, five games to three. As a result, Collins was the toast of Boston.

In 1904 the Red Sox won the pennant again in a very close race with the New York Yankees. But the National League pennant was won by the New York Giants, whose manager, John McGraw, refused to recognize the existence of the younger league and would not play against Collins's Red Sox. Few fans accepted McGraw's complaint that the American League was inferior; the real reason was a matter of several personalities, and thus no World Series was held that year.

Probably because of an aging pitching staff, the Red Sox began to slip after 1904. In 1905 they finished fourth, and in 1906 they were last in the eight-team league. Late that summer Collins was replaced as manager, but he continued to play third base until midseason of the following year when he was traded to the Philadelphia Athletics. He played one more year for Philadelphia and ended his major league career at the end of the 1908 season. He managed minor league clubs for three years, playing part of the time, before retiring from baseball in 1911.

In 1907 Collins had married Sarah Murphy; the couple had two daughters. After his retirement Collins made and lost money in Buffalo real estate and worked several years for the city. He also directed Buffalo's highly regarded amateur baseball league. Collins died in Buffalo.

Comparing Collins's skills with modern third basemen is probably fruitless, but longtime managers John McGraw and Connie Mack, who managed in dead and lively ball eras, both voted him the best they had seen. He was posthumously elected to the Baseball Hall of Fame in 1945.

• Information on Collins can be found at the National Baseball Library in Cooperstown, N.Y. The two best sources on Collins are Martin Appel and Burt Goldblatt, *Baseball's Best: The Hall of Fame Gallery* (1977), and Joseph M. Overfield's entry on Collins in the *Biographical Dictionary of American Sports: Baseball*, ed. David L. Porter (1987). Additional narratives are in Gene Karst, *Who's Who in Professional Baseball* (1973); Lowell Breidenbaugh, *Cooperstown* (1983); and *National Baseball Hall of Fame* (1976). John Thorn and Pete Palmer, eds., *Total Baseball*, 3d ed. (1993), contains Collins's performance data. Obituaries are in the *Buffalo Evening News* and the *New York Times*, both 7 Mar. 1943.

THOMAS L. KARNES

COLLINS, John Anderson (1810–1879), abolitionist and social reformer, was born in Manchester, Vermont. Little is known of his early years. He attended Middlebury College, then left to enter Andover Theological Seminary in Massachusetts. Caught up in the enthusiasm of the early abolitionist movement, Collins left the seminary and became general agent of the Massachusetts Anti-Slavery Society, conducting lecture tours in the late 1830s. He became a loyal lieutenant of abolitionist William Lloyd Garrison and was sent to England to raise money for the American Anti-Slavery Society and its newspaper, the *National Anti-Slavery Standard*, in 1840. Collins's partisan advocacy of the radical Garrisonian position, however, with its anti-clerical overtones, cost him support among members of the British and Foreign Anti-Slavery Society and drew strong criticism from influential British abolitionist Charles Stuart. Having raised only $1,000, Collins had to borrow money for his passage back to the United States in early 1841. Furthermore, his wife had died unexpectedly in 1840, although the circumstances of her death are unknown.

Collins shared Garrison's view that members of the American clergy were obstacles to the abolitionist cause because of their moderate stance on the issue of slavery. He is said to have had a hand in uncovering the so-called "clerical plot," an effort led by abolitionist clergymen Amos A. Phelps and Charles L. Torrey in late 1838 and early 1839 to take control of the board of the Massachusetts Anti-Slavery Society. He earned the enmity of conservative ministers, who accused him of trying to subvert the U.S. government by importing foreign gold. Collins edited the abolitionist *Monthly Garland* from July 1840 to November 1841. He also campaigned in the 1840s to end segregation on Massachusetts rail lines and was a member of the Nonresistance Society of Boston. He traveled widely during the early 1840s in support of the "One Hundred Conventions" movement in the western states, an attempt to spread Garrisonian ideas in regions under the influence of abolitionists advocating the use of political means.

Collins's interest in social reform can be traced to the 1840 World's Anti-Slavery Convention in London, where he became concerned about the plight of the English working classes. He wrote Garrison on 7 December 1840 that the English had the "same prejudice against poverty that we do against color" and that he had come to the conclusion that real progress would not come about "until the entire social structure, from which the state is but an emanation, is completely changed." Collins eventually shifted his primary focus from abolitionism to addressing the fundamental inequities of capitalist society and embraced the utopian ideas of Welsh reformer Robert Owen and French socialist Charles Fourier. An earlier tendency to hold various utopian ideas soon dominated his thinking, and he began to hold meetings promoting Fourierism after his abolitionist lectures.

In 1843 Collins broke ranks with Garrison by forming the Society of Universal Inquiry and Reform. At odds now with most of the abolitionist leadership because of his "no property" views, Collins left New England for Skaneateles, New York, with a handful of enthusiasts who shared his conviction that the crusade against chattel slavery was but a part of a much larger social reformation that would free individuals of all restraints. That year, they began an experiment in communal living on a 300-acre farm at Mottville, two miles north of Skaneateles. Garrison criticized this "Unity in Love" as "the baseless fabric of a benevolent dream." Members of the community held their property in common, denounced revealed religion and all religious creeds, raised their children communally, permitted divorce for those who had "outlived their affections," and advocated universal education, temperance, and vegetarianism. The community broke up due to internal turmoil after two years, however, and Collins left Skaneateles in 1846.

Collins now apparently reverted to conventional views on religion and politics. He supported the Whig party and for a short period of time edited a Whig newspaper in Ohio. Little is known of his last days except that he migrated to California, where in 1865 he was reported to have been involved in mine speculation and land auctions. The circumstances of his death are unknown.

John Collins belongs to that small cohort of American reformers so infected by the spirit of reform sparked by their involvement in the antislavery movement that they became virtual anarchists, suspicious of all government or, even more fundamentally, of any human institution seeking to impose morality on others.

• No collection of Collins's papers exists, but some of his letters are in the papers of William Lloyd Garrison at the Boston Public Library. The most detailed treatment of Collins's utopian experiment is Lester Grosvenor Wells, "The Skaneateles Communal Experiment, 1843–1846," a paper presented to the Onondaga Historical Association, Syracuse, 13 Feb. 1953, and housed at the Onondaga County Public Library. Additional material on the Skaneateles community can be found in John Humphrey Noyes, *History of American Socialisms* (1870), and John L. Thomas, "Antislavery and Utopia," in *The Antislavery Vanguard*, ed. Martin Duberman (1965). A more complete picture of the drift of Collins and other abolitionists toward perfectionist ideas can be found in Lewis Perry, *Radical Abolitionism: Anarchy and the Government of God in Antislavery Thought* (1973), and Carleton Mabee, *Black Freedom: The Nonviolent Abolitionists from 1830 through the Civil War* (1970).

MILTON C. SERNETT

COLLINS, Joseph Lawton (1 May 1896–12 Sept. 1987), army officer, was born in New Orleans, Louisiana, the son of Jeremiah Bernard Collins and Catherine Lawton. His father, an Irish immigrant and a veteran of the Union army, was a grocer and merchant. At age sixteen Joseph entered Louisiana State University but received an appointment to the U.S. Military Academy at West Point the next year. He graduated from West Point in 1917 and was commissioned in the infantry. Ordered to occupation duty in Germany shortly after the World War I armistice, he remained there two years. In 1921, in Koblenz, Germany, he married Gladys Easterbrook, the daughter of a chaplain. They had three children.

From 1921 to 1941 Collins was a student or instructor at most of the army's principal schools, including West Point, the Infantry School, and the Army War College. He also served a tour on the general staff of the Philippine Division from 1933 to 1936. These assignments brought him into association with George C. Marshall and others who would later lead the army, and their consistently superior ratings of his performance as a staff officer, tactician, and strategist marked him as a candidate for high command.

When the United States entered World War II, Collins was a colonel and chief of staff of VII Corps in Birmingham, Alabama. Immediately after the Pearl Harbor attack, he was ordered to Hawaii as chief of staff of the Hawaii Department and was promoted to brigadier general. In May 1942 he received a second star and took command of the "Tropic Lightning" Twenty-fifth Division, which performed magnificently in heavy fighting on Guadalcanal and New Georgia in 1943. His troops gave him the nickname "Lightning Joe" (inspired by the division's name), and he was decorated for personal valor. In January 1944, as planning began for the Allied invasion of Nazi-occupied Europe, Marshall transferred Collins to the European theater. Generals Dwight Eisenhower and Omar Bradley selected Collins to command one of the two army corps that would lead the assault on Normandy.

Collins's VII Corps landed on Utah beach on D-Day (6 June 1944), captured Cherbourg, and in July spearheaded the Allied breakout from Normandy at St.-Lô. Fighting across northern France, Belgium, and into Germany, Collins ordered the attack on Christmas Day 1944 that stopped the deepest German advance during the Battle of the Bulge. In April 1945 his corps linked up with Russian forces at the Elbe River. He possessed a combination of technical skill and nerve that made him relentless on the battlefield. Bradley praised Collins as one of the most successful field commanders of the European campaign.

After the war, Collins moved rapidly up the army chain of command. He served as the army's deputy chief of staff under Eisenhower and then as vice chief of staff of the army under Bradley. He attained four-star rank in 1948. When President Harry Truman named Bradley the first chairman of the Joint Chiefs of Staff (JCS), Collins became army chief of staff. During his term as chief, from 1949 to 1953, Collins supervised profound changes in the army, including its entrance into the North Atlantic Treaty Organization (NATO) forces and its first steps toward racial desegregation. He supported sending U.S. troops into the Korean War and had the responsibility of conveying Washington's limited war strategy to the imperious commander of United Nations forces, General Douglas MacArthur. MacArthur wanted to expand the war in Asia, but Collins and the other chiefs insisted that the United States must maintain its strategic strength and reserves elsewhere in the world and especially in NATO. In March 1951 MacArthur publicly challenged Truman's decision to approve the JCS position, and Collins joined Bradley and the other chiefs in support of the president's removal of MacArthur from command. During the Senate hearings on MacArthur's dismissal in May and June 1951, Collins testified that the JCS had had serious concern that MacArthur might unilaterally violate stated U.S. policies.

As army chief of staff, Collins was an articulate and loyal supporter of both the Truman and Eisenhower administrations' commitment to the containment of Soviet expansion while seeking to avoid a new world war. When Collins's term as chief expired in August 1953, Eisenhower chose him to represent the United States on the Military Committee and Standing Group of NATO, a small group of senior officers who advised NATO's political leaders on military plans and requirements.

Eisenhower again demonstrated his personal confidence in Collins by selecting him to serve as the president's special representative in Vietnam, in effect as ambassador, from November 1954 to May 1955. He was to assess conditions in that war-ravaged country in the wake of its temporary partition the previous July. Collins favored providing U.S. assistance to the new government in South Vietnam, but he declared its prime minister Ngo Dinh Diem unsuited for leadership. Largely because Secretary of State John Foster Dulles could see no promising alternative to the current regime, Washington rejected Collins's counsel and continued to aid Diem. The general dutifully accepted the decision and then left Vietnam to return to his regular NATO duties.

In 1956 Collins retired from the army. He served voluntarily as vice chairman and director of the President's Committee for Hungarian Refugee Relief, which was organized after the Hungarian uprising of 1956. In 1957 he joined Pfizer Pharmaceutical Company as a board member and vice chairman of its International Division, where he remained until 1969. He was also active in several volunteer civic efforts and was on the board of the Society for the Prevention of Blindness and the Institute of International Education. After his retirement from the army, he became a permanent resident of Washington, D.C., and also maintained a cottage on the Chesapeake Bay. He died in Washington.

Collins was one of the small officer corps of West Point graduates who diligently and obscurely served in the regular army during the 1920s and 1930s and who emerged to distinguish themselves with impressive feats of military leadership and organization during World War II. Along with generals like Eisenhower, Bradley, and Matthew Ridgway, Collins helped direct the U.S. victory on the battlefields of Europe during the war and afterward structured the army for its role as part of the American deterrent to a perceived global danger from Soviet ambitions. As army chief of staff during the Korean War, as a senior NATO strategist, and as a special presidential envoy to Vietnam, Collins demonstrated that he was not only a tough soldier, but also an accomplished military statesman. The military in American society had "deep obligations" to the nation's civilian leaders and to the public at large, he reflected in his book, *Lightning Joe: An Autobiography* (1979). His profound sense of duty and honor led him to believe that military leaders were "not only to be skilled in the technical aspects of the profession of arms, but to be men of integrity who have a deep understanding of the human strengths and weaknesses that motivate soldiers under the ultimate test of war."

• Collins's papers are in the Dwight D. Eisenhower Library, Abilene, Kans. Official files relating to his service in World War II, the Korean War, and Vietnam are in the records of the Department of Defense, Department of the Army, and Department of State, National Archives, Washington, D.C. In addition to his autobiography, Collins was the author of *War in Peacetime: The History and Lessons of Korea* (1969). Descriptions of his World War II and Korean War leadership are found in the following official histories published by the U.S. Army Center of Military History: Roy E. Appleman, *South to the Naktong, North to the Yalu* (1960); Martin Blumenson, *European Theater of Operations: Breakout and Pursuit* (1961); Hugh M. Cole, *The Ardennes: Battle of the Bulge* (1965); Kent Roberts Greenfield, *Command Decisions* (1960); Gordon A. Harrison, *European Theater of Operations: Cross-Channel Attack* (1950); Walter G. Hermes, *Truce Tent and Fighting Front* (1966); Charles B. MacDonald, *European Theater of Operations: The Siegfried Line Campaign* (1963); John Miller, Jr., *Guadalcanal: The First Offensive* (1949) and *Cartwheel: The Reduction of Rabaul* (1959); and James F. Schnabel, *Policy and Direction: The First Year* (1971). For Collins's Vietnam service see David L. Anderson, *Trapped by Success:*

The Eisenhower Administration and Vietnam, 1953–1961 (1991). Obituaries are in the *Washington Post*, 13 Sept. 1987, and the *New York Times*, 14 Sept. 1987.

DAVID L. ANDERSON

COLLINS, Napoleon (4 Mar. 1814–9 Aug. 1875), naval officer, was born in Fayette County, Pennsylvania. Little is recorded of his parents or youth. He never married. Appointed a midshipman in 1834, he served with the West Indies Squadron until September 1839. Completing his examinations at the Naval School at Philadelphia, Collins was promoted to passed midshipman in July 1840. He subsequently served aboard the sloop of war *Boston*, then the frigate *Constellation*, the flagship of Commodore Lawrence Kearny. Collins circumnavigated the globe in the *Constellation*, serving off the China coast during the Opium War. After a brief term at the Naval Observatory in Washington, he was promoted to lieutenant in November 1846.

Aboard the sloop of war *Decatur* during the Mexican War, Collins was among the men who disembarked to join Commodore Matthew Perry's expedition up the Tuxpan River in April 1847. In June Collins participated in a similar operation in Tabasco. The next year the *Decatur* sailed to the African coast to patrol against the slave trade. In June 1850 Collins joined the crew of the navy's first iron-hulled warship, the screw steamer *Michigan*, operating on the Great Lakes. After nearly three years of service there, he took command of the supply ship *John P. Kennedy*, which was to accompany the U.S. Surveying Expedition to the North Pacific Ocean. Requiring extensive repairs by the time it reached China, the *Kennedy* had to stay behind, and Collins therefore left his command and returned to the United States. Briefly assigned to the navy yard at Mare Island, California, in 1856, he then joined the *John Adams*, cruising the Pacific and East Indies. In 1858 he returned to the *Michigan* and duty in the Great Lakes. He next reported to the sloop *Vandalia*, which was recalled from the East Indies at the outbreak of the Civil War.

Collins took command of the screw steamer *Anacostia* in the Potomac Flotilla. He participated in the bombardment of Confederate positions at Aquia Creek, Virginia, on 31 May 1861 and supported the blockade at Hampton Roads from early June through late August. He then commanded the *Unadilla*, one of the hurriedly built "90-day" gunboats that joined the South Atlantic Blockading Squadron under Rear Admiral Samuel F. Du Pont. He spent most of the next year in operations along the South Carolina and Georgia coasts, participating in the capture of Forts Walker and Beauregard near Port Royal in early November and afterward commanding naval forces off Beaufort. In January 1862 Collins helped drive off confederate steamers trying to reach Fort Pulaski near Savannah, and in May he captured the English sloop *Mary Teresa*, which was attempting to run the blockade. That July Collins helped repulse a Confederate attack on Port Royal Island, and while patrolling Ossabow

Sound, he captured the British blockade runner *Ladona*.

Promoted to commander in July 1862, Collins in September took command of the screw steamer *Octorara*, part of the "Flying Squadron" under Commodore Charles Wilkes that was searching for the fearsome Confederate commerce raiders *Alabama* and *Florida*. While patrolling in Bahamian waters, Collins captured a dozen ships. These included the British schooner *Mont Blanc*, which was technically inside British territorial waters, being only a mile and a half from an uninhabited sand key. Collins had Wilkes's authorization for taking the ship, but Secretary of State William Seward, eager not to provoke England, pressed Secretary of the Navy Gideon Welles to censure Collins for violating department orders with regard to neutral vessels. A prize court, though, acknowledged that Collins had probable cause for detaining the *Mont Blanc*.

Collins would be at the center of a far more controversial intrusion upon neutral rights after taking command of the screw sloop *Wachusett*. Early in 1864 he had sailed for the coast of Brazil to protect American commerce there from the *Alabama* and the *Florida*. In early October the *Florida*, which had captured thirty-eight merchant ships for losses of over $4 million, entered the harbor at Bahia, Brazil, where the *Wachusett*, coincidentally, lay at anchor. After the Brazilian government rejected the U.S. consul's protest against the *Florida*'s presence, Collins, goaded by the consul, determined to sink it. Early on the morning of 7 October, the *Wachusett* rammed the *Florida* but managed only to cut down its bulwarks and carry away its mizzenmast and main yard. After an exchange of gunfire, however, the *Florida*'s watch officers surrendered the ship, and Collins towed it to sea as Brazilian batteries opened fire. Escaping, Collins took the *Florida* to Hampton Roads, Virginia.

Collins's bold contravening of Brazilian neutrality earned him much praise and also some sharp criticism in the North. The Abraham Lincoln administration was privately loath to return the *Florida* but anxious to mollify the outraged Brazilians. Shortly thereafter, the *Florida* conveniently and most suspiciously sank while in U.S. custody. Collins, in turn, was court-martialed for violating the territorial jurisdiction of a neutral power. Though he claimed he had acted "for the public good," the court found him guilty and ordered him dismissed from the service. After tempers had presumably cooled, however, Secretary Welles disapproved the sentence, ordering Collins back to duty in September 1866.

Promoted to captain, Collins sailed for Africa and the Far East in command of the screw sloop *Sacramento*. Departing Madras, India, on 19 January 1867, the *Sacramento* grounded on a reef. The ship was lost, but all hands were saved. After being suspended from duty, Collins resumed active service at the Norfolk Navy Yard from February 1870 to January 1871, when he was promoted to commodore. In September 1871 he became inspector for the Tenth Lighthouse District, based at Buffalo, New York. Promoted to rear admiral three years later, he took command of the South Pacific Squadron, flying his flag on the steam sloop *Richmond*. With only three ships, Collins patrolled the west coast of South America. He died suddenly in Callao, Peru.

Collins displayed dash and courage in capturing the *Florida*. At least one important observer, Secretary of the Navy Welles, ultimately questioned Collins's merits as a sailor, however. After the wreck of the *Sacramento*, Welles confided to his diary: "Collins is an honest, straightforward, patriotic man. He has not, I think, particular love or aptitude for the service" (Beale, vol. 3, p. 120).

• No known collection of Collins papers exists, but his career can be traced in official naval documents. For his Civil War activities, see *The Official Records of the Union and Confederate Navies in the War of the Rebellion* (30 vols., 1894–1922). Useful insights are in W. J. Morgan et al., *The Autobiography of Rear Admiral Charles Wilkes, U.S. Navy (1798–1877)* (1978), and Howard K. Beale, ed., *The Diary of Gideon Welles* (1960). The capture and sinking of the *Florida* are discussed at length in Frank Lawrence Owsley, Jr., *The C.S.S. Florida: Her Building and Operations* (1965; rev. ed., 1987). For reports of Collins's death and burial and an obituary, see the *Army and Navy Journal*, 28 Aug., 11 Sept., and 18 Sept. 1875 and 17 June 1876.

JOHN B. HATTENDORF
PATRICK G. WILLIAMS

COLMAN, Benjamin (19 Oct. 1673–29 Aug. 1747), Congregationalist minister, was born in Boston, Massachusetts, the son of William Colman and Elizabeth (maiden name unknown), shopkeepers. Colman was greatly influenced in his youth by Increase Mather and Cotton Mather, the ministers of his church, and Ezekiel Cheever, his grammar school instructor whom Cotton Mather made famous as the model of a Puritan teacher who joined piety with learning. The combination of piety with a genteel appreciation of learning became one of the most distinctive features of Colman's life. Harvard College also influenced young Colman, and he later cited the role of its tutors in shaping his own and his generation's attitudes toward piety and intellect.

Colman entered Harvard in 1688 during a period of intense intellectual and religious transformation at the college and in the colony caused by new imperial policies that threatened Puritan domination of the fast-growing colony. Contributing also to the transformation were unresolved theological and ecclesiastical tensions from within Congregationalism between the desire for a pure church of the elect and the need to embrace whole geographical communities. The college attempted to strengthen the founding ideals of the Puritan colony while accommodating many modern and cosmopolitan ways of thinking. Increase Mather, the president of the college, had recently led the college out of a period of doldrums and was the colony's preeminent example of piety and learning. In Colman's freshman year, Mather left for England to preserve Puritan control of the colony and college by making some of his own accommodations. Mather left the college in the charge of two devoted tutors, William Brattle and John Leverett (1662–1724), who were advised by local ministers, especially Charles Morton, a prominent educational reformer among Dissenters in England, textbook author, and philosopher who in 1686 emigrated to New England. Brattle and Leverett inaugurated reforms in logic, ethics, and physics while reinvigorating the spirit of eclectic inquiry and open discussion that had been suffering at Harvard since the 1670s. The tutors were endorsed in their activity by the Mathers and found the intellectual base for their reforms in books and ideas brought from England by Morton. Colman fully imbibed the spirit and teachings of Harvard and so impressed his tutors that they later recommended him to an important new Boston pulpit from which Colman became one of the most prominent ministers of his generation in New England.

After graduating in 1692, Colman supplied the pulpit in Medford for six months, then returned to Harvard. In 1695 he received an A.M. degree and migrated to England. On the way he was captured by French pirates and incarcerated in France. After being ransomed, he arrived in London bereft of money and letters of introduction but soon became part of the interconnected world of American and English Dissenters. Colman had established the beginnings of a successful career in Bath when in 1699 he received letters from his old tutors, his brother, and other prominent New Englanders, asking him to return to America and take charge of a new, fourth Congregational church in Boston, commonly called the Brattle Street Church. The new church was already steeped in controversy because it proposed to implement procedural changes in the Congregational order that had been discussed at Harvard during Colman's undergraduate years and implemented in several non-Boston churches. Experiments within Congregationalism that had been accepted in a spirit of freedom during the past decade became a source of great contention because of a reactionary fear led by Mathers in the midst of heightened political and religious tensions over Increase Mather's position as absentee president at Harvard, Governor Joseph Dudley's lack of commitment to maintaining the distinctive Puritan character of the colony, and fear that levels of piety among Puritans were declining. Colman was a wise choice for minister because he was sympathetic to the ecclesiastical reforms while his piety was well known to the leaders of the new church's opposition.

Upon accepting the post, Colman suffered the virulent antagonism of the Mathers. Because of the intense animosities among the clergy at the time, Colman was advised to take Presbyterian ordination before returning to New England, which he did. Colman did not help matters when, upon his arrival, he and the founders of the new church issued a *Manifesto* (1699) declaring their reforms. Although the *Manifesto* and a subsequent tract, *The Gospel Order Revived*, which

had to be published outside of the colony in 1700, enraged the Mathers, the works show that Colman was at the center of a pious experiment attempting to face modern ecclesiastical problems by reaching back to the ideals of the early church and the founders of Massachusetts Bay.

After tempers calmed and fears concerning the piety and essential Congregational position of the new church subsided, Colman and the Mathers proceeded to reconcile many of their differences. Colman and Cotton Mather remained divided over the leadership of Harvard College, but together with other Boston ministers they supported a dynamic Congregationalism able to embrace new eighteenth-century values imported from British culture while maintaining strong Puritan roots. The architecture of the Brattle Street meeting house symbolized this new compromise with an interior plan designed according to the old New England pattern while adorning its exterior with New England's first tower and steeple in imitation of Christopher Wren's modern London churches. Colman, like his meeting house, remained essentially Puritan while modelling his appearance and sentiments after modern British tastes.

Colman became a master at such compromises in a number of instances throughout his life. One long-lasting concern he faced was Congregationalism's relationship to the Church of England now that imperial policy demanded that they share New England. From the perspective of a local Church of England supporter, the Brattle Street Church maintained "the Devil's work of separation from their mother church," while in the minds of strict Congregationalists Colman and his church appeared too sympathetic to Anglicanism. He was a leader among his generation of Harvard-trained ministers in balancing this tension and creating a tolerant and mutually supportive relationship exemplified by attempts to coordinate missionary endeavors by both churches among various Indian groups. Important individuals in the Anglican Society for the Propagation of the Gospel, such as Bishop White Kennett, relied on Colman's advice so as not to waste resources—especially in keeping missionaries focused on converting Indians and not Congregationalists. Colman even tried to coordinate missionary work with Jesuits on the frontier.

While maintaining a working and sympathetic relationship with Anglicans, Colman favored a distinct separation between Anglicans and Congregationalists. In 1722, for example, Colman abandoned a plan to have Harvard receive a royal charter after his Anglican friend Henry Newman (1670-1743) told him that the royal charter would entail Anglican interference at the college.

Colman, along with many Harvard tutors and other ministers, also hoped to broaden his essential Calvinism by mining the writings of modern English thinkers. Colman was an avid reader of Archbishop Tillotson and the "latitudinarian" wing of Anglican thinkers who emphasized rationality and toleration among Protestants. Colman firmly believed that "religion has reason on its side," and in published sermons such as *God Deals with Us as Rational Creatures* (1723) he taught the rationality of revealed religion. He supported Harvard College's "free air" where many books with Anglican and Roman Catholic sympathies were not censored. Colman modeled his own prose and poetry after modern British tastes, composing one poem to Alexander Pope. Most of his publications are sermons, however; he wrote substantial works of biblical exposition such as *Practical Discourses on the Parable of the Ten Virgins* (1707). Although he wrote a pamphlet on *Some Observations on the New Method of Receiving the Small-Pox* (1721), Colman showed no sustained interest in the scientific and philosophical developments of his era.

Colman was very active in Harvard College affairs as a member of the Corporation and Overseers. He staunchly supported his former tutor, John Leverett, who became president in 1707. After Leverett's death in 1724, Colman was offered but declined the presidency. Colman secured many patrons for Harvard and Yale among rich and prominent Dissenters in England, most importantly Thomas Hollis, who endowed Harvard's first professorships and generously purchased books and equipment. Colman also corresponded extensively with the famous hymn writer and textbook author Issac Watts, who influenced the Harvard curriculum through Colman. As part of a transatlantic network on Nonconformists, many of whom he had impressed as a young man in London, Colman became in 1731 one of several New England ministers who received an honorary doctor of divinity degree from the University of Glasgow.

In the beginning of New England's Great Awakening, Colman encouraged Jonathan Edwards (1703-1758) to write *A Faithful Narrative of the Surprising Work of God* (1737) and invited the evangelist George Whitefield to preach at the Brattle Street Church and at Harvard in 1740. Whitefield contacted Colman when planning his trip to Boston, and Colman helped organize invitations from various pulpits and the college. Whitefield angered some of the clergy and offended the college faculty with insinuating remarks implying lack of religious commitment. Colman found himself mediating between Whitefield and the Harvard faculty, each condemning the other for religious errors. At one point Whitefield attacked the promiscuous reading at Harvard of dubious books, and Colman privately indicated he agreed and wished that many "had never arrived or been read there." However, he continued to give strong support to Edward Wigglesworth (c.1693-1765), the Hollis Professor of Divinity, and the rest of the faculty.

His role in the Great Awakening supporting both the revival and its detractors was in keeping with a life devoted, as his son-in-law explained, to being "all things to all men." Colman's sojourn in England and his continued correspondence with English Dissenters made him a key figure in modeling for New England the role of a cosmopolitan, rational, tolerant, genteel English Protestant. Perry Miller declared that Colman's prose maintained traditional Puritan content but was stylistically influenced by more modern and elegant British taste. A friend and minister in Marblehead, Massachusetts, described Colman as "a most gentlemanly man, of polite aspect and conversation . . . an excellent man in spirit, in faith, in holiness, and charity." Charles Chauncy (1705-1787), whose debate with Jonathan Edwards elicited Colman's mediation, perceptively wrote that Colman's "character would have been greater, could it have been said of him that he excelled as much in strength of reason and firmness of mind, as in many other good qualities."

Colman was married three times: to Jane Clark in 1700, Sarah Crisp Clark, widow of John Leverett, in 1732, and Mary Pepperell, also a widow, in 1745. All three of his children were born to his first wife, and none survived him. One of them, Jane Turell, had a precocious intellect encouraged by her father and became widely praised as a poet. After her early death in 1735, her husband, the Reverend Ebenezer Turell, collected and published her papers, which sold well in Boston and London, as *Memoirs of . . . Mrs. Jane Turell* (1735; repr. 1741). Colman died in Boston.

• The Colman Papers, which include extensive correspondence with English clergy, are at the Massachusetts Historical Society in Boston. Other letters are at the American Antiquarian Society, Worcester, Mass., and sermons are at Harvard University. A sketch biography, an alphabetical list of his numerous published sermons, and citation of other archival sources are in Clifford K. Shipton, *Sibley's Harvard Graduates*, vol. 4 (1933). The standard biography is Ebenezer Turell, *The Life and Character of the Reverend Benjamin Colman* (1749), reprinted with an introduction by Christopher R. Riske (1972). Turell included an appendix of Colman's published sermons in chronological order. See also "Memoir of the Rev. Benjamin Colman, D.D.," *New England Historical and Genealogical Register* 3 (1849): 105–22, 220–32; Samuel K. Lothrop, *A History of the Church in Brattle Street* (1851); Clayton Harding Chapman, "The Life and Influence of Rev. Benjamin Colman, D.D." (Ph.D. diss., Boston Univ., 1948); Howard C. Adams, "Two Sermons and a Poem by Benjamin Colman," *Seventeenth-Century Notes* 34 (1978): 91–93; Anthony Gregg Roeber, "'Her Merchandize . . . Shall Be Holiness to the Lord': The Progress and Decline of Puritan Gentility at the Brattle Street Church, Boston, 1715-1745," *New England Historical and Genealogical Register* 151 (1977): 175–94; Teresa Toulouse, "Syllabical Idolatry: Benjamin Colman's Rhetoric of Balance," *Early American Literature* 18 (1983–1984): 257–274; and the following articles in the *New England Quarterly*: Theodore Hornberger, "Benjamin Colman and the Enlightenment," 12 (1939): 227–40; Clayton H. Chapman, "Benjamin Colman and His Daughters," 32 (1953): 169–92; and Clayton H. Chapman, "Benjamin Colman and Philomela," 42 (1969): 214–31. On the relationship of poetry and theology emphasizing Colman and his daughter Jane Turell, see Laura Henigman, "Coming into Communion: Pastoral Dialogue in Eighteenth Century New England" (Ph.D. diss., Columbia Univ., 1991).

RICK KENNEDY

COLMAN, John (3 Jan. 1670–19 Sept. 1751), merchant, was born in London, England, the son of William Colman and Elizabeth (maiden name unknown). Colman's father was an ensign in an artillery company and a member of the first Board of Overseers of the Poor. Colman immigrated to New England with his parents in 1671. He married Judith Hobbey in 1694; they had fourteen children.

As a prominent merchant, Colman moved among Boston's intellectual and mercantile elite. In 1699 he helped form the Brattle Street Church, the first minister of which was his brother Benjamin. He served in a number of town offices, including selectman and overseer of the poor. In private life, Colman built upon his father's prosperous mercantile business. He owned shares in at least fifteen vessels, occasionally participated in privateering, had a number of warehouses, bought and sold slaves and real estate, and speculated in notes. These activities brought him into frequent contact with other influential members of the colony's mercantile elite. He owned a warehouse on Long Wharf next to that of future governor Jonathan Belcher, and his daughter Sarah married Peter Chardon, one of the wealthiest merchants in the colony.

Colman's business activities led to his concern over the Bay Colony's adverse balance of payments with the mother country and the impact that it had upon the supply of money and the local economy. Because of the policy of mercantilism, colonists generally consumed more than they produced in revenues. Over the long term, payments between the colonies and the mother country tended to come into balance because of indirect expenditures like charges assessed by the carrying trade, local expenses incurred by royal government, and profits obtained from smuggling. Unfortunately, the regulatory structure of the empire still tended to direct the export of specie to the mother country, thereby causing a chronic shortage of money that inhibited colonial commerce. Colman came to believe that commercial activity would increase and prosper if the shortage of money could be alleviated.

In 1714 complaints about currency shortages led to demands for the issue of £50,000 in local Massachusetts notes that could be used as the bases for loans to inhabitants. The existence of the notes would increase the local money supply and thus facilitate local transactions. Fearful of the inflationary and unregulated consequences of the notes, the General Court prohibited the issuing of notes by private banks. In December 1714 Colman, Elisha Cooke, and seven others issued the pamphlet *A Vindication of the Bank of Credit Projected in Boston from the Aspersions of Paul Dudley*, which attacked the reasons for the prohibitions against private banking and the general refusal of the court to expand the money supply. By targeting Dudley, the pamphlet apologist for the bill, the pamphlet prepared by Colman's group reflected the existing political division within Boston's elite. While it is not clear whether Colman was the author of the 1714 tract, many of its ideas resurfaced in 1720 in two similar pamphlets authored by him. The first, *The Distressed State of the Town of Boston etc.*, led to Colman's arrest for libel. The second, a similarly titled revised essay, included a plan for inflating the money supply through notes

backed by land. Shareowners in the Land Bank, as it became known, could issue notes paying 6 percent secured by the value of their property. The interest payments would be reserved and used for the purchase of silver that in turn created a fund to help redeem the loans and generate security for new notes. Because political support had shifted away from Cooke, perhaps the bank's most influential backer, interest in the bank quickly evaporated and was not revived until 1739, the eve of the War of the Austrian Succession.

On 10 March 1740 Colman's name appeared on a broadside with nearly 400 other subscribers announcing their willingness to issue £150,000 in notes secured by land mortgages. Whether Colman actually wrote this broadside is uncertain, but the scheme was very similar to that described in his second *Boston Distressed* pamphlet, and he invested significantly in its operations. Each subscriber could issue Land Bank and Manufactory Notes upon the payment of 40 sterling per £1,000 and provision of sufficient security in land or, in some instances, goods. The 40 sterling was applied to overhead. Interest was set at 3 percent payable annually; and one-twentieth of the principal was to be paid each year. Payment could be either in notes or in various commodities, such as hemp, cordage, or bar or cast iron.

In 1755 opponents to the Land Bank called for the issuance of merchant notes redeemable in silver. These notes were pegged to a schedule of declining prices set against an ounce of silver, which would, in effect, account for the interest. The colony divided; the House and some merchants supported the Land Bank and Governor Belcher, whereas the Council favored the silver scheme. Ultimately Parliament resolved the issue by extending the South Sea Bubble Act of 1720 to the colonies, specifically (if on questionable legal grounds) prohibiting the establishment of the Land Bank. Despite Parliament's action, notes that remained outstanding forced complicated legislation to shut down the bank. Even at that, disputes over the notes and their redemption led to extensive litigation, including a suit by Colman against the directors of the bank.

In proposing a detailed inflationary solution to the tendency toward tight money in the colony, Colman contributed to political controversies that illustrated potential areas of conflict between England and the American colonies. His involvement indicates that divisions between soft and hard money advocates in eighteenth-century Massachusetts did not correspond to poor and rich or debtor and creditor polarities: Colman and his son-in-law Peter Chardon found themselves on the other side of their occasional confidant Governor Belcher. Rather, positions on soft versus hard money reflect an understanding of the commodity value of money, perceptions of economic need, and the comprehension of what impact changes in the money supply might have on personal activities. The Land Bank episode also illustrated the manifold repercussions caused by imperial intervention in relatively common political and economic disputes in Massachusetts. Colman died in Boston.

• A few of Colman's letters may be found in the Colman collection of the Massachusetts Historical Society. His pamphlets and many references to him and his career are in Andrew McFarland Davis, *Currency and Banking in the Province of Massachusetts Bay* (2 vols., 1901), and Davis, *Colonial Currency Reprints, 1682–1751* (4 vols., 1911). Henry H. Edes, "Note on John Colman," *Publications of the Colonial Society of Massachusetts* 69 (1904): 86–89, features an autobiographical note written by Colman that, in 1904, was reported to be in private hands. Other material on Colman and the Land Bank may be found in Herbert L. Osgood, *The American Colonies in the Eighteenth Century*, vol. 3 (1924), and George A. Billias, *The Massachusetts Land Bankers of 1740* (1959). An obituary is in the *Boston Evening Post*, 23 Sept. 1751.

JONATHAN M. CHU

COLMAN, Lucy Newhall (26 July 1817–18 Jan. 1906), abolitionist, women's rights advocate, and freethinker, was born in Sturbridge, Massachusetts, the daughter of Erastus Danforth, a blacksmith, and Hannah Newhall. Her mother died in 1824, and Lucy's aunt, Lois Newhall, acted "in the place of a mother" and in 1833 married Erastus Danforth, officially becoming Lucy's stepmother.

Lucy worked as a teacher before marrying John Maubry Davis in 1835 and moving to Boston, Massachusetts. The couple had no children. Davis died of consumption in 1841, and Lucy returned to teaching. In 1843 she married Luther Coleman, a railroad engineer, and the couple moved to Rochester, New York. Her second husband was killed in a railroad accident in March 1854. Their only child, Gertrude, died in 1862 while attending New England Medical College. During her public career, Lucy Colman used the name of her second husband but altered the spelling from Coleman to Colman.

In 1855 Colman was hired as a teacher for the "colored" school in Rochester. She took the job with the intention of working for the abolition of racially separate schools, which was accomplished in 1856. During her brief teaching career, Colman also protested the unequal salaries of male and female teachers and delivered a controversial speech against corporal punishment at the New York State Teachers Association Convention in 1856, countering biblical arguments in favor of corporal punishment by saying, "If your Bible is a bundle of rods, or a license for adultery, the loss of it will be a blessing."

Colman had been opposed to slavery since she was a child. In the 1850s, encouraged by abolitionist and women's rights advocate Amy Post, Colman began lecturing against slavery in the Rochester area. By late 1856 she was working as a lecturer for the Western Anti-Slavery Society and later as an agent of the American Anti-Slavery Society. For the next four years she traveled extensively through New York, Ohio, Michigan, and as far west as Iowa. In addition to lecturing against slavery, Colman used her lectures and public activities to advocate women's rights and to speak against racial prejudice. In 1858 she joined Frederick Douglass and others in Rochester to oppose capital punishment. A year later she circulated petitions to change the New York state constitution to allow women the right to vote.

Colman was also critical of religious orthodoxy. In her *Reminiscences*, she likened the religious revivalism of the 1820s to "some scourge or plague, so great was the sorrow that followed in its wake." In her early teens Colman, along with others in her family, became a universalist, and by the early 1850s she had adopted spiritualism. The spiritualist leader Andrew Jackson Davis, who had been staying with the Colman family at the time of her husband's death, delivered the address at Luther Coleman's funeral in Rochester. Her identification with spiritualism in the 1850s did not, however, prevent her from criticizing spiritualists for becoming sectarian and forgetting the plight of the slave. Colman later rejected spiritualism for free thought. As she wrote in her autobiography, "Until the majority of the people are emancipated from authority over their minds, we are not safe" (p. 7).

In the summer of 1864 Colman accepted a position as the matron in the National Colored Orphans Asylum of the National Association for the Relief of Destitute Colored Women and Children in Washington, D.C. She soon clashed with the teacher at the orphanage, whom she charged with abusing and starving the children. In her *Reminiscences*, Colman does not name the teacher but says only that she had "a name honored and beloved in Massachusetts." This unidentified teacher was evidently Maria R. Mann, a relative of Horace Mann and the Peabody sisters. Colman claimed to have been successful in having the teacher removed from her office, though Colman resigned her position in September 1864, while Mann remained until January 1865. In 1864 and 1865 Colman worked as a teacher and school superintendent for the National Freedmen's Relief Association in Washington, D.C., and Arlington, Virginia, before returning to Rochester in the summer of 1865.

In October 1864 Colman accompanied Sojourner Truth on her visit to Abraham Lincoln. In a contemporary account published in the *Liberator* (25 Nov. 1865), Colman described Lincoln as polite and cordial and the visit as "quite satisfactory." In her *Reminiscences*, however, Colman was more critical of Lincoln's attitude toward Truth, emphasizing his reluctance to act against slavery. Colman also accompanied Truth on a visit to President Andrew Johnson in 1865.

Around 1870 Colman moved to Syracuse, New York, where she joined her sister Dr. Aurelia F. Raymond. In the 1870s and after she was active in the Radical Club and the John Stuart Mill Liberal League, as well as the New York State Freethinkers Association. Colman died in Syracuse.

• The primary source for Colman's career is her *Reminiscences* (1891), which were originally published as a series of articles in the *Freethinkers' Magazine* 8 (1890). The *Freethinkers' Magazine* 8–9 (1890–1891) includes other autobiographical recollections by Colman not in the *Reminiscences*. A summary of the debate over Colman's speech on corporal punishment in 1856 is included in the *New York Teacher* 5 (1856): 553–56, and Colman's role in ending segregated schools in Rochester is investigated in Judith Ruchkin, "The Abolition of the 'Colored Schools' in Rochester, New York, 1832–1856," *New York History* 51 (1970): 376–93. Colman's activities as an abolitionist lecturer are documented in the *Reminiscences* and in letters from Colman to the *Liberator* (1856–1863). The *Freedman's Advocate* 1 (1865) and *National Freedman* 1 (1865) include information about Colman's activities in Washington in 1865. The National Colored Orphans Asylum in Washington is described in the *Special Report of the Commissioner of Education on the Condition and Improvement of the Public Schools in the District of Columbia* (U.S. Congress, House, 41st Cong., 2d Sess., Exec. Doc. 315). Entries on Colman in Francis Willard and Mary Livermore, *American Women* (1897), and in Samuel P. Putnam, *400 Years of Freethought* (1894), and genealogical information in John J. May, *Danforth Genealogy* (1902), include details on Colman's early life not found in the *Reminiscences*.

CHRISTOPHER DENSMORE

COLMAN, Norman Jay (16 May 1827–3 Nov. 1911), agricultural journalist and first secretary of agriculture, was born near Richfield Springs, New York, the son of Hamilton Colman and Nancy Sprague, farmers. He attended local academies and soon was teaching school himself. In 1847 Colman left home for Kentucky, where plans to open a school in Owensboro were ended by an illness. He recovered and directed a public school in Brandenburg before enrolling at the University of Louisville Law School, earning a degree in 1849. He opened a successful law office in New Albany, Indiana, married Clara Porter in 1851, and in 1852 was elected district attorney. A year later they moved to St. Louis, Missouri, and purchased a farm, although Colman continued to practice law and was elected an alderman within two years. The couple had two children before Clara Colman died in 1863.

As progressive farmers in the Midwest began to show interest in the kind of farm improvements that Colman had known in New York, he became a leading voice for agriculture in Missouri, using his farm to demonstrate new techniques and crops, especially fruit. In 1856 he established the successful St. Louis Nursery, but the cornerstone of Colman's position was the agricultural newspaper he acquired in October 1855, the *Valley Farmer*. It was typical of farm papers, with such regular departments as agriculture, stock, horticulture, the home circle, and letters from readers. Like other editors, Colman lectured widely on farm problems, always promoting the paper as well. He soon added sections on poultry, veterinary questions, and his personal hobbies of fruit production and education. Success followed, with circulation rising toward 10,000 by 1860.

For the next fifty years, Colman the farm journalist was inextricably linked to Colman the organizer of agricultural organizations. Though his journalistic efforts were obviously sincere, they also enabled him to encourage agricultural projects that in turn brought him new subscribers. Thus Colman helped found the St. Louis Agricultural and Mechanical Association (1856), the Missouri State Horticultural Society (1859), and other local farm organizations.

The disruption of the Civil War cut subscriptions by 50 percent. It also propelled Colman into politics as a Unionist Democrat; in 1860 he was an unsuccessful nominee for state representative. In 1864–1865 he served as a lieutenant colonel in the Eighty-fifth Regiment of the Enrolled Missouri Militia. Having demonstrated his loyalty to the Union, Colman was one of the few Democrats elected to the state house of representatives in 1866. He became a leading opposition voice, usually on agricultural subjects but also in challenging Republican corruption and new electoral rules designed to punish Confederate sympathizers and the Democrats by imposing rigid voting requirements. In 1868 he lost a bid for lieutenant governor in a Republican landslide. In 1874 he was a leading candidate for the governor's office but again settled for the Democratic nomination for the lieutenant governor's post. Elected this time, Colman's disappointment about failing to win the gubernatorial nomination left him suspicious of partisan politics.

After the Civil War Colman married Catherine Wright of St. Louis and eventually became a father for a third time. He also revived his paper, renaming it *Colman's Rural World and Valley Farmer*, later shortening it to *Colman's Rural World*. He began to publish the paper weekly in 1868 to accommodate a rising volume of advertising. He added new sections on pigs, dairy, and sorghum, which became an important forage crop thanks to his efforts, and later promoted soybeans, crop rotation, fertilizer, and other techniques to prevent soil depletion. Colman also made the paper a voice for the Grange in the 1870s and for the Farmers' Alliance in the late 1880s.

In 1867 Colman became a director of the Missouri State Board of Agriculture, an affiliation he maintained throughout his life. He expanded his farm, even as he helped organize and support the American Association of Nurserymen, Seedmen, and Florists (1875), the Mississippi Valley Cane Growers' Association (1880), the National Sugar Growers' Association (1885), and the Mississippi Valley Dairy and Creamery Association (1883). He gave most of his attention to establishing an agricultural college in Missouri, which he promoted through the paper and the State Board of Agriculture. In 1870 he was appointed to the first board of curators for the University of Missouri at Columbia, serving until 1885.

Colman's varied background led to his appointment as U.S. commissioner of agriculture by Democratic president Grover Cleveland in 1885. Even a Missouri Republican commented in a letter to the *St. Louis Republican* that "No appointment made in Washington for the last twenty-five years has . . . been so truly a representative one" (Davis and Durrie, p. 407). Colman proved a politically skillful administrator who balanced patronage with competence. As always, he supported practical programs but recognized the value of scientific research. He attempted to replace seed distribution as the department's main activity with programs like the campaign to combat an outbreak of pleuropneumonia among cattle after 1885. During his tenure, the division of entomology was strengthened, and a vegetable pathology section, a division of pomology, and a division of economic ornithology and mammalogy were created. Colman labored steadily to establish agricultural experiment stations, and in 1887 the Hatch Act finally funded this program. His efforts to expand and develop the Agriculture Department culminated in the department being upgraded to cabinet status in February 1889. Appropriately, Colman served as the first secretary of agriculture, although his term ended with Cleveland's a month later. That same year the French government made him an *officier du mérite agricole*.

Colman returned to St. Louis, but his son and trusted editors continued to run *Colman's Rural World*, as they had during his term in Washington. At first Colman devoted time to the Farmer's Alliance, for he had long advocated similar views on the danger of national banks, gold-based currency, and trusts. He broke with the Alliance in 1890, however, over the issue of third-party politics. The agitation in rural areas during the 1890s continued to attract the paper's attention, but eventually agricultural practice returned to the front page. Colman resumed editorial control in 1899.

In his seventies, Colman remained quite active. Even after his wife died in 1897, he helped establish the Missouri State Fair Association in 1899, worked on behalf of the Louisiana Purchase Exposition from 1901 through 1904, and promoted good roads after 1900. His prize-winning trotting horses were his passion, and he was going to see a horse in Plattsburg, Missouri, when he suffered a stroke and died on the train. Famous in Missouri for his involvement in politics and agricultural improvement, and applauded nationally as secretary of agriculture, Colman was honored as the recipient of honorary degrees from several universities. Colman's biographer accurately concluded that "few men have influenced so broadly the development of American agriculture," and others shared this view (Lemmer, p. 126).

• A run of *Colman's Rural World*, along with additional archival material, is held by the State Historical Society of Missouri. Other archival records can be found in the Western Historical Manuscript Collection, University of Missouri-Columbia. The most thorough treatment of Colman's life is George F. Lemmer, *Norman J. Colman and Colman's Rural World: A Study in Agricultural Leadership* (1953); also see Lemmer, "The Agricultural Program of a Leading Farm Periodical, *Colman's Rural World*," *Agricultural History* 23 (Oct. 1949): 245–54. A summary of Colman's career as commissioner of agriculture can be found in Missouri, Board of Agriculture, *44th Annual Report of the Missouri Board of Agriculture* (1911), pp. 28–32; see also T. Swann Harding, *Two Blades of Grass: A History of Scientific Development in the U.S. Department of Agriculture* (1947). A large number of biographical sketches exist, of which the most useful are Walter Bickford Davis and Daniel S. Durie, *An Illustrated History of Missouri* (1876); Floyd G. Summers, "Norman J. Colman, First Secretary of Agriculture," *Missouri Historical Review* 19

(Apr. 1925): 404–8; Lester S. Irving and A. E. Winship, *Fifty Famous Farmers* (1925); William E. Oliver, *Pioneer Agricultural Journalists* (1927); and [unsigned] "Missouri Miniatures: Norman Jay Colman," *Missouri Historical Review* 36 (Oct. 1941): 77–81. Obituaries are in *Colman's Rural World*, 15 Nov. 1911, and the *St. Louis Globe Democrat*, 4 Nov. 1911.

BRUCE E. SEELY

COLMAN, Ronald (9 Feb. 1891–19 May 1958), actor, was born Ronald Charles Colman in Richmond, England, the son of Marjory Read Fraser and Charles Colman, a silk importer. Colman attended the Hadley School at Littlehampton, Sussex, but his formal education ended with his father's death in 1907. At that time Colman became a bookkeeper, and he performed in his spare time with local dramatic groups. In 1914 his brigade was among the first British Expeditionary Forces sent to France. He was wounded and decorated for bravery before his discharge in 1915.

After the war ended in 1918, Colman returned to the London stage, where he played small parts and juvenile leads before acting in the unreleased film *The Live Wire* in 1919. He married that film's leading lady, Thelma Victoria Raye, in September 1919; they would have no children. He made his first film appearance in *The Toilers* in 1919 and appeared in six more films, including his first starring role, in *A Son of David*, before sailing in 1920 to the United States, where his performance in *La Tendresse* on Broadway attracted the attention of director Henry King, who cast him opposite Lillian Gish in *The White Sister* (1923), his first major film role. He was invited to Hollywood in 1924 by producer Samuel Goldwyn, who signed him to a long-term contract after his appearance in *Tarnish* (1924). In 1925 he made eight films, including *Lady Windermere's Fan*, *A Thief in Paradise*, and *The Dark Angel*, which was the first of five enormously popular films featuring Colman and the exotic Vilma Banky as star-crossed lovers. Light romantic comedy was his forté, though his roles in the melodrama *Stella Dallas* (1925) and the Foreign Legion adventure film *Beau Geste* (1926) demonstrated the range of his talents. Colman's dashing good looks and gallant persona earned accolades and fan mail rivaling in volume that of screen idol John Gilbert.

The transition from silent to sound film was a graceful one for Colman, thanks to his silky voice and regal British accent. His first sound picture was the detective film *Bulldog Drummond* (1929), followed by *Condemned* in the same year. For his work in both films he earned an Academy Award nomination for best actor. The following year he appeared as the gentleman crook in *Raffles*, and in 1931 he played a heroic scientist opposite Helen Hayes in director John Ford's *Arrowsmith*.

In 1933 a feud erupted between Colman and Goldwyn, who had, as an advertising strategy for *The Masquerader*, fabricated rumors suggesting that Colman turned out his best performances when inebriated. Furious, Colman responded by suing Goldwyn for libel and $2 million in damages. The case was settled out of court, and Colman never again worked for Goldwyn.

Colman signed with Twentieth Century Pictures, for whom his first picture was *Bulldog Drummond Strikes Back* (1934), a sequel to his successful first sound picture. In 1935 he made what many consider his finest film, *A Tale of Two Cities*. He starred as Sydney Carton, the ill-fated hero of Charles Dickens's French Revolution novel, a role that required him to shave his trademark mustache. That plum role was followed by other memorable performances in *Under Two Flags* (1936), *Lost Horizon* (1937), and *Prisoner of Zenda* (1937).

Having divorced Raye in 1934 after a decade-long separation, he married British actress Benita Hume in 1938; they had one daughter. With the outbreak of World War II in Europe, Colman joined other Hollywood actors in supporting the war effort, establishing with Douglas Fairbanks, Jr., and Charles Boyer the Franco-British War Relief Fund and the British War Relief Association of Southern California, of which he was president.

Colman was also popular on radio, and in 1939 he hosted the talk show program "The Circle," whose celebrity guests included Carole Lombard and Cary Grant. He also appeared in episodes of such broadcasts as "Lux Radio Theater" and "Screen Guild Theatre." Radio broadcasts in which he reprised his most memorable roles, such as *Lost Horizon*, *If I Were King* (both 1938), and *The Light That Failed* (1939), were especially popular at home and with American troops abroad. In 1942 he starred opposite British actress Greer Garson in the popular World War II epic *Random Harvest*. His performance as an amnesiac victim reunited with the woman he loves brought him his second Academy Award nomination for best actor.

After the end of the war, Colman continued to make frequent radio appearances. He hosted and occasionally starred in the successful dramatic series "Favorite Story" and, with Benita, made regular guest appearances on "The Jack Benny Program." He returned to the screen in 1947 to make the comedy *The Late George Apley* and *A Double Life*, in which he played a Broadway actor who blurs the line between his stage roles and his personal life. For this performance he finally won the Academy Award for best actor.

In 1950 he appeared in *Champagne for Caesar*, a spoof of television quiz shows, and narrated a short documentary titled *Shakespeare's Theater: The Globe Playhouse*. However, his energies during this time were directed primarily toward radio and television. From 1950 to 1952 he starred as the president of an Ivy League college in the popular radio series "The Halls of Ivy," which in 1954 moved to television. The show aired on CBS for one year, during which Colman starred opposite his wife Benita. Also in 1954 he appeared in televised episodes of "G. E. Theater" and "Four Star Playhouse," as well as continuing to appear occasionally with Benita on Jack Benny's television program. After a brief cameo in the 1956 all-star spectacle *Around the World in 80 Days*, he made his final appearance on film in *The Story of Mankind* (1957), in which he played the "Spirit of Man." He traveled to England in 1957 for the last time and made a recording of Shakespeare's sonnets there. He died in Santa Barbara, California.

Suave, sophisticated, and erudite, Colman graced screens with a quintessential English style of heroism that garnered millions of fans. He departed from the more flashy swashbuckling flair of Douglas Fairbanks, Jr., and Errol Flynn, taking a more subtle approach that resulted in a style of gentility and cultured dignity. His work inspired and influenced fellow actors Laurence Olivier, David Niven, Rex Harrison, and Gary Cooper, to name but a few. Long after his gentlemanly persona gave way to a rougher hewn American hero, personified by the likes of Humphrey Bogart and Robert Mitchum, the figure of Ronald Colman remains an icon of the grace and civility of Hollywood's "golden age" romantic heroes.

• Further information on Colman can be found in a biography by his daughter, Juliet Benita Colman, *Ronald Colman: A Very Private Person* (1975); Richard Griffith, *Samuel Goldwyn: The Producer and His Films* (1956); Lawrence Quirk, *The Films of Ronald Colman* (1977); R. Dixon Smith, *Ronald Colman, Gentleman of the Cinema: A Biography and Filmography* (1991); and Sam Frank, *Ronald Colman: A Bio-Bibliography* (1996). An obituary is in *Variety*, 21 May 1958.

JENNIFER M. BARKER

COLMAN, Samuel (4 Mar. 1832–27 Mar. 1920), painter and decorative artist, was born in Portland, Maine, the son of Samuel Colman, a publisher, and Pamela Chandler. By 1839 Colman's father had established himself as a successful bookseller and publisher in New York City. The source of Colman's artistic education is unclear; however, he is said to have studied, or at least sketched, with the Hudson River School painter Asher B. Durand. He exhibited for the first time at the National Academy of Design in New York City in 1851. In 1855, with the success of his early paintings such as *Franconia Mountains, New Hampshire* (1853) and *Summer on the River Saco* (1854), he was elected an associate member of the National Academy of Design. In 1860 he traveled to Europe to paint and study works in European collections and to North Africa. Upon his return to the United States in 1862, he married Anne Lawrence Dunham. That year he exhibited paintings of the Hudson River as well as southern Spanish and North African landscapes at the National Academy of Design. In 1864 he was elected to full membership.

Establishing his studio in New York City, he was represented by the private art dealer Samuel P. Avery. Besides painting in oil, Colman worked in watercolor. In 1866 he became the founding president of the American Society of Painters in Water Colors, which became known as the American Water Color Society in 1877. He remained its president until 1870; during this time such artists as Jasper Cropsey, Emanuel Leutze, and Winslow Homer were members. One of the society's major accomplishments under Colman's leadership was to establish an annual public exhibition of its members' work. This exhibition often coincided with that of the National Academy of Design and provided American audiences with some of their earliest opportunities to view watercolors by American artists.

Having firmly established himself in New York with his European and Hudson River landscapes, Colman set out in search of views of the western United States. During his travels he sketched and painted in watercolor, creating finished works as well as drawings that would serve as the basis for later studio productions, such as *Emigrant Train* (1870). After his journey across the United States, Colman turned his thoughts once again to Europe and the Near East. In 1871 he embarked on a four-year tour that took him to France, Holland, Italy, Egypt, Morocco, and Algeria. As was true of his previous European, North African, and American travels, his experiences in the early 1870s served as the basis for many of the works painted upon his return to New York. Among them were works such as *Ruins of the Mosque of Mansowra* and *The Merchants of El Lagouat en route between the Tell and the Desert, Algeria*, which were exhibited at the National Academy of Design in 1876 and 1877, respectively.

Colman's professional activities were not limited to the National Academy of Design and the American Society for Painters in Water Colors. In 1877 he was one of the founders of the Society of American Artists; in 1878 he sent three paintings to the international exhibition in Paris; and by 1878 he was an active member of the New York Etching Club. The subjects of his etchings included not only European sites visited on his travels but also his own collection of Asian and Near Eastern art, which appeared in his etched still lifes. His interest in Eastern art also inspired the wall and ceiling designs that he created with Associated Artists, a group founded in New York City in 1879 by Colman, Louis Comfort Tiffany, Candace Wheeler, and Lockwood de Forest. Colman had met Tiffany in the late 1860s, and in 1869 the two traveled together to North Africa. Colman influenced Tiffany's use of watercolor and introduced him to the material culture of North Africa.

Between 1879 and 1883 Associated Artists significantly influenced interior design style in the eastern United States, and as a result, the firm received numerous commissions. These included the redecoration of the Veterans' Room of the Seventh Regiment Armory building in New York City (1879–1880), the interior design of Mark Twain's home in Hartford, Connecticut (1881), and the redecoration of the East, Blue, and Red rooms and principal dining room of the White House (1882–1883). In addition to these, Associated Artists also received commissions from influential individuals such as Hamilton Fish, Henry de Forest, and John Taylor Johnston. The houses and rooms designed by this firm were discussed in popular contemporary periodicals such as the *Art Amateur, Scribner's Monthly,* and *Harper's New Monthly Magazine.* The work of Associated Artists also appeared in publications such as Clarence Cook's *What Shall We Do with Our Walls?* (1880), which included Colman's and Tiffany's designs for wall and ceiling decorations, and *Artistic Houses* (1883), a volume that contained "a series of Interior Views of a number of the Most Beautiful and Celebrated Homes in the United States." In 1883 Colman and Tiffany left Associated Artists to form Louis C. Tiffany and Company, and the two men continued to work together until around 1890.

Following his success as an interior designer, Colman returned to painting, and in the mid-1880s he traveled to California, Canada, and Mexico. On this trip he painted such popular sites as the Canadian Rockies and Yosemite Valley. His travels back and forth across the North American continent continued well into the 1900s with a break in 1904 to travel to Europe to paint Alpine landscapes. After the death of his first wife, with whom he had no children, Colman married Lillian Margaret Gaffney in 1903; they had one child. In the second decade of the twentieth century Colman began to outline his theories on the application of the unity and harmony of forms found in nature to art and architecture. He published two volumes on the subject with C. Arthur Coan: *Nature's Harmonic Unity: A Treatise on Its Relation to Proportional Form,* in 1912, and *Proportional Form: Further Studies in the Science of Beauty, Being Supplemental to Those Set Forth in "Nature's Harmonic Unity",* in 1920. Active until the end of his life, Colman died in New York City.

Colman enjoyed a sustained and successful career as a painter and interior designer. During his lifetime he was considered by critics and patrons alike as one of the preeminent American landscape painters. With the advent of modernism, however, his influence diminished. His position within the history of American art should be considered in terms of both his artistic production and his leadership. He readily offered encouragement to artists working in alternative media such as watercolor and etching. His commitment to organizations such as the American Watercolor Society, the Society of American Artists, and the New York Etching Club had a positive and lasting influence on artists, critics, and patrons in the American artistic community.

• Colman's work may be found in the following selected collections: National Museum of American Art, Washington, D.C.; Metropolitan Museum of Art; Vassar College Art Gallery, Poughkeepsie, N.Y.; Butler Institute of American Art, Youngstown, Ohio; Museum of Fine Arts, Boston; Hudson River Museum, Yonkers, N.Y.; Cooper-Hewitt Museum, New York City. Biographies of Colman by his contemporaries are included in Henry Tuckerman, *Book of the Artists: American Artist Life* (1867), and in S. G. W. Benjamin, *Our American Artists* (1879). Selected works that focus on specific aspects of Samuel Colman's career are Gerald M. Ackerman, *American Orientalists* (1994), and Sue Welsh Reed and Carol Troyen, *Awash in Color: Homer, Sargent, and the Great American Watercolor* (1993). Wayne Craven provides a more in-depth evaluation of Colman's life and work in his essay,

"Samuel Colman (1832–1920): Rediscovered Painter of Far-Away Places," *American Art Journal* 8, no. 1 (1976): 16–37. An obituary is in the *New York Times*, 30 Mar. 1920.

KATHLEEN L. BUTLER

COLOMBO, Joseph Anthony, Sr. (16 June 1923–22 May 1978), organized crime boss, was born in Brooklyn, New York, the son of Anthony Colombo, who was also connected with organized crime and was garroted while Joseph was still a teenager. His mother's name is unknown. When asked if he ever sought vengeance for his father's murder, Joseph Colombo replied, "Don't they pay policemen for that?" After attending New Utrecht High School, he entered the Coast Guard, from which he was given a medical discharge in 1945 (he allegedly suffered from some sort of "psychoneurosis"). Colombo thereafter balanced a life of crime with legitimate jobs. He began working as a longshoreman soon after leaving the service, while also gaining experience as a small-time criminal, principally involving himself in modest gambling operations. For six years he was a salesman for a Mafia-controlled meat company. Then Colombo became a real estate agent in Bensonhurst, where he continued to work for a $20,000 annual salary throughout his career as an organized crime boss.

After working as a hired killer for Joe Profaci and serving as underboss to Joe Magliocco, Colombo became one of the youngest organized crime bosses in the United States in 1964, when he was given leadership of a Brooklyn "family" that, under his control, eventually comprised 200 members and associates. He had ascended to power by advising puissant Mafia boss Carlo Gambino of a scheme to assassinate Gambino and other highly placed leaders by Joseph Bonanno, who longed to become "boss of all bosses." His plan exposed, Bonanno relinquished his power, and Colombo was rewarded with control of Magliocco's family after the latter died. Colombo also became a member of the powerful Mafia national commission.

Colombo's seven-year reign as an active crime boss was relatively uneventful, as he led his family in such moneymaking activities as loan-sharking, gambling, hijacking, and fencing stolen goods. He also involved himself in licit pursuits, at one time holding interest in at least twenty legitimate businesses in New York City. Preoccupied with his family's image, Colombo angered many men under his command by requiring all to hold down a "real" job.

Colombo became well known outside the underworld for his work in promoting the civil rights of Italian Americans. In the spring of 1970, angered by what he saw as harassment of his son by the Federal Bureau of Investigation, who had arrested the younger Colombo for conspiracy, Joseph Colombo began picketing the FBI offices in Manhattan. He criticized the media and the FBI for using terms such as "Mafia" and "Cosa Nostra," accusing the authorities of blaming unsolved crimes on this created entity to take pressure off themselves. He laughed at his image as an organized crime heavyweight, questioning, "Mafia, what's the Mafia?

There is not a Mafia. Am I head of a family? Yes, my wife [Lucille] and four sons and a daughter. That's my family."

Believing in the existence of a "conspiracy in this country against all Italian people," in 1970 Colombo, in alliance with union organizer Natale Marcone and Colombo's son Anthony, founded the Italian-American Civil Rights League. The league, whose membership reached 45,000 under Colombo's rule (even New York governor Nelson Rockefeller took honorary membership), had more than twenty chapters in the New York City area and many more across the country. Concerned with the public's perception of organized crime in particular and Italian Americans in general, Colombo and the league successfully lobbied the producers of *The Godfather* (1972) to delete all references to a "Mafia" from the film. The TV show "The F.B.I." followed suit. Alka-Seltzer even withdrew its commercial that proclaimed, "Mamma mia, thatsa some spicy meatball."

Despite his activist public image, Colombo did not totally forgo his duties in the Mafia underworld. At the time of the second annual Columbus Circle Italian-American Civil Rights League rally in June 1971, he had been accused of several misdeeds, including income tax evasion. He also stood accused of perjury for not revealing his criminal record (thirteen arrests and three convictions) when applying for his real estate license. He was under indictment for numerous other crimes, the most serious of which involved allegations that he managed a $10 million-a-year gambling organization in three New York counties.

On 28 June 1971, about an hour before the Columbus Circle rally's scheduled start time, Colombo was shot in the head, neck, and jaw. His assailant, Jerome Johnson, a young black man posing as a photographer and holding a rally-issued press pass, was killed almost immediately in the ensuing pandemonium. New York City police denied shooting Johnson, and no one ever claimed responsibility for Johnson's murder. Colombo, critically wounded, was rushed to the hospital for emergency surgery, while the rally continued as scheduled.

Organized crime figures Joseph Gallo and Albert Gallo, who operated under Colombo's leadership, were questioned in connection with the attempt on Colombo's life but were released. Long-standing hostility between the Gallo brothers and Colombo had been revived when the Gallos ordered shops in the area to remain open during the rally in spite of Colombo's mandate to close them. In fact, many Mafia leaders, especially Gambino, who had warned Colombo weeks before the shooting to discontinue his attention-getting activities (supposedly Colombo spat in Gambino's face in response to this admonition), were uneasy about Colombo's ever-expanding ego, his thirst for recognition, and his very public identification with Italian-American rights, not to mention the unwanted notice his picketing of the FBI offices got from law-enforcement agencies. Joseph Gallo's 1972 murder in Little Italy was judged by some a revenge killing, and many believe that Gambino probably hired the Gallos to kill Colombo.

Colombo was left almost totally disabled by the attempt on his life, and he spent his last seven years at the fortress in Blooming Grove, New York, that had formerly been his vacation home. He died of a heart attack at St. Luke's Hospital in Newburgh, New York. After his incapacitation, the Colombo crime family continued under new administration, as did the Italian-American Civil Rights League.

Colombo represents a deviant, perhaps a modern, type of mobster. Eschewing the back-room secrecy of those who preceded him, he was a firebrand when it came to Italian-American rights, a cause in which he no doubt passionately believed. He was unafraid of public scrutiny and brash in his pursuit of attention, in the process angering both the federal authorities and the "family." His rabble-rousing did not blend well with the traditional powers in organized crime, and Colombo became an incendiary that had to be extinguished.

• Information on Colombo is limited. Some background can be found in John H. Davis, *Mafia Dynasty: The Rise and Fall of the Gambino Crime Family* (1993). See also Carl Sifakis, *The Mafia Encyclopedia* (1987), for a short biography. Reports of his shooting are in the *New York Times*, 29, 30 June 1971. An obituary is in the *New York Times*, 24 May 1978. An account of his funeral is in the same newspaper, 27 May 1978.

STACEY HAMILTON

COLPITTS, Edwin Henry (19 Jan. 1872–6 Mar. 1949), communications engineer, was born in Pointe de Bute, New Brunswick, Canada, the son of James Wallace Colpitts and Celia Eliza Trueman, farmers. Intending to become a teacher, Colpitts attended the normal school at Fredericton, New Brunswick. He graduated in 1890, taught for a short time in Newfoundland, then entered Mount Allison University in Sackville, New Brunswick, from which he received a B.A. in science in 1893. He went on to Harvard University for courses in mathematics and physics; there he received a B.A. in 1896 and an M.A. in 1897. For the next two years he was an assistant to John Trowbridge in physics at the Jefferson Physical Laboratory at Harvard.

In 1899 Colpitts began work as a telephone engineer in the mechanical engineering department of American Bell Telephone Company in Boston, Massachusetts. The company had been founded in 1878 by Alexander Graham Bell and his financial associates. Also in 1899 Colpitts married Annie Dove Penney; they had one child.

Under George Ashley Campbell, Colpitts began researching the problem of the loaded telephone line, which is concerned with adjusting the parameters of a transmission line to match those of the circuit that drives it. He demonstrated the practicability of loading, which extended the range of distance for telephones. He made improvements on a newly invented battery supply loading coil for telephone transmission.

This first toroidal repeating coil was standard for twenty years until improved magnetic material made a cheaper alternative practical. He participated in finding ways to send more than one message at a time over a line, and he developed an instrument for balancing cable lines to reduce cross talk. Throughout his career he was noted for developing testing methods and operating standards.

From Boston Colpitts was transferred to New York in 1907 as research engineer and head of the physical laboratory of the engineering department of Western Electric Company, the manufacturing organization of Bell Telephone, and he advanced to head its research branch in 1911. The electronics age in telephone capability began with the development of the vacuum tube. Soon after Lee de Forest's 1906 creation of the three-element vacuum tube that he called the "audion" and that was later called the "triode," engineers at Western Electric Company, directed by Colpitts, investigated ways of using it to amplify signals. Colpitts received a patent for a system of connecting two tubes in tandem as a "push-pull" amplifier to double the amplification of telephone and telegraph signals. He also developed a modulator circuit, in which a vacuum tube superimposes an audio signal on a high-frequency carrier current.

In 1914 Colpitts received a patent for an electromagnetic coil for composite telegraph sets. With his colleague at Western Electric, Harold DeForest Arnold, in 1915 he created a system that allowed transmission by radio telephony between Arlington, Virginia, and Paris, France. After his colleague Ralph Vinton Lyon Hartley devised a stable generator of a single-frequency oscillation using a triode with a tapped coil and a capacitor, Colpitts in 1915 suggested a modification using one coil and two capacitors. Although he had not thought it important at the time, the company persuaded him to apply for a patent in 1918. The device, known as the Colpitts oscillator, proved superior for many purposes and became widely used in radio transmitters and in carrier multiplex circuits.

When alternating current came into use for the propulsion of trains and trolley cars, it interfered with telephone long-distance and local lines. Colpitts led a team effort in cooperation with engineers of Westinghouse Company and of railroad companies to resolve the interference problem, an attempt in which he was noted for his integrity and fair-mindedness. In the course of this process, he took to the field "in rough clothes in the mountains of Pennsylvania or the brush of Georgia or in rubber boots in the winter mud of Indiana," according to his colleagues Frank Baldwin Jewett and E. B. Craft ("E. H. Colpitts Returns to the AT&T Company," *Western Electric News*, May 1924, p. 40).

In 1917 Colpitts was appointed assistant chief engineer in charge of development and research at Western Electric. During the World War I years of 1917–1918 he was on leave from his company to serve on the staff of Brigadier General Edgar Russel, the chief signal officer of the American Expeditionary Forces. Colpitts established a research program to study methods of military communication in Europe and in the United States. After the war he resumed his position at Western Electric, where he took a leadership role in directing and stimulating research of economic significance to the company.

The successor to Bell Telephone was American Telephone and Telegraph Company, located in New York City. Its engineers and those at Western Electric considered the feasibility of radiotelephone use after World War I. In 1919 Colpitts and Craft concluded that radio transmission was not a likely competitor for wire transmission of telephone service in almost all cases, except for moving stations such as ships, airplanes, trains, and trucks, and for "fixed but inaccessible" locations such as "on islands, in deserts and very sparsely settled regions." They did suggest that broadcasting of news, time, and weather signals and warnings could be usefully done by radio (Craft and Colpitts, "Radio Telephony," *Transactions of American Institute of Electrical Engineers* 38 [1919]). Further research on radio transmission for telephones was not pursued actively for about another twenty years.

In 1924 Colpitts became assistant vice president of American Telephone and Telegraph Company to head its department of development and research, which served as a liaison between the research laboratories and operation of the Bell system. In 1925 Bell Telephone Laboratories was organized to combine the engineering and research staffs of AT&T and Western Electric. In 1933 Colpitts became vice president of Bell Telephone Laboratories. By the time of his retirement in 1937, the laboratories had a staff of 4,500 people and a budget of $19 million.

Later in 1937 Colpitts gave a series of lectures on communications in Japan, sponsored by the Iwadare Foundation, and he was awarded the Order of the Rising Sun. Colpitts's wife died in 1940, and soon after he married her sister, Sarah Grace Penney; they had no children.

In September 1940 the National Defense Research Committee (NDRC), at the request of Secretary of the Navy Frank Knox and director of the Naval Research Laboratory Admiral Harold G. Bowen, established a subcommittee to investigate problems of submarine detection and the state of knowledge of antisubmarine warfare. Colpitts was appointed chairman of the subcommittee, which carried out an intense investigation of naval facilities and in January 1941 issued a report on the submarine problem. Known as the Colpitts report, it urged long-range research on all aspects of sound transmission in the ocean. As a result, navy research laboratories were established early in 1941 in New London, Connecticut, and San Diego, California, each involving associated university research laboratories. Continuing with NDRC, in 1943 Colpitts coordinated a project in which charts were prepared for submarine officers that described the acoustical properties of American and Japanese coastal waters. Colpitts received the Medal for Merit in 1948 for his "valuable contribution in the determination of the policies of the Division [Division 6 of the National Defence Research Committee] in the field of sub-surface warfare."

Also in 1948 Colpitts received the Elliott Cresson Medal of the Franklin Institute of Philadelphia for his fundamental contributions to the practical development of long-distance telephone communication. In 1941 he was director of the Engineering Foundation, a joint corporate agency of the country's four major engineering societies.

Colpitts obtained twenty-four patents during his years with the AT&T system, five of them jointly. Their titles included electric circuits, electromagnetic coil, wireless signaling and control devices for it, amplifiers, and multiplex signaling. Jewett and Craft described him as "a pre-eminent executive director and the organizer of a scientific team and its laboratories," a man with "keen analytical ability" and "creative imagination" (*Western Electric News*, May 1924, p. 40). When Colpitts entered the field in 1899, telephones were used by a few people over short distances and were hand-cranked to call an operator; overseas communication was impossible. His engineering contributions and those from laboratories that he directed for AT&T helped lead to worldwide telephone communication. He was an effective team player in a growing organization, and one who worked well with other engineers such as Jewett, so that distinguishing Colpitts's individual efforts from those of others at AT&T in his later years is difficult.

Colpitts died in Orange, New Jersey.

• Archival records of Colpitts are in the AT&T Archives in Warren, N.J., including biographical information. Some biographical sources give Colpitts's date of birth as 9 Jan. instead of 19 Jan., but records at AT&T do not clarify this, nor do they indicate when (or whether) Colpitts became a U.S. citizen. Information on Colpitts's role for the National Defense Research Committee is in Gary E. Weir's *Forged in War* (1993). Background history of AT&T is in M. D. Fagen, ed., *A History of Engineering and Science in the Bell System* (1975); see especially vol. 1: *The Early Years*. An obituary is in the *New York Herald Tribune*, 7 Mar. 1949.

ELIZABETH NOBLE SHOR

COLQUITT, Alfred Holt (20 Apr. 1824–26 Mar. 1894), Confederate military officer and politician, was born in Walton County, Georgia, the son of Walter T. Colquitt, an attorney and later a judge, congressman, and U.S. senator, and Nancy Lane. Graduating from Princeton University in 1844, Colquitt studied law and was admitted to the bar in Georgia in 1846.

Shortly after the Mexican War began in 1846, Colquitt enlisted in the U.S. Army and served throughout the war with the rank of major. After the war ended in 1848, he returned to Georgia and that year married Dorothy Tarver. The couple moved to a cotton plantation in Baker County that Dorothy's father gave to her. As a lawyer, politician, and planter, Colquitt became a prominent member of the gentry of Baker County.

In 1852 Colquitt became a secessionist Democratic candidate for Congress against James Johnson, the incumbent and a member of the Unionist faction of the Georgia Democratic party. Easily winning the election, Colquitt spent one term in Washington as a staunch defender of Southern states' rights and the expansion of slavery in the West. He did not seek reelection because of his wife's poor health. She died in 1855, and that year Colquitt married Sarah Tarver, the sister of his first wife.

Colquitt reentered politics in 1859, when he was elected to the Georgia legislature. A strong secessionist, he served as a presidential elector for the ticket of John C. Breckinridge and Joseph Lane in the 1860 election, representing the southern wing of the Democratic party that demanded an unequivocal endorsement of slavery. The following year Colquitt was elected as a delegate to the Georgia secession convention, which voted to break from the Union in January 1861. When war was declared in April, he enlisted in the Confederate army as a captain of infantry and rose quickly in the ranks to major general. His greatest military success came in 1864 when he commanded infantry at the battle of Olustee, Florida, a humiliating though strategically insignificant defeat for the larger and better-equipped Union army.

After the Civil War Colquitt returned to his Baker County plantation, one of the largest in postbellum Georgia, and resumed his law practice. He was also an industrial promoter of railroads and other industries and invested in the Georgia Pacific Syndicate. Again active in the Georgia Democratic party, he stridently opposed congressional Reconstruction policies. In 1870 he served as president of the Democratic State Convention and later that year was elected president of the state agricultural society.

Widely popular among Georgia Democrats, Colquitt was nominated for governor by the party in 1876 and won handily in the general election against the Republican candidate, Jonathan Norcross, with an unprecedented majority of 111,297 to 33,443. Colquitt, Joseph E. Brown, and John B. Gordon came to be known in Georgia politics as the "Bourbon Triumvirate" for their shared views and domination of the state's governorship and Senate seats from 1872 to 1890. During this period the trio favored sectional reconciliation, industrialization, low taxes, and minimal government. Seeking to advance these principles as governor, Colquitt successfully urged the state legislature to reduce the tax rate and limit government spending. During his six years as governor the state's public debt declined from $11 million to $9.6 million.

Despite its legislative successes, the Colquitt administration was shaken by Democratic infighting and scandal. The drastic reduction of government jobs caused by the administration's fiscal retrenchment created widespread resentment among Democratic office seekers. Colquitt was also denounced for endorsing bonds of the North-Eastern Railroad, which was heavily indebted and on the verge of being sold. In an effort to clear his name, Colquitt demanded that the assembly investigate the transaction. While the investigating committee concluded that accusations against the governor were "vile and slanderous," its findings led to the impeachment and conviction of the comptroller for misappropriation and other illegal practices. Another uproar met Colquitt's appointment of Brown to fill the Senate seat of Gordon, who resigned in May 1880. When Gordon was hired by the Western and Atlantic Railroad, which was then leased by Brown, the "Triumvirate" was charged with perpetrating a corrupt bargain.

Colquitt easily won reelection in 1880 and served a full two-year term. He was then appointed by Governor Alexander H. Stephens to replace U.S. senator Benjamin H. Hill, who had died in office. Colquitt served in the Senate from 1883 until his death. As a senator Colquitt was known for his fierce opposition to protective tariffs. He died in Washington, D.C.

Colquitt was an archetypal member of the Southern ruling class in the nineteenth century. As a planter, secessionist, Confederate officer, and foe of Reconstruction, he was a mainstay of the Old South, yet as an industrialist and laissez faire political leader after the war, he represented the gentry's shift to a modern, bourgeois class.

• The most useful biographical sketch of Colquitt is in James F. Cook, *The Governors of Georgia, 1754–1995* (1995). Amanda Johnson, *Georgia as Colony and State* (1938), contains the best account of the Colquitt administration. C. Vann Woodward, *Tom Watson: Agrarian Rebel* (1938), provides an incisive account of the rivalry between Watson and the "Bourbon Triumvirate." See also Harold H. Martin, *Georgia: A Bicentennial History* (1977), and Joseph H. Parks, *Joseph E. Brown of Georgia* (1977).

THADDEUS RUSSELL

COLT, LeBaron Bradford (25 June 1846–18 Aug. 1924), lawyer and politician, was born in Dedham, Massachusetts, the son of Christopher Colt, a businessman, and Theodora Goujand DeWolf. Colt, the nephew of Samuel Colt of Colt revolver fame, spent much of his childhood at his maternal grandfather's mansion, "Linden Place," in Bristol, Rhode Island. Graduating from Yale College (now Yale University) in 1868, he earned an LL.B from Columbia College Law School in 1870. Following a year of travel in Europe, Colt returned to the United States and began a law practice in Chicago in 1872. There he married Mary Louise Ledyard in 1873; they had six children. In 1875 the Colts decided to make Bristol, Rhode Island, their permanent home. That same year Colt became a law partner of Francis Colwell in Providence.

In addition to law, Colt entered the political arena. Elected to the Rhode Island House of Representatives as a Republican from Bristol in 1879, he served the state legislature until 1881. At that time President James A. Garfield appointed Colt U.S. district judge for the District of Rhode Island. Colt's impressive record led President Chester A. Arthur to appoint him U.S. circuit judge for the First Judicial Circuit in 1884; in 1891 he became the presiding judge of the new Circuit Court of Appeals for the First Circuit. His decisions in the areas of bankruptcy, corporation, and patent law helped contribute to the development of these fields of law. While on the bench, he won the respect of his colleagues for his "impartial decisions and sound judicial temperament" (Schlup, p. 3).

This reputation followed him into national politics. In 1913 Colt accepted his election by the predominantly Republican Rhode Island legislature to the U.S. Senate and won reelection by popular vote in 1918. His peers in the Senate considered him an authority on legal and constitutional questions. He opposed the Panama Canal Toll Bill of 1912 because it contradicted the intent of the Hay-Pauncefote Treaty of 1901. In 1914 Congress repealed this bill. On the other hand, Colt supported the Russian Relief Bill of 1921, which appropriated $20 million to relieve starvation in the Volga region, because he claimed that the Constitution must be "elastic enough to supply the great fundamental wants of society." He believed ardently in American intervention in World War I in 1917 and helped frame the legislation on which U.S. entrance into this war, as well as ensuing wars, depended. Basically, the United States would enter a war if its material and moral interests were endangered.

During the subsequent struggle over the League of Nations, Colt was "one of the most loyal friends of the League of Nations in the Senate" (*New York Times*, 19 Aug. 1924). A mild reservationist, Colt favored the league but recognized the political necessity of adopting some reservations, especially a protection of the Monroe Doctrine and a clarification of the power of the league over domestic issues, such as immigration policy. He firmly advocated the inseparability of the league from the Treaty of Versailles; he insisted that without the league the treaty could not be properly enforced. As he told the Senate, the object of the League of Nations "is to prevent war through international cooperation. . . . Not to try this experiment would leave the world in the same condition of international anarchy as it was before the war." In assessing Colt's role in the fight over the league, political scientist Leonard Schlup claimed that President Woodrow Wilson committed a "serious error in judgment" by not working closely with Colt to secure approval of the covenant with necessary modifications. With the failure of the league in the Senate, Colt threw his support behind the Washington Conference of 1921, particularly the Four Power Treaty, "as an important step in advancing the peace of the world." This treaty among the United States, Great Britain, Japan, and France declared mutual respect for each other's possessions in the Pacific and provided for consultation if problems arose endangering the peace and stability of the area.

While in the Senate Colt served as a member of the Senate Committee on Civil Service and the Senate Judiciary Committee, and he was chair of the Senate Judiciary Subcommittee and of the Senate Committee on Immigration. In the discussion of the Immigration Bills of 1921 and 1924, his colleagues deemed Colt to be "eminently fair-minded" and "sensitive." Colt opposed the adoption of any policy likely to offend or embarrass the people of other nationalities. As a result, he strongly objected to the extreme quota limitations called for in the bills and was one of only two senators who rejected the Japanese exclusion clause of the 1924 measure. Unlike many Americans of his time, Colt did not assume that immigrants imperiled American institutions, habits, customs, and ideals. Despite his stand, however, the majority of his colleagues passed both restrictive bills.

His political philosophy in general during his years as a public figure was progressive. As Senator Thomas Sterling (R.-S.Dak.) stated, "He was liberal in everything that pertained to our national or to human welfare." He favored a loose interpretation of the Constitution and told the Senate he was grateful the document contained abstract provisions such as "general welfare" because such terms were "elastic, and as the country moves and as the world moves these abstract phrases must be interpreted in the light of fundamental conditions of society." Colt believed that the "great problem of government" could be solved with "the common sense of the average man, or the collective sense of the multitude of average men." Throughout his political life, Colt strongly advocated domestic reforms called for by progressives as well as a large international role for the United States in the twentieth century.

Deteriorating health in the summer of 1924 removed Colt from further serious political activity. He died at his home, Linden Place, in Bristol.

• Despite his role in a number of significant national issues, historians have largely overlooked Colt. Perhaps he has remained an enigma to scholars due to the paucity of his political letters and papers. The Colt Family Papers are located at the University of Rhode Island, Special Collections, in Kingston, and include a combination of his private and public papers dealing with his years in the judiciary as well as in the U.S. Senate. Small collections of miscellaneous materials can be found in Providence at the Rhode Island Historical Society, the Rhode Island State House Library, and Brown University. A small but important part of Colt's political legacy, primarily his clandestine political alliance with Taft during the fight over the Treaty of Versailles, can be found in the papers of William Howard Taft, Library of Congress, Washington, D.C. Also significant is Colt's own collection of speeches, *Addresses* (1906). For biographical information, see H. P. Wright, *History of the Class of 1868, Yale College* (1914), and the memorial addresses in the *Congressional Record* (both Senate and House), 68th Cong., 2d sess., 1925. Colt is mentioned in passing in numerous books on the fight over the League of Nations. See also Lloyd E. Ambrosius, *Woodrow Wilson and the American Diplomatic Tradition: The Treaty Fight in Perspective* (1987). Leonard Schlup, "A Senator of Principle: Some Correspondence between LeBaron Bradford Colt and William Howard Taft," *Rhode Island History* 42 (1983): 3–16, analyzes the friendship and political alliance between Colt and Taft during the fight over the treaty and the league. Obituaries are in the *New York Times*, the Bristol *Phoenix*, and the *Providence Journal*, 19 Aug. 1924; and the *Yale University Obituary Record* (1925).

SIMONE M. CARON

COLT, Samuel (19 July 1814–10 Jan. 1862), inventor and industrialist, was born in Hartford, Connecticut, the son of Christopher Colt, a merchant and cotton and wool fabric manufacturer, and Sarah Caldwell. His mother died in 1821, after his father's once-prosperous business failed. Christopher Colt remarried, indentured Samuel at age ten to a farmer, and a year later, sent him to work at a dyeing and bleaching factory in Ware, Massachusetts. Lack of parental supervision made it easy for Samuel to indulge his taste for firearms and explosives: he had acquired a pistol at the age of seven, and at twelve he detonated a spectacular explosion in Ware Pond.

Colt attended Amherst Academy. When his 1830 Independence Day pyrotechnic display set fire to a school building, Colt, anticipating disciplinary action, decamped, and his father dispatched him as a common seaman on a voyage to Calcutta. On the voyage, Colt had whittled a wooden model of a revolving, multi-barrel pistol (a "pepperbox"), not then a novel design. He subsequently realized he could make a much handier weapon with a single barrel and revolving cylinder. Although he devised a mechanism to rotate the cylinder automatically and lock it in place for each successive discharge, he lacked the resources to make a satisfactory prototype.

Colt returned to the Ware dye and bleach works, where he learned some chemistry from the superintendent. At eighteen, under the name of Dr. Coult, he began a successful lecture tour in which he demonstrated nitrous oxide (laughing gas). He used his profits to have models of his revolvers built. On a trip to Europe in 1835 he obtained French and British patents, and in 1836 a U.S. patent, on the revolver principle. That same year, with a group of New Jersey capitalists, he organized the Patent Arms Manufacturing Company in Paterson, New Jersey. The performance of Colt's revolvers in the fighting for Texas independence and the Seminole war brought him recognition. An army board, however, pronounced the weapon too complicated and delicate for adoption in military service, and outside of Texas and Florida few people needed a repeating pistol. Slack business brought the arms company to failure in 1842.

When tension with Britain in 1840 revived government interest in harbor defenses, Colt returned to the design of underwater explosives. He devised a system for electrically detonating mines under hostile ships entering a harbor. Because of his penchant for secrecy and his preoccupation with the (unsuccessful) defense in his brother John's trial for murder, Colt failed to gain acceptance of his invention; he refused to disclose important details of its operation, and without this the government was unwilling to accept it. Nevertheless, the public demonstrations of his underwater mines—several large ships were blown up—gave Colt publicity that helped him launch a successful business manufacturing wire for underwater telegraph lines.

In 1845 federal troops sent to expel the Mexican army from Texas found that Colt revolvers, much favored by the Texas Rangers, were essential weapons.

Captain Samuel Walker, sent to buy more, discovered that Colt had none. Together Walker and Colt drew plans for a heavier, larger-caliber weapon, and in 1847 Colt contracted with Eli Whitney, Jr., to make 1,000 revolvers at Whitney's armory in Whitneyville, Connecticut. Reports of exploits with revolvers in the Mexican war as well as dependence on horseback riding and encounters with many foes by pioneers as they moved onto the plains stimulated demand, and Colt soon had more orders than he could fill. In 1848, determined to apply the new methods of mechanized manufacturing developed by the Whitneys, John Hall, Simeon North, and others, Colt established his own factory in Hartford and hired E. K. Root, the gifted mechanic who had mechanized ax manufacture for the Collins Company, as his superintendent. Root designed new production machines, many of which were soon adopted in other industries.

In 1849 Colt returned from a European trip with an order for 5,000 revolvers from the Turkish government and enlarged his works into the world's biggest private armory by 1850. In 1852 he started plans for a completely new factory suitable for his system of manufacturing. Colt bought land on the flood plain of the Connecticut River and protected it with dikes stabilized with willows (French osiers). His innovations at the armory included hot-air heat, gas lamps, engines built into the building's framing, and washing facilities for workers. Out of gratitude for the Turkish order that had done much to stimulate his business, Colt placed the famous onion-shaped dome atop his armory when operations began in 1856. Colt used inside contractors, and with machine tools, reduced the amount of hand fitting to less than half that common at other works. Always the entrepreneur, Colt recruited willow-ware workers from Europe, built them a German-style village called Potsdam, and set them to work making willow furniture, for which he found a large market in Cuba.

Starting in 1849, Colt spent much time in Europe promoting both his revolvers and American manufacturing methods. His prizewinning display of revolvers at the 1851 London Exhibition and an evening lecture at the Institution of Civil Engineers in London—Colt was the first American to lecture there—stimulated discussion and helped him sell to European customers. To meet European demand and avoid trade restriction in Britain, Colt established a factory in London, which he equipped with American machinery in 1852. Difficulties in supplying their army and navy with sufficient small arms induced the British government to look into Colt's manufacturing techniques, known as the American system. Colt described American methods in testimony before a parliamentary committee in 1853. He was invited to Russia to help modernize arms making there and to sell arms in 1854, 1856, and 1858.

Colt married Elizabeth Jarvis, the daughter of an Episcopal clergyman in Middletown, Connecticut, in 1856 and set off on a honeymoon trip to Russia, where he represented the United States at the coronation of

Czar Alexander. The Colts had four children, though only one lived to maturity. Colt, who began suffering from inflammatory rheumatism in 1858, died in Hartford.

Now chiefly known as the inventor of the revolver, even though others also perfected revolver mechanisms, Colt was a daring and successful entrepreneur. His particular genius and most important contribution was in developing and publicizing new manufacturing techniques. More than anyone, Colt created international markets for American machine tools and made the world aware of the remarkable accomplishments of the Yankee innovators who created the American system of manufactures.

• The principal collections of Colt papers are at the Connecticut State Library, the Connecticut Historical Society, and the Wadsworth Athenaeum, all in Hartford. The biography commissioned by Colt's wife was assembled by Henry Barnard as *Armsmear: The Home, the Arms, and the Armory of Samuel Colt* (1866). Other biographies include Jack Rohan, *Yankee Armsmaker, the Incredible Career of Samuel Colt* (1935), and William B. Edwards, *The Story of Colt's Revolver: The Biography of Col. Samuel Colt* (1953). Philip K. Lundeberg published a detailed study of Colt's harbor defense scheme in "Samuel Colt's Submarine Battery, the Secret and the Enigma," *Smithsonian Studies in History and Technology*, no. 29 (1974). The surviving documents relating to the Colt-Walker revolver were printed by the Connecticut Historical Society as *Sam Colt's Own Record* in 1949. An account of Colt's activities in Britain is in Joseph G. Rosa, *Colonel Colt, London* (1976). Nathan Rosenberg surveys the development of the American manufacturing techniques studied by the British in the introduction of *The American System of Manufactures* (1969), which also contains Colt's testimony before a parliamentary committee. Joseph Bradley, *Guns for the Tsar* (1990), describes Colt's work in introducing American manufacturing techniques in Europe. Numerous books written primarily for collectors describe Colt firearms, including R. L. Wilson, *Colt, an American Legend* (1985).

ROBERT B. GORDON

COLT, Samuel Pomeroy (10 Jan. 1852–13 Aug. 1921), financier and industrialist, was born in Paterson, New Jersey, the son of Christopher Colt, a silk merchant, and Theodora DeWolf. Colt's father died when the boy was very young. Colt then spent his early years at the Hartford, Connecticut home of his uncle, Samuel Colt, the inventor of the Colt revolver. In his early teens Colt, who was known by his middle name, moved with his family to his mother's hometown of Bristol, Rhode Island. Theodora, the daughter of a disgraced member of the town's aristocracy, managed to maneuver herself and her sons back into social prominence. Colt graduated from the Massachusetts Institute of Technology in 1873 and, following a year of travel in Europe, from Columbia Law School in 1876. He entered politics while still in law school, joining the staff of Republican governor Henry Lippitt of Rhode Island in 1875, and was elected to the state's house of representatives in 1876. Colt allied himself with the rising star of Nelson W. Aldrich, at that time a congressman from Rhode Island and soon

to be a powerful and prominent U.S. senator. Colt, with Aldrich's help, secured an appointment as the state's assistant attorney general in 1879, and was elected attorney general in 1882. He was defeated in 1886, partially owing to the flagrant favoritism his office showed to liquor interests.

Colt then devoted his attention to business, building up the two enterprises that would define his public career. He organized the Industrial Trust Company in Providence in 1887 and established it as a sound financial institution despite the inordinately crowded and unprofitable character of the Rhode Island banking industry. Beginning in 1900, Colt began to buy national banks in outlying towns and convert them into branches of Industrial Trust. This move brought high profits and advanced the trust company into the forefront of the state's financial community. The bank's expanded resources allowed him to nurture alliances with such prominent New York financiers as Jacob Schiff of Kuhn, Loeb, and Co., Thomas Ryan of the National Bank of Commerce, and James Stillman of the National City Bank.

Colt began another venture into business when he was appointed receiver of the bankrupt National Rubber Company in Bristol in 1887. By 1892 National Rubber was not only profitable, but was also one of eight companies that merged to create the United States Rubber Company. As a director of U.S. Rubber from the outset and then its president from 1901 to 1918, Colt promoted the vertical integration and diversification of the rubber company, though at the same time he assiduously protected the interests of his original factory in Bristol. The massive size and market dominance of U.S. Rubber during Colt's lifetime earned him high praises, but the company's large indebtedness and excessive number of factories weakened the company in the years following Colt's death.

Colt's marriage to Elizabeth Bullock in 1881 suffered from his absences on business and from the antagonism between Elizabeth and Colt's mother. In 1895 their break was made public in a scandalous divorce trial that revealed that both Colt and his wife had engaged in affairs. The case was settled out of court without an actual divorce. Colt continued to support Elizabeth and their two sons, though they lived apart thereafter.

An attempt by Colt and several allies to take over the *Providence Journal*, the state's leading newspaper, in 1903, stirred the anger of the old elite families of Providence. The takeover effort failed, and Colt's adversaries actively opposed his subsequent move to be elected to the U.S. Senate in 1906. The 1907 legislative session to fill the office was deadlocked among Colt, the incumbent Republican senator, and a fusion Democrat/reform candidate. The session, characterized by vicious political infighting, ended without an election, and Colt withdrew during the summer of 1907. Suffering a nervous breakdown, Colt resigned as president in 1908 and removed himself from public life and day-to-day business activities until 1909. During his absence his political enemies had gained control of Industrial Trust, and Colt, as chairman of the board of directors, began a campaign to wrest the company away from them, finally succeeding in 1912. Having proved his dominance once again in the economic arena, he divided the last ten years of his life between his businesses and the political activities of his brother, Republican LeBaron Colt, a former federal judge who was elected U.S. senator from Rhode Island in 1912. Colt basked in his hometown's appreciation of his patronage of the rubber company as well as his donation of a new high school to the town in his mother's memory. He enjoyed his high stature in Rhode Island economic and social life until he died in Bristol.

• Colt's personal and business papers are in the Colt Family papers in the Special Collections division of the University of Rhode Island library. Other correspondence is included in the Nelson W. Aldrich papers at the Library of Congress. The only comprehensive work on Colt's life is Andrew J. F. Morris, "Restless Ambition: Samuel P. Colt and Turn-of-the-Century Rhode Island" (Honors thesis, Brown Univ., 1991). Other relevant sources include Glenn Babcock, *History of the United States Rubber Company* (1961); George Howe, *Mount Hope: A New England Chronicle* (1959); Fred Piggot, *A History of the Industrial National Bank of Providence, Rhode Island* (1961); and Robert C. Power, "Rhode Island Republican Politics in the Gilded Age" (Honors thesis, Brown Univ., 1972). An obituary is in the *Providence Journal*, 14 Aug. 1921, and in the *Bristol Phoenix*, 16 Aug. 1921.

ANDREW J. F. MORRIS

COLTER, John (c. 1775–Nov. 1813), fur trapper and explorer, was born probably in the vicinity of Staunton, Virginia, the son of John Colter and Ellen Shields, farmers. The Colter family (also spelled Coalter and Coulter) that farmed near the Shenandoah Valley community of Staunton traced its lineage back to Micajah Coalter, a Scots-Irish settler who arrived in Virginia about 1700. Virtually nothing is known about John Colter's youth or early adult years. The earliest record of him dates to 15 October 1803, when Meriwether Lewis, on his way by keelboat from Pittsburgh to St. Louis, stopped at the Ohio River town of Maysville, Kentucky. There Captain Lewis enlisted Colter—then about thirty years of age—and several other men as privates in the Corps of Discovery.

Colter began his service with the Lewis and Clark expedition as a boatman, but excellent marksmanship earned him promotion to hunter by the time the party reached the great falls of the Missouri in 1805. Colter subsequently served as a hunter, scout, and messenger during the outward journey to the Pacific and the return east. In August 1806, while descending the Missouri (in present-day South Dakota), the homeward-bound expedition met two American trappers, Joseph Dixon (or Dickson) and Forest (or Forrest) Hancock. Colter asked permission to join these men, who were headed upstream. William Clark wrote in his journal that the request was granted because "we were disposed to be of service to anyone of our party who had performed their duty as well as Colter had done."

Colter and his new companions spent the winter of 1806–1807 trapping beaver in the upper Missouri drainage. Among the first American trappers to penetrate this far west, they may have included portions of the Yellowstone River drainage in their travels. For unknown reasons, the partnership dissolved the following spring, and Colter resumed his return trip toward St. Louis.

Near the mouth of the Platte in August 1807, Colter encountered the supply-laden boats of St. Louis fur trader Manuel Lisa, who convinced Colter to join his expedition. (One probable factor in Colter's decision to return upstream once again was that Lisa's group included fellow hunter George Drouillard and two other veterans of the Lewis and Clark expedition.) Colter's fame as an explorer and mountain man rests on events that occurred subsequently, during his three-year stint in the upper Missouri basin as one of Lisa's "free trappers."

Perhaps on Colter's recommendation, Lisa established his trading post, Fort Raymond (or Manuel's Fort), not on the Missouri but on the Yellowstone, at the mouth of the Big Horn River. This location (in present-day south-central Montana) lay within the traditional territory of the Crow Indians, a fact that probably angered the Crows' traditional enemies, the Blackfoot Indians. From there Colter set out in November 1807—alone, "with a pack of thirty pounds weight, his gun and some ammunition" (Brackenridge, p. 91)—to visit the Crows in their villages along the upper Yellowstone and encourage them to come trade at Lisa's post. During this winter trek, Colter explored much of present-day northwestern Wyoming. He probably ranged as far west as Jackson Hole and perhaps the upper Snake River's Teton Basin (in present-day Idaho) before returning to Fort Raymond sometime in the spring of 1808.

The only direct testament to Colter's 1807–1808 route is William Clark's 1810 manuscript map. This map contains major inaccuracies (of both scale and location) for the Yellowstone River basin. Clark's cartographic effort (which served as the basis for the famous map that first appeared in Nicholas Biddle's 1814 official *History of the Expedition under the Command of Captains Lewis and Clark*) shows a dashed line marked "Colter's Route," but much of that route is contradicted by the region's actual geography. Historians agree that during his epic winter journey Colter became the first Euro-American to explore portions of present-day Yellowstone National Park. However, the area of hot springs that Colter saw and described—which became known to trappers as Colter's Hell—was located well to the east of Yellowstone, along the Shoshone (or "Stinking Water") River.

In the summer of 1808 Colter traveled west to the Three Forks headwaters of the Missouri. There he met a hunting party of Crow and Flathead Indians. Shortly after Colter joined the group, it was attacked near the Gallatin River by a large party of Blackfoot Indians. Colter fought alongside his companions. (Meriwether Lewis's unfortunate 1806 encounter with a Blackfoot party on the Marias River notwithstanding, many historians trace the origin of the Blackfoot Indians' decades-long enmity toward American trappers to Colter's presence at the 1808 battle.)

Later that year, while trapping on the Jefferson River, Colter and John Potts, another Lewis and Clark veteran, were surprised by Blackfoot Indians. Potts was killed almost immediately. Colter, captured and stripped naked, was permitted to run for his life while pursued by a group of armed young men. Colter's footrace across the cactus-studded plains, between five and six miles to the banks of the Jefferson (or, in one version of the episode, the Madison) River—and his subsequent escape back to Lisa's post—became one of the most durable tales in western American history, immortalized in Washington Irving's *Astoria* and Hiram Chittenden's *Fur Trade of the Far West*.

During the spring of 1810, after another year on the upper Missouri, Colter returned to the Three Forks region as a hunter and guide for Lisa's expanding Missouri Fur Company. Incessant Blackfoot attacks thinned the ranks of company employees. After narrowly escaping death once again, Colter supposedly declared, "I will leave the country day after tomorrow—and damned if I ever come into it again" (James, pp. 65–66). Within a month's time, he canoed to St. Louis. There he provided geographic information to William Clark (used in Clark's 1810 map) and to Wilson Price Hunt, leader of the 1811 Astor overland expedition to the Pacific. He also predicted the feasibility of wagon travel over the passes of the Continental Divide. He never returned to the Far West.

Almost nothing is known of Colter's physical appearance. A fellow trapper simply recalled him as of medium height and build. In 1811 he settled a small farm near the lower Missouri River hamlet of La Charette (where one of his neighbors was octogenarian Kentucky woodsman Daniel Boone). His wife, whom he married in 1811 (and about whom nothing is known but the name Sally, also shown as "Loucy"), possibly was an Indian. Although no birth records document the fact, local tradition asserts that he had a son named Hiram. He died of jaundice in La Charette.

Colter's explorations of the upper Missouri River drainage (specifically the Three Forks and Yellowstone River country) contributed directly to the initial expansion of the American fur trade into that region. It is ironic, then, that Colter's coincidental presence among the Crows in 1808 has been seen as the initial cause for the bitter warfare between Blackfoot Indians and trappers that retarded effective American penetration of the area for a number of years.

For almost two centuries tales of Colter's exploits—especially his solitary winter trek and his desperate race to escape Blackfoot pursuers—have found an appreciative audience among Americans eager to read about dramatic adventures of the mountain men. Colter probably owes at least some of his initial popular fame to the fact that he was the first American trapper of British (that is, not French or Spanish) ancestry to explore the northern Rockies; as such he was ready-made for apotheosis by Washington Irving and other nationalistic nineteenth-century writers. However, the stories of his legendary feats are based on credible testimony about actual events, and doubtless they will continue to provide drama to the history of the Far West fur trade.

• Circumstantial evidence prompts historians to agree that Colter was probably literate; however, other than a December 1813 bill of sale for his estate, no personal papers exist. For Colter's participation in the 1804–1806 Corps of Discovery, see vols. 2 and 5 of *The Journals of the Lewis and Clark Expedition*, ed. Gary Moulton (1986 and 1988). The three primary sources (based on the authors' personal encounters with Colter) about Colter's years in the Rockies are Henry M. Brackenridge, *Views of Louisiana* (1814); John Bradbury, *Travels in the Interior of America* (1817); and Thomas James, *Three Years among the Indians* (1846). Aubrey Haines's concise biographical sketch, in LeRoy Hafen, *The Mountain Men and the Fur Trade of the Far West*, vol. 8 (1971), draws in part on the two classic, if somewhat hagiographic, book-length works about Colter: Stallo Vinton, *John Colter, Discoverer of Yellowstone Park* (1926), and Burton Harris, *John Colter: His Years in the Rockies* (1952; repr. 1993). See also David Lavender's introduction to the 1993 edition of Harris's book.

JEFF LALANDE

COLTER, Mary Elizabeth Jane (4 Apr. 1869–8 Jan. 1958), architect and designer, was born in Pittsburgh, Pennsylvania, the second daughter of William Colter, the owner of a clothing store, and Rebecca Crozier, a milliner. Both parents were Irish immigrants with family ties to St. Paul, Minnesota, to which they returned when Mary was eleven. Mary discovered two major interests in high school: paintings by local Sioux Indians and the drama of railroads opening the West. She treasured the spiritual quality in the former and relished the spectacle of the latter when in 1883 President Chester Arthur and General Ulysses S. Grant came to her town for the ceremony opening the Northern Pacific Railway between St. Paul and Portland, Oregon.

In 1886, on the sudden death of her father, Colter gained her mother's permission to use her small inheritance for art school education in San Francisco as preparation for supporting her family. She chose the California School of Design (later the San Francisco Art Institute) because it had the best program in all design fields and offered a four-year course leading to a teacher's credential. Determined to become an architect, she was apprenticed to an architect through the School of Design, the regular method of study for the profession in the absence of architectural schools in the West. It was a fortunate experience because the area was awakening to the significance and power of regionalism after the longtime imitation of European and East Coast styles, especially their ubiquitous Victorian variations. Colter's teachers talked and wrote about the appropriate site, material, and color—all principles that she embraced and applied in her designs throughout her practice.

At her graduation in 1890, Colter, equipped to teach architecture and drawing, was ready to support her mother and sister. After one year at a small state school, she began a fifteen-year teaching career at Mechanic Arts High School (for boys only) in St. Paul. While teaching freehand and mechanical drawing, she also lectured on world history and architecture in university extension programs, took part in Century Club lectures in Minnesota and Iowa, reviewed books for the *St. Paul Globe*, and took courses in archaeology. She never married, as was the case with the majority of career women of the time.

While visiting the shop of Fred Harvey, a dealer in Indian artifacts, during a vacation in San Francisco, Colter mentioned that she would like to work with Harvey's company to improve its interpretation of Indian materials. To her surprise, once back in Minnesota, a long telegram offered her an immediate position with the Fred Harvey Company. Harvey, an Englishman, had much improved the tourist enterprises of the Santa Fe Railway since 1876 by adding restaurants and hotels at train stops and making visitors aware of the history of the West and the character of the indigenous people. Colter was hired to design, build, decorate, and furnish the train stations. Her work with Harvey ultimately included designing china and pottery for the trains and even giving Indian names to each railway car. Colter adapted from the Mimbres culture (A.D. 1000–2000)—familiar to her from the study of Southwest archaeology—animal designs in maroon, white, and charcoal for the Super Chief, a train in use until 1971. In 1992 a catalog of luxurious gifts from the West listed reproductions of designs by "Indian authority" Mary Colter "that go easily from microwave to dishwasher."

Colter found her opportunity to design important buildings at the Grand Canyon. On the south rim of the canyon she designed and built Hopi House (1905) as a place to display Indian crafts. The whole building was constructed by Hopi tribesmen and tribeswomen who followed her plan, which was a larger version of their own style. Hopi House is across the road from architect Charles Whittlesey's tourist hotel El Tovar, where she designed the cocktail lounge (1905); Colter had earlier done the interior of the Indian Building (1902) at Whittlesey's Alvarado Hotel in Albuquerque. With her own commission, she created in Hopi House a building appropriate to the setting that represented the history of the area and the people who had lived there for centuries. She followed Hopi tradition with flat stone walls fitted together without mortar, each floor set back above the lower one to form ample terraces and porches, ladders of rough trees for stairs, vertical windows of varying heights. Originally some of the Hopis who worked in the building lived on the upper two stories. Interiors were in primitive style with massive plaster walls, ceilings of log beams with smaller branches laid across them, and cement poured to resemble authentic mud floors. Hand-hewn tables displayed Indian baskets and pots, rugs, Kachina dolls, and other religious figures. A Hopi ceremonial altar and a sand painting gave authenticity to the exhibition of Harvey's fine arts collection as well as goods for sale. Hopi artisans were employed to demonstrate their skills in weaving and other crafts, while every

evening at five o'clock they sang traditional songs and performed their own special dances.

After successfully completing Hopi House, Colter returned to teaching in St. Paul. In 1910 she accepted a permanent position with the Fred Harvey Company as architect and designer. During the next thirty-nine years she added twenty more buildings to her credit, six major ones at the Grand Canyon—Lookout, Hermit's Rest, Phantom Ranch, Watchtower, Bright Angel Lodge, and the men's and women's dormitories. Colter never had an independent architectural office of her own. She drew her designs, plans, and elevations and, once approved by the Harvey Company, sent them to the Santa Fe Railway's offices in Los Angeles, where draftsmen made working drawings that she followed on site.

Interior design and remodeling occupied her last years of work, and her retirement was an active period of organizing and placing her collections of Indian ceramics, textiles, and jewelry. She willed more than five hundred pieces of her jewelry to the Mesa Verde Indian Museum, and she added funds for a silver saddle and bridle and for display cases. Her Sioux paintings went to St. Paul, which she believed was their spiritual home. She died in Santa Fe.

Colter exerted a strong influence on the appreciation of Indian arts and buildings. What had been seen as the curiosities of a primitive people was transformed by her art of design and display into serious and reverent work worthy of the respect given to the fine arts. She honored the Indians' sacredness of place and their many crafts skills. In part because of Colter's work the Fred Harvey Company's commercial success legitimized Indian art. Her accomplishment as an architect can be seen most easily at the Grand Canyon, where millions experience the quality of her buildings even when they are not told about the woman who preserved in her work the spirit appropriate to the site.

• A biographical sketch is in the Colter file at the Heard Museum Library and Archives, Phoenix. Some material is in the Colter files in Special Collections, University of Arizona Library; the Grand Canyon National Park Research Library, Grand Canyon, Ariz.; and the Mesa Verde Research Library, Mesa Verde National Park, Colo. The principal source on Colter is Virginia L. Grattan's *Mary Colter: Builder upon the Red Earth* (1980; rev. ed., 1992), which also provides a detailed bibliography. Obituaries are in the *New Mexican*, 8 Jan. 1958, and *Hospitality*, Jan.–Feb. 1958, p. 3.

SARA HOLMES BOUTELLE

COLTON, Calvin (14 Sept. 1789–13 Mar. 1857), clergyman and author, was born in Longmeadow, Massachusetts, the son of Major Luther Colton, a veteran of the American Revolution, and Thankful Woolworth. Educated at Monson Academy, Yale College, and Andover Theological Seminary, Colton was ordained a Presbyterian minister in 1816 and served as pastor of churches in Le Roy and Batavia, in western New York's Burned-Over District, a region profoundly affected by the religious revivalism of the Second Great Awakening. In 1826, bereaved by the untimely death of his wife, Abby North Raymond, and troubled by a persistent throat infection that made preaching difficult, Colton abandoned the pulpit. Soon thereafter he undertook an extensive trip through the frontier regions of the Midwest. His travels led to the publication of *Tour of the American Lakes, and among the Indians of the Northwest Territory in 1830: Disclosing the Character and Prospects of the Indian Race* (1832), a work notable for its appeal for a more honorable and humane Indian policy.

In 1831 Colton settled in England, where he worked for four years as a part-time correspondent for the *New-York Observer*, a nationally circulated Protestant newspaper, and as a freelance writer. He published several books intended to explain and defend American life and culture to the English. *The Americans* (1832) sought to counter Frances Trollope's claim that Americans were uncouth and Captain Basil Hall's assertion that they were lawless. Colton portrayed his countrymen as God-fearing, sober, hardworking, respectful of the rights of property, and basically conservative in their belief in law and order. In *A Manual for Emigrants to America* (1832) Colton celebrated the United States as a land free of class distinctions and abounding in opportunity for the talented and the industrious. However, he warned the lazy and the improvident (among whom he particularly numbered the Irish) that Americans had no sympathy for immigrants deficient in moral character. Colton's *History and Character of Revivals of Religion* (1832) defended the evangelists of the Second Great Awakening against their critics and was notable for its claim that the egalitarian character of American life was particularly conducive to the spread of the Gospel. In *Church and State in America Inscribed to the Bishop of London* (1834) Colton contrasted the vibrant, expanding churches in the United States with the moribund, class-ridden Church of England and defended the principle of separation of church and state.

After returning to the United States in 1835, Colton published *Four Years in Great Britain* (1836), a work critical of both the rigidity of the British class system and the radical egalitarianism of the reform movement in England. Colton's early writings reflected a commitment to a moderate republicanism that accepted both the politics of deference to a ruling, propertied elite and the principle of ultimate accountability of those who governed to the body of people. His essential conservatism was reflected in his praise of the British reverence for tradition and in his defense of the principle that only those with "a stake in society" should be enfranchised. No admirer of democracy in the abstract, Colton maintained that the wide distribution of property and the conservative character of the electorate made democracy safe for America. Soon after his return from England, however, Colton's optimism gave way to a deep loathing for Jacksonian democracy. In *A Voice from America to England*, published anonymously in 1839, Colton warned the British against emulation of the American example. His disaffection was not limited to the political realm.

Shocked by the turbulent spirit and the democratic excesses of the revivalism he had earlier praised as the work of the Holy Spirit, Colton now embraced the principle of ecclesiastical hierarchy and joined the Episcopal church. He served as rector of the Church of the Messiah in New York City in 1836–1837. His aversion to religious innovation was expressed in *Thoughts on the Religious State of the Country* (1836) and *The Genius and Mission of the Protestant Episcopal Church in the United States* (1853). In *Protestant Jesuitism* (1836) he assailed social reformers who invoked religious principles and declared the temperance movement a threat to the nation's health. Abandoning his earlier commitment to the "voluntary principle," Colton called for state support of the conservative denominations as a bulwark against "fanaticism" and "radicalism."

Leaving the ministry a second time, Colton turned his pen to the cause of the Whig party. Writing under the pen name "Junius," he published a series of widely circulated tracts that assailed Jacksonian fiscal policies, promoted a protective tariff and federally chartered national bank, declared abolitionism "a sedition," and portrayed the Whig party as truly democratic and the Jacksonian as demagogic and despotic. His writings on slavery reflected both fear of the disruption of the union and acceptance of the premises of white supremacy and black racial inferiority. Colton's most distinctive contribution to Whig political rhetoric was the doctrine of the unity of interest of all classes. Arguing that the Jacksonians betrayed the workers by promoting class hatred, he declared that in America there was not legitimate conflict between capital and labor, as the highly paid American laborer in time could save enough wages to become a capitalist. "Ours is a country," Colton wrote, "where men start from a humble origin, and from small beginnings rise gradually in the world, as the reward of merit and industry, and where they can attain to the most elevated positions, or acquire a large amount of wealth. . . . This is a country of *self-made men*" (*Labor and Capital* [1844], p. 36).

In 1843 Colton edited the Washington, D.C., *True Whig*. In 1844 he moved to Ashland, Kentucky, to edit the papers of Henry Clay and write Clay's biography. His *Life and Times of Henry Clay* (1846) and *The Last Seven Years in the Life of Henry Clay* (1856) are uncritical and unreliable but do provide a striking example of the use of the myth of the self-made man in political propaganda. Colton's *A Lecture on the Railroad to the Pacific* (1850) invoked religious ideals in justification of American expansionism. His *Public Economy for the United States* (1848), a poorly reasoned and tendentious defense of the protective tariff and of the idea that "labor in America is capital," won the admiration of conservatives throughout the country. It went through three editions and led to the author's appointment to a chair of public economy at Trinity College, Hartford, Connecticut, which he assumed in 1852. He held the position until his death in Savannah, Georgia. A prolific writer, Colton was neither an original thinker nor much of a stylist, but he was influential in his day. His works, though now seldom read, provide invaluable insights into conservative thought in antebellum America.

• Calvin Colton's private papers have not survived. A few of his letters are in the Houghton Library, Harvard University; the Yale University Library; the Henry Clay Papers and the John M. Clayton Papers in the Library of Congress; and the Abner Johnson Leavenworth Papers in the Duke University Library. On his family background, see George W. Colton, *Quarter-Master George Colton and His Descendants, 1611–1911* (1912). Colton's writings are analyzed in Alfred A. Cave, *An American Conservative in the Age of Jackson: The Political and Social Thought of Calvin Colton* (1969); Cave, "The Case of Calvin Colton: White Racism in Northern Anti-Slavery Thought," *New-York Historical Society Quarterly* 53 (July 1969): 215–29; Cave, "Calvin Colton: An Antebellum Conservative Disaffection with the Presbyterian Church," *Journal of Presbyterian History* 50 (Spring 1972): 39–53; Arthur M. Schlesinger, Jr., *The Age of Jackson* (1945); John Ashworth, *Agrarians and Aristocrats* (1983); and Joseph Dorfman, *The Economic Mind in American Civilization* (1946).

ALFRED A. CAVE

COLTON, Elizabeth Avery (30 Dec. 1872–26 Aug. 1924), educator, was born in the Choctaw Nation, Indian Territory, the daughter of James Hooper Colton and Harriet Eloise Avery, missionaries. Colton grew up in a family with a distinguished heritage. Her mother's family had established an eminent history in North Carolina politics, and her father, like his father, was an educator, minister, and college president.

Most of Colton's early education took place in North Carolina after her father's ill health prompted the family's return there. The woman who was destined to become the "foremost authority in the nation on the standards of women's colleges in the South" (Johnson [1956], p. 118) learned early about the condition of such institutions. After receiving an A.B. from a "female college" in Statesville, North Carolina, she was required to engage in an additional year of study before being admitted to Mount Holyoke College as a freshman in 1891. After two years of study, Colton transferred to Teachers College at Columbia University, alternately studying and supporting herself and her family by teaching. She graduated with a B.S. in 1903 and earned an A.M. in 1905.

Colton taught English at Queen's College in Charlotte (1896–1902), North Carolina, and at Wellesley (1905–1908) before accepting the position of head of the Department of English at Meredith College in Raleigh, North Carolina, in 1908. It was her aim that "every student should be able to write reasonably clear and correct English and to read with a certain degree of understanding and appreciation" (Johnson [1956], p. 118). As a teacher she balanced a challenging toughness with encouragement. Students remembered her generous praise and noted that Colton's commendation was worth working for. She was committed to academic excellence and, from her earliest days at Meredith, expressed a concern for raising the college's standards. The year after her arrival she led a move-

ment to increase entrance requirements from 11½ to 14 units. Her work was recognized in a 1911 student parody of a faculty meeting: "It is moved and carried that Miss Colton shall go in behalf of Meredith to impress upon all educational institutions that we *exist*, and by dint of much gnashing of teeth and hard work shall attain to their heights ere long" (Johnson [1956], p. 143).

Colton's activities were not limited to Meredith. In 1903 she joined with other women college graduates to form the Southern Association of College Women (SACW). (In 1921 this group merged with the Association of Collegiate Alumnae to create the American Association of University Women.) Colton was the prominent leader in the SACW's work to raise the standards of education for women in the South, which included efforts to clearly define distinctions between preparatory schools and colleges. Colton engaged in a detailed survey of colleges for women in the South, comparing entrance requirements, courses, libraries, equipment, endowment and fees, and degrees granted. Her first report, "Southern Colleges for Women" (1911), indicted that 90 percent of the institutions were deficient in meeting standards in these areas. Other reports followed: "Improvement in Standards of Southern Colleges since 1900" (1913), "Approximate Value of Recent Degrees of Southern Colleges" (1913), "The Junior College Problem in the South" (1914), and "The Various Types of Southern Colleges for Women" (1916). Chancellor James H. Kirkland of Vanderbilt referred to Colton's papers as "high explosive pamphlets." In fact, many college presidents were outraged by the exposure of their weak institutions, and some threatened lawsuits. Evidently, all were defused by Colton's strong scholarship and her confident manner. According to Colton legend, one principal even threatened to shoot Colton, but when he thrust his hand into his pocket, "Colton looked calmly at him; he dropped his eyes and retired before her steady, honest gaze. Shortly afterward he closed his so-called college" (Tryon [1958], p. 22).

Colton was named president of SACW in 1914 and worked to secure legislation to restrict the indiscriminate chartering of degree-granting institutions. In 1918 only forty-two of the 357 institutions in the South with the legal right to confer baccalaureate and higher degrees conformed to the minimum requirements of standard colleges as formulated by the Southern Association of Colleges. Colton noted that "a large number that have not sufficient equipment to do even good high-school work are (to quote the advertisement of one of them) 'decorating their graduates with the highest college degrees'" (Talbot and Rosenberry [1931], p. 54). Efforts to pass strong legislation in the southern states to redress this situation met with little success. Colton's energies, however, were rewarded in other areas. As vice president of the Association of Colleges and Secondary Schools of the Southern States, she influenced policies for raising standards in higher education, and her efforts to raise the standards of southern women's higher education have been recognized by an AAUW fellowship in her name.

Ill health brought a premature end to Colton's work in 1919. She spent her last three years at Clifton Springs Sanitarium in New York. Perseverance remained a salient characteristic throughout Colton's life. A friend who visited her at Clifton Springs remarked, "She is nothing but a little wisp of courage" (*Meredith College Quarterly Bulletin* [June 1925], p. 61). At the insistence of the president and trustees of Meredith College, Colton did not officially resign there until 1923. The woman who became known as the "valiant crusader for women's education in the South" died in Clifton Springs, New York.

• In addition to papers on standards of women's colleges in the South, Colton published "Changes in English Usage between 1878 and 1902 as Shown in the Textbooks of an American Purist," *Modern Language Notes* 25 (Nov. 1910): 205–9. Biographical information is provided in Mary Lynch Johnson, *Elizabeth Avery Colton*, an undated 16-page pamphlet published by the N.C. Division of the American Association of University Women, and Johnson, *A History of Meredith College* (1956). Also consult Marion Talbot and Lois K. M. Rosenberry, *The History of the American Association of University Women* (1931), and Ruth W. Tryon, comp., *Names Remembered through AAUW Fellowships* (1958). A five-page typed sketch on Colton by Emily Helen Dutton (1930) is in the Schlesinger Library, Radcliffe College. Obituaries are in the *Journal of the AAUW* 18 (Jan. 1925): 17; the *Meredith College Quarterly Bulletin*, June 1925, pp. 60–66; the *Mount Holyoke Alumnae Quarterly*, Apr. 1925; the *News-Herald* (Morganton, N.C.), 28 Aug. and 4 Sept. 1924; and the *Biblical Recorder* (Raleigh, N.C.), 3 Sept. and 10 Sept. 1924.

KAREN L. GRAVES

COLTON, George Radcliffe (10 Apr. 1865–6 Apr. 1916), American colonial administrator, banker, and customs specialist, was born in Galesburg, Illinois, the son of Francis Colton and Frances A. Garey. Nothing is known about his parents' occupations. At seventeen Colton moved west to work on a New Mexico cattle ranch for five years before he entered the banking business in David City, Nebraska, as cashier, manager, and subsequently vice president of the Central Nebraska National Bank. He entered Republican politics in 1889 when he served one term in the Nebraska state legislature. He married Jessie T. McLeod in the same year; they had two children. In 1897 he was a Nebraska state bank examiner and an active member of the National Guard. When the Spanish-American War of 1898 began, Colton helped organize the First Regiment of Nebraska Volunteer Infantry. As lieutenant colonel he served with his regiment in the Philippines. When the war ended President William McKinley appointed him military deputy customs collector for Manila. In 1901 he was promoted to customs collector in Iloilo, the beginning of his distinguished career as an American colonial administrator specializing in tariffs, customs, and banking.

In 1904 the political and economic crisis in the Dominican Republic threatened to precipitate European intervention. President Theodore Roosevelt bought time by establishing an informal naval protectorate. In early 1905, when Roosevelt tried to formalize American control, the Senate regarded the agreement negotiated by naval commander Albert C. Dillingham as a secret treaty intended to diminish the Senate's traditional advise and consent role. Opposition to Roosevelt's Dominican policy reflected Congress's continuing resistance to the president's activist foreign policy.

When Congress deadlocked on the Dominican convention, Roosevelt went ahead anyway. His executive order on 1 April 1905 instituted a modus vivendi that formalized a U.S. naval protectorate, barred foreign intervention and domestic civil war, and put the bankrupt Dominican Republic under U.S. economic receivership. Roosevelt used the Dominican intervention to proclaim the Roosevelt Corollary to the Monroe Doctrine, under which the United States assumed responsibility for Western Hemisphere debt defaults and prohibited unilateral European intervention. Roosevelt appointed Johns Hopkins economist Jacob Hollander as special agent to negotiate a world debt settlement and Colton as the customs collector for the Dominican Republic under U.S. receivership.

Under the terms of the arrangement, Colton and his entire Philippine staff administered the twelve Dominican ports and instituted the first rigorous and honest customs system in the island. As part of the American settlement plan, Dominican revenues were divided, with 45 percent allocated for the expenses of the Dominican internal government and 55 percent to be paid in settling the long-term Dominican debt. This settlement money was deposited in escrow with the City National Bank in New York.

Virtually all of the Dominican revenues came from taxes levied on imports received at the twelve Dominican customs ports. Since 1900 the ports had made attractive targets for armed factions, who seized a port and its revenue until they were overthrown by another armed mob. By securing the ports, the United States ended the incessant war and enabled the island to return to normal economic life. Agriculture flourished and the tobacco crop doubled. With the end of the disastrous system of short-term loans and constant fiscal crisis, the new calm and order encouraged economic productivity. By the end of Colton's first year, revenue collections increased from $1.85 to $2.5 million. Colton's reports to his superior, Secretary of War William Howard Taft, are shrewd assessments of a volatile revolutionary culture from an American who clearly liked and sympathized with his Dominican charges.

Colton's domestic administration complemented Hollander's complex negotiations with American and foreign debtors to settle the Dominican debt for less than 50 percent of its original $41 million amount. Citizens of France, Spain, Belgium, the Netherlands, Great Britain, Germany, Italy, and the United States all held substantial amounts of the debt, which had multiplied after 1900 with compounded unpaid interest. Bondholder groups generally agreed to Hollander's proposal of a 50 percent settlement in cash, and the debt was settled for $17 million.

Colton's ability to end smuggling and honestly administer Dominican revenues assured the Europeans that eventually they would be paid their fair share. The American naval protectorate gave the island a respite from constant civil war. In 1907 Roosevelt and the Senate compromised their dispute, and the United States ended its economic and naval protectorate.

Colton returned to the Philippines as insular collector of customs, 1907–1909, writing a new Philippine tariff, which he convinced a reluctant special session of Congress to pass in 1909, a signal accomplishment. Colton also helped write the new Philippine tariffs in the Payne-Aldrich Tariff Revision Bill of 1909. When Taft succeeded Roosevelt as president, he appointed Colton governor of Puerto Rico, where Colton served until 1913.

In spite of a worldwide sugar recession in 1912, Colton's leadership of Puerto Rico was remarkably successful. He regarded the Puerto Ricans as a "patient, lovable people," whom disease and poverty had reduced to an "indescribably wretched existence." In his 1912 "Report of the Governor of Porto Rico," Colton compared the 1 school building and 26,000 students of 1898 with the 1,180 schools and 161,785 students of 1912. Illiteracy was reduced from 80 to 66 percent; a night school program dramatically reduced illiteracy among adults. The hookworm epidemic that infected almost half of the island was controlled with 60,000 complete cures.

Colton's idealism, superior administrative ability, and the American Progressive reform movement combined to give Puerto Rico a sympathetic and efficient government, reflected in its increased economic productivity. In trade Puerto Rico's exports increased from $8.5 million in 1901 to $49.1 million in 1913, not simply a form of American economic favoritism. Exports to non–U.S. sources equaled all Puerto Rico's exports of 1901. Colton spoke vigorously of the need to maintain quality control in prized Puerto Rican cigars and coffee and rigorously guard against counterfeits or shoddy goods. He was proud that the combined property value of the island doubled in four years. He remained dedicated to the inclusion of native Puerto Ricans in government and was able to make friends with the leading domestic politicians. Although he faced no effective political opposition, he rejected the role of aloof colonial governor.

When a Democratic government came to power in the United States in 1913, Colton's colonial administrative career ended. He returned to private banking in Washington, where he died.

Colton, a product of Roosevelt's Progressive Republican ethos, was a far different American from the stereotypical Yankee entrepreneurial predator. Like Roosevelt, he was sure that American political and economic systems would end colonial poverty and dependence, but both men underestimated the condescension inherent in American colonial paternalism. Colton also erred in his optimism that Progressive capitalism could nurture the tropical paradises he hoped to build, but his idealism and his expertise at least eased some of the problems of a poor region in a difficult transition to modern capitalism.

• Colton's letters to Secretary of War Taft are in the William Howard Taft Papers, Library of Congress. His "Annual Report of the Governor of Porto Rico, 1910–1913," are in *Annual Reports of the War Department* (1911–1914). A brief assessment is in Roberto H. Todd, *Desfile de gobernadores de Puerto Rico, 1898–1943*, 2d ed. (1966). The early biographical material is in George W. Colton, *A Genealogical Record of the Descendants of Quartermaster George Colton* (1912). Obituaries are in the Washington *Evening Star*, 7 Apr. 1916; the *Washington Post*, 8 Apr. 1916; the *New York Times*, 8 Apr. 1916; the San Juan *La Democracia*, 8 Apr. 1916; and the *Bulletin of the Pan-American Union*, Apr. 1916.

RICHARD H. COLLIN

COLTON, Walter (9 May 1797–22 Jan. 1851), clergyman, journalist, and author, was born in Rutland County, Vermont, the son of Walter Colton, a weaver, and Thankful Cobb. The family soon moved to Georgia, Vermont. Colton was apprenticed to a cabinetmaking uncle in Hartford, Connecticut, where in 1816 he joined the Congregational church. He attended classes at the Hartford Grammar School until 1818, entered Yale College, won a prize for excellence in Latin, and graduated as valedictorian poet in 1822. He studied at the Andover Theological Seminary, graduating in 1825. Later that year he became a Congregationalist evangelist and joined the faculty of the Scientific and Military Academy in Middletown, Connecticut, where he taught moral philosophy and belles-lettres and was chaplain. Publishing essays and poems signed "Bertram" in the Middletown *Gazette* provided an entrée into journalism.

In 1830 Colton resigned his professorship, moved to Washington, D.C., and was appointed by the American Board of Commissioners for Foreign Missions to edit the *American Spectator and Washington City Chronicle*. Its opposition to President Andrew Jackson's policy of expelling Indians from Georgia soon caused the paper's demise. But Jackson, friendly to Colton despite his politics, heard him preach, invited him to the White House, and appointed him to a naval chaplaincy. From January to the autumn of 1831 he was aboard the *Vincennes* in the West Indies. From early 1832 until December 1834 he served on the *Constellation* in the Mediterranean. In 1835 Colton became chaplain at the naval station at Charlestown, Massachusetts, and anonymously published *Ship and Shore; or, Leaves from the Journal of a Cruise to the Levant*. The volume was republished at least five times.

In 1837 Colton moved to Washington, D.C., to edit the *Colonization Herald* briefly and to prepare himself to become chaplain and historiographer of the South Sea Surveying and Exploring Squadron, but ill health forced him to resign before the fleet sailed. In early 1838 he was appointed chaplain of the Philadelphia naval yard. He coedited the *Independent North American* in 1841–1842, until its criticism of President John Tyler made his position untenable. In 1844 Colton married Cornelia Colton, a distant relative. (The couple evidently had no children.) The following summer conflict with Mexico loomed, and Colton was ordered to sea on the *Congress*, commanded by Commodore Robert Field Stockton and heading for Monterey, California, to reinforce the Pacific Squadron. Monterey had been seized from Mexico by the time the squadron arrived. In July 1846 Colton was appointed alcalde (chief justice) of Monterey by Commodore John Drake Sloat, civil governor and military commander of American forces in the region. Later that month Stockton replaced the aging Sloat. In August 1846 Colton, with help from Robert Baylor Semple, a rambunctious pioneer, founded the weekly *Californian*, the first newspaper in California. It was printed on a press seized from Mexican officials. When the weekly *California Star* began in Yerba Buena (now San Francisco) and Colton criticized its Mormon leanings, the *Star* editor replied by calling the *Californian* "a dim, dirty little paper" and labeled Colton "a lying sycophant." In September 1846 Colton was one of seven candidates running for alcalde and was confirmed by a plurality of 68 of 368 citizens' votes. In 1847 the *Californian* moved to San Francisco and became the *Alta California*.

Colton was an energetic judge and a versatile mentor. In handling cases of breach of the peace, business obligations, crimes, land-title disputes, and petitions for divorce, he combined California customs and U.S. common-law precedents. In September 1847 he empaneled the first jury assembled in California. Composed equally of Americans, Californians, and Mexicans, it heard a case of alleged theft of lumber, with evidence presented in English, French, and Spanish. At times Colton was required to be legislator and administrator as well as judge. He expressed fear of the absolute power the alcalde wielded and tried to weigh evidence carefully and be tolerant. He designed and supervised the building of the first schoolhouse. Classes were conducted on the first floor, while the second served as Monterey's town hall. Construction costs were defrayed by taxes on grogshops and fines imposed on gamblers, and convicts built the walls of cream-colored stones; the structure, Greek Revival in style, measured seventy feet by thirty feet. Named Colton Hall, it served for a time as the first state capitol. Colton also ordered his convicts to build their own prison, which they did so well that he pardoned several of the ablest workers.

In October and November 1848 Colton visited the southern gold mines, partly in the company of Colonel Richard Barnes Mason, civil governor and military commander of California, and Lieutenant William Tecumseh Sherman, his chief of staff. Colton, quite ill, was transferred in 1849 to the Philadelphia naval yard, published *Deck and Port; or, Incidents of a Cruise in the United States Frigate Congress* (1850; 4th printing, 1888), and completed his influential *Three Years in California, 1846–1849* (1850), dedicated to his friend Mariano Guadalupe Vallejo. In precarious health for some time, Colton died in Philadelphia. His big book on California, sometimes titled *The Land of Gold; or,*

Three Years in California, was often reprinted in the nineteenth century and at least twice in the twentieth.

Popular though they once were, Colton's books about his life as a naval chaplain have little appeal to modern readers. In *Ship and Shore* and *A Visit to Constantinople and Athens* (1836), Colton combines nautical facts, careful descriptions of faraway places, and comments on foreign people and their social and religious customs. *Deck and Port* counterpoints seven chapters of life at sea and seven chapters ashore—including sections on Rio de Janeiro, Valparaiso, Lima, and Honolulu. It is for his *Three Years in California*, however, that Colton will be remembered. In it he not only narrates, in journal form, little incidents and anecdotes in gripping detail—about soldiers, politicians, gold seekers and other laborers, gamblers, women, and convicts—but also reports at ground level events of enduring historical significance in and near Monterey, with its courteous and leisure-loving residents, before California was Americanized. Arriving pro-Anglo-Saxon, Colton soon saw the materialistic Yankee bringing violence and disrespect to an enchanting scene. In the years of its popularity, Colton's classic helped give California a new prominence in the eyes of a national readership, and it remains a valuable source for historians.

• Most of Colton's rather few papers are at the Henry E. Huntington Library, San Marino, Calif.; the libraries at the University of California at Berkeley, Stanford University, and Yale University; and the Historical Society of Pennsylvania, in Philadelphia. Colton's minor writings were collected in *The Sea and the Sailor, Notes on France and Italy, and Other Literary Remains of Rev. Walter Colton* (1851), a spotty miscellany, including poetry, "laconics," and a biographical sketch by Rev. Henry T. Cheever. Edward C. Kemble, *A History of California Newspapers 1846–1858* (1858; repr. 1962), discusses Colton's *Californian*. Laura B. Everett, "A Judge Lindsey of the 'Idle Forties,'" *Survey*, 5 Apr. 1913, pp. 24–27, offers high praise of Colton as alcalde. Colton's brother Gardner Quincy Colton, in *Boyhood and Manhood Recollections* (1897?), discusses his own brief stay in the gold mines. Brief mention of Colton, uniformly laudatory, is made in Hubert Howe Bancroft, *History of California* (7 vols., 1963–1970); David Lavender, *California: Land of New Beginnings* (1972); and Joann Levy, *They Saw the Elephant: Women in the California Gold Rush* (1990). The best extended discussion of Colton is in Kevin Starr, *Americans and the California Dream, 1850–1915* (1973). *California 1847–1852* (1956) reproduces drawings made while Colton was on the West Coast. An obituary is in the *North American and United States Gazette*, 23 Jan. 1851.

ROBERT L. GALE

COLTRANE, John (23 Sept. 1926–17 July 1967), jazz saxophonist and composer, was born John William Coltrane in Hamlet, North Carolina, the son of John Robert Coltrane, a tailor, and Alice Blair. Coltrane grew up in the High Point, North Carolina, home of his maternal grandfather, the Rev. William Blair, a distinguished figure in the African Methodist Episcopal Zion church. Coltrane's mother studied music in college, and his father was a country violinist; at age twelve Coltrane began to play the E-flat horn, then the clarinet in a community band, and he immersed himself in practice and study. In high school he discovered jazz and turned to the alto saxophone, influenced by the recorded work of Johnny Hodges in the Duke Ellington orchestra.

In 1939 Coltrane's father and Blair both died. After graduating from high school in 1943, Coltrane moved to Philadelphia to join his mother, who had migrated there in search of war work. Coltrane continued his musical studies before being drafted into the navy in 1945; he spent a year in the Hawaiian Islands playing clarinet in a military band.

Returning to Philadelphia in 1946, he discovered the bebop insurgency, figuratively led by Charlie Parker and Dizzy Gillespie, and he began working professionally around the city in various jazz and rhythm and blues bands. In 1947 the popular alto saxophonist Eddie "Cleanhead" Vinson hired him for his band on the condition that Coltrane play the tenor saxophone. This new instrument freed Coltrane from the dominant influence of Parker, and "a wider area of listening opened up for me . . . I drew from all the men I heard during this period, beginning with Lester [Young]."

In 1949 Coltrane joined the orchestra of trumpeter Dizzy Gillespie and performed on recordings for the first time. He became addicted to alcohol and heroin during this period, which periodically caused him to be fired from bands for unreliability, although he showed flashes of musical brilliance that won him the esteem of his peers. In 1954 he married Juanita Grubbs, who had changed her name to Naima after embracing the Muslim faith. After brief stints playing in the bands of Earl Bostic, Dizzy Gillespie, and one of his early idols, Johnny Hodges, Coltrane was hired in 1955 by trumpeter Miles Davis, then in the process of assembling the most influential small group of the decade. Despite some outstanding recorded performances during this period, Coltrane was fired yet again for his habits. In early 1957—following a confrontation with the young Philadelphia bassist Reggie Workman, who lamented that such an inspired figure could squander his gifts—Coltrane went into seclusion to battle his addictions and underwent what he later termed a profound spiritual conversion, manifest in the music he created over the remainder of his life.

Reunited with Davis in December 1957, he performed on some of the most influential recordings in modern jazz history, including *Kind of Blue*, an album exploration of Davis's interest in modal music, which opened vast new improvisational terrain. Coltrane's solos wed astonishing technical control with a powerfully innovative harmonic conception and blues feeling. Responding to criticisms of Coltrane's probing introspection, Davis explained: "What he does . . . is to play five notes of a chord and then keep changing it around, trying to see how many different ways it can sound. It's like explaining something five different ways."

By 1959 Coltrane was ready to lead his own group. The album *Giant Steps*—inspired in part by Coltrane's 1957 stint with the extraordinary composer-pianist Thelonious Monk—established him as a formidable creator of original music with surprising popular appeal for a jazz artist. His 1960 recording of the show tune "My Favorite Things" (on which he plays a haunting soprano saxophone) was a commercial hit and provided him with the leverage to support a permanent working quartet consisting of pianist McCoy Tyner, bassist Jimmy Garrison, and drummer Elvin Jones, whose thunderous sonorities provided the ideal counterpoint to Coltrane's exhausting forays into uncharted harmonic landscapes. During 1961–1962 multiple reed player Eric Dolphy often performed with the group; it was not unusual for Dolphy and Coltrane to trade solos lasting upward of three-quarters of an hour. To many listeners their work represented the fulfillment of jazz music's capacity to present the fullest range of human emotions through improvisational flights both highly vocal and of extraordinary technical complexity. To a number of critics, however, Coltrane threatened the conventions of the mainstream jazz that derived from the swing era; writer John Tynan even termed his music "anti-jazz."

Coltrane disdained the politics of jazz criticism and offered his music to a God who transcended denominational or cultural bounds. *A Love Supreme*, perhaps his best-known album recording, is a devotional work in four movements that recapitulates his spiritual journey since 1957. Unexpectedly, he found himself in the vanguard of a broad cultural movement inspired by the mystical traditions of diverse world religions. Coltrane's music was embraced by the 1960s counterculture, and he performed at large arenas to a new generation of fans not ordinarily attracted to jazz. Echoes of his music often appeared in rock songs, most notably in the Byrds' recording of "Eight Miles High." An album of collective free improvisation, *Ascension* (1965), seemed to place him in the camp of Ornette Coleman and other experimenting young musicians who abandoned chordal music and familiar melodic conceptions altogether. The members of his long-term quartet were gradually replaced by younger players committed to the "new thing," including pianist Alice McLeod, whom Coltrane married shortly after divorcing his first wife in 1966, and with whom he had three children. The music grew more mystical and less rooted in traditional jazz; at the same time, however, Coltrane's health deteriorated. He died of liver cancer in Huntington, Long Island.

Coltrane exerted a profound influence over several generations of musicians and listeners. Musically, he combined, as journalist Lawrence Christon explained, "a fierce energy and an affecting poetic tone . . . his technique of arpeggiation, in which he broke chords into their constituent notes and piled them and their variants into voluminous runs of unprecedented height and depth, opened the instrument's range." Saxophonist Archie Shepp, noting Coltrane's stature as the key transitional figure in jazz in the era following that of Charlie Parker, exclaimed that he bridged "the old and new like a colossus."

Coltrane was also a pioneering exponent of "world music," especially the sounds of Africa, India, and the Middle East. His mysticism embraced the contradictory hope and anger many Americans experienced in the 1960s; as Indian sitarist Ravi Shankar put it: "I was much disturbed by his music. Here was a creative person who had become a vegetarian, who was studying yoga and reading the Bhagavad-Gita, yet in whose music I heard much turmoil." Although Coltrane generally abstained from public political statements, his anguish is deeply felt in recordings like "Alabama," dedicated to four young girls killed in 1963 when racists bombed a Birmingham church. A quiet man with a passionate sound, his music, as drummer Roy Haynes put it, "was like a beautiful nightmare." Coltrane's genius, energy, and passion made him a central figure in the tumultuous cultural life of the United States in the 1960s.

• Three biographies of John Coltrane appeared within a year of each other in the mid-1970s. They are highly personal and tend more toward hagiography than criticism; each is valuable, although none can be considered even remotely definitive. See Bill Cole, *John Coltrane* (1976); C. O. Simpkins, *Coltrane: A Biography* (1975); and J. C. Thomas, *Chasin' the Trane: The Music and Mystique of John Coltrane* (1975). See also the brief study by Brian Priestley, *John Coltrane* (1987). For an evaluation of Coltrane's contributions to the jazz avant-garde, see John Litweiler, *The Freedom Principle: Jazz after 1958* (1984).

JAMES TERENCE FISHER

COLUMBO, Russ (14 Jan. 1908–2 Sept. 1934), popular singer, motion-picture star, and radio and recording artist, was born Ruggiero de Rudolpho Columbo in San Francisco, California, the son of Nicholas Columbo, a musician who had immigrated to the United States from his native Naples near the turn of the century, and Mariana or Maria (maiden name unknown). Educated initially in the elementary schools of San Francisco, young Ruggiero Columbo attended high school in Los Angeles, where his parents had relocated in 1921. While at Los Angeles's Belmont High, where he played violin in the school band, he anglicized his first name and became known as Russ Columbo.

An accomplished violinist by age sixteen, Columbo left high school to join a traveling-show band, hoping to follow in his father's footsteps by becoming a professional musician. A teenager with high aspirations, he initially wanted to become a concert violinist (which he tried briefly, but to no great acclaim), although his pleasant singing voice soon led him to consider an operatic career instead. At his father's urging he began studying with a Los Angeles operatic coach, Alexander Bevani, who found promise in the young man's lyric-baritone voice and well-grounded musicianship.

To sustain himself during this period of intense study, Columbo found steady work as a violinist in a number of Los Angeles area hotel dance bands. These

regular and occasionally lucrative engagements allowed him to support his voice lessons while also contributing to the support of his parents' home, which he shared with eleven older brothers and sisters. Often doubling as a violinist and vocalist, Columbo progressed from the orchestras of the Mayfair and Roosevelt hotels to the Cocoanut Grove in Hollywood, where the popular bandleader Gus Arnheim held court. Although Arnheim already had a vocalist on the payroll when Columbo joined the band as a violinist, the rising popularity of Arnheim's singer, Bing Crosby, paved the way for Russ Columbo to replace him when the band toured the United States in 1929–1930.

By the end of the year-long tour Columbo's own star was rapidly ascending, and he left the Arnheim organization to start his own band at the Silver Slipper in Los Angeles. There he met Con Conrad, a published songwriter, who encouraged Columbo to include some of the singer's own compositions on the radio broadcasts that he was performing with his new band. Two of the songs that Columbo wrote yielded immediate dividends: "You Call It Madness (But I Call It Love)" and "Prisoner of Love," both of which were published in 1931. "You Call It Madness" introduced Columbo to East Coast radio audiences that year when he moved to New York, at Con Conrad's urging, and accepted a radio contract from the National Broadcasting Company. "Prisoner of Love" not only served Columbo well on radio and recordings (which he had begun making exclusively for RCA Victor) but was also revived successfully by Perry Como in 1946, and again in 1963 by soul-music pioneer James Brown.

Throughout the early 1930s Columbo and his predecessor with the Gus Arnheim band, Crosby, made highly successful recordings of the same songs, often within months of one another. Some were introduced to the public by Crosby, as was the case with "A Faded Summer Love," which Crosby recorded on the Brunswick label in 1931, and "Temptation," which he introduced in the 1933 film *Going Hollywood*. However, many songs became equally associated with Columbo through his radio broadcasts and Victor recordings. This rivalry, most of which appeared to be friendly, soon gave rise to what the press labeled the "Battle of the Baritones." The rivalry also extended to Hollywood, where Columbo returned in 1932 to appear in the film *Broadway Through a Keyhole*, released the following year. In 1934 he starred in two additional films, *Moulin Rouge* and *Wake Up and Dream*.

Columbo remained in Hollywood after *Wake Up and Dream* was finished, staying with his parents in a lavish home that he had built for them. Now at the height of his career, he anticipated making additional films and radio appearances, though he still harbored operatic aspirations. On Sunday, 2 September 1934, he stopped to see a long-time friend, Hollywood photographer Lansing Brown, with whom he planned to have dinner. As the two sat talking in the photographer's study, Brown was absentmindedly fingering the trigger of a French dueling pistol from an antique gun collection he had bought several years earlier.

Suddenly, a long-forgotten powder charge ignited, disgorging a leaden ball that careened about the room. In an instant, the ball struck Columbo in the forehead and lodged in his brain. He died a few hours later, never regaining consciousness.

• Although Columbo left no memoirs, his career is profiled in Alec Wilder, *American Popular Song: The Great Innovators, 1900–1950* (1972), and Henry Pleasants, *The Great American Popular Singers* (1974). The circumstances of his death were recounted in newspapers coast to coast, the most complete accounts appearing in the *New York Times* and the *Los Angeles Times*, both 3 Sept. 1934.

JAMES A. DRAKE

COLUMBUS, Christopher (?–20 May 1506), explorer, was born in the Republic of Genoa, the son of Domenico Colombo, a weaver, and Susanna Fontanarossa. His early life is poorly documented. A date of birth late in 1451 or 1452 would be consistent with verifiable facts. Brought up in Genoa and Savona, he went to sea, by his own report "at an early age," though in 1472 he was still working in his father's business. In 1478 he was employed by the Lisbon branches of the Centurione and diNigro firms of Genoese merchants, buying sugar for Genoa in Madeira. By that time his normal place of residence was in Lisbon but only romanticized traditions of how he got there survive. Probably toward the end of the 1470s, he married Felipa Moniz Perestrelo, daughter of the deceased explorer and hereditary captain of the island of Porto Santo, Bartolomeu Perestrelo. This was, as far as is known, the first big step in his ascent from the humble rank of society in which he was born.

The extent of his navigation before 1492 is much debated but, by his own accounts, included Iceland, Galway, and (by reasonable inference) Bristol in the north; Chios in the east; the Azores and Madeira group in the Atlantic (to which the Canaries may be added by inference); Tunis; and, in the south, the Portuguese fort of São Jorge da Mina (modern Elmina), founded in 1482 on the Gold Coast.

Also much debated is the chronology of his process of self-education. The earliest date mentioned in the marginal annotations of his surviving books is 1481, though the significance of this has been questioned; the evidence of perusal by the late 1480s is beyond cavil. He never became confident of his own learning and always tended, in debate with savants, to defend himself as a man of practical sagacity or revealed knowledge. But by 1492 he had acquired a certain plausibility and later in the 1490s had a reputation at the Castilian court for erudition in navigation and cosmography. To judge from his surviving books and evidence of the sources of influence on his own writings from 1492 onward, his reading included geography, astronomy and astrology, travel literature, chivalric romance, hagiography, eschatological prophecy, and Scripture.

According to tradition, he began in 1484 to seek patronage in Portugal for a voyage of exploration in the Atlantic. Certainly by the spring of 1486 he was seeking such patronage in Castile; in May of that year he had his first recorded interview with King Ferdinand and Queen Isabella in Cordova. Atlantic exploration had made much progress in the course of the fifteenth century, and projects to extend it were afoot in the 1480s in Bristol and the Azores; the possible objectives were a commonplace subject of speculation among geographers and cartographers. Columbus's own plans had not yet taken definitive form. At different times, addressing different prospective patrons, he seems to have put forward at least three different proposals: first, a journey in search of undiscovered islands, such as had often been made into the Atlantic during the fifteenth century; secondly, an attempt to discover the hypothetical "antipodean" continent, located by some classical authorities (and by humanistic geographers and cartographers) in the western ocean—just such a new continent, indeed, as America ultimately proved to be; and, thirdly, a voyage in search of a direct transoceanic route to the extremities of the Orient, perhaps via the island of Cipangu, reported by Marco Polo.

Of these projects, the first two were of doubtful profitability, the third of doubtful practicality. Among the potential patrons unsuccessfully approached by Columbus and his brother, Bartolomeo (always known in Castilian orthography as Bartolomé), up to 1492 were the monarchs of Portugal, Castile, France, and perhaps England.

During the late 1480s and early 1490s, however, a powerful group of supporters came together at the Castilian court in favor of Columbus, though his own self-image as the hero of a lonely struggle against indifference and derision has obscured the process. His backers included political lobbyists—members of the household of Prince Juan, heir to the throne, and members of the mendicant orders, especially the Observant Franciscans, who were influential at court. Perhaps even more important were the financial investors: Genoese and Florentine merchants and bankers in Seville, and a group of treasury officials concerned with the administration of revenues from the sale of indulgences, from which financiers of Columbus's enterprise would ultimately be indemnified. Some of Columbus's backers had already collaborated in financing conquests in the Canary Islands. He also secured the support and participation of leading members of the Pinzón shipping family of Palos. Martín Alonso and Vicente Yáñez Pinzón were to be unruly fellow captains on the transatlantic voyage. The Castilian monarchs, anxious for new sources of riches, were open to persuasion: their conquest of Granada, completed in January 1492, was costly, and the enviable wealth acquired by Portuguese rivals from access to the African gold trade made a short route to the proverbially lucrative commerce of the East seem attractive.

When Columbus received a royal commission for his Atlantic voyage in April 1492, his objective was vaguely stated to be "islands and mainlands in the Ocean Sea"; it is evident from his own records, however, that he sailed from Palos on 3 August with the conscious purpose of discovering a western route to Asia, "by which," he wrote, "no man, as far as we know, has ever sailed before."

Since the discovery of the outermost islands of the Azores in 1452, various voyages of Atlantic exploration had been commissioned in Portugal, but none made any recorded successes because they were launched from the Azores in the belt of westerly winds. Columbus was bold or foolhardy enough to sail with the wind at his back, via the Canary Islands. Departing after victualing and repairs from San Sebastián de la Gomera on 6 September 1492, he set his course due west and maintained it, assisted for most of the time by the northeast trade winds, for over a month. The voyage into the unknown bred a tense atmosphere in which Columbus quarreled with his fellow officers and feared mutiny. Eventually, under pressure from Martín Alonso Pinzón, he turned southwest on 7 October, making a landfall in the New World very early on the twelfth, probably in the Bahamas or, perhaps, the Turks and Caicos. Claims on behalf of particular islands are not justified by the evidence.

During a cruise of three months in the Caribbean, Columbus made a vivid but often fantastic and romanticized record, substantial fragments of which have survived. He described Cuba and Hispaniola as well as some smaller islands and recorded conflicting perceptions of the inhabitants, seeing them at times as semibestial savages, at others as models of sylvan innocence or dependence on God; at times as potential slaves to be exploited, at others as souls to be saved. Those of Hispaniola (Arawak Taínos) he was inclined to praise as remarkable civilized beings bearing implicit promise of great civilizations near at hand.

Treating as providential the grounding of his flagship on the north coast of Hispaniola on Christmas Day 1492, he left thirty-nine men behind on terms of apparent amity with the locals. The discovery of what seemed exploitable amounts of gold toward the end of his stay was encouraging, but he fell out with Martín Alonso Pinzón and displayed obvious anxiety at his inability to find conclusive evidence of the proximity of Asia. His priorities became increasingly religious as he contemplated the future evangelization of the people he discovered. On 14 February 1493, during a storm-wracked voyage home, he had the first of a series of experiences of the presence of God, when a "celestial voice" comforted him, as it was to do recurrently in future crises of his life.

Martín Alonso died, exhausted by the voyage, almost immediately on reaching Spain; Columbus's return, by contrast, was triumphant. Extricating himself from Portuguese captors in the Azores in February and from the blandishments of the king of Portugal in Lisbon in March, he reached the presence of the monarchs of Castile in Barcelona in April 1493. Though some observers withheld belief that he could have reached Asia after so short a voyage, the exotica he brought aroused universal admiration. The monarchs confirmed his promised titles of *Don* and hereditary Viceroy and Governor and Admiral of the Ocean Sea and commissioned him to return to his discoveries as soon as possible. They published their claims to possess the lands (which Columbus had formally proclaimed on the spot) and initiated appropriate suits at the papal and Portuguese courts.

The return voyage to Hispaniola, departing 25 September 1493 in a large and expensive fleet, was the high point of Columbus's career. Leaving the Canaries behind on 13 October, he essayed a new route to the southwest, more directly in the path of the wind, and reached Dominica on 3 November. As a result of this voyage he established the best routes possible to and from his discoveries: indeed, with only slight modifications, these remained the standard routes throughout the age of sail. He discovered a string of islands in the Lesser Antilles, Puerto Rico, and Jamaica and reconnoitered much of the coasts of Cuba and Hispaniola.

Yet he also proved incompetent as a colonial administrator, shying from his responsibilities, breeding insurrection, and wasting resources. His discoveries, moreover, seemed disappointing. The natives, whose "docility" he had praised, proved hostile; the climate, which he had likened to "spring in Andalusia," proved lethal; the profits uncertain; and Asia elusive.

He returned to Spain to defend himself successfully against growing criticisms in 1496. On a third voyage, commissioned in 1498, he again experimented with a new route, via the Cape Verde Islands, leaving São Tiago on 4 July and reaching Trinidad on the last day of the month. The voyage again produced great discoveries: the mainland of South America, correctly classified by Columbus as an enormous continent; Trinidad; the Orinoco delta; the Pearl Coast of Venezuela. But the colony on Hispaniola was so rebellious that when a royal administrator arrived in the late summer of 1500, Columbus was shipped home in disgrace. This sort of experience was not unusual for a servant of the Castilian monarchy in this period; it was intelligible in Columbus's case in the context of a contemporary campaign of anti-Genoese xenophobia in Spain. And although Columbus never recovered the monarchs' full confidence or favor, he was formally exonerated and—by any standards but his own—amply rewarded.

The rest of his life, however, was clouded by resentment. He argued that he really had got close to Asia; partly on the grounds that he had proved it by his (wildly inaccurate) attempts to measure his longitude by timing eclipses in 1494 and 1498; secondly on the basis of an underestimate by about 25 percent of the true size of the world, justified by garbled reading of evidence, mostly collected in the early fifteenth-century *Imago Mundi* of Pierre d'Ailly; and thirdly on the assumption that his third voyage had taken him to the environs of the earthly paradise (associated with the end of the Orient in medieval cartography and hagiography). He waged a tireless campaign of lobbying for increased rewards, claiming, with some justice, that the monarchs had not fulfilled the contract implied in the terms of their original commission to him.

He grew increasingly religious, compiling in 1500–1501 a collection of mostly biblical prophecies that, he averred, were divine foreshadowings of his own discoveries.

Tired of his importunities, the monarchs commissioned a final voyage, on which Columbus departed from Gran Canaria on 25 May 1502. Though not conclusive, the evidence strongly suggests that Columbus's aim was to leave his earlier discoveries at his stern and go on to reach unquestionably oriental lands. Forbidden to put into harbor at the Hispaniola colony, he survived a hurricane on 30 June and made the first recorded crossing of the Caribbean, arriving off Bonacca Island on 30 July; he was particularly proud of this achievement, which he attributed to celestial navigation, "which is like a kind of prophetic vision." He remained on the coast of the Central American isthmus until 1 May 1503, exploring it as far as the Maracaibo region: the effect, in combination with voyages further east and south by other explorers since 1499, was to establish that the coast of the New World was continuous from the Gulf of Honduras at least as far as Rio de Janeiro. Columbus discovered the gold-rich province of Veragua and the harbor—of future importance—of Porto Bello and professed himself satisfied that he was in a region contiguous with or joined to Asia. Almost throughout the voyage, however, he battled terrible weather and termites holing his ships' hulls. Attempting to cross to Hispaniola, the expedition just made it to Jamaica, where they went aground in St. Ann's Bay on 25 June. They remained marooned until June of the following year, while Columbus contended with mutineers and cajoled food from the natives. The rescue was effected by a subordinate, Diego Méndez, who crossed to Hispaniola by canoe to procure help.

Columbus arrived back in Spain on 7 November 1504, less than three weeks before the death of Queen Isabella of Castile, whom he considered one of his most important patrons. He resumed his lobbying at court, unleashing a series of self-pitying memoranda. His pleas of poverty were much exaggerated, for he was gaining a fortune from his royalty on the gold of Hispaniola. His complaints of ill health, however, were convincing. In May 1505 he managed to make a painful journey to court in person. Ferdinand—now regent in Castile—received him in the early summer but without conceding his claims to enormously inflated rewards. When the new king and queen arrived from Flanders in April 1506, Columbus wrote, promising greater service than ever, but he was already virtually on his deathbed. He died in Valladolid, leaving an heir, Don Diego Colón, and, by a long-lasting liaison with Beatriz Enríquez of Córdova, who also survived him, an illegitimate son, the distinguished man of letters Don Fernando Colón.

Columbus's principal achievement was the discovery of fast, reliable, and exploitable routes both ways across the Atlantic, which linked the shores of the ocean for the rest of the age of sail and inaugurated the continuous history of transatlantic navigation. He was also the founder of the first enduring European colony in the New World and the author of the first written descriptions of the environments of the central Atlantic and of any part of America. As an explorer he was remarkable—indeed, up to his day, unique—for the extent of his navigation and for his additions to geographical tradition.

• The main collections of Columbus's papers, some of which survive only in early copies or abstracts, are in the Biblioteca Nacional and the Archivo de la Casa de Alba, Madrid, and the Archivo General de Indias, Seville. The most reliable biographies are W. D. Phillips and C. R. Phillips, *The Worlds of Christopher Columbus* (1992), and Felipe Fernández-Armesto, *Columbus* (1991). Important contributions have been added by David Henige, *In Search of Columbus* (1991); B. W. Ife, *Letters from America: Columbus's First Accounts of the 1492 Voyage* (1992); V. I. J. Flint, *The Imaginative Landscape of Christopher Columbus* (1992); and Consuelo Varela, *Cristóbal Colón: Retrato de un hombre* (1992). A good review of the vast literature on Columbus is Foster Provost, *Columbus: An Annotated Guide to the Scholarship on His Life and Writings, 1750–1988* (1991).

FELIPE FERNÁNDEZ-ARMESTO

COLVOCORESSES, George Musalas (22 Oct. 1816–3 June 1872), naval officer, was born on the Greek island of Chios, the son of Constantine Colvocoresses and Franka Grimaldi. In 1822 he was kidnapped by Turks, who massacred most of the Greek population of the island, and was taken to Smyrna. His father, who survived the slaughter, ransomed him with the assistance of relatives. Seeing little hope for the boy's future in Greece, the elder Colvocoresses seized an opportunity through the Greek Relief Committee to put his son on board the U.S. brig *Margarita* in company with nine other boys, bound for Baltimore, Maryland. Once in the United States, young George Colvocoresses was received into the family of Captain Alden Partridge, who was head of a military academy in Norwich, Vermont, and was educated in preparation for a naval career.

On 21 February 1832 Colvocoresses was appointed midshipman in the navy and in 1836–1837 was attached to the famous old frigate *United States*, which was part of America's Mediterranean Squadron. In 1838 he was commissioned passed midshipman and in August sailed with Captain Charles Wilkes from Norfolk, Virginia, on the latter's South Seas and Antarctic exploring expedition. Over the next three years he served on the *Porpoise*, *Peacock*, *Vincennes*, and *Oregon* and visited the Cape Verde Islands, various seaports in South America, Tàhiti, Samoa, New South Wales, Antarctica, Fiji, and Hawaii. In 1841 he took part in an overland trek from Vancouver Island to San Francisco as an extension of the Wilkes expedition. Rejoining the squadron at San Francisco, he sailed with Captain Wilkes westward to Manila, Borneo, Singapore, the Cape of Good Hope, and St. Helena Island, finally reaching New York on 10 June 1842. A decade later he published a popular account of his adventures, *Four Years in a Government Exploring Expedition*, that by 1855 had gone through five editions.

On 7 December 1843 Colvocoresses was promoted lieutenant. During the Mexican War, 1844–1846, he served with the Pacific Squadron. In May 1846 he married Eliza Halsey, with whom he had four children. Returning to duty, he was with the Mediterranean Squadron, 1847–1849, then on a vessel off the African coast, 1851–1852, and on shore duty at New York, 1853–1855. That last year he joined the East India Squadron as executive officer of the *Levant*. In November 1856 he commanded a party that captured the barrier forts in the Canton River, below the city of Canton, China. He returned to the United States in 1858, where for the next two years he did duty at Portsmouth Navy Yard. On 1 July 1861, shortly after the outbreak of the Civil War, he was promoted commander and put in charge of the storeship *Supply* off the Atlantic Coast. While on this duty, he captured the Confederate blockade runner *Stephen Hart*, which was laden with arms and military stores. In 1863 he took command of the sloop-of-war *Saratoga* in the South Atlantic Blockading Squadron off the Georgia coast. His ship not being very handy at blockading, he drilled his crew in preparation for harassing raids against tempting enemy installations on shore. A year later, in August 1864, he led his well-trained men in three successful landing parties, capturing fifty-five Confederate soldiers and earning the thanks of his commanding officer, Rear Admiral John A. Dahlgren, in general orders. A month later he was withdrawn from Dahlgren's squadron, over the protests of the admiral.

In 1865 Colvocoresses was sent to the Pacific Squadron off the west coast of South America as commander of the sloop-of-war *St. Mary's*. At Valparaiso, Chile, in 1866, he warned off a Spanish fleet that was threatening to bombard that town, claiming that American property was endangered. Later, while Colvocoresses was otherwise employed, the Spanish fleet, with scant military justification, brutally bombarded Valparaiso but did not affect much damage. On 11 January 1867 he was promoted to captain and retired from active duty.

Colvocoresses settled in Litchfield, Connecticut, with his second wife, Adeline Swasey, whom he had married in 1863 upon the death of Eliza Halsey Colvocoresses. Possessing an appealing personality and a sharp wit, he employed his time over the next five years giving popular lectures on his adventures as a naval officer. He was murdered in Bridgeport, Connecticut, by thieves who gunned him down as he was boarding a coastal steamer for a business trip to New York.

• Correspondence of Colvocoresses during the Civil War is in the *Official Records of the Union and Confederate Navies in the War of the Rebellion*, ser. 1, vols. 2–3, ser. 2, vols. 15–19, 27 (1895–1927). William Arba Ellis, ed., *Norwich University, 1819–1911: Her History, Her Graduates, Her Roll of Honor . . .* , vol. 2 (1911), gives a short sketch of his life. His son, George Partridge Colvocoresses, describes important events in his career in a letter to the *Portsmouth* (Va.) *Star*, 2 May 1923. For the Wilkes expedition, see David B. Tyler, *The Wilkes Expedition: The First United States Exploring Expedition, 1838–1842* (1968), and William Stanton, *The Great United States Exploring Expedition of 1838–1842* (1975). An obituary is in the *New York Herald*, 5 June 1872.

PAUL DAVID NELSON

COLYAR, Arthur St. Clair (23 June 1818–13 Dec. 1907), industrialist and politician, was born in Washington County, Tennessee, the son of Alexander Colyar and Katherine Sevier Sherrill, farmers. As a boy Colyar moved with his parents to Middle Tennessee, where he received a country-school education in Coffee and Franklin counties. He later read law while teaching school and was admitted to the bar in Winchester in 1846. Colyar married Agnes Erskine Estill in 1847; they had eleven children before she died in 1886. In 1888 he married Mary McGuire.

Colyar played a leading role in building the Tennessee Coal and Railroad Company, the firm that eventually developed Birmingham, Alabama, into the largest iron and steel center in the South ("Iron" was added to the name of the company in 1881). Before the Civil War, Colyar forced the company, then named the Sewanee Mining Company, into bankruptcy by bringing suit for nonpayment on behalf of contractors who had built a short rail line. He later bought out other creditors and took charge of the firm.

Colyar was also keenly interested in politics, beginning as an outspoken Whig in a Democratic county. In 1860 he campaigned for the Constitutional Unionist presidential candidate, John Bell, and opposed secession. When Tennessee left the Union, however, he sided with the Confederacy. Although often called Colonel Colyar, he apparently never commanded troops. A member from 1864 of the Confederate House of Representatives, where he served on the Ways and Means Committee, Colyar opposed the Confederate government suspension of habeas corpus in East Tennessee, western North Carolina, and Southwest Virginia and supported enlistment of black troops in the Confederate army and opening peace talks with the Union.

After the war Colyar moved his law practice to Nashville. Taking control of the Tennessee Coal and Railroad Company in 1866, Colyar strengthened its competitive position by leasing state convicts to work in company mines, an arrangement that markedly lowered labor costs. By 1874 TC&RR mines accounted for 45 percent of Tennessee coal production, employed 320 (half of them convicts), and ran twenty-one miles of railroad. Colyar resigned as TC&RR president in 1876 and gave up control of the company in 1881. Also in 1876 Colyar organized a new company in the iron business partly owned by TC&RR and by the Nashville and Chattanooga Railroad Company.

Colyar remained active in politics in the postwar period but held no public office after 1865 except to fill a vacant state legislative seat for a partial term in 1877. During Reconstruction he challenged the Republican city government by persuading a judge to appoint a receiver for the city. Although he was a former Confederate officeholder, he declared in the late 1860s that the Conservative-Democratic party should attract black voters rather than disfranchise them, which could anger northern investors. Nevertheless, until about 1890 he was frequently at odds with powerful Tennessee Democrats, in part because of his Whig background but also because his political views often supported his business interests. Colyar advocated the use of convicts in mines, took an inflationist position on the currency question, preached sectional reconciliation in the interest of industrial development, and urged rapid settlement of the state debt.

In 1870, for example, Colyar was briefly an independent candidate for governor, until the Democratic nominee agreed with him on repudiating secession and allowing the use of convicts as cheap labor in mines. Two years later Colyar allied with Liberal Republicans unhappy with President Ulysses S. Grant's corrupt administration and Reconstruction policy. Colyar again announced as an independent for governor, only to withdraw five weeks later. He supported Andrew Johnson for Congress, telling the ex-president that he wanted to find a middle way between the unreconstructed secessionists and the Radical Republicans.

From 1876 to 1882 Colyar was active in a controversy over the state debt, which had been incurred during the antebellum and Reconstruction periods, first siding against most Democratic leaders, who insisted on paying every dollar. During another unsuccessful race for the Democratic nomination for governor in 1878, Colyar used the rhetoric of party insurgents: he said the real issue was the "money power," which had "made the people jealous and fearful" and wanted "to humiliate, humble, and degrade labor" (*Memphis Avalanche*, 1 Nov. 1878). By 1882 he had moved toward the political center to help reunite the divided party around a compromise position on the debt.

After helping pull Democrats together on the debt issue, however, Colyar resumed his independent ways. With Republican help, he wrecked a new state railroad commission backed by leading Democrats, and being a Methodist and lifelong teetotaler, he campaigned for prohibition, a measure more favored by Republicans than by Democrats, in a statewide referendum in 1887. Colyar was one of the most important Tennessee backers of the New South movement for industrial development. As editor of the *Nashville Union*, he called foes of a New South "a great drawback. They don't want any manufacturing done in the south, because it will put up the price of farm labor. They believe the south ought to have the ways of an aristocracy, money or no money." He praised Governor Robert Love Taylor for favoring a Republican bill for federal aid to education, saying the governor was "in the front rank in the onward march of the new south" (*Nashville Union*, 22 Feb. 1886 and 11 Feb. 1887). His view contrasted with that of the dominant Bourbon faction of Tennessee Democrats. Colyar also fought the agrarian Farmers' Alliance and harshly attacked governor John P. Buhanan, an Alliance member and a

Democrat, blaming him for a protest in 1892, during which free miners released convicts working in mines. Colyar backed Republican H. Clay Evans against a conservative Democrat in a disputed gubernatorial election in 1894.

Although Colyar had promoted immigration of laborers while he was involved in coal mining, he later expressed nativist views, writing after the violent 1886 incident at Haymarket Square in Chicago that immigrants were spreading anarchism. "American institutions must remain American," he declared (*Nashville Union*, 7 May 1886). In the mid-1890s Colyar supported the anti-immigrant American Protective Association, which forced the Democratic party to withdraw a Catholic candidate in Nashville.

Colyar demonstrated as little partisan attachment as any leading Tennessee public figure of his era. He published a laudatory *Life and Times of Andrew Jackson: Soldier—Statesman—President* (1904), which emphasizes the general's military exploits. Why did ex-Whig, sometimes Greenbacker Colyar choose a hard-money Democrat as his hero? Perhaps he admired Jackson for his willingness to confront his foes. When Colyar died in Nashville, his hometown newspaper eulogized him at length but felt compelled to say that a "man of his temperament and views could not escape quarrels and enmities" (*Nashville Tennessean*, 14 Dec. 1907). Despite his career in business, Colyar was not a notably wealthy man at the end of his life.

• Colyar's papers are not collected in one place; a few of his letters are in the Andrew Johnson Papers, Library of Congress. He wrote "Sketch of the Author," in John Haywood, *The Civil and Political History of the State of Tennessee from Its Earliest Settlement up to the Year 1796*, 2d ed. (1891; repr. 1969), and many editorials in the *Nashville Union* in the mid-1880s. Clyde L. Ball, "The Public Career of Colonel A. S. Colyar, 1870–1877," *Tennessee Historical Quarterly* 12 (1953): 23–47, 106–28, 213–38, covers much of Colyar's business and some of his political career. Roger L. Hart, *Redeemers, Bourbons, and Populists: Tennessee, 1870–1896* (1975), touches on several political episodes involving Colyar. An obituary is in the *Nashville Tennessean*, 14 Dec. 1907.

ROGER L. HART

COMAN, Katharine (23 Nov. 1857–11 Jan. 1915), economic historian and social reformer, was born in Newark, Ohio, the daughter of Levi Parsons Coman and Martha Seymour. An abolitionist and leader of a voluntary group serving in the Civil War, Katharine's father held various occupations, including those of teacher, storekeeper, and lawyer. Because of poor health he moved his family to a farm near Hanover, Ohio, after the Civil War. Both of Katharine's parents had college degrees, her father from Hamilton College and her mother from an Ohio seminary. Consequently, they sought good educations for all their children, male and female alike. As a young girl, Katharine took lessons in Latin and mathematics along with her brothers. She first attended Steubenville Female Seminary, but when the school refused to give her more challenging studies, Levi Coman moved his daughter to the high school of the University of Michigan. She later entered the university and received a bachelor of philosophy degree in 1880.

Hired following graduation as a faculty member teaching rhetoric at Wellesley College, Coman advanced to professor of political economy and history by 1883. In 1900 her title changed to professor of economics and sociology when she developed a separate department of economics. During the 1899–1900 school year, Coman also served as dean of the college. In addition to her academic duties, Coman participated in various social reform movements and pioneered the college settlement movement. A great organizer and administrator, Coman met with a number of women graduates in 1887 and founded an organization that would later become the College Settlements Association. She served in the national organization from 1900 to 1907 as president of the electoral board and chairman of the standing committee. In this capacity she was partially responsible for setting up a fellowship program that allowed female college graduates to spend at least a year at an association settlement house.

In 1890 Coman helped to establish a young working girls' club in Boston. As chairman of the Boston Settlement Committee, in 1892, she helped to open Denison House, a settlement house in the city's South End that became a hub for labor organizing. Fixing her attentions on labor activities, Coman also provided work for unemployed seamstresses by setting up a cooperative shop. A member of the executive committee of the Massachusetts Consumers' League from 1899 to 1905, she worked for better conditions for women factory workers by providing the public with information on the conditions and by asking consumers to put pressure on manufacturers. Her quest to improve the lot of laborers brought her to Chicago in 1910. There she joined the striking seamstresses who sought union recognition and chaired the grievance committee of the Women's Trade Union League. Coman then launched a publicity campaign citing the reasons for the strike, which ended in 1911.

Coman also pursued her skills as a writer and editor. With coauthor Elizabeth Kendall, she wrote *The Growth of the English Nation* in 1894 for the Chautauqua Reading Circle series. The two joined forces again in 1899 to produce *A History of England for High Schools and Academies*. In 1902 Coman coedited *English History Told by English Poets* with Katharine Lee Bates. Her writings on economics include a monograph on contract labor in Hawaii, published in 1903 by the American Economic Association, and a textbook titled *The Industrial History of the United States* (1905), which appeared in a number of editions during the next fifteen years. Coman also taught a course on the industrial history of England and America. In 1912 her two-volume work *Economic Beginnings of the Far West* was published. Research for many of her works forced Coman to travel—to England, Alaska, Hawaii, and along the fur trade routes to interview men who had experienced the historic days of the western United States.

An Episcopalian who was temperate in her beliefs, Coman sometimes attended socialist meetings, although she herself was not a socialist. She never married or had children. After illness forced her to retire from Wellesley in 1913, she turned to volunteer work in the National Progressive Service division of the Progressive party. A promoter of old age and unemployment insurance, she traveled to Europe in 1914 to obtain information on how social insurance programs operated in England, Spain, Denmark, and Sweden. Given only months to live, Coman canceled her plans to travel to Germany. Despite her continuing battle with cancer, she returned home to write and published a series of articles in *Survey* magazine. She died of cancer in Wellesley, Massachusetts. *Unemployment Insurance: A Summary of European Systems* was published after her death in 1915. In 1922 Bates, a close friend with whom Coman had lived for many years, published *Yellow Clover*, a collection of sonnets written for Coman.

A family legacy that stressed education prompted Coman to dedicate her life to enlightening young women by teaching them independent thinking and self-reliance. In teaching and outside the academic environment she applied economics to industry, bringing to light the problems facing workers, immigrants, and consumers. Because of her insightful teaching methods many of her graduating students aided the community through social service work. Whether she taught in the classroom or met with the girls in small groups, Coman infused her students with enthusiasm and showed them the human side to economics and history.

• Some of Katharine Coman's letters can be found in the Jane Addams Papers in the Swarthmore College Peace Collection. In addition to the books listed in the text, Coman also authored several articles and reviews, which appeared in a variety of scholarly periodicals. For a sample see "Some Unsettled Problems of Irrigation," *American Economic Review* (Mar. 1911): 1–19. Few biographical sources on Coman exist. Katharine Coman, ed., *Memories of Martha Seymour Coman* (1913), is helpful and offers insights into the author's childhood and later career. See also Alice Henry, *The Trade Union Woman* (1915); Vida Scudder, *On Journey* (1937); Florence Converse, *Wellesley College* (1939); Alice P. Hackett, *Wellesley, Part of the American Story* (1949); Dorothy Burgess, *Dream and Deed: The Story of Katharine Lee Bates* (1952); Mercedes M. Randall, *Improper Bostonian: Emily Greene Balch* (1964); Lois Stiles Edgerly, ed., *Women's Words, Women's Stories* (1994); and Patricia Ann Palmieri, *In Adamless Eden: The Community of Women Faculty at Wellesley* (1995), all of which contain information about Coman's life and career. The yearly reports of the National Consumers' League and the College Settlements Association also offer insight into Coman's reform efforts. An obituary by Olga S. Halsey in *Survey*, 23 Jan. 1915, provides the most valuable biographical information.

MARILYN ELIZABETH PERRY

COMBS, Earle Bryan (14 May 1899–21 July 1976), baseball player and coach, was born in Pebworth, Owsley County, Kentucky, the son of James J. Combs, a farmer, and Nannie Brandenburg. Owsley County, by-passed by the railroads that came to eastern Kentucky in the 1880s, offered little to its residents except a chance to scrape out a living on small, hillside farms. Combs's father encouraged his children to go into teaching, and in 1917 Combs traveled some fifty miles to enter Eastern Kentucky State Normal School in Richmond. He soon became an admired figure there. Personable and a good student, he gained acclaim on the track, basketball, and baseball teams. To finance his education he taught between terms in a one-room Owsley County school. Forty pupils crowded in, rang-ing in age from six to sixteen. Realizing he could earn more by playing semiprofessional baseball than his $37.50 a month teaching salary, Combs in 1921 joined the team in the Harlan County, Kentucky, coal com-pany town of Highsplint. To qualify to play, he went on the company payroll as a carpenter's assistant.

After the 1921 season, Combs also played with a Lexington, Kentucky, semipro team. Attracting the attention of the Louisville Colonels of the American Association, he joined the team in 1922 and was placed in left field by manager Joe McCarthy. Six feet tall and about 180 pounds, Combs quickly became a standout. His skills were raw, but he was a consistent hitter and used his speed to advantage in the outfield. In that same year Combs married Ruth McCollum. The couple were to have three sons.

By 1923 it was assumed that Louisville would sell Combs to the Cleveland Indians, Cincinnati Reds, New York Giants, or New York Yankees, all of which had scouted him. Combs's .380 batting average com-pared favorably with American Association stars Al Simmons and Bill Terry, who also were being watched by major league teams. Early in 1924 the Yankees closed a deal for Combs, giving the Colonels $50,000 and two players for his contract.

A fractured ankle suffered in June cut short Combs's rookie season, and it was not until 1925 that he became a fixture in the New York outfield between Bob Meusel and Babe Ruth. Combs soon became one of the brightest young stars in the American League, batting leadoff and effectively covering Yankee Stadi-um's spacious center field. A weak throwing arm was his one liability. The 1927 Yankees, considered by many to be baseball's greatest team, won the American League championship by 19 games and swept the Pittsburgh Pirates in the World Series. Combs hit .356 while leading the American League in plate appear-ances, hits, and triples. The Yankees won four pen-nants (1926–1928 and 1932) during Combs's nine sea-sons as the team's center fielder. A left-handed hitter, he batted .300 or higher in eight full seasons, and for eight consecutive years he hit more than 30 doubles and scored more than 100 runs.

By 1934 Combs's best years were behind him, and he was moved to left field. In a July 1934 road game against the St. Louis Browns, he crashed into the con-crete outfield wall, fracturing his skull, breaking a col-larbone and arm, and injuring one shoulder. Listed in critical condition, he remained hospitalized for six weeks. He rejoined the Yankees in 1935, but another shoulder injury, sustained when a teammate collided with him in the field, ended his season in August. He retired that November with a .325 career batting aver-age. Combs had not been flamboyant, but he won the admiration of his managers and of sportswriters for his skills, humility, hard play (he was sidelined during his career by four serious injuries), and quiet leadership. He remained with the Yankees as a coach for eight years.

Combs left the Yankees following the 1943 season to return to his home near Richmond, Kentucky. He had long owned farm land there and was involved in other local businesses. In 1947 he returned to baseball as a coach with the St. Louis Browns and then with the Boston Red Sox (1948–1952). He spent a final season as a coach with the Philadelphia Phillies in 1954 before retiring permanently to become more fully involved in business and public service. He was a regional manag-er for an insurance company, served a two-year term as a state banking commissioner, and for many years was a trustee at his alma mater, which became Eastern Kentucky University. A dormitory there is named for him. Elected to the National Baseball Hall of Fame in 1970, he died in Richmond, Kentucky.

• A scrapbook of Combs's career and a small collection of let-ters are located in the archives of Eastern Kentucky Universi-ty. See also John Mosedale, *The Greatest of All: The 1927 New York Yankees* (1974); Ira L. Smith, *Baseball's Famous Out-fielders* (1954); Henry C. Mayer, "A Kentucky Yankee," *Ru-ral Kentuckian*, Apr. 1986; David M. Vance, "From Peb-worth to Cooperstown: The Success of Earle Combs," *Eastern Kentucky University Alumnus*, Spring 1970; and John J. Ward, "The Greatest Lead-Off Man in the American League," *Baseball Magazine*, Dec. 1927. An obituary is in the *New York Times*, 22 July 1976.

LLOYD J. GRAYBAR

COMER, Braxton Bragg (7 Nov. 1848–15 Aug. 1927), industrialist and governor of Alabama, was born at Spring Hill in Barbour County, Alabama, the son of John Fletcher Comer, a planter and lumberman, and Catherine Drewry. Comer was one of the cadets at the University of Alabama who fired on federal troops be-fore they burned the university in the Civil War. He later completed his college training at Emory and Henry, graduating in 1869. In 1872 he married Eva Jane Harris; they had eight children including Donald (born James MacDonald) and Hugh, the sons who took over the family's textile mills. After a brief foray in plantation management, Comer moved to Anniston and organized a wholesale grocery and commission business. Five years later, in 1890, he moved to rapid-ly growing Birmingham. In the "Magic City" he built a grist mill, became a banker, and organized Avondale Mills, which was to become the basis of his fortune.

Attracted to Progressive ideas as a shipper who ob-jected to the exorbitant and discriminatory rates charged by the railroads, Comer was among successful advocates in 1903 of legislation for a stronger Alabama Railroad Commission. The strengthened commission gave no relief, however, and he campaigned successfully for the chairmanship of the commission despite vigorous railroad and press opposition. Frustrated by the resistance of other members of the commission, Comer entered the race for governor in 1906. Most of the press favored his opponent, Russell M. Cunningham, although the Birmingham *News*, with the largest circulation in the state, favored Comer. The railroads, anticipating a Comer victory, focused on electing a legislature opposed to railroad rate reform. Cunningham was an old-style orator, who soothed his audiences with tributes to the beauty of Alabama women and the valor of Confederate soldiers. Recalling his cadet resistance to the Union army at the University of Alabama, Comer countered that he was a Confederate veteran, but he based his campaign on railroad abuses. Despite having been tagged as a "radical" and a wealthy man, quite an anomaly for Alabama, he won decisively.

The 1907 legislature, elected with Comer, was overwhelmingly loyal to the governor and his demands for railroad rate reform. The legislature dutifully passed legislation giving the commission authority to set rates, outlawing free passes, and making other rail reforms. The legislature rejected, however, a Comer proposal, reflecting the governor's puritanical Methodism, to forbid the movement of freight trains on Sunday, except for those carrying perishables. The railroads shifted the fight to the federal courts, where Judge Thomas G. Jones, former governor of Alabama and an apostle of laissez-faire, presided. Jones enjoined the enforcement of the new regulatory laws, declaring unconstitutional the transfer of the legislature's rate-making power to the railroad commission. Jones's injunction was dissolved by the circuit court of appeals, and the U.S. Supreme Court refused to review the decision. Constitutionally ineligible for reelection, Governor Comer returned in 1911 to his business interests until 1914, when he made a new bid for the gubernatorial nomination. His major opponent, Charles Henderson, bested him in the campaign, maintaining that the reduced rail rates were unfair. While Governor Henderson surrendered much of the ground that Comer had won against the railroads, Comer had at least established the principle of regulation.

Comer's achievements in education were equally remarkable. Alabama's educational system was crippled by poverty and an antiquated taxation system. His ambitious program of educational reform raised the appropriations for education substantially and resulted in the designation of Comer as the "education governor." Notable among the governor's achievements was the expansion of the very limited high school system through the creation of county high schools. Substantial increases in appropriations were made for normal schools, higher education, and the medical college in Mobile, an institution newly acquired by the state. The state textbook commission was reorganized, and a uniform series of textbooks was adopted. The governor failed, however, to secure passage of even a mild compulsory education bill—evidently the opposition feared the increased expenses of educating African Americans. The governor's reforms included improvements at mental institutions and the boys' reformatory, and Confederate veterans' pensions were increased. The period of Comer's governorship was one of quiescence in race relations. There is no evidence that he sought fundamental racial reforms and only limited evidence that he sought more generous appropriations for black institutions—a familiar pattern of southern reformers.

Comer's programs were expensive and he soon exhausted the state's financial surplus. As a remedy he secured the creation of a state tax commission to supervise tax assessments and equalize property values. The tax commission greatly increased state revenues. The assessment for taxes in 1910 was about a half billion dollars, up from slightly more than a third of a billion in 1906. Comer was successful in getting a franchise tax passed, but his efforts to place a tax on out-of-state corporations were negated by a Supreme Court decision that the measure was discriminatory. The success of the tax commission was inadequate to balance Comer's budgets, and the state showed constantly increasing deficits.

Despite being a textile manufacturer, Comer signed into law the second Alabama child labor law; its provisions were so mild, however, that national child labor leaders maintained that he was no friend of child labor reform. Even so, Comer's Avondale Mills had above-average working conditions. In 1907 Comer signed another child labor law, increasing the minimum age of employment from ten to twelve and requiring children between the ages of twelve and sixteen to attend school for a minimum of two consecutive months during the school term. Comer also advanced better health conditions by signing into law measures to regulate the practice of medicine, provide for an epilepsy colony, and expand the medical school. Although a bill was approved to establish a sanitarium for tuberculosis patients, the institution was never built because of a shortage of funds. Although Comer showed little interest in court reform, he approved the first juvenile court law for Alabama, thus segregating juvenile offenders from adults. Despite his enthusiasm for the Good Roads movement, Comer believed that road-building was the province of the counties. He approved of legislation, preliminary to the Seventeenth Amendment, favoring popular election of U.S. senators.

A staunch advocate of prohibition, Comer signed a bill for local-option prohibition in 1907. In 1909 he called the legislature into special session to write prohibition into the constitution and to pass a tough enforcement law. In the special election that followed, constitutional prohibition was defeated—an indication of anti-Comerism or the feeling of the electorate that it was surfeited with his reforms. The election was a harbinger of his defeat by Charles Henderson in 1914. In 1920 Governor Thomas E. Kilby appointed Comer to the U.S. Senate to fulfill the unexpired term of Senator John H. Bankhead. Saddened by the death of his wife on the second day of his senatorial service in 1920, he did not attempt to succeed himself. In 1924 he married Mary Carr Gibson of Verbena, Alabama.

Comer enjoyed the political combat of his fights for reform. Appropriately, his favorite sport was hunting wild game. "Whatever trophies I have had in life, either in politics or business," he said, "have come from hard work—the game worth while is above the timber line." Comer was a Progressive in a state relatively little affected by that movement. He died at his home in Birmingham. As historian Allen Going has said, "he was a man of action and not a conciliator." Lacking the forensic arts of the demagogues, Comer was not typical of southern Progressives. A man of great personal wealth and uninterested in some key Progressive goals such as road improvement and judicial reform, he was *sui generis*. He is frequently compared to Theodore Roosevelt as a scrappy, wealthy, patrician reformer.

• Comer's papers are in the Southern Historical Collection at the University of North Carolina at Chapel Hill. Excellent unpublished materials include Owen H. Draper, "Contributions of Comer to Public Education in Alabama" (Ph.D. diss., Univ. of Alabama, 1970), and Allen J. Going, "Governorship of B. B. Comer" (master's thesis, Univ. of Alabama, 1940). See also John C. Stewart, "Braxton Bragg Comer," in his *The Governors of Alabama* (1975), pp. 155–60; Thomas M. Owen's entry on Comer in *History of Alabama and Dictionary of Alabama Biography*, vol. 3 (1921), pp. 384–88; Marie Bankhead Owen's entry on Comer in her *Story of Alabama: A History of the State* (1949); James F. Doster, *Railroads in Alabama Politics, 1875–1914* (1957); and Sheldon Hackney, *Populism to Progressivism in Alabama* (1961). An obituary is in the *Birmingham Age-Herald*, 16 Aug. 1927.

EVANS C. JOHNSON

COMFORT, Will Levington (17 Jan. 1878–2 Nov. 1932), newspaperman, war correspondent, and novelist, was born in Kalamazoo, Michigan, the son of Silas Hopkins Comfort, a Civil War veteran, and Jane Levington. He was raised in Detroit. Comfort later claimed (perhaps falsely) that he was educated at home and "on the street," that he grew up too fast and too hard. He bragged that he had begun writing at age six and drinking at age sixteen. In his autobiographical *Midstream* (1914), Comfort shocked the genteel tradition of literature by writing that his life was "marked" by "maimed homecomings" from war and by women, drink, and dishonor. It is apparently true that, at least in his final years, he became an alcoholic and a believer in the occult, but he started out as a Methodist boy who attended grammar school and high school in Detroit and even completed a part of a semester (1900–1901) in Albion College's preparatory department. He also moved from paperboy to cub reporter on Detroit and Cincinnati newspapers.

Comfort was twenty years old when he indulged in a life of adventure resembling that of Jack London. After the beginning of the Spanish-American War (1898), he enlisted in the Fifth U.S. Cavalry, hoping to be sent to the Philippine Islands theater of operations. Although these hopes were dashed when he fell ill with both malaria and typhoid fever in an army camp in Tampa, Florida, he did get to Cuba, where he received his discharge.

Returning to newspaper work in Detroit in 1898 or 1899, Comfort began freelance writing, but the *Detroit Journal* syndicate sent him to the Philippines as a war correspondent when the Spanish-American War in the Far East turned into the Philippine Insurrection. In 1900 he married Adith Duffie-Mulholland; they had three children. Comfort edited a daily column for the *Pittsburgh Dispatch* and continued to write fiction, using his own experiences as story material. Like London, he was sent to the Far East in 1904 to cover the Russo-Japanese War as a war correspondent, not only for the *Dispatch* but also for other papers via the *Dispatch*'s syndicate.

Comfort's first book was a collection of short stories, *Trooper Tales: A Series of Sketches of the Real American Private Soldier* (1899). The book is a realistic portrayal of the life of enlisted cavalrymen (including the forgotten black troopers) and their mounts, from the Rio Grande border to Cuba's San Juan Hill. To draw this portrait Comfort skillfully mixed fiction with factual material, drawing on his own army experience. His first novel, *Routledge Rides Alone* (1910), revealed a surprising antiwar attitude in the adventurer. The book was enough of a success to turn Comfort into a prolific full-time author, and he began to produce a novel a year. In two of his next novels, *Down among Men* (1913) and *Red Fleece* (1915), he again revealed the pacifist streak in his adventurous nature. Ultimately Comfort wrote twenty novels, one collection of stories, and six other miscellaneous books.

Around 1918 Comfort moved to Los Angeles and made his permanent home in the Highland Park district. Most of his work was behind him by the mid-1920s, at which time his attention turned to East Indian occultism. Critics commented that his mysticism weakened his narrative power, one reviewer dismissing the "new" Comfort as a "scoutmaster" suddenly "discovering Emerson." H. L. Mencken, who liked Comfort's "capital melodramas" and occasional eloquence, dismissed him now as a propagandizer for a Victorian, sentimentalized Bhagavad-Gita.

In 1925 Comfort finally found his proper setting: the desert Southwest. He wrote *Somewhere South in Sonora* that year and followed it with *Apache* in 1931. *Apache* was by far his best and most memorable book, although the merits of *Trooper Tales* endure.

Apache is the fictionalized life of Mangas Coloradas, or Red Sleeves, the first of a line of Apache war chiefs who tried to protect their country against invasion by whites. Comfort avoided all of the traps of sensationalizing, romanticizing, and idealizing the chief of the Mimbreño band of Apaches, and he did not lapse into a sociological or psychological treatment of his subject. Instead he created a remarkably true-to-life portrait of Mangas. An anonymous reviewer in the *Times Literary Supplement* ranked *Apache* in a class with Oliver La Farge's Pulitzer Prize–winning book *Laughing Boy*.

Incredibly, Comfort wrote *Apache* in just eleven weeks after visiting his son John, a newspaperman in Bisbee, Arizona. En route, Comfort stopped off in Tombstone and discovered a file of John P. Clum's newspaper the *Epitaph*. Instead of using its material on outlaws and the O. K. Corral shoot-out, Comfort was inspired to write of the desert's Apache defenders in the hope that the novel might rival *Laughing Boy*. In a testimony to the success of *Apache*, La Farge himself, who was one of its reviewers, said, "It is rare indeed for a white man to penetrate behind the alien mind and . . . state clearly what he has found. . . . He has created for us the real Indian . . . in a manner that few scientists and no other writers have achieved."

J. Frank Dobie, in his *Guide to Life and Literature of the Southwest*, rated *Apache* as the most incisive and moving piece of writing about the Southwest's Indians that he had ever read. Lawrence Clark Powell agreed, designating it one of his *Southwest Classics*.

Comfort followed *Apache* with his last novel, *The Pilot Comes Aboard* (1932), in which he abandoned the desert for a sea setting. He died in Los Angeles, apparently suffering from alcoholism.

• Comfort's few surviving papers are in the Special Collections Department of the library of the University of California, Los Angeles. Sketches of Comfort are in Dan L. Thrapp, comp., *Encyclopedia of Frontier Biography*, vol. 1 (1988); Geoff Sadler, ed., *Twentieth-century Western Writers*, 2d ed. (1991); and *Who's Who in America* (1928–1929). An obituary is in the *New York Times*, 4 Nov. 1932.

RICHARD H. DILLON

COMINGORE, Dorothy (24 Aug. 1913–30 Dec. 1971), actress, was born Margaret Louise Comingore in Los Angeles, California, the daughter of William Paxton Comingore, an electrotyper at the *Los Angeles Times*, and Bernadette Woessner, a seamstress. Around 1923 the family moved to Oakland, where William opened a printing shop. While a student at Castlemont High School, Comingore became active in the school drama society and starred in several plays. She also served as literary editor of the yearbook. After graduating in December 1930, Comingore planned to enroll in college and become a reporter. However, the Great Depression forced a change of plans. She went to work in sales at H. C. Capwell's, a store in Berkeley, but managed to audit classes in literature, art, and philosophy at the University of California, Berkeley. There she met Robert Meltzer, the editor of the acclaimed campus humor magazine *The Pelican*, with whom she lived and traveled for the next several years.

In 1938 Comingore was "discovered" by Charlie Chaplin, whose enthusiastic response to her performances in two productions of the Carmel little theater, *Cradle Song* and *The Night of January 16*, was reported in the press. Warner Bros. subsequently hired her but offered her only "leg shots" and a small role in a film, *Campus Cinderella* (1938), under the name Kay Winters. During the next two years Comingore had minor parts, as Linda Winters, in several films at Columbia, including *Blondie Meets the Boss* (1939), *North of the Yukon* (1939), *Scandal Sheet* (1939), *Pioneers of the Frontier* (1939), *Cafe Hostess* (1939), and *Rockin' through the Rockies* (1939), with the Three Stooges. She also had a small walk-on part in the Frank Capra classic *Mr. Smith Goes to Washington* (1939) and in the forgettable *Trade Winds* (1939), scripted by Dorothy Parker and Alan Campbell. In 1939 Comingore married screenwriter Richard Collins, with whom she had a daughter and a son. A chance date with Orson Welles, arranged for publicity purposes, helped Comingore win a screen test for *Citizen Kane*. The tests were so good that one of them, the El Rancho nightclub interview, was incorporated directly into the finished film.

Citizen Kane opened to critical acclaim in May 1941, and Comingore's gritty performance as the whiny, untalented Susan Alexander Kane established her as a gifted, intelligent actress. The New York Film Critics nominated her for consideration as one of the ten best actresses of 1941, along with Greta Garbo and Joan Fontaine, while *Box Office* magazine voted her an award of merit and the *Hollywood Reporter* predicted that *Kane* "should make this girl a big star!"

Yet there were no major roles forthcoming after *Kane*, and Comingore repeatedly turned down parts she felt were demeaning or otherwise unsuitable. These refusals earned her numerous suspensions and a growing reputation as "difficult." RKO suspended her permanently in the summer of 1942. She did appear in an episode of the radio show *Stars over Hollywood* titled "To Everyone Once" (1942) and played opposite Susan Hayward and William Bendix in a film version of Eugene O'Neill's *The Hairy Ape* (1944). She also performed in an ill-fated Broadway stage show, *Beggars Are Coming to Town* (1945). For the most part, however, she devoted herself to caring for her two young children. In 1946 she divorced Collins and married writer Theodore Strauss, with whom she had a second son.

Besides the difficulty in 1940s Hollywood of combining marriage and motherhood with a career, Comingore's role in *Kane* and her left-wing politics may also have worked against her professional success. Because she played "the Marion Davies character," Comingore was the most vulnerable of all the performers in *Kane* to the ire of William Randolph Hearst, who reportedly felt angriest at the film's negative portrait of his lover. Whether or not Hearst used his considerable influence with conservative Hollywood studio bosses to obstruct Comingore's career, J. Edgar Hoover targeted both Welles and Comingore for surveillance as subversives just months after the opening of *Kane*. The Federal Bureau of Investigation entered charges in her file of "distributing Communist propaganda to Negroes," and Hoover personally ordered her included in his card file of candidates for "custodial detention." In fact, both Welles and Comingore were active in the Hollywood left. During the early 1940s Comingore participated in such left-wing organizations as the Citizens Committee to Defend Mexican-American Youth, later reorganized as the Sleepy

Lagoon Defense Committee, and the Hollywood Anti-Nazi League. She also lent her support to the American Committee for Soviet Friendship and several other groups concerned with fighting racism and promoting U.S.–Soviet relations during World War II. Whether she ever joined the Communist party, as did her first husband, is unclear.

In 1949, after a five-year lapse, Comingore returned to film with a small but affecting cameo role in *Any Number Can Play* (1949), directed by Mervyn LeRoy. Her career appeared to be reviving as she had major parts in a *Fireside TV Theater* production, "Handcuffed" (1951), and in Joseph Losey's last American-made film, *The Big Night* (1951). She was also earning cult status as an actress whose voice and persona may have influenced performers such as Judy Holliday and Marilyn Monroe.

But in the Fall of 1952, recently divorced from her second husband, Comingore suffered a series of devastating losses. In October of that year, with the Hollywood blacklist in effect, she was called to testify before the House Un-American Activities Committee (HUAC). Unlike her former husband Collins, a cooperative HUAC witness, Comingore refused to name names. Instead she delivered an eloquent defense of free speech, immediately ending her career in Hollywood as a result. The following month Comingore lost her two oldest children to Collins in a bitter custody battle in which her politics and noncooperation with HUAC, as well as her alcoholism, were cited as evidence of her "unfitness" as a mother. Six months later she suffered a highly publicized arrest for prostitution.

Comingore's drinking and personal difficulties did not begin with her blacklisting, but they were clearly intensified by the surveillance, suspicion, denunciations, and accusations directed at the Hollywood left. Following her March 1953 arrest, she voluntarily entered Camarillo State Hospital for treatment. Released two years later, Comingore left Los Angeles for the East Coast, spending the last decade of her life in Stonington, a small, conservative town on the coast of Connecticut. She continued to write letters and send whatever support she could to the civil rights, peace, and farmworkers' movements, though she could no longer participate in protests on account of severe neck and back pain. In 1962 she married postal worker John Crowe. Four years later she reunited with her son Michael Comingore Collins, a filmmaker. She had no regrets about her life, acknowledging to a friend that "essentially the problem of becoming a *mensch* remains the same." She died of cancer in Stonington.

• Kirk Crivello, "The Second Mrs. Kane: Dorothy Comingore," *Focus on Film* 9 (Spring 1972), offers a somewhat inaccurate profile and useful filmography. Robert Palm, "Falling Star," *Connecticut Magazine*, June 1980, is a fine elegiac portrait of Comingore. Larry Ceplair and Steven Englund, *The Inquisition in Hollywood: Politics in the Film Community, 1930–1960* (1979), mentions Comingore's activism in the 1940s. Matt Weinstock's column in the *Los Angeles Times*, 12 May 1953, gives a sympathetic account of the "inquisitorial mood" facing Comingore in court. Obituaries are in the *New York Times*, 31 Dec. 1971; the *Washington Post*, 1 Jan. 1972; and the *Los Angeles Times*, 2 Jan. 1972.

ALICE RUTH WEXLER

COMISKEY, Charles Albert (15 Aug. 1859–26 Oct. 1931), professional baseball player and team owner, was born in Chicago, Illinois, the son of John Comiskey, a civil servant, building contractor, and politician, and Mary "Annie" Kearns. He attended St. Ignatius Preparatory School in Chicago before moving on to St. Mary's College in Kansas. Comiskey was a catcher for the baseball team at St. Mary's in 1873. Although he advertised his skills as a pitcher, he attained prominence in professional ball as a first baseman. Historians of the sport cannot agree whether it was Comiskey or Cap Anson of the Chicago White Stockings who developed the strategy of fielding ground balls while playing well off first base, but Comiskey and Theodore P. Sullivan conceived the idea of a "motion" defense on the infield's right side in which the pitcher covered the base on ground balls hit to the right of the first baseman. Sullivan, a forgotten star of the nineteenth-century game, encouraged Comiskey to play baseball as a full-time career and signed him to his first professional contract in 1879 with the Dubuque Rabbits of the Northwestern League. The league collapsed after three years, and Comiskey signed with the St. Louis Browns of the newly formed American Association. The Browns' eccentric owner was Chris Von der Ahe, whose flair for promotion and hucksterism set him apart from more conservative owners. Von der Ahe's commitment to providing first-class accommodations for fans influenced Comiskey in later years. He was to accord the same respect and courtesies to his bleacher patrons as he did to box-seat holders. In 1882 he married Nancy Kelly; they had one child.

Appointed full-time team manager in 1885, Comiskey, while still a regular player, guided the Browns to four consecutive American Association titles (1885–1888). The Browns' 1886 victory over the heavily favored Chicago White Stockings in a forerunner of the modern World Series established Comiskey as a national sporting figure. Although considered to be a management-oriented player, Comiskey bolted the American Association in 1890 to play for the Chicago "brotherhood" team in the short-lived Players League, which consisted of rebellious athletes who had broken away to protest the reserve clause binding a man to one team for life. Comiskey later explained that he had to act in this way to "remain square with the boys."

When the Players League folded after the 1890 season, Comiskey returned to St. Louis, only to witness the demise of the American Association in 1891. With his playing skills eroded by advancing age, he became player-manager of the Cincinnati Reds. While he held the National League in low esteem and correctly blamed the league's owners for driving the American Association and the Players League to insolvency, he reluctantly agreed in 1892 to owner John T. Brush's terms.

Together with Cincinnati sportswriter Ban Johnson, Comiskey forged the American League from an amateur confederation known as the Western League, which Johnson served as president beginning in 1894. In 1895, when his contract with Brush expired, Comiskey purchased the struggling Sioux City, Iowa, team and moved it to St. Paul, Minnesota. The Western League gradually gained strength through the decade, and in 1899 Johnson and Comiskey drew up an ambitious plan to challenge the National League. The key was the transfer of Comiskey's St. Paul team to Chicago, a major city that would help put the Western League on the map. Despite considerable vocal opposition from National League owners, the move was completed in October 1899, and the rechristened American League, with Comiskey's new Chicago White Stockings as the pivot, began play in 1900.

Comiskey spent lavishly to procure established players from National League teams. Playing in a small wooden enclosure on the South Side, he built an enormous following among Chicago's Irish-American residents. With his team's surprise victory over the powerful Cubs in an all-Chicago World Series in 1906, Comiskey established himself as the city's most beloved sports figure—an image that fans held until well after his death.

Comiskey reaped the harvest of a favorable press, an exciting winning ballclub, and the public's admiration. But with the opening of Comiskey Park in 1910, all of his apparent blessings began to change. Comiskey was proud of his palatial steel and concrete stadium, but the ballpark was poorly located and flawed in design. Although it was hailed by Ben Shibe, owner of the Philadelphia A's, and other baseball magnates of the time, as an architectural marvel when it opened, its fortress appearance and massive size that favored pitchers over hitters, as well as the changing ethnic and racial dynamic of the South Side, doomed it to obsolescence. Attendance fell off dramatically in 1928 and continued declining through the years. A losing ball club, coupled with the perception that the racially changing South Side communities were unsafe, were both factors. The White Sox would ponder a move out of Chicago four times: 1968, 1975, 1980, and 1987.

On a celebrated world tour in 1913–1914, Comiskey and John McGraw of the New York Giants took their teams on a goodwill junket to promote baseball in Asia and Europe. It was the last hurrah for Comiskey, who built the greatest White Sox team of them all, only to see it decimated in September 1920 when charges surfaced that eight White Sox players conspired to throw games to the Cincinnati Reds in the 1919 World Series. Other owners, such as Connie Mack and Clark Griffith, had also forced their players to labor under a "plantation" system that required players to have their own uniforms laundered and to accept substandard salaries. Furthermore, the owners had done little to keep gamblers out of their stadiums since the 1870s. In this sense the Black Sox scandal had been simmering for years.

Baseball historians have long regarded Comiskey as a tightfisted misanthrope whose shabby treatment of eight underpaid ballplayers contributed to the scandal. His penury, which may have led to the conspiracy, tarnished his overall career in professional baseball. What is often overlooked by his critics is the warm affection and high regard accorded him by fans during his lifetime. The "Old Roman," as he was commonly known after 1900, commanded the unflagging loyalty of reporters and fans, who adopted the neighborhood baseball park as the focal point of community life.

The scandal deeply affected Comiskey. The eight players were banned from the game for life in 1921 by baseball's first commissioner, Judge Kenesaw Mountain Landis. The White Sox became an also-ran in the 1920s, and increasingly the owner sequestered himself in his northern Wisconsin hunting cottage. Comiskey's wife died in 1922, which led to his slow decline. He did not live to see his White Sox regain the competitive edge they once enjoyed. Not until the early 1950s, when his grandson Charles Comiskey II was in charge, would the team achieve the success of the period from 1900 until 1920.

Comiskey died in Eagle River, Wisconsin. He left a sizable fortune and control of the White Sox to his only son, John Louis. In 1939 he was elected to the Baseball Hall of Fame.

• The only full-length biography is Gustav Axelson's *Commy: The Life Story of Charles A. Comiskey* (1919), a highly sympathetic account of Comiskey's career that reflects prevalent attitudes of the day. The Baseball Hall of Fame Library, Cooperstown, N.Y., contains an extensive file of newspaper and magazine clippings. Written as a historical novel, blending fiction and fact, Eliot Asinof's *Eight Men Out: The Black Sox and the 1919 World Series* (1963), first exposed Comiskey as a petulant, penurious tyrant. Richard C. Lindberg portrays Comiskey as a product of his times in *Stealing First: The White Sox from Comiskey to Reinsdorf* (1994) and *Who's on Third? The Chicago White Sox Story* (1983). Standard White Sox histories discuss Comiskey's career in more general terms. See, for example, Warren Brown, *The Chicago White Sox* (1952), and David Condon, *The Go Go Chicago White Sox* (1960). Anthology collections containing biographical sketches include Lee Allen and Thomas Meany, "Charles Comiskey," in *Kings of the Diamond* (1965), pp. 221–22; Ira L. Smith, "Charles Comiskey," in *Baseball's Famous First Basemen* (1956), pp. 18–26; and Jim Charlton and Mike Shatzkin, eds., *The Ballplayers* (1990), pp. 214–15. Comiskey was profiled or he expressed his own views in many magazines and journals over the years, including issues of *Baseball Magazine*, Apr. 1909, Feb. 1914, Mar. 1915, Feb. 1917, and May 1919; *American Magazine*, Mar. 1911; *Literary Digest*, 8 Apr. 1922; and *Baseball Digest*, Oct. 1942 and Apr. 1945. For a lucid discussion of the Black Sox affair and Comiskey's handling of the scandal, see Harold Seymour, *Baseball: The Golden Years* (1971), and Victor Luhrs, *The Great Baseball Mystery: The 1919 World Series* (1966). For Comiskey's baseball statistics, see Macmillan's *Baseball Encyclopedia*, 9th ed. (1993), and John Thorn and Pete Palmer, eds., *Total*

Baseball, 3d ed. (1993). Concise obituaries appear in the *Chicago Herald and Examiner*, the *Chicago Tribune*, the *Chicago Daily News*, and the *New York Times*, 27 Oct. 1931.

RICHARD C. LINDBERG

COMMONS, John Rogers (13 Oct. 1862–11 May 1945), economist, was born in Hollandsburg, Ohio, the son of John Commons, a marginally successful businessman, and Clara Rogers, a schoolteacher. Commons always regarded himself as an Indiana Hoosier—that is to say, as slightly quaint and peculiar. He was the first child in a family that had formed very late for that era: his father was forty-four and his mother thirty-six at his birth. Theirs was also a religiously mixed marriage—she a strict Presbyterian and he a lapsed Quaker—made more distinctive still by her superior education. She held a bachelor's degree from Oberlin College. In his autobiography *Myself* (1934), Commons credits his mother with anchoring him and the family against the tribulations encountered as the result of his father's limitations as a breadwinner. Their troubled small-town life at various places along the Ohio-Indiana border helped produce the high-strung, inquisitive idealist who spent his adult life trying to pass as a self-effacing, down-to-earth pragmatist.

In 1882 Commons enrolled in his mother's alma mater, supported in part by her undertaking as a boardinghouse keeper and by his own labor as a typesetter. His successful college career was marred, however, in his senior year, when he was disabled by the first in a series of nervous collapses that would afflict his adult life. He withdrew from Oberlin to recover but eventually graduated in 1888. He then enrolled for graduate study at Johns Hopkins University.

Commons came under the powerful influence of Richard T. Ely at Hopkins. Through Ely he came to be familiar with the work of the German historical school and with the critique of classical economics. His commitment to Christian social reform was intensified by Ely's espousal of similar ideas. Commons also developed a taste for social research. As at Oberlin, however, while he created a favorable impression on his professors, he encountered difficulties that resulted in a highly uneven performance. He failed his history examinations and never completed the doctoral degree.

Nonetheless, through recommendations of some of his Hopkins professors, Commons received an instructor's appointment at Wesleyan University in Middletown, Connecticut (1890). Salaried for the first time—at $1,000 per annum—Commons married his Oberlin sweetheart, Ella Brown Downey, and soon became an expectant father; they had a total of three children. However, Wesleyan did not reappoint him because of his shortcomings as a teacher.

Commons had made a deep impression on some of his Oberlin professors: not only had they helped him complete his baccalaureate, but they provided financial support for his graduate studies and awarded him an honorary master of arts degree while he was at Wesleyan. Now they offered him a one-year appointment

as an assistant professor of sociology. He then taught at Indiana University (1892–1895) and Syracuse University (1895–1899), also in sociology. These appointments reflected the blurring of disciplinary lines within the social sciences at the time. The character of a professor's interests rather than the degree held often determined disciplinary affiliation.

Political interests at the time also were not distinct. Thus in 1895 Commons identified himself as "a socialist, a single-taxer, a free-silverite, a greenbacker, a municipal-ownerist, a member of the Congressional Church" (*Myself*, p. 53). This jumble of seemingly incongruous positions rendered such political designations as "populist" and "progressive" as ambiguous as those of a sociologist and political economist.

His teaching failure at Wesleyan had led Commons to abandon the more traditional methods of instruction. Henceforth, instead of organizing course materials in a logical sequence, he took whatever topic he happened to be working on as his starting point and developed his lectures from there. His courses became intellectual explorations in which he strove to find ways to explain the phenomena observed in his researches. Economic theory was but one of the several different approaches he employed. This probably seemed like confused rambling to some of his students, but to others his unrehearsed thinking aloud possessed all the excitement of a voyage of discovery.

During the 1890s Commons published the first of his many books and articles. Even before Commons emerged as an author in his own right, R. T. Ely credited his assistance in preparing *An Introduction to Political Economy* (1889), the premier political economy text of the succeeding generation. Commons's first book, co-written with George W. Knight, was *The History of Higher Education in Ohio* (1891). There followed in rapid succession *The Distribution of Wealth* (1893), *Social Reform and the Church* (1894), and *Proportional Representation* (1896). These titles reflected both Commons's catholic interests and his commitment to reforming society along lines shaped by Christian socialist beliefs. Unfortunately, Syracuse University proved intolerant of his radical views, and he was dismissed. For the next five years, until late 1904, Commons held no university appointment.

Probably no one was more surprised than Commons that he flourished during this period. George H. Shibley privately retained him to prepare an index of weekly prices. Then, the secretary of the United States Industrial Commission, E. D. Durand, a former student, hired him to finish the commission report on immigration. Commons moved to Washington to work on the report. Returning to New York City in 1902, he did labor conciliation work as assistant to Ralph M. Easley in the National Civic Federation. This brought him into contact with many union leaders, and he became a lifelong admirer of Samuel Gompers, the head of the American Federation of Labor. Commons remained at the Civic Federation until Ely invited him to join him at the University of Wisconsin. At Commons's insistence his appointment was in economics rather than sociology. Before taking up his new post he directed a U.S. Department of Labor study on restriction of output (1904).

Commons later characterized these as his "Five Big Years." His work on the Industrial Commission provided the wealth of his evidence on immigrant communities that would subsequently inform the empirical portions of his *Races and Immigrants in America* (1907). His work at the Civic Federation provided the intimate acquaintance with the labor movement and American businessmen that served his editorship of *Trade Unionism and Labor Problems* (1905). But there were woes as well. An infant daughter died; Commons suffered another period collapse.

Joining the Wisconsin faculty in 1904 amounted to a rebirth. At last Commons had found a situation that, besides affording a measure of security, encouraged him to develop and employ the full range of his interests and abilities. For Ely he directed the documents search that culminated in 1910–1911 in the ten-volume *A Documentary History of American Industrial Society*. For Wisconsin Governor Robert La Follette (1855–1925) he drafted the first of a long line of progressive legislative proposals. This effort led to his acquaintance with state legislative reference librarian Charles McCarthy. Their collaboration developed "the Wisconsin idea," that the university as a resource provided the state government with expert advice and research at the same time that it educated the future state citizenry.

During his early years at Wisconsin Commons also supervised the labor investigations that were part of Paul U. Kellogg's Pittsburgh Survey and helped organize the American Association of Labor Legislation (1906), of which he became secretary. He studied and wrote about municipal ownership of utilities and began investigations into tax assessment and utility valuation. His article "American Shoemakers, 1648–1895" (1909) represented one of the first attempts to explain the development of the American labor movement: he characterized unions as defensive worker responses to the competitive pressures unleashed by expanding product markets.

Commons's design of the Wisconsin Industrial Commission in 1911 pioneered the development of the administrative agency in this country. With a broad grant of power from the state legislature, the commission developed and enforced the "working rules" applicable to issues affecting the employment relationship. Several states sought Commons's help in drafting similar legislation, and others introduced variants of his design. He could not, however, convince the labor representatives on the U.S. Commission on Industrial Relations (1913–1915), on which he served as a public member, to endorse the industrial commission idea. This experience helped clarify his thinking about the need for and limits of labor legislation, and it influenced *Principles of Labor Legislation* (1916), which he wrote with John B. Andrews, a former student.

In 1916–1917 Commons suffered another of the nervous collapses that punctuated his life. Still, he was elected president of the American Economics Association (1917) and continued work on the now classic *History of Labour in the United States*, volumes 1 and 2 (1918). The work of many hands under Commons's direction, these volumes recounted in unprecedented detail the struggles of American workers to organize for self-defense and self-help during the nineteenth century. These volumes, supplemented by two later ones prepared by Commons's students and by Selig Perlman's *A Theory of the Labor Movement* (1928), form the core works of the Wisconsin school of American labor history.

Responding to postwar turbulence in industrial relations and the economy, Commons published *Industrial Goodwill* (1919), was coauthor of *Industrial Government* (1921), and edited *Trade Unionism and Labor Problems* (2d ser.) (1921). While seemingly preoccupied with the issues surrounding industrial relations— in 1921 he drafted the first unemployment compensation bill in this country—Commons retained wonderfully diverse interests. His work on inflation and monetary policy led to his election as president of the National Monetary Association (1922–1923). In 1923 he also became president of the National Consumers' League. At the time, Commons had begun an elaborate effort to forge a link between law and economics by tracing and relating the evolution of legal doctrine to the growth and structural change of the American economy. The result was *The Legal Foundations of Capitalism* (1924).

During his years at Wisconsin, Commons trained many students who went on to become leaders in various fields, from public utility regulation to social security. Many of the social policy ideas that he created, adapted, or amplified were carried by students and colleagues into the New Deal. The 1930s marked the high point of his influence on public policies for industrial relations and the American welfare state, and this influence gives him some claim to being a founding father in both realms.

In retirement and alone—his wife died in 1928— Commons continued to write. In 1934 he published both his autobiography, *Myself*, and *Institutional Economics: Its Place in Political Economy*, the most extended and significant statement of his judgment that the study of transactions, not prices, provided the nexus from which economic understanding should proceed. Using this approach he attempted to integrate economics, law, and ethics to illuminate real economic issues, and he simultaneously exposed the inertia and the dynamism inherent in institutions and social systems. Unfortunately, like many others associated with institutionalism, Commons, in his theoretical writings, tended to be overly prolix—as if there were too many variables, relationships, and insights for mere words to handle. Nonetheless, many of his seminal ideas about "going concerns," "working rules," "reasonable value," "negotiational psychology," and "bargaining power" continue to provide starting points in such areas of contemporary economics as industrial relations, game theory, bargaining theory, and industrial organization.

Commons died in Florida but was buried in Madison, Wisconsin.

• The John R. Commons Papers are held in the State Historical Society Library, Madison, Wis. The Richard T. Ely Papers in the same library contain many letters from Commons to Ely. The Memorial Library of the University of Wisconsin in Madison has a collection of Commons's published and unpublished works. An extensive bibliography of his writing appears as an appendix to *The Economics of Collective Action* (1950) and can be supplemented by that which appears in Richard A. Gonce, "The Development of John R. Commons' System of Thought" (Ph.D. diss., Univ. of Wisconsin, 1967).

H. M. GITELMAN

COMO, William Michael (10 Nov. 1925–1 Jan. 1989), editor, was born in Williamstown, Massachusetts, the son of Michael Como and Janet Caporale. In 1944, after graduating from Williamstown High School, Como was inducted into the U.S. Army, serving in the Pacific theater during World War II before his demobilization in 1946. Intent on pursuing an acting career, in 1947 he enrolled in the American Academy of Dramatic Arts in New York City. His course of study included classes with Sara Mildred Strauss, an expert teacher of movement for actors.

From 1948 to 1953 Como acted in New York and California, initially as a member of the touring Clare Tree Major Children's Theatre and later as a player in summer stock companies in Bennington, Vermont, and Stockbridge, Massachusetts. He also served briefly during this period as secretary to the Nobel novelist Sinclair Lewis.

Como's growing interest in dance led to his leaving the acting profession in 1954 to become a receptionist at the New York City offices of *Dance Magazine*, the oldest continuously published periodical on the subject in the world. That same year he was promoted to sales manager, a post he held until 1961, when he was named advertising manager and assistant to the publisher, Rudolf Orthwine. With the July 1968 issue Como added "Public Relations" to his designation on the magazine's masthead. During this period and into the 1970s he also wrote for *Dance Magazine* on a wide range of subjects—from sequins to summer ballet camps to jazz tap—and conducted numerous interviews, a practice that considerably broadened his knowledge of and contacts within the field.

A major change in Como's professional life occurred in 1968, when he became the editor of *After Dark*. Billed as the "National Magazine of Entertainment," the publication was a metamorphosed version of *Ballroom Dance Magazine*, a sister publication of *Dance Magazine*. *After Dark* covered the entertainment spectrum represented by stage, screen, and television. A success from the start, *After Dark* demonstrated Como's editing skills as well as his ability to gauge effectively the interests and expectations of his audience. The publication was described by the German critic Horst Koegler as "a forum for a youthful-hedonistic way of life which demonstrated in a most seductive manner all that was in, chic and sexy at the time in New York."

With the January 1970 issue of *Dance Magazine* Como succeeded Lydia Joel as editor (a position expanded to editor in chief in 1971), simultaneously directing that periodical and *After Dark* until the latter ceased publication in 1979. During his *Dance Magazine* tenure, a post that he held until his death, Como initiated a number of changes designed to give the rather staid publication a more up-to-date appearance, including a gradual revision of its layout and the generous use of dramatic, often openly erotic, photographs. His success in guiding the magazine was reflected in its substantially raised circulation and in increased advertising revenues. Como also adeptly publicized the previously low-key Dance Magazine Awards, granted annually to a number of outstanding members of the profession, and he enjoyed the press attention that accompanied the presentations to such celebrated dancers as Rudolf Nureyev and Mikhail Baryshnikov.

With the January 1978 issue of *Dance Magazine*, Como launched a regular column, "The Editor's Log," which appeared monthly as a record of his travels, social life, and enthusiasms, all of it conducted within the framework of his favorite topic, dance. Once aroused, Como's loyalty was unwavering, and those who particularly benefited from his interest and support include John Neumeier, the American-born director of the Hamburg Ballet in Germany; Eddy Toussaint, the choreographer and founder-director of Montreal's La Compagnie de Danse Eddy Toussaint; Heinz Spoerli, the director of Switzerland's Basel Ballet; and the Bolshoi Ballet defector Alexander Godunov. Como was an ardent champion of Maurice Béjart and his Ballet of the 20th Century, often in the face of the tepid enthusiasm of American critics.

Como candidly assessed his attitude and position in an interview published in Salt Lake City's *Deseret News* on 19 October 1979, as he approached his tenth anniversary as *Dance Magazine*'s editor: "I never grow tired of seeing what's happening in dance around the country," he said, adding, "I have been [sic] become very sharpened in my perspective and I don't mince words. I tell companies to shape up and in what areas they need to do so, and I hit square on. I keep away from puff, and I like to see for myself. . . . I feel I make a major contribution as a behind-the-scenes consultant. I also serve as a sort of informal clearing house for choreographers and dancers, channeling them towards managements that need them."

Among his other activities, Como edited a number of books, including *Raoul Gelabert's Anatomy for the Dancer* (2 vols., 1964–1966), *Celebration* (1971), *The Essence of Béjart* (1972), *Nureyev* (1973), and *Margot Fonteyn* (1973). In the late 1980s he also contributed as a commentator to the radio magazine program "Performance Today," broadcast weekly on National Public Radio.

Como served on many juries and committees and was the recipient of a number of honors, including citations from Dance Masters of America, the Dance Teachers Club of Boston, the American Dance Machine, and the National Association of Dance and Affiliated Artists. Como, who never married, died in New York City.

Perhaps Como's strongest contribution to the arts scene during his years as editor of *Dance Magazine* was his indefatigability in searching out, both in the United States and abroad, and focusing the attention of his readers on lesser-known dancers, choreographers, and companies, among them the San Francisco and Oakland ballets and Salt Lake City's Ballet West. Always sympathetic to the young, he played a pivotal role in the organization in 1979 of the first USA International Ballet Competition in Jackson, Mississippi. His activities on behalf of dance were summed up by the choreographer Donald Saddler at a memorial service conducted at the City Center Theater shortly after Como's death: "Bill chased the muse of Terpsichore to most capitals of the world, every city, town, and hamlet that boasted of a dance company promising a ballerina or a choreographer. It was a constant quest for his true love and obsession, *Dance Magazine*."

• Como's papers, known as the William Como Collection, are at the Harvard Theatre Collection, Harvard University. Another major source of information is in the Dance Collection of the New York Public Library for the Performing Arts, Lincoln Center, the archives of which contain a wide assortment of materials, including photographs, clippings, videos, and audiotaped interviews with Como, as well as computer-accessible references to his writings for *Dance Magazine* and other periodicals. In addition to the standard biographical references, a short entry under his name is included in Horst Koegler, ed., *The Concise Oxford Dictionary of Ballet* (1977; 2nd ed., 1987). Obituaries are in the *New York Times*, 3 Jan. 1989, and *Dance Magazine*, Mar. 1989. *Dance Magazine*, Apr. 1989, published excerpts from appreciations by friends and colleagues at the City Center Theater gathering.

JACQUELINE MASKEY

COMPSON, Betty (18 Mar. 1897–18 Apr. 1974), film actress, was born Eleanor Luicime Compson in a log cabin in a Beaver City, Utah, mining camp, the daughter of Virgil K. Compson and Mary Elizabeth Rauscher. Her father was a mining engineer, then a failed gold prospector in Alaska, and finally the proprietor of a corner grocery store in Salt Lake City. Her mother worked as a domestic and a hotel maid. Compson grew up on the edge of poverty, though her parents were able to provide violin lessons for her. After her father's death in 1912, she played violin in the pit orchestra of a vaudeville and movie theater while attending high school. When one of the vaudeville acts went missing, Compson filled in, hurriedly costumed as a street violinist.

Her success as a replacement led Compson to other vaudeville bookings in western cities, billed as the "Vagabond Violinist." When she played Los Angeles in 1915, she was seen and hired by Al Christie, pro-

ducer of one- and two-reel Christie Comedies. Renamed "Betty Compson" by the producer, she underwent a quick education in film technique as she appeared in dozens of the comedy shorts over the next few years. By 1917 she was attracting attention for her looks and personality on screen: the *New York Dramatic Mirror* reviewer found her "irresistably [*sic*] pretty and vivacious" (17 Feb. 1917).

In 1918 Compson had a falling out with Christie and sought other film work. It was not glamorous work: "[I] appeared in a serial in which I was only an acrobat and, after that, I played a couple of rag-doll heroines" (*Detroit Journal*, 19 Oct. 1919). In December 1918, returning home from a day's filming on location, she learned that director George Loane Tucker wanted to interview her that evening for a part in *The Miracle Man*, a major picture. Still in bedraggled clothes and with makeup in her hairline, she went to the interview by streetcar. "In an effort to find out if I could 'stand up' in a part that required of me a veritable transformation, from . . . the feline creature of the tenderloin that was revealed in the opening of the picture to the awakened and purified woman at the end [through the miracle of a mentor's inspiration,]" Tucker charged at her with questions from all directions, to see her facial expressions (*New York Dramatic Mirror*, 13 Nov. 1920). Her description of how the violin had kept her and her mother going financially after Virgil Compson's death, she felt, won her the part. *The Miracle Man* (1919), starring Thomas Meighan and Lon Chaney, was a great success and made her an overnight favorite of the public.

Offscreen, the cultured, sensitive (and married) Tucker became Compson's mentor as well as lover. She told interviewer Dewitt Bodeen that Tucker introduced her to the "best of literature, music, all the arts, everything." Their romance was cut short when Tucker, directing her in a second film, *Ladies Must Live* (1921), was found to have inoperable cancer. Before his death, he guided her into forming her own production company for further films. These established her as a rising film personality. The *New York Times* reviewer of *Prisoner of Love* (1921), a Compson production, commented that "she is expressive; her looks, gestures, positions mean something, and with the rare quality of expression, she has the even rarer quality of restraint" (17 Jan. 1921).

Compson's fortunes as a movie star fluctuated throughout the 1920s. After signing a starring contract with Paramount, she was not given a scheduled raise because her pictures, standard studio product of the time, were disappointing at the box office. Her roles at Paramount capitalized on her looks and vivaciousness but did not establish a strong star personality, and she complained of inadequate direction. Leaving the studio, she made four films in London. Their box office appeal across the United States brought her back to Paramount with a salary that eventually reached as high as $5,000 a week. When her contract was completed, she went into one-picture contracts with various studios.

Compson never showed the consuming interest in a career that possessed the great stars. To her, it was simply a lucrative line of work. She would sign with a "poverty row" studio if the price was right and never consider the loss of prestige it brought her in Hollywood circles. Also, in 1925 she married director James Cruze and decided that she could cut back on films and "let Jim support me in ease and comfort. In a short time I got fat" (*Films in Review*, Aug.–Sept. 1966).

Strains in the marriage soon developed: Cruze's mercurial, party-loving, extravagant ways were a poor match with Compson's hardworking, dollar-conscious practicality. "From childhood I've had the fear of poverty," she told Bodeen. After they separated, it came out that Cruze had failed to pay federal income taxes for several years, and the government sued Compson as his wife for $150,000, taking her cash and valuables.

Compson, looking for work, found at first that she was considered a has-been. She accepted whatever was offered, even second leads. Her comeback was aided by the arrival of talking pictures. "My voice recorded all right—all those early years playing in vaudeville stood me in good stead," and soon she had more offers than she could accept. Working steadily, she made $180,000 in one year. Moreover, her role as a carnival girl in an early talkie, *The Barker* (1928), brought her an Academy Award nomination as best actress and established her later predominant screen image as a warm, outgoing, wised-up blonde. She and Cruze were divorced in 1930.

Compson kept working steadily through the 1930s and 1940s, though her parts diminished in size and importance. No longer a star, she remained a hardworking professional. In the depths of the depression, when screen jobs became scarce, she toured as the star of a vaudeville show in which she played the violin, danced, sang, and did an imitation of Marlene Dietrich. In 1933 she married Irving Weinberg, who managed her on a yearlong vaudeville tour of the Far East: "I hauled out the violin once more," she told Bodeen. The tour ended to the sound of gunfire in wartorn Shanghai, and the marriage ended in 1937. In 1941 director Alfred Hitchcock gave her a featured role in his *Mr. and Mrs. Smith*; he had been a fledgling art director and assistant director on three of her London films, released in 1923–1924.

Compson's final vaudeville appearance was in 1941, in Billy Rose's Diamond Horseshoe nightclub show featuring old-time stars. During World War II she toured the West Coast in two plays. A performance for servicemen led to a meeting with Silvius Jack Gall, a navy athletic specialist; he became her third husband. A last screen appearance was in *Here Comes Trouble* (1948).

After Gall's death in 1962, Compson took over as manager of his business, which supplied specialty ashtrays to hotels and restaurants. "I've saved money," she told Bodeen, "There will never be a benefit performance for Betty Compson." Death from natural causes came in Glendale, California. Compson stands in movie history as an enduring trouper for thirty-two years and 117 films, who made the most of her opportunities and rose to the top for a while, then made the best of compromises that came with her descent from stardom, and finally made a good life outside the bright lights of Hollywood.

• Materials on the life and career of Betty Compson are in the Billy Rose Theatre Collection at the New York Public Library for the Performing Arts, Lincoln Center. For Compson's views on her career, see Betty Compson, "How It Feels to Be a Star-Producer," *New York Dramatic Mirror*, 13 Nov. 1920. A major biographical source, with photographs and filmography, is Dewitt Bodeen, "Betty Compson," *Films in Review*, Aug.–Sept. 1966. See also Robert M. Yost, Jr., "Rescued from the River, *Photoplay*, Dec. 1919; Dolores Foster, "Too Many Guests," *Photoplay*, Aug. 1930; and Michael Woodward, "Unbeatable Betty," *Photoplay*, Mar. 1931. Portraits and production photographs are in Daniel C. Blum, *A Pictorial History of the Silent Screen* (1953) and *A New Pictorial History of the Talkies* (1968). Obituaries are in the *New York Times*, 24 Apr. 1974, and *Variety*, 1 May 1974.
WILLIAM STEPHENSON

COMPTON, Arthur Holly (10 Sept. 1892–15 Mar. 1962), physicist, was born in Wooster, Ohio, the son of Elias Compton, a Presbyterian minister and professor of philosophy, and Otelia Catherine Augspurger, a graduate of the Western Female Seminary (later Western College for Women) in Oxford, Ohio. Compton and his older brothers Karl Taylor and Wilson Martindale and sister Mary Elesa were brought up in a home that was filled with parental love and emphasized education, discipline, and religious training. All four children became distinguished educators. Karl became president of the Massachusetts Institute of Technology in 1930; Mary and her husband, C. Herbert Rice, spent forty years in India as educational missionaries; Wilson, after a prominent career in business and government, became president of Washington State University in Pullman, Washington, in 1944; and Arthur became chancellor of Washington University in St. Louis in 1945. They and their parents together received more than seventy earned and honorary degrees. They became known as America's first family of learning.

Compton attended the Wooster Elementary and Grammar School (1898–1905), the Wooster Preparatory School (1905–1909), and the College of Wooster (1909–1913). His interest in science was fully awakened as a teenager in 1905 when he observed the constellation Orion and Dog Star, Sirius, in the winter sky. Eventually, he secured his parents' permission to purchase a telescope and photographed Halley's Comet during its appearance in 1910. That same year he built with his own hands a triplane glider with a 27-foot wingspan and flew it successfully for about 185 feet.

In his first years in college, Compton was still uncertain whether to devote his life to science or to the ministry, and only through his father's wise counsel and encouragement did he choose the former for his life's work. In 1913, after receiving his B.S. degree, he followed in his brother Karl's footsteps and entered Princeton University as a graduate student in physics, intending to switch after his first year to engineering as a more directly applied field. Within a few months, however, especially through the brief but strong influence of Owen Willans Richardson, under whom Karl had completed his Ph.D. degree in 1912, he decided to continue his studies in experimental physics. He completed his Ph.D. degree in 1916 under H. Lester Cooke with a thesis on the distribution of electrons in crystals as determined by the angular distribution in intensity of X-rays reflected from them. In 1916 he married Betty Charity McCloskey, a former classmate at Wooster; they had two children.

Compton accepted a position at the University of Minnesota as an instructor in physics for the academic year 1916–1917. There, branching out from his thesis research at Princeton, he reflected X-rays from a magnetite crystal exposed to an external magnetic field, and because he observed no change in the reflected X-ray pattern when the field was turned on and off, he concluded that not the atom as a whole, but the subatomic electron, was the "ultimate magnetic particle." Bearing that conviction in mind, he left Minnesota in the summer of 1917 to work as a research engineer in the Westinghouse Lamp Company in East Pittsburgh. There, shortly after his arrival, he came across a paper by Charles Glover Barkla showing that when high-energy X-rays pass through a thin foil of aluminum they are absorbed to a lesser extent than was expected from Joseph John Thomson's classical theory of scattering. Pondering his Minnesota experiments and Barkla's results, Compton eventually proved theoretically that both could be explained by assuming that the incident X-rays were being scattered by large ring-shaped electrons—some thousand times larger than generally assumed—which were present in the scattering substance.

Compton's increasing desire to return to research in an academic environment prompted him to apply for a National Research Council Fellowship, and in the summer of 1919, after two years at Westinghouse, he received one of the first ones awarded following their establishment after the Great War. His destination was the Cavendish Laboratory in Cambridge, England, where Ernest Rutherford had just succeeded J. J. Thomson as Cavendish Professor of Experimental Physics. There Compton found that the still more energetic gamma rays behaved as strangely as X-rays when scattered by matter, and he resolved to study the phenomenon in detail after taking up a position in the fall of 1920 as Wayman Crow Professor of Physics and head of the Department of Physics at Washington University in St. Louis.

At Washington University Compton embarked on a program of experimental researches that eventually culminated, at the end of 1922, in his decisive proof by means of a Bragg spectrometer that X-rays scattered by carbon undergo a discrete change of wavelength to a higher value, the greater the scattering angle the greater the change. Moreover, to understand this result theoretically, he found that he had to reject all of his past interpretations and assume instead that X-rays (and gamma rays as well) consist of little particles of energy that are scattered by electrons—now viewed as point charges—in a billiard-ball collision process in which both energy and momentum are conserved. Peter Debye in Zurich came to the same conclusion essentially simultaneously, but unlike Compton, Debye had carried out no experiments to support it. This radiation-electron collision process has been known ever since as the Compton effect, and it constitutes Compton's most important discovery in physics.

Compton's discovery thus grew out of a long series of his own experimental and theoretical investigations; it did not follow from an attempt to test Albert Einstein's light-quantum hypothesis, which Einstein had proposed almost two decades earlier in 1905. Until the end of 1922 most physicists, Compton included, viewed Einstein's revolutionary hypothesis with great skepticism. Only after the publication of Compton's discovery in early 1923 did opinion begin to shift more and more, and the Compton effect was seen as the first conclusive proof of the validity of Einstein's hypothesis. As such, it forced physicists to thoroughly reexamine the way in which they thought about the interaction of radiation and matter, and it became a milestone on the way to the creation of modern quantum mechanics in 1925–1926. For his discovery, Compton shared the Nobel Prize in physics for 1927 with Charles Thomson Rees Wilson, the inventor of the cloud chamber. That same year Compton was elected to the National Academy of Sciences. At the age of thirty-five he had reached the apex of his profession.

A few months after the publication of his discovery, in the summer of 1923, Compton left Washington University to accept a position as professor of physics at the University of Chicago, filling a vacancy created by Robert A. Millikan's move to the California Institute of Technology in Pasadena. At Chicago Compton wrote a classic treatise on *X-Rays and Electrons* (1926) and continued to work in this field and supervise doctoral dissertations in it until the end of the 1920s. Both in the classroom and in the laboratory he was throughout his career an inspiring teacher. In 1929 he was appointed Charles H. Swift Distinguished Service Professor at the University of Chicago.

In 1931, stimulated in part by discussions he heard at a conference on nuclear physics in Rome organized by Enrico Fermi, Compton turned to a new area of research, on the highly penetrating radiation striking the earth from outer space that was discovered by the Austrian physicist Viktor Franz Hess in 1911–1912 and was dubbed "cosmic rays" by Millikan. By 1931 the nature of these rays was a matter of dispute. Millikan believed them to consist of high-energy light quanta or photons, while Walther Bothe in Germany, Bruno Rossi in Italy, and others believed them to consist of energetic charged particles. In one of several attempts to settle this question, Compton secured financial support from the Carnegie Institution and organized a world survey of cosmic rays between 1931 and 1934, sending out nine different expeditions—one of which consisted of himself, his wife, and his elder son—to all parts of the globe, each being equipped with identical cosmic-ray detectors. Their goal was to see if the cosmic rays experienced a "latitude effect," arriving at the earth's surface with different intensities at different latitudes owing to their differing deflections in the earth's magnetic field. If such an effect existed, it would be clear evidence that cosmic rays were charged particles; if not, they were quite likely photons. The results of Compton's world survey spoke clearly in favor of the former hypothesis. A long debate that he had carried on with Millikan on the question, which made headlines by pitting one Nobel laureate against another, was settled in Compton's favor. After finishing his world survey, Compton spent the academic year 1934–1935 as George Eastman Visiting Professor and fellow of Balliol College, Oxford.

During the 1930s Compton also turned to much broader areas of human concern. He had visited India on a Guggenheim Fellowship in 1926–1927, and that experience rekindled his lifelong interest in cultural, philosophical, and religious issues. He sought to explore such ancient questions as the nature of free will and man's relationship to God in light of the knowledge gained through modern science, especially quantum and relativity theory. In 1931 he delivered the Terry Lectures at Yale University, dedicating the resulting book to his father, "philosopher and friend," who "taught his students, myself among them, the way toward a rational and satisfying Christian philosophy," thus leaving no doubt about the ultimate source of his beliefs. At the end of the decade, in 1939, he returned to his religious and philosophical concerns in his McNair Lectures at the University of North Carolina.

After the Second World War broke out in Europe in 1939, Compton was called on to put his scientific and administrative talents at the service of the government. Nuclear fission had been discovered in Germany by Otto Hahn and Fritz Strassmann at the end of 1938, and nuclear physicists everywhere rapidly recognized the possibility of producing a chain reaction leading to a weapon capable of enormous destruction. Those in America, who included highly gifted European refugees from nazism and fascism, feared that Adolf Hitler would be the first to possess this terrible weapon. In the face of this threat, Compton was asked in 1941 to chair a committee to determine the feasibility of producing a nuclear weapon, and his committee's positive conclusion, which he transmitted to President Franklin Delano Roosevelt in November of that year, provided a strong impetus in moving the American program to develop an atomic bomb forward. The following year he became director of the Metallurgical Laboratory of the Manhattan Project and brought Enrico Fermi to Chicago to build the first atomic pile, which achieved criticality on 2 December 1942, opening up a new world, the atomic age. In 1945, despite his deep-seated pacifist convictions, Compton voted with the majority of the interim committee appointed by President Harry S. Truman, recommending that the awesome new weapon be used against Japan.

After the end of the war Compton returned to academic life, to Washington University in St. Louis, the site of his most famous discovery. He served as chancellor of Washington University from 1945 to 1953 and as Distinguished Service Professor of Natural Philosophy from 1954 to 1961. His intention to devote the next years of his life as professor at large, dividing his time among Washington University, Wooster College, and the University of California at Berkeley, was cut short by his death in Berkeley.

Compton's exceptional scientific achievements garnered high honors for him. He was only the third American, after Albert Abraham Michelson and R. A. Millikan, to receive the Nobel Prize in physics, and he received numerous honorary degrees and other awards, among them the U.S. Medal for Merit in 1946. Along with other American experimental and theoretical physicists in the 1920s, Compton helped lay the foundation for the scientific symbiosis that developed between them and the European refugees from nazism and fascism in the 1930s. Before the first World War, the United States was a backwater in physics; at the outbreak of the Second World War, America was unexcelled in the field. Compton contributed significantly to this extraordinary transformation in the standing of physics in America.

• Compton's original research notebooks (1919–1941) and other documents are deposited in the Washington University Archives, St. Louis, and duplicate copies of the notebooks are in the Center for History of Physics, American Institute of Physics, College Park, Md. Many of Compton's scientific papers are collected in Robert S. Shankland, ed., *Scientific Papers of Arthur Holly Compton* (1973); those that are not are listed in the bibliography in that work. Most of his nonscientific writings, including his "Personal Reminiscences," can be found in Marjorie Johnston, ed., *The Cosmos of Arthur Holly Compton* (1967). Compton published a revised second edition of his major book with Samuel K. Allison as *X-Rays in Theory and Experiment* (1935). His Terry Lectures were published as *The Freedom of Man* (1935), his McNair Lectures as *The Human Meaning of Science* (1940), and his account of the Manhattan Project as *Atomic Quest: A Personal Narrative* (1956). Compton's family environment is the subject of James R. Blackwood's *The House on College Avenue: The Comptons at Wooster* (1968), and his major discovery is placed in historical context in Roger H. Stuewer's *The Compton Effect: Turning Point in Physics* (1975). An obituary notice is in the *New York Times*, 16 Mar. 1962; another retrospective account of Compton's life and work is Samuel K. Allison, "Arthur Holly Compton," *National Academy of Sciences Biographical Memoirs* (1965).

ROGER H. STUEWER

COMPTON, Karl Taylor (14 Sept. 1887–22 June 1954), physicist and science administrator, was born in Wooster, Ohio, the son of Elias Compton, a professor at the University of Wooster, and Otelia Augspurger. Compton's parents strongly supported their children's intellectual endeavors, and his younger brother, Arthur Holly Compton, enjoyed an even more illustrious scientific career. Like his father, Karl Compton attended the University of Wooster, where he completed a master's degree in physics in 1909. Wooster's science faculty did not offer doctoral training, but as the laboratory assistant in physics, Compton had unlimited access to the teaching apparatus, which included an x-ray generator. Along with an explanation of how the x-ray generator's circuit breaker functioned, Compton developed a knack for the design and manipulation of the electronic apparatus.

Compton went to Princeton for doctoral studies. Since the founding in the late nineteenth century of several American universities that imitated Germany's emphasis on graduate education and research, the older American universities were under competitive pressure to reform. Especially in physics departments, where faculty members felt the need to become current in atomic physics and relativity theory, a scramble was on to acquire the sophistication and rigor of European departments. A common tactic was to import European physicists for a teaching stint.

Compton was a beneficiary of this institutional ferment. He earned his doctorate in 1912 under the English physicist Oliver Richardson, who involved Compton in experiments to test alternatives to Albert Einstein's controversial suggestion of attributing particulate characteristics to light. After a brief stint teaching at Reed College, Compton returned to Princeton and initiated a study of collisions between electrons and gases to determine the "critical potentials" at which an atom or molecule would radiate, ionize, or dissociate. Such measurements seemed meaningful because two different models of atomic structure each partially captured physical reality: Niels Bohr's "dynamical model" explained radiation and ionization of the hydrogen atom but did not account for these phenomena in complex systems and did not address questions of chemical properties; Gilbert Lewis and Irving Langmuir's "static model" qualitatively accounted for chemical combinations without addressing questions of radiation and structural stability. By generating data on phenomena that fell between the successes of these models, Compton hoped to lay the empirical foundations for an integrated viewpoint.

In retrospect, Compton's research was not crucial for finding an internally consistent foundation for atomic theory. But before the momentous conceptual developments that ushered in quantum mechanics in 1925 and 1926, many physicists expected that theoretical enlightenment would be won from an extended period of experimentation. Compton's experimental skills were so highly regarded that his review article on critical potentials was one of the few American publications in atomic physics in the 1920s to be translated into German (Compton and F. L. Mohler, "Critical Potentials," *Bulletin of the National Research Council* 9 [Sept. 1924]). He became chairman of Princeton's physics department in 1929.

Compton's research was significant also for the nonacademic relations it fostered. The interaction of electrons with gases was an interest of the General Electric Research Laboratory because such phenomena were always occurring in light bulbs. Compton became one of the few consultants GE hired. As the advent of quantum mechanics undercut the relevance of Compton's experiments to academic theorists, he found a more technical audience for his studies of electron-gas interactions. By the end of the 1920s, his interests were so close to those of Irving Langmuir, GE's leading physical scientist, that they collaborated on a massive pair of review articles analyzing thirty years of work on ionized gases.

Compton's connections to GE were also critical to a major shift in his career. Gerard Swope, GE's president, was chairman of the Executive Committee of the Massachusetts Institute of Technology Corporation. Along with others, he rightly worried that MIT was not successfully fostering advanced programs in research and graduate education. MIT president Samuel Stratton seemed unsuited by age, temperament, and background to stimulate meaningful reforms. In 1929 Swope offered Compton the MIT presidency. Compton briefly hesitated, then accepted after an additional discussion with Frank Jewett, president of Bell Telephone Laboratories and a member of the MIT Corporation. Compton joked in a 1945 memo about his lack of preparation for the MIT presidency, "While I knew something about the difference between an electron and a proton, I knew much less about the difference between a stock and a bond." However, Compton clearly was not being hired to manage MIT's endowment but to invigorate MIT's research.

Compton had already given conscious thought to how universities should support research. While at Princeton, he had ruminated on the possibility of "departments of a somewhat more flexible nature than those to which we are accustomed" in combination with an administration with the courage and authority to designate favored departments. Such a combination, he reasoned, could impress on faculty the importance of cultivating common interests with colleagues and outside scientists in other disciplines, as Compton had done with GE scientists. At MIT he sought and promoted faculty whose intellectual interests contributed to this social vision.

To push MIT toward his ideal of a research university in which traditional academic specialization did not dominate the organization of research, Compton launched initiatives that required him to negotiate at two levels. At one, he had to convince a distinguished or obviously promising researcher that his professional interests lay less in deepening the foundations of his discipline than in broadening the influence of his field through organizing an intra-MIT program around the appeal of his specialty to other disciplines. At a second level, Compton had to convince a philanthropic foundation that its best contribution to academic research lay less in supporting individual researchers whose projects fit a foundation program than in supporting intra-MIT reforms that experimented with the organization of knowledge and researchers. He made his office an active broker between faculty members and the foundations. When researchers were wary of assuming leadership of an MIT program that lacked secure financing, or foundations were wary of financing an MIT program that lacked nationally recognized leadership, Compton's own scientific reputation helped to break the stalemate.

Compton had several notable successes. The earliest, which helped secure his hold on the MIT presidency, was centered on the physics department. In 1930 he enticed John Slater, a young quantum theorist at Harvard, to sacrifice slow advancement in a secure department to become chairman of MIT's department. Slater drew up a prospectus calling for the development of "deductive atomic theory," by which Slater meant the extension of the new quantum mechanics into atomic and molecular systems that interested chemists, crystallographers, and electrical engineers, as contrasted with the exploration of the inner structure and behavior of the atom's constituents. That prospectus became the centerpiece of a petition from Compton to the Rockefeller Foundation for an MIT research endowment. The foundation, whose finances were feeling the effects of the Great Depression, declined to provide an endowment but did grant MIT a "fluid research fund," which was allocated within MIT by a committee of Compton and selected department chairmen.

A second success originated in the electrical engineering department, where Vannevar Bush and his students had developed an electromechanical machine that graphically generated solutions to differential equations. Bush's stimulus had been the intractability of differential equations encountered in the analysis of electrical power systems, but he recognized the potential of a more powerful, flexible machine that could serve the computational needs of other fields. When Compton became president, Bush, a faculty member who could find common cause with reform-minded scientists, became a superior candidate for institute-wide administration. In 1932 Compton named Bush vice president and supported Bush's efforts to develop his own petition to the Rockefeller Foundation. By then, the foundation had narrowed its focus to supporting projects that promoted the application of physical and chemical techniques to biological issues. However, Bush successfully varied Compton's and Slater's strategy to fit his circumstances. Bush did not mention the industrial origins of his work, called attention to the breadth of areas, including population genetics, where increased computational prowess could prove useful, and argued that the field of mathematical analysis could best be advanced by establishing a Center of Analysis at MIT, where scientists and engineers could pursue their common interest in better computational machines. The foundation noted that Bush's petition fell outside its area of interest but nevertheless made the grant on its merits.

Compton's successful support of efforts to raise external funds for researchers with distinctively multidepartmental interests was complemented by his ac-

tions to resolve intra-MIT administrative difficulties. He set up a professor's fund to support sabbaticals by taxing the consulting fees of faculty members, centralized the administration of industrially sponsored research, and upgraded admission standards for undergraduates. The depression slowed some reforms but also provided a somber backdrop against which his efforts at innovation stood out brightly.

Compton's noteworthy successes at reforming MIT enabled him to use the support of Gerard Swope to move into political circles, where he obtained painful but enlightening lessons. During Franklin D. Roosevelt's first presidential term, Swope's advocacy of industrial self-governance took concrete shape in the National Recovery Administration, and Compton, along with Isaiah Bowman, president of Johns Hopkins University, found support in Roosevelt's cabinet for a "Science Advisory Board" alongside the other boards that the NRA's creation stimulated. The SAB had no authorization to spend government money. Nevertheless, using private funds administered through the National Academy of Sciences and its leaders' abilities to elicit contributions from other prominent, like-minded scientists, the SAB produced two volumes of reports that laid out, bureau by bureau, the prospects for improving the efficiency of government services by using academic scientists to research issues with both academic and policy import.

Report writing did not satisfy Compton and did not make a dent in the depression. He proposed a $10 million government-funded academic research program under the banner "Put Science to Work." That proposal proved to be far more ambitious than the SAB's claim to scientists' loyalties or political legitimacy could bear. Within the National Academy of Sciences, whose members had attained prestige by impressing their disciplinary peers, influential individuals balked at placing unprecedented funds in the hands of reform-minded administrators seeking inspiration in the problems of government agencies. Within the Roosevelt administration, the National Planning Board also sought to enlist natural scientists in studies oriented toward reconsidering the executive branch's organization rather than assisting extant agencies. Compton watched in frustration as intraacademy controversies and continued economic malaise pushed Roosevelt toward the advocates of governmental planning. After two volumes of reports, the SAB went out of business.

In 1938 Vannevar Bush left MIT to become president of the Carnegie Institution of Washington. In promoting Bush's career, Compton extended his influence far more than he could have envisioned. As Roosevelt responded to deteriorating international relations in Europe by cautiously pushing public opinion toward a pro-British stance, Bush was able, in June 1940, to induce Roosevelt to create the National Defense Research Committee under obscure legislative authority granted the presidency during World War I. Bush himself was NDRC chairman, and he elicited the services of Compton along with other research administrators he knew from his MIT activities. Compton thus found himself enmeshed, under the banner of national security rather than economic recovery, in the kind of public administration of research he had hoped to create through the SAB. NDRC members eschewed organizing researchers by academic disciplines or by the missions of the armed services in favor of creating the committee's own categories of military functions. Compton's first NDRC assignment was to survey the armed services' laboratories to determine the areas of general importance that NDRC ought to address.

Compton took charge of the NDRC division for detection. He had previously convinced the financier and amateur physicist Alfred Loomis to support the joint efforts of MIT's electrical engineering and physics departments to create directed radio-wave systems at ever-shorter wavelengths. Compton appointed Loomis chairman of a microwave committee; Edward Bowles of MIT served as secretary. When the committee learned that British scientists had invented a far more powerful generator of microwaves than anything previously available, it opted to establish a central laboratory where academic scientists and engineers could research and develop what came to be known as radar systems. Compton did not directly participate in deciding where to situate the laboratory, but Bowles and Loomis, with Bush's assistance, guided the laboratory to MIT. Compton was instrumental in keeping the MIT "Radiation Laboratory" the center of NDRC's radar program. After Pearl Harbor, Frank Jewett of Bell Telephone Laboratories, with support within the Rad Lab from scientists and engineers who preferred to work independently of each other, urged NDRC to limit the Rad Lab's scope and spread radar activities among more institutions. Compton prepared the memorandum that definitively argued for continued expansion of the Rad Lab on the grounds that radar science and engineering would best be developed by keeping scientists and engineers in constant contact within a single laboratory.

NDRC members found themselves drawn into a variety of other activities. To make research effective during the war, NDRC needed to participate in discussions of military strategy and to supervise the implementation of new equipment on the battlefield. Compton went into the field on several occasions, participated in the difficult discussions over how to use the atomic bomb, and went to Japan shortly after its surrender to assess Japan's wartime scientific developments. His duties took their toll on his vigor. He did not become embroiled, as did Bush, in the political controversies over public support of research in peacetime. Back at MIT, he dealt with the dislocations the war had created, most notably arranging for a new research laboratory in electronics, jointly staffed by members of the physics and electrical engineering departments, to succeed the Radiation Laboratory. He also informed the MIT Corporation of his intention to retire after turning sixty in 1947. He did retire in 1948 and died in New York City six years later.

Compton's career spanned and embodied profound changes in the sociology and political economy of American science. He struggled to harmonize the intellectual need to specialize with a university's need to limit the number of fields it could aggressively support. He inspired innovative attempts to use governmental powers to manage this tension through funding policies. In terms of the structure of the federal government and its relations to the national scientific communities, the postwar legacy of Compton's efforts is ambiguous. Postwar proposals to create a National Science Foundation produced a political stalemate that was not broken until other agencies had established vibrant programs that support academic science. Thus academic science has not had a single, outstanding governmental patron that could combine research funding with assessments of the organization of researchers as Compton had hoped the SAB would do. However, within MIT, Compton's legacy is secure. Multidepartmental research centers, like the Research Laboratory of Electronics, now dot MIT's landscape and span the life and social sciences as well as the physical sciences; MIT's presidents continue to rise to administrative prominence by directing research rather than managing money.

• The MIT archives has an extensive collection of Compton's official papers and correspondence. Other collections of his unpublished writings are housed at Princeton University, the National Academy of Sciences, and the National Archives (Record Group 227). There is no biography of Compton. Information on his early life is available in James R. Blackwood, *The House on College Avenue: The Comptons at Wooster 1891–1913* (1968). A full list of his published works along with tributes from his MIT colleagues was published in *Technology Review* 57 (Dec. 1954).

Compton has figured in many historical works, including A. Hunter Dupree, "The Great Instauration of 1940: The Organization of Scientific Research for War," in *The Twentieth-Century Sciences*, ed. Gerald Holton (1970); Roger L. Geiger, *To Advance Knowledge: The Growth of American Research Universities, 1900–1940* (1986); Joel Genuth, "Groping towards Science Policy in the United States in the 1930s," *Minerva* 25 (1987): 238–68, and "Microwave Radar, the Atomic Bomb, and the Background to U.S. Research Priorities in World War II," *Science, Technology, & Human Values* 13 (1988): 276–89; Henry Guerlac, *Radar in World War II* (1987); Robert Kargon and Elizabeth Hodes, "Karl Compton, Isaiah Bowman, and the Politics of Science in the Great Depression," *Isis* 76 (1985): 301–18; Daniel J. Kevles, *The Physicists* (1978); Robert E. Kohler, *Partners in Science: Foundations and Natural Scientists 1900–1945* (1991); Larry Owens, "Vannevar Bush and the Differential Analyzer: The Text and Context of an Early Computer," *Technology and Culture* 27 (1986): 63–95; Alex S. Pang, "Edward Bowles and Radio Engineering at MIT, 1920–1940," *Historical Studies in the Physical and Biological Sciences* 20 (1990): 313–38; S. S. Schweber, "The Young John Clarke Slater and the Development of Quantum Chemistry," *Historical Studies in the Physical and Biological Sciences* 20 (1990): 339–406; Katherine R. Sopka, *Quantum Physics in America, 1920–1935* (1980); and George Wise, *Willis R. Whitney, General Electric, and the Origins of U.S. Industrial Research* (1985). An obituary is in the *New York Times*, 23 June 1954.

JOEL GENUTH

COMSTOCK, Ada Louise (11 Dec. 1876–12 Dec. 1973), college administrator, was born in Moorhead, Minnesota, the daughter of Solomon G. Comstock, a lawyer, and Sarah Ann Balls. In addition to acting as legal counsel for the Great Northern Railway, Solomon Comstock also served on the state legislature and on the board of regents of the University of Minnesota. The family was well-off, living in an eleven-room house with stables and servants. Both parents recognized the importance of education for all children. Ada was educated at home by her mother for eight years before attending a small private school and then graduating from the local high school at the age of fifteen.

In 1892 Comstock attended the University of Minnesota. Her father arranged for her to lodge with his friend, Dean William Pattee, who warned her that she was overly fond of boys. After two years she transferred to Smith College, receiving her B.L. in 1897. During the next three years Comstock earned a teacher training diploma from Moorhead Normal School, a master's in English, history, and education from Columbia University, and spent a year studying in Paris at the Sorbonne. In 1900 she got her first job as an assistant teacher of English composition at the University of Minnesota, making $225 per year. Her father's influence probably played a role in that appointment, as it did in 1907 when she was appointed the first dean of women at the university, with the chief responsibility of supervising the ever-growing number of female students.

Comstock was concerned that the female students at the University of Minnesota had too little recreation. Rather than seeking off-campus alternatives, she created social outlets within the university, founding the Cap and Gown Society and encouraging afternoon teas. Her major concern was Shevlin Hall, which had been erected in 1906 as a hall for women but was already deteriorating. When Thomas Shevlin, the hall's benefactor, donated more money to the university, Comstock asked President Cyrus Northrup that it be used to renovate Shevlin Hall. When he told her that it was needed for a new chemistry building, she burst into tears. Luckily, Shevlin's daughter, a friend of Comstock's, passed by the room at that point; shortly afterward the family gave an additional $20,000 to renovate Shevlin Hall, providing female students with a meeting place, resting rooms, study halls, and eating facilities. Through her work as dean of women, Comstock managed to integrate female students more fully into the university, all the while fostering a growing general recognition of the importance of higher education for women. In 1910 her achievements at the university were recognized nationally when she was elected president of the Association of Women Deans.

In 1912 Marion Burton, a native Minnesotan and president of Smith College, asked Comstock to assume the position of dean. At Smith, Comstock continued her concern about the living accommodations of the students. She also studied the cost of collegiate education for women and expanded scholarships at Smith. In 1918 she was responsible for the emergency quarantine and nursing needed during the influenza epidemic. In 1916, when Burton returned to Minnesota, he tried to persuade Comstock to move with him but she refused, staying as acting president. Despite her obvious competence, the trustees of Smith preferred to appoint a man as the next president. Comstock formed a close relationship with Burton's successor, William A. Neilson, but she never forgot the slight and in 1923 left Smith to assume the presidency of Radcliffe.

Because Radcliffe had no faculty of its own, Comstock contended with negotiating teaching relationships with Harvard. She established a tutorial system for undergraduate instruction and broadened the student body, instituting regional scholarships and a doctoral program to encourage foreign applicants. To meet vocational needs, she also established a Summer Secretarial School (1931) and a management training program (1937). Without any long-term agreement with Harvard, Comstock struggled with the institution's president, A. Lawrence Lowell, who wished to decrease Harvard's involvement with Radcliffe. He saw the women's college as a "vampire" that drained the intellectual abilities of Harvard's professors. Luckily, Lowell's successor, James Bryant Conant, was more favorable toward Radcliffe, and, before Comstock retired in 1943, Harvard accepted the responsibility for educating Radcliffe women in the liberal arts on a long-term basis.

Comstock was involved in a variety of organizations outside of her professional work. She was the only woman appointed by President Herbert Hoover to the Wickersham Commission of Law Observance and Law Enforcement in 1929, and she recommended the revision, although not the rescinding, of Prohibition. She was also vice chairman of the Institute of Pacific Relations between the wars, visiting Manchuria in 1931 to report on the situation there.

In 1943 Ada succumbed to a 34-year courtship, marrying Wallace Notestein, whom she had first met while dean of women in Minnesota, only a week after her retirement. She then took on a new role: faculty wife. Comstock found the position not without its trials, writing to a friend, "I'm convinced that the superior achievement of men is due in part to their refusals . . . to be distracted by concern for clothes, foods, housekeeping, bill-paying and all the rest" (Smith, p. 224). Her marriage, nevertheless, marked Comstock's permanent retirement from public life.

In 1936 Lotus Coffman, president of the University of Minnesota, awarded Comstock an honorary LL.D., describing her as "Constructive and unselfish in serving the cause of education, constantly widening the intellectual and cultural opportunities of women, vigorously upholding the democratic principles upon which this nation was founded, and tireless in promoting international peace and good will, she has brought honor and distinction to her native state" (unpublished papers, Comstock file, University of Minnesota Archives). Throughout her life Comstock worked successfully to augment higher education for women in the United States, providing them with excellent social and academic opportunities at the university level. Comstock died at her home in New Haven, Connecticut.

• There are published and unpublished materials relating to Ada Comstock in the archives of the University of Minnesota, Smith College, the S. G. Comstock House, and Radcliffe University. See also Susan Smith, "Ada Comstock," in *Women in Minnesota*, ed. Barbara Stuhler and Gretchen Kreuter (1977); Margaret Farrand Thorp, *Neilson of Smith* (1956); and Claire Strom, "Edifices for Educators," *Hennepin History* (Spring 1991): 18–31. For information on Comstock's work on the Wickersham commission and with the Institute of Pacific Relations see various contemporary articles in the *New York Times*. An obituary is in the *New York Times*, 13 Dec. 1973.

CLAIRE STROM

COMSTOCK, Anna Botsford (1 Sept. 1854–24 Aug. 1930), educator and scientific illustrator, was born in a log cabin in Cattaraugus County, New York, the daughter of Marvin Botsford and Phoebe Irish. The Botsfords were prosperous farmers who encouraged Anna in her love of art, literature, and natural history. Her mother, a Hicksite Quaker, shared her love of the natural world with her daughter. From 1871 to 1873 Anna attended the Chamberlain Institute and Female College in nearby Randolph, where she resisted attempts by its faculty to have all students "experience" religion, asserting the moderate beliefs she would retain throughout her life.

In fall 1874, Botsford enrolled in the third class of women at the recently founded Cornell University, majoring in modern languages and literature. In 1875 her life took a decisive turn when she enrolled in the zoology course taught by a young instructor, John Henry Comstock. The two were soon sitting together at meals and taking long nature walks in the surrounding countryside. Botsford left college after two years, returning to her parents' home. In January 1877 she took up wood engraving with tools sent to her by Comstock and began to produce insect illustrations for him. She engraved her well-known piece *The Brook* at this time. After John Henry Comstock was promoted to assistant professor, they were married on 7 October 1878 and set up housekeeping at Fall Creek Cottage on the Cornell campus. Anna Botsford Comstock assumed the traditional duties of a university wife, running the household, supporting her husband's career, and providing a warm social environment for his students and colleagues. In 1906, under the pseudonym Marian Lee, she published her rather pithy observations of university social life in a novel, *Confessions to a Heathen Idol*.

When the hoped-for children did not appear, Comstock focused her energies on her husband's career, assisting him in the laboratory and classroom. She quickly learned much about entomology as she refined her skills as an engraver. The couple left Cornell for two years (1879–1881), when John Henry was appointed chief entomologist at the U.S. Department of Agriculture in Washington. Comstock continued to assist with his work, and in June 1879 she was appointed a clerk in the Bureau of Entomology to perform clerical duties, edit, and produce scientific illustrations of scale insects for the 1880 *Report of the Entomologist*. Her husband lacked the political skills to retain his appointment after a change in administrations, and in 1881 the Comstocks returned to Cornell. Comstock's first paid job and positive reviews of her illustrations encouraged her to develop her skills further, and she resumed her studies at Cornell. The Comstocks hired a maid and took their meals at Sage College to ensure that Comstock had sufficient time for her studies. The couple adopted this strategy at several demanding points in their careers. Based on her research on *Corydalus cornutus*, the dobsonfly, Comstock was awarded a bachelor of science degree in 1885. In 1888 she was one of the first four women to be initiated into Sigma Xi, the national science honor society founded at Cornell in 1886.

In 1885, 1887, and 1890 Comstock studied wood engraving in New York City with John P. Davis of the Cooper Union, developing technical and artistic skills. She joined the Society of American Wood Engravers and exhibited her work in Berlin, San Francisco, at the Chicago World's Fair of 1893, and at the Paris Exposition of 1900. She was awarded prizes at the New York Orleans Exposition of 1885 and the Pan-American Exposition of 1901. When her husband's *Introduction to Entomology* was published in 1888, the title-page credits noted "with many original illustrations drawn and engraved by Anna Botsford Comstock." Comstock's contributions were playing an increasingly important role in her husband's career as he built the premier department of entomology in the country.

As Comstock's scientific and artistic skills matured, she became a full-fledged partner. In *A Manual for the Study of Insects*, a classic textbook published in 1895, she was listed as coauthor with her husband. She prepared more than 800 original drawings as well as descriptions of life histories on such insects as "the clumsy rover, the bumblebee, . . . an old friend of us all." The lively text and beautiful plates distinguished the Comstock textbook from its dry and poorly illustrated competitors. Scientific publications were so central to the Comstocks' career that in 1893 John Henry founded a publishing house, Comstock Publishing Associates. He refused to allow colleagues to reproduce Comstock's drawings, a common practice, arguing that they were valuable, original contributions. Comstock did not, however, play a major role in her husband's theoretical research on the impact of evolutionary theory on insect taxonomy, limiting her work to illustrations and life-history descriptions.

Comstock accompanied her husband, who was also engaged in agricultural extension work, to farmers' institutes where she began teaching classes for farm wives. David Starr Jordan, a friend from their student days and president of the new Stanford University, invited both Comstocks to teach there. During the 1890s they taught in California during winters and at Cornell during the summer and fall.

In 1893 Comstock's career took a new direction that allowed her to combine her interests in teaching, natural history, art, and writing. At the request of the New York Committee for the Promotion of Agriculture, she developed a curriculum in nature study. A recent agricultural depression in New York had forced many young people to abandon farm life. The nature-study curriculum was designed to develop an appreciation for rural life and keep young people on their native farms. In 1896 the New York legislature appropriated $8,000 to the Cornell College of Agriculture for extension work, earmarking part for nature study. Comstock embarked on a career as a teacher, writer, and lecturer. Assisting Liberty Hyde Bailey, a horticulturist, she developed teaching tools for this new, popular area of study. She emphasized experiential learning, influenced greatly by the Pestalozzian method of education. Nature, not the dry textbook, was the teacher. The goal of nature study was to develop an appreciation of the natural world, not conduct scientific research.

Comstock lectured at farmers' institutes and chautauguas nationwide. The Cornell Nature-Study Program developed a national audience for its teacher training and publications. In 1898 she advanced from lecturer to assistant professor of nature study in the Cornell University Extension Division, the first woman appointed to the faculty. The Cornell Board of Trustees, however, revoked President Schurman's action and changed her title to instructor, although she retained the higher salary. She was not advanced to assistant professor until 1913. Two years before her retirement in 1922, she was finally appointed a full professor. Comstock did not protest these actions, believing that protest might jeopardize her husband's career. Although a trailblazer in her work, Comstock was not a political activist for women's rights; indeed, she did not support universal suffrage for women. Through both her actions and example, however, she opened many doors for other women.

During her years on the Cornell faculty, Comstock became a noted writer and editor. In 1903 she published her first book, *The Ways of the Six-Footed*, a compilation of her nature-study essays for children. The following year the Comstocks coauthored a popular volume, *How to Know the Butterflies*, and in 1905 she published *How to Keep Bees*. From 1905 to 1917 she was a contributing editor of the *Nature Study Review* and between 1917 and 1923 served as its editor in chief. From 1924 to 1929 she continued as the *Nature Study Review* editor of *Nature Magazine* after the journals merged. In 1911 she produced her most ambitious work, *Handbook of Nature Study*. Rejected by commercial presses, the 900-page manuscript was published reluctantly by her husband. It proved highly successful, remaining in print through the 1990s, and kept their small press solvent for decades. Designed for a popular audience, it was translated into eight languages and reached twenty-four printings. It introduced readers to nature study through activities in their own backyards.

Although her husband retired from Cornell in 1914, Comstock did not follow suit until 1922, but both continued active careers as professors emeriti until 1926 when her husband suffered a debilitating stroke. Comstock wrote, "this calamity, . . . for us, ended life. All that came after was merely existence." Despite the strain of caring for her husband and her advancing cancer, she continued to teach until August 1930, just a few days before she died in Ithaca. Her husband died within the year.

Anna Botsford Comstock was an internationally noted writer on natural history. She achieved her greatest distinction as an educator, developing innovative curricula for a generation of teachers. Despite her reluctance to assert women's causes, she set an example for generations of younger women.

• The John Henry and Anna Botsford Comstock Papers are located in the Cornell University Libraries, where additional information about Comstock can be found in the Simon H. Gage Papers and the Albert H. Wright Oral History interview. Her autobiography, *The Comstocks of Cornell: John Henry and Anna Botsford Comstock* (1953), recounts their life together. Edward H. Smith, "Anna Botsford Comstock: Artist, Author, and Teacher," *American Entomologist* 36, no. 2 (Summer 1990): 105–13, provides an overview of her career. Arnold Mallis, *American Entomologists* (1971), includes a profile of the Comstocks. James G. Needham, "The Lengthened Shadow of a Man and His Wife," *Scientific Monthly* 62, pts. 1 and 2 (1946): 140–50, 219–29, discusses the Comstocks' careers and their legacy. Pamela M. Henson, "The Comstocks of Cornell: A Marriage of Interests," in *Creative Couples in Science*, ed. H. Pycior et al. (1995), assesses their joint career, and in "Through Books to Nature: Anna Botsford Comstock and the Nature Study Movement," in *Science in the Vernacular: Women Who Have Popularized Science*, ed. B. T. Gates et al. (1997), she focuses on Comstock's role as a nature writer. E. Laurence Palmer, "The Cornell Nature Study Philosophy," *Cornell Rural School Leaflet* (1944), traces the history of nature study. Charlotte Conable, *Women at Cornell: The Myth of Equal Education* (1977), discusses challenges and opportunities for Cornell women, including Comstock. Obituaries are in the *Ithaca (N.Y.) Journal*, 23 Aug. 1930, and *Nature Magazine*, Oct. 1930.

PAMELA M. HENSON

COMSTOCK, Anthony (7 Mar. 1844–21 Sept. 1915), crusader against vice, was born in New Canaan, Connecticut, the son of Thomas Anthony Comstock, a farmer and sawmill owner, and Polly Lockwood. His mother died when Comstock was ten years old; he retained throughout his life a keen sense of her principled expectations. He attended public schools in New Canaan and New Britain. After an older brother died at Gettysburg, Comstock served for two years in the Union army, where he was dismayed by, but staunchly resisted, the raunchiness of camp life. Discharged in the summer of 1865, he held a variety of jobs in New England and the South before moving to New York City. He lived in Brooklyn and in Summit, New Jersey, where he died. In 1871 he married Margaret Hamilton, a woman ten years his senior. After their only child died in infancy, they adopted a daughter.

Throughout his life Comstock was oppressed by the huge disparity between the moral "values" that most Americans, he was confident, deeply believed in, and the behavior that the government, presumably the servant of the people, seemed to tolerate. Even the authorities in the New England town of his youth had failed to suppress a noisome tavern. Much more ominous was the metropolis, large, impersonal, seemingly amoral, and indifferent to the well-being of the innocent young men and women flooding into the city. It sometimes seemed to him that God had posted him at the mouth of a sewer in the middle of a swamp, with the obligation not only to eschew temptation himself but also to alert the government to the abominations he observed. Outraged when government officials ignored crime, he took it upon himself to trap and arrest wrongdoers.

Early in his crusade Comstock won the support of influential gentlemen such as Morris Jesup and William E. Dodge. They not only met some of Comstock's costs but also helped him form a special committee of the Young Men's Christian Association to prosecute a war on vice. When some YMCA members were offended by Comstock's willingness to entrap criminals, Jesup helped form an autonomous committee, the New York Society for the Suppression of Vice, modeled on the British society that had been founded in London earlier in the century. For the rest of his life Comstock served as secretary and principal agent, while Jesup and his friends provided money, upper-class respectability, and influence. In 1873 they helped persuade Congress to make more stringent the law against sending obscene materials through the U.S. mail. Comstock was appointed a special agent of the U.S. Post Office, with broad responsibilities for prosecuting violators of that law. He held this position until his death.

In 1880 Comstock published a 500-page account of a decade of crusading, *Frauds Exposed; or, How the People are Deceived and Robbed, and Youth Corrupted, Being a Full Disclosure of Various Schemes Operated through the Mails, and Unearthed by the Author*, in which he excoriated the lotteries, the bogus banks and brokers, the watch and jewelry frauds, the real estate scams, the astrologically based forecasts, and the bogus plans of medical aid to the poor that infected the mails and the daily newspapers—those "mighty agents [for good or ill] of our present civilization" (*Frauds*, p. 14). In 1887 he described his protracted assault on the racetracks in Brooklyn and Saratoga in *Gambling Outrages; or, Improving the Breed of Horses at the Expense of Public Morals*. In both books Comstock rejected criticism of his methods, including his penchant for devious means of entrapping criminals, his strong-arm arrests ("what are we spared to grow up to be men for, if not to *be men—to act* manly, and do a man's work in a straightforward and heroic manner?" [*Frauds*, p. 378], and his relentless and merciless prosecution in the courts. With breathtaking self-righteousness, he looked forward to being vilified: "I cannot expect," he wrote, "to have better treatment than our blessed Master" (*Frauds*, p. 7). In fact Comstock seems to have enjoyed wide popular support. A special committee of the New York legislature not only absolved him of wrongdoing but went on to conclude that "work such as Mr. Comstock does is vitally essential to the safety and decency of the community" (*Gambling Outrages*, p. 165).

In his later years Comstock was preoccupied with what seemed to him a rising tide of "obscenity." Abhorring both birth control and abortion, he managed to remove tons of pamphlets and "materials" from the U.S. mails. He also secured the prosecution of the prominent abortionist and contraceptionist Madame Restell (Ann Trow Lohman); when she committed suicide rather than face trial, Comstock rejoiced. Comstock was also primarily responsible for the prosecution in 1872–1873 of Victoria Woodhull and her sister Tennessee Claflin for publishing in their *Weekly* an account of Henry Ward Beecher's extramarital adventures.

In Comstock's mind, obscenity and blasphemy were closely linked, as were free love and free thought. In 1878 he secured the jailing of Ezra Heywood, the founder of the New England Free-Love League and the author of *Cupid's Yokes*, a detailed manual for enlightened marriage. Also imprisoned was D. M. Bennett, editor of *The Truth Seeker* and author of an *Open Letter to Jesus Christ*. Congress ignored a petition circulated by Robert Ingersoll and the National Liberal League, and signed by 50,000 citizens, that called for the repeal of all "Comstock laws, State and National."

In the last thirty years of his life, Comstock felt persistently challenged by artists and critics who no longer subscribed to the restraints of the Genteel Tradition. In 1887 he raided an exhibition of reproductions of French paintings, many of them nudes, at Knoedler's Gallery in New York City. The Society of American Artists, including the most distinguished painters and sculptors of the time, condemned, in the name of education, art, and morality, this interference by "incompetent persons." In response, Comstock published a pamphlet, *Morals vs. Art*, declaring that "it requires no expert in art or literature to determine whether a picture tends to awaken lewd thoughts and impure imaginations" (p. 25). Morality was the overriding consideration; art was desirable only insofar as it promoted, or at least did not subvert, morality. Comstock was concerned with the "thousands in the community who can not ever appreciate the nude in art. . . . To young men, cursed as thousands of the present day are, with secret vices, these photographs. . . . [are] a continual menace" (p. 11).

Books were as dangerous as paintings or photographs. In his essay "Vampire Literature" in the *North American Review* (1891), Comstock was concerned with the effect of the wildly popular "dime novels." Less objectionable than the old pornography, this "light literature," he believed, turned many young readers to lives of dissipation and crime. He asserted that many "standard" literary classics should be read only by mature scholars, just as treatises on medicine should be read only by doctors.

Comstock protested against the exotic dancers at the Chicago World's Fair. He tried to block the performance in 1905 in New York of George Bernard Shaw's *Mrs. Warren's Profession*. In 1906 he arrested a bookkeeper and confiscated more than a thousand copies of the New York Art Students League catalog, which included several nude pictures. In 1913 he threatened to arrest an art dealer who displayed Paul Chabas's nude *September Morn*. He was perfectly aware that crusades like his inevitably led to more widespread attention to the offensive art. But he derived immense satisfaction from the thousands of convictions he had won, the fines collected, and the goods confiscated—in sum, the vice suppressed.

In its moral absolutism, Comstock's crusade resembled the abolitionism of many of his forefathers and the prohibitionism of many of his contemporaries. The Society for the Suppression of Vice remained in existence long after his death. He helped form other vice societies; probably the most notable was the New England Watch and Ward Society. Perhaps most importantly, he influenced the federal government and many states to pass more stringent laws against obscenity.

• Comstock's papers have not been collected. The annual reports of the Society for the Suppression of Vice (1873–1915) are in the Library of Congress; they contain numerous handwritten comments by Comstock. Heywood Broun and Margaret Leech, in writing their lively and insightful *Anthony Comstock: Roundsman of the Lord* (1927), drew on Comstock's diary; the present location of the diary is not known. Charles G. Turnbull's uncritical friendship for Comstock limits the value of his biography, *Anthony Comstock: Fighter* (1913). An illustration of the rage Comstock could arouse is D. M. Bennett, *Anthony Comstock: His Cruelty and Crime* (1878; repr. 1971). Two books by Paul Boyer, *Purity in Print* (1968) and *Urban Masses and Moral Order in America* (1978), and Nicola Beisel, *Imperiled Innocents: Anthony Comstock and Family Reproduction in Victorian America* (1997), illuminate the context of Comstock's crusades. Robert Bremner provides a concise and perceptive interpretation of Comstock's career in his introduction to the 1967 repr. of Comstock's *Traps for the Young* (1883). An obituary is in the *New York Times*, 22 Sept. 1915.

ROBERT D. CROSS

COMSTOCK, Cyrus Ballou (3 Feb. 1831–29 May 1910), military engineer, was born in West Wrentham, Massachusetts, the son of Nathan Comstock and Betsey Cook. As a boy Comstock developed an interest in surveys after observing a railroad survey and a party from the Coast Survey, and he served as a rodman and leveler for two Massachusetts railroads. He entered the U.S. Military Academy at West Point in 1851 and graduated in 1855 at the top of his class. Following graduation Comstock supervised fortification construction in Florida and Maryland. From 1859 until July 1861 he served as assistant professor of natural and experimental philosophy at the Military Academy.

During the Civil War Comstock served with the construction of defenses for Washington, D.C., on the engineering staff of the Army of Potomac, and then as senior engineer at the siege and capture of Vicksburg. In September 1863 he was assigned convalescent leave, but his health had recovered by early 1864 when he was appointed an aide-de-camp for General Ulysses S. Grant, with the rank lieutenant colonel of volunteers. He remained as aide to Grant until 1870, although he was detached in early 1865 to assist in the capture of Fort Fisher and the Mobile campaign. The secretary of war awarded Comstock brevet promotions of colonel and brigadier general of volunteers after the assault on Fort Fisher, and for services during the Mobile campaign he earned promotion in 1865 as brevet major general of volunteers. His highest actual rank attained during the war was as major in the Corps of Engineers. In 1869 Comstock married Elizabeth Blair, the granddaughter of journalist and politician, Francis Preston Blair, who had adopted and raised her upon her mother's death. She died giving birth to their daughter in August 1872 (the daughter died the same year), and Comstock never remarried.

In May 1870 Comstock resigned as lieutenant colonel of volunteers and aide to General Grant, and reverted to major in the Corps of Engineers to command the Lake Survey. The Lake Survey had had six directors over the previous thirty years; Comstock served for twelve years and brought the work to a successful conclusion, finishing the survey of the Great Lakes and publishing the first navigation charts. He extended the scientific work of the survey, observing weather, tides, and seiches; established a larger observatory to determine the position of Detroit and assist in determination of the longitude of base stations in Nevada for the Wheeler Survey; and improved the pay of the civilian assistants and increased the size of the operation. He prepared the final "Report upon the Primary Triangulation of the United States Lake Survey," published in 1882 as Professional Paper 24 of the Corps of Engineers.

During his command of the Lake Survey, Comstock spent two periods in Europe: from August to November 1874 to study river engineering technology and military mapping organizations, and from May 1877 to June 1878 to continue those studies. His "Notes on European Surveys" appeared as part of the Chief of Engineers annual report for 1876. While with the survey Comstock also began service on the many boards and commissions that would encompass the remainder of his career. In 1874 and 1875 he served on a board considering the construction of jetties at the mouth of the Mississippi River to improve navigation. Civil engineer James B. Eads proposed these jetties but was opposed by Chief of Engineers A. A. Humphries, who favored a canal. The board, with Comstock in the majority, approved the jetties, and Comstock was appointed to monitor construction by civilian contractors from 1875 to 1877.

In 1875 and again in 1878–1879 Comstock took an active role in the debate about consolidation of the western surveys. As an engineer and leader of the Corps's Lake Survey, he was interested in the fate of the Wheeler Survey, and he shared a Blair family connection to engineer and surveyor G. M. Wheeler; Comstock wrote on federal surveys and testified on mapping procedures at congressional hearings.

Comstock served as one of the initial members of the Mississippi River Commission, established in 1879 to coordinate flood control measures on the river. The first major debate within the commission led to a decision of the majority under Eads to concentrate on building levees to scour out a deeper channel. Comstock and Benjamin Harrison (later U.S. president) opposed the levees-only policy; in 1896 the River Commission moved to dredging after it had become clear that levees only raised the flood level and had to be continually raised. Comstock served on the commission from 1879 to 1895 and as its president for the last five of these years.

In addition to oversight of the Mississippi River Commission, Comstock's final years in the Corps of Engineers included command of the Engineer School of Application at Willet's Point in New York harbor in 1886–1887, command of the Southwestern Division after 1888, and representing the War Department at an international navigation congress in Paris in 1892. After retirement in 1895 he settled in New York City, where he died.

Comstock was elected to the National Academy of Sciences in 1884, but his recognition derived from the application of science to public needs rather than from original research. Most of his publications concerned river and harbor improvements and appeared as appendices to the annual report issued by the Chief of Engineers. He was a member of sixty local engineer boards, and president of twenty-one. Comstock was a dedicated engineer whose efforts improved navigation and flood control throughout the country.

• The best biographical note on Comstock, by fellow army engineer Henry L. Abbot, appeared in essentially the same format in the West Point alumni publication in 1911 and in the National Academy of Sciences, *Biographical Memoirs 7* (1911): 195–201. Recent accounts of his service with the Corps of Engineers appear in Arthur M. Woodford, *Charting the Inland Seas: A History of the U.S. Lake Survey*, U.S. Army Corps of Engineers, Detroit District (1991), and A. E. Cowdrey, *Land's Ends: A History of the New Orleans District, U.S. Army Corps of Engineers* (1971).

PETER L. GUTH

COMSTOCK, Elizabeth Leslie Rous Wright (30 Oct. 1815–3 Aug. 1891), Quaker minister and reformer, was born in Maidenhead, Berkshire, England, the daughter of William Rous, a shopkeeper, and Mary Kekwick. Her parents were Quakers with family ties to the Society of Friends going back to the seventeenth century. They reared her in a strict Quaker atmosphere, an upbringing reinforced by education in Quaker schools at Islington and Croyden. In 1839 Elizabeth Rous returned to Croyden as a teacher; in 1842 she joined the staff of the Friends school at Ack-

worth. She remained there until her marriage in 1848 to Leslie Wright, a Quaker market gardener of Walthamstow in Essex. They had one child. After her husband's death in 1851, Elizabeth Wright kept a shop for a time at Bakewell in Devonshire. In 1854 she immigrated with her daughter and an unmarried sister to Belleville, Ontario. Four years later she married John T. Comstock, a prosperous Quaker farmer of Rollin, Michigan, where Elizabeth Comstock and her daughter moved.

In Rollin, Comstock quickly established herself as a leader in the closely knit Quaker communities of southeastern Michigan. Well known for their antislavery sympathies, she and her husband aided fugitive slaves. In 1861 she was recorded a Quaker minister. Although Friends were not pastoral in practice, Comstock was so highly regarded that she was often called on to minister to non-Quaker neighbors. During the Civil War, Comstock acquired a national reputation in reform circles. She took a particular interest in prison reform. Her visits to them tended to be preaching tours, but she also pressed state officials for more humane treatment of inmates and pleaded the cause of prisoners of whose innocence she was convinced. Her solicitude extended to prisoners of war, army hospital patients, and the freed people, on whose behalf she met with President Abraham Lincoln in October 1864. The meeting began with all present sitting in silent waiting, according to Quaker practice, and ended, by Comstock's account, with the president on his knees beside her as she prayed aloud. Comstock joined with Quakers in New York, Baltimore, Cincinnati, and other cities in educational and Sunday school work to "uplift" the poor. She was an avid temperance advocate, keeping a pledge book in her parlor in case a caller felt led to take the total-abstinence pledge.

Comstock's ties were with the Gurneyite Friends, the largest of the three Quaker groups to emerge from the schisms that splintered American Quakerism between 1827 and 1854. By the 1860s the Gurneyites had moved very close to the evangelical mainstream of American religion, and Comstock was fully in sympathy with this new direction. Her own preaching was highly evangelical. Addressing the Michigan legislature in 1862, for example, she admonished "Righteousness exalteth a nation, but sin is a reproach to any people," and pointed out "the national sins of this nation; slavery, scepticism, infidelity, and covetousness among the higher classes; swearing, drunkenness and depravity among the poor." By the late 1860s much of her time was given to promoting Sunday schools and prayer meetings. In the early 1870s, most of the Gurneyite Friends meetings in the United States were swept by a new wave of revivalism that was largely inspired and led by young Quaker ministers committed to second-experience, instantaneous sanctification or holiness. For a time Comstock united enthusiastically with such work, preaching in revival meetings. By 1880, however, she was moving in a more liberal direction, which put her at odds with the revivalists. She impatiently urged Friends to put aside doctrinal wrangling and devote themselves to more important religious and humanitarian work.

During and after the Civil War, Comstock devoted considerable energy to relief work for the freed people. She became a vocal critic of the Republican party in the 1870s as it edged away from support for black rights. In 1879 Comstock undertook her last great enterprise, made on behalf of the "Exodusters," the numerous black emigrants from the South to Kansas. She toured the country raising funds, tried to interest president James A. Garfield in the cause, and served for two years as secretary of the Kansas Freedmen's Relief Association (1879–1881). A few months after her husband's death in 1884, Comstock moved to Union Springs, New York, where she lived until her death.

• Comstock's papers are not known to have survived. A few letters are in the Joshua L. Baily Papers in the Quaker Collection at Haverford College. The major source for Comstock's life is C[atherine] Hare, *Life and Letters of Elizabeth L. Comstock* (1895). A useful short sketch is in Errol T. Elliott, *Quaker Profiles from the American West* (1972). Family data and information on her life as a Quaker can be found in the abstracts of the records of Rollin Monthly Meeting of Friends in Ann and Conrad Burton, comps., *Michigan Quakers* (1989). Comstock's career is also detailed in Quaker periodicals: the *Friends' Review* (1860–1891), the *Herald of Peace* (1868–1869), the *American Friend* (1867–1868), and the *Christian Worker* (1871–1891). Different estimates of Comstock's relationship to the holiness movement among Friends can be found in Thomas D. Hamm, *The Transformation of American Quakerism: Orthodox Friends, 1800–1907* (1988), and Carole D. Spencer, "Evangelism, Feminism and Social Reform: The Quaker Woman Minister and the Holiness Revival," *Quaker History* 80 (Spring 1991): 24–46.

THOMAS D. HAMM

COMSTOCK, F. Ray (1880–15 Oct. 1949), producer and theatrical impresario, was born and raised in Lynn, Massachusetts, the son of David Comstock and Emma Dean. The family moved to Buffalo, New York, where their son began his career in the theater as an employee of the Star Theatre while still in his early teens. When he was fifteen years old, he struck out on his own, going to New York City, where he found employment as a ticket seller for the producer Charles Dillingham at the Criterion Theatre on Broadway. He next worked as treasurer of the Casino Theatre for the Shubert brothers, who were at the beginning of their aggressive and successful careers as theatrical entrepreneurs. Taking the little capital that he had accumulated from his various employments, he invested it in *The Runaways*, which was produced by Sam Shubert, Samuel Nixon, and J. Frederick Zimmerman at the Casino Theatre, opening in May 1903. Four years later, with the profits he made from its successful Broadway run, he sent the production on the road as an independent manager for three more profitable years. In 1908, he produced a musical comedy, *Bandana Land*, which brought together the best of the black talent of the day to the Broadway stage. The performers included the popular song and dance team of Bert Williams

and George Walker, who later came under his personal management. The musical, one of the earliest to be created entirely by black talent, toured the country for two seasons. Williams went on to become a star of the Ziegfeld *Follies*.

In 1913 Comstock built a tiny theater (299 seats) on West 39th Street, east of Broadway, for the production of one-act plays by young and developing playwrights to be selected by the play agent Elizabeth Marbury. It opened on 14 March 1913 with a bill of serious plays under the direction of Holbrook Blinn, an outstanding dramatic actor of the period. The bill included *The Switchboard*, by Edgar Wallace; *Fear*, by H. R. Le Normand and Jeran D'Auguzan; *Fancy Free*, by Stanley Houghton; *Any Night*, by Edward Ellis; and *A Tragedy of the Future*, by William C. De Mille. Many of the later plays presented by Comstock were in the style of the Grand Guignol, which caused his theater to be known as the "theater of thrills." (Grand Guignol refers to a type of short nineteenth-century horror play of murder and mayhem produced in a theater in Paris of that name.) When the experiment ceased to interest the public, he and Marbury commissioned composer Jerome Kern and playwright Guy Bolton (later joined by playwright P. G. Wodehouse) to put together a musical show for the Princess that would be long on imagination but short on cast, scenery, and expense. The result was *Nobody Home* (1915), and it was successful enough to encourage Comstock to continue with this type of modest musical production. It ultimately engendered a series of intimate Princess Theatre musical comedies, which brought renown to him and his little theater from 1915 to 1918. Among the outstanding successes were *Very Good Eddie* (1915) and *Oh Lady! Lady!* (1918). Another Comstock production, *Leave It to Jane* (1917), which was intended for the Princess Theatre, opened in a Broadway theater because the stage of the Princess was already occupied with *Oh, Boy!* It, too, became a success. The Princess musicals not only developed the talents of their creators but contributed to the maturing of the musical comedy form in America.

In association with producer William A. Brady and, later and more importantly, producer Morris Gest, Comstock presented a series of plays and musicals on Broadway and independently began to acquire leases on theaters in Toledo, Cleveland, Albany, Schenectady, and Chicago, where he could book his own and other productions. With Gest, his most successful collaborator, he was responsible for importing the Moscow Art Theatre to New York in 1923 for an eight-week engagement, Nikita Balieff's *Chauve-Souris* in 1922 (and subsequent years), and Max Reinhardt's production of *The Miracle* in 1924. He also helped to introduce Eleonora Duse to American audiences and was credited with discovering Marion Davies and the Dolly Sisters and bringing them to Broadway. Less flambuoyant than his partner Gest and most of the rest of the producing fraternity of his time, Comstock was considered a level-headed but adventurous business-man who could thread his way through the tangles of

Broadway, always knowing when it was time to retreat or go forward.

In 1929, after a financially rewarding career, Comstock retired from show business to his home in Boston. He closed his career with the statement: "If the American theatre owes me anything, the debt is more than balanced by what I owe it. And what I owe it is thirty years of delightful association with the most fascinating people in the world." He died in Boston. Childless, his only survivor was his wife, Fannie Fiske Comstock. One of the men who early defined the role of the producer in the American theater, Comstock distinguished himself by trying to elevate and broaden the taste of the theater-going public in presenting unpretentious but excellently written musical comedies, talented black performers, and notable European actors and companies.

• There is no published biography of F. Ray Comstock. Some information may be found in the Robinson Locke scrapbook, ser. 3, no. 341, New York Public Library for the Performing Arts; Gerald Bordman, *American Musical Theatre* (1978); and *Who Was Who in America*, vol. 2 (1950), p. 125. His obituary appeared in the *New York Herald Tribune* and the *New York Times*, 16 Oct. 1949, and in *Variety*, 19 Oct. 1949.

MARY C. HENDERSON

COMSTOCK, George Cary (12 Feb. 1855–11 May 1934), astronomer, was born in Madison, Wisconsin, the son of Charles Henry Comstock, a harness maker and later a merchant, and Mercy Bronson. The family moved to Kenosha, Wisconsin, then to Sandusky, Ohio, and then to Adrian, Michigan, where George took the Latin-scientific course in high school. He graduated in 1873 and entered the University of Michigan. Comstock was very good in mathematics and soon attracted the attention of James C. Watson, the professor of astronomy and director of the observatory. From him Comstock learned the classical astronomy of stellar positions and celestial mechanics. At the end of his freshman year the Michigan student, with Watson's support, arranged to go to work as a surveyor for the U.S. Lake Survey for six months each summer, returning to Ann Arbor each winter to continue his schooling. On this job Comstock helped survey Lakes Ontario, Erie, and Superior as well as the upper Mississippi River. After graduating in 1877 he continued this work for a year, then spent a year back at Michigan in graduate work under John M. Schaeberle. Comstock then went to the University of Wisconsin, where Watson had become professor of astronomy and director of the new Washburn Observatory. Comstock was hired as his assistant; but Watson died unexpectedly in 1880, and Edward S. Holden succeeded him as director in 1881.

Comstock continued at Madison as Holden's full-time assistant, but in his "spare time" he studied law at the University of Wisconsin law school, to be prepared for an alternate career possibility if he could not remain in academe. He received his law degree in 1883 and was admitted to the bar, but he never practiced law. Instead, in 1885 he was appointed professor of mathematics and astronomy at Ohio State University. Comstock spent the summer of 1886 at Lick Observatory, then under construction in California, and hoped for a position there when it was completed. In 1885 Holden had left Wisconsin to become president of the University of California, with the understanding that he would give it up for the directorship of Lick as soon as it was ready for operation. Probably he had encouraged Comstock to think in terms of getting a job there.

Comstock, however, was appointed associate director of Washburn Observatory in 1887, after two years at Columbus. Then only thirty-two, Comstock was considered too young to be the director at Wisconsin on his own, and Asaph Hall, of the Naval Observatory staff in Washington, had been named part-time nonresident director. Two years later Comstock became the full director of Washburn. He remained there until he retired in 1922. Thus he spent his entire professional career, except for two years on the Ohio State faculty, at the University of Wisconsin.

All of his research was on positional astronomy, and he considered his most important work to be the measurement of stellar aberration and atmospheric refraction, both of which cause small displacements in the apparent positions of stars. His retiring presidential address to the American Astronomical Society in 1928 was titled "The Atmospheric Refraction," four decades after he had begun working on the problem. Comstock also measured double stars with the Washburn Observatory fifteen-inch refractor.

His main duty at Wisconsin was teaching. Comstock had only a few astronomy students but taught the required course on practical astronomy for civil engineers. He was an expert with every type of sextant and surveyor's instrument, and he wrote the widely used *Text-book of Field Astronomy for Engineers* in 1903, based on this course. It went through several editions, as did his *Text-book of Astronomy*, an elementary text for high school and college courses, first published in 1901.

When Charles R. Van Hise became president of the University of Wisconsin in 1904, he set up its graduate school and named Comstock as its first chairman, later successively titled director, then dean, as it grew. Comstock was a highly effective administrator, and his wide viewpoint—he encouraged the growth of all departments, not just astronomy—did much to build up research at Madison. In 1899 he was the first person to be elected from the University of Wisconsin faculty to the National Academy of Sciences. Comstock never earned a doctoral degree himself, but in 1907 the University of Illinois awarded him an LL.D., and the University of Michigan, his alma mater, awarded him an Sc.D. His own most successful graduate students were Sidney D. Townley, whom he had also taught as an undergraduate, and Joel Stebbins, who came to Wisconsin from the University of Nebraska. Both earned master's degrees at Madison before going on to Ph.D.s elsewhere, and to long and successful careers in astronomy.

Because of his legal training, Comstock was involved as an officer in many scientific societies, ensuring that the societies' by-laws and constitutions were within the law. He drafted the constitution for the Astronomical and Astrophysical Society of America (later changed to the American Astronomical Society), which came into being in 1899, and was the society's first secretary and, later, vice president and then president.

Comstock married Esther Cecile Everett of Madison in 1894, and they had one child. He gave up his post as dean of the graduate school in 1920 and retired two years later. Comstock's advice was no doubt important in bringing Stebbins back to Wisconsin as his successor as professor of astronomy and director of Washburn Observatory. After his retirement Comstock lived in Beloit, Wisconsin, until his death in Madison. He had been an important positional astronomer, teacher, administrator, and astronomical society leader for many years.

• The most complete collections of Comstock's letters are in the George C. Comstock Papers and the Department of Astronomy, College of Letters and Sciences Papers in the University of Wisconsin Archives, Memorial Library, University of Wisconsin, Madison. He published the guiding ideas of his long program of observations of double stars in "Binary Stars," American Academy for the Advancement of Science, *Proceedings* (1894): 27–52, and his measurements of them in "Observations of Double Stars, 1907–1919," Washburn Observatory *Publications* 10, part 4 (1921): 1–167. The best published sources on his life and scientific career are the obituary article by Sidney D. Townley, "George Cary Comstock," Astronomical Society of the Pacific, *Publications* 46 (1934): 171–76, and the memorial biography by Joel Stebbins, "George Cary Comstock, 1855–1934," National Academy of Sciences, *Biographical Memoirs* 20 (1939): 161–82. The latter contains a complete bibliography of Comstock's published scientific papers and books as well as a listing of many of the book reviews he wrote. Two other useful sources are Merle Curti and Vernon Carstensen, *The University of Wisconsin, 1848–1925: A History* (2 vols., 1949), and R. C. Bless, *Washburn Observatory, 1878–1978: University of Wisconsin-Madison* (1978).

DONALD E. OSTERBROCK

COMSTOCK, John Henry (24 Feb. 1849–20 Mar. 1931), entomologist, was born in Janesville, Wisconsin, the son of Ebenezer Comstock, a farmer, and Susan Allen, a nurse. Comstock grew up in upstate New York in a succession of foster homes after his father died en route to the California gold rush. Taken into the home of Lewis Turner, a master of Great Lakes ships, Comstock worked as a ship's cook while pursuing his education. The purchase in 1870 of Thaddeus W. Harris's *Insects Injurious to Vegetation* awakened his interest in insects.

Comstock enrolled in Cornell University in 1869, one year after it opened, working his way through school as a bricklayer, lab assistant, and chimesmaster. Encouraged by his professor, Burt Green Wilder, he developed such expertise in entomology that he was asked to teach a course in that subject while still an undergraduate. During the summer of 1872 Comstock pursued advanced studies in entomology at Harvard University under Hermann August Hagen. He was appointed instructor in entomology at Cornell in 1873, beginning a forty-year tenure. He received the B.S. degree in 1874 and advanced to assistant professor in 1876. His only postgraduate studies were at Yale University in 1875 and at the University of Leipzig, under Rudolf Leuckart, in 1888–1889. He advanced to full professor in 1882 and retired in 1914.

In 1878 Comstock married Anna Botsford, a student at Cornell. During their 52-year marriage, they shared careers devoted to scientific research, writing, and teaching. Anna illustrated Comstock's publications and assisted with his agricultural extension work. The Comstock home on the Cornell campus became the social center for the biology department as well as home to numerous students and colleagues. Although the Comstocks had no children, their home was always filled with an extended Cornell family.

During his first years at Cornell, Comstock became involved in agricultural extension work, teaching farmers about agricultural pests. Economic entomology grew rapidly in the nineteenth century after passage of the Morrill Act of 1862, establishing land grant colleges that taught agriculture, and the Hatch Act of 1887, establishing agricultural extension stations at those land grant colleges. In 1879 Comstock was named U.S. Entomologist at the U.S. Department of Agriculture, replacing C. V. Riley. He outlined an ambitious plan for a national program in entomology, but he lacked the political skills to retain his appointment. In 1881 Riley in turn replaced Comstock as U.S. Entomologist, and Comstock returned to Cornell.

At Cornell Comstock developed the premier department of entomology in the United States, the training ground for most government and university positions in that growing field. His students received broad training in systematic, laboratory, and field entomology. By his retirement in 1914, the entomology faculty had grown from his single position to seventeen. During the 1890s he also established the entomology program at the new Stanford University, at the request of his former student and friend, Stanford's president, David Starr Jordan.

Comstock also had significant impact on entomology through his publications. To fill a need for entomological texts, in 1888 he began publishing textbooks for his students' use. *An Introduction to Entomology* (1888), *A Manual for the Study of Insects* (1895), *The Spider Book* (1912), and *The Elements of Insect Anatomy* (1895) became the standard texts in the field and remained in print through the 1980s. Anna Comstock appeared as coauthor of the texts, which she illustrated. In 1894 Comstock established Comstock Publishing Associates to provide an outlet for his work and that of his colleagues and students. The Comstocks bequeathed the firm to Cornell, and it formed the basis of Cornell University Press.

The Comstocks were also at the center of the nature study movement, with the first Cornell nature study faculty working in Comstock's department. In the 1890s Anna Comstock became a leading figure in the movement, and together the Comstocks published a number of popular works in entomology, including *Insect Life* (1897) and *How to Know the Butterflies* (1904).

During his student years Comstock became intrigued by the questions raised by Charles Darwin in *On the Origin of Species*. Comstock spent the rest of his life trying to unravel the evolutionary history of insects and to formulate a classification of insects that captured their evolutionary relationships. Many historians of science have claimed that in the late nineteenth century, little serious work was done on evolutionary theory; however, Comstock developed and taught a method for evolutionary analysis for systematic biology which looked at variation, sequences of character change, and developmental history. His seminal work, "The Wings of Insects" (1898), appeared as a series of articles in the *American Naturalist*, and applied his methodology to insect wing venation and offered a preliminary evolutionary classification. This complex research program continued throughout Comstock's career and was pursued by many of his students. Comstock taught more than 5,000 students, including such noted biologists as David Starr Jordan, Leland Ossian Howard, and Vernon Lyman Kellogg.

Comstock played a central role in founding the Entomological Society of America, calling its organizational meeting at Cornell in 1906 and serving as its first president. He was an early faculty sponsor of Sigma Xi, the scientific honor society, soon after its founding at Cornell in 1886; he served as its president (1889–1890) and remained active in its affairs throughout his career. Comstock suffered a debilitating stroke in 1926, which ended his research career, and died five years later in Ithaca, New York.

• The John Henry and Anna Botsford Comstock Papers are in the Department of Manuscripts and University Archives, Cornell University Libraries, where additional information about him can be found in the Simon H. Gage Papers and the Albert H. Wright Oral History Interview. The autobiography by Anna Botsford Comstock, *The Comstocks of Cornell: John Henry and Anna Botsford Comstock* (1953), recounts their life together. Pamela M. Henson, "Evolution and Taxonomy: J. H. Comstock's Research School in Evolutionary Entomology at Cornell University, 1874–1930" (Ph.D. diss., Univ. of Maryland, 1990), covers his research and teaching. Arnold Mallis, *American Entomologists* (1971), includes a profile of Comstock. James G. Needham, "The Lengthened Shadow of a Man and His Wife," parts I and II, *Scientific Monthly* 62 (1946): 140–50, 219–29, discusses the Comstocks' careers and their legacy of students and institutions. Obituaries include James G. Needham, "John Henry Comstock," *Science* 73, no. 1894 (1931): 409–10, Glenn W. Herrick, "Professor John Henry Comstock, February 24, 1849–March 20, 1931," *Annals of the Entomological Society of America* 25 (1931): 199–204, and the *New York Times*, 21 Mar. 1931.

PAMELA M. HENSON

CONANT, James Bryant (26 Mar. 1893–11 Feb. 1978), educator and scientist, was born in the Dorchester section of Boston, Massachusetts, the son of James Scott Conant, a photo engraver and real estate developer, and Jennett Orr. Conant attended the Roxbury Latin School, a public boys' six-year examination school in Boston, and subsequently attended graduate school at Harvard University on an academic scholarship, where he studied chemistry with Nobel Prize winner Theodore Richards. He graduated in 1913 and immediately undertook the study of physical chemistry and biological chemistry at Harvard. He completed his doctorate in chemistry in 1916 and in 1917 entered the Chemical Warfare Service Corps of the U.S. Army, where he was placed in charge of manufacturing lewisite, a deadly gas, in Willoughby, Ohio.

After the war, in 1919 Conant returned to Harvard and began work in physical chemistry as an assistant professor. In 1921 he married Grace Richards, the daughter of Theodore Richards; they had two sons. Conant shared only with his wife that he had three ambitions, "to become the leading organic chemist in the United States; after that I would like to be president of Harvard; and after that a Cabinet member, perhaps the Secretary of the Interior" (*My Several Lives*, p. 52).

Between 1919 and 1933, Conant vigorously pursued his academic career. He rose to the rank of full professor in 1927, led the Department of Chemistry from 1931 to 1933, and wrote more than eighty research papers in chemistry. Under his leadership, the Department of Chemistry grew both in prestige and physical plant, and Conant was considered a leading chemist in the arena of reaction mechanisms, electrical chemistry and biochemistry. In particular, he did a considerable amount of research on the chemistry of hemoglobin and chlorophyll. He won the prestigious Nichols Medal (awarded by the American Chemical Society) in 1932 for his work in oxidation-reduction potentials, the Chandler Medal (awarded by Columbia University), in 1932, the Medal of the American Institute of Chemists in 1934, and the American Chemical Society's Priestly Medal in 1944. Conant's intelligence, focus, and ambition coupled with his broad national exposure as a leader in chemistry research and applications made him a figure to be reckoned with in the academic world.

Conant completed his undergraduate education during the academic expansion of the university influenced by the vision of the recently retired Harvard president Charles William Eliot; his professorial career was framed by the building boom sponsored by President A. Lawrence Lowell, which produced the visual and architectural coherence of modern Harvard. Numerous buildings, particularly the undergraduate houses, were constructed during the Lowell presidency; but perhaps the greatest architectural needs of the university were new chemistry laboratories. With Conant, Lowell pressed the agenda for quality academic laboratories, and in 1928 the Mallinckrodt Laboratories were constructed, gaining Conant valuable experience in the art of fundraising.

President Lowell, at age seventy, announced in 1932 his retirement as president of Harvard. He had completed his goal of rebuilding the university and changing the undergraduate curriculum to one based on the Oxford-Cambridge model. The key issues confronting his successor included Harvard's declining reputation for academic rigor, declining enrollment (down 8 percent between 1932 and 1934) due to the depression, and the prospect of a necessary rebuilding of the faculty to reflect the progress in various academic disciplines in the postwar era. The process of selection of a new Harvard president involved Harvard's six-man governing board, the Harvard Corporation, and a complex web of ambition, intrigue, and artful politics. Conant surfaced as a "dark horse" candidate in private conversations with corporation members, where his clarity of thought, quality of intellect and intellectual curiosity, personal discipline and character, and commitment to Harvard emerged in a compelling manner. Other leading candidates were disqualified on the basis of excess ambition (two corporation members), presumed character flaws, lack of Harvard affiliation, or inability to marshal a majority of the corporation. Because, among his achievements, Conant had shown himself to be astutely able to navigate academic politics, the corporation turned to this forward-looking man with nineteenth-century manners to lead Harvard through the depression and the challenges of the twentieth century.

Conant's Harvard presidency spanned the years 1933 to 1953. In the early years, he focused on shaping the student body and faculty of the university by identifying and bringing to Harvard students of great academic promise from across the country and a distinguished faculty from around the world. He planned and executed the Harvard tercentenary celebration in 1936, bringing world attention to issues of free speech. He wanted to solve problems within the graduate schools of the university and began developing a broader view of education, often through the lens afforded by the financially beleaguered Harvard Graduate School of Education. He began to see education as a social instrument to preserve the society rather than merely as an instrument to train the most academically able.

From 1939 to 1946 Conant was deeply involved with the federal Office of Scientific Research and Development, coordinating the federal effort to develop the atomic bomb and other scientific war-related programs. Although he remained the symbolic head of Harvard, he spent little time there, and the real management of the university was left to the provost, Paul Buck. In 1947 Conant returned to Harvard, where his focus was on national issues in education and in international scientific development, and a vision of Harvard as an educational leader through the notion of general education in a free society, rather than as a repository for the most talented students in the United States and the most gifted faculty in the world.

The university that Conant inherited from Lowell was an insular institution of gentleman scholars educated in the elite eastern boarding schools. Intrusions from the surrounding world grew with the deepening economic depression and rising tide of fascism. Conant was well aware of the declining conditions at other universities. For example, "over 60 percent of the freshmen who left the University of Chicago in the fall of 1931 did so for financial reasons. Only 54 percent of those who entered Stanford in 1930–1931 graduated four years later, the highest attrition since World War I" (Levine, *Culture of Aspiration* [1986], p. 188). Coupled with declining enrollment was the emerging criticism that Harvard was declining in intellectual rigor. Frederick Keppel, chair of the Carnegie Corporation, characterized the Lowell-appointed professor as charming and urbane, but he lamented Harvard's elitism, citing the "chilling effects of Harvard's institutional introspection."

Conant sought a solution to Harvard's challenges that combined opportunity and rigor. Arguing that opportunity should be based on merit, he advocated in his first *President's Report* a National Scholar's program based on intellectual merit. Harvard's program was unique in its emphasis on testing, national recruiting, and need-blind admissions. The program was a dramatic intervention in a university where two-thirds of the freshman class came from the North Atlantic states and no student received a full scholarship. Within five years the program expanded throughout the country and Conant had assumed national leadership in espousing his view that democracy required a system of merit in which the academically talented would be identified and given the opportunity to excel regardless of financial need. And excel they did. According to Seymour Harris, more than 65 percent of the scholarship students "in the classes of 1938–1940 graduated Summa or Magna Cum Laude [a rate which exceeded the non-scholarship students by a factor of four]" (*The Economics of Harvard*, p. 99). By the late 1930s, thirty to fifty National Scholars matriculated annually, and the program was being replicated by other universities.

As the 1936 tercentennial of Harvard College approached, Conant had addressed and established a model for the student population for the college. He had also implemented a rigorous evaluation program for the faculty, seeking to bring to Harvard outstanding national and international scholars and to deliberately weed out the junior faculty, retaining only those professors whose futures were unusually bright. Remarkably consistent in his views that the recruitment, promotion, and tenure of faculty should be based on the same meritocratic principles as the recruitment and retention of students, Conant used the opportunity of the Tercentenary to promulgate views on the role of the university in preserving and transforming knowledge. He advocated the creation of a University Professor position as an approach that would allow a superior scholar to "roam" the university in his scholarship and teaching. He used the international plat-

form of the Tercentenary as an opportunity to mobilize funds for his initiatives of university
professorships, national scholarships, and mobile
funds for research. He also spoke out for toleration
and democratic traditions in the university.

During the war years (1939–1946), Conant was
deeply involved with the Office of Scientific Research
and Development led by Vannevar Bush. He chaired
the National Defense Research Council, its new weapons research and development group. Consistent in
his interventionist philosophy, Conant authorized the
"all out" development of an atomic weapon in December 1940. Conant played key national roles, establishing priorities for the expenditure of at least $350–500
million in weapons research. He joined Bush, Henry
Stimson, General George C. Marshall, and President
Franklin D. Roosevelt in the top policy group for the
atomic bomb. He also served a high profile public role
on Roosevelt's Rubber Survey ("Baruch") Committee,
which established the criteria for the domestic allocation of rubber.

Conant believed in "total war," in which the full resources of the nation would be used to justify the
means. Called to serve, he used his full range of university and scientific contacts to mobilize the intellectual resources, the financial resources (through contracting government weapons work directly to
universities), and policy and engineering resources to
develop, test, and use the atom bomb. Present at the
test firing of the atom bomb in Alamogordo, New
Mexico, on 16 July 1945, he was filled with pessimism
and awe:

Then came a burst of white light that seemed to fill the
sky and seemed to last for seconds. I had expected a
relatively quick and bright [light] flash. The enormity
of the light and its length stunned me. My instantaneous reaction was that something had gone wrong. . . .
My first impression remains the most vivid, a cosmic
phenomenon like an eclipse. The whole sky suddenly
full of white light like the end of the world. Perhaps my
impression was only premature on a time scale of years.
(Conant's Diary)

Conant knew that with the bomb's use, the "total war"
would soon be over; he had acted on his belief that the
preservation of democracy was worth the possible destruction of the planet. While Conant and Bush each
favored the internationalization of atomic power, Conant decided to return to university life and explore
the issues of education and the preservation of democracy.

Before the full outbreak of war, Conant had begun
to explore the role of education in a democracy. He
was concerned with identifying leaders who could forward the aims of the democratic tradition. In the postwar years he sought to combine the education and
training of the general population with a system that
saw as its first priority the identification and development of the talented few. Democracy would best be
served, he believed, by an educated elite leading informed and trained masses. Harvard led the explora-

tion of the undergraduate curriculum with the publication and promulgation of *General Education in a Free
Society*, which saw the role of precollegiate education
as training in democratic values and its mission as sorting the college bound from the "vocational classes."

Harvard in the postwar era reflected Conant's early
aspirations. The GI Bill of Rights helped to fill the
university with bright, focused, ambitious students
from every group in American society. Federal money
bolstered the economics of the university. Conant began to use the Harvard presidency as a bully pulpit to
speak out on broader issues in American education,
advocating the social science focus of Harvard's Graduate School of Education as an appropriate model for
sorting and identifying talented leaders from all walks
of American life. A system based on merit should
drive educational opportunity.

After twenty years at the helm of Harvard, Conant
had enormous public stature as a war leader, university president, and educational spokesman. He left Harvard in 1953 and spent the next four years in Germany, where, serving as high commissioner and
ambassador, he managed the occupying military forces, coordinated relief efforts, and provided diplomatic
leadership. In 1957 he returned to the field of education in an attempt to use his prestige and national visibility to strengthen schooling at its core—public education.

While the interpretations of historians differ, the climate surrounding the expansion of high schools in the
1950s reveals many of the crucial and traditional debates about the purpose and constituencies of schooling. In part, the debate was triggered by the vastly expanded numbers of children attending school. In 1945
approximately 6.1 million students enrolled in high
school; by 1959 almost 10 million were enrolled; and
by 1963, 12.375 million students attended high
school. In addition, retention statistics soared. The
prevailing curricular model was "life adjustment" with
the goal of providing civic and vocational coherence in
a diverse society. By the mid-1950s, life adjustment
was attacked by many in the society who felt that the
challenges posed by science and technology required
an enhanced academic curriculum, particularly in
mathematics and science. Critics such as Admiral Hyman Rickover argued that the threat posed by Soviet
expansion required a knowledge-based rather than a
comfortably adjusted response from students and citizens. Conant's approach acknowledged the tradition
of including all of the youth of a community in its comprehensive high school. At the same time he advocated
a separate and more rigorous academic path for academically talented youth.

In 1957 Conant began a two-year study under the
auspices of John Gardner, president of the Carnegie
Corporation, which led to his bestselling book, *The
American High School Today* (1959). In it Conant reported on his visits to numerous schools in the country, as well as his own philosophy of education. Paral-
leling his efforts at Harvard, he described the purpose
of education as fundamentally meritocratic. He be-

lieved that every public school should offer an academic curriculum to all of its students, but he saw as a central purpose of public education identifying and training talented youth in a community-based setting.

In 1959 Conant applied his meritocratic analysis to two groups excluded in previous analyses: youth in slums and in wealthy suburbs. In *Slums and Suburbs* (1961) Conant referred to the developing "social dynamite" accumulating in the nation's large cities and advocated improvement of schools in geographic areas rather than desegregation. Contrasting the lack of opportunity in urban American schools with the gleaming suburban schools of the 1950s, he brought national attention to the issues of urban education; however, his meritocratic analysis simply could not be sustained in an urban environment bereft of basic services. His solution rested on two tracks: identify the academically talented and train them to exercise creativity and leadership; and, defuse the "social dynamite" with the promise of jobs through vocational education. Rather than reviewing the fabric of the society itself, Conant remained focused on the outcomes of education. The results of schools sanctioned their processes.

Conant wrote several additional books on education after 1962, including *The Education of American Teachers* (1963) which continued to reflect his early core views on education. For his entire life, Conant believed in the importance of education to transform an academically talented individual's life. Talent combined with schooling offered the keys of opportunity to the individual and creativity to the nation. Indeed, during his service as Harvard's president, and in his policy efforts on the national level, Conant also began to view the sustenance of public education as essential to the fabric of the national society. Social preservation and individual meritocracy were the cornerstones of his educational philosophy. While his vision of a comprehensive high school became the dominant model of education in the late 1950s and early 1960s, leading to the school consolidation movement and the regional high school, it did not serve the needs of individuals who were economically and socially deprived, and consequently its saliency became limited in the 1960s as the urban problems of the country dominated national debate.

• The Personal and Presidential Papers of James Bryant Conant are in the University Archives, Pusey Library, Harvard University. The Carnegie Corporation, Princeton, N.J., houses many of his educational papers. Other material discussing his service as president of Harvard can be found in the Granville Clark Papers, Baker Library, Dartmouth College. Conant's autobiography, *My Several Lives: Memoirs of a Social Inventor* (1970), is the most comprehensive statement of his life's work. Conant's books on secondary education also include *The Child, the Parent, and the State* (1959). His views on higher education may be found in his annual essays contained in the *Official Registrar of Harvard University, Issue Containing the Report of the President of Harvard College* (1932–1953). Additional statements of his educational philosophy may be found in *Education and Liberty* (1953); *Thomas Jefferson and the Development of American Public Education*

(1962); *Education for a Classless Society*, with Francis T. Spaulding (1940); and the Report of the Harvard Committee, *General Education in a Free Society* (1945). A biography is James Hershberg, *James B. Conant: Harvard to Hiroshima and the Making of the Nuclear Age* (1993). He has also been the subject of five theses. On his educational views, see Jeanne Ellen Amster, "Meritocracy Ascendant: James Bryant Conant and Cultivation of Talent" (Ph.D. diss., Harvard Univ., 1990); Charles deWane Biebel, "Politics, Pedagogues, and Statesmanship: James B. Conant and the Public Schools, 1933–1948" (Ph.D. diss., Univ. of Wisconsin, 1971); and Barry James Teicher, "James Bryant Conant and the American High School Today" (Ph.D. diss., Univ. of Wisconsin, 1977). On his public service, see Hershberg, "James B. Conant, Nuclear Weapons and the Cold War, 1945–1950" (Ph.D. diss., Tufts Univ., 1989), and William McCulloch Tuttle, Jr., "James B. Conant, Pressure Groups and the National Defense, 1933–1945" (Ph.D. diss., Univ. of Wisconsin, 1967).

JEANNE E. AMSTER

CONANT, Roger (1592–19 Nov. 1679), founder of Salem and Beverly, Massachusetts, was born in Budleigh, Devonshire, England, the son of Richard Conant and Agnes Clarke, substantial yeoman farmers. He was baptized at All Saints' Church, East Budleigh, on 9 April 1592. In his teens, he was sent to London to join his brother Christopher, a grocer, and by 1619 he had become a salter, a specialist in the preservation of meat and fish. In November 1618 he married Sarah Horton at St. Ann's, Blackfriars, a center of Puritan lectureships. From 1622 to 1637 nine children were born to the couple in England and America, eight of whom survived infancy.

Conant, his wife, and infant son immigrated to Plymouth Colony, arriving in March 1623. Although evidence is sparse, his apparent intent was to assist Thomas Weston, a London merchant, in establishing the Wessagusett settlement as a base for the colony's fishery. As that venture was failing, he stayed in Plymouth as a "particular" (a person not subject to the Plymouth Colony's financial obligations) until the summer of 1624. Religious and economic tensions between the particulars and the Pilgrims resulted in several of the former being expelled that summer. Although not formally asked to leave, Conant settled at Nantasket with several others to farm and to fish.

Meanwhile, the Reverend John White of Dorchester, a prominent nonseparatist Puritan, assisted by Conant's brother John, who was the minister at nearby Lymington, was attempting to refinance and salvage a Dorchester Company settlement started on Cape Ann in 1623. In 1625 White asked Conant to govern the venture, subject to reorganization. With Conant's and his companions' arrival, the Cape Ann settlement, numbering some fifty, worked to build shelters and prepare a stock of fish for the company. In 1626, in search of better farm lands, Conant moved with about forty men, women, and children to Naumkeag, later Salem. The next year he sent two lieutenants to England to seek a patent for these lands for the company as well. The Dorchester Company, meanwhile, merged into the larger New England Company, which in 1628 dispatched another fifty colonists with John Endecott as the new governor. Wisely, the new company's policy of fully including Conant's followers into the rights and benefits of the new organization allayed initial tensions, which led the colonists to rename the settlement Salem, "in remembrance of a peace," as White later wrote. Sharing similar economic and religious views, as well as common West Country origins, the two groups soon melded into a West Country or Old Planter interest in the face of later, mainly East Anglian, immigrants. These distinctions helped shape Salem's religious and political history at least into the 1660s.

In July 1629 the church at Salem was formed under the direction of Samuel Skelton and Francis Higginson, two recent immigrant Puritan clerics. These founders adopted the congregational organization of the Plymouth church but not its separatist rationale. They also abandoned the Church of England's Book of Common Prayer. Conant's Old Planters, who had used the Book of Common Prayer at Nantasket and Cape Ann, accepted the arrangement as a reasonable adaptation to New World conditions but remained staunchly nonseparatist. However, as the pace of East Anglian migration increased, so did the separatist impulse in Salem. In 1631 Conant and his followers barely prevented the settlement of Roger Williams, a noted separatist, as a replacement for the recently deceased Higginson. In 1633, after Skelton's death, East Anglians, supported by Endecott, were able to bring Williams in as minister, thus initiating one of the more controversial pastorates in the history of Puritan Massachusetts. After Williams's expulsion, he was replaced by the able nonseparatist Hugh Peter in 1636. Nonetheless, Old Planter influence in the Salem church continued to wane.

Conant's and his followers' political influence was also ebbing, albeit more gradually. He was elected to the General Court only once, in 1634. After nearly continuous service as selectman from 1637 to 1643, he served only seven years between 1647 and 1667 as a new group of merchants came to power locally. As their relative power declined, the Old Planters increasingly sought economic and political autonomy. In 1636 Conant and four of his longtime companions each received 200-acre farms in what became Beverly. There Conant also dabbled in the American Indian trade. By 1657 the Old Planters won the right to arbitrate all land disputes in their portion of town. In 1659 the Salem town meeting exempted them from all local taxes, except the minister's rate. In 1664 they were freed of that obligation by settling a young cleric, John Hale, to form a new church. That same year they began petitioning the Massachusetts General Court for status as a separate town. The church was properly formed 20 September 1667. In 1668 the Town of Beverly was formally recognized by the General Court. Conant's last major public service was to survey the new town's boundaries in 1671–1672. He died a widower on his farm in Beverly.

• There are no known surviving Conant papers. However, the earliest chapters of William Hubbard, *A General History of New England, from the Discovery to MDCLXXX* (completed in 1680 but not published until 1815), relies so heavily on interviews with Conant so as nearly to constitute an autobiography. The standard biography is Clifford K. Shipton, *Roger Conant: A Founder of Massachusetts* (1945). Many useful details can be gleaned from Sidney Perley, *The History of Salem, Massachusetts* (3 vols., 1924–1928). Assessments of the Old Planters' role in the development of Salem and Beverly can be found in Richard P. Gildrie, *Salem, Massachusetts, 1626–1683: A Covenant Community* (1975), and in Christine Alice Young, *From "Good Order" to Glorious Revolution: Salem, Massachusetts, 1628–1689* (1980).

RICHARD P. GILDRIE

CONBOY, Martin (28 Aug. 1878–5 Mar. 1944), U.S. attorney and leading Catholic layman, was born in New York City, the son of Martin Conboy, a government worker and police officer, and Bridget Harlow. A graduate of Gonzaga College in Washington, D.C. (A.B. 1898, A.M. 1899), he simultaneously attended Georgetown Law School at night, earning his LL.B. in 1898 and his LL.M. in 1899. In 1900 Conboy joined the firm of Griggs, Baldwin & Baldwin as a law clerk. Admitted to the New York bar in 1903, he remained with the firm until 1929. In 1912 he married Bertha Letitia Mason, with whom he had four children.

Public spirited, Conboy served throughout his life in both government and lay positions while practicing law. In 1918 he served as director of the Selective Service for New York City, supervising the enlistment of nearly 1.5 million soldiers. After serving as director he wrote a lengthy article entitled "What We Found Out about People in the Draft," published in the *American Magazine* in 1920. Very much an anecdotal piece, it was written with spirit and flourish and suggests that nobility and valor were qualities alive and well within the character of the American people. During and after World War I, Conboy held strong anti-Socialist convictions. He served as counsel to the Judiciary Committee of the New York Assembly in 1920 and prosecuted five assemblymen for their Socialist politics. He argued that dissemination of such views posed a threat to property rights, to the stability of family and church, and to the Constitution in general.

Conboy led and acted as an adviser and elder to the lay Catholic community by 1920. His religious convictions deeply influenced his discernment of the common good. He served as president of the Catholic Club (1922–1927), received honors from the Holy See, and was eventually designated as knight commander of the Order of Saint Gregory. On 3 April 1922 the *New York Times* reported that Conboy led a religious-centered attack on national Prohibition as authorized by the Eighteenth Amendment, referring to it as the work of "religious bigots and narrow-minded reformers."

An Independent Democrat, Conboy supported Alfred E. Smith for president in 1924 and at the Democratic National Convention attacked members of the convention for refusing to condemn the Ku Klux Klan by name. Although he was somewhat politically conservative on issues of morality and a strong anti-Socialist, he avidly supported both Franklin D. Roosevelt's governorship and his early presidency. As the *New York Times* reported on 13 April 1938, Conboy saw a strong link between the New Deal programs and papal encyclicals, firmly believing that the Catholic universities "should be able to send corps of men" for whom no problem of government would be "too knotty."

In 1930 Conboy was appointed chairman of Governor Roosevelt's Advisory Committee on Narcotics. In 1932 he acted as a special adviser to Governor Roosevelt in the investigation of the possible criminal activities of Mayor James J. Walker of New York City. In 1933 Conboy was appointed by President Roosevelt as U.S. attorney for the Southern District of New York. Political circles regarded Conboy's appointment as an effort to clean up the Tammany machinery of New York.

Conboy was a strong proponent of legislation to ban "obscene" reading material and films. In 1934 the *New York Times* reported that, after reading James Joyce's *Ulysses* (1922), he found himself so in conflict with a federal court decision that held the book to be a "genuine piece of literature" that he ordered the case appealed. The Second Circuit Court affirmed the lower court despite doubts that the work would be accepted as one of the great works of literature. After the opinion was handed down, Conboy unsuccessfully lobbied the legislature for a "clean book" bill in opposition to what he considered to be the judiciary's loosening of censorship standards. Despite his lack of success in raising censorship standards, Conboy's victories as a U.S. attorney were considerable. This was particularly so in test cases involving the New Deal's antigold-hording legislation and provisions of the National Recovery Act. He resigned as U.S. attorney in 1935 and returned to private practice.

Returning to his firm Conboy, Hewitt, O'Brien & Boardman, Conboy still was able to represent the people as a prosecutor. He served as special prosecutor in the infamous income tax case against mobster Dutch Schultz (Arthur Flegenheimer). He also, however, defended mobster Lucky Luciano (Charles Luciano) on pandering charges. It appears that, as a practicing attorney, he kept distinctly separate the ethics associated with his status as a public spokesman and a defense attorney.

Conboy was also a contributing author for a scholarly volume entitled *Law: A Century of Progress* (1937). His piece was entitled "Federal Criminal Law" and dealt with the cooperative nature of federal and state legislatures in dealing with modern crime. Keeping his hand in public affairs, he served as a member of the Board of Regents of Georgetown University from 1940 until his death. He also acted as coordinating adviser to the New York State director of the Selective Service. Conboy later became a critic of the Roosevelt administration, which he considered coercive in its foreign policy. He also expressed fear about the possibility of sending arms to the Spanish republic on the grounds that strict neutrality and religious faith were the only means by which to avoid war. He died in New York City.

• Very little information about Conboy exists. He wrote "A Keen Character Analysis of the President," *Literary Digest*, 10 Feb. 1934; on maritime law in "The Territorial Seas," *Canadian Bar Review* 11 (1924); and "Trial Experiences," *Georgetown Law Review* 19 (1930). The Howard College Library contains a writing on Conboy's view of whether a Catholic can be president, contained in the *Forum*, p. 77. An interesting article on Conboy also appears in the *Literary Digest*, 7 May 1927, p. 31. The *New York Times*, 13 Mar. 1934, speaks to the Conboy decision to appeal the *Ulysses* lower court decision. Also of interest is the obituary in the *New York Times*, 6 Mar. 1944, which speaks to his defense of alleged members of the Mafia.

TRISHA OLSON

CONBOY, Sara Agnes McLaughlin (3 Apr. 1870–7 Jan. 1928), trade union official, was born in Boston, Massachusetts, the daughter of Michael McLaughlin and Sara Mellyn. Her father died when she was eleven years old, and young Sara, the oldest of several siblings, went to work in a local candy factory. There she earned $2.50 for a sixty-hour workweek. She then worked for a time in a button factory before going to work in a carpet factory in Roxbury, Massachusetts. Still working sixty hours a week, Sara was able to make at most $12 or $13 weekly as a skilled weaver. After only two years of marriage to Joseph P. Conboy, a Boston postal worker, Sara was suddenly left a widow with an infant to support. She returned to the Roxbury Carpet Company, continuing to work long hours and subject to frequent layoffs if looms needed repair or the company had excess stock.

In 1910 the company announced wage cuts of up to one-fourth of current pay scales. At the same time, the company announced the factory would be closed for two weeks. Outraged, Sara Conboy and more than 100 other weavers turned to the Boston Women's Trade Union League for assistance. Thus, Local 721 of the United Textile Workers of America was born, and Conboy's career as a trade unionist began. Assisted by the Boston labor community and the middle- and upper-class women allies of the league, Local 721 waged a successful two-month strike against the Roxbury Carpet Company, winning back their old wages and gaining union recognition.

Another strike took place two years later, and Conboy, as a leader of Local 721, once again played an active role. By that time she had also become involved in trade unionism on the state level, attending the yearly conventions of the Massachusetts State Federation of the American Federation of Labor (AFL) as the delegate from Local 721. In 1913 and again in 1914 Conboy introduced resolutions seeking the support of the state labor organization in the cause of woman suffrage. For Conboy, attaining the right to vote would give working-class women such as herself one more tool in addressing the often exploitative conditions of labor in this period.

But first and foremost, Conboy saw the organization of women as the most effective way of improving work conditions. Her role in the Roxbury strikes brought her to the attention of John Golden, president of the United Textile Workers of America (UTW), who hired her as a general organizer. In 1912 she assisted Golden in the famous Bread and Roses strike in the textile city of Lawrence, Massachusetts. There the UTW, affiliated with the AFL, sought to counteract the growing influence of the more radical Industrial Workers of the World. Concentrating on the skilled, native-born workers, the UTW ignored the needs as well as the demands of the thousands of unskilled textile workers, most of whom were immigrant women. Conboy brought this same conservative approach to the massive strike of silk workers in Paterson, New Jersey, the following year.

However, her conservatism did not prevent Conboy from being an effective organizer for the UTW. In 1914 she spent several weeks in Atlanta, Georgia, where almost a thousand textile workers from the Fulton Bag & Cotton Mill were on strike. Conboy had been particularly moved by the children, some as young as eight years old, who labored in the southern textile mills. A former child laborer herself, she made a passionate appeal to the Massachusetts State Federation for financial assistance. Speaking at their annual convention in the fall of 1914, Conboy showed her fellow trade unionists photographs she had taken of one ten-year-old boy who worked sixty hours a week for thirty-two cents. A compassionate speaker, often armed with photographic evidence, she raised hundreds of thousands of dollars over the years for various UTW strike funds.

In 1915 the UTW recognized Conboy's abilities and her dedication, appointing her secretary-treasurer. Second in command only to the president, Conboy held this position of power for thirteen years during a time when few women were allowed such an opportunity. As secretary-treasurer she continued to be one of the UTW's most successful fundraisers and most effective speakers against child labor. Conboy was also a supporter of protective labor legislation as a way to address some of the worst conditions faced by working women, such as long hours and unsafe work practices. In 1918 Conboy was the sole woman appointed by President Woodrow Wilson to a conference on labor. She also represented labor at the presidential conference on unemployment in 1921. Perhaps Conboy's greatest honor as a woman trade unionist came in 1920 when the AFL appointed her as their representative to the annual British Trades Union Congress.

Known affectionately as "Aunt Sara" to the thousands of working men and women she represented, Conboy remained active in the fight for woman suffrage until passage of the Nineteenth Amendment in 1920. Based in New York City after her appointment as UTW secretary-treasurer, she became a member of the New York State Housing Commission. As a member of the National Committee on Prisons and Prison Labor, she spoke out against the use of prison labor, which trade unionists saw as a threat to the gains made by organized labor. She died in New York City of cerebral hemorrhage after routine throat surgery. Active until her death in a time when few women held positions of power in American trade unions, Sara Conboy was an important exception.

• Information on Conboy's work can be found in the papers of the Massachusetts State Federation, American Federation of Labor, in the W. E. B. Du Bois Library Special Collections, University of Massachusetts at Amherst. An obituary is in the *New York Times*, 9 Jan. 1928.

KATHLEEN BANKS NUTTER

CONDON, Eddie (16 Nov. 1905–4 Aug. 1973), jazz personality and organizer of Chicago-style jazz bands, recording sessions, and concerts, was born Albert Edwin Condon in Goodland, Indiana, the son of John Condon, a small-town saloonkeeper, and Margaret McGrath. As a teenager, Condon played rhythmic dance band accompaniment on the tenor banjo and, once established in jazz, favored the four-string tenor guitar.

The cultural tensions among America's ethnic groups formed a major theme in Condon's life. He also experienced a recurring sense of alienation stemming from intolerant, small-town, midwestern life in Goodland and Momence, Illinois, where his father had been put out of business by the Woman's Christian Temperance Union. With help from his family, Condon launched his career in popular music at age sixteen and rarely looked back, making summer tours of the Midwest with various groups, including Hollis Peavey's Jazz Bandits (1921–1922). In 1923, he moved to Chicago, where he jobbed with famed cornetist Bix Beiderbecke and in many dance-hall, vaudeville, and cabaret bands.

During his Chicago years, Condon frequented such South Side clubs as the Royal Gardens Cafe and the Apex Club where he listened closely to cornetists Louis Armstrong and Joseph "King" Oliver, clarinetists Johnny Dodds and Jimmie Noone, and pianist Earl Hines. In 1927 he co-organized, with William "Red" McKenzie, his breakthrough recording session for the Okeh label with young white musicians whom he named "The Chicagoans." The Chicagoans included the Beiderbecke-influenced cornetist Jimmy McPartland, the creative tenor saxophone stylist Bud Freeman, the bitingly acrid improvisational clarinetist Frank Teschemacher, and a powerful rhythm section made up of string bassist Jimmy Lannigan, drummer Gene Krupa, and pianist Joe Sullivan. Their style combined an intense, rushing-forward rhythm with jagged and often dissonant polyphony.

Condon moved to New York City during the jazz exodus from Chicago in 1928 stimulated by the strict enforcement of Prohibition in the clubs and the centralization in New York of the phonograph, radio, and band-booking businesses. In New York, Condon soon organized and/or played in some pioneering racially integrated recording sessions with black jazz greats such as Armstrong, pianist Fats Waller, and tenor sax-ophonist Coleman Hawkins. The phonograph record and nightclub businesses abruptly declined with the depression, but Condon still managed to play an important role in the exciting recordings made in 1932 by vocalist Billy Banks and the Rhythmmakers.

Condon survived the hard times, all the harder among jazz musicians, by joining McKenzie's Mound City Blue Blowers, a novelty group much in demand among members of the social register on the East Coast. In the late 1930s, Condon often performed at a Greenwich Village club called Nick's in the Village, associating closely with cornetists Bobby Hackett and Muggsy Spanier, clarinetists Pee Wee Russell and Joe Marsala, multi-instrumentalist Brad Gowans, and leading Harlem musicians such as reedman Sidney Bechet, drummer Zutty Singleton, and trumpeter Oran Page. Out of these sessions emerged the excellent recordings of Freeman's Summa Cum Laude Orchestra.

Beginning in February 1942, Condon made his promotional and organizational influence felt when he organized and also emceed—with the assistance of New York City advertising executives Ernest Anderson and Phyllis Smith (whom he married in 1942 and with whom he had two children)—a long-running series of jazz concerts at New York City's Town Hall and Carnegie Hall. Carried by radio wire, these highly improvisational, racially integrated concerts subsequently led to the first televised jazz concert in April 1942, and later to a regular program called "Eddie Condon's Floor Show."

In 1945, Condon opened a jazz club in Greenwich Village called Condon's (said to be a front owned by underworld figures), which remained in business for over twelve years. During the 1950s this club produced one of his best bands that included the incendiary cornetist William "Wild Bill" Davison and the biting clarinet stylist Edmond Hall. These stars led a repertory group of swing-influenced traditionalist jazz musicians in recording, under the joint direction of Condon and Columbia executive George Avakian, several successful long-playing albums for Columbia Records, from 1953 to 1957. These included "Jam Session Coast-to-Coast" (1953), "Jammin' at Condon's," (1954), and "Bixieland" (1955).

Condon's club moved uptown in 1958 and remained in business until 1967. A third nightclub called Condon's, run by Leonard "Red" Balaban, son of vaudeville entrepreneur Barney Balaban, presented small-group improvised music in the Condon manner for many years after the jazzman's death. Condon dictated his autobiography, *We Called It Music: A Generation of Jazz*, to writer Thomas Sugrue; published in 1947, it is considered a classic in the crowded field of jazz autobiography. Thereafter Condon became an established New York City jazz personality whose photo likenesses and acerbic witticisms turned up in most of the mass circulation magazines. He reacted to the publication of Frenchman Hugues Panassie's book of criticism titled *Le Jazz Hot* by asking, "We don't go to France and tell them how to jump on a grape, do we?"

His recipe for a hangover began "Take the juice of two quarts of whiskey. . . . " During the 1950s and 1960s, Condon sometimes played sets at his clubs; he toured Great Britain in 1957 and Australia, New Zealand, and Japan in 1964 with all-star groups.

When the spirit(s) moved him, Condon could play urgent, driving rhythm guitar, but over the length of his career he contributed more as an organizer and jazz personality whose personal magnetism generated club, concert, and recording jobs for many musicians. Thanks to his talent for attracting media attention, Condon projected a slick and ultimately profitable image as a dryly glib, jaunty, late-night libertine who mixed the music of his many excellent small bands with intoxicating doses of Roaring Twenties–style social rebellion. Condon's music and his personal cult of alcoholic abandon helped to fill his clubs and concerts with paying customers who throughout the post–World War II years of bebop, cool, and free jazz sustained a vital traditional style that featured a 1920s repertoire as interpreted by changing mixtures of swing era musicians. This juxtaposition of style elements—the tense twenties beat with the instrumental solo sophistication of the thirties—made Condon's bands an influential force in the post–World War II revival of 1920s jazz.

• For additional information, see Eddie Condon (with Thomas Sugrue), *We Called It Music: A Generation of Jazz* (1947, rev. 1970); Condon and Hank O'Neal, *The Eddie Condon Scrapbook of Jazz* (1973); William Howland Kenney, *Chicago Jazz: A Cultural History, 1904–1930* (1993); Kenney, "Eddie Condon in Illinois: The Roots of a Jazz Personality," *Illinois Historical Journal* 77 (1984): 255–68; and Dan Morgenstern, "Fond Reminiscence with Eddie Condon," *Down Beat* 32 (11 Feb. 1965): 25.

WILLIAM HOWLAND KENNEY

CONDON, Edward Uhler (2 Mar. 1902–26 Mar. 1974), theoretical physicist, was born in Alamogordo, New Mexico, the son of William Edward Condon, a railway engineer, and Caroline Barr. His parents separated when he was six years old. He and his mother moved repeatedly, with Condon attending fourteen different elementary schools. Upon graduation from high school in Oakland, California, young Condon became a reporter for the *Oakland Tribune* newspaper in the summer of 1918. He initially entered the University of California at Berkeley in the fall of 1919 but dropped out. In 1921 he re-enrolled while working part-time in his capacity as a reporter, graduating with an A.B. and highest honors in 1924.

Condon showed a characteristic independence of mind and determination of spirit throughout his life. Several months into his graduate work in physics Condon quantitated a theory of molecular transitions proposed by James Franck, producing a dissertation paper after a long weekend of work. Precipitating an uproar over the acceptability of a "weekend dissertation," Condon received his Ph.D. after one year of study in 1926.

In the fall of 1926 Condon moved to Germany to study in the center of quantum mechanical activity with Professor Arnold Sommerfield. After a year, daunted by the flood of new and difficult ideas in theoretical physics, Condon returned to New York in the fall of 1927 to do public relations for Bell Telephone Laboratories. He spent his time with the Bell research physicists and was soon a popular colloquium speaker at several eastern universities.

Condon's first academic post was as lecturer at Columbia University (1928) in graduate courses in quantum mechanics and the electromagnetic theory of light. He then joined the faculty at Princeton (1928–1937), where he displayed his gift for making complicated things simple and clear in his elementary courses on relativity. At the age of twenty-seven he was appointed full professor of physics at the University of Minnesota but returned to Princeton the following year. During this period Condon made the bulk of his original contributions to the advancement of theoretical physics. His theoretical interpretation of high energy proton-proton scattering clarified the nuclear strong force, serving as the basis for modern nuclear theory and dramatically influencing the development of research in atomic energy. He also made contributions in the mass spectroscopy of molecules and in understanding the quantum mechanical basis of molecular vibrations measured by infrared spectroscopy and the rotation of light by molecules.

Condon joined the Westinghouse Electric and Manufacturing Corporation as associate director of research in Pittsburgh, Pennsylvania, in the summer of 1937, initiating the second phase of his career. He prepared the company to enter the infant field of nuclear energy, strengthening and focusing basic research programs. He set a precedent by attracting bright young scientists to the industry with research fellowships. In the fall of 1940 Condon joined the Radiation Laboratory at MIT, working on development of airborne radar systems for the war effort. He continued to take responsibility for both government and industrial concerns.

Condon was chosen by R. J. Oppenheimer as associate director of the secret Los Alamos laboratories in the winter of 1942 in the hope that he would both make use of his organizational and motivational talents and apply his early work on mass spectroscopy to uranium isotope separation for atomic weapons. Condon struggled with General Leslie Groves, the controversial military leader of Los Alamos, for civilian status for Los Alamos scientists. After six weeks in Los Alamos he returned in the spring of 1943 to Westinghouse briefly to work on microwave radar systems. In August 1943, at the request of E. O. Lawrence, he went to the Radiation Laboratory at Berkeley, California, to work on mass spectrometric uranium isotope separations for the atomic bomb until February 1945. Ironically, the first atomic bomb was exploded near Alamogordo, New Mexico, Condon's birthplace.

After the war ended in August 1945, Condon began the third phase of his career. Like many other scientists awed by the power of nuclear weapons and spurred by Quakerism, Condon entered visibly into public life, writing and speaking to inform the public on policy decisions about the military use of nuclear energy. In the fall of 1945 Condon was named director of the National Bureau of Standards in Washington, D.C. This gave him the opportunity to build the Bureau of Standards into a first-rate research institution as well as the occasion to lobby Congress for civilian control of nuclear energy in the United States. In August 1946 the McMahon-Douglas bill established the civilian Atomic Energy Commission, in part as a result of the educational efforts of Condon. These political involvements drew the attention of the House Committee on Un-American Activities (HUAC). Condon was publicly accused of being a security risk and repeatedly investigated by HUAC and other agencies. He testified at "loyalty-hearings" repeatedly over the next ten years. Little evidence was found against Condon, but HUAC never retracted its allegations and in 1952 issued a report that concluded that Condon was unqualified for any position that entailed access to classified information. At the Bureau of Standards Condon advanced applied mathematics as a tool for government, initiated development of electronic computers, and strengthened the basic physics of atmospheric radiofrequency and microwave transmission. He also put government research to work in the service of the consumer.

Unable to make further progress at the Bureau of Standards in the Cold War climate, Condon accepted the directorship of research at Corning Glass Works in Corning, New York, in the summer of 1951, assisting the company in applications of solid state physics. Dogged by Department of Defense security allegations for the remainder of his career, Condon resigned from Corning in 1954, returning to academe as chairman of physics at Washington University in St. Louis in 1956. As a fellow at the laboratory for astrophysics at the University of Colorado in 1963 he returned to his original love—the theory of atomic spectra. Unfinished with public service, Condon headed a project in 1966 for the Air Force Office of Scientific Research on Unidentified Flying Objects, which culminated in the 1969 Fuller Report concluding a lack of proof of their existence. He retired from the University of Colorado in the summer of 1970.

Condon's multidimensional career spanned fundamental contributions to atomic theory and spectroscopy, guidance of industrial and governmental application of those scientific principles, and, finally, action as a voice of conscience in the control of the power of atomic energy and commitment to the practice of science in the public interest.

Condon's advice was often sought. He served as a member of the S-1 Committee on Military Use of Atomic Energy (1941), scientific adviser to the Special Senate Committee on Atomic Energy (1945–1946), member of the NACA (1945–1951), member of the President's National Evaluation Board, Naval Atomic Bomb Tests (1946), member of the Society for Social

Responsibility in Science (president, 1968–1969), and cochairman of the National Committee for a Sane Nuclear Policy (1970). He was a member of numerous professional societies, including the National Academy of Sciences (1944), American Physical Society (president, 1946), American Association for the Advancement of Science (president, 1953), and American Association of Physics Teachers (president, 1963). He was also editor of *Reviews of Modern Physics* (1957–1968) and was on the board of directors of Annual Reviews, Inc. (1963).

In November 1922 Condon had married Emilie Honzik. Their household, which eventually included three children, served throughout his industrial and academic career as a hub for students and visitors in search of intellectual stimulation, food, and companionship. Condon died in Boulder, Colorado.

• Condon's papers are maintained in the American Philosophical Society Library, Philadelphia, Pa. His publications in the professional literature covered a breadth of topics in atomic and solid-state physics, microwave and radio wave propagation. Books of note are *Franck-Condon Principle in Molecular Spectroscopy* (1926); *Theory of Atomic Spectra* (1935, with George H. Shortley); and *Handbook of Physics* (1958, with Hugh Odishaw). Remembrances of the life and contributions of Condon are presented in *Selected Popular Writings of E. U. Condon*, ed. A. O. Barat et al. (1991), and a companion volume, *Selected Scientific Papers of E. U. Condon*, ed. Barat et al. (1991). Condon's testimony before the House Committee on Un-American Activities (CIS US government document Y4.Un 1/2:C75) and *Study of Unidentified Flying Objects* (1969) detail public aspects of his persecution and contributions in the latter part of his career. A profile by Grace Marmor Spruch can be found in "Reporter Edward Condon," *Saturday Review*, 1 Feb. 1969, pp. 55–62. Another useful source is Jessica Wang, "Science, Security, and the Cold War: The Case of E. U. Condon," *Isis* 83 (1992): 238–69. An obituary is in the *New York Times*, 27 Mar. 1974.

HARRY LEVINE III

CONE, Claribel (14 Nov. 1864–20 Sept. 1929), pathologist and art collector, and **Etta Cone** (30 Nov. 1870–31 Aug. 1949), art collector, were born in Jonesboro, Tennessee, the daughters of Herman Cone, a grocery business owner, and Helen Guggenheimer. The Cone family moved in 1871 to Baltimore, where Herman Cone opened a wholesale grocery business. The business flourished, and the Cones moved to a fashionable neighborhood and engaged in the social life of a large German-Jewish community. By the late 1880s the two eldest sons, Moses and Ceasar, had begun a hugely successful venture into the southern textile industry, so in 1890 the grocery business was dissolved.

Claribel Cone entered the Woman's Medical College in Baltimore in the fall of 1886, despite her parents' misgivings. Claribel was not a feminist; she was motivated by her intellectual interest in medicine and probably her wish to avoid the duties of managing the Cone household. She went on to graduate first in her class in 1890, and she did postgraduate work in 1890–1891. She won a residency at Blockley Hospital for the Insane in Philadelphia, where she worked in 1891–

1892. In 1893 Claribel returned to Baltimore, and from 1893 until 1904 she did pathology research under William Welch at Johns Hopkins Medical School. At the same time she was a professor of pathology at the Woman's Medical College, and in 1900–1901 she was the president of the college. The regally handsome "Dr. Claribel" awed those who knew her with her eccentric independence.

Etta Cone appeared to have been content to defer to Claribel in part because of her sister's elder status. Clever and sensitive to others, Etta cherished close companionship and needed reassurance from others. She graduated from Western Female High School in 1887 and became the capable manager of the Cone household. She devoted many hours to piano playing.

The Cone sisters attended recitals, art lectures, and art exhibitions in Baltimore. Throughout the 1890s Claribel held regular salons at the Cone residence, where colleagues, intellectuals, artists, and musicians would meet for lively discussions. Leo and Gertrude Stein came to live in Baltimore in 1892, and they moved in the same circles as the Cones. Leo Stein became friends with Etta as he shared his deepening interest in art and aesthetics with her.

Perhaps motivated by Leo Stein, Etta was the first of the two sisters to purchase art. She asked her brother Moses to give her money to buy pictures to brighten the family living room, and she purchased five paintings from the March 1898 auction of Theodore Robinson's estate. Etta's purchase of the impressionistic Robinson paintings was a brave move outside of her role as an upper-class, unmarried lady in Victorian-era America. Throughout her life as an art collector, she struggled between her desire to collect modern art and her desire to protect her reputation.

In 1901 Etta took the first of many trips to Europe, traveling with two companions (and also with the Steins at points along the way). Etta's travel diaries reveal in rapturous detail her days in Europe's major art museums and sites, led by Leo Stein. She also described the excitement of her deepening friendship with Gertrude Stein. The last diary entry reveals that she and Gertrude Stein may have had a shipboard affair on their way back to New York.

Claribel and Etta traveled and resided in Europe in 1903–1904 and again for a longer period in 1905–1906. They traveled in Italy and Germany, and Claribel studied at the Senckenberg Institute in Frankfurt during the winters. However, their main center of activity was Paris. They made frequent visits to the Steins' apartment at 24 Rue de Fleurus, where they were introduced to the Steins' circle of artist and writer friends. In September 1905 Etta took an apartment near Leo and Gertrude Stein's older brother, Michael, and his wife Sarah. That October Etta and Claribel visited the Paris Salon d'Automne and saw the newly christened "fauve" work by Henri Matisse. It was their first time seeing avant-garde art, and they responded with disbelief that such crude and distorted work could be taken seriously.

During this period Etta became even closer to Gertrude Stein as she typed the manuscript for Stein's first book, *Three Lives*. In November Stein introduced Etta to Pablo Picasso, and Etta purchased a gouache, or watercolor, and an etching from him. In March 1906 the sisters went to Picasso's studio and purchased eleven drawings and seven etchings. These works are among the most important works by Picasso in the Cone collection. Some are studies for major paintings, such as *Circus Family* and *Boy with a Horse*. Of the 113 works by Picasso in the Cone collection, all except for three major portraits in oil and two sculptures are works on paper or board, and most date from 1905–1906.

In January 1906 Sarah Stein took Etta to meet Matisse, and Etta purchased two of his drawings. She visited Matisse again in February and purchased two fauve watercolors. Etta also purchased prints by Auguste Renoir, Paul Cézanne, and Edouard Manet, influenced, perhaps, by Leo Stein's view that these artists inspired Picasso and Matisse. In an article for the *American Scholar*, Edward T. Cone wrote that Etta later declared "that it was Leo, and not Gertrude, who had developed the real eye for modern art and hence had contributed significantly to her own education." Claribel and Etta Cone departed from Leo Stein's influence in that their appreciation of modern art was based more on subject matter than formalism.

Between 1906 and 1921 the Cones added little art to their collection. In 1908 Claribel departed for Germany for a series of research projects, but Etta, despondent over the death of their brother Moses that year, traveled to Europe infrequently. Claribel lived alone in Munich from 1914 until 1921. Her life there was remarkably undisturbed during the war years; her refusal to leave was characteristic of her steadfast, independent nature.

Gertrude Stein was fascinated by the Cone sisters. In her notes for the manuscript of her nonfiction portrait of them, *Two Women* (1925), she wrote, "Go on with how one of them is more something than the other one . . . what effort they had when they were traveling, how they quarrelled, how they spent money, how they each had what they wanted." In the book she described Claribel as "of a very fortunate make-up" and Etta as "of desperate one."

In 1922 Etta (usually with her companion Nora Kaufman) and Claribel began to make annual spring–summer trips to Europe. The sisters were devoted to each other, but because of the tensions caused by their differences, they often lived and traveled separately. The Cone cotton business had become a financial empire by then, making them even more wealthy. They built their art collection in earnest throughout the 1920s. Michael Stein became the Cones' unofficial art dealer, and he acted as intermediary when they purchased art from Gertrude Stein. Apart from business dealings, they had increasingly less to do with Gertrude Stein, but Michael and Sarah Stein were lifelong friends.

Matisse was the Cones' primary artist. They followed their own tastes when buying Matisse without consulting art professionals or paying attention to critical opinion. The Cones tended to collect Matisse at his most decorous and conservative; they collected fourteen paintings from his "Nice period" (1919–1930, years when he wintered in Nice), which is considered one of his less progressive phases. Among the strongest Matisse paintings in the Cone collection are boldly expressive portraits and still-lifes. Claribel purchased *Woman in Turban* (also known as *The White Turban*), *The Pewter Jug*, and the famous fauve masterpiece *Blue Nude*. Etta's best early Matisse purchase and her favorite was the decorative *Interior, Flowers and Parakeets*. Claribel was more daring in her art purchases than Etta. Claribel bought Cézanne's monumental masterpiece *Mont Sainte-Victoire Seen from the Bibémes Quarry*, while Etta purchased one of Cezanne's *Bathers* studies. Etta bought what she termed "her favorite non-Matisse," Renoir's *Washerwoman*.

In 1927 Claribel bought Vincent Van Gogh's *A Pair of Boots*. In August 1927 she wrote Etta, "I am not so pleased with my Van Gogh—it is so unlike his *better* (more forceful more mad style perhaps) style. A pair of boots will not grace my living room with beauty— however it is a Van Gogh." Claribel's main requirement when purchasing art was to acquire the best of an artist's work and/or the most beautiful. Her taste is also revealed in an earlier letter to Etta (Mar. 1920): "Things are soothing—if they are works of art—most people are over-stimulating."

The sisters purchased art considering how it would look with other works in their collections and how it would physically fit in their separate residences at the Marlborough Apartments on Eutaw Place. During the winters they arranged their collections to form private museums in their small apartments. Etta and Claribel Cone were also compulsive buyers of objets d'art, antiques, and curios of every description, so their small rooms were crowded with art treasures. The stuffy and provincial Baltimorians considered the Cone sisters quite eccentric.

Claribel died suddenly in Lausanne, Switzerland, and Etta deeply mourned her loss for years. Claribel left her collection to Etta, with the wish that their two collections should eventually go to the Baltimore Museum of Art "if the spirit of appreciation of modern art in Baltimore becomes improved." Etta continued her annual visits to Europe through 1938. Each year she paid a visit to her old friend Matisse.

In the 1930s and 1940s Etta appears to have come into her own. She purchased her most important Matisse work, aided by advice from the artist himself. Among the most notable are two portraits, *The Yellow Dress* and *The Blue Eyes*, as well as *Large Reclining Nude* (a rare purchase of abstraction for Etta). She purchased the entire set (250 items) of Matisse's drawings, prints, and copper plates for the illustrated book *Poesies de Stephane Mallarme*. Etta continued to round out her collection historically with work by other French modernists and the nineteenth-century forebears of modernism. Her discerning taste in portraiture is further reflected in her purchase of Picasso's *Mother and Child* and Paul Gauguin's *Woman with Mango*.

The collection became internationally renowned, and Etta graciously opened her door and gave tours to all who wished to see it. She died at a relative's home in Blowing Rock, North Carolina. In her last years Etta had seen enough improvement in Baltimore's appreciation of modern art to consider the Baltimore Museum of Art a worthy home for the collection. In her will she left the Baltimore Museum the full range of art treasures she and Claribel had collected, a total of more than 3,000 items. The Cone sisters had courageously "followed their bliss" and collected modern art when few were doing it. They achieved great breadth in their collection of modern French art, and at the same time they usually chose canvases, drawings, and sculpture that gave them personal pleasure. Their particular pleasure in Matisse led them to purchase paintings from almost every year of Matisse's production between 1917 and 1940. Etta and Claribel Cone's individual tastes are indelibly reflected in the collection and make it truly unique.

• The Cone archive at the Baltimore Museum of Art includes letters between the sisters, account books, travel diaries, notebooks, and clippings. Some of these papers are available on microfilm at the Archives of American Art. Letters from Etta Cone to Gertrude Stein are with the Stein papers at the Yale University Library. Brenda Richardson, *Dr. Claribel and Miss Etta* (1985), is the main biographical source, with extensive treatment of the Cones' relationship with the Steins and the development of the collection. Brenda Wineapple, *Sister Brother: Gertrude and Leo Stein* (1996), is another source for the Cone-Stein relationship. Barbara Pollack, *The Collectors: Dr. Claribel and Miss Etta Cone* (1962), is an earlier full biography. An assessment of the drawings in the Cone collection is provided in Jay M. Fisher, "Drawings from the Collection of Claribel and Etta Cone at the Baltimore Museum of Art," *Drawing* 17 (May–June 1995): 1–6. Reminiscences by Cone family members include Ellen B. Hirschland, "The Cone Sisters and the Stein Family," in the Museum of Modern Art's *Four Americans in Paris: The Collections of Gertrude Stein and Her Family* (1970), and Edward T. Cone, "The Miss Etta Cones, the Steins, and M'sieu Matisse: A Memoir," *American Scholar* 42 (Summer 1973): 441–60. Claribel's obituary is in the *New York Times*, 25 Sept. 1929. Etta's will is printed in a story on the gift of her collection to the Baltimore Museum of Art in the *New York Times*, 14 Sept. 1949.

STEPHANIE MOYE

CONE, Hutchinson Ingham (26 Apr. 1871–12 Feb. 1941), naval engineer and naval officer, was born in Brooklyn, New York, the son of Daniel Newnan Cone and Annette Ingham. The Cone family home was in the country near Lake City, Florida, and his early training and education were at East Florida Military and Agricultural College, from which he graduated in 1889. In September 1890 Cone was appointed a naval cadet at the U.S. Naval Academy. During his four-year course at the Naval Academy, he was vice president of his class, and he opted for training as an engi-

neer cadet his senior year. After graduation from the academy in June 1894, Cone served as a passed engineer cadet on the USS *Atlanta* and was commissioned an assistant engineer on 10 June 1896. Between June 1894 and May 1901, when he was ordered to the Naval Torpedo Station for instruction, Cone served on eight ships, including the USS *Baltimore* during Commodore George Dewey's victory over the Spanish at the battle of Manila Bay in 1898.

In 1897 the Personnel Board, under the chairmanship of Assistant Navy Secretary Theodore Roosevelt, recognized the increasing technological complexity of the 1890s navy. According to Roosevelt, "On the modern war vessel, every officer has to be an engineer." The result was the Amalgamation Act of 1899, which combined engineering officers, like Cone, with the seagoing line officer branch of the navy. The rank of assistant engineer was abolished, and Cone was commissioned an ensign in March 1899. In 1900 he married Patty Selden. They had two children before Patty died in 1922. Cone was assigned to torpedo boat duty, and he advanced to the rank of lieutenant in 1902 and commanded the torpedo boat *Dale* in 1903. In 1907 he commanded the Second Torpedo Flotilla and escorted the battleships of the North Atlantic Squadron to the West Coast via the Straits of Magellan. He was personally commended by President Roosevelt for his leadership and seamanship in shepherding his tiny ships around South America. Cone was promoted to lieutenant commander in 1908 and was selected to serve as fleet engineer of the Atlantic Fleet during the circumnavigating cruise of the Great White Fleet.

Cone's service as fleet engineer brought him to prominence. Rear Admiral C. S. Sperry, the fleet commander, recommended Cone for the next four-year term as engineer in chief of the navy and chief of the Bureau of Steam Engineering. The selection of an officer of such relatively junior rank and age was without precedent. Cone's appointment began on 18 May 1909 and carried with it the temporary rank of rear admiral. As engineer in chief, he supervised the shift from coal to oil fuel to increase the operational radius of the navy in the vast expanse of the strategically important Pacific. He was also involved in the trials of the turbo-electric propulsion system touted by the General Electric Company's William Le Roy Emmet. This system demonstrated many advantages, such as greatly increased fuel economy and smaller size and weight. When the 1916 Naval Act authorized ten superdreadnought battleships and six battlecruisers, the turbo-electric propulsion system was adopted for the new ships.

At the completion of his term as engineer in chief, Cone reverted back to his regular rank of lieutenant commander and became executive officer of the battleship *Utah*. He was promoted to commander in July 1913 and commanded the USS *Dixie* from April 1914 until July 1915, when he became marine superintendent of the Panama Canal. In September 1917 Cone was assigned to U.S. naval forces in Europe and commanded U.S. Naval Aviation Forces, Foreign Service.

In October 1918 the British mail ship *Leinster*, on which Cone was a passenger, was torpedoed. While he was cutting away life rafts, a second torpedo exploded directly underneath Cone. He was rescued after spending two hours in the sea, suffering from compound fractures of his legs and internal injuries. After recovering from his wounds, he became a student at the Naval War College in June 1919. He graduated in 1920 and was promoted to captain, then took command of the battleship *South Dakota* in the Philippines. Cone returned to the United States and retired on 1 July 1922 as "engineer-in-chief, with rank of rear admiral" according to a provision of law relating to officers wounded in wartime.

After retiring from the navy, Cone accepted a position with the Panama Railway Steamship Company. He soon resigned to accept a government appointment as assistant to the president of the U.S. Shipping Board Emergency Fleet Corporation. He advanced to general manager and vice president of the corporation before resigning in November 1925 to become vice president and treasurer of the Daniel Guggenheim Fund for the Promotion of Aeronautics. Cone concentrated on the development of commercial aviation through 1928, when he resigned to accept an invitation from President Calvin Coolidge for a six-year term on the U.S. Shipping Board. Cone worked to expand the U.S. merchant marine, serving with this organization after its incorporation into the Department of Commerce until his resignation in March 1935. In 1930 he married Julia Mattis. They had no children.

Cone's retirement in Washington, D.C., was brief. He accepted the chair of the board of directors of the Moore-McCormick Lines and oversaw efforts to expand their shipping operations to South America.

Cone was awarded the Distinguished Service Medal for his command of naval air forces in Europe during the First World War along with various service and campaign medals. He was also an officer of the Legion of Honor (France), honorary commander of the Order of the British Empire for his lifesaving actions during the sinking of the RMS *Leinster*, recipient of the Distinguished Service Order (Britain), and Cross of Officer of the Order of St. Maurice and St. Lazarus and the Order of Mariziane, both from the Italian government. He died in Orlando, Florida.

• For further information on Cone see Elting E. Morison, *Admiral Sims and the Modern American Navy* (1942). Comprehensive obituaries are in *Transactions of the Society of Naval Architects and Marine Engineers* (1941) and the *Army and Navy Register* (1941).

WILLIAM M. MCBRIDE

CONE, Moses Herman (29 June 1857–8 Dec. 1908), textile entrepreneur, was born in Jonesboro, Tennessee, the son of Herman Kahn, a Jewish wholesale grocery merchant, and Helen Guggenheimer. Cone's father was born in Bavaria, and his mother, though born in Virginia, was of German heritage. When Cone's father moved to the United States, the family name was changed to Cone. Cone was the eldest of thirteen children and spent his formative years in Jonesboro, where his father owned a grocery store. The family moved in 1870 to Baltimore, Maryland, where Cone attended the public schools.

In 1870 Cone's father founded a wholesale grocery supply business, which with the addition of the four oldest sons became H. Cone & Sons in 1878. The firm soon did a sizable business with several southern cotton mills. Moses and his brother Caesar were full partners by 1878 and spent the next twelve years traversing the South in search of sales. They rode trains to the extent possible, but much of their travel was on horseback. The cotton mills in the Carolinas served their employees with mill towns and company stores. It was the company store that was the customer of H. Cone & Sons. Because of the financial difficulties of their customers, the Cones were soon accepting baled textiles and yarn in payment for groceries. The experience gained from the wholesaling of these textile goods led the Cones to become commission sales agents for some of the textile companies. Moses realized that marketing by southern textile mills was limited because their products were not standardized, and they lacked an organized selling organization. He spent much of 1890 attempting to get several southern mills to form a selling organization that would make products more uniform. The result was the 1891 formation of the Cone Export & Commission Company in New York City. The main office was moved to Greensboro, North Carolina, in 1893. About forty-seven mills in the Carolinas and Georgia eventually joined the organization; there were only about fifty mills in the South at that time. The Cones signed five-year contracts with the mills wherein the brothers had exclusive selling rights at a 5 percent commission.

In 1895 Cone and his brother Caesar began a denim mill, Proximity Manufacturing Company, the first of several such mills, on the outskirts of Greensboro. The company was named Proximity because of its close proximity to cotton fields and gins. The Cone mills were soon the world's leading producer of denim, corduroy, and flannel. By the time of Cone's death, his mills were producing one-third of the world's denim. Greensboro was chosen as the site for the mills because of the city's excellent infrastructure (including railroads going in six directions) and the availability of cheap land. The defunct North Carolina Steel and Iron Company had bought thousands of acres of land for a steel mill, but the nearby ore deposits proved unworthy of production. Initially, twenty-five acres were offered free to the Cones. The brothers subsequently bought 2,142 additional acres from the steel company, including land along the main line of the Southern Railway. The brothers bought additional mills throughout North Carolina, including the Ashville Cotton Mills, Salisbury Cotton Mills, and Minneola Manufacturing Company in Gibsonville.

Not only were the mills successful, but the Cones used a portion of their profits to make life better for employees living in the company towns. If anything, it was the attention to employee needs that led to Cone's undying fame. Besides providing subsidized housing, as was characteristic of many mills, the Cones provided large lots for gardens, grape vines, and fruit trees and even free seeds each year. The company plowed the gardens each year and gave prizes for the most attractive yards and best gardens. Schools were also important to the Cones. Before the Proximity mill ever opened, Cone had surveyed the local school situation and found it lacking in both duration and quality. Whereas the local schools in Greensboro had little equipment and were open only four months a year, the school at the mill village was well equipped and open nine months a year. Cone personally urged all employees to send their children to the mill school and offered to buy shoes for any children whose parents could not afford them. To get the best teachers, Cone paid his teachers 50 percent more than did the public schools in Greensboro. The schools were also open at night for the benefit of employees who wanted an education.

In 1903 Cone and Caesar's Greensboro mill, Proximity Manufacturing Company, became the first textile company to hire a social worker, a college graduate named Pearl Wyche, to live with mill families and teach them about sanitation and cooking. Wyche set up a model house in the company town from which employees' families could draw ideas and instruction. Other mill towns soon followed by hiring social workers to teach nutrition, sewing, health, and civics to employees and their families. The Cones also threw huge Fourth of July parties for mill-town residents. At the 1906 party, more than 5,000 attendees ate 2,000 fried chickens, 700 pounds of mutton, 1,000 pounds of ham, 250 gallons of ice cream, and many cases of other foods. The mill band played, residents performed in a minstrel show, and Cone showed workers the latest technology by setting up his Victor talking machine. At the end of the party, employees showed their appreciation by giving each Cone brother a present. An early historian of the company, Carl J. Balliett, stated, "The Cone Mills are communities, not factories. Their success has been based upon a humanitarian policy, upon the development of character, skills and loyalty in the upbuilding of a great organization." Still another author alluded to the fact that the Cones built their empire on goodwill that they earned along with their fortune, rather than on the backs of their employees and customers.

Cone married German-born Bertha M. Lindau of Baltimore in 1888. They had no children. In 1901 the couple acquired a 3,750-acre estate near Blowing Rock, North Carolina, where they grew an apple orchard. By the time of his death in Greensboro, the estate, which later became a state park located off of the Blue Ridge Parkway, had been expanded to 35,000 acres. Cone adopted the Blowing Rock schools and made contributions to what is now Appalachian State University and served on its board. An early death denied Cone the complete fulfillment of all of his ambitions, but his enterprises long stood as enduring monuments to a great name. One of these monuments is the Moses H. Cone Hospital in Greensboro, which was established under the will of Moses Cone. His obituary in the *Charlotte Observer* called him "a benefactor of the best type" (9 Dec. 1908).

• Information about the Cone family's early history and the establishment of the mills is available in Carl J. Balliett, *World Leadership in Denims* (1925); Richard L. Zweigenhaft and G. William Domhoff, *Jews in the Protestant Establishment* (1982); and *Cone: A Century of Excellence* (1991). Information on the Cones' mill towns is available in J. M. Fenster, "The Trouble with Company Towns," *Audacity* 3, no. 3 (Spring 1995): 51–61.

DALE L. FLESHER

CONE, Russell Glenn (22 Mar. 1896–21 Jan. 1961), engineer, was born in Ottumwa, Iowa, the son of Frank Cone, a railroad superintendent, and Alice Haddon. The boy attended public schools in Beardstown, Illinois, and when he was eighteen worked for the Chicago, Burlington and Quincy Railroad near Beardstown for a year. In 1915–1916 he was a rodman on a bridge construction project at Metropolis, Illinois. He then entered the University of Illinois, but his college years were interrupted during World War I, from 1917 to 1919, when he served in France and Germany with the U.S. Army 149th Field Artillery, eventually advancing to the rank of sergeant. He returned to the university, where he took courses in civil engineering from Charles Alton Ellis and received his B.S. in that field in 1922. He married Izetta Lucas in 1922; they had one son.

After graduating, Cone began work as a junior engineer for Modjeski & Chase, founded by Ralph Modjeski and Clement Chase, which was constructing the Delaware River Bridge from Philadelphia, Pennsylvania, to Camden, New Jersey, later named the Benjamin Franklin Bridge. Continuing as assistant engineer from 1923 to 1925 and resident engineer from 1925 to 1927, he dealt especially with the construction of side and central spans of the bridge, which was then the longest suspension bridge in the world. After a few months as general manager of F. J. Ginder, Inc., a construction engineering firm in Philadelphia, he worked from 1927 to 1930 as resident engineer in charge of construction of the Ambassador Bridge in Detroit, Michigan, which was at that time the longest suspension bridge in the world. Both of these bridges, designed by engineer Leon Solomon Moisseif, used a lighter steel framework, which was more aesthetically pleasing, than those of earlier suspension bridges. On the Ambassador Bridge, wrote John Van Der Zee, "Cone, burly and vigorous, was fearless out on the job, climbing catwalks, descending into caissons, unwilling to send anyone to a place he wouldn't go himself" (Van Der Zee, p. 170).

In 1930 Cone became general manager of the Tacony-Palmyra Bridge, a four-lane toll bridge that had just been built by Modjeski & Chase at Philadelphia, across the Delaware River. He was in charge of its maintenance, personnel, toll collecting, and advertising. In the depression years this was a welcome position while he awaited further opportunities in bridge construction.

At that time the Golden Gate Bridge in San Francisco was in the planning stage. Its promoter and senior engineer, Joseph Baermann Strauss, offered Cone a position in 1931. Although Cone had reservations about Strauss, who had fired Ellis from the engineering staff on the bridge about this time although Ellis had done most of the actual design, Cone finally accepted Strauss's offer in 1933. As resident engineer for four years, he supervised ten different contracts and worked simultaneously on the bridge, which was 4,200 feet long, again the longest in the world at the time. It had the highest clearance of any bridge, 220 feet above the water, and was especially difficult to build because of strong ocean currents and severe winds. Cone was "a stickler for on-the-job safety," to the extent of extending a net of manila rope beneath the construction area. Injuries and loss of life—eleven deaths—were much lower than on other major construction jobs of that time. During construction Cone observed that painting would become a continuous maintenance problem because of corrosion from salt fogs, so he designed permanent scaffolds for that purpose.

When the bridge was completed in 1937, Cone helped Strauss prepare the final engineering report and continued as maintenance engineer until 1941. Divorced from his first wife in 1938, he married Jeanne Fozard Hamilton in 1939; they had no children. He was a member of a committee that investigated the collapse in 1940 of the Tacoma-Narrows Bridge in Washington State during high winds four months after it opened. Shortly after that he was abruptly fired by the board of directors of the Golden Gate Bridge, chiefly because he recommended that insurance on that bridge be dropped because of increased insurance costs.

During 1941 Cone carried out an engineering study for a passenger tramway on the mountain above Palm Springs, California. That same year he became general manager of the engineering and construction firm of Silas Mason Company, where he was in charge of construction of four ordnance plants during World War II. In 1951 he became general manager of Mason & Hanger-Silas Mason Company, in New York City. From 1950 to 1953 he was architectural engineer on the construction of the nuclear test site at Frenchman's Flat, Nevada, for the Atomic Energy Commission and was later a participant in designing the rocket and spacecraft facilities at Cape Canaveral (now Cape Kennedy), Florida. In 1956 he returned to bridge building as he supervised the Mason Company contract on the foundations for a bridge at Carquinez Straits on the eastern side of San Francisco Bay. The location was especially difficult over a swift channel, and the project was completed at a considerable financial loss.

Divorced from his second wife, Cone married Pearl Janet Bloomquist in 1957; they had no children. During 1960 Cone was being considered for the position of chief engineer of the Bay Area Rapid Transit District project in San Francisco, but he withdrew his name after suffering a heart attack. He died in Vallejo, California.

Cone demonstrated high competence and administrative responsibility in engineering aspects of major construction projects. He published a number of papers in the *Journal of American Society of Civil Engineers*. For his work on the Golden Gate Bridge and his techniques of its later maintenance, he was awarded the Construction Engineering Prize of the American Society of Civil Engineers in 1940.

• Cone wrote about some of the engineering problems of Golden Gate Bridge in "Battling Storm and Tide in Founding Golden Gate Pier," *Engineering News-Record* 115 (22 Aug. 1935): 245–51. Also see his article "Permanent Painting Scaffolds for the Golden Gate Bridge," *Engineering News-Record* 124 (25 Apr. 1940): 52–53. Information on Cone's role in the construction of the Golden Gate Bridge is in John Van Der Zee, *The Gate: The True Story of the Design and Construction of the Golden Gate Bridge* (1986), which includes biographical material. Obituaries are in the *San Francisco Examiner* and the *New York Times*, 22 Jan. 1961.

ELIZABETH NOBLE SHOR

CONFREY, Zez (3 Apr. 1895–22 Nov. 1971), composer and pianist, was born Edward Elzear Confrey in Peru, Illinois, the son of Thomas J. Confrey, railroad engineer, and Margaret Brown. At age four he began piano lessons after demonstrating the ability to pick out a tune played by an older brother. He conducted and performed with his own orchestra while still in high school; he later graduated from Chicago Musical College where he studied piano and composition. His exposure there to the impressionistic styles of Claude Debussy and Maurice Ravel would influence some of his later pieces. While studying at the college he worked as a drummer in a theater orchestra, and about 1915 he played piano in a touring orchestra he formed with his brother Jim.

During World War I Confrey enlisted in the navy, where he played with a touring show, "Leave It to the Sailors." Here he met and worked with violinist Benny Kabelski, who would go on to fame as Jack Benny.

After the war Confrey began making piano rolls of his arrangements and compositions, turning out some 120 rolls for the QRS Company between 1918 and 1924. He also recorded as piano soloist and with orchestra for several record labels and performed with his own orchestra in vaudeville. During this time Confrey came to the forefront of what was known as novelty piano style, an up-tempo, ragtime-based idiom incorporating flashy "tricks" frequently used in piano roll renditions. His classical training and experience as a percussionist enabled him to pepper his playing with particularly effective pianistic devices such as parallel fourths, tritone-ornamented thirds, and polymetric syncopation. Several of his novelty piano pieces, having appeared first on piano rolls, were published in 1921, and one of them, "Kitten on the Keys," achieved enormous success, selling more than one million sheet music copies in its first year. It went on to become (with "Maple Leaf Rag" and "Twelfth Street Rag") one of the most frequently recorded rags of all time. Over the next decade or so Confrey turned out several more novelty rags, including the popular "Stumbling" (1922) and "Dizzy Fingers" (1923).

By 1923 Confrey had written his *Modern Course in Novelty Piano Playing*, a pedagogical method book presenting novelty devices in several keys and illustrating their application in arrangements. The book, endorsed by five novelty pianists of the day, was quite successful, selling more than 100,000 copies in a matter of weeks and remaining in print for more than forty years.

Confrey's reputation by this time was such that he was invited by bandleader Paul Whiteman to perform some of his compositions and arrangements on the historic Aeolian Hall concert of 1924 at which George Gershwin's *Rhapsody in Blue* was premiered. The concert, advertised as "An Experiment in Modern Music," actually gave Confrey billing above Gershwin.

With the success of his novelty pieces, Confrey's career emphasis shifted away from playing toward composition. However, while the novelty piano style was extremely popular for a number of years, it virtually died out around 1930, as piano sales plummeted and the depression hit. Confrey accordingly changed his compositional style about that time, adopting a smoother and more sophisticated sound, less rhythmically exciting and more harmonically complex, as in "Grandfather's Clock" (1933) and "Arabian Maid" (1935). In 1932 he married Wilhelmina Matthes, who had appeared as a showgirl on the Broadway stage as Gloria Beaumont. They had two children. After World War II he composed mostly pedagogical pieces aimed at children and beginners, such as "Easy Pieces for the Piano" (1948) and "Musical Alphabet Rhymes" (1947). During this time his change of focus was reflected in the use of his full name, Edward E. Confrey, on his pieces. Many of these late works remained unpublished, including a miniature opera, "Thanksgiving" (1947). Also, his compositional activity came to be curtailed by Parkinson's disease. All in all, he wrote more than one hundred pieces in a variety of styles, including songs and more serious compositions. But he was never again able to approach the compositional success he had enjoyed in the 1920s. Confrey spent his last years in Lakewood, New Jersey, where he died.

Confrey is best known as a composer of novelty piano pieces and is often even credited with inventing the idiom. As such he has been denigrated, the style often dismissed as a commercialized degradation of the "legitimate" ragtime of men like Scott Joplin, James Scott, and Tom Turpin, and certainly a step down from the mainstream of black jazz. However, his style, which has come to be regarded as quintessential novelty piano, influenced other novelty composers of the time, including Pete Wendling, Victor Arden, Phil Ohman, and Roy Bargy. Gershwin openly acknowledged Confrey's influence on his own pianistic style. Indeed, Henry Osgood, in *So This Is Jazz* (1926), considered Confrey to be the first real composer of "piano jazz," a genuinely pianistic idiom for jazz. In any case, Confrey's most popular novelty pieces long continued to be played and enjoyed by modern audiences.

• James R. Dossa, "The Novelty Piano Style of Zez Confrey: A Theoretical Analysis of His Piano Solos and Their Relation to Ragtime and Jazz" (Ph.D. diss., Northwestern Univ., 1986), contains some biographical data as well as information on his contributions and their social context. The musical compilation *Zez Confrey: Ragtime, Novelty and Jazz Piano Solos*, ed. Ronny S. Schiff (1982), includes a biographical sketch, "Zez Confrey: Genius Supreme," by David A. Jasen. A slightly abridged version of that material appears in Jasen and Trebor Jay Tichenor, *Rags and Ragtime: A Musical History* (1978). An obituary is in the *New York Times*, 27 Nov. 1971.

WILLIAM G. ELLIOTT

CONGER, Edwin Hurd (7 Mar. 1843–18 May 1907), congressman and diplomat, was born near Galesburg in Knox County, Illinois, the son of Lorentus E. Conger, a prosperous farmer and banker, and Mary Hurd. Edwin graduated from Lombard University in Galesburg in 1862 and immediately enlisted in the 102d Illinois Infantry. He attained the rank of captain and was breveted a major, a title he retained throughout his life. He completed Albany Law School in 1866 and began a law practice in Galesburg. He married Sarah J. Pike in 1866; they had two children.

In 1868 Conger moved to Iowa and began a successful career in livestock raising and banking. He also entered local politics in Madison and Dallas counties and eventually served four years as state treasurer (1881–1884). He was elected to Congress in 1884. During three terms in the House of Representatives, he became chairman of the Committee on Coinage, Weights, and Measures, and he was a member of the conference committee that eliminated the free coinage of silver from the Silver Purchase Act of 1890. In the fall of 1890, he resigned from Congress to become U.S. minister to Brazil. A change of administrations in 1893 caused the Republican Conger to be replaced by a Democrat, but in 1897 his friend and former congressional colleague William McKinley reappointed him to the South American post. His service in Brazil was largely routine, but it provided valuable preparation for his subsequent assignment as U.S. minister to China.

The selection of the experienced Conger as envoy to Beijing (Peking) in 1898 reflected the increased importance of China in U.S. foreign policy, and the appointment was welcomed in American commercial circles. Conger continued his predecessor Charles Denby's practice of supporting specific American enterprises such as railroad projects. He arrived at a time when the Western nations and Japan were moving quickly to claim territorial concessions in China. He supported Secretary of State John Hay's efforts through the Open Door Notes to prevent partition, but he privately and unsuccessfully urged Washington to consider acquiring its own sphere of influence around the port of Tianjin (Tientsin). He viewed an American lease of

Chinese territory as a prudent protection of U.S. interest and as no threat to China. During the war with Spain, he argued for U.S. retention of the Philippines as an entrepôt to the China market.

The dramatic increase in the number of foreign missionaries and merchants in China during the 1890s led to the violent, xenophobic Boxer Rebellion in 1900. Rampaging forces murdered foreigners and destroyed their property across northern China until finally the Boxers entered Beijing and besieged the walled compounds of the diplomatic legations. The conservative empress dowager, the country's de facto ruler, sided for a time with the Boxers. Conger had failed to persuade Washington to make a show of military force earlier, and now he and the rest of the diplomatic corps and their families were cut off from assistance and communication and were in great peril for their lives. For fifty-five days, Conger and the others ate horse meat, fought off assaults, and faced imminent slaughter. Finally an international military force of 18,000 men, including 2,100 American soldiers and marines, rescued them. After the lifting of the siege, the McKinley administration was eager to return the U.S. forces to the Philippines because of fighting there, but Conger prevailed upon Washington to keep its troops in China as part of a temporary occupation force while he and his diplomatic colleagues negotiated with the imperial government. The U.S. military presence provided him tangible leverage against attempts by other ministers to take undue advantage of China's distress. In 1901 he joined with the representatives of ten other nations in signing the Boxer settlement, which extracted new financial and political concessions from China but showed signs of Conger's restraining influence.

Although forced by the foreign concession scramble and the Boxer Rebellion into a militant defense of American lives and economic interests, Conger was in many ways a voice of moderation in the clash between East and West. He always maintained cordial relations with the powerful governor-general of northern China, Li Hongzhang (Li Hung-chang), and other leading Chinese officials. As spreading Russian influence produced frictions that would lead to the Russo-Japanese War, he negotiated protection of U.S. commercial rights in Manchuria in 1903 while avoiding a clash with Russia, Japan, or China over the area. Furthermore his wife established a unique relationship with the empress dowager that opened for the first time social contact between the women of the diplomatic quarter and those of the imperial court. Despite the traumatic Boxer experience, Conger remained a supporter of the prevailing U.S. Open Door Policy in China; that is, he opposed foreign demands on China that would exploit the Chinese and that would dismantle the empire.

In 1905 Conger left China to become U.S. ambassador to Mexico, but he retired from government service after only a few months in that position. He died in Pasadena, California.

• The principal sources on Conger's career are public documents in the *Congressional Record* and in the General Records of the Department of State, National Archives. There is a collection of his papers at the State Historical Society of Iowa, Des Moines. Another significant source of personal information is Sarah P. Conger, *Letters from China* (1909). See also John E. Briggs, "Iowa and the Diplomatic Service," *Iowa Journal of History and Politics* 19 (1921): 321–65; Marilyn B. Young, *The Rhetoric of Empire: American China Policy, 1895–1901* (1968); and Michael H. Hunt, *The Making of a Special Relationship: The United States and China to 1914* (1983). Obituaries are in the *Des Moines Register and Leader* and the *New York Times*, 19 May 1907.

DAVID L. ANDERSON

CONKLIN, Chester (11 Jan. 1888–11 Oct. 1971), actor, was born Jules Cowles in Oskaloosa, Iowa, the son of farmers. He fulfilled many a country boy's dream when, probably sometime between 1905 and 1910, he ran off to join the circus and see the world. He was playing with the Al G. Barnes Circus during the 1912–1913 season, and when the company took up its winter quarters on the West Coast he decided to join the newly formed Keystone company begun by Mack Sennett in the Los Angeles area. By the winter of 1913 Conklin was playing featured parts.

Conklin's work has sometimes been confused with that of other Keystone players, most notably the taller Billy Bevan and the cockeyed Ben Turpin, which is understandable since the costuming of the three share much in common: the oversized faux moustache that hides much of the lower face and accentuates the smallness of the eyes, the jacket fit so tight that it crimps beneath the arms, the high-topped round-toed shoes, and the hat or cap so small it seems to sit atop the head instead of upon it. In its day such costuming would have been familiar from the vaudeville and burlesque, identifying the character as the freshly arrived immigrant, the slightly innocent and often befuddled foreign fellow who cannot quite make his way in a modern, urban America where so much seems to be happening so quickly. It was a variation on this theme with which Conklin first earned his spurs with Sennett and became a highly popular star. Teamed with the bearlike Mack Swain, the diminutive Conklin, sporting a walrus moustache, achieved popularity in the "Ambrose Walrus" series during 1913–1915. In such 1915 two-reelers as *Ambrose and Walrus*, *When Ambrose Dared Walrus*, and *Ambrose's Sour Grapes*, the pair portrayed Eastern European immigrants, with Conklin's wily Walrus character more savvy in the ways of urban life than the duller Ambrose. Ambrose is to Walrus a "greenhorn," a well-meaning if easily abused companion, and abuse him Walrus does, stealing his money, his wife, and virtually anything else not immediately fastened to Ambrose's imposing body.

In addition to such comic villainy, Conklin also took solo roles during this period, primarily as the character Droppington. In such films as *Droppington's Devilish Dream* (1915) and *Droppington's Family Tree* (1915) he plays an immigrant character once again, someone who means to present himself to America as fully equipped to partake in the pleasures and pastimes of middle-class urban life but who rarely succeeds. Machines thwart him; manufactured objects either fail to provide the service for which they were intended or seem to turn on him and put him in peril. Conklin might have risen to stardom in such roles, but others were doing much the same thing, and doing it better. One was Charlie Chaplin.

Chaplin left the British music-hall stage and signed on with Sennett within weeks of Conklin's becoming one of Sennett's featured players. The two became casual friends and sometimes working partners. Conklin appeared in Chaplin's most beloved feature, *The Gold Rush* (1925). In the years to come, long after the era of silent clowns had passed, Chaplin would look to Conklin to play significant parts in two of Chaplin's best sound comedies, *Modern Times* (1936) and *The Great Dictator* (1940). Conklin is also in many of Chaplin's Keystone films, including the first feature comedy ever produced in this country, *Tillie's Punctured Romance* (1914–1915). In a number of other films, including *Dough and Dynamite* (1914), he provided the young Chaplin a splendid partner, perhaps the best Chaplin would have before leaving Keystone and setting out on his own. Seeing them together is much like watching a seasoned dance team in which Chaplin leads and Conklin synchronizes his movement and timing to complement—almost seamlessly—his partner's crazy antics. These films showcase Conklin's greatest strength as a comic performer: his capacity to react, to complement more distinctive and ingenious performers, as his later career would prove.

In 1920 Conklin left Sennett over money, taking a more lucrative salary offer from Fox with the promise of starring in its "Sunshine Comedy" series. He proved out of his depth at Fox when asked to carry a comedy on his own, however, and within a few years he experienced similar disappointments at Universal, MGM, and Paramount as well, though he found his place performing comedic character parts during the conversion to sound in the late 1920s. A number of encyclopedic entries include as only an afterthought anything Conklin did following the advent of sound. In the 1950s rumors spread that he was unemployed and homeless. The truth is that Conklin had the longest motion picture career of any of the initial Keystone players. While the parts he played after talkies arrived were often small, he continued to find work in motion pictures through the mid-1960s, when declining health and old age led him into retirement. His last film was *A Big Hand for the Little Lady* (1966), and the roster of sound comedies in which he made cameo-sized appearances is impressive, as are his performances, particularly those for director Preston Sturges in such American screen classics as *Sullivan's Travels* (1942), *The Miracle of Morgan's Creek* (1944), and *Hail the Conquering Hero* (1944).

In 1965 Conklin married June Gunther, a fellow resident of Woodland Hills Motion Picture Country House, a home for motion picture veterans into which he had moved four years earlier. After their marriage the couple purchased a bungalow in Van Nuys, where they lived until Conklin's death.

• The Margaret Herrick Library of the Academy of Motion Picture Arts and Sciences has the best collection of material on Conklin. Mack Sennett's *King of Comedy* (1990) includes interesting recollections of Conklin; perhaps the most informative work about his Keystone years is Kalton C. Lahue, *Mack Sennett's Keystone* (1971).

JAY BOYER

CONKLIN, Edwin Grant (24 Nov. 1863–21 Nov. 1952), biologist, was born in Waldo, Ohio, the son of Abram Virgil Conklin, physician, and Nancy Maria Hull. Conklin attended a one-room school and received his introduction to natural history while working on the family farm. As the son of a religious family, he entered Ohio Wesleyan University in 1880. There he encountered science for the first time, in natural history classes, on field trips to collect shells, and as an assistant in the museum. During his third year he needed money, so he dropped out to teach in a one-room country school, serving also as janitor and disciplinarian. He returned to graduate from Ohio Wesleyan with a B.S. in 1885 and a B.A. in 1886.

Conklin's strong religious upbringing and his need for a job took him in 1885 to Mississippi where he taught black students at the missionary Rust University (later Rust College). Along with languages and history, he had responsibility for all the sciences. At Rust he also met Belle Adkinson, the daughter of a minister. They were married in 1889, and she remained his close companion until her death in 1940. The couple had three children.

In 1888 Conklin entered the Johns Hopkins University to work with William Keith Brooks on morphology and natural history. As he often recalled, it was among the excellent students and faculty there that he learned to love doing scientific research. His dissertation study of cell lineage in the slipper snail *Crepidula* took him to the U.S. Fish Commission in Woods Hole, Massachusetts, for summer research. There he met Edmund Beecher Wilson, who was working across the street at the Marine Biological Laboratory. An earlier Hopkins graduate, Wilson was also carrying out cell lineage studies, but on a different organism, the annelid worm *Nereis*. Both were tracing in careful detail the exact pattern of each cell division, starting with the one-cell fertilized egg and following the fates of all the cells as they underwent division. By working on different organisms, the two men generated exciting material for comparison and for identifying functional and genealogical parallels among cells across species. They hoped that this would reveal secrets of embryological development as well as help to unlock the evolutionary, or phylogenetic, history of each organism by revealing points of similarity and difference. The classic works by Conklin and Wilson provoked a decade of enthusiasm for cell lineage studies of other organisms. Studies of cell division remained the central focus of Conklin's career in embryology and cytology.

Conklin's work in Woods Hole also introduced him to Charles Otis Whitman, first director of the Marine Biological Laboratory (MBL), who convinced Conklin to join the instructional staff there in 1892. Conklin became a trustee in 1897 and spent nearly all the rest of his summers in Woods Hole as a loyal friend and hard worker for the MBL. In keeping with his interest in marine biology, Conklin also served as president of the Bermuda Biological Station for Research after it was reorganized in 1926; he helped to secure an endowment and a permanent site for the station. In addition, he served on the board of trustees for the Woods Hole Oceanographic Institution.

In 1891, after completing his Ph.D. research but before publishing the final version of his dissertation, Conklin accepted a teaching position at Ohio Wesleyan. There he developed a modern laboratory, and the president of this Methodist institution supported Conklin's freedom to teach the theory of evolution. After three years there, Conklin moved on to Northwestern University in Evanston, Illinois, where he taught from 1894 to 1896. Though the president also backed him there, he left when some local Methodist clergymen began to attack the school by challenging Conklin's teaching of evolution. He moved to the University of Pennsylvania in 1896 and remained there until 1908, becoming an important part of the active Philadelphia scientific community.

In particular, Conklin valued his participation in the venerable American Philosophical Society, of which he became a member in 1897. His participation there had already begun the previous year when he presented his first major public paper in a symposium with Edward Drinker Cope and Liberty Hyde Bailey on "Factors of Organic Evolution." Conklin became very active in the society and worked on many committees, twice serving as president (the first person to do so). He was also active in the Academy of Natural Sciences of Philadelphia and had connections with the Wistar Institute of Anatomy and Biology.

In Philadelphia, Conklin also began to express his religious views more publicly and to address questions about the relations of science, especially evolution, and religion. During his last college year, he and several classmates had received what was called a local preacher's license following a perfunctory test on the Bible and their basic faith. Though he never pursued the ministry formally, in Philadelphia he spoke at various churches and to church congresses about science and religion, even though some members of the Philadelphia Methodist Preachers Meeting vehemently opposed evolution. Conklin felt that evolution was fully consistent with Methodist teachings, but others within the church did not. As a result of that opposition, Conklin never transferred his church membership from Evanston to Philadelphia.

Later, against the background of increasing concern about evolution excited by the Scopes trial in 1925, Conklin worked even harder to articulate the ways in which religion and science, including evolution, are fully compatible. He drew on trends in contemporary liberal theology to demonstrate that the apparently supernatural and miraculous is actually fully natural in origin and character, and that a rich picture of the natural world and of the powers of evolution could provide all the freedom, dignity, and ethical principles that humans seek.

As his career progressed, Conklin devoted greater attention to concerns about nature and man. His *Heredity and Environment* of 1915 looked at humanity's place in nature and at eugenical possibilities for improving that place, as well as at the relative importance of heredity and development in shaping organisms. Conklin accepted the ideals and optimism of eugenics but not the practical suggestions for achieving the goals through genetics. Education and social progress should work with biology to improve the species, Conklin felt.

In 1908 Conklin was elected to the National Academy of Sciences and also moved to Princeton University as professor of biology and chair of the biology department. Princeton was just completing a new modern building for biology and geology, and Conklin's mission was to coordinate previously separate subdisciplines of biology and organize a new biology program. Attracted by Princeton's president Woodrow Wilson, who had urged the development of modern scientific teaching and research, Conklin was frustrated at times after Wilson left to become governor of New Jersey and the new administrations did not always support his requests. Nonetheless, he settled into the Princeton life, holding a regular open house for students and working, until he retired in 1933, to strengthen the biology program and faculty.

Conklin continued his work on various journal boards, including the *Journal of Morphology*, the *Biological Bulletin*, *Genetics*, the *Journal of Experimental Zoology*, and the *Quarterly Review of Biology*. In addition to holding the presidency of the American Philosophical Society, he was elected president of the American Society of Zoologists (1899), the American Society of Naturalists (1912), and the American Association for the Advancement of Science (1936). He served the National Academy of Sciences as first chairman of the new Committee on Zoology for the National Research Council, on the executive committee, and on the council. He also held membership in a number of international societies. This service and professional work was important to Conklin, and as his career progressed the public functions took more and more of his time. During much of his long and productive career, Conklin was one of the most influential biologists in the United States; he remained active until shortly before his death in Princeton, New Jersey.

• Conklin's papers are available in the Manuscripts Collection, Princeton University; unfortunately, they are not cataloged or sorted in any detail. His most important works include "The Embryology of *Crepidula*," *Journal of Morphology* 13 (1897): 1–226; "The Organization and Cell-Lineage of the Ascidian Egg," *Journal of the Academy of Natural Sciences of Philadelphia* 13 (1905): 1–119; *Heredity and Environment in the Development of Man* (1915); *The Direction of Evolution*

(1921); and *Man: Real and Ideal* (1943). The most complete biography, with full bibliography, is E. Newton Harvey, "Edwin Grant Conklin," *Biographical Memoirs, National Academy of Sciences* 31 (1958): 54–91, while A. Richards, "Edwin Grant Conklin," *Bios* 6 (March 1935): 187–211, provides a useful contemporary look. Conklin's autobiographical sketch in *Thirteen Americans: Their Spiritual Biographies*, ed. Louis Finkelstein (1953) gives special insight into his views on religion, ethics, and democracy.

JANE MAIENSCHEIN

CONKLING, Grace Walcott Hazard (7 Feb. 1878–15 Nov. 1958), poet and English professor, was born in New York City, the daughter of Christopher Grant, a Presbyterian minister, and Frances Post Hazard. In 1899 Conkling graduated with a bachelor of letters degree from Smith College, where she returned to teach English in 1914. First, she taught English, Latin, and Greek at Graham School in New York for a year (1901–1902) and then traveled to Europe, where she studied music at the University of Heidelberg in 1902–1903 and languages in Paris during 1903–1904. In 1905 she married Roscoe Platt Conkling, with whom she had two children. The Conklings lived for nearly five years in Mexico. Their daughter Hilda became known as a child prodigy after her mother had two collections of her poetry published, *Poems by a Little Girl* (1920) and *Shoes of the Wind: A Book of Poems* (1922). From the age of four, Hilda apparently told her poems to her mother, who wrote them down.

Grace Conkling published five volumes of her own poetry, much of which had appeared first in such periodicals as the *Century, Poetry*, the *New Republic*, and the *North American Review*. Her collections include *Afternoons of April: A Book of Verse* (1915), *Wilderness Songs* (1920), *Ship's Log and Other Poems* (1924), *Flying Fish: A Book of Songs and Sonnets* (1926), and *Witch and Other Poems* (1929). She also translated the poetry of Spanish author Perez de Ayala's *Prometheus: The Fall of the House of Limon: Sunday Sunlight* for the 1920 English edition and published a book entitled *Imagination and Children's Reading* in 1922. Also in 1922, she was awarded the Poetry Society of South Carolina's Blindman Prize for "Variations on a Theme."

Conkling's lyric poetry often reflected her travels, as in her collection *Witch and Other Poems*, which includes "Poems of Porto Rico," "La Argentine Dances," and "Poems of Mallorca." The title series in *Ship's Log and Other Poems* chronicles a journey across the ocean. Along with detailed observations about nature, Conkling notes others' jaded, uninterested response to the sea. Her long, emotionally intense love poems also incorporate nature imagery. Her poems from 1926 on, collected in *Witch*, are more innovative. The title poem explores the tension for a woman between acquiescing in "the pure / Negation of the stainless air" and risking the consequences of "flying" away from "a winter fierce and brittle."

Conkling's poetry received mixed reviews. Amy Lowell praised her work, saying of *Witch* that "no modern poet is so conversant with nature's moods as Mrs. Conkling," and a review of *Afternoons of April* noted Conkling's "joy in color, joy in sound" (*Poetry* 7 [Oct. 1915–Mar. 1916]: 152). Others were less enthusiastic, however. One reviewer questioned Lowell's awarding the Blindman Prize to Conkling, concluding that Conkling's "words are more to her than the significance of her theme" (*Poetry* 22 [Apr.–Sept. 1923]: 94). Another review referred to the "self-indulgence" of *Flying Fish*, saying that "Mrs. Conkling lacks discipline in the choice of images, and seems unable to reject them even when they hardly serve her purpose," although the reviewer did find a few poems to admire in the volume (*Poetry* 29 [Oct. 1926–Mar. 1927]: 282). Still another said of *Ship's Log* that "all of the poems are delicate, highly colored," but "Mrs. Conkling's subject matter is neither dramatic nor important" (*Poetry* 27 [Oct. 1925–Mar. 1926]: 52–53). The primary criticism of her poetry converges on its presumed old-fashionedness, including her continued use of rhymed couplets and her references to nymphs, dryads, and other classical figures. Yet the strength of Conkling's images and the complex ambivalence toward life that she captures in *Witch*, for example, seem to justify Lowell's more positive opinion of her work.

In addition to her poetry writing and teaching, Conkling lectured on contemporary poetry. In a 1924 inscription in a copy of *Ship's Log*, Conkling wrote, "We are not lonely while a dream endures." She died in Northampton, Massachusetts, where she had been professor emerita of the Smith College English Department.

• The inscription in *Ship's Log* quoted above is in a copy donated to the Michigan State University Library from the library of Catherine Chapin and is dated 13 Nov. 1924. MSU's Special Collections Library has a 1929 copy of *Witch*; the book jacket includes Amy Lowell's review and a brief biographical sketch by the publisher. An obituary and funeral notice are in the *New York Times*, 16 and 20 Nov. 1958.

KATHY D. HADLEY

CONKLING, Roscoe (30 Oct. 1829–18 Apr. 1888), politician, was born in Albany, New York, the son of Eliza Cockburn and Alfred Conkling, a prominent Whig congressman, diplomat, and jurist. Roscoe followed his father into the legal profession but without the formality of a college education. Settling in Utica, he began his legal practice and his political career simultaneously, being named district attorney in 1850. In 1854 he played a role in the organization of his state's Republican party, and the next year he married Julia Seymour, sister of New York's Democratic governor, Horatio Seymour. In 1858 he was elected mayor of Utica and later that same year won a seat in the U.S. House of Representatives, which he would hold, except for a brief hiatus from 1863 to 1865, until he was elevated to the U.S. Senate in 1867.

This rapid ascension was due more to Conkling's personality than to his legislative talents. Even in an era accustomed to flamboyant political leaders, Conkling stood out. Tall, full-bearded, with a carefully arranged blond spitcurl adorning his high forehead, his body strengthened by a strict regimen of exercise, including boxing lessons, Conkling strutted through life with such overwhelming self-assurance that the word most frequently used to describe him was "imperious."

Although Conkling was not totally indifferent to larger issues—he supported Radical Reconstruction and opposed inflationary greenbacks—he was not, throughout his long career, associated with a single legislative measure of major significance. His energies were largely devoted to matters of party organization. "He never interests himself in anything but personal antagonisms," observed John Sherman (1823–1900); "he never rises above a Custom House or a Post Office."

Mastery of the tangled web of New York state politics required just such skills as these. Though scrupulously honest in personal matters (as well as temperate in his use of alcohol), Conkling lived in a world in which political corruption was the norm. Indeed, he scorned the efforts of those "man-milliners and dilletanti," such as George William Curtis, who advocated measures of political purification. "When Dr. [Samuel] Johnson defined patriotism as the last refuge of a scoundrel," Conkling sneered, "he was unconscious of the then undeveloped capabilities and uses of the word reform."

Conkling disdained to adopt the bonhomie exhibited by many political bosses of his era. An aloof, remote figure, he had few personal friends or confidants, preferring to dominate his followers by whiplash sarcasm and implacable hostility to those who dared cross him. Ultimately, few escaped his wrath. James A. Garfield, a prime target of that wrath, correctly appraised him as "a great fighter, inspired more by his hates than his loves." Those hates encompassed not only reformers, such as Curtis, Carl Schurz, and Horace Greeley, but political and personal rivals of any stripe. When James G. Blaine publicly mocked Conkling's "turkey-gobbler strut," the two broke off personal relations and never spoke to each other, though thrown into almost daily contact. Other rivals, such as Rutherford B. Hayes and Garfield, suffered similar excommunication, and even one-time friends, such as Chester A. Arthur and Alonzo Cornell, shared the same fate. Not even his family was immune. His relations with his wife, who seldom accompanied him to Washington, became formal and remote. When his well-publicized affair with Kate Chase Sprague threatened to make him an object of ridicule, he coldly dropped her. He even ceased to speak to his once-beloved daughter (and only child) Bessie after her marriage to a man to whom he objected. Little wonder that he would come to be known as "the great American quarreler."

The only human being to whom Conkling seems to have given unqualified respect and affection was Ulysses S. Grant. Grant reciprocated by funneling all New York state presidential appointments through Conkling, cementing the senator's grip on the state's Republican organization. Grant even offered him the position of chief justice of the United States on the death of Salmon P. Chase, but Conkling declined in the expectation that he would instead follow Grant into the White House.

That hope was dashed at the Republican National Convention of 1876. The supporters of Conkling and Blaine deadlocked, and the convention turned to a dark horse, Hayes of Ohio. Conkling's support for the candidate was lukewarm, and after the disputed election he played an equivocal role in the compromise negotiations that led to Hayes's certification as president.

The new president's acts seemed to justify Conkling's apprehensions. Not only did Hayes appoint Conkling's New York foe, William M. Evarts, as secretary of state, but the new treasury secretary, Sherman, began an investigation into the operations of the New York Custom House, which was under the management of Conkling's henchmen Arthur and Cornell.

With 1,500 jobs at his disposal and with an annual remuneration of almost $100,000, the collector of the Port of New York could provide the means by which Conkling and his friends controlled the party organization of New York State. By challenging that control in the name of civil service reform, the Hayes administration was, in effect, declaring war on Conkling's management of his state political machine. The senator fought back. At the Republican State Convention in September 1877, he led the party into open defiance of the president, and in the Senate he raised the claim of "senatorial courtesy" to defeat Hayes's nominations to replace Arthur and Cornell. Hayes persisted and in a later try succeeded in removing Arthur (who actually had served with reasonable efficiency), replacing him, despite Conkling's objections, with Edwin A. Merritt.

After all this, it was hardly surprising that Conkling should appear at the Republican National Convention of 1880 as the leader of the antiadministration faction, the so-called "Stalwarts." Their candidate was Grant, under whose administration they had prospered and whose name Conkling personally placed in nomination in one of the classic pieces of American political oratory. Although Grant's bid for renomination failed, Conkling could take some satisfaction from having thwarted his rivals, Blaine and Sherman, as well as from the selection of Arthur as the vice presidential candidate. The compromise presidential nominee was more problematic: Garfield, an Ohio congressman with suspiciously close ties to both Sherman and Blaine. Conkling's grudging support in the ensuing presidential campaign would be granted, so he claimed, only upon Garfield's assurance of favoring Conkling's organization in the distribution of presidential patronage.

Garfield's understanding of the agreement was somewhat different. By appointing Blaine to be secretary of state, he seemed to be giving a clear signal as to where his sympathies lay. Conkling insisted that New York was entitled to the equally important office of secretary of the treasury, but Garfield compounded the insult by detaching Thomas L. James from his allegiance to Conkling and offering him the lesser position of postmaster general.

Convinced that his enemies, led by Blaine and *New York Tribune* editor Whitelaw Reid, were planning to use the Garfield administration to supplant his organization, Conkling (with Arthur's support) angrily broke with the newly elected president. Garfield sought some grounds for compromise, but Conkling's arrogant bullying drove the president even closer to Blaine's camp. The last straw was when Garfield, at Blaine's urging, moved Merritt to a diplomatic post and nominated Conkling's prime New York enemy, William H. Robertson, for the critical position of collector of the Port of New York.

Once again Conkling raised the principle of "senatorial courtesy" in an attempt to defeat a nomination by a president of his own party. Garfield countered by elevating what had begun as a patronage squabble to the level of a constitutional confrontation, insisting on the maintenance of presidential prerogatives. The Senate, aware of the growing public support for Garfield's position and unwilling to anger a freshly installed president, failed to support Conkling and confirmed the nomination. In so doing, it helped elevate the prestige of the executive branch after a fifteen-year period during which Capitol Hill had tended to dominate the White House.

Rather than acquiesce, Conkling (along with his junior colleague, Thomas Platt) resigned from the Senate on 14 May 1881, hoping to find vindication in reelection. That consolation was denied him, and an embittered Conkling abandoned public life, even rejecting a tender by Arthur (now president after Garfield's assassination) of an appointment to the Supreme Court.

Conkling devoted his remaining years to the practice of law. His most notable case was *San Mateo County v. Southern Pacific Railroad Company* (1885), in which he argued the historically dubious proposition that he and other Reconstruction congressmen had deliberately framed the Fourteenth Amendment so as to protect corporate property. Though the *San Mateo* case was declared moot, this so-called "conspiracy theory" of the Fourteenth Amendment was accepted both by the courts and by historians until the 1930s.

In March 1888 Conkling was caught in New York City's great blizzard. Disdaining a cab, he plowed through the drifts, collapsing at the entrance of his Gramercy Park town house. He was dead within a month, bringing to an end a spectacular yet essentially empty career, which the *New York Times* summed up in a curiously double-edged assessment as that of "a typical American statesman—a man by whose career and character the future will judge of the political standards of the present."

• No major concentration of Conkling's papers has survived, although there is a small collection at the Library of Congress, and scattered items can be found in various other libraries. Nor is there a totally satisfying biography, though David M. Jordan, *Roscoe Conkling of New York* (1971), is clearly preferable to Donald Barr Chidsey's breezy study, *The Gentleman from New York* (1935). Alfred R. Conkling, *The Life and Letters of Roscoe Conkling* (1889), is a reverential biography by his nephew. Useful biographies of Conkling's contemporaries include Allan Peskin, *Garfield* (1978), and Thomas C. Reeves, *Gentleman Boss: The Life of Chester Alan Arthur* (1975). Political background for Conkling's career can be found in DeAlva Stanwood Alexander, *A Political History of the State of New York* (1909), and H. Wayne Morgan, *From Hayes to McKinley* (1969). Ari Hoogenboom, *Outlawing the Spoils* (1961), clarifies the complexities of the unreformed civil service and the various attempts to reform it. The most substantive obituary is by Robert G. Ingersoll, *Memorial Address on Roscoe Conkling* (1888).

ALLAN PESKIN

CONLAN, Jocko (6 Dec. 1899–16 Apr. 1989), baseball umpire and player, was born John Bertrand Conlan in Chicago, Illinois, the son of Audley Conlan, a policeman, and Mary Ann (last name possibly Clayton). When he was three years old his father died, and the boy was raised along with eight other children by their mother. Growing up on the south side of Chicago, he lived less than a block from the park of a semiprofessional team; when he was seven or eight years of age, he and his young friends laid out a diamond in a nearby vacant lot and attempted to emulate the big boys. About the age of twelve Conlan became a Chicago White Sox bat boy. Not old enough to travel with the team, he worked mornings only and during summer vacation. He picked up bats and stray balls and generally helped out. He also stole a glove, carelessly left in the outfield by coach Kid Gleason, soon to become the unfortunate manager of the infamous "Black Sox" of 1919.

Conlan's mother enrolled him at De La Salle Catholic high school, which he attended for two years. There he made his mark as a cocky and belligerent, but reasonably good, pitcher. He did a little boxing, but he gave that up and happily signed on when a baseball team from the fast Chicago-area semiprofessional Midwest League made him an offer. He graduated quickly to the Western League, signing with Tulsa, Oklahoma, but being traded to Wichita, Kansas, before playing a single game. Just before the end of the 1920 season, missing his family, he went home without permission and incurred a one-year suspension. Violating league rules, he played semiprofessional ball again in 1921, then returned to Wichita for the next two seasons. By this time he was an outfielder, batting and throwing left-handed, and his teammates had begun to call him "Jocko," a sportswriter having nicknamed him after a little-known player with a similar last name. In 1926 he married Ruth Anderson, and the couple would have two children.

Conlan spent about twelve years in the high minor leagues with such teams as Toledo, Ohio; Rochester, New York; and Newark, New Jersey; his one chance to move up to the major leagues failed because of a knee injury. Although he did not star in those years, he was a solid journeyman player. Six times in his nine years of Class AA baseball, then the highest classification in the minor leagues, he hit over .300 and, in his own words, could "Go and get them." But when Montreal released him early in 1933, he decided to retire and perform playground work for the city of Chicago. His highest salary as a player had been $5,200 per year.

In 1934 Conlan's career took an odd turn. Injuries forced the hapless Chicago White Sox to acquire an outfielder in a hurry, and Conlan was instantly available. That year, in a substitute role, he played in 63 games, batting .249. The next year he had batted .286 in 65 games when his occupation was changed for him. The White Sox were in St. Louis playing a July doubleheader against the Browns in 114-degree temperatures, according to Conlan. He was not playing that day because he had injured a thumb in one of his frequent rough but amiable scuffles with Ted Lyons, the White Sox star pitcher and Conlan's best friend. Two umpires were working the first game, but one suffered heat exhaustion and could not continue. Conlan told the two managers that since he could not play he would be willing to umpire. Rogers Hornsby, the Browns' manager, agreed, since one of his men would also work the bases, and Conlan stepped into the vacancy. He umpired so well that he incurred the wrath of his own manager; he then was offered a chance to become a full-time umpire at the end of that season.

Conlan was disappointed to learn that he could not start his umpiring career in the major leagues, but he patiently served two years in the New York–Pennsylvania League and three in the American Association before being promoted to the National League. He umpired in the majors from 1941 through 1967. He received considerable help in the early years from a close friend and dean of umpires, Bill Klem. Conlan was considered too small to umpire in the American League, but height was not a problem to Klem, the National League's chief umpire; both men stood 5'7" tall. Conlan became the first National League umpire to give signals with his left hand and one of the first to wear a large chest protector outside his jacket, prevailing over Klem's objections to these innovations.

Conlan developed a reputation for being honest and tough, and he seemingly enjoyed baseball's many confrontations, which he usually won by throwing his antagonist out of the game. His autobiography would lead the reader to believe that the action provided him with great entertainment. His record substantiates his claim to skill, however. He was called upon to work four National League playoff series, six World Series, and six All-Star Games. Officially he retired in 1964, but he worked occasional games in later years. In 1974 he was elected to the National Baseball Hall of Fame, becoming only the fourth umpire to be so honored. In his later years Conlan spent much time pushing the career of his son, John, who was both a state senator and a U.S. Representative from Arizona.

Conlan's attitude toward umpiring comes clear in his own statements: an umpire must be in charge, respect the players, and demand respect. As he stated in his autobiography, "There is nothing so sad as a weak umpire" (p. 240). He died in Scottsdale, Arizona.

• Archival material on Conlan is at the National Baseball Library in Cooperstown, N.Y. Conlan's autobiography *Jocko*, as told to Robert Creamer (1967), tells a great deal of what Conlan felt about other ball players as well as his own accomplishments, but gives little material about his family life. He had strong opinions about the game and generally felt his views were more sound than those of others. Evidently relying heavily upon Conlan's writings is "Jocko Conlan" in Martin Appel and Burt Goldblatt, *Baseball's Best: The Hall of Fame Gallery* (1974). Most reliable technical data is in John Thorn and Pete Palmer, eds., *Total Baseball* (1993). Also useful is Lowell Reidenbaugh, *Cooperstown: Where Baseball's Legends Live Forever* (1983). Obituaries are in the *New York Times*, 17 Apr. 1989, and *Time*, 1 May 1989, p. 75.

THOMAS L. KARNES

CONNALLY, John Bowden, Jr. (27 Feb. 1917–15 June 1993), U.S. secretary of the treasury, governor of Texas, and U.S. secretary of the navy, was born near Floresville, Texas, the son of John Bowden Connally and Lela Wright, tenant farmers. The family prospered somewhat after resettling in San Antonio in 1926. Connally attended the University of Texas, where he honed his skills as an orator, dabbled in student government, and studied law. Even before receiving his LL.B. in 1941, however, he had gone to work in Washington, D.C., as an aide to Congressman Lyndon B. Johnson. In 1940 he married Idanell "Nellie" Brill. The couple had four children, one of whom died by a self-inflicted gunshot wound.

In his work for Johnson, Connally acquired an early education in such essentials of Texas politics as raising and handling large amounts of cash and managing the machine vote in the Rio Grande Valley. This schooling was interrupted, however, by the Second World War. Commissioned an ensign in the Naval Reserve in 1941, Connally spent several years at desk jobs in Washington and Algiers before being assigned to the aircraft carrier *Essex* in 1944. Directing the carrier's fighters by radio, he served through a number of the deadliest naval engagements of the Pacific war, was promoted to lieutenant commander, and was twice awarded the Bronze Star. Returning to Texas after Japan's surrender, he became general manager of an Austin radio station and practiced law with a local firm. Though no longer a member of Johnson's Washington staff, Connally remained a principal in his organization, running Johnson's 1946 congressional race and the bareknuckled Senate campaign of 1948. Accounts differ as to the extent of Connally's involvement in scaring up the suspect South Texas votes that provided Johnson's very narrow margin of victory.

Through the 1950s Connally worked for oil titan Sid Richardson as legal adviser, lobbyist, and political liaison. Yet he continued to exercise his deft political skills in Johnson's behalf. In 1956, for instance, Connally orchestrated a maneuver by which the Johnson circle made common cause with Texas liberals to undermine the power of a conservative faction within the state party and then turned on its putative allies, depriving them of their share of the spoils. His ruthlessness apparently awed even Johnson, who later remarked on Connally's lack of "even the tiniest trace of compassion. He can leave more dead bodies in the field with less remorse than any politician I ever knew" (Reston, p. 418).

In 1960 Connally oversaw Johnson's bid for the Democratic presidential nomination, in the course of which he publicized rumors concerning John Kennedy's ill health. Nevertheless, the role Texas played in Kennedy's eventual victory and what influence Johnson and Sam Rayburn wielded in the administration earned Connally appointment as secretary of the navy. Connally got along better with military men than with his fellow civilians at the Defense Department, especially those clustered around Secretary Robert McNamara, and tried to ensure that the navy's needs were met in the parceling out of defense funds. However, he already had his gaze fixed on the Texas governorship and after only ten months left the Pentagon post.

In the 1962 Texas race, Connally triumphed over an incumbent governor hobbled by an unpopular sales tax as well as a liberal primary opponent. To ease the bitter factionalism between party liberals and Connally's allies and to raise money in anticipation of the 1964 election, President Kennedy journeyed to Texas early in Connally's first term. Sitting in front of Kennedy in the presidential limousine in Dallas on 22 November 1963, Connally was struck by the gunfire in Dealey Plaza. The Warren Commission's thesis that a single bullet passed through Kennedy's neck and Connally's torso and arm before lodging in the governor's thigh remained implausible to many, including Connally himself, who speculated that Lee Harvey Oswald may have been aiming at him. The former navy Secretary, it seemed, had earlier refused to aid the disgraced marine's efforts to upgrade his discharge.

Connally's wounding and very public recovery have often been cited as reasons for his thumping reelection victories in 1964 and 1966. Yet his imperious charisma and Democratic conservatism were of a sort long favored by many Texas voters. He brought considerably more verve to the office than many earlier governors and made education his special concern. But like many conservative Texans from the nineteenth century onward, his solicitude for public education focused on the state's colleges more than on its primary and secondary schools, which continued to fare poorly by national standards. Connally managed to have faculty salaries raised and strengthened the state university and community college system, but, again like many of his predecessors, the taxes he was willing to impose or to increase in order to cultivate Texas's development were of the most regressive sort. Though he was Johnson's protégé, Connally proved something other than the Great Society's Texas proconsul. He seemed rather unenthusiastic about its social programs, at least if the money appropriated was doled out by federal rather than state officials. While not identifying himself with the truculent resistance of Deep South governors, he criticized the 1964 Civil Rights Act and federal initiatives with respect to voting rights, insisting Texas could make progress unprompted. Connally, by comparison with earlier Texas governors and his counterparts in other southern states, did appoint considerably more African Americans and Latinos to official positions but turned a cold shoulder to efforts at more fundamental change—whether they were Martin Luther King's campaigns or the organizing of Hispanic farm workers in the Rio Grande Valley.

Like Johnson, Connally declined to stand for reelection in 1968, and the following year he joined a Houston law firm, Vinson & Elkins. As he left Texas politics behind, the imperative of maintaining his allegiance to the Democratic party faded. Not in sympathy with Johnson's social agenda, Connally had even less use for the party when it turned its back on Johnson because of the Vietnam War, with respect to which Connally remained an outspoken hawk. He quickly fell in with Richard Nixon, becoming one of the prize trophies in the new president's stalking of conservative southern Democrats. Appointed to a presidential panel on executive reorganization, he subsequently became an unusually close confidant of the president. Henry Kissinger suggested, "Connally's swaggering self-assurance was Nixon's Walter Mitty image of himself" (Kissinger, p. 951).

Named secretary of the treasury in 1971, Connally faced an economy increasingly disordered by inflation, a trade deficit, and dwindling gold reserves (the dollar being convertible into specie and overvalued compared to other currencies). Late that summer the administration took dramatic action that required Nixon and Connally to reverse positions they had previously held. They imposed a ninety-day freeze on wages and prices to be followed by a period, "Phase II," in which a panel led by Connally would attempt to keep inflation contained by other means, chiefly, it turned out, by "jawboning." The United States temporarily ended the conversion of dollars into gold and instituted a surcharge on imports. Connally bargained with European nations and Japan through the balance of the year, leading eventually to an increase in the price of gold and the renegotiation of exchange rates that made American products cheaper abroad. If inflation had yet to be conquered, Connally nevertheless ushered through a significant devaluation of the dollar and a decided shift in the international monetary system.

The fleet-footed Texan left his Treasury post after only a year and afterward headed a Democrats for Nixon organization in the 1972 campaign. The following year he formally pledged allegiance to the GOP and returned to Washington to advise an administration clumsily navigating the currents of Watergate. The scandal might ultimately have worked to Connally's advantage had Nixon been granted his wish to name him vice president in the wake of Spiro Agnew's resignation, but the appointment was scuttled by both the Democrats Connally had spurned and many Republicans not as quick as the president to embrace the convert. Connally instead was almost dragged under in the series of prosecutions of administration figures that followed Watergate. A federal court tried Connally for receiving a $10,000 bribe from a lobbyist in return for supporting continued price supports for milk producers. Because the case rested on the apparently unpersuasive testimony of the putative bribe giver, Connally was acquitted in 1975. He was subsequently appointed to Gerald Ford's Foreign Intelligence Advisory Board, returned to Vinson & Elkins in Houston, and sat on corporate boards.

Connally entertained ambitions both for the Republican vice presidential nomination in 1976 and the presidential nod in 1980. Yet his role in the near-mythic events in Dallas was not sufficient to outweigh his close association with two other presidents not then in good standing with the American public. Connally, furthermore, was neither the first nor the last public figure to demonstrate that a political style that suited Texas did not necessarily suit national audiences. In 1980 he managed the then-remarkable feat of spending some $11 million in the Republican primaries and winning only a single convention delegate.

Afterward, Connally plunged into that combination of real estate development, oil production, and banking that was fueling boom times in Texas. In the overheated atmosphere, he proved incautious—for instance, by making himself personally liable for huge debts. When oil prices and the prosperity they supported collapsed, Connally became, in media eyes, the personification of a swaggering Texas brought low. He declared bankruptcy in 1987 and sat through the widely advertised auctioning of his possessions. Texas's homestead exemption and Connally's many connections in the corporate world ensured that he did not spend his final years destitute, however. He died in Houston.

• The Lyndon Baines Johnson Library in Austin, Tex., holds a comprehensive collection of Connally papers. Connally wrote a memoir with Mickey Herskowitz, *In History's Shadow: An American Odyssey* (1993). James Reston, Jr., *The Lone Star: The Life of John Connally* (1989), is overstuffed and unsympathetic. In addition to biographies of Lyndon Johnson, treatments of the Nixon administration, including Henry Kissinger, *White House Years* (1979), and the vast literature on the Kennedy assassination, see also George N. Green, *The Establishment in Texas Politics: The Primitive Years, 1938–1957* (1979).

PATRICK G. WILLIAMS

CONNALLY, Thomas Terry (19 Aug. 1877–28 Oct. 1963), U.S. senator and congressman, was born near Hewitt, Texas, the son of Jones Connally and Mary Ellen Terry, farmers. The Connallys were better off than many Texas farm families at the time, and young Tom was able to attend Baylor University, graduating in 1896. He then entered the law school of the University of Texas. When war erupted with Spain in 1898, Connally enlisted in the Second Texas Infantry Volunteers. Illness prevented his shipping out, but in his absence the University of Texas awarded him the LL.B.

The following year Connally began practicing law in Marlin, Texas, and he was elected as a Democrat to the Texas House of Representatives in 1900. Reelected two years later, he chaired the Judiciary Committee and helped pass a 1903 law broadening the state's anti-trust provisions. Connally married Louise Clarkson in 1904; the couple had one son. From 1906 to 1910 Connally served as prosecuting attorney for Falls County and thereafter maintained a successful law practice.

A tough and colorful litigator, Connally was elected to the U.S. House of Representatives from his Central Texas district in 1916. He cast an early vote for declaring war against Germany and, volunteering for service in 1918, was commissioned a captain in the army. Again illness kept him at home. Reelected to the House through the subsequent ten years, he was a member of the House Foreign Relations Committee and remained a firm supporter of Woodrow Wilson's foreign policies. He supported U.S. membership in the League of Nations and the World Court. Connally also called for more pacific relations with the nation's Latin American and Caribbean neighbors.

In 1928 Congressman Connally unseated incumbent Texas senator Earle B. Mayfield, who was elected six years before with strong backing from the Ku Klux Klan (KKK). Connally ran a clever but not terribly bold campaign. The Klan was on its last legs in Texas, and Connally's charges that Mayfield had accepted Klan support and then denied having done so managed to both remind those who disliked the KKK of Mayfield's affiliation and suggest to the organization's remaining supporters that the senator had repudiated them. During the first of his four terms, Connally continued to look after his agrarian constituents' interests, opposing higher tariffs and, as the nation's economy worsened, denouncing Herbert Hoover's proposals for a national sales tax.

While seeming to many the very model of the corn pone southern speechifier, with his string tie, linen suit, and locks reaching down toward his collar, Connally proved willing to sanction a more aggressive wielding of federal authority in meeting the economic crisis of the early 1930s. In the case of his home state, the crisis involved not simply the impact of the Great Depression but also the collapse of petroleum prices after the opening of the vast East Texas oilfield. Calling for direct federal spending to relieve hunger and for devaluation of the dollar to boost farm prices, he voted for most major pieces of New Deal legislation during Franklin Roosevelt's first term, with the exception of the National Industrial Recovery Act of 1933 and the Guffey Coal Act of 1935. Though he opposed straightforward federal regulation of the oil industry, he sponsored a federal law, the Connally "Hot Oil" Act of 1935, that prohibited interstate shipment of oil produced in excess of the quotas Texas authorities had set in the attempt to dampen overproduction. He also sponsored legislation that brought direct federal assistance to his state's cotton and cattle raisers. "If the government had not got into business," he declared in

1934, "there would be no business today" (Schlesinger, p. 493).

Yet Connally balked as Roosevelt's innovations began to contemplate more than the revitalization and stabilization of the economic order. Early in Roosevelt's second term, Connally broke with the administration over its plan to reorganize the Supreme Court and from his perch on the Judiciary Committee helped ensure that the "Court packing" scheme went down to defeat. Like other of the routinely reelected white southerners who by that point had accrued so much power in Congress, Connally, through the 1930s and 1940s, firmly opposed accommodation of the interests of more recent parties to the Democratic coalition, particularly African Americans and organized labor. He filibustered against federal antilynching legislation and efforts to prohibit the poll tax and worked hard to see that the South was held to a lesser standard in regard to federal wage and hour laws. He voted to condemn sit-down strikes and, in the 1940s, sponsored legislation giving the government added authority to counter wartime work stoppages. After the war ended, Connally supported the Taft-Hartley Act.

Yet when it came to foreign policy, the old Wilsonian remained in the Roosevelt camp. He played important roles in lifting an isolationist arms embargo in 1939 and in the passage of the Selective Service Act of 1940 and the Lend-Lease Law of 1941. Elevated to the chairmanship of the Foreign Relations Committee in 1941, he introduced the resolution declaring war on Japan at the end of that year. As the Second World War progressed, Connally identified himself with the cause of collective security in the postwar world. Though he offered the Connally Resolution of 1943—which approved U.S. participation in an international peacekeeping organization—only after a very similar resolution penned by J. William Fulbright had passed the House, Connally was thereafter very active in nurturing the United Nations (UN). In 1945 he ushered the UN Charter through the Senate and the same year served as vice chairman of the U.S. delegation to the organization's inaugural gathering in San Francisco. The following year he attended the first meetings of the UN General Assembly as a member of the American delegation and advised Secretary of State James F. Byrnes during early sessions of the Council of Foreign Ministers. But Connally's internationalism had certain limits, and he was careful not to appear to cede too much of the nation's sovereignty. In 1946 he pressed a measure allowing the World Court jurisdiction over the United States only in those cases that the United States determined were not exclusively domestic matters. Though supporting the North Atlantic Treaty and the establishment of the North Atlantic Treaty Organization (NATO) in subsequent years, he managed to soften the language so as to retain congressional discretion in declaring war. Rather than automatically committing the United States to go to war to defend a fellow signatory, the pact, instead, simply pledged every member nation, in the event of an attack on another, to take "such action as it deems necessary, including the use of armed force."

Connally lost the chairmanship of the Foreign Relations Committee when the Republicans took control of Congress after the 1946 elections, but as the Cold War took shape, he continued to cooperate with his GOP counterpart, Senator Arthur Vandenberg, in promoting bipartisanship in foreign policy. In 1947 he played a crucial role in passing legislation aiding Greece and Turkey in accordance with the Truman Doctrine. Connally also firmly supported the Marshall Plan. After reassuming his place at the head of Foreign Relations in 1949, he supported President Harry Truman's deployment of American combat troops in South Korea to stem the North Korean invasion of the following year. Countering the efforts of Senator Robert Taft, Connally worked to assure presidential supremacy in decisions regarding the dispatch of American forces abroad.

Connally was no doubt mindful of the domestic benefits that accrued to the broad international commitments he supported, as his home state enjoyed an outsized role in defense production. As conscientious as he had been in looking after Texas's reigning economic interests, however, Texas oilmen in particular were, by the beginning of the 1950s, looking for a more militant champion. Intent on asserting state, as opposed to federal, control over tideland oil deposits and ready to part with the national Democratic party to assure it, they apparently felt that Connally had become too preoccupied with foreign policy and too close to the unpopular Truman. Seemingly persuaded that he might not prevail over Texas attorney general Price Daniel in the 1952 Democratic primary, Connally did not stand for reelection. He left the Senate early the following year.

Connally stayed on in Washington and resumed the practice of law. A decade earlier, in 1942, he had married Lucile Sanderson Sheppard, the widow of a longtime Senate colleague (Connally's first wife had passed away seven years before). Tom Connally died in Washington, D.C. His career illustrated the paradoxes to which southern Democrats became subject as economic depression, world war, and the Cold War coincided with increasing activism among organized labor and African Americans. Willing to embrace an expanded federal role in managing the economy and increased American commitments abroad, Connally remained steadfastly conservative when it came to the claims of black people and trade unions for greater power and government protection.

• An incomplete collection of Connally papers is at the Library of Congress, Manuscripts Division, Washington, D.C. Connally wrote an autobiography with Alfred Steinberg, *My Name Is Tom Connally* (1954). Useful discussions of various aspects of his career are in Norman Brown, *Hood, Bonnet and Little Brown Jug: Texas Politics, 1921–1928* (1984); Lionel Patenaude, *Texans, Politics and the New Deal* (1983); Arthur Schlesinger, Jr., *The Coming of the New Deal* (1958); George N. Green, *The Establishment in Texas Politics: The Primitive*

Years, 1938–1957 (1979); and Randall B. Woods, *Fulbright: A Biography* (1995). An obituary is in the *New York Times*, 29 Oct. 1963.

PATRICK G. WILLIAMS

CONNELL, Richard (17 Oct. 1893–22 Nov. 1949), short story author and screenwriter, was born in Poughkeepsie, New York, the son of Richard E. Connell, a newspaper editor and congressman, and Mary Elizabeth Miller. A precocious writer, Connell published sports articles at the age of ten in the *Poughkeepsie News-Press*, the newspaper his father edited, and became city editor at sixteen. He attended Georgetown University for a year while serving as secretary to his father who recently had been elected a U.S. congressman. When his father died in 1912, Connell transferred to Harvard University, from which he graduated in 1915, having served as editor of the *Lampoon* and the *Daily Crimson*. In his senior year he wrote an editorial highly critical of the publisher of the *New York American*. As a consequence, the *Crimson* was sued, but Connell was hired by the newspaper. After a year as a reporter, Connell worked in 1916–1917 as an advertising copywriter for the J. Walter Thompson Company. When the United States entered World War I, he enlisted in the army's Twenty-seventh New York Division and was editor of *Gas Attack*, a weekly newspaper; in 1918 he served for a year in France as a private. Following the war Connell took a job as assistant advertising manager of the American Piano Company, and in November 1919 he married Louise Herrick Fox, a writer and editor. They had no children.

The rest of Connell's life can be divided in two. From 1920 until 1936 he was a freelance fiction writer, publishing more than three hundred short stories in *Collier's*, the *Saturday Evening Post*, and many other American and English magazines. Some of these he gathered in four collections: *The Sin of Monsieur Pettipon* (1922), *Apes and Angels* (1924), *Variety* (1925), and *Ironies* (1930). He also published four novels: *The Mad Lover* (1927), *Murder at Sea* (1929), *Playboy* (1936), and *What Ho!* (1937).

Connell is notable for one short story that has achieved immortality as an anthology piece. Entitled "The Most Dangerous Game," it was originally published in *Collier's* in 1924 and was the recipient of that year's O. Henry Memorial Prize. It concerns Rainsford, a famous big game hunter, who, shipwrecked on a Caribbean island, meets General Zaroff, a madman who shares his passion for the sport but who finds only human beings a challenge to hunt. When Rainsford becomes Zaroff's prey, he uses his knowledge of hunting lore to evade Zaroff and eventually kill him.

The fable has found its way into scores of short story collections and has been translated into many foreign languages. More important, it has become a standard piece over several decades in popular high school and college textbooks and, as a result, is now required reading for hundreds of thousands of students in introductory literature courses. The story has been made

into radio plays, television dramas, and at least ten motion pictures: *The Most Dangerous Game* (1932), *A Game of Death* (1945), *Johnny Allegro* (1949), *Kill or Be Killed* (1950), *Run for the Sun* (1956), *The Naked Prey* (1966), *Blood Lust* (1967), *The Hunt* (1975), *Hard Target* (1993), and *Surviving the Game* (1994).

In 1936 Connell moved from Connecticut to California to begin a second career in motion picture scriptwriting. Like other writers from the East who went to Hollywood in the twenties and thirties to make money, he virtually suspended his other writing once he began to work under contract for the studios. During the next thirteen years, he wrote more than a dozen credited screenplays for Paramount, Universal, Metro-Goldwyn-Mayer, and RKO. Although it is difficult to determine what contributions Connell made to these screenplays, from a literary standpoint they are relatively undistinguished. Mostly musical comedies, his films include *The Milky Way* (1936), *Our Relations* (1936), *Dr. Rhythm* (1938), *Hired Wife* (1940), *Nice Girl* (1941), *Rio Rita* (1942), *Presenting Lily Mars* (1943), *Two Girls and a Sailor* (1944), *Thrill of a Romance* (1945), *Her Highness and the Bellboy* (1945), *The Kid from Brooklyn* (1946), and *Luxury Liner* (1948). In addition, a dozen of his stories were made into successful films; these include "A Friend of Napoleon," which received the O. Henry Memorial Prize in 1923 and was filmed as *Seven Faces* (1929), *Brother Orchid* (1940), and *Meet John Doe* (1941). Toward the end of his life Connell appeared to be returning to other forms of writing since he was working on a stage play with Gladys Lehman, his screenplay collaborator, when he died of a heart attack in Beverly Hills, California.

Although his output was considerable, all of Connell's work has been forgotten except "The Most Dangerous Game"; it is probably the most frequently filmed and anthologized American story ever written. Connell will never be regarded as a serious writer whose works meet high literary standards, but he showed unquestionable talent in using plot, character, and suspense to create a story of enduring popular appeal.

• So little has been published about Connell or his work that the best sources of information are a handful of biographical dictionaries, including *National Cyclopedia of American Biography* 36 (1950): 452–53; some obituaries such as the *New York Times*, 24 Nov. 1949; and newspaper articles in the *Poughkeepsie Journal*, esp. 19 June 1960. For information on Connell's screenplays, see the New York Times *Directory of the Film* (1971) and Leslie Halliwell, *The Filmgoer's Companion* (1980).

PETER HAWKES

CONNELLY, Cornelia (15 Jan. 1809–18 Apr. 1879), founder of the Society of the Holy Child Jesus, was born in Philadelphia, Pennsylvania, the daughter of Ralph Peacock, a land speculator and merchant, and Mary Swope Bowen. Very little is known about Cornelia's early childhood, including her education. Like many young women of that time in Philadelphia she probably was educated at home by her mother and possibly tutors. After the death of both her parents, she was raised by her well-to-do half-sister, Isabella Bowen Montgomery, who spared no expense in developing Cornelia's talents. It is uncertain whether she was baptized into the Presbyterian church where her family attended when she was a small child, but records show that Cornelia was baptized into the Episcopal church in February 1831 and married Pierce Connelly, an Episcopalian priest, in December of that year. They had five children.

The newly married couple moved south, as Pierce Connelly had been offered the charge of Trinity Church at Natchez, Mississippi. The anti-Catholicism of that time made a strong impression on the Connellys, and the flood of Roman Catholics immigrating to the United States in the mid-nineteenth century compelled Connelly and her husband to investigate for themselves the claims made against Catholics and Catholicism. Her husband decided to go to Rome to continue his theological studies, and on the way to Italy Connelly abjured Protestantism; she was later accepted (it is unknown if she was rebaptized) into the Roman Catholic church in New Orleans in December 1835. In Rome, her husband was received into the church. In 1838, back in the United States, Connelly began teaching music at the Sacred Heart Convent school in Coteau, Louisiana, and began a path of spiritual development that would continue throughout her life.

In 1840, much to Connelly's initial disappointment, her husband confessed to her his desire to seek ordination in the Roman church, which necessitated that the couple should live henceforth in chastity to better serve the will of God. His calling was officially approved in 1843 but only after the couple met with Pope Gregory XVI so that he might be assured of Connelly's consent to the arrangement. A papal decree of permanent separation was finalized in April 1844, and within days Connelly entered the Sacred Heart Convent in Rome, her two youngest children with her. Husband and wife were permitted weekly visits for the sake of the children. In the summer of 1845 Connelly made her solemn vow of perpetual chastity, and her husband was ordained shortly thereafter.

Encouraged by Father John Grassi, Connelly began taking steps toward establishing a teaching order, and under the sponsorship of Bishop Nicholas Wiseman she went to England, where her husband was already working. This began a very difficult time for the family. The children were put in boarding school, and husband and wife were limited by the superiors of Sacred Heart Convent to only very occasional visits—an order to which Connelly acquiesced but to which her husband did not. Relations between the two quickly deteriorated as his dissatisfaction with the Catholic church escalated. He removed their children from English schools and took them to the Continent without Connelly's consent. Taking advantage of England's marriage laws, he then tried to have his wife returned to his control. His efforts failed, but the personal anguish suffered by Connelly at his hands had a lasting effect, not the least of which was a lifelong estrangement from her children. In 1853 Pierce Connelly returned to Rome as an Episcopalian priest and remained there until his death.

Connelly founded the Society of the Holy Child Jesus in Derby in 1846. Her ambitions were timely as this was a period when Catholicism was experiencing a revival in England. For some time she had been working on an outline of a rule for religious life largely based on the Constitutions and *Spiritual Exercises* of Ignatias Logola, founder of the Jesuits. With this as its foundation, the society's work was to focus on spiritual works of mercy, toward which end the society would be involved in the active duties of the world and not be cloistered. The young society achieved its greatest success with its schools for the poor. A short time after opening, the Poor School at the Derby convent earned a commendation from the visiting government inspector. During her lifetime Mother Connelly, as she was known, oversaw the opening of convents, schools, teacher-training colleges, and orphanages in England, the United States, and France. In addition to many personal hardships, her professional work was constantly overshadowed by financial difficulties, conflicts with Rome, and the withdrawal of support from her once loyal benefactor, Bishop Wiseman. The approbation of her rule, continually delayed by Roman bureaucracy, only came after her death, thus making it very difficult for the society during her lifetime to gain the kind of support it needed, financial and otherwise, to flourish.

Connelly was described by some as a headstrong woman who was sometimes difficult to work with, but most of her students and colleagues remembered a warm, spiritual, indefatigably courageous woman. And in spite of Rome's frequent lack of cooperation and support, she never flagged in her love of the church. Despite the constant trials in her life, she refused to give in to self-pity and continued to have faith that her work was God's will. Largely due to her individual efforts and persistence the society had a strong foundation on which to build when she died in St. Leonards, England, thirty-three years to the day after she first set sail for Rome to begin a new life. The process for her canonization was begun by Rome in 1959.

• Copies of the society's original archives, including Connelly's extant letters, legal and professional documents, journals, and constitutions can be found in the Society of the Holy Child Jesus Archives in Rosemount, Pa. Many of these documents have been collected into the *Positio* (1983), which is required by the church for the canonization process. A documentary study of Connelly's life is Caritas McCarthy, *The Spirituality of Cornelia Connelly* (1986). The biography by Radegunde Flaxman, *A Woman Styled Bold* (1991), is an accessible, well-researched chronological account of Connelly's life.

CARLEEN MANDOLFO

CONNELLY, Henry (1 Sept. 1800–12 Aug. 1866), territorial governor of New Mexico, was born in Fairfax County, Virginia, the son of John Donaldson Connelly and Frances Brent. In 1804 his family moved to Kentucky, where he studied to become a physician. Although several historians have claimed that he graduated from the medical department at Transylvania University in Lexington, Kentucky, that institution has no record of his attendance. In the early 1820s he moved to Liberty, Missouri, and practiced medicine there. Connelly joined a trade caravan to the Mexican province of New Mexico in 1824, traveling over the Santa Fe Trail, and ultimately abandoned the medical profession for the career of an overland merchant.

In 1828 Connelly hauled merchandise to Chihuahua, Mexico, with Missourian Alphonso Wetmore, and over the next two decades continued in the trade there and also for a short time at the mining town of Jesus María, becoming a naturalized Mexican citizen about 1832. He married a Mexican woman (name unknown) at Jesus María, sometime before 1838, and from that union two children survived infancy. In 1839 he was part of a group of Mexican merchants who blazed a trade route from Chihuahua through present-day Texas and Oklahoma to the state of Arkansas, although the difficulties and delays of their expedition and its return the following year revealed the new trail's impracticality.

In 1843 Connelly formed a partnership with Edward James Glasgow, a young merchant from St. Louis. Under the firm name of Connelly & Glasgow; they freighted goods to Chihuahua from Independence, Missouri, until after the outbreak of the Mexican War. Glasgow wrote that Connelly "was moderately well off and in good standing and credit as a merchant of ability, integrity and fair dealing, besides enjoying the personal friendship of many of the influential Mexicans and all of his own countrymen in that city [Chihuahua]" (Gardner, p. 183).

In August 1846 Connelly was in Santa Fe as the Army of the West under General Stephen Watts Kearny was rapidly approaching to seize New Mexico for the United States. Southwest trader James Magoffin, an agent of President James Knox Polk, and a small escort of dragoons arrived in Santa Fe ahead of the army in an attempt to secure a peaceful takeover from New Mexico governor Manuel Armijo. Magoffin sought out Connelly's opinions on the likelihood of armed resistance to the U.S. invasion by Armijo and his second-in-command Colonel Diego Archuleta; after a meeting between Magoffin and Armijo, Connelly traveled with the dragoon escort to Kearny as the governor's "commissioner." But Armijo disbanded his forces soon after and fled to Chihuahua, thereby allowing the American army to enter Santa Fe unopposed.

In October 1846 Connelly and a small party of merchants left their wagons behind and traveled the Chihuahua Trail toward El Paso del Norte (present-day Juárez, Mexico) to see if they could enter their goods there without risk of confiscation. His party was taken prisoner by the Mexicans, however, and they were sent to Chihuahua, where Connelly was held in the custody of two citizens. James Josiah Webb wrote in *Adventures in the Santa Fe Trade, 1844–1847* (1931) that "Dr. Connelly being an American, and a Mexican citizen by naturalization, was looked upon with more suspicion, and suspected if not accused of treasonable designs" (p. 250). Connelly was liberated on 28 February 1847 after the American victory at the battle of Sacramento, eighteen miles north of the city.

After the end of the Mexican War, Connelly moved to New Mexico and married widow Dolores Perea de Chávez (his first wife having died in 1843) and made his residence at her large hacienda near Peralta. They had three children who survived infancy. From 1849 to 1850 he continued his partnership with Glasgow, this time in a wholesale grocery and forwarding and commission business in St. Louis, Missouri. After 1850 he appears to have limited his mercantile pursuits to New Mexico, eventually operating stores (sometimes in partnership with others) at Albuquerque, Santa Fe, Las Vegas, and Peralta. Mercantile Agency credit reports from the mid-1850s rated him one of the wealthiest men in New Mexico Territory.

When an effort was made to gain statehood for New Mexico in 1850, Connelly was elected governor. He was denied that office, however, when the U.S. Congress rejected the statehood bid and subsequently gave New Mexico territorial status. From 1853 to 1858 he served in the territory's legislative council as the elected representative from Bernalillo County. But his greatest political triumph was his appointment as territorial governor by President Abraham Lincoln in 1861 and again in 1864.

The Civil War had commenced by the time Connelly began his term as governor, and Confederate troops from Texas occupied parts of New Mexico. He worked diligently and successfully to ensure that New Mexico remained firmly under Union control, both politically and militarily. When a column of Texas soldiers under Brigadier General Henry H. Sibley advanced up the Rio Grande Valley early in 1862, intent on conquering New Mexico, Connelly traveled with the territorial militia from Santa Fe to Fort Craig (where Union forces planned to confront the Confederate army), personally recruiting volunteers from villages along the way. He was later forced to temporarily move the territorial government from Santa Fe to Las Vegas when the Union army under Colonel E. R. S. Canby failed to stop the Confederates. The Texans ceased to be a threat after the battle of Glorieta Pass in March 1862, after which they retreated from New Mexico.

With New Mexico safe from the Confederacy, Connelly's other major concern was the depredations committed by Apache and Navajo Indians. Together with General James H. Carleton, the military commander of the Department of New Mexico, he advocated forcing the Indians onto a reservation with extermination the alternative for those who would not submit. Carleton relentlessly carried out this policy, but both he and Connelly were criticized for locating the reservation in

Bosque Redondo by New Mexicans resentful of the loss of grazing land. Subsequent overcrowding and insufficient food supplies at the reservation resulted in death and sickness for many of the Indians confined there.

Connelly died in Santa Fe less than a month after the end of his second term as governor. He had been part of a corps of merchants in the 1820s who extended the trade frontier of the United States into northern Mexico and, thus, inadvertently paved the way for the American military conquest of New Mexico in 1846. He played an active role in New Mexico's transition from a conquered province to a territory of the United States, and, when that territory was threatened again by conquest during the Civil War, he demonstrated leadership and fortitude as territorial governor, further strengthening New Mexico's ties to the Union.

• No single comprehensive collection of Connelly's papers exists. His letters, proclamations, and reports as territorial governor are in the Territorial Papers of the U.S. Department of State, National Archives (available on microfilm); the Territorial Archives of New Mexico, New Mexico State Records Center and Archives (available on microfilm); and *The War of the Rebellion: A Compilation of the Official Records of the Union and Confederate Armies* (1880–1901). Biographical sketches can be found in Calvin Horn, *New Mexico's Troubled Years: The Story of the Early Territorial Governors* (1963), and William E. Connelley, *War with Mexico, 1846–1847: Doniphan's Expedition and the Conquest of New Mexico and California* (1907). Connelly's business partnership with Edward James Glasgow is detailed in Mark L. Gardner, ed., *Brothers on the Santa Fe and Chihuahua Trails: Edward James Glasgow and William Henry Glasgow, 1846–1848* (1993). Brief credit reports on Connelly are in the R. G. Dun & Company Collection, Baker Library, Harvard University Graduate School of Business Administration. An obituary is in the *Santa Fe (N.M.) Weekly Gazette,* 18 Aug. 1866.

MARK L. GARDNER

CONNELLY, Marc (13 Dec. 1890–21 Dec. 1980), playwright, screenwriter, and journalist, was born Marcus Cook Connelly in McKeesport, Pennsylvania, the son of Patrick Joseph Connelly and Mabel Fowler Cook. The elder Connelly, as a young man, had been an actor and the manager of a theatrical company. His wife, who had dared the wrath of her parents to elope with him, acted in his company. While they were on tour, their first child, a daughter, died of pneumonia. Believing that this melancholy event might not have occurred had they had a regular home life, they left the stage and settled in McKeesport, where the senior Connelly bought a hotel. Connelly's first experience of theater came at age seven, when his parents took him to nearby Pittsburgh to see Richard Mansfield in *Cyrano de Bergerac*. With this performance as inspiration, Connelly soon began to write sketches for staging in his parents' living room. He also began to attend, with or without the purchase of a ticket, any sort of traveling theatrical entertainment that played McKeesport. It was in these early years that he learned "Spartacus to

the Gladiators," a favorite recitation piece of schools of elocution. Declaiming it with elaborate gestures became his party trick in adult life.

In 1902, the year of his father's death, Connelly was sent to Trinity Hall, a school in Washington, Pennsylvania. His widowed mother built a new hotel in McKeesport, but that same year, in the panic of 1907, she lost it, dashing Connelly's hope of going to Harvard. He moved with her to Pittsburgh and faced with the necessity of supporting himself, went to work at the first of many newspaper jobs: collecting sums owed to the *Pittsburgh Press* for classified ads. From there he moved to the Associated Press as a cub reporter and then to the *Pittsburgh Gazette Times* as both a reporter and the compiler of a Sunday humor column with editorial comment by himself. In exchange for a free membership in the Pittsburgh Athletic Club, he agreed to direct and stage-manage the club's monthly shows. He began to write skits and one-act plays as well, and this activity led to the writing of lyrics for a locally produced musical, *The Lady of Luzon*.

Connelly received a commission to write the libretto and lyrics for a comic opera, with music by Zoel Parenteau, a Pittsburgh composer. They titled it *The Amber Princess*. When it opened in New York in 1916, little of Connelly's work remained in it. Perhaps for that reason the show received poor notices and closed quickly, but, buoyed by the optimism of youth, Connelly determined not to return to his Pittsburgh job. New York City became his permanent home.

From 1916 to 1920 he supported himself by writing, without credit, the lyrics of another unsuccessful musical, *Follow the Girl* (1918); composing verse for *Life*, the popular comic weekly; assisting the scenarist of a film, *The Great Secret*; and, beginning in 1917, gathering items for the daily stage column of the *Morning Telegraph*. His theatrical reporting led to a friendship with George S. Kaufman, the drama editor of the *New York Times*. Both young men were in the habit of dropping in at theaters in the evening, standing at the back of the house, and watching as much of the play on view as held their interest. On 5 May 1919 they spoke to one another for the first time and discovered that they had much in common apart from their being newspapermen: both had lived in Pittsburgh, had already written for the theater, and were now eager to become established on Broadway. It was only reasonable that they should decide to collaborate on a play.

After writing and abandoning the libretto for a musical, the pair took up the suggestion of producer George C. Tyler to fashion a comedy about a fictional character, Dulcinea, the invention of the newspaper columnist Franklin Pierce Adams. In Adams's popular column, "The Conning Tower," Dulcinea supplied humor by conversing only in commonplaces. Typical among the remarks she was "reported" to have made were "When you need a policeman, you can never find one" and, to friends departing for England, "Give my regards to the King." In their play, *Dulcy*, Kaufman and Connelly made her a businessman's wife who manages, bumblingly, to help her husband bring off an important deal. With Lynn Fontanne in the title role, it opened to enthusiastic reviews in 1921.

This success created a bond between the two writers that led to the creation of four more comedies, *To the Ladies* (1922), *Merton of the Movies*, based on the novel of the same name by Harry Leon Wilson (1922), *The Deep, Tangled Wildwood* (1923), and *Beggar on Horseback*, based on a play by the German writer Paul Apel (1924); and two musicals, *Helen of Troy, New York* (1923) and *Be Yourself* (1924). They also contributed sketches to three revues, *No, Sirree!* (1922), *The 49ers* (1922), and *Round the Town* (1924), as well as to the annual entertainments of the Dutch Treat Club, a men's lunch club, and in 1922 supplied *Life* with a comic calendar of bogus anniversaries. Apart from such ephemera, all of their collaborations were humorously satiric views of the business world. Usually a shy or naive young man who is struggling in his career is pushed ahead by a young woman who loves him and encourages him to make the most of his talent. Expressions of affection are rare in the plays. Such passages as do appear in them were supplied by Connelly, for Kaufman had no patience with sentimental dialogue.

Connelly and Kaufman were among the witty young men and women who in the 1920s took lunch regularly at the famed Round Table of the Algonquin Hotel. Although Kaufman often—and unfairly—accused Connelly of laziness, the two remained friends until Kaufman's death in 1961. But after their joint work on *Round the Town*, they brought their partnership to an end. The separation was amicable, but also predictable. They were not a well-matched pair. Connelly was easygoing and comfortably overweight; Kaufman was tense, dour, and lean. Moreover, Connelly, although not indolent, did not share in Kaufman's impatient eagerness to begin work on a new play as soon as the last had opened. Yet he was ready with a new work, *The Wisdom Tooth*, in 1926, a sentimental comedy that achieved a modest success. In the following year he offered another comedy, *The Wild Man of Borneo*, a collaboration with Herman J. Mankiewicz; it lasted a mere two weeks.

Connelly experienced the greatest success of his long career in 1930 with *The Green Pastures*, an adaptation of Roark Bradford's *Ol' Man Adam an' His Chillun*, a collection of tales from the Old Testament told in a black southern dialect. A cast of black actors played it on Broadway for 640 performances and toured with it across the nation for another 1,000 performances. It brought Connelly the Pulitzer Prize, and it triumphed a second time in the film version of 1936.

Hollywood had first taken notice of Connelly's talent much earlier, when movies had not yet learned to speak. The first of the many films on which he lent his writing talent was *Exit Smiling* (1926), a silent comedy starring Beatrice Lillie. The most popular of his films, apart from *The Green Pastures*, was *Captains Courageous* (1937), adapted from the novel of the same name by Rudyard Kipling. For their screenplay he, John Lee Mahin, and Dale Van Every, were nominated for an Academy Award.

Although Connelly continued to write for the stage after *The Green Pastures*, none of his five later plays possessed that work's popular appeal. Only one could be counted a success: *The Farmer Takes a Wife* (1934), on life along the Erie Canal in the 1850s, an adaptation with Frank B. Elser of Walter Edmond's novel *Rome Haul*. *Everywhere I Roam* (1938), a collaboration with Arnold Sundgaard, *The Flowers of Virtue* (1942), *A Story for Strangers* (1948), and *Hunter's Moon* (1958, produced only in London) had only brief runs. Nor did a Broadway revival of *The Green Pastures* in 1951 win an audience; by that date its racial comicality had begun to seem embarrassing. *The Portable Yenberry*, his last play to be staged, was mounted at Purdue University in 1962 with a cast of professional and student actors; a hoped-for Broadway production did not come about. His final play, *The Stitch in Time*, went into rehearsal immediately after his death but was called off for lack of backing.

On occasion Connelly also produced and directed plays and acted in plays and films. As early as 1929 he wrote and appeared in five short film comedies. In 1944 he received praise for his portrayal of the Stage Manager in a New York revival of Thornton Wilder's *Our Town*, a role he repeated two years later in London. He played a priest in the 1957 film *The Spirit of St. Louis*, on Charles Lindbergh's (1859–1924) transatlantic flight. In 1958 in summer stock he played the demanding role of Sheridan Whiteside in *The Man Who Came to Dinner*, the perennially popular comedy by Kaufman and Moss Hart. Howard Lindsay and Russell Crouse gave him a major Broadway role in their comedy *Tall Story* (1959), a role he repeated in the film version.

Connelly also was a prolific contributor of articles on theater and other subjects to magazines and newspapers. He served from 1933 to 1939 as president of the Authors League of America and from 1953 to 1959 as president of the National Institute of Arts and Letters, to which he was elected in 1935. From 1947 to 1951 he taught playwriting at Yale. In 1965 he published a comic suspense novel, *A Souvenir from Qam*, and followed it in 1968 with a volume of memoirs, *Voices Offstage*.

In 1930 Connelly married Madeline Hurlock, an actress. The marriage, which was childless, ended in 1935, when Hurlock left him to marry another playwright, Robert E. Sherwood. Connelly, noted always for his unwavering geniality and essential generosity of spirit, as well as for his ironic humor, refused to allow the breakup of his marriage to cool the friendship that he and Sherwood had enjoyed for many years. Typically, he shrugged the matter off with a joke by saying that his former wife was the only person he knew who had married two Pulitzer Prize playwrights.

In the weeks preceding Connelly's ninetieth birthday, his friends honored him with many celebrations, including a dinner at The Players, the theatrical and literary club of which he had long been a member. There, knowing it was expected of him, but not knowing it would be for the last time, he recited "Spartacus to the Gladiators," complete, as always, with the gestures he had been taught as a child. He died in a New York hospital.

• Connelly's typescripts and other, miscellaneous papers are in the collection of the Wisconsin Center for Theater Research, Madison. The New York Public Library for the Performing Arts has clippings and scrapbooks covering his life and work. Connelly's amusingly written *Voices Offstage* (1968) provides his own estimate of his career. See also Alexander Woollcott, "Two-Eyed Connelly," *New Yorker*, 12 Apr. 1930. For an analysis of his relationship with Kaufman, see Malcolm Goldstein, *George S. Kaufman: His Life, His Theater* (1979). No full-scale biography has appeared to date, although Paul T. Nolan, *Marc Connelly* (1969), presents an overview of his writings. A lengthy obituary appeared in the *New York Times*, 22 Dec. 1980.

MALCOLM GOLDSTEIN

CONNER, David (1792–20 Mar. 1856), naval officer, was born in Harrisburg, Pennsylvania, the son of David Conner, occupation unknown, and Abigail Rhodes. As a boy, he worked at a Philadelphia counting house. On 16 January 1809 he joined the navy with a rank of midshipman. Conner sailed with Captain William Bainbridge aboard the frigate *President* throughout 1810 and the following year transferred to the sloop *Hornet* under Master Commandant James Lawrence. Shortly after the War of 1812 was declared, the *Hornet* captured the British privateer *Dolphin*, on which Conner was appointed prize master. He was captured before reaching port, exchanged, and returned to the *Hornet* in time to participate in the 24 February 1813 victory over the British brig *Peacock*. Promotion to lieutenant followed on 24 July 1813, and he continued aboard the *Hornet* under Master Commandant James Biddle. In this capacity Conner distinguished himself in the 22 January 1815 victory over the British sloop *Penguin*. This was the final confrontation between warships in the War of 1812, and he sustained a dangerous hip wound from grapeshot. For gallant conduct in all of the *Hornet*'s battles, Conner received two congressional silver medals and a sword from his native state.

From 1817 to 1818 Conner accompanied Captain Biddle on the sloop *Ontario* on a long Pacific cruise. Their mission was to reclaim for the United States the Oregon territory that had been captured by the British in 1814 and then restored by the Treaty of Ghent. Following two years of shore duty at Philadelphia, he received his first command, the schooner *Dolphin*, and returned to the Pacific as part of Commodore Charles Stewart's squadron. On 23 March 1825 Conner advanced to commander and took charge of the sloop *Erie* in Commodore Charles G. Ridgley's West India squadron. He subsequently assumed command of the sloop *John Adams* in 1834 as part of Commodore Daniel T. Patterson's Mediterranean squadron. Conner made captain on 3 March 1835 and fulfilled a variety of assignments both afloat and ashore. On 29 July 1841 he gained appointment as one of three navy commissioners, and two years later he headed up the new-

ly created Bureau of Construction, Equipment and Repair. Though declining in health, Conner succeeded Commodore Stewart as senior officer of the West India and home squadrons in December 1843.

The onset of war with Mexico in 1846 found Conner commanding all naval forces in the Gulf and Caribbean regions. His squadron helped transport the army of General Zachary Taylor across the Rio Grande River and subsequently blockaded the Mexican coast. Though hampered by supply shortages and equipped with heavy draught vessels for shallow-water operations, Conner conducted numerous amphibious raids against Alvarado, Tobasco, and Tampico. This last port was captured on 14 November 1846, but Conner was criticized by junior officers for lacking aggressive spirit. Conner felt the caution justified, considering his improper equipment, and he declined to be furloughed. His most important contribution to the war occurred on 9 March 1847, when the fleet landed General Winfield Scott's army at Vera Cruz. This large and complicated amphibious maneuver put 10,000 soldiers ashore in five hours without incident. Conner's fleet then assisted in the reduction of Castle San Juan de Ulloa. On 21 March 1847 Conner was relieved by Commodore Matthew Calbraith Perry, ostensibly for routine reasons but more likely in the quest for more aggressive leadership.

In May 1847 Conner returned to Philadelphia amidst celebrations. He received honorary membership in the Society of the Cincinnati, and President James K. Polk tendered him his old post at the Bureau of Construction, Equipment and Repair. Conner graciously declined, owing to poor health, and spent several years convalescing in Florida. He became commandant of the Philadelphia navy yard in October 1849, but illness necessitated his removal the following June. Following a spate of minor land appointments, Conner was placed on the reserve list in 1855. He died in Philadelphia the following year, survived by his wife, Susan Dillwyn, whom he had married in 1828. They had two sons.

In the pantheon of naval heroes, Conner remains an enigmatic figure. However, he was part of an embryonic naval cadre who distinguished themselves in the War of 1812 and facilitated professionalism in years that followed. As a commanding figure, Conner smoothly oversaw the navy's transition from sail to steam and possessed commendable grasp of the new technology. He was also cognizant of its limitations, which by and large dictated his oft-criticized behavior during the Mexican War. Conner's successful landing at Vera Cruz was a capstone in a long and distinguished career, however, and establishes him as an early practitioner of large-scale amphibious warfare. His prudence was deep-seated and bordered on overcautiousness, but he was a capable officer in a very demanding age.

• Conner's official correspondence is in the Record Group 45, Captains' Letters, National Archives. Large collections of personal papers are at the Manuscript Division, Library of

Congress; the Manuscript Division, New York Public Library; the Beinecke Library, Yale University; and the Franklin D. Roosevelt Library, Hyde Park, N.Y. See also Stanislaus V. Henkels, *The Correspondence of Commodore David Conner* (1914). Panegyrical sketches include "Commodore David Conner," *United Service* 15 (1895): 31–41; Henry Simpson, *Lives of Eminent Philadelphians* (1859); and John H. Brown, *American Naval Heroes* (1899). For greater historical context consult Philip S. P. Conner, *The Home Squadron Under Commodore Conner* (1896), and K. Jack Bauer, *Surfboats and Horse Marines* (1969).

JOHN C. FREDRIKSEN

CONNOLLY, Maureen Catherine (17 Sept. 1934–21 June 1969), tennis player, was born in San Diego, California, the daughter of Martin J. Connolly, a chief petty officer in the navy, and Jassamine Wood, a church organist. Connolly graduated from Cathedral High School in 1951. Although initially passionate about horses, she switched her energies to tennis while on the University Heights playground in San Diego, California. There a local tennis pro, Wilbur Folsom, observed her natural ability. While Folsom changed her into a right-handed player, Eleanor Tennant developed Connolly's talents. Tennant, who had helped develop the tennis talents of champions Alice Marble and Bobby Riggs, called Connolly the perfect pupil because during three- to four-hour practices, five days a week, year-round, the student eagerly learned to execute skills superbly.

The nickname "Little Mo," given to Connolly by the media, aptly described the cannonlike sharpshooting baseline drives that the 5'5", 130-pound Connolly executed off both forehand and backhand sides. She could chop down an opponent with deadly precision, like her namesake the battleship *Missouri*, or "Big Mo," as her groundstrokes consistently landed on or near the sideline. Although she possessed a weak serve and seldom ventured to the net, Connolly still dominated most opponents.

Besides being a well-practiced and precocious player, Connolly learned from Tennant to fear losing while seeking perfection on the court. Connolly's fierce concentration, her cold, calculating court demeanor, and her grim, businesslike approach to the game often alienated her from opposing players and at times the media and fans. Contrastingly, off the court she could be charming.

Connolly won more than fifty junior titles and in 1949 became the youngest female to win the National Junior Championships (at age fourteen). After repeating as singles and doubles champion in 1950 and earning a tenth-best national ranking, she chose not to defend her junior titles but rather to compete in the U.S. Lawn Tennis Association's (USLTA) Women's Championships in Forest Hills, New York. Just two weeks short of her seventeenth birthday, Connolly won the first of three consecutive USLTA titles. Besides being the second youngest (after May Sutton) to win the women's title, she became later that year the youngest player at the time to compete on the U.S. Wightman Cup team against Great Britain. During her four years of Wightman Cup play, she amassed records of 7–0 in singles and 2–0 in doubles. In 1952 the USLTA recognized her notable contributions to tennis in sportsmanship and fellowship by awarding her its Service Bowl.

From 1952 to 1954 Connolly never lost a singles match at the All-England Championships at Wimbledon. By winning at age nineteen the Australian, French (also in 1954), English, and U.S. titles in 1953, she became the first woman to capture the Grand Slam. In Grand Slam singles events, Connolly won three USLTA Championships, three All-England Championships at Wimbledon, two French titles, and one Australian title. Her powerful forehands and backhands combined with her tenacity on the court led to her winning all but one match between September 1951 and July 1954. The Associated Press named her Woman Athlete of the Year three times in a row (1951–1953). A horseback-riding accident prior to the U.S. championships in 1954 crushed her right leg and abruptly ended her competitive tennis career.

In San Diego Connolly met Norman Brinker, a naval officer who had been an equestrian in the 1952 Olympics. After their marriage in 1955, they had two children and lived in Dallas. Besides being a wife and mother, Connolly shared her tennis knowledge through newspaper and magazine articles. In the 1960s she coached British Wightman Cup teams competing in the United States.

The International Tennis Hall of Fame honored her by induction in 1968 as did the Citizens Savings Athletic Foundation for Tennis and the Women's Sports Foundation Hall of Fame (1989). After being diagnosed with terminal cancer, she established in 1969 the Maureen Connolly Brinker Foundation to promote junior tennis. This foundation sponsors international team competition, called the Continental Cup, for girls eighteen years old and under. An award, named for her, is presented annually to the girl at the Nationals who has demonstrated exceptional ability and sportsmanship.

Many tennis experts have speculated that Connolly would have established possibly unequaled records had her career not ended before the age of twenty. Her other noteworthy contributions to the sport were many despite her early death in Dallas.

• There is a file on Connolly at the International Tennis Hall of Fame, Newport, R.I. She wrote two books: one instructional, *Power Tennis* (1954), and the other autobiographical, *Forehand Drive* (1957), with Thomas Gwynne as coauthor. Although almost all books about the history of tennis recount her brief domination of the women's game, the best descriptions of her career are in Allison Danzig and Peter Schwed, eds., *The Fireside Book of Tennis* (1972); Will Grimsley, *Tennis: Its History, People and Events* (1971); Billie Jean King with Cynthia Starr, *We Have Come a Long Way: The Story of Women's Tennis* (1988); and Gwen Robyns, *Wimbledon: The Hidden Drama* (1974).

ANGELA LUMPKIN

CONNOLLY, Thomas Henry, Sr. (31 Dec. 1870–28 Apr. 1961), baseball umpire, was born in Manchester, England, the son of William Connolly and Bridget Cairns. In 1884 the family immigrated to Natick, Massachusetts, where the thirteen-year-old Connolly, an avid cricket player, fell in love with baseball. He served as batboy for a town team and read voraciously about the game. Soon recognized as expert on baseball rules, at age fifteen he began umpiring local sandlot, school, and YMCA games.

Connolly began his professional umpiring career in 1894 with the New England League after an enthusiastic recommendation from Tim Hurst, veteran National League umpire. In 1898 he advanced to the National League. Midway through the 1900 season Connolly resigned, partly because of a physical ailment but primarily because of his frustration at the failure of league president Nicholas Young to support the rulings and disciplinary actions of umpires. The next year President Ban Johnson, acting on the recommendation of Philadelphia Athletics' manager Connie Mack, offered Connolly a position with the newly formed American League. Impressed by Johnson's reputation as a staunch defender of umpires when a minor league executive, Connolly was in uniform at the Cleveland at Chicago game on 24 April 1901, the first game played in the American League's initial season.

For the next half-century Connolly personified American League umpiring. Having been mobbed "plenty of times" in the past, he responded to rowdyism by ejecting ten players in 1901, but he quickly changed to more diplomatic tactics in response to Johnson's strong backing of the staff. Connolly used his Irish wit and brogue in combination with a juridical presence and unparalleled command of the rules to avoid or defuse confrontations. He umpired in a subdued style, believing that the efficient umpire did not call attention to himself or provoke trouble. A fastidious dresser on and off the field who was never seen in public without a starched collar and jeweled stickpin, he was respectfully called "Mr. Connolly" by new players and affectionately known as "Tommy" to veterans, both of whom correctly perceived him as a straitlaced gentleman of unquestioned integrity. During the last ten years of his career he did not eject a single player or manager.

Connolly was in his third decade in the American League when league president Will Harridge, faced with widespread criticism about the deteriorating quality of umpiring, in June 1931 appointed him to the newly created position of umpire in chief. From league headquarters in Chicago the sixty-year-old Connolly supervised current umpires, scouted minor league umpires, and advised Harridge and individual clubs on the interpretation of playing rules. While an active umpire he had made many recommendations regarding situations not covered in rules that subsequently were written into the book, and his expertise was used extensively by the major league rules committee established in 1950. After retiring in January

1954, Connolly continued to serve on the rules committee.

As chief of staff, Connolly was personally responsible for creating a distinctive style of umpiring in the American League, just as Bill Klem, his counterpart in stature and career longevity, did in the National League. Some of his preferences were purely cosmetic, such as the positioning of the field umpires along the foul lines and with a runner at first base; others affected the game itself. Connolly's insistence that his umpires continue to use the inflated outside chest protector after National League umpires followed Klem's lead in adopting the padded protector worn inside the jacket led to the calling of higher strikes in the American League. And although Connolly and Klem were both short and slight in stature, Connolly's preference for big but even-tempered umpires contrasted with Klem's penchant for hiring small and feisty men symbolized the very different philosophies of umpiring in each league. Where Klem ruled by mailed fist and challenged players and managers to behave, Connolly used a velvet glove and conciliation to maintain order. Connolly's attitude toward umpiring found expression in his advice to young umpires: "The public pays to see clubs perform at full strength, so, keep the best players in [the game] as long as you decently can do so. A little diplomacy will go farther than fines and benching."

Connolly's life was umpiring. (His younger brother, Francis, umpired many years in the minor leagues, including eighteen in the American Association; a son, one of seven children from his marriage to Margaret L. Gavin in 1902, umpired briefly in the minor leagues.) During sixty years in the profession, fifty-three in the American League as an umpire or supervisor of umpires, Connolly saw many of the game's legends perform. He umpired eight World Series, including the first in 1903. In recognition of his popularity and reputation, he was frequently assigned to historic games, including the inaugural contests in Chicago's Comiskey Park, Boston's Fenway Park, Philadelphia's Shibe Park, and New York's Hilltop Park and Yankee Stadium. Fittingly, Connolly and Klem were elected to the National Baseball Hall of Fame in 1953, the first umpires to be enshrined in Cooperstown. Connolly died in Carlisle, Massachusetts.

• See the Connolly clippings file at the National Baseball Library, Cooperstown, N.Y. Revealing personal insights may be gleaned from Connolly's "Observations of an Indicator Man," *Baseball Magazine*, Feb. 1909, pp. 31–33. No comprehensive biography has been published, but useful sketches include John W. Ward, "He Ruled the Diamond by Kindness," *Baseball Magazine*, Apr. 1937, pp. 495, 518–19; Lee Allen and Thomas Meany, *Kings of the Diamond* (1965); Martin Appel and Burt Goldblatt, *Baseball's Best: The Hall of Fame Gallery* (1977); and Lee Allen, *The Hot Stove League* (1955). For context and details relating to Connolly's major league career, see James Kahn, *The Umpire Story* (1953). Obituaries are in the *New York Times*, 29 Apr. 1961, and the *Sporting News*, 10 May 1961.

LARRY R. GERLACH

CONNOR, Bull (11 July 1897–10 Mar. 1973), city commissioner and symbol of southern resistance to race reform, was born Theophilus Eugene Connor in Selma, Alabama, the son of Hugh King (or King Edward) Connor, a railroad dispatcher, and Molly Godwin. He spent his childhood years in several cities but each summer lived with relatives in Plantersville, Alabama, where he met Beara Levens, whom he married in 1920. They had one daughter. After attending school in Birmingham and Selma, Connor found employment with Western Union as a telegraph operator. He moved to New Orleans, then Memphis, and later Dallas, where in 1921 a chance to announce a telegraph-reported baseball game altered his life forever. Sportscasting suited Connor, whose ungrammatical expressions and folksy chatter caught the public's fancy. In 1922 he opened a baseball matinee in Birmingham where people paid to hear him read "live" telegraph reports and thus call the games of the local team. An instant hit, Connor's booming style landed him a job selling radios as the "Voice of the Birmingham Barons" and earned him the nickname "Bull."

Connor entered politics in 1934 "to see how many friends I had made as a baseball announcer," he said. Those friends elected him to the Alabama House of Representatives on a conservative platform of fiscal restraint and civil service reform. There he was cultivated by James A. Simpson, a state senator and legal retainer for the U.S. Steel Corporation. For the remainder of his days, Simpson advised Connor. In 1937 Birmingham's industrial and financial elite supported Connor's election to the city commission. As commissioner of public safety—a post he held for six terms, 1937–1953 and 1957–1963—Connor harassed labor leaders and integrationists.

Connor first entered the national spotlight when he forcibly segregated the integrated Southern Conference for Human Welfare during its organizational meeting in Birmingham in November 1938. In protest, First Lady Eleanor Roosevelt pulled her chair into the aisle that separated the white and black delegates to this gathering of southern New Dealers. In 1948 Connor hoisted the Alabama placard and led the state's delegates from the Philadelphia hall when the "Dixiecrats" bolted the Democratic National Convention because of opposition to President Harry S. Truman's civil rights plank. Connor returned as a delegate to the convention in 1956, 1960, 1964, and 1968. Twice a candidate for governor, he placed distantly in 1950 and 1962.

A series of police scandals involving corruption on the force culminated in the December 1951 disclosure of Connor's adulterous relationship with his secretary. Although convicted on charges of moral turpitude, Connor nonetheless survived impeachment in 1952. A grand jury concluded that the former champion of meritocracy had flagrantly used favoritism to advance the obsequious and to punish the disloyal. Connor weathered the damning criticism that called for his resignation, but he chose not to run for reelection in 1953. While managing a filling station, Connor at-

tempted two unsuccessful political comebacks: a 1954 bid to become sheriff of Jefferson County and a 1956 bid to become commissioner of public improvements. Yet the rise of massive resistance to desegregation following the 1954 *Brown v. Board of Education* decision and the 1956 Montgomery bus boycott changed the political climate in the state. A regular speaker on the Citizens' Council circuit, Connor exploited racial tensions to defeat a reformist incumbent by 103 votes and regain the job of commissioner of public safety in 1957. Birmingham's white working class, which profited from segregated lines of promotion in the steel industry and "whites only" jobs, had provided Connor with his margin of victory.

Back in power, Connor set Birmingham on a collision course with the emerging civil rights struggle waged locally by the Reverend Fred L. Shuttlesworth and the Alabama Christian Movement for Human Rights. Connor suppressed a bus boycott in 1958 and student sit-ins in 1960. When the Freedom Riders reached Birmingham on 14 May 1961, a duplicitous Connor arranged for the Ku Klux Klan to attack the black and white integrationists. The ensuing mob scene at the Trailways Bus Station brought national censure to the city and opprobrium to Bull Connor, who disingenuously explained that his policemen had been off duty for Mother's Day. Earlier Connor had won reelection to another four-year term, but negative publicity following his treatment of the Freedom Riders convinced several service economy executives to maneuver Connor from office by changing the form of government from the city commission to a mayor and council. Voters adopted the municipal reform, and Connor lost a race for mayor on 2 April 1963. The next day, Shuttlesworth, assisted by the Reverend Dr. Martin Luther King, Jr., and the Southern Christian Leadership Conference, initiated sit-ins against segregation in the city as the civil rights movement launched its Birmingham campaign.

Refusing to leave office, Connor—assisted by his mentor Simpson—sued to delay the change and, as the courts determined the legal government, remained in charge of the police and fire departments. At first Connor copied Albany, Georgia, police chief Laurie Pritchett's tactics and met the nonviolent demonstrators with polite but firm enforcement of the law. After a protest march on 7 April, he ordered police dogs against unruly black spectators but for the rest of the month kept the dogs at bay. Despite the incarceration of King on 12 April, the civil rights campaign foundered. An uninterested local black community and national media suggested a failure similar to Albany.

In a last-ditch effort to salvage the campaign, movement strategists enlisted black schoolchildren. On 2 May 1963 hundreds of students skipped school and gathered at the Sixteenth Street Baptist Church. Singing and clapping, the youngsters filed out of the sanctuary and headed toward city hall. A perplexed Bull Connor wondered how to respond to this unexpected turn of events. His surveillance had reported a lack of volunteers; yet suddenly hundreds of them appeared.

At first his officers arrested the students and carried them to jail in squad cars, then paddy wagons, and finally school buses. In an effort to fill the jail, the movement leaders resumed the children's crusade the next day. This time an anxious Connor stationed firemen and police dogs around the church. His jail could not hold the hundreds of protesters, so he ordered in the fire hoses. With water pressure that stripped the bark off trees, the firemen's hoses were trained on the young people. Connor again sicced police dogs on the black bystanders. The campaign turned ugly. The climax occurred on 7 May when thousands of activists bounded over police barricades and flooded the business district. Civil order collapsed. Through brute force Connor restored the authority of the police. Yet the massive demonstration convinced Birmingham's white power structure to negotiate an end to the protests. Assisted by the Kennedy administration, black leaders and white businessmen bypassed Connor and on 10 May negotiated a truce that compromised on movement demands. On 23 May the Alabama Supreme Court recognized the legality of the mayor-council government and ordered Connor to vacate city hall, bringing to an unceremonious end his brutal tenure.

To keep him out of city politics, Birmingham businessmen assisted Connor's election to the Alabama Public Service Commission. He was president from 1964 to 1972 and served corporate interests by consistently raising utility bills. A stroke in December 1966 left him partially paralyzed. He died in Birmingham following a second stroke in 1973. President John F. Kennedy attributed the watershed Civil Rights Bill of 1963, which he proposed, to the actions of Bull Connor. (The bill became the Civil Rights Act of 1964 when signed by President Lyndon B. Johnson.)

• Connor's municipal papers are in the Birmingham Public Library Department of Archives and Manuscripts. For a solid biography, see William A. Nunnelley, *Bull Connor* (1991). A contemporary account by Birmingham reporter Irving Beiman is in Robert S. Allen, ed., *Our Fair City* (1947). See also the *Birmingham News-Age-Herald*, 13 Oct. 1931; *Birmingham Post*, 15 Mar. 1949; *Birmingham Post Herald*, 2 Nov. 1953 and 15 Apr. 1957; *Birmingham News*, 31 May 1972; and Connor quoted in the *Birmingham News*, 30 Apr. 1961. On Connor and the civil rights movement, see David J. Garrow, ed., *Birmingham, Alabama, 1956–1963* (1989). An obituary is in the *Birmingham News*, 11 Mar. 1973.

GLENN T. ESKEW

CONNOR, Henry Groves (3 July 1852–23 Nov. 1924), legislator and judge, was born in Wilmington, North Carolina, the son of David Connor, a carpenter, and Mary Catherine Groves. In 1855 the family moved to Wilson, North Carolina, where Connor's father was employed in building the county courthouse. His father's death in 1867 ended Connor's schooling; following a brief stint as a shopkeeper's assistant, he began the study of law in the office of George Howard and George W. Whitfield. After further study with William T. Dortch of Goldsboro, North Carolina, Connor

was licensed to practice law in 1871, while still eighteen years old. It was later said of him that the only law he ever broke was the one requiring lawyers to be at least twenty-one. In November 1871 Connor married Katherine Whitfield, the daughter of his former mentor, with whom he had twelve children, nine of whom survived infancy. Leaving the Roman Catholic religion of his parents, Connor joined the Episcopal church, his wife's denomination.

With hard work and a reputation for earnestness Connor built a successful law practice in Wilson, where in 1877 he formed a partnership with Frederick A. Woodard. Connor's ardent support of Prohibition, locally unpopular, delayed his political career, but running as a Cleveland Democrat in 1884 he was elected to the state senate and promptly became chairman of the judiciary committee. He immediately sponsored an act passed in 1885 that established a new system for recording deeds in the state. Unique among common law jurisdictions, the Connor Act gave effect to the first deed to be recorded, regardless of what might have been known about competing interests, and thereby secured maximum protection, albeit at the expense of occasional injustice in individual cases. Securing titles by eliminating the principal source of legal challenge, the Connor Act facilitated mortgage financing and materially improved credit in the state. In 1885 he resigned from the senate to accept gubernatorial appointment to a newly created superior court judgeship; the following year, running as the incumbent, he was elected for a regular eight-year term.

In 1893 Connor resigned from the superior court to take up the more lucrative duties of executor of the large estate of Alpheus Branch, founder of the Branch Banking Company of Wilson, of which Connor subsequently became president in 1896. In 1894 he declined nomination for a seat on the state supreme court by the Fusion party, composed of Populists and Republicans, although he was attracted by the party's commitment to a nonpartisan judiciary. In 1898, running as a Democrat, Connor was elected to the state house of representatives, forming part of the majority for "white supremacy." In his first term, he was chosen Speaker of the House and was influential in drafting the amendment to the state constitution that largely excluded black voters. Payment of the poll tax was made a qualification for voting, and a literacy test was imposed, although the votes of illiterate whites were preserved by a carefully crafted "grandfather clause." Uncomfortable with public displays of racism, Connor believed that disfranchisement had to be accomplished by lawful means to avoid lawlessness at the polls. Reelected in 1900, Connor supported the progressive wing of his party in an ambitious program to improve public education, but broke with the majority by opposing the impeachment of Fusion supreme court justices because of the damage it could cause to the judicial branch and perhaps also because Connor recalled how close he himself had come to accepting the Fusion nomination.

In 1902 Connor was nominated for the supreme court by the Democratic party despite strong opposition because of his earlier stand against impeachment. Elected to an eight-year term, he quickly distinguished himself by authoring the opinion of the court in *Mial v. Ellington* (1903), which reversed the landmark case of *Hoke v. Henderson* (1834), by which Chief Justice Thomas Ruffin had given state officeholders security against legislative discharge by holding that their offices were a form of property. Although it embodied a concept unique among states at the turn of the century and was by then generally regarded as anachronistic, *Hoke* had recently been reaffirmed by the Fusion judges; their reliance on the precedent in defense of a Republican officeholder was in fact a principal charge in their impeachment.

Although content with his place on the state bench, Connor resigned in 1909 to accept appointment as the United States judge for the Eastern District of North Carolina. Chosen by President William Howard Taft, who took a particular interest in judicial selection, Connor was one of a number of southern Democrats named by the Republican president. These southern Democrats shared with the president a conservative outlook on economic and social problems, evidence of an underlying judicial consensus. In North Carolina, however, Connor's appointment was welcomed as an important step in reconciling white citizens to the federal judiciary, still viewed with suspicion because of Reconstruction. Connor served as federal district judge until his death at his home in Wilson. In the latter years his docket was crowded with cases concerning Prohibition, conscription, and condemnation of land for building the vast army base at Fort Bragg. He had the rare distinction of never having been reversed by the U.S. Supreme Court.

Judicial service seemingly freed Connor to indulge his interest in scholarship. A frequent speaker at formal occasions such as portrait presentations, he specialized in the biographies of southern lawyers and judges; many of his addresses appeared in legal or historical publications or were privately printed. He contributed the essay on William Gaston to the collection *Great American Lawyers* (William Draper Lewis, ed., 1908) and published a biography of the Supreme Court Justice John Archibald Campbell (1920). In collaboration with Joseph B. Cheshire, Jr., he also produced an annotated edition of the North Carolina constitution (1911), for which he prepared a lengthy essay on state constitutional history.

A conscientious lawyer and judge, Connor set a high standard of legal craftsmanship. Raising his large family on a meager judicial salary, he nonetheless devoted long hours to unremunerative scholarship, recording and continuing southern legal culture. His principled public service resulted in lasting contributions to law reform and public education, but also to *de jure* racial segregation.

• Connor's papers, along with those of his son Robert D. W. Connor, are in the Southern Historical Collection at the University of North Carolina, Chapel Hill. A lengthy memorial address by Josephus Daniels appears in 196 *N.C. Reports* at 830 (1929); briefer notices are by R. H. Wettach in 2 *N.C. Law Review* at 228 (1924) and R. W. Winston in 27 *N.C. Bar Association Proceedings* at 102 (1925). Other memorial addresses, printed in pamphlet form, by Frank A. Daniels (1926) and Josiah W. Bailey (1929) are in the collection of the University of North Carolina School of Law. An obituary is in the Raleigh *News and Observer*, 24 Nov. 1924.

JOHN V. ORTH

CONNOR, Patrick Edward (2 Mar. 1820?–17 Dec. 1891), soldier, entrepreneur, and politician, was born Patrick Edward O'Connor in County Kerry, Ireland. His exact birth date and the names of his parents are in question. As a teenager, he emigrated with his parents to New York City, where he probably briefly attended public school.

At age eighteen he joined the First U.S. Dragoons. On his papers he listed his occupation as "laborer" and said he had no parents or guardians with control over him. For the next five years he served on the Iowa and Missouri frontiers. He was honorably discharged in 1844 and returned to New York, where he worked in the mercantile business. He changed his name to P. Edward Connor and became a naturalized citizen possibly at this time.

On 6 May 1846, Connor reenlisted in the army, this time as a member of the First Regiment, Texas Foot Rifles. When his company voted to disband, he enlisted as a first lieutenant in the Texas Volunteers. He was promoted to captain in December. On 22–23 February 1847 "Connor's Company" formed part of 4,500 Americans in battle against General Antonio López de Santa Anna and about 20,000 Mexican troops at the hacienda of Buena Vista. Connor was seriously wounded in the hand and lost much blood but continued in the field. His company was able to repulse Mexican horsemen before reinforcements arrived. He was honorably discharged at Monterrey in May 1847 and is thought to have lived in Santa Fe for the next few years.

Lured by the California gold rush, Connor arrived in Stockton on 22 January 1850. He purchased a ranch with large gravel deposits, which he sold to the city for its roads. Having little success as a gold prospector, he worked variously as a steamship captain, California Ranger, freighter owner, and surveyor.

In 1854 he married Johanna Connor at St. Francis Xavier Church, San Francisco; they became the parents of seven children. Johanna not only had the same last name as Edward but was also from County Kerry. Her family had come to Redwood City by way of Chile. Edward and Johanna Connor settled in Stockton, where they became one of the founding families. He was a successful and innovative general contractor. In 1859 he founded the Stockton waterworks, which he continued to own and operate even after he left Stockton. He became involved in civic affairs and served as president of the board of trustees of the state insane asylum and executive officer of the State Fair Board.

When a volunteer force called the Stockton Blues was formed, he served as first lieutenant and then captain.

When the Civil War erupted in the eastern United States, Californians entered the controversy. The Stockton Blues were disbanded over political disagreements, and Connor became colonel of the Third Regiment, California Infantry. He recruited volunteers in Stockton and at various gold-mining camps. Rather than being sent to Virginia to fight, however, they were sent to Salt Lake City to protect mail routes, emigrant trails, and telegraph lines from Indian attack and to ensure Mormon loyalty. They left on 12 July 1862, established Fort Ruby in eastern Nevada, and arrived in Salt Lake more than three months after their departure. As military commander of the Utah territory, Connor founded Fort Douglas three miles from downtown Salt Lake City. Relations with Mormons were hostile. Mormon leader Brigham Young imposed trade and social restrictions to prevent military intervention in his ecclesiastical governance and fraternization of soldiers with Mormon women.

Destruction of food sources led Shoshoni Indians to beg from settlers or attack farms and emigrant trains. In 1862 Indian attacks had led to the desertion of most mail stations from Fort Bridger to Salt Lake. Connor led some 200 men on a 140-mile frigid march to Bear River, where a battle took place on 29 January 1863. Approximately 250 Shoshonis were massacred, including Chiefs Lehi and Bear Hunter. In battle Connor displayed great personal bravery, established his reputation as the foremost Indian fighter of his time, and was appointed brigadier general on 29 March.

Relations with Mormons continued to be strained. Connor accused Mormons of instigating Indian attacks, while Brigham Young wanted Fort Douglas moved out of the city. Connor decided to fight Mormons by providing protection to non-Mormons and ending Mormon isolationism by attracting a large non-Mormon population to the territory. He established a settlement of Mormon dissidents called Morrisites at Soda Springs, Idaho, and in 1863 began publishing the *Union Vedette*, a weekly, then daily, newspaper that presented non-Mormon and military viewpoints.

In late summer 1863 mining fever struck Camp Douglas when silver was found in Bingham Canyon. Along with others, Connor formed the West Mountain Quartz Mining Company. He allowed his soldiers to prospect as long as prospecting did not interfere with their military duties. Mining, he thought, would open up the territory to non-Mormons. He founded the mining town of Stockton, Utah, and dreamed of a great mineral empire. He led the way in constructing smelters and has been called the "Father of Utah Mining."

In 1865 Connor was given command of the District of the Plains, including Nebraska, Colorado, Utah, and Montana. He planned an all-out war against the Sioux, who, angered over white invasion of buffalo plains, had attacked mail stations. Connor became known as "the exterminator" and at the Battle of Tongue River in Wyoming killed sixty-three Arapaho warriors, captured 500 horses and mules, and destroyed major food supplies. In forty days he opened the overland roads and had stage and telegraph lines operating again.

The American people, particularly in the East, however, wanted an end to high military costs and favored conciliating Native Americans rather than killing them. The District of the Plains was abolished, and Connor returned to command the District of Utah. He was breveted a major general on 19 April and was discharged on 30 April 1866 in Washington, D.C., where he testified to threats posed by Mormon allegiance to church over state and continuation of the practice of polygamy.

Connor returned to Utah as a private citizen involved in mining and fighting Mormon control. While his family settled in Redwood City, California, in 1870, he pursued various business and political interests in California, Nevada, and Utah. Although his Great Basin Silver mine in Utah and Eureka Mining Tunnel in Prospect Mountain, Nevada, ultimately were successful, he never became a wealthy man.

Political office likewise eluded Connor. In 1870 he helped form the Liberal party in Utah to oppose the Mormon power base. He was the symbolic leader of the party but, even after the Liberal victory in the Salt Lake City elections of 1890, did not receive support to obtain office. He had earlier lost the Republican nomination for governor of Nevada and then for Congress when he lived in Eureka, Nevada, in the 1870s. Connor spent his final years alone and in relative poverty. His wife died in 1889. He died in his rooms at Walker House in Salt Lake City and was buried in the Fort Douglas cemetery.

Patrick Edward Connor played an important role in the westward movement from Iowa to Texas to California to Utah and Nevada and in so doing epitomized the individualistic and democratic spirit of the West. A fierce and ruthless soldier, he was an able leader, dedicated to his adopted country and determined to fight those he thought threatened it. His mark on the West has been memorialized by a life-size statue in the Fort Douglas cemetery, the Connor Battlefield State Park in Wyoming, and various geographical sites, including Connor Canyon and Connor Peak in Nevada.

• Connor's personal papers were destroyed in an 1865 fire at Camp Douglas and an 1879 fire at Eureka, Nev. Important sources of information about him are *The War of the Rebellion: A Compilation of the Official Records of the Union and Confederate Armies* (128 vols., 1880–1901) and records and western newspapers in areas where he was active. Two recent biographies of Connor are Brigham D. Madsen, *Glory Hunter: A Biography of Patrick Edward Connor* (1990), and James F. Varley, *Brigham and the Brigadier: General Patrick Connor and His California Volunteers in Utah and along the Overland Trail* (1989). An earlier work that had the assistance of Connor's daughter is Fred B. Rogers, *Soldiers of the Overland: Being Some Account of the Services of General Patrick Edward Connor & His Volunteers in the Old West* (1938). An obituary is in the *Salt Lake Tribune*, 18 Dec. 1891.

ANN ENGAR

CONNOR, Robert Digges Wimberly (26 Sep. 1878–25 Feb. 1950), first archivist of the United States, was born in Wilson, North Carolina, the son of Henry Groves Connor, a state legislator and judge, and Kate Whitfield. Connor attended the University of North Carolina at Chapel Hill and received a Ph.B. in 1899. He taught high school in Winston-Salem (1899–1901) and then became a high school principal within the North Carolina public school system (1902–1904). In 1904 Connor accepted appointment as executive secretary of the Educational Campaign for North Carolina (1904–1907) and subsequently became secretary of the new North Carolina Historical Commission (1907–1921). The commission was charged with developing an archival program within the state, and Connor modeled his program on those that had recently been established in Alabama (1901) and Mississippi (1903).

In order to prepare for a position as professor of history, offered to him in 1920 by his alma mater, Connor undertook graduate work in history at Columbia University in 1920–1921. In 1921 he began teaching as Kenan Professor of history and government at the University of North Carolina, where he remained until 1934.

In the 1920s the American Historical Association (AHA) tried to persuade the federal government to establish an archives agency along the lines of the state archives. J. Franklin Jameson, one of the founders of the AHA and an advocate, saw those hopes come to fruition with the construction of the National Archives Building in 1933–1934. He urged President Franklin D. Roosevelt to appoint Connor to the newly established post of archivist, and Connor was appointed by Roosevelt in 1934.

In his tenure as first archivist of the United States, Connor oversaw the establishment of the archival profession, many of whose leaders came from among his staff and contributed to the formation of the Society of American Archivists in 1936. Connor assumed the presidency of that group from 1941 to 1943. The major tasks of the Connor administration from 1934 to 1941 were to develop procedures for dealing with the great backlog of official federal records that were held in the agencies; to contend with the New Deal period expansion of agencies and consequently of the records generated by Roosevelt's New Deal programs; and to convince old-line agencies, such as the State, War and Treasury Departments, to send their 145-year accumulation of historical records of enduring value to the National Archives. He ultimately won his case, and with the key cabinet agencies showing willingness to part with their historical records, others were quick to follow.

The National Archives staff then had to develop methods for dealing with two major problems: how to catalog, classify, or otherwise organize the materials for research purposes; and how to control and evaluate for retention records that were still in the agencies. The first issue was settled by the end of Connor's tenure as archivist. The second had to await his successor.

The issue of organization involved a choice between the traditional library techniques for the classification of knowledge and cataloging by some unit equivalent to a book; or the acceptance of European "registry" systems for records. Ultimately Connor rejected both alternatives and led the National Archives into the development of a concept of description based on the archival philosophy of "respect for the sources" (*fonds*) of the records and "respect for original order." The concepts of item level control and cataloging were abandoned at Connor's insistence in favor of a process of maintaining records according to the agency of creation and in the file structure employed by the agency at the time. Thus, the two principles of the "record group" (agency or bureau records) and the archival "series" (the structure of records as maintained by the agency) were established with Connor's support. These practices were quickly emulated by state and other archives and defined the distinctive competence of the archival profession.

In 1938 Connor worked with Roosevelt to establish the first of the presidential libraries at Hyde Park, New York. In the middle of his second term, Roosevelt was looking for an alternative to the tradition of depositing the president's papers in the Library of Congress Manuscript Division, which held twenty-eight such collections. Roosevelt's proposal was to combine a donation of land—in his case from his mother's estate in Dutchess County, New York—and a public subscription to fund the construction of a library museum facility. The president would then deed his papers to the federal government to be deposited in the facility (which would also be deeded). Because of his friendship with Connor, his wish to nurture the new archives establishment, and Connor's advice on handling the presidential materials, Roosevelt chose the National Archives to become the permanent administrator of the presidential library. Connor's work with the president, and his acceptance and implementation of the Roosevelt proposal, wrought a major change in the preservation and use of these major governmental documents.

During his seven-year term as archivist of the United States, Connor established both the National Archives as the accepted repository for the records of all executive branch agencies and a system of library/museum/archives institutions as centers for presidential studies (the legislative and judicial branches negotiated deposit agreements in later years). Connor developed the administrative organization pattern for the archives and was instrumental in the development of an archival methodology that initially was unique to the United States but was later adopted by other countries in slightly modified forms.

On retirement from the National Archives in 1941, Connor returned to teaching as Craige Professor of Jurisprudence and History at the University of North Carolina until 1949. He died a year later in Durham, North Carolina.

• Connor's papers (1907–1948) are part of the Southern Historical Collection at the University of North Carolina at Chapel Hill. Connor's major works were *North Carolina: Building an Ancient Commonwealth, 1584–1925* (1929) and two volumes of *Documentary History of the University of North Carolina* (published posthumously in 1953). There is no book-length biography of Connor. Two histories of the National Archives devote space to a discussion of Connor's career at the institution: H. G. Jones, *The Records of a Nation: Their Management, Preservation, and Use* (1969), pp. 16–23, treats Connor's appointment and his administration; Donald R. McCoy, *The National Archives: America's Ministry of Documents, 1934–1968* (1978), provides a more thorough study and covers the early years of the archives and the details of Connor's administration. An obituary by Thad Page, "R. D. W. Connor," is in *American Archivist* 13 (Apr. 1950): 99–101.

FRANK G. BURKE

CONNOR, Roger (1 July 1857–4 Jan. 1931), baseball player, manager, and owner, was born in Waterbury, Connecticut. Nothing is known about his parents except that they were Irish immigrants from County Kerry. His younger brother Joseph was a catcher with five different major league teams. Connor was educated in the Waterbury school system, and he married a local woman, with whom he adopted one child.

Connor first played professionally from 1876 to 1877 as a lefthanded-throwing third baseman with the Waterbury Monitors in the Eastern League. From 1878 to 1879 he played for the Holyoke, Massachusetts, team in the Eastern League, where he hit consistently with power. In 1880 he signed with the Troy Haymakers in the National League. He played third base for the Haymakers through the 1882 season, after which he moved to first base because of a dislocated shoulder. In 1883 the Haymakers became the New York Gothams and then, in 1885, the Giants. Because of his power hitting, the 6'3", 220-pound Connor was a mainstay of New York through 1889. One of his most memorable performances occurred in 1888 when he hit three consecutive homers against Indianapolis. One home run ball hit by Connor traveled completely out of the old Polo Grounds, a total distance of two city blocks. Connor was affectionately known as "Dear Old Roger" by the Giant fans, especially the city's stockbrokers, who contributed $500 toward the purchase of a gold watch for him. His tall stature combined with his broad handlebar mustache made him one of the most notable players of the era.

In 1885 Connor organized the Giants' chapter of baseball's early labor organization, the Brotherhood of Professional Baseball Players. In 1890 Connor switched to the New York club in the ill-fated Players' League, leading the league in home runs with 13. Connor returned to the Giants after the league folded in 1891. After spending the 1892 season with Philadelphia, Connor again played for the Giants in 1893.

During the 1894 season the Giants traded Connor to the St. Louis Browns of the National League. He played for St. Louis until 1897, including 46 games as their manager in 1896. His most productive game oc-

curred on 1 June 1895 against his former Giant teammates, in which he had two doubles, a triple, and three singles in his six times at bat that highlighted a 23–8 rout.

In 1897 Connor purchased the Waterbury club, where he served as the team's manager and first baseman through 1902. With his vision sharpened by spectacles that would have been ridiculed in the major leagues, Connor hit .392 to lead the more friendly and tight-knit Eastern League. After selling the Waterbury franchise in 1902, Connor bought the Springfield, Massachusetts, club and served as player-manager until 1903, when he retired from baseball. In his shoe-string operation, he also coached first base, saving himself two salaries. "And before the games," he once recalled, "I'd stand at the gates and collect tickets. You see there wasn't anything I couldn't do in baseball."

Over the span of an 18-year career, Connor had a lifetime batting average of .318. He hit over .300 eleven times and was the National League batting champion in 1885 with a .371 mark. He led the league in triples twice and ranked fifth in career triples with 233. Connor also had 442 doubles, scored 1,621 runs, and knocked in 1,077 RBIs. Reputed by most historians to have been the most productive power hitter in the dead ball era, Connor liked pitches down by his knees. Later regarded as the "Babe Ruth of the Nineteenth Century," Connor hit 11 to 17 home runs a year when the average hitter had three to four a year. With a total of 136 home runs, Connor held the all-time home run record until Babe Ruth broke it in 1921.

Connor often surprised opposing catchers with his speed, stealing 227 bases. He was known for his "come-up slide," in which he bounced to his feet immediately after a feet-first slide into a base. He also led the league in fielding twice. In 1925 Sam Crane, a sportswriter who played in the big leagues from 1880 to 1890, ranked Connor as the 26th best player in the first 50 years of the game's history. He lauded Connor: "For so big and heavy a man, I think Roger was the best base runner I ever saw, excepting Bill Lange. . . . Roger was both active and nimble. . . . He had a tremendous reach, a good pair of hands and was exceedingly good on pickups, digging the ball out of the dirt. . . . he was a left-handed batter and took a long, free swing." Crane added, "Roger Connor, like all heavy batters of his day, detested the bunt or sacrifice, but he always dropped his individuality for teamwork and was progressive enough to adopt up-to-date methods when the new style of play was found to be best for emergencies."

After his retirement Connor worked for many years in Waterbury's school system as a maintenance inspector. *New York Mirror* sports editor Dan Parker, also a Waterbury native, wrote of Connor, "He had regal dignity and majestic aloofness. The horse and buggy he drove around on tours of inspection might have been a Roman emperor's chariot."

Connor died in Waterbury. In 1976 the Veterans Committee elected him to the Baseball Hall of Fame in Cooperstown, New York. Though it is unfair and unproductive to compare and speculate about different generations, Connor was truly a giant for all times. Had his prodigious swing been used to hit the lively ball of Babe Ruth's era, there is little doubt that he would have been one of the greatest home run hitters in baseball history.

• The National Baseball Library in Cooperstown, N.Y., contains a file on Connor. Information on Connor appears in Mike Shatzkin, ed., *The Ballplayers* (1990); Lowell Reidenbaugh, *Cooperstown: Where Baseball's Legends Live Forever* (1983); and Martin Appel and Burt Goldblatt, *Baseball's Best: The Hall of Fame Gallery* (1977). See also Bob Broeg, "Connor: Real Giant of Early Game," *Sporting News*, 21 Feb. 1976; and Bill Fleischmann, "Aaron Will Join the Immortals, Like Ruth and Old Roger Who," *Sporting News*, 16 Feb. 1974.

WILLIAM A. BORST

CONOVER, Harry Sayles (29 Aug. 1911–21 July 1965), modeling agency founder and businessman, was born in Chicago, Illinois, the son of Harry Conover, Jr., a washing machine salesman, and Claire Byrnes. Conover's parents were divorced soon after his birth, and he spent his first nine years with his maternal grandparents in Chicago, where his grandfather was a prominent lawyer. He moved to Brooklyn in 1920 when his mother married the owner of a tool and die company. From 1923 until his graduation in 1928, he attended Peekskill Military Academy in Peekskill, New York, occasionally vacationing in Palm Beach, Florida, with his family. He was destined for Notre Dame, and perhaps the priesthood, but he rebelled, leaving college on the day he arrived in September 1928.

Conover's early career was spent working in retail stores in Chicago and New York, including a stint on a radio soap opera in New York City and a year as a radio disc jockey on WEXL in Royal Oak, Michigan. In 1935, because of a friend's interest, Conover was introduced to the John Robert Powers Modeling Agency, the nation's leading modeling agency in the thirties. Gifted with the appropriate looks—tall, dark hair, green eyes—he soon became a full-time Powers model. However, it was model management that interested him. In 1939, with approximately $1,000 borrowed from friends, he financed the opening of his own one-room model agency in midtown Manhattan. (Conover's temporary silent partners included Yale law student and part-time model Gerald Ford, who later became president of the United States.)

Using social contacts from Conover's private school years as "scouts" at eastern schools such as Yale, Princeton, and Bates, the Harry Conover Modeling Agency distinguished itself quickly by recruiting natural-looking, "intelligent" coeds, usually young women who had completed two years of college. Conover knew his fresh-faced, photogenic models were perfect for the new photographed magazine covers that previously had been artist-drawn. Soon his "Cover Girls" graced *Mademoiselle, Glamour, Life, Harper's Bazaar, Cosmopolitan,* and *Vogue.* Equally groundbreaking, and in sharp contrast to the nameless Powers models,

Conover created identities for his models, sometimes rechristening them with more memorable first names such as "Choo-Choo," "Dusty," or "Chili."

Conover's commitment to the successful promotion of his "girls" was matched by his enthusiasm for modeling as a profession. Writing prophetically in an agency pamphlet in 1941, he said that "the modeling profession is one of the choicest vocations today an American girl can select. In addition to being a profitable profession, it is one of the few vocations that leads to other fields." The agency's annual publication, *Who Is She?*, was a convenient reference for prospective employers. It provided background information on each of Conover's models, many of whom became stars, such as Shelley Winters, Joan Caulfield, Nina Foch, and radio personality Jinx Falkenburg. Anita Colby, a Conover model, helped produce and appeared in a successful Paramount film named after the agency's copyrighted trademark *Cover Girl,* starring Rita Hayworth and Gene Kelly. Conover served as a technical adviser and provided models for the movie.

The popularity of Conover models increased during the late war years, 1944–1945. Conover, exempted from military service because of hypertension, worked with United Youth for Defense, which was part of the United Service Organizations (USO). Under these auspices "Conover Girls Abroad" entertained servicemen in the South Pacific.

Conover married two of his models. His first marriage in February 1940 to Gloria Dalton by whom he had two daughters, ended in divorce in 1946. His second marriage to Candy Jones, the former Jessica Wilcox, in July 1946 also ended in divorce in May 1959; they had three sons.

Conover's business success was displayed in the agency's twelve-room suite at 52 Vanderbilt Avenue in New York. The agency was grossing about $750,000 annually and showed a profit of $100,000 in 1943. His success was aided by his marriage to Jones, who headed the USO troupe and became his business partner as head of the Candy Jones Career Girl School. Although separate in management from the modeling agency, the school attracted still more young women to Conover by helping them achieve "believable beauty," the natural look he endorsed.

Conover's agency began booking models for television in 1949, grossing $1 million in 1954 for that service alone. His business began to lose ground, however, when the exclusive model-agent relationship, the agency's primary source of funds, was no longer automatic. Freelancing by his models cut into revenues. The agency also received bad publicity in May 1959 because of its failure to pay child models promptly. An investigation caused Conover to lose his license, and the agency was dissolved while his wife's career school continued.

A playboy life-style and consequent inattention to financial detail cost Conover his business. His personal life disintegrated as well with his desertion of Jones in 1958 and their divorce in 1959. Both partners were held legally responsible for some $125,000 owed to more than two hundred models. The case, resolved out of court, gave impetus to 1959 regulations requiring modeling agencies to keep a separate account for client fees.

Conover was arrested for nonpayment of child support and alimony in 1964, having tried without success to regain financial security through the use of his famous name. He suffered a heart attack shortly after his arrival at Reformatory Prison, Hart Island, New York, where he was to serve a two-year sentence, but he was released within a week at the request of his mother. A year later he died on a sidewalk in Elmhurst, New York, from a second heart attack.

Harry Conover, a name that is no longer a household word, changed modeling from a job to a career for American women. The link he established in the forties between the college campus and modeling was institutionalized in the fashion magazines of the fifties. Conover's "Cover Girl" image lives on through innumerable women in the modeling industry who are known by name for their beauty and business acumen.

• The only primary source for Conover is his short pamphlet, *Modeling* (1941). The most complete biographical source is his daughter Carole Conover's *Cover Girls* (1978). For information on Conover's financial problems, see the *New York Times* during May–July 1959; also see his *New York Times* obituary, 25 July 1965. For contemporary modeling see *Entertainment Weekly*, 5 Mar. 1993.

BARBARA MCCARTHY CROFTON

CONRAD, Robert Taylor (10 June 1810–27 June 1858), dramatist and mayor of Philadelphia, was born in Philadelphia, Pennsylvania, the son of John Conrad, a publisher, and Eliza (maiden name unknown). Urged by his father, in 1831 Conrad became an attorney. But he found himself attracted more to journalism and literature than to the legal profession, and from 1831 to 1834 he worked for the *Daily Commercial Intelligencer* and began writing poetry and plays. His first play, *Conrad, King of Naples*, was performed at the famous Arch Street Theater in January 1832. Following the theatrical success of *Conrad*, he wrote a play dealing with the Jack Cade Rebellion of 1450. This blank-verse play was originally named *The Captain of the Commons*, but when it opened at the Walnut Street Theater in December 1835 it appeared as *Aylmere*. The opening performance had to be delayed two evenings because the leading male actor was drunk.

For the next few years Conrad devoted less time to writing. After being appointed criminal sessions court judge in Philadelphia, he became a prominent figure in the legal community. Conrad had not lost interest in the theater, however, and soon rewrote *Aylmere* for the actor Edwin Forrest (1806–1872). On 24 May 1841 the Forrest Theater in New York produced the play. Conrad then changed the title to *Jack Cade*, and the work became one of the most frequently performed plays of the period, later enjoying a brief 1868 run in Europe. Although Forrest was the actor most closely associated with the role of Jack Cade, other leading men such as Edward Eddy and Albert Roberts offered their interpretations as well.

The public's favorable reception of *Jack Cade* made Conrad, widely known for his gracious, scholarly demeanor, one of the leading literary men in Philadelphia. Chairing a committee of literary judges for the *Dollar Magazine*, he was instrumental in awarding Edgar Allan Poe a $100 prize for "The Gold Bug" in 1843. In 1845 he was appointed associate editor of the *North American*, and in 1848 he helped edit *Graham's Magazine*. He revised John Sanderson's *Biography of the Signers of the Declaration of Independence* in 1846, and provided Joseph Reese Fry with information for his 1847 *Life of General Zachary Taylor*. Around this time Conrad again tried his hand at writing poetry. In 1852 a poem entitled "The Sons of the Wilderness," a series of sonnets, and *Jack Cade* were published as *Aylmere, or the Bondman of Kent; and Other Poems*.

Conrad's career as a litterateur was interrupted in 1853 when the Pennsylvania legislature authorized the expansion of the city of Philadelphia. Conrad became a candidate for mayor of the newly enlarged city and, running on the Whig-American party ticket, defeated the Democrat Richard Vaux by more than eight thousand votes in the election of June 1854. A supporter of the Know-Nothing's nativism, he did his best to ensure that all Philadelphia policemen were American-born. A lively orator, Conrad frequently delivered long, rhetorically ornate speeches. Many rivals opposed his tough, no-nonsense style; but these individuals had to endure Conrad's controversial brand of politics only until 1856, when, at the end of Conrad's term, Pennsylvania governor James Pollock appointed him judge of the quarter sessions court. The following year, failing health apparently forced him to step down. Conrad died in Philadelphia.

Various works of his were published posthumously. *Devotional Poems* appeared in 1862, and theater records show that a third play, *The Heretic*, was performed in Boston in June 1863 and later in New York and Philadelphia. No text of either *The Heretic* or *Conrad* exists. Conrad might appear to have been two different people—the often intolerant, impulsive politician and the romantic, pensive writer. Conrad's plays were characteristic of their time in that they were romantic dramas that not only treated the lives of famous historical figures but also relied on a theme that proved most popular with American audiences—the struggle of the individual against tyranny. Thanks to the efforts of various actors, including Edwin Forrest, John McCullough, and Edmund Collier, his plays, especially *Jack Cade*, remained popular well after the Civil War.

• The Historical Society of Pennsylvania in Philadelphia has a collection of Conrad's letters and manuscripts. See also J. T. Scharf and T. Westcott, *A History of Philadelphia* (1884); A. H. Quinn, *The History of the American Drama from the Beginning to the Civil War* (1923); and M. J. Moses, *Representative Plays by American Dramatists* (1925). An obituary is in the Philadelphia *Public Ledger*, 28 June 1858.

MICHAEL L. BURDUCK

CONRIED, Heinrich (13 Sept. 1855–27 Apr. 1909), actor, theatrical director, and impresario, was born Heinrich Cohn in Bielitz, Austrian Silesia, the son of Joseph Cohn, a weaver, and Gretchen (maiden name unknown). It is not known when or why he changed his last name. Conried attended the Oberrealschule in Vienna, but he left school at the age of fifteen to be apprenticed to a weaver. His apprenticeship soon ended, and he secured a position as a bank clerk in Vienna. Attracted to the world of the theater, Conried frequented theaters and cafés where actors congregated. At such a café Conried met August Foerster, the stage manager of the Hofburg Theater, who coached him. Shortly thereafter, around 1870, Conried was cast in minor roles at the Hofburg. He quit his job at the bank and for the first time told his disapproving family of his interest in acting.

After two years at the Hofburg, Conried joined a traveling company in 1872 as leading character actor, and he played in Austria and Germany for two years. In February 1873 he returned to Vienna and became a member of the Hofburg Theater company. Conried acted at the Berlin National Theater in 1874 and at the Leipzig Stadt Theater in 1876. In 1877 he moved to the Stadt Theater in Bremen, where in 1878 he was elected manager by his peers. Conried rescued the theater from financial difficulties, thus beginning a successful career as a theatrical manager. After one profitable season he left for New York, when Adolf Neuendorff, prominent manager of German theater in New York, offered him $200 per month to serve as manager-actor at the Germania Theater. Although Conried's emphasis had shifted to management, he never completely gave up his acting career.

The German theatrical community in New York was quite active during the latter decades of the nineteenth century, invigorated by the presence of many recent German-speaking immigrants. Conried and several partners converted the Bowery Theater into the Thalia Theater, which was operated as a German-language theater. In 1883 the managers inaugurated a season of Viennese operettas, but the venture proved financially unsuccessful. Conried and rival theater manager Gustav Amberg introduced many well-known German actors to the United States, including Adolf von Sonnenthal, Ludwig Barnay, Josephine Gallmeyer, Ernst von Possart, Hedwig Nieman-Raabe, Friedrich Mitterwurzer, and Marie Geistinger. The play brokerage firm of Goldmark & Conried was established in the early 1880s and controlled the American performance rights to such composers as Franz von Suppé, Johann Strauss, Karl Millöcker, and even Richard Wagner, although the weakness of American law in protecting international copyrights made enforcing such contracts difficult. The firm closed in 1894.

In 1884 Conried married Augusta Sperling; they had one child. In 1887 he became a U.S. citizen. In the latter 1880s Conried produced light opera with Rudolph Aronson both at the Casino Theater, where the New York premiere of Mascagni's *Cavalleria Rus-*

ticana was performed in 1891, and with the Conried Opera Company. Conried moved to the German-language Irving Place Theater in 1892, where he remained as manager until 1907. There he developed a superb stock company. Sometimes acting himself, Conried programmed classics and musical performances along with light comedies and farces. The theater became an integral part of the New York German community and the cultural life of the city, gaining respect in both Germany and the United States. There were regular influxes of new actors from Austria and Germany, including Ferdinand Bonn, Agnes Sorma, Georg Engels, and Helene Odilon. Many of the plays presented were of German origin, but German translations of plays written in French, English, and other languages were also given. Conried coveted the prestige of university patronage, believing theatrical life to be an integral part of the literature and culture of a nation, rather than being mere entertainment. Consequently, he delivered lectures at the theater, offered special rates for university students, and lectured and performed at colleges and universities such as Columbia, Yale, Harvard, Vassar, and the University of Pennsylvania.

In 1903 Conried became manager of the Metropolitan Opera following the retirement of Maurice Grau. His appointment aroused some controversy because of his limited experience as an operatic impresario. Nonetheless, the operatic public wanted stars, and Conried successfully arranged for the revivals of established singers such as Emma Calvé, Marcella Sembrich, Emma Eames, Louise Homer, Anton Van Rooy, Marcel Journet, Pol Plançon, Nellie Melba, Lillian Nordica, Antonio Scotti, and Ernestine Schumann-Heink. In November 1903 Enrico Caruso made his Met debut in Verdi's *Rigoletto*. Other stars added to the Metropolitan's crown during Conried's tenure included singers Olive Fremstad, Geraldine Farrar, and Fyodor Chaliapin and conductors Felix Mottl and Gustav Mahler. Probably because of Caruso's presence in the company, Conried emphasized Italian opera. From 1906 to 1910 competition from Oscar Hammerstein's Manhattan Opera House created the second great operatic war in New York, which ended when the Metropolitan bought out Hammerstein. (The first operatic war had occurred when the Met was established in competition with the Academy of Music.) The most memorable operatic events of Conried's tenure at the Metropolitan include the American premiere of Wagner's *Parsifal* in 1903, an artistic and financial triumph accomplished despite the active opposition of the Wagner family, who wanted to preserve a willed proprietary right to restrict performances to Bayreuth; the 1905 American premiere of Engelbert Humperdinck's *Hänsel und Gretel* in the composer's presence; Puccini's attendance at the 1907 introductions of *Manon Lescaut* and *Madama Butterfly*; and the great brouhaha over the single performance of Richard Strauss's *Salomé* in 1907, which was withdrawn at the demand of the board because it offended influential patrons. Other notable events during Conried's period at the Metropolitan include his founding of the Metropolitan Opera School (1903–1908) and the company's survival of the 1906 San Francisco earthquake and fire, although it lost income, sets, wardrobe, and instruments.

After a long illness that had negatively affected his ability to manage the company, Conried resigned from the Metropolitan on 11 February 1908. He did of sciatic neuritis in Meran, Austrian Tyrol. A large public funeral was held on 13 May 1908 at the Metropolitan Opera House. Conried's contributions to the Met during his relatively short five years as manager were fairly limited. He acquired the services of the greatest international stars then available, and he introduced some new operas, but overall little musical new ground was broken. His greatest achievement was his contribution to the German theater in the United States, particularly at the Irving Place Theater. As an intellectual and idealist, he was keenly disappointed that he was unable to realize his dream of establishing a national repertory theater in the United States similar to those in many European countries. Conried demanded much of himself and those he managed, and he produced many high-quality performances during a period of great development in American theater and opera.

• The only full-length biography of Conried is Montrose J. Moses, *The Life of Heinrich Conried* (1916). Three useful contemporary accounts of the Metropolitan Opera are Henry E. Krehbiel, *Chapters of Opera* (1908) and *More Chapters of Opera* (1919), and Henry T. Finck, *My Adventures in the Golden Age of Music in New York* (1926). A good general history of the Metropolitan is Irving Kolodin, *The Metropolitan Opera, 1883–1966: A Candid History* (1968). Obituaries are in the *New York Times* and the *New York Tribune*, both 27 Apr. 1909, and the *New York Dramatic Mirror*, May 1909.

HARVEY R. BRENNEISE

CONROY, Jack (5 Dec. 1898–28 Feb. 1990), author and editor, was born John Wesley Conroy in Monkey Nest, a coal-mining camp near Moberly, Missouri, the son of Thomas E. Conroy, a coal miner and union organizer, and Eliza Jane McCollough McKiernan. Conroy's father was killed in a mine explosion in 1909. Two years later his mother married an unreliable alcoholic; Conroy left school at the age of thirteen to work in a Wabash Railroad car shop in Moberly. He joined two railroad workers' unions and became an officer in one. In his free time he read voraciously, developed a prodigious memory, attended church and rowdy gatherings alike, and enjoyed listening to old timers' yarns. When the United States entered World War I, Conroy, though an anticapitalist pacifist, sought to enlist but was rejected because of a heart murmur.

When peace came, Conroy finished high school, read dozens of the world's classics called "Little Blue Books" published by Haldeman-Julius of Girard, Kansas, and took classes during the fall semester of 1920 at the University of Missouri, Columbia, but soon returned to the car shop. The day after his marriage to Gladys Kelly in 1922 (the couple had three children), the Great Railroad Strike of 1922 began and cost Conroy his job. For three years he traveled, often by boxcar with hoboes, and found dirty, ill-paying work in Des Moines, Iowa; Detroit, Michigan; and Toledo, Ohio. After a year in a grocery store in Moberly, he made rubber heels in a shoe factory in Hannibal, Missouri.

Abandoning any ambition to rise above his "class," Conroy determined to write about it and from within it—as a laboring intellectual. He corresponded with disgruntled Midwestern writers, developed contacts with radical periodicals, and in 1927 saw his first significant poems and essays into print—in *Pegasus*, published in Springfield, Ohio, and *Northern Light*, in Holt, Minnesota. The Sacco-Vanzetti executions that year spurred him to more action. In 1928 he coedited *Spider, the College Radical*, a magazine founded the year before in Columbus, Ohio, to stir campus unrest. Its almost immediate demise convinced Conroy that worker-writers should listen to pro-Soviet propagandists, several of whom he knew, rather than to armchair eastern American liberals. He toiled in a Toledo auto plant until the stock market crash of 1929 reduced him to irregular employment. He and his family returned to Moberly, where he worked for a builder and dug pipeline trenches. He coedited *Unrest: The Rebel Poets Anthology for 1930*, espousing laborers' and women's rights, anti-imperialism, and pacifism and wrote rebel pieces for Michael Gold's *New Masses* and a short story about unemployment for the *American Mercury* (Feb. 1931). H. L. Mencken, its iconoclastic editor, encouraged Conroy to combine his knowledge of the plight of workers, their folk wisdom, and his own wry humor.

Spurred on by Mencken, Conroy wrote his first novel. Artistically uneven, sometimes sentimental, but often solidly realistic, *The Disinherited* (1933) has an episodic, autobiographical plot, with the hero, Larry Donovan of Monkey Nest, reliving Conroy's family and work experiences to the year 1931. It ends with Larry and a friend preparing to organize poverty-stricken farmers. The novel sold only 2,700 copies and earned Conroy only $125; most reviewers, however, admired its honesty and wanted to know about the author. A translation was published in Moscow in 1934 and sold 250,000 copies. Other translations followed. More immediately important was Conroy's ongoing editorial work through the 1930s. He edited *The Rebel Poet: The Internationale of Song* (1931–1932) and coedited it as *The Anvil* from 1933 until it merged with the *Partisan Review* two years later. He published Soviet poetry in translation, editorialized in favor of the Russian experiment, and yet welcomed all protest writing without endorsing any specific movement, or competing with the *New Masses*, or alienating any formal American communist organizations. Conroy and his family suffered horribly during the Great Depression, even as he took part-time jobs and wrote and placed numerous stories, essays, and reviews. He continued to support many Communist party aims but remained independent of its theories. He spoke on "The Worker as Writer" at the first American Writers' Congress, held in New York City in April 1935. Briefly lauded for his hard-work background, he soon lost support because of his maverick ways. One of his most strident critics was the Chicago novelist James T. Farrell, who regarded proletarian novelists, including Conroy, as artless propagandists whose fiction featured lifeless characters. Conroy's friends included the novelists Nelson Algren and Richard Wright, early works by both of whom Conroy had published in his *Anvil*.

Conroy's second (and last) novel, *A World to Win*, was published in April 1935. In it two half-brothers, sons of a vigorous Irishman, separate when one becomes a worker and the other an intellectual. Their ultimate reunion may be seen as an allegory not only of the need in America for unity of diverse elements in the cause of sociopolitical justice but also of Conroy's competing desires to remain an ordinary worker and to write about workers. *A World to Win* was not a success with either the public or the reviewers.

Later in 1935 Conroy received a Guggenheim grant to study workers migrating from the South to such cities as Akron, Ohio; Chicago; and Detroit. Next came employment at the Missouri Writers' Project from 1936 to 1938 in St. Louis. Away from his family, he drank heavily while there. From 1938 to 1941 at the Illinois Writers' Project, where he associated closely with Algren, he wrote industrial folklore narratives and researched unorthodox religious groups. When World War II began, Conroy continued to support the communist cause, although the Nazi-Soviet pact of 1939 made him uneasy. Briefly reviving the *Anvil* as *The New Anvil* (1939–1940), he and Algren solicited work from black writers, including Frank Yerby, as well as white writers, including Karl Shapiro.

In 1940 Conroy and Arna Bontemps, the African-American author, developed a Works Progress Administration project on Illinois blacks, out of which grew *They Seek a City* (1945), their well-received collaborative study of migrations of rural blacks from the South to urban centers in the North. Earlier Conroy and Bontemps had collaborated on a popular folktale for juveniles, *The Fast Sooner Hound* (1942).

Conroy wrote unsigned entries for *The American Peoples' Encyclopedia* simply for a steady income (1943–1966), collaborated with Bontemps on two more books for children (1946, 1951), edited *Midland Humor: A Harvest of Fun and Folklore* (1947), and in 1949 worked at the writers' colony at Yaddo near Saratoga Springs, New York, on a novel never completed. His son committed suicide in 1954. Several friends turned their backs on him, notably Algren, from about 1955. *The Disinherited* was reissued to considerable critical acclaim in 1963. Conroy and Bontemps updated their previous work on southern black laborers in the North in their highly praised *Anyplace but Here* (1966). In the late 1960s Conroy guest-lectured at universities in Alabama, Connecticut, Minnesota, Oregon, Pennsylvania, and Washington. But when requested in October of 1966 to resign from his encyclopedia work for reasons of age (he was sixty-sev-

en), he lacked a pension and had to apply for unemployment compensation. Returning home, he was dubbed "the Sage of Moberly" by old wellwishers and new admirers. He coedited *Writers in Revolt: The Anvil Anthology 1933–1940* (1973). The town declared "Jack Conroy Day" in May 1985. For many years he hoped to write his autobiography but published only five piecemeal fragments (1975–1981). If completed, his autobiography would surely have been a document of great value. He was a nonpareil chronicler of the midwestern proletarian literary movement in the 1930s. Two years after a stroke that left him unable to speak or write, he died in Moberly.

• Conroy's voluminous papers are widely scattered. Substantial collections are in the Newberry Library in Chicago, and in libraries at Augsburg College, the University of Connecticut, the University of Iowa, the University of Missouri, the Ohio State University, the University of Pennsylvania, Pittsburg State University, and Syracuse University. Jack Salzman and David Ray, eds., *The Jack Conroy Reader* (1979), contains two poems, sixteen sketches and stories, eight autobiographical selections, and eleven articles and essays. Frederick J. Hoffman, *The Little Magazine: A History and a Bibliography* (1946), identifies ten magazines that Conroy edited, coedited, or contributed to. Douglas Wixson, *Worker-Writer in America: Jack Conroy and the Tradition of Midwestern Literary Radicalism, 1898–1990* (1994), is an exhaustive biography by Conroy's friend and literary executor, relates Conroy to numerous fellow writers, and contains a full bibliography of his writings. Discussions of *The Disinherited* are in Walter B. Rideout, *The Radical Novel in the United States, 1900–1954* (1956); Erling Larsen, "Jack Conroy's *The Disinherited*, or The Way It Was," in *Proletarian Writers of the Thirties*, ed. David Madden (1968), pp. 85–95; and Laura Hapke, "A Wealth of Possibilities: Workers, Texts, and Reforming the English Department," *Women's Studies Quarterly* 23 (Spring/Summer 1995): 142–54. Daniel Aaron, *Writers on the Left* (1961), touches on Conroy briefly. Obituaries are in the *Chicago Tribune* and the *New York Times*, both 2 Mar. 1990.

ROBERT L. GALE

CONSIDINE, Bob (4 Nov. 1906–25 Sept. 1975), newspaper reporter and author, was born Robert Bernard Considine in Washington, D.C., the son of James Considine, a tinsmith, and Sophie Small. Considine dropped out of high school in 1923 at age seventeen to become a government employee. Over the next four years he worked as a messenger boy in the Census Bureau and in the Bureau of Public Health, a typist in the Treasury Department, and a clerk in the Department of State. During these years, Considine studied journalism in night school at George Washington University.

Considine secured his first job as a journalist by accident. In his twenties he was a fine amateur tennis player, winning the National Public Parks Doubles championship as well as about fifty other state and regional titles. In 1927 the *Washington Herald* misspelled Considine's name in its sports page after he won a match. Complaining to the sports editor that he could do a better job of reporting than they, he was hired on the spot as a part-time sports reporter for the *Herald*.

In 1929 he moved to the *Washington Post* to write a regular tennis column for five dollars per week. In 1931, still doubling as a reporter and a government clerk, he married fellow State Department worker Mildred Anderson. The couple had four children.

In 1933 Considine was offered $60 per week, twice his *Post* salary, to rejoin the *Herald*. There he began his familiar column "On the Line" (named to rhyme with Considine). In January 1937 William Randolph Hearst, Sr., summoned the young reporter to New York City to write for the *New York American* (later the *Journal-American*). He soon took over as sports columnist from the *American*'s star reporter, Damon Runyon. Moving to Hearst's *New York Daily Mirror* in June 1937, Considine first made a name for himself as a newspaperman by producing an award-winning feature article on the second Joe Louis–Max Schmeling heavyweight championship boxing match. Later that same year he began to write for the Hearst syndicate's fledgling International News Service (INS), in direct competition with the AP and UPI wire services. Considine's reporting in these posts cemented his position with the Hearst organization, which employed him for the rest of his life.

At the start of World War II Considine was working full-time for the INS and was rapidly building a reputation as a globetrotting reporter willing to go anywhere for a story. During the war Considine covered many major news stories and personalities, resulting in a number of published works that he either wrote or edited. For example, Considine edited *General Wainwright's Story: The Account of Four Years of Humiliating Defeat, Surrender, and Captivity* (1945), Jonathan Wainwright's memoir of the tragic battles of Bataan and Corregidor in the Philippines in 1942 and his account of his experience as a prisoner of war. Considine also wrote *MacArthur the Magnificent* (1942), an early biography of General Douglas MacArthur, and recounted Captain Ted Lawson's story of James Doolittle's April 1942 air raid over Tokyo in *Thirty Seconds over Tokyo* (1943). Considine also covered the London blitz in the summer of 1943 and the China-Burma-India theater in early 1945. After the war Considine was among a group of top reporters chosen to observe a 20-kiloton A-bomb test at Bikini Atoll in 1946 and then a far more menacing H-bomb test over Eniwetok in 1956. He was also one of three wire-service reporters invited to witness the electrocutions of atomic spies Julius and Ethel Rosenberg at Sing Sing Prison in 1953.

Besides his worldwide news reporting, Considine moonlighted during the 1930s and 1940s as host of several local radio news programs in Washington, D.C., and later for NBC in New York City. He also became part of an experimental television news program for NBC called "America after Dark," which aired for six months in 1952. Considine even made his way to Hollywood as a motion picture screenwriter. His credits include *The Beginning or the End* (1947), dealing with the production of the atomic bomb, and *The Babe Ruth Story* (1948), starring William Bendix as Ruth.

At the height of his career from 1950 to 1975, Considine was part of an elite press contingent that accompanied U.S. presidents on world tours. Highlights of these assignments included President-elect Dwight D. Eisenhower's inspection of wartime Korea in early 1952, President John F. Kennedy's much publicized visit to his family's homeland in Ireland, Vice President Richard M. Nixon's tense confrontation with Nikita Khrushchev in Moscow in 1959, Nixon's later groundbreaking initiatives as the first U.S. president to travel to China and the Soviet Union, and President Lyndon B. Johnson's wartime junkets to Vietnam.

Considine's many high-profile assignments during this period included the elaborate wedding of Monaco's Prince Rainier and Grace Kelly in 1956. He landed an exclusive interview with the Duke and Duchess of Windsor in 1961, when he was invited to spend a weekend with the couple in Paris on the twenty-fifth anniversary of the Duke's abdication of the British throne. He also reported on the deathwatch of Pope Pius XII at Castel Gandolfo in 1958. In addition to his full-time newspaper responsibilities, Considine found time throughout his career to write biographies or ghostwrite books for such colorful American figures as MacArthur, Babe Ruth, Jack Dempsey, Robert Ripley (of Believe-It-or-Not fame), restaurateur Toots Shor, Specs O'Keefe (the man who robbed Brinks), and industrialist Armand Hammer.

Considine's finest moments as a newspaperman came as part of the renowned Hearst Task Force, built on the proposition that the personal prestige of William Randolph Hearst, Jr., could gain access to major news stories when ordinary reporters could not. The heart of the task force, which interviewed dozens of the world's foremost political leaders, consisted of Hearst, top INS reporter Frank Conniff, and Considine. The greatest scoop of Considine's career came when he, Conniff, and Hearst were granted a three-hour and 35-minute interview in November 1957 with Soviet premier Khrushchev in the Kremlin during the height of the Cold War. "It was one of those once-in-a-lifetime exclusives," Considine said in his semiautobiographical *It's All News to Me* (1967). The tense, unrestrained interview gained worldwide attention and solidified Considine's position in the front ranks of distinguished American journalists.

During his 45-year career Considine was one of the most adventurous, wide-ranging, and prolific reporters in the United States. He was extremely popular among his fellow journalists, many of whom remember him as being warm, generous, hard-drinking, and energetic, often working on two typewriters at the same time on two different stories. His award-winning reportorial style was highly descriptive and unfailingly honest. He could not abide hypocrisy or bigotry, but he avoided unnecessarily confrontational questions in most of his high-profile interviews. He was the author or coauthor of twenty-five books and countless magazine articles, news stories, screenplays, and speeches, and his last "On the Line" column for the Hearst-owned King Features was syndicated in 105 newspapers. He gratefully acknowledged in *It's All News to Me* that the Hearsts "bought me a box seat near a world stage whose boards resound to the trod of a cast of characters unmatched in this century." Considine was literally an eyewitness to history, and he reported it faithfully. As a fearless war correspondent and a member of the Hearst Task Force, Considine probably interviewed more celebrities and world leaders in a wider variety of fields and settings than any other reporter before the widespread use of international television as an interviewing device. Considine proclaimed in his final column, "I'll croak in the newspaper business. Is there any better way to go?" He died of a stroke in New York City.

• A significant collection of Considine's papers is at Syracuse University, Syracuse, N.Y. Considine's other major biographies are *Ripley—The Modern Marco Polo* (1961), *Toots* (1969), and *The Remarkable Life of Dr. Armand Hammer* (1975). His other major ghostwritten books are *The Men Who Robbed Brink's* (1950) and *Dempsey—By the Man Himself* (1960). Considine also wrote several historical works, including *The Panama Canal* (1951); *The First Hundred Years: A Portrait of the New York Athletic Club* (1969); *They Rose above It* (1976); *Ask Me Anything: Our Adventures with Khrushchev*, with W. R. Hearst, Jr., and Frank Conniff (1960); and an affectionate history of his ethnic heritage, *It's the Irish* (1961). Considine's career is discussed in *Current Biography*, Dec. 1947, pp. 131–32, and Nov. 1975, p. 43. A warm retrospective of his life is Saul Pett, "Unforgettable Bob Considine," *Reader's Digest*, July 1977, pp. 87–90. Sportswriter Red Smith mentions Considine in "Jack and Bob and the Guys," *New York Times*, 27 Sept. 1975. An obituary is in the *New York Times*, 26 Sept. 1975.

BRUCE L. JANOFF

CONVERSE, Frederick Shepherd (5 Jan. 1871–8 June 1940), composer and educator, was born in Newton, Massachusetts, the son of Edmund Winchester Converse, a Boston dry goods merchant, and Charlotte Augusta Shepherd Albree. Educated in the public schools of his hometown, he entered Harvard College in 1889, where he studied with John Knowles Paine and graduated with highest honors in music in 1893. The next year he married Emma Cecile Tudor, with whom he had seven children. After a year spent working in the family business, Converse quit to pursue a career as a composer. In Boston, he assiduously studied piano with Carl Baermann and composition with George Whitefield Chadwick from 1894 to 1896. At Chadwick's urging, Converse spent two years in Munich at the Royal Academy of Music under Joseph Rheinberger. Upon completion of his course of study in 1898, Converse was honored with a performance of his Symphony in D Minor.

On his return to the United States, Converse was engaged to teach harmony at the New England Conservatory of Music in Boston, of which his erstwhile mentor Chadwick had just been named director. Converse was appointed instructor in 1901 and assistant professor of composition at Harvard in 1904. He re-signed in 1907 and, except for holding office as vice president of the Boston Opera Company from 1911 to 1914, occasional theory and composition teaching, and service as dean at the New England Conservatory (1931–1938), he devoted the rest of his career to composition. In this endeavor he was greatly aided by income from a private inheritance. He and his family settled down on a farm estate in Westwood, Massachusetts, where he cultivated the land, raised chickens, and ran a dairy.

All of Converse's music is carefully crafted. He especially excelled in creating complex sonorities in his works composed during the first two decades of the twentieth century. His orchestral style, which is characterized by great propulsion and expressivity, has been called both modern and Romantic. Cogent examples are his *Romance for Orchestra* (1901); *Endymion's Narrative* (premiered Boston, 1903), after John Keats; and *The Mystic Trumpeter* (Philadelphia, 1905), a "fantasy" after Walt Whitman. The latter contains hints of a more national, less cosmopolitan locution. This tendency becomes dominant in such works of more obvious Americanism as *Flivver Ten Million* (Boston, 1927), a tonal paean to the Model T Ford that incorporates its distinctive raucous horn signal within the orchestral sonority. The symphonic suite *American Sketches* (Boston, 1935), which recollects the title and some of the native musical spirit of Chadwick's *Symphonic Sketches* (1908), is visually inspired rather than poetic. He applies syncopated rhythms to vernacular tunes and freely parallel chords.

Despite these modernisms, Converse rejected abstract or numerical orderings of melody or other uses of serialization. He refused to achieve novelty by the helter-skelter layering of disparate musical elements, one on top of the other, without concern for the harmony of the total effect. Essentially a musical moderate, he summed up his approach to art in 1938: "I am through with the extravagant elements of modern music. No more experimentation of that sort for me. It is already old-fashioned. What we need in our music is deeper, spiritual and emotional significance. Given that, all the rest will take care of itself."

Converse is largely remembered for his operas and vocal-orchestral works, although he composed relatively few of them. *The Pipe of Desire* (Boston, 1906), a pastorale in one act, won a prize of $10,000 from the Metropolitan Opera Company in 1910 and was the first opera by a native-born American to be produced at the Metropolitan Opera House. His second opera, *The Sacrifice* (Boston, 1911), a more stageworthy musical drama dealing with a romantic triangle during the Mexican War, shows remarkable sensitivity to the prosody of English speech. The work also contains convincing action music, passionate vocal melody, and an attempt to create the effect of conflicting ethnicities by means of orchestral color. *Job*, his dramatic poem for soloists, chorus, and orchestra, written for the Worcester Festival in 1907, is an example of a modern oratorio intended for the repertory of choral associations. The Latin text drawn from the Vulgate is set in one continuous movement; vocal passages are separated by expressive orchestral interludes.

Converse was honored for his musical accomplishments early in his career. He was elected to the National Institute of Arts and Letters in 1908 and received the David Bispham Medal from the American Opera Society in 1925, both in response to the favorable reception of his operas. He was elected to the American Academy of Arts and Letters in 1937. He died in Westwood. Converse was versatile and energetic, a New Englander capable of being witty and amused. His self-confidence was borne out by the fact that his music enjoyed wide favor.

• The Converse manuscripts and papers are in the Music Division of the Library of Congress. Based on these and other materials is an admirable scholarly treatment by Robert J. Garofalo, "The Life and Works of Frederick Shepherd Converse, 1871–1940" (Ph.D. diss., Catholic Univ. of America, 1969), which includes a list of Converse's works. Lists are also in *Grove's Dictionary of Music and Musicians*, 5th ed. (1954), and *The New Grove Dictionary of American Music* (1986).

VICTOR FELL YELLIN

CONVERSE, Harriet Maxwell (11 Jan. 1836–18 Nov. 1903), advocate for Native American rights and author, was born Harriet Arnot Maxwell in Elmira, New York, the daughter of Maria (Marie) Purdy and Thomas Maxwell, a lawyer. Both her grandfather and father were adopted by the Seneca in response to their friendship with and advocacy for Native Americans. Her mother died when Harriet was nine, and she was raised and educated in Milan, Ohio, where she lived with an aunt. Converse followed in the footsteps of her father and grandfather and became a widely recognized friend of tribes of the Iroquois nation.

Her first husband was George B. Clarke, a widower and the owner of the Congress Spring in Saratoga. Dates of this marriage are unknown. In 1861 she married a childhood friend, Franklin Buchanan Converse of Westfield, Massachusetts, a musician, writer, and inventor. Her husband had previously lived with Native Americans in the western United States. The Converses traveled in Europe, the United States, Asia, and Africa for five years while Franklin Converse conducted research on native musical instruments. In the early 1860s Harriet Converse contributed several articles and poetry to Scottish and American periodicals, using the pseudonyms "Musidora" and "Salome." Several poems were written in Scottish. The death of her father in 1864 left her with a substantial inheritance and afforded her the freedom to devote her energies to the arts and philanthropic causes.

In 1866 the Converses returned to the United States and lived in New York City. They acted as hosts for numerous Native Americans from all over the country. Both husband and wife served as legal advocates for New York City's small population of Native Americans. Harriet Converse was particularly interested in helping Indians who had moved to the city to find employment and navigate Anglo law.

In 1881 Converse was introduced to General Ely S. Parker, Seneca chief and aid to General Ulysses S. Grant. Parker later served as commissioner of Indian affairs under President Grant. Converse accompanied Parker on visits to reservations throughout New York and Canada. As a result of her tours, she became an active defender of Native American land rights and also developed a strong commitment to the preservation of Native American heritage and artifacts. In 1882 Converse published her first book of poetry, *Sheaves: A Collection of Poems*. In 1884 she published the poem *The Ho-de'-no-sau-nee: The Confederacy of the Iroquois*, which celebrated the culture of the Iroquois Confederacy. The poem was a tribute to her friend Red Jacket. In the opening lines, she salutes him as "sage and warrior," as well as "legislator and commander," and praises his "grave demeanor." Through her poetry she introduced a white readership to a noble, if idealistic, image of Native Americans.

Throughout the 1880s Converse continued to build her friendship with the Seneca tribe and served as an ambassador between Indian and Anglo worlds. On 15 June 1885 she was formally adopted by the Seneca and became the great-granddaughter of Red Jacket. She was given the tribal name of Ga-ya-nes-ha-oh, "bearer of the law." In approximately 1886 she was perhaps the first white woman to be admitted to the secret Little Water Medicine Society.

Converse became more politically active in the early 1890s. In 1891 her lobbying and testimony helped prevent the passage of the Whipple Bill in the New York State legislature. The bill would have replaced tribal land ownership with individual ownership, a move that would have undermined tribal authority and centuries-old traditions of communal ownership. In response to her efforts, the Seneca made her a legal member of the tribe and gave her the name Ya-ie-wa-noh, "she who watches over us." Her husband was also adopted into the clan at this time.

In 1892 Converse was the first white woman to be confirmed as a chief of the Six Nations. Her efforts to defend the Seneca continued at a national level when in 1902 she worked to defeat a federal claim to Seneca lands. Franklin Converse died in September 1902, and Harriet Converse died shortly afterward in New York City.

Converse gave her extensive collection of Indian artifacts to the state of New York, where her donations are on periodic display. In addition to preserving items such as wampum belts and silver brooches, Converse acted as a recorder of Indian myths and legends. In the posthumously published *Myths and Legends of the New York State Iroquois* (1908), Converse relayed stories of creation and provided insight into the world of the Iroquois. She also included a chapter in which she noted the matrilineal nature of Iroquois society: "As the woman of today stands advocate and petitioner of her own cause, she should offer an oblation of gratitude to the memory of the Iroquois Indian who called the earth his 'mighty mother' and who, through a sense of justice, rendered to the mother of his people the rights maternal, political, social, civil, religious and of land" (p. 138). While much of Converse's attention was drawn to the issue of Native American rights, she clearly drew connections to her own life as a white woman. Converse's main contributions were defense of Native American lands and significant efforts to preserve relics and artifacts.

• Converse's letters and papers are in several collections, including the Arthur Caswell Parker Papers at the University of Rochester Rush Rhees Library, Rochester, N.Y.; the Ely S. Parker Papers at the American Philosophical Society Library in Philadelphia; and the Joseph Keppler Papers of the Museum of the American Indian in the Bronx. Converse was the author of numerous anthropological studies of the Iroquois, including a catalog for an exhibition of Iroquois masks (1899) and *The Iroquois Silver Brooches* (1902). She also wrote many articles on the rites and customs of the Seneca.

SARA N. ROMEYN

CONWAY, Katherine Eleanor (6 Sept. 1853–2 Jan. 1927), author and editor, was born in Rochester, New York, the daughter of James Conway and Sarah Agatha (maiden name unknown). Educated at Sacred Heart academies in Rochester and New York City and at St. Mary's Academy in Buffalo, New York, Conway began her writing career in 1875 as a reporter for the *Rochester Daily Union* and in 1880 moved to the *Buffalo Catholic Union Times* as an assistant editor.

In 1883 Conway took a job as an editorial assistant on the *Boston Pilot*, the Irish-American weekly edited by John Boyle O'Reilly and James Jeffrey Roche. Conway was greatly influenced in her writing by the charismatic O'Reilly, and she would later be associated with the so-called "*Boston Pilot* school of Catholic fiction."

After O'Reilly's sudden death in 1890, Roche became editor and Conway became assistant editor of the *Pilot*. They continued the paper's focus on Ireland, the Catholic church, and Democratic party politics. Roche was infirm during many of these years, and Conway often edited and published the paper by herself. Ironically, her name never appeared on the paper's masthead.

In addition to her editorial work, Conway also was a promoter and organizer of adult-education programs that encouraged Catholics to read and support Catholic writers. "The point of all this," she told the World's Catholic Columbian Congress in 1893, "is not only to raise Catholic intellectual standards, but also to create a market for Catholic lectures and writers." Conway also argued that such programs would encourage Catholic self-esteem "by showing them Catholic luminaries in the flesh." Conway was among those Catholic writers speaking to these "summer schools," as she called them.

During the 1890s Conway published six books of poetry and spirituality. These subjects would dominate her writing for the rest of her life. She also produced a collection of short stories and two novels that were well received at the time but are now dated: *The Way of the World and Other Ways* (1900) and *Lalor's Maples* (1901). "Conway's fiction contains a mixture of realism and sentimental romance that is prototypically defining for her Irish-American literary generation," notes historical Charles Fanning. "*Lalor's Maples* is her most realistic book probably because it is based in part on her own life" (*The Irish Voice in America*, p. 153).

Conway became managing editor of the *Pilot* in 1905, but she was dismissed summarily by Archbishop William O'Connell in 1908. Her sudden departure was controversial, and for the next twelve years she wrote several appeals to O'Connell in an effort to gain back pay and other money owed to her by the *Pilot*. O'Connell finally relented in 1920 and sent the funds owed to her.

After leaving the *Pilot*, Conway became managing editor of the *Republic*, a lively Boston paper that had been founded by John F. Fitzgerald, the mayor of Boston from 1908 to 1912. Conway was grateful to Fitzgerald and worked for the *Republic* until it ceased publication in 1926.

She continued to write fiction, poetry, spirituality, and advice books during those years, and her writing won her a significant measure of recognition within American Catholic intellectual circles. In 1907 she received the Laetare Medal from the University of Notre Dame for her outstanding contributions to American Catholicism. Five years later Pope Pius X awarded Conway the papal decoration *Pro Ecclesia et Pontiface* for her contributions in defense of the faith.

From 1911 to 1915 Conway divided her time between her work at the *Republic* in Boston and an appointment as an adjunct professor at St. Mary's College in Notre Dame, Indiana. But ill health and the demands of two jobs were too much for her, and she returned to the *Republic* full time in 1915.

After her return to Boston, Conway became actively involved in the Massachusetts Association Opposed to Woman Suffrage. She disliked the suffrage movement because the vote would overburden women and encourage them to focus on "the morbid consciousness of womanhood" to the exclusion of domestic duties. "It seems so beyond question," Conway wrote, "that woman as woman, can have no vocation to public life. . . . it cannot be necessary, or even useful, that she should try to do what she cannot do." Conway reflected the general ambivalence of Irish-American women toward the vote. These women seemed to seize on those aspects of the suffrage movement that offended them, their religion, and their culture—divorce, birth control, and sexual freedom.

In addition to her editing, writing, and work against suffrage, Conway also was active in several clubs and associations including the Boston Author's Club, the New England Women's Press Association, and the John Boyle O'Reilly Reading Circle. Although she was described as "a frail delicate looking woman," Conway remained active as an editor and author until the mid-1920s, publishing three books in 1918, one in 1925, and a final volume—a collection of her poems—within a year of her death in Boston. She had never married.

Conway's life and career are replete with irony. As a writer and editor, she made a career for herself in a profession dominated by men. Yet her values, as reflected in her writing and social causes, were conservative and encouraged Catholic women to find satisfaction in being wives and mothers. She will be remembered as a transitional figure in Irish-American letters and politics.

• The largest collection of Katherine Conway Papers, two linear feet, can be found in the Special Collections Department at Boston College. Some of her correspondence also can be found in the Archives of the University of Notre Dame. The most substantive study of Conway's life and work is Paula M. Kane, "The Pulpit and the Hearthstone: Katherine Conway and Boston Catholic Women, 1900–1920," *U.S. Catholic Historian* 5 (1986): 355–70. Also see Kane's larger study, *Separatism and Subculture: Boston Catholicism, 1900–1920* (1994). Charles Fanning has produced two brief assessments of Conway's fiction: *The Exiles of Erin* (1987), which he edited, and *The Irish Voice in America* (1990).

TIMOTHY WALCH

CONWAY, Moncure Daniel (17 Mar. 1832–15 Nov. 1907), reformer, minister, and author, was born in Stafford County, Virginia, the son of Walker Peyton Conway, a planter and judge, and Margaret Eleanor Daniel, a self-taught homeopathic doctor. Born to privilege, Conway was expected to emulate powerful, prominent male relatives. But his desire to please his father was exceeded by the influence of his remarkable mother and other female relatives. Together, these women emphasized sharing over hierarchy, personal fulfillment as well as duty, and encouraged, despite his father's disapproval, Conway's love of literature.

Conway graduated from Dickinson College in Carlisle, Pennsylvania, in 1849, having founded a college literary magazine, experienced conversion at a Methodist revival, and studied with an antislavery classics professor, John McClintock. Returning to Virginia, he tried studying law but abandoned it after exposure to Ralph Waldo Emerson's work fortified his determination to seek his own path. On his nineteenth birthday he became a circuit-riding Methodist minister in rural Maryland. There he was impressed by the religious and political beliefs of a Quaker community and disillusioned by Methodist dogma. He wrote to Emerson late in 1851, describing himself as a "Natural Radical" trapped in a family of "talented, conservative Virginians." Emerson responded kindly, encouraging him to be himself. In 1852, after his older brother's death produced more intense paternal pressure, Conway left both Methodism and Virginia. In February 1853 he entered Harvard Divinity School to train for the Unitarian ministry.

In Massachusetts, Conway nourished cosmopolitan cultural tastes and initiated a lasting friendship with Emerson. He also declared himself an abolitionist. Introduced by Wendell Phillips at a rally on 4 July 1854, he denounced Virginia as a place that enslaved blacks physically and whites intellectually. Receiving his B.D. that summer, he was hired by the Unitarian

church in Washington, D.C., by a committee evidently unaware of his growing political radicalism; he was dismissed in October 1856 for antislavery and pro-Republican sermons.

Cincinnati Unitarians immediately hired him for what would be a distinguished six-year engagement. In Cincinnati, Conway found a soulmate in Ellen Dana, daughter of a Unitarian businessman, whom he married in 1858. Their marriage produced three sons and one daughter and seems to have been consistently happy until Ellen's death in 1897. Increased personal stability coincided with still greater boldness in the pulpit. By 1858 Conway was debunking New Testament miracles and doubting Jesus's divinity. He lost over one-third of his congregation but recruited many new members attracted to the religious eclecticism and rationalist emphasis of what he now called his "Free Church."

The Civil War found Conway's pro-Union sister and mother in Pennsylvania, his pro-Confederate father in Richmond, and his two brothers in the Confederate army. He supported the Union on the condition that President Abraham Lincoln show progress toward a policy of emancipation. His views were expounded in two powerful propagandistic books, *The Rejected Stone* (1861) and *The Golden Hour* (1862), prompting Boston abolitionists to make him coeditor of a new antislavery weekly, *The Commonwealth*. Just before moving to Massachusetts in September 1862, Conway rendezvoused in Washington, D.C., with thirty-three slaves newly escaped from his father, and resettled them in Ohio. This, and subsequently the Emancipation Proclamation, raised his spirits momentarily, but increasingly the war anguished and depressed him. With his family divided, his boyhood haunts the scenes of savage fighting, and nationwide emancipation not fully achieved, Conway determined to leave the country. He did so in April 1863 on the pretext of making a speaking tour in England. Shortly thereafter, he sent for his family. He would live in London for the next twenty-two years.

Conway found a rewarding new life in England, thanks to his 1864 engagement as minister by South Place Chapel, London's most distinguished freethought institution. Conway took South Place with him on his intellectual pilgrimage from theism to a kind of pious agnosticism, a stance that combined the reverent tone of the believer with the detachment of the cultural anthropologist. His long South Place ministry (1864–1884) was famous and widely acclaimed in liberal circles; the institution would continue on a more modest scale through the twentieth century as the South Place Ethical Society, meeting after 1929 at Conway Hall in Red Lion Square. During his London years, Conway publicized Eastern religion and advocated a respect for all religions while denouncing the arbitrary dogmas of each. He was also a prolific journalist, writing for English and American magazines and newspapers, working as a war correspondent in France in 1870, and serving as English literary agent for Louisa Alcott, Mark Twain, and Walt Whitman.

Despite his long, productive exile, Conway always thought of himself as American and settled, with his family, in New York in 1885. As early as 1875 he had made a family visit to Virginia, a place for which he always retained affection, but both its cultural isolation and its political conservatism, as well as his wife's inclinations, precluded a move there. For the next seven years he pursued historical scholarship, marked most notably by a highly regarded, still useful biography of Thomas Paine (1892), a transatlantic radical with whom he felt much kinship. After a brief return to South Place between 1893 and 1897, Conway again lived in New York, but immediately on the outbreak of war with Spain, he denounced American militarism and moved to France, which he saw as less belligerent than either Britain or the United States. He divided his last decade between Paris and Greenwich Village, working on his monumental *Autobiography, Memories and Experiences* (1904), one of the most enduring and important nineteenth-century American memoirs. He died in Paris.

Conway's very existence challenges simplistic definitions of the antebellum South. He was the privileged son of a powerful slaveowner, and yet he became a thoroughgoing radical immersed in religious rationalism, abolitionism, feminism, the peace movement, and the drive for racial equality. Outside forces alone, like Emerson or the Maryland Quakers, do not explain this career, which was made possible—unwittingly—by values conveyed to him in Virginia, especially by women. His importance lies partly in his status as the most comprehensively radical upper-class white male produced by the antebellum South. It lies also in the consistency of his "pilgrimage," as he called his life, toward ever-elusive moral, political, spiritual, intellectual, and personal truth. The nineteenth century's growing emphasis on individualism and personal freedom reached an apotheosis in Conway, for whom resistance to all forms of arbitrary authority was life's ultimate purpose. "Those who think at all," he said in his memoirs, "think freely."

• The largest collection of Moncure Conway Papers is in the Butler Library of Columbia University. An important secondary collection is at Dickinson College. In addition to Conway's *Autobiography*, his *My Pilgrimage to the Wise Men of the East* (1906), detailing his 1883–1884 travels in India, is a significant source. After his *Paine*, Conway's most serious scholarly works were *Demonology and Devil-Lore* (1879), *Omitted Chapters of History Disclosed in the Life and Papers of Edmund Randolph* (1888), and *Life of Nathaniel Hawthorne* (1890). His compilation of excerpts from the sacred book of the world's religions, *The Sacred Anthology* (1874), is a pioneering work of its kind. The most analytical biography is John d'Entremont, *Southern Emancipator: Moncure Conway, the American Years, 1832–1865* (1987). Mary Elizabeth Burtis, *Moncure Conway, 1832–1907* (1952), is largely descriptive. Both Burtis and d'Entremont include Conway bibliographies. For his London career, see S. K. Ratcliffe, *The Story of South Place* (1955), Warren Sylvester Smith, *The London Heretics* (1968), and Susan Budd, *Varieties of Unbelief* (1977). An obituary is in the *Times* (London), 19 Nov. 1907.

JOHN D'ENTREMONT

CONWAY, Sarah Crocker (?1834–28 Apr. 1875), theater manager and actress, was born in Litchfield, Connecticut, the daughter of Rev. William A. Crocker, an Episcopal minister. (Her mother's name is unknown.) Two years later, following the death of her father, Crocker moved with her family to New York City. Her older brother worked as an actor to support the family, and in 1845 her older sister Elizabeth also went on the stage.

Sarah Crocker began her acting career by age fifteen with appearances in Brooklyn and Baltimore before her official New York debut in late 1849 at the Chatham Street Theatre, which became known as Purdy's National Theatre in 1850. After more than a year at the National, Crocker joined the company at the Broadway Theatre in 1851. There she met the English actor Frederick Bartlett Conway, whom she married in May 1852. She joined Wallack's company as a leading juvenile for the 1853–1854 season, and she also had the opportunity to assume leading lady roles following Laura Keene's departure from that theater.

In the fall of 1854 Sarah Conway left Wallack's to play an engagement with her husband at the Metropolitan Theatre. For the next ten years the Conways, working together most of the time, toured extensively, played seasons with various stock companies, and accepted shorter engagements in support of other actors. They spent a season in Philadelphia as members of William Wheatley's Arch Street Theatre Company and later played at the Walnut Street Theatre under the management of Sarah Conway's sister, Mrs. D. P. Bowers, during the 1857–1858 season. Conway also had the opportunity to learn more about the business of theater management through her husband's brief managerial stints at Pike's Opera House in Cincinnati and at the Metropolitan in New York in 1859. The Conways traveled to England in 1861 and after a single season resumed touring in the United States.

In April 1864 the Conways arrived in Brooklyn and leased the Park Theatre. At that time Brooklyn did not have a permanent stock company, though visiting stars sometimes appeared at the Academy of Music. First opened on 14 September 1863, the Park Theatre had been built as a home for a professional acting troupe, but the first management quickly failed. The arrival of the Conways, well-known performers with years of professional experience, rekindled local hopes that a permanent theater company could be established in Brooklyn.

With Sarah Conway advertised as "sole directress," the Conways opened on 2 April 1864 with *Ingomar, the Barbarian*. Drawing on such standard pieces from their repertoire as *East Lynne*, *Macbeth*, *The Marble Heart*, and *Peep O'Day*, the Conways changed bills almost nightly in an attempt to draw a crowd. Although the venture lost money at first, Conway saw the potential to create a profitable business by the time the first season ended on 23 July 1864. Determined to succeed in her managerial efforts, Conway reopened the theater as Mrs. F. B. Conway's Park Theatre on 3 September 1864. She ran the Park for the next seven years, leaving it to move to a larger theater built specifically for her.

Conway faced several challenges in establishing a successful company in Brooklyn. Upper-class theater patrons, accustomed to ferrying over to New York City to see plays and their favorite performers, had to be convinced to seek entertainment closer to home. Proximity to New York City also made it difficult for Conway to find good employees. As actors, stage-hands, and musicians also preferred New York City to Brooklyn, she often had to settle for second-rate talent. After gaining experience on her stage, actors sometimes accepted more prestigious contracts across the river.

Conway also attempted to attract a working-class audience to her theater, catering to them especially with melodramatic and spectacular pieces on Saturday nights. Without New York City's large pool of resident and transient theatergoers, Conway had to change the Park's bill of fare often in order to appeal to a variety of tastes and to encourage repeat attendance. At a time when New York City theaters were moving to longer runs, frequent changes of bill meant more work and greater expense. Despite the difficulties, Conway always attempted to run a first-class theater, using the best available talent and maintaining high production standards to appeal to the more sophisticated and knowledgeable theater patrons. On occasion she produced a new work, such as Augustin Daly's adaptation of the French play *Divorce*, that equaled or surpassed a rival production on the New York stage. Visiting stars engaged by Conway to appear at the Park Theatre included Mrs. D. P. (Elizabeth) Bowers, Charlotte Thompson, Lawrence Barrett, John Brougham, E. L. Davenport, Lucille Western, Edwin Adams, and Kate Reignolds.

The Park Theatre had only about 1,000 seats, which limited potential income for popular productions. For several years, Conway's own year-end benefits were held at the larger Academy of Music. In 1871 Conway was able to convince a group of local businessmen to build the 1,500-seat Brooklyn Theatre for her company. On 2 October 1871 Conway opened the new theater with Bulwer-Lytton's *Money*. Despite the excitement generated by a new facility, the change in theaters brought new problems. Audiences, perhaps, had higher expectations for the company in its new home. Certainly critics, now regarding the company as an established fact rather than a fledgling enterprise in need of encouragement, offered harsher criticism of any inferior actors or production elements they noticed. In addition, Conway was presumably distracted from her managerial duties by the serious illness of her husband. The fortunes of the Brooklyn Theatre appeared to improve after a policy of presenting more visiting star performers was instituted. However, Conway did not live to enjoy this change. She died in Brooklyn, following her husband's death on 7 September 1874.

Sarah Conway's daughter Minnie (Marianne), a 21-year-old actress, tried to manage the Brooklyn Theatre after her mother's death. Minnie Conway hoped to maintain the family living quarters above the theater and to support herself, her sister Lillian, age sixteen and also an actress, and her eleven-year-old brother Frederick. However, the theater's owners rescinded debt forgiveness that had been granted Sarah Conway and the venture soon ended.

Sarah Conway is remembered for establishing the first permanent theater company in Brooklyn, a major U.S. city, and was also the first American-born woman to manage a theater for as long as eleven years.

• For details of Conway's managerial career see Jane Kathleen Curry, *Nineteenth-Century American Women Theatre Managers* (1994). See also Joan Weaver, "Sarah Crocker Conway: Actress-Manageress" (master's thesis, Indiana Univ., 1982). For the Brooklyn theater scene see Samuel Louis Leiter, "The Legitimate Theatre in Brooklyn 1861–1898" (Ph.D. diss., New York Univ., 1968). For a complete listing of plays presented by Conway at the Park and Brooklyn theaters see Kathleen Anne Morgan, "Of Stars and Standards: Actress-Managers in New York and Philadelphia, 1850–1880" (Ph.D. diss., Univ. of Illinois, 1989). Regular coverage of both theaters appeared in the *Brooklyn Daily Eagle*. An interview is in the *Spirit of the Times*, 28 Mar. 1874. Background information is available in T. Allston Brown, *History of the American Stage* (1870) and *History of the New York Stage* (1903), and in Gabriel Harrison, "The Progress of the Drama, Opera, Music and Art in Brooklyn," in *The Civil, Political, Professional, and Ecclesiastical History and Commercial and Industrial Record of the County of Kings and the City of Brooklyn, New York, from 1683 to 1884*, ed. Henry R. Stiles (1884). Obituaries are in the *New York Times* and the *Brooklyn Daily Eagle*, 29 Apr. 1875.

J. K. CURRY

CONWAY, Thomas (27 Feb. 1735–1800?), soldier, was born in Ireland. Little is known of his parents. At an early age he was taken to France, where he received an education and in 1749 was enrolled in the French army. Diligent service in his profession, especially in Germany in the early 1760s, led to his promotion to a colonelcy in 1772. Upon the outbreak of the revolutionary war, he offered his services to Silas Deane, an American commissioner in Paris, and was accepted on the strength of his reputation as an artful infantry disciplinarian. He sailed from Bordeaux in April 1777 and on 13 May, shortly after his arrival in America, was commissioned a brigadier general by Congress. Seeing service at the battles of Brandywine and Germantown, he was cast into gloom by the military reverses of 1777 and became critical, at least in private correspondence, of General George Washington's leadership. Probably Conway's negative views reached the commander in chief's ear, for in October Washington strongly opposed Congress's promotion of the Frenchman to major general. Although Conway offered to resign in light of Washington's disfavor, the legislators, who were attempting to assert their independence of Washington's military authority, refused Conway's suggestion and on 14 December advanced him to the higher rank while naming him inspector general of the army.

Meantime, the notorious "Conway Cabal," for which General Conway's name is best remembered, had been exposed by Washington and crushed in its inception. This putative scheme, the aim of which, according to Washington's admirers, was to remove Washington from command of the Continental army in 1777–1778 and replace him with General Horatio Gates, had come to light in early November 1777. At that time, James Wilkinson, an aide to Gates, had told an aide to William Alexander, Lord Stirling, about the contents of a letter Conway had sent Gates. "Heaven has been determin to save your Country," Conway was reputed to have written Gates, "or a weak General and bad Councellors would have ruind it." When Stirling learned of this letter, he immediately informed Washington, and the commander in chief then wrote Conway a frigid note informing him that the correspondence had leaked. Washington also wrote Gates a letter, which he routed through Congress, to let Gates and the legislators know that he was aware of Conway's correspondence with Gates. At that point, consternation reigned among the so-called conspirators, Conway, Gates, and also Thomas Mifflin, but not because they had been found out. The general tone of their subsequent correspondence with each other was bafflement that their private letters, even if critical of Washington, were being construed as evidence of a plot to destroy the man. However, writhing as they were under the withering scorn of Washington, they—but especially Gates—did themselves no good with the ham-handed ineptitude of their explanations.

When Conway arrived at Washington's headquarters to take up his duties as inspector general, he was received coldly by the commander in chief. Therefore, he was glad to learn in early 1778 that Congress had appointed him second in command under the Marquis de Lafayette of a projected winter expedition against Canada. His happiness turned to dismay when Lafayette, a great admirer of Washington who believed that Conway had plotted against his hero, refused his services. Finally Conway joined the expedition in a subordinate position. After the Canadian invasion scheme collapsed, Conway journeyed to Albany and put himself under the command of Major General Alexander McDougall. Unhappy with his situation, he wrote Congress a complaining letter on 22 April offering to resign his commission. Unknown to him, his standing in that body had eroded, and much to his chagrin his resignation was accepted six days later with what seemed to him undue alacrity. Hastening to the seat of power, he explained to the legislators that he had not really meant to quit the service, but his comments went unheeded. Thereupon, he applied for a letter of recommendation, such as all officers received upon termination of their employment. Again he was ignored. Angrily he wrote Gates that "a certain Cabal" consisting of "Mr Samuel Adams and Coll Richard henry Lee" was responsible for his humiliation, but there was nothing Conway could do about it. Although Conway hoped that he might serve under Gates in some future campaign, his hope was in vain.

Feelings among Washington's supporters continued to run high against Conway, and on 4 July 1778, General John Cadwallader, a staunch friend of the commander in chief, challenged Conway to a duel, severely wounding him in the mouth and neck. Believing he was about to die, Conway apologized to Washington for his earlier criticisms, expressing his "sincere grief for having done, written, or said any thing disagreeable to your Excellency." Contrary to his expectations, he was restored to health, but unemployed and in disgrace, he had no option save to depart America for home. In 1779 he served with distinction in the French army in Flanders and two years later was ordered to command a regiment at Pondicherry in the Hindustan. Promoted maréchal-de-camp in 1784, he went on in 1787 to become governor of French possessions in India and to be made a commander of the Order of St. Louis. As governor, he quarreled with Tippoo Saib and thereby (some critics believed) severely hurt his country's prospects in the subcontinent. He returned to France in 1792 and was put in command of a royalist army in the south of France. When the revolution turned radical, he had to flee into exile with his wife, a daughter of Maréchal Baron de Copley. Never allowed to return to France, he died in exile.

• Correspondence between Gates and Conway is in the Horatio Gates Papers, New-York Historical Society. Other documents on the "Conway Cabal" are conveniently printed in Jared Sparks, ed., *The Writings of George Washington*, vol. 5 (1834), and in Edmund C. Burnett, ed., *Letters of Members of the Continental Congress*, vols. 2 and 3 (1923). The best account of the cabal is Bernhard Knollenberg, *Washington and the Revolution, a Reappraisal: Gates, Conway, and the Continental Congress* (1941). Also useful are Paul David Nelson, *General Horatio Gates: A Biography* (1976); Kenneth R. Rossman, "Conway and the Conway Cabal," *South Atlantic Quarterly* 41 (1942): 32–38; and Rossman, *Thomas Mifflin and the Politics of the American Revolution* (1952). In his dubious *Memoirs of My Own Times* (3 vols., 1816), James Wilkinson explains his role. Information on Conway's life is in Joel T. Headley, *Washington and His Generals* (2 vols. 1847).

PAUL DAVID NELSON

CONWELL, Henry (c. 1747–22 Apr. 1842), Roman Catholic bishop, was born in Moneymore, County Derry, Ireland. Little is known of his parentage and life prior to his seminary education. In 1776 Conwell was ordained to the priesthood in Paris, having studied there at the Irish College. Though reputed to be learned in theology and languages, he was not a gifted orator; this deficiency would haunt his later years.

In midlife Conwell apparently considered missionary work in the New World; in 1875 he discussed the possibility with John Carroll, Prefect Apostolic of the United Sates, but he pursued the matter no further. Shortly after, Conwell was assigned as parish priest at Dungannon in the archdiocese of Armagh; a decade later he was appointed vicar-general of Armagh, serving in that capacity for twenty-four years. Outspoken in his criticism of the British government, he was considered too controversial to be made Armagh's archbishop. Instead, the Congregation for the Propagation of the Faith reportedly offered him a bishopric in either Madras, India, or Philadelphia, Pennsylvania. He chose the latter, a conflict-ridden see that had been without a bishop since 1814.

Conwell's understanding of the power and prestige of the episcopacy had been shaped in Europe, and he was ill prepared to deal with the democratic notions of his outspoken and at times obstreperous flock. History would remember Conwell for little more than exacerbating the "lay trustee" conflict that he inherited. At issue were the rights and power of lay trustees versus the jurisdiction of the hierarchy.

Conwell was consecrated second bishop of Philadelphia on 24 September 1820 in London. From the start, some of the city's Catholic elite were disappointed in him: they had hoped for a bishop whose preaching ability would equal, if not outshine, that of the local Protestant ministers. Already on the scene was the young Irish priest William Hogan, a gifted orator whose prowess in the pulpit had endeared him to the trustees and parishioners of St. Mary's, the cathedral church. He delivered the sermon at Conwell's installation on 26 November 1820, taking the occasion to bait the bishop on the trustee issue. Hogan had moved out of the rectory to live alone, and when Conwell ordered him to return to the customary clerical quarters, Hogan refused. He was suspended and, in 1821, excommunicated. There was more at stake than the conflict between an insubordinate cleric and a sometimes obstinate bishop; it was the trustees' powers in the appointment and removal of pastors. In mid-1821 Conwell was shut out of his own cathedral church, and he and his followers were forced to occupy St. Joseph's chapel. Next, the Hogan faction invited all Catholics to schism by forming an independent American church. The conflict peaked on 7 April 1822 during a hotly contested trustee election. A bloody riot broke out on St. Mary's church property, the police had to be called in, and American Catholicism was brought into public disgrace. Legal arbitration validated the Hogan slate, but Pope Pius VII's brief, "Non sine magno," rejected it and set the limits of trustees' power. By 1824 Hogan had left the priesthood; he later used his oratorical talents on the anti-Catholic circuit.

Hogan's exit was not the end of Conwell's trouble with the trustees. In a conciliatory effort, he signed an agreement with them in 1826 that specified the extent of their authority. The canonically troublesome point was Conwell's agreement to be bound by the vote of a predominantly lay committee in resolving disputed pastoral assignments, effectively relinquishing his own authority. This act brought Conwell's troubled administration of Philadelphia to an end. He was called to Rome, and once there he was ordered not to return to Philadelphia. He disregarded the injunction and incurred suspension. To resolve the dilemma, the first plenary council of Baltimore asked Rome to appoint Francis Patrick Kenrick as coadjutor-bishop, stripping Conwell of his governing power. He repented his disobedience; Rome relented and permitted the octo-genarian to save face by retaining the title of bishop of Philadelphia and by officiating at liturgical functions.

Conwell misconstrued this gesture of kindness. For the next twelve years he made Kenrick's life and administration difficult by his refusal to accept the fact that he had no canonical jurisdiction. In his last years, Conwell suffered the loss of his sight and most of his hearing, infirmities he bore with resignation. He died in Philadelphia.

• The Conwell Collection, with correspondence of the bishop with the trustees of St. Mary's Church and with the Congregation de Propaganda Fide (1816–1840), is in the archives of the Philadelphia Archdiocesan Historical Research Center, along with about seventy pamphlets printed during the Hogan schism. Richard H. Clarke, "Right Rev. Henry Conwell, D. D.," in *Lives of the Deceased Bishops of the Catholic Church in the United States* (1888), pp. 310–27, is an early, rather hagiographic essay. Martin I. J. Griffin, "Life of Bishop Conwell of Philadelphia," *Records of the American Catholic Society of Philadelphia* 24–29 (1913–1918), though generally favorable, is more objective. A more recent account of the Conwell era is found in two essays in James F. Connelly, ed., *The History of the Archdiocese of Philadelphia* (1976): Arthur J. Ennis, "The New Diocese," and Hugh J. Nolan, "Francis Patrick Kenrick, First Coadjutor-bishop." A detailed account of the Conwell-Kenrick interaction is in Nolan's *The Most Reverend Francis Patrick Kenrick: Third Bishop of Philadelphia, 1830–1851* (1948). The best study of trusteeism in the United States is in Patrick W. Carey, *People, Priests, and Prelates: Ecclesiastical Democracy and the Tensions of Trusteeism* (1987).

MARGARET M. REHER

CONWELL, Russell Herman (15 Feb. 1843–6 Dec. 1925), lecturer and minister, was born in South Worthington, Massachusetts, the son of Martin Conwell and Miranda Wickham, farmers. Conwell attended Wilbraham (Wesleyan) Academy and Yale University before enlisting in the Union army in 1862. During the war he served as captain of two Massachusetts volunteer units guarding Union installations near New Bern, North Carolina. Although he was dismissed from the military after being charged with deserting his post during a Confederate attack, Conwell claimed to have later been reinstated into the army by General James McPherson, promoted to the rank of lieutenant colonel, and severely wounded at the battle of Kennesaw Mountain in July 1864 (where he was converted to Christianity). No known military records substantiate his claims after his dismissal from the army in May 1864; Conwell maintained that General McPherson died before he could make the reinstatement and promotion official.

After military service Conwell studied law at the Albany University and married Jennie Hayden, in 1865. Over the next several years, Conwell worked as journalist, lecturer, and attorney (numbering among his clients Mary Baker Eddy, founder of Christian Science), first in Minneapolis (1865–1868) and then Boston (1870–1879). During this time Conwell wrote at least ten books, including campaign biographies of Republican party presidential candidates Ulysses S.

Grant, Rutherford B. Hayes, James A. Garfield, and James G. Blaine.

After the death of his wife Jennie (1872) and remarriage to Sarah Sanborn (1874), Conwell began to sense a "call" to the ministry. He abandoned his Boston law practice to become pastor of a struggling Baptist congregation in Lexington, Massachusetts, where he was ordained in 1880. News of Conwell's talents reached Grace Baptist Church of Philadelphia, a congregation founded in 1872 with the help of Baptist philanthropist William Bucknell. Conwell accepted the call to become pastor of Grace Church in 1882. Over the next decade, Grace Church became a leading example of what was known as an "institutional church." Banded together to form the Open and Institutional Church League in 1894 (a predecessor to the Federal Council of Churches, established in 1908), these churches attempted to address the mounting spiritual and social strains of industrialized urban life by providing meaningful worship experiences and community-encompassing ministries (such as education, health care, and vocational training programs) for working-class city dwellers.

By 1891 Conwell's Philadelphia congregation had grown to several thousand members and had erected a new building, which they believed to be "the largest Protestant church in America," with a sanctuary of more than 3,000 seats. This new church, now known as "The Temple," also contained features innovative for the time, such as libraries, leisure and travel clubs, a gymnasium, and a large Sunday school program. Conwell, through The Baptist Temple, also established and served as president of Samaritan, Garretson, and Greatheart hospitals in Philadelphia. Conwell's entire Temple church enterprise attracted large numbers of people because its methods attempted to integrate into one institution the spiritual and social needs that were being fragmented and compartmentalized by the complexities of urban life.

The most enduring legacy of Conwell's institutional church is Temple University, begun as a congregational ministry between 1884 and 1887 when Conwell met in the evenings with workers who desired a higher education but were unable to afford tuition. When "Temple College" was chartered in 1888, Conwell was named president, a position he held for thirty-eight years. From the beginning, Temple was intended to provide low-cost evening education for members of Conwell's congregation as well as Philadelphia area workers. Later Temple expanded to full university status by adding professional schools in law, medicine, pharmacy, and dentistry. By the time of Conwell's death, more than 100,000 students had attended Temple University. When the school became a commonwealth university of Pennsylvania in the 1960s, the Conwell School of Theology left Philadelphia to merge with Gordon Divinity School to form the Gordon-Conwell Theological Seminary, located in South Hamilton, Massachusetts.

Conwell was perhaps best known for his inspirational lecture "Acres of Diamonds," purportedly delivered more than 6,000 times nationwide (between 1873 and 1924), which urged listeners to abandon a vain search for riches in far-off places, for "acres of diamonds" could be found "in your own backyard." Conwell believed it was one's Christian duty to become rich by taking advantage of those very backyard opportunities. When asked, "Why don't you preach the gospel instead of preaching about man's making money?" Conwell replied: "Because to make money honestly *is* to preach the Gospel." He argued that the wealthy were only stewards of the riches entrusted to them by God and that they must use their money for holy purposes. Though Conwell's teachings were not directly influenced by Andrew Carnegie's "Gospel of Wealth," both Conwell and Carnegie reflected the American self-help faith in unlimited opportunity as well as the Puritan doctrine of the stewardship of wealth, though Conwell's gospel was intended to be more "Christian" than was Carnegie's. True to his own sense of stewardship, Conwell gave away most of his earnings to needy students, his church, and college, an act that earned him the title among his followers, "the penniless millionaire."

Conwell's popularized version of the Gospel of Wealth, then, incorporated familiar "Protestant ethic" principles of hard work, honesty, frugality, and stewardship. Yet his message was not simply a Christian baptism for laissez-faire capitalism, intended to legitimate accumulation of massive wealth in the hands of a few industrialists, as was sometimes claimed. Indeed, Conwell feared that the nation's rich—Andrew Carnegie and John D. Rockefeller among them—were conspiring to create an aristocracy that threatened to undermine the foundations of American democracy itself. In contrast, Conwell symbolically transformed the Protestant ethic into democratic language more accessible to urban and rural workers facing radically changing social and economic circumstances in turn-of-the-century America. Judging by the tremendous demand for his lecture among everyday Americans, Conwell's message seemed to express the upwardly mobile aspirations of the emerging American middle class much more than it was used to justify the oppression of workers by unfair labor practices. Nevertheless, Conwell's themes about opportunity and the search for riches influenced later twentieth-century "positive thought" advocates in American religious life (like Bruce Barton and Norman Vincent Peale) as well as those in the "success literature" sector of American business culture (such as Dale Carnegie, Napoleon Hill, and W. Clement Stone).

Conwell remained pastor of Temple Church and continued an active lecture schedule until his health failed shortly before his death in Philadelphia.

• Conwell's personal papers, as well as Temple Church and Temple University archival materials, are in the Conwellana-Templana Collection at Temple University's Samuel Paley Library. Among the more widely read of Conwell's thirty-seven books were *The Life of Charles Haddon Spurgeon* (1892), *How to Live the Christ Life* (1912), *Acres of Diamonds*

(1915), *How a Soldier May Succeed after the War* (1917), and *What You Can Do with Your Will Power* (1917). Five uncritical biographies were written during Conwell's life, the most informative of which is Agnes Rush Burr, *Russell H. Conwell and His Work* (1926). Daniel Bjork, *Victorian Flight: Russell H. Conwell and the Crisis of American Individualism* (1979), is the only scholarly monograph on Conwell to date.

JOHN R. WIMMER

CONYNGHAM, Gustavus (1747–27 Nov. 1819), naval officer, was born in County Donegal, Ireland, the son of Gustavus Conyngham and a cousin of the elder Conyngham, whose maiden name was also Conyngham (first name unknown). In 1763 Conyngham immigrated to Philadelphia and settled in that city with his parents. He shipped in the coastal trade to the West Indies and by the eve of the Revolution he was master of a small vessel. In 1773 he married Ann Hockley, daughter of a Philadelphia merchant; they had no children. Early in the fall of 1775 Conyngham, in command of the *Charming Peggy*, left for Europe to procure military supplies for the newly formed Continental army. He arrived in Holland but British diplomatic pressure on the Dutch prevented him from securing any cargo. Stranded in France, Conyngham came to the notice of William Hodge, a former merchant from Philadelphia, who was in the employ of the American commissioners in Paris.

The commissioners, Benjamin Franklin, Silas Deane, and Arthur Lee, had been sent to France by the Continental Congress to seek aid from the French. Although unwilling to enter into a formal alliance with the Americans, the French government did allow them extraordinary latitude in purchasing arms and commissioning warships. For the latter purpose the Americans had brought with them a number of blank commissions to be filled out as opportunities arose.

It was Hodge's task to find appropriate vessels and captains. He recommended that Conyngham be commissioned to command a small lugger recently purchased by him and renamed *Surprise*. Conyngham's commission was issued on 1 March 1777.

Surprise sailed from Dunkirk on 1 May and in less than a week Conyngham had captured two British vessels and brought them into Dunkirk. British outrage at these "piratical" attacks forced the French to order the prizes returned to their owners. Conyngham himself was arrested and his commission was seized by the authorities and sent to Versailles. His confinement was short-lived and by the end of July he was again at sea, this time in command of the cutter *Revenge* with a new commission dated 2 May 1777. For nearly twenty-two months Conyngham ravaged British shipping in Europe and the Caribbean, capturing or destroying at least sixty vessels. His activities so close to British home waters alarmed the English and embarrassed the Royal Navy. Particularly shameful was the ease with which he captured the *Bristol*, a richly laden vessel bound home from the West Indies. He arrived back in Philadelphia on 21 February 1779.

In April 1779 Conyngham, still in command of *Revenge*, departed Philadelphia and headed north to cruise against enemy shipping. He was captured by the British and after a short confinement in New York he was transferred to England and eventually imprisoned under harsh conditions at the notorious Mill Prison. On his third escape attempt Conyngham managed, along with fifty-three other prisoners, to dig his way to freedom. Making his way to Holland, Conyngham signed on with John Paul Jones aboard the frigate *Alliance*.

His stay aboard *Alliance* was brief and on 17 March 1780 while en route to Philadelphia he was captured again by the British and returned to the misery of Mill Prison. He was finally exchanged in June 1781. He returned to Philadelphia, where he remained for the rest of the war. After the Revolution Conyngham returned to the merchant service, but his principal attention was focused on his appeals to the Congress to recognize his services in the Revolution and to provide compensation. Unfortunately, Conyngham's case was complicated by the fact that his original commission, which had been seized by the French, had never been returned. He was thus forced to provide other evidence of his appointment. Even after being presented with documents sustaining the captain's position Congress determined that the commission granted in France was "temporary" in nature and Conyngham was therefore not entitled to compensation. This untoward reaction to Conyngham had less to do with the captain himself and more to do with the source of his commission. During his stay in Paris, Franklin had liberally, and sometimes carelessly, showered commissions on various applicants. Many were given to people who became mere nuisances to Congress. Albeit unjustly, Conyngham was often unfortunately associated with his less worthy associates. Conyngham continued to press his case while trying, without success, to find his original, now lost, commission. Ironically, shortly before World War I the commission showed up for sale by a print-seller in Paris and was purchased by an American collector. Conyngham died in Philadelphia a disillusioned and embittered man.

• The most important source for Conyngham is Robert W. Neeser, ed., *Letters and Papers Relating to the Cruises of Gustavus Conyngham a Captain of the Continental Navy, 1777–1779* (1915). A good deal of unpublished material relating to Conyngham may be found in the papers of the Continental Congress, located at the National Archives and also available on microfilm.

WILLIAM M. FOWLER, JR.

CONZELMAN, James Gleason (6 Mar. 1898–31 July 1970), football player, coach, and sports executive, was born James Gleason Dunn in St. Louis, Missouri, the son of James Dunn and Margaret Ryan. After his parents divorced and his mother remarried, he took the name of his stepfather. Conzelman attended McKinley High School in St. Louis, where he excelled in sports. In 1916 he enrolled at Washington University in that city, where he played football. The following year he joined the U.S. Navy and served at the Great Lakes

Naval Training Station for two years. During his naval service Conzelman played quarterback for the Great Lakes football team that defeated the Mare Island Marines 17–0 in the Rose Bowl game on 1 January 1919. He was also the middleweight boxing champion at Great Lakes. In the fall of 1919 he returned to Washington University and was an All–Missouri Valley quarterback. Conzelman left school in 1920 to help support his widowed mother, a sister, and two brothers.

In the fall of 1920 Conzelman was recruited to play professional football for the Decatur Staleys, who were coached by his naval shipmate George Halas. After his first year in the newly organized American Professional Football Association, which was renamed the National Football League (NFL) in 1922, Conzelman signed with the Rock Island Independents in 1921. Following the second game of the 1921 season, he was appointed head coach of the Independents, making him along with Earl "Curly" Lambeau of Green Bay at 23 years of age the youngest head coaches in NFL history. Over the next eight years Conzelman was a star player for the Milwaukee Badgers, Detroit Panthers, and the Providence Steamrollers in the NFL. He was also head coach for Milwaukee (1922–1923), Detroit (1925–1926), and Providence (1927–1930). Conzelman also owned the Detroit franchise in 1925–1926 before poor attendance forced him to sell it back to the league. He sued his former teammate Halas, Red Grange, and Grange's manager Charles C. Pyle in 1925 when Grange failed to appear in a contracted game in Detroit as a member of the Chicago Bears. As a player-coach in 1928, Conzelman's Providence team won the NFL championship. A knee injury during the 1929 season ended his NFL playing career, but he continued as Providence coach in 1930. He was named to the All-NFL team as a player on a number of occasions. Conzelman also managed and played catcher for the Rock Island minor league baseball team in 1922. He married Ann Forrestal; they had one son.

In 1930 Conzelman returned to St. Louis and published a suburban newspaper for several years. Beginning in 1932 he coached the Washington University football team for eight seasons. Believing college football should be fun, Conzelman provided ice cream and candy for his players and flew kites with them before games. He turned Washington University into a minor football power, winning three Missouri Valley Conference football championships before he was dismissed as coach after the 1939 season. In 1940 Conzelman was hired to coach the Chicago Cardinals of the NFL. During his first three seasons with the Cardinals, Conzelman did not enjoy much success, his team's record having been 10–22–3. After the beginning of World War II, Conzelman resigned as the Cardinals' coach and joined the St. Louis Browns baseball team as assistant to the president. During his tenure with the club, the Browns won the American League championship in 1944. Conzelman left the Browns organization after the 1945 season.

In 1946 Conzelman returned as coach of the Chicago Cardinals, where he would have his greatest success. At Conzelman's suggestion, Cardinals owner Charlie Bidwill assembled what was termed the "Dream Backfield," which consisted of Paul Christman, Elmer Angsman, Pat Harder, and Charlie Trippi. In 1947 Conzelman's team won the NFL Western Division title with a 9–3 record and then defeated the Philadelphia Eagles 28–21 on an icy field to win the league championship. The following season the Cardinals had an even better division record (11–1) but were defeated by Philadelphia 7–0 in the NFL championship game. Conzelman remained as Chicago's coach until after the 1948 season. His coaching record with the Cardinals was 34–31–3 and his overall NFL record was 82–69–14.

After retiring from coaching, Conzelman was vice president of the D'Arcy Advertising Company in St. Louis until his retirement in the 1960s. In addition to his jobs in football and advertising, Conzelman had many other interests. At one time or another, he was an actor, singer, songwriter, piano player, orchestra leader, writer, sculptor, and highly sought after public speaker. His commencement day speech at the University of Dayton in 1942, "The Young Man's Mental and Physical Approach to War," was so inspiring that it was twice read into the *Congressional Record* and became required reading for students at both the U.S. Military Academy at West Point and the U.S. Naval Academy at Annapolis. An article he wrote for the *Saturday Evening Post*, entitled "I'd Rather Coach the Pro's," was judged the second best magazine sports article of 1946. Conzelman was also a member of the St. Louis Cardinals baseball team's board of directors during the 1950s. He was elected to the Pro Football Hall of Fame in 1964. Conzelman died in St. Louis.

• Materials relating to Conzelman's career are in the Pro Football Hall of Fame, Canton, Ohio. For a survey of Conzelman's career as a professional player and coach, see David S. Neft and Richard M. Cohen, *Pro Football: The Early Years, an Encyclopedic History, 1895–1959* (1987). See also Mike Rathet and Don R. Smith, *Their Deeds and Dogged Faith* (1984); and Dick Reynolds, *The Steam Roller Story* (1988). An obituary is in the *New York Times*, 1 Aug. 1970.

JOHN M. CARROLL

COODE, John (c. 1648–between 27 Feb and 28 Mar. 1709), one of the most colorful and persistent rebels in American colonial history, was born in Penryn, Cornwall, the second son of John Coode, a lawyer, and Grace Robins. Coode matriculated at age sixteen at Exeter College, Oxford. He was ordained as a deacon in July 1668 and later claimed ordination as a priest. Coode served briefly in a chapel under the vicar of St. Gluveas in Cornwall before being turned out of the ministry for unspecified reasons. By early 1672, Coode was in Maryland, first settling in St. George's Hundred where he officiated as a minister on several occasions. Two years later he moved to St. Clement's Hundred after marrying Susannah Slye, the recent widow of a wealthy merchant, Robert Slye, and the daughter of Catholic Thomas Gerard, a powerful land-holder and opponent of the proprietary family. At least fifteen years older than Coode, Susannah was subject to periodic fits of madness exacerbated by the recent deaths of a son, her first husband, and her father. Marriage provided Coode a measure of financial security through his management of the estate Robert Slye had left for his children. Coode devoted considerable attention during the next few years to law suits and other measures to build upon these holdings and to acquire land and wealth of his own.

Control of the Slye estate and Coode's own extensive education, rare among colonists then, brought the attention and patronage of Charles Calvert (1637–1715), the resident governor who would soon become the proprietor. Coode also apparently had a charismatic ability to generate support in the short term, though he rarely could command respect and a following over time. Coode was a militia officer by 1675, with promotion to captain in 1676 and a special assignment to Virginia in response to Bacon's Rebellion. That same summer of 1676, Coode won election to the assembly and an appointment as a county justice. Other local offices quickly followed.

Within three years, however, Coode's home had become a gathering place for persons opposed to the proprietor. The reasons for Coode's disaffection are not clear. He and others resented the growing favoritism shown to Catholics in appointments to the highest offices in the colony, and they disagreed with Calvert on some provincial issues, such as the powers of the elected lower house of the assembly, possible responses to the problems of the tobacco economy, taxes and fees being levied on the colonists, and policies toward Indians within the territory claimed by Maryland. Coode's motivations, however, seem to have derived also from his apparent inability to serve anyone very faithfully for any extended period and from his disruptive behavior. Comments in the 1680s and in later years compare Coode to the leading incendiaries of history. He is described as having an uncontrollable temper and problems with alcohol; possible psychological problems arising from his having a club foot and a disfigured face were also mentioned.

Something prompted Calvert to drop Coode from a new court commission in 1680, although he was reinstated a few weeks later. At the next court, Coode reportedly made a profane and drunken assault on other justices, which again cost him his appointment. Coode soon allied with Josias Fendall, longtime opponent of the Calverts, and both men were arrested in 1681 on charges of sedition. Coode, free on bail, successfully stood for election to an open assembly seat. In an important challenge regarding what constituted legitimate grounds for dismissing an elected representative to an assembly, the lower house withstood Calvert's efforts to bar Coode from sitting. Several months later, the provincial court found insufficient evidence to convict Coode of sedition.

Although free, Coode lost all his appointed offices, and voters did not return him to the next assembly.

For several years, he maintained a lower profile. Susannah Coode died by 1683, leaving Coode with two infant sons and several underage children from her first marriage. Coode later wed a woman named Elizabeth with whom he had another son and three daughters.

As political tensions mounted in the 1680s over the economy, trade regulations, the powers of the legislature and proprietary favoritism and patronage, Coode again emerged to lead discontented planters. He won a by-election in 1688. A year later, when proprietary deputies delayed acknowledging the overthrow of James II and the accession of William and Mary, Coode led Maryland's own "glorious revolution." He organized a militia force in July 1689, which captured the government without bloodshed and removed all Catholic officeholders. A new government of Protestant associators emerged with Coode as the primary military figure and his brother-in-law Kenelm Cheseldyne elected as Speaker of the ruling convention. That body appealed to the new monarchs to make Maryland a royal colony. In 1690, Coode and Cheseldyne sailed for England to defend their revolution. The mission was successful, but Coode personally lost status under the new royal government with disclosure of his misuse of funds and the negative impressions he registered with influential persons in England.

Again an outsider, Coode capitalized a few years later on a power struggle between Governor Lionel Copley and Sir Thomas Lawrence, the provincial secretary and second ranking official in the colony. Siding with Lawrence, Coode regained favor when Copley died in 1693 and the Crown upheld Lawrence's position. A new governor, Francis Nicholson, made Coode a militia colonel and sheriff of St. Mary's County, and his neighbors elected him to the vestry. In a familiar pattern, however, within two years Coode had alienated Nicholson with his poor performance in office, misuse of power, drunken and blasphemous behavior in public, and a challenge to the governor's authority locally as well as a meddlesome correspondence with persons in England to discredit the governor. When Coode won another by-election, Nicholson challenged the seating on the grounds of Coode's earlier ordination as a priest. Coode initially denied the charge under oath and won support from the credentials committee and later the full lower house, but subsequent gloating that he actually had been ordained led his embarrassed defenders to eject him from the assembly.

Judicial proceedings against him initiated by Nicholson prompted Coode to retreat to Virginia where he resided for the next few years. Out of legal reach, Coode conspired with Philip Clarke and others against Nicholson, but the governor squelched the opposition. Upon assuming the governorship of Virginia in 1699, Nicholson issued an order there for Coode's arrest. The exile returned to St. Mary's and surrendered to the new governor, Nathaniel Blakiston. Following imprisonment again, Coode was eventually cleared of sedition for insufficient evidence but was convicted of blasphemy. Blakiston suspended the sentence and later pardoned Coode because of his former services to the colony and his present financial straits.

In 1708, Coode once more challenged authority when he participated in a movement against still another governor, John Seymour, who, like Nicholson, was attempting to reform local government procedures, especially the judiciary, and to hold county officials more accountable. Coode won election to a disgruntled assembly that September, but the entire delegation from St. Mary's was dismissed on the grounds that the sheriff, Coode's son William, had not properly scheduled the time and place of election. Coode was promptly reelected, but this time Seymour challenged Coode's sitting on the same grounds that Nicholson used in 1696, his ordination. The lower house concurred and ruled Coode ineligible. William Coode refused to hold another election until after his father's death.

Coode possessed over 1,000 acres at his death, a tangible mark of economic success for a seventeenth-century immigrant to Maryland. But more important than his worldly gains was Coode's legacy of four decades of prominence in the political life of Maryland, including participation in at least five opposition movements and leadership of the revolution in 1689. As far as is known, he died in St. Mary's County.

• Records of Coode's career in Maryland are available in numerous volumes of the *Archives of Maryland* that cover the years from 1672 to 1709, and in unpublished provincial papers kept at the Hall of Records in Annapolis. The most complete biographical study is David W. Jordan, "John Coode, Perennial Rebel," *Maryland Historical Magazine* 70 (1975): 1–28, with the fullest treatment of the most important period of Coode's career in Lois Green Carr and David William Jordan, *Maryland's Revolution of Government, 1689–1692* (1974).

DAVID W. JORDAN

COOGAN, Jackie (24 Oct. 1914–1 Mar. 1984), actor, was born John Leslie Coogan in Los Angeles, California, the son of John Coogan and Lillian Dolliver, vaudeville performers. Coogan began performing at an early age, with a film to his credit and regular appearances in his father's vaudeville act before the age of three. One performance in Los Angeles was witnessed by film star Charlie Chaplin, who was quite taken by little Jackie's charm and confidence. Chaplin asked Jackie's father for permission to use the child in a motion picture, a request the elder Coogan granted with, "Why, of course you can have the little punk." Thus was launched the project that established Jackie Coogan as the first major child star in American movie history.

Chaplin first tested Coogan in a two-reel film, *A Day's Pleasure* (1919). Liking Coogan's performance, Chaplin built his next feature around the child. The resulting film, *The Kid* (1920), was a big success and catapulted the six-year-old to stardom. Moviegoers embraced the little boy with the big, brown, sorrowful eyes, and Coogan parlayed this success into millions of dollars before the age of ten, following *The Kid* with

the hit films *Peck's Bad Boy* (1921) and *Oliver Twist* (1922), among others. Coogan earned more than $20,000 a week during part of the 1920s, and in 1921 he received a $500,000 bonus to change studios from First National Studios to Metro-Goldwyn-Mayer. The child was named "America's Number One Movie Star" in 1923 (over runners-up Rudolf Valentino and Douglas Fairbanks), and he was in the news for every event in his young life, from a bout with the flu to visits from athletes and celebrities.

Just as stardom and financial success had come suddenly, however, the offers and attention vanished as Jackie approached adolescence. In the mid-1920s his career began to suffer from typical child-into-adolescence transition difficulties, repetitious plotlines, and a wearying insistence on Jackie continuing to play the same "little boy." His "comeback" film versions of *Tom Sawyer* (1930) and *Huckleberry Finn* (1931) were unsuccessful, and Coogan struggled with the perception that his greatest successes in life were behind him when he was not yet eighteen years old.

Matters soon became even worse. Returning from a hunting trip in Mexico in 1935, Coogan was a passenger in a car that slammed into a highway partition. The crash killed the other four occupants of the car, including Coogan's *Tom Sawyer* costar Trent "Junior" Durkin and, more significantly, Jackie's father. From this tragedy even greater troubles arose. After Coogan's twenty-first birthday his mother and her new husband Arthur Bernstein, the family's lawyer, announced that they would not give Jackie any of the millions of dollars he had earned as a child. He had received an allowance of $6.25 per week all of those years, and now that he was of age to receive the rest of his earnings, his mother declared that he was a "bad boy" who could not manage money.

Coogan argued with his mother and stepfather for two years before filing suit to receive the money. The ensuing court battle lasted eighteen months, a bitter time in his life that also saw the dissolution, in 1939, of his brief first marriage to the starlet Betty Grable, whom he had wed in 1937. The lawsuit was eventually settled, but by that time most of the money had vanished, and Coogan received between $35,000 and $100,000.

Because of this total mismanagement of Coogan's considerable wealth, the state of California developed a Child Actors Bill, known informally as the "Coogan Law," which mandated that more than one-half of a child actor's earnings had to be placed in a court-administered trust fund. Passed in 1940, the law came too late for Coogan but has protected young actors ever since.

The next two decades of Coogan's life were a continuous struggle for direction and self-respect. He attended college for a while (at Santa Clara University and the University of Southern California), toured with an orchestra, produced an ice show, and played minor roles in a few low-budget films, while also making news for a series of chorus-girl romances and drunken driving arrests. Gaining weight and losing hair, he looked older than his years and nothing like the adorable child the public remembered fondly. Coogan did distinguish himself in World War II, making hazardous duty flights and receiving the Air Medal for meritorious service. Two more brief marriages occurred during the 1940s, to entertainers Flower Parry in 1941 (they were divorced in 1943) and Ann McCormack in 1946 (divorced in 1951). Each marriage produced one child.

After the war Coogan again sought to find a place in the entertainment world, but the best he could manage was an absurd nightclub act in which he, now over thirty years old, played the part of "The Kid" on his knees to another actor's impersonation of Chaplin. He left the industry for a while and worked in sales, and on his fourth try at marriage he finally found stability, marrying a former dancer, Dorothea Lamphere, in 1952. This union lasted until Coogan's death, and the couple had two children. In the 1950s his career took a bit of an upturn, as he landed several television roles and received an Emmy nomination for his performance as a comical cook on "Playhouse 90." A final unexpected career turn occurred when he gained recognition playing the eccentric Uncle Fester on ABC's "The Addams Family" from 1964 to 1966. His remaining eighteen years after "The Addams Family" were, at long last, his happiest, as he now had a more comfortable financial foundation and a solid marriage. Coogan spent these last years golfing, hunting, making guest appearances in movies and television, and looking back over a career he estimated to include more than 135 films and 850 television programs. He died in Santa Monica, California.

Jackie Coogan will be remembered for one vivid screen portrayal—the orphan with that expressive face and those sad brown eyes in *The Kid*—and for his generally acknowledged position as the first child movie star. Beyond that, the "Coogan Law," which resulted from his mistreatment, will perpetuate his name and story, and he will also live on in reruns of "The Addams Family." Coogan peaked so early in life and suffered for it so publicly later that an air of sadness enters any overall assessment of his life and career, but the actor summed up his own outlook in a 1972 *New York Times* interview: "No matter what I do now, I was the first. Nobody can ever take that away from me."

• Although Coogan gave numerous interviews during his long career in show business, no extensive biographical account has yet been published. Among the articles of value and interest, an appreciation by John Nangle in *Films in Review* (June–July 1984), pp. 347–52, is a concise survey of his life and career, as is the Coogan entry in the *Annual Obituary 1984*. More has been written about Coogan's childhood than about the remaining fifty or sixty years of his life, and accounts of his life and work around the time of *The Kid* may be found in numerous Chaplin biographies as well as in histories of early film. Praise for Coogan's work is found in Ruth Goldstein and Edith Zornow, *The Screen Image of Youth: Movies about Children and Adolescents* (1980), and Coogan himself looks back on his days with Chaplin in Kevin Brownlow, *Hollywood: The Pioneers* (1979), a companion volume to

the Thames Television Series. An interesting and revealing look at the actor can be seen in the Coogan episode of Ralph Edwards's "This Is Your Life" television series, in which Coogan reminisces about the good and bad times of his career and is reunited with friends from his past. The program airs sporadically on the American Movie Classics cable channel and is more compelling than any written account yet published.

ROBERT P. HOLTZCLAW

COOK, Abner Hugh (15 Mar. 1814–22 Feb. 1884), architect and master builder, was born in Rowan County, North Carolina, the son of William Cook and Susanna Hill, farmers. Cook learned the building trades in rural North Carolina, then worked in Macon, Georgia, and Nashville, Tennessee. During his apprenticeship he was exposed to the vernacular version of the Federal style and to high style Greek Revival structures, including Andrew Jackson's "Hermitage," only recently rebuilt with an imposing Grecian portico when Cook arrived in Nashville.

In 1839 Cook became one of the earliest settlers of Austin, the new capital city of the Republic of Texas. His earliest work was for private patrons; his involvement in public projects such as the temporary capitol and the president's house was limited. He was a founder of the local Presbyterian church, to which he belonged for the rest of his life. In 1842 Cook became a partner in a steam sawmill in nearby Bastrop and married Eliza Taylor Logan, a widow. Eliza brought three children to the marriage, and she and Abner had four more. The marriage also made Cook a slaveholder, as his wife owned three slaves. By 1850 the Cooks owned ten slaves, and it seems likely that several of them were trained to work on Cook's buildings.

After Texas joined the United States in 1845, Cook worked on several buildings for the new state government. In 1848 he was appointed first superintendent of the State Penitentiary at Huntsville. When the first building was completed in 1850, he resigned and returned to Austin. In partnership with the carpenter John Brandon, Cook won the contract for the woodwork on the new state capitol (1852–1853). Brandon provided floor plans and an elevation, but authority over the building was split between three capitol commissioners, a chief architect, a superintendent, and contractors and subcontractors for the woodwork and the stonework. The few ornamental notes—four Ionic columns fronting a recessed entry and a pitifully diminutive dome—were derived from Cook's copy of Asher Benjamin's *Practice of Architecture* (1833). The resulting building was so unattractive that a legislative investigation ensued, though the committee was unable to determine who was ultimately responsible.

Cook's earliest documented house, a story-and-a-half wood frame house with a spacious gallery (1846–1847), was for Thomas William Ward, second mayor of Austin and commissioner of the General Land Office. The gallery of the one-story farmhouse for William S. Hotchkiss (now known as the Beriah Graham House, 1851–1853) featured square Doric piers and a railing with x-and-stick balusters, which were to become a Cook trademark.

In 1852–1853 Cook built a house for Samuel G. Haynie, one of the capitol commissioners, on a slight rise just west of the new capitol. When Haynie went bankrupt in 1853, he sold the house to Cook, who lived in it for the rest of his life. The house had five bays with a central porch in which outer Doric piers were paired with inner Ionic columns, all extremely attenuated. A brick house for John Milton Swisher was quite similar, but its portico was entirely Ionic and much better proportioned, though still paired to accentuate the central opening.

Cook's principal accomplishment is a series of two-story brick mansions with full-height porticoes stretching across the facade. In 1854 he built houses with great Ionic porticoes for state treasurer James H. Raymond and for state comptroller James B. Shaw. This became the general scheme for the governor's mansion (1854–1856), for which Raymond, Shaw, and Governor Elisha Marshall Pease served as the building committee. The house was to have wings on both sides of the main block, but these were eliminated to economize. Pease was not only the first occupant of the mansion, but he later bought Shaw's house, named it "Woodlawn," and lived there the rest of his life.

The Washington Hill House (now known as the Neill-Cochran House, 1855–1856) varied the formula by using the Greek Doric for the portico and limestone rubble for the walls. The Mary and Reuben Runner House (now known as "Westhill," 1856) was built into a hillside so that one entered the first floor on the east or the second floor on the west. All of these houses had central passage plans with double parlors and features that Cook found in Minard Lafever's *The Beauties of Modern Architecture* (1835): external doorways framed with Doric piers and internal doorways framed with shouldered architraves.

After the Civil War, professionally trained architects began to move to Austin, and Cook concentrated his efforts on contracting. He worked on a number of projects with Jacob Larmour, including the First National Bank Building (1875–1876). His final project was constructing the west wing of the first building of the University of Texas (1882–1884), designed by F. E. Ruffini. Cook died in Austin.

Cook lacked the professional training and the imagination to be an architect of the first order, but his presence in frontier Austin enriched the beauty of the community through his familiarity with the forms of classical architecture.

• Almost none of Cook's personal papers survives; the most useful primary materials are deed records, state government records, and newspapers. Several of Cook's most important projects are illustrated in Todd Webb and Drury Blakely Alexander, *Texas Homes of the Nineteenth Century* (1966?). A biography of Cook is Kenneth Hafertepe, *Abner Cook: Master Builder on the Texas Frontier* (1992), which contains extensive references.

KENNETH HAFERTEPE

COOK, Clarence (8 Sept. 1828–2 June 1900), art critic and author, was born Clarence Chatham Cook in Dorchester, Massachusetts, the son of Zebedee Cook and Caroline Tuttle. His father was one of the first involved in the insurance business, helped found the Massachusetts Horticultural Society, and served in the Massachusetts House of Representatives. His mother died when he was three. By the time he was ten, Cook and his family had moved to New York City. He studied at the Irving Institute in Tarrytown, New York, and considered himself an iconoclast as a child. He graduated in 1849 from Harvard University, where he had specialized in zoology during his final year. While there he studied under Henry Wadsworth Longfellow, who became a long-term mentor and friend. Cook wrote and published poetry but realized he could not sustain a living that way. He moved to Newburgh, New York, in 1852 to work briefly in the office of architect and horticulturalist Andrew Jackson Downing. On 26 October 1852 Cook married Louisa De Wint Whittemore, a widow, sister of Downing's wife, and great-granddaughter of the second president of the United States, John Adams. None of the couple's children survived past childhood.

From 1854 to 1856 Cook worked as the art critic for the *Independent*. He also started writing for *Putnam's Monthly* by 1855, and his essays appeared in numerous additional publications. Between 1863 and 1864 he served as the editor of the *New Path*, an art journal. Most of his published works do not include his middle name, for he dropped it early on.

Cook became art critic for the *New York Tribune* in 1864, and the influence of his writings grew. Of particular significance were a series of essays criticizing paintings displayed in a loan exhibition at a sanitary fair in New York City. These essays presented a reasoned analysis of art in contrast to more typical contemporary discussions blindly praising or disclaiming art. Cook's caustic remarks proved entertaining to the reader, yet made him a critic artists feared. Cook continued to write columns for the *Tribune* until 1869, when he was sent to Paris as a correspondent. It was at this time that his pamphlet, *A Description of the New York Central Park*, was published. Cook remained in Paris until the beginning of the Franco-Prussian War, when he left for Italy. After some months there he returned to the United States and resumed his position with the *Tribune*.

Cook translated Louis Viardot's *Wonders of Sculpture* and added a chapter on American sculpture in 1873. He wrote the text for a heliotype printing of the sixteenth-century German painter and engraver Albrecht Dürer's *Life of the Virgin*, and he translated art historian Wilhelm Lübke's *Outlines of the History of Art*. Published in 1878 was the book for which he has become best known, *The House Beautiful: Essays on Beds and Tables, Stools and Candlesticks*. Initially published as a series of articles in the periodical *Scribner's Monthly*, *The House Beautiful* served to instruct readers on ways to tastefully furnish their homes. The book explored specific sections of the home—the entrance hall, living room, dining room, bedroom—and concluded with "Words Here and There." In a conversational, yet assured tone, Cook suggested that the objects with which one surrounds oneself reflect the spirit of the person and place: " . . . know first," Cook wrote, " . . . how we ought to live externally, and then . . . surround ourselves with the things best suited for that mode of life, whatever it may be. . . . whoever will try the experiment will find the reward in peace, and serenity, and real comfort, so abounding that it will be no longer a query with him whether he shall continue it or not." Two years later Cook published another manual of taste, *What Shall We Do with Our Walls?*

In 1880 Cook became known for his scathing written attacks on Luigi Palma di Cesnola, the first director of the Metropolitan Museum of Art. Cook questioned the authenticity and provenance of a number of statues from Cyprus on display at the museum that Cesnola had personally been involved in collecting. Letters to the editor of the *New York Times* continued regularly during 1882, and Cook published a pamphlet that year titled *Transformations and Migrations of Certain Statues in the Cesnola Collection.* He argued that Cesnola denied that the statues had been worked on and altered since leaving Cyprus: "The charge made against Mr. Di Cesnola is not at all that he has restored the statues, though we certainly wish he had left them as he found them. It is that he has dishonestly concealed his restoration." Cook gained prestige as an art critic, and he was favored by the public. However, largely because of his criticism of Cesnola, his relationship with the *Tribune* ended in 1883.

Cook continued his attack on Cesnola after founding *The Studio*, a magazine that he edited from its inception in 1884 through 1892. This publication served to introduce new techniques in illustration, including photo-etching. The last issue appeared in November 1894. During its run, Cook also authored a three-volume set titled *Art and Artists of Our Time*, published in 1888.

A favorite drawing room lecturer, Cook established himself as one of the earliest American art critics. His prose encouraged debate in the art world and swayed public opinions. Cook recognized and appreciated the work of the impressionists before most Americans. He also promoted the idea of public museums, and he published a wide variety of discussions of art. His famous book, *The House Beautiful*, helped promote an interest in the past and in antiques that also influenced the development of decorative art collections in American museums. Cook spent a number of years in retirement at his estate in Fishkill Landing, New York, where he later died.

• Personal papers, primarily in the form of letters, are found in a number of archives. For lists of these documents, their locations, and comprehensive records of Cook's published articles, see Jo Ann W. Weiss, *Clarence Cook: His Critical Writings* (Ph.D. diss., Johns Hopkins Univ., 1976), and John P. Simoni, *Art Critics and Criticism in Nineteenth Century America* (Ph.D. diss., Ohio State Univ., 1952). Both provide extensive biographical information as well as analyses of Cook's writings. A general biographical folder in the Harvard University Archives at the Pusey Library includes obituaries and a copy of a letter quoting Cook's thoughts on his middle name; Harvard's archives also contain a brief autobiography Cook wrote in 1849 during his senior year. A posthumously published book of poems, *Poems of Clarence Cook*, ed. Louisa W. Cook (1902), includes introductory material supplied by Cook's wife. Numerous letters to the editor and related articles in the *New York Times* discuss the Cesnola affair, primarily during 1882. For additional information on the controversy see Elizabeth McFadden, *The Glitter and the Gold: A Spirited Account of the Metropolitan Museum of Art's First Director, the Audacious and High-Handed Luigi Palma di Cesnola* (1977). A brief biographical sketch, written by Joseph T. Butler, introduces the 1980 reprint of *The House Beautiful: Essays on Beds and Tables, Stools and Candlesticks.* Significant obituaries are in the *New York Times*, 3 June 1900, and in the *Dorchester (Mass.) Beacon*, 9 June 1900.

KRISTIN HERRON

COOK, Ebenezer (c. 1667–1733?), poet and lawyer, was the son of Andrew Cook, a planter and merchant, and Anne Bowyer. His father owned Cook's Point, at the mouth of the Choptank River, Dorchester County, Maryland. Ebenezer evidently divided his time between Maryland and England. He was living in St. Mary's City, Maryland, in 1694. On 26 September 1700 Edward Ebbitts of Dorchester County delegated his power of attorney to "Ebenezer Cook of the Province of Maryland now Residing in London."

Cook is best known for *The Sot-Weed Factor; or, A Voyage to Maryland. A Satyr* (London, 1708), arguably the best hudibrastic poem of colonial America. Cook's contemporaries would have recognized that it imitated, in content and structure, a popular seventeenth-century anti-American song, "The West-Country Man's Voyage to New England." The English song satirizes America; Cook's poem, however, is a splendid example of American humor, ridiculing the English reader and the English ideas of America. *The Sot-Weed Factor* tells the adventures of a foolish greenhorn who attempts to be a tobacco ("sot-weed") merchant ("factor") in Maryland and is constantly amazed by the lifestyle on the American frontier. The narrator of the *Sot-Weed Factor* has not only suffered disappointments in England, he also loses what little wealth he has to the Marylanders he scorns. Cook, an old Maryland hand long before 1708, wrote that the sot-weed factor crossed a river in a canoe:

> In this most noble Fishing-Boat,
> I boldly put myself a-float;
> Standing Erect, with Legs stretch'd wide,
> We paddled to the other side (65–68)

The English reader, who did not know what a canoe was, would not have realized that Cook was burlesquing the narrator of *The Sot-Weed Factor*, who describes Maryland in unflattering terms. On the other hand, the American reader, who knew that it was absurd to stand in a canoe, would have recognized the satire. The portrait of Maryland as a wild frontier, where the lawyers and judges fight one another, grossly exaggerated the wilderness conditions of the tidewater Chesapeake. Through such strategies Cook's poem mocks anti-American propaganda of the day and British prejudice regarding American society.

After Cook's father's death in 1711, the poet returned to Maryland, where he sold his share of Cook's Point and practiced law. He was also deputy receiver-general for Charles Calvert (1699–1751), fifth Lord Baltimore. When William Parks established a press in Annapolis early in 1726, Ebenezer Cook was the only well-known Maryland literary figure. The earliest extant poem published by Parks was Cook's *Elogy* [sic] *on the Death of Thomas Bordley, Esq* (1727), signed "Ebenezer Cook, Poet-Laureat, of Maryland." Perhaps Cook was indeed the official poet-laureate, but it seems more likely that Thomas Bordley, the leader of Maryland's bar and assembly, had dubbed him the Maryland poet-laureate in some mock ceremony. The Virginia poet John Fox wrote Bordley a poetic epistle early in 1723 asking that Bordley take on Fox as a clerk and promising that, if Bordley did so, Fox would "Dab Cook my Poet Laureate too."

When Henry Lowe, receiver-general for Lord Baltimore, died, Cook published an elegy on him in the *Maryland Gazette* on 24 December 1728. Lowe had been living with his servant, Mary Young, for some years, and evidently Cook thought he should have married her:

But tho' none live so just as to be found
With but some Fault that may their Conscience wound,
It can be said, his Character to blast
He liv'd and dy'd, a Batchelor at last.

For the second and last time, Cook signed himself "Laureat." In 1730, Parks published *Sotweed Redivivus; or, The Planters Looking-Glass by E. C. Gent.* This serious poem dealing with Maryland's economic problems was probably influenced by Richard Lewis's poem "To Mr. Samuel Hastings" (1729), but Lewis's high Horatian mode was not suited to Cook's satiric talent.

In 1731 Parks published Cook's longest work, *The Maryland Muse. Containing I. The History of Colonel Nathaniel Bacon's Rebellion in Virginia. Done into Hudibrastick Verse, from an Old MS. II. The Sotweed Factor.* Cook's poem, based on John Cotton's history of Nathaniel Bacon's Rebellion in Virginia, satirizes everyone in the rebellion. Though the poem is amusing, the burlesque diction often clashes with the subject matter. The poet thus describes a battle in which Hubert Farrell, one of the leaders loyal to the governor, was killed:

Where long they pelted at each other,
Tho' none was kill'd in all this Pother,
Excepting *Hubert*, who i'th'Chase,
Fell once again upon his Face;
When pop came Ball, from Musquet Barrel
That thro' the Back shot Hubert Farrell. (III, 111–16)

Since Parks called this version of *The Sot-Weed Factor* "the third edition," it seems likely that Parks published a second edition (for which drafts of a preface

are extant) about 1728. No copies are extant. Cook's last two known poems, both elegies, appeared in 1732, one on Governor Benedict Leonard Calvert (which does not compare with Richard Lewis's fine celebration of Calvert) and the other on William Lock, a justice of the Maryland provincial court. Cook probably wrote other poems, too, for all his poetry published in Maryland survives in unique copies. No records of him after 1732 have turned up, and he was probably well into his sixties at that time. He spelled his name "Cook" in his publications of 1708, 1727, and 1732, but "Cooke" in 1728 and 1730. In most manuscript references, he and others spell his name "Cook."

In *The Sot-Weed Factor* (1960), John Barth's burlesque history of the colonial Chesapeake area, the modern novelist not only has used Ebenezer Cook as the primary mock-hero of his picaresque fiction but also has quoted Cook's entire poem *The Sot-Weed Factor* within the novel.

• Lawrence C. Wroth, ed., *"Maryland Muse By Ebenezer Cooke," Proceedings of the American Philosophical Society* 44 (1934): 267–335, gathered together a number of facts concerning Cook and printed his *Maryland Muse* in facsimile. Edward H. Cohen, "The Elegies of Ebenezer Cooke," *Early American Literature* 4 (1969): 49–72, printed the texts of the elegies. Cohen also, in "The Second Edition of The Sot-Weed Factor," *American Literature* 42 (1970): 289–303, printed the drafts of Cook's preface for *The Sot-Weed Factor*. Robert D. Arner, "Ebenezer Cook's *The Sot-Weed Factor*: The Structure of Satire," *Southern Literature Journal* 4, no. 1 (1971): 33–47, pointed out that the poem's narrator was not to be confused with Ebenezer Cook and that the poem's whole fictive world was satirical. Arner wrote several additional valuable essays on Cook's poetry (1974, 1975, 1976). J. A. Leo Lemay, *Men of Letters in Colonial Maryland* (1972), added facts concerning Cook and discussed all his poems, showing that Cook burlesqued the narrator of *The Sot-Weed Factor*. Other critical interpretations of note are mentioned in Robert Micklus, "The Case against Ebenezer Cooke's Sot-Weed Factor," *American Literature* 56 (1984): 251–61.

J. A. LEO LEMAY

COOK, Frederick Albert (10 June 1865–5 Aug. 1940), first American explorer of both polar regions and first claimant to the discovery of the North Pole, was born in the Sullivan County, New York, hamlet of Hortonville, the son of Theodore Albert Koch, a German immigrant physician (the spelling of whose name was changed by an immigration clerk), and Magdalene Long. Cook's father died when he was only five years old, and Cook later became breadwinner for his four brothers and sisters, getting up early for a milk route and later working in the Fulton Fish Market after the family moved to New York. Early childhood years were spent in Port Jervis and later Brooklyn, where he attended night classes. In 1885 he entered the College of Physicians and Surgeons, graduating with an M.D. from New York University College of Medicine in 1890.

Cook married Libby Forbes in 1889, and the next year she died in childbirth. The loss of his wife and infant son prompted him to respond to an advertisement placed by a young naval civil engineer, Robert E. Peary, who sought a surgeon for his North Greenland Expedition in 1891. Over the next two decades, Cook would earn a reputation as a doctor afield, interrupting a sporadic medical practice to offer himself as surgeon or leader of eight expeditions "Poleward," a term he often used.

On the North Greenland Expedition Cook earned Peary's praise for "unruffled patience and coolness in an emergency." Cook interrupted his medical practice twice more in Arctic expeditions on the *Zeta* (1893) and the *Miranda* (1894), which were essentially pioneer Arctic "cruises," backed by sportsmen and intended to raise funds for future expeditions.

When an iceberg struck the *Miranda*, the 29-year-old Cook navigated an open boat across ninety miles of polar sea to obtain rescue. The Arctic Club of America was born out of this voyage, and Cook became its second president. He would later preside over the prestigious Explorers Club as well. Cook was married again in 1902, to Marie Fidele Hunt, the widow of another physician; she had a young daughter, Ruth, after whom he named McKinley's largest glacier. They later had another daughter, Helene, who in later years would champion her father's cause.

After a four-year stint of practice and lecturing, the polar quest drew him again, this time as surgeon of the Belgian Antarctic Expedition. The party became locked in the antarctic ice of the Bellingshausen Sea, and its survival was largely attributed to Cook, who was later knighted by the king of the Belgians. Roald Amundsen, the first mate, credited Cook with "unfailing hope and unfaltering courage" in his scheme to free the ship. Amundsen, who would later win the race to the South Pole, in his 1926 autobiography lauded Cook "as the most honest and most dependable man I have ever known."

Returning to the Arctic as surgeon on Peary's 1902 relief expedition, Cook was convinced that the so-called American route through Kane Basin along the west coast of Greenland was unsatisfactory because of open water and excessive ice barriers. In any event, he would never again serve under Peary because of differences that emerged during the earlier Greenland expedition.

Polar historians such as Jean Malaurie contend that Peary first saw Cook as a serious rival dating to 1891. Soon Cook mounted expeditions to Alaska's Mount McKinley, being the first to circumnavigate it in 1903 and making what he claimed to be the first ascent of North America's highest peak in 1906. At a dinner sponsored by the National Geographic Society—with a seething Peary in attendance—Alexander Graham Bell hailed Cook as the conqueror of McKinley and the first American to explore both polar regions.

None of Cook's first seven expeditions ventured into the Queen Elizabeth Islands in Canada's Northwest Territories, but his eighth—his longest, most celebrated, and most controversial—took him into that region for two years. He chose this route because of the game lands found there by the Norwegian explorer

Otto Sverdrup. He sailed north on the schooner *John R. Bradley* in 1907. Leaving his base camp at Annoatuk in northwest Greenland in February 1908 with Rudolph Francke, his German assistant, nine Eskimos, eleven sledges, and 105 dogs, he followed Sverdrup's route for the game lands through Ellesmere and Axel Heiberg islands, reached Cape Stallworthy, and went over the sea due north. His last supporting party turned back after three days' march, and, with two Eskimo companions, Cook fought pressure ridges and ice floes to reach what he determined to be the geographical North Pole on 21 April 1908. "We were the only pulsating creatures in a dead world of ice," he wrote in his diary.

The return journey was an epic in sledge travel—in terms of pure survival, a classic experience. After living in an ancient Eskimo cave on Devon Island through the polar night of 1908–1909, Cook and his party returned to Greenland. Later he received the adulation of the world, first in Copenhagen, then in New York. He was presented with an honorary doctorate by the crown prince of Denmark. Cook's wire that he had reached the pole was sent on 1 September 1909; Peary's announcement followed five days later. The great controversy that began then continued throughout the century.

That Cook's claims soon were treated with incredulity among both the "geographic establishment" and the public has been cited by some historians as an instance of successful media manipulation and defamation. Malaurie called Cook—in regard to his singular quest—a "Bonaparte on the Ice" but also "the most defamed man in Arctic history." The result was an almost absolute Peary victory, which labeled Cook an impostor and the greatest swindler in the history of exploration.

Cook spent almost half his life surrounded by such controversy to the extent that his real fieldwork has largely been overlooked. Neglected are his achievements in Antarctica, his first circumnavigation of McKinley, and the 1907–1909 Arctic expedition, which for a half-century would not be equaled for its extent, duration, and rigors of survival. Cook's unquestioned prior physical description of conditions at the pole and his narrative of then-unknown ice island formations weigh in his favor, providing historical credence to the westward drift of the polar ice.

By 1912 Cook's supporters had pressed for a congressional hearing of his claims, and the explorer went on the lecture circuit. His book *My Attainment of the Pole* (1911) outsold Peary's version, and he continued to gain endorsements from both explorers and politicians. Popular commentators such as Elbert Hubbard wrote in his support. United States entry into World War I shelved Cook's appeal for hearings, however, and Cook left the country for a journey to Borneo and an abortive expedition to Mount Everest.

In 1917 he prospected for oil in Wyoming. A troubled later life included imprisonment in 1923 for falsely promoting Texas oil lands, although they subsequently produced the largest pool of oil in the United States and formed the basis of several oil fortunes. The enrichment of his litigious investors, however, did little for any public vindication of the explorer. Paroled in 1930 and pardoned by President Franklin D. Roosevelt ten years later, Cook died in New Rochelle, New York. Cook wrote three other books on his expeditions, one published posthumously in 1951.

Cook, writing in 1938, expressed his own personal torment: "few men . . . have ever been made to suffer so bitterly and so inexpressibly as I because of the assertion of my achievement." In 1993 an International Symposium on Cook was held at the Byrd Polar Research Center at Ohio State University, with polar explorers and scholars from six nations participating, most favorable to his claims. While controversy continued to swirl around the explorer half a century after his death, the man some termed the "American Dreyfus of the North" now has advocates in science as well as polar history.

• The Frederick A. Cook Papers are in the Library of Congress, with a speciality collection at the Sullivan County (N.Y.) Historical Museum. For Cook's own account, see his first report of the polar quest in *My Attainment of the Pole* as well as his posthumous narrative of the return journey, *Return from the Pole* (1951). For an objective biographical study, see Andrew A. Freeman, *The Case for Doctor Cook* (1960), along with two extensive analytical studies, one by Thomas F. Hall, *Has the North Pole Been Discovered?* (1917), and a later one by Theon Wright, *The Big Nail: The Story of the Cook-Peary Controversy* (1970). For more recent assessments, see Russell W. Gibbons, *An Historical Evaluation of the Cook-Peary Controversy* (1956); Farley Mowat, *The Polar Passion: The Quest for the North Pole* (1968); and a critical summary by Jean Malaurie, *Ultima Thule* (1990). An obituary is in the *New York Times*, 6 Aug. 1940.

RUSSELL W. GIBBONS

COOK, George Cram (7 Oct. 1873–14 Jan. 1924), writer and leading spirit of the Provincetown Players theatrical group, was born in Davenport, Iowa, the son of Edward Everett Cook, a railroad attorney from a prominent local family, and Ellen Katherine Dodge. Fellow students at a private school gave him his lifelong nickname of "Jig." Cook grew up artistic and idealistic in his views. He desired deeply to recapture in modern life the community, simplicity, and depth he found in ancient Greek civilization and drama. In appearance he was a romantic figure: *Modern American Playwrights* describes him as "a classical scholar [who was] also an athlete, tall and powerfully built; he had a classic profile and head, shock of dark hair (early to turn white) sweeping back from a peak on his high forehead; his eyes, from under dark brows, were at once alive and brooding, often mystical in expression." Following study at the University of Iowa and Harvard (A.B., 1893), he traveled in Europe and studied at Heidelberg University (1894) and the University of Geneva (1895).

Returning home, Cook became an instructor in English at the University of Iowa (1895–1899). At the outbreak of the Spanish-American War, he volunteered for military service and was stationed in Flori-

da. He was coauthor of a novel, *In Hampton Roads*, published in 1899. In 1902 he married Sara Herndon Swain of Chicago. They had no children. Following a year as an instructor at Leland Stanford University (1902–1903) he left academic life for the simple life of a farmer. His marriage did not survive this departure from conventionality. In 1903 he published *Roderick Taliaferro*, a novel set in the time of Maximilian's Mexican empire.

Later, Cook was attracted to Socialist views, influenced by the young writer and Socialist Floyd Dell, who worked as a helper on Cook's farm. Together, the two founded the Monist Society in Davenport, promoting "advanced" views to those among the local population who would listen. One of those was an aspiring young writer, Susan Glaspell, eventually Cook's third wife.

In 1908 Cook was married a second time, to Molly A. Price, and the couple had two children. He began contributing articles to magazines. In 1911 he published another novel, *The Chasm*, in which the two main male characters represent Nietzchean and Socialist outlooks on life, contending for the hand of an American heiress. Its ideas caused a literary stir at the time, melodramatic though the plot was. Also in 1911 Cook moved to Chicago to become an associate editor of the Friday Literary Review of the *Chicago Evening Post*.

In Chicago Cook got caught up in the city's dynamic theater scene. A production of *The Trojan Women* at the Little Theater, one of the first presentations of Greek tragedy in the United States, and the repertoire of the Irish Players made powerful impressions on him. Susan Glaspell wrote, "Quite possibly there would have been no Provincetown Players had there not been Irish Players. What he saw done for Irish life he wanted done for American life—no stage conventions in the way of projecting with the humility of true feeling." Glaspell was now in Chicago, and her reunion with Cook brought an end to his second marriage.

In 1913 Cook and Glaspell were married. They had two children and lived in New York's Greenwich Village, spending summers in the artist's and writer's colony of Provincetown, Massachusetts. In 1915 they arrived there with the script of *Suppressed Desires*, a satirical one-act play they had written about the burgeoning vogue for Freudian theories. They put it on at the home of a friend there, together with another one-act play. So successful was the venture that two more one-act plays, including Cook's satire on rival art schools, *Change Your Style*, were presented at an old fishhouse on the wharf. Plans were laid to produce in 1916 a summer of plays of literary and artistic quality. Glaspell in her biography of Cook would quote his statement of inspiration: "Why not write our own plays and put them on ourselves, giving writer, actor, designer, a chance to work together without the commercial thing imposed from without? A whole community working together, developing unexpected talents." The theater would serve as focus and expression of the artistic predilections of the Provincetown colony.

In the summer of 1916 Cook threw himself into work for the new Provincetown Players, including carpentry for the small stage and auditorium of the wharf house. He recognized the talent of a young writer on the fringe of the summer colony, former seaman Eugene O'Neill, and played the leading role in *Bound East for Cardiff*, the first of O'Neill's plays produced by the new theater.

When summer ended, Cook was determined that the work of the group should continue in New York. The organization of the Provincetown Players came in September 1916, to be financed on a shoestring by series subscriptions and membership fees. Cook, elected group president, took a major hand in creating a small theater in the converted parlor of a house on Macdougal Street. Later, a somewhat larger theater was built in a former stable a few doors down.

The subtitle of the group was "The Playwrights' Theatre," an indication that a writer's work and vision were to be presented uncompromised by Broadway tricks. Historian Weldon Durham says it was "the only theatrical producing group in America dedicated exclusively to the production of new American plays. The Players could boast of producing ninety-three new American plays by forty-seven playwrights, and all but two of these playwrights saw their *first* plays produced. . . . In addition, the Provincetown Players must also be recognized for new production practices in this country."

Cook's chief contribution as president was the inspiration and stimulation he gave to others, not his own work as a writer. As his friend Floyd Dell wrote: "Seer more than artist, he had never been fully articulate either in his novels or in his plays, despite the grandeur of their conceptions; meanwhile his creative energies spilled over in talk so luminous and profound, in friendships so stimulating, that they conveyed to all who knew him an impression of true greatness far exceeding his tangible achievement." The Players in 1918 produced an ambitious work by Cook on an antiwar theme. It is described by Ross Wetzteon as "a 30-character drama called *The Athenian Women*, loosely based on *Lysistrata*, cosponsored by the Women's Peace Party, and featuring, as Pericles, none other than the author himself. The fact that the critics reserved their praise for the sets [says something about its reception]."

Gradually, some members of the Players complained that Cook's leadership had become dictatorial and unresponsive. The disaffection of these members crystallized during the 1920 production of O'Neill's play *The Emperor Jones*, when Cook went his own way, regardless of others, in the casting of the title role and the construction of an expensive plaster cyclorama for special lighting effects. The tremendous success of the play worsened the conflicts. Cook was adamantly opposed to moving the production to a Broadway theater. He saw it as caving in to commercial values. The majority of others saw a Broadway success as proof of the value of the work they had done and a reward for it. The move to Broadway was made, and Cook withdrew as leader in 1921. He and his wife were still part of the group, and the Players produced Cook's *The Spring* (1921), a mystical drama of extrasensory perception. It did not succeed. The *New York Times* notice of it called it "less a play than a seance" (6 Feb. 1921).

The Provincetown Players, now split and demoralized, determined that at the end of the 1922 season they would become inactive for a year. Cook and his wife in March 1922 sailed for Greece, land of Cook's dreams. They settled in a primitive dwelling on Mount Parnassus, in the small village of Delphi. Cook found new inspiration in the modern people of Greece, the shepherds and woodcutters who were his mountain neighbors. His attempt to reinstate the ancient drama there failed, but he worked on a modern Greek translation of *The Athenian Women* and wrote poems eventually published in the volume *Greek Coins* (1925). He adopted Greek dress and customs and became the beloved "Kyrios Kouk" (Mr. Cook) of the region's people.

This idyllic period lasted only a short time. In January 1924 Cook gave care to a pet puppy dying of glanders, then caught the disease himself in a rare transmission from animal to human. He died in Delphi before medical aid could arrive from Athens. The Greek government allowed a stone from the sacred ruins of Delphi to be placed on his grave.

• Materials on the life and career of Cook are in the Billy Rose Theatre Collection at the New York Public Library for the Performing Arts, Lincoln Center. Susan Glaspell published *The Road to the Temple* (1927), an outpouring of adoring love for her late husband. Other information on Cook is included in the section on Glaspell in Jean Gould, *Modern American Playwrights* (1966). Two discussions of Cook's stay in Greece are William J. Rapp, "A Self-Made Greek Hero from America," *New York Herald Tribune Magazine*, 3 Jan. 1926, and Ross Wetzteon, "Homage to Delphi: In Search of Jig Cook's Grave," *Village Voice*, 24 Nov. 1992. A history of the Provincetown Players under Cook's leadership and later is in Weldon Durham, ed., *American Theatre Companies: 1888–1930* (1987). An obituary is in the *New York Times*, 15 Jan. 1924.

WILLIAM STEPHENSON

COOK, George Hammell (5 Jan. 1818–22 Sept. 1889), geologist and educator, was born in Hanover, New Jersey, the son of John Cook and Sarah Munn, farmers. Cook received his early schooling in Morris County and studied surveying and geometry at the Old Academy in Chatham. In 1836 Cook worked as a surveyor on the Morris & Essex Railroad and in 1838 on the Canajoharie & Catskill Railroad.

Cook then visited Rensselaer Institute in Troy, New York, looking for work but, finding no jobs available, enrolled at the institute under the tutelage of geologist, biologist, and mineralogist Amos Eaton from December 1838 to March 1839 and received a civil engineering degree. Cook then accepted a teaching job at the Old Academy, where, disliking the low pay and unruly students, he did not last the full school year and again unsuccessfully sought surveying work. Cook returned to Rensselaer as an assistant professor of engineering and surveying while he studied for and received a Bachelor of Natural Science degree in the summer of 1840. He assumed more teaching and administrative responsibility as Eaton's health failed. During the winter of 1840–1841 Cook assisted the science teacher at the Troy Female Seminary and in late 1841 replaced him, teaching during vacation breaks at Rensselaer. When Eaton died in 1842, the young, inexperienced junior professor kept Rensselaer operating. Cook assumed the administrative responsibilities of the school, recruited students to increase enrollment, expanded the curriculum, traveled to Boston to buy laboratory supplies, and persuaded the city of Troy to give the school a building. Throughout, he continued to teach many of the science classes, particularly geology and chemistry, and gave public lectures on chemistry to raise money for the school.

While continuing to teach at the seminary, Cook met, and married in March 1846, Mary Halsey Thomas, a graduate who had returned to teach. They would have eight children, five of whom survived to adulthood. During the winter of 1845–1846 Cook invested in the Albany (N.Y.) Glass Enamel and Porcelain Company, originally a sideline to his two teaching jobs, and resigned from Rensselaer in October 1846 to become the full-time company manager. The company failed after two years, and Cook, on the verge of bankruptcy, returned to teaching, this time at the Albany Academy as professor of mathematics and natural philosophy, then as principal three years later. Concurrently, Cook resumed teaching at the Troy Female Seminary in 1850 two days a week. That same year, the New York State legislature appointed Cook to conduct experiments and analyses of the salt springs at Onondaga for two years. In 1852 he also lectured on general principles of chemistry and inorganic chemistry at the Albany Medical College.

Recruited by Rutgers College in New Brunswick, New Jersey, in 1853 to teach chemistry and natural science, Cook planned to stay for five years. He became active in the Second Dutch Reformed Church, New Brunswick Board of Education, New Brunswick Water Commission, Natural History Society of New Jersey, and the New Jersey Agricultural Society. Seeking other professional opportunities with which to fill his time and purse, Cook inspected and evaluated mining properties and accepted an appointment in 1854 as assistant geologist on the New Jersey Geological Survey, in charge of the southern part of the state. His meticulous stratigraphic mapping of the marl beds and the focus on their economic importance resulted in a report, "The Marls of New Jersey" (*Mining Magazine* 5, no. 2 [Aug. 1855]: 132–46), a paper, "On a Subsidence of the Lands on the Sea-Coast of New Jersey and Long Island" (*American Journal of Science and the Arts* [Nov. 1857]: 341–54), and his report, *The Geology of the County of Cape May, State of New Jersey* (1857). He became the state geologist in 1864, produced the *Geology of New Jersey* (1868), and continued this work until his death.

Cook started a Natural History Society on the Rutgers campus in 1857 and, as its first president, began a museum collection. In addition to pursuing his geological interests, he turned his attention toward agricultural education after the passage of the Morrill Act in 1862. He successfully lobbied for Rutgers to become the land grant college in New Jersey in 1864. Cook became a vice president of the college, became head of the Rutgers Scientific School and experimental farm, and developed the agricultural education curriculum. He delivered a series of agricultural lectures in the counties while supervising the farm, and in June 1867 the college changed his title to professor of chemistry, natural history, and agriculture.

The New Jersey State Geological Survey Board of Managers sent Cook to Europe in 1870 to examine drainage and reclamation operations techniques and practices that he could apply to New Jersey's wetlands. He subsequently spent several years promoting, surveying, and planning wetlands drainage. Cook gradually converted the college farm to an agricultural experiment station, following the models he observed in Europe, and as his cohorts were doing in other states with federal government incentives. His reputation outside the state equaled the esteem he received at home; Professor Alexander Hogg of Alabama Agricultural College, remarked that southerners regarded Cook as the "Father of Agriculture in America" (Bogardus to Cook, 14 Aug. 1874, Cook papers). When the legislature authorized a State Board of Agriculture in 1872, Cook served as secretary until 1877.

Between 1875 and 1888, Cook directed a geological survey project to complete topographical maps for the entire state. He traveled again to Europe as the New Jersey commissioner to the International Geological Congress in Paris in 1878, adding to his knowledge of glaciers and their effects on the landscape. In his annual geological survey reports, Cook wrote about glacial geology, chemical soil analyses, stone quarries, iron and zinc mines, forestry, water supply, and other subjects of practical application. Adding to his heavily burdened workload, Cook purchased one-quarter share in the East Jersey Proprietors in 1877 to reform land claims and earn extra money; while he became their surveyor general, he failed to make a profit.

At the Rutgers farm Cook continued the practical applicability of his research, concentrating on analyzing fertilizers, improving the dairy herd, and discovering beneficial field crops, including soy beans. The Friends of Agricultural Education, later the Association of American Agricultural College and Experiment Stations, named Cook their New Jersey representative in 1871. In 1880 the state legislature authorized the creation of an agricultural experiment station, the third in the nation, and appointed Cook its first director. He lobbied the federal legislature to pass the Hatch Act of 1887 that subsidized agricultural experimentation. By the end of 1889 Cook had published sixty-four regular and ten special bulletins as well as annual reports for the New Jersey Experiment Station.

In 1887 Cook was elected vice president of Section E of the American Association for the Advancement of Science and received his greatest honor, membership in the National Academy of Sciences. Maintaining his frenetic pace eventually took its toll; Cook wrote to his son of fatigue and complained of chest pains to his doctor a few days before he died at home in New Brunswick.

• Cook's papers are in the Special Collections Department, Alexander Library, Rutgers University. The most complete assessment of his life and work is Jean Wilson Sidar, *George Hammell Cook: A Life in Agriculture and Geology* (1976). J. C. F. Tedrow, "George H. Cook: Pioneer Soil Scientist," *Soil Science* 137 (1984): 231–38, focuses on his contributions to soil science. Detailed obituaries are in the *American Geologist* (Dec. 1889): 321–26, *American Journal of Science* (1889): 498–99, and *Bulletin of the Geological Society of America* (1890): 519–20.

SUSAN HAMBURGER

COOK, George William (7 Jan. 1855–20 Aug. 1931), educator and civil rights leader, was born a slave in Winchester, Virginia. The names of his parents are unknown. In May 1862 the Cook family, which included seven children, became war refugees after the Union capture of Winchester. The family eventually settled in Harrisburg, Pennsylvania, where young George Cook's most important early experience as a free person was working as a servant for David D. Mumma, a Pennsylvania state legislator. Permitted to use the Mumma family library, Cook developed the ambition to seek higher education, which would have remained beyond his grasp except for several fortunate events. After he moved to New York in 1871, Cook learned of Howard University from the Reverend Henry Highland Garnet, a black abolitionist and Howard trustee. Then, in the course of working for a physician, Cook met reformer George B. Cheever, a classmate of Henry Wadsworth Longfellow and Oliver Wendell Holmes. Cheever was so impressed by Cook's eagerness for higher education that he paid Cook's tuition to Howard for one year. Cook entered the Preparatory Department (the university's high school) in 1874, graduated three years later, and entered Howard's College Department. Graduating as valedictorian in 1881, he went on to earn an M.A. from Howard in 1886, an LL.B. in 1898, and an LL.M. in 1899.

Widely regarded as "one of the pillars of Howard University," Cook began his career as a tutor of mathematics and as assistant principal of the Normal Department in 1881. Eight years later he became the principal of the Normal Department, a large but very diverse unit of the university. The department reflected the educational improvisation that had responded to the extraordinary needs of the recently emancipated slaves who attended the institution in its early years and included elementary, secondary, and some college-level instruction as well as courses in music, industrial arts, bookkeeping, and typing. In 1899 the university decided to deemphasize precollegiate work and reorganized the Normal Department into a professional Teachers College like the one founded at Columbia University in 1892. Lewis Baxter Moore was appointed dean of the new Teachers College, and Cook, whose major interest was in business education, served from 1899 to 1905 as the dean of the department responsible for commercial subjects. As a professor of civics and commercial law from 1902 to 1928, Cook's primary objective was the development of a stable business college at Howard. It was not realized in his lifetime. The Commercial College was limited to offering secondary-level subjects (1905–1919), and when these courses were terminated in 1919, Cook succeeded in having commercial subjects included in the new Junior College. When the Junior College was abolished in 1925, Cook was appointed professor of commercial law and international law (which he had taught in the Commercial College since its establishment) in the College of Liberal Arts.

Although Cook's ambitions for business education at Howard were thwarted, he nevertheless became a successful administrator of the university. He was appointed business manager in 1908 and a year later secretary of the university and its board of trustees. For a decade he was the highest-ranking black official at Howard. Respected for his business and administrative ability, Cook was also a civic leader. President Theodore Roosevelt appointed him a member of the District of Columbia Board of Charities in 1904, and the District of Columbia Commissioners in 1907 appointed him as the first superintendent of Washington's school for delinquent black children at Blue Plains, D.C. Cook's wife, the former Coralie Franklin, whom he had married in 1899, was a member of the District of Columbia Board of Education.

Cook became a national figure through his work with the National Association for the Advancement of Colored People (NAACP). From 1912 to 1931 he was treasurer of the nation's largest and most active NAACP branch, in Washington, D.C. He was elected to the NAACP's national board of directors in 1914 and served until his death. Cook was at the center of the controversy during World War I to establish a camp for black officers. The War Department had made provisions to train white officers but maintained that no facilities were available for training black officers. Working closely with Joel Spingarn, the white president of the NAACP, Dean William Pickens of Morgan College (now Morgan State University), and George W. Cabaniss of Washington, Cook was the crucial link between the NAACP, the university, and the black civic leadership of Washington. Acting on his own, Cook offered the campus of Howard University as a training camp. After Cook and others organized the Central Committee of Negro College Men, which recruited qualified candidates for the proposed camp, the War Department finally agreed to establish the Colored Officers Training Camp at Fort Des Moines and a Student Army Training Camp at Howard, which trained 1,786 men. Although the army maintained its policy of racial segregation, the NAACP won one of its early public policy victories in the fight for black officers.

Associated with Howard University for fifty-eight years, Cook served under ten presidents and was an important part of the institution's emergence from a Freedmen's Bureau experiment to a respected university. He retired in 1928, was elected secretary of the General Alumni Association, and continued to live on the campus until his death. He died in Philadelphia after a short illness at his summer home in Asbury Park, New Jersey. Funeral services were held in Andrew Rankin Memorial Chapel at Howard on 24 August. He was buried in Lincoln Cemetery, Washington, D.C., and was survived by his wife and a son. Howard named a men's dormitory in Cook's honor in 1940.

• The George W. Cook Papers are in the Manuscript Division of the Moorland-Spingarn Research Center, Howard University. For Cook's important role in the establishment of the Colored Officers Training Camp at Fort Des Moines, see the Joel Spingarn Papers, Moorland-Spingarn Research Center. Two histories of Howard are important sources for Cook's life: Walter Dyson, *Howard University: The Capstone of Negro Education* (1941), and Rayford W. Logan, *Howard University: The First Hundred Years 1867–1967* (1969).

MICHAEL R. WINSTON

COOK, John Francis (1810?–21 Mar. 1855), educator and clergyman, was born a slave in the District of Columbia. His mother was Laurena Browning Cook, but his father's identity is unknown. His mother's sister, Alethia Browning Tanner, was clearly a dominant influence in his early life. Although she was a slave, her owner allowed her to hire out her own time, and by operating a profitable vegetable market in Washington, D.C., she acquired the money to purchase her own freedom as well as that of her sister and about twenty-one other relatives and acquaintances, including her nephew. Freed at the age of sixteen, Cook apprenticed himself to a shoemaker in order to earn the money repay his aunt.

He completed his apprenticeship in 1831 but abandoned shoemaking because of an injured shoulder. He secured a job as a messenger in the office of the United States Land Commissioner where a white employee, John Wilson, recognized his ability and encouraged him to acquire an education. In his spare time Cook learned to read and write. He attended a school for blacks known as Smothers School but was largely self-educated. In 1834 he assumed charge of the Smothers School and changed its name to Union Seminary.

Cook headed the seminary for the next two decades, except for the year 1835 when an outbreak of anti-Negro violence in Washington, D.C., known as the Snow riot, resulted in extensive damage to the school and prompted him and other free blacks to flee the city. For a year he lived near Philadelphia with a friend, businessman and moral reformer William Whipper, whom he had met at various conventions of free blacks who gathered periodically to address the problems of both slaves and freed persons. Cook had made his first appearance as a delegate to such a convention in New York City in 1834. The following year he served as secretary of a similar gathering in Philadelphia, during which delegates petitioned the federal government to extend full rights to free blacks and to grant immediate emancipation to all slaves. The Philadelphia convention also launched the American Moral Reform Society, created to address "education, temperance, economy and universal liberty," an enterprise enthusiastically supported by Cook. Through his participation in the convention movement, Cook became acquainted with prominent free blacks throughout the United States.

After returning to Washington, D.C., in 1836, Cook resumed direction of Union Seminary. The building underwent extensive renovations to repair damage resulting from the Snow riot, and the school's reputation, as well as Cook's, grew in subsequent years. During some years there were more than 100 students in attendance. Among them were the two mulatto daughters of Vice President Richard M. Johnson.

Always a devout, deeply religious individual, Cook increasingly manifested interest in church affairs after his return to Washington. Associated initially with the African Methodist Episcopal (AME) church, he occasionally filled the pulpit of Israel AME Church and was a founder and trustee of Union Bethel AME Church. In 1840, however, Cook withdrew his membership from Union Bethel and became affiliated with the Presbyterian church. The reasons for his transfer of denominational allegiance are unclear, but it appears that the influence of a white friend, John C. Smith, minister of the Fourth Presbyterian Church of Washington, figured in Cook's decision. When racial tensions in the wake of the Snow riot made it impossible for Fourth Presbyterian to hold a Sabbath school for black children, Smith pressed for the establishment of an all-black Presbyterian congregation in the city and promoted Cook as the one to head it. At Smith's urging, the District of Columbia Presbytery approved the organization of a "colored Presbyterian church," and a group of free blacks meeting at Union Seminary late in 1841 chose Cook as pastor. For the next eighteen months he prepared for the rigorous examinations that he had to pass in order to be ordained. In 1843, less than two decades after receiving his freedom, Cook became the first black person in the District of Columbia to be officially ordained as a minister in the Presbyterian church. His congregation was known as the First Colored Presbyterian Church of Washington.

For the rest of his life, Cook devoted his abundant energies to his church and school. In addition to his teaching duties, he presided over his fledgling congregation, preached, held prayer meetings, organized a Sunday school library and abstinence society, assisted in the formation of the first black ministerial association in the District, and engaged in a variety of fundraising activities. The latter enabled the congregation to construct in 1852 a sizable church on Fifteenth Street, and the name was changed to the Fifteenth Street Presbyterian Church. By the time of his death in Washington, D.C., the church had 120 members, including many of the capital city's most prominent people of color.

Despite the demands of running the church and school, Cook was involved in a wide variety of civic and social uplift activities among blacks. A charter member of the local lodge of the Grand United Order of Odd Fellows, he was a prominent figure in the temperance movement and a founder of Harmony Cemetery for blacks in Washington. Widely respected by both blacks and whites, he possessed a reputation for unimpeachable integrity and public spiritedness.

Cook was married twice. With his first wife, Jane Mann, a woman of Afro-Indian ancestry, he had six children. Upon her death, he married Jane Le Count of Philadelphia; they had one child. The children who lived to adulthood became leaders in their own communities. Among them, John F. Cook, Jr., was a public official and reputedly the wealthiest African American in the District of Columbia at that time; George F. T. Cook headed for many years D.C.'s separate colored school system; and Samuel Le Count Cook graduated from the University of Michigan Medical School and was a physician in the District.

• The Cook Family Papers in the Moorland-Spingarn Research Center, Howard University, Washington, D.C., provide the most important source of information about John F. Cook, Sr. Other sources include Willard B. Gatewood, "John Francis Cook: Antebellum Black Presbyterian," *American Presbyterians: Journal of Presbyterian History* 67 (Fall 1989): 221–30, and "History of the Schools for the Colored Population in the District of Columbia," in Special Report of the Commissioner of Education, *Executive Document* 315, 41st Cong., 2d Sess., 1871, pp. 200–204.

WILLARD B. GATEWOOD

COOK, John Francis, Jr. (21 Sept. 1833–20 Jan. 1910), public official and businessman, was born in Washington, D.C., the son of the prominent African-American clergyman and educator John Francis Cook (1810?–1855) and Jane Mann. Educated first at his father's school, Union Seminary, he later attended Oberlin College in Ohio from 1853 to 1855. Upon the death of their father, he and his brother George F. T. Cook, also a student at Oberlin, returned to Washington to assume direction of Union Seminary. Except for a brief tenure in New Orleans as a schoolteacher, John Cook was connected with the seminary until it ceased operation in 1867 after the District of Columbia opened public schools for blacks. While his brother remained in the education field and was for many years superintendent of the "separate colored school system" in the District of Columbia, John Cook embarked upon a career in government service, Republican politics, and business.

In 1867 Cook secured a clerkship in the office of the District tax collector. A staunch advocate of universal manhood suffrage, he was elected the following year to the Washington board of aldermen in the first election in which blacks were allowed to vote. From 1869 to 1876 he also served as a justice of the peace. After 1868 until his death, he wielded considerable influence in local Republican politics and served as a delegate to the party's national conventions in 1872 and 1880. Careful to cultivate influential friends in Congress and the White House, Cook was appointed District tax collector by President Ulysses S. Grant in 1874 and retained the office for the next decade. Although he later served as jury commissioner in 1889 and was a member of the Board of Children's Guardians for almost two decades beginning in 1892, his tenure as a prominent District official ended when he left the tax collector's office.

During his years as a city official Cook began to accumulate what ultimately became a sizable fortune. By the turn of the century he was reputed to be one of the wealthiest black men in the United States. One knowledgeable observer estimated that his net worth in 1895 was in excess of $200,000. Four years later Cook built a large brick and stone home on Sixteenth Street, described as the most commodious house in Washington owned by an African American. Much of his wealth was derived from wise investments in real estate, including some located in the heart of the city's business district. Known as leaders of Washington's "black 400," Cook and his wife continued to be included in the *Elite List,* a forerunner of the *Social Register,* long after other upper-class blacks had been dropped.

Despite occasional criticism voiced in regard to his family's alleged penchant for social exclusiveness, Cook remained solidly identified with the black community and with various efforts to promote its welfare. For many years he was a trustee of the Home for Destitute Colored Women and Children in Washington. Throughout his career Cook was an effective advocate of civil rights and vigorously opposed Jim Crow practices in the District. Although he had abandoned education as a career, he remained deeply interested in educational matters. He used his influence to win greater public support for black schools, especially after his appointment to the District board of education upon its reorganization in 1906, a position he retained until a few months before his death. No educational institution attracted more of his support than Howard University. A member of the university's board of trustees for thirty-five years (1875–1910), Cook served on its executive committee and on several occasions as its chairman.

Cook was associated with various social and cultural organizations in the District. A conspicuous figure in fraternal circles, he was for a dozen years grand master of the Eureka Lodge, the oldest and most prestigious chapter of Prince Hall Freemasonry in the Washington area. Also, like his father, Cook took an active interest in the Harmony Cemetery Association. A man of "refined" musical taste, he served as president of the Coleridge-Taylor Choral Society, an organization chartered in 1903 "to diffuse among the masses a higher musical culture and appreciation for the works that tend to refine and cultivate." The society sponsored American tours in 1904 and 1906 by the Afro-British composer, Samuel Coleridge-Taylor, for whom it was named. Cook took an interest in the preservation of African-American history. As a trustee of the Frederick Douglass Memorial and Historical Association, he labored to preserve the home of Frederick Douglass, "Cedar Hill," as a historic monument. He and his family were staunch members of the church founded by his father, Fifteenth Street Presbyterian.

Cook was married to Helen Elizabeth Appo of an old and well-known Philadelphia family; they had five children. Prominent in the formation of the National Association of Colored Women, Helen Cook was described by Fannie Barrier Williams as "a noted example and inspiration to women of her own social standing in the serious work of social reform." John Cook died in Washington, D.C. Like his father, he was one of the most influential members of the large and expanding African-American community in the nation's capital for a half century.

• The Cook Family Papers in the Moorland-Spingarn Research Center, Howard University, provide important information on John F. Cook, Jr. Also useful are John W. Cromwell, ed., *The Negro in American History* (1914); Willard B. Gatewood, *Aristocrats of Color: The Black Elite, 1880–1920* (1990); and Constance M. Green, *The Secret City: A History of Race Relations in the Nation's Capital* (1967). See the *Washington Bee*, 29 Jan. 1910, for an obituary.

WILLARD B. GATEWOOD

COOK, John Williston (20 Apr. 1844–15 July 1922), educator and university administrator, was born in Oneida County, New York, the son of Henry DeWitt Cook and Joanna Hall. His family moved, when he was seven years old, to a McClean County, Illinois, farm. Two years later his father became a station agent for the Illinois Central Railroad, and the family took up residence in the village of Kappa. While attending Kappa's one-room school, Cook continued to work on the farm, clerk at a store, and assist his father. In 1862 he entered the five-year-old Illinois State Normal University. Graduating three years later, he became principal of a small school in Brimfield, Illinois. He married Lydia Farnham Spofford in Rutland, Vermont, in 1867; they had two children.

Cook established an early and distinguished career in Illinois education and became a national leader of the "normal school movement," which, in the late nineteenth and early twentieth centuries, attempted to professionalize public school teaching by expanding state-financed, institutionalized teacher training in the United States. In 1866 he returned to Illinois State to accept the principalship of the village grammar school, which served as the university's model school for training teachers. He received an appointment as a temporary university faculty member two years later and taught history and geography. When Cook became a permanent instructor in 1869, he taught reading and elocution. His students characterized him as

rigorous; his fine speaking skills dominated the classroom.

Cook began his long administrative career in 1876 as the chair of mathematics and physics. He remained in this post until 1890, when he succeeded Edwin C. Hewett as university president. For the next nine years Cook directed the physical expansion and intellectual growth of Illinois State. He oversaw the construction of numerous buildings and the doubling of enrollment to 700 students. He also hired several faculty members with degrees from prestigious German universities, namely Charles DeGarmo and brothers Frank McMurry and Charles McMurry. They brought Herbartian methods with them to the Normal University. Cook became a staunch advocate of Herbartian methods, a pedagogical system developed by the German philosopher and educator Johann Friedrich Herbart, which emphasized the interests and moral development of elementary school children, and he used his position to spread this approach. He organized the university's model school along Herbartian lines, and by the 1890s Illinois State had assumed national leadership in the systematic study of pedagogy.

In 1899 Cook left the Normal University to accept the presidency at the newly established Northern Illinois State Normal School in DeKalb. He spent the next twenty years formalizing that institution: he organized the physical plant, hired the faculty, and introduced a two-year teaching-training program. Planning to teach and write at Northern until his retirement, he resigned as president in 1919 but suffered a stroke. Williston Hall at Northern Illinois University bears his name.

Cook brought his views on education to a wider audience through his activities as a writer, editor, and public speaker. Throughout his 54-year career, he contributed countless articles to a variety of school journals, and between 1907 and 1914 he delivered seven speeches before the National Education Association (NEA), largely covering the normal school's role in the professional preparation of teachers and his reflections on the public school curriculum. He also wrote prolifically on pedagogy, focusing on math but also touching on music. In 1892 he coauthored an elementary arithmetic series, which was expanded and reprinted through 1904. Cook published the *Educational History of Illinois* in 1912; he edited the *Illinois Schoolmaster* from 1874 to 1876 and the *Illinois School Journal* between 1883 and 1886. He served as president of the Illinois State Teacher's Association in 1880, the NEA's Normal Department in 1896, and ultimately the NEA in 1904.

A lifelong Unitarian and Republican, and a member of the Quadrangle and University clubs, which catered to socially prominent Chicagoans, he died in that city, having never fully recovered from his earlier stroke. Described by his contemporaries as practical, industrious, thorough, indomitable, and earnest, his educational career encouraged the expansion of public schooling in the late nineteenth century and the professionalization of teaching during the Progressive Era.

• The John Williston Cook Collection at Northern Illinois University in DeKalb includes personal and administrative correspondence, genealogical data, speeches, publications, memorabilia, and photographs. It also claims copies of documents housed in the Cook Collection at Illinois State University, which possesses some scattered papers. The *National Education Association Journal of Proceedings and Addresses* contains Cook's speeches to that organization. *Elementary Arithmetic*, the math series published by John W. Cook and "Miss" N. Cropsey, represents another fascinating primary source. See also George Propeck and Irving F. Pearson, *The History of the Illinois Education Association: Its Influence upon the Development of Public Education within the State* (1961); Henry C. Johnson, Jr., and Erwin V. Johanningmeier, *Teachers for the Prairie: The University of Illinois and the Schools, 1868–1945* (1972); and Jurgen Herbst, *And Sadly Teach: Teacher Education and Professionalization in American Culture* (1989).

RICHARD J. ALTENBAUGH

COOK, Joseph (26 Jan. 1838–24 June 1901), public lecturer, was born Flavius Josephus Cook near Ticonderoga, New York, the son of William Henry Cook and Merrette Lamb, farmers. He attended a series of private academies in Vermont and New York from 1851 to 1855, finishing his preparations for college at Phillips Academy in Andover, Massachusetts. In 1858 he entered Yale. His talents for public speaking and for synthesizing complex arguments in religion and philosophy into popular and attractive formulas quickly blossomed at Yale, where he plunged into an exhausting round of study, debate, and the organization of a student periodical, the *University Quarterly*. The strain of these activities triggered a breakdown in 1861 so severe that Cook was committed to the McLean Asylum for the Insane near Boston. After two years, he recovered sufficiently to be admitted to Harvard as a junior. Graduating in 1865, he entered Andover Theological Seminary, where he graduated in 1868 and stayed for another year as a resident licentiate for further study.

Cook's years at Andover were more in the nature of an exploration of a possible vocation in the Congregational ministry than the product of a settled intention to become a clergyman. His success in organizing a series of preaching missions in East Abington, Massachusetts, in January 1869 gave him some inkling that his real milieu might be found more in the role of public evangelist than in that of parish pastor. A one-year stint as supply pastor to the First Congregational Church in Lynn, Massachusetts, further convinced him that he should establish himself as a "scholar evangelist" who would undertake the task of confronting and repelling modern challenges to Protestant evangelical Christianity, translated from academic into popular terms and cast in the form of the lyceum-style public lecture. Cook thus created for himself a niche between the aggressive but unsophisticated evangelism of revivalists like Dwight L. Moody and the elegant entertainments of the literary lecture circuit where Ralph Waldo Emerson, Mark Twain, and Wendell Phillips held positions of considerable cultural eminence.

After two years of study in Germany, Cook established a regular lecture series in Boston under the sponsorship of the Young Men's Christian Association. Scheduled for Mondays at noon, Cook's lectures quickly drew hundreds of listeners to the Tremont Temple; by 1876 he was filling Tremont Temple with 2,000 hearers, and by the spring of 1877 he was scheduling 125 lectures to be given in Boston and throughout Massachusetts. Cook married Georgianna Hemingway in 1877 after a lengthy courtship; they had no children. In 1879 Cook launched his first transcontinental lecture tour, and from 1880 to 1882 he undertook a world tour that saw him delivering lectures in Great Britain, India, Japan, and Australia. With his return to Boston, Cook's lectures took on an institutional life of their own as the Boston Monday Lectureship, running weekly through a season from fall through spring, and in 1888 he founded a new journal, *Our Day*, to act as auxiliary to the lectureship. (In 1895 he sold *Our Day* to the *Altruistic Review*.) He prospered financially as his lectures were gathered and published (beginning with *Biology, with Preludes on Current Events* in 1877), and he was able to rebuild his childhood home at "Cliff Seat," near Ticonderoga, as a summer mansion. In 1888 Cook embarked on a second world tour, but this time his health collapsed in Australia, and the following four years were spent in a painful and slow recovery. He revived the Boston Monday Lectureship in 1900, but he was far short of his old form. When the new lecture series was completed in June 1901, he retreated to Cliff Seat, where he died suddenly.

Part of Cook's success as a popular lecturer was due to his simple power as an orator: he was a large, imposing man in physical terms, with a powerful voice and the energy to sustain a white-hot, emotionally charged delivery. But the other key to his success was his ability to offer audiences made anxious by the challenges of late nineteenth-century science and the tensions of industrial society a stream of reassuring formulas that promised an irenic accommodation between those anxieties and traditional Protestantism. Cook established early in his lecturing career the strategy of beginning each lecture with a brief editorial comment, or "prelude," on some popular issue or event, from politics to theology. Most frequently, the "preludes" espoused a melioristic "social gospel" that emphasized cooperation, self-help, and social legislation as curatives for industrial problems but stopped short of giving any approval to "insane communists and infuriated socialists." With the audience suitably warmed-up, Cook would then begin the lecture on the subject he had adopted for that season (in 1877, for instance, his lectures were devoted to recent developments in biology and their impact on Christian faith; in following years, they were devoted to such topics as labor, heredity, Transcendentalism, and the family). Of the many themes he addressed over the years, none was more critical to Cook than the intellectual challenges being made to Christian orthodoxy in the name of science. However, despite his declaration in the 1877 lecture series on biology that "the false philosophies of the Occident must be judged as the false religions of the Orient, by the true philosophy, the Christian scheme of thought," he preferred to offer satisfying but superficial reconciliations rather than absolute repudiations of science. He was a fundamentally conservative thinker: his lectures sharply criticized New England Unitarianism and defended traditional Trinitarian orthodoxy, and while he was moderately progressive in his ideas on race relations and the need for protective labor legislation, he also attacked the Pullman strikers and Coxey's Army in 1894. He was often strongly anti-Catholic in his utterances.

• Most of Cook's surviving manuscripts and papers are in the Ticonderoga Historical Society and in the Duke University Library, which also possesses a manuscript biography assembled by Georgianna Cook. Fourteen collections of his lectures were published in book form during his lifetime, with *Biology, with Preludes on Current Events* (1877) and *Orthodoxy, with Preludes on Current Events* (1878) containing the most significant material. Cook also published numerous articles in *Our Day* and in the Congregational periodical *The Independent*. Cook's early letters to his parents were collected and published by F. G. Bascom as *Letters of a Ticonderoga Farmer: Selections from the Correspondence of William H. Cook and His Wife with Their Son Joseph* (1946). His involvement with labor issues is discussed through John T. Cumbler's *Working Class Community in Industrial America* (1977) and Cumbler's edition of Cook's Lynn sermons from 1871, *A Moral Response to Industrialism: The Lectures of Reverend Cook in Lynn, Massachusetts* (1982). The most important modern assessments of Cook's career are Steven R. Pointer's "Joseph Cook: Apologetics and Science," *American Presbyterians* 63 (Fall 1985): 299–308, and Pointer's biography, *Joseph Cook, Boston Lecturer and Evangelical Apologist* (1991). Obituaries are in the *New York Times* and the *New York Tribune*, 26 June 1901.

ALLEN C. GUELZO

COOK, Philip (30 July 1817–20 May 1894), soldier and congressman, was born in Twiggs County, Georgia, the son of Philip Cook, a cotton planter and former field officer in the Eighth U.S. Infantry, and Martha Wooten. Cook was educated at a local academy, which he left in 1836 to join a volunteer company recruited for service in Florida during the Seminole Wars. When his enlistment was up, he attended Oglethorpe University in Milledgeville, Georgia, and the law school of the University of Virginia, graduating from the latter in 1841. The following year he married Sara Lumpkin; they had two children. Thereafter, except for three terms in the state legislature, one in the lower house (1854) and two in the senate (1859–1860, 1863–1864), Cook practiced law in the town of Oglethorpe.

A member of a Macon County militia company, Cook accompanied the unit into Confederate service immediately after the April 1861 shelling of Fort Sumter. His military experience, brief as it was, recommended him for a commission, and he was soon elected adjutant of the regiment his company had joined,

the Fourth Georgia Infantry. Early in May 1861 the outfit was sent to Norfolk, Virginia, where it did outpost duty for several months before being transferred to the Virginia Peninsula. The following spring the Fourth Georgia helped block Major General George B. McClellan's advance toward the Confederate capital at Richmond.

At Malvern Hill, 1 July 1862, the last of the Seven Days' battles on the Peninsula, Lieutenant Cook experienced his baptism of fire. Late that afternoon the Fourth Georgia, part of the division of Major General Robert E. Rodes, spearheaded a doomed assault by the Army of Northern Virginia against infantry and artillery atop an elevated plateau along the James River. By great exertion, the Fourth got to within 200 yards of the enemy line, where Lieutenant Cook was wounded by a shell fragment.

During Cook's recuperation, which caused him to miss the campaign of Second Manassas, he was promoted to lieutenant colonel on the unanimous recommendation of his fellow officers. At Sharpsburg, Maryland, on 17 September, the new field officer won the commendation of his immediate superior, Brigadier General George F. Doles, for his "gallant and meritorious conduct" during the bloodiest day of the war. Although it came under artillery fire on 13 December, Cook's outfit was not committed to the principal fighting at Fredericksburg.

During the 2 May 1863 action in the Virginia Wilderness, Cook, now a colonel, and his regiment helped lead Thomas J. "Stonewall" Jackson's offensive against the right flank of the Army of the Potomac. Just before sundown, the Fourth Georgia overwhelmed a sector of the XI Corps line, captured six cannon, and pursued Federals to a second defensive line near the crossroads named Chancellorsville. Charging that position in an attempt to seize additional guns, Cook's leg was broken by a Minié ball.

The wound disabled Cook for three months. After being hospitalized at Richmond, he was invalided back to Georgia. While at home, Cook learned that the voters of his district had returned him to the state senate. He took his seat at Milledgeville, where he served for six weeks. Briefly rejoining the army at Orange Court House, Virginia, he returned to Georgia for the second half of the legislative session, then retook the field in July 1864. At once he assumed command of Doles's brigade, whose leader had been killed the previous month at Cold Harbor. On 5 August Cook was promoted to brigadier general.

During Cook's absence in Georgia, the brigade had accompanied Major General Jubal A. Early from the Petersburg front to the Shenandoah Valley. Now Early was opposed by a Union army under Major General Philip H. Sheridan. The brigade saw hard fighting throughout the summer, and by late September it had been reduced to fewer than 400 effectives. Enlarged somewhat by recruits and returned detachments, the brigade lost heavily on 19 October at Cedar Creek, where an initially successful Confederate drive turned into crushing defeat at Sheridan's hands. At about

4:00 P.M., a Union counterattack caused supporting troops on Cook's left to give way; thereafter, "all was confusion and disorder." Cook and his few unwounded subordinates rallied 200 men, only to be forced into retreat. Despite the outcome, his superiors praised Cook for "great coolness and judgment" in attempting to stem the rout.

Early in 1865 Cook led what remained of his command back to the Petersburg front. During the forlorn attack on Fort Stedman on 25 March, he was for a third time severely wounded. He finished the war in a Petersburg hospital, where he was captured and paroled after the city fell on 3 April.

Returning to Georgia, Cook resumed his law practice, first at Oglethorpe, then in Americus, interrupting it to hold political office on the state and national levels. In late 1865 he was a delegate to the Georgia constitutional convention. In 1872 he was elected to the first of five consecutive terms in the U.S. House of Representatives, where he served as chair of the Committee on Public Buildings. Upon retiring from Congress, he was appointed to a commission that superintended the erection of a new state capitol in Atlanta. In the early 1880s he retired from his law practice and to the life of a gentleman farmer, but in 1890 he was lured back to the public arena as Georgia's secretary of state. He died in office and was succeeded by his son.

By all accounts, Cook was one of the more distinguished regimental and brigade commanders in the Army of Northern Virginia. Yet the quiet, unostentatious Georgian remains an unsung hero of the Confederacy. One reason for his neglect by historians is his relatively brief service in the major theater of the war, the result of long stints in the hospital and the legislature. Whenever in the field, however, he maintained a reputation for effective leadership and "uncommonly meritorious character" that earned him the respect and confidence of superiors, subordinates, and the rank and file. In the civilian realm, Cook's eighteen years in public office were marked by competence, energy, and integrity. A close acquaintance observed, "In every position he discharged the duties belonging to it with fidelity to the State and with credit to himself. . . . [He] had not only the esteem, but the affection of the people of Georgia in as large a measure as any man of his time."

• The few personal papers of Cook that survive are in collections pertaining to James P. Hambleton in the Emory University Library, Atlanta, and to William Jones in the Georgia Historical Society, Savannah. Cook's war service through mid-1863 receives attention in the papers of Lieutenant Colonel David R. E. Winn of the Fourth Georgia, also at Emory University. Biographical accounts include Clement A. Evans, ed., *Confederate Military History*, vol. 6 (11 vols., 1899); William J. Northen, ed., *Men of Mark in Georgia*, vol. 3 (6 vols., 1907–1912); and Douglas Southall Freeman, *Lee's Lieutenants* (3 vols., 1942–1944). A source on his Confederate career is Henry W. Thomas, *History of the Doles-Cook Brigade, Army of Northern Virginia* (1903). Although it contains no battle or campaign reports by Cook, *The War of the Rebellion: A Compilation of the Official Records of the Union and* *Confederate Armies* (128 vols., 1880–1901) sheds some light on his activities at Chancellorsville, Cedar Creek, and elsewhere. A useful obituary is in the *Atlanta Constitution*, 21 May 1894.

EDWARD G. LONGACRE

COOK, Russell Salmon (6 Mar. 1811–4 Sept. 1864), itinerant preacher and religious writer, was born in New Marlborough, Massachusetts, the son of Benjamin W. Cook. His mother's name is unknown. After studying law, he attended Auburn Theological Seminary (1833–1835), where he pursued graduate studies (1835–1836). In 1836 he began work at the Congregational church in Lanesboro, in his native Berkshire County, Massachusetts. He was ordained pastor on 18 January 1837 and married Ann Maria Mills in November. They were later divorced, and she moved to Stonington, Connecticut.

After one year in his pastorate, his voice began to fail, and he ordered several volumes from the New York–based American Tract Society (ATS) to help him in his ministry. Cook soon left his parish ministry and began work for the ATS as a general agent for volume circulation, a project that sought to provide one book or tract for every American household. During his work for the ATS in 1838, he preached nearly fifty sermons; traveled 4,500 miles as he criss-crossed Hartford, Connecticut; Providence, Rhode Island; western New York; and Vermont; and sold nearly 36,000 volumes worth about $8,000. He reported similar successes for an early 1839 southern tour.

In May 1839 the duties of the secretary of ATS were divided, and Cook became corresponding secretary, bearing chief responsibilities for volume circulation, tract visitation, and the publication of the *American Tract Magazine*. His job required him to travel outside of New York City at least three months of every year.

At a special meeting on 17 June 1841, the ATS adopted its system of colportage under Cook's leadership. Taking its name from the French Protestant system of traveling missionary booksellers, colportage employed low-salaried itinerants to distribute the tracts and message of the ATS to towns and cities, to villages and farms, to sailors and soldiers, and to recent immigrants. Increasingly, publications in Danish, Dutch, French, Hungarian, Italian, German, Norwegian, Portuguese, Spanish, Swedish, and Welsh supplemented the hundreds of English-language titles distributed by colporteurs. Under the direction of district superintendents, colporteurs served simultaneously as merchants and evangelists and were frequently called on to preach in less settled areas. The first two American colporteurs were commissioned in June 1841 and began work in August. Fifteen years later the ATS employed 547 full-time colporteurs and 155 summer theological students and reported annual receipts of $415,000.

In 1841 Cook married Harriet Newell Rand of Pompey Hill, New York, who wrote *The Scripture Alphabet of Animals* (1842) and *The Trees, Fruits, and Flowers of the Bible* (1846) for the ATS. She died sometime before the May 1845 meeting of the society, and Cook subsequently married Harriet Ellsworth of Hartford, Connecticut.

In addition to supervising the colportage system, Cook wrote and published extensively for the ATS. In 1843 he merged the bimonthly *Trust Magazine* with his new monthly, *American Messenger*, increasing its circulation from 10,000 to 200,000 copies with an additional 2,500 copies in German. Cook wrote ATS tract No. 493, *Beware of Bad Books* (1847), which presented the "different classes of injurious books, and their evil influence on the mind and character." In 1852 he instituted the *Child's Paper*, which achieved a circulation of 300,000 within two years.

Cook defended the American Tract Society as it came under increasing attack in the early 1850s for its refusal to condemn slavery. Several of its reissued pamphlets dropped any reference to slavery, lest slaveholders be offended, but critics pointed out that the ATS showed no such scruples in condemning alcohol, theater, horse racing, dancing, gambling, and travel on the Sabbath. The issue came to a head in 1858 when the Boston Tract Society declared its independence.

From April to November 1853 Cook traveled throughout Europe, meeting with leaders of tract societies in England, Scotland, France, Switzerland, Germany, and Belgium. After a bout of rheumatic fever in March 1856 he sailed to Switzerland in May and then went on to England and Scotland in October. Returning to Switzerland, he suffered a severe pleuritic attack, forcing him to resign from the ATS in January 1857.

Cook recovered and returned to New York, where in the autumn of 1857 he became corresponding secretary of the newly founded New York Sabbath Committee, organized to promote the Christian observance of Sunday as a day of rest. After a return visit to Europe in July 1858, he published his observations as *The Sabbath in Europe: The Holy Day of Freedom—The Holiday of Despotism* (1858). On one of his trips to Europe, he married the daughter of Caesar Malan of Geneva, Switzerland, the author of more than five volumes of tracts. During the last years of his life, he visited Florida and Maine in vain efforts to forestall his illness. He died in Pleasant Valley, New York.

• Cook wrote frequently for the ATS and the New York Sabbath Committee in his capacity as corresponding secretary, and their publications and annual reports are a valuable source. The ATS report *The American Colporteur System* (1843), reprinted in *The American Tract Society Documents, 1824–1925* (1972), tells of the early years of colportage. His *Report of a Western Tour* includes his recommendations for strengthening the colportage system, and his *Benevolence and Economy of American Colportage* (1859) defends the ATS and its system of colportage against British accusations of financial extravagance. Many of the abolitionist attacks against the ATS mention Cook by name, including William Jay's *Letter to the American Tract Society* (1853) and the *Unanimous Remonstrance of the Fourth Congregational Church, Hartford, Connecticut, against the Policy of the American Tract Society on the Subject of Slavery* (1855).

The dissertation of former ATS general director Stephen Elmer Slocum, Jr., "The American Tract Society, 1825–1975: An Evangelical Effort to Influence the Religious and Moral Life of the United States" (Ph.D. diss., New York Univ., 1975), includes a bibliographic summary and brief survey of the ATS activities during Cook's years. Lawrence Thompson, "The Printing and Publishing Activities of the American Tract Society from 1825 to 1850," *Papers of the Bibliographical Society of America* 35 (1941), covers many of Cook's years at the ATS. A memorial tribute is included in the 1865 *Annual Report of the American Tract Society*, and Cook is listed in the *General Biographical Catalogue of Auburn Theological Seminary* (1918).

DAVID B. McCARTHY

COOK, Vivian E. J. (6 Oct. 1890–28 July 1977), educator, was born Vivian Elma Johnson in Colliersville, Tennessee, the daughter of Spencer Johnson, a farmer, and Caroline Alley, a teacher. One of eight children, she grew up under the enterprising spirit of her parents, both of whom were born in slavery. The fact that her mother was the first black schoolteacher in the Tennessee community of Fayette County set a special standard of achievement for her and her seven siblings. The family moved to Memphis when she was very young and the decision was made to favor the girls with a higher education. All four were to graduate from college, but Vivian, thanks to the financial assistance of a brother, inventor and railway postal clerk Thomas W. Johnson, was able to attend Howard University and later earn a master's degree in English from Columbia University.

In 1912, the year of her graduation from Howard, she accepted a post at Tuskegee Institute under Booker T. Washington, which was the beginning of her teaching career. Over one summer session at Tuskegee, she directed the Children's House, a demonstration school where visiting black educators could observe teaching methods. Though extended an invitation from Washington to return to Tuskegee for a second year, she chose instead to take a post in 1913 in Cincinnati under the principalship of an educator who had observed her at the Children's House. Her year in Cincinnati was followed by several years as an English teacher at Summer High in St. Louis, then one of the leading black high schools in the nation. In 1918 she married Ralph Victor Cook, a graduate in engineering from Cornell and a member of the prominent Cook family of Washington, D.C., whom she had met in graduate school at Columbia in 1918, the summer in which she received her master's degree. The couple had one son, who died in infancy.

Teaching science and English, she joined Ralph Cook, who headed mechanical drawing, at Baltimore's Colored High School, which was later named Frederick Douglass High School. While teaching in Baltimore in 1921, she called a meeting of African-American women to found the Epsilon Omega Chapter, Alpha Kappa Alpha Sorority, the first chapter of this sorority on the East Coast, which she headed for two years. Three years later Cook organized the Baltimore branch of the National Association of College Women and later served as its president for two terms, from 1933 to 1937. Meanwhile, she found time to do additional graduate work at the University of Chicago.

With relatively deep roots in Baltimore by the 1930s, she cofounded, in 1933, the Philomathian Club, which was established to honor outstanding women of color. By then in her early forties, Cook was emerging as a figure of national reputation in black America, exchanging correspondence with Mary McCloud Bethune, perhaps the most distinguished black female educator of the period, and with Mordecai Johnson, the prestigious president of Howard University.

With Ralph Cook a member of the Boule, a social club of black men that boasted the memberships of civil rights pioneer W. E. B. Du Bois and chemist Percy Julian, and with Cook a power in a number of women's organizations, the couple's social network was among the most influential in black America. But both were mainly committed to the uplift of their people. As such, they were members of what Du Bois called "the talented tenth," that minority of gifted blacks who would use their considerable talent to help raise their people as a whole, which was what Cook had in mind when using the word "service."

As a member of the talented tenth, she promoted African-American history and culture before it was fashionable to do so, annually helping sponsor programs for that purpose. Together with other educators in the Baltimore community, Cook brought distinguished students of the arts, such as Alain Locke, the first black Rhodes scholar and a leading theorist of black culture, to Baltimore to lecture. In addition, as chair of the Art Committee of the Cooperative Women's Civic League, she led initiatives for the work of black artists to be exhibited at the Baltimore Museum of Art. Occasionally she saw, but frequently corresponded with, the great storyteller and folklorist William John Faulkner, who was married to a relative of her husband.

She was an elegant woman of regal bearing toward whom others displayed the reserve—admiring from a distance—that she was known to inspire in those around her. Her praise, if only because it seemed to come from such lofty heights, drove home, as did her criticism. Some thought that she moved in circles that were elitist, that there was about her something of the aristocrat in both style and choice of friends, but her example of excellence was placed before such large numbers of blacks over so long a period of time that her influence on social progress was unmistakable.

Despite the barriers of race in the segregated environment in which she worked, she commanded attention and respect from white people. In fact, her pioneering in segregated Baltimore schools, in some respects, transcended race: she was the first woman counselor in the Baltimore school system and went on to become the first black woman to hold an administrative post in a secondary school. In addition, after serving as vice principal and principal of Baltimore schools, she became principal of Dunbar High School, the largest school in Baltimore and the state with its 3,800 students. In her first year as principal of Dunbar, she was given the Future Teachers of America Award of Merit. In 1949 she received the Howard University Alumni Medal for Achievement in Education. During the years of her distinguished principalship at Dunbar, from 1951 to 1956, she was also a member of the National Executive Board of the Association for the Study of Negro Life and History. There could be no better illustration of her stature in those years than when future Supreme Court justice Thurgood Marshall, already with more than twenty victories before the Court, paid tribute to her at Grace Memorial Church in Baltimore on 20 January 1952.

The matriarch of a family in which there were many success stories, she contributed financially to the efforts of numerous family members to prepare for their careers. And for one who subjected herself to discipline at least as stern as that she encouraged in others, no one took greater pride in family accomplishments and no one was more adept than she at surveying the family to determine who was next on the list of those deserving special encouragement.

After her retirement from Dunbar in 1956, she became assistant director of practice teaching in the Teacher-Education Department of Morgan State College in Baltimore. By then she was a widely recognized pioneer in education, in forwarding black history, civil rights, civic affairs, and women's rights. She stands as one of the foremost champions of women's rights not so much by preachment as by having demonstrated that women, despite racial and other odds imposed on them, can perform with brilliance. More than that, she is distinguished for having founded important institutions that have endured after her death in Baltimore, Maryland.

• Cook's papers are housed at the Moorland-Spingarn Collection at Howard University. A useful source is "Vivian E. J. Cook: Pioneer Educator—Civic and Social Leader," appeared in two installments in the magazine section of the *Baltimore Afro-American*, 27–31 Jan. and 3–7 Feb. 1976. An obituary appeared in the *Baltimore Sun*, 1 Aug. 1977.

STERLING STUCKEY

COOK, Walter Wheeler (4 June 1873–7 Nov. 1943), law professor and a principal formulator of the legal realist school of jurisprudence, was born in Columbus, Ohio, the son of Ezekiel Hanson Cook, a school principal and teacher of mathematics, and Clara Wing Coburn, an instructor in French.

Cook attended Columbus public schools, then two schools headed by his father, the Potsdam, New York, State Normal and Preparatory Training School and the Rutgers College Preparatory School. He received an A.B. degree from Columbia University in 1894, winning awards in mechanics and physics. After graduation, he was hired by Columbia as an assistant in mathematics and continued his studies in mathematical physics. He then studied in Germany as a fellow of Columbia.

While in Germany, the intellectual curiosity for which Cook was always known apparently led him to reconsider whether mathematics should be his life work. Immediately upon his return to Columbia, he began to study law and political science. He received an A.M. degree in 1899 and the LL.M. degree in 1901. He married Helen Newman of Washington, D.C., in 1899; they had four children.

In 1901 Cook became an instructor teaching jurisprudence and political science at the University of Nebraska, where he began his association with Roscoe Pound, an important early spokesman for sociological jurisprudence in America and an important influence on Cook for his articulation of the notion that the actual operation of a legal system and the formally stated specification of that system often diverge. Cook became professor of law in two years and remained at the University of Nebraska until 1904, when he rose through a sequence of positions in the hierarchy of prestigious law schools, from the University of Missouri (1904–1906) to the University of Wisconsin (1906–1910), the University of Chicago (1910–1916), Yale (1916–1919), Columbia (1919–1922), where he received the highest salary of any law professor in the United States ($10,000 a year), and, again, Yale (1922–1928).

As a professor, Cook was known for his demanding classroom and conversational style. One scholar concludes that he was an "essentially shy" person "who made up for that shyness with a kind of sustained bluster" (Schlegel, p. 68). Cook's frankness and intensity made him a difficult colleague on occasion; even an admirer acknowledged Cook's "lack of facility in compromise" and wrote that he "offered even his allies only the goad and the hair shirt." Because his theoretical approaches conflicted with those of more traditionally minded persons, Cook often found himself disagreeing with university administrations and traditionalists in his profession. He always insisted that law schools should shape students for the larger duties of the profession—not only for "practicing law," but also for serving as judges, legislators, members of administrative commissions, and active citizens, sufficiently informed about social conditions to factor in such information in all decision-making.

Although he taught and published in several areas, including the procedure in ordinary civil cases and in cases in the "equity" courts, Cook made his primary contribution to the area of conflict of laws. That area concerns the rules courts are to apply when they deal with cases involving transactions, including accidents, contracts, and marriages, that have elements that traverse several states or nations, as when a person is injured in one state and dies in another or when a person barred by one state's law from entering into a contract signs one in another state. When Cook began to write in the field, the prevailing view, articulated most forcefully in the United States by Joseph Beale, was that a court should identify the one state or nation that

has jurisdiction over the entire transaction—for example, because the injury was inflicted or the contract signed there—and then apply that state's rule.

Cook vigorously argued against this view. As he saw it, its proponents were trapped in a world of concepts and purportedly logical deductions. They improperly used, in Cook's eyes, "figurative" or metaphoric language as if the metaphors described real entities. He examined many areas of law to demonstrate both that courts regularly acted in ways inconsistent with the recommendations of Beale and his followers and that the concepts they thought necessarily singled out one state or nation as the proper lawmaker for the transaction actually could rationally be understood in many different ways. Cook called himself a "heretic" in the field, for, as he wrote, he found that "nearly all writers were obsessed with indefensible theories which neither accounted for what the courts were doing nor led to useful decisions if logically applied."

Cook's approach was generally described as destructive. A bit uncomfortable at the charge, Cook nonetheless defended himself as performing a vital ground-clearing function. Drawing on a metaphor from his pastime of gardening, Cook wrote, "until the intellectual garden is freed of the rank weeds in question useful vegetables cannot grow and flourish." Consistent with the tenets of the legal realist jurisprudence that Cook helped create, his critical analyses of existing approaches to conflict of laws pointed in the direction of introducing what he called policy considerations to offset the conceptualism he criticized, but Cook himself did not explore those policy considerations in detail. Cook's writings were an essential part of the background for what came to be known as the revolution in conflict of laws that took hold in the 1950s and 1960s under the influence of Professors David Cavers and Brainerd Currie and Judges Roger Traynor and Stanley Fuld, who acknowledged the contribution Cook made to their endeavors.

Cook's more general jurisprudence was shaped by his early attraction to natural science and by his studies with John Dewey while on the Columbia faculty. He repeatedly urged that law was an empirical social science, which should take the natural sciences rather than deductive mathematics as its model. In recognizing the importance of the scientific method in the processes of gathering and evaluating facts relevant to the law, he sought to make studying law an objective inquiry into an important social institution rather than an unguided set of speculations about what "the law" required. Generalizations in law, as in science, were "working hypotheses, mental devices to which we resort in order to deal more effectively with our experiences." Although Cook had a sophisticated understanding of the scientific method in the natural sciences, his statements about its application to law were often quite unfocused and unhelpful. To settle a new case, he wrote, "our real task is to determine whether the differences involved which make us think of it as new, are as a practical matter, i.e., as tested by their consequences, important for the purpose we have in view." While unexceptionable, these precepts did little to advance the scientific study of law.

While teaching at Columbia and Yale, Cook joined other legal scholars and educators in urging reform in American legal education. Frank Goodnow, the president of the Johns Hopkins University, invited Cook to visit the university and design a school of jurisprudence, to be called the Law Institute of the Johns Hopkins University. Cook spent the years from 1926 to 1928 doing so. Cook brought to the institute an intense interest in improving the lawyer's ability to predict what judges would do, a task he analogized to the scientist's attempt to predict how atoms and electrons would behave. Writing in 1927, Cook sketched out "a university school of law" in which students would learn the scientific method and "study the actual structure and functioning of modern social, economic, and political life," so that they would "not rely upon hit-or-miss information which has been picked up accidentally." The objective was to study "the actual operation of our law."

Cook believed that the Johns Hopkins University Institute could be such a school of law, but his efforts failed, in part because the institute did not develop support within the university and from the Rockefeller Foundation, both of which underwent leadership changes precisely at times when the institute needed their support. He and his colleagues who founded the institute had a naive understanding of what scientific studies of law could actually produce, in part because they were unschooled in the social sciences and proposed a grab-bag of research projects that did not reflect a well-considered intellectual project. The institute's research focused on judicial statistics designed to produce data that would allow the states to manage their judicial systems in a more businesslike way. Cook directed a study of Maryland's civil courts, but this and the institute's other studies were rather far removed from the vision Cook had of a university school of law. Although his vision was to unify a law school with a research institute, the institute actually bore little resemblance to a school for training practicing lawyers. Pursuing his work in jurisprudence and the conflict of laws, Cook remained at the institute until it was dissolved in 1933; having been unsuccessful in obtaining external funding for the institute, the university could no longer support it under the financial strains created by the Great Depression.

In 1931, following the death of his first wife, Cook married Elizabeth Stabler Iddings of Baltimore, who survived him. With the Johns Hopkins Institute's dissolution, Cook managed to obtain a paid though part-time position as the general secretary of the American Association of University Professors, of which he had been a charter member and president (1931–1933). His friends also arranged for him to serve as chair of the Committee on Enrollment and Disbarment of the Treasury Department in Washington, where he reorganized the procedures for licensing attorneys to practice before the department. In 1935 Cook returned to teaching at Northwestern University, where he re-mained until his retirement in 1943. He was a fellow of the American Association for the Advancement of Science, president of the American Association of Law Schools (1916–1917), and a member of numerous other academic associations. He died in the Mercy General Hospital at Tupper Lake, New York.

The critical dimensions of Cook's legal realism were broadly influential, both within the field of conflict of laws and beyond it. His critique of general legal categories led him to insist that traditional approaches to legal analysis concealed the real policy choices that were always part of the law. Those choices should be "based upon considerations of social or economic policy . . . estimating as far as possible the consequences of a decision one way or the other." Commonplace today and not entirely novel when Cook wrote, these views were nonetheless unusual when Cook first articulated them and have become part of the American lawyer's outlook in part because of Cook's work.

• Cook's papers, now held in private hands, are to be deposited at the Northwestern University Law School Library. Other papers related to his teaching are in archives at the Yale University Law School and the Harvard University Law School. His major work in conflict of laws is *The Logical and Legal Bases of Conflict of Laws* (1942). A statement of his personal philosophy is contained in his essay in *My Philosophy of Law: Credos of Sixteen American Scholars* (1941). Biographical information is available in the memorials published in the Association for American Law School *Handbook* (1943) and the *Illinois Law Review*, Mar.–Apr. 1944, by Charles E. Clark, Homer F. Carey, and Hessel E. Yntema. On the Johns Hopkins University Institute and Cook's role in legal realism, see John Henry Schlegel, *American Legal Realism and Empirical Social Science* (1995).

THE EDITORS

COOK, Will Marion (27 Jan. 1869–20 July 1944), composer and librettist, was born in Washington, D.C., the son of John Hartwell Cook, a professor of law at Howard University, and Marion Isabel Lewis, a sewing instructor. He received classical violin training at the Oberlin Conservatory of Music (1884–1887). For approximately the next decade he presumably studied violin and composition with the German violinist Joseph Joachim at the Hochschule für Musik in Berlin (1888–1889?), and he continued harmony and counterpoint training under Antonín Dvořák and John White at the National Conservatory of Music in New York City (1893–1895?).

Cook was a prolific composer whose instrumentals and songs were closely related to the craze for cakewalking and two-stepping. His first musical success began with the show *Clorindy, the Origin of the Cakewalk* (1898), which he originally wrote for the vaudevillian comedians Bert Williams and George Walker, although it was first performed with Ernest Hogan in the lead. This landmark production departed from the minstrel tradition in two ways: first, by employing syncopated ragtime music; and second, by introducing the cakewalk to Broadway audiences. The show, which opened at the Casino Roof Garden Theatre in

New York, emerged along with Bob Cole's *A Trip to Coontown* as one of the first all-black shows to play in a major Broadway theater, and Cook became the first black conductor of a white theater orchestra. The author James Weldon Johnson noted that Cook "was the first competent composer to take what was then known as rag-time and work it out in a musicianly way" (*Black Manhattan*, p. 103). The show's star, Abbie Mitchell, became Cook's wife in 1899. They were divorced in 1906, but continued to work together in show business; they had two children.

Clorindy presented songs that countered minstrel stereotypes. Whereas many of the tunes, notably "Hottes' Coon in Dixie" and "Who Dat Say Chicken in Dis Crowd?", continued in the minstrel tradition, others, such as the choral "On Emancipation Day" and the hauntingly lyrical "Ghost Ship" (unpublished), were stirring tunes that reflected black pride and the pain of middle passage. The production played throughout the summer of 1898 at the Casino in New York. After a brief but successful tour the show was incorporated into the Williams and Walker Company as part of their vaudeville routine.

In the first decade of the twentieth century Cook emerged as an original, if sometimes erratic, genius of musical comedy. He teamed with Paul Laurence Dunbar, Alex Rogers, Joe Jordan, Williams and Walker, Jessie A. Shipp, Cecil Mack, J. Rosamond Johnson, and James Weldon Johnson to produce some of the most popular musical shows, vaudeville, and hit tunes. Cook's next three productions, *The Casino Girl* (1900), *The Policy Players* (1900), and *Jes Lak White Fo'ks* (1900), failed to duplicate his *Clorindy* success, but his fortunes turned upward when he created the music for Williams and Walker's *In Dahomey* (1902–1905), *Abyssinia* (1906–1907), and *Bandana Land* (1907–1909). *In Dahomey* opened successfully in New York, establishing the Williams and Walker Company as the premier black musical comedy troupe for the remainder of the decade. In addition, the show toured throughout Great Britain during the 1903–1904 season.

In 1910 Cook formed the New York Syncopated Orchestra, which toured the United States that same year. He also formed the orchestra known as the Clef Club in 1912, a group of black musicians and entertainers. Both the Syncopated Orchestra and the Clef Club performed a mixture of Cook's music, as well as popular and classical music. His most popular songs, along with those from *Clorindy*, were "Swing Along," a satiric choral piece on relations between blacks and whites, "Mandy Lou," "Red, Red Rose," "Exhortation: A Negro Sermon," "Brown Skin Baby Mine," "Darktown Is Out Tonight," "Nobody Knows the Trouble I See," and "The Rain Song." In 1918 Cook moved his Syncopated Orchestra to Europe, and he was largely instrumental in creating the vogue for black musicians there and in England.

Cook's classical musical education proved a mixed blessing. Endowed with tremendous talent, his refusal to tolerate racism in the white world and show business egos in his own circles alienated him from many friends and colleagues. During the last two decades of his life Cook's productivity declined, but he did compose *In Darkydom* (1914) and fragments of a Negro folk opera called *St. Louis Woman* (1929). He also wrote spirituals, such as "Troubled in Mind" (1929), and during World War II he and his son Will Mercer Cook composed patriotic songs.

Abbie Mitchell referred to him as "a giant in experience, a sincere student of music in spite of all statements to the contrary, notwithstanding his eccentricities, his erratic temperament, which in later years caused him many disappointments, much poverty, loss of influence, contacts and friends and a deep sorrow" (Mercer Cook Papers). He died in New York City's Harlem Hospital.

• Valuable sources of information on Cook include the Mercer Cook Papers, Moorland-Spingarn Research Center, Howard University; the Theatre Museum, London; the Music Division, Library of Congress; and the Billy Rose Theatre Collection at the New York Public Library for the Performing Arts, Lincoln Center. Cook's essay "Clorindy, the Origin of the Cakewalk," *Theatre Arts* 31, no. 9 (Sept. 1947): 61–65, provides a reflective view of the show's opening. Interviews conducted in London include those in *The Tatler*, 20 May 1903, p. 300; and *Daily News* (16 May 1903), p. 6. Also informative are Elton Fax's entry on Cook in the *Dictionary of American Negro Biography* (1982); Thomas L. Riis, *Just Before Jazz* (1989); Riis, *More than Just Minstrel Shows* (1992); Henry T. Sampson, *Blacks in Blackface* (1980); Lester Walton, "Will Marion Cook," *New York Age*, 7 May 1908; and Jeffrey P. Green, "*In Dahomey* in London in 1903," *The Black Perspective in Music* 11, no. 1 (Spring 1983): 22–40. See also Marva Griffin Carter, *The Life and Music of Will Marion Cook* (1988); Eileen Southern, *The Music of Black Americans: A History* (1971); James Weldon Johnson, *Along This Way* (1933); Johnson, *Black Manhattan* (1930); and Bernard L. Peterson, *A Century of Musicals in Black and White* (1993). An obituary is in the *New York Times*, 21 July 1944.

DAVID KRASNER

COOKE, Ebenezer. *See* Cook, Ebenezer.

COOKE, Elisha (16 Sept. 1637–31 Oct. 1715), politician and colonial agent, was born in Boston, Massachusetts, the son of Richard Cooke, a wealthy tailor, and Elizabeth Leverett. Elisha graduated from Harvard in 1657 and began practicing as a physician. He added to his inheritance by accumulating considerable wealth in shares in ships, a saw mill in Maine, and various landholdings. In June 1668 he married Elizabeth Leverett, the daughter of Governor John Leverett and his second wife Sarah. Two children survived to adulthood, including one son, Elisha Cooke, Jr., who succeeded him as leader of Massachusetts's opposition faction. In 1673 he became a freeman and for the next twenty-nine years held numerous positions of influence.

Cooke's political career rested on his sustained defense of the Massachusetts Bay Company Charter. According to Thomas Hutchinson, he "had always adhered stiffly to the old charter and when all the rest of the assistants declined resuming it, he alone was in favor of it." Elected a deputy in 1681, he opposed sending agents to London to defend the charter, believing that any form of negotiation compromised the colony's autonomy. He was so hostile to any infringement on the charter's privileges that Edward Randolph included him among a faction sent to London to answer for high misdemeanors. The popularity of his stance led to a meteoric rise in political influence; he was elected speaker of the house in 1683 and an assistant the following year. Cooke's election to assistant in 1684 displaced Joseph Dudley and marked the beginning of a rivalry that continued into the next generation. The clash between Cooke and Dudley over the charter, with moderates like Increase Mather caught between, illustrated the transformation of political life in Massachusetts as it moved from autonomous colony to an imperial province. Unlike Cooke, Dudley was more amenable to the increases in royal regulation; as his subsequent career indicated, he was ambitious and capable of effectively currying political favor in England. Dudley's ascendancy and Cooke's demise reflected the ways in which the interplay of debate over the charter, the Dominion of New England, and the extent of imperial intervention in colonial affairs altered the bases for political success.

Cooke served as an assistant until the charter was revoked and Dudley was charged with heading the interim government. Subsequently replaced as the head of the Dominion of New England by Sir Edmund Andros, Dudley continued to function as the most influential New Englander in the government, while Cooke was denied appointment to the council. When rumors of the Glorious Revolution arrived in Boston, a committee of safety consisting of Cooke, Simon Bradstreet (the last old charter governor), and a number of others had Andros, and later Dudley, imprisoned pending the arrival of instructions from King William and Queen Mary.

The fall of Andros and Dudley opened up the possibility of restoring the old charter. In 1690 Cooke and Thomas Oakes were sent to London to help Increase Mather and Sir Henry Ashurst press for the return of the old charter. While in London, however, Oakes and Cooke broke with Mather and Ashurst after an important meeting with the lords of trade on 18 April 1690. At the meeting, the lords of trade found the colonial agents evasive, particularly after hearing rejoinders from Andros and Randolph. Mather and Ashurst modified their positions, attempting to shape the draft of a new charter and to salvage what they could for the colony. Cooke and Oakes, however, chose "to save nothing than not to have the old charter."

After his return to Boston, the still popular Cooke was nominated to serve in the council in 1693, but because he had not supported Mather's nominee for governor, Sir William Phips, he was denied office. As Phips, however, began to run into political difficulty the following year, he was forced to accept Cooke's election to the council. Despite his wealth and family connections, Cooke's political success rested on his ability to manage and represent the popular interest in Boston. Ironically, Cooke's power at that point was facilitated by the demise of the religious qualifications for the franchise, a result of the new charter. As tax commissioner, he determined the value of men's property and thus their eligibility to vote. During his term of office as commissioner, the number of voters doubled, with the South End, Cooke's stronghold, dominating elections in the provincial capital. Under a subsequent, more favorably disposed governor, Richard Coote, the earl of Bellomont, Cooke received an appointment as judge of the Superior Court.

Cooke's political career came to an end in 1702 when Joseph Dudley was appointed to replace Bellomont. Dudley's support of Andros and his cultivation over the 1690s of influential politicians had led to a series of positions culminating in the governorship. Although nominated to serve on the council in 1703, Cooke was rejected by the triumphant Dudley, who also deprived him of his judgeship. For the next decade Cooke was continually elected to the council only to be vetoed by Dudley. Finally, in 1715, Dudley relented and quietly assented to his election; Cooke died five months later in Boston.

In his other interests Cooke had more successes than failures, and his business interests seemed to prosper. His wife managed some of his property in Maine, and, in one instance, that of a sawmill, seems to have had more than one willing set of tenants to operate it. Cooke, however, had difficulties in his medical practice. In 1700 he was accused of causing the death of a boy after operating on his skull. Cooke had trepanned, or drilled, through the boy's skull to relieve what he perceived to be an inflammation or swelling of the brain. Cooke's lawyer claimed that the operation was one that was not unusual even if it was rarely undertaken. Moreover, Cooke's actions had met generally acceptable standards. The case seems not to have gotten much farther than a preliminary complaint and answer.

Despite his political popularity, Cooke's defense of the old charter was an anachronism by the time of the Dominion. Being one of the wealthiest men in Boston, connected to one of the colony's most prominent families, and representing a popular position accounted for little. At the heart of Cooke's difficulty was the changed nature of colonial politics. Political success in Massachusetts after the Dominion depended less on decisions within the colony and more on the ability to gain access to prominent patrons in London.

• Primary materials on Cooke are widely scattered. Some important manuscript materials are to be found in the Winthrop, Saltonstall, and Prince papers of the Massachusetts Historical Society. Those dealing with the Dominion of New England have been brought together in Robert Earle Moody et al., eds., *The Glorious Revolution in Massachusetts, 1689–1692, Publications of the Colonial Society of Massachusetts*, vol. 64 (1988). For a contemporary chronicle of Cooke's activities, see M. Halsey Thomas's superb edition of *The Diary of Samuel Sewall 1674–1729* (1973). Secondary accounts of Cooke's political career may be found in Richard R. Johnson,

Adjustment to Empire: The New England Colonies 1675–1715 (1981); J. M. Sosin, *English America and the Revolution of 1688: Royal Administration and the Structure of Provincial Government* (1982), and *English America and Imperial Inconstancy: The Rise of Provincial Autonomy, 1696–1715* (1985); and Michael G. Hall, *The Last American Puritan, The Life of Increase Mather* (1988). See also John Sibley, *Biographical Sketches of Graduates of Harvard College*, vol. 1 (1873), pp. 520–525; and Thomas Hutchinson, *The History of the Province of Massachusetts Bay from the Charter of King William and Queen Mary in 1691 Until the Year 1750* (1767).

JONATHAN M. CHU

COOKE, Elisha, Jr. (20 Dec. 1678–24 Aug. 1737), physician and politician, was born in Massachusetts, probably in Boston, the son of Elisha Cooke, Sr., also a physician and politician. (His mother's name is unknown.) Elisha, Jr., was a grandson of Massachusetts governor John Leverett. A measure of the family's status in Massachusetts is indicated by his first-place rank at Harvard College, the standing reflecting his social position. Cooke graduated from Harvard in 1697 and in 1703 married Jane Middlecott, a descendant of Massachusetts governor Edward Winslow; there is no record of their having children. In addition to his medical career, Cooke had a full career as a politician. He served in the assembly intermittently from 1715 to his death, and in 1717, 1724–1726, and 1728 he was a member of the council. He was also clerk of the supreme court and a judge of the court of common pleas in Suffolk County.

As an assemblyman and opposition leader in Massachusetts, Cooke was intent on protecting traditional rights and advancing the power of the assembly, and hence his own power and that of other provincials, at the expense of the royal prerogative as personified in the governor. His most notorious efforts were during the administration of Samuel Shute. The immediate issue that alienated the two men was a general economic depression that was rampant in Massachusetts when Shute arrived in 1717. The deeper underlying cause was the loss of political autonomy experienced in Massachusetts after the 1684 recall of its charter. A new charter was issued in 1691 that severely limited local privilege while giving extensive power to the governor and council. The Massachusetts assembly was engaged in an ongoing attempt to whittle away at that power.

The first issue that caused a split between Cooke and Shute was financial. To ease a shortage of paper money, Cooke and other potential investors favored the establishment of a private bank to issue paper bills of credit. They were opposed by a group that wanted the assembly to authorize another emission of bills with the money loaned to people with collateral. The interest from the loans was to be applied to the support of government. A third and smaller faction wanted to return to the exclusive use of gold and silver. Shute allied with the group that opposed the bank and urged the assembly to approve the issue of paper money. He also demanded the assembly agree to pay him and succeeding governors a permanent salary, as stipulated in

his Crown instructions. The representatives agreed to Shute's first request and authorized an emission of £100,000 to be offered in loans. The assembly refused Shute the fixed salary, fully realizing that to capitulate would weaken their control of the executive.

Cooke was furious at Shute's rejection of the bank plan and mounted a campaign to convince Massachusetts voters that Shute was determined to reduce their liberties. He was successful because the economy did not improve despite the issue of paper money. Instead, currency depreciated rapidly, particularly hurting those on fixed incomes. The governor, as head of the province, was blamed, and voters and their representatives were receptive to Cooke's antiadministration propaganda.

Cooke and Shute were further divided by a 1718 dispute between Cooke and the Crown surveyor general John Bridger, which pitted local interests against the royal prerogative. Bridger tried to prevent Maine residents from cutting white pines without licenses. Pines were reserved by English law for the exclusive use of the Royal Navy. Cooke, head of the Muscongus Company that owned thirty square miles of land in Maine, stood to profit handsomely from the cutting of white pine on his property. He argued that the right to cut timber was not reserved for the Crown and furthermore charged Bridger with corruption. The governor and his allies supported Bridger while Cooke enlisted the assembly in his cause. The split between the men widened when Shute heard that Cooke had called him a "blockhead." In retaliation Shute removed Cooke from his post as clerk of the supreme court and in 1718 refused to let Cooke serve when the legislature elected him as councillor.

In 1720 the assembly voted Cooke its Speaker, a choice promptly rejected by Shute. Both Cooke and the assembly were furious with what they considered an invasion of the rights of the assembly. Shute ordered the house to make a new selection, but the members adamantly refused and the governor disbanded the assembly. Shute called a new election. When this second assembly met, its first official act was to protest the dissolution of the last assembly and to defend its right to select its Speaker.

The house, which controlled the purse strings, then showed its displeasure by refusing to provide money for defense against invading Penobscot tribes that were threatening the Massachusetts frontiers. Indian war broke out later that year and to conserve expenditures, the assembly, under Cooke's direction, voted to reduce the governor's half-year salary from £600 to £500 in depreciated local currency. In July 1721 the assembly adjourned itself for six days to observe a fast day. Shute insisted he alone had the authority to adjourn the assembly, but the house claimed the same right of self-adjournment enjoyed by the commons.

To weaken the governor's influence with voters, Cooke attacked Shute in the press. One 1720 pamphlet, *A Just and Seasonable Vindication*, insisted on the right of the house to choose its own Speaker and denied the governor's power to veto the actions of the house. A response was written by the minister Cotton Mather, an ally of Shute's, in a pamphlet, *News from Robinson Cruso's Island* (1720), in which Mather referred to Boston as "Insania" and chastised Cooke and his supporters.

Shute returned unexpectedly to England early in 1723 to put the assembly's recalcitrance before the home government. The assembly sent Cooke to England to answer Shute's charges. Cooke's mission was fruitless. The Crown supported its governor and forced the Massachusetts assembly to accept an explanatory charter, which further limited its powers. The explanatory charter explicitly gave the governor the right to veto the house's choice of Speaker, confirmed the Crown's control over Maine land and trees, and limited to two days the time the assembly could adjourn itself. The house feared its charter would be recalled if it refused to accept the amended charter, thereby threatening other privileges. The changes were reluctantly accepted by the assembly by a vote of 48 to 32.

Cooke returned from England to Boston in 1726 and was elected to the assembly in 1728. In the assembly he continued to oppose Crown policy during William Burnet's administration. Burnet arrived in Boston on 13 July 1728 and immediately met resistance when he insisted the assembly pay him a fixed sum for his salary, as stipulated in his instructions. The assembly, under Cooke's direction, refused, and Burnet remained without any salary. Cooke again opposed Burnet when the governor, desperate for revenue for government expenses, tried to impose a fee on shipping. Burnet requested parliamentary intervention to deal with the recalcitrant assembly but died before the matter was considered.

Burnet was succeeded by Massachusetts native son and merchant Jonathan Belcher, who took office in August 1730. In an effort to win Cooke's support, Belcher appointed him in 1731 justice of the court of common pleas in Suffolk County. In accordance with his instructions, Belcher insisted, as had Shute and Burnet, that the assembly establish a fixed salary. Cooke agreed to lend his support for Belcher, who was an old friend, and wrote a bill to give Belcher the same sum every year. The bill was qualified in that it stipulated that this action was not to be seen as a precedent and applied only to Belcher and not to any governor who might succeed him. The bill did not pass the assembly. Cooke's token support of a measure seen by colonists as enhancing the royal prerogative at the expense of local liberties caused him to lose popularity among Boston voters. Cooke won reelection in 1732 by only a few votes. Cooke's lack of fervor in supporting a permanent revenue and his continued opposition to Crown measures also caused him to lose Belcher's favor. In 1733 the governor failed to support Cooke in his bid for reelection to the assembly and removed him from his post as justice in Suffolk County. Nevertheless, Cooke and his adherents won a victory for local privilege when Belcher petitioned the home government to permit him to accept a one-year salary grant.

The privy council agreed, and the permanent salary issue was effectively buried.

Cooke died in Boston. His estate was worth £63,000 and included twelve houses and three warehouses. One of the wealthiest men in Massachusetts, his lavish funeral reflected his status. Cooke's actions, whether in supporting the bank, in which he planned to invest, or in protecting colonists' rights to cut timber on land he personally owned, were undoubtedly self-serving, but he struck a responsive chord. He verbalized and popularized much of the rhetoric in defense of traditional rights and liberties that was adopted by later generations of Americans.

• Many of Elisha Cooke, Jr.'s essays can be found in Massachusetts newspapers such as the *New England Courant*, *New England Weekly Journal*, and the *Boston News-Letter*. See also Noel Sainsbury et al., eds., *Calendar of State Papers, Colonial Series, America and West Indies* (1860–); *Journal of the Commissioners of Trade and Plantations* (1920–1928); William H. Whitmore, *The Massachusetts Civil List for the Colonial and Provincial Periods, 1630–1774* (1870, repr. 1969); and *Journals of the House of Representatives of Massachusetts* (1919–). For early history of Massachusetts that deals in part with Cooke, see Thomas Hutchinson, *History of the Colony and Province of Massachusetts Bay*, ed. Lawrence Shaw Mayo, vol. 2 (1970), and John Gorham Palfrey, *History of New England* (5 vols., 1858–1890). For a biographical sketch of Cooke, see Clifford K. Shipton, *Sibley's Harvard Graduates: Biographical Sketches of Those Who Attended Harvard College*, vol. 1 (1933). For modern works that deal in part with Cooke, see Richard L. Bushman, *King and People in Provincial Massachusetts* (1985), and Kenneth Silverman, *The Life and Times of Cotton Mather* (1984). For a speculative look at Cooke as the possible founder of the Boston political caucus, see Gerard B. Warden, *Boston, 1689–1776* (1970).

MARY LOU LUSTIG

COOKE, Flora Juliette (25 Dec. 1864–21 Feb. 1953), progressive educator, was born in Bainbridge, Ohio, the daughter of Sumner Hannum and Rosetta Ellis. When she was five years old her mother died, and she was sent to live with her mother's close friends, Charles and Luella (Miller) Cooke of Youngstown, Ohio, who legally adopted her in 1881. Cooke attended public schools in Youngstown and, after graduating from high school in 1884, taught school in Ohio for five years. Assigned 125 first graders at the Hellman Street School in Youngstown in 1885, she created activities and games to keep some children busy while she taught others. The principal of the school, Zonia Baber, a recent graduate of the Cook County Normal School in Chicago, not only approved but had helpful suggestions. Since Cooke lived far from the school, in bad weather she boarded with Baber and, as she noted in a speech honoring Baber in 1944, had "two years of intensive professional training (most of it given after midnight)." In 1887 Baber returned to Chicago to head the geography department at the Normal School, leaving Cooke as principal. Two years later Baber persuaded Colonel Francis Parker, a leading progressive reformer, to invite Cooke to study at the Normal School, the most famous teacher-training institution of its time.

Cooke found herself immediately at home with Parker's beliefs that children learn through action, that this action must be motivated by interest, and that a powerful aid in the nurturing of that interest among children is their natural sociability. According to Parker, by the end of one year Cooke was the best primary teacher he had ever known, and after her graduation in 1890 he appointed her critic-teacher of the practice school's first grade. In this role she taught forty children and supervised twenty student teachers who worked with children under her guidance for an hour each day. Continuing on the faculty of the Normal School for ten years, she specialized in the teaching of reading and in 1895 published a popular book for children, *Nature Myths and Stories for Little Children*. During these years she spread Parker's gospel, lecturing in twenty-eight states and teaching an extended summer institute in the new territory of Hawaii.

In 1899 Cooke moved with Parker to the Chicago Institute, which was financed by philanthropist Anita McCormick Blaine to serve as a laboratory for Parker's ideas. In 1901 Blaine provided funds for a new independent school, the Francis W. Parker School, and with Cooke as its principal for the next thirty-three years, it became a national exemplar of progressive education. Cooke's reputation as an educational leader grew as she developed her own ideas. In contrast to Parker, who maintained a paternalistic relationship with his largely female staff, she believed that teachers should have the freedom to work together and to take responsibility for the direction of their teaching. Under her leadership the teachers produced curriculum materials and guides for practice, many of which she edited and published in a twelve-volume series, *The Francis W. Parker Studies in Education* (1912–1934).

Cooke's democratic spirit extended to the belief that the Parker School should serve as a realistic model for public schools and should therefore include students from diverse economic backgrounds. Support from Blaine, who subsidized half of the school's operating expenses for thirty-four years, provided scholarships for children whose parents could not afford the tuition. Cooke's belief in the importance of teachers in the management of the school was limited only by her commitment to students. One teacher recounted that when the school was overcrowded and a teacher proposed the removal of certain children, Cooke said, "If their homes are as sordid as you say and their parents as blind to our vision of education and the children as unpromising, certainly their only hope of glimpsing something better is this school" (Wygant, p. 1).

Cooke saw reading as central to learning and felt that children should learn to read as naturally as they learned to talk, that reading should be integrated into the whole curriculum, and that reading should be a socially meaningful activity. To carry out these principles, she and her teachers encouraged children to talk and then write about activities in which they had engaged, producing illustrated leaflets to be used in place of standard readers.

Though the Parker School stressed the individuality of each student, it was also strongly oriented toward responsible group membership. Cooke and her staff believed that every child should have the opportunity to give "effective, soul-satisfying service" within the school. For example, on the suggestion of a student the school began in 1910 an annual "Santa's Workshop." For ten days each December students were allowed for two periods a day to make and repair toys to be distributed at local settlement houses.

Unlike its forerunners—the practice school at Cook County Normal School and Dewey's Laboratory School—the Parker School always included a high school, and Cooke devoted herself to extending the principles of Parker and John Dewey, the preeminent philosopher of progressive education, to the development of adolescent students. She was concerned that the rigid entrance requirements of most colleges controlled the curriculum of high schools and failed to take into account the artistic, social, and moral qualities promoted by her school and others like it. For this reason, in 1932 she committed the school to the participation in the significant Eight Year Study of High Schools sponsored by the Commission on the Relation of School and College of the Progressive Education Association.

After her retirement in 1934, Cooke served on the board of trustees of the Parker School and continued as a member of liberal organizations such as the Women's International League for Peace and Freedom, the NAACP, and the ACLU. She was instrumental in the founding of the North Shore Country Day School, which was modeled on the Parker School, and Roosevelt University, named for Eleanor Roosevelt and devoted to providing university education for Chicago students who could not afford to attend the distant state university or the expensive private universities in the city. She died in Chicago, having never married.

Cooke was a leading member of a generation of progressive educators who never gave up the hope that the principles they applied in private schools might one day be adopted generally in the public schools, which they saw as trapped in bureaucratic systems that were undemocratic and dehumanizing for students and teachers alike.

• The Flora J. Cooke Papers at the Chicago Historical Society include correspondence, speeches, and printed materials, mostly concerning the Parker School. Materials relating to her work are also located in the Anita McCormick Blaine Papers in the McCormick Collection at the State Historical Society of Wisconsin and in the Chicago Teachers College historical files at Chicago State University. Speeches and articles were published in *Elementary School Teacher* (1912), *NSSE Yearbook* (1926), *Chicago Schools Journal* (1938), *Illinois Teacher* (1936), and *Progressive Education* (1928, 1937). She was the editor of the 1937 edition of Francis W. Parker's *Talks on Pedagogics* (1894). Cooke's approach to the teaching of reading is the subject of an article by Ronald Kellum,

"Reading Education in the Past: The Philosophy and Pedagogy of Flora J. Cooke," *Illinois Reading Council Journal* 14 (Fall 1986): 40–45. For the historical context of her work as a teacher of reading, see Patrick Shannon, *The Struggle to Continue: Progressive Reading Instruction in the United States* (1990). See also Marie Kirchner Stone, ed., *Between Home and Community: Chronicle of the Francis W. Parker School* (1976), and Lawrence Cremin, *The Transformation of the School* (1961; repr. 1964). A tribute by Elsie A. Wygant, a teacher at the Francis Parker School, appeared in the *Bulletin of the National Council of Primary Education* 13 (1930): 1–2. A biographical sketch is Carol Lynn Gilmer, "Flora J. Cooke: Grand Old Lady of Education," *Coronet* (Oct. 1947): 76–84. Obituaries are in the *New York Times* and the *Chicago Tribune*, 22 Feb. 1953.

NANCY S. GREEN

COOKE, George Frederick (17 Apr. 1756?–26 Sept. 1812), actor, was born most likely in Dublin, Ireland (perhaps in military barracks), the son of a British military man (James Moore?) and possibly an Eliza or Allison Renton, although details of Cooke's birth and parentage are not known. Similarly, almost nothing is known about his early life, even though he kept journals and diaries, several of them extant. It seems that he received some education in Berwick-upon-Tweed, England, where he was apprenticed to the printer John Taylor; in 1771 he may have served as a cabin boy on the ship *Brittania*.

His theatrical apprenticeship was one of the longest in the history of the English theater. He spent more than twenty-seven years in the provincial theater before receiving a regular engagement at London's Covent Garden. Most likely his first performances were in Lincolnshire during 1773–1775. In April 1778 he appeared three times during the off-season at London's Haymarket Theatre and twice in February 1779 at the same place, his last London appearances for more than twenty years. Among his notable subsequent provincial engagements are periods in Manchester, Lancaster, Preston, Liverpool, Chester, York (where he first acted with Sarah Siddons in 1786), Hull, Leeds, Newcastle-upon-Tyne, Sheffield, and Buxton.

From 1787, when Cooke joined the Joseph Austin and Charles Whitlock Company in Manchester as a leading player, to the summer of 1794, he rose to the status of a provincial star. More prestigious engagements followed, beginning in Dublin (first as Othello on 19 Nov. 1794), where his success was minimal; nevertheless, by the spring of 1800 the London press had dubbed him the "Dublin Rosius," after the famous actor of the Roman republic. During this long formative period Cooke, who had mastered more than three hundred roles, also developed a major drinking problem and a reputation for unreliability.

Still, in 1800 he was finally invited to join the company at Covent Garden, debuting on 31 October 1800 as Richard III, destined to become his most famous role. Subsequent notable parts in London in 1800 and 1801 included Shylock, Sir Archy MacSarcasm in Charles Macklin's *Love-a-la-Mode*, Iago, Macbeth, Kitely in Ben Jonson's *Everyman in His Humour*, the title role in *The Stranger* by August Friedrich Kotzebue, and Sir Giles Overreach in Philip Massinger's *A New Way to Pay Old Debts*. With the addition of Stukely in *The Gamester* and Sir Pertinax McSychophant in Macklin's *Man of the World*, Cooke's great roles were established by the end of his second London season. Between London engagements he invariably took summer provincial engagements, including several in Scotland and Ireland. From 17 August until 30 December 1807 he was in the Appleby jail in Westmoreland for debts and breach of contract, having failed to appear for a Manchester engagement. Such a consequence is not surprising, for Cooke complicated his finances with his alcoholism and squandered large sums. Returning in March 1808 to Covent Garden, where he continued to compete with leading actor John Philip Kemble, he concluded his London career with two uneven seasons (including performances during the Old Price Riots incited by increased ticket prices after the opening of a new theater building in 1809).

With his career at a low ebb, undermined by a hostile press, Cooke was persuaded by the American actor and comanager of the New York Park Theatre Thomas A. Cooper to appear in the United States. Cooke's debut was on 11 November 1810 as Richard III. Although his reputation for drunkenness and debauchery preceded him, he was generally on his best behavior, looked after by his first biographer, playwright-manager William Dunlap, during his 160 performances in New York, Boston, Baltimore, Philadelphia, and Providence, Rhode Island. In Providence he closed as Sir Giles Overreach on 31 July 1812, his final performance anywhere.

Although Cooke intended to return to London, the War of 1812 and an embargo on foreign-bound ships prevented him. Instead, his health declining, he returned to New York City, where he died of cirrhosis of the liver at the Mechanics' Hall, a well-known tavern. At his side was his American wife, Violet Mary Behn, whom he had married in June 1811. At least two actresses had called themselves Mrs. Cooke before his 1796 marriage to actress Alicia Daniels (annulled by her, July 1801); in 1808 Cooke reportedly married a Miss Lamb, although nothing is known of this union. The number of his children, if any, is unknown.

Cooke's remains, initially placed in the Strangers' Vault of New York's St. Paul's Church, were reburied in 1821 with a monument to his memory erected by the British star and Cooke admirer Edmund Kean during Kean's first American tour.

Cooke, arguably the first British romantic actor, belongs to a select group of great English actors who flourished in the United States in the eighteenth and early nineteenth centuries. He is considered the first major foreign star on the American stage; his two-year presence led to the establishment of the starring system in the United States. In the tradition of predecessors David Garrick and Charles Macklin, Cooke, recognizable by his broad torso and prominent profile, brought a new natural style to the stage (writing

Shakespearean poetry into prose for personal study), although there was a coarseness in both his personal character and his acting. His prominent roles all featured grim humor, specious menace, sardonic sarcasm, baleful guile, or savage ferocity. A contemporary actor noted that seeing Cooke perform the Bard was "like reading Shakespeare thro' a magnifying glass," and nineteenth-century American actor-historian Charles Durang concluded, "He could soar to flights of genius without the aid of declamation, or the usual tricks of the art." Cooke's engagement was remembered long after his final appearances in the United States. His impact on the American theater is incontestable.

• Cooke's diaries and journals are in the Harvard Theatre Collection, with some personal manuscript material in the Billy Rose Theatre Collection of the Library for the Performing Arts at Lincoln Center. The first Cooke biography was William Dunlap, *The Life of George Frederick Cooke* (1813), a pastiche by the aging New York manager who had known Cooke for only eighteen months. Staid and priggish, Dunlap found Cooke's behavior uncouth and immoral. In his rush to complete the book, Dunlap took some facts for granted and chose to ignore others, creating less a biography than a condemnation of his subject's intemperance. His censure of Cooke is even more obvious in *The Diaries of William Dunlap, 1766–1839*, ed. Dorothy Barck (1931). More definitive and balanced are two modern biographies: Arnold Hare, *George Frederick Cooke: The Actor and the Man* (1980), and Don B. Wilmeth, *George Frederick Cooke: Machiavel of the Stage* (1980), the latter providing the most detailed account of the American phase of Cooke's career.

DON B. WILMETH

COOKE, George Willis (23 Apr. 1848–30 Apr. 1923), writer, lecturer, and Unitarian minister, was born in Comstock, Michigan, the son of Hiram Cooke and Susan Jane Earl, farmers. Although he gained wide recognition as a scholar, his formal education was limited. He studied briefly at Olivet College in Michigan, the Jefferson Liberal Institute in Wisconsin, and the Meadville Theological School in Pennsylvania without earning a degree. A voracious reader throughout his life, he was largely self-taught. On 20 June 1872 he was ordained as a Unitarian minister and later that same year married Lucy Nash of Rochester, Wisconsin; the couple had two children. During the next twenty-seven years he served churches in Sheboygan, Wisconsin; Grand Haven, Michigan; Indianapolis, Indiana; Dedham, Sharon, and Lexington, Massachusetts; and Dublin, New Hampshire, at the same time being actively engaged in writing and editorial work. Along with Jenkin Lloyd Jones he was one of the founding editors of *Unity*, established in Chicago in 1878 as the periodical of the radical, humanistic, nontraditional western Unitarians. His first major published work, *Ralph Waldo Emerson: His Life, Writings, and Philosophy*, appeared in 1881, followed two years later by *George Eliot: A Critical Study of Her Life, Writings and Philosophy* and *A Guide-book to the Poetic and Dramatic Works of Robert Browning* in 1891.

In 1899 Cooke retired from the ministry to devote full time to writing, teaching, and lecturing. He was the author or editor of some twenty books covering a wide range of subjects—literary and religious figures, including James Russell Lowell and Theodore Parker; Brook Farm, *The Dial*, and New England Transcendentalism; religious thought; and Unitarian history. In addition to lecturing throughout the United States and Canada, he taught at the Rand School of Social Science in New York City, the Boston School of Social Science, and the New England Institute for the Promotion of Learning. He was an incisive, original thinker, with a great breadth of knowledge and a deep commitment to social reform, particularly economic reform. He considered the capitalistic system of his day to be profoundly unjust and oppressive to all but a favored few. A political independent, he considered himself an evolutionary socialist and advocated a philosophy he termed "collectivism." In practical terms this collectivism meant "in politics, democracy; in industry and in social relations, cooperation; in religion, fellowship."

In 1922 Cooke returned to the ministry, serving a federated Congregational-Unitarian church in Francestown, New Hampshire, while continuing his writing. The following year, his first wife having died, he married the Reverend Mary Lydia Leggett, who also was a Unitarian minister, on his seventy-fifth birthday and her sixty-seventh. One week later he died unexpectedly at Revere, Massachusetts. At the time of his death he had completed the first two volumes of his major life work, a projected four-volume treatise tentatively titled *The Progress of Women in Civilization*.

Interest in Cooke's writings has continued. His *Unitarianism in America* (1902) was for many years a standard denominational history. Reprinted in 1910, 1969, and 1971, it has remained one of the best accounts of nineteenth-century Unitarianism. *The Social Evolution of Religion* (1920), a major work and the last of his books to be published before his death, was reprinted in 1985. However, the chief continuing interest in his thought appears to reside in the literary rather than the religious sphere. During his lifetime he was considered to be the leading authority on New England Transcendentalism, and some of his importance as a writer and critic in this area has persisted, as evidenced by the reprinting of several of his books: *An Historical and Biographical Introduction to Accompany "The Dial"* (1902) in 1961, his study of Emerson and *Poets of Transcendentalism: An Anthology* (1903) in 1971, and *Memorabilia of the Transcendentalists in New England* (1902) and *John Sullivan Dwight: Brook-farmer, Editor and Critic of Music* (1898, 1909) in 1973.

• An extensive appreciation of Cooke, by J. T. Sunderland, including references to his major writings, appeared in *Unity*, 14 June 1923, a shortened version of which was published in the *Christian Register*, 12 July 1923. Obituaries are in the *Unitarian Year Book* (1923–1924), pp. 118–19, and in the *Christian Register*, 10 May and 17 May 1923.

CHARLES A. HOWE

COOKE, Jay (10 Aug. 1821–16 Feb. 1905), banker and financier, was born in Sandusky, Ohio, the son of Eleutheros Cooke, a lawyer, businessman, and politician, and Martha Carswell. Cooke, the third of five children, grew up in a happy and prosperous middle-class frontier family. At age fourteen, with only a modest formal education, Cooke was hired as a clerk in a Sandusky dry goods store. About a year later he was recruited by Mr. Seymour, possibly because of this gentleman's romantic interest in one of Cooke's cousins, to clerk in the dry goods company of Seymour & Bool. This meant leaving home and moving to St. Louis, Missouri, a city that Cooke came to dislike because of its rough frontier character. The financial downturn of 1837 forced Seymour & Bool into bankruptcy, and Cooke returned eagerly to Sandusky—but without a job.

In 1838 William G. Moorhead, Cooke's brother-in-law, offered him a clerk's position with Moorhead's fledgling packet boat company in Philadelphia. This job gave young Cooke an introduction to the city where he would eventually become a leading citizen. His first encounter was not entirely successful, however, because the packet boat company failed. After working a short time as a hotel clerk, Cooke again returned to Sandusky.

Contacts made in Cooke's first jobs in Philadelphia, however, soon paid off as the banking firm of E. W. Clark & Company hired him in 1839. This job launched him into the business of finance. By the age of twenty-one he was a full partner in the rapidly developing banking firm. Cooke bragged to his brother, "I am getting to be a good judge of bank notes, can tell counterfeits at sight, and know all or nearly all the broken banks in the United States of America." These skills partially accounted for his rapid rise in the company.

During a visit to his brother Henry, a student at Allegheny College in Pennsylvania, Cooke met Dorothea Elizabeth Allen, sister of the president of the college. In 1844, several years later, Cooke and Allen were married in Lexington, Kentucky, where the bride's brother was associated with Transylvania University. They had four children.

Cooke was a major force with E. W. Clark & Company marketing bonds for the Mexican War and providing financial support for many railroad ventures. The death of the founder of the company and disputes between members of the family forced Cooke into the role of mediator. By the mid-1850s the national financial condition that led to the panic of 1857 took its toll on E. W. Clark & Company and forced it into bankruptcy. While Cooke continued to oversee some of the investments of the company, particularly its railroad investments, he declined the offer to become a partner in the reorganized company and left in 1858.

In 1861, after several years of partial retirement, Cooke returned to the financial world by opening his own company. Although his brother-in-law, William Moorhead, was a one-third partner in the venture,

Cooke controlled the company and was the managing partner during the lifetime of the company.

Because Jay Cooke & Company was inordinately successful in marketing Civil War bonds, he is often referred to as "the financier of the Civil War." In several instances Jay Cooke & Company took over bond issues whose sales were extremely unsuccessful and in a short time had the issues oversubscribed. Cooke's optimism and aggressive marketing tactics eventually made his company the exclusive agent for many government bond issues. His success was based on an extensive and diverse advertising campaign emphasizing patriotism, the use of a large number of aggressive (some would say high-pressure) sales agents, and his ability to enlist key public figures in the sales efforts.

The best example of Cooke's skills came during the sale of the 5–20 bond issue in 1863–1864 and the 7–30 bond issue in 1865, the latter a period when the Union was in desperate financial condition. The 5–20s were not as desirable as other bond issues because they could be repaid at any time between five and twenty years and only yielded 6 percent interest. The more attractive 7–30s carried 7.3 percent interest and were twenty-year convertible bonds, but by 1864 the public had been saturated with bonds. Nonetheless, Jay Cooke & Company reassembled all its resources and mounted a campaign presaging the World War I bond drives. The momentum generated by this effort oversubscribed the issues and carried into the post-war years when Cooke's agents descended on the South to pressure its citizens into buying bonds as a demonstration of their loyalty to the Union.

With the end of the Civil War, Jay Cooke & Company had to look for new areas of investment. The company expanded to New York in 1866 and opened a house in London in 1870. One project that sought Cooke was the Northern Pacific Railroad—the second transcontinental—a line envisioned to stretch from the Great Lakes to the Pacific Ocean. Cooke initially had doubts about the project but was persuaded after an extensive expedition into the Northwest and an outstanding sales job by backers of the railroad. In exchange for majority ownership in the enterprise, Jay Cooke & Company accepted the challenge of marketing $100 million of bonds for the Northern Pacific Railroad.

Initially sales went well. Cooke used many of the same tactics he used in marketing Civil War bonds, and the name of his company alone was enough to insure an initial scramble for bonds. But the tremendous effort to market Civil War bonds had absorbed much of the excess capital in the United States. Even Jay Cooke & Company's sophisticated pamphlets extolling the potential of the upper Midwest were not enough to sustain sales. Cooke turned his attention to Europe hoping to sell bonds there, but the war between Germany and France, as well as his partner William Moorhead's unenthusiastic presentation of the bond issue to European investors, did not generate adequate sales.

Because Cooke was so convinced that the Northern Pacific would eventually prove profitable, he made some uncharacteristically risky decisions. As the sale of Northern Pacific bonds slowed, construction costs of the railroad increased. Cooke regularly advanced cash to the company, despite warnings from his management staff that such a step was unwise. Unfortunately, not only was the Northern Pacific building into and through areas where little immediate traffic potential existed, but the company was managed poorly, and profits from the land grant from the federal government depended on extensive immigration. Despite Cooke's optimism, even the mighty Jay Cooke & Company did not have the resources to meet these challenges.

Quite suddenly, on 18 September 1873, Jay Cooke & Company closed its doors, causing a tremendous shock in financial circles. The decision to close the company was made by the managers in the New York office with little or no consultation with Cooke—thus reinforcing the image of disagreement among the leaders of the company. The company did not appear to be in hopeless financial condition. Nonetheless, the damage was done. The closing of Jay Cooke & Company initiated a financial panic and eventually a prolonged nationwide depression.

Cooke was extremely discouraged by events surrounding the dissolution of his company. He felt betrayed by many whom he had considered friends. In addition, he had not recovered emotionally from the death of his wife in 1871. His financial downturn forced him to move from his estate into a much smaller house, and he was not allowed to be involved in the reorganization of his company. His son-in-law reopened the firm eventually under the name Charles D. Barney & Company.

Several years after complete withdrawal from the financial world, Cooke gradually reentered it. He invested in silver mines and land in Minnesota. With the proceeds from these and other ventures he repurchased his island resort in Lake Erie and "Ogontz," his estate near Philadelphia. Rather than move back onto the estate, however, he converted it into a prominent school for young ladies and contented himself to live nearby with his daughter, Mrs. Charles D. Barney, and her family.

One of the most satisfying moments of Cooke's later years was an extended trip north to Duluth, Minnesota, and then west on the Northern Pacific Railroad to Tacoma, Washington. At many points on this trip he was received warmly and recognized for his role in the development of the railroad and the Northwest. He continued to live with his daughter until his death. In retrospect, it appears that Cooke's contributions to the financing of the Civil War and to the development of a national banking system outweigh his role in precipitating the panic of 1873.

• The major location of Jay Cooke's correspondence and papers is the Library of the Historical Society of Pennsylvania in Philadelphia. The Ohio Historical Society (Columbus) and the Baker Library of Harvard University also contain additional materials. Jay Cooke is usually given credit for writing *The Northern Pacific Railroad: Its Route, Resources, Progress, and Business* (1871), although his role was probably no more than that of a general editor.

Cooke has not merited much attention from recent historians. The standard biography is still Ellis Paxson Oberholtzer, *Jay Cooke, Financier of the Civil War* (1907; repr. 1970). John L. Harnsberger, *Jay Cooke and Minnesota: The Formative Years of the Northern Pacific Railroad* (1981), provides a detailed look at Cooke's doing and undoing in this major corporate enterprise. An *American Heritage* article by John Steele Gordon, "Paying for the War" (Mar. 1990), and T. J. Grayson, "Salmon P. Chase and Jay Cooke: Financing the Civil War," in Grayson's *Leaders and Periods of American Finance* (1932), provide a review of Cooke's role in that important conflict. The best look at Cooke as a banker is Henrietta Larson, *Jay Cooke, Private Banker* (1936; repr. 1968). An obituary is in the *New York Times*, 17 Feb. 1905.

ROBERT L. FREY

COOKE, John Esten (2 Mar. 1783–19 Oct. 1853), physician and educator, was born in Boston, Massachusetts, the son of Stephen Cooke, a revolutionary war surgeon and Virginia physician, and Catherine Esten. Cooke began his study of medicine under his father and concluded his studies at the University of Pennsylvania, graduating in 1805. He established successful practices first in Warrenton, Fauquier County, Virginia, and later in Winchester, Virginia. During this time he married Lucy Beale; they had ten children. Cooke gained prominence for his singular theory of medicine, namely, that all diseases had a universal cause—cold and miasmata (foul air). This "universal cause," if left untreated, would result in congestion of the vena cava and its branches, affect the heart and especially the liver, and ultimately bring on death. Diseases such as cholera, yellow fever, typhus, and others were merely manifestations of this universal cause. Once Cooke had reduced all diseases to a universal cause, he looked for and found what he considered a universal treatment. Calomel (mercurous chloride), assisted by other purgatives, if taken in sufficient quantity, would, he believed, cure all. "If calomel did not salivate and opium did not constipate," he said, "there is no telling what we could do in the practice of physic" (*American Practitioner* 12: 18).

In 1827 Cooke was offered the chair of theory and practice of medicine at Transylvania University in Lexington, Kentucky, to succeed Daniel Drake, a renowned physician of the West and former classmate of Cooke's at the University of Pennsylvania, who was familiar with and strongly opposed to Cooke's doctrine. In the same year Cooke was appointed coeditor with Charles Wilkins Short of the *Transylvania Journal of Medicine and the Associate Sciences*, the major medical journal of the new frontier. His many articles, mainly expositions of his theory, undoubtedly influenced the medical thinking of the time. His writings were much praised for their clarity and simplicity of style. He was known for editing and reediting his articles, deleting extraneous words, reducing his text so that his explanations could not be misunderstood. In 1828 he published his major, two-volume work *Treatise on Pathology and Therapeutics*, which outlined his universal cause theory. While it brought praise from his students and from those physicians who appreciated his simple method of diagnosis and treatment, it was scorned by prominent medical men such as Elisha Bartlett, who wrote sardonically in his *An Essay on the Philosophy of Medical Science* (1844) that "the Cookeite would be utterly at a loss, in regard to the state of his patient if he should be deprived of the aids which are furnished him by a daily and nightly inspection—ocular and nasal—of the stools. They constitute his guiding star, his rudder and his compass, they shed a clear light on all his pathway which but for them would be darkness and uncertainty itself " (p. 237).

About this time Cooke, a Methodist for eighteen years, abruptly left his denomination to join the Episcopal church. Intensely interested in church doctrine and governance, he had become involved in a theological argument concerning Presbyterian ordination. To explain his sudden move, he wrote *Essay on the Invalidity of the Presbyterian Ordination* (1829). The essay found wide approval among Episcopalians and was considered by many to be one of the best treatises on church governance. When the Episcopal Seminary was established in Lexington in 1832, Cooke was invited to become professor of history and polity of the church there. At Episcopal, in addition to his teaching responsibilities, he built a theological library that was considered to be one of the finest collections of its time. Cooke considered his work with the church to be one of his most important achievements.

In 1837 Transylvania University's medical department merged with Louisville Medical Institute (now University of Louisville), where Cooke became chair of the theory and practice of medicine. It was clear, however, that opposition to Cooke and his doctrine was growing from both inside and outside the institution. Finally in 1843 he was forced into retirement by both the students and faculty, and the chair of the theory and practice of medicine was returned to Drake.

Cooke nevertheless remained true to his doctrine for the remainder of his life. When he was dying of pulmonary disease on his farm near Louisville, he followed his own precepts to the end by prescribing for himself calomel in sufficient quantity.

The view of Cooke and his theories has not changed since his death. His contemporaries understood that his system of medicine was eccentric and flawed, but as a fellow physician observed of his system in a medical journal obituary, "It has not escaped the fate that has attended every other system of medicine hitherto proposed" (*Western Journal of Medicine and Surgery* [1854]: 269). By practicing medicine without any knowledge of the germ theory of disease, Cooke is representative of the many physicians who tried in vain to rationalize the diseases of their patients without benefit of scientific research. He was an active participant in early nineteenth-century medicine both as an educator and author whose simplified system of diagnosis and treatment were carried on by his devoted students

into their own medical practices for another forty years.

• A small collection of Cooke material and the archives of the Louisville Medical Institute as well as other personal papers of Kentucky physicians may be found at the Kornhauser Health Sciences Library, University of Louisville. Among Cooke's publications not already mentioned are *An Account of the Inflammatory Bilious Fever, Which Prevailed in the Summer and Fall of 1804, in the County of Loudon, Va.* (1805) and *Essays on the Autumnal and Winter Epidemics* (1829). Much of the information on Cooke comes from an article by Lunsford P. Yandell in the *American Practitioner* 12 (1875): 1–27. Short biographies are in Emmet Field Horine's *Daniel Drake (1785–1852)* (1961) and *Medicine and Its Development in Kentucky* (1940). James Craik, *Memoir on John Esten Cooke* (1856), and an obituary in the *Western Journal of Medicine and Surgery*, 4th ser., 2 (1854) are two interesting accounts by his contemporaries. F. A. Eberson, "A Great Purging—Cholera or Calomel?" *Filson Club History Quarterly* (Apr. 1976): 28–35, provides a twentieth-century discussion of his system of medicine.

GLEN P. JENKINS

COOKE, John Esten (3 Nov. 1830–27 Sept. 1886), author, was born in Winchester, Virginia, the son of John Rogers Cooke, a lawyer, and Maria Pendleton. Although his father moved his law practice to Richmond in 1840, Cooke always considered the Shenandoah Valley of northern Virginia home. In Richmond, he attended school and participated in the Franklin Debating Society, a literary debating club, apparently in preparation for entering law. Although the family could not afford to finance his further education at the University of Virginia, he managed to earn his law license and in 1851 became a partner in his father's firm.

It quickly became apparent that Cooke was destined for a literary career, like his older brother Philip Pendleton Cooke, a well-known poet. He wrote poems, stories, and essays for the *Southern Literary Messenger* and other publications; within three years he had virtually abandoned law in order to write. In 1854 he published his first novel, *Leather Stocking and Silk*, a frontier romance that drew on the styles of Washington Irving and John Pendleton Kennedy and set the tone for his best-known work. In addition to the title character, based on James Fenimore Cooper's backwoods hunter, the skillfully woven tale's characters include Thomas Fairfax and George Washington. Later the same year, he published *The Virginia Comedians*, a romance of colonial Virginia that received favorable reviews in northern newspapers and magazines. In 1855 he experimented with a social novel in *Ellie*, a Dickensian story contrasting dire poverty and superficial social life in contemporary Richmond. But his audience wanted his romantic descriptions of Colonial Virginia, and he returned to the historical romance in *Henry St. John, Gentleman* (1859).

The Virginia Comedians and *Henry St. John, Gentleman* are set in Virginia before the American Revolution, a period Cooke saw as a golden age of aristocratic splendor. His romantic embellishment of the era and skillful portrayal of the heroic cavalier led the critic and social historian Francis Pendleton Gaines to judge him the "most notable writer of plantation fiction "between [John Pendleton] Kennedy and the postbellum masters."

By now, Cooke's literary reputation was secure, and he had attracted the attention of literary circles in New York. But at the outbreak of the Civil War he quickly turned his back on his hard-won northern readers. Believing that the election of Abraham Lincoln was a catastrophe for the South, he was a strong advocate of secession. When Virginia did secede, he immediately joined the Confederate army as a sergeant. He commanded a gun emplacement at the battle of First Manassas and was quickly promoted to lieutenant. He was later promoted to captain, served on the staff of J. E. B. Stuart, and was present with Robert E. Lee at Appomattox. Although he served throughout the war and won a reputation for remaining steadfast and calm under fire, he was never seriously injured.

Cooke's wartime experiences provided him with a new subject to write about. Amazingly, he managed to write *The Life of Stonewall Jackson*, published in 1863, between military engagements, as well as poems and reports for Richmond newspapers. After the war he returned penniless to northern Virginia and wrote furiously. In 1866 he produced an expanded biography of Jackson and *Surry of Eagle's Nest*, a novel about Jackson's campaigns. He also reworked and expanded his wartime dispatches into full-length histories, *Wearing of the Gray* (1867) and *Hammer and Rapier* (1870). In addition, he published *Mohun*, a novel about Lee's role in the war, in 1869 and a biography of Lee in 1871. The novels were as popular in all regions of the country as *The Virginia Comedians* had been a decade earlier and accounted for most of the $13,000 Cooke earned from his writings from 1873—a substantial sum at the time.

Cooke had married Mary Francis Page in 1867. Had it not been for the marriage, he might have pursued a career in the North, rather than staying in northern Virginia and remaining faithful to his vision of its heritage. He did his writing first at his wife's father's house, and then at their own farm, "The Briars." The substantial earnings from his writing afforded him an opportunity to spend time with his three children, tend to his fields and gardens, entertain many guests, and occasionally travel to New York.

Cooke continued to write prodigiously at The Briars, but his later fiction never matched the popularity of his colonial romances and Civil War novels. Perhaps the most interesting is *The Heir of Gaymount* (1870), a story of a Virginia aristocrat struggling to save his ancestral estate amid the harsh realities of Reconstruction. *Virginia: A History of the People*, published in 1883, was the most influential of his later works, although its grandiose representation of the state's aristocratic heritage seems seriously exaggerated to the modern-day reader. Over the years his reputation faded. When he was suddenly struck down by

typhoid at The Briars, his death occasioned far less comment that it would have two decades earlier.

• Collections of Cooke's papers are at the Duke University Library, the University of Virginia Library, and the Virginia Historical Society. John O. Beaty, *John Esten Cooke, Virginia* (1922), is the only complete biography. Biographical and critical treatments are in Ritchie Devon Watson, Jr., *The Cavalier in Virginia Fiction* (1985), and Watson, "John Esten Cooke," in *Fifty Southern Writers before 1900* (1987), ed. Robert Bain and Joseph M. Flora.

RITCHIE DEVON WATSON, JR.

COOKE, Josiah Parsons, Jr. (12 Oct. 1827–3 Sept. 1894), chemist, was born in Boston, Massachusetts, the son of Josiah Parsons Cooke, a lawyer, and Mary Pratt. The boy's mother died when he was six years old, and he was raised chiefly by a family friend. In early boyhood, after hearing a course of lectures on chemistry by Benjamin Silliman, Sr., Cooke set up a laboratory at home, and, with the aid of *Elements of Chemistry* by Edward Turner, he taught himself considerable chemistry.

Cooke attended Harvard College and received an A.B. in 1848, but the college then offered very little instruction in chemistry. He traveled for a year in Europe and returned to become a tutor in mathematics at Harvard in 1849. The following spring Cooke was appointed instructor in chemistry and mineralogy, under the restriction that he provide "at his own charge the consumable materials necessary in performing chemical experiments."

In his first year Cooke "demonstrated to the satisfaction of the [Harvard] Corporation that he was an efficient and prudent manager in business details, an interesting lecturer, and a zealous and singleminded College official." At the end of 1850, Harvard College appointed Cooke, then twenty-three years old, to the Erving Professorship of Chemistry and Mineralogy, a position that he held until his death.

As recounted by Harvard president Charles William Eliot, who had been his first student in chemistry, "Professor Cooke created the Chemical and Mineralogical Department of Harvard University." He began by offering a class in chemistry for freshmen, using equipment that he provided himself in a small laboratory on the campus, and he ended with a full department and an entire building for his profession.

Cooke's program was with the college and was not part of Harvard's Lawrence Scientific School, which did have a chemistry laboratory. He established a new undergraduate curriculum in chemistry and mineralogy. At his urging, and through his own teaching, the number of undergraduate laboratory courses in his field continuously increased, and so did the equipment. He was at first required also to give lectures at Harvard's Medical College in Boston, which may have been the beginning of laboratory instruction in chemistry for medical students in the United States. When this requirement ended in 1856, Cooke readily withdrew solely to the Cambridge campus. By then he was planning his new building, Boylston Hall, which was completed in 1857, with college funds plus outside contributions that were obtained primarily through his own efforts. The Anatomical Department occupied one-third of the building until 1891, but over the years Cooke obtained all of it for his subjects, including a rooftop addition in 1871.

Cooke was almost as interested in mineralogy as he was in chemistry. In his first year as professor, he employed Benjamin Silliman, Jr., of Yale University to inspect the miscellaneous collection of minerals, fossils, and curiosities at Harvard. Some items were discarded, and the rest became the nucleus of an expanding collection. Cooke picked up some specimens on summer vacation trips, and he purchased others, often with his own money. A significant addition from a trip to Europe was his purchase of the collection of Count Liebener, which contained uncommon minerals from the Tyrolean Alps. He also found donors to contribute funds for the Harvard collection, which was housed in Boylston Hall when its construction was completed. Eventually in 1890, through Cooke's efforts, the mineral collection was moved to the University Museum. Some of his concern by then was that his own Boylston Hall was not fireproof and "was subject to the risks of chemical experimentation."

Cooke's early researches were on specific chemical elements, which were still being defined and distinguished from compounds by various chemists of that day. Early in the nineteenth century, as techniques of analytical chemistry developed rapidly, European chemists began to define the chemical elements according to atomic weight. Cooke's paper titled "The Relation between the Atomic Weights" (*American Journal of Science* 2 [1854]: 387) was among the early efforts in this classification. It included discussion of errors by previous chemists in their determination of atomic weights. He later told Charles Loring Jackson that the high praise that he received for this paper "had a bad effect on his subsequent work for many years, both by keeping him from many excellent researches because they did not promise far-reaching theoretical results, and by making him try to find such results in all the work that he did." During this interval in papers on chemistry Cooke wrote two textbooks, *Elements of Chemical Physics* (1860), which went to three editions through the years, and *Chemical Philosophy* (1868), which had four editions. He then published a book for laymen, *The New Chemistry* (1874), which was continued through five editions in four years and was translated into several other languages. He also wrote several papers describing new minerals. Starting in 1874 he resumed specific researches in chemistry and published on the vermiculites (hydrous silicates of aluminum, magnesium, and iron); on atomic weights of antimony, oxygen, and hydrogen; and on various compounds. His carefully detailed "Revision of the Atomic Weights of Antimony" (*Proceedings of the American Academy of Arts and Sciences* 13 [1877]: 1) was especially significant; he concluded that the determination of antimony's atomic weight had been a study of constant errors, including those made by Jean-Baptiste-André Dumas twenty years earlier.

A devout man, Cooke lectured and wrote on the relationship of religion and science. In line with some of his contemporaries, he attempted to combine his religious views and the concept of evolution. His book *Religion and Chemistry, or Proofs of God's Plan in the Atmosphere and Its Elements* was published in 1864 and as a new edition in 1880. He presented a view of natural theology that was based upon chemical data. His course of lectures on this theme presented in 1887 at the Union Theological Seminary of New York was published the next year as "The Credentials of Science the Warrant of Faith."

Cooke married Mary Hinckley Huntington in 1860; they had no children. He was elected to the National Academy of Sciences in 1872. A member of the American Academy of Arts and Sciences, he served as its librarian for eight years, as its corresponding secretary from 1873 to 1892, and as its president from 1892 until his death, and he established its annual volume of *Proceedings*. Cooke died at his summer home in Newport, Rhode Island.

• Cooke's papers are in the Harvard University Archives. The most detailed biographical account is in *Proceedings of the American Academy of Arts and Sciences* 30 (1895): 513–47, in which five of his close associates describe aspects of his life and accomplishments; it includes a bibliography. Another biography is by Charles L. Jackson in National Academy of Sciences, *Biographical Memoirs* 4 (1902): 175–83, with a selected bibliography.

ELIZABETH NOBLE SHOR

COOKE, Morris Llewellyn (11 May 1872–5 Mar. 1960), consulting management engineer, was born in Carlisle, Pennsylvania, one of eight children born to William Harvey Cooke, a physician, and Elizabeth Richmond Marsden. Morris Cook attended Lehigh University, where he obtained a degree in mechanical engineering in 1895. At age twenty-eight Cooke married Eleanor Bushnell Davis, an heiress who shared his progressive political views. They had no children.

Cooke's work and service history spanned more than sixty years. While in college, he worked as a reporter for the *Philadelphia Press,* the *Denver News,* and the New York *Evening Telegram.* After college he worked as a machinist. During the Spanish-American War (1898) Cooke served as an assistant engineer in the U.S. Navy. After the war he entered the printing business.

In 1903 Cooke met Frederick W. Taylor, another mechanical engineer, who was formulating his influential theories on scientific management. Cooke became one of four engineers designated by Taylor to teach his theories. A lifelong technological liberal, Cooke believed that the application of scientific management principles to industry would benefit all of society. With this in mind, he established his own engineering consultant firm in 1905 and was a freelance consulting engineer until 1911.

Rudolph Blankenburg, Philadelphia's reform mayor, appointed Cooke director of the Department of Public Works (1911–1915), where he changed inefficient management practices in various departments, saving taxpayers thousands of dollars. He forced the powerful Philadelphia Electric utility company to cut its annual rate by over $1 million. During World War I he served on several boards to improve storage of military goods, reorganize the Quartermaster Corps, and provide more electrical service to shipyards. Under Pennsylvania governor Gifford Pinchot, Cooke headed a survey (1923–1925) that emphasized public support for rural electrification and state-directed reorganization of the electric industry.

By 1930 Cooke had moved from being a progressive Republican to the liberal wing of the Democratic party, supporting Franklin D. Roosevelt for president in 1932. President Roosevelt appointed Cooke to several committees, including the Upstream Engineering Conference, the Great Plain Drought Area Committee, and, as chairman, the Mississippi Valley Committee. Most important, however, was Cooke's appointment as director of the newly organized Rural Electrification Administration. This agency was to finance construction of power distribution systems in rural areas where no electricity was available. Cooke had worked toward rural electrification since the 1920s. He served as director from May 1935 until March 1937, when he resigned to be succeeded by his protégé John Carmody.

Cooke returned to federal service in 1940, when he became a technical consultant to the Office of Production Management. In 1942 he went to Mexico to adjudicate conflicting claims between American oil companies and the Mexican government. He also led an American technical mission to Brazil. In 1943 Cooke headed the War Labor Board panel to mediate a coal miners' strike and in 1946–1947 was a member of a committee to survey the patent system. Cooke's last major government assignment came in 1950, when President Harry S. Truman appointed him chairman of the Water Resources Policy Commission. Cooke died in Philadelphia, Pennsylvania.

Cooke considered rural electrification the major achievement of his public service career. His outstanding work also included obtaining inexpensive electricity for residential use, facilitating better labor-management relations, and conservation of land and water resources. To this one can add service to government. Cooke was, foremost, a champion of scientific management. As he wrote in 1913, "We shall never fully realize . . . the dreams of democracy until the principles of scientific management have permeated every nook and cranny of the working world" (quoted in *Business Week*, 18 Apr. 1964, p. 132).

• Cooke's papers are in the Franklin Delano Roosevelt Library, Hyde Park, New York. His papers dealing with the Rural Electrification Administration are available in Record Group 221 in the National Archives, Washington, D.C. A prolific author, Cooke wrote *Our Cities Awake* (1918), *Brazil*

on the March (1944), and, with Philip Murray, *Organized Labor and Production* (1940). Cooke edited several books, among them *Giant Power: Large Scale Electrical Development as a Social Factor* (1925) and *Modern Manufacturing: A Partnership of Idealism and Common Sense* (1919). Pamphlets and reports representative of his work include *Academic and Industrial Efficiency: A Report to the Carnegie Foundation for the Advancement of Teaching* (1910), *Snapping Cords: Comments on the Changing Attitude of American Cities toward the Utility Problem* (1915), and *The Future of the Great Plains: Report of the Great Plains Committee* (1936). Cooke also contributed often to periodicals such as the *New Republic* and *Mechanical Engineering*.

The two biographies of him are Kenneth E. Trombley, *The Life and Times of a Happy Liberal: A Biography of Morris Llewellyn Cooke* (1954), and Jean Christie, *Morris Llewellyn Cooke, Progressive Engineer* (1983). On Cooke, see also "Famous Firsts: Extending the Scientific Gospel," *Business Week*, 19 Apr. 1964, and the obituary notices in the *New York Times*, 6 Mar. 1960, and in *Mechanical Engineering*, June 1960.

SONDRA VAN METER MCCOY

COOKE, Philip Pendleton (26 Oct. 1816–20 Jan. 1850), writer, was born in Martinsburg, Virginia, the son of John Rogers Cooke, a lawyer, and Maria Pendleton. After several years at Princeton College, which he left without a degree in 1834, young Cooke undertook a career in law, although he had previously contemplated a life in literary pursuits. Married at age twenty to Willie Anne Burwell, he engaged thereafter in legal services and plantation management, neither providing sufficient money for a family that eventually included several children. Cooke's local reputation developed mainly because of his authorship and hunting skills.

Dubbed Virginia's "finest poet" by the renowned anthologist of American literature in his day, R. W. Griswold, Cooke's earliest recorded verse and prose sketches appeared in a local newspaper, the *Winchester (Va.) Republican*. In 1833–1834 he published pseudonymously in the newly established *Knickerbocker Magazine*, and beginning in 1835 he contributed primarily to the *Southern Literary Messenger*, although in his last years he brought out several items in the *Illustrated Monthly Courier*. Despite his hope to be appreciated chiefly as a writer of prose, he is now remembered, first, for his poem "Florence Vane," published in *Burton's Gentleman's Magazine* (1840), and *Froissart Ballads and Other Poems* (1847), constituted largely from pieces previously published in periodicals. Cooke's poems often feature a tone of melancholy or ennui that was popular in his day, and some incorporate themes of rousing adventure and violence. Cooke's able handling of narrative, coupled with an equally deft lyrical impulse, recalls similar tendencies in Keats's work. Cooke's interest in antecedent, especially medieval literature and the balladry into which that interest led him, places him in ranks with other nineteenth-century poets such as Henry Wadsworth Longfellow, John Greenleaf Whittier, William Morris, and Algernon Charles Swinburne. Cooke's pictorial skills in verse were pointed out by Henry B. Hirst.

Cooke's critical prose is negligible; his fiction is of greater interest and substance. The critique "English Poetry," serialized in the *Southern Literary Messenger* during 1835 and 1836, reveals his wide acquaintance with, if not always a sophisticated evaluation of, English verse through the eighteenth century. Several works of fiction from his last years also merit disinterring from the periodicals wherein they appeared and deserve studying in light of modern approaches to narrative technique. Cooke's pioneering in the novelette form is evident in tales such as "The Two Country Houses," "The Gregories of Hackwood," and "The Crime of Andrew Blair." All indicate a concern with careful plotting and plausible character creation. These three works ran serially in the *Southern Literary Messenger* from May 1848 to March 1849, but they do not seem to suffer from serial demands as much as other fiction of the era. Among shorter tales, "Captain Guy; or, The Unpardonable Sin," in the *Illustrated Monthly Courier* (2 Oct. 1848), suggests affinities with Nathaniel Hawthorne's work, although the story's setting reveals Cooke's predilection for medievalism, which recurs in several additional tales published during the late 1840s and the uncompleted longer romance, *The Chevalier Merlin*, left unfinished at Cooke's sudden death. In general Cooke's fiction suggests few debts to other fiction writers of his times. "The Turkey-hunter in the Closet," a sketch published posthumously in the *Southern Literary Messenger* (1851), is an exception to Cooke's usual settings; its comic touches are akin to those found in the frontier yarns of the humorists of the Southwest, such as George Washington Harris and Thomas Bangs Thorpe, who were Cooke's contemporaries.

Cooke is also remembered in connection with Edgar Allan Poe, notably because Poe acclaimed "Florence Vane" (perhaps because it treats the death of a beautiful woman as recounted by her wistful lover), as well as other poems by Cooke. Correspondence between Cooke and Poe concerning Poe's tale "Ligeia" has occasioned debate; Poe possibly gulled Cooke, who may have failed to perceive aspects of hoax in that renowned tale. Cooke's critiques of other Poe works such as "The Haunted Palace," "The Fall of the House of Usher," "Morella," "The Murders in the Rue Morgue," and "William Wilson," plus his commentary on Poe's grotesque and arabesque, stand as sympathetic and, in the main, illuminating contemporaneous opinions. Such positive reception was not often elicited at the time by Poe's imaginative writings. After wading an icy stream, Cooke became ill and died suddenly at his home, the "Vineyard," near Winchester.

Cooke's works are derivative in many respects, and thus he never achieved the status of a major author. His brother John Esten Cooke and his cousin John Pendleton Kennedy have overshadowed him in literary history. His collected poems place him among the many versifiers of the second quarter of the nineteenth century who fall just short of major status. Like Stephen C. Foster, Poe, and a host of others, Cooke pro-duced melancholy lyrics featuring blighted love occasioned by the death of the woman involved. Cooke's intentional creation of irregular rhythms in many of his poems, however, marks him as a forerunner of the freedom in American verse that is now commonplace. Moreover, *Froissart Ballads* has been included in a reprint series of works by significant "romantic tradition" writers in nineteenth-century America, and "Florence Vane" and a few other poems have appeared in anthologies, including the Library of America series. Cooke's critical principles, as expressed in magazine essays, offer nothing that was not done better in his own day by, say, Ralph Waldo Emerson or James Kirke Paulding. Nonetheless, accounts left by acquaintances and professional anthologists, as well as his own correspondence, demonstrate that Cooke harbored unflagging interests in the literary climate of his time and that he was respected as a moving force among southern writers by many who knew him or were aware of his work. Therefore, historical interest in him is bound to continue. His fiction alone is worth serious consideration, although locating scattered individual pieces is troublesome.

• Cooke's *Froissart Ballads and Other Poems* was reprinted in 1972 by Arno Press as part of the Romantic Tradition in American Literature series, ed. Harold Bloom. Some of Cooke's poems also appear in John Hollander, ed., *American Poetry: The Nineteenth Century*, vol. 1, *Philip Freneau to Walt Whitman* (1993). For contemporary comment on his career, see [Henry B. Hirst], "Philip Pendleton Cooke," *Illustrated Monthly Courier*, 20 Oct. 1848, pp. 57–58, and [Rufus W. Griswold], "Philip Pendleton Cooke," *International Magazine*, Oct. 1851, pp. 300–303. A biography is John D. Allen, *Philip Pendleton Cooke* (1942). Also useful are Allen, ed., *Philip Pendleton Cooke: Poet, Critic, Novelist* (1969); David K. Jackson, "Philip Pendleton Cooke: Virginia Gentleman, Lawyer, Hunter, and Poet," in *American Studies in Honor of William Kenneth Boyd*, ed. David Kelly Jackson (1940); Edd Winfield Parks, *Ante-bellum Southern Literary Critics* (1962); and Edward L. Tucker, "Philip Pendleton Cooke and the *Southern Literary Messenger*: Letters," *Mississippi Quarterly* 27 (Winter 1973–1974): 79–99.

BENJAMIN F. FISHER

COOKE, Philip St. George (13 June 1809–20 Mar. 1895), soldier and author, was born in Leesburg, Virginia, the son of Stephen Cooke, a physician, and Catherine Esten. Cooke was educated in local schools near his parents' home in Virginia. In 1823 he received an appointment to the U.S. Military Academy at West Point, New York. He graduated in 1827 and was commissioned as a second lieutenant in the infantry. From 1827 to 1833 he served in a variety of infantry assignments on the western frontier, including brief service in the Black Hawk War in 1832. In 1833 he transferred to the cavalry branch, in which he remained for the rest of his military career, and immediately took an assignment with the newly formed First Regiment of Dragoons (a form of mounted infantry). In 1830 he married Rachel Hertzog; they had three children.

During the Mexican War Cooke won a reputation as an independent and resourceful commander. On 30

July 1846 General Stephen Watts Kearny ordered Cooke to Santa Fe, New Mexico (then a part of Mexico), where he took command of a battalion of Mormon volunteers in October 1846. Cooke quickly and vigorously reorganized this outfit and prepared it for a difficult march to southern California, which the James K. Polk administration intended to seize from Mexico. By swift and disciplined marching, Cooke and his command arrived at Tucson on 14 November 1846 and San Diego on 29 January 1847. A noted historian of the Mexican War observed, "The Mormon march was clearly one of the most notable accomplishments of a war in which American soldiers made some of military history's more illustrious marches (Bauer, p. 139). In 1847 Cooke returned to St. Louis with General Kearny and was assured of a bright future within the army for his wartime exploits.

After the Mexican War Cooke advanced steadily in the peacetime army. In 1847 he was promoted to major and transferred to the Second Regiment of Dragoons. In 1853 he was promoted to lieutenant colonel and in 1858 to colonel and commander of that regiment. In addition to frontier duty, he participated in the army expedition to Utah in 1857–1858 and was a military observer of the Franco-Austrian War in Italy in 1859–1860. Just before the outbreak of the Civil War, he published *Cavalry Tactics* (1861), which earned him a reputation as the acknowledged expert on that subject in the U.S. Army.

Because of his expertise, military experience, and reputation, both the Union and the Confederacy wooed Cooke in 1861. His decision to remain loyal to the Union was complicated when his son and both of his sons-in-law chose Virginia over the Union and became Confederate officers. His son, John Rogers Cooke, became a Confederate brigadier general. One of his sons-in-law, J. E. B. Stuart, achieved fame as Robert E. Lee's renowned cavalry commander, which provoked rumors that Cooke did not enthusiastically favor prosecuting the war and eventually contributed to his professional decline.

In late 1861 and early 1862 Cooke was active in assisting General George B. McClellan in organizing the Union Army of the Potomac. On 12 November 1861 he was promoted to brigadier general and assigned the command of the Cavalry Reserve of the Army of the Potomac, which he commanded during the Peninsula campaign in 1862. In June 1862 he failed to prevent General Stuart from leading the Confederate cavalry of General Lee's Army of Northern Virginia completely around the Union army. Throughout the fighting Cooke was slow to react and missed several opportunities to cut off Stuart and prevent his escape. He was severely criticized in northern newspapers at the time, and it was suggested he allowed Stuart's escape because Stuart was his son-in-law. No real evidence supports this conclusion, however, and a better explanation for his poor performance is his age and inability to adapt to the new methods of fighting that emerged during the war.

After the campaign Cooke was eased out of his field command and thereafter assigned to administrative duties. From July 1862 to August 1863 he served on court-martial duty with the Army of the Potomac. From October 1863 to May 1864 he was assigned as commander of the Baton Rouge District in the Department of the Gulf, then a quiet sector of the war. From May 1864 until March 1866 he served as general superintendent of the Recruiting Service of the army. After the war he continued to serve in a succession of administrative posts. He was breveted major general in 1865 and retired from the army in 1873.

After his retirement Cooke devoted himself to family life and writing. He published several revised editions of *Cavalry Tactics*, which continued to be the army's manual for decades after the war, and an earlier work, *Scenes and Adventures in the Army* (1857), a memoir of his antebellum service on the frontier. He also published *The Conquest of New Mexico and California* (1878), a straightforward account of his participation in the Mexican War. He died in Detroit, Michigan.

Cooke was an outstanding cavalry commander and a well-known expert in his field for three decades before the Civil War. He did not adapt, however, to the harsh demands and changing nature of total war that secession unleashed and was quickly shunted away from field command after his first campaign against the Confederates. His extensive writings have remained particularly valuable for understanding the role the army played in U.S. expansion during the era of Manifest Destiny.

• Cooke's Civil War career is covered in *The War of the Rebellion: A Compilation of the Official Records of the Union and Confederate Armies* (128 vols., 1880–1901); see esp. 1st ser., vols. 11 (pts. 1, 2, and 3), 26 (pt. 1), 34 (pts. 2 and 3), and 51 (pt. 1). The best recent account of Cooke's role in the Mexican War is in K. Jack Bauer. *The Mexican War 1846–1848* (1974). His performance in the fighting of 1862 is analyzed in Stephen W. Sears, *To the Gates of Richmond: The Peninsula Campaign* (1992). Also informative are Ezra J. Warner, *Generals in Blue: Lives of the Union Commanders* (1964); and Douglas Southall Freeman, *Lee's Lieutenants*, vol. 1 (1942). An obituary is in the *Bulletin of the Association of Graduates of the U.S. Military Academy* (1895): 79–86.

JAMES K. HOGUE

COOKE, Rose Terry (17 Feb. 1827–18 July 1892), author, was born on a farm near Hartford, Connecticut, the daughter of Henry Wadsworth Terry and Anne Wright Hurlbut. The family lived primarily on wealth inherited from Henry Terry's father, a Hartford banker and member of Congress, and Anne Hurlbut's father, the first New England shipbuilder to sail around the world.

When Cooke (her eventual married name) was six years old, her family moved into her grandmother's large brick house in Hartford. Here the child's education was supervised by Anne Hurlbut, who asked her young daughter to memorize a page of the dictionary each day and to use her new vocabulary in a daily diary. Her mother also inspired her first daughter with her deep piety. Henry Terry drew his daughter out of doors, teaching her to understand and love nature. Finally, the child's imagination and historical interest were fired by her grandmother's memories and her great-grandparents' portraits and clothing from the Revolutionary period, stored in the garret of the old house. She also thoroughly enjoyed observing the family's servants and playing in the house's large, bustling kitchen.

Cooke graduated from the Hartford Female Seminary at age sixteen. In the same year, she had a conversion experience and became a devout, lifelong member of the Congregational church. She taught school and served as a governess for a clergyman's family in New Jersey for three years but returned to Hartford to care for her ailing sister's family. Aided by an inheritance from a great uncle in 1848, she retired permanently from schoolteaching, devoting herself entirely to domestic duties and to writing.

Cooke's first love was poetry. However, despite a facility for verse and the opportunity to publish in such periodicals as the *New York Daily Tribune* and in a collected volume of *Poems* (1860), she did not find sufficient support to continue writing poetry; it did not achieve critical success then or later. She turned instead to short stories, which quickly earned her both critical recognition and popular success: although her first mature story was published in *Putnam's* in June 1855, by 1857 she was asked to write the first story for the premiere issue of the *Atlantic Monthly*. Cooke continued to contribute to the *Atlantic, Harper's Magazine*, and similar periodicals throughout her life. Many of her stories were republished in *Somebody's Neighbors* (1881), *Root-Bound and Other Sketches* (1885), *The Sphinx's Children and Other People's* (1886), and *Huckleberries Gathered from New England Hills* (1891). Cooke's single attempt at a novel, *Steadfast, the Story of a Saint and a Sinner* (1889), was far less successful, as were her didactic children's stories, published in the *Christian Union* and *Youth's Companion* and collected in *Happy Dodd; or, "She Hath Done What She Could"* in 1878.

Cooke's short stories, fictional sketches of New England lives, established her contemporary fame and enduring reputation. Like many other female authors of nineteenth-century New England, Cooke most frequently chose a regional focus for her fiction, working within the genre known as "local-color realism." Centering on impoverished New England towns or barren rural settings, her "historical" sketches explored the hard lives and often dysfunctional relationships of Puritan families. Although her harshest portraits were of greedy, hypocritical deacons of the church who self-righteously starved their wives and children of food and affection, Cooke could also celebrate the faith, strength, and independence of a Puritan farm family or, most notably, an indomitable spinster. Her sharpest criticism was reserved for hypocrisy and dogmatic formalism and for the corrupting, unequal power in traditional patriarchal relationships. Indeed, some of her fiction was affirmative and humorous; she was one of the earliest prose writers to reproduce New England dialect fully and carefully, often for comic effect as well as authenticity. In addition, her short stories were constructed around rich descriptions of the natural wonders and hardships of rural New England. If, as she warned her readers, her fiction rarely portrayed grand or sentimental heroes or heroines, it did offer complicated and interesting sketches of the lives of ordinary New England farm families.

At the time of her mother's death in 1872, Cooke had dedicated a quarter-century to the care of her sister, her sister's children, and then her mother. In 1873, at the age of forty-six, Rose Terry married Rollin H. Cooke, a thirty-year-old widower with two daughters. The family moved to Winsted, Connecticut, where Rose Terry Cooke attended to her step-daughters' needs, supplemented her husband's unsteady income, and rescued her father-in-law from financial ruin. This financial pressure drained her savings and led her to increase the rate of her literary productivity, with mixed results. She died in Pittsfield, Massachusetts.

Throughout her adult life, Rose Terry Cooke was extremely proud of her independence and ability to support herself adequately, if not luxuriously, by her writing. Her local reputation centered on her personal dignity, intelligence, and quick, pungent wit. At the same time, she was devoted to her family and generous with her friends, to whom she often opened her home. Particularly sensitive to the financial and emotional needs of women, Cooke offered her female friends unquestioning support and refuge—she longed to offer the same to Jane Welsh Carlyle, upon reading her letters, and to give Thomas Carlyle a strong piece of her mind. Indeed, her characteristic mixture of sympathy with the oppressed, moral indignation, and honesty pervaded Rose Terry Cooke's best fiction as well as her life; her sketches of New England life still continue to evoke Cooke's own strong personality and beliefs.

• Letters from Cooke are in the Benjamin Holt Ticknor Papers in the Library of Congress Manuscript Division, the Daniel Wadsworth Papers in the Connecticut Historical Society, and the Houghton Library of Harvard University. There is no full-length, published biography of Cooke; the fullest unpublished treatment is Jean Downey, "A Biographical and Critical Study of Rose Terry Cooke" (Ph.D. diss., Univ. of Ottawa, 1956). Harriet Prescott Spofford, who knew Cooke, included many personal reminiscences and quotations from Cooke's letters to her in *A Little Book of Friends* (1916), pp. 143–56, and *Our Famous Women* (1884), pp. 174–206. The most interesting critical studies of Cooke's fiction include Elizabeth Ammons's introduction to Rose Terry Cooke, *How Celia Changed Her Mind* (1986); Katherine Kleitz, "Essence of New England: The Portraits of Rose Terry Cooke," *American Transcendental Quarterly* 47–48 (Summer/Fall 1980): 127–39; Josephine Donovan, *New England Local Color Literature: A Women's Tradition* (1983), pp. 68–81; and Perry D. Westbrook, *Acres of Flint: Sarah Orne Jewett and Her Con-

temporaries, rev. ed. (1981), pp. 78–85, *A Literary History of New England* (1988), pp. 248–54. An obituary is in the *Boston Transcript*, 19 July 1892.

EVE KORNFELD

COOKE, Sam (22 Jan. 1931–11 Dec. 1964), singer-songwriter, was born Samuel Cook in Clarksdale, Mississippi, the son of Charles Cook, a minister in the Church of Christ (Holiness), and Annie May Carl. After Sam's father lost his position as houseboy for a wealthy cotton farmer as a result of the Great Depression, the family migrated to Chicago, where Reverend Cook became assistant pastor of Christ Temple (Holiness) and a laborer in the stockyards. The family lived in Bronzeville, Chicago's severely overcrowded and impoverished black section. Young Sam was educated at nearby schools and gained musical experience by sneaking into taverns to hear pop tunes but mostly by hearing and singing gospel music at church. There he started a gospel group, the Singing Children; later he joined the Teenage Highway QC's and became more widely known throughout the nation. He graduated from Wendell Phillips High School in 1948. About that time he spent ninety days in jail on a morals charge that stemmed from a paternity suit.

Cooke's first major break came when R. H. Harris, lead singer of the famous Soul Stirrers, retired and Cooke replaced him, thus embarking on the possibility of becoming a major gospel star, dressing in elaborate suits and performing as a singing minister to a growing flock of gospel adherents. First there were hurdles to overcome. Cooke's introduction to the Soul Stirrers was a trial-by-fire, as competing groups and highly critical audiences and record promoters were skeptical of his skills. After Cooke became a Soul Stirrer, the group, on Cooke's recommendation, began to aim performances at "Sister Flute," the archetypal black female churchgoer who, once aroused by gospel singing, would ignite the congregation into sacred ecstasy. Cooke's formal, conversational style of singing and his handsome looks initially failed to move older parishioners, but he greatly excited teenage girls, normally an indifferent audience to gospel appeals.

Cooke also had to win over the group's record promoter, Art Rupe of Specialty Records in Los Angeles. Upset that the Soul Stirrers had lost their star, Rupe demanded near perfection during Cooke's first marathon recording session in 1951. The resulting album included Cooke's first hit with the group, "Jesus Gave Me Water," and one of his own songs, "Until Jesus Calls Me Home." Enthusiasm and overwhelming sales brought the group back into the studio a second time in 1952. During this session Cook introduced his trademark "yodel" effect, which would help establish his career. Another first was the birth of a child to his longtime sweetheart, Barbara Campbell, in 1953. Although Cooke acknowledged paternity and paid child support, he did not marry Campbell.

Over the next few years Cooke toured constantly with the Soul Stirrers, singing at churches, stadiums, and religious conventions before pushing on to the next engagement the following day. Cooke's distinctive yodeling of lyrics helped to elevate the group's popularity as never before. At an engagement in Fresno, California, Cooke met Dolorous Mohawk and after a whirlwind romance married her in 1953. Mohawk had a young child from a previous marriage. After they married she moved to Chicago to wait for Cooke while he traveled with the group.

Specialty Records had a very successful line of popular music featuring such innovative stars as Lloyd Price, Percy Mayfield, and, later, Larry Williams and Jesse Belvin. In 1955 Rupe hired Robert "Bumps" Blackwell to sign and arrange new talent, including the immortal Little Richard. The Soul Stirrers continued to sell records in the middle 1950s and celebrated their twenty-fifth anniversary in 1955. Cooke was becoming restless, however, and more keenly interested in making money. In June 1956 he agreed to make some "cross over" pop records for Rupe. During several undistinguished forays into popular music, a personal crisis ensued. His wife, distraught with loneliness, attempted suicide. Cooke went to her side but was soon back on the road. It was also around this time that he added an "e" to his name.

In 1957, after a dispute with Rupe, Cooke and Blackwell, now his manager, took masters of a song called "You Send Me" to a new label, Keen Records. Despite a cover version by white artist Teresa Brewer, Cooke's version sold a reported 1.7 million copies, ascended to the top of the charts, and stayed in the mix for more than six months. Ed Sullivan invited Cooke to appear on his Sunday night show, squeezed him in for only a few seconds before the credits, then received outraged letters from thousands of black Americans. Impressed as well as contrite, Sullivan reinvited Cook for a full performance. Over the next two years Cooke scored with such hits as "I Love You for Sentimental Reasons," "Only Sixteen," "Win Your Love for Me," and even the improbable "Everybody Loves to Cha-Cha-Cha."

Despite his success, Cooke was beset by problems. He divorced his wife, who was later killed in a car accident, and then had a child with another woman. Rupe hit him with numerous lawsuits. A heralded appearance at New York's Copacabana club was a fiasco. At a restaurant on the New Jersey turnpike waitresses refused to serve him, even as his songs were playing on the jukebox. One positive event was a reconciliation with Barbara Campbell, and the two were married.

In 1960, Cook, by now a major star, signed a lucrative contract with RCA. Able to arrange and produce his own songs, Cooke created such pop masterpieces as "Wonderful World," "Chain Gang," "Sad Mood," "Having a Party," "Bring It on Home to Me," "Another Saturday Night," and "Twisting the Night Away." He also produced records for his own label, Sar Records, and ran KAGs Music, a publishing company.

Cooke's second marriage gradually drifted into one of convenience, and while his popularity remained high, his personal life declined. On 11 December 1964 he was shot to death in Hollywood, California, by Bertha Franklin, a motel keeper, under very mysterious circumstances. Although police classified the shooting as self-defense, many black Americans regarded their determination with suspicion. Daniel Wolff, Cooke's biographer, has pointed to a number of discrepancies in the official story and posited alternative explanations.

Cooke's funeral in Chicago was attended by more than 200,000 fans of both gospel and pop. Shortly after his death a new song, "A Change Is Gonna Come," became a big hit and pointed to a fusion of gospel music and social awareness. This style was later successfully broached by such disciples as Marvin Gaye, Otis Redding, and Curtis Mayfield.

• The fullest treatment of Cooke's life is Daniel Wolff, *You Send Me: The Life and Times of Sam Cooke* (1995). Joe McEwen, *Sam Cooke: A Biography in Words and Pictures* (1977), provides a brief sketch of his career and many photographs. Gene Santoro's extensive survey of Cooke's life as a performer, "Sam Cooke," *Nation*, 13 Mar. 1995, details the circumstances of the singer's death. Edward J. Boyer, "The Soulful Legacy of Sam Cooke," *Los Angeles Times*, 23 Dec. 1994, offers a retrospective view of Cooke and his importance to music. Obituaries are in the *New York Times* and the *Los Angeles Times*, both 12 Dec. 1964.

GRAHAM RUSSELL HODGES

COOKE, Terence (1 Mar. 1921–6 Oct. 1983), seventh archbishop of New York, was born on the upper west side of Manhattan, New York, the son of Michael Cooke, a chauffeur, and Margaret Gannon. Cooke's parents were both natives of County Galway, Ireland. Like many lower-middle-class immigrant families in the 1920s, his family joined the exodus from the tenements of Manhattan to the open spaces of the Bronx, where they settled in the still semirural Throgs Neck area. After graduating from the local parochial elementary school in 1934, Cooke entered Cathedral College, a six-year preparatory day seminary, to train for the priesthood. Upon completion of his studies in 1940, he continued his training at St. Joseph's Seminary, Dunwoodie, and was ordained a priest in St. Patrick's Cathedral by Archbishop Francis J. Spellman in December 1945.

After the customary two-year stint as a parish priest and chaplain at an orphanage, Father Cooke resumed his education at the National Catholic School of Social Service at the Catholic University of America in Washington, D.C., where he earned a master's degree in June 1949. For the next five years Cooke had the opportunity to use his degree in social work as a staff member of the Catholic Charities of the archdiocese of New York, the coordinating agency for the church's numerous charitable and social welfare operations. From 1949 to 1956 he also served as an instructor at the Fordham University School of Social Service.

In January 1954 Cooke's career took an abrupt upward turn when he was appointed procurator of St. Joseph's Seminary and became responsible for the financial administration of the institution. His work brought him into frequent contact with Archbishop Francis Cardinal Spellman, who was impressed with Cooke's management of the seminary finances. In 1957 Spellman tapped him to become his private secretary. From that point on, Cooke ascended the ecclesiastical ladder with astonishing rapidity. In August 1957 he became a monsignor; in June 1958, vice-chancellor; in June 1961, chancellor; in February 1965, vicar general; and in September 1965, auxiliary bishop. Spellman's death in 1967 touched off widespread speculation about his successor, but few considered Cooke a serious contender for the post, since he was the youngest of ten auxiliary bishops and an unknown figure outside New York. Many were surprised when Cooke was appointed archbishop of New York in March 1968, and his selection was widely attributed to the Vatican's deference to Spellman's wish that Cooke succeed him.

Cooke's fifteen years as archbishop of New York coincided with unprecedented turmoil in both the Catholic church and American society. On the day of Cooke's installation in St. Patrick's Cathedral in April 1968, Dr. Martin Luther King, Jr., was assassinated in Memphis, precipitating riots in many black ghettos of the United States. That evening Cooke visited a Harlem parish to plead for racial peace and harmony. Continuing a New York tradition, Cooke's installation as archbishop coincided with his appointment as military vicar for the armed forces, which gave him pastoral responsibility for one million Catholics in the armed services and for their Catholic chaplains. One year later, on 28 April 1969, he inherited another New York tradition when he was elevated to the rank of cardinal. Unlike Spellman, Cooke did not play a large role in national or international affairs. The only important post to which he was elected by his fellow bishops was that of chairman of the U.S. Bishops Pro-Life Activities Committee. An innately cautious and prudent person, he generally avoided controversy and confrontation on public issues, preferring instead behind-the-scenes diplomacy and conciliation. A pragmatic conservative in ecclesiastical matters, he accepted loyally, if unenthusiastically, such Vatican II reforms as a vernacular liturgy and an elected senate of priests.

Between 1970 and 1980 the population of New York City declined by 900,000 to 7,071,030, almost half of which consisted of minorities (1,723,124 blacks and 1,405,957 Hispanics). During the Cooke years the Catholic population of the archdiocese remained approximately the same (1,800,000), but this was due to the fact that large numbers of poor Hispanic immigrants replenished the dwindling ranks of middle-class Catholics. At the same time, the number of infant baptisms fell from 50,000 to 31,000 per year, and the number of church weddings slipped from 15,000 to 8,200 per year. Even more ominous was the sharp drop in the number of diocesan priests (from 1,108 to 777). Under such circumstances it was impossible for Cooke to continue the expansionary policies of his predecessors. At the turn of the century Archbishop Corrigan had established ninety-nine new parishes, and Spellman had established forty-five, while Cooke closed several parishes and added a few more, leaving a net gain of four parishes. Cooke excelled, however, in his management of the finances of the archdiocese and in his careful conservation of available resources.

One of his most impressive achievements was the creation of the Inter-Parish Finance Commission, a diocesan agency that taxes more affluent parishes in order to subsidize churches and parochial schools in disadvantaged neighborhoods. Thanks largely to this system, only 31 of the 305 Catholic elementary schools were forced to close during the Cooke administration despite almost a halving of enrollment and the departure from the classrooms of three-quarters of the teaching sisters. Cooke also increased substantially the income from the annual fund-raising campaign, expanded the services of Catholic Charities, consolidated the diocesan offices in a new Catholic Center, established an Office of Pastoral Research and an Office of Black Catholics, organized the Inner-City Scholarship Fund, and appointed the first black and Hispanic auxiliary bishops in the history of the archdiocese. In the summer of 1983 New Yorkers learned that Cardinal Cooke was terminally ill with cancer. During his last six weeks, his faith and courage made a deep impression on the people of the city. At his death the New York *Daily News* summarized the feelings of many: "On Cardinal Cooke's final day a line from Shakespeare seems uniquely appropriate: 'Nothing in his life became him like the leaving of it.' This was a man who showed us all how to pass from time to eternity with courage and grace."

• Cooke's papers are in the Cardinal Cooke Archives, located at St. Joseph's Seminary, Dunwoodie, N.Y. The only biography that has appeared to date is a self-styled "spiritual portrait," written to promote his canonization: Benedict J. Groeschal, CFR, and Terrence L. Weber, *Thy Will Be Done: A Spiritual Portrait of Terence Cardinal Cooke* (1990). Obituaries are in *Catholic New York*, 6 Oct. 1983; the New York *Daily News*, 7 Oct. 1983; and the *New York Times*, 7 Oct. 1983.

THOMAS J. SHELLEY

COOLBRITH, Ina (10 Mar. 1841–29 Feb. 1928), poet, was born Josephine Donna Smith in Nauvoo, Illinois, the daughter of Agnes Coolbrith Moulton and Don Carlos Smith, a farmer and the younger brother of Joseph Smith, founder and prophet of Mormonism. Ina, as her mother called her, was five months old when her father died. In 1844 her uncles Joseph Smith and Hyrum Smith were both murdered in Carthage, Illinois, by anti-Mormons; a third uncle, Samuel Smith, tried to rescue the two victims, failed, and died of exhaustion. In 1846 Ina's mother discontinued her association with Mormons and married William Pickett, a lawyer and printer. The Picketts moved to St. Louis, from which the family undertook an arduous overland journey in 1851 to California, partly guided by the scout James P. Beckwourth. They stopped in Marys-

ville, where Pickett prospected to no avail for gold. Then they moved to San Francisco and, in 1855, to Los Angeles.

While her stepfather began a successful law practice, Coolbrith took her first classes, from 1855 to 1858, at the first public school in Los Angeles. The talented girl published her first poem, "My Childhood Home," in the *Los Angeles Star* (30 Aug. 1856) and followed it with two more juvenile efforts in the *Star* (1856, 1857). She met and quickly married Robert Carsley, a colorful Los Angeles ironworks executive and minstrel performer, in 1858. The marriage soon turned sour. Late in 1861 Carsley returned from a trip to San Francisco, idiotically accused young Ina of being a prostitute, and tried to kill her. In the ensuing argument, her loyal stepfather shot Carsley in the hand, mangling it so severely that it was later amputated. Ina obtained a divorce within weeks, may soon thereafter have borne a child that died, and in 1862 moved with the Picketts to San Francisco. At this point, she began signing her publications Ina Donna Coolbrith.

Coolbrith's first real professional opportunity came in 1868, when the San Francisco bookseller and publisher Anton Roman founded the *Overland Monthly*, a literary journal that aimed to boost California and offer a medium for young regional writers. Its first editor, the local colorist Bret Harte, named Coolbrith and the poet Charles Warren Stoddard coeditors at the journal, where they served until 1871. The three published so regularly in the *Overland* that they were dubbed the "Golden Gate Trinity" and the "Overland Three." Meanwhile, Coolbrith was publishing in such eastern journals as *Harper's Weekly* and *Scribner's Monthly*. She became a happy participant in the bohemianism of the vibrant city. One of her wildest friends was the poet Cincinnatus Hiner Miller, whose name she persuaded him in 1870 to change to Joaquin Miller.

The remainder of Coolbrith's long life was filled with hard work, much misfortune, and less time for writing than she wished. She was saddened by the disappearance early in the 1870s of her stepfather. The death in 1874 of her sister Agnes, married in 1858 but widowed a decade later, obliged Coolbrith to adopt the dead woman's son and daughter. (Two years before, she had opened her home to the irresponsible Miller's natural daughter Calle Shasta.) Later in 1874 Coolbrith began her career as a librarian, at the Oakland Free Library, where she worked twelve hours a day, six days a week. A further hardship was her mother's death in 1876.

Coolbrith was a skillful, innovative, and underpaid librarian until she was dismissed in 1892 over a budget dispute. During those years she wrote and published what she could. More important, she established an informal literary salon in her home and became a valued influence on the lives of many writers and others, including Gertrude Atherton, Mary Austin, Ambrose Bierce, dancer Isadora Duncan, Jack London, Charles Fletcher Lummis, Edwin Markham, naturalist John

Muir, Edward Rowland Sill, George Sterling, and publisher Charles Henry Webb. In 1893 she was honored as a popular West Coast poet at the World's Columbian Exposition in Chicago, visited colleagues in the East, wintered in New York, returned to California, and went on the lecture circuit. When the circuit failed financially, she again did library work, at the Mercantile Library of San Francisco in 1898–1899 and then in a part-time and honorary capacity at the Bohemian Club, where from 1899 until 1907 she was the only woman in the club. She also edited works by a few club members. She was outraged when Stoddard used her as a model for Elaine, the sad and droopy librarian, nicknamed "Our Lady of Pain," in *For the Pleasure of His Company*, his 1903 roman à clef. Although she had begun to write a literary history of California, the San Francisco earthquake and fire of 1906 destroyed everything she owned—not least her manuscripts, notes, and 3,000-book library.

With the help of generous friends, Coolbrith was able to build up her library to a degree and to reestablish her salon. Her inflammatory rheumatism, long a problem, worsened in 1912. In 1915 she organized a meeting of writers for the Panama-Pacific International Exposition and was named poet laureate of California. From 1919 on she obtained helpful medical treatment in New York City and was able to produce new poems. A year before her death, in Berkeley, she discontinued all work on both her literary history and her own autobiography.

Coolbrith was less memorable as a poet than as an inspiration to better writers. Her four books of poetry, *A Perfect Day, and Other Poems* (1881), *The Singer of the Sea* (1894), *Songs from the Golden Gate* (1895), and *Wings of Sunset* (1929), though subjective, thin, and conservatively phrased efforts about love and sorrow, self-pity, and the comforts of beautiful nature, are always sincere and sometimes melodious and moving. Here are several examples: "a sorrow dwells in my young heart— / Its shade is on my brow" (from "To Nelly," 1857); marital love "[t]ransfixed my poor unguarded heart" ("How I Came to Be a Poet," 1859); "What have they brought to me, these many years? / Silence and bitter tears" ("The Years," 1870); to her sister, "It must be sweet, O thou, my dead, to lie / With hands that folded are from every task" ("Beside the Dead," 1875); "The rulers of the World are they / Who make its books and songs" ("In the Library," 1891); and "Below, a sea of stars! / Above, of stars a sea!" ("From Russian Hill," 1915).

• Coolbrith's papers, dating from after the San Francisco fire, are in the libraries of the University of California at Berkeley; Mills College, Oakland, Calif.; Huntington Library, San Marino, Calif.; California Historical Society, San Francisco; Southwest Museum, Los Angeles; State Library, Sacramento; and Oakland Public Library. Ivalu Delpha Stevens published "A Bibliography of Ina Coolbrith" in *News Notes of California Libraries* 27 (Apr. 1932): 105–23. A superb, detailed biography is Josephine DeWitt Rhodehamel and Raymund Francis Wood, *Ina Coolbrith: Librarian and Laureate of California* (1973). Discussions of Coolbrith's friendships with notable people are in Isadora Duncan, *My Life* (1927), Richard O'Connor, *Bret Harte: A Biography* (1966), O. W. Frost, *Joaquin Miller* (1967), and Roger Austen, *Genteel Pagan: The Double Life of Charles Warren Stoddard* (1991). Franklin Walker, *San Francisco's Literary Frontier* (1939; new ed., 1969), definitively places Coolbrith in context. See also William M. Clements, "Overland Monthly," in *American Literary Magazines: The Eighteenth and Nineteenth Centuries*, ed. Edward E. Chielens (1986), pp. 308–13, and Lawrence Ferlinghetti and Nancy J. Peters, *Literary San Francisco: A Pictorial History from the Beginnings to the Present Day* (1980). John E. Findling and Kimberly D. Pelle, eds., *Historical Dictionary of World's Fairs and Expositions, 1851–1988* (1990), includes descriptions of the two expositions in which Coolbrith was active. A brief, slightly inaccurate obituary is in the *New York Times*, 1 Mar. 1928.

ROBERT L. GALE

COOLEY, Charles Horton (17 Aug. 1864–7 May 1929), sociological theorist, was born in Ann Arbor, Michigan, the son of Thomas McIntyre Cooley, a prominent jurist, and Mary Elizabeth Horton. Not a great deal is known about Cooley's early life. Although he kept numerous notebooks, he later destroyed them. It appears from his later comments that his early childhood was not something he particularly wanted to remember and that from the age of eight until he was in his twenties his health was not good. As a youth he was shy and retiring, having few playmates. He liked solitary reading and often daydreamed, featuring himself as a great orator or leader.

Cooley entered the University of Michigan in 1880 at the age of sixteen and, because of his poor health, took seven years to complete his degree in mechanical engineering. His parents were well established and could afford to support him during this lengthy time period. He then worked in Bay City, Michigan, as a draftsman. From the winter of 1889–1890 until 1892 Cooley lived in Washington, D.C., working for the Interstate Commerce Commission and the Census Bureau. While in Washington he decided to pursue his studies in political economy.

In 1890, while working toward his Ph.D. at the University of Michigan, Cooley met and married Elsie Jones, the daughter of the first dean of the Homeopathic Medical College at the University of Michigan; they had a son and two daughters. By 1894 Cooley had finished his doctorate in political economy. His dissertation, "The Theory of Transportation," is considered by one intellectual historian of sociology to be a "pioneering study in human ecology" (Coser, p. 315). Cooley led a very sheltered life at the University of Michigan for the duration of his career. Whereas he was shy and retiring, his wife was outgoing and energetic. She ordered their lives so that he experienced few intrusions. Cooley closely observed the development of his own children. These observations contributed to his theories about the maturation of the self.

From 1892 to 1899 Cooley was an instructor at the University of Michigan. From 1899 to 1904 he was an assistant professor of economics and from 1904 to 1907 he was an associate professor. In 1907 he was appointed as a full professor of sociology. Cooley was a consistently productive writer throughout his lifetime. He wrote "Personal Competition" in 1899, which appeared in *Economic Studies* 4, no. 2 (Apr. 1899); *Human Nature and the Social Order* in 1902; *Social Organization* in 1909; and *Social Process* in 1918. He also wrote an autobiographical account, *Life and the Student*, in 1927, as well as a collection of essays, *Sociological Theory and Social Research* (1930). He wrote some twenty-five journal articles, of which the most important are reprinted in the last book. Despite this productivity, after he had earned advancement from the rank of assistant professor he had to remind the administration that he was due for promotion. This occurred again when he was due to be promoted to full professor. At the University of Michigan he did not like administrative or committee work. Yet he was well respected, particularly by his graduate students. After the publication of *Human Nature and the Social Order*, even his undergraduate courses were well attended. In spite of his own insecurities about his contributions to the emerging discipline of sociology, his status within the sociological profession was secure. In 1910 Franklin H. Giddings offered Cooley a job at Columbia University, which he turned down. He was elected as the president of the American Sociological Society in 1918.

Cooley declared that he had no living teachers in sociology. The writings of Johann Wolfgang von Goethe, Henry David Thoreau, Ralph Waldo Emerson, and Charles Darwin inspired him the most. His major intellectual contribution to the discipline was to focus attention on the plasticity of the human species and on the significance of primary groups in the formation of the self. These twin foci were offered in an age when instinct theory and social Darwinism were well accepted. In contrast to the age-old debate about which came first, the individual or society, Cooley argued that whether one theorized that society or the individual was primary, these were simply different ways of viewing social phenomena. The individual was shaped by social forces such as class, family, and nation as surely as societies were molded by individual persons and their particular characteristics. Cooley wrote that the individual and society were "twinborn."

Perhaps his most important contribution to the emerging discipline of sociology was conceptual: he argued that what makes us truly human is the characteristics acquired in "primary groups." While other theorists hypothesized about the instinctual nature of human "sociability," Cooley developed a whole line of thinking about the nature and origins of this sociability. In his theory, primary groups like the family, the neighborhood, and the play group can develop and nurture sentiments like sympathy, love, and self-feeling in the individual. Primary group sentiments are the basis for all other extended forms of social interaction and, therefore, are the bedrock of complex civilizations. Individuals without primary group attachments do not become fully developed human beings. Primary groups give us our basic "human nature": consciousness of self in relation to others, love of approbation, resentment of censure, emulation, and conscience. Moreover, Cooley believed that the abstract and ethical ideals that we have of love, freedom, and justice come to us not from abstract philosophy but from the simple and widely distributed forms of social relations in the family and play group. As he wrote: "In these relations mankind realizes itself, gratifies its primary needs, in a fairly satisfactory manner, and from the experience forms standards of what it is to expect from more elaborate association. Since groups of this sort are never obliterated from human experience, but flourish more or less under all kinds of institutions, they remain an enduring criterion by which the latter are ultimately judged" (*Social Organization*, p. 32).

Although influenced by James Mark Baldwin and William James, Cooley developed a distinctive notion of the maturation of the self. He argued that human nature was plastic and malleable and not primarily a product of biology and physiology. Biology was a constant in human nature, and history and culture were the variables. What we become as human beings is a product of belonging to different social groups. It is from our participation in the life of groups that we acquire language, human sentiments, and sympathy. In particular, Cooley suggested that we become adults as we develop a "looking-glass self"—that is, an image of how we appear to others, an image of their judgment of our appearance, and some sort of self-feeling. We are constantly dressing ourselves in front of others.

Cooley's critique of turn-of-the-century American capitalism followed from his analysis of primary group sentiments. He argued that we do not have enough primary group sentiments in the larger institutional sectors of society, particularly the economic sector. In this sense he argued, as did Émile Durkheim, the founder of French sociology, that the economy is morally unregulated. In particular, Cooley argued that economists spend too much time on the supply side of economics and not enough on the demand side. Cooley believed that the values manifested on the supply side (for example, economy and efficiency) are not appropriate for other aspects of society.

Like Giambattista Vico, Cooley argued that the social sciences are different from the natural sciences because humans have left a record of their activities. Cooley also believed that symbols have no inherent meaning. Symbols are expressions of different sorts of cultural practices, and they allow us to examine the development, record, and diffusion of meaning. Since humans create meaning over time, they can understand their present consciousness through a study of the past. Since our present meanings emanate from the past, we can use past history to understand our present and future.

As a social and political theorist, Cooley argued that one of the tasks of social science, like art, is to create ideal images. He argued that life is a "dynamic unfinished beauty, not a work of completed art." He asked, "Is not the creation of a fair society the supreme and inclusive art?" (*Life and the Student*, pp. 141, 143). He urged his contemporaries to imagine an ideal democratic society and to hold it up so that others might see how far and in what direction they must travel in order to bring about a fair society. A fair society, according to Cooley, not surprisingly derives its moral impetus from primary group sentiments. "The aspirations of ideal democracy—including, of course, socialism, and whatever else may go by a special name—are those naturally springing from the playground or the local community; embracing equal opportunity, fair play, the loyal service of all in the common good, free discussion, and kindness to the weak" (*Social Organization*, p. 51).

Primary group sentiments constitute the theoretical and normative grounds of Cooley's writings. Human nature is formed in primary groups. In spite of the perversion, stultification, and sublimation of primary group sentiments in many modern institutions, these sentiments endure in language and art and in the formative experiences of most people. Insofar as social scientists participate in the dialogue with language, art, and their own primary sentiments, they can articulate a noble ideal. This ideal not only provides the basis for a critique of modern society but also allows us to articulate a meaningful social practice, one that aligns itself with the sentiments first developed in primary groups.

Cooley's analysis of the looking-glass self passed into the common knowledge of our age, as practically every introductory sociology textbook described this notion and the idea of the primary group. His emphasis on the notion that the social sciences are different from the natural sciences in their methodologies was absorbed by numerous currents in contemporary sociology, including ethnography, symbolic interaction, and ethnomethodology. Cooley died in Ann Arbor, Michigan.

• Special collections of papers on and by Cooley are in the Luther Bernard Papers, Special Collections at the Pennsylvania State University Library, and the Luther Bernard Papers, Special Collections at the University of Chicago Library. For works that feature an assessment of Cooley, see Edward C. Jandy, *Charles Horton Cooley: His Life and His Social Theory* (1942); Robert Gutman, "Cooley: A Perspective," *American Sociological Review* 23 (June 1958): 251–56; Albert J. Reiss, ed., *Cooley's Sociological Analysis* (1968); and Michael D. Clark, "Charles H. Cooley and the Modern Necessity of Tradition," *Modern Age* 36 (Spring 1994): 277–85. Cooley also is treated in various histories of sociology, among them Charles Hunt Page, *Class and American Sociology: From Ward to Ross* (1969); Roscoe C. Hinkle, *Founding Theory of American Sociology, 1881–1915* (1980); Ellsworth R. Fuhrman, *The Sociology of Knowledge in America, 1883–1915* (1980); Lewis A. Coser, *Masters of Sociological Thought: Ideas in Historical and Social Context*, 2d ed. (1977); Glenn Jacobs, "Cooley's Journals: A Study of Sociological Theory Building" (Ph.D. thesis, Temple Univ. 1976).

E. R. FUHRMAN

COOLEY, Mortimer Elwyn (28 Mar. 1855–25 Aug. 1944), engineer and educator, was born near Canandaigua, New York, the son of Albert Blake Cooley and Achsah Bennett Griswold, farmers. After attending the Canandaigua Academy, Cooley taught for a year and then gained admission in 1874 to the U.S. Naval Academy. The navy of the Reconstruction era, poorly financed and overstocked with officers, offered dim prospects for a career, but it gave Cooley a solid education in mathematics and engineering and a habit of command that he kept until the end of his life. Cooley served briefly as a ship's engineer after graduating in 1878. In 1879 he married Caroline Elizabeth Moseley of Fairport, New York; the couple had four daughters. In 1880 he was detailed to teach steam engineering and naval architecture at the University of Michigan under the provisions of a new federal law that sought to give useful work to underemployed officers. The law stipulated that officers on loan to universities should receive the rank of full professor. Thus, Cooley became, at age twenty-six, a full professor at the University of Michigan. He would later claim that he was, at that time, one of only two mechanical engineers in the state. Be this as it may, the University of Michigan needed Cooley much more than did the navy. He resigned his commission in 1885 and, with the exception of brief service as an engineer aboard a blockade ship during the Spanish-American War, spent the rest of his career at Ann Arbor.

Cooley quickly became a popular and well-respected teacher on a campus where personality still mattered more than research accomplishments. His directness, talent for tale-telling and doggerel, and experience in the practical world of engines and boilers appealed to undergraduates, more and more of whom were planning careers in Michigan's booming industrial sector. Cooley himself discovered opportunities to enlarge his knowledge and income as a consultant; during the 1890s he advised state and municipal governments on the construction of power and heating systems for schools, hospitals, and prisons and began to appear with frequency in courtrooms as an expert witness in patent cases and jury trials. An appointment in 1899 as appraiser of the Detroit Street Railways led Cooley into the area in which he would focus much of his professional efforts in the next twenty years—the evaluation of public utilities. Combining extraordinary efficiency with considerable political savvy, Cooley subsequently organized surveys of the railroad properties of the states of Michigan and Wisconsin, of the streetcar systems of Minneapolis, Milwaukee, Chicago, Cleveland, and other major American cities, and of power and light companies in Ohio, Missouri, and other parts of the Midwest. Convinced that accurate tax assessments ought to depend on on-site inspections by engineers rather than simply the review of financial records, Cooley both improved the art of assessment and created new roles for engineers in government.

Colleagues and trustees at the University of Michigan came to appreciate Cooley's efficiency in administration, fairness of mind, and capacity to anticipate the future needs of the school and community. When the state legislature voted funds to expand the engineering college in 1902, Cooley helped plan the new laboratories and superintended construction of a 300-foot-long naval tank that would be the centerpiece for instruction and research in marine engineering. In 1903 he was appointed dean of the College of Engineering, a position he held until 1928. As dean, he guided the college through years in which enrollments more than quintupled and new initiatives were undertaken in highway and automotive engineering, chemical engineering, and electrical engineering. He advocated a broad education in the liberal arts for engineering students, believing that such preparation would stimulate powers of leadership and creative thought in recipients. At the same time, he worked energetically to establish facilities for graduate instruction and research. As part of this effort, he established the Department of Engineering Research in 1920 to undertake work sponsored by government agencies and private industries on a broad range of engineering problems. Cooley did much to transform Michigan's College of Engineering from an institution of modest, primarily local, reputation into a school exercising national leadership.

Cooley's views on engineering education and research were shaped by a conviction that the engineer was destined to play an ever larger role in the governance of American institutions, both public and private. Not only were technologies becoming more complex, so, too, were social organizations and relationships. In Cooley's opinion, the skills of the traditional politician or lawyer were no more adequate to the administration of government than were those of the bookkeeper to assessing the value of public utilities. Effective management called for knowledge and qualities of mind that engineers possessed: experience in the analysis of large systems, a grasp of mathematics and natural science, the habit of thinking undogmatically, and a capacity to elicit cooperation by well-informed straight talk.

Cooley brought his message to the voters of Michigan in 1924, when he was the Democratic candidate for the U.S. Senate. Running a vigorous campaign on the slogan "An Engineer in Congress," Cooley's fact-filled speeches excited little public interest and his resolute nonpartisanship failed to mobilize even the traditional Democratic voters, who then constituted a small minority in the state. On election day, Cooley lost to the incumbent, the liberal Republican James Couzens, by a 3-to-1 margin.

Cooley retired as dean of engineering at Michigan four years after his loss in the Senate race, although he continued to undertake occasional consulting jobs and served in 1933 as state engineer in the Public Works Administration. During a long retirement, he indulged his long-standing interest in the outdoors, taking long canoe trips in the Canadian woods, and continued to improve his collection of Oriental rugs—a hobby that made him familiar to rug dealers throughout the Midwest. Cooley died in Ann Arbor.

The engineer, according to Cooley, should lead an active life. He valued consulting opportunities, not just for the income but also for the direct contact with practical problems they afforded. He encouraged students and junior colleagues to acquire experience in industry and government; he accommodated the curriculum at Michigan to the economic needs of the state. He spoke often, if not always effectively, for a larger role for engineers in public life. While some observers criticized him for subordinating his profession to business, Cooley believed that engineers would be able to maintain their professional independence despite such service. Most of his colleagues and students shared his view. He was president of the American Society of Mechanical Engineers in 1919, of the Society for the Promotion of Engineering Education in 1920–1921, and the American Engineering Council in 1922–1924.

• The University of Michigan Historical Collection holds a large collection of Cooley's papers; additional materials are available in the College of Engineering records. Cooley's autobiography, *Scientific Blacksmith* (1947), yields considerable insight into the author's personality and views on engineering education. On Cooley's work on the evaluation of the value of utilities, see Henry E. Riggs, "Pioneers in Public Utility Regulation: Henry C. Adams and Mortimer E. Cooley," *Michigan Alumnus Quarterly Review* 51 (1954): 297–301; on his campaign for the Senate, see Melvin G. Holli and C. David Tompkins, "Mortimer E. Cooley: Technocrat as Politician," *Michigan History* 52 (Summer 1968): 133–46. See Kenneth E. Trombley, *The Life and Times of a Happy Liberal* (1954), on contemporary criticism of Cooley's views on the relation between engineers and business. Edwin T. Layton, *The Revolt of the Engineers: Social Responsibility and the American Engineering Profession* (1971), and David F. Noble, *America by Design: Science, Technology and the Rise of Corporate Capitalism* (1977), offer broader historical treatments of this issue. An obituary is in the *New York Times*, 26 Aug. 1944.

JOHN W. SERVOS

COOLEY, Spade (17 Dec. 1910–23 Nov. 1969), western swing bandleader and fiddler, was born Donnell Clyde Cooley in or near Pack Saddle Creek, Oklahoma, the son of John Cooley and Emma (maiden name unknown). Some sources indicate that he was born on 22 February 1910 in Grand (or Grande), Oklahoma. The family moved in 1914 to Oregon, where at age seven Cooley received his first musical instruction in classical violin, though soon he was applying his musical talents by fiddling at local dances. As one-quarter Cherokee Indian (from his father's side), Cooley attended Chemawa Indian School, at which he played the cello in the school orchestra. It was also at Chemawa that Cooley acquired his nickname "Spade" during a poker game in which he drew a number of spade flushes.

Cooley's family moved again in 1930 to Modesto, California. Cooley was ambitious to make it as a fiddler and soon headed to Los Angeles to try his luck. But good luck was not his at this point, and he quickly ended up back in Modesto, where for the next few years he worked with several local bands and improved his musicianship while earning little money. In 1934 he headed for Los Angeles again, reportedly with only "his violin and exactly 6 cents in his pocket," but this time things began to click. He met Roy Rogers, the successful cowboy singer who was then being groomed for the movies. Cooley resembled Rogers and was hired to do stand-in work for him. Between this and musical work with various bands, Cooley was able to make a decent living and build a reputation throughout the rest of the 1930s.

By the early 1940s, Cooley was ready for the big time, and Los Angeles was ready for him. Dust-bowl migration and wartime relocation had spread country music and its audience far and wide, and the Los Angeles area, with its thriving defense and entertainment industries, became a hotbed of country music activity. In 1942 Cooley took over leadership of Jimmy Wakely's band at the Venice Pier Ballroom, hiring several new members, including Sollie Paul "Tex" Williams as a vocalist. The band also included three fiddlers, accordionist and arranger Pedro DePaul, and vocalists Smokey Rogers and Deuce Spriggins. The new group was an instant hit and played Venice Pier for eighteen months. Cooley next took his band into the Riverside Rancho Ballroom in Santa Monica, where they played to overflow crowds from 1943 to early 1946. His success as a ballroom attraction reached its pinnacle in 1946, when he leased the prestigious Santa Monica Ballroom for his home venue. It was during these prosperous years that Cooley dubbed himself the "King of Western Swing," apparently the first use of the term that has since been applied broadly to swing jazz–influenced country dance bands.

Meanwhile, Cooley had begun appearing via other media, extending his celebrity to wider audiences. From his first recording session for Columbia in December 1944 came Cooley's biggest hit "Shame on You," which went to number one on the charts in 1945 and became his theme song. He also began to appear in films: he was featured in Warner Bros.'s *Spade Cooley, King of Western Swing* (1945) and given guest spots in a number of westerns, including *The Singing Sheriff* (1944), *Outlaws of the Rockies* (1945), and *Texas Panhandle* (1946). In 1945 Cooley married his second wife, Ella Mae Evans, a vocalist in his band; they had two children. With his first wife, Ann (maiden name unknown), he had had one son. The advent of television provided yet another golden opportunity, and in 1947 Cooley was invited to become the musical host of "The Hoffman Hayride," a variety show sponsored by the Hoffman Company, a regional maker of television sets. Eventually renamed "The Spade Cooley Show," it was broadcast from the Santa Monica Ballroom on station KTLA and quickly became a top-rated show in the Los Angeles area, remaining so for roughly six years.

Cooley's style during this "classic" era reflected multiple influences. Compared to his western swing predecessors Milton Brown and Bob Wills, Cooley's sound was more refined and arranged, perhaps reflecting Cooley's classical training and Los Angeles's entertainment industry. He tended toward large groups (one to two dozen musicians), and the core of his smooth ensemble sound was three to four tightly arranged violins, a pair of accordions and harp, and crooner-style vocals. This smoothness was offset by hot, jazzy steel guitar and guitar solos. Cooley's stage persona embodied the movie-industry version of the flamboyantly elegant cowboy; it is reported that his wardrobe included 100 hand-tailored suits and thirty-six pairs of boots.

By the mid-1950s, however, Cooley's star had begun to fall. Popular music tastes had begun to change, and though he tried different musical formats, by 1955 he was without a recording contract. By 1956 his TV popularity had given way to shows such as "Lawrence Welk" and "I Love Lucy" and he was off the air. In the latter 1950s, Cooley essentially retired from music and turned his ambition, energy, and acquired wealth toward a new project: the development of Water Wonderland, a 1,200-acre recreation area and amusement park near his home in the Antelope Valley. His plans included an eighteen-hole golf course, hotels and restaurants, a complete western town, three man-made lakes, and a 20,000-square-foot ballroom, but personal problems plagued him. He had suffered the first of a series of heart attacks around 1950 and had a growing drinking problem, and his marriage to Ella Mae was deteriorating. Just days after he announced that he was filing for divorce, Cooley's world came crashing down on 3 April 1961. That evening he returned home drunk, argued with Ella Mae, and in an out-of-control rage tortured, beat, and stomped her to death in front of their fourteen-year-old daughter. A week later he was convicted of first-degree murder and sentenced to life in prison. He had had another heart attack during the trial and thus was placed in a medical detention center in Vacaville. Cooley seemed repentant in prison, teaching and performing music with other inmates. As a result, the parole board reviewed his case in 1969, decided to grant him parole to begin in February 1970, and allowed him a short leave to play at a benefit concert sponsored by the Alameda County Sheriff's Association held on 23 November at the Oakland Auditorium. Bruce Henstell described the evening in a 1979 retrospective in *Los Angeles* magazine: "The 59-year-old Cooley played before a crowd of 3,000 and was greeted warmly, at least by those who looked beyond the lingering memory of the murder. He thanked the crowd and the authorities 'for the chance to be free for awhile.' Then he went backstage. There, speaking with friends, he slumped over from yet another heart attack. The show had been a triumph for Spade—but it was his last. The King of Western Swing was dead."

On one level, Cooley's life was a melodrama with a tragic ending: a meteoric rise from poor beginnings to fame and riches, rapid disappearance from the limelight, and a violent and sad ending preyed upon by the media. From a historical viewpoint, though, Cooley is remembered as one of the four key architects of the western swing style, occupying a second-generation position after Milton Brown and Bob Wills and preceding Hank Thompson, and the leader in this style on the West Coast.

• Bowling Green State University has a particularly strong collection of Cooley recordings, including some original issues. Two fine albums of Cooley's "classic" sound from the early to mid-1940s were reissued by Columbia: *Spade Cooley* (1982), and *Spadella: The Essential Spade Cooley* (1994). Presenting a broader repertory but not very accessible are a series of albums on the Club of Spade label: *As They Were* (n.d.); *The Best of Spade Cooley Transcribed Show* (n.d.); *King of Western Swing*, vols. 1–2 (n.d.); *Mr. Music Himself*, vols. 1–3 (n.d.); and *Oklahoma Stomp* (n.d.). For a good discography of old and rare recordings, see also Jerry Osborne, *Country Music Buyers-Sellers Reference Book and Price Guide* (1984). The best biographical article is in Tom Dunbar, *From Bob Wills to Ray Benson: A History of Western Swing Music*, vol. 1 (1988). Another good source is Bruce Henstell, "How the King of Western Swing Reached the End of His Rope," *Los Angeles*, June 1979, pp. 126ff. Helpful on Cooley's early years at Venice Pier are Jimmy Wakely's liner notes to the record *Spade Cooley* (1982). The chapter in Nick Tosches, *Country: The Biggest Music in America* (1977), devoted to Cooley is informative, although it dramatizes Cooley's crime for shock value. Interesting discussion on the origin of the term "western swing" and a comparison of Cooley's and Wills's bands can be found in the letters section of the John Edwards Memorial Foundation's *JEMF Quarterly* 17, nos. 62–64.

DANIEL C. L. JONES

COOLEY, Thomas McIntyre (6 Jan. 1824–12 Sept. 1898), jurist, was born in Genesee County, New York, the son of Thomas Cooley and Rachel Hubbard, farmers. Thomas grew up in the "Burned-Over" district of western New York at a time of religious revivals and anti-Masonic and Whig political ferment. As a young man he appears to have shared his parents' equal-rights Jacksonianism, their "Jeffersonian bias" as one of his friends later wrote. Cooley attended Attica Academy and was inclined to literary interests and the law, although previous generations of Cooleys had been farmers. In 1842 he studied law with Theron Strong, a former Democratic congressman, in Palmyra, New York. In 1843 he went to Michigan, where he settled in Adrian and continued to read law in local offices. He was admitted to the bar in 1846 and married Mary Horton that same year; they had six children. At mid-century Cooley's small legal practice was complemented by literary, journalistic, and political interests. He wrote poems attacking war and slavery and celebrating the European revolutions of 1848. He edited Democratic newspapers and acquired a reputation as a "Progressive Democrat." He also helped organize the Free Soil party in Michigan in 1848 and became a Republican in 1856.

In the 1850s Cooley concentrated more narrowly on the law and began to gain professional recognition. He served as compiler of Michigan statutes, as reporter to the state Supreme Court, and in 1859 became one of the first professors of law at the University of Michigan. He moved from Adrian to Ann Arbor in 1859 and remained there for the rest of his life as an important leader of the community and of the developing University of Michigan. In 1864 he was elected to the Michigan Supreme Court, where he served as the leading justice for twenty years. He was an independ-

ent Republican but considered running for Congress as a Liberal Republican in 1872. As a Mugwump he supported Grover Cleveland in 1884 and again in 1892. His independence may have cost him an appointment to the U.S. Supreme Court, but it also contributed to his 1887 nomination by President Cleveland to the Interstate Commerce Commission, where he emerged as the dominant commissioner. Henry Carter Adams, the young Michigan political economist whom Cooley brought to the commission as its chief statistician, wrote that Cooley's resignation, for health reasons, "was a national calamity." Adams believed that Cooley had begun to develop the meaning of the Interstate Commerce Act by administrative interpretation in the same way that John Marshall had developed the meaning of the Constitution. Ironically, the U.S. Supreme Court in the 1890s was not receptive to Cooley's ideas of administrative law.

In 1868 Cooley's *Treatise on the Constitutional Limitations Which Rest upon the Legislative Power of the States of the American Union* was published. The book went through six editions by 1890 and was probably the best-known legal treatise in the late nineteenth century. Cooley called it a mere "attorney's companion," but it was more than that. Published as the Fourteenth Amendment was being ratified, the treatise, especially Cooley's chapter on the protection of property by the "due process" clause of state constitutions, gained immediate attention because of its substantive, rather than mere procedural, definition of due process. For Cooley, due process meant that the powers of government must be exercised in accord with the "settled maxims" of the common law, especially its safeguards for the protection of individual rights. Cooley's common-law constitutionalism also protected individual liberty from arbitrary regulations that restricted rights "in a manner before unknown to the law." "Established principles," not mere procedure, determined whether a legislative or administrative act was due process.

At a time when American corporations began to look to the courts for protection against legislative regulation, Cooley's restrictive views of due process as based on common law maxims and Jacksonian views of "equal liberty" were regarded by some jurists as justification for "laissez-faire" policies. But Cooley did not intend to offer a constitutional refuge for corporations or unrestrained economic activity. His treatise accepted a broad police power and expressed skepticism of judicial review, a skepticism shared by James Bradley Thayer's criticism of that doctrine. On the Michigan court Cooley denied that due process meant judicial process (*Weimer v. Bunbury*. 30 Mich. 203 [1874]), and when he was on the Interstate Commerce Commission he defended administrative rate-setting against court decisions that said such actions violated due process. Cooley's commitment to individual rights did not extend to a defense of corporate rights. In several decisions on the Michigan court Cooley attacked the Dartmouth College case and its protection of corporate charters (*East Saginaw Manufacturing*

Company v. The City of East Saginaw, 10 Mich. 274 [1869]). He acquired some notoriety with his 1870 opinion in *People v. Salem* (20 Mich. 487), which denied tax aid to private railroad corporations because such aid served no "public purpose" and was "class legislation," inconsistent with the doctrine of "equal rights."

Cooley published articles for the leading journals of the day and was in demand as a lecturer to bar associations and as an arbitrator of trunk-line disputes. Work became something of a narcotic for him, as one of his children said, and in the 1880s overwork contributed to his deteriorating health. Ambivalence, created by his commitment to principles of both equality and liberty, inclined him to a nostalgic conservatism at odds with the political corruption, the concentration of wealth, and the conflict of labor and capital in post–Civil War America. His anxiety was evident in an 1879 lecture on city government in which he remarked that "poverty was never in so much danger of becoming master as when capital unjustly manipulates the legislation of the country."

Cooley enjoyed a close family life in Ann Arbor and was desolate after his wife's death in 1890. His health continued to decline, and, according to his physician son, Thomas, his death in Ann Arbor came as a "long-delayed and much-hoped-for release." His son Charles Cooley, who became a noted sociologist, believed that his father's life had been narrowed by the ideology of the law and that "a nature susceptible and warm enough at the start has been confined by a one-sided development." That may be the case, but Cooley's predicament was also an ironic commentary on tensions between politics and the law and between equality and liberty in American life.

• Thomas Cooley's papers are in the Bentley Historical Collections at the University of Michigan. See two articles by Alan Jones, "Thomas M. Cooley and Laissez-Faire Constitutionalism: A Reconsideration," *Journal of American History* 53 (Mar. 1967): 751–71, and "Law and Economics v. A Democratic Society, The Case of Thomas M. Cooley, Charles H. Cooley, and Henry Carter Adams," *The American Journal of Legal History* 56 (Apr. 1992): 119–38. See also Alan Jones, *Constitutional Conservatism of Thomas McIntyre Cooley: A Study in the History of Ideas* (1987), and Benjamin Twiss, *Lawyers and the Constitution: How Laissez-Faire Came to the Supreme Court* (1942).

ALAN R. JONES

COOLIDGE, Albert Sprague (23 Jan. 1894–31 Aug. 1977), chemical physicist, political activist, and civil libertarian, was born in Chicago, Illinois, the son of Frederic Shurtleff Coolidge, an orthopedic surgeon, and Elizabeth Penn Sprague. His mother was the daughter of Albert Arnold Sprague, a pioneer merchant of Chicago, which made it possible for Sprague Coolidge to be financially independent. He was directly descended from John Coolidge of Watertown, Massachusetts, who emigrated from England in 1630 and whose farm occupied almost all of what is now Cambridge, Massachusetts. His college preparatory education was at the Hill School in Pottstown, Pennsylvania. He graduated summa cum laude with an A.B. from Harvard College in 1915. That year he married Margaret Stewart Coit. They had five children.

Coolidge did research on charcoal for gas masks during the First World War, serving as an enlisted man for the U.S. Army's Chemical Warfare Service. He was discharged in 1919 with the rank of sergeant, first class. He then set up a private laboratory in Pittsfield, Massachusetts, but he found that too isolated. He returned to Harvard in 1920 and received his Ph.D. in chemistry in 1924 under the supervision of Professor George Shannon Forbes with the thesis "The Adsorption of Vapors by Charcoal and Other Papers." At Harvard he was an instructor in chemistry from 1922 to 1930 and a lecturer in chemistry without salary from 1931 until his retirement in 1960. He refused a regular faculty position because he said he did not need the money. He was chair at the inception and for many years afterward of the Committee on the Ph.D. in Chemical Physics, a program that became internationally preeminent.

Coolidge's early publications report experimental researches on charcoal and other topics. In "The Vapor Density and Some Other Properties of Formic Acid," he demonstrated that formic acid exists as a dimer, an associated complex of two molecules (*Journal of the American Chemical Society* 50 [1928]: 2166). About 1930 Coolidge became interested in the emerging revolutionary developments in quantum physics. In his report for his twenty-fifth college reunion he wrote that he "abandoned the laboratory for the library and the computing room."

Using the Schrödinger equation, it is possible to calculate accurately the energetics of one-electron systems such as the hydrogen atom, but this approach fails for more complicated systems because of the complexity of electron-electron interactions. Coolidge made an important scientific breakthrough by demonstrating that approximation methods could be used to gain accurate results on systems with more than one electron. Coolidge and a graduate student, Hubert M. James, did the first quantum calculation on a molecule. Their results on the hydrogen molecule were the most accurate until the time of high speed computers with very large memories. This was the first demonstration that theoretical quantum mechanics could yield molecular energies of great accuracy. Subsequently, Coolidge's work was the conceptual foundation for extensive research by many investigators, and quantum calculations of chemical systems became a significant field within chemistry. In addition to the famous Coolidge and James calculation on the hydrogen molecule ("The Ground State of the Hydrogen Molecule," *Journal of Chemical Physics* 1 [1933]: 825–35), related papers are "Improved Calculation of the Ground State of H_2" (*Physical Review* 43 [1933]: 588) and "A Correction and Addition to the Discussion of the Ground State of H_2" (*Journal of Chemical Physics* 3 [1935]: 129). The approximations involved in the calculation were discussed in "The Approximations Involved in Calculations of Atomic Interactions and Activation Energies" (*Journal of Chemical Physics* 2 [1934]: 811). This method was used in similar quantum calculations on the Li_2 molecule ("Wave Mechanical Treatment of the Li_2 Molecule," *Journal of Chemical Physics* 2 [1934]: 794) and on excited hydrogen ("Wave Functions and Potential Curves for Excited H_2," *Journal of Chemical Physics* 6 [1938]: 730). When his theoretical results on the spectra of hydrogen did not agree with the known experimental data, Coolidge built the experimental equipment necessary to re-examine this question and found data in essential agreement with theory.

Coolidge was active in defense of civil liberties. He was a charter founder of Americans for Democratic Action and served as president of the Massachusetts chapter. He also served as president of the Massachusetts Civil Liberties Union. In that position, on 24 April 1951, he appeared before a committee of the Massachusetts legislature that was investigating "communist activities." He protested vigorously the treatment of two members of the Communist party and a representative of the League of Women Voters. He said that they had been "heckled and bullied and abused" by the committee. A shouting match ensued with demands by legislators for an apology, but Coolidge, who normally was quiet, dignified, and polite, stood his ground. Starting from the "desire to see scientific methods applied to social problems" (Harvard, twenty-fifth reunion class notes), Coolidge became a Socialist and was active politically. He was the Socialist party's candidate for senator from Massachusetts in 1934, and he was a member of the national executive committee from 1932 to 1937.

His mother had endowed the Elizabeth Sprague Coolidge Foundation for support of chamber music at the Library of Congress, and she served on the managing committee of this foundation until her death in 1953. Sprague Coolidge was told that he was the unanimous choice to replace his mother, but the offer later was withdrawn on the grounds that he was a security risk, a result of opposition to Coolidge by Senator Joseph McCarthy. He said at the time that he would not campaign for the $250 per year position but that the decision to deny his appointment "makes the government look ridiculous." The memorial minute to Coolidge by the Harvard faculty, 10 April 1979, notes that Coolidge "did what he thought was interesting and right, whatever others might think."

Coolidge was known well to graduate students in Harvard's chemistry department because he was responsible for administering language examinations. In these examinations, students would report to Coolidge in the Chemistry Library, he would select a journal article, apparently at random, and the student would write a translation. Immediately upon finishing, Coolidge would sit with the student, make corrections, and decide whether the student had passed. One graduate student found Coolidge willing to read a translation into Spanish rather than English.

Like his mother, Coolidge was devoted to chamber music, playing both viola and oboe, and was the first president of the Cambridge Civic Orchestra. At Harvard he presented a celebrated annual lecture on the physics of music, performing on more than a dozen musical instruments. He was an expert photographer, doing his own developing to produce excellent prints. He built and operated elaborate model railroads, an interest that led to his book *Building a Model Railroad* (1929). Noted for his classic automobiles, he owned a 1914 Detroit Electric and two Franklin touring cars, one for Cambridge and one for his summer home in Vermont. Coolidge died at the River Crest Nursing Home in Concord, Massachusetts.

• Copies of a faculty memorial to Coolidge by his chemical physics colleagues and Coolidge's class reports are in the Harvard University Archives, which also has news clippings that cover some of Coolidge's political activities and his actions in defense of civil liberties. A brief biography with an excellent photo of Coolidge is in *National Cyclopedia of American Biography*, vol. 60 (1981), pp. 42–43. A discussion of the James and Coolidge research is found in J. C. Slater, *Quantum Theory of Molecules and Solids*, vol. 1 (1963), pp. 74–79, and chap. 4. A detailed obituary is in the *Boston Globe*, 1 Sept. 1977.

PAUL HAAKE

COOLIDGE, Archibald Cary (6 Mar. 1866–14 Jan. 1928), historian, was born in Boston, Massachusetts, the son of Joseph Randolph Coolidge and Julia Gardner, prominent Bostonians. His father was the great-grandson of Thomas Jefferson; his mother was the daughter of a banking and shipping magnate. Despite their wealth and social position, the Coolidge family was Spartan, staunchly Unitarian, and aloof from much of Boston society.

Coolidge attended Harvard College, graduating summa cum laude in history in 1887 and leaving shortly thereafter to study for a Ph.D. in history at the University of Freiburg, Germany. In Europe Coolidge traveled widely and attempted to broaden his experience beyond the confines of his university. He studied for a number of terms at both the University of Berlin and the École des Sciences Politiques in Paris and mastered a number of European languages, as well as Russian. In the winter of 1890–1891 he worked for six months as acting secretary of the legation in St. Petersburg, and afterward he traveled throughout Russia. The following spring he served as a private secretary to his uncle Thomas Jefferson Coolidge, the American minister to France. By the time Coolidge received his doctorate in 1892, he had grown firm in his belief that a complete education required extensive travel and varied experience. Unlike many of his American contemporaries he continued throughout his life to expose himself to new languages and cultures.

After serving briefly as secretary of the American legation in Vienna, Coolidge returned to Boston and to Harvard, becoming an instructor in history in 1893. Coolidge lavished his attentions on Harvard single-mindedly, undistracted by a family of his own. He proposed and taught Harvard's first course in Russian history and pushed the university to teach Russian and other Slavic languages and literature. He broadened the horizons of the historical discipline in the United States by advancing the study not only of Russia and Northern and Eastern Europe but of other regions long ignored by American historians, including Latin America.

Coolidge sought above all to analyze the past as dispassionately as possible. Unlike many of his peers he maintained a neutral view of Russian expansion and stressed this to his students. Coolidge's desire for historical objectivity steered him away from theory. His most famous book, *The United States as a World Power* (1908), went through ten editions as well as printings in French, German, and Japanese. Yet like his other two books, *Origins of the Triple Alliance* (1917) and *Ten Years of War and Peace* (1927), it was distinguished by its judicious tone rather than by any interpretative breakthroughs. The first two books grew out of a series of public lectures and the third out of a collection of magazine articles. Compared to many of his contemporaries, Coolidge produced few major works of archivally based historical scholarship.

From his elevation to professor in 1908 until his death in Boston, Coolidge continued his efforts to improve Harvard. After President Abbott Lawrence Lowell named him director of the university library in 1910, he overhauled the catalog and classification systems and increased the number and quality of the library's acquisitions. Urging Harvard to "buy first and find the money afterwards" (Byrnes, p. 120) and acting on this dictum, Coolidge personally purchased most of the 30,000 volumes in the university's Slavic collection and paid for their cataloging himself. He was critical in advancing the plans for Widener Library, the centerpiece of the university's famous library system.

Coolidge's lifelong work for Harvard did not prevent him from briefly serving the U.S. government as well. Coolidge was one of the first academics to join "The Inquiry," a research group convened by Colonel Edward M. House in 1917 to prepare the United States for the upcoming peace conference. Coolidge directed the Eastern European division, based in Widener Library, which gathered information about Austria-Hungary, Russia, and Russia's western frontier. In May 1918 he left the group to study conditions in Russia for the Department of State; the following year he spent five months in Vienna reporting on the situation in Central and Eastern Europe for the benefit of American postwar planners. He next joined the American Commission to Negotiate Peace in Paris to help draft the Austrian and Hungarian peace treaties and to assess the Austrian response to Allied proposals. He finished his work for the U.S. government after the war, when at Herbert Hoover's request he headed a liaison division of the American Relief Administration in Russia.

When Coolidge left Russia for Boston in March 1922, he was invited to become the first editor in chief of *Foreign Affairs*, the journal of the newly founded Council on Foreign Relations. Despite his desire to return to teaching and directing the library, Coolidge viewed his six years with the prominent quarterly as important for exposing the informed public to discussions of U.S. foreign policy and international affairs. As editor he outlined the policy that *Foreign Affairs* maintained throughout the remainder of the twentieth century, insisting that the journal "not devote itself to the support of any one cause, however worthy." He consciously sought articles from those he disagreed with, including the isolationist Senator William E. Borah.

Aside from his three books, Coolidge edited three others, wrote sixteen scholarly articles and numerous reviews, and contributed frequently to the *Nation*, the *New York Evening Post*, and *Foreign Affairs*. But Coolidge was not anxious for political influence; he believed strongly that a scholar should provide accurate information without becoming politically involved. Although he helped found one of the most famous journals in international affairs, he was circumspect about advancing his opinion if he thought it might influence political decisions. Reluctant to embroil himself in the debate over U.S. entry into World War I, for example, he avoided publicly announcing his opinion on the war's origins until after the United States had abandoned neutrality. Similarly, despite his formidable expertise on the problems of Central and Eastern Europe, it is unlikely that he significantly influenced the peace process. Coolidge usually preferred to make his contributions unobtrusively, as when he quietly trained students for scholarly or diplomatic careers. This political reticence, like his lack of interest in theory, has perhaps diminished his work in the eyes of recent historians. But by the standards of his day, Coolidge was eminent.

• Coolidge's personal papers, which include his extensive correspondence and several unpublished manuscripts, are in the Harvard University Archives. The most recent biography is Robert F. Byrnes, *Awakening American Education to the World: The Role of Archibald Cary Coolidge, 1866–1928* (1982). Byrnes's invaluable bibliographical essay and bibliography provide an excellent guide for further work on Coolidge. See also Robert A. McCaughey, *International Studies and Academic Enterprise: A chapter in the Enclosure of American Learning* (1984), pp. 74–82. An obituary is in the *New York Times*, 15 Jan. 1928.

EMILY B. HILL

COOLIDGE, Calvin (4 July 1872–5 Jan. 1933), thirtieth president of the United States, was born John Calvin Coolidge in Plymouth Notch, Vermont, the son of John Calvin Coolidge, a storekeeper and farmer, and Victoria Moor. After graduating from Amherst College in 1895, Coolidge read law in Northampton, Massachusetts. He was admitted to the bar in 1897. In 1905 he married Grace Anna Goodhue, a teacher of the deaf; they had two sons.

Coolidge practiced law in Northampton. Steeped in politics by his father, he also engaged in public service. Officeholding eventually became his chief occupation. Although Coolidge was taciturn, his diligence, honesty, reliability, and skillfulness at determining the wishes of his constituents stood him well in climbing the political ladder. In 1898 he was elected to Northampton's city council and thereafter successively served as city solicitor, clerk of Hampshire County's courts, and state representative. Coolidge was elected mayor of Northampton in 1909 and two years later was elected to the Massachusetts Senate. There he attracted statewide notice for his role in settling the great textile strike in Lawrence. In 1914 the Senate elected Coolidge its president. In that office he gained a reputation for efficiency and pithiness, counseling his colleagues to "be brief" and "do the day's work." The voters of Massachusetts elected Coolidge lieutenant governor in 1915 and governor in 1918. By then it was clear that he offered something for everyone so long as it did not cost too much. He was reasonably compassionate with ordinary folk although a promoter of business development, and he was shrewd and effective in discharging his official and political duties.

Governor Coolidge received much credit for his efforts to reorganize the state government, restrain the soaring cost of living, and settle labor-management disputes. Moreover, he championed ratification of the woman's suffrage amendment and favored limiting the workweek for children and women. Coolidge's national reputation came, however, from his role in the highly publicized Boston police strike of 1919. He upheld the city police commissioner's decision to deprive the striking officers of their jobs, which led Samuel Gompers of the American Federation of Labor to dispute the governor. Coolidge's response was, "There is no right to strike against the public safety by anybody, anywhere, any time." This brought him national attention and overwhelming reelection as governor that fall.

He ran for the Republican presidential nomination as a favorite son in 1920. After the convention delegates nominated Senator Warren G. Harding for president, in a surprise move they selected Coolidge to be his running mate. The ticket gained a landslide victory that November. As vice president, Coolidge was hardly noticed. Upon Harding's death, however, he was catapulted into prominence. Coolidge's father swore in his son as president in their rural Vermont home by the light of an oil lamp at 2:47 A.M., 3 August 1923.

Calvin Coolidge presented a great contrast to Harding and every other president then within living memory. As William Allen White wrote, Coolidge was "not like the run of the herd." He was cautious, unpretentious, and parsimonious with money, speech, and time. Pundits widely portrayed him as "Silent Cal," a man whose perfect day was one on which nothing happened. Fortunately for him, his wife, Grace, was vivacious. Moreover, Coolidge had a keen, pointed wit. An example of this was his reply to a woman who told him that she had a bet she could "get more than two words" out of him. "You lose," the president responded.

Coolidge was a caring family man, and he was sympathetic to the ordinary concerns of the people. If he husbanded his energies, he was a conscientious public servant. Coolidge believed the government should seldom act unless necessary, but he also thought that when the government acted, it should do so well. His friend Dwight Morrow provided some insight into him, as reported by a British diplomat. Coolidge was "a man of great simplicity, who never dealt with any subject which he did not understand. If the question of China, for instance, cropped up, he would merely say that he knew nothing about it and refuse personally to rush into the matter."

As chief executive, Coolidge was effective because of his simple, direct, and responsible style. He normally formulated his policies only after consultation and study. Coolidge expected his subordinates to do their jobs efficiently based on those policies and it was clear that if they could not do so, he might replace them. Consequently, the president generally received faithful service from his appointees. He reinforced this by effectively using the Bureau of the Budget to control executive expenditures and programs. If Coolidge did not have a lot to administer compared with later presidents, he administered what he did have exceptionally well. Coolidge was also an excellent spokesman for his administration. He held regular press conferences—his only innovation as president—which he handled like an affable though strict schoolmaster.

Congress was not in session during his first four months in office, so Coolidge was able to study diligently the work of the executive branch and prepare his legislative program. This proved to be an advantage, for in 1924 he would be engaged in combat with Congress.

Harding's administration had been touched by scandals in the Alien Property Custodian's Office and the Veterans Bureau. New scandals emerged in 1924. One problem concerned the ineptitude and corruption surrounding the activities of the attorney general, Harry M. Daugherty. Federal officials and the public quickly lost confidence in him. When Daugherty denied Senate investigators access to Justice Department files, Coolidge promptly demanded, on 27 March, his resignation on the ground that he could not act as both attorney general and his own defense counsel.

Meanwhile, an even greater scandal erupted. Evidence indicated that oil developers Edward Doheny and Harry Sinclair had bribed Albert Fall, when he had been interior secretary, in order to exploit the federal petroleum reserves at Teapot Dome in Wyoming and Elk Hills in California. The press and politicians had a field day; some even charged that Harding's entire cabinet, including Coolidge, had been involved. Coolidge acted expeditiously in dealing with the accusations. He appointed two special counsel, a Republican and a Democrat, to handle the situation. Their work eventually led to the conviction of Fall for receiving bribes and of Sinclair for contempt of court. The Teapot Dome scandal contributed to Daugherty's resignation and to that of Navy Secretary Edwin Denby, although there was no evidence of his culpability. It also led to other congressional investigations.

Coolidge handled these situations skillfully, which explained the attractiveness of his 1924 presidential election slogan, "Keep Cool with Coolidge." With almost indecent haste, the Republican National Convention nominated him for president. He handily defeated his opponents, Democrat John W. Davis (1873–1955) and Progressive Robert M. La Follette (1855–1925), in the November elections, polling almost 55 percent of the votes cast.

Although effective as an administrator, Coolidge was less successful with Congress. This was not for lack of trying, for he made himself available for consultation with senators and representatives of both parties. His problems with Congress had many origins. These included battles over the Harding era scandals, the independence of many Republican legislators, and the ability of Democratic solons to exploit differences among Republicans.

Coolidge's policies differed little from those of Harding. Coolidge championed economical and efficient government and was more concerned with cutting federal taxes and the national debt than with financing new programs. This course, he believed, would promote prosperity as would his administration's encouragement of business development, based on his conviction that the "chief business of America is business." Yet he was interested in a modest expansion of federal programs, so long as it did not jeopardize lowering taxes and reducing the government's debt. Congress had little argument with cutting taxes since government revenues substantially exceeded expenditures. Many legislators wanted, however, to use surplus revenues for existing and new programs, some with political purposes but others with more public-spirited ends. The biggest issues concerned development of Muscle Shoals on the Tennessee River, federal purchase of surplus agricultural commodities and their cheap resale overseas, a bonus for World War I veterans, and flood control projects. The Coolidge administration produced a standoff on the Muscle Shoals issue; major conflict on the McNary-Haugen bills for farm surpluses, which Coolidge vetoed in 1927 and 1928; blockage of a bonus for veterans; and flood control legislation, the cost of which the president greatly reduced.

Most important to Coolidge, he succeeded in protecting his economic program, thus permitting tax cuts in 1926 and 1928 and substantial reduction of the federal debt in order to stimulate business and contain inflation. Nevertheless, he had other victories on Capitol Hill. These included the promotion and regulation of aviation, the regulation of the chaotic radio business with the establishment of the Federal Radio Commission in 1927, and authorization in 1926 of a large program for the construction of federal buildings, including the National Archives. Moreover, the president and Congress agreed on increased funding for, among other things, conciliation of industrial disputes, Indian programs, highway construction, inland water-

ways, and national forests and parks. Coolidge and Congress also agreed that, as he said, "America must be kept American." Thus Congress overwhelmingly passed the restrictionist Immigration Act of 1924.

Coolidge's foreign policy was not adventuresome. His administration worked with some success to improve American relations with China, Mexico, and Nicaragua. The government also increased its cooperation with the League of Nations and supported the Dawes Plan of 1924 to alleviate severe financial distress in Germany. The administration's and private American assistance to Japan after a disastrous earthquake and typhoon in 1923 engendered good feelings there. This neighborliness was negated, however, when Congress, over the administration's strenuous objections, provided no quota for Japanese in the 1924 Immigration Act.

Coolidge was identified with three bold foreign policy initiatives, although they were essentially forced upon him. In 1926 the Senate agreed with his request to ratify American membership on the Permanent Court of International Justice, or World Court. The ratification contained, however, a reservation that the United States would not be bound by the court's advisory opinions, which was unacceptable to most of the court's member nations. The administration also sponsored the Geneva naval arms limitation conference of 1927, but the summit collapsed in disarray. Best known was the Kellogg-Briand Pact of 1928 in which the fifteen signatory nations condemned war and renounced it "as an instrument of national policy in their relations with one another." Unfortunately for world peace, this treaty was ineffective.

Otherwise in foreign affairs, Coolidge pursued policies intended to promote American exports and enhance investment opportunities abroad. His administration was too successful at this, for large favorable trade imbalances and too many risky investments contributed to the coming and the deepening of the Great Depression of the 1930s. Related to this imbalance was the inability of the administration and other governments to resolve the problem of the huge World War I debts they owed to the United States. Americans generally saw forgiveness of the debts of foreign governments as something that would be disastrous to their nation's economy. Coolidge supposedly said, "They hired the money, didn't they?"

Calvin Coolidge was popular with a large majority of Americans. He chose, however, not to run for reelection in 1928. After leaving the White House in March 1929, he retired to Northampton, where he spent his remaining years writing and engaging in occasional business, civic, and political activities. He died in Northampton.

Coolidge faced few crises as president, but he handled satisfactorily those problems that arose during his time in office. He was an outstanding administrator and a skillful politician. If his relations with Congress were often troublesome, he succeeded more often than not in having his way. Coolidge did not expect great things from government; consequently, he sought relatively little from it. This attitude seems to have been in tune with what most Americans wanted then.

• The most significant collections of Calvin Coolidge's papers are in the Library of Congress and the Forbes Library, Northampton, Mass.; scattered records relating to him can be found in the National Archives. The major biographies are Donald R. McCoy, *Calvin Coolidge: The Quiet President* (1967; repr., with new preface, 1988); Claude M. Fuess, *Calvin Coolidge: The Man from Vermont* (1940); and William Allen White, *A Puritan in Babylon: The Story of Calvin Coolidge* (1938). Also useful are Ishbel Ross, *Grace Coolidge and Her Era* (1962), and the occasional publications of the Calvin Coolidge Memorial Foundation, Plymouth, Vt. Among relevant scholarly articles are Robert J. Maddox, "Keeping Cool with Coolidge," *Journal of American History* 52 (1967); John Blair, "Coolidge the Image Maker: The President and the Press, 1923–1929," *New England Quarterly* 46 (1973), and "Calvin Coolidge and the Advent of Radio Politics," *Vermont History* 44 (1976). Pertinent volumes of documents are The Council (Mass.), *Calvin Coolidge, Messages to the General Court, Official Addresses, Proclamations and State Papers* (1920); Howard H. Quint and Robert H. Ferrell, eds., *The Talkative President: The Off-the-Record Press Conferences of Calvin Coolidge* (1964); and Edward Connery Lathem, ed., *Your Son, Calvin Coolidge: A Selection of Letters from Calvin Coolidge to His Father* (1968). Coolidge was the author of numerous articles and volumes; among the most useful are *The Autobiography of Calvin Coolidge* (1929) and *Have Faith in Massachusetts* (1919; 2d ed., 1920). Obituaries and other retrospective material were carried in the country's major newspapers on 5 and 6 Jan. 1933.

DONALD R. McCOY

COOLIDGE, Dane (24 Mar. 1873–8 Aug. 1940), novelist, naturalist, and photographer, was born in Natick, Massachusetts, the son of Francis Coolidge, a corporal in the Civil War and, later, an orange grower in California, and Sophia Upham Whittemore. He moved with his family in 1877 to Los Angeles, where he roamed the fields and mountains around that still-small town and grew up a Republican and a Unitarian. Coolidge graduated from Stanford University in 1898, then studied biology at Harvard University from 1898 to 1899 before returning to the West.

Long before he was a writer, he was a naturalist, first acting as field collector of mammals in Nevada for Stanford University in the summer of 1895. The next summer he collected specimens in Baja California for the British Museum (Natural History) and, in 1897, southern California species for the U.S. Biological Survey. He continued this field work until the turn of the century, for the U.S. National Zoological Park (1898) in both California and Arizona; for the New York (Bronx) Zoo in 1899, collecting live animals, including birds and reptiles; and finally in Italy and France for the U.S. National Museum in 1900.

Who Was Who gives the date of his marriage as 30 July 1906, but the *San Francisco Examiner* carried a marriage notice for Coolidge on 4 October 1909. His wife was a Stanford-trained sociologist-anthropologist, Mary Elizabeth Burroughs Roberts Smith, who had received a Carnegie research grant in 1904. In 1918 Mary E. B. Coolidge was appointed to the faculty of

Mills College in Oakland, California. She was a member of the state board of education, an author in her own right (*Chinese Immigration* [1909]), and an expert on Indian affairs as well as "the Chinese problem." She lectured to women's clubs and the American Association of University Women and was of great help to Coolidge, coauthoring three books with him. The couple had no children.

Dane Coolidge's first novel was *Hidden Water* (1910), and his last, of thirty-seven titles, was *Bear Paw* (1941). All were formula westerns, but his scientific knowledge of flora and fauna made their backgrounds more realistic than those of most potboilers. He was no stylist, but he wrote a straightforward prose without histrionics and with remarkably little violence and bloodshed. He depended on nonstop action, not characterization, to advance his stories, and his heroes were simple, not profound. But they were not just the stereotypes of the westerns of many of his peers. His sheep and cattle wars were ruthless, ugly, and cruel business vendettas of butchered livestock rather than melodramatic shoot-outs at high noon. Occasionally he based his fiction closely on history, as in the case of *Sheriff Killer* (1932), recalling Captain Burton Mossman of the Arizona Rangers, and *Gringo Gold* (1939), calling to mind the legendary California *bandido* Joaquín Murieta.

Coolidge also wrote short stories for popular pulp magazines such as *West* and *Western Story* in the 1920s and early 1930s and contributed travel articles and other light prose to the magazine section of the *San Francisco Chronicle* and to periodicals such as *Overland Monthly*, *Sunset*, and *Westways*.

In the 1930s Coolidge began to write nonfiction books in addition to novels. He coauthored *The Navajo Indians* (1930), *Navajo Rugs* (1933), and *The Last of the Seris* (1939) with his wife. Many readers found the last book fascinating, although its authors were wrong in predicting the extinction of the Seris. The Coolidges lived with the little-known Seri Indians of Mexico's west coast and the island of Tiburón in the Gulf of California for some months, and Coolidge made many photographs there. The book was reprinted in 1991 as a Rio Grande Press Classic.

Fighting Men of the West (1932) and *Death Valley Prospectors* (1937) are collectible today, finding their way into antiquarian booksellers' catalogs much more often than Coolidge's forgotten novels. Some of the information in *Fighting Men* was based on personal interviews, but Ramon F. Adams, always very critical, described Coolidge as a "prolific, though not always accurate author" in his survey *Burs under the Saddle*. Nevertheless, the title was reprinted by Bantam in 1952 as a regional classic and by Corgi in London in 1954.

The most popular and best-remembered books by Coolidge are *Texas Cowboys* (1937), *Arizona Cowboys* (1938), and *Old California Cowboys* (1939). *Arizona Cowboys*, for example, is still of interest for its details of cattle roundups and the feuds between cattlemen and sheepmen, and it is illustrated by Coolidge's own excellent photographs of ranching scenes. Critic J. Frank Dobie, in *Life and Literature of the Southwest*, considered the three cowboy books to be "thin, but genuine." Owen Ulph, in *American West*, wrote that Coolidge's "ironic irreverence" owed more to Ambrose Bierce than to Owen Wister or Emerson Hough, and that his novels were intellectually superior to those of Zane Grey and William McLeod Raine.

Coolidge readily admitted that his novels were entertainment, not sagas or "literature." All of his nonfiction books are superior to his fiction, although popular ("thin") rather than scholarly. Those illustrated by his own photographs are most memorable. But Coolidge accurately recorded a West that was disappearing. He never vulgarized his cowboys, and he refused to imitate the bloody "horse operas" of some of his rivals.

Coolidge's stock as a novelist is low, as a popular historian, only so-so. But he may yet be rediscovered as a talented, although amateur, photographer. His dramatic and picturesque—yet authentic—action pictures (1907–1916) of legitimate cowhands of Arizona's "Cherrycow" (Chiricahua Cattle Company) outfit, for example, are truly extraordinary documents. Coolidge died in Berkeley, California.

• Coolidge's papers, manuscripts, and photos are mostly in the University of California's Bancroft Library in Berkeley, but there is also a fine cache of his Arizona ranching photos in the Special Collections Department of the University of Arizona Library, Tucson. The *San Francisco Chronicle* ran a sketch of his literary career on 25 Dec. 1921. A favorable appreciation of the author's cowboy nonfiction is Owen Ulph, "Dane Coolidge, Western Writer and Photographer," *American West* 14, no. 6 (Nov.–Dec. 1977): 32–46. The best coverage of his entire literary output is Jon Tuska's biobibliography in *Twentieth Century Western Writers* (1991). An obituary is in the *San Francisco Chronicle*, 9 Aug. 1940.

RICHARD H. DILLON

COOLIDGE, Elizabeth Sprague (30 Oct. 1864–4 Nov. 1953), music philanthropist, was born in Chicago, the oldest child of Albert Arnold Sprague, a successful businessman, and Nancy Atwood. She was educated privately and in her youth made several trips abroad in company with her affluent parents, visiting such places as Bayreuth, Egypt, and Russia. At age eleven she began piano lessons with Regina Watson at her School for the Higher Art of Piano Playing in North Chicago and quickly became her "show-pupil," appearing regularly on recital programs from age twelve in performances of music by Joseph Joachim Raff, Felix Mendelssohn, Johann Nepomuk Hummel, and Frédéric Chopin. In 1882, at age eighteen, Coolidge presented her first solo recital.

In 1890 Coolidge began to write music; as her life evolved, composition became principally a source of spiritual consolation in the face of the deafness that began to afflict her in her early thirties. She composed many children's songs as well as several instrumental chamber works, including a Christmas Sextet, a String Quartet in E Minor, and a Sonata for oboe and piano,

which was published by Carl Fischer. For the most part her works were overlooked by critics.

In 1891 she married Frederic Shurtleff Coolidge, an orthopedic surgeon at the Rush Medical College in Chicago; they had one child, born in 1894. Meanwhile, in 1893 she gave two public performances of Robert Schumann's Piano Concerto in A Minor, op. 54—one at the Women's Building of the World's Columbian Exposition in Chicago, the other with the Chicago Symphony under eminent conductor Theodore Thomas.

In 1902 Dr. Coolidge caught an infection while performing surgery. After spending two years in a sanitorium, he opened a practice in Pittsfield, Massachusetts, hoping that the climate there would be favorable to his health. In 1911, however, he contracted tuberculosis and died in May 1915, five months after the death of his wife's father and a few months before the death of her mother.

Coolidge, now a wealthy widow and heiress to the Sprague-Warner Co., began her pursuit of a philanthropic career unparalleled in the twentieth century. She contributed $200,000 for the construction of Sprague Memorial Hall at Yale University in memory of her father, and she gave $100,000 to the Anti-Tuberculosis Association in Pittsfield in memory of her husband. She also agreed to help underwrite, at $50,000 a year for ten years, the Bureau of Educational Experiments run by her cousin Lucy S. Mitchell in New York City, later named the Bank Street College of Education. Coolidge gave her Chicago home to a society of Catholic nurses and her parents' home to Presbyterian nurses. In addition, she established a pension fund for the Chicago Symphony Orchestra and assisted four of the organization's members in forming the Berkshire String Quartet.

As enormous as these benefactions were, her involvements in furthering chamber music most absorbed her for the remainder of her life. In 1918 she established a music colony on South Mountain in Pittsfield, providing a 500-seat hall that she called "The Temple" to house a series that became known as the Berkshire Music Festivals. She then invited the most important people in the world of music to attend a series of five concerts over a three-day period; this turned out to be "the first formal step in expanding her programs which would grow to international dimensions" (Rosenfeld, p. 5). For the dedication of the hall on 16 September 1918, Coolidge herself played piano in Ludwig Thuille's Piano Quintet.

Through the years the South Mountain Festival became increasingly important as, systematically, Coolidge implemented a program to further the composition and performance of chamber music in the twentieth century. The Berkshire Festivals generated many new works especially commissioned by Coolidge from such composers as Arthur Bliss, Ernest Bloch, Frank Bridge, Charles Martin Loeffler, Gian-Francesco Malipiero, Paul Pierné, Ottorino Respighi, Arnold Schoenberg, and Anton Webern. Prizes were given for the best works and occasionally

Coolidge herself performed on festival programs. In 1923, in response to worldwide interest in the festivals, Coolidge began to produce similar events abroad, first in Rome and later in such cities as Naples, Venice, Prague, Paris, and London.

Of all the Berkshire Festivals, the second one (25–27 Sept. 1919) was particularly notable for Coolidge. That year Ernest Bloch's Viola Suite won the Berkshire Prize, and the runner-up prize went to Rebecca Clarke's Sonata for Viola and Piano, a work rediscovered decades later by several younger artists. Most important, however, the occasion marked the inauguration of a long and fruitful friendship between Coolidge and Carl Engel, then head of the Boston Music Company.

By 1925 Coolidge had decided that Pittsfield was no longer adequate for her next scheme to support chamber music on an even larger scale. Since meeting Engel, who had subsequently been appointed as chief of the Music Division of the Library of Congress, she had discussed with him the possibility of establishing the Elizabeth Sprague Coolidge Foundation for the support of chamber music at the Library of Congress. Her aim, she wrote in the *Annual Report of the Librarian of Congress*, was "to make possible, through the Library of Congress, the composition and performance of music in ways which might otherwise be considered too unique or too expensive to be ordinarily undertaken." To implement her plan, she made an initial gift of $60,000 for the construction of the Coolidge Auditorium at the Library of Congress and also endowed the foundation with an annual income of approximately $25,000. The auditorium opened on her sixty-first birthday. Frederick Stock, a longtime friend from Chicago, conducted the premiere of Loeffler's *Canticle of the Sun*, among other works. Later, other important compositions were commissioned by the library's Coolidge Foundation, including pieces by Schoenberg, Igor Stravinsky, Bela Bartok, Aaron Copland, Samuel Barber, George Crumb, and Ned Rorem.

Coolidge's activities as a philanthropist earned her recognition by several educational and cultural institutions in the United States, including a number of honorary degrees. In addition, she received recognition from several European governments for her achievements in the international arena. In 1944, at the conclusion of a three-day festival of chamber music at the Library of Congress in celebration of her eightieth birthday, Coolidge received a "declaration of gratitude" signed by President Franklin D. Roosevelt.

By that time, Coolidge's hearing had failed considerably, and she began to wear a jeweled ear trumpet as part of her attire. She later replaced it with a hearing aid, which she switched off when she did not like the music being played. Coolidge died in Cambridge, Massachusetts. Through her philanthropic activities on behalf of creators and performers of music, she did more than any other citizen to stimulate the love of chamber music in the United States and enriched the lives of countless music lovers throughout the world.

• The Elizabeth Sprague Coolidge Foundation Collection, at the Library of Congress, contains over 300 twentieth-century holographs of such composers as Barber, Bartók, Bloch, Copland, and Stravinsky. In addition to works commissioned by the foundation over the years, the collection includes compositions by Coolidge as well as works dedicated to her. The Library of Congress also holds books from her personal library, several hundred portrait photographs, many of which are inscribed, and correspondence pertaining largely to the commissioning activities of Coolidge and the foundation. The letters are arranged by correspondent and measure fifty linear feet. Other important biographical sources include William C. Bedford, "Elizabeth Sprague Coolidge, the Education of a Patron of Chamber Music: The Early Years" (Ph.D. diss., Univ. of Missouri, 1964); Donald Leavitt and Henri Temianka, "The Boundless Legacy of Elizabeth Sprague Coolidge," *Chamber Music Magazine* 2 (Spring 1985): 14–17; Lucy Sprague Mitchell, *Two Lives* (1953); Carol Neuls-Bates, "Elizabeth Sprague Coolidge, Twentieth-Century Benefactress of Chamber Music," *The Musical Woman*, Vol. 2, *1984–1985* (1987), pp. 136–44; Alan Rich, "A Lady Bountiful," *New York Herald Tribune*, 25 Oct. 1964; and Jay Rosenfeld, *Elizabeth Sprague Coolidge: A Tribute on the One Hundredth Anniversary of Her Birth* (1964). An obituary is in the *New York Times*, 5 Nov. 1953.

S. MARGARET WILLIAM MCCARTHY

COOLIDGE, Grace Anna Goodhue (3 Jan. 1879–8 July 1957), first lady of the United States, was born in Burlington, Vermont, the daughter of Andrew Issachar Goodhue, a steamboat inspector and a mechanical engineer, and Lemira Barrett. Coolidge graduated from the University of Vermont in 1902. After earning her degree, she took additional training for a teaching position at Clarke Institute for the Deaf in Northampton, Massachusetts. During her three years at Clarke she met Calvin Coolidge, an attorney practicing in Northampton; they were married on 4 October 1905. During Calvin Coolidge's early career in local and state politics, Grace Coolidge, who remained in Northampton, devoted her time to domestic responsibilities and to raising two sons.

As wife of the vice president and as first lady, Coolidge's beauty, friendliness, and vivacity balanced the cool austerity of her husband's public personality. Probably in an effort to create an image of grave decorum in contrast to the excesses of the administration of Warren G. Harding and perhaps to shield his family from an aggressive press, Calvin Coolidge prohibited his wife from expressing any political views, from giving interviews, from dancing, and from speaking on radio. Despite these restrictions, Grace Coolidge was admired and respected as first lady, for her warmth and charm were irrepressible. At a luncheon for newspaperwomen, for example, she delighted her audience while remaining mindful of her husband's rule that she not speak to the press—she gave a five-minute speech in sign language. In his study of first ladies, Carl Sferrazza Anthony suggested that, for public relations purposes, the administration consciously exploited Grace Coolidge's popularity to humanize the otherwise stern image of her husband's presidency. There is evidence that she realized that the "first ladyship" was a public role, separate from one's integral self, for she wrote, "This was I and yet not I—this was the wife of the President of the United States and she took precedence over me; my personal likes and dislikes must be subordinated to the consideration of those things which were required of her."

Coolidge did not step out of the traditional domestic and ceremonial role of president's wife, but she did, by her support, draw attention to certain issues. She remained throughout her life an advocate for the education and interests of the deaf. She raised money for the support of Clarke Institute while in the White House and afterward became president of the school's board of trustees. As a former teacher of the hearing impaired, Coolidge addressed their concerns on a professional as well as a humanitarian level.

In search of a project after the 1924 death of her young son from blood poisoning, Coolidge turned her attention to the renovation of the White House, believing that her improvements would provide a legacy to future occupants of the mansion. In the hope of acquiring furniture from the colonial and federal periods, she established an advisory committee of architects, art historians, philanthropists, and businesspeople to consult on questions of authenticity and to raise funds. The remodeling project was not completed during her husband's administration, but Coolidge was instrumental in refurbishing the Green Room in the style of the federal era and in renovating the family quarters, including the construction of a "sky parlor." This third-floor sunroom overlooking Washington provided a restful haven for future residents of the White House.

Although she was not directly involved with feminist causes, Coolidge gave symbolic support to women's issues and achievements. She met personally with women outstanding in politics, education, and the arts. Before photographers, she filled out an absentee ballot on the White House lawn. Through the example of her own healthy lifestyle—she walked five to seven miles per day—Coolidge also exemplified the importance of fitness for women.

The most important organization in Coolidge's life was the first national college sorority, Pi Beta Phi, whose University of Vermont chapter she had helped found. She served as national president in 1915 and corresponded with a group of her sorority sisters throughout her life. This correspondence provides the clearest insight into her thoughts during and after her time as first lady.

Her taste in music, theater, and movies was eclectic, and she invited such diverse artists as Sergei Rachmaninoff and Al Jolson to the White House. With her avid devotion to baseball, her beautiful and fashionable clothes, and her animated personal style, Coolidge both influenced and reflected the popular culture of the 1920s.

After her husband died in 1933, Coolidge continued her volunteer work, especially for the deaf. She published several articles and poems in *Good Housekeeping* and *American Magazine*. Her poems included "The

Open Door" and "The Quest." She also traveled, and was an early public advocate of American involvement in World War II. A 1982 poll of historians ranked Coolidge eighteenth of forty-two first ladies, based on such qualities as integrity, intelligence, accomplishments, and "being one's own woman." Although she spent most of her life in traditional pursuits, she found an autonomous self within that sphere. Her domestic vocation was complementary to but not subservient to her husband's political ambitions. It is unlikely that Calvin Coolidge would have enjoyed the personal popularity he did as president without the warm and lively Grace as his partner.

After leaving Washington D.C., she lived in Northampton, Massachusetts. She died there.

• The Forbes Library, Northampton, Mass., is the major source for material on Grace Coolidge, including many of her letters. Calvin Coolidge's papers are located at the Library of Congress. Ishbel Ross, *Grace Coolidge and Her Era* (1962), is a complete but nonanalytical biography. The best study based on more recent scholarship is Carl Sferrazza Anthony, *First Ladies: The Saga of Presidents' Wives and Their Power, 1789–1961* (1990). Useful insights are included in William Seale, *The President's House: A History*, vol. 2 (1986); Betty Boyd Caroli, *First Ladies* (1987); Myra G. Gutin, *The President's Partner* (1989); and Sol Barzman, *The First Ladies* (1970). Mary Randolph, *Presidents and First Ladies* (1936), and Lillian Rogers Parks, *My Thirty Years Backstairs at the White House* (1961), are memoirs of White House staff members. Bess Furman, *White House Profile* (1951), is a journalist's view of presidential families. Anecdotes are featured in Peter Hay, *All the Presidents' Ladies* (1988), and Paul Boller, *Presidential Wives: An Anecdotal History* (1988). An obituary is in the *New York Times*, 9 July 1957.

MARY WELEK ATWELL

COOLIDGE, Julian Lowell (28 Sept. 1873–5 Mar. 1954), mathematician, was born in Brookline, Massachusetts, the son of John Randolph Coolidge, a lawyer, and Julia Gardner. After graduating summa cum laude from Harvard College in 1895, Coolidge received the first bachelor's degree ever awarded in natural science from Balliol College, Oxford University, in 1897. He then returned to the United States, where he taught at the Groton School in Connecticut for two years. Among his Groton students was Franklin D. Roosevelt, with whom he maintained a lifelong cordial relationship.

In 1899 Coolidge became an instructor at Harvard, where his first publications were devoted to geometric representations of imaginary (complex) numbers and to conic sections. He was made an assistant professor in 1902 and given a two-year leave of absence to study abroad. Using this opportunity to work with a number of Europe's leading mathematicians, he studied with Corrado Segre in Turin and Eduard Study in Bonn. Under the latter, Coolidge completed his doctoral thesis, "Die dual-projektive Geometrie im elliptischen und sphärischen Raume" (Dual-projective geometry in elliptical and spherical spaces) in 1904. Around 1902 he married Theresa Reynolds; they had seven children.

After returning to Harvard, Coolidge steadily advanced from associate professor in 1908 to full professor in 1918. During World War I he served as a major in the U.S. Army, after which he was made liaison officer to the French General Staff. In 1919 he organized courses at the Sorbonne for American servicemen, nearly 2,000 of whom were under his command in Paris, and for which he was made a chevalier of the Légion d'honneur in 1919. Coolidge later returned to Paris as an exchange professor in 1927, and in 1936 he was again honored by the French government when he was named an officer in the Légion.

During the course of his career, Coolidge published four books on various aspects of modern geometry, all of which reflected the influence of Segre and Study: *The Elements of Non-Euclidean Geometry* (1909), *A Treatise on the Circle and the Sphere* (1916), *The Geometry of the Complex Domain* (1924), and *A Treatise on Algebraic Plane Curves* (1931). His *Introduction to Mathematical Probability* (1925), one of the subject's first treatments in English and Coolidge's best-known work, enjoyed considerable popularity at Monte Carlo (according to notices from his publisher). From a strictly mathematical point of view, however, this was a significant work because it defined probability not in terms of ignorance (that is, as a measure of whether an event will occur when it is not known with certainty what will happen) but instead in terms of frequency, thereby making the subject amenable to mathematical applications in the sciences generally.

Coolidge was elected vice president of the Mathematical Association of America in 1924 and became its president the following year. In this role he was instrumental in establishing the association's Chauvenet Prize for outstanding expository writing in mathematics. He was also a member of the Council of the American Mathematical Society from 1911 to 1913 and 1924–1925, serving as the society's vice president in 1918 and as trustee in 1929–1930.

As chairman of the Department of Mathematics at Harvard University in 1927, Coolidge was largely responsible for inaugurating its tutorial system. In 1929, as Harvard underwent a major reorganization under President James Bryant Conant, Coolidge accepted the position of master of Lowell House, where he subsequently resided until his retirement in 1940. As professor emeritus, Coolidge's interests turned to history, and he wrote three important books: *A History of Geometrical Methods* (1940), *A History of the Conic Sections and Quadratic Surfaces* (1943), and *The Mathematics of Great Amateurs* (1949).

In the classroom, Coolidge was known as "an enthusiastic teacher with a flair for witty remarks" (D. J. Struik, *Dictionary of Scientific Biography*, vol. 3 [1970], p. 399). His book reviews could be especially pithy, and at the beginning of one he promised that "we shall cheerfully damn it in detail later on." Coolidge was also a man of considerable athletic prowess. As an undergraduate, he won a gold medal at Harvard for running the mile in less than five minutes, and he also liked to hike and swim. At Oxford he was an oarsman,

and later, back in New England, he enjoyed sailing off the coast of Maine, where he and his wife maintained a summer home. He died in Cambridge, Massachusetts.

As a mathematician, Coolidge was especially important in bringing non-Euclidean geometry and mathematical probability, as well as the ideas of Europeans like Segre and Study, to the attention of American mathematicians. His historical works were pioneering efforts in the United States to take the history of science, and especially the history of mathematics, seriously.

• There are no known collections of Coolidge papers, and published information is scanty. For additional information, see two memorial articles, Mason Hammond et al., "Julian Lowell Coolidge," *Harvard University Gazette* (26 Feb. 1955): 136–38, and D. J. Struik, "Julian Lowell Coolidge. In Memoriam," *American Mathematical Monthly* 62 (1955): 669–82.

JOSEPH W. DAUBEN

COOLIDGE, Susan. *See* Woolsey, Sarah Chauncy.

COOLIDGE, Thomas Jefferson (26 Aug. 1831–17 Nov. 1920), businessman and diplomat, was born in Boston, Massachusetts, the son of Joseph Coolidge, Jr., a businessman, and Eleanora Wayles Randolph. On his father's side Coolidge was descended from John Coolidge, one of the first settlers of Watertown; on his mother's side he was descended from Thomas Jefferson, third president of the United States. His parents were members of the Boston elite, and throughout his life Coolidge moved in the same circles.

Much of Coolidge's early education took place in Europe, as his parents made frequent trips abroad. He attended a boarding school in England, spent five years at a boarding school outside Geneva, Switzerland, while his parents were in China on business, and finished off his secondary education at a Gymnasium in Dresden, Germany. These years were to enrich his diplomatic skills, for he became fluent in French and German.

In 1847 Coolidge returned to the United States and entered Harvard as a sophomore. His rigorous secondary education in Europe and his quickness of mind gave him advantages over his classmates, and he relied on these advantages to carry him through. He described himself as "lazy" while at Harvard, but he nevertheless graduated seventeenth in a class of more than fifty in 1850. In 1853 he was awarded an M.A., and in 1902 Harvard conferred on him an honorary LL.D. Despite his belief that Harvard did not greatly stir him as an undergraduate, Coolidge remained devoted to the university throughout his life. He served on the Harvard Board of Overseers from 1886 to 1897. He donated to Harvard the funds to construct the Jefferson Physical Laboratory, completed in 1884, as well as funds to promote research in the sciences. He also gave the university the resources to construct a small laboratory for chemical research as a memorial to his son, a member of the class of 1884.

Upon completing his education, Coolidge determined that his main responsibility was to make money, and he began a career in business. In 1852, however, his life took a momentous turn. He married Hetty Sullivan Appleton, daughter of William Appleton, who, together with Abbott Lawrence and Nathan Appleton, was largely responsible for creating the Massachusetts textile industry. In 1857 Coolidge's father-in-law prevailed on Coolidge to give up an independent business career and take on a salaried position in one of Appleton's textile firms. In the position of treasurer of the Boott Mills, Coolidge resuscitated the finances of the mills and gained a permanent reputation as a skilled manager of textile operations.

When the Civil War ended in 1865, Coolidge took advantage of the return of peace to give up active participation in business and take his entire family to Europe for three years, hoping thereby to restore his wife's health. When he returned in 1868, he was immediately enlisted by the Boston textile magnates as treasurer of the Lawrence Manufacturing Company. Eight years later he reached the pinnacle of the New England textile world when he became treasurer of the Amoskeag Manufacturing Company, one of the nation's largest textile manufacturing complexes. By custom, the treasurer was the officer most intimately involved in actual operations. Coolidge's financial management of the firm from 1876 to 1898 secured its future.

Coolidge used his now considerable fortune to participate in the great railroad expansion that marked the last quarter of the nineteenth century. In 1876 he joined the board of directors of the Chicago, Burlington and Quincy Railroad and continued to play an important part in the railroad's affairs for many years as a major investor. He was briefly prevailed upon to accept the presidency of the Atchison, Topeka and Santa Fe Railroad, but he resigned the presidency in 1881, after just eighteen months in office.

In the 1880s Coolidge was principally responsible for the reconstitution of the Oregon Railway and Navigation Company, driven into bankruptcy by the speculations of Henry Villard. In 1887 he briefly assumed the presidency of the Boston and Lowell Railway long enough to arrange for its absorption into the Boston and Maine. In the mid-1890s he was one of a group of investors who engineered the reorganization of the Union Pacific Railroad.

Coolidge was also involved in the Boston banking business. He joined the board of directors of the Merchants Bank in 1876 and subsequently served on the boards of the New England Trust Company and the Bay State Trust Company. His chief participation in banking, however, occurred when he and his son jointly founded the Old Colony Trust Company in 1890. His son T. Jefferson Coolidge, Jr., became the president of the bank.

Notwithstanding his remarkable business acumen, Coolidge himself rated his various public roles as much more important. The first major public position

he occupied was as a member of the Boston Parks Commission in 1875–1876. With the advice of Frederick Law Olmsted, the commission laid out the substantial system of parkways that threads through Boston. In 1889 Coolidge was appointed a representative of the United States to the Pan-American Congress, designed to build ties among the various countries of North and South America. At the congress, he defended the gold standard against the prosilver advocacy of nearly all the other participants. In his report he expressed his strong opposition to the proposal of an "international" silver dollar that would circulate freely in all the Americas.

Coolidge himself believed that the peak of his career was reached when he was appointed the American minister to France in 1892. It was a post for which he was ideally suited. His private fortune enabled him to finance the entertaining that was a necessary part of the duties of a diplomatic representative, and his fluency in French and German enabled him to deal effectively with the French government and with the other members of the diplomatic corps stationed in Paris. His tenure in the post lasted less than a year, because in March 1893 the new president, Grover Cleveland, named a Democrat as the new ambassador. It was, however, Coolidge who had persuaded the U.S. government to raise the rank of its representative in Paris. Nevertheless, Coolidge described his year in Paris as "the happiest year of my life."

In 1900 Coolidge assessed his own life in a brief autobiography that he had privately printed in 1902. The forty-eight copies were distributed among his friends and associates. It was subsequently—after his death and with the permission of his family—printed by Houghton and Mifflin as *T. Jefferson Coolidge, 1831–1920: An Autobiography* and copyrighted by the Massachusetts Historical Society in 1923. In the autobiography Coolidge deliberately excludes nearly all material dealing with his business career. In *Who's Who in America* he described himself as a "diplomat," not as a businessman, and his autobiography deals mainly with his numerous travels and his experiences while serving as American minister to France. The autobiography is organized somewhat like a diary and evidently was based on diary notes kept by Coolidge. It is filled with accounts of travels all over America, the Caribbean, Europe, and down the Nile. The Coolidges appear to have been inveterate sightseers. It also makes clear that they had instant entrée to the elites of all the industrialized countries.

After the turn of the century, Coolidge gradually withdrew from active involvement in public or business affairs. He grew increasingly deaf, but his zest for participation was destroyed only when his son died in 1912. His wife had died in 1901, and another of his four children also preceded him in death. He remained physically vigorous until the day of his death in Boston.

Although Coolidge set greater store by his various public roles, the primary encomium passed on his life in the eulogy delivered to the Massachusetts Historical

Society was that, in a time subsequently dubbed the era of the robber barons, Coolidge "was always and wholly without reproach . . . [for he] preferred . . . to carry down-town with him the honorable spirit of a gentleman for daily use in rooms where it did not habitually intrude."

• The records of the Amoskeag Manufacturing Company are preserved in the Manchester (N.H.) Historic Association. The association compiled a record of its Amoskeag holdings, *Guide to the Amoskeag Manufacturing Company Records* (1985). Three volumes of treasurer's reports for the years 1865–1922 cover Coolidge's years as treasurer. In addition, a cubic foot of treasurer's files, including correspondence, legal documents, and the like, for the years 1835–1915 includes Coolidge's operations. Coolidge's report to the Pan-American Congress in 1889 is printed as an appendix to the published version of his autobiography. A few details of Coolidge's business career are in Arthur M. Johnson and Barry E. Supple, *Boston Capitalists and Western Railroads* (1967), and Julius Grodinsky, *Transcontinental Railway Strategy, 1869–1893: A Study of Businessmen* (1967). The customary eulogy delivered to the Massachusetts Historical Society by John T. Morse, Jr., is printed in its *Proceedings* 54 (Jan. 1921): 141–49. It contains a number of details omitted from his autobiography and gives a measured assessment of Coolidge's contributions. An obituary is in the *Boston Globe*, 18 Nov. 1920.

NANCY GORDON

COOLIDGE, William David (23 Oct. 1873–3 Feb. 1975), physicist, inventor, and research director, was born in Hudson, Massachusetts, the son of Albert Edward Coolidge and Martha Shattuck, farmers. He grew up on a farm and briefly dropped out of school to work in a rubber factory; a few months there convinced him he had made a mistake. He completed high school and went on to earn a B.S. in electrical engineering from the Massachusetts Institute of Technology (MIT) in 1896.

On borrowed money and scholarships, Coolidge went to the University of Leipzig, where in 1898 he earned a Ph.D. in physics for work on dielectrics and radio waves under Paul Drude. He long recalled a meeting at Leipzig with Wilhelm Conrad Roentgen, discoverer of X rays. Coolidge had experimented with X rays at MIT, beginning a lifelong participation in this field.

Returning to the United States, Coolidge became a researcher at MIT's newly founded Research Laboratory of Physical Chemistry, working with its director, Arthur A. Noyes, a physical chemist. He and Noyes carried out important experiments on the properties of solutions at high pressures. Coolidge's major contribution was the design and building of the high-pressure apparatus.

A colleague at the MIT laboratory, Willis R. Whitney, served simultaneously as director of the General Electric (GE) Research Laboratory in Schenectady, New York. After repeated entreaties, he convinced Coolidge to join that laboratory in 1905. Coolidge secured an agreement through which he would be allowed time to continue the fundamental research he had begun with Noyes, and he even brought his experimental apparatus with him. However, it languished unused, for Coolidge got fully caught up in the laboratory's major challenge, improving the light bulb.

European companies had begun to replace the cellulose filaments used in light bulbs with metal filaments. This posed a serious threat to GE's competitive position in the incandescent lighting business. Coolidge was given the task of finding a method that was superior to the European inventions (which, just to be on the safe side, GE also licensed). In his first attempt, in 1905–1906 he developed a process for combining tungsten with a cadmium-mercury amalgam. This formed a mixture sufficiently soft to be forced through dies to make filaments. Then the cadmium and mercury were driven off by heating, leaving nearly pure tungsten. The method worked but did not prove to be superior to one of the processes GE had licensed, invented by two Hungarian physicists, Alexander Just and Franz Hanaman. However, in the course of developing his method, Coolidge observed that one of his filaments bent while cold. This suggested that tungsten, normally regarded as one of the most brittle of metals, might be made into a flexible wire if treated in the right way.

Coolidge's next three years from 1906 to 1909 were spent trying to find that right way. Others thought chemical treatments would be the answer, but he chose a combination of heat and mechanical working, first hammering blocks of sintered tungsten above 1,500 degrees Fahrenheit, at which temperature they were soft and malleable, then gradually lowering the temperature as the metal was thinned by rolling and drawing to a wire. He experienced great difficulty finding the right way to apply just the force needed to convert the crystals of tungsten from cubic shapes to longer interlocked fibers without shattering the piece of material. After unsuccessful experiments with conventional mechanical methods, he found the clue he needed on a tour of Connecticut wire mills. He learned to use a swaging machine, a standard wire-making device consisting of many small hammers automatically pounding metal into a die, to reduce the block's diameter to the point where the tungsten can be rolled and pulled through a die to make a wire.

He designed much new equipment, including a new form of hot swaging machine, and steadily improved the process (discovering, for example, that doping the tungsten with small amounts of thorium caused the wire to retain its flexibility longer in use). His method totally replaced other filament-making processes. Rather than squirting out brittle incandescent lamp filaments one at a time, as his predecessors had, Coolidge's process proved capable of turning out hairthin, flexible tungsten wire by the mile. Into the 1990s it remained the process by which virtually all incandescent lamp filaments were made. Lamps using tungsten filaments made by the Coolidge process provided significantly more light per unit of energy input than had their predecessors. In addition, the filaments could be coiled (and the coils in turn coiled), an important property for achieving further efficiency improvements when the vacuum of the lamp was replaced by an inert gas.

Coolidge then applied the metal tungsten to X ray tubes. Combining its superior heat resistance with ideas developed by his GE colleague Irving Langmuir about the use of a high vacuum and pure electron discharge instead of the low vacuum and gas ionization used in previous X ray tubes, he developed a tube that was far more controllable and consistent and that could be operated at far higher voltages than previous X ray tubes. The Coolidge X ray tube became and has remained the world standard.

In subsequent efforts, Coolidge and colleagues steadily increased the voltage at which the tube could be operated, beginning at tens of thousands of volts and eventually surpassing a million volts. Higher-voltage operation meant more penetrating X rays. High-voltage Coolidge tubes increased the capability of X rays for use in therapy and made possible their use for industrial inspection. Coolidge also developed systems for accelerating electrons, carrying out experiments on the biological effects of electron bombardment of plants and seeds.

Coolidge's tungsten and X ray work proved to be the most important of his ninety-four patents and led to his election to the National Inventors' Hall of Fame. He was a member of the National Academy of Sciences and received numerous awards, including the Edison and Faraday medals, for his work on X ray equipment. In 1932 he became director of the GE Research Laboratory, a post he held until his retirement from GE in 1944. While in that post, he launched GE efforts in the field of polymers that helped make the company a world leader in the engineered materials business.

Coolidge also made significant contributions to national defense. During World War I, he invented the "C-tube," a sort of underwater stethoscope for detecting the presence of submarines. It was the most widely used U.S. submarine detection device during the war. In 1941 he served on the Advisory Committee on Uranium, a group assembled by the federal government to assess the feasibility of developing an atomic bomb.

A soft-spoken, gentlemanly leader who was also a remarkably capable experimenter, Coolidge earned great respect from colleagues in the fields of business and science. He was married twice. In 1908 he married Ethel Woodward, with whom he had two children before her death in 1915. The following year he married Dorothy MacHaffie, who died in 1969. Coolidge enjoyed many hobbies, such as photography and travel. He lived in Schenectady until his death there, less than four months before his 102d birthday. His experimental skill had enabled him to give modern form to two of the most pervasive elements of modern technology, the filament of the incandescent lamp and the X ray tube.

• Coolidge's laboratory notebooks are on file at the GE Research and Development Center, Schenectady, N.Y. Coo-

lidge's biographies are John Anderson Miller, *Yankee Scientist* (1963), and Herman A. Liebhafsky, *William David Coolidge: A Centenarian and His Work* (1974). An obituary is in the *New York Times*, 4 Feb. 1975.

GEORGE WISE

COOMARASWAMY, Ananda Kentish (22 Aug. 1877–9 Sept. 1947), historian of the art of Ceylon and India, metaphysician, and champion of Indian culture in the West, was born in Colombo, Ceylon (now Sri Lanka), the son of Sir Mutu Coomaraswamy, a distinguished Ceylonese barrister and legislator, and Elizabeth Clay Beeby, an Englishwoman from a wealthy Kent family. Although his father died during Coomaraswamy's infancy, his wealth, high social position, scholarly learning, and cross-cultural involvement strongly influenced his son. Coomaraswamy was brought to England in 1879, where he lived with his mother until he was sent to Wycliffe College, a preparatory school, at age twelve. In 1897 he entered University College, London, from which he graduated in 1900 with a B.S. in geology and botany. He received a D.Sc. from London University in 1906, writing on Ceylonese mineralogy and other scientific topics. Coomaraswamy was married four times: in 1902 to Ethel Mary Partridge, a weaver and needlewoman; in 1911 to Alice Richardson (also known as Ratan Devī), a singer and performer of Indian music, with whom he had two children; in 1922 to Stella Bloch, a dancer and painter; and in 1930 to Doña Luisa Runstein, a photographer, with whom he had one child. Coomaraswamy's earliest occupation was as director of the Mineralogical Survey of Ceylon (1902–1907), during which time he was also active in nationalistic movements to revitalize traditional Ceylonese culture. This was a concern of his that later broadened to encompass Indian art and culture and remained a lifelong commitment. In 1917 Coomaraswamy came to the United States as curator of Indian art at the Boston Museum of Fine Arts. He remained at the Boston Museum for the remainder of his life, becoming fellow for research in Indian, Persian, and Mohammedan art in 1933.

Coomaraswamy's professional life had four stages. The first, lasting until about 1905, included his university education and geological research. From 1905 until 1917 he wrote on Ceylonese and Indian crafts and arts and became involved in efforts to bring them recognition. From 1917 until the late 1920s Coomaraswamy devoted himself to cataloging collections of Indian art and to detailed art historical scholarship. In his last period he wrote general yet carefully researched essays on Indian art, religion, metaphysics, and culture and their relation to Western, especially medieval, religious thought.

Coomaraswamy's early involvement in the nationalist movement in Ceylon and, later, in India led him to recognize the importance of the artist-craftsman in traditional society, a value that became a permanent part of his outlook on culture and society. His studies of the arts and crafts that date from this period, especially *Medieval Sinhalese Art* (1908) and *The Indian Crafts-*

man (1909), strongly encouraged recognition and study of the traditional folk arts. The arts and crafts movement in England was actively promoting similar objectives at that time, and Coomaraswamy looked to the philosophy of William Morris in support of the idea that art must saturate a society and not be confined to a privileged elite. As his interest in Indian art intensified, Coomaraswamy acquired an authoritative command of this work, which he developed in a series of studies at a time when Indian art was not well understood. He was the first to collect and catalog an important body of Indian art that came out of the Hindu courts in Rajasthan and the Punjab hills, presenting it in a series of publications that culminated in *Rajput Painting* (1916). Coomaraswamy valued this art because, unlike the more worldly Mughal painting, a Muslim art of the court and of portraits, Rajput painting was a broadly based folk art essentially religious in tone that drew on the legends about Krishna and on folk traditions, an art in part erotic yet at the same time embodying the spiritual meaning of love. This interest in the dual presence of the sensuous and the spiritual prefigures an underlying theme in Coomaraswamy's later metaphysical writings. He found in the work of English poet William Blake a kindred spirit who recognized the common presence of both levels of being and who exhibited this in a linear art that bears some resemblance to Rajput.

After his move to the United States Coomaraswamy continued his art historical work in books such as his *History of Indian and Indonesian Art* (1927), and he continued to write iconographic studies of Indian art. Yet his concerns began to shift toward religious and metaphysical issues. As a product of two cultures, Coomaraswamy found a common metaphysical underpinning in the traditional Eastern and Western religions. He explored this in both textual and artistic studies, such as *A New Approach to the Vedas* (1933) and *The Transformation of Nature in Art* (1934). The work that emerged in his last period owed much in style and in content to his admiration of Hindu and Christian scholastic writing. He regularly produced translations and textual studies, and by the mid-1930s he was dividing his writing between scholarly studies of Indian and of Western medieval art, and more popular essays and lectures directed toward a wider audience. Books from this period that reflect these diverse aspects include *Elements of Buddhist Iconography* (1935), *Why Exhibit Works of Art?* (1943), and *Figures of Speech or Figures of Thought: Collected Essays on the Traditional or "Normal" View of Art* (1946). *Am I My Brother's Keeper?* (1947) expressed his concern with the social problems caused by East-West cultural tensions.

Coomaraswamy favored the "anonymous" popular arts of America—the arts of the ordinary people—although he condemned the mass culture of modern industrial society, with its emphasis on materialism, quantity, and repetitive work. He disliked modern art and modern values, so foreign to the transcendent values of a spiritualized culture that he idealized. Central in his religious and metaphysical writing was the contrast of a world of ordinary experience with an intelligible, eternal realm that lies beyond the flux of events but that can be discovered through them. This conviction took various forms in his writing. He understood the self as dual—a particular, mutable self or "I" and a spiritual "Self" that is eternal and identified with the Divine Essence. One had, he often said, to "shatter the image" imprisoned in "name" and "form" (*nāma-rūpa*) in order to discover the spiritual life that cannot be defined. He found this metaphysics also in art, recognizing intelligible meanings and archetypes beyond its sensory surface and symbols. Coomaraswamy supported this view not only with Hindu scriptures but with Platonic philosophy and other sources. His essays, many of which he collected into books, develop their ideas not by argumentation but through the detailed exegesis of Sanskrit terms, heavily documented and expanded in elaborate footnotes, by constructing a complex mosaic of supporting quotations and citations from a large number of Eastern and Western sources, and by constantly returning to first principles.

Coomaraswamy's art historical scholarship, while qualified in places by later scholars, remains a major contribution. His late metaphysical writings, idiosyncratic in his own day, continue to attract those interested in symbol, myth, and Eastern thought. His recognition of the importance of traditional arts and crafts and of integrating them into the general culture gives support to the strong and increasing interest in preserving and practicing them in the United States and abroad. No longer the object of as much widespread attention as when he was actively producing his own works, his contributions continue to influence Indian scholarship and, less directly, the growing awareness of the importance of the traditional arts and crafts. Coomaraswamy died in Boston.

• Coomaraswamy was a prolific author. In addition to the books cited above, he wrote *Buddha and the Gospel of Buddhism* (1916), *The Dance of Siva* (1918), *History of Indian and Indonesian Art* (1927), *Elements of Buddhist Iconography* (1935), *Hinduism and Buddhism* (1943), and *Time and Eternity* (1947). The first two volumes of *Coomaraswamy*, ed. Roger Lipsey (3 vols., 1977), offer collections of his most important papers; the third volume is an excellent biography by Lipsey and also contains a selected bibliography of Coomaraswamy's major writings.

ARNOLD BERLEANT

COON, Carleton Stevens (23 June 1904–3 June 1981), anthropologist, was born in Wakefield, Massachusetts, the son of John Lewis Coon, a Boston importer, and Bessie Carleton. He began studying anthropology as a Harvard College sophomore under Earnest A. Hooton, the preeminent physical anthropologist of his era. Coon graduated in 1925 and continued on with Hooton as a Ph.D. student, receiving that degree just before his twenty-fourth birthday. During this period Hooton characterized Coon as a person who obviously yearned for "the society of the uncivilized and unwashed." Beginning while still an undergraduate, Coon made three research visits to the Rif Berbers of

Morocco, then a remote mountain-living people resisting French and Spanish efforts to enforce colonial rule. He was accompanied on his third visit, in 1926, by his wife, Mary Goodale, whom he had married earlier that year and with whom he later had two children. The data collected on these ventures formed his doctoral dissertation, rewritten and published as *Tribes of the Rif* (1931).

In 1929–1930 Coon and his wife conducted an anthropological survey in what Hooton considered the "wildest spot in Europe, with the toughest and least known population of two-gun men"—northern Albania. He subsequently traveled to Ethiopia and Yemen (1933–1934), and there as well his studies incorporated ethnological, archaeological, and physical anthropological investigations, making him, as it has turned out, one of the last influential anthropologists who both conducted significant field research and published in all three subareas of anthropology.

Beginning in 1927, Coon held a number of minor positions in Harvard's anthropology department, leading in 1935 to an instructorship. He became an assistant professor in 1938 and rose to full professor in 1947. In 1948 he left Harvard to assume an anthropology professorship at the University of Pennsylvania and the position of curator of ethnology in its University Museum. He retired in 1963 to Gloucester, Massachusetts, but maintained nominal appointments at Pennsylvania and Harvard until his death in Gloucester.

Anticipating U.S. entry into World War II, Coon took leave from Harvard in 1941 and volunteered his North African expertise by joining the nascent Office of Coordinator of Information (COI), which within a year became the Office of Strategic Services, the first U.S. secret intelligence and special operations organization. In 1942 he was sent to Morocco under diplomatic cover with the goal of mobilizing Riffian tribesmen in support of the impending landing of Allied troops. Suspicious about Coon's involvement in the assassination of the Vichy chief in French North Africa, Admiral Jean-François Darlan, on Christmas Eve 1942 have not been confirmed, but Coon had trained the man who did the actual shooting (and who was immediately executed), an uncommon gun similar to his was used, and later in Washington he presented his boss, General William J. "Wild Bill" Donovan, with a tract advocating a postwar political assassination squad. For many years Coon was bothered by the effects of a head wound caused by a falling roof tile dislodged in a bombing raid. He was sent home in 1943 to receive a commission as a major in the U.S. Army and saw further military action in Corsica. On discharge in 1945 he received the Legion of Merit. Coon and his wife had divorced, and in 1945, before returning to Harvard, he married Lisa Dougherty Geddes, whom he had met while both were in the army; the couple did not have children.

Although Coon coauthored with Eliot D. Chapple a textbook on social anthropology in 1942, *Principles of Anthropology*, and published an ethnohistorical survey of the Islamic world, *Caravan* (1951), his postwar research and writing focused more on archaeology, later on physical anthropology. (His views on both were set out in a popular introductory text, *The Story of Man* [1954].) Between 1947 and 1965 he excavated prehistoric cave sites in Morocco, Iraq, Iran, Afghanistan, Syria, and Sierra Leone. His excavations in the Middle East were particularly important because he uncovered artifact sequences ranging in time from the Middle Paleolithic to the Neolithic from some very remote and previously undocumented areas. His extraordinary knowledge of ethnographic and archaeological objects, as well as his blustery style, were put to good use from 1949 to 1964, when he was a regular panelist on the weekly Peabody Award–winning CBS television program "What in the World?," in which unusual museum items were identified on sight.

It was in physical anthropology that Coon's contributions were most influential and most controversial. Although he did participate in an expedition in 1959 to southern Chile to investigate the physiology, particularly cold adaptation, of the Alakaluf, and did recover some fragmentary fossil human remains during his many excavations, Coon's interpretations of human evolution emerged from an enormous store of observations—his own and others'—of his fellow humans, living and dead. William W. Howells, Hooton's successor at Harvard, wrote that Coon "knew more about human variation than anyone else in the world."

The earliest synthesis of Coon's knowledge of human population variation was his monumental *The Races of Europe* (1939), a tour de force of the old-style, craniometric-based interpretation of population variation that expired with World War II. His most-lasting contribution was to focus attention on physiological adaptation, particularly to climatic variation, as the basis for the evolution of modern human diversity, which he did primarily in *Races: A Study of the Problems of Race Formation in Man* (1950), written with junior coauthors Stanley M. Garn and Joseph B. Birdsell. While *The Living Races of Man* (1965) and *Racial Adaptations* (1982) reflect Coon's own expansion on this theme, the 1950 *Races* sparked a range of physical anthropology studies, research that has continued in the field. His receipt of the Viking Fund Medal in physical anthropology in 1951 and his election to the National Academy of Sciences attest to his contributions to science.

Coon's *The Origin of Races* (1962) was widely praised for its detailed presentation of the fossil record for human evolution. His notion, however, that the five geographic races he believed exist now probably existed more than 500,000 years ago within the species *Homo erectus* and evolved separately five times into modern *Homo sapiens*'s five races was vigorously disputed by scientists who questioned his understanding of evolutionary mechanisms. Rather pusillanimously, he blamed a copyeditor for the troublesome wording and revised it in later printings.

In the same year, presiding over the annual business meeting of the American Association of Physical Anthropologists, which had elected him president, Coon churlishly resigned in disapproval of a motion that condemned *Race and Reason* (1961), written by a distant relative, Carleton Putnam, which claimed a scientific basis for racial segregation. Ultimately the motion passed, but his resignation was not accepted. This episode, combined with his view expressed in *Origin* that the evolution from *Homo erectus* of the African line until recently "stood still" compared to the Eurasiatic ones, tarnished his image in some eyes, despite his emphatic denials of racism. Coon deserves to be remembered for his felicitous writing, his advocacy of physiological adaptation research, his archaeological discoveries, his delineation of human variation, and his robust enthusiasm for personal engagement in all of anthropology.

• Coon's papers are in the University Museum Archives at the University of Pennsylvania, the Library of the American Philosophical Society in Philadelphia, and the National Anthropological Archives of the Smithsonian Institution's National Museum of Natural History. He wrote two specifically autobiographical books, *Adventures and Discoveries* (1981) and *A North Africa Story* (1982); personal accounts are included in his *The Seven Caves* (1957). *Flesh of the Wild Ox* (1932), *The Riffian* (1933), and *Measuring Ethiopia and Flight into Arabia* (1935) are novelistic chronicles of his African and Arabian travels and the peoples he studied. A personal statement was published in *Annual Review of Anthropology* 6 (1977): 1–10. Earnest A. Hooton describes Coon's early demeanor and adventures in the *Harvard Alumni Bulletin*, 2 Oct. 1930, pp. 34–45. Anthony Cave Brown, *The Last Hero: Wild Bill Donovan* (1982), complements Coon's own account of his OSS activities during World War II. A sense of the arguments against *The Origin of Races*, and Coon's retorts, can be found in *Current Anthropology* 4 (1963): 360–67. Pat Shipman provides a more benign view in her *The Evolution of Racism* (1994). Obituaries are in the *New York Times*, 6 June 1981; by Edward E. Hunt, Jr., in the *American Journal of Physical Anthropology* 58 (1982): 239–41; and by W. W. Howells in National Academy of Sciences, *Biographical Memoirs* 58 (1989): 108–30, which also lists Coon's publications.

EUGENE GILES

COONTZ, Robert Edward (11 June 1864–26 Jan. 1935), naval officer, was born in Hannibal, Missouri, the son of Benton Coontz, a newspaper owner and mayor of Hannibal, and Mary Brewington, schoolmates and neighbors of Samuel Clemens, "Mark Twain." Robert studied at Ingleside and Hannibal Colleges and was appointed to the U.S. Naval Academy in 1881, graduating in 1885. Developing a reputation for a sharp wit and a well-developed sense of humor, Coontz was considered something of a politician at academy. During his second year at the academy, the Naval Committee of the House of Representatives heard testimony from selected midshipmen on the effect of only allowing about one-quarter of a graduating class to secure a commission and that after six years of service. Making an eloquent plea for more commissions, Robert earned the nickname "Senator." In 1887 he continued his unusual advocacy role by becoming secretary of an Ensigns' Committee, a group that supported the causes of young naval officers.

Between 1887 and 1890 Coontz was assigned to the steam sloops *Mohican* and *Juniata*, the steamer *Galena*, and the protected cruiser *Atlanta* prior to becoming a member of the gunboat *Pinta*'s complement in Alaskan waters. He was promoted to ensign in 1887. In 1890, while in Alaska, he married Augusta Cohen. The couple had three children, two of whom survived to adulthood.

Coontz was promoted to lieutenant, junior grade, in September 1896 and participated in the Spanish-American War. With the *Charleston*, which took control of Guam on 20 June 1898, he also saw action at Iloilo, at Subic Bay, and during the Philippine insurrection. With the expansion of the navy, Coontz advanced rapidly, to lieutenant in March 1899, lieutenant commander in January 1905, and commander in 1909. During 1908–1909 he was the executive officer aboard the *Nebraska*, which participated in the world cruise commanded by Admiral Charles S. Sperry.

In 1910 Coontz began pulling ahead of his contemporaries. From 1910 until 1911 he was the commandant of the Naval Academy. During the midshipmen's cruise to Germany in the summer of 1911, he became acquainted with Kaiser Wilhelm II and exchanged correspondence with the German leader for a number of years. Coontz was appointed governor of Guam, serving from 1912 until 1913, and he commanded the battleship *Georgia* from 1913 until 1915. During World War I he commanded the Thirteenth naval District at Puget Sound and was promoted to rear admiral in December 1917.

In late 1918, while the chief of naval operations and his assistant were in London, Coontz temporarily performed the duties of that position, gaining the confidence of Secretary of the Navy Josephus Daniels. Following a tour commanding the Battleship Division of the Atlantic Fleet, Coontz was appointed by Daniels to be chief of naval operations, effective in October 1919.

As the chief of naval operations, Coontz, now an admiral, had the difficult tasks of presiding over the U.S. Navy's demobilization, resisting the efforts of army brigadier general William "Billy" Mitchell to control naval aviation, and establishing the navy's position on international naval limitations negotiations. He headed the group of officers that proposed the famous 5:5:3 ratio for British, American, and Japanese major naval combatants, in which U.S. and Royal Navy battleships were to be identical in number and Japanese battleships were to be ⅗ of that number. This ratio was ultimately accepted and constituted the most controversial naval issue of the 1920s and 1930s. Early in the 1920s Coontz also successfully maneuvered some of the majority congressional Republicans and enough minority Democratic party members to prevent a significant cut in the navy's strength. He accomplished this feat by providing the minority Democrats with confidential Republican papers. Rather than the 67,000-person strength the Republican administration proposed, the 1920–1921 U.S. Navy personnel authorization amounted to 86,000. Additionally, Coontz became a strong supporter of naval aviation, working to give the arm a near-independent status and supporting the building of aircraft carriers. The Atlantic and Pacific fleets were becoming separate entities, estranged from standard navy practices and procedures, so Coontz integrated the great majority of the navy's combatants under a standardized system of operation known as the U.S. Fleet.

Stepping down as chief of naval operations in the summer of 1923, Coontz briefly commanded the U.S. Fleet until October 1925. He was then the commander of the naval district at Norfolk, Virginia, until his retirement in June 1928. In retirement, he became active in politics, supporting the candidacy of Franklin D. Roosevelt, the former assistant secretary of the navy, for high political office. Coontz died in Bremerton, Washington.

Coontz was a key figure in the U.S. Navy's rise to world dominance. His primary contribution was in skillfully guiding the development of the U.S. Navy during a period of reduced naval appropriations. Moreover, his support for naval aviation provided the rationale to thwart General Mitchell's play of the early 1920s and established the essential platform to build America's powerful naval air armada of the 1940s.

• The Coontz family holds a manuscript collection of the admiral's papers that does not cover Coontz's tenure as chief of naval operations. Coontz's memoir, *From the Mississippi to the Sea* (1930), depicts his early life, his naval career, and many of his retirement activities. The best summary of Coontz's entire career and his contributions is in Robert W. Love, Jr., ed., *The Chiefs of Naval Operations* (1980). His obituary is in the *New York Times*, 27 Jan. 1935.

ROD PASCHALL

COOPER, Anna Julia Haywood (1858?–27 Feb. 1964), author, educator, and human rights activist, was born, probably on 10 August 1858, in Raleigh, North Carolina, the daughter of Hannah Stanley, a slave. Though her paternity is uncertain, she believed her mother's master, Dr. Fabius J. Haywood, to have been her father. She later described her ancestry: "The part of my ancestors that did not come over in the Mayflower in 1620 arrived . . . a year earlier in the fateful Dutch trader that put in at Jamestown in 1619. . . . I believe that the third source of my individual stream comes . . . from the vanishing Red Men, which . . . make[s] me a genuine F.F.A. (First Family of America)."

In 1867 Anna entered the new St. Augustine School in Raleigh. Because there were then few teachers for African-American pupils, she became a student-teacher at age nine. Functioning precariously in a former Howard School building, this Episcopal school offered classical and religious training to black youths. Intellectually gifted, Anna graduated in 1877. That year she married another former student-teacher of the school, the Reverend George C. Cooper; two years later he died. Anna then sought a means of continuing her studies. In 1881 she entered Oberlin College, where she struggled to "keep up with my board bills." She achieved her bachelor's degree in 1884. In 1887

Oberlin also awarded her an honorary master's degree.

Cooper's first book, *A Voice from the South by a Black Woman of the South*, a collection of her avant-garde essays on feminist and racial topics, appeared in 1892. In these essays, Cooper expressed her beliefs that black women hold the key to the salvation of the black race and that white women have demonstrated reluctance to work with black women. Intermittently thereafter she published articles and essays and a book on the abolitionist sisters Angelina Emily Grimké and Sarah Moore Grimké, and she lectured on racial, educational, and feminist topics. In 1900 she was a speaker at the London Pan-African Conference, a gathering that launched a world movement of continuing significance.

As she realized the drift of the South toward legal white supremacy, Cooper encountered in her own experience many of the obstacles women and blacks commonly face. She decided to dedicate her life to ensuring blacks an access to higher education at the same time that they acquired marketable skills; unlike the leading black male educators Booker T. Washington and W. E. B. Du Bois, she believed both higher education and vocational competence would be necessary for racial equity.

As a teacher of modern languages, literature, and mathematics at Wilberforce University in Ohio, then as a teacher and principal of the M Street Colored High School in Washington, D.C. (1902–1906), Cooper directed her energies toward educating black youths. The only college preparatory school for blacks in Washington, the M Street school was the most prestigious black public high school in the nation. In 1906, however, Cooper was dismissed from M Street for struggling to preserve college preparatory courses in the face of growing pressure to offer a primarily vocational program. She then taught for four years at Lincoln Institute in Jefferson City, Missouri. When a new administration took over at M Street, she was invited to return, not as principal but as a teacher. She accepted the post, where she remained till her retirement in 1930.

Perhaps partially because of the rejection that her dismissal as M Street principal implied, Cooper's desire to acquire a doctoral degree intensified. She came to exemplify a basic tenet of her own life, that while difficult, it is possible for a black woman to earn a living at the same time that she achieves scholarly goals. During summer vacations, she traveled extensively in Europe, and she took courses designed to meet doctoral requirements. She studied modern languages at La Guilde Internationale in Paris (1911–1913) and undertook courses in modern languages and literature at Columbia University (1914–1916). She also studied independently and participated in conferences.

Le Pèlerinage de Charlemagne, Cooper's translation of an epic poem from ancient to modern French, appeared in Paris in 1925. The same year she wrote two essays in French in partial fulfillment of her doctoral requirement: "Legislative Measures Concerning Slavery in the United States" and "Equality of Races and the Democratic Movement." Later she translated both into English and published them for use in her classes (1941 and 1945, respectively).

Finally in 1925 she was able to transfer credits and to complete her dissertation for a doctoral degree at the Sorbonne in Paris. Her dissertation, "L'Attitude de la France à l'égard de l'esclavage pendant la Révolution" (published in English translation in 1988 as *Slavery and the French Revolutionists, 1788–1805*), was a crowning achievement. In this work, Cooper developed an original interpretation of the French Revolution in its relation to the profitable French colony of St. Domingue (now Haiti) and to world slavery. She pioneered the views that slavery was deeply involved in the French Revolution and that slavery inevitably becomes a matter of international moment.

Upon retirement from the District of Columbia school system in 1930, Cooper devoted her energies for many years to the development of Frelinghuysen University, an institution for the education of working adults (1930–1950). This enterprise presaged the growth of community colleges and state university systems; it operated on the understanding that many students must cover their tuition costs through concurrent employment.

Throughout her long life, Cooper was active in various organizations. She figured prominently in the black women's club movement and in programs to aid black youths. She was active in the National Association of Educators and the National Association for the Advancement of Colored People. An organizer of the Young Women's Christian Association girls' clubs (1911–1915), she maintained a lifetime involvement in the Phillis Wheatley branch of the YWCA. She was also a founding member of the Colored Social Settlement, now the Southwest Settlement House, in Washington, D.C. Early in her life, she had assumed the guardianship of two children, and later she adopted five orphaned young relatives. Cooper died at her home in Washington.

Possessed of endowments once considered unthinkable in a former slave, and particularly in a woman, Cooper devoted herself to serving her race. An articulate feminist, she wrote in 1892 of "that masculine influence which has dominated [the world] for fourteen centuries." Almost sarcastically, she pointed to "our standard of excellence inherited from barbarian ancestors through a long line of male progenitors, the law Salic permitting no feminine modifications." She believed that "so long as woman sat with bandaged eyes and manacled hands, fast bound in the clamps of ignorance and inaction," the world would suffer for want of her insights. Though she failed to achieve a broad currency for these concerns in her lifetime, Cooper alerted the nation to the dangers of sexism and racism.

• Cooper's major archival records, designated as the Anna Julia Cooper Papers, are located in the Manuscript Division, Moorland-Spingarn Research Center, Howard University, Washington, D.C. For a recent edition of her 1892 collection, see Cooper, *A Voice from the South*, ed. and intro. Mary Helen Washington (1988). Important studies on Cooper are Louise Daniel Hutchinson, *Anna J. Cooper, A Voice from the South* (1981); Leona C. Gabel, *From Slavery to the Sorbonne and Beyond: The Life and Writings of Anna J. Cooper* (1981); Sharon Harley, "Anna J. Cooper: A Voice for Black Women," in *The Afro-American Woman: Struggles and Images*, ed. Harley and Rosalyn Terborg-Penn (1978); Karen Baker-Fletcher, "Anna Julia Cooper and the Religious Influences in Her Writings" (Ph.D. diss., Harvard Univ., 1992); Frances Richardson Keller, "The Perspective of a Black American on Slavery and the French Revolution: Anna Julia Cooper," in Cooper, *Slavery and the French Revolutionists, 1788–1805* (1988); Paula Giddings, *When and Where I Enter: The Impact of Black Women on Race and Sex in America* (1984); and Hazel Carby, *Reconstructing Womanhood: The Emergence of the Afro-American Woman Novelist* (1987). An obituary is in the *Washington Post*, 29 Feb. 1964.

FRANCES RICHARDSON KELLER

COOPER, Edward (26 Oct. 1824–25 Feb. 1905), businessman, philanthropist, and politician, was born in New York City, the son of Peter Cooper, a businessman, philanthropist, and public figure, and Sarah Bedell. After attending public school in New York City, the younger Cooper enrolled at Columbia College, but he earned no degree. At Columbia College, Cooper met Abram S. Hewitt. The two men became fast friends, traveled together in Europe during 1844, then survived when the ship returning them to the United States foundered off the East Coast that December. They were lifelong friends, business partners, and, when Hewitt married Cooper's sister Amelia Cooper in 1855, brothers-in-law as well.

Cooper and Hewitt entered the iron business in 1845, building and then managing a mill in Trenton, New Jersey. Their venture was largely made possible by the capital of Peter Cooper, long a leading ironmaster, who had been planning to build in Trenton. Although opposed to partnerships (he never entered one himself), Peter Cooper allowed his son and Hewitt to operate on this basis. Peter Cooper served as president, Hewitt as manager, and Edward Cooper as supervisor of operations of the Trenton Iron Company. Like his father, Edward Cooper was interested in metallurgy and technology. Desiring the widest public benefit from his inventions, he declined to patent them. Within a few years, the young men formed a partnership, Cooper & Hewitt, sometimes called Cooper, Hewitt, and Company, which became the agent for the Trenton mill. They subsequently expanded their business activities as the aging Peter Cooper became less involved in such pursuits. Edward Cooper's enterprises earned him directorships in a range of business firms. Upon the death of his father in 1883, Edward Cooper succeeded to the presidency of the board of Cooper Union, an institute devoted to "the advancement of science and art in their application to the varied and useful purposes of life," which the elder Cooper had founded during the 1850s. Edward Cooper also was active in the affairs of a number of New York City cultural institutions and clubs. In 1863 Cooper married Cornelia Redmond; they had one child.

Although elected to public office only once, Cooper made his political mark in New York City. A Democrat, he served as a delegate to his party's national conventions of 1860 in Charleston, South Carolina, and 1876 in St. Louis. Cooper, Hewitt, Samuel J. Tilden, and others like them were termed Swallowtails (after the form of dress coat preferred by the well to do), businessmen and professionals who sought to influence national and state politics and governmental policies and to perpetuate elite leadership of New York City politics and government against professional politicians and their organizations, which were gaining strength during the 1850s through the 1870s. As a member of the prestigious reform Committee of Seventy, Cooper participated in the overthrow of "Boss" William Marcy Tweed and his corrupt ring during 1871. Four years later Governor Tilden named Cooper to the blue-ribbon Commission to Devise a Plan for the Government of Cities in the State of New York. In 1877 the commission reported a range of reform measures for incorporation in the state constitution, the most controversial of which would create municipal boards of finance to pass on taxes, borrowing, spending, and two key city appointees. Voting for members of and membership on the boards in cities of over 100,000 population would be restricted to taxpayers on property assessed at more than $500 and rent payers of $250 or more per year. Cooper did not sign the report, for reasons that he did not explain, but he lent his name to the effort, ultimately unsuccessful, to win ratification of the amendments.

Following the toppling of the Tweed Ring, Cooper was among the Swallowtails who supported the reformed Tammany Hall, led by "Honest" John Kelly, but like many of the others he ultimately abandoned the organization as Kelly's star rose in Tammany and city government. Indeed, in 1878 Cooper, now an Irving Hall Democrat, won the mayoralty as a fusion candidate, supported by the Republicans and the Independent Germans. He defeated Augustus Schell, the candidate of Tammany Hall and a fellow Swallowtail. (Irving Hall, a Democratic faction, provided Swallowtails with an organization to challenge Tammany Hall.) Cooper's two-year mayoral term was defined by a conflict pitting Cooper and Governor Lucius Robinson against Kelly. Control of the police board figured prominently in the struggle, because the city's politicized police department exerted considerable influence on elections. In the end, Kelly survived the challenge, Robinson failed of reelection in 1879, and Cooper, although judged a successful mayor and considered as a mayoral nominee in 1886 and 1890, never again ran for office. Cooper was among those Swallowtails who, critical of both Tammany and Irving halls, founded the rival New York County Democracy in 1881. Cooper's long prominence in business, philanthropy, and party and factional politics placed him in the first rank of Democratic Swallowtails. Cooper died in New York City.

• Cooper-Hewitt letterpress copybooks in the New-York Historical Society and the Library of Congress include correspondence referring to politics, although business affairs predominate. The New York Municipal Archives and Records Center houses mayoral papers, but one must place primary reliance on newspapers, biases and other shortcomings notwithstanding, in studying the political involvement of Cooper. The *New York Times*, *New York Herald*, and *New York Evening Express* differed in perspective and are especially useful. Such was the closeness of the Hewitts and the Coopers that Allan Nevins, *Abram S. Hewitt: With Some Account of Peter Cooper* (1935), provides the best introduction to Edward Cooper. On the political environment in which Cooper operated, see Iver Bernstein, *The New York City Draft Riots: Their Significance for American Society and Politics in the Age of the Civil War* (1990), and David C. Hammack, *Power and Society: Greater New York at the Turn of the Century* (1982). A thorough obituary is in the *New York Times*, 26 Feb. 1905.

SAMUEL T. McSEVENEY

COOPER, Elias Samuel (25 Nov. 1820–13 Oct. 1862), surgeon, was born near Somerville, Ohio, the son of Jacob Cooper and Elizabeth Walls, farmers. At age sixteen he began studying medicine with his brother who was a physician in Galesburg, Illinois. In 1838 he enrolled in a medical school in Cincinnati, Ohio, but after a short stay he transferred to St. Louis University, where he received an M.D. in 1841.

Cooper immediately opened a medical-surgical practice in Danville, Illinois, which he moved three years later to Peoria, Illinois. He established an infirmary for the treatment of eyes, ears, and clubfoot and also gave dissecting demonstrations to a few surgical students. Word of his skill as a surgeon spread throughout four states, and in 1853 he was elected president of the Knox County (Ill.) Medical Society. A tremendously confident and self-reliant individual, he never married and rarely slept, believing that time spent on any endeavor other than treating patients, teaching medicine, and reading or writing about new medical and surgical techniques was time wasted. Largely because of his single-minded devotion to the practice of medicine, in the early 1850s he developed a mysterious nervous condition that resulted in the partial paralysis of his face. In an effort to restore himself to good health, in 1854 he closed the infirmary and took a tour of London and Paris, although he spent much of his time there examining surgical clinics and learning new techniques.

While in Europe, Cooper evidently became interested in medical developments on the West Coast. Following the discovery of gold at Sutter's Mill in 1848, thousands of people infected with "gold fever" began migrating to the hill country of California. In no time the filthy mining camps in which they lived became fertile breeding grounds for diseases such as rheumatism, dysentery, and fevers of every description, while the mines and creeks where they dug and panned for gold bred broken bones, stabbings, and gunshot wounds. Such a medical "gold mine" attracted physicians and surgeons of every stripe, and they descended upon California by the hundreds. In 1855 they were joined by Cooper, who established an eye, ear, and feet clinic in San Francisco. To what extent he was motivated by the lure of easy wealth is hard to know; although he clearly violated the American Medical Association's Code of Ethics and earned the opprobrium of the local medical community by advertising his services in several languages throughout the state, he also performed surgical operations on Wednesdays and Saturdays at no charge.

Cooper was a gifted surgeon who seemed to draw great inspiration from the rough-and-tumble social and medical conditions that prevailed in San Francisco, which despite its population of approximately 40,000 was essentially a frontier town. He saved one patient's life and gained the admiration of his fellow surgeons by successfully extracting a breechpin from a fowling piece that had lodged itself just under the patient's heart. He saved another's life by tying together the severed halves of the innominate artery, a major artery that branches directly off the aorta to provide blood to the head, and that of a third by removing from under the collarbone a tumor that could not be reached until after the removal of part of the breastbone. As one of the first surgeons to use silver wire to reconnect fractured bones, he successfully rewired broken kneecaps and elbows. His patients rarely suffered from infection because he sterilized his instruments with alcohol before performing surgery, a practice that had yet to be adopted by the medical community at large.

In 1856 Cooper helped to organize the Medical Society of the State of California, which for a brief period published its own medical journal. Two years later he served as the catalyst for the formation of the West Coast's first medical college by bringing together six other physicians and obtaining a charter from the University of the Pacific in San Jose to begin operating a medical department in San Francisco. The first session was held in 1859, and from then until 1862 he taught anatomy and surgery and served as president of the medical faculty. The department was shut down in 1864 but reorganized six years later by Levi Cooper Lane, Cooper's nephew and former partner, as the Medical College of the Pacific. Renamed Cooper Medical College in 1882, it remained an independent entity until 1908, when it was acquired by Stanford University and reorganized as its medical department.

In 1857 Cooper performed the first successful Caesarean section in California's history, although earlier operations of this type had been attempted by Franciscan friars on women who had died during labor without giving birth. Two years later the woman, who seemingly had made a complete recovery, sued Cooper for malpractice, and his technique was severely criticized in the *Pacific Medical and Surgical Journal* by David Wooster, a fellow physician and the journal's coeditor. Outraged by this attack on his professional reputation, Cooper vowed never to submit another article to that publication again and in 1860 founded and served as first editor of the *San Francisco Medical Press*, a rival medical-surgical journal, which also served as the official organ of his medical school. In 1865 financial considerations forced the two publications to merge under the former's name, and they continued to exist in this form until 1917.

In 1862 Cooper's nervous condition worsened to the point that he was forced to rest for several months. After an extended vacation in the Sacramento Valley failed to improve his rapidly deteriorating sight and hearing, he returned to San Francisco, where he fulfilled his many duties as best he could until his death there.

For the last seven years of his life Cooper was widely regarded as the most daring and able surgeon in California. By playing a major role in the establishment of a medical college, a medical society, and two medical journals, he also established his reputation as a pioneer in the development of medicine in the Golden State.

• Cooper's papers are located in the California Historical Society Library in San Francisco. His contributions to the development of medicine in the Pacific West are discussed in Henry Harris, *California's Medical Story* (1932), and Francis R. Packard, *History of Medicine in the United States* (1931; repr. 1963). An obituary is in the *San Francisco Medical Press* (Oct. 1862).

CHARLES W. CAREY, JR.

COOPER, Ezekiel (22 Feb. 1763–21 Feb. 1847), Methodist preacher and publisher, was born in Caroline County, Maryland, the son of Richard Cooper and Ann (maiden name unknown), whom he described as "plain people, in easy and plentiful circumstances of life." He experienced a religious awakening the year of American independence after hearing a young Methodist preacher, Freeborn Garrettson, preach in the Coopers' yard to two companies of militiamen who had been training in the adjacent fields. Cooper's stepfather, an officer in the Continental army, in typical patriot fashion, detested all Methodists as "enemies to the country." But Cooper persisted through several years of religious turmoil, a black servant being his only spiritual companion. Then in September 1781 he had an experience of forgiveness of sins and assurance of salvation that followed a typical Methodist formula for conversion.

Cooper soon felt called to preach. At age twenty, while learning the joiner's trade in Talbot County, he took the first step by accepting appointment by Garrettson as a lay class leader in the Methodist society there. A year later he was present at Barratt's Chapel, Delaware, in November 1784, when Francis Asbury, general assistant of the Methodists in America, met with Thomas Coke to discuss John Wesley's plan for organizing the Methodist societies as a denomination in the newly formed United States. On this same occasion, Cooper hesitantly accepted an appointment by Asbury to succeed the preacher on the Caroline circuit, who had just died. After a two-year trial period, he was accepted into ministerial membership ("full connection") in the Methodist conference and was ordained a deacon on 3 June 1787. After ordination as an elder in December 1788, he could administer the sacrament of Holy Communion.

Cooper spent his ministry along the eastern seaboard during a period that included the massive expansion of the country and Methodism into the west. Although he at times served circuits in New England, New York, New Jersey, Virginia, and South Carolina, he spent most of his ministry in Philadelphia and the Delmarva peninsula. In 1793–1794 Asbury made him a presiding elder (supervisor of preachers) of the Boston circuit, which encompassed four states. Cooper's penchant for following the strict Wesleyan discipline in church polity and practice, such as observing Friday fasts, led him into conflict with Jesse Lee, one of the older leaders, who opened Methodist work in Maine. During Cooper's time in New England, he became engaged to Maria Bemis, but when he was moved to New York City, she declined to follow him, and the itinerant preacher's hope for marriage died.

While serving in Annapolis, Maryland, in the early 1790s, Cooper preached an antislavery sermon on the Fourth of July in a county where nearly half the inhabitants were slaves. His discourse concluded with the question: when shall America indeed be a free country? He subsequently denounced slavery publicly in at least six articles published in Maryland and Virginia newspapers, in which he argued against the idea that African slavery was part of God's design.

Cooper was a notable preacher, a concerned pastor, a careful administrator, and a thoughtful reformer. As an excellent extempore speaker who was well read, especially in history and Scripture, Cooper gained a reputation as an oral disputant said to be unsurpassed among the Methodists of his day. He seems not to have exercised his abilities in popular causes, however, as he often spoke for positions that did not prevail. Matthew Simpson said of him, "His personal appearance embodied a fine illustration of age, intelligence, and piety. . . . He was considered by his ministerial associates a 'living encyclopedia.'" While many fled town during the yellow fever epidemic in Philadelphia, Pennsylvania, he remained there and ministered to the people. When his friend John Dickins succumbed to the disease, Cooper accepted Asbury's appointment to succeed Dickins at the Book Concern as editor and publisher. During his nine years in the post, from 1799 to 1808, Cooper's careful management put the Methodist publishing operation on a solid financial basis.

At the General Conference of 1808, Cooper was named to a Committee of Fourteen. Chaired by Joshua Soule, this committee drafted a constitutional definition of the conference's powers in the form of "Restrictive Rules." Cooper was more interested than Soule in making the bishops amenable to the General Conference. Cooper himself received the second largest number of votes in the episcopal election, which that year chose William McKendree, who favored more independent power for bishops. During the following decade, Cooper became a leader of the Reform party, which favored limiting episcopal power, including transferring the power to select presiding elders from the bishops to the annual conferences.

Poor health kept Cooper from active ministry between 1813 and 1820, but when he returned he negotiated a compromise solution to the presiding elder question at the General Conference of 1820. However, his efforts were overturned by the singular influence of Joshua Soule, who refused to accept election by that conference to the episcopacy under the new circumstances. The Cooper effort at conciliation was rescinded. After 1824, he became silent on the reform issues. The reformers' platform, meanwhile, broadened to include lay representation and began to shift toward the schism that resulted in the formation of the Methodist Protestant church at the end of the decade.

An avid fisherman (his walking cane was made from a fishing rod), Cooper became supernumerary (semi-retired) in 1821 but continued to serve in various appointments in the church, including another stint as presiding elder. In his later years, he became increasingly suspicious of seminary education of ministers and apprehensive about preachers accepting honorary degrees. He fully retired in 1846. He died in Philadelphia, leaving a sizeable estate, much of which was designated to assist the poor.

Cooper's involvement in the major developments within Methodism caused a friend to observe that "he seemed almost like the embodiment of an age." It was an age that had long since passed, however. He had been a faithful leader for many years, but, except in matters of the Book Concern, he never shaped any of the major positions that defined the church of his day.

• Most of Cooper's extant papers are in the Garrett-Evangelical Seminary in Evanston, Ill. Selections were published in George A. Phoebus, *Beams of Light on Early Methodism in America* (1887). Aside from his writings on slavery and his articles in reform journals, Cooper's only published writings were funeral discourses on John Dickins (1799) and Francis Asbury (1819), the latter amounting to a short history of early Methodism in America. A significant article on Cooper is in the *Cyclopaedia of Methodism* (1876). While he receives significant notice in most histories of American Methodism, the only modern biographical study is Lester B. Scherer, *Ezekiel Cooper, 1763–1847: An Early American Methodist Leader* (1965), which includes an extensive listing of his papers.

RICHARD P. HEITZENRATER

COOPER, Gary (7 May 1901–13 May 1961), film actor, was born Frank James Cooper in Helena, Montana, the son of Charles Henry Cooper, a lawyer, and Alice Louise Brazier. The actor, beloved for playing the all-American hero, was raised on a 600-acre ranch near the Big Belt Mountains at a bend in the Missouri River by parents born in Britain. Cooper unreliably attended a one-room schoolhouse his father built on the property and much preferred to play with local Indians and ranch hands. He sometimes swam naked in Andy's Creek with his first girlfriend, Mary Three Feet, standing by. This horrified his mother, who insisted that he and his brother Arthur be schooled in Helena. Cooper's truancy forced the family into a radical course. The boys were enrolled in the Dunstable School in Bedfordshire, England, in 1911 under the watchful eyes of their paternal grandparents. Charles and Alice Cooper remained in Helena, where Charles served as a justice on the state supreme court. During his three years in England their son earned a reputation as headstrong and voluble.

Cooper's late teens seemed to suggest an unremarkable future. Apart from height—he stood over six feet at age sixteen—there was little to distinguish him from other boys. He liked to hunt and fish and became the man around the ranch when his brother entered the army during World War I. Cooper met painter Charles Russell and began dabbling in landscapes. He had no fixed course. The local Marlow Theatre became a favorite haunt. He admired Harry Carey and liked the screen's strong, silent hero. When Cooper broke his hip in a car crash, he took to riding horseback in a stoic recovery. Indolence and injury had gotten Cooper behind in his classes. The efforts of an English teacher named Ida Davis helped him through high school in neighboring Bozeman. He was nineteen at graduation. Davis urged him to consider a career in commercial art. Still uncertain, he agreed to leave his job as tour guide at Yellowstone National Park and enter Grinnell College in Iowa. He was a 21-year-old freshman.

"Cowboy" Cooper's caricatures began appearing in Grinnell's *Scarlet and Black*. He tried out for the school's dramatic club, became tongue-tied, and was rejected. He tried twice more and was rejected. He became art editor of the college yearbook, then quit school in February 1924 to peddle his pictures in Chicago. When that failed, he did the same at the Helena *Independent*. Three months later he had sold seven paintings at five dollars apiece. Then friends wrote from Hollywood that there was money to be made for a man who could ride a horse in the movies. Cooper arrived in Los Angeles on Thanksgiving Day 1924. He registered with central casting, booked appointments for portrait sittings, sold advertising on theater curtains, and became a milkman before getting to ride a horse in a Tom Mix movie. His extra work made him ten dollars a day. Falling from his horse paid five dollars more. Dozens of rides and falls followed.

For Paramount he rode with Jack Holt and Richard Dix. At Fox he supported Buck Jones. He milled about in *Ben-Hur* (1926), was a victim and a survivor in *The Johnstown Flood* (1926), was a tall cossack in Rudolph Valentino's *The Eagle* (1925), and held a horse's hoof in *Drug Store Cowboy* (1925). He estimated he had been in more than fifty films before landing the lead opposite Lightnin' the Super Dog in a two-reeler called *Lightnin' Wins* (1926). It paid him $50 and led him to take his career more seriously. Casting director Nan Collins thought "Frank Cooper" too common and changed his first name to "Gary." She circulated publicity stills and a film test of Cooper on horseback. Henry King hired Cooper for a small part in Samuel Goldwyn's *The Winning of Barbara Worth* (1926), but when the second lead, Herold Goodwin,

could not fulfill his contract, Cooper got the role. The film, starring Ronald Colman and Vilma Banky, was a box-office smash, and Cooper's work was a revelation. *Motion Picture* thought Cooper's easygoing naturalness had stolen the film. *Variety* seemed certain Cooper "will be heard of on the screen." Goldwyn tried to sign Cooper to a long-term contract at $65 a week, but Cooper signed at Paramount for $150.

At Clara Bow's insistence Cooper played a bit part in *It*, a 1927 sex comedy that was a Paramount moneymaker. An affair with Bow put Cooper in the gossip columns. His first starring role came in *Arizona Bound* (1927), a low-budget western. *Variety* liked the "tall youth with the boyish smile." *Exhibitors Daily Review* thought he had the look and "the physique [of a] Western hero." Cooper was paired with Bow in *Children of Divorce* (1927), a familiar love triangle that furthered her career but did little for his. *Film Daily* considered him out of place in a dinner jacket. A small role as a doomed pilot in *Wings*, a 1927 Oscar winner, kept the fan mail coming. Cooper was getting the studio build-up—big parts in small pictures and small parts in big ones. His salary was doubled as he strode harmlessly through *Nevada* (1927) and *The Last Outlaw* (1927). Cooper made eight more silent films, sometimes as star, sometimes as support for Fay Wray, Esther Ralston, and Florence Vidor. Loaned out to First National to play opposite Colleen Moore in *Lilac Time* (1928), he proved himself a budding silent screen star just as the era was ending. *Wolf Song* (1929), a part-talkie, represented Paramount's and Cooper's uneasy transition to sound. *The Virginian* (1929), in which Cooper received the starring role after Richard Dix walked out on the project, established him as an important Paramount property. Owen Wister's romantic portrait of the West sold more than 1 million copies, mainly in the East, and became Hollywood's standard summary of the strong, silent man of action. Victor Fleming's direction and the High Sierras location made more memorable Cooper's reply to the threats of the movie's villain. "If you want to call me that," the Virginian warns, looking Trampas dead in the eye, "smile!" Cooper would never be the "It" boy again. He was becoming America's favorite heroic figure. Paramount boosted his salary to $3,750 a week and over the next eighteen months got their money's worth by rushing him into eleven more movies.

Cooper's appearance as *The Texan* (1930) made him the subject of a Norman Rockwell cover for the *Saturday Evening Post*. His work with Josef von Sternberg and Marlene Dietrich in *Morocco* (1930) brought him his best notices yet. The New York Herald Tribune believed no actor played the role of the hero so expertly. Cooper's underplaying, director Howard Hawks later observed, worked because of its instinctive simplicity. It led audiences to "believe everything that he says or does." Cooper's growing reputation was strengthened in *City Streets* (1931), a Dashiell Hammett crime melodrama directed by Rouben Mamoulian. Exhausted from overwork and suffering from hepatitis, Cooper put his movie work on hold and took a

European vacation. He landed back in the news when he was seen romancing Countess Dorothy di Frasso. When he returned to Hollywood, Cooper took a new interest in managing his career. He fought for *A Tale of Two Cities* but happily settled for *A Farewell to Arms* (1932). *Photoplay* thought his work opposite costar Helen Hayes was the best of Cooper's career. The *Brooklyn Daily Eagle* praised Cooper as an actor of "greater emotional depth." When he was loaned to Metro-Goldwyn-Mayer in exchange for Clark Gable to costar with Joan Crawford in *Today We Live* (1933), it confirmed Cooper's status as a major Hollywood star.

The mid-1930s were good to Cooper. He married socialite Veronica Balfe in 1933, and they bought a ranch overlooking the San Fernando Valley. A daughter was born in 1937. Deft comedic performances in *One Sunday Afternoon* (1933) and Ernst Lubitsch's *Design for Living* (1933) were followed by the swashbuckling success of *The Lives of a Bengal Lancer* (1935). Cooper's characterization of Longfellow Deeds in Frank Capra's *Mr. Deeds Goes to Town* (1936) contained elements of heroic idealism that came to personify the Cooper screen persona. He might be hesitant in speech, reluctant to act, and awkward in manner, but he had virtue on his side and a certain unaffected purity of spirit that appealed to depression-era audiences. His role as Wild Bill Hickok in Cecil B. DeMille's epic *The Plainsman* (1936) solidified Cooper's growing superstar status. *The Times* (London) was immensely impressed by Cooper's work. His quiet strength on-screen was what Americans imagined their "pioneering heroes to be like."

By the close of the 1930s Cooper had joined Clark Gable, Spencer Tracy, and James Cagney as one of the leading box-office stars of Hollywood. A string of monumentally successful films between 1939 and 1943 established him as one of the great stars of twentieth-century cinema. The beautifully mounted, high-spirited *Beau Geste* (1939), directed by William Wellman, was Cooper's final film under his Paramount contract. He could now choose his own material, unencumbered by a studio contract. He was offered his pick of parts. He rejected David Selznick's offer to star as Rhett Butler in *Gone with the Wind* (1939) and instead teamed with William Wyler and Samuel Goldwyn in the immensely popular *The Westerner* (1940). Cooper could now demand half a million dollars per picture. It made him the highest salaried man in America. He could insist on the best directors and most promising properties. *North West Mounted Police* (1940), with DeMille; *Meet John Doe* (1941), with Capra; and *Sergeant York* (1941) and *Ball of Fire* (1941), with Hawks, continued his string of box-office and critical successes. His characterization of World War I hero Alvin York earned him rave reviews, his first Oscar, and the New York Film Critics best actor award. Howard Barnes in the New York *Herald Tribune* considered it "a performance of extraordinary versatility and conviction." Philadelphia's *Public Ledger* thought Cooper dominated the film through "quiet sincerity." The

New York Post failed to see how a screen role could be done better.

Cooper's portrayal of stricken New York Yankees first baseman Lou Gehrig in *Pride of the Yankees* (1942) and fighter against fascism Robert Jordan in Ernest Hemingway's *For Whom the Bell Tolls* (1943) made him the screen's preeminent star. Reviewers wrote of Cooper's uncanny capacity to project the spiritual qualities of the characters he played. His grace under pressure made him the quintessential "unassuming hero to millions" who longed to be like him. Cooper and Hemingway became hunting buddies. They and their wives met annually in Sun Valley, turning the town into a favorite resort for the rich and famous. Cooper was well liked in the Hollywood community and might have made many other masterpieces had he not been committed to other scripts. So John Wayne got *Stagecoach* (1939), Henry Fonda did *The Ox-Bow Incident* (1943), and Cary Grant undertook *Destination Tokyo* (1944). During November and December 1943 Cooper toured military bases in New Guinea, sang "Mairzy Doats," and recited Lou Gehrig's farewell speech for the troops. He was a huge hit.

A new leading man began to develop in postwar Hollywood. He was tough, often embittered, and inexplicably angry in his self-reliance; he trusted no one and was reclusive and cynical. Humphrey Bogart, Alan Ladd, Robert Mitchum, and John Garfield thrived in this new cinematic terrain, and Cooper's laconic hero seemed sadly out of place. *The Story of Dr. Wassell* (1944), for DeMille, was the last real life hero Cooper would play for eleven years. The heroic seemed no longer fashionable. The films that followed failed to match his previous work in artistic achievement or audience appeal. Only *Unconquered* (1947), his final teaming with DeMille, approached the qualities that had made Cooper an American icon. His testimony as a friendly witness before the House Un-American Activities Committee, investigating Communist infiltration in Hollywood moviemaking in 1947, reflected fears in the nation and its film industry and made more headlines than Cooper's increasingly infrequent screen roles.

The trade press now began talking politely of Cooper's need for a "comeback" film. It was difficult to accept Cooper as a self-absorbed architect in *The Fountainhead* (1949), based on Ayn Rand's novel. The film led to Cooper's teaming with newcomer Patricia Neal and their reteaming in *Bright Leaf* (1950). Because of their affair, Cooper separated from his wife. *Dallas* (1950) and *Distant Drums* (1951), a western and an adventure, were low-budget projects that only deepened Cooper's startling decline. Bosley Crowther of the *New York Times* noted, "There is something about the sadness that appears in Mr. Cooper's eyes [and] the slowness and weariness of his walk . . . which reminds [us] that he has been at it a long time." The fading actor's resurrection came from an unlikely source. *High Noon* (1952) was a small-scale western, independently produced, with an unknown Grace Kelly in support and a rapidly aging star who had clearly passed his peak. Preview audiences found the film a bore. The story of a sheriff standing up to a gang that wants to kill him elicited little initial interest. But a reedit, a new song, and shots of a grimly determined Cooper, who was fighting stomach ulcers, a hernia, a bad back, and a painful hip, gave the film a following. Critics were enthusiastic, calling the movie's spare tale of good and evil "a classic." Cooper won his second Oscar and returned to the first rank of Hollywood actors.

Cooper reconciled with his wife. They lived in fashionable Holmby Hills and Southhampton and entertained lavishly. Cooper's personal life had never been happier, but his health was in decline. His years as stuntman and chronic worries now took their toll. He was forced to curb his active lifestyle. The films of Cooper's final decade were hit-and-miss. *Vera Cruz* (1954) showed the rapidly aging star to good advantage, but it was costar Burt Lancaster's picture. Cooper was properly earnest in *The Court-Martial of Billy Mitchell* (1955), but Rod Steiger's flashier role stole the film. *Friendly Persuasion* (1956), under William Wyler's inspired direction, was easily the best film of this period. Cooper underplayed the part of a pacifist Quaker with subtlety and surprising strength.

Cooper was clearly too old to be romancing Audrey Hepburn in Billy Wilder's *Love in the Afternoon* (1957) and appears increasingly haggard in the films that followed. Critics who had been kind to Cooper noted he hardly appeared well enough to be rescuing a much younger Charleton Heston in *The Wreck of the Mary Deare* (1959). It was painful for many of them to watch Cooper taking on physical roles instead of settling into character parts. Cooper's screen persona had always been the resolute man of action. Neither he nor his audiences could accept the fact he was no longer believable in these parts. Cooper tried to break this mold in *The Naked Edge* (1961), playing a morally ambiguous character far from his customary heroic ideal. It was his last film.

Early in 1960 Cooper had prostate surgery. Weeks later, part of his colon was removed. Cancer was diagnosed in the spring of that year. His family kept the news from him, and he kept working. His narration and brief appearance on a television documentary, "The Real West," was warmly received. Radiation treatments failed to check the spread of his disease, however, and in late February 1961 Cooper became aware he would not recover. Only when an emotional James Stewart picked up an honorary Oscar for his friend at the Academy Awards ceremony on 17 April did the press and the public learn of Cooper's condition.

Cooper's final weeks were filled with an outpouring of public sentiment rarely seen for any celebrity. President John F. Kennedy, Queen Elizabeth, and Pope John XXIII joined thousands in lauding an actor whose four decades in films earned the affection of millions worldwide. His death in Los Angeles was an occasion of national mourning. In the decades that followed, analysts of popular culture saw in Cooper's carefully crafted heroic ideal a mid-twentieth-century testimony to what Americans liked to believe about themselves and their collective past. Cooper shared his audience's enthusiasm for the self-actualizing individual who conquers the wilderness, tames its many threats, and makes it a fit place for the creation of a pioneering community. This understanding of the West became a powerful explanation of American exceptionalism and the country's mission and perhaps best explains the special hold Gary Cooper has had on the national imagination.

• Primary materials on the life of Gary Cooper are available through the Montana Historical Society, the UCLA Film and Television Archives, the Wisconsin Center for Film and Theatre Research, the Academy of Motion Picture Arts and Sciences, and the Estate of Gary Cooper. Cooper's daughter, Maria Cooper Janis, and widow served as consultants in the 1989 documentary "Gary Cooper: American Life, American Legend," written by Richard Schickel, which aired on Turner Network Television. Other documentaries on Cooper's life include NBC's "Project 20" series that was narrated by Cooper's friend Walter Brennan and which aired in March 1963 and "Screen Legends: Gary Cooper," produced in 1983 by EMK Productions and appearing on Cinemax. Cooper's remembrances appear in the *Saturday Evening Post*, 18 Feb.– 7 Apr. 1956, and in *McCall's*, Jan. 1961. Early appreciations of Cooper's career appear in *Famous Stars of Filmdom* (1932); *Time*, 3 Mar. 1941; and the *New York Times*, 5 July 1942. Biographies include Lucien Escoube, *Gary Cooper: Le cavalier de l'Quest* (1965); George Carpozi, Jr., *The Gary Cooper Story* (1970); Homer Dickens, *The Films of Gary Cooper* (1970); Rene Jordan, *Gary Cooper* (1974); Hector Arce, *Gary Cooper: An Intimate Biography* (1979); Stuart M. Kaminsky, *Coop: The Life and Legend of Gary Cooper* (1980); and Larry Swindell, *The Last Hero: A Biography of Gary Cooper* (1980). Important biographical sketches appear in David Shipman, *The Great Movie Stars: The Golden Years* (1970); the *Screen Greats Series*, no. 6 (1972); and James Robert Parish and Don E. Stanke, *The All-Americans* (1977). An obituary appears in the *New York Times*, 14 May 1961. Affecting pictorial appreciations appear in *Life*, 26 May 1961; *Esquire*, May 1961; and *Look*, 18 July 1961.

BRUCE J. EVENSEN

COOPER, Henry Ernest (28 Aug. 1857–15 May 1929), lawyer and politician, was born in New Albany, Indiana, the son of William Giles Cooper and Harriet A. Weller. The details of his childhood are unknown. Cooper received his law degree from Boston University in 1878 and was admitted to the bar that same year. Business interests in a railroad took him to San Diego, California, where he married Mary E. Porter in 1883; they had eight children.

Following an 1890 visit to Hawaii, Cooper relocated to the islands with his family in February 1891. In 1892 he applied for his papers of denization, which allowed him to participate in island politics without jeopardizing his American citizenship. In early 1892 Cooper approached Lorrin A. Thurston, a Hawaiian citizen of American parentage, and suggested the creation of an organization opposed to the rule of Queen Liliuokalani and dedicated to the annexation of the Hawaiian Islands by the United States. The conversation led to the formation of the Annexation Club. In January 1893, when Queen Liliuokalani moved to promulgate a new constitution, the Annexation Club responded by forming the Committee of Safety with the intent of overthrowing the queen and forming a government. Cooper selected the committee's member and served as its chairman. On 17 January 1893 Cooper climbed the steps of the government building and read the proclamation that officially established the new government.

His role in the Hawaiian Revolution earned Cooper numerous positions in the Hawaiian government. Although he remained an American citizen, he served on the Advisory Council of the provisional government from January through March 1893. He was appointed a circuit court judge for the First District of the Hawaiian Islands, a position he held until 1895. From 1895 through 1900 Cooper held several public offices, often simultaneously. He served as minister of foreign affairs from 1895 to 1900; as minister of public instruction from 1896 to 1900; as attorney general from March 1899 through June 1900; as minister of the treasury ad interim on three occasions; and as minister of the interior ad interim for four terms.

Political conflict in the Hawaiian Republic centered on the issue of annexation by the United States, a cause that Cooper staunchly supported. When U.S. President Grover Cleveland, who opposed annexation of the islands, reportedly recommended a plebiscite on the matter, Cooper dismissed the suggestion. Realizing that native Hawaiian opposition would defeat an annexation proposal, Cooper argued that a plebiscite violated the Hawaiian constitution, which required only the approval of the Hawaiian senate to ratify treaties, which included annexation agreements. After the November 1896 election of William McKinley to the American presidency, annexationists took heart. Ostensibly on vacation, Cooper traveled immediately to the United States to meet with prominent politicians, including Senator Henry Cabot Lodge and President Cleveland. In December Cooper had an unofficial meeting with President-elect McKinley. Although McKinley refused to commit himself to annexation, Cooper regarded his mission as a success.

Cooper served as acting president from January through March 1898 while President Sanford B. Dole was abroad. During this period the issue of Cooper's American citizenship arose. The Hawaiian constitution required the president to be a Hawaiian citizen. In an attempt to strike at the absent Dole, some legislators argued that Cooper, who retained his American citizenship, could not serve as acting president. The attorney general supported Cooper, who continued in the position until Dole's return.

In his capacity as foreign minister, Cooper became embroiled in an 1897 controversy with Japan over immigration. Cooper and the annexationists saw the conflict as an opportunity to involve the United States and prove that annexation was desirable and necessary. Accordingly, he took an unyielding position in his communications with Japanese diplomats. Japan rec-

ognized the role that the United States played in the negotiations and transferred discussions to Washington, a move Cooper questioned. When Japan agreed to accept a cash settlement, Cooper argued against payment, claiming that Hawaii had acted within its rights. Cooper's protestations were ignored, and the Hawaiian government paid the settlement money.

The United States annexed Hawaii in 1898, and in 1900 Cooper became first secretary of the Territory of Hawaii. He retired from public service in 1903 and practiced law in Honolulu. He chaired the board of regents of the College of Hawaii from 1907 to 1914, and he returned to the bench of the First Circuit Court from 1910 to 1914. Cooper then retired again from public life and spent his final years in California, where he died in Long Beach.

Cooper's prominence during the Hawaiian Revolution and the years of the Hawaiian Republic can be attributed to his political alignments and to his capability. On arriving in Hawaii, Cooper quickly had become affiliated with the powerful minority that would control the islands' affairs in the coming decades. Native Hawaiian antipathy toward Cooper was in part a result of his role as a newcomer and interloper. In the various public offices Cooper held, he acted as an ardent supporter of annexation, a position that ultimately won out. In addition, observers recognized Cooper as capable and effective in office; his abilities earned him the trust of his colleagues and resulted in the numerous appointments he received during his career.

• Cooper has not received significant scholarly attention. The most complete biography is R. S. Kuykendall's sketch in the *Dictionary of American Biography*. He earns brief references in secondary works such as William Adam Russ, Jr., *The Hawaiian Republic, 1894–1898, and Its Struggle to Win Annexation* (1961). J. W. Siddall, ed., *Men of Hawaii*, vol. 2, contains a list of Cooper's achievements; the *New York Times* obituary, 16 March 1929, is largely uninformative.

THOMAS CLARKIN

COOPER, Hugh Lincoln (28 Apr. 1865–24 June 1937), civil engineer, was born in Sheldon, Minnesota, the son of George Washington Cooper, a miller, and Nancy Marion Parshall. He early developed an interest in engineering, and at age seventeen, during a school vacation, he built a timber bridge across Moon Creek for his farmer employer. This bridge, with a span of forty feet, lasted forty years.

Rejecting his father's insistence that he become a millwright, Cooper ran away from home with $50 in his pocket and his 1883 high school completion certificate. He found work at a livery stable, then sold pianos and organs. Pursuing his real interest, in 1884 he found a job in the engineering department of the St. Paul Railroad at $35 monthly, turning down a counter-offer from the piano/organ company for $200 monthly. He assiduously studied blueprints and construction books and seized the opportunity to build a bridge for the company when a building contractor failed and the resident engineer became ill.

In 1885 Cooper moved to the bridge construction firm of Horace E. Horton in Rochester, Minnesota, where he worked as an apprentice. He was promoted to superintend the erection of two bridges over the Mississippi River and in 1889 transferred to Chicago as superintendent and assistant chief engineer for Horton's Chicago Bridge and Iron Works, leaving bridge design to run the company's new shops. In 1891 Cooper became the northwest regional manager for the San Francisco Bridge Co. for which he designed and built bridges, including a 500-foot steel arch railway bridge. The next year he married Frances B. Graves; they had three children.

Cooper became convinced of the growing importance of water power. He bid on some construction projects and became associated with John T. Fleming in water-power studies and construction. Cooper sought work with Stillwell, Bierce and Smith-Bailey Co., a manufacturer of hydroelectric machinery in 1896. He was not hired so he offered to do manual work for nothing so as to learn. After several months he was hired, eventually becoming assistant chief engineer. In the following years he worked for a number of firms, designing and building hydroelectric plants at home and abroad. These firms included Fred Stark Pearson; Viele, Blackwell and Buck; the Mexican Light and Power Company of Montreal, Quebec, Canada, and the Electrical Development Company of Ontario Limited. In 1905 he opened his own firm in New York City.

Between 1902 and 1907 Cooper designed some of his most important dams and introduced significant new ideas. These included a 100,000-horsepower plant at Niagara Falls using the new techniques. His design was so radical that the investors called in British engineers to approve it. One innovation was the design of a tail-race tunnel that discharged directly behind the waters of Horseshoe Falls. Another was a wing dam that went out into the twenty-mile-per hour current. His workers were too frightened to continue work on the dam as it extended into the fast water. Cooper then carried a glass of water to the end of the scaffolding and challenged them to continue working as long as no water spilled from the glass. The dam began operations in 1907.

At McCall Ferry, Pennsylvania, on the Susquehanna River, Cooper designed the dam to be built in sections, like bridge piers, with openings between them that were later completed individually. He also drew from his bridge-building experience in introducing traveling cranes atop the dam to handle the movement of supplies and the pouring of concrete, a technique used widely thereafter.

One of Cooper's most famous projects was the hydroelectric dam at Keokuk, Iowa, on the Mississippi. The low level of the water in combination with the high flood peak posed serious technical problems that had discouraged investors. Cooper arranged the financing and solved the technical problems. He used a combination of bridge and dam construction designs, as he had done at McCall Ferry. He built steel gates between piers, allowing him to raise or lower the height of the dam depending on the water flow, thereby guaranteeing water to the turbines without endangering the dam and bridge at flood times. He again used the traveling cranes, speeding the movement of supplies. There was so much local interest in the project that Cooper built a viewing platform so the public could watch without getting in the way or into danger. He employed many foreign workers and took special care to see they were well treated—particularly that they were paid directly rather than through middlemen. *Engineering News* wrote at the time, "One result was that many skilled and unskilled workers as well as gang foremen stay with the engineering firm which does its own construction." This kind of attention to personnel as well as to machine design, transport issues, materials availability, and constant testing and verification of quality contributed to Cooper's remarkable record for timely and successful construction.

Cooper consulted on two large foreign projects during these years, Lake Biwa for the Japanese government and a power plant design in Aswan on the Nile; this last, while accepted by the Egyptian government, was put aside with the beginning of World War I.

Cooper returned to New York City in 1914 to reopen his own offices. He volunteered to serve when the United States entered the war and in 1917 was commissioned a major of engineers and served in France, making plans for the development of port facilities in Bordeaux. He was promoted to colonel in 1918. For his work in France, Cooper received the Order of the University of Palms, grade of Officier d'Instruction Publique.

In the postwar era Cooper served as the chief engineer and consultant for, among other projects, the Wilson Dam at Muscle Shoals, the V. I. Lenin Dam in Ukraine (known as Dneprostroi), and the Aswan Dam in Egypt. He continued to play a leading role in innovation in construction. At the Wilson Dam Cooper began the use of dry mixed concrete, replacing the wet concrete previously used. At Dneprostroi he had workers doing the "American dance," stomping on the concrete to make it homogeneous and free of air bubbles. He experimented with dampening green concrete in the summer and warming it in the winter and made many changes in the design of the dam, shortening its construction time and reducing costs. He also ordered machinery adapted to the level of the workers' training, even having tools color-coded where they should be held and where they should be used.

While in Russia he also persuaded All-Union inspectors to back him in demanding quality assurance testing so that local political bosses' demands for speed in construction did not compromise the success of the construction. For his consulting work in design and construction the Soviet government awarded Cooper the Order of the Red Banner, the highest civil award for foreigners. The Soviet government recognized the quality of his work by featuring a model of the dam at the 1939 World's Fair in New York, although without recognizing Cooper as engineer. After the dam was demolished during World War II, it was rebuilt exactly as it had been in Cooper's design. Cooper was a strong supporter of trade with the Soviet Union. He served with other U.S. businessmen on the American-Russian Chamber of Commerce and urged President Franklin D. Roosevelt to recognize the USSR to facilitate the expansion of U.S. business opportunities there.

While at Dneprostroi, Cooper spent some time in Egypt consulting on the Aswan Dam. He also carried out extensive work on the St. Lawrence River for navigation, electrical production, and the restoration and preservation of Niagara Falls. At the time of his death in Stamford, Connecticut, he was working on plans for the development of power at the Z-Canyon of the Columbia River, electrical development of the Aswan Dam, and a project in Greece.

Obituaries recognized Cooper's special personal qualities, his "striking and unique personality," and his "intuitive technical knowledge and his broad engineering experience." *Engineering News-Record* described him as "one of those rare men to whom engineering judgment is almost instinctive, men who without formal engineering training have risen to preeminent position in the world by sheer force of native ability and hard work" (1 July 1937).

One of the men who worked under Cooper at Dneprostroi wrote: "He was not only a great [engineer] whom we all admired so much but a wonderful man. I was happy as a young engineer to be priveledged [*sic*] to have known him personally and I can say without reservations that his personality has ever since played a great part in forming my views and judgment as a professional engineer."

• Cooper's papers, which contain some letters, diaries, and photographs, are held by his descendants. The Library of Congress holds nine reports and five addresses written by Cooper or published by him for his firm. A number of obituaries were published in 1937 and 1938 in professional journals and biographical reference books. One of the most complete is in the *Transactions of the American Society of Civil Engineers* 103 (1938): 1772–77. Harold Dorn wrote about Cooper's interest in developing trade with Russia in 1933 in "Hugh Lincoln Cooper and the First Detente," *Technology and Culture* 20 (1979): 322–47. *Engineering News-Record* articles regularly discussed his individual hydroelectric projects.

ANNE D. RASSWEILER

COOPER, Jacob (7 Dec. 1830–31 Jan. 1904), college professor, was born near Somerville, Butler County, Ohio, the son of Jacob Cooper and Elizabeth Walls, farmers. His early years were spent in comparative poverty. Cooper had to work and could only study in the evenings. Entering Yale in 1850 as a junior, he graduated Phi Beta Kappa in 1852. Cooper received his license to preach in the Presbyterian ministry in 1853 and that same year entered the University of Berlin, from which he received his Ph.D. in 1854. His dissertation, *The Eleusinian Mysteries*, was published, with revised editions appearing in 1876 and 1895.

Cooper joined the faculty of Centre College in Danville, Kentucky, in 1855 as professor of Greek. He preached at the Presbyterian church in nearby Harmony, Kentucky. In May 1855 he married Charlotte MacDill of Oxford, Ohio; the couple had one child. His wife died in 1857. Danville had become a center of antislavery activity, and the Presbyterian college was not immune to the controversies that swirled around it. In reaction to the escalating controversy over slavery, several professors at both Centre College and Danville Theological Seminary began the *Danville Quarterly Review* in 1861. Cooper served as editor until 1865, during which time he also contributed numerous articles to the paper on religious and political topics. In 1862 Cooper added the duties of chaplain of the Third Kentucky Infantry to his Civil War activities. He served until the following year, at which time he returned to Centre College. As a result of his wartime experiences Cooper developed an interest in politics that would last for the rest of his life and a deep devotion to the Republican party.

Cooper married Mary Linn of Cincinnati in 1865. They had six children. He accepted the position of professor of Greek at Rutgers College in September 1866. Cooper began his teaching career at Rutgers during the early years of President William Henry Campbell's administration. One of a handful of notable scholars brought to Rutgers by Campbell, Cooper's contribution to the college was significant. On 22 February 1869 he helped found the Phi Beta Kappa chapter. As a lecturer, he was noted for his vitality of speech and depth of knowledge. Awarded a doctorate by the University of Jena in 1874 for his dissertation *The Natural Right to Make a Will* (1874), Cooper also published *Biography of George Duffield, Jr., D.D.* (1889) and *Biography of President Theodore Dwight Woolsey* (1899). Recognition of his talents spread, and on 2 August 1883 the University of Michigan offered him the dual position of professor of metaphysics and ethics and university preacher. Cooper accepted both posts the following January and resigned from Rutgers. The college trustees, however, refused to accept his resignation, and Michigan kept its vacancy open for two years in vain.

Named professor of mental and moral philosophy at Rutgers in 1893, Cooper also served as college pastor and occasionally preached at outside churches as well. His greatest notoriety, however, came from his activities in the college's home community of New Brunswick, New Jersey. A man of strong opinions, Cooper used both written word and speech to campaign against the endemic political corruption of his day. He preached a sermon on 27 February 1894 at St. James Methodist Church in New Brunswick titled "Public Duty, and the Relation of Citizens to the Government," in which he placed the blame for political corruption squarely on the shoulders of apathetic Christian voters. Cooper also advanced his views in frequent letters to the local newspapers during local mayoral races.

Perhaps Cooper's most notable act as a crusader for reform was performed shortly after the assassination of President William McKinley. Outraged by the infamous "yellow journalism" of William Randolph Hearst, Cooper traveled to New York City and delivered a scathing denunciation of Hearst and his paper in front of the *New York Journal* building. Cooper accused Hearst of indirectly inciting the assassination, and when he was later threatened with libel for this act, he dismissed Hearst's agent with the statement, "You may tell Mr. Hearst he can sue me whenever he desires."

Following a short period of declining health, Cooper died at his home in New Brunswick. His house later became the dining hall at Douglass College (the women's division of Rutgers University).

Cooper was one of the leaders of higher education in the late nineteenth century. One of the first academics who held a Ph.D. to teach in an American college, his occasionally strident political activism belied the image of the pedantic professor. While Cooper is somewhat obscure today, politically and socially conscious academics of the recent past might admire both his professional achievements and his public activism.

• A small collection of Cooper material is held at the Rutgers University Archives in New Brunswick, N.J. Information on his life is scarce; the best source of information about his career is William H. S. Demarest, *History of Rutgers College, 1766–1924* (1924). Obituaries are in the *New Brunswick Daily Home News* and the *New York Times*, both 1 Feb. 1904.

EDWARD L. LACH, JR.

COOPER, James Fenimore (15 Sept. 1789–14 Sept. 1851), novelist, was born in Burlington, New Jersey, the son of William Cooper, a land agent and developer, and Elizabeth Fenimore. In 1790 the family moved to Cooperstown, which his father had founded at the foot of Otsego Lake in New York. James ("Fenimore" was not added to his name until 1826) attended the village academy, spent two winters at school in Burlington, and in 1801 was sent to Albany as a boarding student of the Reverend Thomas Ellison. He entered Yale College in February 1803 but was dismissed for misconduct in the summer of 1805. To prepare for a career in the navy, he shipped before the mast in the *Stirling*, a merchant vessel, on a voyage (Oct. 1806–Sept. 1807) that took him to London and Águilas, Spain. Commissioned a midshipman on 1 January 1808, he served for several months on the *Vesuvius*, was stationed at the frontier outpost at Oswego, New York (Aug. 1808–Oct. 1809), and in November was assigned to the *Wasp*, although he spent most of his time recruiting in New York City.

The death of his father in December 1809 brought Cooper a bequest of $50,000 and an interest in the large tracts of land in his father's estate. Cooper found himself financially independent and began to consider leaving the navy, where opportunity seemed limited. His decision was confirmed in 1811 when he married Susan Augusta De Lancey. They had seven children. His resignation from the navy was finally accepted in

January 1813. The Coopers lived first at New Rochelle before moving to Cooperstown, where they planned to settle, but in 1817 they returned to Westchester County to build on a small farm provided by Susan Cooper's father, John Peter De Lancey. Though he lived as a gentleman farmer, involved in the state militia and the local agricultural and Bible societies, Cooper was in financial trouble. His cash legacy was spent, and he was in debt. Worse, his father's estate was unsalable, and claims against it could not be met. The property was eventually lost in a series of forced sales.

To support his growing family, Cooper turned to a literary career. Playfully challenged by his wife's cousin to write a better book than one he was reading aloud, Cooper, after a false start, produced *Precaution* (1820), an imitation of an English novel of manners, which, though weak, brought him to the attention of the New York literary world. Cooper was soon reviewing books for Charles K. Gardner's *The Literary and Scientific Repository, and Critical Review*, and he began a series of moral tales, two of which eventually appeared in *Tales for Fifteen* (1823). Meanwhile, he had begun to write *The Spy*, a tale of the neutral ground in New York during the American Revolution. Published in December 1821, it was a huge success, going rapidly through three editions. For his next book, *The Pioneers* (1823), he turned to the Cooperstown of his youth, described the establishment of a new settlement in the wilderness, introduced the character of Leatherstocking, and began the ambivalent treatment of the westward movement that he would continue for many years. It too was a great success.

In the fall of 1822, Cooper moved to New York City, where he was soon involved in the intellectual life of the town. He founded the Bread and Cheese Lunch, a club that met weekly in the back room of Charles Wiley's bookstore and included among its members William Cullen Bryant, Fitz-Greene Halleck, Samuel F. B. Morse, Chancellor James Kent, and Gulian Verplanck. Cooper's success continued with *The Pilot* (1824), which established him as a novelist of the sea, and though *Lionel Lincoln* (1825), a tale of revolutionary Boston, failed, *The Last of the Mohicans* (1826) was another success. In this book he reintroduced the character of Leatherstocking, setting the tale in 1757 during the French and Indian War. He also began *The Prairie* (1827), which carries the Leatherstocking series, now comprising three novels, to the hero's death on the Great Plains in 1805. Though Cooper's financial problems had been severe, by 1826 he had solved them.

Cooper then fulfilled a longstanding desire to take his family to Europe. He stopped briefly in London to arrange for the publication of the as yet unfinished *Prairie* and went on to Paris, where he remained until February 1828. He completed *The Prairie* there and also wrote *The Red Rover* (1827).

Cooper's reputation had preceded him to Europe, and he soon found himself moving in the best Paris society. He became a close friend of the marquis de Lafayette, at whose repeated request he began his first work of nonfiction, *Notions of the Americans* (1828), a book intended to correct the mistaken views expressed by foreign travelers to the United States. Cooper completed the work during a three-month stay in London early in 1828, where he was much entertained by the Whig aristocracy. In June he took his family for a summer visit to Switzerland, where he wrote little. In October the Coopers traveled to Italy, where they lived for nine months in Florence before moving on to Sorrento, Naples, Rome, and Venice. He published *The Wept of Wish-ton-Wish* (1829) and *The Water-Witch* (1830), the latter printed in Dresden, where the Coopers settled in May 1830.

The July Revolution brought Cooper back to Paris, where he strongly supported republican principles. Through his American Polish Committee, he sought to aid the Poles in their struggle for freedom, and on Lafayette's appeal he was drawn into the Finance Controversy of 1831–1832. In his pamphlet, *Letter . . . to Gen. Lafayette* (1831), and a series of communications to the Paris *Le National* (1832), he sought to show that, contrary to the arguments of conservatives, the expenses of a republic were not greater than those of a monarchy. He was also revising his early books for Richard Bentley's Standard Novels, and he published three romances that were set in Europe and developed liberal themes: *The Bravo* (1831), *The Heidenmauer* (1832), and *The Headsman* (1833). *The Bravo* was especially important because it argued that a moneyed aristocracy could mask its power behind the forms of a republic, a theme with relevance not only to Europe but also to the United States. Cooper expected to be criticized by conservatives in Europe, but he was dismayed to learn that he was under attack in his own country and that American editors were reprinting unfavorable European reviews of his books.

Rejected, as he believed, by his countrymen for having defended American principles in Europe, Cooper resolved to abandon his profession. He returned to New York in November 1833 to find the country much changed. The Jacksonian "revolution" had taken place, and the gentlemanly standards that he valued seemed to have been swept away. Though warmly greeted by close friends, he found his reception in general so cold that he refused a testimonial dinner in his honor. An attack in the Whig press led Cooper to write *A Letter to His Countrymen* (1834), in which he deplored the American practice of deferring to foreign opinion and used the recent reception of his books in the American press as evidence. He also wrote a series of letters signed "A. B. C." for the New York *Evening Post* (1834–1836), in which he discusses the U.S. Constitution and the current state of Franco-American relations, and he published *The Monikins* (1835), a social and political satire on England, France, and the United States that he had begun in Europe.

Cooper resided at first in New York but visited Cooperstown in June 1834 to make a final settlement of his father's estate. Later that summer he bought "Otsego Hall," the family manor, which he planned to renovate. Though he thought at the time to make it only a summer home, it eventually became his permanent residence. Cooper's style of living, however, alienated many of his fellow villagers, and he was soon at odds with them over Three Mile Point, on Otsego Lake, a part of William Cooper's estate that the townspeople used as a park. When a tree was destroyed on the point in July 1837, Cooper gave notice that the land was private property; a public meeting was held to protest his action, and the issue was picked up by the Whig editors in the vicinity. When they refused to retract an abusive editorial, Cooper sued for libel, and his long battle in the courts began. *Homeward Bound* and *Home as Found* (1838) derive from the controversy and satirize the ignorance and presumption of the common man and the arrogance of demagogic leaders. These books incited the Whig editors to further personal attacks.

Between 1836 and 1838, Cooper published five travel volumes based on his experiences in Switzerland, France, England, Italy, and along the Rhine. Although they differ markedly in subject matter and tone, they reveal Cooper's appreciation for picturesque landscape and his understanding of the societies he had observed. In 1838 he also published *The Chronicles of Cooperstown*, a local history, and *The American Democrat*, a brief treatise on government. He was hard at work too on his long-projected *History of the Navy of the United States of America*. During the winter of 1838–1839, the Coopers lived in Philadelphia, where he researched the book. Published in 1839, it is still a valid history, but it too was soon involved in controversy. A feud had long before developed between partisans of Oliver Hazard Perry and those of Jesse Duncan Elliott, his second in command, concerning Elliott's conduct during the battle of Lake Erie. Although Cooper sifted the evidence and tried hard to be impartial, his account did not satisfy Perry's supporters, and Cooper was once again attacked in the Whig press.

Cooper's legal war with the Whig editors—among them, Thurlow Weed, William Leete Stone, James Watson Webb, and Park Benjamin—went on for years. Cooper moved with cool deliberation, most often giving the editors a chance to retract before he sued, while they used every delaying tactic they could muster. The legal actions, begun in 1837, continued into the early 1840s, and one decision was reversed as late as 1845. Meanwhile, the editors carried on their war in the columns of their newspapers and, by reprinting articles from one another's journals, created a large number of libelous items, too many for Cooper to act on. In controlling so much of the press, they had the advantage of Cooper, though he did reply to some of the libels provoked by *Homeward Bound* and *Home as Found* through the series of letters he wrote for *Brother Jonathan*, a New York weekly journal (1841–1842). Cooper won the battles he fought in the courts, for most of the cases were decided in his favor, but he was not successful in accomplishing his larger purpose: curbing journalistic license and awakening his countrymen to the dangers of an irresponsible press.

Cooper's legal actions were not, however, his main concern. During the 1840s he published a large amount of fiction. *The Pathfinder* (1840), in which Cooper mixed forest adventure with exciting maritime episodes on Lake Ontario, revived the character of Leatherstocking. *Mercedes of Castile* (1840), which treats the discovery of America, is, despite its subject, a very dull book, but Cooper followed it with his masterpiece, *The Deerslayer* (1841). The story, set at Otsego Lake in the 1740s, shows a youthful Leatherstocking on his first warpath. These three books launched what was in effect Cooper's second career as a novelist, but under conditions very different from those of the 1820s. The panic of 1837 depressed the book trade into the succeeding decade, and the sums that he could expect for his novels steadily declined.

Cooper's recourse was to write more. In 1842 he published two tales of the sea: *The Two Admirals*, involving the maneuverings of fleets in the English Channel during the Stuart incursion of 1745, and *The Wing-and-Wing*, set in the Mediterranean in 1799. In 1843 he published *Wyandotté*, a dark tale of the American Revolution, and in 1844 *Afloat and Ashore* and *Miles Wallingford*, a double novel of maritime adventure and social criticism, for which he was his own publisher, an experiment that was not financially successful. He wrote as well his *Lives of Distinguished American Naval Officers* for *Graham's Magazine* between 1842 and 1845 (published in book form in 1846); *Le Mouchoir: An Autobiographical Romance* (1843), an attack on commercial values, first published as "Autobiography of a Pocket Handkerchief" in *Graham's*; *The Battle of Lake Erie* (1843); and a review of the court-martial of Alexander Slidell Mackenzie, who had summarily executed accused mutineers on the brig *Somers* (1844). In addition, he edited, as he put it, *Ned Myers* (1843), an account of the life of an old shipmate.

Succeeding years were almost as productive. In 1845–1846 Cooper published three novels attacking the Anti-Rent War, a protest by tenant farmers in New York against the leasehold system under which they held their land. Cooper saw in the struggle a threat to private property and the sanctity of agreements freely arrived at. It struck, in his view, at the heart of society. He was particularly incensed when tenants, disguised as American Indians, resorted to violence. To oppose the movement he published the *Littlepage Manuscripts*, three novels that defend the landlords by showing how the landholding system had originally been formed and how it had developed in succeeding generations. In *Satanstoe* (1845), a tale of colonial New York and one of Cooper's best novels, Corny Littlepage is present as the land is opened for settlement. In *The Chainbearer* (1845), Mordaunt, his son, has problems with squatters. In *The Redskins* (1846), Mordaunt's grandson, Hugh, struggles against the anti-rent agitators of Cooper's own day.

Cooper was to write five more novels. *The Crater* (1847), a Utopia set in the far Pacific, treats many of the issues raised in the Littlepage series, but Cooper sets up his ideal society only to bring it to a catastrophic end. *Jack Tier* (1848), first serialized in *Graham's Magazine* beginning in 1846, is equally somber; it deals with treachery at sea during the Mexican War. On the other hand, *The Oak Openings* (1848), a frontier tale of Michigan during the War of 1812, and *The Sea Lions* (1849), a novel of seal hunting in the Antarctic, are noteworthy for the strong affirmation of Christian belief that they contain. His final novel, *The Ways of the Hour* (1850), is a murder mystery that attacks the jury system, the direct election of judges, and a recently enacted law that gave married women control over their property. While these last books were appearing, Cooper was lightly revising some of his earlier works for a collected edition that G. P. Putnam planned to publish, but the project proved not to be feasible, and only twelve of the novels were issued, between 1849 and 1851.

Cooper attempted no more novels, but he did not stop writing. His only play, *Upside Down* (1850), a social comedy, was performed in New York for four nights in June 1850, and he was at work on two historical books, *The Towns of Manhattan* and a continuation of his naval history, at the time of his death. He also wrote two short pieces: "The Lake Gun," for *The Parthenon* (1850), and "American and European Scenery Compared," published posthumously in *The Home Book of the Picturesque* (1852). As late as the fall of 1850, he seemed to be in vigorous health, but by the following spring he was obviously ill. Though he had long attended the Episcopal church, served it as warden, and represented it at diocesan conventions, he only now formally entered it, receiving baptism and taking communion in the spring of 1851, and receiving confirmation in the summer. He died in Cooperstown.

• Major collections of manuscript materials are in the Beinecke Rare Book and Manuscript Library at Yale; in the American Antiquarian Society, Worcester, Mass.; and in the Clifton Waller Barrett Library at the University of Virginia. Important information may be found in the introductions to the various sections of letters in *The Letters and Journals of James Fenimore Cooper*, ed. James Franklin Beard (6 vols., 1960–1968), and in the historical introductions and textual commentaries in the various volumes of *The Writings of James Fenimore Cooper*, Beard, editor in chief (1980–). Three useful bio-critical studies are James Grossman, *James Fenimore Cooper* (1949), George Dekker, *James Fenimore Cooper: The Novelist* (1967), and Donald A. Ringe, *James Fenimore Cooper, Updated Edition* (1988).

DONALD A. RINGE

COOPER, James Graham (19 June 1830–19 July 1902), naturalist and physician, was born in New York City, the son of William Cooper and Frances Graham. William Cooper (for whom the species commonly known as Cooper's hawk is named) was a founding member of the Lyceum of Natural History of New York and was closely associated with John J. Audubon, Charles Lucien Bonaparte, John Torrey, and other prominent figures in early American science. When James Cooper was seven years old, the family moved to a farm near Slongha, New Jersey. There he came to share his father's love of nature. In 1851 he earned an M.D. from the College of Physicians and Surgeons of New York and worked for two years in the city's hospitals.

In 1853 Spencer Fullerton Baird, then assistant secretary of the Smithsonian Institution, nominated Cooper as surgeon and naturalist for the northernmost of the Pacific Railroad surveys. Baird also gave him instructions for collecting and describing flora and fauna. Led by Isaac Ingalls Stevens, the survey party explored the area west of the Mississippi between the forty-seventh and forty-ninth parallels. Cooper worked under Brevet Captain George B. McClellan, who conducted a reconnaissance in Washington Territory. Starting from Fort Vancouver, Cooper collected animals and plants throughout Washington and along the Columbia River. At the conclusion of the survey in 1854, Cooper remained in the Pacific Northwest and continued to collect specimens in Washington, Oregon, and northern California.

Cooper returned to New York in 1856 and briefly practiced medicine in Orange, New Jersey. The following year he was again in the West, this time as a contract surgeon for a military expedition to survey a wagon road from Fort Kearny, Nebraska, to the Rocky Mountains. Between 1857 and 1861 he traveled extensively along the East Coast, including Florida. Also in this period he deposited in the Smithsonian the specimens obtained on his journeys and, in collaboration with George Suckley, completed the natural history report of the Stevens survey.

Employed once more as a contract surgeon with the army, Cooper in 1860 accompanied troops sent from New York to the Pacific Northwest via the Missouri and Columbia rivers. He collected specimens en route, as well as along the coast from Fort Vancouver to San Francisco, Fort Mojave, and San Diego. In 1862 he moved to Oakland, California. During the last months of the Civil War he served as assistant surgeon, Second California Volunteer Cavalry, at Drum Barracks, near San Pedro.

In 1866 he married Rosa Wells, with whom he had three children. After briefly residing in Santa Cruz, California, he returned to the Bay area and resumed his scientific travels for the state's geological survey. The main result of his observations and collections was volume one of *Ornithology: Land Birds*, published by the survey in 1870 on the land birds of California. Cooper wrote the bird biographies, and Baird edited the work and supplied the technical information. *Land Birds* is considered Cooper's most important contribution to ornithology.

Cooper also wrote on mammals and botany. Among his other early works were studies of the influence of climate on the growth and distribution of vegetation. One was published by the Smithsonian in 1858; another, by the Patent Office, in 1860.

Cooper remained in California, moving to Ventura County in 1872 and to a suburb of Oakland in 1874. The following year he moved to Hayward, where he lived until his death. By the time he moved to Hayward, Cooper had turned his attention primarily to malacology, and the papers of his later years were primarily on the mollusks and shells of the Pacific Coast.

Because of declining health (he suffered from a pulmonary condition), Cooper wrote and traveled less in his last years. Efforts to obtain scientific work with the federal government were unsuccessful, and his medical practice, which he maintained throughout his career as a naturalist, was limited. Nevertheless, he was an active and important member of the California Academy of Sciences and published several papers in its *Proceedings*. Other writings appeared in the *American Journal of Conchology*, *American Naturalist*, *Bulletin of the Nuttall Ornithological Club*, and *The Century*.

Cooper's publications on natural history are not extensive. His works, however, along with his collections, contributed much to the knowledge of the natural history of California and the Far West. Because Cooper was not only among the first naturalists to examine California and other parts of the West Coast but was also one of the first prominent naturalists to take up permanent residence in the state, and because he conducted field studies through which he instructed and encouraged younger naturalists in California, the state's Cooper Ornithological Club, founded in 1893, is named for him.

• Cooper's papers are in the Smithsonian. Cooper and Suckley's report of the Stevens survey was titled *The Natural History of Washington Territory, with Much Relating to Minnesota, Nebraska, Kansas, Oregon, and California* . . . (1860). Eugene Coan, *James Graham Cooper: Pioneer Western Naturalist* (1981), is the most authoritative biography. See also two accounts by W. O. Emerson, "Dr. James G. Cooper: A Sketch," *Bulletin of the Cooper Ornithological Club* 1 (1899): 1–5, and "In Memoriam: Dr. James G. Cooper," *The Condor: A Magazine of Western Ornithology* 4 (1902): 101–3. Also useful are obituaries by William H. Dall in *Science*, n.s., 16 (1902): 268–69, and by J. A. Allen in *The Auk* 19 (1902): 421–22.

MICHAEL J. BRODHEAD

COOPER, John Sherman (23 Aug. 1901–21 Feb. 1991), lawyer, senator, and diplomat, was born in Somerset, Kentucky, the son of John Sherman Cooper and Helen Gertrude Tartar. His father, considered the wealthiest man in town and a leader in Pulaski County, was both a county and a circuit judge, as his father had been before him. It was "assumed that the next generation of Coopers would provide the county its leaders" (Krebs, p. 13). Cooper attended Centre College in Kentucky, then Yale University, where he received his degree in 1923. He began to study law at Harvard but returned to Kentucky in 1925 because his father's death and a recession in 1920 had depleted the family's resources. During the next twenty-five years Cooper assumed financial responsibility for the family and sent his six brothers and sisters to college. He gained admission to the bar in 1928 at age twenty-seven.

Cooper's political career began in 1927 with his election to the Kentucky legislature's lower house for the 1928–1930 term. For the next eight years he was county judge, which gave him administrative experience, a strong hold on patronage, and practice listening to people's problems during the depression. After unsuccessfully running as the Republican candidate for governor in 1939, he practiced law in his home town.

In 1942 Cooper enlisted in the army as a private and subsequently attended officer candidate school. Later, as a captain, he served from July 1944 with General George Patton in Europe. When hostilities ended, Cooper was an adviser on the repatriation of displaced persons and was in charge of reorganizing the court system of Bavaria. He was awarded a Bronze Star.

In 1944 Cooper married Evelyn Pfaff, a nurse. They divorced in 1949. In 1955 Cooper married Lorraine Rowan McAdoo Shevlin. No record exists of any children in either marriage.

Before leaving the army in 1946, Cooper in 1945 was elected in absentia as a circuit judge of Kentucky's Twenty-eighth Judicial District. But he soon resigned from the judicial circuit to begin a Senate career that, with interruptions, would extend from the early Cold War years through the Korean and Vietnam conflicts. Elected in 1946 as a Republican with 53.3 percent of the vote in a Democratic state, he filled out the unexpired term of Democratic senator A. B. "Happy" Chandler, who had become baseball commissioner. Cooper was defeated in the 1948 senatorial election by veteran Democrat Virgil Chapman, but on Chapman's death in 1952, Cooper was elected to fill that unexpired term. In 1954 Cooper lost the Senate race to former vice president Alben W. Barkley. Barkley died in 1956, and Cooper was elected to fill his unexpired term. Cooper won his first full term in 1960. He was reelected in 1966 with the largest electoral majority ever earned by a Kentucky senatorial candidate up to that time, winning 110 of the state's 120 counties.

When Senator Cooper lost his reelection bid after his first two-year term, President Harry Truman asked the Kentuckian to join Warren Austin, Philip Jessup, and Eleanor Roosevelt on the U.S. delegation to the United Nations General Assembly, initiating a concurrent diplomatic career. Cooper was a delegate in 1949, 1950, 1951, 1968, and 1981. In 1950 he also was adviser to Secretary of State Dean Acheson at a London-Brussels North Atlantic Treaty Organization (NATO) conference. Cooper played an important role in the bipartisan foreign policy attempt to deal with post–World War II problems. He emphatically believed that communism was wrong and that closer political and military cooperation between Europe and North America was essential.

After Cooper's 1954 election loss to Barkley, President Dwight Eisenhower appointed Cooper ambassador to India and Nepal, a sensitive battleground area in the Cold War. India lacked confidence in the motives and methods of the United States, and the United States did not understand India's foreign policy of nonalignment. Issues straining relations between the two countries included America's regional defense pacts, which India refused to join; U.S. military aid to Pakistan, perceived by India as a threat to its own security; and the Soviet Union's growing economic and political influence in India. A *New York Times* editorial on 17 January 1955 described Cooper's appointment as "a fortunate one," since he had demonstrated his ability and earned respect.

Cooper had no formal schooling in the art of diplomacy, but in the art of personal relations he was naturally skilled. His experience handling his Kentucky constituents' problems with compassion and genteel modesty transferred well into his conversations with India's prime minister, Jawaharlal Nehru. Cooper quickly learned that Nehru liked to talk, and "all I had to do was listen—and now and then ask a question." Cooper showed sincere sensitivity toward Indian positions and sought Nehru's patience in understanding America's, yet it was always clear that the ambassador represented the interests of the United States. Cooper tried to clarify to the American public and government the subtleties of India's misunderstood policy of nonalignment, explaining that Nehru was expressing Indian independence, "the spirit of nationalism in contrast to Communist imperialism."

In 1956 Cooper left India to resume his Senate career, which would be uninterrupted for the next sixteen years. While a senator, he was also an adviser to the United Nations Educational, Scientific, and Cultural Organization (UNESCO) in 1958 and the conference establishing the Asian Development Bank in 1965. From 1966 to 1972 he was a member of the NATO Parliamentarians Conference.

As a senator, Cooper immediately established a reputation as an independent. His first roll-call vote so irritated the Republican leadership that Senator Robert Taft demanded to know when Cooper was going to "start voting with us." Cooper replied, "If you'll pardon me, I was sent here to represent my constituents, and I intend to vote as I think best." Cooper followed his intention. Although he ardently supported federal aid to education, he consistently opposed any aid that jeopardized the separation of church and state. His liberal voting record on social ills reflected his instinct to explain and try to repair, as well as his personal experience with his Kentucky constituents. He was one of the first Republicans to condemn the tactics of Senator Joseph McCarthy. Cooper addressed the fundamental issue of congressional-presidential powers, opposing U.S. intervention in Vietnam as early as 1954 and persistently trying to discourage military escalation. He voted for the Gulf of Tonkin Resolution in August 1964, hoping it would show a unified resolve to resist attack. Later, as he reflected on the resolution, he concluded that the biggest mistake he made was voting for it, and he continued to speak against increased bombing. Cooper led the way in questioning presidential power to expand the war without congressional authorization, ultimately coauthoring the Cooper-Church Amendment, signed by President Richard Nixon in 1970. By taking legislative steps to restrain presidential war powers, Cooper followed a course he considered "correct and constitutional." He left the Senate in January 1973. In 1974 he was appointed by President Gerald Ford as the first U.S. ambassador to East Germany, where he remained for two years.

Cooper was a poor public speaker who preferred to work quietly and who employed reason rather than rhetoric in persuasion. His ability and integrity won him the confidence of presidents from Truman to Ford, yet he did not surrender his judgment to any president. His independence brought him criticism from the old guard of his party and some constituents, but he answered, "There are many views in both parties and this is part of our free system of government." His philosophy of representation was to consider constituents' problems and ideas and then apply his own best judgment. Typically, Cooper determined his own time to retire from the Senate. The 1970s were a different era with "a whole new set of problems, and they are not as clear . . . as they used to be." He left the new problems for younger minds and joined a Washington law firm, maintaining residences in Somerset, Kentucky, and Washington, D.C. Cooper died in a Washington retirement home.

• Cooper's papers and an oral history project are at the University of Kentucky Library, Special Collections and Archives. His remarks in the Senate are in the *Congressional Record*, 1946–1948, 1952–1954, and 1956–1972. Election statistics are in Malcolm Jewell, *Kentucky Votes* (2 vols., 1963), and Jasper B. Shannon and Ruth McQuown, *Presidential Politics in Kentucky 1824–1948* (1950). Robert Schulman, *John Sherman Cooper: The Global Kentuckian* (1976), credits Cooper's rural background, personal integrity, and openness for his success in dealing with world leaders. Clarice James Mitchiner, *Senator John Sherman Cooper: Consummate Statesman* (1976; repr., 1982), focuses on Cooper as a spokesman for his fellow Kentuckians, his country, and humanity, and the bibliography lists useful articles, books, speeches, interviews, and government publications. Douglas A. Franklin, "The Politician as Diplomat: Kentucky's John Sherman Cooper in India, 1955–56," *Register of the Kentucky Historical Society* 82 (1984): 28–59, uses primary and secondary sources. See also "Ambassador to India," *New York Times*, 17 Jan. 1955; John Pearce, "The Busy Hard Life of the Senate's 'Best Republican,'" *Louisville Courier-Journal*, 19 June 1960; William Cooper, Jr., "John Sherman Cooper: A Senator and His Constituents," *Register of the Kentucky Historical Society* 84 (1986): 192–210; and Richard C. Smoot, "John Sherman Cooper: The Paradox of a Liberal Republican in Kentucky Politics" (Ph.D. diss., Univ. of Kentucky, 1988). Robert F. Maddox, "John Sherman Cooper and the Vietnam War," *Journal of the West Virginia Historical Association* 11 (1987): 52–76, provides essential insight and includes many source notes. Albin Krebs, "John Sherman Cooper Dies at 89," *New York Times*, 23 Feb. 1991, is an informative obituary.

SYLVIA B. LARSON

COOPER, Joseph Alexander (25 Nov. 1823–20 May 1910), farmer and army officer, was born near Cumberland Falls, Whitley County, Kentucky, the son of John Cooper, a farmer. His mother's name is unknown. While Cooper was still a child, his family moved to a farm on Cove Creek in Campbell County,

Tennessee. In 1846 he married Mary J. Hutson; the number of their children, if any, is unknown. The following year he joined the Fourth Tennessee Volunteer Infantry Regiment to fight in the Mexican War. After returning from the war, he took up farming near Jacksboro, Tennessee.

When it came to politics, Cooper was a Whig and, like most of his fellow East Tennesseans, a strong Unionist in the secession crisis of 1861. Elected a delegate to the Knoxville Union convention, he played an active role in that assembly. Thereafter he went to work to recruit and drill Campbell County men for service in the Union army. He was formally mustered into the service in August 1861 in Whitesburg, Kentucky, and commissioned captain of Company A, First Tennessee Volunteer Infantry. During the fall of 1861 and the spring of the following year he served in the mountainous regions of eastern Kentucky and Tennessee. On 19 January 1862 the Union force commanded by General George H. Thomas, of which Cooper was a part, defeated a smaller Confederate force at Logan's Crossroads, near Mill Springs on the Cumberland River in Kentucky. That spring Cooper received authorization from the War Department to raise another regiment of loyal East Tennesseans, and on 18 March this unit was formally mustered in as the Sixth Tennessee, with Cooper as its colonel. The unit then served with the Union garrison at Cumberland Gap, retreated to Ohio to refit, and then joined the Army of the Cumberland. At the battle of Stones River, 31 December 1862–2 January 1863, Cooper's regiment was detailed to cover an ammunition train from Nashville. The Tennesseans fought hard and successfully in preventing Confederate cavalry from striking this vulnerable but vital part of the army's support. Throughout the rest of 1863, Cooper continued to lead his regiment ably through various assignments in the Tullahoma, Chattanooga, and Knoxville campaigns, but during this time the Sixth Tennessee did not become heavily engaged in any of the large battles.

In the spring of 1864 Cooper was given command of a brigade of the XXIII Corps, Army of the Ohio, under General John M. Schofield. Cooper led this brigade throughout the Atlanta campaign, and on 30 July of that year he was promoted to brigadier general of volunteers. When Confederate general John B. Hood led his Army of Tennessee into the state of that name in the fall of 1864, the XXIII Corps (with Cooper) was among the troops sent north to deal with him. On 30 November 1864 Schofield's segment of the Union forces in Tennessee was caught alone by Hood and turned at bay with its back to the Harpeth River at Franklin, Tennessee. Hood launched his army in headlong assaults, only to have it slaughtered before the guns of the XXIII Corps, including Cooper and his brigade. A fortnight later Cooper's brigade took part in the final destruction of Hood's army at the battle of Nashville (15–16 Dec. 1864). For his gallant and meritorious service at this battle, Cooper was breveted major general of volunteers. Thereafter Cooper's brigade was among the troops Schofield took to join General William T. Sherman in North Carolina. Schofield's men traveled by ship to the coast of North Carolina and then marched inland to meet Sherman at Goldsboro. Cooper continued to command his brigade, and from time to time during these last months of the war, as necessity arose, he exercised command of the division.

In January 1866 Cooper was mustered out of the army and went back to farming in East Tennessee. In 1868 he ran for the U.S. Senate but lost. The following year President Ulysses S. Grant made him collector of internal revenue for the Knoxville District. In 1874 Cooper's first wife died, and in January of the following year he married Mary J. Polston. After ten years as tax collector, he resigned and in 1880 moved to Stafford County, Kansas. There, of course, he took up farming. Having been a Baptist for decades and a deacon for thirty-five years, Cooper in 1889 played an active role in organizing the South Central Baptist Association of Kansas. Thereafter he often served as moderator of the association. He died in Stafford, Kansas.

• For further information on Cooper see U.S. War Department, *The War of the Rebellion: A Compilation of the Official Records of the Union and Confederate Armies* (128 vols., 1880–1901); and Ezra J. Warner, *Generals in Blue: The Lives of the Union Commanders* (1964).

STEVEN E. WOODWORTH

COOPER, Kent (22 Mar. 1880–31 Jan. 1965), journalist, was born in Columbus, Indiana, the son of George William Cooper, a lawyer who served as mayor of Columbus and as a U.S. congressman, and Sina Green. Starting as a delivery boy, Cooper worked for Columbus newspapers from the time he was eleven until he entered Indiana University in 1898. In 1899, when his father died and he had to withdraw from college, he returned to reporting, first at the *Indianapolis Press* and then at the *Indianapolis Sun*. In 1903 he was hired as an Indianapolis correspondent by the Scripps-McRae Press Association (SMPA). Two years later he married Daisy McBride; they had one child. When SMPA denied Cooper a raise in 1905, he left and started his own agency; within a year his former employers capitulated and bought him out. At that time, papers that could not afford leased wires received their news by telegraph, generally no more than 500 words per day. In 1906 Cooper negotiated a special rate with the telephone company, permitting his office to make a simultaneous phone call to small papers around the state twice a day and read out the latest news bulletins. In one year Cooper's so-called pony service increased SMPA's Indiana membership by 50 percent.

In 1907 SMPA joined the United Press (UP) news agency. For the next two years Cooper crisscrossed the country, using the pony service idea to win the UP new members. Seeking faster advancement, he moved in 1910 to the UP's rival, the much larger Associated Press (AP). The atmosphere there, he recalled in later years, "reeked with old age," but he thought this could be an advantage. "I had seen few young AP men any-

where. . . . I thought I might have less rivalry at The AP." Starting as a "traveling inspector," Cooper soon worked out a plan for major changes at the agency. The general manager, Melville Stone, ignored his recommendations; but two board members pushed his ideas through, and in 1912, as part of the restructuring, Cooper was made head of the new Traffic Department. The rest of his recommendations were also implemented, some of them saving the agency substantial sums of money. Cooper soon introduced other innovations, including the first teletype machines in 1913, the first employee pension plan in the news industry in 1918, and a system for direct play-by-play transmission of the 1916 World Series to dozens of big-city papers tied into a single 26,000-mile circuit.

Cooper was eager to extend the AP's market around the globe, starting with South America, but Stone held back in deference to a powerful international news cartel. Three European agencies—Britain's Reuters, Germany's Wolff, and France's Havas—had divided the world among them while allocating North America to the AP. South America belonged to the Havas Agency. In addition, most South American papers subscribed to a local agency, La Prensa Asociada, which was secretly funded by the German government. During World War I the obvious bias of Prensa Asociada's reporting opened new possibilities for the AP, and Cooper finally won permission for an exploratory trip in 1918. After gathering applications from twenty-five newspapers in half a dozen South American countries, he persuaded Havas to let him sign them up. Thus, the AP took its first step toward becoming an international service.

Cooper's wife died in 1920, and later that year he married Marian Rothwell. They had no children. Having been named assistant general manager the same year, he began to travel extensively around the United States and abroad. Then in April 1925 he was named general manager. Under his leadership, the number of AP bureaus was increased and the staff greatly expanded. He established "state services" to give member papers more local news, hired the AP's first science editor, and created a new Feature Department. Stone had dismissed human interest stories as "trivialities," but Cooper made them a regular part of the AP service, along with illustrations, political cartoons, recipes, and comic strips. The new style was not universally admired. Journalist Oswald Garrison Villard, noting that Cooper's changes "must have made Melville Stone turn in his grave," argued that the AP now offered too many "light and 'spicy' items of dubious value." Cooper, however, was convinced that broadening the AP's range better enabled it to tell the "true day-to-day story of humanity." Pressing the agency's traditional boundaries further, he initiated a news photo service in 1927. This step led to further innovations, since delivering pictures across the country could take as long as four days. Adopting a new process for transmitting pictures by wire and beating down objections from some AP members who had competing local photo services of their own, Cooper inaugurated the nation's first wire-photo service in 1935. By the end of the next year, the agency was transmitting about forty pictures a day, and its competitors were scrambling to develop equivalent services.

Despite his modernizing zeal, Cooper resisted one emerging trend: unionization. During the 1930s the AP was repeatedly accused of emphasizing news that discredited New Deal labor legislation, interfering with union meetings of its own employees, and punishing staff who engaged in union activities. During the same years, however, Cooper made an important contribution to American journalism by further challenging the cartel that controlled world news, often in line with the political interests of the members' own governments. With his board's support, Cooper broke with the cartel in 1934, setting the AP free to gather news around the globe. This action, which Cooper described in *Barriers Down* (1942), was praised by Villard as "a magnificent crusade" for journalistic freedom.

Cooper was divorced in 1940; two years later he married his longtime executive secretary, Sarah A. Gibbs. They had no children. He retired as general manager in 1948 but served as executive director from 1943 to 1951. His history of press censorship, *The Right to Know*, appeared in 1956, followed by an autobiography, *Kent Cooper and the Associated Press*, three years later. He also continued to pursue his longtime hobby of writing songs. He died in West Palm Beach, Florida. By breaking with the cartel and by his many innovations within the AP, Cooper built his agency into a dominant force in international news gathering. He was, as his colleague Hal Boyle observed, "a tradition-smasher and an applecartupsetter [who] swept through the stodgy newspaper atmosphere of his day like a polar wind."

• Besides the books cited in the text, Cooper wrote a fictionalized biography, *Anna Zenger: Mother of Freedom* (1946). His career is also discussed in Hugh Baillie, *High Tension* (1959), p. 285; Edwin Emery and Michael Emery, *The Press and America* (1978), pp. 300–301; Oliver Gramling, *AP: The Story of News* (1940); Alfred McClung Lee, *The Daily Newspaper in America* (1937); Joe Alex Morris, *Deadline Every Minute* (1957); Richard Schwarzlose, *The Nation's Newsbrokers*, vol. 2 (1990); and Oswald Garrison Villard, *The Disappearing Daily* (1944). An obituary is in the *New York Times*, 31 Jan. 1965.

SANDRA OPDYCKE

COOPER, Merian Coldwell (24 Oct. 1893–21 Apr. 1973), filmmaker and adventurer, was born in Jacksonville, Florida, the son of John C. Cooper, a lawyer, and Mary Coldwell. He attended the U.S. Naval Academy, but resigned in his last year. After a failed attempt to become an aviator early in World War I, he worked for short periods on newspapers and then enlisted in the Georgia National Guard, seeing service in Mexico.

When the United States entered the war, Cooper joined the U.S. Air Service and saw action on the western front. In September 1918 he was shot down behind enemy lines and finished the war in a German hospital. He later served with the American Relief Administration. In 1919 Cooper and Major Cedric Fauntleroy formed the Kosciusko Squadron, a group of American pilots who volunteered to fight the Bolshevik invasion of Poland. Cooper was shot down in July 1920 and taken, under an assumed name, to a Moscow prison. In April 1921 he escaped with two Polish officers to the Latvian border. At the squadron's demobilization, President Pilsudski of Poland awarded Cooper the Cross of the Brave; a statue was erected in his honor in Warsaw.

Returning to the United States, Cooper contributed articles to the *New York Times*. He also wrote a book about the Kosciusko Squadron which was published in Polish as *Faunt-le-Roy i jego Eskadra w Polsce* (Fauntleroy and His Squadron in Poland, 1922). Still restless, Cooper accepted a job as navigator and writer with Captain Edward A. Salisbury and, in September 1922, joined Salisbury's yacht in Singapore. With Salisbury he wrote a book about the voyage, *The Sea Gypsy* (1924).

Cooper and Ernest B. Schoedsack, a photographer on the Salisbury voyage, decided to organize their own filming expedition, and Cooper obtained funding from Marguerite Harrison, whom he had known in Poland. They traveled from Aleppo to Baghdad, stopping at an outpost of the Iraq Desert Patrol. Later they joined the nomadic Bakhtiari tribes of southern Iran and, during the spring of 1924, participated in their annual migration in search of fresh grass. Cooper wrote about the migration *Grass* (1925). After he and Schoedsack edited their film, Cooper accompanied it on lecture engagements. Paramount then released it to theaters as *Grass: A Nation's Battle for Life* (1925), one of the first important feature documentaries. *Grass* received excellent reviews, so Paramount financed another expedition.

In July 1925 Cooper and Schoedsack left for the Nan district of northern Siam (Thailand), returning in December 1926. It was the realization of Cooper's dream to spend a year in the jungle documenting wild animals. The filmmakers personalized the natives' struggle against the jungle by centering on one family and made full use of cinematic techniques. After observing, they wrote a story and recreated events for the camera. They even selected unrelated people to portray the family. This resulted in a kind of staged authenticity which they called "natural drama." The method produced a film of considerable impact. *Variety* called *Chang: A Drama of the Wilderness* (1927) "the best wild animal picture ever made."

When Paramount agreed to back another film, the team further developed their concept of natural drama by adapting A. E. W. Mason's novel, *The Four Feathers*. In spring 1927 they left for East Africa, then moved north to the Sudan, spending a year filming animal action and battle scenes. Back in Hollywood, they directed professional actors, then intercut those shots with the location footage. Later, though, the studio restructured the plot and added several new scenes. *The Four Feathers* (1929) retained its spectacle, but Cooper was disappointed by the changes.

In 1927 Cooper invested his earnings from *Chang* in aviation stocks, and he was elected to the boards of several airlines, including Pan American Airways, Western Air Express, and General Aviation. This kept him in New York from 1929 to 1931, and he became friends with financiers Cornelius Vanderbilt Whitney and John Hay Whitney, as well as naturalist W. Douglas Burden.

Cooper was interested in making a film about African gorillas, and also in filming the Komodo dragon lizards discovered in Indonesia by Douglas Burden. Through editing, he hoped to depict a confrontation between the two creatures. He also wanted to express his belief "that over-civilization destroys people," and he envisioned a dramatic juxtaposition of gorillas and airplanes.

When David O. Selznick became head of production at RKO Radio Pictures in fall 1931, he asked Cooper to evaluate the studio's projects. After viewing footage of animated dinosaur models created by Willis O'Brien, Cooper saw his chance. "I decided I'd make my gorilla picture . . . and make it right here." He outlined the story of *King Kong* (1933) to author Edgar Wallace, who started on a script, and in January 1932 he brought Schoedsack to RKO. Later, writer Ruth Rose (Schoedsack's wife) modeled two of the film's main characters on Cooper and her husband.

While developing *Kong*, Cooper produced a mystery (*The Phantom of Crestwood*, 1932), cowrote the story for an action film set in China (*Roar of the Dragon*, 1932), and had Schoedsack and Irving Pichel codirect the jungle adventure, *The Most Dangerous Game* (1932). For *Kong*, Cooper and Schoedsack shared directorial responsibility; they also played the aviators in the film's climax. In March 1933 *King Kong* played simultaneously at two New York theaters, the Radio City Music Hall and the Roxy, and was a tremendous hit.

Selznick resigned as RKO's vice president on 3 February 1933, and Cooper succeeded him, serving as executive producer on numerous features released between April 1933 and June 1934, including *Little Women* (1933) and *Flying Down to Rio* (1933). Cooper's program was varied, but several films reflect his interests and experiences. Airplanes were often featured, and he depicted such adventurous filmmakers as stuntmen (*Lucky Devils*, 1933) and newsreel cameramen (*Headline Shooter*, 1933). During his tenure as vice president, Cooper impressed others as energetic, sometimes blunt, and always honest.

After seeing a demonstration of Technicolor's new three-color system, Cooper wanted to film *Kong* and *Flying Down to Rio* in the process. When RKO resisted, he acted on his judgment by purchasing stock in the company, along with the Whitneys. In May 1933 he and John Hay Whitney formed Pioneer Pictures to produce films in Technicolor, but at first Cooper remained in the background. Also in May, he married actress Dorothy Jordan; they had three children.

For a time Cooper enjoyed his executive position, but after suffering a heart attack in September 1933, he eased himself out of the studio's daily responsibilities by taking a leave of absence to combine recuperation with a delayed honeymoon. In May 1934 Cooper returned to Hollywood and resigned, but he remained at RKO to produce two films written by Ruth Rose—*She* (1935), from the novel by H. Rider Haggard, and *The Last Days of Pompeii* (1935), which Schoedsack directed. He then turned his attention to Pioneer, which had already made *Becky Sharp* (1935), the first feature in three-color Technicolor. For Pioneer he produced the color musical *Dancing Pirate* (1936). In 1935 the Whitneys and Cooper had invested in Selznick's new company, Selznick International, because the producer agreed to use Technicolor. Selznick International absorbed Pioneer in June 1936, and Cooper continued as vice president and producer. That fall, Cooper helped Selznick convince playwright Sidney Howard to adapt the novel *Gone With the Wind*.

John Ford had contracted with the studio to direct two films; he selected a western story and wanted to cast John Wayne and Claire Trevor. Cooper agreed and, in summer 1937, described the idea to Selznick, who unexpectedly rejected the stars. Cooper angrily resigned and quickly signed with MGM, where he made *The Toy Wife* (1938). He also unofficially produced the western Selznick had rejected, *Stagecoach* (1939); he and Ford then formed the Argosy Corporation, which made Ford's *The Long Voyage Home* (1940).

In May 1941 Cooper reenlisted and at one point flew refugees out of Assam, India. He was chief of U.S. Army Air Corps intelligence and plans in China when, in 1942, he joined Claire Chennault's American Volunteer Group, known as the "Flying Tigers." He became Chennault's chief of staff when the A.V.G. was incorporated into the U.S. Air Corps as the China Air Task Force.

Cooper openly criticized what he and Chennault considered General Joseph W. Stilwell's neglect of China's strategic possibilities, so Stilwell ordered Cooper's return to the United States. In 1943 Cooper began serving with General George Kenney's Fifth Air Force in New Guinea, where he planned the attacks on Wewak and Hollandia that helped destroy Japanese air power in the area. In 1945 he was with Kenney and MacArthur on the battleship *Missouri* when Japan surrendered. Kenney recommended Cooper for promotion several times, but at the war's end he was still a colonel. In 1950, however, he became a brigadier general in the Air Force Reserve.

Cooper and Ford revived Argosy Pictures in spring 1946, with Cooper as president and Ford as chairman of the board. Cooper involved himself in every detail of the company, from casting to advertising. Mainly, though, he handled the finances and organization. *The Fugitive* (1947), Argosy's first film, was shot in Mexico, for RKO release. Argosy then made several westerns, which established the company's financial stability. *Fort Apache* (1948), *She Wore a Yellow Ribbon* (1949), and *Wagon Master* (1950) were released by RKO, and *Three Godfathers* (1948) by MGM. For Republic, Argosy made *Rio Grande* (1950) and *The Quiet Man* (1952); the latter won Academy Awards for direction and color photography. In the same year, Cooper received a special Oscar "for his many innovations and contributions to the art of motion pictures." *The Sun Shines Bright* (1953) was Argosy's last film.

In 1947 Cooper began his own project, *Mighty Joe Young* (1949). Like *Kong*, it featured a giant gorilla, but this one, Cooper said in 1949, "is not out to frighten audiences but to amuse them and to win sympathy and affection." The plot involved "the effects of civilization on animals transported from native habitats to such an incongruous jungle as a Hollywood night club." *Joe* reunited Cooper with several friends and veterans of *Kong*, including director Schoedsack. *Joe* contained impressive scenes, but it lacked the power of *Kong*. Based on Cooper's original story, it included some broad satire of the entertainment business and was his final personal film.

Fellow explorer and showman Lowell Thomas got Cooper involved with the first feature made in Cinerama, a process that used three cameras filming simultaneously; projected on three adjacent, angled screens, the images created a three-dimensional effect. Cooper and Robert Bendick edited and organized documentary footage already shot. Cooper also devised new sequences, including a tour across America filmed from the air. *This Is Cinerama* premiered in 1952. The Cinerama Corporation signed Cooper to a five-year contract as general manager in charge of production, and he announced plans to make four dramatic films. Louis B. Mayer replaced Lowell Thomas as chairman of the board, however, and declared that he had no commitments for productions. The resultant struggle between Mayer and Cooper, along with the company's financial problems, led to the departure of both men in 1954.

Cooper soon joined Cornelius Vanderbilt Whitney in the short-lived C. V. Whitney Productions, for which he produced John Ford's *The Searchers* (1956). In 1958 he formed Merian C. Cooper Enterprises and announced several projects, including a film about Chennault; however, his last film, produced with Thomas Conroy, was *The Best of Cinerama* (1963), an anthology of excerpts from the six previous travelogues.

Around 1968, under treatment for cancer, Cooper spent a year revisiting sites in Europe and elsewhere, then returned to California. His last public appearance was on 30 December 1971, to deliver a eulogy at the funeral of Max Steiner, who had composed the music for *King Kong*. Cooper died in San Diego, California.

• Cooper's papers are in the Harold B. Lee Library, Brigham Young University, Provo, Utah. Rudy Behlmer summarized Cooper's life and career in *Films in Review*, Jan. 1966, pp. 17–35. Orville Goldner and George E. Turner detail his early

adventures in *The Making of King Kong* (1975), and Ronald Haver covers his 1930s film work in *David O. Selznick's Hollywood* (1980).

Marguerite Harrison recounts the *Grass* expedition in *There's Always Tomorrow: The Story of a Checkered Life* (1935); A. J. Siggins recalls the filming of *The Four Feathers* in *Shooting with Rifle and Camera* (1931); and Fay Wray reminisces about *Kong* in *On the Other Hand: A Life Story* (1989). *Grass* and *Chang* are well documented in Kevin Brownlow's *The War, The West, and the Wilderness* (1979). George E. Turner profiles *The Most Dangerous Game* in *The Cinema of Adventure, Romance & Terror* (1989); *The Son of Kong* in *American Cinematographer*, Aug. 1992, pp. 67–71; and *She* in *American Cinematographer*, June 1995, pp. 103–8. Obituaries are in the *New York Times*, 22 Apr. 1973, and *Variety*, 25 Apr. 1973.

PAUL M. JENSEN

COOPER, Myles (Feb 1737–20 May 1785), Anglican priest, president of King's College, and Loyalist, was born near Broughton-Furness, Cumberland County, England, the son of William Cooper and Elizabeth (maiden name unknown). Myles Cooper's date of birth is not known, but he was baptized probably on 19 February 1737 in Cumberland County, England. In 1753 he entered Queen's College, Oxford, earning the B.A. in 1756 and the M.A. in 1760. That year he also taught school in Kent. In 1761 he returned to Queen's College, was appointed chaplain until he was ordained a priest, and published with collaborators *Poems on Several Occasions*, a volume of secular and sentimental verse that celebrated life as viewed by a member of the genteel class of Oxonians whose religious life did not require the self-abnegation common among ardent dissenters.

In 1759 the governors of the Anglican church sponsored King's College (now Columbia University) in New York City. Anticipating President Samuel Johnson's (1696–1772) retirement, they sought from the archbishop of Canterbury the nomination of an Oxonian Anglican cleric as successor. The request was sent to Rev. Edward Bentham of Christ Church, Oxford, who in 1762 selected Cooper, then a curate at a church near Oxford. Though the young Cooper was neither a great scholar nor a memorable preacher, his Oxford degree, his willingness to go to America (rare for an Oxonian), and his gregarious and sociable personality recommended him for the position.

Cooper arrived in New York City on 30 October 1762, and the governors appointed him assistant to President Johnson as well as professor of moral philosophy and fellow of the college. The governors also created a committee to change the college's curriculum and administration. In mid-April 1765, when Cooper replaced President Johnson, the committee Oxfordized King's College by recommending changes that imitated Oxford's rules and curriculum. For example, emphasis was now placed on Aristotelian principles of ethics, poetry, and politics and on Latin and Greek grammar and logic, whereas in the former curriculum science and mathematics had been stressed. In 1774 President Cooper published his lectures in Aristotelian ethics in a thin Latin volume. Oxonian rules of behavior and discipline were now introduced, as President Cooper changed King's College from a reflection of Harvard, Yale, and other American colleges to an imitation of the only university he knew. A fence around the campus, improvements in the library, and enforcement of a strict code of behavior continued the trend. Cooper's energy and enthusiasm helped inspire the governors to enact other changes: James Jay (brother of John Jay [1745–1829]) sought contributions in England; new faculty were appointed; a medical school was begun; land was granted for the college in Gloucester County (part of present-day Vermont); and in the early 1770s the college's enrollment increased.

In the crises leading to the American Revolution, King's College was a bastion of Anglican conservatism in education, imperial politics, and social values. Half the students and alumni plus five of the six faculty (save Robert Harpur) became Loyalists. In 1768–1769 a controversy erupted in New York newspapers between writers led by William Livingston (1732–1790), who penned the "American Whig," and a group of Anglican clergymen led by Cooper, who composed "A Whip for the American Whig." An ardent spokesperson for the Anglican church, Cooper presided at a convention of clergymen of the middle colonies, sought an archbishop for America, defended the Society for the Propagation of the Gospel in Foreign Parts, and attacked such dissenters as George Whitefield. These actions, and his activities countering the political protestors in New York, earned him a reputation as an arch-Loyalist. With the Reverends Charles Inglis, Samuel Seabury (1729–1796), and John Vardill of the college faculty, he monitored and responded to the publications of those who protested British society, values, and imperial policy. Although he wrote probably only a few Loyalist essays and was not as prolific as his accusers claimed, Cooper served as an editor for many Loyalist writers. Therefore, his humorous, satiric, and sarcastic literary touches were evident in many Loyalist essays composed by others.

In 1771 Cooper sailed for England to obtain a charter to convert the college into an Oxford-type "American University." He also sought grants of land for the college, legal privileges comparable to Oxford's and Cambridge's, and royal funding for professorships. He promised that the revamped institution would be a bulwark of educational, church, and political orthodoxy in America. He won more land grants, meager funding for professors' salaries, and a collection of Oxford publications for the college library, plus reduced quitrents on college lands. He did not get a new university charter.

Cooper's active loyalism made him a target for rioters during the years leading to the Revolution. In the middle of the night on 10 May 1775, a mob drove a half-dressed President Cooper out the rear of his house to seek refuge at a friend's home. From that refuge he fled to a British warship and was soon taken to England.

In *Common Sense* Thomas Paine disdainfully referred to "Extract of a Letter from a Gentleman in London, to his Friend in this City," published in New York newspapers in October 1775. The letter sought imperial reconciliation. Cooper's supposed authorship is based on an article in the *New York Gazette* of 16 November by an anonymous correspondent, stating that the style and opinions of "this vile Letter" are those of "Dr. Cooper." Cooper's attempts to disseminate reconciliation sentiments may, therefore, have contributed to the spread of the idea of independence inspired by *Common Sense*. Cooper had fled New York City on 25 May and could have written the letter, dated 26 July. He earned some notoriety by his July 1776 poem that appeared in *Gentleman's Magazine* describing his escapades and by his speech at Oxford on the causes of the Revolution. Cooper was granted a royal pension of £200 per year for life, later reduced by half. He resumed his fellowship and was appointed provost of Queen's College, where he lived for several years. At the end of 1777 he was appointed chaplain of St. Paul's Chapel in Edinburgh and a year later took up an additional post in Shropshire. Cooper remained a bachelor and late in life labored under the self-imposed burden of raising orphaned children in his family.

This man who loved good wine and rich foods died at a luncheon in Edinburgh. Cooper valued a lively social life and material comforts. He was criticized for spending much time dining and drinking rather than in study. A large man of large appetites, Myles Cooper was a worldly, conservative, opinionated, and politically active cleric. His sparkling personality and love of sociability disguised his serious qualities.

• Scattered original materials on Cooper may be found in the Gwathemy (Cabell) collection at the University of Virginia library, the Stuyvesant-Rutherfurd Family Papers at the New-York Historical Society collections, and the Peter Force Papers (Series 8D:79) in the Library of Congress, Manuscript Division. The Clarence Hayden Vance Papers at Columbia University contain materials by and about Myles Cooper and King's College and materials from Vance's unfinished biography of Cooper. The Vance papers form the basis of Vance, "Myles Cooper," *Columbia University Quarterly* 22 (1930): 260–86, and of David C. Humphrey, *From King's College to Columbia, 1746–1800* (1976), which discusses Cooper's career at King's College and as a Loyalist. Humphrey's Ph.D. dissertation was the basis for Robert McCluer Calhoon, "Myles Cooper and the Civilizing of American Society," in Calhoon's *The Loyalists in Revolutionary America, 1760–1781* (1973), pp. 253–56. Cooper's career is considered at various points in the context of the Anglican church's problems in Carl Bridenbaugh, *Mitre and Sceptre: Transatlantic Faiths, Ideas, Personalities, and Politics, 1689–1775* (1962), and Jean Paul Jordan, "The Anglican Establishment in Colonial New York, 1693–1783" (Ph.D. diss., Columbia Univ., 1971). Several references to him also appear in Janice Potter, *The Liberty We Seek: Loyalist Ideology in Colonial New York and Massachusetts* (1983). The probability of Cooper's negative influence on Paine is considered in A. Owen Aldridge, "The

Influence of New York Newspapers on Paine's *Common Sense*," *New-York Historical Society Quarterly* 60 (1976): 53–60.

COOPER, Peter (12 Feb. 1791–4 Apr. 1883), inventor, manufacturer, and civic benefactor, was born in New York City, the son of John Cooper and Margaret Campbell. His father was a struggling merchant who moved the family successively to Peekskill, Catskill, and finally Newburgh, New York, in search of financial success. Assisting his father in a series of occupations (hatter, brewer, shopkeeper, and brickmaker), Cooper obtained valuable practical work experience. Given his family's relative poverty and constant movement, Cooper was only able to obtain a year's worth of formal schooling; this deficiency in his formal education haunted him throughout his life.

At seventeen Cooper was apprenticed to John Woodward, a coachmaker in New York. He so assiduously completed his duties that Woodward voluntarily doubled his pay at the end of his third year of apprenticeship, with another raise coming in the fourth year. After completing his apprenticeship, Cooper was offered a loan by Woodward toward establishing his own business. Given his father's difficulties with debt, Cooper refused the offer and instead took a job with a manufacturer of cloth-shearing machines in Hempstead, Long Island. He subsequently bought the New York rights to the machine while at the same time working to improve its performance. His efforts paid off with the perfection of a new cloth-shearing machine, which he patented and began manufacturing on a full-time basis. Cooper continued this business until profits declined following the War of 1812, at which time he opened a retail grocery business in New York. He took time from his varied endeavors to marry Sarah Bedell of Hempstead in 1813. They had six children. After a period of time he left the grocery firm of Bedell & Cooper (established with his brother-in-law) and struck out on his own in the same field. He also began to invest in real estate.

In 1821 Cooper purchased a glue factory in New York and immediately set out to improve the quality of the glue and the efficiency with which it was manufactured. He experimented with different methods of production and was involved in every facet of the operation. Cooper's glue was equal to the best that France and Great Britain could produce, and he shortly undercut the price of imported glue as well. Soon Cooper added table gelatin and isinglass (a form of gelatin used in making ink, jelly, ice cream, candy, and soup) to his list of products. With this field of business virtually to himself, the basis of Cooper's wealth was secure.

Cooper made a major investment in 1828 when two men from Baltimore invited him to join them in the purchase of a huge plot of commercial property on the Baltimore harborfront. The next year he learned that he had been duped—neither of his partners had contributed a dime toward the purchase price of the prop-

erty. He bought them out, and finding rich iron ore deposits on the property, Cooper founded the Canton Iron Works. In the meantime another crisis developed. The potential value of the land rested on the fortunes of the newly founded Baltimore & Ohio Railroad. It was discovered that existing steam engines could not run on the curved hills of western Maryland, and it appeared that the railroad was doomed. Cooper remained undismayed. He approached the B&O directors and obtained permission to experiment with new designs. His engine—nicknamed the "Tom Thumb"—was the first successful steam engine built in America. Featuring a shorter wheelbase and smaller wheels than its English counterparts, a successful trial run was held between Baltimore and Ellicott's Mills (now Ellicott City), Maryland, in August 1830. Anxious to return to New York, Cooper sold his investment in 1836, taking in payment B&O stock (which soon appreciated). The property was later managed by the Canton Company, which became a leading industrial landholding firm before going out of business in 1981.

In the next few years Cooper's business holdings expanded greatly. He opened three New Jersey operations, a plant that produced wire, wrought iron, and railroad tracks in Trenton; a blast furnace in Phillipsburg; and an iron mine in Andover. His plant in Trenton rolled the first structural iron for "fireproof" (nonwooden) buildings in 1854—a feat that earned Cooper the Bessemer Gold Medal of the Iron and Steel Institute of Great Britain in 1870.

Cooper had a long history of public service. He served on the Board of Aldermen of New York City (assistant alderman, 1828–1831, and alderman, 1840–1841), becoming a tireless advocate of municipal innovations such as professional police and fire departments, public education, and a clean water supply for the city. Becoming conversant with economic issues in his later years, he even ran for president in 1876 as the candidate of the Greenback party.

Cooper was a prolific inventor. In addition to his work on the steam engine and cloth-shearing machine, he also obtained patents on items as diverse as a musical cradle, an endless chain device for towing boats, and an egg desiccator. He was hampered by his lack of formal education, however, and his lack of a scientific background led him to waste much time on inventions that were unworkable or at least impractical. Realizing the deficiency of his education, he sought to help other working-class people better themselves.

The steel from his Trenton plant helped to build Cooper's greatest philanthropic effort, the Cooper Union, a school that opened on 1 July 1859 and featured both scientific and artistic teaching. Free to the public, it offered night classes that enabled working people to further their education, free lectures and concerts, and an excellent library.

One of the most difficult projects in which Cooper became involved was the laying of the transatlantic cable. Approached by Cyrus W. Field for financial assistance, Cooper was elected president of the New York,

Newfoundland & London Telegraph Company upon its founding on 6 May 1854. After years of frustration and enormous cost, the project was finally completed in 1866—after four previously unsuccessful attempts. Cooper had remained faithful to the project even as other investors lost hope. Cooper and Field also foresaw the possibilities of transcontinental telegraph lines, and in 1857 the North American Telegraph Association was founded, with Cooper also serving as president of this firm.

After a long, busy life, Peter Cooper died in New York City and received a funeral commensurate with his standing as a leading citizen. His life stands as an example of the possibilities that were open to men of ambition and drive but limited means and education in early nineteenth-century America.

• The Cooper papers are held at Cooper Union, New York City. The papers of the Canton Company are at the Baltimore Museum of Industry. The *Autobiography of Peter Cooper, 1791–1883* was dictated by Cooper in 1882. Secondary works about Cooper and his career abound; two of the best books are Edward C. Mack, *Peter Cooper: Citizen of New York* (1949), and C. Sumner Spalding, *Peter Cooper: A Critical Biography of His Life and Works* (1941). An obituary is in the *New York Times*, 5 Apr. 1883.

EDWARD L. LACH, JR.

COOPER, Samuel (28 Mar. 1725–29 Dec. 1783), clergyman, was born in Boston, Massachusetts, the son of the Reverend William Cooper and Judith Sewall. He attended Boston Latin School (South Grammar School) and received an A.B. from Harvard in 1743. A period of ministerial studies preceded his receiving an M.A. in 1746. In 1746 he married Judith Bulfinch; they had two daughters. In 1750 Yale awarded him an M.A., and in 1767, upon a recommendation from Benjamin Franklin, he obtained a doctor of divinity from the University of Edinburgh. He served as an overseer of Harvard in 1746 and member of the corporation in 1767; he declined election to the presidency in 1774 to remain with his congregation.

Cooper served as minister of the church in Brattle Street, Boston, usually called the Brattle Street Church, which affirmed the Westminster Confession but did not require the traditional public personal account of one's religious experience. The moderate Calvinism, biblical emphasis, and practical piety, expressed in evangelical and rationalistic terms were hallmarks of this congregation.

The heritage of the Brattle Street Church contributed to Cooper's ministry and he in turn added to its stature. Noted for his eloquence in public speaking during his college years, he was no less so as a minister. He served as the sole minister from 1747 until his death. He was described as the "silver-tongued preacher" and his public prayers were noted for "feeling" and "sensitivity." Within the total context of worship his manner and grace highlighted the experience. A trusted spiritual leader familiar with the religious and community concerns, he nurtured a harmonious pastoral relationship between pulpit and pew. His em-

phasis was to encourage heartfelt practical faith rather than denouncing the sins of the time. Appointed chaplain of the Massachusetts House of Representatives in 1753 and perennial chaplain of either the House or Council, he was able to integrate the religious and political interests of Boston. By 1763, one-fourth of the town merchants sat under his preaching as well as a majority of Boston's selectmen. In 1780 most of the delegates of the state constitutional convention attended his services.

Cooper's public image as a man of peace and reconciliation served him well in the twenty-five years before the outbreak of the American Revolution. During the 1760's, as opposition mounted to British policy, Brattle Street Church remained a neutral sanctuary. Yet in the political debate preceding the war, Cooper and Samuel Adams were at the center of underground activities aimed at royal officials. It was suspected that Cooper anonymously wrote several political essays published in the *Boston Gazette* and *Independent Ledger*. The effect of these efforts was to argue for a return to an earlier period when Massachusetts was virtually independent. Cooper was at the center of an inner circle consisting of James Otis, John Hancock, James Bowdoin, Joseph Warren, and Samuel Adams, who showed outward respect for governor Thomas Hutchinson at the same time they kept agitation against British policy focused. Indeed, Cooper provided former governor Thomas Pownall, then living in England, idealized reports of local Whig activities that made Massachusettites appear as champions of English liberties when such events involved mob activity and forced conformity. In some instances Pownall had these stories printed in the English press.

When the war erupted, Cooper helped transfer a significant portion of Boston's allegiance from a royal to a republican government. In 1777–1778 he was the foremost proponent in New England of a military and diplomatic alliance with France. His cooperation with Benjamin Franklin in achieving that alliance demonstrated his ability to transcend traditional Protestant enmity toward Catholic France. His service in promoting American-French friendship secretly brought him a stipend from Louis XVI, which he received until his death. Criticized by some for his flexibility, he played a major although unobtrusive role in Boston in the success of the American Revolution. His death in Boston was probably caused by a viral infection of the nervous system.

• The largest collection of Cooper's papers is in the Henry E. Huntington Library, San Marino, Calif. Several items are in the New York Public Library. Correspondence with a former Massachusetts governor are "Letters of Samuel Cooper to Thomas Pownall, 1769–1777," edited by Frederick Tuckerman in the *American Historical Review* 6 (Jan. 1930): 301–30. Letters to Cooper from Pownall and Franklin are in the British Library (King's MSS 202–4). Pownall's letters are also in Frederick Griffin's *Junius Discovered* (1854). Franklin–Cooper Correspondence, 1769–1774, is included in *The Papers of Benjamin Franklin*, ed. William B. Willcox, vols. 16–21 (1972–1978). The majority of Franklin–Cooper Letters,

1775–1783, are in the American Philosophical Society. Fragments of Cooper's diaries are in the New-York Historical Society; the Henry E. Huntington Library; and the Massachusetts Historical Society.

For a biography see Charles W. Aker, *The Divine Politician* (1982). See also Clifford K. Shipton's excellent essay on Cooper in *Sibley's Harvard Graduates*, vol. 11 (1960), pp. 192–213. The theological and philosophical content of Cooper's sermons is analyzed in John G. Buchanan, "The Pursuit of Happiness: A Study of the Rev. Dr. Samuel Cooper, 1725–1783" (Ph.D. diss., Duke Univ., 1971).

FREDERICK V. MILLS, SR.

COOPER, Samuel (12 June 1798–3 Dec. 1876), army officer, was born at Hackensack, in the town of Fishkill, New York, the son of Samuel Cooper, a merchant and former major in the Continental army, and Mary Horton. Cooper entered the U.S. Military Academy in 1813 and graduated in 1815. Commissioned a second lieutenant in the Regiment of Light Artillery, he served for the next three years at garrisons on the New England coast. From 1818 to 1825 he was on detached service in the office of the adjutant and inspector general (after 1821 adjutant general) in Washington, D.C., where he received his first experience in the staff duty that would occupy nearly all of his career. During a reduction of the army in 1821, he was assigned to the Fourth Artillery Regiment. Cooper performed garrison duty at St. Augustine, Florida, in 1825–1826 and spent the next two years at the Artillery School of Practice at Fortress Monroe, Virginia. In 1827 he married Sarah Maria Mason, a member of a very influential Virginia family. They had three children.

In May 1828 Cooper was appointed aide-de-camp to Major General Alexander Macomb, the commanding general of the army. For the next eight years the young officer was stationed at army headquarters in Washington, D.C., serving as Macomb's personal secretary and gaining experience in military administration. Under Macomb's supervision, Cooper compiled an instructional manual for militia and volunteer officers, *A Concise System of Instructions and Regulations for the Militia and Volunteers of the United States . . .* (1836), a condensation of the systems of tactics and administration used in the regular army, which was widely adopted by state militia organizations. Promoted to captain in 1836, Cooper served as acting head of the army's Clothing Bureau in 1836, then as chief clerk of the War Department (1837–1838) under Joel R. Poinsett, Martin Van Buren's secretary of war.

As part of a general increase of the staff branches in 1838, Congress added six assistant adjutants general to the Adjutant General's Office, the department charged with the army's central correspondence, record keeping, and general recruiting service. Cooper was appointed the senior assistant adjutant general with the rank of brevet major and remained on duty in the War Department as Poinsett's personal military assistant. An efficient bureau officer with an ingratiating manner, he exercised considerable influence in army administration, on several occasions serving in Poin-

sett's absence as acting secretary of war. Probably because of his association with the Democratic Van Buren administration, Cooper lost his War Department post when the Whigs took control of the government in 1841. During 1841–1842 he served as chief of staff to Colonel William J. Worth, commander in Florida during the last stages of the Second Seminole War, and he saw action in a clash with the Seminoles in April 1842. From 1843 to 1846 Cooper functioned as chief of staff to Brigadier General Edmund P. Gaines, commander of the army's Third Military Department and later Western Division.

In 1846 Cooper returned to duty at the capital as military assistant to William L. Marcy, James K. Polk's secretary of war, and during the Mexican War he supported Marcy's efforts to mobilize American forces and coordinate military operations. He was promoted to lieutenant colonel in 1847 and, in recognition of his wartime services, to brevet colonel the following year. Cooper incurred the enmity of Major General Winfield Scott, the commanding general of the army, who resented his special standing with the War Department. Nevertheless, the veteran staff officer continued as military assistant to George W. Crawford, secretary of war under Zachary Taylor. Assigned to duty as an assistant inspector general in 1850, he conducted an extended inspection tour of the army's Western Division.

On the death of Adjutant General Roger Jones in July 1852, Cooper advanced to the rank of full colonel and adjutant general of the army. In contrast to Jones, who had attempted to formulate policy, Cooper confined himself mainly to the routine administration of his office and the implementation of War Department instructions. During the Franklin Pierce administration (1853–1857), however, he developed an extremely close friendship with Secretary of War Jefferson Davis. The two men associated constantly, and the secretary relied heavily on Cooper's expertise in personnel and administrative matters. Cooper also supported Davis in his acrimonious feud with Scott, and Cooper's relative influence in army administration grew when Scott moved his headquarters to New York City, out of direct contact with the War Department. Under Davis and to a lesser degree Davis's successor, John B. Floyd, the adjutant general functioned in place of the commanding general as unofficial chief of staff of the army.

Although northern-born, Cooper had developed strong southern ties through his marriage and his close association with several southern secretaries of war, and he owned a country estate near Alexandria, Virginia. On 7 March 1861, after the secession of the Lower South, he resigned his commission, then traveled to the Confederate capital at Montgomery, Alabama, and offered his services to his old chief, President Davis. Davis immediately appointed him to the post of adjutant and inspector general of the Confederate army. When the Confederate Congress authorized the rank of full general on 16 May 1861, Davis nominated five men for the grade with Cooper the senior, and the aging veteran remained throughout the war the highest ranking officer of the Confederate army.

Cooper was one of Davis's closest friends and confidants, and their very intimacy suggests that the president consulted the staff officer frequently on military issues. As adjutant and inspector general, however, Cooper followed a conservative path, establishing the basic organization and procedures of the antebellum regular service. Although Davis referred to him as chief of staff of the army, Cooper played little evident role in the formulation of strategy. He confined his office instead to administrative support—maintaining the flow of correspondence and orders between the government's central offices in Richmond and the field armies and keeping army records. Critics claimed that his reliance on prewar methods was ill suited to mass warfare and faulted him for neglecting the inspection functions of his branch. After a debate on staff reform, the government attempted to improve procedures in 1864 by creating a more centralized and professional general staff corps and establishing a separate bureau of inspection within Cooper's department. However, the rapid deterioration of the Confederate military position during 1864–1865 prevented the full implementation of these changes.

Cooper escaped from Richmond with Davis and his cabinet in April 1865, but at Charlotte, North Carolina, he separated from Davis's party because of illness and surrendered to Union authorities, turning over the surviving records of the Confederate War Department. Paroled in early May, he spent his later years at his Alexandria farm, where he died. A quietly competent career staff officer, Cooper played a significant supporting role in the antebellum army as War Department assistant and adjutant general and in the Confederacy as adjutant and inspector general and a member of Davis's inner circle.

• Collections of Cooper's personal papers are preserved at Alderman Library, University of Virginia, Charlottesville, and in the Southern Historical Collection at the University of North Carolina Library, Chapel Hill. The latter collection contains an autobiographical memoir tracing Cooper's career to 1852. His correspondence as adjutant general is in the National Archives, Records of the Office of the Adjutant General (RG 94): Letters Sent by the Office of Adjutant General, 1800–1890, and Reports to the Secretary of War, 1825–1870. Much of Cooper's official Civil War correspondence is published in U.S. War Department, *The War of the Rebellion: A Compilation of the Official Records of the Union and Confederate Armies* (128 vols., 1880–1901). An excellent account of his early career is Matthew B. Veatch, "The Education of a Staff Officer: The Life and Career of Samuel Cooper, 1798–1852" (M.A. thesis, Univ. of Missouri–Kansas City, 1989). For his relationship with Davis, see William C. Davis, *Jefferson Davis: The Man and His Hour* (1991). June I. Gow analyzes Cooper's role in the Confederate war effort in "Theory and Practice in Confederate Military Administration," *Military Affairs* 39 (Oct. 1975): 119–23. For a laudatory assessment of Cooper's career, including a eulogistic letter from Davis, see Fitzhugh Lee, "Sketch of the Late General S. Cooper," *Southern Historical Society Papers* 3 (Jan.–June 1877): 269–76.

WILLIAM B. SKELTON

COOPER, Sarah Brown Ingersoll (12 Dec. 1835–11 Dec. 1896), educator, was born in Cazenovia, New York, the daughter of Samuel Clark Ingersoll, a mechanic, and Laura Case Hopkins. Sarah was only five years old when her mother died, and she and her two sisters were reared by a great aunt. When she was twelve years old, her first article was published in the *Madison County Whig*. Two years later she taught a Sunday school class at nearby Eagle Village. The local Presbyterian elders commended her for her excellent teaching but told her to "go home and lengthen" her skirts.

In 1850 Sarah enrolled at Cazenovia Seminary, one of the first coeducational institutions in the United States; she graduated in 1853. She then took a job as perceptress at the Fayatteville Academy and in 1854 studied at the Troy Female Seminary, founded by Emma Willard. The following year, her abolitionist views notwithstanding, she took a job as governess for the children of Governor William Schley in Augusta, Georgia. Besides her duties with the family, she taught a Bible class for the more than five hundred slaves on the Schley plantation. That September she married Halsey Fenimore Cooper, who had been a classmate of hers at Cazenovia. They had four children, two of whom died in infancy. They settled in Chattanooga, Tennessee, where her husband was editor of the *Chattanooga Advertiser* and customs inspector of the port, an appointment from President Franklin Pierce. At the outbreak of the Civil War, the Coopers went north to New York but returned to the South when President Abraham Lincoln appointed Halsey Cooper internal revenue assessor in Memphis, Tennessee. There Sarah Cooper became president of the Society for the Aid of Refugees and also taught a Bible class for the Union soldiers. In 1864 the Coopers' daughter Mollie died. Sarah Cooper was devastated by the loss of her third child and suffered a nervous breakdown. Three years later, still ill, she went to St. Paul, Minnesota, to convalesce. In 1869 her husband resigned his post, and she rejoined the family. They then moved to San Francisco, California, where Cooper finally regained her health.

Cooper immersed herself in civic activity, social concerns, and writing. She published regularly over the years in the *Overland Monthly*, the *San Francisco Bulletin*, and church magazines, writing about women, children, and education. She also started a Bible class at the Howard Presbyterian Church, which later became the Calvary Presbyterian Church. In 1878 Cooper met Kate Douglas Smith (later Wiggin), who had started a school for poor children called the Silver Street Kindergarten. Inspired by Smith's example and her own social gospel belief in applying Christian principles to all aspects of life, Cooper the following year opened a school on the Barbary Coast, San Francisco's Skid Row. Her Jackson Street Kindergarten gave the children a foundation in the arts as well as an introduction to the various trades. Also in 1879 she wrote a series of articles for the *San Francisco Bulletin*, including one titled "The Kindergarten, a Remedy for Hooliganism," arguing that "ruffianism," or juvenile deliquency, could be reduced by introducing kindergarten education for the masses of poor, neglected, and abandoned children in the nation's cities.

In 1881 Cooper was involved in a controversy that became a cause célèbre. That year the Presbyterian church brought her to trial for denying its doctrine about infant damnation and everlasting punishment. She defended herself with intelligence and great fervor, winning public sympathy both for herself and her work on behalf of children. She resigned from the Presbyterian church and joined the First Congregational Church in San Francisco. There she again taught her popular Bible class, which was attended by Roman Catholics and Jews as well as Protestants.

Over the next several years Cooper opened more kindergartens, which by the time of her death numbered about forty with about 3,600 pupils, ranging in age from two to six years old. In 1884 she organized her schools as the Golden Gate Kindergarten Association. Small in physical stature, she was a personable woman with great organizational ability. She instinctively reached out to the prominent and wealthy of San Francisco society. Phoebe A. Hearst, wife of George Hearst, the mining magnate, donated an office for the association, and Jane Lathrop Stanford, wife of Leland Stanford, the railroad builder and founder of Stanford University, gave a considerable amount of money for Cooper's work. Cooper eventually created an endowment of almost $300,000.

Cooper's husband, who suffered from depression and bouts of mental illness, committed suicide in 1885. Cooper's daughter Harriet, a music teacher, became her secretary and constant companion. As time went on their relationship became more and more ominously codependent.

In 1891 Cooper formed the Golden Gate Kindergarten Free Normal Training School, the first such institution in the United States, to prepare kindergarten teachers. The following year, at a meeting in Saratoga, New York, she became the first president of the newly formed International Kindergarten Union. During this period she continued as one of the prominent civic leaders of San Francisco, serving as director of the Associated Charities of San Francisco. She was also active in the Pacific Coast Women's Press Association and the Century Club, the first women's club in that city, and was treasurer of the General Federation of Women's Clubs (1894–1896).

In 1893 Cooper gave an address at the World's Columbian Exposition in Chicago, Illinois, and was one of only five women delegates from around the world to the Pan-Republic Congress, which met during the fair. By this time she had been won over by the women's rights movement and became a supporter of woman suffrage. Two years later, in San Francisco, she hosted the Woman's Congress, which was attended by, among others, Susan B. Anthony and Anna Howard Shaw. Cooper served as its first president and was vice chair of the committee that pushed unsuccessfully for passage of suffrage reform in California. She was also a frequent speaker throughout the country, addressing such groups as the National Education Association, the National Convention of Charities and Correction, the National Council of Women, and the Chautauqua Association.

Cooper's daughter apparently inherited her father's mental disease and suffered from bouts of depression and paranoia. She made several attempts on her mother's life as well as her own. Cooper disregarded the advice of doctors and friends to have her daughter hospitalized. During the night of 10 December 1896, Harriet Cooper, who shared her mother's bedroom, turned on the gas lamps, asphyxiating herself and her mother. The nation mourned the tragic death of the woman who had done so much to reform education. Flags were flown at half-mast, an honor previously accorded to only two other women.

During her lifetime, Cooper was acknowledged as a woman of "great heroism . . . quiet, magnetic, and exceedingly sensitive and sympathetic." In a tribute after Cooper's death, Gertrude G. Aguirre called Cooper "the best-loved woman in San Francisco . . . [who had] awakened the minds of 18,000 children." Throughout the United States, nearly three hundred schools were established based on Cooper's model of education. She once said that she wanted "to lay the foundation for a better national character by founding free kindergartens for neglected children."

• Cooper's papers are in the Cornell University Archives. See also the first *Annual Report* of the Jackson Street Free Kindergarten (1880); the annual reports of the Golden Gate Kindergarten Association; International Kindergarten Union, *Pioneers of the Kindergarten in America* (1924); and Agnes Snyder, *Dauntless Women in Childhood Education, 1856–1931* (1972). Gertrude G. Aguirre's memorial is "A Woman from Altruria," *Arena*, May 1897. Obituaries are in the *San Francisco Bulletin*, 11 Dec. 1896, and the *San Francisco Chronicle*, 12 and 14 Dec. 1896.

GEOFFREY GNEUHS

COOPER, Stoney (16 Oct. 1918–22 Mar. 1977), fiddler and singer, was born Dale Troy Cooper in Harmon, West Virginia, the son of Kenny Cooper and Stella Raines, schoolteachers. Cooper and his twin brother Dean grew up on a large farm, where they assisted the family in many of the daily chores. As a child Cooper was fascinated by his older brother's fiddle playing. With some help from his brother, Cooper began to teach himself to play. As young Cooper listened to the Grand Ole Opry, he was greatly influenced by the fiddling skills of Arthur Smith (a popular Grand Ole Opry instrumentalist of that era, whose playing strongly reflected jazz influence), and Cooper hoped that some day he could have equal ability. Upon graduation from high school in 1937, he accepted a job with Rusty Hiser and his Green Valley Boys, playing on radio station WMMN in Fairmont, West Virginia. The program was quite successful, but the band decided to move to WMMN in Lynchburg, Virginia. When the group began to have financial difficulties, they disbanded, and Cooper returned to his family's farm.

Cooper's father died in the summer of 1938, so it became the twins' responsibility to operate the farm. During this time the Leary Family, a West Virginia gospel group, needed a fiddler. Impressed with Cooper's playing on WMMN, Jacob Leary traveled to Harmon to invite Cooper to become their fiddler. In 1939 Cooper accepted the position as fiddler and singer with the Leary Family. The family sang only gospel and religious songs; in order to add another dimension to the show, Cooper and Wilma Lee Leary began singing secular duets. Their repertoire included sentimental songs, love ballads, and novelty songs. Both singers had rich, powerful voices, and they complemented each other vocally, achieving a warm blend and nice harmonizations.

Declining an invitation to join the Grand Ole Opry, the Leary Family remained in West Virginia. Shortly afterward in 1941, the Learys accepted an offer to appear regularly on WWVA in Wheeling, West Virginia. That same year Wilma Lee Leary and Stoney Cooper were married. With the birth of their daughter in 1942, the Coopers left the radio station so that Wilma could care for the child and Stoney could seek a better-paying job. For six months Stoney worked long hours at the Vaughn Beverage Company, delivering bottled soft drinks in Wheeling. Within these few months the couple realized they missed their singing careers. They decided to return to the stage, not as part of the Leary Family, but on their own as a duo.

Their first job offer came from station KMMJ in Grand Island, Nebraska, where they performed from the fall of 1942 until the summer of 1943. During this time the station brought the Leary Family to Grand Island and featured the Coopers on six daily programs. With additional members (two sons-in-law) in the Leary Family and a variety of new acts included in their show, the entire family was invited to WIBC in Indianapolis, Indiana, in the summer of 1943. One of the most popular portions of the show was Wilma Lee's renditions of Roy Acuff's songs, accompanied by Stoney playing the dobro. The popularity of the Acuff material created so much demand for the couple on radio shows and in personal appearances that the Coopers decided to put together their own band with Floyd Kirkpatrick on steel guitar and Ab Cole on bass.

During the next several years the duo and their band moved to other stations, including WJJD in Chicago; WMMN in Fairmont, West Virginia; KLCN in Blytheville, Arkansas; and finally WWNC in Asheville, North Carolina, in March 1947. While in Asheville, the Coopers signed their first recording contract with Rich-R-Tone and made their first recording, "This World Can't Stand Long" (1947). Although the company was small and virtually unknown, the recording contract helped the couple win an offer from a 50,000-watt station, WWVA in Wheeling, West Virginia. In July 1947 the Coopers became regular performers on the WWVA Saturday night jamboree. The Coopers stayed with WWVA for the next ten years, sharing the airwaves with some of the biggest names in country music, such as Hawkshaw Hawkins. During

the first years with WWVA, they participated in the Goodwill Tours arranged by the jamboree. They signed a contract with Columbia Records in 1949 and recorded for Columbia for five years. During this period they recorded two of their most requested songs, "Sunny Side of the Mountain" (c. 1950) and "Thirty Pieces of Silver" (c. 1950). Joining the Grand Ole Opry in 1957 brought the Coopers even more success. They maintained a regular schedule with the Opry, in addition to their international tours.

Recording on the Hickory label beginning in 1955, the Coopers had several major hits. These included "Big Midnight Special" (1959) and "Come Walk with Me" (1959), which won awards that year for their placement on Billboard's top-ten charts. "There's a Big Wheel" (1959), written by Don Gibson, was one of the Coopers' most requested and bestselling songs. "Walking My Lord up Calvary Hill" (1958) and "This Ole House" (1960) have become gospel standards.

Stoney and Wilma Lee worked together not only as performers but also as songwriters. Some of their most popular songs were "Cheated, Too" (1956), "He Taught Them How" (1958), "Big Midnight Special" (1959), "Heartbreak Street" (1959), and "Loving You" (1957). The Coopers' music encompassed bluegrass and mountain music, as well as gospel melodies.

The Coopers received many awards and were named "the most authentic mountain singing group in America" by the Harvard University Library of Music in 1950. In 1974 they were honored by the Smithsonian Institution for their contributions to the musical heritage of America and were invited to appear in the American Folk Life Festival (sponsored by the Smithsonian) as representatives of American rural music. As part of the Smithsonian recognition, the Coopers made a two-hour tape featuring their singing and playing. Stoney Cooper was a board member of the Association of Country Entertainers, an organization formed to promote traditional country music. On 2 October 1976 he was honored by the Victory Institute of Lewistown, Ohio, for his outstanding ability and support of traditional mountain and gospel music.

Stoney Cooper was an active performer until the end of his life. Although his health steadily declined following a heart attack in 1963, the Coopers averaged 100,000 miles of travel each year during the 1960s and early 1970s. Throughout his life Stoney aimed to preserve the heritage of country music. He continued to use acoustical instruments, and his playing remained true to the country/bluegrass style. The Coopers have been identified with the "mountain gospel" tradition, which emphasizes clear pronunciation, sustained notes (without embellishments), and simple, diatonic harmony.

As fellow Opry star Grandpa Jones stated, "Stoney was a fellow you'd trust most any where. . . . He was very religious, and on the quiet side—everybody liked Stoney Cooper." This sentiment was echoed by long-time friend Roy Acuff: "[He was] the most humble person I've ever seen." Cooper died in Nashville.

• The personal collections of Carol Lee Cooper, Stoney and Wilma Lee's daughter, and her knowledge of the Coopers' work is a valuable and extensive resource. Nashville researcher and musician Ernie Sykes, Jr., maintains a personal library of materials related to the lives of Stoney and Wilma Lee Cooper. The Summer 1975 issue of the *John Edwards Memorial Foundation Quarterly* contains a lengthy interview and biographical sketch written by Robert Cogswell. Biographical summaries are included in Charles K. Wolfe, *Country and Western Classics: Duets* (1982), and Barry McCloud, *Definitive Country* (1995). Articles and obituaries from newspapers (including the *Tennessean*, the *Roanoke Times and World News*, the *Philadelphia Inquirer*, the *Madison Community News*, and the *Nashville Banner*), as well as promotional biographies, are on file at the Country Music Hall of Fame Library in Nashville.

LINDA P. SHIPLEY

COOPER, Susan Augusta Fenimore (17 April 1813–31 Dec. 1894), writer, was born at Heathcote Hill in Mamaroneck, Westchester County, New York, the daughter of the novelist James Fenimore Cooper and Susan Augusta DeLancey. The Cooper family members were devoted to one another, and the parents saw to it that each child received a fine education. Susan had tutors, attended private schools, spoke and read four languages, and studied American and English literature and history, as well as zoology and botany. She was also skillful in music, drawing, and dancing. She once danced in a great Parisian house to waltzes played by Chopin and Liszt while the hired musicians were eating their dinner.

Because she resembled his favorite older sister, Hannah, Susan seems to have been her father's favorite daughter, and she was always closely associated with him, accompanying him on his travels. She was his copyist, and he wrote of her that she was "meek little Suzy." He once joked that he was her suitor, and he certainly discouraged others from assuming that role.

Susan Cooper never married, possibly because she was too well educated to suit many American men, and most European men did not want an American wife. The Cooper family sailed to England in June 1826 and went from there to Paris. In Paris, James Fenimore Cooper, claiming he wanted to keep his family American, refused a proposal of marriage to Susan from a young, noble, wealthy Frenchman named De Savigny. Frequent visitors in Paris included Sir Walter Scott and Samuel F. B. Morse. The inventor was reportedly attracted to Susan, but her father said that he was too old. After the Cooper family left France in 1833, they lived in New York for three years and finally settled in Cooperstown at "Otsego Hall," the recently refurbished family mansion. It was there that Susan, with her father's encouragement, began to write.

Her first book, *Elinor Wyllys; or, The Young Folk of Longbridge*, published in 1845 under the pen name "Amabel Penfeather," was not successful, according to critics, and it was little read. During the last years of her father's life, she kept a journal, which was the basis of her most important work, *Rural Hours* (1850). She wrote about county fairs, Indians, birds, melting snow, housecleaning, and old Dutch superstitions. William Cullen Bryant called it a "great book." *Rhyme and Reason of Country Life* and *Rural Rambles* were similar nature notes published in 1854, but they were not as popular as their predecessor. Her short story "The Wonderful Cookie" was reprinted several times. She edited the American edition of *Country Rambles* (1853) by the English naturalist John Leonard Knapp. In 1859 she published *Mount Vernon: A Letter to the Children of America*. Because James Fenimore Cooper forbade the use of his papers for a biography, Susan edited *Papers and Pictures from the Writings of James Fenimore Cooper* in 1861.

When James Fenimore Cooper's works were published in the Household edition of 1876–1884, Susan Cooper wrote introductions to fifteen of the novels. She often commented on how her father selected his settings for his books. He had, for example, owned a whaler and on one trip had gone to Newport. He was "much pleased with the town and harbor," and *The Red Rover*'s opening scenes were laid in that port.

Susan Cooper wrote two articles for the *Atlantic Monthly* in 1887, "A Glance Backward," about the writing of *Precaution* and *The Spy*, and "A Second Glance Backward," about the family's European years. Included in the latter article is her father's only surviving poem, an elegy to a naval friend. She also contributed an essay on autumn and autumnal thoughts to a book called *The Home Book of the Picturesque; or, Home Authors and Home Artists* (1852); some of the other contributors were Washington Irving, William Cullen Bryant, and James Fenimore Cooper. Her last work was *William West Skiles, a Sketch of Missionary Life in Valle Crucis in Western North Carolina, 1842–1862* (1890). Susan's memories of her youth, titled "A Small Family Memoir," were published by her nephew (her father's namesake) in *Correspondence of James Fenimore Cooper* (1922). A copy of Susan's remarkable crayon drawing of herself and her four siblings appears on page seventeen of Warren S. Walker's *James Fenimore Cooper: An Introduction and Interpretation* (1962).

At the end of the Civil War, Susan Cooper founded Thanksgiving Hospital, which later merged with the Mary Imogene Bassett Hospital in Cooperstown. She also founded the Orphan House of the Holy Savior in 1873 in Cooperstown. It began with five children and grew under her personal supervision to a several-building institution that housed, fed, and educated nearly a hundred boys and girls.

Susan Cooper died in Cooperstown, and her father's personal journal was buried beside her in the casket. She was extremely pious, and her virtues are illustrated in a stained-glass window of Christ Episcopal Church. In spite of her education, recognition, and achievement, she was opposed to any increase in women's rights.

Most of James Fenimore Cooper's friends were men, many of them famous, but his closest friend and admirer seems to have been his daughter Susan. Her introductions to his novels have been helpful to scholars because of their invaluable background information. She was able to describe the novels' origins and the prototypes of some of the characters because of the close relationship she enjoyed with her father. During her lifetime, she neither sought nor received recognition for her accomplishments as a writer and scholar. She accepted, apparently without complaint, and almost surely with pleasure, the role of interpreting the work of her famous father.

• Susan Fenimore Cooper's papers are in the Research Library of the New York State Historical Association, in Cooperstown. Much of the information about her is obtained from biographies of her father. See, for example, James Grossman, *James Fenimore Cooper* (1949), and Robert Emmet Long, *James Fenimore Cooper* (1990). Rosaly Torna Kurth wrote a thesis at Fordham University in 1974 titled "Susan Fenimore Cooper: A Study of Her Life and Work."

SUE LASLIE KIMBALL

COOPER, Tarzan (30 Aug. 1907–19 Dec. 1980), professional basketball player, was born Charles Theodore in Newark, Delaware, the son of Theodore Cooper and Evelyn (maiden name unknown), occupations unknown. Tarzan, later nicknamed "Tatie" by the press, was a standout for the Central High School basketball team in Philadelphia, where he graduated in 1925. He immediately began a twenty-year career in professional basketball, playing initially with the Philadelphia Panther Pros in 1925, then going on to star for the all-black Philadelphia Giants from 1926 to 1929. Robert Douglas, owner of the famed all-black professional team, the New York Renaissance, spotted Cooper in a game at Philadelphia and signed him the next day to play for his New York Renaissance. Cooper then began an eleven-year career with the Rens, named for their home court, the Renaissance Ballroom in Harlem. Over these eleven years the Rens earned a record of 1,303 wins and 203 losses.

At 6′4″, Cooper was considered a giant for his era. Howie Evans, sports editor of the *New York Amsterdam News*, noted in 1977 that "his hands were like giant shovels, and held more than their share of his 215 pounds." His large size earned him the nickname "Tarzan." Cooper played center and was often considered the Rens's most valuable player. Joe Lapchick, center of the Original Celtics of New York City, considered Tarzan Cooper both the best center in professional basketball and the best center he had ever played against.

In the 1932–1933 season, the Renaissance team earned a record of 127–7, including a winning streak of 88 consecutive games. From 1932 to 1936 just seven players constituted the Renaissance team: Cooper, Eyre "Bruiser" Saitch, James "Pappy" Ricks, William "Wee Willie" Smith, John "Casey" Holt, Bill Yancey, and Clarence "Fats" Jenkins. The "Magnificent Seven," as the Rens were called, consistently defeated the Original Celtics, the top white team of the day. For

example, in 1933 the Rens topped the Original Celtics in seven out of eight meetings.

The teamwork and style of play exhibited by the Rens became their trademark. Known for their passing ability, the Rens rarely dribbled the ball down the court. Instead, their fast breaks consisted of quick passes from player to player, resulting in a scored basket. The Rens were also known for their endurance on the court, rarely calling a time-out in a game. This forced the opposing team to play to exhaustion and use up their own time-outs. The Rens's playing ability attracted crowds of up to 15,000; they remained a popular team among people of all races. Nonetheless, they faced many forms of prejudice and discrimination while on the road.

During the depression of the 1930s the Rens became a barnstorming team traveling to the Midwest and the South to play amateur and professional teams, both black and white. Owner Douglas purchased a custom-made bus for his players to travel in. The bus often served as a restaurant and a hotel for the team, as discrimination prevented the players from being served or housed in many places. In addition, the team would set up headquarters in a large city such as Indianapolis, travel up to 200 miles to a game, and then return to the city afterward. The Rens regularly played and defeated white teams that belonged to the National Basketball League such as Oshkosh, Sheboygan, and Fort Wayne. During Cooper's era professional basketball remained segregated by team, although black and white teams played each other.

Cooper served as the leader of the Rens squad that won the World Professional Championship in 1939. In the 1938–1939 season the Rens had accumulated 112 wins and only seven losses. Having defeated both the New York Yankees basketball team and the Harlem Globetrotters in preliminary games, the Rens became the first World Professional titleholders by defeating the Oshkosh All-Stars, the 1939 NBL Champions, by a score of 34–25.

Gas rationing and travel restrictions during World War II forced Douglas to cut back on the number of away games. Many of the Rens traveled the relatively short distance from New York City to Washington, D.C., on the weekends to play as Washington Bears during the war. In 1943, with Cooper serving as a player-coach, the Bears were 66–0 and entered the World Professional Championship in Chicago. With a 38–30 win over the Dayton Bombers behind them, they defeated the Oshkosh All-Stars 43–31 to win the 1943 title.

In 1963 the famed 1932–1933 Renaissance team, of which Cooper was a member, was inducted into the Naismith Memorial Basketball Hall of Fame in Springfield, Massachusetts. Through the efforts of Eddie Younger, a former Ren, Cooper was the first Renaissance player to be inducted into the Hall of Fame in May 1977. Cooper was nearly seventy years old at his induction ceremony. As witness to his popularity and playing ability forty years earlier, hundreds of supporters traveled to Springfield to witness his induction, including former Rens owner and coach Bob Douglas.

As stated in May 1977 by Howie Evans, sports editor of the *New York Amsterdam News*, "It is because of Tarz, there was a Baylor, a Wilt, a Doctor J, and all the others still to come." Following his professional basketball career, Cooper worked in the Philadelphia Navy Yard. He also volunteered his time as a basketball instructor at the Philadelphia YMCA. Tarzan Cooper died at home in Philadelphia. He was divorced and had no children, but the name of his wife and the dates of their marriage and divorce are unknown.

• Cooper's file is at the Naismith Memorial Basketball Hall of Fame, Springfield, Mass. Important primary sources on Cooper and the Renaissance team include hundreds of articles in the *New York Amsterdam News*, the *Pittsburgh Courier*, the *Chicago Defender*, and other black newspapers. Information on Cooper can also be found in Ocania Chalk, *Pioneers of Black Sport* (1975). For detailed information on the World Professional Championships, see the *Sheboygan Press* and the *Oshkosh Daily Northwestern* newspapers. The best secondary sources include Arthur Ashe, *A Hard Road to Glory: A History of the African-American Athlete, 1919–1945* (1988); Glenn Dickey, *The History of Professional Basketball since 1896* (1982); Robert Peterson, *Cages to Jump Shots: Pro Basketball's Early Years* (1990); and Zander Hollander, *The Modern Encyclopedia of Basketball* (1973). Because there is a lack of detailed information on Cooper and the Renaissance team, see also David L. Porter, ed., *Biographical Dictionary of American Sports: Basketball and Other Indoor Sports* (1989), and Ronald L. Mendell, *Who's Who in Basketball* (1973).

SUSAN J. RAYL

COOPER, Thomas (22 Oct. 1759–11 May 1839), lawyer, chemist, and educator, was born in London, England, the son of Thomas Cooper, a relatively wealthy landowner. The name of his mother is not known. Young Cooper attended University College at Oxford, where he was grounded in the classics. He left the university in 1779, refusing to sign the thirty-nine Articles of Faith required for a formal degree. In that year he married Alice Greenwood and attended medical courses in London in 1780. The couple, who eventually had five children, moved to Manchester. Cooper undertook some clinical work and was active in the Manchester Literary and Philosophical Society; he was elected vice president in 1785. A growing familiarity with chemistry led him to join a firm of calico-printers near Bolton, his subsequent home. The discovery of the bleaching activity of chlorine in 1785 led Cooper to explore the production of the agent with James Watt. He practiced industrial bleaching successfully for some three years before 1793, when a depression in British trade caused the bankruptcy of his firm.

Cooper's early essays for the journal of the "Lit and Phil" ranged from studies on the history of painting to the nature of civil government. His readings of David Hartley and Joseph Priestley evoked essays on philosophical and religious thought. He expressed his belief in both materialism and Christianity and thought Unitarianism was most consistent with reason. Energetic and mobile, Cooper visited London frequently from 1784 to 1787; there he joined the Chapter Coffee House Society to discuss problems of chemistry and natural philosophy. He also attended the Inns of Court in London and subsequently practiced as a barrister in Lancashire.

Early controversy over the French Revolution led to a riot in 1791 in Birmingham that destroyed Priestley's home and laboratory. When the "Lit and Phil" failed to support Priestley, Cooper resigned. He became an active member of the Manchester Constitutional Society, in whose name he addressed the Jacobin Society in Paris in 1792. Edmund Burke castigated his actions in Parliament, and Cooper's angry response, denouncing the "privileged orders," provoked further government warning. In 1793 he visited the United States to prepare a possible haven for English dissenters.

In 1794 Cooper, his reluctant wife, and his family joined the Priestley family in Northumberland, Pennsylvania, after a plan for a site for asylum fell through. Early disagreements over religion and manners between Cooper and an older Priestley were resolved slowly. Cooper became a U.S. citizen, unlike Priestley. Cooper began to farm but failed by 1787 and turned to law and journalism. His newspaper articles assembled in his *Political Essays* (1799), promoted freedom of the press and opposed the Sedition Act. The articles were denounced by Federalists. His political and economic writings became useful to Thomas McKean in the gubernatorial election of 1799 and to Thomas Jefferson in the presidential election of 1800. In 1800, however, Cooper was convicted under the Sedition Act for libeling President John Adams in a 1799 handbill defending Cooper's earlier application for a government position. He was fined and imprisoned for six months, a period in which his wife died. Congress remitted the fine in 1850.

In 1801 Governor McKean appointed Cooper to the Luzerne commission, established to adjudicate claims for lands in Pennsylvania by former settlers from Connecticut and by Pennsylvanians. Cooper's fair and arduous labors from 1801 to 1804 were complimented and in that final year McKean appointed him resident district judge in the state of Pennsylvania.

After the death of Priestley in February 1804, Cooper prepared supplementary appendices to the *Memoirs of Dr. Joseph Priestley to the Year 1795*. The 1806 volume included extensive summaries of Priestley's chemical discoveries, metaphysical writings, and his political and religious works and opinions. Despite his new judicial tasks, Cooper's comprehensive survey of Priestley's chemistry reinvigorated his interest in that discipline. This led to his study of the most recent European advances in chemistry and a reproduction of Davy's isolation of potassium.

Although Cooper's published legal and judicial opinions on problems involving the embargo and commerce received the approbation of Jefferson, he lost the support of radical Republican leaders in Pennsylvania. In 1811 Cooper was removed from office for "injudicious conduct," and his subsequent published comments objected to faults of party-ridden government in both France and Pennsylvania.

In June 1811 the former judge was offered the chair of chemistry at Carlisle (later Dickinson) College. His *Introductory Lecture* (1812) at the college, which affirmed the practicality of chemistry, is recognized as "a remarkable summary of the history of chemistry." In 1812 Cooper married Elizabeth Pratt Hemming; the couple had three children.

Cooper brought much of Priestley's laboratory equipment to Dickinson. In the period 1811–1815 he prepared new laboratory experiments for his students and also annotated several new chemistry texts. During the war with Britain (1812–1814) he edited the journal *Emporium of Arts and Sciences*, designed to instruct Americans on new technology and in political economy. In 1813 he recommended to President Madison the study of Congreve rockets and proposed a new type of shell. His subsequent analysis of rocket fragments earned commendations from the president and the secretary of the treasury, Alexander Dallas. In 1815 he also published the practical treatise *Dyeing*.

As the college failed financially, Cooper undertook in 1815 to teach chemistry and mineralogy at the University of Pennsylvania, where he trained a scion of the du Ponts. He edited and annotated chemical books by Jane Marcet, Frederick Accum, and Thomas Thomson. The latter introduced Dalton's laws of molecular composition to the American scene.

Cooper reported science news in the journal *Port Folio* and also published lectures on chemistry, mineralogy, and plant physiology in that journal. He served as a councilor to the American Philosophical Society and also became an associate of William Maclure in the Academy of Natural Sciences.

Cooper had assisted physicians without recompense, and his many books were relevant to a slowly emerging scientific medicine. In 1818 he was awarded an honorary M.D. degree by the University of New York. Thus armed, he applied for the chair of chemistry in the Medical Department of the University of Pennsylvania. Another candidate, who was appointed, relinquished the role of examining students in chemistry for the medical degree; Cooper's famous essay *Discourse on the Connexion between Chemistry and Medicine* (1818) then stated presciently that chemistry as applied to medicine was in "the infancy of Hercules."

In correspondence with Jefferson, Cooper had described a curriculum possibly suitable for a college in Virginia, and Jefferson subsequently praised Cooper enthusiastically to his associates in a Board of Visitors. In 1819 he was formally elected professor of chemistry, mineralogy, natural philosophy, and law at the college-to-be in Charlottesville. Despite criticism of a "Unitarian" Cooper, the appointment was reaffirmed, but the opening of the college was postponed. He then began to teach chemistry at South Carolina College in Columbia. In 1820 he was also appointed professor of geology and mineralogy and was elected president of the college. His *Introductory Lecture on Chemistry* (1820) emphasized the utilitarian roles of science; his initial *Address to the Graduates of the South-Carolina College* (1821) described religion as a potential force for good citizenship and classical studies as a possible guide to self-improvement. In 1821 he began to serve on a governing board for development of a state lunatic asylum, and in 1822 he pressed for the formation of a medical school in the South. His mineralogical collection became useful in the development of the State Geological Survey.

Cooper had won the favor of many of South Carolina's leading figures in the teaching of states' rights from 1823 to his death. His influential pamphlet *Consolidation* (1824) challenged the constitutionality of federal demands and advocated the sovereign power of the state of South Carolina. Despite earlier opposition to the slave trade and objections to the so-called economic advantages of slavery, he did own slaves and in fact wrote of the biological inferiority of blacks. He denied the doctrines of equality and of natural rights in the Declaration of Independence. Cooper campaigned as a "Nullifier" against a proposed tariff that would affect southern trade. In a speech in 1827 he questioned "the value of the Union," whose demise he had predicted as early as 1815.

After 1830 his battles with clergy over his teaching of an extended age of the earth and of materialist philosophy led to a trial by the Board of Trustees to attempt to remove him from the presidency of the college. In 1832 his spirited defense of the right of free discussion resulted in his clearance. Nevertheless, he resigned his position in 1833 and received the degree of doctor of laws. In 1835 the governor appointed Cooper to compile and edit the statute laws of South Carolina. These were published in five volumes in 1839. He is buried in Trinity Churchyard in Columbia, and the library of the university bears his name.

Cooper was described by Thomas Jefferson as "one of the ablest men in America" and by John Adams as "a learned ingenious scientific and talented madcap." Dumas Malone stated that "modern scientific progress would have been impossible without the freedom of the mind which he championed throughout life."

• Dumas Malone's prize-winning book, *The Public Life of Thomas Cooper, 1783–1839* (1926), contains the most complete compendium of Cooper's publications. Malone's later essay in *The Unforgettable Americans*, ed. John A. Garraty (1960), pp. 97–102, suggests some reconsideration of Cooper. Cooper's contributions to bleaching and dyeing are discussed in A. E. Musson and E. Robinson, *Science and Technology in the Industrial Revolution* (1969), pp. 251–351. Cooper's three volumes of the *Emporium of Arts and Sciences* (1812–1814) contain many of his views of political economy. His economic contributions are summarized by J. Dorfman, *The Economic Mind in American Civilization*, vol. 2 (1946), pp. 527–39, and P. K. Conkin, *Prophets of Prosperity* (1980), pp. 141–52. Cooper's philosophical and religious beliefs and influences are discussed in several texts of the history of philosophy; see P. R. Anderson and M. H. Fisch, *Philosophy in America* (1939), pp. 247–71. His contributions at Dickinson College are described by W. J. Bell, *Journal of the History of Medicine* 8 (1953): 70–87. The reception, then and more recently, of his *Introductory Lecture* at Dickinson is summarized by D. A. Davenport, *Journal of Chemical Education* 57 (1976): 419–22. An account of Cooper's experiences at the University of Pennsylvania is H. S. Klickstein, *Library Chronicle* 96 (1950): 64–80. The events leading to his appointment and its failure at the University of Virginia are found in Malone, *Jefferson and His Time—The Sage of Monticello* (1977; 2d ed., 1981). Cooper's involvements in southern politics have also been discussed extensively by W. W. Freehling, *Prelude to Civil War* (1965, repr. 1966). His career at South Carolina College is described by D. W. Hollis, *University of South Carolina*, vol. 1 (1951), pp. 74–118.

SEYMOUR S. COHEN

COOPER, Thomas Abthorpe (16 Dec. 1775–21 Apr. 1849), actor and theatrical manager, was born at Harrow-on-the-Hill, England, the son of Thomas Cooper, an Irish gentleman trained as a surgeon, and Grace Mary Rae of Wales. Dr. Cooper's prosperous career with the East India Service was cut short with his sudden death at Dacca when young Thomas was eleven. Destitute, Mrs. Cooper had to take a job as a housekeeper, while the son of her first cousin, the philosopher William Godwin, took Thomas as his ward. Expecting the boy to become a writer like himself, Godwin expanded the education he had received at a principal seminary by tutoring him in French, Latin, Italian, and Greek and reading aloud to him all of Shakespeare's plays. Mrs. Cooper's gratitude was mixed with regret for Godwin's abandonment of the Christian ministry and his friendship with the radical revolutionary actor-playwright Thomas Holcroft. So influential were Godwin and his radical circle with the impulsive young Cooper that he almost enlisted in the French Republican army when he was sixteen but was dissuaded in favor of an apprenticeship in the theater instead. Later, writing in 1800 from Washington, where he was starring at the United States' Theatre in the first theatrical production in the new U.S. capital, Cooper would address Godwin as the "father of my mind."

Through Holcroft's assistance, in July 1792, at age sixteen, Cooper began his career with Stephen Kemble's touring company in Edinburgh. He appeared on stage for the first time in the minor role of Mr. Smith in Holcroft's *The Road to Ruin*, but from the beginning he badgered Kemble to let him play leading roles. Finally, in mid-August, Kemble offered him the role of Malcolm in *Macbeth*, and when he forgot the last two lines of the play Kemble took the opportunity to dismiss him. However, he continued in provincial theaters at Portsmouth and Cheshire until the summer of 1795, when he returned to London for intensive coaching by Holcroft, and dancing and fencing lessons. On 19 October at the age of nineteen Cooper made his London debut in the role of Hamlet at the Theatre Royal, Covent Garden. The reviewer for the *Monthly Mirror* wrote that the performance, "for a first appearance before a London audience was, beyond a doubt, unusually brilliant" (Dec. 1795, pp. 45–50). However, when Cooper acted a less ideally suited part as the gallant, gay Lothario in Rowe's comedy *The Fair Penitent* a few weeks later, the harshness of the

criticism from the *Times* seemed to reflect the reviewer's prejudice toward his sponsors' radical politics. Independent and impatient, Cooper turned down a contract that was offered to him for second leads with the Covent Garden Company, where John Philip Kemble was the star. Instead he signed a three-year contract to act leading roles at the Chestnut Street Theatre in Philadelphia under the management of Thomas Wignell.

Cooper is thought to have made his American debut in Baltimore on 11 November 1796 at the "New Theatre" as Penruddock in Richard Cumberland's sentimental comedy *The Wheel of Fortune*. A month later, on 9 December, he first appeared in Philadelphia as Macbeth, which would prove to be his most admired Shakespearean role. He introduced the declamatory "Kemble" style of acting to the American stage, employing formal postures with precise articulation, measured cadence, and frequent pauses, but he used more passion than Kemble, so that on occasion he was faulted for rant. Just under 5'9", with blue eyes, chestnut hair, and rosy English cheeks, the personal qualities that particularly distinguished him as a classical actor were his graceful, perfectly proportioned figure and the notable musicality of his voice. These gifts were matched by enormous physical energy, as well as precise punctuality, and he offered an unusually large repertoire of at least 180 roles in 151 plays. He had a tendency to a careless study of his lines, but his natural generosity made him reluctant to refuse the many requests he received to appear on other performers' benefits, so he sometimes had several new roles to learn in the space of a week.

Cooper captivated the New York audience in his first appearance there on 23 August 1797, as the heroic Pierre in Thomas Otway's *Venice Preserved*, a role with which he became identified. Dissatisfied with a position second to that of James Fennell in the Philadelphia Company, as well as the manager's tardy payment practices, he had taken advantage of a temporary lameness to go to New York. Once he had performed in New York, Wignell had him arrested for breach of contract. Eventually settling the dispute, Cooper agreed to tour regularly between Philadelphia and New York by his own swift horses on alternate nights of the week. His first appearance at the new Park Theatre in New York on 28 February 1798, as Hamlet, was an unqualified triumph. The manager William Dunlap commented that his enactment of the play scene was "the finest thing I ever saw" (*Diary of William Dunlap: The Memoirs of a Dramatist, Theatrical Manager, Painter, Critic, Novelist, and Historian*, vol. 1 [1930], p. 227). Thereafter Cooper was an independent star instead of a stock company actor, the first one so established in America, and he toured every state in the union.

In 1803 Cooper made his first return to England to star at Drury Lane while Kemble was on the Continent. Although he was only twenty-seven years old, the London critics compared him favorably to George Frederick Cooke as Richard the Third and Kemble as Hamlet, both twenty years older. But he explained to

Godwin that he would definitely return to America, for "my fame which is my deity is at its ne plus ultra" (letter to Godwin, 10 June 1802). Indeed, by this time Cooper was the preeminent star of the American stage. His first engagement at the Park Theatre after his return, in November 1804, ran fourteen nights and brought in over $10,000. Noah Mill Ludlow, manager of the American Theatrical Commonwealth Company, who pioneered theater in the South and West, spoke of Cooper's engagement as "about the first instance on record of regular 'starring' in the United States" (*Dramatic Life as I Found It* [1880]).

Cooper became the manager of the Park Theatre in New York in 1806. On 9 January 1808 his first wife, Joanna Johnson Upton, whom he had married soon after his arrival in America, died. Widow of a sea captain, Joanna had three children with Cooper, but only the eldest son, Thomas, survived infancy. That summer Cooper arranged for the businessman Stephen Price to buy a share of his interest in the Park Theatre.

Returning to England in 1810, Cooper made his most successful move as a manager in persuading the great English tragedian Cooke to return with him to America for a tour. Cooke's appearances, some jointly with Cooper, were highly profitable. On 11 June 1812 Cooper married a brilliant belle of New York society, Mary Fairlie, daughter of Major James Fairlie, second secretary of the Order of the Cincinnati, to whom the celebrated writer Washington Irving had introduced him. When he left the management of the Park Theatre in 1815, he moved his family, which eventually included six daughters and a son with Mary, to two adjoining houses on the banks of the Delaware River in Bristol, Pennsylvania. There he enjoyed family life and entertained notable guests in elegant style while continuing to tour indefatigably.

Cooper was the first star to appear in the new English language theater in New Orleans under the management of James H. Caldwell in 1821. In 1822, on a second trip to New Orleans, he presented a new classical character, Damon in *Damon and Pythias* (1821), which became one of his signature roles. Theodore S. Fay, author and coeditor of the *New York Mirror*, said,

His figure, his face, his very voice breathes forth the high-toned grandeur of Roman greatness. It is here we find Mr. [Edmund] Kean is surpassed. He wants the elevated and conscious dignity of Cooper, the power to draw up a noble figure to its full height and look down upon the inferiority of all around—to display might in every limb, greatness and majesty in every motion, and show us in appearance as well as action the great character he personifies. This is the superior power of Cooper, and all this power is brought forward in the play of *Damon and Pythias*. (13 Sept. 1823)

The following year in New York Cooper triumphed with the role of Damon and that of Brutus in John Howard Payne's play of that name, enjoying a new vogue in Roman characters.

Throughout the early 1820s Cooper was unquestionably still America's leading star, but by 1827 a third tour of England lasted only a couple of months. For the next several years he continued the incessant touring in the United States, but by 1833, with the added strain and anxiety resulting from his wife Mary's illness and untimely death at age forty-four, he began to suffer some respiratory weakness. Robert Longface in *The Critic* noted that in a performance of *Othello* in Boston "some of his sentences were lost in his indistinct whispers; his pauses too long." At the time of his retirement Cooper's fortune had also been dissipated, not only by his penchant for gambling and fast horses, but also by his prodigal generosity to family, friends, and strangers. A series of glittering benefits were arranged to provide for his family. The committee for the Cooper Fund was comprised of Charles I. Ingersol and other prominent citizens of Philadelphia, *New York Mirror* editor Colonel George P. Morris, and fellow actors, including Fanny Kemble and Edwin Forrest, who also arranged a benefit in New Orleans.

Three months after his final New York benefit, on 17 February 1834, Cooper introduced his daughter Priscilla to the New York audience. At a benefit at the American Theatre, the Bowery, in Sheridan Knowles's tragedy *Virginius* (1820), Cooper played Virginius, and Priscilla, the role of his daughter Virginia. Priscilla acted with Cooper for four years. The Coopers' last appearance together on record was on 29 October 1838, at the Pearl Street Theatre in Albany as Beatrice and Benedick in Shakespeare's *Much Ado about Nothing*. Priscilla left the stage to marry Robert Tyler, the son of future U.S. president John Tyler of Virginia.

Cooper's final appearance on the New York stage was as Antony in *Julius Caesar* at Bowery Theatre manager Thomas S. Hamblin's benefit on 24 November 1835, although he continued to act on occasion until 1840. In 1841 he was appointed military storekeeper to the Frankford Arsenal in Pennsylvania and thereafter surveyor of the ports of Philadelphia and New York. He died in Bristol, Pennsylvania, at the home of Priscilla and Robert Tyler.

Cooper rose to fame in America at the time when the new nation was forming, and his contemporaries almost invariably noted his passionate espousal of America as his home, unlike most of the imported stars who came and went. Enormously popular, he had a career of long duration as well as influence. At his debut the young Edwin Forrest, the first great American-born star, was hailed as a second Cooper. The distinguished nineteenth-century American actress Charlotte Cushman, who made her debut as Lady Macbeth in 1837, was said to have acquired the majestic quality of her style partly through her admiration for Cooper's acting. In his front-page obituary on Cooper for *The Pennsylvanian*, James Rees, "Colley Cibber," reflected,

Now, even, now, the master-spirit appears, and like some sterling old painting, its beauty still bespeaks the master. Though its colors are somewhat mellowed by the hand of time, his every movement now is grace, every action and attitude show the finished actor, and we turn with sorrow from the too mechanical movement of those around him, to admire still more the model they should study. Cooper *has been great*, and is so still; age has not dimmed the fire of his eye, nor destroyed the energies of his mind; giant-like, he moves along in all the majesty of his collected strength. (26 Apr. 1849)

• Information on Cooper can be found in the records of the India Office Library, London; St. Mary's Church, Harrow; and St. James Church, Bristol, Pa. For Cooper's letters to William Godwin, see the Godwin papers at the Bodleian Library, Oxford University. The Cooper Family Letters are in the University of Alabama Special Collections Library. See also Joseph Norton Ireland, *A Memoir of the Professional Life of Thomas Abthorpe Cooper* (1888); William Dunlap, *History of the American Theatre* (1832); William B. Wood, *Personal Recollections of the Stage* (1855); John Bernard, *Retrospections of America* (1887); George C. D. Odell, *Annals of the New York Stage*, vols. 1–4 (1927–1928); Elizabeth Tyler Coleman, *Priscilla Cooper Tyler and the American Scene 1816–1889* (1955); and Fairlie Arant, "A Biography of the Actor Thomas Abthorpe Cooper (1775–1849)" (Ph.D. diss., Univ. of Minnesota, 1971). A portrait of Cooper by John Jarvis hangs in the Cleveland Museum of Art, and a portrait of the actor by Gilbert Stuart is at the Players Club in New York City, a gift of Cooper's youngest daughter Louisa.

FAIRLIE ARANT MAGINNES

COOPER, William (2 Dec. 1754–22 Dec. 1809), land developer and politician, was born in Byberry (now part of Philadelphia), Pennsylvania, the son of James Cooper and Hannah Hibbs, farmers. Only modestly schooled, in 1774 young Cooper eloped with Elizabeth Fenimore, daughter of the well-to-do Quaker Richard Fenimore of Rancocas, New Jersey. They had twelve children, of whom seven lived to adulthood.

As a Quaker, Cooper took no part in the War for Independence. Instead, this self-confident, poor young man sought his fortune in Burlington, New Jersey, briefly as a wheelwright, storekeeper, and tavern owner, then in land speculation and settlement promotion. His dream soon fixed on lands, no longer threatened by Indians, around Lake Otsego at the headwaters of the Susquehanna River in central New York State, where, in 1786, he founded Cooperstown. These lands had been prematurely opened in the 1760s by the celebrated Indian agent, but failed land speculator, George Croghan. In 1786, by questionable legal means, Cooper acquired title to 29,000 acres, which he quickly and profitably resold to farmers. Thus auspiciously began Cooper's extraordinary career as land proprietor and agent.

Cooper's success owed as much to his pioneering, comparatively equitable, and shrewd business principles, set forth in his *Guide to the Wilderness* (1810), as to his aggressive land grabs and fortunate investment timing. He lived among those to whom he sold property, a civic entrepreneur at home among common people. He insisted on experiencing what his purchasers experienced and worked to establish churches, a seminary, jail, courthouse, newspaper, waterworks, roads,

and bridges. He sold off and did not reserve for himself the choicest properties. To attract settlers, many of them poor, Cooper, unlike many New York landholders who rented to tenant farmers, sold small tracts outright on ten years' credit, taking mortgages for security. To hold settlers, he accepted payments in kind in bad years and marketed settlers' surplus produce, often with great difficulty. "Thus," he wrote in his *Guide*, "by the adoption of a rational plan, it appears that the interest[s] of all parties are made to coincide. The settler sleeps in security, from the certainty of his possession, and the landlord is safe in the mortgages he holds, and the state profits by the success of each, in the increase of its wealth and population." Cooper also represented other American and European speculators, managing and selling their lands. He boasted that, where many others had failed, he had settled as many as 40,000 people on "more acres than any man in America," amounting probably to 750,000 in all.

Not surprisingly, for his own labor and dedication, Cooper won the loyalty of his neighbors. Named presiding judge of the county court of common pleas when Otsego County was formed in 1791, he early became a Federalist, along with such friends and business associates as John Jay, Philip Schuyler, Stephen Van Rensselaer, and his attorney Alexander Hamilton. The segregation of judicial office from partisan activity not yet being established, "The Squire" was a warm and active partisan, involved frequently in conflicts, some physical, with his political opponents and not above pressuring for political support those in debt to him. A wrestler, prodigiously strong and sometimes coarse, he was also recalled by his son, the author James Fenimore Cooper, as "my noble looking, warm hearted, witty father, with his deep laugh, sweet voice, and fine rich eye."

"The Bashaw of Otsego," as Thomas Jefferson disparagingly called him, Cooper served in the U.S. House of Representatives, though still on the bench, from 1795 to 1797 and again from 1799 to 1801, elected by overwhelming majorities. In Congress he proved himself an orthodox Federalist, supporting the implementation of Jay's Treaty (which lessened the British threat to lands like his) and the Alien and Sedition Acts, whose implementation he sought from the bench in the trial and imprisonment of political foes such as assemblyman Jedidiah Peck. Also like most Federalists in Congress, in 1801 he voted for Aaron Burr's election, instead of Jefferson's, when the electoral college deadlocked and the choice of president fell to the House.

Cooper retired from the county court in 1799 and fully from politics in 1801, after declining to seek reelection to Congress. By then he was among the state's, perhaps the nation's, wealthiest men. Though his wife had at first resisted settling upstate, the family came to live an affectionate and comfortable life in "Otsego Hall," their stately home, probably the finest west of the Hudson. At his death, Cooper was worth $700,000 on paper.

The traditional tale that Cooper succumbed from injuries sustained in a political brawl cannot be credited. Instead, he died from natural causes in Albany, survived by his wife and seven children, including James Fenimore Cooper, who modeled Judge Marmaduke Temple in *The Pioneers* after his father.

Cooper was distinctive in becoming an accepted member of New York's landed gentry while retaining the qualities, both fetching and rough, of his common origins. While adhering to eighteenth-century views of paternalism and elite rule, he foreshadowed in much of his life and work the political and cultural triumph of unfettered speculative capitalism and individual enterprise.

• Most of Cooper's papers are at Hartwick College, Oneonta, N.Y. The principal study of his life is Alan Taylor, *William Cooper's Town: Power and Persuasion on the Frontier of the Early American Republic* (1995). The story of Cooper's purported murder is laid to rest in Taylor, "Who Murdered William Cooper?" *New York History* 72 (1991): 260–83. Cooper appears frequently in Alfred F. Young, *The Democratic Republicans of New York: The Origins, 1763–1797* (1967), the best study of New York State's characteristically tangled politics in the early republic.

JAMES M. BANNER, JR.

COOPER, William John (24 Nov. 1882–19 Sept. 1935), educator and U.S. commissioner of education, was born in Sacramento, California, the son of William James Cooper, a painter, and Belle Stanley Leary. Cooper spent most of his childhood in Red Bluff City, California. He received his A.B. in Latin and history from the University of California, Berkeley, in 1906 and was elected to Phi Beta Kappa. In 1908 he married Edna Curtis. They had three children. He later returned to Berkeley for his M.A. in education and history in 1917.

Cooper belonged to the first generation of career educators of the twentieth century. He rose through the ranks of teaching and administration in California to the nation's highest appointment in education. Cooper taught Latin and history at Stockton High School (1907–1910), chaired the history department of the Berkeley junior and senior high schools (1910–1915), and supervised social studies in the Oakland public schools (1915–1918). He served briefly (1917–1918) during World War I as a member of the War Department's Commission on Education and Special Training.

Cooper's administrative appointments included district superintendent of Piedmont (1918–1921) and superintendent of both Fresno (1921–1926) and San Diego (1926–1927) city public schools. In 1927 he accepted Governor C. C. Young's appointment as superintendent of public instruction for California. During his superintendency, Cooper reorganized the state department of education, formed a state educational council to cooperate with the research division of the state department of education, created the first California Curriculum Commission, helped form the Association of California Public School Superintendents, and promoted the creation of junior colleges.

President Calvin Coolidge appointed Cooper eighth U.S. commissioner in 1929, the second Californian to hold that position. The onset of the economic depression during Cooper's tenure (11 Feb. 1929–10 July 1933) significantly altered his views of the federal role in education. Initially, he had described the U.S. Bureau of Education in its traditional capacity, "to interpret education, discover trends, suggest methods of study, and in occasional situations . . . come in and serve as umpire" (*Educational Record*, p. 190). By 1933 he criticized many aspects of local control that, in his opinion, were "handicapping" children. He advocated more cooperation between the state and federal governments to finance public schools (*Scribner's*, p. 131).

In Cooper's era, educators, university professors, reformers, and leaders of private foundations increasingly relied on scientific research and surveys as a policy-making tool. Believing that decisions for the U.S. Bureau of Education should be "based on the best evidence obtainable," Cooper thus initiated three significant surveys while commissioner. The National Survey of Secondary Education represented a comprehensive examination of schools throughout the nation, with an emphasis on "innovational practices." In an effort to upgrade the qualifications of teachers, Cooper also obtained funding for the National Survey of the Education of Teachers. A third study, the National Survey of School Finance (completed by a private university when federal funds were depleted), revealed the vast inequalities among school districts in the various regions of the United States. In contrast to the national attention paid to these larger studies, a smaller survey examining black colleges and universities in 1929 received minimal attention.

In his voluminous written speeches and articles as commissioner, Cooper exemplified the viewpoints of a professional educator and government official. He advocated improvements through cooperation with other government agencies and private organizations. However, he rarely attacked the broader societal evils affecting educational progress. In his only monograph, *Economy in Education* (1933), Cooper argued that through "careful study" and "wise economy" school administrators could stretch the scant money available to depression-era schools.

Although the depression jeopardized school funding throughout the nation, Cooper's early training as a historian helped him see the period as a temporary crisis that should not influence his determination to "press on in the good fight for children's rights" (*Proceedings of the NEA* [1931], p. 734). He analyzed the future of radio and motion pictures as an instructional aid in public school classrooms and for families living in remote areas. Anticipating the problems educators would face later in the twentieth century concerning the proper role of television, he cautioned against radio advertising in classrooms. He also warned of the "passive" nature of learning from radio.

Cooper defined education as a lifelong odyssey of "growth and development." His strong belief in education of the "whole being" shaped his definition of education as something requiring "much effort on the part of others in discovering, nourishing, and directing inherent potentialities." Educators could produce "trained men" and "scientific discoveries," but sociologists, psychologists, and social science research also played an equal role in assisting society. In practical terms, he advocated the hiring of more school psychologists, psychiatrists, and guidance counselors, the creation of nursery schools, and parent education classes.

Cooper enjoyed the respect and admiration of his colleagues in educational circles. He received numerous academic honors and belonged to several professional organizations and societies including the National Educational Association and the American Academy of Political and Social Science. An administrator rather than a scholar, he nonetheless criticized educational bureaucrats who looked after their own interests rather than the child for whom schools were created. He is noted for his numerous speeches (229 official and many more extemporaneous) at educational conferences and meetings throughout the nation while commissioner. Although he increasingly viewed the role of the federal government in schooling as too narrow to meet the educational crisis wrought by the depression, he did not propose any significant reforms. With the exception of his success in convincing Congress of the need for an assistant commissioner of education and the hiring of specialists in newer areas of education, his role as U.S. commissioner of education has had little lasting influence on federal educational policy or administration.

Cooper resigned as commissioner in 1933 to become professor of education at George Washington University. He also taught during the summers at the University of California, the University of Oregon, and the University of Michigan. He died of a stroke while driving to California near Kearney, Nebraska.

• No critical biography of Cooper has been published. Letters, newspaper clippings, copies of speeches, and other materials relating to his tenure as commissioner are available at the U.S. Department of Education, Educational Research Library, Washington, D.C. In addition to his *Annual Reports of the U.S. Commissioner of Education*, the *Proceedings of the National Education Association* contain many of his speeches. Notable articles that reflect his philosophies toward education while commissioner include "Some Responsibilities of the U.S. Bureau of Education," *Education Record* 10 (July 1929): 184–90; " 'Divided Houses' That Endanger Public Education," *Nation's Schools* 8 (Aug. 1931): 31–35; "Knowledge of the Whole Being," *Proceedings of the NEA* 69 (1931): 734–41; "Education—A Definition," *School Life* 16 (Feb. 1931): 110; "The Future of Radio in Education," *Proceedings of the NEA* 70 (1932): 19–22; and "The Crisis in Education: Are We Taking It Out on Our Children?" *Scribner's*, Feb. 1933, 129–131. A comprehensive listing of his writings is in *The Education Index* (1929–1935).

Cooper's educational philosophies are placed within the context of his times in Stephen J. Sniegoski, "The Educational Philosophy and Policy of William John Cooper" *Vitae Scholasticae: The Bulletin of Educational Biography* (Spring 1987): 185–204. His work in California is included in Roy W. Cloud, *Education in California: Leaders, Organizations, and Accomplishments of the First Hundred Years* (1952), esp. pp. 149–52. For an overview of education during the depression, including a discussion of surveys conducted under Cooper's direction, see David Tyack et al., *Public Schools in Hard Times: The Great Depression and Recent Years* (1984). Obituaries are in the *New York Times*, 20 Sept. 1935; *School and Society*, 28 Sept. 1935; and *School Life* 21 (Nov. 1935): 58–59.

VICTORIA-MARÍA MACDONALD

COOTE, Richard (1636–5 Mar. 1701), earl of Bellomont, colonial governor of Massachusetts, New York, and New Hampshire, and British politician, was probably born in Coloony, Ireland, the son of Richard Coote, baron of Coloony, and Mary Rawdon. He married Catherine Nanfan (the date is unknown). Little is known of Coote's early years.

Coote descended from a family with extensive political connections. His uncle Charles Coote translated connection and service into land grants and an Irish peerage, and his father was a member of the Irish Privy Council. Coote's own career rested upon the shifting winds of political fortune in England and America. The second baron of Coloony, he was also a member of the Irish Privy Council. Vast as the family's influence and fortunes in Ireland were, Coote needed to augment his personal holdings to support his ambitions. Although the family had profited from its support of the Stuart restoration, sometime before 1688 Coote, his wife, and his son left Ireland for Holland and entered the service of William of Orange as comptroller of the household. After the Glorious Revolution, which placed William on the British throne, Coote sat in Parliament for Droitwich, became treasurer and receiver general for Queen Mary, and was elevated to the Irish peerage as the earl of Bellomont. With preferment, he received extensive grants of forfeited Irish estates and the favor of a number of prominent Whigs. Among his patrons were the duke of Shrewsbury, the secretary of state for the Northern Department (1689–1690, 1694–1699); and the earl of Somers, Lords Speaker (1693–1700) and lord high chancellor (1697–1700).

Although Coote's Irish lands were extensive, their income was inadequate to his standard of living. When he lost favor with Queen Mary and was deprived of his offices, he was compensated with additional Irish estates. Those additional estates, however, were still inadequate, and his financial condition deteriorated as rents lagged or went uncollected. His title to 77,000 acres was challenged in 1695, and while he prevailed, the delay in the transfer of title hurt. To compensate Coote for his losses, friends arranged for his nomination as the governor of Massachusetts in June 1695. He hesitated in his acceptance until negotiations the next year added the posts of governor of New York and New Hampshire and captain general of the Rhode Island, Connecticut, and Jersey militias and extracted promises from the Lords of Trade for a regular salary as opposed to annual appropriations from the colonial assemblies and an outright grant of £1,200.

Coote's multiple officeholding might have also accomplished the unified governance of the northern colonies that Britain had first attempted in the Dominion of New England. Joining offices in Coote promised to increase military coordination among the northern colonies, enforce the Navigation Acts regulating colonial trade, deal with piracy, and lessen the dependence of imperial administrators on individual colonies. In addition, Coote was to clean up the alleged corruption and lax administration of his predecessor as the governor of New York, Benjamin Fletcher. Coote's brief career as an imperial administrator in North America illustrated how such policies might founder on the shifting hazards of colonial and English political factionalism.

Upon his arrival, Coote encountered the legacy of Leisler's Rebellion in New York. Jacob Leisler's attempt to take over the government in the aftermath of the Glorious Revolution reflected a colony bitterly split between two factions. Coote initially tried to bridge these two factions. Coming as he did as the client of the Whig magnates who had displaced those Tories responsible for the appointment of his predecessor, Coote had strong connections to the Leislerians in England. Still, he tried to appoint anti-Leislerians to his council. Relations with the anti-Leislerians quickly broke down, and he was left to work in New York with the Leislerians and a group of former Tories, among whom was Robert Livingston. At stake was the Leislerian claim that Fletcher had illegally awarded large land grants to anti-Leislerians. Coote moved to invalidate grants larger than a thousand acres while suggesting their subsequent subdivision into smaller units could solve the problems of the colony's labor shortage and the empire's dependence on the Baltic for strategic materials. He recommended the army be encouraged to develop the trade in naval stores. Upon the expiration of their service, soldiers could assume ownership of the small tracts and continue producing naval stores. Retired soldiers would also add to royal support and deter French aggression and colonial rebellion.

While less fractious, Massachusetts's politics also gave Coote difficulty. Arriving in Massachusetts in late May 1699, he faced open challenges to his office and royal authority as the Bay colonists sought to have him replaced with a local resident. Provincial officials insisted that local courts were competent to hear violations of the Navigation Acts, thereby frustrating Coote's instructions to enforce them more effectively. In a direct insult to royal authority, Lieutenant Governor William Stoughton and the General Court had made no provision for the governor to name overseers and had barred Anglicans from serving on the board in the new Harvard College charter. When Coote moved to make piracy a felony punishable by death, several councilors objected to making colonial law consistent with that of England, a violation of the spirit if not letter of the colonial charter. Finally, the assembly reneged on his salary, granting him only £1,000, not the £1,200 agreed upon when he first assumed his American offices. Thus, when he left in the summer of 1700, he had accomplished little in Massachusetts.

Returning to New York, Coote not only faced the rising hostility of the anti-Leislerians, he had to deal with the ebbing power of his patrons in London. William Kidd brought these factors into focus. Before his departure from London for New York, Coote had joined with Kidd, Livingston, and a number of his Whig patrons, among whom were the duke of Shrewsbury and Lord Chancellor Somers, to finance privateering expeditions against pirates. At some point, Kidd's actions seemed to have crossed over the line into technical piracy. By calling for Kidd's arrest and punishment, the anti-Leislerians, the supporters of Fletcher, and English Tories could attack the Whigs and Coote, their placeman. While supporters of Kidd argued for his release, increased Tory criticism forced Coote to send him back to London, where his prosecution discredited British Whigs like Somers and Shrewsbury and undermined their influence.

As the summer wore on, Coote lost ground in New York, as did his patrons in London. The death of the colonial treasurer and his widow's refusal to turn over his records constrained Coote's ability to govern. Differences over the distribution of patronage and the extension of land reform to all grants over a thousand acres led to the defection of moderate supporters like Livingston. Commenting on the loss of men of substance and the appointment of Leislerians, William Blathwayt, secretary to the Lords of Trade, intimated that Coote would precipitate a revolt of the lower orders. Efforts to strengthen intercolonial defense also faltered, as the Iroquois distanced themselves from any alliance with the British while cutbacks in appropriations and the chaos of the colony's system of revenue collection reduced the numbers and morale of British troops along the frontier. Nicholas Bayard, an anti-Leislerian, embarrassed Coote when he returned from London with letters that indiscriminately charged colonial Tories and anti-Leislerians with criminal behavior. At the same time the English solicitor general questioned the invalidation of the large land grants. Buffeted by the attacks of the Leislerians and the defection of his allies, Coote's position was further eroded by rumors that he was to be replaced by Edward Hyde, lord Cornbury, son of the earl of Clarendon, and a representative of the Tory resurgence.

In the midst of his troubles, Coote died in Bowling Green (now southern Manhattan), New York. Like other royal servants, he came to America to revive his fortune, but he stumbled over the difficulties of mediating the bitter political factionalism of early New York, governing multiple jurisdictions, and neutralizing political rivals across the Atlantic. Ultimately, his time in America had little effect. He died with his estate encumbered for sums appropriated for royal troops that had allegedly been diverted to his use, and New York remained divided.

• Primary materials on Coote are in the Bellomont Manuscripts Collection of the New-York Historical Society; the British Colonial Office and Treasury Papers at the Public Record Office, Kew Gardens; and Edmund B. O'Callaghan, ed., *Documentary History of the State of New York* (1849–1851) and *Documents Relative to the Colonial History of the State of New York* (1853–1887). Stanley H. Friedelbaum, "Bellomont: Imperial Administrator during the Seventeenth-century" (Ph.D. diss., Columbia Univ., 1955), provides information on his family and early life. See also William Smith, Jr., *The History of the Province of New York*, ed. Michael Kammen (2 vols., 1972). For a discussion of Coote's colonial activities and N.Y. political factionalism, see Jack M. Sosin, *English America and Imperial Inconstancy: The Rise of Provincial Autonomy, 1696–1715* (1985); Lawrence Leder, *Robert Livingston, 1654–1728, and the Politics of Colonial New York* (1961); John C. Rainbolt, "A 'Great and Usefull Designe': Bellomont's Proposal for New York, 1698–1701," *New-York Historical Society Quarterly* 53 (1969): 333–51; and John D. Runcie, "The Problem of Anglo-American Politics in Bellomont's New York," *William and Mary Quarterly*, 3d ser., 26 (1969): 191–217. On the relations between Kidd and Coote, see Robert C. Ritchie, *Captain Kidd and the War against the Pirates* (1986).

JONATHAN M. CHU

COOTS, J. Fred (2 May 1897–8 Apr. 1985), composer of popular songs, was born John Frederick Coots in Brooklyn, New York. (The names of his parents are unknown.) He learned to play the piano on his own, and at the age of sixteen he started writing songs. About that age he found employment as an accompanist in vaudeville. The young Coots also became a general employee and piano demonstrator in the New York store belonging to Chicago's McKinley Music. He wrote his first Broadway musical, *Sally, Irene and Mary*, with Raymond Klages, in 1922. It ran for two years. From it came Coots's first big hit, "Time Will Tell." In 1923, while a blues fad was at its height, he issued "Hometown Blues," with lyrics by Dave Ringle.

During the remainder of the decade Coots often was employed by the promoters J. J. Shubert and Lee Shubert, and he contributed music to more than a dozen Broadway entertainments, among them *Artists and Models* and *Gay Paree*. Coots's song "A Precious Little Thing Called Love," with lyrics by Lou Davis, was the musical signature of the motion picture *The Shopworn Angel* (1929), in which it was sung by Nancy Carroll. Sheet music of the song sold more than 2 million copies. The musical stage hit of 1929, *Sons O' Guns*, also featured Coots's music to lyrics by Arthur Swanstrom and Benny Davis, with the songs "Cross Your Fingers" and "Why" being particular successes.

Coots worked hard to help Dorothy Fields, the daughter of Lew Fields, of Weber and Fields fame, when she attempted to make her way as a lyricist in the 1920s. She supplied some lyrics for his music while she was still employed as a high school art teacher, and Coots brought her to the attention of several publishers. Fields went on to earn a high reputation after she and Jimmy McHugh formed a writing team.

During the 1930s Coots wrote music for radio, motion pictures, and nightclub entertainers. New compositions evolved in unpredictable ways. For example, the lyricist Benny Davis, thinking up ideas for new songs with Coots, once mentioned that "I Still Get a Thrill" was an excellent title. Coots liked the phrase, and the two men created a song within three hours. Published in 1930, the piece was initially performed by Hal Kemp and his orchestra. Later, a recording by Bing Crosby made it even more popular. Another hit, "Love Letters in the Sand" (1931), was born after Coots read the words as a poem by Nick Kenny, published in the *New York Daily Mirror*. Publishers repeatedly turned down the song until the Irving Berlin firm decided to take a chance. First recorded by Russ Columbo, the song gained wide popularity only after George Hall and his orchestra featured it over the radio and after Pat Boone recorded it (1957).

Listeners heard Coots's superb ballad "For All We Know," lyrics by Sam Lewis, in 1934 on Morton Downey's radio show; it then won a widespread following when recorded by Kay Kyser and by Guy Lombardo. In the same year "Santa Claus Is Comin' to Town" appeared, with lyrics by Haven Gillespie. This novelty number had struggled for two years to find a publisher because it was considered too childish and therefore not salable. Coots, who then was a composer for the Eddie Cantor radio show, tried to get Cantor interested in it, but he failed until Cantor's wife, Ida, urged him to give it a chance. It immediately became a hit. Recorded by Bing Crosby, Perry Como, and many others, it sold more than four million records. Although "You Go to My Head," with lyrics by Haven Gillespie, is considered Coots's finest song, he also sought a publisher for two years before Remick agreed to publish it in 1938. First presented by Kenny Sargent singing with Glen Gray and the Casa Loma Orchestra, the song achieved its greatest popularity after Frank Sinatra recorded it. Coots's ability to respond to swiftly changing situations became evident when, ten days after the Japanese attack on Pearl Harbor, he wrote the music and lyrics to "Goodbye Mama, I'm Off to Yokohama."

Six more of Coots's most successful songs are "Promenade Walk" (1925, lyrics by Al Goodman, Maurice Rubens, and Clifford Grey); "Two Tickets to Georgia" (1933, lyrics by Joe Young and Charles Tobias), first sung by Ted Lewis; "One Minute to One" (1933, lyrics by Sam Lewis), a Harry Richman specialty; "I Want to Ring Bells" (1933, lyrics by Maurice Sigler), a vehicle for Carmen Lombardo; "Beautiful Lady in Blue" (1935, lyrics by Sam Lewis), which Jan Peerce introduced; and "Me and My Teddy Bear" (1953, lyrics by J. Winters), an early hit for Rosemary Clooney.

No unusual style or innovative procedures distinguish Coots's music. His distinction lies in his uncanny ability to know what the song market required at a given moment and then quickly supply a viable product.

Coots was married to Marjorie Jennings and had three children. He died in New York City.

• Coots's sheet music, contracts, playbills, recordings, and other materials are in the Archive Division of the Wisconsin State Historical Society. Published biographical information appears in the *New York Times* obituary, 10 Apr. 1985, and in David Ewen's *All the Years of American Popular Music* (1977). The backgrounds to individual compositions are discussed in David Ewen's *American Popular Songs: From the Revolutionary War to the Present* (1966) and David A. Jasen's *Tin Pan Alley* (1988).

NICHOLAS E. TAWA

COPAS, Cowboy (15 July 1913–5 Mar. 1963), country vocalist and guitarist, was born Lloyd Estel Copas in Adams County, Ohio (he later fabricated the story that he was born on a ranch near Muskogee, Okla.), the son of Eldon Copas and Lola (maiden name unknown), farmers who also played in an amateur country band. Copas was influenced during his early years by Vernon Dalhart, and elements of Dalhart's vocal style can be heard in Copas's singing style. Copas became an accomplished guitarist in the "flatpicked" style and later cut instrumental records featuring his acoustic guitar.

In 1929 Copas worked with promoter Larry Sunbrock in a show that toured the Midwest. There he met fiddle player Lester Storer, who billed himself as "Natchee the Indian." Going onstage in Cincinnati, Copas reportedly heard a man say, "Okay, cowboy, let's see what you can do," and that, apparently, accounted for his nickname. He married Edna Lucille Markins in 1934, and they had three children; his daughter Kathy later followed her father into the entertainment business and recorded some duets with him.

Copas worked on several small stations—WKRC in Cincinnati (1938–1940), WNOX in Knoxville (1940), and WCHS in Charleston, West Virginia (c. 1940)—before moving to WLW in Cincinnati, where he performed on the "Boone County Jamboree." In a self-written publicity release, Copas later asserted that he had performed on 164 radio stations. In 1944 he made his first recordings for the newly formed King Records label, based in Cincinnati. At his first session, Copas recorded "Filipino Baby," a song that was surprisingly forthright about a sailor's passion for a dark-skinned Philippine woman. It became the first hit of any size on King. In the wake of the success of "Filipino Baby" and its follow-up, "Tragic Romance," Copas joined Pee Wee King's band on the Grand Ole Opry in January 1946. He later signed with the show as an individual attraction after King left the Grand Ole Opry to return to Louisville, Kentucky.

The year 1948 was probably Copas's most successful; he reached the country charts with "Signed, Sealed, and Delivered," "Tennessee Waltz," "Breeze," and "Tennessee Moon." Redd Stewart, co-composer of "Tennessee Waltz," one of the most lucrative country music copyrights of the 1950s, later reported that Copas tried to buy his portion of the rights

to the song off him for thirty-five dollars but that the deal fell through because Stewart was holding out for fifty dollars. In mid-August 1948 Copas signed a ten-year contract renewal with both King Records and the Grand Ole Opry. He continued as a top draw in the country music field throughout the early 1950s, but the advent of rock 'n' roll hurt his career. In 1955 he was dropped by King and signed with Dot Records. He tried to record rock 'n' roll for Dot ("Circle Rock" [1957]) but without success. He even tried to record straight popular music with Elliot Lawrence's orchestra, billing himself as Lloyd Copas.

In 1959 Copas was signed to Starday Records. At first his Starday recordings fared no better than his later King recordings, but in 1960 Starday president Don Pierce asked Copas to record a song that would feature his flat-top guitar picking, and in response Copas recorded "Alabam," a song he had written thirty years earlier—and one based on a song called "Coney Isle" by Frank Hutchison. "Alabam" was played regularly by Ralph Emery on his late-night show on radio station WSM, Nashville, and it became the biggest hit of Copas's career, remaining at number one for twelve weeks in the fall of 1960 and peaking at number sixty-three on the pop music charts. Copas reported at the time that he was able to increase his appearance fee from $100 to $400 a night.

Copas continued his run of chart success with "Flat Top" and a remake of "Signed, Sealed and Delivered." He was at a new peak in his career when, on 5 March 1963, he attended a benefit concert for the widow and children of Cactus Jack Call, who had been a disc jockey in Kansas City. He was returning from Kansas City that evening with fellow musicians Hawkshaw Hawkins and Patsy Cline in a private plane piloted by his son-in-law Randy Hughes, when the plane crashed in woodlands five miles west of the Tennessee River near Camden, Tennessee. All of the occupants were killed. The ironically titled "Goodbye Kisses" sold well for Copas after his death.

The late-blooming success of "Alabam" notwithstanding, Copas himself remains known for a series of successful country records in the mid- to late 1940s that featured his deep, expressive baritone voice. His straightforward, accentless singing did not influence many other artists, but it was exceedingly popular at the time and helped to broaden the market for country music.

• Most writing on Copas takes its cue from publicity sheets that Copas himself had a hand in writing, and as a result most are inaccurate. The most accurate article is Rich Kienzle, "Cowboy Copas," *Country Music*, Mar.–Apr. 1990, p. 13. A snapshot description of Copas's reborn career in 1960 is in Pat Anderson, "Boone Gives Copas a Comeback Lift," *Nashville Tennessean*, 23 Oct. 1960. The report of Copas's death and a brief obituary is in the *Nashville Banner*, 6 Mar. 1963.

COLIN ESCOTT

COPE, Arthur Clay (27 June 1909–4 June 1966), chemistry professor and administrator, was born in Dunreith, Indiana, the son of Everett C. Cope and Jennie

Compton, grain storage operators. Cope received the bachelor's degree in chemistry in 1929 from Butler University in Indianapolis. He then worked with Samuel M. McElvain at Wisconsin, where he completed his Ph.D. in 1932. His thesis described the synthesis of compounds for testing as local anaesthetics (one of which became clinically useful) and barbiturates. Three independent papers and two others coauthored with McElvain came out of this research. His interest in medicinal chemistry continued for many years.

After a year as National Research Council fellow at Harvard with Elmer P. Kohler, Cope accepted a teaching position in 1934 at Bryn Mawr, which had a long tradition of excellent teaching and research in organic chemistry. Here he studied the synthesis of novel barbiturates; a few particularly gifted women students assisted him in this research. His meticulous experiments disclosed a new rearrangement reaction involving shift of an allyl group in an all-carbon system. This was a novel discovery in the field of molecular rearrangements and proved to be useful as a synthetic tool in the preparation of complex natural products. Cope investigated it thoroughly, and it became known as the "Cope rearrangement." He received the American Chemical Society Award in Pure Chemistry for this work in 1944.

In 1941 he moved to Columbia University, and during World War II worked on war research dealing with chemical warfare and antimalarial agents. Cope was now recognized as an able and original research chemist and also as a gifted administrator.

Cope's appointment as head of the chemistry department at the Massachusetts Institute of Technology by President Karl T. Compton in 1945 allowed him to show his chemical and administrative talents on a larger scene. Organic chemistry at MIT needed renewal. Cope was given new space and equipment and, most important, was able to hire some brilliant young men, particularly (among organic chemists) John D. Roberts, John C. Sheehan, and Gardner C. Swain. Cope was not a demonstrative person, but he knew how to use power, and he had a rock-like will on essential points. Setting an example by his own research, Cope soon had an outstanding research department at MIT.

In addition to his administrative and research activities at MIT, Cope worked hard for the national community of chemists, many of his activities being associated with Roger Adams of the University of Illinois. He was president (1961) and chairman of the board (1959–1960, 1962–1966) of the American Chemical Society (ACS); he served for nine years as an active member of the important ACS Committee on Professional Training. He was a member of the editorial boards of the annual publication *Organic Syntheses* and the serial publication *Organic Reactions*, and he served as chairman of the organic division of ACS and of the chemical section of the National Academy of Sciences, to which he had been elected in 1947. He was a consultant for Du Pont and for Sharpe and Dohme. These and other activities were demanding even for a person

of his efficiency. Cope and Bernice Mead Abbott, whom he had married in 1930, were divorced in 1963 (with no children). That same year he married Harriet Packard, who brought him a stepson.

Cope's research, in addition to his extensive work on medicinal compounds and rearrangement reactions, dealt with reactions of cyclic carbon compounds, reactions across rings, carbonyl reactions, optical activity in cyclic olefins, and structures of antibiotics. His work was always elegantly executed and clearly described in his papers. Toward the end of his career his research actually became more significant in spite of his many responsibilities. Much of it was in the field of reaction mechanisms. His resolution of *trans*-cycloöctene into optically active forms was a notable experimental feat, providing further support for ideas of three-dimensional arrangements of organic compounds. His work on reactions of platinum, palladium, and cobalt salts with organic compounds to form metal-carbon bonds was novel and important.

Many of the large number of Cope's Ph.D. students and postdoctorates have had outstanding careers in industrial or academic research. Cope relinquished the chairmanship of the MIT department in 1964, becoming a research professor. He received many honors for his research, including membership in the American Philosophical Society and the American Academy of Arts and Sciences, in addition to the National Academy of Sciences.

Cope bequeathed his considerable fortune, resulting from royalties and successful investments, in part to ACS, which has used it to fund annual A. C. Cope awards to chemists for outstanding work. Cope's career combined distinguished scientific research and teaching with valuable public service. He died suddenly in Washington, D.C.

• Cope's career is excellently described by his colleagues John D. Roberts and John C. Sheehan, *Biographical Memoirs, National Academy of Sciences* 60 (1991): 16–30. They list only a few of his 240 scientific papers. A complete list of his publications is available from the archivist, National Academy of Sciences. Personal recollections have entered into the present sketch. Collections of Cope's papers are at MIT; the Roger Adams Papers at the University of Illinois contain much information as well. An obituary by Roger Adams is in *Proceedings of the Welch Foundation*, Conference X (1967): 1–3.

D. STANLEY TARBELL

COPE, Caleb Frederick (18 July 1797–12 May 1888), financier and philanthropist, was born in Greensburg, Westmoreland County, Pennsylvania, the son of William Cope and Elizabeth Rohrer. After his father's death during his early years, Cope was cared for by his mother and his maternal grandfather, Frederick Rohrer. He received only a rudimentary education in a one-room schoolhouse and was apprenticed at the age of twelve or thirteen to John Wells, a storekeeper, with whom he remained for four years.

Cope returned home to his mother (who had since remarried) after completing his apprenticeship. He received a letter from an uncle, Jasper Cope, offering him a home and a place in the mercantile firm that his uncle ran in Philadelphia in partnership with his brothers Israel and Thomas Pine Cope (the latter of whom later established a line of packet ships between Philadelphia and Liverpool, England). The firm of Cope Brothers not only prospered but also enabled Cope to gain valuable experience in business. About 1820 his uncles retired and turned the business over to Cope and his cousin Herman Cope. After his cousin withdrew from the business to accept a position with the Bank of the United States in Cincinnati, Cope formed a series of partnerships that enabled his firm, Caleb Cope & Company, to achieve great success. Specializing in the silk trade, the firm soon became one of the wealthiest of its kind in the United States.

Rapidly rising in prominence in the local business community, Cope became a director of the United States Bank in 1836. He served in that capacity until 1842, and he also served as president pro tempore of the bank during Nicholas Biddle's absence in Washington. He took time from his growing responsibilities to marry a cousin, Abby Ann Cope, in 1835; they had one child before she died in 1845.

Cope became a director of the Philadelphia Savings Fund Society in 1841 and also served as one of the first trustees of the Lehigh Coal & Navigation Company. With continued success of his firm, Cope was able to purchase a large country estate, "Springbrook," located near Holmesburg, Pennsylvania, on the Delaware River. Here he achieved success in yet another field, horticulture; in addition to a magnificent collection of plants, his estate was also the site of the first American appearance of Victoria Regia, the great American water lily. Having produced several flowers of increasingly greater size, Cope was rewarded for his efforts with a gold medal from the Pennsylvania Horticultural Society.

With the continued seeming prosperity of his firm (a new store opened with great fanfare in 1853 on Market Street in Philadelphia), Cope's future appeared bright. The panic of 1857, however, brought distress to a great number of American businesses. Caleb Cope & Company did not prove immune to financial difficulties, and its failure was hastened by dishonesty on the part of Cope's partners. Defrauded of more than $213,000, Cope eventually spent $750,000 to settle his affairs. After selling his estate for a pittance, he moved into the St. Lawrence Hotel. The founder and for several years president of the Merchants Hotel Company, Cope later moved to the Continental Hotel (run by his firm) after its opening in 1861.

The coming of the Civil War opened new opportunities for Cope. Although he turned down the post of European purchasing agent for the North, he did serve on the committee of the Cooper Shop Refreshment Saloon, which provided assistance to Union troops and their families. Active in philanthropic ventures and with his business troubles behind him, Cope found time to serve as a manager of the Pennsylvania Hospital, the Institution for the Instruction of the Blind, and

the Soldiers' Home, among other endeavors. He also served as president of the Pennsylvania Academy of Fine Arts, where he met his second wife, Josephine Porter, whom he married in 1864. The couple had two children.

The latter part of Cope's career was devoted to the leadership of the Philadelphia Savings Fund Society. Familiar with the operations of the fund because of his long service as a director, he was named president pro tempore on 22 December 1863 and assumed the duties of president on 4 January 1864. During his long tenure the fund, which had been founded in 1816 by local merchant Condy Raguet as an institution designed to serve the needs of small savings depositors, grew to become the largest organization of its type in the United States. At the end of his twenty-four years at the head of the firm, nearly 125,000 depositors contributed to an institution that held nearly $30 million in assets.

Cope worked continuously at the fund until February 1888, when his health failed. He died at his Philadelphia residence. During his long life, Cope had lived a rags-to-riches story that was typical of the great men of business in his era. He is best remembered for his role in the growth and development of the Philadelphia Savings Fund Society, a portion of which survives as part of Mellon Bank.

• No organized collection of Caleb Cope's papers is known to have survived; however, the papers of the Philadelphia Savings Fund Society are held at the Hagley Museum and Library in Wilmington, Del. Scant attention has been paid to Cope and his career by scholars; the best secondary source remains James M. Willcox, *A History of the Philadelphia Savings Fund Society, 1816–1916* (1916). An obituary is in the *Philadelphia Public Ledger*, 14 May 1888.

EDWARD L. LACH, JR.

COPE, Edward Drinker (28 July 1840–12 Apr. 1897), biologist and paleontologist, was born in Philadelphia, Pennsylvania, the son of Alfred Cope, a businessman and farmer, and Hannah Edge. The Copes were a wealthy Quaker, mercantile family, and for forty years his father's fortune enabled Cope to pursue independently his studies in natural history. Cope was a precocious child and early demonstrated an interest in nature. His education included private training and one year at the University of Pennsylvania. In 1859 he worked with Spencer Fullerton Baird on the Smithsonian Institution's reptile collections. In the early 1860s he examined collections at Harvard's Museum of Comparative Zoology and later in museums in Europe. He also took advantage of resources in Philadelphia. Beginning in 1859 he recataloged the reptile collections of the Academy of Natural Sciences of Philadelphia and in the early 1860s frequently discussed specimens at Academy meetings and published in its *Proceedings*. Cope's early papers were descriptive studies of fishes, amphibians, and reptiles, though he introduced new criteria for classifying fishes and rearranged the classification of amphibians. From 1864 to 1867 Cope taught zoology at Haverford College. In 1865 he married Annie Pim; they had one child. Although Cope abandoned formal ties to the Quakers, religion continued to influence his interpretation of evolution.

Cope was most famous for his research in vertebrate paleontology. Influenced by his study of recent reptiles, and his association with the Academy of Natural Sciences where Joseph Leidy worked on fossil vertebrates, Cope began examining fossil reptiles in 1865. He subsequently described extinct sea serpents, discovered dinosaur remains, and helped mount the country's first dinosaur skeleton at the Academy. At first, Cope's research concentrated on remains found along the Atlantic seaboard, but in 1871 he made the first of many expeditions to western states and territories in search of extinct animals. His work yielded outstanding results. As indicated in two major studies, "The Vertebrata of the Cretaceous Formations of the West" (*Report of the United States Geological Survey of the Territories* 2 [1875]: 1–302) and "The Vertebrata of the Tertiary Formations of the West" (*Report of the United States Geological Survey of the Territories* 3 [1883]: 1–1009), he described over 1,000 new species and genera of fossil animals, made some of the first American discoveries from the Eocene epoch, and helped to determine the succession of faunas and geological horizons in the American West. Cope, along with his rival Othniel Charles Marsh, found remains of bizarre, horned mammals and gigantic sauropod dinosaurs, organisms previously unknown to science. His papers included not only descriptions and classifications, but also visual representations and dramatic depictions of the habits and habitats of extinct animals.

Cope's descriptions, however, were often brief and hasty; he created many new species or genera on the basis of incomplete material. Yet his work, and Marsh's, brought America to the forefront in vertebrate paleontology.

Cope's work also resulted in a serious controversy with Marsh. Both men, independently wealthy and ambitious, sought to dominate vertebrate paleontology. Their overlapping explorations and competing claims for priority of discoveries led Marsh in 1873 to accuse Cope of having violated the canons of scientific practice. The feud not only produced problems between Cope and Marsh, but it also influenced American vertebrate paleontology for the remainder of the nineteenth century. Both were to blame for the confrontation, though Cope's hastiness and brash tactics reflected a reckless disregard for personal or professional obligations. His aggressiveness on matters of priority, publications, and professionalization later led to controversies with naturalists at the Academy of Natural Sciences and the American Philosophical Society.

The feud soon limited Cope's opportunities for fieldwork in vertebrate paleontology. Though he and Marsh continued to compete for fossils, by the late 1870s Cope had squandered most of his fortune on collecting and a series of poor investments. In 1878 he purchased the *American Naturalist* as a vehicle for his publications, but it too proved a costly venture. Marsh, conversely, was able to draw upon his great wealth to obtain specimens. In addition, Marsh became associated with new leaders in the federal science bureaucracy and was able to isolate Cope from obtaining financial or institutional resources. In 1878 Marsh played an important role in the selection of Clarence King as the first director of the U.S. Geological Survey. In 1882 King's successor, John Wesley Powell, appointed Marsh survey vertebrate paleontologist, thus providing him with access to fossil deposits, the opportunity to publish under government auspices, and a budget that enabled him to maintain a large staff of assistants. Certainly Powell and Marsh had their enemies, and on a number of occasions in the 1880s Cope called on his supporters, notably Henry Fairfield Osborn (1857–1935) and William Berryman Scott, to help dislodge his rival. Those efforts, however, were largely unsuccessful.

Eventually Cope received support for his work. In 1889 he became professor of geology and later zoology at the University of Pennsylvania. In 1892–1893 the Texas Geological Survey and the Academy of Natural Sciences provided him with money to pursue fieldwork in Texas and South Dakota. In 1896 he was elected president of the American Association for the Advancement of Science.

Although he was a committed evolutionist, Cope rejected Charles Darwin's idea that natural selection was the causal mechanism of evolution. In "On the Origin of Genera" (*Proceedings of the Academy of Natural Sciences of Philadelphia* 20 [1868]: 242–300), he argued that modifications in individual embryological development caused important evolutionary changes. Cope did not explain the causes of embryological acceleration or retardation and maintained that God was ultimately responsible for the process and pattern of evolutionary change. By the early 1870s he had moved away from such explicit theism as the cause of variations. Cope constructed a theory, later termed neo-Lamarckism, according to which will or thought led organisms to make choices and in turn to undertake motions, develop habits, and use bodily parts. The growth or atrophy of parts through use or disuse was passed on from an individual organism to its progeny and resulted in evolution. Cope's theory, most fully summed up in *The Origin of the Fittest* (1887) and *The Primary Factors of Organic Evolution* (1896), explained evolution as an additive process. Unlike Darwin, who described a branching tree of life, Cope defined evolution in terms of cumulative, linear patterns of change. By the 1890s the German zoologist August Weismann and other neo-Darwinians were challenging Cope's interpretation of evolution and inheritance. Yet Cope's reliance on nonmaterial factors as the cause of evolution appealed to many who could not accept the materialistic explanation associated with Darwinism. His theory provided a means for explaining adaptation and an interpretation of the data of the fossil record that influenced many American paleontologists until the 1930s.

• The major collection of Cope's papers is in the archives of the Department of Vertebrate Paleontology, American Museum of Natural History, New York City. That collection includes Cope's correspondence with his family and with Henry Fairfield Osborn. A separate collection in that archive includes Cope's diaries from the 1870s, his correspondence with Ferdinand V. Hayden and several collectors, and material pertaining to the American Museum's purchase of Cope's collections. Cope's correspondence with the Academy of Natural Sciences is in Manuscript Collections 80, 566, 567 at the Library of the Academy of Natural Sciences of Philadelphia. The Quaker Collection, Haverford College, includes Cope's correspondence with many prominent scientists. The American Philosophical Society possesses Cope's field notebooks and his correspondence with the society.

Major works by Cope not previously cited include: "Synopsis of the Extinct Batrachia, Reptilia, and Aves of North America," *Transactions of the American Philosophical Society*, n.s., 14 (1870): 1–252; "The Laws of Organic Development," *American Naturalist* 5 (1871): 593–605; "The Method of Creation of Organic Forms," *Proceedings of the American Philosophical Society* 12 (1872): 229–63; and "The Crocodilians, Lizards, and Snakes of North America," *Report of the United States National Museum* (1898): 153–1270.

The best biography of Cope is Henry Fairfield Osborn, *Cope: Master Naturalist. The Life and Writings of Edward Drinker Cope* (1931). That work includes much of Cope's correspondence with his family. "Edward Drinker Cope," *National Academy of Sciences, Biographical Memoirs* 13 (1930): 129–317, is Osborn's shortened version of the Cope biography but includes a more useful bibliography. A favorable view of Cope is presented in William Berryman Scott, *Some Memories of a Palaeontologist* (1939). Joseph M. Maline, "Edward Drinker Cope (1840–1897)" (M.A. thesis, Univ. of Penn., 1974), provides a good overview of his life and an insightful interpretation of his troubles with Marsh.

RONALD RAINGER

COPE, Oliver (15 Aug. 1902–30 Apr. 1994), surgeon and medical educator, was born in Germantown, Pennsylvania, the son of Walter Cope, a prominent architect, and Eliza Middleton Kane. Young Cope was deeply influenced by his family's Quaker principles, particularly their pacifism. He graduated from the Germantown (Quaker) Friends School in 1919 and enrolled at nearby Haverford College, also a Quaker school. After a year, however, he transferred to Harvard and received his A.B. in 1923. That fall he entered Harvard Medical School. After two years he took a leave of absence to travel around the world. He first worked as a correspondent for an English-language newspaper in Beijing, China, and was among the first Western journalists to interview General Chiang Kai-shek. Cope then journeyed along the southern rim of Asia. In Indochina he was followed by the French secret police, who suspected him of being a spy. He traveled through British India and continued westward to the Mediterranean, having walked across great stretches of Persia. The trip left him contemptuous of European imperialism and skeptical of religious missionaries. In the fall of 1926 he returned to the United States in time to re-enroll at Harvard Medical School. He received

an M.D. in 1928 and for the next four years served on the surgical house staff at the Massachusetts General Hospital (MGH) in Boston.

In 1932 Cope married Alice De Normandie of Boston. He had been awarded a Harvard Moseley Traveling Fellowship and planned to do research in Berlin and London, and the couple left immediately for Europe. In Berlin they were so appalled by the growing Nazi persecution of Jews that they left after a short time and went to London, where Cope did research on the pituitary and adrenal glands under the direction of Sir Henry Dale at the National Institute of Medical Research. While in England, Cope and his wife worked to help people who were fleeing Hitler's Germany; the Copes continued their work on behalf of refugees for many years. They had two children.

In 1934 Cope returned to the Massachusetts General Hospital where he worked with E. D. Churchill to study problems of the parathyroid. Cope mapped the location and extent of parathyroid glands and in 1934 published accounts of eleven cases of hyperparathyroidism (HPT), leading to a new understanding and treatment of the disease. He further outlined procedures for the removal of the parathyroid and authored many papers and several textbook chapters on the subject.

After Pearl Harbor, Cope sought to improve and simplify the treatment of burns, a matter of grave concern to army and navy medical authorities. Cope's work was facilitated by tragedy. On 28 November 1942, shortly after Cope had become acting chief of surgery at MGH, a fire engulfed the Coconut Grove night club in Boston. Hundreds died, and thirty-nine were admitted to MGH for severe burns. Cope eschewed the usual treatment of coating the burns with tannic acid and instead administered petroleum jelly to preserve the skin and intravenous fluids to compensate for dehydration. He also recognized the centrality of respiratory failure in burn patients and conducted an intensive study of precisely how burns impaired the entire pulmonary system. The U.S. Office of Naval Research supported Cope's work; his findings were published in the *Annals of Surgery* in 1943. Cope's interest in burns later resulted in the establishment of the Shriner Burn Institute for Children at the MGH; Cope was its first chief of staff.

During his study of burn victims, Cope noticed how frequently a patient's recovery was hindered by depression. He consequently modified burn treatment to include professional counseling on psychological and emotional issues. In subsequent years Cope also found that extensive and disfiguring surgery similarly plunged patients into severe and debilitating depression. Aware of the emotional costs of such surgery, he increasingly criticized surgeons for too readily performing surgery when alternative, less invasive procedures might work as well. In his inaugural address in 1963 as president of the American Surgical Association, Cope urged his colleagues to treat patients' emotional needs as well as their physical ailments. He called on surgeons to work more closely with behavioral and social scientists to devise an approach to medical care that integrated a patient's social, emotional, and physiological needs.

Cope further developed these observations in *Man, Mind and Medicine: The Doctor's Education* (1968), though now he focused on the narrowness of medical training. He recommended that students be educated in the humanities and social sciences and complained that, too often, medical school inculcated in young doctors "a cold-roast attitude in which all that is important is the hard science aspect of diagnosis and treatment." In addition to being inhumane, such an approach was poor medicine, for it impaired a physician's ability to understand a patient's ailments and neglected the emotional component of recovery. He proposed to add segments in psychiatric training as part of the required curriculum in medical schools.

Cope practiced what he preached. He insisted on listening carefully and at length to his patients—sometimes to the annoyance of colleagues, irritated by delayed appointments and late-night meetings. During these long consultations, he was struck by how many women with breast cancer confided that they would rather risk death than countenance the removal of a breast. They were terrified of the radical mastectomy, the operation that removed the entire breast along with surrounding lymphatic and muscle tissue. Worse still, fear of such disfigurement dissuaded thousands of women from seeing a doctor until their cancer had fatally spread beyond the breast. Cope realized that if women were aware of an alternative to breast removal, far more would seek timely medical assistance.

But did alternative treatments work? Data on the subject was mostly unavailable in the United States, where nearly all cancerous breasts were removed by means of the radical mastectomy. Cope therefore tracked the results of foreign research on alternative approaches, such as radiation treatment or more limited surgery such as lumpectomy, which removed the diseased tissue rather than the entire breast. By the mid-1960s he became persuaded that the alternatives, or a combination of them, including chemotherapy, were as effective as radical mastectomies in treating most forms of malignant breast cancer. In 1967 he wrote an article summarizing his conclusions. After a regional surgical journal rejected the piece, Cope permitted articles discussing his ideas to be published in the *Radcliffe Quarterly* as well as in several mass circulation women's magazines. Among other things, he advised women not to submit to radical mastectomies until they had asked their surgeons about alternatives. Many physicians criticized him for taking his case directly to women, but within three months he had received 8,500 letters from women seeking information on alternative approaches. Cope broadened his argument in *The Breast: Its Problems, Benign and Malignant, and How to Deal with Them* (1977).

Although Cope retired from the Harvard Medical School in 1969 and from the Massachusetts General Hospital in 1976, he continued to see patients, especially women with breast cancer. The Copes lived in Lincoln, Massachusetts, for several years after moving from their longtime home in Cambridge, and in 1992 they moved to Woodsville, New Hampshire, where he died.

Cope spent nearly every summer of his life at Crowfield, a family home on Narragansett Bay in Rhode Island, where he and his wife entertained an eclectic gathering of colleagues, refugees, musicians, and friends. Worried that his students were becoming excessively preoccupied with the narrow practice of medicine, Cope regularly invited them to Crowfield, where they were exposed to a restorative dose of broad-minded humanism; students also learned that their eminent professor was an accomplished violinist.

Cope was one of the founders of endocrine surgery and an inspiring teacher of medicine. His humanistic outlook and ability to question entrenched authority and received wisdom enabled him to look at familiar problems in new ways. His suggestions on broadening the education of physicians contributed to some revision of medical school curricula; and his views on the treatment of breast cancer eventually prevailed: by the 1990s most malignancies were treated by alternative therapies such as Cope had championed.

• Cope's papers are located at the Countway Library of the Harvard Medical School. Cope's presidential address to the American Surgical Association appeared in William H. Muller, Jr., ed., *Transactions of the Eighty-Third Meeting of the American Surgical Association* (1963). See also "Oliver Cope: A Founder of Endocrine Surgery," *College and Faculty Bulletin: Supplement to the Annals of the Royal College of Surgeons of England* 77, no. 2 (Mar. 1995). Obituaries appeared in the *New York Times*, 3 May 1994, and the *Boston Globe*, 2 May 1994.

MARK C. CARNES

COPE, Thomas Pym (26 Aug. 1768–22 Nov. 1854), merchant and philanthropist, was born in Lancaster, Pennsylvania, the son of Caleb Cope, a plasterer and town burgess who had come from the family farm in Chester County, and Mary Mendenhall. The third son in a family of seven, Cope received a good education for the time, including study in English, German, Latin, and mathematics. In his diary he describes how an unfair teacher provoked in him such intense concentration that he dreamed mathematical problems and mastered the subject. His diary also reveals a well-trained and wide-ranging mind with a talent for acute, usually sympathetic, observation. During the revolutionary wars, the Quaker pacifism of Cope's parents, and their willingness to house captured British prisoners, drew the attacks of local hotheads. The most famous prisoner that the Copes lodged was Major John André—later executed as a spy for helping Benedict Arnold—who deeply impressed Cope with his charm and urbanity.

Cope went to Philadelphia and was apprenticed to a dry goods merchant in about 1786. He entered into partnership with his uncle Thomas Mendenhall in Philadelphia in 1790, but in 1792, after Mendenhall had involved the firm in speculation in Bank of the

United States scrip, Cope, with the help of friends in the Philadelphia Meeting, forced Mendenhall out and took over the business of the house. He came to Philadelphia, according to his diary, as an "ignorant boy," but as a young man he soon widened his interests and developed an ability to meet and chat with talented people, including Benjamin Franklin and Charles Talleyrand. The Quaker meetings provided Cope's entrée into Philadelphia society. In 1792 he married Mary Drinker, whom he described in his diary as "a female endowed with many attractive qualities of body and mind." They had six children. During the mid-1790s, like Philadelphia generally, he prospered, and by the end of the decade he was sufficiently wealthy and well respected to retire and enter city politics. However, about 1800 his partner lost huge sums and forced Cope to reenter the "drudgery" of business.

Cope gradually reestablished himself, found a better partner, and in 1806 bought his first ship. He was a thorough Federalist and actively lobbied against war with Britain. He wrote in his diary that when the "dark, impenetrable covering . . . enveloping the transactions and intentions of the Government" was finally swept away, he could "scarce credit [his] senses . . . yet the fact is certain . . . Congress have hazarded . . . war." Nevertheless his own uninsured ships returning from China evaded British cruisers off the Delaware and brought home a fortune.

Cope early demonstrated a Quaker social conscience. During the terrible yellow fever epidemics of the 1790s, despite succumbing himself, he remained in the city to help sufferers. The cure for the fever appeared to be better water. Hence in 1798 Philadelphia decided to build the first American steam-powered waterworks to provide clean Schuylkill water. As the leading member of the city watering committee, Cope had to convince skeptical Philadelphians and to discipline the engineers, Benjamin Latrobe and Nicholas Roosevelt. Latrobe, whom Cope heartily distrusted, is usually credited for the works, but Cope understood the technical principles and ensured that Latrobe's extravagant plans were completed at reasonable cost. Although Cope also served in the state legislature in 1807–1880, he refused to run for Congress.

Philadelphia's easy prewar prosperity evaporated after 1815. The Caribbean trade reverted to its old channels, and New York City seized the transatlantic trade. New York's great advantages were ocean packet lines to Liverpool and the Erie Canal. Cope attempted to emulate both of these. First, in 1822, after a false start in 1821, he joined Alexander Brown of Baltimore and his eldest son, William Brown of Liverpool, to establish Philadelphia's first and only long-lasting transatlantic packet line. The line offered a fast, scheduled monthly service to Liverpool for mail, specie, fine British manufactures, and heavier American staples. The line also soon became the standard route for wealthy Pennsylvanians visiting Europe. The Delaware normally added at least two days to the normal transatlantic passage and in severe winters could freeze for weeks, but in the 1820s and 1830s the circuitous route via New York was often equally poor. The conjunction between Cope and the Browns was more than an alliance of simple shipping interests. Alexander Brown was the leading merchant in Baltimore and one of the richest men in the United States; his son William was the leading merchant in Liverpool. These men collectively were among the leaders of Anglo-American commerce in the early nineteenth century.

Cope also contributed to solving Philadelphia's internal communications problems. His main concern for many years was the organization of the Chesapeake and Delaware Canal. He knew DeWitt Clinton and borrowed from his experience on the Erie. He also played a critical role in the early finance and organization of the Pennsylvania Railroad. "Philadelphia," he wrote in his diary, will "be but a village" if Baltimore links with Pittsburgh first. When, however, Asa Whitney invited him in December 1846 to preside over an organizing meeting of the "Railroad to the Pacific," Cope declined; "I felt the scheme too magnificent for the grasp of my intellect," he wrote. The same day he learned that the best ship in his line, the *T. P. Cope*, had been struck by lightning and burned in the Atlantic. Fortunately there was little loss of life, and his sons soon built larger ships for the burgeoning immigrant and grain trades.

Cope was an active director of the Bank of the United States from about 1822 to 1831, was chairman of the committee on branches, and was frequently president pro tempore when the controversial president Nicholas Biddle was traveling. Cope thought the bank was a vital element in Philadelphia's struggle with New York and later argued that Biddle had ruined it. He claimed in his diary that in 1831 he had been told that if he would consent to replacing Biddle as president of the bank, then Andrew Jackson would renew the charter. However, although earlier Cope and Alexander and John Brown had been powers in the bank, by 1831 Cope estimated that Biddle "had taken care to possess himself" of sufficient proxies to control any election. Cope also served as a director of the Insurance Co. of North America.

Cope was an effective and respected civic leader over an astonishingly long period. He had entered city politics before 1800. In middle and old age he was seen as an honest, shrewd, and sanguine merchant with a gift for mediation. Requests to serve in this or that capacity poured in to him. He founded and was president of the Philadelphia Board of Trade (1833–1854) and was president of the Mercantile Library for many years. He was elected to the Select Committee of the City Council (1841–1844) but refused to stand for mayor in 1844. In 1837 he was elected to the state constitutional convention. Frequently invited to stand for state and national office, Cope always refused. "I have neither the taste nor the desire for public life," he wrote. "The path of the politician is strewn with thorns." However, he seems to have enjoyed society and politics but picked and chose his commitments.

Cope hesitated less about philanthropic endeavors. He was president, manager, or a generous supporter of many Philadelphia and Quaker good causes: the Pennsylvania Hospital, the House of Refuge for Coloured Delinquents, the Hospital for the Insane Poor, the Asylum for the Deaf and Dumb, the Quaker appeal for Irish Relief, and the Friend's Indian Society, among others. Many rich Americans of his period financially supported such worthy causes, but Cope gave more personal commitment than most. Like all good Quakers he opposed slavery and supported education—in his case founding Haverford College in 1833. He was executor of the estate of banker and philanthropist Stephen Girard, and he was chairman of the city committee that in 1844 purchased, from the trustees of the defunct Bank of the United States, the "Lemon Hill" estate, which later became Philadelphia's huge Fairmount Park. Cope died at his home in Philadelphia and left about $1.5 million.

Cope's first wife died in 1825, and in 1829 he married Elizabeth Stokes Waln. (This marriage was childless.) Also in 1829 he handed over the shipping line to his sons Henry and Alfred, who, along with their children, continued the line with increasingly larger ships until the 1860s, when it was undercut by steamers. After 1865 the ships were transferred into the long-distance staple trades, but the last was sold in 1882. Unlike many other merchants, the Copes failed to make the transition into manufacturing, modern shipping, or finance. Some of the Cope relatives became rentiers for a time, but Cope's active descendants mostly developed professional interests.

• Thomas Cope's private letter books (1788–1853) are in private hands. Microfilm copies are at the Hagley Museum and Library, Wilmington, Del. The ledgers and letter books of the successive firms in which he was a partner and which were carried on by his sons and grandsons are at the Pennsylvania Historical Society. Many miscellaneous records are at Haverford College. He began his diary in 1800, abandoned it in 1820, and then revived it from 1843 to 1851. The manuscript of the diary is located at Haverford and has been edited by Eliza Cope Harrison into *Philadelphia Merchant: The Diary of Thomas P. Cope, 1800–1851* (1975). Portraits of Cope and his ships are at the Philadelphia Board of Trade, the Mercantile Library, and Haverford College. Eleanor A. Maass, "A Public Watchdog: Thomas Pym Cope and the Philadelphia Waterworks," *Proceedings of the American Philosophical Society* 125 (1981): 134–54, comments on the significance of Cope's work on the Philadelphia Waterworks. Little else has been written on Cope. The best appreciation of him by a contemporary is in Freeman Hunt, *Lives of American Merchants*, vol. 1 (1856), pp. 103–31.

JOHN KILLICK

COPE, Walter (20 Oct. 1860–1 Nov. 1902), architect, was born in Philadelphia, Pennsylvania, the son of Thomas Pim Cope, a none-too-successful shipping company co-owner, and Elizabeth Waln Stokes. Walter Cope's business partner, John Stewardson, was a childhood friend. Both boys were educated in a very traditional Quaker manner, which stressed culture and discipline, at the local Friends' School in Germantown. Choosing architecture over landscape gardening, after graduation Cope applied and was accepted for a position as estimator and draftsman in the office of a Philadelphia architect, Addison Hutton. It was there that Cope received much of his training and was exposed to collegiate building; Hutton was the official architect of Lehigh University and designed works at Bryn Mawr. After Hutton's office, Cope worked for a time in the office of Theophilus P. Chandler, Jr. (It is fairly certain that Stewardson was working for Chandler at the same time.) Chandler was a strong proponent of architectural education, and under his influence Cope and Stewardson formed the T-Square Club, an organization that promoted the study, practice, and appreciation of architecture. Cope enrolled at the Pennsylvania Academy of the Fine Arts in 1883 and was taught painting and drawing by Thomas Eakins and Thomas Anshutz. In March 1884 Cope sailed to Europe and spent fourteen months exploring and sketching in England and France. Upon his return to the United States in 1885, he and Stewardson set up an architectural business together in a small office at 212 South Third Street in Philadelphia. Their firm proved to be one of the busiest with more than two hundred designs in the first five years.

Early in their career Cope and Stewardson tried a variety of styles. They hoped to achieve neither elaborate originality nor banal duplication but the correct and honest application of past styles for modern needs. By their first major commission, Radnor Hall at Bryn Mawr College (1886), Cope and Stewardson had made a firm stylistic choice: English Collegiate Gothic. The modestly Gothic Radnor and subsequent Bryn Mawr works such as Pembroke, East and West, and Denbeigh Halls (1891) would have profound effect on American collegiate architecture. Cope and Stewardson were inspired by Gothic Oxford and Cambridge and thus used this English style to create Americanized collegiate cloisters. Cope married Eliza Middleton Kane in 1893 and settled in Germantown, where he remained for the rest of his life.

In 1895 the firm received an important commission for Princeton University. Blair Hall featured a large, arched tower and flanking dormitories. Contemporary architect Ralph Adams Cram said Blair was "sufficiently British, sufficiently American, a perfect model of sound design and impeccable theories." This was the last of the Cope and Stewardson commissions because John Stewardson accidentally drowned in January 1896. John's brother, Emlyn Lamar Stewardson, joined Cope's firm in 1897. Memorial tablets to Cope and both Stewardsons now reside at Blair Hall.

Other important Princeton commissions included Ivy Club (1897), Stafford Little Hall (1899), and the massive gymnasium (1903). At the University of Pennsylvania, the Cope and Stewardson firm designed the dormitory group, Little Quad and Big Quad (1895–1935), the Georgian-style Law School (1898–1910), and the early Romanesque-style Archeological Museum (1893–1902, completed in 1926 with Frank Miles Day and Wilson Eyre). Perhaps the finest of their collegiate commissions, however, was that of Washington University in St. Louis, Missouri. After winning the commission in 1899, the firm designed thirteen rich pink granite buildings in a tastefully restrained Tudor style. Included in this group is the well-regarded University Hall (1900, used in 1904 as the administration building of the Louisiana Purchase Exposition; later renamed Brookings Hall). Also designed by Cope were Busch and Cupples Halls (1900) and the Ridgeley Library (1902). The various structures were carefully composed to form a large quadrangle replete with gateway tower.

Cope also designed a number of noncollegiate works, and it was in them that his versatility in adapting various styles was most aptly demonstrated. After a trip to Spain in 1895, Cope designed the Pennsylvania State Institute for the Instruction of the Blind in Overbrook, Pennsylvania, in a Spanish Renaissance style. His Municipal Building in Washington, D.C. (completed in 1908), utilized the neoclassical style. In addition, Cope designed an elaborate Gothic chapel, the Lady Chapel of St. Mark's Church, Philadelphia, and a wide variety of domestic works in and around Philadelphia including the "Normandy," the stucco and stone Cassatt House in Rosemont, Pennsylvania (1901).

Cope was made a fellow of the American Institute of Architects in 1893; later he was appointed by the local Philadelphia chapter to chair a committee involved with the restoration of Independence Hall. Reflecting an abiding interest in preservation, Cope was active in restoring a number of local colonial works including Stenton (1722), an Early Georgian home in Germantown.

Cope's love of architecture seemed to stem from a boyhood delight in nature and a noticeable skill working with his hands. He was also accomplished at drawing; he had a precise eye for detail and form. Cope believed that an architect's primary function was to build rather than merely make architectural drawings. This put him squarely in the "hands-on" tradition of William Morris and John Ruskin. Wrote historian Fiske Kimball of Cope and Stewardson, "Their loving study of simple textures was to be perpetuated with richer forms by a whole school . . . and was ultimately, with the complete adoption of the style by Princeton and Yale, to have a wide influence in American universities, as well as in domestic building."

• For an example of Cope's own writing, see "The Relation of Natural to Artificial Beauty in Landscape," *Architectural Review* 9 (Oct. 1902): 270–72. The most complete study of Cope is William Emlyn Stewardson, "Cope and Stewardson" (master's thesis, Princeton Univ., 1960). See also Henry F. Withey, *Biographical Dictionary of American Architects* (1956), and contemporary references by Edgar V. Seeler, "Walter Cope, Architect," *Architecture Review* 9 (Oct. 1902): 289–300; Ralph Adams Cram, "The Work of Messrs. Cope and Stewardson," *Architectural Record* 16 (Oct. 1904): 407–38; Guy Study, "Washington University, St. Louis, Mo.," *Architectural Record* 37 (Jan. 1915): 64–75; and R. Clipston Sturgis, "Walter Cope, Architect," *Outlook* 73 (1903): 773–78. An obituary is in the *A. I. A. Quarterly Bulletin*, Dec. 1902.

ROD A. MILLER

COPELAND, Charles Townsend (27 Apr. 1860–24 July 1952), educator, was born in Calais, Maine, the son of Henry Clay Copeland, a lumber dealer, and Sarah Lowell. A small, shy lad, he attended Calais High School, where he edited and wrote for the school paper. He matriculated at Harvard College in 1878, was an editor of the Harvard *Advocate*, and graduated in 1882 with an A.B. He taught in a private boys' school in Englewood, New Jersey (1882–1883), attended Harvard Law School unhappily (1883–1884), and after a long vacation in Calais worked for a few months in 1885 as a book reviewer for the *Boston Advertiser*. Transferring to the *Boston Post*, he reviewed books and plays for it until 1892. He was usually respectful in discussing books by established authors, but he was also among the first critics to explain the greatness of Rudyard Kipling, Leo Tolstoy, and Ivan Turgenev to Americans. Although Copeland read assiduously, he had ample time to attend plays in Boston, in the course of which he saw stars such as Lawrence Barrett, Sarah Bernhardt, Dion Boucicault, Edwin Booth, Benoit Constant Coquelin, Joseph Jefferson, Fanny Kemble, Lily Langtry, Julia Marlowe, Helena Modjeska, Ada Rehan, and Tommaso Salvini.

In 1893 Copeland returned permanently to Harvard. At first he was an instructor in English A, a required freshman composition course. An eloquent public speaker and reader, he had a deep and resonant voice (early in adulthood he considered becoming an actor but gave up the idea because of his diminutive size). He partly satisfied his desire to be histrionic by giving voluntary lectures on some of his favorite authors to immensely pleased groups until 1896. Both before and after this, he regularly invited swarms of undergraduates to his dormitory rooms, where they listened to his delightful conversation and were encouraged to share their literary insights. Copeland edited *Letters of Thomas Carlyle to His Youngest Sister* (1899), wrote *Life of Edwin Booth* (1901), and coauthored, with Henry Milner Rideout, a friend from Calais and his former pupil, *Freshman English and Theme Correcting in Harvard College* (1901). Copeland's handling of Carlyle's letters was professionally acceptable and included a sound introduction. His biography of Booth, published as part of Mark Antony DeWolfe Howe's brief *Beacon Biographies*, was based on previously published sources but was rendered valuable by Copeland's informed love of the theater. The book on composition was initially a useful text for Copeland's freshman course, given its requirement of daily written essays; but its fame soon spread to campuses nationwide. His own English 12 was also a writing course, in which students prepared weekly 1,000-word compositions and read them to Copeland. Enrollment was limited to thirty students.

Copeland also taught lecture courses on Dr. Samuel Johnson and his contemporaries, Sir Walter Scott, English letter writers, and English Romantic poets. His classes became so popular that as many as 250 students often enrolled in a given course. In the 1905–1906 academic year Copeland felt that his popularity might be due to his lenient grading; so he surprisingly flunked more than half of one class. Since several seniors would immediately be ineligible to graduate, the administration persuaded him to relent.

Copeland's promotion to assistant professor was delayed until 1910 because Harvard president Charles William Eliot called him "unproductive." In 1917 he was promoted to associate professor. In 1925, when he was sixty-five years of age, he was appointed to the coveted position of Boylston Professor of Rhetoric and Oratory. He retired three years later, by which time he was acknowledged as a major professional influence on many students who had gone on or would go on to achieve greater recognition than "Copey" himself, as they dubbed their favorite teacher. His students in English 12 alone included J. Donald Adams, Conrad Aiken, Robert Benchley, Earl Derr Biggers, Van Wyck Brooks, Heywood Broun, Malcolm Cowley, Bernard DeVoto, John Dos Passos, T. S. Eliot, Norman Foerster, Granville Hicks, Oliver La Farge, Walter Lippmann, Haniel Long, Maxwell Evarts Perkins, John Reed, Kermit Roosevelt, Gilbert Seldes, and Robert Sherwood. The most eminent of Copeland's nearby Radcliffe College students, who took writing courses he conducted there for decades, were Rachel Lyman Field, Katherine Fullerton Gerould, and Helen Keller.

Most of his students idolized Copeland. In *The Story of My Life* (1902), Keller waxed ecstatic in describing her response to Copeland's presentation of the Old Testament. On the dedication page of his *Insurgent Mexico* (1914), John Reed named Copeland and wrote: "I never would have seen what I did see had it not been for your teaching me." Maxwell Perkins became his publisher. Some students, however, found both his method and his substance unappealing. They bridled at his emphasis on the beginning and the ending of composition elements, his hatred of long sentences—which he called "swag-bellied"—and his demand for journalistic vividness. Brooks, Dos Passos, and Eliot, for example, went on record as feeling that they had not profited from his classes, while Aiken was put off by what he regarded as Copeland's vanity and demand for adulation.

Copeland never became an outstanding biographer or critic. He devoted his limited physical energy to his teaching and informal, conversational tutoring. He always wrote by hand, slowly and with difficulty, and he was a habitual procrastinator. He spent a great deal of time enjoying food; he once rewrote Alexander Pope's "To err is human, to forgive divine" as "To eat is human, to digest divine," and he was too fond of alcohol, although he said he was a "drinkard" not a "drunkard." Being a lifelong bachelor, he lacked what might well have been a beneficial feminine influence for his professional betterment. In July 1920 he wrote Perkins that he preferred his teaching over anything else in life, that without such work he would be like "a stray cat." For years Perkins hoped that Copeland would write his memoirs, which, however, were forever postponed. Perkins did succeed in encouraging him to assemble, with Thurman Losson Hood, The

Copeland Reader: An Anthology of English Poetry and Prose (1927), a financially successful 1,687-page book of passages lending themselves to oral presentation; and *The Copeland Translations: Mainly in Prose from French, German, Italian and Russian* (1934). Dedicated to Perkins, this 1,080-page book was a financial failure. Copeland planned to follow it with a Greek anthology but delayed and abandoned the idea in 1937, pleading insomnia and tinnitus to Perkins.

In 1928 Copeland went abroad for the first and only time, making pilgrimages to various English and Scottish literary shrines. In 1930 more than 300 friends met at the Harvard Club of New York City to honor him. Beginning in 1931, at the suggestion of Harvard's dean of freshmen, Copeland welcomed to his dormitory quarters, and after 1932 to his Cambridge apartment, two or three especially recommended freshmen for a lively talk each week during the school year; only when well into his eighties did he abandon this pleasure. Until 1937 he rejoiced in attending annual meetings, held every spring in New York, of the Charles Townsend Copeland Association, which had been founded by devoted friends in 1906. His last years were marked by a diminution of mental acuity, and he died in a hospital in Waverly, Massachusetts. Granville Hicks summed up Copeland's contradictory nature by commenting on "his absurd dignity, his amusing poses, his pretended ferocity, and his ironic courtesy." The conclusion of J. Donald Adams that Copeland "left his imprint upon more lives in their budding period than any other American teacher of his time" is more deservedly admiring.

• Copeland's papers are in the archives of Harvard University and in its Houghton Library. Additional correspondence is in the Robert Silliman Hillyer Papers, Syracuse University Library, and the William Stanley Beaumont Papers, University of Virginia Library. J. Donald Adams, *Copey of Harvard: A Biography of Charles Townsend Copeland* (1960), is the most informative biography. Elizabeth Shepley Sergeant, "Charles Townsend Copeland," in her *Fire under the Andes: A Group of North American Portraits* (1927), pp. 125–41; Rollo Walter Brown, "'Copey,'" in his *Harvard Yard in the Golden Age* (1948), pp. 121–37; and David McCord, "Copey at Walpole," in his *In Sight of Sever: Essays from Harvard* (1963), pp. 3–7, all describe Copeland's ability to share his passion for literature with others. "Copey," *Time*, 17 Jan. 1927, discusses the respect accorded to Copeland by students and friends. Granville Hicks, *John Reed: The Making of a Revolutionary* (1937), and Robert A. Rosenstone, *Romantic Revolutionary: A Biography of John Reed* (1975), reveal Reed's admiration for Copeland. Kermit Vanderbilt, *American Literature and the Academy: The Roots, Growth, and Maturity of a Profession* (1986), denigrates Copeland for his meager classroom treatment of American writers. An obituary is in the *New York Times*, 25 July 1952.

ROBERT L. GALE

COPELAND, John Anthony, Jr. (15 Aug. 1834–16 Dec. 1859), abolitionist, was born free in Raleigh, North Carolina, the son of John Anthony Copeland, a carpenter and joiner emancipated in childhood at the death of his white owner-father, and a free-born mulatto, Delilah Evans, a domestic worker. In 1843, impelled by the increasing proscription of free blacks in North Carolina, the Copelands moved to abolitionist Oberlin, a key station on the underground railroad, in northern Ohio. Taking advantage of the exceptional egalitarianism, his parents acquired their own home and reared eight children. The eldest, Copeland attended the preparatory department of Oberlin College in 1854–1855 and pursued his father's trades. A newspaper editor in a neighboring town wrote that young Copeland was regarded as an "orderly and well-disposed citizen."

Regularly attending meetings of blacks in Oberlin to hear fugitive slaves narrate their histories, Copeland expressed "by the deep scowl of his countenance, the moist condition of his eyes and the quivering of his lips, how deeply he was moved," John Mercer Langston, a leading black townsman, recalled in his 1894 autobiography. In September 1858 news that slavecatchers had seized John Price, a Kentucky fugitive, galvanized the community. With rifle in hand, Copeland joined the throng of students and townspeople who surged into nearby Wellington, where Price's captors had taken him into a hotel to await the southbound train. At length, as an angry crowd of some five hundred demanded the fugitive's release, Copeland helped push through armed guards into the hotel where a small company of men wrested Price from the slavecatchers. Later, Copeland reportedly escorted Price to Canada. Copeland was among the thirty-seven men indicted (two of whom, Charles H. Langston and Simeon Bushnell, were convicted) for violating the Fugitive Slave Law in what became known as the Oberlin-Wellington Rescue Case. However, perhaps because his militancy in the rescue as well as his race rendered him particularly vulnerable to prosecution, Copeland refused to surrender.

The rescue intensified black militance and Copeland joined the Oberlin Anti-Slavery Society, part of a new statewide black organization. His fellow society member and kinsman by marriage, Lewis Sheridan Leary, a 24-year-old harnessmaker and an unindicted rescuer himself, exhorted: "Men must suffer for a good cause." In the autumn of 1859 when John Brown signaled his allies of his readiness to launch a direct assault on slavery, Leary, who had met Brown months before in Cleveland, persuaded Copeland to co-enlist. Copeland vowed "to assist in giving that freedom to at least a few of my poor and enslaved brethren who have been most foully and unjustly deprived of their liberty."

Copeland and Leary had barely reached Brown's hideout when he set his plan in motion. On the night of 16 October 1859, Brown led eighteen volunteers, the five black recruits among them, in an attack on the federal arsenal at Harpers Ferry, Virginia. Before midnight, Brown seized the rifle works, a major target, and left his white lieutenant John Henry Kagi and Copeland, later reinforced by Leary, to garrison it. The following afternoon, surrounded and under fierce attack by an overwhelming armed force, the three made a desperate effort to escape across the rapids of the Shenandoah River. Both Kagi and Leary were shot and mortally wounded. Discovered hiding behind jutting rocks in mid-river, Copeland surrendered and was taken into custody, narrowly escaping lynching through the intervention of a local physician.

White northern opinion of the raid was initially divided between Republicans who largely disavowed it and Democrats who pronounced it an abolitionist-Republican conspiracy. Federal marshal Matthew Johnson of Cleveland visited Copeland in jail and emerged with a purported "confession"—actually fabricated from letters found in Brown's hideout—that implicated in Brown's plot prominent figures connected with the Oberlin-Wellington case.

Copeland was convicted of murder and of inciting slaves to rebellion and, like the other captured raiders, was sentenced to death. But just as the imprisoned Brown's eloquence and stoicism helped to transform his own image from madman to Christian martyr, Copeland's conduct challenged racist assumptions of black inferiority. Even the presiding judge and the special prosecutor at his trial, both white Virginians, later would vouch for Copeland's courage and poise, with the latter adding intelligence as well. "There was a dignity to him that I could not help liking," the judge would confess. "He was always manly." The eulogy at a funeral service for Copeland in Oberlin on Christmas Day praised the Supreme Being for granting African Americans a "not less firm, heroic and Christlike champion" at Harpers Ferry than whites had in "the immortal John Brown." African Americans throughout the North applauded, in the words of the Ohio State Anti-Slavery Society, "the noble and Christ-like John Brown and his compatriots."

In poignant letters from prison Copeland urged family and friends to remember that his death was in a holy cause, asserting that he blamed no one for his fate and expressing confidence that history would vindicate his actions. Even though the raid had not succeeded in freeing the slaves, Copeland told his best friend, Elias Green, that it was "the prelude to that great event." Copeland died on the scaffold in Charlestown, Virginia. He never married and had no children.

• Several of Copeland's letters are in the executive papers on the Brown raid in the Virginia State Library and in the Oswald Garrison Villard Collection in the Columbia University Library. Copeland's career is treated in Benjamin Quarles, *Allies for Freedom: Blacks and John Brown* (1974), and William Cheek and Aimee Lee Cheek, *John Mercer Langston and the Fight for Black Freedom* (1989). See also John Mercer Langston, *From the Virginia Plantation to the National Capitol; or, The First and Only Negro Representative in Congress from the Old Dominion* (1894; repr. 1968); and for the Copeland family, William E. Biggleston, *They Stopped in Oberlin: Black Residents and Visitors of the Nineteenth Century* (1981). Of the vast literature on Brown and the raid on Harper's Ferry, one might start with Stephen B. Oates, *To Purge This Land with Blood: A Biography of John Brown* (1970; 2d ed., 1984).

WILLIAM CHEEK
AIMEE LEE CHEEK

COPELAND, Royal Samuel (7 Nov. 1868–17 June 1938), physician and U.S. senator, was born near Dexter, Michigan, the son of Roscoe Pulaski Copeland and Frances Jane Holmes, farmers. Young Copeland was educated in the public schools in the vicinity of Dexter and graduated from Michigan State Normal College at Ypsilanti. Following a brief stint of public school teaching, he attended and, in 1889, graduated from the Medical College, University of Michigan, Ann Arbor. Specializing in ophthalmology and ontology, he practiced medicine in Bay City, Michigan, from 1890 to 1895, leaving that practice to serve as professor at the Homeopathic Medical College at the University of Michigan from 1895 to 1908. Copeland exhibited certain political skills in his profession, rising to the presidency of the American Ophthalmological and Ontological Association. He extended his talents beyond his profession, becoming the Republican mayor of Ann Arbor, Michigan, in 1901 and president of its board of education. He was also active in the Methodist church, serving as a delegate to the Methodist Ecumenical Conference in London in 1900 and three times as a delegate to the Methodist General Conference. In 1908 he married Frances Spalding; they had two children.

Also in 1908 Copeland became dean of the Flower Hospital Medical College in New York City, continuing as a teacher and medical writer, specializing in ophthalmology. His reputation and his articulated experience in bureaucratic and electoral politics caused New York City Democratic mayor John F. Hylan to appoint him commissioner of public health, in which position he helped to double the city's milk consumption and to lower its infant mortality by 60 percent. His office was also credited with the city's relatively low death rate during the influenza epidemic of 1918. His tenure as public health commissioner was somewhat tarnished, however, by an investigation that charged him with permitting excessive influence of Tammany Hall, New York City's Democratic machine, over the department's policies and appointments.

In 1922 Copeland's political fortunes catapulted when Alfred E. Smith and William Randolph Hearst's factions of the state Democratic party selected him as a compromise candidate for U.S. senator from New York. The candidacy was ensured when Smith, running for reelection as governor, refused to accept Hearst as his running mate on the ticket. Copeland, having for some years been converted to the Democratic party, defeated the Republican incumbent, Senator William M. Calder. Copeland's rise to high office was largely attributed to his name recognition in New York City and to the inherent appeal of his rural upbringing, his religious commitment, and his conservative ideology to upstate New York. Although the Republican party in the 1920s survived the "Harding scandals," Copeland continued to ingratiate himself in both New York's upstate and downstate regions, achieving reelection in 1928.

After he became president in 1933, Franklin D. Roosevelt undoubtedly regretted that he had acquiesced in Copeland's Democratic nomination in 1922. Copeland vehemently opposed New Deal measures such as gold devaluation, Philippine Island independence, the St. Lawrence Seaway, Supreme Court reform, and executive branch reorganization. Like many political conservatives (Democrats and Republicans) Copeland seemed to support the New Deal only in its early phase and thereafter only for obvious political needs of his state, such as regulation of fuels and some National Labor Relations Board activity. In 1936, at a New York City anniversary celebration of both the writing of the Declaration of Independence and the founding of Tammany Hall, Senator Copeland stunningly rebuked President Roosevelt, noting that "the inhabitants of the world are living in an atmosphere of dictatorships, remarkable political doctrines and strong economic theories." He questioningly mused, "What would be the attitude of the American people today if one in authority presumed to repeat the acts performed by [the] . . . despot [George III]?" He then listed such "despotic" Rooseveltean acts as making judges dependent on his will alone; erecting a multitude of new offices; taxing the wealth "without consent"; drastically altering the form of government; and investing himself "with power to legislate for use in all cases whatsoever." Copeland concluded, "A prince, whose character is thus marked by every act which may define a tyrant, is unfit to be a ruler of a free people."

Roosevelt reciprocated Copeland's loathing, withholding support from the New York senator's legislative monument, the Copeland-Lea Food, Drug, and Cosmetic Act of 1938. Ironically, the law's tortuous journey from its 1933 introduction to the 1938 enactment epitomized the New Deal's transition to its 1935–1938 "reform" stage. Copeland worked unremittingly for reform in the control of cosmetics and drugs, particularly with regard to regulation of pesticides, color additives, animal drugs, infant formulas, and hazardous substances. He also sought protection against "fake" therapeutic devices, more precise identification of food standards, and increased criminal penalties for violations. It was the nation's first important food and drug legislation since the Wiley Act of 1906, and although amended in years after its passage, the Copeland-Lea Act stood as the principal foundation for federal legislation of the drug industry for over a half-century. Copeland's arduous effort in achieving the bill's passage took its physical toll, with a "general circulatory collapse by a kidney ailment." The senator died in Washington, D.C.

• Some of Copeland's papers are in the Michigan Historical Collection, University of Michigan, Ann Arbor, as well as in sections of the John F. Hylan Papers in the New York Public Library. Copeland coauthored a textbook, *Refraction* (1906), and wrote the *Healthbook* (1924), *Dr. Copeland's Home Medical Book* (1934), and several articles. Of course, the *Congressional Record* is important for his years of U.S. Senate service. The *New York Times* covered well his service as New York

City commissioner of public health and as U.S. senator, the latter of which is also covered by the *Washington Post*. For specific coverage of Copeland's stunning rebuke of Roosevelt, see the *New York Times*, 5 July 1936. For a general discussion of Copeland-Roosevelt relations, see Frank Freidel, *Franklin D. Roosevelt: The Ordeal* (1954) and *The Triumph* (1956); and Alfred B. Rollins, *Roosevelt and Howe* (1956). For information on Copeland and the 1938 Food, Drug, and Cosmetic Act, see "Food, Drugs, and Cosmetics," *New Republic*, 20 July 1938, p. 290, and Henry Wallace [radio address], "The Food, Drug, and Cosmetic Act," *Scientific American*, Nov. 1938, pp. 227–28.

MARTIN L. FAUSOLD

COPLAND, Aaron (14 Nov. 1900–2 Dec. 1990), composer, was born in Brooklyn, New York, the son of Russian Jewish immigrants. His mother, Sarah Mittenthall, and father, Harris Morris Copland, were shopkeepers and had little background in music. Indeed, Copland recalled that when he wanted to take piano lessons "my parents were of a mind that enough money had been invested in the musical training of four older children with meager results and had no intention of squandering further funds on me." His parents relented, however, and Copland began his musical studies, starting piano lessons at age seven. While his pianistic talents were fine, Copland also developed an interest in piano improvisation, a proclivity that, as a teenager, led him into composition.

During his late teens Copland wrote several clever, entertaining works for piano. Although little in these early pieces compared with the innovative styles and harmonies then gaining currency, Copland still succeeded in upsetting his teachers with the harmonic modernity of his music. In 1920, sensing a camaraderie with the artistic avant-garde, and with the opportunity present for travel after the war, Copland went to study in Paris. Outside Paris, in Fontainebleau, Copland met Nadia Boulanger, one of the greatest teachers of musical composition of her day. Copland was her first great pupil. During his studies Copland met such other young artists as Virgil Thomson, Serge Prokofiev, and Igor Stravinsky. Many more Americans followed to Paris where they made up an informal American school of composers who wanted to develop an identifiably American style of musical composition. Copland was its leading figure.

Copland and most of his American colleagues never became part of the circle of Paris expatriates, but, like many of them, he went to Europe and discovered America. As he considered his hope for the development of an identifiably American concert music, he reflected that American popular music—ragtime, blues, and jazz—was already known. Despite subsequent politically based images to the contrary, jazz and other such traditions were not marginalized among the musically literate. Within musical circles of the United States and Europe, artists were well aware of and genuinely enthusiastic about jazz and blues. Ragtime was not only known, it was already passé. Knowing these popular genres, Copland and his colleagues were seeking something more. Copland wanted to weave American musical traditions into a more broadly based language of formal composition. Such appearances of identifiably American fragments in his early compositions had been one of the features that disturbed his teachers back in Brooklyn. But among the Parisians he found people who were fascinated by an American culture that seemed fresh and somewhat exotic, and in Boulanger Copland had a teacher who responded to the incorporation of such materials with encouraging objectivity. She helped Copland discover and develop his own compositional voice. Under Boulanger, Copland also gained greater mastery of the more complex techniques of the craft of composition. Over the next ten years he produced a variety of pieces that were, in differing combinations, technically erudite, thematically popular, and acerbically avant-garde.

Some of the more famous pieces of this phase of Copland's career included *Music for the Theatre* (1925), in which he wove blues and Broadway-style dance themes into a symphonic setting; the jazzy Piano Concerto (1926); *Vitebsk* (1929), an ensemble work in which Copland explored Jewish melodic fragments, one of the few Copland works reflecting his religious background; and a Concerto for Organ and Orchestra (1924). At the premier of the Organ Concerto, conductor Walter Damrosch, fearing that the work's challenging, dissonant harmonies had offended some of the audience, proclaimed from the podium: "If a young man at age twenty-three can write a symphony like that, in five years he will be ready to commit murder." Throughout the decade of the 1920s Copland indeed enjoyed the status of avant-gardist and the parrying that went on between artists, critics, and audiences. As his fame grew, he helped promote modern styles and sponsored concerts for his own and other contemporary works. Copland was disturbed by the knee-jerk conservatism of some of the critics. Sensing a need for a more objective forum, an innovative critic, Minna Lederman, created a new journal, *Modern Music*. There, serious aesthetic issues were discussed without ad hominem rhetoric. Copland's contributions to this journal lent greatly to its prestige. Along similar lines, in 1927 Copland joined with his brilliant colleague Roger Sessions to organize and finance the Copland-Sessions Concerts, a series devoted exclusively to recent compositions.

When the depression came the exchange between the avant-garde and the bourgeois audiences lost much of its earlier fun and frivolity. In the new climate of the early 1930s, Copland turned to the left aesthetically and to some degree politically. Here he wrote some of his most aggressively avant-garde music, such as the bare and clangorous *Piano Variations* (1930); he also wrote some songs "for the masses," such as "Workers Sing!" and "Into the Streets, May First!" This leftist turn led Copland into no revolutionary action, far from it. Nevertheless, in the early 1950s the specter of such a political flirtation in Copland's past led to a cancellation of a performance of some of his music at the first inauguration of Dwight D. Eisenhower. Like many, Copland shifted away from the doctrinaire left when the New Deal portended a unifying national solution to the dilemma of the age, and he became very much an FDR Democrat. This political mainstreaming had an aesthetic counterpoint in Copland. He commented that he felt "an increasing dissatisfaction with the relations of the music-loving public and the living composer. . . . It seemed to me that we composers were in danger of working in a vacuum. . . . I felt that it was worth the effort to see if I couldn't say what I had to say in the simplest possible terms."

As Copland was seeking to speak to a broad national audience, he embarked upon an era of writing that produced his most famous works: *El Salon Mexico* (1936), *Billy the Kid* (1938), *Rodeo* (1942), and *Appalachian Spring* (1944). Whether it was the snap of Latin rhythms in *El Salon*, the slappy, down-home amble of cowboy tunes in *Billy* and *Rodeo*, or the serene, simple melodies of the Pennsylvania Shakers in *Appalachian Spring*, in these masterpieces Copland displayed his uncanny knack for integrating a particular musical style into his own highly personal yet altogether accessible musical language. Melodic lines always unfold gently in Copland. Their entirety only become apparent as the pieces progress, lending a sense of gradual development, evocative of the self-image of a growing country. It is like watching an old fisherman who, with each cast, calmly tosses his line out just a bit further, until at last the length seems just right. The particular flair for rhythm Copland displayed was also key in making the works immensely successful as ballets. Indeed Copland's work with Martha Graham in these pieces marks one of the greatest collaborations in the history of American art. Testimony to his broader melodic as well as rhythmic and instrumental gifts, the works remain even more popular as orchestral suites in the concert and recording literature. With these pieces, Copland gained the recognition of being the greatest of American composers—"the best we have," as composer and critic Virgil Thomson reflected. During the years of the New Deal and World War II Copland extended this musical Americana for which he was renowned with stirring patriotic pieces like *A Lincoln Portrait* and *Fanfare for the Common Man* (both 1942). He also wrote music for Hollywood, composing scores that accompanied such important films as *Of Mice and Men* (1939), *Our Town* (1940), and *The Red Pony* (1949). His music for the movie *The Heiress* won Copland an Oscar in 1949. Copland's many contributions to American culture earned him a Pulitzer Prize in 1945.

Copland's place as *the* American composer was secure by the end of the war, yet he had lived but half of his long life. For the rest he continued to write, generally in the leaner textures and more modern harmonic languages that he had used earlier in his career. None of the pieces he wrote after 1945 gained the acclaim of his orchestral scores and ballets of the late 1930s and early 1940s. Many sympathetic critics and conductors lamented this, but Copland never appeared to be bothered. He continued to write as he wished and to provide support to young talent. For decades he was a

fixture at the summer festivals at Berkshire and Tanglewood. Here he recognized and helped guide the budding talents of many rising musical stars, notably Lukas Foss and Leonard Bernstein, and he championed the music of such neglected American masters as Charles Ives. Of his first meeting with Copland, Bernstein recalled that he had expected some sort of stern, Whitmanesque figure but found instead a highly approachable, almost giggly soul, utterly without pretension. Copland could indeed be disarmingly down-to-earth with most who approached him. He would never suffer fools, but he nurtured any sincere talent with whom he was in contact. This spirit stimulated success in parallel careers for Copland in conducting and guest teaching, notably at Harvard as well as at Berkshire and Tanglewood. He also wrote several important books on music, his *Music and Imagination* (1952) becoming a virtual classic for all music students. He continued to teach and conduct in his late years after he had reached the end of his composing career. An upbeat spirit to the end, he died in North Tarrytown, New York, at the age of ninety, very much his country's chief musical figure of the century his life had spanned.

• Copland's own writings are numerous and provide insights not only into his own music but also into the world of music and the arts that surrounded him: *Copland on Music* (1960), *The New Music* (1968), and *What to Listen for in Music* (1939). Copland assisted scholar Vivian Perlis with two volumes, *Copland, 1900–1942* (1987) and *Copland since 1943* (1990); these are the most encyclopedic works on the composer and the best works particularly on the music and life of the latter part of his career. There is a number of biographies of Copland. The first, published in Chile, is Juan Orrego Salas, *Aaron Copland* (1947). Though the work is obscure to many American audiences, it is also quite thorough, and it is further indicative of the appeal of the composer beyond American shores. Three relatively early works that remain well regarded are Arthur Berger, *Aaron Copland* (1953); Arnold Dobrin, *Aaron Copland, His Life and Times* (1967); and Julia Smith, *Aaron Copland, His Work and Contribution to American Music* (1955). Three other insightful monographs on Copland's life and work are Neil Butterworth, *The Music of Aaron Copland* (1986); Catherine Peare, *Aaron Copland, His Life* (1969); and JoAnn Skowronski, *Aaron Copland* (1985). Two works of broader historical and musical focus that provide useful and interesting chapters on aspects of Copland's music are Alan Levy, *Musical Nationalism* (1983), and Wilfred Mellers, *Music in a New Found Land* (1964). Composer Roger Sessions, *Reflections on the Musical Life in the United States* (1956), and Virgil Thomson, *American Music since 1910* (1970), also give other artists' insights into the major musical figures of the century, including extensive and lucid treatments of Copland. An excellent and lengthy obituary is in the *New York Times*, 3 Dec. 1990.

ALAN LEVY

COPLEY, Ira Clifton (25 Oct. 1864–2 Nov. 1947), newspaper publisher, congressman, public utilities executive, and philanthropist, was born in Copley Township, Knox County, Illinois, the son of Ira Birdsall Copley and Ellen Madeline Whiting, farmers. When Copley was two he was struck with scarlet fever, which left him blind. When he was three, the family moved to Aurora, Illinois, where he received treatment for his eyes. Even with the care of an eye specialist, his complete blindness lasted five years. With the move to Aurora, his father and his mother's brother assumed ownership of the Aurora Illinois Gas Light Company, the beginning of a large utility company that Ira would one day manage.

The eye care Copley received began to help. When he was seven his eyesight returned; however, two episodes of snow blindness resulted in injured vision. Overcoming his handicap, he graduated from West Aurora High School in 1881 and received a bachelor of arts from Yale University in 1887. He studied law at Union College in Chicago but withdrew to assume management of his family's utility company on 2 February 1889. He received an LL.B. from Union in 1889. He was admitted to the Illinois bar shortly thereafter but never practiced law.

In 1892 Copley married Edith Strohn; they had three children, all of whom died in infancy. They adopted two boys. In 1929 Edith Copley died from complications related to surgery for a sinus infection. In 1931 Copley married Chloe Davidson Worley in Paris, France.

While managing the utility company, Copley enlarged the Aurora plant and in 1894 acquired the Joliet, Illinois, Gas Company. The primary business was marketing gas as a fuel. In 1900 he organized the La Grange Gas Company to sell service along the Burlington, North Western, and Milwaukee railroads in Illinois. In 1902 he acquired the competing Aurora Electric Light & Power Company, consolidating all of these enterprises under the name of Western United Gas & Electric Company in 1905. He later started or acquired a steam heating company, two electric plants, a coal product company, a coke oven, three coal mines, and streetcar lines.

Copley purchased the *Aurora Beacon* on 1 December 1905 and the competing paper in 1912 to create the *Aurora Beacon-News*. From this foundation he built a newspaper chain that would eventually own eleven dailies in California and Illinois, eighteen weeklies in Illinois, and seventeen weeklies in California. He acquired the *Elgin* (Ill.) *Daily Courier-News* in 1909; he purchased the *Joliet* (Ill.) *Herald* in 1913 and the *Joliet* (Ill.) *News* in 1915 to create the *Joliet News-Herald*.

Copley entered politics at a young age, serving as a member of the Illinois State Republican League from 1895 to 1898 and as president of the Illinois League of Republican Clubs. He was state park commissioner from 1894 to 1898 and was a member of a commission to build a new state penitentiary from 1905 to 1922.

In 1910 Copley was elected to the U.S. Congress from the Eleventh Illinois District. He was implicated by a competing press in the Lorimer scandal, in which William Lorimer was accused and later found guilty of being elected to the U.S. Senate by corrupt means. Copley was found not to be involved in the scandal, but he was involved in the defeat of Lorimer's opponent, Albert J. Hopkins, using his newspapers to speak out against Hopkins. Copley served six consecutive terms from 1911 to 1923.

In the Sixty-second Congress Copley was a member of the Building and Grounds Committee; in the Sixty-third he was on the Post Office and Post Roads Committee and the Industrial Arts and Expositions Committee; in the Sixty-fourth he served on the Post Office Committee; and in the Sixty-sixth and Sixty-seventh Congresses he was a member of the House Ways and Means Committee. During his service in Congress he sponsored several pieces of legislation primarily related to labor. He contributed significantly to income tax revisions based on a graduated scale according to individual incomes, and he opposed taxes on excess profits. Supporting pensions for mothers, he sponsored the first attempt to prohibit child labor, which was defeated.

In 1920 Copley made up his mind to run for Congress one more time in 1922. He had no political organization and decided to run on the merits of his record. Copley was aware of a general dissatisfaction in farming communities over falling agricultural prices and a beginning resentment of Prohibition. He lost his reelection attempt.

In 1926 Copley sold his utility interests and began his expansion of a newspaper chain. He acquired the *Illinois State Journal* in Springfield in 1928; the *San Diego Union* and *San Diego Tribune* in 1928; and the *Illinois State Register* in Springfield in 1942. In 1928 he bought a newspaper chain in southern California from Frederick W. Kellogg, who between 1920 and 1928 had built a small chain of papers: *Alhambra Post-Advocate, Culver City Star-News, Glendale Press, Hollywood News, Pasadena Post, Redondo Beach Daily Breeze, San Pedro News, Santa Monica Outlook*, and *Venice Vanguard*. Copley newspapers ranked among the top twenty chains in number of newspapers owned, but the primary presence of the chain was felt in Illinois and southern California. He also invested in radio, acquiring a 50 percent interest in WCVS in Springfield in 1937 and in KUSN in San Diego in 1947.

Copley maintained various homes in Aurora, Illinois; Washington, D.C.; and San Diego. Between 1927 and 1942 he spent considerable time on his yacht, *Happy Days*. After the outbreak of World War II, the yacht was sold to the U.S. Navy for use as a training ship and later as a weather ship.

Copley's philanthropic activities included underwriting the building of the Galena Street Home for Children in Aurora, Illinois, and the Aurora Juvenile Protective Association, making it possible for many young men to obtain higher educations through a loan program. After his first wife's death, he bequeathed land and an endowment for a hospital in Aurora. Because of the generous gift, the name of the hospital was changed to Copley Hospital. He also contributed to the Wilmer Ophthalmological Institute in Baltimore, Maryland.

Copley died in Copley Hospital, Aurora, Illinois. He left a lasting legacy in journalism in Illinois and southern California. His utility companies helped promote the growth of industry in Aurora and neighboring communities.

• Sources on Copley include Walter S. J. Swanson, *The Thin Gold Watch: A Personal History of the Newspaper Copleys* (1964); *The Copley Press* (1953); and an obituary in *Editor & Publisher*, 11 Nov. 1947.

EDWARD E. ADAMS

COPLEY, John Singleton (3 July 1738–9 Sept. 1815), painter, was born in Boston, Massachusetts, the son of Irish immigrants Richard Copley and Mary Singleton, tobacconists. Copley's early interest in art received stimulation from his stepfather, Peter Pelham, a successful London mezzotint engraver, whom Mary Copley married in 1748, following the death of her first husband. After Pelham's death in 1751, Copley soon adopted his stepfather's career as a mezzotint engraver, publishing his first portrait, *Reverend William Welsteed* (1753; Museum of Fine Arts, Boston), in his early teens. Copley, however, had the higher artistic ambition of becoming a history painter. To achieve this end, he painted copies of engravings of history paintings on mythological themes, notably *Galatea* (c. 1754; Museum of Fine Arts, Boston), *The Return of Neptune* (c. 1754; Metropolitan Museum of Art), and *The Forge of Vulcan* (c. 1754; private collection), and avidly studied theoretical and anatomical treatises. But history paintings, the highest genre of painting an artist could practice according to contemporary academic orthodoxy, held little interest to patrons in the prerevolutionary colonies, so Copley focused his talents on painting "likenesses," early on attempting complex multiple figural groupings such as *The Brothers and Sisters of Christopher Gore* (c. 1755; Winterthur Museum) and *Mary and Elizabeth Royall* (c. 1758; Museum of Fine Arts, Boston).

In colonial Boston, Copley grew up within a relatively thriving art community. But by the mid-1750s John Smibert and Robert Feke had died, John Greenwood had moved from Boston, and Joseph Badger's mediocre talent posed no threat to Copley's precocity. Only Joseph Blackburn, painting in Boston in the mid-1750s, offered much competition. He had the greatest influence on Copley's emerging portrait style, providing him with firsthand knowledge of the rococo manner in English portraiture.

Copley's colonial portraits demonstrate his preference for bold color and dramatic chiaroscuro. The veneer of elegance in Copley's portraits, whose sitters projected an individual, animated character and whose features were convincingly modeled, assured Copley's popularity among the colonial elite he mostly served. Combining the props, costumes, and settings of eighteenth-century mezzotints of English aristocratic portraits with sensitive psychological studies of his sitters and carefully observed details, Copley soon emerged as the most distinguished artistic talent of the American colonies.

Copley avoided the quality of sameness that often appeared throughout the careers of many colonial American portraitists. For example, his portrait of *Epes Sargent* (1759–1761; National Gallery of Art, Washington, D.C.), with its simplified setting and restrained color combined with the sitter's piercing gaze and swollen hand, presents a poignant picture of age. Other portraits, such as *John Bours* (1758–1761; Worcester Art Museum), picture a casually posed, brooding sitter of melancholic temperament. Copley portrayed *Mrs. Samuel Quincy (Hannah Hill)* (c. 1761; Museum of Fine Arts, Boston) in fancy dress reminiscent of Peter Paul Rubens's portrait of Helena Fourment (c. 1620). Copley also worked in a variety of media and sizes, producing portrait miniatures in oil on copper as early as 1755 and in watercolor on ivory beginning around 1762. He solicited the advice of Jean-Etienne Liotard, and though no evidence survives that suggests the noted Swiss pastelist responded, Copley nonetheless quickly mastered the pastel medium, in which he worked for about ten years, beginning in 1763.

In the early to mid-1760s Copley continued to show his preference for bold color directly applied to a primed canvas, dramatic contrasts of light and dark, and attention to minute detail, but he did so with increasingly flamboyant settings and props. Copley's aptitude for conveying the luster of pearls, the transparency of organza, the sheen of satin, the metallic quality of gold braid or brass tacks on a settee, and the polished surface of a mahogany chair appealed to the largely mercantile and upwardly mobile class he served in Boston. Copley's ability to portray a convincing likeness was perceived by his contemporaries as extraordinary. One wrote in 1764 that Copley's portrait of a father befuddled his one-year-old son, who "sprung to it [the portrait], roared, and schriched, and attempted gripping the hand . . . and when any of us askt him for Papa, he always turned and pointed to the Picture" (Copley-Pelham Letters).

In 1766 Copley-Pelham submitted to the Society of Artists exhibition in London *Boy with a Squirrel* (1765; Museum of Fine Arts, Boston), a pensive portrait of his half brother. The painting earned him election to the Society of Artists. His London debut evinced encouraging comments from Joshua Reynolds and Benjamin West. Both recognized his superior talent and noted that, with academic training abroad, he could develop into one of the "first Painters in the World" (Copley-Pelham Letters). Reynolds, in particular, expressed a concern that "working in [his] little way at Boston" might corrupt his talent, a concern about cultural inferiority that Copley himself had expressed.

Copley recognized that academic training abroad was vital if he were to achieve international stature, and yet he remained in Boston. In 1767 he submitted *Young Lady with a Bird and Dog* (1767; Toledo Museum of Art) to the Society of Artists in London to lesser acclaim. This time, both Reynolds and West were firm in their opinion that Copley would not improve without wide exposure to the European Old Masters. Copley still remained in Boston, however, where he continued to paint Boston and New England merchants, lawyers, clergymen, and artisans, such as Paul Revere (1768; Museum of Fine Arts, Boston). Copley's rising fortune in the colonies, his sense of duty to his family, and his uncertainty about the possibilities for success in London prevented him from risking study abroad until a later date.

Of humble origins, Copley soon demonstrated that his financial and social positions were rising. He felt that his lucrative portrait practice earned him "as much as if I were a Raphael or a Correggio" (Allan Cunningham, *The Lives of the Most Eminent British Painters and Sculptors*, vol. 4 [1868], p. 140). In 1769 he married Susanna Farnham Clarke, the daughter of two wealthy merchant families, the Winslows and Clarkes; the Copleys eventually had six children, three of whom survived childhood. That same year, Copley acquired property on Beacon Hill, where he lived virtually next door to one of his sitters, John Hancock, among the richest men in the colonies.

Copley spent seven months in New York, where he painted, by his own estimate, about thirty-seven portraits. Relinquishing the exuberance of earlier portraits, Copley now preferred to portray figures emerging from dark backgrounds with greater value contrasts and more somber tones. The reduction in the number or size of props and the virtual elimination of landscapes in favor of dark, monochromatic backgrounds heightened the psychological qualities of the sitter in pictures of this period. In New York Copley painted a number of fine works, including *Mrs. Thomas Gage (Margaret Kemble)* (1771; Timken Art Gallery, San Diego), which he described as "beyond Compare the best Lady's portrait I ever Drew" (Copley-Pelham Letters).

After his return to Boston, Copley planned to travel abroad and wrote letters to West and Reynolds soliciting their advice. Given the political turmoil of Boston, which ultimately culminated in the American Revolution, Copley found it increasingly difficult to retain the neutral stance that would allow his portrait trade to continue. Furthermore, his relationship to the Clarkes, whose firm was one of the consignees of the tea eventually dumped in Boston Harbor, guaranteed an atmosphere inhospitable to his line of work, which, by this time, numbered more than three hundred portraits of varying sizes from miniature to full-length. In June 1774 Copley left his family behind and embarked for England.

Arriving in London in July, Copley met both West and Reynolds, who provided entrée to artistic and social circles in London. He traveled in August to Rome by way of Paris and commented on architecture, painting, and sculpture in long letters to his family and friends in Boston and in London that suggest his artistic experience was a "luxury in *seeing*" (Amory, pp. 51–52). In Rome, Copley painted *The Ascension* (1775; Museum of Fine Arts, Boston), his first original history painting, and other works such as a double portrait of *Mr. and Mrs. Ralph Izard (Alice Delancey)* (1775; Museum of Fine Arts, Boston) posed in front of the Colosseum and other popular monuments of the

Grand Tour. Other pictures on religious and mythological themes as well as portraits soon followed on his return to London, where, in October 1775, he joined his wife, father-in-law, and children.

In London, Copley was only one among several superior talents. With astonishing speed he learned how to compose pictures by making numerous preparatory drawings, to square his drawings for transfer to a much larger scale than he had ever worked before, and to absorb the English and Continental method of applying multiple layers of transparent glazes. Beginning in 1776 his entries to the Royal Academy exhibitions brought increased attention to his abilities. He announced his civility and cultural sophistication in the over seven-foot-long portrait of *The Copley Family*, the first and only time he publicly displayed an image of himself (1776–1777; National Gallery of Art, Washington, D.C.). The following year, he presented an even larger and grander family portrait, *Sir William Pepperell and His Family* (1778; North Carolina Museum of Art, Raleigh), and *Watson and the Shark* (1778; National Gallery of Art, Washington, D.C.), the painting that brought Copley the fame he had long craved. Critics and patrons responded to Copley's twist on the large-scale contemporary history paintings made popular by Benjamin West. In *Watson*, Copley challenged the accepted norms of the genre by elevating an ordinary boy's terrifying experience to a realm normally reserved for heroes of exceptional stature and model virtue. The Royal Academy of Arts elected him to full membership in 1779. (He delayed in submitting his diploma picture, *The Tribute Money* [1782; Royal Academy of Arts, London], until 1782, at which point he was promoted to academician.)

At the same time that Copley produced distinguished portraits of American Loyalists, British military figures, and English gentry in a looser, broader manner than in his American career, such as *Admiral Clark Gayton, Admiral of the White* (1779; National Maritime Museum, Greenwich) and his wife, *Mrs. Clark Gayton* (1779; Detroit Institute of Arts), and *Major Hugh Montgomerie, Later Twelfth Earl of Eglinton* (1780; Los Angeles County Museum of Art), he also continued to paint contemporary histories with daring innovations that altered the course of the field. Copley again stretched the limits of contemporary history painting, this time by combining historical event with portraiture in *The Death of the Earl of Chatham* (1781; Tate Gallery, London, on loan to the National Portrait Gallery, London). Here, Copley introduced the novel approach of presenting more than fifty life portraits of lords in dramatic arrangements surrounding the dying hero. Moreover, Copley became the first artist in England to stage a one-picture exhibition, exhibiting *Chatham* not at the Royal Academy but concurrently with that annual exhibition in a rented space where he charged the public a fee and solicited a subscription of the print to be made after the painting. Copley's entrepreneurial spirit, which merged elements of the popular public spectacle with fine art, offended some Academy members. Copley also broke new ground by using the portraits of the lords in *Chatham* as models for later portraits such that the individual pose and expression of a figure in *Chatham* differed little from the later portrait of the same sitter.

In 1784 Copley completed another contemporary history picture, *The Death of Major Peirson, 6 January 1781* (Tate Gallery, London), a major triumph and widely considered the masterpiece of his career. It describes a highly mythologized version of a battle fought three years before between the British and the French on the Isle of Jersey. A dramatic image of death and revenge in the midst of battle, Copley's painting (again displayed in rented rooms to a paying public) earned accolades from the critics. Abigail Adams wrote that she had never seen

painting more expressive than this. I looked upon it until I was faint; you can scarcely believe but you hear the groans of the sergeant, who is wounded, and holding the handkerchief to his side, whilst the blood streams over his hand. (*Letters of Mrs. Adams, the Wife of John Adams*, vol. 2, 3d ed. [1841], pp. 31–32)

Copley even attracted the attention of King George III, who allowed the artist to paint his youngest daughters. *The Three Youngest Daughters of George III* (1785; Collection of Her Majesty Queen Elizabeth II) marked the closest Copley would come to a royal commission. He exhibited a conversation piece similar in spirit but not style in the Royal Academy the following year, *The Sitwell Children* (1786; Sir Reresby Sitwell, Renishaw Hall, Derbyshire), which, as before, attracted hostile reviewers. Copley's playful family portraits did not gain the critical supporters he had for his history paintings.

For the next five years, Copley focused increasingly on *The Siege of Gibraltar* (1791; Guildhall Art Gallery, London), the most important commission of his career as well as the largest, measuring about eighteen by twenty-five feet. Commissioned by the Corporation of the City of London in 1783, *Gibraltar* pictures the British victory over the Spanish and French. Eventually exhibited in 1791 under an enormous tent constructed in Green Park, Copley's eight-year effort, a project that had taken him to Hannover to make studies of the German officers and had involved him in difficult negotiations with the city of London, earned him only the mildest acclaim. According to the artist, however, 60,000 visitors attended the exhibition.

Other pictures of historic English events and religious stories followed, among them *Charles I Demanding in the House of Commons the Five Impeached Members* (1795; Boston Public Library), *Monmouth Before James II Refusing to Give the Names of His Accomplices* (c. 1795, unfinished; Fogg Art Museum, Cambridge, Mass.), *Abraham Offering Up His Son Isaac* (before 1791–1798; unlocated), and *Saul Reproved by Samuel* (1798; Museum of Fine Arts, Boston). None, however, rivaled in composition or innovation his earlier forays in the genre until *The Victory of Lord Duncan* (1799; Camperdown Trustees, Camperdown House and Estate, Dundee), which celebrates a British victo-

ry against the Dutch. As in his previous history pictures, Copley assumed the role of scholar, researching verbal and visual accounts of the battle in order to convey the facts of a dramatic event as correctly as possible. The picture went on view under a tent constructed for the event but attracted only a modest crowd and moderate critical favor. The brochure accompanying the exhibition expressed Copley's beliefs about history painting:

The introduction of portraits in works of this nature must infinitely enhance their value, as well to the present age as to posterity. And here, perhaps, posterity may be mentioned without presumption, since, whatever are the merits of the artist, a painting which records so glorious and splendid an event can never be neglected or forgotten.

Between 1787 and 1796 Copley exhibited only one picture at the Royal Academy, *The Red Cross Knight* (1793; National Gallery of Art, Washington, D.C.), a scene from Edmund Spenser's *Faerie Queene* in which his children posed in the leading roles. But from 1796 to 1812 he faithfully submitted pictures to the academy exhibitions. After *Duncan*, Copley focused on a series of portrait commissions, one of whose complexity and difficult patronage circumstances led to Copley's increasingly weakening reputation. *The Knatchbull Family* (1803; painting cut down), a family portrait once measuring about eleven by seventeen feet, was to include not only the large family but the two former Lady Knatchbulls. Copley was prevented by the owner from showing the picture in the Royal Academy exhibition of 1803; Lord Knatchbull may have heard unfavorable remarks regarding Copley's portrayal of his former wives pictured among angels.

Bitter disputes between Copley and President West about the Royal Academy's power structure as well as petty academy rules alienated the former friends. Copley's failing health and eyesight and erratic behavior won him few supporters. He continued to paint, however, embarking on notable pictures such as an equestrian portrait of *George IV as Prince of Wales* (1810; Museum of Fine Arts, Boston). Often described as bitter and frustrated in his later years by financial difficulties and a waning reputation, Copley died at his home in George Street, London.

Copley was the unrivaled portraitist of the American colonies for almost twenty-five years; his artistic vision, technical mastery, and high ambitions set a standard for the encouragement and development of the arts of North America. Once abroad, Copley negotiated successfully the competitive art market of eighteenth-century London, helping to shape the popularity of contemporary history paintings of heroic deaths and British military victories. His achievements in history painting in his forty-year career in England, which included novel changes in subject matter, composition, and display, were absorbed and disseminated by French artists such as Jacques-Louis David and Théodore Géricault and by the American artist John Trumbull, who advanced the field of history painting in what was a historically indifferent artistic climate for any genre of painting other than portraiture.

• The papers of John Singleton Copley are in the Public Records Office, London. The 1914 Massachusetts Historical Society publication edited by Guernsey Jones, *Letters and Papers of John Singleton Copley and Henry Pelham, 1739–1776*, offers the most accessible edited version of the London holdings. Copley's first extensive biography, *Domestic and Artistic Life of John Singleton Copley* (1882), was written by the artist's granddaughter, Martha Babcock Amory, and includes an anecdotal history of the artist's son, John Copley, Jr., Lord Lyndhurst. The most comprehensive monograph and catalog raisonné remains Jules David Prown, *John Singleton Copley* (2 vols., published for the National Gallery of Art; 1966). Two recent exhibition catalogs offer new information on and interpretations of the artist and his career: Carrie Rebora et al., *John Singleton Copley in America* (Metropolitan Museum of Art; 1995), and Emily Ballew Neff, *John Singleton Copley in England* (Museum of Fine Arts, Houston; 1995).

EMILY BALLEW NEFF

COPLEY, Lionel (1648–9 Sept. 1693), first royal governor of Maryland, was born in Wadsworth, Yorkshire, England, the son of Lionel Copley and Frisalina Ward. Copley matriculated at Brasenose College, Oxford, in 1665, but otherwise little is known about his life before 1676, the year he married Ann Boteler of Walton Woodhall, Hertfordshire; they had three children. That marriage perhaps assisted Copley in acquiring a commission as captain of the royal footguards the same year. He subsequently pursued a military career and by 1681 was stationed at the fortress of Hull under command of the duke of York. His influential patron through this decade was Thomas Osborne, the earl of Danby.

At the outbreak of the Glorious Revolution in 1688, Copley, who had earlier demonstrated anti-Catholic sentiments, secured the Hull area for the new monarchs, William and Mary. His reward was promotion to the rank of colonel and appointment to the post of lieutenant-governor of Hull, serving under Osborne, the new governor, who had also been elevated to marquis of Carmarthen and president of the Privy Council. Osborne soon nominated Copley for appointment as the governor of Maryland, which the new monarchs had decided to bring under royal authority. Osborne no doubt thought it propitious to have Copley out of England because his subordinate was under suspicion for tampering with the mail, an offense that Osborne himself had probably sanctioned. Copley also gained support from William Blathwayt, secretary to the Lords of Trade and secretary of war, who had earlier helped to protect Copley from a suit for indebtedness.

Although named as the governor-designate of Maryland in May 1690 (the commission did not become official until June 1691), Copley did not depart England for almost two years. During this time Copley negotiated for himself as many financial benefits as he could, particularly competing against Sir Thomas Lawrence, who had been named as secretary of the colony and second in authority, and Charles Calvert (1637–

1715), third Lord Baltimore, the former proprietor, for various bureaucratic fees and perquisites. Copley also helped to shape the membership of Maryland's new royal council. These were difficult months financially for Copley, whose sailing for Maryland was almost prevented because of debts. Nonetheless, he did sail in February 1692 with his wife, children, and a retinue of lesser officials.

After reaching Maryland in April 1692, Governor Copley carried out royal instructions for an examination of political developments since the overthrow of the proprietary government in 1689. He also set in motion full implementation of royal authority in the colony, dispensing ample patronage to reward adherents and withholding it to frustrate the ambitions and interests of opponents. The first royal assembly, convened in May 1692, marked a turning point in the colony's political history. Popular local initiatives to reorganize the legislature, long thwarted by the Calverts, were now swiftly implemented with executive sanction; the lower house assumed control of its own membership with legislation stipulating procedures for elections and conditions for eligibility, while the power and independence of the elected branch were extended in numerous ways. Among other laws passed by this assembly was a statute establishing the Church of England in Maryland with a compulsory poll tax for its support. This law ended the Calverts' policy of religious toleration and their insistence that no church receive special privileges.

During these early months in Maryland, Copley negotiated a series of compromises with members of the council and assembly that gave him access to additional revenues and benefits—some expressly forbidden him by royal instructions—while also greatly enriching and empowering some local figures who cooperated in these maneuvers. When Secretary Thomas Lawrence and Edward Randolph, the new collector of customs, reached the province a few months after Copley, they were appalled by his actions. They quickly clashed with the governor over his alleged protection of and patronage for men engaged in illegal trading practices that circumvented the navigation acts and customs duties. Copley had no difficulty marshaling local support against these two imperial placemen, who were intent on upholding English laws despite strong resistance in the colony. Lawrence and Randolph dispatched lengthy reports to England but had little recourse in the local arena. As the power struggle escalated, the council divided. Those men who had reservations about Copley, or who had not enjoyed his full support, aligned with Lawrence. Copley suspended his opponents from the council and imprisoned Lawrence. Randolph, in order to avoid a similar fate, went into hiding.

Copley died in St. Mary's City after a long illness. His wife had died six months before; their children returned to England and had no further contact with the colony. In the jockeying for leadership that followed Copley's death, the anti-Copley faction succeeded in gaining Lawrence's release from prison, and the secretary and his allies were eventually victorious. Proceedings in England largely discredited Copley and vindicated Lawrence and Randolph's positions.

• Copley's tenure as royal governor is documented in the *Archives of Maryland*, especially volumes 8 and 13. Surviving correspondence is found primarily in the William Blathwayt Papers, Colonial Williamsburg, and in the Colonial Office Papers, 5/713 series, at the Public Record Office in London. Many of Copley's letters and other materials about his governorship are condensed and reproduced in *Calendar of State Papers, Colonial Series, America and West Indies*, vols. 1689–1692 and 1693–1696; Lois Green Carr and David William Jordan, *Maryland's Revolution of Government, 1689–1692* (1974); and David W. Jordan, *Foundations of Representative Government in Maryland, 1632–1715* (1987), which discusses Copley's colonial career in detail.

DAVID W. JORDAN

COPLEY, Thomas (1595–1652), Jesuit missionary, is known in many English Jesuit records as Philip Fisher, which name he adopted upon entering the Society of Jesus, following the common Jesuit practice of adopting aliases in Tudor-Stuart England. He was born in Madrid, the son of William Copley, a landholder, and Magdalen Prideaux. His family had come to Madrid by way of Louvain after his grandfather, Thomas Copley of Gatton, a Catholic convert, fled England following the unsuccessful revolt of the northern earls in 1570. They returned to England and the family estate in 1603 after the death of Elizabeth I and the accession of James I. Copley was sent to the English Jesuit school at St. Omers for his education, and then, in 1611, to Louvain. There he conceived the idea of joining the Society of Jesus, which he did by 1616 after administering the family estates for three years. Copley completed his theological training at Louvain and returned to England in 1623.

In London Copley managed the business affairs of the Jesuit Residence, a position that secured his introduction to George Calvert, the first Lord Baltimore and a Roman Catholic convert, who was considering seriously the opportunities for North American colonization. Copley undertook substantial work on Baltimore's Maryland enterprise but remained behind when the *Ark* and the *Dove*, the first ships bound for Maryland, departed in 1633. Copley emigrated to Maryland in 1637. He managed the business affairs of the Jesuit mission, becoming its overall superior in 1641.

In directing the affairs of the mission, Copley concentrated on two fronts. First he sought to secure adequate financial support for the Jesuits' missionary efforts by establishing Jesuit-controlled estates on which tobacco could be produced. Through direct purchase or trade with the Indians and by claiming the fifty-acre headright due for each of the many immigrants the Jesuits sponsored, Copley secured for the order their first two manors, St. Inigoes in St. Mary's County (1641) and St. Thomas in Charles County (1649). The latter manor passed directly into the hands of a lay trustee because of an ongoing controversy between

Copley, the Jesuits, and their lay supporters on the one side and Lord Baltimore and Maryland's proprietary government on the other.

While this conflict seems to have begun close upon Copley's arrival in Maryland, it escalated dramatically in 1638. The following year, Copley negotiated a large donation of land from the Patuxent Indians in return for Jesuit missionary work among them. This grant blatantly violated Baltimore's charter right of ownership of all the land in the province, and Baltimore retaliated by ordering the tract seized in 1640 and by altering the conditions of plantation to prohibit landownership by Jesuits and other corporate groups. In response, Copley lodged a strong protest with his superiors, including the Jesuit superior general, Muzio Vitelleschi, accusing Baltimore of depriving the Catholic church in Maryland of immunities it enjoyed in Catholic countries in Europe and urging his excommunication. Baltimore likewise appealed to Copley's religious superiors; although he feared that the Jesuits might form an opposition party to his proprietary rule, Baltimore also recognized the practical problems of marketing a vigorously Catholic colony to the Protestant immigrants upon whom his hopes for success depended. Following the resolution of the controversy in Baltimore's favor by the superior general, Copley transferred the Jesuit lands in St. Mary's County to lay trusteeship—a practice well known among English Catholics—to prevent Baltimore from claiming them.

Overseeing the religious outreach to English colonists and the local Indians was the second major focus of Copley's efforts. The Indian missions began slowly. By the end of 1639, however, Jesuit efforts under Copley's direction served the Indians from a main base at Mattapany (the land Baltimore would seize in 1640) and other mission stations near St. Mary's City, on Kent Island, and at the Piscattaway settlement of Kittamaquindi. While administering the affairs of the mission prevented Copley from working directly with the Indians, he regularly reported on Jesuit missionary efforts in annual letters to his English superiors. Copley also supervised Jesuit work among the English colonists. He made sure that the Jesuits preached sermons on the principal feast days, catechized on Sundays, and provided for the regular participation of Maryland Catholics in the sacraments of their church. Copley's annual letters also reflect satisfaction with the Jesuit ministrations to Maryland's Protestant majority.

Except for about two and one-half years between 1645 and 1648, Copley spent the remainder of his life in the Maryland mission. In 1645 the Maryland colony and the Jesuit missions within it were disrupted by Richard Ingle, a parliamentary buccaneer intent upon establishing parliamentary authority in the Catholic proprietor's domain. Ingle seized control of the colony's government, sacked the Jesuit mission, scattered its priests, and took Copley and Father Andrew White (a Jesuit who had come to Maryland with the original settlers) back to England in chains. Escaping the capital offense of being a Roman Catholic priest and returning to England by arguing that he had not come of his own accord, Copley returned to Maryland by early 1648, shortly after Governor Leonard Calvert succeeded in reasserting proprietary authority over the colony. For the next several years Copley pieced the mission back together, recovering its property and its servants. Now, however, proprietary restraints on Jesuit activities; a shortage of priests, brothers, and servants; and growing suspicions about the Indians forced Copley to refocus the mission's work exclusively on the English settlers. By 1652, the year of Copley's death, the Jesuits controlled through lay trustees the two manors of St. Inigoes and St. Thomas, maintained a residence and chapel in St. Mary's City, and operated a school for the colonists, probably at Newtown Manor in St. Mary's County.

• Primary sources pertinent to the career of Thomas Copley may be found in Maryland Historical Society, *The Calvert Papers* (1889), and Thomas Hughes, *The History of the Society of Jesus in North America* (4 vols., 1907–1917), which also contains other information on Copley. The only book-length biography of Copley is Katherine C. Dorsey, *Life of Father Thomas Copley* (1885). An excellent short account of his background, personality, and career is Edwin W. Beitzell, "'Thomas Copley, Gentleman,'" *Maryland Historical Magazine* 47 (1952): 209–23. A useful description of the early Jesuit mission in Maryland is Gerald P. Fogarty, "The Origins of the Mission, 1634–1773," in *The Maryland Jesuits, 1634–1833*, ed. Gerald P. Fogarty, Joseph T. Durkin, and R. Emmet Curran (1976).

MICHAEL GRAHAM

COPPIN, Fanny Jackson (1837–21 Jan. 1913), educator, civic and religious leader, and feminist, was born a slave in Washington, D.C., the daughter of Lucy Jackson. Her father's name and the details of her early childhood are unknown. However, by the time she was age ten, her aunt Sarah Orr Clark had purchased her freedom, and Jackson went to live with relatives in New Bedford, Massachusetts. By 1851 she and her relatives had moved to Newport, Rhode Island, where Jackson was employed as a domestic by George Henry Calvert, a descendant of Lord Baltimore, the settler of Maryland. Jackson's salary enabled her to afford one hour of private tutoring three times a week. Near the end of her six-year stay with the Calverts, she briefly attended the segregated public schools of Newport. In 1859 Jackson enrolled at the Rhode Island State Normal School in Bristol. In addition to the normal course, she also studied French privately. Funded by her aunt Sarah and scholarships from Bishop Daniel Payne of the African Methodist Episcopal (AME) church and Oberlin College, Jackson was able to enroll in the ladies department of Oberlin in 1860. She also helped to pay for her education by working during her years at Oberlin. By 1861 Jackson transferred into the collegiate department at Oberlin, where she distinguished herself and actively participated in student life. Her outstanding academic achievements resulted in her being chosen as the first African-American student teacher of Oberlin's preparatory department. In

addition, Jackson was chosen as class poet and graduated in 1865 with an A.B. degree, becoming the second African-American woman in the nation to receive such a degree.

After graduating from Oberlin, Jackson accepted the position of principal of the female department of the prestigious Institute for Colored Youth (ICY) in Philadelphia. Founded by the Society of Friends in 1837 as a high school for African Americans, the ICY offered a preparatory department, separate secondary-school departments for males and females, and a teacher training course. Jackson's ability as a teacher and as a principal was immediately recognized by the Quaker managers as well as the African-American community. Her skills in public speaking and elocution were reflected in the improved speaking of the female students. By the end of her first year, the enrollment of the girls' secondary school nearly doubled from forty-two to eighty, and the school reported fewer dropouts. By 1869, when Ebenezer Bassett, the principal for the entire school, was appointed U.S. minister to Haiti by President Ulysses S. Grant, Jackson was promoted to head the entire school. This promotion was extremely significant because no woman at this time headed a coeducational institution that had both male and female faculty.

Immediately after Jackson became principal of the ICY, many changes that reflected her educational and personal philosophies began to appear at the school. She believed that if respect were given to students it would be returned by the students to the teachers. Thus, she abolished corporal punishment at the school. Academic performance at the school was so high that the institution averaged thirty visitors a week in 1869. Jackson also believed in fostering close relationships between the faculty, students, managers, and parents. She began sending monthly conduct papers to parents to inform them of their children's character, attendance, and recitations. Monthly meetings were also held with parents of ICY students. Managers began sponsoring teas for the school's upper-level students and teachers to stimulate conversation and fellowship.

In 1878 Jackson began a regular column titled "Women's Department" in the *Christian Recorder*, the newspaper of the AME church. Through her column she was able to reach African-American women of all income levels. She reported the achievements of women in education, employment, and other areas and also discussed cases of discrimination against black women. Jackson was always concerned about gender discrimination as well as racial discrimination and stressed to her female readers that they should pursue the same professions and occupations as men and not simply enter traditional female-dominated fields. In 1881 Jackson married Levi Jenkins Coppin, an AME minister at least fifteen years her junior. Her devotion to the ICY was so great that she remained as principal for the next twenty-one years.

Coppin's greatest contribution to the ICY was the establishment of an industrial department. She was stimulated to take action after visiting the Centennial Exposition in Philadelphia (1876), which emphasized education and national progress; she was particularly impressed by the exhibition of the Moscow Imperial Technical School's Victor Della Vos, who demonstrated his newly developed approaches to the teaching of the mechanical arts. She became acutely aware of the need to prepare African-American youth for an increasingly industrial nation, and so she began to campaign for a department of industrial arts at the ICY. Her idea, though, was a hard sell. The Quaker managers did not want to incur additional expenses for expansion of the institution, and African Americans were apprehensive about what was being proposed by Coppin. Many of the leading families in Philadelphia who sent their children to the ICY had a tradition of classical education and affiliations with prestigious literary societies, and they were reluctant to embrace a form of education that appeared more practical in nature. Nevertheless, the industrial department finally opened in 1889, although it failed to offer the advanced classes that Coppin had proposed, such as mechanical drawing and engineering. Instead, the department offered only carpentry, bricklaying, shoemaking, printing, and plastering for men, and millinery, dressmaking, and cooking for women. By 1892 typing and stenography were added to the curriculum. The industrial department was a great success. As the only institution in Philadelphia to offer industrial training for African Americans, the ICY had eighty-seven students enrolled in the new department and 325 on a waiting list just two months after the department opened.

During Coppin's tenure as principal of the ICY, her normal students were so sought after that most were able to successfully pass teacher examinations and secure employment after only two years in secondary school. By 1890 three-fourths of the African-American teachers in Philadelphia and Camden, New Jersey, were ICY graduates. Many of the institute's students also pursued the professions.

In addition to her school work, Coppin was extremely active in the African Methodist Episcopal church. She was elected president of the local Women's Mite Missionary Society and later became national president of the Women's Home and Foreign Missionary Society. In addition, she was on the board of managers of the Home for the Aged and Infirm Colored People in Philadelphia for over thirty years (1881–1913), and she was elected vice president of the National Association of Colored Women in 1897.

In 1902 Coppin retired from the institute and accompanied her husband, who had been elected bishop of the Fourteenth Episcopal District of South Africa in 1900, to Capetown. They returned to Philadelphia in the spring of 1904. Bishop Coppin was then appointed to the Seventh Episcopal District, which encompassed South Carolina and Alabama. Coppin, who had frequently traveled with her husband, made the trip to South Carolina; however, the South African trip had severely impacted her health, and by 1905 her health had deteriorated to such an extent that she was primarily confined to her Philadelphia home for the remaining years of her life. She died in Philadelphia.

• Primary documents concerning Coppin's Oberlin years are available in the Oberlin College Archives. Documents from her years as principal at the ICY are available at the Friend's Historical Library, Swarthmore College. The *Christian Recorder* carried articles by Coppin and about her community, school, and church activities from 1865 until her death in 1913. Published materials on Coppin include an autobiography, *Reminiscences of School Life, and Hints on Teaching* (1913), which provides scant information on her family and personal life; and Levi Jenkins Coppin's autobiography, *Unwritten History* (1919; repr. 1968), which briefly mentions Fanny Coppin's devotion to ICY and about her relationship with her students. Linda M. Perkins's *Fanny Jackson Coppin and the Institute for Colored Youth, 1865–1902* (1987) is a full-length biography. Biographical entries include Dorothy Drinkard-Hawkshawe, "Fannie Jackson Coppin," in *Dictionary of American Negro Biography*, ed. Rayford W. Logan and Michael R. Winston (1982); Leslie H. Fishel, Jr., "Fanny Jackson Coppin," in *Notable American Women*, vol. 1, ed. Edward T. James (1971); and Linda M. Perkins's entry on Fanny Jackson Coppin in *Notable Black Women* (1991). An obituary is in the *Philadelphia Tribune*, 1 Feb. 1913.

LINDA M. PERKINS

COPWAY, George (1818–Jan. 1869), North American Indian writer and lecturer, known in Ojibwa (or Chippewa) as Kahgegagahbowh, was born near the mouth of the Trenton River (near present-day Trenton), Ontario, Canada, the son of John Copway, an Ojibwa chief, and his Ojibwa wife (name unknown). Shortly after his parents accepted Christianity, in 1830 George Copway also adopted the new faith. After briefly attending the Methodist-run mission school at Rice Lake, Upper Canada (present-day Ontario), the sixteen-year-old boy left to be a Methodist mission worker to the Lake Superior Ojibwa in 1834. The missionaries highly regarded their ambitious Indian convert, who advanced quickly from interpreter and teacher to preacher. In 1837 the Methodists sent him for two years of study at the Ebenezer Manual Labor School, located near Jacksonville, Illinois.

Immediately before taking up his appointment as a missionary in the Upper Mississippi district, Copway, anxious to see more of the world, visited the eastern United States and his family in Upper Canada. At the Credit River Indian mission just west of Toronto, the young Ojibwa preacher met Elizabeth Howell, the daughter of an English settler. Five months after their first meeting they married in June 1840. Evidently her parents did not approve of the union as no member of her large family acted as a witness at the wedding. They had several children, although apparently only a son and a daughter lived to adulthood.

The Copways spent two years at Methodist Indian missions in Minnesota, eventually settling at Fond du Lac at the head of Lake Superior. Rev. William Boutwell, an American missionary in the area, met the Canadian Indian missionary at this time. He later commented that he found him full of "vanity, self-confidence, and [a] disposition to be headstrong." Unhappy in the United States, Copway accepted an invitation from the Upper Canadian Methodists to return home.

Initially the Canadian Methodists held their new recruit in high esteem as "an exceedingly clever man and good speaker, both in Indian and English." His casual handling of money, however, cost him his church's support. In 1846, two Upper Canadian Ojibwa communities, including his own reservation at Rice Lake, accused him of embezzlement of their band funds. According to Thomas G. Anderson, superintendent of Indian Affairs, Copway earlier that year had "been in Jail for some time past where he was lodged for debts due to White People." The Upper Canadian Methodists expelled the Ojibwa missionary.

Shortly after his release from prison the defrocked minister left for the United States. Energetically he began, no doubt with considerable help from his well-educated English wife, to write a book, *The Life, History, and Travels, of Kah-ge-ga-gah-bowh (George Copway). A Young Indian Chief of the Ojebwa Nation, a Convert to the Christian Faith, and a Missionary to his People for Twelve Years.* The fact that he was not a chief of a Canadian Indian reservation or any longer a Methodist missionary did not deter him from inferring that he was both. He knew his eastern American readers' preconceptions and what they wanted to hear. In his book he presented himself as "one of nature's children": "I have always admired her; she shall be my glory; her features—her robes, and the wreath about her brow—the seasons—her stately oaks, and the evergreen—her hair—ringlets over the earth, all contribute to my enduring love of her; and whenever I see her, emotions of pleasure roll in my breast, and swell and burst like waves on the shores of the ocean, in prayer and praise to Him, who has placed me in her hand." To help sell his book Copway began a series of public lectures on North American Indian and temperance themes. Throughout 1847 and 1848 the Indian Christian convert spoke in cities along the Atlantic seaboard. By the end of 1848 his autobiography had gone through seven printings.

Conscious of the need to add a new theme to his repertoire, Copway revealed in 1848 his plan for an all-Indian territory to be established west of the Mississippi, to be called "Kahgega," which meant "Ever-to-be." Although several prominent eastern American politicians endorsed the idea, it gained little popular support. Wisely the Indian celebrity now concentrated on his preparation of another manuscript.

Both Henry Wadsworth Longfellow and Francis Parkman encouraged Copway with his writing. In 1850 he published his *Traditional History and Characteristic Sketches of the Ojibway Nation*, the first volume on the history of an Indian tribe written by a North American Indian. The book, in a discursive fashion, reviewed the Ojibwas' legends, customs, language, and history. The following year Copway's last book appeared, *Running Sketches of Men and Places*, an ac-

count of his European travels on his way to and from the World Peace Conference at Frankfurt, Germany.

By 1851 Francis Parkman and others who had befriended Copway lost interest in him as his novelty diminished and his requests for financial assistance increased. The summer of 1851 proved a trying time for him as he struggled to bring out a weekly newspaper in New York City, *Copway's American Indian*; without adequate financial backing, it failed after three months.

The Indian writer descended further and further into poverty and obscurity in the years to follow. Apparently he continued to live in New York City in the 1850s and gave occasional lectures in eastern American cities to diminishing audiences. His wife and infant daughter left him in the 1860s. During the Civil War he collected a bounty for enlisting Canadian Indians in the Union army. After the war he worked as an Indian root doctor in Detroit. Finally, in 1868, he moved to the Roman Catholic Indian mission at the Lake of Two Mountains, just west of Montreal. There, just before his death, he declared that he had been a "pagan" and converted to Roman Catholicism.

In retrospect George Copway lived a life full of tragedy. For one brief period in the late 1840s he achieved extraordinary fame in the eastern United States, but he quickly lost it. The first North American Indian to write a history of his people died away from his reservation, where he had been accused of embezzlement, and separated from his English wife and his family.

• See Donald B. Smith, "The Life of George Copway or Kah-ge-ga-gah-bowh (1818–1869)—and a Review of His Writings," *Journal of Canadian Studies* 23, no. 3 (1988): 5–38. Also see A. LaVonne Brown Ruoff, "George Copway: Nineteenth-Century American Indian Autobiographer," *Auto-Biography* 3, no. 2 (1987): 6–17. A commemorative edition of the 150th anniversary of George Copway's *The Life, History, and Travels of Kah-ge-ga-gah-bowh (George Copway)* (1847), was published as *Life, Letters, and Speeches*, ed. by A. LaVonne Brown Ruoff and Donald B. Smith (1997).

DONALD B. SMITH

CORAM, Thomas (1668–29 Mar. 1751), philanthropist and colony promoter, was born in the Dorsetshire coast village of Lyme Regis, England, the son of John Coram, a mariner, and Spes (maiden name unknown). Coram was primarily self-educated. He went to sea from age eleven to sixteen and was then apprenticed to a shipwright. Coram's steady rise from humble birth to prominent merchant was due to his great vigor, ambition, and trustworthiness. In 1694 a group of London merchants sent him to Boston as head of a team of shipwrights in order to establish a shipyard. The new governor, William Phips, apparently encouraged the project; in the newly reorganized colony Anglican businessmen such as Coram were increasingly integrated into Boston's society. Coram married Eunice Wayte (Wait), the daughter of a prominent Congregationalist family, in 1700. Eunice continued her nonconformity for the rest of her life while her husband remained committed to the Church of England. After

1700 Coram also formed a close friendship with Benjamin Colman, a Congregationalist minister. Colman and Coram shared interests in humanitarianism and humanitarian institutions.

The success of his Boston shipyard led Coram to establish another shipyard in Taunton, Massachusetts, in 1697 or 1698. Apparently the citizens of Taunton were less tolerant of Anglican newcomers than were Bostonians. Also, as at other times in his life, Coram offended some people in Taunton with his forthright speech: "free from all hypocrisy, he spoke what he thought with vehemence" (McClure, p. 26). Between 1697 and 1700 five ships were built at the new shipyard and a new industry established there, but after 1699 Coram regularly contended with broken contracts, confiscated materials, and unresponsive local officials and courts. In 1702 the superior court upheld Coram's complaint against Taunton's deputy sheriff, but soon after Coram was ambushed and nearly shot. In 1703 Coram donated fifty-nine acres in Taunton to Boston's King's Chapel so that an Anglican church could be built in the town that treated him so badly. The town of Taunton refused to act on the gift for many years. In 1703 he also chose to return to England, after addressing a memorial to Governor Joseph Dudley describing the "barbarous treatment" he received in Taunton.

Coram never returned to America, but America never left his mind. Throughout his life he supported all sorts of charitable, missionary, and educational causes in America. Economically he was a mercantilist who considered America merely a colonial support for the mother country. Philanthropically he considered America a land of opportunity for the disadvantaged in England. Around 1713 Coram devised a humanitarian plan to relocate English soldiers returning from the War of the Spanish Succession to the Province of Massachusetts, in what is now northern Maine. The Board of Trade supported the plan as advantageous to England and America, but opposition in Massachusetts and in the English bureaucracy buried it.

Throughout the subsequent decade Coram's connections in philanthropic and missionary circles steadily expanded. Through his friendship with the churchman philanthropist Thomas Bray, Coram was involved in creating parochial libraries and encouraging education throughout the empire, including among African Americans. Like Bray, Coram did not do much hands-on work among the disadvantaged; rather, he zealously solicited benefactors and consistently exemplified the ideal gentleman of conscience.

Through Bray, Coram was brought into the humanitarian project of founding the colony of Georgia. After Bray's death, Coram remained in "Dr. Bray's Associates," a group (including James Oglethorpe) initially dedicated in part to resettling persecuted European Protestants to America. The Board of Trustees that was chartered in 1732 to oversee the development of Georgia grew out of Dr. Bray's Associates and included Coram. As always, Coram took his position seriously and was among the most active trustees. In 1735,

however, Coram was censured by the other trustees for publicly advocating that females in Georgia should have the right to inherit land. After the censure he had little to do with the subsequent trustees and therefore had little to do with the subsequent erosion of the trustees' ban on slavery in Georgia.

Blocked in one humanitarian project, Coram always found others to champion. A Reverend Samuel Smith wrote to Benjamin Colman that "Mr. Coram is animated with so generous and extensive a Zeal, that he has a share in forwarding the Progress of almost every good Undertaking, that is set on Foot by publick spirited Persons amongst us." In the 1730s Coram helped two Mohegans from Connecticut, who were defrauded of tribal lands, to receive compensation. He also advocated a plan for educating Indian girls in America. In 1735 Coram devised another humanitarian colony in Nova Scotia for out-of-work tradesmen in London. This plan was eventually buried in bureaucracy, but Lord Halifax's successful scheme in the late 1740s for a colony in Nova Scotia was built on the foundation of Coram's plan.

Although the possibilities America offered were often in Coram's mind, his most influential work had nothing to do with America. Coram founded the first philanthropic corporation. He expanded the long tradition of individual benevolence in England into chartered institutional benevolence on the model of joint stock companies. "The genius of Thomas Coram," writes Ruth K. McClure, "was that he gave to this increasingly commercial and industrial world the most appropriate charitable structure possible." Coram accomplished this innovation in the long process of establishing the Foundling Hospital in London.

Beginning in 1722 Coram worked for seventeen years to establish a home for orphans who were living and dying on the streets of London. An endowment from an individual or the church seemed impossible so Coram decided to adapt the corporate structure that had been very popular. Unfortunately the fiasco of the South Sea Bubble had made the government wary of granting new experimental charters after 1720. Coram eventually succeeded by enlisting the support of aristocratic ladies. The idea that noble women should play a special role in the Foundling Hospital came from Thomas Bray, but Coram extended the idea by soliciting them to petition the king. The duchess of Somerset was the first to sign the Ladies' Petition in 1729. Ten years later the Foundling Hospital opened its doors, becoming a successful model for many subsequent philanthropic institutions.

Coram had no children, and his wife died in 1740. Coram subsequently neglected his own business affairs and fell into poverty. An annual subscription of friends and the prince of Wales gave him financial security. Although he continued to be an active philanthropist, much of his time was devoted to the children at the hospital. Coram was in London when he "passed from doing to enjoying Good" and was buried under the Foundling Hospital Chapel.

- Many Coram letters are at the Massachusetts Historical Society in Boston in the Colman papers, the Colonel Edward Hutchinson Papers, and in Miscellaneous Bound Items. A selection of these is published in the *Proceedings of the Massachusetts Historical Society*, vol. 56 (1922–1923), pp. 15–56. Other manuscript sources and secondary sources are listed in the bibliography in Ruth K. McClure, *Coram's Children: The London Foundling Hospital in the Eighteenth Century* (1981), which devotes two chapters to Coram's life. See also Richard Brocklesby, *Private Virtue and Publick Spirit Display'd in a Succinct Essay on the Character of Capt. Thomas Coram* (1751); Herbert F. B. Compston, *Thomas Coram, Churchman, Empire Builder, and Philanthropist* (1918); and Hamilton Andrews Hill, "Thomas Coram in Boston and Taunton," *Proceedings of the American Antiquarian Society*, vol. 8 (1892–1893), pp. 133–48.

RICK KENNEDY

CORBETT, Harvey Wiley (8 Jan. 1873–21 Apr. 1954), architect, was born in San Francisco, California, the son of Samuel James Corbett and Elizabeth Jane Wiley, physicians. He received a B.S. in engineering from the University of California, Berkeley, in 1895. In 1896 he went to Paris, where he studied at the École des Beaux-Arts, receiving his diploma in 1900. Afterward he traveled throughout Europe and eventually became a lecturer in architecture at Columbia University (1907–1909).

As was the custom of Beaux-Arts architects of the time, Corbett began his career with historicist leanings, first as draftsman in 1901–1903 for architect Cass Gilbert, and later in his own practice in New York, designing variations of the classical style from 1903 through the teens. In 1905 he married sculptor Gail Sherman; they had two children and lived in New York near Columbia University. He broke with the classical style and in the early 1920s designed the thirty-story Manhattan Bush Terminal (1924, extant) and Bush House, London (1927, extant).

Corbett was one of the first architects to embrace fully the new design configurations dictated by the New York City zoning and setback laws of 1916, understanding the aesthetic and social considerations of the setback skyscraper. With architectural delineator Hugh Ferriss, a fellow convert from the Beaux-Arts style to art deco *moderne*, Corbett published his theoretical models of the shapes of the tall buildings of the future, titled *Evolution of the Set-Back Building*. Although the theory was based in Corbett's ideas, the highly expressionistic drawings were Ferriss's, and it is Ferriss who has historically been credited with the project. In his own time, however, Corbett was well known within architectural circles in New York and London, enjoying a reputation as an architectural theorist, teacher, urban planner, and builder of tall, sleek buildings. Perhaps his major contribution to American architecture, and to New York architecture in particular, was in his finding an aesthetic within the strictures of skyscraper zoning, proving that a city could be both tall and monumental while preserving urban amenities of space, light, and air. Thus he pointed to an important modern direction for architectural think-

ing, based in finding the solution within the problem. In architecture and urban design, he illustrated that constraint can lead to creativity.

Corbett was finding his true style concurrent with the advent of the American skyscraper. He was one of the designers of the Roerich Museum and Master Apartments on Riverside Drive (1928–1929, extant) and Rockefeller Center (1928–1937, extant) and worked on the plans for the United Nations Headquarters (late 1940s–1950), all composed of tall, modern buildings for Manhattan. Rockefeller Center and the UN were two of the most significant urban projects of the first half of the twentieth century, projects that together would shape the concept of the modern city. He is especially remembered for his contribution to Rockefeller Center, a team project in which it is difficult to credit individual architects, so complex and reworked was the scheme over time. The Fifth Avenue site, purchased from Columbia University by John D. Rockefeller during the 1920s, was built during the Great Depression. Corbett's firm, then called Corbett, Harrison & MacMurray, submitted plans, with renderings by Ferriss. These plans foreshadowed many of the features one now associates with Rockefeller Center: symmetrical buildings ranging from low-rise to skyscraper heights, arranged about reconfigured traffic plans and plazas, in a simplified art deco *moderne* style.

Corbett headed the planning committees of the 1939 New York World's Fair, the New York Regional Plan Association, and the United Nations Headquarters—massive projects calling for cooperation among numerous architects and planners. Corbett, the visionary, created utopian illustrations of a city reconstructed in megabuildings and tiered streets; as the pragmatist he suggested the need for the tunnels under the Hudson River that now link Manhattan Island to the metropolitan region. He was able to conceive of the city of the future and engineer it as well.

Corbett's success with commercial projects such as Rockefeller Center did not dim his personal interest in the social values of architecture and urban planning. During the depression, he headed a committee to aid the many unemployed of the architectural profession. After World War II he became involved in the pressing needs for low-income housing, designing the Amsterdam House projects in New York in 1947. A fellow of both the American Institute of Architects and the Royal Institute of British Architects, he died in New York.

- Illustrations of Corbett's urban visions appear in Hugh Ferriss, *The Metropolis of Tomorrow* (1929). Corbett's brief summary of his futurist city plans may be found in "New York in 1999, Five Predictions, Architects and City Planners Look into the Crystal Ball and Tell What They See," *New York Times Magazine*, 6 Feb. 1949, p. 18. For a discussion of his role in the building of Rockefeller Center see Carol Herselle Krinsky, *Rockefeller Center* (1978), based on material in the Rockefeller Family Archives. See also Thomas Adams, *The Building of a City*, vol. 2 (1931), and William Jordy, *American*

Buildings and Their Architects: The Impact of European Modernism in the Mid-Twentieth Century (1972). An obituary is in the *New York Times*, 22 Apr. 1954.

LESLIE HUMM CORMIER

CORBETT, Henry Winslow (18 Feb. 1827–31 Mar. 1903), banker, capitalist, and politician, was born in Westboro, Massachusetts, the son of Elijah Corbett, a mechanic and businessman, and Melinda Forbush. Reared in a large family in Washington County, New York, Corbett attended Cambridge Academy and later clerked. In 1843 he moved to New York City and took employment with Williams, Bradford & Company. Confident of his business acumen, the company sent him by sea to Oregon to sell merchandise, and in February 1851 Corbett arrived in Portland, a village hacked out of the timber. While awaiting the arrival of his goods, the ambitious young merchant rode up the Willamette Valley to discover what pioneer farmers wanted to buy, and he found a strong demand for shoes, nails, sugar, coffee, tobacco, cloth, and brooms. Thus Corbett began a lifetime practice of seeking market opportunities. He opened a Portland store near the Willamette River, slept in the store's loft, made a remarkable $20,000 profit in about fourteen months, and then rejoined his employers in New York.

In 1853 Corbett married Caroline E. Jagger of Albany, New York. The newlyweds decided to move to Portland, where, as an independent, Henry would have better economic opportunities. In Portland, Corbett immediately plunged into a quest for wealth and influence. Like his competitors he received produce—including pork, butter, eggs, and potatoes—in payment and sold them in Portland or San Francisco. Unlike his competitors, however, Corbett bought most of his goods in New York City because San Francisco prices were too high. Corbett sold a variety of goods to farmers (in the mid-1850s he began selling McCormick reapers), to volunteer soldiers serving in regional Indian wars that lasted into the 1860s, and to miners. He outfitted the miners and supplied their remote camps in Oregon, British Columbia, Idaho, and Montana. The significant increase in Oregon's population—from 52,000 to 414,000 between 1860 and 1900—provided Corbett with continuing financial opportunities.

Corbett participated in Oregon's emerging industries by distributing woolens regionally and selling salmon in New York City. He invested in Portland property, a telegraph company, a steamboat operation, a stagecoach line, and railroads, including the Northern Pacific and the Oregon and California. In 1869 he and competitor Henry Failing obtained control of the First National Bank of Portland; it would become the Pacific Northwest's leading financial institution. In 1871 the two men, who had been linked through a marriage, merged their lucrative businesses and specialized in wholesale hardware as Corbett-Failing and Company.

Caroline Corbett had died in 1865, leaving two children. In 1867 Corbett had married Emma L. Ruggles, a young woman who became a renowned hostess as she made her mansion into a popular social center. They had no children together.

Meanwhile, Corbett realized his political ambitions. Like Lincoln he had admired Henry Clay and the Whig party. No Oregonian worked more zealously than Corbett to build Oregon's Republican party in the 1850s. He and his first wife enthusiastically supported the Union during the Civil War, and he led the local movement to combine the Republican and War Democrats into the Union party. In 1866 Republicans rewarded Corbett by selecting him as a U.S. senator. In this office he sought federal assistance for his state's economic development, including a Portland bridge, new roads, improved river navigation, and expanded mail service. Corbett played no real role in the Senate's impeachment trial of President Andrew Johnson, but he voted guilty. He was much more involved in the economic issues of Reconstruction—he favored the gold standard, defended protective tariffs, approved the utilization of liquor and tobacco taxes and the termination of wartime stamp taxes, and proposed funding the nation's war debt at a low interest rate. He opposed the eight-hour workday concept and argued that the proposed Fifteenth Amendment should state that "Chinamen" born abroad could not be naturalized.

Corbett had no patience with woman suffrage, but he battled to improve the conditions of reservation Indians. As a member of the Senate's Committee on Indian Affairs, he wanted good, well-paid Christians to serve as Indian agents (under questioning he admitted that he could not judge a "good Christian"), insisted that improved salaries would attract better state Indian superintendents, sought to avoid costly wars with reservation Indians by providing them with sufficient appropriations, and proposed a new Department of Indian Affairs.

Although many Republicans applauded Corbett's political record, transportation mogul Ben Holladay and his supporters—who were seeking the realization of a sweeping economic and political agenda in Oregon—prevented Corbett's reelection. To fight this rival, Corbett bought control of the *Oregonian*, the region's leading newspaper. Holladay's financial collapse in 1876 allowed Corbett, Failing, and their Portland allies to restore much of their political power and once again become the city's social and economic leaders.

Corbett supported Portland's schools, public library, Presbyterian church, board of trade, Young Men's Christian Association, and the Lewis and Clark expedition. A congenial companion, a clever businessman, a devoted Republican, and a persistent booster of his beloved Portland, Corbett has been called "the epitome of the frontier tycoon" (Clark, vol. 1, p. xix) and "the most significant and complex of the successful frontier merchants" (MacColl, p. 360). His estate, valued at more than $2 million, proved the wisdom of his move to frontier Portland. Corbett's will, which bequeathed funds to various cultural institutions and charities, demonstrated his continuing concern for the advancement of the city in which he lived most of his life and in which he died.

• Corbett's papers are in the Oregon Historical Society, Portland. His U.S. Senate record is in the *Congressional Globe* for the Fortieth, Forty-first, and Forty-second congresses. An adequate biography has yet to be published, but useful assessments by Corbett's contemporaries are Harvey W. Scott, *History of the Oregon Country* (1924), and Malcolm Clark, Jr., ed., *Pharisee among Philistines: The Diary of Judge Matthew P. Deady, 1871–1892* (1975). See also Arthur L. Throckmorton, *Oregon Argonauts: Merchant Adventurers on the Western Frontier* (1961), on Corbett's career as a frontier merchant, and E. Kimbark MacColl, *Merchants, Money and Power: The Portland Establishment, 1843–1913* (1988), on his economic, political, and social activities.

G. Thomas Edwards

CORBETT, James John (1 Sept. 1866–18 Feb. 1933), boxer, was born in San Francisco, California, the son of Patrick J. Corbett, an Irish-born owner of a livery stable, and Katherine McDonald. He received some secondary education, first at St. Ignatius College and then at Sacred Heart College, before being expelled from the latter for fighting. At age 13 he became a messenger for the Nevada Bank of San Francisco and by the age of 19 had risen to the post of assistant receiving teller.

As a boy Corbett aspired to become a professional baseball player but gave up the sport after badly injuring a hand. He then turned seriously to boxing. Under the guidance of Walter Watson, the boxing instructor of the Olympic Athletic Club, he became its middleweight and heavyweight champion. He remained an amateur until 1889 except for two paid fights, one each in Utah and Wyoming, under an assumed name. At maturity he stood 6′1″ and weighed between 180 and 190 pounds.

Corbett's keenest amateur rival was Joe Choynski who, in 1889, was also his first professional opponent. Because professional boxing was illegal in California, it was necessary to hold fights in secrecy. Corbett's and Choynski's first meeting took place in a barn on 30 May, but it was soon halted by the local sheriff. The following week another fight was held on a barge in San Francisco Bay, with Corbett winning by a 27-round knockout after a grueling fight that he later said was his most punishing. Corbett claimed to have "invented" the left hook punch in this fight, and afterward he may have been the first to consistently use it. Managed by William Brady and trained by Billy Delaney, Corbett thus commenced a career that would involve few fights but would last until 1903.

Corbett's success in two important fights made him the foremost heavyweight title contender. In 1890 he defeated Jake Kilrain, who had fought champion John L. Sullivan in the previous year. In 1891 he met Peter Jackson, the great black fighter, in San Francisco in a fight that was supposed to last until one of the partici-

pants could no longer continue. The referee declared the fight "no contest" in the 61st round. According to Corbett, this action was taken to save the bets that the referee's gambling friends had made on Jackson. Corbett was very tired but capable of continuing the fight, while Jackson collapsed on his way to the dressing room after leaving the ring.

On 7 September 1892 Corbett knocked out Sullivan in 21 rounds in New Orleans to become the first heavyweight boxing champion to win the title while wearing gloves and fighting under the rules of the marquis of Queensberry. This fight has often been regarded as the beginning of modern boxing. Sullivan was a crude slugger, as had been almost all bareknuckle fighters, but Corbett's methods were entirely different. He was described by James P. Dawson as "a straight standup fighter [with] a style peculiarly his own. His idea was to hit and get away, rather than to go tearing into a rival pell-mell. . . . Corbett specialized in speed of foot and hand and a trigger brain that worked in perfect harmony with his legs and feet and arms and fists." In the terminology of the time, Corbett was the first well-known "scientific boxer." Corbett beat Sullivan so decisively that his superiority could not be questioned. He broke Sullivan's nose in the third round, outboxed him in every round, and ended the fight with a clean knockout. However, Corbett's clever, unaggressive tactics were widely disapproved by sportswriters and boxing fans, who preferred the crude old-time slugging.

Corbett held the heavyweight championship for nearly six years but made only one successful defense, knocking out Charlie Mitchell of England in three rounds at Jacksonville, Florida, in 1894. His second defense was against Bob Fitzsimmons of New Zealand in Carson City, Nevada, on 17 March 1897. Corbett was winning the fight easily until Fitzsimmons landed a powerful blow below the heart, the so-called "solar plexus" blow, and won by a knockout in the 14th round.

After losing on a foul to heavyweight contender Tom Sharkey in 1898, Corbett attempted to regain the heavyweight title from Fitzsimmons's conqueror, James J. Jeffries. They met on 11 May 1900 at Coney Island, New York, and Corbett won nearly every round of a scheduled 25 until the 23rd, when Jeffries scored a one-punch knockout. Later that year Corbett scored a five-round knockout over the former middleweight champion, Kid McCoy, in New York City, which was widely reported as a "fake." Corbett always claimed afterward that he fought honestly, but McCoy was notoriously devious, and it is likely that he feigned the knockout to achieve a betting coup. Dissatisfaction with the outcome of this fight was largely responsible for public boxing promotions being made illegal in New York from 1901 until 1911.

In 1903 Corbett once again attempted to regain the heavyweight title, fighting Jeffries for a second time in San Francisco. A terrific body blow floored Corbett for a nine-count in the second round, after which he took a terrific beating. Floored five more times, Corbett fought on until the 10th round, when he was put down twice more, and his second threw the sponge into the ring, bringing the fight and his boxing career to an end. This fight better than any other showed his gameness under adverse conditions, but emphasized his comparative fragility.

Corbett's demeanor outside the ring was as different from most contemporary boxers as his style within it. Polished, intelligent, and well spoken, he was often called "Gentleman Jim." After his retirement, he had many friends and acquaintances in politics, acting, and journalism. Corbett spent a great deal of time on the stage, first in *After Dark*, following his fight with Peter Jackson, and later in a play entitled *Gentleman Jack*, written especially for him, after the Fitzsimmons defeat. He also developed and delivered witty monologues for vaudeville. In later years many ghostwritten articles on boxing were published under his name, but these caused him some embarrassment when the authors consistently picked the losing fighters to win.

In 1886 Corbett married Olive Lake. He was divorced from her in 1895 and later that year married Jessie Taylor, an actress, known theatrically as Vera Stanwood. Corbett had no children. For his last thirty years he lived in Bayside, New York, where he died. His life was the subject of the 1942 film *Gentleman Jim*, in which Errol Flynn played Corbett. He was elected to the International Boxing Hall of Fame in 1990. Corbett was the boxer most responsible for transforming boxing from an exhibition of crude slugging to a sport of skill, in which clever tactics and the use of a variety of different blows prevailed. He introduced innovative defensive techniques and made it respectable for a boxer to avoid punishment by nimble footwork. Stylistically he was the forerunner of such great fighters as Jack Johnson, Jack Britton, Benny Leonard, and Gene Tunney. Furthermore, his gentlemanly demeanor and the respectability of his manager contributed greatly to the replacement of bare-knuckle prizefighting and its image of brutality by the more socially acceptable form of boxing with padded gloves.

• Corbett's autobiography, *The Roar of the Crowd* (1925), is the best source of information about him. He also published a book of anecdotes, *Jabs: Being an Account of the Remarkable Experiences of "Handsome Jim"* (1907). Nat Fleischer, *"Gentleman Jim": The Story of James J. Corbett* (1942), is useful and accurate. Corbett's record in the ring may be found in Herbert Goldman, ed., *The Ring Record Book* (1986–1987 ed.). A cinematic record of Corbett's boxing style in 1894 exists in the form of his exhibition with Peter Courtney, the first boxing to be put on film. His role in the transformation of boxing is described in Elliott J. Gorn, *The Manly Art: Bare-Knuckle Prize Fighting in America* (1986). An obituary by James P. Dawson is in the *New York Times*, 19 Feb. 1933.

LUCKETT V. DAVIS

CORBIN, Austin (11 July 1827–4 June 1896), financier, real estate developer, and railroad executive, was born in Newport, New Hampshire, the son of Austin Corbin, a farmer and politician, and Mary Chase. Corbin had little formal education. He attended the common schools in Newport and taught there briefly as a young man. He read law under two New England attorneys and then enrolled in Harvard Law School, graduating in 1849. Corbin was not an active member of the bar for very long. For two years he practiced law in Newport with Ralph Metcalf. In 1851 he moved to Davenport, Iowa, and continued as an attorney for three more years. In 1853 he married Hannah Maria Wheeler of Newport; they had four children.

In 1854 Corbin shifted from law to finance when he formed with Louis A. Macklot the bank of Macklot & Corbin in Davenport. The firm invested the money of Corbin's eastern associates in Iowa farm mortgages. The partnership flourished and was one of the few banks in the state to survive the panic of 1857, a point of particular pride for Corbin. In 1863 he organized the First National Bank of Davenport, one of the earliest federally chartered banks. He moved to New York City in 1865 and established the banking house of Austin Corbin & Company (in 1874 incorporated as the Corbin Banking Company).

In 1873 Corbin began his long involvement with Long Island by chance when a doctor instructed Corbin to take his ill son to Coney Island for the sea air. Corbin quickly realized the potential of the area as a resort and in concert with friends purchased land on Manhattan Beach. During 1876–1877 he built (in cooperation with his brother Daniel Chase Corbin) the New York & Manhattan Beach Railway to take vacationers quickly from New York City to the development. Corbin opened two lavish hotels, the Manhattan Beach in 1877 and the Oriental in 1880. Also in 1880 he purchased securities of the insolvent Long Island Rail Road and was named as its receiver. The following year he became the railroad's president, a position that he would hold until his death. Corbin quickly reorganized and expanded the railroad. The Long Island purchased new equipment, increased standards of train and track maintenance, and started new services aimed at attracting a wealthy clientele. It was during this period that the development of Long Island as an exclusive suburb for the affluent began. The railroad paid dividends every year under Corbin's management.

From his involvement with the Long Island Rail Road (and in 1874 the reorganization of the Indiana, Bloomington & Western Railroad), he gained a reputation in financial circles as an expert in rehabilitating weak railroads. In 1886 J. Pierpont Morgan asked him to become president of the bankrupt Philadelphia & Reading Railroad. It was the company's second receivership since 1880, and Morgan had lost confidence in the ability of Franklin Benjamin Gowen, its president, to reorganize it. Morgan and Corbin created a voting trust that controlled the stock of the Reading for five years, during which time Corbin directed the revitalization of the railroad. Corbin and his assistant Archibald A. McLeod rationalized the Reading's debt and rebuilt its physical plant under Morgan's supervision. In 1888 Corbin organized a syndicate that took control of the bankrupt Central Railroad Company of

New Jersey, the line that provided the Reading with access to New York City. In 1890 he resigned as president of the Reading, and McLeod took his place.

After Corbin finished his work on the Reading, he divided his time between his adopted home of New York City and his childhood home in Newport. His last major railroad projects were his attempts to establish a deep water port on the Long Island Rail Road for transatlantic shipping and to build a subway system for New York City in the 1890s. The port was never completed, and construction on the subway did not begin until well after his death. He also created a 26,000-acre game preserve near Newport, which he stocked with wild animals from around the world. Corbin died at his Newport home after being thrown from his carriage when the horses bolted.

Although Corbin had a successful and highly profitable career, few of his achievements survived him, and thus he is little remembered. The Reading slipped back into bankruptcy under the management of McLeod less than three years after Corbin resigned its presidency, when it overextended itself in an attempt to complete a line from Boston to Chicago. The Long Island Rail Road ceased to pay dividends soon after his death and was acquired by the Pennsylvania Railroad in 1900 as part of the Pennsylvania's expansion into Manhattan. Corbin's most lasting accomplishment was the establishment of Coney Island as a resort, but even there his vision was not quite realized. His Manhattan Beach was an up-market haven for the wealthy, not the amusement park for the masses that Coney Island became. Perhaps rather than for any specific project, Corbin should be remembered as a successful investment banker who first channeled the funds of wealthy friends into Iowa, then Coney Island, and finally various railroads. His career is representative of the key positions held by financiers in the changing American business environment of the late nineteenth century.

• The largest collection of Corbin's correspondence to survive is in the Reading Company Files at the Hagley Library and Museum, but it relates essentially to the reorganization of that railroad. Details of his business involvements can be found in John F. Kasson, *Amusing the Million: Coney Island at the Turn of the Century* (1978); Ron Ziel and George Foster, *Steel Rails to the Sunrise: The Long Island Rail Road* (1965); George H. Burgess and Miles C. Kennedy, *Centennial History of the Pennsylvania Railroad Company* (1949); and James L. Holton, *The Reading Railroad: History of a Coal Age Empire*, vol. 1 (1989). Obituaries are in the *New York Times* and the *Philadelphia Evening Bulletin*, both 5 June 1896.

JOHN H. HEPP IV

CORBIN, Margaret Cochran (12 Nov. 1752–c. 1800), was a revolutionary war heroine. The details of her early life are based on an undocumented source that indicates she was born in Pennsylvania in what is now Franklin County, the daughter of Robert Cochran. Her mother's name is not known. In 1756, Native Americans killed her father and abducted her mother. Margaret and her brother John, who might have been visiting their mother's brother, escaped capture and were subsequently raised by their uncle. She was probably still living in Pennsylvania when she married John Corbin, a Virginian by birth, in about 1772. Although a 1782 source referred to a son being killed in the Revolution, the couple apparently had no children. When John went to war, Margaret, who at about five feet eight inches was tall for the era, accompanied him.

Pennsylvania records reveal that John Corbin, an artilleryman, was killed at the battle of Fort Washington, which took place near New York City on 16 November 1776. In June 1779, Pennsylvania's Supreme Executive Council described what had happened to the Corbins. Margaret, the council reported, was "wounded and utterly disabled by three Grape shott, while she filled with distinguished Bravery the post of her Husband, who was Killed by her side, serving a piece of Artillery at Fort Washington." (When an army surgeon examined Corbin's remains in 1926, he noted that her left shoulder bones showed evidence of being injured; this supports the often-reported statement that the grape shot hit her in the shoulder and breast.) After fierce fighting, Corbin and over 2,000 other Americans were captured. Contemporary documents do not reveal if she received any preferential treatment while a prisoner.

By June 1779, Corbin had somehow managed to gain her freedom and had returned to Pennsylvania. Facing hard times, she petitioned the state for assistance. The Supreme Executive Council, emphasizing how "heroically" Corbin had acted, directed that she be given $30 "to relieve her present necessities." Despite claims to the contrary, Pennsylvania never pensioned Corbin. However, in addition to providing immediate relief, the council took action that led to her becoming a pensioner. It recommended that the Congress's Board of War help Corbin because, "notwithstanding the rations which have been allowed her, she is not Provided for as her helpless situation really requires" (*Pennsylvania Colonial Records*, vol. 12, pp. 34–35). After apparently doing some investigating, the board responded quickly. In its report of 3 July, the board spoke of "many circumstances" in addition to the recommendation of the council that caused the board to support her petition for relief. The board observed that "as she had fortitude & virtue enough to supply the place of her husband after his fall in the service of his Country, and in the execution of that task received the dangerous wound under which she now labours, the board can but consider her as entitled to the same grateful return which would be made to a soldier in circumstances equally unfortunate." On 6 July, Congress, following the specific recommendations of the board, ordered that Corbin be given a complete suit of clothes or its cash equivalent. Moreover, as long as she remained disabled, she would receive half the monthly pay of "a soldier in the service of these states." Thus, as an army officer later remarked, Margaret Corbin became "a pensioner of Congress."

Immediately following Congress's action, Corbin was enrolled in the Corps of Invalids, a regiment created by Congress in 1777. As the name implies, this regiment consisted of soldiers who, due to wounds or other disorders, could not march onto a field of battle but who could perform garrison duties.

In spite of these actions, the Board of War reported in 1780 that she "still remains in a deplorable situation in consequence of her wound, by which she is deprived of the use of one arm, and in other respects much disabled and probably will continue a cripple during her life." Considering this, the board resolved that, in addition to the half-pay pension authorized by Congress, Corbin would also annually receive either a complete suit of clothes or its equivalent in cash.

Corbin probably remained in or near Philadelphia until late 1781 when the Invalid Regiment officially become part of the garrison at West Point. A brief report prepared by Captain Samuel Shaw, who was then stationed at West Point, indicates that Corbin had remarried by September 1782. This marriage to a man whose name is not given—and curiously by which Corbin was not thereafter known—did not improve her situation. As Shaw phrased it, perhaps using Corbin's own words, "her present husband is a poor crippled invalid who is no service to her but rather adds to her trouble." Faced with mounting difficulties, Corbin made a special application. Probably drawing on Corbin's words, Captain Shaw noted that, "hers being so singular a case," Corbin "thinks" she ought again to receive the normal rum allowance that had been cut off, apparently as of January 1782. "With this back allowance," the argument went, "she will be able to procure sundry necessaries that will render her present wretchedness a little more tolerable" (Hall, p. 21). Corbin's request was granted. In April 1783, along with the other members of the Invalid Regiment, she was officially discharged from military service.

Records prepared by military officials, who by the mid-1780s simply referred to her as "Captain Molly," demonstrate that Corbin continued to live in the vicinity of West Point at Highland Falls and that she depended on the federal government for support. Although the records are silent on the fate of her second husband, the fact that Corbin was placed in various private homes to be maintained at a fixed rate suggests that he may have died or otherwise disappeared. West Point officials, who occasionally provided additional aid for Corbin, clearly believed that they and the government had a special duty to continue to assist her. However, they also found their task increasingly troublesome. In January 1786, William Price, the base commissary, observed that "Captain Molly . . . is such an offensive person that people are unwilling to take her in charge." In 1787, the West Point commander described "Captain Molly" as "a disagreeable object to take care of" (Hall, pp. 27, 28). Although the Board of War's 1780 observations about Corbin's disabilities are suggestive, what made caring for her so "offensive" and "disagreeable" remains unclear.

The last references in the West Point commissary books to "Captain Molly" indicate that she stayed with Mrs. Elizabeth Randal in Highland Falls from late 1786 through 24 August 1789. On that date Corbin disappears from the documentary record. Remembrances recorded decades later or passed on from generation to generation of Highland Falls residents provide what is known of Corbin's later years. Based on those accounts, Corbin was an Irish woman who was not fastidious about her appearance, who could be acerbic, but who was also respectfully addressed as "Captain Molly." For about a decade, she reportedly lived alone near the village of Highlands Falls and was buried near there when she died in about 1800. In 1926, through efforts coordinated by the Daughters of the American Revolution, Corbin's remains were exhumed, examined by medical authorities, and reinterred at West Point. The bronze tablet on her monument depicts a resolute woman firing a cannon and also gives a brief history of this "Heroine of the Revolution."

During the nineteenth century, Margaret Corbin's story became entangled with accounts of Mary McCauley—the "Molly Pitcher" who supposedly replaced her husband and helped keep a cannon in action during the 28 June 1778 battle of Monmouth. Mary McCauley may have done so, but contemporary records do not document that fact. No such questions cloud the story of Margaret Corbin's heroism. She did replace her husband when he was killed in battle in 1776; she did help keep a cannon firing, at least until three grape shot tore into her. Having been made a disabled cripple by her war wounds, "Captain Molly" depended on government help to subsist. Her life after the battle of Fort Washington was difficult and, it seems, often lonely. Measured by any standard, Margaret Corbin paid a heavy price for helping to create a new nation. The government of her native state and of the fledgling nation acknowledged that fact and her special status by treating Corbin as what she was: a combat soldier who became disabled by wounds "in the service of these states."

• No collection of Corbin papers is known to exist. Despite the claim in the *Index of Revolutionary War Pension Applications in the National Archives: Bicentennial Edition (Revised and Enlarged)* (1976, p. 124), the Deborah Gannett pension file does not contain correspondence relating to Corbin. Documents about Corbin are printed in the *Pennsylvania Archives*, 5th ser., vol. 4, pp. 40, 59, 65, 79, 90 and vol. 6, p. 65; the *Pennsylvania Colonial Records*, vol. 12, pp. 34–35; and the *Journals of the Continental Congress*, vol. 14, p. 805 and vol. 17, p. 664. The important 3 July 1779 Board of War report is in the Papers of the Continental Congress, item 147 in vol. 3 (pp. 501–4) available on roll 158 of the microfilm edition of the papers. All published accounts of Corbin's early years ultimately rest on William Henry Egle, ed., *Notes and Queries: Historical, Biographical and Genealogical: Relating Chiefly to Interior Pennsylvania*, 4th ser., 1 (1893): 264–65. The essential work is Edward H. Hall, *Margaret Corbin: Heroine of the Battle of Fort Washington 16 November 1776* (1932). Hall convincingly corrects most errors that appear in other works; he also reprints, albeit with modernized capitalization, sections of key documents from the 1770s and 1780s. Information on the medical examination of Corbin's remains appears in Amelia C. Parker, "Revolutionary Heroine Interred in West Point Cemetery," *Daughters of the American Revolution Magazine*, June 1926, pp. 347–52. An undocumented and unconvincing claim that Corbin resided in Pennsylvania after the war is advanced in Egle, *Notes and Queries*, and in Randolph Keim, "Heroines of the Revolution," *Journal of American History* 16 (Jan. 1922): 31–35. On the intertwining of the stories of Corbin and "Molly Pitcher," in addition to Hall's coverage, see D. W. Thompson and Merri Lou Schaumann, "Goodbye, Molly Pitcher," *Cumberland County History* 6 (Summer 1989): 3–26.

JOHN K. ALEXANDER

CORBY, William (2 Oct. 1833–28 Dec. 1897), Roman Catholic priest and educator, was born in Detroit, Michigan, the son of Daniel Corby, a real estate dealer, and Elizabeth Stapleton. After working for four years in his father's real estate firm, Corby entered the University of Notre Dame in 1853. He joined the Congregation of Holy Cross, a religious order, in 1854 and continued his studies at Notre Dame until 1860, when he was ordained a priest. Soon afterward, he was appointed director of the Manual Labor School at Notre Dame, Indiana, and served as pastor of a parish in South Bend, Indiana.

Shortly after the outbreak of the Civil War, Corby traveled to Washington, D.C., to minister to the spiritual needs of Roman Catholic soldiers in the Union army. In December 1861 he was commissioned chaplain of the Eighty-eighth New York Regiment, one of the units of the famed Irish Brigade. While he faithfully performed the pastoral and liturgical functions of a priest for nearly three years, his most notable wartime achievement occurred on 2 July 1863 during the battle of Gettysburg. Immediately prior to the Irish Brigade's entering combat, Corby climbed onto a boulder near the center of the Union line, stood erect, raised his right hand, and pronounced a general absolution on the hundreds of soldiers massed in front of him. This dramatic demonstration of religious faith and bravery under fire was eventually commemorated in one of the few monuments honoring a chaplain's service in the Civil War. Following Corby's death, St. Clair Mulholland, the former commander of a regiment in the Irish Brigade, began a fundraising campaign to memorialize the priest's heroism. Mulholland's efforts came to fruition in 1910 when a bronze statue of Corby was unveiled at the spot on the battlefield where he had blessed the troops.

In the fall of 1864, when the end of the war seemed near, the superior of Corby's order asked him to resign from the army and return to Notre Dame. Corby was installed as vice president of the university in 1865 and, following the president's untimely death, was named president the next year. He served as president of Notre Dame until 1872, when his order dispatched him to Watertown, Wisconsin, to take charge of Sacred Heart College there. During his tenure as president of Sacred Heart, Corby not only helped place a struggling educational institution on solid financial ground but also exercised a pastorate at the local parish church. When the situation at Sacred Heart was stabilized, Corby was recalled to serve a second term as president of Notre Dame. He greatly expanded the university between 1877 and 1881, adding new academic departments and strengthening the school's overall educational standards. After a devastating fire virtually destroyed the campus in 1879, he organized an impressive rebuilding program. In 1881 Corby retired from the presidency and returned to Watertown to work as a parish priest. Five years later he was elected provincial general of the Congregation of the Holy Cross and once more moved back to Notre Dame, a residence he maintained until his death.

During the last decade of his life, Corby was active in veterans' affairs, founding a Grand Army of the Republic post composed entirely of Roman Catholic priests and religious brothers. An invitation to participate in the twenty-fifth anniversary of the battle of Gettysburg inspired him to compose *Memoirs of Chaplain Life* (1893; 2d ed., 1894), a book that described both homey aspects of life in camp and moments of danger and excitement in battle. Corby was also highly conscious of making his book a forum for educating Protestants about the patriotic virtues Roman Catholic soldiers and chaplains had displayed throughout the Civil War. In an era when anti-Catholicism and nativism were still pervasive forces within American culture, he used the experiences of soldiers he had known to demonstrate that their Roman Catholic faith had been a key element in the contributions they made to Union victory. In fact, so strong was his emotional attachment to the Irish Brigade that, at the time of his death, his casket was wrapped in his regiment's flag and carried to the cemetery, not by priests of the Congregation of Holy Cross (as was customary), but by a group of aging Civil War veterans.

Corby was one of the most popular and successful priests of the Roman Catholic church in the second half of the nineteenth century. He came to prominence as a chaplain during the Civil War and enjoyed an illustrious career in education in the 1870s. His writings confronted anti-Catholic prejudice in the United States, and his leadership as a college president helped establish Notre Dame as a premier institution of American higher education.

• Corby's papers are in the University of Notre Dame Archives and at the Province Archives Center of the Priests of Holy Cross (Indiana Province) in Notre Dame. The "Corby Memorial Number" of the *Notre Dame Scholastic* 31 (1898): 245–76 contains basic biographical information and assessments of Corby's character compiled at the time of his death. Historian Lawrence Frederick Kohl provides a useful, modern introduction to Corby's career in the facsimile of the 1893 edition of *Memoirs of Chaplain Life: Three Years with the Irish Brigade in the Army of the Potomac* (1992), which he edited. Kohl has also edited a reprint of David P. Conyngham, *The Irish Brigade and Its Campaigns* (1867; repr. 1994), a serviceable if dated history of Corby's Civil War unit.

GARDINER H. SHATTUCK, JR.

CORCORAN, James Andrew (30 Mar. 1820–16 July 1889), Catholic theologian and editor, was born in Charleston, South Carolina, the son of Jane O'Farrell and John Corcoran, Irish immigrants and grocers. John Corcoran immigrated to Charleston in 1817 and died there in 1819 at the age of thirty-five, five months before James was born. James's mother Jane took over the family grocery business and raised his older brother John and him until she, too, died in 1832, leaving her two sons to the care of a hired maid. John England, who had been appointed the first Catholic bishop of Charleston in 1820, took an interest in James, enrolling him in the classical college that England had established. Because England considered the orphaned James to be precocious and to have a vocation to the priesthood, he sent him, at the age of thirteen, to the Urban College of the Propaganda in Rome to study for the priesthood. From 1833 to 1842 James studied ancient and modern languages, philosophy, and theology, receiving his doctorate in theology in 1842, when he was also ordained to the priesthood.

Upon his return to Charleston in 1843, he became a professor in England's seminary and served congregations in the city. From 1850 until the beginning of the Civil War in 1861, he was also editor of the *United States Catholic Miscellany*, the first Catholic newspaper in the United States to have a national distribution. He used the *Miscellany* to comment on various events in American Catholic history and to criticize what he considered to be the revolutionary liberties of European and American reform movements. An apologist for the Catholic church, he asserted the importance of authority in the state as well as in the church. As editor he also demonstrated periodically his attachments to southern culture, his states' rights view of government, his hatred for the abolitionists, and his disdain for President Abraham Lincoln's election, which he saw as the final insult to the South and the culmination of forces creating a split between the two sections of the country.

From 1861 to 1868, after the newspaper was destroyed during the Civil War, he became a pastor in Wilmington, North Carolina, and served as vicar-general of the Diocese of Charleston. Corcoran was considered one of the best-educated Catholic theologians and canonists in the United States and was frequently used as a theological advisor to the bishops at the Baltimore provincial councils in the 1840s and 1850s, and he was the theological expert at the national plenary councils of American Catholic bishops in 1866 and 1884. In 1868 Baltimore's archbishop Martin John Spalding chose him as the theological representative of American bishops to assist in the preparations for the First Vatican Council (1869–1870). During the preparatory sessions for the council, Corcoran became disturbed by what he told Archbishop Spalding was proposed legislation on church and state issues that would, if accepted by a council, condemn "the fundamental principles of our [American and common sense] political doctrine." Although the council eventually defined papal infallibility, a position Corcoran

defended, it did not address the church-state issue as Corcoran feared.

After his return from the First Vatican Council, Corcoran became a professor of theology at St. Charles Borromeo Seminary in Philadelphia, becoming rector from 1872 to 1873. In 1876, he became the founding editor of and a regular contributor to the *American Catholic Quarterly Review*, a general journal of Catholic opinion on theological, historical, social, literary, political, and ethical issues. The journal, one of only two journals of Catholic opinion, provided American Catholics with an organ for intellectual expression that was rare in the immigrant Catholic community. In 1889 Corcoran was the first theologian to be invited to join the faculty of the American bishops' newly established Catholic University of America in Washington, D.C., but he refused the appointment because of age.

Within the American Catholic community Corcoran was a conservative ultramontane theologian whose national sympathies were with the South, even the defeated South after the Civil War. Although he upheld traditional values of authority, community, and unity, he was also American in his acceptance of democratic government, separation of church and state, and religious liberty. He was extremely critical of the new evolutionary theories, the rising biblical criticism, and the Protestant ecclesiastical propensity toward ever increasing diversity and disintegration. Although he was a theological educator and considered by many to be brilliant, his students considered him routine and dull. He was a leading Catholic theologian in the country, but he was never a creative publishing scholar. He was an occasional essayist who was more interested in attacking his opponents' positions than in developing creative alternatives.

Corcoran was never in good health, and when he became sick with Bright's disease in 1885, he never fully recovered, dying in Philadelphia.

• Corcoran's letters and other unpublished papers are located primarily in the archives of the Diocese of Charleston and of the archdioceses of Baltimore, New York, and Philadelphia. His theological perspectives are evident in his *Stock Misrepresentations of Catholic Doctrines* (1902) and in numerous articles of the *American Catholic Quarterly Review* (1876–1889). There is no published critical biography of Corcoran, but useful biographical information and an analysis of his life and works are found in Mary Marcian Lowman, "James Andrew Corcoran: Editor, Theologian, Scholar (1820–1889)" (Ph.D. diss., St. Louis Univ., 1958), and John J. Keane, "Monsignor Corcoran," *American Catholic Quarterly Review* 14 (1889): 738–47.

PATRICK W. CAREY

CORCORAN, Thomas Gardiner (29 Dec. 1900–6 Dec. 1981), government official and presidential adviser, was born in Pawtucket, Rhode Island, into an affluent, teetotaling, self-consciously "lace-curtain" Irish family. His father, Patrick, was a Democrat who served briefly in the Rhode Island legislature; his mother, Mary O'Keefe, was from a prosperous Republican family that looked with some contempt on the "cheap" political activities of the "damned Shanty Irish." In his youth, at least, Corcoran shared something of his mother's distaste for "politicians," if not for politics, and ultimately he brought to his own public career a conviction that, while elected officials were necessary, the best sources of public wisdom were intelligent, highly educated administrators like (he chose to believe) himself.

Corcoran excelled at Brown University, where he graduated as valedictorian, and at Harvard Law School, where he became an editor of the law review. Along with other exceptionally bright young law students, he attracted (and prudently reciprocated) the attention of Professor Felix Frankfurter, who was known for his ability to place his protégés in positions of influence. When Corcoran left Harvard in 1926, Frankfurter secured for him a coveted clerkship with Associate Justice of the Supreme Court Oliver Wendell Holmes (1841–1935). His year at the Court left Corcoran with a deep and enduring reverence for Holmes and passion for the work of government.

Corcoran spent the five years after his clerkship practicing law in the Wall Street firm of Cotton, Franklin, where he developed an expertise in securities law and underwriting. He returned to Washington in March 1932 to work on the legal staff of the Reconstruction Finance Corporation, a newly created federal lending and investment agency. Corcoran remained with the RFC after Franklin D. Roosevelt became president in 1933 and, except for temporary service in the Justice Department in 1934, stayed there until 1940. Despite his relatively inconspicuous official position, he quickly became an important figure in the Roosevelt administration. During the first three years of the New Deal, his position was largely a result of his close relationship with Frankfurter, who used his personal friendship with Roosevelt to expand his influence in Washington and who came to consider Corcoran his unofficial "agent" in the capital. When Frankfurter received a request for assistance from the president, more often than not he directed it to Corcoran. Among other things, he recruited Corcoran to help draft the legislation that created the Securities and Exchange Commission in 1933 and, two years later, to draw up the controversial Public Utilities Holding Company bill (the so-called "death sentence," designed to break up utilities monopolies). Corcoran also played a role in writing the Tennessee Valley Authority Act in 1933 and the Fair Labor Standards Act of 1938.

Gradually, however, Corcoran established a significant power base apart from Frankfurter by virtue of his energy, his intellect, his personal charm, and his own success in recruiting bright young men (from Harvard Law School and elsewhere) for important posts in the administration. By 1935 he was the unofficial leader of a group of young, mostly unmarried New Dealers, many of whom lived together for a time in a house in Georgetown and who occupied important, if secondary, positions in New Deal agencies and shared a commitment to defining a new and more aggressive

liberalism for the administration. He had a particularly important relationship with Benjamin V. Cohen, another Frankfurter protégé from Harvard, who, like Corcoran, came to wield considerable power from relatively minor official positions. Indeed, Corcoran and Cohen worked together intimately on almost all their legislative projects and developed as well a close friendship that continued throughout their lives.

Corcoran's relationship with the president was the subject of much speculation. Roosevelt clearly liked him and enjoyed his company. He also admired Corcoran's skills as a writer and came increasingly to rely on him to put a "lilt" in his speeches. Corcoran was, for example, one of the principal draftsmen of the president's dramatic 1936 acceptance speech in Philadelphia and the author of Roosevelt's celebrated phrase a "rendezvous with destiny." Whether Corcoran often shaped Roosevelt's positions on policy in any fundamental way is less clear, but there is little to suggest that he ever exercised the sort of influence over the president that both friends and enemies often attributed to him. Corcoran, however, did nothing to discourage such beliefs; indeed, he traded openly and at times somewhat dishonestly on the widespread assumption that he was acting as the president's agent.

Like the president himself, Corcoran suffered politically during Roosevelt's second term from his association with a series of controversial measures. He was an energetic and conspicuous supporter of the president's unsuccessful court-packing plan of 1937, and he was one of the architects of Roosevelt's equally unsuccessful effort to purge the Senate of influential conservative Democrats in 1938 by campaigning on behalf of their opponents in the primaries. (He claimed later that he had privately opposed both measures but had promoted them out of loyalty to the president.) He was also one of the leaders of the covert effort to nominate Roosevelt for a third term in 1940. In the process, he deeply antagonized a powerful group of conservative Democrats, some of whom had hoped to run for president themselves.

Corcoran resigned from the RFC in 1940 to allow himself to work openly for Roosevelt's reelection. When the campaign was over, however, the president did not bring him back into the administration—partly because of the strong hostility Corcoran had evoked from many members of Congress, and partly because he had fallen out with Frankfurter, who declined to support his effort to be appointed solicitor general. Out of government, Corcoran maintained a cordial, if increasingly strained, personal relationship with the president, served him at times as an informal adviser, and continued to hope for appointment to a major post. But the appointment never came. His public career had effectively ended.

Corcoran had other reasons for leaving government. In 1940 he had married his longtime secretary, Margaret Dowd, and early in 1941 the first of their four children was born. Eager to increase his income, he entered a lucrative private law practice through which he established himself as one of the first and most successful of a new breed of lobbyists, using political connections to represent clients in their dealings with the government. His private activities quickly became almost as controversial as his public ones. Late in 1941 a Senate committee subpoenaed him to answer charges of illegal "influence-peddling"; similar accusations bedeviled him for the next forty years as he accumulated substantial wealth and an imposing list of corporate clients. No one ever demonstrated that he had done anything illegal, but the energy and aggressiveness he brought to his work for private interests, so like the energy and aggressiveness he had once brought to his work for Roosevelt, persuaded even some of his longstanding friends that he had abandoned his political principles. Still, few people could dislike the ingratiating "Tommy the Cork" for long, and he remained a popular and at times influential figure in Democratic politics until his death in Washington, D.C.

• Corcoran's papers are housed in the Manuscript Division of the Library of Congress. There is no published biography. Lynne Niznik, "Thomas G. Corcoran" (Ph.D. diss., Univ. of Notre Dame, 1981), is the most extensive study of his life. Joseph P. Lash, *Dreamers and Dealers* (1988), also gives significant attention to Corcoran's career.

ALAN BRINKLEY

CORCORAN, William Wilson (27 Dec. 1798–24 Feb. 1888), banker, investor, and philanthropist, was born in Georgetown, District of Columbia, the son of Thomas Corcoran, an Irish-born merchant, real estate seller, and local politician, and Hannah Lemmon. Corcoran, who is usually referred to as "W. W." rather than William, was educated in local Georgetown schools and spent one year at Georgetown College (now Georgetown University). In 1815 he left college to go into the business of operating a dry goods store with his two older brothers, James and Thomas, Jr. In 1817 Corcoran opened a branch store, and by 1820, the three brothers expanded their interests to include an auction and commission house. After the company went bankrupt in a financial panic in 1823, Corcoran worked until 1847 to pay off all their creditors in full, an act that demonstrated his views regarding honor.

After losing his business, Corcoran became a real estate investor and worked as a clerk for the Bank of Columbia. The latter job ended when the bank failed, and in 1828 its assets and Corcoran's job were transferred to the Washington branch of the Bank of the United States. At the BUS Corcoran became manager of real estate accounts and of suspended debts. After seven years at his post, Corcoran eloped in 1835 with fifteen-year-old Louise Amory Morris, daughter of Navy Commander Charles Morris; they had three children, two of whom died in infancy. After his wife's death in 1841, Corcoran never remarried.

When the BUS federal charter expired in 1836, Corcoran and others began to offer services formerly monopolized by the bank. In 1837 he opened a brokerage firm and in 1840 formed a banking firm, Corcoran & Riggs, which he partnered with George Washington Riggs, the son of New York banker Elisha Riggs. Corcoran & Riggs did not issue banknotes, choosing instead to concentrate on investing in U.S. Treasury notes to resell to investors. The firm turned a large profit even in its first year, benefiting from a close relationship with Treasury Secretary Levi Woodbury, who kept Corcoran apprised of competitors' bids on treasury notes. In the economic free-for-all that characterized nineteenth-century banking, such cooperation was not viewed as unethical or illegal; it did lead to bad feelings among other bidders, but it also served the Treasury by assuring the government lower costs. The firm also expanded its interests into New York City and Baltimore, Maryland.

The change of administration after the 1840 presidential election had little effect on Corcoran & Riggs. Because it was an exchange bank paying specie and did not issue banknotes, Corcoran & Riggs supported key aspects of Andrew Jackson's economic plan; that support continued under the fiscally conservative Whig president John Tyler as well. By 1845, as the Democrats resumed control of the White House and Corcoran's growing social circle included political allies from both parties, the firm became the principal depository of government funds. In 1846 Corcoran's fortune was made as Corcoran & Riggs almost singlehandedly financed the Mexican-American War. The U.S. Treasury floated two loans in the spring of 1847, for $18 million and $16 million. Corcoran & Riggs held $14.7 million of the first loan. The bonds sold well to American investors, and Corcoran & Riggs's profit was $250,000. The second loan, of which Corcoran & Riggs held $14 million, sold less well in a skittish market. Corcoran gained authorization as an American agent for the U.S. Treasury from Robert Walker, the secretary of the treasury under James K. Polk, and traveled to England to try to spark interest in the bonds, which he succeeded in selling. By 1851, the market rebounded, and with the loan's final liquidation, Corcoran had made well over $1 million in profit. He had, along the way, lost his far more cautious partner; George Riggs was replaced by his son, Elisha Riggs, Jr.

The election of Zachary Taylor in 1848 put the Whigs back in office and began the move to an independent treasury system and away from the practice of using private banking firms. Corcoran's longstanding political friendships, however, postponed the final removal of funds for some time; not until the tenure of Democrat Franklin Pierce's treasury secretary, James Guthrie, were government deposits completely removed from private firms.

The severing of the firm's government tie, the deaths in 1853 of both Elisha Riggs, Sr., and his son Joseph Riggs, who had served Corcoran & Riggs's New York City interests, and Corcoran's long-held ambition to play the role of a wealthy gentleman of leisure, led him to retire in 1854. He continued to invest in armaments with the Maynard Arms Company; in government bonds, railroads, and land grants; and in real estate in Manhattan, St. Louis, and the District of Columbia, where, by the 1860s, he had become the largest single landowner. He maintained his connection to the political world by pursuing claims against the government on behalf of individuals who desired an effective spokesman on their behalf. He pursued this activity largely for his own amusement: by the mid-1880s, he was lobbying Congress to pay small claims that were over a half-century old, from which he might receive a nominal 5 to 10 percent commission. He also funded various Democratic politicians, including James Buchanan, who won the presidency in 1856. But Buchanan's failure to support southern demands during the secession crisis during his last months in office turned Corcoran against the president, and Abraham Lincoln's assumption of office in March 1861 turned Corcoran against the Union. Corcoran's antipathy was solidified in November 1861 as the Union stopped the British mail packet *Trent* and seized Confederate commissioners James Mason and John Slidell, along with Slidell's private secretary, George Eustis, Jr., Corcoran's son-in-law, and his daughter, Louise, traveling with her husband and the commissioners to Europe. All were imprisoned at Fort Warren outside Boston until released when the Lincoln administration realized Britain might go to war to preserve the principle of freedom of the seas. Corcoran decided to join his daughter and son-in-law in France and expatriated over $1 million in cash and securities to Europe, smuggling out silver plate with the help of the French ambassador to the United States. He remained in France until Louise's death from tuberculosis in December 1867.

In retaliation for Corcoran's expatriation of such massive sums of money, his subsequent avoidance of wartime taxes, as well as his work serving the Confederacy by giving financial advice and carrying messages, in 1863 Secretary of War Edwin Stanton seized some of Corcoran's Washington properties and confiscated some of his rents. In 1859 Corcoran had begun the Corcoran Gallery of Art. The Civil War interrupted the work, and the building at Pennsylvania Avenue and 17th Street was seized and occupied by Quartermaster General Montgomery Meigs and his officers during the war. After Corcoran took the loyalty oath and returned to the United States in 1868, his properties were restored, and work resumed on the gallery. On 24 May 1870 the gallery was incorporated by an act of Congress and Corcoran was reimbursed for its use during the war. The gallery opened to the public in 1872; the nucleus of its collection came from Corcoran's own. In 1897 the gallery moved to 17th Street between E Street and New York Avenue.

The gallery was one of many charitable and intellectual concerns of Corcoran. In 1869 he founded the "Louise Home," named for his daughter, to provide support for gentlewomen who had suffered financial reverses. He gave generous gifts to the University of Virginia, the College of William and Mary, Virginia Military Institute, and Washington and Lee University, as well as various church institutions. He also served as vice president of the Washington Monument

Society and loaned the concern funds to speed completion of its work.

The exclusion of Democrats from the seat of power in Washington after the Civil War precluded Corcoran from reviving any political power. He contributed to Democratic campaign funds and funded the Democratic newspaper, the Washington *Union*, to reverse the trend. In 1884, with the return of the Democrats to the White House, the 86-year-old philanthropist found himself back in the social circles of power. He died in Washington, D.C.

• Corcoran's papers are in the Library of Congress. Additional financial papers of Corcoran & Riggs and Riggs & Company are in the archives of the Riggs National Bank in Washington, D.C. *A Grandfather's Legacy*, Corcoran's autobiography, was published in 1879. The standard biography of Corcoran is Henry Cohen, *Business and Politics from the Age of Jackson to the Civil War: The Career Biography of W. W. Corcoran* (1971); see also Robert T. Sweet, *Selected Correspondence of the Banking Firm of Corcoran & Riggs* (1982). An important article on the nature and degree of Corcoran's political influence is Irving Katz, "Confidant at the Capital: William W. Corcoran's Role in Nineteenth-Century American Politics," *Historian* 29 (1967): 546–64.

JANET L. CORYELL

CORD, Errett Lobban (20 July 1894–2 Jan. 1974), automaker and financier, was born in Warrensburg, Missouri, the son of Charles W. Cord, a storekeeper, and Ida Lobban. Throughout his life Cord was known simply by his initials, "E. L." In the early 1900s his family moved to Los Angeles, where Cord attended high school but left before finishing his final year. As a teenager he showed a passion for automobiles, rebuilding old cars and racing them on dirt tracks in California and Oregon. Cord operated a garage and a trucking firm in California, the latter in Death Valley. He also established the short-lived Cord Auto Washing Company, worked as a truck driver, and sold and raced cars in Phoenix, Arizona. In 1914 Cord married Helen Marie Frische of Cincinnati. They had two sons.

In 1918, when Cord left Phoenix for Chicago, he was virtually penniless, but he became a successful salesman for the Moon Automobile Agency. He returned to California briefly in a failed attempt to sell a new type of domestic heater, repaired to Chicago, and was soon promoted to sales manager of the Chicago Moon distributorship. His sales commissions were spectacular, often exceeding $30,000 a year. Yearning to leave sales and engage in automobile manufacturing, he saved $100,000 and in 1924 took his first steps toward building a financial empire by visiting the troubled Auburn Automobile Company (AAC) in Indiana. The company, struggling to overcome the effects of a 1922 recession, was making only $10,000 a year in profits and had produced a mere 175 cars in 1923.

In 1924 Cord moved to Auburn and, instead of accepting a $36,000-a-year salary at AAC, asked for 20 percent of company profits plus stock options; he was also made vice president and general manager of the company. His first task was to work off the company's inventory of 700 unsold cars; he spruced up these cars with new paint jobs and nickel plating and managed to sell all of them. He also proposed to liquidate the surplus of parts and instead develop an all-new automobile. The new car, the Auburn 8–63, was painted in bright colors and became the first American automobile to be outfitted with a Lycoming-built straight-eight cylinder engine. It was promoted in a creative *Saturday Evening Post* advertising campaign. Cord personally supervised the design of the new Auburn car, which also earned a record as the first American stock car to break the 100-m.p.h. barrier, a record he established with himself at the wheel. The new car sold briskly and became one of the most sporty, prestigious cars in the country.

Cord effected a remarkable turnaround at AAC. In 1924, his first full year at the company, AAC produced 2,000 cars and made a profit of over $200,000. He created markets for the cars not only throughout the United States but also overseas, establishing distributorships in European cities. By 1928, AAC was exporting 17 percent of its cars. Cord, who was still in his twenties when he came to AAC, hired a raft of young, ingenious designers to develop new cars, including Alan Leamy, who designed the Auburn cars of the late 1920s and early 1930s and who styled the innovative Cord L-29 automobile, and his successor, Gordon Buehrig, who designed the Cord 810 automobile with its distinctive "coffin-nose" hood. He also cut red tape by abolishing AAC's board of trustees and its receiving department, moves that saved the company an estimated $100,000 a year.

Cord became president of AAC and, exercising his stock option, gained controlling interest of the company. He soon began an expansion. In 1926 he purchased the Duesenberg Automobile and Motors Corporation, an Indianapolis firm that built incomparable luxury vehicles and record-setting sports cars. The marriage of Cord's corporation with that of Duesenberg soon yielded the Duesenberg Model J, one of the most powerful and elegant automobiles of its day. Owners of Duesenbergs included movie celebrities, such as James Cagney, Gary Cooper, and Clark Gable. In 1929 Cord opened a branch plant in Connorsville, Indiana, to manufacture more automobiles. During the same year the L-29 Cord automobile premiered, the first mass-produced car with four-wheel drive. The model was discontinued after 1932 because of sluggish sales.

AAC offered a wide range of cars to the American consumer, from the Auburn Brougham that sold for less than $1,000 to more expensive Cords to the Duesenbergs, which went for $20,000 or more. In 1929 the Cord Corporation was created, which comprised the Auburn, Cord, and Duesenberg family of automobiles, for which E. L. Cord was renowned; it was also a conglomerate holding company with sixty diverse subsidiaries, including Century Air Lines and Century Pacific Air Lines (which were not only commuter airlines but also among the country's first air mail carriers); the Checkered Cab Company of Kalamazoo, Michigan; the Lycoming Manufacturing Company of Williamsport, Pennsylvania, which built engines that Cord used in his cars; the New York Ship Building Company, builder of luxury liners and navy cruisers; the Stinson Aircraft Corporation of Wayne, Michigan; and many other automotive component, aviation, and shipbuilding interests. After his first wife died of cancer in 1930, in 1931 Cord married Virginia Kirk Tharpe of Los Angeles. They had three daughters.

AAC enjoyed its peak year of prosperity in 1931, when it built 34,000 cars, ranked thirteenth in sales among American automobile manufacturers, and made a net profit of over $3.5 million. But the Great Depression quickly broke the company's momentum after that year by robbing consumers of their ability to purchase luxury cars. The company struggled for the next several years, never showing a profit, even though in 1936 the front-wheel drive Cord 810 was introduced as part of an effort to resuscitate AAC. This new model boasted many avant-garde features, including advanced streamlining, retractable headlights, a concealed gas cap, full wheel covers, and the elimination of running boards. In 1937 Cord sold the entire Cord Corporation to a group of Manhattan bankers for $2.63 million. AAC halted production in 1937 and officially went bankrupt two years later. The Great Depression, which swept like a scythe through the American automobile industry, had claimed AAC as one of its many victims.

By the early 1930s Cord had made his name synonymous with success and wealth. But with fame and fortune came kidnapping threats directed at his children. An intensely private man, Cord left Auburn in May 1934 and took his family to Europe. They stayed there for the summer and returned to the United States in September, at which time they relocated to California. Ostensibly the Cords sojourned abroad because of Cord's concern for the safety of his children, but that explanation may have been more apparent than real. Cord was also seeking to escape the growing controversy stemming from the far-flung, variegated nature of Cord Corporation holdings, which were attracting attention from the Securities and Exchange Commission (SEC). The SEC later named Cord in a 1936 investigation, and the following year a federal court order enjoined him from any violations of SEC antimanipulation rules in his financial activities.

By the time he sold his Cord Corporation, Cord had invested in other areas, especially in aviation and in the Los Angeles real estate market; in 1931 he had also built a 62-room mansion, "Cord Haven," in Beverly Hills, California. He later sold the mansion and in 1939 moved to Nevada, where he owned a 3,400-acre ranch in Esmeralda County, plus 30,000 acres of cattle land elsewhere in the state.

Over the next two decades Cord continued his business activities, and his profile in Nevada increased. In 1952 he found himself at the center of controversy when he and the U.S. Bureau of Land Management ordered about seventy-five persons evicted from federal land in Nevada where he had a grazing lease. In 1954 he and ten other businessmen pooled their resources to buy a uranium mine in Utah for $500,000; they sold it three years later for $17 million. In 1956 Cord was elected to the Nevada State Senate from Esmeralda County. He served one term and was a major presence in the state's Democratic politics.

Cord owned three large ranches in Nevada and spent most of his time at a home in Reno, Nevada. He was also owner of the KCRL television-radio station in Reno and had extensive property holdings in Southern California, including tungsten mines and the 31-acre Pan Pacific Auditorium in Los Angeles. Cord died in Reno.

• The Auburn-Cord-Duesenberg Museum of Auburn, Ind., which opened in 1974, occupies the original factory showroom building of the Auburn Automobile Company. The museum houses many Auburn, Cord, and Duesenberg automobiles and contains exhibits that honor the life and work of E. L. Cord. The Blommel Historic Auto Data Collection of Connersville, Ind., has collections devoted to the history of the Cord Corporation, including original accounting journal photographs as well as company documents. The National Automotive History Collection of the Detroit Public Library maintains a file on Cord. At the apex of Cord's automobile manufacturing career *Time* magazine featured him in two cover stories, "Motion for Sale," 18 Jan. 1932, and "Farlay's Deal," 23 Apr. 1934. Cord was also the subject of "Down to the Sea and Ships Via Auto and Airplane," *Newsweek,* 12 Aug. 1933. Four books feature Cord and his automobiles. They are Griffith Borgeson, *Errett Lobban Cord, His Empire, His Motor Cars: Auburn, Cord, Duesenberg* (1983); Don Butler, *Auburn, Cord, Duesenberg* (1992); Josh B. Malks, *Cord 810 and 812: The Timeless Classics* (1995); and Lee Beck and Malks, *Auburn and Cord* (1996). Cord is the subject of an article by Beverly Rae Kimes, "E. L.: His Cord and His Empire," *Automobile Quarterly* 28, no. 2 (Second Quarter, 1980): 192. Obituaries are in the *(Auburn, Ind.) Evening Star,* 3 Jan. 1974, the *New York Times,* 4 Jan. 1974, and the *Reno (Nev.) Evening Gazette,* 3 Jan. 1974.

YANEK MIECZKOWSKI

COREY, Giles (1612?–16 Sept. 1692), farmer, was born in England, probably of a farm family. His parents' names and occupations are not known. Little is known of Corey's early life, and he appears in Massachusetts records only in court cases and contemporary accounts of his death. Corey was apparently married twice, the first time to Mary (maiden name unknown), the second time to Martha Rich. She had an illegitimate mulatto son, who lived with the family in Salem Town just across the dividing line from Salem Village, the center of the upheaval over the witches. Two sons-in-law are mentioned in Giles Corey's will, and Giles and Martha may have had a third daughter as well. Martha Corey was a member of the church in Salem Village; Giles was not until late in his life.

Giles Corey was a successful, even prosperous farmer who at the time of his death owned his own land. His will mentions land, meadow, cattle, clothing, "household stuffe," and "brass peauter" (pewter). But as the records of several court cases reveal, he had a reputation for unlawful and sometimes violent behavior. Indeed, the records of the Essex County Court are filled with accounts of quarrels, usually in suits and countersuits against neighbors. In 1670 Corey was fined for theft, in 1676 for beating Jacob Goodell. The spring of 1678 saw him in court in a cluster of suits involving neighbors. Several people living nearby testified that Corey had stolen wood and tools from them and had threatened to burn their homes and orchards. The called him a "very quarrelsome and contentious bad neighbor" (*Records of . . . Essex,* vol. 7, p. 91). These cases continued well beyond the spring and ended when Mary, Corey's first wife, was fined for drunkenness, cursing, and "abusive speeches." Giles Corey escaped punishment, though his reputation as a deviant grew during these years.

When the witchcraft accusations were first made in Salem by a group of young girls, Giles Corey's name did not appear among those charged. But soon it did. A most difficult man, Corey was a natural target. He was arrested in April 1692. The warrant issued for his arrest cited complaints of "Sundry acts of Witchcraft." Fourteen witnesses, twelve of them female, testified against him. One reported that his "apparition" had beaten, punched, and choked her. (Witches, according to the prevailing theory of the time, had made a covenant with the Devil, and their agreement allowed the Devil to use their shapes, or apparitions, to afflict the innocent.) Others made similar accusations against Corey, all insisting that he was a wizard in league with Satan.

One of the ironies in Giles Corey's case involved his wife, Martha, who was, as far as the records tell, a godly and thoughtful woman. She had been questioned by the judges after she had indicated some skepticism about the validity of the charges brought by the girls in Salem. During her interrogation she said, "We must not believe all that these distracted children say" (*Salem Witchcraft Papers,* vol. 1, p. 250). Giles Corey, however, was of a different mind and testified against his wife before she was arrested in March. By this time his old age may have dimmed his understanding, and in the initial hearings he seemed awed, almost cowed, by the court and the tumultuous behavior of the accusers, who shrieked and cried out in what were considered to be fits induced by the invisible presence of the witches. In his testimony Corey reported that he could not pray while Martha was nearby and that she sometimes sat up after he went to bed and then kneeled at the hearth as if she were praying. But, Corey stated, he heard her say nothing.

Martha Corey was found guilty and executed in September 1692. To all the accusations she responded that she was a "gospel woman" and that her accusers were nothing but "poor, distracted children." Giles Corey had been pressed to death the week before because he refused to plead to the charges; something had aroused his spirit, which had seemed to be broken in the spring. Refusal to plead, however, brought a procedure called *peine forte et dure,* with the sheriff piling stones on his chest demanding that he plead. But

Corey said nothing and thereby protected his property for his heirs, for property could not be condemned before a trial that brought conviction. Corey died instead, lying in a field with one heavy stone after another being stacked on his chest. His courage probably impressed the watchers of his agony and may have persuaded some to rethink the basis for New England's belief in witchcraft in Salem.

• Most of the unpublished documents concerning the Salem witchcraft trials are housed at the Essex County Courthouse in Salem, Mass. An important source for our knowledge of Salem witchcraft is Paul Boyer and Stephen Nissenbaum, eds., *The Salem Witchcraft Papers: Verbatim Transcripts of the Legal Documents of the Salem Witchcraft Outbreak of 1692* (3 vols., 1977). For other revealing documents and records, see Boyer and Nissenbaum, eds., *Salem Village Witchcraft: A Documentary Record of Local Conflict in Colonial New England* (1972), and *Records and Files of the Quarterly Courts of Essex County, Massachusetts* (8 vols., 1911–1921). Among the many studies, Marion L. Starkey, *The Devil in Massachusetts* (1961); Boyer and Nissenbaum, *Salem Possessed: The Social Origins of Witchcraft* (1974); and David T. Konig, *Law and Society in Puritan Massachusetts, 1629–1692* (1979), are helpful.

ROBERT MIDDLEKAUFF

COREY, Martha (c. 1625–22 Sept. 1692), Salem "witch," was born in England in the late 1620s and subsequently migrated to Massachusetts. Nothing is known of her parents or early life. As Martha Rich, widow, she married Giles Corey (or Cory) in Salem, probably in the 1680s. Giles Corey was a huge, bumbling, eccentric man who owned a hundred or so acres of valuable farmland near Salem. Martha joined the Salem church in 1690; because of the distance from the Corey farm to Salem Town, she attended the Salem Village church, most faithfully. In 1691 her husband joined the church and took his membership very seriously.

In 1692 Salem was convulsed by witchcraft hysteria. In the winter of 1691–1692, Tituba, a slave owned by the Reverend Samuel Parris of Salem Village, inflamed the imaginations of several young girls—including Parris's daughter Elizabeth (age nine) and her friends Mercy Lewis (a seventeen-year-old orphan servant in the home of Thomas and Ann Putnam), Ann Putnam, Jr. (age twelve), Abigail Williams (Elizabeth Parris's eleven-year-old cousin), and Elizabeth Hubbard (age seventeen and a servant of her great-aunt, the wife of Dr. William Griggs)—by telling voodoo stories from her native Barbados. Some of the girls soon fell ill and began having fits, crawling about, and contorting their bodies. Griggs, when consulted by a group of ministers including Parris, opined that the girls' troubles were caused by witchcraft. The girls claimed to be haunted and tortured.

The witch-hunt then began. When Giles Corey expressed a desire to be present at the subsequent hearings, Martha Corey hid his saddle to prevent him from doing so; but he insisted, and the two began to attend the examinations of the first suspects held by a group of magistrates at the meetinghouse. Martha Corey,

among a few others, doubted the veracity of the girls who had brought charges, and she unfortunately said so in public, relying on her well-established reputation for piety to keep her out of trouble. When the girls learned of Corey's skeptical and derogatory remarks, however, Ann Putnam accused her of tormenting them, asserted that she had seen Corey with other witches, and insisted that Corey had often afflicted her. Two respected citizens of the town went to the Corey farm to question Martha on 12 March. At first she was courteous but soon stated in a mocking tone that Ann Putnam and her idle playmates might well have been persuaded by the devil to discommode the whole community. Two days later, she amiably visited the Putnam home, but on seeing her, Ann suffered a fit for which she loudly blamed Corey. Meanwhile, other adults, including John and Elizabeth Proctor, were also indicted for witchcraft. Tituba was jailed, confessed to various witchcraft crimes, implicated others, and thus escaped hanging.

On 21 March Martha Corey was arrested and questioned. The leading magistrate was John Hathorne, novelist Nathaniel Hawthorne's great-great-grandfather. To his opening questions, she replied that she had not tormented the girls and did not know who had done so. At this, the afflicted girls cried out that Corey was scratching, biting, and choking them at that moment, and, further, that Corey's apparition was holding out a book for them to sign. When Corey said that she knew of no such book, one girl asserted that Corey was suckling a yellow bird while holding it between her fingers. When queried, Corey said that she knew of no such bird and stated that she was a "gospel woman." The girls said she was a "gospel witch." When Ann Putnam said that she had seen Martha Corey and another "witch" praying to the devil outside the Putnam house, Corey urged Hathorne to regard all of the girls as distracted. When Corey bit her lip to concentrate on formulating an answer, one girl displayed bleeding lips and blamed Corey. When Corey clasped her hands together, the girls said that she was pinching them. When Corey nervously moved her feet, the girls stamped their own feet in pain. A matron in the audience, accusing Corey of causing her pain in the bowels, hit her in the head with a shoe. One girl said that the Black Man was standing beside Corey and was whispering answers to her during the examination. Another girl said that Martha Corey and the devil had signed a ten-year pact, with four years to go. Giles Corey, growing suspicious of his wife, testified that she prayed too fluently to suit him and that he was puzzled when he found her quietly kneeling on their hearth late one night. Thus, he hurt her cause and, to make matters worse, damaged his own reputation by speaking critically of the afflicted girls. Hathorne concluded the hearings against Corey and ordered her confined in the Salem jail, from which she was soon transferred, because of overcrowding there, to the Boston jail.

On 2 June, before the Court of Oyer and Terminer, Ann Putnam, Sr., and another person accused Martha Corey of murder by witchcraft. On 30 June another woman testified that in a vision she had seen Corey commit a double murder by witchcraft. On 5 September a medical panel was ordered to search Corey's body for marks of the devil's hand and possibly an extra teat with which she might suckle imps. On 9 September she was condemned to death. On 11 September she was taken to the Salem church and excommunicated. On 22 September, after delivering a brief but eloquent prayer attesting to her innocence, she was hanged on Gallows Hill.

On 18 April a complaint had been filed against Giles Corey. The next day he was arrested, questioned, and jailed. On 5 September his person also was searched by physicians for devil marks. On 7 September, after damning preliminary testimony, he was indicted, chose to stand mute, and could therefore not be legally tried. On 19 September, three days before his wife's execution, he was placed on his back in a field and was pressed to death by having heavy weights placed on his chest. Alice Parker, accused by the magistrates of witchcraft and hanged on 22 September 1692, may have been one of Giles Corey's daughters from a previous marriage, and hence Martha Corey's stepdaughter.

In 1693 Governor Sir William Phips ordered the release of all prisoners, including Tituba, who were being jailed as witches. Parris, when charged by his church, confessed that his accusations had all been groundless and left Salem in 1693. His successor, the Reverend Joseph Green, reconciled factions in the church and succeeded in revoking the excommunication of Martha Corey in 1707 and in 1712 that of Giles Corey, who had also been excommunicated.

• The most influential contemporary "intellectual" during the Salem hysteria was Cotton Mather, whose *The Wonders of the Invisible World* (1693) contains the official report of the 1692 Salem witchcraft trials. Kenneth Silverman, *The Life and Times of Cotton Mather* (1984), explains Mather's part in the craze. The following books treat events in Salem at the time and include information on Martha and Giles Corey: W. Elliot Woodward, *Records of Salem Witchcraft, Copied from the Original Documents* (2 vols., 1864); Samuel G. Drake, *Annals of Witchcraft in New England and Elsewhere in the United States, from Their First Settlement* (1869); George Lincoln Burr, *Narratives of the Witchcraft Cases, 1648–1706* (1914); Marion L. Starkey, *The Devil in Massachusetts: A Modern Inquiry into the Salem Witch Trials* (1949); Leo Bonfanti, *The Witchcraft Hysteria of 1692* (1971); Paul Boyer and Stephen Nissenbaum, eds., *The Salem Witchcraft Papers: Verbatim Transcripts of the Legal Documents of the Salem Witchcraft Outbreak of 1692* (3 vols., 1977); Carol F. Karlsen, *The Devil in the Shape of a Woman: Witchcraft in Colonial New England* (1987); and Enders A. Robinson, *The Devil Discovered: Salem Witchcraft 1692* (1991). Among the many authors who have written about the Salem witchcraft craze are Nathaniel Hawthorne, Henry Wadsworth Longfellow, Arthur Miller, John Updike, and John Greenleaf Whittier.

ROBERT L. GALE

COREY, Robert Brainard (19 Aug. 1897–23 Apr. 1971), protein crystallographer, was born in Springfield, Massachusetts, the son of Fred Brainard Corey, an electrical engineer, and Caroline Louise Heberd. Robert attended a private elementary academy, Brown School, in Schenectady, New York. In 1914 his father moved the family to Pittsburgh, and Robert attended high school in Edgewood, Pennsylvania. In the great polio epidemic that swept the United States during the second decade of the twentieth century, Corey contracted infantile paralysis that caused crippling effects that he was eventually able to mitigate. His remaining disabilities did not prevent him from hiking and playing baseball and tennis. Quiet and shy, Corey was attracted to science; the experimental approach to reality became the foundation of his career and colored his outlook on life. Having decided to study chemistry, he entered the University of Pittsburgh, from which he received a bachelor's degree in 1919. He went on to Cornell University, undertaking studies in inorganic chemistry under Louis Munroe Dennis.

In his ambitious graduate project, Corey, working with R. W. Moore, a fellow student, constructed the first all-glass vacuum apparatus in the United States and used it in synthesizing several germanium hydrides. Their work established that germanium closely resembled silicon in its ability to form a homologous series. After receiving his Ph.D. in 1924, Corey continued at Cornell as an instructor in quantitative and qualitative analysis. During this time he became fascinated by a General Electric X-ray spectrometer that Ralph Wyckoff had used when he had been a Cornell graduate student a few years before. Corey refurbished this machine and used it to study the structures of various molecules, commencing an interest that would dominate the rest of his life. This research led to his leaving Cornell in 1928 to join Wyckoff in the Department of Biophysics at the Rockefeller Institute for Medical Research in New York City.

The eight-year collaboration of Corey and Wyckoff was extremely fruitful. Corey was able to design and construct an excellent X-ray ionization spectrometer to measure the weak beams of X rays reflected from the small organic crystals that he and Wyckoff were investigating. Their ultimate goal was to study crystalline proteins, but because these substances were very complex, they thought it reasonable first to establish the structures of several simple compounds possessing the carbon-carbon and carbon-nitrogen bonds characteristic of proteins. Thus they investigated several substituted ureas (urea is the major nitrogenous end product of protein metabolism).

Corey married Dorothy Gertrude Paddon in 1930; their marriage produced no children but was a happy one. Corey's wife watched over her husband's fragile health while he dedicated his energies to proteins.

An important step toward obtaining good X-ray pictures from single protein crystals occurred when Wyckoff and Corey discovered how to crystallize hemoglobin in their new air-driven ultracentrifuge. Other scientists used their technique to concentrate and purify many plant and animal viruses, and they themselves used it to study two fibrous proteins—collagen and keratin.

Wyckoff and Corey eventually decided that their spectrometric studies had matured sufficiently that they could begin investigations of amino acids, the building blocks of proteins. Corey began collecting data on glycine, the simplest amino acid, but the Rockefeller Institute, for economic reasons, eliminated their biophysics laboratory. In 1937 Corey went to the California Institute of Technology (Caltech) to work with Linus Pauling. Initially Corey's position in Pasadena was temporary, with the Rockefeller Institute paying his salary and allowing him to bring his own equipment. Pauling admired Corey's work on proteins, a field that deeply interested him.

During the summer before Corey's arrival in Pasadena, Pauling, an inveterate theorizer, had attempted to construct a sensible model for the way in which the polypeptide chain of proteins might be folded, but he failed, concluding that some unusual structural feature must still be eluding scientists. After Corey's arrival they jointly decided that Corey should continue the work he had been doing on the structure of glycine, because no scientist had yet determined the structure for any crystal of an amino acid. The plan was to then determine other amino-acid structures, followed by determinations of combinations of two amino acids (dipeptides), followed by other, more complex peptides in a step-by-step fashion.

By using improved methods and techniques, including punched-card calculations, Corey and his collaborators were able during the next ten years to work out the structures of several amino acids and peptides. In 1939 Corey and Gustav Albrecht published the structure for alpha-glycine, the first correct determination of an amino acid. Corey was also the first to publish the structure of a dipeptide—diketopiperazine—whose cyclic structure revealed the partial double-bond character of the compound's carbon-nitrogen bond.

World War II interrupted Corey's systematic studies on protein structure, and from 1942 to 1946 he was on leave from Caltech to direct a research team that, under contracts with the Office of Scientific Research and Development and the U.S. Navy, carried out work on propellant powders for rockets. So conscientiously did Corey devote himself to this and other projects that his health was seriously impaired. In 1947 he was awarded a joint War and Navy Department Certificate of Appreciation.

After the war Corey was an important contributor to the development of new crystallographic techniques. He worked with Pauling and others to develop space-filling molecular models. The CPK (Corey-Pauling-Koltun) models represent different atoms by various colors, such as black for carbon, blue for nitrogen, and red for oxygen. These models became an indispensable aid in modern chemistry and molecular biology.

By the end of 1947, when Pauling left Pasadena to assume the George Eastman Professorship at Oxford University, he was convinced from Corey's work on amino acids and simple peptides that nothing surprising had been found about the bond lengths and angles in these components of proteins. During the spring of 1948, by manipulating a paper on which he had sketched a polypeptide chain of amino acids, he discovered a way to construct a structurally satisfactory helical configuration for proteins, but because his model, which contained a nonintegral number of amino-acid residues per turn of the helix, appeared to contradict experimental data from X-ray crystallography, he did not write Corey about it and did not tell him until he returned to California in the summer of 1948. Pauling put Herman Branson, an African-American physicist, to work exploring possible helical conformations of the polypeptide chain. The helical model that Branson came up with impressed Corey, and Pauling, believing that the structure was too good not to be true, eventually overcame his qualms about publishing a structure that the available evidence actually contradicted. In 1950 Pauling and Corey published a note in the *Journal of the American Chemical Society* (1950) in which they described what came to be known as the alpha helix, a twisting conformation that contains approximately three and two-thirds amino-acid residues to each turn, or about eleven residues in three turns of the helix. Most scientists accepted the structure when the details of the work of Pauling, Corey, and Branson finally appeared in April 1951 in the *Proceedings of the National Academy of Sciences*.

This was soon followed by a series of seven papers on protein structure by Pauling and Corey, which the managing editor of the journal called "the scientifically most distinguished of the first fifty volumes." In what was essentially a monograph on protein structure, Pauling and Corey gave additional information about the alpha and gamma helices; they also described the beta pleated sheet, a new layer configuration resulting from the formation of hydrogen bonds between different polypeptide chains. They went on to discuss the structures of collagen and hemoglobin as well as the structures of hair, muscle, and related proteins. This tour de force of protein crystallography made news around the world.

Experimental evidence confirming the alpha helix eventually appeared when X-ray pictures were published on synthetic polypeptides constructed from a large number of identical amino acids. Later, John Kendrew corroborated that about 75 percent of the protein in whale muscle myoglobin existed in the alpha-helical conformation, and Max Perutz obtained diffraction patterns from hemoglobin crystals that strongly supported the Pauling-Corey-Branson model. Further studies of the structures of a number of proteins revealed that the helices in actual proteins are somewhat distorted from the idealized arrangement in the 1951 model of the alpha helix.

Because of the spectacular success of the alpha helix, scientists began to search for hydrogen-bonded helices in other biological substances. Pauling and Corey believed that molecules such as deoxyribonucleic acid (DNA) might also have a helical configuration. In 1952, working with poor X-ray photographs and defective data about DNA, they came up with a three-strand model for the genetic material. Prevented by political problems from attending scientific meetings abroad, Pauling had to rely on Corey to publicize the alpha helix and to discover what work was being done on DNA structure in England. Unlike Pauling, Corey did not enjoy playing the showman or the detective, but in May 1952, while attending a Royal Society protein meeting in London, he visited King's College and learned about the work of Maurice Wilkins and Rosalind Franklin on DNA. Wilkins, however, declined to provide copies of their good X-ray pictures of DNA. Pauling and Corey therefore did not understand that DNA actually had two forms, wet and dry, and they consequently were confused about DNA's density. Early in 1953 they published an inaccurate triple helix model, with the large bases projected outward from the central core formed by the backbone of phosphate and sugar groups. Corey realized that there were problems with this structure and immediately went to work on a revised model, but it was not a radical revision. When James Watson and Francis Crick published their double helix model for DNA later in 1953, Corey perceived that this structure was not only correct but one of the most beautiful structures of a biological molecule ever determined.

In the years following the discovery of the alpha and double helices, Corey continued to disseminate his and Pauling's work on protein structure. In 1955 he made a round-the-world trip during which he lectured on the alpha helix, the pleated sheet, and other protein structures. After 1956 Corey focused his efforts on crystalline proteins, especially enzymes, focusing on lysozyme. He developed new techniques and helped to set up a new protein-structure laboratory at Caltech, profoundly influencing American protein crystallography. He embarked on a program to use large complexes of tantalum and niobium as phase-determining groups in structure analysis. Difficulties with this approach prevented him from solving the structure of lysozyme, but the experimental techniques he advanced bore fruit in the work of others.

After Corey's retirement in 1968, he was named emeritus professor of structural chemistry and continued his research on protein structure. He died in Pasadena. He had been a member of the Caltech faculty for thirty-four years.

Corey is best remembered for determining the structures of several amino acids and peptides and for pioneering work on the basic structures of proteins. Corey once told a colleague that he felt his mission in life was to keep the theoretician Pauling honest by providing him with facts. Shy and reluctant to express publicly his personal feelings about his colleagues, he nonetheless had misgivings about Pauling's getting the lion's share of the credit for their long collaboration. However, according to Norman Davidson, a Caltech colleague who knew both well, Corey was basically happy and fulfilled despite playing second fiddle to Pauling for most of his career. From Pauling's perspective, Corey was a good and sincere man who found happiness in scientific research, the activity that he enjoyed the most. Corey was, however, honored in his own right. He was awarded a Guggenheim fellowship in 1951; he was a fellow of the American Chemical Society and of the American Association for the Advancement of Science, and in 1970 he was elected to the National Academy of Sciences.

• Some of Corey's papers are in the archives of the California Institute of Technology and in the Ava Helen and Linus Pauling Papers at Oregon State University. Some material on Corey is in the Rare and Manuscript Collections of the Carl A. Krogh Library, Cornell University. This article also used material from interviews with Pauling, Herman Branson, Norman Davidson, and Albert Washington Laubengayer. The most substantial biographical article on Corey is by Richard E. Marsh in National Academy of Sciences, *Biographical Memoirs* 72 (1997): 51–68, which contains a three-page selected bibliography of Corey's principal scientific papers. Books containing biographical material on Corey and analysis of his work include Robert C. Olby, *The Path to the Double Helix* (1974); Dan McLachlan, Jr., and Jenny P. Glusker, eds., *Crystallography in North America* (1983); and Thomas Hager, *Force of Nature: The Life of Linus Pauling* (1995). The most extensive obituary is in *Engineering and Science* 34 (June 1971): 25.

ROBERT J. PARADOWSKI

COREY, William Ellis (4 May 1866–11 May 1934), steel industrialist, was born in Braddock, Pennsylvania, the son of Alfred Adams Corey, a moderately successful coal merchant, and Adaline Fritz. Young Corey attended the local public schools but evinced little interest in schooling other than in the opportunity it gave for him to participate in athletics. His success on the football field, however, did not provide enough motivation to keep him in school. Eager to marry his classmate, Laura Cook, the daughter of a coal miner, and to find employment in the steel mills of Braddock, Corey left high school at the age of sixteen, even though his father's financial situation had not necessitated the boy's early employment. A year later, in 1883, he married Cook; they had one child.

His first job as a tippler in his uncle's coal yards was only a temporary stopgap until Corey could persuade the Edgar Thomson steel plant to hire him at one dollar a day as little more than an errand boy in the research laboratory. Here he educated himself in those subjects that truly interested him—chemistry and metallurgy. He also attended night classes in business management at a local commercial college. Such industry and high motivation soon caught the attention of the plant's chief engineer, Charles M. Schwab, and from that moment on Corey's and Schwab's individual careers within the steel industry were inextricably enmeshed. Corey had the good sense to tie his own destiny to that of his mentor, and when Schwab was asked to take over the Homestead (Pennsylvania) plant after the tragic strike of 1892, he took Corey with him. Soon thereafter, Schwab appointed Corey to head up the armor plate division. Corey quickly proved the wisdom of this appointment by developing a radically new process of reforging armor plate, making it more resistant to fired missiles while at the same time being lighter in weight. Within a decade the Corey processed plate was the preferred armor among the major navies of the world. For this accomplishment Corey won the favor of Andrew Carnegie and a partnership in Carnegie Steel.

Meteoric as was Schwab's rise within the company, Corey's own advancement kept pace. He was always to be one rung below his leader as the two men climbed the ladder of preeminence within the industry. When Schwab in 1897 became president of Carnegie Steel, Corey succeeded him as general superintendent of all the company's mills. In 1901 Schwab negotiated the deal by which the J. P. Morgan syndicate purchased Carnegie Steel. Schwab's reward was to be the first president of the resulting United States Steel Corporation. Corey stepped up to the vacated spot as head of the Carnegie Steel division within the corporation. Within two years, Schwab had engendered so much bad publicity because of his outside interest in Bethlehem Steel and its ties with the bankrupt U.S. Shipbuilding Company that he was forced to resign the presidency. There waiting to accept his mantle of power was Corey, who at thirty-seven became president of America's largest corporation. Young as Corey was, his appointment was neither unwarranted nor unexpected, for with the exception of Schwab himself, no one in the industry was more knowledgeable about the making and marketing of steel or more adept in large-scale business management. Lacking Schwab's conviviality and warm personal charm, Corey compensated for these deficiencies by the intensity of his drive to succeed and his dedication to the tasks at hand.

As was true of several of Carnegie's "boys" who had suddenly found their small partnership percentages within Carnegie Steel to be worth millions after the 1901 sale, Corey did not conduct his personal life with, if not the decorum, at least the discretion that society expected. In 1905 he became enamored of a young musical comedy star, Mabelle Gilman, and deserted his wife and young son. Mrs. Corey reluctantly obtained a divorce, and in May 1907 Corey married Gilman. Hostile criticism from the nation's pulpits and press made Corey a marked man within the company he had served with such distinction. The new Mrs. Corey's extravagant lifestyle—a château in France and expensive gowns, jewels, and furs, all reported with great relish by the press—kept the scandal alive for the next several years. In January 1911 Corey, like his predecessor, was forced to resign as president of United States Steel.

The next few years marked a period of drift in Corey's life. He was on the board of directors of several major corporations, but as his wife refused to live in the United States, he spent much of his time shuttling between his Wall Street office and the château in France. It was not until 1915, when he accepted the presidency of the Midvale Steel and Ordnance Company, that Corey came to life again. He had reentered the steel industry at a most propitious time. With the embattled Allied nations clamoring for the matériel of war, Corey was able to expand and modernize Midvale's modest production facilities as orders for millions of rifles and thousands of tons of steel armor plate poured in. He acquired iron ore fields in Cuba, purchased the Remington Arms and Worth Brothers steel companies, and in 1916, in his biggest coup, secured control of the old and highly regarded Cambria Steel Company. By the conclusion of the war in 1918, Midvale Steel had become the third-largest producer of steel in the country. His former colleague, Charles Schwab, now president of Bethlehem Steel, thus became his arch-rival.

Peace brought an abrupt end to this prosperity. Midvale's net earnings declined 143 percent by 1921. Corey's efforts to find salvation through combination with the also ailing Lackawanna, Republic, and Youngstown Steel companies came to naught. Facing bankruptcy, Midvale had no option but to accept Bethlehem's offer of purchase in 1923. The long saga of cooperation and rivalry between Corey and Schwab had ended with Schwab firmly entrenched on the top rung, leaving Corey with no higher step to climb.

In that same year, Mabelle Corey divorced her husband. Perhaps in the vain hope that he might win her back, Corey announced soon afterward that he was leaving the United States and would spend the rest of his life in France. Within five months, however, he was back home. During the next decade, he served as board director for some eleven companies, ranging from the Baldwin Locomotive Works to the International Motor Truck Company. He had, however, become an exile from the steel industry to which he had contributed much over the previous forty years in both technology and management, the only pursuit that had given meaning to his life. Since his youth an avid hunter, Corey's only interest outside business was the promotion of legislation for the conservation of wildlife in America. He died in his Fifth Avenue home in New York and was buried in Downington, Pennsylvania. He left the bulk of his estate to his only child, with whom he had become reconciled after his second divorce.

• There is no collection of Corey papers extant. Business letters from and to him may be found in various collections, including the Andrew Carnegie Papers in the Library of Congress, the archives of the Bethlehem Steel Corporation, and the Helen Clay Frick Archives in Pittsburgh. A full-length biography of Corey is yet to be written. Some useful information on his business activities can be found in related biographies, including Robert Hessen, *Steel Titan: The Life of Charles M. Schwab* (1975); Burton J. Hendrick, *The Life of Andrew Carnegie* (1932); Ida M. Tarbell, *The Life of Elbert H. Gary* (1925); and Joseph F. Wall, *Andrew Carnegie* (1970). See also William B. Dickson, *History of the Carnegie Veterans Association* (1938). Two articles written shortly after Corey became president of United States Steel are Ralph D. Paine, "William Ellis Corey," *World's Work* 6 (1903): 4025–27, and William R. Stewart, "Captains of Industry: William Ellis Corey," *Cosmopolitan* 36 (1904): 479–82. The editorial comment in *Outlook* 83 (1906): 825–26 is an example of the barrage of criticism leveled against Corey because of his marital scandal.

The *New York Times* files for 1906 and 1907 also provide detailed information on this incident. An obituary is in the *New York Times*, 12 May 1934.

JOSEPH FRAZIER WALL

CORI, Carl Ferdinand (5 Dec. 1896–20 Oct. 1984), and **Gerty Theresa Radnitz Cori** (15 Aug. 1896–26 Oct. 1957), biochemists, were born in Prague, Austria-Hungary. Carl was the son of Carl Cori, a physician, and Martha Lippich. Gerty was the daughter of Otto Radnitz, a successful businessman, and Martha Neustadt.

Gerty was privately tutored at home until she entered a Gymnasium in Tetschen (later Decin). Carl spent most of his youth in Trieste, where his father became the director of the Marine Biological Station. As a youth, Carl explored nearby caves, where he collected specialized insects, and enjoyed hiking, swimming, skiing, and tennis, hobbies that he pursued throughout his life.

In late 1914, after the outbreak of World War I, the Cori family returned to Prague, where Carl entered the medical school in the German University. Here he became acquainted with fellow student Gerty Radnitz, and they quickly developed a warm friendship. Carl, however, was soon drafted into the Austrian army and, after a period of service in the ski corps, was transferred to the sanitary corps, for which he set up a laboratory in Trieste. When the war ended he returned to Prague and completed his studies for the M.D. in 1920, while at the same time Gerty completed her M.D. Carl and Gerty married in 1920 and both worked in Viennese clinics for a time.

During this period Carl also began to study the effect of the vagus nerve on the heart in the Pharmacological Institute. His work came to the attention of Otto Loewi, who had been studying the same problem for a decade and would receive the Nobel Prize in medicine (or physiology) in 1936. Loewi invited Carl to Graz to assist him in his research on the chemical transmission of nerve impulses to the heart. Gerty remained in Vienna at the Karolinen Children's Hospital.

After almost a year in Graz, Carl received an offer to join the State Institute for the Study of Malignant Diseases (now the Roswell Park Memorial Institute) in Buffalo, New York. After careful deliberation, the couple moved to the United States and settled in Buffalo. Both pursued metabolic research, feeling no desire to be involved in medical practice.

At Buffalo the Coris' scientific interests became focused on the intermediary metabolism of carbohydrates in the animal body, the subject of their research during the rest of their lives. Carbohydrates are present in many foods and range in complexity from glucose and fructose (monosaccharides), sucrose and lactose (disaccharides composed of two simple sugar units), and polysaccharides containing many simple sugar units. The Coris began by examining the problem of how the simple sugar, glucose, is metabolized. They examined the overall processes of sugar metabolism, determining what percentage of ingested glucose was oxidized and what amount was converted to fat and stored. From the 1920s on, the Coris and their students explored the nature of these intermediate changes in moving from the carbohydrates molecules to successive intermediate products.

In 1931 the Coris accepted positions at the Washington University School of Medicine in St. Louis. Carl joined the faculty as professor of pharmacology and in 1942 was made professor of biochemistry. Gerty was a research associate until 1947, when she also became a professor of biochemistry. Both became U.S. citizens in 1928. In 1936 their only child was born.

At St. Louis the Coris turned from animal studies to in vitro experiments. They accidentally recognized that minced and washed frog muscles, when incubated in a solution containing inorganic phosphate, yielded a compound not known to them. On isolation it proved to be glucose-1-phosphate, later called the Cori ester. The glucose portion of the ester had to come from glycogen and the phosphate from inorganic phosphate solution, since the muscle had been washed free of sugars and organic phosphates. They recognized that the washing procedure had removed enzymes that react with glucose-1-phosphate to prevent its accumulation and soon found that one of these enzymes, phosphoglucomutase, converts glucose-1-phosphate to glucose-6-phosphate, known as the Robison ester.

The Coris also crystallized an enzyme, which they named "phosphorylase." This enzyme catalyzed the reaction of glucose-1-phosphate with glycogen to add a unit of glucose to the straight chain region of the glycogen, while creating inorganic phosphate or, in the case of different concentrations, catalyzing the reverse reaction.

While studying the influence of the hormones insulin and epinephrine, the Coris discovered that conversion of glucose to muscle glycogen was increased by insulin but the same enzyme decreased conversion to liver glycogen. Epinephrine, however, had an opposite effect. The Cori team concluded that another intermediate must be formed from muscle glycogen before conversion to liver glycogen, because muscle glycogen did not contribute glucose to the blood. They ultimately demonstrated that lactic acid was this intermediate in what ultimately became known as the Cori cycle:

Muscle glycogen → blood lactic acid → liver glycogen → blood glucose and → to muscle glycogen.

The studies were initiated at Buffalo but continued at St. Louis with the aid of students and postdoctoral fellows. Their success in clarifying the nature of carbohydrate metabolism led to a succession of honors, including in 1947 the Nobel Prize for physiology or medicine (which was shared with Bernardo Hussay of Argentina). Gerty Cori was only the third woman to receive a Nobel science award and was the first American woman to receive a Nobel Prize in any category of science. By that time she had begun to suffer an incurable type of anemia; she continued her research with her husband almost to the end and died in St. Louis, Missouri. As a scientific team from 1920, the couple had published certain studies separately, but the majority of their papers had been published jointly.

In 1960 Carl married Anne Fitz-Gerald Jones, who shared many of his interests outside the laboratory. He continued a heavy research program with coworkers until 1966, when he officially retired from his chairmanship of the biochemistry department at Washington University and moved to Cambridge, Massachusetts. There, Harvard University provided space in a laboratory of the Massachusetts General Hospital, where he pursued research in genetics. He died in Cambridge.

The careers of Carl and Gerty Cori reflect a deep dedication to clarification of basic biochemical problems, coupled with a deep enjoyment of nature, books, and art.

• For more information see B. A. Houssay, "Carl and Gerty T. Cori," *Biochemica et Biophisica Acta*, Apr. 1956; and John T. Edsall, "Carl Ferdinand Cori (1896–1984)," *American Philosophical Society Yearbook* (1985), pp. 109–16. The best and most comprehensive biography of Carl Cori is by his student Mildred Cohn in National Academy of Sciences, *Biographical Memoirs* 61 (1992): 79–109, which includes a portrait and bibliography. The same edition contains a biography, portrait, and bibliography of Gerty Cori by Joseph Larner, pp. 111–35. On Gerty also see Joseph S. Fruton's entry in *Dictionary of Scientific Biography*, vol. 3, pp. 415–16, and S. Ochoa and H. M. Kalckar, "Gerty Cori, Biochemist," *Science* 128 (1958): 16–17.

AARON J. IHDE

CORIAT, Isador Henry (10 Dec. 1875–26 May 1943), psychoanalyst, was born in Philadelphia, Pennsylvania, the son of Harry Coriat, a Jewish native of Morocco who emigrated to the United States from France in 1867, and Clara Einstein. When Isador was about four years old, the family moved to Boston, where his father established a cigar-manufacturing business. Isador attended public schools in Boston and graduated with an M.D. from Tufts Medical College in 1900. Immediately after graduating from Tufts, Coriat accepted an offer from Adolph Meyer—one of the preeminent figures in American clinical psychiatry during the early twentieth century—to join the medical staff at the Worcester (Mass.) State Hospital for the insane. Coriat spent five years at Worcester, building his credentials as a neurologist and psychiatrist. He married Etta Dann in 1904; they had no children.

In 1905 Coriat moved back to Boston, where he established a private practice and worked as a neurologist at both Boston City Hospital and Mt. Sinai Hospital. He resigned his appointment at Mt. Sinai in 1914 and accepted a part-time position as an instructor in neurology at Tufts, teaching there for two academic years. In 1919 he left behind his position at Boston City Hospital and accepted appointments as a consulting neurologist at Chelsea Memorial Hospital and Beth Israel Hospital, holding both positions until

1928. In the midst of these various transitions, Coriat also held an appointment as a neuropsychiatrist at the Forsyth Dental Infirmary from 1913 through 1929.

In 1909 Coriat attended a series of five lectures delivered by Sigmund Freud at Clarkson University in Worcester. Coriat had gained a rudimentary understanding of Freud's theories through the initial American proselytizers, Bostonian James J. Putnam and A. A. Brill of New York, but hearing Freud for himself was instrumental in Coriat's conversion. Almost three decades later Coriat recalled that "these lectures crystallized a latent interest in psychoanalysis. . . . A new planet had swum into the ken of psychology and psychiatry." Coriat's conversion would eventually be complete, but it was not immediate. He went on to recall that Freud's "revelations" at Clarkson "were so revolutionary that for the time being some of us found it difficult to either assimilate or believe this new science from Vienna" ("Some Personal Reminiscences," p. 4).

During the decade following that experience Coriat became increasingly convinced of the complete correctness of psychoanalytic theory and technique. Along the way, he produced a number of publications based on Freud's thinking, including *The Hysteria of Lady Macbeth* (1912), which was the first American application of psychoanalytic theory to literary criticism. Coriat also wrote three books during this period that were explicitly intended to bring Freud's ideas to a broad American audience: *The Meaning of Dreams* (1915), *What Is Psychoanalysis?* (1917), and *Repressed Emotions* (1920).

After Putnam died in 1918, Coriat was left alone as the only committed Freudian in the Boston area for several years. In the mid-1930s Coriat recalled the travails of this period: "It is very difficult to reanimate the antagonism, resistance, and worst of all, the ambivalence which psychoanalysis met . . . among the medical profession" ("Some Personal Reminiscences," p. 6). But Coriat persevered, giving a large share of the credit to his wife.

By 1924 a small cadre of Freudians had begun to arise in Boston, and Coriat emerged as its natural leader. Initially, this group held informal but fruitful monthly meetings at Coriat's home. In 1930 the loose confederation of local followers of Freud became more officially organized as the Boston Psychoanalytic Society. Coriat played an instrumental role in founding this organization and served as the society's first president (1930–1932). He had already served as the president of the American Psychoanalytic Association several years earlier (1924–1925).

In 1935 Coriat once again stepped forward to play a crucial role in further establishing Boston as a center for psychoanalytic thought, training, and practice when he was among the founders of the Boston Psychoanalytic Institute. He served as a part-time faculty member and trustee at the institute until his death.

Shortly after the founding of the training center, Coriat served once again as the president of the American Psychoanalytic Association (1936–1937). He also served one more term as the president of the Boston Psychoanalytic Society. As this additional term came to an end in 1943, Coriat's colleagues reelected him to yet another term as a further affirmation of Coriat's central place in the pantheon of early Freudian psychiatrists in Boston and the entire United States. He died in Boston one day after this final reelection took place at a banquet meeting of the Boston Psychoanalytic Society.

• Coriat's recollections are recorded in "Some Personal Reminiscences of Psychoanalysis in Boston: An Autobiographical Note," *Psychoanalytic Review* 32 (1945): 1–8, a posthumously published text that was reprinted from the manuscript of a speech that Coriat gave on 6 May 1936 before the Boston Psychoanalytic Society. Coriat is mentioned in Nathan G. Hale, Jr., *Freud and the Americans: The Beginnings of Psychoanalysis in the United States, 1876–1917* (1971), a comprehensive history of Freud's early reception in America. Also see Ives Hendrick, ed., *The Birth of an Institute: The Twenty-fifth Anniversary, the Boston Psychoanalytic Institute* (1961). Significant biographical pieces published on the occasion of Coriat's death include George B. Wilbur, "Isador Henry Coriat," *Psychoanalytic Review* 30 (1943): 479–83, and A. A. Brill, "Isador Henry Coriat," *Psychoanalytic Quarterly* 12 (1943): 400–402.

JON M. HARKNESS

CORITA (20 Nov. 1918–18 Sept. 1986), artist, was born Frances Elizabeth Kent in Fort Dodge, Iowa, the daughter of Robert Vincent Kent, a businessman, and Edith Genevieve Sanders. The Kent family moved several times, first to Vancouver, Canada, then again to Hollywood, California, where the family settled. In 1936 she entered the religious order Sisters of the Immaculate Heart of Mary (IHM), taking the religious name Sister Mary Corita. In 1941 she received her B.A. from Immaculate Heart College, after which she was assigned to the IHM convent in British Columbia. There she taught grade school, including more than one year at a school on an American Indian reservation. She returned to Los Angeles to teach art at Immaculate Heart College (IHC), receiving her master's degree in art history from the University of Southern California in 1951. She taught art at IHC from 1951 until 1968, serving as chair of the art department from 1964 until 1968.

In 1951 Corita learned the art of printmaking from a course at USC and from Mrs. Alfredo Martinez, widow of the famed Mexican muralist. Printmaking and the creation of serigraphs became Corita's primary means of artistic expression. In 1952 she added colors to a black and white print she had made as part of her master's project at USC, creating a new print that she titled *The Lord Is with Thee*. The print won first prize at the Los Angeles County Museum Show and the California State Fair. Corita's early art treated traditional religious themes in a nontraditional expressionistic manner. In another early print, *Benedictio*, she used words in her print, an innovation that was well received and which became a standard part of her serigraphs. During this early period Corita was sig-

nificantly influenced by two professors at IHC, Alois Schardt and Charles Eames.

Corita spent each school year teaching, and she earned a reputation as a brilliant and demanding teacher. During the summer months she would create a new set of prints. During the 1950s Corita produced shows that exhibited not only her own work, but the work of her students as well, often in the form of a group project. As a result, her fame and that of the art department at IHC began to grow. By the end of the 1950s Corita was much in demand to produce shows and give lectures, which she did, traveling extensively throughout the United States. In 1958 she and her students produced a banner exhibit for the National Gallery in Washington, D.C.

By the early 1960s Corita was at the forefront of the pop art movement, using bright colors, simple forms, and simple sayings and openly embracing modern popular culture. She made frequent use of advertising slogans and billboard motifs in her serigraphs, attempting to illustrate the often hidden beauty of modern culture. In 1963 Corita created the IBM corporation's Christmas exhibit in New York City, *Peace on Earth, Good Will Towards Men*, using large decorated boxes. The following year she produced a forty-foot mural, the *Beatitude Wall*, for the Vatican Pavillion at the New York World's Fair. By 1966 her fame was clearly established as she was featured in several popular magazines. Westinghouse began commissioning one of her prints each year, which they published in mass circulation magazines such as *Time* and *Newsweek*. These publications gave Corita's work wide circulation.

Inspired by changes wrought by the Second Vatican Council in Rome (1962–1965), Corita was also in the forefront of changes occurring within the Catholic church in the United States. In 1964 she transformed IHC's traditional Mary's Day, which honored the Mother of God, from a traditional, staid affair to a vibrant celebration, which included colorful banners carried in a procession with balloons, flowers, dancing, and concluding with a simple meal. These innovations brought her (or at least IHC) into conflict with James Francis McIntyre, the archbishop of Los Angeles, as did some of her "religious art," most notably her print that referred to Mary as "the juiciest tomato of them all." Corita was either "adored or abhorred" in Catholic circles. Her promotion of spontaneous celebrations culminated in her instigation of "happenings" in the late 1960s in which instant celebrations were created at traditionally mordant gatherings such as business meetings or conventions.

Two priests greatly influenced Corita in the mid-1960s, Daniel Berrigan and Robert Giguere. Berrigan introduced Corita to the struggle for social justice, and her prints took on an increasingly political edge with prints protesting the Vietnam War, such as *Stop the Bombing*. She created others in support of the civil rights movement, Cesar Chavez and the United Farm Workers, and other causes, most notably Physicians for Social Responsibility, for which she created a famous billboard in 1984. It read, "We can create life without war." Though she never engaged in protest marches herself, Harvey Cox called her a "guerilla with a paint brush," as her art served as her form of protest. Giguere served as Corita's spiritual guide and most intimate confidant, assisting her in dealing with her inner anguish as an artist during a traumatic era for the church and nation.

In 1968 Corita's intense work schedule—printmaking, teaching, lecturing, producing shows nationwide—combined with the struggles her order was facing with local church authorities prompted her to leave the sisterhood and the Catholic church. In 1968, while taking a sabbatical in Cape Cod, Massachusetts, she decided not to return to Los Angeles. She resettled in Boston, retired from teaching, and devoted herself completely to her art. She retained her religious name "Corita" and continued making prints. She supported herself by accepting commissions, most notably her creation of a 150-foot rainbow mural that adorned a natural gas tank in Boston for the Boston Gas Company. Equally famous was the production of her "Love" stamp for the U.S. Postal Service, which became the bestselling postal stamp of all time. The stamp was classic Corita with six lined splashes of color and the word "Love" drawn at the bottom of the stamp.

In the 1970s Corita was diagnosed with cancer and underwent two operations. She waged a noble fight against the disease until succumbing to it. She died in Boston. Corita was a major influence in the Catholic church during the 1960s, striking out boldly into new areas in the spirit of Vatican II. She also made major contributions to the American art scene, blurring the distinction between commercial and fine art. Her art is currently housed in more than thirty-five major museums, including the Museum of Modern Art in New York City and the Art Institute of Chicago.

• Corita's papers are housed at the Schlesinger Library in Boston, Mass. The University of California at Los Angeles Oral History Project has made transcripts of interviews with Corita available in Bernard Galm, *Los Angeles Art Community: Group Portrait: Corita Kent* (1977). A film biography produced by Jeffrey Hayden is *Primary Colors: The Story of Corita* (1990). See also Mary Bruno, "Portrait of an Artist," *Newsweek*, 17 Dec. 1984. An obituary is in the *New York Times*, 19 Sept. 1986.

JEFFREY M. BURNS

CORLE, Edwin (7 May 1906–11 June 1956), author, was born in Wildwood, New Jersey, the son of Samuel Edwin Corle and Marie Gertrude Dever. Corle learned to read at four and began building his own library at eight (by the time of his death, he had accumulated more than six thousand volumes). His love for writing led him to record every adjective in "The Fall of the House of Usher." His family moved to California when he was seventeen. Corle attended the University of California at Los Angeles, receiving a bachelor of arts degree in English in 1928. He spent the next two years in graduate school at the College of Fine Arts at Yale University, where he studied playwriting. In

1930 he returned to California and worked as a radio writer for two years. In 1932 he married Helen Freeman, whom he later divorced.

Corle's earliest publication, a short story entitled "Amethyst," appeared in the *Atlantic Monthly* in March 1933 and was included in *The Best Short Stories of 1934*. For several years Corle contributed to such magazines as *Forum, Scribner's, New Yorker, Harper's,* and *Esquire*. His first book, *Mojave: A Book of Stories* (1934), was critically well received. While working on *Mojave*, Corle became interested in Juanito Razon, a Cahuilla Indian from southern California. His novel about him, *Fig Tree John*, was published in 1935. Written in twelve weeks, it is considered his finest work.

Corle spent the summers of 1935 and 1936 on Indian reservations. He conducted research and studied the southern Athapascan language. The Navajos named him Hosteen Ay Doh-Klish, which translates into "Mr. Blue Shirt." These summers led to the publication of *People on the Earth* in 1937, a novel that won a silver medal from the Commonwealth Club of San Francisco. His next novel, *Burro Alley*, was published in 1938. It portrays the lives of Mexicans living in and around Santa Fe. Although it received good reviews, it was compared unfavorably with John Steinbeck's earlier novel, *Tortilla Flat* (1935).

In 1938 Corle traveled through Europe, writing newspaper articles on the political climate of the time. His travels provided much of the material for his later novel *Three Ways to Mecca*. In Geneva, Corle met Clarence Streit, author of *Union Now* (1938), a book proposing a world government. His ideas prompted Corle to found the Hollywood Committee of Inter-Democracy Federal Unionists in 1940 on his return home. That same year he published the novel *Solitaire*. A play based on the book opened in New York in January 1942.

Desert Country, Corle's first nonfiction book, appeared in 1941. The study surveys the history of southern California, Nevada, Arizona, and Utah and the people who passed through these regions. Also in 1941 Corle received a Guggenheim Fellowship for creative writing. With this fellowship, he left for Mexico and South America. He returned in 1942 and published *Coarse Gold*, named for the ghost town where the novel takes place. In March 1943 Corle joined the Army Air Corps. In 1944 he married his second wife, Jean Armstrong, who gave birth to his only child.

Corle finished *Listen, Bright Angel* in 1946, a novel begun before he joined the service. Like *Desert Country*, this novel gives a geographical history of the Grand Canyon region and a history of the people who traveled there. It was well received. R. L. Duffus of the *New York Times* said that Corle included "every kind of thing that can exist or happen in a desert." The publication in 1947 of *Three Ways to Mecca* led to a play, *The Man in the Dog Suit*, by Albert Beich and William H. Wright. This three-part novel is considered his weakest achievement. The book's main character, Oliver Walling, insists on wearing a dog costume, an action that draws attention away from the story's plot.

Corle's seventh novel, *In Winter Light* (1949), is again set on a Navajo reservation. The narrative style resembles *Burro Alley*. His last book, *Billy the Kid*, was published in 1953. The book, a fictionalized biography based on Corle's research, was hard to classify, and so was unpopular with contemporary critics. Corle lived his last years at Hope Ranch in Santa Barbara, California, where he died of a heart attack.

Corle's depiction of Native Americans was not stereotypical or steeped in sentimentality. At a time when most white people romanticized the Native American, Corle was objective and convincing. He was one of the first white writers who tried to understand the psychological and social problems of Native Americans as they tried to adapt to white culture. His accurate depiction of this plight provides a significant contribution to the appraisal of Native Americans and their culture.

• Corle's books and papers were donated by his widow to the library at the University of California at Los Angeles. Other books written by Corle include *John Studebaker, an American Dream* (1948), *The Royal Highway (El Camino Real)* (1949), and *The Gila, River of the Southwest* (1951). For other fiction, see also "One More Hero," *Forum and the Century*, Apr. 1934, pp. 250–52; "The Great Manta," *New Yorker*, 5 May 1934, pp. 23–25; "McGuire's Kitty," *New Yorker*, 4 Aug. 1934, pp. 15–18; "Last Boat," *New Yorker*, 7 Dec. 1935, pp. 38–42; "Doing the Mud Dance," *Esquire*, Dec. 1937, pp. 142, 326–27; "Good Morning Friends," *New Yorker*, 11 Dec. 1937, pp. 28–31; "Quejo the Killer," *American Mercury*, Jan. 1941, pp. 94–101; "The Widow," *Yale Review*, Dec. 1949, pp. 337–43; and "Patron of the Arts: A Story," *American Mercury*, Nov. 1951, pp. 42–49. For other nonfiction, see also "Calico Days," *Yale Review*, Mar. 1941, pp. 549–59; "The Ghost Town of Rhyolite," *Esquire*, May 1941, pp. 34, 165–67; "Seeing the Southwest," *Harper's*, Oct. 1941, pp. 490–500; "Tungsten over Darwin," *Atlantic Monthly*, May 1942, pp. 642–44; and "There's Something about a Soldier," *Virginia Quarterly Review*, Aug. 1943, pp. 575–92. William T. Pilkington, *My Blood's Country; Studies in Southwestern Literature* (1973), takes a critical look at Corle's novels dealing with Native Americans. See also Carl R. Shirley, "Edwin Corle and the White Man's Indian," *Arizona Quarterly* (Spring 1986): 68–76, for an evaluation of the depiction of Native Americans in *People on the Earth* contrasted with previous stereotypical depictions in literature.

ELIZABETH A. ARCHULETA
SUSAN E. GUNTER

CORLISS, George Henry (2 June 1817–21 Feb. 1888), inventor and manufacturer, was born in Easton, Washington County, New York, the son of Hiram Corliss, a country doctor, and Susan Sheldon. When Corliss was eight his family moved to nearby Greenwich, where he attended school until he was fourteen. While working for William Mowry & Company (the first cotton cloth factory in New York), Corliss, an ingenious lad of eighteen, gathered volunteers after the swollen Batten Kill swept away the town's bridge and in ten days built a temporary bridge that pedestrians and wagons could cross. In 1838 he gradu-

ated from Castleton Seminary in Vermont, where he had spent three years. Returning to Greenwich, Corliss formed a partnership with his father and started a general store. In 1839 he married Phoebe F. Frost, with whom he had two children. She died in 1859, and in 1866 he married Emily A. Shaw. There were no children from his second marriage.

His customers' complaints that their shoes ripped where they had been sewn challenged Corliss to find a solution. In December 1843, three years before Elias Howe patented his sewing machine, Corliss secured a patent for his "sewing engine." The next year, hoping to secure financial backing to produce his invention, Corliss sold out his interest in the store and visited Providence, Rhode Island. There he later obtained a job as a draftsman for Fairbanks, Bancroft, & Company, put aside plans for manufacturing his sewing engine, and devoted his energies to improving and manufacturing steam engines. At thirty-one years of age he was president of the company, whose name had become Corliss, Nightingale & Company; he retained that position for the rest of his life. In 1856 the firm moved to a new plant and the next year changed its name to the Corliss Steam Engine Company.

With neither formal nor theoretical training, Corliss consulted Alexis Caswell, professor of mathematics and natural philosophy at Brown University, for a better understanding of the scientific principles utilized in the steam engine. Corliss invented a governor "with an automatic variable cut-off, which made it possible for the engine to use only that amount of steam necessary to produce the required power with no loss of speed" (Kenny, p. 52). In 1848 he built two successful steam engines incorporating his invention, which he patented the following year. Between 1850 and 1880 he took out six more patents on the improvements he devised for his engine. Corliss produced "the most efficient power unit of the day" just when New England's demand for steam power was at its peak (Holding, p. 6).

Throughout his working years Corliss received numerous awards. These included a gold medal at the 1867 Paris Exhibition, where more than a hundred engines competed, and in 1870 the coveted, seldom-given Rumford medals (one gold and one silver) from the American Academy of Arts and Sciences for enhancing the efficiency of the steam engine more than anyone since James Watt invented the modern condensing steam engine. Like most inventors, Corliss combined, refined, and adapted the innovations of others until they became his own. And like most inventors he battled those who claimed he had infringed on their inventions and those he claimed had infringed on his inventions. On the whole, he was successful in his litigation. During his lifetime Corliss spent over $100,000 on legal fees and at one time sued ninety manufacturers of engines using the Corliss cutoff for infringement of his patent rights.

During the Civil War Corliss rendered a special service to the Union navy. It was hurriedly completing the *Monitor* to challenge the Confederate ironclad *Vir-*

ginia (the former *Merrimac*), and there was no place in New York to machine its large bearing, on which the revolving turret mechanism for its guns depended. When Corliss said his factory could handle it, rail lines were cleared, and the gigantic ring was transported to Providence, where it was machined and returned to Brooklyn the same day.

The 1,400-horsepower steam engine Corliss made for the Philadelphia Centennial Exhibition became its symbol and the nation's icon in the age of industry. Towering more than forty feet in the air and weighing more than 700 tons, it attracted more attention than did anything else at the nation's birthday celebration. Shipped to Philadelphia on seventy-one flat railroad cars (some of which had been reinforced to bear extra weight), the gigantic engine was a working exhibit, furnishing power for the 8,000 machines in the thirteen-acre Machinery Hall. Everyone described the great Corliss engine in human terms. Novelist William Dean Howells called it "an athlete of steel and iron," and Frédéric Auguste Bartholdi, the sculptor of the Statue of Liberty, thought it "grand and beautiful" with "almost the grace of the human form" (Brown, p. 130; Holding, p. 15). Having spent $100,000 of his own money to construct the colossal engine, Corliss was there to show President Ulysses S. Grant and Emperor Dom Pedro II of Brazil which silver levers to turn to start it on "its work with an almost human intelligence" (Holding, p. 15).

After the exhibition's duration of six-months, during which the Corliss engine ran continuously except on Sundays, when Corliss insisted it be closed down, the engine was put into storage. In 1880 George M. Pullman purchased it for $62,000 and shipped it to Illinois, where he made it his company town's focal point and his sleeping car manufacturing plant's sole source of power. Adding to the nine million who had seen it at the Centennial Exhibition, visitors constantly milled around the base of this working icon. In 1905, when the introduction of electrically powered machines ended the great engine's usefulness, it was sold as scrap for $7,892.

When in the early 1880s his wife's doctor insisted that she winter in Bermuda, Corliss created "a Bermuda" for her. Acting as his own architect, he designed a mansion that was probably the first radiantly heated, thermostatically controlled home in the nation (later used as the Brown University Admissions Office). In the stable behind his new house he installed a small Corliss engine to drive a fan that blew air over steam-heated pipes and through a tunnel into the house, where it circulated through ducts built into the walls, before returning to the stable to be reheated and again circulated.

When Corliss died suddenly in Providence, he was in the midst of reorganizing his factory to mass produce uniform parts for steam engines. Sixty-seven patents were issued in his name, including vertical and horizontal pumps, an elevator, and a number of technical appliances and machine tools. Besides the steam engines he made in his factory (the largest employer in

Rhode Island, having at one time over 1,000 workers), hundreds more were made by licensed manufacturers; and when his patents expired, the Corliss valve and engine were copied and sold all over the world.

• The Corliss papers are at Brown University. Especially helpful are three articles in *Rhode Island History*: Robert S. Holding, "George H. Corliss of Providence, Inventor," 5 (1946): 1–17; Robert W. Kenny, "George H. Corliss: Engineer, Architect, Philanthropist," 40 (1981): 48–61; and Charles Hoffmann and Tess Hoffmann, "From Watt to Allen to Corliss: One Hundred Years of Letting Off Steam," 44 (1985): 19–27. Also see Dian O. Belanger, "The Corliss at Pullman," *Technology and Culture* 25 (1984): 83–90. For a beautifully printed memorial biography, illustrated with first-rate pictures of Corliss and his steam engine, see American Historical Society, Inc., *The Life and Work of George H. Corliss* (1930). For the impact of the Corliss engine at the Centennial celebration, see Dee Brown, *The Year of the Century: 1876* (1966). Obituaries are in the *Providence Evening Bulletin* and the *New York Times* both 22 Feb. 1888.

OLIVE HOOGENBOOM

CORNBURY, Viscount (28 Nov. 1661–31 Mar. 1723), colonial governor, was born Edward Hyde in England, the son of Henry Hyde, the second earl of Clarendon and a prominent High Church Tory leader, and Theodosia Capell. Cornbury, who later succeeded his father as the third earl of Clarendon, was the eldest son of one of England's most distinguished noble families. His grandfather, Edward Hyde, the first earl of Clarendon, was the celebrated founder of the Tory party and distinguished historian of the English Civil War. Among Cornbury's numerous influential relatives were his royal cousins, Queen Mary and Queen Anne.

Cornbury matriculated at Oxford but stayed only a year. A staunch Tory, he entered Parliament in 1685 and became a colonel of the Royal Regiment of Dragoons. In 1688 he clandestinely married Lady Catherine O'Brien; they had only one child who reached adulthood. In 1688 Cornbury led the first major defection of English troops to the Prince of Orange, but his subsequent vote in the Convention Parliament for a regency deprived him of any preferment in England from William and Mary for his services during the Glorious Revolution. During the next decade the personally extravagant Cornbury fell ever more deeply into debt, and it was primarily to improve his financial situation that he accepted appointments as royal governor of New York from King William in 1701 and as royal governor of New Jersey from Queen Anne in 1702.

Cornbury's personal corruption and arbitrary ways made him generally unpopular in New York. Aligning himself with the anti-Leislerian party (the more Tory-oriented faction), Cornbury was widely suspected of systematic peculation of public funds, which inspired the New York Assembly to strive successfully for extensive legislative control of provincial finances during his administration, an effort that in the end gravely weakened royal authority in the colony. Cornbury further compounded his unpopularity among New

York's predominantly Dissenting population by using coercive methods to further the cause of the province's small Anglican minority, forcibly ejecting a Presbyterian minister from a Jamaica, Long Island, church in favor of an Anglican missionary and having the itinerant Presbyterian minister Francis Makemie prosecuted for preaching without a license. Cornbury's personal extravagance, which led him to contract private debts in excess of £7,000 with various local creditors, and his fondness for appearing in public dressed in female attire, a peculiarity that seems to have been triggered by his wife's death in 1706, completed the alienation of the New York political world. As early as 1707 New York political leaders began to lobby with imperial authorities for Cornbury's recall, and in 1708 the New York Assembly condemned his administration in a grand remonstrance.

A similar pattern of maladministration and misfeasance marked Cornbury's tenure as governor of New Jersey. After balancing precariously between the colony's proprietary and antiproprietary parties, Cornbury threw his support to the latter in return for a substantial bribe. In order to ensure his allies' control over the New Jersey Assembly, Cornbury arbitrarily excluded three Quaker representatives from it and called on the imperial administration to deny Friends the right to hold public office in New Jersey. He also subverted the East Jersey Board of Proprietors and the West Jersey Council of Proprietors, so that a corrupt clique of his favorites could control the distribution of land and the collection of quitrents in New Jersey. By 1707 Cornbury was so unpopular in New Jersey that a newly elected assembly approved a grand remonstrance condemning his administration, refused to provide his government with financial support, and petitioned Queen Anne for his removal.

The fall from power of the Tories—and with them Cornbury's most important English patrons—and the formation of a Whig ministry led the English government early in 1708 to replace Cornbury as governor of New York and New Jersey with John Hurley, Baron Lovelace. Upon Lovelace's arrival in December 1708, Cornbury was imprisoned for debt in New York; he was released when news came in 1710 that his father had died and he had succeeded to his father's title. Returning to England, Cornbury became a member of the Privy Council and in 1714 served as Queen Anne's envoy extraordinary to the Hanoverian court. After Anne's death in that year and the accession to power of George I and his Whig allies, Cornbury was consigned to political oblivion for the rest of his life. According to his obituary he died in Chelsea, England, "in obscurity and deeply in debt." His name long endured in colonial America as a symbol of arbitrary and corrupt royal government.

• Cornbury's gubernatorial papers are in Edmund B. O'Callaghan, ed., *Documents Relative to the Colonial History of the State of New York* (15 vols., 1856–1887), vols. 3 and 4, and William A. Whitehead et al., eds., *Archives of the State of New Jersey* (43 vols., 1880–1949), vol. 3. There is also valuable information about him in the Clarendon papers in the British Library, London, and the John Carter Brown Library, Providence, R.I. See also George E. Cokayne et al., *The Complete Peerage* (12 vols., 1910–1959), vol. 3; Charles W. Spencer, "The Cornbury Legend," New York State Historical Association, *Proceedings* 13 (1914); Arthur D. Pierce, "A Governor in Skirts," New Jersey Historical Society, *Proceedings* 83 (1965); and Eugene R. Sheridan, *Lewis Morris, 1671–1746: A Study in Early American Politics* (1981). A more sympathetic view of Cornbury, and one that refutes the accusation that he dressed as a woman, is found in Patricia U. Bonomi, *The Lord Cornbury Scandal: The Politics of Reputation in British America* (1998).

EUGENE R. SHERIDAN

CORNELL, Alonzo Barton (22 Jan. 1832–15 Oct. 1904), businessman and governor of New York, was born in Ithaca, New York, the son of Ezra Cornell, the capitalist and founder of Cornell University, and Mary Ann Wood. At the age of fifteen Cornell withdrew from the Ithaca Academy, left home, and moved to Troy, New York, where he worked as a telegrapher. From there he moved to Montreal, Quebec, then to Buffalo, New York, and Cleveland, Ohio, to take various managerial jobs with telegraph companies. In 1851 Cornell returned to Ithaca, where he worked as an officer of the Tompkins County Bank. The following year he married Elen Augusta Covert. In 1855 he moved to New York City to take a job as a telegraph manager on Wall Street.

Four years later Cornell returned to Ithaca, where he became active in the Republican party and rose to the chairmanship of the Republican Central Committee of Tompkins County in 1858. He participated in establishing the First National Bank of Ithaca, serving as cashier of the bank from 1864 to 1866. He worked with the First National Bank until 1868, when he was hired as a director of the Western Union Telegraph Company, a company cofounded by his father, who was also a director. At the 1868 Republican State Convention, Cornell was nominated for lieutenant governor with John A. Griswold for governor. Running on a platform to curtail state spending on public works, Cornell and Griswold lost the general election to a Democratic ticket headed by John T. Hoffman.

By the time Cornell joined Western Union, the company had acquired control of its major competitors and established a near-monopoly of the telegraph industry in the United States, though it faced increasing competition from a Jay Gould company in the 1870s. In 1871 Cornell was named the company's vice president. The following year Western Union acquired the Gold and Stock Telegraph Company, the nation's leading commercial news and market-reporting company, and operated it as a subsidiary. Cornell remained with the company until the end of the century, retaining his position as director and vice president after Gould acquired Western Union in 1881.

During his time with Western Union, Cornell rose rapidly in the New York Republican party. In 1870 he was elected chairman of the state committee. As chairman he led a successful effort to reorganize the Republican General Committee and district associations of New York City, which he charged with being "subsidized by Tammany plunderers." In 1872 Cornell ran a successful campaign for assemblyman for the Eleventh District of New York County. Largely as a reward for his reform of the New York City party, he was elected Speaker of the New York Assembly shortly after joining the legislature in 1873.

In 1874 Cornell declined to seek reelection for his assembly seat in order to devote more time to his duties with Western Union. In 1877 President Ulysses S. Grant appointed Cornell naval officer of customs at the Port of New York, where he remained until 1879. President Rutherford B. Hayes suspended him for refusing to relinquish his chairmanship of the New York Republican party as required by Hayes's executive order barring federal officials from holding offices with political parties. Largely in protest against Hayes's action and the Senate's confirmation of Cornell's successor, the New York Republican party nominated Cornell for governor at its 1879 convention. He won easily in the general election, with a plurality of 40,000 votes over his leading competitor.

Cornell's tenure as governor was marked by its relative absence of scandal and by Cornell's liberal use of the veto. During his four years in office he returned three hundred acts for amendment and sustained vetoes against four hundred others. Many of these vetoes were aimed at alleged attempts to supply New York City's political bosses with funds for their machine operations. Despite Cornell's intransigence on many issues, he did sign into law several significant measures, including subsidies for the real estate industry, taxation of corporations, and various electoral reforms designed to curb manipulation by Tammany Hall in New York City. In 1881 Cornell suffered the wrath of many New York Republicans when he refused to take a public stand on the resignations of both U.S. senators from New York, Roscoe Conkling and Thomas Platt, who left their offices in protest against a patronage decision by President James Garfield. The dispute revolved around a factional struggle within the party, as Conkling and Platt were leaders of the "Stalwart" wing and Garfield represented the "Half-Breed" faction, which supported Maine senator James G. Blaine.

In part because of the enmity he had incurred from the Stalwart faction, Cornell was defeated in his bid for renomination at the 1882 Republican State Convention, losing by a sizable margin to Charles J. Folger. Following his defeat at the convention, Cornell dropped out of politics. He returned to work with Western Union and wrote a biography of his father, which was published in 1884 as *"True and Firm": Biography of Ezra Cornell, Founder of the Cornell University*. Cornell died in Ithaca.

Cornell's tangible accomplishments as governor of New York were limited, but he was one of the first major politicians of the post-Reconstruction period to make earnest attempts at "modern" political reform. Particularly notable are his attacks on Tammany Hall

and his public scorn for petty factionalism in his own party.

• A collection of Alonzo Cornell's papers is at Cornell University, Ithaca, N.Y. A useful though highly laudatory account of Cornell's life through his governorship (possibly coauthored by Cornell) is in P. A. Chadbourne, *Public Service of the State of New York* (1882). For background on N.Y. Republican party politics in the 1870s and 1880s, see James C. Mohr, *The Radical Republicans and Reform in New York during Reconstruction* (1973), and Daniel Barr Chidsey, *The Gentleman from New York: The Life of Roscoe Conkling* (1935).

THADDEUS RUSSELL

CORNELL, Ezra (11 Jan. 1807–9 Dec. 1874), entrepreneur and founder of Cornell University, was born at Westchester Landing (now the Bronx), New York, the son of Elijah Cornell, a potter and schoolteacher, and Eunice Barnard. Both parents were Quakers, and his father struggled to make a modest living in various communities around New York City. Seeking to better their fortune, the family moved in late 1818 to a previously purchased farm in the community of De Ruyter, in upstate New York. Establishing themselves in a Quaker enclave on the outskirts of town, Cornell's father tried his hand at farming and also taught during the winter at the local school. Ezra Cornell assisted his father in his work and also sporadically attended school, finishing his formal education in De Ruyter at the age of seventeen. Having learned the carpenter's trade and after achieving some success locally, Cornell then became a journeyman carpenter. He spent the next few years traveling throughout upstate New York, working in a number of communities, including Syracuse and Homer. Learning of the prosperity that existed in the town of Ithaca, Cornell arrived in what would become his lifelong home in April 1828.

After a short period as a journeyman in his adopted community, Cornell met Colonel Jeremiah S. Beebe, who offered him the position of foreman at his mill. The business ground grain as well as wall plaster, and "Plaster" Cornell (as he came to be known by the townspeople) made many improvements to the operation. He constructed an enlarged flour mill, replaced an outmoded wooden flume with a tunnel that he drilled through solid rock, and constructed a dam to ensure an adequate supply of water for the mill. Successful in his new position, Cornell married Mary Ann Wood at Dryden, New York, in 1831. They had eleven children, one of whom, Alonzo, later became governor of New York. The marriage was not without controversy, for his new wife was an Episcopalian. Excommunicated by his Quaker meeting, Cornell demonstrated the resolve that he would call on again and again in his future dealings. When offered reinstatement by the meeting on the condition of his apology, Cornell refused; in his view, he could not see the logic in apologizing for what he considered to be the best act of his life. Although he remained religious throughout his life, his experience with the meeting may have influenced his later actions at Cornell.

Beebe's business flourished until conditions following the panic of 1837 forced him to sell. Consequently unemployed at the beginning of 1839, Cornell resumed farming in the spring of that year and also began a grocery store partnership. While the grocery venture was short-lived, his farm became a model operation, and soon thereafter Cornell led a revival of the local Agricultural Society. Still searching for opportunity, he purchased the patent rights to a new invention—a double moldboard farm plow—for the states of Maine and Georgia. Traveling first to Maine, he met F. O. J. Smith, a lawyer and U.S. congressman, who also published the *Maine Farmer*. After an unsuccessful business trip to Georgia, Cornell returned to Maine, where he found Smith in his office reviewing plans for a ditch-digging machine that was intended for use with another new invention—the telegraph.

Smith had subcontracted with Samuel Morse, the inventor of the telegraph, to lay underground telegraph lines between Washington, D.C., and Baltimore prior to the original test of the system. Cornell designed a machine that worked efficiently. The initial testing was complicated, however, by the discovery that the underground wires lacked sufficient insulation. Morse discovered the difficulty only after the pipeline was nearly completed, and fearing the loss of congressional funding for the project if the malfunction was discovered by the public, he urged Cornell to create a delay that would allow him time to correct the problem. Cornell obliged Morse by deliberately wrecking his invention, then assisted Morse in devising a new, effective method of insulation. The decision was also made to place the wires on overhead poles, rather than underground as before. The first line was completed, and on 24 May 1844 the famous first message, "What hath God wrought?" traveled across the wires. Cornell saw the immense potential of the telegraph; he wrote to his wife, "I hardly know how to arrange matters for the future. . . . The Telegraph will ultimately go on and when it does I shall go with it."

Cornell's entry into the embryonic telegraph field placed him squarely in the middle of all its attendant opportunities and controversies. In a highly competitive environment that featured individuals possessing equal portions of innovation, greed, and mutual distrust—and marked by a constant struggle to obtain adequate capital and by casually worded contractual agreements that virtually invited litigation—Cornell ultimately profited due to his foresight and his belief in the inevitable success of the venture. His initial involvement consisted of exhibitions of the new device in Boston and New York, which attracted some attention but little of the hoped-for investment capital. In May 1845 he subscribed to $500 worth of stock in the newly founded Magnetic Telegraph Company and then supervised (along with Dr. A. C. Goell) the construction of the telegraph line between New York and Philadelphia. Dropped from the payroll of the company in January 1846 due to petty jealousies, Cornell then supervised the building of the telegraph line between Albany, New York, and New York City, which

resulted in a $6,000 profit. Having supervised its construction, Cornell became line superintendent in October 1846, only to see his appointment terminated in January 1847 due to quarrels with the line's owner, Theodore Faxton.

Cornell then set his sights westward, having previously formed a partnership with Ithaca neighbor John James Speed, Jr. Founding the Erie & Michigan Telegraph Company in 1847, Cornell also built lines northward into Quebec through Vermont. After a constant battle with weather and material shortages—and litigation from a rival line headed by Henry O'Reilly—the line, completed in 1848, stretched from Buffalo to Milwaukee. Ignoring the possibility of overextension, Cornell then founded in the spring of 1848 the New York & Erie line, which was designed to link up the Erie & Michigan line with New York City. Cornell also undertook the simultaneous construction of numerous short spur lines as well.

Unfortunately for Cornell, the New York & Erie was a financial disaster. Cost overruns and cutthroat competition from numerous rivals left Cornell deeply in debt by 1851, and his financial condition was salvaged only by the consolidation of several lines into the Western Union Telegraph Company in 1856. Cornell remained as a director (as well as the largest single stockholder) of the company but retired from active management within the industry. His dogged faith in the future of the telegram finally paid off; his stock share, originally valued at $50,000—barely enough to pay his debts—rose rapidly in value. Cornell was at last a wealthy man.

Returning to Ithaca finally able to adequately provide for his family, Cornell then pursued other interests. He served in the New York state legislature (the house from 1861 to 1863, and the senate from 1863 to 1867), reestablished a model farm, became president of the State Agricultural Society in 1862, and donated $100,000 toward the establishment of a free public library in Ithaca in 1863. He also served as a trustee of the stillborn State Agricultural College at Ovid, New York.

Service in the state senate led to Cornell's most enduring contribution. His proposal that funds received by New York State under terms of the Morrill Act (which provided for higher instruction in agriculture and the mechanic arts) be divided between the school at Ovid and a competing institution in Montour Falls met with opposition from a new state senator from Syracuse, Andrew D. White. Negotiations led them from acrimony to friendship, and the two men joined forces, with Cornell ultimately offering a $500,000 endowment to a new institution, contingent on its location in Ithaca. Opening in 1868, Cornell University had an original mission statement that strongly reflected the beliefs of Cornell and White. Instruction was provided in agriculture and mechanical sciences as well as the classics, to poor men as well as rich, and, starting in 1872, to women as well as men. Perhaps remembering his own doctrinal difficulties with the Quakers, Cornell imposed religious requirements on neither faculty nor student. Cornell selected White as the school's first president, and his stubborn refusal to prematurely sell off the school's land grant (the financial responsibility for which he had assumed) ultimately led to a rich endowment for the university.

Cornell's later years were filled with controversy and reverses. Steering the bill chartering Cornell University through the state legislature had created enemies, and he was forced to deal with unjust accusations of financial impropriety. Unwise railroad speculation and litigation also depleted much of his wealth. The effort required to start a major institution of higher learning from scratch took its toll and contributed to his death at his home in Ithaca.

Cornell rose from modest beginnings to wealth through hard work, stubborn tenacity, and not a little luck. He then used his wealth in the best tradition of nineteenth-century altruism and created several lasting contributions to his community, the greatest of which remains Cornell University.

• The papers of Ezra Cornell are divided between the Cornell University Archives, Ithaca, N.Y.; the New-York Historical Society, New York City; and the De Witt Historical Society of Tompkins County, N.Y. Several good biographies of Cornell exist; the most balanced is Philip Dorf, *The Builder: A Biography of Ezra Cornell* (1952). A more cynical view of Cornell is provided by Carl Becker (at his iconoclastic best) in *Cornell University: Founders and the Founding* (1943). An obituary is in the *New York Times*, 10 Dec. 1874.

EDWARD L. LACH, JR.

CORNELL, Katharine (16 Feb. 1893–9 June 1974), actress and producer, was born in Berlin, Germany, the daughter of Peter Cornell, a physician, and Alice Gardner Plimpton. Cornell's family was prominent in Buffalo, New York, society, where she grew up. At age thirty-six her father abandoned his medical practice to manage the Star Theatre in Buffalo.

Despite her family's wealth and prominence, Cornell's youth was not happy. A domineering father, an alcoholic mother, and self-consciousness about her looks engendered a nagging sense of inadequacy. She found some compensation in athletics, becoming an accomplished swimmer and tennis player, and in the make-believe world of drama, which was a pervasive part of the family's life. Moreover, at the private schools she attended, first St. Margaret's Episcopal school in Buffalo, and then Oaksmere, a finishing school on Long Island, she was extensively involved in drama. Cornell later wrote that she determined on a stage career after seeing Maude Adams fly across the stage in *Peter Pan* in 1906.

She graduated from Oaksmere in 1911. Hindered by a diffidence that prevented immediate pursuit of her dream, however, she remained there for five years as drama instructor and athletics coach. The time was not unproductive, as she learned much about staging plays and met theater people such as Edward Goodman, a founder of the Washington Square Players. In 1916 she took up his offer to get in touch with him when she decided to begin her career. Her New York debut, at age twenty-three, came in the fall of 1916 with a single line to recite in *Bushido*. A more substantial role followed in 1917 in *Plots and Playwrights*. Reviewing the play, critic Burns Mantle proclaimed Cornell "the most promising actress of the present season." For the next two years she played a variety of supporting roles with the Washington Square Players.

Jesse Bonstelle, one of America's most successful stock company managers, next furthered Cornell's career. Since her company played half of each season in Cornell's father's Buffalo theater, Bonstelle had known her as a child and had encouraged her aspirations. In 1918 Bonstelle invited her to join her summer stock company, in which Cornell was introduced to the rigors of ten performances a week, a constant round of polishing one play while beginning to learn the next, and a potpourri of roles. For Cornell (who was a slow study) it was a tutorial in the fundamentals of her art. Her hometown debut naturally evoked much interest. But in Detroit as well (where the Bonstelle company performed the other half-summer), Cornell attracted the critic's attention no matter how small her part.

In the fall of 1918 she joined her first touring company, *The Man Who Came Back*, and experienced the demands of the road. "Junk towns; bad hotels; awful food; 3:30 calls to catch a train at four o'clock on a zero morning; traveling all night in hermetically sealed day-coaches," she remembered. Nevertheless, she loved it and retained a strong commitment to touring.

Back with Bonstelle's stock company after the tour ended, Cornell essayed the role of Jo in *Little Women*, which the company presented to appreciative London audiences in 1919. The following summer—her last with Bonstelle—she met Guthrie McClintic, a young director hired by Bonstelle. A romance quickly ensued, culminating in a 1921 marriage. Cornell chose to end her one pregnancy with an abortion. Thus, apart from their love of the theater, Cornell and McClintic appeared to have little in common. Yet their forty-year marriage was marked by both devotion and an artistic synergism. Cornell, who seemed the more imposing of the two, drew much of her inspiration from her husband; indeed, once she became a star he directed all of her plays and became an important theatrical figure in his own right.

Cornell, who seemed pulled along almost reluctantly in her career, even turning down an early offer of star billing, now felt ready to tackle Broadway. For the second and last time in her career she made the rounds of the theatrical agencies seeking a job. She landed a spot in Rachel Crothers's look at the flapper generation, *Nice People*, followed that same year (1921) by a featured role as Sydney Fairchild in *A Bill of Divorcement* (a "problem play" typical of that age's drama, in this case dealing with inherited insanity). After a slow start it became a hit, and the critical enthusiasm for Cornell's performance set her on the course to stardom.

Still, a series of unmemorable plays followed—*Will Shakespeare*, *Casanova*, and *The Outsider* among them—useful primarily in helping Cornell refine her art. An exception to these mundane dramas was her title performance in the Actors' Theatre production of George Bernard Shaw's *Candida* (1924). Where to this point, as biographer Tad Mosel notes, Cornell's performances had been of "maladjusted, physically flawed, mentally tainted, sexually boisterous, neurotically driven females," *Candida* offered a role of stability and strength, one which Cornell would revive periodically in repertory and make a signature piece.

But Cornell's breakthrough to stardom was in yet another bit of melodramatic fluff, Michael Arlen's *The Green Hat* (1925). Her role as Iris March, the quietly defiant flapper whose manner belied an underlying idealism, epitomized female sophistication of the 1920s. In New York and on tour it ran for two years, and for the first time Katharine Cornell's name went above the title. Through the rest of the decade Cornell continued to play, as theater historian Paul Myers phrased it, "femme fatale" parts, in *The Letter* (1927), as Ellen Olenska in an adaptation of Edith Wharton's *The Age of Innocence* (1928), and in *Dishonored Lady* (1930). Although the dramas were of uneven quality, Cornell's star appeal and McClintic's direction made all three plays successful.

Despite her popularity, some critics complained that she was squandering her talent on second-rate drama. In the 1930s she began to attempt more challenging and enduring theater. The role with which she is linked most memorably, Elizabeth Barrett Browning in Rudolf Besier's *The Barretts of Wimpole Street* (1931), represented the greatest challenge of her career to that point. Physically demanding, forced as she was to lie on a couch for much of the play and yet project her voice to the balcony, the play also seemed to violate the unwritten law that stars have the best lines. A different kind of challenge was posed when friends convinced her to form her own production company. In so doing she became the last in the distinguished tradition of actor-managers. Cornell and McClintic Productions would ultimately gross more than $12 million, but the enterprise thrust increased responsibilities on her. Yet with her remarkable ability to focus on her role whatever the outside distractions or physical ailments, Cornell made *The Barretts of Wimpole Street* among Broadway's most successful dramas of the 1930s, revived frequently, including a barnstorming tour for U.S. servicemen in Europe during World War II.

Although an established star, Cornell could not ignore the accepted wisdom that theatrical greatness demanded an attempt at Shakespearean roles. Thus, at age forty she assumed the persona of a fourteen-year-old Juliet. Her company (which included Basil Rathbone and Orson Welles) made *Romeo and Juliet* part of a three-play repertory cycle that in 1933–1934 they took across the United States. The 17,000 mile, 75-city tour marked a significant revival of theatrical touring, which had virtually died in the 1920s. In the acclaimed Broadway run that followed (1934), Cornell's passionate and youthful Juliet, together with McClintic's un-

precedented restoration of nearly the entire text, inspired a modest Shakespearean renascence on the New York stage.

Two years later Cornell scored a triumph in Shaw's *Saint Joan*. Supported by a cast featuring Maurice Evans and Brian Aherne, she again proved able to portray a young girl with, as one critic wrote, the "spiritual exaltation of a transcendent heroine."

Now at the height of her career, Cornell mixed revivals of her successes with a series of new plays, almost all of which were well-received. Most notably she created the role of Oparre in Maxwell Anderson's *The Wingless Victory* (1936), showcased an infrequently displayed talent for comedy as Linda Esterbrook in S. N. Behrman's *No Time for Comedy* (1939), remained with comedy in Shaw's *The Doctor's Dilemma* (1941), and joined Ruth Gordon and Judith Anderson in Chekhov's *The Three Sisters* (1942), making it the longest U.S. run that any Chekhov play had known.

Despite an occasional flop, Cornell retained an incredible box-office appeal through World War II. But advancing age, which limited her choice of roles, and changes in theatrical fashion in the postwar years tempered public enthusiasm. Essentially a romantic in the roles she played and in how she played them, the new style of Method acting with its psychological realism made her technique seem dated. In the 1950s most of her productions were commercial failures.

And yet there were successes during these years. Her *Antony and Cleopatra* (1947) had the longest run the play has ever enjoyed. And Somerset Maugham's comedy *The Constant Wife* (1951) gave her the vehicle for her one commercial success of the 1950s. Moreover, she continued to revive her old standbys, *Candida* and *The Barretts of Wimpole Street* (including a television version in 1955). Even some money losers were artistically interesting, such as her production of Jean Anouilh's modern-dress version of *Antigone* (1946). Her final stage appearance came in *Dear Liar* (1959). With the death of her husband in 1961 she lost all desire to continue on stage, choosing an active retirement at her home on Martha's Vineyard, where she died.

Cornell belonged to that shrinking group of stars who eschewed Hollywood's enticements to remain on the stage. (She made only the briefest foray into the movies, a vignette from *Romeo and Juliet* for the wartime film *Stage Door Canteen*.) A commitment to live theater and to a thoroughly professional approach to her craft marked her career. Few actresses have created so many notable and varied roles. Not pretty in a conventional sense, she had, according to one critic, a "dark, ivory-colored beauty that is almost Amerindian in its quality." Her stage presence was magnificent, abetted by a "resonant, liquid voice, even a sigh of which could rouse a sleeper in the end seat of the last row in the top balcony" (Mosel, p. 114). Cornell was loved not only by her public, but by others in the theater. Considerate of her cast, modest in self-estimation, and lacking affectation, she stands alongside Ethel Barrymore, Helen Hayes, and Lynn Fontanne as one of the first women of the twentieth-century American stage.

• The largest collection of Cornell materials is located in the Billy Rose Theatre Collection of the New York Public Library. Other collections can be found at the Smith College and State University of New York, Buffalo, libraries and at the Hoblitzelle Theatre Arts Library, Humanities Research Center, University of Texas at Austin. Cornell's autobiography, *I Wanted to Be an Actress* (1938), covers only the first half of her career, but in *Actors Talk About Acting*, ed. Lewis Funke and John Booth (1961), she reflects more deeply over the entire course of her career. McClintic's reminiscences, *Me and Kit*, adds another perspective. Cornell's only full-length biography, *Leading Lady* (1978), by Tad Mosel with Gertrude Macy, is perceptive and entertaining. An obituary is in the *New York Times*, 10 June 1974.

BENJAMIN MCARTHUR

CORNER, George Washington (12 Dec. 1889–28 Sept. 1981), anatomist, endocrinologist, and medical historian, was born in Baltimore, Maryland, the son of George Washington Corner II, a merchant, and Florence Evans. He attended the Boys Latin School, from which he graduated with honors in six subjects, and entered the Johns Hopkins University in 1906. His original intention was to study languages. Within a year, however, he discovered he was more inclined to biological studies. In 1909 he graduated with an A.B. and entered the Johns Hopkins Medical School. Corner's years at Johns Hopkins were those of the great founders, William Henry Welch, William S. Halsted, and Howard A. Kelly. Corner also had memories of William Osler (who had addressed his class), Franklin P. Mall, Lewellis Barker, Harvey Cushing, and Florence Sabin.

Corner's serious research began in the anatomy department at Johns Hopkins when he studied the development of the pancreas of the pig. After earning an M.D. in 1913, Corner spent one year as an assistant in anatomy under Mall and an additional year as a house officer on the gynecology service of Howard A. Kelly. In 1913 Corner's research focus was shifted by Mall's suggestion to study the development of the corpus luteum of the mammalian ovary. As a result of these studies, Corner would spend thirty fruitful years studying the anatomy, physiology, biochemistry, and embryology of the female reproductive system. His initial work in the field of endocrinology, however, failed to answer the question proposed by Mall: when did the embryo start developing after the ovary released its egg? Corner later commented that of the 240 papers he published in scientific journals the one he published on the development of the embryo was the one he "most willingly" wished blotted out.

At the invitation of endocrinologist Herbert McLain Evans, Corner moved to the University of California at Berkeley in 1915 to be an assistant professor of anatomy, an action that diverted him permanently from his plans to practice medicine to a career of academic research. After his transfer to Berkeley, Corner continued his investigation of ovulation and found that it oc-

cured in the sow on the first or second day of estrus and was independent of mating.

In 1919 Lewis H. Weed succeeded Mall, who had died two years earlier, as chairman of anatomy at the Johns Hopkins Medical School, and that year Weed invited Corner back to Baltimore. Corner returned to Johns Hopkins as an associate professor of anatomy. Corner set for himself two research goals at Hopkins: to complete the study of the full three-week cycle of estrus in the sow and to carry out a similar study in female primates. By 1921 he had completed his studies on the estrus cycle of the sow. In his published results, he described the fate of the unfertilized egg, the cyclic rise and fall of the corpus luteum, and the changes in the uterine wall that occur in preparation for a pregnancy. At the time of publication, he initiated a study of the primate menstrual cycle in the rhesus monkey, since it differed from the estrus cycle in the sow and resembled that of humans. In 1923 Corner published evidence (in the *American Journal of Anatomy* 31) that ovulation occurs midway between menstrual cycles and menstruation can occur without ovulation.

In 1923 Corner was chosen to head the Department of Anatomy at the newly founded medical school at the University of Rochester, where he remained as chairman for seventeen years and continued his studies on the menstrual cycle of the rhesus monkey. In 1926 Corner had set out to find the hormone of the corpus luteum that controlled this process. A stimulus to Corner's work was the discovery in 1923 by Edgar Allen and Edwin Adelbert Doisy of estrogen, which controlled female sex characteristics. In his work to discover the hormone controlling development of corpus luteum, Corner was aided by Willard Allen, and in 1929 the two announced that they had discovered the hormone, which they named progestin. Progestin was crystallized almost simultaneously by Allen and by Oskar Wintersteiner of Columbia University in 1929, and the availability of pure samples of estrogen and progestin permitted more meaningful studies of the factors controlling the female reproductive cycle in mammals. Later, using progestin prepared by Corner's methods, A. W. Makepeace, Maurice H. Friedman, and George Louis Weinstein found progestin suppressed ovulation. This discovery was the key to the development of the birth control pill.

Corner felt that the public should have a clear understanding of the reproductive process, and to accomplish this he wrote several lucid books that explained reproduction to laypersons: *Attaining Manhood* (1938), *Attaining Womanhood* (1939), *Ourselves Unborn* (1941), and the *Hormones in Human Reproduction* (1942). In 1940 he returned to Baltimore as director of the Department of Embryology of the Carnegie Institution of Washington, a position he retained until 1956.

Corner's interest in history dated from his years as a student at the Johns Hopkins Medical School, where he wrote "Mithridatium and Theriac, the Most Famous Remedies of Old Medicine" for the Johns Hopkins Medical History Club in 1915. He later organized a similar medical history club when he joined the faculty of the Rochester Medical School. In his history papers, Corner gave a broad view, as he was never satisfied in merely telling the story of the life of a medical hero or recounting how a discovery was made. Corner's brief history of anatomy, which appeared in Rudolph Hoeber's *Clio Medica* series in 1938, sold more copies than any other in the set.

Corner's membership in the American Philosophical Society (1940) gave him further opportunities to pursue medical history, and with the availability of this vast collection of primary material his interest shifted from medieval medicine to nineteenth-century American medical history. In 1943 the American Philosophical Society purchased the manuscript of the autobiography of Benjamin Rush, and Professor William E. Lingleback invited Corner to edit this important historical work. Corner's edition of *The Autobiography of Benjamin Rush*, published in 1948, drew praise from scholars for its careful and "unobtrusive" annotations.

Corner had married Betsy Lyon Copping, a schoolteacher, in 1915; they had two children. When she became interested in the life of William Shippen, Jr., an anatomist, midwifery professor, surgeon, and founder of the University of Pennsylvania School of Medicine, Corner aided his wife in translating Shippen's Edinburgh Latin thesis into English. He also completed with Dr. Christopher C. Booth the John Fothergill biography, *Chains of Friendship*, that his wife had begun but was unable to complete in 1955 because of illness. In 1954 and 1955 Corner was president of the American Association of the History of Medicine. In 1955 Dr. Detlev W. Bronk asked Corner to write a history of the Rockefeller Institute. He accepted this challenge and moved to New York City for five years to master this complicated history of the institute that was the site of a large amount of early medical research in the United States. In this period, Corner also completed two additional books, *George Hoyt Whipple and His Friends* (1963) and *Two Centuries of Medicine: A History of the School of Medicine of the University of Pennsylvania*, prepared for the bicentennial of the medical school in 1965.

In 1960 Corner became the executive officer of the American Philosophical Society. In addition to overseeing the affairs of the society, he wrote numerous biographical memoirs for the *Year Book of the American Philosophical Society*, as well as for the National Academy of Sciences, *Biographical Memoirs*. At the age of eighty-eight, Corner relinquished some of his duties as the executive officer of the American Philosophical Society but retained the post of editor and chairman of the committee on research. Corner's wife died in 1976, and four years later he gave up these appointments as well and moved to live with his son, a professor of obstetrics and gynecology at the Medical School of Northern Alabama in Huntsville. In the spare time made available to him after leaving Philadelphia, Corner wrote his autobiography, *The Seven Ages of a Medical Scientist* (1981), which expressed with gentle humor his long life of accomplishments. Corner died in Huntsville, Alabama.

• Fifty boxes of Corner's papers are preserved at the American Philosophical Society, Philadelphia, Pa. Corner's books include *Dr. Kane of the Arctic Seas* (1972). A memoir of Corner is Jane Oppenheimer and Whitfield Bell, "George Washington Corner (1889–1981)," *Year Book of the American Philosophical Society* (1982): 460–68. Other sources include L. G. Stevenson, "George Washington Corner's Eightieth Birthday," *Bulletin of the History of Medicine* 43 (Nov. 1969): 497–500; Whitfield J. Bell, "George Washington Corner," *Journal of the History of Medicine and Allied Sciences* 37 (Jan. 1982): 77–78; and Jonathan E. Rhoads, "Memoir of George Washington Corner, M.D.: 1889–1981," in *Transactions and Studies of the College of Physicians of Philadelphia* 4 (June 1982): 162–65. An obituary is in the *New York Times*, 1 Oct. 1981.

DAVID Y. COOPER

CORNING, Erastus (14 Dec. 1794–9 Apr. 1872), manufacturer and railroad executive, was born in Norwich, Connecticut, the son of Bliss Corning and Lucinda Smith. About 1805 the family moved to Chatham, New York, a few miles southeast of Albany. Erastus completed a common school education and, at about age thirteen, moved to nearby Troy to work in his uncle Benjamin Smith's hardware business. Smith was particularly helpful to Erastus, perhaps because an injury in infancy had left the boy with a lifelong reliance on crutches.

In 1814 Corning moved to Albany. Within little more than a decade Albany, as the eastern terminus of the Erie Canal, had become an important entrepôt for trade between New York City and the West. Corning, a clerk for John Spencer and Company, a mercantile firm that had done business with his uncle, began a rapid rise to success. In 1819 he wed Harriet Weld; they had five children, of whom only two lived to adulthood. In 1824 Corning became a partner in the firm and, with the death of the senior partner a few months later, became the owner.

In 1826 Corning purchased an ironworks and began the manufacture of nails. He also invested in banks and insurance companies. In the 1830s Corning held directorships in several companies and was president of the Albany City Bank and the Mutual Insurance Company. Then he entered politics as a Jacksonian Democrat and became an important member of the Albany-based machine known as the Regency, initially limiting his political participation to intraparty activities. Changing tactics in 1833, however, he was elected mayor of Albany, a post in which he served three one-year terms.

Before becoming mayor Corning was named vice president of the Mohawk & Hudson Railroad, a line linking Albany and Schenectady. The railroad, the first in New York state, was one of several that Corning later brought together to form the New York Central. Within three months of becoming Mohawk & Hudson vice president, Corning was named president of the Utica & Schenectady Railroad. Incorporated in 1833, the Utica & Schenectady's track paralleled the

Erie Canal for all of the railroad's eighty miles. As testimony to Corning's leadership skill, the railroad prospered despite competition from the canal. The Utica & Schenectady provided Corning with experience for his later railroad ventures, and it offered a market for goods produced by Corning's iron business.

The output of Corning's Albany Nail Factory consisted largely of nails, iron rods, and plate iron. With the coming of the railroads, however, the factory began producing iron for the new roads. Demand was strong enough by 1837 for Corning to bring skilled ironmaker John Winslow in as a partner in the renamed Albany Iron Works. The burst of railroad building in the 1840s and 1850s provided a ready market for the output of the ironworks. The eastern railroads were converting to the new iron *i* and *t* rails fastened to wooden crossties by iron spikes. Corning's Albany Iron Works manufactured the spikes, and Erastus Corning & Company, his mercantile firm, imported rails from England, the chief source at the time.

As the rail lines pushed west of Buffalo, Corning also looked to western land as an outlet for his capital. Since he had invested in Michigan lands, he was attracted to the Michigan Central Railroad. In March 1846 Corning was among the buyers of the yet-unfinished road, as was the prominent Boston financier John Murray Forbes. Within three years of its sale the Michigan Central reached Lake Michigan and was connected by ferry service to Chicago. Then the Michigan Central men began to search for a route between Buffalo and Detroit. They soon found it in the Great Western, an underdeveloped Canadian line that followed a straight route through Ontario's lower peninsula from Niagara Falls to Windsor, across the border from Detroit. Funds were pumped into the Great Western by American investors, among them Corning and Forbes, and both men were added to the line's board of directors. The railroad became the connecting link between the Michigan Central and the New York Central, the amalgamation of New York railroads achieved by Corning in 1853. Corning left the Great Western's board in 1854.

By mid-century Corning's investments had made him a wealthy man. In addition to his holdings in factories and railroads, Corning also speculated in land. His largest land purchases were in New York, Iowa, Michigan, and Wisconsin. In 1835 he and eight others bought nearly 2,000 acres along the Chemung River in southwestern New York. The village of Corning was founded on the riverbanks and became widely known for its major industry, Corning Glass. In addition to his purchases along the Chemung, Corning bought a tract at the mouth of the Cattaraugus Creek on Lake Erie, thirty miles south of Buffalo. He also invested in real estate in Auburn, New York, twenty-five miles west of Syracuse. Among Corning's investment partners was Martin Van Buren, then vice president of the United States.

In 1835 Corning was among the organizers of the American Land Company. During the speculation fever that swept the United States preceding the panic of 1837, the American Land Company bought land in nine states, mainly in the Midwest and the South. Between 1845 and 1861 Corning received regular dividends of 5 percent or more on this investment. Corning also owned 25 percent of the New York Land Company, whose holdings were in Iowa, and in 1855 he became a principal in the Fox and Wisconsin Improvement Company. Although the improvement company was a failure, due in part to the panic of 1857, Corning's involvement in the firm paved the way for his role in the St. Mary's Falls Ship Canal Company. This company built a canal around the falls of the St. Marys River, the water passage between Lakes Superior and Huron. Corning was elected company president in 1853. Ten years later the company was dissolved, and the 750,000 acres of Michigan land it owned were sold at public auction. Corning purchased nearly 100,000 acres to be added to the 2,700 acres he already owned in Michigan. It was little wonder that the Albany merchant was keenly interested in improving rail connections between his home city and the Midwest.

In 1842 Albany finally was linked to Buffalo by rail. It had taken eleven years to build the seven rail lines that crossed central New York. Still, for the next eleven years it was necessary to change railroads five times in making the 300-mile trip across the state. Consolidation was needed, and Corning was the man to accomplish it. As president of the Utica & Schenectady, he led the drive to bring together the several roads across New York.

Perhaps the chief factor in prompting the consolidation of the central New York lines was the completion in the early 1850s of a number of railroads from the Atlantic seaboard that competed for the western traffic. The central railroads of New York state had to act or lose their share of the western trade to these new rivals. At Corning's urging, a meeting was held on 12 February 1851 in Albany, where it was decided to petition the state legislature for permission to combine into a single railroad company. During the two years that it took to convince the state's lawmakers, Corning was the leading lobbyist for the railroads. The New York Central Consolidation Act was passed on 2 April 1853.

At the first stockholders' meeting of the new $23 million corporation in July, Corning was elected president. This made him one of the leading railroad executives in the country. Because of stock he held in the old member companies, Corning netted about a $100,000 profit from the merger. Also, as the New York Central almost immediately began construction of a second track between Albany and Buffalo, nearly $700,000 was spent for the purchase of the rails, the agent for which was Erastus Corning & Company. Spikes and wheel sets were purchased from Corning's Albany Iron Works for the sum of $155,000. Thus, the man who spearheaded the consolidation of the railroads between Albany and Buffalo profited very well from the union. Corning continued in the New York Central's presidency until April 1864. From 1857 to 1859 he also served in the U.S. Congress.

By 1860 Corning's Albany Iron Works employed about 750 workers. With the outbreak of the Civil War the following year, the company bid for government war contracts. Corning, elected for a second time in 1860, was a member of Congress during the first two years of hostilities, but he did not personally seek the contracts, leaving that to his partner Winslow. Iron from the works went into the manufacture of railroad equipment, cannons, and other war material, including iron plate for the USS *Monitor* and several other ironclads.

In 1867 Corning bought out Winslow's interest and became sole owner of Albany Iron Works. Simultaneously, he was involved in the nearby Rensselaer Iron Works that by the end of the Civil War was pioneering the improved Bessemer steelmaking process in the United States. After 1864 Corning remained a member of the New York Central's directorate and also had a vested interest in twelve other railroads. But the rigors of managing such a large and diverse portfolio began to tell on him. In 1869 Corning was bedridden for several months. He died at his home in Albany.

• Erastus Corning's papers are in the Albany Institute of History and Art. For additional information on his life and career, see Joel Munsell, *Annals of Albany* (1859); Frank W. Stevens, *The Beginnings of the New York Central Railroad* (1926); Edward Hungerford, *Men and Iron: The History of the New York Central* (1938); Alvin F. Harlow, *The Road of the Century: The Story of the New York Central* (1947); and Irene D. Neu, *Erastus Corning: Merchant and Financier, 1794–1872* (1960). An obituary is in the *New York Times*, 10 Apr. 1872.

F. DANIEL LARKIN

CORNISH, Nellie Centennial (9 July 1876–7 Apr. 1956), pianist and arts educator, was born in Greenwood, Nebraska, the daughter of Nathan Cornish, a businessman, and Jeannette Simpson. The U.S. centennial in 1876 was the source of her middle name. She founded the Cornish School of Music, now Cornish College of the Arts, a pioneer institution in the teaching of dance, music, and theater in the Pacific Northwest.

By the time Cornish reached adolescence, her mother had died and her father was suffering serious business reverses. She had shown an early aptitude for the piano and when she was fifteen began to teach the instrument. When her father's business failed, she left the family home in Portland, Oregon, and became a salesperson in a Seattle music store. This job proved unappealing, and she again took to giving piano lessons.

Realizing her need for further training, Cornish borrowed money in 1904 and went to Boston where she learned a new method of educating kindergarten children from Ellen Fletcher-Copp. Seven years later, she made a similar pilgrimage to Los Angeles and studied with Calvin Brainard, whose concept of educating the total individual through music was to have a lifelong effect on her teaching.

Despite the onset of World War I in 1914, Cornish decided to open her own school in Seattle. Its nascence was extremely modest. She borrowed $300 from her father and rented a single room in which she placed a grand piano, a blackboard, and a kindergarten table and chairs. She called it the Cornish School of Music and taught theory there. Piano lessons took place in the children's homes. Cornish gave herself a salary of $2.50 per week. By the following year, the school had one hundred students. Folk dance and voice were added to the curriculum. A dance recital in 1917 so stimulated enrollment that she was able to occupy a whole floor and engage an office staff. By 1918, the school even had a marionette department. It also fostered a touring theater and regular recitals by the distinguished Cornish Trio whose members taught at the school.

In 1921, the same year that the famed Russian choreographer Adolph Bolm staged his *Gargoyles of Notre Dame* for the Cornish dance students, the school finally acquired its own building. It was constructed according to Cornish's ideas and contained a penthouse apartment where "Miss Aunt Nellie," as she was called, entertained both students and dignitaries. The school also housed a small but charming theater.

The organization had no endowment, which made it seriously vulnerable in the Great Depression. In 1932 the board of directors unwisely voted to save money by disbanding the Cornish Trio, and in 1936 they voted a budget so stringent that Cornish went without a salary for a year rather than compromise the quality of the faculty, which over the years had included such luminaries as Martha Graham, Louis Horst, and John Cage. Three years later, after a quarter century of leadership, Cornish retired. She subsequently engaged in other musical activities, including the planning of children's radio programs in Los Angeles and directing the Pittsfield, Massachusetts, Community Music School. She died in Seattle; she had never married.

"Miss Aunt Nellie," as she was fondly called by her students and colleagues, was a small, rotund, energetic woman of Scottish, Irish, and English stock with a genius for spotting gifted teachers. She brimmed with innovative ideas in the arts and intrepidly found ways to bring them to fruition despite recurring financial limitations.

• See Nellie Centennial Cornish, *Miss Aunt Nellie: The Autobiography of Nellie C. Cornish* (1964). Obituaries are in the *Seattle Times*, 24 Apr. 1956, and the *Seattle Post-Intelligencer*, 25 Apr. 1956.

DORIS HERING

CORNISH, Samuel Eli (c. 1795–6 Nov. 1858), clergyman and newspaper editor, was born in Sussex County, Delaware, the son of free black parents. Cornish was educated after 1815 in Philadelphia, where he studied for the ministry with John Gloucester, pastor of the First African Presbyterian Church. During Gloucester's illness, Cornish served as minister to the church for a year. In this brief tenure Cornish learned much about the tenuous finances of black churches, knowledge that would serve him later. Cornish gained a probationary license to preach from the Presbyterian synod in 1819. He then spent six months as missionary to slaves on Maryland's Eastern Shore, where his license gave him greater credibility than most black preachers enjoyed. In 1821 he moved to New York City, where he worked in the blighted ghetto around Bancker Street and organized the first black Presbyterian congregation in New York, the New Demeter Street Presbyterian Church. Ordained in 1822, Cornish preached at New Demeter until 1828, while itinerating among blacks in New York and New Jersey. In 1824 he married Jane Livingston; they had four children.

In 1827 Cornish and John Russwurm established *Freedom's Journal,* the first black newspaper in the United States. The editors combined local news and black history with condemnations of slavery and colonization. After several months, Cornish resigned to devote more time to his ministry. Russwurm operated the newspaper until he left abruptly for Africa in 1829. The same year, Cornish initiated *Rights of All,* which lasted less than a year. Eight years later, Cornish became editor of the *Colored American,* remaining in that post until 1839.

In his newspaper editorials, ministry, and personal life, Cornish emphasized the importance of education, hard work, thrift, and agricultural labor for the progress of African Americans. He first advocated agriculture for black uplift in 1827 in the *Colored American.* He offered to distribute 2,000 acres of land on the banks of the Delaware River in New Jersey to blacks willing to leave the city to become independent farmers. Vehemently opposed to colonization, in 1840 he coauthored with Theodore S. Wright a lengthy diatribe against the American Colonization Society entitled *The Colonization Scheme Considered, in Its Rejection by the Coloured People—in Its Tendency to Uphold Caste—in Its Unfitness for Christianizing and Civilizing the Aborigines of Africa and for Putting a Stop to the African Slave Trade.*

Cornish was a key participant in many of the reform movements of the antebellum period, serving as agent for the New York African Free Schools (1827–1829), member of the executive committees of the American Anti-Slavery Society and the New York State Vigilance Committee, manager of the American Bible Society (1835) and Union Missionary Society (1842), and a founder, executive committee member, and vice president of the American Missionary Society (1848–1858). A founder of the New York City Phoenix Society for mutual aid and education of urban blacks, Cornish had an active role in the early black national convention movement.

Cornish often disagreed with his colleagues. Although an organizer of the American Moral Reform Society, he left it because he felt it acted too slowly on racial issues. While active in the New York City Vigilance Committee, he opposed the controversial methods of one of its leaders, David Ruggles. In 1838

Ruggles used the pages of the *Colored American* without Cornish's permission to accuse a black New York City landlord of slave trading. A resulting lawsuit for libel threatened the financial viability of the newspaper. Cornish blamed Ruggles for the incident, which badly divided the local antislavery community. In 1840 he forced Ruggles to resign as head of the New York State Vigilance Committee.

In the late 1830s and 1840s Cornish took a number of controversial positions. He objected to William Lloyd Garrison's anticlerical tone and left the American Anti-Slavery Society for the American and Foreign Anti-Slavery Society. Later he left the AFASS over its support of the Liberty party because it would not back black political candidates. In 1839 he opposed the formation of an antislavery political party. In the late 1840s he disagreed strongly with the development of exclusively black conventions and political activity because he did not believe in racially separate movements. He disdained the Pan-African movement of the 1850s because of its support of colonization.

Cornish's Presbyterian affiliation caused problems for him. As the denomination grew more conservative and identified with colonization projects, Cornish sought refuge as an activist minister. In addition to his tenure at New Demeter, Cornish was pastor of Gloucester's Philadelphia church from 1831 to 1832 and in 1843 ministered to the activist Negro Presbyterian Church in Newark. In 1845 he organized and pastored the Emmanuel Church in New York City, where he remained until 1847.

In his personal life, Cornish suffered discrimination and tragedy. Although he regarded New York City as his home, racial discrimination against his children forced his departure in 1838 for Belleville, New Jersey, and then in 1840 for Newark. Cornish outlived his wife and three of his children. In 1855 he moved to Brooklyn, where he died. Despite his individualized politics and membership in a conservative denomination, Cornish sustained black abolitionist institutions while pioneering black journalism.

• Cornish's papers can be found in C. Peter Ripley et al., eds., *The Black Abolitionist Papers,* microfilm ed. (1981–1983). The fullest biographies of Cornish are in David Everett Swift, *Black Prophets of Justice: Activist Clergy before the Civil War* (1989), and Jane H. Pease and William H. Pease, *Bound with Them in Chains: A Biographical History of the Antislavery Movement* (1972). For summary information on Cornish's newspapers, see I. Garland Penn, *The Afro-American Press and Its Editors* (1891).

GRAHAM RUSSELL HODGES

CORNPLANTER (1740?–18 Feb. 1836), Seneca chief, had the Seneca name Gyantwakia but was also known as John O'Bail. He was born at Conawaugus (now Avon, N.Y.), the son of John Abeel, a Dutch trader from Albany, and Gahhononeh, a Seneca matron of the Wolf clan. Among the Seneca, maternal relatives were more important than paternal, and Cornplanter's uncle (his mother's brother), at least in the classificatory sense of Seneca kinship, was the important chief and diplomat Guyasuta.

The relationship between Cornplanter's parents was transitory, with John Abeel returning to Albany. Cornplanter as a youth may have been present (as part of the French-Indian force) at the defeat of British general Edward Braddock at the forks of Ohio in 1755 during the French and Indian War. After the outbreak of the American Revolution both he and Guyasuta are said to have argued that the Iroquois confederacy should maintain neutrality in the conflict. By 1777, however, Indians were drawn into the war on the side of the British. Traditionally, a metaphorical silver chain ("the Covenant Chain") bound the Iroquois confederacy to the Crown, and the British Indian Department had resources to support Iroquois warriors in the field and their families at home. The Crown was also seen by the Iroquois as a barrier against loss of lands to non-Indian settlement. Cornplanter and the aged chief Old Smoke were the principal war chiefs of the Seneca who allied themselves with British and Loyalist forces.

Cornplanter was at the August 1777 siege of Fort Stanwix (Rome, N.Y.). When the Mohawk Valley militia attempted to raise the siege, Cornplanter was among the largely Indian force that repulsed them in the bloody engagement at Oriskany. Seneca losses were heavy in this battle, with approximately thirty-five killed (of a total British-Indian loss of fifty). American casualties have been estimated from 200 to 500 killed. Despite this victory, Fort Stanwix did not fall since the British did not have sufficient artillery to capture it.

Cornplanter led the Seneca contingent in the one-sided battle of Wyoming in Pennsylvania on 3 July 1778. Four hundred soldiers from Forty Fort were outflanked and routed, with 300 dying in the battle (Indian-British losses were fewer than ten). Eight forts in the Wyoming Valley were destroyed, as were a thousand houses, but no civilians were killed. Later that year, Cornplanter led his Seneca warriors to help repel invaders of the Delaware country at Wyalusing in September. Cornplanter was the leading Seneca in the force commanded by Loyalist captain Walter Butler that ravaged Cherry Valley in New York in November 1778.

Food shortages in the Seneca country resulted from the large portion of men absent on military service. Cornplanter's participation in the July 1779 expedition into the Susquehanna Valley (in which Fort Freeland surrendered) was motivated at least in part by the desire to capture livestock to feed his people. The victorious Indians and Loyalists left the valley with 116 head of cattle.

The Americans under General John Sullivan took the offensive against the Iroquois with an army numbering 3,000 and an artillery train of eleven pieces that summer. Cornplanter was part of the greatly outnumbered Indian and Loyalist force defeated at the battle of Newtown (28 Aug. 1779). Sullivan's army then burned forty Seneca, Cayuga, and Delaware towns and destroyed the fields and orchards in the Seneca and Cayuga country. Sullivan claimed to have destroyed 160,000 bushels of corn. However, he did not advance as far as Conawaugus, Cornplanter's home village.

Although Sullivan's invasion caused hardship, the Seneca under Cornplanter were back in the field the next summer, helping to attack Canajoharie and the Schoharie Valley. In the former raid, the Seneca chief's father, John Abeel, was among those captured, but Cornplanter set him free.

Offensive operations in the war then ceased as the British and Americans negotiated peace, finally achieved with the Treaty of Paris of 1783. The British ignored their Indian allies in that treaty, leaving those (including the Seneca) living south of the Great Lakes to cope with the new American government. Cornplanter was at the forefront of Seneca chiefs in negotiations with New York, Pennsylvania, and the U.S. governments of the next two decades, and he presided, sometimes reluctantly, in the paring away of Iroquois lands. He was present at treaties or land sales concluded at Fort Stanwix (1784), Buffalo Creek (1788), Fort Harmar (1789), Canandaigua (1794), and Big Tree (1797). He headed delegations carrying Seneca grievances over land issues, squatters, and their behavior to the Continental Congress in New York in 1786 and to President George Washington in Philadelphia in 1790–1791.

While the Seneca had negotiated peace with the Americans, the Indians in Ohio country continued their military resistance. Cornplanter was sent in 1792 by the Americans to urge the Ohio Indians to seek peace, but the Seneca delegation was rebuffed with contempt by the Shawnee and others in Ohio. With fear for their own safety, the Seneca returned to their homes.

Because of Cornplanter's role in peace negotiations, Pennsylvania awarded to him a personal land grant on the Allegheny River, just south of the New York State border. Cornplanter resided there from 1791 until his death. It was there in 1799 that Cornplanter's half brother, Handsome Lake, experienced a vision that led to a revitalization of the Iroquois traditional religion with its ceremonial cycle geared to the agricultural year. A dispute between the brothers and a factional split within the community led Handsome Lake and others to move from the Cornplanter grant to Coldspring on the Allegany Reservation in 1807. At this same time Cornplanter was removed from his position as chief, but he was soon restored to office.

Although Handsome Lake preached against participation in the War of 1812, Cornplanter offered his services to the United States. The offer was declined, but Cornplanter's son Henry O'Bail led Seneca forces in battles along the Niagara frontier. Henry was born to Cornplanter's first wife, shortly before or during the American Revolution. Cornplanter had at least five more children by a second wife, most likely Ke-koi-no-us.

Late in his life Cornplanter himself experienced a vision calling on him to burn memorabilia of his military and diplomatic activities in his service to whites. He was at the same time resisting attempts by local authorities in Pennsylvania to tax the lands of the Cornplanter grant. The period of his preaching a religious message was brief, but he did obtain tax-exempt status for the Cornplanter grant as long as it remained in the hands of himself or his descendants.

Cornplanter was buried on his grant, and a marble monument was placed on his grave in 1866. A century later both the monument and the remains beneath it were moved, for the entire Cornplanter grant had been taken to be flooded by the Allegheny River Reservoir behind the Kinzua Dam built by the U.S. Army Corps of Engineers.

• Record of Cornplanter can be found in the microfilm publication Francis Jennings, ed., *Iroquois Indians: A Documentary History of the Six Nations and Their League* (1984). Notable among archival collections are the Joseph Brant Papers, Draper manuscripts, State Historical Society of Wisconsin. Some of his speeches are published in *American State Papers: Indian Affairs* (1823–1861). Cornplanter figures prominently in Anthony F. C. Wallace, *Death and Rebirth of the Seneca* (1970); Barbara Graymont, *The Iroquois in the American Revolution* (1972); and Thomas S. Abler, ed., *Chainbreaker: The Revolutionary War Memoirs of Governor Blacksnake* (1989). The longest published biography of Cornplanter is found in C. Hale Sipe, *The Indian Chiefs of Pennsylvania* (1926).

THOMAS S. ABLER

CORNSTALK (?–Nov. 1777), Shawnee leader, had the Indian name Hokoleskwa, meaning "a blade of corn"; his original name was also rendered in the white settlers' records as Colesqua, Keightughque, and Semachquaan. His early life is obscure. A document of 1764 identifies him with Tawnamebuck, a Shawnee who attended the council at Lancaster, Pennsylvania, in 1748, but is probably in error. In a speech of 1775 Cornstalk seems to describe himself as the son of White Fish, but Matthew Arbuckle, who knew them both, implies otherwise in a letter of December 1776. Records of the Moravian missionaries, who knew Cornstalk well, indicate that he was the son or grandson of the noted headman Paxinosa, and there are circumstances that suggest that this was true. Cornstalk may have spent part of his youth on the Wyoming, near present-day Plymouth, Pennsylvania, where Paxinosa's band was living from the late 1720s. Although some members of this village appear to have been Pekowi Shawnee, Cornstalk belonged to the Mekoche division, which supplied the tribal civil chief. Paxinosa was friendly to the British, enjoyed a good relationship with the Moravians, and did not aid the French when the Seven Years' War began. Instead, he moved closer to the neutral Iroquois peoples, in 1756 to the site of present-day Athens, Pennsylvania, and then to what is now Canisteo, New York. For this reason it is difficult to credit statements made long afterward that Cornstalk led a raid upon Carr's Creek, Virginia, in 1759.

Even Paxinosa grew suspicious of British land hunger, and in 1760 he withdrew westward into Ohio, in due course establishing himself on the Scioto River, where Cornstalk and many other Shawnees were also living in 1773. Cornstalk may have participated in "Pontiac's uprising" against the British in 1763 and is said to have led the war party that ravaged settlements on the headwaters of the Kanawha (now in W.V.), killing and capturing up to 100 people. However, the first clear contemporary reference to the chief shows him to have been a participant in the peace talks with Colonel Henry Bouquet in October and November 1764. He was one of five hostages surrendered by the tribe, but fearful for his safety Cornstalk soon absconded from Pittsburgh and made his way home. Despite this interlude, throughout his life Cornstalk generally sought friendly relationships with whites and continued to visit the Moravian settlements.

Cornstalk is best remembered for his part in Lord Dunmore's war of 1774 and as the martyred advocate of Indian neutrality during the American Revolution. His position among the Shawnees at this time has not been explained. Since Moravian records refer to Hardman, the leading Shawnee, as being deposed in the summer of 1774, it has been suggested that Cornstalk superseded him as head civil chief. More probably the record alluded to the transfer of primacy from the head civil to the principal war chief at a time when conflict was imminent. During wartime Shawnee war chiefs assumed the direction of affairs, and Cornstalk probably held the office of head warrior. He was then at his peak. Described as "a noble portly-looking Indian," he was a courageous soldier and a powerful orator. Two sons, Cutemwha (The Wolf) and Allanawissica, had reached maturity; a brother, Silver Heels, and a sister, Non-hel-e-ma, known to whites as "the Grenadier Squaw," both held positions of authority among the Shawnee.

The roots of the war conducted by Dunmore (John Murray, 1732–1809) lay in the treaty of Fort Stanwix (1768), by which the Iroquois ceded what is now Kentucky to the British. The Shawnees, who used the territory for hunting, were not consulted, and expansionists and speculators such as Sir William Johnson eagerly embraced the Iroquois' misleading claims to have owned the land. From 1769, hunters, surveyors, and settlers penetrated the disputed area, and the Shawnees began forming an intertribal confederacy to defend it. Ultimately, the tribe was preparing for war. How far Cornstalk was involved in this strategy is not known, but in June 1773 he told one of the surveyors, Thomas Bullitt, who had visited the Shawnee town of Chillicothe on the Scioto, that whites should not proceed farther down the Ohio. Judging him by his later conduct, it is probable that Cornstalk represented moderate opinion among the Shawnee and hoped to avert hostilities.

In 1773 the governor of Virginia, the earl of Dunmore, who was associated with the speculators, sent an unscrupulous deputy, John Connolly (c. 1743–1813), to take charge at Pittsburgh. Both were eager to clear the Indians from the path of white settlement. In April 1774 the murder of a trader by Cherokees encouraged Connolly to call upon the frontiersmen to prepare for war. Several attacks were made upon friendly Indians, a Shawnee was murdered at Grave Creek, and at the mouth of Yellow Creek ten Mingoes, including noncombatants, were slaughtered and a child abducted. The kin of the victims retaliated, according to native custom, but the Shawnees were not ready for war, and Cornstalk tried to forestall a general conflict. On 28 May he sent word to Connolly that his warriors were being restrained until he learned "whether it is the intention of the white people in general to fall on us," and he sent his brother, Silver Heels, to escort the British traders from the Scioto to Pittsburgh. This gesture was futile. Connolly, backed by Dunmore, raised the militia, Silver Heels was fired upon and wounded, and full-scale hostilities developed. Cornstalk did the best he could, confronting impossible odds. His emissaries solicited aid from the Lakes Indians, the Iroquois, and the peoples of the Wabash and the South, but so effectively did British officials isolate the Shawnee that there was little direct help. With only about 500 Shawnee and Mingo warriors at his disposal, Cornstalk faced two invading armies, one descending the Ohio under Dunmore and the other under Colonel Andrew Lewis marching from West Virginia. In an attempt to prevent them joining, Cornstalk struck at Lewis's force of 1,100 men at Point Pleasant at the mouth of the Kanawha on 10 October 1774. Both sides fought furiously, but although the Indians inflicted 140 casualties, they could not dislodge the Virginians and eventually withdrew.

To protect their villages on the Scioto the Shawnees were now forced to retreat. At Camp Charlotte, Cornstalk reluctantly surrendered four hostages (one his son, Cutemwha) to Dunmore, promised to restore prisoners and captured property to the Virginians, and apparently acknowledged the loss of Kentucky. The tribe remained embittered, nevertheless, and in the next few years their favor was sought by both belligerents in the revolutionary war. Understandably, many Shawnees saw an opportunity to employ British aid to attack American settlements in Kentucky, but Cornstalk, ever pursuing a policy of peace, advocated Indian neutrality. To this end he maintained good relations with the Americans, returning stolen horses, and in September and October 1775 visiting Pittsburgh to secure the release of the remaining Shawnee hostages, affirm peace, and discuss outstanding problems. Cornstalk insisted upon attending this conference despite rumors that the Americans intended treachery. He assisted William Wilson, an American agent, to speak to the Wyandots on the Detroit-River the following August, and in October 1776 he was again in Pittsburgh. Cornstalk also courted the British, presenting them a wampum belt of friendship at Detroit in the summer of 1776, but he increasingly feared retaliation from Indians committed to an active British alliance. Before the end of 1776 he resolved to break with the militant Shawnees and move his immediate

following to the neutral Delaware town of Coshocton on the Tuscarawas River.

In October 1777 Cornstalk visited the American post of Fort Randolph at Point Pleasant to investigate rumors that the Virginians intended to invade the Indian country. Captain Matthew Arbuckle unwisely detained him with other Shawnees as hostages. About 10 November a militiaman was killed by Indians in the vicinity of the fort, and his enraged companions murdered Cornstalk, his son Allanawissica (who was visiting his father), and the two other hostages. According to one present, when the Indians learned the intentions of the mob Allanawissica "trembled exceedingly," but "his father encouraged him, told him not to be afraid for the Great Spirit above had sent him there to be killed. The men advanced to the door, the Corn Stalk arose and met them. Seven or eight bullets were fired into him, and his son was shot dead as he sat upon a stool."

The significance of Cornstalk's death has been misinterpreted. It did not swing the Shawnees toward war. Most Shawnees had already decided on that course, and Cornstalk's own faction still moved to Coshocton in 1778. However, it robbed the Americans of an influential supporter of peace, diverted Indian attention from the victory at Saratoga, and convinced many Indians that the Americans were not to be trusted. Governor Patrick Henry tried to appease the Shawnees but predictably failed to secure the punishment of Cornstalk's killers. Cornstalk left the memory of an honorable, moderate man whose efforts to preserve peace between the races in adverse circumstances were constantly frustrated by the violence, greed, and mistrust on the eighteenth-century frontier.

• Lyman C. Draper, "Sketch of Cornstalk," *Ohio Archaeological and Historical Society Publications* 21 (1912): 245–62, is valuable but rambling and not always reliable. Many of the stories about Cornstalk can be traced to John Stuart, "Memoir of Indian Wars and Other Occurrences," *Collections of the Virginia Historical and Philosophical Society* 1 (1833): 35–68. Most of the primary material is printed in Peter Force, ed., *American Archives, 4th series* (6 vols., 1837–1843) and *5th series* (3 vols., 1848–1853); *Minutes of the Provincial Council of Pennsylvania*, vol. 9 (1852); Reuben G. Thwaites and Louise P. Kellogg, eds., *Documentary History of Dunmore's War* (1905), *The Revolution on the Upper Ohio* (1908), and *Frontier Defense on the Upper Ohio* (1912); and Carl J. Fliegel, comp., *Index to the Records of the Moravian Missions* (1970). The recollections of Samuel Murphy, Draper Manuscripts, State Historical Society of Wisconsin, Madison, ser. S, vol. 32, p. 2–67, contain useful details but must be used with caution. Of secondary accounts the most complete is Paul Lawrence Stevens, "His Majesty's 'Savage' Allies" (Ph.D. diss., State Univ. of New York, 1984). Valuable additional commentary is provided by Virgil A. Lewis, *History of the Battle of Point Pleasant* (1909); Randolph C. Downes, *Council Fires on the Upper Ohio* (1940); Jack M. Sosin, "The British Indian Department and Dunmore's War," *Virginia Magazine of History and Biography* 74 (1966): 34–50; Erminie Wheeler-Voegelin and Helen Hornbeck Tanner, *Indians of Ohio and Indiana*

Prior to 1795 (2 vols., 1974); Richard White, *The Middle Ground* (1991); and Michael N. McConnell, *A Country Between* (1992).

JOHN SUGDEN

CORNWALLIS, Charles (31 Dec. 1738–5 Oct. 1805), commanding general of British forces in the southern campaign in the American Revolution, was born in London, England, the son of Charles, the first earl Cornwallis, and Elizabeth Townshend. Known as Lord Brome, Charles was educated at Eton and began his military career in 1756. Rising rapidly, he served on the Continent during the Seven Years' War, participating in several major battles as regimental commander. On the death of his father in 1762, he became the second earl Cornwallis and took his seat in the House of Lords, where he allied with the duke of Newcastle and with the Rockingham Whigs. In 1768 he married Jemima Tullikens; they had two children. Initially sympathetic to the colonists' struggle with Parliament, Cornwallis nevertheless offered his services to the Crown during the American rebellion, sailing with his regiments to the colonies in 1776.

Audacious and brave in battle, Cornwallis won the admiration of his soldiers, first in an abortive attack on Charleston, South Carolina, and subsequently on Long Island and at White Plains. In the New Jersey campaign, he failed to catch General George Washington at Trenton or to prevent the American attack at Princeton. He was at his best as a field commander rather than as a strategist, and his tactics at Brandywine Creek, September 1777, crushed the American forces, opening Philadelphia to British occupation. After a leave in England, he returned as lieutenant general, second in command under Sir Henry Clinton, a position leading to constant friction and an enduring personal hostility. Disheartened with Clinton's desultory leadership and with his own failed assault at the battle of Monmouth, Cornwallis left for England.

In 1779 the death of his wife brought Cornwallis, ambitious and restless, back to the American military scene. He enthusiastically endorsed plans to conquer the southern colonies and sought action and fame with an independent command. By invading South Carolina, he intended to crush the rebellion while rekindling loyalty to Britain. Challenged by General Horatio Gates, the earl daringly attacked and destroyed Gates's army at Camden, South Carolina, on 16 August 1780. Yet Cornwallis overestimated that victory's impact in evoking Loyalist support and in subduing the resilient patriots.

Despite continued manpower losses, disruptive partisan patriot activity, and the Loyalist defeat at Kings Mountain, Cornwallis remained convinced that he could subdue the rebels in battle. He boldly moved into North Carolina in January 1781. Spurred by the unexpected British losses at Cowpens, he pursued General Nathanael Greene's forces, rashly engaging them with his small army at Guilford Court House. Innovative in the battle and fearless despite being wounded, he did not achieve his anticipated victory.

To recoup British fortunes, Cornwallis marched into Virginia, convinced that "If we mean an offensive war in America, we must abandon New York and bring our whole force into Virginia" (Ross, ed., vol. 1, p. 87). No longer able to operate independently against converging American and French forces, the embittered general yielded to Clinton's orders to establish a defensive base. Despite reinforcements and fortifications at Yorktown, Cornwallis was forced to surrender his besieged army to General Washington on 19 October 1781, effectively ending the war in America. Cornwallis explained to Clinton, "I thought it would have been . . . inhuman to the last degree to sacrifice the lives of this small body of gallant soldiers. . . . I therefore proposed to capitulate" (Benjamin F. Stevens, ed., *The Campaign in Virginia 1781* . . . , vol. 2 [1888], p. 213).

Cornwallis remained popular with the public on his return to England in 1782 and was held blameless by George III and the government for the Yorktown debacle and its ultimate effect in ending the war. Offered the governor generalship of the East India Company, he reluctantly accepted, arriving in Bengal in 1786. Essentially an administrative and military reformer, he grappled with the abysmal quality of the company's European and native troops, financial ills, and rampant fraud in the governmental system. Between 1789 and 1793 an honest, sober Cornwallis struggled to enlarge the British hold on India, making notable improvements in the civil service, eliminating dishonest officials, and reforming the judicial system.

Attacked by Tipu Sultan, the aggressive maharaja of Mysore, Cornwallis engaged in extensive but inconclusive campaigns until, in 1792, his siege of Seringapatam led to a negotiated peace, effectively undermining Tipu's power. Rewarded with a marquisate, he was sent to the European continent in 1794 to strengthen Britain's anti-French coalition and was appointed master general of ordnance with a seat in the cabinet. In 1798 he was granted extraordinary powers as viceroy and commander of the British forces to cope with the Irish rebellion. Repressing a French invasion, he dispersed the Irish rebels and treated all but the leaders leniently. He endeavored to alleviate the Irish situation by supporting the Act of Union but resigned on the failure of Catholic emancipation. Still an activist, he gave up retirement in 1805 to return to India, again as governor general, but shortly after his arrival he died at Ghazipur.

A complex individual whose strength of character and deeply pervasive sense of aristocratic duty to country have often been obscured, Cornwallis was outstanding though not brilliant as a general in the American campaigns. His major contributions were made, however, after Yorktown.

• Extensive manuscript collections are in the Public Records Office, the British Museum, and the British War Office, London. The Sir Henry Clinton Papers at the William L. Clements Library, University of Michigan, are revealing about Cornwallis's decisions and actions in the American campaign. For information on Cornwallis, Clinton, and the British war effort see *The Correspondence of Charles, First Marquis Cornwallis*, ed. Charles Ross (3 vols., 1859); *The Cornwallis Papers, Abstracts of Americana*, comp. George H. Reese (1970); and Henry Lee, *Memoirs of the War in the Southern Department of the United States* (1827).

A comprehensive biography of Cornwallis is the two-volume study by Franklin Wickwire and Mary Wickwire, *Cornwallis: The American Adventure* (1970), which focuses on his actions during the American Revolution, and *Cornwallis: The Imperial Years* (1980), which deals with his later career in India and in British politics. Secondary sources relating to the Revolution in the South and Cornwallis's part in it include William B. Willcox, *Portrait of a General: Sir Henry Clinton in the War of Independence* (1964), and Hugh F. Rankin, "Charles Lord Cornwallis: A Study in Frustration," in *George Washington's Opponents: British Generals and Admirals in the American Revolution*, ed. George A. Billias (1969). Willcox, "The British Road to Yorktown: A Study in Divided Command," *American Historical Review* 52 (1946), offers a judicious appraisal.

WINFRED E. A. BERNHARD

CORONADO, Francisco Vázquez de (1510–22 Sept. 1554), explorer and governor, was born in Salamanca, Spain, the son of the nobleman Juan Vázquez de Coronado and doña Isabel de Lujan. Coronado was the youngest of six brothers and two sisters, and, under the laws of primogeniture, the entire *mayorazgo*, or entailed estate, went to the eldest son, Gonzalo Vázquez de Coronado, when their father died. The younger brothers received substantial financial settlements, and endowments were made to convents where the two sisters had become nuns. Coronado and his other brothers were forced to seek their fortunes elsewhere. One brother, Juan Vázquez de Coronado, became an *adelantado* (governor-general) in Costa Rica. Similarly, Coronado sought his fortunes in the viceroyalty of Mexico.

Coronado arrived in New Spain in October 1535 as a member of Viceroy Antonio Mendoza's entourage. As a favorite of Mendoza, Coronado gained prominence in Mexico City. In 1537 the viceroy sent him to Amatepeque in western Mexico to quell a rebellion by African slave miners, which Coronado quickly suppressed by hanging some rebels. With his star on the rise, Coronado was appointed a member of the city council of Mexico City in June 1538, a post he held for the remainder of his life. He also became a member of the *Hermandad del Santísimo Sacramento de la Caridad*, a lay charity society founded in 1538 to help the needy and educate orphan girls in Mexico City. In 1538 Coronado's land holdings expanded when he bought from conqueror Juan de Burgos, who wanted to return to Spain, the privately held half of Teutenango (thirty-one miles southwest of Mexico City) and Cuzamala (122 miles southwest of Mexico City), which contained twenty-two *sujetos* in 1570. In August 1538 Mendoza appointed Coronado to succeed Nuño de Guzmán, conqueror of the Gran Chichimeca, as governor of Nueva Galicia. During his governorship (1539–1544) Coronado acquired more land in Mexico. In the early 1540s he shared *encomiendas* with Alvaro

de Bracamonte at Aguacatlán, Xala, Amaxáque, Tepuzcuacán, Amatlán, Xalancingo, Istimitique, Atengoychan, Cacalotlán, and Guaxacatlán (seventy to eighty-five miles west of Guadalajara, containing perhaps 3,000 total tributaries c. 1548). As a partner in the *encomiendas*, Coronado received an equal part of the tribute collected from these Indian towns and benefited from the forced labor when the tribute could not be paid. In 1544 the Coronado share reverted to the Crown. He also held Guazamoto (sixty miles east-southeast of Durango). It was later transferred to the Portuguese *poblador* Gonzalo Martín, a settler from Compostela, Mexico.

In 1537 Coronado married a wealthy heiress, Beatríz de Estrada, daughter of the deceased Alonso de Estrada, the royal treasurer in New Spain. It had been rumored that Estrada was the illegitimate son of King Ferdinand. In dowry from her mother, doña María Gutiérrez Flores de la Caballería, Beatríz de Estrada received half of Tlapa (140 miles south-southeast of Mexico City), which contained 6,802 tributaries in 1548. Coronado and doña Beatríz had five children. After their only son died young, Coronado at his death was succeeded in his estate by his eldest daughter, doña Isabel de Lujan, who married Bernardino Pacheco de Bocanegra. Childless, she was succeeded around 1570 by a sister married to Nuño de Chaves de Bocanegra, Bernardino Pacheco's brother. In 1597, forty-three years after Coronado's death, doña Beatríz was still listed as *encomendera* of half of Tlapa.

In 1540 Coronado embarked on his most famous undertaking, the expedition to Cíbola, which covered more than 2,000 miles from Culiacán in western Mexico through the present U.S. states of Arizona, New Mexico, Texas, Oklahoma, and Kansas. With a force of 285 Spaniards, 225 of whom were mounted, and perhaps 800 Indian auxiliaries supported by a large supply train, Coronado sought the Seven Cities of Gold and Quivira. The fabled Seven Cities of Cíbola, as they were called, failed to materialize, and Coronado found no mineral riches. His inventory of lands visited did, however, invite subsequent exploration, conquest, settlement, and proselytization. Contemporaneous with the expeditions of Hernando de Soto in Florida and Juan Rodríguez Cabrillo along the California and Oregon coasts, Coronado's explorations resulted in substantial cartographical and geographical knowledge of North America's interior. During his explorations, Europeans caught their first descriptive glimpses of the Grand Canyon, Zuni Pueblo, the Sky City at Acoma, the southern Rocky Mountains, the Rio Grande and the many Indian pueblos along it from Taos to Isleta, Cicuye on the Pecos River, Cañon Blanco and Palo Duro Canyon in the Texas Panhandle, the Great Plains with its millions of buffalo and, at the time, stone-age Athapascans and other tribes who lived off the land, and the Great Bend of the Arkansas River in central Kansas. During the expedition Coronado suffered a tremendous head injury after falling off his horse in a race. Injured and disappointed, Coronado returned to Mexico following the same route through Arizona and Sonora. The legacy of the expedition is threefold. Aside from the knowledge gained about the land and people of the North American interior, the expeditionary personnel began a written tradition of the area from western California to central Kansas, and it inspired subsequent exploring expeditions northward, including the founding expedition of New Mexico led by Juan de Oñate in 1598 with 200 settlers. The chronicles of the Coronado expedition by Juan de Jaramillo and Pedro de Castañeda as well as letters to the king by Coronado form the earliest literary descriptions of the greater Southwest and are part of the national stories of the United States and Mexico.

The expedition to Cíbola became the subject of investigation by the Crown after charges of mismanagement and cruelty to Indians were brought against Coronado and several of his lieutenants. The abuse of Indian burden bearers on the expedition, the attack on Zuni Pueblo as well as pueblos on the Rio Grande, and the torture of certain Indian headmen were allegations investigated by the commission under Judge Lorenzo de Tejada. Between the conquest of Tiguex, a large Indian district on the Rio Grande in New Mexico in 1541, and the investigation of it in 1544 by Spanish authorities in Mexico City, the inescapable conclusion was that Spanish-Indian relations in New Mexico had been damaged. As the leader of the expedition, Coronado was charged with having given orders to burn Indians alive during the Tiguex War of 1541 against the pueblos of Alcanfor, Moho, and Arenal. In the end the board of inquiry absolved Coronado of all charges against him. His second in command, García López de Cárdenas, however, was not as fortunate. He ultimately served seven years in prison, six of them in the fortress at Pinto, Spain, and one year at Vélez-Málaga, Spain.

After the expedition Coronado's life returned to that of socialite, politician, and landowner. He lived in Mexico City and served as *regidor* (alderman) in the *cabildo* of Mexico City and testified in behalf of Viceroy Mendoza in a fact-finding commission engineered by the disgruntled Hernán Cortés, conquerer of Mexico and Mendoza's archrival, in the *visita secreta* (secret investigation) presided over by Tello Salazar, a royal judge. Coronado died in 1554 and was buried in the Iglesia de Santo Domingo in Mexico City.

Francisco Vázquez de Coronado is remembered as the leader of the expedition to Cíbola, which explored from the eastern edge of California to central Kansas a mere forty-eight years after Christopher Columbus's first voyage of discovery.

• Microfilm and photostatic copies of documents related to the Coronado expedition from Spanish and Mexican archives are located in the Spanish Colonial Research Center Collection and Special Collections in the Zimmerman Library at the University of New Mexico, Albuquerque. George P. Hammond and Agapito Rey, eds. and trans., *Narratives of the Coronado Expedition* (1940), includes a number of translated accounts, correspondence, and reports of the Coronado expedition from Spanish colonial archives in Mexico and Spain.

Herbert Eugene Bolton, *Coronado: Knight of Pueblos and Plains* (1949), is the definitive study of the Coronado expedition.

JOSEPH P. SÁNCHEZ

CORRIGAN, Michael Augustine (13 Aug. 1839–5 May 1902), third Catholic archbishop of New York, was born in Newark, New Jersey, the son of Mary English and Thomas Corrigan, a prosperous wholesale grocer and real estate dealer who emigrated from Ireland in 1829. By the 1850s he had become one of the wealthiest Catholics in Newark, enabling his son Michael to attend private schools in Newark and Wilmington, Delaware. In 1855 Michael matriculated at Mount St. Mary's College at Emmitsburg, Maryland, and graduated in 1859. From 1857 to 1858, in the middle of his college career, the Corrigans sent him on a grand tour of Europe to broaden his experience and cultural education. After he decided to study for the priesthood, Newark's bishop James Roosevelt Bayley sent him to the newly established North American College in Rome. Upon ordination there in 1863, Michael continued his education for another year, receiving a doctorate in theology. In 1864 Corrigan returned to the Diocese of Newark to teach Scripture and dogmatic theology at Seton Hall College and Seminary in South Orange, New Jersey. He became president of the college from 1868 to 1876 and in 1873 was ordained bishop of Newark. During his seven-year episcopacy, he consolidated the administration of church properties, fought losing battles to obtain state funds for Catholic institutions, instituted a solemn, Roman-style liturgy, increased the number of Catholic schools and other ecclesiastical institutions, and, because of the growing number of Catholics in the state of New Jersey, provided for the establishment of a new diocese in Trenton.

In 1880 he was appointed to New York, where he became coadjutor archbishop and in 1885 archbishop, succeeding Cardinal John McCloskey. By 1880 New York was the largest and wealthiest Catholic diocese in the United States, with a substantial middle-class population and an emerging Irish political leadership. It was also the central port of entry for a new flood of poor Eastern and Southern European Catholic immigrants, who swelled the already overburdened and overpopulated churches and other ecclesiastical institutions. In the midst of the immigrant influx Corrigan continued to develop charitable institutions for the poor, actively seeking missionary support, especially for the large number of Italian immigrants. He also continued the educational efforts of Archbishop John Hughes, who required that Catholic schools be built, even before churches, to educate the Catholic immigrants and to provide for their religious and ethnic solidarity and identity in American society. During Corrigan's episcopacy, from 1880 to 1902, the number of Catholics in the New York diocese increased by 600,000, churches by 78, priests by 296, colleges and academies by 22, parish schools by 89, and industrial and reform schools by 18.

After the Third Plenary Council of Baltimore in 1884, Corrigan and Bernard J. McQuaid—the first bishop of Rochester, New York, and a personal friend from their early priestly ministry in Newark—became the national leaders of a conservative party in the Catholic church. They rejected the accommodationist stance toward American values and institutions that characterized the pastoral efforts of Americanizing archbishops such as John Ireland (1838–1918) of St. Paul and John Joseph Keane of Dubuque. The American Catholic accommodationists proposed, for example, that immigrants learn English and adopt American cultural values, that Catholics develop their educational institutions according to American models, and that labor unions be accepted as movements toward social justice. Corrigan, in particular, petitioned Rome to condemn the Knights of Labor as a secret society and suspended Edward McGlynn, the popular pastor of St. Stephen's Church, when, in violation of canonical legislation, he campaigned for the populist and (in Corrigan's view) "socialist" Henry George (1839–1897), a candidate for mayor of New York City in 1886. Corrigan also criticized and rejected the establishment of the Catholic University of America at Washington, D.C., fearing its liberal leadership, and was adamantly opposed to Archbishop Ireland's attempts to create a rapprochement between public and Catholic schools. Corrigan believed that Catholics who supported these programs were undermining the specific identity of Catholicism, weakening its authority, and confusing its religious aims with specific political and cultural programs and agendas. Corrigan held that American Catholicism could preserve its identity only by staying out of political and social issues, concentrating upon its religious mission and institutional developments, and reinforcing ecclesiastical and civil authority as a primary means for maintaining the unity and stability of church and society.

Between 1886 and 1899 Corrigan periodically complained to Rome that the pastoral approaches of the "liberal" Americanizing bishops were threatening the foundations of Catholicism in the United States. In 1899, when Pope Leo XIII issued his encyclical *Testem Benevolentiae*, condemning the so-called heresy of Americanism, Corrigan rejoiced that ecclesiastical authority had finally intervened to dam up the flood of a false Americanism that, he believed, without a forceful rebuke, would have drowned the American Catholic church. Although Corrigan was an ultramontane authoritarian bishop, he used his authority in ways that helped immigrants adjust to American society from a position of communal strength. He supported American religious liberty and separation of church and state and the dynamics of a moderate capitalism, but he adamantly opposed the populist, reforming, and progressive movements in late nineteenth-century American society. He preferred to work almost exclusively within the church and surreptitiously behind the scenes of ecclesiastical and civil politics rather than in the open exchange of public life. His friends admired him for his maintenance of order and stability, and his

enemies saw him as intransigent and belligerently hostile to change and reform. In February of 1902 he ruptured a blood vessel in his foot, and his health rapidly declined thereafter; he contracted pneumonia in April and died the following month at his home in New York City.

• Corrigan's letters and unpublished papers are located primarily in the archives of the archdioceses of New York and Baltimore, the dioceses of Newark and Rochester, and Propaganda Fide (Rome). His diary and some of his correspondence have been published in Joseph F. Mahoney and Peter J. Wosh, eds., *The Diocesan Journal of Michael Augustine Corrigan* (1987), and Frederick M. Zwierlein, ed., *The Letters of Archbishop Corrigan to Bishop McQuaid and Allied Documents* (1946). There is no scholarly biography of Corrigan, but biographical information and an analysis of his thought and policies are available in Robert Emmet Curran, *Michael Augustine Corrigan and the Shaping of Conservative Catholicism in America, 1878–1902* (1978), and Stephen DiGiovanni, *Corrigan, the Vatican, and the Italian Immigrants* (1990). An obituary is in the *New York Times*, 6 May 1902.

PATRICK W. CAREY

CORRINGTON, John William (28 Oct. 1932–24 Nov. 1988), short story writer, novelist, and poet, was born in Cleveland, Ohio, the son of John Wesley Corrington, an insurance adjuster, and Viva Shelley. In 1942 the family moved to Shreveport, Louisiana, where he began his formal education in the third grade.

"My great ambition in life," Corrington told William Parrill, "was to play lead trumpet in the Glenn Miller orchestra" (*Southern Man of Letters*, p. 182). After two years as a music major at Centenary College of Louisiana, he switched to English and decided to become a writer. "Because of my slow reflexes, I knew I would never become a 'great' trumpet player," he explained to friends.

In 1956 Corrington received a B.A. and entered Rice University in Houston as a graduate fellow. Late that fall he married Floice Rhodes Smith of Knoxville, Tennessee, but the marriage ended in divorce in 1957. He completed the course work for a Ph.D., but opted to take an M.A. in Renaissance literature instead. His decision was based on a personality conflict and philosophical differences with Jackson I. Cope, a professor of English, who informed Corrington that his choice of a twentieth-century topic for his dissertation would never be approved.

In 1960 Corrington married Joyce Elaine Hooper, a chemical engineer. They had four children. The Corringtons moved to Baton Rouge, Louisiana, where he accepted an appointment as instructor in English at Louisiana State University. Corrington wrote prolifically, publishing poetry and literary criticism in the leading little magazines of the day. In 1962 he received the Charioteer Poetry Prize for the volume *Where We Are*.

Taking a leave of absence from LSU in 1963, Corrington journeyed to England, where he wrote his dissertation on James Joyce under the direction of David Daiches at the University of Sussex. He was awarded the D.Phil. in 1965. During the year abroad he also completed the first of four novels, *And Wait for the Night*, published by Putnam's in New York and Anthony Blond in London in 1964. In the same year, two other collections of poetry appeared: *The Anatomy of Love and Other Poems* and *Mr. Clean and Other Poems*.

Returning to LSU, Corrington was promoted to assistant professor. A fourth collection of poetry, *Lines to the South*, appeared in 1965. When Corrington and poet Miller Williams were not appointed editors of the *Southern Review* as they expected to be, Corrington left LSU for an appointment as associate professor and chairman of English at Loyola University, New Orleans, Louisiana. A second novel, *The Upper Hand*, was published and was cited by Nelson Algren as "the darkest, funniest American novel since *Catch-22*" (*Dallas Morning News*, 2 July 1967).

With Williams, Corrington founded the *New Orleans Review* in 1968, and the National Endowment for the Arts recognized Corrington's short story, "To Carthage Then I Came," with an award of $1,000. Although fiction claimed Corrington's major attention, he continued to contribute poetry as before; some of these poems were anthologized in such collections as *Poets of Today* (1964), *19 Poetas de hoy en los Estados Unidos* in Chile (1966), and *Black and White Culture in America* (1969).

In addition to this recognition, critics observed that, although much of his writing is devoted to themes of or relating to the South, there is also a universality in regard to myth and history. Granville Hicks, in the *Saturday Review* (23 May 1964), mentioned Corrington's awareness of the past and his devotion to it as a defining element of identity.

In 1968 Corrington accepted a visiting professorship in modern literature at the University of California at Berkeley. Although his conservative views did not match those of his liberal students, they gave him standing ovations at the close of the three courses he taught there.

Returning to Loyola, Corrington began another novel and a career change as well. Movie producer and director Roger Corman offered Corrington the opportunity to write screenplays. The first was *Von Richthofen and Brown* (1969), which followed his first collection of short stories, *The Lonesome Traveller and Other Stories* (1968). *The Omega Man* was completed while he finished work on the novel *The Bombardier* (1970). A third movie, *Boxcar Bertha*, was written for Corman in 1971. *The Arena*, his fourth script, was produced in 1972. When his strong recommendation for tenure of a professor in his department was overruled by the Loyola administration, Corrington resigned. Because of an interest in the law for many years and as a tribute to his father, who had been a member of the Tennessee bar, it seemed to Corrington an appropriate time to enroll in Tulane University School of Law while continuing to write screenplays for *The Battle for the Planet of the Apes* (1973) and *The Killer Bees* (1974).

Graduating with a J.D. in 1975, Corrington practiced law until 1978. Several of his short stories were included in *Best Short Stories* of 1973, 1976, and 1977, and in the *O. Henry Award Stories* of 1976. Furthermore, two new collections appeared in 1978 and 1981, respectively: *The Actes and Monuments* and *The Southern Reporter and Other Stories*. His fourth novel, *Shad Sentell*, was published in 1984.

Venturing into yet another medium, he formed Corrington Productions, Ltd., and began writing for television programs such as "Search for Tomorrow," "Texas," "General Hospital," "Capitol," and "One Life to Live." He also produced and wrote "Superior Court" (1986–1988).

In commenting on his own writing to William Parrill, Corrington remarked that he did "what a writer is *supposed* to do, which is to listen to his people talking and be able to describe what they see" (*Southern Man of Letters*, p. 193).

Commitments in television became so overwhelming that Corrington moved to California, purchasing a house and twenty-six acres in Malibu. From this house he wrote two novellas, "Decoration Day" and "The Rizi's Wife," both published in the volume *All My Trials* (1987), and, with his wife, wrote a series of detective novels for Viking: *So Small a Carnival* (1986), *A Project Named Desire* (1987), and *A Civil Death* (1987).

Corrington died in Malibu. After his death, *The Collected Stories of John William Corrington* was published in 1990. His works have been translated into Danish, Italian, Japanese, German, Portuguese, and Spanish.

In commenting on Corrington's fiction, Lewis P. Simpson points out that "confidence in the possibilities of history is more positive in [Corrington's work] . . . than in Percy's. . . . Corrington harks back to a vision of history proclaimed by the defeated South: history must be an overriding scheme of justice." Simpson observes further that Corrington's use of the grotesque and the absurd "brings into focus a southern metaphysic of 'grace as history transcendent'" (pp. 183–84). With regard to a writing "style," which Corrington likened to an instrument, he made an early decision not to develop one. In this way, he reasoned, rather than twisting the material to the instrument, the material in his writing would be treated truthfully and honestly. His work is the epitome of pure prose wearing poetic shoes. His reputation as a craftsman of the short story and the novella certainly ranks him among the most polished of the second half of the twentieth century.

• John William Corrington's papers, including his manuscripts, are in the Peters Research Center, Centenary College, Shreveport, La. The most complete critical assessment of his fiction, poetry, and scripts is William Mills, ed., *John William Corrington: Southern Man of Letters* (1994). See also Thomas N. Walters, "The Lonesome Traveler and Other Stories," *Literary Annual*, ed. Frank N. Magill (1970), for his attitude toward the South and the Southerner, and William Parrill, "An Interview with John William Corrington," *Louisiana Literature* (Fall 1985): 5–14, for his assessment of art versus commercialism in New York publishing, literary tradition, and influences on his writing. To explore his youth and middle teen years, see Lloyd Halliburton, "Autobiography in the Fiction of John William Corrington," *Southern Literary Journal* 1 (1992): 118–28; and also on the decade of the sixties and a biographical and critical analysis of his poetic relationship with Charles Bukowski, "Corrington, Bukowski, and the Loujon Press," *Louisiana Literature* (Spring 1996): 103–9. Lewis P. Simpson, "Southern Fiction," in *Harvard Guide to Contemporary American Writing*, ed. Daniel Hoffman (1979), pp. 179–84, examines Corrington's place in relationship to Flannery O'Connor and Walker Percy, the nature of the self's being, and the movement out of history toward the absolute. William Domnarski, "Will the Defendant Please Rise," *Virginia Quarterly Review* 3 (1983): 530–31, gives an analysis of his contribution to legal fiction as contrasted with other lawyer-writers. William Mills, "Risking the Bait: John William Corrington," *Southern Review* 3 (1989): 586–94, is the best critical biography.

LLOYD HALLIBURTON

CORROTHERS, James David (2 July 1869–12 Feb. 1917), journalist, poet, and clergyman, was born in Chain Lake Settlement, Cass County, Michigan, a colony first settled by fugitive slaves in the 1840s. His parents were James Richard Carruthers (spelling later changed by Corrothers), a black soldier in the Union army, and Maggie Churchman, of French and Madagascan descent, who died when Corrothers was born. Corrothers was legally adopted by his nonblack paternal grandfather, a pious and respected man of Cherokee and Scotch-Irish origins, who raised young Corrothers in relative poverty. They lived in several roughneck towns along the eastern shore of Lake Michigan, where Corrothers attended school and became aware of racial hostility. In his boyhood family members introduced him to a rich vein of African-American folk tales that he would later draw upon for a number of his dialect sketches.

Working in his teens variously as a sawmill hand, hotel menial, coachman, pantryman on a lake steamer, and bootblack in Chicago, Corrothers also managed a vigorous program of literary self-education. Settling in Chicago in the early 1890s, he was first befriended by the crusading journalist Henry D. Lloyd and then by the temperance reformer Frances E. Willard. Sponsored by Willard, he sporadically attended a preparatory school at Northwestern University for two years and then spent a year at Bennett College in Greensboro, North Carolina. By this time he was beginning his own first tentative efforts as a poet.

Returning to Chicago, Corrothers married Fannie Clemens in 1894; they had two children. In a profession where opportunities to write for the black press were scant and white editors were distinctly inhospitable to an aspiring black journalist, Corrothers struggled to establish his career as a freelance writer for various Chicago newspapers. Overcoming his initial distaste for dialect speech and spurred by the example of his friend Paul Laurence Dunbar, he took advantage of an offer in 1896 to write a series of prose sketches and poems in black dialect for the *Chicago Evening Journal*.

Unable to find sufficient newspaper employment because of his color, Corrothers accepted a call to enter the ministry in the African Methodist Episcopal church in 1898. In the same year, as he embarked on his first pastorate in Bath, New York, he lost his wife and youngest son to consumption. At this time he also undertook his literary career in earnest, placing a dialect poem in *The Century*. With the interest and support of the editor Richard Watson Gilder, he received some modest recognition by publishing his poetry with some regularity in that magazine. Over a period of several years at the turn of the century, his poems also appeared in the *Colored American*, the *Criterion*, the *Southern Workman*, the *New York Sunday Herald*, and the *Philadelphia Inquirer*. This achievement culminated in 1902 with the publication by Funk and Wagnalls of *The Black Cat Club*, his best known work.

At the same time Corrothers continued his career in the ministry. After several pastoral appointments in New Jersey, he was accused of an inappropriate relationship with a young woman in the congregation and of plotting, as he said, "to ruin my bishop's good name." This incident led to his expulsion from the church in 1902, followed by an interval of extreme despair and irregular employment in the New York City area. Subsequently he became a Baptist, and in the period from 1904 to about 1914 he pursued an active ministry in that faith with a series of pastorates in Virginia; Michigan; Washington, D.C.; and Massachusetts. In 1906 he married Rosina B. Harvey; they had one son.

Along with his clerical responsibilities, Corrothers sustained a busy literary life as a poet. Although today his reputation has been overshadowed by the prominence of contemporaries like Charles Chesnutt, W. E. B. Du Bois, James Weldon Johnson, and Dunbar, in his time he earned more than modest celebrity for his dialect poetry. Converting to the Presbyterian faith, he was appointed in 1915 to a parish in West Chester, Pennsylvania, where he finally found a degree of calm and stability. In 1916 he published his autobiography, *In Spite of the Handicap*. A year later he died of a stroke in West Chester at the age of forty-seven.

Although best known as a dialect poet and often excelling in that form, Corrothers was never entirely comfortable in the role. Educated mainly among white children, he observed that before his introduction to black life in Chicago he was "not used to colored people" and "never talked Negro dialect." He was particularly sensitive at the beginning of his literary career to the invidious distinction between what he referred to as the "dis" and "dat" of black vernacular speech and his own strong preference for refined standard English. Needing income, however, Corrothers sought to take advantage of the popularity of the fashion of dialect writing. To accomplish this, he describes how he was obliged to learn literary dialect when he began publishing the prose sketches and verse that were collected in *The Black Cat Club*. Although he later expressed his regret for having produced that material, he developed an uncanny range within the dialect, from the shallow doggerel of pieces like "De Cahvin'" (the bloody carvings of a razor fight) to the moving lyrical appeal of poems like "Way in de Woods and Nobody Dah" to social resistance pieces like "An Indignation Dinner." He continued to publish dialect poems even when he came under the influence of Swinburne and focused the latter part of his career on what he termed "a higher class of work" in "literary English." The non-dialectal works that he wrote later in his career, including two volumes of poems he is alleged to have written but that have not been recovered, were little noticed. More recently, his autobiography has been criticized for its tendency to harshly characterize other African Americans, while his dialect poetry, despite the cultural and social limits that the genre poses from a contemporary perspective, is thought to rank among the best of its kind.

Writing at the turn of the century in an era of extreme racial prejudice and discrimination, he was pessimistic about his chances for success. His own turn to a sustaining religious faith was repeatedly tested by racial hostility and by what he increasingly came to believe was spiteful behavior among his own people, especially in his painful experiences with the church. Although tempered by expressions of sentimental feeling and a strong commitment to the values of respectful behavior and intellectual accomplishment, his autobiography clearly reveals these underlying tensions.

• Corrothers's autobiography, *In Spite of the Handicap* (1916), is the chief source of information about his life. See also James Weldon Johnson, *The Book of Negro Poetry* (1931); "A New Negro Poet," *Southern Workman*, Dec. 1899; Eugene B. Redmond, *Drumvoices: The Mission of Afro-American Poetry, a Critical History* (1983); and Dickson D. Bruce, *Black American Writing from the Nadir* (1989).

WILLIAM C. FISCHER

CORSE, John Murray (27 Apr. 1835–27 Apr. 1893), soldier and politician, was born in Pittsburgh, Pennsylvania, the son of John L. Corse, a stationer, and Sarah Murray. At age seven he moved with his family to Burlington, Iowa, where he worked in and later helped manage his father's business. After spending two years (1853–1855) at the U.S. Military Academy, he returned to Iowa to practice law and dabble in local politics. He married Ellen Edwards Prince in 1856. Corse's political horizons soon expanded: in the election of 1860 he was the unsuccessful Democratic candidate for Iowa secretary of state. His prominence as a Democrat who supported the war effort, along with his family's political connections (his father was a six-term mayor of Burlington), brought Corse to the attention of state officials when the Civil War broke out. On 13 July 1861 he was appointed major of the sixth Iowa Volunteer Infantry.

An officer of youth, energy, and intelligence, Corse made a favorable impression on Brigadier General John Pope when the latter gained an important command in the western armies early in 1862. During Pope's campaign along the upper Mississippi, Corse served as his inspector general. Under fire at New Madrid (13 Mar.) and Island Number 10 (7 Apr.), he earned praise for his cool-headed efficiency. Soon after rising to lieutenant colonel of his regiment on 21 May, he began an association with an even more successful superior, Major General William T. Sherman. Under Sherman, Corse did garrison duty at Memphis, Tennessee, and served ably in the October campaigning around Corinth, Mississippi. He managed to avoid Sherman's December debacle at Chickasaw Bluffs.

Corse continued to distinguish himself in Ulysses S. Grant's campaign against Vicksburg in the spring and summer of 1863, especially on 16 July at Jackson, Mississippi, where he commanded the skirmish forces in Brigadier General William Sooy Smith's division, Sixteenth Corps, Army of the Tennessee. "At the designated signal," Corse declared in his after-action report of the engagement, "the men dashed forward with a shout, met the line of the enemy's skirmishers and pickets, drove them back, capturing some 18 or 20, and killed as many more. . . . The enemy were driven from two pieces [of artillery] at the point of the bayonet." His division leader described Corse's conduct on that day as "daring that could not be excelled."

Such service, and the high-level appreciation it received, brought tangible rewards to the young Iowan. By early August he was a brigadier general of volunteers in command of a Fifteenth Corps brigade. The following month he accompanied most of the army that had captured Vicksburg under Grant and Sherman to the relief of Chattanooga. En route Corse's command drove a rebel force out of Trenton, Tennessee; once at Chattanooga it helped wrest commanding positions from the Confederates besieging the city. Leading an assault along Sherman's right center at sunrise on 25 November, Corse's brigade captured a heavily defended ridge in front of Braxton Bragg's main line atop Missionary Ridge and held it against over an hour's worth of counterattacks. He was seriously wounded in the fighting.

Only two months after his "great gallantry" at Chattanooga, the recovering Corse was chagrined to find himself assigned by the adjutant general's office to command a draft rendezvous in Illinois. The intercession of Sherman, however, secured his return to the Army of the Tennessee early in February 1864. Upon Corse's arrival, Sherman appointed him an acting inspector general and sent him on a series of missions up and down the Mississippi aimed at strengthening outposts against the cavalry raiders of Nathan Bedford Forrest and expediting the return of a part of Sherman's command sent to support the Red River campaign of Major General Nathaniel P. Banks.

Rejoining Sherman in time for the Atlanta campaign, from early May until late July Corse discharged the myriad of duties incumbent upon a troubleshooter at the headquarters of the Military Division of the Mississippi. On 26 July he returned to field duty at the head of the Fourth Division, Sixteenth Corps, one day after its irascible, hard-drinking commander, Brigadier General Thomas W. Sweeny, provoked a fistfight with his immediate superior, Major General Grenville M. Dodge. As Sherman and Dodge anticipated, Corse proved fully equal to divisional command, without displaying his predecessor's temper. He won praise for his leadership at Ezra Church (28 July) and especially at Jonesboro (31 Aug.), where his troops tossed back a succession of attacks lasting all afternoon.

After the capture of Atlanta, Sherman assigned Corse the difficult job of guarding communications in northwestern Georgia. The Iowan reached the pinnacle of his career on 5 October at Allatoona, site of a fortified supply depot on the Western & Atlantic Railroad, whose retention was critical to Sherman's ability to subsist his troops in Georgia. With a small portion of his division, Corse reinforced the vulnerable garrison just in time to thwart an assault by twice as many Confederates under Major General Samuel G. French. Though virtually surrounded, Corse spurned his enemy's offer to surrender and thus "avoid a needless effusion of blood." Enjoined by Sherman to hang on until reinforcements arrived (a plea later corrupted into the phrase "Hold the fort!" which inspired a famous song of that title), Corse repelled a succession of assaults through his masterful disposition of limited forces and despite sustaining a wound in the cheek. A frustrated French called off his attack and retreated before Sherman's additions could arrive. Casualties had run unusually high: more than 700 of the 2,000-man Union garrison and as many as 650 of the 4,000 Confederate attackers.

Returning to Atlanta in mid-November as a brevet major general, Corse was transferred to the command of the Fourth Division in the Fifteenth Corps, which he led on the March to the Sea and throughout the Carolinas campaign. From Atlanta to Goldsborough (now Goldsboro), his division wrecked miles of railroads, freed hundreds of slaves, and drove thousands of enemy troops from its path. Its service culminated on the last day of the battle of Bentonville (21 Mar. 1865), when it seized a hotly contested line of works along the Confederate left.

In the postwar army, Corse sought to remain with Sherman but instead was assigned to a military department headed by his old superior, Pope. In late August 1865 Corse took command of the District of Minnesota at St. Paul, where he spent most of his time protecting outlying settlers from the Sioux. Frontier duty proved not to his liking; in April 1866 he left the volunteer service and declined a lieutenant colonelcy in the regular army. For some years he worked as a civil engineer in the Northwest before moving to Massachusetts and reentering political life as chairman of that state's Democratic committee. He served as postmaster of Boston during Grover Cleveland's first administration, making that office a nationally recognized model of governmental efficiency. In 1882 he married Frances McNeil. It is not known when his first wife died or if he had any children by either marriage. He died in Winchester, Massachusetts.

Corse was one of those solid, dependable, sometimes extraordinary officers whose emergence in 1863–1865 made the Union armies in the West consistently successful. He was both a talented aide and a gifted field leader; in either capacity he enjoyed the utmost confidence of Sherman and Grant. A man of steady habits and unswerving morality, he could not refrain from lecturing his troops on the rules of right living. He frequently enjoined them to overcome the "debasing influences of camp vices" through harmless entertainments and physical exercise. (He was one of very few commanders to establish gymnasiums in his camps.) His men were made to understand that "it is disgraceful to get drunk, to quarrel, to use profane and coarse language; that they are regarded as gentlemen, and should bear themselves as such." He saved his harshest rhetoric for "marauding and lawlessness," especially when committed against helpless citizens. Such utterances were prompted by Corse's belief that the profession of soldiering was "the most dignified and honorable in the world" and the cause of the Union "the most sacred in which man ever embarked."

• Corse's life and career cannot be traced through any known collection of personal letters. The only biographical work is William Salter, "Major-General John M. Corse," *Annals of Iowa* 3, no. 2 (1895–1896): 1–19, 105–45, 278–304. *The War of the Rebellion: A Compilation of the Official Records of the Union and Confederate Armies* (128 vols., 1880–1901) includes several of his battle and campaign reports (see ser. 1, vols. 24, pt. 2; 38, pt. 3; 39, pt. 1; 44; and 47, pt. 1) as well as some of his paternalistic admonitions to his troops (ser. 1, vol. 38, pts. 3 and 5). Corse's stint as regimental commander is chronicled in two unit histories: Lurton D. Ingersoll, *Sixth Iowa Infantry* (n.d.), and Henry Haviland Wright, *A History of the Sixth Iowa Infantry* (1923). He also receives attention in two works by Victor Hicken, *Illinois in the Civil War* (1966) and "The Battle of Allatoona," *Civil War Times Illustrated* 7 (June 1968): 18–27; and in Albert Castel, *Decision in the West: The Atlanta Campaign of 1864* (1992).

EDWARD G. LONGACRE

CORSI, Edward (29 Dec. 1896–13 Dec. 1965), public official, was born in the village of Capestrano in the Abruzzi region of Italy, the son of Filippo Corsi and Julia Pantano. His father had served in the Italian House of Deputies, and Corsi had grown up attending political rallies and listening to his father's fiery speeches demanding individual liberties and democratic institutions. Forced to flee to Switzerland in 1903 because of his radical views, Filippo Corsi died two years later. Corsi's mother remarried, and in 1907, when Edward Corsi was ten, the family emigrated to the United States, where they settled in the noisy, congested, and dreary atmosphere of New York's East Side. The family was so poor that at times Corsi was forced to go without food. His mother did not stay long in New York. Plagued by illness and plunged into deep despair in sordid tenement rooms, she returned to Italy in 1910 and died there one year later. Few experiences in Corsi's life were to be as painful as the hardship of his early years in New York.

Corsi was studious and energetic. He did well in public school and eventually attended St. Francis Xavier College, graduating in 1917. To support himself, he held a variety of after-school jobs, from lamplighter to clerk in a telegraph office. He graduated from Fordham University Law School in 1922. In his youth Corsi was very much influenced by Theodore Roosevelt, whose commitment to good government and social justice for the urban masses encouraged Corsi to organize a Roosevelt Club on the East Side and to win over Italian-American voters to liberal Republican politics. Corsi called himself a progressive Republican and throughout his life saw himself as faithful to Roosevelt's causes such as political reform and the ideal of public service. In the years following his graduation from law school, Corsi became director of Haarlem House, located on East 116th Street in the heart of Harlem's Little Italy. Haarlem House offered a wide variety of social and educational services designed to prepare Italian immigrants for citizenship. It also functioned as a protective wall against discrimination. Haarlem House educated Corsi in the techniques of dealing with the problems of the underprivileged; it also renewed his hope in America as a land of opportunity. Committed to its ideals, Corsi was executive director of its successor organization, La Guardia Memorial House, at the time of his death.

By the early 1920s Corsi had established himself as something of an intellectual. He was well aware of the growing hostility toward immigrants of southern and eastern European backgrounds and was anxious to communicate the sources of their fears and aspirations to the general public. He turned to journalism, writing with great passion in newspaper and magazine articles about the damaging effects of intolerance as well as the contributions immigrants had made to the cultural and material development of the nation. In 1923 Corsi went to Mexico as a correspondent for *Outlook* magazine; five years later he was in Italy, where he reported on the fascist revolution for the *New York World*. He returned to New York with a hatred of fascism and an urgent determination to combat the threat of its appeal among Italians in the United States. In 1926 Corsi had married Emma Gilles, with whom he had one child.

Corsi made his first move into public affairs in 1930 when he served as Manhattan supervisor of the federal census. The following year President Herbert Hoover appointed him U.S. commissioner of immigration at Ellis Island. Corsi's service as immigration commissioner coincided with a dark time in American immigration policy. Overzealous government officials organized raids on immigrant communities, arrested thousands of men and women, and sent them to Ellis Island for deportation. Corsi, who privately disapproved of the administration's policy, tried to alleviate the harsh treatment of deportees on the island and lobbied immigration officials in Washington to stop the worst abuses connected with the deportation process. In 1933 President Franklin Roosevelt reappointed Corsi. Corsi's major achievement over the next year was in obtaining $1.5 million in government funds from Congress to finance the renovation of the rapidly deteriorating buildings on Ellis Island. After resigning as commissioner in January 1934, Corsi published an anecdotal account of his experience on Ellis Island, *In the Shadow of Liberty*, in which he called for new legislation to liberalize the nation's immigration and naturalization policy.

In New York's political circles, Corsi had become very close friends with Fiorello La Guardia, who in the summer of 1933 had received the nomination for mayor from the Fusion party, an anti-Tammany coalition of good government reformers, businessmen, and liberal Republicans. The fusionists' organization, led by Corsi and Vito Marcantonio, a La Guardia aide from East Harlem, worked furiously to widen La Guardia's support among the city's ethnic minorities, a significant number of whom were Italian Americans. Corsi's involvement in the campaign contributed significantly to La Guardia's victory.

After the election Corsi accepted the job as director of New York City's Emergency Home Relief Bureau and later was named deputy commissioner of welfare. Corsi made his first bid for political office when he ran unsuccessfully as the Republican candidate for the U.S. Senate in 1938. Two years later he left the welfare department to head the East Coast campaign of the Republican presidential candidate, Wendell Willkie. In 1943 Governor Thomas Dewey appointed Corsi industrial commissioner for the state of New York, a position he held for eleven years. Corsi called for the liberalization of unemployment insurance and became known to workers throughout the state as a dedicated and fair-minded administrator who had a sympathetic understanding of their concerns and grievances. Corsi made another try at political office in 1950, losing as the Republican candidate for mayor of New York in a bitter three-way race.

In 1954 Secretary of State John Foster Dulles named Corsi as his special assistant on refugee and immigration problems. The job was a difficult one. In July 1953, under pressure from the Eisenhower administration, Congress had passed the Refugee Relief Act, which authorized the State Department to admit 214,000 nonquota refugees over the next three years. The national hysteria generated by Cold War hostilities and the McCarthy red scare had grown so intense, however, that eighteen months after passage of the Refugee Relief Act only 13,056 European refugees had been admitted. Corsi was determined to break the impasse. But his appointment provoked strong reactions in Congress, most prominently from Representative Francis E. Walter, chairman of the House Subcommittee on Immigration and cosponsor of the 1952 McCarran–Walter Immigration Act, which had retained the national origins quota system of the 1924 legislation. Walter accused Corsi of having been a member of various Communist front organizations in the 1930s, a charge Corsi vigorously denied.

For Corsi, the opposition of Walter and his allies in Congress was followed by another disappointment, the decision by Dulles to dismiss him from his position in surrender to the intimidating pressure of Walter's red-baiting tactics in the spring of 1955. Many influential Americans thought that Corsi had been treated unjustly. Among them was New York governor E. A. Harriman, who appointed Corsi to the state's Committee on Refugees (1954–1955) and to the State Unemployment Insurance Appeal Board (1958–1965). Through much of his career Corsi maintained his interest in bringing to the public a greater awareness and a more profound appreciation of the nation's extraordinary experience with mass immigration. Among his projects was an effort to persuade Congress to turn Ellis Island into a national monument. He died in an automobile accident in upstate New York.

• Although there is a very large collection of Corsi papers at Syracuse University, his biography has yet to be published. Corsi continued to write books on historical subjects during his years of public service in New York, including *Poland: Land of the White Eagle* (1933) and *Paths to the New World: American Immigration— Yesterday, Today and Tomorrow* (1953). A number of studies on various topics contain useful information on Corsi's life and career, in particular, Arthur Mann, *La Guardia Comes to Power: 1933* (1965) and *La Guardia, a Fighter against His Times, 1882–1933* (1959). See also Thomas Kessner, *Fiorello H. La Guardia and the Making of Modern New York* (1989); *The Italians of New York, a Survey Prepared by Workers of the Federal Writers' Project* (1938); Chris McNickle, *To Be Mayor of New York* (1993); Michael Musmanno, *The Story of the Italians in America* (1965); Charles Garrett, *The La Guardia Years: Machine and Reform Politics in New York City* (1961); Ann Novotny, *Strangers at the Door: Ellis Island, Castle Garden, and the Great Migration to America* (1971); Barbara Benton, *Ellis Island, a Pictorial History* (1985); Herbert S. Parmet, *Eisenhower and the Great Crusades* (1972); and Gil Loescher and John A. Scanlan, *Calculated Kindness: Refugees and America's Half-Open Door, 1945 to the Present* (1986). An obituary is in the *New York Times*, 14 Dec. 1965.

FELICE A. BONADIO

CORSON, Juliet (13 Jan. 1841?–18 June 1897), founder of the New York Cooking School and pioneer in the scientific cookery movement, was born in Mount Pleasant, Massachusetts, the daughter of Peter Ross Corson, a prosperous produce merchant, and Mary Ann Henderson. (Although most obituaries and biographical sources give Corson's birth date as 1842, the Vital Records of Roxbury, Massachusetts, give the date as 1841.) Corson's family moved to New York City when she was six years old. In New York her uncle, Alfred Upham, helped to raise her and provided her with a classical education. She began to support herself in her late teens after her mother's death.

Corson's first jobs introduced her to the world of female philanthropic and educational organizations, which would later offer institutional support and opportunities when she began her work in scientific cookery. One of her first positions was at the Working Women's Library in New York City, where she received four dollars a week and her room. She supplemented her income by writing book reviews, verse, and articles about women. Between 1863 and 1870 she wrote for the *New York Leader* and the *Courier*.

In 1873 Corson became secretary of another female philanthropic organization in New York, the Wom-

en's Educational and Industrial Society. Founded in response to the economic panic of 1873, the organization offered courses at a free training school for women, which was dedicated to providing them with skills to make them employable. Initially, training classes were held in Corson's home. Leaders of the organization instructed young women first in sewing and in skills appropriate to white-collar employment—shorthand, bookkeeping, and proofreading. Soon realizing that there were not enough white-collar positions available, instructors at the school began to offer courses that would prepare young women for domestic service.

In 1874 the free training school began classes in the various domestic arts. In the cooking class, Corson lectured while a chef cooked. In 1876 Corson founded her own institution, the New York Cooking School. There she taught New York women of all economic classes how to cook healthful and economical meals. She charged for her courses on a sliding scale, according to the means of her pupils. In 1877 Corson published her first book on cooking, *The Cooking School Manual of Practical Directions for Economical Every-day Cookery*. She stressed economy in her classes and her recipes, reminding students in her book that "in cooking, this fact should be remembered above all others; *a good cook never wastes.*"

Corson believed that a central part of her mission was to teach the poor how to eat nutritiously. She wrote in *The Cooking School Manual*, "The question of the hour is 'How well can we live, if we are moderately poor?' The author of *The Cooking School Manual* is doing her best to answer it satisfactorily." Her concern with feeding the poor brought her to public notice in 1877, when, responding to the railroad strikes of that year, she offered laboring men and women free copies of her pamphlet *Fifteen-cent Dinners for Workingmen's Families* in a 19 August letter to the editor of the *New York Times*. In her letter, Corson offered free copies of the pamphlet and noted that "the conflict between capital and labor, which has so lately threatened our national prosperity, is far from being settled. . . . The leaders of all the strikes declared that their action was taken only because they could not support their families upon the wages received by them. The question of feeding his family is the most difficult one the working man has to answer." Corson paid for the printing of 50,000 copies of *Fifteen-cent Dinners*, which became very popular. She subsequently received threats from socialists who believed that if she succeeded in teaching workers to live on less, employers would further reduce their wages.

Corson was not only interested in helping poor people eat better and more economically; she also wanted to raise the status of cooking as a field. She realized that cooking was held in low regard, but she hoped to alter that image by making it a more scientific discipline with codified principles. In *The Cooking School Manual* she claimed, "Food is concentrated force. The manipulation of a motive power capable of invigorating both body and mind, is an occupation worthy to employ intelligence and skill."

Corson worked to introduce scientific cooking and domestic economy into the curriculum of schools and colleges. She advised teachers on how to present these subjects in a systematic fashion and during the 1870s and 1880s offered instruction in Montreal and at the University of Minnesota, the Lake Erie Seminary in Ohio, Miss Porter's School in Connecticut, and schools in California. The U.S. commissioner of education had asked her to spread her knowledge around the country and became a great supporter of her work. Corson succeeded in introducing cooking education into many public schools in the United States, and she lectured widely in cities such as Peoria, Cleveland, Indianapolis, Washington, D.C., and Boston. Additionally, she instructed nurses at training schools on the proper diet for invalids and also wrote a book on the topic. The French consul in New York asked her to write down her principles in order to offer them to public schools in France.

Corson received much public praise for her efforts. A glowing article in *Harper's New Monthly Magazine* reported in 1879 that Corson was the "benefactor of the working classes, for she teaches them how to make two dishes where formerly they made but one; and the friend of women, for she has shown them the way to a useful and honorable profession." Further recognition came in 1892, when Corson was asked to organize the New York State Cooking Exhibition at the World's Fair. There, she received an award for her work in scientific cooking and dietetics. She died of uremia in New York City.

Although some of Corson's ideas about cooking seem odd and outdated, many principles she espoused have been confirmed by later nutritionists. For instance, while she recommended dishes such as eggs with burnt butter, she reminded her less-fortunate readers that it was more economical to serve several dishes instead of a single costly one, and specifically suggested in *The Cooking School Manual* that they should serve soup, fish, vegetables, and bread rather than "heavy joints of meat." In her other cookbooks she suggested lentils as a meat substitute and recommended pastas and polenta.

Corson addressed the daily economic difficulties of the industrial classes in nineteenth-century America. Although some of her contemporaries clearly resented her efforts and worried that her work ultimately might benefit the wealthy and not the poor, her recipes and free instruction were not offered with this aim in mind. She was a reformer, not a revolutionary, and while she could not resolve the conflict between labor and capital, she could offer advice in an effort to help the underpaid and the underfed.

• The University of Minnesota published lectures that Corson had delivered as part of the university's Farmers' Lecture Course in *A Course of Lectures on the Principles of Domestic Economy and Cookery* (1886?). In addition to her books mentioned above, she published many others, including *Meals for the Millions: The People's Cookbook* (1882), *Diet for Invalids and Children* (1886), and *Family Living on $500 a Year: A Daily Reference-Book for Young and Inexperienced Housewives* (1887). See also Mary J. Lincoln, "The Pioneers of Scientific Cookery," *Good Housekeeping*, Oct. 1910. For information on the free training schools of the Women's Educational and Industrial Society, see their annual reports in the *New York Times*, 8 Nov. 1874 and 26 Apr. 1875. An obituary appears in the *New York Times*, 20 June 1897.

SUSAN MATT

CORTELYOU, George Bruce (26 July 1862–23 Oct. 1940), presidential aide, cabinet secretary, and businessman, was born in New York City, the son of Peter Crolius Cortelyou, a businessman and Rose Seary. Educated at public and private schools, he graduated from the Massachusetts State Normal School in 1882. He studied music in Boston before going back to New York to learn stenography and court reporting. He married Lilly Morris Hinds in 1888; they had five children.

During the early 1890s Cortelyou went to work as a secretary to the surveyor of the Port of New York. His administrative talents soon took him to Washington, D.C., as an aide to the fourth assistant postmaster general. In 1895 he became stenographer to President Grover Cleveland. Meanwhile, he studied law at Georgetown University and Columbian College (now George Washington University).

During William McKinley's presidency, Cortelyou emerged as a valued White House official. His efficiency and tact made him indispensable to the president during the war with Spain in 1898. Named secretary to the president by McKinley in 1900, Cortelyou managed White House press relations, organized the frequent trips that McKinley made, and supervised the release of official presidential statements. By 1901 he had become the forerunner of the modern White House staff member. A journalist described him as "always by the President's side, acting as an intermediary between him and the people" (Barry, p. 3339). Cortelyou's discretion was legendary. A cartoon depicted him sitting silently at his desk under the caption "Can't-Tell-You" (Ford, p. 270).

When McKinley was shot on 6 September 1901 in Buffalo, New York, Cortelyou managed the president's care and then supervised the transition of power to Theodore Roosevelt (1858–1919) with cool efficiency when McKinley died eight days later. Cortelyou was McKinley's literary executor, and his shorthand diaries of his dealings with the president are a valuable source for the inner workings of the administration.

During the early years of Roosevelt's presidency, Cortelyou filled the same role for the new chief executive. According to contemporary accounts, he created an "atmosphere of courtesy" around "the loud-voiced and impetuous" Roosevelt ("Suavity," p. 443). By 1903 Roosevelt decided to appoint Cortelyou to head the newly created Department of Commerce and Labor. Cortelyou proved adept at organizing the department and was well liked within the business community. He advised Roosevelt on the trust issue, patronage, and the issue of union power in the Government Printing Office. His stand in favor of the open shop at the printing office brought him opposition from organized labor.

As the 1904 presidential election neared, Roosevelt decided that Cortelyou should manage his campaign for a full term in the White House. The president believed that Cortelyou had "the requisite capacity and integrity to make him direct a strong square campaign" (Gould, p. 134). Roosevelt secured Cortelyou's appointment as chair of the Republican National Committee at the party's national convention in June 1904. During the campaign, Cortelyou proved to be a skilled organizer and effective fundraiser. Toward the end of October 1904, the Democratic candidate, Alton B. Parker, charged that Cortelyou had capitalized on the information gained from his cabinet service to extort campaign funds from large corporations. The Democrats claimed that "Cortelyouism" had brought the GOP its large campaign war chest, and the controversy enlivened the last days of an otherwise dull election. Both Cortelyou and Roosevelt denied the allegations heatedly. The Republicans had secured large donations from the business world, but there was no credible evidence at that time that money had been secured because of implied threats from Cortelyou.

Following his victory, Roosevelt returned Cortelyou to the cabinet as postmaster general. Cortelyou reorganized the operations of the department and emphasized the merit system in making appointments. After two years, he was named secretary of the treasury. The major crisis of his tenure arose during the banking "panic" that occurred in October 1907, when the collapse of major financial institutions in New York threatened the stability of the nation's banking system. Cortelyou responded with deposits of Treasury funds into banks across the country that preserved their liquidity. He took similar actions in the weeks that followed with funds from Panama Canal bonds and Treasury deposits. Cortelyou's policies freed funds for the purpose of moving crops from agricultural regions to their markets. His actions also alleviated the financial stringency and bolstered international confidence in the American economy.

There was talk of a Cortelyou presidential candidacy in 1908, especially after his record of success with the panic of 1907. Once Roosevelt made clear his preference for William Howard Taft, the Cortelyou "boom" collapsed. Taft did not wish him to serve in the succeeding administration, so the secretary stayed until the end of Roosevelt's term and prepared to enter private business in March 1909. He told a friend that "when I leave here I am going to have the satisfaction of not having compromised my conscience" (Ford, p. 261).

For the rest of his active career, Cortelyou was associated with a precursor of the Consolidated Edison Company, the New York Consolidated Gas Company, a firm that supplied power to millions of consumers in the New York metropolitan area. By one estimate,

Cortelyou managed a corporation worth nearly $1 billion. Until his retirement in 1935, Cortelyou was a successful, enlightened executive who stressed benefits for his employees and efficient service to his customers. "I consider that in a way I am still in the public service," he told an interviewer in 1932 (McConnell, p. 275). He died in Huntington, Long Island.

Cortelyou was a key figure in the institutional development of the twentieth-century presidency. For both McKinley and Roosevelt, he devised practices in the management of press relations, presidential tours, and the flow of official documents that became significant precedents for the White House staff members who followed him. The modern form of the internal operations of the American presidency descends directly from Cortelyou's work in the White House between 1897 and 1903.

• The Cortelyou papers, with his diary, are at the Library of Congress. Other Cortelyou letters and documents are in the William McKinley Papers, the Theodore Roosevelt Papers, and the William Howard Taft Papers, Library of Congress. For Cortelyou's own writings, see "Some Agencies for the Extension of Our Domestic and Foreign Trade," *Annals of the American Academy of Political and Social Science*, July 1904, pp. 1–12, and "Frauds in the Mail," *North American Review*, Apr. 1907, pp. 808–17. For contemporary assessments, see David S. Barry, "George Bruce Cortelyou," *World's Work*, Apr. 1903, pp. 3337–40; anon., "Suavity and Stenography," *Stenographer*, Aug. 1904, pp. 442–44; James Creelman, "Mr. Cortelyou Explains President McKinley," *Pearson's Magazine*, June 1908, pp. 569–86; and Burt M. McConnell, "The President of a $1,000,000,000 Corporation on 'Choosing a Profession,'" *Gregg Writer*, Feb. 1932, pp. 275–76, 307. The only biographical study is Benjamin Temple Ford, "A Duty to Serve: The Governmental Career of George Bruce Cortelyou" (Ph.D. diss., Columbia Univ., 1963). See also Lewis L. Gould, *The Presidency of William McKinley* (1980) and *The Presidency of Theodore Roosevelt* (1991). Information about the Cortelyou family is in John Van Zandt Cortelyou, *The Cortelyou Genealogy* (1942). The *New York Times*, 24 Oct. 1940, has an informative obituary.

LEWIS L. GOULD

CORTEZ LIRA, Gregorio (22 June 1875–28 Feb. 1916), cowboy and Mexican-American folk hero, was born in the state of Tamaulipas, Mexico, near the U.S.–Mexico border, the son of Roman Cortez Garza, a rancher, and Rosalia Lira Cortinas. In 1887 his family moved to Manor, Texas, near Austin. Two years later Cortez joined his older brother, Romaldo Cortez, in finding seasonal employment on the farms and ranches of South Texas. Some time in this period, Cortez married Leonor Díaz; they had four children. After eleven years as vaqueros, or cowboys, and farmhands, Cortez and his brother settled on a farm in Karnes County, Texas, renting land from a local rancher. Cortez and his first wife divorced in 1903, and in 1905 he married Estéfana Garza. They had no children and later separated.

At the time that Cortez and his family had immigrated to South Texas, Anglos had also begun to penetrate the region in increasing numbers, particularly with the arrival of the railroad. As political and economic power shifted to the newcomers, most Mexican Americans, like Cortez, lived as hired agricultural workers or as tenant farmers. Class and ethnicity relegated them to the bottom of a discriminatory Anglo-dominated Texas society. Thus, in 1901, when a horse was reported stolen by a "Mexican" and Cortez was known to have recently traded a mare, Sheriff W. T. Morris assumed there was a connection. The following blunders, Cortez's flight from the law, and his subsequent arrest and trial transformed the obscure farmer into an enduring symbol of Mexican-American pride and resistance.

On 12 June 1901 Sheriff Morris and two deputies arrived at Cortez's farm. Only one of the lawmen, Boone Choate, spoke Spanish, but he was far from fluent. Relying on Choate's misinterpretations of Cortez's idiomatic Spanish, Morris was led to believe in Cortez's guilt and ordered his arrest. Cortez protested in words that Choate took to mean that he was resisting arrest. In the confusion that followed, Morris shot and wounded Cortez's brother Romaldo and then fired at Cortez. Unscathed, Cortez returned fire, fatally wounding the sheriff. The deputies withdrew, and Cortez and his family abandoned the farm. Sending his wife and children ahead by road to the nearby community of Kenedy, Cortez hid in the brush with Romaldo. Later that night, Cortez slipped into Kenedy, left his wounded brother in the care of his family, and fled north on foot to evade a posse already combing the area.

When one of Cortez's family members was later captured and intensely questioned, he revealed Cortez's probable whereabouts. Using this information, Sheriff Robert M. Glover of Gonzales County and another posse surprised Cortez at the home of his friend, Martin Robledo. The posse attacked the house, and Cortez shot and killed Sheriff Glover and once more eluded capture. Heading south to the border with Mexico, Cortez picked up a mount at the home of another friend. After riding this horse into the ground, he found another and continued on his journey, all the while just managing to stay beyond the reach of numerous posses on his trail. When his second horse gave out, too, Cortez was some thirty miles from the border and safety. Mindful of the thousand-dollar reward posted for Cortez's capture, Jesus Gonzalez, a local vaquero, recognized the fugitive and notified a party of Texas Rangers of his location. On 22 June 1901 Cortez, after a ten-day chase that had led scores of lawmen over 500 miles, was finally apprehended.

Immediately, Mexicans from both sides of the border began to subscribe to Cortez's defense, an effort coordinated by members of the Mexican-American press of San Antonio. Nevertheless, a Gonzalez County jury, facing a gallery full of lawmen indignant at the death of Glover, found Cortez guilty of second degree murder for the death of a posse member named Schnabel and sentenced him to fifty years in prison. Other trials and convictions followed for the deaths of Sheriffs Morris and Glover and for horse theft. Troubled by conflicting testimony during the trials, the Texas Court of Criminal Appeals overturned all the verdicts, except for the conviction for Sheriff Glover's murder. On 1 January 1905, after three and a half years of legal battles, Cortez entered the Huntsville penitentiary to serve a life sentence for murder. Efforts to secure his pardon commenced immediately. Impressed by Cortez's demeanor during his incarceration, various law enforcement and prison personnel concurred. On 7 July 1913 Governor O. B. Colquitt pardoned Cortez, who soon afterward retired to Nuevo Laredo, Mexico. Cortez became involved in the Mexican Revolution and suffered a wound while fighting for the forces of Victoriano Huerta. Returning to Texas, he eventually settled in Anson, Jones County, where he died of pneumonia. In 1916, just before his death, Cortez married again, possibly to Esther Martínez.

Sensationalistic reports in the Anglo-Texan press avidly followed the doings of Cortez and his "gang" throughout his long ride. Soon after his capture anonymous balladeers composed *corridos* that cast Cortez's exploits in the tradition of the border Mexicans' conflict with the *rinches*, especially the despised Texas Rangers. In these ballads, Cortez emerges as the ideal man—skilled and self-assured yet modest and restrained—forced into flight by Anglo injustice. Struck by Cortez's determination and conviction, even his pursuers grow to admire his fortitude, and, fittingly, they effect his capture through betrayal. In other variants, Cortez's death results from poisoning, a last act of treachery that in no way invalidates his ultimate victory. Thus, Cortez the folk hero, symbolizing his people's resistance against an unjust but ever-encroaching Anglo-Texas society, overshadows Cortez the man.

• Drawing extensively on Cortez family interviews, Americo Paredes, *"With His Pistol in His Hand"—A Border Ballad and Its Hero* (1958), provides the most complete biographical information on Cortez and contains a comprehensive discussion of the *corrido* and its variants. See also Paredes, "The Problem of Identity in a Changing Culture: Popular Expressions of Culture Conflict along the Lower Rio Grande Border," in *Folklore and Culture on the Texas-Mexican Border*, ed. Richard Bauman (1993). Although it relies heavily on Paredes, Robert J. Rosenbaum, *Mexicano Resistance in the Southwest: "The Sacred Right of Self-Reservation"* (1981), places Cortez in the context of cross-border social banditry and conflict. David Montejano, *Anglos and Mexicans in the Making of Texas, 1836–1986* (1987), is the best critical study of South Texas interethnic social relations.

JOSEPH C. JASTRZEMBSKI

CORTINA, Juan Nepomuceno (16 May 1824–30 Oct. 1892), revolutionary, politician, Mexican governor, and rancher, was born in Camargo, Tamaulipas, Mexico, the son of Trinidad Cortina, the town mayor and an important landowner, and María Estéfana Goseascochea. Little is known of Juan Cortina's early life and education. Upon the death of his father in the early 1840s, his family moved to the Espíritu Santo grant, part of the area between the Nueces and Río Grande claimed by both Mexico and Texas and the future site of the city of Brownsville, Texas. This land belonged to Cortina's mother. Cortina associated with *vaqueros*, or herdsmen, who gave him the nickname "Cheno," and he endeared himself to these Mexicans by resenting their mistreatment by non-Hispanic Texans, called Anglos.

During the Mexican-American War Cortina fought against General Zachary Taylor's troops at the battles of Palo Alto and Resaca de la Palma. After the war he served briefly in the U.S. Quartermaster Corps and started a cattle ranch on part of his mother's land. The Cortina family became American citizens under the provisions of the Treaty of Guadalupe Hidalgo (1848). In the early 1850s Cortina was involved in several filibustering expeditions financed by local Anglo merchants who wanted to form the Republic of the Sierra Madre out of the Texas Río Grande region. In the late 1850s Cortina became active in local politics and gained some power in the local Democratic party as leader of the Mexican-American vote. Cortina was sympathetic to the economic and social plight of Mexicans living in the lower Río Grande area, and he also opposed slavery. For these reasons he was popular with the Mexican common people.

Relations between Anglo and Hispanic Texans, called *Tejanos*, had deteriorated following the Texas War for Independence, and the Mexican War further increased racial animosity. Anglos soon dominated county and city politics and through adverse court rulings and lawyers' fees paid in land reduced Mexican Americans to a second-class status. Anglo land speculators gained control of land in the Río Grande valley from the old Mexican landholding families. The Cortina family's title to the Espíritu Santo grant was among those challenged by the Anglos, further embittering Juan Cortina.

Cortina gained his reputation as a champion of Mexican-American rights when on 13 July 1859 he witnessed a Brownsville city marshal brutally beat a Mexican who had once worked on the Cortina ranch. Cortina reproached the marshal, who then insulted and angered him. After firing a warning shot, Cortina wounded the marshal in the shoulder and carried the Mexican ranch hand to Cortina's mother's Santa Rita Ranch west of town. On 28 and 29 September 1859 Cortina raided Brownsville to punish the Anglos who had persecuted and robbed the Mexican people of their land. He did not rob or steal when he was in the city. In a published proclamation he cited his reasons for seeking revenge against the injustices suffered by Mexicans at the hands of the Anglo Texans. On 23 November 1859 he published another proclamation, again outlining the crimes that had been committed against local Mexicans, and called for granting Mexicans their rights guaranteed by the Treaty of Guadalupe Hidalgo. Following his raid on Brownsville, Cortina defeated a group of Texas Rangers. Despite protests to Mexican authorities, he was not prosecuted by Mexico, since he was a U.S. citizen. Cortina engaged federal troops in a battle near Río Grande City on 27 December 1859, but he was defeated and fled

with his men into Mexico. All this was part of the so-called Cortina War, which lasted a decade, during which Cortina raided South Texas from Brownsville to Río Grande City. He defied capture, constantly eluding his pursuers, including Robert E. Lee, who led expeditions against him.

Although Cortina, a devout Catholic, had sympathized with the Conservatives in the war of the reform, in 1860 he joined the army of the Liberal forces in support of President Benito Juárez. Cortina quickly rose through the ranks to become Juárez's military commander at Matamoros, Tamaulipas, Mexico, and from 1861 to 1867 helped defend the state against the French. Settling in Tamaulipas he served briefly as its military governor as well as a general in the Mexican army.

Cortina became a victim of a smear campaign by Anglo Texans during the years 1870 to 1873. Most likely because he was sympathetic to the Union during the American Civil War, he was branded a cattle thief. This charge thwarted efforts to gain him a pardon from the Texas state legislature. Cortina was cleared of the alleged crime of cattle stealing in the Río Grande valley by the Mexican investigation committee sent to the border to investigate the charges. In 1875 he was arrested by the Mexican government under pressure from the United States on charges of shipping stolen cattle, but he was not brought to trial for these charges. Escaping from Mexico City, Cortina returned to the border, where he was apprehended by Mexican forces. After he was court-martialed and sentenced to be shot, Porfirio Díaz, president of Mexico, kept him under arrest for the rest of his life. When Cortina died in Mexico City, he was buried with full military honors.

• Cortina's life can be traced in José T. Canales, *Juan N. Cortina Presents His Motion for a New Trial* (1951); Charles W. Goldfinch, *Juan N. Cortina 1824–1892: A Re-Appraisal* (1974); Lyman Woodman, *Cortina: Rogue of the Rio Grande* (1950); *Difficulties on the Southwestern Frontier*, 36th Cong., 1st sess., 1860, H. Doc. 52; and *Troubles on the Texas Frontier*, 36th Cong., 1st sess., 1860, H. Doc. 81.

ZARAGOSA VARGAS

CORTISSOZ, Royal (10 Feb. 1869–17 Oct. 1948), art critic, was born in Brooklyn, New York, the son of Francisco Emanuel Cortissoz, an English native of Spanish descent, and Julia da Costa Mauri, a native of Martinique. He attended public schools in Brooklyn, but otherwise he was self-educated, and he began to write in his early teens, submitting his first articles to the *Kansas City (Mo.) Courier*. In 1883 he started work as an office boy at the architectural firm of McKim, Mead and White in New York City. In later years he credited Charles Follen McKim with having influenced his career by teaching him art history and forming his taste for work in the classical tradition. Indeed, McKim took Cortissoz with him to Italy to help choose sculptures to be reproduced in plaster for the World's Columbian Exposition in Chicago in 1893.

After leaving McKim, Mead and White in 1889, Cortissoz went to work as an art critic for the *New York Commercial Advertiser*. In 1891 he joined the staff of the *New York Tribune* (later the *Herald Tribune*) and remained its art editor for the next fifty-three years, covering hundreds of exhibitions annually both in the United States and Europe. On occasion in his earlier years, he also wrote music and theater reviews. Throughout the 1890s, in addition to working for the *Tribune*, Cortissoz contributed essays on art to periodicals such as *Harper's* and *Century*—one of his articles, for example, was a lengthy report on the holdings of the Prado Museum and the Hispanic Society Museum in New York that attests to his love of Spanish painting ("Spanish Art in Spain and Elsewhere," repr. in *American Artists*, pp. 249–333). Cortissoz was married in 1897 to Ellen Mackay Hutchinson, literary editor of the *Tribune*, and from then to about 1913 shared the literary editorship with his wife. They had no children.

The first of Cortissoz's several books were monographs on artists he considered upholders of the classical tradition: *Augustus Saint-Gaudens* (1907) and *John La Farge: A Memoir and a Study* (1911). Texts for Whitney Museum of American Art publications on his other favorite artists, *Arthur B. Davies* (1931) and *Guy Pène du Bois* (1931), eventually followed. All four are included in the bibliographical notes of Oliver W. Larkin's much-respected survey *Art and Life in America* (rev. ed., 1960). Cortissoz also wrote texts for a number of catalogs of exhibitions of American artists, and contributed chapters to the catalogue raisonné of the work of Gilbert Stuart, published in 1926, and to a new edition of Samuel Isham's *The History of American Painting* (1927). Cortissoz's best-known works are probably the collections of his longer reviews and essays: *Art and Common Sense* (1913), *American Artists* (1923), *Personalities in Art* (1925), and *The Painter's Craft* (1930), which give evidence of his breadth of knowledge of European and American art and architecture from the Renaissance on. Cortissoz's books also included the two-volume *Life of Whitelaw Reid* (1921), a biography of the *New York Herald Tribune* publisher commissioned by Mrs. Reid; a brief history of the paper, *The New York Tribune: Incidents and Personalities in Its History* (1923); and, as a devoted golfer himself, *Nine Holes of Golf* (1922).

Despite his "remorseless writing schedule" (Morgan, p. 98), which led to a breakdown in the 1920s and subsequent psychosomatic ailments, Cortissoz's style was always polished and felicitous, marked by its clarity, wit, and urbanity—and it was much praised by his colleagues and even those later commentators (such as the art historian Milton W. Brown) who have deplored his rigidly traditionalist views. His aim throughout was to make an appreciation of art an integral part of American life, as an antidote to materialism. His reviews were thus addressed to an interested but nonspecialist audience, and he avoided technical language and an art-historical approach. As a result, he was widely read and accepted as an understandable, relia-

ble guide. According to H. Wayne Morgan, in his study of the work of Cortissoz and his contemporaries Kenyon Cox and Frank Jewett Mather, Jr., of the three arch-conservative critics, Cortissoz exerted the strongest influence on American attitudes toward (and suspicion of) modern art. He was, in Morgan's phrase, "a traditionalist for every man," who judged art in light of the conviction that it "should embody an idea, that it should be beautiful, and that it should show sound craftsmanship" (quoted in *New York Herald Tribune* obituary). Enlarging on this concept elsewhere, Cortissoz maintained that "good worksmanship [is] the very life-blood of art" (*The Painter's Craft*, p. 13) and that by beauty he meant a design that pleases the eye, intrigues the mind, and produces a sense of harmony and order.

Thus, Cortissoz's response to the landmark Armory Show in New York in 1913 was largely negative. Granting the worth of its purpose, which was to introduce the work of contemporary European and American artists, he concluded that most of it posed a threat to the acceptance of art by the average viewer, who would perceive these artists as bizarre eccentrics. He was particularly scornful of Vincent Van Gogh, an "egotist" who "spoiled a lot of canvas with crude, quite unimportant pictures," Henri Matisse (to whom the critic had a particular antipathy) and his "*gauche puerilities*," and the cubists, who "give us not pictures but so many square yards of wallpaper" (*Personalities in Art*, p. 320; Brown, *Story of the Armory Show*, pp. 142, 147). Years later he simply declared of "non-objective" art: "I'm not interested; I think it leads to an impasse" (*New York Herald Tribune*, 13 Dec. 1936). Of such comments Milton Brown remarked that Cortissoz's "invective was frequently caustic [but] it always wore the guise of rational probity and moral rectitude" (*Story of the Armory Show*, p. 131). And he went on to note that Cortissoz "remained until his death a peculiar phenomenon of American art life, a critic who viewed . . . the passing art scene for over fifty years only to remain completely impervious to the march of events" (*American Painting*, p. 85).

In 1941 Cortissoz's half-century at the *Tribune* was celebrated by his many friends in the international art world with a gala exhibition at the Knoedler Gallery in New York. Paintings, chosen and hung by Cortissoz himself, were lent by public and private collections. It was a grouping that represented the critic's catholicity of taste, including old masters as well as works by his favorite American artists. Cortissoz kept writing indefatigably for three more years until a heart condition forced his retirement in 1944. He died in his New York home, and he was buried at the Church of the Ascension, for which his much-admired friend La Farge had painted his masterpiece, the *Ascension* mural.

A frequent lecturer over the years at universities and museums, Cortissoz was a chevalier of the Order of Leopold (of Belgium) and in 1924 was elected to the American Academy of Arts and Letters. In addition, Cortissoz served as a trustee of the American Academy in Rome and the Hispanic Society of America, and he was an honorary fellow of the Metropolitan Museum of Art, the American Institute of Architects, and the National Sculpture Society. In 1931 he received the medal of the Art Dealers Association of America for distinguished service in the fine arts.

• Royal Cortissoz's extensive correspondence with members of the international art world (Alfred Stieglitz and the art historian Bernard Berenson among them) is housed in the Yale Collection of American Literature in the Beinecke Rare Book and Manuscript Library at Yale University. Files of clippings of his reviews and some autobiographical material are also housed there. Another collection of scrapbooks of his clippings is in the Archives of American Art at the Smithsonian Institution. H. Wayne Morgan, *Keepers of Culture: The Art-Thought of Kenyon Cox, Royal Cortissoz, and Frank Jewett Mather, Jr.* (1989), contains biographical information in addition to a summary and discussion of his critical opinions. The most detailed discussion of his antagonism to modern art—specifically in relation to the Armory Show—is in Milton W. Brown, *American Painting from the Armory Show to the Depression* (1955) and *The Story of the Armory Show* (1963). The exhibition catalog accompanying the Knoedler & Company show, *Loan Exhibition in Honor of Royal Cortissoz and His Fifty Years of Criticism in the New York Herald Tribune, December 1 to December 20, 1941* (1941), not only illustrates his tastes in terms of the pictures chosen but is evidence of his standing with collectors; his own foreword to the catalog expresses the philosophy by which he was guided. Obituaries are in the *New York Herald Tribune* and the *New York Times*, both 18 Oct. 1948.

ELEANOR F. WEDGE

CORWIN, Edward Samuel (19 Jan. 1878–29 Apr. 1963), professor of public law and jurisprudence, was born in Plymouth, Michigan, the son of Frank Adelbert Corwin and Cora C. Lyndon, farmers. He studied history as an undergraduate at the University of Michigan, graduating Phi Beta Kappa in 1900. He did graduate work at the University of Pennsylvania and received the doctorate in 1905. His doctoral dissertation was on the French-American Alliance during the War for Independence, under the direction of John Bach McMaster, and was published in 1916 as *French Policy and the American Alliance of 1778*. His formal training in history influenced his writing on American constitutional development and set the modern standard against which historical-doctrinal research in public law scholarship is measured. In 1909 Corwin married Mildred Sutcliffe Smith; they had no children.

Corwin joined Princeton University in 1905 as one of the original preceptors (assistant professors who led small discussion groups with students) assembled by then-university president Woodrow Wilson. Corwin was preceptor in history, politics, and economics until 1911, the year he was promoted to full professor of politics. In 1918 he was named McCormick Professor of Jurisprudence, the chair first held by Wilson and the one Corwin held until his retirement in 1946. In 1924, the year a separate department of politics was created, Corwin became the department's first chairperson, serving until 1935.

Corwin's courses quickly became part of the Princeton mythology. His course on constitutional interpretation had the reputation of being both the most difficult and the most valuable. Known affectionately among his students as "The General," Corwin was a dedicated teacher who reached out to all students and encouraged them to reach their potential.

What characterized Corwin's work and assured its enduring quality was its emphasis on constitutional development in a broader context of social and political change. His research revealed that constitutional development and social change in the United States were inextricably linked, and that the nature of the relationship depended upon judicial review. Incremental growth through the process of judicial review makes the Constitution an instrument of permanent—and mostly peaceful—revolution in a world where the only constant is change. Corwin understood well that the Supreme Court played an important role in this process, mediating colliding values in society and serving as a kind of continuous constitutional convention. He also understood that judicial review raised the central political issues of legitimacy, subjectivity, and accountability in a democratic republic. Despite its antidemocratic character, Corwin was not totally opposed to judicial review. Instead he favored the notion that judicial review, guided by "rational and objective principles," could be made to protect democracy from itself by giving meaning to the values of federalism, separation of powers, and individual rights.

Corwin's scholarship advanced the frontier of knowledge in several other areas of constitutional inquiry. What distinguished his works on American federalism, separation of powers, presidential power, and due process of law was the way he always returned to the conclusion of his research on judicial review, namely, that courts and judges were the backstops to other political safeguards built into the constitutional system. The Constitution, he argued, is the supreme law of the land. Letting judges have the last word on the meaning of the Constitution is the best way to protect democracy from majoritarian abuses.

Corwin's knowledge and skills also were valued outside the ivy-covered walls of Princeton. In 1931 he served as president of the American Political Science Association. In 1935 he extended his service outside of academia as adviser to the Public Works Administration on constitutional questions. In 1936–1937 he was special consultant to Homer S. Cummings, U.S. attorney general. When President Roosevelt sent his "court-packing plan" to Congress, Corwin entered the fray, testifying passionately in favor of the bill before the Senate Judiciary Committee. Corwin identified the problem and, as was his style, cut straight to the heart of the issue:

The present situation is not due to the inadequacy of the Constitution, but is due to interpretations of the Constitution by the Court which do not meet present-day needs . . . [T]he President's proposal . . . was required to correct a serious unbalance in the Constitution, resulting from the undue extension of judicial review. (Senate Judiciary Committee, Hearings on S. 1392, 75th Cong., 1st sess., 1937, 169)

Though the president's proposal was eventually withdrawn, Corwin did not shy away from controversial issues and continued to play a part in public affairs. In 1954 he chaired the national committee against the proposed Bricker Amendment to the Constitution, restricting the president's treaty-making power. Corwin helped to forge, along with Charles G. Haines (University of California, Los Angeles), Alpheus T. Mason (Princeton University), and Carl Swisher (Johns Hopkins University), what has been called a "golden era of constitutional scholarship." Works by Corwin from this golden era continue to be widely read and cited. A *WestLaw* search of all Supreme Court opinions in the twentieth century identified nineteen separate cases in which works by Corwin were quoted and cited. Of all his works, *The President: Office and Powers* was referred to the most by the Supreme Court. Corwin's approach to the study of the American presidency emphasizes the historical development of the office and its checks and balances in the Constitution. What makes this study of the formal powers of the presidency a classic is Corwin's perspicacious analysis of history and Supreme Court doctrine.

Corwin's influence on American constitutional law went well beyond the number of citations in the U.S. Reports. His insights live on, framing the central debates over constitutional theory and doctrine in the classroom, in the scholarly literature, and in the chambers of justices on the highest court in the land.

Corwin died at Princeton after a long and distinguished career as teacher and writer. He was one of the greatest scholars of American constitutional law and of the Supreme Court. His legacy stems from the more than twenty books he wrote and the generation of students he trained, many of whom went on to become leading public law scholars themselves.

• Corwin's papers are in the Firestone Library at Princeton University. For more information about Corwin and his contribution to public law scholarship, see Robert E. Newton, "Edward S. Corwin and American Constitutional Law," *Journal of Public Law* 14 (1965): 198–212; and Gerald Garvey, "Corwin on the Constitution: The Content and Context of Modern American Constitutional Theory" (Ph.D. diss., Princeton Univ., 1962). For a complete listing of Corwin's work, see the fourteen-page bibliography appended to Alpheus T. Mason and Gerald Garvey, eds., *American Constitutional History: Essays by Edward S. Corwin* (1964). A select listing of Corwin's major works would certainly include *National Supremacy—Treaty Power vs. State Power* (1913), *The Constitution and What It Means Today*, rev. ed. (1920), *The Twilight of the Supreme Court* (1934), *The Commerce Power versus States' Rights* (1936), *Court over Constitution: A Study of Judicial Review as an Instrument of Popular Government* (1938), *The President: Office and Powers* (1940; rev. ed. 1957), and *Liberty against Government* (1948). From 1949 to 1952, Corwin served as editor of the Library of Congress's Legislative Reference Division, where he directed the preparation of *The Constitution Annotated: Analysis and Interpretation*. Of all his articles, "The Doctrine of Due Process of Law

before the Civil War," *Harvard Law Review* 24 (1910–1911): 366–85, 460–79; "The Basic Doctrine of American Constitutional Law," *Michigan Law Review* 12 (1913–1914): 247–76; "The 'Higher Law' Background of American Constitutional Law," *Harvard Law Review* 42 (1928–1929): 149–85, 365–409; and "The Passing of Dual Federalism," *Virginia Law Review* 36 (1950): 1–24 are cited the most in scholarly literature. An obituary is in the *New York Times*, 30 Apr. 1963. An "in memoriam" written by Mason is in the *American Political Science Review* 57 (1963): 789–90.

MICHAEL C. TOLLEY

CORWIN, Edward Tanjore (12 July 1834–22 June 1914), minister and historian, was born in New York City, the son of Edward Callwell Corwin and Mary Ann Shuart. Descended on his father's side from English founders of New Haven, Connecticut, Corwin seems to have been more influenced by his mother's ethnic heritage. Her ancestors were Dutch, early settlers in New Amsterdam, and the whole family found sustenance in Reformed theological traditions. In 1853 Corwin graduated first in his class from the Free Academy, a school soon to be named College of the City of New York. Three years later he graduated from New Brunswick Theological Seminary in New Brunswick, New Jersey, the oldest and best Dutch Reformed ministerial academy in the country. In 1856 he was also licensed by the church in Bergen, New Jersey. Staying a fourth year at the seminary, he received ordination at Paramus, New Jersey, in 1857. That same year Corwin began his first pastorate in Paramus, devoting himself to ministerial duties there until 1863. In 1861 he married Mary Esther Kipp; the couple had four children, two of whom survived to adulthood.

The Dutch Reformed church in Millstone, New Jersey, called Corwin to minister there in 1863. From then until 1888 he labored in this Hillsborough Township setting in the center of the state. On occasion (1883–1884) he also served as instructor in Greek, Hebrew, and Old Testament exegesis at his old seminary in nearby New Brunswick. Between 1888 and 1895 he concentrated fully on work at the seminary, lecturing as needed and presiding continuously as rector of Hertzog Hall. During this appointment, in 1891, he also served as president of the American Dutch Reformed General Synod. A third pastorate followed to round out this part of his career. Corwin was minister (1895–1897) of a church in Greendale, New York, a hamlet in the Hudson Valley township of Greenport.

Corwin's activities as a historian began modestly and developed slowly. Upon moving to a new parish, he always investigated historical lore related to his own church and to churches in surrounding parts of the county. He also helped organize centennial proceedings and Commemoratives for New Brunswick Theological Seminary. These activities in local history eventually drew notice from his denominational colleagues, and their recognition led to work on a broader scale. In 1897 the General Synod named him official historiographer of the Reformed Church in America, and Corwin spent a full year as the denomination's agent in Holland. While in the Netherlands he collected documents related to Dutch churches in the colonies, especially New York and New Jersey. The result of his search for "American correspondence" in Amsterdam archives was a valuable selection of materials that placed Dutch American ecclesiastical history on solid documentary grounds. Corwin edited historical sources for his denomination from 1897 until 1905; between 1901 and 1914 he also worked as an assistant to the state historian of New York, preparing documents to publish with the aid of legislative appropriations.

A listing of major publications associated with Corwin's name indicates how valuable and durable his contributions were to this segment of historical studies. Beginning in 1859 he brought out four editions of the *Manual of the Reformed Dutch Church in North America*, an indispensable collection of information regarding churches, ministers, and denominational institutions. The fifth edition of this compendium, appearing in 1922, was dedicated to his memory. In 1895 Corwin's balanced and accurate *History of the Reformed Church, Dutch* appeared in volume 8 of the influential American Church History series. Beginning in 1901 he was instrumental in producing *Ecclesiastical Records of the State of New York*, a series whose culminating seventh volume was printed in 1916. This collection has been singled out for praise by generations of historians as a model of scholarly archival research. Corwin's fourth contribution, *Digest of the Constitutional and Synodical Legislation of the Reformed Church in America*, appeared in 1906 and addresses a narrow topic of limited value, but one sustained by the author's consistently high professional standards.

Corwin continued to work on galley proofs of the index volume to the records of the ecclesiastical archives in Holland to the end of his life, which occurred at his son's home in North Branch, New Jersey.

• All of Corwin's major publications are mentioned in the text. Meager references to his life and career can be found in the *National Cyclopedia of American Biography*, vol. 23, and the *Dictionary of American Biography*, vol. 2. An obituary is in the *New York Times*, 24 June 1914. Several references, including the *New York Times*, erroneously report that Corwin died on 23 June, but newspapers in New Brunswick verify that his death occurred the previous day.

HENRY WARNER BOWDEN

CORWIN, Thomas (29 July 1794–18 Dec. 1865), politician, was born in Bourbon County, Kentucky, the son of Matthias Corwin, a legislator and farmer, and Patience Halleck. In 1798 the Corwins moved to Lebanon, Ohio, where Thomas, one of nine children, worked on the family farm. He read law in Lebanon, Ohio, under attorney Joshia Collett and was admitted to the bar in 1817. In 1818 he was appointed prosecuting attorney of Warren County. In 1822 he married Sarah Ross, with whom he had five children. During the 1820s he concentrated on his law practice and served three one-year terms in the Ohio legislature.

Corwin's political career began in earnest in 1830, when he ran for Congress as a National Republican,

identifying closely with the Henry Clay–John Quincy Adams party against the Jacksonian Democrats. He was reelected four times and, during his years in the House, consistently supported Henry Clay's program of a national bank, protective tariffs, and federal aid for internal improvements. Affectionately nicknamed "the Wagon Boy," Corwin emerged as one of the best known and most effective stump speakers in Ohio, for he could successfully combine satire and wit and thus frequently overwhelm his political opponents. He defended Ohio's claim in its boundary dispute with Michigan and, in an 1840 House debate, bested Democrat Isaac E. Crary in his defense of Whig presidential candidate William Henry Harrison. Corwin's speech led John Quincy Adams to describe his colleague's vanquished opponent as "the late Mr. Crary of Michigan" (Morrow, p. 32).

In 1840 Ohio Whigs nominated Corwin for governor to oppose the popular Democratic incumbent, Wilson Shannon. Corwin's oratorical skills on the stump helped produce an impressive victory, but with no veto and few other powers as governor, he found himself ineffective in persuading the legislature to enact his proposals, especially those relating to banking. He noted sarcastically that his principal duties as governor were "to appoint notaries public and pardon convicts in the penitentiary" (Morrow, p. 39). In 1842 the Democrats, who controlled the legislature, enacted their banking plan, and Corwin was defeated by Shannon in the fall gubernatorial race.

When Ohio Whigs won control of the state legislature in 1844, they elected Corwin to the U.S. Senate, and in this arena his reputation as an orator and politician peaked. During the presidency of James K. Polk, Corwin emerged as the leading Whig critic of the Mexican War effort. Arguing that the disputed area along the Texas-Mexico boundary belonged to Mexico, he attacked the morality of the administration's war policy and described it as stealing a neighbor's territory. In his memorable speech on 11 February 1847, he concluded: "If I were a Mexican I would tell you: Have you not room in your own country to bury your dead men? If you come into mine we will greet you with bloody hands and welcome you to hospitable graves" (*Congressional Globe*, 29th Cong., 2d sess., app., pp. 216–17). This speech made him an immediate center of controversy, with most northern Whigs defending his efforts and Democrats in the Ohio legislature demanding he be removed for what they regarded as unpatriotic attacks on the Polk administration.

The senator's opposition to the war coincided with rising northern antislavery sentiment, which insisted that the purpose of southerners and the administration was to acquire additional slave territory. The Wilmot Proviso, which sought to ban slavery in any territory taken from Mexico, was then under debate in Congress. Because of Corwin's opposition to the war, some northerners began to urge his candidacy for the presidency in 1848. Liberty leaders like Salmon P. Chase and antislavery Whigs, including Joshua Giddings and Charles Sumner, believed he could unite those opposed to slavery. Corwin quickly dashed their hopes by denying any interest in a nomination and by suggesting that his opposition to the war had more to do with the immorality of the war in general than with support for the Wilmot Proviso. Rather than supporting a ban on slavery, the senator preferred for Whigs to take a position renouncing the acquisition of any territory from Mexico. A conservative on economic issues, Corwin had little interest in the antislavery movement. He was more concerned with uniting his fellow Whigs, North and South, to save the Union, which he believed was in peril because of the explosive sectional issues. When the Whigs nominated Zachary Taylor in 1848, Corwin loyally led the Whig campaign for the general in Ohio. Fearing the impact of the Free Soil party, with its endorsement of the Wilmot Proviso, on Whig support, he argued that, if elected, Taylor would favor the northern position on territorial slavery.

Following the war, Corwin supported Clay's compromise measures in 1850. With President Taylor's death in July of that year, Millard Fillmore appointed Corwin secretary of the treasury, a position he held until the end of Fillmore's term in 1853. Taking no part in the 1854 Kansas-Nebraska controversy, Corwin was slow to abandon the dying Whig party, for he preferred its emphasis on economic issues over the antislavery priorities of the new Republican organization. He only reluctantly and belatedly endorsed John C. Frémont, the Republican candidate for president in 1856. In 1858 Corwin won election to the House of Representatives as a Republican, but his reentry into politics was an attempt to move the party away from its emphasis on the containment of slavery and to convince voters in both the North and the South that Republicans were not controlled by antislavery crusaders. Instead, he argued, they were a conservative group dedicated to conciliating sectional differences. He thus disappointed antislavery advocates by endorsing enforcement of the controversial Fugitive Slave Act of 1850, an action that especially angered his Ohio colleague Giddings. In 1860 he supported Supreme Court justice John McLean of Ohio for the Republican presidential nomination and in early 1861 chaired the House Committee of Thirty-three, which, in an effort at sectional compromise, endorsed a constitutional amendment guaranteeing slavery where it already existed.

President Abraham Lincoln appointed Corwin minister to Mexico in March 1861, in part because the Ohioan's earlier opposition to the Mexican War assured him a friendly reception in Mexico City. In his new post, Corwin labored successfully to prevent Mexican support of the Confederacy. He vehemently protested French involvement in Mexico but could do little to prevent it. In May 1864, just prior to the arrival of the French puppet, Maximilian of Austria, Corwin returned to Washington to practice law. He died there suddenly.

Corwin's primary significance is as an outspoken opponent of the Mexican War. Disappointing anti-slavery leaders, he remained a conservative voice whose chief concern was party loyalty and preservation of the Union.

• Corwin's papers relating to his years heading the Treasury Department are in the Library of Congress. His speeches in Congress can be found in the *Congressional Globe*, 22d–26th, 28th–30th, and 34th Congs. Many of his letters are published in Belle L. Hamlin, ed., "Selections from the Follett Papers," *Quarterly Publication of the Historical and Philosophical Society of Ohio* 9 (1914): 71–100; and Hamlin, ed., "Selections from the William Greene Papers," *Quarterly Publication of the Historical and Philosophical Society of Ohio* 13 (1918): 4–38. Josiah Morrow's laudatory *Life and Speeches of Thomas Corwin, Orator, Lawyer and Statesman* (1896) is the best of the older studies.

Corwin's role in national and Ohio politics in the 1840s and 1850s is covered in several studies, including E. A. Holt, *Party Politics in Ohio, 1840–1850* (1930); and Stephen E. Maizlish, *The Triumph of Sectionalism: The Transformation of Ohio Politics, 1844–1856* (1983). Two volumes in Carl Wittke, ed., *The History of the State of Ohio*, cover important aspects of Corwin's activities: Francis P. Weisenburger, *The Passing of the Frontier* (1941), and Eugene H. Roseboom, *The Civil War Era, 1850–1873* (1944). Four articles covering important aspects of Corwin's career are Hal W. Bochin, "Tom Corwin's Speech against the Mexican War: Courageous but Misunderstood," *Ohio History* 90 (1981): 33–54; Norman Graebner, "Thomas Corwin and the Election of 1848: A Study in Conservative Politics," *Journal of Southern History* 17 (1951): 162–79; J. Jeffrey Auer, "Lincoln's Minister to Mexico," *Ohio State Archaeological and Historical Quarterly* 59 (1950): 115–28; and Daryl Pendergraft, "Thomas Corwin and the Conservative Republican Reaction, 1858–1861," *Ohio State Archaeological and Historical Quarterly* 57 (1948): 1–23. An obituary is in the *New York Tribune*, 18 Dec. 1865.

FREDERICK J. BLUE

CORY, Charles Barney (31 Jan. 1857–29 July 1921), ornithologist, was born in Boston, Massachusetts, the son of Barney Cory, a successful importer, and Eliza Ann Bell Glynn. From his early youth Cory engaged in a variety of sports, achieving competence in such diverse activities as billiards, pistol-shooting, golf, fencing, boxing, and riding. An avid outdoorsman, he was particularly fond of hunting and bird-collecting, and the latter interest eventually led to his career as a naturalist and ornithologist. From 1876 to 1878 he attended the Lawrence Scientific School at Harvard, where he met Joel A. Allen, curator of birds and mammals at Harvard's Museum of Comparative Zoology. He also met ornithologist William Brewster and in 1878 joined the Nuttall Ornithological Club of Cambridge. Cory did not graduate from the Lawrence Scientific School; in the fall of 1878 he briefly attended the Boston Law School. Subsequently he studied physiology and psychology in London and Paris, eventually returning to Boston in 1880. He married Harriet W. Peterson of Duxbury, Massachusetts, in 1883; they had two children.

Because of his family's wealth, Cory was able to devote more than thirty years to his scientific interests, traveling extensively and conducting worldwide ornithological studies. From 1875, while he was still a student at Harvard, until he lost his fortune, he explored and collected birds in Florida, the West Indies, Europe, Africa, and Mexico. Having taken disastrous advice on some speculative investments, in 1906 Cory lost almost everything. Consequently, he accepted the salaried position of curator of zoology at the Field Museum of Natural History in Chicago, where he spent most of the remainder of his life engaged in ornithological research. He had established his relationship with the Field Museum when it was founded in 1893 under the name of the Field Columbian Museum. At that time Cory had been named curator of ornithology for life, in recognition of his having donated his enormous bird collection to the institution. He was also a member of the Boston Society of Natural History and its curator of birds from 1887 to 1905. Cory was an important leader in the American Ornithologists' Union, having been among the founding members of the organization in 1883 and serving subsequently as treasurer (1886–1887), vice president (1898–1903), and president (1903–1905).

Cory's voluminous production of natural history literature began in 1878, when he published *A Naturalist in the Magdalen Islands*, based on his exploration in the Gulf of St. Lawrence in July and August 1878. From December 1878 through July 1879 he visited the Bahamas and began his emergence as the acknowledged authority on the birds of the West Indies. From his personal fieldwork and review of previous data, Cory published several major works on the region, including *Birds of the Bahama Islands* (1880), *The Birds of Haiti and San Domingo* (1885), and *The Birds of the West Indies* (1889). His greatest ornithological effort, done primarily in later years at the Field Museum, was the multivolume *Catalogue of the Birds of the Americas* (1918–1949). The final volumes were published after his death by the museum, with Cory appearing as sole author of only two volumes (1918 and 1919). Cory labored on volumes three and four up until his death, but the final work was completed largely by Carl Edward Hellmayr.

Cory wrote more than one hundred scientific papers, published mainly in the *Bulletin of the Nuttall Ornithological Club* and *The Auk*. His other book-length publications include *Beautiful and Curious Birds of the World* (1880–1883), *Birds of Illinois and Wisconsin* (1909), *Mammals of Illinois and Wisconsin* (1912), *Southern Rambles* (1881), *Hunting and Fishing in Florida* (1896), and *Catalogue of the Birds of Eastern North America* (1893). He also produced a number of popular field guides, such as *Key to the Water Birds of Florida* (1896), *How to Know the Ducks, Geese and Swans* (1898), *How to Know the Shorebirds* (1898), and *Birds of Eastern North America* (1899, 1900). These were illustrated using small woodcuts of heads, feet, or other parts of birds—a technique that was described as being "as near foolproof as anything that has been devised for the identification of birds" (Osgood, p. 159).

Cory's diverse talents and interests extended far beyond his zoological career. A skilled golfer, he won many prizes for his championship golf tournament play in the United States. He also wrote articles on golf, designed clubs, and researched the history of the game. He was interested in hypnotism, serving as chairman of the committee on hypnotism of the American Society of Psychical Research and publishing *Hypnotism or Mesmerism* (1888). Noted for his strong baritone voice, Cory was a founder of the Boston Glee Club and wrote several light opera librettos, including *The Corsair* (1887), *The Mermaid; or, the Curse of Cape Cod* (1888), *A Dress Rehearsal* (1891), and *An Amazon King* (1893). He also wrote the lyrics of "A Dream," a popular song among vocalists, including Enrico Caruso. His literary activities included fiction as well, reflected in a collection of short stories, *Montezuma's Castle and Other Weird Tales* (1899). Although an avid hunter and bird collector, Cory established one of the first bird sanctuaries in the United States at his estate in Hyannis on Cape Cod, where he lived and maintained a spacious game park. In Florida he founded the Florida Museum of Natural History at Palm Beach.

A stroke in November 1920 left Cory partially paralyzed. He attempted to continue work on his *Catalogue* at home, then moved to a resort in July 1921. He died in Ashland, Wisconsin, without completing his projected work.

Cory was admired and respected by his colleagues, both for his scientific abilities and for his character. Witmer Stone of the Academy of Natural Sciences in Philadelphia noted Cory's "kind and generous disposition," "keen sense of humor," and remarkable "strength of character." Another friend commented on his "great capacity for discovering the humorous side of every situation" and observed that he freely directed this humor at himself whenever possible. Frank M. Chapman claimed that he had "never met a man so gifted as Charles Cory." In recognition of his contributions, Cory's Shearwater, Cory's Least Bittern, and the Florida cougar (*Felis coryi*; later a subspecies of *Felis concolor*) were named in his honor.

• The bulk of Cory's specimens and papers are the Field Museum of Natural History in Chicago and at the Academy of Natural Sciences in Philadelphia; his correspondence is widely scattered at archival collections in American natural history museums. Major sources on Cory include Barbara Mearns and Richard Mearns, *Audubon to Xantus* (1992), pp. 155–59; W. E. Davis, "Early Years, 1873–1919," *History of the Nuttall Ornithological Club 1873–1986*, Memoirs of the Nuttall Ornithological Club, no. 11 (1987): 9–30; and Wilfred H. Osgood, "In Memoriam: Charles Barney Cory," *The Auk* 39 (1922): 151–66.

MARCUS B. SIMPSON, JR.

CORYELL, Charles DuBois (21 Feb. 1912–7 Jan. 1971), chemist, was born in Los Angeles, California, the son of William Harlan Coryell, an accountant, and Florence Elizabeth Cook. After attending public schools in Alhambra, California, Coryell received his B.S. in 1932 and his Ph.D. in 1935, both from the California Institute of Technology (Caltech). He spent a year of his graduate studies as an American-German exchange fellow at the Technische Hochschule in Munich. He stayed at Caltech as a research associate with Linus Pauling until 1938. From 1937 to 1939, he was also an instructor at Deep Springs (Calif.) Junior College. In 1938 he joined the chemistry department of the University of California at Los Angeles (UCLA) as an instructor, rising to assistant professor in 1940 and associate professor in 1944. While on the UCLA faculty, he directed the research of three doctoral candidates.

From 1942 to 1946 Coryell was on leave from UCLA to participate in the Manhattan Project, working in the Metallurgical Laboratory at the University of Chicago (1942–1943) and at the Clinton Laboratories in Oak Ridge, Tennessee (1943–1946) as chief of the fission products section. He left to become professor of chemistry at the Massachusetts Institute of Technology (MIT), a post he held until his death. He also remained a consultant to the U.S. Atomic Energy Commission laboratories until his death.

Coryell's graduate training was in physical and inorganic chemistry, dealing with the electrochemistry of vanadium, the reactions of divalent silver, and (at the Technische Hochschule) the fluorescence of organic vapors. His work with Linus Pauling resulted in a series of papers on the magnetic properties of hemoglobin and its addition products with oxygen, carbon monoxide, and cyanide. Intended to obtain information about the nature of the bonding involved, the research showed that the products were not the result of some nonspecific physical attraction, but that a covalent bond formed between the iron of the hemoglobin and the added species. This discovery led to a greater understanding of the oxygenation/deoxygenation cycle of hemoglobin and the transport of oxygen through the body by the blood. It was a pioneering study, showing that physical chemical measurements, hitherto thought to be useful only on simple inorganic or organic compounds, could be made on complex, biological materials.

Coryell's group in the Manhattan Project had to determine the identities and yields of the nuclides formed during fission. Many of these turned out to lie in the rare earth group of elements, and Coryell contributed to the development of ion-exchange methods for separating these elements. In 1945, during this work, J. A. Marinsky and L. F. Glendenin, working under Coryell, discovered and isolated isotopes of the missing rare earth element now called promethium. In 1949 the International Union of Pure and Applied Chemistry officially recognized this and accepted the name suggested by Coryell's wife, Grace Mary. Coryell withheld his name from the paper announcing this discovery because he felt his part in the work did not warrant a claim to coauthorship.

With Glendenin and R. R. Edwards, Coryell deduced how nuclear charge is distributed among fission products. He also systematized the energetics of beta-decay so as to predict the masses of unstable nuclear species. This led to his hypothesis that the heavy chemical elements in the solar system originated in the explosion of one or more stars more than five billion years ago, an idea made public in his address to the American Chemical Society in 1960 on the occasion of his receiving its award for applications of nuclear chemistry. An outgrowth of this work was his suggestion that the abundance of rare earths in rocks and minerals could be better understood if they were normalized against a standard provided by averaging the abundances in several chondrite meteorites.

At MIT Coryell introduced lecture and laboratory courses in radiochemistry, as well as guiding a productive graduate research group. He helped to create the Gordon Research Conferences in Nuclear Chemistry, cochairing the first with Glen Seaborg in 1952 and chairing the second in 1953.

Coryell was active in promoting nuclear science for peaceful rather than military purposes. He helped to prepare a petition that Oak Ridge scientists presented to President Truman, asking that the atomic bomb be demonstrated to the Japanese before being used against them. He played an important role in the effort to put atomic energy under civilian control, and he helped Pauling with a petition submitted to the United Nations in 1958 calling for an immediate ban on nuclear weapons tests. A letter he wrote to the State Department passport division helped Pauling obtain a passport to go to Sweden to receive the Nobel Peace Prize in 1962. He was active in the Federation of American Scientists, the United World Federalists, and the Committee for a Sane Nuclear Policy. At one time Coryell thought a million people would die in atomic warfare before a thousand were saved through research using radioactive isotopes, but when he received an Atomic Energy Commission Citation in 1970, he thanked the AEC for the extension of his and other cancer victims' lives made possible by radiotherapy.

In 1953 and 1954 Coryell was Louis Lipsky Fellow at the Weizmann Institute of Science in Rehovoth, Israel; in 1963 he was a Guggenheim Fellow and Fulbright lecturer at the Institute de Radium in Paris, France. Coryell was on the board of trustees of Windham College, Putney, Vermont (1963–1969), and the board of directors of Mark Hopkins College, Brattleboro, Vermont (1964–1971). He was associated with Middle East Technical University in Ankara, Turkey, to which he made a site visit for the Ford Foundation (1968).

Coryell married Meta Patricia Seward in 1930. They divorced in 1936, and Coryell married Grace Mary Seeley in 1937. After her death in 1965, he married Barbara Ogilvie Buchman in 1968. There was one child from each of the first two marriages. Coryell died in Boston, Massachusetts, after a five-year battle with cancer.

• A biographical sketch of Coryell is in Ralph A. Horne, "Charles Dubois Coryell," *American Chemists and Chemical Engineers*, ed. Wyndham Miles (1976), pp. 95–96. Coryell's obituary by Glen E. Gordon, *Journal of Inorganic Nuclear Chemistry* 34 (1972): 1–11, lists Coryell's ninety-eight papers and the forty-three doctoral theses he supervised at MIT and UCLA. Obituaries are also in the *New York Times*, 9 Jan. 1971, and *Chemical and Engineering News*, 25 Jan. 1971.

RUSSELL F. TRIMBLE

COSBY, William (c. 1690–10 Mar. 1736), royal governor of New York and New Jersey, was born at Stradbally Hall, Ireland, the son of Alexander Cosby, a gentleman, and Elizabeth L'Estrige. There is no information about Cosby's early life and education. Cosby married Grace Montague, the sister of the earl of Halifax and cousin to the duke of Newcastle, both prominent British figures. The date of the marriage is unknown; it produced three children. Like other members of the Anglo-Irish ascendancy, Cosby entered the British army, procuring a commission in Spain under the command of General James Stanhope. He rose to the rank of colonel and in 1718 attained the governorship of the Mediterranean island of Minorca, recently won in the War of the Spanish Succession. He administered the island for ten years during a relatively peaceful period. Nevertheless, Cosby's brazenly illegal seizure of a Portuguese vessel—an attempt to confiscate the valuable cargo of snuff for himself—resulted in a £10,000 judgment against the governor, leaving him in dire financial straits. After his return to England, Cosby relied on the duke of Newcastle's patronage to procure another political plum, turning down the governorship of the Leeward Islands in the West Indies for that of the healthier and potentially more profitable colonies of New York and New Jersey. He arrived in New York on 1 August 1732, eager to recoup his fading fortunes.

Cosby's presence in New York sent political tremors through the province after several months. Provincial politics, although relatively quiet for the preceding few years, had often proved contentious, as different Anglo and Anglo-Dutch families attempted to dominate the government. Governors required strong administrative and political skills to deal with the normally factious province. Cosby's rash and arbitrary temper, combined with a strong venal streak, illustrated his unsuitability for the post. Although able to win the loyalty of the sitting assembly by refusing to call new elections and thereby acquiring a five-year grant of support, Cosby's undiplomatic utterances and very apparent avarice hardened opinion against him. Cosby squeezed an extra £250 from the assembly by inviting opponents to dinner where "he Damn'd them & asked them why they did not make their Present in pounds, shillings, and pennies" (Colden, p. 288). People complained too about the governor's generally boorish behavior. Cosby's first major crisis arose when he clashed with Rip Van Dam, the previous acting governor, and demanded that his predecessor turn over half the salary he had collected for filling the governor's office. Van Dam refused unless Cosby turned over half of the profits of office he had pocketed while in England. This deadlock prompted Cosby to initiate a court action against Van Dam, asking the Supreme Court of New York to sit as a court of equity, hence eliminating the need for a jury. Such courts had an odious reputation among the colonists; critics deemed them the equivalent of a star chamber designed to fortify executive power. On 9 April 1733 Chief Justice Lewis Morris, already concerned about the tone of the governor's administration, threw out Cosby's case against Van Dam on legal grounds. Cosby retaliated and removed Morris from his position in August 1733.

An energized Morris joined forces with James Alexander, William Smith, Sr., and other government critics to comprise a "country" party to counteract Cosby and his court party supporters in the administration. The formation of an opposition newspaper, the *New York Weekly Journal*, in November 1733 under the editorship of Alexander and printed by John Peter Zenger, roiled the political waters further. Barbed articles from the paper attacked Cosby over the Van Dam affair, ridiculed his decisions, questioned his judgments, and lampooned him in general. Other essays in the paper championed the rights and liberties of true Englishmen. Of equal significance was the paper's stimulation of a new tone of political warfare, creating the basis for a lively opposition—the first time a provincial newspaper in New York had been employed in such fashion. Pamphleteers bemoaned Cosby's policies, urging ordinary people to resist the governor and his court party of supporters. Elections held in 1734 went against Cosby as the Morrisite faction won seats in the New York City Council. What Cosby had earlier labeled political insubordination to his superiors in England exploded into a constant barrage of criticism against him and his political henchmen, so severe in fact that Cosby had Zenger arrested for seditious libel on 17 November 1734, hoping to quell the opposition newspaper.

This heavy-handed measure led to the now famous trial of John Peter Zenger. Justice James Delancy, a Cosby supporter, attempted to neutralize the defense by disbarring Zenger's lawyers, James Alexander and William Smith, Sr. Cosby's opponents turned instead to Andrew Hamilton, a well-known Philadelphia attorney, and the jury ruled in favor of Zenger. Nevertheless, Hamilton's remarks to the jury had furnished weak legal and historical precedents, crafted to play more on their sentiments and fears of arbitrary government. What the decision did establish, however, was the removal of the courts as the chief weapon against free speech; instead, the assembly would become a possible tool for prosecution of seditious libel in the future history of colonial New York. This still marked an important improvement overall. Legislatures tied to the popular will by elections were less likely to act in an arbitrary fashion to hamper the freedom of speech than appointed judges. Yet, despite the loss of the case, Cosby retained control of the council, removing Van Dam and making George Clarke, Cosby's right-hand man, the heir-apparent to the governorship. He had been embarrassed but not destroyed.

In New Jersey, by contrast, Governor Cosby had a relatively quiet administration, calling the assembly only once in 1734 and receiving a £200 bonus from them. He was the last governor to head the united provinces of New York and New Jersey. Tuberculosis debilitated Cosby, however, during the winter of 1735, finally causing his death in New York City.

Cosby's administration of the province inspired an unusual degree of factionalism even by middle colony standards. His overbearing temperament and haughty attitude toward colonists in general, and his efforts to enrich himself and his family in particular, aroused widespread revulsion toward him and his court party cronies. Even considering the partisan nature of the attacks on him, there is little reason to believe that Cosby was anything but a strong-willed military official with a grasping, venal disposition. What he did stimulate, inadvertently however, was the popularization of politics: ordinary individuals found their services summoned by upper-class individuals as a counterforce to the governor's policies. This was perhaps Cosby's most significant legacy for colonial New York.

• No Cosby manuscript collections have been discovered. A biography of Cosby has yet to be published, but many of his letters to superiors in England can be found in E. B. O'Callaghan and Berthold Fernow, eds., *Documents Relative to the Colonial History of the State of New York*, vols. 5 and 6 (1855). Cosby's background can be traced in J. B. Burke, *Genealogical and Heraldic History of the Landed Gentry of Ireland* (1912). Useful histories by contemporaries, although heavily biased against the governor, include Cadwallader Colden, *History of Gov. William Cosby's Administration and of Lt.-Gov. George Clarke's Administration through 1737*, New-York Historical Society Collections, vol. 68 (1935), pp. 283–355, and William Smith, Jr., *History of the Province of New York*, ed. Michael Kammen (2 vols., 1972), whereas James Alexander, *A Brief Narrative of the Case and Trial of John Peter Zenger*, ed. Stanley N. Katz (1963), has an explanation of the case by the editor. Letters written by politicos during this period can be found in the Rutherford Collection, New-York Historical Society. Useful secondary sources for assessing Cosby's policies and their political context, imperial and domestic, include Herbert L. Osgood, *The American Colonies in the Eighteenth Century*, vol. 2 (1924); Stanley Katz, *Newcastle's New York: Anglo-American Politics, 1732–1753* (1968); Patricia U. Bonomi, *A Factious People: Politics and Society in Colonial New York* (1971); and James A. Henretta, *Salutary Neglect: Colonial Administration under the Duke of Newcastle* (1972). These can be supplemented by Eugene R. Sheridan, *Lewis Morris, 1671–1746: A Study in Early American Politics* (1981), for a look at one of Cosby's main opponents, and Gary Nash, *The Urban Crucible: Social Change, Political Consciousness, and the Origins of the American Revolution* (1979), for the political class dynamics that Cosby's policies unleashed.

ROBERT E. CRAY, JR.

COSELL, Howard (25 Mar. 1920–23 Apr. 1995), radio and television sportscaster, was born Howard William Cohen in Winston-Salem, North Carolina, the son of Polish-Jewish immigrants Isidore (or Isadore) Cohen and Nellie (maiden name unknown). Cosell's father, an accountant at a credit clothier, moved his family to Brooklyn, New York, where Howard attended public schools. He graduated from Alexander Hamilton High School with an outstanding academic record in 1938. Cosell, who ran track and played varsity basketball, served as the sports editor of the high school newspaper. After graduating from high school, he wanted to become a newspaper reporter, but his parents persuaded him to pursue a law career instead.

By age twenty-one Cosell had completed both a bachelor's degree in English literature and a law degree at New York University. As an undergraduate he changed his last name from Cohen, the name given to his family by immigration officials, to the original family name of Cosell. He served as the editor of the *New York University Law School Review* and, in 1941, gained admission to the New York bar. During World War II Cosell graduated from Officer Candidate School and served in the U.S. Army Transportation Corps, stationed at the New York Port of Embarkation. There he supervised a 50,000-civilian workforce, excelling in transportation planning and industrial negotiation. Cosell eventually rose to the rank of major. In 1944 he married Mary Edith "Emmy" Abrams, the daughter of Norman Ross Abrams, a prominent Protestant industrialist. The couple would have two daughters. After World War II Cosell opened a law practice in Manhattan, specializing in sports and entertainment law. His clients included baseball superstar Willie Mays of the New York Giants, for whom he handled general legal and tax matters.

Cosell's career in sports journalism grew out of his lifelong interest in baseball. After he prepared the charter for the New York Little League, the American Broadcasting Company (ABC) asked him to participate in the production of a radio program that featured Little Leaguers interviewing major league baseball players. In 1953 ABC signed Cosell to a six-week contract to host the program. The show gained instant popularity, mainly because he provided the youngsters with leading questions such as "Coach, you once called your team a load of garbage. Now what did you mean by that?" After hosting the Little League show for three years without pay, Cosell abandoned his lucrative law practice and, in 1956, signed a contract with ABC radio to become a full-time reporter and sports commentator. With the advent of television, Cosell also hosted "Sports Focus," a nightly ABC television show. Unlike other sports shows of the day, in which sportscasters typically either served as cheerleaders or simply read results without any commentary, "Sports Focus" allowed Cosell to examine the issues affecting sport, showing how sport reflected larger social and political concerns.

Cosell gained national recognition with his coverage of boxing for ABC radio and television. He reported the world championship heavyweight bout, in which Ingemar Johansson unexpectedly upset Floyd Patterson in June 1959. Cosell's career as a boxing commentator, especially on ABC's "Wide World of Sports," accelerated in 1962, after conducting his first interview with Cassius Clay, the 1960 Olympic light heavyweight champion who would defeat Sonny Liston for the world heavyweight championship in 1964. This interview led to a symbiotic association between Cosell and Clay that proved beneficial to both in terms of promoting their television celebrity. Television viewers perceived their relationship as controversial and turbulent, especially after Clay became a Black Muslim and changed his name to Muhammad Ali. Cosell, in respect of Ali's wishes, addressed him by his new title, rather than his former "slave name." After the New York State Boxing Commission stripped Ali of his world heavyweight title for refusing to serve in the U.S. Army on the grounds of conscientious objection to the Vietnam War in 1967, Cosell criticized the commission's actions as "imbecilic," maintaining that the government's treatment of Ali "was inhuman and illegal under the Fifth and Fourteenth Amendments." Cosell's defense of Ali drew ferocious viewer response, as he received hate mail and life threatening telephone calls.

In 1961 Cosell began a ten-year stint as the sports anchor for the WABC-TV nightly news program in New York. With the formation of the New York Mets baseball team in 1962, the Mets organization selected Cosell and Ralph Branca to cover the games over ABC radio. After two years, however, the Mets fired the duo because Cosell refused to cheer for the hometown team. Determined "to tell it like it is," he formed his own company, Legend Productions, to create sports documentaries for television in 1963. Narrated by Cosell, the first documentary, "A Look behind the Legend," critically examined the life and career of Babe Ruth. Sportswriter Red Smith of the *New York Times* praised the show as "a study of the man and the legend which, for faithful reporting, affectionate honesty and all-around literate excellence, sets a television record as valid as the Babe's sixty home runs in 1927." Cosell produced seven subsequent shows, the most highly acclaimed being "Run to Daylight," about the Green Bay Packers football team and its coach Vince Lombardi, which contributed to shaping the Lombardi coaching legend. Cosell's favorite, "One Hundred Yards to Glory," profiled Grambling College, the small African-American Louisiana college with an exceptional football team coached by Eddie Robinson.

In an effort to improve ABC's primetime ratings, the network entered into an agreement with National Football League commissioner Pete Rozell to introduce "Monday Night Football" in 1970. Keith Jackson, and later Frank Gifford, gave the play-by-play, Don Meredith analyzed the videotape instant replays, and Cosell provided color commentary. Roone Arledge, the producer of ABC Sports, purposely played the caustic Cosell off against the glib Meredith in order to popularize the show and to boost ratings. At the end of its first season "Monday Night Football" was a great success, as Meredith won an Emmy Award and Cosell became in demand as a public speaker. Nevertheless, he received bundles of hate mail and his phone rang with threatening calls for his irreverent remarks about football players and teams. Cosell, who had a knack for generating controversy, fueled "Monday Night Football" for thirteen years. In 1983 he called Alvin Garrett, the elusive wide receiver of the Washington Redskins, a "little monkey" in a game against the Dallas Cowboys. Cosell later commented during the show that his remark only referred to Garrett's size, not his race. Despite protests from African Americans who insisted that Cosell was insensitive to the racial implications of the remark, he never apologized for his words. Nevertheless, Cosell left "Monday Night Football" at the end of the 1983 football season, as his contract had expired at that time. For three months in 1984 he hosted ABC's "Sports Beat," a sports talk show in which Cosell candidly interviewed sports figures, before the network dropped the show in response to his critical remarks of his former "Monday Night Football" colleagues in his book *I Never Played the Game*, written with Peter Bonventre (1985). Until his retirement from broadcasting in 1992, Cosell conducted "Speaking of Sports," a weekly radio show. In 1991 he was hospitalized for the removal of a malignant chest tumor. Cosell died of a heart embolism in a Manhattan hospital.

Perhaps more than any other sportscaster of the twentieth century, Cosell revolutionized the way in which sports were presented to the American public. Since the early twentieth century, especially the 1920s, sports journalists and broadcasters had cast athletes as larger than life—as flawless superheroes whose deeds both on and off the playing field displayed only virtue. Through his reporting, Cosell knocked the sports hero off the pedestal that he had so reverently occupied. More importantly, Cosell was part of a larger effort by Roone Aldridge, who during the 1960s and 1970s revolutionized the way in which Americans would view and appreciate sports through the televised media, with Olympic Games broadcasts, "Wide World of Sports," and "Monday Night Football." While Cosell's effort to "tell it like it is" won high ratings and accolades for ABC Sports, his style made him a cheerleader for the underdog, as demonstrated by his unabashed support of Ali. On the other hand, his impromptu verbiage on "Monday Night Football" tarnished his reputation as an unabashed supporter of civil rights, as a slip of the tongue resulted in what many perceived as a retractable racial slur. At any rate, Cosell was among the first sports journalists and broadcasters to hold a mirror to sport, forcing Americans to take an honest look at themselves.

• In addition to the book mentioned above, Cosell wrote *Cosell* (1973) and *Like It Is* (1974). Profiles of Cosell include those in the *New York Post*, 14 May 1966 and 11 Dec. 1971; *Sports Illustrated*, 13 Mar. 1967 and 25 Oct. 1971; *New York Sunday News*, 11 Apr. 1971; *Esquire*, Oct. 1971; the *Washington Post*, 11 Nov. 1971 and 19 Sept. 1972; *Playboy*, May 1972; *Newsweek*, 2 Oct. 1972; and the *New York Times*, 17 Feb. 1995. For historical examination of the impact of television on sports, see especially Benjamin G. Rader, *In Its Own Image: How Television Has Transformed Sports* (1984); Randy Roberts and James Olsen, *Winning Is the Only Thing: Sports in America since 1945* (1989); and Elliot J. Gorn and Warren Goldstein, *A Brief History of American Sports* (1993). For ABC and Cosell's role in particular, see Bert Randolph Sugar, *"The Thrill of Victory:" The Inside Story of ABC* (1978). Jeffrey T. Sammons's *Beyond the Ring: The Role of Boxing in*

American Society (1988) is an analysis of boxing in twentieth-century America that includes a discussion of the relationship between Cosell and Muhammad Ali. Obituaries are in *Current Biography*, July 1995, and the *New York Times*, 24 Apr. 1995.

ADAM R. HORNBUCKLE

COSTA, David (1825–6 May 1873), dancer and choreographer, was born Davide Costa in Italy and trained in Milan by La Scala's ballet master, Carlo Blasis, in his private school. Costa's name first appears as a dancer at various provincial French and Italian opera houses. In 1843, for instance, he was a dancer for the choreographer Ferdinando Rugali at the Teatro Carlo Felice in Genoa, and in 1845 he appeared at the Teatro Comunale in Bologna. In 1856 Costa appeared in the ballet *Forced Insanity*, choreographed by Antonio Pallerini, at the Teatro Risoluti in Florence.

During the early years of his career Costa also worked as a choreographer. In 1853 he devised the dances of *Semiramide on the Throne of Assyria*, a ballet performed by Amina Boschetti in Florence at the Teatro della Pergola to music by Gioacchino Rossini. Other ballets followed: *Ataliba* (Palermo, Teatro Carolino, 1855); *Edmondo Dantes; or, The Count of Oglata* (Rome, Teatro Argentina, autumn 1856); *The Gypsy*, to music by Giuseppe Giaquinto; and *The Wayward Daughter* (Rome, autumn 1857); *Pelagio and Loretta the Seer*, to music by Giaquinto (Naples, Teatro San Carlo, 1859); *Megilla and Folgore; or, The Seductive Demon* (Naples, Teatro San Carlo, winter 1861); *The Count of Montecristo* (Palermo, Teatro Bellini, 1862); *Benvenuto Cellini* (Rome, Teatro Argentina, autumn 1862); and *Oronos* (Milan, La Scala, autumn 1864).

In 1856, while Costa was ballet master at Palermo, he choreographed his own version of *La Sylphide*. Like most choreographers recreating this well-known ballet, he made some changes in the story. Costa moved the ballet's location from Scotland to China and rechristened the role of James as Zabi, which he danced himself.

The publication *Dramatic Esthetic Musical Gifts* (Rome, 1857), noted, "[Costa] is cutting the ho-hum-type scenes from ballet, taking out the insipid minuets and polkas that bore today's public. Though his ballets are full of many kinds of dances, they evoke applause by their lightness, simplicity, and innovativeness. His ballet 'Edmondo Dantes' (presented with great success in Rome) is a prime example of these qualities." The journal further noted that "his dancing is so perfect he has nothing to fear by comparison with his peers."

In February 1866, while working in London, Costa and his wife, a costumer, were hired by the American theatrical managers Henry Jarrett and A. M. Palmer to take part in a large-scale spectacular ballet in New York, *La Biche au Bois*. The production, based on the legend of Sleeping Beauty, was scheduled to open in the fall of 1866 at the Academy of Music. However, following the academy's destruction by fire on 21 May 1866, Jarrett and Palmer altered their plans, changing the production to *The Black Crook*, a spectacular melodrama by Charles Barras, and moving to Niblo's Garden Theater.

Costa, his wife, and the principal dancers arrived in New York on 21 August 1866 on the steamer *The City of London*. Although Costa registered his nationality as French when he went through immigration proceedings, he was Italian, and, at forty-one, considerably older than most of the other dancers.

The Black Crook was an enormous success, achieving a record-breaking run of 474 performances. Much of this success was a response to the dances, which Costa devised and in which he performed, and to the excellence of the Italian and French ballerinas he partnered. With ballerina Maria Bonfanti he performed a "Pas de Démons," considered scandalous because of the brevity of the ballerinas' costumes. The tutu worn by Bonfanti and the puff-drawers and sleeveless tops worn by the four supporting soloists, considered standard fare in European opera houses, were referred to in the American press as exposures of "fraudulent nudity."

In fact, the controversy over the morality of the production drew large and enthusiastic audiences to Niblo's and lengthened the run of *The Black Crook*. Costa was frequently called on to add new choreography to the production as the audience tired of the familiar; and the *Crook* was so loosely structured that the subject matter of the dances was not as important as their novelty. In May 1867, for instance, he premiered a "Pas de Chinois" for himself and Bonfanti.

Following the close of *The Black Crook* in January 1868, Costa remained at Niblo's to choreograph *The White Fawn*, based on *La Biche au Bois*. Costa composed for himself and Bonfanti a duet, "Jealousy," in which he portrayed a disreputable old Turk and she a slave. He also devised a new solo for her, "The Light of the Harem," and an elaborately patterned "Amazonian March" for the supernumeraries. Costa excelled at maneuvering masses of dancers in such marches and in cancans.

When *Fawn* closed in October 1868, Costa was much in demand as a choreographer at other theaters. He took his wife and several principal dancers from Niblo's to join the cast of *The Second Volume (Bound to Please) of Humpty Dumpty*, starring the famed American pantomime and clown George L. Fox. The production opened on 25 January 1869 at New York's Olympic Theatre. Realizing that the best way to bring the ballet into a more prominent position in the production was to include Fox in the dances, Costa choreographed two new ballets featuring the clown with Rita Sangalli, an Italian colleague. Together they performed a "Scandinavian Polka," in which half the women in the corps de ballet carried small wood and straw musical instruments on which they played while the remaining dancers whirled in and out of picturesque groupings, and "Costa's Fancy Dress Ball, Dance of Deportment," in which Fox and Sangalli were featured satirizing the ballroom conventions of the day.

Costa's wife, who took care of the costumes originally designed in Europe for *The Black Crook* and was responsible for costuming the additions and novelties
added to the production during its long run, also designed the costumes for *Humpty Dumpty*. Her costumes for the finale, which consisted of ornamental
papier-mâché work, cost several thousand dollars, and
the dance for this section of the evening was particularly successful. To ensure that audiences would see both
of the Costas' handiwork, Fox inserted a program note
that warned, "[Humpty Dumpty] without wishing to
be intrusive (which is not one of his small vices) ventures upon a mere suggestion to his generous friends.
Please keep your seat until the curtain falls upon The
Gorgeous Fairy Scene."

According to theater producer Bolossy Kiralfy, by
1870 Costa was New York's most successful choreographer, producing French-style spectaculars with
English and American casts. He had the backing of the
infamous Jim Fisk, who owned the Grand Opera
House. However, on a tour to Havana, Cuba, where
he was performing at the Tacon Theatre in 1873, Costa contracted yellow fever and died.

David Costa brought the Italian traditions of spectacular ballet, featuring sophisticated ballerinas surrounded by marching, posing, parading armies, to the
popular theaters of New York. He also brought a
knowledge of the traditional post-Romantic repertory
of European theaters and translated it to the American
stage in the years following the Civil War.

• For listings of the New York productions in which Costa
appeared, see George Odell, *Annals of the New York Stage*,
vol. 8 (1865–1870) and vol. 9 (1870–1875). For discussions of
his appearances in *The Black Crook*, see Barbara Barker, *Ballet or Ballyhoo* (1984).

BARBARA M. BARKER

COSTAIN, Thomas Bertram (8 May 1885–8 Oct.
1965), editor and author, was born in Brantford, Ontario, Canada, the son of John Herbert Costain, a carpenter and building contractor, and Mary Schultz.
Costain attended Brantford public schools, where he
developed an early love for history and biography. Aspiring to become a writer at an early age, he wrote four
novels while still in high school. Because these early
attempts were rejected, his ambitions were sidetracked
for many years into reporting and editing.

After leaving school at seventeen, Costain began
working as a reporter for the *Brantford Courier*, earning five dollars a week. He was offered this position
after a mystery story he wrote was accepted for publication by the magazine. In 1908 Costain moved to
Guelph, Ontario, where he became an editor for the
Guelph Daily Mercury, a position he held until 1910. In
Guelph he met his future wife, Ida Randolph Spragge,
after seeing her in a production of *The Pirates of Pen-
zance*. The two were married in January 1910; they
had two children. That same year Costain joined the
Maclean Publishing Company, where he edited the
trade magazines *Plumber and Steamfitter*, *Hardware*

and Metal, and *Milliner and Drygoods*. He also became
the editor of *Maclean's Magazine*, a position he held
until 1920.

In 1920 Costain moved to the United States. He was
hired by the Curtis Publishing Company in Philadelphia to be the chief associate editor for George Horace
Lorimer of the *Saturday Evening Post*. He became naturalized as a U.S. citizen later that same year. In 1934
Costain began working for the Twentieth Century–
Fox film corporation as an eastern story editor. Along
with E. H. Ellis and P. Hal Sims, he cofounded and
edited a literary magazine in 1937 called *American
Cavalcade*. But the enterprise was not a success; after
only seven issues, the magazine ceased publication in
1939.

From 1939 to 1946 Costain worked for Doubleday,
Doran as a part-time advisory editor. With more time
on his hands, Costain began a writing career at the age
of fifty-five. Following his own advice to other writers,
he wrote about what he knew. From his study and love
of history he compiled sketches of forgotten historical
characters and offered them as a book, which he called
"Stepchildren of History." When his editor suggested
that Costain turn the material into six books rather
than one, he responded by producing three historical
novels: *For My Great Folly* (1942), *Ride with Me*
(1944), and *The Black Rose* (1945). The books depicted the lives of John Ward, a seventeenth-century pirate; Francis Ellery, publisher of a London paper
called the *Tablet* and advocate for a free press during
the Napoleonic Wars; and Bayan of the Hundred
Eyes, a Mongolian warrior, respectively. Costain also
collaborated with Rogers MacVeagh in 1943 to write
Joshua: Leader of a United People.

The Black Rose became a Literary Guild selection
the year it was published and stayed on the bestseller
list for a year. A film version of the book was made in
1950 by Twentieth Century–Fox. Costain retired in
1946 from Doubleday to begin a full-time writing career. His next novel, *The Moneyman* (1947), was
equally successful. It became a Book-of-the-Month
Club selection and reached second place on the bestseller list. Written in the same style as his first three
novels, *The Moneyman* tells the story of Jaques Coeur,
a fifteenth-century Frenchman living during the reign
of Charles VII, who is said to be the originator of the
department store. As in most of his novels, Costain
projected his own mid-twentieth century sensibilities
onto a distant past.

With all his historical novels, Costain's work began
only after conducting extensive research on the time
period of his text. He continued to check his facts even
while writing. He felt it was the duty of the historical
novelist to present a full and unified picture of the time
period that served as a background for the narrative.
He consulted over one thousand books when he wrote
The Silver Chalice (1952), a novel about the artist who
made the silver chalice that would hold Christ's cup
from the Last Supper, which Warner Bros. made into
a movie in 1954 starring Paul Newman. While normally conducting research on his own, Costain obtained

the help of his niece to translate French sources for *The Moneyman*, and he had a Chinese student help him with *The Black Rose*.

Costain also wrote historical nonfiction. His series entitled "The Pageant of England" contains four volumes that cover the years 1066–1485. This series, along with the book *The Conquerors* (1949), a history of England in the Middle Ages, was praised by historians. He also wrote a series on Canadian history called *The White and the Gold* (1954). In 1965 he was the recipient of the Canadian Club award. He died in New York City.

Costain brought history into the lives of millions of readers. Aware that history books did not sell and convinced that history was taught poorly in public schools, he made it his goal to bring history to life. He also set the pattern for many historical novelists by devoting attention to careful research, rich detail, and dramatic action.

• Costain's manuscripts and documents can be located at the University of California at San Diego, the University of Pennsylvania, and the University of Texas. His other books include *High Towers* (1949), *Son of a Hundred Kings* (1950), *The Magnificent Century* (1951), *The Tontine* and *The Mississippi Bubble* (1955), *Below the Salt* (1957), *The Three Edwards* (1958) *The Darkness and the Dawn* and *William the Conqueror* (1959), *The Chord of Steel* (1960), *The Last Plantagenets* (1962), and *The Last Love* (1963). For additional information see John T. Frederick, "Costain and Company: The Historical Novel Today," *College English* 15 (Apr. 1954): 373–79, and an interview in the *New York Times Book Review*, 17 Aug. 1952. An obituary is in the *New York Times*, intl. ed., 9–10 Oct. 1965.

ELIZABETH ARCHULETA
SUSAN GUNTER

COSTELLO, Frank (26 Jan. 1891–18 Feb. 1973), criminal entrepreneur, was born Francesco Castiglia in Lauropoli, near Cosenza in Calabria, southern Italy, the son of Luigi Castiglia and Maria (maiden name unknown), farmers. At age four Costello moved to New York City with his father; his mother and the rest of his immediate family followed two years later. The Castiglias settled in Manhattan's East Harlem Italian district, where they eked out a subsistence living running a small grocery shop. Despite being considered one of the neighborhood's brightest boys, Costello turned to crime after finishing elementary school. Americanizing his name with a useful touch of Irish, Costello became the leader of the Italian 104th Street gang and gained a reputation as one of the toughest young hoodlums in the area.

By 1911 Costello had been arrested twice and twice freed on charges of assault and robbery. After an attempted robbery at age twenty-four, he was convicted of carrying a gun and sentenced to a year in prison. Despite his reputation he was released after ten months for good behavior. In 1914 he married a Jewish woman named Loretta Geigerman. His experience in prison convinced him of the need to operate beyond public scrutiny, and he started to develop legitimate business fronts and cultivate New York politicians while pursuing bootlegging and gambling ventures. In August 1919, with Harry Horowitz, Costello formed the Harry Horowitz Novelty Company and cashed in on the punchboard craze that was sweeping the country.

Throughout his career Costello ignored traditional ethnic divisions within the underworld, entering lucrative partnerships with Italian, Jewish, and Irish racketeers alike; these included Charles "Lucky" Luciano, Arnold Rothstein, Meyer Lansky, and "Big Bill" Dwyer. During the 1920s Costello and Dwyer exploited the profitable opportunities created by Prohibition. Their activities soon made them millionaires, although the partnership ended in 1925 when they were indicted for bribery and rum-running. Costello survived the indictments and prospered, teaming up in brewing and bootlegging with Owney "The Killer" Madden. Wealth from bootlegging enhanced Costello's hold over New York politics, particularly in the city's Midtown area. Yet while other criminals maintained a high public profile, Costello remained quiet and dignified. He shunned unnecessary violence and acted as a go-between for the underworld and Tammany Hall politicians.

During the late 1920s and early 1930s Costello forged a partnership with former Rothstein Wall Street operator "Dandy Phil" Kastel, increasing his stake in gambling and the legal liquor business. In 1931 Costello and Kastel obtained the New York territory from the Mills Novelty Company of Chicago, the largest makers of slot machines in the country. During its first year, Triangle Mint Company, the company they set up to handle their slot machine business, placed 5,186 slots around the city and made profits estimated between $18 million and $36 million. In 1934 Costello's business became the target of reform mayor Fiorello La Guardia, who began a campaign against slot machines in New York. La Guardia's attention encouraged Costello to move the operation to New Orleans, where its safety was guaranteed by Senator Huey P. Long.

Despite the end of Prohibition Costello continued to profit from distributing alcohol. He and Kastel became agents for Alliance Distributors, Inc., a New York corporation formed at the time of repeal in December 1933. In 1938 Costello provided financial backing for Kastel to purchase all the stock of J. G. Turney and Sons, Ltd., of London. Costello was appointed the personal agent for Turney and Sons in the United States and given a $25,000-a-year salary. Costello also increased his gambling interests in 1947 by investing in the Flamingo Hotel casino in Nevada.

During the late 1940s increasingly exaggerated claims were being made concerning the extent of Costello's grip over organized crime in America. Despite his efforts to keep a low public profile, by 1949 he had become a national celebrity, appearing on the cover of *Time* (17 Oct.) and *Newsweek* (21 Nov.). Costello was seen as a master criminal who ruled a vast mysterious empire and was duly nicknamed the Prime Minister of the Underworld. Nevertheless, the news magazines could find little evidence to confirm such popular suspicion. Costello had substantial legally declared real estate investments and earnings from liquor distributorship. These may have been legacies of bootlegging, but they were nonetheless legitimate.

In March 1951 Costello endured a grueling interrogation before the Senate Crime Investigating Committee, chaired by Senator Estes Kefauver. The committee adopted the popular contemporary perception of Costello as the most influential underworld leader in America. In an attempt to preserve what was left of his anonymity, Costello refused to show his face at the televised hearings. Instead he permitted only his hands to be filmed. On many occasions he invoked the Fifth Amendment, answering other questions in the gruff whisper that had characterized his voice since he had undergone a botched throat operation as a child. The impression created by Costello's nervous hand movements, combined with the voice one commentator described as the death rattle of a seagull, seemed to add weight to his status as the underworld's kingpin. Costello was convicted for contempt and started to serve an eighteen-month sentence on 22 August 1952. In April 1954 Costello was convicted of income tax evasion and in May 1956 began serving an eleven-month prison sentence.

In 1957 Costello survived a gang assassination attempt inspired by Vito Genovese. He then decided to retire, but evidence found at the scene linking him to the Tropicana Casino in Nevada resulted in another prison sentence. In June 1961, after serving forty-two months of a five-year term, Costello was released. His years of retirement were spent fighting the attempts of the Immigration and Naturalization Service to deport him to Italy. In his old age Costello maintained some links with the underworld and enjoyed providing advice to those who asked for the benefit of his great experience. Costello died in New York City.

Costello was an extremely successful mobster whose approach to racketeering brought some order to the business of crime. However, his overstated image as the leader of the underworld merely provided the media and law enforcement authorities with a convenient scapegoat for the problem of organized crime in America.

• The best sources on Costello remain the biographies by Leonard Katz, *Uncle Frank* (1973), and George Wolf and Joseph Dimona, *Frank Costello: Prime Minister of the Underworld* (1974). For an accurate portrayal of Costello's place within organized crime in America, see Michael Woodiwiss, *Crime Crusades and Corruption: Prohibitions in the United States, 1900–1987* (1988). An insight into Costello's popular image can be found in Estes Kefauver, *Crime in America* (1952). An obituary and follow-up article can be found in the *New York Times*, 19 and 22 Feb. 1973.

DAVID R. BEWLEY-TAYLOR

COSTELLO, Lou. *See* Abbott, Bud, and Lou Costello.

COSTIGAN, Edward Prentiss (1 July 1874–17 Jan. 1939), lawyer and U.S. senator, was born in King William County, Virginia, the son of Emilie Sigur and George Purcell Costigan, Sr., a lawyer and judge. His father successfully invested in mining ventures, and the family settled in Denver, Colorado. Illness interrupted his studies at Harvard University. Joining his brother, George, Jr., in Salt Lake City, he studied law and was admitted to the bar in 1897. He completed his Harvard A.B. in 1899 and began practice in Denver in 1900. In 1903 he married Mabel Cory; childless, they became lifetime personal and political companions.

A municipal reformer and progressive Republican, Costigan was a founder and attorney for both Denver's Honest Election League, from 1903 to 1906, and the Law Enforcement League, from 1906 to 1908, and he was president of the Civil Service Reform Association. Personally and politically prohibitionist, he argued a local option case before the Colorado Supreme Court for the Anti-Saloon League, and in 1910 he became chairman of the Dry Denver Campaign Committee. He helped organize the Direct Primary and Direct Legislation Leagues of Colorado. He was a founder of the Citizen's party, which carried Denver in 1912 and instituted a commission government.

Costigan was at the center of the Colorado Progressive Republican League's challenge to President William Howard Taft in 1912. He supported Robert La Follette's (1855–1925) presidential nomination until it appeared hopeless. Shifting his allegiance to Theodore Roosevelt (1858–1919), he followed him into the Bull Moose movement and headed the unsuccessful Colorado Progressive party ticket as candidate for governor in 1912 and 1914.

In 1914 Costigan served as legal counsel for the United Mine Workers during and after a bitter, bloody strike. The remnants of the Colorado Progressive party split into supporters of Costigan and anti-striker "law and order" challengers, largely from the embattled counties. Charging coal operators with law violations before and during the strike and demanding law, order, and justice, he maintained party control but lost more than half his previous gubernatorial support.

In 1916 Roosevelt, distracted by World War I, maneuvered the Progressive party into endorsing the Republican candidate for president. Costigan endorsed Woodrow Wilson, however, praising his progressive record.

In 1917 Costigan joined the newly formed Tariff Commission as an independent Wilson appointee. Disturbed by Republican appointments that undermined the commission, he led an open fight to reduce the sugar schedule in 1924 and precipitated a 1926 Senate investigation, during which he attacked the changes in the commission and recommended its overhaul. In 1928, with a bitter blast, he resigned from the Tariff Commission.

Becoming a Democrat in 1930, he was elected senator from Colorado. When the new session began, Costigan and Senator Robert La Follette, Jr., (1895–1953) had already prepared a bill for federal grants in aid to state relief programs; passage of comparable legislation followed the election of President Franklin D.

Roosevelt in 1932. Costigan was a consistent New Dealer, joining other progressives in promoting a more liberal agenda. He supported federal relief for strikers, anathema to antiunion conservatives. He endorsed legislation to prohibit National Labor Relations Board recognition of company unions, which were promoted and financed by corporations. When congressional investigators revealed that millionaires had paid no income tax, he called for publicity of income tax returns. Yet most of his attention was focused on two bills: the Jones-Costigan sugar amendment to the Agricultural Adjustment Act, which reorganized the world sugar market by trading quota access to the American market for limited production, and the Costigan-Wagner Antilynching Bill, which, had it been enacted, would have imposed stiff financial penalties on counties that permitted lynching.

As 1936 approached, pundits mistakenly expected a conservative Democratic challenge to Costigan. However, coronary problems forced Costigan to withdraw from politics; he died three years later in Denver.

Throughout his lifetime Costigan was a respected principal progressive. Accustomed in Denver to working closely with progressive Democrats, when he left the Republican party in 1912 he never returned, supporting La Follette in 1924 and Alfred E. Smith in 1928. An impressive platform and radio speaker with a clear understanding of legislative detail, he quickly became a leading senator during his single term. His sudden departure was a loss to progressivism, particularly in Colorado.

• Costigan's papers are at the University of Colorado. See also Ray Tucker and Frederick Barkley, *Sons of the Wild Jackass* (1932); John Franklin Carter, *American Messiahs* (1935); Colin B. Goodykoontz, ed., *Papers of Edward P. Costigan Relating to the Progressive Movement in Colorado, 1902–1917* (1941); and Fred Greenbaum, *Fighting Progressive: A Biography of Edward P. Costigan* (1971). An obituary is in the *New York Times*, 8 Jan. 1939.

FRED GREENBAUM

COTTEN, Elizabeth (c. 5 Jan. 1893–29 June 1987), folksinger, was born near Chapel Hill, North Carolina, the daughter of George Nevills, a day laborer and part-time farmer, and Louise (maiden name unknown), a domestic worker. Her parents' blue-collar jobs were tied to the largely agrarian economy that supported the black community in Orange County. One of five children, "Libba" Cotten's formal education did not extend beyond elementary school. She was attracted to music as a child. She began playing her older brother Claude's banjo and guitar shortly after the turn of the century and taught herself to tune and play both instruments left-handed (upside-down). She was exposed to a wide variety of music during a fruitful and creative period for southern music. Blues was just beginning to emerge, and the ballads that developed in the United States, country dance tunes, minstrel show songs, and sacred songs were all commonly heard.

Around this time Cotten wrote two songs—"Freight Train" and "I'm Going Away"—for which she later became famous.

She remained involved with music making for her family and neighbors until 1906, when she joined the Baptist church. A year later she married a local man, Frank Cotten; they had one child. Just shy of her fifteenth birthday Elizabeth Cotten put down her instruments and settled into a conventional domestic life of housework and child rearing.

Cotten and her family made Chapel Hill their home until 1940, when they journeyed northward, settling in Washington, D.C., the mecca for so many black Americans from central North Carolina. After working in a series of short-term domestic jobs Cotten providentially met Ruth Crawford Seeger, who invited her to become her family's housekeeper. Seeger's family included her husband, famed music ethnologist Charles Seeger, and their children, Peter, Mike, and Peggy. For over forty years Cotten had not played music at all, but in the company of the Seeger family her talents were eventually uncovered.

For many years Cotten occasionally played a guitar around the Seeger household, usually for her own amusement but sometimes for visitors. Two of the children, Peggy and Mike, became involved with learning and playing different styles of folk music. By the mid-1950s, at the dawn of the "folk revival," they began to build professional music careers and sometimes included songs—most notably "Freight Train"—as part of their repertoire. During a 1957 tour of England, Peggy regularly played "Freight Train," and the song quickly circulated among local singers. Startled to hear her music performed outside her immediate circle of friends and encouraged by the burgeoning market for folk musicians, Cotten launched her own professional music career when she was in her mid-sixties. In 1958 Mike Seeger recorded her on an album called *Folksongs and Instrumentals with Guitar* for Folkways Records.

By 1960 Cotten had established herself as a regular performer at folk festivals throughout the United States and Canada and was identified with "Freight Train." During this period Cotten recorded *Negro Folk Songs and Tunes* for Folkways and *Freight Train and Other North Carolina Folk Songs and Tunes* for Smithsonian/Folkways. She often appeared at the early folk festivals at UCLA and the University of Chicago and at clubs such as the Gas Light Coffee House and Gerdes Folk City in New York City.

Cotten continued performing into the early 1980s as one of the few black women on the folk music circuit. She received a Heritage Fellowship from the National Endowment for the Arts in 1984. In 1985 she recorded *Elizabeth Cotten Alive* (Arhoolie), which won a Grammy Award for best traditional folk album. Washington, D.C., remained her home until she moved to Syracuse, New York, in the early 1980s to be closer to relatives. Cotten remained in upstate New York until her death in Syracuse.

• For more information on Cotten, see Carol Coy, "Elizabeth Cotten," *Folk Scene*, Apr. 1974, pp. 14–17; Sheldon Harrison, *Blues Who's Who* (1979), p. 130; and Mike Seeger's liner notes to *Freight Train and Other North Carolina Folk Songs and Tunes* (reissue, Smithsonian/Folkways Records SF 40009, 1989). An obituary is in the *Washington Post*, 30 June 1987.

KIP LORNELL

COTTEN, Joseph (15 May 1905–6 Feb. 1994), actor, was born in Petersburg, Virginia, the son of Joseph Chesire Cotten, Sr., the superintendent of mails for Petersburg, and Sally Willson. After graduating from a local high school in 1923, Cotten attended the Hickman School of Expression in Washington, D.C., for one year. He then tried his luck as an actor in New York but found no success. In 1925 Cotten moved to Miami, Florida, where he worked as a newspaper advertising salesman and as an occasional theater reviewer for the *Miami Herald*. He was also involved in a number of failed business ventures. While living in Miami, Cotten often performed with the Miami Civic Theatre, and in 1930 a patron of the theater gave Cotten a letter of introduction to *New York Daily News* theater critic Burns Mantle. Returning to New York, Cotten presented the letter to Mantle, who recommended Cotten to producer David Belasco. Cotten was immediately hired as an assistant stage manager for Belasco's production of *Dancing Partner* (1930). He then understudied for Melvyn Douglas in Belasco's *Tonight or Never* (1930) and spent the 1931–1932 season as a member of the acting company at the Copley Theatre in Boston. In October 1931 Cotten married Lenore Kipp, whom he had known in Miami. The couple had no children, although Kipp had a daughter from a previous marriage.

After returning to Broadway, Cotten had parts in *Absent Father* (1932), *Jezebel* (1933), *Loose Moments* (1935), and *The Postman Always Rings Twice* (1936). He also supplemented his income by acting in short industrial films and on radio. Tall and slim, with blue eyes and curly blond hair, Cotten also found work as a photographer's model. In the mid-1930s, while working on CBS radio's "School of the Air," he was introduced to a young actor named Orson Welles, who was also participating in the program. During a rehearsal for the broadcast, both Cotten and Welles found a line in the dramatic script that was unintentionally humorous and began laughing. From that point on, they formed a close friendship.

In 1936 Welles organized the government-funded Federal Theatre Project (FTP) company and asked Cotten to join. While working in Welles's FTP company, Cotten starred in *Horse Eats Hat* (1936), an adaptation of the French farce *An Italian Straw Hat*. He was also "Second Scholar" in Christopher Marlowe's *Doctor Faustus* (1937). Concerned that this relatively comfortable financial situation disqualified him from work in an unemployment relief project, Cotten appeared in *Doctor Faustus* under the name of Joseph Wooll. In 1937 Welles established his own independ-

ent acting company, the Mercury Theatre. Cotten was Publius in the Mercury Theatre's highly praised modern dress version of Shakespeare's *Julius Caesar* (1937). He also appeared in the Mercury Theatre's productions of Thomas Dekker's *The Shoemaker's Holiday* (1938), Georg Buchner's *Danton's Death* (1938), and William Gillette's farce *Too Much Johnson* (summer try-out performances only, Stony Creek, Conn., 1938).

Cotten's good looks and laconic style drew the attention of Katharine Hepburn, who requested that he play opposite her in Philip Barry's *The Philadelphia Story*. In this popular comedy, which opened at Broadway's Shubert Theatre on 28 March 1939, playboy C. K. Dexter Haven, played by Cotten, wins back his former wife, the high-spirited young socialite Tracy Lord, played by Hepburn, just as she is about to marry another man. Hepburn repeated her role as Tracy Lord in the hugely successful 1940 screen version, but Cotten lost his former role to Cary Grant.

It was Cotten's friendship with Welles however, that took him to Hollywood. In the now classic *Citizen Kane* (1941), directed by and starring Welles, Cotten was the idealistic theatre critic, Jedidiah Leland, the friend and "conscience" of newspaper magnate Charles Foster Kane played by Welles. After touring with the national company of *The Philadelphia Story*, Cotten returned to films with major parts in two Welles projects: *The Magnificent Ambersons* (1942) and *Journey into Fear* (1942). Cotten continued to appear in films and was under contract to independent producer David O. Selznick for most of the 1940s. The affable, easygoing Cotten became a close friend of Selznick and his wife, actress Jennifer Jones. Cotten appeared with Jones in *Since You Went Away* (1944); *Love Letters* (1945); *Duel in the Sun* (1946), also featuring Gregory Peck; and *Portrait of Jennie* (1948). Handsome and convincing, if somewhat lacking in charisma, Cotten was a suitable leading man to female stars and reliable second lead to male stars. Other notable films include *Shadow of a Doubt* (1943), a highly regarded suspense thriller directed by Alfred Hitchcock; *Gaslight* (1944), costarring Ingrid Bergman and Charles Boyer; *The Farmer's Daughter* (1947), with Loretta Young; *The Third Man* (1949), directed by Carol Reed and costarring Welles; *Under Capricorn* (1949), which reunited Cotten with both Hitchcock and Bergman; *September Affair* (1950), with Joan Fontaine; *Niagara* (1953), with Marilyn Monroe; and *The Angel Wore Red* (1960), with Ava Gardner and Dirk Bogarde. Cotten also made brief appearances in two more films directed by his old friend Welles, *Othello* (1952) and *Touch of Evil* (1958).

When his screen career began to decline in the 1950s, Cotten returned to Broadway and enjoyed a major success in Samuel Taylor's comedy *Sabrina Fair* (1953). The featherweight concoction featured Cotten as a serious-minded businessman who is secretly adored by his chauffeur's daughter, played by Margaret Sullavan. "Mr. Cotten gives a most attractive performance. It is masculine, gravel-voiced, cynical and romantic, too. For Mr. Cotten is not limited to one dimension," wrote critic Brooks Atkinson in the *New York Times* (12 Nov. 1953). Cotten later appeared on Broadway in *Once More with Feeling* (1958), a somewhat successful comedy with Arlene Francis, and *Calculated Risk* (1962), a moderately popular murder mystery costarring his second wife, Patricia Medina, whom he had married in October 1960 after the death of Kipp from leukemia in January of the same year. They had no children.

From 1955 to 1956 Cotten served as host of the "20th Century–Fox Hour," an anthology series. For the next three years, Cotten also hosted and occasionally starred in television episodes of "The Joseph Cotten Show," another dramatic anthology series (originally titled "On Trial") that based its stories on actual legal cases from different parts of the world and from various periods in history. Later he appeared on "Hollywood and the Stars" (1963–1964), which presented half-hour documentaries about the motion picture industry.

In his later years, the gray-haired but still trim and debonair Cotten was regularly employed as a character actor in films, including *Hush, Hush, Sweet Charlotte* (1965), a popular southern gothic horror film starring Bette Davis and Olivia De Havilland; *Petulia* (1968), a comedy/drama costarring George C. Scott, Julie Christie, and Richard Chamberlain, with Cotten as Chamberlain's father; *Tora! Tora! Tora!* (1970), a film about the bombing of Pearl Harbor, with Cotten as Secretary of War Henry Stimson; *A Delicate Balance* (1973), a screen version of the Edward Albee Play featuring Katharine Hepburn and Paul Scofield; and *Airport '77* (1977), a star-studded disaster film.

Cotten made his last major screen appearance as the "Reverend Doctor" in *Heaven's Gate* (1980), an infamously over-budget western directed by Michael Cimino. A stroke, which left his speech impaired, ended Cotten's acting career a year later. Cotten died at his home in Los Angeles.

• Scrapbooks and other material on Cotten's film and stage career are at the Cinema and Television Library, University of Southern California. Cotten's autobiography is *Vanity Will Get You Somewhere* (1987). Ronald Bowers, *The Selznick Players* (1976), offers a detailed essay on Cotten's career. See also Theodore Strauss, "Mr. Cotten Batting," *New York Times*, 17 Jan. 1943, and Alton Cook, "Versatility Keynote to Cotten's Success in Pictures," *New York World-Telegram*, 24 July 1943. Simon Callow, *Orson Welles* (1996), establishes a context for Cotten's radio career. An obituary is in the *New York Times*, 7 Feb. 1994.

MARY C. KALFATOVIC

COTTEN, Sallie Swepson Sims Southall (13 June 1846–4 May 1929), advocate of women's education and the women's club movement in North Carolina, was born in Lawrenceville, Virginia, the daughter of Thomas Southall and Susan Sims. Because of her father's precarious fortunes as planter and hotelkeeper, she came to Murfreesboro, North Carolina, at the age of thirteen to live with her father's wealthy cousin. She attended Wesleyan Female College and Greensboro Female College, graduating in 1863. While teaching in Edgecombe County, North Carolina, in 1864, she met Robert Randolph Cotten, a Confederate cavalryman. They were married in 1866.

In 1868 Robert Cotten bought 1,000 acres of land in Pitt County, North Carolina, and established there the plantation "Cottendale," which would be the couple's home until their deaths. Before 1890 Sallie Cotten was occupied as plantation wife and mother. Six Cotten children grew to maturity. The eldest son, Robert, drowned on his fifteenth birthday; in his memory, Sallie Cotten wore the white, gray, lavender, and black of half-mourning for the rest of her life.

From childhood on Sallie Cotten had believed that women were not treated fairly in their educational and career choices. Letters in the early 1880s show a growing feminist outlook based on extensive reading and thought, despite her rural isolation. She became a published writer in *Demorest's*, a women's magazine, in the mid-1880s.

In 1890 she was chosen as one of three North Carolina women to serve on the Board of Lady Managers for the Chicago World's Fair of 1893. The board was the first official U.S. government body to be made up of women. Cotten's work for the fair proved to be an education in leadership for her, made her known to women's leaders across the nation, and established her as a public figure in North Carolina. In the next few years she gained a national reputation as a public speaker on the need for women's education. The national press delighted in presenting her as that anomaly, a progressive southern lady. She also wrote, published, and gave public recitations of a long narrative poem, *The White Doe*, which was based on a legend about the death of Virginia Dare.

Sallie Cotten's most enduring contribution to the education of North Carolina women was her introduction of women's clubs to the state. In the 1890s these groups, virtually unknown in the state at the time, offered an alternative form of higher education for women socially discouraged from attending college. In clubs, women could discuss and write papers on books they had read; many clubs went on to work for civic improvements inspired by their discussions. Cotten helped organize women's clubs across North Carolina. She was one of the founders of the North Carolina Federation of Women's Clubs in 1902 and served as its president from 1911 to 1913. Nationally, she was a pioneer member of the General Federation of Women's Clubs (founded in 1890) and of the National Congress of Mothers (founded in 1897); she held various offices in both organizations. She published a *History of the North Carolina Federation of Women's Clubs* in 1925.

With her crown of white hair and clothes of mourning colors, Sallie Cotten presented herself in public as the traditional figure of a southern lady—one that conservative people in her state would accept. Yet women's groups knew her as a tenacious fighter for women's advancement. To younger women she was "Mother" Cotten, wise guide and adviser. The writer

Hope Summerell Chamberlain of North Carolina summed her up as a "woman of remarkable insight, well known and highly regarded. She had wrought nobly, accomplishing a great change in the ideas of the women of our State, organizing the women's club movement, standing for betterment projects all over the land. [She] looked like the portrait of white-haired womanly aristocracy, and possessed in herself the fiery soul of the reformer, joined with a statesmanlike conception of just how fast, or how slow she must move for the best interest of her cause."

Cotten died in Winchester, Massachusetts, where she had gone to live with a daughter after her husband's death.

• Various collections of the correspondence, writings, papers, and memorabilia of Sallie Southall Cotten and her family are located in the Southern Historical Collection, University of North Carolina at Chapel Hill. Her extensive and revealing correspondence with a longtime friend, General William LeDuc, can be found in the William Gates LeDuc Papers, Minnesota Historical Society. A full-length biography is William E. Stephenson, *Sallie Southall Cotten: A Woman's Life in North Carolina* (1987); a biographical article was written by Henry Groves Connor for the *Biographical History of North Carolina*, vol. 8 (1917), pp. 122–32. Her family life is extensively covered in a memoir by her son Bruce Cotten, *As We Were* (1935). Hope Summerell Chamberlain's discussion of Cotten's effect on club women is in "What's Done and Past," typescript, Manuscript Collection, Perkins Library Duke University, Durham, N.C.

WILLIAM E. STEPHENSON

COTTER, Joseph Seamon, Sr. (2 Feb. 1861–14 Mar. 1949), teacher, author, and civic leader, was born in Bardstown, Kentucky, the son of Michael (also spelled Micheil) Cotter, a boarding house owner, and Martha Vaughn. Although his father was known as an avid reader, Cotter was raised largely by his mother, a freeborn woman of mixed English, Cherokee, and African blood. It was from her naturally dramatic manner—she orally composed poems and plays as she worked at chores—that he acquired his love of language and stories. Having taught herself, she also taught Cotter to read and enrolled him in school, but at age eight economic necessity forced him to drop out and begin working at various jobs: in a brickyard, then a distillery, and finally as a ragpicker and a teamster. Until age twenty-two, manual labor consumed much of Cotter's life.

The friendship of prominent black Louisville educator Dr. William T. Peyton, who sensed Cotter's natural intelligence, inspired his enrollment in night school in 1883. His talent and discipline are indicated by the fact that after less than a year of studies he was teaching. He began his career as an educator in Cloverport, Kentucky, staying there until 1887; he then conducted a private school for two years. After next teaching at the Western Colored School in Louisville, Kentucky, from 1889 to 1893, Cotter founded and served as principal of the Paul Laurence Dunbar School in Louisville. He remained there until 1911—during his most fruitful years as a poet—and then became principal of the Samuel Coleridge-Taylor School, where he remained until his 1942 retirement.

Cotter would be remembered in Louisville primarily as an educator, but his life held much more, both privately and professionally. In 1891 he married Maria Cox of Louisville. And, despite the demands of his teaching and administrative chores, he began to work more diligently at the poetry that would be the source of his national reputation. His first published work, *A Rhyming* (1895), showed the strong influence of early English lyrics, including the ballad and the sonnet, but by the time this volume saw print, Cotter was moving in a different direction. On Thanksgiving of 1894, having already acquired a burgeoning reputation as a local poet, Cotter hosted fellow African-American poet Paul Laurence Dunbar (namesake of his school) on his first visit to the South and discovered not only an enduring friendship but also a new style that would both distinguish him individually and link him to a larger tradition. Excited by Dunbar's incorporation of African-American dialect into poetry, Cotter—sensing the appropriateness of this language to the oral storytelling tradition into which he had been born—often followed the same practice in his own career, beginning with his second collection, *Links of Friendship* (1898). He also adopted Dunbar's practice of writing poems in praise of African-American leaders, as in "Frederick Douglass," "Dr. Booker T. Washington to the National Negro Business League," and "The Race Welcomes Dr. W. E. B. Du Bois As Its Leader." Cotter never entirely gave up experimenting with more established English forms and language, however; and if in his era African-American poetry fell into three schools—the dialect poetry of Dunbar, the protest tradition of W. E. B. Du Bois, and "literary" work that was couched in European forms and expressed noble sentiments—he ultimately participated in all three.

Cotter experimented with other genres as well. *Caleb, the Degenerate* (1903), his only play, was written in blank verse and was practically unperformable; it attempted to express dramatically many of the views endorsed by Booker T. Washington in his conservative 1895 Atlanta Exposition speech, which encouraged African Americans to be content with their current lot as laborers and to concentrate on vocational education. Cotter's *Negro Tales* (1912), a mixture of prose genres that constituted his only fiction outside of newspapers, came immediately after his prolific period at the Dunbar School; it was one of only four collections of fiction by African-American writers to appear nationally between 1906 and 1922. Then, while moving in new political directions in the second half of his life, he embraced the fundamentally different Du Bois and his call for African-American intellectual achievement. He published his *Collected Poems* (1938) and *Sequel to "The Pied Piper of Hamelin" and Other Poems* (1939)—on the whole, his best work—near the end of his teaching career.

Cotter was without family in his last years. His first-born son, who bore his name, had been a promising poet before his death from tuberculosis at age twenty-three; Cotter's two other children also predeceased him, as did his wife. But he lost himself in his community. Aside from his teaching and writing, he was also active in the NAACP, the Kentucky Negro Educational Association, the Story-Tellers League, and the Authors League of America, and he served as director of the Louisville Colored Orphans Home Society. He helped to organize African-American neighborhoods in Louisville, and his initiation of storytelling contests for local children grew into a national movement and earned him a place in *Who's Who in America* in 1919, during an era when African-Americans were rare in those ranks. The teacher-poet was remembered in Louisville as a humanitarian who devoted himself to the younger generation, as when in writing a community creed he advised his fellow citizens: "Let us lose ourselves in the welfare of our children." Even more characteristically, in "The Negro Child and the Story Book" (*Collected Poems*, 1938) he praised the power of the imagination in the lives of the young.

He died at his home in Louisville, a pillar of his community and a minor but essential figure in his field. Although the aesthetic quality of his work is inconsistent, he combined wide-ranging formal and stylistic approaches with a thematic concern for both the universal human condition and the particular needs of his race. During the seemingly fallow period between the turn-of-the-century eclipse of figures such as Dunbar and Charles Chesnutt and the beginnings of the Harlem Renaissance, he held the small but already significant ground that had been gained in the field of African-American letters.

• Cotter's papers are in the Western Branch of the Louisville Free Public Library. Two significant works by Cotter not mentioned in the text are *A White Song and a Black One* (1909) and *Negroes and Others at Work and Play* (1947). Ann Allen Shockley, "Joseph S. Cotter, Sr.: Biographical Sketch of a Black Louisville Bard," *CLA Journal* 18 (Mar. 1975): 327–40, is a thorough chronicle of the author's life; the relevant sections of Joan R. Sherman, *Invisible Poets: Afro-American Writers of the Nineteenth Century* (1974), and Eugene Redmond, *Drumvoices: The Mission of Afro-American Poetry* (1976), focus on Cotter's work in verse, placing it in the context of the larger African-American tradition.

W. FARRELL O'GORMAN

COTTON, Henry Andrews (18 May 1876–8 May 1933), psychiatrist, was born in Norfolk, Virginia, the son of George Adolphus Cotton, occupation unknown, and Mary Delha Biggs (daughter of U.S. senator Asa Biggs). He studied medicine at Johns Hopkins and the University of Maryland (M.D., 1899). After six months of service as a private in the Army Medical Corps and at the Baltimore City Lunatic Asylum, Cotton was recruited in 1900 by Adolf Meyer as an assistant physician at the Worcester (Mass.) State Hospital. Three years later he transferred to a similar but better paying post at the Danvers (Mass.) State Hospital and married Alice Della Keys of Baltimore. The couple had two children.

Like other ambitious physicians of his generation, Cotton sought to obtain advanced training in Germany, and with Meyer's sponsorship he was able to spend a year in Munich (1905–1906), where he studied under Alois Alzheimer and Emil Kraepelin. In 1907, with strong professional credentials and the enthusiastic support of his mentor, he was appointed as superintendent of the New Jersey State Hospital in Trenton, in the aftermath of a scandal about brutality and mistreatment of patients. Within two months he had eliminated all mechanical restraint, freeing ninety-six patients from their shackles and tossing aside more than 700 restraining devices.

Cotton also introduced a series of administrative reforms at the hospital. These changes, however, were clearly subordinate to his primary concern—the introduction of modern medicine into the asylum. Convinced, as he later explained, that "even if we did not have the evidence of cortical lesions in the 'functional' psychoses, we would have to assume their existence, if we accept modern biological teachings" ("The Relation of Chronic Sepsis," p. 436), he pursued any and all means of physical treatment: hydrotherapy; salvarsan for syphilitics, injected intraspinally or intracranially; the use of glandular extracts—all without result.

In 1916, however, Cotton became convinced of the importance of focal sepsis in the etiology of mental disorders. The idea that low-level chronic bacterial infections might account for a variety of puzzling, poorly understood, and intractable diseases enjoyed considerable vogue in general medicine in the first quarter of the twentieth century. Cotton was not the first to adopt this theory to account for psychosis, but he rapidly became its most prominent and aggressive exponent. Concentrating at first on the removal of decayed teeth, he soon insisted that it was essential "to literally 'clean up' our patients of all foci of chronic sepsis" ("The Relation of Chronic Sepsis," p. 438) and extended his attention to the tonsils and then the gastrointestinal and genitourinary tracts. Equally aggressive in seeking professional and lay attention to his work, he claimed that this application of modern medical science proved the biological origins of all serious mental disorders and had spectacular effects on cure rates, which he alleged were as high as 85 percent of those treated.

Professional reaction to Cotton's claims was mixed. Though he attracted some enthusiastic American disciples and an ambiguously worded endorsement from Meyer, others were skeptical or openly hostile. In Britain, the response was more uniformly enthusiastic, and in 1923 (and again in 1927) Cotton crossed the Atlantic to bask in the acclaim of his British peers.

By 1924, as controversy over Cotton's work grew in North America, the Trenton trustees sought to forestall a potentially hostile inquiry by asking Adolf Meyer, now professor of psychiatry at Johns Hopkins, to evaluate his protégé's claims. Meyer delegated the investigation to one of his assistants, Phyllis Greenacre, whose research, conducted over eighteen months, conclusively showed that Cotton's treatments were not merely wholly ineffectual, but highly dangerous. (The death rate for patients he subjected to abdominal surgery, for example, exceeded 40 percent.) Cotton, however, who had suffered a brief mental breakdown of his own during the investigation, refused to accept Greenacre's findings, and when Meyer rewarded his recalcitrance by suppressing her report, Cotton was able to resume his surgical assault on psychosis.

In 1930 Cotton finally lost his position as superintendent at Trenton, after local physicians complained that, while a full-time state employee, he had simultaneously developed an extensive and lucrative private practice operating on well-to-do mental patients. Awarded the honorific title of director of research at his former institution (which continued to proclaim its loyalty to his doctrines), Cotton persevered with his war on sepsis, though his therapeutic efforts were now perforce concentrated solely in the private sector. Three years later, in the midst of a public campaign to reintroduce colectomies at the state hospital, he dropped dead while lunching at his club.

Continuing to disguise what he knew about the actual effects of Cotton's work, Meyer eulogized him in the *American Journal of Psychiatry* in 1934, praising "a most remarkable achievement of the pioneer spirit . . . [by] one of the most stimulating figures of our generation." At least in the United States, however, Cotton's death essentially marked the end of experiments with surgical treatment for focal sepsis and the demise of his particular claims about the biological origins of mental disorder.

• There is no known repository of Cotton's papers. Among his most important publications are *The Defective, Delinquent, and Insane; the Relation of Focal Infections to Their Causation, Treatment and Prevention* (1921); "The Etiology and Treatment of the So-Called Functional Psychoses," *American Journal of Psychiatry* 79 (1922): 157–94; and "The Relation of Chronic Sepsis to the So-Called Functional Mental Disorders," *Journal of Mental Science* 69 (1923): 434–65. A critical assessment of Cotton's approach is in N. Kopeloff and C. O. Cheyney, "Studies in Focal Infection: Its Presence and Elimination in the Functional Psychoses," *American Journal of Psychiatry* 79 (1922): 139–56. A retrospective assessment is given in Andrew Scull, "Desperate Remedies: A Gothic Tale of Madness and Modern Medicine," *Psychological Medicine* 17 (1987): 561–77. Memoria include Thomas Chivers Graves, "Obituary: Henry Andrews Cotton, M.A., M.D.," *Journal of Mental Science* 79 (1934): 178–80, and Adolf Meyer, "In Memoriam: Henry A. Cotton," *American Journal of Psychiatry* 90 (1934): 921–23.

ANDREW SCULL

COTTON, John (4 Dec. 1584–23 Dec. 1652), clergyman, was born in Derby, Derbyshire, England, the son of Roland Cotton, a lawyer, and Mary Hurlbert. A serious and talented student, he matriculated at Trinity College, Cambridge, at the age of thirteen. He received his B.A. in 1603 and his M.A. in 1606, the year he became a fellow at Emmanuel College. He remained there until 1612, serving as lecturer, catechist, dean, and tutor while acquiring a reputation as both an able disputant and a remarkable preacher. At first his preaching was in the learned and ornate style, but after

being spiritually affected in 1609 by the preaching of Richard Sibbes, he adopted the plain Puritan style. Although this change was received with dismay by many of his admirers in Cambridge, it was responsible for the conversion of John Preston, later master of Emmanuel and an eminent Puritan divine. Cotton was ordained in 1610, and in 1613 he received the B.D. His first call was as vicar of St. Botolph's Church in Boston, Lincolnshire, where he served from 1612 until shortly before his departure for New England in 1633. In 1613 Cotton married Elizabeth Horrocks, sister of a Lancashire minister. During his Lincolnshire ministry, Cotton ran an informal seminary for recent Cambridge graduates. Young Dutch and German exiles from the war on the Continent also lived with the Cottons, so that, as his contemporary John Norton noted, Cotton "had his house full of Auditors." Although an opposing faction disapproved of his strict Calvinist beliefs and Puritan practice, he became notable among his fellow Puritans for his ability to avoid stern ecclesiastical punishment despite his nonconformity in prescribed forms of worship, such as making the sign of the cross, wearing the surplice, and kneeling to receive communion. Cotton endured temporary suspensions by successive bishops in 1615 and early 1621, but the protection of influential citizens such as the Boston alderman Thomas Leverett, together with Cotton's own posture as an earnest seeker after God's truth, led each time to his restoration. Samuel Ward, a well-known Cambridge Puritan, said he envied Cotton above all others "for he does nothing in the way of conformity, and yet hath his liberty, and I do everything that way, and cannot enjoy mine."

By the end of the decade, Cotton's ministry was increasingly threatened, partly because his shield, Bishop John Williams, was not well liked by King Charles. Cotton's early interest in New England colonization was signaled by his Southampton departure sermon, *Gods Promise to His Plantation* (1630), to the founding émigrés of the Massachusetts Bay Colony, led by John Winthrop. The end of Cotton's Lincolnshire ministry may have been delayed by a long bout of ague in 1630–1631. In April 1631 Cotton's wife died, after a childless marriage of eighteen years. Cotton married Sarah Hawkredd Story, widow of William Story, in April 1632. They had six children. One daughter, Maria, married Increase Mather and became the mother of Cotton Mather.

Though he had friends among the titled gentry, they were no longer able to protect him from the increasing ecclesiastical pressure to conform. He went into hiding in the fall of 1632 and was temporarily separated from his new wife and her ten-year-old daughter, Elizabeth. Reunited before the end of the year, they were concealed by Puritan friends, including John Dod. Early in 1633 Cotton was cited to appear before the Court of High Commission. During this period, Cotton is said to have converted John Davenport, Thomas Goodwin, Philip Nye, and Henry Whitfield to nonconformity. On 7 May 1633 Cotton resigned his vicarage in Boston, regretting that "neither my bodily health, nor the peace of the church will now stand with my continuance there." The crucial issue of conformity had been the central factor, as he explained to Bishop Williams: "howsoever I doe highly prize and much prefer other mens judgment and learning, and wisdome, and piety, yet in thinges pertaining to God and his worship, still, I must (as I ought) live by mine own fayth, not theirs." Along with Puritan ministers Thomas Hooker and Samuel Stone and their families, Cotton sailed for New England on the *Griffin* on 13 July 1633. During the voyage, Sarah delivered their first child, aptly named Seaborn Cotton.

Although Cotton, who arrived at the new Boston in September, was well established as an intellectual and spiritual leader of the Puritan movement, his career as a published author lay ahead of him. In the years following emigration, his writings began to be published, especially in the 1640s as the Puritans gained positions of authority in church, university, and state. His sermons retained an audience in old as well as New England. Early sermon series appeared as *The Way of Life* (1641), *A Brief Exposition of the Whole Book of Canticles* (1642), *Christ the Fountain of Life* (1651), *A Brief Exposition . . . of Ecclesiastes* (1654), and *A Practical Commentary . . . upon the First Epistle Generall of John* (1656). Works written and preached by Cotton in New England included *An Exposition upon the Thirteenth Chapter of the Revelation* (1655) and *The Powring Out of the Seven Vials* (1642), both millennialist and vehemently anti-Catholic works. As was common with popular preachers of this era, Cotton's sermons were often taken down in shorthand or other abbreviated form by auditors whose notes were later published without the author's knowledge or permission.

Soon after arriving in Boston, Cotton was chosen teacher of the first church in Boston, of which John Wilson was already pastor. Cotton thus enjoyed a prominent position in the only church in what was to become the principal town of New England. His reputation for piety, learning, and insight, together with the respect paid to the minister in a community based on a desire to worship "in the purity of the ordinances," gave him immediate influence. He was therefore in an uncomfortable and unaccustomed position when he sided with those accused of "antinomianism" in the years 1636–1638. John Wheelwright, a Lincolnshire minister who had arrived after Cotton; Anne Hutchinson, Wheelwright's sister-in-law and a Lincolnshire follower of Cotton who led discussions in her home at which she presented a theology of "free grace"; and Henry Vane, a gentleman who lived in Cotton's house and was elected governor of the colony for one year, 1636–1637, led numerous followers in Boston's first church in dismissing the importance of good works as primary evidence of saving faith while emphasizing the belief that an individual's access to God's grace is direct, thus minimizing the role of the minister as the mediator between the sinner and God's mercy. Wheelwright and Cotton were opposed by most of the clergy in the colony, including especially

Wilson, Hooker, Shepard, and Peter Bulkeley, as well as the magistrates and sometime governors John Winthrop and Thomas Dudley. Cotton's thoughts on the central issue appear in his sermons in *The New Covenant* (1654) and its longer version, *A Treatise of the Covenant of Grace* (1659). His retrospective construction of the controversy is in *The Way of Congregational Churches Cleared* (1648), a response to the Scottish churchman Robert Baillie's anti-Congregationalist attack in *A Dissuasive against the Errours of the Time* (1645). During a 1637 synod, Cotton became aware that the antinomian faction, while claiming him as their chief authority, held opinions that were "blasphemous: some of them, heretical, many of them erroneous." He distanced himself from Hutchinson and Wheelwright, both of whom were exiled from the colony following court trials during 1637 and 1638. Correspondence as late as 1640 shows Cotton still trying to persuade Wheelwright to soften his outspoken charges that ministers and magistrates overemphasized works at the expense of grace and to admit that he did "overvalue . . . an heretical and seditious faction." It was a period of unaccustomed agitation that put Cotton in the minority and on the defensive in the area in which he had been assumed to be a preeminent authority—the life of the spirit.

He eventually recovered from his sense of personal loss and pain to resume a position as key spokesman for the New England polity. In the 1640s many in England wrote to New England asking for clear statements on church practice, often implying or stating disagreement with what they saw as overly strict requirements for membership in New England churches. Cotton himself had opposed the separatism of Roger Williams, who was banished from the colony in 1635. These two strongly principled men engaged in a debate about toleration and conscience known as the "Bloody Tenent Controversy," named after the chief published products of the debate, Williams's *The Bloudy Tenent of Persecution* (1644), Cotton's reply, *The Bloudy Tenent, Washed and Made White in the Bloud of the Lamb* (1647), and Williams's final rejoinder, *The Bloody Tenent Yet More Bloody* (1652). In this involved and protracted debate, Cotton argued that when a dissenter publicly disagrees with generally held views of the community, it is sometimes necessary that the dissenter be punished, as Williams was.

Along with John Davenport and Thomas Hooker, Cotton was invited by members of Parliament to return to London to represent New England in the Westminster Assembly, an invitation all three declined. Cotton did help to define what became known as the New England Way. Although Cotton's draft, *The Keyes of the Kingdom of Heaven* (1644), saw several printings, it was his *The Way of the Churches of Christ in New-England* (1645) that he wanted to represent his views. While this work and *The Grounds and Ends of the Baptisme of the Children of the Faithfull* (1647) were meant to satisfy the inquiries of brethren in his "native country" about New England church practice, he wrote also for his neighbors in their everyday lives, including his catechism for children called *Milk for Babes: Drawn Out of the Breasts of Both Testaments* (1646) and *Singing of Psalmes a Gospel-Ordinance* (1647). The latter remains the chief statement on the use of the psalms in worship by a Puritan of his generation. He also had a major role in the translation of the psalms by several New England ministers, which produced the *Bay Psalm Book* (1640), the first book published in America.

Cotton corresponded with a wide array of contemporaries. Although only a small portion has survived—about one hundred letters to and by Cotton—we know of many other letters through his own and his contemporaries' references to them. He sometimes complained of having his time and energies sapped by his multiple duties, including his need to reply to many letters. He wrote that it is "a foolish conceit of ignorant people, that think Ministers and Schollers eat the bread of idleness" or "come easily by their living. No calling more wasteth and grieveth him that is occupied therein, then theirs doth" (*A Brief Exposition of . . . Ecclesiastes*, p. 33).

Cotton's death in Boston acquired mythological status by being associated with a comet that appeared in early December and disappeared shortly after his death. One of his earliest biographers calls the comet a "monitory Apparition" and says that Cotton himself, when asked about it on his deathbed, "thought it portended great changes in the churches" (Norton, pp. 47, 48).

Cotton was one of the most influential leaders of the Puritan movement in England and in the first generation of New England's settlement. He brought a scholar's erudition to his practice as preacher, biblical interpreter, disputant, and analyst of spiritual experience.

• Cotton manuscript items, chiefly letters, are in the Boston Public Library, the Massachusetts State Archives, the Massachusetts Historical Society, Pilgrim Hall in Plymouth, Mass., the New England Historic Genealogical Society, the American Antiquarian Society, the Hawthorne-Longfellow Library at Bowdoin College, the Bodleian Library, the British Library, and the Gemeente Archief, Leyden, the Netherlands. Additional important works include *A Letter of Mr. John Cottons . . . to Mr. Williams* (1643), *The Controversie Concerning Liberty of Conscience in Matters of Religion* (1646), and *Of the Holinesse of Church-Members* (1650). Several writings appear in David D. Hall, ed., *The Antinomian Controversy, 1636–1638: A Documentary History* (1968; rev. ed. 1990). Three books are printed in modern format in Larzer Ziff, ed., *John Cotton on the Churches of New England* (1968). For complete primary bibliographies, see Julius H. Tuttle, "The Writings of Rev. John Cotton," in *Bibliographical Essays: A Tribute to Wilberforce Eames* (1924), and Everett Emerson, *John Cotton*, 2d ed. (1990), which gives known or estimated dates of composition. For a thorough listing of works on Cotton up to 1975, see Edward J. Gallagher and Thomas Werge, *Early Puritan Writers: A Reference Guide* (1976), pp. 59–97. The most complete treatment of his life is Ziff, *The Career of John Cotton: Puritanism and the American Experience* (1962), though three early biographies are indispensable: Samuel Whiting, "Concerning the Life of the Famous Mr. Cotton. . . . ," in *Chronicles of the First Planters of the Colony of Massachusetts Bay, from 1623 to 1636*, ed. Alexander Young

(1846), John Norton, *Abel Being Dead yet Speaketh; or, The Life & Death of . . . John Cotton* (1658), and Cotton Mather, "Cottonus Redivivus," in bk. 3 of *Magnalia Christi Americana* (1702), first published in *Johannes in Eremo* (1695). Sargent Bush has provided "John Cotton's Correspondence: A Census," *Early American Literature* 24 (1989): 91–111, anticipating his edition of the letters. See also William K. B. Stoever, *"A Faire and Easie Way to Heaven": Covenant Theology and Antinomianism in Early Massachusetts* (1978), for discussion of Cotton's theology as it relates to the antinomian controversy. Darrett B. Rutman, *Winthrop's Boston: A Portrait of a Puritan Town, 1630–1649* (1965), contains much that is relevant to Cotton's New England career. On his relation to the Puritan movement in England, see Bush, "Epistolary Counseling in the Puritan Movement: The Example of John Cotton," in *Puritanism: Transatlantic Perspectives on a Seventeenth-Century Anglo-American Faith*, ed. Francis J. Bremer (1993). On the Williams-Cotton controversy, see Jesper Rosenmeier, "The Teacher and the Witness: John Cotton and Roger Williams," *William and Mary Quarterly* 25 (1968): 408–31; Sacvan Bercovitch, "Typology in Puritan New England: The Williams-Cotton Controversy Reassessed," *American Quarterly* 19 (1967): 166–91; and Irwin H. Polishook, *Roger Williams, John Cotton and Religious Freedom: A Controversy in New and Old England* (1967). Valuable chapters on Cotton's thought appear in Teresa Toulouse, *The Art of Prophesying: New England Sermons and the Shaping of Belief* (1987), and Theodore Dwight Bozeman, *To Live Ancient Lives: The Primitivist Dimension in Puritanism* (1988).

SARGENT BUSH, JR.

COTTON, Joseph Potter (22 July 1875–10 Mar. 1931), corporate lawyer and public official, was born in Newport, Rhode Island, the son of Joseph Cotton and Isabella Cole. Following a public education in Newport, Cotton attended Harvard College, graduating in 1896. He taught English at Harvard in 1896–1897, earned an A.M. in 1897, and then entered Harvard Law School in the fall of 1897. A distinguished student, he became editor in chief of the *Harvard Law Review* and graduated in 1900 at the top of his class.

Cotton moved to New York City after graduation and joined the office of Cravath, Henderson, and De Gersdorff, where he became a partner in 1906, an uncharacteristically quick advancement in his profession. In 1905 he married Jessie Isabel Child; they had two children. Although engaged in the reorganization of railroads, public utilities, and industrial corporations, he found time to edit and publish *The Constitutional Decisions of John Marshall* in 1905. Cotton resigned his partnership in 1907 and practiced alone until 1910.

Cotton's first effort to employ his legal expertise on behalf of social justice occurred during this three-year period of solitary practice. At the request of Governor Charles Hughes, he worked with New York's Workmen's Compensation Commission, the Wainwright commission, in a pioneering attempt to establish a more just code of injury compensation to replace the antiquated common law system. Although the bill he helped author passed in the legislature, it was struck down by New York's conservative Court of Appeals in *Ives v. South Buffalo Ry. Co.* (1911).

In 1910, through an introduction from fellow progressive lawyer George Rublee, Cotton formed a partnership with ex-senator John C. Spooner of Wisconsin. While with Spooner, Cotton was involved with some of the larger railroad reorganizations of the day, such as Metropolitan Street Railway Co., Wabash Railway Co., Chicago and Eastern Illinois Railway Co., and the St. Louis–San Francisco Railway Co. Despite his workload, Cotton continued to be involved with progressive reform issues. He contributed informally to Louis Brandeis's defense of Gifford Pinchot before Congress and signed with Brandeis the brief prepared by Rublee.

Later in 1910 Cotton and Rublee managed the gubernatorial campaign of progressive Republican Robert Perkins Bass of New Hampshire, a friend of Cotton's from Harvard. Following Bass's victory, the only successful Republican gubernatorial race east of the Mississippi River that year, Cotton helped the Bass administration draft a workmen's compensation act and establish a public service commission to supervise public utilities.

Cotton next, with Rublee and Judge Learned Hand, advised Theodore Roosevelt during the early months of his 1912 presidential campaign. Cotton was the principal author of Roosevelt's March 1912 Carnegie Hall speech. Rublee, who had introduced Cotton to Roosevelt, described Cotton as the brightest young lawyer in New York and a man who "believes in the rule of the people and places human rights above property rights." Cotton's liberal inclinations never conflicted with his respect for law and order. Writing to Felix Frankfurter during this period, Cotton stipulated that he advocated an "orderly progress" that was bereft of "any social, industrial, or political disturbance."

Through the influence of Brandeis and Rublee, who relied on the gifted young lawyer to help advance progressive reform issues, Cotton was assigned to several important posts in the Woodrow Wilson administration. Serving first as advisory counsel on the *First National Bank v. Union Trust Co.* case, Cotton helped sustain the constitutionality of the Federal Reserve Act. He next became counsel for the Alaska Engineering Commission at the invitation of Interior Secretary Franklin Lane.

During the summer of 1917 Cotton served as counsel to General George Goethals, general manager of the U.S. Shipping Board's Emergency Fleet Corporation. Cotton drafted plans to commandeer ships for war service. He was next invited to work with Herbert Hoover in the Food Administration, where he supervised the meat-packing industry and formulated regulations for price maintenance and food distribution. In July 1918 Hoover appointed Cotton to represent the Food Administration on a program committee of the Allied Maritime Transport Council sitting in London. There he worked with representatives from Britain, France, and Italy to adjust national import schedules to meet available Allied tonnage and arranged financial transactions for the purchase of American agricul-

tural products. He was decorated by both France and Italy for this service, which increased his own interest in international affairs.

Having spent most of the decade engaged in various sorts of public work, Cotton turned his attention to his private practice after the war. He formed a partnership with former secretary of the treasury William McAdoo and longtime friend George Franklin. In the course of the 1920s, Cotton reorganized Goodyear Tire and Rubber Co., the Willys Corporation, and several railroad companies. He was involved in the organization of the Radio Corporation of America and International Harvester as well as the merger of Dodge and Chrysler.

On 24 May 1929 President Hoover appointed Cotton under secretary of state to Secretary Henry L. Stimson. Cotton's accumulated experience with large organizations, government agencies, and international bodies in concert with his stellar reputation among men of influence allowed him to perform his duties with great dispatch and ingenuity. His competence permitted Stimson to become directly involved with such important events as the 1930 London Naval Conference. The conference period, 21 January–22 April, was likely Cotton's most stressful phase of public work. Acting as the primary line of communication between Hoover and Stimson, Cotton had a difficult time when Ambassador Dwight Morrow and Rublee influenced Stimson to offer, contrary to Hoover's original intention, a consultative pact with France to keep the French at the negotiation table. It was much a rematch of the 1918 armistice period, in which Hoover had met opposition from Cotton, Morrow, and Rublee over American relations with Europe.

In the two years that Cotton was with the State Department, he helped set the stage for stronger U.S.–Latin American relations by transferring some of the department's most qualified men to Latin American posts, previously less prestigious appointments. He was also noted for working fervently against slavery in Liberia and for preventing the use of slaves by an American firm in Abyssinia.

Cotton's rising influence and leadership as a public official came to a tragic end in March 1931, when he developed blood poisoning following surgery to remove a tumor from his spinal cord. He died in Baltimore, Maryland. Morgan partner Thomas Lamont remarked at the New York Harvard Club that Cotton had been "the guide, counselor, and friend of his seniors, his contemporaries, and his juniors." Secretary Stimson, speaking to a friend after Cotton's funeral, exclaimed: "You can't realize what a loss to the country Joe's death is. He is the only man who could do anything with the President."

• Unpublished sources referring to Cotton's work include "The Reminiscences of George Rublee," Columbia University Oral History Office (microfilm); the Dwight W. Morrow Papers at the Amherst College Library (microfilm); and the Henry L. Stimson Papers at Yale University (microfilm). Published sources include Gerald Gunther, *Learned Hand:*

The Man and the Judge (1994); Elting Morison, *Turmoil and Tradition: A Study of the Life and Times of Henry L. Stimson* (1960); and Raymond O'Connor, *Perilous Equilibrium: The United States and the London Naval Conference of 1930* (1962). An obituary is in the *New York Times*, 11 Mar. 1931.

MARC MCCLURE

COTTRELL, Frederick Gardner (10 Jan. 1877–16 Nov. 1948), chemist and inventor, was born in Oakland, California, the son of Henry Cottrell, a confidential secretary to a San Francisco ship broker, and Cynthia Durfee. Cottrell's boyhood in California coincided with the spread of the electrical power industry, and during those years he conducted many electrical experiments in his home laboratory-workshop. After graduating from the University of California, Berkeley, in 1896 with a B.S. in chemistry, Cottrell taught chemistry at Oakland High School. Finding this too restrictive for his imaginative talents and wanting to continue his studies in the new field of physical chemistry, Cottrell traveled to Europe where the laboratories and graduate research training in science were then most advanced. Cottrell studied with Wilhelm Ostwald in Leipzig, receiving the Ph.D. with highest honors in 1902.

Upon returning to the United States, Cottrell accepted a position at the University of California, Berkeley, and in 1904 married Jessie May Fulton; they had no children. At Berkeley he wrote several articles on the recently developed air liquefaction process (1905–1906) and installed the West Coast's first liquid air machine. The oxygen distilled from the liquid air enabled him to investigate the use of oxygen-enriched air in various metallurgical processes. After the 1906 earthquake devastated his laboratory, Cottrell left the university and worked with the Du Pont Company on the problem of arsenic poisoning of the metal catalyst used in the industrial production of sulfuric acid.

About this time Cottrell began to think about electrostatic precipitation to reduce atmospheric pollution. Electrostatic precipitation was not original with Cottrell, but by skillfully incorporating the recent advances in electrical power engineering, he made its industrial application a reality. M. Hohlfeld in Germany in 1824, and in England C. F. Guitard in 1850 and Oliver Lodge in 1905, had described electrostatic precipitation, yet it remained a laboratory novelty because voltages high enough for industrial application were unavailable until about 1886 when George Westinghouse developed transformers that produced high voltages. Cottrell used as much as 30,000 volts, and by 1907 he had demonstrated the industrial feasibility of electrical precipitation. That year he filed for a patent on an electrostatic precipitator that effectively removed dust particles from industrial smokestacks, receiving it on 11 August 1908. In the Cottrell process particles from the escaping waste gases passed through a high-potential electrostatic field where they acquired an electrical charge and were attracted to an oppositely charged collecting or precipitating electrode that discharged and deposited them as dust in the bottom of the precipitator. Cottrell secured sufficient financial backing from several associates in California, and in 1907 they established the International Precipitation Company and the Western Precipitation Company for commercial development of the electrostatic precipitator. Their first operational precipitator was at Du Pont's Pinole, California, plant, and within two years American Smelting and Refining Company, Anaconda Copper, and Portland Cement Company were using Cottrell's precipitator.

In 1910 Joseph Holmes, head of the U.S. Bureau of Mines, asked Cottrell to join the bureau and establish a West Coast office in San Francisco. Cottrell agreed but saw a potential conflict of interest resulting from the bureau's having to regulate polluting industries that could reduce their atmospheric emissions by installing his precipitator. Before leaving Berkeley, Cottrell therefore assigned his patent rights to the Smithsonian Institution subject to one condition: that it establish a nonprofit foundation for the purpose of awarding future royalties from his and any other assigned patents to investigators needing funds to bring their scientific ideas to practical application. The Research Corporation was the foundation established in 1912 to carry out Cottrell's plan. Many universities and private industries financially assisted scientists in their research, but the Research Corporation was the first independent agency whose sole mission was to support the research and development of scientific ideas considered most beneficial to society.

Cottrell remained with the Bureau of Mines until 1921, first as an assistant director and then as director. He served as chairman of the Division of Chemistry and Chemical Technology of the National Research Council in 1921 before leaving to become director of the Department of Agriculture's Fixed Nitrogen Research Laboratory. Under Cottrell's directorship the Fixed Nitrogen Laboratory emerged as the leading U.S. center for research on nitrogen-based fertilizers and explosives. He resigned in 1930 to become a consultant to the Research Corporation, and in 1935 when the Research Corporation established Research Associates, Inc., Cottrell served as its director for three years before financial problems forced Research Associates to shut down. During its brief existence Research Associates tested ideas submitted to the Research Corporation and promoted projects having both industrial and social significance. The two organizations were the embodiment of Cottrell's lifelong belief that scientists had a special responsibility to society for both the benefits and the consequences of their research. He lived according to this principle and left in the Research Corporation a testament to all the scientists who donated the patents that have sustained its operation to this day. They include Robert Williams at Bell Laboratories, who synthesized vitamin B_1 (thiamine), and Morris Kharasch at the University of Chicago, who synthesized ergotinate, a drug used to control hemorrhaging, and mercurochrome, an antiseptic. Kharasch's patents were the first since Cottrell's to yield significant royalties. Other noteworthy projects that the Research Corporation supported were E. O. Lawrence's cyclotron at the University of California, Robert Van de Graaff's generator at the Massachusetts Institute of Technology, and Harold Urey's isotope research at Columbia.

Cottrell's last major scientific interest was the construction of a high-temperature pebble bed furnace for the conversion of atmospheric nitrogen and oxygen to nitric acid, a compound used for the production of fertilizers and explosives. Although technically promising, the process could not compete with the more economical high-pressure Haber process and never became a commercial success.

Cottrell received several prestigious awards for his scientific contributions. Among the most notable were the Perkin Medal, applied chemistry's highest honor (1919), the Willard Gibbs Medal from the Chicago section of the American Chemical Society (1920), the Gold Medal of the Mining and Metallurgical Society (1925), the Holley Medal of the American Society of Mechanical Engineers (1937), the American Institute of Chemists Medal (1938), and election to the National Academy of Sciences (1939).

Cottrell's death occurred unexpectedly at a National Academy of Sciences meeting in Berkeley. He had attended a session reporting on E. O. Lawrence's latest cyclotron that the Research Corporation had funded. Sitting between two old friends, chemists Joel Hildebrand and Farrington Daniels, he slumped in his chair and died.

Cottrell was an American physical chemist and air pollution control pioneer. He invented the Cottrell Precipitator and contributed to the development of a regenerative high-temperature pebble bed furnace. Known as the "samaritan of science" for his benevolence, Cottrell established the Research Corporation, the first American foundation wholly dedicated to the advancement of science.

• Cottrell's papers are in the Library of Congress, Manuscript Division. Cottrell's publications include "Separating Suspended Particles from Gaseous Bodies," U.S. Patent No. 895,729 (11 Aug. 1908); "The Electrical Precipitation of Suspended Particles," *Journal of Industrial Engineering and Chemistry* 3 (1911): 542–50; "The Research Corporation, an Experiment in Public Administration of Patent Rights," *Journal of Industrial Engineering and Chemistry* 4 (1912): 864–67; and "Patent Experience of the Research Corporation," *Transactions of the American Institute of Chemical Engineering* 28 (1932): 222–25. The only biography is Frank Cameron's *Cottrell, Samaritan of Science* (1952). A shorter biographical article is Vannevar Bush, "Frederick Gardner Cottrell," National Academy of Sciences *Biographical Memoirs* 27 (1952): 1–11. For more recent articles on Cottrell and on the Research Corporation see California State College, *Cottrell Centennial Symposium* (1977); Harry J. White, "Centenary of Frederick Gardner Cottrell," *Journal of Electrostatics* 4 (1977–1978): 1–34; Michelangelo de Maria and Robert W. Seidel, "Lo scienziato e l'inventore: L'inizio dell'integrazione sistematica fra scienza e industria in USA durante la Prima Guerra Mondiale," *Testi Contesti* 4 (1979): 5–32; A. B. Costa, "A Matter of Life and Breath: Frederick Gardner Cottrell and the Research Corporation," *Journal of Chemical Educa-* *tion* 62 (1985): 135–36; and J. L. Heilbron and Robert W. Seidel, *Lawrence and His Laboratory*, vol. 1 (1990). An obituary is in the *Yearbook of the American Philosophical Society* (1950), pp. 272–77.

ANTHONY N. STRANGES
RICHARD C. JONES

COTTRELLY, Mathil de (17 Feb. 1851–15 June 1933), actress, was born in Hamburg, Germany, the daughter of August W. Meyer, conductor of the Hamburg State Opera Company, and Johanna Guilden. Cottrelly's 66-year career as a performer began at the age of eight, when she had her stage debut in Hamburg, and embraced the genres of light opera, circus, vaudeville, and drama. Born into a family that was prominent in the German opera, Cottrelly was taught at home by her father and largely raised, after her mother's death, by her older sister, Clementina Meyer, who was an actress. She emerged as a child prodigy, playing leading parts in touring companies throughout Europe by the time she was fourteen. When she was sixteen, she began singing coloratura soprano in light operas, such as Donizetti's *La Fille du Régiment* and *La Belle Hélène*.

She met her future husband, well-known English circus acrobat George Cottrell, at age fifteen, while playing vaudeville in Berlin. After marrying him at sixteen, she took his stage name of Cottrelly and became an equestrian circus performer. They went to Russia to perform together in the Hinne-Ciniselli Circus, where they often performed before the czar. After her husband was killed in a fall during a performance in Russia, Cottrelly returned to Germany in 1870, touring Europe in comedies and light operas for five years. She appeared for the first time in New York on 5 October 1875 at the Irving Place Theatre in *Ehrliche Arbeit*, a German light opera, touring the next year in Philadelphia, St. Louis, and San Francisco, where she met Buffalo Bill, who was to be a lifetime friend.

In the 1880s Cottrelly starred in such vehicles as Johann Strauss's *Die Fledermaus* at the Thalia Theatre in the Bowery and became a partner in the McCaull Opera Company, where she was reputed to be the highest-salaried American actress as well as an occasional director, costume designer, and wardrobe mistress. Her productions there included *Clover, The Queen's Lace Handkerchief, The Beggar Student*, and *The Begum*. Among her fellow actors in the company were Lillian Russell, Chauncey Olcott, DeWolf Hopper, and Francis Russell. Cottrelly also appeared in a number of revues with Russell's Comedians. During the 1890s Cottrelly gave up singing for straight dramatic roles. In 1895 she played Mme. Vinard in the original American production of *Trilby* starring Wilton Lackaye as Svengali, and she played a minor role in the 1899 London production of Israel Zangwill's *The Children of the Ghetto*, with Mackaye as Reb Shemuel.

After the turn of the century, Cottrelly gradually remade herself into a respected character actress. She appeared with Maxine Elliot in *The Great Match* and with Maude Adams in *The Jester*. She played the title role in *Die Frau Gretl* in 1911. In her sixties and seventies, Cottrelly made a specialty of Jewish character roles. She played Mrs. Isaac Cohen, the kindly Jewish neighbor who ends up cooking a ham for the young interfaith couple, in the Broadway production of *Abie's Irish Rose*, which ran for 2,327 performances after its premiere in 1922. She starred opposite Ludwig Satz as Rosie Potash in *Potash and Perlmutter, Detectives, or Poisoned by Pictures* in 1926, a popular comedy featuring Motague Glass's beloved schlemiels. This was her last professional appearance on the stage.

Cottrelly had one son with George Cottrell. After her first husband's death, she married Thomas J. Wilson, a businessman, whose death preceded hers by more than ten years; they had no children. Until the end of her life, Cottrelly was a beloved figure in the entertainment world, known for her generosity to others in the profession. Even after her retirement, she continued to act, appearing as late as 1931 in private performances of the Troupers, a Hollywood stage group. She died in Tuckerton, New Jersey.

• Cottrelly's New York career is chronicled in G. C. D. Odell, *Annals of the New York Stage*, vols. 10–15 (1938–1949). An obituary appears in the *New York Times*, 17 June 1933.

BRENDA MURPHY

COTZIAS, George C. (16 June 1918–13 June 1977), physician and neuroscientist, was born in Canea, Crete, the son of Constantin Cotzias, and Katherine Strumpuli. He began his early schooling and his initial medical studies in Athens, Greece. With the outbreak of World War II, he joined the Greek Royal Army, but because his father, then the mayor of Athens, was a leader in the Greek resistance against the Germans, he and his family fled to the United States in 1941.

Despite his limited English, Cotzias impressed Harvard Medical School sufficiently to be admitted to its second-year medical class and graduated cum laude with an M.D. in 1943. He was an intern in pathology at the Peter Bent Brigham Hospital and resident in neurology and medicine at the Massachusetts General Hospital. He began a career in research, joining the famous D. D. Van Slyke in 1944 at the Rockefeller Institute, where Cotzias, as senior scientist and head of the physiology division, developed enzyme assays and discovered that monoamine oxidase was concentrated in the mitochondria of cells. He followed Van Slyke when the latter moved in 1953 to Brookhaven National Laboratory; there Cotzias was appointed senior scientist and head of the physiology division. In 1951 he married Betty Ghinos; they had one son. In 1952 Cotzias became a naturalized U.S. citizen.

Cotzias became a pioneer in the area of research on biogenic amines in the brain, the physicochemical effects of metallic ions, and the effects of polyvalent ions on mitochondrial pumps. He pioneered the use of radioisotopic tracers in biological research. Because of his important early studies of manganese metabolism in the brain, in 1962 at the request of the World Health Organization, he joined a team investigating neurological symptoms in Chilean manganese miners. Cotzias noted they suffered symptoms similar to Parkinson's disease. He showed that manganese accumulated more in some tissues, causing selective damage to the pigmented cells in the substantia nigra of the brain, and that the damage persisted after the manganese levels returned to normal. This work led him in 1964–1967 to study the brains of Parkinson's patients, which had low melanin concentrations in the substantia nigra, the same area affected in the Chilean miners. He and his co-workers were interested in the possible beneficial effects of a melanocyte-stimulating hormone, which proved disappointing, and in the effect of L-dopa.

At this time A. Carlsson in Sweden and Oleh Hornykiewicz in Austria were showing the depletion of the neurotransmitter dopamine in the brain of Parkinson's patients. Andre Barbeau in Canada and Walther Birkmayer and Hornykiewicz in Vienna tried dopa in these patients with variable but essentially disappointing results. Cotzias, putting aside these results, administered D,L-dopa, and later l-dopa, but administered gradually increasing doses to high levels, as he recognized that it was necessary to saturate the enzymes in the vascular system to allow enough to enter the brain and be converted into active metabolites. He achieved remarkable results in eight of sixteen Parkinson patients he treated, with some improvement in two others, which he reported, with M. H. van Woert and L. M. Schiffer, in the *New England Journal of Medicine* ("Aromatic Amino Acids and Modification of Parkinson's Disease" 276, no. 7 [1967]: 374–79). This publication created great excitement in the medical world and within the year confirmatory studies were reported by others at major neurological meetings in Edinburgh and Washington, D.C. The use of L-dopa in Parkinson's disease has been said to be one of the most important medical discoveries of our age.

Thirty years later l-dopa drugs remained the most important drugs in the treatment of Parkinson's disease, even though other agents and new forms of surgery had been developed. Influencing more than just the therapeutic advance in Parkinson's Disease, Cotzias's now classic 1967 paper with van Woert and Schiffer has stimulated major advances in brain research and therapy of other neurological diseases.

While carrying on this research at the Brookhaven National Laboratory, in 1966 Cotzias became head of the Hospital and Medical Research Center. In 1970 he became professor of neurology at Mount Sinai Medical School, professor of medicine at State University of New York at Stonybrook, and attending physician at New York Hospital. In 1974 he and his team moved to the New York Hospital–Cornell Medical Center, where he simultaneously held appointments at Memorial Sloan-Kettering Cancer Center and the Rockefeller University.

Regarded as a warm, but challenging leader, who displayed great intelligence, skeptical curiosity, and quiet strength, Cotzias was described by his colleagues as a giant of a man, both physically and in his personality. He inspired loyalty and could excite others both with his ideas and with the belief that research should go from observations at the bedside to the laboratory and back to the bedside to benefit people suffering with illness.

Cotzias's contributions to neurochemistry and the hope he brought to many thousands of patients with Parkinson's disease were acknowledged through his many honors. He was decorated Commander in the Greek Royal Order of Phoenix and received the Albert Lasker Award for clinical research in 1969; the Citation and Gold Medal of the Atomic Energy Commission, the Borden Award of the American Association of Medical Colleges, and the Oscar Hunter Award of the Society of Clinical Pharmacology and Therapeutics in 1972; the award for distinguished contribution in medical science of the American College of Physicians in 1974; and the A. Cressy Morrison Award of the New York Academy of Sciences in 1954. He was elected to the National Academy of Sciences and was a fellow of the American Academy of Arts and Sciences and the New York Academy of Sciences. He was a member of the Association of American Physicians, the American Society for Clinical Investigation, and the American Physiological Society.

Cotzias was diagnosed in 1973 with lung cancer, which was treated by surgery and chemotherapy. Despite his illness, he continued his busy research schedule, and in order to be closer to his physicians as he worked, he moved to Cornell University Medical College in New York. He also acted as the special assistant to the director of Memorial Sloan-Kettering Cancer Center in 1974. Cotzias worked on the development of new drugs for Parkinson's disease and the effect of the brain on the metabolic effects of other body tissues until his death, in New York City. Following his death the American Academy of Neurology established in 1978 one of their most prestigious awards in his name, the Cotzias Award and Lecture.

• A description of the pathways that led to the discoveries about dopamine in the brain and the depletion in the basal ganglia in Parkinson's disease is in Oleh Hornykiewicz's memoir, "From Dopamine to Parkinson's Disease: A Personal Research Record," in *The Neurosciences: Paths of Discovery*, vol. 2, ed. F. Sampson and G. Adelman (1992). Personal views of Cotzias's life and work are provided by his friend Fred Plum in an obituary in the *Annals of Neurology* 2, no. 6 (1977): 540, and by longtime research colleague Lily C. Tang in "A Personal and Scientific Biography of Dr. George C. Cotzias," *Neurotoxicology* 5, no. 1 (Spring 1984): 5–12. An obituary is in the *New York Times*, 14 June 1977.

JOCK MURRAY

COUCH, Darius Nash (23 July 1822–12 Feb. 1897), soldier, was born in the town of Southeast, Putnam County, New York, the son of Jonathan Couch, a farmer. His mother's name is unknown. Couch entered the U.S. Military Academy at West Point on 1 July 1842 and graduated thirteenth of fifty-nine in the class of 1846. He served as a lieutenant of artillery in the Mexican War and received one brevet promotion on

23 February 1847 for gallantry and meritorious conduct at the battle of Buena Vista. At the conclusion of the war Couch served at various posts on the East Coast, including brief service in 1849 against the Seminole Indians in Florida. In 1843–1854 he collected zoological specimens for the Smithsonian Institution as part of a surveying expedition in northern Mexico. Couch married Mary Caroline Crocker in 1854, and on 30 April 1855 he resigned from the army and took employment with a Massachusetts copper company owned by his wife's family.

Couch reentered the army on 15 June 1861 as colonel of the Seventh Massachusetts Infantry. He escorted his regiment to Washington, D.C., in July and there received an antedated promotion to brigadier general of volunteers, effective 17 May 1861. He was assigned as a brigade commander in Major General George B. McClellan's Army of the Potomac. During the Peninsula campaign of March–August 1862, Couch led a division of the IV Corps that saw heavy fighting in front of the Confederate defensive lines at Williamsburg, Virginia. Couch's division was the first to discover that the enemy had evacuated the line during the predawn hours of 6 May. During the battle of Fair Oaks on 1 June 1862, Couch's division maintained itself without reinforcements against superior numbers and retired in order only after receiving positive orders. His division also held a large portion of the Federal line at Malvern Hill on 1 July. For his adept handling of troops in battle during the campaign, Couch was promoted to major general of volunteers on 4 July 1862.

In the latter months of 1862 Couch assumed command of the Army's II Corps headquartered at Harpers Ferry, West Virginia. Although portions of the II Corps saw action at the battle of Antietam, Maryland, on 17 September 1862, Couch arrived with additional troops too late to join in the fighting. At the battle of Fredericksburg, Virginia, Couch's corps crossed the Rappahannock River by pontoon boats under enemy fire on 11 December 1862 and participated in the doomed assault on Marye's Heights on 13 December. Always known for his blunt, succinct statements, Couch signaled Major General Ambrose E. Burnside: "I am losing. Send two rifle batteries."

In February 1863 Couch became the senior corps commander of the Army of the Potomac, now commanded by Major General Joseph Hooker. On the final day of the battle of Chancellorsville (1–4 May 1863), Couch was summoned by the disabled Hooker to take command of the army and withdraw it. Hooker's inept performance and rash statements during the fight were not lost on his senior commander; after the battle Couch wrote that "it hardly seemed possible that a sane General could have talked in this manner" (unpublished letter). Couch asked to be relieved from further duty under Hooker and scoffed at the suggestion of President Abraham Lincoln that he himself be placed in command. Couch did not desire to have an army command, and he furthermore looked forward to serving under Major General George Meade, whom he suggested as Hooker's replacement.

In view of the threatened invasion of Pennsylvania, the Department of the Susquehanna was formed on 11 June 1863, with Couch as its commander. Within a few days Confederate cavalry entered the state, and Couch turned to the task of assembling 37,000 volunteer and militia troops to meet the emergency. During the next three weeks, units of Couch's department repeatedly engaged Confederate forces during the Gettysburg campaign. Remaining in command of the department after the Confederate invasion, Couch was in charge of ceremonies at the national cemetery during which Lincoln delivered the Gettysburg Address on 19 November 1863. During the next twelve months Couch continued to organize the Pennsylvania militia for the state's defense.

In December 1864 Couch was ordered to Nashville, Tennessee, to command a division in the hastily organized army of Major General George H. Thomas. Couch led the division during the battle of Nashville on 15 and 16 December 1864. At war's end he was a division commander with Major General William T. Sherman's army in the Carolinas. He resigned from the army on 26 May 1865.

Couch ran unsuccessfully as the Democratic candidate for governor of Massachusetts in 1865. Following that he served briefly as collector of the port of Boston, but his appointment was not confirmed by the Republican Senate. He then turned away from politics and served as president of a manufacturing and mining company in Virginia. He moved to Norwalk, Connecticut, in 1870 and became quartermaster general of the state from 1876 to 1878; he was adjutant general of the state of Connecticut in 1883. Couch died at Norwalk.

Couch is best remembered as an able division and corps commander in the Army of the Potomac. His career occasionally was marred by personal traits of impatience and temper directed at both subordinates and superiors. He also suffered from prolonged bouts of ill health, which led to his acceptance of the post of department commander. Although in this administrative position Couch greatly aided in the repulse of the Confederate invasion of Pennsylvania, he undoubtedly would have performed greater service as a commander in the field.

• The Couch papers covering the period 1861–1872 are housed in the manuscript collections of the New York Public Library. Couch wrote two accounts of his wartime experiences for Robert Underwood Johnson and Clarence Clough Buel, eds., *Battles and Leaders of the Civil War* (1884). These monographs cover the battles of Fredericksburg and Chancellorsville. Couch's war dispatches and correspondence are in *The War of the Rebellion: A Compilation of the Official Records of the Union and Confederate Armies* (128 vols., 1880–1901). A biographical sketch is William Farrus Smith, "In Memoriam of General Darius Nash Couch," *Bulletin of the Association of Graduates of the Military Academy* (1897). A close examination of his best year in combat is in Francis A.

Walker, *History of the Second Army Corps* (1886). A substantive report on Couch's death is in the *New York Times*, 13 Feb. 1897.

HERMAN HATTAWAY
MICHAEL D. SMITH

COUCH, Harvey Crowley (21 Aug. 1877–30 July 1941), entrepreneur, was born in Calhoun, Arkansas, the son of Thomas Gratham Couch, a preacher and farmer, and Manie Heard. The Couches were of Welsh extraction. Harvey Couch grew up in rural poverty with little formal schooling until the illness of his father led the family to give up farming and move to Magnolia, Arkansas, where at age seventeen Couch completed his education at the Magnolia Academy. He credited his education to a teacher, Pat Neff, later a governor of Texas.

From an early age Couch displayed both acquisitive instincts and an interest in machinery. After seeing his first railroad train, he built his own model out of scraps. His first business venture involved buying guinea hens and selling the eggs. In Magnolia he worked in Dr. H. L. Longino's drugstore before becoming a railway mail clerk in 1898. Besides sorting the mail, Couch bought eggs from local farmers and sold them in the Memphis market.

Couch was still employed as a clerk by the "Cotton Belt" (the St. Louis and Southwestern Railroad) when he learned of the telephone and foresaw an opportunity. In 1903 Couch and a partner formed the North Louisiana Telephone Company and linked the towns of Bienville, Louisiana, and McNeil, Arkansas. In 1904, with money supplied by his former employer, Longino, Couch bought out his partner and rapidly expanded into four states, constructing 1,500 miles of wire and servicing fifty exchanges. When the powerful Bell interests tried to make his system incompatible by refusing long-distance service, Couch convinced the Arkansas legislature to require connections. In October 1904 he married Jessie Johnson; they had five children.

In 1911 Couch sold out to the Bell interests for $1.2 million and turned his attention to electricity by purchasing bankrupt companies in the Arkansas cities of Malvern and Arkadelphia. A system builder, Couch formed Arkansas Light and Power (AL&P) in 1914, acquired thirty-three local companies, and tied them together into a unit. To promote consumption he encouraged rice farmers to use electricity for pumps and in 1922 opened Arkansas's first radio station, WOK, in Pine Bluff.

During World War I Couch served as fuel administrator for Arkansas. Wartime inflation hurt the company, so Couch recruited C. Hamilton Moses, a skilled attorney, to oversee the creation of the Arkansas Corporation Commission to regulate utilities. The commission promptly released AL&P from its long-term contracts. Moses henceforth handled an ever-growing network of patronage and lobbying. These measures included making sure local newspapers received large advertising accounts as a reward for their support, keeping the legislature friendly through timely financial support, and packing state regulatory bodies with stockholder-friends. After the war Couch expanded to neighboring states, creating the Mississippi Power and Light Company in 1923 and the Louisiana Power Company in 1924.

Couch believed in hydroelectric power and in 1924 built Remmel Dam (named for Arkansas Republican Harmon L. Remmel) on the Ouachita River. Carpenter Dam, also on the Ouachita River, came in 1931. These two dams allowed the company to eliminate fifty-two small power plants.

During the mid-1920s Couch actively battled Electric Bond and Share Company, a subsidiary of General Electric. In 1926 the two firms joined with AL&P, renamed Arkansas Power and Light (AP&L), as an operating unit in the system. Couch remained nominally in charge, but his energies were applied mostly to promoting electric use in Arkansas. He maintained his love of trains and used them to transport industrialists to Arkansas under the banner "Helping Build Arkansas."

Couch acquired the North Louisiana and Arkansas Railroad (NL&A) and as president of the Kansas City Southern Railroad (KCS) merged the two lines in 1937, thus giving the KCS an outlet to New Orleans. To promote the new opportunity he created a luxury passenger service, the "Southern Belle."

Couch engaged in a variety of civic and business endeavors. He served as chairman of the Arkansas State Chamber of Commerce and directed relief efforts for the Red Cross in the flood of 1927. A director of the Chase National Bank of New York, Banker's Trust Company of Little Rock, and Simmons National Bank of Pine Bluff, Couch also had extensive interests in natural gas fields in Louisiana. A nominal Democrat, he was a delegate and an alternate to the national conventions in 1924 and 1928.

At the outset of the Great Depression Couch was appointed to the Reconstruction Finance Corporation, serving from 1932 to 1934. He approved a controversial loan to General Charles G. Dawes's bank and later wrote an account of his involvement in the decision, which was apparently never published.

Couch returned to Arkansas during the late 1930s and promoted rural electrification. AP&L engineer Ralph Pittman devised a way to build electric lines for $750 a mile, or half the standard cost. However, the political climate of the times did not favor private power interests, and local farmers lacked the capital to finance the building of their own private lines even at a reduced cost. The Public Utility Holding Act of 1935 broke up Electric Bond and Share, and AP&L became, along with Mississippi Power and Light, Louisiana Power and Light, and New Orleans Public Service, a part of Middle South Utilities.

Couch was eased from power, his plan for another hydroelectric plant at the Blakely Mountain dam was derailed, and the investment bankers who now controlled the company replaced him with Moses. In addition, a new generation of New Deal political leaders

such as Arkansas congressman Clyde Ellis disliked AP&L's power and patronage system and favored public power. Some observers might call Couch the father of rural electrification, but public power, notably the Tennessee Valley Authority and its spawn, the electric cooperatives, took electricity to the outback over the opposition of private power interests.

Couch died at "Couchwood," the home he had erected on Lake Catherine, outside of Hot Springs, Arkansas. He typified industrialists who were more promoters than scientists or technicians. His success in building an electric empire included large amounts of speculative financing, political jobbery, and high-pressure tactics. After the 1920s utilities replaced railroads as the chief lobbyists and became, according to its critics, the center of corruption in state politics. Louisiana's governor, Huey Long, was the first to exploit popular discontent against utilities, forcing Couch, hat in hand, to defend his empire. By the time of Couch's death, private utilities were on the defensive in the South, and a new generation of corporate men had replaced flamboyant promoters like Couch.

• Harvey Couch's scrapbooks are in the corporate files of Arkansas Power and Light. A useful authorized biographical sketch appears in D. Y. Thomas, ed., *Arkansas and Its People*, vol. 3 (1930). Two laudatory biographies, Winston P. Wilson, *Harvey Couch: The Master Builder* (1947), and Stephen Wilson, *Harvey Couch: An Entrepreneur Brings Electricity to Arkansas* (1986), highlight his personality and gloss over the means he utilized to obtain his goals. A brief corporate history of Arkansas Power and Light is in *Arkansas Times*, 15 Sept. 1994. Also useful is James E. P. Griner, "The Growth of Manufactures in Arkansas, 1900–1950" (Ph.D. diss., George Peabody College for Teachers, 1957). A lengthy obituary appears in the *Little Rock Arkansas Gazette*, 31 July 1941.

MICHAEL B. DOUGAN

COUDERT, Frederic René (1 Mar. 1832–20 Dec. 1903), international lawyer, was born in New York City, the son of Charles Coudert and Jeanne Clarisse du Champs. His father, a native of Bordeaux, France, and an army officer under Napoleon I, was convicted and sentenced to death for his role in the conspiracy to place Napoleon II on the throne. Through a technicality in his trial, the sentence was postponed. He was imprisoned twice but escaped and in 1824 made his way to the United States. In New York City he set up a school for boys that became well known. Frederic Coudert received his early education at this school. At the age of fourteen Frederic entered Columbia College and in 1850 was awarded an A.B. with highest honors. His commencement address at that occasion attracted attention from the press. While still in college he gave Spanish and French lessons to a large class of boys.

For the next two years he apprenticed in the law offices of Edward Curtis and Edward Sandford, at the end of which he was admitted to the New York bar in 1853. He began to practice law and formed a partnership with his two brothers, Louis Leonce and Charles, Jr.; the partnership became the nucleus of the family firm of Coudert Brothers, which with its Paris branch soon became one of the most reputable firms in the city, transacting a huge business and numbering among its clients many European governments.

Coudert's practice included a wide range of civil, commercial, and criminal cases. In addition, the firm and its branches handled a large volume of patent, trademark, and extradition cases. Over time it was recognized as one of the country's leading specialists in international law. In the estimation of his colleagues Coudert was a brilliant courtroom lawyer with the ability to make quick recoveries during trials if the facts suddenly changed or if the evidence seemed to go against his client. He had great natural gifts as an advocate—intuitive insight, clear and logical statement of argument, and originality in presentation. He is said to have possessed a withering power of sarcasm but was equally capable of an unexpected transition to humor.

The Couderts were pioneers in the slowly emerging field of modern international law. Frederic was initiated into this field as an associate of Reverdy Johnson trying blockading cases during the Civil War, which formerly had been a specialty closely tied in with admiralty law. The U.S. Congress still had to look overseas for the rules on navigation and maritime collisions. Few New York firms had either the connections, linguistic talent, or resources that the Couderts could use. Frederic Coudert was U.S. counsel to the French, Italian, and Spanish governments.

When well established in his law practice Coudert married Elizabeth McCredy. Their only child, Frederic René, was born in 1871. Like his father he was destined for a distinguished career as an international lawyer.

The times called for lawyers to take an active part in civic affairs, and Coudert was much sought after as a public speaker. He gave the principal address to the French delegates at the dedication of the Statue of Liberty in New York in June 1885. He was able to command the attention of his audiences with the clarity of his style and his ready wit. One of the high points in his career was the address he delivered at the centennial celebrations of Columbia College in 1887.

Apart from his legal work and public lectures, many of which were donated to charitable causes, Coudert contributed numerous articles and essays to periodicals of the day, often on subjects unrelated to his profession. While still a young law student he had contributed to his own support by writing for newspapers and magazines, in particular for Porter's *Spirit of the Times*—the leading sporting journal of the period.

Throughout his adult life Coudert was interested and involved in politics at national, state, and local levels. Then, as now, lawyers were in the midst of politics everywhere. He believed it was a civic duty at some stage to become active in government, but he thought this could be more effectively achieved by those who ask or expect no reward or salary from the public treasury.

Coudert was prominent in New York City politics, where his services as a party worker and speaker were in constant demand, especially after he became the seventh president of the Association of the Bar of the City of New York. Most nineteenth-century lawyers belonged to the Republican party, but Coudert was an Independent Democrat. He supported William R. Grace for mayor in both his campaigns and played a key role in the election of Grover Cleveland to the presidency in 1884, often speaking under the auspices of the Lawyers' Campaign Club, of which he was president. He also accepted the presidency of the Young Men's Democratic Club and the Manhattan Club. Coudert used his influence to ensure that the Democratic party was restored to power at the national level and was proud to call Cleveland, the first Democrat elected president since 1856, his friend.

In the presidential campaign of 1876 he supported the Democratic candidate Samuel Tilden, and after the election Coudert was sent to New Orleans by the Democratic National Committee to investigate and resolve the disputed Louisiana returns. In 1892 he again led the move by New York's Independent Democrats to win the renomination of Grover Cleveland. For his services to the party he might have been rewarded with some influential position, but he consistently declined public office, including appointment to the New York Court of Appeals.

Following the death of Supreme Court justice Samuel Blatchford in the summer of 1893, Cleveland named William B. Hornblower to succeed him. But the appointment soon ran into trouble. One of its opponents, David B. Hill, the senior New York senator, was a friend of Isaac H. Maynard. Two years earlier Maynard, as deputy attorney general and acting counsel for the board of state canvassers, had robbed public records to destroy election returns from Dutchess County, New York, to ensure Democratic control of the state senate. The State Bar Association appointed a committee to investigate the outrage: its members included Hornblower, Elihu Root, James C. Carter, and Coudert. The committee's report, released in 1892, was scathing. It held both Hill and Maynard guilty of a crime. When Maynard was subsequently nominated for the New York Court of Appeals, he was defeated by a plurality of more than 100,000. In retaliation Hill rallied all his friends against Hornblower's appointment, which was lost.

In defiance, Cleveland nominated Wheeler H. Peckham, but he too became the victim of a hostile cabal organized by Hill. Once again the Independents called on Cleveland to keep up the fight and urged him to nominate Coudert. Few lawyers have been able to resist the offer of a seat on the Supreme Court, but Coudert declined the nomination for business reasons. After his refusal, Cleveland gave up the fight and nominated Senator Edward D. White of Louisiana, who was confirmed. In 1895, on the death of Justice Howell E. Jackson, Coudert was again offered the nomination, but again he refused. Rufus W. Peckham, an able New York attorney and the last of Cleveland's four appointees to the Supreme Court, was commissioned in 1896, following eight years of service on the New York Court of Appeals.

In spite of his refusal to accept public office, Coudert was the recipient of many honors and positions of trust. In 1877 he was a delegate of the New York Chamber of Commerce to the Antwerp Conference, called to revise the international rules of trade and general average. In 1880 he was a member of the International Conference held at Berne for codification of the law of nations. He joined Edward J. Phelps and James C. Carter in July 1893 to appear as counsel for the United States before a jury of arbitration in Paris to argue the American claim in the Anglo-American dispute over fur seal hunting rights in the Bering Sea. An international tribunal of judges from Italy, France, and Sweden ruled against the American claim to a closed sea, and sealing was prohibited during specified periods each year around the Pribilof Islands. In January 1896 President Cleveland again appointed Coudert to serve on the High Commission to investigate and report on the boundary dispute between Venezuela and British Guyana.

Coudert, a warm friend of educational institutions, served as trustee for Seton Hall College in Newark and for Barnard College and Columbia College in New York. Until a year before he died he was president of the Columbia College Alumni Association. He served ten years as president of the French Benevolent Society, and he became the first president of the American Catholic Historical Society, an office he held for several terms.

Not surprisingly he was the recipient of many honors from foreign governments, including the medal of the French Legion of Honor during the presidency of Marshal McMahon. He was made an officer of the Crown of Italy for services rendered to the Italian diplomatic mission in Washington. The honors of an officer of the Order of Bolivar were conferred on him by the government of Venezuela in recognition of the address he delivered at the dedication of the statue of Simon Bolívar in New York's Central Park.

Coudert died at his residence in New York City.

• Information about Coudert is sparse. He left no body of personal papers. Some material on him can be found in the papers left by his son to the Special Collections Department of the Columbia University Library. Especially useful is "The Reminiscences of Frederic Coudert," based on the interviews his son gave Allan Nevins and Owen Bombard in 1949–1950. See his *Addresses: Historical-Political-Sociological* (1905), with an introductory note by Paul Fuller, and the memorial by Judge Edward Patterson in the *Report* of the Association of the Bar of the City of New York (1905). Fuller's tribute to Coudert in U.S. Catholic Historical Society, *Historical Records and Studies* 3 (Dec. 1904). A brief but informative sketch of his early life is in David McAdam et al., eds., *The History of the Bench and Bar of New York*, vol. 2 (1897), pp. 102–4, which includes a full-length portrait. An obituary is in the *New York Times*, 21 Dec. 1903.

MARIAN C. MCKENNA

COUDERT, Frederic René, II (11 Feb. 1871–1 Apr. 1955), international lawyer, was born in New York City, the son of Elizabeth McCredy and Frederic René Coudert, founder of the New York law firm Coudert Brothers, established in 1853. He graduated from Columbia College in 1890 and from Columbia School of Law in 1891, gaining admission to the New York bar a year later. While still a student of law in 1892, Coudert accompanied his father to Paris, where the elder Coudert served with James C. Carter as counsel for the United States in the Bering Sea fur seal arbitration with Great Britain. This was young Coudert's first introduction to an important controversy in international law. Thousands of pages of evidence were submitted in the case, and arguments lasted several months before settlement. Later, as a respected specialist in the field, Coudert wrote, "If I had ever cherished any illusions about the exceptional nature of international law, they would have been shattered then and there."

In 1894 Coudert earned a Ph.D. in political science at Columbia University. He joined the family law firm in 1895 and was admitted to practice before the U.S. Supreme Court in 1897. That same year he married Alice Tracy Wilmerding. They had four sons, three of whom joined the family firm and one of whom was elected from New York to the House of Representatives. Coudert's law work was interrupted in the spring of 1898 by active service until the end of the Spanish-American War as a volunteer first lieutenant. He commanded Troop A, New York Cavalry, under General Nelson A. Miles when his captain became ill.

During more than a half-century of practice, in which he argued many cases before the U.S. Supreme Court and other tribunals, Coudert established himself as one of the foremost authorities on alien property rights, consular privileges under treaties, and admiralty law, including the international law of prize. At the outset he maintained a general and miscellaneous law practice, justifying his proposition that the trained lawyer's reasoning and knowledge of precedents should be drawn from almost every department of law. Successful litigation, he believed, required the drudgery incident to the making of any kind of lawyer. International law cases could best be dealt with by lawyers with general experience and a wide practice; overspecialization was a dangerous thing, often preventing a catholicity of view and a breadth of concept.

Coudert argued his first case before the Supreme Court at the age of twenty-six, defending a U.S. citizen who was arrested in New York and who was also the consul general of Turkey in Boston, where he was wanted on a charge of embezzlement. The issue in the case, *Iasagi v. Van De Carr* (1897), became moot when Consul Joseph A. Iasagi was removed from office by the government of Turkey. In this first appearance before the Court, Coudert admitted he was "somewhat nervous" but said he was reassured by the fixed attention of the justices.

One of Coudert's cases involving the duties, privileges, and powers of civil officers and military commanders in accordance with international law established an important precedent in American law. The case involved a Venezuelan, José Manuel Hernandez, arrested in New York and charged by an American businessman, George F. Underhill, for his actions during a successful revolution in the Venezuelan state of Bolivar. Underhill was detained during the fighting to continue operating the country's waterworks, was denied a passport to leave the country, and was subjected to alleged assaults and affronts by soldiers. When the case went before the Supreme Court with Coudert representing General Hernandez, the Court in *Underhill v. Hernandez* (1897) ruled that the general's acts were those of a de facto government (the 'acts of state' doctrine) and, as such, were not properly the subject of adjudication in the courts of another country.

The most celebrated cases Coudert argued before the Supreme Court were the *Insular* cases (1900–1904), which clarified the statuses of the Philippines and Puerto Rico. In *DeLima v. Bidwell* (1901) he represented the firm of DeLima & Co. and won a judgment for recovery of duties exacted and paid at the port of New York on sugar imported from San Juan in the fall of 1899, subsequent to the cession of the island to the United States. Puerto Rico no longer came under the terms of the Dingley tariff.

Between 1913 and 1914 Coudert was special assistant to the U.S. attorney general. Over the next five years he was legal adviser to the British ambassador, involved with legal problems arising from the British naval blockade during the period of American neutrality (1914–1917) in World War I. He collaborated closely with the U.S. State Department to settle Anglo-American conflicts over ship seizures and the definition of contraband. It was his intention to be a buffer between the State Department and the Allied governments and to absorb as much of the shock as possible. In this he had limited success.

A 1917 case that became a cause célèbre during World War I involved the capture by the German cruiser *Moewe* of the British ship *Appam*, which was taken to a Virginia port as a prize of war to lay up for an indefinite period out of fear of recapture. The British ship's owners, represented by Coudert, went to court to recover and won a decree. On appeal to the Supreme Court, almost every known precedent from the earliest history of international law was adduced to support arguments. The Germans claimed the right to use American ports under an old treaty of 1799. Coudert argued that the German captor's failure to bring the proceedings with due diligence into a competent prize court for adjudication was in itself grounds for release of the vessel to its original owners. In a unanimous ruling, the Court held that the German vessel had violated American neutrality laws and ordered the *Appam* returned to its owners.

In 1925 Coudert won important cases for the British government and for Chinese merchants. He was a frequent contributor to legal journals and much sought after as a speaker. At the outbreak of both world wars he grew impatient with American neutrality policies,

actively identifying himself with pro-British interests. After the first war he championed the League of Nations, and in response to its failure, he became one of the original members of the Committee to Defend America by Aiding the Allies in 1940. From 1942 to 1946 he was president of the American Society of International Law and a member of the Institut de Droit International.

Coudert Brothers had opened an office in Paris in 1879, and the firm was frequently retained in cases involving questions of French and American private international law. France decorated Coudert as commander of the Legion of Honor, he was an officer of the Crown of Belgium, and he was an honorary member of the International Olympic Committee. For forty years he served as a trustee of Columbia University, resigning from the board the year before his death. In private life he was a fencer and played golf. He made his permanent home at Cove Neck, Oyster Bay. Coudert died at his New York City residence. The publication of his papers a year earlier was dedicated "To My Three Sons—Frederic R., Jr., Ferdinand and Alexis, the Present Coudert Brothers."

Coudert ably enlarged the foundations of the family firm established in 1853; in the late twentieth century it had offices in more than a dozen countries and a reputation as one of the world's leading specialists in international law. Coudert's strengths were in admiralty law and arbitration and as an adviser on the legal aspects of foreign policy. He took a strong personal interest as a result of his war experiences in the Spanish islands acquired by the United States after 1898–1900. His most notable contribution was in the landmark *Insular* cases that, among other things, clarified the status of Puerto Rico. His interest and influence on international law and foreign policy spanned more than five decades.

• A collection of Coudert's papers, addresses, and correspondence is in the Special Collections Division of the Columbia University Library and includes "The Reminiscences of Frederic René Coudert," based on interviews with Allan Nevins and Owen Bombard in 1949–1950. This valuable autobiographical source has been reproduced on microfilm as *Reminiscences* (1972). Insight into the literary and philosophical interests of Coudert, with speeches and occasional papers concerning his legal work, is in his collection *A Half Century of International Problems: A Lawyer's View* (1954), with an introduction by Philip C. Jessup. The range of subjects that interested him is illustrated in his earlier volume, *Certainty and Justice* (1913), which includes his views on the American legal system. A brief autobiographical chapter is in Francis L. Wellman et al., *Success in Court* (1941). An obituary is in the *New York Times*, 2 Apr. 1955.

MARIAN C. MCKENNA

COUES, Elliott (9 Sept. 1842–25 Dec. 1899), naturalist and historian, was born in Portsmouth, New Hampshire, the son of Samuel Elliott Coues and Charlotte Haven Ladd. His father, a prominent peace advocate, received a position in the U.S. Patent Office and moved the family to Washington, D.C., in 1854. There, under the tutelage of Spencer Fullerton

Baird, assistant secretary of the Smithsonian Institution, young Coues developed into an accomplished student of natural history. His first major field experience was as a member of an expedition to Labrador in 1860. While a teenager he began publishing papers on ornithology in leading scientific journals. He attended Washington Seminary (Gonzaga College); earned bachelor's (1861) and master's degrees (1862) and a Ph.D. (1869) at Columbian College (now George Washington University); and graduated in 1863 with an M.D. from the National Medical College, the medical department at Columbian College.

Commissioned an assistant surgeon in the army in 1864, Coues was sent to Fort Whipple, Arizona, where he served as post surgeon. Here and elsewhere in the Southwest Coues did much collecting and writing on birds, mammals, and reptiles; he described, as well, many species previously unknown to science. He returned to the East at the close of the war and, choosing to stay in the army, served in a succession of southern posts. The appearance of the first edition of his *Key to North American Birds* in 1872 assured him a prominent place among the nation's naturalists. During 1873–1876 he served as surgeon and naturalist to the Northern Boundary Commission, in which capacity he did much to advance knowledge of the biota of Dakota and Montana territories.

In 1876 he became secretary and naturalist of Ferdinand V. Hayden's U.S. Geological and Geographical Survey of the Territories. This proved to be the most fulfilling period of his career. One of his first duties was to conduct a reconnaissance in Wyoming and Colorado. The survey published his *Birds of the Northwest* (1874), *Birds of the Colorado Valley* (1878, containing the first of four installments of his monumental bibliography of ornithology), *Fur-bearing Animals* (1877), *Monographs of North American Rodentia* (1877, with Joel A. Allen), and several monographs in the Survey's *Bulletin*, of which he was editor. The army ended its generous treatment of Coues in 1880, sending him to Arizona for routine medical duties. He angrily resigned his commission the following year.

He then found employment as professor of anatomy at his alma mater, the National Medical College (1881–1887). In 1884 he traveled in Britain and Europe, where many leading scientists honored him. Coues shocked many of his scientific colleagues by embracing Theosophy and spiritualism, an interest that began about this time. Although he had an acrimonious falling out with the founder of Theosophy, Helena Blavatsky, he retained a lively interest in psychic research for the remainder of his life. He also championed equality for women.

Coues's professional energy found still other outlets. He served as natural history editor of the *Century Dictionary* and supplied entries for the American supplement to the *Encyclopaedia Britannica*. Coues also continued to publish a multitude of articles, notes, and reviews in scientific and popular periodicals. All told, he produced over 800 titles.

Coues was a member of the Nuttall Ornithological Club and was one of the founders of the American Ornithologists' Union. He served as an associate editor of the journals of both organizations and as the AOU's vice president (1883–1890) and president (1892–1895). Coues also served on the AOU Council in 1890–1892 and 1895–1896.

In his last decade he plunged into the editing of western exploration and travel accounts, beginning with the Lewis and Clark journals. Later came his editions of the journals of Zebulon Montgomery Pike, Alexander Henry, Charles Larpenteur, and Francisco Garcés. All contained voluminous annotation displaying his considerable knowledge of the West. In the midst of these labors he learned that he was dying of cancer. He died at Johns Hopkins Hospital in Baltimore after an unsuccessful operation.

Coues was capable of charm and kindness, and he helped nurture the careers of several younger naturalists, notably that of Louis Agassiz Fuertes. He could also be an unrelenting foe. Among his more heated battles was that with Thomas Mayo Brewer over the introduction of the English sparrow into North America, which Coues opposed. Neither friend nor foe denied his intellectual powers.

Thrice-married, Coues also had liaisons with several other women. His first marriage (1864), to Sarah A. Richardson, was annulled after six months. With his second wife, Jane "Jeannie" A. McKinney (1867), he had five children. They divorced in 1886, and in the following year he married a wealthy widow, Mary Emily Bates, who survived him.

• Some of the more important Coues papers are to be found in the Records of the Secretary's Office, Smithsonian Archives, and (for his historical projects) in the Coues-F. P. Harper correspondence, Yale University Library. The only book-length study of his life is Paul Russell Cutright and Michael J. Brodhead, *Elliott Coues: Naturalist and Frontier Historian* (1981). Convenient shorter accounts include J. A. Allen, "Biographical Memoir of Elliott Coues, 1842–1899," *Biographical Memoirs, National Academy of Sciences* 6 (June 1909): 397–446; D. G. Elliot, "In Memoriam: Elliott Coues," *Auk* 18 (Jan. 1901): 1–11; and Edgar E. Hume, *Ornithologists of the U.S. Army Medical Corps* (1942), pp. 52–89.

MICHAEL J. BRODHEAD

COUGHLIN, Charles Edward (25 Oct. 1891–27 Oct. 1979), Catholic priest, radio personality, and political insurgent, was born in Hamilton, Ontario, the son of Thomas Coughlin and Amelia Mahoney, devout Catholics of Irish descent. Thomas Coughlin was the sexton of the Catholic cathedral in Hamilton; Amelia attended mass daily and dreamed of seeing her only child enter the priesthood. Throughout his youth Charles was surrounded by the institutions of the church. His family lived on the cathedral grounds, and he attended local parish schools. At age twelve he entered St. Michael's, a secondary school and college run by the Basilian order and intended to prepare young boys to enter the clergy. Coughlin remained at St. Michael's through college and in 1911 entered St.

Basil's Seminary to begin formal training for the priesthood. He was ordained in 1916, at the age of twenty-three. After teaching at Basilian schools in Canada for seven years, Coughlin left the order in 1923 and moved to Michigan to become a parish priest. Three years later he was assigned to a new parish in the Detroit suburb of Royal Oak, where he spent the rest of his life. He named his church the Shrine of the Little Flower, for the recently canonized Ste. Thérèse.

Coughlin's early months in Royal Oak were difficult ones. The new church, located in a community where there were still few Catholics, was struggling financially and was being harassed by the local Ku Klux Klan. In October 1926 Coughlin asked the owner of a local radio station (a fellow Irish Catholic) for time to air his Sunday sermons. He hoped that they would attract attention (and money) to his parish. His broadcasts were immediately successful and soon became a weekly fixture on the station, whose strong signal allowed Coughlin to be heard well beyond Detroit. By 1930 his popularity had grown to the point that CBS radio began to broadcast "The Golden Hour of the Little Flower" over its national network each week. According to some estimates, Coughlin now reached an audience of over forty million people every Sunday. Mail flowed into Royal Oak in astonishing amounts, much of it containing small contributions. The money defrayed the cost of Coughlin's broadcasts and his expanding public activities. It also helped finance construction of a lavish new church building of striking Art Deco design and comfortable homes in Royal Oak for Coughlin and his parents. There is no evidence that Coughlin was financially corrupt, however, in spite of repeated efforts by his critics to prove otherwise.

Coughlin's early sermons were largely nonpolitical and uncontroversial appeals for religious tolerance, moral lessons for children, or meditations on the Bible. His initial success was a result less of the content of his broadcasts than of his rich, magnetic voice (with its affected Irish brogue) and his impressive dramatic ability to simulate a wide range of emotions within a single speech. But as the Great Depression began to reach out into the communities of ethnic auto workers from which Coughlin drew his parishioners, he began speaking increasingly about economics and politics. Although he initially warned of the dangers of communism, he soon turned his attention to what he claimed was the greater danger: the "predatory capitalists" whose greed and corruption had created and sustained the economic crisis. He was particularly critical of the influence of powerful bankers and financiers, whom he blamed for the "tyranny of the gold standard." Like many American dissidents before him, he sought a solution to the nation's problems in a reform of the currency—although his prescription for that reform often changed. At various times he advocated issuing greenbacks, remonetizing silver, and nationalizing the banking system.

Coughlin's political beliefs were not, however, a product of the native populist traditions that influenced other American inflationists. He was, rather, drawing primarily from social ideas that had been growing within the Catholic church ever since Pope Leo XIII had issued his famous 1893 encyclical *Rerum Novarum*, an appeal for balancing the rights of capital against the needs of the community. Coughlin's rhetoric was filled with references to the encyclical and to the idea that, while ownership of property might be absolute, the ways in which owners used their property must be adjusted to the needs of the community. Control of the money supply, he insisted, was not a "property right," but a legitimate public function. Allowing that control to fall into the hands of a few "Wall Street financiers" and "international bankers" was, he argued, a betrayal of democracy. Whatever the sources of Coughlin's own beliefs, however, he succeeded in tapping deep popular resentments of the modern industrial order, resentments inflamed by, but not new to, the Great Depression. His popularity demonstrated the survival of a populist challenge to corporate capitalism, but the flimsiness of his proposals (and what eventually turned out to be the thinness of his popular support) also illustrated the limits of that challenge.

By the early 1930s, Coughlin had accumulated a remarkable amount of political and financial autonomy for a Catholic priest. That he was able to do so was in large part because he had the warm support of his bishop, Michael Gallagher, who was himself a veteran of Catholic social activism in Europe and who apparently saw Coughlin as a spokesman for many of his own beliefs. Coughlin called Gallagher "the most beloved man in his life" next to his own father.

In 1932 Coughlin met and began a personal and political relationship with Franklin D. Roosevelt, for whom he apparently developed an immediate admiration. He did not formally endorse Roosevelt's presidential candidacy, but he spoke about him enthusiastically in his weekly broadcasts. Once Roosevelt was in the White House, Coughlin publicly lavished praise on the New Deal and privately maneuvered for access to the president and his staff. He evidently expected to play a major role in the administration—an expectation the president and his advisers did not share. Disenchantment was inevitable. By mid-1934, the White House staff was beginning to distance itself from Coughlin. They believed the priest was acting presumptuously in claiming to speak for the president, and they were becoming uncomfortable with Coughlin's increasingly drastic financial proposals, which diverged from the administration's policies more than Coughlin was willing to admit. Coughlin, for his part, now sprinkled occasional attacks on the administration among his usual florid tributes. He continued to vacillate in his attitude toward the president for much of the next two years, at times denouncing Roosevelt for his failure to "drive the money changers from the temple," at other times insisting that the American people still faced a choice between "Roosevelt or ruin." In 1935 he created his own national organization, the National Union for Social Justice (NUSJ), whose purpose was to mobilize popular support for Coughlin's program. The NUSJ had no formal membership and no organized activities, so it is difficult to gauge the size or power of the movement. Coughlin did not at first respond to speculation that he intended it to be the genesis of a new political party.

Whatever the weaknesses of his organization or the vagueness of his political intentions, however, Coughlin clearly had substantial popular influence. When Roosevelt sent a treaty to the Senate early in 1935 that called for American membership in the World Court, Coughlin summoned his supporters to oppose it—arguing that it was the first step toward "handing over our national sovereignty" to Europe and the "international bankers." He generated so many telegrams and letters to members of the Senate that, when the treaty unexpectedly failed, many believed Coughlin's hostility had made the difference. In the meantime, he extended his influence in other areas. He allied himself with several labor organizations in the Detroit area and began a cautious flirtation with other dissident leaders, such as Huey Long (the Louisiana senator who had launched a dissident political movement of his own, the Share-Our-Wealth Society) and Francis Townsend (a California physician who had launched a national movement to demand government pensions for the elderly).

By the end of 1935 Coughlin was clearly losing patience with the Roosevelt administration—with what he considered the slow pace of its reform efforts and with what he recognized was his own waning influence within it. He began speaking cryptically about the need for a new political party and hinting that he would play some role in creating it. Finally, in December 1935, he told his radio audience, "I humbly stand before the American people to admit that I have been in error." The principles of the New Deal, he confessed, were "unalterably opposed" to those of the National Union for Social Justice.

In May 1936 he announced the formation of the new Union party, and a month later he designated William Lemke, a little-known second-term congressman from North Dakota, as the party's presidential nominee. At about the same time, he reached an agreement with Francis Townsend and Gerald L. K. Smith (an unstable associate of Huey Long who, after Long's assassination in September 1935, implausibly claimed to have assumed leadership of the Share-Our-Wealth movement). Townsend and Smith would support the new party as well. Squabbling among the leaders began almost immediately and plagued the party throughout the election year. Coughlin had promised that if he could not deliver at least nine million votes to the Union party he would abandon his broadcasting career. In the end, Lemke's drab candidacy attracted fewer than 900,000 votes. A few days after the election, Coughlin disbanded both the party and the NUSJ and tearfully announced his withdrawal from public life.

His retirement was a brief one. Early in 1937 he returned to the airwaves and began to deliver increasingly strident attacks on Roosevelt and the New Deal for "dictatorial" and "communistic" policies. Although he retained an audience, it was neither as large nor as intense as the following he had attracted before 1936, and it seemed to dwindle by the month. Coughlin's position grew weaker, too, as a result of the death of Bishop Gallagher in 1937 and the Vatican's appointment of the much less sympathetic Edward Mooney to replace him.

Desperate to revive his flagging fortunes, he turned in new and unsavory directions. Early in 1938 an overt anti-Semitism began to appear, first in Coughlin's weekly newspaper, *Social Justice*, and gradually in his radio sermons as well. Some critics had detected hints of anti-Semitism in Coughlin's public statements in earlier years, and there is evidence that Coughlin had long harbored private prejudices toward Jews. But the strident, public anti-Semitism of his statements in 1938 and after was new and disturbing even to many of his erstwhile admirers. Coughlin soon drove away most of his traditional supporters. He retained a significant, but much-diminished constituency in which bigots and crackpots were disproportionately represented. In 1939 Coughlin urged his supporters to organize again, this time into a vaguely military organization that he ultimately named the Christian Front. The front was never large, and it remained confined mainly to a few northeastern cities with large Catholic populations. But it became notorious, nevertheless, for the thuggishness of its members, who on occasion smashed windows in stores owned by Jewish merchants and engaged in Nazi-like street brawls with Jews.

When war began in Europe, Coughlin became a strident advocate of American isolationism, accompanying his stance with increasingly admiring statements about Hitler and the Nazi party. Radio station owners became reluctant to broadcast his sermons, and by early 1940 he found himself almost completely cut off from the airwaves. He continued to publish *Social Justice* for another two years, but after Pearl Harbor the government moved to have it banned from the mails as seditious. Finally, the attorney general warned Archbishop Mooney that Coughlin might face formal federal charges of sedition if his public activities continued, and in May 1942 Coughlin announced that he had "bowed to orders from Church superiors" and would cease all political activities. He returned to his duties as pastor of the Shrine of the Little Flower and remained there until his retirement in 1966. He spent his remaining years in obscurity in a comfortable home in a nearby Detroit suburb, where he died.

• There are no significant collections of Coughlin papers, although the University of Michigan and the Catholic Archdiocese of Detroit have possession of some documents pertaining to him. The Radio League of the Little Flower published a series of volumes of Coughlin's sermons in the early 1930s; beginning in 1936, the sermons were published in Coughlin's newspaper, *Social Justice*. Biographies include Charles J. Tull, *Father Coughlin and the New Deal* (1965), and Sheldon Marcus, *Father Coughlin* (1973); neither is definitive. Alan

Brinkley, *Voices of Protest* (1982), chronicles the rise of Coughlin's political career, and David Bennett, *Demagogues in the Depression* (1969), charts its decline.

ALAN BRINKLEY

COULDOCK, Charles Walter (26 Apr. 1815–27 Nov. 1898), actor, was born in London, England, the son of a composer who died when Charles was four. The names of his parents are unknown. He lived with his paternal grandmother for five years and then with his mother and stepfather, into whose carpentry shop young Charles was apprenticed. At age thirteen he obtained a position in a silk warehouse, where he remained for nearly nine years. He decided on a theatrical career after seeing William Charles Macready play in Byron's *Werner* at Drury Lane, but his desire to study acting was frustrated by his grandmother. After her death on his twenty-first birthday, however, he was free to indulge his passion and in 1837 made his London stage debut as Othello at Sadler's Wells Theatre. In search of further training, Couldock left London for the provinces and was soon acting with an itinerant company in Surrey and with stock companies from Edinburgh to Southampton. The English provinces provided an intensive training ground for young actors, who had to learn dozens of roles, often memorizing new parts overnight. Paltry salaries, hazardous theaters, barely tolerable housing, and the demands of travel convinced Couldock in 1845 to opt for a less transient life. For four years he took leading roles at the Theatre Royal, Birmingham, and the Theatre Royal, Liverpool, acting with all the famous actors and actresses of his day, including his theatrical idol, Macready.

He also met American actress Charlotte Cushman, who in the summer of 1849 persuaded him to join her company in New York. Cushman's return to the United States with Couldock in tow was a triumphal one, despite her worries that the American public had irrevocably linked her name with the Astor Place riot of the previous May. This disastrous event, which left a score of people dead in the streets of New York City, had been caused by a venomous professional rivalry between Macready and American actor Edwin Forrest. Cushman had been professionally associated with Macready; moreover, Forrest had harshly criticized Cushman as "anti-American" for engaging the foreign-born Couldock, who refused to enter the fray. Couldock made his American debut on 8 October 1849 in the title role of *The Stranger*, opposite Cushman's Mrs. Haller, at the Broadway Theatre in New York. The production was an immediate success. Later in the 1849–1850 season, Couldock played Mercutio to the Romeo of Cushman, who often used her masculine appearance and powerful voice to advantage in male parts. A brief tour with Cushman's company followed. Between 1850 and 1855 Couldock was leading man in the stock company of Philadelphia's Walnut Street Theatre, appearing in Shakespeare one night (*Othello, Macbeth, King Lear, Hamlet, Henry VIII, As You Like It,* and *Much Ado about Nothing*) and romantic melodramas the next (*The Wife, The Hunchback, The Honeymoon,* and *Louis XI*).

His was the old-school, sentimental style of acting that required great emotive power and a command of the sweeping gesture. He was not at his best in heroic tragedy, but in maudlin domestic pieces he gave convincing life to a gallery of uniquely American stage characters. In 1852 Couldock undertook the role of Luke Fielding, a farmer driven mad by what he believes is his daughter's betrayal of the family's good name, in *The Willow Copse*, a creaky five-act melodrama that was one of Dion Boucicault's early adaptations. Couldock's engagement at the Walnut Street Theatre was followed by an extensive tour of this play, in which his daughter Eliza also appeared. (He had at least two daughters and one son, although the name of his wife and the date of their marriage are unknown.) His visits to towns across the United States brought him to the attention of a broad range of audiences and assured his reputation. In 1858 he became a member of Laura Keene's company, where he originated the role of Abel Murcott in the first American production of Tom Taylor's *Our American Cousin*, one of the biggest comedy hits of its time. (Couldock was not a member of Keene's company on the night of 14 April 1865, when Abraham Lincoln was assassinated at Ford's Theatre during a performance of this play.)

Following a season in New Orleans, he resumed touring. Between American engagements, Couldock found time to visit Canada, where his portrayals of virtuous rustic characters made him an audience favorite. He paid regular visits to Toronto between 1851 and 1858 and returned several times between 1874 and 1879 to appear in the Grand Opera House stock company managed by his daughter Charlotte. In 1880 he created his most famous role, Dunstan Kirke, an iron-willed miller who disowns his daughter when she marries against his wishes, in Steele MacKaye's *Hazel Kirke*. Billed by its author as a domestic comedy-drama in four acts, this production opened at the new Madison Square Theatre and enjoyed the longest run, up to that time, of any nonmusical play on an American stage: 486 performances. In 1883 Couldock embarked on a tour with *Hazel Kirke* under the management of Daniel Frohman. In 1885 the seventy-year-old Couldock reprised his role of Luke Fielding at the Madison Square Theatre. Tastes had changed drastically in the thirty-three years since he had first appeared in the part, however, and this revival of *The Willow Copse* met with a hostile critical reception. The play's contrived plot and Couldock's expansive acting style were considered hopelessly outdated relics of a past theatrical age, with little relevance to modern life as it was lived in the last decades of the nineteenth century. Audiences, however, received him warmly, and the production lasted four weeks largely because of the personal esteem in which he was held by the American public. Despite his advanced age, Couldock managed a year-long tour of this production after it closed in New York.

A leading man who had become a widely admired character actor, Couldock successfully interpreted a wide range of roles in his distinguished career. His heavy build and curly hair gave him an ursine aspect that he used to good effect when playing sincere or comic American rustics. His popularity among American theater audiences was no surprise to his peers, who honored his energetic efforts on behalf of their profession with several benefit performances, including one in 1887 that celebrated his fiftieth year on the stage and another in 1895 that netted the actor more than $6,000. He was loved for his convivial manner and gentle good humor, which had, over the years, tamed a youthful hot temper. He counted many leading actors, including Joseph Jefferson and Edwin Booth, among his closest friends. Critic William Winter, who particularly admired Couldock's Louis XI, called him a "powerful and versatile" actor and one of the "shining names" that "brightly spangled" the American theater in the last half of the nineteenth century. Couldock retired in 1896 after nearly five decades as one of the country's most beloved stars. He died at his home in New York City, and, as fellow actor Nat C. Goodwin observed, a "sterling old player" passed from the scene.

• Although recognized as an important theatrical figure both in his own time and in ours, Couldock has not received sustained scholarly attention from historians of the American theater. He is briefly mentioned in Garff B. Wilson's *A History of American Acting* (1966), where it is observed that Couldock was a leading example of a classical tradition that flourished for several decades in the middle of the nineteenth century. His career can be pieced together from newspaper reviews of his performances and from other contemporary accounts, including the memoirs of the more famous actors with whom he worked. Especially relevant material can be found in T. Allston Brown, *History of the American Stage* (1870), and Laurence Hutton, *Plays and Players* (1875). Detailed obituaries recounting Couldock's career are in the *New York Clipper*, 3 Dec. 1898, and the *New York Times*, 28 Nov. 1898.

KRISTAN A. TETENS

COULON, Johnny (12 Feb. 1889–29 Oct. 1973), prizefighter, was born in Toronto, Ontario, Canada, the son of Emile "Pop" Coulon. (His mother's name is unknown.) His family immigrated to Chicago, Illinois, when Coulon was three years old, and he lived there for the remainder of his life. He began amateur boxing in 1904 and won all 12 of his bouts. The following year he won his first professional bout with a sixth-round knockout of "Young Bennie" in Chicago. With his father as manager, he quickly rose to prominence by winning his first 26 professional fights. During that time, while in New York City for a bout, he saved a boy from drowning in the East River and was awarded the Congressional Gold Medal.

In 1906 Jimmy Walsh, the world bantamweight champion, moved up in class to challenge Abe Attell for the world featherweight title and consequently abandoned his bantamweight title. During the next few years several boxers claimed the vacant title. One

such fighter, Kid Murphy (Peter Frascella), was matched with Coulon in March 1907 in Milwaukee, Wisconsin; Murphy won the fight in a 10-round decision, allowing him to claim the bantamweight title. On 8 January 1908 Coulon met Murphy in a rematch in Peoria, Illinois. Although he weighed only 105 pounds, Coulon won in another 10-round decision, claiming the 116-pound American bantamweight title. He also claimed the 105-pound title and was recognized by Tom S. Andrews, editor of the leading boxing record book at that time, as the first paperweight champion of America—a weight class that did not survive the next generation. Coulon established his supremacy over Murphy by defeating him twice more in 1908 and 1909.

In 1910 Coulon traveled to New Orleans and won three bouts in January and February. He then met Englishman Jim Kendrick in a bout advertised for the world bantamweight championship despite the fact that two weeks earlier Frankie Conley defeated Monte Attell in a fight billed for the same boxing title. Coulon stopped Kendrick in the 19th round and claimed the title along with Conley. A year later the two met in a 20-round bout in New Orleans; Coulon solidified his title claim by defeating Conley by decision. He again defeated Conley by a 20-round decision on 3 February 1912 in Vernon, California. Two weeks later, back in New Orleans, Coulon successfully defended his title by defeating Frankie Burns in 20 rounds.

On 9 June 1914 Coulon was knocked out in the third round by Kid Williams (Johnny Gutenko) in a title fight in Vernon. After a 22-month layoff, he resumed boxing in 1916 and continued through 1917 when he was stopped by the then champion, Pete "Kid" Herman, in three rounds in a nontitle bout. Coulon then joined the U.S. Army as a boxing instructor and remained in the service until 1919. He attempted a brief comeback in 1920 in Paris, but, after winning one bout, he was knocked out in six rounds by European bantamweight champion Charles Ledoux on 16 March, terminating his boxing career.

Coulon invested his ring earnings wisely in real estate and other ventures, his most successful being a gymnasium that he opened in 1923 on Chicago's South Side. The many well-known boxers who worked out in his gym over the next 50 years included Joe Louis, Ray Robinson, Sonny Liston, Max Baer, Tony Zale, and Barney Ross. Along with his wife Marie Maloney, a female boxing matchmaker who had set up more than 10,000 matches, he promoted amateur boxing shows in the Chicago area. (He and Maloney had married in 1921; they had no children.)

Coulon also developed a specialty act in which he challenged people to lift him off his feet. As he was only five feet tall and weighed no more than 120 pounds it seemed to be a simple task. Yet by placing his finger on a nerve on his opponent's neck he could prevent being lifted by all who accepted the challenge. Having learned this trick as a schoolboy, he gained more money, fame, and publicity from this stunt than he had as a boxer. (He estimated that he made more than $150,000 in his lifetime performing his act.) During the 1920s he toured Europe under the management of promoter Leon See, who was also the manager of heavyweight champion Primo Carnera; Coulon appeared in 11 nations and gave a command performance for King Albert and Queen Elizabeth of Belgium. During the 1950s he made several television appearances and went on a world tour with the Harlem Globetrotters basketball team in which he performed his specialty during the half-time intermission. Coulon claimed he was lifted only once—on a train in Switzerland when he let some young women try to lift him and later found that they had lifted his wallet instead.

From 1961 to 1973 Coulon managed boxer Eddie Perkins's career and led him to the world junior welterweight title. Perkins held the title from 1962 until 1965 and won championship bouts in Italy, the Philippines, Japan, and Jamaica before losing on an extremely poor decision to Venezuelan Carlos Hernandez in Caracas. The Venezuelan newspapers strongly criticized the decision. One column in the newspaper *El Universal* stated, "The patriotic judges covered themselves with the flag and the national anthem in order to strip the world title from Perkins in an unjust decision." Although shorn of his title, Perkins remained one of the top contenders for the next decade thanks to Coulon's efforts as manager.

Coulon died in a nursing home in Chicago. In 97 total professional fights his record was 56 victories (24 by knockout), only four losses, four draws, one no-contest, and 32 no-decisions. He was elected to *The Ring* Boxing Hall of Fame in 1965.

• The best source for Coulon's complete ring record is Herbert G. Goldman, *The Ring 1985 Record Book and Boxing Encyclopedia* (1985); the 1986–1987 version erroneously omitted Coulon's record. A magazine article that discusses Coulon's relationship with Eddie Perkins is Perkins (as told to Lester Bromberg), "Coulon Made Me What I Am Today," *The Ring*, Jan. 1963, pp. 24–26, 45. His specialty act is discussed in Joe Woodman, "The Big Lift," *Boxing and Wrestling*, Sept. 1956, pp. 26–27, 74–75. His gymnasium, which he managed with his wife, is written about in Neil Milbert, "They Don't Make 'em Like Coulon's Anymore," *The Ring*, May 1972, pp. 26–27, 38; and in Charles Chamberlain, "The High Priest and Priestess of Boxing," *Boxing and Wrestling*, Dec. 1962, pp. 72–79. An obituary appears in Peter Heller, "Old-time Bantam King Coulon Dies," *The Ring*, Feb. 1974.

JOHN GRASSO

COULTER, Ellis Merton (20 July 1890–5 July 1981), professor and historian, was born in Catawba County, North Carolina, the son of John Ellis Coulter, a farmer and businessman, and Lucy Ann Propst. He grew up in Connally Spring, North Carolina, and attended the University of North Carolina (A.B., 1913), where he majored in history and published his first historical article, "Early Life and Regulations at the University of North Carolina," in *University of North Carolina Magazine* (n.s., 29, no. 4 [Feb. 1912]). After graduation he taught school in Glen Alpine, North Carolina, for one year and then enrolled at the University of Wisconsin,

where he worked with Professor Carl Russell Fish and earned an M.A. in 1915 and a Ph.D. in 1917. Coulter delivered his first professional paper at the 1916 meeting of the Mississippi Valley Historical Association. In 1917 he became professor of history and political science at Marietta College in Marietta, Ohio. Two years later he was appointed associate professor of history at the University of Georgia. He became full professor in 1923, regents professor in 1948, and professor emeritus in 1958. He served as department head from 1941 to 1958. He was also a visiting professor at thirteen other institutions, including the University of Texas, National University in Mexico City, and the Hebrew University of Jerusalem.

Coulter was a popular teacher because his engaging lectures brought history to life and because he taught subjects that were popular in the South. He usually had large classes, and students remembered him fondly throughout their lives. His most popular courses were antebellum South, Civil War, and Georgia history. He taught some ten thousand students during his career, a number of whom went on to graduate school and became faculty members in southern colleges and universities.

In his early years at the University of Georgia, Coulter was one of the few publishing scholars and set an example for other faculty in the history department and throughout the university. He helped to begin a doctoral program at the university and was a founder and long-time (1939–1958) board member of the University of Georgia Press. He also backed the founding of the *Georgia Review*, the university's literary periodical, and was an editorial board member from 1947 to 1963. His colleagues in the College of Arts and Sciences named him distinguished professor of the year in 1952. In 1980 he was the recipient of the Georgia Association of Historians Distinguished Service Award.

As a scholar, Coulter's main interest was in southern and Georgia history, and he wrote almost forty books and over a hundred articles, which were mainly based on research in primary sources, on these fields. In 1921 he published his first work in Georgia history, "The Nullification Movement in Georgia," in the *Georgia Historical Quarterly*. In the same year he became a member of the *Quarterly*'s board of editors. His most influential book, *A Short History of Georgia* (1933), which was reissued as *Georgia: A Short History* (1947; repr. 1960), sold over twenty thousand copies and was used as a textbook in courses in Georgia history for forty-four years. *College Life in the Old South* (1928; repr. 1983) was one of his most popular books and won wide readership. He was coeditor of *A History of the South* series and wrote two volumes in it: *The Confederate States of America* (1950) and *The South during the Reconstruction* (1947). He was a founder and the first president from 1929 to 1930 of the Southern Historical Association. As editor of the *Georgia Historical Quarterly* from 1934 to 1973, Coulter made it a leading state historical publication and was a frequent member of the Board of Curators of the Georgia Historical Society, the sponsor of the *Quarterly*.

He secured a great number of manuscripts, newspapers, and books on Georgia and southern history for the University of Georgia Library, thus adding to its research resources. At his death he left his considerable collections of material in these fields to the university library.

Coulter's history was strong on narrative and short on analysis, but it was always interestingly written and appealed to both scholars and laypeople. He believed that people and civilizations were formed from their past and viewed history with the attitude of a southerner of the early twentieth century. By the time of his death, some scholars felt that Coulter's methods and viewpoints were outdated and his writings contained too much detail, but others disagreed.

Coulter was unmarried and always said that his books were his children. At his death he had just finished a biography of Abraham Baldwin, Georgia's leader in the Constitutional Convention of 1787 and the founder of the University of Georgia. This book was published in 1987. Coulter enjoyed an active social life and was popular with faculty, townspeople, and members of the Georgia Historical Society. He traveled extensively in the United States and abroad, liked to hike in the Georgia and Carolina mountains, listened to classical music, and took photographs of the landscape and historical buildings, including every courthouse in Georgia.

He died in Athens, Georgia, and was buried in Connally Springs, North Carolina. By his teaching, writing, and editorial work he did more to encourage study and research in Georgia history than anyone else during his lifetime. He was truly "Mr. Georgia History."

• Coulter's papers are in the Hargrett Library of the University of Georgia in Athens. Useful sources on his life include Ellis Merton Coulter, *John Ellis Coulter, Small-Town Business Man of Tarheelia* (1962); Horace Montgomery, ed., *Georgians in Profile: Historical Essays in Honor of Ellis Merton Coulter* (1958); Kenneth Coleman, "Ellis Merton Coulter," in Georgia Association of Historians *Proceedings and Papers* (1981); a special section on Coulter in *Georgia Historical Quarterly* 58 (1974): 1–23; and Michael Vaughan Woodward, "The Publications of Ellis Merton Coulter to 1 July 1977," *Georgia Historical Quarterly* 61 (1977): 268–78. Obituaries are in the *Atlanta Constitution*, 6 July 1981, and the *Athens Banner-Herald*, 6, 7, and 12 July 1981.

KENNETH COLEMAN

COULTER, Ernest Kent (14 Nov. 1871–1 May 1952), reformer and lawyer, was born in Columbus, Ohio, the son of James Hervey Coulter and Emily J. Erwin. His parents' exact occupations are not known, although a biographical listing shows his father as Dr. Coulter. After attending local schools, Coulter graduated from Ohio State University in 1893. He worked briefly as tri-state editor for the *Pittsburgh Dispatch* and then completed a course of study at New York Law School in 1894. Returning to journalism, Coulter worked in the editorial department of the *New York*

Telegram, served as a correspondent for the *New York Herald* in Cuba and Puerto Rico during the Spanish-American War, and in 1900 became assistant city editor of the *New York Evening Sun*. Coulter returned to New York Law School a few years later, receiving the LL.B. degree in 1904.

During these years reformers in several U.S. cities were working to establish children's courts, so that young offenders could be kept separate from adult criminals. Coulter joined the effort in New York City, and in 1902, when the Court of Special Sessions established a separate section for juvenile cases, he became clerk of the court. Coulter was deeply moved by the children he encountered, and he became convinced that their problems were attributable to the degradation and neglect they experienced during their formative years. In 1904 he spoke to the Men's Club of a local Presbyterian church about a boy soon to be sent to a reformatory, where his character was likely to grow worse rather than better. There was only one way to save him, said Coulter. "That is to have some earnest, true man volunteer to be his big brother, to look after him, help him to do right" (Beiswinger, p. 9). When Coulter called for a volunteer, nearly every man in the room responded. This was not the first program in which middle-class men had reached out to youngsters in trouble, but Coulter appears to have been the first to use the term "big brother" in connection with such a project. He built an organization around the idea, launching the Big Brother movement.

Over the next several years the Big Brother movement spread across New York City, supported by the Young Men's Christian Association and a number of church groups. By 1909 the group leaders estimated that they had served 1,000 children. That year Coulter and his colleagues established Big Brothers as a charitable corporation "to organize and direct a body of men of good will whose purpose shall be to interest themselves individually in the welfare and improvement of children who have been arraigned before the Children's Court of the City of New York and similar courts throughout the United States" (Beiswinger, p. 11). Coulter was elected president of the new corporation, a headquarters was established, and branches were set up around the city. Soon the program also began to help disadvantaged boys who had not yet entered the court system.

Volunteers were required to see their Little Brothers at least twice a month and to report periodically on their progress. Because of the brutal poverty in which many of the children lived, some volunteers felt compelled to offer financial assistance, but Coulter stressed that their most important contribution was personal, not monetary. He advised, "Just be a brother and a companion to your boy. Invite him to your office and to your home, take him to the ball game, a concert, or a good, clean show. . . . Give the boy his individual chance to be honest and to grow up into a useful citizen" (Beiswinger, p. 11).

In addition to his work with Big Brothers, Coulter helped organize a clinic to study the behavior of delinquent children and helped found the Boy Scouts of America, on whose national council he served for many years. He also produced numerous lectures and magazine articles, reinforcing the idea that delinquency was the product of bad social conditions and that it could be prevented by steps like the creation of children's courts, the suppression of movies glamorizing crime, and the criminalization of narcotics. In the latter cause Coulter helped win passage in 1914 of the Harrison Act, which for the first time outlawed the purchase of certain drugs. Coulter summarized his views in *The Children in the Shadow* (1913), for which the renowned urban reformer Jacob Riis wrote the preface. He resigned from his clerk's position at Children's Court in 1912 and established a private law practice with Charles G. Bond, but he remained active in Big Brothers and undertook a nationwide lecture tour on its behalf in 1914. That same year he became general manager and assistant to the president of the New York Society for the Prevention of Cruelty to Children (NYSPCC).

During World War I Coulter went overseas with the American Expeditionary Force (AEF). Rising from major to colonel, he served as AEF historical officer, taking photographs and movies as well as writing. He was at the front during several battles, after which he moved to the historical section of the Office of the Quartermaster General. When the war ended Coulter returned to his NYSPCC position, where he remained until his retirement in 1936. Besides being an honorary member of England's National Society for Prevention of Cruelty to Children until his death, he served on the boards of the American Humane Association, the Campfire Girls, and the Federated Boys Clubs. Meanwhile, he continued to follow the activities of Big Brothers and helped to arrange its merger with the Big Sisters movement in 1917. The two organizations split in 1937 but were reunited some years after Coulter's death. In 1946 he married Ora May Malone; they had no children. He died in Santa Barbara, California.

American approaches to social welfare underwent dramatic changes during the course of Coulter's long life, but the movement that he launched as a young man continued to flourish long after he was gone. The idea that privileged Americans could make a difference by reaching out individually to help impoverished youngsters continued to resonate with later generations, and by the end of the twentieth century Big Brothers/Big Sisters of America had more than 500 agencies, covering all fifty states as well as the District of Columbia, Guam, and the Virgin Islands.

• Besides his book, Coulter wrote a number of articles, including "Psychiatric Bunk," *Outlook*, 7 Oct. 1931. He left no papers, but information about the activities of Big Brothers/ Big Sisters sheds important light on his career. See the organization files in Philadelphia as well as George L. Beiswinger, *One to One: The Story of the Big Brothers/Big Sisters Movement in America* (1985). Further information appears in "Little Father of the Big Brothers," *Hampton's Magazine*, July 1910, and William D. Murray, *History of the Boy Scouts of America* (1937). An obituary is in the *New York Times*, 3 May 1952.

SANDRA OPDYCKE

COULTER, John Merle (20 Nov. 1851–23 Dec. 1928), botanist, was born in Ningpo, China, the son of Moses Stanley Coulter and Caroline Crowe, Presbyterian missionaries. When Coulter was just two years of age, his father died in China. His mother, with her two young children, returned shortly thereafter to her father's home in Hanover, Indiana, where Coulter spent the remainder of his childhood. His interest in the natural sciences, and especially botany, were evident by his early boyhood as he and his younger brother Stanley explored geologic and botanical formations in nearby areas.

In 1870 Coulter received a bachelor's degree from Hanover College, having studied primarily classics, but also the natural sciences. He immediately became a teacher of Latin at the Presbyterian Academy at Logansport, Indiana. In 1872 he was given the post of assistant geologist in the two-year Hayden Survey of Yellowstone, but Coulter so impressed the leader, Ferdinand Vandeveer Hayden, with his botanical knowledge, that Hayden appointed him as the exploration's botanist. This vote of confidence changed Coulter's life; he decided at that point that he would pursue the natural sciences full time. While still in a classical course of study at Hanover (he received his master's degree in 1873), Coulter slowly began to make his life-transition to the study of natural sciences with a special interest in botany following his experience on the survey. With his brother Stanley, he founded a modest publication titled "Botanical Bulletin." In deference to the title of the "Bulletin of the Torrey Botanical Club," the Coulters changed the name of the second volume of their journal to the *Botanical Gazette*, which John Merle edited until 1926. On New Year's Day 1874 he married a childhood acquaintance, Georgiana M. Gaylord; they had six children, four of whom grew to adulthood.

In his subsequent career, Coulter was associated with several scientific and administrative positions at universities and other institutions. From 1874 to 1879 he was professor of natural sciences at Hanover. He was then professor of biology at Wabash College from 1879 to 1891. In 1882 he received a Ph.D. in systematic botany from the University of Indiana, while still teaching at Wabash. In 1891 he became president and professor of botany at the University of Indiana, largely on the advice of his close friend David Starr Jordan, who himself had become president of Stanford University. In 1893 he moved to Lake Forest University, where he again served as president until taking the position in 1896 of head of the new department of botany at the University of Chicago, from which he retired in 1925. His last institutional affiliation was with the Boyce Thompson Institute for Plant Research in Yonkers, New York, where he went in 1925 to help organize the institution and serve on the board of directors.

Coulter's scientific interests followed the development of American botany to an amazing degree, beginning with his initial interest in exploration and systematic botany, and growing to include newer areas of research in morphology and plant evolution that were part of the "New Botany" making its way to the United States from Germany. In supporting these botanical reforms at the turn of the century, Coulter ranked alongside Charles E. Bessey as a reformer of American botanical practice, helping to convert it from a descriptive and taxonomic study to a more rigorous laboratory-oriented practice.

Coulter's publication career began with his taxonomic work from the Hayden Survey. In 1874 he published a *Synopsis of the Flora of Colorado* (with the aid of T. C. Porter), followed in 1875 by a major article describing the flora of Montana, Idaho, Wyoming, and Utah, titled "Botany [of Montana, Idaho, Wyoming, and Utah]," in *Hayden's Geological Survey of the Territories*, pp. 747–92. In 1885 he published his *Manual of the Botany of the Rocky Mountain Region*. In this phase of his career he became especially well known for his work on the Umbelliferae (the celery family). As an outgrowth of his interest in systematic botany, Coulter's interests turned to the newer fields of functional morphology, development, and plant evolution, as microscopy and laboratory practice were introduced to botany. He became a pioneer in these fields, and his next publications, *Morphology of Spermatophytes* (1901), followed by *Morphology of the Angiosperms* (1903), and finally, *Morphology of the Gymnosperms* (1910) with C. J. Chamberlain as his collaborator, became compulsory readings for students of botany. Other projects included introductory textbooks in botany for high school students, study of the sexuality and life-histories of plants, and the study of plant breeding. In 1916 he wrote a book on evolution titled *Evolution, Heredity, and Eugenics*. In later years his interests widened even further to include general issues of science in *Ideals of Science* (1919), as well as the relationship between science and religion in *Where Evolution and Religion Meet* (1924). Coulter's interests were so broad, and he so grew to appreciate the diversity of botanical sciences, that he become one of the outstanding botanists and leading botanical spokespersons of his time. This no doubt gave him the necessary vision to edit the *Botanical Gazette*, the organ for promoting future directions in botanical and scientific research. He also became one of the most sought-after speakers for university and college functions.

Coulter is probably best known, however, for influencing the development of his field by producing more Ph.D. students in botany than any other individual of his time. He was an inspiring lecturer and sympathetic teacher who attracted able students to the study of botany. It is estimated that he produced some 175 Ph.D. students while at the University of Chicago alone (nearly as many received their master's degrees). At the university's quarter centennial in 1916, eighty-one of his former doctoral students presented him with *A Record of the Doctors in Botany of the University of Chicago 1897–1916 Presented to John Merle Coulter Professor and Head of the Department of Botany* (1916), which devoted a biographical page to each student. Its dedication page stated "The achievements of the Department of Botany of the University of Chicago are your achievements." Because these students were the first generation to be trained as botanists in the United States, rather than in Germany, England or France, the University of Chicago and Coulter's laboratory became one of the premier centers of botanical instruction in the country. Coulter's name, more than any other, is therefore associated with a "school" of American botany.

Among his honors, Coulter was elected to foreign membership of the Linnean Society of London in 1921 and to membership in the National Academy of Sciences. In 1897 he was president of the Botanical Society of America (he served as president again in 1915; he was also a charter member), and in 1918 he served as president of the American Association for the Advancement of Science.

Coulter was a lifelong member of the Presbyterian church and published numerous small articles on religious matters for religious journals. He died in Yonkers, New York. His influence in botany continued to be felt decades later, primarily through the *Botanical Gazette*, his morphological classics written with C. J. Chamberlain, and the work of his numerous academic progeny who went on to lead in American botany.

• Coulter's papers and correspondence are largely scattered among well-known botanical collections in the United States. The documents are described in detail and listed in the excellent biography by Andrew Denny Rodgers, *John Merle Coulter: Missionary in Science* (1944). For discussion on Coulter and the history of the *Botanical Gazette*, see H. C. Cowles, *Botanical Gazette* 87 (1929): 211–17. For a biographical sketch and complete list of publications compiled by J. C. Arthur, see William Trelease, "John Merle Coulter, 1851–1928," National Academy of Sciences, *Biographical Memoirs* 14 (1932–1934): 97–123. Coulter is discussed in Harry Baker Humphrey, *Makers of North American Botany* (1967). For an overview of Coulter and his role in American botany see Joseph Ewan, ed., *A Short History of Botany in the United States* (1969). One copy of the book listing his graduate students at the University of Chicago is located in the Mann Library at Cornell University. Obituaries include those by O. W. Caldwell et al. in *Science* 70 (1929): 299–301, and G. D. Fuller in *Science* 69 (1929): 177–80.

VASSILIKI BETTY SMOCOVITIS

COUNCILL, William Hooper (12 July 1848–17 Apr. 1909), black educator, was born in Fayetteville, North Carolina, the son of William Councill and Mary Jane (maiden name unknown), both slaves. In 1854 Councill's father escaped to freedom in Canada, leaving his wife and children to be dispersed in the South by slave traders. In 1863 young William, his mother, and his youngest brother escaped from a plantation in northern Alabama to a U.S. Army camp in Chattanooga, Tennessee. Councill attended a freedmen's school in Stevenson, Alabama, from 1865 to 1867 and later was tutored at night in Latin, physics, chemistry, and mathematics. In 1867 he established a school for freedmen in Jackson County and in 1869 began another in Madison County, laboring under the constant threat of Ku Klux Klan violence.

As a young man, Councill made contacts and received appointments that established him as an emerging black Republican leader in Alabama. He was active in the state's African Methodist Episcopal church, the Prince Hall Masons, and the Independent Order of Immaculates and the Pallbearers. Councill also organized branches of the National Labor Union, served as secretary of the 1873 National Equal Rights convention, and attended the 1874 Chattanooga Convention of Republicans. Ambitious for political office, he served as chief enrolling clerk of the Alabama legislature from 1872 to 1874 and narrowly lost his bid for a seat in the legislature in 1874. That same year Councill abandoned the Republican party, an action that alienated him from most Alabama blacks and even provoked death threats. Councill nevertheless believed that blacks should work with Democrats rather than simply distrusting them. "The republican party will grow tired of you," he warned, "and like the bat who was disowned by the beasts and not recognized by the birds, you will find favor with neither democrats or republicans" (Sherer, p. 34). In order to woo him back into the Republican ranks, President Ulysses S. Grant appointed Councill receiver-general of the Land Office of the Northern District of Alabama in 1875. He refused the post.

Councill's star ascended as a Democrat. In 1875 he became the first principal of the State Normal and Industrial School in Huntsville, Alabama, a school that preceded and rivaled Booker T. Washington's Tuskegee Institute, which was founded six years later. From 1877 to 1884, Councill also published the *Huntsville Herald* in an effort to espouse his political opinions. In 1879 he attended the National Conference of Colored Men in Nashville. During these years he read law and was admitted to the Alabama bar in 1883, although he never actually practiced. More accommodating to whites than Washington, Councill thrived until April 1885, when he was accused of raping a twelve-year-old student and then assaulting her uncle. Although he was later acquitted, Hunstville blacks, already dissatisfied with Councill's accommodationism, called for his expulsion. He retained his position, but as a result of the controversy, northern philanthropists shifted their support from Huntsville to Tuskegee.

In 1887 Councill became involved in two other crises that ultimately forced him to resign. In the first he filed a suit before the Interstate Commerce Commission (ICC) against the Atlantic Railroad Company for excluding him from a first-class coach on a trip between Tennessee and Georgia. While the ICC sided with Councill, ordering separate if equal treatment on railroads, this ruling went unenforced. The second case resulted when several of Councill's students attempted to sit in the first-class coach on a trip between Huntsville and Decatur. Whites accused Councill "of forcing social equality," and he resigned under pressure from Huntsville Normal, only to be reappointed principal in 1888.

These incidents convinced Councill of the importance of placating whites. Afterward he espoused accommodationist views openly, without Washington's long-term political agendas. Whereas Washington looked to northern philanthropists for support, Councill sought the largesse of white southerners. He believed that once blacks "proved" themselves, whites would treat them fairly. "Councill's error," according to historian Robert G. Sherer, "was betting on the wrong horse, not gambling" (Sherer, p. 41). Still, for a time Councill's strategy worked.

Huntsville Normal, not Tuskegee, first received funds from the 1890 Morrill Act, and in 1891 the school relocated to Normal, north of Huntsville, and was renamed Alabama State Agricultural and Mechanical College for Negroes. (In 1948 it became Alabama Agricultural and Mechanical College.) Gradually, after 1895, however, Washington outmaneuvered Councill for state funds, and in 1896 Tuskegee acquired Alabama's state's agricultural experiment station for blacks. By 1900 Washington, who reaped large donations for Tuskegee from northerners, distanced himself from Councill because of his "reputation of simply toadying to the Southern white people" (Meier, p. 110).

White supremacists, however, applauded Councill as a "good" Negro. In 1900 John Temple Graves described him as "the wisest, the most thoughtful and the most eloquent Negro of his time—as discreet as [Booker T.] Washington, a deeper thinker and a much more eloquent man. But for one hour of the Atlanta Exposition, Councill would stand to-day where Washington stands—as the recognized leader of his race" (*Race Problems of the South* [1900], p. 50). In 1905 William Benjamin Smith likewise praised Councill as "that most able and eloquent Negroid," one who admitted that whites never would grant blacks equal economic, political, social, and civil rights (*The Color Line* [1905], p. xiii).

Vacillating between the promotion of industrial training and literary education, as well as between accommodationism and militancy, Councill never became a race leader of Washington's stature. Nevertheless, he published *The Negro Laborer—A Word to Him* (1887), *Lamp of Wisdom, or, Race History Illuminated* (1898), *Negro Development in the South* (1901), *Bright Side of the Southern Question* (1903), and *The Young Negro of 1864; the Young Negro of 1904: The Problem Then; the Problem Now* (1904), as well as many articles concerning questions of race.

Councill's accommodationism and "unctuous sycophancy" (Meier, p. 77) toward whites concealed his anger at the circumscribed world of late nineteenth-century blacks. As early as 1893, he expressed bitterness at the limited avenues for racial progress, encouraging blacks to immigrate to Africa. Four years later he attacked lynching and longed for the return of racial harmony that allegedly existed under slavery. In 1899

Councill blamed the new generation of whites for inhibiting black progress. Evaluating Councill out of context, historians have often overvalued his opportunism and undervalued both his realism and his ideological and financial commitment to his school and blacks in general. In 1901, for example, Councill explained "that the salvation of the negro in this country depends upon drawing the social lines tighter, . . . North and South. The moment they become slack the white man becomes brutal—the negro goes down forever" (quoted in Sheldon Hackney, *Populism to Progressivism in Alabama* [1969], p. 185). Nonetheless, Councill, who died in Normal, is remembered for his pragmatic accommodationism, one that encouraged blacks to trust and cooperate with whites, a strategy that ultimately guaranteed their second-class citizenship.

• Some of Councill's letters are deposited in the Governor's Office Records at the Alabama Department of Archives and History and in the Booker T. Washington Papers at the Library of Congress. In addition to his books, Councill published many articles that chart his changing racial and educational thought. See, for example, "The Future of the Negro," *Forum* 27 (1899): 570–77; "Important Papers at the Industrial Convention," *Chattanooga Times*, 20 May 1900; and "Kindness as a Necessary Element in Leadership," *Colored American Magazine* 11 (1906): 403. Contemporary sketches include Gustav Kobbé, "Once Slave—Now Teacher," *Harper's Weekly*, 21 May 1892, pp. 500–501; A. W. McKinney, "Professor William H. Councill as I Knew Him and I Knew Him Well," *The Normal Index* (8 May 1920); and McKinney, "Professor W. H. Councill," *The Normal Index* 4 (May 1927): 156. More analytical appraisals of Councill are Charles Walter Orr, "The Educational Philosophy of William H. Councill" (master's thesis, Fisk Univ., 1939); Horace Mann Bond, *Negro Education in Alabama: A Study in Cotton and Steel* (1939); Earl Endris Thorpe, "William Hooper Councill," *Negro History Bulletin* 19 (1956): 85–86, 89; and August Meier, *Negro Thought in America, 1880–1915: Racial Ideologies in the Age of Booker T. Washington* (1963). The most complete and balanced assessment of Councill is Robert G. Sherer, *Subordination or Liberation? The Development and Conflicting Theories of Black Education in Nineteenth Century Alabama* (1977).

JOHN DAVID SMITH

COUNCILMAN, William Thomas (1 Jan. 1854–26 May 1933), pathologist, was born in Pikesville, Maryland, the son of John F. Councilman, a physician and farmer, and Christiana Drummond Mitchell. Councilman grew up on a busy farm where he began cultivating his powers of observation and an interest in plants. He attended St. John's College in Annapolis, Maryland, for his freshman and sophomore years but then left to engage in jobbing coffee and in other business enterprises. Around 1876 Councilman decided to go into medicine and enrolled in the University of Maryland. While there he lived at home, dissected animals, and built up a large collection of skulls and other bones. He received his M.D. in 1878.

After graduation, Councilman successfully applied for a fellowship in Henry Newell Martin's physiology laboratory at Johns Hopkins University. After a few months he left for the Quarantine Hospital to become an assistant to a friend who was the resident physician there. For the next few years Councilman alternated between the Quarantine and Martin's laboratory and also worked at the Bay View Asylum, Baltimore's almshouse and hospital. Here he performed many autopsies, began his interest in pathology, and started saving for a trip to Europe, where pathology was more advanced than it was in the United States.

While in Martin's laboratory, Councilman investigated inflammation of the cornea. A paper he wrote on the topic won him the Baltimore Academy of Medicine's $100 prize. In 1880 this became his first publication. Traveling to Europe, he studied in Vienna, Leipzig, Strassburg, and Prague from late 1880 to early 1883. During this time he worked primarily with pathologists such as Cohnheim and von Recklinghausen.

Back in Martin's laboratory, Councilman confirmed Laveran's discovery of the malarial parasite, being the first in the U.S. to describe and picture it. He sent his sketchbooks to William Henry Welch, professor of pathology at Johns Hopkins, who was in Europe at that time. Both Welch and the European pathologists to whom he showed the sketchbooks were impressed by Councilman's skills. Councilman did excellent original work on the diagnosis of the various forms of malaria, his interest in this disease resulting from the many cases he had seen at the Quarantine Hospital. He later wrote several more publications on this subject.

With Martin's support Councilman returned briefly to Prague in the summer of 1883 to obtain pathological specimens for Johns Hopkins. During the 1880s he wrote definitions for John Shaw Billings's *National Medical Dictionary* and entries for various encyclopedias. In this decade Councilman spent much time at Bay View and also taught at both of Baltimore's medical schools. For a year he also served as coroner's physician to the city of Baltimore. Despite this crowded schedule he became an enthusiastic fan of the Baltimore Orioles baseball team.

In 1884 Councilman was appointed associate in pathology by Hopkins, and in 1888 he was promoted to associate professor. Becoming Welch's right-hand man, he handled most of the autopsies and took care of the Department of Pathology's business matters. He helped develop postgraduate courses in pathology and in 1886 became an original member of the Association of American Physicians, which then had a strong leaning toward pathology. When the Johns Hopkins Hospital opened in 1889, Councilman was appointed resident pathologist.

At William Osler's suggestion, Councilman turned his attention to the disease he ultimately named amoebic dysentery. He made detailed studies of it and its parasite with H. A. Lafleur. Their monograph of 1891, with its detailed observations and reports, also contained Councilman's drawings.

In 1892 Councilman accepted the position of Shattuck Professor of Pathological Anatomy at the Harvard Medical School in Boston. Diphtheria, cerebrospinal meningitis, nephritis, and smallpox became the subjects of significant and original research by Councilman, both alone and with his colleagues. He helped build strong departments of pathology at Boston City and Massachusetts General hospitals, which in turn raised the level of teaching and research at Harvard.

After producing several editions of a syllabus for his medical-student course Councilman wrote and had published in 1912 a textbook, *Pathology, a Manual for Teachers and Students*. The following year the Peter Bent Brigham Hospital opened with Councilman as its pathologist in chief.

Councilman had earlier been married to a woman named Anne; her last name and the date of their marriage are unknown. On 17 December 1894 he married Isabella Coolidge; the couple had three daughters, the youngest of whom, Elizabeth, became a physician.

To encourage research and teaching in pathology Councilman helped found the American Association of Pathologists and Bacteriologists in 1901 and was elected its first president. He also served the American Medical Association, representing pathology on its Council on Medical Education (1904–1909) and as a member of its Board of Trustees (1909–1917; chairman, 1913–1917). In 1916 Councilman joined Hamilton Rice's expedition to the sources of the Amazon and was able to study both tropical diseases and plants. The completion of the trip was delayed, however, and Councilman became ill. During the remaining seventeen years of his life he was troubled increasingly by attacks of angina pectoris.

He retired from Harvard in 1922 and the next year went to China as a visiting professor at the Union Medical College in Peiping, accompanied by his wife. The Councilmans turned this opportunity into a round-the-world trip and a botanical treasure hunt. They then settled in York Village, Maine, in the house where they had spent their summers since 1906. There he devoted the remainder of his life to his splendid gardens.

An exceptionally competent investigator and teacher, Councilman firmly believed that the two could progress only if they were combined. The National Academy of Sciences elected him to membership in 1904. A short, stocky man with a florid countenance, he had a wide variety of interests, an inquiring mind, and a whimsical sense of humor. Councilman died in York Village.

Councilman's original investigations in infectious diseases and the associated major publications stimulated the scientific growth of pathology in the United States. His skills as a teacher and in the motivation of his colleagues added substantially to the undergraduate and graduate development of the field. Ultimately Councilman is noted for having created, along with Welch, a place for modern European pathology in the American medical school.

• The Countway Library of Medicine at Harvard University has a collection of Councilman material, consisting primarily of lectures, but also including some letters and his European sketchbooks. The Alan Mason Chesney Medical Archives at Johns Hopkins University also has some letters. His unpublished autobiography and his accounts of his Chinese travels are in private hands.

A major publication on Councilman is Harvey Cushing, National Academy of Sciences, *Biographical Memoirs* 18 (1936): 157–74, which includes a bibliography of his writings. Also of interest are obituaries by S. B. Wolbach in *Archives of Pathology* 16 (July 1933): 114–19, and by William G. MacCallum in *Bulletin of the Johns Hopkins Hospital* 53 (1933): 159–61. A brief but helpful source is William H. Welch, "Remarks at Dinner in Honor of William T. Councilman" (13 May 1915), in *Papers and Addresses by William Henry Welch*, vol. 3 (1920), pp. 423–25. Additional information, much of it personal, appears in A. McGehee Harvey, "Amebic Dysentery Gets Its Name: The Story of William Thomas Councilman," *Johns Hopkins Medical Journal* 146 (1980): 185–201, and Councilman's final lecture in pathology to his medical students, which was privately printed in 1921.

WILLIAM K. BEATTY

COUPER, James Hamilton (4 Mar. 1794–3 June 1866), planter, was born in Georgia, perhaps in Liberty County, the son of John Couper, a planter, and Rebecca Maxwell. John Couper had come from Scotland to Georgia in 1775 and in 1805 purchased, with lifelong friend and fellow émigré James Hamilton, 2,000 acres along the southern bank of the Altamaha River, about sixteen miles from Brunswick. They developed this land into Hopeton Plantation, which soon was expanded to 4,500 acres, with 659 slaves (many of whom came directly from Africa) to prepare the fields first for sea island or long-staple cotton, then sugar, and finally rice as the principal crops. In 1818 James Hamilton Couper (Hamilton's namesake), following graduation from Yale and after studying Dutch methods of water control in Holland, became manager of the Hopeton estate.

The partnership of James Hamilton and John Couper ended in 1826. Earlier difficulties plus the virtual loss of two cotton crops in 1824 and 1825 convinced Couper to sell his share to Hamilton, which Hamilton then resold to James Hamilton Couper in 1827, with Couper remaining as manager of the plantation. In addition to his half-interest in Hopeton, Couper would ultimately own outright three other plantations: Cannon's Point, which he inherited from his father, and Hamilton—both on St. Simon's Island—and Barrett's Island on the Altamaha River. By 1860 these four plantations comprised 2,600 acres of improved rice land and a work force of 1,142 slaves.

Couper was not only one of the largest rice planters in the South; he was also one of the most skilled. Following the cotton losses of 1824 and 1825, he shifted Hopeton mainly to rice until 1830, when sugar was made the principal crop—in 1829 the three crops were planted on roughly the same amount of acreage (246 in cotton, 234 in rice, and 202 in sugar), a diversification of crops that probably was not replicated on any other plantation in the South. Hopeton's diking and drainage system, developed by Couper on the Dutch model, became the envy of rice planters everywhere. Too, the estate's rice-milling facilities were of the most advanced quality, perhaps the best in Georgia. After Couper made sugar the main crop at Hopeton, he built a state-of-the-art sugar mill in the South. J. D. Legare, famous editor of the *Southern Agriculturist* (Charleston), visited Hopeton in 1832 and later described it in his magazine as probably the best plantation in the South, adding that in terms of the amount of acreage, the variety of crops, and the number of workers who had to be supervised, Hopeton could be favorably compared with any other like establishment in the nation. Sugar, however, was never produced with much success in Georgia because of its short frost-free season. By 1834 Couper had shifted most of Hopeton's land back to rice, and by 1838 cotton had been discontinued entirely and sugar reduced to a mere forty acres (for provisions for the slaves). By 1860 some 800 acres were being planted in rice, and the plantation worked about 500 slaves.

Couper was ever ready to experiment with the production of new commodities. He developed the grove of olive trees that his father had planted at Cannon's Point and thereby demonstrated that olives and olive oil were feasible products of the island despite intermittent losses caused by heavy frosts. He was a pioneer as well in the production of oil from cotton seed. According to the U.S. Census, the first cotton seed oil mill was established in 1837; however, the Couper papers show that in 1834 Couper was operating two such mills, one in Mobile, Alabama, the other in Natchez, Mississippi. He experimented early with Bermuda grass, proving its feasibility. All of this led to Couper's being considered a scientific farmer, experimenter, and geologist of the first order and his election to the British Royal Geological Society.

Couper's fame as a planter was widespread—a number of foreigners visited the plantation. Beyond the grandeur of the plantation (Hopeton had beautiful gardens and orchards, a 24-room mansion, and a splendid library of 5,000 well-chosen books), visitors were most interested in his skill in managing slaves. Couper was genuinely interested in the welfare of his slaves (never selling any except the ones who were impossible to control and maintaining one of the best slave hospitals in the South), and he was well served in this respect by a number of superb overseers and slave drivers, especially Old Tom (also known as African Tom); the son of an African prince, he served as a driver from roughly 1840 to 1860 and during that time was as able as—if not more able than—any others in the South.

The Civil War would of course change everything. Although Couper was opposed to secession, all five of his sons served in the Confederate army; two were killed. (Couper had married Caroline Wylly in 1827, to which union at least eight children had been born.) The war ravaged Couper's plantations—all had to be abandoned eventually—but emancipation dealt the harshest blow. At the time of his death, which occurred on St. Simons Island, Couper was attempting to recover his fortunes (to no avail) and to deal with the more burdensome and expensive free-labor system. He was buried at Frederica on St. Simon's Island.

• The Couper papers are in the Southern Historical Collection of the University of North Carolina at Chapel Hill. The papers of Francis Porteus Corbin, who was half-owner of Hopeton through his wife, James Hamilton's daughter, are at Duke University and the New York Public Library; they contain much information on Couper's planting, especially in the 1850s. Sir Charles Lyell, *Second Visit to the United States of North America*, vol. 1 (1849), chapters 18 and 19, presents a complete survey of the Couper plantations. For an extensive contemporary account of Hopeton Plantation, see J. D. Legare, "Account of an Agricultural Excursion Made into the South of Georgia in the Winter of 1832," *Southern Agriculturist* 6 (June–Aug. 1833), pp. 243–48, 297–304, 358–67, 410–16, 460–66, 515–29, and 571–77. For a more recent treatment of Hopeton, see James M. Clifton, "Hopeton, Model Plantation of the Antebellum South," *Georgia Historical Quarterly* 66 (Winter 1982): 429–49. References to Couper and his work are in Fredrika Bremer, *The Homes of the New World*, vol. 3 (1853); Frances Anne Kemble, *Journal of a Residence on a Georgian Plantation in 1838–1839* (1863); and Frances Butler Leigh, *Ten Years on a Georgian Plantation* (1883).

JAMES M. CLIFTON

COURANT, Richard (8 Jan. 1888–27 Jan. 1972), mathematician and educator, was born in Lublinitz, Upper Silesia (then Germany), the son of Siegmund Courant, an unsuccessful small businessman, and Martha Freund. By the age of fourteen, Courant was living alone in Breslau and supporting himself by tutoring. At nineteen he followed enthusiastic friends to Göttingen, where the mathematician Felix Klein had gathered a brilliant constellation of scientists and philosophers around his younger colleague, the mathematician David Hilbert. Contact with this scientifically electric atmosphere was the determining event in Courant's life as mathematician, teacher, writer, administrator, and tireless promotor of the unity of the mathematical sciences.

Courant earned his Ph.D. under Hilbert in 1910 with a thesis on conformal mapping that applied a simplified and modified version of Hilbert's work on the Dirichlet principle to fundamental problems in geometric function theory. That principle and questions of mathematical existence were to fascinate him throughout his career. In 1912, after a required stint in the army reserve, Courant became a private lecturer in Göttingen and married Nelly Neumann, a mathematician who had been one of his Breslau students. The childless marriage ended in divorce in 1916.

As an infantry officer at the beginning of the First World War, Courant saw heavy trench combat and developed a device to transmit telegraphic signals through the earth. After being wounded, he was transferred to the general staff of the wireless command. Although the acceptance of his telegraphic device came too late for general use, in this latter position he discovered that he had unsuspected entrepreneurial talents and a gift for relating to people of all classes, including the rich and powerful.

In 1917 Courant convinced the publisher Ferdinand Springer that there would be an urgent need after the war for advanced texts on contemporary developments in mathematics with emphasis on applications. Between 1919 and 1938 he edited almost fifty volumes in Springer's influential "Grundlehren der mathematischen Wissenschaften" series and contributed three classic volumes of his own. In December 1918 he returned to Göttingen and the following month married Nerina Runge (daughter of the mathematician Carl Runge), who shared his passionate love of music; they had four children.

In 1920, after a semester as a professor at Münster, Courant succeeded Felix Klein at Göttingen, a condition of his appointment being that he would continue to promote Klein's educational and mathematical interests as they pertained to the postwar situation at the university level. In a system that had consisted entirely of lectures, Courant set up an innovative "Praktikum" in which older students helped younger ones with assigned problems and acted as "talent scouts," drawing gifted newcomers into a mathematical family that shared such activities as skiing and music making.

Mathematically Courant directed his attention to the partial differential equations of mathematical physics and the transformation of methods based on physical intuition into rigorous mathematical tools. In 1924 he combined his own new work with notes from Hilbert's lectures for *Methoden der mathematischen Physik*, which was published under both their names. Appearing two years before the invention of quantum mechanics, for which it provided the needed modern mathematical methods, the work has been called "one of the most dramatic anticipations in the history of mathematical physics" (E. T. Bell, *The Development of Mathematics* [1940; 3d ed., 1992], p. 494).

Courant's intuition about mathematics that would prove useful, as well as about the abilities of young people, is exemplified by the 1928 collaboration with his students K. O. Friedrichs and Hans Lewy on finite difference equations. The work was to play an unexpectedly important role in numerical analysis after the invention of the computer in the Second World War.

At Courant's memorial service, Friedrichs said, "One cannot appreciate Courant's scientific achievements simply by enumerating his published work. . . . [The work] was original, significant, beautiful [but] it was always connected with problems and methods of other fields of science, drawing inspiration from them and in turn inspiring them."

Courant was attracted to people who were his opposite in personality and character, such as the historian of ancient mathematics Otto Neugebauer, whom he once described—with characteristic wit—as "having all the virtues of pedantry and none of the vices." Under Courant's leadership, and with Neugebauer as his chief aide, Göttingen quickly regained its prewar position as the popularly known "mecca of mathematics." In 1929 a grant from the Rockefeller Foundation, matched by the German government, made possible a building that brought together all mathematical activities at the university—the prototype of now ubiquitous mathematical institutes.

Courant had many devoted students and friends, including influential foreigners, but he also had detractors in many different quarters. In 1933, when the Nazis came to power, he was one of the first Jewish professors dismissed, although his military service should have exempted him, even under the new laws.

In the fall of 1934 Courant accepted a modest position at New York University. The move, which freed him to devote himself again to mathematics, resulted in some of his finest work: a new approach to the recently solved problem of Plateau concerning surfaces of smallest area spanned by any closed curve in space.

In New York Courant quickly adopted the view that its young first-generation Americans were an untapped "reservoir of talent." After 1937, joined by Friedrichs and the American mathematician James J. Stoker, both of whom were as unlike him in character and personality as Neugebauer, he began to adapt to NYU the philosophy he had absorbed in Göttingen, seeing it as his task "to restore . . . easy communication" between mathematics and its applications and "to bring mathematics back into the mainstream of science." In 1940, convinced that applied mathematics was being dangerously neglected, he campaigned brashly but unsuccessfully for a national institute of the mathematical sciences. He was more successful in 1941 with a collaboration with Herbert Robbins that set out his view of mathematics, *What Is Mathematics?*, which inspired many young people to become mathematicians.

During World War II Courant was appointed to the Applied Mathematics Panel of the U.S. Office of Scientific Research and Development. Funding for war-related research became available for his group at NYU, and he began to play a more active role nationally in science.

After the war Courant returned as soon as possible to Germany to help. Thereafter, according to the German mathematician Klaus Müller, "for more than a quarter of a century he was a never failing friend of the mathematical and scientific institutions in Germany," but he never considered returning permanently.

As he became increasingly involved in the activities and concerns of the scientific community, Courant's published research declined, but his mathematical interests continued to be broad, extending even to the mathematics of traffic flow. In 1953 increased support for scientific research and selection of NYU as the site for the Atomic Energy Commission's computer resulted in a "mathematics institute" at NYU. In 1965 this outstanding center of applied mathematics became the Courant Institute of Mathematical Sciences.

Courant was a complex individual, capable of embracing contradictory views and philosophies. In Neugebauer's opinion, however, "his ability to create a feeling of mutual confidence in those who knew him intimately [lay] at the foundation of his success and influence." He also inspired confidence in men of affairs who scarcely knew him. Yet, in America as in Germany, many distrusted his entrepreneurial approach, feeling that he worked only to advance himself and his group. Courant died in New Rochelle, New York.

The impact of Courant's immediate small group on American mathematics can be gauged by the number of its members elected to the National Academy of Sciences: Courant, Friedrichs, Stoker, Fritz John, Harold Grad, Joseph Keller, Louis Nirenberg, Peter Lax, and Cathleen Morawetz. Owing in large part to Courant's tireless efforts, American mathematicians increasingly cross over between "pure" and "applied," and the institute that bears his name is no longer, as it was for many years, the only place in the country where applied mathematicians are being trained.

• Courant's papers are at the Courant Institute and with his family. All of his books have been translated into English, but revised editions in German and translations into English often differ substantially from the originals. (Dates here are for first editions and German titles are abbreviated.) *Functionentheorie* (1922), published with Adolf Hurwitz, contains an influential chapter by Courant on geometric function theory. The second volume of *Methoden der mathematischen Physik* (1937), written with Friedrichs's assistance, includes a particularly influential chapter on existence proofs. The two volumes of *Calculus* (1930, 1931), based on Courant's lectures in Göttingen, present a unified view of the subject with emphasis on applications. The Courant-Friedrichs *Supersonic Flow and Shock Waves* (1948) is a comprehensive treatment of wartime collaboration at NYU. *Dirichlet's Principle, Conformal Mapping, and Minimal Surfaces* (1950) has been described as the most "Courantian" of Courant's books. An obituary of Klein in *Naturwissenschaften* 13 (1926) 765–72, is interesting for Courant's empathetic view of his great predecessor. The Courant-Friedrichs-Lewy paper was originally published in German in *Mathematische Annalen* 100 (1928): 32–74; it was republished in English as "On the Partial Difference Equations of Mathematical Physics," in *IBM Journal of Research and Development* 1, no. 2 (Mar. 1967): 215–34. There is no published bibliography. A biography, *Courant in Göttingen and New York: The Story of an Improbable Mathematician* (1976), has been written by Constance Reid with the cooperation of K. O. Friedrichs. An obituary is in the *New York Times*, 29 Jan. 1972.

CONSTANCE REID

COURNAND, André Frédéric (24 Sept. 1895–19 Feb. 1988), physician and scientist, was born in Paris, France, the son of Jules Cournand, a dentist, and Marguérite Weber. He entered the Lycée Condorcet at the age of five, although he credits his mother with teaching him to read before he entered school. In 1913 Cournand received his bachelor's degree at the Sorbonne, and in 1914 he took the diploma of physics, chemistry, and biology of the Faculté des Sciences. He then started his medical studies but left school after one year to serve in the French army in the First World War. He became a battalion surgeon, was gassed and wounded, and was awarded the Croix de Guerre with three bronze stars. After the end of the war, Cournand returned to his medical training. He became interne des hôpitaux de Paris in 1925 and was awarded an M.D. from the Faculté de Médecine de Paris in 1930, with a thesis on acute disseminated sclerosis. Cournand befriended a number of modern artists, such as the sculptor Jacques Lipschitz.

Cournand moved to the United States, where he was first a resident and then chief resident on the Tuberculosis Service of the Columbia University Division of Bellevue Hospital in New York City. Cournand performed most of his investigations in the Bellevue Hospital Cardio-Pulmonary Laboratory. His academic appointments went from instructor (1934) to professor of medicine (1956) at Columbia University. He became an American citizen in 1941.

Cournand is best known for his role in the development of cardiac catheterization. The heart is a pump that circulates blood throughout the body. In 1929 the German physician Werner Forssmann described the passage of a small tube, called a catheter, into his own heart. Forssmann hoped to find a way to inject drugs into the central circulation so that the drugs could have a more immediate effect, but he did little further investigation on the technique. In 1932, as chief resident at Bellevue Hospital, Cournand started to collaborate with Dickinson Richards, then at the Columbia-Presbyterian Medical Center, on studies of the heart and circulation. Cournand and Richards worked together from February 1932 until February 1973, a remarkably sustained period of collaboration. They initially wanted to study the lungs but found that to understand the treatment of lung diseases they needed to know more about what was happening within the heart. Cournand returned to Paris in 1936 to learn how to pass a catheter into the right auricle, the cardiac chamber that collects blood returning from the body to the heart. Back in New York, Cournand, Richards, and their colleagues spent four years establishing that the passage of catheters into laboratory animals' hearts caused no significant ill effects.

In early 1940s Cournand and his co-investigators gradually became bolder and passed their catheters farther and farther into the right side of the human heart, then extending through the heart and into the lungs. Some of this work was sparked by that of other investigators who were using the ballistocardiograph, an instrument that recorded the motion of the body caused by the heartbeat, to measure the heart's output. These researchers wanted to compare their results with another method of determining the cardiac output, such as could be accomplished with Cournand's catheter. Technical advances by Cournand, Richards, and their colleagues enabled them to obtain increasing amounts of information from their studies. The danger of passing tubes into the human heart engendered relatively little opposition, perhaps because they were studying shock, a subject of great wartime importance. The federal Committee on Medical Research provided funds to study more than 100 critically ill patients. Cournand and Richards described the profound effects of reducing circulating blood volume on cardiac output and on blood flow to peripheral organs and to the kidney; they also described how the condition could be reversed by appropriate volume replacement.

Cardiac catheterization rapidly became central to much of the study of human disease. Cournand did additional work on using catheters to diagnose congenital heart disease as well as to further the study of lung diseases. By 1949 more than 10,000 catheterizations had been performed throughout the world. Using catheterization to measure accurately the pressure and blood flow in various chambers of the heart, and utilizing the heart-lung machine, surgeons found that they could repair congenital defects and correct faulty heart valves. By the 1990s the passing of catheters into the heart for diagnosis had become a routine procedure, one for which patients might not even spend the night in a hospital. Physicians had begun to use catheters not only to diagnose disease but also to treat it, both by instilling medicine directly into the heart and by using special catheters to expand a constricted blood vessel or to ablate a diseased part of the heart. The techniques of Cournand, Richards, and Forssmann have become central to both the diagnosis and the treatment of almost every type of heart disease. Catheters within the heart are also used routinely to monitor people who are seriously ill even if they do not have disease primarily of the heart; indeed, the technique holds implications for all manner of medical care.

Cournand enjoyed pushing the boundaries of the possible in fields as diverse as modern art, mountain climbing, and science. As evidenced by the outpouring of sentiment on the occasion of a memorial service held for Cournand at Columbia University on 17 March 1988, those who knew him found him an inspiring person to be with.

Cournand received many honors, most notably the 1956 Nobel Prize in Medicine or Physiology, which he shared with Richards and Forssmann. Cournand was married in 1924 to Sibylle Blumer, who died in 1959. Cournand adopted her son, who was killed in action in France in 1944, and they had three children together. In 1963 Cournand married Ruth Fabian, who died in 1973. In 1975 he married Beatrice Bishop Berle, who died in 1993. He died in Great Barrington, Massachusetts.

• Cournand described his work in several useful places, including André Cournand and A. Ranges, "Catheterization of the Right Auricle in Man," *Proceedings of the Society for Experimental Biology and Medicine* 46 (1941): 462–66; Cournand, "The Historical Development of the Concepts of Pulmonary Circulation," in *Pulmonary Circulation: An International Symposium*, ed. Wright Adams and Ilza Veith (1959); Cournand, "Control of the Pulmonary Circulation in Man, with Some Remarks on Methodology," in *Nobel Lectures, Physiology or Medicine, 1942–1962* (1964); Cournand, "Cardiac Catheterization: Development of the Technique, Its Contributions to Experimental Medicine, and Its Initial Applications in Man," *Acta Medica Scandinavica*, supp. 579 (1975): 7–32; and Cournand, *From Roots to Late Budding: The Intellectual Adventures of a Medical Scientist* (1986).

For useful discussions of Cournand's life and the importance of his work, see Stanley E. Bradley, *André Cournand, 1895–1988: Remarks Delivered at the Memorial Service, St. Paul's Chapel, Columbia University, 17 March 1988* (1988), pp. 5–9; Steven L. Johnson, *The History of Cardiac Surgery, 1896–1955* (1970); Allen B. Weisse, "André Cournand," in *Conversations in Medicine: The Story of Twentieth-Century American Medicine in the Words of Those Who Created It* (1984); Robert H. Franch, "André Cournand, Father of Clinical Cardiopulmonary Physiology," *Clinical Cardiology* 9 (1986): 82–86; and J. Lequime, "André Cournand (1895–1988): His Role in the Development of Modern Cardiology," *Acta Cardiologica* 43 (1988): 437–42. An obituary is in the *Washington Post*, 21 Feb. 1988.

JOEL D. HOWELL

COURNOS, John (6 Mar. 1881–27 Aug. 1966), writer and critic, was born Johann Gregorievitch Korshoon in Zhitomir, Russia, the son of Gregory Korshoon and Euphrosyne Khatavner. His parents divorced, and when he was three his mother married Bernard Cournos, a Hasidic Jew who had first been introduced into the family as a tutor. They moved to Boyarka, a village ten miles from Kiev, where Cournos was educated by tutors and governesses, learning German and Hebrew. Financial difficulty and obligatory army service for Cournos precipitated the family's move to the United States. His stepfather refused to leave Russia; nevertheless, Cournos's mother moved the children to Philadelphia because she read that it was "famed for its philanthropic and educational institutions."

Cournos was enrolled in public school at age ten, even though he had no knowledge of English. He attended Sunday school at a German Lutheran Church. At age thirteen he left school to educate himself and help his mother support his family as a newsboy and as a mill hand in a woolen mill. He worked fourteen years for the *Philadelphia Record*, beginning as an office boy. He mastered English through reading, and at age seventeen he was promoted to the position of assistant Sunday editor. Determined to become a journalist, Cournos began reporting and contributing articles on art criticism to the *Record*, until contact with students at the Pennsylvania Academy of Fine Arts inspired him to experiment with creative writing. In 1912 he moved to London. Commissioned by the *New York Times Book Review*, Cournos interviewed H. G. Wells, Gordon Craig, John Masefield, and G. K. Chesterton.

Cournos's literary career took off after he met expatriate Ezra Pound in London through his membership on Craig's Committee of the School of the Theatre. In his *Autobiography*, Cournos described his first impression of Pound: "The Englishman as an individual is an incalculable quantity, a mystery. . . . Compared to these, Ezra Pound, the American, is a glass-house, with all the furnishings of his mind visible" (p. 235). Pound introduced Cournos to Violet Hunt, W. B. Yeats, and two men who contributed to the founding of imagism, Ford Madox Ford and T. E. Hulme. Influenced by the imagist aesthetic and entrance into high literary circles, Cournos began writing poetry with the encouragement of his new colleagues.

In 1914 Pound published one of Cournos's prose poems in his *Des Imagistes: An Anthology* (1914), which also included contributions from H. D. (Hilda Doolittle), Amy Lowell, William Carlos Williams, and Pound. Between 1915 and 1920 Cournos published art criticism and poetry in the *Egoist, Anglo-Italian Review, New World, Coterie, Voices, New Europe, New Leader, Nation* (London), *Poetry, Little Review, American Hebrew,* and the *Dial.* In 1923 his poems were collected and published with the title *In Exile.* Like many of Cournos's later publications, the poems from *In Exile* drew on his experiences with the imagists. The collection ends with his translations of the works of Russian poets such as Feodor Sologub. Two of Cournos's poems, "Shylock's Choice" and "God's Face," appeared in Aldington's *Imagist Anthology 1930* (1930).

Cournos aided the British government during World War I at Marconi House in London, England, by decoding news sent from the Russian government. The British Foreign Office appointed Cournos, as well as novelist Hugh Walpole, to spend six months of 1918 in Petrograd during the Bolshevik Revolution as a member of an Anglo-Russian Commission. On his return Cournos wrote for the Russian Liberation Committee, *London under the Bolsheviks: A Londoner's Dream on Returning from Petrograd* (1919). He continued to work for the British government as a member of the British Ministry of Information and later as part of the political intelligence department of the foreign office until 1920. In 1920 he visited slums, schools, and hospitals in famine-stricken areas of Central Europe as a member of a commission for London's Save the Children Fund. In 1924 he married Helen Kestner Satterthwaite, an American divorcee in London and mother of two; the couple had no other children. Their romance is reflected in Cournos's satirical novel, *The New Candide* (1924).

Cournos wrote seven novels for which he received much praise but reaped little monetary reward. *The Mask* (1919), *The Wall* (1921), and *Babel* (1922) form a semiautobiographical trilogy featuring a character based on himself, John Gombarov, and another, the tragic hero Seymon Gombarov, based on his stepfather Bernard Cournos. *The Mask,* which loosely traces Cournos's life in Russia to his relocation in Philadelphia, remained his most successful fictional effort. Cournos was prematurely awarded the British Hawthornden Prize for *The Mask* in 1920 but could not accept because of his American citizenship. *Miranda Masters* (1926), dedicated to his mother, is loosely based on Cournos's relationship with H. D., Richard Aldington, and Pound. His final novel, *Face of Death* (1934), a commercial failure, was published under the pseudonym Mark Gault. In 1935 Cournos published *Autobiography,* which was praised by Van Wyck Brooks and Sherwood Anderson. Cournos titled the first section "I Decide To Be Born" and explained, "I decided to be born because the blind will in the germ which was myself (though an unconscious self) suc-

cessfully contended for life with a multitude of other germs in my mother's womb" (p. 6).

Cournos, inspired by his childhood appreciation for Russian poets and by his desire to master English, began translating Russian literature as early as 1915. He introduced to the English-speaking world works by well-known Russian writers, such as Feodor Sologub, Alexei Remizov, and Andrey Biely. Cournos edited six volumes of *British Short Stories of 1922–1927,* an anthology of imagist poems entitled *Shylock's Choice* (1930), *American Short Stories of the Nineteenth Century* (1930, 1960), and, in 1943, the anthology, *A Treasury of Russian Life and Humor,* reprinted in 1962 as *A Treasure of Classic Russian Literature.*

In the late 1930s Cournos was forced to sell his correspondence with notable literary figures such as D. H. Lawrence, Edwin Arlington Robinson, Robert Frost, and Pound in order to earn an income. He moved to New York City, where he wrote book reviews and collaborated on publications with his wife, who wrote under the names John Hawk and Sybil Norton. They jointly edited a number of collections, including *Famous Modern American Novelists, Famous British Novelists,* and *Best World Short Stories of 1947.* They also collaborated on juvenile biographies of Roger Williams (1953), Daniel Webster (1953), and John Adams (1954). In addition to submitting regular reviews to the *New York Sun,* Cournos lectured at New York University and Bryn Mawr. The deterioration of his career was followed by the failure of his marriage. His wife committed suicide in 1959. He died in New York City.

• Cournos's correspondence with Ezra Pound is in the Beinecke Library at Yale University. See his *Autobiography* (1935), which covers his life from his birth to 1924. An obituary is in the *New York Times,* 28 Aug. 1966.

BARBARA L. CICCARELLI

COURTENAY, William (19 June 1875–20 Apr. 1933), actor, was born William Leonard Courtenay in Worcester, Massachusetts. Although no biographical sources name his parents, Courtenay reported that they came to the United States from Ireland weeks before his birth. He was ambiguous about his father, who died when Courtenay was fifteen, stating only that he was connected with the law in some way. After attending Holy Cross College in Worcester until 1892, Courtenay joined an amateur touring production of *Ten Nights in a Barroom.* Professional touring engagements followed over the next three years. In 1894 he also appeared as the lead in a "picture play," *Miss Jerry.* This lyceum attraction, a series of coordinated slides with accompanying spoken narration, figures in film histories as a precursor to the movies' visual storytelling.

In 1896 Courtenay became a member of Richard Mansfield's theatrical company and appeared in a number of roles, including the part of Christian in the first English-language production of *Cyrano de Bergerac.* Next he worked with Daniel Frohman's Lyceum

Theatre stock company for two seasons and then with Charles Frohman's Empire Theatre stock company, also for two seasons. In 1902 he joined the theatrical company of Virginia Harned for two seasons, playing romantic leads with her in *Iris*, *Camile*, and various other plays.

Courtenay's first individual success came in the comedy *Mrs. Leffingwell's Boots* (1905). In this production he played a young man-about-town in whose room a married woman's bedroom "boots" are found, causing a scandal. Seeing him at this time, Oliver Morosco found "he had all the requisites of a star. His voice was perfectly modulated and his poise admirable. He knew how to reach a climax, how to put over comedy. . . . He was about six feet tall, slight and very handsome" (Helen M. Morosco and Leonard P. Dugger, *The Oracle of Broadway: The Life of Oliver Morosco* [1944], p. 171). Further stage successes both in comedy and drama came in *The Secret Orchard* (1907), *The Wolf* (1908), and *Arsene Lupin* (1909). Courtenay toured again with Harned during the 1910–1911 season, playing in *Anna Karenina* and *An American Widow*. The play *Ready Money* (1912) brought him further success as another dashing young man-about-town.

Early in 1913 Courtenay (known as "Billy" to his friends) was married in a secret ceremony to Virginia Harned, formerly the wife of E. H. Sothern. They had no children. Later that year he was in one of the period's great stage hits, *Romance*, in which he played an aging bishop who relives his youthful love affair with an Italian opera star. More successful appearances followed: *The Girl and the Pennant* (1913), *Under Cover* (1914), and *Under Fire* (1915). Articles of the time emphasized his good looks and his ability to play romantic lovers. Ada Patterson in *Green Book* (Aug. 1914) spoke of his "lithe figure . . . comely face, regular featured and with fine fresh color . . . eyes, large and blue . . . a mop of curly black hair . . . lips [that] are full and mobile." Mary Morgan declared, "William Courtenay stands nearly alone in the art of stage love-making" (*Theatre Magazine*, July 1914). Interviews convey the impression that offstage he was easygoing and eager to charm, a man of surfaces rather than of depths who worked hard to portray the dashing, virile hero convincingly on stage.

From 1915 to 1917 Courtenay appeared in seven silent films, notably the melodrama *Kick In* (1917), in which he took the role originated on stage by John Barrymore. The screen was never as congenial to Courtenay as the stage, however. Returning to the theater, he appeared in a series of successes opposite comedian Thomas Wise: *Pals First* (1917), *General Post* (1917), and *Cappy Ricks* (1920). Thereafter his career declined, as a new generation of playgoers found his mannerisms stale. A review of his appearance in *Honors Are Even* (1921) spoke of his "mellifluous and rather smug voice" as unsuitable to the part. The *New York Times* critic said he performed his role in *The Lawbreakers* (1922) "with precisely the same manner and method that have sustained him in similar roles these many years. Which fact is reported as a hearty

reassurance to those who admire Mr. Courtenay as an actor and a gentle warning to those who do not" (7 Feb. 1922).

After playing in *The Harem* (1924), Courtenay disappeared from the stage for years. In 1929–1930 he took character roles in five talking pictures, notably *Three Faces East* (1930), with Constance Bennett and Erich von Stroheim. His last stage appearance, ending a career of forty years, came in 1932. He played Governor Hazleton, an official who has the power to pardon a young condemned man, in a crime drama titled *The Inside Story*. The following year he died at his country home in Rye, New York, after succumbing to a heart condition. In the view of critics, he never advanced beyond the status of a good-looking matinee idol. As such, however, says theater historian Gerald Bordman, he was "one of the handsomest and most durable."

• Scrapbooks and other materials on the career of Courtenay are in the Billy Rose Theatre Collection at the New York Public Library for the Performing Arts, Lincoln Center. A list of his stage appearances is in *Who Was Who in the Theatre 1912–1976* (1978). An index of his film appearances is in *The American Film Institute Catalog*, vols. 1921–1930, ed. Kenneth Munden (1971), and 1931–1940, ed. Patricia King Hanson (1992). Three articles discussing his demeanor as an actor are Mary Morgan, "William Courtenay, the Stage Lover," *Theatre Magazine*, July 1914; Ada Patterson, "Making Stage Love-Making Pay," *Green Book Magazine*, Aug. 1914; and Thoda Cocroft, "William Courtenay," *National Magazine* (Boston), May 1922. Numerous portraits in contemporary publication are indexed in Frederick Faxon et al., eds., *The Cumulated Dramatic Index 1909–1949*. His obituary is in the *New York Times*, 21 Apr. 1933.

WILLIAM STEPHENSON

COUSIN ALICE. *See* Haven, Emily Bradley Neal.

COUSIN EMMY (1903–11 Apr. 1980), country singer, banjoist, and comedian, was born Cynthia May Carver near Lamb, a hamlet in south central Kentucky near Glasgow. The youngest of eight children, she grew up in a log cabin while her father tried to make ends meet working as a sharecropper raising tobacco. Her family was musical, and she learned old English and Scottish ballads from her great-grandmother. As she grew up, she became proficient on a number of instruments, ranging from the orthodox (fiddle, banjo, guitar) to the unusual (the rubber glove, the Jew's harp, the hand saw). A natural "show off" and entertainer, by around 1915 she was leaving the farm and trying her hand at entertaining in nearby towns. Having no real interest in school, she taught herself to read by studying mail order catalogues.

By the time she came of age, Carver had become fascinated with the work of two of her cousins, Noble "Bozo" Carver and Warner Carver; they had a well-known string band, the Carver Boys, which became one of the first string bands from the area to make records. The Carver Boys were early professionals and established their reputation while playing in the Midwest on the radio. Carver soon joined them as a banjo player and singer, performing over Kansas City radio station WHB. In 1935 her brashness won her a spot on a more local radio station, WHAS in Louisville, where she became, in her own words, "the biggest thing to hit any man's radio station." She stayed at WHAS until 1937.

During the next decade Carver, who began using the name Cousin Emmy as early as 1937, became one of the most popular rural radio stars, male or female. She was one of the first of a new breed of entertainers who established their reputations primarily through broadcasting; indeed, she would not make any commercial phonograph records until the late 1940s. With her cascades of platinum blonde hair, wide, Martha Raye–like mouth, and brassy voice, she was a natural bandleader and specialist in up-tempo "shout" songs like "Groundhog" and "Raise a Ruckus Tonight." By 1938 she had formed her own show troupe, which did radio shows and then traveled to personal appearances in a huge old Cadillac. In the early 1940s she told a reporter from *Time* magazine why she had become one of radio's most popular acts:

First I hits it up on my banjo, and I wow'em. Then I do a number with the *guit*-ar and play the French harp and sing, all at the same time. Then somebody hollers, "Let's see her yodel," and I obliges. And then somebody hollers, "Let's see her dance," and I obliges. After that we come to the sweetest part of the program—hymns.

By 1937 Cousin Emmy was working at the WWVA "Jamboree" in Wheeling, West Virginia, where she met Louis "Grandpa" Jones; she taught him how to play her style of banjo, the old Kentucky "clawhammer" style, which during the 1940s became the Grandpa Jones trademark on the Grand Ole Opry. By 1941 she was on KMOX in St. Louis as Cousin Emmy and Her Kinfolks, attracting an audience that ranged from Canada to Mexico and included at times more than 2.5 million listeners. During World War II she was popular enough to win a Hollywood film contract, appearing in Columbia's musical *Swing in the Saddle*. In 1947 noted folklorist Alan Lomax recorded a 78-rpm album of eight of her songs, *Kentucky Mountain Ballads*; about the same time she recorded a more commercial effort for Decca, a driving banjo song called "Ruby (Are You Mad at Your Man?)," which became popular on southern juke boxes and later was made into a bluegrass standard by the Osborne Brothers.

With the demise of live radio in the 1950s, Cousin Emmy's career took a different turn. She found work on the West Coast, taking a nonmusical role in the 1955 film *The Second Greatest Sex*. By the early 1960s she was appearing at Disneyland, singing her classic songs and impressing a new generation of listeners. This led, in turn, to a comeback of sorts, in which she appeared at a number of folk festivals (including the well-known festival at Newport, Rhode Island) and on television shows, playing her banjo and singing many of her old songs. In 1968 she joined forces with the

New Lost City Ramblers, the leading string band of the folk revival, for a new Folkways LP, *The New Lost City Ramblers with Cousin Emmy*.

Cousin Emmy died in Sherman Oaks, California. Scholars and critics hailed her as one of the first women performers in professional country music and one of the first women to organize her own touring troupes and radio shows. She became a role model for dozens of other women in country music and was one of the most accomplished traditional musicians of her time.

• For more information on Cousin Emmy, see Charles Wolfe, *Folk and Country Music of Kentucky* (1982), and Mary A. Bufwack and Robert K. Oermann, *Finding Her Voice: The Saga of Women in Country Music* (1993).

CHARLES K. WOLFE

COUSINS, Norman (24 June 1915–30 Nov. 1990), author, editor, and peace advocate, was born in Union Hill, New Jersey, the son of Samuel Cousins and Sara Miller, owners of a dry goods store. Soon after his birth the family moved to New York City. In his youth Cousins excelled in English composition and was a fine baseball player. After graduating from Columbia University Teachers College in 1933, he secured an editorial position as an education writer for the *New York Evening Post*. Three years later he joined *Current History* magazine as literary and managing editor. He married Ellen Kopf in 1939; they had four children and adopted another who had survived the atomic bombing of Hiroshima. In 1940 Cousins joined the staff of the *Saturday Review of Literature* as executive editor; two years later, at the age of twenty-seven, he became its editor. He shortened the magazine's title and broadened its scope to encompass the arts, current events, science, travel, education, and contemporary society, and circulation grew to 650,000. Cousins remained as editor of the *Saturday Review* until 1971, when he resigned over disagreements with its new owners. He returned as editor and owner from 1973 to 1978, when he retired.

During World War II Cousins served as a member of the editorial board for the Overseas Bureau of the Office of War Information. He was also cochairman of the 1943 Victory Book Campaign. At the same time, he threw himself into a lifelong effort to revitalize what he considered the main values of Western civilization through the construction of a working world federal system. In his *Saturday Review* editorials, he championed world government through world citizenship. During the war he joined a group, Americans United for World Organization, that helped shape public opinion in favor of the United Nations. It was the atomic bomb, however, that gave the fullest urgency and scope to his thinking. "The need for world government was clear before August 6, 1945," Cousins declared in the *Saturday Review*, "but Hiroshima and Nagasaki raise that need to such dimensions that it can no longer be ignored" (*Modern Man Is Obsolete*, p. 23). National sovereignty was "preposterous now."

Cousins tried to sort out his hopes and his fears of the nuclear age in an editorial, "Modern Man Is Obsolete" (18 Aug. 1945). His secular sermon drew a tremendous response. Viewed as one of the most prophetic statements of its time, it became the most widely quoted editorial of the infant atomic age; when it was expanded and published as a book, it appeared briefly on the bestseller list. Immediately after the bombings, Cousins went on a barnstorming lecture tour, trying to educate the American people about the effects of nuclear war and the nuclear arms race. Calling for a world federal government with limited but definite and adequate powers to prevent war, he joined with other influential Americans in the attempt to galvanize a popular movement in that cause. In February 1947 the United World Federalists was founded, and Cousins served as one of its vice presidents and later as president (1952–1954).

His involvement with the victims of the Hiroshima blast prompted Cousins to arrange for twenty-four young Japanese women, called the "Hiroshima Maidens," to come to the United States for medical treatment, funded by contributions from *Saturday Review* readers. Later the magazine also sponsored the "Ravensbruck Lapins," thirty-five Polish victims of medical experimentation in a Nazi concentration camp.

In the mid-1950s Cousins became intensely concerned with the health hazards associated with atmospheric nuclear testing. He believed that testing had to be brought under control: it powered the arms race, abetted the spread of nuclear weapons, and menaced children and the unborn. In an editorial in the *Saturday Review* (5 June 1957), Cousins urged the United States to undertake a unilateral suspension of tests in the belief that "world public opinion will compel all other nations to do likewise." In the spring of 1957 he joined with other nuclear pacifists to form the National Committee for a Sane Nuclear Policy (SANE) and became its cochairman and most prominent spokesperson. Cousins was particularly influential in getting the partial nuclear test-ban treaty approved in September 1963, even acting as unofficial liaison between President John F. Kennedy and Soviet premier Nikita S. Khrushchev and helping to break an impasse in the negotiations. Afterward, Cousins resigned from the chairmanship of SANE (although he remained on its national board) and returned under the title of honorary president to the United World Federalists.

An early and persistent critic of American military intervention in Vietnam, Cousins believed that the United Nations should effect a cease-fire and move the conflict from the battlefield. In December 1965 he traveled with Vice President Hubert Humphrey on a trip to Vietnam in the hope of encouraging a negotiated settlement. According to the White House Asian affairs adviser Chester Cooper, Cousins was among the most reliable, responsible, and highly regarded citizen-diplomats who assisted Washington's peacemaking efforts. As the war dragged on, Cousins continued to call for negotiations and for a UN resolution of the war. However, his attempts to multilateralize the diplomacy of the war failed to confront the depths of Washington's determination to win in Indochina. His

declining influence among other peacemakers reflected that reality.

Throughout the Vietnam years Cousins consistently maintained that the first responsibility of peacemakers was in the fight against nuclear war. In an editorial in the *Saturday Review* (17 Apr. 1976), "The Nightmare That Won't Go Away," he reminded his readers that "the nuclear threat is still alive, ugly, more menacing than ever." In order to reignite discussion and debate on the nuclear issue, in 1976 Cousins resumed the presidency of the United World Federalists (now called the World Federalist Association) and argued that its program posed the only convincing alternative to mutual annihilation.

After retiring from the *Saturday Review* in 1978, Cousins joined the faculty of the University of California–Los Angeles School of Medicine, where he taught ethics and medical literature and researched his theories about the link between mental attitude and health by working with cancer patients. He also wrote two very popular books on his remarkable recoveries from serious illness: *Anatomy of an Illness as Perceived by the Patient* (1979) and *The Healing Heart* (1983). These books, along with more than a dozen books on the ills of nations, reflect Cousins's broad interest in searching for ways of healing humankind and its world. He died in Los Angeles.

In June 1983 Cousins told the graduating class of Harvard Medical School that the "conquest of war and the pursuit of social justice . . . must become our grand preoccupation and magnificent obsession." These certainly were the concerns that obsessed him throughout his life, and over the years he battled through his writings and actions to make them matters of more general concern. Driven by the shock and portent of Hiroshima, he worked to combat unchecked nationalism, promote federalism, and build a sense of world citizenship, in the belief that people as a whole might yet construct a new world order of peace and justice. His optimism, intellectual curiosity, and commitment to the preservation of human life were equally unquenchable. Indeed, the journalist Bill Moyers observed in the *Saturday Review* (11 Nov. 1967), Cousins was one of the few men who lived through an incredible era and was not consumed by it.

• Cousins's papers are in the Special Collections Library at the University of California, Los Angeles. He assembled two autobiographical collections, *Present Tense: An American Editor's Odyssey* (1967) and *Human Options: An Autobiographical Notebook* (1981). Among his many writings, Cousins most impressively set down his thinking about issues of war and peace in *The Good Inheritance* (1942), *Modern Man Is Obsolete* (1945), *Dr. Schweitzer of Lambaréné* (1960), *The Improbable Triumvirate: John F. Kennedy, Pope John, Nikita Khrushchev* (1972), and *The Pathology of Power* (1987). In *Who Speaks for Man?* (1953), Cousins anticipated the globalization of world problems and argued for the development of world institutions in the human interest; *In Place of Folly* (1961) considers the implications of modern mass warfare and proposes arms control. Biographical information is in Milton S. Katz, "Norman Cousins: Peace Advocate and World Citizen" in *Peace*

Heroes in Twentieth-Century America, ed. Charles DeBenedetti (1986). A revealing portrait is Bill Moyers, "An American Editor's Odyssey: N.C.'s Twenty-five Years at S.R.," *Saturday Review*, 11 Nov. 1967, p. 30. An obituary is in the *New York Times*, 1 Dec. 1990.

MILTON S. KATZ

COUZENS, James (26 Aug. 1872–22 Oct. 1936), businessman, mayor of Detroit, and U.S. senator, was born in Chatham, Ontario, Canada, the son of James J. Couzens and Emma Clift, an immigrant couple from England. Raised in a stern Presbyterian household and a lower-income family that lived on the "muddiest" street in town, young Couzens's education was capped by two years of bookkeeping study at Chatham's Canada Business College. He worked as a newsboy and then stirring smelly, boiling vats for his father, who had parlayed his skills as a soapmaker and salesman into ownership of a small soap-making factory. Displaying an assertive independence, which contemporaries noted that he had inherited from his stern-willed father, young Couzens set off for Detroit to test his mettle in the larger world and in 1890 was taken on as a railroad car–checker for the Michigan Central. Five years later he became an assistant bookkeeper for Alex Malcomson's coal business, which brought him into contact with a mechanical tinkerer and automobile pioneer named Henry Ford.

Ford in his many attempts to become an automobile manufacturer sought financing from Malcomson, and Couzens, sensing opportunity, borrowed, begged, and scraped together $2,500 of his and his sister's money to put into this speculative enterprise. Shortly thereafter Couzens joined the Ford company as a manager, partly because investor Malcomson wanted Couzens to direct Ford's mechanical genius to profit-making. An astute accountant, Couzens helped keep the business solvent by forcing the sales of cars that Ford wished to tinker with further to perfect. Couzens could later claim some credit for helping turn a small-time motorcar assembly shop into a profitable mammoth manufacturing corporation.

In 1898 Couzens married Margaret Manning, a Roman Catholic, despite their religious differences. The couple had five children, who were all raised as Catholics. Their son Frank Couzens later became mayor of Detroit, serving from 1933 to 1938.

Couzens's own interest in politics and civic duty prompted him in 1913 to take on the chairmanship of Detroit's public transportation system, which was known as the Detroit Street Railway Commission. It also stirred in him a burning passion to carry to completion the goals of one of his political idols, Detroit mayor Hazen S. Pingree, which was to bring about municipal ownership of the street railway system. In 1916 Couzens was appointed police commissioner and became known as a demanding, uncompromising, and impeccably honest police official. The year before he had had a dispute with Ford over business matters and a dislike of Ford's prewar pacifism and had resigned from his managerial job; in 1919 Couzens sold out his original investment, which netted a princely $30 million. Now independently wealthy, he could give full rein to his political ideas. He ran for and won the mayoralty of Detroit in 1918 and was reelected in 1921, becoming the city's first executive under its "strong" mayor charter. Strong-willed and bulldog stubborn, Couzens pulled out all stops with his war with the privately owned street railway company, its backers, and a resistant city council. After a four-year political battle, Couzens brought about municipal ownership for Detroit transportation in 1922.

The same year Couzens, a Republican, was appointed to fill the unexpired term of U.S. senator Truman Newberry, who had resigned because of a scandal caused by election irregularities. Thereafter followed a tempestuous fourteen years in the Senate in which the abrasive and independent-minded Couzens sometimes seemed to be a political party unto himself. This unconventional politician continued to live by his old mayoral campaign slogan: "I will reward no friends and punish no enemies." He had few of the former and increasing numbers of the latter.

In the Senate Couzens never mastered the art of oratory or diplomacy and continued to behave like a Ford Motor Company executive instead of an elected representative of the people. Yet he endeared himself to a larger public and the liberal progressives in Congress when he openly opposed his old partner Henry Ford's efforts to buy publicly owned Muscle Shoals and when he sponsored a "soak the rich" surtax on the wealthy. Couzens made something of a career attacking Republican secretary of the treasury Andrew Mellon for his tax cuts for the wealthy. Always an outsider with populistic instincts, Couzens took puckish delight in deflating the egos of Detroit millionaires and his social betters, who had never accepted Couzens into their circles. During the depression of the 1930s he opposed some liberal measures such as federal funding for public housing. He supported most of President Franklin D. Roosevelt's work and welfare programs from 1933 to 1935, however, and he became known as a New Deal Republican, a label that Couzens did not especially like. He resisted all efforts of the Democrats to recruit him into their party in the 1930s.

Couzens's hodgepodge of support and opposition to New Deal measures never fit into a clear ideology. What he seemed to dislike was authoritarianism, whether it came from individuals or from the states. He tended to support measures that he perceived as helping the little man, which he had once been himself. Even so, President Roosevelt paid special attention to Couzens and sent him as a U.S. representative to the World Economic and Monetary Conference in London in 1933. When the national bank crisis began in Detroit that same year, Couzens, a member of the Senate banking committee, was in the thick of the frantic efforts to find a solution. When none was found and the Detroit banks were closed by the state and then by a national bank holiday ordered by the president, Couzens was widely blamed for the bank collapse.

Couzens was accused of not applying political pressure on the Reconstruction Finance Corporation, a federal agency, to loan money to the foundering Detroit system. His critics said he was trying to get even with the "old money" of Detroit for not accepting him into its ranks. Couzens's biographer Harry Barnard has gone to some lengths to exonerate the senator of that charge. A more recent study by Donald Davis, however, finds the charge not only plausible but also asserts that Couzens delighted in avenging slights of the past. The fact that the bank crisis wiped out the economic influence of the premotorcar elite in Detroit lends credence to the argument. It would appear that Couzens had gone back on the second part of his old campaign slogan: "punish no enemies."

Despite his sometimes irascible persona, Couzens had a soft spot in his heart for children, especially those of the poor and handicapped, and he spent a sizable portion of his private fortune on public health efforts such as the establishment of the Children's Fund of Michigan in 1934. He also built at his own expense residence halls for nursing students and did many other good deeds. His beneficence totaled about $30 million, a stupendous sum in the depression year of 1936. Yet he wanted no monuments or memorials to attest to his philanthropy and also refused to permit his name to be used for the children's fund. Moreover, Couzens insisted that all of the money of the fund must be expended by 1954, which it would be, thus leaving no lasting impression of his generosity. He had come to Michigan as a penniless car-checker, and he seemed to want to leave as he had entered.

Turning down an invitation to run for the Senate as a Democrat in 1936, Couzens entered the Republican primary and was defeated in September. The next month he died in Detroit.

• Couzens's papers are in the Library of Congress. Other papers, scrapbooks, and related items can be found in the Burton Historical Collection of the Detroit Public Library. His authoritative biography is Harry Barnard, *Independent Man: The Life of Senator James Couzens* (1958). Information on the bank crisis and other aspects of Couzens's life is in Donald F. Davis, *Conspicuous Production: Automobiles and Elites in Detroit, 1899–1933* (1988). For the background of political issues that motivated Couzens, see Melvin G. Holli, *Reform in Detroit* (1969), and John M. T. Chavis, "James Couzens: Mayor of Detroit, 1919–1922" (Ph.D. diss., Michigan State Univ., 1970). An obituary is in the *Detroit News*, 23 Oct. 1936.

MELVIN G. HOLLI

COUZINS, Phoebe Wilson (8 Sept. 1839?–6 Dec. 1913), lawyer, suffragist, and lecturer, was born in St. Louis, Missouri, the daughter of John Edward Decker Couzins, a carpenter and builder, and Adaline Weston. Her parents were both politically active. Her father held the posts of chief of police of St. Louis and U.S. marshal for the Eastern District of Missouri. Her mother served as a nurse to the Western Sanitary Commission during the Civil War where she provided aid to wounded and sick soldiers. Both parents instilled in their daughter an activist spirit.

At age fifteen Couzins graduated from a St. Louis public high school. While assisting her mother as a volunteer aide for the Sanitary Commission, she began to develop her ideas on women's rights. She felt that war and the miseries stemming from such conflicts could be prevented if women had political power. In 1869 she founded the Woman's Franchise Organization in St. Louis and also became a member of the Missouri Woman Suffrage Association. Through these organizations Couzins began to construct a role for herself as an impassioned supporter of women's rights.

In 1868, at the urging of woman's rights advocate and family friend Judge John M. Krum, Couzins applied to the law school of Washington University. She was accepted as the first woman in the law school, later graduating and gaining admission to the Missouri bar in 1871. Although she never practiced law, she was admitted to the bars of Missouri, Arkansas, Utah, Kansas, and the federal courts of the Dakota Territory. She was appointed by her father as his deputy while he served as U.S. marshal. Upon his death in 1887, she was made interim marshal for two months, the first woman to hold such a post.

Couzins cleverly used the skills, discipline, and knowledge she acquired in studying the American legal system and constitutional law to undergird her arguments in favor of suffrage for women. She became a prominent figure in the women's rights movement. In a letter to the *Revolution*, Elizabeth Cady Stanton specifically noted that Phoebe Couzins was a young woman of great beauty who was a gifted writer and speaker. At the anniversary of the American Equal Rights Association in 1869, Couzins, as a delegate from Missouri, spoke eloquently on her opposition to passage of the Fifteenth Amendment. She felt that black women's issues were being overlooked, stating that the condition of black women was and always had been far worse than that of black men. She argued that passage of the Fifteenth Amendment would reinforce the inferiority of all women.

Dissension over passage of the Fifteenth Amendment caused a split in the Equal Rights Association. Along with Susan B. Anthony, Elizabeth Cady Stanton, and others, Couzins left the Equal Rights Association and formed the National Woman Suffrage Association (NWSA). She was deeply influenced by Anthony and began to lecture extensively on women's rights. She served as a vice president of the NWSA and as a member of its Resolutions Committee. In addition to her support for women's rights, Couzins was an advocate for populist reforms and the temperance movement.

Couzins held many appointed positions. She served as commissioner for Missouri on the National Board of Charities and Correction. Around 1890 she was also appointed manager of the division of mortgage indebtedness for the city of St. Louis. In July 1890 Couzins became a commissioner for Missouri to the Board of Lady Managers of the World Columbian Exposition in Chicago. She was eventually elected to the paid position of secretary of that group, a position that she was eager to take because of her dire financial circumstances. Couzins suffered from arthritis and was intermittently forced to use a wheelchair. Her concern with finding a cure, as well as her taste for expensive clothes, worsened her financial need.

Couzins alienated many women in the suffrage movement because of her support for the more radical organizations in the women's movement and disdain for the younger, more affluent women coming into the movement. She was eventually dismissed from the Board of Lady Managers because of her efforts to overpower the chairperson and other members. She unsuccessfully fought her dismissal in the case *Couzins v. Palmer et al.* (1891).

Remaining unmarried all her life, Couzins was allegedly engaged to the silver millionaire and former Nevada senator James G. Fair. In her later years, Couzins abandoned the causes of woman suffrage and temperance and became a lobbyist for the United Brewers' Association. This change was attributed in part to her bitterness over not being able to achieve the stature in her career that she had envisioned. She eventually lost her prestige and died in poverty in St. Louis.

• Manuscript collections that contain some of Couzins's correspondence and speeches include the J. E. D. Couzins Papers, Missouri Historical Society, St. Louis. Elizabeth Cady Stanton et al., eds., *A History of Woman Suffrage* (1969), has many references to Couzins throughout the multiple volumes. Volume three contains an engraving and excerpts from several of Couzins's speeches. Passages from her speeches and a brief biography are in Lana Rakow and Cheris Kramarae, *The Revolution in Words: Righting Women, 1868–1871* (1990). Another brief biographical sketch is found in Frances E. Willard and Mary A. Livermore, eds., *American Women*, vol. 1 (1973). References to Couzins are in Barbara Andolsen, *"Daughters of Jefferson, Daughters of Bootblacks": Racism and American Feminism* (1976), Oscar Lewis, *Silver Kings* (1947), and Judith Papachristou, *Women Together: A History in Documents of the Women's Movement in the United States* (1976). An obituary is in the *St. Louis Republic*, 7–9 Dec. 1913.

MAMIE E. LOCKE

COVELESKI, Stanley Anthony (13 July 1889–20 Mar. 1984), baseball player, was born Stanislaus Kowalewski in Shamokin, Pennsylvania, the son of Polish immigrants. (The name is sometimes also spelled "Coveleskie" and "Covaleskie.") Little is known of Coveleski's parents except that his father worked in the coal mines and that they had five sons, all of whom played baseball. Stan, the youngest, had but a few years of schooling before entering the mines with the rest of his family. At age 12 he earned five cents an hour and often worked six 12-hour days a week. To his family, baseball seemed the only way out of its economic difficulties, and Coveleski spent many hours perfecting his control by throwing rocks at tin cans swinging from a tree. His occasional game at the mines

persuaded the Shamokin team of the Atlantic League to sign him. His pitching record for 1908 was 6–2, and he was promoted the next year to Lancaster in the Tri-State League. Enjoying immediate success, he led the league in 1909 with 23 wins against only 11 losses. The next year Coveleski was almost as productive, with a 15–8 record. Although he slipped to a 15–19 record in 1911, he demonstrated his fine control that season by allowing only 65 walks in 272 innings.

Coveleski spent part of the 1912 season with Atlantic City of the same league. In September he was given a trial with the Philadelphia Athletics of the American League, compiling a 2–1 record and pitching a shutout in his first major league game. Having an abundance of quality pitchers, however, the Athletics farmed Coveleski to Spokane and then Portland of the Pacific Coast League. In all he spent eight seasons in the minor leagues before joining the Cleveland Indians in 1916. He remained in the majors through 1928.

About 1915 Coveleski mastered control of the spitball, a most difficult ball to hit because in most varieties it dropped sharply as it approached home plate. The pitch was outlawed in 1920 in the major leagues, but Coveleski and sixteen other pitchers were exempted from the rule because the pitch was considered essential to the livelihood of those men. After his retirement from baseball Coveleski was quoted as disclaiming his frequent use of the strange pitch; instead, he said, the threat of its use greatly served to keep batters off balance. His real stock in trade was his control. Probably possessing the best control of all the spitball pitchers, Coveleski walked only 58 hitters in 232 innings during his first year at Cleveland. One biographer claimed that in one game Coveleski threw every pitch for a strike during the first seven innings, a scarcely believable performance.

During his nine seasons with the Indians, Coveleski compiled a 172–123 record and won at least 20 games for four consecutive seasons. He also led the league in a number of categories, including strikeouts and lowest opponents' batting averages in 1920, and lowest earned run average in 1923. In 1925 Coveleski was traded to the Washington Senators, where he again led the league in earned run average. He also had the highest victory percentage—.800, based on a 20–5 record. He spent three years with Washington and one with the New York Yankees before retiring from baseball in 1928.

Coveleski appeared in two World Series. In 1920 he defeated the Brooklyn Dodgers three times without a loss, as the Indians won the series five games to two. In the series Coveleski allowed only two runs in 27 innings and walked only two men in those three games. He gave up just five hits in each game, and his earned run average was a minuscule 0.67. In 1925 he pitched reasonably well against the Pittsburgh Pirates, who won the series four games to three, but lost both games that he started.

In his 14-year career Coveleski won 215 games and lost 142, and he suffered only two losing seasons. His earned run average was 2.89. He struck out 981 and walked 802. Hitters averaged fewer than five home runs a year against him. He won 20 or more games five times and pitched 38 shutouts. Even his last season was victorious, as he compiled a 5–1 record. In 1969 he was elected to the National Baseball Hall of Fame.

Coveleski settled in South Bend, Indiana, after leaving baseball, and for several years he managed a service station. He had married Frances D. Shivetts, and the couple had one son. The Coveleskis were a close, quiet family. Although the opportunity arose several times, he and his brother Harry, who had a brief but successful career with the Detroit Tigers, had always refused management's urging that they pitch against one another. He died in a nursing home in South Bend.

• A clipping file on Coveleski is at the National Baseball Library in Cooperstown, N.Y. Satisfactory sketches on him are in Martin Appel and Burt Goldblatt, *Baseball's Best: The Hall of Fame Gallery* (1977); and Lowell Reidenbaugh, *Cooperstown* (1983). Coveleski's pitching statistics and achievements are thoroughly covered in John Thorn and Pete Palmer, eds., *Total Baseball*, 3d ed. (1993). An obituary is in the *New York Times*, 21 Mar. 1984.

THOMAS L. KARNES

COVELLO, Leonard (26 Nov. 1887–19 Aug. 1982), educator, was born Leonardo Coviello in Avigliano, Italy, the son of Pietro Coviello, a skilled artisan, and Clementina Assunta Genovese. In 1890 Covello's father emigrated to the United States and settled in New York City, where his wife and children joined him in 1896. Covello was raised in the immigrant enclave of East Harlem, which exerted a strong influence on him that lasted throughout his life. Almost immediately, Covello was placed in a local school run by the Female Guardian Society of America, a Protestant mission group that ministered to the needs of immigrants and, like most philanthropic organizations of the time, aimed principally to Americanize immigrant children. Covello spent two years at the school, finished his elementary education at Public School No. 83, and entered Morris High School in 1902. (His name was changed to Leonard Covello while he was in the public school system.) In high school Covello won a Pulitzer Scholarship to attend Columbia University. He graduated in 1911 from Columbia College and took a position as a teacher of French and Spanish at De Witt Clinton High School in New York City. In 1913 he married Mary Accurso, who died in 1914. In 1923 he married Rose Accurso, who predeceased him in 1969. Both marriages were childless.

During World War I Covello first served as a volunteer with the Farm Cadet Bureau, and in December 1917 he enlisted as a private in the U.S. Army Artillery Corps. In France he became an interpreter for the Corps of Intelligence Police. Contacts made during World War I enabled Covello to obtain a postwar position with a midwestern clearinghouse for foreign advertising. He returned in 1920 to his former position at De Witt Clinton High School and served as head of the De Witt Clinton Italian Department from 1922 to

1934. In 1926 he was appointed first assistant in modern languages, a position he held until 1934.

In East Harlem Covello was influenced by the social reform ideas of Anna C. Ruddy, a settlement house worker who came to East Harlem from Canada in 1890 and devoted her life to working with Italian immigrant families. Covello was also influenced by the social activism of Norman Thomas, whose Presbyterian mission church in East Harlem Covello joined. Covello sought to ease the transition of immigrant school children into American life and to facilitate their acculturation without separating them from their native culture and communities. He earned a Ph.D. in educational sociology from New York University in 1944 with a thesis titled "The Social Background of the Italo-American School Child." Research for the thesis had taken him to southern Italy and had engaged him for more than a decade. Originally published in Leiden, the Netherlands, in 1967, this classic sociocultural study appeared in the United States in 1972.

Covello was actively involved in virtually every organization and activity related to the city's Italian immigrant community. In 1910 he and his friend John Shedd organized the Lincoln Club of Little Italy in East Harlem, and in 1914 Covello began to sponsor a *Circolo Italiano* at De Witt Clinton High School. He also participated in the work of the Italian League for Social Service (organized in 1915) and the Young Men's Italian Educational League (organized in 1916), and from its inception in 1912, he served as vice president of the New York City Italian Teachers Association, which encouraged the study of the Italian language. In 1927 he was instrumental in founding the Italian Parents Association, which promoted interaction between the schools and the Italian community. It was Covello's strategic deployment of the influence of the Order of the Sons of Italy that helped lead in 1922 to the New York City Board of Education granting parity to Italian with other modern languages in the city schools. Covello also participated in the work of the Italian Educational League, the Italy-America Society, the Casa Italiana Educational Bureau, and the Istituto di Cultura Italiana (later the Casa Italiana of Columbia University). In the mid-1960s he provided the major impetus for the founding of the American Italian Historical Association, whose operating expenses he assumed for some years.

During his years at De Witt Clinton, Covello was aware of the need for a senior high school in East Harlem, and for a number of years he led a campaign in the community for the high school. In 1934, with the help of New York congressman Vito Marcantonio and New York mayor Fiorello La Guardia, he was finally successful in establishing Benjamin Franklin High School in East Harlem. Covello was appointed principal of the new 4,000-student, all-male high school, a position he held until his retirement in 1957.

As principal of Benjamin Franklin (and James Otis Junior High School, a sending school), Covello implemented many of his innovative ideas and turned Benjamin Franklin into one of the national examples of the community-centered school. This concept, based on the recognition that the public school was the one social agency that touched nearly all families, called for almost complete interaction between the school and the community. Working through the school's Community Advisory Council, which consisted of teachers, parents, students, and business and civic leaders, he initiated intensive programs to strengthen the East Harlem community. Efforts included housing and sanitation campaigns, the establishment of social and educational centers in the community, citizenship campaigns, adult education programs and summer school programs as well as a number of other educational and community improvement programs. In about 1935 an intercultural education program designed to teach students to understand and appreciate other ethnic and cultural groups was added. Covello also taught courses at New York University (1932–1948) and at Fairleigh Dickinson University (1957–1963) on the community-centered school, ethnic and cultural communities, and the social background of the Italian-American schoolchild in the New York City schools.

As East Harlem began to change with an influx of Puerto Rican immigrants during the 1940s and 1950s, Covello implemented programs for Puerto Rican students at Benjamin Franklin High School that were similar to those that had proved so successful among Italian immigrants. He also instituted major programs for the Puerto Rican community at large, such as literacy and language campaigns, work with Puerto Rican organizations, conferences and workshops on Puerto Rican needs, and a continuing effort to awaken pride in Puerto Rican history and culture. After his retirement in 1957, Covello accepted an appointment as educational consultant to the Migration Division of the Commonwealth of Puerto Rico.

Covello was also deeply involved in work with the senior citizens in East Harlem. A founder in 1952 of the East Harlem Day Care Center for Older Persons (renamed the Leonard Covello Senior Center for East Harlem in 1969), Covello also helped form the East Harlem Committee on Aging in the early 1960s and served as chairman of its Directing Committee from 1960 to 1967.

Covello contributed many articles to scholarly and popular journals and to newspapers. His most significant works include his published thesis, *The Social Background of the Italo-American School Child*; his autobiography, *The Heart Is the Teacher*; and an unpublished manuscript, "The Benjamin Franklin High School," which he wrote between 1953 and 1955.

In 1972 Covello joined the Sicilian social reformer Danilo Dolci to work as a consultant with Dolci's Center for Study and Action in Western Sicily. Covello died in Messina, Sicily.

• Covello's papers are deposited at the Balch Institute For Ethnic Studies, Philadelphia. The main source for Covello's life is his autobiography, *The Heart Is the Teacher* (1958; repr. as *Teacher in the Urban Community*, 1970). See also

Robert Peebles, *Leonard Covello: An Immigrant's Contribution to New York City* (1978), and Francesco Cordasco, ed., *Studies in Italian American Social History: Essays in Honor of Leonard Covello* (1975). For the East Harlem community, see Francesco Cordasco and Rocco Galatioto, "Ethnic Displacement in the Interstitial Community: The East Harlem (New York City) Experience," *Phylon: The Atlanta University Review of Race and Culture* 31 (Fall 1970): 302–12. An obituary is in the *New York Times*, 20 Aug. 1982.

FRANCESCO CORDASCO

COVICI, Pascal Avram (4 Nov. 1885–14 Oct. 1964), book publisher and editor, was born in Botosani, Romania, the son of Wolf Covici, a vintner, and Schfra Barish. When he was twelve years old Covici, who went by "Pat," immigrated with his parents and his sister to Chicago, where his six brothers owned half a dozen retail stores. He attended the University of Michigan and the University of Chicago but did not graduate from either and then worked as a manager of his brothers' stores. In 1915 he married Dorothy Soll of Chicago; they had one son.

Before he opened a bookstore and publishing house in Chicago with his first partner, Billy McGee, in 1922, Covici spent four years in Bradenton, Florida, where he was a manager and the publisher of a monthly newspaper at Waterbury Grapefruit Groves. Covici, who had taken literature courses in college, was noted for his enthusiasm for books. Covici and McGee published many lavish and expensive limited editions intended for collectors, and their bookstore became a meeting place for writers and artists. The *Chicago Literary Times* was published there in 1923–1924. One of the first books published under the Covici-McGee imprint was Ben Hecht's memoir *1001 Afternoons in Chicago* (1922). Hecht's *Fantazius Mallare: A Mysterious Oath* (1922), a Covici-McGee limited edition, was declared obscene and confiscated by postal officials. The publishers, the author, and the illustrator, Wallace Smith, were all arrested; each pleaded no contest and paid a $1,000 fine.

Health problems forced McGee to leave the business in 1924, and starting in 1925, Covici began to publish under the imprint of Pascal Covici, Inc. Three years later he formed a new publishing firm with Donald Friede in New York. Covici, Friede wrote later, was a "flamboyant Rumanian" with a "shock of white hair," the head of a poet, and the body of a football player. Their working relationship was "effectively harmonious" in a way "that made life enjoyable and exciting" (p. 80). Like Covici's earlier enterprises, Covici-Friede specialized in limited editions featuring lush illustrations and expensive papers and bindings. *The Front Page*, a play by Hecht and Charles MacArthur, brought the firm immediate success in 1928, as did Radclyffe Hall's novel *The Well of Loneliness*. The novel's portrayal of lesbianism, however, incurred the wrath of the New York Society for the Suppression of Vice, and copies of the book were seized as obscene in January 1929. Covici and Friede were found guilty by a magistrate, but their convictions were later reversed and the case dismissed by an appeals court, which ruled that a book could not be declared obscene simply because of its theme.

The Covici-Friede list also included works by Gene Fowler, Wyndham Lewis, Clifford Odets, and Nathanael West. The firm's most important author, however, was John Steinbeck, who was a virtual unknown when Covici signed him in 1934. Chicago bookseller Ben Abramson had recommended to Covici, his friend, that he read Steinbeck's *The Pastures of Heaven* (1932), a commercial failure that was being sold on a remainder table at Abramson's bookshop. Covici paid ten cents for the novel and, after reading it, wrote to Steinbeck and asked to be his publisher. In addition to publishing Steinbeck's fourth—and first successful—novel, *Tortilla Flat*, in 1935, Covici-Friede brought out four other new works in 1936 and 1937 and reissued his earlier works.

In 1935 Friede sold his share of the firm, which by then had run up substantial debts, especially to printers and binders. Its financial problems led in 1938 to its dissolution in order to satisfy creditors. Covici then became a senior editor at Viking Press, persuading Steinbeck to join him there. In 1939 Viking published Steinbeck's *The Grapes of Wrath* in a big first printing that Covici recommended. It won a Pulitzer Prize in 1940. In addition to being Steinbeck's editor, Covici supervised the editing of the Viking Portable Library and worked with other major writers of nonfiction and fiction, including Joseph Campbell, Gilbert Highet, Lionel Trilling, Arthur Miller, and Saul Bellow, who dedicated his novel *Herzog* (1964) to Covici, "a great editor, and better yet, a generous friend." Bellow was not unusual. More than thirty authors dedicated books to Covici. It was at Viking that Covici, not wanting to appear older than fifty when he joined the firm, first began to list his birth year as 1888, a date that continued to be cited even after his death.

The relationship between Covici and Steinbeck was extraordinary both in terms of its length and its mutuality. Steinbeck described their association as "singularly blessed" (*Journal of a Novel*, p. 179) and Covici as his collaborator and conscience (*New York Times*, 15 Oct. 1964). For his part, Covici called Steinbeck "my rarest experience" (1941 letter quoted in Fensch, p. 29). While writing *East of Eden* in 1951, Steinbeck kept a daily journal for Covici, which was later published as a separate work, and he dedicated the novel to his editor. He also gave Covici the manuscript of the novel as a Christmas gift; it came in a mahogany box that Steinbeck had built as he wrote the novel. Covici died in New York City. He had great instincts for good writing but was esteemed as well for his ability to motivate writers in a manner that was demanding but never demeaning.

• Covici's papers have not been collected. Correspondence between Covici and Steinbeck is in the John Steinbeck Collection, Humanities Research Center, University of Texas–Austin. The Covici-Steinbeck relationship is given a full treatment in Thomas Fensch, *Steinbeck and Covici: The Story of a Friendship* (1979). Other valuable sources are *Journal of a Novel: The East of Eden Letters* (1969) and *Steinbeck: A Life in Letters*, ed. Elaine Steinbeck and Robert Wallsten (1975). The Covici-Friede association is recalled in Donald Friede, *The Mechanical Angel* (1948). Morris Ernst and Alan U. Schwartz, *Censorship: The Search for the Obscene* (1964), includes an account of the legal fight over *The Well of Loneliness*. On Covici's Chicago days, see Ben Hecht, *A Child of the Century* (1954). On Covici as publisher and editor, see Charles Madison, *Book Publishing in America* (1966) and *Irving to Irving: Author-Publisher Relations, 1800–1974* (1974). In 1964 Viking Press published a limited-edition memorial volume, *Pascal Covici, 1888–1964*, which contains eulogies and evaluations by authors Covici edited and by others with whom he worked. Obituaries are in the *New York Times*, 15 Oct. 1964, and *Publishers Weekly*, 26 Oct. 1964.

RONALD S. MARMARELLI

COVODE, John (18 Mar. 1808–11 Jan. 1871), member of Congress, was born near West Fairfield in Westmoreland County, Pennsylvania, the son of Jacob Covode and Ann Updegraff, farmers. Covode worked on the family farm and as an apprentice blacksmith as a young man, receiving some elementary education in the local public schools. In 1829 he married Sara Hay; they had six children. At an unknown later date he married Margaret Peale; they had three children.

Covode learned the woolen manufacturing business at a woolen mill in Lockport, and in the 1840s he owned and operated a woolen mill. He worked as a canal construction contractor, then as owner of a section boat on the canal from Philadelphia to Ohio. He was also a promoter of the Pennsylvania Central Railroad and helped organize the Westmoreland Coal Company, which during the 1840s and 1850s grew into the largest supplier of coal for the production of illuminating gas.

As a justice of the peace Covode earned the nickname "Honest John." He served two terms in the Pennsylvania House of Representatives as a Whig, and he ran unsuccessfully for the state senate twice. In 1854 Covode was elected to Congress as an Anti-Masonic Whig and then as a Republican to the next three Congresses, serving from March 1855 through March 1863. Like many other northern Whigs who became Republicans, he stood for protective tariffs, and he was directly and explicitly opposed to the extension of slavery. In 1858 he delivered a speech attacking the proslavery Lecompton constitution of the Kansas Territory and roundly criticizing James Buchanan for his proslavery stance. He claimed in his speech that Buchanan had been "trimming between the extremes of North and South, until he ascertained that the slave interest predominated in the Democratic Party." Then, Covode charged, Buchanan "at once threw himself into the arms of the slavery propagandists; and today his position is more ultra-southern than that of Mr. Calhoun was at the day of his death."

Covode distinguished between the "theoretical" concept of popular sovereignty, which suggested that the first settlers in a territory could set the laws and governance of the territory, and a more "practical" popular sovereignty, in which Congress might consider accepting a proposition from the people of a territory for admission to the Union. In other words, he would limit the sovereignty of territorial residents to the ability to apply for admission to the Union and would not extend it to include the writing of fundamental law for the territory. He believed that within a few years not only Kansas but Minnesota and Oregon would be ready to be admitted as states without slavery. He predicted that slavery would soon diminish and come close to vanishing in Arkansas and Maryland. He argued that slaves were kept in ignorance as a "necessary police regulation" and that, therefore, they were suited only to the most common labor. As a consequence, southern agriculture could never flourish or compete with northern agriculture, and southern agriculture was bound to wither away.

In 1860 Covode introduced a resolution to Congress calling for an investigation into whether or not President Buchanan had bribed members of Congress in connection with the Lecompton constitution and into alleged corruption at the Philadelphia Navy Yard. He was appointed to head the Select Committee on Alleged Corruptions in Government, called the Covode investigation committee, set up to investigate those charges, and in that connection he gained national attention. In 1860 his committee issued an 800-page anti-Buchanan report, which was authored by committee member Charles Train, although the conclusions are attributed to Covode. Among other charges, the committee established that financial assessments had been made against employees at the navy yard for political purposes. Further, the Covode committee report concluded that Buchanan had offered bribes to members of Congress to approve the Lecompton constitution. However, Congress took no action on the charges. Since Covode served as a member of the Republican Executive Congressional Committee during the election of 1860, his charges had a partisan flavor. Furthermore, President Buchanan had earlier charged that bribery was extensively used in the Pennsylvania congressional races of 1858, leading some to suspect a more personal motive for Covode's charges against the president. The Covode investigation drew national attention partly because it served as a focal point for attacking Buchanan and for discrediting, more generally, the tactics of the proslavery forces. Furthermore, it was an early example of the use of congressional power to investigate the executive department.

During the Civil War, Covode was a strong supporter of Abraham Lincoln and served as a member of the Joint Committee on the Conduct of the War. After his retirement from Congress in 1863, he was appointed in 1865 by the War Department to investigate the governance of the federally controlled regions in the Mississippi Valley. Upon Covode's return, President Andrew Johnson rejected his report, which recommended the dismissal of the appointed governor of Louisiana and urged retaining federal troops in the former Confederacy.

Covode was reelected to Congress in 1866 and 1868, joining with the Radical Republicans in opposing Johnson's Reconstruction plans and supporting Congressional Reconstruction. He introduced the measure calling for the impeachment of Johnson. Through his attacks on Buchanan in 1858–1860 and his opposition to Andrew Johnson in 1868, Covode clearly emerged as a firmly committed antislavery Radical Republican, although he was never regarded as a major national leader of the faction. Covode's election in 1868 was contested by Henry D. Foster, and neither Covode nor Foster was certified by the Pennsylvania governor as elected. The House of Representatives finally declared Covode duly elected and seated him in February 1870. He declined to run for reelection in 1870 but served in Congress until his death in Harrisburg, Pennsylvania.

Covode's fame derives from his charges against Buchanan and from his reputation as a strongly antislavery Republican from Pennsylvania during the Civil War and early Reconstruction periods. Continually active in Pennsylvania Republican politics, he served as president of the 1860 state convention of the party and as chairman of the Republican State Committee from 1869 until his death.

• Some Covode papers are at the Historical Society of Pennsylvania, and papers relating to the Westmoreland Coal Company are at the Hagley Museum in Wilmington, Del. Covode's writings include the pamphlet *Kansas—The Lecompton Constitution—Popular Sovereignty, Theoretical and Practical* (1858). Sources on Covode include Edward W. Chester, "The Impact of the Covode Congressional Investigation," *Western Pennsylvania Historical Magazine* 42 (Dec. 1959): 343–50. For information on Pa. politics, see John Coleman, *The Disruption of the Pennsylvania Democracy 1848–1860* (1975). An obituary is in the *Philadelphia Press*, 12 Jan. 1871.

RODNEY P. CARLISLE

COWAN, Clyde Lorrain, Jr. (6 Dec. 1919–24 May 1974), physicist, was born in Detroit, Michigan, the son of Clyde Lorrain Cowan, a metallurgist, and Esther May Koenig. The family subsequently moved to St. Louis, Missouri, where Clyde Jr. received his early education in the public schools. He attended Missouri School of Mines and Metallurgy (later the University of Missouri—Rolla), where he was a member of the Reserve Officers' Training Corps and received a B.S. in chemical engineering in 1940. Following graduation he worked in industrial positions as a chemical engineer and as a chemist until 1942, when he received his commission as a second lieutenant in the Chemical Warfare Service and was assigned to the U.S. Army Air Forces. He served as a chemical warfare officer with the Eighth Air Force stationed in London, later as a staff member of the British branch of the Massachusetts Institute of Technology Radiation Laboratory, and subsequently as a liaison officer between the Royal Air Force and the U.S. Army Technical Service Corps. He was married in Woodford, England, in 1943 to Betty Eleanor Dunham. The couple reared three of their own children and adopted two others.

After leaving active duty in 1946 with the rank of captain, Cowan entered graduate study in physics at Washington University, St. Louis, from which he received an M.S. in 1947 and a Ph.D. in 1949. Following completion of his graduate work, Cowan joined the nuclear weapons test division of the Los Alamos Scientific Laboratory, in which he served as group leader, division J, from 1953 to 1955. From 1955 until 1957 he was a group leader in the physics division at Los Alamos. In 1951 he and Frederick Reines also began a search for a postulated elementary particle called the neutrino.

Early studies of beta decay, in which a radioactive atom undergoes transmutation by emission of an electron, had led to a puzzle: this kind of decay did not appear to conserve either energy or intrinsic angular momentum. In 1930 Wolfgang Pauli proposed a "desperate" solution, suggesting that beta decay involved not only the emission of an electron but also of a second particle, uncharged and of small mass, which became known as the neutrino. This second particle carried away part of the energy, and since it had never been observed, it was assumed that it rarely interacted with matter. Further work by Enrico Fermi indicated that the mass of the neutrino was either zero or very small compared to the mass of the electron; at the time Cowan and Reines undertook their experiments, many scientists felt that the neutrino could never be detected.

Although the first proposal by Cowan and Reines involved use of a large scintillation counter to detect a small number of the many neutrinos from a nuclear explosion, they soon decided on a nuclear reactor as the neutrino source. They hoped to observe inverse beta decay, in which a neutrino from the reactor interacted with a proton to produce a neutron and a positive electron, as the signature reaction to identify the neutrino. Their first attempts, at a Hanford reactor in 1953, were not conclusive due to a large background. They subsequently developed a new target and detector system, two targets, of 200 liters each, sandwiched between three detector sections, each of which contained 1,400 liters of liquid scintillator viewed by 110 photomultiplier tubes. The site of the measurements was moved to the larger Savannah River reactor near Aiken, South Carolina (which produced a flux of 10^{13} neutrinos per square centimeter per second in the target region of the detector). At this location they were able to place the target-detector system twelve meters below ground in a massive building, thus reducing the background flux. In measurements completed in June 1956, the signal rate observed was about 1.8 events per hour with the reactor operating, falling to one-fifth of this rate with the reactor off. This experiment provided definitive evidence for the existence of what is now known as the electron antineutrino, one of six members of this important class of elementary particles.

Cowan left Los Alamos in 1957 to teach at George Washington University in Washington, D.C. In 1957–1958 he also served as an organizer of scientific exhibits for the second Atoms for Peace conference held in Geneva, Switzerland. In 1958 he joined the faculty at the Catholic University of America as professor of physics, a post he held for the remainder of his life. There, in addition to his teaching, he coauthored a textbook of modern physics and undertook a number of difficult measurements aimed at studying the properties of extraterrestrial neutrinos.

Honors received by Cowan include a bronze star for his wartime work on radar, a Guggenheim Fellowship (1957), and election as fellow of the American Physical Society and of the American Association for the Advancement of Science. He also received a Distinguished Alumni Award from Washington University (1962). He died in Bethesda, Maryland. He will be remembered for the research with Frederick Reines, which led to the detection of the neutrino and for which Reines received the 1995 Nobel Prize in physics.

• Accounts of the neutrino discovery, along with references to Cowan's most important publications, appear in Clyde L. Cowan, "Anatomy of an Experiment: An Account of the Discovery of the Neutrino," in *Annual Report of the Smithsonian Institution* (1964); Frederick Reines, "The Early Days of Experimental Neutrino Physics," *Science* 203 (5 Jan. 1979): 11–16; and Frederick Reines, "Detection of the Neutrino," in *Pions to Quarks: Particle Physics in the 1950s*, ed. Laurie M. Brown, et al. (1989). An obituary is in the *New York Times*, 26 May 1974.

ROBERT G. ARNS

COWAN, Edgar A. (19 Sept. 1815–29 Aug. 1878), senator, was born in Greensburg, Pennsylvania. His parents' names are unknown, but they were apparently very poor. Cowan was brought up by his grandfather, Captain William Cowan. He worked as a boat's carpenter in Allegheny County and managed to save enough money to enter Greensburg Academy. He attended Franklin College in New Athens, Ohio, graduating in 1839 at the top of his class. In 1842 he married Lucetta Oliver, with whom he had three children.

Cowan read law with Henry D. Foster in Greensburg. He was admitted to the bar in Westmoreland County in 1842 and quickly became known as a forceful orator. He established a successful practice both as a defender and later as a prosecutor, winning difficult cases against experienced and well-known lawyers. Although early in his career he was a Jackson Democrat, he allied himself with the Whig party in 1840. In 1856 Cowan joined the new Republican party and supported John C. Frémont's bid for the presidency. Although Cowan held strong beliefs on the sanctity of constitutional protection of property rights, he was also opposed to the extension of slavery into the territories and so supported Abraham Lincoln in the 1860 presidential election, serving as a Republican elector. The following year Cowan was elected U.S. senator. Although still relatively unknown, he was believed to be more conservative than his arch rival, David Wilmot.

As a senator, Cowan was true to his conservative reputation. He supported conciliation, argued for civilized warfare, and was a careful defender of the Constitution. When President Lincoln called a special session of Congress on 4 July 1861, Cowan, like most moderates, supported the war effort by voting for troop and supply bills but sought to contain the severity of legislation for the punishment of rebels. Explicit in his stance that the war was for the restoration of the Union and not a war for conquest, he consistently voted against legislation he considered too harsh or contrary to the international laws of war. He was criticized both by his fellow congressmen and in the popular press, and this criticism became especially vehement during the regular session of Congress in the winter of 1861–1862. During proceedings to expel Senator Jesse Bright of Indiana, who had been accused of treason for writing a letter to Jefferson Davis, Cowan defended Bright. Republican senator Benjamin F. Wade saddled Cowan with a derogatory nickname, "the watchdog of slavery," which haunted him for the rest of his political life. The following spring a special meeting of Republicans in Pennsylvania published a series of resolutions censuring him.

Cowan, predictably, also vigorously opposed confiscation legislation on the grounds that it was unconstitutional and would forever destroy any possibility of peaceful reunion with the seceded states. He believed that the confiscation of private property was contrary to the law of nations, and he was the only Republican in Congress to oppose the First Confiscation Act. Throughout the war he attempted to mitigate any punitive legislation proposed by Radical Republicans, convinced that such acts would eventually result in the destruction of the federal government and would liberate all slaves, regardless of the limits the more moderate Republicans in Congress sought to impose upon the legislation.

Despite the disapproval heaped on him, Cowan continued to adhere to his view that "the Constitution is the charter of our liberties and the covenant of the Union which we are all so anxious to defend. I will stand upon it to the last despite every necessity." He supported the suspension of habeas corpus and voted for the Homestead Act of 1862. He also voted for the Thirteenth Amendment, abolishing slavery, in 1864.

Throughout the war years, Cowan supported the administration on fiscal measures that were intended to support the war effort, such as floating loans, increasing taxes, and internal revenue. But he voted against the legal tender measures and the National Bank Act as being unconstitutional. Cowan aligned himself consistently with the Democratic opposition and by doing so lost the support of the Republican party in his home state. In 1866 the Pennsylvania state legislature and the Union State Convention passed resolutions requesting Cowan's resignation.

In 1866 Cowan opposed the Freedman's Bureau Bill while insisting that he remained a "friend of the Negro." This statement, coming after his longstanding opposition to measures for emancipation and black suffrage, caused an uproar on the floor of the Senate and drew down on him an avalanche of denunciation.

In Congress as well as in the public press in Pennsylvania, he was excoriated as a supporter of the slave power and was called by the *Pittsburgh Gazette* an "ingrate who had so basely deceived his political friends."

During the early years of Reconstruction Cowan caused another sensation by proposing, in 1866, an amendment granting black women the right to vote. His action caused a debacle on the floor of the Senate, where he was accused of submitting the bill as a joke. He defended himself against this charge, but he nevertheless failed in his attempt. The Senate defeated the bill on the grounds that white women did not have suffrage.

Cowan was an ardent and loyal supporter of President Andrew Johnson during the impeachment proceedings. He served on the Judiciary Committee, the Committee for Indian Affairs, the Committee on the Patent Office, and the Finance Committee. Johnson appointed Cowan as minister to Austria, but because of the latter's unpopular opinions and Johnson's subsequent impeachment, his appointment was never confirmed by the Senate. Pennsylvania Democrats nominated Cowan for the Senate in 1867, but he was defeated by Simon Cameron. After leaving Washington, Cowan resumed his law practice in Greensburg, where he died.

Known as a classical scholar, Cowan was considered a great orator and was respected in his legal profession. Standing 6′4″, he was called by the *Pittsburgh Gazette*, in a friendlier mood, "gigantic in stature and also gigantic in intellect." He was a man of firm if unpopular convictions, which he clung to despite the sometimes fierce disapproval of his fellow party members and the popular press in his own state.

• Some of Cowan's letters are preserved in manuscript collections in the Library of Congress. A biographical sketch is in J. M. Gresham and S. T. Wiley, *Biographical and Historical Cyclopedia of Westmoreland County, Pennsylvania* (1890). A brief assessment of Cowan's political career is in B. F. Pershing, "Senator Edgar A. Cowan," *Western Pennsylvania Historical Magazine* 4, no. 4 (Oct. 1921). For a discussion of Cowan's political career, consult Erwin Stanley Bradley, *The Triumph of Militant Republicanism* (1964). For Cowan's activities as senator, see the *Congressional Globe* for the 37th Congress. Cowan's obituary is in the *New York Times*, 30 Aug. 1885.

SILVANA SIDDALI

COWAN, Louis George (?16 Dec. 1909–18 Nov. 1976), radio and television producer, was born in Chicago, Illinois, the son of Jacob Cohen, a salesman, and Hetty Smitz. Graduating in 1931 from the University of Chicago, where he studied with Harold Lasswell, he soon started his own public relations firm, plugging such clients as Kay Kyser's band and Chicago's Steven's Hotel. That same year he also changed his name to Cowan. In 1939 he married Pauline "Polly" Spiegel, the daughter of the head of the giant midwestern mail order house. They had four children. In 1940 Cowan had his first major radio success, when his show "The Quiz Kids" became a hit over the NBC network. The program featured a group of prodigies, none older than sixteen, who fielded questions sent in by listeners. The program was the first in Cowan's attempts to create shows with intellectual content for a popular audience.

Cowan invested some of the money he made from "The Quiz Kids" in his new show "Fighting Senator" (1946), which chronicled the adventures of a principled populist state senator who battled corruption. This program failed to achieve popularity and was soon canceled.

During World War II Cowan was a consultant and director of Domestic Affairs in the Office of War Information. One of his assignments during that period was to try to convince radio producers to include more African-American characters in their programs to publicize the war's egalitarian goals. As a result of his efforts, the soap opera "Our Gal Sunday" (1942) created the character of Franklin Brown, a young African American in military training. Another show, "The Romance of Helen Trent" (1933–1960), portrayed the heroine's rescue by an African-American doctor, for whom she later found a position in a wartime factory.

Cowan was also responsible for overseeing the attempt by network executives to create more favorable images of military personnel. In response, one radio soap opera producer launched a show called "Chaplain Jim" (1942), whose title character was the military equivalent of such perennial do-gooder radio favorites as "Ma Perkins" and "David Harum." On another assignment, one that would have significant long-term consequences, he was given the task of briefing newly appointed psychological warfare officer and former CBS president William S. Paley on the role of the program.

After the war Cowan rebuilt his company Louis G. Cowan Productions, Inc. Its first big postwar hit was "Stop the Music" (1948) on the newly formed ABC network. Hosted by Bert Parks, the show tested musical knowledge and awarded prizes during live telephone calls to contestants. The show's popularity was so great that it caused the cancellation of several competing programs, particularly in 1950 "The Fred Allen Show," a favorite of many critics and intellectuals.

In 1952 Cowan was a consultant in the presidential campaign of Adlai Stevenson, whom he unsuccessfully advised to use television more aggressively. This failure was especially disastrous to Stevenson's campaign because his opponent, General Dwight D. Eisenhower, made full use of the advertising agency Batten, Barton, Durstine and Osborne, which created a highly influential series of ads for their client during the election.

In 1955 Cowan developed for CBS "The $64,000 Question," which was sponsored by the Revlon cosmetics company. The show presented contestants who were apparently experts in their field answering questions of increasing difficulty and doubling their winnings after each correct answer. When the stakes increased past a certain point, the contestants were placed in an isolation booth and could stop at any point along the way or go on to the $64,000 plateau. The show's popular appeal was based on audience identification with ordinary contestants like shoemakers who were experts on opera and Marine captains who were authorities on Shakespeare. The longer contestants were on the show the more the audience came to identify with them, and within a matter of months the show rocketed to the top of the Nielsen ratings. It spawned a whole host of imitators, so that by 1957 no fewer than three high stakes quiz shows received top ten Nielsen rankings.

Furthermore, the program undeniably proved the advertising potential of television. Revlon, which had been one of the nation's smaller cosmetics companies, became one of the industry's giants as a result of its sponsorship of "The $64,000 Question." Cowan chose to see the program as affirming knowledge and information, whereas others saw it as the celebration of greed.

But Cowan's career blossomed, and in 1955 he was asked to join CBS as its vice president for creative services. While he was obliged in that role to support shows such as "The Beverly Hillbillies," he was also able to champion a number of more creative programs. Perhaps his most long-lived, prestigious success was the children's program "Captain Kangaroo," which lasted for twenty-four years (1955–1984) and for which he won two Peabody awards. He also created "Rawhide" (1959–1965).

Unfortunately, in 1958, shortly after Cowan had been appointed president of CBS by Paley, the roof fell in on the high stakes quiz shows, with the disclosure of cheating on programs such as NBC's "Twenty-One." The scandal reached a climax when Professor Charles Van Doren of Columbia, who had catapulted to international fame as a result of his appearances on the show, confessed before a congressional committee to having been given answers to questions.

"The $64,000 Question" was also implicated in the scandal when some of its contestants admitted to being given answers. Looking for a scapegoat, CBS forced Cowan to resign. Before becoming CBS president, Cowan had severed all ties with "The $64,000 Question," and all cheating on the show occurred after he had left. Illness prevented him from testifying in his own defense at congressional hearings convened to investigate the scandal, but he always maintained his innocence of any wrong-doing on "The $64,000 Question."

The quiz show scandals brought to an abrupt end Cowan's career as a producer of television and radio shows. Nevertheless, he still maintained links to broadcasting, teaching first in the communications program at Brandeis University and then in Columbia University's Graduate School of Journalism. In addition, he started his own publishing company, the Chilmark Press, and was cofounder of the American Jewish Committee's William E. Weiner Oral History Library.

Cowan was a pioneer in broadcasting who felt that the medium could be used to educate as well as entertain. One of his major goals as a producer was to connect programs with educational content to popular entertainment. His tragedy was that others were less scrupulous in combining the two. Cowan and his wife died in an accidental fire, possibly caused by faulty wiring in their television set, which started in their New York City apartment.

• Cowan's son Paul wrote extensively about his father's life in *An Orphan in History: Retrieving a Jewish Legacy* (1982). Erik Barnouw, *A History of Broadcasting in the United States*, vols. 2 and 3 (1968, 1970), contain important material both on Cowan's career during the 1930s and 1940s and on "The $64,000 Question." Richard Goodwin was counsel for the congressional committee investigating the quiz show scandal, and his *Remembering America: A Voice from the Sixties* (1988) has an excellent chapter on the investigation.

ALBERT AUSTER

COWARD, Noël (16 Dec. 1899–26 Mar. 1973), playwright, songwriter, and performer, was born Noël Peirce Coward in Teddington, England, the son of Arthur Sabin Coward, a generally unsuccessful traveling piano salesman, and Violet Agnes Veitch. Coward's American connections began at age sixteen as an extra in a D. W. Griffith film being shot in England. After small parts in London musicals, an unhappy term in the English army, and the writing of several unremarked plays, he "formed a fixed resolution to go to America," where he believed all English actors would be welcomed with opened arms.

His first visit to New York in 1921 was permanently influential. Buoyed by the insouciance, rhythm, and taste of Fred Astaire and Adele Astaire and Eubie Blake's music for *Shuffle Along*, he wrote, "In New York, they have always taken light music seriously. There it is, as it should be, saluted as a specialised form of creative art, and is secure in its own right." Coward also spent a knockabout weekend at the home of Hartley Manners that he later refashioned into *Hay Fever* (1925), his earliest success in the field of straight comedy.

Back home, beginning with *London Calling*, his first revue in 1923 for André Charlot, he brought to the form bite and freshness, wit and irony, social satire and a light, poignant, and oddly personal kind of tune. (He credited himself with a "musical ear" but was unable to write down his music or play it on the piano.) At the time, his own frail singing was less admired, though his dancing, coached by Astaire himself, passed muster. With Charlot, he made British revue the standard of the world. The best parts of *London Calling* were merged with an earlier revue and brought to New York in 1924 as *Charlot's London Revue*; Coward did not appear in this show. In London he wrote plays in an astonishing flurry; these were terse, world-weary, entertaining, and on "sophisticated" subject matter frequently outrageous for their time. When another *Charlot's Revue* appeared on Broadway in late 1925, it found four Coward plays in residence: *Still Life, Fallen Angels, Easy Virtue*, and *The Vortex*. Soon *Hay Fever* was added.

Traveling the world and collecting celebrity friends, he continued his creative explosion. His 1928 revue, *This Year of Grace*, encapsulating in "Dance, Little Lady" the accelerating frenzy of the flapper era, caused the American humorist-critic Robert Benchley to write, "It is the kind of revue that one might dream of writing for a completely civilized world. . . . unless someone in America is able to do something that approximates Mr. Coward's feat we shall always feel that it was a mistake to break away from England back there in 1776."

Sensing a change in the mood of the times, Coward switched to operetta and in *Bitter Sweet* (1929) evoked with songs such as "I'll See You Again" the sentimental works of the turn of the century. Ironically, it was his most enduring musical. His 1930 play with music *Private Lives*, including "Somewhere I'll Find You" and the brilliantly cool romantic dialogue that made him a prime subject for parody, was equally enduring. It stamped him a major performer of his own words and confirmed his childhood friend, Gertrude Lawrence, as a major dramatic actress. They teamed again in *Tonight at Eight-Thirty* in 1936, by which time he had come to epitomize for Americans the understated, razor-sharp quality of British wit. Aside his fellow Americanophile P. G. Wodehouse, he was responsible for a series of stereotypes of fusty British loonies, including the colonials of his song "Mad Dogs and Englishmen," the only ones in the tropics who "go out in the midday sun."

During World War II, largely spent in Britain, his sentimentality and patriotism again rose high, as did his admiration for the monarchy; he wrote and performed in films such as *In Which We Serve, Brief Encounter* and *This Happy Breed*. His breezy supernatural comedy *Blithe Spirit* (1941) was popular in both Britain and the United States.

He remained prolific (ultimately he wrote nearly forty plays), but in the austere British postwar years the popularity of his theatrical output declined, and in 1951 he made his first appearance in London cabaret. After the failure in 1954 of his nostalgic musicalization of *Lady Windermere's Fan* by Oscar Wilde, *After the Ball*, he resolved, according to Sheridan Morley, "henceforth to take all his scores across the Atlantic for proper professional treatment from the musical authorities around Broadway" (*Spread a Little Happiness*, pp. 136–37). Later that year, following the death of his mother, who nurtured his theatrical ambitions, Coward embarked on a remarkable two-year parade of personal triumphs as singer and actor in the showrooms of Las Vegas and on American television. Recordings of these performances helped restore him to international prominence and confirm him for Americans as the essence of urbanity. When the National Theatre (now the Royal National Theatre) was formed in Great Britain in 1963, its first production of a living dramatist's work was *Hay Fever*, which Coward, a perfectionist, directed.

Coward, who never married, had published acclaimed volumes of autobiography in 1937 and 1954.

In his later years, spent largely for tax purposes in Jamaica or Switzerland, he continued his gossipy diaries (which end in 1969) and wrote short stories and a novel. He was knighted in 1970, and by 1972, the year before his death in Jamaica, staged collections of his theatrical songs were appearing in London and on Broadway. Although in plays, songs, and performance he gave the world a series of indelible impressions of Englishness, Coward was perhaps even more popular in the United States, where his "talent to amuse" has been extravagantly praised. His reputation as a consummately entertaining epigrammist and chronicler of his times seems secure.

• Although there are many biographies of Noël Coward, including very personal works written by his lifelong companions, for tone, control, self-awareness, and entertainment value nothing rivals Coward's autobiographical works, *Present Indicative, Future Indefinite*, and the unfinished *Past Conditional*, collected by Sheridan Morley in *Noël Coward: Autobiography* (1986). *The Noël Coward Diaries* (1982), edited by Morley and Graham Payn, were called in 1993 by the *Guardian* the century's best in that highly personal form especially cherished by the British. There is no end of Cowardiana in the memoirs and biographies of his contemporaries. A full portrait of this versatile personality is needed.

JAMES ROSS MOORE

COWDERY, Oliver (3 Oct. 1806–3 Mar. 1850), Mormon leader, was born at Wells, Vermont, the son of William Cowdery, Jr., and Rebecca Fuller, farmers. When Oliver was three, his mother died, and the family moved to Poultney, Vermont, where his father remarried. Oliver lived and worked on the farm until joining his brothers in western New York in 1825. In New York he worked successively as a general store clerk, a blacksmith, and a farmer before embarking on the course that would lead him into the midst of the formation of the Church of Jesus Christ of Latter-day Saints and thereby the beginnings of Mormonism.

In 1828 Cowdery began teaching in a rural school in Manchester Township. He boarded with the family of Joseph Smith, Sr., through whom he heard about a purportedly ancient record that Joseph Smith, Jr., was in the process of translating. Cowdery felt inspired to join Smith and assist him in this work. They met in Harmony, Pennsylvania, and on 7 April 1829 Cowdery began to serve as Smith's scribe, recording the translated message as Smith dictated it to him. Smith and Cowdery interrupted their work only to return to New York and move in with the Peter Whitmer family on their farm near Fayette.

Upon completion of the translation in late June 1829, the manuscript was taken to a printer in nearby Palmyra, where Cowdery, acting on Smith's instructions, oversaw printing. Smith's translation was published on 26 March 1830 as the Book of Mormon, a spiritual and historical record of pre-Columbian peoples in the Americas that covers a period of 1,000 years and includes a chronicle of Jesus Christ's personal ministry among these ancient peoples shortly after his death and resurrection. Cowdery was chosen, along with David Whitmer and Martin Harris, as one of the Three Witnesses of the Book of Mormon. The combined sworn testimony and the names of Cowdery, Whitmer, and Harris are printed in each copy of the book that is published, affirming Smith's claims regarding the divine origin of the book and its mode of translation.

The Church of Jesus Christ of Latter-day Saints, commonly known as the Mormon church, was organized under Smith's direction on 6 April 1830 at Fayette. Cowdery, present at the group's founding, was ordained by Smith as second elder of the church. Five days later Cowdery delivered the first public sermon of the new church at the Whitmer home in Fayette to a large group, thus commencing the public ministry of the church. That fall he led the church's first major mission, teaching as he and two others traveled some 1,500 miles through Ohio to Jackson County in western Missouri; there he presented the Book of Mormon to Native Americans, the descendants of pre-Columbian peoples. In 1832 Cowdery married Elizabeth Ann Whitmer. They would have six children, only one of whom, Maria Louise, would live to maturity.

In 1833, while serving as one of the leaders of a local branch of the church in Missouri, Cowdery was among the 1,200 Latter-day Saints who were expelled from Jackson County by mob force. He then made his way to Kirtland, Ohio, a small town east of Cleveland, where the church had since established its headquarters. In December 1834 at Kirtland, Cowdery was ordained assistant president of the church. The following February, with the two other Book of Mormon witnesses, he officiated over the selection, instruction, and ordination of the church's Quorum of Twelve Apostles, who act as standing witnesses of Jesus Christ and form a governing body second in authority only to the first presidency. He was the first church historian, and as a printer and publisher for the church, he helped Smith prepare the church revelations for printing, which were published in 1835 as *The Doctrine and Covenants*. He also edited several church newspapers, including the *Messenger and Advocate*, and prepared instructional materials for children. In April 1836 Cowdery played a prominent role in the dedication proceedings of the Kirtland Temple.

During the latter part of 1837 and into 1838, however, Cowdery, who had moved back to Missouri, this time to Far West, opposed Smith on some issues of church policy, among them how lands would be provided for members arriving in Missouri. Cowdery was planning to sell land at a profit as the headquarters of the church and its members relocated there, having been forced to leave Kirtland. Smith's communitarian revelations called for a bridling of the speculative spirit, but Cowdery persisted in trying to profit through land speculation, and ultimately he resigned from the church. Tried by a church tribunal, he was found to be out of harmony with the church and excommunicated on 12 April 1838. Cowdery would later explain that it was not a dispute over doctrine or belief that caused him to leave the church but, rather, matters pertaining to "the outward government of this church" (Gunn, p. 155).

A short time after his excommunication, Cowdery returned to Kirtland, where he taught school and studied law and involved himself in political and civic affairs. After completing his law study, he was given the editorship of a newspaper sponsored by local members of the Democratic party in Tiffin, Ohio. Soon after he relocated to Tiffin in 1840, it was discovered that he had been a witness to the creation of the Book of Mormon. Cowdery affirmed his role in the establishment of the Mormon religion even though it cost him the editorship of the paper.

Cowdery practiced law in Tiffin for seven years and during that time rose to local prominence through his political activities and civic service as well as his legal acumen. An ardent Democrat, he was chosen as a county delegate to various conventions; he also served on the board of school examiners, which certified local schoolteachers, and he tested candidates for admission to the bar. Suffering from a lung ailment and seeking a better climate, Cowdery took his brother Lyman's advice and moved in 1847 to Elkhorn, Wisconsin, where he became a partner in his brother's law firm and began to consider a reconciliation with the church he still believed in and had helped to form.

A brother-in-law, Phineas H. Young, had written to Cowdery suggesting that he ask to rejoin the church. The Mormons, having been forced by political pressure and by mob activity to leave Nauvoo, Illinois, were, in 1846, scattered in various encampments across Iowa as part of the great migration being led by Brigham Young to the Salt Lake Valley. In late 1848 Cowdery and his family left Elkhorn and traveled to Council Bluffs, Iowa, where, in an emotional assembly, he reiterated his witness and asked to be readmitted to the church. Cowdery was rebaptized on 12 November 1848. He held no high office after rejoining the church, although he might have if he had lived longer.

Hoping to migrate to the Salt Lake Valley the next spring, the Cowderys traveled to Richmond, Missouri, to visit Elizabeth Cowdery's family and to prepare for the journey. Before they could leave, however, Cowdery's health failed, and he died in Richmond of tuberculosis. Both Mormons and non-Mormons mourned his death. The Richmond Circuit Court noted that the legal profession had lost, "an accomplished member, and the community a reliable and worthy citizen." John Breslin, who knew Cowdery while he lived at Tiffin, described Cowdery as having been "a man of more than ordinary ability" who "endeared himself to all who knew him in the private and social walks of life" (quoted in Anderson pp. 46–47). He was buried at Richmond, where a monument commemorates his role as one of the Three Witnesses of the Book of Mormon and thus as one of the earliest eyewitnesses to the events of the founding and early development of what has since become a worldwide religious movement.

• The main repositories of primary documents related to Cowdery are the historical archives of the Church of Jesus Christ of Latter-day Saints, Salt Lake City, Utah, and of the Reorganized Church of Jesus Christ of Latter Day Saints, Independence, Mo. Good secondary sources are the seven-volume *History of the Church of Jesus Christ of Latter-day Saints* (repr. 1976), and B. H. Robert's six-volume *A Comprehensive History of the Church of Jesus Christ of Latter-day Saints* (repr. 1975). Book-length biographies are Stanley R. Gunn, *Oliver Cowdery: Second Elder and Scribe* (1962), and Phillip R. Legg, *Oliver Cowdery: The Elusive Second Elder of the Restoration* (1989). A more accessible source for many readers will be the detailed sketch of Cowdery's life and contributions that can be found in Daniel H. Ludlow, ed., *The Encyclopedia of Mormonism*, vol. 1 (1992). Other sources are Richard Lloyd Anderson, *Investigating the Book of Mormon Witnesses* (1981); Leonard J. Arrington, "Oliver Cowdery's Kirtland, Ohio, 'Sketch Book,'" *BYU Studies* 12 (Summer 1972): 410–26; and Preston Nibley, *The Witnesses of the Book of Mormon* (1973).

RANDALL CLUFF

COWEN, Esek (24 Jan. 1787–11 Feb. 1844), jurist, was born in Rhode Island, the son of Joseph Cowen, a farmer. His mother's name is not known. His family moved to Greenfield, Saratoga County, and four years later to Hartford, Washington County, both in New York. Aside from about six months' attendance at a common school, Cowen was self-educated. Reportedly, part of this learning was gained by being read to as he labored in his father's field, which had the effect of building up what became a phenomenal memory and a remarkable physique. He even learned Greek and Latin. In any event, Cowen was teaching school at age fifteen to support his study of the law, which he began in Roger Skinner's Sandy Hill office the following year, and was admitted to the bar in 1810. That same year he began practice with Gardner Stowe, in Northumberland, Saratoga County. In 1811 he married widow Martha Berry Rogers; they had three children.

The couple moved to Saratoga Springs in 1812, where Cowen was an active participant in that community's affairs for the rest of his life. It was not uncommon for him to deliver commemorative addresses, as for the groundbreaking of the Saratoga & Schenectady Railroad, which would set the town's course as the primary resort community of northern New York over neighboring Ballston Spa, in 1831. An unsuccessful assembly candidate in 1815, Cowen served on local and regional school commitees and was a justice of the peace from 1815 on. In 1821 he published his first edition of *A Treatise on the Civil Jurisdiction of a Justice of the Peace, in the State of New-York*, which stands as a model composite of common sense and erudition; a second, two-volume edition appeared in 1841. He was a co-founder of one of the nation's first temperance organizations at Northumberland in 1812, and in 1817 he financially supported the founding of the *Saratoga Springs Sentinal*. He also personally financed the construction costs of Saratoga Springs' Episcopal Chapel (1832).

Cowen took aspiring lawyers under his direction and published in 1839 *Cowen's Treatise and the Notes on Phillipps' Evidence*, a four-volume work, which while bearing his name was the joint effort of Nicholas Hill, William L. F. Warren, and Cowen. He boasted that his law library was larger than any north of Albany and also had "a good, large miscellaneous library." But Cowen's talent and learning would have gone for naught without the right political connections. His legal mentor, Roger Skinner, was a leading lieutenant in Van Buren's "Bucktail" faction, and presumedly helped further Cowen's interests. In any event, the two "Bucktails" on the committee selected a state court reporter, Lieutenant Governor Erastus Root and Chief Justice John Savage outvoted Chancellor James Kent, to replace Kent's friend William Johnson with Cowen. Cowen remained reporter until 1828 when he was appointed by Governor Nathaniel Pitcher to replace Reuben Hyde Walworth as fourth circuit judge, on Walworth's elevation to chancellor, and in 1836 he was elevated to the state supreme court by Governor William L. Marcy, where he served the rest of his life.

Contemporaries often compared Cowen to the English jurist Mansfield. In Cowen's case, however, there are indications that such praise was based on reality rather than the hyperbole of local pride. Perhaps one of the most thorough and astute twentieth-century observers of the American judiciary, Karl N. Llewellyn, ranked Cowen among the foremost practitioners of what he calls the "grand style"—the ability to keep the law current with the times. However, Llewellyn did not consider Cowen's most controversial opinion—*People v. McLeod* (1841).

Alexander McLeod, a British national had been part of a force organized by the British government in Canada to destroy the steam boat *Caroline*, which had been engaged in supporting a combined force of Americans and Canadians against the royal government. In the course of the attack in December 1837, the boat was burned and an American citizen killed. McLeod was subsequently arrested and indicted by an Erie County grand jury, and the question for the New York Supreme Court was whether he could be tried. The case had become an international *cause célèbre*, with both the British government and U.S. State Department opposed to such a course. Cowen, in his unanimous opinion for the three-member court maintained that McLeod had to stand trial, on the ground that courts were independent of other branches of government, and the attack on the *Caroline* could only render McLeod immune if an actual state of war existed between the United States and Great Britain. Cowen's opinion was attacked and defended with equal vigor (Secretary of State Daniel Webster was livid), but that battle became moot when McLeod was acquitted at trial. Like many persons north of Albany, Cowen had been supportive of the Canadian rebels, but this point was not made in the attacks on his opinion. He died in Albany a short time before he reached the mandatory retirement age of sixty.

• For the scant biographical material on Cowen, see William L. Stone, *Reminiscences of Saratoga and Ballston* (n.d.). See also Karl N. Llewellyn, *The Common Law Tradition Deciding Appeals* (1960). For the McLeod case controversy, see *Washington National Intelligencer*, 11 Feb. 1842, and "Review of the Opinion of Judge Cowen," 26 Wendell Reports (N.Y., 1841), p. 663, and "The Supreme Court of New York and Mr. Webster, on the McLeod Question," *United States Magazine and Democratic Review* 10 (1842): 487. Cowen's opinion is at 25 Wendell Reports (N.Y., 1841), pp. 483 and 567.

DONALD M. ROPER

COWEN, Joshua Lionel (25 Aug. 1877–8 Sept. 1965), inventor and manufacturer, was born in New York City, the son of Hymen Nathan Cowen, a hat maker and real-estate dealer, and Rebecca Kantrowitz, a shopkeeper. Cowen's love for tinkering became apparent early in his life, when he would break apart toys to see how they worked. Unfortunately for his sisters, their dolls were not immune from these investigations. Curious why the dolls' eyes opened and shut, young Joshua broke open their bisque heads to find the answer. Unwilling to surrender himself to the discipline of school, he often skipped classes. Valuing education too highly to let him drop out, his father enrolled him in the Peter Cooper Institute (later Cooper Union). There he was able to work with electricity and even invented what he claimed was the first doorbell. His unimpressed instructor told Cowen that nothing would ever replace the simple act of knocking on a door to announce one's arrival.

In September 1893 Cowen entered the City College of New York. Within a short time he dropped out, reenrolled, dropped out again, and then entered Columbia University. After one semester of classes there, Cowen left to work as an apprentice at Henner and Anderson, which manufactured one of the first dry-cell batteries in the United States. He then moved on to the Acme Electric Lamp Company, where he assembled battery lamps. Often staying on after hours to pursue his own ideas, it was there that he developed the skills that he would need in the near future.

On 6 June 1899 Cowen filed his first patent, a "flash lamp," which used dry-cell batteries to ignite photographers' magnesium flash powder. Its design, a cylinder that held the dry-cell batteries with a threaded cap on one end, resembles the everyday flashlight, which Cowen also claimed to have invented. According to Cowen, he saw it strictly as a novelty item and failed to see its usefulness as a hand-held portable light. The light, which malfunctioned occasionally, was abandoned by Cowen.

During this time Cowen convinced the Navy Department that his flash lamp, with slight modifications, could act as a fuse to detonate submarine mines. The contract resulted in another patent for Cowen, for "improvements in electric explosion fuses," and a $12,000 profit. In the wake of his successful navy contract, on 5 September 1900 Cowen and a colleague, Harry C. Grant, filed to conduct business as the Lionel Manufacturing Company, its purpose being "the manufacture of electrical novelties."

Around 1901 Cowen built a small, battery-run electric fan. "It ran like a dream and it had only one thing wrong with it," he recalled. "You could stand a foot away from the thing and not feel any breeze." He saw little use for this invention as it was and pondered how this device could be made into something useful. While gazing into a lower Manhattan shop window, an idea suddenly came to Cowen. He would fasten the fan motor to the bottom of a miniature wooden railroad flatcar. This would run on a small circle of miniature railroad tracks made from brass strips mounted on wooden ties. The batteries that powered the train would connect directly to the tracks. The cars and tracks, Cowen reasoned, would be ideal for use in shop display windows, where they would both attract customers and carry featured merchandise.

Orders from shop owners came immediately. As the volume of orders grew, however, sales to private individuals overtook those to store owners. This was the era when railroads built America, when trains moved the nation's raw materials and manufactured goods. Naturally enough, children were drawn to the excitement of the locomotive, and toy trains quickly became a popular Christmas gift. In 1920 Lionel's sales were fifteen times those of 1910. Before the beginning of World War I the company built a 450,000-square-foot factory in Irvington, New Jersey. Lionel's continued growth made necessary its reorganization as the Lionel Corporation in 1918.

Cowen, ever the tinkerer and innovator, steadily introduced new elements into his world of model trains. The first major addition was the transformer, which eliminated the need for cumbersome batteries. Patents were also issued for an automatic train control device (1917), panels that gave greater strength to car and locomotive bodies (1918), insulated fiber frogs on switches (1925), die-cast wheels with nickeled steel rim over the tread (1925), "lockon" track connections (1925), and headlights with individual switches (1925).

Lionel manufactured railroad cars with specialized functions such as milk cars, log cars, and cranes. Great stress was placed on manufacturing model trains that were not only durable and safe but accurate representations of real trains. Some Lionel locomotives were even designed to bear the same number of rivets as the locomotives after which they were modeled. Likewise, years were spent perfecting model trains that could give off realistic smoke and make authentic chugging sounds.

Cowen married Cecilia Liberman in 1904; the couple had his only two children. In 1949, three years after the death of his first wife, Cowen married Lillian Appel Herman.

During the early 1950s Cowen's son, Lawrence, gradually took over the management of Lionel. By 1954 annual sales reached $33 million, propelled in part by the postwar "baby boom." This was not to last, however. The late 1950s ushered in drastic changes. The coming of television as family entertainment left less time for toy trains. This brought on a steady decline in Lionel sales, which mirrored the demise of America's great railroads during the same time. In the early 1960s the Cowens lost control of the company and were bought out by a group led by Roy Cohn, Cowen's great-nephew and the former legal counsel for Senator Joseph McCarthy. Joshua Lionel Cowen died in Palm Beach, Florida.

To several generations of American children, Lionel trains were as much a part of Christmas as Santa Claus. They were by far the most popular toy trains available. Cowen did more than design and build model trains; he freed the imaginations and dreams of the children (and grownups) everywhere who played with these trains.

• The most comprehensive work about Cowen is Ron Hollander, *All Aboard: The Story of Joshua Lionel Cowen and His Lionel Train Company* (1981). Of additional help is Robert Lewis Taylor, "Profiles: High Railers and Full Scalers," *New Yorker*, 13 Dec. 1947, pp. 38–42, and D. Wharton, "He Put Tracks beneath the Christmas Tree," *Reader's Digest*, Jan. 1954, pp. 133–35. An obituary is in the *New York Times*, 9 Sept. 1965.

DANIEL M. DUMYCH

COWL, Jane (14 Dec. 1884–22 June 1950), actor, producer, and writer, was born Grace Bailey in Boston, Massachusetts, the daughter of Charles A. Bailey, a provision dealer and clerk, and Grace Avery, a singer and voice teacher. Around 1887 the family moved to Brooklyn, where Jane published verses in *Brooklyn Life* and attended the public schools. She studied for two years at Erasmus Hall and took some classes at Columbia College.

She asserted that she was driven from the start by "a dire and stressful poverty" that made her "more serious than [her] years" (Cowl, "Personal Reminiscences," p. 270). Taking the stage name Jane Cowl, she began acting small parts in David Belasco's theater, starting with *Sweet Kitty Bellairs* (1903). In 1904 she met and befriended fellow player Jane Murfin during rehearsals for *The Music Master*. Cowl and Murfin went on to co-write several successful plays, but in the meantime Cowl continued to pursue her acting career—a career plagued with stage fright but enriched by a variety of compelling roles. In 1906 she married Adolph Klauber, a critic for the *New York Times*.

Cowl received her first big break as Fanny Perry in Belasco's production of *Is Matrimony a Failure?* by Leo Ditrichstein (1909). Critics praised her beauty and her comic timing, but Cowl was not content. She continued to hone her craft, joining the Hudson Theatre stock company in Union Hill, New Jersey—an experience that led her to remark that, "as a practical school of acting, two years in a well-directed stock company, to a girl who has already collected a mass of undigested dramatic ideas, is worth ten seasons' general stage experience" ("Personal Reminiscences," p. 271).

The autumn of 1910 began inauspiciously for Cowl as *The Upstart* failed after only three performances. Charles Klein's *The Gamblers* next brought the actress strong reviews. Her theatrical stock continued to rise as she starred as Mary Turner in Bayard Veiller's popular melodrama, *Within the Law* (1912). During the 1915–1916 season she took on *Common Clay*, by Cleves Kinkead, thereby cementing her standing as a powerful leading lady.

The season of 1916–1917 saw *Lilac Time*, Cowl's first collaboration with Murfin, on the Broadway stage. Cowl's husband, Klauber, produced the successful war play. Later in 1917 Cowl appeared in Samuel Goldwyn's *The Spreading Dawn* in her first motion picture role. In 1918 Murfin and Cowl got a taste of failure with *Information Please*, in which Cowl was nonetheless lauded for her comic abilities. Later the same year she starred in the Edgar Selwyn–Channing Pollock production *The Crowded Hour*.

Smilin' Through was Cowl's next big hit and marks the apex of her career, both as a playwright and as an actress. Though Cowl and Murfin again collaborated on this venture, they concocted the pen name Alan Langdon Martin for it, suspecting that the failure of *Information Please* was due in part to prejudice against female authors. The pseudonym certainly did not hurt; *Smilin' Through* ran from 30 December 1919 to 1922.

With reputation and finances secure, Cowl looked for a change of pace. She played the title role in the short-lived *Malvaloca*, opposite Rollo Peters, then undertook one of her most celebrated characterizations, Juliet in *Romeo and Juliet*. The production ran 174 consecutive performances at the Henry Miller theater, then went on the road, where the company set a record for consecutive performances of Shakespeare (856). So popular was the production that, at the final New York performance of the show, 2,000 people were turned away at the box office, and 3,000 fans gathered in the street to cheer the actress. Crosby Gaige noted that Cowl had "charm, beauty and dramatic power and all the attributes we now carelessly wrap up in the convenient word 'glamour'" (p. 88). These qualities, combined with her melodic voice and gracefulness, made Cowl an ideal Juliet for the 1920s.

She next appeared in two unsatisfying productions, as the female leads in Maeterlinck's *Pelleas and Melisande* (1923) and Shakespeare's *Antony and Cleopatra* (1924). But in late 1925 another hit—and a fresh concentration on comedy in Cowl's repertoire—emerged in the form of Noël Coward's *Easy Virtue*, which opened first in New York, then in London in early 1926. A little vaudeville and a successful run as Amytis in Robert Sherwood's playful *The Road to Rome* followed. Several disappointments, including Cowl's coauthorship with Theodore Charles of *The Jealous Moon*, were next. In 1930 she played Viola in Shakespeare's *Twelfth Night*—a production for which she also suggested the design and which ran in repertory with Levy's spirited comedy *Art and Mrs. Bottle*. She returned to melodrama in 1931 with *The Lady of the Camellias*.

In 1933 Cowl's husband, who had produced many of his wife's plays, died. Cowl rebounded from his death and in 1934 brilliantly portrayed the disingenuous Lucy Wayne in George S. Kaufman and Katherine Dayton's *First Lady*. Four years later she created the effervescent matchmaker Dolly Levi in Thornton Wilder's *The Merchant of Yonkers*—a play that later became the phenomenally popular *Hello, Dolly!* After a successful run of John Van Druten's *Old Acquaintance* (1940–1941) Cowl played a few revivals, including *The First Mrs. Fraser* (1947) and *Candida* (1942). But she spent much of her time during World War II as codirector of the Stage Door Canteen in New York.

Cowl's huge box-office appeal dwindled, but she continued to work. She began to accept offers from the motion picture industry, including a job playing herself in *Stage Door Canteen* (1943), as well as roles in *Once More My Darling*, *The Lie*, and *The Secret Fury*. Cowl died in Santa Monica, California. She had no children.

Like her mentor, David Belasco, Cowl was not above throwing her weight around, but—also like Belasco—she demanded theatrical perfection from herself and others, even in less-than-perfect vehicles. Cowl wrote of her own experiences in various magazines, hoping that other theatrical aspirants might learn from her mistakes as well as her successes. As vice president of Actor's Equity in 1927, Cowl devoted herself to all aspects of the theater. On occasion she oversaw production of costumes and sets, and she often took the role of playwright when good women's roles were lacking. Cowl should be remembered as much for the passion she gave to her profession, as for her glamour, her longevity, and her stunning Juliet.

• The Billy Rose Theatre Collection at the New York Public Library for the Performing Arts, Lincoln Center, contains scrapbooks, clippings, photographs, and programs, as well as voluminous correspondence and an incomplete but substantial portion of an autobiography. Other useful sources include Joseph Verner Reed, *The Curtain Falls* (1935), which has a lengthy section on the author's interaction with Cowl regarding planning for *Twelfth Night*. Crosby Gaige, *Footlights and Highlights* (1948), has a similar anecdotal tone, as do all of Cowl's own magazine essays, such as "Personal Reminiscences," *Theatre* 24 (Nov. 1916): 270–71. For a more complete list of sources by and about Cowl, see Stephen Archer, *American Actors and Actresses: A Guide to Information Sources* (1983). An obituary is in the *New York Times*, 23 June 1950.

CYNTHIA M. GENDRICH

COWLES, Betsey Mix (9 Feb. 1810–25 July 1876), educator and reformer, was born in Bristol, Connecticut, the daughter of Giles Hooker Cowles, a Congregationalist minister, and Sally White. To support their family of eight children, Cowles's parents moved the family to the fledgling town of Austinburg in Ohio's western reserve shortly after her birth. Two more children came along later. Cowles's early education took place in subscription schools. Before the spread of state-funded public schools, parents who wished to educate their children had to make arrangements with traveling schoolmasters. Cowles herself joined the ranks of such teachers at age sixteen and taught in many communities throughout northeastern Ohio and western New York.

In the early 1830s Cowles began experimenting with innovative teaching methods. She sought training in the new techniques of infant schools that focused on the education of children aged four to six through the use of songs, rhymes, and visual aids. In addition to teaching, Cowles helped organize the Ashtabula County Female Anti-Slavery Society in 1835. As its secretary she helped to establish local societies within the county's townships.

In 1838 Cowles, increasingly interested in teaching as a profession, decided at age twenty-eight to enter Oberlin College. She completed the abbreviated ladies' course, graduating in 1840 with a "literary degree." At that time, the leaders of Oberlin College were committed to making education available to women, an ambition Cowles shared. In 1839 she wrote her sister Cornelia that "woman in point of intellect does not occupy the station which was designed by her maker; & she never will until the standard of female education is elevated." In 1842 Cowles obtained her first professional position as an instructor at the Portsmouth Female Seminary in Scioto County, Ohio. While there she earned the town's enmity by establishing a Sabbath school for both black and white children. White parents refused to send their children to such a school. Cowles moved back home to Austinburg the next year to become the first woman to head the women's department at the Grand River Institute, a private school affiliated with the town's Congregational church.

While in Austinburg, Cowles entered the most active phase of her career as a reformer, engaging in abolition work through the Western Anti-Slavery Society (WASS). During these years she worked closely with the prominent abolitionist Abby Kelley, who encouraged her to lecture about her views. Cowles instead turned her attention to the organization of sewing circles. Under her leadership women produced clothing for escaped slaves and quilts for sale at fairs to help finance local and state antislavery activities. In the late 1840s Cowles organized many such fairs in addition to distributing abolition literature and serving as a business committee member and recording secretary for WASS.

Cowles left the Grand River Institute in 1848, moving to the Canton, Ohio, area to participate in the changes in education taking place there as the spread of free public schools culminated in their modern form of organization. New graded schools allowed students to attend a primary school first, followed by grammar school and high school. Cowles took a teaching post at the new Massillon Union School but had a falling out with local townspeople over her strong advocacy of a movement to repeal Ohio's Black Laws and her attempts to keep African-American students in her classes despite local pressure to exclude them. Still respected by education leaders, however, she was ap-

pointed as the superintendent of the girls' grammar and high schools in Canton in 1850.

While in Canton, Cowles made a brief foray into the arena of women's rights. She was the president of the first Ohio Women's Rights Convention, held in 1850, and served on the business committee for the next year's convention. For the 1851 meeting she prepared and read a report comparing the differences in men's and women's wages. In 1852 Cowles served on the executive committee of Ohio's newly established Woman's Rights Association.

In 1856 Cowles turned her attention to the field of teacher training, taking charge of the new McNeely Normal School in Hopedale, Ohio, one of the earliest normal schools established in the United States. Precipitated by the spread of graded schools, normal schools had their origins in a movement for professional training for teachers in their own areas of specialization. Two years later she moved for a short time to the Illinois State Normal University in Bloomington. She left this post in 1858 for the challenge of serving in Painesville, Ohio, as the superintendent of public schools, a position very few women held in Ohio at that time. But during her Painesville stay she developed trouble with her eyes and resigned after only two years. Cowles then took a teaching position in Delhi, New York, from 1860 to 1863, before retiring from teaching permanently because of her worsening eyesight. After a dynamic teaching career of more than three decades, Cowles spent her last years back home in Austinburg, where she died. She concerned herself with local rather than state and national affairs.

Betsey Mix Cowles spent most of her life on the move, relocating whenever a new challenge and opportunity to grow presented itself. These opportunities presented themselves often because of the wide renown she enjoyed among Ohio's education leaders. Cowles was a woman of wide-ranging interests as shown by the contents of a newspaper scrapbook she kept. She collected Spanish and Russian poetry as well as poetry written by soldiers. She compiled a series of articles dealing with Native Americans, Polish history, motherhood, and female education. In a lighter vein, she enjoyed a series of stories titled "Popular Tales."

Cowles's life demonstrates that lacking the right to vote did not preclude women from having an impact on and participating in the public sphere of nineteenth-century American life. While at Oberlin in 1839, she wrote to her sister Cornelia that "I do hope the time is not far distant when females will feel & act that they are made for something more than to flutter or to serve."

• Cowles's papers are located in the Department of Special Collections at Kent State University. She published a few articles and letters about education in *Child's Friend and Family Magazine* in 1846 and 1847 and about Ohio's Black Laws in the *Anti-Slavery Bugle* (Salem, Ohio) in 1848 and 1849. Her "Report of Labor" is published in the *Proceedings of the Woman's Rights Convention Held in Akron, Ohio, 28 and 29 May 1851* (1851). The Western Reserve Historical Society published Linda L. Geary, *Balanced in the Wind: A Biography of*

Betsey Mix Cowles (1989). See also Donna Marie DeBlasio, "Her Own Society: The Life and Times of Betsey Mix Cowles, 1810–1876" (Ph.D. diss., Kent State Univ., 1980). Cowles's activities are commented on briefly in Frances Juliette Hosford, *Father Shipherd's Magna Charta: A Century of Coeducation in Oberlin College* (1937); Robert Samuel Fletcher, *A History of Oberlin College: From Its Foundation through the Civil War* (1943); and William W. Williams, *History of Ashtabula County, Ohio* (1878). Dorothy Sterling comments briefly on Cowles's relationship with Abby Kelley in *Ahead of Her Time: Abby Kelley and the Politics of Antislavery* (1991). An obituary is in the *Cleveland Leader*, 29 July 1876.

KIM M. GRUENWALD

COWLES, Gardner (28 Feb. 1861–28 Feb. 1946), newspaper publisher, was born in Oskaloosa, Iowa, the son of William Fletcher Cowles, a Methodist minister, and Maria Elizabeth LaMonte. His mother died when he was twelve. Because Cowles's father held pastorates in a number of Iowa towns, the family (which pronounced its name "coles") moved frequently. Cowles's college experience was as peripatetic as his childhood. After starting as a freshman at Penn College in Oskaloosa, he moved on to two years at Grinnell College and finally graduated in 1882 from Iowa Wesleyan. During his college years Cowles supported himself by teaching school, and after graduating he worked for two years as superintendent of schools in Algona, Iowa. In 1884 he married an Algona teacher, Florence Maud Call; they had six children. In 1885 he earned a master of arts degree at Iowa Wesleyan.

During his years as superintendent, Cowles helped publish a weekly paper, the *Algona Republican*; for a brief period he also edited the weekly *Advance*. But from 1885 to 1903 he devoted himself to business. Iowa was developing rapidly, and Cowles's prosperity expanded with the area's expanding economy. He bought and sold land, arranged loans on land, managed investments, and gradually moved into banking. By the turn of the century, he controlled ten banks in the northern part of the state. From 1899 to 1903 he also served as a Republican member of the state house of representatives.

While publishing the *Algona Republican*, Cowles became friends with Harvey Ingham, who edited a rival paper. Twenty years later, in 1903, Cowles was approached by Ingham, who had become associate editor for the *Des Moines Register and Leader* as well as a minority stockholder in the Register and Leader Co. that published the paper. Learning that majority ownership in the company was for sale, Ingham persuaded Cowles to buy it, though at the time the paper was $180,000 in debt and its circulation was only 14,000. Cowles threw himself into building up the paper, working long hours and personally responding to customer complaints. His efforts were supported by the area's growing population and by its spreading rail network, which could get early editions from Des Moines to every corner of the state by 8 A.M. By 1906 Cowles had reduced the company debt and nearly doubled the paper's circulation. Two years later he bought a small afternoon paper, the *Des Moines Eve-*

ning Tribune, and changed his company's name to the Register and Tribune Co., becoming both president and treasurer. Cowles placed particular emphasis on home delivery. For many years—unlike most American newspapers—his company received more revenue from circulation than from advertising. By 1913 the *Register* and the *Tribune* had a combined readership of about 55,000, more than half of it outside Des Moines. Remaining interested in politics, Cowles served as a delegate to the Republican convention in 1916.

During the 1920s Cowles eliminated his remaining competition by acquiring the *Daily News* from the Scripps-McRae League in 1924 and the *Capital* in 1927, combining both of them with the *Tribune*. This left Des Moines with just three papers, all controlled by Cowles: the morning *Register*, the afternoon *Tribune*, and the *Sunday Register*. At this point Cowles became chairman of the board of directors of the Register and Tribune Co., while his son Gardner assumed the company presidency. By then, with a combined circulation of about 350,000 on weekdays and 425,000 on Sundays, the three papers exerted a dominant influence around the state.

During the 1920s the Cowles papers pioneered the use of readership surveys, using the services of George Gallup, then a young graduate student at the University of Iowa who was exploring the new field of public opinion polling. The organization also became one of the first newspaper publishers to establish employees' group insurance and retirement and stock purchase plans. In 1928 Cowles entered the new field of news broadcasting, acquiring radio stations in Des Moines; Yankton, South Dakota; and Washington, D.C. No matter what the innovations, however, getting out the daily Des Moines papers remained the heart of the Cowles operation. By 1935 the company employed 56 circulation managers, 90 supervisors, a fleet of trucks, and 4,820 carriers to sustain its large circulation across the state. Each day, the paper was changed as many as twenty times, to ensure that in each community the front page featured news of local interest.

During the 1930s the Cowles empire bought the major Minneapolis papers, and in 1937 it established *Look* magazine. By this time Cowles's sons Gardner and John were taking increasing responsibility for the family business. Cowles began to travel extensively, played frequent golf, and served on the boards of several banks, the Iowa Methodist Hospital, and two local colleges, including his alma mater. In 1929 he was appointed by President Herbert Hoover to the U.S. Commission on Conservation and Administration of the Public Domain. He also served from 1932 to 1933 as a director and then briefly as chair of the Reconstruction Finance Corporation (RFC), one of Hoover's most ambitious efforts to revive the national economy. Cowles left the RFC when the new president, Franklin D. Roosevelt, took office in the spring of 1933. In 1934 Cowles and his wife established the Gardner Cowles Foundation, created to support twenty-eight colleges in Iowa as well as other major charitable institutions in the state. By the time of Cowles's death, the foundation had given away nearly $1 million; one of the largest gifts was a $100,000 donation for a black community center in Des Moines, named for Wendell Willkie.

Cowles died in Des Moines. The organization he had built over nearly half a century had achieved commercial success and wide influence, while its high standards were reflected in its many Pulitzer Prizes and other awards. It is a tribute to the power of the enterprise Cowles founded that, fifteen years after his death, when journalism educators were asked to choose the best morning/evening paper combination in America published by the same organization, both second and third places went to Cowles papers—in Minneapolis and Des Moines, respectively.

• A memorial book published by the Register and Tribune Co., *Gardner Cowles: 1861–1946* (1946), includes many of the news articles, editorials, and tributes published after Cowles's death. See also Alfred McClung Lee, *The Daily Newspaper in America* (1937); Frank Luther Mott, *American Journalism* (1962), p. 663; and Robert A. Rutland, *The Newsmongers* (1973). An obituary is in the *New York Times*, 1 Mar. 1946.

SANDRA OPDYCKE

COWLES, Gardner, Jr. (31 Jan. 1903–8 July 1985), publisher and media executive, was born in Algona, Iowa, the son of Gardner Cowles, a banker, and Florence Call. In 1903 the senior Cowles bought the *Des Moines Register and Leader*, which within a few years after his acquisition of the *Tribune* (by 1908), became known as the *Des Moines Register and Tribune*, a statewide newspaper and one of the most important in the Midwest. Mike, as Gardner, Jr., was known, attended Phillips Exeter Academy and Harvard University, where he received his B.A. in 1925.

After graduating Cowles became the city editor of his father's paper, then news editor, associate managing editor, managing editor, and executive editor, all before he was thirty. Among the innovations that he espoused were using an airplane (named *Good News*) to cover the news of the state, increasing the rotogravure section by using photo essays, and launching the Gallup poll to tell people what their neighbors were thinking. He also initiated a news service to twenty-six newspapers in the United States. In the early 1930s Cowles began buying radio stations—the first was in Fort Dodge, Iowa, the second in Des Moines—and became president of both IA Broadcasting Company and SD Broadcasting Company. In 1935 he and his brother John bought the *Minneapolis Star*.

Cowles was intrigued with the idea of developing a "picture language," and noting the popularity of photo essays in his newspapers he began plans for an illustrated magazine that would contain little text. Reportedly Henry Luce showed him a dummy for Luce's forthcoming *Life* magazine, and Cowles felt there would be no competition with his magazine, *Look*, because he intended to use human interest photographs only, not to report the news as Luce wanted to do. However, *Look* and *Life* were fiercely competitive

from the first to the last. *Life* debuted in 1936, and *Look*'s debut issue appeared on 5 January 1937. *Look* was immediately popular. It featured personalities (especially movie stars), fashion, cute children and animals, health fads, sports, popular science, and "oddities and curiosities," which included bloody accidents and grisly murders. Critics called the magazine sensational, charging that it relied on sex and gore to sell. Cowles responded by cutting much of the gore, romanticizing the sex, gradually adding editorial content, and finally using "hard" news. Through the use of polls and questionnaires, he kept in touch with his readers and their tastes.

Cowles was a liberal Republican, an internationalist who toured Russia with presidential hopeful Wendell Willkie in 1942. During World War II he directed the domestic division of the Office of War Information, which produced propaganda for the home front. After less than a year he was accused of trying to manage the news and resigned in 1943. During the 1950s Cowles criticized President Dwight D. Eisenhower's foreign policy, called for recognition of Red China, and actively opposed the Cold War. He brought national attention to the civil rights movement through the pages of *Look* during the early 1960s.

In 1959 Cowles founded Puerto Rico's first English-language daily newspaper, the *San Juan Star*, which immediately won a Pulitzer Prize for editorial writing. Soon afterward he bought *Family Circle*, a full-color magazine filled with advertising and domestic advice, which was sold in supermarkets. Then he branched into television, buying several stations in Florida in addition to several Florida newspapers. During the 1960s *Look*, *Life*, and other illustrated magazines lost both circulation and advertising revenue because of the increasing power of television. *Look* stopped publishing in 1971, on "the most difficult day of my life," according to Cowles. In 1978 he dissolved Cowles Communications, his umbrella media group, and from then until his death he directed his energy to overseeing the Cowles Charitable Trust.

Cowles married four times. His first wife was Helen Curtis whom he married in 1926; they were divorced in 1930. In 1933 he married Lois Thornburg, a graduate of the University of Iowa School of Journalism and a reporter with the *Register*. They had three children before they divorced in 1946. That same year he married Fleur Fenton, an advertising executive known for "promotional razzmatazz." Fleur Cowles developed an arty, highly innovative, and expensive fashion magazine called *Flair*, which lasted for twelve issues, while Cowles experimented with a pocket-sized news magazine, *Quick*, which also failed after a few issues. The couple was divorced in 1955, and in 1956 he married Jan Streat Cox, with whom he had one child and raised a stepchild. He died in Southampton, Long Island, New York.

Cowles helped define the mass-circulation, general-interest magazine so popular in the 1940s and 1950s. He did not require his subscribers to think or to analyze but merely to react to images that were quirky, sentimental, sensational, or artistic. By seeking out new technologies and new techniques in communications, he encouraged the development of the American mass media in all its expressions.

• Some of Cowles's papers are at Drake University and the Iowa Historical Society. Biographical data can be found in *Current Biography* (1943) and the *New York Times Biographical Service*, vol. 16 (1985). His career can be traced through *Business Week*, *Time*, and *Newsweek*, among other periodicals. An obituary is in the *New York Times*, 9 July 1985.

BETTY BURNETT

COWLES, Henry Chandler (27 Feb. 1869–12 Sept. 1939), botanist, was born in Kensington, Connecticut, the son of Henry Martyn Cowles and Eliza Whittlesey, farmers. He graduated from New Britain High School and then entered Oberlin College, receiving an A.B. degree in 1893. From 1894 to 1895 he taught natural science at Gates College in Nebraska. Cowles next turned to graduate studies at the University of Chicago. At first he studied geology, where he was influenced by T. C. Chamberlin and R. D. Salisbury, who were advocates of the dynamic point of view. When John Merle Coulter was appointed professor of botany, Cowles became a member of the first group of graduate students in that department, and was appointed a graduate assistant in 1897. His classic dissertation, "The Ecological Relations of the Vegetation on the Sand Dunes of Lake Michigan," was the first major study of dunes in America and the first to show the relationships between vegetation and physiography. Cowles completed his studies, earning a Ph.D., in 1898. In 1900 he married Elizabeth L. Waller. They had one child.

Cowles remained at the University of Chicago for his entire career, advancing from assistant to associate professor of botany, then becoming professor of botany in 1911 and chairman of the department from 1925 until his retirement in 1934. His dissertation, published in the *Botanical Gazette* (1899), was followed by a more comprehensive study, "The Physiographic Ecology of Chicago and Vicinity," published in the 1901 issue of the same journal. Later papers included "The Fundamental Causes of Succession among Plant Associations" (1909) and "The Causes of Vegetative Cycles" (1911). Of major importance also was his volume on ecology in *A Textbook of Botany for Colleges and Universities* (2 vols., 1911), which emphasized the development and stabilization of the individual organism with its environment (autecology). The other authors of the textbook were J. M. Coulter and C. R. Barnes; it is regarded as having been influential in raising American botany to European standards.

Even though Cowles was not a prolific writer, his influence was of great significance for American science. Along with Frederic Clements of the University of Nebraska, he was a pioneer in dynamic plant ecology. The aim of his theories was to show that the plant world was not a group of static communities, but communities in active development and change. In vegetation studies, Cowles emphasized the idea of "succes-

sional development." By relating this to landforms, he was able to produce a physiographic ecology that took into account the effects of local landforms in deflecting or retarding normal plant succession. His theories were very much influenced by the writing of the Danish botanist Eugenius Warming, whose 1895 work, *Plantesamfund* (translated into German as *Lehrbuch der ökologischen Pflanzengeographie* [1896]), established the concept of a plant community determined by its habitat. In his study of the vegetation growing along the sandy shores of Lake Michigan, Cowles was able to apply successfully the Warming theories of succession and climax formation, showing, for example, that an observer walking inland from the water's edge could trace a pattern of ecological succession in space that paralleled the development of vegetation in time. From the water-tolerant plant communities, succession went back through the dune societies, eventually arriving at the inland oak woods that represented the climax formation. According to Cowles, this climax formation would never cover the area as long as the lake existed but would be retarded by the unique local physiographic character of the beaches and dunes.

In his career at Chicago, Cowles was essentially a field teacher who used the laboratory of outdoors to bring his students directly to nature. From his early years, he attracted groups of enthusiastic young graduate students who joined him in the development of the new field of dynamic ecology. Many future teachers learned how to use the "natural classrooms" as a setting for learning; among the original investigators of American vegetation he trained were V. E. Shelford, W. S. Cooper, G. D. Fuller, and G. E. Nichols. From all accounts, Cowles was an inspiring teacher; when plans for a special dedicatory number of *Ecology* were announced, more than three hundred students and colleagues responded with letters of admiration and esteem.

Outside of the university community, Cowles was active in a great number of professional affairs. In 1910 he was elected president of the American Association of Geographers. In 1914, along with some of his former students, he founded the Ecological Society of America, was its first secretary-treasurer, and became president in 1917. He was president of the Botanical Society in 1922, and vice president of the biological sciences section of the American Association for the Advancement of Science in 1913. In 1930 he was made president of the section on phytogeography and ecology of the International Botanical Congress in Cambridge, England. For many years, Cowles was president of the Chicago Academy of Sciences. He was also an active supporter of the Illinois State Academy of Science and president, patron, and trustee of the Geographic Society of Chicago. In the area of conservation, he was influential in establishing the state park system of Illinois, and the forest preserves of Cook County, Illinois.

In the last ten years of his life, Cowles was hampered in his work by arteriosclerosis, and he lived quietly after his retirement in 1934 in Chicago, where he died. The best word of description for him is pioneer. When the British Ecological Society awarded him an honorary life membership in 1934, it was "in recognition of the extreme value of [his] pioneer work in Ecology." One of his old students, W. S. Cooper, wrote, in the 1935 issue of *Ecology*, "He laid the foundation for a new and useful branch of science, he constructively influenced the thought of hundreds of investigators and teachers, and in his professional and personal contacts he made for himself a multitude of devoted friends."

• Papers and materials regarding Cowles are at the Charles C. Adams Center for Ecological Studies at Western Michigan University. For a discussion of Cowles and the early history of the ecological sciences, see Donald Worster, *Nature's Economy: A History of Ecological Ideas* (1977). The 1935 issue of *Ecology* 16, no. 3, dedicated to Cowles, contains a biographical essay by William S. Cooper. Additional biographical information is in E. J. Krause, "Henry Chandler Cowles," *Botanical Gazette* 101 (1939): 241–42; George D. Fuller, "Henry Chandler Cowles," *Science* 90 (1939): 363–64; W. M. Davis, *Annals of the Association of American Geographers* (1924): 203–5. Many references to Cowles and his work are in A. D. Rodgers III, *John Merle Coulter: Missionary in Science* (1944). An obituary is in the *Journal of Ecology* 28 (1940): 450–52.

ROBERT F. ERICKSON

COWLEY, Malcolm (24 Aug. 1898–28 Mar. 1989), literary critic and editor, was born in a farmhouse near Belsano, Pennsylvania, the son of William Cowley, a homeopathic physician, and Josephine Hutmacher. After attending Pittsburgh public schools, in which he began a lifelong friendship with the critic Kenneth Burke, Cowley entered Harvard in 1915. He studied under the renowned professor Charles Townsend Copeland and associated with Conrad Aiken, an alumnus, E. E. Cummings, a graduate student, and other literary persons. He also attended the salon of the poet Amy Lowell, who praised his early efforts at writing poetry. He withdrew to drive munitions trucks for the Camion Corps of the American Field Service in France during World War I and was often under bombardment. He returned to Harvard in 1918, edited the *Harvard Advocate*, a literary magazine, but left again to join the U.S. Army, training in Kentucky. He married the painter Marguerite "Peggy" Frances Baird in 1919, returned to Harvard, and graduated in 1920. The couple had no children. After leading a hand-to-mouth existence in New York's Greenwich Village as a freelance book reviewer, advertisement writer, and poet (1920–1921), he and his wife went to France, where he studied French literature on fellowships at the University of Montpellier and received his diploma in 1922, placed poems and essays in periodicals back home, visited Paris occasionally, and associated with a number of writers, including the Dadaists Tristan Tzara and Louis Aragon, and American expatriates such as Ernest Hemingway, Ezra Pound, and Gertrude Stein. Cowley moved back to Greenwich Village in 1923 to freelance; at that time he met Hart Crane, Allen Tate, and Matthew Josephson among other writers.

In 1925 Cowley determined to range through many literatures, be a productive freelancer, and extend his intellectual limits. He and Josephson coedited the avant-garde magazine *Broom* (1923–1924). Among other French works, Cowley translated Paul Valéry's 1924 *Variété* (1927). In 1927 he and his wife bought a farm home in New York, across the border from Sherman, Connecticut, partly with money from his prizewinning poem "The Urn" (*Poetry: A Magazine of Verse* 29 [Nov. 1926]: 70), which celebrates one's never lost sense of home. In 1929 he published *Blue Juniata*, meditative poems on his emotional and intellectual development in France. He succeeded Edmund Wilson as literary editor of the *New Republic* (1929–1940).

The bohemian and unfaithful Peggy Cowley obtained a divorce in Mexico in 1931, after which her enigmatic relationship with the homosexual Crane ended with his suicide in 1932. Cowley, back from reporting on coalminers' bitter strikes in Kentucky, married Muriel Maurer, a New York fashion editor, in 1932; they had one child. He published *Exile's Return: A Narrative of Ideas* (1934), which details post–World War I activities of deracinated American expatriates in France. The depression caused Cowley to look with some favor on Marxist explanations of U.S. political and economic shortcomings, although he always had reservations about both the theory and the practice of the Communist party, which he never joined. In 1935 Cowley co-organized the liberal League of American Writers and a year later bought a farmhouse in Sherman, Connecticut. In 1937 he attended the World Congress of Writers in Madrid and edited and contributed parts of *After the Genteel Tradition* (1937) and *Books That Changed Our Minds* (1939), with the Marxist Bernard Smith, on standard studies in economics, history, politics, psychology, and sociology. Although Cowley in 1940 resigned from the League of American Writers because of its Communist affiliations, trouble still came. Having accepted a high position in the Office of Facts and Figures, under his friend Archibald MacLeish, in Washington, D.C. (1941), Cowley was soon monitored by the Federal Bureau of Investigation, attacked by the journalists Whittaker Chambers and Westbrook Pegler for radicalism in 1942, and smeared by the Texas congressman Martin Dies for having Communist connections. Cowley resigned in 1942, vowing not to write on politics again.

Enormous success followed. Cowley received a long-term Mary Mellon Fellowship grant (1943–1948), which enabled him to read, write, and publish at his own pace. He translated André Gide's 1942 *Interviews Imaginaires* in 1944, Aragon's war poetry in 1945, and other French works. He prepared Viking Portable Library volumes on Ernest Hemingway in 1944, William Faulkner in 1946, and Nathaniel Hawthorne in 1948—all with distinguished critical introductions. *The Faulkner-Cowley File*, assembled and published in 1966, explains Cowley's part in rescuing Faulkner from undeserved neglect two decades earlier. Cowley's judicious editing of the popular *Portable Faulkner* started the Faulkner revival and played a considerable, if indirect, part in Faulkner's being awarded the 1949 Nobel Prize in literature. In 1949 Cowley impugned Chambers by testifying at the trials of Alger Hiss, the State Department official accused of being a Communist spy. Cowley taught at the University of Washington, Stanford University, the University of Michigan, Yale, Berkeley, and Warwick, England (1950–1966, 1973). He edited a revised version of F. Scott Fitzgerald's *Tender Is the Night* based on a reconsideration of manuscripts in 1951 and wrote critical introductions to new editions of Walt Whitman's 1855 *Leaves of Grass* in 1959 and Sherwood Anderson's 1919 classic *Winesburg, Ohio* in 1960. Cowley published his study of post–World War II American literature titled *The Literary Situation* in 1954 and assembled some of his 1930s *New Republic* articles as *Think Back on Us . . . A Contemporary Chronicle of the 1930's* in 1967.

Seven major books followed, often reprinting earlier essays. They are *Blue Juniata: Collected Poems* (1968), with much new verse; *A Many-Windowed House: Collected Essays on American Writers and American Writing* (1970); *A Second Flowering: Works and Days of the Lost Generation* (1973), presenting 1920s writers as self-doubting heroes; *—And I Worked at the Writer's Trade* (1978), anecdotal memoirs; *The Dream of the Golden Mountains: Remembering the 1930s* (1980); *The View from 80* (1980), on growing old nicely; and *The Flower and the Leaf: A Contemporary Record of American Writing since 1941* (1985). Meanwhile, Cowley, a member of the National Institute of Arts and Letters from 1950, served as chancellor of the American Academy of Arts and Letters (1966–1976) and helped Jack Kerouac, Ken Kesey, and other young writers get published by Viking Press. Cowley died in New Milford, Connecticut.

Cowley began his career as a crisp, judicious book reviewer (ultimately publishing 542 reviews), as a poet of clarity and precision, and as a skillful translator of meritorious French books. He was briefly in trouble as a radical polemicist but mellowed in due time. Having seen much and having known many authors, he wrote valuable memoirs—best when on cultural developments of the 1920s and 1930s. Publishing over a period of seven decades, he evolved into a literary critic, editor, and historian of major significance. He will be best remembered for his autobiographical histories of the 1920s "lost generation," for seeking to explain the place of a European tradition within American literature, and for encouraging interest in several major writers, among them William Faulkner.

• Most of Cowley's papers are in the Newberry Library in Chicago. Diane U. Eisenberg, *Malcolm Cowley: A Checklist of His Writings, 1916–1973* (1975), lists 1,171 works, long and short, by Cowley and is definitive to its date. James Michael Kempf, *The Early Career of Malcolm Cowley: A Humanist among the Moderns* (1985), is a short, pioneering biographical study, while Hans Bak, *Malcolm Cowley: The Formative Years* (1993), which covers the period 1898–1930, is far longer and is massively annotated. Thomas Daniel Young's edition of *Conversations with Malcolm Cowley* (1986) includes numerous interviews, even the FBI's grilling of Cowley. For *The Portable Malcolm Cowley* (1990), the editor Donald W. Faulkner provides a splendid introduction, notes, and a chronology. Lewis P. Simpson, "Malcolm Cowley and the American Writer," *Sewanee Review* 84 (Spring 1976): 221–47, discusses Cowley's comments on writers' attitudes toward home and exile, independence and loneliness, and sense of community. Philip Young, "For Malcolm Cowley: Critic, Poet, 1898–," *Southern Review* 9 (Autumn 1973): 778–95, is an informal, partly anecdotal tribute to Cowley's varied accomplishments. "Malcolm Cowley, Writer, Is Dead at 90," is a six-column obituary in the *New York Times*, 29 Mar. 1989.

ROBERT L. GALE

COX, Allyn (5 June 1896–26 Sept. 1982), muralist, was born in New York City, the son of Kenyon Cox, a painter and art critic, and Louise Howland King, a painter. Cox's education included study at the National Academy of Design and the Art Students League (1915–1916) and a fellowship in painting from the American Academy in Rome (1916). Before leaving for Rome, he assisted his father, a noted muralist, on several commissions, including a mural for the Wisconsin state capitol's supreme court room. In Italy Cox studied Renaissance and baroque painting and served from 1917 to 1918 as a first lieutenant with the American Red Cross in Italy.

After returning to New York City in 1921, Cox, no doubt aided by his family's social and artistic connections, immediately received numerous commissions to decorate private homes. Most of these early projects consisted of Italian baroque–style landscapes, still lifes, and grisaille figures (monochromatic figures painted to resemble sculpture). His clients during the 1920s included the wives of W. K. Vanderbilt, Sr., Charles Tiffany, and John Innes Kane and Vincent Astor and his wife, all of New York City; the wife of Andrew Calhoun of Atlanta; and the Dumbarton Oaks house in Washington, D.C.

Cox's commissions for public buildings included a series of ceiling murals titled *Parnassus* and *All for Love* for the W. A. Clark Memorial Library at the University of California, Los Angeles, completed in 1927. With their trompe l'oeil decorations, dramatic compositions, and muscular figures, the paintings resemble works by the Italian painters Michelangelo and the Carracci family. In 1927 Cox married Ethel Howard Potter, who later assisted him with several commissions; they had no children.

Painted between 1931 and 1934 for the law building of the University of Virginia in Charlottesville, *Moses with the Law* and *The Trial from the Shield of Achilles* depict epochal themes of justice and continue Cox's heroic classical style. Other public commissions include the Continental Bank (1932), the lingerie department at Lord and Taylor's (1938), the ballroom of the Cosmopolitan Club (1940), and the Guaranty Trust Company branch at Radio City (1945), all in New York City, and the *S. S. America* for United States Lines (1940). Between 1940 and 1941 Cox taught at the Art Students League.

Cox's first major fresco restoration was for the 110-year-old Alsop House in Middletown, Connecticut, owned by Wesleyan University. Originally intended to be surrounded by statues, the exterior of the mansion was instead decorated with trompe l'oeil figures and urns. In 1949 Cox sealed the outside deteriorated paintings with hot wax and covered them with his own replicas painted on waterproof plywood.

The only "true fresco" Cox said he ever did—"buon fresco" is the application of pigment on lime-plaster ground—was the completion of the frieze in the rotunda of the U.S. Capitol in Washington, D.C. Begun in 1877 by Italian-born artist Constantino Brumidi, the frieze represents important events in American history, starting with Columbus's landing in 1492 and ending with the discovery of gold in California in 1848. After Brumidi died in 1880, the painter Filippo Costaggini completed the remaining images based on the original design, but when he finished in 1888, he left more than thirty feet empty. As a child Cox was taken by his mother to the Capitol and saw Brumidi's frieze for the first time. "I decided then and there," Cox later told a reporter, "that I'd like to round out those thirty-two feet" (*New Yorker*, 7 Mar. 1953, p. 22).

In August 1950 Congress passed legislation to fill the gap with scenes depicting the Civil War, the Spanish-American War, and the birth of aviation. Cox's designs were accepted by the Joint Committee on the Library (a congressional committee that manages art in the Capitol), and he began work on the commission in 1951. After completing his portion in 1953, he cleaned the entire original frieze. Little critical comment or interpretation followed its unveiling in 1954. Reported, however, was President Dwight D. Eisenhower's earlier directive that Cox's panels not contain any reference to the atomic or hydrogen bombs. Instead, the additions were to depict progress "that brings happiness to humans" (*Washington Post*, 12 May 1954).

Painted in a grisaille style, Cox's figures blend in easily with the older images. Located to the right of Brumidi's portrayal of the Forty-niners is Cox's representation of the Civil War, consisting of a Union and a Confederate soldier stiffly shaking hands (he had been asked not to depict any fighting). The middle section, on the Spanish-American War, shows a naval crew of eight men preparing a salvo for fire. The *Birth of Flight* includes scenes of the Wright Brothers and their plane; aviation pioneers Leonardo da Vinci, Samuel Pierpont Langley, and Octave Chanute; and an eagle, that image connecting the modern event with Brumidi's depiction of Columbus.

A member of the Royal Arch Chapter of the Freemasons, Cox completed a large number of decorations for the George Washington Masonic Memorial in Alexandria, Virginia, in 1958. The two largest works (each measures about 48 feet in length), *George Washington Laying the Cornerstone of the National Capitol* and *George Washington and Brethren in Saint John's Day Observance*, depict the titled historical events in a stoically classical manner and include portraits of the participants. The Royal Arch Room contains Hebrew-

and Egyptian-inspired decorations to represent King Solomon's Temple. For the Cryptic Room, Cox recreated the feel of a crypt within the confines of Solomon's Temple with murals depicting the Masonic legends of the Degrees as well as a scene from the court of Babylonian king Nebuchadnezzar.

Through the late 1950s and into the 1960s Cox completed several government and private commissions, including a portrait of Senator Henry Clay (1958), now located in the vice president's reception room in the Capitol. He also cleaned and restored Brumidi's 1865 fresco *The Apotheosis of Washington*, located inside the Capitol dome (1959). Working outside his usual domain of fresco and paint, Cox designed nine mosaics for St. Paul Hospital in Dallas, Texas (1963), three stained glass windows for St. Bartholomew's Church in New York City (1964–1967), and three mosaics for the General Grant National Memorial (Grant's Tomb), also in New York (1966). From 1960 to 1961 Cox taught mural classes at the National Academy of Design, which in 1962 elected him to academician status.

Cox's last and most-ambitious projects were for the Senate and House corridors of the U.S. Capitol. In 1974 he added a painting of America's first moon landing to Brumidi's corridors on the Senate side. On the House side, Cox's Hall of Capitols, completed in July 1974, represents the history of the U.S. Capitol, including its architects and several precursors, such as earlier capitols in New York and Philadelphia. The Great Experiment Hall, finished in 1982, depicts the development of American democracy, starting with the Mayflower Compact of 1620 and ending with a woman suffrage parade in 1917. His designs for the Westward Expansion Hall, scenes depicting the discovery and settlement of the country, were completed posthumously in 1993.

A marked lack of criticism of Cox's work underlines the meager recognition of his role in twentieth-century art history. Unlike twentieth-century mural painter Thomas Hart Benton and other artists whose work was underwritten by the depression-era Works Progress Administration, Cox rarely brought a modern aesthetic to his vision—a conscious choice in a period when the prevailing artistic mood was toward progress, abstraction, and invention. On the other hand, his conservative style and technical abilities were rewarded with a long and prosperous career of private and government commissions. Cox died in a Washington, D.C., hospital five months after his retirement and just five days after he was recognized at a special ceremony held in National Statuary Hall in the U.S. Captol.

• The most-thorough source of materials on Cox is the Archives of American Art in Washington, D.C. Extensive records are also located in the office of the curator, architect of the Capitol, Washington, D.C. *The American Story in Art: The Mural of Allyn Cox in the U.S. Capitol* (1986), published by the National Society of the Daughters of the American Revolution and the United States Capitol Historical Society, includes color reproductions from the Hall of Capitols and the Great Experiment Hall. Also see "Allyn Cox: A New Mural for the Capitol," *American Artist*, Dec. 1974; Henry Hope Reed, "An Interview with Allyn Cox," *Classical America* 3 (1973): 27–36; and Cox's two-part article on the Capitol rotunda frieze and the dome canopy in *Museum News*, Feb. 1961 and Mar. 1976. Informative obituaries are in the *New York Times* and the *Washington Post*, both 28 Sept. 1982, and the *Los Angeles Times*, 29 Sept. 1982.

PHILIP H. VILES, JR.
N. ELIZABETH SCHLATTER

COX, Elbert Frank (5 Dec. 1895–28 Nov. 1969), mathematician, was born in Evansville, Indiana, the son of Johnson D. Cox, a high school principal, and Eugenia D. Talbot. From an early age he demonstrated tremendous talent as a violinist and was offered a scholarship to study in Europe at the Prague Conservatory of Music. Instead, he opted for a career in mathematics and received an A.B. from Indiana University in 1917. He became assistant principal and mathematics teacher at Alves Street School in Henderson, Kentucky, but resigned the next year to enlist in the U.S. Army. He spent the last six months of World War I in France as a clerk and was discharged in 1919 with the rank of sergeant.

That same year Cox was appointed chairman of the Department of Natural Sciences at Shaw University in Raleigh, North Carolina. In 1922 he left Shaw to enroll at Cornell University, where he was awarded a graduate scholarship in mathematics that same year and an Erastus Brooks Fellowship two years later. He spent the fall semester of 1924 as a traveling fellow at Canada's McGill University in order to work with William Lloyd Garrison Williams, a former Cornell professor who was his dissertation committee chairman. His doctoral work focused on the polynomial solutions of the difference equation $af(x+1) + bf(x) = \Phi(x)$, where "$\Phi(x)$" represents the Euler function, the number of integers that are not greater than x and that share no common factor with x other than 1. To this end he adopted the symbolic methods of the Danish mathematician Niels Erik Nörlund and the French mathematician Edouard Lucas concerning Bernoulli numbers, which take the form $B_0 + B_1 x/1! + B_2 x^2/2! + \ldots$ and are used as coefficients in power series of the form $a_0 + a_1 x + a_2 x^2 + \ldots + a_n x^n + \ldots$, where a represents a Bernoulli number.

In 1925 Cox's dissertation was accepted by Cornell. As a result of Williams's efforts, it was also accepted by the Imperial University in Sendai, Japan, thus making Cox the first person of African descent in the world to receive a Ph.D. in pure mathematics. This achievement is all the more impressive when one considers that by 1925 fewer than fifty African Americans had received doctorates of any kind. Moreover, prevailing racial attitudes in the United States had forced many of them to go abroad to undertake their graduate studies. His accomplishment helped to make it possible for other black mathematicians, such as Dudley Welcon Woodard, William Waldron Shiefflin Claytor, Marjorie Lee Brown, Evelyn Boyd Granville, and Da-

vid Blackwell, to receive their doctorates from American universities. By becoming the second black to receive a doctorate from Cornell (Thomas Wyatt Turner, who received his Ph.D. in biology in 1921, was the first), Cox also helped to open the door a little wider for black doctoral candidates at that school. By 1943 an additional twenty-three blacks had received doctorates from Cornell, including seven who received their degrees in either mathematics or physics.

In 1925 Cox accepted a position as a professor of physics at West Virginia State College, at the time a poorly funded segregated institution without a science library. In 1928, the year after he married Beulah P. Kaufman, with whom he had three children, he taught both physics and mathematics but left the next year to become an associate professor of mathematics at Howard University. During World War II he contributed to the American war effort by teaching engineering science and war management at Howard from 1942 to 1944 and by serving as head of a specialized training program for the army from 1943 to 1945. In 1947, the same year he was promoted to full professor, he assisted in overhauling Howard's grading system. In 1949 he served briefly as head of the mathematics department and assumed the chairmanship again in 1956. In 1957 the departments of mathematics and physics were merged, and Cox chaired the combined department until 1961. He retired in 1966 with the reputation of having supervised more master's theses than any other member of Howard's faculty.

Throughout his academic career Cox carried a heavy teaching load as well as substantial administrative and advising duties. These factors effectively prevented him from publishing anything more than "The Polynomial Solution of the Difference Equation $af(x+1) + bf(x) = \Phi(x)$" (*Tohoku Mathematical Journal* 39 [1934]: 327–48), a revised version of his dissertation that offered a better understanding of generalized Euler polynomials of both higher and lower order. He planned to spend his retirement years writing about mathematics, but health considerations prevented him from doing so. He died in Washington, D.C.

Cox was a member of the American Mathematical Society, the American Physical Society, the American Physics Institute, and Beta Kappa Chi, Pi Mu Epsilon, and Sigma Pi Sigma education fraternities. Although he was a very private person, he possessed an excellent speaking voice and often served as an after-dinner speaker.

By becoming the first African American to earn a doctorate in pure mathematics, Cox helped to open the door to a career in that discipline for many other black scholars. As a teacher and thesis adviser he inspired and helped dozens of promising young black mathematicians to achieve success in their chosen field.

• Cox's papers have not been located. Biographies are Leonard C. Bruno, "Elbert Frank Cox," *Notable Twentieth Century Scientists*, ed. Emily J. McMurray (1995), pp. 418–19, and James D. Cox, "Questions/Answers Relating to Dr. Elbert F. Cox" (unpublished ms., Mathematics Library, Cornell

Univ.). His contributions as a mathematician and as a black doctorate-earner are addressed in Jacqueline Giles-Giron, "Black Pioneers in Mathematics: Brown, Granville, Cox, Claytor, and Blackwell," *MAA Focus* (Jan.–Feb. 1991): 18, 21; Virginia K. Newell et al., eds., *Black Mathematicians and Their Works* (1980); and Harry W. Greene, *Holders of Doctorates among American Negroes: An Educational and Social Study of Negroes Who Have Earned Doctoral Degrees in Course, 1876–1943* (1947). An obituary is in the *Washington Post*, 2 Dec. 1969.

CHARLES W. CAREY, JR.

COX, George Barnesdale (29 Apr. 1853–20 May 1916), political leader and "boss" of Cincinnati, was born in Cincinnati, Ohio, the son of George Barnesdale Cox, a recent English immigrant and laborer. Cox's mother, whose family name was Stitt, was born in Canada. At his father's death eight years later, Cox left school to help support his impoverished family. He did the kind of work available to a young boy in the crowded mid-nineteenth century city, including selling newspapers and blacking boots. He progressed to "looking-out" at gambling houses, delivering groceries, tending bar, and selling tobacco before acquiring his own saloon, Dead Man's Corner, in the 1870s.

From this base Cox built the relationships through which he made the turn-of-the-century transition from ward boss to citywide boss, capable of controlling his party and securing its electoral victories over an extended period of time. Cox and his "gang" drew the attention of the national muckraking press, who called him in 1904 "Proprietor of Cincinnati," in 1911 "The Biggest Boss of Them All," and in 1912 "The Thing above the Law." Cox worked his way up in the Republican party from election-day vote challenger to boss during the last quarter of the nineteenth century, a period of dramatic changes in American cities. In Cincinnati and elsewhere, the traditional densely populated walking city gave way to the "new city," with its defined central business district and residential areas. The elite moved their homes to the suburbs, leaving the poorest residents just beyond the center and the upwardly mobile occupying the space between the suburbs and the central city. Over time Cox's political coalition drew together elements of all three residential components of the new city.

Cox won election to the city council as a representative of his transitional, central city Eighteenth Ward in 1879. After reelection to a second term, he sold his saloon to focus, he said, "on real estate and other business enterprises" (*Cincinnati Enquirer*, 15 May 1911). Cox constructed the first phase of his political "enterprise" as a ward leader who could be counted on to deliver his delegates in Republican city nominating conventions and his constituency in city and county elections. He became a local party authority with his selection to manage James G. Blaine's 1884 presidential campaign in Hamilton County. Together with a white suburban lawyer and an African-American leader in the West End, he organized the Young Men's Blaine Club, which served as Cox's base of political operations for the rest of his career. He ran unsuccess-

fully for county clerk in 1885 and 1888, but he gained the confidence of Ohio governor Joseph B. Foraker, who appointed him state oil inspector in 1888. He continued to strengthen his position within the factionalized Republican party, despite the resistance of the city's elite. In 1890 Cox married Caroline Schill; they had no children.

As late as the city elections of 1889 Charles P. Taft's *Times-Star* attacked the unnamed (Cox) "Conspiracy." Just two years later Taft accepted Cox, expecting him "to secure a 'New Order' for Cincinnati." Gas company president Andrew Hickenlooper retained Cox's services at a rate of $3,500 annually, which Cox viewed as comparable to an attorney's retainer. Cox continued to nominate candidates for patronage jobs and to expect their voting loyalty. He also maintained decorum in city conventions, eliminated multiple voting, and accepted the nomination and election of reform business candidates for mayor. His party's candidate for mayor was elected for all but two of the next fourteen years. Under Cox's leadership, this coalition was "able to bring positive government to Cincinnati and to mitigate the chaos which accompanied the emergence of the new city" (Miller, *Boss Cox's Cincinnati*, p. 239). With some justification, Cox boasted of his "achievement of taking the schools, Police, and Fire Departments out of politics" and insisted that "a boss is not necessarily a public enemy" (*Cincinnati Enquirer*, 15 May 1911).

Reformers outside the machine, who alleged corrupt practices, including compulsory party assessment of patronage workers, formed a successful third-party reform ticket in 1897. Reformers within the machine, however, found themselves unable to succeed without the boss and accepted him back in 1899. In 1906, after another Republican loss in the 1905 municipal election, the state of Ohio launched the Drake Committee, whose investigation revealed that interest on Hamilton County funds amounting to $214,998.76 had been retained by county officers. Cox testified before the grand jury that he had not personally received any of those funds. In 1911 reformers outside the machine obtained an indictment against Cox that charged him with committing perjury in his 1906 grand jury statement. The *Cincinnati Post* predicted that the indictment of "the last of the old-time bosses . . . Means downfall of Gang rule in Cincinnati and Hamilton co." (22 Feb. 1911). The prediction was only half-right. While Cox managed to have the charge dismissed, he found himself unable to reclaim his authority and reluctantly left politics. However, his chief lieutenants, August Herrmann and Rudolph Hynicka, continued to maintain the political machine for nearly another decade.

Cox spent the last five years of his life in the impressive home he had built in suburban Clifton. He focused his formidable executive skills and fortune on banking and theater, including the World Film Corporation and the Shubert, Loew, and Keith theater businesses. He died in Cincinnati.

Cox's machine helped bridge the gaps among diverse elements in the new city and establish relatively stable politics that fostered effective government. While his perseverance is remarkable, so too is the fragility of the political coalition that supported him. His alliance with the central city ward bosses ultimately moved him beyond the tolerance of city government reformers.

• No collection of Cox papers exists. He gave few interviews, but his lengthy statement to the *New York World*, 14 May 1911, was published in the *Cincinnati Enquirer*, 15 May 1911, and gives his account of his own life. The definitive analyses of Cox are by Zane L. Miller, *Boss Cox's Cincinnati: Urban Politics in the Progressive Era* (1968) and "Boss Cox's Cincinnati: A Study in Urbanization and Politics, 1880–1914," *Journal of American History* 54 (Mar. 1968): 823–38. See Gustav J. Karger, "George Barnesdale Cox: Proprietor of Cincinnati," *Frank Leslie's Popular Monthly*, Jan. 1904, pp. 273–78; Lincoln Steffens, "Ohio: A Tale of Two Cities," *McClure's Magazine*, June 1905, pp. 293–311; Frank Parker Stockbridge, "The Biggest Boss of Them All," *Hampton's Magazine*, Jan.–June 1911, pp. 616–29; and George Kibbe Turner, "The Thing above the Law: The Rise and Rule of George B. Cox, and His Overthrow by Young Hunt and the Fighting Idealists of Cincinnati," *McClure's Magazine*, Mar. 1912, pp. 575–91. For Cox's life after his retirement from political life, see his obituaries in the *Cincinnati Enquirer* and the *Cincinnati Times-Star*, 20 May 1916, and an account of the funeral, including a listing of those who sent flowers, in the *Cincinnati Enquirer*, 23 May 1916.

JUDITH SPRAUL-SCHMIDT

COX, Gertrude Mary (13 Jan. 1900–17 Oct. 1978), statistician, was born near Dayton, Iowa, the daughter of John William Allen Cox and Emmaline Maddy, farmers. After graduating from high school in 1918, she spent the next seven years in social work, including a stint as housemother at a Montana orphanage. Hoping that a college degree would help her become superintendent of the orphanage, in 1925 she matriculated at Iowa State College. She received her B.S. in mathematics in 1929 and, in 1931, the first M.S. granted by the college in statistics. From 1931 to 1933 she studied psychological statistics at the University of California at Berkeley.

In 1933 she accepted a position with the newly created Statistical Laboratory at Iowa State, the first of its kind in the United States. The laboratory was established to help experimental scientists interpret their results, but it soon became clear that many experiments were being conducted in such a way that statisticians could infer nothing from the results. Consequently, Cox devoted herself to promoting experimental design. By involving statisticians in the planning stages of experiments, when they could get the experimenter to define the objectives of the experiment, describe it in detail, and devise a plan for analyzing the data before beginning the experiment, she hoped to enhance significantly the usefulness of the results. Her expertise in experimental design led to her promotion to research assistant professor in 1939, and in 1940 she was named head of the newly created Department of Experimental Statistics at the North Carolina State College School of Agriculture, a position she held until 1949. Under her direction, the department supported research in agriculture and worked closely with the U.S. Bureau of Agricultural Economics in general and its Raleigh-based Division of Agricultural Statistics in particular. In 1945 she started a graduate program to provide training in statistical theory as well as methods.

In an effort to make applied statistics more accessible to southern researchers in agriculture, biology, and medicine, in 1944 Cox obtained a grant from John D. Rockefeller's General Education Board that allowed her to establish the Consolidated University of North Carolina Institute of Statistics. As first director of the Institute, she implemented a series of short working conferences on how to apply statistics to such fields as plant and animal sciences, quality control, agricultural economics, plant genetics, agronomy and horticulture, and soil science. She also helped to establish at the University of North Carolina–Chapel Hill School of Public Health a department of biostatistics, a social science statistical laboratory, and a psychometric laboratory. In addition, she played a major role in establishing the Southern Regional Education Board's Committee on Statistics to further regional cooperation in statistical teaching, research, and consulting. Much of this success resulted from her skill at obtaining grants; in all, she received three large grants from the General Education Board as well as funds from the Ford and Rockefeller foundations. Her accomplishments as director are all the more impressive given that most of the institute's original staff had little formal training in statistics. Because few statisticians were available for her to hire, she sought out graduates trained in agricultural disciplines who had minored in statistics and then helped them to become proficient statisticians.

Cox was a driving force in the creation of the Research Triangle Institute (RTI). Devoted to consulting and research, RTI melded the capabilities of three major universities in the Raleigh-Durham-Chapel Hill area and served as the nucleus around which an important high-tech business community would grow. In 1960 she retired from North Carolina State and the Institute of Statistics to become director of RTI's first operating unit, the Statistics Research Division (SRD). Because eighteen of RTI's first twenty research contracts dealt with statistics, her ability to complete these contracts successfully greatly enhanced the fledgling organization's reputation. Under her leadership, SRD evolved into an international center for statistics as she avidly promoted international cooperation in the development of statistical programs.

In fact, Cox's global view of statistics predated SRD. In 1947 she had helped to found the International Biometrics Society (IBS), and from 1947 to 1955 she edited its journal, *Biometrics*. In 1949 she became the first female member of the International Statistical Institute and served as treasurer (1955–1961) and education committee chair (1962–1968). In 1950 she co-published *Experimental Designs* as a reference work for researchers around the world who knew a little but not much about statistics; the book was adopted by a number of schools as a text on the design and analysis of replicated experiments. In 1964 she helped to establish the Institute of Statistics at the University of Cairo, Egypt, and in 1970–1971 she promoted statistical assistance programs in Thailand. From 1968 to 1969 she served as president of IBS.

Cox's contributions to statistics were recognized in a number of ways. In 1956 she was elected president of the American Statistical Association. In 1959 she received the O. Max Gardner Award for outstanding service to the University of North Carolina System. In 1960 she received Gamma Sigma Delta's International Award for Distinguished Service to Agriculture. In 1964 she was made an Honorary Life Member of IBS. In 1970 North Carolina State named its new statistics building in her honor, and in 1977 her former students created the Gertrude M. Cox Fellowship Fund for outstanding graduate students in statistics at that school. She was elected to the National Academy of Sciences in 1975.

Cox possessed enormous energy and self-confidence. She never married, largely because she regarded her staff and their families as her own relations. She was particularly close to Richard Anderson, a former classmate at Iowa State and colleague in North Carolina, and his wife and children. She died in Durham, North Carolina.

Throughout her career Cox believed that the value of statistical research could be measured only by the degree to which it contributed to progress in other fields, and she devoted her career to making experimentation more fruitful. As a teacher and consultant she recognized and then helped others to recognize the importance of experimental design. As a fundraiser and administrator she developed and implemented programs to enhance research via statistics in the South and around the world.

• Cox's papers are located in the North Carolina State University Archives, D. H. Hill Library. An excellent biography of Cox and a complete bibliography of her work appear in Richard L. Anderson, "Gertrude Mary Cox," National Academy of Sciences, *Biographical Memoirs* 59 (1990): 117–32. Peter W. M. John, "Industrial Experimentation (1955–1965)," and Boyd Harshbarger, "History of the Early Developments of Modern Statistics in America (1920–1944)," both in *On the History of Statistics and Probability*, ed. D. B. Owen (1976), discuss the pioneering aspects of Cox's work in statistics. Charles X. Larrabee, *Many Missions: Research Triangle Institute's First 31 Years* (1991), assesses the importance of her contribution to RTI. Other useful works are Louise S. Grinstein and Paul J. Campbell, eds., *Women of Mathematics: A Bibliographic Sourcebook* (1987), and Richard L. Anderson et al., "Gertrude M. Cox—A Modern Pioneer in Statistics," *Biometrics* 35 (Mar. 1979): 3–7.

CHARLES W. CAREY, JR.

COX, Ida (25 Feb. 1896–10 Nov. 1967), blues singer, was born Ida Prather in Toccoa, Stephens County, Georgia, of parents whose names have not been recorded. In Cedartown, Georgia, where she spent her childhood, Prather sang in the African Methodist church choir. At age fourteen she left home to tour with the White and Clark Black & Tan Minstrels, playing "Topsy" roles; she subsequently joined other companies, including the Rabbit Foot Minstrels and Pete Werley's Florida Cotton Blossom Minstrels. She married three times. Her first husband, Adler Cox, whom she married about 1916, was a trumpeter with the Florida Blossoms Minstrel Show; he died in the First World War. The date of her second marriage, to Eugene Williams, is unknown; the couple had a daughter. Her third husband was Texan Jesse ("Tiny") Crump, a pianist and organist who may be heard performing on some of her recordings and who also shared management responsibilities with her.

By 1922 Cox was solidly established as a star performer. With Crump, she led her own touring tent show throughout the South from 1929 into the 1930s. That revue, *Raisin' Cain*, was chosen to be the first show from the Theatre Owners Booking Circuit to open at New York's Apollo Theater. Difficult times after the stock market crash forced Cox and Crump to reorganize and seek bookings as far away as the West Coast before bringing the show, under the title *Darktown Scandals*, to the Midwest. Still, Cox never ceased barnstorming through the South in the late 1930s and into the 1940s.

Her performances always maintained a high-class tone. They were constructed on a simple formula: three letters in each name (i.e., Cox, Ida), three jokes between songs, and three songs. With regal bearing, dignity, and a beauty that combined glamor and sophistication, she came across as a blues queen in every way. Audiences saw her as "always a lady," even though her often salty lyrics were laced with sexual allusions and sly humor directed at men. The most distinctive aspect of her work was the frequent use of macabre formulas; her work has been characterized as death-focused blues. Though she could be imperious and demanding, she was known as a fair employer and a good manager.

Working the clubs and theaters over the course of a quarter century, mostly in the Southeast, she performed with headliners such as Jelly Roll Morton, in Atlanta, c. 1920; King Oliver, in Chicago; and Bessie Smith, in the 1934 revue *Fan Waves*. At the invitation of John Hammond, she took part in the 1939 Carnegie Hall concert *From Spirituals to Swing*.

From 1923 to 1929 she recorded extensively for Paramount with pianist Lovie Austin ("Any Woman's Blues") but not exclusively, as the company claimed; under an assortment of aliases—Julia/Julius Powers, Jane Smith, Velma Bradley, Kate Lewis—she also cut sides for Harmograph and Silvertone. Her output includes more than seventy titles. These early recordings suffer from inferior sound, but backed up by Austin and her Blues Serenaders, as well as other outstanding musicians such as Tommy Ladnier and Jim Bryant—and later Coleman Hawkins and Fletcher Henderson—they reveal a high level of artistry.

In her phrasing she had an expressive habit of displacing the normal word stress in a way that intensified the rhythmic pulse and held the listener's attention. Outstanding titles from the 1923 and 1924 sessions include "Death Letter Blues," "Chicago Monkey Man Blues," "Wild Women Don't Have the Blues," and "Kentucky Man Blues." By 1925 and 1926, at her artistic peak, she recorded "Mississippi River Blues," "Coffin Blues," and "Rambling Blues." Following a ten-year hiatus, she recorded for Vocalion-Okeh, with Lionel Hampton, Hot Lips Page, J. C. Higginbotham, James P. Johnson, and Charlie Christian ("Four Day Creep").

Following a stroke in 1945, she retired to Knoxville, Tennessee (1949), where she lived with her daughter until her death. Between 1940 and 1960 Cox performed only intermittently and reluctantly, as she became increasingly active in church work. After a hiatus of more than twenty years, she returned to the recording studio in 1961 for a final album, *Blues for Rampart Street*, with an all-star band including Coleman Hawkins and Roy Eldridge (Riverside). The album featured a persuasive new version of "Death Letter Blues." Even though her voice had faded, the *New York Times* reviewer John Wilson praised the greater "artfulness of her phrasing" (10 Sept. 1961). Sammy Price, the blues pianist who took the place of Crump on that final recording, commented on her "flowing blues sound," the "good melodic lines, words that make sense, decent diction" (Harrison, p. 238). The brief revival of her career ended when she suffered another stroke in 1965 in Knoxville.

A classic blues singer known in the 1920s and 1930s for the ability to communicate feeling and bring out her own personality in performance, Cox was sometimes billed as the Uncrowned Queen of the Blues and the Sepia Mae West. Possessed of a regal stage presence and a strong, resonant voice with a touch of nasal quality, coupled with a "salty cynicism all her own," she was most effective in traditional-form blues songs, notably her own blues compositions and those of Austin, with whom she regularly performed and recorded in the early 1920s.

• For additional information on Cox, see Ian Carr et al., *Jazz, the Essential Companion* (1987); Daphne D. Harrison, "Ida Cox 'Queen of the Blues,'" in *Notable Black American Women*, ed. Jessie Carney Smith (1992), and Harrison, *Black Pearls: Blues Queens of the 1920s* (1988); Suzanne Flandreau, "Ida Cox," in *Black Women in America: An Historical Encyclopedia*, ed. Darlene Clark Hine (1993); Paul Oliver, *Conversation with the Blues* (1965); and D. Stewart-Baxter, *Ma Rainey and the Classic Blues Singers* (1970). The liner notes from *Ida Cox 1923 Recordings* (Fountain Vintage Blues 301, 1973) are also useful. An interview of Cox is "Yes Yes Yes Yes," *New Yorker*, 29 Apr. 1961, pp. 30–31. A three-volume set of CDs, *Ida Cox: Complete Recorded Works*, was released in 1995. Sheldon Harris, *Blues Who's Who: A Biographical Dictionary of Blues Singers* (1979), contains a brief biography of Cox, as well as a song list. An obituary is in the *New York Times*, 12 Nov. 1967.

LOUIS E. AULD

COX, Jacob Dolson (27 Oct. 1828–8 Aug. 1900), Union general and Republican political figure, was born in Montreal, Canada, the son of Jacob Dolson Cox, Sr. (whose family name was originally Koch), a New York builder, and Thedia Redelia Kenyon. Cox's family had moved to Montreal, where his father supervised construction of the Basilica of Notre Dame; they returned to New York City shortly after Jacob's birth. The family's financial reverses in the wake of the depression of 1837 forced young Cox to curtail his formal education. He clerked for New York City lawyers and bankers while pursuing a rigorous course of self-study, which by 1846 prepared him to enter Oberlin College. Cox was drawn to Oberlin by Professor (soon to be President) Charles G. Finney, then America's preeminent evangelist. In 1849 that relationship was cemented by Cox's marriage to Finney's recently widowed daughter, Helen Finney Cochran; they had seven children, including the artist, Kenyon Cox. His relationship with Finney was severely strained when, shortly before his 1851 graduation, Cox decided he had lost his ministerial vocation and accepted a position as superintendent of schools at nearby Warren, Ohio.

At Warren, the young superintendent studied to enter the Ohio bar and also dabbled in politics, helping to organize the state's Republican party. In 1859, without his prior knowledge or consent, Cox was nominated and subsequently elected to the Ohio Senate. There he and his roommate, James A. Garfield, won reputations as outspoken foes of slavery expansion.

After the outbreak of the Civil War, both became officers in the Union army. Commissioned a brigadier general in May 1861, Cox was assigned to western Virginia and in 1862 fought at South Mountain and Antietam, where he commanded the Ninth Corps in its assault on the Burnside Bridge. After serving as district commander in West Virginia and then as commander of the District of Ohio during John Hunt Morgan's raid, he was assigned, at his request, to more active duty, participating in the Atlanta campaign, the March to the Sea, and the battles of Franklin and Nashville. He received a belated promotion to major general in December 1864.

In June 1865 Cox received the unanimous nomination of the Union party for governor of Ohio. During the campaign, Cox offended his Radical supporters by issuing the so-called Oberlin Letter, which opposed African-American suffrage and advocated racial separation. Despite the controversy, he easily defeated the Democratic challenger, General George W. Morgan.

After a relatively uneventful gubernatorial term, Cox declined to run again. He moved to Cincinnati to resume his law practice but was called to Washington, D.C., by newly elected President Ulysses S. Grant to serve as secretary of the interior. In that capacity, he implemented Grant's "peace policy" toward the American Indians, which aimed at eventual assimilation through the establishment of reservations rather than warfare or forced relocation. His most striking innovation was the introduction of civil service reforms, such as promotion by merit, permanence of tenure, and competitive exams. These practices aroused the opposition of Republican spoilsmen, such as Michigan senator Zachariah Chandler. Cox, assuming (perhaps rashly) that President Grant was behind these attacks, precipitately resigned on 5 October 1870. His "martyrdom" gave publicity to the cause of civil service reform and impetus to the creation of the Liberal Republican party, a movement that Cox at first encouraged but which he abandoned because of his disapproval of its 1872 presidential nominee, Horace Greeley.

After a term in Congress representing Ohio's Sixth District (Toledo) from 1877 to 1879, Cox abandoned politics for other pursuits. He had already resumed his legal practice, and one of his clients, the Toledo & Wabash & Western Railroad, was so impressed with his services that it made him its president from 1873 to 1877, during which term he led the company out of bankruptcy. In 1881 Cox embarked on yet another career, as dean of the Cincinnati Law School, a post he held for sixteen years, four of which (1885–1889) were spent doing double duty as president of the University of Cincinnati.

In 1897 Cox declined an opportunity to become U.S. minister to Spain, preferring to devote his retirement years to intellectual pursuits. Those pursuits were varied and productive. He was a connoisseur of European cathedrals, an interest derived from his father. An amateur microscopist, he won a gold medal for photomicroscopy at the Antwerp Exposition of 1891, bringing to his hobby, according to his colleague C. M. Vorce, "that painstaking thoroughness and striking power of logical analysis which he displayed in all his works in every walk of life" (p. 202). As a man of letters, Cox focused his literary output on the central event of his own life, the Civil War, regularly reviewing books on that subject for the *Nation* and writing his own book-length accounts of the March to the Sea and the battles of Atlanta, Franklin, and Nashville. His magnum opus, the two-volume *Military Reminiscences of the Civil War* (1900), was completed shortly before his death at Magnolia, Massachusetts.

Living in an era before the demands of specialization would make such versatility unlikely, Cox was master of an astonishing variety of endeavors—law, theology, education, warfare, business, government, science, literature, and art—a true nineteenth-century American Renaissance man.

• The largest collection of Cox papers is at the Oberlin College Library. Other significant groups of letters are in the James A. Garfield Papers and the John M. Schofield Papers, both at the Library of Congress. Cox is the subject of two comprehensive unpublished dissertations: Eugene D. Schmiel, "The Career of Jacob Dolson Cox . . . " (Ph.D. diss., Ohio State Univ., 1969), and Jerry Lee Bower, "The Civil War Career of Jacob Dolson Cox" (Ph.D. diss., Michigan State Univ., 1970), the scope of which is wider than its title indicates. Briefer sketches can be found in James R. Ewing, *Public Services of Jacob Dolson Cox . . .* (1902), and the obituary by C. M. Vorce in the *Transactions of the American Microscopical Society* (1901), pp. 197–202.

ALLAN PESKIN

COX, James Middleton (31 Mar. 1870–15 July 1957), newspaper publisher and politician, was born in Jacksonburg, Ohio, the son of Eliza Andrews and Gilbert Cox, farmers. He attended a one-room school until he was sixteen. His parents divorced, and in 1886 Cox moved to nearby Middletown to live with his mother. Cox's brother-in-law John Q. Baker, who published the *Middletown Weekly Signal*, introduced him to journalism. After an apprenticeship of several years, Cox was hired by the *Cincinnati Enquirer* in 1892 to cover railroad news. In 1893 he married Mayme Simpson Harding; they had three children, one of whom died in infancy.

In 1894 Middletown paper manufacturer Paul J. Sorg was elected to Congress, and he hired Cox as his assistant. With Sorg's help, Cox in 1898 purchased the *Dayton Daily News*. He introduced modern journalistic techniques into the growing Dayton market. The *News* became the city's leading afternoon paper and succeeded in driving its afternoon competition out of business in 1905. In that same year Cox purchased the *Springfield (Ohio) Daily News*. His newspapers prospered, and Cox thus turned to electoral politics.

Elected to Congress as a Democrat from the Third Ohio District in 1908, Cox served two terms and became part of the reform coalition transforming national politics. In 1912 he was elected governor of Ohio in a three-way race, in which he won 41.5 percent of the vote. Serving three terms (1913–1914, 1917–1921), he presided over a massive restructuring of Ohio government. His first marriage ended in divorce in 1912, and in 1917 he married Margaretta Blair. They had two children.

Under Cox's leadership, Ohio legislators established an Industrial Relations Commission, created a mandatory "no fault" workmen's compensation program, and passed a child labor law. In addition, Cox instituted a civil service system, modernized the state's schools, began building a unified state highway system, allowed home rule charters for cities, and adopted electoral reforms, including the initiative and referendum, recall of elected officials, and a short ballot law. The Ohio reformers dealt with the alcoholic beverage issue with regulations and a state licensing system. Dissatisfied prohibitionists, opponents of the workmen's compensation law, and critics of the other reforms successfully worked to deny Cox reelection in 1914.

Cox was victorious over the Republican incumbent governor, Frank B. Willis, in 1916, and in his second term he focused on the nation's involvement in World War I. He created a "war cabinet" that promoted voluntary cooperation between business, labor, and government, and as the war deepened, he implemented federal mandates. Following Cox's reelection to an unprecedented third term in 1918, Ohio legislators ratified the Prohibition and Woman Suffrage amendments to the U.S. Constitution. Cox's ability to win in the Republican stronghold of Ohio when most Democrats were going down to defeat made him a viable candidate for the presidency.

The Democratic party was in disarray in the aftermath of World War I. The Republicans won control of Congress in the 1918 elections, President Woodrow Wilson's stroke left him incapacitated, and the postwar economic and social unrest left political leaders uncertain about policy for the future. Wilson wanted the election of 1920 to serve as a referendum on U.S. entrance into the League of Nations. The Democrats were divided on the League of Nations issue, with some of them supporting a list of reservations to the treaty before Senate ratification. Cox supported the League of Nations but remained silent on the question of amendments to the treaty.

The 1920 Democratic convention met in San Francisco in the midst of the post–World War I economic reconstruction and xenophobia. Mired in conflicts, the convention deadlocked over the candidacies of A. Mitchell Palmer, William Gibbs McAdoo, and Cox. Supported by a coalition of delegates from the urban-industrial Northeast and Midwest, Cox also had numerous second choice pledges. He was nominated on the forty-fourth ballot. Before naming Assistant Secretary of the Navy Franklin Delano Roosevelt as his running mate, Cox gave Charles Murphy of New York's Tammany Hall, a leader of the coalition that nominated him, the right to veto that choice. In contrast to Republican Warren G. Harding, who ran a "front porch" campaign and called for a return to "normalcy," Cox waged an energetic, activist campaign. He traveled 22,000 miles, visited 36 states, and delivered 394 speeches to some 2 million people. In August and September, campaigning in the Midwest and West, Cox focused on domestic concerns. As unemployment and inflation mounted, he proposed lower income taxes and an end to the excess profits tax on business. Instead, he called for a value-added tax of "one or one-and-a-half per cent on going concerns." To end unrest in the workplace, he supported national collective bargaining legislation. Widely perceived as "wet" on the Prohibition issue, Cox pledged to enforce the Volstead Act. To counter ethnic discontent over the Palmer raids and calls for immigration restrictions, the Democrat urged expanded Americanization programs to foster loyalty to the United States. In sum, Cox wanted to shape the postwar reconstruction with an activist federal government.

Cox's program failed to capture the imagination of the electorate and aroused the ire of the Wilsonians, who viewed the election as a referendum on the League of Nations. In October, as his campaign train moved east of the Mississippi River, Cox stressed foreign policy issues. Favoring U.S. membership in the League of Nations, he pledged to amend the league treaty to guarantee congressional approval of U.S. military action under the agreement. Responding to these remarks, a concerned Woodrow Wilson told a group of journalists that Article X of the League of Nations Charter was "a specific pledge" to resist aggression.

The Democrats were overwhelmingly defeated. Harding won 16,152,200 votes to 9,141,353 for Cox. Socialist Eugene V. Debs, imprisoned in the Atlanta, Georgia, federal penitentiary, received 919,799 votes. The Republicans also gained control of both houses of Congress. "The war," Cox concluded, "brought so many reactions that the landslide was inevitable."

Cox never again ran for public office. However, when the 1924 Democratic convention deadlocked, Cox went to New York and helped work out a compromise that led to the nomination of John W. Davis of West Virginia but gave control of the party machinery to its urban wing. A member of the Al Smith wing of the Democratic party, Cox joined the "Stop Roosevelt" effort in 1932, but, unlike many Democratic leaders from the 1920s, he campaigned for Roosevelt and remained loyal to the New Deal, although he turned down several presidential appointments.

During the interwar period, Cox broadened his communications empire. In journalism, the Cox chain expanded to include the *Miami Daily News* (1923), the *Canton Daily News* (1923), the *Atlanta Journal* (1939), and the *Atlanta Constitution* (1950). By the end of the 1930s, Cox communications stretched from the Great Lakes to the Gulf of Mexico. At the age of seventy-six Cox published his memoir, *Journey through My Years* (1946). He died at "Trailsend," his home of more than forty years, in Dayton, Ohio.

• Cox's personal papers are at Wright State University in Dayton, Ohio. His official papers from his time as governor of Ohio are at the Ohio Historical Society in Columbus, Ohio. The most complete study of Cox's life is James E. Cebula, *James M. Cox: Journalist and Politician* (1985). Hoyt Landon Warner, *Progressivism in Ohio: 1897–1917* (1964), is the most detailed account of the reforms Cox implemented as governor. Wesley M. Bagby, *The Road to Normalcy: The Presidential Campaign and Election of 1920* (1962), is the most detailed account of the election of 1920. An obituary is in the *New York Times*, 16 July 1957.

JAMES CEBULA

COX, Kenyon (27 Oct. 1856–17 Mar. 1919), artist and critic, was born in Warren, Ohio, the son of Jacob Dolson Cox, later a Union general in the Civil War, governor of Ohio, secretary of the interior for President Ulysses S. Grant, attorney, and legal educator, and Helen Finney, daughter of the famous evangelist Charles Grandison Finney. Cox desired to be an artist from an early age, and as a youth he studied at the McMicken School of Design in Cincinnati and the Pennsylvania Academy of the Fine Arts. In Paris from 1877 to 1882 he studied first with Carolus-Duran, then at the Académie Julian, then with Alexandre Cabanel, and finally with Jean-Léon Gérôme, the latter two at the École des Beaux-Arts. Cox did not adopt Gérôme's style or subject matter but appreciated his insistence on disciplined drawing and painting. Cox became a master draftsman and also enjoyed work in oils. Essentially a formalist, he was nonetheless capable of delightful informal works and steeped himself in the traditional art he saw in Parisian collections and in northern Italy during a brief but intense tour of the region in 1878.

Cox returned to Ohio before he moved to New York City in the fall of 1883, determined to succeed in the nation's art capital. He immediately secured work as an illustrator for magazines, a common occupation among artists. Both dependable and talented, he pleased publishers and succeeded in making a modest name for himself among fellow artists, his illustrations appearing in influential magazines such as *Century*, *Scribner's*, and *Harper's*. He also instructed in life drawing, chiefly women's classes, at the Art Students League from 1884 to 1909; taught anatomy, some men's life drawing, and instructed individual painting students; and in 1885 wrote exhibition reviews for the *New York Evening Post*, some of which were reprinted in the *Nation*. He always expressed his views bluntly and was easier to respect than to like. His acerbic reviews antagonized a good many fellow painters, whose works he considered inferior. Cox quit writing these reviews in 1886 after receiving an important commission to make a series of figurative illustrations from *grisaille* paintings for a special edition of Dante Gabriel Rossetti's poem *The Blessed Damozel*. Although this work brought him considerable critical acclaim, he declined to illustrate other books because he wanted to focus on easel figure painting.

Cox did not think so, but he was an excellent landscapist and also produced quality portraits of friends, family, and fellow artists. His first love, however, was figure painting rooted in classical modes, whose unifying ideals he hoped to update for a modern society. In the mid-1880s he produced several large allegorical paintings in the tradition of European salons; these works gained him a reputation for breadth of thought and ability to paint but not a living. He continued to rely on illustration, teaching, and writing for a basic income. Cox wrote with great clarity and conciseness, whether in analyzing complex ideas and figures from art history or in surveying contemporary art writing, as in his book review essays for the *Nation*. By the end of the century he was a well-known cultural spokesman in genteel circles. The magazines that used his illustrations also published his criticism. Cox was always concerned with ideas and emotions in painting as well as its forms. He was a powerful spokesman for those aspects of painting and appreciation that both expanded the individual observer's mind and unified society while at the same time enhancing the artist's special vision. He was also a familiar figure in the affairs, and as a juryman, of art organizations such as the National Academy of Design and the Society of American Artists. He exhibited works at all the major exhibitions in the East and abroad in 1889 at the Paris Universal Exposition, where he received a bronze medal.

His ideas and artistic abilities, especially at figure paintings, made Cox important in the mural movement from the mid-1890s to the First World War. This period witnessed a flowering of arts, crafts, and architecture based on Italian Renaissance models. Architects received many commissions for public buildings, apartment houses, offices, and private dwellings suitable for mural decoration. This muralism encompassed several subjects and approaches: historical scenes, current events, abstract depiction of social forces, and classicism modeled on the Renaissance. Cox became a leader in this last approach, using a style of painting that attempted to make lofty ideals readily accessible to all kinds of viewers through easily read symbols, such as idealized female figures. Cox created large mural commissions for numerous buildings, including the Walker Art Gallery at Bowdoin College (1894), the Library of Congress (1896), and the state capitols of Minnesota (1904), Iowa (1906), and Wisconsin (1912–1915). He also produced designs for stained glass, statuary, and external stone decorations, such as those for the University Club in New York City and the Boston Public Library. He also produced classical designs for magazine covers, diplomas, and other documents as well as the back of the $100 federal reserve bank note of 1914.

Cox's reputation as a traditionalist made him a logical foe of the emerging trend toward modernism. Intensely devoted to art as thoughtful personal expression and as unifying cultural force, he could not be moderate about work he thought was purely personal or idiosyncratic, as most modernism seemed to be to him. His acerbic reviews of the historic Armory Show of 1913, and other widely read criticism, separated him from the coming generation, though he believed that his artistic and cultural ideals would triumph in the long run.

Cox had married Louise Howland King, whom he had instructed at the Art Students League, in 1892; the couple had two sons and a daughter. Although he may have been formidable in his public roles, Cox was an affectionate husband and father. He could even be whimsical as when he made special drawings of mythical animals to accompany nonsense verse for his children, published as *Mixed Beasts* (1904). The family spent most summers after the late 1890s in the artist colony in Cornish, New Hampshire. Mural commissions ceased with the coming of the world war in 1914, and Cox spent his last years in poor health and some emotional depression over modernism, which he could not understand or accept but whose momentary triumph he sensed. He died of tuberculosis at his apartment in New York City.

• In the 1950s Cox's son, Allyn, who became a noted decorator, gathered his father's papers and disposed of his residual paintings and drawings. The papers formed the Kenyon Cox Collection at the Avery Architectural and Fine Arts Library, Columbia University. Material relating to Cox's mural commissions appears in several other collections, such as the Cass Gilbert Papers at the New-York Historical Society and the respective capitol commission records at the Minnesota Historical Society and the State Historical Society of Wisconsin. Some other letters are in the holdings of the Archives of American Art, Smithsonian Institution, Washington, D.C., and other collections. The Cooper Hewitt Museum in New

York City is the chief repository of his residual drawings and designs. His paintings are in several major museums. Allyn Cox bequeathed other easel works, sketchbooks, and drawings to numerous regional museums. Cox's own major writings, though not his exhibition or book reviews, are collected in *Old Masters and New* (1905); *Painters and Sculptors* (1907); *The Classic Point of View* (1911), an elegant summary of his ideas; *Artist and Public* (1914); and *Concerning Painting* (1917). He is the subject of several works by H. Wayne Morgan: *Keepers of Culture: The Art-Thought of Kenyon Cox, Royal Cortissoz and Frank Jewett Mather, Jr.* (1989); two volumes of letters, *An American Art Student in Paris: The Letters of Kenyon Cox 1877–1882* (1986) and *An Artist of the American Renaissance: The Letters of Kenyon Cox 1883–1919* (1995); and a full biography, *Kenyon Cox, 1856–1919: A Life in American Art* (1994).

H. WAYNE MORGAN

COX, Palmer (28 Apr. 1840–24 July 1924), author and illustrator, was born in Granby, Canada, some sixty miles east of Montreal in Quebec Province, the son of Michael Cox and Sarah Miller, farmers. Young Palmer attended local schools and received a secondary education at Granby Academy. In his late teens, following graduation, he struck out on his own; by 1863 he had settled in San Francisco. After working for several years as a clerk in a railway office, he became a ship carpenter and pursued that occupation for nearly a decade.

In his spare time, seeking relief from daily toil that never fully engaged him, Cox began to write humorous verse and draw cartoons. In the early 1870s he began submitting his efforts to area periodicals, and two of them, *Golden Era* and the *Alta Californian*, printed some of his work. Cox wrote and drew pictures for *Squibs of California, or Everyday Life Illustrated*, a collection of brief observations of the local scene that was published as a book in 1875. That same year, despite general indifference to his artistic output, Cox gave up his carpentry job and moved to New York City to pursue a career as a writer and an illustrator.

In Manhattan, Cox was hired by a struggling comic weekly, *Wild Oats*, and remained on its staff until the paper's demise five years later. During this time he published three humorous verse narratives that he also illustrated: *Hans Von Pelter's Trip to Gotham* (1876), *How Columbus Found America* (1877), and *That Stanley!* (1878), a satire of the widely publicized African expedition of Henry Morton Stanley to find David Livingstone. When *Wild Oats* folded in 1880, Cox was hired as an illustrator for the monthly *St. Nicholas Magazine*, the nation's leading periodical for children, to which he also began contributing his own illustrated verses.

At *St. Nicholas* Cox discovered his life's calling. Children responded enthusiastically to his work and clamored for more, and Cox in turn found enormous pleasure in entertaining them. He wanted to create a series of interconnected stories for *St. Nicholas* that would engage the continuing attention of its young readers. Harking back to his own childhood, Cox remembered folktales of Scotland's Grampian Hills that

he had heard from his family and friends in Granby. Adapting the fairylike protagonists of those tales to nineteenth-century life, Cox created the Brownies, a race of humorous elfin creatures who, in their creator's words, did good "just for the sake of doing good, and not for the sake of any reward."

Cox's Brownie stories were an immediate success, and young readers of *St. Nicholas* demanded more. Over the next four decades, Cox created hundreds of wholesome adventures for the Brownies, nearly all in verse. Not long before his death he estimated that he had drawn more than a million of the tiny creatures; no two were exactly alike, although each was distinguished by spindly legs, pointed feet, a long beard, and a potbelly. Cox always adhered to the rule he had set for himself when he began the series: the residents of Brownieland were never allowed to perform any task more than once.

Following their publication in the magazine, Cox's Brownie stories were published in book form. The first, *The Brownies, Their Book*, appeared in 1887; this was followed by thirteen more volumes: *Queer People* (1888), *Queer People with Wings and Stings* (1888), *Queer People with Paws and Claws* (1888), *Another Brownie Book* (1890), *The Brownies at Home* (1893), *The Brownies around the World* (1894), *The Brownies through the Union* (1895), *The Brownies Abroad* (1899), *The Brownies in the Philippines* (1904), *The Palmer Cox Brownie Primer* (1906), *Brownie Clown in Brownie Town* (1907), *The Brownies' Latest Adventures* (1910), and *The Brownies' Many More Nights* (1913). Cox also wrote *The Brownies in Fairyland* (1895), a two-act cantata, and *Palmer Cox's Brownies* (1895), a three-act play that ran for nearly five years in New York City. During Cox's lifetime more than a million copies of his Brownie books were sold as "Brownie-mania" swept the nation. Merchandise tie-ins were also in vogue as millions of young consumers and their parents bought Brownie toys and Brownie-adorned items that ranged from pencil boxes to clothing to wallpaper.

Cox's Brownies made him a wealthy man. Around the turn of the century he returned to his birthplace and built an enormous house that he named "Brownie Castle." Thereafter he spent his summers in Canada, residing during the rest of each year on Long Island. Cox, who never married, died at Brownie Castle. An editorial tribute in the *New York Times* on the day after his death lauded Cox as a peer of Robert Louis Stevenson, J. M. Barrie, and Lewis Carroll in contributing "the richest and tenderest creations" to "the realm of the young imagination."

Today literary historians pay tribute to Cox for his pioneering role in the creation of nondidactic children's literature. Cox's purpose in creating the Brownies was to entertain, not teach; thus his books never moralized, although they do offer ethical lessons by example. Cox is also considered one of the founders of the genre of children's fantasy, and his Brownies have been viewed as precursors of J. R. R. Tolkien's Hobbits.

• Biographical information on Palmer Cox can be found in Roger W. Cummins, *Humorous but Wholesome: A History of Palmer Cox and the Brownies* (1973); Malcolm Douglas, "Palmer Cox, the Brownie Man," *St. Nicholas Magazine*, Oct. 1924, p. 1288; Joyce Kilmer, "Palmer Cox of Brownie Castle," *New York Times Magazine*, 16 Jan. 1916, pp. 19–20; and Stanley J. Kunitz and Howard Haycraft, eds., *American Authors, 1600–1900* (1938). An obituary and an editorial are in the *New York Times*, 25 July 1924.

ANN T. KEENE

COX, Samuel Hanson (25 Aug. 1793–2 Oct. 1880), New School Presbyterian minister and educator, was born in Rahway, New Jersey, the son of James Cox, a merchant, and Elizabeth Shepard. The Coxes were Quakers, descended from a family that had immigrated to Maryland from England in the seventeenth century. Cox grew up in Philadelphia and received his early education at the Friends' Academy in Westtown, Pennsylvania. After working briefly as a store clerk, he studied to become a lawyer in Newark, New Jersey. During the War of 1812, he saw combat sporadically as a volunteer rifleman.

A defining moment in Cox's life occurred in 1813, when a study of the Bible led him to renounce Quakerism in favor of Presbyterianism. He was baptized in the Second Presbyterian Church of Newark on 7 March 1813. His religious struggle was later discussed in his vituperative polemical tome, *Quakerism Not Christianity* (1833).

Less than one year after his baptism, Cox began to study theology, first in Newark, then, in Philadelphia, Pennsylvania. In 1816 he was licensed by the presbytery of New York. On 1 July 1817 he was ordained and became pastor of the Presbyterian Church of Mendham, New Jersey. An impressive orator whose eloquence was somewhat strained by a predilection for long words interlaced with Latin phrases, Cox drew large audiences to hear his fiercely evangelical sermons. He was married in April 1817 to Abia Hyde Cleveland; they had fifteen children. They moved to New York City, where he enjoyed even greater pastoral successes at Spring Street (1820–1825) and Laight Street Presbyterian churches (1825–1835).

Cox was a key figure in the development and institutionalization in the 1820s and 1830s of "New School Presbyterianism," a pro-revivalist faction that can be viewed theologically as a weakening of the traditional Calvinist beliefs of total human depravity and bondage of the will. At the outset of Cox's career (1816), he was refused employment by the Young Men's Missionary Society of New York, because of his devotion to the modified Calvinism of Samuel Hopkins. This slight, and the possible discomfort Cox felt from never having earned an academic degree, made him a lifelong champion of Presbyterian education that reflected New School tendencies. During the 1820s he became a founder of New York University and Chi Alpha, a ministerial association. As Chi Alpha's first president in 1829, he conceived a plan to train ministers in New York City. This proposal resulted in the establishment of Union Theological Seminary in 1836. Through a

brief tenure as professor of biblical and ecclesiastical history and a much longer term of thirty-six years on Union's directing board, Cox placed an indelible imprint on the seminary's early history. Understanding the importance of the press as a vehicle of religious advocacy, he also played an important role in the start of the *New York Observer*, a Presbyterian periodical.

For Cox, controversy accompanied prominence. Reflecting the moralistic evangelical spirit of the day, he opposed the consumption of liquor and tobacco. He also wrote increasingly scathing tracts against the growing Catholic number of "Papists" (that is, Catholic immigrants) who were settling on the eastern seaboard of the United States. This unsavory nativist spirit was reflected in Cox's revised edition of Archibald Bower's anti-Catholic *History of the Popes* (1844–1847) and his role in founding the Society for the Promotion of Collegiate and Theological Education in the West (1844). Obstensibly concerned with the financial assistance of Protestant colleges in the Midwest, the organization's greater objective was to impede Catholic expansion into the region.

The greatest controversy to consume Cox was slavery. The complexities of the issue caused him to shift his stand on slavery several times during the course of his career. After attending the annual meeting of the London Missionary Society as a foreign delegate in 1833, Cox became an advocate of the antislavery cause. His pronouncements drew such anger from New York City's riotous antiabolitionist contingent that he was forced to remove himself from the city for a time to assume the chair of sacred rhetoric and pastoral theology at Auburn Theological Seminary (1835–1837) in western New York State. In opposition to radical abolitionism, however, Cox later fought an attempt to bar slaveholders from the London meeting of the new Evangelical Alliance in 1846.

In 1837, in the midst of denominational strife during which the Old School Presbyterians acted procedurally to rein in the influence of the New School Presbyterians at a national meeting, Cox returned from his "Auburn exile" to assume the pastorship of First Presbyterian Church, Brooklyn, New York. He remained pastor of the Brooklyn church for seventeen years (1837–1854) and successfully convinced his congregation to affiliate with the New School faction in 1838. His leadership within the faction culminated in 1846 when he became moderator of its General Assembly. No strict sectarian, however, he was thoroughly involved in numerous interdenominational benevolent and mission societies like the Society for the Promotion of Christian Union, which he helped found with Samuel Schmucker in 1839. It was a source of considerable chagrin to Cox that his eldest child, Arthur Cleveland Coxe, left Presbyterianism to become a member, and eventually a prominent scholar and bishop, in the Episcopal church. Four more of Cox's children followed Arthur's example.

Chronic laryngitis forced Cox to resign his Brooklyn pastorate in 1854 and move to Oswego in western New York. Two years later he came out of retirement to serve as president, from 1856 to 1863, of Ingham Collegiate Institute, a girls' school (later Ingham University) in Le Roy, New York.

On 16 November 1869, four years after the death of his first wife, Cox married Anna Fosdick Bacon, of Hartford, Connecticut. The couple lived in Bronxville, New York, where Cox died. His literary corpus also included *Interviews, Memorable and Useful* (1853).

Cox personified the extremes of the nineteenth-century "Evangelical Empire." On the one hand, his strong moralism and revivalistic piety made him the organizer of numerous reforming institutions, societies, and causes. On the other hand, his triumphalism tended to exclude and excoriate many nonevangelical groups from his own vision of Christian America.

• Autobiographical information is in a lengthy statement in Cox's *Quakerism Not Christianity* (1833). George L. Prentiss, *The Union Theological Seminary in the City of New York* (1889), contains an eight-page sketch of the life of Cox. The best account of his Brooklyn pastorate is Ralph F. Weld, *A Tower on the Heights* (1946). Two nineteenth-century essays that focus on Cox as a contemporary are the unsigned "Rev. Samuel H. Cox, D.D. (with a Portrait)," *Marsh's Athenaeum Magazine* 1 (Feb. 1854): 2–7, and Henry Fowler, *The American Pulpit* (1854). A significant work that examines Cox's attitude toward slavery is Dwyn Mecklin Mounger, "Bondage and Benevolence: An Evangelical Calvinist Approaches Slavery—Samuel Hanson Cox" (Ph.D. diss., Union Theological Seminary, 1975). An abridged version of Mounger's dissertation appears in "Samuel Hanson Cox: Anti-Catholic, Anti-Anglican, Anti-Congregational Ecumenist," *Journal of Presbyterian History* 55, no. 4 (Winter 1977): 347–61. The Quakerism of Cox is the focus of H. Larry Ingle, "Samuel Hanson Cox, Quakers and the Hicksite Separation," *American Presbyterians* 64, no. 4 (Winter 1986): 259–63. Cox's contribution to higher education is covered in Prentiss and is mentioned in Theodore F. Jones, *New York University, 1832–1932* (1933), and John Quincy Adams, *A History of Auburn Theological Seminary 1818–1918* (1918). An obituary is in Wendell Prime, ed., *Samuel Irenaeus Prime* (1888).

ROBERT H. KRAPOHL

COX, Samuel Sullivan (30 Sept. 1824–10 Sept. 1889), congressman, was born in Zanesville, Ohio, the son of Ezekiel Taylor Cox, a publisher, and Mary Matilda Sullivan. After graduating from Brown University in 1846 Cox returned to Ohio to practice law in Cincinnati. In 1849 he married Julia Ann Buckingham, the daughter of a Zanesville merchant. Their exceptionally happy (though childless) marriage commenced with a European honeymoon, which provided material for the first of his ten books, *A Buckeye Abroad* (1852).

Tiring of his legal practice, Cox took up journalism, moving to Columbus in 1853 and purchasing a controlling interest in the *Ohio Statesman*, a Democratic party organ. It was in its pages, on 19 May 1853, that he published the effusive description of a sunset that won him the nickname "Sunset," which so fortuitously matched his own initials.

After an abortive diplomatic appointment to Peru that illness prevented him from assuming, Cox began his political career in 1856 with election to the House of Representatives, where he would sit (with occasional interruptions) for the rest of his life. He entered the House at the height of the Kansas controversy. A follower of Stephen A. Douglas, he strongly opposed imposing the proslavery Lecompton Constitution on Kansas but prudently supported the compromise English Bill to get back into President James Buchanan's good graces. As sectional tensions mounted he urged compromise, but when that failed he stood with Douglas in supporting the Union cause.

During the Civil War Cox, now a leader of his party in the House, had to walk a tightrope delicately. Overt opposition to the war could smear his party with the derogatory label of "copperhead"; uncritical support of the Lincoln administration could blur the party lines and deprive the Democrats of their unique identity. His solution was to support the war insofar as it aimed at the restoration of the Union but to oppose the "despotic" President Lincoln for his efforts to emancipate the slaves and violate the civil liberties of dissenters such as Cox's friend, Clement Vallandigham. Although Cox voted against the Thirteenth Amendment and remained a staunch opponent of racial equality, he was convinced that the Democratic party had to throw off its proslavery stigma and he therefore quietly persuaded enough other Democrats to abstain so that the amendment could pass the House. Secretary of State William Seward (a personal friend) handsomely acknowledged this assistance, saying that "more than any other member" Cox was due credit for the amendment's passage. Cox was also responsible, near the end of the Thirty-eighth Congress, for the long-overdue measure that split off banking and appropriations functions from the unwieldy Ways and Means Committee into separate committees of their own.

By that time Cox was a lame duck, having been defeated for reelection after the gerrymandering of his district. He moved to New York City and in 1868, with the support of Tammany Hall, was elected to Congress to represent his new hometown. As spokesman for the minority party, he opposed Radical Reconstruction and high tariffs and advocated amnesty for former rebels, displaying an eloquence and wit that were highly praised in his day though their charms have since faded with changing tastes.

In addition to defending his party, Cox adopted two causes as his own. One was the Life Saving Service (now part of the Coast Guard), which rescued shipwrecked sailors. Cox labored assiduously to regularize this organization and to improve its pay and benefits, winning the title "Father of the Life Saving Service" for his efforts. His dedication to his other cause won him the appellation "The Letter Carriers' Friend" for his advocacy of increased salary, shorter hours, and paid vacations for the nation's mail carriers. In gratitude, they erected a bronze statue in his honor in New York's Astor Plaza (since removed to Tompkins Square Park).

In 1872 Cox was again gerrymandered out of his congressional district. He ran for election as congressman-at-large but was defeated. The next year, however, he was elected to fill the Lower East Side seat made vacant by the death of James Brooks. The economic downturn of that year revived the political fortunes of the Democratic party, bringing them control of the House of Representatives. From 1874 on, Cox enjoyed the pleasures of working with the congressional majority, rather than enduring the frustrations of leading the opposition. He expected that his seniority and long record of party service would entitle him to the Speakership, but his colleagues wanted someone more forceful than the genial Cox, turning instead to Indiana's Michael C. Kerr. During Kerr's protracted illness, however, Cox usually occupied the chair, making him Speaker in fact, if not in name.

Cox's congressional activities while in the majority were less significant than when he had been a spokesman for the loyal opposition. Although he chaired some major committees, such as Banking and Currency, Census, and Naval Affairs, little significant legislation emerged from that service. This was in keeping with his party's then-regnant political philosophy that deeply distrusted governmental activism at the federal level. Cox shared the Democratic party's nostalgic agrarianism, its dogmatic faith in free trade, as well as its commitment to white supremacy—these views inhibited him from pursuing a positive legislative agenda.

In 1885 President Grover Cleveland appointed Cox minister to Turkey. Despite his love of exotic places, Cox resigned the post in 1886 to return to the House of Representatives, serving until his death in New York City.

In an era when few congressmen served more than two terms, Cox's lengthy tenure, spanning three and a half decades, marked him as a dependable fixture in the House he so loved. His parliamentary skill, his ready wit, and his concern for civil rights (except for black Americans) made him an ideal gadfly when in the minority. If his positive accomplishments seem modest by later standards, that is because he subscribed to the belief, common in his time, that the function of government was not to make things better but to keep things running.

• The most substantial collection of Cox's papers can be found at Brown University Library; it contains more than 1,000 items, mostly of a political nature. Smaller collections can be found at the Ohio Historical Society and the New York Public Library, especially in the Madigan Collection of George B. McClellan correspondence. Cox, who wrote extensively, considered *Three Decades of Federal Legislation* (1885) to be his most substantial work, but more of Cox the man emerges from *Why We Laugh* (1876) and his half-dozen travel accounts ranging from *A Buckeye Abroad* (1852) to *The Isle of the Princes* (1888). William Van Zandt Cox and Milton H. Northrup, *Life of Samuel Sullivan Cox* (1899), is a reverential family biography, while David Lindsey, *"Sunset" Cox: Irrepressible Democrat* (1959), provides a workmanlike twentieth-century study.

ALLAN PESKIN

COX, William Ruffin (11 Mar. 1832–26 Dec. 1919), army officer and politician, was born at Scotland Neck, Halifax County, North Carolina, the son of Thomas Cox, a businessman and planter, and Olivia Norfleet. He graduated from Franklin College and studied law at Lebanon College, both in Tennessee. Thereafter he practiced law for some years in that state before returning to North Carolina in 1857 to marry Penelope Battle. The marriage brought a fine plantation in Edgecombe County, where he took up his abode.

Cox became somewhat of a fire-eater in politics, favoring southern secession. To be prepared for all manner of Yankee perfidy, he raised a volunteer military company and equipped it out of his own pocket. Having then devoted himself to the study of military tactics, he was well prepared when the Civil War broke out. Appointed by the governor as major of the Second North Carolina Regiment, 8 May 1861, Cox served first in the vicinity of Fredericksburg, Virginia, and then in the defenses of Wilmington, North Carolina. When Robert E. Lee drew together maximum Confederate forces from throughout the eastern seaboard to resist Union general George B. McClellan's drive up the Virginia Peninsula toward Richmond, the Second North Carolina was one of the regiments that went north. Cox was to serve the remainder of his Civil War career under Lee, being separated from Lee's immediate command only for a few months during the summer and fall of 1864.

Cox participated in the Seven Days' battles and the battles of South Mountain and Antietam during the summer of 1862. For the last of these, he was promoted to lieutenant colonel of the Second, to rank from 17 September, the day of the battle. That winter came the battle of Fredericksburg (13 Dec.). The following spring, Cox became colonel of the Second North Carolina (21 Mar. 1863). On the third day of the battle of Chancellorsville (1–4 May 1863), Cox's regiment was engaged in fierce fighting, losing 75 percent of its numbers in fifteen minutes and losing its colors when every member of the color guard was hit. Cox himself that day received five of the total of eleven wounds he would suffer during the war. Nevertheless, he was able to return to his regiment by 1 August, having missed the battle of Gettysburg. He participated in the army's unsuccessful Bristoe Station campaign in October, and when an abortive advance by the Union Army of the Potomac generated combat at Kelly's Ford on the Rappahannock River on 7 November, Cox collected two more of his wounds.

The following spring General Ulysses S. Grant directed northern armies in a relentless offensive. In Virginia the Union drive resulted in fierce battles at the Wilderness, Spotsylvania, Cold Harbor, and Petersburg within a six-week period, beginning in early May. At Spotsylvania Cox displayed outstanding courage and for this service was promoted to brigadier general and command of the North Carolina brigade previously led by Stephen Dodson Ramseur (4 June 1864). Shortly thereafter, Cox's brigade was among the troops—under the overall command of General Jubal A. Early—dispatched to the Shenandoah Valley by Lee in hopes of breaking Grant's stranglehold on the Army of Northern Virginia. With Early, Cox served through a series of hard-fought battles: Monocacy (just outside Washington, D.C.), Third Winchester, Fisher's Hill, and Cedar Creek. That winter his unit rejoined Lee's main army, now pinned by Grant's force within the entrenched defenses of Petersburg and Richmond. On 2 April 1865 the army's lines collapsed, and it fled westward. When Lee's army surrendered at Appomattox Court House one week later, Cox was among the remnant still with the colors. Indeed, he had led the army's last attack in the vain attempt to break out of Grant's encirclement.

After the war Cox returned to North Carolina and practiced law in Raleigh. He soon became involved in politics, for which his impressive war record was a definite asset. In 1868 he successfully ran for solicitor in Raleigh, despite the district's heavily Radical Republican composition and his own much different views. He held the office until 1874, when he became North Carolina state Democratic party chairman. Over the next three years he applied the drive, discipline, and toughness he had displayed in the army to his efforts for the "redemption" of the state (that is, its return to white Democratic rule). He succeeded and in 1876 was appointed a district judge. This office he in turn resigned in order to be elected to the first of three consecutive terms in the U.S. House of Representatives in 1880. His first wife died shortly after the war, and in 1883 he married Fannie Augusta Lyman. They had two children. From 1893 to 1900 he served as secretary of the Senate. Also during these years he held important positions in the Masonic Order, the Episcopal church, and the North Carolina Agricultural Society. His second wife died, and in 1905 he married a widow, whose name is not known. Cox died in Richmond, Virginia.

• For further information on Cox see William C. Davis, ed., *The Confederate General* (1991); Douglas Southall Freeman, *Lee's Lieutenants: A Study in Command* (3 vols., 1942–1944); Gary W. Gallagher, *Stephen Dodson Ramseur: Lee's Gallant General* (1985); U.S. War Department, *The War of the Rebellion: A Compilation of the Official Records of the Union and Confederate Armies* (128 vols., 1880–1901); and Ezra J. Warner, *Generals in Gray: The Lives of the Confederate Commanders* (1959).

STEVEN E. WOODWORTH

COXE, Arthur Cleveland (10 May 1818–20 July 1896), Episcopal bishop and leader of the Anglo-Catholic movement, was born in Mendham, New Jersey, the son of Samuel Hanson Cox, a Presbyterian minister, and Lucy Todd. As a youth Cox moved to New York City. There he lived in the home of his uncle, Dr. Abraham Cox, a prominent New York physician and Episcopalian who led his nephew into the Episcopal church in 1829. He subsequently changed his name to what he deemed to be an earlier, and English, spelling of his name—Coxe.

Coxe received his undergraduate degree from the University of New York in 1838 and his theological degree from the General Theological Seminary in New York in 1841. He was ordained a deacon in the Episcopal church in 1841 and a priest in 1842. Thereafter he served a number of parishes as rector, including Grace Church in Baltimore, Maryland, from 1854 to 1863, and Calvary Church in New York City, from 1863 to 1865. In 1865 he was elected second bishop of the Episcopal diocese of western New York, to succeed William Heathcote DeLancey, one of the prominent leaders of the Episcopal House of Bishops.

From his time as seminarian, Coxe was deeply influenced by and served as one of the leaders and theologians of the Anglo-Catholic revival in the Episcopal church, a direct outgrowth of the Tractarian (or first) phase of the Oxford Movement, which began in England in 1833. The Oxford Movement sought to restore the practice and belief of Catholicism to the Church of England. The movement brought not only a renewed sacramental life and enriched liturgies but also a deeper understanding of the church's concern for all people. These two emphases shaped all the practical ministry and scholarship of Coxe.

One of the leaders of the Oxford Movement had urged in particular that the Anglo-Catholic movement should focus on modern cities, rather than on the parishes of the rural countryside. Bishop Coxe successfully translated this teaching to western New York, moving the seat of the diocese from Batavia to Buffalo in 1866. In 1870 he transformed St. Paul's Church, the largest parish in Buffalo, into the cathedral of the diocese, a place of vivid worship, focusing on the weekly celebration of the Holy Eucharist as the regular form of Sunday worship.

One of the principles of the Oxford Movement was to look back to the church of the patristic era as a model of what the modern church could become. Thus in 1885 Coxe organized the Christian Literature Company for the publication of the writings of patristic theologians, and in 1885–1886 he published *The Ante-Nicene Fathers: Translations of the Writings of the Fathers Down to A.D. 325.* Another thrust of the movement was to begin a dialogue with the Roman Catholic church. With this in mind, Coxe published in 1852 an English translation of a key work of a liberal German theologian, Johann von Hirscher, under the title *Sympathies of the Continent*, as well as a *Letter to Pius IX* on the calling of the First Vatican Council, which was translated into French, German, Greek, Bohemian, and Italian.

In all of these activities Coxe brought a characteristic style of episcopacy in New York that had also marked two previous bishops of the nineteenth century, John Henry Hobart and William DeLancey: a vigorous apologetic for the Episcopal church as an embodiment of the apostolic Christian faith of the past that could at the same time adapt easily to the new cultural dynamic of American democracy. He saw Buffalo as an urban, industrial center where such adaptation could readily take place. He died at Clifton Springs, New York.

• Coxe's papers, including extensive correspondence with leaders of the Episcopal church and manuscript sermons and poems, are in the library of the General Theological Seminary in New York City. Two short biographical accounts of Coxe may be found in Henry C. Potter, *Reminiscences of Bishops and Archbishops* (1906), and Herman G. Batterson, *Sketch-Book of the American Episcopate* (1891), which also includes a complete and valuable bibliography of Coxe's eighty-one publications. For the larger context of the Episcopal church in the time and region of Coxe see Robert Bruce Mullin, *Episcopal Vision/American Reality* (1986), and Diana Butler, *Standing against the Whirlwind: Evangelical Episcopalians in Nineteenth-Century America* (1995).

R. WILLIAM FRANKLIN

COXE, Daniel (Aug. 1673–25 Apr. 1739), landowner and New Jersey politician, was born in London, England, the son of Daniel Coxe and Rebecca Coldham. The elder Daniel Coxe (c. 1640–1730) served as royal physician at the courts of King Charles II and Queen Anne. Dr. Coxe also ranked as the largest shareholder in the West Jersey proprietorship by 1687, and he acted as that colony's absentee governor from then until he sold his proprietary interest in 1692.

The senior Coxe retained large landownings in New Jersey, and his son emigrated to Burlington, New Jersey, in 1702, for the apparent purpose of developing them. Daniel Coxe, Jr., immediately became embroiled in controversy with the Quaker proprietors who controlled government in the counties that had formerly been West Jersey. His anti-Quaker activities arose partly from his efforts to establish title over certain tracts of land claimed by both his family and the Quaker-dominated West Jersey Council of Proprietors. As an ardent High Church Tory who believed dissenters from the Church of England should be ineligible to vote and hold office, he also wanted to end the Quakers' political ascendancy. Coxe energetically supported missionary efforts to draw nonconformists back into the Anglican fold, and he mobilized his fellow parishioners at St. Mary's Church of Burlington into a formidable phalanx of anti-Quaker voters.

Coxe soon emerged as the most prominent leader of West Jersey's non-Quaker population, which was growing rapidly because of immigration and defections from Quaker meetings. His entrance into politics coincided with the arrival of New Jersey's first royal governor, Edward Hyde (1661–1723), Lord Cornbury, in 1702. The governor shared Coxe's High Church prejudices and appointed him to the provincial council in 1705 and to the Supreme Court in 1706. Cornbury also assisted Coxe's attempts to establish his family's title to several land grants by forbidding the West Jersey Council of Proprietors to sell any tracts whose ownership was disputed, and ordering them to surrender their deeds and surveys to one of Coxe's political allies.

Corruption, blatant favoritism toward Anglicans, and abuses of power pervaded Cornbury's administra-

tion. Opposing his policies were a coalition of West Jersey's Quaker proprietors and members of the East Jersey Board of Proprietors, most of whom were former Scots belonging to Britain's established (or Episcopal) church, who favored political rights for dissenters. This proprietary party found itself barred from appointment to high office by Cornbury and battled the governor's followers for the assembly's control.

Following Cornbury's dismissal in 1708, Coxe became the foremost antiproprietary spokesman. Badly discredited for having acquiesced in Cornbury's misgovernment, Coxe's party nevertheless rebuilt its reputation by exploiting widespread anxiety over the colony's exposure to seaborne attack during the War of the Spanish Succession (1702–1713). Because French and Spanish privateers regularly menaced the colony's coasts, and sometimes landed raiding parties, many voters abandoned the proprietary party out of fear that its pacifist Quaker members, who constituted the largest voting bloc in the assembly, would obstruct measures needed to defend the province. From 1708 to 1710 public opinion swung back toward Coxe's antiproprietary alliance, which comprised a majority of the provincial council, and away from the proprietary party, which had held the assembly since 1707.

The antiproprietary coalition suffered a serious setback when Robert Hunter (1666–1734) became governor in 1710. Hunter was a Whig who favored admitting Quakers and other dissenters into government, and, like most of the proprietary party's East Jersey leaders, he was a Scot. Hunter not only appointed Quakers and East Jersey proprietors to vacancies on the provincial council but also advised the Board of Trade to remove Coxe and three of his supporters from that body. Coxe's Tory connections in London initially blocked Hunter's proposals, but in 1713 he was discharged from the council and from the Supreme Court.

Coxe and his supporters had meanwhile increased their support among the voters and stood poised to capture the assembly. Hunter intended to postpone elections indefinitely but was forced to end the legislature's tenure when Queen Anne died, since British law mandated that all lawmakers be chosen under writs issued in the name of the reigning monarch. Coxe's followers inflicted a major defeat on the proprietary party in 1714. Hunter nullified their victory in 1715 by ordering a new election, which also went against the governor's backers; he then called a third vote, which cut the antiproprietary party's majority to one seat, but their margin of victory had been accomplished only because Coxe had run in two constituencies and triumphed in both.

The assembly made Coxe its Speaker and adjourned while awaiting the by-election of a replacement to take the second seat that he had won. The special ballot of 1716 went against Coxe's party and tipped control of the house to their antagonists. Coxe's supporters tried to prevent a quorum in the house by absenting themselves, but this maneuver failed when their opponents compelled attendance by enough members to convene a session. The proprietary party stripped Coxe of his speakership, expelled him and nine other members, and declared the former members ineligible for reelection.

The expulsion of Coxe and his followers decisively altered the balance of political power in New Jersey. Having lost control of every branch of the government, the antiproprietary party fell into disarray, and Coxe fled the province in apprehension that he would be arrested. Coxe sailed to London in July 1716 to petition the Board of Trade for Hunter's removal as governor but discovered that Hunter's influence at the Whig court far exceeded that of his own Tory patrons. After Coxe's failure in London, the antiproprietary party lost all realistic hopes of regaining power and rapidly disintegrated as a political force.

Coxe returned to New Jersey but never again played a major role in government. He ran for the assembly in 1725 and was defeated. He gained reappointment to the Supreme Court in 1734 only because Governor William Cosby was bitterly hostile to the proprietary party. When Cosby died two years later, Coxe's influence again waned. Coxe also failed in his legal struggle to win title over the lands in western Jersey he claimed as part of his father's estate.

Daniel Coxe had eloped with Sarah Eckley in 1707 after her Quaker father forbade their marriage; the couple had four children. He became the first American deputized as a Masonic Grand Master in 1730. Daniel Coxe moved to Trenton in the 1730s and died there.

• Correspondence by and about Coxe is in vols. 3–5 in William A. Whitehead et al., eds., *Archives of the State of New Jersey*, 1st ser. (43 vols., 1880–1949), and vol. 29 of Great Britain, Public Record Office, *Calendar of State Papers, Colonial Series: America and West Indies, 1574–1738* (44 vols., 1860–1969). See also Donald L. Kemmerer, *Path to Freedom: The Struggle for Self-Government in Colonial New Jersey, 1703–1776* (1940), pp. 50–106, and a biographical sketch in Hamilton Schuyler, *A History of St. Mary's Church, Trenton: In the Diocese of New Jersey from Its Foundation in the Year of Our Lord 1703 to 1926* (1926).

THOMAS L. PURVIS

COXE, John Redman (16 Sept. 1773–22 Mar. 1864), physician, medical educator, and writer, was born in Trenton, New Jersey, the son of Daniel Coxe, an attorney, and Sarah Redman. Coxe's father, a zealous Loyalist, moved to New York in 1777 and remained there through the course of the revolutionary war. John's upbringing became the responsibility of his grandfather, John Redman, the noted Philadelphia physician. Coxe went to school in Philadelphia and, joining his parents in England after the war, received a classical education in London and Edinburgh. In 1789–1790 he attended courses in anatomy and chemistry at London Hospital. He then returned to the United States and studied medicine under the preceptorship of Dr. Benjamin Rush, with whom he worked diligently during the yellow fever epidemic of 1793. After receiving an M.D. from the University of Penn-

sylvania in 1794, Coxe traveled to London, Edinburgh, and Paris, furthering his medical education. He returned to Philadelphia to set up a medical practice in 1796. Two years later he married Sarah Cox; they had ten children.

In 1797 Coxe was resident physician in Philadelphia's Bush Hill Hospital, and in 1798 he served as the city's port physician. From 1802 to 1807 he was a physician at the Pennsylvania Hospital and also served as physician of the Philadelphia Dispensary. He did much to break down the prejudice against vaccination and was one of the first to use the procedure in Philadelphia. In 1801 he vaccinated himself and his 23-day-old son. He was responsible also for what was called "Coxe's Hive Syrup," a syrup of squill that the *Dispensatory of the United States* (1843) called a "very popular preparation" and which the *Chicago Medical Journal* (1864) said had made Coxe's name a "household word" for more than a half-century. It was used chiefly as an emetic, expectorant, and diaphoretic.

Coxe described his practice, which included a drugstore, as "lucrative," but in 1809 he "closed his drug business" when he was elected to the chair of chemistry at the medical school of the University of Pennsylvania. In applying for the position Coxe pointed to his study of chemistry abroad and to his being "one of the first . . . in the [1792] establishment of the Chemical Society" of Philadelphia, to which he was elected one of the lecturers and later president. (Coxe had been a member of the university's board of trustees since 1806—probably through the influence of his grandfather, John Redman—but resigned in 1809, the year he was appointed to the professorship.) He was not successful as a teacher of chemistry, however, and in 1881 he applied for and received the professorship of materia medica and pharmacy.

In 1821 the University's board of trustees, at Coxe's urging, offered a "master of pharmacy" diploma. City pharmacists, however, who felt threatened by the prospect of being subjected to the controls of a medical faculty, established their own Philadelphia College of Apothecaries (later Philadelphia College of Pharmacy) in the same year. Although no pharmacy student ever attended lectures at the university, and Coxe's program failed, his efforts did provide the impetus for the beginnings of pharmaceutical education in the United States.

In 1835, at the behest of the faculty, Coxe was removed from his post, "without a trial, without a hearing," as he put it. His colleagues declared that materia medica and pharmacy were of too little importance to require the full time of a professor and charged him with incompetence in fulfilling his duties, as did his students. Coxe was outraged and published *An Appeal to the Public, and Especially to the Medical Public, from the Proceedings of the Trustees of the University of Pennsylvania, Vacating the Chair of Materia Medica and Pharmacy* (1835), a 68-page tract in which he castigated the "scandalous violence of young men" and the "insidious artifices of older men." Coxe claimed to have taught the "doctrines which I deemed the wisest and the best"; his critics contended that he gave "too exclusive an exposition" of the "doctrines and opinions of earlier fathers of Physic" and was not giving "proper significance to the facts of the humoral physiology and pathology" then gaining ground. Coxe held no teaching post thereafter.

Coxe's major contributions were in medical editing and writing. In 1805 he inaugurated and edited the *Philadelphia Medical Museum*, a substantial journal that covered all aspects of medicine and was issued in four "numbers" per year. The journal met with early success, but its conservatism eventually lost it favor, and publication ceased in 1811. It was the first such regular medical periodical publication in Philadelphia. Another attempt, the *Emporium of Arts and Sciences*, lasted only from 1812 to 1814.

Although eleven of his papers gained the distinction of being listed in the *Catalogue of Scientific Papers* of the Royal Society of London, Coxe was not essentially a medical investigator. His writings, which began with *An Inaugural Dissertation on Inflammation* (1794), and included several journal publications such as "Some Observations on the Wounds of the Heart" (*American Journal of the Medical Sciences 4* [1829]) and pamphlets such as *Observations on Combustion & Acidification: With a New Theory of Those Processes Founded on a Conjunction of Phlogistic and Antiphlogistic Doctrines* (1811), tended to be review articles of the literature from the ancients on. They demonstrated a knowledge of the literature and languages, but their impact was antiquarian. He also wrote briefly on telegraphy in Thomas Thomson's *Annals of Philosophy* in 1816.

Coxe's first book, *Practical Observation on Vaccination, or Inoculation for the Cow-pock* (1802), probably his most original effort, brought attention from other parts of the country along with requests for samples of the virus and directions for its use. In 1808 he issued *The Philadelphia Medical Dictionary*, which, Coxe acknowledged, was based on "Dr. Fox's 'New Medical Dictionary, revised and augmented by Dr. Bradley,'" with extensive additions by Coxe, and which was reprinted in 1817. In 1834 he published *An Inquiry into the Claims of Doctor William Harvey to the Discovery of the Circulation of the Blood*, which displayed considerable erudition, but which the noted surgeon Samuel Gross said, was "met with much ridicule and much caustic criticism." *The Writings of Hippocrates and Galen, Epitomized from the Original Latin Translations*, which he published in 1846, indicated the conservative bent for which he had been criticized by his faculty colleagues but was hailed by Gross as "a valuable addition to our medical literature."

The most significant of Coxe's publications was the *American Dispensatory* (1806), the first such dispensatory compiled under American authorship. The work was "committed to the public with little deviation from the Edinburgh copy," that is, the *Edinburgh New Dispensatory*, of which four issues had already appeared in the United States. Indeed, although Coxe did a good deal of rearranging and added some American materials, much was lifted verbatim from the Edinburgh

work. Later, James Thacher, whose *American New Dispensatory* first appeared in 1810, contended that Coxe's third edition (1814) copied some forty pages from him "not designated by the customary marks of quotation." Coxe's work, nevertheless, met with considerable success; its ninth edition was published in 1831. Coxe also edited, in 1817, with notes and additions, William Henry's *The Elements of Experimental Chemistry*, and in 1818 he translated from the French Matthieu Orfila's *Practical Chemistry*.

A member of the American Philosophical Society from 1799 on, he listed as his other professional connections the Royal Medical Society and the Royal Society of Sciences of Copenhagen and the Batavian Society of Sciences at Haarlem. Coxe's learning was acknowledged by his contemporaries, such as Samuel Gross, who considered Coxe "one of the ablest Greek and Latin scholars that our country has ever produced." Coxe's library contained almost 5,000 volumes at the time of his death in Philadelphia.

• No collected papers of Coxe are known to exist. Both the library of the College of Physicians of Philadelphia and the Rare Book and Manuscript Collections of Cornell University Library have papers relating to his estate. The most complete biographical sketch is by his granddaughter Mary Clapier Coxe, "A Biographical Sketch of John Redman Coxe, M.D. and John Redman, M.D.," *University of Pennsylvania Medical Bulletin* (Feb. 1908): 294–301. It must be used with caution. "Cato" included Coxe in his series titled "Sketches of Eminent Living Physicians" in *Boston Medical and Surgical Journal* 41 (1849): 156–59. Alexander Du Bin, *Coxe Family* (1936), gives a full account of Coxe's ancestors and descendants.

DAVID L. COWEN

COXE, Tench (22 May 1755–16 July 1824), promoter of American industrial growth and journalist, was born in Philadelphia, Pennsylvania, the son of William Coxe, a landowner and merchant, and Mary Francis. His great-grandfather Daniel Coxe, besides securing the family's fortune as the principal proprietor of colonial New Jersey, apparently bequeathed to his great-grandson an intense appetite for land speculation. At age six Tench was enrolled in the academy division of the Philadelphia College and Academy (later the University of Pennsylvania), where he appears to have been an indifferent student. In 1772, after attending college for only a brief time (it is not clear what he studied), Coxe opened a small trading business. Four years later he became a partner in his father's commercial firm, Coxe, Furman, and Coxe. Active in the social world of Philadelphia's elite, Coxe also became a member in 1775 of the United Company of Philadelphia for Promoting American Manufactures, one of the nation's earliest joint stock manufacturing companies.

Although he considered himself to be a neutral during the American Revolution, Coxe could at best be called an opportunist. In the summer of 1776, rather than take an active part in the revolution, Coxe resigned his commission in the Fourth Pennsylvania

Regiment. A few months later, confronted by a rising tide of violence against suspected Tories that included an attack on a carriage in which he was riding, Coxe fled Philadelphia and sought refuge in New York City, then under English control. A year later he returned to Philadelphia "triumphantly," according to his critics, when British troops commanded by Lord Charles Cornwallis took over the city.

Narrowly avoiding conviction for treason in May 1778, Coxe spent the next several years rebuilding his business and personal life. Just a few months earlier, Coxe had married Catherine McCall, the daughter of a leading Philadelphia merchant. Coxe's married life with Catherine was brief. Ill at the time of her wedding, possibly with tuberculosis, Catherine died on 22 July 1778. In January 1782 Coxe married his first cousin Rebecca Coxe, with whom he had ten children. Although Coxe remained active in commerce, his real wealth came in the 1780s from land speculation, especially in extensive tracks of mineral-rich land in western Pennsylvania and Virginia.

Coxe was often at the center of political economic debates in early America. By the time of the drafting of the Constitution (which he considered to be an indispensable prerequisite for a strong and independent national economy), he had emerged as a leading advocate of a balanced economy "nourished particularly by the encouragement of manufactures." As a charter member of the Pennsylvania Society for the Encouragement of Manufactures and Useful Arts (PSEMUA), founded in 1787, Coxe was instrumental in the opening by the society of a textile manufactory in the fall of its first year. The PSEMUA intended its mill both to provide employment for the poor and, coincidentally, to demonstrate the economic value of cotton manufacture. After an enthusiastic start, this early effort to stimulate manufacturing failed when, in March 1790, the society's mill burned to the ground.

An avowed economic nationalist, Coxe actively supported the financial program of Secretary of the Treasury Alexander Hamilton, particularly Hamilton's efforts to establish a national bank. In May 1790 Hamilton named Coxe to be his assistant secretary of the treasury. Hamilton used Coxe's research in preparing his report on manufactures (1791), and the assistant secretary's "Plan for a Manufacturing Society" was the basis for the Society for Establishing Useful Manufactures (SEUM), a government-promoted attempt to harness private capital on behalf of developing a "national manufactory." After sufficient funds had been raised, the SEUM received a charter from the New Jersey legislature on 22 November 1791 to develop a model industrial town at a site that became Paterson, New Jersey. Five years later, with many of its directors in bankruptcy as a result of the panic of 1792 and with almost all of its attempted manufactures failing, the SEUM's directors suspended operations.

To its many opponents the National Manufactory represented a sinister intrusion of government into the private sphere. Responding to these critics, Coxe rejected the idea that the SEUM was a "dangerous scheme." National self-sufficiency, which was a primary objective for Coxe, required that government vigorously promote economic growth. Coxe's ideas on the role of government are precursors to the economic theories identified in the nineteenth century with "American School" economists such as Daniel Raymond and Henry Carey.

Always a devoted promoter of manufactures, Coxe nevertheless took for granted that America's self-sufficiency and material prosperity required an interdependent national economy. A diversity of economic pursuits was necessary in his view to produce a natural balance of interests. Yet, for Coxe, without manufacturing the endless potential of America's vast natural resources would remain untapped. The growth of manufacturing was essential if America was to realize its national destiny.

During the 1790s Coxe began to express misgivings about Hamilton's economic program. Unlike Hamilton, whose main objective was to bind the wealthy elite to the new government, Coxe believed in the need to sustain economic opportunity for all citizens, and he expressed greater sympathy as well for popular participation in politics. By the close of the century, Coxe had formally broken with the Federalist party over the Jay Treaty and had joined the Republican party.

Despite the high regard of his contemporaries for his administrative ability and intelligence, Coxe could not free himself from the taint left by his Tory sympathies during the revolutionary war. Even though he served the new nation as both commissioner of revenue (1792–1797) and purveyor of public supplies (1803–1812), Coxe never held—much to his regret and despite his best efforts—a political office that he believed was commensurate with his abilities.

Successful as a merchant and land speculator, Coxe made his lasting mark as a political economist and publicist. In *A View of the United States of America* and "A Brief Examination of Lord Sheffield's Observations on the Commerce of the United States," as well as in his many works as a journalist, Coxe provided an optimistic blueprint for America's economic future. Coxe died at his home in Philadelphia.

• Michael Brewster Folsom and Steven D. Lubar, eds., *The Philosophy of Manufactures: Early Debates over Industrialization in the United States* (1982), is an accessible source for brief selections from Coxe's writings. See also Tench Coxe, *A View of the United States of America, in a Series of Papers, Written at Various Times between the Years 1787 and 1794 . . .* (repr. 1965). Joseph Stancliffe Davis, *Essays in the Earlier History of American Corporations*, vol. 1 (1917), contains valuable sources on the SEUM. Jacob E. Cooke, *Tench Coxe and the Early Republic* (1978), is the standard biography. Also useful for understanding Coxe and his times are Harold Hutcheson, *Tench Coxe: A Study in American Economic Development* (1938); Joseph Dorfman, *Economic Mind in American Civilization, 1608–1865*, vol. 2 (1946); Leo Marx, *The Machine in the Garden: Technology and the Pastoral Ideal in America* (1964); Samuel Rezneck, "The Rise and Early Development of Industrial Consciousness in the United States, 1760–1830," *Journal of Economic and Business History* 4

(1932): 784–810; and John R. Nelson, Jr., *Liberty and Property: Political Economy and Policymaking in the New Nation, 1789–1812* (1987).

BRIAN GREENBERG

COXEY, Jacob Sechler (16 Apr. 1854–18 May 1951), businessman, politician, and head of "Coxey's Army" of the unemployed, was born in Selinsgrove, Pennsylvania, the son of Thomas Coxey, a stationary engineer, and Mary Sechler. Six years later his family moved twenty miles farther north to Danville, in Montour County, where his father worked in an iron-rolling mill. Young Jake attended public school for eight years and, at age sixteen, took a summer job as a water boy in the mill with his father. He quickly advanced to machine oiler and then boiler tender. By the time he left the mill at the age of twenty-four he had become a stationary engineer like his father.

An uncle living near Harrisburg launched Coxey's career in business when he invited his nephew to join his scrap-metal firm. Three years later, in May 1881, Jake made a trip to Massillon, Ohio, to purchase an abandoned blast furnace for scrap. He liked the Ohio community and returned the following month to buy a farm and a small, unprofitable sandstone quarry. Erecting a crushing mill, Coxey produced a special type of sand needed by the steel, glass, and pottery industries then enjoying boom times. He proved to be an excellent salesman, and demand for his white sand increased in Pittsburgh and throughout the Ohio Valley. The young businessman's career seemed assured. By the early 1890s he had expanded his holdings to include a stock farm near Massillon and ranches near Lexington, Kentucky, and Guthrie, Oklahoma, where he raised several dozen blooded race horses. Coxey Silica Sand Company operated from 1881 until 1929 when he sold the business and retired. He also founded a steel mill at Mount Vernon, Ohio, in 1899 that he sold in 1909. Beginning in the 1920s he concocted and sold an elixir called "Cox-e-lax."

Beginning in his teenage years, Coxey spent much time reading and thinking about the money question, arguing endlessly about politics, interest rates, paper money, and bank credit. He boldly advanced two novel ideas of his own. The first, which came to him in late 1891, was to put the nation's unemployed to work building roads, which were then in a generally terrible condition throughout the United States. This proposal was first introduced in Congress in 1892. It was to further interest in the idea that Coxey formed his Good Roads Association, one of dozens of similar organizations popular during the decade.

Two years later, in early January 1894, Coxey announced a plan whereby federal lawmakers could finance his jobs and good-roads program by issuing noninterest-bearing bonds, a complicated financial arrangement that would enable local governments to construct schools, courthouses, libraries, museums, and other public buildings in addition to streets and highways. His program would, in effect, use fiat money to prime the economic pump during periods of economic depression.

A flamboyant associate, Carl Browne, originated the idea of a march on Washington as a way to publicize and impress upon Congress the need to approve Coxey's twin proposals for good roads and temporary public-works jobs. Browne, a self-described professional agitator from California, would play a brief but decisive role in Coxey's life. The two first met in Chicago at the World's Columbian Exposition in 1893 and became immediate friends as a result of their shared interest in monetary reform. Coxey invited Browne to spend the following winter at his home in Massillon where the two worked out details of their grand protest march. To many in Coxey's family, the eccentric Californian exercised a strange, even sinister power over Coxey. Browne, who believed in reincarnation, converted Coxey, a nominal Episcopalian, to his occult theology. Even worse in the eyes of Coxey's family and friends, Browne had convinced him to squander large sums of money on the bizarre march to Washington.

Among those most worried about Browne's influence was Coxey's former wife, Caroline Amerman, who held the second mortgage on his sandstone quarry. Their fourteen-year marriage had broken up in 1888, apparently as a result of Coxey's passion for owning and racing horses. They had four children. Two years later he married Henrietta Sophia Jones, a former maid in his home, who was more accepting of his foibles. At the time of the march they had two children, the youngest being named Legal Tender. Two more children were born afterwards.

"Coxey's Army," the first national crusade against unemployment, briefly attracted more newspaper coverage than almost any event between the Civil War and Spanish-American War. The daily press often carried the story on page one, and rare was the country weekly that did not print some news of the march. The flood of publicity inspired formation of additional contingents of "Coxey's Army," primarily in the Far West. "General" Coxey's name became a household word, although he personally shunned the military terminology used by the press to describe the movement. He preferred to style himself simply as president of the J. S. Coxey Good Roads Association of the United States and ex officio of the Commonweal of Christ, the name organizers formally gave the protest movement.

Two to three hundred marchers accompanied Coxey on a 400-mile long, six-week odyssey from Massillon, Ohio, to Washington, D.C., in March and April 1894 to demand that Congress fund public-works jobs. Hundreds more joined them on 1 May 1894, when they marched down Pennsylvania Avenue to present Congress with their unusual "petition in boots," but certainly there were not the 500,000 protesters Coxey had once predicted. As many as 30,000 spectators lined the way, some drawn by sympathy but most by curiosity and a desire to see what would happen next in a drama that had captivated national attention since late March.

Coxey planned to give a brief speech summarizing their grievances, but police arrested the Ohioan before he could address the several thousand onlookers gathered at the base of the Capitol steps. They charged him with violating laws that prohibited walking on the grass or displaying banners on the grounds, although Coxey's only "banner" was the small American flag pinned to his lapel. For this crime a judge sentenced Coxey and Browne to twenty days in jail.

If Coxey ever had cause to regret his association with Browne, it was not because the Californian spent too much of his money or caused him to be denounced as a "crank," but because Browne secretly courted his eighteen-year-old daughter behind his back. When reporters announced that they had been quietly wed in mid-1895, Coxey broke ties with them both. That is probably a primary reason why Coxey did not lead another march to Washington that year as he had earlier planned to do.

After his 1894 march, Coxey returned to Ohio where he campaigned often for public office—distinguishing himself primarily as an indefatigable monetary reformer—and lost, with the one exception of being elected mayor of Massillon in 1931 as a Republican. The following year he ran for president as the Farmer-Labor party candidate and received 7,309 votes. Party labels meant little to Coxey, who also ran for office as a Democrat, Greenbacker, and Populist.

Coxey returned to Washington in 1914 and this time spoke legally from the Capitol steps. On 1 May 1944, on the occasion of the fiftieth anniversary of the great march and in the ninetieth year of Coxey's long life, the elder statesman of American reform again mounted the Capitol steps and, with the permission of Speaker Sam Rayburn and Vice President Henry A. Wallace, completed the protest speech he had attempted to deliver there once before. His 200 listeners were mostly federal employees and servicemen who happened to be there and were curious.

Although Coxey's jobs and money proposals were never enacted into law, by 1944 the idea of temporary public-works jobs for unemployed Americans during times of economic depression was no longer considered radical, and Coxey had attained the status of historical curiosity. Two generations of Americans after 1894 used the epithet "Coxey's Army" to describe any disorganized undertaking, although, in fact, Coxey's followers had generally been well organized and well disciplined. Coxey died in Massillon, Ohio.

• Newspapers devoted thousands of column-inches of space to Coxey and his protest crusade in 1894. Probably the best dispatches were filed by Ray Stannard Baker for the *Chicago Record* and are available on microfilm. Henry Vincent, a reform journalist, authored *The Story of the Commonweal* (1894), a tract sold to raise money for the marchers. Coxey figures prominently in two books that detail the history of the movement: Donald L. McMurry, *Coxey's Army: A Study of the Industrial Army Movement of 1894* (1929), and Carlos A. Schwantes, *Coxey's Army: An American Odyssey* (1985). A collection of Coxey memorabilia is preserved at the Massillon Museum and also on microfilm at the Ohio Historical Society in Columbus. See also Embrey Bernard Howson, "Jacob Sechler Coxey: A Biography of a Monetary Reformer" (Ph.D. diss., Ohio State Univ., 1973), and Michael Barkun, "'Coxey's Army' as a Millennial Movement," *Religion* 18 (1988): 363–89.

CARLOS A. SCHWANTES

COXHEAD, Ernest Albert (1863–27 Mar. 1933), architect, was born in Eastbourne, Sussex, England, the son of William Palmer Coxhead, a schoolmaster and, later, a lodging-house keeper, and Mary Maria Wadley. The fourth of six children, Coxhead was raised in boarding houses run by his parents. At an early age he showed an interest in design and at fifteen was articled to a local civil engineer, George Wallis. Five years later, in 1883, he moved to London, entering the office of architect Frederic Chancellor. While employed by Chancellor, Coxhead was admitted to the Royal Academy of Fine Arts, where he remained for three years (1883–1886). Simultaneously he attended classes at the Architectural Association.

For reasons that remain unknown, Coxhead left England and by January 1887 established an independent architectural practice in Los Angeles, California. He was assisted by his older brother Almeric, who apparently had no previous training in architecture. The office was moved to San Francisco in 1889. Soon thereafter, Almeric became a partner, a position he retained until his death. Subsequently Ernest continued to practice on his own for about two years. Throughout their association, Almeric managed the business and assisted in supervising projects under construction. Ernest had full responsibility for design and, since the office always was small, did most of that work himself.

Virtually from the start of independent practice, Coxhead pursued a personal style, which, while reflecting a sound knowledge of historic precedent, embodied a highly inventive, sometimes eccentric, use of form, space, and scale. Between 1887 and 1892 much of his energy focused on designs for Episcopal churches both in southern and northern California. Divergent historical references often were juxtaposed in unorthodox ways to give the scheme a commanding presence even if the actual dimensions were not large. Among the most notable examples is the Church of St. John the Evangelist (1890–1891) in San Francisco, a rambunctious assemblage of allusions to Romanesque and Byzantine as well as high-style and vernacular precedent.

After 1892 the great majority of Coxhead's realized work was residential. He designed several large city houses, including ones for Reginald Knight Smith (1895), Alonzo McFarland (1895), and Sarah Spooner (1899–1900) in San Francisco and Edwin Tobias Earl (c. 1895–1898) in Los Angeles. Most commissions were for dwellings of more modest size, including those for his family (1893) and Charles Murdock (1893) in San Francisco, E. Wiler Churchill in Napa (1892), and Andrew Corrigan in San Anselmo (1892). Collectively, this work exhibits unusual breadth of expression that encompassed innovative interpretations of elaborate classical sources as well as vernacular postmedieval ones. The results at once reflect Coxhead's English background and knowledge of then current English design, and a sensitivity to the terrain as well as the cultural climate of the Bay Area.

Coxhead married Helen Browning Hawes in 1898; she died giving birth to their third child, around 1905. The loss appears to have affected him deeply, as did repeated failures to secure the large-scale projects he coveted such as the Sub-Treasury Building or the Panama-Pacific International Exposition in San Francisco. By the mid-1900s, Coxhead's work had lost much of its originality, and the unconventional attributes that remained seemed ever more forced. The volume of work also began to diminish. Coxhead produced little of consequence after 1910. Once considered a leading architect in the region, he had become virtually forgotten by many colleagues when he died at his house in Berkeley.

• Most of Coxhead's surviving papers are in the estate of John Beach in San Francisco and have yet to be placed in a repository to which the public has ready access. Drawings for several projects are at the Bancroft Library, University of California, Berkeley. The most detailed account of Coxhead's career is Richard Longstreth, *On the Edge of the World: Four Architects in San Francisco at the Turn of the Century* (1983). See also Sally Woodbridge, ed., *Bay Area Houses* (1976).

RICHARD LONGSTRETH

COY, Ted (24 May 1888–8 Sept. 1935), college athlete, coach, and sportswriter, was born Edward Harris Coy in Andover, Massachusetts, the son of Edward Gustin Coy, a master of Phillips Andover Academy, and Helen Eliza Marsh. He graduated from the Hotchkiss School in 1906, two years after his father, its first headmaster, died. Coy earned a B.A. degree in 1910 from Yale College, which had been attended by his father, brother, and two uncles, one of whom was former college president Timothy Dwight. He captained the Yale freshman football team. As varsity fullback for three years and captain his senior year, the six-foot, 195-pound, blond-haired Coy was dubbed a "Frank Merriwell hero" after the fictional all-around football player. Coy, propelled by high knee action, became one of Yale's and the college game's greatest running backs, frequently gaining fifty or more yards. A strong punter, he often reached sixty yards. By using his instep instead of his toe, he proved an effective dropkicker. Coy also lettered in baseball, as first baseman, and in track, in which he placed at meets in the shotput, hammer throw, and high jump.

From 1907 to 1909 the Yale varsity football team lost only once (4–0 against Harvard University in 1908) and tied twice (0–0 with the U.S. Military Academy in 1907 and 10–10 with Brown University in 1908). In a 1907 game, Princeton University led Yale at the half, 10–0. Coy, however, scored two successive touchdowns as Yale rallied to win by two points. He again tallied two touchdowns against Harvard in the Elis' 12–0 victory, clinching the Big Three championship. Yale was ranked number one nationally. In 1908 Coy scored the only touchdown in victories of 5–0 over Syracuse University and 6–0 over Army and tied Brown with his 25-yard field goal. In 1908 Princeton led Yale 0–6 until Coy returned to fullback from end, where Coach Walter Camp had placed him, and scored two touchdowns for an 11–6 win. The next week, however, Yale's 42-game streak, including 39 wins and 3 ties, ended with their first loss to Harvard since 1901. In 1909 the removal of his appendix sidelined Coy the first four games, but his dropkick field goals and passes helped Yale record an undefeated season. Yale scored 209 points and shut out all opponents, none of whom penetrated beyond the Elis' 25 yard line. Coy contributed a 30-yard pass for a touchdown in Yale's 17–0 win over Army, a touchdown and a field goal to its 17–0 victory over Princeton, and two field goals in its 8–0 defeat of Harvard. With six first team and three second team All-America players, the 1909 Elis represented Yale's football zenith.

His honors included selection by Camp as an All-America fullback for the second team in 1907 and for the first team in both 1908 and 1909 and being named the 1909 Citizens Savings Player of the Year. He was chosen as fullback on four All-Time All-Player teams: by Camp in 1910, by Bill Edwards and by John W. Heisman, respectively, in the 1930 and 1932 *Illustrated Football Annual*, and by Jim Thorpe in a 1942 syndicated Associated Press article. Coy ranked among both the punters and the backs on Allison Danzig's all-time specialists list. In 1951 he was elected to the National Football Foundation and the Helms Athletic Foundation College Football Halls of Fame.

Coy's undergraduate activities included membership in Delta Kappa Epsilon fraternity and Skull and Bones, an elite senior society. According to the Eli custom of graduate coaching, the 1910 football team captain appointed Coy head coach. Coy sought advice from more than seventy former players, but he recorded only five wins as head coach. When Yale lost to Army and Brown and was held to a scoreless tie by Vanderbilt, Thomas L. Shevlin, a 1906 graduate, replaced him.

Coy worked in various jobs, including assistant sales manager of the Durham Coal and Iron Company, Chattanooga, Tennessee, from 1911 to 1913; bond manager at Munsey Trust Company, Washington, D.C.; financial editor of the *Washington Times*; office manager and member of the New York City stock exchange firm of Davies, Thomas and Company from 1915 to 1924; a Fuller Brush Company field manager from 1929 to 1931; and a solicitor at Smyth, Sanford and Gerard, New York City insurance agents, from 1931 to 1935. He filed a bankruptcy petition in U.S. District Court in New York City, on 3 March 1933, showing assets of $750 and liabilities of $13,872. "All a man can do is the best he can and then take his medicine," acknowledged Coy. While "repudiating no debts or obligations," he promised that, given "a chance to work on unhampered," he would "come through all right."

Coy, involved in civic activities, volunteered with the New York City mounted police during World War I and later was a special investigator for the Department of Justice (1920–1922). He served as a Yale alumni fund agent, a treasurer and executive committee member of the Girl Scouts, an athletic director at New York City's Lenox Hill Settlement House, and a member of the Ivy Republican Club. He wrote articles, chiefly about football, for *St. Nicholas Magazine* (1910–1911), the *New York World*, and several other newspapers. In 1928 Coy was special sports critic for the *San Francisco News* and contributed "Eastern and Western Football" to *Game and Gossip*.

Coy was married three times, first to Sophie d'Antignac Meldrim of Savannah, Georgia, in 1913; she divorced him in 1925 and obtained custody of their two children. His 1925 marriage to actress Jeanne (Amelia Jean) Eagles lasted three years before also ending in divorce. Three weeks later, Coy married Lottie Bruhn in El Paso, Texas. He had no children with either of his last two wives. Following a heart attack on 5 September 1935, he died of pneumonia in New York City. Never as successful off the field as on, Coy was ranked with Ernest Alonzo "Ernie" Nevers of Stanford University and Felix Anthony "Doc" Blanchard, Jr., of Army as one of the greatest college fullbacks.

• Detailed biographical sketches of Coy are in *History of the Class of 1910, Yale College* albums (1910, 1917, 1926, and 1935). Another helpful reference is Albert Beecher Crawford, ed., *Football Y Men—Men of Yale Series*, vol. 1 (1962). For Coy's football career, the best secondary sources are Tim Cohane, *The Yale Football Story* (1951), and Marcia G. Synnott, "Edward Harris Coy," *Biographical Dictionary of American Sports: Football*, ed. David L. Porter (1987). His football achievements are noted in L. H. Baker, *Football: Facts and Figures* (1945); Thomas Bergin, *The Game: The Harvard-Yale Football Rivalry, 1875–1983* (1984); Allison Danzig, *The History of American Football: Its Great Teams, Players, and Coaches* (1956) and *Oh, How They Played the Game: The Early Days of Football and the Heroes Who Made It Great* (1971); and John McCallum, *Ivy League Football since 1872* (1977). For a wealth of information on Yale football, see Arnold Guyot Dana, "Yale Old and New," reel 16, microfilm, and William Charles Wurtenberg, comp., scrapbook (c. 1902–1915), Manuscripts and Archives, Yale University Library. An obituary is in the *New York Times*, 9 Sept. 1935.

MARCIA G. SYNNOTT

COYLE, Grace Longwell (22 Mar. 1892–10 Mar. 1962), social work theorist, was born in North Adams, Massachusetts, the daughter of John Patterson Coyle, a Congregationalist minister, and Mary Allerton Cushman. She attended Wellesley College, where she was elected to Phi Beta Kappa, and graduated in 1914 with an A.B. Coyle later cited the writings of Jane Addams, the founder of Hull-House in Chicago, Mary Follett, and John Dewey and the progressive education movement as early influences. In 1915 she earned a certificate from the New York School of Philanthropy (now Columbia University's School of Social Work). Coyle entered social work as a settlement worker in the coal

mining regions around Wilkes-Barre, Pennsylvania. After three years she returned to New York City to work in the Industrial Women's Department of the Young Women's Christian Association (YWCA). Coyle held a part-time position in the late 1920s with a New York organization, The Inquiry, which was dedicated to reducing racial and national conflict through group discussion. This brought her into contact with a number of prominent intellectuals and social reformers, including William H. Kilpatrick, John Dewey, Harrison Elliott, Alfred Sheffield, Herbert Croly, and Eduard C. Lindeman.

Coyle earned her master's degree in economics (1928) and her doctorate in sociology (1931) from Columbia University. Her published dissertation, *Social Progress in Organized Groups* (1930), is an analysis of universal processes that occur in small groups. Coyle's special interests included conditions of group cohesion, morale, and the role of ritual and symbol in modern society. In 1930 she rejoined the YWCA on the National Board as executive director of the Laboratory (research and program) Division.

Case Western Reserve University hired Coyle in 1934 as an assistant professor of group work in the School of Applied Social Sciences. Extremely popular with her students, many of whom later remembered her as the inspiration for their own careers in social work, Coyle remained at Case Western until her death, except for two years during World War II when she worked with the War Relocation Authority.

Coyle's reputation rests primarily on her writings and theoretical work. Her paper "Group Work and Social Change," given at the National Conference of Social Work in 1935 in Montreal, won the Pugsley Award as the paper that made the most important contribution to social work. In two important articles, "Case Work and Group Work: Where the Two Areas Meet and Contribute to Each Other" (*Survey*, Apr. 1937) and "Social Group Work as an Aspect of Social Work Practice" (*Journal of Social Issues*, 1939), Coyle argued for a closer connection to be made between group work and social case work, whereas previously there had been a sharp differentiation between the two. Group work had been done primarily in community organizations like the YWCA, the Young Men's Christian Association (YMCA), and settlement houses; social case work had been directed at severely troubled patients and had focused on their problems as individuals rather than on their problems interacting in groups. Coyle helped to expand the scope of group work, bringing it into hospitals, clinics, and children's institutions, and to move the conception of its purpose away from its recreational or educational benefits and toward social rehabilitation and integration.

In 1940 Coyle became president of the National Conference of Social Work. From 1942 to 1944 she held the presidency of the American Association of Social Workers. Her major publications in the late 1940s include *Group Experience and Democratic Values* (1947), the article "On Becoming Professional" in *Towards Professional Standards* (1947), and her third book, *Group Work with American Youth: A Guide to the Practice of Leadership* (1948).

In later life, in addition to teaching, Coyle served as president of the Council on Social Work Education (1958–1960) and authored the monographs *Social Science in the Professional Education of the Social Worker* (1958) and *Social Process, Community and Group* (1958). In 1961 the Grace Longwell Coyle Professorship was established at Case Western. She never married but lived with her long-term companion, Abbie Graham. Neither woman had children of her own, but upon the death of Coyle's sister-in-law Coyle took over the care of her brother's three young children. She died in Cleveland, Ohio.

A leading figure in social work because of her pioneering efforts in group work, Grace Coyle was the first to argue for the integration of social case work and group therapy. Social group work, as Coyle saw it, is "an educational process aiming at the development and social adjustment of individuals through voluntary group association." Emerging from her early experiences in settlement houses and with immigrant populations, Coyle's theory of group work was rooted in a set of political beliefs that argue that the integration of citizens into society is a critical prerequisite for effective democracy. Positive group experiences, according to Coyle, both encourage good citizenship and can help to counter the alienating influence of modern technology. Her writings blend educational and sociological methods with more conventional social work and psychological theory.

• Coyle authored six books and monographs and twenty-six articles. A collection of her personal papers, including manuscripts, course outlines, and correspondence, can be found in the Archives of Case Western Reserve University in Cleveland, Ohio. Posthumous tributes to Coyle appear in *Social Casework* 43, no. 7 (July 1962): 376, and in the *American Sociological Review* 28, no. 1 (Feb. 1963): 136. An obituary is in the *New York Times*, 10 Nov. 1962.

ELIZABETH ZOE VICARY

COZZENS, Frederick Swartwout (11 Mar. 1818–23 Dec. 1869), author and wine merchant, was born in New York City, the son of Frederick Cozzens, a chemist, naturalist, geologist, and mineralogist. His mother's name is unknown. Cozzens's maternal grandmother was from Carlisle on the Scottish border; as a child he enjoyed a "passionate love of poetry," a result of hearing his grandmother's retelling of the old Border ballads and legends in verse.

Cozzens became enamored with study and reading at an early age, collecting minerals, shells, coins, and Indian curiosities. By the time he was fifteen, he had already studied anatomy and chemistry and performed a number of scientific experiments. In addition, he was fond of theatrical performances. He also studied mechanics and spent three years working in the machine branch of bank-note engraving.

When he was twenty-one, he went into the grocery and wine business in Vesey Street, an activity that he followed for almost thirty years, until the business failed in 1868. During this period he was considered a prominent wine merchant, having been the first to introduce native wines (the Longworth wines of Ohio) in New York for sale. In 1854 he began the publication of the *Wine Press*, a monthly periodical principally devoted to the introduction of native wines. He continued to edit the paper for seven years; the publication of *Wine Press* was brought to an end by the outbreak of war. When his business failed, he and his wife, Susan Meyers of Philadelphia, retired to Rahway, New Jersey. The couple had at least one child.

In the meantime, however, Cozzens had become internationally known as a writer, a reputation based primarily on his humorous works. His first publications appeared in 1847: a humorous imitation of Edmund Spenser and "Mythology History of the Heavens" in *Yankee Doodle*. In the same year he also published a short, religious poem titled "Worship" in the *Knickerbocker Magazine*. He contributed a number of essays, sketches, and poems to the *Knickerbocker Magazine*, most published anonymously, during the next eight years. A number of these pieces were published in *Prismatics* in 1853 under the pseudonym Richard Haywarde (an adaptation of the name of one of his ancestors) in a volume that the author characterized as "beautifully illustrated" by Elliott, Darley, Kensett, Hicks, and Rossiter.

Cozzens's second profession was kept quite distinct from his first. As he noted in a brief autobiographical sketch introducing *Sayings, Wise and Otherwise* (1880), "People often ask how I managed to find time to write as much as I did? The secret was this: I always put aside business when I went home, and always put aside literature when I went to business." Still, he found ample time to pursue his avocation. Cozzens had a gift for making friends, and as one of the original 100 members of the Century Club he had the opportunity to meet many of the literati. For instance, William Cullen Bryant introduced him to Washington Irving, and subsequently, at about the time that he moved to Yonkers in 1852, he met William Makepeace Thackeray, who was on his first tour of the United States.

In 1854 Cozzens published a series of sketches, humorously exaggerated accounts of his personal experiences at "Chestnut Cottage," his summer home in Yonkers on the Hudson River. These sketches, recounting the adventures of a city man in a rural atmosphere, which were published in *Putnam's Monthly*, became the first chapters of *The Sparrowgrass Papers; or, Living in the Country* (1856). The volume was an immediate success, selling 5,000 copies in the first week. It also established Cozzens as a humorist and was reprinted in at least five editions through 1870. This passage from "Early Rising" in the *Sparrowgrass Papers* provides a representative sample of the writer's style:

A friend recommended me to send to the south side of Long Island for some very prolific potatoes—the real hippopotamus breed. Down went my man, and what with the expenses of horse-hire, tavern bills, toll-gates, and breaking a wagon, the hippopotami cost as much apiece as pine-apples. They were fine potatoes, though, with comely features, and large, languishing eyes, that promised increase of family without delay. As I worked my own garden (for which I hired a landscape gardener, at $2.00 per day, to give me instructions), I concluded that the object of my first experiment in early rising should be the planting of the hippopotamuses. I accordingly arose the next morning at five, and it rained! The next, and it rained! It rained for two weeks! We had splendid potatoes every day for dinner. "My dear," said I to Mrs. Sparrowgrass, "Where did you get these fine potatoes?" "Why," said she, innocently, "Out of that basket from Long Island."

In an article in *Putnam's Monthly* in 1908, Mary Ross, commenting on *Sparrowgrass Papers*, noted that a "whole nation once responded to their mild-drawn pleasantries—the beginning of the suburban joke!"

Cozzens gave the concluding lecture of the Second Chorus of the session before the Mercantile Library Association at Clinson Hall, Astor-Place, on 27 January 1857. He discussed wit and humor and determined that humor could be united with exquisite pathos, but in no sense could wit be pathetic. (*New York Daily Times*, 28 Jan. 1857). The distinction between the quality of pathos and the emotional reaction of the pathetic is similar to the difference between tragedy and melodrama. Charlie Chaplin's tramp figure who can turn imminent starvation into a game, as in *The Gold Rush*, is an illustration of this principle of the transforming power of wit. Cozzens seldom dealt with situations involving true pathos—his subject matter was the minor tragedy of Mrs. Sparrowgrass's cooking those prize seed potatoes for dinner—but he also seldom used the pathetic as a source of his humor.

In 1858 the New York Publishers Association sent Cozzens as a representative to the Copyright Congress in Brussels, Belgium. In the following year Cozzens published the less widely read *Acadia; or, A Month with the Blue Noses*, an account of his tour of Nova Scotia. That same year he also published his 52-chapter "True History of New Plymouth" in the *New York Ledger*. *The Sayings of Dr. Bushwhacker and Other Learned Men*, published in 1867, was an anthology of entertaining and instructive essays on various topics that Cozzens and others had written for publication in the *Wine Press*. Additional fugitive pieces included "Memorial of the Late Peter A. Porter" (1865), "Memorial of Fitz-Greene Halleck" (6 Jan. 1868), and "Bunker Hill: An Old-Time Ballad."

Among his contemporaries, Cozzens was well regarded. Donald G. Mitchell, the editor of *Hearth and Home Journal*, for example, was entranced by the writer's "smacking humor"; he could rouse a great, uproarious laugh, according to Mitchell. The poet Halleck wrote that Cozzens possessed the "'faculty-divine,' the power of invention, the wit, the wisdom, the stories of miscellaneous, [sic] literature," and concluded that the humorist was "the best, or among the best, writers of our time in any language."

Cozzens died from an asthmatic attack while visiting a relative in Brooklyn.

While Cozzens's amusing anecdotes were widely read and even imitated during the third quarter of the nineteenth century to the extent that he was considered a noted humorist, his fame and even recognition of his name had faded by the beginning of the twentieth century. Still, his unaffected style, together with the entertaining nature of his tales, continued to make his works enjoyable.

• A collection of Cozzens's correspondence is at the New-York Historical Society. *Sayings, Wise and Otherwise* (1880) is autobiographical and contains an introductory note by Donald G. Mitchell. A bibliography of his writings is in Jacob Blanck, comp., *Bibliography of American Literature*, vol. 2 (1957). James Grant Wilson, *Bryant and His Friends: Some Reminiscences of the Knickerbocker Writers* (1886), includes a sketch, as does Arthur D. F. Randolph, "Leaves from the Journal of Frederick S. Cozzens," *Lippincott's Magazine*, May 1890, pp. 739–48. See also J. G. Wilson, *Life and Letters of Fitz-Greene Halleck* (1869). Obituaries are in the *New York Herald*, 25–28 Dec. 1869, and the *New York World*, 28 Dec. 1869.

STEVEN H. GALE

COZZENS, James Gould (19 Aug. 1903–9 Aug. 1979), author, was born in Chicago, Illinois, during an extended visit to that city by his wealthy parents, Henry William Cozzens and Bertha Wood. In 1906, when his father accepted a high-income executive post in New York, the family settled on Staten Island, where they enjoyed rural life in an area of sizable estates with room for growing vegetables, raising poultry, and keeping small dairy herds. At age eleven, while attending Staten Island Academy, Cozzens contributed a poem, "The Andes," to the school paper. Later, at Kent School in Connecticut, he wrote several prose pieces for the *Kent Quarterly*, served a term as its editor, and had an article, "A Democratic School" (about Kent), published in the *Atlantic Monthly*. He enrolled at Harvard in 1922 but left in his second year after missing too many classes while writing both poetry and prose for the *Advocate* and completing his first novel, *Confusion*, which was published in April 1924. The novel lacked essential conflict, but Cozzens realistically portrayed upper-class society, as he would later do with steadily increasing skill.

While visiting relatives in Nova Scotia, Cozzens wrote his second novel, *Michael Scarlett* (1925), which was set in sixteenth-century England and contained plenty of the conflict lacking in *Confusion*. By then he was a committed novelist though still in need of income from other sources to support himself. A year in Cuba, 1925–1926, tutoring children of Americans working in a large sugar mill, provided Cozzens the material for two books, *Cock Pit* (1928) and *Son of Perdition* (1929), both of which portrayed the American sugar industry as a titan dehumanizing all it touched. In 1927 he became librarian for the New York Athletic Club, and on the last day of that same year, he married Bernice Baumgarten, a literary agent who continued her career. With her steady income to count on, Cozzens sought greater privacy and found it in Lambertville, New Jersey, in surroundings like those of his boyhood on Staten Island. In a 1936 letter he told of the pleasure he derived from growing his own vegetables, and proceeded to offer his philosophy about creative writing: "I have no theories about literature and other people's irk me. . . . The view I have of writing is that a writer does well to write in a clear and unobtrusive way, trying not to be dull, and being careful to avoid obvious untruths and general nonsense."

During the 1920s and 1930s Cozzens managed to turn out a good many short stories and a novel almost every year. *The S.S. San Pedro* (1931), based on the tragic sinking of the *Vestris*, won a $2000 prize offered by Scribner's. In 1933 Cozzens's career reached a gratifying new level with *The Last Adam*, the first of a series of novels closely examining single professions—beginning with medicine. It was his first Book-of-the-Month Club selection and was made into a motion picture, *Dr. Bull* (1933), starring Will Rogers. *Men and Brethren* (1936) concerns the clergy, in the person of the Reverend Ernest Cudlipp—Episcopalian like Cozzens himself. *Ask Me Tomorrow* (1940) portrays a young writer whose pride needs tempering by age and reason. In the final two books about professions, Cozzens reached his peak as an author: *The Just and the Unjust*, about the practice of law, and *Guard of Honor*, about the military.

Each is compact, with the action limited to half a week. In *The Just and the Unjust* (1942), the central character is Abner Coates, an assistant district attorney, for whom sordid details disclosed during a murder trial prompt him to wonder whether he really wants to become a D.A. himself. His bedridden father, a former judge, has no advice to offer in that matter, but through the father Cozzens offers the view that all members of society, like it or not, must share responsibility for what happens to them each day. This view is more dramatically projected in *Guard of Honor* (1948), which was awarded the Pulitzer Prize for fiction in 1949 and is widely regarded as the finest American novel about World War II. It owed much to Cozzens's experience in the U.S. Air Force, from 1942 to 1945, in which he rose to the rank of major. His first assignment was to a school of applied tactics, in Florida, and his last to the Pentagon. His wide range of experience enabled him to describe accurately the various military personnel, procedures, and emergencies that could be found on an air base within a three day span. Readers are left wondering whether Bus Beal, youngest major general of the Air Force, will win the supreme command for which he is being considered. But that is only one thread in this compact fictional pattern. One other is the conflict between white and black airmen, while yet another is the extent to which the entire base suffers from the obvious incompetence of its commanding officer.

Of Cozzens's final half dozen books, *By Love Possessed* (1957) was his most successful: it was a Book-of-the-Month Club selection, a condensed version was published in *Reader's Digest*, and the motion picture rights yielded $250,000. It was also the most controversial. *Time* put him on its cover for an issue, with strong misrepresentation of his position on critical issues. Even highly regarded individuals, he insisted in this novel, are not immune from passion and would be less than complete without it. An important subtheme, moreover, defends a character's misappropriation of trust funds to protect investors from total ruin. Cozzens was sufficiently annoyed by *Time*'s criticism to refute it point by point, and in 1965 insisted, in response to a query from *Contemporary Authors*, "I don't defend anything; I don't eagerly assert anything."

From Lambertville, Cozzens and his wife moved three times: to Belle Haven, Virginia, in 1957; to Williamstown, Massachusetts, in 1958; and finally in 1973 to Stuart, Florida, where he died. He had set for himself demanding standards, and kept raising them, with results welcomed by judicious readers. What the mass audience hoped for was no concern of his. Although American fiction has often dealt with criminals, clowns, antiheroes, and amusing prodigies, Cozzens, for the most part, dealt with mature men possessed of the power to shape and move the quality of American life. With such a goal, he could hardly have offered concessions to average readers.

• Cozzens's manuscripts and other papers are held by the Princeton University Library. Matthew Bruccoli, *Just Representations: A James Gould Cozzens Reader* (1978), includes essays by Cozzens himself with autobiographical content. He is given extended attention also in vol. 9 of the *Dictionary of Literary Biography* (1981), wherein Leland H. Cox, Jr., reviews all Cozzens's fiction. See also James A. Parrish, Jr., "James Gould Cozzens: A Critical Study" (Ph.D. diss., Florida State Univ., 1955). An interview with Cozzens by Robert Van Gelder is in the *New York Times Book Review*, 23 June 1940. The attack on Cozzens by *Time*, titled "The Hermit of Lambertville," is in its issue of 2 Sept. 1957.

WILLIAM PEIRCE RANDEL

CRABBE, Buster (7 Feb. 1908–23 Apr. 1983), athlete and motion picture actor, was born Clarence Linden Crabbe in Oakland, California, the son of Edward Crabbe and Agnes McNamara. When Crabbe was two, the family moved to Hawaii, where his father was overseer of a pineapple plantation. There Crabbe's natural abilities in many sports brought him the lifelong nickname of "Buster." He earned sixteen sports letters in high school, set thirty-five national and sixteen world swimming records during his years in sports competition, and was a member of the U.S. swimming team for the Olympics of 1928 (Amsterdam) and 1932 (Los Angeles). He received a B.A. from the University of Southern California in Los Angeles in 1932. In the Olympics that same year he crowned his athletic career by winning the gold medal for the 400-meter freestyle event, coming in first by one-tenth of a second. "That one-tenth of a second changed my life," he said (*Philadelphia Inquirer*, 24 Apr. 1983).

With his good looks and splendid physique, Crabbe had already done stunt and extra work in motion pictures since 1930 as a way of earning money toward the law degree he contemplated. The publicity that came with his gold medal focused Hollywood's interest on him as a potential movie personality. He was given a screen test, along with many other Olympic athletes, and was the choice of twenty-four out of twenty-five Paramount studio secretaries to play the loincloth-clad lead in *King of the Jungle* (1933), a near clone of MGM's Tarzan pictures. "I had an edge," Crabbe said later. "I was used to running around just in swim trunks for practice, though we still wore tops for public meets. The test was made with what amounted to a slightly enlarged G-string, and it didn't bother me, but I do think it bothered the other guys." Other low-budget action pictures followed, and the idea of a law career was abandoned. In 1933 Crabbe married Adah Virginia Held; they had three children.

Although initially Crabbe hoped to be cast in major films, he found himself typecast in action roles in B pictures. He considered his role as a cocky young marine in *Lady Be Careful* (1936) the best indication of what he might have done as an actor. That year, however, Paramount loaned him out to the Universal studio to play the lead in an action serial, *Flash Gordon*, based on a popular science-fiction comic strip of the day. To match the comic-strip Flash Gordon's appearance, Crabbe had to have his hair bleached to a bright blonde. He took to wearing a hat at all times, even in the presence of women. "I was just so ashamed by that bleach job," he told an interviewer. "I didn't give a damn if they were all ladies—my hat stayed on. . . . And to have guys whistle at you—that really burned me up."

The serial's great success made Crabbe the idol of young boys at Saturday movie matinees but also completely pigeonholed him in Hollywood's eyes as a hero of low-budget serials and action pictures. He starred in two more Flash Gordon serials, in 1938 and 1940, and in 1939 he played the lead in *Buck Rogers*, a serial based on another science-fiction comic strip. Other serials included *Red Barry* (1938), *The Sea Hound* (1947), *Pirates of the High Seas* (1950), and *King of the Congo* (1952). Crabbe also appeared as a two-fisted cowboy in several dozen program westerns from the 1930s into the 1960s. His last two films, *The Bounty Killers* and *Arizona Raiders*, appeared in 1965.

Crabbe did not tie his fortunes entirely to moviemaking. He knew his value as an Olympic gold medalist. It brought him a starring position in the Aquacade at the New York World's Fair of 1940; later he toured with his own Buster Crabbe Aquacade. He knew his value as a lifelong practitioner and exponent of physical fitness who kept his weight always within three pounds of what it was at the 1932 Olympics. Moving from Hollywood to New York in the 1950s, he became athletic director at a large resort hotel in the state. He promoted Buster Crabbe swimming pools for a New Jersey company and presented an exercise show on television. In 1976 he published *Energistics*, a book about

exercise for people over fifty; he also lectured on fitness and made personal appearances at fitness conventions.

Crabbe further knew his value as a figure of nostalgic appeal to a legion of movie serial buffs. He made personal appearances at nostalgia conventions and acted as host of a television program that showed his old films and serials, commenting on his memories of them. He did occasional cameos on drama anthologies and was star and producer of the television adventure serial "Captain Gallant of the French Foreign Legion" (1955–1957; appeared in syndicated reruns as "Foreign Legionnaire"), which also included Crabbe's son Cullen. His final television appearance was in 1980, playing Buck Rogers's father in an episode of "Buck Rogers in the 25th Century."

Before his death, Crabbe was engaged in promoting the 1984 Los Angeles Olympics. He died suddenly of a heart attack at his home in Scottsdale, Arizona. He had shrewdly made a lifetime career of exploiting and perpetuating the fame that "one-tenth of a second" in 1932 had brought him. His serials have given him an enduring place in the annals of movie nostalgia. Jim Harmon and Donald F. Glut, in *The Great Movie Serials* (1973), wrote that he had "the distinction of being one of the only actors who literally looked like a comic strip hero and who played the role with total believability. Crabbe was *the* serial hero, showing the zenith in bravery and sheer determination to vanquish evil from Earth or anywhere."

• Materials on the life of Crabbe are in the Billy Rose Theatre Collection at the New York Public Library for the Performing Arts, Lincoln Center. A list of his films is in the *International Dictionary of Films and Filmmakers*, 2d ed., vol. 3 (1992). Interviews include "Kaleidoscope Interviews Buster Crabbe," *Kaleidoscope* 2, no. 2 (1966): 4–11; "Me Buster, You Jane," *New York Times*, 23 May 1976; and Robert A. Cutter, "The Man Who Fell to Mars," *Saga*, Feb. 1977, pp. 44–45, 69, 71–72. Obituaries are in the *Philadelphia Inquirer* and the *Los Angeles Times*, both 24 Apr. 1983, and the *New York Times*, 25 Apr. 1983.

WILLIAM STEPHENSON

CRABTREE, Lotta (7 Nov. 1847–25 Sept. 1924), actress and theater producer, was born Charlotte Crabtree in New York City, the daughter of John Ashworth Crabtree and Mary Ann Livesey, both immigrants from England. At the age of six Crabtree went with her mother to search for her wayward father, who had abandoned his family in the East for the attraction of California gold. They arrived in San Francisco in 1853 and quickly became acquainted with the booming theatrical ventures of the city. In particular, child performers seemed to be the rage. Kate and Ellen Bateman, ages eleven and nine, were famous for their miniaturized performances of *Hamlet* and *The Merchant of Venice*; they were taken on a European tour by P. T. Barnum in 1851.

Crabtree's mother, a strong woman faced with impending poverty and an unreliable husband, having seen other child performers of the time, realized the potential of a stage career for her daughter. After locating her husband in Grass Valley, a mining town in the Sierras, she settled there to run a boardinghouse. Despite Grass Valley's small size, it boasted a troupe of child performers, a theater company, a number of saloons with stages for evening entertainment, and a playhouse.

Grass Valley served the family well as a base from which to launch Crabtree's theater career. Not only was she able to perform regularly in the town, she also had the opportunity to learn from other performers who passed through. For a period of time Lola Montez, the dancer and notorious femme fatale, resided in Grass Valley, and Crabtree took dancing lessons from her. By the age of eight she was touring the mining camps and performing solo song-and-dance routines to a pleasure-starved, rowdy male audience.

Child performers were extremely popular in nineteenth-century theater, but in the male-dominated mining camps of the West they were celebrated with frenzied enthusiasm. Crabtree's theatrical apprenticeship took her on extensive tours of the rough and rowdy camps, where she danced and sang her way into the hearts of the brutalized, childless miners. Young boy rascals and saucy, gaminlike waifs figured among her popular characters; she made the image of orphanhood a personal triumph, and on more than one occasion her solo numbers—usually featured on a bill with other performers in a variety-style format—elicited such pleasure from the spectators that they threw coins and gold nuggets on the stage in appreciation.

By the time she was a favorite among the mining camps, Crabtree was known simply as "Lotta." Her success continued when she moved to San Francisco, where between 1859 and 1864 she became "Miss Lotta, the San Francisco Favorite" and gradually achieved star billing in various legitimate theaters. Her performance specialty was comedy that included singing, dancing, farce, and minstrel-show routines. So well known was Crabtree that Adah Isaacs Menken, one of the highest-paid performers of her day, struck up a friendship with the young performer during her 1863 tour of the West.

In 1864 Crabtree headed for New York City, the essential road for any performer seeking national fame. After a rocky start that included tours to Chicago, Ohio, Boston, and New Orleans, her first major New York success was in John Brougham's stage adaptation of Charles Dickens's *The Old Curiosity Shop* in 1867. This free adaptation, titled *Little Nell and the Marchioness* and commissioned by Crabtree, featured her in a delightful dual role that she embodied with stunning speed and alacrity, evoking the pathos of Little Nell, then returning to the stage in a matter of minutes as the comic, ludicrous marchioness.

Wallack's Theatre was packed every night, and the two-week summer engagement was extended. The box office averaged $1,100 a night, and after twenty-eight days Crabtree's share reached almost $10,000, a staggering sum in those days. She had previously depended on existing dramatic material, ranging from

comic parodies such as *Jenny Lind* (or *Jenny Leatherlungs*) in 1863 to the perennial favorite of the 1860s, *Uncle Tom's Cabin*, in which she performed in 1866. The success of *Little Nell*, which she kept in her repertoire for twenty-five years, led to numerous commissions to established playwrights to create "star vehicles" for her. Crabtree began performing in full-length scripted plays, but she still maintained elements of variety-style performance by inserting songs and dance numbers. Her specialty was to grab a banjo and perform a "break-down," an energetic dance that mixed the Highland jig with clog dancing.

The majority of Crabtree's central roles were waiflike children, separated from their rightful parents and usually unaware of their own identities. She was adept at playing both genders and in 1869 in *The Ticket of Leave Man*, an early "convict drama" set in the slums of London, she played a fifteen-year-old boy. In addition to her music and dance expertise, she was known for being able to capture a naive innocence in her child characters while at the same time offering comic, exuberant humor. Her popularity not only produced numerous imitators, but at the height of her fame people all over the country danced the "Lotta Polka" and the "Lotta Gallop."

In addition to commissioning her own plays, Crabtree assembled her own company of actors to perform with in New York and on her numerous tours. Avoiding the standard gossip of the day concerning the "loose morals" of those in the theater profession, Crabtree and her company were above reproach. Her mother, who had sheltered her daughter from the taint of immorality that so persistently haunted other women performers, allowed her no theatrical friends. She controlled all of Crabtree's finances and most of the hiring, made sure that potential company members were thoroughly screened, and monitored her daughter's every move.

When the mania for equestrian performance (known as hippo drama) hit New York, Edmund Falconer adapted *Under Two Flags* for Crabtree in 1868 with a new title, *Firefly*. Along with her usual singing and dancing, Crabtree led a regiment and rode a horse speedily across a desert. Falconer also wrote *Heartsease* for her; it became her major new production in 1870. The play was unusual in that, unlike the majority of Crabtree's other vehicles, it had an American locale and theme that was close to her own experience in the California mining camps.

One of Crabtree's more fascinating collaborations was with David Belasco, a soon-to-be theater producer and impresario. In 1879 in San Francisco the young Belasco had performed with Crabtree in the role of Foxey Joe in a revival of *Little Nell and the Marchioness*. Several years later she commissioned Belasco and Clay Greene to write a play for her. She had promised them $5,000 for the script, of which $1,000 was a down payment. Both authors traveled to the opening of their play, *Pawn Ticket 210*, in Chicago in 1887. When Belasco saw the devastating reviews, he felt so embarrassed at the thought of facing Crabtree the next morning that he was prepared to forgo the remaining commission. To his astonishment Crabtree greeted him cheerfully and assured him that all of her plays had received bad reviews, but that the public always came. *Pawn Ticket 210* had a profitable run for her.

In 1891, near the end of one her most successful tours, Crabtree fell on her back during a performance, fracturing a vertebra. The final performances were cancelled. After recovering in 1892, she started performing again, but after six weeks of pain during performances the tour was cancelled. Crabtree never acted again, despite requests from numerous friends and dignitaries; against common theater practice of the day, she never mounted a farewell tour.

When Crabtree ended her enterprising and productive career at the age of forty-five, she retired as the wealthiest actress of her generation to have earned her own fortune. She gave generously during her lifetime to numerous charity organizations, including the Audubon Society, the American Society for the Prevention of Cruelty to Animals, and charities for retired actors who had fallen on hard times. One of her acts of philanthropy was to build a fountain in San Francisco, the city that made her famous. At her death in Boston, Massachusetts, she left $4 million, with more than half of it pledged to charity. Because she never married and all of her close relatives were dead, her will was contested by numerous people claiming to be related to the once-famous star.

Crabtree's fame and personal fortune was derived from playing versions of her eight-year-old self for nearly forty years; her theater career stands out as one of the leading examples of popular entertainment in the second half of the nineteenth century.

• Several libraries have considerable Crabtree memorabilia, reviews, and photos, including the New York Public Library at Lincoln Center; the Theater Collection at the Houghton Library, Harvard University; the Allen A. Brown Collection at the Boston Public Library; the Theater Collection at the Sterling Library, Yale University; and the Museum of the City of New York. Constance Rourke, *Troupers of the Gold Coast; or, The Rise of Lotta Crabtree* (1928), focuses on Crabtree's early tours in the West. A convincing case is made for Crabtree's work as an important early source for the American musical in Irene Comer, "*Little Nell and the Marchioness*: Milestone in the Development of the American Musical Comedy" (Ph.D. diss., Tufts Univ., 1979). David Dempsey, *The Triumphs and Trials of Lotta Crabtree* (1968), offers a fine examination of her life and career as well as sections that focus on the attacks made on her estate. Helen Marie Bates's *Lotta's Last Season* (1940), is a first-person account by an actress who worked with Crabtree on her last successful tour. Claudia D. Johnson, *American Actress: Perspective on the Nineteenth Century* (1984), has a chapter on Crabtree's talents as a comedienne. Lesley Ferris, *Acting Women: Images of Women in Theatre* (1990), explores the image of the "golden girl" in the career of Crabtree. An obituary is in the *New York Times*, 26 Sept. 1924.

LESLEY FERRIS

CRAFT, Ellen (1826?–1891), abolitionist and educator, was born on a plantation in Clinton, Georgia, the daughter of Major James Smith, a wealthy cotton planter, and Maria, his slave. At the age of eleven Ellen was given by her mistress (whose "incessant cruelty" Craft was later to recall) as a wedding present to Ellen's half sister Eliza on the young woman's marriage to Robert Collins of Macon, Georgia. Ellen became a skilled seamstress and ladies' maid, esteemed for her grace, intelligence, and sweetness of temper. In Macon she met another slave two years her senior, William Craft, to whom she was legally wed in 1846. William's owner had mortgaged him to a bank and then later sold him to a bank cashier, who hired him out to a cabinetmaker.

Because "the laws under which we lived did not recognize her to be a woman, but a mere chattel, to be bought and sold," as William wrote in the couple's autobiographical narrative, they devised a plan of escape. Ellen made a pair of men's trousers, while William worked a second job as a waiter to purchase their tickets for the North. On 21 December 1848, after obtaining Christmas passes from their owners, Ellen and William made their escape. Wearing a man's suit and green spectacles, the "almost white" Ellen disguised herself as "a most respectable looking gentleman," journeying North with William acting as her manservant. When Ellen attempted to book passage on a steamer out of Charleston, the ticket master insisted that she sign the register, but she could neither read nor write; fortunately, a young military officer stepped forward and offered to sign for the "gentleman."

During their journey by train, steamer, and ferry boat "Mr. William Johnson and slave" were constantly in danger of discovery by suspicious passengers and officials. Pretending to be an invalid, her face partially covered with poultices and her arm in a sling, Ellen Craft spoke little and kept to herself, while her "loyal servant" attended to his deaf and rheumatoid master during the day and slept in the baggage car at night. On Christmas Day the runaways reached Philadelphia, where they were welcomed by abolitionists, including William Still, who described their escape in *The Underground Rail Road* (1872), and a Quaker family, who offered them a home and taught them to read and write their names.

After a few weeks the fugitives went on to Boston, accompanied by another ex-slave, William Wells Brown, whose 1853 novel, *Clotel; or, The President's Daughter*, was inspired by the Crafts' story. With the support of abolitionists William Lloyd Garrison and Wendell Phillips, the Crafts obtained housing and employment, Ellen as a seamstress and William as a cabinetmaker. During their two-year sojourn in Boston, the couple appeared frequently at antislavery rallies. On 7 November 1850 they were remarried by Unitarian minister Theodore Parker. A month later, they fled Boston when members of the Vigilance Committee of Boston warned that their former owners, emboldened by the Fugitive Slave Act of 1850, had sent two slave catchers to arrest them. Although Ellen was ill at the time, the Crafts went to Maine and then to Nova Scotia, where they boarded a steamer for Liverpool, England.

In England, they studied writing, grammar, and scriptures at Ockham School, a trade school founded in Surrey by Lady Noel Byron. Ellen taught needlework and William taught cabinetmaking at the school. Although they were offered positions as matron and superintendent in the school's industrial department, they moved instead to London to open a boardinghouse and to organize an import-export business. With their friend Brown they joined the antislavery lecture circuit, traveling for six months throughout England and Scotland. Their home in the London suburb of Hammersmith, where they entertained prominent Britains and African Americans such as Sarah Remond, became a center of abolitionist activity.

Ellen, who had recoiled at the thought of bearing a child "to linger out a miserable existence under the wretched system of American slavery," gave birth to five children in England. And it was there, in 1860, that the Crafts published their slave narrative, which recounted the dramatic story of their escape from bondage. Between 1862 and 1867, William Craft made two trips to Dahomey, Africa, to persuade the African king to eliminate human sacrifice, abolish the slave trade, and sell cotton to the British. He was unsuccessful in this effort. In London, Ellen, who was active in the Women's Suffrage Association and the British and Foreign Freed-men's Aid Society, raised money to support the school that her husband founded in Dahomey. In 1865, with the help of British philanthropists, Ellen brought her mother, from whom she had been separated for thirty years, to London to live.

After nineteen years in England, Ellen, William, and three of their children returned in 1869 to Boston, leaving two children behind to continue their education. After a brief visit in Boston, they moved south and opened an industrial school at "Hickory Hill," a plantation in South Carolina just across the Georgia state line, where Ellen and her daughter taught a day session for children and a night class for adults. When the school was burned down by night riders in the fall of 1870, the Crafts moved to Savannah to help their son operate a boardinghouse, which they abandoned six months later after incurring considerable financial losses. In early 1871, the couple bought "Woodville," a plantation in Bryan County, and opened the Woodville Co-operative Farm School. While William was away fundraising, Ellen taught sewing and domestic arts and managed the plantation, which by 1874 included seventy-five acres of rice, cotton, and peas. They moved the school from a barn to a one-and-a-half-story frame building, but finally, mounting debts, insufficient capital, and the enmity of white farmers forced them to close the school in the 1880s.

Ellen Craft then moved to Charleston, South Carolina, to live with their daughter, Ellen, and son-in-law, William Demos Crum, a physician and later minister to Liberia. Her husband likely remained at Woodville, struggling to hold on to the property. Ellen died in Charleston and was buried under a tree on her Georgia plantation; her husband died three years later. One of the most celebrated African-American women of the

nineteenth century, Ellen Craft was noted for her daring escape from slavery and for her antislavery activities.

• Besides the Crafts' autobiographical narrative *Running a Thousand Miles for Freedom; or, The Escape of William and Ellen Craft from Slavery* (1860), the most complete accounts of Ellen Craft's life appear in Dorothy Sterling, *Black Foremothers: Three Lives* (1979), and R. J. M. Blackett, *Beating against the Barriers: Biographical Essays in Nineteenth-Century Afro-American History* (1986). In *The Underground Rail Road* (1872), William Still recounts the Crafts' escape and reprints their letters and articles from the *Liberator*. Other details about the Crafts appear in John Blassingame, ed., *Slave Testimony: Two Centuries of Letters, Speeches, Interviews, and Autobiographies* (1977), and Benjamin Quarles, *Black Abolitionists* (1969). Carter G. Woodson, *The Mind of the Negro as Reflected in Letters Written during the Crisis, 1800–1860* (1926), reproduces letters about the Crafts, while Larry Gara, "Ellen Craft," *Notable American Women*, vol. 1 (1971), pp. 396–98, provides bibliographic references.

MIRIAM DeCOSTA-WILLIS

CRAFT, William (1824–28 Jan. 1900), runaway slave and abolitionist lecturer, was born in Georgia, where he was a slave for the first twenty-four years of his life. In 1841 his owner, also named Craft, mortgaged William and his sister Sarah to a Macon bank. Later, when the slaveholder could not make the payments, the bank sold the slaves at an auction. Craft's new owner permitted him to hire himself out as a carpenter, and Craft was allowed to keep earnings over $220 annually. In 1846 William married Ellen, the daughter of a slave named Maria and her owner, James Smith. Two years later William and Ellen planned their escape from slavery. Ellen informed her mistress that she needed a few days to be with her "dying" mother, who lived twelve miles from Macon, and William begged his owner for permission to accompany his wife. Disguised as a white man traveling with a servant, the couple left Macon with a five-day pass on 21 December 1848. Besides dressing in men's clothing and cutting her hair, Ellen, who was illiterate, kept her right hand in a sling to make certain that she would not be asked for her signature. A large bandage covered one side of her face, making their pretext of traveling to see a specialist in Philadelphia believable, while green tinted glasses hid her eyes.

Using money they had secretly saved, the Crafts traveled by train to Savannah, by steamboat to Charleston, by boat to Wilmington, North Carolina, and by train through Virginia and Maryland. In Baltimore a railroad clerk suspected that she was an abolitionist attempting to help a slave escape, but Ellen's believable portrayal of an arrogant, wealthy slave owner allayed his suspicions. When William and Ellen reached Philadelphia on Christmas Day, their 1,000-mile journey elated abolitionists. "No other escape, with the possible exception of Frederick Douglass' and Josiah Henson's, created such a stir in antebellum America," according to historian R. J. M. Blackett (1986, p. 87). The *Boston Chronotype* hailed the couple's ingenuity (Blackett, p. 89, note 6).

In late January 1849 William Wells Brown, himself a runaway slave, escorted the Crafts to Boston, where William, who was prevented from practicing carpentry by discriminatory artisans, opened a secondhand furniture store. The publicity generated by their escape brought the couple to the attention of slave catchers after Congress enacted the Fugitive Slave Law in September 1850. In October two agents of the Crafts' owner spent a week in Boston trying to capture the runaways but were repulsed by the League of Freedom, a black association formed for their protection, and a revitalized Boston Vigilance Committee. The Crafts' former owner then petitioned President Millard Fillmore for assistance. His decision to make the Crafts a symbol of the federal government's support for the Fugitive Slave Law forced them to flee to England. Before their departure, the Reverend Theodore Parker married them on 7 December 1850, granting them the religious ceremony they had been denied in the South.

For three years the Crafts attended Ockham School, an agricultural school in Surrey, England, where they studied English, music, the Bible, printing, basket making, and farming. William taught cabinet making, and Ellen taught needlework. Later, they modeled schools in Dahomey (present-day Benin), Africa, and Georgia after Ockham. During this time, the first of their five children was born. In 1859 they helped organize the London Emancipation Society, and in 1860 they published *Running a Thousand Miles for Freedom*, a narrative of their escape from slavery. They joined William Wells Brown, Frederick Douglass, and others on a lecture circuit throughout England. In these antislavery tours, William Craft in particular worked to refute the myth that American slaves were docile and unwilling to rebel. He also pressed British religious leaders to urge their American counterparts to challenge Christian apologists for slavery. His confidence as a lecturer grew as he spoke throughout the British Isles. In 1863 he criticized John Crawfund, president of the Ethnological Society, and James Hunt of the Anthropological Society for their assertion that blacks were intellectually inferior to Europeans.

Craft supported the free-produce movement to make slavery unprofitable by urging consumers to boycott slave-produced goods in favor of goods produced by free blacks in West Africa, a crusade espoused in 1850 by Henry Highland Garnet, Frederick Douglass, Charles Lenox Remond, and Nathaniel Paul. From 1865 to 1867, Craft labored in Whydah, Dahomey, as an agent for the African Aid Society, a British-based effort to encourage the production of free-labor cotton.

The Crafts returned to the United States in 1869, first to Boston and then to "Hickory Hill," a plantation they purchased in Georgia. In 1870, however, night riders burned their house and barn and completely destroyed their crops. They then moved to Savannah, where they ran a boardinghouse with the help of their son. Severe financial losses forced them to take a three-year lease on "Woodville," a plantation twenty miles

from Savannah. Here Ellen managed a school, and William solicited money to operate it. However, William's participation in Reconstruction politics as chairman of the 1874 Republican congressional convention for the local district and as a candidate for the state senate made him a target of further hostility. After he was accused of raising funds under false pretenses and could not account for $7,000 in contributions, the school at Woodville was forced to close in 1878.

The Crafts spent their last years at the Charleston home of their daughter and her husband. The *Charleston Enquirer* declared upon William's death that "he was an unassuming genial gentleman, and reared a family that has proven a credit to the race." William and Ellen Craft were extraordinary individuals who in their defiance of American law were pioneers in the African-American tradition of civil disobedience.

• The best sources on William and Ellen Craft are R. J. M. Blackett, *Beating against the Barriers: Biographical Essays in Nineteenth-Century Afro-American History* (1986), and *Building an Antislavery Wall: Black Americans in the Atlantic Abolitionist Movement*, 1830–1860 (1983); Florence B. Freedman, *Two Tickets to Freedom: The True Story of Ellen and William Craft, Fugitive Slaves* (1971); C. Peter Ripley et al., eds., *The Black Abolitionist Papers*, vol. 1 (1985); Mary Shepard, *The Disguise* (1972); and Dorothy Sterling, *Black Foremothers: Three Lives* (1979). Letters of the Crafts are in the *Journal of Negro History* 10, no. 3 (1925): 446–48. An obituary from the *Charleston Enquirer* is reprinted in the *Savannah Tribune*, 17 Feb. 1900.

WILLIAM SERAILE

CRAFTS, James Mason (4 Mar. 1839–20 June 1917), chemist and professor, was born in Boston, Massachusetts, the son of Royal Altemont Crafts, a New England woolen merchant and manufacturer, and Marianne Mason, the daughter of Jeremiah Mason, a U.S. senator from New Hampshire. As a child growing up in a prosperous Boston family, Crafts had opportunities to meet community leaders such as William Barton Rogers, a founder and first president of Massachusetts Institute of Technology. His early education was in the Boston Latin School. He then entered Harvard's Lawrence Scientific School and completed the B.S. in 1858. He had become interested in mining and stayed on another year to pursue graduate work in the field. In 1860 he spent a year in Freiberg in Saxony, where he studied metallurgy with Karl F. Plattner. After Plattner's death he studied in Heidelberg under Robert Bunsen during the period when R. W. Bunsen and G. R. Kirchhoff were developing the spectroscope. After two years, however, he enrolled in the École de Médicin in Paris as a student of Charles-Adolphe Wurtz. It was here that he became acquainted with Charles Friedel, a young faculty member talented in organic chemistry and mineralogy, with whom he studied the close relation between the hydrogen compounds of carbon and silicon.

Upon his return to the United States in 1865, Crafts spent a year as an inspector of mines in Mexico and in California. In 1868 he became a chemistry professor at the newly founded Cornell University, where he taught qualitative analysis and organic chemistry and served as chairman of the department. Crafts was a strong proponent of laboratory work as a supplement to theoretical lectures at a time when most American universities omitted laboratory work in favor of lecture room demonstrations by the professor. In 1869 he published *A Short Course in Qualitative Analysis with the New Notation*. The book subsequently went through five editions. In June Crafts married Clémencine Haggerty of New York City; they had four children.

In 1871, Crafts accepted a position in the chemistry department at MIT, which had been chartered a decade earlier. Here he introduced laboratory innovations that brought analytical chemistry to a new level of accomplishment. His balances and optical apparatus were placed in a separate room free of dust and fumes, and laboratory ventilation was installed. Each laboratory bench was provided with water suction pumps, and steam tables were provided for evaporating solutions. Crafts had observed the suction pumps in Bunsen's laboratory in Heidelberg and was one of the first to introduce them in American laboratories. Crafts was also and innovator in the organic chemistry course. Providing a list of the most advanced textbooks, he allowed students to choose the one they themselves preferred. He also encouraged students to develop a research attitude by extending their experiments beyond the preparation of an assigned compound.

After four years at MIT Crafts's declining health forced him to take a leave of absence. Returning to Paris, he carried out research in Friedel's laboratory. The collaboration led to discovery in 1877 of the general reaction that became known as the Friedel-Crafts reaction. The basic reaction involved the use of anhydrous aluminum chloride to catalyze the combination of an aromatic hydrocarbon such as benzene with an alkyl chloride such as methyl chloride. The reaction eliminated hydrogen chloride and formed a compound of the aromatic and alkyl residues such as toluene, also known as methyl benzene. Extensive studies by Friedel and Crafts revealed that the reaction was a very general one that involved a great variety of aromatic compounds (benzene, substituted benzenes, napthalenes, heterocylclic compounds, etc.); alkylating agents (alkyl halides including bromides and iodides, alcohols, esters); and anhydrous catalysts ($AlCl_3$, $AlBr_3$, BF_3, HF, H_2SO_4, $ZnCl_2$, $SnCl_4$). Besides being a useful procedure for synthesis of hydrocarbons, the reaction has been adapted to the synthesis of aromatic ketones, aldehydes, amides, and various other types of compounds. Crafts remained in Paris from 1874 to 1888, working much of the time with Friedel in exploring many variants of the reaction. He also carried on studies of the density of halogens at high temperatures, and thermometry.

In 1888 Crafts returned to the United States. Although he had resigned from MIT in 1880, when the new reaction was under serious study, he was quickly restored to his position in the institute and took over the instruction of organic chemistry. In 1897, following the sudden death of President Walker, Crafts was chosen to be the new president of MIT. He retained the position for less than three years because he wanted to have more time for research. He continued his research in a private laboratory at the institute until 1911, when neuritic problems made physical work impossible. His last years were spent in preparing earlier studies for publication, mostly in French journals. These final publications did not deal with the Friedel-Crafts reaction but concerned, instead, earlier work on thermometry and vapor tension. By this time many organic chemists were extending their studies of the Friedel-Crafts reaction in directions that went well beyond the scope pursued by the original collaborators. Crafts died in Boston.

• The principal early papers by Friedel and Crafts appear in *Comptes Rendus Hebdomadaires des Séances de l'Académie des Sciences* 84 (1877): 1292 and 1450. Charles R. Cross, "James Mason Crafts," *Biographical Memoirs of the National Academy of Sciences* 9 (1920): 159–77, provides a list of Crafts's scientific publications. See also Avery A. Ashdown, "James Mason Crafts," *Journal of Chemical Education* 5 (1928): 911–21. Alexander R. Surrey, *Name Reactions in Organic Chemistry* (1954), pp. 72–74, has a brief discussion of the Friedel-Crafts reaction. C. C. Price's and E. Berliner's review of the modern applications of the reaction appear in *Organic Reactions*, ed. Roger Adams: vol. 3 (1946), pp. 1–82, and vol. 5 (1949), p. 229. See also H. C. Brown and H. W. Pearsall, *Journal of the American Chemical Society* 74 (1952): 191, and C. A. Thomas, *Anhydrous Aluminum Chloride in Organic Chemistry* (1941). An obituary is in *Proceedings of the American Academy of Arts and Sciences* 53 (1917–1918): 801–4.

AARON J. IHDE

CRAFTS, William (24 Jan. 1787–23 Sept. 1826), author and lawyer, was born in Charleston, South Carolina, the son of William Crafts, an affluent merchant, and Margaret Tébout. The handsome and precocious Crafts studied under Charleston tutors and then went to Harvard College, entering in 1802 as a sophomore. Young Crafts's geniality and his ease in learning foreign languages brought him popularity and a reputation for both wit and scholarship. After graduation in 1805, he studied law in Charleston at the office of Ford and DeSaussure; but after three years and apparently with only superficial knowledge he returned to Cambridge to pursue a master's degree.

Admitted to the South Carolina bar in 1809, Crafts, though gifted, never attained widespread fame as a lawyer apparently because he shunned tasks that demanded exacting knowledge and sustained effort. He was more successful in criminal cases by swaying juries with his oratorical skills. His style was brilliant; his substance was deficient. Entering politics as a Federalist, he was elected to the state house of representatives in 1810, failed at reelection, and was elected again two years later. He served in the state senate the last six years of his life. Three years before his death Crafts married his cousin, Caroline Homes of Boston.

Crafts's literary and political careers were concurrent, though he attained more contemporary success as an author than as a lawyer. He and the more talented Hugh Swinton Legaré were the most conspicuous Charleston lawyer-authors of the period. Before William Gilmore Simms became Charleston's most outstanding author, Crafts and Legaré reigned over the literary circles in that city. Crafts's greatest appeal, however, was in his oratory. An oration he delivered while a graduate student at Harvard College was enthusiastically received, despite its faulty Latin, and added to his growing reputation as an eloquent speaker in demand for public occasions. Later in Charleston, his *Eulogy on the Late Rev. James Dewar Simons, Rector of St. Philip's* (1814) was acclaimed locally as a masterpiece in eloquence. Always loyal to Harvard, in 1817 he gave the Phi Beta Kappa address, "The Influence of Moral Causes on National Character." The *Charleston Courier* printed a number of his speeches, including one to the New England Society of Charleston and his most famous one before the legislature in November 1813, in which he adamantly rebuffed opponents of the Free School Act. Some passages are striking, but the speeches as a whole are vitiated by poetic bombast, a trait not uncommon in southern oratory of the era. Legaré wrote that Crafts thought only of an impression he might make before an audience. His manner "reminded one of an undergraduate at a college exhibition."

Many of Crafts's essays in the *Courier* reflect the graceful, urbane, and gently humorous literary style of English essayist Joseph Addison, whether Crafts is castigating British critics on America—as in "Literary Sparring"—or describing Charleston, the theater, Sullivan's Island, and the city's popular Race Week.

Some of the faults and merits of his prose may also be found in his poetry, including the two small volumes of verse he published in Charleston: *The Raciad and Other Occasional Poems* (1810) and *Sullivan's Island, The Raciad, and Other Poems* (1820). Composed too hastily, these poems are blemished with imitativeness and are generally lacking in substance. The adverse influence of the Irish poet Thomas Moore is evident in some of Crafts's Anacreontic love poems. Typical short poems—"The Infidel Girl," "A Dying Mother to Her Erring Daughter," and "To a Friend at Sea"—are didactic and sentimental. A few of Crafts's poems borrow subjects from his essays. His description of "Sullivan's Island" is a slavish imitation of Alexander Pope's "Windsor Forest," whereas "The Raciad," his best poem, written in the manner of Pope's "The Rape of the Lock," recounts the ambiance of Charlestonians during their favorite sporting week.

During the last few years of his life, Crafts experienced many disappointments and increasingly debilitating illness. His professional business had dwindled greatly, his influence in the legislature was on the wane, and he had failed to attain any eminence in his profession. In search of health, he journeyed to Lebanon Springs, New York, where he died. He was buried in Boston in the King's Chapel churchyard.

Critics have given little attention to Crafts. Jay B. Hubbell's essay in *The South in American Literature* (1954) remains the most judicious appraisal. Recent scholars have not attempted to rekindle enthusiasm for Crafts's accomplishments. In *The History of Southern Literature* (1985) modern scholars accord Crafts only passing notice as a minor writer of the Old South. Hubbell aptly summarized Crafts as "a facile dabbler in literary trifles" but conceded that in selecting the lighter side of antebellum Charleston for materials he tried "to portray a most interesting aspect of American life which the abler Southern writers who followed him left almost untouched."

• Crafts's original papers have disappeared, but miscellaneous pieces and clippings are housed in the South Caroliniana Library, University of South Carolina, Columbia, and in the Charleston County Library, Charleston. For additional writings, see *The Sea Serpent; or, Gloucester Hoax; A Dramatic Jeu d'Esprit in Three Sets* (1819) and *A Selection, in Prose and Poetry, from the Miscellaneous Writings of the Late William Crafts*, ed., with a memoir, by Samuel Gilman (1828). For critiques, consult Hugh Swinton Legaré, "Crafts's Fugitive Writings, *Southern Review* 1 (May 1828: 503–29; repr. in *Writings of Hugh Swinton Legaré*, vol. 2, 1845); J. M. and W. F. Crafts, *The Crafts Family* (1893); V. L. Parrington, *Main Currents in American Thought*, vol. 2 (1927); and Jay B. Hubbell, *The South in American Literature* (1954).

RAY M. ATCHISON

CRAIG, Elisabeth May Adams (19 Dec. 1888–15 July 1975), journalist, was born in Coosaw Mines, Beaufort County, South Carolina, daughter of Alexander Adams, a phosphate miner, and Elizabeth Ann Essery. Her mother died when she was four, and two years later she was taken in by Frances and William Weymouth, owners of the phosphate mines that employed her father.

Elisabeth moved with the Weymouths to Washington, D.C., when she was twelve, attended Washington Central High School, and wrote for the school newspaper. She briefly attended nursing school at George Washington Hospital and in 1909 married Donald Alexander Craig, a columnist with the Washington bureau of the *New York Herald*. Her attendance at nursing school and her marriage caused a break with her foster parents, who felt they could no longer control her. As a young wife and mother of a daughter and son, Craig was active in the suffrage movement and worked for reform in education: proudly marching in "Mrs. Harvey Wiley's homemakers' section" in the suffragist parade at Woodrow Wilson's inaugural; founding a society for young mothers; circulating sample issues of "Junior News," an unsuccessful newspaper for children she co-wrote; and organizing and serving as the first president of the Parent-Teacher Association at Washington's Bryant School.

Craig first gained serious attention in journalism with a feature article for the *New York World* about how "silent Cal Coolidge" dictated correspondence to his secretary. After Donald Craig's serious injury in 1923 in an automobile accident as he was traveling with the press following President Warren G. Harding in Colorado, Craig began work with her husband on the column, "On the Inside in Washington," for the Guy Gannett Publishing Company, with her own by-line first appearing with the column in 1931. In addition, in 1931 she formed a news bureau with Buck Bryant, a member of the *New York World*'s Washington bureau before the newspaper stopped publication early that year. She covered the Capitol beat and was syndicated in newspapers in Maine, Montana, New York, and North Carolina. Craig's husband died in 1936, and she renegotiated with Gannett to give her a Washington correspondent byline and column, "Inside in Washington," for the chain's Maine newspapers. Gannett later publicized her column as "a breakfast-table habit of Maine readers."

During the 1930's Craig's columns and occasional pieces for *Independent Woman* included "society news" about Washington personages and events but primarily concentrated on New Deal politics and policies. Craig saw the New Deal as a "long overdue" social movement and argued, "We can't just use the word 'democracy' and expect the world to kow-tow. We've got to justify our form of government by making it work for all the people" (*Portland Press Herald*, 30 Nov. 1940). At the same time, Craig never claimed a political party affiliation and didn't vote because of her belief in the "Fourth Estate being the Fourth Estate."

Throughout her career, Craig was actively involved in journalism organizations. She joined the American Newspaper Guild when it originated in 1933 and was an active opponent of "left-wing" domination. As an early member of the Washington Newspaper Guild, she served on its executive committee, including two terms as president. She was a founder of Eleanor Roosevelt's Press Conference Association, and she served as president of the Women's National Press Club of America in 1943–1945. Craig made it a point each year to seek admission to the male-only dinner of the White House Press Correspondents' Association.

During World War II, Craig received accreditation as a war correspondent and from 1944 to 1946 filed dispatches about London V-bomb raids, the Normandy campaign, the liberation of Paris, and the advance of the Allied army into Germany. "Khaki-clad," she "heated water in an old tin can over bonfires, and washed her feet in her helmet" (Montgomery, p. 13), and in 1946 she was decorated with a "theater ribbon" for service as a war correspondent by the War Department. Following Germany's surrender, Craig continued to cover stories from Greece, Italy, Palestine, and Egypt.

After World War II Craig continued to publish her Maine column and in 1946 became one of the first journalists to appear on the radio and later television program, "Meet the Press." Gannett publicized Craig as a woman who had "the world as her beat." Strongly anticommunist, she covered Cold War stories about the Good Neighbor Policy, traveling in South and Central America. She was the only woman reporter on the press plane to accompany President Truman to the 1947 Inter-American Security Conference in Brazil. In a widely publicized incident Craig informed the Navy of her intention to return from the conference with her twenty-five male correspondents aboard the USS *Missouri*. Despite wide support she was refused. Two years later, however, she became the first newspaper correspondent on a combat ship at sea, covering air-sea maneuvers on the aircraft carrier *Midway*. She interviewed Fidel Castro just after he had successfully overthrown the Batista regime in Cuba. Between 1949 and 1952 Craig flew on a "coal-carrying" plane in the Berlin airlift; circled the globe on Military Air Transport by invitation of the Air Force; and, during the Korean War, became the first woman correspondent to stay aboard a battleship and to cover the Kaesong truce talks. She was the only woman on the first flight by reporters over the North Pole. On the home front, Craig wrote about Washington politics and followed the presidential campaign trail.

Craig became a "celebrity" journalist who was often photographed and interviewed, achieving a popular culture status as the subject of a *New Yorker* cartoon in 1959. Her newsworthiness came partly because of numerous examples of her "firsts" as an establishment woman journalist with a reputation as a "visible, vocal feminist," and her "irrepressible" and "toughest questions" at presidential press conferences. Craig's early notoriety came when she defended her profession after Franklin Roosevelt castigated the press corps for not adequately informing the public, with the *New York World-Telegram* observing that "the female of the species is more deadly than the male." She led assaults before the Senate and House of Representatives committees to install the first "ladies rooms" in the press galleries and shortly after was elected in 1944 to the Standing Committee of Correspondents (which governs the press galleries) as its first woman member. She was also made the unfortunate subject of "recurring jokes" because of her exchange of "jibes" challenging President Kennedy about the controversial "woman question" at press conferences in the early 1960s, so that when the word "sex" was added as an amendment to Title VII of the Civil Rights Act of 1964 Capitol Hill insiders referred to the measure as the "May Craig Amendment." Craig also received publicity because she cultivated what some referred to as the "stereotype of a precise school teacher" in appearance and manner. The "raspy" voice that called out "Mr. President! Mr. President!" from her first or second row position at presidential press conferences became as famous as her blue suits, pink jewelry, "un-bobbed hair tied in an old-fashioned knot" under pink hats "with a hat pin."

She retired at age seventy-six after one of her last widely circulated columns was published in 1964. "Decline of the United States—and Fall," reprinted in *U.S. News and World Report* under the headline, "A Woman Writer Takes a Critical Look at America," questioned the strength of the national character and will, both public and private. She singled out American conduct in the Vietnam War for some of her harshest remarks. Craig had begun work on her unfinished autobiography, which she titled "From the Sidelines" prior to retirement.

Craig died in a nursing home in Silver Spring, Maryland, from complications of cardiovascular disease. Upon her death, the senator from Maine, Edmund Muskie, noted that "her personal characteristics were annoying and endearing at one and the same time. She was peppery, undaunted in her questioning and yet one never really resented it. She had an eye for the great issues and the key figures in the unfolding scene."

Craig's significance lies in her struggle, which began before World War I, to achieve equality for women in journalism. She earned a column byline presenting "a woman's view" of the news during the founding years of the political column on the American scene, and she kept it for more than thirty years. A wife and mother, "Miss May" was part of the mainstream establishments of government and journalism, who nonetheless successfully reduced barriers placed on how women could report the news, whether in Washington or around the world.

• The Library of Congress holds Craig's papers, including early drafts and outlines of her uncompleted autobiography, scrapbooks, clippings, and correspondence. The Franklin D. Roosevelt, Harry S. Truman, Dwight D. Eisenhower, John F. Kennedy, and Lyndon B. Johnson presidential libraries have small collections of correspondence and other items related to Craig. Correspondence between Craig and Eleanor Roosevelt is also found in the Franklin D. Roosevelt Library. Clippings and biographical materials are held by the Guy Gannett Publishing Company and the NBC News, Washington, D.C., archives of "Meet the Press." Biographical articles include Eleanor Harris, "May Craig: TV's Most Unusual Star," *Look*, 26 Apr. 1962, pp. 109–10; Patricia Schroth, "Meet May Craig," *Down East*, Aug. 1959, pp. 32–35; and Ruth Montgomery, "'Little Woman in Blue' Who Outquips President," *Washington Times-Herald*, 7 Jan. 1945, p. 13. For brief sketches and references to Craig's significance in the struggle for women's rights see Blanche Linden-Ward and Carol Hurd Green, *American Women in the 1960s: Changing the Future* (1991), and Maurine H. Beasley and Sheila J. Gibbons, *Taking Their Place: A Documentary History of Women and Journalism* (1993). Obituaries are in the *New York Times* and *Portland Press Herald*, both 16 July 1975.

JENNIFER L. TEBBE

CRAIG, Isaac (1742–14 June 1826), American revolutionary officer and Pittsburgh business and civic leader, was born in Hillsborough, Ireland, to parents whose names and occupations are not known. He came to Philadelphia in late 1765 and worked in that city for about ten years as a master carpenter and builder. He became a patriot and in November 1775 was appointed as a first lieutenant in the first company of marines. That year Craig served on the *Andrew Doria*, a ship in the squadron of Commodore Esek Hopkins and a vessel known for its successful assaults that year against British forts in the West Indies at Montagu and Nassau.

After Craig's return to Philadelphia in 1776, he became active in the Continental army. That year Craig was promoted to the rank of captain and served in the marine corp of Major Samuel Nichols. After Nichols's corp was ordered to join the army as infantrymen, Craig and other members of this newly created army contingent took part in the capture of the Hessians at Trenton on Christmas night 1776. Craig also fought in the battle of Princeton in late December 1776 and early January 1777. He was appointed on 3 March 1777 as a captain in Colonel Thomas Proctor's regiment, took part with this regiment that year in the battle of Brandywine, and was slightly injured during it. In 1777 Craig also commanded the company that cannonaded the Chew House during the battle of Germantown and spent the winter of 1777–1778 with George Washington's army in one of the log huts at Valley Forge. In April 1778 Craig was sent with four other officers to Carlisle to learn from a Captain Coren about the preparation of munitions and the manufacturing of gunpowder. In late April 1779 Craig was ordered to Billingsport, a town along the Delaware just south of Philadelphia, and served during June and July of that year as commander of the town's fort. He also served in 1779 at Easton under General John Sullivan, assumed a position of leadership in this campaign against the Indians of the Six Nations, and then spent the winter of 1779–1780 in Morristown, New Jersey.

From the spring of 1780 until the end of the War of Independence, Craig became an important revolutionary leader in western Pennsylvania. In late April 1780 he was ordered to move artillery and military stores from Carlisle to Pittsburgh and the next month completed this major task. Craig was named as commander of Fort Pitt in the early summer of 1780 and in late July of the following year led troops from Fort Pitt to Detroit to assist George Rogers Clark in his expedition against the British. After his return from the Detroit expedition in December 1781, Craig was promoted to the rank of major. In 1782 he took measures to bolster defenses at Fort Pitt and to protect the American position at the forks of the Ohio River from attacks by the British and their Indian allies. The same year Craig conducted an expedition to the mouth of the Cuyahoga River to investigate British activities in the Western Reserve and then filed a detailed report about British posts in this region.

After the American Revolution, Craig became part of the aristocracy of early Pittsburgh. He formed in 1784 with Colonel Stephen Bayard a real estate partnership, selling land parcels to settlers coming to the vicinity. Craig married Amelia Neville on 1 February 1785; they had five sons. Six years later Craig was appointed as deputy quartermaster general and military storekeeper of Pittsburgh. As deputy quartermaster he was invested with many significant responsibilities. Craig was empowered to send troops, arms, and provisions to forts located between the Ohio and Mississippi rivers and was delegated powers to build flatboats and ships for the national government, to supervise mail service in the upper Ohio valley, and to erect new forts in that region. In carrying out his responsibilities, Craig led federal troops against the rebels during the 1794 Whisky Rebellion and that same year headed an expedition to assist "Mad" Anthony Wayne in his campaign against the Indians. Four years later he ordered the launching of two ships, the *President Adams* and the *Senator Ross*, to protect American positions in the lower Mississippi River valley.

In addition to his work in real estate and encouragement of the river trade, Craig promoted commercial activity in other ways. In 1797 he established with James O'Hara the first glass factory west of the Alleghenies and thus became involved in the profitable manufacturing of window glass and bottles in early Pittsburgh. He was named in 1786 as one of the incorporators of the First Presbyterian Church of Pittsburgh, was a charter member in 1785 of Pittsburgh Masonic Lodge No. 45, contributed in 1787 to the creation of the Pittsburgh Academy (which later became the University of Pittsburgh), and was elected in 1787 to the American Philosophical Society. Craig also made significant contributions during the War of 1812, helping to prepare munitions for American armies located in western Pennsylvania. He retired in 1815 to a large farm on Montour Island, located about nine miles from Pittsburgh in the Ohio River, where he died.

The career of Craig reflects much about revolutionary America and the early republic. Having distinguished himself during the War of Independence, Craig became part of the aristocracy of early Pittsburgh. He played a prominent part as a loyal Federalist, maintaining western forts and suppressing the Whiskey Insurrection. Craig, too, promoted commercial activities in frontier Pittsburgh; he helped to develop boating as a major industry in the town, encouraged trade with other towns along the Ohio and Mississippi rivers, and fostered its glass industry. In other ways, he displayed leadership in early Pittsburgh.

• The Craig papers are housed in the Carnegie Library in Pittsburgh and contain ledgers and valuable letters concerning his business career. A terse account of Craig's early life and of his contributions to the American Revolution appears in *Memoirs of Allegheny County Pennsylvania*, vol. 1 (1904), pp. 357–58. *The Sketch of the Life and Services of Isaac Craig* (1854), which was written by his son Neville B. Craig, is the most comprehensive study and contains lengthy sections regarding Craig's achievements during the American Revolution. Leland D. Baldwin, *Whiskey Rebels* (1939), and Thomas P. Slaughter, *The Whiskey Rebellion* (1986), well assess Craig's role in this episode. Craig's career as a businessman is evaluated in Solon J. Buck and Elizabeth H. Buck, *The Planting of Civilization in Western Pennsylvania* (1939); Leland D. Baldwin, *The Keelboat Age on Western Waters* (1941); and Lowell Innes, *Early Glass of the Pittsburgh District* (1950).

WILLIAM WEISBERGER

CRAIG, Malin (5 Aug. 1875–25 July 1945), chief of staff of the U.S. Army, was born in St. Joseph, Missouri, the son of Louis Aleck Craig, an army officer, and

Georgie Malin. Craig's youth was typical of children in army families, moving frequently to new posts in Kansas, Arizona, and New Mexico. Family heritage drew Craig toward a military career. Along with his father, both grandfathers had been army officers. Craig's younger brother, Louis Aleck Craig, Jr., also entered military service, retiring as inspector general of the U.S. Army in 1952.

After a solid academic preparation at the Georgetown School and College in Washington, D.C., Craig received an appointment to the U.S. Military Academy in West Point, New York, from the District of Columbia and enrolled in 1894. He graduated in 1898, standing thirty-third in a class of fifty-nine, and he was commissioned as a second lieutenant in the Fourth Infantry. Craig, however, preferred mounted service, and when the army expanded during the Spanish-American War, he transferred to the Sixth Cavalry, with which he participated in the Santiago campaign.

Craig's career between 1898 and 1910 was active and varied but nonetheless typical for army officers of the time. From 1898 through 1900 he rode with the Fourth Cavalry in Wyoming and Oklahoma. In 1900 he went overseas with the China Relief Expedition. Posted next in the Philippines, Craig found an intellectual mentor and professional role model in General J. Franklin Bell, under whom he served as aide-de-camp. When Bell became commandant of the Infantry and Cavalry School at Fort Leavenworth, Craig soon won an assignment there, and he graduated near the top of his class in 1904. His high standing admitted him to the Army Staff College, also at Fort Leavenworth, from which he graduated in 1905. Craig then returned to active duty and served until 1910 with cavalry units in western garrisons, and he served a second tour in the Philippines. Accompanying him was his wife, Genevieve Woodruff, whom he had married in 1901; together they had one child.

Beginning in 1910 Craig's assignments revealed his superiors' growing awareness of his pronounced capacities for planning and staff work. He did so well as a student at the Army War College, from which he graduated in 1910, that he was retained as an instructor for the next academic year. He took special interest in creating complex map exercises, notable both for their realism—he drew on genuine historical situations for inspiration—and for their intellectual rigor. Assignment to the General Staff followed, and Craig served as chief of staff for the Maneuver Division in 1911 and as assistant to the chief of staff of the Western Division in 1911–1912. Officially assigned to the First Cavalry from 1912 to 1916, Craig shuttled between troop duties and detached service, including a six-month stint as chief of staff of General Bell's Second Division on the Texas-Mexico border. From 1916 until the United States entered World War I, Craig served as an instructor at the Leavenworth schools.

Promoted to major in May 1917 and to lieutenant colonel soon after, Craig quickly obtained important assignments with the new American Expeditionary Force. In August he became chief of staff of General

Hunter Liggett's Forty-first Division. After arriving in France in December, Liggett was elevated to command of the U.S. I Corps, and Craig accompanied him, serving as chief of staff on the corps level through the Marne, St.-Mihiel, and Meuse-Argonne campaigns. For his services Craig won a number of citations, most notably the Distinguished Service Medal, for his "personal influence, aggressiveness, and untiring efforts" during operations at Chateau Thierry, Ourcq, and Vesle, and especially for his part in helping to plan the rescue of the famous "Lost Battalion" of the Seventy-seventh Division. Known for his frank appraisals of subordinate officers and their capacity for responsible command, Craig was promoted to colonel in February 1918 and to brigadier general in the wartime National Army in June. He ended his overseas tour in 1919 as chief of staff of the Third Army, the U.S. contingent in the Army of Occupation.

Like most career officers who held temporary National Army commissions during the war emergency, Craig reverted to his regular army rank of major during the demobilization. His talents had not gone unobserved, however. He was again promoted to brigadier general, this time in the regular army, in April 1921. For the next fourteen years Craig served in a variety of senior command and staff positions at home and abroad, including important stints as chief of cavalry, commander of the Panama Canal Department, and commandant of the Army War College.

In 1935 Craig succeeded General Douglas MacArthur as chief of staff of the U.S. Army. His selection came as somewhat of a surprise to insiders. Craig had never been touted as a leading candidate, and he had not actively campaigned for the position. He won the post primarily on his merits and his demonstrated professionalism in not seeking the assignment. He inherited an understaffed and underfunded force in an increasingly dangerous world. Nonetheless, MacArthur had also handed over a five-year plan for rearming and recruiting men into a larger U.S. Army. Craig was faced with intraservice clashes over the allocation of funds and intense congressional scrutiny of nearly all military expenditures, but he succeeded in revealing that the nation's military preparedness was in such a low state of readiness that its army could only be called "an unfinished and unassembled machine."

During Craig's tenure as chief of staff, no detail concerning military efficiency escaped his attention. Believing that "new devices for war are of critical importance" for an army to win on the battlefield, Craig actively supported weapons development in many areas. He stood in the forefront of the move to adopt the semiautomatic M1 Garand rifle, destined to become the standard arm of the World War II infantryman. Armor and air power interested Craig greatly, but he did not support their expansion at the expense of the arms. An astute observer of military events in China and Spain, Craig concluded that neither tanks nor planes were "decisive in land operations. They are auxiliaries . . . to the Infantry," he warned. He opposed the tendency of armor proponents to detach their forces for independent operations instead of using them in hard-hitting thrusts that supported decisive actions. An advocate of motorization, mechanization, and modernization, Craig also pushed for standardization of equipment to facilitate logistics. Craig's challenges were formidable; even when he left the chief of staff's position in 1939, he still felt that he had not done enough in antitank weapons, coast defense, and many other areas.

Craig's concerns were not limited to matériel problems. He criticized the army's war plans as unrealistic, complaining that they relied too much on paper units and conjectural supply while completely ignoring the element of time. He wanted the army school system to pay greater attention to the application of theories of mobility and firepower rather than obsessing about the validity of the theories themselves. He urged greater attention to industrial preparedness, which he believed "must go hand in hand with military effort." Craig endorsed a controversial plan to sell American-built planes to the British as a way to help the U.S. Army Air Corps by supporting the struggling American aircraft industry. Perhaps his greatest concern was manpower. He tried to find ways to fill the ranks of the newly approved 168,000-man regular army. At the same time, he was a great supporter of the National Guard; Reserve Officer Training Corps programs expanded during his time as chief of staff; and the corps of cadets at West Point increased by one-third. By 1939 Craig had advanced the Protective Mobilization Plan, which called for a quick expansion in time of war—from about 150,000 soldiers in the U.S. Army to 400,000 in one month's time, with growth to one million to follow—a program reminiscent of John C. Calhoun's "expansible army" plan proposed over a hundred years earlier. Still, even with all these accomplishments, in 1939 Craig complained that he continued to lack a "clear definition of what constituted adequacy in normal military defense." On the eve of Germany's invasion of Poland, Craig left the army in August 1939 when he reached the mandatory retirement age of sixty-four.

Craig was not out of uniform for long. Even before the Japanese attack on Pearl Harbor in December 1941, he was recalled to head the secretary of war's Personnel Board, which helped to allocate American manpower among the armed services and critical war industries. He served tirelessly in this position, despite increasingly severe health problems caused by arteriosclerosis. He died in Washington, D.C., and was buried at Arlington National Cemetery without the rendering of formal honors, according to his wishes.

Craig was a modest and extremely capable soldier, perhaps almost a prototype of the modern officer, whose skills shine brightly both in the staff room and in the field. His stern demeanor hid a sharp sense of humor, which he usually revealed only to family and to that select circle of brother officers with whom he felt most comfortable. He was also a private man who left little personal or professional correspondence that might expound upon his contributions to the U.S. Army. His admirers—and they were legion—preferred simply to remember him as "the father of World War II mobilization planning."

• Craig left no personal or professional papers, which explains in part why no lengthy biographical works have yet appeared. Only a painstaking search for papers in appropriate segments of the records of the AEF or of the Office of the Chief of Staff, reinforced by gleanings from the personal papers of Craig's contemporaries, will in time reveal the full dimensions of Craig. The most useful assessment of his contributions as chief of staff is in Mark S. Watson, *Chief of Staff: Prewar Plans and Preparations*, The U.S. Army in World War II (1950), a volume in the U.S. Army's "green book series." An obituary is in the *New York Times*, 26 July 1945.

CAROL REARDON

CRAIG, Thomas (20 Dec. 1855–8 May 1900), mathematician, was born in Pittston, Pennsylvania, the son of Scottish immigrants Alexander Craig, a mining engineer, and Mary Hall. Craig entered Lafayette College in Easton, Pennsylvania, in 1871 with the intention of following his father into a career in engineering. He graduated in 1875 with a degree in civil engineering but took, as his first job, a position as a high school teacher in Newtown, New Jersey. During the year he spent in Newtown, Craig continued his mathematical studies in his spare time. To guide him in his reading, he sought and followed the advice of two distinguished scientists, Harvard mathematician Benjamin Peirce and University of Edinburgh physicist Peter Guthrie Tait. Their counsel and his diligence and self-motivation stood the young Craig in good stead in the spring of 1876.

Word of the founding and organization of the Johns Hopkins University spread rapidly in the United States and in Great Britain. Craig, who had read not only that the eminent British mathematician James Joseph Sylvester would hold the first chair in mathematics but also that ten $500 fellowships would be awarded to incoming graduate students, wrote directly to the first Hopkins president, Daniel Coit Gilman, for further information. Gilman invited Craig to come to Baltimore for an interview and was so favorably impressed that he arranged for the young man to meet with his science adviser, Simon Newcomb, the director of the Naval Observatory in Washington, D.C. Newcomb confirmed Gilman's opinion, and Craig became one of the ten original Hopkins fellows.

Because of the extent and depth of his prior preparation, Craig taught several courses during his first year at Hopkins: an undergraduate course in differential and integral calculus and, most surprisingly, graduate-level classes in mechanics and the theory of definite integrals. He continued to supplement the offerings in the department while he worked on a dissertation in differential geometry, for which he earned the first Hopkins Ph.D. in mathematics in 1878. Though nominally a student of Sylvester, Craig probably drew less inspiration from the algebraically inclined Sylvester than from the geometrically minded

teaching associate in charge of the Hopkins undergraduate mathematics program, William E. Story.

Craig stayed on at Hopkins as a fellow for the 1878–1879 academic year and served on a part-time basis as assistant (1879–1880) and lecturer (1880–1881) in mathematics while working as a mathematician on the staff of the U.S. Coast and Geodetic Survey in Washington, D.C., from 1879 to 1881. He held the full-time, teaching-intensive post of associate from 1881 to 1883 and in 1883 was appointed to an associate professorship. His promotion to full professor came nine years later in 1892. In 1880 he married Louise Alvord; they had two children.

At Johns Hopkins University, Craig came into his own as an original mathematical researcher. His early work centered on geometry and resulted in several papers, most notably those between 1880 and 1882 in the pages of the *American Journal of Mathematics*, America's first research-level journal and a publication partially underwritten by the Johns Hopkins University. In 1882 Craig incorporated some of the research from his thesis into *A Treatise on Projections*, a book intended to meet the geometrical needs of the mathematicians at the U.S. Coast and Geodetic Survey. Also in 1882 he succeeded in bringing his work before the standard-setting German mathematical public when he published his paper on differential geometry, "On the Parallel Surface to an Ellipsoid," in the prestigious *Journal für die reine und angewandte Mathematik* (93 [1882]: 251–70). After 1882 his interests increasingly turned to the theory of elliptic functions and to differential equations. His most important work in the latter area, *A Treatise on Linear Differential Equations* (1889), was an advanced course text based on his Hopkins lectures.

Craig's mathematical tastes ran to the applications-oriented areas of function theory, differential equations, and fluid mechanics as well as to geometry, and throughout his career on the Hopkins faculty he taught courses on these and other topics. In the classroom, he tended to lecture at an advanced level and at a quick pace, which often made it difficult for all but the best students to keep up. This did not suggest an insensitivity toward his students, however. Especially during the first part of his career, Craig enjoyed teaching and the interaction that it brought with young and eager minds. In fact, he and his wife occasionally held mathematical soirées in their home for his students. During the 1890s, as general ill health and alcoholism increasingly consumed his energies, Craig became more distant and withdrawn. In his annual report on the university in 1900, Gilman wrote that "[t]hose who knew Dr. Craig only in his declining years, need to be told of the enthusiasm, the diligence, and the learning which for a long period were his distinguishing characteristics." Craig died of heart failure in Baltimore, Maryland.

As a mathematician, Craig was certainly not in the first rank, but he was a member of the first generation of American mathematicians who, committed to the ideals of research, established a community of mathematical researchers in the nation. In 1884–1885 he served as assistant then associate editor of the *American Journal of Mathematics* and from 1894 to 1898 worked tirelessly as the journal's editor to secure quality submissions both from home and abroad. He also supported the efforts of the American Mathematical Society (founded as the New York Mathematical Society in 1888) through his membership and through his service on its governing council between 1894 and 1896.

• The Milton S. Eisenhower Library of the Johns Hopkins University holds a number of materials that relate to Craig's association with the university, and the Johns Hopkins University Circulars are a gold mine of information on the teaching and professional activities of Craig and his colleagues. Additional biographical information is in F. P. Matz, "Professor Thomas Craig, C.E., Ph.D.," *American Mathematical Monthly* 8 (1901): 183–87. J. C. Poggendorff provides a partial list of Craig's publications in *Biographisch-Literarisches Handwörterbuch*, vol. 4 (1904), p. 279. On the mathematical environment in which Craig participated at Johns Hopkins, see Karen Hunger Parshall and David E. Rowe, *The Emergence of the American Mathematical Research Community 1876–1900: J. J. Sylvester, Felix Klein, and E. H. Moore* (1994). Hugh Hawkins places Craig within the broader framework of the university in *Pioneer: A History of the Johns Hopkins University, 1874–1889* (1960). For a sense of Craig's place in the American mathematical community, consult David Eugene Smith and Jekuthiel Ginsburg, *A History of Mathematics in America before 1900* (1934; repr. 1980).

KAREN HUNGER PARSHALL

CRAIGIE, Andrew (22 Feb. 1754–19 Sept. 1819), druggist, entrepreneur, and speculator, was born in Boston, Massachusetts, the son of Andrew Craigie, a ship captain and merchant, and Elizabeth Gardner. He attended Boston Latin School for an undetermined period starting in 1763; there is no information as to his further education. Indeed, there seems to be no further record of him until 1775, when the Massachusetts Committee of Safety appointed him to take care of medical stores and the Provincial Congress named him "medical commissary and apothecary for the Massachusetts army." This and his subsequent activity in the Continental army suggest that he had had some background in pharmacy or the wholesale drug business. There is nothing known of Craigie's background or later activity that would warrant the appellation "Doctor" frequently accorded him.

The Continental Congress appointed Craigie apothecary general of the Northern Department in 1777 and (chief) "apothecary" in 1780. He remained chief apothecary throughout the war, and although records indicate that he was mustered out in November 1783, he was still signing official documents pertaining to military medical supplies as "Andrew Craigie, Apothecary" in May 1784 and still held in his possession "articles out of the Public Medicines" in August 1785. He was a member of the Society of the Cincinnati.

Craigie's pharmaceutical duties included the procurement of drugs, the providing and oversight of the medical supplies at the army hospitals, and the establishment of a "laboratory" for the compounding of

drugs and the making-up of medicine chests. At Carlisle, Pennsylvania, Craigie established an "Elaboratory and Stores for the reception of medicines &c. belonging to the military hospitals."

Craigie spent most of his war service in Carlisle and Philadelphia. His biographers agree that he came out of the war a wealthy man. At times he acted as a private wholesaler of drugs while in service, without a suggestion of any conflict of interest. He was likely among the Continental officers who "trafficked in specie"; at least by 1784 he was a "heavy dealer" in public securities. In 1780, when Congress was about to reorganize the medical department of the Continental army, and Craigie's reappointment was in question, his character and service received the approbation of Dr. John Cochran, and George Washington recommended him to Congress (although Washington did not know Craigie personally). Later Dr. Benjamin Rush was to attest to Craigie's character "as a man, as a public officer, and as a whig."

After the war, Craigie entered the wholesale drug business with Francis Wainwright in New York, but by 1789 he had given it up, having "lost very considerably." He did not stop speculating in securities and in land, and in fact was among the first rank of the postwar speculators. He was to become a director of the first Bank of the United States, a subscriber to the (New Jersey) Society for Establishing Useful Manufactures, and a subscriber to the abortive Connecticut Manufacturing Society. Among his many business associates, most important was William Duer. Duer, outstanding speculator and prime mover in many land ventures, was politically well placed. Craigie consulted Duer often, paid him great deference, and profited much from their association. Yet Craigie, despite the insolvency of his New York business agents, weathered the panic of 1792 that landed Duer into debtor's prison.

Craigie invested heavily in state paper, buying South Carolina certificates, for example, late in 1789—at a time when Duer was assistant to Secretary of the Treasury Alexander Hamilton (1755–1804). Craigie was also involved in speculations that went beyond the domestic market and included, unsuccessfully, international schemes for gaining control of the debt of the United States to France. These speculations reached major proportions. For example, in September 1788 Craigie sent $400,000 worth of securities abroad to British and French correspondents.

Craigie's land dealings, usually conducted in secrecy if not in a conspiratorial manner, extended from Georgia to Vermont and west to Indiana. As a joint trustee of the Scioto Associates, with Duer and Royal Flint, he was a major participant in the machinations and activities of that venture—a venture that deviously procured an option to buy almost five million acres of land in Ohio and that ended in default to the government because of unexpectedly poor sales in France and because of the panic of 1792. Some 500 Frenchmen found that they had acquired only options to buy the land they had been led to believe they were purchasing. Craigie's culpability in this "debacle" has been reduced, aptly, to the charge of being "negatively acquiescent in a doubtful project."

In 1791 Craigie purchased the Vassall House and estate in Cambridge, Massachusetts, and left New York somewhat later. His speculating activities continued and included a new interest in Cambridge real estate. From 1795 to 1807 he quietly bought up parcels of land in East Cambridge, and in 1808 the Massachusetts legislature authorized the building of a bridge by Craigie and his associates from Boston to Cambridge. The "Canal Bridge," or "Craigie Bridge," was opened on 30 August 1809, eventually to be replaced by the Charles River Dam.

The Vassall House, enriched to become the "Craigie Mansion," was an elegant and extravagant center of social life in Boston, especially after Craigie's marriage to the young Elizabeth Shaw in 1793. The marriage, however, proved to be unhappy, and husband and wife took up separate quarters in the mansion. There were no children.

Craigie's fortunes began to wane: he is reported to have said that the authorization to build the bridge "made him a beggar." He found himself so fearful of debtor's prison that he seldom ventured out of the house. He died of "apoplexy" in Cambridge. Mrs. Craigie, who lived until 1841, was left in such straightened circumstances that she took in lodgers. The last was Henry Wadsworth Longfellow, and the house, which became Longfellow's, has become the Longfellow National Historic Site.

• Scattered documents pertaining to Craigie's military service as apothecary are to be found in the National Archives. The voluminous Craigie papers, consisting of his correspondence, military pharmaceutical records, and business records and accounts are in the American Antiquarian Society, Worcester, Massachusetts. These papers were intensively used by Joseph S. Davis in his "William Duer, Entrepreneur," in his *Essays in the Earlier History of American Corporations: Numbers I–III* (1917), and by Robert F. Jones in his *"The King of the Alley": William Duer, Politician, Entrepreneur, and Speculator* (1992). Both recount details of Craigie's activities. Archer B. Hulbert has covered the Scioto affair in his "The Methods and Operations of the Scioto Group of Speculators," *Mississippi Valley Historical Review* 1 (1914–1915): 502–15 and 2 (1915–1916): 56–73, and in his "Andrew Craigie and the Scioto Associates," *Proceedings of the American Antiquarian Society* 23 (1913): 222–36. Biographical sketches of Craigie are in Frederick H. Pratt, *The Craigies* (1942); Lyman F. Kebler, "Andrew Craigie, the First Apothecary General of the United States," *Journal of the American Pharmaceutical Association* 17 (1928): 63–74, 167–78; and John Holmes, "Andrew Craigie," *Publications of the Colonial Society of Massachusetts* 7 (1902): 403–7.

DAVID L. COWEN

CRAIK, James (1730–6 Feb. 1814), physician and military surgeon, was born on his father's estate near Dumfries, Scotland, the son of Robert Craik, a member of the British Parliament; the name of his mother is unknown. Little information about his early life is available. Although his parents were apparently not married, he was acknowledged by his father, who assumed responsibility for his education. After studying medicine at the University of Edinburgh, he joined the British army as a surgeon. Shortly after being sent to the West Indies, he resigned his position and sailed for Virginia in 1751. After a short period in the Norfolk area, he moved to Winchester, Virginia.

In 1754 Craik became surgeon of the Virginia Provincial Regiment, then commanded by Colonel Joshua Fry and later, after Fry's death, by George Washington. During this period he and Washington formed a close and lasting friendship. Craik served under the British general Edward Braddock during the French and Indian War. After Braddock was wounded on 9 July 1755, Craik cared for him until his death four days later. Craik served with Washington and the provincial forces under Washington's command from 1755 to 1758. When the unit was disbanded in November 1758, Craik bought an estate at Port Tobacco, Maryland, opening a medical practice and building an impressive mansion there.

In 1760 Craik married Marianne Ewell of Prince William County, Virginia; they had nine children, all of whom predeceased him. His friendship with Washington remained active during this period, and in 1770 he joined his friend on a journey west to survey lands offered by the British to participants in the French and Indian War.

Craik was active among the colonists angered by British restrictions on trade and in 1774 played a leading role among citizens of Port Tobacco who protested the British blockade of Boston. In 1777 after Washington asked him to join the Continental army's hospital department (or medical department), he chose to serve as assistant director general, responsible for the care of troops serving between the Potomac and Hudson rivers. Like all of the army's physicians, he was technically a civilian and, as a result, was not given official rank. He cared for the wounded in many of the major battles involving forces personally led by Washington. Among his patients after the battle on the Brandywine Creek in Pennsylvania in September 1777 was the marquis de Lafayette.

In 1777 Craik informed Washington of a plot to replace him as commander in chief of the Continental army, the so-called Conway Cabal. In the summer of 1780, on Washington's orders and despite the opposition of much of the citizenry who saw hospitals as hotbeds of infection and disease, he persuaded Rhode Island College in Providence (now Brown University) to allow him to establish a facility in college buildings for French forces arriving to help the Continental army. Later the same year a reorganization of the hospital department resulted in Craik's promotion to the third highest position in that organization. The following year, on the resignation of the department's head, Craik was promoted to the second highest position.

In the spring of 1783 he became one of the founding members of the Society of the Cincinnati. After being present for the British surrender at Yorktown, Craik left military service on 23 December 1783 at the conclusion of the war. He initially returned to his home at Port Tobacco, but at Washington's urging soon moved to Alexandria, where he could be near his friend and care for those who fell ill at Mount Vernon. When Washington journeyed west in 1784, Craik again accompanied him, traveling through the Appalachian Mountains to the Ohio and Monongahela rivers and back.

On 19 July 1798, after fear of a possible war with France led to plans to call up another army with Washington at its head, Craik was appointed chief medical officer. Both Craik and Washington returned home in 1799, before the army was officially disbanded. When Washington fell seriously ill with what may have been a streptococcal infection of his throat, Craik was called to his side. He used all the major weapons in the medical armory of his time, including blistering, repeated bleeding, and drugs that caused purging and vomiting. Without the benefit of the insights of modern medicine, even calling in two eminent physicians to serve as consultants did not enable him to save his patient. Craik's only known published writing followed this tragic event, when he and one of the consultants collaborated to explain Washington's illness and their treatment of it in an appendix to a sermon inspired by Washington's death.

Craik was officially mustered out of the army on 15 June 1800. Although he retained his physical vigor into his old age, he retired from practice not long thereafter and moved to his estate outside Alexandria, where he lived until his death with his wife and the widow of the only one of their sons who had married.

Craik served as one of the leaders of the Continental army's hospital department effectively and honorably without being caught up in the acrimonious and divisive wrangling that characterized that organization almost from the day of its creation. Unfortunately, he may be best known as the physician who attended the nation's first president on his deathbed and whose ministrations, though typical of the practice of his time, may have hastened Washington's demise. In a 1789 letter to physician James McHenry, Washington himself wrote of his complete confidence in Craik's professional skills, noting that Craik was "the man of choice in all cases of sickness" and that he would "with cheerfulness trust my life in his hands."

• Although letters from Craik can be found in the papers of some of his contemporaries, including George Washington, no collection of his papers is known to exist. The various articles that have been written about Craik differ slightly about minor details of his early life. Since James Thacher was a contemporary of Craik's, his *American Medical Biography; or Memoirs of Eminent Physicians Who Have Flourished in America*, vol. 1 (1828), is particularly interesting. Considerably greater detail concerning Craik's life after his arrival in Virginia is in Wyndham B. Blanton, *Medicine in Virginia in the Eighteenth Century* (1931), although this material is contained in several different locations throughout the volume. Also worthwhile are James Evelyn Pilcher, "The Surgeon Generals of the Army: James Craik, Physician General of the United States Army, 1798–1800," *Journal of the Association of Military Surgeons of the United States* 14 (1904): 189–93, and J. M. Toner, "A Sketch of the Life and Character of Dr. James Craik, of Alexandria, Va.," *Transactions of the Tenth Annual Session of the Medical Society of Virginia* 3 (1879): 95–105. Material can also be found in Pilcher, *The Surgeon-Generals of the Army of the U.S.A.* (1905), and James M. Phalen, *Chiefs of the Medical Department, United States Army 1775–1940* (1940).

MARY C. GILLETT

CRAIN, Gustavus Dedman, Jr. (19 Nov. 1885–15 Dec. 1973), publisher, was born in Lawrenceburg, Kentucky, the son of Gustavus Dedman, Sr., a salesman, and Anna Edwards. "G. D." Crain, as he later called himself (he hated his first name), attended public schools in Louisville, Kentucky. He later accepted a scholarship to Centre College in Danville, Kentucky, where he earned bachelor's and master's degrees in English. Immediately after graduating from Centre College in 1904, Crain became a reporter for the *Louisville Herald*. He was told that he would receive pay for his services only if he showed he was capable of handling the assignments; two weeks later Crain was earning $10 a week. While at the *Herald*, Crain served first as city editor and then as sports editor.

Eventually, Crain left the *Herald* to start his own Louisville-based editorial service. He had begun to investigate this growing trade of independent "stringers," or correspondents, while still at the *Herald*. His company submitted news and features to about a hundred business publications in a variety of fields, including banking and finance, lumber, and manufacturing. In 1916, at the age of thirty, Crain sold his editorial service to his two employees. He then formally entered the publishing business, a long-held dream. Crain first founded a trade publication serving hospital administrators. "My original choice was *Hospital Management* because I discovered there was only one [other] important publication in the field at that time," he later said. Because advertising was slow to develop for *Hospital Management*, Crain started a second publication, *Class*, exclusively devoted to specialized advertising in business publications, which served in part to promote *Hospital Management*. *Class*, a business publication designed to interest manufacturers and advertising agencies, was "a modest success from the beginning."

Later in 1916 Crain decided to relocate his offices from Louisville to Chicago. It was in this new location, on the eighth floor of the Transportation Building in the heart of the city's "Printer's Row" district, that Crain's publishing business was destined to thrive. The company began publishing the annual *Crain's Market Data Book and Directory of Class, Trade, and Technical Publications* as a spin-off of the successful *Class* (later, *Class and Industrial Advertising*) in 1921. *Hospital Management* also began to gain strength in the mid-1920s around the same time Crain hired the then fifteen-year-old Sidney Bernstein, who later became editor and publisher of *Advertising Age*, as well as chairman of the executive committee of Crain Communications. In 1922, after some ten years of marriage, Crain's wife, the former Ailiene Ferris, died, leaving Crain to raise their two daughters.

Despite the stock market crash of 1929, Crain went forward with his plans and launched *Advertising Age*. *Advertising Age* was different from other advertising journals at the time because it devoted more space to news developments. In its premiere issue the weekly carried stories such as the death of Edward W. Bok, the longtime editor of *Ladies' Home Journal*, various activities of industry giants, and worker legislation, including the winning of the five-day work week by printers and engravers. Despite initial shaky advertiser support, within a year *Advertising Age* broke even in a depressed economy, partly because it was the first publication of its kind covering the advertising industry. Crain worked harder than ever promoting his newest publication as the depression wore on. *Class and Industrial Marketing* was eventually subsumed into *Advertising Age* as a cost-cutting maneuver. Finally by 1934 *Advertising Age* began to pick up considerable business until just prior to World War II. In 1936 Crain married Gertrude Ramsay.

The year 1938 was to see another sweeping business turndown; *Advertising Age*'s advertisement volume plummeted some 600 pages from the previous year's level. The following year brought both the good news of economic recovery after the 1938 dip and the bad news of the war in Europe. Crain, who always had a penchant for dispensing advice, ordered editorials written about the impact of the European war on U.S. business and made several speeches himself on the subject. By this time *Advertising Age*'s issue length had grown to between eighty and one hundred pages and had firmly established itself as a dynamic advocate and defender of business-to-business advertising. By 1940 Crain had turned over his editorial duties for *Advertising Age* to Bernstein, previously the director of research and promotions. The second half of the 1940s also saw the inception of *Advertising Age*'s influential annual ranking of advertising agencies by billings.

Crain Publications continued to flourish and produce a number of new titles: *Advertising Requirements* (1953; changed to *Advertising and Sales Promotion* in 1961), *Advertising Agency* (1961), *Marketing Insights* and *Business Insurance* (1967), *Automotive News* (1971), and *Pensions and Investments*, *American Laundry Digest*, *American Dry Cleaner*, *American Coin Op*, and *American Clean Car* (1973).

In 1969 Crain's company became known as Crain Communications, Inc. Crain was officially the company's chairman of the board from 1969 until his death, although he gradually spent less and less time in the office. Throughout his career Crain was honored by numerous organizations, such as the Chicago Industrial Advertiser's Association, the Chicago Business Publications Association, Dentsu Advertising, and the American Business Press, for his contributions to advertising.

Crain Communications continued on as a family business after his death. Gertrude Crain became chairperson and led the company as it eventually acquired and managed twenty-four publications, a radio station, more than 1,000 employees, extensive computerization in all departments, and offices in New York, Detroit, Chicago, Los Angeles, Dallas, Washington, Cleveland, Akron, and London, in addition to correspondents and advertising representatives in many cities both in the United States and abroad by 1990.

During the 1970s *Advertising Age*'s influence could be felt nationally. Once read exclusively by industry insiders, the publication was now read by members of Congress, corporate executives, and the financial community. *Advertising Age* broadened its coverage to include fashion, sports, and show business, which also helped to increase its readership and sphere of influence. By the beginning of the 1980s circulation of the publication stood at 77,000. In 1990 *Advertising Age* ranked its own company, Crain Communications, as ninety-ninth out of the 100 largest U.S. media companies with net revenues of $150.1 million. Crain Communications flourished as a privately-owned company, a testament to the man who created it.

• Biographical information concerning Crain as well as a detailed chronicling of the Crain empire can be found in Robert Goldsborough, *The Crain Adventure: The Making and Building of a Family Publishing Company* (1992).

CATHERINE GOLDBERG

CRAM, Ralph Adams (16 Dec. 1863–22 Sept. 1942), architect and cultural critic, was born in Hampton Falls, New Hampshire, the son of William Augustine Cram, a Unitarian minister, and Sarah Elizabeth Blake. Cram's early career was strongly affected by his father's decision to abandon his profession and return to the family farm in New Hampshire to care for his elderly parents. As a result, the young Cram received no formal education after completing high school in 1880; instead, he was formed by a combination of apprenticeship in the office of the Boston, Massachusetts, architectural firm of Rotch and Tilden; extensive travel abroad, financed in part through prizes won in architectural competitions; and voluminous personal reading.

Cram was first of all an architect, forming his first partnership with Charles Francis Wentworth in 1890. This firm was transformed in 1895 into Cram, Wentworth & Goodhue in 1895 with the addition of the gifted young draftsman Bertram Grosvenor Goodhue. Although the two parted company in 1913, much of Cram's finest work was enhanced through Goodhue's talent for ornamental detail as well as the contributions of the gifted craftsmen the two recruited, including the sculptor Lee Lawrie and the stained-glass artist Charles Connick. The firm's name was changed to Cram, Goodhue & Ferguson in 1899 when Frank Ferguson succeeded the deceased Wentworth; at the time of Goodhue's departure, it became Cram and Ferguson. In 1900 Cram married Elizabeth Carrington Read; they had three children.

Although Cram designed several houses in the Boston area during his early career, it soon became clear that ecclesiastical architecture was his true vocation, and that the Anglo-Catholic wing of the Episcopal church, to which he had been converted in 1888 while attending a Midnight Mass in Rome, was to be his primary object of professional and artistic interest. One of his earliest churches, All Saints', Ashmont, in the Boston suburb of Dorchester (1892), demonstrated his penchant for adapting the Medieval English parish church into a contemporary idiom. Later, more ambitious works, such as St. Thomas Episcopal Church on Fifth Avenue in Manhattan (1914) and the Cathedral Church of St. John the Divine, taken over by Cram in 1911 and never completed, illustrate his appropriation of French Gothic elements as well as the fruits of his collaboration with Goodhue and their circle of artists and craftsmen.

Although his commissions generally followed his theological and liturgical bent, Cram occasionally undertook projects for other denominations such as East Liberty Presbyterian (1931–1935) in Pittsburgh, Pennsylvania, and the Polish Catholic St. Florian's in Hamtramck (Detroit), Michigan (1925–1928). He also ventured into collegiate architecture on various occasions, most notably in his collaboration with Goodhue on the fortresslike campus of West Point (1903), an eclectic foray at Rice (1909), and a long-term appointment by Woodrow Wilson as supervising architect of Princeton's Gothic revival campus beginning in 1907. All of those buildings are extant.

In both thought and action, Cram worked to correlate his architectural practice with a broader scheme of social and cultural transformation based on an ideology of medieval restorationism he developed in nearly countless books and articles. His early writing was more literary than architectural and emerged from the bohemian subculture of fin de siècle Boston. During these years he collaborated with other young and "decadent" literati such as Goodhue, Fred Day, and Louise Imogen Guiney in the production of *The Knight Errant* (1892), a short-lived periodical.

Cram wrote in a variety of genres, including the ghost story *Spirits Black and White* (1895). In later years he turned to historical and cultural criticism, relentlessly castigating the wrong turnings of Western civilization wrought by the Renaissance, the Reformation, and the French and Industrial Revolutions. In *The Gothic Quest* (1907), *The Substance of Gothic* (1917), *Walled Towns* (1919), and other works, he criticized the linked decline of aesthetics and spirituality in the modern West. He called for a restoration of medievally inspired architecture, such as his own churches, and social institutions based on the principles of hierarchy and interdependence, which he saw in the craft guild and the (Anglo-) Catholic church.

Cram served as chairman of the City Planning Board of Boston from 1914 to 1922, and as head of the Department of Architecture at MIT from 1914 to 1921 despite his lack of the usual academic credentials. He received considerable recognition from contemporaries, appearing on the cover of *Time* (13 Dec. 1926). In addition he was one of the founders of the influential lay Roman Catholic journal *Commonweal* (1924) and the Mediaeval Academy of America (1925). He died in Boston and is buried next to his self-designed chapel on the grounds of his estate, "Whitehall," in Sudbury, Massachusetts.

Cram's legacy is problematic. His churches have often been acclaimed as masterpieces of the latter phase of the Gothic revival in the United States, which influenced other religious architects in their concentration on design essentials. Cram himself saw his work as progressive, in the tradition of Henry Hobson Richardson in reaction to the fussiness of Victorian excess. Revivalism of any sort, though, was even during his career overshadowed in both popular taste and elite practice by the forces of modernism represented by native practitioners such as Frank Lloyd Wright and his Prairie School and emigrés such as Walter Gropius of the Bauhaus. The Anglo-Catholic wing of the Episcopal church with which he was affiliated never managed to do more than survive as an option within that tradition, and the costs of building following World War II, together with changes in taste, demographics, and liturgical theology converged against Cram's Gothicism. Elements of his critique of modern civilization were more memorably expressed by Henry Adams, T. S. Eliot, and others, so that little of his published work remains in print or of interest to other than intellectual historians. Almost all of his architectural work has endured, however, and still plays a major role in the cityscape of Manhattan and many other, primarily northeastern, locales. Although hardly triumphant on his own terms, Cram nevertheless left an enduring legacy in the built environment of American religion.

• Cram's personal and professional papers, including the records of the firm of Cram and Ferguson, are in the Cram and Goodhue papers at the Boston Public Library. The papers of Cram's long-time partner, Bertram Grosvenor Goodhue, are in the care of the Avery Library at Columbia University. For a bibliography, see Lamia Doumato, *Ralph Adams Cram* (1981). Two major studies of Cram are Robert Muccigrosso, *American Gothic: The Mind and Art of Ralph Adams Cram* (1980), and Douglass Shand-Tucci, *Boston Bohemia, 1881–1900* (1995). An extensive study of Cram's architectural work is Ann Miner Daniel, "The Early Architecture of Ralph Adams Cram, 1889–1902" (Ph.D. diss., Univ. of North Carolina at Chapel Hill, 1978). Illustrations of Cram's architectural work are in *Contemporary American Architects: Ralph Adams Cram, Cram and Ferguson* (1931) and *The Work of Cram and Ferguson Architects* (1929). Discussions of Cram include Albert Bush-Brown, "Cram and Gropius: Traditionalism and Progressivism," *New England Quarterly* 35, no. 1 (1952): 3–22; James F. White, "Theology and Architecture in America: A Study of Three Leaders," in *A Miscellany of American Christianity*, ed. Stuart C. Henry (1963); Peter W. Williams, "A Mirror for Unitarians: Catholicism and Culture in Nineteenth Century New England Literature" (Ph.D. diss., Yale Univ., 1970); T. J. Jackson Lears, *No Place of Grace* (1981); and Richard Guy Wilson, "Ralph Adams Cram: Dreamer of the Medieval," in *Medievalism in American Culture*, ed. Bernard Rosenthal and Paul E. Szarmach (1989). Also relevant is Richard Oliver, *Bertram Grosvenor Goodhue* (1983), a biography of Cram's principal collaborator.

PETER W. WILLIAMS

CRAMP, Arthur Joseph (10 Sept. 1872–25 Nov. 1951), American Medical Association investigator and critic of health quackery, was born in London, England, the son of Joseph Cramp and Mary Ann Jackson. About 1891 Cramp migrated to Missouri, attending Maryville Seminary and in 1897 marrying Lillian Caroline Torrey. From 1894 to 1902 he taught science in Milwaukee high schools and served as principal of the Wisconsin Industrial School for Boys at Waukesha.

The death of Cramp's only child, a three-year-old daughter, while being treated by a man recognized only afterward as a charlatan changed her father's career. He enrolled in the Wisconsin College of Physicians and Surgeons in Milwaukee, teaching chemistry while pursuing an M.D., acquired in 1906. Private practice in Waukesha proved uncongenial to Cramp, and in December 1906 he became an editorial assistant on the staff of the *Journal of the American Medical Association* (*JAMA*) in Chicago.

Cramp's coming to the American Medical Association (AMA) coincided with rising concern among physicians about fraudulent medications marketed to both the medical profession and the lay public. Intensifying antiquackery efforts was the Food and Drugs Act of 1906, which went into effect in 1907, with its provisions aimed at controlling misbranded and harmful nostrums. Cramp's role at the AMA immediately became that of chief exposer of quackery's many dimensions. He developed the Propaganda for Reform Department, renamed the Bureau of Investigation in 1925, which he directed until his retirement following a heart attack in 1935.

Cramp prepared factual studies of individual cases of fraud, including drugs, devices, practitioners, and institutes. He assembled advertising and other types of promotion, had analyses made, consulted with medical specialists, and occasionally played the role of patient seeking treatment. Then, the facts assembled, Cramp, after reading a chapter of *Alice in Wonderland* to get himself into the requisite mood of fantasy, wrote his profile of the quack, his sketch couched in a tone of indignation and irony. Sometimes the irony could have a humorous overlay, as when Cramp reported that ads three years apart had given credit to Nuxated Iron for Jess Willard's boxing victory over Frank Moran, then Jack Dempsey's victory over Willard. Cramp drew the moral: "Ain't science wonderful!"

First publication of Cramp's sketches came in *JAMA* in 1907. Case histories were then cumulated in blue-bound pamphlets according to theme: cancer, consumption, deafness, diabetes, epilepsy, kidney disease, female weakness, and male inadequacy. The AMA had sold two million such pamphlets at cheap prices by 1933. Cramp further compiled his cases into green-bound volumes, *Nostrums and Quackery*, issued by the AMA in 1911, 1921, and—his final project—

1936. His bureau also distributed posters and lantern slides.

The persons and companies attacked in AMA publications often countercharged in print and threatened to do so in court. Some libel suits were filed, but, as of 1933, only two went to trial. One case the AMA won. The other, brought by the makers of Wine of Cardui, a female remedy that Cramp had termed a "vicious fraud" because it could not lift up a fallen womb as advertised, the AMA lost. The association considered the verdict a "moral triumph" nonetheless, because damages assessed were only one cent.

Cramp and regulatory officials at the Department of Agriculture and the Post Office Department were in constant contact, he publishing their enforcement results, they tapping his database while developing cases. Many other inquirers sought information from Cramp's expanding archives: better business bureaus, newspapers, physicians, members of the general public, and foreign nationals worried about American patent medicines for sale in their countries.

Cramp hoped to educate consumers to be wary about fraudulent promotions. He gave many lectures, but he was more comfortable with the written than the spoken word, and he wrote incessantly. Besides his profiles, he explained the broad pattern of quackery: why nostrums got credit for nature's cures, how testimonials were usually deceptive and sometimes tragically wrong, and how nostrum ingredients ranged from the inert to the life threatening. He did not deny a role for self-medication in the case of simple ailments, urging that instead of commercial nostrums the public get at the drugstore cheaper standard medications listed in the *United States Pharmacopeia* and the *National Formulary*. Cramp's articles were a mainstay of the AMA's health magazine for the lay public, *Hygeia*, launched in 1923. He published in numerous other journals, ranging from *American Mercury* to the *New England Journal of Medicine*. During the First World War, Cramp furnished educational material to the armed services to help protect the troops from venereal disease. One of Cramp's continuing themes was the need for strengthening laws against quackery. He gave his strong support for the campaign during the New Deal to secure what became the Food, Drug, and Cosmetic Act of 1938.

Cramp was slight in build, shy, dignified, and fastidious in his dress and habits. His hobbies included hiking, photography, and ornithology. In retirement he moved to Hendersonville, North Carolina, where he died.

• Cramp's importance rests in his writings, especially the three *Nostrums and Quackery* volumes published by the American Medical Association in 1911 (expanded ed. 1912), 1921, and 1936. Several of his magazine articles were gathered into a pamphlet, *Patent Medicines*, issued by the AMA in 1923 or 1924. Accounts of Cramp's activities appear in his own article, "The Work of the Bureau of Investigation," *Law and Contemporary Problems* 1 (1933): 51–54, and in Bliss O. Halling, "Bureau of Investigation," in *A History of the American Medical Association, 1847 to 1947*, ed. Morris Fishbein

(1947); James G. Burrow, *AMA: Voice of American Medicine* (1963); and James Harvey Young, *The Medical Messiahs: A Social History of Health Quackery in Twentieth-Century America* (1967). An index to the archives that Cramp began to assemble has been published by the AMA: Arthur W. Hafner et al., eds., *Guide to the American Medical Association Historical Health Fraud and Alternative Medicine Collection* (1992). A brief obituary of Cramp is in the *Journal of the American Medical Association* 147 (29 Dec. 1951): 1773.

JAMES HARVEY YOUNG

CRAMP, William (22 Sept. 1807–6 July 1879), shipbuilder, was born in Kensington, Pennsylvania, a suburb later incorporated into northeastern Philadelphia; his parents' names are unknown. After attending public schools, he studied under the naval architect Samuel Grice. He married Sophia Miller in 1827; they had eleven children. In 1830 Cramp established his own shipbuilding firm on the Delaware River, first in Kensington and then in a larger facility in Richmond. Over the next decades this shipyard grew to become one of the most important in the United States, constructing wood, ironclad, iron, and eventually steel ships. He remained president of the firm for forty-nine years, from its founding until his death in Atlantic City, New Jersey.

Cramp constantly modernized his equipment to adapt to changes in ship construction. The ability of the Cramp firm to adapt to the changing technology of shipbuilding and ship propulsion through the mid-nineteenth century brought both Cramp and his company lasting fame. As sail power gave way to steam-powered paddle wheels and then propeller-driven vessels, Cramp developed steam-engine facilities. During the Civil War he provided the Union navy steam-propelled ironclads, which played crucial roles in blockade duty and sea engagements. Following the Civil War iron construction replaced wooden hulls through the 1870s. The firm was ready for the revolution of the 1880s, which brought steel-hulled ships into the naval and merchant fleets of the world. During his lifetime Cramp personally oversaw the construction of more than 200 ships.

In 1862 the Cramp company constructed for the Union navy *New Ironsides*, the largest ironclad warship of the Civil War and the one that saw more engagements than any other. Other warships constructed by Cramp in this period included gunboats and ironclads, and the first-class cruiser *Chattanooga*. In the early 1870s the Cramp yard turned to all-iron construction, producing four passenger ships for the Philadelphia-based American Steamship Line. Each of the vessels was about 3,000 tons, and they were launched within a few months of one another.

Cramp brought his sons into the business, admitting Charles H. Cramp as a partner. In 1872 he changed the name of the firm to William Cramp and Sons' Ship and Engine Building Company. The company won contracts to build warships for several foreign navies, including those of Russia and Venezuela. The performance of Cramp ships in the Russian fleet in the war between Turkey and Russia (1876–1878)

enhanced the reputation of the Cramp firm as a constructor of warships. As the U.S. Navy pressed for expansion of the fleet in the 1870s and 1880s, the firm of William Cramp and Sons played a role both in advocacy of the new navalism, and in construction of the steel ships of the new navy.

Cramp understood both merchant and naval shipbuilding as matters of national pride and national power, anticipating in his own way the later doctrine of Alfred Thayer Mahan that linked national power to a strong navy. He articulated a doctrine of shipbuilding—in competition with the British in particular—which was intensely nationalistic. He claimed that the long British supremacy in shipbuilding had given them a sense of proprietary right to the sea, and a right to the carrying trade of the United States. The British, he claimed, were so arrogant that they resented any effort to build an American passenger fleet as a usurpation of their prerogatives. With the construction of the iron ships of the 1870s for the American Steamship Line, he laid the groundwork for later expansion in liners by Cramp and Sons in the 1890s. Similarly, the construction of ships for Russia paved the way for the warships needed in naval expansion in the United States at the end of the century.

The William Cramp and Sons Ship and Engine Company was a major contributor to the growth of Delaware River shipbuilding in the late nineteenth century, concentrating manpower, skills, technological capability, facilities, and political power. In addition to Cramp's firm and the Philadelphia Navy Yard, many shipbuilding companies on both the Pennsylvania and New Jersey sides of the river converted this fifteen-mile stretch of the Delaware into one of the major shipbuilding centers of the United States in the late nineteenth and early twentieth centuries.

• A small collection of Cramp's papers is at the Special Collections of Temple University Library, Philadelphia, which includes a list of all the engines built between 1867 and 1901, as well as ship plans, memoranda, and ballistic tests on armor plate. Sources include *History of Cramp's Shipyard*, published by the company in several editions from 1894 through 1910, and Gail E. Farr, *Shipbuilding at Cramp & Sons* (1991). An obituary is in the *Philadelphia Enquirer*, 7 July 1879.

RODNEY P. CARLISLE

CRANCH, Christopher Pearse (8 Mar. 1813–20 Jan. 1892), Transcendentalist poet and artist, was born in Alexandria, District of Columbia (now Va.), the son of William Cranch, chief judge of the District of Columbia Circuit Court, and Nancy Greenleaf. He was graduated from Columbian College (now George Washington University) in 1832 and Harvard Divinity School in 1835. Cranch was never ordained, though he served as a Unitarian missionary in New England and the Midwest for a few years.

Cranch became associated with the New England Transcendentalists while at Harvard. Between 1836 and 1839 he assisted James Freeman Clarke in the editing of the Transcendentalist *Western Messenger* in Louisville, Kentucky, contributing prose and poetry and editing several issues. Returning to the Boston area, he contributed regularly to the *Dial* and often visited (though never actually joined) the Brook Farm community.

In 1843 Cranch married Elizabeth De Windt of Fishkill, New York. They settled in New York City, where they operated a boardinghouse. They had three children. Cranch wrote frequently for such periodicals as the *Democratic Review*, *Graham's Magazine*, and the *Harbinger*; in 1844 he published his *Poems*. About this time he turned his attention to painting and for a number of years was regularly represented in the annual exhibits of the National Academy of Design. Looked upon as a member of the Hudson River School, he specialized in American landscapes. A number of his oils may be seen in the Fruitlands Museum in Harvard, Massachusetts.

Cranch traveled frequently to Europe, spending some years in Italy, where he associated with such prominent members of the English-American colony there as Robert Browning, William Wetmore Story, and Henry James, Jr. He also lived for shorter periods in Paris and London. In later years he settled in Cambridge, Massachusetts, where he renewed his ties with such friends as Ralph Waldo Emerson, James Russell Lowell, and Henry Wadsworth Longfellow. He died in Cambridge.

Cranch published several other volumes of poetry, including *Satan: A Libretto* (1874), *The Bird and the Bell* (1875), and *Ariel and Caliban* (1887). Two books for children, *The Last of the Huggermuggers* (1856) and its sequel *Kobboltozo* (1857), achieved wide popularity through the rest of the century. Although now almost completely forgotten, they reflect Cranch's vivid imaginative powers. His translation into blank verse of Virgil's *Aeneid* was published in 1872 in James R. Osgood's prestigious series of classics in translation.

Cranch had a charming, witty personality that won him wide friendship during his lifetime, but his literary reputation has faded. His best known poem, "Enosis" (persistently misspelled as "Gnosis"), is appreciated as a concise statement of the Transcendentalist philosophy. Oddly he is now best known for a series of cartoons facetiously illustrating some of the writings of his Transcendentalist friends; his depiction of Emerson as a "transparent eyeball" is particularly popular. Most were not published until 1951, when they were rediscovered by F. DeWolfe Miller. Cranch's light-hearted whimsicality often causes him to be dismissed as a dilettante, a "jack-of-all-trades and master of none," but his sense of humor often serves as a welcome antidote to the oversolemnity and vapidness of some of the lesser Transcendentalists. Much of his charm lives on in his cartoons, his juveniles, and a handful of his poems.

• Cranch's manuscripts are widely scattered, with a large collection at the University of Wyoming and others at Harvard, the Massachusetts Historical Society, the Boston Public Library, Andover-Harvard Theological Library, and the Albany (N.Y.) Institute of History and Art. Most of his poetry is included in *Collected Poems of Christopher Pearse Cranch*, ed. Joseph M. DeFalco (1971). A biography is Leonora Cranch Scott, *The Life and Letters of Christopher Pearse Cranch* (1917), by his daughter. F. DeWolfe Miller, *Christopher Pearse Cranch and His Caricatures of New England Transcendentalism* (1951), reproduces and evaluates his cartoons. The most comprehensive bibliography of Cranch's writings is Miller's "Christopher Pearse Cranch: New England Transcendentalist" (Ph.D. diss., Univ. of Virginia, 1942). The best survey and evaluation of Cranch's work and of Cranch studies is David Robinson, "The Career and Reputation of Christopher Pearse Cranch: An Essay in Biography and Bibliography," *Studies in the American Renaissance* (1978).

WALTER HARDING

CRANCH, William (17 July 1769–1 Sept. 1855), jurist and Supreme Court reporter, was born in Weymouth, Massachusetts, the son of Richard Cranch, a watchmaker, judge, and legislator, and Mary Smith. His mother was Abigail Adams's sister. Graduated from Harvard at the age of nineteen, Cranch was a classmate there of his cousin John Quincy Adams. After being admitted to the bar in 1790, he practiced briefly and served as justice of the peace for Essex County. In 1794 he moved to the new federal capital city then under construction as legal agent for a real estate speculation syndicate, whose collapse led to his financial ruin. Although discharged of indebtedness by the insolvency laws, he ultimately settled all the claims against him. The real estate debacle itself became the subject of a Supreme Court case, *Pratt v. Carroll* (1814), reported by Cranch himself. A further, happier result of the venture was his 1795 marriage to Nancy Greenleaf, sister of one of the real estate operators. They had five children.

In 1800 Cranch was appointed a commissioner of public buildings in the federal capital by his well-placed uncle, President John Adams. A year later Adams named him assistant judge of the newly created District of Columbia Circuit Court. The act of 8 March 1802, intended to sweep out Adams's "midnight judges," made no mention of Cranch's court. Spared of the Jeffersonian purge, Cranch became chief judge in 1805, serving on the court, in all, for fifty-four years.

In the meantime, Cranch had begun to report the decisions of the Supreme Court upon its translation, with the rest of the federal government, to the new capital city. Although the older histories occasionally refer to Cranch as the court's first "regularly appointed" reporter, no confirming entry appears in the court's minutes, nor did Congress or the court provide for such an appointment by statute or rule. Probably Cranch, like his predecessor, Alexander James Dallas, appointed himself.

The enterprise, absent any government subsidy, was strictly entrepreneurial. Besides the illusory prospect of financial gain, Cranch seems to have been spurred by the closeness of Washington's small legal community and a keen appreciation of the importance of the task. In the preface to the first volume of his reports, he wrote

Much of that *uncertainty of the law*, which is so frequently, and perhaps so justly, the subject of complaint in this country, may be attributed to the want of American reports. . . . One of the effects, expected from the establishment of a national judiciary, was the uniformity of judicial decision; therefore, to report the cases decided by the Supreme Court of the United States, can not need an apology.

In all, Cranch published nine volumes of Supreme Court reports, covering decisions from 1801 through 1815. On the completeness and accuracy of Cranch's reports, the verdict is mixed. Justice Joseph Story complained that several volumes were "particularly & painfully erroneous," but others were more favourable. Undoubtedly, the reports are notable for containing many of the most fundamental constitutional decisions of the Marshall court, beginning with *Marbury v. Madison* (1803).

The great complaint against Cranch's Supreme Court reporting was his lack of timeliness, involving in later volumes up to a five-year delay in relaying to the bench and bar the decisions of the nation's highest court. By 1815 Story and others were urging Cranch's replacement. Although Cranch's final volume did not appear until 1817, his duties as reporter were assumed, beginning with the February 1816 term, by Henry Wheaton, who brought to the task both greater scholarly capacity and the requisite promptness in publication. The following year Congress made the reporter a salaried official of the court.

Cranch, however, continued his public service in other roles. In 1818 he presented to Congress, at its invitation, a draft code of laws for the District of Columbia to replace those of Maryland and Virginia. While ultimately not adopted, Cranch's code anticipated many ameliorative reforms, including total abolition of capital punishment. He also published a memoir of his uncle John Adams and taught at Columbian College (now George Washington University), helping to establish there the first law school in the city.

Most important, Cranch continued his work as chief judge of the District of Columbia Circuit Court (whose cases he reported in six volumes). As a jurist, he was known for his modesty, integrity, and industry. To cite one early example, in a dissenting opinion maintaining, against both presidential pressure and popular clamor, that the arrest of Aaron Burr's accomplices was unjustifiable under the treason clause of the Constitution, Cranch wrote

In times like these, when the public mind is agitated, . . . it is the duty of a court to be peculiarly watchful lest the public feeling should reach to the seat of justice, and thereby precedents be established which may become the ready tools of action in times more disastrous. . . . Dangerous precedents occur in dangerous times. It then becomes the duty of the judiciary calmly to poise the scales of justice, unmoved by the arm of power, undisturbed by the clamor of the multitude. . . . In cases of emergency it is for the executive department of the government to act upon its own responsibility, and to rely upon the necessity of the case for its justification; but this court is bound by the law and the constitution in all events. (*United States v. Bollman & Swartwout* [1807])

Cranch had the satisfaction of seeing the majority reversed by Chief Justice John Marshall himself in *Ex Parte Bollman & Swartwout* (1807).

Cranch died in Washington, D.C., after six decades in residence in what had begun as a "dismal swamp," having contributed admirably to the jurisprudence both of the district and of the new American nation.

• Cranch's papers are scattered in repositories, including the Massachusetts Historical Society, the Boston Public Library, the Library of Congress Manuscript Division, and the Cincinnati Historical Society. His life is the subject of Alexander Burton Hagner, "William Cranch, 1769–1855," in *Great American Lawyers*, vol. 3, ed. William Draper Lewis (1907); Helen Newman, "William Cranch, Judge, Law School Professor and Reporter," *Law Library Journal* 26 (1933): 74–91; and Morris L. Cohen and Sharon Hamby O'Connor, "William Cranch," in *A Guide to the Early Reports of the Supreme Court of the United States* (1995).

CRAIG JOYCE

CRANDALL, Ella Phillips (16 Sept. 1871–24 Oct. 1938), public health nurse and educator, was born in Wellsville, New York, the daughter of Herbert A. Crandall, a manufacturer, and Alice Phillips, a seamstress. She grew up in Dayton, Ohio, to which her father moved in 1872 to work with the railroad. The Crandalls were Presbyterians, and Crandall's father served on Dayton's school and health boards.

Crandall did not become interested in nursing until several years after she graduated from high school in 1890. She enrolled in a two-year course at the Philadelphia General Hospital School of Nursing, known as "Old Blockley." After graduating in 1897, she returned to Dayton and worked in supervisory positions in local hospitals. By 1899 she was assistant superintendent of the Miami Valley Hospital. Crandall also served as director of the hospital's recently established school of nursing. Her childhood friend, S. Lillian Clayton, was the hospital's superintendent, and together they transformed the hospital into a modern institution. Crandall was on the executive committee of the Society of Superintendents of Training Schools for Nurses and president of the Ohio State Association for Graduate Nurses.

Becoming increasingly influential in her profession, Crandall moved to New York City in 1909 to serve as the supervisor of the visiting nurse service in Lillian Wald's Henry Street Settlement House. She also enrolled in a postgraduate class at the New York School of Philanthropy (later the New York School of Social Work). With Mary Adelaide Nutting, Crandall developed courses in public health nursing for the Department of Nursing and Health at the Teachers College of Columbia University and served as an instructor on the graduate nursing faculty until 1912. Influenced by Wald and Nutting, Crandall participated in the early professionalization of public health nursing. She insisted that nurses take courses in sociology, economics, and psychology as well as nursing subjects to prepare them to meet health care demands. She worried that lowering standards would result in a poor quality of nurses.

Crandall was especially concerned about how people living in small towns and slums could cope with diseases. In 1911 she suggested at the annual meeting of the Association for the Prevention of Infant Mortality that the American Red Cross become responsible for nursing in rural areas, and in the next year the Red Cross Rural Nursing Service was established. Newly available Ford automobiles helped transport nurses affordably and reliably. Meanwhile, in urban areas, poor sanitation and outbreaks of tuberculosis prompted health departments to request more qualified nurses.

As demand for public health nursing increased, more nurses had to be adequately trained for home care services. In 1911 Crandall initiated a letter campaign to determine public health nurses' interest in forming a national organization. She served on a commission formed by the American Nurses' Association and the Society of Superintendents of Training Schools to study the need for organized public health work and to standardize the role of nurses in the public health field. The commission resulted in the founding of the National Organization for Public Health Nursing in June 1912. Crandall was selected as the group's first executive secretary. A capable administrator known for her "forceful leadership," she sought to enhance the esteem of public health nursing and secure professional respect and recognition by implementing high standards. She insisted that members be graduates of a two-year course at a nursing hospital with a minimum of fifty beds, and she barred nurses lacking this credential despite their practical experience.

Crandall opened the organization's headquarters in New York City and managed a staff of twenty. She transformed the Cleveland Visiting Nurse Association magazine into a monthly professional journal, *Public Health Nurse*, and began visiting and observing nurses throughout the United States, traveling thousands of miles and giving almost a hundred lectures a year. Especially concerned about nurses working in isolation, whether in slums or the wilderness, Crandall sought to unify all public health nurses and to share their experiences. She advised nurses and encouraged standardization of methods, improving the quality of services and securing public support. She returned to Dayton in March 1913 to supervise nurses conducting sanitary inspections during Ohio floods, and around the country her presence was a catalyst, sparking the will to improve and expand public health nursing. Attempting to incorporate the nursing profession as an important component of the public health movement, she demanded that nursing be considered a social service with "status and autonomy." She secured external funding, including $30,000 from the Rockefeller

Foundation, the largest contribution to a nurses' group at that time.

Crandall wrote articles for newspapers and professional journals, and in 1914 she published *Organization and Administration of Public Health Nursing* for New York City's State Charities Aid Association's Committee for the Prevention of Tuberculosis. She was a member of the American Nurses' Association's board of directors and the American Red Cross Committee on Nursing between 1913 and 1920. During World War I, Crandall moved to Washington, D.C., to act as executive secretary of three nursing committees for the Council of National Defense: the General Committee on Nursing, the Sub-Committee on Public Health Nursing of the Committee on Hygiene and Sanitation, and the Committee on Home Nursing. On the National Emergency Committee on Nursing she ensured that enough nurses were available to serve domestically and for the military while maintaining standards. She coordinated nursing war work at home and abroad, directed a national census of nurses, and drafted a resolution to recognize army nurses with rank. Worried about preventing the spread of communicable diseases at home, Crandall wrote visiting nurses' associations, asking every public health nurse to "remain at her post." A contemporary noted that Crandall's vision and devotion were "epitomized" during that difficult period.

After the war, Crandall urged nurses to help with the influenza epidemic and serve their communities through health care. Her *New York Times* article, "Teaching the People How to Keep Well" (26 Jan. 1919), stressed the "care and conservation of health" and the responsibility of public health nurses to teach patients "how to keep well and prevent illness" for the stability of the community and nation. She also asked for financial support to help nurses seek the necessary education to pursue public health service.

Crandall resigned from the National Organization for Public Health Nursing in 1920. The pioneering phase of the organization had ended, and Crandall believed it was time for new leaders. During her administration, the organization had expanded its services and opened new offices. Also, she disagreed with the Red Cross's unprofessional nursing practices and vowed she would be a "thorn in the flesh of them" and protect public health nursing from the Red Cross "menace," limiting the Red Cross to "simple experimentation and demonstrations" in public health nursing while promoting state and federal health services.

Crandall next focused on charitable groups that assisted impoverished women to seek health care for themselves and their children. She investigated the possibility of low-cost nursing services through the Maternity Center Association, the New York Association for Improving the Condition of the Poor, and the Committee to Study Community Organization for Self Support for Health Work for Women and Young Children. From 1922 to 1925 she was associate director of the American Child Health Association. In "Education in Health: The Importance of a Program in the

Schools Is Emphasized" (*New York Times*, 6 Sept. 1924), she warned that "inadequate health education can produce disastrous results" such as typhoid fever. "Pure water, clean milk, perfect sanitary conditions," she added, "have incomplete significance to a community until each individual within that community has been so educated as to make a proper use of all the civic health provisions and to apply the principles of personal health."

In 1927 Crandall became executive secretary for the Payne Fund, established by her friend, philanthropist and congresswoman Frances Payne Bolton, to provide peace education for children. An outspoken advocate for social reform, Crandall also studied sociology and psychology and enjoyed cultural and musical activities. She never married and devoted herself to her work, having little time for friendships, even with fellow nurses. Although she contributed to the advancement of women professionals, Crandall could be considered more a humanist than a feminist, being concerned about the well-being of all people.

Crandall died of pneumonia in New York City's Roosevelt Hospital. The *American Journal of Nursing* (38 [Dec. 1938]: 1406–9) eulogized that Crandall's extraordinary career pushed her to the "forefront of new movements" in public health nursing.

• Crandall's archival records are located in the Red Cross Collection and Army Nurse Corps Historical Files at the National Archives, in the M. Adelaide Nutting Historical Nursing Collection at Teachers College, Columbia University, in the Visiting Nurse Association of Boston Records at Boston University, and in the Mary Gardner Papers, Schlesinger Library, Radcliffe College. Other sources on Crandall's contributions include Annie M. Brainard, *The Evolution of Public Health Nursing* (1922; repr. 1985); Karen Buhler-Wilkerson, *False Dawn: The Rise and Decline of Public Health Nursing, 1900–1930* (1989); and Sandra Beth Lewenson, *Taking Charge: Nursing, Suffrage, and Feminism in America, 1873–1920* (1993).

ELIZABETH D. SCHAFER

CRANDALL, Prudence (3 Sept. 1803–28 Jan. 1890), abolitionist and teacher, was born in Hopkinton, Rhode Island, the daughter of Pardon Crandall, a Quaker farmer, and Esther Carpenter. When Crandall was ten her family moved to another farm in Canterbury, Connecticut. As a young woman she spent a few years (1825–1826, 1827–1830) at the New England Friends' Boarding School in Providence and also taught school for a time in Plainfield, Connecticut.

In 1831 the leading citizens of Canterbury hired Crandall to organize a school for girls. The Canterbury Female Seminary opened with twenty students and ran smoothly for about a year. But controversy—and a chance to make history—arose in the fall of 1832, when Sarah Harris, the daughter of a prosperous African-American farmer, sought admission. She wanted to get an education, she said, so that she could teach children of her own race. Crandall, who had recently begun reading William Lloyd Garrison's abolitionist

newspaper, *The Liberator*, concluded that if she denied this black woman a chance for advancement, she would be no better than a slaveholder herself. So she accepted Sarah Harris.

Most of the parents opposed Crandall's decision, and when it became clear that she would not reverse it, a number withdrew their children from the school. Meanwhile, Crandall took an even more dramatic step. In February 1833 she announced that her school was to be reorganized as a teacher-training institution for young African-American women. This decision brought on a storm of criticism. When Crandall offered to set up her school in a less central location, the town authorities told her that no such institution could be established anywhere in the state.

Defying the town's ruling, Crandall opened her school in April 1833, recruiting students from prosperous black families as far away as Boston and New York. The people of Canterbury then united to force her surrender. Merchants stopped selling her food, physicians refused to treat anyone in her household, the Congregational church barred her and her students from attending services, and the local authorities tried to prosecute her pupils as paupers and vagrants. The school's windows were broken, its well befouled, and the building nearly set on fire. When Crandall still held her ground, the town sought legislative relief through the political influence of Andrew Judson, her next-door neighbor. Judson, a well-connected lawyer, persuaded the state legislature in May 1833 to pass the "Black Law" forbidding any Connecticut school to admit African Americans from outside the state and requiring that if black students were accepted from outside town limits, they must be approved by the town selectmen. Crandall ignored the new law and was arrested in August 1833.

A Unitarian minister, Rev. Samuel J. May of nearby Brooklyn, was one of Crandall's few local supporters, but the broader abolitionist community offered her important support. Arthur Tappan, a wealthy evangelical Protestant, paid for her legal defense, and Garrison gave her case extensive publicity in *The Liberator*; indeed, Garrison's language was so intemperate that Crandall suggested that he moderate his tone. Other abolitionist publications also defended Crandall's position.

Outside support did Crandall little good in Canterbury. Her first trial (in which her neighbor Judson led the prosecution) ended in a hung jury, but she was retried and this time she was convicted. Although her lawyer argued that under the Constitution out-of-state pupils had equal rights to the privileges enjoyed by Connecticut residents, the court held that since African Americans were not citizens, they could not make that claim. Crandall's conviction was reversed on appeal in July 1834 but not on the merits of the case—the state supreme court merely ruled that the prosecution had offered insufficient evidence. The citizens of Canterbury had lost their legal fight against the school, but they continued their physical attacks. Finally, after the building was set upon by a mob in

September 1834, Crandall gave in and closed the school.

One month earlier, Crandall had married Rev. Calvin Philleo, a Baptist minister from New York State. Soon after the school was closed, she, her new husband, and two children from his previous marriage moved to Boonville in upstate New York. The marriage was an unhappy one; Crandall's husband was sixteen years older than she, unstable in temperament, given to long absences, and increasingly dependent on her financially. The family moved back to Canterbury in 1839, and three years later Crandall set out on her own for Troy Grove, Illinois, to settle with her brother on land that had belonged to her father. There she opened a school, the Philleo Academy, and won a kind of local fame for her combination of upright behavior and radical thinking. Even after her husband rejoined her in 1847, Crandall continued to pursue her own interests, including temperance, woman suffrage, and spiritualism.

In 1865 the couple relocated to Cordova, Illinois, where Crandall's husband died in 1874. Two years later, she and her brother—though both in their seventies—gambled on exchanging the Cordova farm for another they had never seen in Elk Falls, Kansas. Besides working on the new farm, Crandall took up a new interest, Christian Science. In 1886, in belated acknowledgment of past debts, the Connecticut state legislature voted her a small pension. She died in Elk Falls four years later.

Prudence Crandall was barely thirty when the battle for which she is best known ended. Yet looking back on her career fifty years later, she told an interviewer: "My whole life has been one of opposition. I never could find anyone near me to agree with me." From her youthful decision to defy the most influential men in her community to the independent life she built for herself despite a disappointing marriage, the choices Crandall made often ran counter to the expectations of her times. But choose she did, and her life exemplifies both the rewards and the costs of those choices. "She had deep convictions of right," said a friend at her funeral, and "neither death, life, angels, principalities, things present, things to come, heights, depth, nor any other creature could keep her from following her convictions."

• Prudence Crandall's papers are in the Connecticut State Library in Hartford and in the library of Connecticut College in New London. Correspondence with her can also be found in the papers of Florence Woolsey Hazzard at Cornell University, Alma Lutz at Radcliffe College, and Elizabeth Yates at Emporia State University, Emporia, Kans. Discussions of her life and work include Susan Strane, *A Whole-Souled Woman: Prudence Crandall and the Education of Black Women* (1990); Leon Stein, *Lives to Remember* (1974); Philip S. Foner and Josephine Pacheco, *Three Who Dared: Prudence Crandall, Margaret Douglass, Myrtilla Miner: Champions of Antebellum Black Education* (1984); Henrietta Buckmaster, *Women Who Shaped History* (1966); and a biography for young people, Elizabeth Yates, *Prudence Crandall: Woman of Courage* (1955). See also Bertram Wyatt-Brown, *Lewis Tappan and the Evangelistic War against Slavery* (1969); Louis Ruchames, *The Abolitionists: A Collection of Their Writings* (1963); and Russel B. Nye, *William Lloyd Garrison and the Humanitarian Reformers* (1955). Cornell University has a portrait of Crandall painted by Francis Alexander.

SANDRA OPDYCKE

CRANE, Anne Moncure (7 Jan. 1838–10 Dec. 1872), novelist, was born in Baltimore, Maryland, the daughter of William Crane, a leather merchant, and Jean Niven Daniel, his second wife. Crane's private education, supervised by Reverend N. A. Morrison, ended in 1855. Her writing career began in 1858, when a group of her friends decided that they should each write a novel; she was the only one to complete a manuscript, which was published anonymously in 1864 as *Emily Chester*. The novel details the fortunes of its eponymous heroine who falls in love with a man but remains faithful to her husband, a good and stable man for whom she feels no sexual passion. *Emily Chester* was an immediate success, going through three editions in the first year of its publication—it eventually went to a total of ten editions; it was also pirated in England, translated into German, and adapted for the stage. The influence of *Emily Chester* was grudgingly acknowledged in Crane's death notice in *The Nation* (30 Jan. 1873): "Its example was not without influence on many of its author's young countrywomen, and there was at once a rise in the market value of the young heroine who was wavering between two gentlemen, for one of whom she feels 'an affinity,' and to the other of whom she is bound by common or statute law."

Crane's second novel, *Opportunity* (1867), is primarily a character study of two men—one self-confident and deliberate, the other selfish and attractive to women—and the novel's heroine, Harvey Berney, who is attracted to both but who ultimately marries neither. Harvey, like her predecessor Emily, is a forthright, independent-minded young woman who charmed her female readers and enraged male critics. Henry James described her as shrewish, pert, pedantic, and puerile, while the editor of *Lippincott's Magazine* grumbled that "the thing least to be endured with patience in a novel is a heroine scarcely out of pinafores, . . . running about and disposing of grave and vexed questions with a flippant assurance deserving of nothing so much as boxed ears" (quoted in Habegger, p. 112).

During the time Crane wrote this novel, she renewed her childhood friendship with Augustus Seemuller (or Seemüller), a well-to-do merchant who had left Baltimore to travel in Europe. They married in 1869 and moved to New York, where she was exposed to such "fearful" things that she felt impelled to speak out against them. Her third novel, *Reginald Archer* (1871), published under her married name, was the result of her experience in New York.

Christie Macalaster, the heroine of *Reginald Archer*, is a rich young heiress whose ideas of life and love have been shaped by reading poetry and novels. She easily falls victim to the morally dissolute Reginald Archer, who marries her for her fortune. Faced with proof that her husband is continuing an affair with a mistress, Christie seeks refuge with Tom, a businessman who deeply loves her. The interest of the novel lies in Crane's analysis of female sexuality and her depiction of Christie's moral ambiguity—Christie is briefly tempted to follow her husband's example and take a lover. Crane's frankness shocked and revolted male critics into condemning her for failing to punish with a sad and painful death those female characters who had sinned.

The scholar Alfred Habegger argues convincingly that the young Henry James was both fascinated and scandalized by Crane's heroines and that he devoted much of his fiction to rewriting those heroines into noble women who choose the moral high road. Certainly the predicament of James's Isabel Archer in *The Portrait of a Lady* (1881) mirrors that of Christie Macalaster Archer.

Crane's psychological insight animates her writing. Here is the self-deprecating heroine of Crane's 1866 short story "My Courtship":

The truth was I was watching and waiting for my hero to appear, whose slave and queen I was equally to become, as soon as I beheld him; and that for ordinary mortals to even aspire to his place, was an insult and impertinence to him, which I resented with all my heart. I think now, my ideal man was the incarnation of an archangel and a steam-engine combined; of some highest ethereal essence conjoined to the lowest material force. But such as he was I worshipped him in spirit, and waited for his revealing.

Crane's real significance, however, resides in her willingness to examine women's issues honestly and frankly in the face of moral outrage and condemnation. This sense of outrage is apparent in Crane's obituary in *The Nation*, in which the anonymous writer notes that a "characteristic motto" of Crane's work is "Nature is to be studied in her monstrosities." However, Crane's own words, taken from her 1866 essay "Novelists' Poetry," more accurately describe the aim of her fiction: "Those who have the gift of speech will always utter their thought in the way in which it demands to be spoken; but at no time can it do harm to make an effort to call things by their own name."

Shortly after the publication of *Reginald Archer*, the Seemullers traveled throughout Europe; this trip has been variously explained as Crane's attempt to escape the storm of criticism occasioned by the novel or to regain her failing health, which may have been damaged by paint she ate as a child. Crane died in Stuttgart, Germany.

Although Crane's fiction went out of print after her death, she is significant as one of several influential female novelists writing at the middle of the nineteenth century—a group that included Louisa May Alcott, Rebecca Harding Davis, and Elizabeth Stoddard—whose novels explored women's issues realistically and candidly. These women rejected the pat "lived-happily-ever-after" formula of popular fiction and instead focused on the plight of their passionate, intelligent, articulate heroines who are oppressed by marriage.

• The William Conant Church Papers at the New York Public Library contain some of Crane's letters. In addition to the works noted above, Crane wrote two other essays—"Private Bohemias" (1868) and "Colored Photographs" (1872); two more short stories—"My Note-Book" (1868) and "Little Bopeep" (1869)—both published in *Galaxy*. *Galaxy* also published Crane's poems, which include "Arbutus," "Barbarossa and Bismarck," "Edwin Booth," "Winter Wind," and "Words to a 'Lied ohne Worte.'" Alfred Habegger, *Henry James and the "Woman Business"* (1989), devotes chapter 5, "Anne Moncure Crane Seemuller: Henry James's Jocasta," to an analysis of Crane's fiction and her influence on James. Habegger also provides a detailed list of biographical sources on Crane. Entries on Crane can be found in Esmeralda Boyle, *Biographical Sketches of Distinguished Marylanders* (1877), and Henry Elliott Shepherd, *The Representative Authors of Maryland* (1911).

JUDITH E. FUNSTON

CRANE, Bob (13 July 1928–29 June 1978), actor, was born Bob Edward Crane in Waterbury, Connecticut, the son of Alfred T. Crane and Rosemary Senich. Following graduation from high school, Crane studied music in Waterbury with plans to become a professional drummer. He played with the Connecticut Symphony from 1944 until 1946, when he left to perform with several dance bands touring the East Coast. Following a stint with the Connecticut national guard from 1948 until 1950, he became a radio disc jockey with a reputation for humor and a glib manner. Between 1950 and 1956 he worked for radio stations in New York and Connecticut before moving to station KNX in Hollywood, California, where he remained until 1965. His humor and clowning made the show a quick success.

In 1960 he began his acting career with a guest appearance on "The Lucy Show," which was followed by performances on "G.E. Theater," "The Dick Van Dyke Show," "The Alfred Hitchcock Hour," and "Channing." Appearances in two episodes of "The Donna Reed Show" in 1963 led to a part in the series during the 1964–1965 season; Crane played Reed's next-door neighbor. During this period he also acted for the large screen. In 1961 he appeared in minor roles in two movies, *Mantrap* and *Return to Peyton Place*. In neither did his acting receive critical attention.

During these brief excursions into television and film he retained his on-the-air job at KNX, but the offer of a leading role in a new television comedy series convinced him to give up the security and good pay of radio broadcasting and devote himself to acting. The concept for this series—a comedy about prisoners of war in a Nazi prison camp who make life difficult for their captors—seemed risky, but Crane and his fellow actors made this series one of the most popular on television for the next five years. "Hogan's Heroes" premiered on CBS on 17 September 1965 and ran until 4 July 1971. In Stalag 13, a fictitious German POW camp run by the inept Colonel Klink, the real power is held by Colonel Robert Hogan of the U.S. Air Corps—the role played by Crane. Hogan (code-named Papa Bear) and his men run a spy system for the Allies and a World War II version of the Underground Railroad, assisting downed Allied fliers to escape to England. Hogan uses wit, charm, and audacity to befuddle and confuse the Germans, who never catch on to the subterfuge practiced by their prisoners. The humor was usually broad and played with a slapstick panache.

Produced by Bing Crosby Productions, "Hogan's Heroes" ranked ninth in the Nielsen ratings its first season. The following year it was seventeenth and then fell out of the top twenty, but it remained popular. Crane was nominated for an Emmy in both the 1965–1966 and 1966–1967 seasons as best actor in a leading role in a comedy series. The series itself was nominated as best comedy series three times. After its cancellation the show went into syndication, entertaining new audiences on cable television.

Crane never again received the acclaim accorded him in "Hogan's Heroes." In 1969 Crane played a leading role in yet another television adaptation of *Arsenic and Old Lace*, costarring with Helen Hayes and Lillian Gish on ABC. He made guest appearances in episodes of many of the popular TV series of the day, including "Love, American Style," "The Doris Day Show," "Police Woman," and "Ellery Queen," and on two variety shows, "Make Mine Red, White and Blue" with Fred Astaire for NBC (1972) and Mitzi Gaynor's "Mitzi and a Hundred Guys" on CBS (1975). He also had a minor role in a television film, *The Delphi Bureau* (1972/NBC).

Crane's career seemed to be on the rise again with a starring role in the 1974 Disney film *Superdad* and, in 1975, his own series on NBC. In "The Bob Crane Show" he played Bob Wilcox, a 42-year-old insurance salesman who gives up his job and old lifestyle to go to medical school. The show was canceled after only thirteen episodes. The following year he had a small role in another Disney film, *Gus*, a minor and forgettable movie. His last television appearance was on an episode of "The Love Boat" (ABC) in 1978. In his later years he toured regional and dinner theaters in a variety of roles, with little professional success.

Crane married Anne Terzian, his childhood sweetheart, in 1949. They had three children and divorced in 1970. Soon after the divorce Crane married Patricia Olson, who had appeared in "Hogan's Heroes" under her stage name, Sigrid Valdis. They had one son. Crane and Olson were estranged at the time of his death.

On 29 June 1978 Crane was brutally murdered in an apartment in Scottsdale, Arizona. He was appearing in a local dinner theater, which maintained the apartment for its visiting actors. Sometime during the night he was tied up and beaten to death. Fourteen years later, in June 1992, a longtime friend of Crane's, John Henry Carpenter, was arrested for the murder. Police claimed that Crane and the man often engaged in bizarre sex with various women Crane met through the theater. Crane frequently videotaped his sexual encounters, and the tapes present a different image of a man often believed to be ebullient and giving. In October 1994 Carpenter's trial ended in his acquittal.

Crane's only significant professional role was that of Colonel Hogan, but he turned that character into an icon of American culture. Hogan/Crane's wit, breezy attitude, and cocky confidence contributed in a major way to the show's success, but "Hogan's Heroes" was popular for reasons other than Crane's acting. As director Howard Morris put it, the show dealt with "a bunch of guys outwitting authority." Hogan was an officer who refused to take the military seriously, while at the same time accepting his duty and responsibilities. Crane's character represented the protest against authority, especially military authority, which helped to define the 1960s in the United States.

• Crane was listed in *Who's Who in America* (1974). His television career is documented in Vincent Terrace, *Encyclopedia of Television: Series, Pilots, and Specials* (1986). An obituary is in the *New York Times*, 30 June 1978. Further discussion of his murder can be found in the *Arizona Republic*, especially the issue of 6 June 1992.

ROBERT A. ARMOUR

CRANE, Hart (21 July 1899–27 Apr. 1932), poet, was born Harold Hart Crane in Garrettsville, Ohio, the son of Clarence Arthur Crane, a wealthy candy manufacturer and retailer, and Grace Hart. The Cranes' marriage was troubled, ending in divorce in 1917, and Hart Crane, an only child whose formal education ended in high school, became a pawn in their turbulent relationship. Forced to choose sides, he eventually became more and more estranged from his father and devoted to his mother, whose surname he honored by dropping Harold from the name he was known by professionally.

Crane had hopes of being a poet from his earliest adolescence, and so he was an avid student of the emerging schools of modernism in the various arts. He was particularly encouraged by Helen Moody, the widow of the poet William Vaughan Moody, whom he had met through family connections. Crane was barely seventeen when his first published poem, "C33," on Oscar Wilde, appeared in *Bruno's Weekly* in 1916. Encouraged by this early success, in the same year he left for New York City, where he soon became a member of a growing bohemian coterie that included poet and editor Alfred Kreymborg and poet and novelist Maxwell Bodenheim, and he saw more of his work accepted by such avant-garde magazines as the *Pagan* and the *Little Review*.

In other early poems like "North Labrador" (1917), "My Grandmother's Love Letters" (1919), "Black Tambourine" (1921), "Chaplinesque" (1921), and "Praise for an Urn" (1922), the thematic and stylistic features that have come to characterize Crane's poetry emerge. These are all lyric poems of no more than four or five stanzas, but they combine an intensity of vision with a verbal density that often borders on the opaque, or the merely clever. In their very experimentalism, however, they explore aspects of time and perception and personality in uniquely modernist ways. Crane's tone hovers between a romantic sentimentality and a bittersweet sense of irony, but his was not a drawing room poetry intended to titillate the hyperliterary. There was an unmistakable seriousness of commitment and execution even in these early poems that made it abundantly clear that they were not mere wordplay. "A poem is at least a stab at the truth, . . . a single, new *word*," Crane wrote in his essay "General Aims and Theories" (1925), addressing an abiding interest in the metaphysical as much as the lexical aspects of poetry writing.

Crane first essayed the long poem in the three-part "For the Marriage of Faustus and Helen" (1923). On his return to Ohio from New York in 1919, he studied and wrote poetry while working at various of his father's candy stores in Cleveland and Akron, where the poem is set. Using jazz rhythms and the verbal aerobatics typical of his work—"corymbulous formation of mechanics" is a description of fighter planes in a chevron formation—the poem was an attempt to "unbind our throats of fear and pity" by celebrating rather than denigrating or bemoaning the modern world, a vision in direct contradiction to the pessimism that Eliot's famous poem *The Waste Land* seemed to be encouraging. For his part, Crane viewed Eliot's poem as "good, of course, but so damned dead."

The Bridge was the direct result of Crane's resolve to celebrate the modern. From the first, it was to be, in its affirmations, the Holy Grail of Modernist poetics—the long poem—for theory at the time held that the modern experience was too chaotically manifold and fragmented to lend itself to the sort of necessary harmonies and balances the long poem, or sustained epic, required.

Crane began talking about a poem that would have the Brooklyn Bridge as its primary iconic reference point in 1923 after he moved back to New York and took a job as a copywriter with the J. Walter Thompson Advertising Company. By 1924 he had moved into the same Columbia Heights apartment that the crippled architect John A. Roebling had occupied during the Brooklyn Bridge's construction.

Crane had become the center of a New York literary circle that included Gorham Munson, editor of the *Pagan*, the poet and critic Waldo Frank, poet Allen Tate of Fugitive movement fame, Matthew Josephson, Slater Brown, and Malcolm Cowley, who would later devote a chapter to Crane in his study of the American expatriate scene, *Exile's Return: A Literary Odyssey of the 1920s* (1934; rev. ed. 1951). Young men like himself, they anticipated the completion of Crane's great epic with much excitement, and he continuously shared thoughts and comments on its progress in his correspondence with them, particularly as completed sections emerged in 1926. This sudden spurt of productivity occurred largely through the generosity of banker and art patron Otto Kahn, who advanced Crane $1,000, with the promise of an additional $1,000, so that he might leave his job as an ad-

vertising copywriter with Sweet's Catalogue Service to devote his attention full-time to *The Bridge*.

In the meantime, Crane's career was advancing on other fronts as well. In December 1926 Boni and Liveright brought out *White Buildings*, his first book of poems. Included in this remarkable first volume, along with many of the early lyrics and "For the Marriage of Faustus and Helen," were several of Crane's most beautiful and complex lyrical poems, including "Lachrymae Christi" (1924), "The Wine Menagerie" (1925), and "At Melville's Tomb" (1926), which required an explication in the form of a letter from Crane to editor Harriet Monroe before she published it in *Poetry* in 1926.

Crane lived with the same intensity with which he wrote, often writing while drinking wine and listening to Ravel's *Bolero* on the phonograph. He was also a homosexual, frequently indulging a predilection for sexual adventurism.

A six-poem sequence of love lyrics, "Voyages," concluded *White Buildings*. Written between 1921 and 1924, these lyrics were first published in the *Little Review* in 1926 and are addressed to an absent sailor lover. For the rhapsodic melody of their sweeping verbal images of the sea and the night sky, each betokening the lover's sense of his separation from his beloved, this sequence comprises some of the most beautiful love poetry written in English in the twentieth century.

Crane had spent from April to November 1926 sojourning at the family's vacation home on the Isle of Pines off the island of Cuba. Although the retreat was shortened by a painful ear infection and by a devastating hurricane, he was extremely productive, composing during July more than half of the individual poems that make up the completed *Bridge*, including "To Brooklyn Bridge," "Ave Maria," "Harbor Dawn," "Cutty Sark," "Three Songs," and the final section, "Atlantis"—much of the poem's most lyrical passages and the heart of its visionary core. Always a meticulous editor of his own work, he revised continually but did publish individual sections as they reached final shape.

After several more years had passed, however, the magnum opus was still not completed and appeared to be bogged down. Crane joined the American expatriate scene in Paris from December 1928 to July 1929; there he gained a considerable notoriety by indulging in assorted debaucheries. Back in New York, he finally rushed the long-awaited *Bridge* to completion, and it was published in a limited edition in Paris by the Black Sun Press in February 1930 and by Liveright in New York in April, receiving a mixed critical response.

In its final form, the work is a progressing series of interrelated lyrics arranged in an order suggesting a narrative sequence. The reader begins at the foot of the Brooklyn Bridge in contemporary Manhattan and then is transported back in time to the deck of the *Santa María* as Columbus approaches discovery of the New World. The remainder of the poem is a sometimes frenzied lyrico-mythical passage through American history, bringing the reader back to contemporary New York for a visionary finale that sees both the Orphean poet and the enspirited nation fulfilling themselves, through the concrete manifestation of the Brooklyn Bridge, as the mystical realization of the New Atlantis.

There is perhaps no more sustained or ambitious a poetic undertaking from that period of American literature, and yet *The Bridge* has generally continued to be received as a flawed epic, grander in the scope of its design and of its central metaphor of America as the dynamic "bridge" between past and future than in its execution. Crane later commented in a letter to Allen Tate: "So many true things have a way of coming out all the better without the strain to sum up the universe in one impressive little pellet."

In March 1931 Crane received a Guggenheim Fellowship and sailed for Mexico with the intention of writing a poetic drama on Montezuma and the conquest of Mexico. He settled in an artists' colony near Mexico City along with fiction writer Katherine Anne Porter and the painter David Alfaro Siqueiros. Crane's high hopes dissipated, however, and for much of the year he did little more than drink heavily, threaten suicide, and indulge in sexual adventures. By early 1932, however, he had become involved in his first heterosexual love affair, with Peggy Baird, the wife of Malcolm Cowley, and he wrote a number of lyrics that he planned to include in a new volume to be called "Key West: An Island Sheaf." Most of these poems remained unpublished at the time of his death. Among them was one last great lyric love poem, "The Broken Tower," which might almost serve as a summation of the frustrations of his poetic career to date as well as of his enduring commitment to "trace the visionary company of love." Returning to New York with Baird in April 1932 to settle his father's estate, the lovers quarreled, and Crane apparently committed suicide by leaping from the stern of their ship, the SS *Orizaba*, into the Atlantic Ocean somewhere north of Cuba.

Largely because of the efforts of Crane's mother, Philip Horton brought out a full-length biographical tribute, *Hart Crane: The Life of an American Poet*, in 1937, and Cowley's later chapter in *Exile's Return*, along with the editorial efforts of critic Brom Weber, kept Crane's critical reputation and work current well into the 1960s.

On the basis of his major achievement, *The Bridge*, it is reasonable to view Crane as a poet whose commitment led to his settling on the apotheosis of the American experience as a theme equal to his talents and ambitions as a modernist poet. Through his commitment to that poetic vision, he has come to occupy an enduring place in the American literary canon.

• Crane's papers are in the Rare Books and Manuscripts Collection at Columbia University. In addition to the Cowley memoir and the Horton biography, John Unterecker's *Voyager: A Life of Hart Crane* (1969) provides an exhaustive study of the poet's life, and Brom Weber has edited the most authoritative edition of his poetry, *The Complete Poems and Selected Letters and Prose of Hart Crane* (1966), as well as *The Letters of Hart Crane, 1916–1932* (1952). Major critical studies of Crane's poetry include Weber's *Hart Crane: A Biographical and Critical Study* (1948); Monroe K. Spears, *Hart Crane* (1965); R. W. B. Lewis, *The Poetry of Hart Crane: A Critical Study* (1967); M. D. Uroff [Margaret Dickie], *Hart Crane: The Patterns of His Poetry* (1974). L. S. Dembo, *Hart Crane's Sanskrit Charge* (1960); and R. W. Butterfield, *The Broken Arc: A Study of Hart Crane* (1969). *The Bridge* is given special attention in Sherman Paul's *Hart's Bridge* (1972) and Edward Brunner's *Hart Crane and the Making of "The Bridge"* (1984).

RUSSELL ELLIOTT MURPHY

CRANE, John (7 Dec. 1744–21 Aug. 1805), soldier and patriot, was born in Braintree, Massachusetts, the son of Abijah Crane and Sarah Beverly. Crane entered into his profession of soldiering at an early age. In 1759 he volunteered to serve in the French and Indian War in the place of his father, who had been drafted. Nothing specific is known of his service in that war. He returned from the conflict and learned the trade of housewright. In 1767 he married Mehitable Wheeler. That same year he set up a shop with his brother on Tremont Street in Boston and soon became associated with the organization of the Sons of Liberty. It is not known whether Crane wrestled with the competing notions of loyalty to the king and patriotism for Massachusetts, but in 1773 some members of the group that undertook the Boston Tea Party met at his shop and dressed themselves as Indians prior to the event. Crane went to the tea ships with his fellows, and while in the hold of one of the three ships, he was knocked unconscious when a tea chest fell on him. His companions took him to be dead and left him buried underneath a pile of wood shavings in a carpenter's shop near the wharf, but Crane recovered.

Crane moved to Providence, Rhode Island, in 1774, following a serious drop off in his business due to the Boston Port Bill, one of the Coercive or Intolerable Acts that came about as a result of the Boston Tea Party. When the American Revolution began in April 1775, Crane, who already had some knowledge of guns and artillery, became a company commander in the Rhode Island "Army of Observation" that was sent to participate in the siege of Boston (1775–1776). Following the battle of Bunker Hill (17 June 1775), Crane's artillery unit was loosely joined with the artillery of Richard Gridley, another veteran of the French and Indian War. On 8 July 1775 Crane led a successful attack against one of the advance posts of the British defenders of Boston.

When the Continental army was organized in the fall of 1775, Crane was appointed the first major of Henry Knox's artillery regiment (10 Dec. 1775). Crane suffered a wound in his foot during an artillery duel with a British ship at Corlear's Hook in September 1776. On 1 January 1777 he was promoted to colonel and given command of the new Third Continental Artillery Regiment, to be made up of troops from Massachusetts and Rhode Island. He raised and recruited nine companies of men, and another three companies came from Ebenezer Stevens's provisional artillery battalion.

Sections of Crane's regiment fought in the battles of Germantown, Brandywine, Red Bank, and Monmouth. Crane is known to have participated in the campaign to take British-held Newport, Rhode Island, in 1778, because he was mentioned in the dispatches. A notion has long existed that Crane served at Saratoga, but this seems very unlikely. However, Crane did serve for the duration of the war, and his name has remained prominent in the records as an important member of the early artillery corps of the army.

Crane took command of the newly formed Corps of Artillery on 17 June 1783, thereby succeeding Major General Knox as the head of American artillery forces. He received a brevet promotion to brigadier general on 30 September 1783, but he resigned from the army in November 1783 to reenter the world of business. He opened a lumber business on Passamaquoddy Bay in Massachusetts (now Maine), but he failed in that endeavor. Crane then moved to a 200-acre plot of land in Whiting, Maine, that had been granted to him by the Massachusetts legislature for his military service. In 1790 Massachusetts governor John Hancock appointed Crane a judge of the court of common pleas, and he remained in this position for the rest of his life.

Crane was an excellent example of the generation that made the transition from the late colonial to early national periods. Having served in the last of the French and Indian wars and having experienced a life in Boston that was in some respects similar to that of Paul Revere (craftsman, Son of Liberty, patriot), Crane was ready to participate in the Revolution with all of his energy. The same spirit that animated Crane in his younger years had moved the young John Adams to exclaim, "Oh to be a soldier!" When the Revolution began in 1775, few people understood how ghastly warfare could be. Although little serves to distinguish Crane among early revolutionary officers, his experience nonetheless provides lessons for the historian of that time period. The efforts of common people such as Crane and his associates led to the Boston Tea Party, the siege of Boston, and the British evacuation of Boston in 1776. Unlike many New Englanders, who viewed their task as finished when the British left Boston, Crane endured and served until the end of the war in 1783. The longevity of his service and his dedication distinguish him as one of the many heroes who sustained the cause of liberty from the start to the conclusion. Lacking such a dedication, the Revolution would have been doomed to be a purely regional movement rather than a national one.

• A manuscript memoir by George H. Allan is in the library of the New England Historical and Genealogical Society in Boston. Information on Crane is in Thomas J. Abernethy, "Crane's Rhode Island Company of Artillery," *Rhode Island History* 29 (1970): 46–51; Robert K. Wright, Jr., *The Continental Army* (1983); and Francis B. Heitman, *Historical Register of Officers of the Continental Army* (1914). See also Francis S. Drake, *Tea Leaves* (1884); Albert Crane, *Henry Crane of Milton, Massachusetts* (1893); *Massachusetts Soldiers and Sailors of the Revolutionary War* (1896–1898); and "Heath Papers," in *Massachusetts Historical Society Collections*, ser. 5, vol. 4 (1878).

SAMUEL WILLARD CROMPTON

CRANE, Richard Teller (15 May 1832–8 Jan. 1912), manufacturer, was born in Paterson, New Jersey, the son of Timothy Crane, a builder and architect, and Maria Ryerson. He received three years of formal education, but his family's precarious finances forced him to go work in a Paterson cotton factory at age nine. When he was fifteen he moved to Brooklyn, where he found employment in a brass and iron foundry and lived with his brother. He subsequently worked in shops building locomotives and printing presses. In 1855 he moved to Chicago and went to work for his uncle Martin Ryerson, the steel magnate, who at the time owned a lumberyard. Two years later Crane married Mary Josephine Prentice. They had nine children, two of whom died in childhood.

In 1859 Crane built a small brass foundry in a corner of his uncle's lumberyard and began to cast couplings and parts for lightning rods. He invited his brother Charles to join him, and together they established the firm R. T. Crane and Brother. They quickly diversified their operations, producing parts for railroad cars and locomotives as well as steam-heating radiators for homes and offices. They secured county and state contracts to heat several large public buildings. The brothers built an iron foundry, which expanded rapidly during the Civil War as they won government contracts to produce a wide variety of metal items. After the war the Cranes used their profits to build a large factory to make steam engines and cast-iron fittings. They incorporated, calling their new business the Northwestern Manufacturing Company.

As Chicago rebuilt after the fire of 1871, the company began producing steam freight and passenger elevators. Through the subsidiary company that he established, Richard Crane played an important role in this field until he sold Crane Elevator in 1895. The new homes built to replace the thousands destroyed by the 1871 fire also provided a market for other goods made at the foundry, chiefly pipes and plumbing fixtures. In 1872 the company changed its name once again, becoming the Crane Brothers Manufacturing Company. Richard was its president and, on his brother's retirement, its sole head. By 1880 the company employed more than 1,500 people, and the Crane factory was one of the biggest in Chicago. The firm became the largest maker of plumbing fixtures in the United States, a position it held until the 1950s. By the mid-1880s the company had established a number of branch operations outside Chicago, including one in Los Angeles. Richard Crane remained an innovator, investing in research, bringing ever more sophisticated use of machinery to industrial production, and meeting the demands of building construction and power production on an increasingly massive scale. At the same time, his firm—known after 1890 simply as Crane Company—was credited with treating its employees with respect.

Besides being a business leader, Crane became involved in Chicago reform movements in the 1880s, helping to found the Citizens Association and Improvement League. This organization allied with the Republican party, with Crane enlisting in the fight against city hall corruption and Mayor Carter Harrison's Democratic machine. He advocated civil service reform, open bidding on city contracts, and temperance. Crane refused to run against Harrison as the Republican candidate in 1883 but two years later launched a brief, unsuccessful independent campaign for mayor. None of the reforms he advocated came to pass in these years, but his son Charles eventually became president of the Municipal Voters League, the most successful of Chicago reform groups in the first decade of the twentieth century.

Crane also devoted himself to improving education. In 1884 he contributed money to help the board of education develop the Chicago Manual Training School and served on the school's board of directors from that time until shortly before his death twenty-eight years later. Crane funded scholarships for students interested in becoming industrial arts teachers but insisted he would rather put his money into spreading smallpox than support a school teaching art, literature, or philosophy. He saw job training as the public schools' chief mission, believing that vocational education increased society's wealth, while a liberal education diverted students from life's true purpose—making things and selling them.

Perhaps because he had had no opportunities for higher education, Crane hated colleges and universities and denounced them for fostering contempt for labor and disrespect for parents. To prove his contention that higher education encouraged moral degeneracy he even hired a private detective to investigate student life at Harvard, Columbia, and Princeton Universities. In *The Demoralization of College Life*, a pamphlet privately published in 1911, Crane reported his spy's findings that at the most distinguished U.S. institutions of higher learning more than 90 percent of students drank hard liquor on a regular basis, and more than 65 percent combined "wine" with "bad women." His attacks had little long-term effect on colleges and universities or American attitudes toward higher education, but they did catch the attention of the nation for a brief moment during the presidential campaign of 1912. President William Howard Taft, a Yale graduate, and candidate Woodrow Wilson, formerly the president of Princeton, issued statements assuring Americans that higher education was not "the great curse of our country" but actually promoted economic growth.

Crane's first wife had died in 1885, and two years later he had married her younger sister, Eliza Ann. After Eliza's death in 1902 Crane married Emily S. Hutchinson. In his last years, Crane spent much of his time playing solitaire, bitter and lonely. He had apparently quarreled with his Yale-educated son over business and family affairs. He died in Chicago.

Despite his status as a leading industrialist, Richard Crane believed his work in supporting education was his greatest gift to Chicago. The first two-year college operated by the city was named after him. Naturally, Crane Tech (now Malcolm X College) specialized in vocational training.

• There are no accessible archival sources or company papers. *The Autobiography of Richard Teller Crane* (1927) contains very little information about Crane's private life. His career in industry, however, is discussed in the essay on Crane Co. in Paula Kepos, ed., *International Directory of Company Histories*, vol. 8 (1994). Abigail Loomis and Franklin Court, "Richard Teller Crane's War with the Colleges," *Chicago History* 11 (1981): 204–13, describes Crane's views on education. For a picture and brief biography, see James Currey, *Chicago: Its History and Its Builders*, vol. 5 (1912). An obituary is in the *Chicago Tribune*, 9 Jan. 1912.

LESLIE V. TISCHAUSER

CRANE, Royston Campbell (22 Nov. 1901–7 July 1977), cartoonist, was born in Abilene, Texas, and raised in Sweetwater, forty miles west, the son of Royston Crane, an attorney, and Mamie Douthit. After graduating from high school in 1918, Crane entered Hardin-Simmons University in Abilene, transferring to the University of Texas at Austin the next year. In 1920 he went to the Chicago Academy of Fine Arts, where he met a fellow Texan, Leslie Turner, with whom, after only six months of classes, he returned to Texas, hopping freight trains and riding the rails throughout the Southwest for a season—an adventure that Crane would recall later in his most celebrated comic strip, *Wash Tubbs*.

When he eventually returned to Texas in 1921, Crane went to work for the *Austin American* as a reporter. He also tried the University of Texas again but left in 1922 and went to sea. He shipped on a freighter that went to Europe and back, and when it docked in New York, Crane jumped ship and joined the art department of the *New York World*, where he stayed for the next two years. When Turner came to New York in 1923 to pursue a career in illustration, the two resumed their friendship. After failing to find a market with a panel cartoon, *Music to the Ear*, Crane sold a comic strip to the Newspaper Enterprise Association (NEA) in Cleveland.

Washington Tubbs II debuted on 21 April 1924. Destined to be the first adventure story comic strip, there was little in the inaugural comedy sequences to suggest that *Wash Tubbs* was in the vanguard of a new genre in the medium. Wash was a diminutive fellow with spectacles and a curly wad of hair who emerged as a slang-slinging, girl-chasing opportunist, a brash version of movie comic Harold Lloyd, always on the lookout for a quick buck. Playing the strip for laughs, Crane soon wearied of Wash's playboy antics. He dreamed of the excitement of his seafaring days, and since he could not go to sea again himself, he sent

Wash. The pallid daily punchlines disappeared from the strip: Wash had harrowing adventures instead, capering breathlessly from one exotic locale to another. Crane drew in a comically exaggerative, "big-foot" style, and his pictures and the irrepressible ebullience of his hero gave his adventure yarns a decidedly humorous complexion. Secure now in a career, Crane married Evelyn Hatcher in 1927; they would have two children.

In early 1928 Wash met Bull Dawson, a villainous brute of murderous cunning, whose presence in the strip added an ingredient vital to an adventure story: he made the threat of danger seem real. But Wash was too frolicsome a personality to sustain the feeling of reality over the long haul, nor was he bright enough or rugged enough physically to overcome the dangers he now encountered. Then on 6 May 1929 Crane introduced the character who could match wits or fists with all comers, and Captain Easy completed the transformation of the strip from comedy to adventure. Easy (no first name) was the classic soldier of fortune—beachcomber, boxer, cook, aviator, seaman, explorer, and soldier of artillery, infantry, and cavalry (Easy's own description of himself). And champion brawler. Thereafter, the exuberant Wash, always leaping before he looked (for another buried treasure or for one or another of an endless succession of plumply curving damsels), got the duo into trouble; Easy got them out.

The strip was boisterous, rollicking, and fun-loving, full of last-minute dashes, free-for-all fisticuffs, galloping horse chases, pretty girls, and flamboyant sound effects—Bam, Pow, Boom, Sok, Lickety-whop. When Crane's characters ran, they ran all-out—knees up to their chins. When they were knocked down in a fight, they flipped over backward, head-over-heels. These old-fashioned cartoon conventions gave the action the pace of a headlong dash. And Crane enhanced the aura of adventure with backgrounds that became increasingly realistic. His seascapes were dramatic renderings, the water a brooding solid black with white foam flecking the caps of the waves; his mountain ranges, majestic sprawls of rock, etched black by deposits of wind-blown snow. Experimenting with graphic techniques, Crane mastered the use of Craftint, a coated art board that could be treated by chemicals to develop two shades of reproducible gray. He was soon creating pictures of remarkable depth with photographic tonal quality. *Wash Tubbs*'s combination of the fantastic and the authentic—comic figures cavorting through realistic scenes, whimsical plots jammed with life-threatening dangers, humorous heroes with real feelings—made it unique on the comics page.

Captain Easy soon eclipsed Wash as the strip's central character, and in 1933 Crane retitled the Sunday page *Captain Easy—Soldier of Fortune*; here, Crane concentrated his energy on producing imaginative layouts and knockabout action sequences, and although he wrote the weekday installments, he left much of the drawing to assistants. In 1937 he took an extended six-week vacation, entrusting the strip to his old friend,

Turner, who remained Crane's assistant for the rest of Crane's tenure on the strip. The next year, the two friends moved to Orlando, Florida, the first of the NEA stable to work outside the Cleveland office.

In the summer of 1943 Crane left Wash and Easy to create a new strip for William Randolph Hearst's King Features Syndicate. Hearst, following his established practice, had lured Crane away with a better offer, including ownership of his new creation, a nearly unprecedented arrangement at the time. (Turner stayed with Wash and Easy until retiring in 1969.) Crane launched *Buz Sawyer* on 1 November 1943. Taking advantage of the opportunities for action and adventure afforded by World War II, Crane put Buz in the U.S. Navy as a pilot, gave him a picturesque partner in Roscoe Sweeny, and continued telling stories in much the same lively vein as before. The strip was a military strip for most of its run, with Buz in naval intelligence after the war. The navy recognized Crane's public relations value, awarding him its gold medal for distinguished public service in 1957. A member of the National Cartoonists Society, Crane received its Reuben as "outstanding cartoonist of the year" in 1950. In 1974 he was given the Yellow Kid Award by the Salone Internazionale dei Comics in Lucca, Italy.

Long before his death in Orlando, Crane had relinquished most of the work on the strip to his assistants, Edwin Granberry and Henry Schlensker. *Buz Sawyer* was an accomplished work by a master of the medium, but Crane broke little new ground here compared to the vistas he had opened in the 1930s. Undoubtedly the most unsung of those who shaped the medium, Crane set the pace for a generation of cartoonists, who, as they felt their way in developing techniques for telling adventure stories in comic strips, looked to Crane's *Wash Tubbs* for inspiration.

• Crane's papers (1918–1965), including some original drawings, are archived at the George Arents Research Library of Special Collections at Syracuse University. All of his *Wash Tubbs and Captain Easy* (1924–1943) has been reprinted in eighteen quarterly volumes (1987–1992) by Nantier, Beall, Minoustchine Publishing, N.Y. Bill Blackbeard's prefatory notes in some of these volumes include biographical as well as historical information (sometimes rather speculative). The only other biographical material on Crane is in *The Adventurous Decade* (1975) by Ron Goulart. A sympathetic and insightful appreciation of *Wash Tubbs* can be found in Coulton Waugh's classic, *The Comics* (1947; rpt. 1991).

ROBERT C. HARVEY

CRANE, Stephen (1 Nov. 1871–5 June 1900), writer, was born in Newark, New Jersey, the son of Jonathan Townley Crane, a prominent Methodist minister and author of books denouncing popular amusements, and Mary Helen Peck, a Methodist church writer. The youngest of fourteen children, Crane rebelled against the ecclesiastical/moral tendencies of his elders, indulging in such forbidden activities as baseball, smoking, drinking, going to the theater, and reading novels. Among his favorite "respectable" activities were bicycle riding and horsemanship.

Crane's upbringing was largely in the hands of his sister Agnes, to whom he was devoted. Fifteen years his senior, Agnes encouraged Crane to write. She was also, like him, a rebel. Around the time she died, in 1884, Crane, who recalled enjoying "church and prayer meetings when I was a kid," turned away from "the lake of fire and the rest of the sideshows." He never returned to the fold, but, as many readers have noted, the Bible exerted a lifelong influence on his writing. His poetry in particular attests to his ongoing concern with eschatological questions.

After early schooling in a New Jersey seminary (1885–1887), Crane attended a quasi-military academy where he gained some sense of martial life. In 1890 he briefly attended Lafayette College (Pennsylvania) before switching to Syracuse University, where he was in residence for a little more than a semester in 1891, displaying more prowess as a baseball catcher and shortstop than as a scholar. He reported on college and city affairs for the *New York Tribune*, being especially intrigued by the red-light district and the police court, and wrote the first version of *Maggie: A Girl of the Streets*. At this time he became involved with Helen Trent, an already engaged singer from an established New York family. In Asbury Park, New Jersey, where he reported on resort activities for his brother Townley, local bureau chief for the *New York Tribune*, Crane met and fell in love with Lily Brandon Munroe, an unhappily married woman who returned his affection but, on the advice of her family, decided not to elope with him. In Asbury Park Crane had a memorable meeting with Hamlin Garland, who quickly became an enthusiast of his writing.

Crane's sketches and tales of Sullivan County began appearing in print in 1892 (a complete collection was not published until 1968). While they are slight treatments of outdoor life in upstate New York, some of the pieces already demonstrate the author's skill and vision. In "Killing His Bear" the paradigmatic figure of the Little Man, a combative egotist, tests himself against a variety of challenges, the biggest of which are the game of pursuit and the emotional impact of bringing the bear to a violent end. In "The Mesmeric Mountain" the Little Man, feeling threatened by the mountain of the title, climbs to the top to show that he cannot be cowed. About midyear, having forsworn the clever, Kiplingesque style that he had previously employed, Crane reported on the contrast between the bent, workworn marchers in an Asbury Park parade and the affluent spectators. Rival journalists accused him of satirizing organized labor, their aim being to embarrass *Tribune* editor Whitelaw Reid, who was running for vice president on the Republican ticket.

Fired by his newspaper, Crane settled into a New York boardinghouse where in 1892 he wrote poems, revised *Maggie*, and further familiarized himself with urban life. The ensuing sketches are among the most enduring of his early productions. In "The Men in the Storm" the down and out are exposed to the harshness of the elements, while "An Experiment in Misery" portrays a nightmarish stay in a flophouse.

Failing to find a publisher for *Maggie*, Crane paid for the publication of the book in 1893 (it cost $700), but the book had virtually no sales. It offers a glaring representation of social conflict in a modern urban environment, ending with the death of Maggie, either as a suicide or as a murder victim, depending upon the textual reconstruction. William Dean Howells found in it the sense of tragic fate characteristic of ancient Greek tragedy. *Maggie* is the only 1890s slum novel that is still read because Crane portrayed graphically and colorfully the realities of big-city "lowlife," balancing compassion for the abused heroine with the detachment necessary for conscientious reporting.

In 1894 Crane completed *George's Mother* and presented Garland with a manuscript of *The Red Badge of Courage*, the conception of which probably goes back to his boast, in 1891, that he could write a better battle story than Zola's *La Débâcle*. A short version of Crane's war novel was published in newspapers in 1894, and a complete version appeared the following year. His most popular work, and the classic American treatment of the Civil War, it interprets military experience through the perspective of an untried volunteer who receives his wound-badge while fleeing from a battle but eventually proves himself by fighting bravely. The book was so convincing that a Union colonel said he recalled serving with Crane at Antietam.

The epic sweep of the novel arises in part from Crane's ability to convey a common soldier's rite of passage from fear to confidence. It also arises from Crane's ability to blend a variety of literary modes, including irony, the mock-heroic, comedy, and the grotesque. Crane's strikingly original use of colors, partly inspired by Goethe and already on display in *Maggie*, became a trademark, as did his penchant for offbeat insights and arresting turns of phrase. The autumn 1895 publication of *The Red Badge of Courage* in the United States and England brought Crane international fame as the book went into fourteen printings within the year.

It is widely accepted that *Maggie*, *The Red Badge of Courage*, and other prose works, especially the major tales, strongly influenced other writers identified with realism, signifying concretely rendered, vividly detailed representations of everyday life. These writers include, among direct contemporaries, Frank Norris, Willa Cather, and Joseph Conrad and, among successors, Theodore Dreiser, James T. Farrell, John R. Dos Passos, Andrew Lytle, and perhaps most notably, Ernest Hemingway.

In 1895 Crane traveled in the West and Mexico. In Nebraska he described the harsh conditions of the plains later used in "The Blue Hotel," "The Bride Comes to Yellow Sky," and other Western tales. From her meeting with the young reporter, Willa Cather recalled Crane's observation that in the first place he wrote "the matter that pleased himself" and secondarily "any sort of stuff that would sell." Crane's experiences in Mexico resulted in "The Five White Mice," an underrated tale of American expatriates.

The same year saw the publication of his first book of poems, *Black Riders and Other Lines*. Crane thought highly of his "lines," including those contained in the later collection *War Is Kind* (1899). He thought they best expressed his leading ideas about life as a whole, in contrast with *The Red Badge of Courage*, which he termed "a mere episode." Variously received at first, the poems deploy, with a surprising degree of technical resourcefulness, perspectives that shift with whatever narrative, expository, or lyric locus Crane chose to adopt at a given time; they resemble his mature writings in prose.

In 1895 Crane was attracted by an Ohio girl, Nellie Crouse, whom he idealized but who rejected him. During October he composed *The Third Violet*, a romance about an aspiring young artist and his passion for a New York heiress. Like *Active Service* (1899), a lengthier exercise in the same general mode but transported to exotic locales, this was "any sort of stuff that would sell."

The following year Crane published a revised version of *Maggie, The Little Regiment and Other Episodes of the American Civil War, George's Mother*, and a serialized *The Third Violet*. *The Little Regiment* is a moderately successful attempt to wrest another major work from the same kinds of materials that informed *The Red Badge of Courage*. *George's Mother* comes closer to being a genuine sequel. It returns to the scene of *Maggie* to trace the disintegration of the urban nuclear family and the decline of social solidarity and sense of fraternity that remained among Crane's most cherished values.

A run-in with the New York police and their commissioner, Theodore Roosevelt (1858–1919), marked 1896 as a year of notoriety and tribulation. When two women were arrested for an act of soliciting of which he knew them to be innocent, Crane testified in a well-publicized court against the police charges. Perhaps because of his involvement in the seamier side of New York, Crane emerged from the episode, despite conduct bordering on the chivalric, as something of a notorious character.

Crane tended to repeat the pattern (first emphasized by John Berryman) of rescuing the fallen female when he became involved with another woman of "doubtful" reputation, Cora Taylor, a twice-married woman five years his elder, who became, for practical purposes, Mrs. Stephen Crane. He met Taylor, operator of a Jacksonville, Florida, house of assignation, while he waited to find passage on a ship involved in American filibustering, or gun-running, to Cuba. The two were soon in love, though Crane at the time was corresponding with a drama critic, Amy Leslie, with whom he had an affair.

For Crane the public highlight of 1897 was the January sinking of the *Commodore*, the filibustering ship he was finally able to board, and his ordeal at sea in an open lifeboat with three of the ship's crew. Crane wrote a gripping news dispatch describing the tragedy, but the event entered world literature in the form of the much-anthologized masterpiece "The Open Boat," a brooding, ironic study of the heroism of which ordinary persons are capable when confronted with life-or-death crises.

Crane's dispatches on the Greco-Turkish War supplied material for *Active Service* (1899), in which a New York editor flies to the rescue of a beautiful American girl stranded abroad, and for "Death and the Child," which depicts war from the perspective of a young Greek boy. Arriving in England in June 1897 Crane and Taylor took up residence in Oxted, Surrey. In October Crane was introduced to Joseph Conrad, who became a close friend. Other friends in England included Henry James (1843–1916), Harold Fredric, Ford Madox Ford, and H. G. Wells, all of whom at one time lived within some thirty miles of Crane.

Crane covered the Spanish-American War from April to November 1898 for the *New York World* and the *New York Journal*, producing some of the best news reporting ever written by an American war correspondent. Examples include "Regulars Get No Glory" and "The Red Badge of Courage Was His Wig-Wag Flag." When he returned to New York to enlist in the navy after the sinking of the *Maine*, Crane was rejected as physically unfit.

Magazine readers could meanwhile peruse major stories such as "The Blue Hotel" and "The Bride Comes to Yellow Sky" and the short social novel *The Monster*, all of which appeared in periodical form in 1898. "The Blue Hotel" is to "The Open Boat" as a nightmare is to a dream. One of the most difficult of Crane's stories, its depiction of gratuitous violence suggests the fragility of human existence in a bleak natural world. "The Bride Comes to Yellow Sky" delineates the impact on a Western town of its sheriff's marriage to a "lady" who represents the advent of a new West in which civil behavior will be the order of the day as the old Wild West fades into oblivion. In Cuba Crane covered the landing of U.S. marines at Guantanamo and the famous charge up San Juan Hill. In one of his best stories from the Cuban-American conflict, "A Mystery of Heroism," a soldier reminiscent of the Little Man risks his life to bring water to a fallen officer who dies before the soldier reaches him, after which two larking lieutenants spill the contents of the bucket. Before writing the story Crane himself risked death by delivering water to thirsty U.S. troops under siege. His surprise meeting with a gravely wounded former schoolmate found its way into the moving sketch "War Memories."

Settling in at Brede Place, Sussex, Crane and Taylor lived a lavish social life that they could not begin to afford. As a consequence Crane struggled to write himself out of debt, producing in 1899 such potboilers as *Active Service and Battles of the World*, but also a collection of poems, *War Is Kind*, which was published in May. *The Monster and Other Stories* appeared in December. *The Monster* explores, as do most of Crane's best tales, a community in crisis, here precipitated by a black servant whose death-defying heroism saves the son of the local doctor. When disfiguring injuries turn the man into the monster of the title, both the servant and the family are ostracized. Although Crane elsewhere succumbs to the ethnic and racial stereotypes of his age, *The Monster* is one of the most forceful fictional inquiries into racism in the United States.

In his brief career Crane demonstrated his belief that by adopting different perspectives on his experiences, and by registering concretely the impressions that persons, things, and events made on him, he would be (to quote from a letter) "unmistakable." That he did this so early and so consistently accounts to a large degree for his almost immediate success among his contemporaries and for the fact that his writings continue to appeal to the general reader as well as to the scholar.

Suffering from a tubercular infection apparently complicated by malaria contracted in Cuba, Crane lived to see the serialization of *Whilomville Stories*, in which he portrayed sentimentally, and mock-heroically, the vicissitudes of American childhood. He was transported to a sanitarium in Badenweiler, Germany, where, with Taylor at his side, he passed away. He was buried in the Evergreen Cemetery in Hillside, New Jersey. Obituaries were published in leading newspapers and magazines, including the *New York Tribune*, *World*, and *Journal*; the *Philistine*; and the London *Spectator*. His Cuban experiences were published as *Wounds in the Rain* (1900). *Great Battles of the World*, partly written by Kate Lyon (Mrs. Harold Fredric), was published in 1901. An anthology, *Last Words* (1902), put together by Cora Taylor, contained early pieces as well as unpublished tales and sketches (two of which she completed herself). The Irish swashbuckler novel, *The O'Ruddy*, was completed by Robert Barr and appeared in 1903.

• Crane materials are in the university libraries of Columbia, Connecticut, Dartmouth, Indiana, Lafayette (Penn.), Minnesota, New York, Ohio State, Syracuse, and Virginia; the Library of Congress, the Newark Public Library, and the New York Public Library; and private collections. (For a complete list of locations and information about letters from and to Crane, see Wertheim and Sorrentino, below.) Corwin K. Linson, *My Stephen Crane*, ed. Edwin H. Cady (1958), contains valuable information from the perspective of a friend. The first biography, *Stephen Crane: A Study in American Letters*, by the novelist Thomas Beer (1923), though sometimes unreliable, is still readable; John Berryman, *Stephen Crane* (1950), remains a seminal study; more fully researched, if uneven, is *Stephen Crane: A Biography*, rev. ed., by R. W. Stallman (1973). James B. Colvert, *Stephen Crane* (1984), is a cogent biography with illustrations. In 1960 Stallman and Lillian Gilkes published *Stephen Crane: Letters*, which was surpassed by *The Correspondence of Stephen Crane* (2 vols.), ed. Stanley Wertheim and Paul Sorrentino (1988), containing nearly 400 items not in Stallman and Gilkes. The standard edition of primary works is Fredson Bowers, ed., *The Works of Stephen Crane* (10 vols., 1969–1976), superseding Wilson Follett's popular edition *The Work of Stephen Crane* (12 vols., 1925–1927).

Daniel G. Hoffman, *The Poetry of Stephen Crane* (1957), is the first major study of the verse. See also Joseph Katz, *The Poems of Stephen Crane: A Critical Edition* (1971). Crane's development is studied by Eric Solomon in *Stephen Crane: From Parody to Realism* (1966). Chester L. Wolford, *The Anger of Stephen Crane: Fiction and the Epic Tradition* (1983), inquires into the influence of epic. Marston La France, *A Reading of Stephen Crane* (1971), offers a general analysis, as do Frank Bergon, *Stephen Crane's Artistry* (1975), and Bettina L. Knapp, *Stephen Crane* (1987). Donald B. Gibson, "*The Red Badge of Courage*": *Redefining the Hero* (1988), studies Crane's concept of heroism, and Michael Fried, *Realism, Writing, Disfiguration: On Thomas Eakins and Stephen Crane* (1987), ventures an art-historical approach. Other interpretations include David Halliburton, *The Color of the Sky: A Study of Stephen Crane* (1989), and Christopher Benfey, *The Double Life of Stephen Crane* (1992).

DAVID HALLIBURTON

CRANE, Thomas Frederick (12 July 1844–9 Dec. 1927), linguist, scholar, and educator, was born in New York City, the son of Thomas Sexton, a successful merchant, and Charlotte Nuttman. His early life was spent traveling between New York and New Orleans, where his father's business was based. He had little formal education during these years, but his mother taught him to read. He enjoyed the New Orleans Municipal Library, and his father always brought back books for him when he returned home.

In 1853, at the age of nine, Crane was sent to live with his maternal grandmother in Ithaca, New York. Here he attended the Ithaca Public School and, later, the Ithaca Academy. After a year on his retired father's farm in Elizabeth, New Jersey, Crane enrolled in the College of New Jersey (Princeton), graduating in 1864. He went on to receive the degrees of A.M. in 1867, Ph.D. in 1883, and Litt.D. in 1903, from the same institution. While in college, Crane studied a set academic course that included no foreign languages, although he managed to learn a little French from a member of the faculty.

In 1864 he began studying law at Columbia Law School. Here he made friends with a young minister, Frederick Parmenter, who began to teach Crane German, thus setting him on his career path. During a visit to Ithaca in January 1865 to see an ailing relative, he agreed to join the law firm of Boardman and Finch.

The law office became involved in 1866 with Mr. Ezra Cornell's plans for a university (both members of the firm eventually became deans of the Cornell University Law School). During the process of founding the university, Crane acted as secretary to Finch and Cornell. Independently, he continued to study German and began to learn Spanish. By 1868 his Spanish was so competent that he was being asked to review Spanish books for the *Nation*. Despite this proficiency in languages, Dr. Andrew D. White, the first president of Cornell University, discouraged him from pursuing a teaching career in linguistics.

However, when the university formally opened in October 1868, a German professor, Dr. Willard Fiske, who was in Egypt, informed White that he would not return until January. In desperation White asked Crane if he would be willing to organize the department and keep things going in the interim. Crane accepted the position of librarian and instructor of Spanish and German for a salary of $800.

Crane enjoyed his new position so much that in 1869, after Fiske's return, he sailed for Europe and spent the next year and a half in Germany, Italy, Spain, and France, perfecting his language skills. On his return, he resumed his assistant professorship in north European languages. Shortly before the 1870 schoolyear began, James Morgan Hart, assistant professor of south European languages, suggested to Crane that they swap chairs. From then on, Crane taught French, Spanish, and Italian.

Crane spent the rest of his career at Cornell University. In July 1872 Crane married Sarah Fay Tourtellot, daughter of Jeremiah Tourtellot of Ithaca; they had one daughter. In 1882 he was appointed professor of romance languages and literatures and department head. He held this position until his retirement in 1909 with the title professor emeritus. He served as dean of the college of arts from 1896 until 1902 and dean of the university faculty from 1902 to 1909. He returned after his retirement to serve as acting president of the university for a brief period in 1899 and for a year from 1912 to 1913.

Despite his linguistic skills, Crane was not a popular teacher in his early years and was universally known as "Vinegar Crane." However, his popularity increased as he aged, and he became the "Grand Old Man of Cornell" to undergraduates and homecoming alumni.

Crane's academic interests were in folklore and medieval literature (one of his most popular courses was on Dante). He contributed numerous articles to the *Nation* and the *North American Review* and was a member of the board of editors for the initial volumes of the *Journal of American Folklore* from 1888 to 1892. He edited a large number of European works, including *The Exempla; or, Illustrative Stories from the Sermones Vulgares of Jacques de Vitry* (1890), *Liber de Miraculis Sanctae Dei Genitricis Mariae, Published at Vienna, in 1731 by B. Pez* (1925), and *Italian Popular Tales* (1885). He also wrote books on European culture, including *Italian Social Customs of the Sixteenth Century* (1920). Much of his research and writing after his retirement was funded by Andrew Carnegie.

Crane's presence at Cornell helped to establish the institution as one of the foremost educational establishments in the world. He also helped the institution materially, donating several hundred volumes of rare and valuable works on French and Italian society in the sixteenth and seventeenth centuries to the university library in 1896. Crane died in Deland, Florida.

• Most of the information on Crane's early career is from his own article, "How I Became a Professor," *The Cornell Era* 41 (Jan. 1909): 149–58. His career at Cornell and his importance to that institution is documented in Morris Bishop, *A History of Cornell* (1962), and Waterman Thomas Hewett, *Cornell University: A History* (1905). See also the preface to *Italian Social Customs of the Sixteenth Century and Their Influence on the Literatures of Europe* (1920). Obituaries are in the *New York Times*, 11 Dec. 1927, and the *Nation*, 18 Jan. 1928.

CLAIRE STROM

CRANE, William Henry (30 Apr. 1845–7 Mar. 1928), actor, was born in Leicester, Massachusetts, the son of Amaziah Brito Crane, a locksmith and bell hanger, and Mary Sophia Masters. Crane grew up with his family in and near Boston, which in his successful years happily embraced him as a native son. While attending the Brimmer School, Crane participated in school and amateur theatrical and choral groups. In 1863 Crane attended a performance of the Holman Opera and Dramatic Troupe, a traveling family group that included four siblings near his own age. Crane reported: "I simply went crazy. I wanted to be, if not like them, as like them as it was possible to be" (*Footlights and Echoes*, p. 33). That same year, Crane's professional life began with a grueling apprenticeship with the Holmans during which he performed in "character" and comic roles suited to his untrained bass voice. The company settled for a series of consecutive seasons beginning in 1866 in Toronto, where their repertory up to the time of Crane's departure in 1870 included more than forty titles. From the Holmans, Crane moved directly to the Oates Opera Troupe, another touring company. In 1870 Crane married Ella Chloe Myers, whom he had met in Utica, New York, when first appearing with the Holmans. He wrote that: "Mrs. Crane joined the company with me the next night in Providence, and has been traveling . . . ever since. She has managed and mothered not only me, but my whole company. The whole profession has come to know her as Aunt Ella" (*Footlights and Echoes*, p. 48). The couple did not have children. Also in this first season with the Oates company, Crane began his long friendship with his distinguished fellow performer Joseph Jefferson III.

Never a trained musician, Crane's professional interests focused increasingly on acting instead of singing. In 1874 Crane joined Hooley's Stock Company. With Hooley, Crane went to San Francisco and afterward enjoyed success at several western theaters. Crane began a decade-long association with the actor Stuart Robson when they appeared together in 1877 in *Our Boarding House*, Crane in the role of Colonel M. T. Elevator. Although they mounted successful productions of *Comedy of Errors*, *The Merry Wives of Windsor*, and *She Stoops to Conquer*, Crane indicated in his biography that they were more interested in playing comedies by American authors. This preoccupation absorbed Crane for the rest of his career. Their most successful joint venture was also their last. They opened together in 1887 in Bronson Howard's *The Henrietta*, a comedy of Wall Street life and stock market dealings, and enjoyed a two-year run after which they parted by mutual agreement to pursue their own ventures.

For Crane, that venture provided the role with which he was to be associated for the rest of his life.

After preliminary outings at various sites, *The Senator* opened on 13 January 1890 and ran for more than 200 performances in its first year at the Star Theatre in New York City. Crane played this role almost exclusively in many cities for a total of five years and frequently thereafter. Though some critics faulted the play itself—comparable to many star vehicle plays then and now, it has more theatrical than literary merit—praise for Crane's portrayal was unreserved from all quarters. The *New York Times* declared:

Mr. Crane has added appreciably to the merriment of his time by his impersonation of Senator Hannibal Rivers, one of the new millionaire statesmen from the breezy West. There is less of caricature in this personage than in . . . the well-remembered Sellers [a famous "stage American from the Southern States" in *The Gilded Age*] of Mark Twain. Outwardly he is an every-day sort of fellow, lacking the polish and refinement that come from association with polite society, though his heart is, of course, sound and his honesty is unimpeachable. . . . The part of Rivers affords Mr. Crane an opportunity to exhibit genuine feeling as well as exuberant humor. (19 Jan. 1890)

Crane claimed and it is true that: "I became so identified with the part that people I met for the first time called me senator, and it was a common thing in newspapers to speak of me as Senator Crane" (*Footlights and Echoes*, p. 133).

With *The Senator*, Crane assumed the status of a star performer. He had engaged Joseph Brooks to manage his company, and together they presented many successful vehicles for Crane that toured the country every year. None, however, was as popular as *The Senator*, which was always retained in the repertory. In the spring of 1896 he joined Jefferson and other luminaries in a well-remembered, all-star production of Sheridan's *The Rivals*. In 1899 Crane turned to Charles Frohman, who managed Crane for the next nine years. Their fruitful partnership began with the production of *David Harum*, based on a well-known rural character. After the usual preliminary engagements, *David Harum* opened at the Garrick Theatre in New York City on 1 October 1900. If not his greatest financial success, Crane's Harum was frequently cited as his most artistic creation. In 1913, with his old manager Brooks, Crane assembled an updated version of *The Henrietta*, called *The New Henrietta*, which featured Crane and Douglas Fairbanks, who would soon begin his film career. *The New Henrietta* lasted three popular seasons and was made into a movie called *The Saphead*. Crane retired to Hollywood, California, after *The New Henrietta*, giving only occasional benefit performances, mostly on the West Coast.

His final illness and death, in the presence of his wife in his Hollywood hotel room, were widely chronicled. During his long career, Crane was well-acquainted not only with many of the foremost of his professional colleagues but also with many notable persons from American society and politics. Besides creating a series of popular American characters, he was an active supporter of American playwrights and a thoughtful commentator on American arts. At the turn of the century, he was one of the most successful comedians in the United States and a much-admired promoter of American values in the theater. In Crane there was a conflation of personal and character values. Lewis Strang noted that: "He is a character comedian, whose one character is himself. His is a whole-souled, frank, and genial personality, a personality that suggests shrewdness and generosity, keen good sense, and tender-hearted chivalry. In a word, he realises to a degree the American ideal of what a man should be" (*Famous Actors*, p. 149).

• Crane's autobiography, *Footprints and Echoes* (1927), is an indispensable source. Brief overviews are provided by William C. Young, *Famous Actors and Actresses on the American Stage* (1975), and Lewis Strang, *Famous Actors of the Day in America* (1900). The *Illustrated American*, 6 Dec. 1890, pp. 603–17, has a detailed, illustrated synopsis of Crane's production of *The Senator*. An obituary is in the *New York Times*, 8 Mar. 1928.

MAARTEN REILINGH

CRANE, William Montgomery (1 Feb. 1784–18 Mar. 1846), naval officer, was born in Elizabeth, New Jersey, the son of William Crane and Abigail Miller. His father was a revolutionary war colonel distinguished at the siege of Quebec. Crane became a midshipman on 23 May 1799 and spent several years aboard the frigate *United States*. He sailed under Captain John Barry in the Quasi-War with France and was commissioned a lieutenant on 20 July 1803. Crane assumed command of the schooner *Vixen* during the Tripolitan War and later directed gunboats during the 7 August 1804 bombardment of Tripoli. He was present aboard the frigate *Chesapeake* under Captain James Barron during the infamous *Leopard* affair of 1807, and subsequently he testified against Barron when that officer was court-martialed for failing to prepare the *Chesapeake* for battle.

The renewal of war with Great Britain in June 1812 found Crane in New York commanding the schooner *Nautilus*. In this capacity, he enjoyed the dubious honor of losing the first U.S. Navy vessel to the enemy. Crane sailed from New York on 1 July and soon encountered the blockading squadron of Commodore Philip V. Broke. He lightened the *Nautilus* and threw his lee guns overboard in an attempt to escape but finally surrendered to HMS *Shannon* after a six-hour pursuit. Crane was taken to Halifax as a prisoner and, following a brief internment, was exchanged and became commanding officer of the Charlestown Navy Yard in November 1812. He remained in Boston until February 1813 when orders arrived directing him to the frigate *John Adams* in New York. There he received promotion to commander on 4 March 1813.

Crane's tenure aboard the *John Adams* proved uneventful, and he was shortly after transferred with his crew to Sackets Harbor, New York, as part of Commodore Isaac Chauncey's Lake Ontario squadron. He took charge of the sloop *Madison* and fought in numerous skirmishes throughout the summer and fall of 1813. The following spring he assumed command of the brig *General Pike* and was promoted to captain on 22 November 1814. Crane remained on Lake Ontario until the advent of peace in January 1815.

Crane's postwar career was extremely active and varied. In the summer of 1815 he captained the ship-of-the-line *Independence*, flagship of Commodore William Bainbridge's squadron, and sailed against Algiers. The following year he transferred his flag to the sloop *Erie* and made additional demonstrations against the North African coast. Following several years at sea, Crane returned to command the Charlestown Navy Yard from 6 April 1825 to 5 May 1827, when he was succeeded by Commodore John Morris. In June 1827 he hoisted his pennant aboard the battleship *Delaware* as commander of the Mediterranean Squadron and assisted Consul David Offley in negotiating a commercial treaty with the Ottoman Empire. Crane later commanded the navy yard in Portsmouth, New Hampshire, from 1832 to 1840, and the following year he was appointed to the Board of Navy Commissioners in Washington, D.C.

In 1842 Crane became chief of the Bureau of Ordnance and Hydrology. The navy was then experiencing a transition to more modern technology, and he was responsible for the testing of metals and explosives and other matters relating to weapons. When the navies of Britain and France began simplifying shipboard ordnance by standardizing the calibers mounted, Crane dispatched several officers to Europe to study the changes. He lacked authority, however, to prevent individuals like Captain Robert F. Stockton from experimenting with their own pieces. When Stockton had an immense twelve-inch bore cannon cast in England to his own specifications, Crane refused to attend the firing trials. On 28 February 1844 this weapon, the so-called "Peacemaker," exploded during an exhibition aboard the steam frigate *Princeton*. Eight people died, including Secretary of State Abel P. Upshur and Secretary of the Navy Thomas W. Gilmer. Though not held responsible for the accident, Crane grew increasingly despondent over it. On 18 March 1846 he locked himself in his Washington, D.C., office and committed suicide by cutting his own throat.

Crane was survived by his wife, Erza King. The date of their marriage and the number of their children, if any, are unknown. Despite an untimely demise, Crane was a fine sailor and administrator who rendered valuable services to the country in several wars. Unlike many contemporaries, he proved himself equally adept on the deck of a ship, at the negotiating table, or behind a bureau desk. Crane's career personifies the professionalism of the nineteenth-century naval officer corps.

• Crane's official correspondence is in RG 45, Captains' Letters, National Archives. Other material is in the Smith Naval Collection, Clements Library, University of Michigan, and the New-York Historical Society. His regulation book for the USS *Madison* is preserved at the New York State Historical Association, Cooperstown. Items relating to Crane's career are in Dudley W. Knox, ed., *Naval Documents Related to the Quasi War* (7 vols., 1935–1938) and *Documents Related to the United States Wars with the Barbary Powers* (6 vols., 1939–1944); William S. Dudley, ed., *The Naval War of 1812* (2 vols., 1985–1990); J. F. Goodwyn, "Ship's Orders: 1815," United States Naval Institute, *Proceedings* 66 (1940): 78–82; and Edwin V. Bearss, *Charlestown Navy Yard* (2 vols., 1984). For insight into Crane's diplomatic ventures see David F. Long, *Gold Braid and Foreign Relations* (1988). Crane's role as naval administrator is discussed in Geoffrey S. Smith, "An Uncertain Passage: The Bureaus Run the Navy," in *In Peace and War*, ed. Kenneth Hagan (1984), pp. 70–106, and Spencer C. Tucker, *Arming the Fleet* (1989).

JOHN C. FREDRIKSEN

CRANE, Winthrop Murray (23 Apr. 1853–2 Oct. 1920), industrialist, governor of Massachusetts, and U.S. senator, was born in Dalton, Massachusetts, the son of Zenas Marshall Crane, a paper manufacturer, and Louise Fanny Laflin. A member of a wealthy and politically prominent western Massachusetts family, Crane attended Wesleyan Academy (later Wilbraham Academy) in Wilbraham, Massachusetts, and Williston Seminary in Easthampton. He left school in 1870 to work in his family's paper mills. After trying every job from floor sweeper to mill superintendent, he found his niche in sales.

Through resourcefulness and dogged persistence, Crane developed into the family firm's crack salesman. He secured the business of the Winchester Arms Company in 1875 by designing and producing "Bullet Patch," a special cartridge paper needed for the breech-loading rifles the gun merchant sold abroad and in the American West. Crane's second major sales coup came in 1879, when he outmaneuvered the politically connected representatives of three larger firms and captured an exclusive contract with the federal government for currency and bond paper. In 1880 he married Mary Benner; she died after the birth of their only child in 1884.

Murray Crane advanced into management in the 1880s and, after the deaths of his father (1887) and uncle (1891), emerged as the leader of the next Crane generation. While his brother and cousin tended to the operation of the company mills, he took charge of the family's stock portfolio. His shrewd investing expanded the already considerable Crane fortune and involved him in the affairs of booming late nineteenth-century enterprises such as the American Telephone and Telegraph Company, the Boston & Albany Railroad, the Otis Elevator Company, and Western Union. These activities made him a familiar figure in financial circles in Boston and New York.

After the death of his wife, most of Crane's life outside of business was taken up with philanthropic and political activities. Following his family's paternalistic tradition, he personally came to the aid of ill and injured workers and needy families in Dalton, established substantial scholarships for local students, and even underwrote loans for slumping businesses in western Massachusetts. In addition, the Congregational church, hospitals, and the temperance movement were regular recipients of his generosity.

Crane also contributed significant sums of money to the Republican party, which his father had joined in its infancy. He sought a more active role in party affairs in 1892, accepting a place on the slate of Massachusetts delegates to the Republican National Convention. At the conclave in Minneapolis he was elected the Massachusetts national committeeman by his fellow delegates, who thought his financial connections would be useful for the post's principal task: fundraising. He served on the National Committee for twenty-four of the next twenty-seven years.

Beyond filling Republican coffers, Crane used his National Committee job to win party support for his own ambition "to direct larger affairs." When he launched his candidacy for lieutenant governor in 1896, all of the major factions of the Massachusetts GOP came together and helped him defeat a formidable rival at the state convention. He was then elected easily in a national and statewide Republican sweep and was reelected in 1897 and 1898. In 1899 he moved up the party escalator to the governorship and served three one-year terms.

The watchwords of Crane's conservative, business-oriented governorship were balance and stability. Crane moved to aid the commercial interests of Massachusetts in 1900 by arranging the lease of the Fitchburg Railroad to the home-based Boston & Maine, making the latter competitive with the out-of-state New York Central, which had just absorbed the Boston & Albany line. A year later he vetoed special interest legislation giving another Bay State enterprise, the Boston Elevated Railway Company, the right to build a new subway line in Boston and an exclusive lease to run it for fifty years. In the latter case, he believed the long lease transgressed traditional state policy and was detrimental to the city.

Crane supported mild reform legislation to end interlocking directorates of savings and national banks and to require railroads to share the cost of eliminating hazardous grade crossings. The Republican-dominated legislature under Crane also passed laws strengthening food inspection, requiring compulsory vaccination, and loosening blue laws. At the same time, the conservative governor and his allies in the Massachusetts house and senate scuttled what they viewed as more radical progressive efforts to improve labor conditions, provide for public ownership of utilities, and institute direct primaries for state officials.

Crane gained national stature in 1902, when he settled a crippling three-day teamsters' strike by assembling business and labor leaders in separate rooms at the state house, shuttling between the two sides, and mediating a stopgap agreement in two hours. Hailed as a sage on labor matters, Crane was called in for consultation by President Theodore Roosevelt on the prolonged national anthracite coal strike. Subsequently, a labor-management conference, similar to the one that had ended the teamsters' strike, was arranged and led to an agreement.

After turning down a number of high posts in the Roosevelt administration, including the secretaryship of the Treasury, Crane accepted the appointment of his friend Governor John L. Bates to fill the Massachusetts seat in the U.S. Senate left vacant by the death of George Frisbie Hoar in 1904. Crane fit easily into the probusiness "Old Guard" faction of the Republican Senate majority headed by Nelson W. Aldrich of Rhode Island. As Aldrich's lieutenant, he opposed the Hepburn Act of 1906 and other efforts at railroad regulation from his seat on the Commerce Committee and most often voted with his leader against other progressive reforms. Although the once dominant Old Guard had come under fierce attack by the muckraking press and an increasingly activist President Roosevelt, Crane retained his popularity in Massachusetts and was elected to a full term by the legislature in 1907. In 1906 he married Josephine Porter Boardman, who was twenty years his junior; they had three children.

In 1908 Crane, who had broken with President Roosevelt a year earlier, opposed the nomination of Roosevelt's handpicked successor, Secretary of War William Howard Taft. After Taft's election, however, Crane found the new president less progressive and more sympathetic to congressional prerogatives than his predecessor. The two became close confidants and social friends.

Taft's reliance on the advice of Crane and other members of the Republican Old Guard and his tilt toward conservatism on matters of the tariff and conservation won him the bitter opposition of progressives and Roosevelt. After the retirement of Aldrich in 1911, Crane became Taft's chief adviser and troubleshooter. The Massachusetts senator helped the president push his Canadian Reciprocity Treaty through the Senate and, at the request of the White House, attempted unsuccessfully to convince Interior secretary Richard A. Ballinger, a particular target of progressives, to leave his post and run for the U.S. Senate in the state of Washington. In 1912 Crane was a member of the Republican National Committee panel that threw out challenges by progressives to the seating of 235 Taft delegates and ensured the president's victory over former president Roosevelt at the GOP convention in Chicago. Roosevelt then used his defeat at the hands of Crane and other Old Guard "bosses" as an issue in his third-party campaign.

Crane retired at the end of his term and returned to Dalton. Remaining in close touch with significant developments in national and state politics, he often helped his fellow conservatives formulate strategies to advance the interests of the large corporate entities with which he was associated and to combat the reform efforts of the Woodrow Wilson administration. In Massachusetts Crane influenced the election of a protégé, Calvin Coolidge, to the presidency of the state senate in 1913 and took great satisfaction in Coolidge's ascent to the governorship and the vice presidential nomination.

In his last political battle, Crane fought to have the Republican party support U.S. entry into the League of Nations. Believing, with most of the financial community, that the league was the answer to the disorder brought about by World War I, Crane convinced the Massachusetts Republican state convention to endorse his position in 1919. Crane's effort embarrassed his former colleague Henry Cabot Lodge, who opposed the league as propounded by the Democratic president Wilson. Even after the Republican-controlled Senate rejected the league, Crane continued his quixotic effort, seeking support at the 1920 GOP National Convention. A few months after he lost this last battle with Lodge, Crane died in Dalton.

A remarkable figure in Massachusetts history, Crane won six elections without making a speech and was held in higher political esteem than his more visible Brahmin rival, Lodge, for twenty years. The taciturn Yankee businessman's paternalism, commitment to traditional standards, and behind-the-scenes skills made him a master of the political game in his home state. Nationally, however, his corporate conservatism and secretive ways ran counter to the progressive tide. As a result, Crane is remembered principally as the provincial mentor of Coolidge.

• The Winthrop Murray Crane Papers are in family hands. Important Crane letters are in the collections of William Howard Taft in the Library of Congress and Henry Cabot Lodge at the Massachusetts Historical Society. Carolyn W. Johnson, *Winthrop Murray Crane: A Study in Republican Leadership, 1892–1920* (1967), is a recent biographical study. Solomon Bulkley Griffin, *W. Murray Crane, a Man and Brother* (1926), and John Lewis Bates, "Hon. Winthrop Murray Crane," *New England Historical and Genealogical Register* 77 (Jan. 1923): 3–9, are memoirs by friends and political associates. See also Michael E. Hennessy, *Twenty-five Years of Massachusetts Politics, 1890–1915* (1917), on the electoral history of the Crane era, and Richard M. Abrams, *Conservatism in a Progressive Era: Massachusetts Politics, 1900–1912* (1964), for a discussion of Crane's career in historical context. An obituary is in the *Springfield* (Mass.) *Republican*, 3 Oct. 1920.

RICHARD H. GENTILE

CRANSTON, Samuel (7 Aug. 1659–26 Apr. 1727), governor of Rhode Island, was born in Newport, Rhode Island, the son of John Cranston, an earlier governor who had various occupations, and Mary Clarke. Samuel Cranston probably had as much formal schooling as was available in Newport. It is said that he learned the trade of a goldsmith and also went to sea for a few years—he was called "Captain"—and engaged in commerce, but his record of holding public office was so extensive as to make him the first man in Rhode Island to make governmental service a career. In 1680 he married Mary Hart, daughter of Thomas Hart, a shipmaster, and of Freeborn Williams, a daughter of Roger Williams. They had seven children.

Cranston rose to high office at least by 1695, when he was elected an assistant for his colony. The ten assistants, together with the governor and deputy governor, composed the upper house of the legislature, the council of war, and the bench of the high court. Upon the resignation of his uncle, Walter Clarke, in March 1698, Cranston was chosen governor by the General Assembly and elected by the freemen the following May to his first full term. He was reelected annually twenty-eight times. During his administration he also filled many other positions in the town government of Newport and in organizations of proprietors of common lands. In all capacities, he acted energetically and displayed an evenhanded, forthright character. At first over-confident and somewhat clumsy in his handling of public business, he gained self-control and wisdom over the years. Never one to shrink from a fight, he preferred to reconcile opponents by his talents of persuasion.

Rhode Island changed enormously during Cranston's years as governor, but there is little evidence revealing how much he steered events. The government solved several long-standing problems that had hampered the colony in the seventeenth century. It settled some bitterly contested boundaries between towns, made some progress in exerting a tax authority, ended the conflict over ownership and jurisdiction in the region west of Narragansett Bay, and won a long-sought definition of the boundary with Connecticut. Cranston had a strong hand in at least the last two of these achievements. He also did much to end old conflicts over common lands and push forward the work of dividing them into individual holdings. These successes made possible Rhode Island's rapid growth in population and prosperity during the eighteenth century. The growth was further stimulated by extension of the transportation network, which he favored, and the issuance of paper currency, which he opposed.

Cranston engineered a sharp break with the colony's past in other ways. Faced with the last two of several campaigns by the Board of Trade and Privy Council to abolish the colony's charter government, he skillfully frustrated them by some compromises and by improving the colonial government in ways that imperial officials said would not get done without installing a royal governor. Rhode Island became responsive to the imperial administration and willing to admit a few royal officials, such as a vice admiralty judge and a customs collector.

The most important compromise, and one plainly near Cranston's heart, was military cooperation in the imperial wars. Pacifist Baptists and Quakers in the past had avoided armed force almost entirely, so he had to reverse a settled disposition. By 1705 he received the votes for sizable military forces—eventually more than London asked for—to join under royal commanders for action against the French in Nova Scotia and Canada. It followed that Newport had to be fortified for the first time. Well after the war he contended with an often unwilling General Assembly to maintain military preparedness.

The heavy military expenditures of Queen Anne's War led to the first issue of paper currency, and the depression that followed peace led both to widespread settler refusal to pay property taxes to retire it and demands for the issuance of more currency in the land bank fashion. Cranston opposed this policy and as a consequence saw some of his most effective colleagues form an opposition to him that gained control of the General Assembly by 1715 and enacted the relief measures. He took no part in the administration of the land banks. His opponents probably did not want to unseat him; surely they never succeeded in doing so. But he became more of a presiding figure than a leading one, a skilled administrator rather than a planner.

In 1710, during the most demanding years of his long administration, Cranston's first wife died. The next year he married Judith (Parrett or Parrott) Cranston, widow of his brother Caleb. She brought two young nieces into the household but bore no more children. Samuel Cranston died in Newport, much honored for his diplomacy and compromises. In retrospect, his outstanding accomplishment was in preserving Rhode Island's charter privileges while establishing smoother and enduring relationships with Crown officials.

• Few papers by Samuel Cranston are in generally accessible repositories. The state archives in Providence has a few of his administration papers, and there is a small collection of personal materials under his name at the Rhode Island Historical Society in Providence. Other documents are scattered there in other collections, in the Winthrop papers at the Massachusetts Historical Society in Boston, and in the file papers of the General Court of Trials at the Rhode Island Supreme Court Judicial Center, Pawtucket. The only valuable published account of his life and accomplishments is in Sydney V. James, *Colonial Rhode Island—A History* (1975).

SYDNEY V. JAMES

CRAPSEY, Adelaide (9 Sep. 1878–8 Oct. 1914), poet, was born in New York City, the daughter of Rev. Algernon Sidney Crapsey, an Episcopal clergyman whose own small fame came from his trial for heresy in 1906, and Adelaide Trowbridge. At the time of Crapsey's birth, her father was on the staff of Trinity Parish in New York City. The family moved to Rochester in 1879 where he was the rector of St. Andrews.

Adelaide Crapsey was the third of nine children, and the only child mentioned in Rev. Crapsey's autobiography, *The Last of the Heretics* (1924). Short, small, and athletic, she was a brilliant student at Kemper Hall, her prep school in Kenosha, Wisconsin. She went on to college at Vassar, graduating in 1901. Her poetry at this time was light-hearted, often poking fun at the young men she met in her social and collegiate life.

From 1903 through 1905 she taught history and literature at Kemper Hall, and from 1905 to 1906 she attended the School of Archaeology in Rome. Returning to the United States in 1907, she worked until the following year as an instructor in literature and history at Miss Lowe's Preparatory School in Stamford, Connecticut.

A severe illness in 1908 was not diagnosed as tuberculosis, and in 1909 Crapsey decided to travel alone to Europe to recuperate and study English metrics and art. By 1911 she was back in the United States and able to teach again. She taught poetics at Smith College until 1913, when her health collapsed again. This time her already established tuberculosis was discovered, and she went to Saranac Lake, New York, where America's first tuberculosis sanitarium had been created and where many chose to recuperate.

Ironically, her room overlooked a local graveyard, which she dubbed "Trudeau's Garden" (Edward Livingston Trudeau was the founder of the Sanitarium). One of her most revealing poems was written here, entitled, "To the Dead in the Grave-Yard Under My Window:—Written in a Moment of Exasperation."

Her health did not improve in the year she spent at Saranac, and she returned home to Rochester, dying there at the age of thirty-six.

The great works of Crapsey's life were her study of the metrics of the English language and her original verse form, which she named the "cinquain." Her work on metrics was a scholarly study of the relations between monosyllabic and polysyllabic words and was intended to refute the notion that English prose evolved from a lower to a higher state. Concurrent with this research was the development of the cinquain, a five-line verse with (generally) twenty-two syllables, presenting the maximum of idea with the minimum of words. She brought the form to perfection during her time at Saranac, where she personally selected the poems she wished published after her death.

Crapsey stood out among her peers and within her family with both self-deprecating humor and, paradoxically, restrained self-assurance. This was especially evident in the poems written during her confinement at Saranac. The title of one reads, "Lines Addressed to My Left Lung Inconveniently Enamoured of Plant-life." In addition, sometime before she started teaching at Smith College, she began wearing dull colors, such as gray and brown, even to the point of using only gray pencils. This preference was also reflected in her poetry, which rarely spoke of color; only gray, black, and silver are mentioned.

None of Crapsey's poems were published during her lifetime, except in school annuals and newspapers. Her closest friends—Jean Webster, playwright and grandniece of Mark Twain, and Esther Lowenthal, an economics instructor at Smith College—supported Adelaide's work and saw to it that her poems were made available after her death. It was Lowenthal who arranged for the publication of her work on metrics; titled *A Study in English Metrics*, it appeared posthumously in 1918.

Claude Bragdon, a Rochester publisher, was responsible for bringing Crapsey's poems to the public. Her poems were collected in a volume called *Verse*, published in 1915. An expanded version appeared in 1922, and both editions have brought Adelaide Crapsey the small fame she enjoys among devotees of American poetry. Carl Sandburg, for example, spoke highly of the originality of her poetic voice.

She is especially revered by those who study poetry written by women. Her association with female friends brought her the most personal satisfaction and essential support. This is especially true during the last, fatal illness, which robbed her of the poetic opportunities and well-deserved fame a longer life would have brought her.

• The University of Rochester houses Adelaide Crapsey's papers, consisting of correspondence, drafts of her poems and study of metrics, reading notes, published and unpublished articles about Crapsey, photographs, memorabilia, and scrapbooks covering the period 1878–1934. Additional primary source material is held in the Alumnae Collection of Vassar College. Biographies include Mary Elizabeth Osborn, *Adelaide Crapsey* (1933); Edward Butscher, *Adelaide Crapsey* (1979); and Karen Alkalay-Gut, *Alone in the Dawn: the Life of Adelaide Crapsey* (1988). Further background on Crapsey's life can be found in her father's autobiography, *The Last of the Heretics* (1924).

The definitive work on Crapsey and her poetry is found in Susan Sutton Smith, *The Complete Poems and Collected Letters of Adelaide Crapsey* (1977). Additional secondary sources are Robert Taylor, *Saranac* (1986), and William Drake, *The First Wave: Women Poets in America, 1915–1945* (1987). A poem by Carl Sandburg about Crapsey appears in *Cornhuskers* (1918).

LYNN DOWNEY

CRAPSEY, Algernon Sidney (28 June 1847–31 Dec. 1927), religious leader, was born in Fairmount, Ohio, the son of Jacob Tompkins Crapsey, a lawyer, and Rachel Morris. His father's declining legal practice forced Crapsey at age eleven to seek employment in a dry goods store. During the Civil War he served for four months as a private in the Ohio Infantry but was discharged when he was diagnosed as having a hypertrophied heart. He moved to New York City in the mid-1860s, became a bookkeeper, and joined the Episcopal church. Soon after he felt a call to ministry, studied at St. Stephen's (later Bard) College from 1867 to 1869 and graduated from General Theological Seminary in 1872. He was ordained a priest of the Episcopal church in 1873 and served on the staff of Trinity Church in Manhattan. In 1875 he married Adelaide Trowbridge; they had nine children.

In 1879 Crapsey accepted the pastorate of St. Andrew's Church in Rochester, New York. Under his leadership the small, struggling congregation maintained parochial and industrial schools and was recognized throughout the Episcopal church for its application of the Christian gospel to social issues. Crapsey became well known in Rochester for his involvement in civic affairs and for his work with Walter Rauschenbusch, a professor at Rochester Theological Seminary and the most prominent theologian of the Social Gospel. Crapsey also became a popular speaker, retreat leader, and writer.

A volume of his lectures, *Religion and Politics*, embroiled him in conflict in 1905. In one lecture he stated:

In the light of scientific research, the Founder of Christianity . . . no longer stands apart from the common destiny of man in life and death, but He is in all things physical like as we are, born as we are born, dying as we die, and both in life and death in the keeping of that same Divine Power, that heavenly Fatherhood, which delivers us from the womb and carries us down to the grave. (pp. 288–89)

In stressing Jesus' humanity, Crapsey sought to motivate Christians to follow Jesus' example and become more responsive to the suffering of others. More concerned about moral reform than adherence to doctrine, he emphasized the spiritual meaning of the creeds rather than their historical veracity.

Others in the Episcopal church disagreed. In 1906 Crapsey was brought up on heresy charges by the Right Reverend William David Walker, bishop of western New York, accused of denying central Christian doctrines of the virgin birth and the divinity of Jesus. Crapsey's views were similar to those of other clergy, but Walker may have wanted to show others what would happen if a priest spoke and acted without regard for clerical hierarchy. Despite the support of his congregation and Episcopal clergy and professors, Crapsey was convicted. Although he appealed the verdict, it was upheld in a higher church court. When the bishop requested that he recant his views, he refused. He was deposed from the priesthood and resigned from St. Andrew's.

After his departure from the priesthood, Crapsey had little influence in the Episcopal church. No other heresy trials, resignations in protest, or repercussions in seminaries followed his exit. He remained in Rochester but did not enter the ministry of another denomination. He wrote several books and lectured widely. He served as a delegate to the International Peace Conference at the Hague in 1907 and in 1914 was appointed a New York state parole officer. He died in Rochester.

To the end of his life Crapsey was committed to beliefs that placed him on the outskirts of Christendom. In the final chapter of his autobiography, *The Last of the Heretics* (1924), he wrote:

When I am asked in these days what my religion is, I hesitate and stumble, and men go away thinking that I have no religion. But I have a religion and if asked to give it a name I should say I am a Pantheistic Humanist, and if one were to ask, "What is a Pantheistic Humanist?" I should say one who believes in the divinity of a telegraph pole. . . . When I thought on these things I said if my Christ has in Him the divinity of a telegraph pole, then he is divine enough for me. (pp. 292–93)

Crapsey's heresy trial was one of several conducted by Protestant denominations at the turn of the century, among them, those of Presbyterian Charles Briggs, Southern Baptist Crawford Toy, and Methodist Borden Bowne. These trials reflected the growing polarization between conservative and liberal theologies and culminated in the 1925 Scopes "monkey" trial in Dayton, Tennessee. However, unlike the heresy trials in other denominations, Crapsey's case did not focus on biblical literalism but on faithfulness to the historical creeds of the church. His case tested the limits of the freedom of individual clergy to interpret creeds against ecclesiastical authority to enforce a particular interpretation. Crapsey's career provoked discussion of these issues but did not resolve them.

• The best contemporary source on Crapsey's life is his autobiography. His other published works include a novel, *The Greater Love* (1902), a historical interpretation of modern social problems, *The Rise of the Working Class* (1914), and a second volume of lectures, *The Rebirth of Religion* (1907). On the trial proceedings, see *Arguments for Presenters and Defence of Reverend A.S. Crapsey before the Court of Review of the Protestant Episcopal Church upon His Appeal from the Judgment of the Court of the Diocese of Western New York* (1906). Modern treatments include Carolyn Swanton, "Dr. Algernon S. Crapsey, Religious Reformer," *Rochester History* 42, no. 1 (1980): 1–24, and Hugh M. Jansen, Jr., "Algernon Sidney Crapsey: Heresy at Rochester," in *American Religious Heretics*, ed. George Shriver (1966). On the impact of the case on the Episcopal church, see W. Dudley F. Hughes, "Agreement on Fundamentals: Correspondence between Dr. Huntington and Dr. Manning on the Crapsey Case, 1906," *Historical Magazine of the Protestant Episcopal Church* 25, no. 3 (1956): 263–76. An obituary is in the *New York Times*, 1 Jan. 1928.

EVELYN A. KIRKLEY

CRARY, Isaac Edwin (2 Oct. 1804–8 May 1854), congressman and educator, was born in Preston, Connecticut, the son of Elisha Crary and Nabby Avery, farmers. He graduated from Trinity College in 1827 and spent two years practicing law in Hartford, Connecticut. In 1832 Crary moved to Marshall, Michigan, where he established that town's first law firm. While law remained Crary's profession, the advancement of education was his avocation, and he was instrumental in making Michigan a leader in the field of public education during the nineteenth century.

Shortly after arriving in Marshall, Crary developed a friendship with John Pierce, a traveling missionary of the American Home Mission Society, who had come to Marshall in 1831. According to one historian, Crary and Pierce, who "seemed to understand each other thoroughly," were impressed with a translation of Victor Cousin's report on the Prussian school system and believed Michigan's school system should be centralized and controlled by state officials.

On 5 April 1835 Crary was elected as a delegate to Michigan's first constitutional convention. When the convention opened in Detroit that May, Crary was appointed chairman of the Committee on Education. Article X of the constitution, as drafted by Crary's committee and adopted without substantive change, provided for the gubernatorial appointment of a superintendent of public instruction. At that time no other state in the Union made a constitutional provision for a superintendent of public instruction. The article also established safeguards for federal lands granted to the states for educational purposes and provided for the foundation of a state university. The founding of the University of Michigan in 1841 fulfilled this latter obligation. At the end of the convention, the delegates, at Crary's suggestion, adopted a petition requesting that Congress grant section sixteen of each township into a state school fund, rather than to the township, that would distribute revenues from the sale of these lands among the schools.

Elected Michigan's first congressman on 5 October 1835, Crary, a Democrat, was denied the right to take his seat in Congress until the border dispute with Ohio was resolved. He did, however, persuade Congress to adopt the state's constitutional provision regarding the section sixteen school lands. This innovation, which was enacted when Michigan was admitted into the Union in January 1837, allowed the state to realize "far more income" from the sale of these lands, which totaled over one million acres, than any other state in the Old Northwest had generated for support of schools. Once Michigan's stormy entrance into the Union was achieved, Crary formally took his seat in Congress in 1837.

Crary was reelected to Congress in 1836 and 1838. As Michigan's lone representative, he advocated harbor and river improvements, specifically urging support for surveys of the Great Lakes to aid navigation and commerce. Crary's most outspoken comments in his six years in Congress were against the U.S. Naval Board, which he described as "worse than useless." On 19 February 1839 Crary unleashed a tirade, declaring the board was "a hindrance to the navy and its efficient construction" and demanding the board's appropriations be ended. The reasons behind Crary's comments remain a mystery.

Despite being in Washington, Crary did not forget about education in Michigan. In 1836 Governor Stephens T. Mason, at Crary's suggestion, appointed Pierce the state's first superintendent of public instruction. Although Crary laid the foundations for Michigan public education, Pierce organized the system. Crary left Congress at the end of his term on 4 March 1841.

Back in Michigan, Crary was elected to the state house of representatives in 1842, 1844, and 1846. He served as chairman of the Committee on Education and, during the 1846 session, as Speaker. Crary was also a member of the 1850 state constitutional convention, and during that same year he was appointed to fill a vacancy on the state board of education. In 1852 he was elected to a six-year term on the board.

Crary's first wife, Jane Hitchcock, died in 1839. He married Bellona Pratt in 1841. Apparently he had no children. He died in Marshall, Michigan.

• Sources on Crary include Richard Carver, *A History of Marshall* (1993); Floyd Dain, *Education in the Wilderness* (1968); and Harold C. Brooks, "Founding of the Michigan Public School System," *Michigan History Magazine* (1949). See also James V. Campbell, *Outlines of the Political History of Michigan* (1876), and George N. Fuller, ed., *Historic Michigan* (2 vols., 1924).

ROGER L. ROSENTRETER

CRASKE, Margaret (26 Nov. 1892–18 Feb. 1990), ballet dancer and teacher, was born in Kirkley, England, the daughter of Edmund George Craske, a coal merchant, and Hannah Bishop. At the age of eighteen Craske began formal ballet study in London with a Madame Van Dyck and the expatriate Russian ballerina Serafina Astafieva. Having been warned against studying with Enrico Cecchetti, a former dancer and ballet master with Serge Diaghilev, because he was considered too old to teach, Craske visited his studio in 1918 out of curiosity. She later recalled, "There was a lion teaching, not an old man at all" (*Dance News*, Nov. 1982). Craske expressed interest in studying with him, and Cecchetti accepted her as a student.

Two years later, Diaghilev invited Craske to join his Ballets Russes corps de ballet. She danced two seasons, under the name Krasnova, until she injured an Achilles tendon. In the meantime she completed the required Cecchetti examinations and received a certificate as a teacher of his method. Craske taught at his school until 1923, at which time Cecchetti turned the school over to her. In a 1924 letter to Craske from Milan, Cecchetti called her "the only one who knows my method and who knows how to give lessons."

Craske's reputation as a teacher in the 1920s and 1930s was affirmed by critic Cyril Beaumont in a June 1950 *Dancing Times* article, in which he praised "that other great nursery of dancers, the studio of Margaret Craske, in my opinion still the greatest English teacher of dancing we have so far produced." The noted dancers whom Craske taught include Peggy Van Praagh, later director of the Australian Ballet, and Mary Skeaping, later director of the Royal Swedish Ballet.

In addition to teaching at her school, Craske continued to dance occasionally, with the Ninette de Valois troupe in London variety halls and as a principal with the Royal Italian Ballet at Covent Garden in 1924. In 1928 dancer Mabel Ryan became her teaching partner, and the name of the school was changed to the Craske-Ryan School.

Teaching and furthering the development of ballet in England became Craske's main focus. In 1920 she coauthored with Beaumont *The Theory and Practice of Allegro in Classical Ballet (Cecchetti Method)*, still a standard reference. She was a founder of the Cecchetti Society, the Camargo Society and the Ballet Club. Craske also taught guest classes at de Valois's Vic-Wells Ballet Company at the Old Vic Theatre, and she was one of the earliest teachers at the Sadler's Wells (later Royal) Ballet company at Covent Garden in London. She choreographed for the Carl Rosa Opera and was ballet mistress for Antony Tudor's London Ballet in 1938–1939.

In the fall of 1939, only weeks after the outbreak of World War II, Craske gave her school over to Van Praagh and sailed for India to spend seven years with her spiritual master, Meher Baba, whom she had met in London in 1931.

Craske returned to England in mid-1946, shortly before the Ballet Theatre company came from New York to appear in a Royal Opera House production. Tudor, who had left London in 1939 to become the company's choreographer, suggested to Lucia Chase, the Ballet Theatre's director, that Craske be engaged as the company's ballet mistress. Craske arrived in the United States in December 1946 and served as ballet mistress through 1950, the year the company, renamed American Ballet Theatre, contracted to direct for a year the Metropolitan Opera's ballets. When the company left the Met in 1951, Craske stayed on as associate director of the Metropolitan's school of ballet, and Tudor became its director. Concurrently, Craske served on the faculty of the Juilliard School's dance division (1951–1966) and taught during the summers at Ted Shawn's Jacob's Pillow school and festival near Lee, Massachusetts, through the late 1960s. In 1956, with Frederica Derra de Moroda, a student of Cecchetti and a teacher and dance writer, Craske wrote *The Theory and Practice of Advanced Allegro in Classical Ballet*, based on the Cecchetti technique.

Craske was a strict but patient teacher. She said that when she began teaching she thought "one had to be cruel" to be a good teacher, and she spoke at times of "whipping a dancer into shape." Her attitude soon changed, and she came to see the teacher's role as akin to that of a sculptor, charged with molding raw material. Her seriousness became well seasoned with humor, sharp wit, and an irrepressible love of repartee. The world of dance had changed after World War II, as had the rest of the world, and dance students were no longer willing to spend the years required to learn the Cecchetti technique and pass its stepping stone exams to certification. Craske realized this and accordingly condensed the Cecchetti technique. Nonetheless, she remained devoted to the attainment of correctness and balance, qualities that she believed enabled a dancer to do anything a choreographer asked. "The movement must have meaning," she declared, but she detected a lack of this in many dancers, whom she described as running around the stage and kicking themselves in the ear. From Craske's American classes emerged such notable dancers as Nora Kaye, Melissa Hayden, and Sallie Wilson.

Craske's working relations with Tudor deteriorated in disagreements over teaching methods, and she felt that the Met had lost interest in the school. She consequently resigned in 1968 and began to teach at Robert Ossorio's Manhattan School of Dance. The Manhattan school closed in 1984, and, not ready to retire, Craske then taught at Diana Byer's Ballet School NY and coached its companies. Craske retired in 1987 and moved to the Meher Spiritual Center in Myrtle Beach, South Carolina, where she died. She had never married.

Craske is generally regarded as one of the great ballet teachers. Her students respected her for her air of authority, her integrity in insisting on what she saw as correctness, and her refusal to put acrobatic flash before quality of technique. Her focus on fundamentals also drew to her classes a number of what choreographer Twyla Tharp has called "crossover dancers," modern dancers such as herself, Paul Taylor, Carolyn Brown, and Helen McGehee. The same focus was criticized by some teachers and dancers over the years as being outdated and too restrictive. But choreographer Don Mahler, one of Craske's students during the late 1940s and 1950s, remarked, "As time goes on I realize more and more how right what she taught was and how pertinent it still is" (taped interview with Ann Conlon, 24 Nov. 1990). With hundreds of former students teaching at schools and coaching companies around the world, Craske's "technique-before-flash" philosophy continues to influence the ballet world.

• Good overviews of Craske's career are Klasina Vander Werf, "Uncompromising Champion," *Ballet News*, Jan. 1983, pp. 28–31, and Joseph Gale, *Behind Barres: The Mystique of Masterly Teaching* (1980). A portrait of Craske as a teacher and mentor is in Christopher Sexton, *Peggy Van Praagh: A Life of Dance* (1985). Obituaries are in the *New York Times*, 23 Feb. 1990, and the London *Independent*, 22 Feb. 1990.

ANN CONLON

CRATTY, Mabel (30 June 1868–27 Feb. 1928), administrator of the Young Women's Christian Association, was born in Bellaire, Ohio, the daughter of Charles Campbell Cratty, a tanner, merchant, and insurance agent, and Mary Thoburn. Cratty credited her maternal grandfather, Matthew Thoburn, with instilling a Christian sense of mission and regard for the welfare of other human beings in his ten children, who expressed their mission through service in the Methodist Episcopal church. Cratty's maternal uncle James Thoburn became a bishop for the Methodist church in India. Her maternal aunt Isabella Thoburn became the first unmarried female American missionary to serve in a foreign country (India) and thus exemplified for Cratty the independent public life that educated single women could pursue beginning in the late nineteenth century.

Upon her high school graduation in 1884, Cratty enrolled in Lake Erie College in Painesville, Ohio, where she studied for one year until a diphtheria epidemic closed the college down. After she returned home, her father died. At age seventeen, Cratty, the oldest of five children, then helped her mother move the family to Delaware, Ohio, where Cratty attended Ohio Wesleyan University. She graduated with honors from Ohio Wesleyan and received a bachelor of law degree in 1890.

Although Cratty had dreamed of beginning mission work in India with her Aunt Isabella, Cratty put her family's needs first and became a teacher so that she could work near her home. Her first teaching position was at a private girls' school in West Virginia. After one year she returned to Ohio, where she taught Latin and worked as a principal in public schools until 1904. Cratty would not have chosen teaching, but other professional opportunities for women were scarce at the time.

In 1902 Cratty began her association with the Young Women's Christian Association (YWCA) by attending a summer training institute for female social activists that was run by the American Committee of the YWCA. The committee required evangelical Protestant church membership, promoted overseas mission work, and spread Christian morality among local student and professional female populations. In 1904 Cratty joined the national staff of the American Committee of the YWCA, which was headquartered in Chicago, as an associate general secretary. In 1906 the committee merged with its eastern US regional counterpart, the International Board of the YWCA, and became the Young Women's Christian Association of the USA. At that time Cratty moved to New York City and became the chief executive of the YWCA Home Department, where she developed policy for the YWCAs that operated in the United States. Soon thereafter, she became the general secretary of the YWCA of the USA in New York City and supervised policymaking in the Home Department and Foreign Division. She held the position of YWCA general secretary from 1906 until her death.

Cratty proved to be a skilled leader who oversaw and assisted a period of remarkable growth and development in the YWCA. In 1906 the organization consisted of fewer than 300 local associations in the United States with a total membership of about 143,000 women. At Cratty's death in 1928 there were 1,300 local associations with a total membership of approximately 600,000 women. Cratty strove to break down economic, racial, and social barriers within the YWCA organization because "she had [a] genuine vision of the way in which a Christian organization should move" (Burton, p. 71). Cratty promoted the adoption of the Social Gospel movement's credo, the "Social Ideals of the Churches," in 1920. She redirected the social orientation of the YWCA mission to better serve the needs of working-class, minority, and recent immigrant women. Cratty demonstrated her commitment to increasing the YWCA's inclusiveness through her leadership as a dedicated and involved administrator who cared personally about the intellectual and social growth and development of all her staff members. She encouraged collaborative decision making at all levels of the YWCA organization through her personal willingness to subordinate the interests of her own ego in group meetings and because she recognized that each individual had a unique and valuable contribution to make to the whole.

In the post–World War I period Cratty also contributed to the growth of international organizations that promoted social and economic justice as a means of achieving world peace. She attended international conferences for the world YWCA organization and the Institute of Pacific Relations. She served on the boards of directors of the Camp Fire Girls, the National Social Work Council, the Federal Council of Churches, and the National Committee on the Cause and Cure of War.

Cratty never married. She died of pneumonia in New York City. Friends and colleagues from around the world sent more than three hundred cables expressing their grief to the YWCA headquarters in New York. Cratty contributed to the development of the American YWCA's cooperative and inclusive character during its formative years. Under her stewardship the YWCA became one of the leading organizations of female social activists in the United States in the early twentieth century.

• The Sophia Smith Manuscript Collection at Smith College contains the organizational papers of the YWCA of the USA and a variety of documents pertaining to Cratty as well as copies of the YWCA publication the *Womans Press*. The YWCA printed three special issue pamphlets to honor Cratty's service to the organization: "Mabel Cratty: She Is Forever Here," Bulletin No. 1, 10 Dec. 1928; "Mabel Cratty: The Woman of God," Bulletin No. 2, 12 Jan. 1929; and "Mabel Cratty: The Good Administrator," Bulletin No. 3, 5 Feb. 1929. All are available in the Sophia Smith Collection. The most complete biography of Cratty, which includes excerpts from her published writing and personal correspondence, is Margaret E. Burton, *Mabel Cratty, Leader in the Art of Leadership* (1929). Information regarding the early organizational history of the YWCA of the USA and Cratty's role in its history can be found in Marion O. Robinson, *Eight Women of the YWCA* (1966). An obituary appears in the *New York Times*, 28 Feb. 1928, and an editorial in the same paper, 29 Feb. 1928, is a tribute to Cratty.

KAREN GARNER

CRAVATH, Paul Drennan (14 July 1861–1 July 1940), lawyer, was born in Berlin Heights, Ohio, the son of Erastus Milo Cravath, a minister and educator who was the first president of Fisk University, and Ruthanna Jackson. His father's extensive travel gave Paul a highly diverse background; he attended secondary school at the Brooklyn Polytechnic Institute and the Collège de Genève, and then Oberlin College, from which he earned his A.B. in 1882. After reading law briefly in Minneapolis, he attended Columbia University Law School. He received his LL.B. and was admitted to the New York bar in 1886. Cravath married Agnes Huntington, an operetta star, in 1892. They had one child and separated in 1926. Cravath traveled widely after the separation but kept for the rest of his life his residences in New York City and Locust Valley, New York, where he died.

After law school, Cravath clerked for Carter, Hornblower & Byrne. The firm dissolved in 1887, and Cravath joined the law firm of Carter & Hughes. In 1888 he became a partner in Carter, Hughes & Cravath. His talents were organizational and transactional rather than as a trial lawyer and proved well suited to an elite corporate clientele. This work led him to elaborate some of Walter Carter's ideas on training young attorneys into the "Cravath system" of law firm organization, designed for the explosion of demand for legal services by the large U.S. corporations of the 1890s. In 1891 he left the Carter firm to organize Cravath & Houston, which dissolved in 1899, but was able to implement his system only when

he joined the long-established firm of Seward, Guthrie & Steele in 1899. Cravath became head of the firm in 1906, and, as late as the end of the twentieth century, it still flourished as Cravath, Swaine & Moore.

The Cravath system transformed the firm from a handful of partners and apprentice lawyers—normal even for Wall Street practice at the time—into a hierarchical organization, which by the end of Cravath's career included more than seventy-five lawyers and a larger number of support personnel. The firm hired substantial numbers of top law school graduates, who worked on corporate transactions and litigation under the supervision of a comparatively small number of partners. After several years' service, the firm chose a few as partners, while the rest went on to other law firms or to work inhouse for corporate clients. The system also made innovative use of a large, permanent support staff for services such as stenography and proofreading, and it enabled the firm to assemble teams to work around the clock if necessary to provide extensive, high-quality legal services on short notice. The system's ability to handle massive transactions and litigation, combined with the financial leverage created by the firm's pyramidal structure, made it extremely profitable for the partners. The firm's size and its lawyers' frenetic lifestyle gave rise to persisting criticism—some lawyers spoke of it as "the Factory" as late as the 1950s, although other law firms had reached comparable size—but its success led to widespread emulation.

Cravath and his firm played important parts in the life cycle of major U.S. corporations, acting as legal advisers, drafting organizational and financial documents (particularly in connection with the issuance of securities), and negotiating major transactions. Cravath's dominant personality and organizational skills helped him to play a leading role in organizing and financing corporations such as RCA, Bethlehem Steel, and Westinghouse, where he served as general counsel for over thirty-five years and chairman of the board from 1927 to 1929.

Even more significantly, Cravath expanded on the work of his predecessors at Seward, Guthrie to pioneer methods for reorganizing financially troubled corporations. Originally, corporations that defaulted on their obligations faced liquidation. As investment in U.S. corporations grew enormously during the late nineteenth century, investors and their professional advisers sought alternatives to liquidation that would keep troubled but still viable businesses in operation. This was especially true for enterprises such as railroads, whose continued operations were important to the general public as well as to their investors and employees. Corporate lawyers began using the common-law receivership to reorganize troubled railroads as early as the 1870s. Cravath played a leading role in developing railroad reorganization techniques, including the use of creditors' committees and new securities, and expanded their use to troubled enterprises of all types. His major reorganizations included those of the Baltimore & Ohio Railroad (1899), the Missouri Pacific

Railroad (1916), International Harvester (1918), and Goodyear Tire & Rubber (1921).

In the 1910s Cravath's international business interests ripened into a significant role in international politics and diplomacy. He actively supported U.S. entry into World War I, visiting Allied forces in France and writing a series of articles for the *New York Times* that were published in book form as *Great Britain's Part* in 1917. When the United States entered the war, he went to Europe as counsel to Edward M. House's U.S. mission to the Inter–Allied Council, and he continued as advisory counsel to the U.S. mission to the Inter–Allied Council on War Purchases and Finance. In this position he played a significant role in organizing financial and logistical support for the Allied war effort. After the war his international interests continued in both the public and private spheres. In 1921 he helped to found the Council on Foreign Relations and was active in the liberal, internationalist wing of the Republican party. In this capacity, he publicly opposed the Treaty of Versailles as unduly punitive and unworkable, supported the League of Nations, expressed dismay at the U.S. retreat toward isolation, and early recognition of the Soviet Union.

Cravath was also a noted art collector, and his musical interests led him to become a director of the New York Symphony Society and the Metropolitan Opera. In 1931, as the Met faced financial crisis under the impact of the Great Depression, he served (until 1938) as its chairman and president and for two years more just as president, applying his experience in corporate reorganization to rescue it from insolvency. His successful restructuring of its finances included introducing commercial radio broadcasts of its productions.

Cravath is best known as the chief architect of the modern large corporate law firm. He transformed his own firm from a small, traditional partnership into a major institution well suited to the increasingly complex needs of corporate clients, both in transactions and litigation. It survived him, and the Cravath model, with various adaptations, continues to form the organizational framework for most large corporate law firms in New York and other U.S. financial centers.

Cravath's other most influential work was his role in developing the process of reorganization for financially troubled corporations. The methods that he helped to develop were important evolutionary steps in the development of modern out-of-court financial restructurings and of the more formal court-supervised reorganization methods now embodied in Chapter 11 of the U.S. Bankruptcy Code.

• There is no critical biography of Cravath. His partner, Robert T. Swaine, made extensive use of primary sources held privately at Cravath, Swaine & Moore in his chronicle, *The Cravath Firm* (3 vols., 1948), which remains the largest source of information on Cravath's career and has long been the starting place for secondary works on the growth of Wall Street law firms. The best of these, with important insights on the Cravath system of law firm organization, is Erwin O. Smigel's sociological study, *The Wall Street Lawyer: Professional Organization Man?* (1964). The best account of

Cravath's personality is Milton Mackaye's profile in the *New Yorker*, 2 Jan. 1932, in connection with Cravath's chairmanship of the Metropolitan Opera. Cravath's own writings provide some further insight into his work; for example, the essay "The Reorganization of Corporations," in *Some Legal Phases of Corporate Financing, Reorganization and Regulation*, ed. Cravath et al. (1917), is an early landmark in the field. An obituary is in the *New York Times*, 2 July 1940.

RICHARD E. MENDALES

CRAVEN, Braxton (22 Aug. 1822–7 Nov. 1882), clergyman and college president, was born near Buffalo Ford, Randolph County, North Carolina, the son of Ann Craven and an unknown father. Details of his early life are sketchy, but by the age of seven he was under the care of Nathan Cox, a Quaker farmer who also ran a sawmill and a distillery. Brief trips to the market provided occasional relief from the arduous farm work, and on one such trip a fall from a horse led to Craven's introduction to formal learning. While Craven recuperated from his injuries, a shopkeeper provided him with a spelling book. This initial exposure to learning inspired a brief period of study at local schools, and by the age of sixteen Craven was running his own subscription school in Randolph County.

Although a Methodist, Craven obtained the endorsement of several Quaker neighbors and attended the New Garden Boarding School (now Guilford College) in Greensboro, North Carolina, from 1839 until 1841. He studied Latin, Greek, philosophy, mathematics, and history and also received a license to preach at the Poplar Springs Church in 1840. After two academic terms at New Garden, he came to the attention of a committee from the Union Institute, a school that had been founded in Randolph County in 1838 by both Methodists and Quakers. Hired as an assistant teacher in November 1840, he succeeded Brantley York as principal after the latter's resignation in 1842. The institute had begun on a modest basis, and Craven sought to improve its level of instruction. Recognizing the problem of deficient teacher training in North Carolina, Craven began a program of instruction in that area. Remembering all too well his own struggle to balance the twin demands of work and education, Craven also began a night school at the institute and conducted the classes free of charge.

While attending to a sick student, Craven met Irene Leach, a teacher at the institute who had also been its first female graduate. They were married in 1844 and had four children. In 1849 Craven passed an examination at Randolph-Macon College, from which he was awarded an honorary A.B. Fired with enthusiasm for education, Craven lost few opportunities to advance his views on common schools and teacher training. His vision of normal schools placed them on a more equal footing with "academic colleges." He was critical of both the Prussian system and of Horace Mann's efforts in New England. He accused Mann of setting up a virtual "caste system" by pigeonholing teacher-training candidates into a narrow vocational mold. Although Craven was clearly far less successful in implementing his vision than was Mann during his lifetime, the evolution of former normal schools into modern-day universities seems to have confirmed his vision. Craven began the *Southern Index* in 1850 with Reuben H. Brown. Originally founded as an educational journal, it soon became *The Evergreen*, a literary magazine. During the brief, twelve-issue life of *The Evergreen*, Craven serialized two novels, *Mary Barker* and *Naomi Wise*, that he later published, under the pseudonym Charlie Vernon.

Craven's years of effort began to bear fruit in January 1851, when he succeeded in getting the North Carolina general assembly to pass a bill that incorporated Union Institute as Normal College. While the bill contained provisions for financial support, the legislators refused to grant any funds. The most immediate benefit of the charter was to allow the school to grant teacher certifications. Craven also sought, without success, to have the state establish scholarships for prospective teachers. While the charter was amended in 1853 to make Normal College a state school, the only financial assistance received was a $10,000 loan from the state Literary Fund, which Craven eventually ended up paying back out of his own pocket.

Frustrated in his attempts to gain state support for the school and concerned with the poor quality of its first graduates, Craven turned to the North Carolina Conference of the Methodist Episcopal Church, South, for help. In 1856 he persuaded that body to adopt Normal College as its own. With Craven serving as its first president, the school became Trinity College in 1859.

With the advent of the Civil War in 1861, Craven organized the Trinity Guard, to maintain order during the crisis. A program of military training began in the summer of 1861, and later in the year Craven and the guard were posted to the Confederate military prison at Salisbury, North Carolina. Craven returned to Trinity after about a month, having maintained his presidency, and the college remained open throughout the turbulent war years. A schism within the North Carolina Conference led to internal bickering and criticism relating to Craven's advocacy of continued support of Trinity College (in lieu of support of other schools) and the rate at which Trinity's debts were being discharged. Craven resigned as president on 1 January 1864, taking his first and only pastorate at the Edenton Street Methodist Church in Raleigh, North Carolina.

Following the end of the war, Craven was persuaded to return as president of Trinity. The college, which had admitted females as students in 1864, had finally closed in April 1865. Craven resumed his duties in January 1866, taking over from president pro tempore William T. Gannaway, and the college reopened. For the following seventeen years Craven held a relatively uneventful presidency. The never ending struggles over funding and administrative duties wore heavily, however, and after a brief period of poor health he died in the town of Trinity, which had grown up around the college. The institution Craven had built later became Duke University.

Craven's life and career remain an example of the possibilities open to men of drive and ambition in the nineteenth century. Possessing few advantages at birth, he was a self-educated and self-made man whose career illustrates the struggle for educational opportunities, especially for individuals of limited means, in the antebellum South. The existence of what is now Duke University, as well as the widespread availability of quality teacher training programs at other institutions of higher learning, are a tribute to his perseverance.

• Craven's papers are held at the Duke University Archives, Durham, N.C. His career at New Garden receives mention in Dorothy Lloyd Gilbert, *Guilford: A Quaker College* (1937). The best source of information on his life and career is Jerome Dowd, *Life of Braxton Craven* (1896), by a former student of Craven. Additional information can be found concerning his years at Trinity in Nora C. Chaffin, *Trinity College, 1839–1892* (1950). An obituary is in the *Raleigh News and Observer*, 9 Nov. 1882.

EDWARD L. LACH, JR.

CRAVEN, Frank (24 Aug. 1880?–1 Sept. 1945), actor and playwright, was born in Boston, Massachusetts, the son of John T. Craven and Ella Mayer. Craven's parents, both repertory theater actors, were members of the Boston Theatre Company at the time of his birth. It was in that company's production of Henry Arthur Jones's *The Silver King* that young Craven, age three, made his two-line theatrical debut in Providence, Rhode Island, while "hanging on to my mother's dress." He continued to play small roles, but the rigors of repertory and touring precluded traditional schooling. Craven was taught by his mother up to the age of nine; he then spent a year in school in Silver Lake on Cape Cod and "picked up some more learning" while living in Reading, Massachusetts. Leaving school "for good and all" when he was fourteen years old, he helped to tend a sawmill in Reading and worked for a time in a tack factory. After nine months as a mail clerk in a Boston insurance company, Craven realized he was not cut out for business and returned to the stage. He joined his father in a Baltimore stock company and was cast as an old man in *The Silver King*, the same play he had debuted in some fifteen years earlier.

From imitating famous ball players and dancing hornpipes between acts to performing "turkey shows" (fill-in performances on holidays like Christmas and Thanksgiving) at Boston's Dudley Street Opera, Craven learned the skills of his craft. Although he would have preferred to be a "boss carpenter" rather than an actor, he followed the family tradition playing repertory in Baltimore, Philadelphia, Boston, Cleveland, and Detroit.

Craven's New York City acting debut was in the play *Artie* (1907), and his career as a playwright began the next winter when he contributed a skit for the annual "Gambol" at New York City's theatrical club, the

Lambs. Titled *The Curse of Cains* (Cains was the storehouse where producers "buried" the sets and props of theatrical failures), the sketch was followed by others, including *Up in Minnie's Room*, *Little Stranger*, and *Honor among Thieves*. The last two pieces became staples in vaudeville for years.

Craven's first success as an actor came in the 1911 hit *Bought and Paid For*, in which he played the resourceful shipping clerk Jimmy Gilley. After a New York run of more than a year, an American tour, and playing the role in London, it was out of desperation that Craven began writing his first full-length play. The domestic comedy was successfully produced by William A. Brady in 1914 as *Too Many Cooks*. Also that year Craven married actress Mary Blyth; their son John, who later acted with his father in such plays as *Our Town*, was born in 1916.

By the age of thirty-five Craven had clearly established the trademark of both his acting and playwriting styles. Focusing on the homespun virtues of the American scene, Craven possessed "an uncanny appreciation of the commonness, the bread-and-butter reality of middle-class America, of representing . . . what George M. Cohan terms the 'regular fellow'" (*New York Dramatic Mirror*, 30 Sept. 1916, p. 5).

Encouraged by the success of *Too Many Cooks*, Craven's goal was to quit acting altogether to pursue a full-time writing career. However, he quickly found that producers and audiences would not accept the shows that he wrote unless he starred in them. His writing debut was followed by the comedy *This Way Out* (1917), the libretto and lyrics for *The Girl from Home* (1920), and his smash hit *The First Year* (1920), which ran for 725 performances. The last production teamed Craven with producer John Golden, an association that was to last more than twenty-five years. In the 1922 production of his *Spite Corner*, the actor-playwright began his directing career in earnest, while Craven's 1924 *New Brooms* added producing to his other credits. Although the failure of *Money from Home* (1927) was partially offset by the moderately successful lampoon on people's obsession with golf in *The Nineteenth Hole* (1927), it was evident that his earlier box-office successes were difficult to replicate.

However, Craven soon found that his folksy image would sell in Hollywood. His first foray to the West Coast was brief: roles in the films *We Americans* (1928) and *The Very Idea* (1929). Starring roles in Dan Jarrett's *Salt Water* (1929) and his own *That's Gratitude!* (1930) brought Craven back to New York where he directed the comedy melodrama *Whistling in the Dark* (1932) and the mystery *Riddle Me This* (1932). By the early 1930s, however, Craven had essentially abandoned New York City in favor of California where he wrote screenplays, penned dialogue for Laurel and Hardy films, acted, and directed. His credits include the 1933 *State Fair* (screenwriting and acting), as well as adapting his own comedy, *That's Gratitude* (1934), for film.

In 1935 Craven was put "on loan" to John Golden by 20th Century–Fox to direct the Broadway plays *For Valor* and *A Touch of Brimstone*. Neither was a success, however, and Craven retreated to Hollywood to continue working in film. It would be another three years before producer Jed Harris and playwright Thornton Wilder lured him back to star in the ground-breaking drama *Our Town* (1938), a performance that renewed Craven's theatrical reputation. With Craven playing the Stage Manager, a role that became synonymous with the actor's folksy, relaxed style, the drama won a Pulitzer Prize and a place in modern American theater history. Upon his return to Hollywood, he shared writing credit for the film version of *Our Town* (1940), as well as reprising his Broadway role. Craven was wooed back to Broadway only twice more: to co-produce and star in *Village Green* (1941); and, in his final stage appearance, to star opposite Billie Burke in Zoë Akins's comedy *Mrs. January and Mr. Ex* (1944). Back in California, Craven maintained a prodigious schedule of films up to the last weeks before his death in Beverly Hills.

Critic Brooks Atkinson once referred to Craven as "the best pipe and pants-pocket actor in the business." That his pipe-smoking, hands-in-the-pocket image reached iconographic proportions with the American people is evidenced by the use of Craven's photo and name in advertising various products over the years: the Romelink Swinging Couch Hammock with "Cravenette" finish (1918) and the Drinkless Kaywoodie Pipe (1927).

Craven appeared in thirty-eight films in addition to garnering several screenwriting and film-directing credits. Of the more than 250 stage roles that he estimated he had played throughout the years, he claimed that only once (and that time with disastrous results) did he depart from light roles. Those light roles, however, left an indelible mark on more than three decades of theater patrons and film viewers. Brought up in what he called "the honest-to-goodness" school of acting, Craven's stage persona exemplified the ordinary man-on-the-street while his plays delineated the homey truths of domestic life.

• Many of Frank Craven's scrapbooks and clipping files are in the Billy Rose Theatre Collection at the New York Public Library for the Performing Arts, Lincoln Center. Although numerous articles on Craven are scattered throughout the theatrical and popular publications of the period, the most informative include *New York Dramatic Mirror*, 30 Sept. 1916; *Theatre* (June 1914): 296–98 and *Theatre* (Sept. 1917): 146–47, 168. An extensive article is in the *New York Tribune*, 6 Mar. 1932. Reviews of his work in Hollywood can be found in the published volumes of the *New York Times Film Reviews*. The chronology of his parents' careers in the Boston Theatre Company can be gleaned from Eugene Tompkins, *The History of the Boston Theatre, 1854–1901* (1908). Obituaries are in the *New York Times* and the *New York Herald Tribune*, both 2 Sept. 1945.

JANE T. PETERSON

CRAVEN, Thomas Tingey (20 Dec. 1808–23 Aug. 1887), naval officer, was born in the District of Columbia, the son of Tunis Craven, who held minor posts in the navy, including purser and naval storekeeper at the navy yards in Portsmouth, New Hampshire, and Brooklyn, New York, and Hannah Tingey. His grandfather on his mother's side was Commodore Thomas Tingey, a distinguished American naval officer. His younger brother was Tunis Augustus Mac-Donough Craven, also a naval officer, who was killed during the battle of Mobile Bay in August 1864. On 1 May 1822, while his father was serving at Portsmouth, Thomas entered the navy as a midshipman appointed from New Hampshire.

Craven became a passed midshipman on 24 May 1828 and was detached to the sloop of war *Erie* as sailing master on 9 August 1828. He remained on the *Erie* one year, and on 10 August 1829 he was put on leave. While on leave he was promoted to lieutenant, 7 June 1830, and on 24 November 1831 he reported to the receiving ship *New York*. One month later he was ordered to the sloop of war *Peacock*, then on the Brazil Station. He sailed on the schooner *Boxer* and joined the *Peacock* on station. He returned to the United States in the summer of 1834.

After returning from duty on the *Peacock*, Craven went on a six-month leave. He reported to the receiving ship *New York* in February 1835. He went back on leave in July and remained in that status until September 1837, when he was ordered to the frigate *John Adams*, then undergoing repairs at Hampton Roads. He stayed there until 6 April 1838, when he was assigned as first lieutenant aboard the sloop of war *Vincennes*, the flagship of the U.S. exploring expedition preparing to sail under the command of Lieutenant Charles Wilkes. He remained aboard the *Vincennes* until 13 February 1840, when he once more took leave.

During the 1840s Craven served in a variety of posts, including as an officer with Matthew C. Perry's squadron on the West African slave patrol. During his service with Perry he served aboard the frigate *Macedonian* and commanded the brig *Porpoise*. He also served for six months on board the ship of the line *Independence* (May 1849–Dec. 1850) while it was cruising in the Mediterranean. On 3 June 1850 he was appointed commandant of midshipmen at Annapolis. With the exception of the time he commanded the frigate *Congress* (24 May 1855–14 Jan. 1858), Craven remained as commandant until the outbreak of the Civil War.

On 20 April 1861 Craven was ordered to Portland, Maine, on recruiting duty. On 28 June he was given command of the Potomac River flotilla and on 14 August was promoted to captain. On 29 November 1861 Craven was given command of the steam sloop *Brooklyn*, serving in David G. Farragut's squadron. As captain of the *Brooklyn* Craven saw action at Head of the Passes, Mississippi, that resulted in the capture of Forts Philip and Jackson (15 Feb. 1862), opening the way for Farragut's squadron to steam up the Mississippi and capture New Orleans (24 Apr. 1862). During the battle at the forts, *Brooklyn* took a position immediately behind the flagship *Hartford*, where she suffered heavy enemy fire. After the fall of New Orle-

ans, *Brooklyn* continued to operate on the river, moving upstream to bombard Grand Gulf (26 May 1862) and Vicksburg (28 June 1862). Having failed, however, to capture either position, *Brooklyn* and the rest of the squadron returned downstream. During these battles Craven distinguished himself as an able officer.

After Craven was detached from the *Brooklyn* on 11 August 1862, a shortage of suitable commands left him inactive for nearly a full year. In June 1863 he was ordered to command the ironclad steamer *New Ironsides*. However, those orders were revoked, and on 26 August he was promoted to commodore and given command of the steam frigate *Niagara*. The *Niagara* was assigned to European waters, patrolling for Confederate raiders. Operating from Antwerp, the ship sailed in the English Channel and along the coasts of France and Portugal. On 15 August 1864 it captured the Confederate raider *Georgia* off the coast of Portugal.

Early in 1865 Union intelligence learned that the iron ram *Stonewall* was preparing to sail from El Ferrol, Spain. On 11 February the *Niagara*, accompanied by the steamer *Sacramento*, took up a position at the port of Corunna, only nine miles from El Ferrol. On 24 March 1865 the *Stonewall* steamed out of El Ferrol. Craven declined to engage it, later claiming that, if he had, "the *Niagara* would most undoubtedly have been easily and promptly destroyed."

Craven's decision brought heavy criticism. He was court-martialed on charges of "failing to do his utmost to overtake and capture or destroy a vessel which it was his duty to encounter." The court found him guilty and ordered him suspended with "leave pay" for two years. Given the nature of the offense, which would nominally have carried the penalty of death, Secretary of the Navy Gideon Welles was perplexed by the light sentence. Upon reviewing the case, Welles referred to the court's judgment as "inexplicable." He set the decision aside and returned Craven to duty. Although he returned Craven to duty, Welles, along with many of Craven's fellow officers, viewed his actions as those of an overly cautious officer, a reputation well deserved.

Following the war Craven was promoted to rear admiral (10 Oct. 1866). He commanded the Mare Island Navy Yard from 11 July 1866 to 5 October 1869 with a short break (1 Aug. 1868–13 Mar. 1869), during which time he commanded the North Pacific Squadron. From Mare Island Craven was detached to become port admiral at San Francisco. He was placed on the retired list on 30 December 1869 but remained as port admiral until 13 September 1870. After retirement Craven returned east and died at the Boston Navy Yard.

Craven was married twice. His first wife was Virginia Wingate, with whom he had no children. His second wife was Emily Truxtun Henderson, with whom he had eight children.

• Craven's professional career is best followed in the "Z" files at the Naval Historical Center. For his Civil War years see *The Official Records of the Union and Confederate Navies in the*

War of the Rebellion (30 vols., 1894–1922); and William M. Fowler, Jr., *Under Two Flags: The American Navy in the Civil War* (1990).

WILLIAM M. FOWLER, JR.

CRAVEN, Tunis Augustus MacDonough (11 Jan. 1813–5 Aug. 1864), naval officer, was born in Portsmouth, New Hampshire, the son of Tunis Craven, a merchant, navy purser, and storekeeper, and Hannah Tingey. After his father became a storekeeper at the Brooklyn Navy Yard, Craven attended grammar school at Columbia College in New York City. Craven's maternal grandfather was Commodore Thomas Tingey, so considering the family's connection with the navy, it is hardly surprising that both Tunis and his older brother Thomas Tingey Craven chose careers as naval officers.

Tunis Craven was appointed a midshipman in 1829. At the time of his promotion to passed midshipman in 1835, he was doing work in surveying and hydrography for the Coast Survey. In 1838 he married Mary Carter, who died five years later. Craven's second marriage was to Marie Stevenson. Survey duties continued following Craven's promotion to lieutenant in 1841, and in 1845–1846 he served as an editor of the *United States Nautical Magazine*. During the war with Mexico, he participated in naval operations in California aboard the sloop *Dale*. Craven's reputation as a scientist was well established as a result of more than twenty years of employment with the U.S. Coast Survey. He became one of the navy's most distinguished surveyors and hydrographers. In 1857 he was chosen to command an expedition to survey a projected ship canal route from the Atlantic to the Pacific through the Isthmus of Panama. While commanding the steamer *Mohawk* of the Home Squadron off the coast of Cuba from 1859 to 1861, Craven was credited with the capture of a vessel engaged in the illegal African slave trade, and while on the same station, the men of the *Mohawk* rescued the crew from a Spanish shipwreck. Craven was awarded a gold medal from the Queen of Spain and received a letter of commendation from the New York Board of Underwriters.

After the Civil War began, Craven commended the *Crusader*, enforcing the blockade off Key West. Promotion to commander that year brought with it command of the sloop *Tuscarora*. Craven spent more than a year in a frustrating search for Confederate commerce raiders. When the *Tuscarora* finally caught up with the commerce raider *Sumter* at Gibraltar, the *Sumter* was no longer being used by the Confederates. Major mechanical problems and general wear caused by months at sea had resulted in its decommissioning. In the summer of 1863 he was placed in command of the newly built ironclad *Tecumseh*, which was initially part of the James River flotilla until Craven received orders to take it to Mobile to join Admiral David G. Farragut's naval force there. The *Tecumseh* arrived in time to participate in Farragut's attack on Fort Morgan and the small Confederate naval force defending Mobile. Warned of the torpedoes the Confederates

had placed in the bay, Craven responded, "I don't care a pinch of snuff for them." As the attack began on 5 August 1864, Farragut suffered his first major setback. The *Tecumseh* struck a mine and sank within minutes after the explosion, killing 93 of its 114 officers and crew. At the moment of the explosion, Craven and the ironclad's pilot hurried from the pilothouse to the ladder leading to the top of the turret, where Craven held back, telling the pilot to go first. His consideration for the other man cost Craven his life, as the pilot was among the few survivors of the disaster. Later, commenting on the "terrible catastrophe" that had befallen a brother officer, Admiral Samuel du Pont noted gravely that the navy had lost "one of the smartest men in that fleet."

• Craven's Mexican War journal was published as "Naval Conquest in the Pacific: The Journal of Lieutenant Tunis Augustus MacDonough Craven, USN, during a Cruise to the Pacific in the Sloop of War *Dale*, 1846–49," ed. John H. Kemble, *California Historical Quarterly* 20, no. 3 (Sept. 1941): 193–234. Craven's official survey report of 1857–1858 is in 46th Cong., 2d sess., H. Exec. Doc. 63. His official Civil War correspondence is in *The Official Records of the Union and Confederate Navies in the War of the Rebellion*, ser. 1, vol. 21 (30 vols., 1894–1922). See also Loyall Farragut, *The Life of David Glasgow Farragut, First Admiral of the United States Navy, Embodying His Journal and Letters* (1879). An obituary is in the *Army and Navy Journal*, 20 Aug. 1864.

NORMAN C. DELANEY

CRAVEN, Wesley F. (19 May 1905–10 Feb. 1981), historian and educator, was born in Conway, North Carolina, the son of W. F. Craven, a Methodist minister, and Elizabeth Turner. Craven earned B.A. and M.A. degrees from Trinity College, Duke University, and then went on to Cornell University, where he earned a Ph.D. in history in 1928. His doctoral dissertation was titled "The Life of Robert Rich, Second Earl of Warwick, to 1642." In 1932 he married Helen McDaniel, the daughter of Methodist missionaries to China. They would have two daughters.

Craven began his teaching career at New York University in 1928. He remained in the Department of History for twenty-two years, except for a three-year assignment in the U.S. Army Air Corps during World War II. At NYU he rose through the academic ranks to professor of history. For his service in the army he was discharged at the rank of lieutenant colonel. In 1950 he moved to Princeton University, where he became the Jonathan Edwards Professor of History, succeeding the distinguished Thomas Jefferson Wertenbaker. In 1964 he became the first holder of the Davis Professorship in History at Princeton, named for George Henry Davis, class of 1886. He retired after twenty-three years, in 1973.

Craven's historical writing both set new standards in the field and opened new areas of investigation. His seven-volume *History of the Army Air Forces in World War II* (with J. L. Cate, 1948) set the standard for the writing of military history. His reinterpretation of American colonial studies, in which he stressed the importance of the development of the Chesapeake Bay region, began new efforts to broaden colonial research. His own publications, particularly *The Colonies in Transition 1660–1713* (1968) and *White, Red, and Black* (1970), illustrated the new questions in the field. Craven differed from previous historians, for instance, in asserting that at the beginning of the eighteenth century, colonial Americans were content to remain within the British Empire, for they had learned to fashion and exploit political institutions within the colonies to their own good. He also believed that the conflicts that arose between whites and Indians arose primarily from a misunderstanding of Indian cultures, rather than a lust for lands. On the important issue of slavery, Craven held that racial discrimination emerged slowly in the eighteenth century only as the number of slaves increased dramatically. The colonial Negro's status in law was not well-defined at the end of the seventeenth century.

Craven's leadership in American colonial studies won him wide recognition. In addition to serving on the editorial boards of the *Journal of Modern History*, the *Journal of Southern History*, the *William and Mary Quarterly*, and the *American Historical Review*, he was a founding member of the Council of the Institute of Early American History and Culture at Colonial Williamsburg. His historiographical lectures at the Stokes Foundation in 1956 placed him in the forefront of colonial American historians. In 1964 he gave a widely acclaimed public lecture at Princeton to inaugurate the Davis Chair in American history, and in 1970 he delivered the James W. Richard Lectures at the University of Virginia. He was a member of the American Philosophical Society and the American Academy of Arts and Sciences, as well as chairman of the Princeton University Bicentennial Committee.

Craven was esteemed as a classroom teacher, especially the undergraduate course "Origins of the United States" and his graduate seminar, "The Colonies and the American Revolution," both handled without lecture notes. His professional colleagues applauded his transparent honesty and his quiet sense of humor.

In retirement Craven edited the *Biographical Dictionary of Princetonians*, contributing more than 100 articles of his own. He died at his home in Princeton.

• Papers relating to Craven are found in the Princeton University Archives. His major books not mentioned above include *Introduction to the History of Bermuda* (1938), *The Southern Colonies in the Seventeenth Century* (1949), *The Legend of the Founding Fathers* (1956), *The Virginia Company of London 1606–1624* (1957), and *New Jersey and the English Colonization of North America* (1964). An obituary is in the *New York Times*, 13 Feb. 1981.

WILLIAM H. BRACKNEY

CRAWFORD, Broderick (9 Dec. 1911–26 Apr. 1986), actor, was born William Broderick Crawford in Philadelphia, Pennsylvania, the son of Lester Robert Crawford, a vaudevillian, and Helen Broderick, a comedienne and musical performer. As a child he often accompanied his parents on vaudeville tours and occa-

sionally played bit parts in short pants in their comedy skits. He was a student and popular athlete at Dean Academy in Franklin, Massachusetts, beginning in 1924 and graduating in 1928. At his parents' insistence, he enrolled at Harvard University but withdrew after three weeks. He held a succession of jobs, as New York City waterfront stevedore, professional boxer, and able-bodied seaman aboard tankers. He was intermittently a radio actor (1930–1934), at one point playing a Marx Brothers' stooge.

In 1932 Crawford made his legitimate stage debut cast as a football player in *She Loves Me Not* at the Adelphi Theatre in London. Although the play soon failed, Noël Coward admired his work and gave him a bit part in the 1935 Broadway production of his *Point Valaine*, which starred Alfred Lunt and Lynn Fontanne. Crawford acted for a couple of seasons in stock and then went to Hollywood. He appeared as a comic butler in the film *Woman Chases Man* (1937), starring Miriam Hopkins; was featured with Pat O'Brien and George Raft in *Submarine D-1* (1937); and appeared with Jimmy Durante in the college movie *Start Cheering* (1938).

In 1937 Crawford read John Steinbeck's *Of Mice and Men* during a trip by railroad to New York. He appealed to George S. Kaufman, director of the projected Broadway adaptation of Steinbeck's classic, for the role in it of Lennie, the essentially gentle, doomed simpleton. After visiting mental institutions to observe the behavior of patients challenged like poor Lennie, Crawford rehearsed brilliantly and obtained the part. The spectacular success of the play owed much to Crawford's sensitively modulated performance. He returned to Hollywood, hoping to obtain the role of Lennie in the movie version. But the part went instead to Lon Chaney, Jr. For the next several years Crawford played mostly supporting roles in more B movies—as a burly, mean-faced bank robber; gunman; legionnaire; prisoner; western gunslinger; bodyguard; brawler; and con artist. He began to feel typed as an abrasive, gravel-voiced thug.

As U.S. involvement in World War II deepened, Crawford in 1942 enlisted in the U.S. Army and served as a sergeant in the Air Corps. Overseas for eighteen months, he acted briefly as master of ceremonies with the Glenn Miller Band in London and fought in France during the Battle of the Bulge. After he returned to Hollywood, he was featured in nine more B movies from 1946 through 1949, including *Night unto Night* (1949) with Ronald Reagan.

When Robert Rossen began casting for the film version of *All the King's Men*, the 1946 Pulitzer Prize–winning novel by Robert Penn Warren, he wanted Crawford for the leading role of Willie Stark, based on the Louisiana demogogue Huey Long. Columbia studio executives preferred Spencer Tracy, but Rossen held out for Crawford because he could be more hateful on screen, whereas it was feared that Tracy would come across as too likable. Crawford won an Oscar as best actor of 1949 and the New York Critics Award as well, while the movie was accorded the Oscar for best picture. Crawford was relegated to several more B movies full of action but then performed memorably opposite Judy Holliday as Harry Brock, the millionaire junk dealer, in the film adaptation of the Broadway hit *Born Yesterday* (1950). Crawford had been sought for the stage role, but Paul Douglas was cast instead. Generally mediocre roles followed for Crawford, with few exceptions. So he went to Italy, where he was excellent as a thief trying to reform in Federico Fellini's comedy caper *Il Bidone* (The swindle, 1955); his dialogue was dubbed in Italian.

Crawford returned to the United States and appeared in several more movies, but he gained unique fame as Captain Dan Matthews in *Highway Patrol*, the pioneering syndicated television police-drama series in 156 thirty-minute episodes (1955–1959). Less popular was his TV work in the crime-drama series *King of Diamonds* (1961–1962), the medical-drama series *The Interns* (1970–1971), and a few later efforts. Meanwhile, and on through 1981, he shuttled back and forth to Europe to appear in several movies filmed in Italy, Yugoslavia, Spain, and Germany. In 1974 he played the part of the coach in the London stage presentation of *That Championship Season*.

In 1977 Crawford enjoyed his final outstanding American success with his portrayal of the enigmatic Federal Bureau of Investigation director in *The Private Files of J. Edgar Hoover*. Crawford meticulously prepared for the role, read everything available about Hoover, studied film clips of the man, and learned to mimic his head gestures, clipped speech, and private smoking and drinking manners. In 1932, five years before he appeared in Broadway in *Of Mice and Men*, Crawford had met Hoover briefly at a party in Washington, D.C. When they met again, Hoover immediately named Crawford, the location and date of their earlier meeting, their hostess at the time, and even some of the other guests. In the movie, Crawford tried to depict what he defined as a patriotic but awesome "egomaniac" with a "diabolical memory." *Liar's Moon* (1982), Crawford's last movie, was filmed in Hollywood.

Crawford never had a high opinion either of moviemaking or of his acting ability. He said that he relied on instinct to present his varied roles with as much sensitivity as possible. He was willing to appear before the camera for any purpose, even to advertise scouring pads on TV, and once described how liquor relieved the pain of being between jobs and waiting for the next telephone call from a movie producer or director. He once remarked that he was glad his mother was dead and hence out of the "rat race" of theatrical employment. In private he was known as a barroom brawler and a heavy drinker. He was married four times. He and Joan Tabor, his first wife, were married in 1940 and had one child; their marriage ended in 1955. He and Kay Griffith, his second wife, were married in 1962 and had two children; their marriage ended in 1967. Details of his last two marriages are unavailable. Crawford, who suffered a series of strokes beginning

on New Year's Eve 1984, died in Rancho Mirage, California.

• Tony Thomas, *The Films of Ronald Reagan* (1980), includes photographs of Crawford in coverage of *Night unto Night*. Gary Carey, *Judy Holliday: An Intimate Life Story* (1982), and Will Holtzman, *Judy Holliday* (1982), discuss Holliday's friendship with Crawford and her preference for him over Paul Douglas. Ephraim Katz, *The Film Encyclopedia* (1994), lists seventy-seven movies in which Crawford appeared; David Quinlan, *Quinlan's Illustrated Directory of Film Stars*, 4th ed. (1996), lists ninety-six, including seven made for television. Tom Burke, "Broderick Crawford—From Huey Long to J. Edgar Hoover," *New York Times*, 16 Jan. 1977, is a revealing interview. Obituaries are in the *New York Times*, 27 Apr. 1986, and in *Variety Obituaries, 1984–1986* (1988).

ROBERT L. GALE

CRAWFORD, Cheryl (24 Sept. 1902–7 Oct. 1986), theatrical producer, was born in Akron, Ohio, the daughter of Robert K. Crawford, a real estate agent, and Luella Elizabeth Parker. Her interest in the theater was kindled when she performed in amateur productions as a teenager and enhanced during her undergraduate years at Smith College, where she was able to gain experience in virtually all aspects of production before graduating with a B.A., cum laude, in 1925. Her broad interests in the theater and a growing admiration for plays from many exciting "new" genres being imported from overseas led her naturally to enroll almost immediately in the Theatre Guild's drama school. She also began the customary round of auditions and made her Broadway debut as an actress in the role of Madame Barrio in *Juarez and Maximilian* in 1926. Meanwhile, the Theatre Guild recognized her versatility and employed her in a number of capacities, especially as an assistant stage manager. She moved up the ladder fast, and by age twenty-seven she held the title of assistant to the board of managers of the Theatre Guild, which in reality meant that she was the organization's casting director.

Crawford was a part of the group of Theatre Guild associates who believed fervently that the guild should establish a permanent acting company. Under the leadership of Harold Clurman, this group of dissidents undertook a series of events in 1931 that finally led in 1932 to the establishment of the Group Theatre, a theatrical collective shaped in the image of the Moscow Art Theatre and other European theaters that followed in its footprints. By this time Crawford had abandoned any hopes she may have had of becoming an actress, concentrating instead on the business aspects of the theater and the behind-the-scenes preparations of both scripts and productions. She was very much committed to the Group Theatre's approach to acting and to its philosophy of improving the quality of drama being produced on the American stage. However, she left the Group in 1937 after a group of dissident actors had criticized the decisions of the directors.

Her strongly held convictions continued to guide Crawford's selection of plays throughout her career, even as an independent producer, the occupation that would dominate her career despite several ventures into projects that would help shape the American theater of the twentieth century. Her first independent effort was a 1938 production of *All the Living*, directed by Lee Strasberg. This effort, like much of her early work, was a succès d'estime, and it was not until she brought in a production of *The Second Mrs. Tanqueray* (1940), starring Tallulah Bankhead, that one of her productions found enough favor with the public to be a financial success. She continued to tackle projects that run-of-the-mill producers shunned—revivals of *Porgy and Bess* (1941, 1942, 1944); the quirky musical *One Touch of Venus* (1943); Margaret Webster's production of *The Tempest* (1945), starring black actor Canada Lee; and a production of the religious drama *Family Portrait* (1939), starring Judith Anderson, for example. During these years she also became the producer for the Maplewood Theatre in New Jersey, an organization that featured a large stock company.

She never forgot her dream of a permanent repertory company for the United States, and in 1945 she joined forces with Margaret Webster and Eva Le Gallienne to make it happen. The result was the moderately successful American Repertory Theatre, originally designed as a company of thirty actors who would be asked to make a commitment for a minimum of two seasons. The company was dedicated to producing the best of the modern theater as well as the classics at affordable prices, and many of its successful productions—including *Henry VIII* (1946), *What Every Woman Knows* (1946), and *Alice in Wonderland* (1947)—benefited from Crawford's touch as either director or producer.

By the time the American Repertory Theatre closed in 1948, Crawford had already left to help Elia Kazan and Robert Lewis found the Actors Studio in 1947, serving for the next few years as executive producer for many of their productions. She remained associated with the Actors Studio, at least as a trusted observer and friend, until her death. This important organization was committed to a method of acting, based on the work of Konstantin Stanislavski, that was to dominate American theater for decades. In 1950 Crawford also became the general director, with Robert Breen, of a series of new plays and revivals produced by the American National Theatre and Academy at its recently purchased ANTA Theatre.

During these same years Crawford continued her work as an independent producer, bringing to New York City successful musicals such as *Brigadoon* (1947) and *Yentl* (1975). She was the producer for *Brecht on Brecht* (1962) and four of Tennessee Williams's plays, *The Rose Tattoo*, which won the Tony in 1951, *Camino Real* (1953), *Sweet Bird of Youth* (1959), and *Period of Adjustment* (1960). She was involved in one way or another with more than 100 productions and remained active up to her death in New York City.

This unprepossessing and tough-minded woman is relatively unsung and undervalued by historians who have assessed the American theater. Very quietly she managed to play an integral role in the most important theatrical projects of the twentieth century: the Theatre Guild, the Group Theatre, the American Repertory Theatre, and the Actors Studio. Perhaps it is because Crawford was usually behind the scenes that her contributions are overlooked. In her *New York Times* obituary, Sidney Kingsley writes that "though she always wanted [her contribution] to be artistic, [it] really was den mother and producer. She was good at raising money and settling disputes." No doubt this rare combination of talents was fundamental to the success of the projects and organizations with which she became involved. Through them and through the individual plays she produced, she was determined to prove that serious works of art were compatible with successful commercial theater. This she accomplished at an unparalleled level in an environment often hostile not only to her concepts but also to her gender.

• Crawford's autobiography, *One Naked Individual*, was published in 1977. Extremely useful information about her contributions to the Group Theatre are in Harold Clurman's *Lies Like Truth* (1958) and *All People Are Famous* (1974). See also Wendy Smith, *Real Life Drama: The Group Theatre and America, 1930–1940* (1990); W. P. Eaton, *The Theatre Guild: The First Ten Years* (1929); and R. A. Schanke, *Shattered Applause: The Lives of Eva Le Gallienne* (1992). An obituary is in the *New York Times*, 8 Oct. 1986.

LARRY CLARK

CRAWFORD, F. Marion (2 Aug. 1854–9 Apr. 1909), novelist and historian, was born Francis Marion Crawford in Bagni di Lucca, Italy, the son of Thomas Crawford, an American sculptor, and Louisa Cutler Ward. The family lived in Rome, where Crawford began a cosmopolitan education in places that would later form the settings of his novels. Crawford's parents made certain that their children never lost sight of their American roots. After her husband's death in 1857 Louisa married Luther Terry, an American painter, and continued to make her home in Rome. Crawford's early education was conducted mainly by private tutors until 1866 when he was sent to St. Paul's School in Concord, New Hampshire. After his return to Rome in 1869, he studied in a variety of places: Rome, England, Germany, and India. He left India in 1880, returned to Rome, and the following year came to Boston to seek literary employment and perhaps to enter politics.

With the advice of his uncle, Sam Ward, the well-known gourmet and lobbyist, Crawford wrote some articles and his first novel, *Mr. Isaacs: A Tale of Modern India* (1882), based on the life of Alexander M. Jacob, a jewel merchant whom Crawford had met while editing a newspaper in Simla, India. Encouraged by the novel's instant success, he wrote in quick succession *Doctor Claudius* (1883), *To Leeward* (1883), and *A Roman Singer* (1884).

Promising as this beginning was, Crawford still had not decided to devote himself to fictional writing. Rather, he hoped to enter American politics, unaware of how little he was suited to political life, a point underscored by his *An American Politician: A Novel* (1885). Crawford knew very little about American politics, having lived in the United States only briefly. His outlook was European, and he was essentially aristocratic. Meanwhile, his mother felt that he should marry. At her prompting Crawford went to Constantinople to pay court to Elizabeth Christophers Berdan, the daughter of General Hiram Berdan, a weapons expert and gun inventor. In 1884, Crawford and Miss Berdan were married in the French Catholic church in Pera (the European quarter of Constantinople), with the entire diplomatic corps in attendance. They would have four children.

For a time Crawford and his wife resided in Rome with his mother, but often they enjoyed the pleasures of Sorrento, where Crawford sailed his felucca in the Bay of Naples. Contracts for more novels and the birth of a daughter led him to realize that his career lay in the writing of fiction in Italy. In 1887 he purchased a magnificent villa on a cliff in Sant' Agnello di Sorrento to be his permanent home.

In the decade between 1885 and 1895, Crawford wrote much of his best work, including *A Tale of a Lonely Parish* (1886), *Saracinesca* (1887), *Marzio's Crucifix* (1887), *Paul Patoff* (1887), *The Witch of Prague* (1891), *Don Orsino* (1892), *Pietro Ghisleri* (1893), *Katherine Lauderdale* (1894), *The Ralstons* (1895), *Casa Braccio* (1895), and *Corleone: A Tale of Sicily* (1896). These novels, issued simultaneously in New York and London, established Crawford during these years as a major American writer.

By 1896 more than 600,000 books by Crawford had been sold in the United States, and he estimated that more than a million had been sold worldwide. In writing fiction Crawford first sketched a plot in its general outlines. He then filled it in with episodes imagined as he wrote. Each character spoke as Crawford himself would have in the same situation. He wrote rapidly, revising very little, and often in his almost microscopic handwriting put as many as 2,200 words on a single sheet about the size of modern typewriter paper.

The Saracinesca trilogy is representative of his best work. In *Saracinesca* Don Giovanni Saracinesca falls in love with Corona, the Duchesa d'Astrardente and wife of the Duca d'Astrardente, a "broken-down and worn-out dandy of sixty." Giovanni's resolve to keep his feelings to himself suddenly breaks down; but although Corona has married the old duke to save her father from financial ruin, she will not betray her husband. Not until the death of the duke does she reveal her love for Giovanni and are the lovers united in marriage. In *Sant' Ilario*, the second volume, the happiness of their union is disturbed by a variety of incidents. *Don Orsino*, the final volume, concentrates on Giovanni and Corona's son, a young man growing up in a united Italy. Political and social conditions have changed, and Orsino finds many difficulties in his way. At the end of the novel he has yet to find a vocation in life, but he has learned the value of true love.

In 1893 Crawford published a defense of his work in *The Novel: What It Is*. In it he declared that the novel was an intellectual luxury, a commodity, whose purpose is not to instruct but to entertain. In opposition to William Dean Howells's *Criticism and Fiction* (1891), Crawford argued that the novel must show men and women as they could or should be, not as they are in real life. Realism in fiction produced vulgar, if not dirty, pictures of boring, ordinary life. Crawford wanted his novel to be, in his phrase, a "pocket theatre" that one could read for amusement. Thus he became the spokesman for the literature of entertainment in the genteel tradition.

During the 1890s, prompted by the growing needs of his wife and children in Sorrento, Crawford made frequent trips to the United States to write novels, plays, and articles as well as to lecture and to oversee the claims of the Berdan Firearms Company against the government. He also renewed his long friendship with Boston socialite and art collector Isabella Stewart Gardner. His letters to her and to his wife in these years form a valuable commentary on his activities.

Eventually, as Crawford's enthusiasm for fiction abated, he turned to historical writing. In two years he published two popular histories, *Ave Roma Immortalis* (1898) and *The Rulers of the South: Sicily, Calabria, Malta* (1900), and two historical novels, *Via Crucis* (1899) and *In the Palace of the King* (1900). In addition his lecture tour in the United States (1897–1898) contained a great deal of Italian historical material, including Italian Renaissance life and the biography of Pope Leo XIII. In 1905 he published the last of his histories, *Salve Venetia: Gleanings from Venetian History*. He left a history of Rome unfinished at his death in Sant' Agnello di Sorrento.

Crawford's more than forty novels tell compelling stories of love and adventure among the nobility in distant countries. He was one of the first writers in the United States to defend the romance as a fictional form. He increased its popularity and began a long line of popular novels of entertainment that has remained solidly in the mainstream of American fiction.

• The largest single collection of Crawford letters and manuscripts is in the Houghton Library of Harvard University. Important letters are also held by the Isabella Stewart Gardner Museum (Boston), the Library of Congress, and the New York Public Library. Manuscripts of his novels are in the Library of Congress, Harvard University, Yale University, Princeton University, and the University of Pennsylvania. Additional material may be found in the F. Marion Crawford Memorial Society, Nashville, Tenn. Among Crawford's novels not mentioned in this essay but noteworthy are *A Cigarette-Maker's Romance* (1890), *Marion Darche* (1893), *Taquisara* (1896), *The Heart of Rome* (1903), *Fair Margaret* (1905), *Arethusa* (1907), *The Primadonna: A Sequel to "Fair Margaret"* (1908), *The Diva's Ruby: A Sequel to "Primadonna" and "Fair Margaret"* (1908), and *The White Sister* (1909). The fullest bibliographical listing is found in John C. Moran, *An F. Marion Crawford Companion* (1981). The most complete biographical treatment and modern assessment is John Pilkington, Jr., *Francis Marion Crawford* (1964). Valuable information about Crawford and his career may be found in Vittoria Colonna, Duchess of Sermoneta, *Things Past* (1929); Maud Howe Elliott, *My Cousin: F. Marion Crawford* (1934);

Louise Hall Tharp, *Three Saints and a Sinner* (1956); Pilkington, "F. Marion Crawford's Lecture Tour, 1897–1898," *University of Mississippi Studies in English* 1 (1960): 66–85; John C. Moran, *Seeking Refuge in Torre San Nicola* (1980); Alessandra Contenti, "La topografia del rimpianto: Roma al tempo di pio IX nei romanzi de F. Marion Crawford," *Rivista di Studi Anglo Americani* 5 (1990): 315–26; Gordon Poole, ed., *The Magnificent Crawford: Writer by Trade: Acts of the International Conference Held in Sant' Agnello on May 7–8–9, 1988* (1990); and Alessandra Contenti, *Esercizi di nostalgia: La Roma sparita de F. Marion Crawford* (1992). Numerous articles about Crawford have appeared in the volumes of the *Romantist*, a journal published by the F. Marion Crawford Society, Nashville, Tenn.

JOHN PILKINGTON, JR.

CRAWFORD, George Washington (4 June 1861–6 Apr. 1935), industrialist, was born in Venango County, Pennsylvania, two years after the discovery of petroleum in the region, to Ebenezer Crawford, a businessman, and Elizabeth Wilson. After completing his education in local public schools, Crawford took a business course at Eastman College in Poughkeepsie, New York. At age nineteen he worked briefly in the oil and gas fields around Venango County. For a short time he then operated a hardware and oil and gas supply business in Bolivar, New York. Finally, he returned to Venango County where for about nine years he worked for the family firm, E. Crawford & Sons, which operated a network of pipelines bringing oil from wellheads to railroads for shipment to refineries. In 1891 he transferred to another pipeline company and succeeded in obtaining a right-of-way from the oil field near Bradford, Pennsylvania, to Wilkes-Barre.

Two years later, at thirty-two, Crawford entered into a lifelong partnership with his sister's husband, Milo Clinton Treat, who was twenty years his senior and a developer of western Pennsylvania's natural gas and oil. The Treat & Crawford partnership established its headquarters in Pittsburgh in 1901 and organized numerous corporations to exploit the natural gas and oil resources of western Pennsylvania, Ohio, West Virginia, Kentucky, and Indiana. Their efforts resulted in making cheap natural gas available, which influenced the expansion of the glass industry in and around Pittsburgh.

Treat retired from active management of partnership affairs in 1913, but Crawford continued to merge their various enterprises and to take over others until 1925 when Treat died. In the following year Crawford consolidated the former partnership's holdings as the Columbia Gas & Electric Corporation. This new company owned property valued at $500 million and served almost 1.5 million customers in and around the Ohio River Valley. Although its operations centered on natural gas, Columbia Gas & Electric was generally considered one of the nation's leading public service systems. It also sold oil, gasoline, electricity, water, and steam, and operated street railways and other utilities.

The impact of this consolidation and its later development was notable. In the early 1920s coal provided 75 percent of the energy used in the United States, with natural gas barely visible on the chart. By the 1940s coal use was down to 50 percent, and natural gas consumption had risen to 10 percent. In the late 1950s natural gas passed coal at a bit above coal's 25 percent. In 1990 the conglomerate created by Crawford was still operating through numerous subsidiaries as the Columbia Gas System, Inc., with assets of almost $6 billion.

In 1927, the year after creating Columbia Gas, Crawford married Annie Laurie Warmack, daughter of a St. Louis shoe manufacturer. They had one daughter.

In addition to their partnership activities, Crawford and Treat had engaged in ventures independently of each other. Crawford's encompassed the development of oil and gas fields in Illinois, Colombia, and Canada. Although these were moderately successful, none achieved the scope of Columbia Gas. Crawford also served as a director of the Mellon and several other important Pittsburgh banks.

Because of his retiring disposition and constant attention to business affairs, there is little material from which to describe Crawford personally. Close associates considered him a man of dignified bearing with a kindly and a personally sensitive nature. All credited him with being a keen businessman, a man of vision, and an exceptionally talented manager and executive. He died in Pittsburgh.

• There is no full biography of Crawford. The following may prove useful on Pennsylvania oil and natural gas: Paul Henry Giddens, *Early Days of Oil* (1948); J. A. Clark et al., *The Chronological History of the Petroleum and Natural Gas Industries* (1963); E. D. Thoenen, *The History of the Oil and Gas Industry in West Virginia* (1964); J. H. Herbert, *Clean Cheap Heat* (1992); and Glenn E. McLauglin, *The Growth of American Manufacturing Areas: A Comparative Analysis with Special Emphasis on Trends in the Pittsburgh District* (1970). A few brief notices of Crawford and Columbia Gas activities appeared in the *New York Times*, 8 Feb. 1935, p. 33; 7 Mar. 1935, p. 37; 8 Mar. 1935, p. 33; and 30 Jan. 1936, p. 27. His obituary is in the *New York Times*, 7 Apr. 1935. Treat's obituary appears in the *New York Times* of 21 Dec. 1925.

NICHOLAS VARGA

CRAWFORD, Joan (23 Mar. 1904–10 May 1977), actress, was born Lucille Fay LeSueur in San Antonio, Texas, the daughter of French-Canadian Thomas LeSueur, a laborer, and Irish-Scandinavian Anna Bell Johnson, a waitress. Crawford was fond of saying, "We can skip my childhood. I didn't have any. Everything I have in life, Hollywood gave me. I never went beyond the fifth grade. Pictures gave me all my education." Her father deserted the family before she was born. Her mother then married Henry Cassin, a hotel and theater operator, and Lucille changed her name to Billie Cassin. When Crawford was eleven, Henry Cassin left the family after having been accused of theft.

Crawford entered Stephens College in Columbia, Missouri, paying her tuition by waiting tables, but she dropped out during her first term. Plump and unsure of her appearance, she entered dance contests. In 1923 Broadway producer David Belasco hired her as a chorus girl for a tour that took her to Chicago and Detroit. When the tour ended she was hired by Ernie Young, who sent her to work as a chorus girl in Detroit, where impresario J. J. Shubert saw her. He hired her as a dancer for his Broadway shows. "She had something I couldn't define, but she stood out. She wasn't particularly sexy, but she enjoyed herself onstage . . . and the audience, especially the men, stared."

Harry Rapf, a Metro-Goldwyn-Mayer (MGM) supervisor of B pictures, signed her as Lucille LeSueur to a five-year, $75-a-week contract. She arrived in Hollywood in January 1925 and was promptly fired. Rapf thought she had strong possibilities and fought to keep her. Studio chief Louis B. Mayer decided that her "surname sounded too close to sewer," and a nationwide contest to come up with a new name ensued. Crawford later said the contest was a sham and "Joan Crawford" had been preselected.

Crawford did bit parts, learning her craft by sneaking onto other film sets and observing MGM's stars. She noted that Lon Chaney, with whom she appeared in *The Unknown* (1927), "gave me a real insight into the business of acting." At night she worked as an exhibition dancer in speakeasies and clubs. After *Our Dancing Daughters* (1928), she graduated to star billing. She appeared in twenty-two silents opposite such leading men as Francis X. Bushman, John Gilbert, and Ramon Novarro.

Crawford easily made the transition to the talkies. In *Hollywood Revue of 1929*, in which she displayed a pleasant singing voice, she was introduced as "the personification of youth, beauty, and joy and happiness." In two to three films a year, usually as "the hard-to-get broad," she displayed an icy sexuality. *Dance, Fools, Dance* (1931) teamed her with Clark Gable for the first time. She was Fred Astaire's first screen dancing partner in *Dancing Lady* (1933). *Grand Hotel* (1932), *The Women* (1939), and *Susan and God* (1940) were among her early hits.

In 1929 Crawford married Douglas Fairbanks, Jr. He transformed Crawford's flapper image into that of a "dashingly chic, conservative woman of tomorrow," but his family never accepted her. The couple divorced in 1933, and Crawford began an on-again, off-again affair with Clark Gable.

MGM had the motto, "Beautiful pictures for beautiful people." Crawford did not quite meet Mayer's dream factory glamour queen image. "I came to work well dressed, I thought," Crawford said. "I had on slacks, with my hair pulled back and wrapped in a scarf. L. B. took one look and ordered me to go home and dress as a star. He said, 'Never look the way *any* woman could!'" Mayer made Crawford the first product of the studio's star system, where mystique was cultivated into an art form. Soon men ogled and women emulated her. The actress was quoted as saying, "I never go out unless I expect and anticipate and hope and pray that I'll be recognized, that someone will ask for my autograph. When they do, I'm ready and as

well-dressed as I possibly can be. When somebody says, 'There's Joan Crawford,' I say, 'It sure the hell is!'"

Crawford enjoyed star treatment. Photographer Laszlo Willinger told how Crawford insisted a limousine take her from her dressing room to his studio, a few hundred yards away. When asked why, she replied, "It's in my contract." On the soundstage, she shrewdly demanded the best costume designers, lighting directors, makeup artists, and hair stylists.

In 1935 Crawford wed Franchot Tone, a member of New York's Group Theatre (and later the Actors Studio), who attempted to teach her method acting. Theirs was the "perfect" marriage until she caught him being unfaithful. They divorced in 1938 or 1939 but remained friends. She then married the relatively unknown actor Phillip Terry in 1942; they divorced in 1946. In 1939 Crawford said that though she was "the ultimate career woman, something is missing in my life." She adopted a six-week-old French-Irish girl, naming her Joan Crawford, Jr. The child was legally named Christina in 1940. Later Crawford adopted three other children. In her autobiography, she wrote, "I had something to go home to—my babies. That miracle had come to pass, what I had long prayed for, a family."

Despite such solid hits as *Mannequin* (1938), *Strange Cargo* (1940), *A Woman's Face* (1941), and *Above Suspicion* (1943), movie houses considered Crawford "box-office poison." Unhappy with films offered by MGM, she asked to be released. She then signed with Warner Bros. The studio purchased a popular James M. Cain novel, which Bette Davis and Barbara Stanwyck turned down. Producer Jerry Wald suggested Crawford to director Michael Curtiz. Concerned about her reputation and box-office appeal, Curtiz insisted on a screen test, and although Crawford considered that requirement an insult she stunned everyone and agreed. Curtiz was impressed, and *Mildred Pierce* (1945), a drama about a resourceful waitress and mother who uses brains and energy to become a restaurant entrepreneur, won her the Academy Award. She left Warner Bros. in 1951.

After her 1955 marriage to Alfred N. Steele, president of Pepsi-Cola, Crawford became a company spokesperson, starring at press conferences, plant openings, and conventions. Steele died of heart failure in 1959. Crawford's life became more frugal when her Pepsi contract was not renewed. She turned more and more to alcohol and Christian Science.

Crawford and Bette Davis struck paydirt when they made *Whatever Happened to Baby Jane?* (1962), a horror comedy about two former film star sisters living in vengeful propinquity with a secret. Though both denied a feud, their costarring was described as a "cannibal's banquet." Davis later told an interviewer that she delighted in causing Crawford aggravation; Christina Crawford said, "Mother would only have to hear Bette's name to start a tirade." *Baby Jane* became the actresses' most successful film and a cult classic. Crawford took less of an advance and negotiated a larger percentage of the gross but fumed when Davis was nominated for her tenth Academy Award (a record then). It was predicted that Davis would win an unprecedented third Oscar, but, when the award went to an absent Anne Bancroft, Crawford stole the evening by accepting it for her.

During the mid-1960s Crawford appeared mostly in films of the horror genre. Starting in 1953 she made numerous television appearances, including a role in the 1969 pilot of Rod Serling's series "Night Gallery." On one of these Steven Spielberg made his directorial debut. As he became famous, Crawford took much credit for "discovering" him, but Christina Crawford recalled that "Mother was furious with Universal Studios for assigning a kid (to direct her) who'd never done anything."

Other films in which Crawford starred were *Rain* (1932), *Chained* (1934), *The Bride Wore Red* (1937), *Humoresque* (1946), *Possessed* (1947; Oscar nomination), *Daisy Kenyon* (1947), *Flamingo Road* (1949), *The Damned Don't Cry* (1950), *Harriet Craig* (1950), *Goodbye, My Fancy* (1951), *Sudden Fear* (1952; Oscar nomination), *Torch Song* (1953), the off-beat western *Johnny Guitar* (1954), and *Autumn Leaves* (1956). *Trog*, made in 1970, was her last film. She made eighty-one films between 1925 and 1970.

In 1974, after seeing "horrid" pictures of herself after a tribute, Crawford became a virtual recluse in her small, antiseptic Manhattan apartment. "Inactivity is one of life's great indignities," she said. "I need to work." Diagnosed with stomach cancer and on edge when she quit smoking and drinking, Crawford lost weight rapidly. She died in New York City.

Of working-class origins, she was able to rise through the ranks to personify the glamour of Hollywood's golden era. Through endless endeavor, she developed admirable talent, made the transition from flapper and silent pictures to the talkies, and developed a screen presence that was tenacious, passionate, and strangely alluring. Like her rival, Bette Davis, she was a star of much greater magnitude than most of her contemporaries in Hollywood.

• Crawford's autobiography *A Portrait of Joan* (1962), written with Jane Kesner Ardmore, touches few revealing aspects of her life. Her *My Way of Life* (1971) deals with health and beauty tips. Alexander Walker, *Joan Crawford, the Ultimate Star* (1983), is richly illustrated and definitive with an excellent filmography. Books on such Hollywood moguls as Louis B. Mayer and Irving Thalberg and directors George Cukor and Joshua Logan include anecdotes about Crawford. See also Cindy Adams, *Lee Strasberg, the Imperfect Genius of the Actors Studio* (1980); Larry Carr's photography book, *Four Fabulous Faces* (1970); Jane Ellen Wayne, *Crawford's Men* (1988); Bob Thomas, *Joan Crawford* (1978); Roy Newquist, *Conversations with Joan Crawford* (1980); Lawrence J. Quirk, *The Films of Joan Crawford* (1968); and Shaun Considine, *Bette and Joan: The Divine Feud* (1989). Christina Crawford, *Mommie Dearest* (1978), an account of Crawford's daughter's love-hate relationship with her mother and of her turbulent family upbringing, caused shock and disbelief. An obituary is in the *New York Times*, 11 May 1977.

ELLIS NASSOUR

CRAWFORD, John (3 May 1746–9 May 1813), physician, was born in northern Ireland. His father was a nonsubscribing Presbyterian minister in Crumlin, County Antrim, but the names of his parents are not known. At the age of seventeen he was sent to Trinity College at Dublin for a classical education and apparently began medical studies there. He was practicing medicine before 1770, but not until 1791 did he receive an M.D. degree, from St. Andrews. In 1794, at the age of forty-eight, he received a more respectable medical degree from the University of Leiden in the Netherlands.

Early in his career Crawford made two voyages to the East Indies as a surgeon in the service of the East India Company. His first publication, *An Essay on the Nature, Cause and Cure of a Disease Incident to the Liver Hitherto but Little Known, Though Very Frequent and Fatal in Hot Climates* (1772), grew out of his experience in this service. In 1778, shortly after his marriage to the daughter (whose first name is not known) of John and Deborah O'Donnell of Limerick, he was appointed physician to the hospital at Barbados, where he remained until ill health forced him to return to England in 1782. He returned to Barbados, but in 1790 he accepted the position of surgeon-major to the colony of Demerara, then under Dutch control. There he was in charge of the military hospital where he was afforded the opportunity of performing a large number of autopsies, and of studying entomology and botany. The last was indicated in his "Observations on Native Camphor," which appeared in the Edinburgh *Medical Commentaries* of 1793. Ill health again forced him to return to England in 1794.

In 1796 Crawford migrated with his two small children—his wife had died, probably on his first voyage back to England—to the United States. He settled in Baltimore and quickly established himself. In 1798 he was already planning a dispensary in Baltimore modeled on that of Benjamin Rush's in Philadelphia. The dispensary, which finally opened in 1801, owed its origin to Crawford, and he continued active in its affairs until his death.

In 1800 Crawford received some smallpox vaccine from England on a "cotton thread rolled up in paper and covered with a varnish which excluded air." This was the first vaccine to reach Maryland, roughly at the same time as Dr. Benjamin Waterhouse was introducing it in Cambridge. While there is but a single record to his having used the procedure, in 1807 Crawford wrote that "the inoculation of the kine-pox has rendered it [smallpox] nearly harmless."

Crawford was consulting physician to the Baltimore Board of Health and City Hospital, was chairman of the Faculty of Medicine of Baltimore, and served as vice president of the medical society of the city. In 1804 he lectured, on invitation, before the Medical and Chirurgical Faculty of Medicine, but no published version of the lecture has been found. His plan to offer a course of lectures, published as *A Lecture Introductory* in 1811, proved abortive; only one lecture was given. An appointment as lecturer on natural history by the regents of the medical college also proved only nominal.

Crawford made medical history, however, by being the first in the United States to expound at length on the doctrine of *contagium vivum*. His concept of insects and animalcules attacking the human organism suggest a Darwinian approach to the interspecies struggle for survival. Insects, their eggs and their larvae, many invisible to the human eye—Crawford did not mention microorganisms—preyed on man for sustenance and were the cause of disease. These infectious agents, moreover, were specific to each disease. "Diseases," he wrote, "are propagated from a cause in every instance varying in nature and qualities." Every disease thus "must be, in the beginning, local," and he questioned the validity of "the doctrine long prevalent in the schools, that most fevers are diseases of the whole system." From these ideas he completely rejected the role of contagion and considered quarantine useless. "If diseases," he reasoned, "are occasioned by a living principle which attacks and preys upon its fellow mortal, how can a quarantine obviate the difficulty?" Indeed, he concluded, "It is impossible to foresee how far the successful management of diseases may be managed."

Crawford's ideas were propounded originally in the *Observer and Repertory of Original and Selected Essays*, a local journal (edited by his daughter and founded by him in 1804, originally edited by him under the nom de plume Edward Easy and under the title of the *Companion and Weekly Miscellany*). "Remarks on Quarantines" and "Dr. Crawford's Theory" appeared in short essays in twenty-five issues in 1806 and 1807. In 1809 his ideas were presented in three installments in a new and short-lived medical journal, the *Baltimore Medical and Physical Recorder*, put out by his friend Dr. Tobias Watkins. In 1811 he expounded his ideas in a 51-page pamphlet titled *A Lecture, Introductory to a Course of Lectures on the Cause, Seat and Cure of Diseases Proposed to Be Delivered in the City of Baltimore.*

In these essays, Crawford presented long reviews of the work of Jan Swammerdam and Athanasius Kircher. His ideas were not, and could not then have been, based on experimentation, although he cited Kircher's "experiments" that noted the presence of "worms of various sizes" visible under the microscope when flesh was permitted to putrefy. His presentation was logical and detailed, and he relied on his profound knowledge of entomology. He was to write that he labored fifteen years over these matters and "often wasted the midnight lamp." He was aware that his ideas were not consistent with medical thinking and pointed out that *contagium animatum* was not mentioned by William Cullen, Hermann Boerhaave, and Gerhard van Swieten and that John Pringle mentioned it only once.

Although Crawford was a member of the board of examiners of the Medical and Surgical Faculty of Maryland, a member of its publications committee, and once its orator, his ideas were derided by his fellow physicians to the point, as he put it, of "contempt" and "obloquy." Early in 1806, even before his ideas were published, he wrote to Benjamin Rush that the "premature disclosure" of his opinions had led the "envious and malignant" to generate prejudice against him, "so as to deprive me of all the valuable practice in this City." (In 1808 Rush noted in his diary that during a visit to him, Crawford had confided that at the age of sixty-two, he was "not worth a cent, but in debt.") The New York *Medical Repository* of 1807 made note of Crawford's ideas and politely dismissed them with the comment, "For ourselves, who are believers in the chemical theory, we must refer such of our readers as wish further proofs of Dr. C.'s learning and ingenuity, to his original dissertation."

Crawford was active in civic affairs in addition to his work with the dispensary. He was involved in the creation of the Maryland Society for Promoting Useful and Ornamental Knowledge in 1800; he was associated with the Hibernian Society of Baltimore from its beginnings and held offices in that society; the state penitentiary was established in 1804 largely through his efforts; he was one of the founders of the Bible Society dedicated to the spread of the gospel; and he was director of the Baltimore Library. A very prominent and active Mason, he became grand master of the Grand Lodge of Maryland in 1801. Except for one year at his own request, he held that post until his death, and some of his addresses and his writings were published and disseminated nationally.

Crawford had an extensive library, including books in medicine, pharmacy, dentistry, and nursing. The books were in six languages; on one list the earliest bore the date of 1565 and the latest 1811. The Crawford collection, numbering 569 volumes, now forms the cornerstone of the Historical Collections Room of the Health Sciences Library of the University of Maryland at Baltimore. Crawford died in Baltimore.

Crawford, one of the pioneers in the introduction of vaccination into the United States, was hardly an ordinary practitioner of medicine. Well versed in medical literature and possessed of an impressive knowledge of entomology, he propounded his ideas in the face of considerable opposition. These ideas suggested an approach to etiology that occasionally showed glimpses of modern thinking, and, if nothing else, pointed up the inadequacies of the knowledge of disease and its causes of the times.

• The Health Sciences Library of the University of Maryland at Baltimore has miscellaneous Crawford papers. Crawford's letters to Benjamin Rush are in the Rush papers in the collections of the Library Company of Philadelphia. The best biographical sketch is J. E. Wilson, "An Early Baltimore Physician and His Medical Library," in *Annals of Medical History*, 3d ser., 4 (1942): 63–80. It includes an imposing selected list of books in Crawford's library. Eugene F. Cordell earlier published two biographical sketches of Crawford: in the *Johns Hopkins Hospital Bulletin* 10 (1899): 158–62 and in *The Medical Annals of Maryland, 1799–1899* (1903), pp. 758–70.

R. A. Doestch has analyzed Crawford's ideas in "John Crawford and His Contribution to the Doctrine of *Contagium Vivum,*" *Bacteriological Reviews* 28 (1964): 87–96.

DAVID L. COWEN

CRAWFORD, John Randolph (4 Aug. 1915–14 Feb. 1976), bridge champion, born in Bryn Mawr, Pennsylvania, the son of Andrew Wright Crawford, an architect, and Clotilde (maiden name unknown), became an expert at bridge and other games as a teenager. In 1934 he and Robert McPherran, who was a year younger, became famous, indeed notorious, for imaginative play and psychic, or bluff, bidding. "Don't you ever make a normal bid?" an official asked Crawford, who was soon known in Philadelphia bridge circles as "the Boy Wonder," a description given earlier to an equally famous bridge star, Oswald Jacoby.

While still in his teens Crawford was welcomed into a group of established Philadelphia players that included Charles Goren, B. Jay Becker, Charles Solomon, Olive Peterson, and Sidney Silodor. In 1937 the twenty-two year old won his first national title at a younger age than any other American player. The tourney was the Board-a-Match Teams, today called the Reisinger, which he was to win ten times, a record, during the next twenty-four years.

The Board-a-Match Teams was then, and still is, one of the three most important events on the bridge calendar, along with the Spingold Knockout and the Vanderbilt Knockout. In 1939 Crawford became Life Master #19 at the age of twenty-four, the youngest at that time to achieve the rank. (This was highly meaningful in his day, but it has diminished in importance because of reduced qualifying requirements.)

In the same year that he became a Life Master Crawford married Marie Blackburn Washington, fifth-generation niece of George Washington and a niece of Admiral Richard Byrd. This marriage, the first of three for Crawford, produced three daughters. He cut short his honeymoon to fly to Pittsburgh, where he helped his team win a third straight victory in the Board-a-Match Teams.

An expert who knew Crawford well at this time said: "He is like a magician who wishes to distract your attention from his real purpose and lead you on." Said another: "He's endlessly resourceful and always looks for the hidden angle." Some of his "angles" skirted the game's ethical borderline. For example, he was known for his habit of staring at his opponent, hoping to disconcert him or obtain a psychological clue. One opponent reportedly objected: "I ain't gonna bid until Crawford takes his eyeballs outta my lap."

In 1941 Crawford scored the first of nine victories in the Vanderbilt, and in 1943 he collected his first of five Spingold titles. He joined the army in 1943, served with a chemical-mortar battalion in France, endured the Battle of the Bulge, and received a campaign ribbon. With official encouragement, he lectured to the troops on how to avoid being cheated at cards, drawing on his experience at many games, particularly poker and gin rummy.

When World War II ended in 1945, he was discharged, resumed his life in Philadelphia, and supported himself by playing and writing. Most of his income came from playing bridge, backgammon, and gin rummy for high stakes. At this time he claimed, with only slight exaggeration, to be the world's best player at all three games. He wrote a regular column for *Elks Magazine* and books on bridge, canasta, samba, and other card games. His last book, published in 1970, was written jointly with Oswald Jacoby and was on backgammon.

The decade from 1948 through 1957 saw a string of remarkable successes for Crawford. In 1950, 1951, and 1953 he was a member of an American team that won the first three postwar world bridge championships, which were played in Bermuda, Naples, and New York City. In 1957 he achieved a unique grand slam by simultaneously holding all five major national team titles: Vanderbilt, Spingold, Board-a-Match Teams, Men's Teams, and Mixed Teams. In 1958 and 1960 he returned to Italy to represent the United States in world championship play. His team was second in Como and third in Turin, where a side trip proved profitable; a hot streak in a casino forced management to open the vault to pay him his considerable winnings.

In 1958 Crawford was divorced, and he moved to New York City the following year. About 1960 he married Lesley Bogert, and this marriage also ended in divorce. His tournament appearances from that point on were less frequent, and less successful. Some brilliant young players were making a mark, introducing new bidding methods with which he was unfamiliar.

About 1973, Crawford married Carol Stolkin, who survived him. In that year he became a center of controversy. He made a speech to the American Contract Bridge League's board of governors on the subject of cheating, which he described as a pressing threat to the game. He claimed that he had been cheated not only in a world championship fifteen years earlier, but also in a Vanderbilt match the previous day. He did not name the two players concerned, but it was well-known who they were, and the authorities took notice. Since such accusations are supposed to be made to officials in private, Crawford was suspended from tournament play for six months. Eleven months after his death from a heart attack on Valentine's Day 1976, he was vindicated. The two players he had accused resigned from the national organization in the face of serious allegations of impropriety, matching those he had alleged.

• An account of Crawford's early bridge career appears under the title "Buccaneer" in *Championship Bridge as Played by the Experts* (1949), by J. Patrick Dunne and Albert A. Ostrow. See also *Official Encyclopedia of Bridge,* 4th ed. (1984). An obituary is in the *New York Times,* 15 Feb. 1976.

ALAN TRUSCOTT

CRAWFORD, John Wallace (4 Mar. 1847–28 Feb. 1917), army scout and playwright, known as "Captain Jack, the Poet Scout," was born in Donegal, Ireland, the son of John Austin Crawford, a tailor, and Susie Wallace. In 1854 his father moved to the United States and found work in the coal mines of Minersville, Pennsylvania. He was joined by his wife in 1858 and by his children in 1860. Three weeks after their arrival he enlisted in the Union army, and his boys had to go to work in the coal mines.

Young Crawford tried to enlist in the army twice before he was fifteen years old, and in 1863 he joined Company F of the Forty-eighth Pennsylvania Volunteer Infantry. He was wounded twice, first on 12 May 1864 at Spottsylvania and then on 2 April 1865 at Petersburg. After his first injury he was hospitalized in Washington, D.C., before being transferred to Saterlee Hospital in West Philadelphia. There he was taught to read and write by a sister of charity. Honorably discharged in 1865, he returned home to find his parents dying. Shortly before his mother died, he promised her that he would never drink alcohol. Crawford often described this touching scene in his later prohibition lectures.

In 1869 Crawford married Anna Marie Stokes, with whom he had five children. For most of the first ten years of his married life Crawford lived on the frontier, while his family remained behind in Pennsylvania. During the 1870s he served as an army scout and as a prospector; and he helped found the frontier towns of Deadwood, Custer City, Crook, and Spearfish. In 1876 Crawford left scouting to costar with William F. ("Buffalo Bill") Cody in his Wild West melodramas. Crawford was wounded during a performance and while recuperating wrote his first play, *Fonda; or, The Trapper's Dream*. The play was so successful that he toured California with it and was invited to take it to Australia. When he could not raise money for the trip, he returned to scouting.

Crawford's first collection of poetry, *The Poet Scout*, was published in 1879, and throughout the 1880s and 1890s he continued to spend his time producing plays, writing poetry and plays, prospecting, and lecturing. He also traveled to England to investigate an inheritance and to Alaska to set up a mining operation that failed. In 1903 Crawford left his family, who had joined him in 1881 at Fort Craig, New Mexico, and established residence in Brooklyn, New York, where he coauthored a play with Marie Madison titled *Colonel Bob* (1908) and continued to publish poetry.

Crawford's most important works are his plays, in which he created the myth of the western hero—and which reveal his concept of himself as such a hero. During his lifetime, however, he did not receive the recognition as a playwright and creator of the American hero that he felt he deserved. His poetry was more renowned than his plays, and his popularity was based on his acting and his lectures that proclaimed him as a Civil War veteran and patriot and as a "great scout" and teetotaler. Crawford died at his home in Brooklyn.

• Crawford's other play, not mentioned in the text, is *The Mighty Truth; or, In Clouds or Sunshine* (1896). For a commentary on his plays, see Paul T. Nolan, *Three Plays by J. W. (Capt. Jack) Crawford: An Experiment in Myth-Making* (1966). Crawford's other collections of poetry include *Camp Fire-Sparks* (1893); *Lariattes: A Book of Poems and Favorite Recitations* (1904); *The Broncho Book: Being Buck-Jumps in Verse* (1908); and *Whar' the Hand of God Is Seen and Other Poems* (1911). For more on Crawford and a bibliography of works by and about him, see Paul T. Nolan, *John Wallace Crawford* (1981). Obituaries are in the *New York Times*, 28 Feb. 1917, and *Literary Digest* 54 (24 Mar. 1917): 13.

PAUL T. NOLAN

CRAWFORD, Ralston (25 Sept. 1906–27 Apr. 1978), painter and photographer, was born George Ralston Crawford in St. Catharines, Ontario, Canada, the son of George Burson Crawford, a ship's captain, and Lucy Colvin. In 1910 the family moved to Buffalo, New York, where Crawford grew up. In high school his flair for illustration drew encouragement from teachers; for two years following his graduation in 1924 he remained at the school to take additional art courses. In 1926 he shipped out from New York City on a United Fruit Company vessel and sailed on tramp steamers for a year until he decided to stay in Los Angeles to continue his training in art. After a brief stint at Walt Disney's studio, he attended the Otis Art Institute through the spring of 1927.

Later in 1927 Crawford enrolled at the Philadelphia Academy of Art. He also went to lectures at the Barnes Foundation in Merion, Pennsylvania, and studied Dr. Albert C. Barnes's collection of modern European art. The influence of Picasso, Gris, Matisse, and especially Cézanne is evident in Crawford's student paintings, which reveal talent but not a personal style. On completing art school in 1930 he moved to New York City. In 1931 he married Margaret Stone, whose well-to-do family sent them on a six-month tour of Europe. They were to have two children.

The couple settled in Greenwich Village, a haven for experimental American painters at the time. Although he and his wife had means, Crawford struggled to establish his career in an era of severe economic crisis. The depression awakened his social consciousness, reflected in his involvement in the Artists Union and the American Artists Congress. Although Crawford advocated a more rational, humane socio-economic order, he did not ardently embrace left-wing causes and soon became disenchanted with Stalinism.

As Crawford's characteristic style developed during the 1930s, he adopted a kind of super-realism suggesting the angularity of the cubists. His subject matter was increasingly the engineered landscapes of modern America, largely unpeopled scenes of bridges, storage facilities, docks, power lines, and the like. As a result, he was identified with the Precisionists, a somewhat older generation of artists who cast the industrial world in sharply delineated images.

Crawford had his first one-man show in 1934 at the Maryland Institute of Art in Baltimore, but his breakthrough as an artist to be noticed occurred in 1936, when Philip Boyer's private gallery in Philadelphia exhibited Crawford's work of the previous two years. The following year, Crawford completed a frequently reproduced painting, *Steel Foundry, Coatesville, Pa.* (1936–1937; Whitney Museum of American Art), in which an unadorned foundry building looms in solid color and shadow above a wall, a lower fence, and telephone lines in the foreground.

Crawford's best-known painting dates from this period too. *Overseas Highway* made him a celebrity, thanks to its color reproduction in the February 1939 issue of *Life* magazine soon after the work was finished. The components are simple: massive unblemished concrete pavement recedes from the foreground into infinity; the sides of the highway are girded with steel; to the sides a field of dark blue represents the sea; and in a bright blue sky a shelf of white cloud broadens out. The shapes are cleanly defined; the contrast between light and shadow is almost absolute. Here Crawford fulfills his basic aesthetic principle: the essence of painting emerges from the dynamic interplay of structural forms.

During the late 1930s Crawford and his family lived in Exton, Pennsylvania. Following his divorce in 1939, he went back to New York City, which remained his home for the rest of his life, even though he became an inveterate world traveler. In 1942 he married Peggy Frank, with whom he had three children. That same year he joined the Visual Presentation Unit of the U.S. Army Air Force's Weather Division and for the rest of the war was in charge of converting meteorological data into pictures of weather formations and flight patterns.

In 1946, on assignment for *Fortune* magazine, Crawford witnessed an atom bomb test on the Pacific atoll of Bikini and portrayed the event in *Test Able* (1946; Georgia Museum of Art, Athens, Ga.), a painting unlike his previous work. Where once he would have presented fully representational, pristine shapes set in perspective, he created a nearly abstract plane of jagged forms that convey a fracturing of coherent order. Henceforth his paintings typically transform real objects into complex patterns of motifs that have to be "read" more on their own terms than with reference to the images from which he worked—airplanes, ruins of a bombed city, lobster traps, ship's rigging, or the Third Avenue El. The geometric character of his earlier work is still present, but the fields of color often have a darker tone. In any event, he was never to waver from his original artistic credo: " . . . what is there [on the canvas], however abstract, grows out of something I've seen" (*New York Times*, 2 May 1978).

But the ascendancy of abstract expressionism in postwar American art eclipsed Crawford's career as a painter. The abstract expressionists' powerful spontaneity and emotional drive, rendered in vivid brushstrokes and spatterings, were alien to his style of "cool," deliberately formed shapes and patterns. While critics and the art market favored Jackson Pollock, Willem de Kooning, and similarly inclined artists, Crawford could rarely sell a painting of his own.

Much of his income came from visiting appointments at art schools and universities around the country. He also profited by turning to print-making. Often based on his paintings, his lithographs steadily attracted collectors of prints.

From the late 1930s onward Crawford kept a camera at hand in lieu of a sketchbook. A visit to New Orleans in 1948, however, inspired him to make photographs radically different from his work on canvas. Fascinated by the world of poor blacks, he took pictures in jazz clubs and seedy neighborhoods. His photographic portraits have a startling warmth and sense of immediacy; they catch a moment in time rather than suggest the atemporal world of his paintings. Even so, many of his other photographs highlight the texture and geometry of architectural forms.

Crawford's absences and his abrasive nature estranged his wife, who separated from him in 1970. Two years later, he was diagnosed as having terminal cancer. Yet he was not deterred from continuing to travel extensively over the next six years. At the time of his death, he was in Houston to help mount an exhibition of his work. As he had requested, a traditional jazz funeral was held for him in New Orleans, where he was buried in one of the old cemeteries.

Despite his fall from favor, Crawford never lost faith in his genius. Retrospectives, such as the show at the Whitney Museum of American Art in 1985–1986, prompted fresh reassessments, but future praise is unlikely to carry him into the front rank of American artists of his time. Regardless of his artistic weaknesses, Crawford succeeded in painting enduring images that are distinctly his own.

• The Ralston Crawford estate retains most of his papers. His paintings, prints, and photographs are located in numerous collections around the United States, including the Art Institute of Chicago; the Los Angeles County Museum of Art; the Metropolitan Museum of Art, the Museum of Modern Art, and the Whitney Museum of American Art in New York; the Philadelphia Museum of Art; and the Hirshhorn Museum, the Library of Congress, and the Phillips Collection in Washington, D.C. His life and his work as a painter are informatively discussed in three books with the same title, *Ralston Crawford*, by Richard B. Freeman (1953), William C. Agee (1983), and Barbara Haskell (1985). The Hirschl & Adler Galleries have issued reproductions of his work in *Ralston Crawford and the Sea*, with an introduction by Carter Ratcliff (1991), and *Ralston Crawford: Images of War* (1993). For his photographic work, see *Music in the Street: Photographs of New Orleans by Ralston Crawford*, with introductions by Curtis D. Jerde and John H. Lawrence (1983), and *Ralston Crawford: Photographs/Art and Process*, exhibit catalog for a show at the University of Maryland, College Park, organized by Edith A. Touelli and John Gossage (1983). An obituary is in the *New York Times*, 2 May 1978.

PAUL BETZ

CRAWFORD, Sam (18 Apr. 1880–15 June 1968), baseball player also known as Wahoo Sam, was born Samuel Earl Crawford in Wahoo, Nebraska, the son of Stephen Orlando Crawford, a Civil War veteran who had settled in Wahoo in the 1870s, and Ellen Ann "Nellie"

Blanchard. Stephen Crawford, who had a war disability pension, raised three boys and a girl working as a part-time real estate broker.

Crawford left school after the fifth grade to take up barbering. He became the star of the local baseball team and in 1897 left home to become a baseball player, making stops in Chatham, Ontario; Columbus; and Grand Rapids, reaching the major leagues with Cincinnati at the end of his initial season in professional baseball. By 1901 he was a star batting .330 and leading the majors with sixteen home runs, and in 1902 he hit .333 and led the league with twenty-three triples. In 1903, exploiting the bidding rivalry between the National League and the recently established American League, he jumped clubs, going to the Detroit Tigers for a salary of $3,500.

Although Crawford had a banner year in 1904 for Detroit, batting .355, the Tigers cut his salary to $3,000, noting that the "war years" between the leagues were over—the two leagues had agreed to end their bidding on baseball talent—and that the club was losing money. Crawford, who had married Ada Lattin, the daughter of a prosperous Wahoo farmer in 1901, was not allowed, as he had in the past, to take his wife to spring training, and he was now charged for his uniform. He carefully saved his baseball earnings, rarely going to night spots. He was respected as the "Rockefeller of the Tigers" and as a "tight proposition" for his frugal ways. (It was not until the 1920s that baseball stars were expected to spend their money lavishly.)

Crawford was a favorite of the fans, who loved his long drives against, and occasionally over, the fences. From 1903 to 1907 he was the subject of many feature stories in the Detroit press, including one with a caption under his photo that read: "After all is said and done the crowd loves the slugger."

Crawford resented Ty Cobb, the brash, brilliant outfielder who joined the Tigers at the end of the 1905 season and who by 1906 was not only grabbing the headlines of the Detroit sports sections but also had caused Crawford to be moved from right field to center field. In 1906 the Detroit veterans subjected Cobb, a rookie, to extensive hazing; this was considered a proper rite of passage for young players becoming major leaguers, but Cobb thought it was unnecessarily cruel and saw Crawford as the chief instigator. Crawford, on the other hand, felt that Cobb's overreaction to what he considered harmless pranks revealed an unbalanced mind. Moreover Crawford was frustrated at seeing Cobb's salary soar well above his own, and each spring during contract negotiations he exchanged bitter letters with Frank Navin, the general manager and part owner of the Tigers. Although the two never became friends Crawford and Cobb constituted, with Bobby Veach, baseball's first murders' row. Crawford posted a career-high .378 batting average in 1911 only to finish second in the league to Cobb's .420. Despite their personal enmity, Crawford and Cobb led Detroit to pennants in 1907, 1908, and 1909. In the Tigers'

three World Series defeats of those years, Crawford batted only .243.

Crawford was a pioneer in bringing major league baseball to the West Coast. At the end of the 1905 season he took several Detroit players to California and organized an All–American League team that played a series of exhibition games against the All–National League team.

After being released from his contract in 1919, Crawford, who left Detroit blasting Cobb's individualistic style of play and the Tiger management for never fully compensating him for his immense achievements, moved from Wahoo, where he had kept his off-season home, and settled in Peco, California. He was a star in the Pacific Coast League for four years, retiring in 1921. He stayed on the coast doing a number of odd jobs and in 1935 became an umpire in the Pacific Coast League, a job he hated and from which he retired in 1938, the year Ada Crawford died. They had had two children. In 1943 he married Mary Blazer, a widow.

In 1951 Crawford returned to Detroit for the All-Star game and had a partial reconciliation with Cobb at the funeral of teammate Harry Heilmann. However, while Cobb wrote letters to influential sportswriters, such as J. G. Taylor Spink, the editor of the *Sporting News*, urging them to support Crawford's election to the National Baseball Hall of fame, he also continued to complain about Crawford's role in the hazing incidents of 1906.

Although he had had little formal education, Crawford was a relatively cultured man who read serious books and wrote elegant and charming letters. He began his baseball career at a time when baseball players were accorded little respect, and in his old age he made disparaging remarks about the profession of his youth. His baseball savings depleted, he spent his last years as a semirecluse. He was elected to the Hall of Fame in 1957 and later died in Hollywood, California.

Crawford was a long ball hitter in the dead ball era, when it was nearly impossible to drive a baseball over the fences. H. G. Salsinger, a Detroit sportswriter who covered the Tigers from 1909 to 1951, thought the left-handed Crawford could have matched Babe Ruth's home run records if he had played in the live ball era. Cobb shared these sentiments. During his nineteen-year career, Crawford hit 97 home runs, led the league in triples a record six times (312 total), hit 457 doubles, drove in 1,525 runs, amassed 2,964 hits, and posted a .309 batting average with a .453 slugging percentage.

• For more information on Crawford, see the *Detroit Tigers Letter Books*, 10 Feb. 1904 and 12 Dec. 1904, Ernie Harwell Collection (part of the Burton Historical Collection), in the main branch of the Detroit Public Library. The letter books contain copies of letters sent from the Detroit Baseball Club to players discussing contracts, training, and general baseball gossip. The letters, signed by Ed Barrow, "Cousin Ed," through 1904 and then by Frank Navin, who replaced Barrow as general manager, not only provide information about salaries but also give insights into negotiating strategies of that era. For the genealogy of the Crawford family, see the file put together by Gladys Cajka in the Saunders County Historical Society of Wahoo, Nebr., which houses a collection of birth and marriage certificates on various members of the family. Feature stories about Crawford in the *Detroit News*, 17 June 1905 and 8 Sept. 1907, illustrate how highly he was regarded and how much he was liked at the peak of his career. Lawrence Ritter, *The Glory of Their Times* (1966), provides an interview with Crawford that displays his lively mind and intelligence. Ty Cobb, with Al Stump, *My Life in Baseball—The True Record* (1961), while giving credit to Crawford's skills, is full of bitterness against the man who was involved in the hazing of the young Cobb. Frederick G. Lieb, *The Detroit Tigers* (1946), gives Crawford a prominent place in the history of the Detroit Tigers. Lieb, as a journalist, covered much of Crawford's career. Obituaries are in the *Evening Journal & Nebraska State Journal*, 17 June 1968, which includes interesting Wahoo anecdotes, and the *Sporting News*, 29 June 1968, which gives a balanced account of his career.

A. J. PAPALAS

CRAWFORD, Samuel Johnson (10 Apr. 1835–21 Oct. 1913), politician and soldier, was born near Bedford, Lawrence County, Indiana, the son of William Crawford and Jane Morrow, farmers. Crawford attended public schools and an academy in Bedford before reading law in the office of a local attorney. In 1857 he entered the Law School of Cincinnati College, from which he graduated in 1858.

In 1859 Crawford migrated to Garnett, the county seat of Anderson County, in territorial Kansas, where he practiced law. In anticipation of statehood, on 6 December 1859 Crawford, a Republican, was elected to the prospective Kansas House of Representatives. Kansas was finally admitted to statehood on 21 January 1861, following the walkout of senators from the secessionist South, and Representative Crawford took his seat in the Kansas legislature on 26 March.

Soon after southern gunners opened fire on Fort Sumter and President Abraham Lincoln called for ninety-day volunteers, Crawford took a leave of absence from the legislature and recruited a company of soldiers from his district. The company, with Crawford as its captain, became part of the Second Kansas Volunteer Infantry, which was bloodied at the battle of Wilson's Creek, Missouri, on 10 August 1861.

Crawford participated in the organization of the Second Kansas Cavalry and was appointed captain. After an uneventful 2,000-mile trek to New Mexico, the unit was active in engagements in northwest Arkansas in 1862, including Maysville (Old Fort Wayne), 22 October, Cane Hill, 28 November, and a major battle at Prairie Grove, 7 December. Crawford won praise for his bravery in each of the engagements while serving as battalion and acting regimental commander.

Promotion to colonel came with Crawford's acceptance of the command of the Second Kansas Colored Infantry. Under threat of the Confederacy's "black flag policy" of taking no black prisoners, Crawford's men fought well, especially at Jenkins's Ferry, Arkansas, on 30 April 1864. Crawford served as volunteer aide-de-camp to General Samuel Curtis during Sterling Price's raid in the fall of 1864. He was involved at Westport, Missouri, 23 October, and he was instrumental in the coup de grâce administered to Price's Confederate army at Mine Creek, Kansas, 25 October.

In September 1864 the 29-year-old war hero was handed the Republican nomination for governor of Kansas. Representatives of the Kansas regiments and Senator James H. Lane (1814–1866) appear to have engineered his surprise nomination. His successful defense of Kansas against the Price expedition negated the necessity for Crawford to campaign, and he was elected by a large majority.

The new governor complained, after his inaugural on 9 January 1865, that the state had nothing "except the State Seal, a lease on some leaky buildings, and quite an assortment of bills payable" (Crawford, p. 226). After the war ended, however, the economy expanded rapidly, and his administration established a state university, agricultural college, and normal school; enlarged the penitentiary; and commenced building a capitol.

Lane was reelected in January 1865 with Crawford's support, and the senator continued to dominate Kansas politics until his suicide in 1866. Governor Crawford reached outside the established competing political factions to appoint a friend from the army, Edmund G. Ross, to fill the vacant U.S. Senate seat. With no organized opposition in the Republican party, Crawford was reelected by more than a two-to-one majority in 1866. Soon after the election, the governor married Isabel Marshall Chase. They had two children.

During his second term, Crawford promoted land settlement and railroad building at the expense of the American Indians. The governor shared the view of the settlers of the fast-growing state that the Indians should be removed because, as he stated in his 1866 Annual Message, they "will neither improve nor cultivate the lands, and their occupancy prevents others from doing it." Although he attended the Indian peace meetings at Medicine Lodge in 1867, Crawford opposed the "soft" Indian policy of the government. When the U.S. Army failed to protect the settlers in western Kansas, Crawford organized the state militia to expel the Indians.

As Crawford's second term neared an end, he unsuccessfully challenged incumbent Sidney Clarke for the Republican nomination for congressman-at-large. Crawford's popularity with the Republican party had been weakened by factionalism, his "lame duck" status, and the "not guilty" vote of his appointee, Senator Ross, in the impeachment trial of President Andrew Johnson. On 4 November 1868, after Clarke's reelection, Crawford submitted his resignation as governor and assumed command of the Nineteenth Kansas Regiment, which he had previously commissioned to aid General Phil Sheridan in a winter campaign against the Indians. Although Sheridan succeeded in punishing the Indians for their alleged treaty violations, Crawford's expedition was thwarted by a ten-inch snowfall in northwest Indian Territory. Crawford resigned the command on 12 February 1869, six weeks before the unit was mustered out of service.

At age thirty-four, the former governor moved to Emporia and joined a real estate firm while seeking to revive his political career. Crawford abandoned the Republican party after his bid for the U.S. Senate seat in 1871 was thwarted by bribery. Alexander Caldwell was elected, but a Senate committee found him "not duly and legally elected" after an investigation that concluded in 1873. Crawford made unsuccessful bids for the U.S. Senate as a Liberal Republican in 1873 and as an Independent Greenback candidate for Congress in 1876 and 1878.

In 1877 Crawford returned to Topeka and joined his brother-in-law in a law firm. Ironically, Crawford became wealthy after he was appointed "state agent" for land and monetary claims against the federal government by a Republican legislature and as a legal representative of certain American Indian tribes.

In retirement, with homes in Baxter Springs and Topeka, Crawford published his memoirs in 1911 and basked in his status as one of the last surviving Civil War governors. He died at his home in Topeka.

• Crawford's gubernatorial papers are in the archives of the Kansas State Historical Society in Topeka. His memoir, *Kansas in the Sixties* (1911), is a useful source. The only biography is Mark A. Plummer, *Frontier Governor: Samuel J. Crawford of Kansas* (1971). An obituary is in the Topeka *Daily Capital*, 22 Oct. 1913.

MARK A. PLUMMER

CRAWFORD, Thomas (22 Mar. 1813?–10 Oct. 1857), sculptor, was born in New York City, the son of Aaron Crawford, evidently a waiter and laborer, and Mary Gibson, both of whom were Irish immigrants. His father had wanted him to become an office clerk, but from his earliest years Crawford wanted to be a sculptor. Consequently, he apprenticed himself to a wood carver, made drawings of plaster casts of ancient sculpture at the American Academy of Fine Arts, and studied art informally at the National Academy of Design. When he was about nineteen years of age, Crawford obtained a position in the firm of the sculptors John Frazee and Robert Launitz. Frazee, a bricklayer who taught himself to carve wood and stone, is said to have been the first native-born sculptor to create a marble portrait bust in the United States (in 1824). Russian-born Launitz had studied sculpture in Rome under Bertel Thorvaldsen, the Danish neoclassical sculptor, before emigrating to New York in 1828. Crawford demonstrated such competence in carving ornate floral mantels that his supervisors put him to work on busts of four important patrons, including Chief Justice John Marshall.

In 1835 Crawford took steps to fulfill the dream of his youth, which was to study in Rome. After a tedious crossing on a merchantman, he disembarked at Leghorn and was soon in the Eternal City. Thorvaldsen welcomed Launitz's recommended protégé and let him work in one of his three studios, during his first year abroad. Crawford soon made the acquaintance of George Washington Greene, the American consul in Rome. Crawford energetically sketched nudes at the French Academy and studied classical sculpture at the Vatican galleries, copied antique statues for some American patrons, and modeled portrait busts in clay to be put into marble for others. According to his friend the painter and biographer Thomas Hicks, Crawford modeled seventeen portrait busts in ten weeks early in 1837; he also planned several original ideal figures.

In 1839 Crawford began his first momentous work, a life-sized *Orpheus*. The three-headed dog Cerberus is at his feet, his lyre is in his left hand, and his right hand shades his eyes, as he peers into Hell, searching for his lost Eurydice. Charles Sumner, the future senator, was vacationing in Europe in 1839 and Greene took him to Crawford's studio. Sumner admired the *Orpheus* and wrote fellow well-to-do Bostonians and patrons about Crawford and his work. On returning to Boston the next spring, Sumner arranged for the Athenaeum to commission the *Orpheus* in marble. After a long bout of fever and a brief visit in mid-1840 to the American sculptors Horatio Greenough and Hiram Powers in Florence, Crawford returned to his work, which included several new orders. He worried when his promised payment of $2,500 for what he called "Sir Orfeo" was delayed, but in mid-1843 he shipped the finished marble to Boston, where it arrived broken in several places. Skillfully restored by the sculptor Henry Dexter, the work was triumphantly exhibited in Boston early in 1844, together with other works by Crawford—*Anacreon* (1841, Boston Athenaeum), *Bride of Abydos* (1842, private collection), *Christ Blessing the Children* (1843, not located), *Hyperion* (1841, Carnegie Museum of Art, Pittsburgh), and a bust of Sumner (1842, Boston Museum of Fine Arts). Crawford's future seemed assured.

In the winter of 1843–1844, Samuel Gridley Howe, the heroic reformer, paid a visit to Crawford's studio in Rome, as many traveling Americans were in the habit of doing. With him were his wife Julia Ward Howe, author of "The Battle Hymn of the Republic" and much else, and Julia's beautiful young sister Louisa Ward. Although the wealthy and socially ambitious Ward family raised preliminary objections, Crawford and Louisa Ward were married in New York in 1844. During this time, Crawford garnered new orders in New York, Boston, Washington, D.C., and elsewhere. Crawford was especially fortunate in his commission for a portrait bust of Josiah Quincy (1772–1864), Harvard's retiring president. Crawford and his wife returned to Rome to establish a permanent residence there in 1845. Their social circle in the bustling American art colony soon included the sculptors Mary Louisa Lander and William Wetmore Story and the painters William Page, Luther Terry, and Cephas Giovanni Thompson in addition to many visitors and several potential clients.

Crawford opened a series of studios at the Villa Negroni, between what are now the Piazza dei Termini and the Piazza Esquilino. He was busily occupied with portrait busts but was more happily so with biblical and mythological statues and genre figures, mainly of children, including *Dancing Girl* (by 1850, now in the Tulane University Art Collection), *Babes in the Woods* (c. 1850, now at the Metropolitan Museum of Art, New York), *Boy with Broken Tambourine* (by 1854, stolen from Tulane Art Collection around 1968, present location not known), and *Boy and Goat* (by 1857, not now located). In 1849 the Crawfords visited the United States because Louisa was heartsick to see her family.

While in Boston, Crawford read in a newspaper about a competition for a monument honoring George Washington that was to be erected in Richmond by the state of Virginia. Crawford quickly submitted an equestrian model, was awarded the commission in 1850, and returned jubilantly with his family to his Roman studios to plan to first work in bronze. In addition to the central figure on horseback, there were to be standing figures of Patrick Henry and Thomas Jefferson, two shields, and thirteen wreaths and stars. The price offered was $52,975, in staggered payments, out of which Crawford paid for the expensive casting in bronze, by Ferdinand von Müller of Munich. In 1856 Crawford contracted to add standing figures of John Marshall, Thomas Nelson, George Mason, and General Andrew Lewis, for an additional $9,000 each. All figures were to be presented naturalistically, in contemporary dress.

Meanwhile, Crawford accepted commissions for other public monuments. These commissions included a huge bronze *Beethoven* for the Boston Music Hall, modeled in 1853 and cast later, and the marble Amos Binney monument for the Mount Auburn Cemetery in nearby Cambridge (1847–1850). More important, he agreed to fill several large orders for the embellishment of the Capitol in Washington, D.C. Captain Montgomery C. Meigs, a career officer and the engineer in charge of enlarging and decorating the Capitol, wrote Crawford in 1853 with a number of suggestions and a request for other ideas. The result of months of communication was that Crawford signed contracts to provide *The Progress of Civilization* in marble for the pediment of the east wing of the Senate building, bronze doors for the Senate, bronze doors for the House of Representatives, allegorical figures of Justice and History for the Senate doorhead, and a bronze entitled *Armed Freedom* for the Capitol dome.

The Progress of Civilization, one of Crawford's finest works in marble, contains fourteen figures plus accessories, all planned in detail in 1853. The central statue is that of a draped goddess representing America, with a symbolic rock, ocean waves, an eagle, and a rising sun. On her left are a backwoodsman with an axe, a young Indian hunter, a gloomy Indian chief (nude and seated), an Indian mother and baby, and a grave. To America's right are a revolutionary war soldier, a merchant, a pair of lads, a teacher with a pupil, a mechanic with tools, and sheaves of corn. Crawford asked

$20,000 for the pediment and promised plaster casts within thirty months.

Even as this work, which was to measure twelve feet in height at the center and sixty feet in length, was steadily advancing, Crawford began additional plans in 1855. He developed ideas for the Senate doors, somewhat after Lorenzo Ghiberti's fabulous baptistry "Gates of Paradise" in Florence. Crawford proposed revolutionary war scenes (Bunker Hill, Monmouth, Yorktown) for the right valve and peacetime scenes (events in George Washington's postwar career) for the left, plus allegorical and symbolic items. He asked a modest $6,000 for the work. Plans for the Capitol dome followed. Crawford proposed a draped female figure, 19′6″ in height, with a wreath of wheat and laurel, a sword and an olive branch, and a national shield. Crawford then sketched out his plans for the House of Representatives door: the left valve would be devoted to depictions of revolutionary war battles and deaths; the right, to scenes of independence and peaceful pursuits. He also planned his Justice and History figures. In August 1855 Crawford wrote Meigs, offering to prepare models for a proposed 9-by-300-foot interior Capitol rotunda frieze for $50,000. This project came to naught.

With dozens of skillful Italian works under his supervision at his studios near the Villa Negroni, Crawford felt free to take a quick trip to Paris and London; he returned to Rome early in 1856 to see his wife and their four children (including Francis Marion Crawford, the novelist) off to New York. Crawford continued his studio work and then joined his family in the summer for what proved to be his final business trip to the United States. In Boston, he worked out details for a large marble statue of James Otis, and in Washington he conferred with Meigs about his numerous Capitol embellishments. Louisa and the children decided to prolong their stay; so Crawford persuaded his sister Jenny Crawford Campbell to return to Rome with him. She was delighted and proved of inestimable help when tragedy struck Crawford. He experienced a swelling in his left eye, consulted two American physicians in Rome, and went to Paris early in 1857, accompanied by his painter friend Luther Terry. Crawford's wife joined them in Paris and took Crawford to specialists in London, where, despite the removal of a cancerous brain tumor and the affected eye, he soon died.

Crawford's widow supervised the completion of his major unfinished works. The sculptor Randolph Rogers was selected to handle unfinished elements in the Richmond group, and the sculptor William Henry Rinehart oversaw completion of the bronze doors. Crawford's *Armed Freedom* bronze, weighing 14,985 pounds, and the marble *Progress of Civilization* were set in place in 1863; the Senate doors, in 1868; the House doors, not until 1905. The marble *Justice* and *History* deteriorated irreparably when exposed to the elements beginning in 1863; replicas were ordered and set in position in 1974.

Crawford's artistic accomplishment was prodigious—no fewer than twenty-nine portrait busts, 103 ideal works, and eight commissioned public monuments. Crawford worked in a modified neoclassical style, produced popular biblical, literary, and genre works during his middle phase, and toward the end of his life moved toward more robustly naturalistic efforts in his austere public monuments.

• Some 127 letters from Crawford to his wife are in the National Archives, Washington, D.C. Lauretta Dimmick, "A Catalogue of the Portrait Busts and Ideal Works of Thomas Crawford (1813?–1857), American Sculptor in Rome" (Ph.D. diss., Univ. of Pittsburgh, 1986), provides a definitive descriptive listing of Crawford's portrait busts, statues, bas-reliefs, funerary pieces, and public monuments. Dimmick discusses the influence of artists in Italy on Crawford in "Veiled Memories, or, Thomas Crawford in Rome," in *The Italian Presence in American Art, 1760–1860*, ed. Irma B. Jaffe (1969). Biographical studies of Crawford include Thomas Hicks, *Thomas Crawford: His Career, Character, and Works . . .* (1858); George Washington Greene, *Biographical Studies* (1860); and Robert L. Gale, *Thomas Crawford, American Sculptor* (1964). Studies placing Crawford in his era and tradition are Margaret Ferrand Thorp, *The Literary Sculptors* (1965); Wayne Craven, *Sculpture in America* (1968; repr. 1984); Sylvia E. Crane, *White Silence: Greenough, Powers, and Crawford, American Sculptors in Nineteenth-Century Italy* (1972); and William H. Gerdts, *American Neoclassic Sculpture: The Marble Resurrection* (1973). Crawford's federally commissioned works are discussed and illustrated in *Art in the United States Capitol: Prepared by the Architect of the Capitol under the Joint Committee on the Library* (1976). Obituary notices appeared in numerous newspapers, including the New York *Evening Transcript*, 2 Nov. 1857.

ROBERT L. GALE

CRAWFORD, William (1732–11 June 1782), soldier, was born in Frederick County, Virginia, the son of William Crawford and Onora Grimes, farmers. After Crawford's father died in 1736, Crawford's mother married Richard Stephenson. A resident of Frederick County, Virginia, Crawford was a surveyor and land speculator who served with his friend George Washington in the Virginia militia. In 1755 he was an ensign on General Edward Braddock's ill-fated western expedition against the French at Fort Duquesne. He served directly under Washington as a captain in the more successful British military operation led by General John Forbes.

Crawford's experience on the western frontier plus the lure of potential profits from land speculation may have led him in 1765 to settle in the valley of the Youghiogheny River, a territory then claimed by both Pennsylvania and Virginia. He located at Stewart's Crossing, near present-day Connellsville, Pennsylvania. Two years after Crawford's migration west, Washington wrote to him for help in identifying potentially lucrative tracts, not only for Washington and his brothers but also for the veterans of Washington's Virginia regiment with land claims from the French and Indian War. In 1770, when Washington journeyed west to inspect his lands and those of the regi-

ment, he stayed with Crawford, his wife Hannah Vance, and their three children. At that time Crawford served as a justice of the peace in Cumberland County, Virginia, which disputed Pennsylvania for the area west of Charles Mason and Jeremiah Dixon's boundary for Pennsylvania and Maryland. Crawford seems to have followed the shifting territorial currents; he served as a justice of the peace for Bedford County, Pennsylvania, in 1771 and for Westmoreland County, Pennsylvania, in 1773.

Crawford and Washington along with six other explorers guided by two Native Americans descended the Ohio River as far as the Kanawha River in 1770. When Virginia's governor, the earl of Dunmore, organized an expedition against the Shawnee in 1774, Crawford was one of those recommended by Washington to the governor for his military leadership and frontier expertise. Although Crawford's troops did not participate in the battle at Point Pleasant, they advanced up the Hocking River and eventually destroyed a small Mingo (western Seneca) village known as Salt Licks Town. Crawford's detachment captured fourteen, killed six, freed two prisoners, and seized baggage, horses, and guns later sold at auction for £400.

Crawford's loyalty to his birthplace ultimately led to his enlistment in the Continental troops raised by Virginia early in the American Revolution. He was commissioned as lieutenant colonel of the Fifth Virginia Regiment. After service under Washington at the battles of Long Island, Trenton, and Princeton, he transferred west to aid in the defense of the Fort Pitt frontier. His residence nearby, his knowledge of the terrain, and his familiarity with the Indian trade fit him almost ideally for this task. He was present at Fort Pitt in the fall of 1778, when a treaty was signed by several Delaware leaders, including Captain Pipe, or the Pipe, a later opponent who was present at Crawford's death. As a colonel of the Thirteenth Virginia Regiment stationed at Fort Pitt, Crawford was intimately familiar with the bloody frontier warfare. Indian soldiers repeatedly attacked the frontiersmen poised to cross the Ohio in search of Indian lands. Like most frontier leaders, Crawford blamed the raids on the influence of British agents, especially those operating from Detroit and in the Native American villages located in present-day Northwest Ohio.

In the spring of 1782 the Continental military authorities approved an expedition into the Ohio country, and Crawford was one of those experienced officers willing to volunteer. Aware of the dangers inherent in such a venture, the fifty-year-old Crawford drew up his will with careful consideration for his wife and children. Colonel Crawford and his men then met the other forces from western Pennsylvania on the bank of the Ohio River at Mingo Bottom; there he was voted commander of the expedition. His closest rival, Colonel David Williamson, emphatically reminded his supporters that Crawford was the commander and would remain so until the expedition was completed.

As the 468 troops marched west, they encountered few Indians, only deserted villages. When they neared the upper reaches of the Sandusky River, they were running low on rations and were about to turn homeward. At that point they engaged in their first skirmishes; a substantial engagement erupted as more warriors and then British irregulars arrived. In danger of being destroyed, the Americans took advantage of nightfall to begin retreating. In that maneuver, Crawford and John Knight, a surgeon's mate who had served under Crawford during the Revolution and who was on loan to the expedition from the Fort Pitt garrison, were separated from the main body of retreating frontiersmen. Unfortunately, the two were captured.

The longstanding antipathy between the Ohio native peoples and the American frontiersmen had been whipped to a fever pitch by the preceding eight years of warfare (since 1774) and then driven higher by a bloody event several months before Crawford's expedition. In March a party of Christian Delawares had returned temporarily to their old settlement at Gnadenhutten, where they were captured by a band of Pennsylvania militiamen commanded by Colonel Williamson, Crawford's second in command on the Sandusky expedition. When the issue was put to a vote, the militia chose to kill the Delawares rather than return them to Fort Pitt as prisoners. Word of the massacre spread across the frontier. Thus, when the commander of another military expedition fell into the hands of the native peoples, there was a loud cry for retaliation. The decision was taken to burn Crawford at the stake, and this occurred near present-day Upper Sandusky, Ohio. Given the emotions generated by this cruel death by fire and torture, no completely dispassionate account exists. His comrade who escaped, Surgeon's Mate Knight, often called Dr. Knight, later retold the tale for publication in the most graphic, anti-Indian, anti-British details. Secondary accounts from British sources attempted to lay responsibility for the execution on the Indians or on the savage excesses of the American frontiersmen. When Washington learned of his friend's death, he described Crawford as "an officer of much care and prudence; brave, experienced, and active."

• Consul W. Butterfield sketched Crawford's life and the Sandusky expedition in *An Historical Account of the Expedition against Sandusky under Col. William Crawford in 1782 . . .* (1873). Butterfield published substantial amounts of documentary material in *The Washington Crawford Letters . . .* (1877), correspondence primarily about land speculation matters, and in *The Washington-Irvine Correspondence . . .* (1882), which includes several references to Crawford. Knight's eyewitness description of Crawford's death is in John Knight, *A Remarkable Narrative of an Expedition against the Indians, with an Account of the Barbarous Execution of Col. Crawford and Dr. Knight's Escape from Captivity* (1782). Maps showing Crawford's route as well as the location of the several villages against which he advanced are in Helen Hornbeck Tanner, *Atlas of Great Lakes Indian History* (1987). The most up-to-date material, however, is scattered through the text and notes of *The Papers of George Washington, Colonial Series, June 1767–December 1771*, vol. 8, ed. William W. Abbott et al. (1993), and *The Diaries of George Washington, 1766–1770*, vol. 2, ed. Donald Jackson et al. (1976).

JAMES H. O'DONNELL III

CRAWFORD, William Harris (24 Feb. 1772–15 Sept. 1834), U.S. senator, cabinet member, and presidential candidate, was born in Amherst County, Virginia, the son of Joel Crawford and Fanny Harris, farmers. In 1779 financial reverses led the Crawfords to move to the Edgefield District of South Carolina and four years later to Kiokee Creek, near Appling, Georgia. Joel Crawford valued education, and his children attended the field schools that served families in rural areas. After Joel's death in 1788, young William Harris helped out on the farm while teaching at the field school he had recently attended. In 1794, at the age of twenty-two, Crawford enrolled for two years in Moses Waddel's Carmel Academy near Appling. He left in July 1796 to teach English at the Richmond Academy in Augusta, where he formed a close friendship and lifelong political ties with Charles Tait, the rector, and met his future wife, Susanna Gerardin, a student at the academy. During his last year at the academy he studied law, and in the spring of 1799 he began to practice in Lexington, Oglethorpe County.

Crawford's skill in arguing cases and his sincere but forceful manner in court made him an immediate success in his new profession. His impact on juries was so compelling that he reputedly never lost a case in which he made the closing argument. His law practice brought him into contact with local and state politicians, who were immediately impressed with his political potential. He had a fine logical mind, an excellent command of English, a good sense of humor, and genuine amiability. Given the rough nature of Georgia society, he had the polish and self-confidence needed for leadership. His political connections bore fruit in December 1799, when he was appointed to serve on a committee to prepare a one-volume digest of the Georgia laws. In 1803 he was elected to the state legislature. The following year he purchased an estate, "Woodlawn," near Lexington and married Gerardin. They had eight children. By 1804 he had became the most active lawyer on the western circuit and a rising figure in the Georgia Republican party.

The political world that Crawford entered was treacherous, violent, and sometimes deadly. By 1800 the Federalists, never very strong in Georgia, had nearly vanished as a political force, leaving the Jeffersonian Republicans in complete control of the state government. With but one effective party in the state, politics became factional and bitterly personal. The factional alignments depended largely on social and economic factors and on the personalities of particular leaders. Crawford entered politics as a member of the faction headed by James Jackson, who opposed the wing of the party led by John Clark. The reasons for their rivalry are difficult to define, but the bitterness on both sides was extreme and unrelenting. Violence was an accepted part of this political culture, and rivals often settled their differences on the dueling ground. In 1802 Crawford, who was known not to be proficient with pistols, was challenged by a Clark supporter, who apparently expected him to refuse and thus ruin himself politically. A man who would not defend his honor with his life could not command the respect and support of voters at the polls. But Crawford accepted and killed his challenger. Four years later he fought a duel with Clark himself and emerged from the encounter with a badly wounded left wrist. Far from damaging his reputation, the duels won him respect and added to his growing prestige.

Crawford's reputation and influence spread rapidly throughout the state. From 1803 to 1807 he served on numerous committees of the legislature, working to improve education, the judicial system, and the electoral process. He supported measures for the construction of bridges and voted to improve navigation on state waterways. Although a slaveholder himself, he successfully opposed the importation of slaves into Georgia from abroad and from other states. In November 1807 the legislature recognized his services to the state by choosing him to fill the vacancy in the U.S. Senate created by the death of Abraham Baldwin. Crawford's rise in only eight years from country lawyer to U.S. senator can be attributed in part to the vagaries of factional politics but even more to his recognized ability, political skill, and personal magnetism. These same qualities made him a key player on the national political scene for almost two decades.

When Crawford entered the Senate late in 1807, both the country and Congress were divided over President Thomas Jefferson's call for an embargo to deal with British and French violations of American neutral rights on the high seas. Crawford favored strong measures to uphold American rights, but he doubted that a general embargo was the right measure. So he opposed it against the wishes of the president and a majority of his own party. But instead of claiming political credit for having been right when the embargo backfired and became massively unpopular, he led the opposition to its repeal on the grounds that abandonment of the embargo would leave the country no alternative but war to redress its grievances. Having committed itself to an embargo, the United States had to stand firm or risk losing all credibility with foreign governments. Crawford's principled stand, both for and against the embargo, won him the respect of even those who disagreed with him. His willingness to put public interest first turned out to be good politics as well, because it earned him national recognition as an emerging party leader.

Crawford's conduct during the embargo debates brought him recognition, but his vigorous defense of the Bank of the United States established his preeminence in the Senate. The bank's charter would expire in March 1811 unless Congress voted to renew it. Although its establishment in 1791 had been one of the defining issues between Jefferson and Alexander Hamilton, many Jeffersonian Republicans came to recognize the bank as a useful institution. Nevertheless, a majority of the party, principally in the South and West, opposed the bank, maintaining that nothing in the Constitution expressly authorized Congress to create such an institution. During 1810 the state banks, which hoped to take over the bank's government business, waged an intense and largely successful campaign to arouse public opinion against recharter. Convinced that the bank was good for the economy and indispensable to the government, Crawford led the fight to renew its charter. In an exchange with Henry Clay, who argued, rather lamely, against the constitutionality of the bank, Crawford embraced the implied powers doctrine, arguing that the Constitution was dynamic and should be interpreted according to present needs. His brilliance during the debates brought what seemed to be a lost cause almost to the point of victory. But in the end the Senate deadlocked, 17–17, and Vice President George Clinton cast the deciding vote that killed the measure. Crawford later had the satisfaction of seeing most of his opponents of 1811 vote to reestablish the bank in 1816.

Although he lost the bank fight, Crawford's efforts won him the respect of the Senate. In March 1811 he was elected president pro tempore, and the death of Vice President Clinton a month later made him the regular presiding officer. His relations with the James Madison administration were marked by the same independence that brought him recognition in the Senate. He staunchly defended the administration when he thought it was right but did not hesitate to criticize its mistakes and shortcomings. He supported the War of 1812 but refused to serve as secretary of war because his experience did not qualify him for the position in wartime. His refusal did not prevent Madison from appointing him minister to France with instructions to improve relations with that country while the United States was at war with Great Britain and to secure indemnification for American ships and cargoes illegally seized by the French. Crawford accepted the appointment and did not return to the United States until the war was over.

Crawford's mission produced mixed results. Relations with France were stabilized, but he could make no progress on the indemnification issue. Before Crawford returned to the United States in June 1815, Madison appointed him secretary of war, and this time he accepted the appointment. He spent nearly the next decade as a member of Madison's and James Monroe's cabinets. Although Crawford stayed at the War Department only until October 1816, he made some notable innovations. He reorganized the department, making its operations more efficient; inaugurated a program of coastal fortification; and improved the quality of education at West Point by requiring cadets to pass an entrance examination. He also incurred the enmity of Andrew Jackson by ordering the general to renegotiate a treaty he had concluded with the Creek nation. Crawford determined that the Creek land cession included lands belonging to the Cherokee nation, and he required Jackson to make boundary adjustments between them.

Early in 1816 Crawford emerged as the favorite of most Republicans in Congress to succeed Madison as president. The leading contender was Monroe, who had Madison's support, but many in the party objected to electing another Virginian. The sentiment for Crawford in Congress was important, because party candidates were traditionally chosen by the Republican caucus. But Crawford refused to become a candidate and instead endorsed Monroe for the sake of party unity. Nevertheless, Crawford fell only eleven ballots short of Monroe when the caucus voted. If he had made the slightest effort, he would have won the nomination. In October 1816 Crawford moved to the Treasury Department, serving there during the two terms of the Monroe administration. Treasury was by far the largest department of the federal government and badly in need of reorganization when Crawford took charge. He overhauled the administrative machinery completely, introduced a new inspectional system to monitor government operations, and insisted on strict accountability from those who handled public funds. His innovations left the department with fewer employees doing more work at less cost to the government than any time since 1801.

After 1820 intense intraparty rivalry broke out over who would succeed Monroe. Besides Crawford, the leading contenders were John Quincy Adams, Clay, Jackson, and for a time John C. Calhoun and William Lowndes. Crawford, as the front-runner, was attacked by the supporters of his rivals, but his prospects remained bright until he suffered a paralytic stroke in the fall of 1823. Nearly blind and hardly able to articulate, he was unable to contend effectively against his rivals. Although his condition gradually improved, the damage to his presidential prospects was irreparable. His rivals, aware that he still had strong support in Congress, now made the caucus system the target of their attacks, charging that it was undemocratic to exclude the rest of the party from the nominating process. Crawford got 64 of the 68 votes cast when the caucus met in February 1824, but the refusal of the other 261 senators and representatives to participate made the nomination virtually meaningless. Crawford's health greatly improved during the summer of 1824, but doubts about his condition cut into his support in all parts of the country. When the electoral votes were cast in November, he finished a poor third behind Jackson and Adams but ahead of Clay. Since no candidate had an electoral majority, the election went to the House of Representatives, where Adams, with the support of Clay, was chosen on the first ballot. The next day Adams requested that Crawford remain as secretary of the treasury, but the offer was refused. Returning to Georgia, Crawford served as a state superior court judge until his death.

Crawford never fully recovered from his catastrophic illness, but he turned out to be a remarkably able judge, presiding over the annual meetings of the superior court judges during his tenure on the bench. In 1830 he precipitated a rift between Jackson and Calhoun by disclosing in a letter that Calhoun had proposed at a cabinet meeting in 1818 that Jackson should be disciplined for seizing Spanish Florida and executing two British subjects. Crawford died at the home of a friend in Elbert County, Georgia, while on his way to open the September session of the superior court for that county. Contemporary estimates of his career varied greatly. John Quincy Adams regarded Crawford as an archintriguer, blind to everything but his own ambition, but Albert Gallatin thought him the most able and principled Republican since Jefferson. Although he did not intervene in the campaign, Jefferson favored Crawford's candidacy in 1824, and Madison, Martin Van Buren, and John Randolph worked for his election. Before disaster struck, he was one of the most capable leaders of the Republican party and was as qualified as any of his rivals for the presidency. He was the last candidate nominated by the Republican caucus, and his removal from the political scene marked the beginning of the party realignment that ended the Jeffersonian era.

• John E. D. Shipp, *Giant Days; or, The Life and Times of William H. Crawford* (1909), was the first sustained effort to organize the scattered and fragmentary data into a comprehensive account of Crawford's remarkable career. Shipp's eulogistic treatment has many flaws, but it had the salutary effect of rescuing Crawford from obscurity and calumny. Philip J. Green, *The Life of William Harris Crawford* (1965), includes material not found in Shipp's biography. Chase C. Mooney, *William H. Crawford, 1772–1834* (1974), is a balanced, carefully researched work, fully documented and with an excellent bibliography. Information on particular aspects of Crawford's career is in two articles by Green, "William H. Crawford and the Bank of the United States," *Georgia Historical Quarterly* 23 (1939): 337–50, and "William H. Crawford and the War of 1812," *Georgia Historical Quarterly* 26 (1942): 16–39. For the Ga. phase of his career, see Ulrich B. Phillips, *Georgia and State Rights* (1902), and Alvin L. Duckett, *John Forsyth, Political Tactician* (1962). Significant events of his national career are covered in Irving Brant, *James Madison* (6 vols., 1941–1961); Harry Ammon, *James Monroe: The Quest for National Identity* (1971); and Leonard D. White, *The Jeffersonians: A Study in Administrative History* (1951). Contemporary press reports of his death are in the *Georgia Messenger*, 25 Sept. 1834, and the *National Intelligencer*, 26 Sept. 1834.

EDGAR J. MCMANUS

CRAWFORD-SEEGER, Ruth Porter (3 July 1901–18 Nov. 1953), composer, teacher, and scholar of American folk music, was born in East Liverpool, Ohio, the daughter of Clark Crawford, a Methodist minister, and Clara Alletta Graves. Her father moved the family to Jacksonville, Florida, in 1911. After his death in 1914, the family supported itself by running a rooming house. Crawford-Seeger began piano study in Jacksonville with her mother and later studied at the city's School of Musical Art. In 1920 she enrolled at the American Conservatory in Chicago, where she studied piano with Heniot Levy and Louise Robyn, and theory and composition with John Palmer and Adolf Weidig. After a year at the conservatory, she earned a teaching certificate and continued her composition studies with Weidig, earning a master's degree in 1929. During this period, Crawford-Seeger continued her piano study with Djane Lavoie-Herz and became a member of the faculty at both the conservatory and Elmhurst College of Music near Chicago. The children of poet Carl Sandburg were among her Elmhurst College students, and she composed piano accompaniments for some of the songs in his *American Songbag* (1927). She also composed a number of works for the keyboard, including the Four Preludes for Piano (1927–1928), which attracted the attention of modernist composer Henry Cowell, who published the work in his journal, *New Music*.

Crawford-Seeger was honored with residence at the MacDowell Colony in New Hampshire in the summer of 1929 and moved to New York in September of that year. Through Cowell, she met composer Charles Seeger, who encouraged the modernist and experimental aspects of her style. In 1930, with the help of a Guggenheim Foundation fellowship, Crawford-Seeger studied with several composers in Paris and Berlin, and she received encouragement from Bartók, Berg, and Ravel. Returning to New York in November 1931, she continued to compose. She married Seeger the following year; they had four children together. After her marriage she began a new phase of her musical career, one that included political activity and developing her interests in folk music and music for children.

As a member of the Composers' Collective in New York, Crawford-Seeger participated in serious discussions on the role of music in society with her husband, John Lomax (1867–1948), Alan Lomax, Cowell, Aaron Copland, Earl Robinson, and others. Her songs "Sacco, Vanzetti," "Chinaman, Laundryman," and "Prayers of Steel," all with texts on contemporary political and social issues, were selected for performance at the 1933 festival of the International Society of Contemporary Music. She collaborated with the Lomaxes on the 1941 anthology *Our Singing Country* and published her own books of songs for children, *American Folk Songs for Children in Home, School and Nursery School* (1948), *Animal Folk Songs for Children* (1950), and *American Folk Songs for Christmas* (1953). She brought the music that she discovered and transcribed from the Library of Congress's Archive of Folk Song to children by teaching in the public schools in the Washington, D.C., area.

Crawford-Seeger's compositional style was distinctly dissonant and modern. Toward the end of her career, she began to incorporate elements of the folk music she had studied into her compositional style. Her last two completed works were "Rissolty, Rossolty" (1940) and the Suite for Wind Quintet (1952). Although her personal style was described by Charles Seeger as "uncompromisingly and successfully radical," she contributed to an awakening interest in local and regional folk music through her transcribing and publishing activities and the involvement in folk music

performance of her children. She died in Chevy Chase, Maryland.

• Crawford-Seeger's diaries are held by her daughters Barbara and Penelope; letters to her mother are held by her brother Carl; and letters to her husband are part of the Charles Seeger estate. For a biography and discussion of her works, see Matilda Gaume, "Ruth Crawford Seeger: Her Life and Works" (Ph.D. diss., Indiana Univ., 1973), and Judith Tick, *Ruth Crawford Seeger: A Composer's Search for American Music* (1997). See also Paul Rosenfeld, *An Hour With American Music* (1929); Marion Bauer, *Twentieth Century Music* (1933); Charles Seeger, "Ruth Crawford," in Henry Cowell, ed., *American Composers on American Music* (1933); George Perle, "Atonality and the Twelve-Note System in the United States," *The Score* (July 1960); John Rockwell, "Musical Spotlight Puts Ruth Seeger in Focus Sharply," *New York Times*, 21 Feb. 1975; and B. Jepson, "Ruth Crawford-Seeger: A Study in Mixed Accents," *Feminist Art Journal* (1977).

BARBARA L. TISCHLER

CRAYON, Porte. *See* Strother, David Hunter.

CRAZY HORSE (c. 1840–5 Sept. 1877), Oglala Lakota war chief, was born near Bear Butte in present-day South Dakota, the son of Crazy Horse, a noted Oglala warrior and medicine man, and (according to some sources) Rattle Blanket Woman, a Minicoujou Lakota of the prestigious Lone Horn family. By 1861 the boy had inherited the name Crazy Horse from his father. Believing himself informed by visions and protected by war medicines prepared by Horn Chips, a respected Oglala *wicasa wakan* or holy man, Crazy Horse was an extraordinarily courageous warrior who commanded the respect of both his own people and his enemies. During Oglala leader Red Cloud's war against wagon roads, army forts, and other white incursions on Lakota lands in Wyoming and Montana in the mid-1860s, Crazy Horse demonstrated courage and remarkable skill as a leader of warriors in the Fetterman Fight at Fort Phil Kearny, the Hayfield Fight, and the Wagon Box Fight. Lakota resistance persuaded the government to cease fighting and begin the difficult negotiations that led to the 1868 Treaty of Fort Laramie, establishing a reservation in South Dakota. However, although Red Cloud and some Lakota chiefs signed the treaty, Crazy Horse and other Lakota leaders rejected it.

Crazy Horse's triumphs as a warrior and as a war leader earned him admiration among all of the Lakota tribes as well as among the northern Cheyenne, with whom he lived periodically, which helped to strengthen the alliance between the Cheyenne and the Lakota. His stature and unyielding resistance to the U.S. government made him a central figure among the nontreaty Lakota, who increasingly looked to him for leadership. Compared to other leading warriors, Crazy Horse was a quiet, modest, sometimes reclusive man. To outsiders—and even to some of his own people—these qualities made him appear unorthodox, yet his people fully accepted him because his behavior and his steadfast assurance sprang from dreams and visions, which, in traditional Lakota culture, guided one's conduct.

In 1868 Crazy Horse earned the highest formal honor from his people. A large camp of Lakota gathered in northeast Wyoming where, a witness recalled, leaders selected Crazy Horse and three other young warriors as head warriors or "shirt wearers," who "represented in their commands and acts the entire power of the nation." Crazy Horse remained a shirt wearer until 1870, when a dispute arose after a Lakota woman, whose name was Black Buffalo Woman, left her husband for Crazy Horse. Lakota women had the right to end one marriage and begin another; however, in this instance, the husband shot Crazy Horse in the face with a pistol. The Lakota expected their chiefs to be above personal matters, and this quarrel cost Crazy Horse his formal position as a shirt wearer.

By the mid-1870s government officials and army officers recognized Crazy Horse as one of the most prominent leaders of the Lakota resistance to the whites. During the conflict with the U.S. government over the Black Hills region of South Dakota and Lakota hunting grounds in the Yellowstone River basin, areas assigned to the Lakota in the 1868 treaty, many Lakota turned to Crazy Horse for leadership. In 1874 gold had been discovered in the Black Hills, and by 1875 Lakota leaders on and off the reservations were angry and alarmed about the growing number of prospectors and miners moving into the Black Hills, trespassing on Lakota land. Negotiations failed because the Lakota rejected a government proposal to lease the Black Hills, and the army was reluctant to keep the miners out of the area, thus angering the Lakota.

In December 1875 the government ordered the Lakota bands living in the Yellowstone and Powder rivers area to report to the reservations in Nebraska or on the Missouri River within six weeks or face punitive military action. The ultimatum was absurd because even if the nontreaty Lakota had intended to comply, and most did not, they would have been reluctant to move their families and villages to the reservations because of the difficulty of traveling during the winter months. Some Lakota and northern Cheyenne had decided to wait for spring and then go to the reservations so that they could decide what to do after they had seen the situation there. Contemporaries of Crazy Horse have claimed that in the early winter months of 1876 he had adopted a similar attitude toward the government's demands.

After the army attacked a northern Cheyenne village in March 1876, however, Crazy Horse and other Lakota and northern Cheyenne chiefs prepared for war against the army. A rare leader whose reputation and personality permitted him to maintain his authority over a large number of warriors from other tribes, Crazy Horse, along with Sitting Bull, a Hunkpapa Lakota, emerged during 1876 as the most conspicuous leaders of the Lakota-Cheyenne alliance.

Crazy Horse was a central figure in the two most significant battles of the Sioux War of 1876. On 17 June 1876 he was one of the leaders of a force of approximately 1,500 warriors in an attack on a 1,300-man military column led by Brigadier General George Crook along Rosebud Creek in southern Montana. Crazy Horse helped coordinate the warriors' attack, which resulted in a strategic victory for the Indians. On 25 June Lieutenant Colonel George A. Custer and units of the Seventh Cavalry attacked the Lakota-Cheyenne village in the battle of the Little Bighorn. Crazy Horse was conspicuous in leading his warriors in charges that destroyed Custer and his immediate command.

The Indian victories spurred the army to relentlessly pursue the Lakota and the Cheyenne in the Yellowstone River country during the winter of 1876–1877. The increased force convinced many warriors to move their families to the reservations. Recognizing that further fighting would be futile, on 7 May 1877 Crazy Horse and his followers surrendered at Camp Robinson, Nebraska.

Despite his disdain for reservation life, Crazy Horse hoped to live quietly on the reservation. Because he had been the pivotal leader of the Lakota in their fight against the army, government officials and army officers were anxious to meet the chief who had been such a skillful adversary. This attention caused jealousy among other Oglala and Sicangu chiefs, who spread rumors that Crazy Horse intended to escape from the reservation. Junior army officers believed the malicious gossip and reported it to their superiors as fact. By September 1877 the rumors convinced army officers to arrest Crazy Horse. On 5 September 1877 during an attempt to imprison him at Camp Robinson, a soldier bayoneted Crazy Horse, who died a few hours later.

In 1871 Crazy Horse married Black Shawl Woman, an Oglala. The couple had his only child, a daughter named They Are Afraid of Her. The girl died around 1873. Always somewhat reclusive, Crazy Horse devoted his life to warfare after the death of his daughter, when he created the Last Child Society, whose members were the last-born boys of their families. Crazy Horse remained married to Black Shawl Woman until his death. In 1877 he also took Nellie Laravie as his wife. Both wives survived him. Black Shawl Woman never remarried. She lived on the Pine Ridge Reservation until her death circa 1927. Nellie Laravie remarried, and she lived on the Rosebud Reservation.

The valor and skill with which Crazy Horse led the Lakota marked him as a great Native-American leader, and the passage of more than a century has not diminished his stature.

• Although Crazy Horse left behind no personal correspondence or memoirs, his contemporaries, Indian and non-Indian, have documented their recollections of him. The Eli S. Ricker Collection at the Nebraska State Historical Society in Lincoln contains numerous interviews conducted by Ricker with contemporaries of Crazy Horse. Other works based at least in part on interviews with Lakota who had been associated with Crazy Horse include John G. Bourke, *On the Border with Crook* (1891); E. A. Brininstool, *Crazy Horse, the Invincible Ogalalla Chief* (1949); John M. Carroll, ed., *The Eleanor H. Hinman Interviews on the Life and Death of Crazy Horse*

(1976); and Amos Bad Heart Bull with Helen H. Blish, *A Pictographic History of the Oglala Sioux* (1967). The Walter M. Camp interviews are in manuscript collections at Indiana University, Bloomington, and Brigham Young University, Provo, Utah. Mari Sandoz, *Crazy Horse: The Strange Man of the Oglalas* (1942), remains the most comprehensive biography. A good recent guide is Richard G. Hardorff, *The Oglala Lakota Crazy Horse: A Preliminary Genealogical Study and an Annotated Listing of Primary Sources* (1985).

JOSEPH C. PORTER

CRAZY SNAKE. *See* Harjo, Chitto.

CREEFT, José de. *See* De Creeft, José.

CREEL, George Edward (1 Dec. 1876–2 Oct. 1953), journalist and government administrator, was born in Lafayette County, Missouri, the son of Henry Clay Creel and Virginia Fackler, farmers. He grew up in the Missouri towns of Independence and Odessa, where his mother supported the family by sewing, gardening, and operating a boarding house, because his father was often drunk and unemployed. As a teenager, Creel ran away from home to follow county fairs, then to roam the Southwest. In 1896 he was hired as a cub reporter by the *Kansas City World*, a Scripps paper, at four dollars a week. In 1898 he hopped a cattle car for New York, where he shoveled snow and sold newspapers before being hired by the comic supplement of William Randolph Hearst's *New York American*.

In 1899, with his wealthy friend Arthur Grissom, Creel established a weekly, the *Kansas City Independent*, and soon became full owner, editor, and publisher. An aggressive reformer, he fought the political machine of Thomas Pendergast while promoting such causes as single tax, women's rights, public ownership of utilities, direct primaries, and the commission form of government. In 1904, already skilled in developing publicity, Creel helped elect Democratic reformer Joseph Folk as governor. He received national visibility by calling for the lynching of eleven state senators who opposed municipal ownership of Denver's water company.

Creel was editorial writer for the *Denver Post* in 1909–1910, during which time he helped organize a Citizen's party for the city. When his own employers manipulated the party slate, in the process gutting much of its reformist thrust, Creel moved to New York, where in 1911 he worked for Hearst's *Cosmopolitan*. Back in Denver later that year, he became editorial writer for the *Rocky Mountain News*, where he ardently supported the policies of Woodrow Wilson. In 1912 he married Blanche Bates, a leading actress who died in 1941. They had two children.

From 1912 to 1913 Creel served as police commissioner of Denver, but when he accused the policemen of frequenting saloons, Mayor Henry Arnold dismissed him. Creel had already been strongly attacked for recommending that the city's prostitutes be rehabilitated at a city-supported farm. Leaving Denver, he

returned to New York, where he wrote muckraking articles for *Harper's Weekly*, *Century*, and *Everybody's*. In 1914, along with Judge Benjamin Lindsey and poet Edwin Markham, he wrote *Children of Bondage*, an exposé of child labor that he later said was "more rhetorical than factual." In 1916 he organized a committee of authors and publicists to back Wilson's reelection and published a campaign tract, *Wilson and the Issues*, in which he strongly defended the president's neutrality policies and social reforms.

On 14 April 1917, eight days after the United States entered World War I, Wilson appointed Creel chairman of the Committee on Public Information (CPI), the most gigantic propaganda effort in American history to that date. In its campaign to promote the war effort at home and overseas, the committee engaged in what Creel called "a vast enterprise in salesmanship, the world's greatest adventure in advertising." It published 75 million pamphlets, 6,000 press releases, and 14,000 drawings and sponsored 75,000 public speakers, often called Four-Minute Men because of the brevity of their addresses. It printed the first government daily, entitled *Official Bulletin*, which was posted in every military camp and some 54,000 post offices. Its sixteen-page bimonthly, the *National Service Bulletin*, reached 600,000 schools. Creel tried to avoid sensationalist accounts of alleged atrocities, but some committee publicists were irresponsible. Creel attempted to suppress "dangerous" material, whether pro-German or pro-Bolshevik, and to stop any book that was not "pro-American" from leaving the United States.

Creel's acerbic tongue created powerful enemies. He once compared the mind of Senator Henry Cabot Lodge (R.-Mass.) to the soil of New England: "highly cultivated but naturally sterile." When asked about the loyalty of Congress, he snapped back that he did not go slumming. Only Wilson's direct intervention kept him in office, though the president, Creel later said, put a "padlock on my lips." Creel accompanied Wilson to the Paris Peace Conference of 1919, and while in Europe, he visited Czechoslovakia, Poland, and Ireland on behalf of the president.

In 1920 Creel joined *Collier's* as a feature writer and began writing various nonfiction works. Six years later he moved to San Francisco. When the New Deal was launched, Creel was firmly in the camp of President Franklin D. Roosevelt. In 1933 he chaired the Regional Labor Board for California, Utah, and Nevada. He also directed the West Coast office of the National Recovery Administration. He left both posts in 1934 to seek the Democratic nomination for governor of California, where he was backed by the party establishment. After losing the primary heavily to muckraking novelist Upton Sinclair, he rejoined *Collier's*, serving as Washington correspondent. In 1935 he briefly chaired the National Advisory Committee of Harry Hopkins's Works Progress Administration. In 1939 Roosevelt appointed him U.S. commissioner of the Golden Gate International Exposition in San Francisco. Possessing strong misgivings over the president's spending and prounion policies, he began to sour over the New Deal around 1939 but never formally broke with the president.

When World War II broke out, Creel sought again to direct war publicity but was rebuffed. In this and subsequent twentieth-century wars nothing like the "Creel Committee" was attempted. In 1943 he married Alice May Rosseter, who died in 1948. In his book *War Criminals and Punishment* (1944), he advocated harsh treatment of Germany and Japan, saying of the Germans, "After centuries of deliberate, systematic poisoning, there is no health in them."

Creel was a prolific writer. In 1908 he wrote *Quatrains of Christ*, an effort to offer a "Christian answer" to the *Rubaiyat of Omar Khayyam*. In *Ireland's Fight for Freedom* (1919) Creel offered a strong indictment of British policy and called for Ulster's union with the rest of Ireland. *The War, the World, and Wilson* (1920) defends the Fourteen Points, the Versailles treaty, and the League of Nations. His *People Next Door: An Interpretive History of Mexico and the Mexicans* (1926) expresses strong sympathy for that nation's budding nationalism. *Sons of the Eagle: Soaring Figures from America's Past* (1927), a collection of essays originally printed in *Collier's*, treats such figures as Daniel Boone and Sam Houston with superlatives, and *Tom Paine—Liberty Bell* (1932) covers its subject in a similar fashion. *Russia's Race of Asia* (1949) claims that the Chinese Communists were mere puppets of the Soviet Union and that Chiang Kai-shek was a great and often betrayed leader. Creel also collaborated with Vice Admiral Ross T. McIntire, Roosevelt's medical doctor, in *White House Physician* (1946).

The postwar years reveal Creel as a man obsessed with conspiracy. In his memoirs, *Rebel at Large: Recollections of Fifty Crowded Years* (1947), he claimed that V. I. Lenin and Leon Trotsky were German agents, accused Roosevelt of betraying the Atlantic Charter at the Teheran and Yalta conferences, and linked President Harry S. Truman to the corruption of Kansas City's Pendergast machine. In 1951 he endorsed Senator Robert A. Taft (R.-Ohio) for the presidency and in 1952 backed the red-hunting efforts of Senator Joseph R. McCarthy, saying he "stems from the same sturdy Americanism that led plain men to risk all at Lexington and Concord." Creel died in San Francisco.

Creel's name will ever be synonymous with government propaganda of a heavy-handed nature. Yet to link him with the excesses of the Creel Committee and to forget his entire record is something of an injustice, for his career was a rich one.

• Creel's papers are at the Library of Congress. Major Creel correspondence relating to the CPI is in the Records of the Committee of Public Information, RG 63, National Archives, and the papers of Woodrow Wilson and Josephus Daniels, both in the Library of Congress. Creel's *How We Advertised America* (1920) is a firsthand account of his experience with the CPI. A superior short sketch is Warren T. Francke, "George Creel," in *American Newspaper Journalists*, ed. Perry J. Ashley (1984). For a most perceptive treatment,

see Frank Annunziata, "The Progressive as Conservative: George Creel's Quarrel with New Deal Liberalism," *Wisconsin Magazine of History* 57 (Spring 1974): 220–33. For favorable views of Creel and the CPI, see James R. Mock and Cedric Larson, *Words That Won the War* (1939), and Walton Bean, "George Creel and His Critics: A Study of the Attacks on the Committee on Public Information, 1917–1919" (Ph.D. diss., Univ. of California at Berkeley, 1941). For a more critical treatment, see Stephen Vaughn, *Holding Fast the Inner Lines: Democracy, Nationalism, and the Committee on Public Information* (1980). For Creel's political battle of 1934, see Greg Mitchell, *The Campaign of the Century: Upton Sinclair's Race for Governor of California and the Birth of Media Politics* (1992). In William L. Chenery, *So It Seemed* (1952), a former *Collier's* editor tells of his association with Creel. Creel's obituary is in the *New York Times*, 3 Oct. 1953.

JUSTUS D. DOENECKE

CREELMAN, James (12 Nov. 1859–12 Feb. 1915), journalist, was born in Montreal, Canada, the son of Matthew Creelman, a boiler inspector, and Martha Dunwoodie. Creelman attended Montreal's Royal Arthur primary school before leaving home in 1872 for New York City, where he attracted the attention and patronage of the prominent divine Thomas DeWitt Talmage, with whom he studied at the Lay Theological College, and Republican party boss Roscoe Conking, who tutored him in the law. The Reverend William Muhlenburg likewise counseled the young man and found him his first employment in the print shop of the Episcopalian church newspaper *Church and State*. During Creelman's later stint in the print shop of the Brooklyn *Eagle*, editor Thomas Kinsella discouraged him from becoming a poet. Undaunted in his determination to become a writer, Creelman joined James Gordon Bennett, Jr.'s New York *Herald* as a reporter in 1876.

Creelman's journalistic technique developed quickly and was marked by extensive travel in pursuit of stories coupled with a willingness to take great personal risks. He traveled the Yellowstone and Mississippi river systems with adventurer Paul Boyton, was shot at while reporting on the Hatfield/McCoy feud, interviewed Sitting Bull as well as other Indian chiefs, and broke his arm while making a balloon ascent in Montreal. In spite of the absence of bylines in the *Herald*, several of Creelman's articles brought him to public attention, provoking controversy along with legal and legislative action. An 1879 New York *Herald* article documenting illegal ocean dumping off New York prompted a court trial featuring the young reporter as the star witness. An 1883 feature on the Broadway railway fraud likewise resulted in legal action, while an 1888 expose of the immigrant recruiting practices of steamship companies resulted in a congressional hearing at which Creelman played a major role.

By 1887 Creelman was editing the Sunday *Herald* while writing editorials for the daily *Herald*. In 1889 Bennett ordered Creelman to take charge of the floundering London edition of the *Herald*. Failing to salvage the paper, he took up editing and reporting duties with the Paris *Herald* the following year. While writing for the Paris *Herald* Creelman developed as an interview journalist with a preference for difficult and elusive subjects. He secured interviews with, among others, Louis Kossuth and Leo Tolstoy. He was the first English-speaking non-Catholic reporter to interview Pope Leo XIII. Creelman also investigated the Mafia for his newspaper and the U.S. Department of State in late spring 1891.

In 1891 Creelman briefly assumed the editorship of the *Herald*'s late edition, the *Evening Telegram*, later returning to the *Herald*, from which, among other assignments, he was dispatched to Haiti to report on its politics and culture. Also in 1891 Creelman married Alice L. Buell of Marietta, Ohio, an artist and society writer with the Paris *Herald*; they had three children. In 1893 Creelman wrote a series of articles for the *Herald* championing the music of Antonín Dvořák, then director of the National Conservatory of Music in New York. His articles discussed the possibilities of an "American school of music" and Dvořák's newly completed symphony, *From the New World*, the premiere of which Creelman attended with the composer at Carnegie Hall. Creelman left the *Herald* in 1893 and worked briefly for *Illustrated American* and *Cosmopolitan* magazines, attempting unsuccessfully to establish a London edition for the latter publication. Creelman was hired in 1894 by Joseph Pulitzer's New York *World* to cover the war between Japan and China. Accompanying the Japanese army, he reported on the aftermath of hostilities at Pyongyang and the Yalu River naval engagement, and interviewed the king of Korea. (At one point, Creelman disappeared and was reported beheaded by the Chinese.) Creelman's coverage of the battle of Port Arthur and his claim of atrocities (including the brutal murders of women and children) committed by Japanese soldiers, with whom he initially sympathized, gained him substantial attention. Though his story was supported by Pulitzer and subsequently verified by fellow journalist Julian Ralph and others, including the Japanese foreign minister, Creelman's graphic account of slaughter was initially disbelieved and denounced by many American newspapers, among them the *Herald*. Before leaving the *World* in 1896, Creelman earned an expulsion order from the Spanish government for his reporting on the rebels in Cuba.

In 1897 William Randolph Hearst recruited Creelman as a special correspondent for his New York *Journal* at the huge annual salary of $8,000. Dispatched to London as the *Journal*'s European bureau editor, he interviewed statesmen and covered the Turkish-Greek War before being recalled to travel to Cuba with Hearst and other *Journal* staff after war with Spain was declared in 1898. In Cuba Creelman was assigned to cover General Chaffee's regiments, joining up with the Twelfth Infantry during its 1 July assault on the Spanish fort at El Caney. Having scouted the surrounding terrain, Creelman suggested tactics that resulted in the seizure of the fort. He also captured the Spanish flag but was wounded in the shoulder as he taunted the remaining Spanish soldiers with the war trophy. Hearst

discovered his correspondent in a field hospital and took down his story of the battle for publication in the *Journal*. (It was Creelman who, in his 1901 book of reminiscences, *On the Great Highway*, reported Hearst's response to artist Frederic Remington, bored with his assignment in Cuba: "You furnish the pictures and I'll furnish the war." While years later Hearst strongly denied he had ever said such a thing, the quote is still attributed to him.)

After publishing the novel *Eagle Blood* in 1902, Creelman returned to work for Pulitzer, with whom he remained until 1906 when he joined *Pearson's Magazine* as an associate editor. There he specialized in feature interview profiles on individuals as diverse as Thomas Edison, Theodore Roosevelt (1858–1919), William Howard Taft, and President Diaz of Mexico. The Diaz interview (which Creelman subsequently turned into the 1912 book *Diaz, Master of Mexico*) has been credited with contributing to events leading to the Mexican Revolution (Ronald Atkin, *Revolution! Mexico 1910–1920* [1969], pp. 45 and 52).

Creelman's relationship with his employers Bennett, Pulitzer, and Hearst was stormy at times, but each found in him a valuable writer. Hearst also took advantage of Creelman's shrewd political sense and contacts by involving him in his various political activities. They also served together on the executive committee of the National Association of Democratic Clubs. In 1911 a close friend, New York mayor William J. Gaynor, appointed Creelman to the presidency of the city's Civil Service Commission. His eighteen-month tenure in that position was followed by a brief stint on the city's school board. True to character, he resigned both positions, disillusioned by the lack of independence and his inability to gain acceptance for needed reforms.

The latter part of Creelman's life was plagued by ill health that frequently affected his career. His "nervous temperament" was compounded by muscular spasms brought on by the wound received at El Caney. Like his father he was afflicted with Bright's disease and was also diagnosed with other health problems, including heart disease and nicotine poisoning brought on by a thirty-cigars-a-day habit. He died in Berlin, Germany, waiting to interview Kaiser Wilhelm II for Hearst. He had carried with him to Germany a confidential message from Secretary of State William Jennings Bryan to the German government.

Creelman steadfastly believed that good newspaper reporting was a potent vehicle for social change. Like Hearst and Pulitzer, he was an unapologetic proponent of "journalism that acts." His vivid, personal, and highly subjective writing nearly always mirrored his own beliefs and personality regardless of who employed him and foreshadowed the style of modern investigative and interview journalists.

• James Creelman's papers, including both professional and personal documents, are at the Libraries of Ohio State University, Special Collections Division. Other important sources, including letters, photographs, and a diary, remain in the possession of the Creelman family. Creelman's *On the Great Highway: The Wanderings and Adventures of a Special Correspondent* (1901) is one of the few descriptions of his newspaper career written in his own words. In addition to his other works he wrote *Why We Love Lincoln* (1909). Two colorful and invaluable profiles appearing in Creelman's lifetime are "Character Sketch: Mr. James Creelman, War Correspondent," *Review of Reviews* (London), 1 Oct. 1898, and "Men of Our Day, Mr. James Creelman," *Our Day*, Aug. 1897. Creelman's Cuban coverage is discussed in Joyce Milton, *The Yellow Kids* (1989), while two articles representative of his style are reprinted along with an assessment of his work in *The Great Reporters*, ed. Wm. David Sloan et al. (1992). Useful obituaries are in the *New York Times* and the Brooklyn *Eagle*, 13 Feb. 1915.

JOHN E. CREELMAN

CREESY, Josiah Perkins (23 Mar. 1814–5 June 1871), sea captain, was born in Marblehead, Massachusetts, the son of Josiah P. Creesy and Mary Woolridge. As a youngster he sailed borrowed dories to nearby Salem to admire the ships called East Indiamen at the wharves, and in his teens he shipped out on one as a foremast hand. Rapidly working his way up, he became a captain at age twenty-three.

In 1851 his fast voyages as skipper of the *Oneida* in the China trade won him the coveted appointment as captain of Donald McKay's newest and largest clipper ship, *Flying Cloud*. Despite two partial dismastings, which he repaired on the run, and a sabotage attempt by frightened crewmen, Creesy raced the *Cloud* from New York to San Francisco (anchor to anchor) in eighty-nine days, twenty-one hours, bettering the previous record by a full week. This passage remained unchallenged until 1854 when Creesy, again in the *Cloud*, bettered it himself by thirteen hours.

Creesy's wife, Eleanor H. Prentiss, accompanied him on most of his voyages; a student of Matthew Maury's *Wind and Current Charts*, she was an excellent navigator. Unlike some nineteenth-century captains, Creesy paid special attention to the recruiting and training of his crews. After one San Francisco run he praised them: "They worked like one man, and that man a hero." But he drove them hard. While returning from San Francisco by way of China on the *Flying Cloud*'s fourth voyage, the clipper ran onto a coral reef. The thrifty Creesy decided against the estimated $30,000 cost for repairs and brought the *Cloud* home with the crew constantly at the pumps.

Between 1851 and 1855 Creesy commanded the *Flying Cloud* on five runs to San Francisco at the height of the clipper ship races to the gold fields, with an average time of just over 100 days. When he claimed that the *Cloud* needed an overhaul before its sixth voyage, the owners, Grinnell, Minturn & Co., refused. So Creesy went home to Salem. The *Cloud*'s new captain was forced to put into Rio de Janeiro for repairs before continuing to San Francisco, where more repairs were made. Creesy went to San Francisco and brought the *Cloud* home in ninety-one days. Creesy retired in 1857, but with the outbreak of the Civil War he volunteered for the Union navy. He was appointed acting lieutenant in 1861 and given command of the newly armed ten-year-old clipper *Ino*, which he took from Boston to Cadiz, Spain, in a record twelve days while searching for the Confederate raider *Sumter*. A grizzled, gray-bearded, stubborn veteran of his own quarterdeck, Creesy found the navy rank-consciousness galling; he disobeyed orders from a superior and was discharged. He returned to sea again to take the clipper ship *Archer* to China twice. He then retired permanently to Salem, where he died.

• For information about ships and life at sea in Creesy's time, see Arthur H. Clark, *The Clipper Ship Era* (1910); Carl Cutler, *Greyhounds of the Sea* (1930; repr. 1984; see especially Appendix V: abstract log of the *Flying Cloud*'s maiden voyage); Octavius T. Howe and Frederick C. Matthews, *American Clipper Ships, 1833–1858* (2 vols., 1967); and A. B. C. Whipple, *The Challenge* (1987).

A. B. C. WHIPPLE

CREIGHTON, Edward (31 Aug. 1820–5 Nov. 1874), pioneer telegraph builder, banker, and philanthropist, was born in Belmont County, Ohio (near the present town of Barnesville), the son of James Creighton and Bridget Hughes, farmers. Creighton's father had emigrated in 1805 from County Dungannon, Ireland, to the United States. In 1830 the Creighton family moved to a farm in Licking County, Ohio. Edward Creighton began full-time employment on the family farm and as a wagoner at the age of fourteen. In these early years he worked on the pike roads of Ohio with the young Philip Sheridan, later the highly decorated Civil War general. Creighton's first large contract was the construction of a stage highway from Wheeling, West Virginia, to Springfield, Ohio.

Creighton developed business relationships with important telegraph magnates of his day, especially Jeptha H. Wade and Hiram Sibley. He built telegraph lines in the Midwest and Southwest, a labor that earned him a reputation for being a pioneer telegraph builder. Sibley sent Creighton to make a perfunctory survey of the South, a performance later dubbed "the lemon-squeezer" because Creighton's activity frightened a rival company into yielding a coveted lease necessary to build the Western Union. In 1854 his brother, John Andrew Creighton, joined him in the Pacific Telegraph Company, then located in Omaha City, an outfitting point for pioneers crossing the Nebraska Territory. Creighton was made general manager of the Western Union Telegraph Company by Sibley and was asked to survey a cross-country telegraph route by way of Memphis, Tennessee, and another by Fort Smith, Arkansas. In anticipation of a profitable future, Creighton invested much of his personal wealth in Western Union. During the period 1847–1856 Creighton considered two other settlements: Mexico, Missouri, and Keokuk, Iowa, before difficulties stemming from unprofitable engineering contracts led him to join family members in Omaha, Nebraska. He returned briefly to Dayton, Ohio, to marry Mary Lucretia Wareham in 1856; they had one son, who died as a young child.

During the spring of 1857 Creighton loaded a steamer with lumber, which he shipped to Omaha and used to build a house. Settling in Omaha with his brothers John Andrew and Joseph and his cousin James, Edward acquired financial interests in silver and gold mines and cattle ranches; profits from these ventures enriched a growing fortune. Creighton rehearsed a more substantial venture in telegraph building by constructing a link between Omaha and St. Joseph, Missouri, linking St. Joseph for the first time with eastern settlements by way of St. Louis. About the same time, Creighton raised the necessary capital to construct a telegraph line from Omaha to Fort Smith.

In 1860, after several years of deliberations by competing telegraph companies, Creighton was employed to make preliminary surveys for an overland coast-to-coast telegraph line. At the time of his survey, there were short lines in virtually every state, and most of the principal cities east of the Mississippi River were linked. The situation was drastically different in the western United States, where the California State Telegraph Company had managed to extend a line eastward to Fort Churchill, Nevada. The men responsible for laying the great Atlantic cable connecting Europe with the eastern United States had twice tried and failed to construct a transcontinental overland line. With the financial backing of eastern investors Henry O'Reilly and Jeptha Wade, Creighton surveyed a path from Omaha to Salt Lake City (through Fort Kearny; Laramie; South Pass; Julesburg, Colorado; and the Sierra Nevadas to Sacramento and San Francisco) during the winter of 1860. Creighton had the help of Brigham Young while he covered the entire stretch on muleback. Creighton reported to Sibley on 12 April 1861 that he was prepared to begin construction to Salt Lake City.

The year after his initial survey (1861), Congress appropriated a $400,000 subsidy over ten years to the Pacific Telegraph Company, which would construct the telegraph link. Work commenced on 4 July 1861. Creighton's contractors sought to build westward to Salt Lake City from Julesburg, a distance of 1,100 miles, while the California Telegraph Company pushed eastward a distance of 450 miles. Creighton arrived in Salt Lake City seven days ahead of the California group. The joining of the wires (eight years before the completion of the transcontinental railroad) was accomplished near Fort Bridger, Utah, on 24 October 1861 and by 15 November 1861 the line was operational. Creighton's investment in the venture realized him a great fortune. Creighton's exploits were deemed worthy of a Hollywood film production; in 1941 20th Century–Fox produced *Western Union*, a film directed by Fritz Lang that starred Dean Jagger in the role of Edward Creighton.

After completion of the line, Creighton was the organizer and president of the First National Bank in Omaha, the pioneering banking institution of that section. A devout Roman Catholic, Creighton frequently proclaimed his intention to provide a free Catholic

school for higher education. At fifty-four, Creighton was stricken with paralysis and died in Omaha. John Andrew Creighton inherited Edward's entire fortune; his will provided $150,000 to establish an institution of higher education. Combining his own money with funds from Edward's estate, in 1878 John Andrew endowed Creighton University in Omaha. The following year, the university was turned over to the Society of Jesus and incorporated.

Creighton has been celebrated, both in popular culture and in the institutional history of Creighton University, as a pioneer whose self-reliant industry appeared to confirm the expansionist doctrines of Manifest Destiny.

• A biographical sketch of Creighton by Alfred Sorensen is in *Nebraska History* 17 (July–Sept. 1936): 163–69. The best source on his life remains a sequence of articles that appeared in the university newspaper, the *Creighton Courier*, between 1 July and 15 Dec. 1912. The text of the telegram Creighton sent his wife in Salt Lake City from the completion point of the telegraph in Fort Bridger was published in the *Creighton Courier*, 15 Oct. 1912. See also an article on Creighton in the *Omaha (Nebr.) Journal Telegraph*, 1 June 1870, and P. A. Mullens, *Creighton* (1901).

CHRISTOPHER D. FELKER

CREIGHTON, James Edwin (8 Apr. 1861–8 Oct. 1924), philosopher and educator, was born in Pictou, Nova Scotia, Canada, the son of John Creighton and Mary O'Brien. Creighton attended Dalhousie College in Halifax, Nova Scotia, graduating with an A.B. in 1887. At Dalhousie, Creighton studied with Jacob Gould Schurman, a scholar of philosopher Immanuel Kant, and followed Schurman to Cornell University in 1888. During his graduate career, Creighton studied in Leipzig and Berlin and then returned to Cornell. He received his Ph.D. in 1892 with the thesis "The Will; Its Structure and Mode of Operation." In the same year Creighton married Katherine F. McLean, also of Pictou; the couple had no children. Creighton began his teaching career as an instructor in philosophy at Cornell in 1889. He became assistant professor of modern philosophy in 1892 and Sage Professor of Logic and Metaphysics in 1895, filling that chair until his death. Creighton also served as dean of the Graduate School of Cornell from 1914 to 1923 and was on the board of trustees from 1922 to 1923.

Creighton believed that "intellectual life is a form of experience which can be realized only in common with others through membership in a social community" ("The Social Nature of Thinking," p. 46). Creighton dedicated much of his career to fostering intellectual community both at Cornell and among American and European philosophers. Creighton's leadership, from 1892 until his death, established the Sage School at Cornell as one of the premier graduate training programs in philosophy. Creighton sought to encourage intellectual seriousness in students, arguing that philosophy teachers need not concern themselves with pedagogy but must engage students directly in the philosophical process. Creighton revealed his personal delight in teaching, remarking "to join with youthful minds in the keen pursuit of truth is a perpetual joy and refreshment of the spirit" ("The Social Nature of Thinking," p. 70). Creighton's students clearly valued his insight and guidance; to celebrate twenty-five years of teaching, twenty-two of Creighton's students honored him with a festschrift, *Philosophical Essays in Honor of James Edwin Creighton* (1917).

Creighton's service as dean of the Graduate School also reflected his ideals of socially engaged scholarship. Upon Creighton's retirement, the Cornell faculty drafted a resolution commending Creighton for holding to the "loftiest and most inspiring ideals of scholarship, . . . [and] an indomitable courage coupled with absolute fairness and generous consideration of points of view opposed to his own" (*Cornell Alumni News*, 28 June 1923). Creighton promoted the need for the American Philosophical Association, over the objections of philosophers as prominent as William James, on the grounds that "thinking is the outcome of the functioning of a society of minds," and he served as the association's first president in 1902 ("The Social Nature of Thinking," p. 51). Creighton helped found the *Philosophical Review*, one of the first scholarly philosophical journals in America, and coedited the journal from 1893 until 1924. He was also the American editor of *Kant-Studien* from 1896 until 1924.

Creighton used the term "speculative idealism" to describe his own philosophical view. The influence of Creighton's study in Germany can be seen both in his commitment to idealism and in his requirement that the philosopher see his own intellectual activity within a social and historical context. Philosophy must begin from the standpoint of experience as it "has been developed and defined by reflection of the past" ("Two Types of Idealism," p. 265). Progress toward truth, which Creighton held to be the goal of philosophical activity, must build upon a thorough knowledge of the history of philosophy. Creighton developed his own views as critical responses to British empiricism, to Kantian critical philosophy, and to the pragmatism of Henry James and John Dewey. According to Creighton, all these views fail to explain the "true nature of experience."

Creighton rejected the central question of seventeenth- and eighteenth-century epistemology—how the mind or subject, though different and separate from the rest of reality, can nonetheless come to know and understand the external world—on the grounds that this way of framing the problem distorts the nature of experience. From the standpoint of experience "we do not first have a mind and then become conscious of our relations to objects, but *to have a mind* is just to stand in those self-conscious relations to the objective realities" ("The Standpoint of Experience," p. 79).

But although "the mind is already in touch with reality," subject and object are not, as the pragmatists held, peer entities, equal partners constituting experience ("Two Types of Idealism," p. 266). Experience is from the first "in the clutches of thought, moulded by the mind's conceptions and presuppositions" ("The Standpoint of Experience," p. 75). We only know objects through self-consciousness; thus, philosophy must recognize that the ideal includes and subordinates the real. But we need not conclude from this, as Sir George Berkeley did, that all real existences are mental existences; Creighton's subjective idealism admits that the physical and the mental function together within an organically unified experience.

For Creighton, subjective idealism was both a philosophical theory and a defense of commitments that shaped his life. Reality, including nature, ourselves, and our fellows, has meaning and significance in relation to consciousness. The "characteristic mark of idealism . . . is its direct acceptance" of this meaning or value ("Two Types of Idealism," p. 258). As a philosopher, the subjective idealist interprets experience by showing "its relation to the ideals and purposes of a rational self-consciousness" ("The Standpoint of Experience," p. 92). But philosophy's interpretive task is not merely to describe the relation of experience to consciousness; philosophy has a dynamic role in testing and criticizing the many ways mind meets its objects and draws them into its purposes. Mind is "the continuous principle of criticism" in life, and philosophy is the element of "absolutely free inquiry" with purposes inherently practical and social ("Two Types of Idealism," pp. 275–76). Philosophy thus continuously shapes experience, and experience is incomplete without philosophy.

Creighton's importance lies in part in the clarity of his written work, particularly in his critical accounts of the state of American philosophy in his time. But he also modeled a philosophical life, living his theoretical belief in the social nature of thought as a teacher and leader of the academic and philosophical communities of his time. Creighton expressed his own beliefs perhaps most succinctly when he borrowed the motto of the Phi Beta Kappa society, "Philosophy is the pilot of life," to point up the mutual dependence of scholarship and social living ("Knowledge and Practice," p. 24). At the time of his death Creighton was preparing to deliver the Carus Lectures. He died in Ithaca, New York.

• All the articles cited in this essay are collected in *Studies in Speculative Philosophy*, ed. Harold Smart (1925), containing a select bibliography of works by and about Creighton. Creighton's written works also include *An Introductory Logic* (1898), which went through five editions; a translation with E. B. Titchener of W. Wundt's *Lectures on Human and Animal Psychology* (1894); a translation with Albert Lefevre of *Immanuel Kant: His Life and Doctrine* (1902); and numerous articles and book reviews for the *Philosophical Review*, the *Journal of Philosophy*, *Kant-Studien*, and *Science*, as well as entries in *Encyclopedia Americana* and *Hasting's Encyclopedia of Religion and Ethics*. Works on Creighton's philosophical views and his influence on American philosophy as a teacher, administrator, and editor include Joseph Blau, *Men and Movements in American Philosophy* (1952), which contains an extended discussion; G. Watts Cunningham, *The Idealist Argument in Recent British and American Philosophy* (1933); Harvey G.

Townsend, *Philosophical Ideas in the US* (1934). G. W. Cunningham wrote an obituary in *International Journal of Ethics*, Jan. 1925.

SUZANNE SENAY

CREIGHTON, William (29 Oct. 1778–1 Oct. 1851), congressman and political leader in early Ohio, was born in Berkeley County, Virginia (now W.Va.), the son of William Creighton (his mother's identity is unknown). Creighton graduated from Dickinson College in Carlisle, Pennsylvania, in 1795, studied law in Martinsburg, Virginia (now W.Va.), and migrated to the Scioto Valley in the Northwest Territory in 1799. There he built a reputation as a lawyer and as a caustic opponent of popular rule in general and the territorial government in particular. Creighton was more interested in the economic development of the Scioto Valley than in social equality or political democracy; not surprisingly, this conservative Jeffersonian Republican became a stalwart Whig.

Creighton was a young man in a hurry, and he deeply resented Governor Arthur St. Clair's control of patronage and disdain for the wishes of local leaders. Creighton formed an alliance with Thomas Worthington and Nathaniel Massie, prominent figures in South-Central Ohio. With their support, he was selected Ohio's first secretary of state in 1803. Two years later he married Massie's sister-in-law, Elizabeth Meade. In December 1808 Creighton resigned. In 1809, through the influence of Worthington, he was appointed U.S. district attorney. He served in that office until 1811.

With the removal of the territorial hierarchy, however, the inherently conservative Creighton increasingly found himself at odds with the more democratic Worthington and his brother-in-law Edward Tiffin. Now they were the aristocracy standing in the way of younger men of talents. In the winter of 1808–1809, Creighton defied Worthington by acting as an attorney in the impeachment trial of two supreme court justices for declaring an act of the state legislature unconstitutional. They were acquitted. He then opposed the Republican effort to remove judges through legislative action as well as attempts to regularize partisan behavior through the formation of secret organizations such as the Tammany Society. The split became personal as well as ideological, with Creighton leading a schism in the Methodist church in Chillicothe, which pitted him against Worthington and Tiffin.

Ultimately, Creighton and more conservative Republicans emerged from the struggle stronger than their opponents. Upon the resignation of Congressman Duncan McArthur in March 1813, Creighton was chosen to take his place. He was reelected in 1814 but lost an 1815 bid for the U.S. Senate. Voters in the Chillicothe area sent Creighton back to Congress in 1827 as a strong supporter of John Quincy Adams. The president returned the favor by nominating him for a federal district judgeship in August 1828, but the Senate declined to confirm the appointment. Creighton, who had resigned in anticipation of his new job,

was elected to fill out his own term in March 1829. He was a reliable National Republican backbencher until his retirement from politics in 1833. Despite these elections, Creighton was never again as influential politically as he had been in the first decade of Ohio statehood.

Creighton became a director of the branch of the Bank of the United States in Chillicothe in October 1817. In his capacity as president of the board of directors, he resisted agents of the state of Ohio when they arrived on 17 September 1819 to collect a tax levied on the branch; the tax was collected but later returned, and in 1824 it was declared unconstitutional by the U.S. Supreme Court. In most respects, Creighton was simply a solid citizen of Chillicothe. He was the epitome of the local notables in the small towns of the nineteenth-century Middle West who dominated the interlocked economic, social, and political networks of the region. Creighton was never a man of the people; he served the interests of businessmen and professionals concerned with the progressive development of the United States. He died in Chillicothe.

• There is no collection of Creighton papers, but there are a considerable number of his letters in the papers of Worthington, Massie, and other early Ohio politicians in the Ohio Historical Society in Columbus. See Linda Elise Kalette, ed., *The Papers of Thirteen Early Ohio Political Leaders* (1977). References to Creighton, as well as discussions of the relevant political context, can be found in Andrew R. L. Cayton, *The Frontier Republic: Ideology and Politics in the Ohio Country, 1780–1825* (1986); Donald J. Ratcliffe, "The Experience of Revolution and the Beginnings of Party Politics in Ohio, 1776–1816," *Ohio History* 85 (1976): 186–230; Alfred Byron Sears, *Thomas Worthington, Father of Ohio Statehood* (1958); and William T. Utter, *The Frontier State: 1803–1825*, vol. 2 of *The History of the State of Ohio* (1942).

ANDREW CAYTON

CREMIN, Lawrence Arthur (31 Oct. 1925–4 Sept. 1990), educator, was born Lawrence Cremin in New York City, the son of Arthur T. Cremin and Theresa Borowick, music school proprietors. Early in his career Cremin took his father's first name as his middle name, a reflection of the close relationship between them. To use one of his favorite words, Cremin was a "quintessential" New Yorker, a product of its public schools for high-achieving students: the Model School of Hunter College; Townsend Harris High School, where he received his diploma at the age of fifteen; and the College of the City of New York, where he earned a B.S. in social science in 1946. Cremin's father wished him to enter the family music business, but while studying music education at Teachers College, Columbia University, he encountered George S. Counts and his colleagues in the Department of Social and Philosophical Foundations of Education. Cremin switched his emphasis to the history of education and received his A.M. in 1947 and his Ph.D. in 1949 from Columbia University. His doctoral thesis became the basis for his first book, *The American Common School* (1951). Except for brief service in the Army Air Corps

(1944–1945) in Georgia and sabbatical years in Madison, Wisconsin; Palo Alto, California; and Princeton, New Jersey, Cremin spent his whole life in Manhattan. Offers from other universities tempted him, but in the end he could not bear to leave New York.

Cremin's entire professional career centered on Teachers College, whose faculty he joined as a graduate student in 1948, remaining until his death. At the time of his death he was Frederick A. P. Barnard Professor of Education, an endowed chair he had received in 1961 after publication of his best-known book, *The Transformation of the School*, which received the Bancroft Prize in American history in 1962. In 1961 he also became a member of the Department of History at Columbia University, a rare acknowledgement by the Columbia faculty of the accomplishments of a colleague at Teachers College.

As a teacher Cremin was superb. Both in the large lecture course on the history of American education that he gave for many years and in intense, individual sessions, he exuded knowledge and enthusiasm for issues of America's educational past. One of his former students, Diane Ravitch, captured these qualities in a memoir in *American Scholar* (Winter 1992). "He defined his role as critic in a way that kept me from becoming his clone," she wrote. "I knew that I would always be able to turn to him for advice the way that other people turn to psychics and priests." Cremin described himself as a "charismatic listener."

However, Cremin was more widely known as an extraordinarily productive author, primarily of books and articles dealing with the history of American education from its precolonial origins to its contemporary policy dilemmas. His monumental work was his three-volume collection *American Education*, published between 1970 and 1988. *The National Experience, 1783–1876*, volume two of the series, won Cremin the Pulitzer Prize for history in 1981. Each volume contains an extraordinary bibliography, and together these bibliographies represent one of the widest collections of sources related to education and culture in America. The texts also illustrate two principal characteristics of his scholarship: his expansive definition of education and his commitment to placing education within the political, social, and intellectual context of its period. His definition of education for the three volumes was "the deliberate, systematic, and sustained effort to transmit, evoke, or acquire knowledge, values, attitudes, skills, and sensibilities, as well as any learning that results from that effort, direct or indirect, intended or unintended." His readers condensed this elaborate definition to the single idea for which he was best known: "Many agencies educate."

Cremin's second goal, to reduce the isolation of historical studies of education from broader themes of American history, was foreshadowed in *The Transformation of the School*. In that earlier text, Cremin had argued that the progressive education reform movement was the educational embodiment of political progressivism from 1876 to 1955. The three volumes further illustrate the close links between education and its historical context. He intended his final book, *Popular Education and Its Discontents* (1990), to be a coda to the three historical volumes, and in it he assesses contemporary education and its relationship to American democracy. At the time of his death, Cremin was beginning a biography of John Dewey.

In addition to his career as a teacher and author, Cremin was also president of Teachers College from 1974 to 1984. Cremin brought to this administrative position the same commitment to a broad definition of education and to rigorous, disciplinary-based scholarship. Nevertheless, with the myriad academic and professional programs that reflected Cremin's multifaceted definition of education, Teachers College experienced financial constraints during Cremin's presidency that made it difficult for him to academically strengthen its programs as much as he wished. The publication of the National Commission on Excellence in Education's report to the secretary of education, *A Nation at Risk* (1983), however, narrowed the national education agenda to issues of schooling, a constriction that Cremin rejected intellectually and that made sustenance of Teachers College, which had reduced dramatically its attention to school matters, more challenging.

From 1985 until the year of his death Cremin served as president of the Spencer Foundation, on whose board he had served since 1973. The foundation, which provides funds for research about education, gave Cremin more opportunities to fulfill his intellectual priorities than the more constraining circumstances at Teachers College had allowed.

In addition to his full agenda of teaching, writing, and administering, Cremin also managed to serve on the boards of several not-for-profit organizations broadly related to education. Cremin had married Charlotte Raup, the daughter of one of his former professors and later a colleague at Teachers College, in 1956; they had two children. Cremin suffered a massive heart attack and died across the street from Teachers College.

• Cremin's papers are located at Teachers College, Columbia University, and at the Spencer Foundation archives in Chicago, Ill. In addition to the works cited above, Cremin was also the author of *The Republic and the School: Horace Mann on the Education of Free Men* (1957), *The Wonderful World of Ellwood Patterson Cubberley* (1965), *The Genius of American Education* (1965), *Public Education* (1965), and *Traditions of American Education* (1977). He was coauthor of *A History of Education in American Culture* (1953), *A History of Teachers College, Columbia University* (1954), *Public Education and the Future of America* (1955), *Public Schools in Our Democracy* (1956), and *Research for Tomorrow's Schools: Disciplined Inquiry for Education* (1969). Cremin also edited the Classics in Education series at Teachers College, which included more than fifty volumes. Ellen Condliffe Lagemann and Patricia Albjerg Graham prepared a biographical memoir for the National Academy of Education, of which Cremin was a founder and former president. The memoir also appeared as "Lawrence A. Cremin: A Biographical Memoir," *Teachers College Record* 96, no. 1 (Fall 1994): 102–13.

PATRICIA ALBJERG GRAHAM

CRESAP, Michael (29 June 1742–18 Oct. 1775), frontiersman and soldier, was born in Old Town, Maryland, the son of Thomas Cresap, a frontier trader and a member of the Ohio Company of Virginia, and Hannah Johnson. Michael attended school in Baltimore County, and shortly after leaving school he married Mary Whitehead, of Philadelphia, in 1764; they had five children. Cresap began his career as a merchant in Old Town. He failed in this endeavor. In an attempt to provide for his growing family Cresap decided to "improve" western lands, intent on selling them to future settlers. After hiring some men, Cresap traveled westward in the spring of 1774. The party took Nemacolin's Path to Redstone (present-day Brownsville, Pa.), and then traveled the Mingo Path southwesterly past Wheeling (present-day Wheeling, W. Va.).

Cresap's fame, or infamy, results from his actions in Lord Dunmore's War. Cresap is often blamed for beginning the war and for killing the family of the Mingo war chief Tah-gah-jute (known to whites as Logan) during the conflict. While Cresap was clearing land south of Wheeling, a series of skirmishes between settlers and some Shawnee warriors occurred in Kentucky. These were the first skirmishes of Dunmore's War. Cresap's immediate reaction to the outbreak of violence was to counsel restraint. Shortly thereafter, in April 1774 Cresap received reports implying a frontier war had begun to the north. Believing himself surrounded, Cresap and his men prepared for war. He and his men attacked a canoe carrying two warriors, one Delaware and the other Shawnee. These Indians were actually employees of a Pittsburgh trader, but Cresap and his mean either did not know, or chose not to care. In either case the Delaware and Shawnee were scalped, an Algonquian declaration of war. Cresap's small force then attacked a party of Shawnee warriors. This attack was later confused with the attack on Logan's family. After attacking the Shawnee, Cresap and his men returned to Wheeling.

Cresap's actions, along with those of his men, were a small part of Lord Dunmore's War, occurring after earlier skirmishes, and were not, as some have argued, the start of the war. After a short stay at Wheeling, Cresap returned to Old Town, where he raised a company of rangers to fight in the war. Before the troops could go into action, Virginia's royal governor Lord Dunmore at the head of a Virginian army had defeated the Shawnee at the battle of Point Pleasant (where the Kanahwa River enters the Ohio) in October 1774. Shawnee leaders then negotiated a settlement with the Virginians that effectively opened Kentucky to colonial settlement.

It was while Cresap was at Wheeling that Logan's family was killed. Part of the confusion over Cresap's role in the Yellow Creek event centers around Cresap's military actions while at Wheeling. Cresap led volunteers on scouting actions and did some skirmishing while at Wheeling. Some of Cresap's followers suggested an attack on Logan's Mingo village at Yellow Creek. Evidence suggests Cresap talked the men out of the attack. Blame for the massacre at Yellow Creek rests with the Virginian Daniel Greathouse.

The first mention of Cresap's role in the Logan family massacre occurred when the Shawnee and Virginians negotiated an end to the war. At the treaty conference, John Gibson spoke for Logan since the latter refused to attend the conference. In a speech to Dunmore, Gibson charged Cresap with the murder of Logan's family. Gibson's speech was included in the conference minutes, but Gibson had the speech ascribed to Logan, not himself. The *Virginia Gazette* reprinted the speech in 1775 and attributed it to the Mingo warrior. When Logan learned who Gibson had blamed for the murders of his family, he flatly disavowed Gibson's assertion. Nevertheless, Logan's supposed speech had taken on a life of its own, fostered first by Gibson, who became John Heckewelder's source of information regarding the American Indians and events of the period in question, and later by Thomas Jefferson.

Jefferson also blamed the Yellow Creek massacre on Cresap. In his *Notes on the State of Virginia* Jefferson correctly mentioned two colonial parties fighting along the frontier at the time in question. One party was Cresap's, the other was led by Greathouse. Greathouse's party operated along Baker's Bottom, along the Yellow Creek, and this is where the murders took place. The evidence suggests Greathouse was the leader of the party that killed Logan's family. Nevertheless, Jefferson blamed Cresap for the act.

It is possible that Jefferson blamed Cresap because the speech that appeared in the *Virginia Gazette* contained a reference to "Colonel Cresap" (Jefferson, pp. 60–61 and app. 4). Colonel Cresap was Michael Cresap's father. Michael Cresap was referred to as Captain Cresap. Jefferson probably did not know this and confused the reference to Thomas Cresap with Michael Cresap. By inserting the speech into the record, Gibson convinced many citizens that Cresap was responsible for the murders. Most of Cresap's contemporaries did not believe the charges made against him, as was evidenced by events at the beginning of the American Revolution.

Shortly after peace returned to the frontier, Cresap returned with more men to the Ohio River, again intent on developing lands. Before Cresap could benefit from his improvements on the land, war again erupted—this time between colonists and the Crown. In June 1775 the Second Continental Congress requested that individual colonies raise troops for the struggle against England; the Maryland assembly sought two rifle companies from Frederick County, Cresap's home. The local Committee of Correspondence named Cresap captain of one of the regiments. Cresap accepted the appointment, and in August, after raising the requisite number of men, marched with them 550 miles in twenty-five days, joining the Continental army at Boston. By the fall of 1775 Cresap had become too sick to continue his military service and was discharged. He died while en route home, in New York City.

Cresap's fame rests on his actions along the colonial frontier on the eve of the American Revolution. While Virginians blamed Cresap for the hostilities of 1774, Pennsylvanians and Marylanders did not. They saw the Virginians' actions as an attempt to shift blame and responsibility. Cresap's reputation within the community was so great that the rifle company he captained called itself "Cresap's Rifles" even after his death. Cresap's life illustrates how colonial frontiersmen operated in a world that pitted not only colonist against Indian but also colonies against each other.

• Cresap died while relatively young; there are thus no "Michael Cresap Papers" as such. There are a few references to Cresap in *The Papers of Sir William Johnson* (14 vols. 1921–1965) and *Documents Relative to the Colonial History of the State of New York* (1856–1861). Cresap is not nearly as famous today as he was in the nineteenth century. As a result, many of the most famous studies on him are a century old, including the one full-length biography that exists, John J. Jacob, *A Biographical Sketch of the Life of the Late Captain Michael Cresap* (1826; repr. 1866). A shorter study of Cresap is M. L. Stevenson, "Captain Michael Cresap and the Indian Logan," *West Virginia Historical and Antiquarian Society* 3, no. 2 (Apr. 1903). Another short piece is (anonymous) "Michael Cresap: A Brief Sketch of a Revolutionary Hero" (1928). The Cresap Society (Gallatin, Tenn.) has prepared a useful history of the Cresap family, Joseph Ord and Bernarr Cresap, comps., *The History of the Cresaps*, rev. ed. (1987). One of the most cited works concerning Cresap and the events surrounding the murders at Baker's Bottom is Theopile Conneau, *Tah-gah-jute; or Logan and Cresap, an Historical Essay* (1867). For the Virginian perspective see Thomas Jefferson, *Notes on the State of Virginia*, ed. Thomas Perkins Abernethy (1964).

MICHAEL J. MULLIN

CRESSON, Margaret French (3 Aug. 1889–1 Oct. 1973), sculptor, was born in Concord, Massachusetts, the daughter of the noted sculptor Daniel Chester French and his wife and first cousin, Mary Adams French. Cresson grew up in New York City, where her father had his studio, and in Stockbridge, Massachusetts, where the family spent its summers. She was educated at the Clarke Private School and the Brearley School in New York. She made her debut into society in the winter of 1909, and the next several years were largely given over to social activity; her father recalled that "the vanities of life seemed to be Margaret's sole occupation."

Cresson early displayed a talent for drawing and studied at the New York School of Applied Design for Women in 1912. She often saw her father at work and fancied that she herself could sculpt, although she had never done anything in that medium. On a dare from a friend she attempted to copy Desiderio's bust of the Infant Jesus, doing the work in her father's Stockbridge studio. She had more difficulty than she had anticipated, "and a very chastened young woman came back to the house that day for lunch." However, she was attracted to the art of sculpture and determined to take it up professionally. She received her first lessons from her father and subsequently studied with sculptors Abastenia St. Leger Eberle and George Demetrios. Daniel Chester French remained her dominant influence, however, and he often critiqued her work.

Both because of her deepening interest in sculpture and the outbreak of World War I, Cresson largely gave up the socializing that had dominated her life. In addition to her studies she was involved in the war effort and served for a time as secretary of the Duryea War Relief; she also worked for the American Red Cross. A few pieces survive from this period, but the majority of her sculptures date from after 1919.

In 1921 she married author and diplomat William Penn Cresson in a twelfth-century monastery in Taormina, Sicily, where she and her parents were spending the winter. As a wedding present Daniel Chester French gave the couple a small house called "the Dormouse," located near his own home, "Chesterwood," near Stockbridge. The Cressons had no children.

Margaret Cresson was very active as a sculptor during the 1920s. She specialized in portrait busts and memorial plaques, and she depicted many prominent individuals. What are probably her best-known works date from this decade, including busts of Admiral Richard Evelyn Byrd (1927, bronze; Corcoran Gallery of Art) and President James Monroe (1926, bronze; James Monroe Museum, Fredericksburg, Va.). The bust of Admiral Byrd is a sensitive likeness that well captures the personality of the famous explorer. It is a worthy successor to the portrait busts executed by her father and, like French's work, far transcends perfunctory realism to reach a level of vigorous naturalism. The bust of President Monroe is surprisingly lifelike, given that the subject had been dead for nearly a century when Cresson undertook his portrait. She was further handicapped by having to work from paintings, as no bust of Monroe modeled from life was known to exist. Her main source appears to have been Gilbert Stuart's portrait, and she may also have consulted paintings by John Vanderlyn and Rembrandt Peale and a death mask by John H. I. Browere. Despite the lack of a living model, she produced a lively and accurate likeness that succeeds both in depicting Monroe's features and in capturing his intelligence. Her inspiration undoubtedly was due in part to the fact that her husband was at that time writing a biography of the fifth president.

Other outstanding works from the 1920s include portrait busts of her father (1924, bronze; Corporation of Yaddo) and husband (1923, bronze; Chesterwood) and a portrait relief of her mother (1925, marble; Chesterwood). Cresson also assisted her father on several of his commissions, doing the lettering for both the Edward Mallinckrodt Memorial Tablet at Harvard University (1928) and the Bashford Dean Memorial Tablet at the Metropolitan Museum of Art (1930). She also completed French's memorial to Daniel Webster, a bronze bust erected at the statesman's birthplace in Franklin, New Hampshire, and dedicated in 1932.

Daniel Chester French died in 1931, followed by William Penn Cresson in 1932 and Mary Adams French in 1939. Cresson inherited Chesterwood, and although she continued to work as a sculptor, her primary focus thereafter was the preservation of her father's artistic legacy. For the next thirty years she acquired as much of his work as she could—in James Biddle's words, "rescuing, whenever possible, original plasters from museums all too willing to deaccession them." She helped organize the Daniel Chester French Foundation, which initally managed Chesterwood and its collections. In 1969 ownership was transferred to the National Trust for Historic Preservation, which continues researching the life and work of her father. In 1947 Cresson published *Journey into Fame: The Life of Daniel Chester French*, a well-written, informal biography.

Cresson's later sculptures include busts of her friend sculptor Ivan Mestrovic (1948, plaster; Chesterwood) and his wife Olga (1948, terra-cotta; Chesterwood) and a bust of a former neighbor, Dr. George C. Merrill, Jr., of Baltimore (1948, plaster; Chesterwood). She in fact did three busts of Merrill at ten-year intervals, depicting him in 1928, when he was seventeen, and again in 1938. In 1960 she designed the Daniel Chester French Medal for the National Academy of Design, awarded by the academy since 1961 for sculpture executed in the classic tradition. She had been elected an associate of the academy in 1942 and became a full academician in 1959. She also sculpted her father's tombstone (1934) in Sleepy Hollow Cemetery, Concord, Massachusetts, and a memorial tablet to her husband (1939) in Saint Paul's Episcopal Church in Stockbridge.

Cresson remained an active member of the Stockbridge community until the end of her life. She died during a dinner party at Chesterwood. She was devoted to the art of sculpture and, commented her friend sculptor Walker Hancock, "wanted full recognition for the sculptors and proper respect for their work." She felt, as had her father, that sculpture often took a backseat to painting in museum and gallery exhibitions, and she worked to correct the misapprehension that it was an inferior art.

• Collections of Margaret French Cresson's papers are owned by the Library of Congress (French Family Papers) and Chesterwood, the National Trust for Historic Preservation. The largest collection of her work is at Chesterwood. She is also represented in the collections of the Corcoran Gallery of Art, Washington, D.C.; the James Monroe Museum, Fredericksburg, Va.; the National Academy of Design, New York; the Corporation of Yaddo, Saratoga Springs, N.Y.; and Dartmouth College. Chesterwood owns nineteen portraits of her, including paintings and drawings by Daniel Chester French, Violet Oakley, John C. Johansen, and Robert Vonnoh and two busts by Evelyn Beatrice Longman. A sculpture of her by Ivan Mestrovic belongs to the Berkshire Museum, Pittsfield, Mass. An unpublished four-page autobiographical sketch is in the Chesterwood Archives. She wrote of her relationship with her father in *Journey into Fame*, and she is mentioned frequently in her mother's book, *Memories of a Sculptor's Wife* (1928). The *Chesterwood Pedestal* 7, no. 1 (1974), includes a brief biographical account, reminiscences by friends and associates, a checklist of her work in the Chesterwood collection and a partial listing of her work elsewhere,

a checklist of the portraits of her, and a list of some of her published and unpublished writings. She is also mentioned in Michael Richman, *Daniel Chester French: An American Sculptor* (1976).

DAVID MESCHUTT

CRESWELL, John Angel James (18 Nov. 1828–23 Dec. 1891), lawyer and politician, was born in Port Deposit, Maryland, the son of John G. Creswell and Rebecca E. Webb. In 1848 he graduated from Dickinson with honors, and two years later he passed the bar. Not long afterward he married Hannah J. Richardson; they had no children.

Originally a Whig, when the party broke up Creswell shifted allegiances to the Democratic party for a short while and in 1856 was a delegate to its presidential nominating convention. In the secession winter of 1860–1861, he declared for the Union, and as a member of the House of Delegates, he served to keep Maryland from seceding in 1861. The following year he was appointed assistant adjutant general for the state. In the fall of 1862 he won election as a Republican to Congress, beating incumbent John W. Crisfield. Creswell sided with the Radical Republicans in Maryland as an ally of Henry Winter Davis and played an important role in securing passage of emancipation in that state in 1864. That year he lost his bid for reelection. He served out Thomas Hicks's term in the U.S. Senate starting in 1865 but failed to secure election in his own right in 1867. Supporting congressional Reconstruction measures, he advocated the impeachment of President Andrew Johnson. In 1864 and 1868 he served as a delegate to the Republican presidential nominating conventions.

In 1869 Ulysses S. Grant named Creswell postmaster general—the only Republican from a southern state in Grant's first cabinet. Creswell managed to be effective and to avoid the taint of scandal that touched some of his colleagues. He worked to make the postal service faster and less expensive, especially international mail. He reduced the cost of carrying mail by steam and rail, increased the number of mail routes and postal employees, introduced the penny postal card, and worked with Secretary of State Hamilton Fish to revise postal treaties. His willingness to attack the franking system and his advocacy of a postal telegraph sparked opposition from both congressmen and Western Union. However, he did not play a significant role in the politics of Grant's first term, maintaining a low profile in the intraparty feuds that resulted in the Liberal Republican bolt of 1872. Rather, Creswell administered his charge with an eye to promoting both efficiency and the Republican party's fortunes through the appointment of loyal party supporters as postmasters. With unwavering loyalty to the president, he supported Grant's plan to annex the Dominican Republic and advocated American intervention in Cuba. He reaffirmed his Radical credentials in supporting additional Reconstruction measures. In 1874 he was one of only two cabinet members who advised Grant to veto the so-called Inflation Bill. Leaving

Grant's cabinet later that year under circumstances left unclear, Creswell served as the American counsel for the *Alabama* claims and supervised the closing of the Freedmen's Bank. Returning to private legal practice after December 1876, he served as president of the Citizens National Bank in Maryland. His last notable political activity was on behalf of the effort to nominate Grant for a third term in 1880. He died in Elkton, Maryland.

• Creswell's papers are in the Library of Congress and the Pennsylvania State Library. Additional information is in Robert V. Friedenberg, "John A. J. Creswell of Maryland: Reformer in the Post Office," *Maryland Historical Magazine* 64, no. 2 (1969): 133–43. He is the subject of Elizabeth M. Grimes's master's thesis (Columbia Univ. 1931) and Michael C. Hodgson's master's thesis (Catholic Univ., 1951). See also Dorothy G. Fowler, *The Cabinet Politician: The Postmasters General, 1829–1909* (1943), for a summary of Creswell's political activities. An obituary is in the supplementary issue of the *Baltimore Son*, 26 Dec. 1891.

BROOKS D. SIMPSON

CRET, Paul Philippe (23 Oct. 1876–8 Sept. 1945), architect and educator, was born in Lyons, France, the son of Paul Adolphe Cret and Ann Caroline Durand, both possibly employed in the silk industry, although after his father's death, his mother became a dressmaker. His education began in the office of his uncle, an architect, and was continued at the École des Beaux-Arts in Lyons. In 1896 he was awarded the Paris Prize, enabling him to move to Paris to attend the École there and to enroll in the Atelier Pascal. Even in a larger and more competitive venue Cret gained attention, winning the Rougevin Prize in 1901. Cret's life, however, changed in 1903, when Paul Armon Davis III, himself a former student in the Atelier Pascal, put out a call to University of Pennsylvania alumni pursuing their architectural studies abroad to nominate a candidate for professor of architectural design at the university. The alumni chose Cret, who was at first hired as an assistant professor. Then twenty-seven years of age, Cret could little know the effect that his arrival in the United States would have on the architectural community, both in Philadelphia and in the nation. Soon he was acting as patron, not only for the atelier at the University of Pennsylvania, but also for one held in the evenings under the auspices of the T-Square Club of Philadelphia. Under his direction students from the Philadelphia Atelier excelled in national competitions; beginning in 1911 Cret's students took the Paris Prize, administered by the Society of Beaux-Arts Architects, for four consecutive years. Theo B. White, one of Cret's architectural design students, described Cret's working method: "Cret's criticism was made largely on rolls of tracing paper spread over the student's problem, drawing with a soft pencil and with a minimum of talk (quite different from the modern critic)" (White, p. 29).

Although Cret's success as a design critic no doubt enhanced his local reputation, it was initially through his participation and success in nationally advertised architectural competitions that he became known outside of Philadelphia. A few years after arriving in the United States Cret entered the first of a number of architectural competitions in which he participated. For the first, the 1907 competition for the building of the International Bureau of American Republics (the Pan-American Union Building, construction completed 1910), Cret collaborated with Philadelphia architect Albert Kelsey. This venture was successful, with the temporary partnership carrying off the first prize. Cret continued to enter national competitions, eventually participating in the Robert Fulton Memorial Competition of 1909, in which he took third place; the Perry Memorial competition of 1911 (third place); the Indianapolis Public Library competition of 1914 (construction completed 1917), which he won in collaboration with architects Zantzinger, Borie & Medary; the Nebraska State Capitol Competition, which he lost to Bertram G. Goodhue; and the Kansas City Liberty Memorial Competition of 1923, which he lost to H. Van Buren Magonigle. All of these competitions, as well as the independent designs created by the firm of Paul P. Cret, Architect, which he established in Philadelphia, emphasized a Beaux-Arts classicism now known as modern classicism.

Soon after World War I Cret was presented with another opportunity to establish his version of Beaux-Arts classicism as a national style. Cret spent World War I in the army in France, receiving the croix de guerre and being made an officer in the Legion of Honor. Before returning to Philadelphia after his discharge, however, he was asked to design a memorial for Quentin Roosevelt, who had been killed in the war in France. Located at Charnery, France, this 1919 memorial marked the beginning of Cret's association with monuments erected for Americans killed in military actions abroad. From 1923 until his death in 1945 Cret served as consulting architect for the American Battle Monuments Commission, a role in which he affected the image of the United States around the world as it was projected in monuments, cemeteries, and chapels. As Elizabeth Grossman has pointed out, Cret's designs for the Pennsylvania Battle Monument Commission and for the American Battle Monuments Commission "reaffirmed, in his new modern classical idiom, Cret's belief in the robustness of classicism" ("Architecture for a Public Client," p. 143).

Nor was Cret's taste for classicism limited to civic designs. His Barnes Foundation Gallery in Merion, Pennsylvania, and the Folger Shakespeare Library (1928–1931) in Washington, D.C., attest to the continuing popularity of his style. In fact, although his office completed few residential designs, the 1920s and 1930s, a time of stylistic controversy in the United States, found several commercial structures, as well as bridges and academic buildings, on the boards. He produced office buildings and interiors for the Integrity Trust Co. in Philadelphia during the 1920s, and during the 1930s and early 1940s Cret's firm even produced several designs for the new streamlined trains, including the California Zephyr. Bridge designs included the Delaware River Bridge in Philadelphia, a collaboration with engineer Ralph Modjeski, and the Market Street Bridge in Harrisburg, Pennsylvania. Eventually Cret's designs spread to the Midwest and South and included the John Herron Art Institute in Indianapolis, the Detroit Institute of Arts, the Hartford County Building, Hartford, Connecticut, and the campus plan for the University of Texas in Austin. From his University of Pennsylvania students, Cret had chosen John F. Harbeson, William Hough, William Livingston, and Roy Larson to work in his independent firm. After his death in Philadelphia, the younger men continued working as Harbeson, Hough, Livingston & Larson (later called H2L2).

Cret's architectural career had been launched when he won the Paris Prize, which enabled him to attend the École des Beaux Arts in Paris. He would continue to gain honors throughout his long career, including the Gold Medal awarded by the American Institute of Architects in 1938.

By the time of Cret's death in 1945, the world of American architecture had changed, but even among young architects more influenced by Bauhaus design, he was venerated as both an educator and an architect. Although he came to the United States in 1903 as one of a flock of Beaux-Arts–trained architects who would influence the departments of architectural design in universities across the country, he quickly distinguished himself from the rest by the level of his own success in national competitions and by the success of his students in competing for celebrated Paris and Rome prizes. Furthermore, as an outstanding practitioner of modern classicism as an acceptable permutation of the Beaux-Arts style, he influenced the design of America's civic architecture, creating a public face for American construction that can be seen both in the United States and abroad.

• Major collections of the drawings of Paul P. Cret are in the Athenaeum of Philadelphia and the Architectural Archives of the University of Pennsylvania. Smaller collections of individual buildings and other records are at the Detroit Institute of Arts, the Folger Shakespeare Library, the Avery Architectural Library at Columbia University, and the Archives of American Art. Accounts of his life and work are in Theo B. White, *Paul Philippe Cret, Architect and Teacher* (1973). Elizabeth Grossman's work on Cret includes "Paul Philippe Cret: Rationalism and Imagery in American Architecture" (Ph.D. diss., Brown Univ., 1980), *The Civic Architecture of Paul Cret* (1996), and two articles, "Architecture for a Public Client: The Monuments and Chapels of the American Battle Monuments Commission," *Journal of the Society of Architectural Historians* 43 (May 1984): 119–45, and "Two Postwar Competitions: The Nebraska State Capitol and the Kansas City Liberty Memorial," *Journal of the Society of Architectural Historians* 45 (Sept. 1986): 244–69. For a discussion of the impact of Cret's modern classicism on the District of Columbia, see Richard Guy Wilson, "Modernized Classicism and Washington, D.C.," *American Public Architecture: European Roots and Native Expressions*, Pennsylvania State University *Papers in Art History* 5 (1989): 273–303, and Travis C. McDonald, "Modernized Classicism: The Architecture of Paul Philippe Cret in Washington, D.C." (M.A. thesis, Univ. of Virginia, 1980). An account of Cret's impact on city planning in Philadelphia can be found in David B. Brownlee, *Building the City Beautiful: The Benjamin Franklin Parkway and the Philadelphia Museum of Art* (1989). See also S. L. Tatman and R. W. Moss, *Biographical Dictionary of Philadelphia Architects 1700–1930* (1985). An obituary is in the *New York Times*, 9 Sept. 1945.

SANDRA TATMAN

CRETIN, Joseph (10 Dec. 1799–22 Feb. 1857), first Roman Catholic bishop of St. Paul, Minnesota, was born in Montluel in the department of Ain, France, the son of Joseph Crétin, a prosperous baker and innkeeper, and Jeanne-Marie Mery. During the revolution his mother was imprisoned briefly for protesting the government's persecution of Catholics. Joseph was enrolled in the presbyteral school in Montluel in 1812. He made his classical studies at the minor seminary of Meximieux, where his future friend Mathias Loras was teacher and rector, and his philosophy courses at the minor seminary of L'Argentière. He spent only a year at the major seminary of Alix before entering the prestigious seminary of St. Sulpice in Paris in 1820. He was ordained a priest on 20 December 1823 by Bishop Alexandre Devie of Belley, in whose diocese he served first as curate and then as pastor of Ferney, near the Swiss border. There he founded in 1826 a boarding college to counter the rationalistic tendencies in this former home of Voltaire. In 1829 he received the degree of bachelor of letters from the University of France. In 1830 he refused to offer prayers for the new king, Louis Philippe, which put him in disfavor with the government.

In the fall of 1838 Loras, now the newly ordained bishop of Dubuque, Iowa, visited Ferney and invited his former pupil to join him in that frontier diocese. Cretin arrived in Dubuque on 18 April 1839 and was immediately appointed vicar general. For the rest of his life he remained Bishop Loras's closest friend and most trusted adviser. In 1841 he was sent to serve the largely French-Canadian community at Prairie du Chien, which in 1843 became a part of the diocese of Milwaukee. He took under his charge the Winnebago Indians of upper Iowa, whose difficult language he mastered perhaps even better than he did English. The recommendation of the federal agent and others that he be appointed principal of the school established for the Winnebago was ignored by the governor, who in 1845 also forbade Cretin to erect a mission school desired by the Indians. In 1846, at Loras's request, Cretin went to Europe to recruit priests, especially Irish ones, for the growing diocese but was able to obtain only five French seminarians. In 1849 he wished to accompany those Catholics drawn to the California gold fields but was dissuaded.

In 1849 the American bishops, meeting in Baltimore, petitioned the Holy See to make a diocese of the newly created territory of Minnesota (detached from the state of Iowa) with St. Paul, the territorial capital, as its see and Cretin its bishop. On 23 July 1850 the Holy See appointed Cretin bishop. He then traveled to France, where he was consecrated by Bishop Devie on 26 January 1851 in the cathedral of Belley. He returned with six clerics to a diocese where he found only the veteran Indian missionary Augustin Ravoux and a log chapel he made his cathedral. There were, he informed a mission-aid society in Europe, some 3,000 Catholics in the new diocese, including Dakota (Sioux), Ojibway (Chippewa), and Winnebago Indians.

Before 1851 was out, Cretin erected a three-story building that served as cathedral, residence, seminary, and boys' school. John Ireland, later archbishop of St. Paul, attended both the boys' school and seminary. The old log cathedral was made first a temporary school for girls staffed by the Sisters of St. Joseph of Carondolet, whom Cretin had persuaded to come to St. Paul, and then a dispensary where the same sisters nursed cholera victims. In 1854 Cretin opened St. Joseph's Hospital, the first charitable institution in Minnesota.

Irish, Canadian, and German Catholics entered the diocese in large numbers, some 20,000 in 1855 alone. The Germans came partly as a result of appeals sent to eastern United States and European newspapers by Father Franz Pierz, who had come to Minnesota in 1852 to serve the Chippewa. So much of Pierz's time was given to building churches for the Germans that he persuaded the bishop to invite Benedictine priests from Germany to come to Minnesota to serve them. They came in 1856 to establish a priory near St. Cloud. That year Cretin also laid the cornerstone for a new cathedral.

Cretin lived simply. He made his own bed, swept his own floor, and split his own firewood. Though he ate sparingly, he fretted over a bulging waistline. He, like his mentor Bishop Loras, was a great advocate of temperance. He founded in 1852 the Catholic Temperance Society of St. Paul. When the Minnesota legislature voted a strict law prohibiting the sale of liquor, Cretin had the bells of the cathedral rung in joyous approval. He was also a musician who played the organ and delighted in hymn singing. Throughout his four and a half years in St. Paul he remained a pioneer bishop, constantly worried by chronic shortages of money and personnel. Shortly before his death at the cathedral rectory, he composed a report for one of the mission-aid societies of Europe that helped keep the diocese afloat. In it he claimed for a Catholic population of 50,000 only nineteen priests and some twenty structures that could be called churches.

• Cretin's letters and a life by Archbishop John Ireland can be found in the St. Paul's Catholic Historical Society's *Acta et Dicta*, vols. 1–5 (1907–1918). Cretin's letters to the Leopoldinen-Stiftung are in that society's *Berichte*, vols. 25 and 26 (1853, 1854). Important biographical material is in M. M. Hoffmann, *Church Founders of the Northwest: Loras and Cretin and Other Captains of Christ* (1937).

THOMAS W. SPALDING

CRÈVECOEUR, J. Hector St. John de (31 Jan. 1735–12 Nov. 1813), writer and government official, was born in Caen, Normandy, where, in the parish of St. Jean, he was baptized Michel-Guillaume Jean de Crèvecoeur. He was the elder son of Guillaume-Augustin Jean de Crèvecoeur and Marie-Anne-Thérèse Blouet, his father a substantial landowner and his mother also of the provincial nobility of Normandy. Crèvecoeur grew up in the manor house of Pierrepont, near the village of Creully. At the Jesuit Collège Royal de Bourbon at Caen, Crèvecoeur studied practical mathematics, learned surveying and cartography, and was graduated with distinction in literature and languages in 1750. He continued his education in Salisbury, England, and probably visited Lisbon, about which he wrote several times.

During the French and Indian War, Crèvecoeur surveyed and mapped French lands in Canada. As a cadet in colonial troops, he fought in the battle at Fort George in 1757; the next year he was commissioned lieutenant in a French regiment. In 1759, when Louis XV praised a battle site map and fort plan Crèvecoeur had made for General Montcalm, the *Gazette de France* reported that Crèvecoeur had made "beaucoup de réputation" for his bravery and talents. A few months later, during the English siege of Quebec, Crèvecoeur was wounded and hospitalized.

Instead of returning to France with the defeated troops, Crèvecoeur resigned his commission and accepted passage on a British ship to New York, where, on arrival in December 1759, he changed his name to J. Hector St. John and his language to English. He made his living first as a trader, explorer, and surveyor in the coastal settlements and uncharted woods of eastern North America, trading with and often guided by Native Americans. In a single year he visited all the colonies from New Hampshire to Virginia and made extensive notes on them. For five months he voyaged down the Ohio and Mississippi rivers as far as St. Louis, and returned to the East via the Great Lakes. His explorations and observations of the continent and its settlements made him one of the most knowledgeable people of his time concerning America and American civilization.

In 1765 Crèvecoeur was naturalized as a citizen of the colony of New York. A resident of Ulster County, in 1769 he married Mehitable Tippet, daughter of a prominent Dutchess County family. That year he also purchased 120 acres in Orange County, which became the setting of his classic *Letters from an American Farmer* (1782), fictionally placed in Pennsylvania. The couple had a daughter and two sons.

Crèvecoeur turned his lands into a productive farm with an ample house and quarters for the farmhands who worked with him. He was in his element as a scientific agriculturist and a citizen-observer of a country where he saw European paupers being "regenerate[d]" by "new laws, new modes of living, a new social system." He led a county project to drain the swampy Greycourt Meadows in his neighborhood and provide acres of new farmland. He continued to travel occasionally, observing flora, fauna, and natural phenomena and conversing with people he met. His idyllic life during the decade from 1769 to 1779 is described with charm and grace in *Letters from an American Farmer*, in which his penetrating observations on America and its developing civilization are attractively blended.

The coming of the Revolution was a disaster for Crèvecoeur, a pacifist who credited Great Britain with the mild government of its American colonies. The conflict between Loyalists and revolutionaries destroyed his euphoric participation in "the most perfect society . . . in the world." During the years from 1775 to 1779 his neutrality brought him fines, imprisonments, and alienation. In addition, Orange County was the hard-hit site of revolutionary battles, Tory-Indian raids, and incendiary pillaging as civil order failed.

In 1778 Crèvecoeur requested permission to return to France to establish his children's legitimacy (unrecognized there because his marriage and the children's baptisms were Protestant) and their right to inherit the family lands in Normandy. In February 1779 he and his six-year-old son left Orange County. While waiting in New York for a ship, Crèvecoeur was arrested by the British as a suspected patriot collaborator. Though innocent, he could not get a hearing for three months; imprisoned unjustly and treated with inhumanity, he quickly lost his admiration of British rule. He was released in September and reunited with his son, only to endure the deadly cold winter of 1779–1780 with inadequate food, clothing, and shelter. The two finally sailed in September 1780 but were shipwrecked off Ireland and reached Dublin with little more than the clothes they wore. Seven months later Crèvecoeur sold a collection of fifteen epistolary essays to publishers in London.

Crèvecoeur reached Normandy in August 1781. Within a week he met several American seamen stranded after escaping from British prisons; Crèvecoeur arranged with Benjamin Franklin (1706–1790), the American minister to France, to return them to America. In January 1782 he published a treatise in French on the cultivation of potatoes to improve nutrition and land productivity in Normandy. This work anticipated the diversification of French agriculture that prevented the recurrence after 1790 of bread famines. Crèvecoeur was introduced into social, governmental, and intellectual circles in Paris by several family friends, most notably the countess d'Houdetot (Jean-Jacques Rousseau's "Héloïse"), who adopted him as her American "noble savage."

Early in 1782 Davies and Davis published *Letters from an American Farmer*, Crèvecoeur's composite answer to his inspired question, "What is an American?" He had composed the insightful *Letters* from the journals of his American years, in which he had nightly recorded observations on his experiences of the day. *Letters* became an international bestseller, the first American book to receive such respect. It was followed quickly by a flurry of reviews and excerpts in periodicals, three subsequent English and Irish editions, and German and Dutch translations, all by 1784.

Although he wrote much else, *Letters* remains Crèvecoeur's most important work, an informative and humane exploration of a wide range of modes of living in the different American colonies. The book found popularity quickly because it answered European needs for down-to-earth information on America; many of the thousands who emigrated to America were influenced by *Letters*. But there is much more to the book than information; it is a work of literature, a collection of familiar essays on topics organized around the life of a thoughtful, scientific farmer. Unified as a series of letters from the farmer and ostensibly written to a cultivated European friend, it is partly autobiographical, partly fictional. It tells the story of the farmer's happy life in peacetime America, deteriorating into his struggles in the revolutionary war. The letters also include accounts of the farmer's travels to other sections of America, of nature and customs he observes, anecdotes of animals and people, and his original, often philosophical comments.

In his most famous essay Crèvecoeur asks, "What then is the American, this new man?" In Crèvecoeur's manuscript, the answer is "either a European or the descendant of a European" who, "leaving behind him all his ancient prejudices and manners, receives new ones from the new mode of life he has embraced, the new government he obeys, the new rank he holds." Crèvecoeur was the first to conceive and describe America as a melting pot when he concluded succinctly, "Here individuals of all nations are melted into a new one."

At Mme d'Houdetot's urging he prepared a French version of *Letters*, published in 1784, expanded to two volumes then and to three in 1787. Late-twentieth-century critics' readings of *Letters* as a protonovel underscore the strength of its story line and characters. In making the multivolume French versions of *Letters*, however, Crèvecoeur added more, and more purely autobiographical, historical, and geographic material to the compact and moderately coherent English original, and rearranged the chapters somewhat randomly, but without accommodating the original Farmer James material and the later expository material to each other. The French versions thus became a collection of essays with some unity of subject, but lacking the sequence and coherence to constitute a novel. Since Crèvecoeur often referred to the French and English versions as one and the same book, it is clear that he did not consider it a literary form structured by a plot.

By 1783 Crèvecoeur was recognized in Europe as an authority on America. During the multinational peace negotiations held at Versailles that year to close the American Revolution, the minister of the French navy, Marshal de Castries, commissioned Crèvecoeur to provide comprehensive information on the geography, resources, industries, and commerce of America. His report so impressed Louis XVI that he appointed him consul to New York, New Jersey, and Connecticut.

Crèvecoeur crossed the Atlantic on the ship that carried the first copy of the Treaty of Paris to the United States and reached New York in November 1783, just before George Washington entered the city in triumph. Crèvecoeur then learned that his home had been burned and his wife had died in 1781 and the two children with her had been saved from famine by a Boston relative of a seaman whom he had assisted in France.

Crèvecoeur's foremost consular duty was to increase American importation of French goods. He initiated regular transportation and communication by establishing packet boat service between France and America, and he established scientific and cultural exchanges between his two countries. He also fostered the establishment in America of projects important to both countries including pioneering botanical gardens, a medical school, and the first Catholic church in New York.

From 1785 to 1787 he had leave in France, where he worked effectively to promote Franco-American trade. He cofounded with Jacques-Pierre Brissot the Société Gallo-Américaine, which worked for a duty-free French port and a central bureau of information about exporting to America. Crèvecoeur formed a close working relationship with Thomas Jefferson, then American minister to France, which became a long-term friendship. He also had extensive relations with the marquis de Lafayette, first in support of American interests and then on a personal and family basis. In 1786 Crèvecoeur published a paper on the American acacia, which inspired many of the locust-lined avenues now found all over Europe, and for it he was elected to the Royal Agricultural Society in Paris.

Back at his New York post, Crèvecoeur became more of a public figure: he corresponded on mutual interests with many national figures including Washington and James Madison (1751–1836), assisted John Fitch's experiments with steam navigation, was honored by several American cities and states (Vermont named St. Johnsbury for him), and in 1789 was elected to the American Philosophical Society. His children and prominent French friends sometimes received honors with him, and Crèvecoeur sent the published reports to France to establish the children's heritage by showing that those French nobles accepted them as his legitimate offspring.

In May 1790 Crèvecoeur was granted another leave in France, this time for his health. His friends there were on all sides of revolution and royalism; some emigrated; others met imprisonment or death. Fearing to make himself conspicuous, Crèvecoeur remained in obscurity. Still unwell in 1792, he retired without pension and shared crowded quarters in Paris with his daughter and her family. During the Reign of Terror, both of his sons emigrated, one to settle in Hamburg and one to farm in New Jersey. Crèvecoeur visited the elder in Hamburg in 1795–1796.

In 1796, when the French Academy was reorganized as the Institut, Crèvecoeur was elected to membership, and in 1801 his *Voyage dans la haute Pensylvanie et dans l'état de New-York* was published in three volumes in Paris. It received little attention and was not published in English until 1964. Crèvecoeur spent his last years enjoying a farmer's life at Lesches, east of Paris, sometimes with his children, and visiting friends and family around France and elsewhere in Europe. He spent three years, from 1806 to 1809, in Munich, where his son-in-law was French minister to Bavaria. When Austria abruptly declared war on Bavaria and the Austrian army advanced on Munich, Crèvecoeur and his daughter and granddaughter fled to Paris. He wrote articles on agriculture and technology for European journals, an appreciation of Mme d'Houdetot, and other essays. He died at his son-in-law's house in Sarcelles, near Paris.

Crèvecoeur's *Letters from an American Farmer* is still an indispensable source of information and understanding of prerevolutionary and revolutionary America, and in the twentieth century it has again been widely read. It is now recognized as both a highly important work of literature and a rich source of information about many aspects of American life in the years before the Revolution. *Letters* has sometimes been read skeptically because of its naive narrator or other fictional elements. But research into questioned statements by Crèvecoeur has, more often than not, found them based on the extensive knowledge that his contemporaries credited to him. The soundest judgment remains that of Jefferson, who wrote of him, "His veracity may be relied on"; and "You may rely certainly on the author's facts, and you will be easily able to separate from them his reflections."

• Crèvecoeur's English manuscripts are at the Library of Congress in three large, bound volumes. English essays not included in *Letters from an American Farmer* are collected in *More Letters from an American Farmer*, ed. Dennis Moore (1995). There are significant holdings of Crèvecoeur's consular papers in the Archives Nationales and other archives of government departments in Paris, and in the Bibliothèque Municipale in Mantes, France. Some personal correspondence and papers are scattered in France and the United States. Other manuscripts of particular interest are "Mémoire sur la région située à l'ouest des Montagnes d'Alléghany," Archives Nationales, Marine, Paris; and "Voyage aux Grandes Salines de Reichenhall . . . 1809," Deutsches Museum, Arkiv, Munich. Bernard Chevignard provides a census of personal letters and extensive primary and secondary bibliographies in *Saint John de Crèvecoeur: "Letters from an American Farmer" et "Letters d'un Cultivateur Américain": Genèse d'une oeuvre franco-américaine* (1989), a facing-page edition of the published English and French texts. Chevignard has also edited "Esquisse de ma vie depuis ma sortie à New York . . . 1779 jusques à mon retour . . . comme consul de France . . . 1783," *Annales de Normandie* 33 (1983): 164–73; and "Souvenirs consacrés à la mémoire de Mme la Comtesse de Houdetot," *Dix-huitième Siècle* 14 (1982): 246–62.

Although there is no full and reliable biography, Robert de Crèvecoeur, great-grandson of the author, wrote a biography still of considerable value, *Saint John de Crèvecoeur: sa vie et ses ouvrages* (1883); it includes texts, selections, or French translation of many of Crèvecoeur's papers. Other valuable sources are Julia P. Mitchell, *St. Jean de Crèvecoeur* (1916), and Howard C. Rice, *Le cultivateur américain: Etude sur l'oeuvre de Saint John de Crèvecoeur* (1933). Some new information (and misinformation) is in Gay Wilson Allen and Roger Asselineau, *St. John de Crèvecoeur: The Life of an American Farmer* (1987). Thomas Philbrick, *St. John de Crèvecoeur* (1970), is a good critical study.

KATHERINE EMERSON
EVERETT EMERSON

CREW, Henry (4 June 1859–17 Feb. 1953), physicist, was born in Richmond, Ohio, the son of William H. Crew, a general store owner and manager, and Deborah Ann Hargrave. His parents were devout Quakers, and he was raised in that faith. Crew's father died when Henry was eleven years old, providing in his will that he and his two sisters each receive a "classical education." Crew attended high school in Wilmington, Ohio, where his mother had moved with her children, and then Princeton University, where he studied Latin, Greek, and mathematics. In his last two years he also took science courses and was especially inspired by physicist C. F. Brackett and astrophysicist Charles A. Young. Crew graduated in 1882 with an A.B., remained at Princeton one more year as a graduate student in physics, and then went to Berlin, where he attended lectures in physics by Hermann von Helmholtz, Heinrich Kayser, and Gustav Kirchhoff. In 1884 he returned to the United States to become a physics graduate student at Johns Hopkins University under Henry Rowland. Crew did his thesis on the spectrographic measurement of the velocity of rotation of the sun as a function of latitude and received his Ph.D. in 1887.

Crew continued at Johns Hopkins for another year, as assistant in charge of the undergraduate physics laboratory, and then went to Haverford College in 1888 as instructor in physics and head of the department. In 1890 he married Helen C. Coale, whom he had met in Baltimore. They had three children. In 1891 Crew left Haverford to accept a position as an assistant astronomer at Lick Observatory, the University of California research station on Mount Hamilton, California. There he worked with the 36-inch refractor, using a Rowland concave-grating spectrograph of his own design for stellar spectroscopy. His spectrograph was not well suited for astronomy, and after a year he had published no papers based on his observations. After his one year at Lick he accepted an appointment at Northwestern University as professor of physics and head of the department. He remained a faculty member at Northwestern until he retired in 1933. From 1930 until his retirement Crew was on leave as chief of the Division of Basic Sciences at the Century of Progress International Exposition, better known as the Chicago World's Fair of 1933.

In his early years at Northwestern, Crew did laboratory spectroscopic research and published several papers in this field. He was an associate editor of the *Astrophysical Journal* for many years, specializing in the atomic-spectroscopy papers it published. However, his main interest was in teaching physics, which was what was expected of him at Haverford and Northwestern. Recognizing a real need for better textbooks, Crew wrote *The Elements of Physics: For Use in High Schools* (1899), *General Physics: An Elementary Textbook for Colleges* (1908), and *The Principles of Mechanics: For Students of Physics and Engineering* (1908), all three of which were widely used and went through many editions. More than two decades later he published a more advanced version of the third, *Mechanics for Students of Physics and Engineering* (1930).

Very soon after arriving at Haverford in the late 1880s, Crew had begun teaching a night extension course in electricity for students who already had jobs in the new and rapidly developing field. In this, as in his regular college courses, Crew liked to use demonstration experiments. He insisted that they be as simple as possible, work without fail, and clearly show the principle "in such a way as to leave no doubts in the mind of the student regarding their meaning or their validity." If possible the demonstrations should be "new and exciting" but never "some form of legerdemain." He was considered a very good teacher by his students, particularly the best of them who went on to graduate work and their own careers in physics.

Crew was a pioneer in using the historical approach in teaching physics. As part of a series of scientific memoirs edited by Joseph S. Ames, his friend and one of his instructors at Johns Hopkins, Crew edited a volume on *The Wave Theory of Light* (1900), containing long research papers by Thomas Young, Christiaan Huygens, and Augustin Fresnel (he translated Huygen's and Fresnel's work from French). Some years later (1914) he translated into English Galileo's *Dialogues Concerning the Two New Sciences*. Crew's classical education stood him in good stead; he translated the parts in Latin, and his collaborator, Alfonso de Salvio, translated those in Italian. Their translation was widely used in physical science survey courses throughout the United States for many years, in many editions. One of Crew's most important books was *The Rise of Modern Physics* (1928), beginning with Greek and Roman science and ending with the rise of modern spectroscopy and the new theory of atomic structure just then being developed by Niels Bohr. The book was highly successful, and Crew published a second, updated edition in 1935. In all his books, texts as well as historical efforts, he presented physics as a live, developing subject, done by vital human beings in the real world, rather than as a cold-blooded collection of theories and experiments.

The culmination of Crew's career as a teacher was the Chicago World's Fair, devoted to the theme of progress through science and technology. He was responsible for all the exhibits in the giant Hall of Science in the fairgrounds on the Lake Michigan shore. Crew handed the details over to subordinates, several of them his own former students, but he emphasized (and enforced) the general policy of interesting working demonstrations, remotely controlled whenever possible by the viewer, which clearly, vividly, and faultlessly taught the principles of all the natural sciences. Many of these demonstrations were moved to the Museum of Science and Industry after the fair closed, and the descendants of many of them, improved and modernized over the years, were still on display there in the 1990s.

After his retirement Crew lived on in Evanston, keenly interested in physics, and he attended colloquia at Northwestern and meetings in Chicago until nearly the year of his death in the Evanston Hospital. He had been an important educator who greatly influenced the teaching of physics in the United States.

• The main collection of Crew's letters is in the Northwestern University Archives, Evanston, Ill. With them are two autobiographical sketches that he wrote at different stages of his life, as well as a biographical sketch of him written by his son, also a physicist. There is also a smaller collection of Crew's correspondence, mostly with astronomers, in the Mary Lea Shane Archives of the Lick Observatory, in the University of California, Santa Cruz, Library. A published memorial biography is William F. Meggers, "Henry Crew," National Academy of Sciences, *Biographical Memoirs* 37 (1964): 33–54, which contains a bibliography of all of Crew's scientific papers and books. It also includes some of his more important publications on teaching physics and on the history of science; one of the best is "Galileo, the Physicist," *Science* 37 (1913): 463–70. Crew's short career as an observational astrophysicist is described, with full references, in Donald E. Osterbrock, "Failure and Success: Two Early Experiments with Concave Gratings in Stellar Spectroscopy," *Journal for the History of Astronomy* 17 (1984): 119–29. Xu Qiaozhen and Robert C. Michaelson, "Henry Crew, a Successful Teacher of Physics," *Physics Teacher* 25 (1987): 362–66, tells the story of his educational efforts and contains references to many of Crew's published papers and articles in this field. A. A. Knowlton, "Henry Crew (1859–1953)," *Isis* 45 (1954): 169–74, describes his contributions to the field of history of science and gives a complete bibliography of his published work in that field.

DONALD E. OSTERBROCK

CREWS, Laura Hope (12 Dec. 1879–13 Nov. 1942), actress, was born in San Francisco, California, the daughter of John Thomas Crews, a carpenter, and Angelena Lockwood, a stock company actress. Crews first appeared on the San Francisco stage at the age of four, in *Bootle's Baby*, and at six toured West Coast cities as Editha in *Editha's Burglar*. She retired from child parts to attend school, completing her education in 1898 at the State Normal School in San Jose, California. Immediately afterward she joined the Alcazar Stock Company in San Francisco as an actress.

Crews went to New York City in 1900 to join the Henry V. Donnelly Stock Company at the Murray Hill Theatre, rising from small parts to leads in three years. In 1904 she made her Broadway debut performing a supporting role in *Merely Mary Ann*. Her potential as an ingenue who could play comedy impressed a leading actor-manager, Henry Miller, and he cast her in several of his productions, beginning in 1904. In his highly successful production of *The Great Divide*, which ran from 1906 to 1909 in New York and on tour

and had a London production in 1909, Crews scored with critics and public. The *Chicago Record* reviewer said she gave "a deliciously piquant sketch of a satirical Puritan minx with a touch of the devil in her—she has some of [the author's] best lines" (17 Dec. 1907). In these years Crews and Miller began a close association that would last until his death in 1926, though she did not act exclusively in his productions.

With her round face and roly-poly body, Crews was not ideally suited physically to play dramatic leads, though Miller sometimes cast her in such parts. Her own preference was for comedy roles, and she proved to have few peers as a comedienne. Her next great success was in *Her Husband's Wife* (1910), playing the role of a sweet, fluttery hypochondriac convinced (completely in error) that she will die young, who sets out to choose her husband's next spouse. *Vogue*'s reviewer declared that she "bore away the honors of an admirable performance, and established herself in the front rank of present-day comediennes . . . past the shaft of criticism" (15 June 1910). Critic Walter Prichard Eaton pointed out the artistry of her comic acting in the smallest details, such as "the trick of talking just after she has taken a dose of medicine in such a way as to suggest a puckery taste" ("Practice and the Young Player").

After several subsequent plays had failed to please the public and a venture into Shakespearean comedy with John Drew in *Much Ado about Nothing* (1913), Crews had another major success in *The Phantom Rival* (1914) playing a wife who daydreams about a former suitor as several kinds of hero, only to bump up against reality when the man visits her husband. The reviewer for the *New York Times* wrote that Crews "establishes herself more firmly than ever as a comedienne of rare gifts. The most delicate humor of the comedy finds fine and full expression in her performance which is superb from first to last" (7 Oct. 1914).

In 1915 Crews made a few silent films for Famous Players–Lasky without notable success, then returned to stage work. For the next few years she played comedy roles in New York and on tour, including Mistress Page to Sir Herbert Beerbohm Tree's Falstaff in *The Merry Wives of Windsor* (1916). Her range as an actress was perhaps too limited to make her a true star. Able to choose her parts, she typecast herself as a dithery, fluttery wife in one play after another. She positively refused to consider parts that would have her portray "evil women or crying women or fallen women," she told an interviewer (*Theatre Magazine*, Dec. 1921).

Crews's next two outstanding portrayals were both comic wives, in *Mr. Pim Passes By* (1921) and *Hay Fever* (1925). A variation of the role in the latter play was that the wife was a famous actress, apt to go into past stage characters in moments of family crisis. The *New York Times* commented, "In the part of Mrs. Bliss, Miss Crews made these changes in tempo skillfully, with the most absurd and amusing results. She simpered, smirked, looked arch, looked noble, all by turns, and came in and out of her former stage parts without leaving a wrinkle in the general pattern of her performance" (5 Oct. 1925).

Only in *The Silver Cord* (1926) did Crews assume a serious role, that of a smotheringly possessive mother whose "devotion" to her sons has a baleful effect on their lives and loves. Even here, critics said, she slipped at times into comedy mannerisms. Crews repeated the role in a motion picture version in 1933. Also in 1933 she played a "juggernaut aunt," a character role, on the New York stage, in *Her Master's Voice*. "Miss Crews has long been the mistress of this style of comedy," said the *New York Times* (24 Oct. 1933). She appeared in a screen version of the play in 1936.

For the most part, the 1930s saw Crews in motion pictures. She had been brought to Hollywood as a dramatic coach for Norma Talmadge in 1929, when many silent screen stars were trying to master the new art of talking pictures. That same year she provided coaching for Gloria Swanson in *The Trespasser* with such success that the Pathe studio signed Crews to a contract, calling her an "associate producer." Her job was to suggest suitable dramatic vehicles for the studio's female stars and to coach them in their roles. Her contract ended in 1933.

Now in her fifties and never married, Crews was content to live comfortably in Beverly Hills and visit New York between character roles in films. Two notable screen performances were as the raucous Prudence in *Camille* (1937) and the clairvoyant Madame Zuleika in *Idiot's Delight* (1939). The great comic performance of her film career came in *Gone with the Wind* (1939), in which she played the swooning Aunt Pittypat. Her final film role was in *One Foot in Heaven* (1941). She joined the cast of the long-running stage farce *Arsenic and Old Lace* in 1942, playing one of the two sweetly murderous old ladies of the play, for a final Broadway appearance. A kidney ailment forced her to leave the cast in October of that year, and she died a month later in New York City.

On stage or on screen, Crews was inimitable in her particular comedy persona of the scatterbrained innocent with fluttering hands, quivering voice, and looks of wide-eyed surprise. William Lindesmith has noted that just as Clark Gable was considered the only choice to play Rhett Butler in *Gone with the Wind*, "Crews was virtually the only serious candidate for the role of Pittypat Hamilton." Offstage, Crews was highly respected in her profession as a capable, dependable character comedienne. Walter Prichard Eaton had written in 1913: "All the niceties of high comedy suggestion—the right emphasis, the proper pause, the quick transition of mood, the stabbing dart of seriousness or sincerity, the shimmer of varying moods over a ground pattern of laughter, are at Miss Crews's command" ("Carrying on the Torch"). The same could be said of her all the way to her final performance three decades later.

• Materials on the life and career of Crews are in the Billy Rose Theatre Collection, New York Public Library for the Performing Arts, Lincoln Center. A biographical sketch by

William Lindesmith is in *Notable Women in the American Theatre*. Stage and talking film appearances to early 1939 are listed in *Who Was Who in the Theatre, 1912–1976*, though the list omits her first appearance in *Her Husband's Wife* at the Garrick Theatre, New York City, 9 May 1910. Her stage artistry is discussed by Walter Prichard Eaton in "Practice and the Young Player," *American Magazine*, Sept. 1910, and "Carrying on the Torch," *American Magazine*, Oct. 1913. For her self-limitation in choosing roles, see Carol Bird, "Scarlet Roles Objectionable to Women," *Theatre Magazine*, Dec. 1921. Her work as a dramatic coach for film actresses is discussed in Harry Lang, "Glory by Proxy," *Photoplay*, June 1930. Portraits and production photographs are in Daniel C. Blum, *A Pictorial History of the American Theatre* (1960) and *A Pictorial History of the Talkies* (1968). Obituaries are in the *New York Times* and *New York Herald Tribune*, both 14 Nov. 1942, and in *Variety*, 18 Nov. 1942.

WILLIAM STEPHENSON

CRILE, George Washington (11 Nov. 1864–7 Jan. 1943), surgeon and medical researcher, was born in Chili, Ohio, the son of Michael Crile and Margaret Dietz, farmers. He received his early education at the Crawford Township public schools and earned an A.B. (1885) and an A.M. (1888) from Northwestern Ohio Normal School (later Ohio Northern University). While in college he taught school in Coon's Nest, Ohio, for two years before becoming principal of the Plainfield (Ohio) School.

In 1886 Crile enrolled at the University of Wooster Medical School in Cleveland, Ohio (later merged with Western Reserve University School of Medicine), where he paid a physician-preceptor for the privilege of reading his medical books. He earned his M.D. in 1887 and served his internship at University Hospital of Cleveland the following year. Crile then became an assistant to Dr. Frank Weed, dean of Wooster Medical School, who had an active private practice specializing in treating injuries from industrial and railroad accidents and burns from tenement fires. Following Weed's sudden death in 1891, Crile and fellow assistant Frank Bunts bought Weed's practice and were later joined by Crile's cousin, William Lower.

Crile joined the Wooster staff as a lecturer and demonstrator of histology (1889–1890), professor of physiology (1890–1893), and professor of principles and practice of surgery (1893–1900). In 1900 he married Grace McBride; they would have four children. That same year he became clinical professor of surgery at Western Reserve University School of Medicine, and he was professor of surgery from 1911 to 1924. He also served on the surgical staffs at St. Alexis, Lutheran, and Lakeside hospitals. In 1921 Drs. Crile, Bunts, Lower, and John Phillips formed the Cleveland Clinic Foundation, and in 1924 they opened the Cleveland Clinic, a group medical practice modeled after the Mayo brothers' practice in Rochester, Minnesota.

Crile's service as a lieutenant and brigade surgeon with the U.S. Army Medical Corps in Puerto Rico and Cuba during the Spanish-American War resulted in a longstanding interest in military surgery. During World War I he served as surgical director of the

Western Reserve Medical Unit, an innovative civilian group hospital system designed by Crile, stationed at the American Ambulance Hospital in Neuilly, France, in 1915 and operated by the American Red Cross. Known as the Lakeside Unit, it was the first American forces hospital unit ordered to active duty in France.

Commissioned as a major in the army's medical reserve corps, Crile served as director in chief of the professional staff until May 1918, when he became senior consultant in surgical research for the American Expeditionary Forces, serving the AEF until January 1919. He was promoted to lieutenant colonel in June 1918 and colonel in November, and he was awarded the U.S. Distinguished Service Medal in 1919. He stressed the importance of safe anesthesia, wide debridement, adequate drainage for wounds, and whole blood transfusions. Working in the hospitals, he experimented with various means of resuscitating patients, including blood transfusions and the administration of oxygen under pressure for gas casualties.

Crile was an innovator in the field of surgery and pioneered in researching the effects of physiology and emotional factors on successful surgery. At the time when he started practicing surgery was still relatively unsophisticated. Anesthesia was crude and infection rates for surgical wounds were just starting to decline as surgeons began adopting aseptic surgical techniques.

Early on Crile became interested in the surgery of the head, neck, and respiratory system. He was a pioneer in the surgery of the endocrine system, with emphasis on the surgical treatment of the thyroid and parathyroid glands. He performed one of the earliest laryngectomies and was the first to recognize the need to excise the lymphatic gland-bearing tissues in treating cancers of the head and neck.

In 1888, while serving as an intern at University Hospital, Crile witnessed the death of a fellow student, William Lyndman, caused by the onset of shock following surgery. This experience motivated Crile to begin researching the causative factors of shock and its treatment. He made trips to Europe in 1892 and 1895 to study special problems of shock and performed extensive experiments on laboratory animals to observe the effects of physical stress, hemorrhage, and anesthesia in the onset of shock. His first monograph on shock (1897) was an important early attempt to identify its nature, causes, and treatment.

Crile's continued work on shock and its related problems in surgery resulted in numerous advanced conclusions that were insufficiently appreciated at the time. He was among the first to recognize the need to monitor a patient's blood pressure during surgery; that hemorrhaging was only one of many variables in shock; and that prevention of shock was of greater importance than treatment. As a result he promoted atraumatic and bloodless surgery combined with safe anesthesia. To that end he developed a pressure suit for clinical use that restored blood to the circulation system through the application of external pressure.

In 1903 Crile originated the nerve block system of anesthesia that made it possible to use local anesthesia to shut off the operated area from the brain, thus confining trauma and shock and protecting the brain and nervous system as a whole. In 1908 he organized the first formal school of anesthesiology at Lakeside Hospital. By 1905 he had demonstrated that respiration could be restored to apparently dead patients by the administration of adrenaline and that year made the first recorded direct donor-to-patient blood transfusion.

A man of tremendous curiosity and imagination, Crile's wide-ranging interests led him into many different areas of medicine and to numerous controversial concepts, such as the radio-electric theory of life that he championed during his later years. Most of his contributions to medicine came through his pioneering research in the field of surgical physiology, which helped to transform the practice of surgery from its primitive and rudimentary origins into an applied scientific discipline. Crile died in Cleveland.

• The bulk of Crile's papers are at the Western Reserve Historical Society, on seventy-one reels of microfilm and in several other manuscript collections. In addition to the records relating to the founding and early operation of the Cleveland Clinic, the Cleveland Clinic Archives has approximately eighty linear feet of Crile family papers. The records of the Lakeside Unit during World War I are at the University Hospitals of Cleveland Archives. The best source of information on Crile's personal life is *George Crile: An Autobiography* (2 vols., 1947), edited by his wife, Grace Crile, who also provides sidelights to her husband's memoirs. A review of Crile's work and his contributions to medical science is Floyd Loop, "Dr. George W. Crile: The Father of Physiologic Surgery," *Cleveland Clinic Journal of Medicine* (Jan.–Feb. 1993), pp. 75–80. Peter C. English, *Shock, Physiological Surgery, and George Washington Crile: Medical Innovation in the Progressive Era* (1980), looks at Crile's contributions to medical research in the context of his time. Obituaries are in the *Cleveland Press* and *Cleveland Plain Dealer*, both 8 Jan. 1943.

WILLIAM BECKER

CRISLER, Fritz (12 Jan. 1899–19 Aug. 1982), football coach and athletic administrator, was born Herbert Orin Crisler outside Earlville, Illinois, the son of Albert Crisler, a farmer, and Catherine Thompson. Since Crisler was small in stature, he did not play football at Mendota High School. In 1917 he was admitted to the University of Chicago with an academic scholarship. Crisler's college sports career came about accidentally. While walking along the sidelines, he collided with Amos Alonzo Stagg, Chicago's fabled football coach from 1892 to 1932. Coach Stagg suggested that Crisler come out for the team. A long and close relationship between coach and player began, as Stagg challenged Crisler to improve his skills as an athlete.

World War I interrupted Crisler's education when he enlisted and was sent to infantry officers' candidate school at Camp MacArthur in Waco, Texas. However, the war ended before he saw action, and he returned to the University of Chicago in early 1920. His army training, one season of physical conditioning in college football, and his determination to prove himself to Coach Stagg all propelled him to a remarkable career in his three remaining college years. He won nine varsity letters, three each in football, basketball, and baseball. As an end, Crisler was an all-Western Conference selection and a third team All-America in 1921. The 1921 Chicago team had a 6–1 won-lost record, losing only to Ohio State. Crisler pitched for the baseball team, which toured Japan in 1920, and was offered a major league contract with the Chicago White Sox.

After his graduation in 1922 with a degree in psychology, he dropped out of medical school for financial reasons. In 1923 he married Dorothy Adams; the couple had one child. Crisler then served as an assistant coach under Coach Stagg for eight years. In 1930–1931 he was head football coach and athletic director at the University of Minnesota, but in 1932 he left to become head coach at Princeton University, the first non-Princeton graduate to hold that position. Crisler quickly turned around a losing program and made Princeton a national powerhouse. In his six years there, his teams won 35, lost 9, and tied five. His 1933 and 1935 teams were unbeaten, giving up a combined total of only 40 points, and the 1934 team lost only to Yale by a touchdown.

Crisler's success at Princeton brought him to the attention of the University of Michigan athletic department. From 1934 through 1937 the once-mighty Michigan teams had suffered through the worst seasons in their history. Convinced he could reverse Michigan's fortunes, Crisler was invited to name his own terms for the position. They included a free hand in selecting assistant coaches, an annual salary of $15,000, and promotion to athletic director when Fielding H. Yost retired in 1941. Michigan accepted Crisler's terms, and he came to Ann Arbor to begin his reclamation project in 1938. His team that season was 6–1–1. During ten seasons as head coach, his teams featured explosive offenses and stingy defenses and compiled a 71–16–3 record. The culmination of Crisler's coaching career came in 1947, when his team went undefeated, scored better than seven points to its opponents' one, and beat Southern California in the Rose Bowl, 49–0. Although undefeated Notre Dame had been rated the top team in the nation at the end of the regular season and had beaten Southern California 32–0, the Associated Press held a supplementary poll after the bowl games and ranked Michigan first.

As a coach, Crisler relied on a modernized single-wing offense that featured careful execution and precision timing, effective deception, and a multiplicity of offensive formation and plays. This system produced such All-America players as Tom Harmon, Bob Westfall, Bill Daley, and Bob Chappuis. Crisler also devised and developed the two-platoon system after 1945, using separate squads for offense and defense. His overall coaching record was an outstanding 116–32–9. In his influential chairing role of the National Collegiate Athletic Association's Football Rules Committee he helped to bring about the two-point conversion after touchdowns (1958), intended partly to reduce the number of tie games, and the widening of the goalposts (1959), which brought added excitement and scoring to the college game.

In March 1948 at the height of his success, Crisler resigned as head coach and directed his energies and organizational acumen toward his role as Michigan's athletic director. During his twenty-seven years in that position he developed one of the nation's most successful intercollegiate athletic programs, with outstanding physical facilities and alumni support. He also was a full professor and head of the physical education department. In his multiple roles he obtained finances for new sports facilities, directed to stadium expansions, and saw to the construction of an all-events building that was named the Crisler Arena. At the national level he was a persuasive proponent of rules changes to increase the sport's safety, such as improvement of the helmet and the 1964 rule that made head-spearing a personal foul. His coaching clinics attracted participants from throughout the state and indirectly served as an effective means of recruitment. Convinced of the social and personal values of competitive sports, he was committed to integrity and honesty in recruiting and supporting athletes within NCAA rules.

He retired in 1968 after thirty years at Michigan. He died in Ann Arbor, recognized as one of the most important individuals who influenced and directed the development of college football.

• Crisler's papers, covering 1925 to 1978, are located in the Michigan Historical Collections at the Bentley Historical Library, University of Michigan. Biographical information can be found in *Current Biography* (1948); Stanley Frank, "Football's Supersalesman," *Saturday Evening Post*, 27 Oct. 1945; and Gerald Holland, "The Man Who Changed Football," *Sports Illustrated*, 3 Feb. 1964. Information on his coaching career from 1922 through 1947 is available in Tim Cohane, *Great College Football Coaches of the Twenties and Thirties* (1973); Allison Danzig, *The History of American Football: Its Great Teams, Players, and Coaches* (1956); Mervin D. Hyman and Gordon S. White, Jr., *Big Ten Footfall: Its Life and Times, Great Coaches, Players, and Games* (1977); Tom Perrin, *Football: A College History* (1987); and Will Perry, *The Wolverines: A Story of Michigan Football* (1974). Articles on Crisler in the *Detroit News*, 21, 22, and 23 Aug. 1982, are also a valuable source of information. An obituary appeared in the *New York Times*, 21 Aug. 1982.

DOUGLAS A. NOVERR

CRISP, Charles Frederick (29 Jan. 1845–23 Oct. 1896), Speaker of the U.S. House of Representatives, was born in Sheffield, England, the son of William Crisp and Elizabeth (maiden name unknown), Shakespearean actors. His parents were American citizens, but his mother was visiting England when Crisp was born, which made him ineligible to run for vice president or president. Charles was seven months old when he and his mother returned to the United States. The family settled in Savannah, Georgia, where Charles was educated in the public school system.

Only sixteen when the Civil War erupted, Crisp volunteered in the tenth Virginia Infantry, Company K, and was soon made a lieutenant. He was captured on 12 May 1864 at the battle of Spottsylvania and spent the remainder of the war as a Federal prisoner. He was incarcerated at Fort Delaware, moved to Morris Island, then to Fort Pulaski, and finally returned to Fort Delaware. He was allowed to study law during his last few months as a prisoner.

Crisp returned to Georgia after the war. In 1866 he passed the bar and opened a practice in Ellaville. In 1867 he married Clara Belle Burton; they had two sons and two daughters. Crisp became politically active in the resistance to the rule of African-American Republicans during Reconstruction. He was appointed solicitor general of the South West Judicial Circuit in 1872 and judge of the superior court in 1877. In 1882 he ran for the U.S. Congress in the Third Georgia District and was elected.

Crisp served in Congress from the Forty-eighth Congress, 1883, until his death. He held several important committee assignments, including Pacific Railroads, Commerce, Manufactures, and Ordinance and Gunnery. He was also the chair of the Committee on Elections. The Interstate Commerce Act of 1887 was among the most important measures that Crisp helped to guide through Congress. The law sought to curb abuses in the railroad industry by forbidding rebates to favored customers, charges that unreasonably discriminated between places, and collusive pooling between competing lines. In response to protests at home, Crisp asserted that this measure would not result in the mixing of races but would provide for equal services.

Crisp increasingly found himself opposing the positions of the Republican Speaker of the House, Thomas Reed, who favored high protective tariffs and the gold standard. Crisp called for tariff reduction and favored the free coinage of silver. An early contention centered around Reed's changes in the House rules, which Reed pushed through the Fifty-first Congress as a method of reducing inefficiency and eliminating unnecessary delays. Throughout the debates on Reed's changes, Crisp was an active and vocal opponent. Especially controversial was Reed's practice of including in quorum any member who was present but did not offer a vocal response to the roll call.

Crisp was elected Speaker in 1891, when the Democrats became the majority party. Opposed by Roger Mills and William Springer, Crisp received his party's nomination for Speaker only by the slimmest of margins on the thirtieth ballot, even though southern Democrats constituted a significant percentage of the congressional Democrats. Southern Democrats subsequently became the majority faction within the party, and Crisp won reelection as Speaker handily, serving until 1895.

Democrats and Republicans engaged in a heated partisan war throughout Crisp's years in Congress. The majority in the House changed hands between the two parties often, and the Speaker increasingly became more of a leader of the majority party than a leader of the entire House of Representatives. Crisp quickly acted to repeal the rules adopted under Reed's Speakership.

Reed, now the leader of the minority Republicans, continued to clash frequently with Crisp. In 1892, when Reed made a speech supporting the rates of the McKinley Tariff Act of 1890, Crisp's response was to turn the chair over to another member and vociferously condemn the Republican tariff. Democrats linked protectionist tariffs, which assessed additional duties on raw goods and materials such as steel, glass, sugar, and cotton, to high consumer prices and corporate monopolies and called for their reduction. Crisp stated, "No amount of juggling, no amount of sophistry, no amount of theory will prevent them from understanding really what this Protective system is; that its effect is to take from one class to give to another, to take from the mass to give to a class; and when they do understand it they will speedily repudiate its authors" ("Protection," p. 171).

The silver issue rose to the forefront of national politics while Crisp was Speaker. Silver prices had been on a steady decline, and Congress sought to end the fall with the Bland-Allison Act of 1878 and the Sherman Silver Purchase Act of 1890. The cry for bimetallism (the use of both gold and silver as a monetary standard) was associated with a call for higher prices on agricultural goods. The Sherman Silver Purchase Act was repealed in 1893 while Crisp was Speaker. Many members feared that act would end the gold standard and felt that it had an adverse effect on the gold reserve. Crisp supported the repeal of the act, though he had hoped for the inclusion of a measure that would provide for the unlimited coinage of silver. In the end the repeal was signed without the coinage measure.

In 1894 Crisp was offered an appointment to fill an unexpired Senate seat, which he turned down, feeling obligated to fulfill his duties in the House. He became minority leader when the Republicans regained the majority in the Fifty-fourth Congress. His old adversary Reed once again became Speaker and soon reimposed the House rules of his previous leadership.

Crisp decided to run for the Senate in 1896 using the free coinage of silver as his campaign issue. That summer a series of debates were held on the issue between Crisp and his opponent, Hoke Smith, secretary of the interior for President Grover Cleveland, and Crisp seemed assured an easy victory. However, a heart attack unexpectedly took his life in Atlanta. In his time of fierce partisan conflicts between the Democrats and Republicans, Crisp was widely regarded as an able debater and a more than adequate match for his Republican opponents.

• No collection of Crisp's manuscripts exists. Crisp published two articles, "Protection: A Help to Few, a Hindrance to Many," *American Journal of Politics* 1 (Aug. 1892): 160–71, and "How Congress Votes Money: A Rejoinder," *North American Review* 162 (Jan. 1896): 14–20. A thorough biography of Crisp is Preston St. Clair Malone, "The Political Career of Charles F. Crisp" (Ph.D. diss., Univ. of Georgia, 1962). S. Walter Martin, "Charles F. Crisp, Speaker of the House," *Georgia Review*, Summer 1954, pp. 167–77, contains important information about Crisp as a young man, especially his Civil War career. Donald Kennon, *The Speakers of the U.S. House of Representatives: A Bibliography* (1985), includes a brief overview on Crisp's life and lists all of his writings as well as sources about him. Lucian Lamar Knight, *Reminiscences of Famous Georgians* (1908), also provides a good overview of Crisp's life and political career. Ronald Peters's works, *The Speaker Leadership in the U.S. House of Representatives* (1994) and *The American Speakership* (1990), help place Crisp's tenure as Speaker in a larger historical context.

LAURA RUNDELL

CRISS, Sonny (23 Oct. 1927–19 Nov. 1977), jazz alto saxophonist, was born William Criss in Memphis, Tennessee, the son of Lucy B.; her maiden name and her husband's name are unknown. Criss began playing saxophone at age eleven. In 1942 his family moved to Los Angeles, where he attended Jefferson High School and performed with fellow students Hampton Hawes, a pianist, and Cecil (later known as "Big Jay") McNeely, a tenor saxophonist. Criss studied music with Samuel Browne, who also taught trumpeter Art Farmer and tenor saxophonist Dexter Gordon. He transferred to the Polytechnic High School, again with Hawes, and while in school worked with the pianist in a quartet at the Last Word, a nightclub. Criss may have married in the mid-1940s. Details are unknown, apart from his mention of a son who returned from service in Vietnam around 1966.

Around 1945 Criss first toured, going to Chicago to play with rhythm-and-blues drummer Johnny Otis's band. From February to March 1946 he sat in with alto saxophonist Charlie Parker's quintet, which included Miles Davis, at Club Finale, and he was also a member, along with Parker and tenor saxophonist Teddy Edwards, of trumpeter Howard McGhee's band at the same club from March through May 1946, at Billy Berg's Swing Club early in July, and then at the Hi-De-Ho Club.

Criss joined trumpeter Al Killian's band at Billy Berg's in April 1947. His early recordings include solos on "Groovin' High" and "Hot House," made as a member of McGhee's All Stars at Gene Norman's Just Jazz concert in Pasadena on 29 April 1947, and "The Hunt," "Bopera," "Jeronimo," and "Bop after Hours," as a member of the Bopland Boys, a nine-piece group including tenor saxophonist Wardell Gray, McGhee, Gordon, and Hawes, performing at a Hollywood Jazz Concert on 6 July 1947. During this period Criss toured with Killian to Portland, Oregon, Seattle, and San Francisco before returning to Los Angeles, where the group recorded with singer Billy Eckstine.

Criss left Killian's band early in 1948. He began rehearsing with trumpeter Gerald Wilson's orchestra in autumn 1948 but soon left when the opportunity arose to tour nationally with Jazz at the Philharmonic from November 1948 through June 1949; during breaks

from this affiliation, Criss concurrently toured the East Coast from New York to Miami Beach in a small group with tenor saxophonist Flip Phillips, a long-term member of Jazz at the Philharmonic. In mid-June 1949 he worked with Phillips in Chicago.

Returning to the West Coast, Criss recorded in Los Angeles as the leader of a quartet including Hawes in September 1949. In the fall he joined Edwards, Gordon, and Hawes as a member of the house band at Bop City in San Francisco, and through the latter part of 1949 he performed at the Lighthouse in Hermosa Beach, California, in a quintet with Edwards, Hawes, bassist Howard Rumsey, and drummer Larry Bunker. He was one of Gray's Los Angeles All Stars at the Hula-Hut Club in Los Angeles in August 1950.

In association with Jazz at the Philharmonic, Criss toured nationally from 1950 to 1951 in a distinguished septet comprising trumpeter Joe Newman, trombonist Benny Green, saxophonists Criss and Eddie "Lock-jaw" Davis, pianist Bobby Tucker, bassist Tommy Potter, and drummer Kenny Clarke. The septet accompanied Eckstine but also performed on its own, and one such performance was recorded in concert on 12 October 1951. An almost maniacally inspired Criss dominates this session, released posthumously as *Intermission Riff* under his own name, on the strength of his playing.

Early in 1952 Criss was among a rotating pool of musicians who played with baritone saxophonist Gerry Mulligan on Monday nights at the Haig club on Wilshire Boulevard. That summer he was heard at the Trade Wind Club in Inglewood, California; surviving recordings also include Parker, trumpeter Chet Baker, and pianist Al Haig. Severely impaired by alcoholism, Criss struggled for work over the next few years, at times performing in striptease houses. After joining Stan Kenton's Jazz Showcase package tour in 1955 (not as a member of Kenton's band), he toured with drummer Buddy Rich on and off for five years. Rich's quintet, which at times included pianist Wynton Kelly or Kenny Drew, often worked in resort areas, including Miami Beach.

Late in 1959 or early the next year Criss returned to Los Angeles. He made a guest appearance with Hawes's trio on an episode of the "Jazz on Stage" television series, c. 1960. In 1961 he failed to find any work, and the following year he traveled to Europe. As a fresh face on the European jazz scene, Criss performed with Clarke in the film *Le glaive et la balance* (1962) and with pianist Henri Renaud at the Trois Mailletz nightclub in Paris (1963), but by 1964 he was again struggling for work. These problems continued early in 1965 with his return to Los Angeles, where his scant earnings came from occasional performances at Shelly's Manne-Hole and Redd Foxx's club, and early in 1966, at Marty's nightclub.

Criss's career moved forward in 1966 when he signed a contract with Prestige Records. His first album, *This Is Criss!*, was recorded in October 1966 and helped him secure engagements in New York at the Village Vanguard and the Museum of Modern Art.

Further albums included *Up, up and Away* from 1967 and *Sonny's Dream (New Birth of the Cool)* from 1968, and in the latter year he performed at the Newport Jazz Festival. His contract with Prestige was abruptly cancelled when he showed up drunk for his eighth session in 1969.

From 1970 through 1974 Criss was devoted to community service, giving concerts for schoolchildren at the Hollywood Bowl and working as an alcohol rehabilitation counselor. He also toured Europe in 1973 and 1974, and he began to make further recordings, including the albums *Crisscraft*, *Saturday Morning*, and *Out of Nowhere*, all from 1975. Shortly before a scheduled performance in Tokyo, he committed suicide with a gun at his home in Los Angeles. Given his recent success, after a career impeded by alcohol and other personal problems and after decades of struggle for opportunities to perform, this action seemed inexplicable. Eleven years later Criss's mother revealed that he had been suffering from stomach cancer but told no one and kept playing until finally he could no longer face the pain.

Writer Thomas Owens called Criss "another of Parker's disciples," noting that the saxophonist borrowed certain melodic phrases from Parker but had a sweeter tone and a "fast and automatically applied vibrato [that] was more typical of swing than of bebop. . . . The chief source of tension in his playing was his disconcerting unconcern for, or perhaps inability to keep track of, the meter. . . . Eventually, however, he solved his rhythmic and harmonic problems and developed into an excellent soloist" (pp. 48–50). Unlike many who received Parker's technically minded musical message, Criss also shared Parker's deep feeling for blues phrases, which he inserted into any manner of tune. The ballad "Sweet Lorraine" on his album *At the Crossroads* (1959) provides a particularly striking example. Within the erudite context of the bop tradition, he delivered these blues formulas in a somewhat rawer form than did Parker himself. On mature recordings from the mid-1960s and mid-1970s, Criss was most creative when improvising at a leisurely pace, as for example in his renditions of "Black Coffee" on *This Is Criss!*, "Willow Weep for Me" on *Up, Up, and Away*, and "Blues in My Heart" on *Crisscraft*.

• Interviews and surveys are by Harvey Siders, "One Horn Man," *Down Beat*, 19 May 1966, pp. 27–29; Bob Porter and Mark Gardner, "The Californian Cats: Sonny Criss," *Jazz Monthly*, no. 158 (Apr. 1968): 7–10, and no. 159 (May 1968): 6–8; Howard Mandel, "Up from the Underground," *Down Beat*, 10 March 1977, pp. 20, 40–41, 48; J. Detro, "Sonny Criss Fund Set: Hard Truth Revealed by Sonny's Mother," *Jazz Times*, Aug. 1988, p. 6; and Ted Gioia, *West Coast Jazz: Modern Jazz in California, 1945–1960* (1992), pp. 121–29. For a detailed account of Criss's career from 1943 to 1953 see Dieter Salemann et al., *Sonny Criss: Solography, Discographical Informations [sic], Band Routes, Engagements in Chronological Order* (1987). See also Robert Gordon, *Jazz West Coast: the Los Angeles Jazz Scene of the 1950s* (1986). For musical analysis, see Thomas Owens, *Bebop: The Music and Its Players* (1995). Gardner prepared a catalog of recordings,

"Sonny Criss Discography," *Discographical Forum*, no. 16 (Jan. 1970): 9–12; no. 17 (March 1970): 3–6; no. 18 (May 1970): 3–4, 19–20; and no. 21 (Nov. 1970): 19. Obituaries are in the *Los Angeles Times*, 20 Nov. 1977, *New York Times*, 21 Nov. 1977, *Down Beat*, 26 Jan. 1978, p. 10, and *Jazz Journal International* 31 (Jan.–Feb. 1978): 49.

BARRY KERNFELD

CRITTENDEN, George Bibb (20 Mar. 1812–27 Nov. 1880), soldier, was born in Russellville, Kentucky, the son of John Jordan Crittenden, a statesman, and Sarah Lee. Although growing up in near-frontier conditions, he received a good education. He was an apt pupil, and his tutor, George Clark, praised him to his father in 1827. Securing admission to the U.S. Military Academy, Crittenden graduated in 1832, served as brevet second lieutenant in the Black Hawk War, then was relegated to garrison duty in Georgia and Alabama. Tiring of military routine, he resigned from the army on 30 April 1833 to take up the study of law, first with his father and later at Transylvania University. He also grew bored with the practice of law and in 1842 volunteered for service with Colonel William S. Fisher's Texas forces in a border war with Mexico. Crittenden and his company were captured the following year at Meir, taken to Mexico City, and confined in a dirty prison. After a failed escape attempt, he and his fellows were compelled to draw lots to determine who would be shot in retaliation. Luckily, Crittenden drew two favorable beans, thus saving himself and a friend who had a family. He and his surviving comrades were released almost a year later, owing to the intervention of his father, who was a U.S. senator; American secretary of state Daniel Webster; and Waddy Thompson, U.S. minister to Mexico.

At the commencement of the Mexican War in 1846, Crittenden again volunteered for military service as captain of a company of mounted riflemen. He joined General Winfield Scott's expedition against Mexico City in the following year. Distinguishing himself in the battles of Contreras and Churubusco, he was brevetted major and was one of the first Americans to enter the Mexican capital. On 15 April 1848 he was appointed major in the regular army but fell into difficulties because of his drinking and was court-martialed and suspended. His father, now governor of Kentucky, once again intervened, asking former Senate colleagues, particularly Thomas Hart Benton (1782–1858), to help his son. In 1849, with the assistance of these high-placed friends, Crittenden's court-martial was declared illegal, and he was reinstated. For a time, he flirted with the idea of migrating to California but finally retained his commission and, over the next few years, served in various posts on the frontier. He was promoted to lieutenant colonel on 30 December 1856. Five years later, when the Civil War broke out, he was doing duty in the territory of New Mexico.

On 10 June 1861, despite his father's wishes, Crittenden resigned his Federal commission and joined the Confederate army with the rank of brigadier general. Given command at Knoxville, Tennessee, he was quickly promoted to major general and in November 1861 was ordered by President Jefferson Davis to supersede General Felix Zollicoffer as commander of Confederate forces in southeastern Kentucky. In mid-January 1862 he was entrenched in a camp at Beech Grove, on the north bank of the Cumberland River, with an army of 4,000 men, when he learned that Union general George H. Thomas was marching in his direction with 7,000 poorly trained soldiers. On the evening of the 18th, Crittenden decided to attack the approaching enemy and thus ordered his army to advance southward across the Cumberland River. The following morning the Confederates attempted to surprise Thomas's troops at Fishing Creek. In the ensuing battle of Mill Springs, or Logan's Crossroads, which lasted about three hours, both commanders managed to get about 4,000 soldiers into the fight. When General Zollicoffer was killed, Crittenden's men lost heart, and the Confederate left was broken. Crittenden was compelled to abandon his artillery and retreat across the Cumberland. Halting only temporarily in his fortified camp at Beech Grove, he quickly proceeded on to Gainesboro, Tennessee. In early February he rested his army at Camp Fogg, then upon orders from General Albert Sidney Johnston, he finally marched to Murfreesboro.

Crittenden's military reputation was ruined by his defeat at Mill Springs. Southern newspapers, referring to the battle as "Crittenden's gross blunder," accused the general of being drunk at the time, and even his father, who viewed him as something of a black sheep in the family, complained about his son's "occasional habit of intemperance" (Myers, pp. 112–23). Some editorial writers went so far as to charge Crittenden with cowardice and treason. Hence, he was arrested and tried by a military court of inquiry; but he was finally released, and the matter was dropped. His ability to command troops irrevocably impaired, he resigned his commission in October 1862, joined the staff of General John Stuart Williams as a volunteer, and served the remainder of the war as a trusted adviser of that officer.

After the war Crittenden lived in Frankfort, Kentucky. In 1867 he was appointed by the legislature as state librarian and was annually reelected to that post until 1874. Shortly before his death, he wrote Davis a letter, attributing his loss of the battle of Mill Springs to "the inferiority of our arms and the untimely fall of General Zollicoffer." He insisted that the battle was "a necessity" but would not defend his own handling of it. On that point, he said wryly, he had "nothing further to say" (Myers, p. 116). Never married, he died in Danville.

• Important information about Crittenden is in the John Jordan Crittenden Papers, Library of Congress. For a guide, see *Calendar of the Papers of John Jordan Crittenden* (1913). Crittenden's Civil War correspondence is in *The War of the Rebellion: A Compilation of the Official Records of the Union and Confederate Armies*, ser. 1, vols. 4–52, ser. 2, vol. 1, ser. 4, vol. 1 (128 vols., 1880–1901). Information on his life is in Ann Mary Butler Coleman, *The Life of John J. Crittenden,*

with Selections from His Correspondence and Speeches (1871); Richard H. Collins, *History of Kentucky*, vol. 1 (1874); and Albert D. Kirwan, *John J. Crittenden: The Struggle for the Union* (1962). For his role in the Texas border wars, see Paul Horgan, *Great River: The Rio Grande in North American History*, vol. 2 (1954). His Civil War service is surveyed in R. M. Kelly, "Holding Kentucky for the Union," in *Battles and Leaders of the Civil War*, vol. 1, ed. Robert Underwood Johnson and Clarence Clough Buel (1884–1887); R. Gerald McMurtry, "Zollicoffer and the Battle of Mill Springs," *Filson Club History Quarterly* 29 (1955): 303–19; Raymond E. Myers, *The Zollie Tree* (1964); Lowell H. Harrison, *The Civil War in Kentucky* (1975); and C. David Dalton, "Zollicoffer, Crittenden, and the Mill Springs Campaign," *Filson Club History Quarterly* 60 (1986): 463–71.

PAUL DAVID NELSON

CRITTENDEN, John Jordan (10 Sept. 1786–26 July 1863), U.S. senator, U.S. attorney general, and governor of Kentucky, was born in Woodford County, Kentucky, the son of John Crittenden, a landholder, and Judith Harris. His father served with Morgan's Riflemen and later with General George Rogers Clark during the Revolution, before moving to a portion of his vast land holdings near Versailles, Kentucky. Crittenden attended nearby Pisgah Academy and then an area boarding school before studying law in Lexington, Kentucky, under George M. Bibb, a family friend.

To broaden his knowledge, Crittenden enrolled at Washington Academy (now Washington and Lee University) in Lexington, Virginia, and later at the College of William and Mary, where he was schooled in a Jeffersonian curriculum that stressed Enlightenment philosophers and Republican thought; he graduated in 1807. After briefly practicing law at home in Woodford County, Crittenden moved to the important town of Russellville, the county seat of Logan County, in the southwestern part of the state. An acquaintanceship with Ninian Edwards there led to Crittenden's appointment as attorney general of Illinois Territory under Edwards, who been named governor of the territory in 1809. Back in Logan County in 1811, Crittenden was elected to the first of six consecutive terms in the state legislature. That year he married Sarah O. Lee, a daughter of revolutionary war soldier John Lee of Woodford County. The couple would have seven children.

Crittenden's budding political career was interrupted by the War of 1812, during which he served on the staffs of General Sam Hopkins and Governor Isaac Shelby, commander of Kentucky forces. His war service and superior legal and oratorical skills made him increasingly popular among the state's leaders; so much so that he was offered a U.S. Senate seat by Shelby in 1814 before it was learned that Crittenden, at age twenty-seven, was too young to serve. Crittenden resumed his legislative career after the war; he served as speaker of the state house in 1815 and 1816, and he had been elected speaker in 1817 before being selected to fill a vacant U.S. Senate seat.

Leaving the Senate at the end of the term in 1819, Crittenden returned to Kentucky and moved to

Frankfort to expand his law practice to the more lucrative state capital. He quickly became a successful defense and appeals court attorney, building a reputation that attracted the attention of other successful lawyers of the day. His clients included former presidents James Madison and James Monroe, and Henry Clay, who would become his political mentor. In 1820 the state of Kentucky appointed Crittenden, along with John Rowan, to negotiate a solution to the longstanding boundary dispute with the state of Tennessee. Although negotiations failed, Crittenden subsequently recommended a solution to the state legislature, which was accepted by both states.

Crittenden's reputation as a calming, nonpartisan leader was tested during the Old Court–New Court crisis in the state of the 1820s, as the contending groups divided into parties. Forced to choose, Crittenden took the conservative, Old Court view, which cost him local political standing for a time. He was again elected to the legislature in 1825, lost in 1826, and won again in 1829, serving until 1832. Throughout this period Crittenden was a trusted aide to Clay at a time when state legislatures elected U.S. senators. He supported his mentor for the presidency in the election of 1824, which was decided by the House of Representatives when none of the candidates secured a majority in the electoral college. After Clay used his influence to elect John Quincy Adams, Crittenden urged him to accept Adams's offer to appoint him secretary of state. Clay followed the advice and was appointed. This resulted in the charge of a "corrupt bargain" in which Clay had exchanged his support for the cabinet position.

His first wife having died in 1824, in 1826 Crittenden married the widowed Mrs. Maria K. Innes Todd, the daughter of Judge Harry Innes; the couple had two children. The following year Adams appointed Crittenden a U.S. district attorney, but he was removed in 1829 under President Andrew Jackson's spoils system. Crittenden was serving as Kentucky secretary of state in 1834—having been appointed by Governor James T. Morehead—when he was again elected to the U.S. Senate. He served until the end of the term on 3 March 1841, when he was appointed U.S. attorney general by President William Henry Harrison. Harrison sent him to New York to manage events surrounding the murder trial of British citizen Alexander McLeod, which was quickly becoming an international incident. Following Harrison's death in April and the ensuing dispute with new president John Tyler, Crittenden resigned with all other members of Harrison's cabinet, except Daniel Webster. He returned home to acclaim and the belief by party members that he had sacrificed his Senate seat for the Whig party. Perhaps to repay Crittenden, the state legislature elected him to Clay's vacated Senate seat, to which he was reelected in 1842.

Supporting Clay for the presidency in 1844, Crittenden agreed with his opposition to Texas annexation. After Clay's defeat, Crittenden opposed the admission of Texas into the Union and the subsequent Mexican War. Supporting the war effort, however, Crittenden

corresponded often with General Zachary Taylor, a kinsman of Crittenden's first wife, Sarah Lee Crittenden. He supported Taylor's nomination for the presidency in 1848, a move that alienated him from Clay and ended their political association. They reconciled toward the end of Clay's life.

Crittenden resigned from the Senate and stood as a candidate for governor of Kentucky, in an effort to carry the state for Taylor and the Whigs, which he did. Given his choice of cabinet positions by the president-elect, Crittenden refused them all, perhaps to take office as governor, perhaps out of deference to Clay. After Taylor's death Crittenden resigned the governorship in 1850 to accept President Millard Fillmore's appointment as U.S. attorney general. As the Whigs declined, Crittenden only half-heartedly supported the Know Nothings, although he agreed with their advocacy of prohibiting non-naturalized immigrants from voting. Crittenden's second wife had died in 1851, and in 1853 he married the widowed Mrs. Elizabeth Moss Ashley; they had no children.

Elected to the Senate again in 1854, Crittenden strove against the resurgence of the slavery issue brought about by the Kansas-Nebraska Act. Assuming the role of the deceased Clay, Crittenden attempted to alleviate sectional tension with conciliation. He spoke thoughtfully and eloquently on the need for compromise and an end to the growing stridency of his fellow senators. He helped found the Constitutional Union party that nominated John Bell for president in 1860.

In December 1860, one month after Abraham Lincoln's election, Crittenden introduced his "Crittenden Compromise" proposal to restore and extend the Missouri Compromise line to the Pacific Ocean. Its terms included that slavery would be protected south, and prohibited north of the 36° 30′ line; new states could exercise popular sovereignty; and Congress would be prohibited from either abolishing slavery in the District of Columbia or regulating the interstate transport of slaves. The proposal was rejected, seven to six, by a special "Committee of Thirteen," a group of senators appointed to consider it. Ironically, its defeat was secured by a coalition of southerners and antislavery Republicans.

Crittenden left the Senate and returned to Kentucky in 1861, arguing successfully for his state not to join the secessionist movement and participating in a border-state convention seeking compromise. Reflective of the times, of Crittenden's sons who joined the war, two attained the rank of major general: George Bibb Crittenden for the Confederacy, Thomas Leonidas Crittenden for the Union. "I am inflexibly for the Union," he wrote Thomas Crittenden in 1862. "I can never subscribe to a separation of the United States—It is possible that I may be obliged to submit to it, but I cannot assent to it. It will be in itself, the surrender and destruction [sic] of our great country" (quoted in Kirwan, p. 459).

Elected to a special session of Congress that met in July 1861, Crittenden secured the passage of resolutions stating that the purpose of the war was to preserve the Union and the Constitution, not to subjugate the South. In accordance with this belief, he opposed federal acts such as the admission of West Virginia as a state, the enlistment of black troops, the Emancipation Proclamation, and military rule in Kentucky. He was a candidate for reelection to the House at the time he died in Frankfort.

• Crittenden records are numerous, but they are located primarily at the Library of Congress; Duke University; the Kentucky Historical Society in Frankfort, Ky.; the Filson Club in Louisville, Ky.; and the University of Kentucky. The best published source is Albert D. Kirwan, *John J. Crittenden: The Struggle for the Union* (1962). Also, Ann Mary Crittenden Coleman, *The Life of John J. Crittenden* (1871), is a collection of letters and speeches edited by Crittenden's daughter.

THOMAS E. STEPHENS

CRITTENDEN, Thomas Leonidas (15 May 1819–23 Oct. 1893), lawyer and soldier, was born in Russellville, Kentucky, the son of John J. Crittenden, a lawyer and statesman, and Sarah "Sally" Lee. After unsuccessful business ventures in New Orleans and with a brother-in-law in Louisville, he studied law and was admitted to the Kentucky bar in 1840. Appointed a commonwealth's attorney in 1843, he occasionally opposed his famous father in courtroom appearances. Crittenden married his stepsister Kittie Todd, probably in 1840. Their only son, Lieutenant John J. Crittenden, was killed with George A. Custer at Little Big Horn in 1876.

Crittenden had brief duty as a private in the Kentucky Infantry in 1836 when war with Mexico seemed possible. During the Mexican War a decade later, as an aide on the staff of General Zachary Taylor, Crittenden was selected to carry news of the victory at Buena Vista to President James K. Polk. Crittenden then served as lieutenant colonel of the Third Kentucky Infantry in which John C. Breckinridge was major. The regiment joined General Winfield Scott's army after Mexico City was captured. Crittenden's standing with Taylor was enhanced in 1848 when his father abandoned his friend Henry Clay and helped General Taylor win the presidency. Thomas Crittenden then secured the lucrative consulship at Liverpool in 1849. Returning to Kentucky in 1853, he practiced law and engaged in business undertakings. He was appointed colonel of a volunteer Kentucky regiment in 1858, but the "Mormon War" ended before the troops could be sent to Utah.

In 1861 Crittenden commanded and reorganized the state militia after numerous Kentuckians left the state to join the Confederacy. Among them was his brother George Bibb Crittenden, who ultimately became a Confederate major general. Commissioned a brigadier general of volunteers on 27 September 1861, Thomas Crittenden saw his first important action on the second day at Shiloh (7 Apr. 1862), where he commanded a division in Don Carlos Buell's Army of the Ohio. His service there earned promotion to major general on 17 July 1862. Crittenden commanded Bu-

ell's Second Corps during the 1862 Confederate invasion of Kentucky. At Perryville on 8 October freakish atmospheric conditions prevented him from hearing the sounds of battle a few miles away, and he waited in vain for orders to attack. At Stones River (Murfreesboro) at the end of 1862, he commanded the three-division left wing of General William S. Rosecrans's Army of the Cumberland. His assault on the Confederate right on 31 December was halted when the Confederates broke the Union right wing. Crittenden's stout defense helped prevent disaster. His effective use of massed artillery on 2 January 1863 broke up a Confederate attack. During the battle he was described as "cheerful and full of hope" as he rode the line to direct and inspire his men. Rosecrans commended him as one "whose heart is that of a true soldier and patriot." Aware of his lack of formal military training, Crittenden usually accepted the advice of more experienced colleagues. On 2 March 1867 he was brevetted brigadier general in the regular army for his Stones River performance.

Crittenden directed the Twenty-first Corps during the campaign leading to the battle of Chickamauga. On 20 September 1863 Rosecrans's mistake in moving troops created a gap in the Union line that James Longstreet's assault penetrated with devastating results. Several of Crittenden's units had been shifted to support other parts of the line, and he was unable to rally those that remained with him. Convinced that the battle was lost, Crittenden joined the flight to Chattanooga that Rosecrans led, but George H. Thomas held his position. Rosecrans sought to share the blame by charging generals Crittenden, Alexander McCook, and James S. Negley with misconduct, and Crittenden was relieved of command on 29 September. But on 23 February 1864 a court of inquiry concluded that Crittenden's "whole conduct was most credible." He had gone to Rossville and Chattanooga after doing all that he could to rally his troops and was declared "not censurable for this act."

Crittenden's usefulness in the western theater was impaired, and on 12 May 1864 he assumed command of the First Division in Ambrose E. Burnside's IX Corps in the Army of the Potomac. He was not comfortable in the eastern army, and his pride was hurt because his rank required more than a divisional command. Relieved on 7 June 1864 at his request, the Kentuckian was not given another command, and he resigned from the service on 13 December. In January 1866 he accepted the position of Kentucky state treasurer but soon resigned when President Andrew Johnson offered him a colonelcy in the regular army. Crittenden served with the Thirty-second and Seventeenth Infantry regiments at a number of western posts and at Governor's Island, where he retired on 19 May 1881. He lived at Annandale, Staten Island, until his death there.

• Some correspondence is in the Crittenden papers in the Library of Congress and at Duke University. No biography exists, but information is available in Albert D. Kirwan, *John*

J. Crittenden: The Struggle for the Union (1962); Mrs. Chapman Coleman, *The Life of John J. Crittenden* (2 vols., 1871); Lewis Collins and Richard Collins, *History of Kentucky* (2 vols., 1874); and William M. Lamers, *The Edge of Glory: A Biography of General William S. Rosecrans* (1961). Henry Cist, *The Army of the Cumberland* (1882), has numerous references to Crittenden, as do the *Official Records* and the many accounts of the major battles and campaigns in which he participated. Obituaries are in the *New York Times* and the Louisville *Courier-Journal*, 24 Oct. 1893.

LOWELL H. HARRISON

CRITTENDEN, Thomas Theodore (1 Jan. 1832–29 May 1909), congressman and governor, was born near Shelbyville, Shelby County, Kentucky, the son of Henry Crittenden and Anna Maria Allen, farmers. After attending local schools in Cloverport, he graduated in 1855 from Centre College in Danville, Kentucky. His uncle, U.S. senator John J. Crittenden, a prominent Frankfort attorney, former governor, and cabinet official, supervised the youth's preparation in law. In 1856 Crittenden, then the registrar of Franklin County, was admitted to the bar. In the fall of that year he married Carrie W. Jackson, with whom he had four children, one of whom died in childhood.

Crittenden relocated in 1857 to Lexington, Missouri, where he formed a law partnership with Judge John A. S. Tutt. After the outbreak of the Civil War, Crittenden sided with the Union. He secured an appointment from Governor Hamilton R. Gamble as a captain and later became lieutenant colonel of the Seventh Missouri Cavalry Militia Regiment, commanded by Colonel John F. Philips. Crittenden served honorably in Arkansas and Missouri from 1862 to 1864, when Governor Willard P. Hall appointed him state's attorney general, a vacancy occasioned by the death of Aikman Welch. The next year Crittenden formed a law partnership in Warrensburg with Francis M. Cockrell, who later served as U.S. senator from 1875 to 1905.

Crittenden's political career seesawed in the 1870s. In 1872, Crittenden, a former Whig, was elected as a Democrat to the Forty-third Congress, serving from 1873 to 1875. Believing that the Civil War had been a military conflict to preserve the Union rather than to subjugate the South to a permanent minority status, Crittenden opposed harsh Reconstruction policies. During his congressional terms, he sponsored bills for the free circulation of weekly newspapers through the mail and proposals to amend and liberalize pension laws, among other measures. His speech in the Forty-third Congress on the wealth and wants of the West was a masterful account of the region's vast natural resources, potential, and importance to the nation. He was narrowly defeated for renomination in 1874 by his former commander, Colonel Philips, a one-time Sedalia mayor and lawyer. In 1876 Crittenden again received his party's nomination and won election by a large majority. He represented Missouri's Seventh Congressional District from 1877 to 1879, during which time he supported the free coinage of silver and

became a loyal ally of Congressman Richard P. "Silver Dick" Bland of Missouri.

Nominated by his party in 1880 for governor of Missouri, Crittenden easily defeated the Republican challenger, David P. Dyer. His term, lasting from 1881 to 1885, was noteworthy in that the state successfully instituted a suit against the Hannibal and St. Joseph Railroad for payment of an old loan, an action that upheld the credit of the state. The governor also curtailed outlawry and train robbing, succeeding most importantly in putting down the Jesse James gang, which had preyed on the populace for more than a decade.

After the expiration of his gubernatorial term, Crittenden moved to Kansas City, Missouri, where he practiced law. In April 1893 President Grover Cleveland appointed him to the post of U.S. consul general at Mexico City. While serving there he became familiar with Mexican finance and with that nation's economy. His experience in Mexico, a silver-standard country, changed his thinking about the silver issue in the United States. He believed that the silver standard was responsible for Mexico's weak economic condition.

By the time of the 1896 presidential campaign in the United States, Crittenden was committed to sound money. He urged silverites to be moderate in their demands, fearing that if extremists gained control of the Democratic party, a Republican victory would result. "No party in the United States can ever succeed which turns its guns on itself," he stated (Mexico City *Mexican Herald*, 15 Nov. 1895). Cognizant that Democrats did not hold together as cohesively as did Republicans, Crittenden wanted his party to reach a compromise on the vexatious currency issue. When William Jennings Bryan, an advocate of free coinage, captured the Democratic presidential nomination, a disappointed Crittenden expressed his disgust. He believed it was a blow as serious as the party split of 1860. Crittenden accurately predicted the electoral triumph of William McKinley, the Republican presidential nominee.

Because he was a loyal Democrat, Crittenden opposed the actions of bolting Democrats, who convened at Indianapolis and selected Senator John M. Palmer for their presidential candidate on a sound-money platform. On this score he parted company with his close friend, General Joseph O. Shelby, U.S. marshal in Missouri, who joined the Gold Democrats on the premise that Bryan's candidacy betrayed traditional Democratic ideals. Crittenden countered by arguing that Bryan did possess common sense and that his speeches were revealing conservative signs. Believing that Bryan posed no threat to the American way of life, Crittenden announced his support of the Democratic nominee, contending that the presidency would have a stabilizing influence on Bryan.

On 4 March 1897, the day of McKinley's inauguration as president, Crittenden tendered his resignation as consul general. He returned to Kansas City, where he served as a federal bankruptcy referee for the U.S. district court from 1898 until his death in Kansas City. An astute observer of people and events, Crittenden was a farsighted Missouri politician and a prominent member of a noted American political family.

• Crittenden's papers are in the Western Historical Manuscripts Collection at the University of Missouri at Columbia. Many of his letters may also be found in the manuscript collections of John J. Crittenden and Grover Cleveland at the Library of Congress. An excellent primary source is H. H. Crittenden, *The Crittenden Memoirs* (1936). The major articles on Crittenden are P. Joseph Powers, "'Yours Very Truly, Thos. T. Crittenden': A Missouri Democrat's Observations of the Election of 1896," *Missouri Historical Review* 68 (1974): 186–203; and Walter V. Scholes, "Mexico in 1896 as Viewed by an American Consul," *Hispanic American Historical Review* 30 (1950): 250–57. Other useful sources include Francis M. Cockrell II, *The Senator from Missouri: The Life and Times of Francis Marion Cockrell* (1962), and Maynard G. Redfield, "The Political Campaign of 1896 in Missouri" (M.A. thesis, Univ. of Missouri at Columbia, 1946). Obituaries are in the *Kansas City Star*, 29 May 1909, and the *St. Louis Republic*, 30 May 1909.

LEONARD SCHLUP

CROCE, Jim (10 Jan. 1943–20 Sept. 1973), singer and songwriter, was born James Joseph Croce in Philadelphia, Pennsylvania, the son of James Croce and Flora (maiden name unknown). Croce grew up in South Philadelphia, the eldest son in a middle-class traditional Italian Catholic family. His initial musical training began at the age of six with accordion lessons. Croce learned to play the guitar at the age of sixteen or eighteen, after he purchased his first twelve-string guitar with money he earned working in a toy store.

Croce attended Villanova University (the first in his family to attend college) and graduated with a degree in psychology in 1965. During college, he began playing guitar and singing in a college group called the Coventry Lads. He also was master of ceremonies for a folk and blues radio show on the school station. While folk and blues were his primary interests, the different bands he formed during his years at Villanova played everything from rock music to folk and pop ballads. Croce met Ingrid Jacobson while serving as a judge at a hootenanny in Philadelphia. Shortly after they met, the two formed a folk duo, singing at local coffeehouses and colleges for several years.

At the end of 1965, while still enrolled at Villanova, an employee of the State Department heard Croce sing and arranged for him to go on tour in the Middle East and Africa. As a result, after graduation he traveled for the State Department as a "musical" cultural liaison. In 1966 he married Jacobson. They had one son. Shortly after they were wed, Croce joined the Army National Guard and attended boot camp at Fort Jackson, South Carolina. When he was discharged from the National Guard he became a special education teacher at an inner-city junior high school in Chester, Pennsylvania.

Stardom was far from instant for Croce, and he struggled to support himself and his family for many years. The years between 1965 and 1970 were his "dues-paying" years, and he supported his family with a series of jobs as a laborer. At one point Croce's financial situation became so bad that he was forced to pawn off his guitars and seek work in the construction business.

Hoping for better luck, Croce and his wife moved to New York City in 1968 and began performing in Greenwich Village coffeehouses. That same year the couple recorded *Jim and Ingrid Croce* on Capitol Records, but it failed to generate substantial sales. Discouraged with the music business, the Croces then moved back to Pennsylvania, settling in rural Lyndell. The primary job he held during those lean years was truck driving. As a truck driver, Croce had time alone to think and to write songs, many of which later became hits. Traveling the country while working, he played at coffeehouses and on college campuses.

In 1971 his old college friend Tommy West, a record producer, convinced Croce to return to New York City to record an album. The result, *You Don't Mess Around with Jim*, was released by ABC Records in May 1972, and by the end of the year the title track had gone top ten, and "Operator (That's Not the Way It Feels)" hit the top twenty. Following this success, a second album was released in early 1973, *Life and Times*, giving Croce his first number-one single, "Bad, Bad Leroy Brown."

Just as his career was starting to peak, Croce, only thirty, was killed when his chartered private plane crashed on takeoff at Natchitoches, Louisiana. Soon after his death, his single "I've Got a Name" moved into the top ten. In late 1973 "Time in a Bottle," with the ironic lyric, "There never seems to be enough time to do the things you want to do," rose to number one.

After Croce's death his records continued to grow in popularity. Early in 1974 his eighth single release, "I Have to Say I Love You in a Song," remained on the charts for well over four months. By mid-1974 both of his albums had sold more than half a million copies. Two posthumous albums followed, *I've Got a Name*, which was completed before his death, and *Photographs and Memories*, a compilation of his hits. No other recordings were made before his death. However, in 1990, a live album, *The Final Tour*, appeared.

Croce will be best remembered for his gentle love songs and his humorous character songs. He was, according to *Time* magazine, a "lean, needling, fun-poking man in work boots and work shirts . . . He took a mad kind of joy in the commonplace, and tomorrow was always the best of all possible times" (11 Feb. 1974). Croce's voice was characterized by a slightly nasal tenor, and most of his songs featured tight melodies that combined folk, blues, and pop styles. Critics generally agree that his best work was probably still ahead of him. According to Tommy West, as quoted in *Jim Croce: His Life and Times*, "He sure could learn from people, and give it back in song: songs about bars, about truck drivers, and 'Bad, Bad Leroy Brown.'"

• Ingrid Croce published a cookbook/memoir about her life and her years with Jim Croce, *Thyme in a Bottle* (1996). Jim Croce gave an extensive interview for a songbook in his *Jim Croce: His Life and Music*, ed. Josh Mills (1974). Most biographical information on Croce can be found in musical reference sources such as Irwin Stambler and Grelun Landon, *The Encyclopedia of Folk, Country, and Western Music* (1974), and George T. Simon, *The Best of the Music Makers* (1979). Additional biographical information can be found in "Epitaph for Jim," *Time*, 11 Feb. 1974, and J. Jorst, "Jim Croce Craze Lives On," *Biography News*, May 1974.

JUDITH B. GERBER

CROCKER, Alvah (14 Oct. 1801–26 Dec. 1874), manufacturer, railroad promoter, and congressman, was born in Leominster, Massachusetts, the son of Samuel Crocker and Comfort Jones. His parents were among the founders of the Baptist church in Leominster, and they imparted a strong work ethic to their seven sons, of whom Alvah was the eldest. He went to work at the age of eight in a Leominster paper mill, where he earned twenty-five cents for each twelve-hour day. He received little formal education (one year at Groton Academy at age sixteen), but he read widely on his own, and his letters displayed a bent toward literature and rhetoric. He subsequently worked in other paper mills in Franklin, New Hampshire, and Fitchburg, Massachusetts, before he started his first industrial concern, a paper manufactory in Fitchburg in 1826.

Crocker experienced financial and personal hardships in the early years of his business. Tales of his honesty, devotion, and good-heartedness parallel the stories told about the young Abraham Lincoln in Illinois. There seems to be little doubt that Crocker was exceptionally industrious, cheerful, and vigorous in his work life. He persevered in his business and began to achieve financial prosperity during the 1830s, the same decade in which he entered local and state politics. In 1850 Crocker reorganized his paper-making factory, calling it Crocker Burbank & Company; by that time it had become one of the largest industrial concerns of its type in New England.

Crocker was elected as a tithingman in 1831, and he went on to serve in the Massachusetts House of Representatives for three terms commencing in 1836, 1842, and 1843. A loyal Whig during these years, Crocker would later join the Republican party. Business success combined with political service made Crocker quite visible in the affairs of north-central Massachusetts, the area that he would identify with and seek to serve throughout the rest of his life.

Crocker became an avid proponent of railroad building during the 1830s and 1840s. He was a member of the board of directors of the Boston and Fitchburg Railroad, and in 1842 he went to England to purchase iron rails for the project. After the completion of the railroad in 1845 (which connected north-central Massachusetts with Boston), Crocker and other industrialists moved to extend the iron rail farther west. The resulting Brattleboro and Fitchburg Railroad was built between 1845 and 1849.

Dreaming of a railroad that would extend from western Massachusetts to upstate New York, Crocker gave hundreds of speeches on the subject throughout New York and New England. His vision was grandiose: to connect Massachusetts with the Erie Canal and thereby reach the markets and goods of the far American West. Crocker's speeches and activities pushed forward the ambitious Hoosac Tunnel project, which conquered the Berkshire hills and allowed for a strong connection between western and central Massachusetts for the first time; he was the commissioner in charge for the state from 1869 until his death.

Flush with success in business and transportation, Crocker turned his attention to town development. He organized the Turners Falls Company in 1866 (it later became the Western Massachusetts Electric Company) to move forward the development of the small village of Turners Falls. Seeking to emulate the success of milltowns such as Holyoke and Lowell, Massachusetts, Crocker intended to make Turners Falls into a planned industrial town where people could live, work, and play, all within walking distance. He was instrumental in the design and construction of a power canal that quickly drew several large paper, cutlery, and textile mills to Turners Falls, whose citizens continuously regarded Crocker as the town's founding father and visionary spirit.

In 1872 Crocker was elected to fill a vacancy created in the U.S. House of Representatives. He served as a Republican congressman from 2 January 1872 until his death. His speeches in Congress were principally concerned with business matters—shipping, commerce, and the tariff. He died in Leominster while at home on vacation from Congress. Crocker had married Abigail Fox in 1829; the couple had five children before her death in 1848. Crocker subsequently married Lucy A. Fay in 1851, and after her death he married Minerva Cushing in 1872.

Crocker was both a practical businessman and a gifted visionary. He was among a handful of prominent New England industrialists who foresaw the power and the potential of the railroad. Although his inspiration in many matters may have come from his religious upbringing, Crocker was essentially a secular thinker; in his view the expansion of industries, towns, and railroads symbolized the acme of development. Among his numerous enterprises, the most impressive were the Boston and Fitchburg Railroad, the Hoosac Tunnel, and the development of Turners Falls. In all these matters Crocker was faithful to his central vision of development, which he aptly expressed in the summation of his address, as a businessman, to the Massachusetts legislature in 1862: "Massachusetts is small in territory, her soil is sandy, sterile, rock-bound. . . . If you would have her maintain her high position, her noble pre-eminence and prestige . . . you must give to her every section, north as well as south, the best facilities for a full development of her resources, the means for the quickest transit and intercommunication, grappling with any and every obstacle which stands in the way, or in any way bars her from sustaining the most dense, active, industrious, and therefore virtuous population."

• Information on Crocker and his activities is in the Fitchburg Historical Society and the Pioneer Valley Studies Program at Greenfield Community College. A good deal of information exists regarding Crocker's business affairs; less detail is available regarding his personal life. William Bond Wheelwright, *Life and Times of Alvah Crocker* (1923), comes close to hagiography, but the use of primary sources, particularly from Crocker's speeches, is excellent. Information on Turners Falls and the Hoosac Tunnel can be found in several sources, notably N. H. Egleston, "The Story of the Hoosac Tunnel," *Atlantic Monthly*, Mar. 1882, pp. 289–304; Terrence E. Coyne, "The Hoosac Tunnel: Massachusetts' Western Gateway," *Historical Journal of Massachusetts* 23 (Winter 1995): 1–20; and Robert L. Merriam et al., *The History of the John Russell Cutlery Company* (1976).

SAMUEL WILLARD CROMPTON

CROCKER, Charles (14 Sept. 1822–14 Aug. 1888), railroad executive, was born in Troy, New York, the son of Isaac Crocker, a struggling merchant, and Eliza (maiden name unknown). Charles "Charlie" Crocker grew up in a very poor family. His father failed as a merchant in Oswego and then in Troy. Charlie was forced to work from an early age. As he recalled, "I had no 'nursery' days. I commenced selling apples and oranges at nine years of age." By age twelve he was working full time, as errand boy and distributor of the New York *Transcript*. While still in his teens, with some $300 in savings, he moved to rural Indiana, where he worked as a sawyer and eventually bought an iron forge. Moderately prosperous ("I was always apt at trade"), he headed west when news of the 1849 California gold strikes reached Indiana.

In 1850 he set out overland with brothers Clark and Henry and four laborers from his forge. After a grueling, 100-day trip that cost him most of his savings, Crocker ended up working in someone else's mine near El Dorado City, saving every penny he earned. In 1851 he and his brother Clark opened a general store near Sacramento. While Clark clerked, Charlie did the stock buying and also teamstered merchandise throughout the mining district for sale. They prospered and soon had a branch store.

In 1852 Crocker bought a half interest in a larger store in downtown Sacramento, then soon bought out his partner and renamed the business Crocker & Bro. Also in 1852, while back in Indiana buying stock, he married Mary A. Deming. They had four children and adopted another. Returning to Sacramento he found that his store—and much of the city—had been consumed by the "Great Fire," but he and Clark rebuilt the establishment—in brick—on the same site and were soon doing a thriving business. Within a few years he was sole proprietor of a high-volume retail outlet, for Clark had moved to San Francisco.

In 1855 Crocker helped found the California Republican party and, almost against his will, was soon elected as a Sacramento alderman, forming a close friendship with Republican councilman Mark Hopkins. Through the new party he also became acquainted with Leland P. Stanford and Collis Huntington. The future "Big Four" of the railroad industry were

thus in place by 1856. Like Hopkins, Huntington, and Stanford, Crocker was a substantial businessman, but he alone fairly radiated strength and dynamism. A bear of a man, standing over six feet and weighing 260 pounds, he abstained from tobacco and alcohol. An insomniac, he habitually arose at four and worked until he was exhausted.

By 1860, the year he was elected to the state legislature, Crocker was showing interest in the idea of a transcontinental railroad, thanks to the efforts of a brilliant, messianic young engineer, Theodore Dehone Judah. The engineer had been propagandizing the feasibility of such a railroad, doing route surveys and writing persuasive pamphlets, and Crocker, Huntington, Stanford, and Hopkins were interested. Although they knew nothing about railroads per se, they scented potentially huge profits. In mid-1861 the four became majority shareholders in Judah's Central Pacific (CP) Railroad. Crocker, who was worth a quarter of a million dollars, was willing to speculate. Like the others of the Big Four, he subscribed $150,000 in company stock, paying the legal minimum of 10 percent down. The $15,000 subscribed by each of the Big Four, plus lesser amounts from a handful of others, would a decade later balloon into the greatest aggregation of industrial capital in the history of the nation to that point.

When President Abraham Lincoln signed the Pacific Railway Act the following year, providing substantial government aid, the cash-poor company began to move. In December it awarded a construction contract for the first eighteen miles of rail line—from Sacramento to the foothills of the rugged Sierra Nevadas—to C. Crocker & Co., in which all the Big Four had quietly invested. Crocker, who often bragged that he "knew how to manage men," was, given his energy, the obvious choice for construction boss, but when he unwisely subcontracted the work in one-mile stretches to inept contractors, his company went bankrupt.

Reborn as the Contract & Finance Co., Crocker's firm cast about for capital and loans to get the work underway. With the help of ex-governor Stanford, "we got some state aid bills passed," but most of the operating capital, of both the CP and the construction company, came through personal loans, for the banking community had no faith in the project. "We bought the first 50 miles of iron on our own personal obligations," Crocker wrote later, admitting that "I owed everybody that would trust me." Construction, and hence the federal aid that was tied to completed mileage, was agonizingly slow, and both companies' treasuries were chronically empty. In the first three years a paltry fifty miles of track were laid. Bankruptcy was a constant threat. Crocker later wrote, with little hyperbole, that "I would have been glad, when we had 30 miles of road built, to have got a clean shirt and absolution from my debts. I would have been willing to give up everything I had in the world, in order to cancel my debts."

But the work in the daunting Sierras continued, driving eastward to link up with the rails of the Union

Pacific (UP), which was pushing west from Omaha. Crocker, at first beset with a labor shortage, imported Irish immigrants from the East, but they often ran off to prospect for gold. In 1866, as an experiment, he hired a gang of Chinese and was soon touting "the superiority of the Chinese to whites as laborers," hiring them by the thousands. Although the Chinese were looked down upon and discriminated against in California, Crocker treated them fairly. They were paid well, on time, and in gold coin. Many later used the skills they gained working with Crocker and the CP to work on the Southern Pacific, Canadian Pacific, and other railroad construction projects. Crocker was criticized by bigots, but his desperate need for efficient labor led him to employ more than 10,000 Chinese workers during times of peak construction.

From 1865 to 1869 Crocker was almost constantly in the field with his engineers and his workers, bossing, cajoling, inspiring, and threatening. "I used to go up and down the road in my car like a mad bull," he later recalled. By 1868 Crocker was overseeing what had become a mad construction race with the UP; each mile of progress meant considerable federal aid—and future profits from the sale of lands allotted by Congress to the companies. As the tracks advanced eastward, the Big Four began an orgy of acquisitions, somehow buying on credit a network of other railroads, vineyards, an ice company, and more. The CP—guided by the Big Four—soon became the cornerstone for a vast network of railroads that dominated the American West, and federal land grants were parlayed into the largest real estate empire in American history.

Charlie Crocker's "Celestials," as he called his Chinese workers, were in perpetual motion, and, on a wager with the UP, on 28 April 1869, in Utah, they set a record that stands today: ten miles and 185 feet of track laid during the sunlight hours of a single day! Less than two weeks later, at Promontory, Utah, a golden spike united the rails of the two companies, finishing the greatest engineering feat of nineteenth-century America.

Although Crocker soon sold his construction company to his colleagues (for $1.8 million), he retained his CP stock and shares in diverse companies that the Big Four had acquired. He now lived in opulent style in a 12,000-square-foot French Renaissance mansion in Sacramento. By the late 1870s the CP's average net profits were about $9 million, of which Crocker's share was more than $1.5 million. One of his brothers, E. B. Crocker, owned even more, but apparently his name was merely being used by Crocker as a front, for E. B. had been deranged for years.

Both the CP and the UP became objects of congressional investigation in the 1870s and 1880s, and several times the CP's account books (and those of the Contract & Finance Co.) were subpoenaed. Mark Hopkins, the Big Four's accountant, claimed that the books in question had been mysteriously "lost," and, questioned under oath about the alleged excess profits of his construction company, Crocker merely shrugged: "I was not familiar with the finances." That, from the man who putatively had owned the largest construction company in the United States! Although he openly admitted to having bribed government officials on all levels, Crocker was never contrite. "You can get any man to be unfriendly with a railroad *after* it is built," he said. "It is a 'great monopoly' as soon as it wants pay for serving the public."

Crocker remained involved in the railroad business until his death in Sacramento; court documents reveal that he left an estate valued at more than $20 million (plus $8.5 million in promissory notes), but, as a newspaper obituary lamented, "Mr. Crocker gave nothing to charity, nothing to the park, nothing to public institutions of any kind."

Crocker accomplished what had seemed impossible. Admitting that in 1862 "We had no idea how we were going to build the road," and spurned by experienced investors, he and the others of the Big Four borrowed the money to build a railroad that was to cost nearly $100 million in an act of sheer financial legerdemain. Crocker, who had never supervised the work of more than a dozen men before 1862, four years later was orchestrating the largest single labor force in North America. His vision, his unflagging energy, and his determination fundamentally altered nineteenth-century America.

• Much of Charlie Crocker's correspondence can be found in two major California research repositories: the Bancroft Library at the University of California, Berkeley, and the Huntington Library in San Marino. There is no published collection of his papers, nor is there a true biography, but biographical material can be found in a number of railroad histories. The best of these are Lucius Beebe, *The Central Pacific and the Southern Pacific Railroads* (1963); John Debo Galloway, *The First Transcontinental Railroad: Central Pacific, Union Pacific* (1950); James McCague, *Moguls and Iron Men: The Story of the First Transcontinental Railroad* (1964); David Mountfield, *The Railway Barons* (1979); and John Hoyt Williams, *A Great and Shining Road: The Epic Story of the Transcontinental Railroad* (1988). Although it is a biography of Collis P. Huntington, David Lavender's *The Great Persuader* (1970) has reliable information on Crocker.

JOHN HOYT WILLIAMS

CROCKER, Hannah Mather (27 June 1752–11 July 1829), author, was born in Roxbury, Massachusetts, the daughter of Samuel Mather, a minister, and Hannah Hutchinson. Her father was the son of Cotton Mather, the famous Puritan divine; her mother, the sister of Thomas Hutchinson, a royal governor of Massachusetts. In 1779 she married Joseph Crocker, then a military officer and later a shopkeeper, by whom she had ten children, the first being born in 1780 and the last in 1795. Her husband died in 1797.

Crocker was an early female defender of Masonry, publishing her thoughts about it in *A Series of Letters on Free Masonry* (1815), "By a Lady of Boston." Dedicated to "the present Officers and Members of the Grand Lodge of Massachusetts . . . with the most ardent wish of benevolence, that every worthy member may square his conduct by the line of integrity" (the

Masons had obviously been misbehaving), this slender book contains three letters from A. P. Americana in Boston, all dated 1810, and a response to each from her correspondent, Enquirer, in Montpelier, Vermont, who is debating whether to join the Masons. Americana convinces him to join by arguing that although an occasional Mason behaves badly, Masonry itself is good because it is based on the principles of wisdom, strength, and beauty. But Crocker (as Americana) wishes most to discuss not Masonry but women, specifically the manner in which society treats them. In Americana's first letter, Crocker bristles at how easily the female intellect is dismissed, observing that society deems as adequate the ability of women barely to write their name and read. She wants women to be trained in literature and science, a goal that women help frustrate by spending time visiting one another and reading novels.

If Crocker defended the Masons in 1815, the next year she criticized another group: sailors. Responding to an observation by an anonymous male that a woman would probably succeed better than a man in convincing sailors to pursue a regular, moral life, she attempts to do so in *The School of Reform; or, Seaman's Safe Pilot to the Cape of Good Hope*, where on the title page she styles herself "the seaman's friend/ H. M. Crocker." In a heavily moralistic manner, she attempts to convince sailors to conduct themselves well in sentences such as this: "If, then, the righteous shall hardly dare appear in the divine presence, where shall the drunkard and ungodly hide their heads?" Perhaps surprisingly in such a tract, Crocker argues only for temperance, not for abstinence from drink. She concludes her composition, which she signs Prudentia Americana, with these lines from a didactic poem linking sobriety and success:

> All hands on deck ! with hearts sincere,
> Well man the yards, with heads quite clear,
> Then steady, steady boys you'll see
> Return with bless'd prosperity.

In 1818 Crocker, writing as H. Mather Crocker, published her longest and most important book, *Observations on the Real Rights of Women, with Their Appropriate Duties, Agreeable to Scripture, Reason and Common Sense*, "the first feministic book by an American woman" (Riegel, p. 7). "Printed for the author," this volume was delayed by an illness that prohibited Crocker from gaining subscribers to pay for publication. In this book dedicated to Hannah More, English author of *Strictures on the Modern System of Female Education* (1799), Crocker supports her argument that men and women are intellectual equals by citing Isaac Watts, Lady Montagu, and others who share her opinion. She illustrates her point by detailing the accomplishments of such women as the biblical Deborah, Queen Elizabeth, Mary Wollstonecraft, Sarah Wentworth Morton, and Mercy Otis Warren, among others. Yet Crocker continues to reflect the cultural biases of her time, stating that women

must still estimate the rights of men, and own it their prerogative exclusively to contend for public honours and preferment, either in church or state, and females may console themselves and feel happy, that by the moral distinction of the sexes they are called to move in a sphere of life remote from those masculine contentions, although they hold equal right with them of studying every branch of science, even jurisprudence (pp. 19–20).

Because of her pronouncements in favor of women, Crocker holds a small but significant place in the history of American feminist literature. She probably died in Roxbury, Massachusetts; she is interred in the Mather tomb on Copp's Hill in Boston.

• Crocker's papers are in the New England Historical and Genealogical Society in Boston. One of the few critics to discuss Crocker is Robert E. Riegel in *American Feminists* (1963).

BENJAMIN FRANKLIN V

CROCKER, Lucretia (31 Dec. 1829–9 Oct. 1886), educator, was born in Barnstable, Massachusetts, the daughter of Henry Crocker and Lydia E. Farris. The family moved about 1848 to Boston where her father worked in the insurance business. Crocker attended the Normal School for Girls, the pioneering training school for teachers in West Newton, Massachusetts (later the State Normal School at Framingham), and graduated in April 1850. The following fall she joined the small faculty of the Normal School as instructor in geography, mathematics, and natural sciences and taught there for four years before resigning, apparently for reasons of health. Her invitation to Louis Agassiz to lecture to her classes led him to become a staunch supporter of her educational ideas; he, in turn, encouraged Crocker to devote much of her own life to teaching about nature and allowed her to attend his lectures at Harvard.

Crocker's reputation as an unusually effective teacher at the Normal School led Horace Mann to offer her, in 1857, a faculty position at Antioch College in Yellow Springs, Ohio. There she taught astronomy and mathematics, thus becoming one of very few women teaching science to both men and women. A former student there recalled that Crocker was admired for her expertise by a group of advanced students who had been explicitly critical of her male predecessor while at the same time she found time to work patiently with those for whom mathematics was not easy. When Horace Mann died in 1859, however, she returned to Boston to care for her aging parents and rejoin friends involved in other educational activities.

Crocker's clarity in writing led her to produce, over the course of her life, a number of textbooks and manuals for teachers dealing with science education. She assisted her former student Mary L. Hall in writing a textbook on geography entitled *Our World* (1864). In the early 1870s she encouraged Alpheus Hyatt of the Boston Society of Natural History to develop the Teachers' School of Science, a lecture series for public school teachers, and worked with him to develop curricular materials. That program provided a model for other museums across the country as they became interested in reaching a school-age audience. She also published *Methods of Teaching Geography: Notes on Lessons* (1883) to bring current theories into the classroom. Geography, she argued, must begin with knowledge of the physical earth, but it should always include the adaptation of its resources to the needs of humans; that is, geography should make the connection between physical conditions and the lives of different cultural groups. This theme was also evident in the widely read and republished books, particularly *Seven Little Sisters Who Live on the Round Ball That Floats in the Air* (1861), of her student Jane Andrews. Always active in the Unitarian church, Crocker presided for a number of years over a committee of the American Unitarian Association to select books for Sunday school libraries.

Crocker's educational interests were wide ranging and often focused on the underprivileged. Within a year after the end of the Civil War, Crocker became active as a member of the New England Freedmen's Aid Society, serving from 1866 to 1873 on the Teachers' Committee that selected, advised, and coordinated the curriculum for teachers working in the southern schools. In her memoir of Crocker, Ednah Dow Cheney recalled, "She never betrayed any remnants of race prejudice or any distrust of the Negro's power to rise to the full stature of a man. She felt a peculiar value in this labor among the freedmen, not only for the great opportunities opened to them, but for the new experience it offered in education, since each teacher was thrown mainly upon her own resources" (p. 28). In 1869 the society sent her to inspect the schools it sponsored; Crocker's enthusiasm helped sustain the program until 1875. She was also secretary and chair of the executive committee of the Boston School for Deaf-Mutes, supporting the innovative methods of its principal, Sarah Fuller. In 1873 she developed the science department of the Society to Encourage Studies at Home, a correspondence program to augment women's educational opportunities. Colleagues remembered her as a catalyst who brought order and direction to the ideas and activities of others, inspiring them to do their best work.

Crocker is most often cited as one of the first four women elected to the Boston School Committee, the result of vigorous campaigning by the New England Women's Club and her friend Ednah Dow Cheney; those elected in 1873 were not allowed to take their seats. So, in 1874, the club lobbied for a legislative act that declared women eligible for school committees in the state of Massachusetts. In December of that year, six women, including Crocker, were elected and seated. When the school administrative system was reorganized in 1876, Crocker was elected by the committee to be one of six supervisors to visit schools, make recommendations about the curriculum, and advise on particular subjects; Crocker was made responsible for the natural sciences. Continuing her efforts with the Boston Society of Natural History as well as with faculty from Harvard and the Massachusetts Institute of Technology, she worked to provide training courses for teachers in the Teachers' School of Science, specimens and laboratory equipment for classrooms, and an updated curriculum. With Ellen Swallow Richards, she developed a model course in mineralogy for teachers in the Boston area, and she regularly attended and taught in the Saturday program for teachers at the Boston Museum of Natural History. Alpheus Hyatt, director of the museum, noted that she was a "true friend and tireless associate" who raised funds, encouraged teachers, gave advice on course development, and taught classes.

Crocker was a woman whose life was devoted to her multifaceted educational work. She maintained a quiet and self-effacing demeanor that matched contemporary expectations of women and was inevitably described in terms that emphasized delicacy, refinement, charm, and empathy. However, she held a deep-seated set of convictions that led her boldly to promote science as part of the educational curriculum for girls and boys, visit schools for freed black people in the South, and join other women who campaigned for the Boston School Board in 1873. Records on her life are sparse, probably because so much of her influence was exercised personally and directly on teachers, colleagues, and the influential and philanthropic Bostonians who shared her interest in educational causes. Her life reflected her commitment to educate women and to teach science to pupils at every level, particularly through the public systems. She died of pneumonia at her home in Rutland Square in Boston. A public school in Boston and a dormitory at the State College at Framingham were named for Crocker, as were a scholarship at Woods Hole Oceanographic Center and, in 1986, the Lucretia Crocker Fellowships for experienced teachers in Massachusetts.

• For additional information on Crocker see Ednah Dow Cheney, *Memoirs of Lucretia Crocker and Abby W. May* (1893); Frances Zirngiebel, "Teachers' School of Science," *Appleton's Popular Science Monthly*, Aug.-Sept. 1899, pp. 451–65; 640–52; "In Memory of Miss Lucretia Crocker," a three-page circular letter concerning Lucretia Crocker scholarship at the marine biological laboratory, Boston (188?). There are various references to Crocker in Norma Kidd Green, *A Forgotten Chapter in American Education: Jane Andrews of Newburyport* (1961). Also worth consulting are Sally Gregory Kohlstedt, "From Learned Society to Public Museum: The Boston Society of Natural History," in *The Organization of Knowledge in Modern America, 1860–1920*, ed. Alexandra Oleson and John Voss (1979); and Charles F. Hopkins, "A Study of Teacher Empowerment: Lucretia Crocker Fellows in Massachusetts" (Ed.D. diss., Univ. of Massachusetts, 1991).

SALLY GREGORY KOHLSTEDT

CROCKER, William (27 Jan. 1874–11 Feb. 1950), plant physiologist, was born on a farm in Montville, Ohio, the son of Charles David Crocker, a farmer and carpenter, and Catherine House. He left home at age fourteen and attended the preparatory school of Baldwin University in Berea, Ohio. From there he went to Illinois Normal College, graduating in 1898; his next period of formal education was at the University of Illinois, from which he received a B.A. in 1902 and an M.A. in 1903. In the ten years preceding his M.A., Crocker taught at various country schools, and after graduating he took a teaching job in biology at Northern Illinois Normal School. This lasted two years, and he then turned to further graduate studies at the University of Chicago, receiving a Ph.D. in 1906. His principal professor at Chicago was John Merle Coulter, and Crocker eventually gained the rank of associate professor (1915–1921) in Coulter's famous department. In addition, from 1913 to 1918 Crocker held an appointment as a plant physiologist in the U.S. Department of Agriculture. In 1910 Crocker married Persis Dorothy Smallwood, and they had two children. Crocker was well established in Chicago and might have stayed in the academic world for the remainder of his career had it not been for the establishment of a unique, private scientific institution, the Boyce Thompson Institute for Plant Research in Yonkers, New York.

Colonel William Boyce Thompson was a millionaire mine developer and financier with a powerful interest in using his fortune to expand knowledge and promote the welfare of humanity. He concluded that a scientific organization for plant studies would be the object of his philanthropy. His scientific counselor, Raymond Bacon of the Mellon Institute, recommended that he consult J. M. Coulter, who, in turn, asked Crocker to draw up a plan for plant research work and the organization of the institute. This proposal was given to Thompson in 1920 and was accepted by him, and Crocker was appointed director in 1921.

Crocker was responsible for planning and equipping the laboratories, selecting the scientific staff, planning the research programs, and for the overall administration. In 1921–1922 he traveled in Europe visiting biological laboratories and experiment stations and consulting prominent biologists. He also purchased the nucleus of the institute's library, obtaining complete bound sets of German, English, and French periodicals in botany, biology, and chemistry, a complete set of Justus Liebig's *Annalen*, and several thousand German dissertations. In the fall of 1924 at Yonkers, adjoining the Thompson estate, the institute was officially opened. On that occasion, Coulter said, "In my judgment, this Institute stands for an epoch in the history of botanical science in this country."

A pioneer in team research, the Boyce Thompson Institute initiated research in a variety of subjects, including seed dormancy, insecticides and fumigants, plant hormones, plant growth and controlled environmental conditions, and the life span of seeds. The institute emphasized prompt publication of results, well-equipped laboratories employing the latest technology, and the use of numerous laboratory assistants. One of its most important reference projects was the *Bibliography of Seeds*, begun by Crocker.

Along with his administrative responsibilities, Crocker was able to continue as a research botanist and made significant contributions in the study of seed dormancy, lifespan, and germination. He developed a storage method that preserved seeds for future use. Another field of inquiry was that of the toxicity to plants of various gases such as sulfur dioxide, carbon monoxide, and mercury vapor. Nearly all of his research was directed to the solution of practical problems such as the use of fertilizers and the causes of plant injuries and deficiencies. His research papers were published in the *Botanical Gazette*, the *Journal of Agricultural Research*, *Contributions from Boyce Thompson Institute*, and others. His published books are *Growth of Plants* (1948), *Physiology of Seeds* (1953), and *Twenty Years of Seed Research at Boyce Thompson Institute for Plant Research* (1948), both of the latter with Lela V. Barton.

Outside the institute, Crocker was active in both professional and public affairs. He took a strong interest in the city of Yonkers, especially its schools, and was both a member and president of the board of education. He was chair of the Division of Agriculture and Biology of the National Research Council and a member of the Advisory Committee on Gerontology of the U.S. Public Health Service. He was also a fellow of the American Association for the Advancement of Science and, in 1924, president of the Botanical Society of America. He was the recipient of the A. Cressy Morrison prize in experimental biology from the New York Academy of Science and of a medal from the Institute of Arts and Sciences of New York.

William Crocker's major contribution to American science was the Boyce Thompson Institute itself. In a memorial address, Edmund W. Sinnott described him as a "great botanist" and also as a "great administrator" who possessed the qualities of imagination and leadership and who also had the ability to inspire others with his enthusiasm and his vision. Sinnott said, "The Institute, as we know it, is the outcome of the imaginative enthusiasm of its first Director." Crocker's wife died in 1948. He died in Athens, Ohio, just hours after marrying Neva Ray Brown Ankenbrand.

• Some of Crocker's personal papers and newspaper articles about him are at the Boyce Thompson Institute. For information about the establishment of the institute and Crocker's role, there is a detailed discussion in A. D. Rodgers III, *John Merle Coulter, Missionary in Science* (1944). There is much additional information in the introduction to W. Crocker, *Growth of Plants: Twenty Years Research at Boyce Thompson Institute* (1948). In *Yearbook of the American Philosophical Society* (1950), Otto Kunkel lists Crocker's honors. E. W. Sinnott's memorial address, "William Crocker, the Man and Scientist," was published in *Contributions from Boyce Thompson Institute* 16 (Jan.–Mar. 1950): 1–3. His obituary is in the *New York Times*, 12 Feb. 1950.

ROBERT F. ERICKSON

CROCKETT, Davy (17 Aug. 1786–6 Mar. 1836), frontiersman, Tennessee and U.S. congressman, and folk hero, was born David Crockett in Greene County,

East Tennessee, the son of John Crockett, a magistrate, unsuccessful land speculator, and tavern owner, and Rebecca Hawkins. John Crockett hired his son out to Jacob Siler in 1798 to help on a cattle drive to Rockbridge County, Virginia, and Siler tried forcibly to detain young Crockett after the completion of the job. The boy ran away at night, however, and arrived home in late 1798 or early 1799. Preferring to play hooky rather than attend school, he ran away from home to escape his father's wrath. His "strategic withdrawal," as he called it, lasted about thirty months while he worked at odd jobs and as a laborer and a wagon driver. When he returned home in 1802, he had grown so much that his family at first did not recognize him. He soon found that all was forgiven and reciprocated their generosity by working for a year to settle the debts that his father had incurred.

Crockett married Mary "Polly" Finley in August 1806 in Jefferson County, Tennessee, and they remained in the mountains of East Tennessee for just over five years while he supported their growing family as a farmer and a hunter. In the fall of 1811 the Crocketts and their two sons, John Wesley and William, settled in Lincoln County, Tennessee, but in 1813 they moved again, this time to near the present Alabama border in Franklin County, Tennessee. Crockett enlisted twice as a volunteer in the Indian wars in the southeastern United States from 1813 to 1815, seeing action mainly in Alabama and Florida. Soon after his discharge, Polly gave birth to Margaret, their third child, and David was elected a lieutenant in the Thirty-second Militia Regiment of Franklin County in 1815. Polly died that summer, and a year later he married Elizabeth Patton, a widow with two children, and they moved to Lawrence County, Tennessee, in the fall of 1817.

Although Crockett served as a justice of the peace and town commissioner of Lawrenceburg and was eventually elected colonel of the Fifty-seventh Militia Regiment of Lawrence County by 1818, he was still a relatively unknown backwoods hunter with a talent for storytelling until his election to the Tennessee legislature in 1821 as the representative of Lawrence and Hickman counties. From the start, he took an active interest in public land policy regarding the West. Reelected in 1823 but defeated in 1825, he won election to the U.S. House of Representatives in 1827. He had promoted himself as a simple, honest country boy who was an extraordinary hunter and marksman, someone who was in every sense a "straight shooter." Reelected to a second term in 1829, he split with President Andrew Jackson and the Tennessee delegation headed by James K. Polk on several important issues including land reform and the Indian removal bill. Crockett was defeated for a bid for a third term when he openly and vehemently opposed Jackson's policies, but he was reelected in 1833.

Political notoriety had given his image a life of its own, and by 1831 Crockett had become the model for Nimrod Wildfire, the hero of James Kirke Paulding's play *The Lion of the West*, as well as the subject of articles and books. Crockett said he was compelled to publish his autobiography, *A Narrative of the Life of David Crockett of the State of Tennessee*, which was written in 1834 with the help of Thomas Chilton, to counteract the outlandish stories printed under Crockett's name as the *Sketches and Eccentricities of Colonel David Crockett of West Tennessee* a year earlier. A good deal of the information in *Sketches and Eccentricities*, however, was likely supplied by Crockett. He clearly recognized the power of his popular image and sought to manipulate it for political gain. The more outrageous stories were taken up and expanded by the anonymous eastern hack writers who spun tall tales for the *Crockett Almanacs* (1835–1856). In their hands the fictional Davy Crockett became the apotheosis of the backwoods screamer, and with the death of the historical Crockett at the Alamo in 1836, the floodgates were loosed for the full-blown expansion of legend. He could not only "run faster, –jump higher, –squat lower, –dive deeper, –stay under longer, –and come out drier, than any man in the whole country" (*Crockett Almanac* [1835], p. 2) but could save the world by unfreezing the sun and the earth from their axes and ride his pet alligator up Niagara Falls.

Crockett's "corrective" *Narrative* can also be viewed as the first presidential campaign autobiography, since he was being touted by the Whigs as the candidate who would oppose Jackson's handpicked successor, Martin Van Buren, in the election of 1836. Jackson and Governor William Carroll of Tennessee helped to engineer Crockett's defeat in his bid to be returned to Congress in 1835. The election of Adam Huntsman, a peg-legged lawyer, in his stead ended Crockett's presidential ambitions and, temporarily disenchanted with politics and his constituents, he made the now famous remark, "Since you have chosen to elect a man with a timber toe to succeed me, you may all go to hell and I will go to Texas." His last surviving letters spoke of his confidence that Texas would allow him to rejuvenate his political career and finally make his fortune. He intended to become land agent for the territory that was in revolt against its Mexican rulers and saw the future of an independent Texas as intertwined with his own.

Crockett and his men joined Colonel William B. Travis at San Antonio De Bexar in early February 1836. Mexican general Antonio Lopez de Santa Anna arrived on 20 February and laid siege to the Alamo garrison. In the defense of the Alamo Travis wrote that during the first bombardment that Crockett was everywhere in the Alamo, "animating the men to do their duty." The siege of thirteen days ended on 6 March 1836 when the Alamo was overrun at about six o'clock that morning. According to the eyewitness account in the diary of Lieutenant Jose Enrique de la Pena, Crockett and five or six other survivors were captured. Several Mexican officers asked that they be spared, but Santa Anna had the prisoners bayoneted and then shot.

Many thought that Crockett deserved a better end and provided it, from thrilling fictions of his clubbing Mexicans with his empty rifle until cut down by a flurry of bullets or bayonets or both—stories that under-girded the movie portrayals by Fess Parker and John Wayne—to his survival as a slave in a salt mine in Mexico. No matter what the past or future directions of the legendary Crockett, however, it is quite clear that the historical Crockett proved a formidable cultural hero in his own right and attained a continuing preeminence in the American mind as the representative of frontier independence and virtue.

• The best bibliography of primary and secondary materials is Miles Tanenbaum, "Following Davy's Trail: A Crockett Bibliography," in *Crockett at Two Hundred: New Perspectives on the Man and the Myth*, ed. Michael A. Lofaro and Joe Cummings (1989). The best biography is James Atkins Shackford, *David Crockett: The Man and the Legend* (1956; rev. eds. 1981, 1986, 1994). Other works that appeared under Crockett's name, but which he did not author, are *An Account of Colonel Crockett's Tour to the North and Down East* (1835), *The Life of Martin Van Buren* (1835), and *Col. Crockett's Exploits and Adventures in Texas* (1836).

MICHAEL A. LOFARO

CROGHAN, George (?–31 Aug. 1782), Indian agent and land speculator, was born in Dublin, Ireland. Croghan's early life is obscure. Scholars do not know who George Croghan's parents were, or even the name of his European wife. We do know that he had one European daughter, Susannah, and at least one daughter from a union with a Mohawk woman. In 1741 Croghan immigrated to Pennsylvania, where he entered the fur trade. Between 1741 and 1754 Croghan became one of the most successful fur traders in Pennsylvania because he refused to wait for the Indians to bring their furs to his trading post. Instead he emulated French traders and traded with the Indians at their villages. During this time Croghan came to appreciate his Indian trading partners and their society. His letters are filled with defenses of Indian society. He learned their languages (he knew Delaware and at least one of the Six Nations' languages, probably Mohawk) and their customs.

By going west, Croghan extended the English fur trading sphere beyond its traditional boundaries. Croghan was one of the first Englishmen to visit Kentucky. He also traded along the Great Lakes and in the Ohio and Illinois valleys, regions claimed by France. During the 1740s the Ohio and Illinois fur trade offered enormous profits for traders like Croghan, and with those profits he began building a trading empire. By 1754 Croghan maintained four trading or storehouses at various locations along the Frankstown path. The Frankstown path was a major artery in the Pennsylvania fur trade and ran from Paxtang (present-day Harrisburg) through Frankstown to Kittanning and then to either Chartier's Town (present-day Tarentum) or the beginning of the Ohio River (present-day Pittsburgh). Each of Croghan's storehouses had an employee stationed at it. The houses eased some of the rigors and dangers associated with the fur trade. The posts allowed Croghan to store trade goods and furs at each location. This allowed Croghan to stay in the field

longer and provide a greater variety of goods than his competitors. In this manner Croghan's trading empire grew. It also made Croghan more susceptible to the economic problems of the fur trade—warfare, stolen goods, and imperial rivalry. These problems combined to bankrupt Croghan in 1753. Croghan's trading empire made him one of the first economic casualties of the Seven Years' War, which began a year later.

During the Seven Years' War, Sir William Johnson, superintendent of Indian affairs for the northern colonies, chose Croghan as his deputy superintendent for the northern district. His appointment confirmed in 1756, Croghan kept this position until he resigned in 1772. As deputy superintendent, Croghan dealt with those Indian groups living west of the Six Nations and north of the Ohio River, primarily the Shawnees, Delawares, Miamis, Wyandots, and Ottawas. These were the Indian polities he had traded with in the 1740s. Croghan was headquartered at Fort Pitt for most of the Seven Years' War (1754–1760 in America). When the war ended, Croghan had to inform the Indians formerly allied with France that France had relinquished its claims to the interior of North America to England. Croghan also played a significant role in negotiating an end to the Anglo-Indian War of 1763.

The war began when Sir Jeffery Amherst ordered Croghan and others to curtail their practice of providing the Indians with gifts, as custom dictated. Croghan understood the dire consequences of such an order and tried to forestall hostilities by providing the Indians with the presents they expected out of his deputy superintendent salary. The extraordinary expense associated with Indian affairs led Croghan to propose resigning his position in 1762 and 1763. His superiors rejected Croghan's resignation and he remained deputy superintendent. Nevertheless, warriors from Seneca country in the east to the Illinois Indians along the Mississippi River in the west, and from Shawnees along the tributaries of the Ohio River to Ottawas along the Great Lakes tried to drive the English out of the territory recently ceded by France. The underlying cause of the war was colonial expansion westward. The Crown realized this and tried to solve the problem by issuing the Proclamation of 1763, an act that forbade most settlement west of the Appalachian Mountains.

By the spring of 1764 the fighting was nearly finished, and Croghan traveled to England. Although Indian affairs were part of the reason for the trip, Croghan also hoped to secure a land patent for 200,000 acres in New York. In 1768 the Crown granted Croghan a patent for 10,000 acres bordering the western side of Lake Ostego. While in London, Croghan also submitted a series of proposals made by Johnson regarding colonial-Indian relations. The proposals asked the Board of Trade to reaffirm its commitment to the Indian superintendent system, which the board did. The proposals Croghan carried also restructured how the Indian trade was to be conducted, placing it under the direction of the Crown rather than the colonies. The Board of Trade integrated Croghan's analysis of the trade and its role in colonial-Indian relations into their plan for the future management of Indian affairs. With his work in London complete, Croghan returned to Pennsylvania and his deputy superintendent position.

As deputy superintendent Croghan's task was to negotiate a formal end to the Anglo-Indian War of 1763. Croghan's duties took him into the Ohio and Illinois valleys in 1765 and into 1766. In the end he secured the Indians' acceptance of British rule for the region. During the negotiations Croghan also informed the Indians of the Illinois region that British troops would finally take control of French outposts in the region such as Fort de Chartres. These British troops had been unable to secure these forts due to the war. Royal officials and officers praised Croghan for the success of his trip.

In 1767 Croghan again attempted to resign because he understood that London officials were losing interest in colonial-Indian relations. Events along the seaboard had taken center stage in the colonial-imperial relationship. From Croghan's perspective this meant trouble since it was the Crown that mediated colonist-Indian disputes. This time Johnson convinced Croghan to withdraw his resignation letter. At the same time, Croghan turned his attention to land speculation, although he remained deputy superintendent until 1772.

Croghan's interest in the West did not concern just Indian affairs. It also involved land speculation. Throughout his career Croghan attempted to secure huge tracts of Indian land for future sale. Croghan's proximity to the frontier made him a leading figure in Pennsylvania, New York, and Virginia land schemes. By 1751 Croghan had patented 1,400 acres by Harris's Ferry, along the Susquehanna River. In 1751 Harris's Ferry sat along a major road connecting Pennsylvania and Virginia. By 1763 Croghan had two tracts of land at the Forks of the Ohio River, the center of Virginia and Pennsylvania's boundary dispute. Croghan also negotiated directly with the Indians for land. In 1767 Croghan and his associates claimed to have purchased 40,000 acres from the Six Nations. Just before the Treaty of Fort Stanwix (1768) began, Croghan and his associates secured a land grant totaling 2.5 million acres from the Indians who were at Stanwix to negotiate a boundary between the colonists and the Indians. The grant, known as the "Indiana Grant," was ostensibly to offset the losses Croghan and other traders had suffered during the past Indian wars. The Indiana grant—which involved the land bounded by the southern boundary of Pennsylvania and the Ohio, the Little Kanawha, and the Monongahela rivers—was purposely incorporated into the boundary settlement reached at Fort Stanwix. Virginians opposed the Indiana grant for this reason and asked the Board of Trade to invalidate the sale. When Lord Dunmore's War broke out in 1774, the issue was once again western lands—and the war convinced the Board of Trade to once again postpone any decision regarding the Indiana grant. By this time, however, Croghan had cast his

lot with the proponents of a new western colony, Vandalia. Croghan owned a proprietary share in the Vandalia enterprise, a pending claim to colonize an estimated 20 million acres. The Vandalia proposal incorporated much of Croghan's Indiana grant within its bounds, and Croghan supported this latter group because it had the backing of Virginia politicians, which the Indiana grant lacked. Croghan also owned shares in some of the other land companies of the day, most noticeably the Illinois and the Grand Ohio companies. Croghan's speculative activities regarding land illustrate the interconnectedness between Indian affairs and land speculation. While Croghan might defend the Native Americans against unlawful land encroachments, he fully expected colonists to supersede the Indians as owners of the lands in question. Croghan hoped to profit from this transition.

Unfortunately for Croghan, his creditors called in his debts before these companies had capitalized on the lands' potential wealth. To meet his obligations he sold some of his shares in the companies and much of the land he already owned. Compounding Croghan's financial problems was the decision by London officials not to create Vandalia colony in 1774. As had been the case with the Indiana grant, Lord Dunmore's War convinced the British government that these western land schemes had created Indian uneasiness. Since England and the colonies were embroiled in a bitter struggle that ultimately led to war, the Board of Trade believed good Indian relations were more important than western colonies. As a result, Croghan found his western landholdings a financial drain.

George Croghan had paid little attention to the colonial-imperial struggles from 1763 onward; nevertheless he decided to cast his lot with the colonists in 1775. Initially Croghan chaired a local committee of correspondence. His neighbors, however, believed that Croghan was a Tory sympathizer, and they forced his resignation in 1777. In part their distrust of Croghan stemmed from the fact that most Indian Department personnel had remained loyal to the Crown. Moreover, Croghan's son-in-law, Augustine Prevost, was a commissioned British officer. In 1778 Croghan's name appeared on a list of traitors. His neighbors brought Croghan to trial for the crime of treason in June 1779, but he was acquitted. Nevertheless, the charge effectively ended his association with the American Revolution.

Croghan spent the rest of the war settling outstanding debts and securing titles to those lands he still held. Most of his efforts were unsuccessful. By 1780 Croghan had sold all of his lands in New York to meet his financial debts. He was living in poverty, and he depended on the generosity of previous business associates to survive. The American Revolution ended all of Croghan's hopes for developing western lands. No state government was willing to recognize the validity of his Indiana or Vandalia grants since they had been secured under the British government.

Croghan's career illustrates certain problems royal officials faced in colonial America. As deputy superintendent, Croghan's successes or failures were often tied to London's willingness or unwillingness to pay the costs involved. Nowhere was this more evident than in the early 1760s. When officials in London decided to reduce the available funds for Indian affairs, colonial-Indian relations deteriorated. The result was the Anglo-Indian War of 1763. When royal officials placed the funding of the Indian Department in colonial hands, intercolonial disputes quickly appeared. This was evidenced by Virginia's opposition to Croghan's Indiana patent. This resulted in increased competition for Indian lands, more violence, and jurisdictional disputes over land already being settled.

Croghan's career also illustrates the importance of credit in the colonial economy and Indian affairs in particular. Many of Croghan's economic problems were the result of a decided lack of specie in colonial America. Croghan built his empire on credit, and when creditors called in those debts, Croghan ran into trouble. Indeed, when he died, his personal property was reckoned to be worth only £50 13s. 6d.

Croghan's life was intertwined with two important forces in eighteenth-century North America: the fur trade and western expansion. Croghan's life illustrates the difficulties most participants in the Indian trade encountered. Hard work was not enough to secure one's future on the western frontier of colonial America. In part he failed because he could not reconcile his appreciation of Indian society with his desire to profit from their demise. Croghan defended Indian culture, religion, and customs in his letters, yet he worked to secure special land cessions from them. He exploited them through his trade practices and worked tirelessly to settle the West with colonists. His importance in Indian affairs was recognized by his contemporaries, but political importance did not translate into economic security. Croghan died a pauper in Passyunk, Pennsylvania, now within the Philadelphia city limits.

• Many of George Croghan's records are in the holdings of the Historical Society of Pennsylvania. The George Croghan Papers and the Gratz collection contain essential information regarding Croghan's career. Many of Croghan's letters are found in *The Papers of Sir William Johnson*, ed. James Sullivan (14 vols., 1921–1965). Two full-length biographies of Croghan exist: Albert T. Volwiler, *George Croghan and the Westward Movement, 1741–1782* (1926), and Nicholas B. Wainwright, *George Croghan: Wilderness Diplomat* (1959). Randolph C. Downes, *Council Fires on the Upper Ohio* (1940), discusses Croghan's role in Anglo-Indian relations in the Ohio and Illinois valleys. Recent works that discuss Croghan's career and emphasize the Native Americans' experience are Michael N. McConnell, *A Country Between: The Upper Ohio Valley and Its Peoples, 1724–1774* (1992), and Richard White, *The Middle Ground: Indians, Empires, and Republics in the Great Lakes Region, 1650–1815* (1991).

MICHAEL J. MULLIN

CROGHAN, George (15 Nov. 1791–8 Jan. 1849), inspector general of the U.S. Army, was born at the family's country seat, "Locust Grove," on the Ohio River east of Louisville, Kentucky, the son of Major William Croghan, a surveyor and entrepreneur, and Lucy Clark. His mother was the sister of both the explorer William Clark and the western military leader in the American Revolution George Rogers Clark, who resided in the Croghan household from 1809 to 1818.

Croghan (pronounced Crawn by his descendants) was classically educated before entering the College of William and Mary in Williamsburg, Virginia, in 1808. Graduating in 1810, he briefly studied law but returned to Locust Grove to read and hunt before volunteering in 1811 as a dragoon to fight Indians in the Northwest Territory. In November 1811 he served as an aide-de-camp to John P. Boyd at the battle of Tippecanoe and became part of the army in the spring of 1812, soon being promoted to captain and then major. He was placed in charge of Fort Stephenson near the head of the Sandusky River but was ordered to evacuate and burn the fort in late July 1813. Major Croghan defiantly notified General William Henry Harrison, "We have determined to maintain this place, and by heavens we can." On 1 and 2 August Croghan's 160 men repulsed a much larger British and Indian force, commanded by Henry Proctor, with considerable enemy loss. Croghan was recognized with a sword (and in 1835 by a congressional medal) for his valor, but his relationship with Harrison became quite cold.

As the conflict came to a conclusion in the Northwest, Lieutenant Colonel Croghan and his Locust Grove neighbor Major Zachary Taylor were requested by Secretary of War James Monroe to organize a corps of Kentucky volunteers to defend New Orleans. The war ended before this task was completed. In June 1816 Croghan was relieved of his command by his future brother-in-law, Major Thomas S. Jesup, and he traveled to New York determined to leave the military and farm. He married Serena Eliza Livingston, daughter of J. R. Livingston of New York, in 1817. The couple had seven children. Serena Livingston's uncle Edward lived in New Orleans, and the Croghans resided there extensively, traveling between New Orleans and New York. In July 1824 Croghan became postmaster of New Orleans, only to leave the office in considerable debt when he was appointed in late 1825 as inspector general of the U.S. Army. In this capacity, his responsibility was to conduct annual tours of the military installations that were spread along the country's borders and on the western frontier beyond the Mississippi River. Croghan made reports of his findings and recommendations to the general in chief of the army. According to Francis Paul Prucha, who published selections from these official reports in *Army Life on the Western Frontier* (1958), Croghan made inspection tours in every year between 1826 and 1845, except in 1830 and 1832 when members of his family were sick, in 1835 when cholera was a significant threat, and in 1837 when he was mustering troops for the Florida war. Croghan's conduct during these tours when away from his wife and family was less than exemplary. Intoxication and gambling were frequently noted, to the despair of his family. He was always in debt, and in many instances he applied for and received double payment for his services. With insufficient money to pay his debts, he borrowed from fellow officers, while his brothers would make restitution to protect their family's name. As recompense, he sometimes worked at Mammoth Cave overseeing construction for his brother John Croghan, who was its proprietor. On 5 May 1845 President James K. Polk ordered a general court-martial to be convened at Fort Monroe, Virginia, to consider numerous double payment charges brought against Croghan by Major General Winfield Scott. Again, Croghan's brothers and his brother-in-law, Quartermaster General Jesup, intervened. His wife filed for a legal separation to protect her possessions. Under scrutiny, Croghan toured the western posts for the last time in the fall of 1845. After mustering volunteer troops to fight in the Mexican War, the next year found him in Monterrey, Mexico, fighting under his old friend and neighbor Zachary Taylor. He returned sick but evidently retaining his title as inspector general. He died of cholera in New Orleans. On 2 August 1906 his remains were reinterred in Fremont, Ohio, the site of his Fort Stephenson victory.

• Many of Croghan's papers are in the Library of Congress and the Henry E. Huntington Library, San Marino, Calif. Published biographical sketches include the *Port Folio* 4 (Mar. 1815): 214; C. R. Williams, "George Croghan," *Ohio Archaeological and Historical Publications* 12 (1903): 375–409; Thomas W. Parsons, "George Croghan in the War of 1812," *Northwest Ohio Quarterly* 20 (1948): 192–202; and Samuel W. Thomas, "George Croghan (1791–1849): A Study of the Non-Military Life of the Inspector General of the United States Army," *Filson Club History Quarterly* 41 (1967): 304–22.

SAMUEL W. THOMAS

CROIX, Teodore de. *See* De Croix, Teodore.

CROKER, Richard (23 Nov. 1843–29 Apr. 1922), New York City political leader, was born in County Cork, Ireland, the son of Eyre Coote Croker, a blacksmith and veterinarian. Little is known of his mother, except that her maiden name was Wellstead. In 1846 the Crokers immigrated to the United States and, after a short sojourn in Cincinnati, settled in New York City. Richard attended public school intermittently until he was thirteen years old, when he began an apprenticeship as a machinist for the Harlem Railroad. Young Croker's prowess with his fists won the admiration of neighborhood street gang members, and he became leader of the Fourth Avenue Tunnel Gang.

As gang leader, he attracted the notice of local Democratic politicians, becoming the protégé of Alderman Jimmy O'Brien. In 1868 O'Brien won the office of sheriff, and Croker took his place on the board of aldermen, where he joined the "reform" faction opposed to the powerful boss of the Tammany Hall Democrats, William M. Tweed. When John "Honest John" Kelly succeeded the discredited Tweed as boss of Tammany in 1872, Croker became his loyal lieutenant. In 1873 he married Elizabeth Frazier; they had nine children. That same year a grateful Kelly secured

Croker's election as coroner, a lucrative position earning the holder ample fees, but the rising young politician soon suffered a setback. An election-day scuffle between Croker's followers and those of a rival leader resulted in the fatal shooting of one of Croker's foes, and the coroner was charged with murder. In the ensuing trial, the jury was unable to agree on a verdict, and the prosecution did not attempt to retry Croker. The murder charge, however, damaged Croker's reputation, and a local newspaper called him a "bad odor to the party." After a few years of withdrawal from politics, in 1883 Croker was appointed fire commissioner and gradually reestablished himself as a political force. When Kelly died in 1886, Croker assumed leadership of Tammany Hall, a position he held for the next sixteen years.

As "boss" of Tammany, Croker proved much more successful than Kelly. He commanded an army of 90,000 party workers and generally kept firm control over Tammany's thirty-five district leaders. During the late 1880s and early 1890s he eliminated the rival Democratic factions that had prevented Kelly from assuming absolute sway over the party machinery in New York City. Consequently, in one election after another he was able to place Tammany loyalists in the mayor's seat. Among his closest henchmen were mayors Hugh Grant and Thomas Gilroy, who generally could be counted on to carry out Croker's wishes. Croker was unabashed in his devotion to monopolizing government jobs for his loyal followers. He admitted that the "logical result" of his views "would be that all the employees of the city government, from the Mayor to the porter who makes the fire in his office, should be members of the Tammany organization." Following revelations of gross corruption in the Tammany-dominated police department, a reform coalition momentarily won control of city hall in the mid-1890s. But in the election of 1897, Croker's handpicked mayoral candidate, Robert Van Wyck, triumphed, and for the next four years the Tammany chieftain was unquestionably the power behind the throne, dispensing the extensive patronage and favors associated with New York City government. At this time an unhappy opponent of Tammany commented, "It is no mere jest when people call Richard Croker the King of the City of New York."

Profiting from his political power, Croker became a rich man during the late 1880s and the 1890s. He did not steal directly from the municipal treasury, but through his political influence he ensured that the city awarded lucrative contracts to businesses in which he held an interest. In one of a series of state investigations into corruption in New York City government, a hostile questioner asked Croker, "Then you are working for your pocket, are you not?" "All the time; the same as you," replied the candid Tammany boss. Mounting dissatisfaction with evidence of malfeasance in the Van Wyck administration, however, resulted in Tammany's defeat in the election of 1901. Reformer Seth Low won the mayor's office, and the vanquished

Croker lost control of the Tammany organization and of New York City politics.

Since the early 1890s Croker had been spending an increasing amount of time in Europe, and following Low's victory he retired to an English manor, where he devoted himself to the breeding and racing of horses. He proved as successful at this as he had been at politics, and in 1907 a horse from his stable won the vaunted English Derby. However, his private life became increasingly troubled. In 1897 the Crokers separated, and soon after his wife's death in 1914 the former Tammany boss married Bula Benton Edmondson, a 23-year-old Cherokee Indian. During the early 1920s his children by his first marriage tried unsuccessfully to have Croker declared incompetent in order to wrest away control of his fortune. At the time of Croker's death in Ireland, this bitter conflict over his wealth remained unsettled.

His Irish immigrant status, his early life as a gang leader, his willingness to profit from politics, and his calculating, behind-the-scenes string pulling made Croker a stereotypical urban boss. Because of his limited education and rather harsh voice, he did not excel at public speaking but instead was known for his sullen reserve. He was not the flashy frontman of politics, wooing the masses with his oratory. He was the manager of electoral victories who ensured that Tammany garnered the requisite number of votes and that loyal party workers were rewarded. During his life and for years after, reformers deplored the fact that a figure like Croker amassed such political clout and made of him a symbol of the wrongs wreaked by Tammany. For better or worse, however, Croker proved an effective political organizer, refining a party machine that was unequaled in its ability to seize control of the levers of urban government.

• The principal biography of Croker is Lothrop Stoddard, *Master of Manhattan: The Life of Richard Croker* (1931). Alfred Henry Lewis, *Richard Croker* (1901), is an adulatory work of little value that compares the political boss to Cromwell, Napoleon, and Caesar. A critical account of Croker is found in William Allen White, *Masks in a Pageant* (1928). More useful are Harold Zink, *City Bosses in the United States: A Study of Twenty Municipal Bosses* (1930); M. R. Werner, *Tammany Hall* (1928); and Alfred Connable and Edward Silberfarb, *Tigers of Tammany: Nine Men Who Ran New York* (1967). An obituary is in the *New York Times*, 30 Apr. 1922.

JON C. TEAFORD

CROLY, David Goodman (3 Nov. 1829–29 Apr. 1889), journalist and social thinker, was born in County Cork, Ireland, the son of Patrick Croly and Elizabeth (maiden name unknown), Irish Protestants; the family moved to New York City when David was an infant. Although a poor man, Croly's father collected books and read widely in history, theology, and letters. As a youth David served an apprenticeship to a silversmith but found his real pleasure in reading, thinking, writing, and debating. He attended New York University (then called the University of the City of New York) for a year, receiving a "special diploma" in 1854. In 1855 he became a reporter for the *New York Evening Post* but quickly moved to the *Herald*, where he worked until 1858.

In 1856 Croly married Jane Cunningham, an English-born journalist who was beginning her own spectacular career; using the pseudonym "Jennie June," she wrote on women's topics and over the next three decades attracted a huge audience of devoted readers. The couple had five children, among them Herbert Croly, the political philosopher and editor. Despite evidence that the Crolys' marriage was stormy on both personal and intellectual grounds, David and Jane Croly never separated. In 1858 they moved to Rockford, Illinois, where they bought and tried unsuccessfully to revive a small newspaper, the *Rockford Democratic Standard* (whose title they changed to the *Daily News*). By 1860 they were back in New York City, where they spent the remainder of their lives.

David Croly joined the *New York World* and in 1862 became its managing editor. Thus for a decade he, together with owner Manton Marble, had much to do with setting the policy of the leading Democratic newspaper in the United States. In 1872 Croly left the paper after disagreements erupted with Marble over the *World*'s handling of the tariff issue, the Franco-Prussian War, and the accusations made against "Boss" William Marcy Tweed. A year later Croly helped found the *Daily Graphic*, the nation's first illustrated daily, which he edited until 1878. In 1868, with his best friend Clinton W. Sweet, Croly also started a successful trade paper, the *Real Estate Record and Builders' Guide*, which he edited from time to time and where he deposited some of his most characteristic and revealing personal views.

Those views from the start were highly unorthodox. An avid reader of "advanced" social philosophy, Croly admired Herbert Spencer, John Stuart Mill, Thomas Huxley, Frederic Harrison, John Fiske, and other "radicals." He was above all, however, a loyal follower of the French thinker Auguste Comte, and other adherents of Comte credited Croly with doing effective work in spreading Comte's teachings, including the Frenchman's controversial Religion of Humanity, among an influential circle of New York intellectuals. He expressed his radicalism in another short-lived venture, a periodical called the *Modern Thinker*, which ran only two bizarre issues, one in 1871 and the second in 1873 (the magazine appeared with variously colored pages printed with colored inks). Croly gave his Comtism the most direct expression in *A Positivist Primer* (1871), written in his favorite style—an extended conversation with various interlocutors, each representing a particular position and putting questions to a teacher.

In addition to these literary activities, Croly embarked on other unusual projects. He and George Wakeman, another *World* journalist, perpetrated a wild hoax with a book, *Miscegenation* (1864), which they published anonymously, hoping to embarrass the Republicans by slyly creating the impression that the party favored race-mixing. The authors are credited with inventing the term *miscegenation*. Four years later Croly wrote the Democratic campaign biography, *Seymour and Blair: Their Lives and Services*. If this were not enough, he published *The Truth about Love* (1872), a remarkably frank exploration of sexuality and "the passion of Love." Finally, Croly, who thought of himself as a prophet of future events, collected some of his predictions in *Glimpses of the Future* (1888).

Croly was a warm, gregarious, talkative, leisurely, and affectionate man. Known in the offices of the *New York World* as "the Great Suggester," he poured out ideas faster than he could follow through on them. Many coworkers would have agreed with the assessment of the well-known journalist Montgomery Schuyler: "His was the most prolific mind I ever knew. For . . . seven years my association with him was daily, and during all that period he teemed with suggestions. He was never at a loss for assignments to unoccupied reporters or for topics to editorial writers." His last years were a constant struggle against sickness, and he eventually died of nephritis at his home in New York City.

• No collection of David Goodman Croly Papers exists. His ideas are most easily approached through his books. Two Ph.D. dissertations contain biographical information, David W. Levy, "The Life and Thought of Herbert Croly" (Univ. of Wisconsin, 1967), and J. M. Bloch, "The Rise of the New York *World* during the Civil War Decade" (Harvard Univ., 1941). Also useful is James M. Bolquerin, "An Investigation of the Contributions of David, Jane, and Herbert Croly to American Life" (M.A. thesis, Univ. of Missouri, 1948). See also Sidney Kaplan, "The Miscegenation Issue in the Election of 1864," *Journal of Negro History* 34 (1949): 274–343; Carl Bode, "Columbia's Carnal Bed," *American Quarterly* 15 (1963): 52–64; and Gillis J. Harp, *Positivist Republic: Auguste Comte and the Reconstruction of American Liberalism, 1865–1920* (1995). Two helpful biographical memorials appeared in the *Real Estate Record and Builders' Guide* at his death; see the issues of 4 May and 18 May 1889.

DAVID W. LEVY

CROLY, Herbert David (23 Jan. 1869–17 May 1930), political philosopher and editor, was born in New York City, the son of David Goodman Croly and Jane Cunningham (Jane C. Croly), two famous journalists. His mother was a widely read writer on women's topics. His father was an experienced newspaperman, a writer of unorthodox views, and a follower of the French thinker Auguste Comte. From early childhood Herbert received instruction from his father, who was surely the chief influence in his life. No doubt growing up in a home of such intense intellectual activity predisposed Croly to a life of reading, thinking, and writing.

He attended New York City private schools and, after a year at City College in New York, entered Harvard in the fall of 1886. His career there was highly unusual. After two years of study (1886–1888), he returned to New York City to tend his ailing father. Upon David Croly's death in 1889, Herbert went to work for two periodicals that his father had started, the

Real Estate Record and Builders' Guide and the *Architectural Record*. On 30 May 1892 he wed Louise Emory, whom he had met when she was a student at Radcliffe; they had no children. The couple returned to Harvard in the fall, but this time Croly dropped out before midsemester because of a somewhat mysterious mental breakdown. He returned to Harvard in 1895, intending to become a professor of philosophy. For a variety of personal, economic, and intellectual reasons, however, he abandoned that ambition and left college in 1899, still without his degree.

He returned to New York City to serve as an editor of the *Architectural Record*. Under his own name, and under various pseudonyms (especially "A. C. David"), he wrote dozens of articles on architectural style, municipal reform, and urban planning. With fellow editor Harry W. Desmond, Croly published *Stately Homes in America from Colonial Times to the Present Day* (1903) and a collection of his own articles, *Houses for Town and Country* (1907), under the name "William Herbert." Although he contributed to the *Architectural Record* until the end of his life, Croly loosened his editorial connection with it in the summer of 1905 to devote himself to the book that would make his reputation and establish him as perhaps the leading political philosopher of the progressive movement.

That work, *The Promise of American Life*, appeared in November 1909. It combined striking historical, political, and economic analysis with somewhat turgid and difficult prose, and offered views on a score of American problems. At its heart was the contention that the modern industrial world required Americans to surrender their devotion both to unbridled individualism and to the Jeffersonian tradition of a limited federal government. For the former, Croly wished to substitute a community-minded, socially conscious citizenry; for the latter, a Hamiltonian central government, energetically pursuing the national interest by entering into the life of the nation in unprecedented ways. Croly scorned the attempt to break the "trusts" into small competing units and advocated instead federal regulation of them in the interest of the nation.

Dozens of newspapers and periodicals reviewed the book enthusiastically, and numerous political leaders and reformers discussed its arguments. Most important, Theodore Roosevelt (1858–1919), the former president, found many of his own ideas confirmed in its pages and struck up a friendship with Croly. Naturally, Croly supported Roosevelt in his Progressive campaign of 1912 (Roosevelt's slogan, "the new nationalism," had first appeared in Croly's book) and performed a few literary chores in the campaign. To maintain his independence, however, he refused to become an official of the Progressive party.

Because of Croly's new prominence, Mark Hanna's family commissioned him to write a biography of the Republican political boss; the perceptive, but overly sympathetic *Marcus Alonzo Hanna* appeared in 1912. Croly's sudden fame also resulted in an invitation to deliver Harvard's prestigious Godkin lectures in late 1913 and early 1914. These lectures, published as *Progressive Democracy* in 1914, never received the praise and respect accorded to *The Promise of American Life*. The book reflected both the influence of the pragmatism of William James and John Dewey and the optimism Croly derived from the early successes of progressive reform. It attacked Woodrow Wilson's progressive vision as inadequate.

Croly's ideas attracted the attention of Willard Straight and Dorothy Straight, a wealthy and philanthropic couple with reform leanings. They soon agreed to provide funds for a weekly journal of political opinion under Croly's editorship. After a year of planning and gathering together a brilliant staff, the first issue of the *New Republic* appeared in November 1914. After the death of Willard Straight in 1918 (Croly published a lengthy biography of him in 1924), Dorothy Straight continued to support the magazine generously. Croly served as its principal editor until his death. From the beginning, the *New Republic* earned a reputation for clearheaded and forceful advocacy and for attracting writers of high intelligence and reputation. Under Croly, the journal enjoyed a far greater influence than might have been suggested by its modest circulation figures.

During its first five years, Croly's magazine was absorbed by World War I and its aftermath. It slowly came to espouse American preparedness and in 1916 endorsed both Wilson's general position and his presidential candidacy. Alongside war-related articles and editorials, the *New Republic* pressed for greater authority for the central government and for a wide range of progressive reform measures. The announcement of the Treaty of Versailles struck Croly with enormous force. He regarded the agreement as a great betrayal of enlightenment principles, an unconscionable retreat from the idealism Wilson had enunciated, and a document whose general harshness and specific provisions were likely to be the source of further international problems. He and the other editors—sacrificing both subscriptions and their deepest desires to wield influence as Washington "insiders"—forthrightly, instantly, and bitterly denounced both the treaty and Wilson himself.

During the 1920s the *New Republic* fought a rearguard action to protect old progressive reforms and to challenge a rising tide of reactionary conservatism. In the 1924 presidential campaign, the journal supported Progressive candidate Robert La Follette (1855–1925) with enthusiasm and, in 1928, the Democrat Alfred E. Smith. Frustrated by the political atmosphere of the 1920s, Croly shifted the focus of the journal—still a vehicle for some of the most talented and original writers in the United States and England—toward literary, artistic, and philosophic concerns.

During the last ten years of his life, Croly suffered a pessimism caused by steadily declining health and by the disappointment of the political and editorial hopes of earlier days. He expressed his gloom in another book, *The Breach in Civilization*, and in an autobiographical fragment, neither of which he published. The frustrations of the 1920s brought forward a mysti-

cal strain in his nature that had always been present, but not always so visibly. He became interested in social Christianity and, for a time, was a follower of the European mystic G. I. Gurdjieff and his disciple, A. R. Orage. In the autumn of 1928 Croly suffered a massive stroke, which left him permanently disabled and enfeebled. His wife moved him to Santa Barbara, California, where he died. He was buried in a small cemetery near Cornish, New Hampshire, where he and his wife maintained a summer home.

Croly was painfully shy. He almost never made a speech; meeting new people and conventional socializing were sometimes excruciatingly painful for him. Nevertheless, by a force of will, he denied himself the life of a recluse; he had a number of close and loyal friends who enjoyed his conversation and admired his searching honesty and intellectual integrity, the purity of his motives, and the quality of his intelligence.

• There is no collection of Croly manuscripts, but letters may be found in the Felix Frankfurter Papers at the Library of Congress and in the Learned Hand Papers at the Harvard Law School. See also a memorial supplement in the 16 July 1930 issue of the *New Republic*. The only full-length biography is David W. Levy, *Herbert Croly of the New Republic: The Life and Thought of an American Progressive* (1985). Also valuable are Charles Forcey, *The Crossroads of Liberalism: Croly, Weyl, Lippmann and the Progressive Era, 1900–1925* (1961); David Noble, "Herbert Croly and American Progressive Thought," *Western Political Quarterly* 7 (1954): 537–53; James A. Neuchterlein, "The Dream of Scientific Liberalism: *The New Republic* and American Progressive Thought, 1914–1920," *Review of Politics* 42 (1980): 167–90; and Suzanne Stephens, "Architecture Criticism in a Historical Context: The Case of Herbert Croly," in *The Architectural Historian in America*, ed. Elisabeth Blair MacDougall (1990).

DAVID W. LEVY

CROLY, Jane Cunningham (19 Dec. 1829–23 Dec. 1901), writer and women's club leader, was born in Market Harborough, Leicestershire, England, the daughter of Joseph Howes Cunningham, a Unitarian preacher, and Jane Scott. Croly's family emigrated to the United States from England in 1841, perhaps prompted by the unpopularity of her father's extreme Unitarianism and his efforts to educate workers. She was twelve years old when they settled in Poughkeepsie, New York, and then in Wappinger's Falls, New York. She kept house for her Congregationalist minister brother and acquired enough learning to teach district school and write a semimonthly newspaper for her brother's parishioners.

At the age of twenty-five she moved to New York City. There she began her career as a professional journalist on James Gordon Bennett's (1795–1872) *New York Herald*. She wrote a regular column for women there and in the *Sunday Times and Noah's Weekly Messenger*. By 1857, under the pen name Jennie June, she became one of the earliest syndicated women columnists. Her work was carried in other newspapers in New Orleans, Richmond, Baltimore, and Louisville. In 1856 she married David Goodman Croly, an Irish immigrant and *New York Herald* staff writer. They were married until he died in 1889, at the age of sixty, from a decade-long struggle with Bright's Disease. Together they had five children, including Herbert Croly, the first editor of the *New Republic*.

In 1859 the Crolys moved to Rockford, Illinois, the home of Jane's sister Mary, to publish and edit the *Rockford Daily News*. Jane seems to have carried more than her fair share of the journalistic responsibilities. M. J. Bolquerin notes that "she edited the paper and he played chess."

The following year the Croly family returned to Manhattan, where both Jane and David wrote for the *New York World*. There she managed the woman's department (1862–1872), wrote for the *Weekly Times*, and became chief staff writer for *Mme. Demorest's Mirror of Fashions*, later *Demorest's Monthly Magazine*, from 1860 to 1887. She also published three collections of her columns: *Jennie Juneiana: Talks on Women's Topics* (1869), *For Better or Worse* (1875), and *Thrown on Her Own Resources* (1891). In addition, she wrote four guides to needlework and a cookbook. When her husband left the *New York World* in 1877 to spread the doctrine of Auguste Comte's positivism, her income supported the family.

Since the thrust of her advice to middle-class women readers concerned the absurdity of devoting one's full time to housework and fashion, it is not surprising that she advocated women's increased participation in public life. She taught journalism to women and founded the New York Women's Press Club in 1889, serving as its president for many years. Incensed at the exclusion of women journalists from the mostly male New York Press Club celebration to honor Charles Dickens in 1868, she was inspired to create the most influential early woman's club in post–Civil War America. Her New York City women's club was named Sorosis, a botanical term referring to a flowering plant that bears fruit. The organization attracted pioneer career women from the entire region, including Vassar astronomy professor Maria Mitchell, physician Mary Putnam Jacobi, Universalist minister Phebe Hanaford, and many writers and journalists of distinction, including poet Alice Cary, novelist Louisa May Alcott, and newspaperwoman Kate Field. Sorosis's luncheon meetings at Delmonico's fashionable restaurant provided a forum for members' formal delivery of speeches on historical, literary, and current events topics. Debates sometimes led to social action, including the support of women's education and improved conditions for working women. Inspiring participants' mental stimulation and social responsibility, the club's structure was widely emulated in cities and towns throughout the nation.

Croly worked through additional associations at encouraging other women to stretch their minds and challenge the constraining traditions that limited women's activity to housekeeping and homemaking. To that end she helped found the Association for the Advancement of Women (1873–1897) and the General Federation of Women's Clubs in 1890. Her efforts to unite women's clubs to effect change succeeded in winning public parks, playgrounds, vocational training, street lights, health care, improved working conditions, scholarships for girls, employment opportunities for women, and a wide variety of other reforms for multitudes of cities and towns where women's clubs formed, decades before women won a public voice via the suffrage.

Croly devoted her professional skills to attracting national interest in women's clubs. She edited their periodicals, *Woman's Cycle* (1889–1893), *Home-Maker* (1890–1893), and *New Cycle* (1893–96), as well as a massive compilation of local women's club histories. Her *History of the Woman's Club Movement in America* (1898) is the strongest source of turn-of-the-century club activity by women.

Croly's extraordinary ability to organize women created a formidable force in American culture and reform. For this, she was deified by the clubwomen she inspired and was honored at club gatherings she attended and those she did not. She broke her hip in 1898 and her health declined thereafter. She died a few years later in New York City of cardiac dilation. She is buried in a cemetery in Lakewood, New Jersey.

• Croly burned her own papers, but sparse materials are collected at the Schlesinger Library, Radcliffe College; in the Sorosis Papers, Sophia Smith Collection, Smith College Library; and in the Caroline M. Severance Papers, Henry E. Huntington Library, San Marino, Calif. In addition to those works mentioned above, Croly wrote *Ladies Fancy Work* (1886), *Needle Work: a Manual* (1885), *Jennie June's American Cookery Book* (1866), *Knitting and Crochet* (1885), and *Sorosis, Its Origin and History* (1886). See also Henry Ladd Smith, "The Beauteous Jennie June: Pioneer Woman Journalist," *Journalism Quarterly* 40 (Spring 1963): 169–74; Karen J. Blair, *The Clubwoman as Feminist: True Womanhood Redefined, 1868–1914* (1980); Mildred White Wells, *Unity in Diversity* (1953), pp. 47–51; Elizabeth Bancroft Schlesinger, "The Nineteenth-Century Woman's Dilemma and Jennie June," *New York History* 42 (Oct. 1961): 365–79; Frank L. Mott, *History of American Magazines*, vol. 4 (1957); M. J. Bolquerin, "An Investigation of the Contributions of David, June [*sic*] and Herbert Croly to American Life—with Emphasis on the Influence of the Father on the Son" (M.A. thesis, Univ. of Missouri, 1948); and M. D. Winant, *A Century of Sorosis, 1868–1968* (1968). Obituaries are in the *New York Times*, 24 Dec. 1901, and in *Woman's Journal*, 4 Jan. 1902 and 11 Jan. 1902.

KAREN J. BLAIR

CROMPTON, George (23 Mar. 1829–29 Dec. 1886), inventor and manufacturer, was born at Holcombe, Tottingham, Lancashire, England, the son of William Crompton, a textile inventor, and Sarah Low. After immigrating to the United States in 1836, William Crompton brought his family in 1839 from England to Taunton, Massachusetts. There Crompton attended local schools before going to Millbury Academy. He then worked as a bookkeeper in his father's office and as a mechanic with the Colt Company in Hartford, Connecticut. From an early age he displayed an uncommon mechanical aptitude and a desire to see a mechanical problem through from start to completion.

William Crompton, who had invented the first fancy power loom (1837), became incapacitated in 1849, and in that year Crompton went to Washington, D.C., in order to renew his father's loom patent. Having accomplished this, Crompton formed a partnership with Merrill E. Furbush in 1851; the two men began to manufacture looms in Worcester, Massachusetts, which became the seat of Crompton's personal and professional life.

In 1854 a fire destroyed the loom works, and Crompton and Furbush moved their location to the site that later became the Crompton & Knowles Company in Worcester. From 1851 until 1857 the partners focused on making "narrow looms," but in 1857 Crompton brought out a fast-operating broad fancy loom, with twenty-four harnesses and three boxes at each end. With this new loom, which was able to reach the speed of eighty-five picks per minute, almost doubling the speed of the most efficient of its predecessors, Crompton had succeeded in improving upon his father's work, and his future looked especially bright.

In 1859 the Crompton and Furbush partnership was dissolved, and Crompton established his sole proprietorship, the Crompton Loom Works, on Green Street in Worcester. During the Civil War the need for uniforms and blankets for the U.S. Army was so great that Crompton and his workers could not meet the demands for loom-building, but these frenetic years also laid the foundation for Crompton's personal prosperity. In 1862 he purchased a dozen acres on Providence Street in Worcester; this land, centered around an Elizabethan-style mansion known as "Mariemont," became his estate. Here Crompton, his wife Mary Christina Pratt, whom he had married in 1853, and their nine children lived in sober splendor.

One of the great coups of Crompton's business career came in 1867, when he brought his looms to the Paris Exhibition. Although the Crompton looms had competition from English, Belgian, Saxon, Prussian, and French looms, Crompton's products won first prize and a medal, presented to Crompton by Emperor Napoleon III. This event, coupled with the reception of Crompton's looms at the Centennial Exhibition in Philadelphia in 1876, made his name and his product famous throughout the world of manufacturing. The judges at the Centennial Exposition reported that "the original and well-known Crompton loom has been modified and improved from time to time by successive inventions until it covers a wide range of figured or fancy-woven fabrics, and is a thoroughly well-built, trustworthy and adaptable machine."

Although he was principally an inventor (he eventually came to hold more than 100 patents), Crompton was involved in a number of other areas of business and civic interest in Worcester. President of the Crompton Carpet Company, Crompton paid a debt of over $137,000 when the company failed in 1878. He was also a director of the Worcester National Bank, the Worcester Gas Light Company, and the Hartford Steam Boiler Insurance Company. He served as an alderman in 1863–1864 and was a member of the common council of Worcester in 1860–1861. Perhaps the greatest setback to his personal and political ambitions came in 1871, when he lost the Worcester mayoral election (he was running as the Republican candidate). Remaining involved, nevertheless, in civic affairs, he made the presentation speech at the dedication of the Soldiers' Monument in Worcester in 1874. Upon his death at home, the Worcester community conceded that it had lost one of its leading lights and that Crompton's work had had a good deal to do with the transformation of Worcester from the "pretty New England town" that English writer Charles Dickens had witnessed in 1842 to the industrial city it had become by 1880.

In the footsteps of his father, William Crompton, George Crompton brought an English trade to America: textile weaving. It was men such as Crompton who brought New England towns such as Worcester, Lowell, Lawrence, and Holyoke fully into the industrial age during the mid-nineteenth century. Although Crompton was truly a man of one town (Worcester), his influence in mechanical matters spread far beyond the confines of his chosen location. As a result of his rather modest demeanor, Crompton never became a member of the pantheon of celebrated American inventors, but his work stood for itself. The Crompton loom, patented in 1857, became the standard of its type throughout the United States for many years.

• There is not a great deal of information available on Crompton in standard histories. Biographical information is provided in the writings of Crompton's son, George Crompton, *The Crompton Loom: William and George Crompton* (1949) and *Mariemont* (1952). The Crompton loom is discussed briefly in Steve Dunwell, *The Run of the Mill: A Pictorial Narrative of the Expansion, Dominion, Decline and Enduring Impact of the New England Textile Industry* (1978). Crompton's success in Philadelphia in 1876 is described in Francis A. Walker, ed., *United States Centennial Commission International Exhibition 1876: Reports and Awards*, vol. 5 (1880), p. 21. Older but still valuable works are S. N. D. North, *The New England Wool Manufacture* (1897), and Charles G. Washburn, *Industrial Worcester* (1917).

SAMUEL WILLARD CROMPTON

CROMWELL, Dean Bartlett (20 Sept. 1879–3 Aug. 1962), track and field coach, was born in Turner, Oregon, the son of William Cromwell, the owner of a sawmill and a small ranch, and Emma (maiden name unknown). Following his father's death in 1891, Cromwell, his mother, and four siblings moved to southern California, where Cromwell became a premier athlete while attending Occidental College Prep in Los Angeles. His athletic prowess at Occidental College won him recognition in 1901 as the Helms Athletic Foundation athlete of the year in southern California. At Occidental he played first base in baseball and right halfback in football. A versatile track performer, he ran the 50- and 100-yard dashes and the quarter mile. He also competed in the pole vault, high jump, shot put, and hammer throw as well as in bicycle racing. Following his college years, he represented the Los Angeles Young Men's Christian Association in 1904 and 1905 at YMCA national meets, placing in the high jump, shot put, and hammer throw.

Cromwell worked with the contracts division of the telephone company in southern California before accepting head coaching positions in football and track at the University of Southern California in 1908. He coached football for five seasons, compiling a 21–8–6 record, including an undefeated 1910 season. His tenure as track and field coach continued until 1948 when he was elected track and field coach for the American Olympic team.

At Southern California Cromwell developed the most successful programs in the country. USC joined the prestigious Intercollegiate Association of Amateur Athletics of America conference in 1924. They won nine IC-4A championships, including seven in a row, before USC elected to leave the largely eastern-based conference in 1939. Cromwell's teams also won 12 National Collegiate Athletic Association national championships, including nine consecutive championships from 1935 to 1943.

Cromwell recruited the great athletes of California. Critics and competing coaches believed that Cromwell had a "star fixation," centering his attention only on highly skilled athletes. Cromwell believed that championships were won with "champions not with just a lot of fine, tall, handsome boys." He believed that champions and world record holders brought other champions to his program. The "star system" brought immediate international recognition to Cromwell and USC. Southern California squads generally had around thirty-five members, small when compared to other teams, which carried about a hundred athletes. Cromwell focused his attention on the talented athlete who could score significant points in any type of meet, then won meets and championships because his smaller number of athletes accumulated large point totals.

Competing coaches underestimated Cromwell's ability to foster athletic prowess, instead believing that any coach could be successful in southern California, where superior athletes abounded. They thought that Cromwell was not a strong coach, because he had neither a specific philosophy nor a specific technique that fostered success. Cromwell's success was based neither on his technical competence nor a strict regimen of training. As a coach, "the Dean" focused his attention on the talents and innate abilities of individual athletes and on an appreciation of the specific skills and styles that an athlete brought to each event. He observed each athlete for hours, refusing to change the idiosyncrasies of the athlete's style, preferring to improve performance through enhancing the individual's natural or chosen methods. One criticism of Cromwell's coaching was that he had little patience with athletes who could not be highly competitive. Such young men felt ignored and often quit his squads.

In addition, Cromwell achieved success with athletes through positive reinforcement, believing that neither an athlete nor an athletic team would perform better when subjected to overt criticism. Those who participated on Cromwell-coached teams came to believe that they could defeat any competition. To reinforce this concept Cromwell addressed each of his athletes as "Champ." This mannerism and his ability to produce Olympic quality athletes earned him his nickname, "Maker of Champions."

Few coaches in any sport had the long-term success that Cromwell experienced. In every Olympic games between 1912 and 1948 a Cromwell-coached athlete won a gold medal, accumulating twelve Olympic gold medals. Thirty-six different Southern California track stars competed in the Olympic games during these years. Cromwell-coached athletes held 13 individual world records, while relay teams held three world records. His athletes held 34 National Collegiate Athletic Association individual event titles, 40 IC-4A, and 39 Amateur Athletic Union titles. It was alleged but never verified that Cromwell had remarked during the 1936 Berlin Olympics that black athletes were not doing the sport any good.

Cromwell retired in 1948 to become the Olympic track coach for the United States. Yet his election was controversial. Cromwell's relationship with other coaches sometimes appeared strained. He may not have been elected to the coaching post, in fact, had the U.S. Olympic Committee panel unified on the choice of Emil Von Elling of New York University. But a few eastern voters split on the Von Elling candidacy. Cromwell was elected because there was no consensus on a candidate from the east. Eastern journalists in 1948 attempted to subvert Cromwell's candidacy by accusing him of racism (based on the alleged remarks during the 1936 Olympics). Black athletes who competed for the Maker of Champions staunchly defended Cromwell's support of all athletes, citing instances when Cromwell refused to allow the entire team to stay in eastern hotels or eat in eastern restaurants that refused to serve all members of the team.

By the end of his career Cromwell owned apartment buildings and rental properties in Los Angeles, as well as apple orchards in Oregon. Cromwell was married twice, first to Cora (no other details are available), with whom he had one child, and then in 1907 to Gertrude Potter, with whom he had two children. After retirement, he became the sideline announcer for Los Angeles Rams home football games, an adviser to track programs throughout the country, and a well-recognized figure in sports throughout southern California. He was buried in Turner, Oregon, following his death in Los Angeles.

• Clippings files on Cromwell are available in the Sports Information Office of the University of Southern California, at the *Sporting News*, and at the Helms Foundation Library, Los Angeles. Useful articles include Quentin Reynolds, "The Perfect Track Man," *Colliers*, 12 Jan. 1935, p. 20; Pete Martin, "Wizard of the Cinders," *Saturday Evening Post*, 20 Mar. 1948, pp. 34–35, 116, 118–20, 122; and Al Stump, "Track Coaches," *Sportfolio*, Apr. 1948, pp. 73–82. Obituaries are in *Track and Field News*, Aug. 1962, and the *New York Times*, 4 Aug. 1962.

HARRY JEBSEN, JR.

CROMWELL, Gladys (28 Nov. 1885–19 Jan. 1919), poet, was born Gladys Louise Husted Cromwell in Brooklyn, New York, the daughter of Frederick Cromwell, a businessman, and Esther Whitmore Husted. Her parents were prominent in New York society. She was educated at Brearley, a private school, and traveled throughout Europe. Cromwell began writing poetry at an early age, but her family became disturbed when she began to publish her poems. Publication was deemed "an unwelcome invasion of family privacy" (Drake, p. 45). She published several poems in a number of magazines including *Poetry* and *New Republic*. Her first volume of poetry, *The Gates of Utterance and Other Poems*, was published in 1915.

Cromwell's blossoming publishing career was interrupted by the entry of the United States into World War I. In January 1918 she and her twin sister, Dorothea, joined the Red Cross. They spent several months as canteen workers in France at Chalons-sur-Marne and later transferred to work at evacuation hospitals. By the war's end they had experienced the strain of air raids and continuous gunfire, and when they boarded the French liner *La Lorraine* in Bordeaux to sail for New York, other Red Cross personnel were concerned about the sisters' mental and physical condition. Dr. C. L. Purnell described them as tired, nervous, and hysterical.

Although Purnell gave the women sedatives, his efforts did not prevent their suicide the following day. Edward Pemberton, a sentry, saw the sisters walking on the deck at about 7:00 P.M. on 19 January. He did not pay them too much attention until suddenly one woman put her foot on the rail and proceeded to jump off. The other followed suit. Pemberton recovered from his momentary surprise and reported the event to his superiors. However, by the time the report reached the captain, the ship was twenty minutes and five miles from the point of their fatal jump. It was both too late and too hazardous to attempt a rescue.

The sisters left behind three notes: one to Major James C. Sherman, the senior Red Cross officer, one to their brother Seymour L. Cromwell, and the third to their sister-in-law. The contents of the letters were not revealed, but their wills suggest that they may have anticipated suicide. Both wills were dated 2 January 1919 and included the clause, "If my sister and myself die in or as the result of any common disaster or catastrophe, whether simultaneously or otherwise" (*New York Times*, 5 Mar. 1919). Although the women advised their brother of their impending return and asked that he have their apartment prepared for their arrival, the sisters appear to have entertained a different kind of homecoming.

A memorial service was held for the sisters on 5 February 1919 at St. Bartholomew's Church in New York. The bodies were not recovered until three months later. Both were buried in France with military honors. The sisters were posthumously awarded the Croix de Guerre and the Médaille de Reconaissance française.

A second volume of Cromwell's verse was published after her death. *Poems* (1919) included poems from her previous book, poems previously published in magazines, and unpublished poems. *Poems* shared the 1920 prize awarded by the Poetry Society of America with John G. Neihardt's *The Song of Three Friends*. Although Cromwell's poetry is not as well known as that of her contemporaries, it was well received at the time. In a review in the *New Republic* (8 Mar. 1919) of her first book, Padraic Colum describes her as "a younger sister of the great poets." In her biographical note in *Poems*, Anne Dunne states that *The Gates of Utterance* "was obviously a first book: but it was the first book of a poet."

Colum describes Cromwell's poetry as being touched with a "tragic vision of life" in his introduction to her *Poems*. Perhaps it is this tragic vision that led to her own tragic ending. "The Actor-Soldier" appears to reflect on Cromwell's service with the Red Cross:

> Ah, yes, I appeared heroic,
> Unflinching, true and brave;
> I wore the look of a stoic;—
> All hurts I forgave.

The speaker of the poem has put on a brave face, but it is revealed to be merely a masquerade as she hears a refrain in the rain: "O Masquerader, come!" The tone of the poem is rather melancholic. This somberness is also seen in "The Mould." The speaker begins by acknowledging that some supreme force has "vanquished Death / And foiled oblivion," but the speaker, described as "this indifferent clay," still feels "death as though it were / A shadowy caress." Although many of Cromwell's poems are brooding and pensive, they are not always pessimistic. For example, a number of her poems contemplate what it means to be a poet. "The Gates of Utterance" describes Cromwell's desire to join the ranks of poets:

> But when a lyric theme invites,
>   I reach outlying bowers
>
> Where dwell the bards of quiet years;
>   I join my song to theirs;
> My glad, unfettered spirit hears
>   The melody it shares.

"The Gates of Utterance" describes the desire to be a poet, while "The Poet" considers the hard work involved:

O tell me, tell me,
Melody's price—
Is it work, is it pain,
Is it sacrifice?

Cromwell reveals the power and importance of words in her poem "Words." The poem opens with the line: "Words are the stones I use in building." The question now is what did Cromwell manage to build? Although she is largely a forgotten figure, Cromwell and her contemporaries were part of a burgeoning period for women poets.

• Although it is known that Cromwell kept a war diary, the whereabouts of the diary and her other papers are unknown. Louis Untermeyer, *Modern American Poetry* (1925), includes a brief commentary about Cromwell's life and work. A modern critical assessment can be found in William Drake, *The First Wave: Women Poets in America 1915–1945* (1987). For an account of Cromwell's suicide and posthumous honors, see the *New York Times*, 25, 26, 29, and 30 Jan.; 6 Feb.; 5 Mar.; 8 and 9 May; 31 Aug.; and 7 Oct. 1919.

VENETRIA K. PATTON

CROMWELL, John (23 Dec. 1887–26 Sept. 1979), actor and director, was born Elwood Dager Cromwell in Toledo, Ohio, the son of George Oliver Cromwell, a businessman, and Helen Sheeler. Cromwell attended the Howe School in Howe, Indiana, graduating in 1905. While a student Cromwell made his stage debut as a clerk in the school's production of *His Excellency, the Governor* and later performed in *The Dictator* and *Dorothy Vernon of Haden Hall*. Determined to become a professional actor, Cromwell spent the next several years doing touring productions and summer stock. Beginning in 1907 he toured in *If I Were King* and *The Girl Who Looks Like Me*, joining the R. C. Herz stock company based at the Colonial Theatre in Cleveland, Ohio, as both an actor and stage manager. Cromwell then teamed up with William A. Brady's company during the 1908–1909 season, touring in *Classmates* and the following season in *A Woman's Way*. He also spent summers at the Lakewood Theatre in Skowhegan, Maine.

When Brady built the Playhouse Theatre in New York, Cromwell joined him, making his New York City debut as the policeman in *Baby Mine* in August 1910. After a tryout tour of *Sauce for the Goose*, Cromwell appeared in the production when it opened in New York in April at the Playhouse Theatre. After a brief tour of *Baby Mine*, Cromwell took over the role of Jimmy in *Bought and Paid For* at the Playhouse Theatre in September 1911. In October 1912 Cromwell appeared as John Brooke in *Little Women* at the Playhouse, his first appearance using the stage name John.

Cromwell made his Broadway directing debut with *The Painted Woman*, which opened in March 1913 at the Playhouse Theatre. Brady encouraged him to continue directing, so Cromwell subsequently directed *The Family Cupboard* at the Playhouse Theatre (Aug. 1913); *The Things That Count* at the Maxine Elliott

Theatre (Dec. 1913); *Too Many Cooks*, in which he starred and codirected with author Frank Craven at the Thirty-ninth Street Theatre (Feb. 1914); and *Life*, which he codirected with William A. Brady and Frank Hatch at the Manhattan Opera House (Oct. 1914). In January 1914 Cromwell married actress Alice Indahl; they had no children. Cromwell served in the U.S. Army during World War I.

For the next fourteen years, Cromwell continued to act, direct, and produce theater productions in the United States and London. In 1915 Cromwell joined Grace George's New York Repertory Theatre, performing as Archibald Coke in *The Liars*, William Sudley in *The New York Idea*, Joe Garfield in *Sinners*, Captain Hamlin Kearney in *Captain Brassbound's Conversion*, Roger Morrish in *The Earth*, Charles Lomax in *Major Barbara*, and Jules in *L'Elévation*. He then directed *The Man Who Came Back* (1916) and *L'Elévation* (1917). Three years later Cromwell again directed *The Man Who Came Back* at the Oxford Theatre in London, followed by *The "Ruined" Lady* at the Comedy Theatre. Cromwell's first wife died in 1918, and in 1920 he married another actress, Marie Goff. The couple divorced in 1922. In 1928 Cromwell married actress Kay Johnson, and they had one son, who also became an actor.

After success on Broadway, Cromwell moved to Hollywood in 1928 at a time when the movie studios were actively searching for directors for the new "talking" movies. He acted in *The Dummy* (1929), but just as he had in the theatre Cromwell soon turned to film direction. He codirected his first two films, *Close Harmony* and *The Dance of Life* (both 1929), with Edward Sutherland. At RKO Pictures, Cromwell worked closely with producer David O. Selznick, content to do as the powerful producer instructed. According to Cromwell, they "were at odds only because of his [Selznick's] love of lush sentimentality. I would always underplay that—I would never let an actor sneak a quiver into his voice." Of the forty-five films Cromwell directed, the most notable successes were *Of Human Bondage* (1934), starring Leslie Howard and Bette Davis; *Banjo on My Knee* (1936); *Prisoner of Zenda* (1937), starring Douglas Fairbanks, Jr., and containing one of the most famous film duels; *Algiers* (1938), starring Charles Boyer and Hedy Lamarr; *Abe Lincoln in Illinois* (1940); *Since You Went Away* (1944), starring Claudette Colbert, Jennifer Jones, and Shirley Temple; *Dead Reckoning* (1947), starring Humphrey Bogart and Lizbeth Scott; and *The Racket* (1951), starring Robert Mitchum and Robert Ryan.

In 1946 Cromwell divorced his third wife and a little over a month later married another actress, Ruth Nelson. From 1944 through 1945 Cromwell served as founding member and president of the Screen Directors' Guild and received the U.S. Treasury Award for patriotic service from 1941 to 1945. In spite of such an honor, in 1951 Cromwell returned to the stage after a falling out with the head of RKO studios, Howard Hughes, in part because Hughes suspected Cromwell of being a leftist. Thus, during the McCarthy era Cromwell was blacklisted though he denied any communist connection. A friend said Cromwell was "hounded out of Hollywood because he had been active in the unions" (*New York Times*, 28 Sept. 1979). Few offers for film came his way due to the blacklisting, and consequently Cromwell returned to the stage.

Cromwell's return to the New York stage after such a long absence proved successful; in 1951 he appeared as John Gray in *Point of No Return* at the Alvin Theatre and received a Tony Award for the performance. The critic for the *Herald-Tribune* called his portrayal a "special delight," and likewise Richard Watts, Jr., of the *New York Post* praised Cromwell's "exceptionally delightful characterization." Cromwell then played Linus Larrabee in *Sabrina Fair* at the National Theatre in 1953, and a year later he also directed the play in its London debut. In 1963 Cromwell joined the Minnesota Theatre Company in Minneapolis, remaining with the company until 1966 and playing such roles as Anselme in *The Miser*, Player King in *Hamlet*, Ben in *Death of a Salesman*, Exeter in *Henry V*, De Courcelles in *Saint Joan*, Brackenbury in *Richard III*, and Avocatore in *Volpone*. In 1970 and 1971 he played at the Yale Repertory Theatre, the Long Wharf Theatre in New Haven, Connecticut, and at the Cleveland Playhouse. Cromwell finished his career in film, appearing in two Robert Altman films: *3 Women* (1977), in which he and his wife played the parents of Sissy Spacek; and *A Wedding* (1978), in which he played a cardinal. Cromwell died in Santa Barbara, California.

As an actor Cromwell was known for his meticulous yet natural style. As a director his respect for the text led him to concentrate on a truthful and dignified transference of the text to the screen without the imposition of his own style or interpretation. His own experience enabled him to be particularly sensitive to the actors he directed on stage and in film—a sensitivity that made him capable of bringing out the best performances in his actors. Cromwell believed his work as a director should be invisible. He admitted that "for a while the director was all powerful in Hollywood, but I've always considered him a member of the team . . . When the director attracts too much attention it's usually because there's something wrong with the story" (*New York Times*, 28 Sept. 1979). Cromwell insisted on giving his actors full rehearsals with camera before the shooting took place, believing strongly that doing so enhanced the quality of performances and took days off a shooting schedule.

Cromwell came into film at a time when the neophyte talking film began demanding more from the performers and directors than the silent film. Cromwell's vast stage experience allowed him to play an important part in this development through his attention to text and characterization and his adeptness at working with actors.

• Information on Cromwell's theater work is in *Who's Who in the Theatre* (1981) and *The Biographical Encyclopaedia and Who's Who of the American Theatre* (1966), which includes a complete listing of Cromwell's stage performances. Information on Cromwell's film work is in Larry Langman, *A Guide to American Film Directors—The Sound Era 1929–1979* (1981); David Quinlan, *Illustrated Guide to Film Directors* (1983); Ephraim Katz, *The Film Encyclopedia* (1979); *World Encyclopedia of Film* (1972); and David Thomson, *Biographical Dictionary of Film* (1979). An interview conducted by David Lyons appears in *Interview*, Feb. 1972, and one by Leonard Maltin appears in *Action*, May–June 1973. Obituaries are in the *New York Times*, 28 Sept. 1979; *Cinéma*, Mar. 1980; and *Image et son*, Oct. 1979.

MELISSA VICKERY-BAREFORD

CROMWELL, John Wesley (5 Sept. 1846–14 Apr. 1927), lawyer and historian, was born a slave in Portsmouth, Virginia, the son of Willis Hodges Cromwell, a ferry operator, and Elizabeth Carney. In 1851 Cromwell's father purchased the family's freedom and moved to West Philadelphia, Pennsylvania, where Cromwell entered the public schools. In 1856 he was admitted to the Preparatory Department of the Institute of Colored Youth. Graduating in 1864, he embarked on a teaching career. He taught in Columbia, Pennsylvania, and in 1865 opened a private school in Portsmouth, Virginia. Cromwell left teaching temporarily after an assault in which he was shot at and his school burned down. He returned to Philadelphia and was employed by the Baltimore Association for the Moral and Intellectual Improvement of Colored People. Then he served as an agent for the American Missionary Association and went back to Virginia. He became active in local politics, serving as a delegate to the first Republican convention in Richmond in 1867.

After his short political career, Cromwell returned to teaching. He taught in Withersville, Richmond, Southhampton, and Columbia, Virginia. In 1871 he moved to Washington, D.C., and enrolled in Howard University's law school. While at Howard, he passed the civil service examination for the Treasury Department. In 1873 Cromwell married Lucy A. McGuinn of Richmond; they had seven children. In 1874 he graduated and was admitted to the bar. He also accepted a position as chief examiner of the money order department and later become the registrar of money order accounts, a position he held until 1885. Cromwell practiced law from his admission to the bar until 1892, and he earned the distinction of being the first African American to argue a case before the Interstate Commerce Commission. In 1895 he was appointed by Blanche K. Bruce, an African American from Mississippi who served in the U.S. Senate during Reconstruction, as honorary commissioner of the department of colored exhibits in the Cotton Centennial Exhibition at New Orleans. Despite his governmental duties, Cromwell actively engaged in social and educational causes. In 1875 he founded the Virginia Educational Organization, consisting of black teachers throughout the state, to whom he delivered "An Address on the Difficulties of the Colored Youth in Obtaining an Education in the Virginias" in Richmond; he served as president of this organization for eight years. In 1876 he founded *People's Advocate*, a weekly newspaper in Alexandria. The paper moved to Washington, D.C., in 1877, and Cromwell ran the paper until 1884. During these years he argued that African Americans should patronize black tradespeople exclusively, that black students and teachers would perform best in all-black schools, and that industrial education should be fostered.

In the 1880s, Cromwell became involved in the nascent black history movement. In 1881 he joined Daniel Alexander Payne, a bishop in the African Methodist Episcopal Church, in founding the Bethel Literary and Historical Association. A forum in which black intellectuals discussed issues of black advancement, the Bethel Literary and Historical Association's membership included many of the District's most prominent black citizens. Cromwell later wrote the organization's history, *History of the Bethel Literary and Historical Association* (1896).

In 1897 Cromwell played a prominent role in establishing the American Negro Academy. Founded by Alexander Crummell, a classical scholar and minister educated at Cambridge University, the American Negro Academy (ANA) sought to promote scholarship, educate youth, establish an archive to document the work of black authors, and publish an annual anthology to foster increased intellectual production by black scholars. Present at the founding meeting of the organization on 5 March 1897, Cromwell served as the organization's corresponding secretary from 1897 to 1919. In this capacity, he handled all materials printed and distributed by the organization and used his position to promote the publication of the annual. From 1901 to 1909, despite teaching and serving as principal of several District schools, including Briggs, Garnet, Banneker, and Crummell, Cromwell also found time to edit the *Washington Record*, a Washington weekly newspaper. In 1910 he and James Robert Lincoln Diggs, a Baltimore businessman, established the American Negro Monograph Company. Although this publishing concern lasted only eleven months, it managed to publish four papers—two of which were written by members of the ANA. In 1919 Cromwell became president of the ANA, but his advanced age and the members' waning interest in the organization's goals forced him to resign by 1920.

Cromwell's reputation as a writer and amateur historian blossomed during the first two decades of the twentieth century. He occasionally published papers for the ANA—for example, "The Early Negro Convention Movement" (1904), an overview of the convention movement among African Americans from 1817 to the 1860s; and "The Challenge of the Disfranchised: A Plea for the Enforcement of the Fifteenth Amendment" (1924), an analysis of African American disfranchisement from the end of Reconstruction through the early 1920s. In 1914 he published his first full-length monograph, *The Negro in American History*. It covered the history of African Americans from the slave trade through Reconstruction and its aftermath. The second portion of the text featured biographical sketches of notable African Americans such as Phillis Wheatley, Benjamin Banneker, Sojourner Truth, and Frederick Douglass.

After Carter G. Woodson founded the Association for the Study of Negro Life and History in 1915 and its organ, the *Journal of Negro History* (*JNH*) in 1916, Cromwell published two articles in the *JNH*: "The Aftermath of Nat Turner's Insurrection" (1920), an assessment of the effect Nat Turner's 1831 Slave Rebellion in Southampton, Virginia, had on the social, political, and economic control of slaves in the South; and "First Negro Churches in the District of Columbia" (1922), a survey of the development of black churches in the District of Columbia from colonial times until the 1920s. Cromwell died at his home in Washington, D.C. He was survived by his second wife, Annie E. Cromwell, whom he had married in 1892, and his seven children.

Cromwell thrived as both a self-made man and a race man, combining advocacy for the collective uplift of African Americans with a belief in educational advancement and intellectual achievement. His historical work placed him at the nexus of the preprofessional and professional milieus in African-American scholarship.

• The main corpus of Cromwell's papers is in the possession of Dr. Adelaide Cromwell, director of the Afro-American Studies Center, Boston University. Another, smaller collection is housed at the Moorland Spingarn Research Center, Howard University, Washington, D.C. An excellent example of Cromwell's writing on racial advancement is his *Jim Crow Negro* (1904). There are no biographies of Cromwell, thus the standard biographical source remains William J. Simmon, *Men of Mark: Eminent, Progressive and Rising* (1887), 898–907. The most complete modern assessments of Cromwell's life is August Meier, *Negro Thought in America, 1880–1915* (1968), which discusses various aspects of Cromwell's participation in social and educational organizations; Tony Martin's essay, "Bibliophiles, Activists and Race Men" in *Black Bibliophiles and Collectors: Preservers of Black History*, ed. Elinor Des Verney Sinnette, W. Paul Coates, and Thomas C. Battle (1990), also provides information on Cromwell's contributions to the early black history movement. Alfred Moss, *The American Negro Academy: Voice of the Talented Tenth* (1981), provides the fullest description of Cromwell's involvement with the American Negro Academy between 1897 and 1920. Obituaries include "Notes," *Journal of Negro History* 12 (July 1927): 563–66 and *Washington Evening Star*, 15 Apr. 1927.

STEPHEN GILROY HALL

CROMWELL, William Nelson (17 Jan. 1854–19 July 1948), lawyer, was born in Brooklyn, New York, the son of John Nelson Cromwell and Sarah M. Brokaw. In the late 1850s the family moved to Peoria, Illinois. During the Civil War, John Nelson Cromwell, a Union colonel in the Forty-seventh Illinois Volunteers, was killed during Ulysses S. Grant's advance on Vicksburg in 1863. The family returned to Brooklyn in straitened circumstances and often faced financial hardship. Cromwell was educated in the public schools and graduated from high school at the age of seventeen. He would have liked to go on to college, but conditions at home required that he work to support his mother and brother. For several years he was an accountant in a railroad office, and his superiors thought he was the best one the railroad had ever had. In 1874 Cromwell secured an accounting position with the New York law firm of Sullivan, Kobbe and Fowler.

The firm's senior partner, Algernon Sydney Sullivan, an experienced trial lawyer from Cincinnati, was quick to spot Cromwell's exceptional ability and offered to put him through law school. Eagerly accepting, Cromwell kept his daytime bookkeeping job while attending Columbia Law School part-time. He was in the last class to be admitted without an undergraduate degree and received an LL.B. in 1876 at the age of twenty-one. With the presentation of his diploma, he was admitted to the New York bar; the diploma in those days was regarded as conclusive evidence of the holder's fitness to practice law. Two years later he was well established in Sullivan's firm, and on Christmas Eve 1878 he married Jennie Osgood Nichols, a widow with one son. They had no other children. They were Episcopalians, and his wife was for many years active in the charitable work of St. Bartholomew's Dorcas Society in Manhattan.

In 1879 Herman Kobbe and Robert Ludlow Fowler withdrew from the firm, and that same year Sullivan paid his protégé Cromwell, only three years out of law school, a high compliment by inviting him to become his partner with a one-third interest in all fees. Cromwell was then twenty-five years old. The firm has since been known as Sullivan and Cromwell. The two partners, who got along famously, complimented each other—Sullivan had a polished courtroom style, and Cromwell had a head for figures. Endowed with boundless energy, Cromwell made a striking appearance with his ruddy complexion, bright blue eyes, and full mane of hair cascading over his collar. When Sullivan died in 1887, Cromwell, who then became the senior partner, was so devastated that he temporarily went into seclusion in a state of almost complete physical collapse.

With a specialization in corporation and international law, the Sullivan and Cromwell firm enjoyed continuous success. As the United States came of age and, in particular, as New York increasingly became a center of finance, commerce, and industry, a comparable legal need arose. It was the genius of Cromwell to see and respond to changing requirements, among them a breakthrough from law practices that were routine, parochial, and unnecessarily restrictive of the creative impulses of the era. Through an imaginative approach and purposeful action, he and his successors won the transitory successes of juries' verdicts and also blazed new trails that others could follow.

Cromwell worked for some of the country's most notorious "robber barons." At various times the firm's clients included E. H. Harriman, J. P. Morgan, Henry Villard, John H. Flagler, and Harrison Williams. Cromwell had a reputation for shrewd economic analysis and a flair for fast-talking argument. He supplied

sound legal advice to client-directors of increasingly complex forms of business organization, developed innovative ways to allow his clients to prosper, and helped them formulate schemes for building great industrial empires. From the outset Sullivan was quick to recognize Cromwell's wizardry with figures. Skills in accounting were a valuable asset, unusual in lawyers of that day, who were generally trained in logic, rhetoric, philosophy, the classics, and to some extent the natural and mathematical sciences.

By the time of Sullivan's death the firm had one of the most modern law offices in the country. Firms of more than three partners were rare before the Civil War, but after 1900 they became common on Wall Street. By 1902 Sullivan and Cromwell employed at least a dozen lawyers and six stenographers. Under Cromwell's organization, three associates worked for each partner, a ratio that prevailed a century later in the major corporate law firms. When Arthur Dean published its history in 1957, the firm, which at one time or another employed such lawyers as Allen Dulles, John Foster Dulles, Harlan Fiske Stone, and Robert E. Olds, had grown into what some termed a "law factory," with thirty-one partners and fifty-three associates. John Foster Dulles, offered his first job with the firm in August 1911, was hired at $50 a month. Until that time law students and beginning lawyers worked for nothing, on the theory that what they learned was far more valuable than anything they could contribute. At the end of the nineteenth century, under the new "Cravath system," all lawyers who worked in Cromwell's office were paid. Beginners received $30 a month.

Much of the firm's legal work was in organizing large corporations and putting them on a sound financial basis. In 1899 Cromwell directed the consolidation of sixteen of the largest tube manufacturing concerns in the United States into the National Tube Company with a capitalization of $80 million. Another merger organized that year was the American Cotton Oil Company, one of the first to incorporate under New Jersey's new and very permissive incorporation law. While at work putting together the Cotton Oil trust, Cromwell reportedly locked himself in a room with his client at 6:00 P.M., drew up 175 agreements, and had them signed and registered by the next morning. His fee for the night's work was $50,000. His firm was also one of the organizers of U.S. Steel. As a corporation lawyer par excellence, Cromwell unraveled complicated legal tangles and received many millions of dollars in fees for doing so.

Cromwell's railroad work related primarily to financing equipment, development of railroad mortgages, and reorganization. He was appointed assignee to the Northern Pacific when it went into receivership in 1893; the plan for its reorganization was largely his creation. He directed the two-year legal and proxy battle against Stuyvesant Fish and won for his client, Harriman, control of the Illinois Central in 1908. During World War I his firm reorganized Brazil's entire railway system.

Cromwell became known in the corporate world as "the physician of Wall Street," a lawyer adept at salvaging wrecked business enterprises. He made an important contribution to the practice of American business law with what became known as "the Cromwell Plan," a method of rescuing businesses in distress and protecting their assets from creditors. Within the framework of the state's insolvency laws, a business in financial difficulty arranged a voluntary agreement among its creditors allowing it to reorganize, continue to operate, and fulfill its obligations without going through a sacrifice sale of assets during economic downturns, when values were depressed. The Cromwell Plan, originally developed in 1890–1891, was first employed to save the failing brokerage house of Decker, Howell and Company, which had liabilities in excess of $10 million. Under Cromwell's direction the New York banking house paid off the entire debt within three months. The plan's basic premise was to hold off creditors as long as possible while waiting for an economic upturn. To a large extent the scheme relied for success on the confidence that Cromwell was able to inspire, and it offered creditors the promise of receiving more than they could expect in an immediate, drastic liquidation. The plan was used to rescue other businesses facing ruin in the panic of 1907.

In the international arena, Cromwell's most famous work was in directing the legal phase of transferring the Panama Canal route and rescuing the project from French control. He was first engaged in 1896 as general counsel for the New Panama Canal Company of France. During more than eight years of lobbying, legal maneuvering, and public relations work, he utilized his firm's influence and his connections with high-ranking people in public life, financial circles, and the press to win support for his objectives. The Nicaraguan route was rejected, and the governments of Colombia and France agreed to transfer the New Panama Canal Company's property in Panama and the company itself to the United States for a price of $40 million. The United States negotiated new treaties with Nicaragua, Colombia, and Panama. The Spooner Bill, authorizing the Panama route, was passed by Congress and signed in June 1902 by President Theodore Roosevelt, who later boasted, "I took Panama," referring to the "little revolution" in 1903.

Cromwell did not escape severe criticism for his role in this affair. He was attacked for using his political connections and financial wizardry to secure the transfer of the isthmian canal from Nicaragua to Panama, thus benefiting a French client. In the words of one hostile critic, he was "the man whose masterful mind, whetted on the grindstone of corporation cunning, conceived and carried out the rape of the Isthmus" (Miner, p. 76).

After the First World War Cromwell retired from active practice and took extended trips abroad. He resided for long periods of time in France, a country he admired, and he financed the reconstruction of the hand-lace industry at Valenciennes. He also took an interest in the welfare of the blind. Under his supervision, books, journals, and music were printed in Braille and distributed throughout the United States, France, and other countries of Europe. For his philanthropic work the French government awarded him the cross of the Legion of Honor. Later Cromwell was instrumental in establishing the Legion of Honor Museum. For his contribution to relief measures for the children of Romania after the war, he was made a commander of the Order of the Crown.

Perhaps because his childhood experiences in a financially strapped, single-parent household remained vivid in his mind, Cromwell was always a strong believer in decent wages and reasonable hours and working conditions. Although he had been a staunch Republican all his life, giving conspicuous support to President William Howard Taft in his 1908 and 1912 campaigns, Cromwell recognized the extent of the economic dislocation of the Great Depression. Apart from the National Industrial Recovery Act, which he thought impeded economic recovery, he supported the initial economic reforms introduced by President Franklin D. Roosevelt's New Deal. Cromwell recommended a realistic examination of the economic plight of workers and stockholders. His partner Dean participated in drafting the Securities Act of 1933, and Cromwell approved of the creation in 1934 of the Securities Exchange Commission. Unexpectedly for a Wall Street lawyer of his stature, he was not in the least dismayed at the idea that a society had to take emergency measures to meet unusual situations. He believed that lawyers were frequently unrealistic in their somewhat technical approach to the urgent practical problems that face a government and business in such emergency situations.

Cromwell rarely worked out of the elegant office maintained for him at the firm's headquarters at 47-48 Wall Street, in what was then the U.S. Trust Building. He preferred working at home at 12 West Forty-ninth Street in his mid-Victorian mansion, crowded with tapestries, paintings, and statuary acquired on his European trips. Time after time the Rockefeller interests tried to persuade him to sell this real estate, which they wanted for Rockefeller Center, but he refused to do so. As a youth he had been organist at the Pilgrim Church in Brooklyn, and on his mansion's ground floor was a huge pipe organ, which he loved to play in his leisure hours.

Cromwell's wife died in 1931. On his ninetieth birthday he was awarded a plaque by Helen Keller on behalf of the blind people he had helped, both at home and abroad. When he died at home in New York City, leaving no heirs, the bulk of his $19 million estate went to charitable causes. Included was a $5 million bequest to law schools, bar associations, and legal research centers. The Cromwell Library at the headquarters of the American Bar Foundation in Chicago, dedicated on 22 February 1955, formed part of what was, for its time, the largest sum ever bequeathed by an individual to the legal profession.

• The richest source for study of Cromwell is the history written by Sullivan and Cromwell partner Arthur H. Dean, *William Nelson Cromwell, 1854–1948: An American Pioneer in Corporation, Comparative and International Law* (1957). For details on Cromwell's role in the Panama Canal negotiations, see Dwight C. Miner, *The Fight for the Panama Route: The Story of the Spooner Act and the Hay-Herrán Treaty*, chaps. 3, 4, 8, and 10 (1940). For a more recent treatment, see Walter LaFeber, *The Panama Canal: The Crisis in Historical Perspective* (1978). A more critical approach to the firm is in Nancy Lisagor and Frank Lipsius, *A Law unto Itself: The Untold Story of the Law Firm of Sullivan and Cromwell* (1988). Some interesting material on Sullivan and Cromwell is in Joseph S. Auerbach, *The Bar of Other Days* (1940), and Lawrence M. Friedman, *A History of American Law* (1973). An obituary is in the *New York Times*, 20 July 1948.

MARIAN C. McKENNA

CRONIN, Joe (12 Oct. 1906–7 Sept. 1984), baseball player, manager, and executive, was born Joseph Edward Cronin in San Francisco, California, the son of Jeremiah Cronin, an Irish-born horse team driver, and Mary Carolin. Cronin played baseball and basketball in high school and captured a city junior tennis championship in 1920. He worked as a bank clerk and played shortstop for the Columbia Park Boys Club, winners of the 1923 city championship, and for the semipro Napa team in 1924. St. Mary's College in Oakland offered Cronin an athletic scholarship, but Pittsburgh Pirates' scout Joe Devine signed him in September 1924 for a $200 bonus and a monthly salary of $400.

Cronin played for Johnstown, Pennsylvania, of the Middle Atlantic League in 1925 and for New Haven of the Eastern League in 1926. The Pirates promoted Cronin that spring and used him as a reserve shortstop behind Glenn Wright for the 1927 National League champions. Cronin's contract was sold in 1928 to the Kansas City Blues of the American Association, where he impressed Washington Senators' scout Joe Engel. In late July 1928 the Washington club signed him. An off-season conditioning program brought his weight to 180 pounds on a 6' frame.

From 1929 to 1934 Cronin starred at shortstop for Washington. In 1930 he earned *Sporting News* player of the year honors, attained career highs in batting average (.346) and runs batted in (126), and helped the Senators finish in second place. Cronin ranked among the American League's most feared clutch hitters. As well as driving in 126 runs in 1931, he led the league in triples in 1932 and doubles in 1933. Defensively, he possessed a strong throwing arm and ranked among the premier major league shortstops of his day.

In October 1932 Washington owner Clark Griffith fired Walter Johnson as manager and named the intelligent, gentlemanly 26-year-old Cronin player-manager. In 1933 Cronin batted .309 and guided Washington to its first American League pennant in nine years. The New York Giants, however, defeated Washington in the five-game World Series, marking the Senators' last Series appearance. In 1934 the injury-riddled Senators tumbled to seventh place. Cronin played short-

stop in the first major league All-Star game in 1933 and was Carl Hubbell's fifth consecutive strikeout victim in the 1934 All-Star Game.

Cronin married Mildred Robertson, Griffith's niece and a Washington club secretary, on 27 September 1934; they had four children. A month after the wedding, Griffith traded Cronin to the Boston Red Sox for shortstop Lyn Lary and $250,000. That sum set an existing record as the highest amount paid for a single player. Tom Yawkey, the young millionaire Boston owner, signed Cronin to a five-year, $50,000-a-year contract as Red Sox player-manager. Cronin played for Boston until he fractured his right leg in April 1945, the accident forcing his retirement. He enjoyed hitting in Fenway Park, batting over .300 seven times between 1937 and 1945, hitting a career-high 24 home runs in 1940 and displaying impressive run production. Johnny Pesky replaced him as Boston's regular shortstop in 1942, but in 1943 Cronin set an American League record by hitting five pinch-hit home runs. During 20 major league seasons he batted .301 with 2,285 hits, 515 doubles, 118 triples, 170 home runs, 1,424 runs batted in, and a .468 slugging percentage in 2,124 career games. He batted in more than 100 runs per season eight times and appeared in seven All-Star Games.

Cronin managed the Red Sox until 1947. During his managerial tenure, Boston initially suffered from weak pitching, but Cronin molded the team into a pennant contender by 1938. From 1938 to 1942 the Red Sox finished second to the New York Yankees four times and led the American League in team batting three times. Boston added first baseman Jimmie Foxx to its roster in 1936, second baseman Bobby Doerr in 1937, third baseman Jim Tabor in 1938, outfielder Ted Williams in 1939, outfielder Dom DiMaggio in 1940, and shortstop Pesky in 1942. The 1946 Red Sox dominated the American League with a 104–50 record and captured their first pennant in 28 years. The St. Louis Cardinals, however, defeated Boston in a dramatic, hard-fought, seven-game World Series. Cronin managed for 15 seasons, his teams recording 1,236 career victories and winning 54 percent of its games.

Yawkey promoted Cronin to general manager, vice president, and treasurer in 1948. He was a hard-working, paternalistic, able, and friendly executive. Besides being a shrewd trader, he was scrupulously honest and fair to his players and staff. In 1956 he was elected to the National Baseball Hall of Fame.

On 31 January 1959, Cronin became the first former player to be elected president of the American League, succeeding Will Harridge. He remained president until January 1974, during which time the league expanded from eight to twelve teams. The California Angels and Washington Senators joined the American League in 1961, while the Kansas City Royals and Seattle Pilots were added in 1969. Cronin administered the transfer of franchises from Washington, D.C., to Minnesota in 1961, Kansas City to Oakland in 1968, Seattle to Milwaukee in 1970, and a second Washington club to Texas in 1972. In 1968 Cronin dismissed umpires Al Salerno and Bill Valentine on learning that they were trying to form a union. Nevertheless, the Major League Umpires Association was formed and signed a contract with the major leagues in 1970. The American League added divisional playoffs in 1969 and the controversial designated hitter rule in 1973. It is widely thought that the designated hitter rule, which Cronin lobbied for behind the scenes, helped the American League set a new attendance record. In December 1973 Cronin blocked New York Yankee's owner George Steinbrenner's attempt to hire Dick Williams of the Oakland Athletics as manager. Cronin ruled that Williams was still under contract to Oakland, but he allowed Detroit to sign Ralph Houk of the Yankees as the Tigers' manager.

After retiring, Cronin chaired the American League's board of directors from 1973 to 1984. He also became a director of the National Baseball Hall of Fame in 1959, chairman of its Veterans Committee in 1970, and president of the Baseball Players Association of America in 1977. Cronin died in Osterville, Massachusetts.

• The National Baseball Library in Cooperstown, N.Y., houses material on Cronin's life. Al Hirshberg, *From Sandlots to League President* (1962), provides the fullest biographical account. The Ellery Clark, Jr., Red Sox Analytical Letter Collection, Annapolis, Maryland, has some of his correspondence, while the Ellery Clark, Jr., Red Sox Interviews contain Cronin's reflections on his baseball career. Cronin's statistical accomplishments are detailed in *The Baseball Encyclopedia* (8th ed., 1990). For Cronin's roles as player and manager, see Shirley Povich, *The Washington Senators* (1954); Frederick G. Lieb, *The Boston Red Sox* (1947); and Ellery H. Clark, Jr., *Boston Red Sox: 75th Anniversary History* (1975). Dan Shaughnessy, *The Curse of the Bambino* (1990), adeptly summarizes the Red Sox story during Cronin's era. An obituary appears in the *New York Times*, 8 Sept. 1984.

DAVID L. PORTER

CRONKHITE, Bernice Brown (23 July 1893–3 Aug. 1983), college dean and vice president, was born Bernice Veazey Brown in Calais, Maine, the daughter of James Edmund Brown, a physician, and Grace Veazey. After her mother's death from appendicitis in 1898, the family moved to Providence, Rhode Island, where her father raised Bernice and her brother with the aid of relatives. She entered Radcliffe College in 1912, having spent two summers as a volunteer working with immigrants and one year as a teacher in a one-room rural school. She concentrated in government and twice won prizes for essays on municipal government. After receiving her A.B. (1916), she enrolled as a graduate student at Radcliffe, while working half time as a bibliographer in Harvard's Bureau for Municipal Research. At the time she was appointed the first woman teaching assistant in the government department at Harvard on the understanding that "there was no male candidate available and that it was for one year only."

With the United States' entry into World War I, her interest shifted from municipal to international government. She studied at Yale Law School on an award from the Carnegie Endowment for International Peace and received her A.M. (1918) and Ph.D. (1920) from Radcliffe in political science. She spent the next year abroad on a fellowship from the Commission for Relief in Belgium. In 1921 she was appointed director of the School for Public Service, established by the Boston Women's Municipal League to train women for government service.

In 1923 Ada Louise Comstock, the new president of Radcliffe College, appointed Cronkhite dean, the youngest in the history of Radcliffe and in the United States at that time. Thus began a harmonious partnership that stretched through the presidencies of Comstock and Wilbur K. Jordan. The dean, wrote Comstock, "is like Kipling's engineer, charged with keeping a complicated mechanism in smooth operation." During this period Radcliffe was a coordinate college with Harvard University, responsible for its own admissions, administration, and students. The Harvard faculty directed educational policy and provided all the teaching. Radcliffe undergraduates were taught in separate classrooms, but graduate students and upperclasswomen were able to attend some Harvard graduate courses. Cronkhite was responsible for all aspects of the lives of undergraduates and graduates until 1934, when she was appointed dean of the newly formed Radcliffe Graduate School. She was married in 1933 to Leonard Wolsey Cronkhite and was stepmother to his two children.

Although not herself a scholar, Cronkhite recruited, inspired, and counseled young scholars from all over the world. Under her leadership, the graduate school came to grant more doctorates to women than any other university in the United States except Columbia University. Among new initiatives instituted during her deanship was the joint Harvard-Radcliffe Bureau of International Research (1925–1959), which fostered graduate studies in international issues, the Master of Arts in Teaching (1936), designed to ensure that teachers received advanced training in subject specialties as well as education courses, and an extracurricular course in the problems and methods of college teaching, which she organized in 1947. Cronkhite established funds for research fellowships to provide college teachers and postdoctoral scholars with the freedom to pursue advanced research, and, in a foreshadowing of the Bunting Institute founded by President Mary Bunting in 1960, contemplated a program to train women for reentry into the academic market. Cronkhite's most lasting legacy was to spearhead the fundraising for, and shape the design of, the graduate center, which provided a social and living center for young scholars and which was fittingly named for her in 1971.

Little, however, could be done to ameliorate the poor prospects for women in academia. A report on graduate education at Radcliffe edited by Cronkhite presented a discouraging account of the experience of graduates. The book, *Graduate Education for Women: The Radcliffe Ph.D.* (1956), based on surveys of the career paths of holders of the Radcliffe Ph.D., came to the conclusion that few had received tenure at major research universities, that their scholarly output was low, due partly to heavy teaching loads and family commitments, and that the number of Radcliffe women entering the academic profession was decreasing.

Although avoiding pressure tactics or confrontation with Harvard, Cronkhite welcomed the increased access to the university's facilities when a new contractual tie in 1943 opened all Harvard courses to graduate women, reduced the fees, and made possible more generous use of the library. She was instrumental in persuading Samuel Zemurray to endow a Radcliffe professorship to be held by a woman in any department of the Faculty of Arts and Sciences. This led to the appointment of the first tenured woman professor at Harvard in 1947. Although she regretted the closing of the Radcliffe Graduate School in 1962, three years after her retirement, and the ending of its effective support system for students, she generously acknowledged that the simultaneous opening of the Harvard Graduate School of Arts and Sciences to women provided key advantages of more scholarship aid and the Harvard degree.

Cronkhite held numerous positions in educational organizations. As a member of the Board of Foreign Scholarships, she flew around the world in 1957 interviewing candidates and reforging connections with Radcliffe alumnae. Her many awards included the Radcliffe Graduate Chapter Medal (1952), the Alumnae Achievement Award (1956), the Founder's Award (1967), and honorary degrees from Radcliffe (1978) and five other institutions. She died in Cambridge, Massachusetts.

Cronkhite was a revered dean and the model of a wise and gracious woman, a gifted planner with a flair for design who left a tangible mark on the buildings and landscape of the college, and, in the course of her long tenure as dean and vice president, the principal architect of the expansion of graduate education for women at Radcliffe and Harvard. "At a time when women's place was deemed to be primarily in the home," said Radcliffe president Matina Horner, Cronkhite "dared to act on her firm belief that women had the right as well as the responsibility to develop and contribute their intellectual talents for the betterment of society."

• Cronkhite's personal and professional papers are in the Schlesinger Library, Radcliffe College, and the Radcliffe College Archives. The Schlesinger Library has a small collection of her speeches and reports; her letters are in many other collections of the library, notably that of Ada Louise Comstock. Her official dean's papers in the Radcliffe College Archives illustrate her relationship with Harvard departments, her continuing links with alumnae, and the successful campaign to raise funds for and build the graduate center. Also in the archives is a collection of affectionate and grateful letters from graduates, the transcript of an oral history interview with Mary Manson (1976), an article by Ada Louise Comstock about Cronkhite's deanship in *Radcliffe Quarterly* 33

(Feb. 1949): 4–6, and a biographical file of questionnaires, clippings, and obituaries.

Cronkhite also edited *A Handbook for College Teachers* (1950). Her memoir, *The Times of My Life*, was published in 1982. Her articles include "Grave Alice," about Alice Mary Longfellow, *Radcliffe Quarterly* 49 (Nov. 1965): 11–14; "Here We Are Given Not Only a Pattern, But a Compass and a Star," for her fiftieth class reunion, *Radcliffe Quarterly* 50 (Aug.–Sept. 1966): 10–11; and "Time for Freedom," about aging, *Radcliffe Quarterly* 61 (Mar. 1975): 2–3. Her speeches and reports were regularly covered by the college magazines and newspapers, and her annual reports as dean of the college and the graduate school are published in the *Annual Reports of Radcliffe College*. An obituary is in the *New York Times*, 5 Aug. 1983.

JANE S. KNOWLES

CROOK, George (8 Sept. 1828–21 Mar. 1890), soldier, was born near Taylorsville, Ohio, the son of Elizabeth Matthews and Thomas Crook, farmers. Entering the U.S. Military Academy in 1848, Crook graduated in 1852 and served until 1861 in California and Oregon fighting hostile American Indians. Fascinated by American Indians, Crook's studious interest helped him in combat against them where other officers failed. Most important, he learned and appreciated that American Indians fought to preserve their cultures and lands.

Crook was a prominent Union officer during the Civil War, who by April 1865 was a major general of volunteers; he had earned regular army brevet (or honorary promotions for valor) up to and including that of major general. By late 1862 he was a brigadier general, leading a brigade at the battle of Antietam on 17 September. After serving in West Virginia, he was in the Tullahoma campaign in June 1863 and fought in the battle of Chickamauga on 20 September 1863. General Ulysses Grant ordered him east, and after commanding the Department of West Virginia in 1864, Crook led the Eighth Corps in Philip Sheridan's Army of the Shenandoah. Crook skillfully commanded the Eighth Corps during the battle of Winchester, 19 September, and the battle of Fisher's Hill, 22 September, but Confederate general Jubal A. Early routed the Eighth Corps at the battle of Cedar Creek on 19 October 1864. The goals of the Union campaign in the Shenandoah Valley presaged the strategies that Sheridan and Crook later employed against the western American Indian tribes.

Confederate guerrillas captured Crook in his quarters on 21 February 1865. After his exchange, he commanded the cavalry of the Army of the Potomac until war's end. On 22 August 1865 he married Mary Daily, sister of a guerrilla in the Confederate unit that had captured Crook. They had no children.

Civil War service left its mark upon Generals Sherman, Sheridan, Crook, and others who fought against the American Indians after 1865. Their primary goal against the Confederates and the American Indians was to obliterate the economic and resource foundation of the enemy, realizing that this wrecked the enemy's ability to fight and destroyed the morale not only of the warriors but of their families. In the West this meant the destruction of stores of food in American Indian villages, the disruption of nomadic hunting patterns crucial to getting more food, and the eradication of buffalo herds.

In the 1866 reorganization of the army Crook became a lieutenant colonel, returning west to fight American Indians in Idaho, Oregon, and California. An innovator at logistics, he replaced slow wagons with pack-trains of surefooted mules to supply his troops in the field. Mule-based units were very mobile, capable of following American Indian war parties anywhere. The U.S. Army still used Crook's system of mule pack-trains in mountainous areas during World War II.

After 1865 increasing numbers of migrants pushed into the West, triggering American Indian wars. The Apache tribes were formidable opponents, and in 1871 the army ordered Crook to Arizona. He discerned that the Apaches consisted of various tribes that fought each other. Realizing that soldiers were incapable of defeating the Apaches, Crook enlisted hundreds of Apaches in the army and sent mixed units of warriors and soldiers after the hostile Apaches. He let his warriors use American Indian tactics to fight other American Indians, and by 1875 most of the Apaches were at peace. He made every effort to meet his agreements with the Apaches, which earned Crook the respect of his former enemies.

The army promoted Lieutenant Colonel Crook to brigadier general in 1873, and in 1875 he was ordered to command of the Military Department of the Platte in Omaha, Nebraska. The predicament facing the army arose from the Black Hills of South Dakota and hunting grounds in Montana and Wyoming, lands assigned to the Lakotas and their allies in treaties. After prospectors discovered gold in the Black Hills, the government wanted the area, but the Lakotas refused to relinquish it.

In December 1875 the government ordered the army to move Lakotas and Cheyennes from the Powder River watershed of Montana and Wyoming to American Indian reservations in Nebraska. Crook and other officers designed a winter campaign because the mobile Plains Indians settled in villages during the winter. The villages were, in effect, warehouses storing tons of food, hundreds of buffalo robes, and ammunition, all essential for survival during the winter months. Destroying one of these villages rendered the tribe destitute, especially during the winter. Critics charged that attacks on villages killed women, children, and old people, who starved, froze, or died in the fighting. Crook and other strategists, however, had successfully used this tactic in the Civil War, and in 1876 they used it against the American Indians.

Crook's forces entered Wyoming, and on 17 March an officer from Crook's command led an attack on a Cheyenne village. The soldiers destroyed the village but were then forced to retreat during a furious Cheyenne counterattack. The battle only stiffened the resolve of Cheyennes and Lakotas for war against the

army. On 17 June 1876 Crook's Wyoming Column with 1,300 fighting men (including 175 Crow and 86 Shoshone warriors) fought approximately 1,500 Lakota and Cheyenne warriors led by Crazy Horse in the fierce six-hour battle of the Rosebud, Montana. Crook claimed victory, but Crazy Horse had stopped Crook's advance.

Eight days later Crazy Horse and Lakota and Cheyenne warriors annihilated Lieutenant Colonel George Custer (who served in Brigadier General Alfred H. Terry's Dakota Column) and his immediate command in the battle of the Little Bighorn. Crook and other officers campaigned throughout 1876 and early 1877, destroying more American Indian villages and disrupting the hunt, and their pressure compelled the nontreaty Lakotas and Cheyennes to surrender by the summer of 1877.

Believing that American Indians fought to protect their rights, Crook advocated civil rights for American Indians, including the franchise. In 1878 the government ordered Crook to arrest members of the Ponca tribe, who walked to their Nebraska homeland from the Indian Territory. Believing his orders terribly unjust, Crook convinced others to initiate a lawsuit to stay his orders. In the resulting *Standing Bear v. Crook*, the judge decided for the first time in American history that "an Indian is a person within the laws of the United States."

Returning to Arizona in 1882, Crook achieved his finest military accomplishment in 1883, when with nearly 200 western Apache scouts and about 50 soldiers and officers, he went into Mexico to search for the Chiricahuas, who were raiding from their sanctuaries in the Sierra Madre. Crook found the Chiricahuas, and after one skirmish, he negotiated their peaceful return to the Arizona reservations. Disgruntled with reservation life, Geronimo and some other Chiricahuas left the reservation in 1885, thrusting Crook into the most controversial years of his career. The southwestern press vilified Crook for his evenhanded treatment of the Apaches.

His superior, General Sheridan, questioned Crook's wisdom in using Apaches to fight other Apaches, and other officers, especially Brigadier General Nelson A. Miles, criticized Crook. His relations with Sheridan deteriorated, and in 1886 Crook asked to be replaced in Arizona. Crook returned to the Department of the Platte until 1888 when he became a major general and moved to Chicago to command the Military Division of the Missouri. In 1889 he convinced the Lakota tribes of South Dakota to relinquish 11 million acres of their reservation land, candidly telling the Lakotas that the government would simply take the land if they did not accept proffered terms. To his fury and anguish, the government cut beef rations to the Lakotas after they relinquished the land, triggering the starvation and ensuing crisis behind the Ghost Dance movement and the Wounded Knee massacre in 1890.

Crook continued to fight for American Indian rights, especially those of the Chiricahua prisoners of war. Crook's replacement in Arizona arrested the entire Chiricahua tribe, including hundreds who had been peaceful since 1883 and scouts still in the army hunting Geronimo, their own relative. Miles sent the desert and mountain Chiricahuas to prisoner-of-war camps in Florida, where many died in the humid climate. Outraged, Crook publicly denounced the imprisonment and rallied support for the Chiricahuas. He organized a major political and newspaper crusade in their behalf, which he planned to launch in March 1890, but he died that month in Chicago. The Chiricahuas would remain prisoners until 1913.

The significance of Crook's life was revealed by those who most deeply felt his passing. General Sherman called him the greatest American Indian fighter and manager that the army ever had. Some Apaches mourned Crook as one of their own. The Oglala chief Red Cloud said, "General Crook came; he, at least, had never lied to us. His words gave the people hope. He died. Their hope died again. Despair came again."

• There are Crook manuscript collections at the Rutherford B. Hayes Library in Fremont, Ohio, and in Special Collections, University of Oregon Library, Eugene, Ore. There is a great deal of material related to Crook in the John Gregory Bourke Collection, Nebraska State Historical Society, Lincoln, Neb., and in the 124 volumes of John Gregory Bourke's Diaries, 1872–1896, Library of the U.S. Military Academy, West Point, N.Y. Martin Schmitt, ed., *General George Crook: His Autobiography* (1986), is most useful in detailing Crook's Civil War career and his years in the West until 1876. Bourke, *On the Border with Crook* (1891; repr. 1950), remains an invaluable source on Crook's career in the American West as seen through the eyes of his longtime staff aide. Charles King, *Campaigning with Crook* (1890; repr. 1964), treats Crook's role during the Sioux War of 1876. See also Joseph C. Porter, *Paper Medicine Man: John Gregory Bourke and His American West* (1986). Jerome A. Greene, "George Crook," in *Soldier's West: Biographies from the Military Frontier*, ed. Paul Hutton (1987), is an excellent essay-length study of Crook.

JOSEPH C. PORTER

CROPSEY, Jasper Francis (18 Feb. 1823–22 June 1900), artist, was born in Rossville, Staten Island, New York, the son of Jacob Rezeau Cropsey and Elizabeth Hilyer Cortelyou, farmers and devout members of the Dutch Reformed church. As a boy, Cropsey worked with his parents on the family farm after school. But because he was a frail child and often too ill (possibly with asthma) to work or study, he took up drawing. According to the artist's unpublished reminiscences (1846), his subjects "were mostly of the landscape and architectural tendency—seldom many figures." This proved to be the rule throughout his mature career as well.

At the age of fourteen, Cropsey was awarded diplomas from the New York Mechanics' Institute and the American Institute of the City of New York for an elaborately detailed model of a house, the product of two years' work. Soon after this, the New York architect Joseph Trench offered Cropsey a five-year apprenticeship in his office, encouraging the young man's talent for drafting and painting by supplying him with artists' materials. In 1840 Trench hired British painter Edward Maury to further Cropsey's skill at rendering landscape backgrounds in architectural presentation drawings by giving him lessons in watercolor painting. Cropsey later recollected that this instruction "rekindled the passion for pictures," and he began reading books on painting. This instruction, along with several classes in life drawing at the National Academy of Design, constituted Cropsey's formal artistic education. His earliest watercolor and oil paintings, from the early 1840s, depict Italian landscapes and Dutch-type scenes of peasants and rural cottages, revealing his reliance on books and prints for subject matter.

Cropsey opened his own architectural practice in New York in about 1843. That year, he designed a church for the Moravian church in New Dorp, Staten Island, and exhibited a painting for the first time at the National Academy of Design. The inscription on his business card—"Architect and Landscape Painter"—documents the integration of his two occupations. The painter William Sidney Mount gave Cropsey some friendly instruction and advised him to use nature as his model; by late 1845, Cropsey was devoting himself entirely to landscape painting. He was honored in August of that year with an invitation to speak on "Natural Art" at the New York Art Re-Union, where he told his audience that, in his opinion, "those [artists] that have produced the greatest works . . . have been the most attentive to nature." Cropsey's own favorite spot for communing with nature was Greenwood Lake, New Jersey. His paintings of that site won him an associate membership at the National Academy in 1844 (he became a full member in 1851), and it was at Greenwood Lake that he met Maria Cooley, whom he married in May 1847; they had two children.

Cropsey took his bride on a two-year honeymoon trip to Italy. After a short sojourn through England, he rented Thomas Cole's former studio in Rome and began sketching and painting picturesque compositions that show the influence of French landscape painter Claude Lorrain. Cropsey also studied the landscape on trips to Tivoli, Albano, Sorrento, Lake Nemi, Naples, Pisa, and Genoa. When he returned to New York in 1849, he set to work producing paintings from his travel sketches, but soon returned to American scenery. Over the next few years his paintings documented his travels in New Jersey, the White Mountains of New Hampshire, and New York's Hudson River valley. The style, technique, and subject matter of Cropsey's paintings from the early 1850s, such as *Hawking Party in the Time of Queen Elizabeth* (1853; Collection of Mrs. John C. Newington) and *Catskill Mountain House* (1855; Minneapolis Institute of Arts), reveal the strong influence of Cole, although he never studied with the artist himself. Cropsey's philosophy of art, which he expounded upon in his essay "Up Among the Clouds" (*The Crayon*, Aug. 1855), was clearly inspired by Asher B. Durand, whose "Letters on Landscape Painting" appeared in the same publication earlier that year.

By the mid-1850s, Cropsey had developed an expressive, imaginative painting style without forsaking his ideas about the importance of working directly from nature. From 1856 to 1863 he lived in England. Though he sketched on the English coast and in the countryside, American scenery remained his forte. His American scenes were so popular in London that Gambert and Company, Lithographers, commissioned thirty-six views from him, of which sixteen were finally printed. In May 1857 he exhibited *An Indian Summer Morning in the White Mountains* (1857; Currier Gallery of Art), and his rendering of the ragged cliffs bathed in warm, autumnal hues was a great success. *Autumn on the Hudson River* (1860; National Gallery of Art, Washington, D.C.) so impressed the London press, as well as Queen Victoria, with its brilliant coloration and vast scope, that Cropsey became something of a celebrity. An American friend reportedly sent real autumn leaves for Cropsey to exhibit alongside the painting as proof for English viewers who were skeptical that trees actually blazed red and orange. Cropsey exhibited the painting at several venues and the rave reviews preceded him back across the Atlantic. His reputation as America's best painter of autumn scenery endured through the 1860s.

Cropsey painted a large oil of the Gettysburg battlefield (the picture was destroyed by fire in 1875) but for the most part maintained his artistic focus upon idyllic landscapes. In 1864 he began work on *Valley of the Wyoming* (Metropolitan Museum of Art), an expansive canvas showing the fertile Pennsylvania countryside. Commissioned by Milton Courtright, a prosperous civil engineer who was born in the Wyoming valley, the painting was finished in time for the National Academy's 1865 exhibition. The *New York Times* called it "a monument of patient and accurate labor, . . . a topographical survey of a highly picturesque and romantic region."

At about the same time, Cropsey was at work on *Starrucca Viaduct, Pennsylvania* (1865; Toledo Museum of Art), featuring the engineering marvel that crossed the Starrucca Creek and Starrucca valley at Lanesboro, Pennsylvania. Cropsey's vantage point, the highest point across the valley from the viaduct, was a scheduled stop along the Erie Railroad. His view combines rich, natural landscape drenched in autumn colors with an important emblem of progress, the train. The painting was so popular that he painted it again, on canvas reportedly eight by fourteen feet, for a raffle at the Crosby Opera House in Chicago. That enormous painting was destroyed in the Chicago fire of 1871.

Cropsey's financial success during the mid-1860s enabled him in 1867 to begin and build a magnificent Hudson River villa in Warwick, New York. The house, which he named "Aladdin," was a two-year project and proved quite costly to maintain. As Cropsey's painting career was becoming progressively less lucrative, he returned to architecture to support his family. Despite several notable commissions, among them a villa for inventor George Pullman and station houses for the Gilbert Elevated Railway Stations in New York, Cropsey was forced to sell Aladdin in 1884.

The next year, Cropsey moved his family to a house in Hastings-on-Hudson, New York, where the artist replicated his high-ceilinged Aladdin studio as an addition. (The house, called "Ever Rest," is maintained as a historic property and can be visited by appointment.) While Cropsey's work from the last fifteen years of his life was considered old-fashioned by art critics and more progressive painters, he maintained his talent and his enthusiasm for the idealized American landscape long after the market for painting of the Hudson River School type had almost disappeared. He died at his home in Hastings-on-Hudson.

• The bulk of Cropsey's papers are owned by the Newington-Cropsey Foundation, Hastings-on-Hudson, N.Y., and are accessible on microfilm through the Archives of American Art. In these papers, Cropsey's "Reminiscences of My Own Time" (1846), prepared for C. Edwards Lester's *Artists of America*, and the untitled autobiographical sketch (1867) he wrote for Henry T. Tuckerman's *Book of the Artists*, are especially useful. The most important secondary source is William S. Talbot, *Jasper F. Cropsey: 1823–1900* (1977), which includes an extensive catalogue of the artist's work. The following exhibition catalogues also include valuable information: William S. Talbot, *Jasper F. Cropsey: 1823–1900* (National Collection of Fine Art, Washington, D.C., 1980); Kenneth W. Maddox, *An Unprejudiced Eye: The Drawings of Jasper F. Cropsey* (Hudson River Museum, Yonkers, N.Y., 1980); Carrie Rebora, *Jasper Cropsey Watercolors* (National Academy of Design, 1985); Ella Foshay et al., *Jasper F. Cropsey: Artist and Architect* (New-York Historical Society, 1987); and John K. Howat et al., *American Paradise: The World of the Hudson River School* (Metropolitan Museum of Art, 1987).

CARRIE REBORA

CROSBY, Bing (3 May 1903–14 Oct. 1977), singer of popular music, was born Harry Lillis Crosby in Tacoma, Washington, the son of Harry Lowe Crosby, a plant accountant, and Catherine Harrigan. His father was an easy-going descendant of Edmund Brewster, one of the Puritan signers of the Mayflower Compact. His mother, an Irish Catholic, was a strict disciplinarian. Early in his life the family moved to Spokane, Washington, where Crosby grew up. At age six he entered Webster Elementary School (1909–1917), where he received the nickname "Bing." In 1921 he graduated from the rigidly Jesuit-run Gongaza High School and entered Gongaza University (1921–1925), where he prepared for a law career.

As a high school and university student Crosby did a variety of odd jobs to put some spending money in his pocket. His hobbies were swimming, basketball, fishing, and hunting. His parents loved music and instilled this love in their children. Crosby's father sang in local Gilbert and Sullivan productions, and on Sunday evenings the family gathered around the piano to sing together and to listen to Catherine Crosby sing Irish folk songs in her light, warm soprano voice. Bing Crosby liked listening to recordings by Al Jolson,

John McCrae, and contemporary jazz groups. He also played the drums. He joined the Musicaladers, a dance band that played at high school hops and social functions. In 1925 he dropped out of law school to pursue a musical career. He teamed up with Alton Rinker, and the two played as a duo in West Coast vaudeville theaters. In 1926 they arrived in Los Angeles and in October of that year were booked with the Paul Whiteman band, the most popular orchestra in the country at that time. They went with the orchestra on a cross-country tour that wound up in 1927 in New York. The duo act of Crosby and Rinker was transformed there into a trio and renamed the Rhythm Boys, with Harry Barris as the third singer. They developed a light, easygoing style that within a year became the Whiteman band's signature. Crosby was given a chance to solo, gathering in the process his own following. In 1930 the Whiteman band was hired to appear in a major Hollywood movie, *The King of Jazz*. After the movie was completed, Crosby persuaded the Rhythm Boys to leave the Whiteman band and stay in Los Angeles, where they began working with the Gus Arnheim Orchestra at the fashionable Coconut Grove night spot.

In September 1930 Crosby married Dixie Lee (born Wilma Winfred Wyatt), a Twentieth Century–Fox studio actress who had already starred in six films. At the same time producer Mack Sennett hired Crosby to appear in a series of two-reel shorts in which he sang some of the songs that he had recorded with the Arnheim orchestra. Crosby also played bit parts as a singer in two full-length feature films, *Reaching for the Moon* (1930) and *Confessions of a Coed* (1931).

In 1931 CBS chairman William S. Paley offered Crosby a network contract, the biggest boost to his career so far. The offer did not include the remaining Rhythm Boys, and the trio broke up. Crosby's fifteen-minute CBS program began in September 1931 and was an instant success. The radio show continued well into the 1950s. In 1934 Crosby signed with Decca Records as a recording artist. Between 1935 and 1946 he also hosted the Kraft Show.

His film career gained momentum when in 1932 Paramount Pictures gave him a contract and assigned him his first lead role in *The Big Broadcast* (1932), co-starring George Burns and Gracie Allen. As Paramount continued to cast Crosby in light musicals, his singing voice made him the studio's biggest money-maker next to Mae West. Between 1932 and 1939 Crosby starred in nineteen films. Two songs dating from this period, "Love in Bloom" from the film *She Loves Me Not* (1934) and "Pennies from Heaven" from the 1936 film of the same name, were nominated for Academy Awards. The song "Sweet Leilani" from the film *Waikiki Wedding* (1937) received an Oscar.

A turning point in Crosby's life took place in 1940 when he teamed with Bob Hope and Dorothy Lamour in *The Road to Singapore*. The film was so well received that Paramount went on to produce a whole series of "Road" films: *The Road to Zanzibar* (1941), *The Road to Morocco* (1942), *The Road to Utopia* (1946),

The Road to Rio (1947), and *The Road to Bali* (1952). Ten years after their previous Road film the trio made the celebratory *Road to Hong Kong* (1962), with five prominent stars—Frank Sinatra, Dean Martin, David Niven, Peter Sellers, and Jerry Colona—in cameo roles.

Throughout this time Crosby continued to make box-office blockbuster films for Paramount and to sell millions of his song recordings for Decca. Nominated for Academy Awards were the songs "Only Forever" from the film *Rhythm on the River* (1940), "Accentuate the Positive" from *Here Come the WAVES* (1944), "Aren't You Glad You Are You?" from *The Bells of St. Mary's* (1945), "Zing a Little Zong" from *Just for You* (1952), "Count Your Blessings" from *White Christmas* (1954), "True Love" from *High Society* (1956), and "The Second Time Around" from *High Time* (1960). Receiving Academy Awards were the songs "White Christmas" from Irving Berlin's classic film *Holiday Inn* (1942), "Swingin' on a Star" from *Going My Way* (1944), "You Keep Coming Back Like a Song" from *Blue Skies* (1945), and "In the Cool, Cool, Cool of the Evening" from *Here Comes the Groom* (1951).

In 1956 Crosby made his last film for Paramount, *Anything Goes*. He then began freelancing as an actor. By that time his screen image was well established in the pantheon of American entertainment. Wearing a straw hat and carrying a cane, often clothed in white slacks and a gold-buttoned navy blue jacket, he exuded a sympathetic warmth and a relaxed joy of life. He cultivated a style of equanimity, a civilized quality of virtue, restraint, and unassuming modesty. Offscreen he was often pictured puffing a pipe, attending a tennis match, or barbecuing for his family in his backyard. This self-possessed ease of manner and rhythm did not come to him without long hours of hard work and practice, forever polishing that casual charm.

During the 1950s and 1960s, a new musical sound and a new young generation of singers displaced the old crooners on the charts. Crosby, while still singing in films and on radio and selling millions of his songs on records, adapted himself quickly to the new taste of filmgoers, who now demanded more realism on the screen. Almost overnight he transformed himself from a popular singer to a serious actor—and a good one at that. For a number of years Crosby had been seeking dramatic roles and deemphasizing his image as a successful crooner. He had first attained this status as early as 1944, when he received an Academy Award as best actor for his lead role in *Going My Way*, the story of a well-meaning Father Chuck O'Malley, who is called by the cardinal of the New York archdiocese to fix up the failing finances of Saint Dominic's Church. *The Bells of St. Mary's* (1945) reintroduced Father O'Malley, this time on a mission to St. Mary's to fix its failing finances. In *The Country Girl* (1954), Crosby demonstrated his unsuspected, emotional reserves as a straight dramatic actor. He gave a powerful performance as an alcoholic stage actor who receives a second chance from a director and former fan, played by William Holden, and thereby saves his career and his marriage. Crosby's assured performance mingled seriousness with sentimentality and earned him an Academy Award nomination as best actor.

Changes occurred also in Crosby's private life. His wife of twenty-two years died in 1952. In 1957 he married actress ingenue Kathryn Grant. He was fifty-four years old; she was twenty-four. Crosby had four children with his first wife, and three children with his second wife.

In the mid-1960s Crosby began dedicating all of his time to television. He briefly starred in a Bing Crosby weekly show (1964–1965) with family members and guests. For a number of years he produced and starred in his own annual Christmas shows with a string of illustrious guest stars. He also made numerous appearances on other shows. He formed his own television production company, which created such hit series as "Ben Casey" (1961–1966), "The Wild, Wild, West" (1965–1970), and "Hogan's Heroes" (1965–1971).

Crosby became one of the richest men in the history of show business. He had investments in real estate, mines, oil wells, cattle ranches, race horses, music publishing, baseball teams, and television. He made a fabulous fortune from the Minute Maid Orange Juice Corporation, in which he was a principal stockholder.

In 1974 Crosby underwent a major surgery that cost him part of his left lung. That did not seem to hurt his performance as a singer, as between 1974 and 1977 he cut ten new albums that sold in the millions. In 1977, at age seventy-four, he went on an international singing tour that took him from Broadway to the London Palladium. His wife and their three children traveled with him. After the tour they went to Spain to relax. Finishing a game of golf outside Madrid, Crosby suddenly collapsed of a heart attack and died before reaching the hospital.

In his lifetime Crosby made over seventy feature films and sold over 500 million albums on which were recorded more than 1,600 different songs ("White Christmas" alone sold 40 million copies). He had about twenty cameo parts and made numerous guest appearances on television. His hit songs were so numerous that yet more should be cited besides those already mentioned: "Down the Old Ox Road" (1933), "Love Is Just around the Corner" (1934), "It's Easy to Remember" (1935), "Soon" (1935), "I Wished on the Moon" (1935), "Blue Hawaii" (1937), "Small Fry" (1938), and "The Waiter and the Porter and the Upstairs Maid" (1941). With his songs Crosby changed the sound of American popular music. His easygoing, moderately paced, mellow renditions influenced a whole generation of popular singers, including Frank Sinatra, Dean Martin, Perry Como, and Tony Bennett.

• Crosby's autobiography, *Call Me Lucky* (1953), was published when he still had an important part of his career ahead of him. *Bing: The Authorized Biography* (1975), on which he worked closely with Charles Thompson, covers most of the subsequent years of his life. Several biographies of Crosby published after his death portray him in a negative light;

Donald Shepard and Robert F. Slatzer, *Bing Crosby: The Hollow Man* (1980), is representative. Family members tell their stories in Gary Crosby and Rose Firestone, *Going My Way* (1983). Although after his death Crosby's older sons complained bitterly about their father's harsh disciplinary methods, they became more sympathetic and even applied some of those methods to their own children. A chapter devoted to Crosby is in John Fisher, *Call Them Irreplaceable* (1976). For additional sources of information, see J. Roger Osterholm, *Bing Crosby: A Bio-bibliography* (1994). Illustrated albums with detailed biographical texts include Robert Bookbinder, *The Films of Bing Crosby* (1977), and Ken Barnes, *The Crosby Years* (1980). Obituaries appear in the *Los Angeles Times* and the *New York Times*, both 15 Oct. 1977, and in all of the trade papers of the motion picture and recording industries.

SHOSHANA KLEBANOFF

CROSBY, Bob (25 Aug. 1913–9 Mar. 1993), jazz and popular bandleader and singer, and radio, film, and television personality, was born George Robert Crosby in Spokane, Washington, the son of Harry Lowe Crosby, a bookkeeper at the Inland Products Canning Company, and Catherine "Kate" Helen Harrigan. He attended Webster High School, North Central High School, and Gonzaga, a Jesuit high school and university. Not a remarkable student, he excelled at sports but chose instead to pursue a career as a singer, following his famous brother, Bing Crosby.

On Bing's recommendation, Bob joined Anson Weeks's dance orchestra from around 1933 to 1934. After working briefly in July 1934 in a duo with singer Lee Wiley at the Paramount Theater in New York, he joined the new Dorsey Brothers Orchestra. Like many people, Crosby did not get along with Tommy Dorsey. He recorded "I'm Getting Sentimental over You" (Aug. 1934), but Tommy disliked his singing and allowed him to participate only marginally in the band's several residencies in the New York area.

Crosby happily transferred to a new band that saxophonist and musical director Gil Rodin had organized from ex-members of Ben Pollack's band. The new leader served as a lively master of ceremonies, and he sang, although his contributions in the latter area were consistently undistinguished. (Dorsey was tactless but right.) The Bob Crosby Orchestra opened at the Roseland Ballroom in New York in June 1935. Rodin recalled, "Crosby didn't know how to beat tempo, but we didn't mind. We just started." His band's ensuing activities involved extensive touring, with many residencies in hotel ballrooms.

The Bob Crosby Orchestra strove to make contemporary (that is to say, mid-1930s, swing-oriented) big-band arrangements of small-group jazz of the 1920s. Recorded examples include "Dixieland Shuffle" and "Royal Garden Blues" (both 1936) and "South Rampart Street Parade" and "Dogtown Blues" (both 1937). Writer John Chilton reported that early on the orchestra received a review in the *Philadelphia Evening Bulletin* that was meant to be critical but instead confirmed, to the members' satisfaction, that they were achieving what they were after: "The Crosby swing music is indeed jazz at about its lowest level, with none of the later Paul Whiteman refinements."

From April 1937 on Crosby was also the nominal leader of the Bob Cats, an eight-piece Dixieland band-within-the-band. At various times its membership included trumpeter Yank Lawson or Billy Butterfield, clarinetist Matty Matlock or Irving Fazola, tenor saxophonist Eddie Miller, pianist Bob Zurke, guitarist Nappy Lamare, bassist Bob Haggart, and drummer Ray Bauduc. Their recordings include "Who's Sorry Now?" (1937) and "March of the Bob Cats," recorded in mid-March 1938, shortly before the orchestra and the Bob Cats began the first of several stays at the Blackhawk Restaurant in Chicago.

Crosby had earlier been married to Marie (maiden name unknown). In 1938 he married June Audrey Kuhn, who became a successful writer on cooking; they had five children. During this year the orchestra performed "South Rampart Street Parade" and "Pagan Love Song" in film shorts, and Haggart and Bauduc had a hit recording under Crosby's name with their novelty duo, "The Big Noise from Winnetka." In addition to hybrid swing-Dixie material, Crosby's group performed many ballads and swing tunes, including Haggart's ballad "I'm Free," later retitled and popularized as "What's New."

Later recordings included "Rose of Washington Square" (1939), "Spain" (1940), and "Jazz Me Blues" (1940). In June 1939 they secured a place on the Camel Caravan radio show, broadcasting nationally every Tuesday night, and beginning in January 1940 the band took Benny Goodman's place on the Saturday night edition of the show. Later that year the band appeared in the film *Let's Make Music*. New members in 1940 included trumpeter Muggsy Spanier and, only briefly, singer Doris Day. During this period the Dixieland component was pushed into the background in favor of contemporary pop themes; hence while reaching a wider audience, Crosby lost some of his most devoted fans.

Crosby's group recorded "Milenberg Joys" (1942) and performed in the movies *Presenting Lily Mars* and *Reveille with Beverly* (both 1943), after which time he disbanded. In 1944 he made an effort to become a movie actor, starring in *The Singing Sheriff*, a film that caused him considerable embarrassment, and holding lesser roles in *See Here, Private Hargrove* and *Pardon My Rhythm*. Before the year ended he became a lieutenant in the U.S. Marines. Running an entertainment unit based in Honolulu, he toured the Pacific War Zone. He completed his military career in the fall of 1945 as master of ceremonies for the Armed Forces Radio show "Swingtime."

Crosby led a new band from late 1945 to the spring of 1947. He then began to work regularly as a host on broadcasts, first on radio and then on television, while continuing to lead bands and to hold roles in a few feature films, including *Two Tickets to Broadway* (1951), in which he comically imitates his brother Bing, singing "Let's Make Comparisons." After a business venture in Honolulu failed in 1961, he resumed bandleading, performing at first mainly in Las Vegas but also touring the Far East and Australia in 1964 and later working at Lake Tahoe and in New York. He continued leading bands until 1992, the year before his death in La Jolla, California.

Although he was never a distinguished singer, and his activities in film and broadcasting are of only modest importance, at the height of the swing era, in the late 1930s and early 1940s, Crosby as a bandleader was rated alongside Benny Goodman, Glenn Miller, Duke Ellington, Artie Shaw, and the Dorseys in fan popularity polls. His band's swing-Dixie hybrid proved not to have the same widespread, lasting attraction as the styles of these other ensembles, and his records were never big sellers by comparison. Instead, Crosby's music in later decades found a different historical niche, coming to be perceived as arguably the first step toward the subsequent international revival of New Orleans jazz.

• Some useful sources on Crosby are John Chilton, *Stomp Off, Let's Go!: The Story of Bob Crosby's Bob Cats & Big Band* (1983); Ian Crosbie, "That Dixieland Jazz," *Jazz Journal* 23 (Mar. 1970): 12–15; Frank Littler, "I Just Blew in from Winnetka . . . " *Jazz Monthly* 6 (June 1960): 12–13; Albert McCarthy, *Big Band Jazz* (1974); Leonard Feather, *The Pleasures of Jazz* (1976); and George T. Simon, *The Big Bands*, 4th ed. (1981). For musical analysis, see Gunther Schuller, *The Swing Era: The Development of Jazz, 1930–1945* (1989). Obituaries are in the *Los Angeles Times*, 10 Mar. 1993, and the *New York Times*, 11 Mar. 1993.

BARRY KERNFELD

CROSBY, Dixi (7 Feb. 1800–26 Sept. 1873), surgeon, was born in Sandwich, New Hampshire, the son of Asa Crosby, a physician, and Betsy Hoit. Crosby spent his youth working on a farm and acquiring an education in public schools in Sandwich and in an academy at Gilmanton, New Hampshire. As a young adult he taught in a country school and pursued, unsuccessfully, business ventures in New York and New Orleans.

In 1821, on the recommendation of his father, Crosby committed himself to the study of medicine. For the next three years he energetically pursued medical training, focusing on anatomy. He engaged in adventurous intrigues to secure cadavers, studying them in all-night, solitary dissection sessions. He was once caught by Gilmanton residents on a grave-robbing expedition, seriously undermining his reputation in the community. On another occasion, though still a student, he convinced a patient who had been deemed an inappropriate candidate for surgery to allow him to perform his first limb amputation, much to the disgust of local physicians. In another student incident, he reportedly employed a carving knife and a carpenter's saw and chisel to amputate a leg. Crosby received his M.D. from New Hampshire Medical Institution (later Dartmouth Medical School) in 1824 and began his medical practice in Gilmanton, moving then to Laconia, and later to Hanover, New Hampshire. In 1827 he married Mary Jane Moody; they had two children.

In 1838 he was appointed to the chairs of surgery and obstetrics at Dartmouth College, positions he held until 1868 and 1870 respectively.

Crosby acquired his national reputation primarily as a result of his extensive and innovative surgical practice. At the height of his career at mid-century he was considered the leading surgeon in New Hampshire. For much of his life he traveled widely and regularly on horseback throughout the state, as well as through Vermont and Connecticut, to further his surgical practice. Although he taught at a medical school, he devoted scant attention to scholarly literature or academic developments, relying instead on his own experience and intuition. His teaching focused on practical rather than theoretical principles and was characterized by directness, certitude, and a celebration of self-reliance. He advised aspiring physicians: "Take no man's diagnosis, but see with your own eyes, feel with your own fingers, judge with your own judgment, and be the disciple of no man" (quoted in Frost, p. 110).

Boldness and confidence, even when acting in conflict with prevailing professional and academic opinion, were the hallmarks of Crosby's career. His most celebrated triumph involved the removal in one operation of a patient's shoulder joint, clavicle, and scapula in order to excise a cancerous tumor. The 1836 operation was the first of its kind in the United States and had been declined by some of the most eminent surgeons in the country. Crosby successfully completed the procedure, and the patient survived for more than two years. In addition, very early in his career, Crosby pioneered a novel method of relocating dislocations of the thumb and finger. Crosby performed all the major operations recognized by contemporary surgeons during his working lifetime, often soon after their introduction, and frequently before he had witnessed their completion by other surgeons. His aggressive approach to practice was seemingly untouched by the conservative surgery movement of the mid-nineteenth century that aimed to limit surgical experimentation and intervention.

Although Crosby was considered one of the most talented surgeons of his age, he wrote and published little. His most significant published contribution (Crosby, 1854) recounts his experience with what is often thought to be the first medical malpractice suit filed against a consulting physician. In 1845 Crosby had offered advice in a fracture case, and in 1853 he was initially found negligent by a trial jury. He appealed the case and was eventually absolved of liability. Although a relatively routine case legally, the lawsuit commanded national attention because of Crosby's involvement, because he chose to publicize the case, and because it seemed to illustrate the plight of the medical community, then in the throes of the country's first spate of malpractice suits.

Crosby was an active member of the local, state, and national medical societies. He served as president of both the New Hampshire society and of the American Medical Society's convention of teachers of medicine. He was a member of the state militia and a surgeon in the provost marshal's office during the Civil War. Crosby was twice elected to the state legislature. He was also active in local government and was particularly instrumental in urging the enforcement of liquor laws. His support of the temperance movement was buttressed by his studies concerning the impact of alcohol on the stomach.

Crosby practiced until he was nearly seventy years old, his professional career spanning fifty years of dramatic change in surgery. He entered medicine before the introduction of anesthesia and left the field on the eve of the introduction of antiseptic and aseptic techniques and the first major forays into body-cavity surgery. His style of practice, based almost solely on technical competence and boldness, would soon, however, become a thing of the past. By the end of the century leading surgeons would have to combine technical proficiency with scientific medicine, a full understanding of the disease process, and an appreciation for emerging laboratory methods. Crosby died in Hanover.

• A frank portrait of Crosby, based in part on personal recollections is Carlton P. Frost, "In Memory of Dixi Crosby," *Transactions of the New Hampshire Medical Society* (1874): 105–19. A factually rich yet more celebratory account, also based in part on personal acquaintance, is James A. Spalding, "Dixi Crosby," in *American Medical Biographies*, ed. Howard A. Kelly and Walter L. Burrage (1920): 261–63. Crosby's account of the malpractice suit is *Report of a Trial for Alleged Mal-practice* (1854).

KENNETH ALLEN DE VILLE

CROSBY, Elizabeth Caroline (25 Oct. 1888–28 July 1983), neuroanatomist, was born in Petersburg, Michigan, the daughter of Lewis Frederick Crosby and Frances Kreps. Crosby attended public grade school and high school in Petersburg. Promised four years of college by her father for her good grades, she enrolled in Adrian College in Adrian, Michigan, completing the requirements for the B.S. degree (1910) in only three years. Taking her fourth year of college support and the advice of a chemistry and physics professor, she traveled to the University of Chicago with plans to study under C. Judson Herrick. Although initially discouraged by Herrick, Crosby convinced him to give her a chance. She enrolled in neuroanatomy and gross anatomy courses, did her graduate work with distinction, and went on to receive the M.A. (1912) and Ph.D. (1915, magna cum laude) degrees from the University of Chicago.

To be near her aging parents, Crosby, who never married, returned to Petersburg in the fall of 1915 and took a position in the public school system, teaching Latin, zoology, and mathematics and also coaching the boys' basketball team. In 1916 she became principal of the high school, and in 1918 superintendent of schools.

Feeling the need for scholarly and academic advancement, Crosby in 1920 approached G. Carl Huber, professor of anatomy and director of the anatomical laboratories at the University of Michigan, about the possibility of doing research in his laboratory. There followed a formal offer, and Crosby became an instructor in anatomy at the university. She was promoted to assistant professor of anatomy in 1926, became an associate professor of anatomy in 1929, and in 1936 was the first woman to be promoted to the rank of professor at the University of Michigan. She was also lecturer in anatomy at Marischal College of the University of Aberdeen in Scotland (1939–1940, returning in 1960 as senior research fellow) and was a visiting professor at the University of Puerto Rico (1949).

Crosby's first paper, "The Forebrain of *Alligator Mississippiensis*" (*Journal of Comparative Neurology* 27 [1917]: 325–402), was the result of her Ph.D. dissertation. In this manuscript Crosby was first to suggest that the cortex of submammalian vertebrates may have a neopallium. This observation provided evidence that parts of the reptilian forebrain (the neopallium) were structurally comparable to the six-layered neocortex of the mammalian brain. A series of dissections conducted while she was a graduate student were incorporated into her first book, *A Laboratory Outline of Neurology* (with C. J. Herrick, 1918). These two early writings exemplified the contributions that would characterize her career: excellence in basic research on the brain and excellence in teaching.

In the period from 1920 to 1934 Crosby and Huber collaborated on a series of papers on the diencephalon (a group of nerve cells that receives input from wide areas of the neuraxis and relates to the overlying cerebral cortex) and on the midbrain with emphasis on the optic tectum (the part of the midbrain most intimately associated with visual function). During a trip abroad in 1926, Crosby met the great Dutch neuroanatomist C. U. Ariëns Kappers; he invited her to collaborate on a translation of his famous work, *Die Vergleichende Anatomie des Nervensystems der Wirbeltiere und des Menschen*. Upon Crosby's return Huber also joined this project, which, based on a growing body of new information, soon evolved into a totally new work. Crosby, as acknowledged by Ariëns Kappers, was the moving force behind this huge project, and the untimely illness and death of Huber in 1934 threw the entire load on her. The two-volume edition, *The Comparative Anatomy of the Nervous System of Vertebrates, Including Man*, appeared in 1936, received international acclaim, and established Crosby as a leading authority on brain morphology.

From 1937 to around 1950, Crosby, with her students and co-workers, published on the olfactory system, on telencephalic structures, and especially on the midbrain, using a broad comparative approach. Although continuing her basic studies on brain structure, beginning about 1950 Crosby enlarged her research to include studies on the clinical application of basic neuroanatomical observations. An extension of this effort came to fruition in 1955 when Crosby appeared as a coauthor of the highly regarded book *Correlative Neurosurgery*, with Edgar A. Kahn, Richard C. Schneider, and James A. Taren.

In 1959 Crosby became professor emeritus of anatomy at the University of Michigan, but she immediately continued working as consultant in neurosurgery at Michigan and also held the position of professor emeritus of anatomy and consultant (1964–1981) at the University of Alabama. Her research activity continued unabated and now shifted more to functional neuroanatomy and clinical issues. Her textbook *Correlative Anatomy of the Nervous System* (with Humphrey and Lauer, 1962) was immediately recognized as one of the most up-to-date, best-illustrated, and most detailed presentations on the functional anatomy of the human brain. Numerous papers issued from her laboratories at Michigan and Alabama; second (1969) and third (1982) editions of *Correlative Neurosurgery* appeared; and in 1968 contracts were signed for two, and eventually four, additional books on vertebrate neuroanatomy. (Owing to unforseen delays, only the first book in this series, *Comparative Correlative Neuroanatomy of the Vertebrate Telencephalon* [1982] was published.) In addition to her fundamental discoveries on the structure of the vertebrate brain, Crosby also made contributions to the understanding of clinical problems such as syringomyelia, cerebral palsy, the Korsakoff syndrome, the control and regulation of eye movement, and the brain's influence on abnormal motor activity.

During her career Crosby received numerous awards and honorary degrees and was a member of many professional organizations. Most notable among her awards were the Solis Prize (1926), the Karl Spencer Lashley Award from the American Philosophical Society (1969), and the Henry Gray Award from the American Association of Anatomists (1972). When presented with the Gray Award, Crosby was cited as "unquestionably the foremost authority on the anatomy of the nervous system." In 1980 Crosby received the National Medal of Science, presented by President Carter, for her "outstanding contributions to comparative and human neural anatomy." She was a member of numerous organizations, including the American Association of Anatomists, International Brain Research Organization, and the Society for Neuroscience. She was also elected an honorary member of prestigious clinical societies, such as the American Association of Neurological Surgeons, the American Neurological Association, and the Société Française de Neurologie. She served on the editorial boards of the *Journal of Comparative Neurology* (1940–1969), *Experimental Neurology* (1959–1970), and the *Journal für Hirnforschung*.

Like many scientists and scholars, Crosby never really retired; she was as active in the quarter century after her retirement as she was before. At the time of her death, at the home of her adopted daughter in Dexter, Michigan, Crosby was widely recognized as one of the most influential neuroanatomists in the middle fifty years of the twentieth century.

• Documents relating to Crosby are in the Bentley Historical Library of the University of Michigan. Information on her life and career is in E. G. Hamel, "Elizabeth Caroline Crosby, 1888–1983," *Journal für Hirnforschung* 25 (1985): 361–63; "Elizabeth Crosby: Laying the Foundations of Neuroscience," *Research News* (Univ. of Michigan), Aug.–Sept. 1983, pp. 1–23; E. C. Sensenig and T. Humphrey, "Elizabeth C. Crosby," *Alabama Journal of Medical Science* 6 (1969): 357–63; S. M. Burns, "Elizabeth C. Crosby, a Biography," *Alabama Journal of Medical Science* 22 (1985): 317–23; C. J. Herrick, "Elizabeth Caroline Crosby," *Journal of Comparative Neurology* 112 (1959): 13–17; R. T. Woodburne, "Elizabeth C. Crosby, a Biographical Sketch," *Journal of Comparative Neurology* 112 (1959): 19–29; and Woodburne, "Elizabeth Caroline Crosby, 1888–1983," *Anatomical Record* 210 (1984): 175–77.

DUANE E. HAINES

CROSBY, Ernest Howard (4 Nov. 1856–3 Jan. 1907), attorney, social reformer, and writer, was born in New York City, the son of Howard Crosby and Margaret Evertson Givan. His father was the pastor of the prestigious Fourth Avenue Presbyterian Church from 1863 to 1891, chancellor of New York University, founder of the city's Society for the Prevention of Crime, and a critic of the labor movement and single tax reform. Crosby was educated at Mohegan Lake School in Westchester County and at New York University, from which he graduated with first honors in his class of 1876. Two years later Crosby graduated with honors from Columbia University's law school and was admitted to the bar. He practiced law for ten years and became a major in the National Guard. In 1881 Crosby married Fanny Kendall Schieffelin, the daughter of a wealthy New York importer. They became the parents of two children.

In 1887 Crosby was elected to New York's state assembly from a district previously represented by Theodore Roosevelt. In Albany he followed his father's conservative reform instincts, introducing and promoting a "high license" liquor control bill, which sought to control consumption of liquor by increasing its cost. The bill passed both houses of the legislature three times and was three times vetoed by Governor David Bennett Hill. In 1889 Crosby retired from the legislature and moved to Egypt when President Benjamin Harrison nominated him and the khedive, the hereditary pasha of Egypt, appointed him to a lifetime position as a judge on the international court at Alexandria. In 1892 Crosby contributed to the relief of famine-stricken Russian peasants and began corresponding with the family of Count Leo Tolstoy. During an unhappy crisis of religious and self-doubt early in 1894, his reading of Tolstoy's *My Life* worked a revolution in his life. "Love others" was the Russian author's message, said Crosby's poetic recollection:

> "love them calmly, strongly, profoundly,
> And you will find your immortal soul."
> I leaned back in my arm-chair, letting my hand fall
>   with the volume in my lap,
> And with closed eyes and half a smile on my face
>   I made the experiment and tried to love.

Crosby resigned from the court and was decorated by the khedive as a Knight of Medjediah of the third class.

In May 1894 Crosby toured Europe and visited Tolstoy at his estate, "Yasnaya Polyana." The two-day visit with Tolstoy and immersion in his thought confirmed the change in Crosby's life. When he returned to New York in the summer of 1894, he attended a meeting of Baptist social gospel theologian Walter Rauschenbusch's Brotherhood of the Kingdom at Marlboro, New York, and announced his determination to live by Tolstoy's creed. Thereafter, he led a small but influential group of Tolstoy's American admirers, such as Rauschenbusch, Jane Addams, John Haynes Holmes, William Dean Howells, and Edward A. Steiner. Abandoning both elective politics and his legal practice, Crosby and his wife moved to a 700-acre estate at Rhinebeck-on-the-Hudson, New York. There, like the Russian aristocrat, he lived as austerely as his wife's wealth allowed, farmed, and wrote. Between 1895 and 1906 his articles appeared in such journals as *Arena, Coming Age, The Comrade, Cosmopolitan, The Independent, The Kingdom, National Single Taxer, North American Review, The Outlook, Progressive Review, Review of Reviews, Single Tax Review,* and *Social Gospel.*

Mrs. Crosby acquired the Rhinebeck estate in hopes that her husband would accept the life of a gentleman farmer. Her plan failed. Crosby took a modest apartment on New York's East Side, contacted Henry George, and became an advocate of his single tax. In November 1894 he founded and was the first president of the Social Reform Club of New York City. Like both his father and his "pre-Tolstoyan" self, Crosby was again active in moral and social reform. Alienated from old associates and calling for revolutionary changes in society, he became the "universal reformer" of his generation, an advocate of anti-imperialism and antimilitarism, child labor laws, industrial arbitration and labor reform, nonviolence and racial reform, immigration and social settlements, the single tax, and vegetarianism.

In 1900 Crosby founded and became the first president of the Anti-Imperialism League of New York. In the Social Reform Club and the Anti-Imperialism League he drew together a network of New York reformers that included Howells, Episcopal bishop Henry Codman Potter, the Ethical Culture Society's Felix Adler, organized labor's Samuel Gompers, and social reformer Mary White Ovington. Crosby became the most prolific of anti-imperialist writers of the era. His satirical novel, *Captain Jinks, Hero* (1902), sought to expose the folly of military heroism. His books of free verse, *Plain Talk in Psalm and Parable* (1899), *Swords and Plowshares* (1902), and *Broad-Cast* (1905), were somewhat more successful artistically. His more numerous nonfiction prose titles, *Edward Carpenter: Poet and Prophet* (1901), *Shakespeare's Attitude toward the Working Classes* (1902), *Tolstoy and His Message* (1903), *Tolstoy as a School-Master* (1904), *William Lloyd Garrison, Non-Resistant and Abolitionist* (1905), and *Golden Rule Jones, Mayor of Toledo* (1906), reflected the range of his interests in literature and social reform.

Crosby's radical associates deeply disturbed his family. At the request of Emma Goldman and Jacob Schwab, he appealed unsuccessfully to Andrew Carnegie for clemency for the anarchist Alexander Berkman, who had attempted to assassinate steel magnate Henry Clay Frick. In 1906 Howells and Mark Twain withdrew their sponsorship of a banquet for Maxim Gorky when it was learned that the Russian radical was accompanied by his mistress. When Crosby played host to Gorky and his paramour, his family feared that he was "becoming a communist."

Crosby died suddenly of pneumonia in Baltimore, Maryland. His memorial service at Cooper Union on 7 March 1907 was sponsored by such figures as Addams, Adler, Gompers, Howells, William Jennings Bryan, Abraham Cahan, Clarence Darrow, Hamlin Garland, William Lloyd Garrison, Jr., Henry George, Jr., Thomas Wentworth Higginson, William James, and Booker T. Washington. His wife and family felt so disgraced by the universal reformer's career after 1894 that mention of his name was banned from their conversation for a generation after his death. Never the captive of any ideology, however, Crosby was instinctively a large-hearted individualist who hated social injustice. His friend Leonard Abbott was closer to the truth in depicting Crosby as "a leader of forlorn hopes."

• The Ernest Howard Crosby Papers are at Michigan State University. Absent an autobiography, see Ernest Howard Crosby, "The Crosby Family of New York," *New York Genealogical and Biographical Record* (Oct. 1898–July 1899). See also the following tributes with biographical information: Leonard Abbott, "Some Reminiscences of Ernest Crosby," *Mother Earth* 1 (Feb. 1907): 22–27, expanded and published as Abbott, *Ernest Crosby: A Valuation and a Tribute* (1907); *Addresses in Memory of Ernest Howard Crosby* (1907); Benjamin Orange Flower, "Ernest Howard Crosby: Prophet of Peace and Apostle of Social Righteousness," *Arena* 37 (Mar. 1907): 259–71; "The Late Ernest Crosby," *Single Tax Review* 6 (15 Apr. 1907): 7–15; and Hamlin Garland, "Ernest Howard Crosby and His Message," *Twentieth Century Magazine* 1 (Oct. 1909): 27–28. Secondary sources on Crosby include Fred H. Harrington, "The Literary Aspects of American Anti-Imperialism," *New England Quarterly* 10 (Dec. 1937): 650–67; Louis Filler, *Crusaders for American Liberalism* (1939); Perry E. Gianakos, "Ernest Howard Crosby: A Forgotten Tolstoyan Anti-Militarist and Anti-Imperialist," *American Studies* 13 (Spring 1972): 11–29; Peter J. Frederick, "A Life of Principle: Ernest Howard Crosby and the Frustrations of the Intellectual as Reformer," *New York History* 54 (Oct. 1973): 396–423; and Frederick, *Knights of the Golden Rule: The Intellectual as Christian Social Reformer in the 1890s* (1976).

RALPH E. LUKER

CROSBY, Fanny (24 Mar. 1820–12 Feb. 1915), poet and author of gospel hymn texts, was born Frances Jane Crosby in Putnam County, New York, the daughter of John Crosby and Mercy Crosby, farmers. (Her mother's maiden name and married name were the same.) At the age of six weeks, she developed an eye infection, for which a man falsely claiming to be a physician prescribed the application of hot poultices; the tragic result was permanent blindness. That same year her father died, and her mother went to work as a maid. Fanny was first sent to live with her grandmother, and later with a Mrs. Hawley, who realized the child's precociousness and set her to memorizing much of the Bible. Within two years, Fanny had committed the entire Pentateuch (complete with genealogies), most of the poetic books, and the four Gospels to memory.

In 1835 Crosby entered the newly founded New York Institution for the Blind, where she quickly mastered studies in history, science, and philosophy. She so loved grammar that she could recite the entire text of *Brown's Grammar* word for word until the day of her death. Crosby hated math, however, and had difficulty learning braille, which she rarely used.

While attending the institute, Crosby developed an unusual gift for poetry. She could, almost instantly, construct fairly elaborate poems, a talent that school officials used to impress visiting dignitaries and potential donors. Although not always eager to versify on command, Fanny's unusual gift earned her a considerable reputation as "the Blind Poetess" and provided her the opportunity to meet many important people, such as Grover Cleveland, who as a young man worked at the institution and became a lifelong friend.

In 1847 Crosby became a teacher of grammar, rhetoric, and history at the institution. A regular contributor to various New York City newspapers and magazines, including the *Saturday Evening Post*, she enjoyed a growing stature as a published poet. Four books of her poetry were also published. Crosby often collaborated with the composer and music educator George F. Root, providing texts for many of his successful pre–Civil War songs: "Hazel Dell" (1852), "There's Music in the Air" (1854), and "Rosalie, the Prairie Flower" (1858). For these lyrics, she received the standard fee of one or two dollars each.

Crosby left the institute in 1858 upon her marriage to Alexander Van Alsteine, Jr., another blind teacher at the school. A year later, she bore a child that lived only a short time. She continued to use her maiden name after marriage, resorting to "Van Alstyne" (Crosby's preferred spelling) only as a poetic pseudonym. Whereas Crosby preferred to live in crowded tenement houses and give away all money not needed for essentials, Van (as he was known) gravitated toward the more affluent members of society, and eventually the couple separated. They remained apart until Van's death in 1902.

Although she had received a traditional Calvinistic religious upbringing, Crosby experienced a profound "born again" conversion in 1850 while attending revival meetings at New York City's Methodist Broadway Tabernacle. Fourteen years later, the somewhat mystical poet received a vision revealing that her new purpose in life was to write hymns. Shortly afterward she submitted her first hymn to William Bradbury, a leading composer/publisher of popular Sunday school songs. Bradbury was impressed and launched Crosby's career.

Over the next four decades, Crosby wrote approximately 9,000 hymn texts, most originally intended for Sunday school use. However, with the rise of urban revivalism in the 1870s, as led by Dwight L. Moody and Ira D. Sankey, Crosby's hymns became revivalistic paradigms and entered the Protestant mainstream as gospel hymns. Their success arose from the poet's ability to speak directly to both the uneducated working classes with whom she lived and the affluent, many of whom she numbered among her friends. Whether hymns of praise, prayer, or repentance, Crosby's songs quickly came to epitomize the musical message of nineteenth-century revivalism with its emphasis on individual sin and the good news (gospel) of God's forgiveness through Jesus Christ.

Although most of Crosby's hymns were penned for Biglow and Main Publishing (the successor to Bradbury's company), nearly 1,000 were written expressly for the leading gospel song composers of the day, such as William J. Kirkpatrick and William H. Doane, Crosby's most successful collaborators. She was so prolific that her publishers asked her to disguise their heavy reliance on her material by using over 200 pen names. By the mid-1870s Crosby had written the majority of her hymns that were to gain widespread popularity. Yet her fame did not wane in succeeding decades, as missionaries carried her songs around the world, translating them into hundreds of languages.

Nearly fifty of Crosby's hymns are published in modern English hymnals, over a dozen of which are still widely sung. Her most popular include "Jesus, Keep Me Near the Cross" (1869), "Praise Him, Praise Him" (1869), "Safe in the Arms of Jesus" (1869), "Pass Me Not, O Gentle Savior" (1870), "Rescue the Perishing" (1870), "Blessed Assurance" (1873), "All the Way My Savior Leads Me" (1875), "Draw Me Nearer," (1875), and "To God Be the Glory" (1875).

In addition to her hymn writing, Crosby was a tireless social worker in missions along New York's Lower East Side, a popular religious speaker, and one of the most prominent figures in American evangelical life. She considered her blindness to be a gift from God and not a handicap: "It was the best thing that could have happened to me; how could I have lived such a helpful life had I not been blind?" When Fanny Crosby died in Bridgeport, Connecticut, at the age of ninety-four, she was generally considered the most significant writer in the history of the phenomenally popular gospel song. A century later, her songs not only epitomized the genre of gospel hymnody but also continued to be sung by millions of people who found in them a vital and personal experience reflecting the good news of the gospel.

• Crosby's papers are housed in the Music Division of the New York Public Library at Lincoln Center. Her secular poetry is published in four collections: *The Blind Girl and Other Poems* (1844), *Monterey and Other Poems* (1851), *A Wreath of Columbia's Flowers* (1858), and *Bells at Evening and Other Voices* (1897). Her most famous hymns are published in the American revival collection *Gospel Hymns and Sacred Songs* (6 vols., 1875–1894). Donald P. Hustad, ed., *Fanny Crosby Speaks Again* (1977), includes recently discovered, unpublished hymns. The definitive biography is Bernard Ruffin, *Fanny Crosby* (1976), while earlier and less scholarly works include Will Carleton, ed., *Fanny Crosby's Life-Story, by Her-*self (1903); Fanny Crosby and Adelbert White, eds., *Memories of Eighty Years* (1906); and Samuel Jackson, *An Evening of Song and Story with Fanny Crosby, the Blind Poetess* (1912). For decades, John Julian, ed., *A Dictionary of Hymnology* (1892), had been the standard reference source for Crosby (listed under Van Alstyne), but recent scholarship is reflected in Harry Eskew, "Gospel Music, I," in the *New Grove Dictionary of Music and Musicians*, ed. H. Wiley Hitchcock and Stanley Sadie (1980), and Mel R. Wilhoit, "Fanny Crosby," in the *New Grove Dictionary of American Music* (1986). An obituary is in the *New York Times*, 13 Feb. 1915.

MEL R. WILHOIT

CROSBY, James Morris (12 May 1927–10 Apr. 1986), businessman and entertainment entrepreneur, was born in Great Neck, Long Island, New York, the son of John F. Crosby, an attorney, and Emily M. (maiden name unknown). After attending preparatory school in Lawrenceville, New Jersey, he went to Franklin and Marshall College in 1945. From that year to 1946, he served in the U.S. Navy, but 1946 found him back stateside, attending Bucknell College. He enrolled in Georgetown University later that year, graduating in 1948 with a degree in economics. He attended Georgetown Law School from 1948 to 1949. From 1949 to 1951 he was a shipping representative for the International Paint Company of New York City.

In 1951 he became an investment banker on Wall Street, working for Smith Barney Harris Upham & Company. After his father and Thomas E. Dewey joined other investors to buy the Mary Carter Paint Company in 1958, 31-year-old Crosby became the company's new president. With boundless energy, high expectations, and long hours of work, he reorganized the business. It evolved into the Unexcelled Chemical Corporation of New Jersey. He remained president and chief executive officer of Unexcelled until 1967. During his tenure he diversified the company greatly, leading it into the real estate business, focusing particularly on resort hotels and gambling casinos.

In 1968 Crosby dropped the paint business altogether and reorganized the company as Resorts International with its headquarters in Miami, Florida. He opened the first Resorts International on Paradise Island in the Bahamas. As it was developing into a billion-dollar business in the late 1960s and early 1970s, Crosby opened new Resorts casinos in various areas and, most notably, started buying up real estate in Atlantic City, New Jersey, before the state's voters approved a gambling referendum in 1976. In 1978 Crosby accomplished a first in the modern American gambling industry: He opened the first legal casino-hotel outside Nevada, the 750-room Resorts International Casino in Atlantic City. Continuing to buy land, Crosby by 1985 owned 280 acres of developed or developable land in Atlantic City, making Resorts International the largest landholder in town. Virtually all businessmen who wished to open a casino-hotel had to deal with Crosby, either buying or leasing land from him. For example, when the Showboat Casino opened in 1986, it agreed to pay Crosby $6 million a year in rent.

Throughout the 1970s and 1980s Crosby made a fortune in the gambling industry although he never gambled. He once averred that he found the practice boring. And to paraphrase his own rhetorical question: Since the house always has the "odds," why should an individual gamble against it?

Crosby eventually invested hundreds of millions of dollars acquiring undeveloped real estate in the Bahamas, Miami, Nevada, and elsewhere. Crosby and his family controlled about 60 percent of Resorts International's voting stock; thus he was free to make all decisions about the future. Crosby became one of the richest men in the United States and shuttled between homes in Miami, Manhattan, Atlantic City, and Paradise Island. In 1983 total revenues from his casinos were $468 million, the number growing to $483.9 million in 1984.

By 1985 Crosby was finishing his most ambitious project in Atlantic City. Resorts II soon opened to the public. It was a $400 million hotel-casino complex. The 42-story, 1,200-room hotel also featured an 80,000-square-foot exhibit hall and two ballrooms. It was virtually a self-contained "city" and played host to many conventions. The adjacent casino had 120,000 square feet of space for its games.

Crosby was occasionally the focus of controversy. For example, in 1978 allegations surfaced that Resorts International had ties to the mob or "underworld" figures. There followed an investigation by the New Jersey Division of Gaming Enforcement, but the agency cleared Crosby. However, his critics still maintained that, indeed, the mob was flourishing in Crosby's business circles.

Another controversy soon followed. Always called a "freewheeler," Crosby in 1983 risked $93 million from the Resorts' coffers to buy metal futures. Selling out the next year, he lost $24 million. Criticized by many experts, Crosby had to face thousands of shareholders of Resorts International.

In 1985 Crosby saw yet another troublesome issue arise. A government investigation substantiated that Resorts International had paid hundreds of thousands of dollars to two lawyers, the money later being given to a Resorts "consultant" and ultimately passed on to the sitting prime minister of the Bahamas. Because of such actions, the New Jersey attorney general's staff gave a spirited argument against renewing Resorts International's license. But Crosby's organization was too strong. Voting three to one to renew his license, the New Jersey Casino Control Commission accepted Crosby's statement that he and other executives knew nothing whatsoever about such payoffs. Logic and legality aside, the entrepreneur continued running his gambling empire and amassing a bigger fortune.

After these controversies Crosby's health became a bigger problem. Although only fifty-eight years old in 1986, he had always been a heavy smoker and had suffered from emphysema for years. A single man who had no children, he died in New York City during surgery at New York University Medical Center.

• The *New York Times* ran articles on Crosby and his empire; see especially 16 Apr.; 17 Sept.; 2, 18 Oct.; and 7 Nov. 1986. For Crosby and his billion dollar gambling empire, see also E. S. Ely, "Big Deal in Atlantic City," *Financial World* 154 (1–14 May 1985): 93–95; Judith Waldrop, "Atlantic City Makeover," *American Demographics* 16 (Sept. 1994): 4; and David Johnston, *Temples of Chance: How America Inc. Bought Out Murder Inc. to Win Control of the Casino Business* (1992). An obituary is in the *New York Times*, 12 Apr. 1986.

JAMES M. SMALLWOOD

CROSBY, John Schuyler (19 Sept. 1839–8 Aug. 1914), military officer and government official, was born in Albany County, New York, the son of Clarkson Floyd Crosby, who was independently wealthy, and Angelica Schuyler. Crosby attended the University of the City of New York in 1855–1856 but left for a grand tour of the Far East and South America. In 1863 he married Harriet Van Rensselaer; they had two children.

Early in the Civil War, in 1861, Crosby joined the army as a second lieutenant of the First U.S. Artillery. He served with distinction and valor in numerous battles, receiving promotions that culminated in 1865 with the rank of brevet lieutenant colonel. Of particular note during the war was his service as a courier behind enemy lines, for which he received the thanks of President Abraham Lincoln. Near the end of the war he joined the staff of Major General Philip H. Sheridan, acting as assistant inspector general of the Military Division. For the rest of his military career, Crosby was closely associated with Sheridan and participated in Sheridan's American Indian campaigns in the West. After serving from 1869 to 1870 as a lieutenant colonel and aide-de-camp to Sheridan, Crosby completed his military career in December 1870. After leaving the army, Crosby worked as an engineer on coastal lighthouses and breakwaters.

In 1876 Crosby, a war hero, successful diplomat, and Republican activist, was appointed U.S. consul at Florence, Italy, where he served until 1882. As consul, he encouraged skilled, experienced American artists to go to Florence but warned neophytes of the hardships there. He was also active in drives to raise money from visiting and resident Americans to aid the poor in Florence, especially during the harsh winter of 1880. In 1881 the Italian government made him an officer of the Order of the Crown of Italy for his assistance to the Italian government in capturing a band of forgers with American connections.

In 1882 President Chester A. Arthur appointed Crosby, his friend and fellow New Yorker, territorial governor of Montana. Crosby arrived in Montana in January 1883, and his earlier service with Sheridan in the West made the elite New Yorker more acceptable to Montanans. The new governor was a dedicated Republican, who, like his two predecessors, sought to transfer Montana from the Democratic to the Republican column. To gain credibility, he made investments in the territory, including banks, a ranch, and one of the first steamboats on the upper Missouri River.

Crosby proved to be an assertive governor. Although his term lasted less than two years, he vetoed eleven bills, of which only three were overturned by the territorial legislature. His most important veto was a bill to establish a territorial agency of cattle commissioners and inspectors, earning him the animosity of cattle raisers. He took a popular, firm stand on crime by refusing to grant many pardons, and he stopped the importation of cattle with Texas fever.

Although a hunter himself, Crosby was greatly concerned about the preservation of wildlife in Yellowstone National Park and particularly decried the sportsmen who were randomly and ruthlessly decimating buffalo and other wildlife. He set up a meeting with the governors of Wyoming, Idaho, and Dakota to take action to protect wildlife in the national park, a gathering that he later claimed led to the passage of some protective laws. He lobbied the federal government to station a company of cavalry at Yellowstone to protect wildlife and other natural resources and resisted attempts of the Yellowstone National Park Improvement Company to develop the park commercially. Crosby further antagonized cattle raisers by attempting to stop them from gaining grazing venues in the park. He also called for the protection of timber resources in the territory and proposed the appointment of government officials to advance this goal.

Crosby supported politically popular but harsh proposals for dealing with Native Americans and Mormons. He proposed granting 160 acres to each Native American head of household with an additional 80 acres for each child. The rest of the vast Native-American lands in Montana would be sold off to settlers, with the proceeds going to a Native-American fund. Crosby justified this proposal by "that irresistible law of nature under which a lower must yield to a higher civilization" (*Message of Governor Jno. Schuyler Crosby of the Territory of Montana* [1883], p. 8). The governor was anxious to keep Mormons out of the territory, objecting to their practice of polygamy. He proposed that Mormons be disfranchised and barred from settling on public lands.

Crosby continued his friendship with President Arthur and accompanied him on his tour of Yellowstone in August 1883. In November 1884 Arthur appointed Crosby assistant postmaster general, a position he held for the last four months of the Arthur administration. From 1889 until 1893 he served as a school commissioner in New York City. He protested the limited amount of time given to the study of American history in the schools. Following a period of declining health that was worsened by a violent attack on Crosby by one of his servants, Crosby died in Newport, Rhode Island, while on a yachting trip.

Because Crosby was independently wealthy from his family fortune and that of his wife, he was thus able to accept numerous appointments in public service. He was one of the heroic Civil War officers that the Republicans successfully placed in public offices in the late nineteenth century to keep alive the image of the party as the defender of the Union.

• The John Schuyler Crosby Personal Clippings Scrapbooks covering the period of his consulate in Florence and his territorial governorship in Mont. are in the Houghton Library, Harvard University. For his military career, see Francis B. Heitman, *Historical Register and Dictionary of the United States Army, from Its Organization, September 29, 1789, to March 2, 1903* (1903). For his governorship, see Clark C. Spence, *Territorial Politics and Government in Montana, 1864–1889* (1975). To place Crosby in context with other territorial governors, see Thomas A. McMullin and David Walker, *Biographical Directory of American Territorial Governors* (1984). An obituary is in the *New York Times*, 9 Aug. 1914.

THOMAS A. MCMULLIN

CROSBY, Sylvester Sage (2 Sept. 1831–18 Aug. 1914), watchmaker and numismatist, was born in Charlestown, New Hampshire, the son of Jaazaniah Crosby, a Unitarian minister, and Holdah Robinson Sage. At the age of seventeen Crosby established a watchmaking business in Charlestown, New Hampshire. To be with other family members, he later moved to Boston, where he opened a watchmaking business. In 1855 he married Mary Elizabeth Capelle of Lexington, Massachusetts; she died in 1874, and the next year he married Mehitabel "Hittie" Ackers. Crosby had no children.

Crosby's interest in coins as a collector began in 1857. In 1869 he wrote a variety study of the U.S. cents of 1793, which was published in the *American Journal of Numismatics*. This work introduced one of Crosby's major innovations, which has continued to be used—the designation of a coin's obverse die variety with a number and its reverse die variety with a letter. This method of listing is particularly helpful in distinguishing between coins whose dies were often prepared by hand punching. Crosby's study was updated and expanded to include the half cents of 1793 and republished in 1897 (in a 200-copy printing) as *The United States Coinage of 1793: Cents and Half Cents*, which was reprinted in 1933 and 1962. Crosby created a reputation for numismatic perfection. In 1879 Edward Frossard, a cent specialist, maintained that "in only one instance and that in the description of a reverse apparently unknown when Mr. Crosby wrote his article have we been able to add any information not previous conveyed by him." When the New England Numismatic and Archeological Society was formed in 1866, Crosby was named its curator.

In 1869 the New England society appointed Crosby chairman of a committee of six to publish a book on early American coins. The committee proved of little assistance to Crosby, who by November 1872 had substantially completed the task. *The Early Coins of America* (1875) was printed in twelve parts (the last two were combined) from 1873 to 1875 with a few chapters appearing in the *American Journal of Numismatics*. "I intend no exaggeration," Crosby wrote, "in stating that I have long anticipated the day that should witness the completion of my labors, as the day that would bring me relief from the greatest care with which I have been burdened; a care I would never have accepted had I entertained the most remote idea that the whole labor and responsibility would devolve upon me." Crosby's book was the first major numismatic volume with a comprehensive coverage of American colonial coins and tokens as well as Washington pieces and other pattern and trial pieces. Sales of the book, whose printing was financed by Crosby himself, were hampered by the panic of 1873. Only 160 subscriptions were purchased of the original printing (variously stated to be 350 or 500). A testament to the enduring quality of this numismatic masterpiece is that it has been reprinted many times without editing (1945, 1970, 1974, and 1981).

Crosby's scholarly contribution was recognized immediately, but its importance grew with time. For many years, he continued to write articles for the *American Journal of Numismatics*. These included studies on early Fugio patterns, Somers Islands (Bermuda) coins, and the 1804 dollar. In 1876 Crosby was made an honorary member of the American Numismatic Society (which struck medals of him at that time and in 1869 when he was a corresponding member); he was also made an honorary member of the American Numismatic Association (1907) and the Boston Numismatic Society (1908). He died in Cambridge, Massachusetts, where he had lived for forty-two years, and was buried in a Lexington cemetery next to his first wife. When the American Numismatic Society expanded its building in 1930, Crosby was the only American among the six numismatic scholars honored by having their names cut into the frieze of the building's front facade. He was elected posthumously to the American Numismatic Association's Hall of Fame in 1970.

Crosby began an important era in American numismatic research with his painstakingly accurate and comprehensive work, which proved a model for later scholars. His astounding contribution—all the more noteworthy because he was a numismatist by avocation only—assisted in establishing American numismatics as a field for systematic, scientific inquiry.

• There are no papers left regarding Crosby's numismatic studies except for the run of articles in the *American Journal of Numismatics*. Apart from the cent and half-cent articles, which were nicely condensed in his 1897 book, "Notes on an Undescribed Trial Piece Bearing Impressions of Two Hubs for a Fugio Pattern," *American Journal of Numismatics* 36 (Jan. 1902): 76–80, and "The Somer Island Coins," *American Journal of Numismatics* 18 (Oct. 1883): 30–31, round out his work on early American coins. Crosby also added his voice to the enigma surrounding 1804 dollars with his article "United States Coinage for 1804," *American Journal of Numismatics* 25 (Apr. 1891): 100–101. The pair of articles by Robert I. Wester, "The Search for Crosby the Man," *Colonial Newsletter* 27 (July 1987): 982–96, and "The Crosbys of Charlestown, New Hampshire," *The Asylum* 2 (Spring 1982): 1–4, are excellent on his family history and personal life. Also worth consulting is Pete Smith, *American Numismatic Biographies* (1992). Eric Newman's introduction to the 1975 edition of *Early Coins of America* provides some further information on the prepara-

tion and printing of that volume. See also Edward Frossard, *Monograph of United States Cents and Half Cents 1793–1857* (1879). An obituary is in *The Numismatist*, Sept. 1914.

ERIC P. NEWMAN

CROSBY, William Otis (14 Jan. 1850–31 Dec. 1925), economic and engineering geologist, was born in Decatur, Ohio, the son of Francis William Crosby, a mining manager, and Hannah Everett Ballard. His father, originally a schoolteacher, served under General Sherman during the Civil War; while on campaign he became acquainted with the gold mine at Concord, North Carolina, of which he became superintendent in 1868. Here young Crosby developed a deep-seated interest in geology and a familiarity with the practical geological concerns of managing mining operations, backed by extensive reading on geological subjects. During the summer of 1871 he moved with his father to Colorado, where they operated a small silver mill at Georgetown. Together they built two Ballard furnaces, designed by the elder Crosby, for smelting gold and silver ores. Meanwhile, the younger Crosby explored the countryside and visited local mining operations, acquiring a reputation for knowledge of the local geological region. After he served as a guide in the area for a Massachusetts Institute of Technology (MIT) field excursion of twelve students and four professors, the president of the university, John D. Runkle, enticed Crosby to complete his formal education at MIT by promising to waive his first year's tuition and to pay him a modest salary if he would build two Ballard furnaces and a stamp mill, and offer some practical advice for the Institute's new metallurgy laboratory.

Between 1871 and 1876 Crosby studied for his B.Sc. in natural history. After taking a hiatus from the 1872–1873 school year to earn some money by working at his father's silver mill in Colorado, he attended Louis Agassiz's new summer school for science teachers on the Pekinese Islands. There he honed the observational, collection, and taxonomic skills that became the hallmarks of his professional career. Resuming his studies, Crosby so impressed Alpheus Hyatt, professor of paleontology, that he was appointed Hyatt's assistant at the Museum of the Boston Society of Natural History in 1874, and as a student assistant in paleontology at MIT during his senior year. Crosby finished his degree in June 1876; his bachelor's thesis, "Geology of Eastern Massachusetts," was the first geology thesis written at MIT. In September 1876 he married his first cousin, Alice Alzina Ballard of Lansing, Michigan; they would have two children, one of whom died in infancy.

After graduation Crosby continued to work at the museum as assistant curator of geology and mineralogy. He was responsible for the expansion, reorganization, and presentation of various collections that had been in a serious state of disarray. So effective was he in presenting thematically-organized, educational displays for the public, and so useful were the numerous guidebooks he wrote on the collections for the public's benefit, that a Boston schoolteacher is quoted as saying, "These collections Professor Crosby made into a demonstration of the evolutionary processes of inorganic nature. To the teacher they were an illuminating guide, to the child a story that goes right on" (Shimer and Lindgren, p. 37). Also under the museum's auspices he conducted an intensive investigation of the geology of eastern Massachusetts, which culminated in the publication of the three-volumes *Geology of the Boston Basin* (1893–1900) and numerous shorter publications. He contributed to the popularization and dissemination of geological knowledge at the museum by frequently offering popular lecture series and guiding field excursions for science teachers and the general public.

While working at the Boston Museum Crosby was hired by MIT as an assistant in paleontology, eventually rising to become director of the department of geology (1902–1904) and full professor (1906). An engaging speaker whose enthusiasm for his subject was infectious, he punctuated his meticulously-organized lectures with references to poetry and drew on his vast firsthand experiences throughout the United States, Canada, Trinidad, Cuba, Panama, Venezuela, and Spain. He also complemented his lectures by leading field trips, conducting laboratories, making available his extensive collections of minerals, rocks, and fossils, and writing a number of textbooks and laboratory manuals. As a researcher he was indefatigable and thorough; as a writer he was comprehensive and prolific. During his life he produced more than 150 publications on a wide variety of geological subjects and wrote numerous other private reports as a geological consultant. When he was forced to retire in 1907 by a partial loss of hearing, he became more active as an economic and engineering geological consultant.

As an economic geologist Crosby capitalized on his personal experience when hired as a consultant for mining operations in the western United States, Massachusetts, Missouri, New York and New Jersey, as well as at the Alaskan Treadwill mines and the Michipicoten mines in Canada. These travels provided him with opportunities to increase his ever-growing geological collections, as well as fresh material for his extensive publications on such subjects in economic geology as rare minerals, geological classification of deposits (by origin and structure), and gold, silver, and copper deposits.

Most important, though, was Crosby's work as an engineering geologist. Along with his friend and fellow classmate at MIT, the civil engineer John R. Freeman, Crosby was one of the first Americans to recognize the importance of geology for civil engineering and to resolve practical problems of water storage and supply. He was first introduced to this field in 1895, when he was hired at a meager $10 per day as consultant to the Metropolitan Water Commission of Boston to study the foundations of the Wachussett Dam, the North Dike, and the route of the aqueduct tunnel; he later worked on the Boston Dry Dock, continuing until 1903. As an expert not only on mineral deposits but also on building stones, construction materials, and

underground structures, he was in high demand as a consultant for new dam-building projects, including the Muscle Shoals Dam in Alabama, the Arrow Rock Dam in Idaho (then the highest dam in the world), the Sun River Dam in Montana, the dam across the Mississippi at Keokuk, Iowa, three dams in Spain (including the highest in Europe at the time, on the Pallaresa River), and the largest dam in Mexico, La Boquilla. While working for the Board of Water Supply of New York City (1906–1912) he advised on the conditions for the Ashokan and Kenisko dams and the siphons on the Hudson River, as well as the construction of aqueducts, such as the Catskill in New York, and the excavation of sewage and subway systems for the cities of Boston and New York. His importance to the history of engineering geology cannot be overestimated; he was one of the first geologists to work closely with engineers, and many of his projects were enormous in both sheer physical size and financial outlay. He was also called on to solve problems related to clay, coal, kaolin, oil, and various ore deposits, and his expert testimony was sought to resolve legal disputes that revolved around geological factors.

Crosby's achievements were recognized both in his lifetime and after his death. He was elected to membership in numerous societies and received many awards, including a silver medal for his role as collector at the 1900 Paris Exposition. Eight years later a 4,000-foot peak on Atka Island in the Aleutians was named Mount Crosby in his honor. He was both a geologist and an enthusiastic mountain-climber, so this was singularly appropriate. Finally, MIT's William Otis Crosby Lectureship was established in 1961 at the bequest of his son, also a geologist. Crosby died of pneumonia at his home in the Boston area of Jamaica Plain.

• A fairly comprehensive collection of Crosby's published and unpublished papers is in the MIT Institute Archives; included are lecture notes, laboratory guides, fieldnotes, an unpublished record of his ancestors written by P. W. Pringle in 1970, and a journal of his experiences in Colorado during the summer of 1871. The most comprehensive works on Crosby are Robert R. Shrock, *The Geologists Crosby of Boston* (1972), which contains a copy of his 1871 journal in the appendix; and Shrock, *Geology at M.I.T., 1865–1965: A History of the First Hundred Years of Geology at the Massachusetts Institute of Technology*, vol. 1 (1977), pp. 271–300. Also illuminating are obituaries including W. H. Niles, "A Sketch of Professor Crosby's Work," *Technology Review* 9 (1907): 174–77; D. W. Johnson, "William Otis Crosby," *Science* 63 (1926): 609–10; H. W. Shimer and W. Lindgren, "Memorial to William Otis Crosby," *Geological Society of America Bulletin* 38 (1927): 34–45; and A. C. Lane, "William Otis Crosby," *Proceedings of the American Academy of Arts and Sciences* 64 (1930): 518–26.

TRENT A. MITCHELL

CROSMAN, Henrietta Foster (2 Sept. 1861–31 Oct. 1944), stage and film actress, was born in Wheeling, West Virginia, the daughter of Major George H. Crosman, a commander of an army post, and Mary Wick, a relative of the composer Stephen Collins Foster. After being educated until about age fifteen in Wheeling and studying voice in Paris, where faulty training methods ruined her singing voice, Crosman sought an acting career. She petitioned her great-uncle Morrison Foster (a brother of the composer), who sent her to his friend, John A. Ellsler, then the manager of the Grand Opera House in Pittsburgh. Ellsler cast her in the minor role of Letty Lee in Bartley Campbell's *The White Slave*, in which she debuted in August 1883 at the Windsor Theatre in New York City.

After the young actress spent several years eking out a living on tour, Augustin Daly hired her in 1889 for his stock company. There she had her first substantial success, playing Celia to Ada Rehan as Rosalind in *As You Like It* that year. Crosman considered Daly a great teacher but felt he hampered her originality and ambition, so she moved to Daniel Frohman's company at the Lyceum, debuting on 9 April 1890 and subsequently appearing opposite many of the leading men of the day. There followed an engagement with Charles Frohman, and she soon became the leading lady of Charles Frohman's Comedians, playing roles in such forgotten plays as *Mr. Wilkinson's Widows* (1891) and *The Junior Partner* (1891–1892).

In 1886 Crosman married Sedley Brown, a director, with whom she had one child. She divorced Brown in 1896, retaining custody of their child. The same year she married Maurice Campbell, a theatrical press agent turned producer, who determined to make her a star. They had one child. Crosman scored her first smash hit in the title role of *Mistress Nell* by George Hazelton. The script was weak and funding difficult to secure, but she opened in New York despite the opposition of the Theatrical Syndicate, which at that time held a near-monopoly on the American theater. Crosman's portrayal of the Restoration actress Nell Gwyn became the hit of the 1900–1901 season in New York. The critic Lewis C. Strang spoke glowingly of Crosman's "magical prettiness" and called her work "the art of the light comedian at its best . . . spontaneous, free, and natural. . . . Miss Crosman lived Nell Gwyn." Praising her versatility, Strang lauded Crosman's "voice that interprets while it charms." Her third-act curtain line—"Gentlemen—to hell with you!"—may have been the first time an actress had uttered such an oath on the Victorian stage, but most audiences seemed to find the line amusing rather than shocking. The role elevated her to stardom; the drama critic John Ranken Towse praised her performance for "its variety, its animation, its delightful deviltry, and its general fascination." According to several interviewers, she retained those qualities into old age.

Crosman followed *Nell* with Shakespearean roles in productions that her husband produced. In 1901 she appeared in New York City as Rosalind and was immediately acclaimed as the role's foremost interpreter of her time. The critic William Winter cited her qualifications for Rosalind as "a slender, lithe, boy-like figure, a handsome face, a blithe temperament, cheery spirits, physical alacrity, aptitude for playful banter, and artistic skill to indicate sentiment marked by levi-

ty." Towse considered Rosalind to be Crosman's greatest artistic achievement, one of the most satisfying expositions of character he had ever seen. She played the role for one hundred nights, then a record for Shakespearean comedy. A contemporary English script, *The Sword of the King* (1902), won her more plaudits, followed by *Sweet Kitty Belairs* (1903), in which she was selected to star by David Belasco.

She later appeared in such productions as *Getting Married* (1916), *The Merry Wives of Windsor* (1916), *The School for Scandal* (1925), and *Trelawney of the Wells* (1927). When she appeared as Mistress Page in James K. Hackett's revival of *Merry Wives*, she was considered a fine comedian but one who had become somewhat hardened and embittered, even cynical. Winter spoke of a tart, subacid tone in her voice, while praising her precision and poise.

Crosman began to appear in silent films in 1913 and continued to do so until 1927. In 1930 she appeared in her first sound movie, *The Royal Family of Broadway*, based on a play by Edna Ferber and George S. Kaufman. Several other films ensued, most notably John Ford's *Pilgrimage* in 1933, as well as such trifles as *Charlie Chan's Secret* in 1934.

After a few more stage performances she moved to her Pelham Manor home in New York State, where she lived with her son and daughter-in-law until her death. Her husband, who had become a federal Prohibition administrator in the 1920s, died in 1942.

Towse suggested that Crosman never received the appreciation she deserved, calling her "an exceedingly bright and capable performer, of considerable range and much technical expertness. Spontaneous vivacity [was] one of the potent charms in her various embodiments." Towse compared her work to that of Helena Modjeska and Ada Rehan, actresses at the top rank of their profession. Unfortunately, Crosman's two most successful roles, Nell and Rosalind, came early in her career; she never again achieved that level of success, either critical or popular.

• Considerable archival material may be found in the Locke Scrapbooks in the Theatre Collection at the New York Public Library for the Performing Arts, Lincoln Center. Her only attempt at autobiography was "My Stage Struggles and Triumphs," *Metropolitan*, Dec. 1900, pp. 661–67. Her other publications include "After the Matinee," *Green Book Album*, May 1910, pp. 1085–89; "The Gentle Art of Comedy," *Theatre*, Mar. 1917, pp. 160–61; "The Hardships of Stage Life," *Theatre*, Dec. 1902, pp. 18–19; "The Plays an Actress Never Plays," *Green Book Album*, Jan. 1910, pp. 98–103; "Stage-Struck Youth and the Dramatic School," *Hampton's Magazine*, Aug. 1910, pp. 239–48; and "The Story of 'Mistress Nell,'" *Harper's*, Feb. 1938, pp. 279–90. See also Lorraine Hollis, "With Rosalind in Arden, An Interview with Henrietta Crosman," *Theatre*, Aug. 1903, pp. 195–97. Obituaries are in *Variety*, 8 Nov. 1944, and the *New York Times* and *New York Herald Tribune*, 1 Nov. 1944.

STEPHEN M. ARCHER

CROSS, Arthur Lyon (14 Nov. 1873–21 June 1940), historian and educator, was born in Portland, Maine, the son of Emerlous D. Cross, a tailor and merchant, and

Charlotte Noyes. The family moved to Boston in 1877 and settled at Beachmont. Following his graduation from Chelsea High School, Arthur won a scholarship to Harvard College from which he was graduated with a B.A. in 1895. Originally intent on studying for the Episcopal priesthood but not being overly fond of the prospect of working with people as a pastor, he stayed on for graduate study at Harvard. He studied with the renowned historians Edward Channing and Albert Bushnell Hart, obtaining his M.A. in 1896.

Cross was drawn to the Anglican religious heritage of the American people, and he focused his doctoral research on the evolution of a religious institution through the political crises that led to the American Revolution. He investigated the role of the bishop of London in the colonies, a topic suggested by Channing, his mentor. He tested the popular thesis advanced by Jonathan Boucher in 1797 that attempts to establish an American episcopate constituted a major cause of the Revolution. Cross found instead that, while there was a longstanding nonconformity in the colonies, political alienation preceded religious antagonism and that religious freedom was a corollary to political independence. He demonstrated that following the Revolution the Anglican church was successfully reorganized with an episcopacy. Cross's work was pioneering because it opened a new area of historical investigation using religious institutions to assess political and social events. It also established a new approach to American religious history that stressed the Americanization of religious values. Following a travel fellowship in 1897–1898, during which he studied at the University of Berlin and the University of Freiburg, Cross received his Ph.D. in 1899. His dissertation won the Toppan Prize in that year and in 1902 was published as *The Anglican Episcopate and the American Colonies*. It was reissued in 1964 in recognition of its historiographical significance.

Except for an assistantship at Harvard in 1895–1897, Cross's teaching career was wholly spent at the University of Michigan in Ann Arbor. Attracted to Michigan by president James B. Angell who affirmed New England values in higher education, Cross was hired as an instructor in 1899, became assistant professor in 1904, junior professor in 1907, and professor of history in 1911. His affection for the Anglican church during this period led to his publication of the *History of St. Andrews Church* (1906), which concerned his local parish in Ann Arbor. In 1916 he was named Richard Hudson Professor of English History in recognition of his contribution to British historical studies. He was a pivotal figure in the development of that discipline in the United States, producing textbooks and integrating historical courses in related curricula in the university.

Cross made several advances in English historical scholarship. Following several years of research in British libraries, he produced in 1914 *A History of England and Greater Britain*, a comprehensive textbook intended for use in American institutions. This text, which included a major chapter on the American Revolution, became the most widely used textbook in its field in U.S. universities and was hailed by a reviewer as "the best of all the textbook histories." It won the respect of the British historical community because of its solid attention to detail. Cross's careful investigation of such original sources as the Shelburne Manuscripts led to further pioneering contributions. His monograph, *Eighteenth-Century Documents Relating to the Royal Forests, the Sheriffs, and Smuggling* (1928), proved his depth and diversity as a historian. Cross's explanatory notes were considered a model of documentary scholarship. Although scholarly journals during his career included many short essays and notes by him, much of his work, which was presented in lectures and classroom presentations, went unpublished.

Under Cross's leadership as head of the history department, the University of Michigan became nationally regarded; he attracted top faculty and advanced students to its ranks during his tenure. Before formal graduate schools had evolved, Cross directed numerous students in English history and did as much to stimulate in others the writing of English history as any scholar west of the Alleghenies. His own lectures in English constitutional history, particularly his study of the "benefit of clergy," were a foundation for many law students, and his humorous lecture style won many adherents in the Ann Arbor community.

A beloved teacher and resolute New Englander, Cross was a bachelor. Known as "Uncle Artie," he was short in stature and invited caricature. His contemporaries recalled him as a cultured man, a person of broad and catholic learning and lively wit. He died in Ann Arbor and was buried in Newton Center, Massachusetts.

• Personal papers relating to Cross are in the archives at the University of Michigan. He revised his 1914 work in 1920 as *A Shorter History of England and Greater Britain*. His essay, "Benefit of Clergy in the American Criminal Law," *Proceedings of the Massachusetts Historical Society* 61 (1928): 154–81, is still useful in constitutional law bibliography. An obituary is in *American Historical Review* 46 (Oct. 1940): 256.

WILLIAM H. BRACKNEY

CROSS, Charles Whitman (1 Sept. 1854–20 Apr. 1949), geologist, was born in Amherst, Massachusetts, the son of the Reverend Moses Kimball Cross, a Congregational minister, and Maria Mason, a teacher. In 1875 he received the degree of bachelor of sciences at Amherst College, where he was the first student in their new Scientific Course, thereby avoiding "the study of dead languages" he found objectionable. He pursued advanced studies in petrography at Göttingen and then under Ferdinand Zirkel at Leipzig where he was awarded the doctor of philosophy degree in 1880. He immediately joined the U.S. Geological Survey, where he remained for forty-five years.

Cross is praised primarily for his time-tested geological mapping of more than 3,800 square miles of southwestern and central Colorado. His initial interests were in specific minerals of that region, which included the zeolites in Table Mountain basalt, cryolite, hypersthene in andesite, sanidine and topaz in nevadite, alunite, and the new mineral ptilolite, now considered equivalent to mordenite. His attention then turned to the mining districts of Rico, Silverton, Telluride, Ouray, Lake City, and Creede. The spectacular scenery of these primitive areas in the San Juan Mountains captivated Cross as he traveled on foot or horseback. His field parties provided the training for many associates, such as A. C. Spencer, Albert Johannsen, E. S. Larsen, J. C. Hunter, and C. S. Ross, all of whom became prominent geologists. In addition, he studied the rocks of Pikes Peak and the mines at nearby Cripple Creek and Silver Cliff to the south and examined a wide array of laccoliths in several states, the unusually alkali-rich rocks of the Leucite Hills, Wyoming, and the modern volcanic rocks of Hawaii.

As a result of his wide experiences with rocks, he was assigned to three committees in the U.S. Geological Survey dealing with the classification of igneous rocks, petrography, and nomenclature. With these interests, he joined Joseph P. Iddings, Louis V. Pirsson, and Henry S. Washington in devising a system of rock classification in 1902 on a quantitative chemical-mineralogical basis. Cross, with his usual modesty, gave much of the credit for this exceptional contribution to petrology primarily to Iddings and Washington, but it is evident that the talents of all were required to generate this perceptive and imaginative system. Using the chemical analysis of a rock, they calculated a set of theoretical, end-member minerals that closely represented the actual minerals that had (or would have, if glassy) crystallized in the rocks. These "normative" minerals thereby approximated the mode, that is, the actual minerals observed when due consideration was given to solid solutions. The normative scheme was particularly useful in deducing the relationships among associated rocks and provided a base for the experimental determination of those relationships by means of simplified systems composed of the normative minerals. The method of calculation was widely adopted, even though the nomenclature assigned by the authors was abandoned, and has continued to influence petrologic thought greatly. The system is usually described as the CIPW norm devised from the first letter of the last name of each collaborator.

Cross was a major contributor to the organizations supporting geologists. He was the first co-secretary of the Geological Society of Washington in 1893 and served as its president in 1899. He helped organize the Petrologists' Club, and the meetings from 1910 to 1922 were held predominantly in his large library at home. As a member of the famous Committee of Eight, he contributed to the formulation in 1903 of the initial program of scientific study for the Geophysical Laboratory that was formed as a department of the Carnegie Institution of Washington in 1905. Cross was elected to the National Academy of Sciences in 1908 and served as treasurer from 1911 to 1919. He was also active in the organization of its National Research Council, serving as a member of its council and as

treasurer and vice chairman of the Division of Geology and Geography. He also was a member of the committee that surveyed the landslide problems plaguing the Panama Canal in the Culebra Cut. Cross was a member of the Geological Society of America (president, 1918), the American Philosophical Society, and the Washington Academy of Sciences; a corresponding member of the Academy of Natural Science of Philadelphia; and a foreign member of the Geological Society of London.

After his mandatory retirement in 1925, Cross moved to a home with considerable grounds in Chevy Chase, Maryland, where he began a study of rose culture. He developed new varieties that were adopted commercially under the names "Mrs. Whitman Cross" and "Hon. Lady Lindsay" (after the British ambassador's wife). Cross's garden, containing about 2,000 rose bushes, became a major neighborhood attraction. His other hobbies included golf and financial investments.

Cross was a friendly, sympathetic, and generous person who was particularly attentive to detail. He meticulously documented his specimens, over 2,000 of which were transferred to the Smithsonian Institution. He was equally meticulous in the selection of a campsite for its view, convenience, and comfort. His ready smile and modesty were two characteristics noted by friends. Cross married late at age forty-one; he and his wife, the former Virginia Stevens, had one son, Richard Stevens Cross, and a grandson carries his name.

The mineral crossite, a sodium amphibole, was named after him by Charles Palache in 1894. At the time of Cross's death in Rockville, Maryland, he was the oldest living member of the National Academy of Sciences and the oldest alumnus of Amherst College. Whitman Cross was not only one of the leading petrologists of his generation but also an outstanding field geologist.

• Cross's field notebooks are in the National Archives. His diaries, letters, autobiography, and a biographical manuscript are in the hands of his grandson. The personal letters between Cross and his wife were destroyed by the family. An example of the nine quadrangles that Cross mapped is the Silverton Quadrangle, Col. (with E. Howe and F. L. Ransome), no. 120 of the U.S. Geological Survey Folios. Some of Cross's other important regional petrology studies are "Igneous Rocks of the Leucite Hills and Pilot Butte, Wyoming," *American Journal of Science* 4 (1897): 115–41; *Lavas of Hawaii and Their Relations*, U.S. Geological Survey Professional Paper no. 88 (1915); and "The Laccolitic Mountain Groups of Colorado, Utah, and Arizona," *U.S. Geological Survey Annual Report* 14, pt. 2 (1894): 157–241. Cross's mineral studies are represented by "On the Occurrence of Topaz and Garnet in Lithophyses of Rhyolite," *American Journal of Science* 32 (1887): 117–21; "On the Minerals, Mainly Zeolites, Occurring in the Basalt of Table Mountain, near Golden, Colorado," *American Journal of Science* 23 (1882): 452–58, and 24 (1983): 129–38; and "On Alunite and Diaspore from Rosita Hills, Colorado," *American Journal of Science* 41 (1891): 466–75. The papers that record some of Cross's studies of landslides are "The Cimmarron Landslide," *Colorado Scientific Society Proceedings* 2 (1887): 116–26, and "Historical Sketch of the Landslides of Gaillar Cut (Panama Canal)," *National Academy of Science Memoirs* 18 (1924): 23–43. Examples of important Cross papers on other topics are "Wind Erosion in the Plateau Country," *Bulletin of the Geological Society of America* 19 (1908): 53–62; "Geological Formations versus Lithologic Individuals," *Journal of Geology* 10 (1902): 223–44; "Geology in the World War and After," *Bulletin of the Geological Society of America* 30 (1919): 165–88; and "The Development of Systematic Petrography in the Nineteenth Century," *Journal of Geology* 10 (1902): 332–76, 451–99. A complete bibliography for Cross is given by E. S. Larsen, Jr., "Charles Whitman Cross, 1854–1949," National Academy of Sciences, *Biographical Memoirs* 32 (1958): 100–112. N. L. Bowen wrote a short biography of Cross in the *Quarterly Journal of the Geological Society* 105 (1950): lv–lvi. An obituary by Clarence S. Ross is in the *Journal of the Washington Academy of Sciences* 39 (1949): 347–48.

H. S. YODER, JR.

CROSS, Edward (11 Nov. 1798–6 Apr. 1887), U.S. congressman and jurist, was born in Hawkins City, Tennessee, the son of Robert Cross, a revolutionary war soldier and a farmer of Welsh stock from Virginia. (His mother's name is unrecorded.) Cross grew up on a farm in Cumberland County, Kentucky, and received an education in the local schools. He moved to Overton County, Tennessee, in 1820 to read law with Adam Huntsman. Admitted to the bar in 1822, Cross practiced law in Tennessee until 1826, when he moved to Washington, Arkansas Territory, to practice law in partnership with Daniel Ringo, later chief justice of the Arkansas Supreme Court. Cross also became involved in Democratic politics and in 1828 joined Governor George Izard's staff in charge of forming the territorial militia. In 1831 he married Laura Frances Elliott; they had eight children.

Cross's judicial career began with an appointment from President Andrew Jackson to the U.S. Superior Court for the Territory of Arkansas in 1832. While on the territorial bench, Cross wrote several important opinions for the fledgling territory. In *Grande v. Foy* (1831), Cross found that the English common law was the law of the territory either by statutory provision or by common consent. This finding, based on sometimes confused legislative actions and longstanding proceedings in court, was important because it validated the action of ejectment. In a territory with Spanish, French, and American claims to land, Cross provided litigants with a method for trying title to land. Ejectment was a familiar common-law action to try title to land, thereby quieting titles and increasing their marketability. In *Cocke v. Henson* (1832), Cross confronted an issue of first impression in the territory: whether the court had the discretion to require that costs of prior litigation now nonsuited but before the court be paid prior to proceeding with the pending suit. Cross found that this procedural ploy, designed to force the defendant to assume "heavy bills of costs" and drive him to "insolvency or elopement," was vexatious. Under the circumstances, the court did have the discretion to have the moving party pay costs before proceeding. Further, in *Fletcher v. Ellis* (1836), Cross

demanded precision in pleadings by openly criticizing counsel in the case as "an extremely careless pleader." As a territorial supreme court judge, Cross sought to establish procedure as a means of enabling dispute resolution and thereby justice. He continued on the court until 1836, when Arkansas became a state, at which time he was appointed U.S. surveyor-general of the public lands.

In 1838 Cross won the Democratic nomination for Arkansas's single seat in the U.S. House of Representatives. He was elected to the Twenty-sixth Congress and was reelected to two additional terms. Cross was chair of the Committee on Private Land Claims in the Twenty-eighth Congress and consistently supported appropriations for an increased cavalry presence in the West, arguing that mounted forces were far more effective than infantry against plains tribes. Cross also contributed to the settlement of private land claims in Arkansas under House Bill No. 55, April 1844.

Although Cross was a Martin Van Buren delegate to the Democratic National Convention in Baltimore in 1844, he cast his ballot for James K. Polk because of the publication of a Van Buren letter to Silas Wright condemning the annexation of Texas. When Cross returned to Arkansas, his switch to Polk was ratified by his party members.

In 1852 Cross won emergency appointment by the governor to a special justiceship of the Arkansas Supreme Court. In 1853 Cross left the court to become one of the promoters of the Cairo and Fulton Railroad, designed to connect Cairo, Illinois, with St. Louis and ultimately Texas. Cross became president of the railroad in 1855 and continued in that capacity until the company became bankrupt in 1862.

During the Civil War, Cross was the Arkansas agent for the Confederacy's depository and handled thousands of dollars for the state. After the war, he returned to politics but was successful only in 1874 as Arkansas attorney general. In private life he maintained Millbrook farm in Hempstead County. Cross died in Little Rock.

• Cross papers, which include incoming correspondence from 1838 to 1843 as well as other items, are housed in the John E. Conner Museum, Texas A&I University, Kingsville, Tex. A copy is held by the University of Arkansas. For Cross's decisions as Arkansas Territory supreme court justice, see Samuel H. Hempstead, *Reports of Cases Argued and Determined in the United States Superior Court for the Territory of Arkansas from 1820 to 1836; the United States District Court for the District of Arkansas, in the Ninth Circuit, from 1839 to 1856, with Notes and References and Rules of Court* (1856). Government sources on Cross include Bicentennial Committee of the Judicial Conference of the United States, *Judges of the United States*, 2d ed. (1983), and U.S. Congress, Senate, *Biographical Directory of the United States Congress, 1774–1989*, 100th Cong., 2d sess., 1989, S. Doc. 34. Other sources on Cross include Morris S. Arnold, *Unequal Laws unto a Savage Race: European Legal Traditions in Arkansas, 1686–1836* (1985); Michael B. Dougan, *Confederate Arkansas* (1976); and Lonnie J. White, *Politics on the Southwestern Frontier: Arkansas Territory, 1819–1836* (1964).

GORDON MORRIS BAKKEN

CROSS, Milton (16 Apr. 1897–3 Jan. 1975), radio announcer, was born Milton John Cross in New York City, the son of Robert Cross, American Bible Society employee, and Margaret Lockhard. He received his education in the city's schools. After the Latin discipline of the classical program at De Witt Clinton High School, Cross went on to the Damrosch Institute of Musical Art (later the Juilliard School), where he studied music theory and singing with the aim of pursuing an educational career as a music supervisor. To finance his studies he sang on weekends in the chorus of the First Presbyterian Church in New York and the quartet of a Brooklyn synagogue.

Cross's interest in radio began when he was introduced one evening in 1921 to an electrically minded acquaintance in East Orange, New Jersey, who had succeeded in picking up broadcasts of the pioneer Westinghouse station WJZ. Cross was fascinated and wondered if the radio people could use a singer on their programs. He sent a letter to WJZ outlining his qualifications and within a few days found himself in the studio, which was a portion of the women's restroom at the Westinghouse factory that had been partitioned off for broadcast purposes. His accompanist was the young woman he would marry four years later, Lilian Ellegood; they had one child.

A month later Cross was hired as an announcer, working a 4:30 to 10:30 P.M. shift. In this capacity he found himself serving as a jack-of-all-trades, reading Uncle Wiggly stories to the children at 5 P.M. if author Howard Garris failed to show up, or filling in for artists who didn't appear on schedule (a common occurrence in the days when talent wasn't paid) by playing records or singing to mechanical accompaniment.

In due course WJZ moved its operations to the old Waldorf-Astoria Hotel at Thirty-fourth Street and Fifth Avenue in Manhattan and later to the old Aeolian Hall on Forty-second Street. In 1926 the station merged with WEAF to form the parent station of the National Broadcasting Company (NBC), and Cross became associated with the cultural side of network broadcasting.

When NBC moved to Radio City in the early 1930s, he became host of *The Magic Key*, which featured a number of prominent opera singers. Previously he had served as announcer for opera broadcasts originating from the Chicago Auditorium, where he and the engineers were stationed in the cellar with no way of knowing what was happening on stage. On one memorable evening that was to feature a performance of Verdi's *Il Trovatore* he was compelled to ad lib for thirty minutes about the opera and participating artists while utilities mogul Samuel Insull, the underwriter of Chicago Opera in that period, delivered an extended financial report that was not intended for broadcast from the stage. After this experience he always kept ready a substantial amount of filler material for his Met presentations and was upset when the perfect opportunity to use it seemed at hand some years later as Giovanni Martinelli became prostrate with acute indigestion just as he began to sing "Celeste Aida." Cross prepared to

improvise only to have the program returned to the studio where an ensemble filled the time gap caused by the interrupted performance.

On Christmas Day in 1931, the historic first broadcast of a Metropolitan Opera matinee performance, the traditional holiday season treat of Humperdinck's *Hansel and Gretel* was presented by NBC with Milton Cross as the announcer. The commentary was initially handled by Deems Taylor, composer and ubiquitous personality in presentation on performing arts, and diva Geraldine Farrar. But Cross gradually assumed all the functions of host for the series and remained in that capacity until his death, which occurred on the day before his scheduled announcing of Rossini's *The Italian Girl in Algiers*.

In the forty-three years of his weekly appearances on the series Cross missed only two broadcasts. Both followed the death of his wife Lilian in February 1973. WQXR announcer Peter Allen filled in for him on both occasions and was his able successor.

Apart from the Saturday matinee opera broadcasts, Cross officiated at the Metropolitan Opera Auditions of the Air when these were introduced in the early 1940s. He was also NBC's announcer for the Radio City Music Hall and Town Hall series, a children's Sunday morning program, *Coast to Coast on a Bus*, and later the *Information Please* quiz program. In a change of pace from his classical assignments, he was made "chairman" of the weekly jazz and blues sessions of the Chamber Music Society of Lower Basin Street in which Dinah Shore was the original featured vocalist.

However, it was as host of the Met matinees that he made his lasting impact. Opera had traditionally been the private preserve of the wealthy and an intellectual elite, but Cross's lucid explanations of the intricacies of opera plots and affable introductions to a broad range of operatic personalities did much to popularize the art form.

On a single Saturday afternoon the performance of an opera on the Met stage was shared by a radio audience that was estimated at 10,000,000 listeners in the early years and grew to upwards of 15,000,000 subsequently. This intensely loyal listenership responded promptly and generously to appeals for financial help from the Metropolitan Opera Guild, organized by Mrs. August Belmont, the resourceful former actress Eleanor Robson, in 1936 to see the beleaguered opera association through the financial storms of the depression.

At the time of Cross's death the broadcasts were carried by 120 commercial and ninety college radio stations, and his voice was one of the most familiar on the air. Variously described as mellifluous and resonant, it conveyed an attractive impression of dignity and heartfelt friendliness. In a tribute on the broadcast marking the fortieth anniversary of his association with the program, assistant manager Francis Robinson jokingly suggested that even Milton's ordinary speech sounded operatic.

In 1929 Cross received the gold medal of the American Academy of Arts and Letters for good diction. Forty years later he was awarded the Handel Medallion of the City of New York for his contributions to the arts.

Cross prepared meticulously for his radio presentations, attending the rehearsals of new productions and even studying the sets beforehand in order to be completely accurate in his descriptions. In serving the institution of the Metropolitan Opera he became a veritable institution himself. Francis Robinson observed on more than one occasion that large numbers of listeners assumed he owned the opera house.

Summing up his own feelings as a "forty-year man," Milton Cross commented, "To be the story and stage-action guide from the Met has given me a feeling of camaraderie with the radio audience. I always try to help my listeners hear, and see in their mind's eye, some of the beauty and joy of these great productions, which mean so much to me."

• The best sources of information on Milton Cross as host of the Metropolitan Opera broadcasts are a series of articles that appeared over the span of his career in this capacity in *Opera News*, the magazine published by the Metropolitan Opera Guild containing features about the opera world. These include "Milton Cross and His 20,000,000 Ears," 1 Jan. 1940, pp. 11–14; Lilian E. Foerster, "Milton Cross: The Speaking Voice of Opera," 17 Apr. 1944, pp. 8–9; and the reminiscences of Cross himself, "Forty-Year Man," 5 Dec. 1970, pp. 8–11. Francis Robinson's tribute to Cross was presented at the beginning of his fortieth season with the Met broadcasts as the "Biographies in Music" intermission feature on 26 Dec. 1940. Peter Allen also paid tribute to his predecessor in his article on broadcasting in David Hamilton, ed., *The Metropolitan Opera Encyclopedia* (1987). An obituary is in the *New York Times*, 4 Jan. 1975.

ALBERT O. WEISSBERG

CROSS, Wilbur Lucius (10 Apr. 1862–5 Oct. 1948), scholar and governor of Connecticut, was born in Gurleyville, Connecticut, the son of Samuel Cross, a farmer, miller, and manufacturer, and Harriet Maria Gurley. With considerable accuracy, Cross dubbed himself a "Connecticut Yankee." His family had lived in the state for more than two hundred years. From early on, he embraced the political faith of his father and by age eight had proudly proclaimed to a local politician in Gurleyville, "I am a Democrat" (Cross, p. 35).

Cross began studies at Yale in 1881 during an exciting period in the college's history. One of his favorite instructors, William Graham Sumner, "then in the very prime of his life," was a professor in the budding field of political economy (Cross, p. 70). Cross's speeches in the 1920s and 1930s assailing the "paternalism" of national Prohibition would echo many of the ideas he had learned in Sumner's classes. Although his interest in political and economic questions never flagged, Cross increasingly concentrated on his first love, English literature.

After earning a B.A. in 1885, Cross found employment as principal of Staples High School in Westport,

Connecticut. He returned to Yale one year later on a fellowship for advanced studies in English literature. His Ph.D. dissertation, which was completed under Professor Henry Beers in 1889, dealt with the relationship between French and English literature. After completing his studies at Yale, Cross taught for five years at a prep school, the Shady Side Academy, in Pittsburgh, Pennsylvania. In 1889 he married Helen Baldwin Avery; they had four children. He accepted a position as instructor in English at the Sheffield Scientific School of Yale in 1894. He advanced in short order to assistant professor of English and then, in 1902, to full professor.

This period was an extremely productive one for Cross. He authored *The Development of the English Novel* (1899), which was based on a series of lectures; wrote numerous articles on English literature for the *International Encyclopedia* (1903–1904); and completed *The Life and Times of Laurence Sterne* (1909). He was also hard at work on a grand study that was eventually published in three volumes as *The History of Henry Fielding* (1918), still the standard work on the subject. It included painstaking research and helped to restore Fielding's reputation as a novelist of the first rank. Cross convincingly challenged the traditional assessment of Fielding, the author of *The History of Tom Jones* (1749), as a "dissipated rake." Instead, he emphasized that "Fielding, who knew men and women in all stations, knew exactly what he was doing. His was a wonderfully penetrating mind" (Cross, *History of Henry Fielding*, p. 366).

At the suggestion of President Arthur Hadley, Cross took over as editor of the *Yale Review* in 1911. It soon blossomed into one of the nation's foremost journals on literary and public affairs. He also served as dean of the Yale Graduate School from 1916 until 1930, when he reached the mandatory retirement age of sixty-eight.

The year 1930 witnessed yet another turning point for Cross. He won the Democratic nomination for governor of Connecticut despite the opposition of the "Old Guard" in the party. Starting as an underdog, he rapidly proved his mettle as an adept campaigner. As John W. Jeffries, a historian of Connecticut politics, has noted, Cross's "upbringing plus time spent as a youth around courtroom and country store provided him with a fund of cracker-barrel wit and stories that he used to good effect in politics" (Jeffries, p. 24). He won a comfortable majority against a Republican opponent, who had the backing of the entrenched John Henry Roraback machine.

Cross was a popular and, by and large, effective governor and was easily reelected. He more than held his own against the machinations of the veteran politicians who dominated the state legislature.

At first Cross reacted to the emerging New Deal with skepticism. His instincts were those of a Grover Cleveland Democrat who would have preferred a regime of limited government and states' rights. In the election campaign of 1932, for example, he urged the mayor of Bridgeport to hold off seeking aid from the Reconstruction Finance Corporation "unless absolutely necessary" (Roth, p. 196).

Despite these small-government preferences, Cross did not swim against the rising tide of the New Deal. He not only gave his support to the essentials of Franklin D. Roosevelt's policies but reluctantly laid aside "the unsubstantial ghost of state sovereignty" and requested federal dollars for Connecticut. "During the next six years," wrote historian David M. Roth, "New Deal money flowed into Connecticut like water downhill" (Roth, p. 197). In 1934 alone the state received $15 million in subsidies from Washington. Among the policies enacted during Cross's tenure in office were increased spending on public works projects for the unemployed, abolition of child labor, enactment of minimum wages for women, and old-age pensions. It was said later by his supporters that he introduced a "little New Deal" to Connecticut.

Cross faced an uphill struggle when he sought a fourth two-year term in 1938. The Republicans conducted a vigorous campaign under the leadership of a much younger candidate, Raymond E. Baldwin. In addition, the popular Socialist mayor of Bridgeport, Jasper McLevy, waged a spirited third-party challenge. Baldwin and McLevy both scored points by stressing Cross's advanced age of seventy-six and by pledging to enact governmental economies. The final tally was close, but Baldwin edged out a victory. In great part, Cross owed his defeat to the national GOP resurgence and a strong Socialist showing that split the traditional Democratic vote. Cross died in New Haven.

• Cross's papers are at the Yale University Library. The most detailed published source remains his *Connecticut Yankee: An Autobiography* (1943). For additional information, see *Commemorative Tributes of the American Academy of Arts and Letters, 1942–1951* (1951). On Cross's political career, see Robert L. Woodbury, "Wilbur L. Cross: New Deal Ambassador to a Yankee Culture," *New England Quarterly* 41 (Sept. 1968): 323–40; David M. Roth, *Connecticut: A Bicentennial History* (1979); and John W. Jeffries, *Testing the Roosevelt Coalition: Connecticut Society and Politics in the Era of World War II* (1979).

DAVID T. BEITO

CROSSKEY, William Winslow (14 June 1894–6 Jan. 1968), lawyer and law professor, was born in Chicago, Illinois, the son of William Crosskey and Margaret Campbell. He grew up in Connecticut, and after graduating from high school in 1912 and assuming financial responsibility for his family, worked his way through Yale College (now University) selling aluminum. He earned his A.B. from Yale in 1923 and then entered Yale Law School in 1923, earning his LL.B. in 1926. He married Cecelia Moryks in 1924, and they had one child. Crosskey's brilliant record at Yale led to his appointment as secretary to Chief Justice William Howard Taft in 1926–1927. He returned to join the New York law firm of Davis, Polk and briefly worked as a corporation counsel. While working independently for John W. Davis, Crosskey was unable to accept a

professorship at Yale Law School but was offered a position at the University of Chicago in 1935, where he taught for the rest of his career.

Crosskey specialized in securities regulation while a Wall Street lawyer and was brought to the University of Chicago to teach courses in federal taxation and public utilities. He began to undertake study of constitutional problems associated with these issues, particularly Congress's power to regulate interstate commerce. The culmination of this research was the massive work *Politics and the Constitution in the History of the United States*, the first two volumes of which were published in 1953.

Crosskey was an ardent nationalist, whose life work was spent arguing that the Constitution provided Congress with nearly absolute power to legislate for the general welfare of the American people. He maintained that the entire course of American constitutional history was a distortion of the original plan of the framers of the Constitution and that generations of further misinterpretation by the Supreme Court necessitated a painstaking immersion in eighteenth-century documents and doctrines to recover the original meaning. He thus compiled what he called a "specialized dictionary" to recapture eighteenth-century usage. The primary responsibility for the distortion of the Constitution rested with Thomas Jefferson and states' rights interests, especially slavery, but James Madison occupied a particularly prominent place in the story. Crosskey believed that Madison betrayed his original beliefs after the constitutional convention, lied (or "bluffed") in *The Federalist* to win approval for the document, and then spent the rest of his career distorting the Constitution, ultimately forging his notes on the convention. Crosskey portrayed Chief Justice John Marshall, usually regarded as a vigorous nationalist, as at best an equivocal, beleaguered defender of the Constitution's original plan.

Politics and the Constitution provoked a storm of criticism. It drew an unusually large number of scathing reviews from prominent legal academics, and a smaller number of defenders. Though Crosskey staked his entire thesis on an appeal to the historical record, academic historians paid little attention to the work. It is safe to say that the monumental work has never recovered from this initial critical response.

The year after the publication of *Politics and the Constitution*, Crosskey entered another controversial area of constitutional interpretation, responding to Charles Fairman's attack on Hugo Black's argument that the Fourteenth Amendment had "incorporated" the Bill of Rights against infringement by the states. While most of Crosskey's argument in his monumental work is either neglected or rejected by scholars, his position in the incorporation debate is more widely supported, with good arguments still made on either side of this question. Nevertheless, Fairman got the better of the historical argument with Crosskey, and the proincorporation argument has appealed to other authorities than him.

The hostile reaction to Crosskey's scholarship was the result of bad timing and personality, in addition to faulty methodology. When he undertook his researches in the mid-1930s, the issues of congressional power to legislate for the general welfare were important and controversial. After the Supreme Court acceded to the New Deal in 1937–1938 and certainly by the time *Politics and the Constitution* was published in 1953, the timeliness of Crosskey's argument had passed. Crosskey dedicated the book "To the Congress of the United States in the hope that it may be led to claim and exercise for the common good of the country the powers justly belonging to it under the Constitution," but, in a further irony, Crosskey's work appeared on the eve of the Warren Court revolution, and the next generation would be a period in which the Supreme Court rather than and often despite Congress would lead the nationalization of political and constitutional questions. Crosskey took a dim view of the Supreme Court, especially in its exercise of judicial review of acts of Congress, which he regarded as illegitimate.

Crosskey was a legal positivist, recognizing nothing above the will of the sovereign as a rule for politics, and there is a certain logic to the idea of legislative supremacy, and even omnipotence, in a regime of popular sovereignty. But he was too determined to find the framers of the Constitution to have been fellow positivists. The complexities of the founding were too manifold to fit into Crosskey's rigid mold.

Temperament also played a part in the controversy over Crosskey's work. Crosskey was a famous curmudgeon, with even his closest friends and colleagues attesting to his impatience with formalities and academic politics. Always the iconoclast, Crosskey presented a bold, even revolutionary thesis and needed a sympathetic reception for which he apparently did nothing to prepare. Though appearing at the high point of the liberal nationalist period in American constitutional law and historiography, Crosskey nevertheless alienated the academic community for which he wrote.

In the final analysis, Crosskey's work suffered from fundamentally flawed methods of research and presentation. Essentially, Crosskey approached his work in the style of an advocate rather than as a disinterested judge, and he wrote what is often characterized as "law office history." His appeal to the original materials was a sound approach, and his spadework was formidable, but his "originalism" was largely textual, without consideration of some of the more obvious historical context. Thus he was led into a risky conspiracy theory regarding Madison and *The Federalist*, which has proven to be a dead end. Historians have continued to pay little attention to the work, and legal academics, including those who base their constitutionalism on "original intent" grounds, have gone elsewhere for inspiration. While his work contained many valuable insights and contributions, they were overshadowed by his more outlandish claims, and these contributions were not enough to carry the entire work.

Crosskey continued teaching and working on more volumes of *Politics and the Constitution*, until severe arthritis forced him into retirement. After leaving the University of Chicago, he taught for a year at Howard University. He died in Connecticut. One further volume was completed by William Jeffrey, Jr., and was published posthumously in 1980.

Crosskey will most likely stand as a monument to the enduring attraction of historical justification for constitutional argument. Like many American political thinkers, Crosskey had a vision of a rational, orderly, and simple Constitution, which would accomplish everything that he wanted the American government to accomplish, and he imagined that if we could but sweep away a century and a half of juridical distortion, we would find that our vision was the vision of the framers of the Constitution.

• The *University of Chicago Law Review* 35 (1968), which was dedicated to Crosskey, contains several reminiscences of colleagues and students. Crosskey's other published work consists of "Charles Fairman, 'Legislative History,' and the Constitutional Limitations on State Authority," *University of Chicago Law Review* 22 (1954): 1–143, with Fairman's reply, 144–56; and his essay, "Mr. Chief Justice John Marshall," in Allison Dunham and Philip B. Kurland, eds., *Mr. Justice* (1964). An index to reviews of *Politics and the Constitution* can be found in William Jeffrey, Jr., "American Legal History, 1952–54," *1954 Annual Survey of American Law* (1955): 866–80. Recent work that considers Crosskey's contribution includes Larry Arnhart, "William Crosskey and the Common Law," *Loyola University of Los Angeles Law Review* 9 (1976): 544–95; Leonard R. Sorenson, *Madison on the "General Welfare" of America: His Consistent Constitutional Vision* (1995). See also George Anastaplo, *The Constitutionalist* (1971), and his "Mr. Crosskey, the American Constitution and the Nature of Things," *Loyola University Law Journal* 15 (1984): 181–260.

PAUL MORENO

CROSSWAITH, Frank Rudolph (16 July 1892–17 June 1965), labor leader, was born in Frederiksted, St. Croix, Virgin Islands, the son of William Ignatius Crosswaith, a painter, and Anne Eliza (maiden name unknown). He left school at thirteen and immigrated in 1910 to the United States, where he joined the U.S. Navy as a messboy. In 1915 he married Alma E. Besard; they had four children. Settling in New York City, Crosswaith worked as an elevator operator during the day and at night attended the Rand School of Social Science, a socialist educational center.

While at the Rand School, Crosswaith encountered two influences that changed his life: the teachings of socialist leader Eugene V. Debs and the radical politics of the "New Negroes," a group of young African Americans in Harlem who had begun speaking out against the accommodating policies of their elders. Upon his graduation in 1918 Crosswaith began a long career of socialist political activity and part-time teaching at the Rand School.

Crosswaith was convinced that if black workers could win acceptance in labor unions, job competition among the races would end, and all workers could unite against their common enemies. In pursuit of this goal he devoted much of his career to a succession of organizations, many short-lived and underfunded, designed to introduce black workers to the labor movement and persuade white unions to accept them. The first such effort was the Friends of Negro Freedom (FNF), which Crosswaith joined in 1920. The FNF provided a useful discussion forum for Crosswaith and other black activists, but it had little effect, and after campaigning against black nationalist Marcus Garvey in 1922 it disbanded.

Next came the Trade Union Committee for Organizing Negro Workers (TUC), set up in 1925 with the backing of the New York Urban League, the Garland Fund, the National Association for the Advancement of Colored People, and several socialist unions. Crosswaith became executive secretary; one historian calls him "the real sparkplug" of the organization. The TUC managed to persuade a few unions to accept a handful of black members, and it started to organize the city's 30,000 laundry workers, two-thirds of whom were black women. It also stirred Harlem with a campaign for housing reform, but with insufficient funding and minimal support from mainstream labor leaders the TUC dissolved in 1926.

By then Crosswaith had become involved in a new undertaking, the Brotherhood of Sleeping Car Porters (BSCP). A. Philip Randolph, the founder, hired Crosswaith part time as his special assistant in 1925. A year later, when the TUC closed down, Crosswaith began to work for the BSCP full time as its first professional organizer. His association with the union ended in October 1928 when he and another employee accused the secretary-treasurer of taking BSCP funds and implied that Randolph had known about the wrongdoing. An investigation cleared the official, and both Crosswaith and his ally were forced to resign. Crosswaith then became an organizer for the International Ladies' Garment Workers' Union (ILGWU), a position he held for the rest of his career.

Crosswaith polled few votes in his repeated campaigns on the Socialist party ticket for Harlem's congressional seat and various state offices; furthermore, the United Colored Socialists of America that he established in 1928 soon dissolved. Nevertheless, Crosswaith won recognition within the party, earning the title "the Negro Debs." His impassioned oratory made him, according to a contemporary, "one of the most effective Socialist speakers in the party," and he made many national lecture tours. He also wrote a column in the *Chicago Defender*, contributed articles and reviews to the *Messenger*, and in 1931 published a pamphlet, *The Negro and Socialism*, which was one of the few party publications aimed specifically at blacks.

Crosswaith continued to battle union discrimination, urging not only membership for blacks but equal treatment once they were admitted. He edited the Negro Labor News Service from 1932 to 1934 and in 1935 was chosen to head the Negro Labor Committee (NLC), created by the ILGWU to open American Federation of Labor (AFL) unions to black workers.

Crosswaith made progress in several trades, including meat cutters, painters, and cafeteria employees. He also played a major role in the Socialist party's National Negro Work Committee (NNWC) and ran the NNWC's Harlem Labor Center, established in 1937 to educate black workers about unionism. Nevertheless, even in the more open atmosphere created by the National Labor Relations Act, most unions remained racially exclusive.

In 1941 Crosswaith joined Randolph in planning a march on Washington to protest discrimination in defense work; he was among those who met with President Franklin D. Roosevelt and were told that their plan was a "bad and unintelligent" idea. However, the group held its ground, calling the march off only after Roosevelt issued an executive order prohibiting discrimination in defense industries. In 1942, when Randolph was unable to accept Mayor Fiorello LaGuardia's offer of a position on the New York City Housing Authority, Crosswaith was chosen to serve instead.

During these years Crosswaith became increasingly concerned about communist influence in the labor movement. He opposed the Congress of Industrial Organization (CIO) and the National Negro Congress because of their left-wing connections. Having joined the American Labor party (ALP) in 1936, he resigned from the Socialist party in 1941 and helped found the anticommunist Union for Democratic Action. Then, along with other anticommunists, he left the ALP in 1944 for the new Liberal party. In 1952 he chaired a new national Negro Labor Committee, USA, organized by seventy-five unions both to promote black unionism and to counter communist agitation among blacks. He died in New York City.

Crosswaith spent most of his life trying to bring black workers into the American labor movement. He faced formidable obstacles in the resistance of most unions to integration and in the Socialist party's reluctance to highlight the unique problems of black workers. His anticommunism in later life cut him off from some potential allies, but for more than three decades he enriched American dialogue by testifying in word and deed to the fundamental connection of two compelling goals: working-class solidarity and racial justice.

• Information about Crosswaith's career is in the papers of the Negro Labor Committee at the Schomburg Branch of the New York Public Library and of the Socialist Party of America at Duke University, Durham, N.C. His writings include "The Trade Union Committee for Organizing Negro Workers," *Messenger* (Aug. 1925); "Sound Principle and Unsound Policy," *Opportunity* (Feb. 1934); *Negro and White Labor Unite for True Freedom*, with Alfred B. Lewis (1942); and *Negro Labor Committee: Ten Years of Struggle* (1946). See also Theodore Kornweibel, Jr., *No Crystal Stair: Black Life and the "Messenger," 1917–1928* (1975); Irwin M. Marcus, "Frank Crosswaith: Black Socialist, Labor Leader, and Reformer," *Negro History Bulletin* 37 (Aug.–Sept. 1974): 287–88; Philip Foner, *Organized Labor and the Black Worker* (1974); Foner, *American Socialism and Black Americans*

(1977); Gilbert Osofsky, *Harlem: The Making of a Ghetto*, 2d ed. (1971); and Foner and Ronald L. Lewis, eds., *Black Workers: A Documentary History from Colonial Times to the Present* (1989). On Crosswaith's involvement with the Brotherhood of Sleeping Car Porters, see Jervis Anderson, *A. Philip Randolph: A Biographical Portrait* (1973); Brailsford Brazeal, *The Brotherhood of Sleeping Car Porters: Its Origins and Development* (1946); and William H. Harris, *Keeping the Faith* (1977). A *New York Times* obituary appears on 18 June 1965.

SANDRA OPDYCKE

CROSTHWAIT, David Nelson, Jr. (27 May 1898–25 Feb. 1976), mechanical engineer, was born in Nashville, Tennessee, the son of Dr. David Nelson Crosthwait, and Minnie Harris. He attended elementary school and graduated from high school in Kansas City, Missouri.

Crosthwait received a Bachelor of Science degree in mechanical engineering from Purdue University in 1913. That same year he began lifelong employment with the C. A. Dunham Company (later Dunham-Bush) in Chicago, where he distinguished himself nationally in the field of heating, ventilation, and air-conditioning (HVAC) technology. By 1915 he had been appointed to the position of engineering supervisor, and by 1919 he had risen to the position of research engineer. In 1920 Crosthwait received a Master of Science degree in engineering from Purdue University.

In 1925 Crosthwait became director of research at Dunham, overseeing heat transfer research, steam transport research, and temperature control systems. In 1930 he was designated a senior technical consultant and advisor at the Dunham-Bush Co. Crosthwait married E. Madolyn Towels in 1930; they had one son, who died at age six. After the death of his wife, he married Blanche Ford in 1941.

Between 1930 and 1969, when he retired, Crosthwait conducted research on heating systems. He developed techniques to reduce noise caused by steam and noncondensable gases in heating systems. A signal achievement was his design of the heating system for the seventy-story Radio City Music Hall at Rockefeller Center in New York City.

Crosthwait received thirty-four U.S. patents and eighty foreign patents relating to the design, installation, and testing of heating, ventilation, and air-conditioning systems for large buildings. His U.S. patents included: Apparatus for returning water to boiling (1920); Method and apparatus for setting thermostats (1928); Differential vacuum pump (1930); Freezing temperature indicator (1932); Method of steam heating from central station (1934); Vacuum heating system (1935); One pipe heating system (1937); Heat balances (1940); Unit heater and air-conditioner (1941); Window thermostat (1944); and Balance resistance type temperature control (1947).

Crosthwait's achievements and contributions to the HVAC field were recognized with the award of a medal by the National Technical Association in 1936. In 1971 he became the first African American to be elect-

ed a fellow of the American Society of Heating, Refrigerating and Air-Conditioning Engineers.

As a recognized specialist in his field, Crosthwait contributed to the HVAC literature. His first article, "Heating System Vacuum," was published in *Power* in 1919. He was a contributor to chapters in the 1939, 1959, and 1967 editions of the *American Society of Heating and Ventilation Engineers Guide*. His technical writings also appeared in the *Heating and Ventilation* magazine and in other industrial engineering publications.

Professionally, Crosthwait was active in the National Society of Professional Engineers and the American Association for the Advancement of Science. In community and civic affairs he served on the Executive Committee of the North West Comprehensive Health Planning Commission (Michigan City, Ind.) and as president of the Michigan City Redevelopment Commission. On his retirement from Dunham-Bush in 1969, Crosthwait became an instructor at Purdue University, where he taught a course on steam heat theory and applications. He died, after a brief hospital stay, in Michigan City, Indiana.

• Crosthwait is discussed in Harry A. Ploski and James Williams, *The Negro Almanac: A Reference Work on the Afro American* (1976), and *American Men and Women of Science*, 12th ed. (1971). An obituary is in the *Michigan City (Ind.) News Dispatch*, 25 Feb. 1976.

ROBERT C. HAYDEN

CROSWELL, Andrew (30 Jan. 1709–12 Apr. 1785), Congregational minister and revivalist, was born in Charlestown, Massachusetts, the son of Caleb Croswell and Abigail Stimpson. He trained for the ministry at Harvard, receiving a B.A. in 1728 and an M.A. in 1731. He was called to the Second Church of Groton, Connecticut, in 1736, and there he was drawn into the emergent world of evangelical Protestantism. Revivals of religion had rippled down the Connecticut River valley in the mid-1730s from Jonathan Edwards's parish in Northampton, and Groton's Congregational pastors, Croswell and John Owen, had shared in this awakening. Also about this time, in or around 1736, Croswell married Rebecca Holmes; they had two children.

Croswell was drawn further into the revivalist fold after the New England swing of the heralded English evangelist George Whitefield in 1740. As controversy began to mount around the practices of itinerants like Whitefield and his host of colonial imitators, Croswell rose to the defense of the new evangelism in his first published tract, *An Answer to the Rev. Mr. Garden's Three First Letters to the Rev. Mr. Whitefield* (1741), a blast at the Anglican commissary of South Carolina, Alexander Garden. Soon Croswell had moved into the orbit of radical New Lights like James Davenport and became the chief polemicist for this fiery, ecstatic, and kinetic brand of the gospel. Taking Davenport as his mentor and model, he moved about the New England countryside, preaching furiously and singing the revival's praises at every turn. His style was fervent, uncompromising, and divisive; like other radicals, he solemnly pronounced judgment on those ministers and lay persons he considered unconverted or unregenerate. He also raised the hackles of the established churches through his encouragement of lay preachers or exhorters, claiming to have been the first in New England to have promoted such unlettered evangelists, his brother Joseph among them. The democratizing or leveling potentialities of such itinerant preaching and lay exhortation were lost on few, whether opponents or supporters.

Croswell continued his defense of the revivals in one pamphlet after another in the 1740s. Unlike most radical proponents of the awakening, Croswell cooled little in his ardor as the movement ebbed. When Davenport repented of his excesses in 1743, Croswell failed miserably with his own confession and instead soon furthered controversy with additional tracts that were perceived as unqualified and unwavering in their support for revivalistic extremism. He made matters worse in 1746 by moving to Boston, where he took charge of a congregation of evangelical separatists and where he established himself as a resident irritant to Boston's established churches and to his alma mater, Harvard, which he saw as sunk in liberalism and apostasy.

Laboring over this upstart church in Boston for the rest of his life, Croswell preserved much of his former temper and style. He also continued to codify his evangelical version of Calvinist theology and piety in periodic publications. He emphasized a sudden and instantaneous experience of conversion or new birth, arguing that the new evangelical piety cut through all the traditional stages of preparation for salvation. In his view, this intensely experiential and joyful faith freed Christians from what he saw as the gloom, fear, and anxiety of New England's Puritan piety. He thus placed considerable emphasis on the full assurance of salvation—a theological rhetoric that his critics saw as arrogant and antinomian but that he saw as a cure for spiritual melancholia. This comforting antidote was a consistent theme in his ministry and his writing; it emerges in a range of works, notably *What Is Christ to Me, If He Is Not Mine?* (1745), *Comfort in Christ* (1767), and *A Discourse, from the First Epistle of Thessalonians* (1784).

By the end of Croswell's life, his Boston church had dwindled dramatically and new itinerants and sectaries had stolen much of his thunder. His wife died in 1779, and in his last years his remaining opponents simply dismissed him as a lonely, disillusioned, and half-blind curmudgeon whose lingering prayers for a renewed awakening were of little note or consequence. He died in Boston.

Notwithstanding the crumbling of his ministry during the years of the American Revolution, Croswell had been a crucial player in the advent and perpetuation of the evangelical movement in New England, especially in its radical separatist form. He helped legitimize new patterns of ministry and evangelism that pointed ahead to the democratic ferment in the religious world of the early republic. He also helped provide theological articulation for an evangelical piety of dramatic new birth and full assurance, pushing aside Puritan anxiety and pilgrimage and pointing ahead to the world of nineteenth-century revivalists like Charles Grandison Finney who similarly saw little place for Puritan doubt in evangelical spirituality. Few other radicals matched Croswell's polemical output or were such consistent gadflies of New England's standing order.

• Only a smattering of Croswell's manuscripts survive. Small collections of his correspondence are at the Massachusetts Historical Society and in the Eleazar Wheelock Papers at Dartmouth College. His published writings were rarely lengthy or sustained discourses; they consisted mostly of letters, sermons, and short replies to his critics, squibs fired off in battle. See, for example, *The Apostle's Advice to the Jaylor Improved* (1744), *Heaven Shut against All Arminians and Antinomians* (1747), *A Narrative of the Founding and Settling the New-Gathered Congregational Church in Boston* (1749), *Free Forgiveness of Spiritual Debts* (1766), *Brief Remarks on the Satyrical Drollery at Cambridge* (1771), and *Mr. Murray Unmask'd* (1775). For an assessment of Croswell's ministry and theology see Leigh Eric Schmidt, "'A Second and Glorious Reformation': The New Light Extremism of Andrew Croswell," *William and Mary Quarterly* 43 (1986): 214–44. For the wider world of evangelical firebrands in which he moved see Harry S. Stout and Peter Onuf, "James Davenport and the Great Awakening in New London," *Journal of American History* 70 (1983): 556–78, and C. C. Goen, *Revivalism and Separatism in New England, 1740–1800: Strict Congregationalists and Separate Baptists in the Great Awakening* (1962).

LEIGH E. SCHMIDT

CROTHERS, Rachel (12 Dec. 1870–5 July 1958), playwright and director, was born in Bloomington, Illinois, the daughter of Eli Kirk Crothers and Marie Louise De Pew, both physicians. Crothers's birth date is sometimes given as 1878, but the 1870 date is confirmed by both her death certificate and the U.S. Census. She was the youngest in a prosperous family of English and Scottish descent. When Crothers was six, her mother began taking medical courses, eventually becoming the first female doctor in the Bloomington area. Crothers's plays would later be populated by many women endeavoring, like her mother, to reconcile professional and maternal roles.

Crothers began writing, producing, and acting in plays as a child, composing a four-act melodrama (*Every Cloud Has a Silver Lining*) at the age of thirteen and founding the Bloomington Dramatic Society. After graduating from the Normal University High School in 1891, she went on to receive a certificate in elocution after one semester at Boston's New England School of Dramatic Instruction. To her family's dismay, Crothers was determined to launch a theatrical career in New York; in 1897, following her father's death four years earlier, she gave up teaching elocution in Bloomington and once again headed east.

Crothers spent three months as a student and then four years as an instructor at the Stanhope-Wheatcroft

School of Acting. During this period she made her debut as a professional actor and appeared for several seasons with the Lyceum Stock Company. More important, writing and directing one-act plays for her students apprenticed Crothers in the start-to-finish supervision of dramatic works, anticipating her thorough involvement with the staging of her plays in subsequent decades. These early productions foreshadowed other developments as well; the writer protagonist of *Criss-Cross* (1899), for example, gave an early indication of Crothers's penchant for centering her plots on strong female characters.

In 1906 *The Three of Us* opened at the Madison Square Theater. It was Crothers's first full-length play to be produced professionally; running for over 200 performances in New York before moving on to London, it was also the first of her many commercial successes. Critics admired the uncluttered realism of *The Three of Us*, and a few even saw in it the makings of a national theater that was only emergent at this time. As in *Criss-Cross*, its heroine, Rhy, evoked the controversial New Woman—a "young Amazon" who speaks her mind and scorns the sexual double standard. Defying popular opinion, Rhy refuses to consider herself ruined by an innocent visit to a man's room at midnight. By including this scene (though bending her heroine to a traditional destiny in the play's final act), Crothers, too, began her career in defiance of both theatrical and social norms.

From 1908 through 1913 Crothers continued to chronicle the New Woman's challenge to discriminatory sexual mores and to explore the conflict between her professional ambitions and her family loyalties. *A Man's World* (1909), though unsuccessful at the box office, provoked praise, as well as debate, for, in the words of Walter Prichard Eaton, its "though[t]ful, sympathetic, intelligent comment" on the feminist movement. Its central figure, the female novelist and reformer Frank Ware, is one of the few Crothers heroines who chooses independence and integrity over love. Not so the heroine in *He and She* (1911), a Shavian "discussion play" in which the sculptor Ann Herford finally sacrifices her work, hoping to soothe the ego of her sculptor husband and attend to their troubled teenage daughter. Crothers denied, however, that *He and She* simply endorsed sacrifice, and critic Alexander Woollcott for one saw the play's 1920 revival as less a profamily comedy than a tragedy in which "something fine and strong dies in the last act . . . the hope, the ambition and all the future work of a genius." This prewar phase of Crothers's social problem plays peaked and closed with *Ourselves* (1913). Crothers's only work in what she called a "photographic" style, it chides bourgeois women for attempting to reform prostitutes instead of their own husbands.

In 1917 Crothers established the Stage Women's War Relief Fund (she would organize similar relief efforts during the Great Depression and World War II), and the social comedies Crothers produced between 1914 and 1937 are in some sense analogous to these charitable projects. Unlike the high seriousness of

American art theater in the 1920s, and contrary to the politically engaged theater of the 1930s and of Crothers's own early period, she now turned from confronting audiences to diverting them; the plays belonging to this second phase of her career performed a kind of comic relief work. After a spate of sentimental and nostalgic pieces, Crothers became known in the 1920s and 1930s for her witty and wealthy sophisticates who work out marital and generational conflicts in glamorous, urban settings. Often, small-town honesty and homespun values seem to triumph over newfangled theories and aspirations, and the predominant effect is to chasten the modern woman. *A Little Journey* (1918) and *Nice People* (1921) both involve citified heroines who are brought back to their senses by decent, down-to-earth men. *A Lady's Virtue* (1925), *Let Us Be Gay* (1929), and *As Husbands Go* (1931) all portray discontented wives who ultimately find that marital fidelity is preferable to freedom. At the same time, male characters are held to an identical sexual standard, and the restlessness of female characters is portrayed with significant sympathy; occasionally it is played out by a secondary figure whose departure contrasts with the heroine's return home (Dierdre in *Let Us Be Gay* and Emmie in *As Husbands Go*). *When Ladies Meet* (1932), winner of the Megrue Prize for comedy and generally considered one of Crothers's best plays, is particularly unconventional in its solution to a classic love triangle: when wife and mistress meet, the result is not a cat fight but rather mutual compassion and a decision by both to leave their two-timing man. Crothers's relation to the New Woman is, in short, ambiguous during this later phase, yet there is no doubt that women's issues—the desire for sexual equity and economic independence, the difficulty of reconciling love and autonomy—remain key to her work.

If Crothers's dramatic treatment of feminism was mixed, her success as a woman playwright and director was not. With a play on Broadway almost every year for more than thirty years—her notable hits include *A Little Journey* (1918), *Nice People* (1921), *Expressing Willie* (1924), *Susan and God* (1937)—Crothers was not only the foremost female dramatist, but also the most prolific American playwright of her day. Her casts were invariably star-studded, and many of her plays were later adapted for the screen. *When Ladies Meet* and *Susan and God* each won the Theater Club's gold cup for best play of the season. Moreover, despite the mutual antipathy between Crothers and the art theater crowd, her dramatic achievement exceeded the simply commercial. At a time when there were numerous "lady playwrights" but few were taken seriously, Crothers received respectful critical attention from the start. Her extraordinary technical prowess, which seemed slick to some, was also widely admired, and in 1928 she was invited by the University of Pennsylvania to lecture on "The Construction of a Play." Notwithstanding her preference for Broadway over Bohemia, Crothers's realism—the directness and economy of presentation she derived from Ibsen—helped modern American theater develop beyond nineteenth-century claptrap and stylization. And notwithstanding her contradictory statements about feminism, Crothers's total commitment to her art—she never married—helped American women develop beyond the Victorian domestic ideal. She died in Danbury, Connecticut.

• Collections of clippings pertaining to Crothers are available on microfilm at the University of Chicago Library; in special collections at the Illinois State University Library, Normal; at the Withers Public Library, Bloomington, Ill.; and in the Billy Rose Theatre Collection of the New York Public Library for the Performing Arts, which also has numerous typescripts. A small collection of letters is in the Library of the American Academy of Arts and Letters, New York City. Crothers's lecture, "The Construction of a Play," is in *The Art of Playwriting* (1928), pp. 115–34. Interviews with Crothers include Ada Patterson, "Woman Must Live Out Her Destiny," *The Theater* 40 (May 1910): (unsigned) "Future of American Stage Depends on Directors," *New York Times Magazine*, 3 Dec. 1916; Djuna Barnes, "The Tireless Rachel Crothers," *Theater Guild Magazine* 8 (May 1931); and Charlotte Hughes, "Women Playmakers," *New York Times Magazine*, 4 May 1941. Walter Prichard Eaton's comments on *A Man's World* appeared in *At the New Theater and Others: The American Stage, Its Problems and Performances, 1908–1910* (1910), pp. 155–61. Alexander Woollcott made his remark about *He and She* in the *New York Times*, 13 Feb. 1920, p. 16. A biography is Lois C. Gottlieb, *Rachel Crothers* (1979), which includes a bibliography. Before Gottlieb's, the only full-length study of Crothers was Irving Abrahamson, "The Career of Rachel Crothers in the American Drama" (Ph.D. diss., Univ. of Chicago, 1956). See also Arthur H. Quinn, *A History of the American Drama from the Civil War to the Present Day*, vol. 2 (1936), pp. 50–61; Sharon Friedman, "Feminism as Theme in Twentieth-Century American Women's Drama," *American Studies* 25, no. 1 (1984): 69–89; and Doris Abramson, "Rachel Crothers: Broadway Feminist," in *Modern American Drama: The Female Canon*, ed. June Schlueter (1990), pp. 55–65. An obituary is in the *New York Times*, 6 July 1958. See also Sherman Day Wakefield's letter to the editor, *New York Times*, 12 July 1958.

SUSAN FRAIMAN

CROTHERS, Thomas Davison (21 Sept. 1842–12 Jan. 1918), pioneer physician in the medical treatment of inebriety, temperance advocate, and editor, was born in West Charlton, New York, the son of Robert Crothers and Electra Smith. Members of Crothers's family had taught surgery and medicine at Edinburgh University since the eighteenth century, and, with this influence, after attending the Fort Edward Seminary, he enrolled in Albany Medical College in 1862. With the outbreak of the Civil War Crothers signed on as a medical cadet at the Ira Harris Military College. Awarded his M.D. in 1865, Crothers continued his studies at Long Island College Hospital until he began his medical practice in West Galway, New York, in 1866. Four years later Crothers left West Galway for Albany, where, at his alma mater, he became assistant to the chair of the practice of medicine, lecturer on hygiene, and instructor in physical diagnosis. In 1875 he married Sarah Walton; the couple had no children. He also took a new position in Binghamton, New York, home of the

nation's first hospital for inebriates, the New York State Inebriate Asylum. There Crothers received his formal introduction to the medical treatment of inebriety. In 1878 he established his own private inebriate asylum in Hartford, Connecticut, the Walnut Hill Asylum (known after 1880 as the Walnut Lodge Hospital).

From his asylum in Hartford, Crothers became the leading spokesman for the medical treatment of inebriety in turn-of-the-century America. He was particularly well positioned to reach a large audience, serving the American Association for the Cure of Inebriates as the editor of the organization's *Quarterly Journal of Inebriety* for the duration of the periodical's existence, 1876 to 1914. Crothers was also secretary to the American Medical Temperance Association, an organization dedicated to eliminating alcohol from the physician's therapeutic arsenal, between 1891 and 1904, its entire lifetime. In addition, as president of the Medico-Legal Society of New York, an office he held at the time of his death, Crothers ably addressed his interests in the legal consequences of viewing alcoholism as a disease.

Crothers's activities in the inebriety field were not limited to mainstream medicine or the United States. For many years he worked with the National Women's Christian Temperance Union, helping to develop its scientific temperance curriculum for public schools. The first courses on alcoholism in the United States were offered by Crothers at Albany Medical College and the University of Vermont in 1888 and 1889. In 1897 he was a member, along with Joseph Parrish, of the American delegation to the International Temperance Congress in London. There Crothers was feted by his British colleagues for his outstanding contributions to the scientific research underpinning the disease concept of inebriety. So great was Crothers's reputation in England that he was invited in 1905, some eight years later, to deliver the Norman Kerr Memorial Lecture to the British Society for the Study of Inebriety. In 1909, when the U.S. government appointed the first commission to attend the International Congress on Alcoholism, Crothers was selected as part of the U.S. delegation.

Contemporary alcohol researchers frequently dismiss the work of Crothers and his turn-of-the-century colleagues for its want of scientific rigor. Yet, a closer examination of the writings of Crothers, in particular, reveals a sophisticated understanding of inebriety's etiology and a relatively comprehensive classification scheme for the different varieties of inebriety—indeed, one that resembles the alpha, beta, gamma, delta, epsilon system developed by E. M. Jellinek, the modern "rediscoverer" of the disease concept of alcoholism. Crothers's work might have born the stamp of nineteenth-century class and ethnic prejudices, but he did allow for multifactoral etiological explanations for alcohol and opiate addiction, and he did distinguish between acute, chronic, and periodic inebriates. One view, however, that distinguished Crothers from his contemporaries was his understanding of women's drinking. Contrary to the prevailing late nineteenth- and early twentieth-century hue and cry over women's drinking as a distressing sign of her deviation from the traditional female role of nurturer, Crothers argued that women's drinking was actually on the decrease and would all but vanish when women were given full civil rights. It is impossible to know if Crothers's views were correct, but they were based in part on both clinical observations (a decline in women patients) and cultural observations (fewer women drinking in public, more women taking strong roles in the anti-drink campaigns).

At the time of Crothers's death in Hartford, he was in the process of organizing the thousands of patient case files and data that he had accumulated over the years at the Walnut Lodge Hospital. It was his dream that this data would form the basis for the Research Institute of Hartford, a foundation he established in his last years to pursue original research on the alcohol question. His death was noted in a variety of major medical journals, who mourned the passing of "one of the most cheerful and optimistic of men, gentle, courteous, an adventurous, far-seeing . . . possess[ing] a mind stored with literary and scientific wealth—prolific, keen, original, serious in thought, careful in judgement, and charitable in everything" (McCuen).

• There is no official body of Crothers papers. For the best modern assessment of Crothers, see Mark Lender, "Thomas Davison Crothers," *Dictionary of American Temperance Biography: From Temperance Reform to Alcohol Research, the 1600s to the 1980s* (1984), which also includes a list of Crothers's publications. Lender also points out the similarities between the modern disease concept of alcoholism and that developed by Crothers in "Jellinek's Typology of Alcoholism, Some Historical Antecedents," *Journal of Studies on Alcohol* 40, no. 5 (1979): 361–75. For contemporary reviews and portraits of Crothers's work, see "The Death of Dr. Crothers," *American Medicine*, n.s., 13, no. 2 (1918): 77; "Thomas Davison Crothers," in *The Standard Encyclopedia of the Alcohol Problem*, vol. 2, ed. Ernest Cherrington (1924); Leslie McCuen, "In Memoriam," *Medico Legal Journal* 35, no. 1 (1918): 10; the pamphlet *Colonial and International Congress on Inebriety, London, England—Papers and Addresses by Delegates from the United States of America, Also a Report of a Reception Given to T. D. Crothers, M.D.* (1887); and "Dr. T. D. Crothers," in *Hartford in 1912: Story of the Capital City, Present and Prospective: Its Resources, Achievements, Opportunities, and Ambitions in Which Is Incorporated Illustrated Biographies of the Leading Representatives in Finance, Insurance, Educational, Religious, Legal, and Industrial Life of Hartford* (1913). The most informative of the early sketches of his life is an obituary in the *Hartford Daily Courant*, 14 Jan. 1918.

SARAH W. TRACY

CROUSE, Russel McKinley (20 Feb. 1893–3 Apr. 1966), journalist, playwright, and screenwriter, was born in Findlay, Ohio, the son of Hiram Powers Crouse, a newspaper editor and publisher, and Sarah Schumacher. Crouse was educated in public schools in Toledo, Ohio, and Enid, Oklahoma, and as a teenager he began working on his father's newspaper, the *Enid Morning News*. During his last year of high school, he

received an alternate congressional appointment to Annapolis but failed the mathematics portion of the entrance examination and had to leave.

Returning to Cincinnati, he found work as a reporter for the *Cincinnati Commercial Tribune*. By his early twenties he had already spent nine years as a reporter, sports writer, and theater reviewer for the *Enid Morning News*, the *Commercial Tribune*, and the *Kansas City Star*. He had also worked for four years as Kansas City correspondent for the New York–based *Variety*, and in 1917 he was a political reporter for the *Cincinnati Post*. After serving in World War I at the Great Lakes Naval Training Station as yeoman second class in the U.S. Navy from 1917 and 1919, he again returned to journalism.

Crouse moved to New York City in 1919 and began work as a reporter for the *Globe*, where he remained until it folded in 1923. That year he married Alison Smith, a New York drama critic. They had no children and divorced in 1929, but their generally amicable relationship lasted until her death in 1943. After leaving the *Globe*, Crouse served a brief term as a reporter for the *Evening Mail* before joining the *Evening Post* as a reporter and columnist. He also wrote the *New Yorker* columns "Talk of the Town," "That Was New York," and "They Were New Yorkers." Crouse acted on stage briefly in 1928, playing the reporter Bellflower in Ward Morehouse's *Gentlemen of the Press*, and soon after leaving the *Evening Post* in 1931, he began work as a press agent for the Theatre Guild (1932–1937).

In the early 1930s, Crouse wrote several books, including *Mr. Currier and Mr. Ives* (1930), *The American Keepsake* (1932), and *Murder Won't Out* (1932). In 1931 he collaborated with Morrie Ryskind and Oscar Hammerstein II on a musical comedy, *The Gang's All Here*. It closed shortly after its 18 February opening, but the project solidified the course of the rest of Crouse's professional life–collaboration on musicals and plays for the New York theater. Crouse's own adaptation of his novel *It Seems Like Yesterday* (1931), a musical comedy called *Hold Your Horses*, premiered two years later. Corey Ford helped him on the book, and Robert Russell Bennett wrote the score. Critical reception was mixed, but the show played for half a year at the Winter Garden.

Crouse's lifelong partnership with Howard Lindsay began in 1934 when producer Vinton Freedley's *Bon Voyage*—a new musical comedy written by P. G. Wodehouse and Guy Bolton—urgently needed a major rewrite as it was going into rehearsals: the USS *Morro Castle* had sunk, killing many and making the new play's comic shipwreck inappropriate. The authors were in Europe and therefore unavailable, so Freedley hired Lindsay, who in turn brought in Crouse as another writer for the project. The show, renamed *Anything Goes*, starred Ethel Merman and became the hit of the season.

On their next collaborations, Crouse and Lindsay refined their working method. Their musical comedies *Red, Hot, and Blue* (1936), with Ethel Merman,

Jimmy Durante, and Bob Hope, and *Hooray for What!* (1937), with Ed Wynn, each played for half a year and helped establish them permanently on Broadway. Their nostalgic three-act comedy *Life with Father* (1939), based on Clarence Day's *New Yorker* reminiscences of his irascible father and unflappable mother, ran for a record 3,224 performances, making it the longest running Broadway show in history until *Fiddler on the Roof*, which opened twenty-five years later.

Early in *Life with Father*'s eight-year run, Lindsay and Crouse produced (with some of their own revisions) John Kesserling's *Arsenic and Old Lace* (1941) starring Boris Karloff, and it became a solid hit. Then came their less popular comedy, *Strip for Action* (1942), about a burlesque troupe's visit to an army base, as well as their production of John Patrick's *The Hasty Heart* (1945).

Crouse married Anna Erskine in 1945, and they had two children. He would coauthor two books with his wife: *Peter Stuyvesant of Old New York* (1954) and *Alexander Hamilton and Aaron Burr* (1958).

Crouse and Lindsay's next hit was the political satire *State of the Union* (1945), starring Ralph Bellamy and Ruth Hussey. It won the 1946 Pulitzer Prize for its portrayal of a virtuous industrialist who refuses the Republican party's 1948 presidential nomination rather than sacrificing his liberal political ideals to reactionary forces. *Life with Mother* (1948), the inevitable sequel to their most popular play, was warmly received but had only a modest run. They then produced Sidney Kingsley's *Detective Story* (1949) and *Call Me Madam* (1950), a musical starring Ethel Merman that ran a year and a half. Their comedy-mystery *Remains to Be Seen* (1951), starring Jackie Cooper and Janis Paige, ran half a year. Next, Crouse and Lindsay produced *One Bright Day* (1952) and *The Prescott Proposals* (1953), but both had only short runs. *The Great Sebastians* (1956), with Alfred Lunt and Lynn Fontanne as a pair of mind readers performing in Eastern Europe, was more warmly received.

Their next offerings were *Happy Hunting* (1956), a musical starring Ethel Merman, and *Tall Story* (1959), a short-lived comedy about an attempt to bribe a basketball player. Neither received critical acclaim, and perhaps their lack of success can be attributed to Crouse and Lindsay's preoccupation with their next work—an adaptation of Maria Augusta Trapp's autobiographical *The Trapp Family Singers*, which told the story of a family of musicians who fled Austria on foot to escape the Nazis. Ironically, Lindsay and Crouse are often overlooked as authors of the book *The Sound of Music* (1959), one of their best known and most popular works, with music by Richard Rodgers and lyrics by Oscar Hammerstein II.

The writing team's final collaboration was *Mr. President* (1962), which featured a score by Irving Berlin. Despite failing health, they rushed to meet production deadlines, knowing that it simply was not ready to open. Nevertheless, because of the popularity of the authors and the immense preshow publicity, it ran for over half a year.

Early in his career as a playwright, Crouse also began writing screenplays for Hollywood. His works include *Mountain Music* (1937), *The Big Broadcast of 1938* (1938), and *The Great Victor Herbert* (cowritten with R. Lively, 1939). During most of the 1940s and 1950s, Crouse wrote film adaptations of plays with Lindsay, including *Anything Goes* (1936; remake 1956), *Artists and Models Abroad* (cowritten with Ken Englund, 1938), *Life with Father* (1947), *State of the Union* (1948), *Call Me Madam* (1953), and *Remains to Be Seen* (1953).

In an intensely competitive business, "Buck" Crouse was widely respected for his gentle wit, his generosity and kindness, and his careful attention to production details throughout the run of his shows. In his many collaborations with Lindsay, Crouse wrote and produced some of the twentieth century's most well-received theater productions. His best works were masterful examples of the popular theater. Crouse died in New York City.

• A collection of Crouse's papers is in the State Historical Society of Wisconsin, Madison. For a book-length treatment of his life and works, see Cornelia Otis Skinner, *Life with Lindsay and Crouse* (1976). An article on Crouse and Lindsay was published in the *New York Times*, 7 May 1946, following their receipt of the 1946 Pulitzer Prize. An obituary appears in the *New York Times*, 4 Apr. 1966.

ROBERT NELSON

CROWDER, Enoch Herbert (11 Apr. 1859–7 May 1932), soldier, diplomat, and jurist, was born in Grundy County, Missouri, the son of John Herbert Crowder and Mary Weller, farmers. Crowder graduated from the U.S. Military Academy in 1881 in the bottom half of his class. Commissioned a second lieutenant in the Eighth Cavalry, he was stationed at Fort Brown in Texas. While there he read law in Brownsville, and by 1884 he was admitted to practice in Texas, Missouri, and federal courts. That year Crowder was transferred to Jefferson Barracks in Missouri. Between 1885 and 1889 he served as a professor of military science and commandant of the cadet corps at the University of Missouri. He also continued to study law both at the university and with a Kansas City law firm and earned his LL.B. in 1886. That summer he played a bit part in the campaign against Geronimo in New Mexico. Transferred to Fort Yates in North Dakota three years later, he in 1890 helped save the Indian policemen whose botched arrest of Sitting Bull led to the Lakota leader's death. Crowder thereafter put his legal training to better use, being assigned acting judge advocate for the Department of the Platte in 1891. Headquartered at Omaha, he was promoted in 1895 from captain to major and formally transferred to the Judge Advocate General's Department, which administered the military justice system and performed the army's legal work.

If Crowder had chiefly tagged along in the army's final pacification of the West, he would play a far more important role as the military's task turned to projecting American influence overseas. During the Spanish-

American War, he went to the Philippines as a judge advocate on General Wesley Merritt's staff and helped draw up the terms for Manila's surrender. As the postwar struggle against Philippine nationalists developed, Crowder served the military government established in the islands by the United States. He presided over a board hearing Filipino claims against the United States, acted as associate justice of the civil branch of the Philippine Supreme Court, and forged a new code of criminal procedure for the islands. In 1900 Crowder became secretary to the military governor, General Arthur MacArthur. The appointment, in effect, made him responsible for much of the civil administration of the Philippines. He oversaw such departments as Treasury, Public Instruction, Justice, and Public Works and dealt with matters as varied as currency stabilization, public health, the enforcement of Chinese exclusion laws, and church-state relations.

Leaving the Philippines in 1901, Crowder served the Judge Advocate General's Department in Washington and Chicago. Promoted to colonel in 1903, he was named chief of the First Division of the newly formed General Staff. Crowder spent 1904–1905 in Manchuria observing the Russo-Japanese War. In 1906 he was called to Cuba. The United States had not annexed the island but that year exercised its right under the Platt Amendment, which was passed by Congress in 1901 and incorporated into the Cuban constitution in 1903, to intervene for "the maintenance of a government adequate for the protection of life, property, and individual liberty." Transferred to Cuba, Crowder acted as legal adviser to the provisional government the Americans set up and supervised Cuba's Departments of State and Justice. He also led the Advisory Law Commission that framed a number of fundamental statutes governing national, provincial, and municipal administration; the judiciary; the military; elections; and taxation. After overseeing the elections in 1908, Crowder returned home.

Crowder served as first assistant in Washington until 1911, when he became judge advocate general of the army with the rank of brigadier general. Reappointed to the post in 1915 and 1919, he streamlined the Articles of War and retooled the court-martial and penal system with an eye toward greater uniformity, the rehabilitation of erring soldiers, and the establishment of various procedural safeguards.

Shortly before the United States entered World War I in April 1917, Secretary of War Newton D. Baker instructed Crowder to frame a conscription measure, the Wilson administration having decided against raising a wartime army chiefly through volunteer enlistment. The bill that Crowder and his staff drew up became law in May, and soon afterward he was placed in charge of the draft as provost marshal general. He became a major general that autumn. The Selective Service System that Crowder created and administered provided for the registration of men between twenty-one and thirty and their induction for the duration of the conflict. It did away with unsavory elements of the Civil War draft, particularly substitution, but allowed

for deferments for men with dependents and those at work in essential industrial or agricultural production. The law also provided for noncombatant service for some conscientious objectors. The most noteworthy and enduring feature of Crowder's system, however, was its administration by more than 4,000 local draft boards staffed, as Crowder put it, by "the friends and neighbors of the men to be affected" (Crowder, *The Spirit of Selective Service*, p. 120). The decentralized, largely civilian apparatus may have reconciled many Americans to this most fundamental exercise of federal authority or at least tempered opposition to it, but the system also permitted irregularity and outright discrimination in induction and deferment decisions.

Eventually expanded to cover men from eighteen to forty-five, the Selective Service System in a year and a half registered about 24 million men and drafted almost 3 million, providing over 70 percent of the army's servicemen during the war. In using conscription to raise such a large part of its fighting force, the United States departed from its practice in earlier wars and set a precedent that endured through the Vietnam War. In addition, Selective Service facilitated management of manpower at home. The progressive elimination of voluntary enlistment, the more careful classification of registrants, and Crowder's "work or fight" order of May 1918, which promised speedy induction of those not otherwise employed in the war effort, increased the government's ability to direct men to where they might be most valuable, whether on the western front, in factories, or on the farm.

With the war's end, Crowder reprised his role as lawgiver to Spain's former colonies. With political unrest again troubling Cuba, Crowder in 1919 was dispatched to craft a new electoral code. His laws, however, were honored chiefly in the breach. The resulting turmoil, as well as a downturn in Cuba's sugar-based economy, prompted the United States to a vigorous, if novel, exercise of its powers under the Platt Amendment. Rather than resorting to military occupation and the formal abrogation of Cuban sovereignty, the American government instead sent Crowder back in January 1921 to act as stern preceptor. Officially the personal representative of President Woodrow Wilson and later President Warren G. Harding, Crowder—headquartered aboard an American battleship in Havana Harbor—pressed upon Cuban leaders the necessity of cutting the budget, developing new sources of revenue, and rooting out corruption. In a series of memoranda to President Alfredo Zayas he also presumed to make more specific demands with respect to commercial relations, banking, the national lottery, public works, and constitutional changes. The power of the United States to block a much-needed loan from J. P. Morgan & Co. gave Crowder ample means to enforce his will on the Cubans. His so-called "moralization program" climaxed in 1922 with the ouster of the Cuban cabinet, which was replaced by men of Crowder's choosing.

Crowder left the army in 1923 to become the first U.S. ambassador to Cuba. After securing the Morgan loan, Zayas was less disposed to defer to Crowder. But policymakers in Washington, with Cuba's debt provided for and stability the priority, found less occasion for aggressive meddling in the name of political reform. Therefore, Crowder settled down to a more pacific relationship with Zayas's successor, Gerardo Machado. Crowder left Cuba in 1927 to practice law in Chicago, where his clients included firms dealing in Cuban sugar. He retired in 1931. Crowder, who never married, died in Washington, D.C. He did much to extend the federal government's reach at home and leave America's imprint abroad.

• The main body of Crowder papers is in the Western Historical Manuscripts Collection at the University of Missouri, Columbia. The National Archives holds official correspondence in the Records of the Office of the Judge Advocate General (Army) (RG 153); Records of the Office of the Provost Marshal General, 1917–1919 (RG 163); and, for the Cuban years, General Records of the Department of State (RG 59). Some diplomatic material has been reprinted in the volumes of *Papers Relating to the Foreign Relations of the United States* covering 1919 to 1927 (1934–1942). Crowder issued several reports on conscription, *Report of the Provost Marshal General to the Secretary of War on the First Draft under the Selective Service Act, 1917* (1918), *Second Report of the Provost Marshal General to the Secretary of War on the Operations of the Selective Service System to December 20, 1918* (1919), and *Final Report of the Provost Marshal General to the Secretary of War on the Operations of the Selective Service System to July 15, 1919* (1920). He also published a more personal book, *The Spirit of Selective Service* (1920). For a biography, see David Lockmiller, *Enoch H. Crowder: Soldier, Lawyer and Statesman* (1955). Useful discussions of various aspects of Crowder's career are in John Whiteclay Chambers II, *To Raise an Army: The Draft Comes to Modern America* (1987); David Kennedy, *Over Here: The First World War and American Society* (1980); Louis A. Pérez, Jr., *Cuba under the Platt Amendment 1902–1934* (1986); and Robert F. Smith, *The United States and Cuba: Business and Diplomacy, 1917–1960* (1960).

PATRICK G. WILLIAMS

CROWE, Francis Trenholm (12 Oct. 1882–26 Feb. 1946), civil engineer, was born in Trenholmville, Quebec, Canada, the son of John Crowe, a woolen mill operator, and Emma Jane Wilkinson. Because of his father's career, he grew up in a succession of mill towns—Trenholmville; Fairfield, Iowa; Kezar Falls, Maine; Picton, New Jersey; and Byfield, Massachusetts—and his own career proved to be equally peripatetic. After graduating from Governor Dummer Academy in South Byfield in 1901, he matriculated at the University of Maine to study civil engineering. During his junior year he was so impressed by a lecture about the Wild West and the efforts of the U.S. Reclamation Service to tame it that he obtained a summer job with the service as a surveyor along the lower Yellowstone River in Montana. The rugged outdoor life and the scope and importance of the work to be done in the West captivated him, and upon receiving his B.S. degree in civil engineering in 1905 he went to work full time for the service.

Crowe returned to the lower Yellowstone as an engineering aide and instrument handler but left after a year to become the superintendent of construction for James Munn and Company, a construction firm in Deadwood City, South Dakota, that specialized in building concrete water-containment structures. He rejoined the Reclamation Service in 1908 as an engineer and was put in charge of the construction of an irrigation pumping station in Minidoka, Idaho. In 1910 he embarked on his life's work, the construction of high concrete dams, when he became the engineer and then the superintendent of construction of Jackson Lake Dam in Wyoming. In 1911 he married Marie Sass, who died within months of the wedding. Later that year he became assistant superintendent of construction of Arrowrock Dam in Idaho. He overcame the difficulty of delivering concrete to all sections of the 349-foot masonry structure by developing both an overhead cableway system and a method of pumping concrete pneumatically via a pipe grid. By the time the project was finished two years later, he was the superintendent of construction and Arrowrock was the highest dam in the world.

In 1913 Crowe married Linnie Kortz and they had two children. After the completion of Arrowrock, he was project manager for various projects in Idaho, Wyoming, and Montana until 1920, when he became a partner in the Missoula, Montana, contracting firm of Rich, Markhus and Crowe. He returned to the Reclamation Service the next year to become construction engineer of Tieton Dam in Washington, a project he completed in 1924. He was then made general superintendent of construction for the renamed Bureau of Reclamation's Office of the Chief Engineer in Denver, Colorado, a position that gave him oversight of all bureau construction projects in seventeen western states. He resigned this position a year later and left the agency for the last time when the bureau decided to abandon the construction business in favor of contracting the work to private firms. He joined the Morrison-Knudsen Company that same year and, as the on-site superintendent of construction, oversaw the completion of Guernsey Dam in Wyoming in 1927, Coombe Dam in California in 1928, and Deadwood Dam in Idaho in 1930.

Crowe is best remembered for the role he played in the construction of Hoover Dam, the supreme engineering feat of its day. Since its inception in 1902, the bureau had been investigating the possibility of bringing the unpredictable and disastrous flooding of the Colorado River under control, and Crowe had been anticipating eagerly the opportunity to dam the river at Black Canyon, the site of Hoover Dam, since 1919 when he worked up a rough cost estimate for his superior at the bureau. When the bid documents for the project were released in 1931, they called for an arched concrete structure 1,244 feet long at the crest and 726 feet high, more than twice the height of Arrowrock, the highest dam in the world at the time. Moreover, because Black Canyon was in the middle of a scorching desert and could not be reached except by horse or small boat and because its high sheer walls made moving workers and equipment onto the river bottom extremely difficult, the entire project was considered by many knowledgeable engineers to be an impossible task. Crowe, who was widely acclaimed as the most knowledgeable builder of dams in the country, saw the project as the supreme challenge of his engineering and managerial skills and wanted more than anything else to accept that challenge. He convinced the owners of Morrison-Knudsen to put together Six Companies, Inc., a syndicate of six western construction companies, to capitalize the project. He worked up the successful bid of almost $49 million, an extraordinary amount of money for a depression-era construction project.

In 1931 Crowe became the superintendent of construction for Six Companies, Inc. His duties included overseeing the construction of the dam itself as well as a number of auxiliary projects such as diversion tunnels and access roads; a twenty-mile railroad to the dam site; the town of Boulder City, Nevada, which housed most of the project's 5,000 workers and their families; and water, power, and telephone systems and lines for the town and the dam. Christened "Hurry Up" by the bureau's construction engineer, he was always on the lookout for a faster way to accomplish any task. Instead of using horses and mules to move rock and dirt, the standard practice at the major construction sites of the day, he employed electric shovels and dump trucks almost exclusively. He developed an elaborate aerial cableway system, patterned after the one he had first used at Arrowrock and subsequently improved upon at succeeding dam sites, capable of delivering workers, tools, and concrete to virtually any point of the vast construction site within a few minutes. When concrete delivered deep into the "glory holes," the tunnels by which the Colorado was diverted around the dam site, hardened before it could be worked, he solved the problem by mounting a portable agitator in the concrete bucket to keep it from setting up en route. As a result of these and other innovations and his own keen leadership abilities, the massive project was completed in 1936, more than two years ahead of schedule. Bonuses and profit-sharing from the project made him a wealthy man.

Neither the glory nor the money Crowe received as a result of damming the mighty Colorado River diminished his enthusiasm for building more dams. From 1936 to 1938 he supervised the construction of Parker Dam, 155 miles downstream from Black Canyon. Its reservoir, Lake Havasu, provides drinking water for the cities of southern California and its foundation extends 253 feet below the riverbed, at the time the deepest submerged section of any dam in the world. After quickly completing Copper Basin and Gene Wash dams, two small structures in California, in 1938 he signed on as general superintendent of Pacific Constructors, Inc., the general contractor for the 602-foot Shasta Dam in California. Designed to provide irrigation water for that state's incredibly fertile Central Valley, its 3,500-foot length at the crest make it twice as long as Hoover Dam, and at the time of its completion

in 1944 it was the second-highest and second-largest dam in the world.

In 1945 the U.S. Department of War offered Crowe the assignment of organizing and directing all reconstruction work in the American Zone of Occupation in Germany. Although he saw the job as a new and intriguing challenge, his failing health, caused mostly by the fact that he never took a vacation or even a weekend off during the construction of one of "his" dams, forced him to turn down the offer and retire to his 20,000-acre cattle ranch near Shasta Dam in Redding, California, where he died.

Crowe received several awards including an honorary membership in the American Society of Civil Engineers in 1943 and the 1944 annual award of the Moles, a New York organization of tunnel and heavy construction engineers. In the course of his career, he built nineteen dams, including three that at the time of their completion were either the world's highest, largest, or deepest. Much of his success was due to the fact that he inspired loyalty in his workers to the point that most of his foremen and many of his laborers followed him from job to job. In some cases fathers brought their sons to build dams with "The Old Man," as he was known to those who dug the dirt, hauled the rock, and poured the concrete. His ability to motivate and direct their activities in the most efficient way possible earned him a reputation as the finest field engineer in the world and the best dam builder of his generation.

• Crowe's papers have not been located. A biography is S. O. Harper et al., "Memoir of Francis Trenholm Crowe," *Transactions of the American Society of Civil Engineers* 113 (1948): 1397–403. Additional biographical material is in Joseph E. Stevens, *Hoover Dam: An American Adventure* (1988). Obituaries are in the *New York Times*, 28 Feb. 1946, and *Newsweek* and *Time*, both 11 Mar. 1946.

CHARLES W. CAREY, JR.

CROWELL, Henry Parsons (27 Jan. 1855–23 Oct. 1944), businessman, was born in Cleveland, Ohio, the son of Henry Luther Crowell, a wholesale shoe merchant, and Anna Eliza Parsons. Due to ill health, Henry left school at seventeen to work in the family business. While in Cleveland he attended a Dwight L. Moody revival, which so inspired him that he vowed to God that he would make a great deal of money and use it to finance Christian evangelism. In 1874 he left for Denver and for the next seven years traveled throughout the West in an effort to regain his health. In 1878 he bought a ranch outside Fargo, North Dakota, which he later sold at a profit in order to buy another in partnership with an uncle in South Dakota. There they raised wheat and Percheron horses. When his crop failed, Crowell moved back to Ohio and became a partner in an oat mill in Ravenna, sixteen miles east of Akron. It was then, in 1881, that Crowell wrote out his plan for creating a worldwide organization that would sell the best quality oatmeal that technology could make.

Crowell speculated that advertising would be the key to securing a national market for oatmeal. In 1882, however, advertising agencies did not exist; in fact, advertising was considered an activity for charlatans. Crowell initiated the theory and practice of modern consumer advertising by using packaging not only as a convenient and sanitary means of shipping but also as a sales lure. He was thus the first to market and promote a breakfast cereal nationally. In 1882 Crowell married his childhood sweetheart, Lillie Augusta Wick. The couple had one child, but Mrs. Crowell died in 1885.

By the mid-1880s the Ravenna Mill's Quaker brand oatmeal was well established east of the Rocky Mountains. There were, however, at least twenty other oat mills in the same area, which all together produced almost twice as much meal as the market could absorb. In an attempt to stabilize oat sales, by the end of 1886 the twenty-one largest companies had come together to form the Oatmeal Millers' Association. The group lasted about six months and then reorganized as the Consolidated Oatmeal Company, a pool chartered in the state of Illinois and capitalized at $50,000. Crowell served as its president. In the summer of 1888 he married Susan Coffin Coleman and that autumn when the Oatmeal Millers' Association moved its general offices to Chicago, the Crowells followed. There their son, Henry Coleman Crowell, later executive vice president of the Moody Bible Institute, was born.

The goal of the newly reorganized Consolidated Oatmeal Company was control of members' outputs and pricing. Price-fixing was discussed openly and recorded in the minutes. The company, however, could not control the establishment of new mills, nor could it afford to buy or purchase all of them. For those reasons and because new laws were being instituted state by state against pooling agreements, Consolidated Oatmeal collapsed in 1889.

Anticipating the company's demise, seven of the members secured a West Virginia charter for a holding company, called the American Cereal Company. By then Crowell was visualizing an international market for their product, despite the uncertainty of many of the company's directors. When American was incorporated in Ohio in 1891, Crowell was named vice president and general manager.

The company chose to promote the "Quaker" brand most heavily. To create a demand and then satisfy it, Crowell built his campaigns on soundly conceived estimates of human reactions, particularly those of mothers. He designed red, yellow, and blue boxes for each of the products and filled them with oats and gift premiums. Promotions were created to keep the Quaker name before the public constantly. Half-ounce sample boxes were distributed door to door from the East Coast to the West. Murals, billboards, metal signs, window displays, calendars, blotters, flyers, cookbooks, and even ads in church bulletins announced the wholesomeness of Quaker Oats. Scientific endorsements, customer testimonials, contests, market testing, giveaways, and boxtop premiums created an enthusiastic public response. Crowell educat-

ed the consumer to ask for the Quaker brand and thus forced the retailer to stock it.

In 1896 American Cereal experienced its first operating loss, and at the next annual meeting in February 1897 the president, Frederick Schumacher, requested the resignation of Robert Stuart, secretary and treasurer. This undermined Crowell's position, and he retired in February 1898. A proxy fight ensued. For the rest of the year, he and Stuart purchased American Cereal stock until they had a holding almost equal to Schumacher's. When Schumacher unwittingly sold 3,000 of his shares to them, the Crowell group had the majority. Three days before the 1899 annual meeting, the American Cereal Company had formally consolidated with several other millers, resulting in the Stuart-Douglas-Crowell-Andrews-Cormack combination, a $33 million New Jersey holding company. Crowell was elected president. In 1901 "The Quaker Oats Company" was set up as a holding company. It became an operating company in 1906 after acquiring the remainder of American Cereal's assets.

Crowell exercised his business acumen in another venture, which he began in 1888 when he organized the Cleveland Foundry Company in partnership with Francis Edson Drury, to make oil cooking stoves. Standard Oil of Ohio sold the stoves in conjunction with their coal oil. Crowell then organized the Cleveland Factory Company and the Cleveland Metal Products Company, which merged with the Cleveland Foundry Company in 1917, becoming the Perfection Stove Company in October 1925. Using the same advertising techniques that he employed for oatmeal, Crowell created a powerful consumer demand for his stoves. From this and his other enterprises Crowell became a millionaire and one of the most important businessmen in Cleveland and Chicago.

The second phase of Crowell's life began in 1898 when he and his wife renewed their commitment to Christian evangelism. The "Christian businessman" now became the "Christian statesman" (Day, p. 155). In 1901 the Crowells moved to Winnetka, Illinois, when he was named to the board of trustees of the Moody Bible Institute; he was elected president in 1904, an office that he held until 1944. Through his leadership the institution was placed on a solid business footing and achieved an excellent financial standing. Crowell Hall, the institute's administration building, was later named for him.

In 1910 Crowell was elected vice president of the Bible Institute Colportage Association, and in 1941 he became director of the Colportage Division of the Moody Bible Institute when the two organizations merged.

During his years with the Moody Bible Institute, Crowell acquired a winter home in Augusta, Georgia, called "Green Court." He also acquired the Wyoming Hereford Ranch east of Cheyenne, Wyoming, in 1920, turning it into a nonprofit institution devoted solely to improving beef cattle. In 1922 Mrs. Crowell died from a heart ailment. In 1939 he established a trust to provide for the operation of the ranch for twenty-five years after his death. He had already established the Henry Parsons Crowell and Susan Coleman Crowell Trust, with the provision that the interest would be distributed from time to time to evangelical Christian organizations that could guarantee loyalty to the conservative Christian beliefs to which Crowell subscribed.

Crowell also headed the Layman's Evangelistic Council of Chicago in the early years of the twentieth century and in 1907 helped to organize the Committee of Five dedicated to the eradication of vice in Chicago. This committee also included Julius Rosenwald, Harold H. Swift, Medill McCormick, and Clifford W. Barnes. Crowell was instrumental in the passage of the Mann Act of 1908 and remained a member of the committee until his death. He was also a charter member of the City Crime Commission.

In May 1940 Crowell retired as chairman of the board of Quaker Oats and was immediately appointed honorary chairman. He died in Chicago. Often referred to as an "autocrat," he was noted for his patience, gentleness, and relentlessness. He is remembered as one of the creators of modern advertising and was also among the first of the nineteenth-century industrialists to use a theory of business as his guide rather than depending on trial and error. In his personal life Crowell fulfilled his youthful vow, for nearly fifty years dedicating 65 percent of his annual earnings to Christian causes.

• The standard published works on the history of the Quaker Oats Company and Henry Parsons Crowell's contributions are Arthur F. Marquette, *Brands, Trademarks and Good Will, The Story of the Quaker Oats Company* (1967), and Harrison John Thornton, *The History of the Quaker Oats Company* (1933). Crowell's biography, *A Christian in Big Business* (1946), was written by Richard Ellsworth Day. See also Lewis Nordyke, "Angel of the Range," *Saturday Evening Post* 218 (3 Nov. 1945): 26–27, 69–71.

CYNTHIA L. OGOREK

CROWLEY, James H. *See* Four Horsemen of Notre Dame.

CROWLEY, Patrick Francis (23 Sept. 1911–20 Nov. 1974), Catholic layman and a founder of the Christian Family Movement (CFM), was born in Chicago, Illinois, the son of Jerome J. Crowley, a lawyer, and Henrietta Louise O'Brien. He received a B.A. from the University of Notre Dame in 1933 and a J.D. from Loyola University of Chicago in 1937. In 1937 he married Patricia "Patty" Caron. Having passed the Illinois bar examination, he joined a law firm, working as a business lawyer and as a director and counsel to several companies, including Caron International, KAR Products, and the O'Brien Corporation. Eventually he became a senior partner of Crowley, Barrett, and Karaba. He and his wife had five children of their own and adopted one, and in the course of their married life they took care of more than fifty foster children who came from several countries.

Having been attracted by the inquiry method of Joseph Cardijn, the Belgian founder of the Young Christian Workers (Jeunesse Ouvrière Chrétienne, known as Jocists), and by Pope Pius XII's encyclical *Mystici Corporis,* Crowley and five other married men began to meet regularly in his law office in Chicago with Father Louis Putz, a Holy Cross priest who taught them the Jocist technique, and with Monsignor Reynold H. Hillenbrand, who instructed them in the theology of the Mystical Body of Christ, emphasizing the role of the laity in the liturgy. They decided to focus their attention on marriage and the family as their common interests and created a body of experts who were willing to assist anyone considering a divorce. The original cell was multiplied sixfold.

Now calling itself the Catholic Action Federation, the organization published the first issue of a quarterly titled *Act* in 1946. Some of the members' wives formed a cell of their own with a priest as chaplain and began to meet weekly; they were engaged in serious discussions and practical activities. The Crowleys started the first mixed group in their parish, St. Joseph's in Wilmette, in 1947. By the end of 1948 cells of Catholic men and women were active in the "family apostolate" in at least twenty cities in the United States. In Chicago the Catholic Action Federation was renamed Christian Family Action in order to accommodate couples in mixed marriages. In 1949 Crowley was elected its president. In the same year a conference of more than sixty representatives of Catholic action groups, held in Wheeling, Illinois, decided to establish a national coordinating committee and to make the Crowleys temporary chairs. At the second meeting, held in Lisle, Illinois, in 1950, it was resolved that the name of the organization should be the Christian Family Movement. The Crowleys were again chosen to head the movement as executive secretary couple and were ex officio chairs of the executive committee of the National Coordinating Committee. They also edited until 1955 the movement's organ, *Act,* which was increased in frequency to six issues a year in 1952. Crowley and his wife, along with other leaders, propagated the movement by speaking before meetings held in many places throughout the country with the permission of the local ecclesiastical authorities. They addressed not only married people but also seminarians, and they recruited chaplains among the clergy of the various dioceses that they visited. In 1956 the Crowleys made a six-week tour of the world to visit groups that had formed abroad; a decade later they were elected president couple of the International Confederation of Christian Family Movements and began to issue a newsletter.

In 1964 the Crowleys were appointed to Pope Paul VI's Special Study Group on Population and Birth Control. They gathered the opinions of hundreds of couples in the United States and Canada who belonged to the movement and reported to Rome the frequently expressed desire for a modification of the church's traditional teaching on artificial contraception. Having been asked to investigate for the pastoral section of the

806 • CROWN

commission the experience of CFM couples with the rhythm method, they sent out two questionnaires to thousands of active members. In keeping with the desires of 78 percent of the respondents, Crowley and his wife argued against the condemnation of all forms of family limitation beyond the rhythm method. They agreed with the majority of the study group who maintained that the doctrine stated in Pius XI's encyclical *Casti Connubii* did not pertain to the infallible magisterium. After Paul VI issued his encyclical *Humanae Vitae* in 1968, reaffirming the teaching of his predecessors, the Crowleys publicly expressed their dissent and thereby lost the support of the archbishop of Chicago, Cardinal John Cody, and of their chaplain, Hillenbrand.

This episode proved to be one of the causes of the rapid decline of the Christian Family Movement. Another was the admission of non-Catholic couples to the movement in 1968, with the consequent omission of references to papal encyclicals from the movement's manuals. Thus the doctrinal foundation of the movement was eroded, and its spirituality was left unsupported since, as a nondenominational organization it could not be affiliated with a Catholic parish or diocese. Many members became dissatisfied with the growing Focus on social and political issues such as race relations and international affairs; in addition, some reckless ecumenical ventures at CFM conventions alienated many bishops, priests, and laypeople from the movement. The last cause of the decline was the rise of another movement, Marriage Encounter, which the Crowleys had helped to introduce to the United States from Spain in 1968. Aggravating the difficulties of the CFM was a growing financial crisis. The Crowleys resigned as executive secretary couple in August 1970, but they retained the presidency of the International Confederation of Christian Family Movements, which had a membership of about 135,000, until Patrick's death.

Besides his work with the CFM, Crowley was also a director of the Center for the Study of Democratic Institutions in Santa Barbara, the Fund for the Republic, the Little Brothers of the Poor, and Catholic Scholarships for Negroes. He was president of the Family Institute of Chicago, treasurer of the Foundation for International Co-operation, and a trustee of several educational institutions. In 1968 he served as director of Eugene McCarthy's presidential campaign in Illinois but became disillusioned with political activity thereafter.

Crowley and his wife were widely acclaimed for their work. They received the Pro Ecclesia et Pontifice Medal in 1957, when they attended the Second World Congress of the Laity in Rome. They were presented with awards from the Chicago Commission on Human Relations and the Conference of Christians and Jews. In 1966 they received the Laetare Medal of the University of Notre Dame, the first couple so honored. He died in Chicago.

• Crowley's papers are in the archives of the University of Notre Dame. See also John N. Kotre, *Simple Gifts: The Lives of Pat and Patty Crowley* (1979), and Robert McClory, *Turning Point* (1995).

ROBERT TRISCO

CROWN, Henry (13 June 1896–14 Aug. 1990), entrepreneur and philanthropist, was born Henry Krinsky in Chicago, the son of Arie Krinsky, a Lithuanian immigrant garment worker, and his wife Ida Gordon. At some point they changed their name to Crown. To help his poor family, Crown took a job at age fourteen as clerk at the Chicago Firebrick Company. In 1912 he began work at the Union Drop Forge Company, while taking night courses in accounting. In 1915 he and his two older brothers, Sol and Irving, formed a small steel-brokerage company, S. A. Crown and Company, and Crown quickly established a local reputation as an aggressive and reliable deal maker with a discerning eye for opportunity, a striking power of recall, and an acute sense of timing.

In 1919 the brothers invested their savings—about $10,000—into their company and renamed it Material Services Corporation. With Henry as president, treasurer, and general manager, Material Services flourished, quickly becoming the leading sand and gravel supply firm in Chicago. The basis of the firm's success was Crown's support from local bankers, who supplied him unsecured loans; the purchase of a large tract of land from the city of Chicago that contained easily accessible deposits of sand, rock, and limestone; and Crown's vigorous strategy of integration and diversification, including buying out rival suppliers and establishing the company's own trucking and barge firms, brick works, and coal mines. Because of his private and reserved manner and his many dealings with the government, Crown was accused of becoming successful mainly through his political contacts, especially with the Democratic party in Chicago. He denied such charges, once saying that "a man does not have to pay bribes to run a business successfully."

By World War II, the fortunes of Material Services and of the Crown family were secure. During the war, Crown accepted a colonel's commission, serving as chief of procurement in the Great Lakes Division of the Army Corps of Engineers. For his role in securing $1 billion in scarce construction materials for military projects, Crown received numerous citations from Allied governments. At war's end, Colonel Crown, as he was now widely known, expanded Material Services. In 1951, as the world's largest cement distributor, it returned $45 million on sales of $115 million. Crown extended his investment portfolio beyond the Chicago area, purchasing large or controlling shares of railroads, coal mines, sugar plantations, and real estate ventures, including the Chicago, Rock Island & Pacific Railroad, the Empire State Building in New York City, and Hilton Hotels.

Throughout all these dealings, Crown reinforced his reputation as a formidable deal maker with an uncanny ability to find low-cost investment opportunities and quickly enhance their values. It was once said that "when the Colonel gets into a deal he knows the size of your underwear." He always kept detailed data on his holdings close at hand and spent much of his day on the telephone, monitoring his investments and pursuing new ones. Considered elusive and secretive, Crown conferred only with close friends and associates, avoided the publicity and social functions of America's business elite, and had a relatively modest lifestyle, describing himself as "a sand and gravel man." He was known particularly for his skill at minimizing tax liability through forming partnerships, holding companies, and family trusts; his inclination toward real estate; and his deep reluctance to give up—even at great profit—control over investments he had nurtured.

The central deal of Crown's life—the 1959 merger between Material Services and General Dynamics Corporation—was the first time Crown was bettered; the deal almost destroyed his treasured Material Services. General Dynamics, builder of warplanes, missiles, battle tanks, and nuclear-powered submarines, had been consistently among the nation's top three military contractors. In the year of the merger, however, General Dynamics stock was slipping due to losses at its Convair commercial air transport division in San Diego. Nevertheless, its Electric Boat submarine works at Groton, Connecticut, Canadair in Montreal, and the Atlas missile and military aircraft business in Fort Worth, along with other strong divisions, made the firm seem a good buy. Crown was misled and deceived, however, by Convair executives, who misrepresented the firm's losses on the development of a new jet airliner, and only after the deal was finalized did Crown learn the extent of Convair's problems. Cash from Material Services eventually covered the drain of nearly $425 million, the greatest American corporate loss to that time. An indignant Crown took personal control of General Dynamics, restructured it, ousted incompetent executives, and arranged new credit that kept the conglomerate afloat until it won a large U.S. Air Force contract for the new F-111 fighter-bomber in late 1962.

The F-111 project was steeped in the sort of controversy, cost overruns, and charges of political favoritism that also characterized work in General Dynamics' submarine division. These problems may have been exacerbated by Crown's enigmatic business manner and the suspicions of political favoritism that had plagued him throughout his career. In 1966 Crown's opponents mobilized to force him out of General Dynamics and Material Services; however, he regained control in 1970. He then directed the corporation through a small executive committee, marginalizing the board of directors, until the mid-1980s, when the aging Crown increasingly passed responsibility on to his son Lester.

At the time of his death in Chicago, Crown's stake in General Dynamics was worth nearly $1 billion, which constituted only half the estimated worth of the family fortune. Since 1966, Crown had managed and amply supplemented his assets through a holding company, Henry Crown and Company, based in Chicago. Over the years, its diverse portfolio came to include shares in First Chicago Bank, Burlington Northern, Swift and Company, Pennzoil, Aspen Skiing, the Chicago Bulls, and the New York Yankees, as well as key real estate properties in Chicago and Manhattan and large tracts of farm and ranch lands in Florida, Arizona, and California. The company also dispensed some $80 million in philanthropy, most notably to the Chicago Boys Clubs; the Chicago Museum of Science and Industry; Evanston Hospital; Northwestern, Stanford, and Brandeis Universities; and the U.S. Naval Academy.

Crown was married to Rebecca Kranz in 1920. They had three sons. She died in 1943, and in 1946 he married Gladys Kay. Crown's fifteen grandchildren and ten great-grandchildren make up one of the wealthiest families in America.

• Accounts of Crown's life consist mainly of journalistic reports. See Roger Franklin, *The Defender: The Story of General Dynamics* (1986); Patrick Tyler, *Running Critical: The Silent War, Rickover, and General Dynamics* (1986); "The Crown Family Empire," *Businessweek*, 31 Mar. 1986, 50–53; and *Biographical Dictionary of American Business Leaders* (1983). Obituaries are in the *Chicago Tribune*, 15 Aug. 1990, and the *New York Times*, 16 Aug. 1990.

JACOB A. VANDER MEULEN

CROWNINSHIELD, Benjamin Williams (27 Dec. 1772–3 Feb. 1851), merchant and politician, was born in Salem, Massachusetts, the son of George Crowninshield, a sea captain and merchant, and Mary Derby, daughter of another prominent shipping family. Young Benjamin received a common school education and then was put into his father's shipping business, George Crowninshield and Sons, to learn navigation and the clerical details of the business. He went to sea at a very early age and may even have captained a ship himself. In 1804 he married Mary Boardman, who was also from a prominent shipping family; they had no children.

The death in 1809 of Crowninshield's brother Jacob, perhaps the most outstanding of the brothers, was a blow to the company and to the family. The business, however, was reorganized and continued to prosper, especially during the War of 1812 when the company outfitted several privateers, including the *America*, that preyed on British commerce very successfully.

The Crowninshields were uncompromising supporters of Jeffersonian policies, and Benjamin followed in his brother Jacob's footsteps as the family politician. Jacob had served with great credit in the Eighth, Ninth, and Tenth Congresses before his death. Benjamin Crowninshield served in the Massachusetts House of Representatives in 1811 and then in the state senate in 1812. In December 1814 President James Madison chose Crowninshield to replace William Jones as secretary of the navy. Crowninshield declined the appointment but two days later changed his mind and accepted. The reasons for his vacillation are unknown, but he may have been reluctant to leave his family in Massachusetts and take up residence in Washington, D.C. He was mostly an absentee secretary, remaining in Washington only when Congress was in session.

Crowninshield took up his duties as secretary of the navy on 16 January 1815, shortly before news of the end of the War of 1812 arrived. Jones, the former secretary of the navy, had successfully urged Congress to establish a three-man Board of Naval Commissioners, which was created in February 1815. One of Crowninshield's duties was to develop a relationship between the board and the secretary of the navy that would assist the department in the disposition of the fleet, the supervision of the construction of warships, the procurement of naval stores, and other matters relating to its affairs. Crowninshield possessed in a high degree the disposition to accommodate the strong personalities on the naval board, who at first insisted on their independence of the secretary's direction. Firm but not contentious, Crowninshield insisted on his prerogatives in running the department, and he was supported by President Madison.

When James Monroe became president, he was satisfied enough to retain Crowninshield in office. There is little to point to in the way of accomplishments during Crowninshield's tenure in office. Congress did, however, during this period begin a naval building program to enlarge the navy. The naval regulations of 1800 were also revised and brought up to date. The "Rules, Regulations, and Instructions for the Naval Service," issued in April 1818, outlined in detail the duties and responsibilities of commissioned and noncommissioned officers, even to their supervision of floggings.

Crowninshield, apparently growing weary of the frequent travel from New England to Washington, D.C., as well as the vexations of dealing with the naval board, resigned as secretary of the navy on 1 October 1818. His father's death in 1815 and another brother's death in 1817 led to the dissolution of the Crowninshield shipping firm. Crowninshield's business interests were changing in any event. In 1811 he had become the president of Merchants Bank of Salem, and he was more interested in merchandising than shipping. Nevertheless, he still held an interest in politics. He was chosen as a presidential elector in 1820, casting his vote for Monroe. In 1821 he was again chosen to serve in the Massachusetts House of Representatives, and in 1823 he was elected to the Eighteenth Congress. He was reelected to the Nineteenth, Twentieth, and Twenty-first Congresses. During this period he was a strong supporter of John Quincy Adams, but his career as a congressman was largely undistinguished. In 1830 Crowninshield was defeated by the prominent young attorney Rufus Choate.

Crowninshield's political career was not over, however, for he was elected for a third time to the Massachusetts House of Representatives. He served only one term and then retired to Boston where he remained until his death.

Crowninshield was an individual on whom duty was thrust. He lacked ambition and had only modest abilities, but because of his position in a financially secure and distinguished family he had a notable career in politics and even gained appointment to high office. He performed his duties adequately but without great distinction.

• There is no collection of Crowninshield papers, and information about his life and career is scant and not easily available. His letters may be found in the papers of many of his contemporaries in the Library of Congress, Manuscript Division; in the Essex Institute, Salem, Mass.; and in the Massachusetts Historical Society. A biography of Crowninshield has yet to be published. Information about his career as secretary of the navy may be found in Harold D. Langley, *Social Reform in the U.S. Navy, 1798–1862* (1967) and Charles O. Paullin, *Paullin's History of Naval Administration, 1775–1911* (1968). Crowninshield's relationship with John Quincy Adams during Crowninshield's period in Congress may be found in Charles F. Adams, ed., *Memoirs of John Quincy Adams* (12 vols., 1874–1877).

C. EDWARD SKEEN

CROWNINSHIELD, Frank (24 June 1872–28 Dec. 1947), editor, was born Francis Welch Crowninshield in Paris, France, the son of Frederic Crowninshield, an artist, and Helen S. Fairbanks. The surname is an anglicized version of the German name von Kronensheldt, adapted when a German ancestor settled in Salem in 1670. At the time of Crowninshield's birth, his father was specializing in watercolors and studying in Europe. The family returned to Boston in 1878. Francis was educated mostly by private tutors, until he enrolled at Lyons Academy in New York City, where the family had moved in 1886.

Crowninshield thrived in the metropolis. In 1890, after studying art for two years at the University of Rome, he returned to Manhattan, determined to pursue a career in publishing. He approached Major George Haven Putnam, head of the publishing house and bookstore that bore his name. Crowninshield is said to have asked for a job that entailed reading manuscripts, socializing with authors, and generally dabbling in the publishing end of the business. Such tasks would later define his life and historic significance, but he appeared presumptuous at the time. "Very sorry, but that's what I do myself," replied Putnam, according to the *New Yorker* (19 Sept. 1942). Crowninshield was put to work as a clerk in the bookstore.

Crowninshield soon acquired the experience and skills necessary to become an accomplished editor. He worked as publisher of the *Bookman* (1895–1900), assistant editor of *Metropolitan Magazine* (1900–1902), assistant editor of *Munsey's Magazine* (1903–1907), a literary agent (1908–1909), and art editor of *Century Magazine* (1910–1913).

Near the end of his tenure with *Century*, Crowninshield was approached by publisher Condé Nast about a new magazine to be titled *Dress and Vanity Fair*.

Crowninshield, asked to comment on the project, remarked that no magazine in existence covered what people discussed at lunches and parties—"the arts, sports, theatre, humor, and so forth." Intrigued by the possibility of such a publication, Crowninshield told Nast that he would edit the magazine only if the title were shortened to *Vanity Fair* and if women's fashions were excluded from the content. Nast agreed, and thus was born one of America's most successful magazines, covering sophisticated fare on arts, entertainment, and social opinion.

Crowninshield's editorial savvy helped *Vanity Fair* achieve a distinction on par with the other so-called "smart" magazines, such as the *New Yorker*, *Life*, and *Esquire*. These were publications that the literary elite read and were influenced by, establishing New York City as the arts and intellectual capital of the world. Crowninshield was especially suited to such a milieu because of his love of art. His artistic sensibilities were shaped by his father, his experiences and studies abroad, and the 1913 Armory Show in New York City which introduced European avant-garde art styles to some 300,000 Americans. Crowninshield's criticism in *Vanity Fair* often introduced new art styles to readers, and his patronage helped the careers of many artists, especially the French moderns. Crowninshield was also an avid collector of art. On his seventy-first birthday he said it would be "a frightful mess" if he were to die and leave his many artworks unbequeathed. Consequently, he scheduled a three-day auction at Parke-Bernet Galleries and fetched $181,747 for his collection—a sizable amount for the time.

Unlike millions, Crowninshield lived comfortably during the Great Depression. He had become wealthy as an editor of *Vanity Fair*, owing to the successful fulfillment of its mission, as it was reported in a March 1914 editorial penned by Crowninshield: "first, to believe in the progress and promise of American life, and second, to chronicle that progress cheerfully, truthfully and entertainingly." Such an editorial concept suited the 1920s era, when optimism reigned, especially on Wall Street. The vision, however, was inappropriate in the years following the October 1929 stock market crash.

Crowninshield maintained his urbane lifestyle through good times and bad, collecting art and socializing in Manhattan clubs. But in 1932 Nast decided that the previously successful concept of *Vanity Fair* needed to be changed and appointed two editorial consultants, who recommended less emphasis on the arts and more on politics and economics, the pressing concerns of the day.

Because of the struggling economy, *Vanity Fair* continued to lose advertising support. In 1936 it was merged with a new Nast magazine, *Vogue*, and Crowninshield was reassigned within the company. He spent his remaining years as art editor of *Vogue* and literary adviser to Condé Nast Publications, Inc.

Crowninshield died in New York City. Shortly before he died, his doctor asked Crowninshield if there was anything he could do for him. A bachelor and teetotaler all of his life, Crowninshield replied, "Yes, get me a wife exactly like yours" (Hellman, p. 80). After his death, a family member found a note bequeathing the doctor a bottle of champagne—a typical gallant gesture and a symbol of what Crowninshield's life and career represented: wit, good humor, and style.

• There is no record of Crowninshield's personal papers or professional correspondence. Crowninshield wrote a short book—*The Unofficial Palace of New York* (1939)—about the Waldorf-Astoria hotel and published two books under the pseudonym Arthur Loring Bruce, *Manners for the Metropolis* (1908) and *The Bridge Fiend* (1909). The best sources on Crowninshield are three comprehensive pieces by Geoffrey T. Hellman in the *New Yorker*: a two-part profile titled "Last of the Species," 19 and 26 Sept. 1942, and an obituary in the 14 Feb. 1948 issue. Insightful material about the life, times, and editing of Crowninshield is found in George H. Douglas, *The Smart Magazine* (1991). Crowninshield is also mentioned briefly in *Magazines in the Twentieth Century* (1964) and *American Mass-Market Magazines* (1990). A lengthy obituary with a picture appears in the *New York Times*, 29 Dec. 1947.

MICHAEL J. BUGEJA

CROWNINSHIELD, George, Jr. (27 May 1766–26 Nov. 1817), merchant and yachtsman, was born in Salem, Massachusetts, the son of George Crowninshield, a merchant, and Mary Derby. Though never married, he had one daughter, Clarissa (called Clara), whose mother was Elizabeth Rowell. The Crowninshields, among the richest Salem merchant families, gained their wealth through privateering and in the Far Eastern trade for which Salem was famed in the later eighteenth and early nineteenth centuries. After studying navigation and going to sea as a captain's clerk, Crowninshield commanded a ship to the West Indies in 1790 and, according to records, commanded the *Belisarius* to the East Indies four years later. Crowninshield's work was largely in the outfitting of ships, but he was known around Salem for his extracurricular activities, such as driving around the city in his bright yellow curricle, dressed in ostentatious style. He also chased fires, but rescuing people from ships in distress, for the purpose of which he maintained a vessel, was a passion.

In 1813 the American *Chesapeake* was defeated off Marblehead by HMS *Shannon*. Captain James Lawrence (of "don't give up the ship" fame) and a Lieutenant Ludlow were killed in the action, and their bodies were buried by the British in Halifax, Nova Scotia. Crowninshield captained the family ship that brought their bodies back for a ceremonious reburial in Salem and final interment in New York. Though the idea had not been his and the costs were shared by prominent Salemites, he was lavishly praised for the deed.

Crowninshield gained a measure of national and international fame (or notoriety) with his *Cleopatra's Barge*, the first American vessel built solely as a pleasure yacht. Launched in 1816, this barkentine was 83 feet long at the waterline and 23 feet in beam and was built for speed. The elaborately painted and gilded vessel boasted a sumptuous interior. Its $50,000 cost of construction was probably matched by the expense of equipping and provisioning; everything about it was calculated to awe and impress.

Setting sail from Salem on 30 March 1817 with fourteen men and 300 letters of recommendation from prominent Americans, the yacht touched at the Azores and went on to Gibraltar, where Crowninshield hoped to receive the Princess of Wales aboard. That was the first of a series of disappointments: though *Cleopatra's Barge* attracted huge crowds of sensation-seekers at various ports around the Mediterranean, Crowninshield was unable to attract the royalty he had envisioned entertaining. The diary kept by his cynical cousin, "Philosopher Ben" Crowninshield, refers to the throngs of curiosity seekers as "canaille." It records scenes of crowded disorder, drunkenness, seasickness, and uproar.

At Florence, George Crowninshield sought daily an introduction to the Empress Marie Louise, wife of Napoleon—then in exile on St. Helena. He had to settle for common souvenirs of the great man. At Elba he managed to acquire a piece of carpet and some tile fragments from Napoleon's rooms as well as a pair of boots supposedly left behind by the fallen emperor because they were too small. At Rome, Bonaparte relatives managed to fob off on the gullible American a supposed adopted son of Napoleon. Not until the yacht was at sea did it become clear that the young man was merely a penniless nuisance. He and his four companions disappeared after their free passage to the United States.

By 3 October 1817 *Cleopatra's Barge* had returned to Salem, and two months later Crowninshield died there of a heart attack. He had been contemplating a similar cruise to northern Europe. The *Barge* went on to become the personal yacht of Kamehameha II, king of Hawaii, its intimacy with royalty coming only after the death of the man who thought that American wealth and ostentation could gain him entrée to the titled society of the Old World.

• Most of the Crowninshield family papers are in the Essex Institute and the Peabody Museum, both in Salem. A reconstruction of the interior of *Cleopatra's Barge* is also at the Peabody Museum. A rich source of information is Peter Smith, ed., *The Diary of William Bentley* (4 vols., 1962). James Duncan Phillips, *Salem and the Indies: The Story of the Great Commercial Era of the City* (1947), mentions Crowninshield a number of times. David L. Ferguson, *Cleopatra's Barge: The Crowninshield Story* (1976), is both deeply researched and entertaining to read.

HASKELL SPRINGER

CROWTHER, Bosley (13 July 1905–7 Mar. 1981), newspaper film reviewer, was born Francis Bosley Crowther in Lutherville, Maryland, the son of F. Bosley Crowther and Eliza Leisenring. His father was a wholesale grocer, but the family was clearly of the middle class. Crowther's earliest public schooling took place in Lutherville, near Baltimore. When his parents moved to Winston-Salem, North Carolina, he attend-

ed grade school there, and after another family move he finished his high school education in Washington, D.C. He then spent a postgraduate year at the Woodberry Forest school in Virginia.

In 1924 Crowther began four years at Princeton University, from which he graduated with an honors degree in history and the goal of pursuing a career in law or diplomacy. During college he served as editor of the *Daily Princetonian*, and in his senior year he won a current events competition sponsored by the *New York Times*. After a four-month stay in Europe at the newspaper's expense, he took a job on the *Times* news staff.

As a nightside cub reporter, Crowther covered the Brooklyn police beat and other borough activities. He gained the respect of the city desk editors as a fast, efficient writer. Away from his job, he tried his hand as a dramatist. *East of the Sun* (written with William Du Bois) got as far as Philadelphia tryouts; *Royal Stuff*, a romantic comedy, went into rehearsals but was canceled before a Broadway opening.

Crowther was named assistant drama editor of the *Times* in September 1932. In January 1933 he married Florence Marks, a one-time *Times* staffer; they had three children. Crowther remained at the drama desk until 1937, when he shifted to a slot as assistant motion picture editor under the veteran Frank Nugent. Three years later, he succeeded Nugent as chief film editor and reviewer.

Crowther presided in that position, with the prestige and influence of the *New York Times* behind him, for the next twenty-seven years. Under his supervision the paper increased its news reporting on the U.S. and foreign film industries, while it widened its coverage of New York film openings by eventually employing six regular reviewers. Crowther himself wrote about half of the approximately four hundred reviews that appeared in the *Times* each year; he also contributed a prominently featured article in each Sunday's edition, which had a far wider circulation than the weekday paper. Without question, during the 1940s and 1950s, Crowther was the most important motion picture reviewer in the country and a major influence on the opinions and tastes of American filmgoers.

Crowther never spelled out a specific agenda of his interests in films and filmmaking. However, during his quarter-century in charge, certain issues and themes recurred on the newspaper's cinema pages. For one, Crowther was usually on top of new motion picture techniques. He felt that the two key advances in motion picture history were the additions of sound and of color to moving images. Improvements in these areas were welcomed. But Crowther was skeptical of the spate of innovations that flourished during the early 1950s in Hollywood's vain efforts to counter the increasing competition of television for once-reliable film audiences. Stereoscopy (3-D) he viewed as a gimmick that did virtually nothing to enhance the realistic qualities of color. Similarly, the introduction of wider and wider theater screens struck him as irrelevant, since attempts to manipulate moviegoers with "optical stunts," as he called them, were futile "unless those stunts make for better telling of better stories."

Crowther always strongly opposed film censorship; he supported free expression as vital to a free social order. Such a stance caused him to speak out against the postwar blacklisting of Hollywood film figures who allegedly were communist sympathizers. He likewise criticized Senator Joseph R. McCarthy and others for their scattershot accusations of disloyalty.

Although he was a churchgoing Roman Catholic, Crowther opposed the Catholic Legion of Decency by defending the right of filmmakers to present such controversial pictures as *Forever Amber* (1947), *Stromboli* (1950), *The Miracle* (1951), and *La Ronde* (1954). He did advocate an important proviso in his discussion of censoring films, however. His review of *Blackboard Jungle* (1955), a dramatization of delinquent behavior in urban public schools, called for that film—or any other—to present an honest portrayal of the conditions being depicted. If those details were "misrepresented and sensationalized," he noted, the picture's content was "irresponsible and fraught with peril." On the other hand, if *Blackboard Jungle* could be considered "a true and valid picture," then the moment had come "for drastic social action."

Such statements embody Crowther's approach to film criticism, but they also reveal his bias and limitations. Crowther was usually at the forefront among reviewers of his era. He enthusiastically endorsed Orson Welles's *Citizen Kane* on its 1941 release, and he supported the postwar Italian neorealist films of directors Roberto Rossellini and Vittorio de Sica. Yet at heart in his writings he was didactic and rigid, convinced that films should primarily dramatize social problems and bring about social betterment.

Motion pictures for Crowther, according to one observer, "should be morally instructive," and reviewers should endorse or condemn filmmakers' "visions of reality." To Crowther, his own visions of reality were the themes that "serious" films explored. Thus, when *An American in Paris* received the Academy Award for best picture in 1951, winning over Crowther's own favorite, *A Place in the Sun*, he lashed out at Academy members for being "so insensitive to the excellence of motion-picture art that they would vote for a frivolous musical picture over a powerful and poignant tragedy." Only a decade later, a new breed of filmgoers fully committed to "motion picture art" would look upon such scoldings as pompous curiosities.

By 1960, when that new breed had come to the fore, Crowther's career dictates were rejected as simplistic and old-fashioned, or, worse, he was ignored altogether. In film circles at the end of the twentieth century, he was remembered as little more than an exemplar of bygone days.

Still, as the nation's principal film reviewer for so many years, Crowther's achievements ought to be acknowledged. He demonstrated to his readers that motion pictures were the twentieth century's newest art form, and he encouraged them to watch films thoughtfully. He tirelessly heralded the best of imported foreign films. The expanded staff he forged gave the *Times* nearly comprehensive coverage of the motion picture industry, and his reviewers seldom missed any of the hundreds of films that played in New York City each year. On three occasions he was elected president of the New York Film Critics. And the Directors Guild of America paid him the unusual compliment of honoring the quality of his reviews with a special award. While maintaining his active schedule, he also published two worthwhile books on the Hollywood film industry.

A year after Crowther's retirement in 1967, the *Times* named him critic emeritus. During his retirement years he occasionally lectured, and he compiled several film anthologies. He died in Mount Kisco, New York.

• A biography by Frank Beaver, *Bosley Crowther: Social Critic of the Film*, was published in 1974. Besides his film reviews, feature articles, and news stories in the *Times* from 1937 until 1967, Crowther's published writings include his historical study of Metro-Goldwyn-Mayer, *The Lion's Share: The Story of an Entertainment Empire* (1957); *Hollywood Rajah: The Life and Times of Louis B. Mayer* (1960); *The Great Films: Fifty Golden Years of Motion Pictures* (1967); *Vintage Films* (1977); and *Reruns* (1978). An obituary is in the *New York Times*, 8 Mar. 1981.

ROBERT MIRANDON

CROZET, Claudius (31 Dec. 1789?–29 Jan. 1864), engineer and educator, was born Benoît Crozet in Villefranche in southeastern France, the son of François Crozet, a wholesale wine merchant, and Pierrette Varion. He and his family may have lived for a time in New York when he was a child. Benoît Crozet graduated from the École Polytechnique in Paris in 1807, completed two years of advanced study at the Imperial Artillery School in Metz in 1809, and then entered the Napoleonic Wars. Sometime after he finished school he adopted the name Claudius; some people knew him as Claude. Commissioned a second lieutenant in a battalion of bridge builders in the Imperial Artillery Corps, he spent one year in Germany and two years in Holland. Then, promoted to captain, he participated in Napoleon Bonaparte's invasion of Russia in July 1812 but was captured at Borodino, just west of Moscow, in September and spent nearly two years in Russia as a prisoner of war. After his release and return to France he resigned from the army in April 1816, married Agathe DeCamp in June, and soon departed France with his bride for the United States, where they lived the rest of their lives and raised three children. For the next forty-five years Crozet lived in New York, Virginia, or Louisiana and altered between education and transportation as his major spheres of activity.

In September 1816 Crozet began teaching engineering as an assistant professor at the U.S. Military Academy at West Point, New York. Within a year he had been promoted to professor, a position he held for six years. The academy, founded only in 1802, was still a young institution, and Crozet had a profound influence on its engineering curriculum. He brought to it the best civil and military engineering known in Europe at the time. To teach his students engineering, he found he had to begin by teaching them mathematics, and he brought in related matters like architecture, fortifications, and military science. He also shouldered the task of teaching other courses for which he saw strong need but for which there was no other instructor, including artillery and topography. He taught cadets, many of them destined for the U.S. Army Corps of Engineers, how to build bridges, buildings, fortifications, canals, and roads.

And yet Virginia attracted Crozet's attention as a better place of employment. Hearing about the new University of Virginia, he wrote Thomas Jefferson in 1821 to inquire about a professorship there but was told that no school yet existed. Another opportunity arose, however, when the Virginia Board of Public Works, established in 1816 to promote transportation improvements, developed a vacancy for a principal engineer. From 1823 to 1832 Crozet filled that position. His assignments included surveying routes for possible roads, canals, and eventually railroads as well as rendering technical advice on how to choose among various projects and then execute the choice. On the most central and pressing line of improvements, he came to favor a water route from Richmond west to Lynchburg but preferred a railway from Lynchburg through western Virginia to the Ohio Valley. The legislature, to whom he reported, was dominated by eastern interests that had no wish to see the west thrive. Local rivalries and legislative interference led him to resign his position and look for a more promising place to deploy his talents and experience.

Louisiana beckoned, partly because of the French culture and the presence of Crozet's siblings but largely because it was preparing to inaugurate state-sponsored transportation improvements. There, much as Virginia had in 1816, the legislature in 1832 established an internal improvements fund and authorized the appointment of a civil engineer. Crozet secured the position and went to work on surveys of rivers and bayous and possible new roads and railroads. Thinking in strategic terms, Crozet envisioned a great railway from the Mississippi River to the District of Columbia through Virginia's Shenandoah Valley. Frustrated as much in Louisiana as he had been in Virginia by his inability to command the favorable attention of the state legislature, Crozet resigned as state engineer and obtained appointment as president of Jefferson College, a state-supported school in Convent, Louisiana, where classes began in 1834. In early 1836 he left that position, too, returned to New Orleans, and worked for the city government surveying street drainage problems.

In 1837 Crozet accepted an invitation to return to his old position as principal engineer for the Virginia Board of Public Works. For a time he perceived progress in promoting turnpikes, waterways, and railroads in the Old Dominion, but in 1843 the legislature terminated his position. In the meantime he had taken a major role in developing a new school in Lexington, the Virginia Military Institute, where the legislature wished to convert the state arsenal into a military college. He served as president of the board of visitors from its beginning in 1837 to 1845 and greatly influenced its curriculum, which emphasized military and engineering studies, from the beginning of its operations in 1839. From 1845 through 1849 he served as principal of another school, the Richmond Academy.

In 1849 Crozet returned to engineering work. That year the legislature incorporated the Blue Ridge Railroad and the Virginia and Tennessee, both of them lines that Crozet had championed during his tenure as the state's principal engineer. Certain that he wanted to direct construction of one of the two lines, he applied for and obtained appointment as chief engineer of the Blue Ridge Railroad Company. That line would traverse the Blue Ridge Mountains between Charlottesville and Staunton and would require tunnels, cuts, and an iron bridge through extremely difficult terrain. Eight years later, the project successfully completed, Crozet moved to the District of Columbia, where he worked from 1857 to 1859 with Montgomery C. Meigs on the Washington aqueduct, a system designed to supply Georgetown and Washington with water from the Great Falls of the Potomac River. Crozet's final position, in 1860 and 1861, was as chief engineer of the Virginia and Kentucky Railroad, a line intended to push west from a point in southwestern Virginia on the Virginia and Tennessee Railroad.

Already in his seventies when the Civil War began, Crozet played no active role in it, though he offered in various ways to support Virginia's efforts in the Confederacy. He died in Midlothian, Virginia. Crozet brought cutting-edge technology and engineering to America in the aftermath of the Napoleonic Wars and their American offshoot the War of 1812, and during his many years in America he applied his advanced technical training to his varied work. His career displayed the close relationship between civil engineering and military affairs in the nineteenth century, and it also displayed the significant state sponsorship, in the South much as in the North, of education and transportation improvements in the pre–Civil War years. He had his major impact on the engineering curricula at West Point and at Virginia Military Institute and on public works in Virginia. After his death he was honored for his work in education and transportation. A building at Virginia Military Institute was named after him, and a station, later a town, on the Blue Ridge Railroad (later the Chesapeake and Ohio) was named Crozet in 1876.

• The Claudius Crozet Papers are in the Preston Library at the Virginia Military Institute, Lexington. Crozet's publications include *A Treatise on Descriptive Geometry, for the Use of the Cadets of the United States Military Academy* (1821), *An Arithmetic for Colleges and Schools* (1848), and many papers in the annual reports of the Virginia Board of Public Works between the 1820s and the 1840s. Biographies of him are William Couper, *Claudius Crozet: Soldier—Scholar—Educator—*

Engineer (1789–1864) (1936), and Robert F. Hunter and Edwin L. Dooley, Jr., *Claudius Crozet: French Engineer in America, 1790–1864* (1989).

PETER WALLENSTEIN

CROZIER, William (19 Feb. 1855–10 Nov. 1942), army officer and technologist, was born in Carrollton, Ohio, the son of Robert Crozier, a jurist and U.S. senator, and Margaret Atkinson. Appointed from Kansas to the U.S. Military Academy at West Point in 1872, Crozier graduated in 1876 with an outstanding scholarly record. His service over the next three years as a second lieutenant of artillery on the frontier included campaigns against the Sioux and the Bannocks.

Thus seasoned in traditional soldiering, Crozier returned in 1879 to West Point for a five-year stint teaching mathematics. A permanent transfer from the artillery to the Ordnance Department in 1881 brought him a promotion to first lieutenant. From 1884 to 1888, while assigned first to Watertown Arsenal in Massachusetts and then to the Office of the Chief of Ordnance in Washington, D.C., he assiduously applied his technical bent, attacking problems of ordnance engineering, designing artillery guns, and publishing a series of notable technical papers.

After Congress in 1888 approved the rehabilitation of coast defenses, Crozier spent a year in Europe studying technological advances. He was unable to find a good disappearing gun carriage that would protect guns and crews from the increasing threat of battleships, but he returned to the Office of the Chief of Ordnance in December 1889 undaunted. Promoted to captain in 1890, he reworked an unimplemented, twenty-year-old American design. The army in 1894 adopted the resultant Buffington-Crozier disappearing carriage, which remained standard for several decades.

Immersion in technical matters filled most of Crozier's fin-de-siècle decade. Assignment to the War Department's evaluative Board of Ordnance and Fortification at Sandy Hook Proving Ground, New Jersey, from 1892 to 1896 was followed by further service in Washington. As a temporary major inspecting and instructing at domestic seacoast fortifications during the Spanish-American War, he issued a widely noted, critical report on the state of the coast defenses. Growing respect for his abilities led to his appointment in 1899 as U.S. military delegate to the International Peace Conference at The Hague, where he worked in concert with navy delegate Captain Alfred Thayer Mahan to minimize concessions affecting U.S. military strength.

Crozier had not been near combat for more than twenty years, and he next sought an assignment that would take him to it. From the fall of 1899 until the following July, he served as a staff officer in the campaign against Philippine nationalists in southern Luzon. When the United States sent troops as part of an international expedition against anti-foreign Chinese "Boxers," who had besieged legations in Peking, he saw action as the chief U.S. ordnance officer until the relief of the city in August 1900.

After returning to Washington and declining a prestigious lieutenant colonelcy on the West Point faculty, Crozier was still a captain when in November 1901 Secretary of War Elihu Root picked him, over many officers more senior, for the brigadier general's position of chief of ordnance. The Ordnance Department had grown rigid and insular, selecting weapons with little regard for the opinions of the officers of the line who had to use them. Root wanted the department's "ablest, strongest, most broad-minded, vigorous, and competent administrator"—and a man with recent field service—to repair relations with the using arms (57th Cong., 1st sess., 1902, S. Doc. 387, p. 2).

Over the next fifteen years, combat arms officers' influence in the weapons selection process seemed to increase, as Crozier included infantry and artillery officers in various weapons evaluation panels. The chief of ordnance even spent a potentially broadening ten months in 1912–1913 as president of the Army War College, a bastion of line officers. Yet he actually paid little more than polite attention to the opinions of the line, and the locus of decision-making power did not shift. Crozier's belief in the efficacy of the military technician's knowledge ran deep. Controlling the choice of arms was a means for technical officers to assert a professional parity with line officers, who equated soldierly professionalism with fighting and not with logistical support functions.

Crozier did show some willingness to open his department to outside influence when Congress pressed him to reduce costs at his manufacturing arsenals. From 1909 to 1913 Crozier employed followers of Frederick Winslow Taylor to install scientific management at Watertown Arsenal. Ordnance officers commanding the other arsenals were receptive to the new methods, but they insisted on implementing their own variations without the direct aid of outside experts. The chief of ordnance, despite his enthusiasm for the results at Watertown, condoned this wariness of control by civilian management engineers. Opposition by organized labor brought congressional restriction of scientific management at the arsenals in 1915.

By that time European nations were fighting World War I, and Crozier had begun to warn an unreceptive Congress of the need to prepare for greatly expanded munitions production that his arsenals and the rest of his small peacetime department were not equipped to undertake. A large-scale, industrial-based war, he realized, would require production by a great number of civilian contractors. He understood that overall civilian coordination of competing military procurement agencies (the navy's and four army bureaus besides his own) was needed to ensure a balanced distribution of contracts lest unbridled purchasing skew production priorities and badly inflate prices.

Crozier diluted his congressional warnings by failing to alter his own cautious peacetime approach to planning for weapons procurement, and when the United States entered the war in April 1917, he found it difficult to translate his comprehension of mobilization necessities into effective action. He was enmeshed in detail and initially frustrated by a slow-moving appropriations process. As appropriations burgeoned to billions of dollars expended on thousands of contracts in the second half of 1917, tremendous growth in the size of the Ordnance Department inexorably pulled from his hands peacetime's close, comfortable control. Inundated within his department by civilians newly uniformed, he resisted intervention by external civilian mobilization agencies as a further diminution of his authority. When Secretary of War Newton D. Baker relayed one such proposal of civilian assistance in September, Crozier responded to his superior as would a schoolmaster to a student. "I explained to the Secretary of War," he noted for the official record, "that this Department intended to exercise a follow-up system on production, and that such a follow-up would be exercised by the Department as a contracting agency on behalf of the United States" (file 334.8/319, General Correspondence, 1915–1931, Records of the Office of the Chief of Ordnance, National Archives).

Crozier's promotion to major general in October 1917 came despite organizational problems in the Ordnance Department and inefficiencies in munitions production. Legal and administrative impediments stemming from the government's slow shift to a war footing contributed much to production delays but could not bear the full causative weight that the chief of ordnance sought to put on them. While Crozier was in the midst of highly publicized, defensive testimony in December before a hostile Senate committee investigating War Department performance, Baker appointed him to a newly created War Council and ended his responsibility for running the Ordnance Department.

The War Council, composed of senior War Department officials, had a vague charter to deal with "larger problems," including relations with the American Expeditionary Forces in France. At Baker's direction, Crozier spent from late January through May 1918 on a fact-finding trip to Europe, which conveniently removed him from involvement in home front controversy. Crozier retained the title of chief of ordnance until July 1918, when he was appointed a major general of the line and assigned to command the Northeastern Department.

After retiring in January 1919, he defended his stewardship of the Ordnance Department in *Ordnance and the World War: A Contribution to the History of American Preparedness* (1920). Long accustomed to a social life among eminent civilians, he maintained such contacts widely over the next two decades, traveling frequently about the world with his wife, Mary Hoyt Williams, whom he had married in 1913. (They had no children.) He died in the locale of his greatest prominence as a soldier, Washington, D.C.

Crozier attained the leadership of the Ordnance Department on the basis of his brilliance as a technologist, his administrative ability, and the breadth of his military experience. Like most of his peers, however,

he did not transcend professional intraservice rivalry. His legitimate concerns over the place of the technical officer in the modern army led him to rigid behavior rather than toward a useful accommodation with line officers. During his unexceeded seventeen-year tenure as chief of ordnance, he sought to enhance his professional status by dominating his department and exerting power over the combat arms. At ease in civilian society, he was nonetheless protective against significant civilian penetration of his professional military preserve, which existed between traditional soldiering and the civilian business-technical world. As modern war took on greater organizational and economic complexity, Crozier's concern for professional status hindered him in working with other elements of the army and industrial experts. His fall in the face of the challenges of World War I thus has come to seem the result not just of personal shortcomings and national unpreparedness but of tensions within the military profession.

• No known collection of Crozier's personal papers exists. Official material is in the Records of the Office of the Chief of Ordnance and other U.S. Army records in the National Archives. Details of his service are in George W. Cullum, *Biographical Register of the Officers and Graduates of the U.S. Military Academy . . .*, vols. 3–6 (1891–1920). On particular aspects of his career, see Calvin DeArmond Davis, *The United States and the First Hague Peace Conference* (1962); U.S. Congress, Senate, *Report from the Secretary of War Giving the Reasons for the Selection of Captain Crozier to Be Chief of Ordnance*, 57th Cong., 1st sess., 1902, S. Doc. 387; and Hugh G. J. Aitken, *Taylorism at Watertown Arsenal: Scientific Management in Action, 1908–1915* (1960). His tenure as chief of ordnance is covered in his annual War Department *Report of the Chief of Ordnance* (1902–1917) and more briefly and critically in Constance McLaughlin Green et al., *The Ordnance Department: Planning Munitions for War*, United States Army in World War II series (1955); Harvey A. DeWeerd, *President Wilson Fights His War: World War I and the American Intervention* (1968); and Edward M. Coffman, *The War to End All Wars: The American Military Experience in World War I* (1968). Obituaries highlighting his technical achievements and his personality, respectively, appear in *Army Ordnance*, Jan.–Feb. 1943, pp. 77, 80; and *Assembly*, Jan. 1944, insert, pp. 3–4.

TERRENCE J. GOUGH

CROZIER, William John (24 May 1892–2 Nov. 1955), biologist, was born in New York City, the son of William George Crozier and Bessie Mackay. He attended local public schools and City College, where he demonstrated a strong interest in chemistry and biology and was voted "ablest man" in the class of 1912. During this time he also worked as a laboratory assistant in the U.S. Bureau of Fisheries, and began a long friendship with Selig Hecht.

Crozier did his graduate work in the Harvard University Zoology Department under George Howard Parker, a pioneer in experimental analysis of the functions of the invertebrate nervous system and a believer in the application of physics and chemistry to biological problems. Following completion of his

Ph.D. in 1915, he spent a short period in France, where he assisted the idiosyncratic Cleveland surgeon George Washington Crile in developing techniques to manage surgical shock. On his return he married Blanche Benjamin in June 1915; they had two children. Crozier served from 1915 to 1918 as resident naturalist at Harvard's Bermuda Biological Station. He then worked as assistant professor of physiology at the University of Illinois College of Medicine (1918–1919), assistant professor of zoology at the University of Chicago (1919–1920), and, beginning in 1920, professor of zoology at Rutgers College. In 1925 Parker brought him back to Harvard as associate professor to build a program in general physiology.

In the 1920s general physiology was a promising but vague scientific rubric promoted most vigorously by the Rockefeller Institute biologist Jacques Loeb. It signified an aggressively experimental attack on the fundamental problems of biology and behavior, utilizing physical chemistry to predict and control changes in a wide range of biological systems, from bacteria to vertebrates. Crozier identified himself closely with Loeb. He studied the responses of marine invertebrates to chemical changes in their environments, tropisms in both invertebrates and in mammals, and the effects of temperature on the rate of response in cold-blooded organisms. He sought to demonstrate that the functions of whole organisms were determinate and strove to deduce the contours of the chemical reactions that controlled vital processes from patterns of responses. He believed that this form of physiology offered the possibility of bypassing the seemingly endless analytic programs of cytologists and biochemists to attain a reductionistic account of life.

Crozier's research program appealed to influential senior biologists, foundation executives, and Harvard graduate students. On Loeb's death in 1924, Crozier became coeditor of Loeb's *Journal of General Physiology*. Three years later, after declining T. H. Morgan's offer to organize a physiology program at Caltech, he became a full professor at Harvard. There, as head of the construction committee (1928–1932), he coordinated a Rockefeller-funded, multimillion-dollar project to consolidate the university's life science programs through construction of new biological laboratories. Utilizing the resources of Harvard and the National Research Council, Crozier brought a number of young researchers into his Laboratory of General Physiology, where he encouraged individual creativity, interdisciplinary research, and the belief that the major problems of biology could quickly be solved through strategic problem choice, energetic experimentation, and quantitative analysis. In some cases, this approach worked. Crozier fostered B. F. Skinner's first work on operant conditioning, Gregory Pincus's explorations of in vitro fertilization and artificial parthenogenesis in mammals, and the investigations of the dynamics of photosynthesis made by E. S. Castle, William Arnold, and Tracy French.

Crozier's scientific advocacy was bound to a narrowly personal ambition, and his antagonism toward intellectual conservatives was to a considerable degree an expression of lower-class resentment toward the social superiority of many of his Harvard colleagues. These characteristics became problematic in the aftermath of a personal and institutional midlife crisis. In 1933 Crozier obtained a divorce and in 1934 married his junior colleague Hudson Hoagland's sister Louise; they had one child. At the same time he sought to make a new beginning in science. He gave up his administrative responsibilities for an unencumbered research professorship and began a new experimental program on visual perception.

This second scientific career did not work out as he had hoped. His perceptual research was superficial and had little impact. Moreover, he soon lost all institutional influence at Harvard. One of the colleagues he had alienated in the 1920s was James Bryant Conant, a Bostonian who believed in tradition and hierarchy, and an organic chemist who studied photosynthesis from a structural perspective that clashed with that of Crozier's group. In 1936, as Harvard's president, Conant presided over a reorganization of the biology program, a key element of which was the elimination of the Department of General Physiology.

Crozier spent World War II in the Pacific as an operations analyst with the rank of colonel. On his return to Harvard he initiated a long series of experiments on visual perception in humans, using his wife as the primary subject. He published nothing in the five years before his death in Belmont, Massachusetts, from heart disease.

Although he had limited success as a scientist, Crozier was important both for pioneering a reductionist program in biology and for exploring how to be an independent scientific intellectual within the modern university. B. F. Skinner fictionalized this latter problem in *Walden Two*; his character T. E. Frazier, the irascible, alienated, and messianic designer of the community, was largely modeled on Crozier.

• A substantial and illuminating collection of Crozier's correspondence is in the Harvard University Archives. Crozier published more than 300 scientific papers. He provided a general orientation to his perspective in W. J. Crozier and Hudson Hoagland, "The Study of Living Organisms," in *The Handbook of General Experimental Psychology*, ed. Carl Murchison (1934), pp. 3–108. See also W. J. Crozier, *Déterminisme et variabilité dans le comportement des organismes*, trans. Jacques Monod (1935). The only biography is Hudson Hoagland and R. T. Mitchell, "William John Crozier: 1892–1955," *American Journal of Psychology* 69 (1956): 135–38. General physiology at Harvard is discussed in Philip J. Pauly, *Controlling Life: Jacques Loeb and the Engineering Ideal in Biology* (1987).

PHILIP J. PAULY

CRUDUP, Arthur (24 Aug. 1905–28 Mar. 1974), blues singer and songwriter, was born Arthur Crudup in Forest, Mississippi, between Jackson and Meridian, the son of Minnie Louise Crudup, an unmarried domestic worker. His father was reputed to be a musician, but Crudup recalled seeing him only twice.

Raised by his mother and growing up in poverty, Crudup began singing both blues and religious music around age ten. In 1916 he and his mother moved to Indianapolis. After she became ill, Crudup dropped out of school and took a job in a foundry at age thirteen.

By his own account Crudup did not start playing guitar until around 1937, by which time he had returned to the South, married and divorced his first wife, Annie Bell Reed, and taken work as a farm hand. Supposedly, he found a guitar with only two strings, and one by one added the other four while picking up rudimentary chords from a local musician known as "Papa Harvey." Despite his limited skills on guitar, Crudup found musical employment, supplementing his weekday job by playing at weekend dances.

In 1939 or 1940 he went to Chicago, possibly on tour with a gospel group. Unable to find a steady job, he took to music in desperation, playing the streets for handouts. In 1941, as he was trying to make enough money to return south, recording artist Peter "Doctor" Clayton heard him playing on the street and summoned veteran race-record producer Lester Melrose to hear him. Melrose offered Crudup $10 to play a "house party" that evening. The house party, actually an audition, included Tampa Red, Big Bill Broonzy, Lil Green, Lonnie Johnson, Memphis Minnie, Washboard Sam, and others—the cream of Chicago blues talent at that time. After the audition Melrose signed Crudup to two contracts, one as recording artist, the other as songwriter. On 11 September 1941 Crudup cut his first four sides for RCA Victor's Bluebird subsidiary. He played an acoustic guitar and was accompanied by Joe McCoy, who did a vocal imitation of a bass. Three of the sides, "Death Valley Blues," "If I Get Lucky," and "Black Pony Blues," are now considered classic examples of down-home blues.

The records sold well, and on 15 April 1942 Crudup was called back for a second Bluebird session, this time playing an electric guitar and accompanied by noted session bassist Ransom Knowling. The session yielded six issued sides, including one of the greatest of all train blues, "Mean Old 'Frisco Blues." A 15 December 1944 Chicago session with drummer Melvin Draper produced another blues that would become traditional, "Rock Me Mama."

During World War II, Crudup was one of the only blues artists included in the U.S. Armed Forces Radio Services transcription series—although his songs were wrongly credited to "Art Crudux."

A postwar session in February 1946 with drummer Armand "Jump" Jackson yielded "So Glad You're Mine" and "Ethel Mae," also considered classics, released on RCA Victor. A September 1946 session, teaming Crudup with bassist Knowling and drummer Judge Riley, produced Crudup's best-known song, "That's All Right [Mama]"—a candidate, according to some critics, for the first rock and roll recording. The successful trio stayed together through 1952, putting out notable hits, "Train Fare Blues," "Hand Me Down My Walking Cane" (also known as "Look on Yonder Wall"), "Shout, Sister, Shout," and "My Baby Left Me."

Crudup received payments for each session, but the money from record sales went to Melrose and RCA, so from 1941 to 1945 Crudup alternated between menial day jobs in Chicago and farm work in Mississippi.

While in Chicago he married again, but little is known about his second wife. Crudup told family members years later that she had been murdered. On one of his trips back to Forest, Mississippi, after the death of his second wife, he bumped into Annie Bell, his first wife, whose second husband also had died under violent circumstances. A year later, probably around 1945, Crudup moved back to Mississippi, remarried Annie Bell, and resumed full-time farming. With seven children from Annie Bell's second marriage, the Crudups went on to have five children of their own (one of whom died in infancy) and remained together until Annie Bell died in 1963. Crudup remained a part-time musician, performing on "King Biscuit Time," a popular midday show on KFFA Radio in Helena, Arkansas, in the mid-1940s. He struck up an informal musical collaboration with "King Biscuit" star Sonny Boy Williamson No. 2 and in 1948 met slide guitarist Elmore James, who was living in Belzoni. Crudup, Williamson, and James began playing together informally in what must have been one of the most formidable blues trios ever assembled.

Crudup did further recording in the South in 1952, 1953, and 1954, but his style was dated and the records met with minimal success. Discouraged, he withdrew from recording. Ironically, at that same time, Elvis Presley remade "That's All Right Mama," helping to touch off the rock-and-roll revolution that Crudup is thought by some to have fathered.

Around 1954 Crudup left Mississippi and began contracting and transporting migrant labor for seasonal farm work near Orlando, Florida, and Franktown, Virginia, where he eventually settled. In 1959 he recorded an album, *Mean Ol' Frisco*, released on the Fire label, but it did little for Crudup, and Fire went bankrupt soon after. As the 1960s began, he continued to live in Franktown on Virginia's Delmarva Peninsula, performing every so often in his own small dance hall, built next to his house, or sitting in with his sons' band, the Malibus.

As the nationwide blues revival gathered steam in the 1960s, Robert Koester, who had been recording rediscovered blues artists, wrote Crudup to propose a session in Chicago. Crudup accepted and went to Chicago in 1967 to appear at the University of Chicago's Rhythm and Blues Festival and record for Koester's Delmark label. Signing with Dick Waterman's booking agency, Crudup successfully made the transition to the blues-revival festival circuit, playing major U.S. festivals and touring Europe and Australia to much acclaim.

Meanwhile, Waterman, the American Guild of Artists and Composers and other concerned parties sought to help Crudup collect royalties he was long due. Although no final settlement was ever reached,

Broadcast Music, Incorporated (BMI) did make a substantial payment to Crudup. Ironically the end of his poverty coincided with the end of his life. Diagnosed with insulin-dependent diabetes in 1972, he suffered a series of small heart attacks starting about that same time. He was being treated for heart trouble at a hospital in Nassawadox, Virginia, when he suffered a fatal heart attack. He was buried in Franktown.

Best known in rock history as Elvis Presley's idol, Arthur "Big Boy" Crudup was a transitional artist whose recordings bridged the era of down-home Delta blues and the dawn of electric blues. If he had a larger role in the beginnings of rock, it was in bringing electric-guitar blues to the forefront as a marketable sound for the recording industry. In his heyday Crudup recorded more than eighty sides, which sold primarily to the African-American blues and rhythm-and-blues markets. A limited guitarist who favored the key of E, he tended to rework the same instrumental figures time and again, which for better or for worse made his music consistent and predictable.

Despite his hulking size, Crudup had a keen, high-pitched voice that retained traces of the field holler. With early help from Tampa Red, Crudup found that he had a remarkable talent for blues composition. Although Crudup himself became a symbol of economic exploitation and racial injustice, his songs became staples for blues, rock, and even country artists, including Presley, Creedence Clearwater Revival, and B. B. King.

• For more information about Crudup, see Margaret McKee and Fred Chisenhall, *Beale Black and Blue: Life and Music on Black America's Main Street* (1981), and Sheldon Harris, *Blues Who's Who: A Biographical Dictionary of Blues Singers* (1989). For an interview, see Mike Leadbitter, "Big Boy Crudup," *Blues Unlimited*, no. 75 (Sept. 1970): 16–18, no. 76 (Oct. 1970): 18–19, and no. 77 (Nov. 1970): 19. For a discography, see Robert M. W. Dixon and John Godrich, *Blues and Gospel Records: 1902–1943* (1982), and Leadbitter and Neil Slaven, *Blues Records, 1943–1966* (1968). For a sample of his music, try *Arthur "Big Boy" Crudup: That's All Right Mama* (RCA Heritage Bluebird 61043-2) and *Arthur Big Boy Crudup: Mean Old Frisco* (Charley Blues Masterworks, vol. 50, CDBM50). For a discussion of Crudup's financial problems, see Bruce Cook, *Listen to the Blues* (1973). An obituary is in *Living Blues*, no. 16 (Spring 1974): 5.

BILL McCULLOCH
BARRY LEE PEARSON

CRUGER, Henry, Jr. (22 Nov. 1739–24 Apr. 1827), merchant, member of Parliament, mayor of Bristol, England, and New York state senator, was born in New York City, the son of Henry Cruger and Elizabeth Harris. The Cruger family had long been prominent in the economic and political life of New York, and Henry Cruger, Jr., enjoyed an assured position in the Atlantic community throughout his career. His paternal grandfather had migrated in 1698 from Bristol, England, to New York, where he became a prosperous merchant and shipowner and also an alderman and mayor. His father was also a merchant and shipowner trading between England, North America, and the

West Indies as well as a member of the provincial assembly and the governor's council. John Cruger, his uncle, was the first president of the New York Chamber of Commerce, an alderman and mayor of New York, a member and speaker of the provincial assembly, and a delegate to the Stamp Act Congress of 1765. John Harris Cruger, an older brother, succeeded their father as a member of the governor's council.

Cruger entered King's College (now Columbia University) in the class of 1758 but left before graduation. In 1757 his father placed him in the counting house of Henry Cruger and Company in Bristol, England, so that he might become familiar with the family firm engaged in the American trade. Becoming an energetic and enterprising merchant, he married in 1765 Hannah Peach, the daughter of Samuel Peach, a wealthy Bristol linen merchant who fostered his son-in-law's political interests. In 1765 Cruger was elected to the Common Council of Bristol and was named sheriff of the city in 1766–1767. Because his family business was adversely affected by American non-importation agreements in response to the Stamp Act, Cruger served in a delegation of Bristol merchants appearing before Parliament to protest that act. On that occasion Cruger was shocked by the ignorance concerning trade and American affairs evidenced by members of Parliament.

During the late 1760s and early 1770s, Cruger and his father-in-law became identified with the radical movement in Bristol against Parliament and the ministry. He supported John Wilkes, which caused Lord North to dub him "a hot Wilkite," and he espoused such measures as annual Parliaments and the instruction of members of Parliament by their constituents when voting on legislation. When Cruger stood for election to the House of Commons from Bristol in 1774 as an opposition candidate to the ministry, he was enthusiastically supported by the poorer classes, which included artisans, Methodists, and what his opponents called the "alehouse gang" and "vagabond tradesmen." He declined to stand with Edmund Burke, a candidate for the other Bristol seat, though many of his supporters also voted for Burke, whose followers had exploited Cruger's popularity as the other opposition candidate. In the bitterly fought election, during which Cruger's personal appearance and manners as well as his "youthful follies" were condemned, he nevertheless received the largest number of votes and took his seat in Commons along with Burke. The canard that Cruger in a postelection address at Bristol exclaimed, "I say ditto to Mr. Burke," has been disproved. Even though one of Burke's prominent supporters recognized Cruger as being "a proper colleague" and "a man of spirit and understanding in commercial affairs," the two men were uncongenial. Burke had befriended Cruger's family while agent for the colony of New York, but Cruger held that Burke had been an unsatisfactory agent, had failed to offer any friendly advice or useful information to the colony, and was, furthermore, "crafty and selfish." Moreover, differences in political philosophy could not be bridged between Burke, the conservative Whig with aristocratic connections, and Cruger, the American colonial with radical associations. Thus the lack of cooperation between the two men in Commons contributed to both being defeated in 1780.

In Parliament Cruger did not support radical measures nor join the opposition but took an independent and moderate stand. Repelled apparently by the language and tactics of his radical colleagues, he resolved to join none of the violent parties and to be prudent in his opposition. Cruger may also have thought that a less strident stand might influence the government to take a more moderate position on the American question. He recognized the need for the superintending and regulating power of Parliament in imperial matters, but he questioned the wisdom of taxing American colonials. He deplored, however, many of the proceedings in America against British authority and defended the conduct of the Loyalists, several of whom were members of his family. In 1775 his father left New York and settled in Bristol. His uncle John Cruger remained in America but withdrew from New York City and public life for the duration of the War for Independence. John Harris Cruger, his older brother, was a lieutenant colonel of Brigadier Oliver De Lancey's First Battalion and fought valiantly with the British forces in South Carolina. But despite the loyalism of the Cruger family, Henry Cruger, Jr., continued to seek peace and reconciliation between Britain and America and by 1780 had concluded that American independence should be granted.

Even though Cruger was popular with his constituents and had diligently attended to their interests, he was defeated in the parliamentary election of 1780. Cruger attributed the defeat to his American ties, but Burke's friends contributed by withholding their support in revenge for Cruger's refusal to stand with Burke in 1774. Defeated again in a by-election in 1781, Cruger served as mayor of Bristol in 1781–1782. With the coming of Anglo-American peace in 1783, Cruger's loyalty to Britain did not prevent his congratulating the Americans, whom he still called his "countrymen," for having won their "liberty and independence." Owing to the depletion of his personal fortune during what he termed the "accursed war," he hastened to advise his former clients in the United States that his firm would again welcome their trade.

In 1784 Cruger, as a follower of William Pitt, was again returned to Parliament, where he supported Pitt's efforts for financial and parliamentary reform and sought to promote trade between Great Britain and the United States. With much of the American trade shifting from Bristol to Liverpool, Cruger's efforts did not help him recover the losses he had suffered during the war. In straitened circumstances, he applied to Pitt in 1789 for a consular appointment in the United States. Disappointed in this effort, he decided to leave England, for as he had written his brother-in-law in 1788, "my heart still cleaves to New York." Advising his Bristol constituents in March 1790 that he would not stand again for election to Par-

liament, he left England in April while still a member of Parliament. Without ever having renounced his allegiance to the king, Cruger was elected as a Federalist to the New York State Senate in 1792 and served for one term. Having retired from the mercantile and shipping business, he lived quietly and obscurely in New York City until his death there.

Cruger's career is striking because it appears to be one of irreconcilable loyalties. As a native American he faithfully represented a major British port in Parliament while defending American interests and rights during and after the War for Independence. To Cruger, whose motto was "Cruger, Trade and Liberty," loyalty to an interdependent Atlantic community was the best guarantee of freedom, peace, and prosperity, and transcended parochial loyalties.

With his first wife, Hannah Peach, who died in 1767, Cruger had one son. With his second wife, Elizabeth Blair, whom he married sometime before leaving England and who died soon after his return to the United States, he had one daughter. He married in 1799 Caroline Smith, who survived him and with whom he had four children.

• Although there is no collection of Cruger papers, Henry C. Van Schaack's *Henry Cruger: The Colleague of Edmund Burke* (1859) contains several letters and parliamentary speeches by Cruger as well as important information about the family. The most comprehensive account of Henry Cruger, Jr., is the sketch by John Brooke in *The House of Commons, 1754–1790*, ed. Sir Lewis Namier and John Brooke, vol. 2 (2 vols., 1964); the political history of the Bristol constituency by J. A. Cannon in vol. 1 of the same work provides valuable background. P. T. Underdown, "Henry Cruger and Edmund Burke: Colleagues and Rivals at the Bristol Election of 1774," in the *William and Mary Quarterly*, 3d ser., 15 (1958): 14–34, throws much light on Cruger and his political career in England. Lorenzo Sabine, *Biographical Sketches of Loyalists of the American Revolution* (2 vols., 1864), and Gregory Palmer, *Biographical Sketches of Loyalists of the American Revolution* (1984), contain information pertaining to other members of the Cruger family who were Loyalists.

MALCOLM LESTER

CRUMBINE, Samuel Jay (17 Sept. 1862–12 July 1954), physician and public health reformer, was born in Venango County, Pennsylvania, the son of Samuel Jacob Krumbine and Sarah Mull. Crumbine's father, a blacksmith and small-scale farmer, served in the 101st Pennsylvania Infantry during the Civil War, was captured, and died in Libby Prison. Crumbine and his mother lived with his maternal grandmother until, at the age of eight, he entered the Soldiers Orphan School in Mercer, Pennsylvania. Because schoolmates called him "Crummie," he began spelling his last name with a *C*. After his graduation in 1878, Crumbine worked for a local physician and pharmacist and then moved to Cincinnati, Ohio, where he studied medicine with Dr. W. E. Lewis. Upon the completion of his medical studies in the mid-1880s he moved to Spearville, Kansas, acquired a half-interest in a drugstore, and practiced medicine. He then furthered his medical education at the Cincinnati College of Medicine, where he graduated first in his class in 1889. The following year he married Katherine Zuercher. The couple settled first in Spearville and then moved to Dodge City, where Crumbine entered private practice; they had two children.

In 1899 Crumbine received an appointment to the Kansas State Board of Health. He served as a board member until 1904, when he was named its secretary and executive director, necessitating a move to Topeka. By 1907 he had abandoned his private practice and devoted all his time to his public health work.

Crumbine had few precedents to guide him as he began his work as head of the state board of health (part time, 1904–1907; full time, 1907–1923), giving him the opportunity to shape the direction of public health work in Kansas. His approach to public health rested on his ability to capture the attention of the public and keep politics out of the board of health. He generated support for his public health crusades through the cultivation and skillful use of support from different places, including local women's clubs, individual newspaper editors, Boy Scout troups, medical groups, universities, and the state legislature.

One of his earliest programs grew out of a report published on the spread of typhoid fever among soldiers during the Spanish-American War. That report identified the fly as a carrier of typhoid fever. The Fly-Control Campaign, as it was first called, was preceded by a survey to collect information on the state's fly population. Armed with the knowledge gained from the survey, the board of health launched an intensive public health education program dubbed "Swat the Fly" in 1905, focusing on the fly and its relation to the public's health. The fly swatter made its debut into American life during this campaign. A Boy Scout troop leader from Weir City, Kansas, attached a square of wire screening to an advertising stick. His scout troop delivered one of these contraptions to every household so that Weir City residents could swipe at the fly with the "fly bat." "Swat the Fly" captured the imagination of his fellow Kansans and was adopted by other health departments around the country.

The basic components of this campaign became the model for other public health drives launched during Crumbine's years with the state board of health and, ultimately, helped him acquire a national reputation in the field of public health. Other catch phrases associated with his efforts to improve the health of Kansas citizens that were often adopted nationwide were "Bat the Rat," "Don't Spit on the Sidewalk," and "Sleep with Your Window Open."

In addition to using slogans, Crumbine devised other projects to bring health information to the public. The board of health distributed monthly bulletins identifying various health problems and discussing the elimination or reduction of these problems. Crumbine also disseminated information through newspaper articles and songs.

In 1915 the board of health established one of the earliest state child hygiene divisions in the country. Focused on the role of maternal education in reducing infant mortality, the division sponsored the appointment of juvenile health officers, the establishment of Better Baby Clinics and Little Mother's Leagues, and participation in the 1918 national Children's Year Campaign. Other important campaigns during Crumbine's tenure on the board of health included an antituberculosis crusade (1906); the drive for food, drug, water, sewage (1907), and mining district (1917) regulations; and the establishment of a visiting nurse program.

From 1911 to 1919 Crumbine served as dean of the Kansas Medical School. In 1915 he held the presidency of the Association of American Dairy, Food and Drug Officials. During World War I he served on the state Council of Defense and oversaw the War Department's efforts to control venereal disease in six western states. Crumbine's efforts to provide public information in Kansas on the existence and prevention of venereal disease provoked a public outcry. The controversy exploded just as the state entered into a period of political turmoil. The intrusion of politics into the staffing and operation of the state board of health forced his resignation as director.

Crumbine then moved to New York City to work with the American Child Health Association (ACHA), which was established when the American Association for the Study and Prevention of Infant Mortality merged with the Child Health Organization of America in 1923. Under the leadership of Secretary of Commerce Herbert Hoover, the new organization transformed the parent groups into a dynamic association for the promotion of child health and welfare. Crumbine came to ACHA as head of the Division of Public Health Relations. By 1925 he was the general executive of ACHA. A pioneering study of child health programs in eighty-six cities, which resulted in the development of a checklist for community child health activities, a School Health Study that evaluated school health programs, and an investigation of conditions relating to child health in Puerto Rico, were among the projects carried out by ACHA under his leadership.

After ACHA discontinued operation in 1936, Crumbine went into semiretirement, serving as a consultant for the Save the Children Federation and the Paper Cup and Container Institute until his death in Jackson Heights (Queens), New York. Throughout his professional life, Crumbine played an important role in the popularization of health information and was well known for his ability to stir public action on important health issues.

• A collection of materials relating both to Crumbine's Kansas years and his work with the American Child Health Association is in the Samuel J. Crumbine Collection of the Clendening History of Medicine Library at the University of Kansas Medical Center. Information about his work with the American Child Health Association can be found in the American Child Health Association papers in the Herbert Hoover Presidential Library, West Branch, Iowa. In addition to his autobiography, *Frontier Doctor: The Autobiography of a Pioneer on the Frontier of Public Health* (1948), his publications include *Graded Lessons in Physiology and Hygiene*, written with William C. Krohn (1912); *The Most Nearly Perfect Food: The Story of Milk*, written with James A. Tobey (1929); and *The Historical Background of Public Health in Kansas* (1946). An extended discussion of Crumbine and his place in the history of public health in Kansas can be found in Thomas N. Bonner, *The Kansas Doctor: A Century of Pioneering* (1959). Obituaries are in the *Kansas City Star*, 17 July 1954; the *New York Times*, 14 July 1954; and the *New York State Journal of Medicine* (15 Aug. 1954).

PATRICIA MOONEY-MELVIN

CRUMMELL, Alexander (3 Mar. 1819–10 Sept. 1898), clergyman, activist, and Pan-Africanist, was born in New York City, the son of Charity Hicks, a freeborn woman of Long Island, New York, and Boston Crummell, an African of the Temne people, probably from the region that is now Sierra Leone. Boston Crummell had been captured and brought to the United States as a youth. The circumstances of his emancipation are not clear, but it is said that he simply refused to serve his New York owners any longer after reaching adulthood. Boston Crummell established a small oyster house in the African Quarter of New York. Alexander Crummell received his basic education at the African Free School in Manhattan. In 1835 he traveled to Canaan, New Hampshire, along with his friends Thomas Sidney and Henry Highland Garnet, to attend the newly established Noyes Academy, but shortly after their arrival, the school was destroyed by local residents, who were angered by its policy of integration. He resumed his education at the Oneida Institute, established by the reformer Beriah Green in Upstate New York. Encouraged by his pastor, Rev. Peter Williams, Jr., an Episcopal priest, Crummell applied for admission to the General Theological Seminary of the Protestant Episcopal church in New York City. Rejected for purely racial reasons, Crummell sought out private instruction from sympathetic clergymen in Providence and Boston, attended lectures unofficially at Yale University, and was elevated to the status of deacon in 1842.

Crummell was ordained a priest in 1844, but there were few among the Episcopal clergy who accorded him the respect due his office. As a young pastor in Providence, Rhode Island, during 1841 and 1842, he began to show the stubbornness, pride, and intellectual toughness that were his prime temperamental traits. The exact date of his first marriage to Sarah Mabitt Elston is unknown, but probably took place sometime in 1841. Also uncertain are the exact birth dates of their children, who numbered at least five. Their first child was born and died during the scant year the Crummells spent in attempting to develop a congregation in Philadelphia in 1844. The young couple moved to New York in 1845 but was continually dogged by poverty, hunger, and racial discrimination.

Crummell had participated in the antislavery movement from the time he was a boy, when he worked in the New York offices of the American Anti-Slavery Society. In 1838, along with his brother Henry, he represented the Eleventh Ward in a public meeting called by the black community of New York, and he represented the same constituency at a meeting of the New York State Anti-Slavery Society in Utica that same year. He worked as the New England correspondent for the *Colored American* in the early 1840s. During these same years he participated in the convention movement among black Americans. Like Samuel Cornish, the esteemed leader of black New Yorkers who had cofounded *Freedom's Journal* in 1827, Crummell opposed efforts to replace the black convention movement with the American Moral Reform Society. He belonged to that faction of black activists who identified themselves as "race men," working through separate organizations for the specific interests of people of African descent.

In 1847 the rooms in which Crummell's congregation, the Church of the Messiah, worshipped were destroyed by fire, and he went to England to raise funds for a new church by lecturing on the antislavery circuit. With the support of a committee of distinguished British philanthropists, he established a fund for the church, but he also set up a separate fund to support his apparently longstanding ambition to study at Oxford or Cambridge. He immediately began reviewing classical languages with retired clergyman Thomas Fry of Bath. He also began making arrangements to bring over his wife and children, lending credence to the accusation that his plans from the beginning were more ambitious than a mere fundraising tour.

Crummell's experiences in England were comparatively pleasant despite poverty, illness, and the minor humiliations and thoughtless condescensions he and his family occasionally experienced. Admitted to Queens' College, Cambridge, he attended lectures on moral philosophy by William Whewell, the famous scientist and polymath. Crummell's studies were disrupted by ill health, the difficult pregnancies of his wife, and the death of one of his children. He was further distracted by his travels on the antislavery circuit, which extended far from Cambridge. While uncompromisingly militant in his opposition to slavery, he did not present himself as an authority on the conditions of the slaves, often preferring to focus his lectures on the problem of "caste" encountered by the free black community.

Crummell's preaching and lecturing career advanced splendidly, but his academic performance suffered. His achievements in classical and biblical languages were not uniformly excellent, and his work in mathematics was less than mediocre. He was awarded the bachelor's degree by special examination in the spring of 1853, as were a number of other students. Early that summer, he surprised many of his supporters when he left for Liberia, West Africa, as a missionary of the Protestant Episcopal Church of the United States and under the financial sponsorship of that body. Crummell's opposition to colonization was well known, but he explained that he wished to bring up his children "amid the political institutions of black men."

Crummell's prickly disposition and contentious temperament were not improved by the rigors of frontier life. He suffered from heart ailments, fevers, varicose veins, and "liver complaint." Nonetheless he demonstrated tremendous energy, often embarking on long treks into the bush, working variously as a farmer, preacher, schoolmaster, politician, and small businessman, and toiling over vitriolic lucubrations regarding his enemies. He quarreled constantly and bitterly with his bishop, John Payne, a white man from Virginia, accusing him of color prejudice and condescension. Payne accused Crummell of conspiring to usurp his authority and of refusing to work with the native population. True, Crummell preferred to work in the capital, Monrovia, rather than in isolated missionary outposts. It is said, however, that he was an effective preacher before native audiences, and that as administrator of the agricultural school at Cape Palmas, he met with remarkable success.

Although Crummell claimed he had no political ambitions, it is clear he hoped to have an influence on the political philosophy and intellectual life of the society. He envisioned a career as a scholar statesman and pinned his hopes on the new college that was to be erected in Monrovia. His cultural ideals and political ideology were revealed in speeches delivered in Liberia over the next decade. In "God and the Nation" (1854), he revealed an almost theocratic conception of the state. His Anglocentric biases were revealed in "The English Language in Liberia" (1860) and "The Progress of Civilization along the West Coast of Africa" (1861). "The Relations and Duty of Free Colored Men in America to Africa" (1860) is an excellent illustration of his Christian black nationalist sentiments. Another essay, "The Responsibility of the First Fathers of a Country for Its Future Life and Destiny" (1863), reveals Crummell's vision of himself as a founding father of the republic. Crummell's uplift ideology was consistent with ideas expressed in the Constitution of the African Civilization Society drafted by American black nationalists in 1861 and anticipated the aims of Marcus Garvey's Universal Negro Improvement movement of the 1920s.

Crummell's marriage, never a happy one, continued to suffer after the death of yet a third child shortly after the family's arrival in Liberia, and he was frequently alienated from his wife and children. At the time of Sarah's death in 1878 she was living separately from him in New York. Crummell's dealings with associates, both clerical and lay, went no better than his domestic affairs during these years. He nonetheless continued to produce letters, sermons, and public addresses in a style both graceful and strong, which are among the most polished examples of African-American literature in the nineteenth century.

From 4 April 1861 to 4 October 1862, Crummell toured and lectured widely in the United States on behalf of the American Colonization Society and in support of the nascent Liberia College that was to be opened as soon as funds and faculty could be assembled. He returned to Liberia despite the issuance of the Emancipation Proclamation and was appointed to the professorship of English and moral philosophy at Liberia College. Crummell was not happy with the prevailing definition of a professor's life, which involved the social supervision of high-spirited youth. Furthermore, he deeply resented the college's president, J. J. Roberts, the former president of Liberia, who meticulously logged the faculty's comings and goings. Crummell left the college for several months in 1865, claiming the need to look after the fortunes of his daughters who were studying at Oberlin College in Ohio. He also used the occasion to embark on another speaking tour in the United States, and on his return, he was relieved of his professorial duties.

Frustrated in his ambitions as a scholar, cleric, and intellectual leader, Crummell submitted to the discipline of the church hierarchy during his final years in Liberia and turned his attention to missionary work outside Monrovia. He published occasional letters in the Episcopal journal, *Spirit of Missions*, describing his preaching and travels in the back country. Crummell was committed to a policy of educating and intermarrying with the native population. He supported the assimilationist policies of President Edward James Roye, opposing Roberts and the Republican party, whom he denounced as a venal mulatto elite dedicated to keeping the natives in a permanently inferior status. Crummell's Liberian career came to an end in 1871, when Liberia experienced its first coup, led by the Roberts faction. Roye was assassinated, and Crummell, fearing for his life, was forced to flee the country.

Returning to the United States in 1872, Crummell became rector of St. Mary's Church in Washington, D.C. Seven years later he established the congregation of St. Luke's, which he served until his retirement in 1894. During this time, he was often embroiled in ecclesiastical controversies but continued to write on a variety of social and religious issues. His essay, "The Black Woman of the South: Her Neglects and Her Needs" (1883), outlines a program of moral and industrial education for the masses of black peasant women to compensate for the ravages of slavery, anticipating the issues addressed by Mary Church Terrell, president of the National Association of Colored Women, in her essay, "Club Work of Colored Women," in *Southern Workman* (Aug. 1901). In another address, "The Assassination of President Garfield" (1881), he stated his admiration for "that great political prophet, Alexander Hamilton," and expressed grave concern that "one of the deep undercurrents of American thought, in responsible circles, has been with regard to the drift of society to lawless freedom." Always an advocate of strong central government in the tradition of Hamilton and John Jay, he was critical of the democratic principles of Thomas Jefferson. In an undated sermon written in the 1880s, he expressed the opinion that "the nation's existence is endangered by insane political excitements." He believed it was the destiny of African Americans to offer a conservative balance to the radical tendencies of certain European immigrant groups.

Crummell was married in 1880 to Jennie Simpson, who played an active role in his church and social life.

After his retirement from St. Luke's, Crummell was granted a lectureship at Howard University. He served as president of the Colored Minister's Union of Washington, D.C., and worked actively in the Episcopal church on behalf of its African-American membership. Again traveling and lecturing widely, he spoke at the Atlanta and Cotton States Exposition of 1895 on the need to train indigenous African missionaries and on "Civilization as a Collateral and Indispensable Instrumentality in Planting the Christian Church in Africa." His address "The Solution of Problems, the Duty and Destiny of Man" at Wilberforce University in 1895 was a call for ceaseless intellectual struggle. In *The Souls of Black Folk* (1903), W. E. B. Du Bois recalled the impression Crummell made at Wilberforce: "Instinctively I bowed before this man, as one bows before the prophets of the world. Some seer he seemed, that came not from the crimson Past or the gray To-come, but from the pulsing Now" (p. 216).

In 1897 Crummell founded the American Negro Academy, an institution opposed to the educational policies of Booker T. Washington and committed to the vindication of the African race through scholarly publication. Although Crummell was an advocate of industrial education, he was just as strong a proponent of classical studies, the social sciences, and the liberal arts. The American Negro Academy program reflected Crummell's dedication to the development of independent black institutions, the promotion of stable nuclear families, and the development of individual character. Two of Crummell's protégés, John E. Bruce and William H. Ferris, also members of the academy, became active in the Garvey movement and continued to promote Pan-Africanism and self-help.

Crummell remained intellectually active until his death at Red Bank, New Jersey. His essays and addresses, written in a style described by John Greenleaf Whittier as "clear, classic, and chaste," provide a unique if somewhat sardonic perspective on nineteenth-century intellectual life. While Crummell contributed substantially to the African-American protest tradition, it would diminish the importance of his legacy to view him primarily as a racial protest writer. His writings, for the most part addressed to black audiences, are most often concerned with the relationship of human nature to the concept of authority, the importance of traditions and institutions to human existence, and the defense of literary culture.

• Crummell's sermons have been preserved in the collections of the Schomburg Research Center of the New York Public Library and are readily available on microfilm. His letters to the Domestic and Foreign Missionary Society are in the Archives of the Episcopal Church in Austin, Tex., and another copy is at Cuttington University College in Liberia. The Library of Congress has microfilmed Crummell's letters to the American Colonization Society, and a valuable collection of his letters is in the Jay Family Papers at Columbia University. Crummell published three books during his lifetime: *The Future of Africa* (1862), *The Greatness of Christ and Other Sermons* (1882), and *Africa and America* (1891). The best summation of his racial chauvinism is his sermon on "The Destined Superiority of the Negro" (1877). Biographies of Crummell include Luckson Ejofodomi, "The Missionary Career of Alexander Crummell in Liberia, 1853–1877" (Ph.D. diss., Boston Univ., 1974); a pamphlet by Otey M. Scruggs, *We the Children of Africa in This Land: Alexander Crummell* (1972); Gregory Rigsby, *Alexander Crummell: Pioneer in Nineteenth-Century Pan-African Thought* (1987); Wilson J. Moses, *Alexander Crummell: A Study of Civilization and Discontent* (1989); and John Oldfield, *Alexander Crummell and the Creation of an African-American Church in Liberia* (1990). An obituary by John E. Bruce is in the *Colored American*, 24 Sept. 1898.
WILSON J. MOSES

CRUMP, Edward Hull (2 Oct. 1874–16 Oct. 1954), political boss, was born in Holly Springs, Mississippi, the son of Edward Hull Crump, a Confederate veteran and planter, and Mary C. Nelms. Crump's father died when Crump was three years old, and the family, struggling against poverty, gave up the plantation and moved into town. As a young man, Crump worked in a variety of odd jobs, including plowing with a team of oxen, selling fruit to passengers on the railroad, and working as a printer's assistant. At the age of sixteen he became a bookkeeper in a country store in Lula, Mississippi, and at age seventeen he moved to Memphis.

Initially Crump worked in a harness shop, and after eight years he bought out the owners. In 1902 he married Bessie Byrd McLean; they had three children. As a popular young man in the rough city of Memphis, he soon developed a following and served as a delegate to the Democratic state conventions in 1902 and 1904. He ran successfully for city council in 1905 and served as a member of the Memphis Board of Public Works that year and as fire and police commissioner in 1907. He campaigned on a reform platform, fighting against the corrupt combination of public utilities and city government.

In 1909 Crump was elected mayor of Memphis, serving from 1910 to 1916. W. C. Handy, "Father of the Blues," composed a marching song for Crump that was later known as the "Memphis Blues." Crump used the political machine he built to support various candidates over the next forty years, sometimes holding paid political office himself. In 1920 he established an insurance, investment, mortgage loan, and real estate business, the E. H. Crump Company, which maintained its offices in downtown Memphis near city hall. A delegate to the Democratic national conventions in 1912, 1924, 1928, 1936, 1940, and 1948, he was also treasurer of Shelby County, 1917–1923; a member of the Democratic National Committee, 1936–1945; and a member the Seventy-second and Seventy-third Congresses, 1931–1935. In 1939 he was again elected mayor of Memphis, but one minute after being sworn in on 1 January 1940, he resigned to turn the post over to a Crump loyalist, Walter Chandler, who had been unable to run because at election time he was a member of Congress.

Crump brought many improvements to Memphis, including a diminished crime rate and a system of municipally owned public utilities. In the 1910s Memphis was known as a wide-open town with flourishing speakeasies and brothels, but in the late 1930s, when Crump moved against public vice, the city became more respectable. Crump drew considerable public attention, particularly in his later years, with his curly white hair, straw hat, and bushy black eyebrows. His critics charged him with repeatedly using corrupt methods, such as false registrations of deceased voters, to "deliver" 40,000–60,000 votes in Shelby County to his selected and approved candidates. His supporters and more objective observers claimed that his methods were far more ethical, based simply on a natural Democratic majority and a core of African-American voters who supported the ticket.

Crump remained in the public eye with annual charity events, participation in civic affairs, and frequent printed attacks on opposition candidates. In 1948 his criticism of Congressman Estes Kefauver as resembling a thieving raccoon led Kefauver to adopt the coonskin cap as a symbol of his election campaign for the U.S. Senate.

From the late 1930s through the early 1950s Crump was often criticized in the local and national press as a living representative of a particular type of American urban boss more characteristic of an earlier era. While Memphis had been cleaned up, both physically and in terms of civic peace, voters there found that candidates supported by Crump almost always won by huge majorities. Those who spoke out against him were defeated or fired. The choice, opponents charged, was Crump's, not the people's.

Although the Crump machine regularly collected contributions to support candidates, Crump prided himself on never using the funds for his personal benefit. However, critics charged, his insurance and real estate operations thrived because many local supporters believed doing business with Crump helped assure political advancement. Nevertheless, Crump always insisted on efficiency and honesty in the expenditure of public funds.

Crump vigorously opposed the Ku Klux Klan at the peak of the organization's power in 1924, a position he remained proud of for the rest of his life. He supported the Democratic ticket nationally, putting his organization behind presidential candidates Alfred Smith and Franklin Roosevelt. However, in later years, he opposed President Harry Truman and his civil rights activities and criticized what he saw as the left wing of the party, represented by Eleanor Roosevelt. In his attacks on Kefauver and other politicians and on Congress of Industrial Organizations (CIO) union organizers, he frequently employed virulent accusations of Communist affiliation or sympathy.

Crump's activities inspired many local legends. He worked to increase the bird population of Memphis, took personal note of areas that needed cleaning up, and initiated a campaign to reduce noise in the city, virtually banning the use of car horns downtown, and under his guidance the city required all utility poles to be painted green to blend with foliage. He maintained a card index on all voters and made it a practice to remember the names of thousands of supporters, speaking to them often in public.

Crump's power in Shelby County, Tennessee's largest, was crucial in statewide elections. For example, in 1936 the Crump organization supported gubernatorial candidate Gordon Browning, who earned a 60,000-vote majority in Shelby County. Over the next two years, however, Browning and Crump had a falling out, because Crump charged Browning with corruption in office. In 1938 Browning lost the statewide election, losing Shelby County by 60,000 votes. Senators Tom Stewart and Kenneth McKellar and most West Tennessee members of Congress during the 1940s and early 1950s owed their seats to the Shelby County votes.

Toward the end of Crump's life, his statewide influence declined, particularly with the election of Kefauver to the U.S. Senate in 1948 and the Democratic nomination of Browning for governor that year. Both had won support by specifically directing their attacks against Crump. Involved in planning political activities to the end, Crump died at his home in Memphis.

• Material on Crump is in the Memphis Public Library. William D. Miller, *Mr. Crump of Memphis* (1964), is based on Crump's records, then stored in the Crump Company Building in Memphis. See also "Ring-Tailed Tooter," *Time*, 27 May 1946; Alfred Steinberg, *The Bosses* (1972); R. Biles, "Ed Crump vs. the Unions," *Labor History* 25 (Fall 1984): 533–52; Robert S. Allen, *Our Fair City* (1947); Allen H. Kitchens, "Political Upheaval in Tennessee: Boss Crump and the Senatorial Election of 1948," *West Tennessee Historical Society Papers* 16 (1962): 104–26; Allen Bussel, "The Fight against Boss Crump: Editor Meeman's Turn," *Journalism Quarterly* 44 (1967): 252–56; and Virginia Emerson Lewis, "Fifty Years of Politics in Memphis, 1900–1950" (Ph.D. diss., New York Univ., 1955). An obituary is in the *New York Times*, 17 Oct. 1954.

RODNEY P. CARLISLE

CRUMPLER, Rebecca Davis Lee (8 Feb. 1831–9 Mar. 1895), physician, was born in Delaware, the daughter of Absolum Davis and Matilda Webber. Little is known of her early life, except that she was raised in Pennsylvania by an aunt who was often sought out by sick neighbors and whose kind attention to the sufferings of others had a great impact on her appreciative and impressionable niece. By 1852 Crumpler had moved to Charlestown, Massachusetts (near Cambridge), and for the proceeding eight years worked as a nurse for various doctors there. Her lack of formal training did not distinguish her from other nurses at the time, as the first U.S. school for nurses did not open until 1873. In 1860, bearing letters of recommendation from her physician-employers, Crumpler sought admittance to the M.D. program at New England Female Medical College (NEFMC). The first black medical school in the United States would not open until 1868, and in antebellum America medical school administrators routinely denied entrance to blacks, both male and female. Yet the trustees of New England Female Medical College admitted Crumpler to their four-year medical curriculum in 1860. The school had opened in 1848 under the name Boston Female Medical College, the first women's medical college in the world.

In 1860 only about 300 of the 54,543 physicians in the United States were women with medical degrees. None were black women. American physicians were only gradually finding medical degrees necessary to their work; many still trained in apprenticeships, and most states had no licensing requirements. No records remain of Crumpler's first three years at NEFMC, or of the struggles she may have endured to gain admittance or to remain enrolled. Her later writings give no indication that she was aware of her status as the first black woman M.D. in the United States; indeed, until the late twentieth century, scholars had assigned that distinction to Rebecca Cole, who received her degree from the Woman's Medical College of Pennsylvania in 1867, three years behind Crumpler. It seems likely that Crumpler attended medical school less to enable her to practice as a physician than to improve her nursing skills. She would later argue, for example, that "woman should study the mechanism of the human structure . . . before assuming the office of nurse" (Crumpler, p. 3).

On 24 February 1864 Crumpler and her two white classmates, Mary Lockwood Allen and Elizabeth Kimball, came before the four faculty members to undergo their final, oral examinations. Each candidate had had at least three years of preparatory coursework, written a thesis, and paid her graduation fees, all standard for the time. At the conclusion of the exam, the faculty voted to recommend Crumpler and her two classmates to the board of trustees, but they recorded some hesitation with regard to Lee's recommendation. "Deficiencies" in Crumpler's education and what the faculty regarded as her "slow progress" in medical school led the faculty to note that "*some* of us have hesitated very seriously in recommending her." In spite of their reservations, the faculty deferred to "the wishes of the Trustees & the present state of public feeling," suggesting that the faculty had felt pressured to pass Crumpler. The minutes of that meeting offer no further explanation. It is possible that the doctors for whom Crumpler had worked before entering medical school had put pressure on the faculty. Nevertheless, on the first of March the trustees conferred the "Doctress of Medicine" degree upon Crumpler. The trustees identified her as "Mrs. Rebecca Lee, negress," suggesting Crumpler had been married while in school, though nothing more is known of her husband. According to NEFMC statistics, in this period only about 35 percent of all women who attended the college completed the degree program. With Crumpler's graduation, the number of NEFMC graduates totaled forty-eight women. The college would close in 1873 without graduating another black woman. At around the time of her graduation she married Arthur Crumpler, but further details about him or their marriage are unknown except that Arthur outlived Rebecca.

Crumpler remained in Boston after graduation to practice and for a time sought additional training at an unspecified location in the "British Dominion." She specialized in caring for women and children, particularly poor ones. At the end of the Civil War she moved to Richmond, Virginia, to do what she considered "real missionary work," treating black patients through an arrangement with the Freedmen's Bureau (Crumpler, p. 3). Many southern blacks, particularly former slaves, found themselves without medical care after leaving the plantation. The resulting need led Crumpler and other black physicians to offer such care; it also encouraged many more blacks to seek formal medical training. White missionary groups as well as black community groups were instrumental in founding, in the late nineteenth century, the first black medical schools in the United States. Yet despite the need for them, black practitioners were not usually welcome in the postwar south. There is some indication that Crumpler herself was not well received in Richmond. One source suggests that "men doctors snubbed her, druggists balked at filling her prescriptions, and some people wisecracked that the M.D. behind her name stood for nothing more than 'Mule Driver'" ("Outstanding Women Doctors," p. 68).

By 1869 Crumpler had returned to Boston, where she practiced with "renewed vigor," perhaps because she felt more at home in the community where she had been trained. She lived, for a time at least, at 67 Joy Street on Beacon Hill, then a predominantly black neighborhood. By 1880 she and her husband had moved to Hyde Park, Massachusetts, where the residents apparently were less in need of her services. She appears not to have been in active practice in 1883, the year she published *A Book of Medical Discourses* to advise women on medical care for themselves and their children. That she dedicated the volume to mothers and nurses seems a further indication that she viewed her medical training primarily as preparation for her nursing work. According to her death certificate, she died in Fairview, Massachusetts, still a resident of Hyde Park.

Over the course of the nineteenth century, American medical education began to open to many groups that previously had been excluded. David John Peck, the first black man to receive a medical degree in the United States, did so in 1847; in 1849 Elizabeth Blackwell became the first American woman to earn a medical degree, and in 1879 Mary E. P. Mahoney became the first black graduate of a U.S. nursing school. By 1920 there were sixty-five black women doctors in the United States. Each of these pioneers had to overcome serious obstacles, many of which continue to face women and minorities hoping to enter medicine. The lives of many of these trailblazers have been ably documented by historians. Although much of Rebecca Lee Crumpler's life remains hidden, and in spite of her exclusion from most histories of American medicine, many have drawn inspiration from her achievements, as evidenced by the name of one of the first medical societies for black women: the Rebecca Lee Society.

Additional research into her life would no doubt increase our understanding of the obstacles as well as the opportunities brought about by the spread of formal medical training in the United States.

• Lee apparently left no personal papers. Records of her education at NEFMC are held at the Boston University Archives. A meager bit of information on Lee is available at the Archives and Special Collections on Women in Medicine at the Medical College of Pennsylvania and was gathered as part of the Black Women Physicians Project. Lee's only known publication, and a source of much of the information on her life, is *A Book of Medical Discourses in Two Parts* (1883). Copies are held at the National Library of Medicine in Washington, D.C., and at Countway Medical Library at Harvard University Medical School. Although little information is available on her life, Crumpler's role as the first black woman M.D. in the United States has made her the subject of many entries in biographical dictionaries. Brief mention of her is made in "Outstanding Women Doctors," *Ebony*, May 1964, pp. 68–76; W. Montague Cobb, "The Black in American Medicine," *Journal of the National Medical Association* 73 supp. (Dec. 1981): 1208; and Frederick C. Waite, *History of the New England Female Medical College, 1848–1874* (1950), pp. 56, 88, 122.

SARAH K. A. PFATTEICHER

CUBBERLEY, Ellwood Patterson (6 June 1868–14 Sept. 1941), educator and historian, was born in Andrews (then called Antioch), Indiana, the son of Edwin Blanchard Cubberley, a pharmacist, and Catherine Biles. His father owned a small drugstore where Cubberley, by the age of twelve, worked long hours. His father assumed that he would eventually take over the family business and prepared him accordingly. He attended public school in Andrews and in 1885 entered nearby Purdue University to study pharmacology. In the summer of 1886 he attended a lecture by David Starr Jordan, then president of Indiana University, titled "The Value of a College Education" and was deeply moved by Jordan's wisdom. By the fall of 1886 he had persuaded his parents to allow him to enroll in Indiana University, where he set off to be a natural scientist, majoring in physics. During his undergraduate years at Indiana, Cubberley developed an interest in teaching. He also developed a close relationship with Jordan, who would later recommend him for all the key appointments he secured.

After his sophomore year Cubberley took a year's leave from Indiana to teach at a rural one-room school. In the spring of his senior year he accepted a post as instructor in science and French at the Ridgeville Baptist College. After graduation in 1891 he accepted a professorship at Indiana's Vincennes University, where he taught physics, botany, mathematics, and European history and directed the laboratory. In 1892 Cubberley married Helen Van Uxem, and shortly after their honeymoon that summer, he accepted the offer of the presidency of Vincennes. The couple had no children. For the next three years he reorganized the curriculum, following Charles Eliot's initiatives at Harvard and Jordan's at Indiana that called for more science. Putting to use the business skills he learned in

his father's pharmacy, Cubberley put the struggling institution on firm financial ground, wiping out the deficit and reorganizing the administration. Energetic, disciplined, and confident, Cubberley also taught a full load alongside the other twelve faculty, lectured widely, and worked on a geography textbook.

In 1896, on the recommendation of Jordan, who was now the president of Stanford, Cubberley left Vincennes and accepted a post as the superintendent of schools in the city of San Diego. He was chosen over a local candidate, and his appointment was controversial. Nevertheless, he endured the local politics and established order in the curriculum and the administration. Unhappy in this job, however, when the local School board voted to close the high school in San Diego, Cubberley decided to resume scientific and scholarly work, accepting a position in 1898 as assistant professor of education and acting head of the department of education at Stanford University. Although his stay in San Diego had proved to be less than ideal, his administrative experiences there would serve him well in the emerging field of educational administration.

At Stanford, Cubberley's task was to make the department respectable. He developed the education curriculum and taught the theory and practice of teaching, the history of education in Europe and the United States, and the organization, supervision, and administration of schools. Having successfully transferred his ambition from becoming a scientist to studying schooling, Cubberley invested his time and energies in mastering educational administration and history.

After three years at Stanford, Cubberley took a leave of absence to pursue a master's degree in school administration at Teachers College, Columbia University, which he earned in 1902. His master's thesis, a 300-page treatise titled *Syllabus of Lectures on the History of Education*, published that same year, was his first educational work. He returned to Stanford to teach and direct the department of education and then went back to Teachers College in 1904 to complete his doctorate, resuming his efforts under the guidance of Paul Monroe, Edward L. Thorndike, and James E. Russell and working swiftly to complete his dissertation. In less than three months, Cubberley had completed his study. Unlike his master's thesis, which was historical, his doctoral thesis, *School Funds and Their Apportionment*, contributed to the new field of educational administration. According to his biographer Richard Thursfield, *School Funds* was the first scientific study of state school finance. In it Cubberley concluded that schools were inefficient because they were seriously underfunded and lacked uniformity in allocation of revenue. To make schools productive he called on state government to increase and equalize expenditures to local districts. It was a theme he would return to many times over his career.

After completing his doctorate, Cubberley returned to Stanford, where he taught, wrote, consulted, and edited for the next thirty-five years. In 1906 he was promoted to full professor and in 1917 was named dean of Stanford's new School of Education. His work at Teachers College, which resulted in his first two book-length publications, placed him in command of two emerging fields of scholarship—educational administration and American educational history. Along with George Strayer of Teachers College, Cubberley oversaw the construction of the "New Educational Hierarchy" (Newman, "Ellwood P. Cubberley," p. 161), a comprehensive system for teacher education and public school administration, featuring a top-down flow of knowledge and influence. At the apex of Cubberley's hierarchy was the new cadre of educational professionals who developed graduate schools of educational administration at three universities: Columbia in the East, Chicago in the Midwest, and Stanford in the West. At the next level were "professional" superintendents, many of whom received their graduate training in educational administration programs, which were spreading steadily to other universities. Next came high school principals, followed by elementary school principals. Classroom teachers appeared on the lowest rung of Cubberley's hierarchy.

Cubberley's design was predicated on the idea that oversized local boards of education were ill equipped to carry on the daily functions of a rapidly expanding system of public schools. He argued that after setting general policy, lay boards must step aside to leave the responsibilities of managing schools to the experts. According to Cubberley, who relied heavily on management developments in industry (particularly Frederick Taylor's theory of scientific management), schools needed efficiency experts. His model quickly became the standard, and local school boards across the nation acceded power to professional administrators. Critics of his model have noted that the hierarchical organization of schools required subordination, which, in practice, meant the subordination of female teachers to the authority of male administrators. Cubberley, Strayer, John Bobbitt of Chicago, Edward Elliott at Wisconsin, and Frank Spaulding at Yale were the most influential leaders in educational administration in the early twentieth century. Cubberley published more than twenty books and reports, edited numerous textbook series, consulted with state and local authorities, and lectured widely.

Cubberley was equally influential in the field of educational history. Although he had no formal training in historical writing, between 1902 and 1934 he published seven books and wrote scores of articles and speeches on the history of education. His best-known books, *Public Education in the United States* (1919; rev., 1934) and *History of Education* (1920), together had a circulation of more than 165,000 copies. His educational histories celebrated education and sought to instill teachers with professional zeal. Characterizing the horizontal and vertical expansion of schooling as "a triumph of good over evil" (Newman, "Ellwood P. Cubberley," p. 167), Cubberley applauded and encouraged the proliferation of the education enterprise and viewed it as vitally linked to the stability of democracy in the United States. His optimistic writings reaffirmed and augmented the view that Americans must put their faith in schools as the best hope for a greater society. One historian writing in the 1960s said that Cubberley's historical writing "ha[d] become so pervasive that we are largely unaware of them; yet they profoundly affect private practice, professional pronouncement and public policy" (Cremin, p. 2). Critics of Cubberley's historical work have charged that he confused education with "schooling." Others charge that he ignored the darker side of the expansion of schooling and failed to assess the impact of the system on blacks, females, immigrants, and the poor.

In 1933, at age sixty-five, Cubberley retired from Stanford. Always frugal and an able investor of his editing proceeds and royalties, Cubberley and his wife donated nearly $775,000 in gifts to Stanford while in retirement. He died in Palo Alto. Like many reformers of his day, Cubberley held paternalistic attitudes toward those outside the mainstream. He supported efforts to Americanize immigrants, to scientifically classify and sort pupils, and to "get the politics out of schooling." He developed an empirical knowledge base in educational administration and trained an entire generation of "schoolmen" who would carry out his design. His administrative and historical views of the educational system became embedded in the system he helped to build. As a key architect of the "educational hierarchy," Cubberley designed and provided a comprehensive basis for a system of universal schooling that became the standard worldwide.

• The key repository for primary materials relating to the life and work of Ellwood Patterson Cubberley is the Department of Special Collections, Stanford University Libraries. For a biography on Cubberley and an extensive list of primary sources, including his writings and papers, see Jesse Sears and Adin Henderson, *Cubberley of Stanford* (1957). Also see Richard Thursfield, "Ellwood Patterson Cubberley," *Harvard Educational Review* 9 (1939): 43–62; Harold Benjamin, "Ellwood Patterson Cubberley, a Biographical Sketch," in *Modern School Administration*, ed. John C. Almack (1933); George E. Arnstein, "Cubberley: The Wizard of Stanford," *History of Education Journal* 5 (1953–1954): 73–81. For critical accounts see Raymond Callahan, *Education and the Cult of Efficiency* (1962), chapter 8; Lawrence Cremin, *The Wonderful World of Ellwood Patterson Cubberley* (1965); David B. Tyack, *The One Best System* (1974); Joseph W. Newman, "Ellwood P. Cubberley, Architect of the New Educational Hierarchy," *Teaching Education* 4 (1992): 161–68, and *America's Teachers*, 2d ed. (1994), chapter 6.

THOMAS V. O'BRIEN

CUDAHY, Edward Aloysius, Jr. (22 Aug. 1885–8 Jan. 1966), meat packer, was born in Chicago, Illinois, the son of Edward Aloysius Cudahy, a meatpacking plant supervisor, and Elizabeth Murphy. In 1887 his father, his uncle Michael, and Philip D. Armour purchased from Sir Thomas J. Lipton a new, small packing plant in South Omaha, Nebraska, with a capacity of a thousand hogs a day. Edward, Sr., moved with his family to South Omaha to manage the plant. Thus, Edward, Jr., grew up in Omaha, where he attended public schools. Meanwhile, his father and uncle Michael bought out Armour in 1890, renamed the company Cudahy Packing Company, and built it into one of the four major packing houses, ranking with Swift, Armour, and Morris.

On the evening of 18 December 1900, as 15-year-old Edward was returning books to a neighbor, James Callahan and Pat Crowe kidnapped him, holding him in chains for twenty-four hours. Crowe, a "garrulous swindler and train robber," whom Cudahy's father had helped financially on occasion, threatened to blind the boy with acid; his father paid a $25,000 ransom in gold. Edward was released, unharmed; Crowe escaped and spent the money before surrendering. Because Nebraska had no law against kidnapping an adolescent, Callahan and Crowe were indicted for robbery, and Crowe was also indicated for felonious assault; both were acquitted. Crowe then pursued a career lecturing on the evils of law-breaking, wrote an autobiography, and had the audacity to send Cudahy a congratulatory telegram when Cudahy announced his engagement in 1919. After the kidnapping Cudahy moved to Chicago and attended Chicago Latin School and then Creighton University, graduating in 1904.

In 1905 Edward began working at the Cudahy plant in Omaha, learning the business from the ground up. When his uncle Michael, who had served as company president since 1890, died in 1910, Edward's father became president and moved his family to Chicago. Edward, Jr., then had the opportunity to learn the business from the top down, when in 1916 he was promoted to first vice president.

After serving in World War I as a captain in the army, commanding a machine-gun company in the Coast Artillery, he returned to the company and began playing a wider role in management, gradually taking over from his father. In 1919 the Federal Trade Commission charged the meat packers with price fixing and attempted monopolization of the food industry; in February 1920 the five major packers—Armour, Cudahy, Morris, Swift, and Wilson—signed a consent decree under which they were barred from participation in retailing and cold storage businesses and thus restricted to the wholesale meat business. (The decree remained in force until 23 November 1981, nearly a decade after a precipitous decline of these old-line meat packers.) At the same time, Cudahy earned public derision when he blamed high meat prices on public demand for expensive cuts such as steaks and roast; he urged people to eat corned beef. In 1920 he married Margaret Carry; they had two sons and a daughter.

In January 1926 Cudahy's father stepped aside as president (remaining as chairman of the board), and Edward, Jr., assumed the position. At the time the company operated nine packing plants, maintained nearly 100 distribution facilities around the country, and operated a fleet of railway cars and trucks; in addition to the meat business, it made Old Dutch Cleanser, soap, and cottonseed oil. Sales were $232 million; profits were $4 million.

With the depression, the company saw sales and profits shrink (in spite of imposing two 10 percent wage cuts on employees) and then disappear in 1937 and 1938. Unable to gain a modification of the 1920 consent decree, Cudahy had no clear ideas of how to move the company in new directions. And under the economic pressures of the Great Depression, the company, confronting increasing labor conflicts, in 1939 was ordered to disband its company union. Then, in 1941 Cudahy and others faced federal indictments for fixing hog prices in Iowa and Nebraska and for fixing prices of Easter hams nationally. But World War II intervened, bringing renewed profits; the indictments were dropped in 1949.

Cudahy himself was reducing his involvement in company management by 1942; he divorced his first wife that year and began wintering in Phoenix, Arizona. On 25 January 1944 he married Eleanor Peabody Cochran; they had no children. Later that year he stepped down as president, remaining as chairman of the board. During his chairmanship, which ran to 1962, the company declined dramatically. Riding the wave of postwar prosperity, sales peaked in 1947 at $573 million with strong profits of $7.1 million, but in 1948 a bitter two-month strike damaged the company and led to a loss of $4.7 million in 1949. In 1954 Cudahy lost $7.2 million on sales of $455 million; by 1956 sales had fallen to $291 million. By 1962 the firm was seventh among packers and was among the last to confront the need to close obsolete plants and modernize its remaining ones. In 1962, the year Cudahy resigned from the chairmanship, the company suspended dividends on its preferred stock. This financial failing reflected profound disarray, a company with no personnel policy, no job descriptions, and no research capability. Its management was ingrown, narrow-minded, and top-heavy; its marketing had ignored the growing chain supermarkets and private labels, relying instead on independent grocers, which forced it to maintain an extensive, expensive distribution system. *Business Week* observed that Cudahy was "a sickly shadow of its once robust self." Cudahy himself moved to Phoenix, where he died.

In 1971 General Host, frustrated in an effort to buy Armour, acquired Cudahy; in 1982 *Fortune* characterized the acquisition "an unmitigated disaster," one which cost General Host millions in losses. In 1981 most Cudahy assets were acquired in a management buyout by the newly-organized Bar-S Foods of Phoenix; the remaining assets were sold in 1984, effectively ending the history of the once-proud Cudahy company.

• There are apparently no extant company records; there are extensive labor records relating to the industry and Cudahy in the large United Packinghouse, Food, and Allied Workers collection in the State Historical Society of Wisconsin. This collection includes Arthur Kampfert's five-volume manuscript history of the unions in the meatpacking industry. The Minnesota Historical Society has a significant set of files on the 1948 packing house strikes. Other material on Cudahy and his company are available in Cudahy Packing Company,

Annual Report (1943–1957); *Yearbook* (1925–1932); Patrick T. Crowe, *Spreading Evil: Pat Crowe's Autobiography* (1927); William Terence Kane, *The Education of Edward Cudahy* (1941); "Young Blood Puts Life into an Old Packer," *Business Week*, 13 Feb. 1965, pp. 142–44; "Businessmen in the News," *Fortune*, Feb. 1963, p. 53, and 3 May 1982, pp. 84–89; and the *New York Times*, 9 Jan. 1966.

For information on the history of the meatpacking industry, consult Rudolf A. Clemen, *The American Livestock and Meat Industry* (1923); Jimmy M. Skaggs, *Prime Cut: Livestock Raising and Meatpacking in the United States: 1607–1983* (1986); and Mary Yeager, *Competition and Regulation: The Development of Oligopoly in the Meat Packing Industry* (1981).

FRED CARSTENSEN

CUDAHY, Michael (7 Dec. 1841–27 Nov. 1910), meat packer and businessman, was born in Callan, County Kilkenny, Ireland, the son of Patrick Cudahy and Elizabeth Shaw. He immigrated with his parents to Milwaukee in 1849, where his father worked at various occupations in brickyards and in the produce business. Leaving grammar school at age fourteen, Michael went to work for Layton and Plankinton, Milwaukee's largest meat-packing concern, and rose rapidly through the employee ranks. Between 1859 and 1866 he was employed by the meat-packing firm of Edward Roddis. In 1866 Cudahy temporarily went into business for himself and married Catherine Sullivan; they had seven children.

Through the intervention of packing pioneer Frederick Layton, Cudahy was appointed meat inspector for the Milwaukee Board of Trade in 1866, the same year that he joined Layton's firm as a private inspector. In these combined capacities, Cudahy initiated a painstaking scientific study of the chemistry of meat preservation, an investigation that helped to make him one of the foremost advocates for raising the quality of American dressed meats. In 1869 he was appointed superintendent of the Plankinton and Armour packing-house in Milwaukee, a position that he filled so well that Philip D. Armour offered Cudahy a partnership in Armour and Company of Chicago in 1875. From that point until his withdrawal from the enterprise in 1890, Cudahy functioned as the supervisor of Armour's Union Stockyards, overseeing both the slaughtering and meat-packing operations.

While in Milwaukee and Chicago, Cudahy experimented with methods for curing meats in the summer using refrigeration. Prior to Cudahy's innovation, fresh meat was only available during the coldest months of the year, and consumers were forced to eat salted or otherwise preserved meats during warmer weather when the danger of spoilage was virtually endemic. Meat-packing plants typically closed during the summer months. By storing ice in cribs, Cudahy was able to reduce the temperature within the packinghouse to near-winter conditions, thereby allowing fresh meat to be processed year-round. This innovation helped revolutionize the meat-packing industry by greatly increasing productivity and profits, preventing the premature deterioration of numerous perishable products, enabling meat packers to signif-

icantly expand the geographical boundaries of their markets, and providing them with a powerful incentive to integrate the industry "vertically" from the point of production to that of ultimate consumption.

Cudahy's further contribution to the "revolution in refrigeration" of the late 1870s was at the production end of the business: he popularized the utilization of stationary refrigeration in his cold-storage warehouses or "coolers." On the transportation side of the revolution, Cudahy soon joined other packers, chiefly Swift and Company, in using refrigerated railroad cars. He also helped to set other trends in the meat-packing industry such as moving his operations farther west in order to be closer to the source of cattle, acquiring financial interests in and ownership of stockyards, and establishing branch houses throughout the United States and, eventually, in foreign countries.

In 1887 Cudahy joined his younger brother Edward and Armour in purchasing a small packing plant in South Omaha, Nebraska, which became the foundation of the Armour-Cudahy Packing Company. Its phenomenal success induced several other major packing companies to set up shop in Omaha, making it the third largest livestock market and packing center in the United States by 1894. In 1890 Cudahy sold his interest in the firm of Armour and Company and purchased Armour's share of the Armour-Cudahy Company, thereby establishing the Cudahy Packing Company. Over the next three decades, the new company expanded from a single plant with 700 employees and an annual payroll of $300,000 to a concern of eight plants, with a floor area of 110 acres and cold-storage facilities covering twenty-five acres. It possessed a daily slaughtering, curing, and preparing capacity for 15,000 hogs, 4,000 cattle, and 10,000 sheep, employed 9,000 people, and boasted an annual payroll of more than $10 million. Staunchly independent, the Cudahy brothers retained all of the stock in the company and declined to join the giant National Packing Company combine owned by Armour, Gustavus F. Swift, and Edward Morris and financed by the investment banking house of Kuhn, Loeb. They did, however, generally follow the conglomerate's lead on pricing and production quotas and benefited from its disseminated information on "dressed" costs, closing prices, and margins. By the turn of the century, Cudahy ranked fourth among the "Big Six" companies of the meat-packing industry. Cudahy remained president of the company until his death, and he also served as the president of the North American Transportation and Trading Company.

Active in civic and philanthropic activities, Cudahy was also a trustee of the Catholic University of America and the chairman of the committee in charge of solicitations from meat packers for the World's Columbian Exposition, held in Chicago in 1893. Upon his death in Chicago, he left an estate estimated at between $11 and $20 million dollars, most of which went to his family. He also bequeathed substantial sums to several Catholic orphanages and hospitals in both Milwaukee and Chicago.

• There are many useful references to Cudahy in *Patrick Cudahy: His Life* (1912), the autobiography written by his brother, the founder of the meat-packing company in Cudahy, Wis. Cudahy's contributions to the evolution of the meat-packing industry are detailed in Rudolph A. Clemen, *The American Livestock and Meat Industry* (1923), and Alfred D. Chandler, *The Visible Hand: The Managerial Revolution in American Business* (1977). Obituaries are in the *New York Times* and the *Chicago Tribune*, both 28 Nov. 1910.

JOHN D. BUENKER

CUFFE, Paul (17 Jan. 1759–7 Sept. 1817), entrepreneur and Pan-Africanist, was born Paul Slocum on Cuttyhunk Island near New Bedford, Massachusetts, the son of Coffe Slocum, a freedman from West Africa, and Ruth Moses, a Wampanoag Native American. Cuffe moved with his family from insular Cuttyhunk and Martha's Vineyard to mainland Dartmouth, a bustling maritime community. After his father's death, Cuffe shipped out on local vessels bound for the Caribbean. He was twice jailed, once in New York during the American Revolution, when the British blockade captured the vessel he was on, and later in Massachusetts, when Dartmouth selectmen ordered him and his older brother John confined for tax evasion. Unable to vote because of their color, they had unsuccessfully petitioned the Massachusetts legislature not to tax them.

Successful blockade runs to Nantucket in his own boat launched Cuffe in the maritime trade. By the end of the Revolution he had married Alice, a "Pequit" (in 1783), with whom he had seven children. Adopting his father's Akan name, Cuffe, or "Kofi" (born on Friday), he then returned to sea and became a boat-building partner of Michael Wainer, his sister Mary's Indian husband. Together, the two families built and predominantly staffed three schooners, the *Sunfish* and *Mary*, completed by 1792, and the *Ranger*, completed four years later. Personally and publicly identified as a black captain of vessels with all-black crews, Cuffe frequently confronted racism. When he sailed the *Ranger* to Vienna, along Maryland's eastern shore, slaveholders there, fearful of a slave revolt, tried to keep his free black crew members from landing, but Cuffe prevailed, and they were allowed ashore. In Massachusetts, so that his and other black children might obtain the formal education he lacked, Cuffe founded Cuff's School.

Cuffe was on his way to becoming the wealthiest African American of his time. By 1808 he owned property valued at approximately $20,000. As his bark *Hero* entered East African whaling grounds, construction of two more vessels was under way at his Westport yards, the 268-ton ship *Alpha* and the brig *Traveller*. Commanding the *Alpha* himself, Cuffe headed for the Baltic Sea with a cargo taken on at Wilmington, Delaware, and Savannah, Georgia. After returning home, accompanied by his Swedish apprentice, Cuffe found that the United States had abolished the transatlantic slave trade (1808) but that Congress had passed the Embargo Act (1807), restricting European trade. Cuffe was publicized as an abolitionist "African cap-

tain" both in an article written in Delaware for a British publication and by a transatlantic correspondence network. When Cuffe joined the Westport Friends' Meeting in 1808, he was asked to assist in making the black settlers in Sierra Leone, England's West African asylum for former slaves, more industrious. He sailed twice to Africa, first in 1811–1812 and then in 1815.

Cuffe's missions to Sierra Leone increased his interest in Africa and his spiritual leanings, both nurtured in his childhood. After meeting with the governor, British merchants, and black settlers, he cautiously concluded that a local British merchant monopoly excluded the settlers from profit making. He sailed for Liverpool carrying to Parliament a settlers' petition requesting protection. Philanthropists in the African Institution and members of Parliament praised him but took no action. Cuffe's Quaker host William Allen, however, agreed to organize a society "to encourage black settlers." Cuffe returned to Africa, where he formed the mercantile-oriented Friendly Society of Sierra Leone before embarking for home. Future institutions among African Americans, working with like-minded societies in Sierra Leone and England, he hoped, would promote a legitimate triangular trade among the three continents in order to discourage slave trading and encourage emigration. But back in the United States he found that anti-British sentiments made cooperation with Great Britain impossible. So intense were hostilities that Cuffe had to call on President James Madison personally before his "British" cargo was released.

During the War of 1812, while directing and financing reconstruction of the Westport Friends' Meeting House, Cuffe petitioned the president and Congress to permit a peaceful emigration voyage to Sierra Leone. The resulting bill failed by seven votes in the House of Representatives, although proponents had argued that the proposed mission might "invite the emigration of free blacks, a part of our population which we could well spare." In contrast, influential free urban blacks in the United States, among them James Forten, applauded Cuffe's vision.

At the war's end Cuffe took nine families to Sierra Leone and paid for their settlement there, but failure of promised reimbursements doomed further voyages. News in the summer of 1816 of the brutal repression of slave uprisings in the South convinced Cuffe that blacks would arise more safely in Africa than in the United States. In 1817, before his death in Westport, Massachusetts, Cuffe endorsed the newly established American Colonization Society, which advocated the colonization of "free" blacks wishing passage to Africa. Throughout his life Cuffe served as a mediator between disparate groups on three continents "for the family of Africa," an idea far ahead of its time.

• The most complete collection of Cuffe's papers, including his maritime log for 1811–1812, is at the New Bedford Free Public Library in New Bedford, Mass. Additional manuscript collections can be found at the Historical Society of Pennsylvania, the Library Company of Philadelphia, the

Massachusetts Historical Society, the Massachusetts State Archives, the Old Dartmouth Historical Society, the Rhode Island Historical Society, and the National Archives. Valuable collections in England are at the London Public Record Office, the Society of Friends House Library, and Allen and Hanbury, Ltd. A Wilmington, Del., memoir first appeared in the British *Monthly Repository of Theology and General Literature* (Apr. 1807); its contents were copied in the *Liverpool Mercury*, 4 and 11 Oct. 1811, which included an interview with Cuffe; and the *Freedman's Journal* (1827) reprinted it as well. Secondary works include Lamont Thomas, *Rise to Be a People* (1986), retitled in paperback *Paul Cuffe: Black Entrepreneur and Pan-Africanist* (1988); Sheldon Harris, *Paul Cuffe: Black America and the African Return* (1972); George Salvador, *Paul Cuffe: The Black Yankee* (1969); and Arthur Diamond, *Merchant and Abolitionist* (1989). An obituary is in the *New Bedford Mercury*, 12 Sept. 1817.

LAMONT D. THOMAS

CUGAT, Xavier (1 Jan. 1900–27 Oct. 1990), bandleader, was born in Gerona, near Barcelona, Spain, the son of Juan Cugat, an electrician, and Mingall de Bru y Deulofeo. His full name was Francisco de Asis Javier Cugat Mingall de Bru y Deulofeo. When he was two or three years old, his family moved to Cuba. His musical career is reported to have begun when a neighbor who was a violinmaker gave young Cugat a miniature violin. His first appearance with the Cuban Symphony was at age six.

Although Cugat became famous as the bandleader who popularized Latin rhythms in the United States during the 1930s and 1940s, he began as a concert violinist, touring throughout Europe and the United States. He gave two recitals at Carnegie Hall, accompanying the celebrated tenor Enrico Caruso at the age of sixteen; he studied violin with Franz Kneisel and appeared as a soloist with the Los Angeles Philharmonic Orchestra. He was said to have been the first to play the violin for the radio in the United States, with a performance in December 1921 (one source gives the date as 1917) in Camden, New Jersey. Cugat immigrated to the United States in 1921. Some sources on his life mention an early marriage to Rita Montaner, of whom little is known.

Cugat decided to abandon his concert career because of its uncertain income; he had also received some bad reviews. In the mid-1920s he joined the dance orchestra of Vincent Lopez in New York City, then tried unsuccessfully to revive a concert career in Los Angeles. He tried his hand at producing films in 1928 with an early sound picture in Spanish, but he lost his investment because there were no sound projectors yet in Latin America. He also drew caricatures for a living, finding a job with the *Los Angeles Times* in 1927.

Cugat met singer Carmen Castillo while he was drawing her caricature. Married in 1929, they divorced in 1947. Castillo encouraged Cugat to return to performing, as the leader (as well as violinist and singer) of a seven-piece dance band. The band, Xavier Cugat and His Gigolos, rose from relief band to featured performers at the Waldorf Astoria Hotel in New York

City during the period from 1933 to 1949. They also toured the nation's top nightclubs, and beginning in 1934 they appeared on "Let's Dance," a weekly, three-hour network radio program broadcast nationwide. Latin entertainers such as Desi Arnaz, Rita Hayworth, Lina Romay, and Miguelito Valdes became well known as performers in Cugat's band. He introduced Latin American rhythms to the American public and became known as the "King of the Rhumba"; he titled his autobiography, *Rhumba Is My Life*. Cugat is also credited with the invention of the congat, a hybrid of bongo and conga drums.

Cugat's band was a regular feature of one of the most popular radio programs of the 1940s, "The Camel Caravan"; this led to appearances in fourteen Hollywood films from 1942 to 1949. Many were musicals starring swimmer and actress Esther Williams, including *Bathing Beauty*, *On an Island with You*, and *Neptune's Daughter*. Cugat also recorded regularly for RCA Victor until 1937 and then with Columbia. He constructed a memorable stage persona, cultivating a thin moustache and conducting while cradling a chihuahua in his arms and wearing a large South American hat.

In 1947, Cugat divorced Castillo and married actress Lorraine Allen. They divorced in 1950, and Cugat married a singer in his band, Abbe Lane, in 1952; they divorced in 1964. Cugat's last wife was Spanish singer, dancer, and guitarist Charo (Maria Rosario Pilar Martinez Molina Baeza), whom he married in 1966.

Cugat's later career included cameo appearances in films—*The Monitors* (1969) and *The Phynx* (1969). He recorded his last album, *Spanish Eyes*, in 1972. A number of his albums recorded in the 1940s and 1950s, such as *Continental Hits* and *To All My Friends*, were reissued in the 1980s.

Cugat continued his interest in art through his hobbies of painting murals and theater curtains. He retired from performing after a stroke in 1971. He invested in entertainment projects, such as Brazilian films, and appeared in the 1987 television documentary "Images/Imagenes: Latin Music Special." He died in Barcelona. There were no children from any of his marriages.

• The best source of information on Cugat is his autobiography, *Rhumba Is My Life* (1948). For his contributions to American music in the 1940s, see "Good-Will Set to Music," *New York Times*, 20 July 1941. Biographical Sketches appear in *The Guinness Encyclopedia of Popular Music* (1992) and in Ephraim Katz, *The Film Encyclopedia*, which includes a list of films in which Cugat appeared. Obituaries are in the *New York Times*, 28 Oct. 1990, and *Variety*, 5 Nov. 1990.

Among Cugat's many albums, including many of his own compositions, are *Xavier Cugat's Favorite Collection of Tangos and Rhumbas* (1936), *The Other Americas* (1938), *New Album of Xavier Cugat's Best Compositions and Other Latin American Favorites* (1941), *Xavier Cugat's Folio* (1942), *Xavier Cugat's Collection of Pan-American Songs* (1942, 1947), *Meet Mr. Cugat* (1943), *Xavier Cugat's Favorite Hits* (1943), *Xavier Cugat's Mambo-land* (1953), *Viva Cugat* (1958), *Continental Hits* (1959, 1984), and *To All My Friends* (reissued 1986).

MARIANNE FEDUNKIW STEVENS

CUKOR, George (7 July 1899–24 Jan. 1983), motion picture director, was born George Dewey Cukor in New York City, the son of Victor Cukor, a lawyer and assistant district attorney, and Helen Gross; both were immigrants of Hungarian-Jewish origin. Cukor graduated from De Witt Clinton High School in 1917 and at age nineteen got a job working backstage on touring productions for the theatrical producers Klaw & Erlanger. In 1920 he began working in summer stock in Rochester, New York, and by the summer of 1922 had become general manager of the Lyceum Players in that city. This led to a position as stage manager of East Coast tryout tours and Broadway productions for the Charles Frohman organization. By 1925 Cukor was directing plays on Broadway, among them, *The Great Gatsby* (1926).

In the late 1920s experienced theater personnel were sought by the Hollywood studios to write scripts and to assist actors in speaking dialogue. Paramount signed Cukor in February 1929, brought him to California, and gave him a job as dialogue director. Cukor was loaned out to Universal to serve in this capacity on the prestigious production of *All Quiet on the Western Front* (1930). Paramount promoted Cukor to the role of co-director, in charge of a film's actors, in 1930. His third film, *The Royal Family of Broadway*, based on an Edna Ferber and George S. Kaufman play, led to a salary increase, a contract extension, and promotion to full director. Cukor's first solo effort was *Tarnished Lady* (1931), starring Tallulah Bankhead; it was the first of seven collaborations with screenwriter Donald Ogden Stewart. *Girls about Town* (1931), a prototype for later Cukor films, is a romantic comedy about a group of gold-digging women whose desperation lurks just below the surface.

In 1931 Cukor was assigned to direct *One Hour with You*, a chic musical comedy starring Maurice Chevalier and Jeanette MacDonald. Ernst Lubitsch, the film's producer, participated extensively in the production and was awarded sole director credit. The resulting acrimony allowed Cukor to terminate his contract and move to RKO. Cukor completed six films at RKO over the next four years, three each with Constance Bennett and newcomer Katharine Hepburn. *What Price Hollywood?* (1932) parallels the rise to movie stardom of a naive actress (played by Bennett) with the decline of her mentor, a veteran director. This Pygmalion-like theme of an experienced teacher leading the education and transformation of a younger protégée is a virtual standard in Cukor's film career. Cukor himself became a mentor, to Hepburn, in *A Bill of Divorcement* (1932). This motion picture marked her film debut as well as a collaboration that extended to ten films over the next fifty years, the longest director-star relationship of the Hollywood studio era.

In early 1933 producer David O. Selznick abruptly left RKO for Metro-Goldwyn-Mayer and arranged for Cukor to sign a two-year contract with MGM provided that he return to RKO later to complete two more pictures. Cukor immediately began work on a highly suc-

cessful film version of another Kaufman and Ferber play, *Dinner at Eight*, which follows a stylish group of dinner party guests. That same year, back at RKO, Cukor directed a film version of Louisa May Alcott's *Little Women*, with an Academy Award–winning script by Victor Heerman and Sarah Y. Mason. The film, starring Hepburn as the independent and imaginative Jo, was RKO's most-successful moneymaker of the era, and it received Academy Award nominations for Cukor as best director and for best picture. Cukor directed another adaptation of a literary classic, *David Copperfield*, for MGM and Selznick in 1935. The lengthy motion picture was a box office success; it also received a nomination for best picture and was the third straight Cukor-directed film to make *Film Daily*'s Ten Best list. Cukor fulfilled his obligation to RKO with *Sylvia Scarlett* (1936), starring Hepburn and Cary Grant. For part of the film Hepburn's character is disguised as a boy, a challenge to traditional gender roles that Cukor and Hepburn would explore again in their postwar films.

In 1935 Selznick left MGM to form his own independent production company. Cukor signed contracts with both Selznick and MGM that guaranteed him $4,000 per week. In 1936, assisted by MGM's Irving Thalberg, Cukor directed Shakespeare's *Romeo and Juliet* and *Camille*, the latter starring Greta Garbo. These films received respectful reviews and, in the case of *Romeo and Juliet*, a best picture nomination.

After Thalberg's death, Cukor returned to work for Selznick. They spent 1937 preparing to film *Gone with the Wind*, doing research and casting, with Cukor shooting numerous screen tests. Amid much publicity, filming on *Gone with the Wind* finally commenced in December 1938. Pressures resulting from an expanding budget and an unfinished script frayed the long-standing relationship between producer and director, and Selznick dismissed Cukor from the film after less than two months of shooting. The few scenes Cukor completed remain in the picture.

Cukor, who had often been referred to in studio publicity and the press as a "woman's director" owing to his special rapport with such talents as Hepburn and Garbo, returned immediately to MGM to direct *The Women* (1939). Another romantic comedy with desperate undertones, the film exemplifies Cukor's preoccupation with the imaginative lives of his characters; men are much discussed and fought over but never seen on screen. Philip Barry's play *The Philadelphia Story* had marked Hepburn's victorious return to the stage. For the 1940 MGM film, which starred Hepburn, James Stewart, and Cary Grant, Joseph L. Mankiewicz produced and Cukor directed. Another Cukor portrayal of crumbling relationships against a backdrop of high society, the film received six Academy Award nominations, including ones for best picture and best director. Comedic moments and the hopeful ending balance the pessimism in one of Cukor's most popular films.

Cukor's first "film noir" was *A Woman's Face* (1941), which featured Joan Crawford as a scarred outcast who is remade by a surgeon into a beauty and challenged to stop her criminal ways. The Pygmalion theme is repeated here but with the most horrifying slant it would ever take: Crawford's character must be dissuaded from murdering a child. Cukor's next two films were the final films for two of MGM's biggest stars. *Two-Faced Woman* (1941), starring Garbo, was a complete disaster; the critics dismissed it, the Catholic church condemned it, and European audiences, so important to the Swedish-born actress, were preoccupied with the war. *Her Cardboard Lover* (1942), based on a play that Cukor had previously staged on Broadway, was a quieter failure; it featured Norma Shearer.

At the end of 1942 Cukor enlisted as a private in the U.S. Army Signal Corps; he directed a training film and was discharged after six months. (He had wanted an officer's commission but did not receive one, so he was entitled to a discharge on account of his age.) MGM then signed him to a seven-year contract, and in 1944 he directed *Gaslight*, his most successful film of the era. Previous Cukor themes—a collapsing marriage, a plush but confining mansion, and a Pygmalion relationship—turn sinister in this story of a husband who tries to drive his wife crazy. Ingrid Bergman won an Academy Award for her performance. The next few years were marked by several unsuccessful projects; Cukor left *Desire Me* (1947) before its completion and after extensive preparations was unable to shoot *The Razor's Edge*.

Edward, My Son (1949), shot in Britain, was Cukor's most extreme cinematic stylistic attempt. Following Alfred Hitchcock's *Rope* (1948), Cukor shot the film with extended long takes in a series of flashbacks that trace the rise of a ruthless industrialist who destroys his personal life while acquiring an empire. The title character is never seen. That same year Cukor shot *Adam's Rib*, a film in which he found the perfect material and collaborators. Written by Garson Kanin and Ruth Gordon and introducing Judy Holliday, the film, starring Hepburn and Spencer Tracy, concerns husband-and-wife lawyers on opposite sides of a domestic dispute case. The humor and imagination of the script balance the more serious elements of attempted murder, divorce, and suicide. *Adam's Rib*, which deals directly with the issue of women's rights, was a minor hit at the time but has since become one of the most meaningful comedies of the studio era.

Cukor received his third Academy Award nomination for *Born Yesterday* (1950). Adapted from a play by Kanin, the film was a smash for Columbia. It too tells a kind of Pygmalion story; here, the "dumb blonde" mistress (played by Judy Holliday, who won an Academy Award) of a crude tycoon is educated by a reported into fighting against corruption in Washington, D.C. As in *Adam's Rib*, the film's serious elements, including political corruption and brutality, are complemented by wit, style, and optimism. In 1952 Cukor directed two other Gordon and Kanin original screenplays, *The Marrying Kind*, for Columbia, again with Holliday, and *Pat and Mike*, for MGM, with Hepburn and Tracy. Both films combined a realistic shooting style with dream sequences as well as serious drama with comic elements. *The Actress* (1953), which Gordon scripted from her own autobiographical play, starred Jean Simmons as a World War I–era stage-struck youth who dreams of a theatrical career. The desire to be famous was also at the heart of *It Should Happen to You* (1954). From a Kanin script for Columbia, the film, which introduced Jack Lemmon, was the last of Cukor's small, personal, black and white comedy-dramas.

As the studio era ended, film companies turned to gimmicks and blockbusters in an attempt to draw audiences away from their television sets and back into movie theaters. *A Star Is Born* (1954), Cukor's first completed film in color and widescreen as well as his first musical, was expected to be a smash hit and singer Judy Garland's comeback. Warner Bros., however, drastically shortened the finished film, and it enjoyed only mild success, though Cukor did receive an Academy Award nomination. With a new contract from MGM, Cukor directed another widescreen, color film, *Bhowani Junction* (1956), with an obligatory cast of thousands, on location in India. *Les Girls* (1957), also in widescreen and color and shot primarily in Europe, was Cukor's second musical film; it featured MGM's dance star Gene Kelly and an original score by Cole Porter.

Wild Is the Wind (1957) was Cukor's last film in black and white. In it, Anna Magnani's character comes from the old country to marry her sister's widower (played by Anthony Quinn), a sheep rancher in Nevada. Shot in a neorealist style, the film begins Cukor's examination of aging lead characters, where coming to terms with the past is as important as finding a partner. *Heller in Pink Tights* (1960), with Quinn and another Italian legend, Sophia Loren, was Cukor's only western. From a story by Louis L'Amour, the film has the classical elements of gunfighters and Indian attacks, but the action is seen through the experiences of a traveling theater troupe.

Cukor's unparalleled reputation for bringing the best out of actresses no doubt landed him his next film, the musical *Let's Make Love* (1960), with Marilyn Monroe. This was followed, also in the early 1960s, by two unsuccessful projects, *Lady L* and *Goodbye Charlie*, both of which were later filmed by others. *The Chapman Report* (1962), from a fiction bestseller that sensationalized the Kinsey Report on sexual activity, was heavily cut and not a success. This was followed by a complete disaster; Cukor began *Something's Got to Give* for Fox, but it was abandoned with the dismissal and subsequent death of Marilyn Monroe.

Now in his sixties, and with few recent successes, Cukor seemed to be at the end of his creative career. Yet there was one more triumph, *My Fair Lady* (1964), Cukor's bona fide Pygmalion story. Produced by Warner Bros. as exquisitely and artificially as any from the studio era, the film swept the Academy Awards, including Oscars for best picture, best actor (Rex Harrison), and best director.

Cukor suffered through the longest unproductive period of his film career after *My Fair Lady*. His contemporaries from the studio era had all departed the scene, and the American film industry appeared moribund. He did complete *Justine* (1969), based on the novels by Laurence Durrell, for Fox and *Travels with My Aunt* (1972), from the novel by Graham Greene, for MGM. The latter film, shot on location in Spain, received four Academy Award nominations, winning for best costumes. It illustrates many of Cukor's characteristic preoccupations, including the Pygmalion situation and a *Sylvia Scarlett*–like journey in which social roles are less confining and sexual experimentation is permitted. *Travels with My Aunt* was the first of three late Cukor films to examine old age and its particular problems involving sexuality and failing powers, memory and regret.

Cukor became one of the few veteran theatrical feature film directors to work in made-for-television movies, shooting *Love among the Ruins* for the ABC television network in 1975. Laurence Olivier plays a lawyer who defends aging star Katharine Hepburn in a breach-of-promise suit. In this ironic reversal of the standard gold-digging plot the courtroom becomes the stage on which subjective visions of beauty and sex appeal vie to be called the truth. The film received an Emmy Award. *The Corn Is Green* (1979), another television movie, was Cukor's last collaboration with Hepburn, who plays an aging mentor to a talented youth. It was also Cukor's last treatment of the Pygmalion situation. His final film, *Rich and Famous* (1981), shot for MGM, made Cukor Hollywood's oldest working filmmaker. He died in Los Angeles two years later.

Of the Hollywood directors whose careers began with sound, Cukor is unique. For five decades he directed memorable films with noted performances. He was MGM's leading filmmaker throughout the studio era, and he made use of all the major cinematic trends of the poststudio era. His collaborations with actors and writers were some of the most productive in the history of Hollywood. Cukor's characteristic situations, his focus on the role of women in society, and his exploration of questions of sexuality from youth to old age have kept his films relevant to modern audiences. Able to balance a surface of romantic comedy with an underlying treatment of serious personal and social issues, and exemplifying a traditional, sophisticated style but willing to adapt innovative technique and technology, Cukor exemplified the virtues of the classic Hollywood filmmaker of the studio era.

• Cukor's personal papers and letters are on deposit at the Margaret Herrick Library of the Academy of Motion Picture Arts and Sciences in Los Angeles. *George Cukor, A Double Life* (1991), a biography by Patrick McGilligan, is the best source on his film career; it also examines his private life and includes a well-researched discussion of his homosexuality. Cukor is the subject of several book-length studies, including Gary Carey's *Cukor & Co.* (1971); Carlos Clarens's *George Cukor* (1976); Gene D. Phillips's *George Cukor* (1982), which contains the most-detailed discussions of the films; and Emanuel Levy's *George Cukor, Master of Elegance* (1994).

James Bernardoni, *George Cukor: A Critical Study and Filmography* (1985), analyzes eight films from throughout Cukor's career. Allen Estrin, *The Hollywood Professionals*, vol. 6, *Frank Capra, George Cukor, Clarence Brown* (1980), presents the director's themes concisely and briefly discusses many of his key films. Cukor was interviewed on numerous occasions; Gavin Lambert's *On Cukor* (1972) has the most-complete published interview. Jonathan Kuntz, "The Films of George Cukor" (Ph.D. diss., UCLA, 1982), contains a detailed discussion of virtually every one of Cukor's films.

JONATHAN KUNTZ

CULBERSON, Charles Allen (10 June 1855–19 Mar. 1925), lawyer, governor, and U.S. senator, was born in Dadeville, Alabama, the son of David Browning Culberson, a lawyer, and Eugenia Kimbal. His parents moved to Texas when he was young, and he grew up in Jefferson. He attended Virginia Military Institute, from which he graduated in 1874. After studying law with his father, he received a law degree from the University of Virginia in 1877. He married Sallie Harrison in 1882; they had one daughter. While practicing law in Jefferson, Culberson served briefly as county attorney. His father, in the meantime, had become an influential Democratic member of the U.S. House of Representatives. A brother recalled that Culberson "took a drink now and then and played an occasional game of poker or whist" (Madden, p. 7).

Culberson's first statewide race came in 1890, when he ran for the Democratic nomination for attorney general at the suggestion of James S. Hogg, who was a candidate for governor. Hogg's victory helped Culberson gain the nomination, and he won the general election easily in solidly Democratic Texas. Culberson appeared in court to defend the constitutionality of the state's railroad commission statute (*Reagan v. Farmers' Loan and Trust*, 1894) and represented the state in other cases involving railroad policy and a boundary dispute with Oklahoma. He won reelection in 1892.

In 1894 Culberson sought the Democratic nomination for governor. His campaign manager was Edward M. House, whose strategy of winning early endorsements for his candidate gave Culberson a decisive lead. Although Culberson supported Hogg's policies to regulate railroads and out-of-state corporations, he was not as identified with the free coinage of silver or opposition to President Grover Cleveland as were many Texas Democrats. He had to overcome the opposition of former senator John H. Reagan and to compromise on the silver question, but in the end Culberson secured the nomination. In a hotly contested race that focused on the issue of silver, he defeated the Populist candidate, Thomas L. Nugent, in the fall election by nearly 60,000 votes.

Culberson's first term was not distinguished. He emphasized economy in government and vetoed unneeded legislation. His most celebrated achievement was a special session to prevent a heavyweight prize fight in the state. He shared the prevailing opinion that boxing in public was a vulgar display. One disgruntled Democrat called him "a foolish snob" who had "none of Hogg's . . . sympathy for the poor and oppressed"

(Barr, p. 169). Despite a strong Populist campaign against him, Culberson won a second term in 1896. About this time, Culberson developed a drinking problem that affected him for the rest of his life.

In 1898 Culberson moved on to the U.S. Senate. The incumbent, Roger Q. Mills, announced for reelection and then withdrew in the face of Culberson's strength. Culberson was an effective orator at this stage of his career, but characteristic caution had already become his trademark. His senatorial colleague, Joseph Weldon Bailey, said of him in 1900, "Charlie would be all right if he had a little more iron down his backbone" (Gould, p. 13). In Washington, D.C., Culberson attended to his Senate duties and spent time at health resorts and spas. Critics called him "the sick man of the Senate." One opponent said in 1910 that he "had been in a comatose state for five years" (Gould, p. 13).

On policy issues Culberson supported some aspects of overseas expansion but attacked Theodore Roosevelt's (1858–1919) policy on Panama in 1904. He charged that the president's administration had "distinguished itself in shame by adding to multiplied offenses against law the grossest moral delinquencies" (*Address of Senator Culberson*, p. 2). During a period of relative sobriety, he was elected to the largely symbolic post of minority leader of the Senate by his Democratic colleagues in December 1907.

Culberson became chairman of the Senate Judiciary Committee in 1913 and was lobbied by President Woodrow Wilson to support the 1916 nomination of Louis D. Brandeis to the U.S. Supreme Court. Culberson worked for enactment of the Clayton Antitrust Act of 1914 and other progressive legislation of the Wilson years.

The senator faced no opposition for reelection in 1904 and 1910, but his deteriorating health, which now included Bright's disease, made him vulnerable in 1916. He had well-publicized episodes of bad health in 1913 and 1915, and he had to regain sobriety "in a small secluded place in Maine" (Gould, p. 175). At the urging of friends, he announced in early 1916, "I am not strong enough to make a campaign of the State" and that he would have to leave his chances "largely to my friends" (Gould, p. 175). Soon there were Culberson clubs that were informed, "Culberson is a better dead man than his opponents are alive" (Gould, p. 176). Letters from his doctor assured voters that his "mentality is good. The tremor which he has had for some time is functional" (Gould, p. 176). Despite these weaknesses, he gained the second spot in the Democratic primary and faced former governor Oscar B. Colquitt in the runoff.

Because of Colquitt's connections with the German Americans and their opposition to the president, the Wilson administration strongly endorsed Culberson, and that support carried the incumbent to a decisive reelection victory. His fourth term repeated the pattern of his earlier career. He endorsed most of the Wilson administration's measures, such as the Treaty of Versailles, but opposed Prohibition on the ground of states' rights. When it came time for him to run again in 1922, his secretary argued that the senator's health demanded another race. "His life depends on keeping this last interest alive, his work in the Senate" (Brown, p. 90). Once again, he told the voters in a newspaper statement, "I am not strong enough to make a canvass of the State" (Brown, p. 91). Without the special conditions that had existed in 1916, the senator was a wounded incumbent. Newspaper photographs disclosed what time and alcohol had done to him. He finished third in the Democratic primary. After his term ended, he lived in Washington, where he died.

Culberson was a leading example of the workings of Democratic politics in the "Solid South" during the first quarter of the twentieth century. A capable lawmaker when healthy, he was a hopeless invalid for much of his career. Nevertheless, because of the one-party system and the absence of genuine partisan competition, Culberson served four terms in the Senate. He was a cautious, bland, mildly conservative figure, who capitalized on luck and good looks to achieve a position of some importance within the national Democratic party.

• Culberson's personal papers were destroyed after his death. The few letters from him that remain are terse and unrevealing. His official letterbooks and executive correspondence as governor are in the Archives Division, Texas State Library, Austin. The James S. Hogg Papers, Center for American History, University of Texas at Austin, and the Edward M. House Papers, Yale University, have helpful items about Culberson. The Oscar B. Colquitt Papers, Center for American History, document the 1916 campaign. *Address of Senator Charles A. Culberson at the Iroquois Club Banquet, April 13, 1904* (1904) gives a good sense of Culberson's style. James William Madden, *Charles Allen Culberson: His Life, Character and Public Service* (1929), is the only biography. Robert L. Wagner, "The Gubernatorial Career of Charles Allen Culberson" (M.A. thesis, Univ. of Texas, 1954) is balanced; Pollyana B. Hughes and Elizabeth B. Harrison, "Charles A. Culberson: Not a Shadow of Hogg," *East Texas Historical Journal* 11 (1973): 41–52, defend Culberson's record. For overviews of his career, see Alwyn Barr, *Reconstruction to Reform: Texas Politics, 1876–1906* (1971); Lewis L. Gould, *Progressives and Prohibitionists: Texas Democrats in the Wilson Era* (1973); and Norman D. Brown, *Hood, Bonnet, and Little Brown Jug: Texas Politics, 1921–1928* (1984). There is an obituary in the *Dallas Morning News*, 30 Mar. 1925.

LEWIS L. GOULD

CULBERSON, David Browning (29 Sept. 1830–7 May 1900), attorney and U.S. congressman, was born in Troup County, Georgia, the son of David B. Culberson, a Baptist minister, and Lucy Wilkinson. He attended Brownwood Institute in La Grange, Georgia. After moving to Tuskegee, Alabama, he studied law with William P. Chilton, the chief justice of the Alabama Supreme Court. Following his admittance to the bar in 1851, he began to practice law in Dadeville, Alabama. In 1852 he married Eugenia Kimbal. They had two children who survived and four children who died at early ages. In 1856 the Culbersons migrated west to Upshur County, Texas, where he resumed his career as an attorney.

Culberson considered himself a member of the Whig party before it collapsed in the mid-1850s. He won election to the Texas House of Representatives in 1859 as a supporter of Sam Houston, who was elected governor as a Unionist Democrat. During the presidential election of 1860 Culberson favored the Constitutional Union party. When some Texans organized a secession convention in early 1861, he remained an opponent of withdrawing from the Union and gave up his seat in the legislature.

As the Civil War began Culberson moved to Jefferson, Texas, to practice law. In 1861 he joined the Confederate army as an enlisted man. The following year he helped recruit men for the Eighteenth Texas Infantry, which he served as lieutenant colonel. He became colonel of the regiment, which fought as part of a division under John George Walker, first in Arkansas and later in Louisiana. Because of health problems, he left active duty in 1863, then Governor Pendleton Murrah assigned him to be state adjutant and inspector general. He again won election to the state house of representatives during 1864.

When the Civil War ended, Culberson resumed his career as an attorney and achieved prominence because of his success in the courtroom. He returned to politics as a presidential elector for the Democratic party in 1868 and then won election as a member of the Texas Senate in 1873. The following year he ran successfully for the U.S. House of Representatives. Beginning with the Forty-fourth Congress in 1875, he served eleven terms through early 1897. In the 1870s, when most farming regions favored expanded currency and credit, Culberson voted for repeal of specie resumption but faced opposition for reelection from a Greenback party candidate in 1878. He actively supported a Prohibition amendment to the Texas constitution that met defeat in a hotly contested election in 1887. During the 1880s he voted for lower tariffs and railroad regulation, positions favored by his agricultural constituents. After creation of the Interstate Commerce Commission, Culberson in 1890 refused a position as a commissioner.

Culberson served for many years on the House Judiciary Committee. After he became chair of the committee in 1887, he presented and defended antitrust legislation in the House that won adoption in 1890. The following year he was one of the three leading candidates for a U.S. Senate seat from Texas but lost. In the 1890s he chaired the Judiciary Committee twice. He also supported free coinage of silver, a proposal favored by farmers who wanted cheaper currency to pay debts, especially as a depression began.

In 1894 Culberson withdrew from a contest with Horace Chilton for a U.S. Senate seat from Texas in the hope that Governor James S. Hogg, who supported Chilton, might then favor Charles A. Culberson, David Culberson's son, for the Democratic gubernatorial nomination. (Hogg took a neutral position in the race, but Charles Culberson still won the nomination.) After David Culberson retired from Congress in 1897, President William McKinley asked him to serve on the

commission that codified U.S. laws, which Culberson did until his death. He lived to see his son Charles move from governor of Texas to the U.S. Senate in 1899. Culberson died in Jefferson, Texas.

• No collections of Culberson's papers have survived. Some biographical information on Culberson is in the biography of his son by James William Madden, *Charles Allen Culberson: His Life, Character, and Public Service* (1929). Aspects of his career are noted in Llerena Friend, *Sam Houston: The Great Designer* (1954); Tommy Yett, comp., *Members of the Legislature of the State of Texas from 1846 to 1939* (1939); J. P. Blessington, *The Campaigns of Walker's Texas Division* (1875); Ernest William Winkler, *Platforms of Political Parties in Texas* (1916); Alwyn Barr, *Reconstruction to Reform: Texas Politics, 1876–1906* (1971); and Robert C. Cotner, *James Stephen Hogg: A Biography* (1959). Obituaries are in the *Dallas Morning News* and the *Houston Daily Post*, 7 May 1900, and the *New York Times*, 8 May 1900.

ALWYN BARR

CULBERTSON, Ely (22 July 1891–27 Dec. 1955), authority on bridge, was born in the village of Poiana di Verbilao, near Ploesti, Romania, the son of Almon Culbertson, an American mining engineer, and Xenia Rogoznaya, the daughter of a Cossack general. He studied at gymnasia in Russia and briefly at Yale (1908), Cornell (1910), the Sorbonne (1913–1914), and the University of Geneva (1915). But he was largely self-educated, with an extensive knowledge of political writings. He was a remarkable linguist, speaking seven languages fluently and able to read six others, including Latin and Greek.

According to his autobiography, Culbertson became a revolutionary at the age of sixteen. At age seventeen he was almost shot by the authorities in Sochi, Russia, on the Black Sea, but was saved by his American citizenship. Culbertson's subsequent years were action-packed. In Manhattan he was a panhandler, a newsboy, and a helper in a bar. He led a strike of Ukrainian railroad workers in Edmonton, Alberta, Canada, and then he crossed the western United States as a hobo on the railroads. In 1912 he was a revolutionary in Mexico and Spain and was expelled from both countries, again saved by his American status.

During World War I Culbertson lived in Paris, supporting himself by playing auction bridge. When the war was over he visited London, England; Berlin, Germany; and then Brussels, Belgium, from which he was expelled for being a bridge teacher. He then crossed the Atlantic ocean as a seaman, and resumed his bridge activities.

In 1923 Culbertson married Josephine Murphy Dillon, who was apparently the highest-paid bridge teacher of the period; the couple would have two children. They quickly acquired a major reputation as players. When contract bridge was introduced in 1926 and began to displace auction bridge, Culbertson seized the opportunity and within six years had become the acknowledged authority on the new game, outshining his rivals with a well-planned campaign. He established *The Bridge World* magazine in 1929, and issued a series of books on the game, starting with the *Contract Bridge Blue Book* in 1930. His "Approach Forcing" System, based on honor-trick valuation and forcing two opening bids with strong hands, became standard in North America for the next twenty years, and were popular throughout the world. Although honor-tricks and the forcing fell out of favor, the structure of bidding that he recommended became the basis for modern bidding. One-over-one suit responses as preliminary forcing moves were popularized by him. He also invented the Grand Slam Force, usually credited to his wife.

In 1930 Culbertson took a team to London and earned wide publicity by defeating an English team in the first international match ever played. He repeated this effort in 1933 and 1934, capturing the Schwab Cup. On all three occasions he was partnered by his wife, with two of his closest associates completing the team.

As he had planned, Culbertson and his wife were now public figures, constantly in the news. She was beautiful, and always elegantly dressed. Later in 1930 Culbertson challenged the old guard of auction bridge experts to play a match of 150 rubbers at contract. The challenge was accepted by Sidney Lenz, who played with two different partners. Culbertson played mainly with his wife, but there were several substitutes. The Culbertson-Lenz match was played in Manhattan and was front-page news throughout North America; the Associated Press gave play-by-play coverage. Culbertson won by 8,980 points, and as a result he and his system became firmly established in the public mind. He negotiated lucrative contracts for syndicated newspaper articles and radio broadcasts.

After his team won the Vanderbilt Cup in 1930, Culbertson avoided open competition and turned down challenges from even stronger players, notably the "Four Aces" team. In 1935 he accepted a challenge from P. Hal Sims and his wife, Dorothy Rice Sims, and duly won a match of 150 rubbers by 16,130 points. His last major effort came in 1937, when he selected his own team to represent his United States Bridge Association in the first World Championships, played in Budapest, Hungary. His team reached the final, but then lost to Austria by 4,740 points in a match of 100 deals. The year 1937 represented Culbertson's peak as a bridge entrepreneur. His organization, which included an association of bridge teachers with 6,000 members, World Bridge Olympic contests, and the sale of Kem plastic cards, grossed more than $1,000,000 that year. He had an efficient staff which did almost all the writing and other work involved.

In 1938 Culbertson and his wife were divorced. That same year, with war imminent in Europe, he lost interest in bridge and returned to his original love, political science. He spoke in favor of international control of decisive weapons and a quota for each nation in tactical forces. He also proposed a world federation, in which each nation would be required to give up the "sovereign right" to wage war. The federation would have its own army, recruited from the small nations

who had most to gain. Culbertson wrote two books to this effect, *Total Peace* (1943) and *Must We Fight Russia?* (1946). Bertrand Russell, who had similar objectives, described Culbertson as "The most remarkable, or at any rate the most psychologically interesting, man it has ever been my good fortune to know."

Culbertson also wrote articles for the *Reader's Digest*, of which the most important were "The Truman Doctrine Is Not Enough" (July 1947), and "The ABC Plan for World Peace" (July 1948). He received support from a wide range of thinkers, including Dorothy Thompson and Norman Thomas. In 1948 he sought Congressional support, and in April of that year sixteen senators and fourteen congressmen, including Richard Nixon, Estes Kefauver, and Mike Mansfield, agreed to put his plan before Congress. In May the House Foreign Affairs Committee conducted two weeks of public hearings on United Nations reform. During these hearings John Foster Dulles expressed his support for Culbertson's resolution, which featured elimination of the veto, limitation of the arms race, and an international police force, but nothing came of it. The resolution was shelved as the 1948 election campaign drew greater attention. Culbertson wrote one further article for *Reader's Digest*, "We Can Really Have an Effective U.N. Police Force" (Dec. 1950).

In 1947 Culbertson had married 21-year-old Dorothy Renata Baehne; they had two children before their divorce in 1954. Culbertson suffered from emphysema and died in Brattleboro, Vermont, when he caught a cold that aggravated his lung problems.

• The Albert Morehead Memorial Library at the American Contract Bridge League in Memphis, Tennessee, has some of Culbertson's papers, including the unfinished sequel to his autobiography. Culbertson's autobiography is *Strange Lives of One Man* (1940). A modern biography is *Culbertson—The Man Who Made Contract Bridge* (1985). See also *Official Encyclopedia of Bridge*, 5th ed. (1994). An obituary is in the *New York Times*, 28 Dec. 1955.

ALAN TRUSCOTT

CULLEN, Countée (30 May 1903?–9 Jan. 1946), poet and playwright, was the son of Elizabeth Thomas Lucas. The name of his father is not known. The place of his birth has been variously cited as Louisville, Kentucky, New York City, and Baltimore, Maryland. Although in later years Cullen claimed to have been born in New York City, it probably was Louisville, which he consistently named as his birthplace in his youth and which he wrote on his registration form for New York University. His mother died in Louisville in 1940.

In 1916 Cullen was enrolled in Public School Number 27 in the Bronx, New York, under the name of Countee L. Porter, with no accent on the first "e." At that time he was living with Amanda Porter, who generally is assumed to have been his grandmother. Shortly after she died in October 1917, Countee went to live with the Reverend Frederick Asbury Cullen, pastor of Salem Methodist Episcopal Church in Harlem, and his wife, the former Carolyn Belle Mitchell. Countee was never formally adopted by the Cullens, but he later claimed them as his natural parents and in 1918 assumed the name Countée P. (Porter) Cullen. In 1925 he dropped the middle initial.

Cullen was an outstanding student in every school he attended. He entered the respected, almost exclusively white, Dewitt Clinton High School for boys in Manhattan in 1918. He became a member of the Arista honor society, and in his senior year he received the Magpie Cup in recognition of his achievements. He served as vice president of the senior class and was associate editor of the 1921 *Magpie*, the school's literary magazine, and editor of the *Clinton News*. He won an oratorical contest sponsored by the film actor Douglas Fairbanks and served as treasurer of the Inter–High School Poetry Society and as chairperson of the Senior Publications Committee. His poetry appeared regularly in school publications and he received wider public recognition in 1921 when his poem, "I Have a Rendezvous with Life," won first prize in a citywide contest sponsored by the Empire Federation of Women's Clubs. At New York University, which Cullen attended on a New York State Regents scholarship, he was elected to Phi Beta Kappa in his junior year and received a bachelor's degree in 1925. His poems were published frequently in the school magazine, *The Arch*, of which he eventually became poetry editor. In 1926 he received a master's degree from Harvard University and won the *Crisis* magazine award in poetry.

When Cullen's first collection of poetry, *Color*, was published in 1925 during his senior year at New York University, he had already achieved national fame. His poems had been published in *Bookman*, *American Mercury*, *Harper's*, *Century*, *Nation*, *Poetry*, *Crisis*, the *Messenger*, *Palms*, and *Opportunity*. He had won second prize in 1923 in the Witter Bynner Undergraduate Poetry Contest sponsored by the Poetry Society of America. He placed second in that contest again in 1924 but won first prize in 1925, when he also won the John Reed Memorial Prize awarded by *Poetry* magazine.

Color received universal critical acclaim. Alain Locke wrote in *Opportunity* (Jan. 1926): "Ladies and Gentlemen! A genius! Posterity will laugh at us if we do not proclaim him now. COLOR transcends all of the limiting qualifications that might be brought forward if it were merely a work of talent." The volume contains epitaphs, only two of which could be considered racial; love poems; and poems on other traditional subjects. But the significant theme—as the title implies—was race, and it was the poems dealing with racial subjects that captured the attention of the critics. Cullen was praised for portraying the experience of African Americans in the vocabulary and poetic forms of the classical tradition but with a personal intimacy. His second volume of poetry, *Copper Sun*, published in 1927 also by Harper and Brothers (the publisher of all his books), won first prize in literature from the Harmon Foundation. There are fewer racial poems in this collection than in *Color*, however, they express an

anger that was not so pronounced in the earlier volume. The majority of the poems in *Copper Sun* deal with life and love and other traditional themes of nineteenth-century poetry.

Cullen edited the October 1926 special issue of *Palms* devoted to African-American poets, and he collected and edited *Caroling Dusk* in 1927, an anthology of poetry by African Americans. Cullen was by this time generally recognized by critics and the public as the leading literary figure of the Harlem Renaissance. Gerald Early in *My Soul's High Song* (1991), Cullen's collected writings, said, "He was, indeed, a boy wonder, a young handsome black Ariel ascending, a boyish, brown-skinned titan who, in the early and mid-twenties, embodied many of the hopes, aspirations, and maturing expressive possibilities of his people."

Cullen said that he wanted to be known as a poet, not a "Negro poet." This did not affect his popularity, although some Harlem Renaissance writers, including Langston Hughes, interpreted this to mean that he wanted to deny his race, an interpretation endorsed by some later scholars. A reading of his poetry reveals this view to be unfounded. In fact his major poems, and most of those still being printed in anthologies, have racial themes. Cullen expounded his view in the *Brooklyn Eagle* (10 Feb. 1924):

If I am going to be a poet at all, I am going to be POET and not NEGRO POET. This is what has hindered the development of artists among us. Their one note has been the concern with their race. That is all very well, none of us can get away from it. I cannot at times. You will see it in my verse. The consciousness of this is too poignant at times. I cannot escape it. But what I mean is this: I shall not write of negro subjects for the purpose of propaganda. That is not what a poet is concerned with. Of course, when the emotion rising out of the fact that I am a negro is strong, I express it. But that is another matter.

From 1926 to 1928, Cullen was assistant editor to Charles S. Johnson of *Opportunity* (subtitled "A Journal of Negro Life") for which he also wrote a feature column, "The Dark Tower." On the one hand, in his reviews and commentaries, he called upon African-American writers to create a representative and respectable race literature, and on the other insisted that the African-American artist should not be bound by race or restricted to racial themes.

The year 1928 was a watershed for Cullen. He received a Guggenheim Fellowship to study in Paris, the third volume of his poetry, *The Ballad of a Brown Girl*, was published, and, after a long courtship, he married Nina Yolande Du Bois. Her father, W. E. B. Du Bois, the exponent of the "Talented Tenth" concept, rejoiced at bringing the young genius into his family. The wedding, performed by Cullen's foster father, was the social event of the decade in Harlem. After a brief honeymoon in Philadelphia, Cullen left for Paris and was soon joined by his bride. The couple experienced difficulties from the beginning. Finally, after informing her father that Cullen had confessed that he was sexually attracted to men, Nina Yolande sued for divorce, which was obtained in Paris in 1930.

Cullen continued to write and publish after 1928, but his works were no longer universally acclaimed. *The Black Christ and Other Poems*, completed under the Guggenheim Fellowship, was published in 1929 while he was abroad. His only novel, *One Way to Heaven*, was published in 1932, and *The Medea and Some Poems* in 1935. He wrote two books for juveniles, *The Lost Zoo* (1940) and *My Lives and How I Lost Them* (1942). His stage adaptation of *One Way to Heaven* was produced by several amateur and professional theater groups but remained one of his several unpublished plays. Critics gave these works mixed reviews at best.

Cullen's reputation as a writer rests on his poetry. His novel is not an important work, and it received little attention from the critics. He rejected so-called jazz and free-style as inappropriate forms of poetic expression. He was a romantic lyric poet and a great admirer of John Keats and Edna St. Vincent Millay. While his arch traditionalism and lack of originality in style had been seen in *Color* as minor flaws, they came to be viewed as major deficiencies in his later works.

Cullen's fall from grace with the critics had little effect on his popularity. He remained much in demand for lectures and readings by both white and black groups. In 1931 alone he read his poetry and lectured in various institutions in seventeen states and Canada. Some of his poems were set to music by Charles Marsh, Virgil Thomson, William Schuman, William Lawrence, Margaret Bonds, Clarence Cameron White, Emerson Whithorne, and Noel DaCosta. However, even though he continued to live with his foster father, royalties and lecture fees were insufficient income for subsistence. He searched for academic positions and was offered professorships at Sam Huston College (named for an Iowa farmer, not the Texas senator), Dillard University, Fisk University, Tougaloo College, and West Virginia State College. There is no clear explanation of why he did not accept any of the positions. In 1932 he became a substitute teacher in New York public schools and became a full-time teacher of English and French at Frederick Douglass Junior High School in 1934, a position he held until his death (caused by complications of high blood pressure) in New York City, and where he taught and inspired the future novelist and essayist James Baldwin.

Cullen married Ida Mae Roberson in 1940, and they apparently enjoyed a happy married life. Cullen's chief creative interest during the last year of his life was in writing the script for *St. Louis Woman*, a musical based on Arna Bontemps's novel *God Sends Sunday*. With music by Harold Arlen and lyrics by Johnny Mercer, *St. Louis Woman* opened on Broadway on 30 March 1946. Although the production was opposed by Walter White of the National Association for the Advancement of Colored People and some other civil rights activists as an unfavorable representation of African Americans, it ran for four months and was re-vived several times by amateurs and one professional group between 1959 and 1980.

On These I Stand, a collection of poems that Cullen had selected as his best, was published posthumously in 1947. The 135th Street Branch of the New York Public Library was named for Cullen in 1951, and a public school in New York City and one in Chicago also bear his name. For a few brief years Cullen was the most celebrated African-American writer in the nation and by many accounts is considered one of the major voices of the Harlem Renaissance.

• Countée Cullen's personal papers (1921–1969, c. 4,400 manuscripts and photographs and thirty-nine volumes) are in the Amistad Research Center at Tulane University; microfilm copies of that collection are in other repositories. The James Weldon Johnson Collection in Beinecke Library at Yale University contains more than 900 letters written by and to Cullen and other writings by and about him. One of the best biographies is Michael L. Lomax, "Countée Cullen: From the Dark Tower" (Ph.D. diss., Emory Univ., 1984). Also valuable is the biographical introduction to *My Soul's High Song: The Collected Writings of Countee Cullen, Voice of the Harlem Renaissance*, ed. Gerald Early (1991). This volume contains reprints of all Cullen's published books except *Caroling Dusk, The Lost Zoo, My Lives and How I Lost Them*, and *On These I Stand*; it also contains some of Cullen's uncollected poems, speeches, and essays. See also Blanche E. Ferguson, *Countee Cullen and the Negro Renaissance* (1966); Margaret Perry, *A Bio-Bibliography of Countée P. Cullen, 1903–1946* (1971); and Alan R. Shucard, *Countee Cullen* (1984), for biographical studies. For critical studies of Cullen's poetry, see Houston A. Baker, Jr., "A Many-Colored Coat of Dreams: The Poetry of Countee Cullen," in his *Afro-American Poetics: Revisions of Harlem and the Black Aesthetic* (1988), pp. 45–87; Isaac William Brumfield, "Race Consciousness in the Poetry and Fiction of Countee Cullen" (Ph.D. diss., Univ. of Illinois at Champaign-Urbana, 1977); Nicholas Canaday, Jr., "Major Themes in the Poetry of Countee Cullen," in *The Harlem Renaissance Remembered*, ed. Arna Bontemps (1972), pp. 103–25; Eugenia W. Collier, "I Do Not Marvel, Countee Cullen," in *Modern Black Poets*, ed. Donald B. Gibson (1973), pp. 69–83; Arthur P. Davis, "The Alien-and-Exile Theme in Countee Cullen's Racial Poems," *Phylon* 14 (Fourth Quarter 1953): 390–400; Robert E. Fennell, "The Death Figure in Countee Cullen's Poetry" (M.A. thesis, Howard Univ., 1970); and David Kirby, "Countee Cullen's Heritage: A Black Waste Land," *South Atlantic Bulletin* 4 (1971): 14–20. Of value also is James Baldwin, "Rendezvous with Life: An Interview with Countee Cullen," *Magpie* 26 (Winter 1942): 19–21. For an extensive discussion of Cullen's impact on Baldwin, see David Leeming, *Baldwin* (1994). Obituaries and related articles are in the *New York Herald Tribune*, 10 Jan. 1946; the *New York Times*, 10 and 12 Jan. 1946, and the *Negro History Bulletin* 14 (Feb. 1946): 98.

CLIFTON H. JOHNSON

CULLEN, Hugh Roy (3 July 1881–4 July 1957), oilman and philanthropist, was born in Denton County, Texas, the son of Cicero Cullen, a businessman whose father was a hero of the Texan struggle for independence, and Louise Beck, who came from a plantation-owning family of South Carolinians. When Cullen was in his early childhood his parents separated, and he moved with his mother to San Antonio where he completed his elementary education. At seventeen he was employed by a cotton broker, but after a six-year apprenticeship he set up his own cotton brokerage firm and vowed never to be someone else's employee. In 1903 he married Lillie Cranz; they had five children.

The cotton market depression of 1911 prompted Cullen to move his family to newly developing Houston where he turned to dealing in real estate. His enterprises prospered modestly, but they also resulted in a lifelong rivalry with another Houston real estate operator, Jesse Jones. The Cullen-Jones rivalry extended beyond business into politics and philanthropy.

In 1917, at the invitation of a business acquaintance, Cullen got out of Houston real estate and into west Texas oil, where during the next two decades he discovered and developed fields worth billions of dollars. Although Cullen's spectacular success earned him the popular title of "king of the wildcatters," his early ventures were partially backed by Gulf and Standard Oil. Cullen explained his good fortune by an undefined "creekology," by which he apparently meant a close personal examination of the lay of terrain supplemented with geological and geophysical data. In addition, he was able to tap oil pools below previously abandoned fields by drilling deeper, by using water instead of mud around the drill bit, and by using heavy pipe to smash through a stratum called "heaving shale" that had stymied his competitors. None of these methods were new, but the combination had not been applied to the rock formations Cullen attacked.

Cullen's major philanthropic activities began in 1936 when he was fifty-five and after his only son was killed in an oil field accident. He and his wife donated $260,000 to the recently chartered University of Houston for a classroom building named in their son's honor. The sole condition was that the university must remain "a college for working men and women and their sons and daughters." Eventually their gifts to the institution totaled more than $30 million, which helped convert a small, struggling school into a major regional university.

In 1945 Cullen and his wife began making generous gifts to various Houston hospitals and schools, culminating in the Texas Medical Center at Baylor University. In 1947 they established the Cullen Foundation by endowing it with oil fields valued at more than $160 million, which made it the third largest U.S. foundation. Their only stipulation was that foundation grants had to be spent in Texas; otherwise, decisions were left to trustees, who included three of their daughters. Shortly before his death, Cullen estimated that he had already disposed of 93 percent of his wealth. This was the result of a "desire to spend all the money I possibly can during my life, so that I may get a selfish pleasure out of spending it."

The other significant facet of Cullen's life was politics. He was a Democrat until 1928 when Jesse Jones scored a personal triumph by bringing the Democratic party's national convention to Houston, at which Al-

fred E. Smith was nominated. This move by his rival drove Cullen into the Republican party, which was then committed to a high tariff that he favored to protect American workers from foreign competition. Idiosyncratically he urged Republican presidential candidates during the 1930s and 1940s to promote a national policy encouraging large corporations to pay part of workers' wages in stock to give them a personal stake in America's industrial development, but his prompting went without notable success. Cullen does not appear to have implemented this policy in his own corporations.

Although he personally favored Senator Robert Taft over other Republican presidential candidates in the early 1940s, Cullen became convinced that Taft could not win in Texas or in any other southern state. From 1948 on he worked diligently for the nomination of Dwight Eisenhower because he saw Ike and the Republican party as bulwarks against "creeping socialism" and as guarantors of states' rights. He contributed funds widely to the election campaigns of congressional and senatorial candidates—some of whom won.

A knowledgeable observer described Cullen as "by turns impulsive, sentimental, opinionated, sharp-tongued and folksy, and as tactful as a Texas steer stampeding through a glass works." But, the observer added, only one word captured his spirit: "generous." He died in Houston. Cullen may be considered one of the pioneers in the movement toward a two-party South and for a Republican party more fully committed to a conservative ideology, but probably his most lasting impact may be found in his philanthropies.

• A biography by Edward W. Kilman and Theon Wright, *Hugh Roy Cullen: A Story of American Opportunity* (1954), was published before Cullen's death. There is no explicit evidence of Cullen's involvement except that the book includes many extensive quotations from his correspondence. The milieu in which Cullen operated is covered in George M. Fuermann, *Houston: Land of the Big Rich* (1951); David G. McComb, *Houston, Bayou City* (1969); Richard O'Connor, *The Oil Barons* (1971); Theodore H. White, "Texas: Land of Wealth and Fear," *The Reporter*, 25 May 1954, pp. 10–17; and Cleveland Amory, "Oil Folks at Home," *Holiday*, Feb. 1957, pp. 52–57. Cullen's philanthropies were the subject of articles in the *New York Times*, 19 Mar. 1947, p. 17, and the *Christian Science Monitor*, 7 May 1947, p. 11, as well as "Words of Wrath," *Newsweek*, 9 Feb. 1948, pp. 20–21; "A Man So Rich," *Time*, 7 Apr. 1948, p. 29; and "A Man Who Likes to Give Away Millions," *U.S. News & World Report*, 11 Feb. 1955, pp. 68–72. An obituary is in the *New York Times*, 5 July 1957.

NICHOLAS VARGA

CULLINAN, Joseph Stephen (31 Dec. 1860–11 Mar. 1937), oil industry executive, was born near Sharon, Pennsylvania, the son of John Francis Cullinan, an oil field worker, and Mary Considine. Joseph's parents, who were both Irish immigrants, moved the family to Oil Creek, Pennsylvania, when he was eight. When he was fourteen, Joseph left school to help support the family. Working in the oil fields of western Pennsylvania, he gained valuable experience in the industry. In

1882 he joined Standard Oil's major transportation affiliate, the National Transit Company of Oil City, Pennsylvania, and soon became a foreman. He was reassigned to Lima, Ohio, in 1888 and became a superintendent in Standard Oil's major transportation affiliate in the Ohio-Indiana region, the Buckeye Pipe Line Company. It was in Lima that Cullinan met Lucie Halm, a merchant's daughter, whom he married in 1891. They had two sons and three daughters.

In 1893 Cullinan returned to Pennsylvania as a superintendent of another Standard Oil affiliate, the Southwestern Pennsylvania Pipe Line Company. In 1895 he left Standard Oil after thirteen years of service to the company and formed his own concern, the Petroleum Iron Works, headquartered in Washington, Pennsylvania, and devoted to manufacturing oil equipment such as storage tanks and steam boilers. Cullinan turned this firm into a lucrative enterprise. His legend as an oil industry chieftain also began to grow, with workers calling him "Buckskin Joe" because his toughness as a leader reminded them of the leather in work gloves and shoes.

In 1897 a seminal event in Cullinan's life occurred when city officials of Corsicana, Texas, a small city near Dallas, invited him to that city to appraise the growing oil industry there. Oil had been discovered at Corsicana in 1894, but the nascent industry needed more capital and more rigorous, experienced management if it was to realize its potential. Cullinan visited Corsicana for three weeks as a stop on a planned trip to California. Recognizing the enormous potential of the oil industry at Corsicana, he scrapped his California travel plans and settled in Corsicana, where he embarked on a whirlwind of activities.

Cullinan helped to solve many of the vexing dilemmas that were impeding the growth of the Corsicana oil industry. To provide badly needed field storage, he immediately began construction of the oil field's largest storage facility and eventually built three more storage tanks, the largest two holding 36,000 barrels of oil each. In 1898, in order to secure more capital for the industry, Cullinan formed a partnership, J. S. Cullinan & Company, with two of his former Standard Oil associates. The same year he also reached a contract agreement with the three largest oil producers in Corsicana to purchase their crude oil. This arrangement put Cullinan in control of most of the crude coming from Corsicana's fields. Cullinan also found new ideas for the use of crude. He sold crude to the city of Corsicana so that it could be spread on dirt roads to control dust; other Texas cities soon followed this practice. Cullinan also began the natural gas industry in Texas. Whereas oil drillers had considered natural gas—which was found above oil deposits—worthless and simply let it burn at the field, Cullinan piped the gas to households and businesses in Corsicana, making it the first city in Texas to have natural gas.

In 1898 Cullinan took a major step toward integrating oil operations in Corsicana by building a refinery. One of the most technologically advanced in Texas, it was soon refining 1,000 barrels of crude a day. The following year Cullinan formed the Corsicana Petroleum Company to direct oil and natural gas production in that city; he served as president of the new firm.

What Cullinan accomplished in fewer than five years at Corsicana was astounding. He gave Corsicana operations the direction and expertise they badly needed, solved many of the problems they faced—such as field storage and outlets for crude oil and natural gas—and established a model for integrated operations in the Texas oil industry.

By the early 1900s Corsicana oil fields had already reached their peak production and were on the wane. The locus of the Texas oil industry began to shift to the Gulf Coast, especially with the prolific oil discovery at Spindletop, near Beaumont, Texas. The prodigious output there almost instantly made Texas the premier oil-producing state in America and stimulated the growth of new oil companies. The Texas oil boom helped to tear down Standard Oil's monopoly even before the landmark 1911 Supreme Court decision that dismantled Standard Oil.

Cullinan was eager to become involved with operations at Spindletop, and with his sterling reputation in the Texas petroleum industry, local officials were just as eager to draw on his experience and knowledge. In 1901 Cullinan formed the Texas Fuel Company (TFC), a pipeline and refining concern that purchased the crude oil produced at Spindletop. He also formed a business arrangement with the Hogg-Swayne Syndicate, one of Spindletop's most important oil prospecting companies, headed by former Texas governor James Hogg, Fort Worth attorney James Swayne, and several other Texas lawyers. The arrangement, whereby Cullinan built more storage facilities and marketed Hogg-Swayne products, allowed Cullinan to make further inroads in Spindletop oil operations; he became so absorbed in business there that in 1902 he resigned from his Corsicana business interests.

In 1902 Cullinan helped found the Producers Oil Company, a production company in which he held 100,000 shares. Devoted to exploring for and producing crude oil, Producers Oil was the complement to TFC that helped Cullinan have an integrated oil operation at Spindletop, just as he had at Corsicana.

Because the capitalization of TFC was too small and its scope of operations limited, in 1902 Cullinan helped to found a new company, the Texas Company (TC), devoted to both production and pipeline facilities and headquartered at Beaumont, Texas. Named president of the new company, Cullinan recruited experienced oil industry associates, raided the rosters of Standard Oil workers, and lured key executives to TC with high salaries and promises of quick promotions. He also secured needed capital from eastern stockholders. TC soon purchased an 865-acre tract at Sour Lake, which proved to be a prolific source of oil, soon producing 50,000 to 60,000 barrels of oil a day. In 1903 TC opened a large refinery at Port Arthur, which by 1906 was refining over 800,000 barrels a year.

TC increased its operations with the completion of an Oklahoma pipeline in 1908, which connected the

Port Arthur refinery with Glenn Pool, Oklahoma. There lucrative oil fields were struck in 1906, a discovery critical to Cullinan since the Gulf Coast fields had peaked and were on the decline. The Texas Company changed its name to Texaco in 1907 and built a new refinery at West Dallas, later purchasing an asphalt processing plant at Port Neches, Texas. The company's three refineries turned out a wide variety of petroleum products—lubricating oils, road oil, roofing materials, gasoline, and more. Texaco was booming under Cullinan's direction, and in its first ten years of operation its only major setback came in 1905, when an attempt to merge the company with the Guffey-Gulf Companies (also formed at Spindletop) failed because of Texas antitrust laws.

Texaco began to suffer economic reversals in 1911 and 1912, and many of its directors grew disenchanted with Cullinan's leadership. Cullinan, too, was greatly disturbed by the increasing number of easterners among Texaco's stockholders, for he believed the company was a Texas company and should reflect the state's ideals with greater Texan control. Cullinan and Texaco's directors could not resolve their differences, and in 1913 Cullinan was forced to resign. In part he was a victim of his own management style. He practiced tight, highly personal control over the company, but the company had become too large for one-man rule and was ready for further growth; only shared decision-making and shared company responsibility could foster such growth, and Cullinan was averse to adopt such a management style.

After leaving Texaco, Cullinan traveled to California briefly but returned to Houston, a city that he now considered home. From 1913 to 1919 he served as president of the Houston Chamber of Commerce; one of the more notable achievements of his tenure was his successful fight to obtain federal money to build and maintain the Houston Ship Channel.

Cullinan's foremost activity continued to involve the oil industry. In 1914 he organized the Farmers Petroleum Company, which operated five productive wells. After this company dissolved in 1916, Cullinan organized and was president of the American Republics Company, a holding company for several subsidiaries, the most important of which were the Republic Production Company, the Federal Petroleum Company (operating in Los Angeles), and the Papoose Oil Company (operating in Oklahoma). During World War I Cullinan also served as an advisor to the Food Administration, in which capacity he met Herbert Hoover, the future U.S. president, who became a lifelong friend. After the war demonstrated the invaluable importance of oil, Cullinan grew more emphatic in his fight for the conservation of oil and natural gas and argued for federal control of the oil industry.

In 1929 Cullinan successfully countered a stockholder challenge to his leadership of the American Republics Company, but in that same year he voluntarily handed the presidency over to his son Craig. The elder Cullinan was later reelected but relinquished the office again in 1936, this time permanently, and Craig once

again became president. During this time, from 1928 to 1933 Cullinan also served as chairman of the Mount Rushmore National Memorial Committee.

Cullinan spent his entire working life in the oil industry, rising from an oil field laborer to become a manager in the Standard Oil Company. He eventually founded oil companies on his own, including Texaco, which became one of the largest oil companies in Texas. Although his highly individualized executive style eventually proved inadequate for the burgeoning Texaco, he left on indelible imprint on the embryonic Texas oil industry. He drew on a wide circle of friends and associates in the oil industry to attract eastern capital to the state. An aggressive, visionary leader, he provided the managerial and technical direction necessary to bring Texas's oil industry to national prominence. It was with good reason that he was regarded as "the dean of the oil fraternity." Cullinan died in Palo Alto, California, during a planned trip to visit former president Herbert Hoover.

• The Joseph Stephen Cullinan Papers in the Texas Gulf Coast Historical Association Archives at the University of Houston include both personal correspondence and business records. They are valuable in tracing the organization and development of the Texas Company during Cullinan's presidency. The Texaco Archives, located at company headquarters in New York City, contain extensive material covering Cullinan's tenure as corporation president. The Texas and Local History Collection of the Houston Public Library has a large clipping file on Cullinan. The James Lockhart Autry Papers at Rice University also provide insight into Cullinan's business practices (Autry was legal counsel to Cullinan from 1897 to 1920). A valuable biography is John O. King, *Joseph Stephen Cullinan: A Study of Leadership in the Texas Petroleum Industry, 1897–1937* (1970). Four other books yielding information on Cullinan are James Clark and Michel Halbouty, *Spindletop* (1952), Marquis James, *The Texaco Story* (1953), Charles Warner, *Texas Oil and Gas Since 1543* (1939), and Harold Williamson and Arnold Daum, *The American Petroleum Industry: The Age of Energy, 1899–1959* (1963). Obituaries are in the *Houston Chronicle* and the *Houston Post*, both 11 Mar. 1937, and in the *New York Times*, 12 Mar. 1937.

YANEK MIECZKOWSKI

CULLOM, Shelby Moore (22 Nov. 1829–28 Jan. 1914), politician, was born in Wayne County, Kentucky, the seventh of the twelve children of Richard Northcraft Cullom and Elizabeth Coffey, farmers. Within a year the family moved to Tazewell County, Illinois, and Richard Cullom eventually achieved enough prominence to serve two terms in the lower house of the Illinois General Assembly and two in the state senate as a Whig between 1836 and 1854. The rigors of farm work and a stint of country-school teaching helped crystallize in young Shelby a desire to study law. In 1853, following two years of indifferent schooling at the Rock River Seminary at Mount Morris, Cullom moved to Springfield, sought advice from Abraham Lincoln, a political friend of his father, and began to read law. In 1855 Cullom was admitted to the bar and elected to his first office, city attorney. A political career marked by longevity, a rural outlook, and party devotion was thereby launched.

As was the case with many late nineteenth-century public figures, the Civil War became the moral reference point for Cullom's political career. Unlike most others, he spent the war years as a Republican politician, not a soldier. Initially wary of the radical image of the new party, Cullom supported Millard Fillmore in 1856 and was elected to the state legislature on a combined Fillmore–Free Soil ticket. Then in 1858, he took the biggest (and perhaps the only) gamble of his career by hitching his fortunes to Lincoln and the Republicans. Cullom returned to the Illinois General Assembly in 1861 and served as Speaker of the lower house. He moved on to the U.S. House of Representatives in early 1865 and remained in office until 1871. Cullom returned to the Illinois General Assembly from 1873 to 1875, again holding the post of speaker from 1873 to 1874. Two terms as governor of Illinois followed between 1877 and 1883. Finally, in 1883 Cullom began the first of five consecutive terms in the U.S. Senate lasting until 1913. Throughout his tenure he clung to the image of Lincoln and the dictates of the Republican party. At the outset of his national political career, Cullom was a member of Lincoln's funeral party. At the close of Cullom's public life following his defeat in the 1912 Illinois Republican senatorial primary, he was awarded a sinecure on the Lincoln Memorial Commission. During the intervening half-century, Cullom waved the bloody shirt, memorialized the "boys in blue," and became so closely linked with the GOP in Illinois that he developed into a visible symbol of the party's heroic past, "the man who looked like Lincoln."

Cullom's national reputation grew out of his thirty-year career in the Senate. Generally a cautious and unimaginative lawmaker, in his first term Cullom made his greatest contribution to American government as the chief senatorial architect of the Interstate Commerce Commission (created in 1887). As an Illinois representative in 1873, Cullom had participated in the creation of the state Railroad and Warehouse Commission and then oversaw its operation while governor. Although unfamiliar with railroad economics, Cullom brought to the Senate a conviction that federal regulation of interstate carriers was necessary and that an appointive commission was the proper regulatory apparatus. Political realism and legislative circumspection shaped this viewpoint. Complaints of railroad rate discrimination from shippers and agricultural groups indicated the need for regulation of interstate commerce, but Cullom believed the courts had discouraged states from undertaking such initiatives. Congressional action was necessary, yet Cullom disliked Representative John Reagan's proposal to prohibit rebates and pooling, regulate long-haul and short-haul rates, and rely on the courts for enforcement. Cullom favored a more general law that gave a commission of experts the freedom to establish reasonable guidelines, thus providing more effective regulation that would

not disrupt business. Cullom submitted a bill to the Senate in 1884 authorizing the creation of such a commission; became the head of a select commission investigating interstate commerce in 1885; helped steer the Interstate Commerce Act, which combined parts of the Reagan bill with the essence of Cullom's bill, through Congress in 1887; and then chaired the Senate Committee on Interstate Commerce until 1901.

Cullom became one of the Senate's experts on railroads, but characteristically he wavered over the merits of pooling, on the one hand recognizing its role in stabilizing rates but, on the other, hesitating to endorse monopoly. In other matters he was a moderate expansionist, supporting the war with Spain and the acquisition of canal rights in Panama, chairing the commission that drew up the territorial government of Hawaii, endorsing and later regretting the annexation of the Philippines. He was also a defender of Republican tariff policy, despite personal doubts, and a fervent opponent of polygamy among the Mormons of Utah.

Bland, reticent, and uninspiring, Cullom rose to a position of power in the Senate by biding his time, refraining from public criticism of his colleagues, and trimming his own beliefs to fit the platform of his party. As such, he was a fitting symbol of the organizational politics of the late nineteenth century. He used senatorial patronage to build a loyal organization in Illinois, which returned him to Washington every six years. Often enmeshed in factional squabbles, Cullom almost always closed ranks with his party at election time. Four times he headed the Illinois delegation at GOP national conventions, and after 1911 he chaired the Senate Republican caucus. Cullom, however, viewed office as a legitimate reward for party service. In 1888 and again in 1896 he put in modest presidential bids and was hurt when his overtures were rebuffed. In 1901 he demanded by right of seniority the chairmanship of the Senate Foreign Relations Committee and held onto the post until he left the Senate, thereby enraging his talented and ambitious rival for the position, Henry Cabot Lodge.

Cullom's final years were unhappy. Twice married (to Hannah M. Fisher from 1855 until her death in 1861 and then to her sister Julia from 1863 until she died in 1909), Cullom had to bear the deaths of both wives and of his two daughters. Likewise, his senatorial colleagues died one by one. He found the political mood and issues of the Progressive Era baffling and unattractive. Cullom developed a dislike for Theodore Roosevelt (1858–1919), especially after his Bull Moose apostasy in 1912, and considered many of the new senators inconsiderate and ill tempered. In that same year, Illinois Republicans determined it was time for "Uncle Shelby" to retire. In truth, Cullom had outlived the world with which he was familiar. His memoirs, *Fifty Years of Public Service* (1911), surprised contemporaries with their candor and occasioned a minor uproar because of Cullom's skeptical remarks about the possibility of an afterlife. Besieged by clergymen, Cullom recanted and returned to Methodist orthodoxy before his death, observing one final time the lifelong habits of a practical and talented politician. He died in Washington, D.C.

• The Shelby Moore Cullom Papers are housed at the Illinois State Historical Library in Springfield. In addition to Cullom's memoirs, there is a biography by James W. Neilson, *Shelby M. Cullom: Prairie State Republican* (1962). Cullom's talents as an organizational politician are recounted in James W. Fullinwider, "The Governor and the Senator: Executive Power and the Structure of the Illinois Republican Party, 1880–1917" (Ph.D. diss. Washington Univ. 1974).

THOMAS R. PEGRAM

CULLUM, George Washington (25 Feb. 1809–28 Feb. 1892), army officer and author, was born in New York City, the son of Arthur Cullum, a coach maker, and Harriet Sturges. In 1817 Cullum's family moved to Meadville, Pennsylvania, where his father served as an agent of a land company and practiced law. Young Cullum entered the U.S. Military Academy in 1829 and graduated in 1833.

Commissioned a second lieutenant in the Corps of Engineers, Cullum spent his early career supervising the construction of seacoast fortifications and harbor improvements along the New England coast. He was promoted to captain in 1838, and during the Mexican War he helped raise and equip an elite company of sappers, miners, and pontoniers that had been added to the Corps of Engineers. On assignment at the Military Academy during 1847–1850, he drafted a treatise on pontoon bridges and served as instructor of practical military engineering. Because of poor health, Cullum went on extended leave from 1850 to 1852 and traveled in Europe, the Middle East, and the West Indies. On his return, he served a second tour as instructor at the Military Academy and commanded the company of engineering troops stationed there. During 1855–1861 he again supervised fortification projects and civil works, mainly in the Carolinas, New York, and New England.

In April 1861, just before the outbreak of the Civil War, Cullum was promoted to lieutenant colonel and aide-de-camp to Lieutenant General Winfield Scott, the commanding general of the army. Advanced to brigadier general of volunteers in November 1861, he served as chief engineer and chief of staff to Major General Henry Wager Halleck, commander of the Departments of Missouri and the Mississippi. While stationed at Cairo, Illinois, in early 1862, Cullum supported Brigadier General Ulysses S. Grant's campaign against Fort Donelson on the Cumberland River, and he worked closely with Halleck during the subsequent offensive against the Confederate railroad center at Corinth, Mississippi. In July 1862 President Abraham Lincoln appointed Halleck to the post of commanding general of the army, and Cullum accompanied Halleck to Washington, D.C., continuing as his chief of staff. Throughout the critical middle stages of the Civil War, the veteran engineer worked at the hub of the northern war effort, helping to handle his chief's correspondence and supporting Halleck's efforts to coordinate overall Union strategy. Cullum also served on military boards and undertook frequent special assignments, and from 1861 to 1864 he was a member of the U.S. Sanitary Commission.

In March 1864 the Lincoln administration replaced Halleck with Grant as commanding general, though Halleck continued to advise the government in the new and anomalous office of chief of staff of the army. Cullum remained as Halleck's assistant until September, when he was appointed to head the U.S. Military Academy. The new superintendent faced a difficult situation. The demands of the war had led to a shortage of effective officer-instructors at West Point; consequently, hazing and other disciplinary problems and dismissals for academic failure had reached new heights. To raise morale and encourage academic achievement, Cullum moderated some of the stringent rules traditionally imposed on the cadets and authorized badges and special chevrons for those who excelled in their studies and military duties. Together with other engineer officers, he lobbied to preserve the Corps of Engineers' longstanding control of the Military Academy, but in 1866 Congress opened the superintendent's position to officers of all branches of the army. Cullum ended his West Point tour in August 1866, and the following month he was mustered out of volunteer service and returned to his regular grade of lieutenant colonel of engineers. Until his mandatory retirement in 1874, he served on various engineering boards engaged in seacoast fortification and harbor and river improvements. In 1875 he married Elizabeth Hamilton Halleck, the widow of his former commander. The couple had no children.

Cullum was a military intellectual—representative of a growing professional culture in the nineteenth-century officer corps—and he published treatises and articles on military engineering, policy, and history. Recurring themes of his writings were the superiority of regulars over citizen soldiers and the critical importance of formal military education. In particular, he was a staunch defender of West Point, and his most notable achievement was the compilation of his monumental biographical register of the officers and graduates of the U.S. Military Academy. Cullum began this project while stationed at the academy in 1847, apparently acting on Superintendent Henry Brewerton's desire to demonstrate the value of the institution and thus strengthen its popular image. The first edition, published in 1850, consisted only of lists of academy officers and brief summaries of graduates' service records. For Cullum, however, the register became a lifelong labor of love, and in the decades that followed he engaged in a major research effort, poring through archives and sending out thousands of letters of inquiry. The second edition appeared in 1868 and contained much fuller data on the military and civilian careers of West Point officers and graduates as well as substantial biographical sketches of many. Interestingly, Cullum said nothing of the Civil War services of graduates who had supported the Confederacy, noting only that they had "joined in the Rebellion of 1861–66 against the

United States." Published in 1891, the third edition consisted of three lengthy volumes and covered graduates through the class of 1889.

During his retirement, Cullum lived in New York City. Supporting philanthropic and scientific causes, he was especially active in the American Geographical Society and served as a vice president from 1877 to 1892. His marriage had brought him a large fortune, and his will left sizable sums to both the Geographical Society and the Military Academy, including funding for subsequent editions of his register. A dedicated career soldier and a strong advocate of professional military education, Cullum played a significant secondary role as a staff officer during the Civil War, and his magnificent West Point register remains an invaluable source for the history of the U.S. Army. He died in New York City.

• A collection of Cullum's personal papers, correspondence relating to his register, and letterbooks and other records pertaining to his superintendency of West Point are preserved at the U.S. Military Academy Library, West Point, N.Y. Cullum included a detailed record of his military service and a list of his professional publications in the third edition of the register: *Biographical Register of the Officers and Graduates of the U.S. Military Academy at West Point, N.Y., from Its Establishment in 1802, to 1890* (1891). Among his other works are *Description of a System of Military Bridges, with India-Rubber Pontons* (1849); *Campaigns of the War of 1812–1815, against Great Britain, Sketched and Criticized; with Brief Biographies of the American Engineers* (1879); and a translation of Nicholas Edouard Delabarre-Duparcq's *Elements of Military Art and History* (1863). Data on his Civil War service may be gleaned from U.S. War Department, *The War of the Rebellion: A Compilation of the Official Records of the Union and Confederate Armies* (128 vols., 1880–1901). For his West Point administration, see James L. Morrison, Jr., *"The Best School in the World": West Point, the Pre–Civil War Years, 1833–1866* (1986); and George S. Pappas, *To the Point: The United States Military Academy, 1802–1902* (1993). Russell F. Weigley briefly analyzes Cullum's professional thought in *Towards an American Army: Military Thought from Washington to Marshall* (1962). An obituary and excerpts from his will are in *Twenty-third Annual Reunion of the Association of the Graduates of the United States Military Academy* (1892).

WILLIAM B. SKELTON

CULPEPER, John (1644–1693), proprietary official and rebellion leader, first appears in the records of Barbados in 1663 when at age nineteen he wrote the will of a neighbor and served as the overseer of his estate. The same document also mentions a Margaret Culpeper, who was surely related to him. By February 1671 Culpeper had arrived in southern Carolina with a slave, and at the end of the year his wife, Judith, joined him, accompanied by a woman servant. Within a month of his arrival in Charles Town, the able Culpeper had replaced the inadequate surveyor of the province. His extant map of Charles Town was the first accurate plat of the settlement. A year later his commission from the lords proprietor as surveyor general, dated 30 December 1671, was received about the time he was elected to the provincial assembly. By the

end of 1672, in addition to his 2-acre town lot where he was residing, Culpeper was granted a 370-acre plantation.

It is not known what happened from January 1673, when Governor Sir John Yeamans described Culpeper as a person of "good fame and credit," to June, when he and others were forced to flee the colony under threat of the death penalty for alleged rebellious action. A law designed to prevent debtors from escaping their obligations required all persons leaving the colony to have the permission of the government or face capital punishment, and there is some evidence that the precipitous flight of Culpeper and his partners was simply a matter of a commercial debt. Later he was characterized by a political opponent as having fled southern Carolina for "indeavouring to sett the poor people to plunder the rich," but this allegation can be explained by the bitterness engendered by the political conflicts in which Culpeper was involved at the time.

Whatever the circumstances of his departure from Charles Town, Culpeper was by November 1673 in the northern Carolina Albemarle County settlement, where his life has been confused with another John Culpeper (b. 1633), of Virginia, the brother of Dame Frances Culpeper, who was the wife of Sir William Berkeley, the governor of Virginia. While the Virginia John Culpeper did conduct business for the Berkeleys in Albemarle County by appearing in court, he never resided there.

In Albemarle County, Culpeper became a planter and a merchant handling goods in the West Indian and the coastal trade through New England shippers. At the time of his location in Albemarle County, the colony was entering a prolonged period of political unrest, unmatched in any other colony, that was primarily caused by internal factional power struggles, uncertain land policy, and the adverse effects of the Plantation Duty Act of 1673, which imposed a burdensome duty on tobacco, the colony's chief cash crop. In 1677 the acting governor, Thomas Miller, began systematic suppression of his political opposition through arbitrary arrests and seizure of property for alleged customs violations. His arrests in December of a New England trader, Zachariah Gillam, and George Durant, a local opponent of Miller, forced their supporters to organize an armed band, including Culpeper, that released Gillam and Durant, seized the colony's official records, and arrested Miller and several of his supporters. Culpeper also authored the "Remonstrance," a call for revolt that rallied support throughout the settlement. Miller managed to escape to Virginia in 1679, but a rebel assembly and council, with Colonel John Jenkins as the acting president, took control of the government.

During the assembly Culpeper was a key adviser and served as its secretary. Although some historians have claimed that Culpeper became the rebel governor, there is no evidence that he served in any capacity beyond that of collector of customs. The rebels successfully governed the colony for a year and a half, and when the Carolina proprietors appointed acting governors they chose local planters acceptable to the rebel council. In December 1679, while Culpeper was in England to represent the rebel case to the proprietors, the testimony of his opponents led to his arrest and trial for treason by the Crown. Anxious to minimize the importance of the rebellion in order to head off Crown proceedings against their charter, the proprietors successfully defended Culpeper and secured his acquittal. Culpeper's trial appears to be the primary reason the rebellion is named for him. With many of the rebels remaining in office, their influence continued long after a legal government was reestablished in 1679 with the appointment of John Harvey as governor.

Upon Culpeper's return to Albemarle in 1680 he settled back into his life as a merchant and planter in Pasquotank precinct with connections in New England and New York. Apparently the trial for treason, which could have resulted in his execution, convinced him to stay away from the often turbulent political affairs of the colony. A widower, Culpeper married Margaret Bird in 1680, and following her death he married Sarah Mayo on 23 August 1688. When his estate was settled in 1694, children who were apparently from this last marriage were mentioned. It is not known what Culpeper's religious inclination was, but his surviving wife and a daughter were Quakers.

• The only document related to Culpeper in Barbados is the will of Armell Gould, 27 Dec. 1663, Barbados Archives, Black Rock. The several years that Culpeper spent in South Carolina are well documented in Agnes Baldwin, comp., *First Settlers of South Carolina, 1670–1680* (1969); Langdon Cheves, ed., "The Shaftesbury Papers . . . ," in *Collections of the South Carolina Historical Society*, vol. 5 (1897); and Alexander S. Salley, Jr., ed., *Records of the Secretary of the Province and the Register of the Province of South Carolina, 1671–1675* (1944) and *Warrants for Land in South Carolina* (1973). Background for South Carolina is in Edward McCrady, *The History of South Carolina under the Proprietary Government, 1670–1719* (1897). Official records of Culpeper's North Carolina life and the Culpeper Rebellion are in Mattie E. E. Parker, ed., *North Carolina Higher-Court Records, 1670–1696* (1968) and *1697–1701* (1971); and William L. Saunders, ed., *The Colonial Records of North Carolina*, vol. 1 (1887). Useful for background on Culpeper's Rebellion are Hugh F. Rankin, *Upheaval in Albemarle: The Story of Culpeper's Rebellion* (1962); Lindley S. Butler, "The Governors of Albemarle County, 1663–1689," *North Carolina Historical Review* 46 (1969): 281–99, and "Culpeper's Rebellion: Testing the Proprietors," in *The North Carolina Experience: An Interpretive and Documentary History*, ed. Lindley S. Butler and Alan D. Watson (1984); Mattie E. E. Parker, "Legal Aspects of 'Culpeper's Rebellion.'" *North Carolina Historical Review* 45 (1968): 111–27; and William S. Smith, Jr., "Culpeper's Rebellion: New Data and Old Problems" (M.A. thesis, North Carolina State Univ., 1990).

LINDLEY S. BUTLER

CULPEPER, Thomas (1635–27 Jan. 1689), colonial governor of Virginia and second Lord Culpeper, was born in England, the son of the first Lord Culpeper, John, a landed aristocrat, and his second wife, Judith Culpeper, the daughter of Sir Thomas Culpeper.

Upon his father's death he assumed the title of second Lord Culpeper and inherited the family estate, which included Leeds Castle in Kent. He was given a share in the proprietorship of the Northern Neck of Virginia, consisting of 5.7 million acres, under a patent issued in 1649 and reconfirmed in 1669. He married Margaretta van Hesse in The Hague in 1659; they had one daughter. He also had two daughters with his mistress Susanna Willis; he lived openly with her in London while his wife remained at Leeds Castle. Because he had helped King Charles II to secure the English throne in 1660, he became a favorite of the monarch. He was appointed captain and later governor of the Isle of Wight and in 1671 was named to the Council for Foreign Plantations. Two years later he and Henry Bennett, earl of Arlington, were granted the quitrents of the entire colony of Virginia for thirty-one years. In the early 1680s Culpeper enlarged his Virginia proprietorships by buying out Arlington and the surviving patentees of the Northern Neck lands. Although Culpeper and Arlington had neither the desire nor the resources to assert their claims, the Virginians looked upon these favorites of the king as troublesome adventurers.

In July 1675 Culpeper was commissioned by King Charles to serve as governor of Virginia for life, with the understanding that his appointment was to become effective when the sitting governor, William Berkeley, either died or was removed. Following Berkeley's death in 1677, Culpeper, a pleasure-loving gentleman who vastly preferred England to Virginia, remained at home and sent Henry Chichely and Herbert Jeffreys to administer the colony. In 1680 King Charles forced Culpeper to assume the government in person by threatening to rescind his commission; thus, in May 1680 he arrived in the colony. Quickly he made himself popular with Virginians by allowing the general assembly to pass an act of indemnity for offenses committed during Bacon's Rebellion four years earlier. Also passed were acts to empower the governor to naturalize residents, to regulate slave assemblies, and to give the king control over certain export revenues. So popular was Culpeper that the assembly voted him a special grant of £500 sterling, despite the fact that his salary and living allowance were more than triple the amount that Berkeley had enjoyed (£3,150 as compared to £1,000). Despite his financial rewards, Culpeper missed the finer things of English life. After only a few months' residence in Jamestown he departed for home, leaving Chichely to administer the colony.

In 1682 Culpeper's repose in England was disturbed by news that Virginia was roiling in civil unrest caused by men destroying tobacco plants to protest overproduction. King Charles II demanded to know why Culpeper had left the colony without royal consent and also why he had taken money from the assembly, thus compromising his independence as governor. Ordered back to Virginia with harsh instructions from the King to stabilize the colony and increase the king's revenues, Culpeper arrived in December 1682 a disgruntled man. He threw off the mask of amiability that he had worn earlier, insisting that settlers pay quitrents and implementing a number of unpopular measures. He dealt harshly with the destroyers of tobacco, hanging a few of the worst offenders. Ordering the price of tobacco to be raised without assembly action, he declared that this measure would enrich the king and assure his own salary. He attempted to modify legislation proposed by the assembly and, acting on the king's instructions, announced that he alone would draft laws, receiving advice only from the Council of Foreign Plantations. He also ended the right of the House of Burgesses to entertain appeals from the lower courts jointly with the council and tried to establish the precedent that the speaker of the House of Burgesses should hold office upon his suffrance. Culpeper made life difficult for Robert Beverley, clerk of the House, by threatening to disenfranchise and arrest him when he would not surrender the journals of the House of Burgesses to the governor. Finally, Culpeper dissolved the assembly and declared that he would rule for the Crown without that body.

Having made himself thoroughly despised by Virginians, Culpeper departed the colony for the last time in September 1683, leaving Nicholas Spencer, president of the council, to administer his government. When Culpeper arrived in London, he found himself thoroughly out of favor with King Charles II for having left his colony a second time without royal permission. He was arrested and put on trial for this crime and also for supposed bribery and extortion in having earlier accepted gifts from the Virginia General Assembly. Although deprived of his commission, he managed to avoid the bribery and extortion charges by agreeing to sell to the Crown all his proprietary rights in Virginia, except for the Northern Neck lands, in return for a lump sum payment of £700 and an annual pension of £600 for twenty-one years. Meanwhile he retained all of his English estates, consisting of manors in Kent and lands on the Isle of Wight. In 1688 he lent support to the claims of William and Mary to the throne of England. He died in London.

• Primary sources on Culpeper's life are William Waller Hening, *The Statutes at Large, Being a Collection of All the Laws of Virginia*, vol. 2 (1823); Henry R. McIlwaine and W. L. Hall, eds., *Executive Journals of the Council of Colonial Virginia, 1680–1754*, vol. 1 (1925); and Warren M. Billings, ed., *The Old Dominion in the Seventeenth Century: A Documentary History of Virginia, 1606–1789* (1975). See also "Culpeper's Report on Virginia in 1683," *Virginia Magazine of History and Biography* 3 (1896): 225–38. Information on Culpeper's ancestry is in George Edward Cokayne, ed., *The Complete Peerage of England*, vol. 3 (1913); and Fairfax Harrison, comp., *The Proprietors of the Northern Neck: Chapters of Culpeper Genealogy* (1926). Charles M. Andrews, *The Colonial Period of American History*, vol. 2 (1936), describes Culpeper's proprietary interests. For his gubernatorial administration, see Herbert L. Osgood, *The American Colonies in the Seventeenth Century*, vol. 3 (1907); Thomas J. Wertenbaker, *Virginia under the Stuarts, 1607–88* (1914); Percy Scott Flippen, *The Royal Government in Virginia, 1624–1775* (1919); and Wesley Frank Craven, *The Colonies in Transition, 1660–1713* (1968). For historical background, see Matthew Page Andrews, *Virginia, the Old Dominion* (1937); Craven, *The Southern Colonies in the Seventeenth Century, 1607–1689* (1949); and Richard L. Morton, *Colonial Virginia*, vol. 1 (1960). For more recent views, see Edmund S. Morgan, *American Freedom, American Slavery: The Ordeal of Colonial Virginia* (1975), and Stephen Saunders Webb, *The Governors General: The English Army and the Definition of the Empire, 1569–1681* (1979).

PAUL DAVID NELSON

CUMING, Sir Alexander (c. 1690/1692–Aug. 1775), leader of a Cherokee delegation from America to England, was born in Culter, Aberdeenshire, Scotland, the son of Sir Alexander Cuming, M.P., the first baronet of Culter, Aberdeenshire, and Elizabeth Swinton. The visionary if erratic second baronet of Culter had a varied career. Called to the Scottish bar in 1714, he also held captain's rank in the Russian army. He left the law when he received a pension of £300, bestowed by the government at Christmas 1718 for services either done by his family or to be performed by him. Cuming lost the pension three years later, either because he was thought unable to provide the expected services or, according to Cuming, because Sir Robert Walpole, just named first lord of the treasury and chancellor of the exchequer, had been angered by the elder Cuming's opposition in Parliament.

On 30 June 1720 Cuming was elected to the Royal Society, remaining as a member until 9 June 1757, when he was removed for failing to pay the annual fee. He married Amy Whitehall, the daughter of Lancelot Whitehall, a customs commissioner in Scotland. The couple had two children.

Cuming is best known for an unusual journey taken on his own responsibility to the Cherokee Indians in 1730, resulting in Cuming naming a Cherokee "emperor," himself receiving a crown, and then escorting the first Cherokee delegation to England, where a treaty important to British interests was concluded. The journey to North America is said to have originated in a dream of Lady Cuming. On 13 September 1729 he set sail for Charleston. He arrived on 5 December in a colony that had overthrown its proprietors ten years earlier and that had just become a royal colony. Cuming attempted to establish a bank by issuing promissory notes to Carolinians in exchange for their deposits.

While in Carolina, Cuming learned about the unsettled relations with the Indian nations, including the Cherokees. On 13 March 1730 he set out for Cherokee country, inquiring about, inspecting, and collecting chunks of iron ore and other minerals, useful herbs, and other "natural curiosities." The Cherokees were a numerous people living in sixty or so towns stretched east-west from the upper reaches of the Savannah River to the Tennessee River valley, 300 miles from Charleston. When Cuming arrived at the Cherokee town of Nequassee, having been assisted by resident Carolina traders, he received a warm welcome, made more so by his bold actions and appearance. Making clear that he acted unofficially, Cuming called on Cherokee leaders of other towns to meet with him.

The Cherokees concurred in his "nomination" of Moytoy of Tellico as emperor and brought forth from Tennessee their crown, which they bestowed on Cuming along with five eagle tails and four scalps, which were to be "laid at the feet" of the English king.

Cuming returned to Charleston, completing the several-hundred-mile trip on 13 April. He quickly embarked on the *Fox* for England with seven Cherokees, including the future leader Attakullakulla, known to the English as Little Carpenter, and trader/interpreter Eleazar Wiggan, who had first settled among the Cherokees in 1711 and was affectionately known as "The Old Rabbit." Apparently Cuming also departed from Charleston with his "bank's" assets. Concerned depositors broke into his bank, found it empty, and immediately dispatched letters to London accusing Cuming of defrauding the depositors, charges he never answered. The *Fox* anchored at Dover on 5 June.

The Cherokee delegates sparked great interest in England and were shown the sights and entertained at the expense of the Crown. They were presented to the king at Windsor on 18 June and four days later laid the eagle tails and scalps at his feet, signifying their power over their enemies, while Cuming tendered his crown. All public excursions drew large and curious crowds. Cuming, however, was increasingly ignored, perhaps because even though he had created an opportunity for the British government, he was no longer needed. The Cherokee delegates were eventually put under the supervision of South Carolina's new governor, Robert Johnson. On 9 September six delegates agreed to a treaty, although they made clear their displeasure at the excluding of their "friend" Cuming from the proceedings.

By the Treaty of 1730, in return for guns, powder, and other goods, the Cherokees acknowledged British sovereignty and agreed to trade only with the English and to allow no one but the English to reside among them. They also promised to return any fugitive slaves and to surrender any Cherokees accused of murdering English colonists. The delegation, accompanied by Johnson, departed in October and arrived safely home laden with numerous goods provided in the treaty.

The next decades found the English continually having to shore up their relations with the Cherokees, who with other interior tribes received overtures from the French. Increasingly annoyed by pressures on their lands, and never as tightly controlled by their leaders as Europeans assumed and hoped, tribes posed persistent problems for colonial governments. Cuming's role in British-Cherokee relations was fortuitous and fit into an unsteady relationship made more difficult by trader excesses for two years before he arrived. His nomination of a Cherokee emperor echoed an arrangement negotiated by Governor Francis Nicholson in 1721. The Cherokee delegation he brought to England was the first for that people, but twenty years earlier a delegation of Mohawks had come to England, and in 1725 a delegation of Indians from the Illinois Country visited Louis XV in Paris. It seems likely that Cuming may have been influenced by these events.

After 1730 Cuming continued to concoct schemes, proposing at one point a plan to enrich the British treasury by settling 300,000 Jewish families in Cherokee country. Official London viewed as impractical this and schemes to address colonial taxation problems. Cuming never escaped the shadow of the failed bank scheme. As a debtor, from 1737 to 1765 he was confined in London's Fleet prison and was supported by the contributions of friends. Lady Cuming died in 1743. In 1762 Cuming interpreted for a second delegation of Cherokees in London under the auspices of Virginia. In 1766 he was appointed a pensioner in the Charterhouse, a charitable institution in London, by Archbishop Thomas Secker; Cuming died there.

• Reports on the Cherokee delegation appeared in the London *Daily Courant*, *Daily Post*, and *Daily Journal*, June–Oct. 1730; see also Carolyn Foreman, *Indians Abroad* (1943). Robert L. Meriwether, *The Expansion of South Carolina, 1729–1765* (1940; repr. 1974), is helpful on South Carolina in 1729–1730. Cuming's journal appears in Samuel Cole Williams, ed., *Early Travels in the Tennessee Country, 1540–1800* (1928), pp. 112–43. For a twentieth-century discussion, see Verner Crane, *The Southern Frontier, 1670–1732* (1928; repr. 1956), pp. 276–80 and 294–302. Critical to understanding Cuming's efforts among the Cherokees are James Mooney, *Historical Sketch of the Cherokee* (repr. 1975) and *Myths of the Cherokee* (1900; repr. 1972); Henry T. Malone, *Cherokees of the Old South: A People in Transition* (1956); David H. Corkran, *The Cherokee Frontier Conflict and Survival, 1740–62* (1962); and Theda Perdue, *Slavery and the Evolution of Cherokee Society, 1540–1866* (1979). For Cuming's reemergence in 1762, see Samuel Cole Williams, ed., *Lieut. Henry Timberlake's Memoirs, 1756–1765* (1927; repr. 1971).

DOUGLAS D. MARTIN

CUMMING, Alfred (4 Sept. 1802–9 Oct. 1873), territorial governor of Utah, was born in Augusta, Georgia, the son of Thomas Cumming, a politically prominent Georgian, and Ann Clay, a Georgia socialite. Originally making their home in Savannah, Thomas and Ann later moved to Augusta, where they became prominent landowners, merchants, bankers, railroad builders, and developers. Thomas was the first intendant (mayor) of Augusta after it was incorporated in 1798. Alfred's older brother William was a major (later colonel) in the War of 1812. In 1835, while studying in Boston, Alfred married Elizabeth Wells Randall, a great-granddaughter of patriot Samuel Adams (1722–1803) and daughter of an eminent Boston physician. The couple was childless.

Cumming was mayor of Augusta in 1839 and was acclaimed for his efficiency and boldness in attacking the yellow fever epidemic of that year. He was a sutler in the army of General Winfield Scott during the Mexican War (1846–1847). In the early 1850s he was superintendent of Indian Affairs on the Upper Missouri.

In May 1857 President James Buchanan, inaccurately informed by some federal appointees to Utah that the Mormons were, in the words of the secretary of war, John B. Floyd, in a state of "substantial rebellion against the laws and authority of the United States," appointed Cumming to replace Brigham

Young, leader of the Mormons, as governor of Utah. Buchanan also ordered a major segment of the U.S. Army to Utah to escort and install the new governor. Cumming and other appointed territorial officials arrived with the main body of Colonel Albert Sidney Johnston's army at what had been Fort Bridger (renamed Camp Scott), in southwestern Wyoming, in November 1857. On 21 November Cumming issued a proclamation, declaring Utah in a state of revolt, calling on its militia to disband, and promising, if laws were obeyed, a friendly administration. Mormon guerrillas, however, had succeeded in burning three supply trains and capturing some of their livestock, and the army was unable to move until the spring of 1858.

In the meantime, Thomas L. Kane, a prominent Philadelphia friend of the Mormons, had journeyed to Utah by way of Panama and southern California. After conferring with Young in Salt Lake City, Kane arrived incognito at Camp Scott on 12 March 1858 to negotiate with Cumming. Over the fierce objections of Colonel Johnston, who thirsted for confrontation, Cumming was persuaded by Kane's plea for peaceful accommodation and set out with him for Salt Lake City on 5 April 1858. When they arrived in the territorial capital a week later, Young surrendered the executive seal and yielded the reigns of government to Cumming. Despite Cumming's report to Johnston that peace was restored and the army was no longer necessary, Johnston moved forward in June with replenished supplies and transport.

The Mormons, fearful of a repetition of the abuse from the military they had experienced in Illinois and Missouri in the 1830s and 1840s, abandoned their homes in Salt Lake City and northern Utah and moved south. When Johnston marched through Salt Lake City on 26 June with 2,500 regular troops and 500 teamsters, herdsmen, blacksmiths, laundresses, and other civilians, he found deserted buildings and streets. Moving forty miles south of Salt Lake City, the army established Camp Floyd at Cedar Valley, west of Utah Lake. Observing good order among the troops, the Mormons returned to their homes in July. Federal "peace commissioners," supportive of Cumming, arranged for a "full and free" pardon for Young and his 35,000 followers, and "peace" seemed to be assured.

As governor, Cumming sought to prevent incidents that would lead to confrontations between the military and civilians; prohibited military officers from actions that might provoke hostilities; and allowed Brigham Young to function as de facto leader of Utah's Mormon settlers. Mormon colonization and development proceeded without interference, and Cumming was respectful of local rights. When Colonel Johnston and the hard-line judges who came with him attempted to impose martial rule in the city of Provo, Cumming used his authority to prevent the action. He was sustained by Attorney General Jeremiah S. Black, who, in a decision rendered 17 May 1859, declared that Cumming was the supreme authority.

Johnston left the territory the following spring. Most of the troops were reassigned to Arizona and New Mexico later in 1860, and in July 1861 the remainder went East, some to join the Confederacy, some the Union army. With the election of Abraham Lincoln, Cumming resigned and returned to Augusta. He lived a life of retirement until his death in Augusta. Although somewhat pompous, Cumming discounted the vicious rumors directed against the Mormons and proved to be a fair and effective governor during a difficult period.

• The Alfred Cumming Papers, 1857–1861, are in the William R. Perkins Library, Duke University, Durham, N.C. The family background and Georgia sojourn are told in William J. Northen, ed., *Men of Mark in Georgia*, vol. 3 (1974), pp. 454–57. The Cummings' trip to and experiences in Utah are described in Ray R. Canning and Beverly Beeton, eds., *The Genteel Gentile: Letters of Elizabeth Cumming, 1857–1858* (1977). Cumming's service as territorial governor is traced in Charles S. Peterson, "A Historical Analysis of Territorial Government in Utah under Alfred Cumming, 1857–1861" (master's thesis, Brigham Young Univ., 1958). The Utah War is discussed in Richard D. Poll, "The Mormon Question, 1850–65" (Ph.D. diss., Univ. of California, Berkeley, 1948); Norman F. Furniss, *The Mormon Conflict, 1850–59* (1960); and Leonard J. Arrington, *Great Basin Kingdom: An Economic History of the Latter-day Saints, 1830–1900*, 2d ed. (1993), especially pp. 161–94. A collection of diaries, letters, and other documents pertaining to the Utah expedition is published in LeRoy R. Hafen and Ann W. Hafen, eds., *The Utah Expedition, 1857–1858: A Documentary Account* (1958). See also Oscar O. Winther, ed., *The Private Papers and Diary of Thomas Leiper Kane, A Friend of the Mormons* (1937). An obituary is in the *New York Tribune*, 13 Oct. 1873.

LEONARD J. ARRINGTON

CUMMINGS, Bob (9 June 1910–1 Dec. 1990), screen, television, and stage actor, was born Charles Clarence Robert Orville Cummings in Joplin, Missouri, the son of Charles Cummings, a physician, and Ruth Kraft, a minister in the Church of Religious Science. The year of his birth is said by some sources to be 1908. After graduating from Joplin High School in 1927, Cummings attended several colleges, including the Carnegie Institute of Technology, with hopes of becoming an aeronautical engineer. Although forced by hard times to quit school, he nevertheless learned while there to pilot an airplane.

In 1930 he was admitted to the American Academy of Dramatic Arts in New York. Advised that he was "too American" to suit the current Broadway trend for English leading men, he went to London where he tried to develop a West End accent. He returned to New York a year later and appeared in *The Roof*, using the stage name Blade Stanhope Conway. While playing a romantic character in the Ziegfeld Follies of 1933, he met Vivian Janis, a dancer whom he married but soon divorced. (He had been married earlier to Edma Emma Myers, his high school sweetheart; presumably, they were divorced.)

In the mid-1930s Cummings left Broadway for Hollywood, appearing in roles calling for a suave leading man or romantic type in dozens of films including *So Red the Rose* (1935), *The Devil and Miss Jones* (1941), and *Kings Row* (1941). His most notable films were both thrillers directed by Alfred Hitchcock: *Saboteur* (1942) and *Dial M for Murder* (1954). But such serious dramatic acting was unusual. One critic described him as "the movies' perennial college boy."

Cummings remained an avid aviation enthusiast throughout his life, owning an airplane and maintaining a commercial pilot's license. During World War II, considered too old for combat service, he became a flight instructor in the U.S. Army Air Corps, eventually receiving an honorary commission as a colonel in the California Air National Guard. He was also active in War Bond drives.

In March 1945 Cummings married Mary Elliot Daniels, with whom he had five children. Daniels, a former actress, took over management of Cummings's business affairs and collaborated with him on various projects. The family resided in Beverly Hills, and Cummings became well known in the movie community. After the war he appeared in such films as *The Lost Moment* (1947), with Susan Hayward; *The Accused* (1949), opposite Loretta Young; and Hitchcock's *Dial M for Murder*, in which he costarred with Grace Kelly and Ray Milland.

But Cummings soon shifted his career toward television. In 1954 he won an Emmy Award for "Best Actor in a Single Performance" in "12 Angry Men," a taut courtroom drama presented by CBS on the live anthology series "Studio One." When the script was later adapted into a feature film, however, Henry Fonda was cast in the role that Cummings had created.

Although Cummings had appeared in scores of pictures, he would be best remembered as the star of a weekly television series. Always most at home in romantic light comedy roles, he found a suitable vehicle in "The Bob Cummings Show," which premiered on NBC in 1955 and ran for four seasons. Cummings played Bob Collins, a Hollywood photographer and bachelor-about-town, whose busy social life is complicated when his widowed sister and her son arrive from Joplin to share his house. Cummings won *Billboard*'s "Best Comedy Actor" award for 1955 and was nominated for Emmies during each of the show's seasons. He also directed many episodes of the series, which has been shown in syndicated reruns as "Love That Bob."

In 1960, attempting to capitalize on his TV notoriety, Cummings brought out a book, *How to Stay Young and Vital*. But his later attempts at television series were less than successful, and his career began to falter. In 1961 a new "Bob Cummings Show" premiered on CBS, featuring the star as Bob Carson, a charter airplane pilot and detective; it was canceled during its first season. In "My Living Doll" (CBS, 1964) Cummings played Dr. Robert McDonald, an Air Force psychiatrist in charge of a robot played by Julie Newmar. This series also failed to win renewal. Film roles became fewer; they included appearances in such

lightweight comedies as *My Geisha* (1962) and *Beach Party* (1963).

As Cummings reached his sixties, his career, indeed his life, took a series of bizarre turns, all apparently traceable to an inability to cope with advancing age. In 1969 he was sued for divorce by his wife of twenty-five years. In the divorce complaint he was accused of both adultery and habitual use of methadrine, commonly known as "speed," which can effect the appearance of youthful energy. In 1971 he married his secretary, Regini "GiGi" Fong, a 32-year-old immigrant from Portuguese Macao. The couple had one child.

No longer able to find parts in movies or television, Cummings attempted a new career in marketing products designed to make their users look and feel more youthful. In 1971 he was named vice president of Holiday Magic, a cosmetics firm, and a year later he founded Bob Cummings, Inc., a company specializing in dietary supplements. Neither business was successful. In 1975 Cummings was arrested for making $4,500 in long distance telephone calls by use of an illegal "blue box" device. Though the case was thrown out of court on a technicality, he paid out-of-court damages to the phone company.

During the last years of his life Cummings was a regular subject of tabloid press stories concerning miraculous antidotes to the effects of aging. He told reporters that he took as many as 174 nutritional supplements daily and described athletic workout schedules that seemed far too rigorous for a man in his seventies. According to the *New York Times* obituary, in 1989 he married (presumably after divorcing his previous wife, GiGi) a woman identified only as Janie. Cummings died in Woodland Hills, California.

• For details on Cummings's life and career beyond the standard film reference works, see Walter Rigdon, ed., *The Biographical Encyclopedia and Who's Who of the American Theatre* (1966); Cleveland Amory, ed., *International Celebrity Register* (1959); and *Current Biography* (1956). An account of his divorce troubles with Daniels appears in the *Los Angeles Times*, 29 Oct. 1969. The *Los Angeles Herald-Examiner*, 2 Dec. 1975, and the *Los Angeles Times*, 15 Apr. 1977, cover his arrest and out-of-court settlement for illegal phone use. An obituary is in the *New York Times*, 3 Dec. 1990.

DAVID MARC

CUMMINGS, Edward (20 Apr. 1861–2 Nov. 1926), sociologist and Unitarian minister, was born in Colebrook, New Hampshire, the son of Edward Norris Cummings, the part owner of a general store, and Lucretia F. Merrill. As a high school student in Woburn, Massachusetts, he worked alongside master carpenters following the failure of his father's business, an experience that doubtless colored his later understanding of theology and sociology.

Cummings entered Harvard in 1879. He graduated magna cum laude, in 1883 and then studied at the Harvard Divinity School, where he developed an interest in social science while studying under Francis G. Peabody, the pioneering teacher of Christian social ethics. He received an A.M. in 1887 and joined the

Department of English as an instructor, which allowed him to devote time to the study of sociology. The July number that year of the first volume of the *Quarterly Journal of Economics* carried his article "Action under the Labor Arbitration Acts," in which he concluded that the legal arbitration of labor disputes in various states had largely failed. In 1888 he became the first holder of the Robert Treat Paine Fellowship, which enabled him to study social problems abroad.

From 1888 to 1891 Cummings studied the working classes in Italy, Germany, France, and Great Britain, looking particularly at co-operatives, labor unions, mutual aid societies, and friendly societies. In Germany, he studied at the University of Berlin and in France at the Collège de France, the Sorbonne, and the École Libre des Sciences Politiques. In Britain he spent a year in residence at the Toynbee Hall settlement in London's East End and was able to witness at first hand Charles Booth's methods of compiling statistics for *Life and Labour of the People in London.*

Between 1889 and 1890 Cummings published articles on trade unionism in England, co-operative production in England and France, and the Paris Exposition display of social economy. On his return to the United States in 1891 he became instructor in sociology in the Harvard Department of Political Economy. In June he married Rebecca Clark; they had two children. Appointed assistant professor in 1893, he remained on the Harvard faculty until 1900.

Cummings taught courses on the principles of sociology, the working classes in Europe and the United States, and utopian and socialist schemes. Occasionally he lectured to Peabody's social ethics class, although he was now more interested than Peabody in social reform measures and sociological research. His European experience had convinced him of the need for systematic empirical investigation of social conditions.

Cummings's reverence for facts informed both his teaching and his research. If unplanned benevolence had no place in his social theory, neither did the speculative systems of Spencer or Comte. Instead he encouraged his students to study facts. In the *Quarterly Journal of Economics*—of which he became editor—he surveyed American co-operative stores and tabulated fine distinctions among labor practices. He was never able to integrate his findings into a larger explanatory theory of society, but he rejected collectivism and socialism as contrary to the American character and to labor unionism. He thought unions properly functioned as benevolent societies, exemplifying the progressive tendencies of voluntary co-operation and prudence, and he viewed the workhouse as another case where social evolution harmonized with social co-operation. The workhouse allowed the able to return to work, and it alleviated the hereditary burden of disease and pauperism by keeping the feeble childless.

Rationalizing in the face of social upheaval rather than reasoning about the process of social change, Cummings wrote no book, founded no school, and directed just two dissertations. In 1900, in circumstanc-

es that remain unclear, his assistant professorship was not renewed. But he had never been content to be a cloistered academic. Even before his departure from Harvard he had presided over the Harvard Co-operative Society and worked in the Hale House settlement. It was probably there that the Unitarian minister of the South Congregational Church, Edward Everett Hale, suggested that Cummings join him in his ministry.

Cummings was ordained in October 1900 and remained at the South Church until its merger with the First Church in 1925. His sympathy with the liberal theology of Boston Unitarianism made his career change less radical than it might appear. He had first addressed his thoughts on charity and progress to a Unitarian conference, and in his 1919 sermon "The Laymen's Answer" he told his congregation that the "study of social, political and economic problems" had driven him into the pulpit after "ordinary divinity school studies" had kept him out. He distinguished the "religion of the cross"—conservative evangelicalism—from the "religion of the star of Bethlehem." The Crucifixion, he explained in 1913, had been a "terrible mistake," occasioning superstitions about resurrection and the afterlife. The religion of the star, foreshadowed by Plato, taught by Jesus, and exemplified by such worthies as Emerson and Lincoln, proclaimed that the Kingdom of Heaven could be built by the "family law of co-operation" and "democratic opportunity."

Cummings regarded these social gospel ideals as globally applicable. In 1910 the publishing magnate Edwin Ginn appointed him as a founding trustee of his World Peace Foundation, dedicated to educating the peoples of the world to the destructiveness of war and the promotion of peace and justice. The foundation became the center of his philanthropic activities. The war in Europe divided the foundation, but Cummings argued that the duty to promote peace required America to make war. In April 1917 he told the Boston City Club that the Allied Powers were on the side of democracy, tolerance, and progress.

Six months later, Cummings learned that the French military had incarcerated his son, the poet E. E. Cummings, because, based on scant and faulty evidence, they considered him pro-German. He angrily wrote to President Woodrow Wilson, but neither his son's experience nor the wider disillusion that followed the peace of Versailles destroyed his idealism. He traveled to Europe to assist in postwar relief and continued to devote his energies to the World Peace Foundation, especially in its efforts on behalf of the League of Nations. The year after his retirement from the ministry, he died when a train hit his car during a snowstorm in the Ossipee Mountains in New Hampshire.

Cummings proved unequal to the task of establishing his own tradition of sociology at Harvard; his sociological writings were pedestrian; his sermons could be facile. But his ceaseless activity in reform institutions, his anxiety to discover the "facts" about industrial society, and his readiness to adopt new forms of religious and scholarly language in order to preserve an older vision of America as a harmonious moral community mark him out as typical of his era.

• Cummings's papers and sermons are in the Houghton Library at Harvard University and the Harry Ransom Humanities Research Center at the University of Texas at Austin. Sociology articles and reviews by Cummings are in volumes 1, 3, 4, 6, 7, 9, 11, and 12 of the *Quarterly Journal of Economics*. Richard S. Kennedy's *Dreams in the Mirror: A Biography of E. E. Cummings* (1980) contains a comprehensive biographical picture of Edward Cummings. For Cummings's thinking on sociology, see Robert L. Church, "The Economists Study Society: Sociology at Harvard 1891–1902," in *Social Sciences at Harvard 1860–1920: From Inculcation to the Open Mind*, ed. Paul H. Buck (1965). E. E. Cummings's understanding of his father can be found in *I: six nonlectures* (1953) and his 1939 poem *my father moved through dooms of love*. Obituaries are in the *Harvard Graduates Magazine*, Mar. 1927, and in the 1927–1928 *Unitarian Year Book*.

JONATHAN DAVIS

CUMMINGS, E. E. (14 Oct. 1894–3 Sept. 1962), poet and painter, was born Edward Estlin Cummings in Cambridge, Massachusetts, the son of Edward Cummings, a Unitarian minister of the South Congregational Church in Boston, and Rebecca Haswell Clarke. Cummings's mother encouraged him from an early age to write verse and to keep a journal. He was educated at the Cambridge Latin School and at Harvard College, where in 1915 he received his A.B., graduating magna cum laude in Greek and English; he received his A.M. from Harvard in 1916. In his last year of college, he became intensely interested in the new movements in the arts through his association with John Dos Passos, S. Foster Damon, and Scofield Thayer and began to experiment with free verse and to develop as a self-taught cubist painter. The first book appearance of his poems was in *Eight Harvard Poets* (1917).

When the United States entered World War I in 1917, Cummings volunteered for the Norton-Harjes Ambulance Corps, serving in France for five months before he and his friend William Slater Brown were arrested on suspicion of espionage because Brown's letters had expressed pacifist views. Cummings's experiences in the Depôt de Triage, a concentration camp at La Ferté-Macé, became the subject of his first autobiographical work, *The Enormous Room* (1922). Released from prison after four months, he was sent back to the United States, where he was drafted into the army. He served in the 73d Infantry Division at Camp Devens, Massachusetts, until November 1918.

After the war Cummings moved to New York, entering his cubist paintings in yearly exhibitions and attaining celebrity for the unusual poems he published in the *Dial* and other avant-garde magazines in the 1920s. In college he had followed the Imagist principles for poetry laid down by Ezra Pound: to use the rhythms of common speech rather than metrical regularity, to strive for compression and precision in language, to avoid worn-out poetic diction, and to make poetic statement by means of images. But by 1918

Cummings had created his own poetic style. Because he was a painter as well as a poet, he had developed a unique form of literary cubism: he broke up his material on the page to present it in a new, visually directed way. Some of his poems had to be seen in their printed arrangement before they could be completely understood. "The day of the spoken lyric is past," he proclaimed. "The poem which has at last taken its place does not sing itself; it builds itself, three dimensionally, gradually, subtly, in the consciousness of the experiencer."

In addition, Cummings expressed ideas through new grammatical usage: he employed verbs as nouns, and other locutions as new linguistic creations (for example, "wherelings, whenlings / daughters of ifbut offspring of hopefear / sons of unless and children of almost / never shall guess"). He indulged in free play with punctuation and capitalization. Lowercase letters were the rule; capitals were used only for special emphasis; punctuation marks were omitted for ambiguous statement; others were introduced for jarring effects. His use of the lowercase letter "i" not only became a well-known means of self-reference in his work, but also reflected a role that he created for himself: he was the underling, the unnoticed dreamer, the downtrodden one, the child in the man; yet by asserting his individuality in this way, he thrust himself forward and established a memorable persona.

His first manuscript book of poems, "Tulips & Chimneys," was a gathering of work in traditional verse forms as well as in his newest unconventional forms of expressiveness. It included lush lyrics from his Harvard years, tender love poems, erotic epigrams, sonnets (some crammed with literary allusion, others merely attempting to depict ordinary scenes of life—on city streets, in cafés, in rooming houses), celebrations of the beauties of the natural world, and harsh satires directed at politicians, generals, professors, the clergy, and national leaders. The publishing world was not yet ready for some of Cummings's poems about drunks, prostitutes, Salvation Army workers, gangsters, or bums. Thus, the original version of Cummings's manuscript did not survive the forbidding selectivity of editors, and it eventually emerged as three books: *Tulips and Chimneys* (1923), *XLI Poems* (1925), and (privately printed) *&* (1925).

In 1924 Cummings married Elaine Orr, the former wife of his mentor, Scofield Thayer, editor of *The Dial*; they had one child, Nancy, born while Elaine was still married to Thayer. Elaine divorced Cummings within the year, to marry an Irish banker and politician, taking Nancy with her to Ireland and blocking Cummings from seeing his child. His second marriage, to Anne Barton in 1929, also ended in divorce, in 1932. These marital disasters affected Cummings's personality so much that by the 1930s he had changed from a vivacious young celebrant of life to a cynical, hard-hitting critic of American culture. These attitudes are increasingly evident in his volumes of poems *Is 5* (1926), *ViVa* (1931), and *No Thanks* (1935).

Cummings's travels in Europe and extended stays in Paris in the 1920s brought him in touch with the Dada and Surrealist movements in the arts, influences that appear in his increasing experiment with language and ventures into irrational modes of expression in his poems. "The Symbol of all Art is the Prism," he declared. "The goal is destructive. To break up the white light of objective realism into the secret glories it contains." In a play, *Him* (1927), Cummings attempted to include the unconscious thoughts of its two principal characters, Him, a playwright, and Me, his girlfriend. The plunge into the unconscious was represented by a series of vaudeville skits and circus acts, so that Cummings's jokes and verbal nonsense made for a highly entertaining but not very coherent work.

His six-week visit to Soviet Russia in 1931 led him to compose *Eimi* (1933), an autobiographical narrative based on his travel diary. He recorded his train travel, three weeks in Moscow, and two weeks in Kiev and Odessa in highly idiosyncratic prose as the travels of an American, Comrade Kem-min-kz. His disappointment with and hostility to the Communist world is organized into a structure based on Dante's descent into the Inferno. Comrade K eventually passes through the Purgatorio (Turkey) and at length reaches the Paradiso (Paris). The result, despite the difficulties it poses for a reader, is Cummings's most powerful achievement, concluding with a transcendental experience, a mystical union of the narrator, the artist, with the creative force in the universe.

Cummings's third wife, the fashion model Marion Morehouse, lived with him as his common-law wife from 1934 until the end of his life. A change of tone in his next three volumes of verse, *50 Poems* (1940), *1 X 1* (1944), and *Xaipe* (1950), reflects not only the happiness that this relationship brought, but also the fact that Cummings was spending more time at his summer home in Madison, New Hampshire, "Joy Farm," absorbing the natural landscape and the benevolence of the rural seasons. These books express more clearly the individualistic philosophy of life that Cummings had developed out of his dedication to art and his casting off the restraints of society. What emerges is his affirmation of life in all its essential forms, but especially in whatever is natural, unpretentious, and unique. His philosophy entailed a rejection of social forces that hinder the expression of individualism, especially whatever encourages group behavior, conformity, imitation, or artificiality. It valued whatever is instinctively human and promoted feeling and imagination; it rejoiced in romantic and sexual love; and it thrust aside the products, both material and spiritual, of an overly organized, emotionally anesthetized, technologically quantified civilization. His painting changed too: he became representational in technique as he turned to still lifes, portraits, nude figures, and landscapes.

In 1946 Cummings was able to bring about a reunion with his daughter, Nancy, who was now living in the United States and married to Willard Roosevelt, a grandson of President Theodore Roosevelt (1858–1919). While painting her portrait, he revealed to her astonishment that he was her father, and as a consequence a fresh relationship between father, daughter, and grandchildren emerged. The mere reentry of Nancy into Cummings's world gave rise to his most successful play, *Santa Claus* (1946), a Christmas fantasy that represents his belief in the joys of love and giving and his rejection of the materialism and false expectation that he associated with "Science." In the end, Santa Claus without his mask is revealed to be a young man, who is then reunited with an adoring woman and a child whom he had lost.

In the 1950s Cummings undertook an additional career as a reader of his poetry to audiences in New York and on college campuses, becoming, after Robert Frost, the most popular performer on the academic circuit. This venture led ultimately to his holding the Charles Eliot Norton lectureship at Harvard during 1952–1953. His lectures and readings at Harvard became the autobiographical work *i: six nonlectures* (1953), which recounts aspects of his early life and his development as a poet.

In these last years, honors came to Cummings in many forms: a Guggenheim fellowship in 1951; a collected edition of his poetical works, *Poems, 1923–1954* (1954), which earned a special citation from the National Book Award Committee in 1955; appointment as the festival poet for the Boston Arts Festival in 1957; the Bollingen Prize in 1958; and a two-year grant of $15,000 from the Ford Foundation in 1959.

A serene volume of verse, *95 Poems* (1958), extolled the wonders of the natural world, honored a number of very ordinary individuals, recorded Cummings's outrage at the disastrous outcome of the Hungarian revolution, reflected memories of childhood, and meditated on birth, time, and death. It was a fitting close to the poet's career. Cummings died at a hospital in North Conway, New Hampshire, after suffering a stroke at Joy Farm.

E. E. Cummings was a combination of an unabashed Romantic in his view of life and an avant-garde modernist seeking to explore unusual means of expression. His poetry developed from boyhood imitations of Longfellow to the linguistic surprises he brought to the literary scene in the 1920s. He continued to write sonnets all his life, often traditional in theme—a tribute to love, an address to the moon, the praise of a church, a prayer of thanks for the ability to respond to life—but sometimes he chose "unpoetic" subjects—a nightclub dancer, the gurgle of water going down a sink, brothels and their customers, a denunciation of salesmen, a politician giving a hypocritical patriotic speech, a mélange of play with advertising slogans.

His visually directed free verse shows an even greater variety of subject and mood. It ranges from children's songs and romantic lyrics through antiwar satires and epigrammatic attacks on his contemporaries to realistic vignettes of city life and delighted responses to the natural objects of earth and the heavens. Cummings produced a large body of work, and although he allowed himself to publish some trivia, he continued to produce poems of wit and ingenuity, of vigorous satire, and of beauty and delicacy well into his seventh decade. He is principally renowned for his linguistic exuberance, which delighted in continual innovation in form and technique. Cummings was a central figure in that remarkable generation of American writers, including Ezra Pound, Gertrude Stein, T. S. Eliot, John Dos Passos, and William Faulkner, who carried out a revolution in literary expression in the twentieth century.

• The lines from "wherelings, whenlings" quoted above are used by kind permission of Liveright Publishing Corporation. Cummings's letters, diaries, sketchbooks, manuscripts, personal library, and miscellaneous papers are in the Houghton Library, Harvard University. Additional manuscripts are in the Humanities Research Center, University of Texas; the Clifton Waller Barrett Library, University of Virginia; the Sibley Watson Collection, Rochester, N.Y.; the Beinecke Library, Yale University; and the Princeton University Library. Poems found among his papers after his death are in *73 Poems* (1963) and *Etcetera* (1983). The only collection of his letters is F. W. Dupee and George Stade, eds., *Selected Letters of E. E. Cummings* (1969). Two important bibliographies are George Firmage, Jr., *E. E. Cummings: A Bibliography* (1960), and Guy Rotella, *E. E. Cummings: A Reference Guide* (1979). The definitive biography is Richard S. Kennedy, *Dreams in the Mirror: A Biography of E. E. Cummings* (1980); see also Charles Norman, *E. E. Cummings: The Magic Maker* (1958). The best critical studies are Norman Friedman, *E. E. Cummings: The Art of His Poetry* (1960) and *E. E. Cummings: The Growth of a Writer* (1964), and Rushworth Kidder, *E. E. Cummings: An Introduction to the Poetry* (1979). For Cummings's work as a painter, see Milton Cohen, *Poet and Painter: The Aesthetics of E. E. Cummings's Early Works* (1987). For a linguistic perspective, see Irene Fairley, *E. E. Cummings and Ungrammar: A Study of Syntactic Deviance in His Poems* (1975). See also Nicholas Joost, *Scofield Thayer and the Dial* (1964), and George Wickes, *Americans in Paris, 1903–1939* (1969). A front-page obituary is in the *New York Times*, 4 Sept. 1962.

RICHARD S. KENNEDY

CUMMINGS, Homer Stillé (30 Apr. 1870–10 Sept. 1956), attorney, Democratic party leader, and attorney general of the United States, was born in Chicago, Illinois, the son of Uriah C. Cummings, a businessman, and Audie Schuyler Stillé. Educated at the Heathcote School in upstate New York, the Sheffield School of Engineering of Yale University, and the Yale Law School, from which he graduated in 1893, Cummings opened a legal practice in Stamford, Connecticut, soon thereafter and formed a partnership with Charles D. Lockwood that lasted until he joined the Roosevelt administration in 1933. In 1897 Cummings married Helen W. Smith; they had one child (his only offspring) before their divorce in 1907. Although he commanded a reputation as an outstanding litigator with a showy courtroom style, Cummings's first and enduring passion remained politics. A silver Democrat who supported lower tariffs, the income tax, and antimonopoly efforts, Cummings campaigned for William Jennings Bryan in 1896 and ran for secretary of state on the party's Connecticut ticket. Like Bryan, he went down to

defeat in his first campaign. Four years later, however, he was elected to his first of three terms as mayor of Stamford.

As mayor of Stamford in the Progressive era, Cummings never attracted the national attention that other reform-minded city executives did, such as Tom Johnson, Hazen Pingree, and Seth Low, who waged war against political machines, predatory public utilities, and padded city contracts from San Francisco to New York City. He did refurbish the city's infrastructure, however, and removed the police and fire departments from partisan politics. His local political success was not sufficient to win him either a seat in the House of Representatives in 1902 or the United States Senate in 1910 or 1916, but it did catapult him to the post of state's attorney in Fairfield County for more than a decade from 1914 to 1924. In 1909 he married Marguerite T. Owings; they divorced in 1928.

Cummings had considerably more success building a power base within the national Democratic party organization. From 1900, when he first served as a committeeman from Connecticut, through his service as national chairman (1914–1920), Cummings moved steadily up the ladder of the party's bureaucracy. A frequent delegate at the Democrat's quadrennial national conventions, he also held posts as director of the party's speaker's bureau and vice chairman between 1913 and 1919.

Remaining faithful to the Bryan wing of the party, Cummings backed Woodrow Wilson's son-in-law, William Gibbs McAdoo, against New York governor Alfred E. Smith at the Democrats' 1924 convention. His efforts as head of the platform committee to craft a compromise plank on the issues of prohibition and the Ku Klux Klan failed to bridge the gap between the McAdoo and Smith forces, however, and the party remained deeply divided, turning at last to John W. Davis, a Wall Street lawyer, as its presidential candidate. In 1929 Cummings married Mary Cecilia Waterbury.

In 1932, with the country mired in economic depression and President Herbert Hoover stumbling toward defeat, Cummings backed a winner: Franklin Roosevelt, the governor of New York, who secured enough support from all major factions to gain the Democratic nomination. Cummings helped manage Roosevelt's delegate search at the Chicago convention and delivered a seconding speech on his behalf. In return for his loyal service, President-elect Roosevelt offered Cummings the governor-generalship of the Philippine Islands. On the eve of Roosevelt's inauguration, however, Cummings received a promotion when attorney general–designate Thomas Walsh of Massachusetts died suddenly, and Roosevelt offered the job to the Connecticut Democrat.

Cummings's tenure as attorney general from 1933 until 1939, the longest since William Wirt's in the early 1800s, was more notable for administrative and statutory innovations touching the Department of Justice and the scope of federal criminal jurisdiction than for success in defending the controversial programs of the New Deal before the courts.

In many areas of social and economic life, the New Deal extended the role of the federal government into activities traditionally reserved to the states or private organizations, activities such as securities regulation, labor-management relations, aid to the unemployed, and social security. Attorney General Cummings pursued an equally expansive program with respect to the federal role in fighting crime. At his urging, Congress added a wide range of offenses to the United States Code by expanding the penalties for kidnapping, bank robbery, illegal possession of certain firearms, and crossing state lines to avoid prosecution. Like most attorneys general before and after, Cummings augmented the power of FBI director J. Edgar Hoover.

Cummings's record in fending off judicial attacks on the New Deal's economic reforms was far less impressive. He faced not only a federal judiciary staffed with Republican appointees hostile to change, but a Department of Justice with many second-rate attorneys whose political connections usually exceeded their legal acumen. This was especially the case in the office of the solicitor general, charged with defending the government's actions, where Postmaster General James A. Farley had played a larger role in filling vacancies during the early years of the New Deal than law professors such as Felix Frankfurter.

Cummings scored a notable victory in the *Gold Clause* cases of 1935, when the Supreme Court narrowly upheld the authority of Congress to manage the nation's monetary system by nationalizing gold and prohibiting the payment of public and private obligations in the metal. That triumph, however, was soon erased in 1935–1936 by a series of eight judicial reversals of the central programs of the New Deal, including the National Recovery Act, the Agricultural Adjustment Act, and the Guffey Coal Act.

Like Roosevelt, flushed with an overwhelming victory at the polls in 1936, Cummings burned for revenge against his judicial tormentors on the Supreme Court. At the president's urging, but without the advice of the administration's leading legal minds, Cummings drafted the fateful Judicial Reorganization Act. This measure, soon the center of conflict in Congress, would have permitted the president to appoint an additional federal judge (including justices of the Supreme Court) for every sitting jurist who reached the age of seventy and did not retire within six months.

Cummings and Roosevelt continued to push the so-called court-packing plan, even in the face of substantial opposition from Democrats in Congress, more tolerant Supreme Court decisions upholding New Deal measures, and the retirement of at least one justice who had consistently opposed the president's programs. The Senate finally killed the plan by voting to return it to committee. Roosevelt's stubbornness, however, had fractured his own party and emboldened his enemies, who blocked additional New Deal reforms and attacked existing ones.

Cummings stepped down as attorney general in 1939. His third wife having died, he married Julia Alter in 1942. He practiced law in Washington, D.C.,

and continued to dabble in Connecticut politics until his death in Washington.

• Cummings's extensive manuscripts are housed in the Alderman Library at the University of Virginia. Carl B. Swisher edited *The Selected Papers of Homer Cummings* (1939). Cummings himself wrote *We Can Prevent Crime: The American Program* (1937) and, with Carl McFarland, *Federal Justice: Chapters in the History of Justice and the Federal Executive* (1937). His role in the New Deal can be explored in Peter H. Irons, *The New Deal Lawyers* (1982); Joseph P. Lash, *Dealers and Dreamers: A New Look at the New Deal* (1988); and Joseph Alsop and Turner Catledge, *The 168 Days* (1938). Obituaries are in the *New York Times* and the *Stamford Advocate*, both 11 Sept. 1956.

MICHAEL E. PARRISH

CUMMINS, Albert Baird (15 Feb. 1850–30 July 1926), Iowa governor and U.S. senator, was born in Carmichaels, Pennsylvania, the son of Thomas L. Cummins, a carpenter and farmer, and Sarah Baird Flenniken. Raised in a Scotch-Irish Presbyterian tradition that valued both individual independence and education, the nineteen-year-old Cummins faced a serious moral dilemma during his last year at Waynesburg College and left without a diploma when he supported the class valedictorian's right to express an opinion, probably in support of Darwinism, that was repugnant to the institution's president.

Following an uncle to Elkader, Iowa, in 1869, he became a clerk in the Clayton County recorder's office and also worked as a carpenter. Moving to Allen County, Indiana, in 1871, Cummins labored variously as a railway clerk, railroad construction engineer, express company manager, and deputy county surveyor before relocating to Chicago where he clerked in an attorney's office and studied law. In 1874 he married Ida Lucette Gallery, with whom he had one daughter.

Admitted to the Illinois bar in 1875, Cummins practiced law in Chicago for three years before taking up permanent residence in Des Moines, Iowa. Specializing in railroad and patent law, Cummins gained a measure of fame and a reputation as a champion of the "common man" against "the interests" by representing the Iowa Farmers' Protective Association against the "barbed wire trust."

Becoming active in Republican politics, he was a delegate to every state and national convention from 1880 to 1924, a state legislator from 1888 to 1890, a presidential elector in 1892, and a member of the national committee from 1896 to 1900. Gradually, he emerged as a leader of the insurgent or progressive faction of the Iowa GOP that was challenging the leadership of the prorailroad, probusiness regulars headed by U.S. Senator William Boyd Allison and Congressmen David B. Henderson and William P. Hepburn. Defeated in a campaign for the U.S. Senate in 1894 and 1900, Cummins was elected governor of Iowa in 1901 and served three consecutive terms. Associating himself with the insurgent movement that was beginning to build in the Midwest, he ran on an antimonopoly, populist platform that stressed increased railroad taxation and regulation and support for the "Iowa Idea"—the removal of tariff protection for any industry dominated by a "trust." As governor, he pressed for a prohibition of free railroad passes to public office holders, a two-cents-per-mile limit on railroad fares, the regulation of insurance and investment companies, prison reform, a pure food law, the curtailment of child labor, primary elections, and the selection of U.S. senators by popular vote. A believer in party competition, he unsuccessfully opposed adoption of the "Des Moines Plan" for a nonpartisan commission form of municipal government.

Defeated as a candidate for the U.S. Senate by the legislature in 1908, Cummins won the Republican nomination in a primary election that same year and was selected by the legislature to fill the vacancy caused by the death of William B. Allison. In the Senate, he quickly became an important part of the insurgent movement, led by Wisconsin's Robert M. La Follette (1855–1925). The insurgents challenged the administration of President William Howard Taft and the "Standpat" Republican leadership by supporting tariff reductions, the federal income tax, the inclusion of a recall provision in the Arizona state constitution, and Chief Forester Gifford Pinchot in his public-land dispute with Secretary of the Interior Richard Ballinger, while opposing trade reciprocity with Canada. In 1911 Cummins participated in the formation of the National Progressive Republican League, designed to support a Progressive challenger, most likely La Follette, against Taft in 1912. However, Cummins and several of his cohorts switched their allegiance to Theodore Roosevelt (1858–1919), creating a rift between themselves and La Follette that gradually destroyed insurgent solidarity. In spite of his personal support for Roosevelt, Cummins refused to leave the Republican party.

Although personally affronted by President Woodrow Wilson's manner and his highly partisan tactics in pushing legislation through Congress, Cummins eventually supported many of the landmark measures of the New Freedom, authoring the "Magna Carta" provision of the Clayton Antitrust Act: "The labor of human beings is not a commodity or article of commerce." Although this provision supposedly exempted labor unions from prosecution as "combinations in restraint of trade" under the antitrust laws and recognized their right to organize, bargain collectively, and strike, it failed to permit secondary boycotts and was vague enough to allow antilabor judges great latitude in issuing injunctions. Always a strong supporter of the railroad brotherhoods, he opposed the Adamson Eight-Hour-Day Act as too weak.

For neutrality and opposed to Wilson's efforts to strengthen U.S. military forces with the outbreak of World War I, Cummins was one of what Wilson called that "little group of willful men" who filibustered against the arming of merchant ships in 1917. Although he voted for Wilson's declaration of war and supported the conduct of the war, the Iowan was part of the "loyal opposition" that demanded strict account-ing, restraints on governmental authority, and measures to restrict profiteering. He was one of the "Irreconcilables" who opposed U.S. membership in the League of Nations. His role in the drafting of the 1920 transportation act that bears his name greatly upset fellow insurgents, liberals, and the unions by returning the railroads to private operation, ending their wartime control by the federal government.

A personal friend and golfing companion of President Warren G. Harding, Cummins increasingly sided with New Era Republicanism and denounced La Follette's Progressive party candidacy in 1924, although he was a staunch supporter of the McNary-Haugen bill championed by the "farm bloc." His growing conservatism cost Cummins a great deal of political support in his native state, and he lost the 1926 Republican primary to La Follette's protégé, Smith Brookhart. Cummins died in Des Moines.

During a political career that spanned more than four decades, Cummins virtually personified the tensions that existed within midwestern Republicanism during those years. Breaking with the regular leadership of the party in the 1890s, he emerged as a key figure in the insurgent movement that split the party in state and nation by 1912. Isolationist by conviction, he opposed military preparedness and membership in the League of Nations, but supported the war effort. Republican to the core, he refused to bolt to the Progressive party in either 1912 or 1924, preferring even the conservatism of Calvin Coolidge to the advanced progressivism of La Follette in the latter year.

• Cummins's papers are housed in the Iowa State Department of History and Archives in Des Moines. They comprise the major source for the only full-scale biography, Ralph Mills Sayre, "Albert Baird Cummins and the Progressive Movement in Iowa" (Ph.D. diss., Columbia Univ., 1958). Elbert W. Harrington has written helpful analyses of two important aspects of Cummins's career, "Albert Baird Cummins as a Public Speaker," *Iowa Journal of History and Politics* 43 (1945): 209–53; and "The Political Ideas of Albert B. Cummins," *Iowa Journal of History and Politics* 39 (1941): 339–86. Important insights into Cummins's activities and ideas can also be gained from James Holt, *Congressional Insurgents and the Party System, 1900–1916* (1967); Thomas Richard Ross, *Jonathon Prentiss Dolliver: A Study in Political Integrity and Independence* (1958); and Kenneth W. Hechler, *Insurgency: Personalities and Politics of the Taft Era* (1964).

JOHN D. BUENKER

CUMMINS, George David (11 Dec. 1822–26 June 1876), Episcopal bishop and founder of the Reformed Episcopal church, was born near Smyrna, Delaware, the son of George Cummins and his second wife, Maria Durborow, wealthy landowners. Although Cummins's family had long associations with the Protestant Episcopal church, the early death of his father and his mother's remarriage to a Methodist itinerant brought Cummins under the religious influence of the Methodists. He entered Dickinson College in approximately 1837, and in April 1839, in the midst of an evangelical revival in the college, "he gave his heart to God, and joined the Methodist Episcopal Church, entering on a life of earnest love and faithful labor for Christ." On 2 March 1843 he was received into the "itinerant communion" of the Methodist Episcopal church, under license from the Baltimore Conference, and began riding and preaching on the Bladensburg (Md.) circuit.

However, in 1845 Cummins withdrew from itinerant preaching and returned to the Episcopal church. He studied briefly under the Evangelical bishop of Delaware, Alfred Lee, and was ordained deacon by Lee on 26 October 1845. He served as curate at Christ Church, Baltimore, in 1846–1847 under the tutelage of the fiery Evangelical Episcopal priest, Henry Van Dyke Johns. In June 1847 he married Alexandrine Macomb Balch; they would have three children. After his ordination to the priesthood that July, he became rector of Christ Church, Norfolk, Virginia. In 1853 he moved to St. James's Church, Richmond, Virginia, and a year later to Trinity Church, Washington, D.C. He moved once more to St. Peter's Church, Baltimore, in 1858 and then took up his last parish in the Episcopal church in 1863 as rector of Trinity Church, Chicago, Illinois. His training and religious convictions placed him squarely within the Evangelical party of the Episcopal church, which in the 1840s claimed a substantial portion of the clergy and laity. True religion, declared Cummins in 1865, "is to be saved by trust in the Good Shepherd, by simple reliance on the infinite sacrifice of Jesus—by committing his soul to Him who loved him and gave himself for him." This was to be no "mere cold act of the intellect" or the "simple assent of the mind to certain propositions." It was instead "the whole being surrendered to another, the soul of the sinner committed to the Savior to be possessed, dwelt in, moulded and transformed by Him."

It was not Cummins's Evangelical commitment so much as his talent as a reconciler that brought him to prominence in the Episcopal church. Throughout most of the 1860s, Cummins held up the evangelicalism of the Episcopal church as a model for ecumenical union among American churches, and he was an admirer of William Augustus Muhlenberg's "evangelical Catholicism." At the church's 1865 general convention, Cummins offered the motion that welcomed the former Confederate delegates back into communion with the Episcopal church. Largely in response to this motion, the Diocese of Kentucky elected him as its assistant bishop on 1 June 1866, and he was consecrated in Christ Church, Louisville, on 15 November 1866. The diocesan bishop, Benjamin Bosworth Smith, was an Evangelical but elderly and feeble, so Cummins inherited de facto episcopal oversight of the entire diocese. This, unfortunately, involved Cummins in a conflict that pitted his instincts for reconciliation against his Evangelicalism. The ritualism of the Oxford movement, a revival of Catholic doctrine and practice that began in the Church of England in the 1830s and that spread to the Protestant Episcopal church in the United States in the mid-1840s. The movement appeared in Kentucky in 1868, and Cummins considered those practices a betrayal of Protestant principles. "*Superstition* is its name," Cummins announced. "A religion more of form than of spirit. A religion that substitutes penance for penitence—that rends the garments and not the heart." Lacking any effective power to suppress the growth of "Anglo-Catholicism" in Kentucky, Cummins became a sponsor of the American Church Missionary Society, an independent Episcopal agency organized to filter Evangelical curates into strategic parishes. He eventually lent his support to Evangelical protest meetings and calls for revisions of the Episcopal church's Book of Common Prayer, such as the elimination of all references to *regeneration* in the baptismal office and the substitution of the term *presbyter* (elder) for *priest*.

These efforts did little to slow the growth of Anglo-Catholicism, and by 1873 it was apparent that some sort of schismatic movement was imminent. The occasion for that break came, ironically, in the midst of one of the most important ecumenical events in nineteenth-century America, the 1873 international convention of the Evangelical Alliance in New York City. Cummins addressed the alliance on "Roman and Reformed Doctrines of Justification Contrasted," in which he reviewed the classic formulae on justification in the major Protestant confessions, contrasted them with Roman Catholicism, and hailed them as the source of all "real unity of all Protestant Christendom." He then participated in a joint Communion service with other non-Episcopal Protestant clergy. Cummins was promptly denounced by Anglo-Catholics for a "breach of ecclesiastical order." It was not clear whether he could actually have been tried for any specific offense, but the embarrassment and outrage he felt over the accusations "for joining fellowship [with] believers around the Table of the Lord" provoked Cummins into resigning his episcopate on 10 November 1873. He announced that he now intended to "transfer my work and office to another sphere," and on 15 November he issued a "Call to Organize" a new Protestant and Evangelical Episcopal church. A small number of Episcopal Evangelicals rallied behind him, and on 2 December 1873, at a public meeting at Association Hall in New York City, Cummins presided over the organization of the Reformed Episcopal church and drafted its "Declaration of Principles." This "Declaration," based at many points on Muhlenberg's famous *Memorial* to the 1853 General Convention of the Protestant Episcopal Church, stated the commitment of the Reformed Episcopalians to the authority of the Bible and the creeds and articulated Cummins's opposition to the Anglo-Catholic concept that "the Church of Christ exists in only one form of ecclesiastical polity." The "Declaration" also renounced any belief in an "inseparable" connection between baptism and spiritual regeneration, any definition of "the Lord's table" as an "altar," and any idea that "the presence of Christ in the Lord's Supper is a presence in the elements of bread and wine."

In addition to founding the new movement, Cummins established a Reformed Episcopal parish in New York City (the First Reformed Episcopal Church) and directed the growth of the Reformed Episcopal church as its presiding bishop. The strain of these responsibilities, along with the difficulty of settling his affairs in Kentucky, broke his health. Thus forced to resign the New York parish, he found a more congenial residence in the Baltimore suburb of Lutherville, which allowed him to be nearer to the centers of Reformed Episcopal growth on the East Coast. The incessant grind of travel and the strain of carrying the new Reformed Episcopal church on his own shoulders continued to wear him down. In June 1876, after fulfilling an emergency call in Baltimore, Cummins caught a mild cold, and on 21 June he suffered the first in a series of heart attacks. He lingered for four days, conscious but in "such suffering . . . as to require the unremitting services of those around him." He died in Lutherville and was buried in the Loudon cemetery in Baltimore.

Cummins's death was a severe blow to the growth of the Reformed Episcopal church. Once he was gone, protracted internal divisions erupted within the church, making it less and less appealing to Cummins's erstwhile Episcopal Evangelical colleagues as a possible refuge from the aggressiveness of Anglo-Catholic influence in the Episcopal church. The Reformed Episcopalians never reached a higher total of communicant members than the 11,000 they numbered between 1915 and 1921, and in 1990 the Reformed Episcopal church contained only about 6,000 members in the United States and Canada. Ironically, Cummins's writings and life are not very well known within the Reformed Episcopal church, although the "Declaration of Principles" remains the official doctrinal statement of the Reformed Episcopalians.

• Cummins left few papers, but the Bishop Cummins Memorial Reformed Episcopal Church, Catonsville, Md., owns a bound collection of Cummins's sermon manuscripts from the early days of his parish ministry in Maryland, Virginia, and Illinois. Cummins's letters can be found in a number of Episcopal archives, most notably in the Maryland Diocesan Archives, Baltimore. The original copy of Cummins's "Call to Organize" the Reformed Episcopal church is in the Reformed Episcopal Archives, Philadelphia Theological Seminary, Philadelphia, Pa. Cummins published numerous sermons and wrote a biography of an Evangelical Episcopal missionary, *The Life of Mrs. Virginia Hale Hoffman* (1859). His address to the Evangelical Alliance in 1873 was published in *History, Essays, Orations, and Other Documents of the Sixth General Conference of the Evangelical Alliance Held in New York, October 2–12, 1873* (1874). In 1884 the Reformed Episcopal Publication Society issued a slim volume of *Sermons by Bishop Cummins.* The only biography is Alexandrine Cummins, *Memoir of George David Cummins, D.D., First Bishop of the Reformed Episcopal Church* (1878).

ALLEN C. GUELZO

CUMMINS, Maria Susanna (9 Apr. 1827–1 Oct. 1866), novelist, was born in Salem, Massachusetts, the daughter of the Honorable David Cummins (sometimes spelled Cummings), a lawyer and judge, and Maria F. Kittredge, his third wife. Inaccuracy has long existed regarding the identity of Cummins's mother, with Mehitable Cave often being cited. Cave was actually the novelist's grandmother; that she was married to David Cummin[g]s the elder probably initiated the lasting confusion.

Maria Cummins's father enjoyed high standing in Dorchester, Massachusetts, where—after a brief spell in Springfield when Maria was a girl—he served for nearly thirty years as judge of the Court of Common Pleas in Norfolk County. He guided his daughter's early education, training her well in belles-lettres. Having cultivated Maria's precocious writing skills, he eventually enrolled her in Mrs. Charles Sedgwick's Young Ladies School in Lenox, Massachusetts, where she continued her adolescent studies. While attending this progressive and select boarding school, Cummins met Catharine Sedgwick, the renowned author of *Hope Leslie* (1827) and other tales, who often gave readings there and apparently influenced the future novelist.

Between her return, upon completing school, to the family homestead in Dorchester and the publication, in March 1854, of *The Lamplighter*, Cummins wrote and anonymously published short fiction (still unidentified) in New England periodicals. Anonymous authorship in no way restricted the phenomenal sales of *The Lamplighter*, a novel that captivated both American and European readers. Domestic sales at the end of twenty days reached 20,000 copies; by year's end the total had swelled to 73,000, and translations in French, German, Danish, and Italian followed suit, along with pirated editions in England. In the 1850s *Uncle Tom's Cabin* was the only novel to outsell *The Lamplighter* in the United States.

Cummins's achievement prompted Nathaniel Hawthorne to write an oft-quoted letter to his publisher William Ticknor, in which Hawthorne denounced America's "d——d mob of scribbling women," characterized their fiction as "trash," and pondered "the mystery of these innumerable editions of the 'Lamplighter,' and other books neither better nor worse." Marion Harland, another contemporary novelist and an acquaintance of Cummins, expressed a positive view of the fuss surrounding her colleague: "In 1855, no other woman writer was so prominently before the reading public. *The Lamplighter* was in every home, and gossip of the personality of the author was seized upon greedily by press and readers. . . . [Maria Cummins was] quietly refined in manner and speech, and incredibly unspoiled by the flood of popular favor that had taken [her] by surprise" (Harland, pp. 284–85).

Conventionally termed a sentimental novel, *The Lamplighter* traces the growth of Gerty, a destitute and neglected eight-year-old orphan, into a fully realized young woman who attains moral, emotional, material, and spiritual fulfillment. Key figures in her evolution include her mentor and friend Emily Graham, her fiancé Willie, and Trueman Flint, the benevolent lamplighter who initiates Gerty's rise in the world by being the first to befriend the forlorn girl. Interspersed throughout the novel's ingenious plot are didactic asides that reflect either on Gerty's development into a woman of shining virtue, or on other topics. For example, the narrator discusses Willie's departure by sea to make his fortune:

Among [such New England] wanderers, we hope,—ay, we *believe* that there is many a one who is actuated, not by the love of gold, the love of change, the love of adventure, but by the love he bears his *mother*,—the earnest longing of his heart to save her from a life of toil and poverty. Blessings and prosperity to him who goes forth with such a motive! And, if he fail, he has not lived in vain; for, though stricken by disease or violence at the very threshold of his labors, he dies in attestation of the truth that there are sons worthy of a mother's love, a love which is the highest, the holiest, the purest type of God on earth.

Cummins's second novel, *Mabel Vaughan*, appeared in 1857 and focuses on the career of a fashionable woman who watches in dismay as the fortunes of her family and relations, assailed by dissipation and bad luck, deteriorate. Mabel's inner strength responds to the challenge of helping her remaining loved ones rebuild their lives in rural Illinois. *El Fureidîs* (1860), a romance situated in Syria, tells the story of Havilah, the beautiful "Oriental" heroine, and Meredith, the roaming Englishman who wins both her heart and, by way of Western ingenuity, the devotion of her Palestinian brethren. Although commended by many critics, *El Fureidîs* fared poorly with the reading public, as did Cummins's last novel, *Haunted Hearts* (1864), a murder mystery in which the female protagonist suffers for years until the crime, which implicates her absent lover, is solved. So highly rated were Cummins's first three novels that the Tauchnitz Library of British and American Authors selected them as part of their distinguished series.

Cummins's travels have proven difficult to verify, but one scholar believes internal evidence in *Mabel Vaughan* indicates firsthand knowledge of Niagara Falls. Two long essays by Cummins in the *Atlantic Monthly*—"A Talk about Guides" (June 1864) and "Around Mull" (July 1865)—discuss visits to England, Scotland, and "a brief sojourn in Alpine regions," as well as a "second Alpine excursion" (her passport confirms entry into France in 1860). These few journeys aside, the well-loved novelist, who never married, spent her adult years in the delightful family manse and domain on Bowdoin Street in Dorchester, where she was a member of the Unitarian church and taught Sunday school. Cummins's health failed soon after her tour abroad; a protracted bout of "abdominal disease" caused her death at her home in Dorchester at the age of thirty-nine. An obituary declared, "She was,—she *is*,—so intensely *living*, that the thought of her and of death cannot rest in our minds together" (*Boston Semi-Weekly Advertiser*, 3 Oct. 1866).

A new edition in 1988 of *The Lamplighter* demonstrates this novel's durability. Even though the other three texts failed to match the commercial impact of her debut, Maria Cummins's importance as the author of an archetypal American romance remains secure.

• The Cummins Family Papers are located in the Peabody Essex Museum, Salem, Mass. Other early sources about Maria Cummins are Nathaniel Hall's *A Sermon Preached in the First Church, Dorchester, on the Sunday Following the Decease of Maria S. Cummins* (1866), a pamphlet that may be read (but not photocopied) at the Phillips Library of the Peabody Essex Museum; George Mooar, *The Cummings Memorial: A Genealogical History of the Descendants of Issac Cummings, an Early Settler of Topsfield, Massachusetts* (1903); and Albert Oren Cummins, *Cummings Genealogy: Issac Cummings 1601–1677 of Ipswich in 1638 and Some of His Descendants* (1904). See also *Vital Records of Andover, Massachusetts, to the End of the Year 1849* (1912) and *Vital Records of Salem, Massachusetts, to the End of the Year 1849* (1916–1925). A firsthand view of Cummins is related in *Marion Harland's Autobiography: The Story of a Long Life* (1910), pp. 284–87. For criticism of *The Lamplighter* and the sentimental genre, see Donald A. Koch's edition (1968), Nina Baym's edition (1988), and Baym's *Woman's Fiction: A Guide to Novels by and about Women in America, 1820–1870* (1978). Annette Kolodny analyzes *Mabel Vaughan* in *The Land before Her: Fantasy and Experience of the American Frontiers, 1630–1860* (1984). Kimberly Devlin, "The Romance Heroine Exposed: 'Nausicaa' and *The Lamplighter*," *James Joyce Quarterly* 22, no. 4 (1985): 383–96, probes Joyce's parodic use of Gerty in *Ulysses*.

STEVE HAMELMAN

CUNNINGHAM, Alfred Austell (8 Mar. 1882–27 May 1939), U.S. Marine Corps officer and aviator, was born in Atlanta, Georgia, the son of John D. Cunningham, an attorney, and Cornelia Dobbins. At the outbreak of the Spanish-American War in 1898, the sixteen-year-old Cunningham left Gordon Institute, a military preparatory school in Barnsville, Georgia, and joined the second Georgia Infantry Volunteers. He served in Cuba but did not see combat and was discharged as a corporal.

Cunningham worked as a bank clerk and sold real estate in Atlanta until 1908, when he applied for and received a commission in the U.S. Marine Corps. Enamored with flight since an ascent in a balloon in 1903, Cunningham secured orders in 1912 to the navy's new aviation camp at Annapolis. He was the first marine corps officer to be assigned to aviation duty, and the date that he reported to Annapolis—22 May—is considered the birthdate of marine aviation.

After a brief stay at Annapolis, Cunningham was sent to the factory of the Burgess Company in Marblehead, Massachusetts, for flight training. He made his first solo flight on 1 August 1912. Between October 1912 and July 1913, following his return to Annapolis, Cunningham logged nearly 400 flights in a Wright B-1 biplane, reaching a maximum altitude of 800 feet.

In August 1913 Cunningham asked to be detached from flight duty because his fiancée would not consent to marry him unless he gave up flying. After his request was granted, Cunningham married Josephine Jeffries. Apparently he managed to reassure his new wife about the hazards of aviation. In April 1915 he reported to Pensacola, Florida, for refresher training and flight duty.

Marine corps aviation languished before U.S. entry into World War I. At the end of 1916 Cunningham was one of only five officers who, together with eighteen enlisted men, constituted the entire marine corps aviation contingent. In February 1917, as American involvement grew more likely, Cunningham was ordered to form an aviation company for the Advanced Base Force. This was the first formal marine corps aviation organization.

The marine corps expanded rapidly after the United States declared war on Germany in April 1917. Cunningham, acting as the de facto head of marine aviation, led a campaign by aviation enthusiasts to ensure that the marines' air component received a generous share of the new manpower.

In November 1917 Cunningham traveled to Europe in search of a role for his growing aviation force. Discovering a need for bombers to attack German submarines that operated from bases on the coast of Belgium, he returned to the United States in January 1918 and urged the General Board to assign four marine corps squadrons to the bombing mission. The board approved his proposal and ordered the formation of the Northern Bombing Group. In March Cunningham was asked to organize and command the First Marine Aviation Force of the projected group.

The initial marine contingent reached France in July 1918. As the marines did not yet have airplanes, Cunningham arranged for his aviators to fly with British units. In October the First Marine Aviation Force flew its own DeHavilland DH-4Bs in support of the Allied advance. In all, Cunningham's men conducted forty-three missions with the British and fourteen independent missions, dropping fourteen tons of bombs on the enemy.

At the end of the war the marine corps had 282 officers and 2,180 enlisted men assigned to aviation duty. However, aviators still lacked a permanent status. Cunningham became the main lobbyist for marine aviation, testifying before the General Board and writing articles about the value of marine aviation. He defined the mission of marine aviation in terms of supporting ground troops. Its main purpose, he wrote in 1920, was to assist troops on the ground "to successfully carry out their operation."

After an eighteen-month legislative battle, Congress in 1920 established the manpower of the postwar marine corps at 27,400 officers and men, with 1,020 personnel designated for aviation service. Cunningham remained head of marine aviation until December 1920, when he was replaced by his bureaucratic rival, Major Thomas C. Turner.

Cunningham commanded the First Marine Squadron in Santo Domingo for the next year and a half and then returned to ground duty in accordance with a policy (which he supported) of giving all aviators ground assignments after five years of flying. In 1928 Cunningham requested aviation duty but was turned down. Cunningham retired because of physical disability on 1 August 1935. He died four years later of coronary thrombosis in Sarasota, Florida.

The first marine corps flyer, Cunningham was the central figure in marine aviation between 1912 and 1920. As contemporary Ford O. Rogers later commented, "Without him, there never would have been any [marine corps] aviation." Although in 1920 he fell victim to an internal power struggle, his contributions to marine aviation had been fixed. Having firmly attached an aircraft component to the organization of the corps, he had earned the title "Father of Marine Aviation."

• The U.S. Marine Corps Historical Research Center, Washington, D.C., has a biographical file on Cunningham and a small collection of his personal papers. Graham A. Cosmas has edited the diary that Cunningham kept during his visit to France in 1917–1918, *Marine Flyer in France* (1974). Cunningham's contributions to marine aviation are documented in Edward C. Johnson, *Marine Corps Aviation: The Early Years, 1912–1940* (1977), and Robert Sherrod, *History of Marine Corps Aviation in World War II* (1952).

WILLIAM M. LEARY

CUNNINGHAM, Ann Pamela (15 Aug. 1816–1 May 1875), founder and first president of the Mount Vernon Ladies' Association, was born at "Rosemont" plantation, Laurens County, South Carolina, the daughter of Robert Cunningham and Louisa Bird, plantation owners. The only girl among four children of a prominent southern cotton planting family, Cunningham was pretty, bright, imaginative, persuasive, and strong-willed. She was educated at home and "finished" at the South Carolina Female Institute (Barhamville) near Columbia, South Carolina. At the age of seventeen she was thrown from a horse, which permanently injured her spinal cord and made her a lifelong invalid. Her mother often took her to Philadelphia for prolonged medical treatments.

In 1853, on a return trip by steamboat on the Potomac, Cunningham's mother observed Mount Vernon in its dilapidated condition. It had been a losing venture even at the time that it was owned by President George Washington and had financially drained generations of the family. The current owner, John Augustine Washington, Jr., a great-grandnephew of George Washington, had been approached to sell it and had been offered $300,000. The would-be purchasers intended to use it for a resort hotel, in one instance, and for industrial development in another. He refused both offers. Its fate had been of widespread public concern for some time. His unsuccessful attempts to sell for the lesser sum of $200,000 to the federal government and to the Commonwealth of Virginia had aroused public criticism. Shocked by the low estate to which the home of the first president had fallen, Louisa Cunningham wrote her daughter a letter asking whether the women of this country might keep Washington's home in repair if the men could not?

Cunningham took up her mother's challenge. She began in December 1853 with a letter to the *Charleston Mercury*, which solicited help and money to buy Washington's home and preserve it for the nation. Because it was considered improper for a lady to take part in public affairs, she signed it "A Southern Matron." She also wrote Washington's descendants asking them not to sell Mount Vernon until the women of the South had tried to raise money to buy it. An organizational meeting at the Presbyterian church to which the Cunninghams belonged collected $294, of which Louisa Cunningham contributed $100. In 1856 Cunningham and her associates, most notably Anna Cora Ogden Mowatt Ritchie (Anna Cora Mowatt) of Richmond, persuaded the Virginia legislature after considerable effort to grant a state charter to her organization, The Mount Vernon Ladies' Association of the Union. Edward Everett, a former governor of Massachusetts, president of Harvard University, and noted orator, agreed to donate the proceeds of what became a series of lectures on George Washington; these drew large audiences and raised over $69,000. Cunningham also arranged for the well-known Washington banker George W. Riggs to serve as treasurer and financial adviser to the association.

Cunningham drew upon her family's connections with the Virginia gentry to try to persuade Mount Vernon's owner to sell the estate to her association. Washington, however, did not believe that the association could raise the funds, resented the publicity that he had received, and was suspicious of the motives of the ladies. He remained distrustful until Cunningham paid him a personal visit, in which she expressed her sympathy for his ill treatment in the press and suggested that the charter be amended by the legislature to recognize his contribution. Finding his earlier suspicions groundless, Washington reversed his position and agreed that the Mount Vernon Ladies' Association of the Union could purchase the estate for $200,000. At the same time, the association moved to allay sectional tensions by accepting responsibility for Mount Vernon and its surrounding 200 acres in its own right, rather than merely administering it for the Commonwealth of Virginia. A new state charter was granted the association in 1858.

The Mount Vernon Ladies' Association of the Union had organized itself along lines that proved successful. In 1856, as newly installed regent, Cunningham appointed viceregents for each of the participating states and "lady managers" at the country and town level, who were chosen for their social standing, abilities, and financial resources. This new form of organization raised the money to buy Mount Vernon through public lectures, benefit performances, sales of copies of Washington's and Everett's portraits, and solicitation of funds. Cunningham herself proved an able fundraiser and organizer and published a monthly paper, the *Illustrated Mount Vernon Record*, from July 1858 to June 1860 in Philadelphia, where she moved temporarily for medical treatment. At Everett's insistence she made her identity public in the first issue. By 1860 the association had enough money to take formal possession of Mount Vernon, more than two years earlier than called for in the contract.

During the Civil War, the association maintained a strict neutrality under Cunningham, in spite of her mother's wish that she declare for the Confederacy. She appointed a northerner, Sarah Tracy, as first secretary of the association, and Upton H. Herbert, a distant relative and friend of Washington, as resident director. He volunteered for neither the Union nor the Confederate army, but living at Mount Vernon throughout the war he protected it and oversaw its refurbishing. Cunningham spent the Civil War managing the family plantation after her father's death, while trying simultaneously to aid the association. From 1867 to 1874 she was resident director at Mount Vernon and lobbied successfully for compensation from the United States for the wartime seizure of the association's steamboat, which had brought tourists and their admission fees to Mount Vernon. Most of that money was spent on rebuilding the greenhouse.

During this period her physical condition declined, and she suffered from rheumatism, convulsions, and constant pain. She was often bedridden and became increasingly dependent on the opiate laudanum. This affected her personality and her managerial skills. The viceregents removed her from all financial and administrative affairs in 1872 and asked her not to reside at Mount Vernon. She resigned as regent in 1874 and died at Rosemont the following year. She was buried in Columbia, South Carolina, and her native state honored her by placing her portrait among those of other distinguished citizens in the senate chamber of the capitol. The Mount Vernon Ladies' Association continues to carry out Cunningham's charge to perpetuate the memory of George Washington by keeping his home intact and unchanged for the public. It also maintains an administration building adjacent to the mansion in which it displays photographs of Cunningham in the meeting rooms.

Cunningham was a pioneer of the historic preservation movement and an early organizer in what later became known as the women's club movement. She and other American women proved that a privately controlled, self-perpetuating cultural organization could preserve historic places. Her organization was the first women's patriotic society in the United States. Her methods of organization at the local, state, and national levels have served as models for other successful groups. She stands out as a most persuasive advocate, able to recruit support in both the North and South at a time when sectional differences were splitting the Union and when women rarely wrote, spoke, or acted in the political arena.

• Letters and minutes are found in the Library of the Mount Vernon Ladies' Association. The fullest account of Cunningham's contributions is Elswyth Thane, *Mount Vernon Is Ours: The Story of the Preservation and Restoration of Washington's Home* (1966). Thane's is a popular account without footnotes and with few specific attributions of sources. See also chapter 2 of Charles B. Hosmer, Jr., *Presence of the Past: A History of the Preservation Movement in the U.S. before Williamsburg* (1965). A pamphlet is by Marion R. Wilkes, *Rosemont and Its Famous Daughter* (1947). Works that deal with the role of the Mount Vernon Ladies' Association in the historic preservation movement are William J. Murtach, *Keeping Time: The History and Theory of Preservation in America* (1988), and Susan Porter Benson, Stephen Brier, and Roy

Rosenzweig, *Presenting the Past: Essays on History and the Public* (1986). An obituary is in the *New York Times*, 10 May 1875.

VIRGINIA W. LEONARD

CUNNINGHAM, Glenn V. (4 Aug. 1909–10 Mar. 1988), track and field athlete, was born in Atlanta, Kansas, the son of H. Clint Cunningham, a water well driller and odd-jobsman. His mother's name is unknown. At age seven, Glenn and his thirteen-year-old brother Floyd were engulfed in a schoolhouse fire. Floyd received severe burns to his entire body and died days later. Glenn survived the fire but sustained near-crippling burns to his legs. After being bedridden for nearly six weeks, during which time doctors almost amputated his legs, Cunningham recovered his mobility through daily massage from his mother to restore the circulation to his badly scarred legs. Once he was able to walk again, he soon began running. As a result Cunningham increased his physical endurance and easily outran boys twice his age. A county mile-run champion at age thirteen, he excelled at the distance on the high school track team in Elkhart, Kansas. Cunningham reigned as the nation's best high school miler in 1930, winning the event in the Kansas Relays (Interscholastic Division) in a national high school record of 4:31.4. He won the high school state championship in the mile and lowered the record to 4:28.4. As a final measure of his ability, Cunningham lowered the record to 4:24.7, winning the national interscholastic mile championship.

Cunningham graduated from high school and entered the University of Kansas in 1930. As a member of the track team, he developed into the nation's leading middle-distance runner. In 1932 Cunningham won the first of three consecutive indoor and outdoor Big Six (later Big 12) Conference mile run titles and the 1,500 meters in the National Collegiate Athletic Association (NCAA) Track and Field Championships. That year he edged out veteran miler Gene Venzke for the third and final position in the 1,500 meters on the U.S. Olympic Team. At the Summer Olympic Games in Los Angeles, California, Cunningham and Canada's Philip Edwards forged a huge lead early in the race, only to succumb to Italy's Luigi Beccali and Britain's John Cornes in the homestretch. Cunningham finished fourth, as Beccali, Cornes, and Edwards took the gold, silver, and bronze medals, respectively. Known as the "Kansas Iron Horse" for his courageous front-running, Cunningham won the NCAA mile title and the 800 and the 1,500 meters in the Amateur Athletic Union (AAU) Track and Field Championships in 1933, an achievement that earned him the Sullivan Award as the nation's top amateur athlete. In addition to winning the AAU outdoor 1,500 meter title from 1935 to 1938, he also captured four AAU indoor 1,500 meter championships in 1934, 1935, 1938, and 1939.

In 1934 Cunningham enjoyed one of his most successful yet disappointing seasons. After establishing indoor world records of 3:53.2 in the 1,500 meters and 4:08.4 in the mile, he recorded an outdoor world record of 4:06.7 for the mile at the Princeton University Invitational. In the latter, Cunningham triumphed over East Coast rival Billy Bonthron, who in turn defeated the front-running Kansan in the NCAA mile and AAU 1,500 meter championships later that year. Cunningham, who lowered the indoor world record in the 1,500 meters to 3:50.5 in 1935, won the 1,500 meters at the U.S. Olympic Trials in 1936. At the Summer Olympic Games in Berlin, Germany, his front-running tactics failed to secure the gold medal, as New Zealand's Jack Lovelock ran in Cunningham's shadow and outsprinted him in the final lap. Cunningham's second place time of 3:48.4 eclipsed Bonthron's 1934 world record by .4 seconds. (Lovelock established a new 1,500 meter world record of 3:47.8.) In 1936 Cunningham also set a world record of 1:49.7 in the 800 meters.

Cunningham posted his fastest times in the years following the 1936 Olympic Games. Undefeated in the mile and the 1,500 meters indoors in 1938, he established a world record of 3:48.4 in the 1,500 meters in winning the AAU indoor title that year. Within a week after his AAU triumph, Cunningham ran the mile in 4:04.4 at Dartmouth College. This remarkable performance, however, did not qualify as an indoor world record because he was aided by pacers on an oversized track. His fastest outdoor time for 1,500 meters, 3:48.0, came in the final race of his career, the 1940 AAU championships.

Cunningham earned a bachelor's degree from the University of Kansas in 1934 and a master's degree from the University of Iowa in 1936. He completed a Ph.D. in education at New York University in 1938 and then became the director of physical education at Cornell College in Mount Vernon, Iowa, in 1940. Cunningham left Cornell College in 1944 and served in the U.S. Navy for two years during World War II. In 1947 he married Ruth Sheffield and, instead of returning to his position at Cornell College, settled on an 840-acre ranch near Burns, Kansas, where they established the Glenn Cunningham Youth Ranch for orphans, juvenile delinquents, and underprivileged youths. Cunningham, who did not accept any federal or state funds, supported the enterprise through his income as an inspirational speaker. In 1960 he moved the ranch to Augusta, Kansas. Financial troubles exacerbated by his wife's failing health forced Cunningham to close the ranch in 1978. For over thirty years, the Cunninghams, who raised twelve children of their own, took care of nearly 10,000 youngsters at the ranch. In 1985 two Arkansas couples who wished to continue the Cunninghams' work reopened the ranch and hired Glenn and Ruth as advisers. On 28 February 1988 Cunningham returned to New York City's Madison Square Garden, where he had won twenty-one of thirty-one mile races, for the 100th anniversary of the Mobil/USA (formerly AAU) Indoor Track and Field Championships, and participated in a relay race of former champions. He died of a heart attack at his farm for exotic animals near his home in Menifee, Arkansas, less than two weeks later.

Cunningham overcame a near-crippling childhood accident to became the nation's premier middle-distance runner in the 1930s, winning ten national titles and setting three world records in the mile and the 800 and 1,500 meters. The last American to hold the outdoor world record in the mile until another Kansan, Jim Ryun, claimed it in 1966, Cunningham was one of several international performers capable of breaking the world record in either the 1,500 meters or the mile under the right conditions. His 4:04.4 mile indoor performance at Dartmouth in 1938 caused track and field experts to begin thinking that a sub-four-minute performance was indeed possible. The true measure of Cunningham's personal significance, however, is not his fastest mile, but in the thousands of children raised by him and his wife at the Glenn Cunningham Youth Ranch.

• The Alumni Association, Archives, and Sports Information Department of the University of Kansas all have extensive material on Cunningham. Cunningham published an autobiography, *But Never Quit*, with George X. Sand (1981). Statistical information on Cunningham's performances is in Frank G. Menke, *The Encyclopedia of Sports*, 4th rev. ed. (1969), and David Wallechinsky, *The Complete Book of the Olympic Games*, rev. ed. (1988). For Cunningham's place in the history of athletics, see Roberto L. Quercetani, *A World History of Track and Field Athletics* (1964). Obituaries include the *New York Times* and the *Kansas City Times*, both 11 Mar. 1988, and *Kansas Alumni*, Apr. 1988.

ADAM R. HORNBUCKLE

CUNNINGHAM, Imogen (12 Apr. 1883–23 June 1976), photographer, was born in Portland, Oregon, the daughter of Isaac Burns Cunningham, a farmer and small businessman, and Susan Elizabeth Johnson. Cunningham grew up the fifth of ten children in a poor working-class family. Most of her childhood was spent on her parents' remote farm near Seattle, Washington. Getting an education was difficult due to the family's isolation, but she succeeded in finishing high school. Before venturing off to college, Cunningham expressed to her father her interest in becoming a photographer. Even though he preferred teaching as a career for his daughter, Isaac Cunningham supported her choice and built a darkroom in their woodshed. By 1901 Cunningham had a 4″ × 5″ camera and a book of instructions from the International Correspondence School in Scranton, Pennsylvania. She began developing pictures in the woodshed made light-tight by tar-papered walls.

Cunningham entered the University of Washington in the fall of 1899. She wanted to major in art, but at that time the university did not have an art department. She chose chemistry instead and graduated with honors in three and a half years. After graduation she worked in the Seattle studio of Edward S. Curtis, who was compiling an important photography portfolio on American Indians. She spent eight years at his studio and learned the difficult process of platinum printing. In 1909 she received a scholarship for postgraduate study of photographic chemistry at the Technische

Hochschule in Dresden, Germany. She returned to Seattle the following year and set up her own portrait studio.

Cunningham's early work consisted mostly of soft-focus portraits and nudes. She was inspired by an enthusiasm for Pre-Raphaelite poetry and would dress friends in exotic costumes and have them act out scenes from romantic poems in the forests around her studio. This was, for Seattle, hardly the average commercial portrait studio. With her blue draperies on the walls and statues of the *Winged Victory* and the *Venus de Milo* on the mantle, Cunningham escaped what she called the "conventionalities that surround photography."

Although her earliest works were technically proficient, they represented nothing revolutionary. Cunningham showed, however, a rebellious and independent spirit when she wrote a short manifesto published by the University of Washington Press in 1913, *Photography as a Profession for Women*. This work demonstrated her unmistakable commitment to feminism. She called for the inclusion of women not only in the photographic profession but in all areas of the arts and industry, saying that modern times allowed women to work with no disgrace attached to it and without their being regarded as eccentric.

In 1915 Cunningham married etcher Roi Partridge. That same year she published a series of photographs of him posed nude on Mount Ranier. These pictures so shocked the Seattle community that she took them out of print for many years. The couple had three sons, and Cunningham successfully combined her career with raising a family. In 1917 they moved to San Francisco; three years later, to neighboring Oakland. During this time Roi Partridge was teaching art at Mills College. The move from Seattle resulted in a major change in Cunningham's photographic style. In California she found inspiration in the modernist movement and in the work of photographers such as Alfred Stieglitz and Edward Weston. These two men produced tightly focused, highly detailed pictures with strongly contrasting shades of black and white. They also began to seek out new subject matter that had been ignored in the past. Cunningham embraced these ideals and began making close-up studies of flowers and other botanical specimens. She made highly contrasting photographs of flowers and their inner structures, capturing an aspect of the flower that had previously been of interest only to botanists. Many of her best-known photographs were made in her own backyard, in part out of necessity because she stayed home with the children and did not have a driver's license. One example of her work during this time is *Magnolia Blossom* (1925), which her son Padraic recalled was of a flower brought home and put in a vase where it was left for at least three days before being photographed. Cunningham's flower photographs brought her recognition and are now considered some of her most important work.

Though her work was appreciated in the photographic community on the West Coast and she had several successful exhibitions dating back as early as 1912, Cunningham did not earn a national reputation until the 1930s, when she contributed photographs of celebrities such as Cary Grant, Spencer Tracy, and dancer Martha Graham to *Vanity Fair* and *Life* magazines. She gained further recognition by her involvement with Group f/64, an informal art society founded by Ansel Adams and Willard Van Dyke and influenced by Edward Weston. This group, named after the aperture setting on a camera lens that secures the greatest sharpness in the image, promoted "straight" photography and protested against academic pictorialism. The members also wanted recognition for West Coast photography similar to that achieved by Stieglitz in New York. Cunningham joined Group f/64 in 1932 but eventually left in order to experiment with techniques such as double exposure and collage.

Nevertheless, from the 1930s to the 1960s Cunningham remained primarily a portrait photographer. Her ability to "penetrate the mask" of a sitter gave her portraits the quality of art. In a 1973 review of her work, Hilton Kramer said, "She really gives herself to the subject—there is no question of turning the subject into 'a Cunningham'" (*New York Times*, 26 June 1976).

Cunningham photographed both the famous and the unknown. During World War II her studio attracted many servicemen who wanted portraits before going overseas. These types of portraits remained traditional so that she could continue to compete in the commercial market. But Cunningham's mischievous nature came into play when she photographed the famous. For example, in a 1953 photograph of Ansel Adams, she caught him gesturing skyward from a perch on a rock, looking as if he were delivering the word of God.

From 1947 until her death Cunningham operated a successful portrait studio in San Francisco; she had moved back there after a 1934 divorce from Partridge. After 1945, supported by grants and fellowships, she began teaching photography to a new generation of artists. Her tutelage was in high demand, and the number of her students increased significantly in the 1950s and 1960s. Despite the demands of teaching and her advancing age, Cunningham continued to work on new projects. She applied for a Guggenheim Fellowship at age eighty-one to photograph "the grand dames of England," women who were well established in the art world. She was turned down but received a fellowship six years later. By that time she felt unable to travel abroad, so she requested the grant to print some of her older work. Much of that work was published in *Imogen! Imogen Cunningham Photographs, 1910–1973* (1973), her second book of photography.

Cunningham's last project was a series of photographs of people aged ninety years or older; she began this project when she herself was ninety-two. She died in San Francisco before the work was completed, but it was published posthumously as *After Ninety* (1977). In the introduction to this book, Margarette Mitchell wrote, "No words can describe old age as well as the

photographs reproduced in *After Ninety*, which is a direct result of Imogen's own confrontation with life after ninety. This is surely one of the most unusual projects ever undertaken by a photographer . . . because in our culture it is the rare artist of any age whose work confronts this stage of life without fear, without condescension, but with self-identification and compassion."

Imogen Cunningham's work spanned seventy-five years and mirrored the evolution of twentieth-century photography. Her work was shown at galleries and museums across the country, including the Metropolitan Museum of Art in New York, the San Francisco Museum of Modern Art, and the Oakland Museum of Art. Her flower and plant photographs taken in the 1920s were hailed by some critics as her most celebrated pictures, while others found her portraiture most memorable. In her last interview in the spring of 1976, Cunningham said of her portrait work, "You must be able to gain an understanding at short notice and at close range of the beauties of character, intellect, and spirit, so as to be able to draw out the best qualities and make them show in the face of the sitter."

• Imogen Cunningham's papers are held by the Smithsonian Institution's Archives of American Art. Her first book of photographs is *Imogen Cunningham: Photographs* (1970). Amy Rule, ed., *Imogen Cunningham: Selected Texts and Bibliography* (1992), contains a number of articles and critical essays on Cunningham and her work. It also includes a short biographical essay. Richard Lorenz, *Imogen Cunningham: Ideas without End* (1993), is a detailed biography. The bibliography in *After Ninety* provides a list of articles about Cunningham. Three films were made about Cunningham: Fred Padula's *Two Photographers: Imogen Cunningham and Wynn Bullock* (1966), John Korty's *Imogen Cunningham, Photographer* (1967), and Ann Hershey's *Never Give Up: Imogen Cunningham* (1975). An obituary is in the *New York Times*, 26 June 1976.

DEBBIE GRIGGS CARTER
LISABETH G. SVENDSGAARD

CUNNINGHAM, Minnie Fisher (19 Mar. 1882–9 Dec. 1964), suffragist and political activist, was born in New Waverly, Texas, the daughter of Horatio White Fisher and Sallie Comer Abercrombie, farmers. She was educated at home and passed a teacher certification examination. Rather than teach, however, she decided to enroll in the pharmacy program at the University of Texas Medical Branch at Galveston. She graduated in 1901, one of the first women in Texas to earn a pharmacy degree, and worked as a prescription clerk in San Antonio and Huntsville. Discovering that she was being paid only half as much as less-qualified male co-workers, she recalled years later, was the seed of her commitment to suffrage and women's rights.

Following the conventions of the time, Minnie Fisher relinquished paid work after marrying Beverly Jean Cunningham, a lawyer, in November 1902; they had no children. Interested in politics since childhood, when she had tagged along to political meetings with her father, she entered enthusiastically into her city-bred husband's campaign for county attorney in 1904 and helped him carry a majority of the rural districts. After the couple's move to Galveston in 1907, Minnie Fisher Cunningham became involved in women's voluntary association politics through the Woman's Health Protective Association; by 1913 she had become chair of its School Hygiene Committee. Her deepest interest, however, was in the rising suffrage movement. She joined the Galveston Equal Suffrage Association at its inception in 1912 and was elected president in 1914, at the same time serving as an unofficial state organizer.

Elected president of the Texas Equal Suffrage Association in 1915, Cunningham soon proved herself an uncommonly capable politician. She was the behind-the-scenes organizer and secretary of the Woman's Campaign for Good Government, which during 1917 helped build sentiment in favor of impeaching the demagogic governor, James E. Ferguson, an implacable suffrage foe. When his attempt at a political comeback split the Democratic party, Cunningham quietly persuaded the legislative leaders of the progressive wing that the surest way of stopping Ferguson was to enfranchise women. In return for a bill that gave women the right to vote in primary elections (tantamount to full suffrage in one-party Texas) Cunningham spearheaded a campaign that registered 386,000 women voters in seventeen days and helped elect the progressive faction's candidate for governor, William P. Hobby, by a landslide in 1918.

During World War I Cunningham organized and led the Texas Women's Anti-Vice Committee that pressured state and local officials to protect young recruits by creating "white zones" free of liquor and prostitution around military training camps; served on the Texas Military Welfare Commission; and chaired the state's Fourth Liberty Loan drive. By 1918 she was also separated from her husband and dividing her time between Texas and Washington as she became increasingly prominent in the national suffrage movement. As secretary of the National American Woman Suffrage Association's Congressional Committee, she was part of the core group who lobbied the Nineteenth Amendment through Congress in 1919. She traveled in the western states urging its ratification and in 1920 was elected a delegate-at-large from Texas to the Democratic National Convention.

Cunningham helped organize NAWSA's successor, the League of Women Voters, and served as its executive secretary in Washington from 1921 through 1923. She urged women to become active in politics; twenty years later Eleanor Roosevelt still remembered her eloquence at the league's 1921 convention. In 1924 she was elected second vice president of the LWV and chaired its national "Get Out the Vote" campaign. Simultaneously, she was becoming visible in "women's work" within the Democratic party, helping found the Woman's National Democratic Club in 1923 and training women organizers. Late in 1925 Cunningham became executive secretary of the Woman's National Democratic Club, charged with "poking up," as she

said, the lethargic party women who were depressed by the Republican victory in 1924. She revived the organization's newsletter, *The Bulletin* (subsequently the *Democratic Bulletin* and later the *Democratic Digest*), and during 1926–1927 also substituted for Emily Newell Blair as vice chair of the Democratic National Committee.

In 1928 Cunningham returned permanently to Texas and became the state's first woman candidate for the U.S. Senate. Running on a platform that opposed the Ku Klux Klan and supported prohibition, farm relief, and tax and tariff reduction, she drew good crowds and favorable press coverage but finished fifth in a field of six candidates. "[I]f compliments had counted in the election I would have won hands down," she wrote afterward, "but always the finale was the same 'she can't be elected because she's a woman.'" Financially pressed and temporarily disillusioned with politics, she accepted an editorial position in mid-1930 with the Agricultural Extension Service at Texas A&M University, where she remained for the next decade.

From 1939 to 1943 Cunningham was again in Washington, D.C., as a public information specialist in the women's division of the Agricultural Adjustment Administration. Although she resigned after a conflict with administrators whom she believed were hostile to the information program for the food production effort, Cunningham remained a strong supporter of the New Deal and President Franklin D. Roosevelt. When anti-Roosevelt Democrats took over the Texas Democratic Convention in 1944, Cunningham, who chaired her county's delegation, was among those who bolted and held a rump convention; it elected her parliamentarian. As a further protest against the conservative governor, Coke Stevenson, who was expected to lead the delegation to the national convention, 62-year-old "Minnie Fish" entered the race for governor as the liberals' standard bearer. Her campaign forced Stevenson to stay home, and although he won by a substantial margin Cunningham finished well ahead of the other seven candidates.

That year she also began writing a political column for the weekly *State Observer* (subsequently the *Texas Observer*) and a decade later, when the paper faced sale to a conservative buyer, rallied a group of fellow liberals to the financial rescue by offering to mortgage part of her farm property. Disgusted by the defection of prominent Texas Democrats to Dwight Eisenhower in 1952, Cunningham helped organize the Texas Democratic Women's State Committee and was elected treasurer. She was still serving when she died in Conroe, Texas. A lifelong political activist, Cunningham was one of few suffrage leaders able to wrest voting rights from a southern legislature and was part of the pioneering generation of women who attempted to carve a niche for themselves in politics in the postsuffrage decades.

• Cunningham's papers are at the Houston Public Library. Substantial correspondence from the 1920s and her unpublished account of the 1928 Senate race are in the Dorothy Kirchwey Brown Papers at the Schlesinger Library, Radcliffe College. Other correspondence is in the Jane Y. McCallum Family Papers at the Austin Public Library; the Carrie Chapman Catt Papers, the National American Woman Suffrage Association Papers, and the League of Women Voters Papers at the Library of Congress; the Maud Wood Park Papers at the Schlesinger Library; and the Jessie Jack Hooper Papers at the Wisconsin Historical Society. The League of Women Voters in Washington, D.C., has a file of clippings on Cunningham. Two long interviews with her are in the *Austin American*, 24 May 1946, and the *Texas Observer*, 21 Nov. 1958. On her suffrage activity, see Glenn K. Polan, "Minnie Fisher Cunningham" (M.A. thesis, Sam Houston State Univ., 1968); John Carroll Eudy, "The Vote and Lone Star Women: Minnie Fisher Cunningham and the Texas Equal Suffrage Association," *East Texas Historical Journal* 14 (1976): 52–59; and Judith N. McArthur, "Motherhood and Reform in the New South: Texas Women's Political Culture in the Progressive Era" (Ph.D. diss., Univ. of Texas at Austin, 1992), which documents the suffrage bargain. Patricia Ellen Cunningham has described the gubernatorial campaign in "Too Gallant a Walk: Minnie Fisher Cunningham and Her Race for Governor of Texas in 1944" (M.A. thesis, Univ. of Texas at Austin, 1985) and "Bonnet in the Ring: Minnie Fisher Cunningham's Campaign for Governor," in *Women and Texas History: Selected Essays*, ed. Fane Downs and Nancy Baker Jones (1993). An obituary is in the *Washington Post*, 14 Dec. 1964.

JUDITH N. McARTHUR

CUNNINGHAM, William (fl. 1774–1800), British provost marshal during the American Revolution, was born in Ireland. No reliable information exists concerning Cunningham's parentage or youth. He arrived in New York City during 1774. Originally, his intended destination was Albany, but he appears to have been waylaid in New York City by the problems caused in America by the Intolerable Acts. At first he seemed friendly to the views of the New York Sons of Liberty. However, he changed his position and urged that the Continental Association be violated, a pro-British stance. Supporters of the Sons of Liberty charged that he was currying favor with friends of the British government and military men in order to gain preferment.

At the public meeting of 6 March 1775, the people of New York City called for the creation of a provincial convention to pick a congressional delegation. What little dissent there was came from colonial officials, military men, and some others among whom were John Hill, an Irish tavernkeeper, and Cunningham. After the meeting ended, the two Irishmen were confronted by a mob angry at them for their support of the British. Cunningham was ordered to kneel and "damn his Popish king George." When Cunningham responded "God bless King George," the mob set upon him, stealing his watch and ripping his clothing. Hill received the same treatment. Although supporters of the Sons denied Cunningham's charges, even an observer such as John Pintard, who later became the patriots' agent for New York prisoners of war, attributed the cause of Cunningham's cruelty during the war years to this abuse.

When fighting broke out, Cunningham fled to Boston, which was controlled by the British. There, General Thomas Gage, impressed by Cunningham's loyalty, gave him a captain's commission and made him the provost marshal. Undoubtedly, Gage was happy to find someone to take the position. The job entailed not only caring for prisoners of war but also executions and disciplining of soldiers, unpleasant duties not appealing to many.

Cunningham would also serve as provost marshal in New York and for part of the British occupation of Philadelphia as well. On 14 November 1777 General George Washington complained to the British commander, General Sir William Howe, about the treatment of American prisoners in Philadelphia. Washington commented that "many of the cruelties exercised towards Prisoners, are said to proceed from the inhumanity of Mr. Cunningham." Soon after, Howe sent Cunningham back to New York, where he remained for the rest of the war.

The treatment meted out to American prisoners of war in occupied New York City is what made Cunningham's name synonymous with cruelty among Americans who supported the Revolution. The provost jail, which was operated by Cunningham, was a place of evil. Indiscriminate beatings were the rule, no doubt an echo of what the Sons of Liberty had done to Cunningham. Requesting additional water during hot weather was an offense punishable by confinement in a dark and unhealthy cell. Sometimes, slowness in retiring for the night merited the same punishment. Other times, a prisoner might be left for a long period in a dank cell for no offense whatsoever. Most of this cruelty was blamed by the prisoners themselves on a Sergeant Keath, or Keiff, who was the jailkeeper and so in daily contact with the captives. All those who encountered him seem agreed that the man was a fiend.

Yet Cunningham's role seems plain enough. John Adlum, an American prisoner not in the provost jail, was warned by a British sergeant familiar with the jail that Cunningham might not turn over specially delivered provisions to the men in his charge. Some food that was given to the captives in the provost was contaminated with vermin.

Additional information about Cunningham's culpability was unearthed in February 1778, when Elias Boudinot investigated the provost jail for the patriots. He learned that Cunningham had himself beaten two rebel captives to death. The murder weapon was the prison's key. Other stories about Cunningham that Boudinot believed he termed too repulsive to write about. Boudinot's complaint to British general James Robertson resulted in a restriction of the jailkeeper's authority. There is no report of Cunningham being disciplined, and he retained his position.

After the Revolution, according to an alleged confession by Cunningham, he became a forger after leaving the army and was hung in 1791. However, this confession is not credible. The publication that printed this item in 1792, the *American Apollo*, emphasized moral essays, of which the confession was almost certainly one. It has the wrong number of sons. The confession's statement that Cunningham secretly executed more than 200 Americans late at night is sheer fantasy. The confession has Cunningham begging God for pardon, which is just what a moral essay would emphasize.

Not surprisingly, Cunningham was reported alive in 1799 and was in Gloucester, England, as a prison's governor. He had finally mellowed in Gloucester and was no longer acting like a savage.

Cunningham was married, probably more than once, although the name of his wife (or wives) is unknown. By 1784 he had at least five children.

• There are no Cunningham letters. His claim for compensation is in the British Public Record Office, under AO 12/100, no. 288. A microfilm copy is at the New-York Historical Society, New York, Frank Moore, *Diary of the American Revolution*, vol. 1 (1860), pp. 36–37, 45–48, reprints newspaper accounts of Cunningham and the Sons of Liberty. Kenneth Scott, comp., "Rivington's New York Newspaper: Excerpts from a Loyalist Press, 1773–1783," New-York Historical Society, *Collections* 84 (1973), has references to him. On the provost jail, see David L. Sterling, ed., "American Prisoners of War in New York: A Report by Elias Boudinot," *William and Mary Quarterly*, 3d ser., 13 (1956): 376–93; Helen Jordan, ed., "Colonel Elias Boudinot in New York City, February, 1778," *Pennsylvania Magazine of History and Biography* 24 (1900): 453–66; Howard H. Peckham, ed., *Memoirs of the Life of John Adlum in the Revolutionary War* (1968); and Charles I. Bushnell, ed., *The Narrative of Major Abraham Leggett* (1865). The alleged confession is in the *American Apollo* 1, no. 7, pt. 2 (1792): 68–69. There is no biography. See Philip Ranlet, *The New York Loyalists* (1986), and George Adams Boyd, *Elias Boudinot* (1952), for Cunningham's conduct. For Cunningham at the Gloucester prison in 1799, see John W. Jackson, *With the British Army in Philadelphia, 1777–1778* (1979).

PHILIP RANLET

CUPPLES, Samuel (13 Sept. 1831–6 Jan. 1912), merchant, manufacturer, and philanthropist, was born in Harrisburg, Pennsylvania, the son of James Cupples, an educator who had immigrated to the United States from County Down, Ireland, in 1814, and Elizabeth Bigham. Cupples was chiefly educated by his father, who operated a business school in Pittsburgh. At age twelve Cupples began his working life in a grocery store in Pittsburgh and, five years later, moved to Cincinnati, Ohio, where he was employed by Albert O. Tyler, a pioneer, midwestern manufacturer, and wholesaler of woodenware.

In 1851 Cupples moved to St. Louis and, with Tyler as a silent partner, established his own woodenware business. St. Louis became the major center for the manufacture and distribution of woodenware throughout the West and the firm of Samuel Cupples & Company was a leader in this development. In 1871, the brothers Robert S. Brookings and Harry Brookings were made partners in the firm; although they had only worked in Cupples's firm for a few years, they had demonstrated great ability and were contemplating establishing their own company. From 1872, Rob-

ert Brookings, who was then only twenty-two, became the virtual operating head of the company. Cupples's judgment was not misplaced; by the 1880s the Cupples company had expanded to become the biggest enterprise of its kind in the country. In 1895 the company constructed Cupples Station in St. Louis, a giant complex of fifty warehouses, each with its own railroad siding. The complex was an immediate economic success because it overcame the problems of freight congestion and inadequate warehousing facilities in the rapidly growing city.

In 1848, after the death of his father, Cupples had assumed responsibility for the support of his mother and sister. In the same year he also had joined the Southern Methodist Episcopal church. In 1854 he married Amelia Kells, also a Methodist, with whom he had at least one child. In 1867 the Cupples became charter members of St. John's Methodist Church in St. Louis. He was an active member of the Southern Methodist church throughout his life and attended annual and general conferences.

Like many of his generation who acquired large fortunes in the second half of the nineteenth century, Cupples developed an interest in philanthropy as he grew older. A semi-invalid for the last thirty years of his life, his philanthropies came to be his predominant interest. The major beneficiaries of his generosity were the Southern Methodist church and Washington University in St. Louis. His wife's death in 1894 prompted him to donate $100,000 to erect a modern building in her memory for the Methodist Children's Home of Missouri, which she had helped to endow. Cupples also donated funds to the Central Methodist College in Fayetteville, Missouri, the St. Louis Provident Fund, the Orphans' Home, the Girls' Industrial Home, the St. Louis City Mission, and the Church Extension Society, which promoted the establishment of Southern Methodist churches and congregations.

Cupples's interest in educational philanthropy arose out of his interest in manual training. With the cooperation of other philanthropists he had established the St. Louis Training School of Washington University, which attracted favorable attention both within the United States and abroad. Stimulated by his business partner, Robert Brookings, who was also an active philanthropist and served as president of the Washington University Corporation, Cupples began to take an interest in broader university education and, particularly, in the upgrading of Washington University, an undistinguished pre–Civil War institution in his adopted city. In 1900 Cupples and Brookings donated the Cupples Station property to Washington University as an endowment. Cupples also underwrote the establishment of the School of Engineering and Architecture and established special scholarships to encourage graduates of the Manual Training School to undertake tertiary education. He also contributed to Vanderbilt University in Nashville, Tennessee. In all, Cupples donated approximately $1.25 million to various activities of the Southern Methodist church and $1.75 million to Washington University. Cupples died in St. Louis, where he lived in a house that is renowned for its romanesque architectural style.

• For additional information see the entry on Cupples in the *Encyclopedia of World Methodism* (1974), vol. 1, p. 615. On the construction of Cupples Station see William Hyde and Howard L. Conard, eds., *Encyclopedia of the History of St. Louis* (1899), vol. 1, p. 535, and on the subsequent donation to Washington University see *Encyclopedia Americana*, vol. 8 (1924), p. 304. On the architecture of the Cupples house see Maurice B. McNamee, *Cupples House: a Richardsonian Romanesque Mansion* (1986), and Elinor Martineau Coyle, *The Cupples House: A Turn of the Century Romanesque Mansion* (1980). For contemporary obituaries and eulogies see the St. Louis *Globe-Democrat*, 7–8 Jan. 1912; *Manual Training Magazine*, Oct. 1912, 46; and Washington University, *Bulletin*, July 1912.

WILLIAM J. BREEN

CUPPY, William Jacob (23 Aug. 1884–19 Sept. 1949), humorist and critic, was born in Auburn, Indiana, the son of Thomas Jefferson Cuppy and Mary Frances Stahl. His father worked as a grain trader, farm implements dealer, and railroad employee, his mother as a seamstress. His childhood summers were spent on his grandparents' farm in South Whitley, Indiana, where he acquired an interest in "the birds and the flowers and all the other aspects of animate nature" that later served as objects of his satire. Cuppy entered the University of Chicago in 1902 and graduated five years later with a B.A. in philosophy. He remained on campus for another seven years as a graduate student, "taking courses in practically everything, with or without bothering to go to examinations." In 1908 the editor of the university press asked Cuppy, a member of Phi Gamma Delta, to concoct some fraternity "traditions" similar to those of the Ivy League schools. The result was *Maroon Tales* (1910).

Cuppy supported himself throughout his school years by working as a reporter for the *Chicago Daily News* and the *Chicago Record-Herald*. In that capacity, he met Burton Rascoe, a fellow student and freshman reporter for the *Herald*, who later became his editor at the *New York Herald Tribune*. In 1914 Cuppy converted his extensive doctoral research on Elizabethan prose writers into a master's thesis in English and moved to New York City to become a playwright. During World War I Second Lieutenant Cuppy served as a publicity writer with the Motor Transport Corps stationed in Washington D.C. In 1921 he wrote Rascoe, then the literary editor for the *New York Herald Tribune*, "a very droll letter" about Aldous Huxley's *Crome Yellow*. Rascoe pressed the reluctant Cuppy into service as a critic of popular literature for the *Herald's* new book review section. Cuppy's first weekly column, "Light Reading," was changed to "Mystery and Adventure" in 1926. From then on he read and reviewed four to six mystery and detective novels a week and between 1943 and 1946 edited three anthologies of murder and mystery stories.

Cuppy, a lifelong bachelor, moved to a small shack on Jones Island, south of Long Island, New York, in 1921 to gain some relief from allergies and people. In 1929 he forged several previously published essays about his reclusive lifestyle into his first major success, *How to Be a Hermit*, which went through six printings in six months. It earned Cuppy national recognition as a humorist and the nickname the "Hermit of Jones Island." Two years later he converted his prodigious research in zoology into the first of a trilogy of books that in the guise of natural history satirized human behavior. In each volume, *How to Tell Your Friends from the Apes* (1931), *How to Become Extinct* (1941), and *How to Attract the Wombat* (1949), he lampooned the "crown of creation" through short explications of insects, birds, and mammals. "House flies are full of germs and bad manners," Cuppy writes in *How to Attract the Wombat*. "They come to the table and act something awful. They have a positive gift for the wrong gesture at all times and places." As with all of his books, Cuppy packed additional research plus much of his humor into trenchant footnotes, a trademark of his writing. Walter Sellar and Robert Yeatman hired Cuppy specifically to "footnote" their parody on gardening, *Garden Rubbish and Other Country Bumps* (1937).

After leaving his Jones Island shack in 1929, Cuppy moved into a Greenwich Village apartment that he crammed with books. Threatened with eviction during a bout of depression, Cuppy ended his life in his apartment with an overdose of pills. His friend and editor Fred Feldkamp assembled the final chapters of *The Decline and Fall of Practically Everybody* (1950), a historical burlesque over which Cuppy had struggled for the last sixteen years of his life. The misanthropic Cuppy skewered well-known historical figures with studied acumen and then salted the wounds with copious footnotes. At one point he coaxes the reader to look at Nero's good side: "Try to remember he didn't murder his mother until he was twenty-one years old." *Decline and Fall* quickly became the most popular of all Cuppy's books; it was translated into dozens of languages and was still in print almost fifty years after his death. Feldkamp assembled another book, *How to Get from January to December* (1951), by selecting the best of 200,000 note cards on which Cuppy stored quotes, quips, and comments for future works.

Cuppy was a perfectionist, a nighthawk, a fan of hamburgers and cigarettes, and a recluse with a gregarious streak who could form "spontaneous friendships with ease," yet for the most part he kept his life solitary and his sexual preferences carefully closeted from even his closest heterosexual friends. Although a world-renowned humorist, Cuppy chronically doubted his talent, avoided writing by doing constant research, and was painfully sensitive to criticism. Yet five decades later, his research still holds true, and his pugnacious wit remains fresh and timely.

• The papers of Will Cuppy are in the Regenstein Library at the University of Chicago. Additional information was graciously provided by Phyllis Feldkamp of Ardmore, Pa., from research gathered by both her late husband and Thomas Maeder. *How to Tell Your Friends from the Apes* and *How to Become Extinct* were reissued together as *The Great Bustard and Other People* (1944). Analysis of Cuppy's comic style is in Norris Yates, *The American Humorist: Conscience of the Twentieth Century* (1964). Fred Feldkamp describes Cuppy's work habits in the foreword to *The Decline and Fall of Practically Everybody*, as does Burton Rascoe in *Before I Forget* (1937). Also see Maeder's afterword in the 1984 reprint of *The Decline and Fall*. For a brief sketch of Cuppy and his associates at the *New York Herald Tribune* see *Publishers Weekly*, 30 Sept. 1939. See also Al Castle, "Naturalist Humor in Will Cuppy's *How to Tell Your Friends from the Apes*," *Studies in American Humor* 3 (Winter 1984–1985): 330–36. A memorial is in the *New York Herald Tribune Book Review*, 20 Nov. 1949, and an obituary is in the *New York Times*, 20 Sept. 1949.

WILLIAM S. PUGSLEY III

CURLEY, James Michael (20 Nov. 1874–12 Nov. 1958), mayor of Boston and governor of Massachusetts, was born in Boston, the son of Irish immigrants Michael Curley, a laborer, and Sarah Clancy, a washerwoman. The death of his father, when Curley was ten, marked the boy's childhood. Forced to enter the paid workforce in his teens, Curley worked as a store clerk and in a variety of other jobs before becoming active in the ward politics of his Roxbury neighborhood. To advance his political career, he joined a series of Irish fraternal organizations, became active in Catholic lay affairs, and developed his skills as a public speaker. In 1897 he failed on his first attempt to win a seat on the Common Council of Boston, but he prevailed two years later.

In 1901 Curley won election to the lower house of the Massachusetts legislature and worked to gain control of the Democratic organization in the neighborhood of Roxbury. To solidify his base of support, he founded the following year a political club that modeled itself by name and operation after New York City's Tammany Hall. Like its namesake, this Curley-dominated organization sought to gain influence by providing job referrals, direct relief, and other services to constituents, many of whom were recently arrived European immigrants. Later that same year Curley took a federal civil service examination on behalf of a constituent and supporter that led to his indictment on federal fraud charges. Despite a guilty conviction and a jail sentence, Curley managed to turn this issue to his advantage and win election as a city alderman in 1903. Serving as an alderman until 1909, Curley won a seat that year on a restructured Boston City Council.

In 1910 Curley gained election to the U.S. House of Representatives. Appointed to the Foreign Relations Committee, he opposed measures that restricted immigration and favored legislation that abrogated commercial treaties with Russia in order to protest that country's record of pogroms against Jews. He lobbied for increased naval expenditures at the Boston Navy Yard. In 1912 he supported the unsuccessful bid of House Speaker Champ Clark to secure the Democratic party's presidential nomination.

Elected the mayor of Boston in 1914, Curley began his term in office by criticizing the administration of his predecessor, John F. Fitzgerald, for reckless spending as well as political favoritism in the awarding of municipal contracts and jobs. His administration's first measures included a round of budget cuts, removal of a number of senior Fitzgerald appointees, and other economy measures, and political reformers initially greeted Curley's actions as mayor with skepticism, surprise, and even grudging admiration. But after narrowly surviving a recall election in 1915, Curley abandoned efforts to appeal to the upper-class-dominated good-government wing of the electorate and emphasized policies that aided Boston's immigrant communities. He stressed the need to devote greater resources to social welfare institutions, increased the wages for the lowest-paid municipal workers, and supported legislation that improved housing conditions. In the interest of both patronage and charity, as mayor he regularly met with people seeking employment and tried to find appropriate positions for them in government or business.

Other Irish Americans had been elected to the Boston city hall before Curley, but few governed as flamboyantly. A controversial figure throughout his career, Curley appealed to ethnic chauvinism and anxieties as part of his political arsenal. In an era that often placed few ethical or legal barriers to using public office for private gain, few outdid Curley. His conspicuously lavish lifestyle was signaled in 1915 by his building of a mansion in the fashionable Jamaica Plains section of the city. In running Boston, he clashed frequently with efforts by the Massachusetts state legislature to limit his authority. Even before Curley assumed the mayoralty, the growing Irish-Catholic dominance of Boston politics led to increasing efforts by the Protestant-dominated state government to place limits on the city's autonomy, especially with regard to municipal finance and control of the police force. In all four of his terms as mayor, Curley opposed state governmental oversight as well as the limitations placed on the taxing and bonding authority of the city.

Although he lost a bid for another term in 1917, Curley remained an anathema to political reformers of Massachusetts. In a move aimed at frustrating Curley's political ambitions, his successor as mayor, Andrew J. Peters, convinced the state legislature to amend the charter to prohibit Boston mayors from succeeding themselves. But after Peters mishandled the Boston police strike and the economic downturns of 1921, Curley recaptured city hall in 1921. Under his second administration, Curley embarked on a major building program that poured millions into the City Hospital, schools, parks, and other public facilities. In an era of political conservatism on the national level, Curley advocated an activist role for government to help ensure the economic and social well-being of the average citizen.

Prohibited from running for a successive term, Curley turned his attention to statewide office and ran unsuccessfully for governor in 1924. His linking his name to Alfred E. Smith's Democratic presidential campaign in 1928, however, helped win Curley a third term as mayor of Boston shortly after the 1929 stock market crash. During the first years of the Great Depression, Mayor Curley advocated massive public works to deal with unemployment both in Boston and in the entire nation. Contrary to the Massachusetts Democratic party establishment, he favored Franklin D. Roosevelt over Alfred E. Smith for the 1932 Democratic presidential nomination, waging an unsuccessful primary bid in Massachusetts on Roosevelt's behalf. Denied a place in the Massachusetts delegation to the Democratic National Convention, Curley attended the convention, in place of an ill delegate, as leader of the Puerto Rican delegation.

The disappointment of not receiving a cabinet or major ambassadorial appointment in 1933 strained Curley's relationship with the Roosevelt administration, however. Granted only limited political spoils from Washington, Curley had little influence over New Deal public-works spending in Massachusetts. During the 1930s he offered tacit support to the raucous populist Father Charles E. Coughlin and even lent some organizational support to the priest's quasi-fascist movement. Again unable to serve a successive term as mayor, Curley ran for governor of Massachusetts in 1934, and this time he won. Over the course of his term, Curley's extravagant personal spending and expensive vacations showed, however, that he had lost touch with his constituents. A series of scandals rocked his administration, including the involvement of his state limousine in several traffic accidents, the alleged sale of pardons to state convicts, and the appointment of scores of poorly qualified individuals to public offices.

In the late 1930s Curley's political fortunes began to ebb. Denied Roosevelt's endorsement in the 1936 senatorial election, he lost against a moderate Republican, Henry Cabot Lodge, Jr. In 1937 and 1940 one of Curley's former political confidants, Maurice J. Tobin, twice defeated him for the Boston mayoralty, and in 1938 Leverett Saltonstall turned back Curley's attempt to recapture the Massachusetts governorship. After leaving the office of governor, he squandered a substantial sum of money in unsuccessful investments in Nevada gold mines; then he lost a civil suit brought by the Suffolk County prosecutor that forced him to forfeit to the city of Boston the amount of money he received from General Equipment Company for "fixing" a damage claim settlement.

In 1942, however, Curley managed to revive his faltering career by returning to Congress. In defeating Thomas H. Eliot, a former New Deal attorney with an exemplary voting record on behalf of the Roosevelt administration, Curley based his campaign on appeals to ethnic and religious pride. Once back in Congress, he compiled a voting record that matched his former opponent's in support of the Roosevelt administration's social agenda.

Curley's popularity within Boston remained high—despite even a felony indictment in 1943 for influence peddling, which stemmed from his involvement with a consulting firm seeking to secure defense contracts. On the slogan "Curley Gets Things Done" he won an unprecedented fourth term as mayor of Boston in 1945. A federal jury then found him guilty of the felony charges, but he remained mayor even after he entered a federal penitentiary in 1947. To prevent his political rival Tobin from emerging against Curley, Republican governor Robert F. Bradford helped pass special legislation that made John B. Hynes, the city clerk, acting mayor of Boston in place of the president of the City Council. After President Harry Truman commuted his sentence, in part out of political expediency and because of pressure from the Massachusetts congressional delegation, Curley returned to Boston and resumed the duties of office.

Changes in Boston's charter had permitted Curley to run for reelection in 1949. Hynes defeated him, however, in an election that heralded the growing ascendancy of the middle-class ethnic voter who wanted political leaders that portrayed an image of personal honesty, professionalism, and efficiency. In 1951 and 1955 Curley made two final unsuccessful bids for the mayoralty. In retirement he personified in the public imagination the last of the ethnic ward politicians, who were giving way to the modern age of television-dominated middle-class politics. Curley's fictional counterpart is the Tammany Hall–style politician Frank Skeffington in Edwin O'Connor's novel of the time, *The Last Hurrah* (1956). The former mayor's death in Boston led to one of the largest funerals in the city's history.

A devoted family man, Curley was first married in 1906 to Mary Emelda Herlihy, who died in 1930. Seven of their nine children predeceased him, several under tragic circumstances. In 1937 Curley was remarried, this time to a widow, Gertrude Casey Dennis. His public identity was shaped by his devotion to Roman Catholicism, pride in his Irish ancestry, and love of politics and campaigning. In assessing the career of James Curley one can easily fault him for his demagoguery and his personal corruption. A self-styled "Mayor of the Poor," as he wanted to be remembered, Curley symbolized the later stages of an era of ethnic ward politics and augured the growing presence of Irish Americans in the national political arena.

• Before his death, Curley destroyed many of his personal papers, but he deposited a large collection of scrapbooks containing newspaper clippings, photographs, and other documents in the Holy Cross College Library, Worcester, Mass. Some of Curley's surviving correspondence can be found in the Franklin D. Roosevelt Library. The year before he died, he published an autobiography, *I'd Do It Again: A Record of All My Uproarious Years* (1957). Joseph F. Dinneen, *The Purple Shamrock: The Hon. James Michael Curley of Boston* (1949), offers a contemporary journalistic account. Jack Beatty, *The Rascal King: The Life and Times of James Michael Curley, 1874–1958* (1992), is the definitive biography. Important aspects of Curley's career are examined in Thomas H.

O'Connor, *The Boston Irish: A Political History* (1995); Ronald P. Formisano and Constance K. Burns, ed., *Boston 1700–1980: The Evolution of Urban Politics* (1984); Charles H. Trout, *Boston, the Great Depression, and the New Deal* (1977); and Herbert Marshall Zolot, "The Issue of Good Government and James Michael Curley: Curley and the Boston Scene from 1897–1918" (Ph.D. diss., SUNY at Stony Brook, 1975). Articles about his death and his career are in the *New York Times*, 13, 15, 16 Nov. 1958.

G. KURT PIEHLER

CURLEY, Michael Joseph (12 Oct. 1879–16 May 1947), archbishop of Baltimore, was born in Athlone, county Westmeath, Ireland, the son of Michael Curley, a prosperous farmer, and Maria Ward. In 1885 he entered Mungret College, Ireland, to study for the priesthood and in 1900 transferred to the Urban College of the Propaganda in Rome to become a missionary. On 19 March 1904 he was ordained a priest in Rome and was sent to Florida, then an underdeveloped part of the Catholic world, where he was given charge of a parish that comprised 7,200 square miles in the diocese of St. Augustine. He lived in a rented room above a store and ate in a diner where a $5 ticket bought him twenty-one meals. For a brief time he was chancellor and secretary to Bishop William J. Kenny.

On 3 April 1914 Curley was named by the Holy See bishop of St. Augustine, Florida, and on 30 June was raised to the episcopacy. As bishop he attracted national attention by battling a convent inspection bill and a law forbidding Catholic sisters to teach black children. On 10 August 1921 he was appointed archbishop of Baltimore. He took possession of the oldest American Catholic see on 21 November.

In his first years in Baltimore Curley's principal energies were devoted to the work of consolidation, centralization, and creation of an efficient bureaucracy, goals neglected, for the most part, by his predecessor, Cardinal James Gibbons. Though perhaps the nation's most popular Catholic prelate, Gibbons had not been an active administrator. Throughout his years in Baltimore Curley would live in Gibbon's shadow. In 1922 Curley organized the archdiocesan Office of Education, in 1923 the Bureau of Catholic Charities, and in 1925 the Society for the Propagation of the Faith for home and foreign missions. His most notable achievements were in education, having begun in his first year the annual teachers' institute. In 1926 he would boast, "I defy any system of grammar school education in the United States to prove itself superior to the system that is being maintained in the Archdiocese of Baltimore." An impressive building program was halted by the Great Depression but resumed in the postwar years.

Curley encouraged the growth of such lay organizations as the Holy Name Society, Knights of Columbus, Catholic Daughters of America, and International Federation of Catholic Alumnae, entrusting to them such tasks as the promotion of Catholic education, relief of the poor, and defense of the church. In his twenty-five and a half years as archbishop of Baltimore the archdiocese, which included the District of Columbia, nearly doubled in population, personnel, and institu-

tions. On 22 July 1939 Curley was named archbishop of the newly created archdiocese of Washington but continued to govern the two archdioceses as a single unit.

Curley was a crusader as well as a builder. From about 1926 until 1941 he was the most active of the American bishops in the battles he joined. He campaigned with vigor and boldness against the Catholic Foundation movement to establish Catholic centers at secular universities, the anticlerical governments of Mexico and Spain, and "dirty" movies. He was the first American Catholic bishop to speak out forcefully against communism, persuading the bishops in 1936 to conduct a study of its influence in the nation. He organized labor schools in Baltimore and Washington to promote papal teachings on social justice and to counter the activities of the Communist party in local labor unions. Curley was quick to demand apologies for what he considered slurs upon the Catholic church, conducting a bitter campaign against the Baltimore *Sun* when one of its reporters compared Adolf Hitler to Ignatius of Loyola.

Though he had little to do with local politics, Curley was outspoken in his criticism of the administration of Franklin D. Roosevelt. Unaware of the bombing of Pearl Harbor, he responded to a reporter in a flippant manner concerning what he thought was simply the sinking of another American vessel as a result of Roosevelt's policy. Those who wished the archbishop silenced seized upon the interview to have the Holy See admonish him. Pained by the rebuke, he refrained thereafter from any pronouncements of a political nature.

Curley was the first archbishop of Baltimore not to be recognized as leader of the Catholic church in the United States. He had, in fact, no close friends in the American hierarchy. He was often at odds with the policies of the administrative committee of the National Catholic Welfare Conference, his public statements often proving a source of embarrassment to that body. As chancellor of the Catholic University of America, however, he played a role of national importance but was forced by the Holy See to accept a rector he judged unequipped to raise the standards of the institution.

Curley had a genuine sympathy for victims of discrimination, the poor, immigrants, African Americans, and Jews. He served for several years as spiritual director of the Federated Colored Catholics and broke with anticommunists who proved anti-Semitic. He was, perhaps, the poorest bishop in the United States, accepting an annual salary of only $1,200 and immediately bestowing upon the needy any gifts he received. He was honest and forthright. Even his critics admired his directness and candor as they complained of his lack of tact. He was a tireless administrator, though he spent the summer months in his childhood home in Ireland. He suffered without complaint a variety of ailments, conducting much of the business of the archdiocese in the second half of his administration in Baltimore from a hospital bed. Two years before his death in Baltimore he was blinded by one of a series of strokes. An overflow of ten thousand mourners stood in the rain outside the cathedral during his funeral.

• The Curley papers are in the archives of the archdiocese of Baltimore. A popular biography spanning less than a third of his Baltimore years is Vincent de Paul Fitzpatrick, *Life of Archbishop Curley: Champion of Catholic Education* (1929). His career, however, is well covered in the Baltimore *Catholic Review*. See also Thomas W. Spalding, *The Premier See: A History of the Archdiocese of Baltimore, 1789–1989* (1989), and Joseph Bernard Code, *Dictionary of the American Hierarchy (1789–1964)* (1964). An obituary is in the Baltimore *Sun*, 18 May 1947.

THOMAS W. SPALDING

CURME, George Oliver (14 Jan. 1860–29 Apr. 1948), college professor, was born in Richmond, Indiana, the son of Arthur Allen Curme, a clergyman and business-man, and Elizabeth Jane Nicholas. He attended public schools in his home town and also received tutoring in both Latin and Greek. In 1876 he enrolled at DePauw University, but his father's financial reverses forced him to leave school. Money problems persisted until he transferred to the University of Michigan at Ann Arbor in 1881. In that same year, he married Caroline Chenoweth Smith; they had four children.

Curme shifted from the classical course to the study of the German language after receiving encourage-ment from faculty members in the field. He graduated from Michigan with a B.A. in 1882 and immediately began a teaching career at the Jennings Seminary in Aurora, Illinois, where for two years he provided in-struction in both French and German before moving to the University of Washington in 1884. In 1885 he received a master's degree from DePauw. He re-mained in Seattle for two years as professor of modern languages before again relocating, this time to Cornell College in Mount Vernon, Iowa.

Promoted to professor of German language and lit-erature in 1887, Curme published his first book, *Se-lected Poems from Premières et Nouvelles Méditations of Lamartine*, in 1888. Although the work reflected Curme's broad range of linguistic interests, he soon fo-cused his scholarly efforts on German and English grammar. His first effort in the field, *Lessing's Nathan der Weise*, appeared in 1898. In 1886 he had begun work on the book that would establish his worldwide academic reputation, *Grammar of the German Lan-guage*. Published in 1905 after years of careful rewrit-ing and study, including a year (1890) spent in residence at the University of Berlin, it served as a standard text in the subject for generations. Featuring original quotations from literary works and newspa-pers, the book was enormously popular, with an en-larged second edition appearing in 1922. In the interim, Curme moved yet again, this time to North-western University. Appointed professor of German philology in 1896, he remained at the school until his retirement in 1934.

Curme continued to write, producing *Grillparzer's Libussa* in 1913. In that same year he also published his follow-up to *Grammar*, an elementary textbook ti-tled *A First German Grammar*, although it was too scholarly in nature to duplicate the success of *Gram-mar*. Curme remained undaunted, but he began to de-vote an ever-increasing portion of his efforts to the study of English grammar. His first work in the field, *College English Grammar*, was published in 1925. His most famous work in the area, *Grammar of the English Language*, appeared in two volumes, *Syntax* in 1931 and *Parts of Speech and Accidence* in 1935. These pub-lications, which competed with existing European studies on the subject, proved slower than his German language works in gaining acceptance and only be-came influential after his death.

Despite the mixed response to his latest efforts, Curme was at the height of his career. A lifetime mem-ber of the Modern Language Association of America, he served as president of the western branch of that organization for a year and as national president in 1931. He also held memberships in the National Insti-tute of Social Sciences, the Linguistic Society of Amer-ica, the Simplified Spelling Board of America, as well as Phi Beta Kappa. He lectured in German at the Uni-versity of Southern California following his retirement from Northwestern until 1939, when he moved to White Plains, New York. Curme and his wife separat-ed after their children reached adulthood. A son, George Oliver Curme, Jr., achieved prominence as an industrial chemist. Curme lived quietly with a daugh-ter, producing one final publication, *Principles and Practices of English Grammar* (1946), until his death in White Plains.

Curme made substantial contributions to the schol-arship and scholarly treatment of modern languages. He was one of the last of a generation of academics to prosper without an earned Ph.D., and his work in both German and English grammar set the standard for scholarship in those areas for many years.

• The archives at Northwestern University in Evanston, Ill., holds a small collection of material on the life and career of Curme. He has received surprisingly little scholarly attention in recent years; the best secondary sources remain James Taft Hatfield et al., eds., *Curme Volume of Linguistic Studies* (1930), and the introduction to the 1952 reprint of his *Gram-mar of the German Language*. An obituary is in the *New York Times*, 30 Apr. 1948.

EDWARD L. LACH, JR.

CURME, George Oliver, Jr. (24 Dec. 1888–28 July 1976), chemist, was born in Mount Vernon, Iowa, the son of George Oliver Curme, a college professor, and Caroline Chenoweth Smith. In 1896 Curme's family moved to Evanston, Illinois, where his father taught German at Northwestern University. Curme received his B.S. from Northwestern in 1909, then studied briefly at Harvard University before receiving his Ph.D. in organic chemistry from the University of Chicago in 1913. He spent the year after graduation studying chemistry in Germany at the Kaiser Wilhelm Institute and the University of Berlin, and returned to the United States just before the outbreak of World War I. In 1916 he married Lillian Grace Hale; they had five children.

In the early twentieth century, American science and technology were for the most part separate enterprises. Most scientists pursued knowledge for its own sake, while many industrialists regarded scientists as dangerous meddlers whose research threatened to render their physical plants and production methods obsolete. Curme disagreed with both views. Having seen the developing field of synthetic organic chemistry in Germany, he determined to find practical applications for this knowledge in the United States, because he believed "science was so wonderful that the public ought to be given a chance to benefit by it" (Kinzel, p. 122). His first opportunity came in 1914, when the Mellon Institute of Industrial Research hired him as a research fellow to find a cheaper way for the Prest-O-Lite Company, which made headlamps for bicycles and automobiles, to produce acetylene, a colorless gas used for illumination. In 1915 Curme discovered that by boiling crude oil, he could produce large amounts of acetylene as well as ethylene, a flammable hydrocarbon gas. Today ethylene is perhaps the most important petrochemical. Its simple molecular structure allows it to react easily with inexpensive reagents such as water, oxygen, and chlorine to make a number of valuable commercial chemicals used in the production of such things as thermoplastics, synthetic rubber and fibers, and industrial solvents. At the time of Curme's discovery, however, it had no known application.

Curme determined to find a use for this by-product in order to make his method of producing acetylene more attractive financially. Under the auspices of the Mellon Institute, he continued his research for Prest-O-Lite until 1917, when that company merged with several others to form the Union Carbide and Carbon Corporation (UCC); after 1917 Curme worked for the new conglomerate. By 1920 he had discovered six different uses for ethylene and propylene, another hydrocarbon gas by-product of oil-boiling. He convinced UCC's upper management that products derived from these gases could take the place of many products of the existing chemical industry. Accordingly, that same year UCC created the Union Carbide and Carbon Chemical Corporation, with Curme as manager, chief chemist, and salesman, and a plant in an old gasoline compressor station in Clendennin, West Virginia. By 1922 Curme was producing, and shipping in railroad tank cars, Pyrofax propane for use as an inexpensive fuel for home cooking and heating. In 1925 a new plant was built in South Charleston, West Virginia, to make ethylene glycol, most of which was used in Prestone antifreeze for water-cooled automobile engines.

In 1929 Curme was made vice president and director of research of the Chemical Corporation; in 1938 he was promoted to vice president of UCC's Research Laboratories. All the while, he continued to create new compounds by combining various hydrocarbon gases with a variety of chemical reagents. Among the new chemical compounds his laboratories developed were butadiene for use in synthetic rubber, acetic acid for use in synthetic fibers, polyethylene for use as a plastic coating, and a variety of agricultural chemicals. Curme himself held twenty-nine U.S. patents for the preparation of such hydrocarbon-based chemical compounds as acetaldehyde, acetic acid, acetone, alkyl chloride, benzoic acid, ethylene diamide, ethylene dichloride, ethylene and propylene chlorhydrin, ethylene and propylene glycol, isopropyl alcohol, isopropyl chloride, and propylene dichloride.

Curme made significant contributions to the American war effort during World War II. Initially he was a consultant to the War Production Board and the National Defense Research Committee. Later, because of his ability to bring new products rapidly from the experimental stage to full-scale manufacture, he was appointed to the five-man Planning Board of the Office of Scientific Research and Development (later part of the Manhattan Project), in effect making him partially responsible for designing and constructing the facility in which the world's first atomic bomb was built.

In 1951 Curme became UCC's vice president of research, and the following year he was elected to the company's board of directors. He also served as vice president of two of UCC's subsidiaries—the Bakelite Company, a plastics manufacturer (1939–1951), and Carbide and Carbon Chemical Limited (1944–1955). He retired to Martha's Vineyard, Massachusetts, in 1955, but he remained on UCC's board until 1961.

Curme received a number of awards, including Columbia University's Chandler Medal (1933), the Society of the Chemical Industry's Perkin Medal (1935), the Franklin Institute's Elliott Cresson Medal (1936), the National Association of Manufacturers' National Modern Pioneer Award (1940), and the American Chemical Society's Willard Gibbs Medal (1944). He was elected to the National Academy of Sciences in 1944. He died in Oak Bluffs, Massachusetts.

In the words of the Gibbs Medal citation, Curme was "the father, grandfather, and great-grandfather of ethylene and her numerous progeny." As such, he created the modern petrochemical industry in the United States. His research led to the production of a number of industrial chemicals and contributed significantly to the development of a vast number of products integral to modern life.

• Curme's papers are located in the corporate files of the Union Carbide Corporation in New York City. A good biography of Curme, including a complete bibliography of his works and a list of his patents, is Augustus B. Kinzel, "George Oliver Curme, Jr.," National Academy of Sciences, *Biographical Memoirs* 52 (1980): 121–37.

CHARLES W. CAREY, JR.

CURRAN, Joseph Edwin (1 Mar. 1906–14 Aug. 1981), labor leader, was born in New York City, the son of Eugene Curran, who died before Curran was born, and Ida Cohan, a cook. His mother soon remarried, and Curran was placed with a foster family. He left school in the seventh grade, did a variety of odd jobs, and in 1922 became a sailor. Rising to the rank of boat-swain, Curran earned the nickname "No Coffee-Time Joe" for his toughness. One legacy of his years at sea was a pair of scars on his back from the night a shipmate attacked him with an ax.

In 1935 Curran joined the International Seaman's Union (ISU), which was affiliated with the American Federation of Labor (AFL). Crews on East Coast ships had staged a number of walkouts to obtain the better pay scales and work conditions that West Coast sailors enjoyed, and in 1936, while his ship, the *California*, was docked in San Pedro, California, Curran organized a sit-down strike to press these demands. The strikers went back to work after Secretary of Labor Frances Perkins promised they would get a fair hearing in New York, but as soon as they landed all sixty-four men were fired and blacklisted. In the wave of strikes that followed, East Coast sailors made few gains in part because they were systematically undermined by their union leaders.

Curran's activism in the strike, which crystallized years of dissatisfaction with bad conditions and ISU's corrupt leadership, made him a hero with ordinary seamen. Organizing his fellow insurgents as the Rank-and-File Committee, Curran initiated a series of job actions so disruptive that they convinced employers the ISU could no longer control its members. In May 1937 one major shipping line agreed to recruit its sailors from Curran's hiring hall. Immediately Curran announced the formation of the National Maritime Union (NMU). At the founding convention two months later, 35,000 former ISU seamen elected Curran president and voted to affiliate with the Congress of Industrial Organizations (CIO). The ISU rashly demanded dozens of union elections, nearly all of which it lost; within a year the NMU had contracts with more than sixty shippers. Abandoning the discredited ISU, the AFL organized a new organization, the Seafarers International Union (SIU), but it made little headway against the NMU on the East Coast.

In 1939 Curran married Retta Toble; they had one child. Meanwhile, the NMU established itself as a militant and progressive union. Internally the organization was a model of participatory democracy, and internationally it made a point of showing solidarity with workers in other countries, for example, by observing their picket lines in foreign ports. Curran also fought owners, ships' officers, and sometimes his own members to win equal employment rights for black seamen. In one 1942 case, when black NMU members were refused employment, he wired a protest to President Franklin Roosevelt, whose response demanding equal treatment set an important precedent.

Communists played a powerful role within the NMU; one estimate suggests that in 1947 they held three-quarters of the top union offices. The party's influence within the union attracted criticism (particularly from the House Un-American Activities Committee, which was investigating left-wing influence in the labor movement, in 1939), but during the NMU's early years Communists provided the union with invaluable talent, organizational support, and a progressive orientation that proved highly popular with the members. Observers differ as to whether Curran himself was a Communist—he always denied it—but until after World War II he worked harmoniously with those who were, and he tended to align himself with party policy on political matters by, for example, opposing war mobilization and Lend-Lease until Germany attacked the Soviet Union in 1941.

Once the Soviet Union aligned itself with the Allies, Curran threw himself into the war effort, holding the union to a no-strike pledge and serving on the Wartime Manpower Commission. Contention continued to follow him, however. The NMU filed $4 million worth of libel suits over charges that union seamen failed to do their job at the battle of Guadalcanal. Curran's draft status was also controversial; he was granted a deferment (over his objections, he maintained) on the grounds of his essential work with the U.S. Merchant Marines, but when his deferment lapsed in 1943 it took Roosevelt's personal intervention to extend it until Curran's birthday put him beyond draft age.

During these years, Curran gained stature in the broader labor movement. In 1940 he was elected president of the Greater New York Industrial Union Council, an association of the 118 CIO locals in the New York area. That same year he ran unsuccessfully for Congress on the American Labor party ticket, and in 1941 he became a CIO vice president. After the war he represented the CIO at a series of international labor conferences, and he joined the first American labor delegation to the Soviet Union since 1927. Maintaining his connection with rank-and-filers, he also supported the New York longshoremen's strike of 1945 despite the opposition of their leaders. When the AFL and the CIO were reunited in 1955, Curran became a vice president and a member of the AFL-CIO executive council.

When Soviet-American relations chilled after the war, the NMU, like many other American labor unions, launched a purge of its left-wing members. Curran led the attack, though he insisted that he was only targeting individual Communists who sought to undermine the union. By 1950 the NMU had barred "Communists, Nazis and Fascists, and other subversive organizations" from membership and had forced out virtually all the men who had helped Curran build the union. During the years that followed, the NMU steadily lost ground, suffering both from an era of scandals and waning democracy within the union and from the overall decline of the American merchant fleet. Curran's first wife died in 1963, and he married Florence Stetler two years later; they had no children. He retired as president of the union in 1973 and settled in Boca Raton, Florida. Shortly before his death there, he defeated a suit by union dissidents to challenge his million-dollar pension, but he was required to repay NMU funds that he had spent on personal expenses.

A contemporary described the six-foot two-inch Curran as having "a head like a block of granite, a loud, angry voice, and the attitude of someone struggling against an impulse towards mayhem." These qualities served him well, reinforcing his standing as a militant voice for the ordinary sailor. Although Curran lost sight of that vision in his later years, the example of the NMU in its best days remains an important legacy.

• An oral history about Curran was produced for the Columbia University oral History Project in 1964. NMU publications covering his career include *On a True Course: The Story of the National Maritime Union AFL-CIO* (1967) and the monthly *Pilot*, in which Curran wrote a regular column for many years. See also Irving Bernstein, *The Turbulent Years: History of the American Worker 1933-1941* (1970); Joseph Goldberg, *The Maritime Story: A Study in Labor-Management Relations* (1958); Philip Foner, *Organized Labor and the Black Worker, 1619-1973* (1974); Bruce Nelson, *Workers on the Waterfront: Seamen, Longshoremen, and Unionism in the 1930s* (1988); and Helen Lawrenson, "Covering the Waterfront," *Harper's*, Apr. 1975. An obituary is in the *New York Times*, 15 Aug. 1981.

SANDRA OPDYCKE

CURRIER, Charles Warren (22 Mar. 1857–23 Sept. 1918), bishop and author, was born on St. Thomas, West Indies, and raised on St. Eustatius and St. Kitts, the son of Warren Green Currier of New York City and Deborah Heyliger of the Netherlands. At fourteen he sailed to the Netherlands to attend Assumption College in Roermond. Professed a Redemptorist in 1875, he taught from 1876 to 1877 and pursued advanced studies to a Ph.D. in religious philosophy at the Redemptorist seminary at Wittem. He was ordained a Catholic priest by Bishop Henry Schaap (vicar apostolic of Dutch Guiana) in Amsterdam on 22 November 1880. Currier knew Greek and Hebrew and was fluent in Latin, English, Dutch, Spanish, French, German, and Italian.

In January 1881 he arrived in Surinam for his first missionary assignment. In February 1882 he sailed to the United States. His preaching drew crowds in Boston, New York, and Baltimore, and he began to publish. "The History of the Church of Our Lady of Perpetual Succor in Boston," his 1888 lecture before the American Catholic Historical Society of Philadelphia, was printed in the second volume of the society's journal. In 1935 Philip H. Frohman, architect of the National Episcopal Cathedral in Washington, began plans for the restoration of the first Carmelite foundation in the English colonies, near Port Tobacco, Maryland. His most valuable source, for its sketch of the 1800 "Monastery," was Currier's *Carmel in America* (1890). Currier noted the "encouragement and aid" of historian John Gilmary Shea and on assignments in southern Maryland explored sites, recorded recollections, and consulted materials in private hands. For the Carmelite bicentennial in 1990, a facsimile of *Carmel* was published as the inaugural volume of the Carmelite Sources series.

In November 1891 Currier was released from his Redemptorist obligations and thereafter served the Baltimore Archdiocese in a variety of capacities. His contributions to a wide range of periodicals proliferated, and he acted as foreign correspondent, both while in the United States and abroad. Reissued six times in twenty years, *History of Religious Orders* (1894) was the most popular of his eight books. His first novel, *Dimitrios and Irene* (1894), drew an unsubstantiated charge of plagiarism from Lew Wallace; the author of *Ben Hur* had just published *Prince of India* (1893), a romance also unfolding during the fall of Byzantium. *The Rose of Alhama* (1897) was Currier's second and last novel.

Currier promoted education. His Maryland Catholic Summer School, founded in 1900, was later absorbed into the Cliff Haven Summer School at Plattsburgh, New York. As pastor of St. Mary's Church in the U.S. capital from 1900 to 1905, he worked for better understanding between the Americas and among Spanish-speaking nations. He often presented papers at the International Congress of Americanists, in Europe and in the Americas, representing the United States government, the Smithsonian Institution, and the Catholic University of America. He was commissioned by the State Department to be U.S. delegate at congresses held during the centennial celebrations of independence in Argentina and Mexico in 1910. His *Lands of the Southern Cross* (1911) was issued by the Spanish-American Publication Society. Published articles on writers from several Spanish-speaking countries indicate that his unfinished *History of Spanish Literature* would have included Latin American authors.

"Indian Languages in the United States" was Currier's 1904 presentation before the Americanists in Stuttgart, and in 1905 he was named assistant director of the Bureau of Catholic Indian Missions. His lectures and publications raised consciousness, consciences, and money as he recalled the "blood-stained pages" of history from the Arctic to the Antarctic circle and drew attention to conditions—particularly of the schools—on North American reservations. He collaborated with Secretary of the Navy Charles J. Bonaparte, who as legal counsel to the U.S. Board of Indian Commissioners (by appointment of President Theodore Roosevelt) had tried to eradicate corruption among government field agents and had advocated federal funds for missions. At Currier's suggestion, Bonaparte in Washington, Francis J. Kirby in Baltimore, and prominent citizens in other cities and locales helped establish branches of the Marquette League for Indian support. Currier's eulogy of Chief Hollow Horn Bear (whose image appeared on U.S. postage stamps in 1923 and 1931 and on the $10 Military Payment Certificate 1970-1973), given at St. Paul's Church in Washington, D.C., is printed in *The Indian Sentinel* (1914). In the presence of officials such as Secretary of the Interior Franklin K. Lane and Acting Commissioner of Indian Affairs F. H. Abbott, Currier summarized his views on the plight of the Indians and government obligations to them.

Unfamiliar with the Philippines, Currier in 1910 had declined the nomination by Pope Pius X to become bishop of Zamboanga, writing articles to James Cardinal Gibbons that it would be "a calamity." But he had published articles on Cuban history, and in Rome, on 6 July 1913 he was consecrated first bishop of Matanzas, Cuba. He held his first diocesan synod in January 1915 but resigned his bishopric the following month for reasons of health. Named titular bishop of Hetalonia, he assisted Cardinal Gibbons of Baltimore until his death on a train nearing Baltimore. Currier was buried from the Baltimore cathedral with Cardinal Gibbons presiding.

Praised as an outstanding orator and a scholar of international reputation, Currier held progressive views on education and global relations that helped further Pan-American understanding and cooperation as well as the crusade to improve the situation of American Indians. His religious and fictional works are of less interest than his historical investigations, for he had an eye for gaps in published records and a knack for finding unpublished manuscripts.

• Currier's papers are scattered. Some are in the archives of the Baltimore Archdiocese and of the Redemptorist Order, Brooklyn, N.Y., in the Marquette University Archives, and in the possession of Francis F. Burch. An incomplete bibliography fills a page in the *National Union Catalog*. Obituaries are in the *New York Times* and the *Baltimore Sun*, both 24 Sept. 1918, and in the *Bulletin of the Pan-American Union*, Oct. 1918.

FRANCIS F. BURCH

CURRIER, Nathaniel (27 Mar. 1813–20 Nov. 1888), lithographer and founder of the firm Currier & Ives, was born in Roxbury, Massachusetts, the son of Nathaniel Currier and Hannah (maiden name unknown). He was educated in public schools until the age of fifteen, when he became an apprentice to the Boston printing firm of William S. and John Pendleton. The Pendleton company, the first in America to make successful use of the relatively new process of lithography, imported equipment, artists, and workers from Europe, where the process had been invented at the end of the eighteenth century. Currier learned the technique at the firm in Boston, moved to Philadelphia to work with lithographer M. E. D. Brown in 1833, and relocated to New York in 1834. He had planned to go into business in New York with John Pendleton, but Pendleton changed his plans and sold his interest in the business to Currier. The resulting firm of Currier & Stodart lasted about a year. In 1835, at the age of twenty-two, Currier established his own lithographic printing business, N. Currier, which printed letterheads, handbills, business cards, and the like.

In 1835 Currier issued a print illustrating a recent fire, "*Ruins of the Merchant's Exchange N.Y. after the Destructive Conflagration of Decbr 16 & 17, 1835.* The print, published four days after the fire as an addition to the *New York Sun*, was an early example of an illustrated news story. Currier's first large success documented a similar event in 1840. A print titled *Awful Conflagration of the Steam Boat 'Lexington' in Long Island Sound on Monday Eveg Jany 13th 1840, by Which Melancholy Occurrence Over 100 Persons Perished* appeared as a supplement in the *New York Sun* three days after the fire. Many thousands of copies of the print were sold, demonstrating the sales potential of detailed pictorial information about current newsworthy events. While continuing to publish and successfully market prints of such incidents, the printmaker also expanded his range of subjects. In 1857 Currier made James Merritt Ives, who had joined the firm as bookkeeper in 1850, a full partner in the enterprise, which was then renamed Currier & Ives.

The company, located at 152 Nassau Street in New York, prospered. In the course of the firm's history more than 7,000 different prints were produced, many of them reproduced by the thousands. The cost was low, ranging from fifteen cents to three dollars retail. The distribution was widespread, with prints marketed at the New York store, at dealers throughout the United States and Europe, by traveling sales representatives, and through mail order. Costs were kept low by establishing a production line at the firm's plant at 33 Spruce Street, where skilled artists, lithographers, printers, and hand-colorists all worked to mass-produce the pictures. Although many of the prints were not signed, and many were the product of several different hands, some well-known artists worked for the firm, including Louis Maurer, Thomas Worth, Arthur Fitzwilliam Tait, and George Henry Durrie. Frances "Fanny" Bond Palmer, a British woman employed by Currier & Ives for more than twenty years, was one of the firm's most prolific and versatile designers. Both Currier and Ives were closely involved in the production of the prints. The main reason for the firm's success, however, was the partners' ability to select subjects of great popular appeal. The company produced landscapes, rural and pioneer scenes, political cartoons and banners, humorous scenes, portraits, depictions of events from American history, religious pictures, and views of the Mississippi River, the railroads, western settlement, horses, and sporting events, as well as sheet music. The variety of subjects appealed to virtually every popular interest and taste, and Currier & Ives became the most successful American printmakers in history.

Currier was married twice. With his first wife, Eliza West Farnsworth, he had one child, a son. After her death, he married Lura Ormsbee in 1847. His second marriage was childless. Currier was acquainted with many of the prominent figures of his time, including Henry Ward Beecher, Horace Greeley, P. T. Barnum, and John Greenleaf Whittier. He maintained a town house in New York and a summer residence in Amesbury, Massachusetts.

At the time of his retirement from the firm in 1880—turning his interest over to his son, Edward West Currier—Currier had worked in the lithography business for fifty-two years; for forty-six of those years he had run his own company. He died in New York eight years after retiring. The firm continued operations until 1907, but by that time, the hand processes employed by Currier & Ives had been supplanted by chromolithography, photoengraving, and photography, which its competitors were using. The enormous success of Currier & Ives in its prime, however, is a testament to Currier's technical skills, his shrewd business sense, and his awareness of public taste. Indeed, Currier & Ives prints continue to be of great interest to collectors, and some of the images that the firm produced are still used in decorative arts and advertising. The rural scenes—landscape, marine, and sporting prints in particular—are highly valued by collectors. The prints, which once sold for less than three dollars can now, depending on condition and rarity, command prices in the hundreds or thousands of dollars. Some of the winter scenes, like *Central-Park, Winter: The Skating Pond*, *The Road: Winter*, and *Home to Thanksgiving*, have been reproduced so frequently on cards and calendars that they have become part of the iconography of the Christmas and Thanksgiving holidays in the United States. Taken as a whole, the prints document in vivid detail nineteenth-century American history, culture, and values and thus constitute an important pictorial record of their time.

• Major collections of Currier & Ives prints are held at the Library of Congress and the Museum of the City of New York. Harry T. Peters, *Currier & Ives: Printmakers to the American People* (1942), is an authoritative source on the history of the company and the partners. Walton Rawls, *The Great Book of Currier & Ives' America* (1979), and *Russel Crouse, Mr. Currier and Mr. Ives* (1930), describe the historical context of the firm's work. *Currier & Ives: A Catalogue Raisonné*, ed. C. Carter Smith and Cathy Coshion (1984), lists all known Currier & Ives prints.

LINDA S. CHASE

CURRY, Daniel (26 Nov. 1809–17 Aug. 1887), Methodist pastor, college president, and editor, was born near Peekskill, New York; the names of his parents are not known. An industrious youth who received a good preparatory education, Curry graduated in 1837 from Wesleyan University in Middletown, Connecticut. He spent the next two years as the principal of the Troy Conference Academy in West Poultney, Vermont. From 1839 to 1845 he labored in Georgia, first as a professor at Georgia Female College in Macon and then, after being received on probation as a Methodist minister in 1841, as the pastor of congregations in Athens, Lexington, Savannah, and Columbus.

Curry's vocal opposition to slavery, especially to biblical defenses of it, hampered his ministry. When differences over slavery caused Methodists to split into separate northern and southern branches in 1845, Curry took a church in New York City. During this and several other short pastorates in New Haven, Connecticut (1846–1847), Brooklyn (1848–1849), New York City (1850–1851), and Hartford, Connecticut (1852–1853), he continued to battle against slavery. He later became active in the Antislavery Society of New York. From 1855 to 1857 he served as the president of Indiana Asbury (later DePauw) University. His intense, impulsive personality and inflexibility made his tenure there short.

Following several more brief stints in Methodist congregations, Curry became in 1864 the editor of the *Christian Advocate*, the leading Methodist weekly journal, which was headquartered in New York City. Curry's keen mind, wide reading, and theological acuity equipped him well for this position. But Curry exercised rigid control over the journal, publishing many of his own long essays on doctrine and polity, usually choosing contributed articles that expressed views with which he agreed, and frequently interjecting editorial comments into the midst of printed articles that advocated views contrary to his own. The ex cathedra tone of his essays and editorials led many outside the denomination to accept his views as official statements of Methodist policies. Opposition to his editorship arose on the ground that the *Advocate* had become his personal organ.

In 1876 Curry became the editor of the *Ladies' Repository*, a prominent religious journal that soon changed its title to the *National Repository*. From 1880 to 1884, while serving several brief pastorates in New York, he wrote many articles for Methodist and other Protestant periodicals and edited a new edition of the New Testament portion of Adam Clarke's *Commentary*. The 1884 General Conference of the Methodist Episcopal church elected him the editor of its principal theological journal, the *Methodist Review*. Under his leadership, the review continued the policy of his predecessor, Daniel Whedon, and sought to inform Methodists about the theological implications of Darwinism, biblical criticism, European philosophy, and other current developments. Although in his mid-seventies, Curry wrote with vigor, and his views on polity and doctrine helped make the review successful.

Curry wrote approximately sixty articles and editorials for religious journals, many of which were printed in *Fragments, Religious and Theological: A Collection of Independent Papers Relating to Various Points of Christian Life and Doctrine* (1880) and *Platform Papers: Addresses, Discussions, and Essays on Social, Moral, and Religious Discussions* (1880). In these volumes Curry analyzed Arminianism (a theology that opposes the Calvinist doctrines of unconditional election and the irresistibility of grace); predestination; the inspiration of the Bible; the American nation; the origins of Methodism; public education; civil government; and the relationship between faith and culture. He edited Robert Southey's *Life of Wesley* (1847) and published *New York: A Historical Sketch* (1853), *Life Story of Rev. D. W. Clark* (1873), and *The Book of Job, According to the Revised Version; With an Expository and Practical Commentary* (1888).

Theologically, Curry was an advocate of the liberal evangelicalism that was prominent in the Methodist denomination in the second half of the nineteenth century and espoused by church leaders Daniel Whedon, William F. Warren, Randolph Foster, and John Miley. Curry was one of the few who objected to the prevailing Methodist view on the freedom of the will. He saw more value in the Calvinist doctrine of divine sovereignty than did most of the denomination's theologians. While most Methodists insisted that the effect of original sin was primarily that of deprivation, Curry maintained that it also produced a depraved nature. An insightful critic, he did not make any major theological advances, but he stimulated the thinking of many fellow Methodists.

Curry was a complex person. One colleague argued that he came from "that Scotch-Irish ancestry which lives long, works hard, fights well, reasons closely, loves intensely, dislikes strongly, and has underneath the firm rock of religious conviction" (Goodsell, p. 809). His husky voice, serious manner, lofty language, philosophical method, didactic discourse, and emphasis on logical reasoning did not appeal to lay audiences. This preaching style, coupled with his stern, argumentative nature, made his pastorates short. He was at his best when preaching on special themes and occasions, especially when speaking at the funerals of colleagues, delivering sermons to ministerial groups, and debating. At meetings of local Methodist ministers' associations and of the Methodist Annual or General Conferences, his views commanded respect. In the heat of debate he usually exercised the judgment and tact he sometimes lacked in interpersonal relations, and his courage, determination, and intelligence were displayed in this setting.

In the years following the Civil War, Curry was an advocate of foreign missions, a defender of revivals, a proponent of black uplift, and—as an editor and author of articles for Methodist publications—an astute analyst of political and cultural issues. A pastor, professor, college president, journalist, and commentator, he was considered a maverick by most of his contemporaries; yet, as one colleague put it, "as an intellectual guidepost no man in Methodism has been his superior" (Goodsell, p. 811). He died in New York City.

• Curry compiled *The Life of John Wycliffe* (1846) and *Young People's Scrapbook, Containing Selections, Narratives, Descriptive Pieces, Natural History, Scenes and Places, Personal Sketches, and Illustrated Poems* (1884). His other works include *Christian Education* (1889); "The Dangers of Apostasy," *Methodist Review* 67 (Sept. 1885): 727–42; "Present Necessity for a Restatement of Christian Belief," *Methodist Review* 68 (Sept. 1886): 750–60; and "Polity of the Methodist Episcopal Church," *Methodist Review* 68 (May 1886): 425–44. The principal sources of information on Curry's career, philosophy, and personality are D. A. Goodsell, "In Memoriam—Daniel Curry," *Methodist Review* 69 (Nov. 1887): 809–24; and "A Powerful Personality Withdrawn," *Christian Advocate* 62 (25 Aug. 1887): 545. See also Matthew Simpson, ed., *Cyclopedia of Methodism* (1878), and W. H. Daniels, ed., *The Illustrated History of Methodism in Great Britain, America, and Australia* (1893). Robert E. Chiles, *Theological Transition in American Methodism, 1790–1935* (1965), analyzes Curry's theological views. Emory S. Bucke, ed., *The History of American Methodism*, vol. 2 (1964), discusses many of his contributions to the denomination.

GARY SCOTT SMITH

CURRY, Jabez Lamar Monroe (5 June 1825–12 Feb. 1903), politician and educational reformer, was born in Lincoln County, Georgia, the son of William Curry and Susan Winn, planters. He attended school in Lincoln County until his family moved to Talladega County, Alabama, in 1838. In 1839 he entered Franklin College (now the University of Georgia) in Athens, Georgia. He graduated from Franklin in 1843 and then enrolled in the Law School of Harvard College. He received his law degree in 1845 and returned to Talladega, where he read law and then joined the bar. In 1847 Curry married Ann Alexander Bowie; they had four children, two of whom died in infancy.

Curry began his political career in 1847 by being elected to the state legislature. He did not run for reelection but did run again, successfully, for election to the legislature in 1855. He was then active in a fight to establish a public school system in Alabama. In 1856 he worked for the election of Democratic Presidential nominee James Buchanan. The next year he ran successfully for the U.S. House of Representatives from the Seventh District of Alabama; he was reelected in 1859.

In 1861, as secession loomed, Curry resigned from the U.S. Congress and was soon elected to the Confederate Congress. After being defeated in his bid for reelection, he served in a variety of positions in the Confederate Army, notably as an aide to General Joseph E. Johnston. When the war ended, he returned to Talladega.

Prevented from running for office because of his Confederate military service, Curry looked to his Baptist religion as a new outlet for his energies. In 1865 he was chosen president of the Alabama Baptist Convention and president of Howard College in Marion, Alabama. He was soon ordained as a Baptist minister and began to preach widely in the state. In sermons and public lectures, he advocated religion and education as the roads for the rehabilitation of his defeated and nearly destitute state. His first wife had died in 1865, and in 1867 he married Mary Wortham Thomas; they had no children. In 1868 he resigned the presidency of Howard and moved to Richmond, Virginia.

In October 1868 Curry became professor of history and English literature at Richmond College. He was a popular teacher as well as an educational and civic leader in the city and state. As an Alabama minister and educator and as a Richmond professor he had preached the gospel of publicly funded education for all citizens, including the recently freed slaves.

This activity led to Curry's being chosen in 1881 to succeed Barnas Sears as general agent of the Peabody Fund for Education in the South. He is best remembered for his twenty-three years of activity on behalf of this fund and in cooperation with other philanthropic efforts for education, such as those of the John F. Slater Fund, the Conference for Education in the South, and the General Education Board. He is credited with facilitating the establishment of state normal schools and graded schools throughout the South. In that period he became by far the most influential figure in Southern education. His gentlemanly ways, religious commitment, and political experience no doubt enhanced his effectiveness.

Twice in the midst of his educational reform efforts, in 1885 and in 1902, Curry accepted diplomatic appointments as minister to Spain. In both cases he served successfully but quickly returned to his educational endeavors.

Curry was an indefatigable advocate for free public education for both whites and blacks in the late-nineteenth-century South. He spoke enthusiastically for the Blair Bill in the early 1880s and lobbied Southern congressmen on its behalf. Sponsored by a congressman from New Hampshire, the Blair Bill sought federal aid for education and was designed especially to help education in poorer states—like most of the South—where the evils of illiteracy were most apparent. Curry's advocacy of federal aid was markedly opposed to his generally laissez-faire approach to economic and social life and his firm belief in limited government. He was generally conservative in his attitudes toward labor and was firmly opposed to the political and economic changes sought by the white farmers of the Farmers' Alliance and, subsequently, the Populist party. His conservative economic views included opposition to Southern states' repudiation of war debt. His conservatism convinced his Northern philanthropic sponsors, wealthy industrialists, that he was with them on the major issues of the era.

Although he had defended slavery as an Alabama Congressman and had served the Confederacy, Curry spent much of his later years as an advocate of education for freed slaves and spoke out against lynching. As agent for the Peabody Fund, he threatened to deny support to Southern communities that refused to educate their black children on the ground that blacks paid little or nothing in taxes. His advocacy, however, was carefully couched and calibrated not to offend either the white Southern aristocracy to which he belonged or the Northern philanthropists who sponsored his activities. He knew Booker T. Washington and was a firm advocate of the industrial education that Washington had learned at Hampton Institute in Virginia and pioneered at Tuskegee Institute in Alabama.

Personally, Curry thought that enfranchisement of African Americans after emancipation had been a mistake, and he believed that there were firm limits to what the black race could accomplish, even with increased educational privileges. Thus, although Curry worked assiduously for the education of freed slaves, he was firm in his commitment to continued segregation in schools. He never advocated biracial education, and this almost certainly reflected his own personal views as well as the desires of the white aristocracy of North and South.

Thus, Curry's reputation as an educational reformer was well earned but also subject to the distinct limits that he and his sponsors put on the achievement of the freed people. He died in Asheville, North Carolina.

• The main collection of Curry's papers is housed in the Library of Congress. Curry published several books, most notably *A Brief Sketch of George Peabody and a History of the Peabody Education Fund through Thirty Years* (1898); other publications include *Constitutional Government in Spain* (1889), *William Ewart Gladstone* (1891), and *Civil History of the Government of the United States* (1901). There is a smaller collection at the Alabama Department of Archives and History in Montgomery. On Curry's life, see Edwin A. Alderman, *J. L. M. Curry: A Biography* (1911), and Jessie Pearl Rice, *J. L. M. Curry: Southerner, Statesman, and Educator* (1949). Also helpful is W. Porter Kellam, "Reminiscences of Franklin College by Jabez Lamar Monroe Curry, Class of 1843; with a Biographical Sketch of the Author and Notes," *Georgia Historical Quarterly* 52 (1985): 211–28.

WAYNE URBAN

CURRY, John Steuart (14 Nov. 1897–29 Aug. 1946), artist, was born near Dunavant, Kansas, the son of Smith Curry and Margaret Steuart, farmers. He took an early interest in drawing and began to take art lessons in 1909. Resolving to pursue a career as an artist, Curry left home in 1916 for three years of art study, beginning at the Kansas City Art Institute and continuing at the Art Institute of Chicago and at Geneva College in Pennsylvania. In 1919 he moved to Leonia, New Jersey, to receive instruction in illustration from artist Harvey Dunn. Shortly thereafter he began to achieve modest success as a professional illustrator, publishing his work in western novels and popular magazines, such as *Boy's Life*, *St. Nicholas*, *Country Gentleman*, *Wayside Tales*, and the *Saturday Evening Post*. In 1923 he married Clara Derrick; they had no children. By the following year his earnings allowed him to purchase his own studio in Westport, Connecticut. But Curry began to grow weary of producing illustrations to other people's specifications, and in an effort to take his career to a higher level, he sought further training in art. He traveled to Paris in 1926 to study with Basil Schoukhaieff at the Russian Academy art school and returned to the United States the following year for instruction in lithography at the Art Students League. Only then, in 1928, did he come back to Westport, determined to make his mark as a painter.

Success came to Curry remarkably quickly. His breakthrough painting was *Baptism in Kansas*, which was exhibited at the Corcoran Gallery of Art in Washington, D.C., that autumn. It received high praise from *New York Times* art critic Edward Alden Jewell, who declared that in Curry "Kansas has found her Homer" (7 Dec. 1930). It also so impressed Gertrude Vanderbilt Whitney that she awarded Curry a weekly stipend of $50 to support him for the next two years, and in 1930 she purchased the painting for the Whitney Museum of American Art, which would open in New York the following year.

While nearly all of Curry's works of this period were concerned with Kansas themes, he tended to ignore the tranquil side of his native state, favoring instead dramatic or even violent subject matter, as in his *Tornado over Kansas* (1929) and the oil painting *Hogs Killing a Rattlesnake* (1930). Perhaps as a result of this emphasis, a 1931 solo exhibition of Curry's work that traveled throughout his home state was not well received. Though stung by this rebuff, Curry nonetheless claimed to find it understandable, noting, "Why should Kansas want any of my work? It has Kansas" (*Kansas City Star*, 30 June 1937).

In 1932 Curry's wife died. Two years later he married Kathleen Muriel Gould; though they had no children, Curry became a stepfather, as his wife had a child from a previous marriage.

In 1934 the U.S. government initiated a national mural project, part of the Federal Art Project, in which American artists were appointed to create works of art for the walls of government buildings across the country. Curry received many of the most prestigious of these commissions, and over the next few years he completed murals in several prominent public buildings, including the Department of Justice building (for which he produced *Westward Migration* and *Justice Defeating Mob Violence*) and the Department of the Interior building (for which he painted *The Homestead*, depicting the activities of a farm family, and *Oklahoma Land Rush*), both in Washington, D.C.

In 1936 Curry was appointed artist in residence at the University of Wisconsin at Madison, the first artist ever to obtain such a position at an American university. He held this post for the rest of his life, and he painted several murals in buildings on the campus and in the town of Madison. In 1939, working at his studio at the University of Wisconsin, Curry completed *Wisconsin Landscape*, which later won first prize in the New York Metropolitan Museum's Artists for Victory exhibition in 1942.

By the following year Curry had largely finished two murals that he had been commissioned to paint for the capitol building of his home state of Kansas. While Curry had intended to paint eight smaller panels in addition to the two large works he did manage to execute, he was not allowed to do so. The official reason given was that the Kansas legislative committee overseeing the project refused to authorize the removal of some Italian marble slabs to make room for Curry's work. Unofficially, the reason seems to have been that the committee was displeased with one of the large murals, *The Tragic Prelude*. The committee, on issuing the invitation to Curry to paint the murals, had insisted that he depict Kansas in a "sane and sensible manner" (*Art Digest* [1 Aug. 1937]). Instead, Curry gave them a violent, compelling mural featuring a tornado, a prairie fire, and several dead soldiers. At the center, dominating the scene, is the gigantic presence of John Brown, towering over all other figures, depicted with his arms outstretched, holding a rifle in one hand and a Bible in the other. His hair and beard whip in the wind, and he has a look of righteous indignation on his face. Though the committee may have been displeased, Curry himself felt that "in the panel of John Brown, I have accomplished the greatest painting I have yet done" (*Topeka Daily Capitol*, 23 May 1942), an opinion shared by many critics.

In the final four years of his life, Curry painted few important works, though he did illustrate several books and make many drawings and lithographs—all activities that he had also done at earlier times in his career without, however, ever receiving the same recognition for them that he had achieved for his easel and mural paintings. He died of a heart attack in Madison, Wisconsin.

Curry is remembered as a major representative of an art movement called "regionalism." The movement was characterized by its subject matter (the American scene, especially when set in small towns and rural areas of the Midwest), by its attitude (celebratory rather than critical—though many of Curry's works have been thought to contain some satirical content), and by its style (realistic, in opposition to the modernist abstraction then on the ascendancy in Europe). Regionalism was a popular style in the 1930s, and one in which scores of artists worked with some success. Curry is regarded, along with Thomas Hart Benton of Missouri and Grant Wood of Iowa, as one of its three leaders.

At the height of its popularity, Curry's work was described by sculptor Harry Wicker as fulfilling "Walt Whitman's hope and prophecy of a truly great native art growing out of American life" (Schmeckebier, p. 347). Although the regionalism movement and Curry's work in particular are often considered in the late twentieth century to be overblown and unsophisticated, it is still too early to determine the nature of his lasting reputation. Since many of his finest paintings are on the walls of public buildings, the general public, which once thrilled to Curry's gigantic, dramatic compositions, will have ample time to consider returning to its earlier judgment.

• Curry's papers, including more than 4,000 items, are located at the Archives of American Art, Smithsonian Institution. A brief statement by Curry on his approach to art is his "What Should the American Artist Paint?" *Art Digest* (Sept. 1935), which is reprinted, along with much other material on Curry, in Joseph S. Czestochowski, ed., *John Steuart Curry and Grant Wood: A Portrait of Rural America* (1981). The most comprehensive work on Curry, encompassing both biographical information and an extensive evaluation of his art, is Laurence E. Schmeckebier, *John Steuart Curry's Pageant of America* (1943). A more recent study, focusing especially on Curry's Kansas murals, is M. Sue Kendall, *Rethinking Regionalism: John Steuart Curry and the Kansas Mural Controversy* (1986). An annotated bibliography on Curry and the two other major regionalists is Mary Scholz Guedon, *Regionalist Art: Thomas Hart Benton, John Steuart Curry, and Grant Wood: A Guide to the Literature* (1982). An obituary is in the *New York Times*, 30 Aug. 1946.

DAVID DETMER

CURTI, Margaret Wooster (18 Feb. 1892–19 Sept. 1961), psychologist, was born in Silver Creek, Nebraska, the daughter of Charles Wooster, a newspaper publisher and progressive politician, and Lillie M. Todd. At the University of Nebraska (B.A., 1913, A.M., 1915) she learned experimental psychology from Harry Kirke Wolfe, served as his laboratory assistant, and lived with his family. In her master's thesis ("An Experimental Study of Bright and Dull Children") she concluded that intelligence was a unitary psychological quality that could be assessed by simple sensory-motor tasks. Without proper assessment and remediation, she warned, a child of low intelligence could "become permanently discouraged and left without hope or initiative, through repeated failure in school work and the scorn of his companions." After a year and a half of teaching in rural Nebraska, Curti continued her graduate studies at the University of Chicago (Ph.D., 1920), where she became converted to pragmatism and to the biological functionalism of her adviser Harvey Carr.

From 1920 to 1922 Curti taught at Beloit College in Wisconsin, where she reestablished psychology as a separate, laboratory-based discipline. After two years, however, she confided to her parents that she would "rather be one of many in a big important department than the only one in a small one." Initially accepting a position at the University of Texas, she moved instead to Smith College, where she could both pursue her career and be near Merle Curti, a historian whom she had met at Beloit. They married in 1925, and she mothered two daughters while advancing from assistant to associate professor at Smith (1922–1937). Following her husband to Columbia University, she was a research associate and occasional instructor at Teachers College (1937–1942). Next, Curti and her family moved to Madison, Wisconsin, where she was a visiting lecturer at the University of Wisconsin (1943–1944) and taught elsewhere for summer sessions.

As a researcher and writer, Curti centered her work on the relative roles of native endowment and experience in animals and children. In 1926 she added her voice to the growing criticism of the belief that delinquency and criminality are caused by the inheritance of subnormal intelligence. Summarizing the evidence that the scoring standards for intelligence tests mislabeled 30 to 50 percent of U.S. adults as feebleminded, Curti argued that accurate test norms would reveal delinquent children to be of the same intelligence as others ("The Intelligence of Delinquents in the Light of Recent Research," *Scientific Monthly* 22 [1926]: 132–38). In "The New Lombrosianism" (*Journal of Criminal Law and Criminology* 17 [1926]: 246–53), she expanded this argument into a critique of social uses of hereditarian thought.

Conservative educators, judges, and social agencies, Curti charged, used the alleged "mental inferiority of the delinquent 'class'" as a "rationalization of the status quo." Proposing that "anti-social acts are due chiefly to the conditions of living," she challenged the social elite (herself included) to help develop "the potential strength and goodness that . . . most human beings have." She campaigned for progressivist and socialist causes locally and in 1935 organized a nursery school for poor children in Northampton. A 1930 visit to Moscow and Leningrad (where she toured psychological institutes and conferred with Pavlov, Kras-

nogorski, and others) strengthened her faith in the psychological benefits of social reorganization.

In the 1930s Curti joined Otto Klineberg and others in attacking the validity of comparisons of the intelligence of different groups defined by race. In 1935 she published a reinterpretation of a 1929 study that had found the performance of black children in Kingston, Jamaica, inferior to that of white children living in New Haven, Connecticut. After a five-week trip to see how and where the Jamaican children had been tested, Curti rescored their answers and showed that the race differences were not striking and in some cases favored the Jamaicans. Stressing the variability of the Jamaicans' responses, she attributed it to nutrition, income, and other environmental causes and to the lack of a black test administrator. In 1939 Curti again wrote on the issue of cultural bias in testing, describing her adaptation of the Minnesota Preschool Tests for use with Mayan children in Yucatán, Mexico. Finally, in 1960 and 1964 her attempts to show no relation between race, skin color, and intelligence in Jamaican children were published in the *Journal of Psychology* (49 [1960]: 13–27) and the *Journal of Social Psychology* (62 [1964]: 181–88).

Curti's greatest influence may have been through her widely used college text, *Child Psychology* (1930; 2d ed., 1938). In it she described testing hypotheses on her young daughter, appealed to the common sense and experience of her readers, and showed an appreciation for sources ranging from baby biographies to experimental research. The result was an articulate, theoretically eclectic, and nonsectarian treatment of developmental psychology. She praised the conceptual innovations of behaviorist John Watson, for example, but criticized his insensitivity to the context in which behavior is elicited. In analyzing intelligence, she asserted that its expression and modification in children was dependent upon environmental influences. "When we see two people whom we know to be equally gifted by nature [and who are] so different in their response to the world and in their ability to enjoy life," she asserted, "we need no statistics to prove to us the importance of environment" (p. 175). Because it relied upon logical and moral arguments as much as research data, Curti's text illustrates the ideological shift toward environmentalism that transformed the U.S. social sciences at the end of the 1920s.

Curti was a lifelong pacifist and socialist, and she championed civil liberties from the time of the First World War (when she protested university censorship of antiwar students) to the McCarthy era (when she collected signatures on "Joe Must Go" petitions). Although she suffered from poor health her entire life, she enjoyed nature and travel, accompanying her husband on his many trips abroad. A lover of poetry and literature, Curti helped her husband edit his many books; she was also responsible for statistical analyses in his influential *The Making of an American Community* (1959). She was widely known as a devoted mother and wife, combining marriage with a professional career at a time when many felt obligated to choose one or the other. She died in Madison, Wisconsin.

• Most of Curti's papers are divided between the Sophia Smith Collection, Smith College, and the Archives of the History of American Psychology, University of Akron. There is also correspondence with her father in the Charles Wooster Papers, Nebraska Historical Society; a few letters in the Beloit College Archives; and research data at the Jamaica Institute, Kingston, Jamaica. Her dissertation was published as *Certain Factors in the Development of a New Spatial Coordination*, Psychological Monographs, no. 146 (1923), for the American Psychological Association by the Psychological Review Company; it is briefly evaluated in I. P. Howard and W. B. Templeton, *Human Spatial Orientation* (1966). Her major study of animals was *Native Fear Response of White Rats in the Presence of Cats*, Psychological Monographs, no. 210 (1935), pp. 78–98. Her most successful articles on race, culture, and psychological testing appeared in the *Journal of Comparative Psychology* 20 (1935): 125–56; and 28 (1939): 207–22. For a hereditarian's statistical critique of her final study of the subject, see Audrey M. Shuey, *The Testing of Negro Intelligence*, 2d ed. (1966). An intellectual self-analysis and autobiography is in *Psychological Bulletin* 31 (1934): 438–49, and Ludy T. Benjamin, *Harry Kirke Wolfe: Pioneer in Psychology* (1991), provides clues to her early professional and political development. For the context in which her views on criminality, race, and intelligence developed, see Leila Zenderland, *Measuring Minds: Henry Herbert Goddard and the Origins of American Intelligence Testing* (1997).

BENJAMIN HARRIS
MERLE CURTI

CURTICE, Harlow Herbert (15 Aug. 1893–3 Nov. 1962), automotive executive, was born in Petrieville, Michigan, the son of Marion Joel Curtice, a fruit commission merchant, and Mary Ellen Eckhart. His early schooling was in the Eaton Rapids public schools, where he was remembered as a serious, freckle-faced boy nicknamed "Red," who "blushed easily and often." While working as a clerk at the Horner Woolen Mills in Eaton Rapids, Michigan, he completed a two-year business course at Ferris Institute in Big Rapids.

After completing his business course, Curtice secured a job as a shipping clerk with the Standard Rule Company in Flint, Michigan. In 1914, when Standard Rule was bought out and left town, he answered the blind ad of an employment agency for a bookkeeper, which turned out to be with the Champion Ignition Company. This was the first step in his General Motors (GM) career.

Three years later, Curtice found himself in the U.S. Army in France in World War I. In the service he supplied equipment for horse-drawn units of artillery.

After his discharge, Curtice returned to Champion Ignition (which had since become the AC Division of GM). He earned rapid promotions to assistant general manager and vice president, and in 1929 he became the company's youngest president.

Curtice married Dorothy Biggs in 1927; they had three daughters. Even during his honeymoon in Europe, AC was not far from his thoughts. Several accounts of his life mention that the couple planned their trip so that they could be in Paris for the arrival of

Charles Lindbergh's historic transatlantic flight, which made the trip equipped with AC spark plugs.

By all reports, Curtice was successful in each of his assignments and moved steadily up GM's corporate ladder. In the early fall of 1933 Curtice was called to Detroit by William S. Knudsen, GM executive vice president. Knudsen told him of a planned reorganization of the corporation and offered Curtice the job of president and general manager of Buick operations in Flint. Curtice accepted what proved to be the most challenging assignment thus far in his career.

Buick sales were at a twenty-year low. The overall economic depression, combined with a product that had failed to remain competitive, had tumbled Buick from its former place of industry leadership within its class.

Curtice's training had been primarily in accounting and finance, but he was also knowledgeable in GM's engineering, style, and sales objectives. Working under the tenet "higher speed and lower price," the company built a new line, the 1934 Series 40, which cost between $855 and $925. Buick doubled its sales volume in 1934 and produced 78,757 cars (far more than the previous year's 46,924).

Market share continued to increase with the introduction of another lower-priced model for 1936. Buick Special and Roadmaster joined other traditional names in the Buick line of cars: Super, Century, and Limited. Production in 1936 reached 168,596 cars; at the end of the year Curtice was told by a happy GM central office executive that Buick was finally "off relief."

Production for 1937 was expected to exceed the previous year's. A 15 November 1936 article in the *Detroit News* quoted Curtice: "Nothing can stop business in 1937." But Curtice failed to foresee the growing number of grievances of many GM employees at Flint's Fisher Body Plant and other sites. On 30 December 1936 members of the United Automobile Workers (UAW) organized a sit-down strike at the Fisher plant, which resulted in the shutting down of Buick's final-assembly operations the following day.

When the strike ended on 11 February 1937, Buick employees were quickly called back to work, and final assembly resumed on 17 February. Buick's climb to the top of the automotive industry reached a prewar peak in 1941 with the production of 377,428 cars.

In February 1942, with the advent of World War II, Buick stopped producing cars and aimed its resources toward the war effort. Curtice took personal charge of Buick's war production team. Curtice and Buick eventually completed more than thirty military assignments, including the development and production of the M-18 "Hellcat" tank destroyer. Curtice's efforts during the war earned him the Medal of Merit, which he received from President Harry Truman on 26 January 1949 for his "outstanding and meritorious conduct."

After the war and coincident with the production of Buick's five millionth vehicle in 1948, Curtice was named executive vice president of GM in charge of general staff activities. On 2 February 1953 he was named GM president, replacing C. E. Wilson, who became President Dwight Eisenhower's secretary of defense.

Curtice's success was rooted in his masterly understanding of consumer tastes and his ability to develop products that satisfied them. He was a superb salesman whose years as president of Buick and GM were marked by an aggressive marketing campaign that continued well after his 1958 retirement. After retiring, he remained an active member of the board of directors until his death at his Flint home.

Curtice took a positive approach to problem solving and often was motivated by the gloomy predictions of market analysts. "Do it the hard way!" he once said in a commencement address at Olivet College in Olivet, Michigan. "Think ahead of your job. Then nothing in the world can keep the job ahead from reaching out for you. . . . Be bold, knowing that finally no one can cheat you but yourself."

• The key repository for primary materials on Curtice is the Harlow H. Curtice Collection in the GMI Alumni Foundation Collection of Industrial History in Flint, Mich. Secondary materials include Alfred P. Sloan, Jr., *My Years with General Motors* (1964); Lawrence Gustin and Terry Dunham, *The Buick: A Complete History* (1980); Ed Cray, *Chrome Colossus* (1969); Robert Sheehan, "How Harlow Curtice Earns His $750,000," *Fortune*, Nov. 1947; "Autos: The Battle of Detroit," *Time*, 1 Nov. 1954; "The Biggest Business—and Harlow Curtice, the Salesman-Optimist," *Newsweek*, 7 Nov. 1955; and "Man of the Year: First among Equals," *Time*, 2 Jan. 1956.

RICHARD P. SCHARCHBURG

CURTIN, Andrew Gregg (22 Apr. 1815–7 Oct. 1894), lawyer, politician, and diplomat, was born in Bellefonte, Pennsylvania, the son of Roland Curtin, an iron manufacturer and county coroner and sheriff, and Jane Gregg, the daughter of U.S. congressman and senator Andrew Gregg. After attending private academies near his home, Curtin studied law with W. W. Potter of Bellefonte and with Judge John Reed at Dickinson College Law School. Admitted to the Centre County bar in April 1837, he soon entered into a partnership with John Blanchard.

The extensive political and social connections of his mother's family, and his father's wealth, provided Curtin with unusual advantages. His almost immediate success as a lawyer, and later in political life, were also attributed to his commanding presence; he had a tall, well-proportioned figure, a strikingly handsome countenance, a kindly smile, and a genial yet dignified volubility and ready wit that captivated jurors and voters alike.

Curtin's oratorical abilities and his Whig partisanship led to his involvement in political campaigns, beginning with William H. Harrison's successful presidential race in 1840. On 30 May 1844 he married Catherine Irvine Wilson; they had seven children. That year Curtin delivered speeches in nearly every county of Pennsylvania for Henry Clay, and in 1848 he

worked with equal ardor for Zachary Taylor for President. In 1852 he once again made speeches throughout the state, this time for Winfield Scott. In the two latter campaigns, he was a Whig presidential elector. Curtin was instrumental in achieving the election of James Pollock as governor of Pennsylvania in 1854. His reward was an appointment as secretary of the commonwealth, with additional duties as superintendent of public instruction, in which capacity he obtained increased legislative funding for public schools and authorization to establish a system of state normal schools for training teachers.

In 1854 the Pennsylvania legislature balloted inconclusively to try to fill a vacancy in the U.S. Senate. The candidacy of Simon Cameron of Harrisburg to recapture the office he had held as a Democrat during the previous decade was vigorously opposed by Curtin and his political allies. This contest concluded with Cameron's selection as a Republican (with Democratic votes) in time to take his Senate seat on 4 March 1857, and it began one of the most intense intraparty political feuds in American history, lasting more than twenty years. At the February 1860 state convention of the Pennsylvania People's Party (the local Republican organization), Curtin won the gubernatorial nomination over Congressman John Covode, who was Cameron's candidate, but Cameron was conpensated with an endorsement for the presidential nomination at the Republican national convention.

Although not an elected delegate, Curtin attended the Republican convention at Chicago in May 1860, and there he influenced most members of the Pennsylvania delegation to abandon Cameron and join with politicians from several other states in a movement to derail the candidacy of New York Senator William H. Seward, the clear favorite for the presidential nomination at the outset of the convention. Seward's detractors believed that his well-publicized reference to a "higher law" than those protecting slavery and to the "irrepressible conflict" between slaveholding and free societies rendered his candidacy controversial enough to endanger their own prospects of election should he head the Republican ticket. Hence they sought a more "available" (less well-known) nominee. The result of these machinations was the choice of Abraham Lincoln as the Republican presidential candidate and a commitment by Lincoln's floor managers to propose Cameron for a Cabinet position, while Cameron was to assist Curtin's election in October. All went as planned: Lincoln won the presidency, Cameron became his secretary of war, and Curtin was sworn in as governor of Pennsylvania, serving in that office from 15 January 1861 until 15 January 1867.

As the state's chief magistrate during the Civil War, Curtin energetically recruited troops and procured supplies and equipment for the Union armies. After the Northern defeat on 21 July 1861, at Bull Run (First Manassas), a reserve militia force from Pennsylvania protected Washington, D.C., from Confederate assault. In September 1862, although suffering from one of many serious illnesses that impeded his duties as governor much of his tenure, Curtin initiated a meeting of Northern governors at Altoona, Pennsylvania; out of this came a declaration of support for two controversial steps about to be taken by the Lincoln administration—emancipation of Southern slaves and a military draft of civilians. As the Civil War intensified, Curtin devoted his flagging energies mostly to caring for the logistical and personal needs of the soldiers from his state, including increased funding and staffing for hospitals and financial support and schooling for war orphans. He was reelected by a large margin in 1863.

Notwithstanding his popularity—he was known among veterans and their families as "the Soldiers' Friend"—Curtin failed after leaving the governor's office to win the backing of the Pennsylvania legislature for a seat in the U.S. Senate, which went instead to his rival Cameron. In 1868 Curtin was again blocked by Cameron's partisans when he sought the vice presidential nomination on the Republican national ticket with Ulysses S. Grant. In 1869, however, Grant appointed Curtin as U.S. minister to Russia, where he served creditably until poor health compelled him to resign in 1872. That autumn, disillusioned with Grant, he publicly backed the Democratic candidate for president, Horace Greeley, and soon thereafter announced his departure from the Republican party.

Defeated as a candidate for Congress on the Democratic ticket in 1878, Curtin was successful in gaining election in 1880 and thereafter served three terms in the U.S. House of Representatives, on one occasion chairing the foreign relations committee. He retired on 3 March 1887. For a while he practiced law in Bellefonte, where he died.

• Publications treating Curtin's life tend to be eulogistic. Alexander K. McClure, a close friend and political associate of Curtin's, provided much of the material for such writings in his *Abraham Lincoln and Men of War-Times* (1892), *Recollections of Half a Century* (1902), and *Old-Time Notes of Pennsylvania* (1905). Laudatory essays dealing with aspects of Curtin's life are in William H. Egle, ed., *Life and Times of Andrew Gregg Curtin* (1896). Two more recent assessments are Rebecca G. Albright, "The Civil War Career of Andrew Gregg Curtin, Governor of Pennsylvania," *Western Pennsylvania Historical Magazine* 47 (1964): 323–41, and 48 (1965): 151–73; and Paul B. Beers, "Andrew Gregg Curtin," *Civil War Times Illustrated* 6 (May 1967): 12–20. See also Erwin S. Bradley, *The Triumph of Militant Republicanism: A Study of Pennsylvania and Presidential Politics, 1860–1872* (1964), and Stanton L. Davis, "Pennsylvania Politics, 1860–1863" (Ph.D. diss., Western Reserve Univ., 1935). An obituary is in the Philadelphia *Times*, 8 Oct. 1894.

NORMAN B. FERRIS

CURTIS, Austin Maurice (15 Jan. 1868–13 July 1939), physician and surgeon, was born in Raleigh, North Carolina, the son of Alexander Curtis and Eleanora Patilla Smith. One of nine children, Curtis attended the Raleigh public schools and went north to college, graduating from Lincoln University in Pennsylvania in 1888. He received his medical degree from Northwestern University in 1891 and became the first intern hired by Chicago's fledgling Provident Hospital. The first voluntary black hospital, Provident opened the doors of its two-story frame building a few months before Curtis started his internship. Provident Hospital boasted an interracial medical staff as well as the first training school for black nurses. There Curtis formed alliances with two individuals who would influence the rest of his life. The first was Daniel Hale Williams, a renowned black physician and one of the founders of Provident Hospital, who hired Curtis for the Provident internship. The second was seventeen-year-old Namahyoke "Nama" Sockum, whom Curtis married in either 1888 or 1891. They would have four children and would become one of the most prominent and active couples in black society of their time.

After his one-year internship at Provident, Curtis opened a private general surgical practice in Chicago. His wife continued her volunteer activities; for example, she helped organize Colored American Day at the 1893 World's Columbian Exposition in Chicago and became active with the National Republican Committee. Within three years of opening his medical practice, Curtis had made a name for himself among Chicago physicians and in the community. For example, the 1895 *Chicago Journal and Evening Press* carried a report of a man who suffered a blow to his head by an irate cook wielding a butcher's cleaver. Curtis was called to the hospital to save the man's life and on arriving discovered that he had treated this patient twice in the past, once repairing damage done to the man's head by a pitchfork and another time patching wounds from a blow with a beer bottle. Despite the extensive injuries caused by the cleaver attack, Curtis managed to perform the delicate operation necessary to save the patient's life.

Curtis also participated in a number of charity endeavors and belonged to the Chicago Society Baseball League. He helped found the city's Civic League, as he said, not only to "help worthy colored people attain to a higher mode of life, but to suppress crime."

When the city commission decided in 1895 that it was time to appoint a black man to the medical staff of Cook County Hospital, Curtis's name was among the first considered. At the time no black man had ever been asked to join the staff of a nonsegregated hospital. But that year Theodore W. Jones, himself a black man, had been elected to the post of city commissioner. Among the many duties of the city commissioner was filling positions on the medical and surgical staff of Cook County Hospital. Jones convened a committee of twelve local physicians to select the newest addition to the hospital's surgical staff, and the group agreed that the time had come to integrate the staff. A tight battle ensued, with the group nearly equally divided between Curtis and another physician, but they finally chose Curtis.

Curtis maintained that job, along with his growing private surgical practice, until 1898 when his old mentor Williams stepped down from the post of surgeon in chief of Freedman's Hospital in Washington, D.C. Among those suggested for the job was Curtis. At first it did not look as though Curtis would win the much-coveted position. He finished second in the civil service examination required for all applicants, and many black newspapers throughout the country lobbied ardently for a different candidate. Nevertheless, Curtis was eventually offered the post, an offer that some speculated owed more to his wife's political connections than to his qualifications.

However, once Curtis moved to Washington and assumed the post, the rumors and controversy quieted. Curtis was acutely aware of the role that the hospital, founded in the midst of the Civil War, played in the minds of the country's black population. He defended the institution in a report he wrote in 1899 to the secretary of the interior, whose office oversaw its operations and who, in an earlier report, had made staffing and regulation suggestions. "To the negro race especially Freedman's Hospital means a great deal more, both from a philanthropic and scientific standpoint, than can be made to appear in such a brief statement as this necessarily is," Curtis wrote. He helped usher the hospital into the twentieth century, overseeing the installation of a modern telephone system, a new children's ward, and the expansion of the nurses' home. In the four years he served as surgeon in chief, 428 surgeries were performed, among which there were only five deaths.

Although Curtis resigned from the post of surgeon in chief in 1902, he remained on the surgical faculty of Freedman's Hospital until 1938. From 1911 to 1912 Curtis served as president of the National Medical Association, the professional association for black physicians. He was known among the students at Howard University Medical School, with which Freedman's Hospital was affiliated, for his careful and extensive explanations in the surgical theater and his powers of observation. He drilled into these students his favorite surgical saying, "Diagnosis must depend upon the preponderance of symptoms." Howard students were not the only ones to enjoy the benefit of his teachings. He offered frequent demonstration clinics in West Virginia and elsewhere throughout the South. Among his favorite students were his three sons, all of whom became doctors and trained at Howard University. To distinguish him from his second son, who bore his name, Curtis's colleagues gave him the nickname "Pop." Curtis remained close to all his sons and opened a private surgical hospital in Washington with the eldest, Arthur Leo.

Over the years Nama continued to follow her activist instincts. During the Spanish-American War she played an instrumental role in helping the military recruit African-American nurses who had already had yellow fever to join the ranks of those caring for ill soldiers in Cuba and throughout the United States. She traveled to Louisiana, Alabama, and Florida and persuaded more than thirty immune blacks to sign up. Although she herself was not a trained nurse, she volunteered with the American Red Cross after floods had devastated Galveston, Texas, and in 1906 she journeyed to San Francisco to lend a hand with the earth-quake relief project. In recognition of her wartime service, she was buried in Arlington National Cemetery when she died in 1935. Curtis died in Washington, D.C.

• For the most complete biography of Curtis, see William Montague Cobb's account in the "Medical History" section of the *Journal of the National Medical Association* 46 (1954): 294–98. Rayford Logan, *Howard University: The First Hundred Years, 1867–1967* (1969), contains an account of Curtis's years at Howard. For more on Nama Curtis's life, see Gerri Majors with Doris E. Saunders, *Black Society* (1976), and Mary Elizabeth Carnegie, *The Path We Tread: Blacks in Nursing, 1854–1984* (1986).

SHARI RUDAVSKY

CURTIS, Benjamin Robbins (4 Nov. 1809–15 Sept. 1874), jurist, was born in Watertown, Massachusetts, the son of Benjamin Curtis III, a merchant marine officer, and Lois Robbins. Curtis was five years old when his father died abroad on a trading voyage. Curtis's mother managed to send Benjamin and his younger brother George Ticknor Curtis to nearby Harvard College, where Benjamin received an A.B. in 1829. That year he entered Harvard Law School, but he left eighteen months later, enticed by the prospect of eventually inheriting the practice of an old-fashioned country lawyer in western Massachusetts. Returning briefly during 1832 to complete his Bachelor of Laws, Curtis built a comfortable if limited rural practice at Northfield. In 1833 he married his cousin Eliza Maria Woodward. They had five children, including a son and daughter who both died in 1842. After three years in this "narrow arena," however, he accepted an offer back in Boston from Charles Pelham Curtis, a distant relative whose legal firm catered to some of the city's most substantial merchants.

Benjamin Curtis soon gained experience across a wide-ranging state and federal practice. As early as 1836 he took on his first slave case, *Commonwealth v. Aves*, in which lawyers representing the Boston Female Anti-Slavery Society argued a black child named Med had been emancipated by accompanying her mistress into a free state. Curtis shared the fears of local leaders that unless something was done to check militant abolitionism and reassure slaveholders, sectional strife would tear the Union apart. In an argument invoking comity between states, he contended southerners visiting Massachusetts temporarily could restrain slave attendants for the purpose of returning them to the domiciles of their owners.

Although Curtis lost the Med case, his impressive argument, while controversial, enhanced his growing professional reputation. Over the next decade this articulate junior partner emerged as one of Boston's leading young attorneys. Introduced to Whig society by his Brahmin half uncle George Ticknor, he joined the fashionable King's Chapel and in 1843 became a proprietor of the Boston Athenaeum. In January 1844 he published an exhaustive treatise for Baring Brothers, the influential London banking house, supporting Daniel Webster's argument that states could not repudiate their public debts. Curtis's first wife died in 1844. Two years later he married Anna Wroe Curtis, his partner's eldest daughter. They had three children.

Curtis became a respected member of the state's Whig establishment, succeeding Justice Joseph Story on the Harvard Corporation in 1846 and serving in the lower house of the Massachusetts legislature during the 1849 and 1851 terms. Primarily concerned with court reform, he also spoke out on issues ranging from slavery to foreign affairs. The veteran Whig still did not consider himself a politician, but after seventeen years at the bar his lucid forensic style impressed even Webster. In the debate over Henry Clay's Compromise of 1850, Webster recruited distinguished jurists like Curtis and Rufus Choate to defend the new Fugitive Slave Act. Convinced an opinion Curtis wrote for federal authorities would "silence the small lawyers," Webster recommended that U.S. attorney George Lunt employ him in slave rescue cases.

Curtis acknowledged that runaways had natural rights but cautioned that aiding their escape might well ignite a civil war. Following his reelection to the state legislature, he defended an arrest warrant in the case of Thomas Sims, a fugitive seized in Boston, and publicly challenged the legality of the political bargain that elected antislavery advocate Charles Sumner to the U.S. Senate.

Associate Justice Levi Woodbury's death in 1851 created a vacancy on the Supreme Court. Hoping to appoint an accomplished young Whig, Millard Fillmore wrote Webster: "I have . . . formed a very high opinion of Mr. B. R. Curtis. What do you say of him? What is his age? constitution? & legal attainments? Does he fill the measure of my wishes?" Once Webster assured him that Curtis met these criteria, Fillmore made the appointment.

Although Judge Curtis spent six terms on a Court dominated by southern Democrats, he wrote fifty-three majority opinions and dissented only thirteen times. Near the outset he spoke for a 6 to 3 majority in *Cooley v. Board of Wardens* (1851), an interstate commerce case that upheld a Pennsylvania statute governing pilotage in the port of Philadelphia. Finding a middle ground between federal and local authority, Curtis argued the Constitution gave states some power over commercial matters where no national regulations existed. Subsequent opinions broadened the scope of federal admiralty jurisdiction, recognized corporations engaged in interstate commerce as citizens of the state where they were incorporated, and restricted the meaning of due process by upholding the authority of the Solicitor of the Treasury to collect debts from a defaulting customs official without a court order. On circuit duty, meanwhile, his involvement with the Shadrach and Anthony Burns rescue cases prompted attacks from northern abolitionists. Curtis was not a Massachusetts judge, the *New York Tribune* (9 Apr. 1855) railed, "he is a slave-catching Judge, appointed to office as a reward for his professional support given to the Fugitive Slave bill."

Curtis later surprised these critics by dissenting in *Dred Scott v. Sandford* (1857). Both Benjamin Curtis and George T. Curtis, who helped represent Dred Scott, continued to advocate enforcement of the unpopular Fugitive Slave Law. But, as George Curtis explained in his biography of Benjamin, "when the demands of the slave interest . . . extended beyond that stipulation, and claimed for slavery a position which [Curtis] believed neither the Constitution nor the system of the Union had given to it, his mind was . . . just as capable of an unbiased and impartial examination of those demands as if he had never contended for a Southern right." One of two dissents in *Dred Scott*, Curtis's opinion challenged Chief Justice Roger B. Taney and the Court majority by arguing that the black citizens of a state were automatically citizens of the United States and that Congress had complete constitutional authority to regulate slavery in the territories. Curtis rejected the argument that because Scott was a black he could not be a citizen. Claiming five states had recognized free blacks as citizens by 1787, he asserted that under the Articles of Confederation and then the Constitution, U.S. citizenship derived from state citizenship. Thus Scott was a citizen and entitled to sue in federal courts.

Curtis used English precedent, state law, and the Missouri Compromise to show that Scott's residence in Illinois and the Wisconsin Territory had made him a free man. In the process he defended the right of Congress to exclude slavery from the northern part of the Louisiana Purchase. As support for his argument he cited John Marshall concerning federal power over the territories and pointed out fourteen distinct instances of congressional legislation on slavery in the territories between 1789 and 1848. Contrary to Taney's majority opinion, he concluded, the Missouri Compromise line was constitutional and valid.

While Curtis agreed with Republicans on the power of Congress to prohibit slavery in the territories, his opinion was racially conservative. In establishing Scott's right to sue in federal court, he emphasized that citizenship under the Constitution did not necessarily imply equal political or civil rights. Far from taking an antislavery position, he argued it was up to the states to define the rights of their citizens. "To what citizens the elective franchise shall be confided," he wrote, "is a question to be determined by each State in accordance with its own views of the necessities or expediencies of its condition. What civil rights shall be enjoyed by its citizens, and whether all shall enjoy the same, or how they may be gained or lost, are to be determined in the same way."

Since Curtis was better organized and less partisan than John McLean, the second dissenter in *Dred Scott*, his opinion had more of an impact. The *Law Reporter* (June 1857) said it was by common consent the strongest and clearest as well as the most thorough and elaborate of the opinions. John Appleton, an associate justice on the Maine Supreme Court, wrote his former student: "I think you have exhausted the subject and with unanswerable logic. . . . The opinion is worthy of Marshall."

Many scholarly works, on the other hand, maintain the dissenters forced Taney into a broader and more inflammatory opinion. Samuel Nelson's initial effort sidestepped the Missouri Compromise issue, but according to one constitutional history, by insisting on introducing it into their dissents, McLean and Curtis put great pressure on the majority to do likewise. In what two justices claimed was a direct response to this pressure, the majority set aside the Nelson opinion and adopted a motion from Judge James M. Wayne, a southern Democrat, to take up all aspects of the case.

Curtis reportedly provided his own account of the deliberations in a conversation with Clement Hugh Hill during the winter of 1873–1874. Looking back in 1878, Hill remembered his friend saying that if Nelson had prevailed, the opinions in *Dred Scott* would have been devoid of all the bitterness to which the case ultimately gave rise. Hill, a former assistant attorney general of the United States, recalled their conversation in some detail. Curtis claimed that, after Nelson completed his opinion, Judge Wayne convinced the Court to address the troubling question of slavery in the territories and persuaded Taney to take over the case. As for his own role, Curtis always said he wrote his dissent in response to the chief justice. When Taney accused him of hurriedly publishing his opinion to gain political advantage, he answered, "It is a sufficient reply for me to declare that I have no connection whatever with any political party, and have no political or partisan purpose in view, and no purpose whatever, save a determination to avoid misconstruction and misapprehension, from which I have suffered enough in times past."

Overall the evidence tends to support Curtis. Nothing in his background or opinion suggests he was trying to force the Court into a broad decision on the constitutionality of the Missouri Compromise. While the statements of Justices Robert Cooper Grier and John Catron about the provocative stand of the two dissenters might seem credible with respect to McLean, the historian Allan Nevins noted, they were quite incredible as to Curtis: "That conservative Whig of the Daniel Webster school, who had protested against Sumner's election, who had endorsed the Seventh of March speech, who had long represented the views of State Street business circles, was one of the last men in the country to act a radical part" (Nevins, *The Emergence of Lincoln* [2 vols., 1950], p. 475). A remark by Wayne taking credit for changing the majority strategy cast further doubt on the assertion that McLean and Curtis were primarily responsible. Another study concluded in 1978 that the best explanation of the shift may be the most obvious one, that the change of plan spelled victory for those justices who had wanted all along to issue an emphatically prosouthern decision.

The *Dred Scott* case ended Curtis's judicial career. Already concerned about supporting a large family, he complained he could never again feel the confidence in the Court and the willingness to cooperate that were essential to the satisfactory discharge of his duties. Charging that the justices were influenced by political considerations, he resigned on 1 September 1857 and opened a law office in Boston.

After leaving the bench, Curtis resumed his role as a conservative spokesman. During the administration of James Buchanan, he warned that any forcible interference with slavery was a "gross and barbarous wrong," called for the repeal of legislation designed to thwart the Fugitive Slave Act, and endorsed a sectional compromise developed by Kentucky congressman John J. Crittenden. His second wife, Anna, died before Abraham Lincoln's election in 1860. In 1861 Curtis married Maria Malleville Allen, a resident of Pittsfield, Massachusetts, where the Curtises maintained their country estate. They had four children, three of whom died in childhood.

With the onset of the Civil War Curtis had agreed to support the established government and especially President Lincoln "so long and so far, and by all ways and means possible to a good citizen." Toward the end of 1862, however, he began to criticize Lincoln for exceeding his constitutional authority in issuing the preliminary Emancipation Proclamation and suspending habeas corpus. The day the final proclamation took effect Curtis wrote from Washington: "I have seen a good many eminent men today, . . . & I have not seen one who does not say the country is ruined & that its ruin is attributable largely to the utter incompetence of the Prest. & to the radicals, *who have subdued him utterly.*" In the 1864 election Curtis supported Lincoln's Democratic opponent, General George B. McClellan.

Curtis's criticism of the administration attracted the attention of Orville Browning, a moderate Republican who had opposed the second Confiscation Act (July 1862) and the Emancipation Proclamation. When Chief Justice Taney died on 12 October 1864, Browning considered backing Curtis for the post but realized the president would never appoint him. In 1866 Browning invited Curtis to attend the National Union Convention, aimed at uniting moderates from both sections behind Andrew Johnson's Reconstruction policies, including the immediate readmission of the southern states. Curtis, though unable to attend, sent a statement to the effect that organizing new governments did not require congressional approval. As commander in chief and the chief executive officer, he concluded, the president had the official duty to know if a rebellion had been suppressed and if the authority of the Constitution and laws had been restored.

In the impeachment trial in 1868, Curtis served as a counsel for President Johnson, along with William M. Evarts, Henry Stanbery, and William S. Groesbeck. On 9 and 10 April Curtis delivered an impressive opening argument that lasted five hours. Reminding the senators that party spirit, political schemes, foregone conclusions, and outrageous biases had no place in a judicial proceeding, he launched into a characteristically clear and unemotional argument. He argued that the president had considered removing a Lincoln appointee before Congress passed the Tenure of Office

Act, that because Secretary of War Edwin Stanton was appointed by Lincoln rather than Johnson he was not covered by this legislation, and that, in any event, Johnson had the right to test its constitutionality. As one journalist recounted: "The clearness of his statements, the accuracy of his logic, and the precision and steadiness with which he advanced from every premise he established to conclusions, needed . . . no fiery oratory to enhance the effect. If his tones did not often thrill the heart, they reached the brain." Another observer wrote Curtis's wife after returning from the Senate chamber, "For power and condensation of thought, and for dignity and persuasiveness of delivery, it was indeed a glorious effort." Even House manager Benjamin F. Butler conceded that those who followed Curtis added nothing substantial to his argument.

Within weeks of Johnson's acquittal Curtis refused an offer to succeed Stanbery as attorney general. Citing obligations to his clients and family, he informed the president he would not willingly accept any public office. He continued at the bar another five years, arguing twenty-two cases before the Supreme Court, twelve before the Supreme Judicial Court of Massachusetts, and many in lower courts. Upon returning from a trip to Europe in 1871, he declined appointment as a counsel to the international board arbitrating outstanding differences between the United States and Great Britain under the Treaty of Washington. According to his brother, he scarcely felt equal to another voyage across the Atlantic.

During the next couple of years Curtis taught at Harvard Law School and was put on a commission to revise the Boston city charter. After the death of Sumner in 1874, Massachusetts Democrats unsuccessfully supported Curtis for Sumner's Senate seat. In late June Curtis went to spend the summer months at a villa the family had rented in Newport, Rhode Island. Around 1 July his health began to fail, and he rarely ventured out except to take an occasional carriage ride. He died in Newport.

A meeting commemorating Curtis in the U.S. Circuit Court for Massachusetts lauded him for a fullness, breadth, and accuracy of learning unsurpassed at the bar or on the bench of his time, an almost intuitive capacity to discern the points on which a case hinged, and a power of simple, clear, comprehensive statement that gave to his enunciation of legal principles something of the beauty and precision of the exact sciences. Perhaps he had not made such contributions to the law as Judge Story, added Republican congressman E. R. Hoar, but for clearness, steadiness, and uprightness he had left a judicial fame anyone might envy. Butler was closest to the mark when he claimed: "There is one contribution of Judge Curtis . . . which shall live long and be reckoned in the judgments of Lord Mansfield on kindred subjects. The Dred Scott opinion was the opening of a legal thought which has since been embodied in the constitution of the country." Despite his conservative record and the limited scope of his opinion, Curtis is largely remembered as a dissenter in *Dred Scott*.

• Curtis's papers are at the Library of Congress, the American Antiquarian Society, and the Harvard Law School Library. The Harvard University Archives includes a biographical file and several student papers, including his 1828 Bowdoin Prize dissertation, "How Far May Political Ignorance in the People Be Relied on for the Security of Absolute Government in Europe?" While on the Supreme Court, Curtis edited *Reports of Cases in the Circuit Courts of the United States* (1854) and *Decisions of the Supreme Court of the United States* (1856). His son, also named Benjamin R. Curtis, edited *Life and Writings of Benjamin Robbins Curtis* (2 vols., 1879). The first volume, written by George Ticknor Curtis, is a sympathetic biography filled with letters, articles, and opinions. The second volume contains miscellaneous writings and speeches, including his argument in the Med case; the paper "Debts of the States," first published in the *North American Review*, Jan. 1844; and *Executive Power*, an 1862 pamphlet attacking Lincoln's war policies. Chandler Robbins added some useful personal information in his "Memoir of the Hon. Benjamin Robbins Curtis, LL.D.," *Proceedings of the Massachusetts Historical Society* 16 (1879): 16–35. A balanced full-length biography is Richard H. Leach, "Benjamin R. Curtis: Case Study of a Supreme Court Justice" (Ph.D. diss., Princeton Univ., 1951). William Gillette wrote on Curtis in *The Justices of the United States Supreme Court 1789–1969*, vol. 2, ed. Leon Friedman and Fred L. Israel (1969). Major reassessments of his role in *Dred Scott* include Don E. Fehrenbacher, *The "Dred Scott" Case* (1978), and Kenneth M. Stampp, *America in 1857* (1990). On the impeachment proceedings see Benjamin F. Butler, *Butler's Book* (1892); Eric L. McKitrick, *Andrew Johnson and Reconstruction* (1960); and Hans L. Trefousse, *Andrew Johnson* (1989).

ROBERT C. MORRIS

CURTIS, Charles (25 Jan. 1860–8 Feb. 1936), congressman, senator, and vice president of the United States, was born in North Topeka, Kansas, the son of Orren Arms Curtis, a soldier, and Ellen Gonville Pappan, a quarter-blood member of the Kansa (Kaw) Indian tribe. The only person of Indian blood to be elected to the second highest office in the land, Curtis traced his ancestry on the maternal side to Kansa chief White Plume, who married a daughter of the renowned Osage chief Pawhuska, thus providing Curtis with a modest Osage heritage as well. Left to others by the death of his mother in 1863 and the roving habits of his father, young Charles was raised mainly by his paternal grandmother, Permelia Hubbard Curtis.

At the age of six Curtis was placed in custody of his half-blood Indian grandmother, Julie Gonville Pappan, at the Kaw Indian reservation near Council Grove, Kansas. In 1868 the impending removal of the Kaw tribe to Indian Territory and the closing of the Friends reservation school (which Charles attended) prompted his return to North Topeka and the home of his grandmother Curtis. He later exaggerated and exploited his brief reservation experience in terms of his own Indianness and consequent special understanding of Indian needs in the face of emerging government policy for tribal dissolution following the Civil War.

Curtis attended the common schools of North Topeka, while working on weekends as a hack driver and fruit peddler to passengers arriving by train near his grandfather's hotel. During the summer months from 1869 to 1875, he was a jockey at county fairs in Kansas and at race tracks in Indian Territory and Texas. He entered Topeka High School in 1876, and in 1879 he began reading law under a Topeka attorney. Two years later, at the age of twenty-one, Curtis was admitted to the Kansas bar, and as a practicing attorney, he specialized in criminal law. He married Anna E. Baird in 1884, to which union were born three children.

Local town promoters, including his grandfather, William Curtis, encouraged him to pursue real estate development. The young mixed-blood enjoyed special opportunity, for by the Kansa land cession treaty of 1825, his Indian grandmother had been awarded a fee-simple allotment that in part was willed to Charles on the death of his mother. Curtis turned his inheritance along the railroad line in North Topeka into a profitable enterprise and in later years often cited his business acumen as proof that the allotment of Indian reservations was a vital instrument in the acculturation and assimilation of Indian people.

Like most ambitious attorneys in post–Civil War Topeka, Curtis became an avid Republican. The influence of his grandmother Curtis is apparent as well, for according to Curtis's half-sister, Dolly Gann, she "regarded being both a Methodist and a Republican as essential to anyone who expected to go to heaven." In his autobiography, Curtis recalled "that whatever I am, and all that I have in the way of success, I owe to . . . my Grandmother Curtis."

Curtis's formal political career began in 1884 when he was elected county attorney in Shawnee County, Kansas. Five years earlier Kansas had amended their state constitution in favor of Prohibition, and the young county attorney made the most of it by shutting down most of the bootleg bars that continued to dispense alcohol in the shadow of the state capitol. In 1892 Curtis was elected to the U.S. Congress from Kansas's old Fourth District, in an election that saw the state support Populist James B. Weaver for president and elect a Populist governor. It was a dramatic victory for the conservative Republican and a testimony to his capacity for working the human side of politics. In his 1946 autobiography, William Allen White, who knew Curtis well, remarked, "Issues never bothered him. . . . I never saw a man who could go into a hostile audience, smile, shake hands, and talk before and after the meeting so plausibly that what he said on his feet was completely eclipsed as a human being."

There was another side to the Curtis popularity, what the political pundits called his "confusing mixed-bloodedness." Because he did not join his tribe on the Indian Territory reservation in 1873 or take part in tribal affairs, Curtis was expelled from Kaw membership in 1878. Yet as a member of committees dealing with tribal annuities, Indian Territory legislation, and public lands, and after 1903 as chairman of the powerful House Committee on Indian Affairs, Curtis assumed a leadership role in the destiny of the American Indian. He sponsored the Curtis Act of 1898, which abolished tribal courts, led to the dissolution of the Five Civilized Tribes, and laid the foundation for Oklahoma statehood. He fought for the rights of Indian women and mixed-blood children while at the same time serving as attorney for energy companies that were cheating tribal governments out of their natural resources. He played a personal role in the allotment of his own tribe, a role that led to his regaining tribal membership in time to share in the Kaw allotment distribution in 1902. In most of these activities he worked behind the scenes, for to him formal debate was a waste of time; getting things done without a fuss was his preference. "As a fixer," concluded one observer, "Charley is truly one of the best in the business" ("Heap Big Chief," *American Mercury*, Aug. 1929, p. 410). Others called him Washington's best whisperer.

For his hard work and regularity, including what one critic termed his deference to the trinity of the high protective tariff, the grand army of the Republic, and the Republican party, Curtis was reelected to the House of Representatives until 1907. Then the state legislature chose him to fill the unexpired term of Joseph R. Burton, a full six-year term in the U.S. Senate. He was defeated for reelection in 1912. By popular vote in 1914, however, he was returned to the Senate, where he served continuously until he became vice president of the United States in 1929.

In the Senate, where he headed the Rules Committee and became party whip under majority leader Henry Cabot Lodge, Curtis supported conservative farm policies, high protective tariffs, diplomatic isolation, veterans' benefits, Prohibition, the economic interests of his home state, and the Nineteenth Amendment. He took great pride in being one of the first legislators at the national level to advocate women's rights, and he was no less dedicated to fair labor practices for children.

Upon Lodge's death in November 1924, Curtis was chosen majority leader of the Senate. It was clear by 1928 that he had his eye on the White House, if for no other reason than as a reward for his long and dedicated work for the Republican party on Capitol Hill. In his campaign for the presidential nomination, Curtis contended that the front-running candidate, Herbert Hoover (1874–1964), would place a "hopeless burden" on their party, apparently reflecting the belief that Hoover could not win. Hoover easily won the nomination at the Republican National Convention in 1928, however, and Curtis was selected to run for vice president. They won the election handily in November over Democrats Alfred E. Smith and Joseph T. Robinson.

As vice president, Curtis grudgingly wielded the Senate gavel and hosted hundreds of official dinner parties, but he exerted no significant influence in the Hoover administration. While he did attend most cabinet meetings, his advice was seldom sought; perhaps, as one critic noted, he had little to offer. He criticized the Federal Reserve System as too speculative, continued to push for high protective tariffs as the panacea for economic ills, and viewed the worsening depression as a natural occurrence that would run its course and eventually give way to even greater prosperity. In the 5 July 1930 *New York Times* he decried "the wave that is sweeping the country which disregards law and order and the Constitution." By the end of his public career, brought on by the victory of Franklin D. Roosevelt and John Nance Garner in 1932, Curtis was clearly a disillusioned man. He returned to his law practice until his death in Washington, D.C. Other than performing the routine duties of office, Curtis's contribution as vice president was minimal. More important were his Republican regularity in Congress and his unwavering support of federal allotment policy for Indians, Prohibition, women's suffrage, farm and veterans' benefits, high tariffs, parliamentary reform in the Senate, and economy in government.

• A small collection of Curtis manuscripts and an unpublished autobiography are in the Kansas State Historical Society; a more complete version of the Curtis autobiography is in private hands. Other manuscripts are the William Allen White Papers, Library of Congress; the William A. Jones Papers in the State Historical Society of Wisconsin; the Kaw Indian Agency Collection, University of Oklahoma Library; the Kaw Files, Oklahoma Historical Society; the Kansas and Osage Agency Letters Received, RG 75, M 234, National Archives; and the Osage Miscellaneous Files, RG 75, Federal Records Center, Fort Worth, Tex. The only critical biography is William E. Unrau, *Mixed-Bloods and Tribal Dissolution: Charles Curtis and the Quest for Indian Identity* (1989). Don C. Seitz, *From Kaw Teepee to Capitol: The Life Story of Charles Curtis, Indian* (1928), is a hurried campaign sheet with numerous errors in fact and interpretation, while Marvin Ewy, "Charles Curtis of Kansas: Vice President of the United States, 1929–1933," *Emporia State Research Studies* 10 (1961): 1–58, emphasizes Curtis's later political career. An obituary is in the *New York Times*, 9 Feb. 1936.

WILLIAM E. UNRAU

CURTIS, Charlotte Murray (19 Dec. 1928–16 Apr. 1987), journalist, was born in Chicago, Illinois, the daughter of George Morris Curtis, a physician, and Lucile Atcherson, a foreign diplomat. Curtis and her family moved to Columbus, Ohio, when she was three years old. Born into a family of privilege, Curtis was active in the Junior League and other charitable organizations as a young woman. In 1946 she enrolled as a freshman at Vassar College, where she majored in American history. Curtis would later say that her real "alma mater" was the Columbus *Citizen*, her hometown newspaper where she worked during the summers while she was in college. In 1950, the year she graduated from Vassar, Curtis began as a society writer at the *Citizen*, a job she would hold until 1961, when she became a society and women's news writer for the *New York Times*. It was at the *Citizen*, Curtis said, that she developed a love of writing and a passion for newspaper journalism.

A society writer at the *New York Times* until 1965, Curtis then served as the *Times* women's-news editor until 1974, editing the section as well as continuing to write for it. Curtis believed that women's and society news should be treated in the same manner as hard news. Thus, during her tenure on the women's pages, society reporting—wedding announcements in particular, which in most newspapers had been written in a flowery style—was treated as "news." Curtis once explained her philosophy in an interview: "It was as though all wedding stories were written, 'And the beautiful bride wore, etc.' Well, I'm sorry, but that doesn't have anything to do with reality. Some brides are not beautiful."

Curtis's frank and sharp-tongued reporting of the excesses of some wealthy Americans was hailed as unique and unorthodox, especially for the staid *Times*. In one article, for example, she noted that a wealthy family had installed marble floors so that their dogs could keep cool during the warm months. Curtis's treatment of the wealthy and well-to-do was often biting and irreverent, quite different from the treatment they received in the society pages of most daily newspapers. A *Newsweek* reporter went so far as to compare her to F. Scott Fitzgerald: "Charlotte Curtis has been serving up such delicious slices of upper-crust life in a style that combines a Fitzgeraldian sense of mood with a reporter's eye for detail" (28 Sept. 1964, p. 62).

One of Curtis's most famous stories was an account of a 1970 fundraiser held by conductor Leonard Bernstein for the radical Black Panther party. In her story, printed 15 Jan. 1970, Curtis mocked both sides, Bernstein and his guests as well as members of the Panther party, portraying the latter as naive and harmless and Bernstein and his friends as naive as well as hypocritical, both in their *noblesse oblige* and in their uncritical acceptance of the Panther philosophy. Curtis described how Bernstein had attempted to "become" one of the Panthers by donning their dress and mode of speech and how, in response to one member of the party telling him that the U.S. government should be overthrown, he coolly agreed, saying, "I dig absolutely." This story illustrates well Curtis's early penchant for ridiculing her subjects simply by quoting them precisely.

As women's-news editor, Curtis ran fewer fashion, recipe, and "how-to" stories—conventional "women's-page" fare—and more social and news stories about such topics as abortion, feminism, and single-parent families. She thus set the trend for other newspapers around the country to change the content of their women's pages. Curtis was no radical feminist, however. Running the women's pages at the beginning of the so-called women's liberation movement, she was open to news stories about women's issues but was put off by the demonstrations, sit-ins, and fundraisers that were prevalent at the time, and she opposed the use of "Ms." in the *Times* to replace "Mrs." and "Miss." Curtis often said she believed that the feminist movement tried to turn women into men and that there were reasons for the differences between the sexes, but she was a firm believer in equal pay for women and men, and she believed that women were just as capable as men of participating in the workplace. Her criticisms of feminism notwithstanding, Curtis became a role model for many women who began to question their being limited to the roles of wife and mother. For most of her life, Curtis's job was her top priority, and the change in tone of her women's pages led many women to believe that there was more to think about than weddings and recipes.

In 1972, at age forty-four, Curtis married William E. Hunt, a neurologic surgeon at Ohio State University Hospitals. The two maintained a commuter marriage, with Curtis based in New York City and Hunt in Columbus, Ohio.

In 1974 Curtis was named the *Times* op-ed editor, responsible for editing and selecting guest columns for the page opposite the editorial page. In this capacity, she also was named associate editor of the newspaper and became the first woman to appear on the *Times* masthead. Many readers and employees were surprised by the promotion. The op-ed page had been designed and edited by former foreign correspondent and Pulitzer Prize–winning writer Harrison Salisbury, who had filled it with commentary about world affairs and politics. It was not a job for a women's-page writer, some people believed. Under Curtis, the page became much more eclectic. Columnists discussed the future of the mini-skirt, books, and even the joys of eating at McDonald's. While world leaders and scholars continued to contribute to the page, so did more popular figures, such as author Erica Jong, filmmaker and musician Yoko Ono, and political activist Tom Hayden.

Curtis's reviews as op-ed editor were mixed. Some readers thought she had destroyed the intellectual integrity of the page, whereas others thought she had opened it up to a greater variety of readers. She remained in the post until 1982, when she became a weekly columnist for the *Times*. In her column she focused on social commentary and profiles of famous New Yorkers, but her tone and voice had changed over the years. Gone was the subtlety and satiric subtext of her stories as a society reporter, and her irreverent attitude had all but disappeared.

Many of Curtis's friends, who admitted that the column was disappointing, later learned that she had been ill during much of her tenure as columnist. Breast cancer that had developed in the mid-1970s had returned, greatly debilitating her during those years. In 1986 she was forced to return to her home in Columbus, where she died a year later.

• Curtis's papers are at the Schlesinger Women's Studies Library at Radcliffe College in Cambridge, Mass. An interview conducted on 21 June 1983 is part of the *New York Times* Oral History Project in New York City. A compilation of her writings was published in 1976 under the title *The Rich and Other Atrocities*. She also authored *First Lady* (1963), a biography of then first lady Jacqueline Kennedy. A full biography is Marilyn Greenwald, "The Life and Career of Journalist Charlotte Curtis: A Rhetorical Biography" (Ph.D. diss., Ohio State Univ., 1991). Biographical sketches include Julie Baumgold, "Charlotte: Star Reporter," *New York*, 6 Oct. 1969, pp. 39–44, 46, 48–49; "Charlotte Curtis," *Vogue*, June 1975, p. 116; Jane Howard, "Charlotte Curtis: First Lady of the *New York Times*," *Cosmopolitan*, Jan. 1975, pp. 60, 158; Lois Melina, "*Times* Editor Doubts Social Responsibility of the Nation's Rich," Muncie (Ind.) *Star*, 8 Oct. 1977, p. 1; and "Upper Crust," *Newsweek*, 28 Sept. 1964, p. 62. The *New York Times* obituary of 17 Apr. 1987 describes Curtis's irreverent reporting on the excesses of well-to-do New Yorkers.

MARILYN GREENWALD

CURTIS, Cyrus H. K. (18 June 1850–7 June 1933), publisher, was born Cyrus Hermann Kotzschmar Curtis in Portland, Maine, the son of Cyrus Libby Curtis, a salesman, and Salome Ann Cummings. Forced by economic necessity to leave school after completing the ninth grade, Curtis often recalled that he began his publishing career as a newsboy for the *Courier* in order to earn money to buy fireworks. He bought papers and sold them, his greatest success occurring during the Civil War, when he sold newspapers to news-starved soldiers at nearby Fort Prebel. He was then hired by the *Portland Press* but soon moved to the *Portland Argus*, which offered him more money. On 5 April 1865 Curtis began the newspaper *Young America*, which he printed and distributed as well as wrote. The format was simple, containing book news, fiction, and riddles. It sold for two cents a copy. Because printing by an outside source cost more than Curtis's profit on the newspaper, he got enough money together to buy his own press and thus began his lifelong practice of having control over all aspects of his publishing business.

Curtis's plant was destroyed in the great Portland fire of 1866, and three years later he moved to Boston, where in 1872 he started a weekly magazine for businessmen called the *People's Ledger*. His success was cut short that same year, again by fire, and he lost everything he owned. After unsuccessfully trying to continue publishing the magazine out of temporary quarters, in 1876 he decided to go to Philadelphia, hoping that he would be able to move his publishing business there. He discovered that he could get printing work done for fifteen hundred dollars less per year in Philadelphia, and because of these savings, he decided to try his luck in the new location. Unfortunately, the magazine failed in 1878, and Curtis was forced to find a job. He took one as an advertising solicitor at the *Philadelphia Press*, where he eventually became advertising manager.

In 1879 Curtis borrowed enough money to start the *Tribune and Farmer*, which is seen as the beginning of Curtis Publishing Co. (formally organized in July 1890), of which he was president from 1891 to 1922. When the former Louisa Knapp, whom he had married in 1875, objected to the fact that he was writing the column "Women at Home," he gave the job to her. Under her editorship, the column grew first to a page and then to a supplement; ultimately it became *Ladies' Home Journal*, which toward the end of the century boasted a circulation of five million. Their only child,

Mary Louise Bok Zimbalist, would later found and endow the Curtis Institute of Music in Philadelphia.

In 1897, against the advice of family and friends, Curtis bought the failing *Saturday Evening Post* for $1,000. Friends told him he had made a grave mistake, but undaunted, he continued to put money into the ailing magazine. After hiring George Horace Lorimer as editor in 1898, his perseverance was finally rewarded as the publication began to thrive, in time becoming one of the most prestigious in the country, with such renowned writers as Ring Lardner and Sinclair Lewis and illustrators such as Norman Rockwell all vying to be included between—and on—its covers. By 1962 this "grave mistake" reached a peak circulation of 6,652,000. In 1911, the year after the death of Louisa Curtis and his marriage to Kate Stanwood Cutter Pillsbury (a second cousin), he began another huge success, the *Country Gentleman*.

Curtis was less successful in the publishing of newspapers. His first purchase was the *Philadelphia Public Ledger* in 1913. He next purchased both the *Philadelphia Press* and the *Philadelphia North American*, which he combined with the *Public Ledger* in 1920. He also bought the *New York Evening Post* in 1923 and *Philadelphia Inquirer* in 1930. All lost money, hindered by inefficient management and a lack of editorial vision and direction. The evening edition of the *Public Ledger* was sold, along with the *Evening Post* and the *Inquirer*.

From the beginning, Curtis's greatest strengths lay in his attitude toward advertising and his willingness to let editors—Lorimer at the *Saturday Evening Post* and Edward W. Bok (who became his son-in-law) at *Ladies' Home Journal*—be editors with minimal interference on his part. He recognized early on that publishing success rested on strong advertising revenues and sound editorial policy. One fed the other, in a continuous loop. A crusader for honest advertising long before it became the norm, Curtis forced his own high standard on others and thereby gave legitimacy to magazine advertising. He first banned the advertising of proprietary medicine in his magazines in 1889 and, following that bold, unheard of act, next banned financial advertising. Curtis strongly believed in truth in advertising and stood behind the advertisements that appeared in his magazines, a fact that the reading public came to know and appreciate. Both bans were therefore editorially and economically wise, as the public perception that the magazine cared about its readers led them to trust the magazine and renew their subscriptions. As history has shown, Curtis's perception was accurate, and the banning of this type of advertising paid vast dividends. Curtis died at his home in Wyncate, Pennsylvania, eleven days before his eighty-third birthday.

• Edward W. Bok's *A Man from Maine* (1923) is an excellent source written by his son-in-law. See also Matthew J. Culligan, *The Curtis-Culligan Story: From Cyrus to Horace, to Joe* (1970), and Walter Deane Fuller, *The Life and Times of Cyrus H. K. Curtis (1850–1933)* (address delivered during a national Newcomer dinner held in New York on 19 Feb. 1948). Obituaries and memorial articles are in *Newsweek*, 17 June 1933, and the *Nation*, 21 June 1933.

BARBARA L. FLYNN

CURTIS, Edward Sheriff (19 Feb. 1868–19 Oct. 1952), photographer, was born near Whitewater, Wisconsin, the son of Johnson Asahel Curtis, a poor farmer and part-time minister, and Ellen Sheriff. When he was a young boy, his family moved to Cordova, Minnesota, where he attended elementary school. Teaching himself photography with the help of popular manuals, Curtis took his first job with a St. Paul photographic studio. In 1887 he moved with his family to Sidney (now Port Orchard) on Puget Sound in Washington Territory. He settled in Seattle in 1891 and the following year married Clara J. Phillips; they had four children. After several years of partnerships, Curtis opened his own photography studio in 1897 and was soon highly sought after for his society portraits.

The turning point in Curtis's career came in 1898 through a chance encounter with a group of stranded scientists on Mount Rainier. Among the distinguished company were C. Hart Merriam, chief of the U.S. Biological Survey, and George Bird Grinnell, editor of *Field and Stream* magazine. Through their efforts, the following year Curtis was appointed the official photographer on railroad magnate E. H. Harriman's expedition to Alaska. Having photographed local Indians since around 1896, Curtis accompanied Grinnell to Montana in 1900 to witness the Blackfoot Sun Dance. With Grinnell's encouragement, Curtis resolved to create a comprehensive visual record of the American Indian. Describing "the need that has inspired" his work, Curtis wrote, "The passing of every old man or woman means the passage of some tradition, some knowledge of sacred rite possessed by no other; consequently, the information that is to be gathered, for the benefit of future generations, respecting the modes of life of one of the greatest races of mankind, must be collected at once or the opportunity will be lost for all time." This project would occupy him for the next three decades. Working mostly with a 6 × 8-inch reflex camera, he produced a total of over 40,000 sepia-toned images; he also made over 10,000 cylinder recordings of American Indian music. Curtis was aided in this immense project by William E. Myers, a former journalist, who was largely responsible for interviewing and written documentation, and by photographer Adolph F. Muhr, who managed the studio where the photographs were developed and printed. Smithsonian archaeologist Frederick W. Hodge edited the accompanying text.

Curtis's work began to attract national attention. President Theodore Roosevelt, favorably impressed with his work, chose him to photograph his family in 1904. In 1906 the president introduced Curtis to financier J. Pierpont Morgan, whose family ultimately contributed nearly $400,000 toward the project's total cost of over $1,500,000. Privately printed in a lavish edition of twenty volumes with associated portfolios, *The*

North American Indian (1907–1930) contained approximately 2,200 photogravure images. Curtis's subjects ranged broadly; while he favored portraits, the volumes include scenes of daily life, ceremonies, architecture and artifacts, and landscapes. Seeking to depict tribes that "still retained to a considerable degree their primitive customs and traditions," Curtis emphasized Native Americans west of the Mississippi. The work was offered by subscription, and only about half of the limited edition of 500 sets were sold.

After the Morgan money ran out, Curtis struggled to raise the funds to keep the project going. In 1911 and 1912 he toured the country with a "musicale," a lecture program, illustrated with slides and film drawn from the entire project, and accompanied by orchestral transcriptions of Indian songs. In 1914 he premiered a feature-length film, *In the Land of the Head Hunters*, a fictionalized story of the Kwakiutl Indians of British Columbia, but it failed to attract the attention that Curtis had hoped for.

The difficulties of completing *The North American Indian* and its lack of success led to increasing personal and professional problems for Curtis. Because of his extended absences from home, his wife divorced him in 1919. Moving to Los Angeles, he worked in Hollywood during the next decade as a movie cameraman and still photographer. All the while, Curtis strove to complete his magnum opus. His last years were marked by illness and a succession of failed mining and writing projects: prospecting for gold and zircon, and writing books about gold and Northwest Coast Indians for a popular audience. Curtis died in Los Angeles, largely forgotten, his work buried in rare book libraries.

Curtis's photographs were rediscovered in the early 1970s as a partial result of the counterculture's interest in American Indian culture. He is now by far the most popular and well-known photographer of the American Indian, even though his images have been criticized for their use of re-creation and staging. Nevertheless, his photographs are masterpieces of pictorialist photography, and they remain the most vivid expressions of the misplaced concept of the "Vanishing Indian," which was common in his day.

• Curtis's correspondence and manuscripts are in the Southwest Museum in Los Angeles, the Seaver Center of the Los Angeles Museum of Natural History, the Seattle Public Library, the University of Washington Library, and the Morgan Library in New York City. In the absence of an adequate biography, the following should be consulted: A. D. Coleman and T. C. McLuhan, Introduction, Curtis, *Portraits from North American Indian Life* (1972); Florence Curtis Graybill and Victor Boesen, *Edward Sheriff Curtis: Visions of a Vanishing Race* (1976); Christopher M. Lyman, *The Vanishing Race and Other Illusions: Photographs of Indians by Edward S. Curtis* (1982); Bill Holm and George Irving Quimby, *Edward S. Curtis in the Land of the War Canoes: A Pioneer Cinematographer in the Pacific Northwest* (1980); and Barbara Davis, *Edward S. Curtis: The Life and Times of a Shadow Catcher* (1985).

IRA JACKNIS

CURTIS, Edwin Upton (26 Mar. 1861–28 Mar. 1922), police commissioner and mayor of Boston, was born in Roxbury, Massachusetts, the son of George Curtis, a lumber merchant and Republican politician, and Martha Ann Upton. Curtis attended the Roxbury public grammar and Latin schools and Bowdoin College (A.B. 1882; A.M. 1885; LL.D. 1914). He read law at a Boston firm and attended Boston University Law School. Admitted to the bar in 1885, he practiced law and in 1888 became secretary of the Boston Republican City Committee. Elected city clerk of Boston in 1889, he served for two years.

Boston was largely a Democratic stronghold, made up of a coalition led by ex-Mugwump Yankee Democrats and Irish and ethnic followers. The Republican-controlled state government continually sought to curb the growing power of the Hub's Democrats. In 1894 Curtis ran for mayor and defeated Democrat Francis Peabody, Jr., by 2,500 votes. During his year in office Curtis pursued a program of cost cutting and business efficiency that did not endear him to the working classes. Curtis successfully pushed charter reform through the state legislature, a measure that he had hoped would give Republicans more power. The 1895 Charter reform provided for a two-year term for mayor, set up a new board of electoral commissioners, created a new system for city departments to be run by a commissioner, and revised the financing of the public schools. The *Boston Globe* of 5 December 1895 complained "of the recent amendments to the charter of this city, which were prepared by Mayor Curtis, and by the legislature [and] forced down the throats of the citizens of Boston." In addition to the Republican-Democratic power struggle, during Curtis's administration severe xenophobia gripped the city, resulting in a Yankee-Irish riot on Independence Day. Curtis lost his reelection bid by 4,400 votes to Brahmin Democrat Josiah Quincy, who had the support of Irish ward bosses.

On 27 October 1897 Curtis married Margaret Maude Waterman of Thomaston, Maine, who bore him two daughters. He returned to the practice of law until 1906, when he became assistant U.S. treasurer in Boston. Curtis served as collector of customs from 1909 to 1913. Throughout these years he was a member of the Metropolitan Park Commission (1896–1916).

A Republican governor, Samuel McCall, appointed Curtis as police commissioner of Boston in 1918. In 1885, because of the election of an Irish-born Democrat, Hugh O'Brien, the state legislature had amended the city charter to take away the mayor's police powers. Thereafter, the governor appointed the police commissioners (three at first, and later, one). This blatant political interference by the state came to a dramatic climax in the 1919 police strike.

The year 1919 was one of extreme turbulence and unrest across the nation. With over 2,600 strikes that year, rabid antiunion sentiment pervaded the land. The Boston police suffered with low pay and poor working conditions. Francis Russell, in his *City in*

Terror (1975), reported that the police found Curtis to be "cold and unapproachable" (p. 56). To redress their grievances, the Boston police sought affiliation with the American Federation of Labor (AFL). Commissioner Curtis responded by publishing a general order forbidding members of the force from associating with any organization outside the police department. "I desire to say to the members of the force that I am firmly of the opinion that a police officer cannot consistently belong to a police union and perform his sworn duty." He threatened to dismiss those who violated this order. The police voted to join the AFL, and Curtis immediately suspended nineteen union leaders, threatening to dismiss them from the force. Mayor Andrew Peters, a Yankee Democrat, fearing a strike, attempted to mediate the situation. He asked Curtis to postpone the firing of the police leaders. Peters then appointed a blue-ribbon committee headed by a noted Republican, James Jackson Storrow, to look into the matter.

Commissioner Curtis made it clear that he and he alone was legally in control. "What right has the mayor of Boston to send me a letter asking for a continuance?" The Storrow Committee came up with a compromise. Affiliation with an outside union was out of the question, but the police would be allowed their own union organization. An appointed citizens committee would adjudicate unresolved grievances. Mayor Peters approved the solution, as did most Boston newspapers and the business community. The adamant Curtis rejected the compromise on the basis that it violated "his prescribed legal duties." He dismissed the newly elected officers of the police union. On 9 September 1919 the police went on strike.

The fearful Mayor Peters asked Republican governor Calvin Coolidge to call out the state militia. Curtis assured Peters and Coolidge that only a small number of policemen would strike and that the police commissioner had matters under control. Governor Coolidge informed Mayor Peters that he could not intervene legally as long as Commissioner Curtis was in control of the situation. Moreover, based on a little-known statute, in case of "tumult, riot or mob," the mayor could call out local militia units if he so desired. Curtis assured the mayor that he "had the situation well in hand." After three-fourths of the police went out, mobs began forming, and serious violence and looting began. Finally, realizing he could not control the situation, Curtis reported the situation to the mayor. Peters then called out the local state guard. By doing so, Mayor Peters officially took charge over the police department. After three days of mob rioting, the militia effectively restored order. At this point Governor Coolidge entered the fray. Coolidge called out the entire state guard, thus removing Peters from any legal control of the situation. One can only speculate that the Republican governor finally responded so that the Democratic mayor would not receive credit for ending the disturbances.

Coolidge restored Curtis to office. The police commissioner then fired all 1,147 striking policemen. Praised for his stance against union recognition, Curtis received full community support in his reorganization of the department.

In office until his death, Curtis remained a figure of public note. Only later did criticism of Curtis's actions emerge. Writing in 1940, historian Claude Fuess termed Curtis as "fair-minded" (p. 204) but "not prepared for the emergency when it arrived" (p. 220). Curtis's harshest critic has been Francis Russell, who in 1975 dubbed the commissioner an "uncompromising martinet with no previous experience in police administration and no great affection for the Boston Irish" (p. 43). An old guard Republican Yankee, Curtis was unable to fathom the needs of the largely Irish-Catholic policemen under his control. Curtis (and Coolidge) had reacted to a crisis situation based on years of class and ethnic conflict in Boston.

• The only unpublished material on Curtis and the strike is a collection of four bound volumes of letters received by Curtis on his handling of the strike, the papers of Mayor Andrew J. Peters, both at the Boston Public Library, and 244 items addressed to General Samuel D. Parker of the state national guard at the Houghton Library, Harvard University. Curtis gave his views on the strike in an official report, "Fourteenth Annual Report of the Police Commissioner for the City of Boston" (1920). Contemporary periodical support for Curtis can be found in [unsigned] "Harvard Men in the Boston Police Strike," *School and Society* 10 (1919): 524–25; Gregory Mason, "No Bolshevism for Boston," *Outlook* 123 (1919): 124–25; [unsigned] "Police Strike in Boston and Other Labor Problems," *Current History* 11 (1919): 54–57; and [unsigned] "Policemen's Right to Strike," *Literary Digest* 62 (1919): 7, 8. See Randolph Bartlett, "Anarchy in Boston," *American Mercury* 26 (1935): 456–64, and Richard L. Lyons, "The Boston Police Strike of 1919," *New England Quarterly* 20 (1947): 147–68, for articles critical of both Curtis and Coolidge. The only book written about the strike is Francis Russell, *A City in Terror: The 1919 Boston Police Strike* (1975). Several works on Coolidge mention Curtis and the strike. The most important are Claude M. Fuess, *Calvin Coolidge: The Man from Vermont* (1940), and William Allen White, *A Puritan in Babylon: the Story of Calvin Coolidge* (1938). All the Boston newspapers wrote highly favorable obituaries of Curtis on 29 Mar. 1922.

JACK TAGER

CURTIS, George Ticknor (28 Nov. 1812–28 Mar. 1894), lawyer and historian, was born in Watertown, Massachusetts, the son of Benjamin Curtis, a master in the merchant marine, and Lois Robbins. After his father died abroad, his mother raised him and his brother Benjamin Robbins Curtis, later a U.S. Supreme Court justice, in her parents' house. George graduated from Harvard College in 1832, then attended Harvard Law School and read law in the Boston office of Charles Pelham Curtis, a distant cousin. He was admitted to the bar in 1836 and immediately established a Boston practice. In 1844 Curtis married Mary Oliver Story, the daughter of Supreme Court Justice Joseph Story; they had two children. Mary Curtis died in 1848, and in 1851 Curtis married Louise A. Nyström; they had six children.

Curtis served as a Whig in the Massachusetts House from 1840 to 1843. His views on constitutional law were shaped by the nullification controversy of the early 1830s; he believed that southern challenges to the assertion of national authority in an area clearly committed to Congress—foreign trade—were a threat to the Constitution's premises. In 1852, as a United States commissioner, Curtis presided over the fugitive slave hearing for Thomas Sims of Georgia; his decision against Sims was one of the first upholding the constitutionality of the 1850 Fugitive Slave Law that significantly reduced the burdens placed on slaveowners attempting to reclaim slaves who had fled to northern states.

Like Daniel Webster, whose political leadership and constitutional theories he admired, Curtis believed that the Constitution conferred a limited range of powers on the national government but that those powers were plenary within that range. On this ground he defended the Missouri Compromise by representing Dred Scott before the Supreme Court in 1856–1857. Although the Court rejected Curtis's argument that Congress had complete power to determine what property relationships would be allowed in the territories, Curtis remained committed to the view that national power under the Constitution was extensive. Also, like Webster, Curtis believed that Congress would be imprudent to exercise all the power the Constitution conferred on it. In criticizing expansive theories of national power that emerged during the Civil War, Curtis's 1862 Fourth of July oration nonetheless defended the use of arms against the South, whose rebellion rested on what he regarded as an erroneous theory of the relationship between the states and the Union.

In 1862 Curtis moved to New York where he participated behind the scenes in Democratic party politics, urging the party to insist on reunification as a war aim, while he renounced Republican efforts to make slavery's abolition a condition of reunification. He became a leading patent lawyer, defending the interests of major inventors such as Samuel F. B. Morse and Cyrus McCormick. Shortly before retiring from active practice in 1888, Curtis delivered an eloquent plea for religious liberty on behalf of Utah's Mormons in a case designed to test how severely the national laws against polygamy and cohabitation would be applied (*Snow v. United States* [1886]; *Ex parte Snow* [1887]). After dismissing one appeal on jurisdictional grounds, the Supreme Court limited the statute's reach by holding that cohabitation was a continuous act. This defeated the government's effort to multiply the punishments it could impose on Mormons by prosecuting them for each year (or even day) of cohabitation.

Curtis published treatises on admiralty, patents, copyrights, and the jurisdiction of the federal courts, and numerous legal pamphlets. He dabbled in literature, writing a novel of the Civil War, and he wrote a philosophical examination of evolution. He also wrote a *Memoir of Benjamin Robbins Curtis* (1879) and two important biographies, the *Life of Daniel Webster*

(1870) and the *Life of James Buchanan* (1883). Written on the nineteenth-century model of biographies of public figures and concentrating on their activities in political life, these works are useful presentations of the Old Whig interpretation of antebellum history, arguing that the most valuable achievement of antebellum politicians was establishing that national power could be exercised broadly while maintaining in practice a prudent balance between the states and the nation.

Curtis's most enduring work, *Constitutional History of the United States* (1854–1858), was based on his Lowell Lectures, delivered in Boston. In 1889 Curtis revised *Constitutional History*'s treatment of the period up to independence and was working on another volume dealing with the period after 1789 at the time of his death in New York; the volume was edited by J. C. Clayton and published in 1896. The second edition of *Constitutional History* remained focused on the constitutional theories underlying the Civil War. Curtis believed that because abolitionist constitutional theories defended the actual exercise of expansive power by the national government, abolitionists bore responsibility for the Civil War. For Curtis, more prudent leaders like Webster understood better that the Union southerners were moving to challenge had to have extensive constitutional power to meet the demands placed on a powerful nation but needed to exercise that power only in the most urgent cases. Following Webster even after the Civil War, Curtis rejected the southern defense of secession as an act within the Constitution, seeing it instead as a repudiation of the agreement made on entering the Union. To Curtis, if the South believed that the national government had exceeded the limits the Constitution placed on its power, the only remedies were constitutional amendment or the exercise of the natural right of revolution in the face of intolerable oppression.

Curtis's works are clear and competent. The first edition of *Constitutional History* presents a view of the Constitution that had become outdated when the second edition appeared; the Reconstruction amendments had complicated American federalism in ways that Curtis's views could not explain. Curtis criticized Reconstruction as a betrayal of the war aim of preserving the Union. Some passing phrases in his works suggest that Curtis glimpsed the transformation in constitutional theory occasioned by the Civil War and Reconstruction, which made extensive assertions of national power common although still contested, but he never grappled with that transformation. The war's legacy was the revitalization of Jacksonian constitutionalism, with its focus on individual rights and antimonopoly secured through vigorous assertions of government power.

The states' rights controversies that shaped Curtis's vision of the Constitution took a new shape. Curtis did not understand that the new issues were whether the national government should override states' rights to protect individual rights, not whether it should override them to advance national unity and commercial power. Significantly, the second edition draft of *Constitutional History* contained a chapter heading for "judicial construction" of the Reconstruction amendments, which presumably would have dealt with those amendments' proper interpretation, but Curtis left no notes for that chapter. Within a generation, theories like Curtis's, which combined claims for national power with a desire for its prudent exercise, were displaced by theories defending extensive exercise of national power, either by courts defending individual rights of property and contract or by legislatures defending individual rights against the economically powerful.

• Some letters are reprinted in Curtis's *Memoir of Benjamin Robbins Curtis* (1879), which also describes the family's background; a few other letters are in the George McClellan Papers at the Library of Congress. Curtis's involvement in the Dred Scott case is described briefly in Don E. Fehrenbacher, *The Dred Scott Case: Its Significance in American Law and Politics* (1978). The *Snow* case and its importance are discussed in Edwin B. Firmage and Richard C. Mangrum, *Zion in the Courts: A Legal History of the Church of Jesus Christ of Latter-day Saints, 1830–1900* (1988).

MARK V. TUSHNET

CURTIS, George William (25 Feb. 1824–31 Aug. 1892), writer, editor, and orator, was born in Providence, Rhode Island, the son of George Curtis, a banker and businessman, and Mary Elizabeth Burrill, whose father had been a U.S. senator from and chief justice of Rhode Island. After his mother died in 1826, Curtis and his older brother James Burrill Curtis were cared for by their father and relatives for four years and then attended a boarding school in Jamaica Plains, Massachusetts. In 1835 their father married Julia B. Bridgham, aged twenty-four, and the boys joined them in Providence. Four years later the family moved to New York City, where Curtis was tutored for a short time and then became a counting-house clerk. He and his brother participated in the Brook Farm communal experiment at West Roxbury, outside Boston (1842–1843), returned home for a year, and became farmhands in Concord (1844–1846). During these years, Curtis made enormous intellectual strides through contact with Bronson Alcott, Ellery Channing, Ralph Waldo Emerson, Margaret Fuller, Nathaniel Hawthorne, George Ripley, and Henry David Thoreau. Accompanied part of the time by his brother, Curtis traveled abroad as a *New York Tribune* correspondent (1846–1850). He wrote with special zest about the Middle East.

During his long career, Curtis distinguished himself as a writer, editor, and popular lecturer. His books about his travels in Egypt and Syria, *Nile Notes of a Howadji* (1851) and *The Howadji in Syria* (1852—*Howadji* being Arabic for "traveler"), were widely acclaimed in America and England for their lush descriptions. He placed essays on art and music in the *Tribune*, for which he also wrote pieces about traveling in the eastern United States and which he assembled into *Lotus-Eating: A Summer Book* (1852). Curtis was extraordinarily busy in 1853. He became associate edi-

tor of *Putnam's Monthly Magazine*, lectured successfully through New York State, and wrote the first of his popular "Easy Chair" columns, on dozens of subjects and in several styles, for *Harper's New Monthly* (until 1892). He and his editorial confreres George Palmer Putnam, George Frederick Briggs, and Parke Godwin began to make *Putnam's Monthly* the outlet for such eminent writers as William Cullen Bryant, Emerson, Henry Wadsworth Longfellow, James Russell Lowell, Herman Melville, Thoreau, and John Greenleaf Whittier. Curtis contributed essays on George Bancroft, Emerson, Longfellow, and Hawthorne as part of Putnam's *Homes of American Authors*. He also published *The Potiphar Papers* (1853), a set of sketches satirizing footloose New York plutocrats with too little education and too much pretentious vulgarity.

Another especially full year for Curtis was 1856. During that year he actively campaigned for John C. Frémont, the Republican party's unsuccessful antislavery candidate for president. Also in 1856 he married Anna Shaw of Staten Island, with whom he had three children. He delivered the first of his three finest orations (all often repeated), "The Duty of the American Scholar to Politics and the Times." (This stirring speech was followed by "The Present Aspect of the Slavery Question" in 1859 and "Political Infidelity" in 1864.) And he assembled some fictional sketches in a collection titled *Prue and I* (Prue being the sentimental, didactic narrator's wife).

In 1857 *Putnam's Monthly*, which was too sophisticated to sell well, went bankrupt. Although not legally obligated to do so, Curtis shouldered a staggering debt in an act of impressive personal probity. It took him sixteen years of tireless writing, lecturing, and abstemious living to repay all creditors in full. Some of his sizable earnings came from "The Lounger" columns—entertaining but light—that he wrote for *Harper's Weekly* from 1857 to 1863. He also serialized *Trumps*, his only novel, in *Harper's Weekly* (1859–1860). It was published in book form in 1861. Though popular, *Trumps* dismally combines social and political realism, romantic sentimentality, and a needlessly sad ending. Curtis was an effective Republican party campaigner for Abraham Lincoln in 1860. In 1863 Curtis became political editor of *Harper's Weekly* and continued in that capacity until 1892, despite occasional internal squabbles, mainly with the "immoderate" cartoonist Thomas Nast.

Appointed a regent of the University of the State of New York in 1864, Curtis helped supervise New York's educational system and sought to implement adult extension studies. He tried but failed to obtain the Republican nomination for U.S. senator from New York in 1866. He served as a delegate to a convention formed to revise the state's constitution in 1867–1868. The Republicans nominated him by acclamation to be New York's secretary of state, but he declined the job as well as an invitation to be the editor of the *New York Times* in 1869. After teaching briefly at Cornell University, he sought but failed to obtain the Republican nomination for New York governor in

1870. President Ulysses S. Grant appointed him to chair a seven-man commission to study measures for civil-service reform in 1871–1873. Amid these and other activities, Curtis spoke far and wide in favor of free speech, organized labor, common sense in government, and woman suffrage. His recommendations for civil-service reform, mainly to replace the spoils system by appointing government workers for approved merit, were largely ignored by Grant but were implemented by Presidents Rutherford B. Hayes and James Garfield.

Curtis remained active in his last decade of life. In 1884 he and several other influential political thinkers deserted the Republican party, formed the independent "Mugwumps," and shifted their support to Democrat Grover Cleveland, the successful candidate for president. Two years later Curtis was appointed vice chancellor of the University of the State of New York; in 1890 he was named chancellor. He wrote at his Staten Island home and his summer residence at Ashfield, Massachusetts. He died in his home on Staten Island.

In all, Curtis wrote about forty books and pamphlets, two dozen poems, and more than sixty periodical articles and stories (in addition to innumerable columns and several miscellaneous pieces). He edited the American historian John Lothrop Motley's correspondence. But better than any of Curtis's writings was his inspiring example. He willingly sacrificed a promising career in literature to serve his fellow citizens by writing and speaking out about the momentous issues of the day.

• Curtis's letters are widely scattered, and many libraries own major collections. In addition to the institutions listed in J. Albert Robbins, ed., *American Literary Manuscripts*, 2d ed. (1977), Curtis's manuscripts are held by the Fruitland Museum, Harvard University, and the Paulist Fathers, New York City. An old-fashioned laudatory biography is Edward Cary, *George William Curtis* (1894). Gordon Milne's excellent *George William Curtis and the Genteel Tradition* (1956) includes an exhaustive primary and secondary bibliography. William Morton Payne has a fine chapter on Curtis in his *Leading American Essayists* (1910). Frank Luther Mott in *A History of American Magazines, 1850–1865* and in *A History of American Magazines, 1865–1885* (both 1938) points out the power and influence of Curtis as an editor of and contributor to leading American magazines of his time. William W. Stowe, *Going Abroad: European Travel in Nineteenth-Century American Culture* (1994), offers excellent comments on Curtis's *Potiphar's Papers*. Alexander Cowie in *The Rise of the American Novel* (1951) astutely analyzes the political features of *Trumps*. An extended eulogistic obituary is Curtis's close friend Parke Godwin's *George William Curtis: A Commemorative Address* (1893).

ROBERT L. GALE

CURTIS, Heber Doust (27 June 1872–9 June 1942), astronomer, was born in Muskegon, Michigan, the son of Blair Curtis, a one-armed Union army veteran, schoolteacher, editor, and customs official, and Sarah Eliza Doust. The family moved to Detroit when Heber was seven years old, and he received a classical education at Detroit High School. He was good in mathe-

matics but showed little interest in science. After high school he entered the University of Michigan at Ann Arbor, where he was elected to Phi Beta Kappa and earned his A.B. in three years (1892) and his A.M. one year later. Curtis had decided to be a teacher of classical languages, and he took all the Latin and Greek courses then offered at Michigan, as well as two years of Hebrew, two of Assyrian, and one of Sanskrit. In his four years at Michigan he never entered the astronomical observatory, but he was interested in machine-tool work from boyhood.

After graduation Curtis taught Latin at Detroit High School for six months and then was offered a position in 1894 as professor of Latin and Greek at Napa College, a small Methodist institution near San Francisco. The school had a small refracting telescope, and he became interested in astronomy. In 1895 Curtis married Mary D. Raper, with whom he had four children. In 1896 Napa College merged with the College of the Pacific, then located in San Jose, and within one year Curtis made a highly unusual career switch to become professor of mathematics and astronomy. He spent six weeks of his summer vacation of 1897 at nearby Lick Observatory as a special student and volunteer assistant to supplement his own independent study in astronomy. Its director, Edward S. Holden, encouraged Curtis's interest and welcomed him to the mountain-top observatory. Curtis spent the next summer at Lick as well and the summer of 1899 back in Ann Arbor studying celestial mechanics.

In 1900 he joined the Lick expedition, headed by research astronomer W. Wallace Campbell, to Thomaston, Georgia, to observe the total solar eclipse. Curtis's ability and resourcefulness in helping set up, test, and use the eclipse apparatus made a strong impression on Campbell, who encouraged Curtis's desire to go back to graduate school and recommended him strongly to the University of Virginia. Curtis took his family to Charlottesville as a reentry student in the fall, with a fellowship paying $350 per year. He received his Ph.D. in 1902 and was immediately hired on the Lick Observatory staff by Campbell, who by then had succeeded to the directorship.

Curtis's eighteen years at Lick were the most productive of his career. At first he worked as an assistant to Campbell on his new radial-velocity program. But Curtis did not limit himself to the 36-inch refractor and its spectrograph; he familiarized himself with all the instruments at the observatory and suggested improvements to many of them, based on his mechanical skills. Campbell sent Curtis to take charge of the Lick southern station at Santiago, Chile, in 1906 and to measure the radial velocities of the stars in the southern sky. As always, Curtis succeeded in obtaining large amounts of high-quality data for his chief. When he returned to Lick at Mount Hamilton in 1910, Campbell assigned him to take over the Crossley 36-inch reflecting telescope and the program of nebular research that James E. Keeler had begun and Charles D. Perrine had continued.

In the next ten years, with the Crossley telescope, Curtis made his greatest contributions to astronomy. He was a skilled, highly intelligent observer, with the ability to recognize important problems, frame creative hypotheses, and test them at the telescope. He obtained excellent photographs of all kinds of nebulae, classified them, and described their forms. His pioneering photographic survey of planetary nebulae established that many of them have structures with axial rather than spherical symmetry. He recognized as "peculiar" objects such as the Crab nebula and the "jet" (as it is now known) in the elliptical "nebula" M87, both found years later to be among the strongest radio sources in the sky.

Curtis was a great pioneer in the study of nebulae and galaxies, which he recognized for what they were by his careful observations and creative thinking. His greatest triumph was his recognition that the spiral "nebulae" that Keeler had found to be so numerous in the sky, actually were galaxies—remote star systems or "island universe." Between 1911 and 1917 Curtis reached this conclusion from his study of the long-exposure photographs he obtained at the Crossley reflector. From then he came to understand that the dark markings, so prominent in the nearly edge-on objects, result from obscuring material within the galaxies, "interstellar dust" in current terminology. Curtis recognized the analogy between our Milky Way and edge-on spirals and suspected that they, and hence all spiral "nebulae," are star systems. In 1917 George Willis Ritchey discovered a faint "new" star on a photograph he had taken of a spiral with the 60-inch Mount Wilson reflector and followed it up with several more discoveries from earlier photographs of similar objects. Curtis immediately realized that this result provided the direct, quantitative proof that he had been seeking that the spirals *are* galaxies and that they are far distant from our own galaxy, because the new stars in them appear so much fainter than those in our system.

In a perceptive 1919 paper Curtis summarized the evidence that spiral "nebulae" are actually remote star systems like our galaxy. He was invited to lecture summarizing this picture before the National Academy of Sciences in 1920 in what came to be called "the Great Debate." Harlow Shapley took the opposite point of view, that the spirals are nebulae within our galaxy. A few years later Edwin Hubble's evidence, gained with the 100-inch Mount Wilson reflector, convinced even Shapley that he had been wrong.

Curtis left Lick Observatory in 1920 to become the director of the Allegheny Observatory of the University of Pittsburgh. He had hoped to continue his observational studies with the Allegheny's 30-inch reflector, but he soon learned that the light and smoke pollution of the big city made this impossible. He devoted himself to an ongoing parallax program, to instrumentation, to eclipse expeditions, and to writing an excellent review article on nebulae for the *Handbuch der Astrophysik* (1933). In 1930 Curtis returned to his alma mater, the University of Michigan, as director of its

observatory. He had plans for a large reflecting telescope, which he secretly hoped to locate in California, with its much better observing climate than Michigan's, but the Great Depression destroyed any possibility of raising the funds. The later years of Curtis's life were troubled by a serious thyroid disease, of which he died in Ann Arbor.

• Curtis's papers are in the Heber D. Curtis Papers and the Department of Astronomy Papers in the Bentley Historical Library, University of Michigan, Ann Arbor; in the Allegheny Observatory Papers in the Archives of Industrial Society, Hillman Library, University of Pittsburgh; and in the Mary Lea Shane Archives of the Lick Observatory, University Library, University of California, Santa Cruz. Published memorial biographies are Robert R. McMath, "Heber Doust Curtis 1872–1942," *Publications of the Astronomical Society of the Pacific* 54 (1942): 69–71; H. Spencer Jones, "Heber Doust Curtis," *Monthly Notices of the Royal Astronomical Society* 103 (1943): 73–75; and Robert G. Aitken, "Heber Doust Curtis 1872–1942," National Academy of Sciences, *Biographical Memoirs* 22 (1943): 275–94. The last contains a complete bibliography of Curtis's published scientific papers and books. A more informal reminiscence is Joel Stebbins, "Heber D. Curtis and the Michigan Telescope," *Publications of the University of Michigan Observatory* 10 (1951): 1–5. Other useful articles dealing with Curtis's research are two by M. A. Hoskin in *Journal for the History of Astronomy* 7 (1976), "Ritchey, Curtis, and the Discovery of Novae in Spiral Nebulae," pp. 45–53, and "The 'Great Debate': What Really Happened," pp. 169–82, and Donald E. Osterbrock, "The Observational Approach to Cosmology: U.S. Observatories Pre–World War II" in *Modern Cosmology in Retrospect*, ed. B. Bertotti et al. (1990). Also excellent is Robert W. Smith, *The Expanding Universe: Astronomy's "Great Debate," 1900–1931* (1982).

DONALD E. OSTERBROCK

CURTIS, John Green (29 Oct. 1844–20 Sept. 1913), physiologist, surgeon, and medical educator, was born in New York City, the son of George Curtis, president of the Continental Bank, and Julia B. Bridgham. Curtis attended private schools as a child and received private tutoring to prepare him for Harvard College. He graduated from that institution in 1866 with an A.B. and again in 1869 with an M.A. On 1 April 1869 Bellevue Hospital appointed him junior assistant physician for six months, then senior assistant for six additional months, and finally house surgeon for six months. In 1870 Curtis received his medical degree from the College of Physicians and Surgeons. After graduation from medical school he entered private practice and became a junior partner with Henry B. Sands. Curtis married Martha McCook Davis in 1871.

In 1870 the College of Physicians and Surgeons, which was associated with Columbia College and which became part of Columbia in 1891, appointed Curtis assistant demonstrator in anatomy—a post he held for five years until his appointment as adjunct lecturer in the physiology department headed by John Call Dalton. The following year Curtis was promoted to adjunct professor of physiology. He also served as attending surgeon at Bellevue from 1876 to 1880. When Dalton became dean of the medical school in

1883, Curtis succeeded him as professor of physiology and gave up clinical medicine entirely. He held the post until his retirement as an emeritus professor in 1909. Curtis was secretary of the faculty at Columbia University from 1876 to 1890 and was dean of the medical school for one year. Although not actively engaged in experimental work, Curtis equipped the physiology laboratory at the medical school—which moved in the 1880s from Twenty-third Street to Fifty-ninth Street—with apparatus he purchased while traveling in Europe. The funds for the equipment came from a $10,000 donation in the memory of Foster Swift, an 1857 graduate of the college. In 1890 Curtis petitioned the president of Columbia, James McLane, to provide a full-time assistant to facilitate the introduction of experimental physiology into the curriculum of the college. Previously Curtis supported an assistant, Warren Lombard, from personal funds. As Dalton had incorporated Claude Bernard's approach to physiology for a previous generation, so Curtis assimilated Carl Ludwig's approach for his generation.

Curtis was instrumental in the rise and professionalization of experimental physiology in the United States. At a meeting held on 30 December 1887 in his laboratory at Columbia, Curtis, along with Henry Pickering Bowditch, Russell Henry Chittenden, Henry Newell Martin, and Silas Weir Mitchell, founded the American Physiological Society. He served for six years on the first council of the society and attended the society's annual meetings. Curtis was also active in addressing the charges of antivivisectionists. In 1883 Curtis submitted a report of the committee on experimental medicine that defended the use of living animals for scientific medicine. He also contributed to the *American Text-Book of Physiology*, published in 1896 and edited by William Henry Howell, professor of physiology at the Johns Hopkins University Medical School. Curtis wrote part one of the chapter on circulation titled "The Mechanics of the Circulation of the Blood and of the Movement of the Lymph." Beginning with the anatomy of the vascular system, Curtis reviewed the physical forces involved in the circulation of blood and lymph throughout that system. He also covered the cardiac cycle, including the heart sounds. He concluded his contribution by discussing the arterial pulse. His section not only included the latest research on circulatory physiology but also was sympathetic to the historical origins and development of physiological concepts. The second part of the circulation chapter was "The Innervation of the Heart" by William T. Porter.

Besides his effort to establish experimental physiology at Columbia, Curtis also delved into the history of physiology. He studied and translated sections from ancient Greek and Latin texts by writers in the life sciences—a skill he acquired while a student at Harvard. In 1900 Curtis gave the Cartwright Lectures at the New York Academy of Medicine. The title of his lecture was "The Discovery of the Nerves and Their Function." At the time of his death at his country home in Chatham, Massachusetts, Curtis left a number of unpublished manuscripts on the history of physiology. One such manuscript was a lecture on William Harvey that he delivered in 1907 to the Johns Hopkins Hospital Historical Club. Frederic S. Lee, his successor to the chair of physiology at Columbia, published posthumously Curtis's lecture as *Harvey's Views of the Use of the Circulation of the Blood* (1915). "If [Curtis's] work is to be summarized in a single sentence," wrote Lee in prefatory remarks, "it may be said that he has shown Harvey to be a disciple more of Aristotle than of Galen" (Lee, p. vii).

In a tribute to his mentor published in the *Columbia University Quarterly*, Lee stated that Curtis "was a man of a lovable personality, of a superior culture, always the gentleman, a lover of high thoughts, a follower of noble ideals, a hater of sham and pretense, generous to others, and considerate of others' shortcomings" (p. 54). Certainly Curtis contributed much to the rise of science, as well as to the advance of medicine, in the United States.

• The Curtis papers are at the Augustus C. Long Health Sciences Library, Columbia University. For biographical information on Curtis, as well as relevant background, see John Shrady, ed., *The College of Physicians and Surgeons, New York, and Its Founders, Officers, Instructors, Benefactors and Alumni: A History*, vol. 2 (n.d.); Frederic S. Lee, "John Green Curtis," *Columbia University Quarterly* (Dec. 1913): 54–57; William Henry Howell, "The American Physiological Society during Its First Twenty-five Years," in *History of the American Physiological Society: Semicentennial, 1887–1937* (1938); Toby A. Appel, "Founding," in *History of the American Physiological Society: The First Century, 1887–1987*, ed. John R. Brobeck et al. (1987); and W. Bruce Fye, *The Development of American Physiology: Scientific Medicine in the Nineteenth Century* (1987).

JAMES A. MARCUM

CURTIS, King (7 Feb. 1934–13 Aug. 1971), saxophonist, was born Curtis Ousley in Fort Worth, Texas, and adopted by William Ousley, a guitarist, and Ethel (maiden name unknown) of Mansfield, Texas. He began playing saxophone at about the age of twelve, initially playing alto saxophone, but later switching to tenor, which remained his principal instrument. He performed in the school band at I. M. Terrell High School, where he also learned baritone saxophone. Around the age of fifteen he began leading his own group, playing at the Paradise Inn in Fort Worth and becoming a protégé of its proprietor Aaron Watkins. In 1952, on a visit to an uncle in New York City, he twice won the amateur contest at the Harlem Apollo Theatre. On this visit he also made his first issued recordings with the Doc Pomus All Stars, including Mickey Baker, and the Doc Kent Band.

Curtis subsequently toured with a band that included Lester Young, then returned to Texas to continue his education; he had offers of scholarships from Bishop College and Wyley College. He made further records in Fort Worth, most of which feature vocalist Melvin Daniels, and performed with a band led by Red Connor, which also included Ornette Coleman and David "Fathead" Newman. In 1953 he joined Lionel Hampton's orchestra when they passed through Fort Worth, staying for several months and leaving in New York City, where he had arranged to study saxophone with jazz musician Garvin Bushell.

In New York City Curtis worked a variety of musical jobs including engagements with the society bands of Art Mooney and Lester Lanin, as well as many jazz and rhythm and blues dates, including with Doc Pomus and guitarist Mickey Baker at Snooky's in Manhattan. He formed his own trio, initially with pianist Horace Silver and drummer Osie Johnson, later replaced by Earl Knight and Lenny McBrowne respectively. As a result of this exposure, he was able to embark on a career as a session musician, which began on 14 December 1955 when he recorded with "Mr. Bear" (Teddy McRae) for RCA's Groove subsidiary.

For the remainder of his life Curtis was in constant demand as an accompanist and recorded for many record companies with hundreds of performers. They included jazz, blues, and rhythm and blues artists, such as Sammy Price, Joe Turner, Ruth Brown, LaVern Baker, and Mickey & Sylvia (Mickey Baker and Sylvia Vanderpool), and also popular vocalists, among them Buddy Holly and, later, John Lennon, and vocal groups, including the Isley Brothers, The Drifters, and The Coasters. He even worked occasionally behind country and western performers, including Lester Flatt and Earl Scruggs on a CBS TV special in 1961. He is featured on numerous pop hits of which The Coasters' *Yakety Yak* (1958) is perhaps the best known.

Away from the studios, Curtis led a quintet that held residencies at the Club Baby Grand in Brooklyn and Small's Paradise in Harlem. He also became involved in the development of rock and roll, appearing in Alan Freed's show at the Brooklyn Paramount (30 Aug.–8 Sept. 1957). At Small's Paradise he was heard by record producer Bobby Robinson, under whose direction he began to achieve popular hits under his own name, such as *Soul Twist* (1962). On some of these records he also sang. In the wake of this success, his groups appeared regularly during the 1960s at prestigious New York City venues such as the Harlem Apollo, Birdland, and the Village Gate. In 1965 Curtis and his orchestra were chosen to be the feature attraction supporting the British pop group The Beatles on their American tour that began at Shea Stadium, New York City, on 15 August.

In the 1960s Curtis's session work was mainly for Atlantic Records, and he accompanied many of their star blues, soul, and popular singers, including Freddie King, Wilson Pickett, Roberta Flack, and Aretha Franklin. His own band recorded extensively as King Curtis & The Kingpins after a brief incarnation as The Noble Knights. In this period he began doubling on the saxello, a variant of the soprano saxophone.

In 1971 Curtis became Aretha Franklin's musical director and accompanied her on a European tour in June, during which he also played and recorded at the Montreux Jazz Festival in Switzerland. He returned to the United States the following month, and at the time of his death he was musical director of the Channel 13 TV show *Soul*, for which he wrote the musical theme *Soulful 13*. He died in New York City of stab wounds received during a fight that developed when he tried to drive off two drug addicts who were blocking access to a building that he owned at 50 West Eighty-sixth Street. He was survived by his wife Ethelynn, from whom he had been estranged for seven years, and a son.

Curtis belonged to the group of jazz tenor saxophonists often referred to as the Southwestern school and played in an intense, full-toned, muscular style related to that of Arnett Cobb and Illinois Jacquet. His musical reputation suffered in his lifetime from his extensive involvement with commercial and novelty music, but his best recorded work, much of which is to be found in his accompaniments to blues singers such as Roosevelt Sykes, Sunnyland Slim, and Champion Jack Dupree, shows him a worthy and inspired representative of the style. He is also regarded as one of the most significant instrumentalists in the rock and roll and soul idioms.

• Roy Simonds, *King Curtis, A Discography* (1984), is a comprehensive listing of his work in all musical idioms. Simonds edited a magazine devoted to Curtis's work under the names the *Sound* (issues 2–7, 1985–1986) and *Boss* (issues 8–19, 1986–1988), which included extensive supplements to the discography as well as much other material on Curtis's life and work. His jazz, blues, and rhythm-and-blues records only can also be found in Walter Bruyninckx, *70 Years of Recorded Jazz, 1917–1987* (1987–). There is an assessment by Joël Dufour in *Soul Bag* 65 (Jan. 1978): 13–25. Obituaries are in the *New York Times*, 15 Aug. 1971, and the *Fort Worth Telegram*, 19 Aug. 1971.

HOWARD RYE

CURTIS, Moses Ashley (11 May 1808–10 Apr. 1872), botanist and Episcopal minister, was born in Stockbridge, Massachusetts, the son of Jared Curtis, a teacher and prison chaplain, and Thankful Ashley, the daughter of revolutionary war general Moses Ashley. Young Curtis received his early education at home and at Stockbridge Academy, a private school where his father was preceptor. He first became interested in botany at the age of nine, when public lectures on the subject were given in his home town by Amos Eaton. Curtis enrolled at Williams College in 1823 and graduated with an A.B. in 1827. He studied at Auburn Theological Seminary in 1827 and 1828 and worked as a teacher in Malden and Waterboro, Massachusetts, in 1829 and 1830.

In October 1830 Curtis moved to Wilmington, North Carolina, to serve as a tutor in the household of General Edward B. Dudley, later governor of North Carolina. Although he had no botanical training, Curtis soon developed an enthusiasm for collecting and classifying plants. Encouraged by James F. McRee, a local physician and botanist, Curtis began a study of the rich flora of the southeastern coastal plain around Wilmington. He acquired a copy of Stephen Elliott's multivolume *A Sketch of the Botany of South Carolina and Georgia* (1816–1824) and began corresponding with botanist William Darlington of West Chester, Pennsylvania. By 1833 Curtis had decided to become an Episcopal minister; he returned to Massachusetts to pursue his new career. On his way north he visited Darlington in Philadelphia and, in New York City, met John Torrey and Asa Gray, who were to emerge as the leaders of American botany during the middle of the nineteenth century. In 1834 Curtis returned to Wilmington and marked the occasion of his first botanical publication, "Enumeration of Plants Growing Spontaneously around Wilmington, N.C.," which listed more than 1,000 species recorded within a two-mile radius of the city. Curtis married Mary Jane de Rosset in 1834; they had ten children.

Ordained to the ministry in 1835, Curtis was assigned to mission work in western North Carolina, where his constant traveling on behalf of the church provided him an opportunity to explore portions of the botanically diverse southern Blue Ridge Mountains. From 1837 to 1839 he was a teacher and headmaster of the Episcopal School in Raleigh, North Carolina, where he began corresponding with New England botanist Edward Tuckerman, who received lichens from Curtis over the following decades. The rigorous demands of the Episcopal School proved too much for Curtis, and he resigned in the spring of 1839 because of poor health. He was ordained to the priesthood in May of the same year and spent much of the summer exploring and collecting plants in the southern Blue Ridge in an effort to regain his strength. The mountain sojourn enabled Curtis to search a region made famous by the earlier botanical labors of William Bartram, André Michaux, John Fraser, and John Lyon. From 1840 to 1841 Curtis was assigned to mission work in Washington, North Carolina, where he continued his local plant studies and began corresponding with George Engelmann, a botanist in St. Louis, Missouri.

In 1841 Curtis was appointed minister of St. Matthews Episcopal Church in Hillsboro (later Hillsborough), North Carolina. Determined to make a major contribution to American botany, Curtis decided in 1846 that he should turn his energies to mycology, the study of fungi, which remained a comparatively unexplored discipline in the United States. Gray informed Curtis that any assistance in this field would have to be sought abroad; therefore, in 1847 Curtis initiated correspondence with the Reverend Miles Joseph Berkeley, the renowned English mycologist. Their exchange of specimens and data and their personal and professional association combined to establish a solid scientific basis for North American mycology. Curtis also began correspondence with other scientists during this period, including botanist A. W. Chapman and mycologists Henry William Ravenel of South Carolina and Elias Fries of Upsala, Sweden.

Curtis left Hillsboro in 1847 to assume the pastoral duties at the Episcopal church in Society Hill, South Carolina, where he remained until 1856. During this time, Captain Charles Wilkes asked Curtis to assist in identifying the plants obtained by the U.S. Exploring Expedition to the Pacific islands and Pacific rim of 1838–1842. Curtis declined to work on the entire collection but agreed to examine the fungi, which were sent to him for review in 1849 and 1850. In 1848 his first paper dealing with fungi was published, appearing in the *American Journal of Science and Arts*; in 1849 he was elected to membership in the American Association for the Advancement of Science. While living in Society Hill, Curtis was able to devote considerable time and effort to mycology, and he and Berkeley determined to produce a landmark publication on the fungi of North America. A critical step in the process was for Curtis to review the enormous collection of Lewis David von Schweinitz, whose pioneering labors in the field remained the high watermark of American mycology at that time. In 1851 Curtis was able to visit Philadelphia and begin his examination of the von Schweinitz herbarium, which was housed at the Academy of Natural Sciences. Realizing that the vast collection could not be reviewed in the little time that he had available, Curtis negotiated an arrangement with the academy that permitted him to remove duplicate specimens that would then be analyzed at his leisure at home. By 1852 Curtis was immersed in the study of the duplicate von Schweinitz fungi, an effort that continued jointly with Berkeley for many years. Curtis did not limit his natural history activities to plants, however, as he sent many mammal skins to Spencer F. Baird at the Smithsonian Institution in 1855 and 1856.

Curtis resigned from his pastorate in Society Hill in 1856, and in 1857 he returned to be minister of St. Matthews Church in Hillsboro, where he remained until his death. In 1857 he was selected to help organize the University of the South at Sewanee, Tennessee, and in the same year he and Berkeley began analysis of the fungi collected by Charles Wright on the Pacific Exploring Expedition. From 1859 to 1863 Curtis served as botanist and zoologist under Ebenezer Emmons, director of the North Carolina Geological Survey, who hired Curtis specifically to write a comprehensive flora and fauna of the state. The first portion, Curtis's *Catalogue of the Plants of the State*, was printed in 1860, but the onset of the Civil War effectively prevented any further publication until after the termination of hostilities. In 1867 Curtis produced the second portion of his flora of North Carolina, the *Catalogue of the Indigenous and Naturalized Plants of the State*, which contained accounts of more than 4,800 species, including both flowering plants and fungi. The *Catalogue* was widely hailed as one of the most comprehensive and authoritative state floras published to that time. Although Curtis had finished the manuscript on the quadrupeds of North Carolina and was drafting the text for the birds of the state, the economic situation in the years following the war precluded any funding to see these works into print, and they remain unpublished. Curtis sent many zoological specimens to Baird at the Smithsonian during this time; unfortunately many of his bird skins were later destroyed by family members after his death. Curtis had also developed an illustrated manuscript on edible fungi, as he believed that many species could be used to provide nutrition for Confederate troops and for the civilian population. After the Civil War Curtis resumed correspondence with Gray, Baird, Berkeley, and other colleagues who had been unable to contact him during the conflict. Although Curtis and Berkeley continued their plans for a great "Mycologia Americana," the project had not materialized at the time of Curtis's sudden death. The bulk of his collaborative efforts with Berkeley were subsequently published by Berkeley, with credit to Curtis, as "Notices of North American Fungi," appearing in London from 1872 to 1876 in volumes one through four of *Grevillea*.

Curtis was widely admired and respected in the scientific world and within the Episcopal church. He was noted particularly for his insistence on the highest possible standards of accuracy and clarity in scientific research and publishing. Harvard botanist Gray noted his "unremitting and well-directed labors" and his "honored and faithful professional life." Considering that Curtis was almost entirely self-taught in botanical matters, his accomplishments are the more remarkable, particularly Gray's comment that Curtis had become the "highest American authority" in the extraordinarily difficult field of mycology. A. W. Chapman dedicated his *Flora of the Southern United States* (1860) to Curtis. Curtis was also a skilled musician and composer, who wrote a number of hymns and sermons. Curtis died in Hillsboro.

• The major repository of Curtis's manuscripts is the Southern Historical Collection at the University of North Carolina, Chapel Hill; other important manuscript material is in the Spencer F. Baird Papers at the Smithsonian Institution Archives, the Asa Gray Papers at Harvard University's Arnold Arboretum, the John Torrey Papers at the New York Botanical Garden, and the Miles Joseph Berkeley Papers at the Museum of Natural History in London. Among the more important publications by Curtis are his *Geological and Natural History Survey of North Carolina: Part III, Botany: Containing a Catalogue of the Plants of the State, with Descriptions and History of the Trees, Shrubs, and Woody Vines* (1860); *Geological and Natural History Survey of North Carolina: Part III, Botany: Containing a Catalogue of the Indigenous and Naturalized Plants of the State* (1867); and M. J. Berkeley and M. A. Curtis, "Contributions to the Mycology of North America," *American Journal of Science and Arts*, 2d ser., 8 (1849): 401–3; 9 (1850): 171–75; 10 (1850): 185–88; and 11 (1851): 93–95. The major reference on Curtis and his botanical work is Edmund Berkeley and Dorothy S. Berkeley, *A Yankee Botanist in the Carolinas: The Reverend Moses Ashley Curtis, D.D. (1808–1872)* (1986), which contains a portrait, an extended bibliography, a list of manuscript repositories, and details of herbarial collections containing specimens collected by Curtis. The extensive correspondence between Curtis and Berkeley is found in Ronald H. Petersen, *The Mycological Association of M. J. Berkeley and M. A. Curtis* (1980). For a review of zoological contributions made by Curtis, see Marcus B. Simpson, Jr., and Sallie W. Simpson, "Moses Ashley Curtis (1808–1872): Contributions to Carolina Ornithology," *North Carolina Historical Review* 60 (1983): 137–70. Other important sources on Curtis include William S. Powell, *Moses Ashley Curtis 1808–1872: Teacher-Priest-Scientist* (1958); Asa

Gray, "Moses Ashley Curtis," *American Journal of Science and Arts* 5 (1873): 351–53; Frans A. Stafleu and R. S. Cowan, *Taxonomic Literature*, vol. 1 (1976); Thomas F. Wood, "A Sketch of the Botanical Work of the Rev. Moses Ashley Curtis, D.D.," *Journal of the Elisha Mitchell Scientific Society* 2 (1884–1885): 9–31; and C. L. Shear and Neil E. Stevens, "The Mycological Work of Moses Ashley Curtis," *Mycologia* 11 (1919): 181–201. Major collections of Curtis's plants are in the Farlow herbarium at Harvard and in the botany department at the University of North Carolina at Chapel Hill. A contemporary obituary is in the *American Journal of Science and Arts*, 3d ser. (1873).

MARCUS B. SIMPSON

CURTIS, Natalie (26 Apr. 1875–23 Oct. 1921), ethnomusicologist, was born in New York City, the daughter of Edward Curtis, a physician, and Augusta Lawler Stacey. She studied piano with Arthur Friedheim in New York, and later with Ferruccio Busoni in Berlin, Alfred-August Giraudet in Paris, Leonhard Wolff in Bonn, and Julius Kniese in Bayreuth. After her return to the United States around 1900, Curtis visited her brother in Arizona and encountered the songs and ceremonies of Native Americans. Fearing that this music was in immediate danger of vanishing forever, she decided to postpone her career as a pianist and composer in favor of recording the music and songs of the Indian tribes.

At the time, however, the U.S. government's policy of Indian assimilation prohibited the singing of tribal songs in federal schools, so Curtis made a personal appeal to President Theodore Roosevelt. His lifting of the ban enabled Curtis to pursue her research in the field, where with phonograph cylinders and written notation, she recorded the musical melodies and songs of at least eighteen tribes, particularly the Apache, Hopi, Navajo, Pima, Pueblo, and Yuma tribes of the Southwest, and the Arapaho, Cheyenne, Dakota, Kiowa, and Pawnee tribes of the Great Plains. This research culminated in the publication of *The Indians' Book* (1907), which contained transcriptions of some 200 songs collected from these tribes, as well as illustrations and contextual information on the tribes' folklore and cultural beliefs.

Although preservation had been Curtis's primary concern initially, she continued her field research in part to promote the wider cause of Native Americans. In "A Plea for Our Native Art," published in *Musical Quarterly* (Apr. 1920), she urged her fellow citizens "to fight at home for rights not political merely, but spiritual and cultural as well—the right of the American Indian to *be himself*; to express his own ideals of beauty and fitness in his religion, his customs, his dress and in his art." Accordingly, Curtis continued to visit Indian reservations, particularly among the Pueblos of the Southwest, in order to share with them the results of her ethnomusicological fieldwork.

Meanwhile, Curtis was also extending her efforts to the cause of African-American music and culture. A few years after the publication of *The Indians' Book*, she was instrumental in 1911–1912 in establishing in Harlem the Music School Settlement for Colored People, which was intended not only to preserve African-American music but, moreover, to serve as a social and educational center for its expression. Curtis also was credited with organizing, as a fundraiser for the school, perhaps the first formal concert of African-American music intended for a white audience. Defying the skepticism of New York society, Curtis and Elbridge L. Adams, president of the Music School Settlement, brought Harlem's Clef Club Orchestra featuring conductor James Reese Europe to Carnegie Hall for a sellout performance in May 1912. Several observers have credited that concert with establishing the vogue for African-American music that flowered after World War I during the Harlem Renaissance.

As a result of her success and obvious enthusiasm in promoting non-European music in the United States, Curtis was invited by the heads of the most prestigious African-American educational institutions to move south and "do for the black race what she had accomplished for the Indian." Curtis accepted the offer and established herself in residence at the Hampton Institute (now Hampton University) in Virginia, where she recorded and transcribed the spirituals, work songs, and play songs of both African and African-American students there. The results of her research appeared initially in several articles in musical as well as general-interest periodicals before culminating in the *Hampton Series Negro Folk-Songs* (4 vols., 1918–1919) and *Songs and Tales from the Dark Continent* (1920). The former consists of transcriptions Curtis made from spirituals and secular songs recorded in 1915 by two male quartets at Hampton, as well as an analysis of their harmonic improvisation; the latter examines the music and folklore of Kamba Simango (Ndau tribe) and Madikane Cele (Zulu tribe), two native African students at Hampton.

In the summer of 1921 Curtis traveled to Europe with her husband, the artist Paul Burlin, whom she had married in 1917. Several of her publications were being translated into French and German, and she was scheduled to give recitals of the songs she had collected. A few days after speaking on American folk music at the International Congress of Art History at the Sorbonne, she was fatally injured when struck by an automobile on a Paris street. Curtis is probably best remembered today for her pioneering work in the recording and transcribing of traditional songs and texts with which few other scholars at the time, much less classically trained musicians, were concerned. Although her recordings and observations have since been supplanted by more complete fieldwork, her enthusiasm and sympathy for her subjects helped inspire further such endeavors, bringing much-needed attention to the music of Native Americans and African Americans.

• The most extensive collection of Curtis's personal papers, including correspondence, clippings, musical compositions, and publications, is found at the University Archives of Hampton University. Also there are cassette tapes made from her recordings of African and African-American music. The Music Division at the Library of Congress holds four boxes of Curtis's handwritten transcriptions of songs, mostly Native American, organized according to tribe. The Denver Art Museum Library has a small collection of her field notes and music manuscripts. Wax cylinders of recordings made by Curtis of Native Americans and African Americans are found at both the Federal Cylinder Project in the Library of Congress and the Archives of Traditional Music at Indiana University. No biographies of Curtis have been published, but for appreciations of her life see Frances R. Grant, "World Loses Ardent Seeker of Truth in Natalie Curtis-Burlin," *Musical America* 35 (5 Nov. 1921): 47; Richard Aldrich, "Music," *New York Times*, 6 Nov. 1921; "Natalie Curtis Burlin," *Outlook* 129 (23 Nov. 1921): 458–59; "Natalie Curtis," *Southern Workman* 55 (Mar. 1926): 127–40; and Alfred R. Bredenberg, "Natalie Curtis Burlin (1875–1921): A Pioneer in the Study of American Minority Cultures," *Connecticut Review* 16 (Spring 1994): 1–15.

JAMES DEUTSCH

CURTIS, Olin Alfred (10 Dec. 1850–8 Jan. 1918), pastor and educator, was born in Frankfort, Maine, the son of Reuben Curtis, a minister, and Mary Gilbert. During his youth Curtis's family moved from Maine to Wisconsin, and as a young man he worked in business in Chicago, Illinois. Deeply influenced by the preaching of evangelist Dwight L. Moody, Curtis decided to prepare for the ministry. He graduated from Lawrence University in Appleton, Wisconsin, in 1877 and three years later received his B.D. from Boston University School of Theology. While in Boston the preaching of Episcopal rector Phillips Brooks and the lectures of reformer Wendell Phillips had a substantial influence on his theological and social views.

After pastoring Methodist congregations in Janesville (1880–1883) and Milwaukee (1883–1886), Wisconsin, Curtis studied theology for two years at the University of Leipzig in Germany. While serving the First Methodist Church, Englewood, in Chicago, he received an unexpected call in 1889 to be the chair of systematic theology at Boston University. During the six years he taught at the seminary, he did further graduate work in theology and philosophy at Erlangen in 1890, Marburg in 1893, and Edinburgh in 1894. Prompted by his growing uncertainty about his own theological position, Curtis resigned from Boston University in 1895 and spent time in Europe in a personal reexamination of his own theological convictions. Upon his return to the United States, he was elected in 1896 to succeed John Miley, a noted Methodist theologian, as professor of systematic theology at Drew Theological Seminary in Madison, New Jersey.

Through his eighteen-year tenure at Drew and through his many publications, Curtis had a significant impact on Methodist thought in the United States. Along with Milton Terry, Wilbur Tillett, Henry Sheldon, and Albert Knudson, he was an advocate of evangelical liberalism, a widely espoused position among Methodists that sought to reconcile the findings of biblical criticism with traditional Christian beliefs in the deity of Christ, the necessity of Christ's atonement for sin, the authority of the Bible, and the importance of personal conversion. Church historian John Faulkner, Curtis's colleague at Drew, contended that Curtis's approach to theology was both conservative and progressive; while still defending historic Christian faith, Curtis sought to inspire students not to simply accept Curtis's convictions but to develop their own understanding of God and the Scriptures through critical reflection and prayerful searching.

Curtis's thorough knowledge of the history of doctrine, his extensive study in German theology, his passion for English and American literature, his deep, personal interest in his students, and his inspiring and effective lectures combined to make him an outstanding professor. Although he was a rather thin, frail man whose health was never good, his lectures conveyed a spiritual and intellectual energy that powerfully challenged students and often left him feeling exhausted. One observer insisted that Curtis had an "unrivaled power of making systematic theology a commanding and vital matter in the lives of students" (Hough, p. 687). Hough maintained that through his teaching, Curtis made theology vivid, human, cosmopolitan, and dynamic.

In his major theological work, *The Christian Faith* (1905), Curtis acknowledged his debt to English writer Thomas Carlyle, who helped him to appreciate the ethical teachings of the Old Testament prophets, and to Methodist theologians Daniel Whedon, who convinced him that determinism could not be defended in either ethics or psychology, and Borden Bowne, who enabled him to understand the cosmic significance of personality. Curtis's theological treatise rested upon two primary ideas: personal responsibility and solidarity of all human beings. Every individual, he argued, was a responsible moral person, but no individual was complete by himself; each was created by God as a component of the larger human race. In this book Curtis sought to "exhibit the Christian faith as one mighty organic whole" by showing the underlying philosophical connections among biblical doctrines.

A man of wide-ranging interests, Curtis had a passion for baseball, classical music, horticulture, great novels, and books on Christian spirituality. Curtis strongly endorsed the U.S. war with Spain in 1898, and despite his poor health he served as a chaplain in the navy during the conflict. He carefully monitored American political life and enjoyed spending election nights with the crowd in Times Square. An admirer of Theodore Roosevelt, Curtis supported him as a Republican in 1904 and as a Progressive in 1912. Curtis was married three times. In 1880 he wed Eva Farlin, who died in 1883. He married Ellen Hunt in 1889. After her death in 1895, he married Ida Gorham in 1906. He had two daughters. Curtis died in Leonia, New Jersey.

Curtis was one of Methodism's leading theologians during the late nineteenth and early twentieth centuries. He was widely respected for his teachings and publications, and his theology was Christocentric. He insisted that the Bible "should be interpreted organically, out from the center, which is the atoning death

of Jesus Christ." Curtis prodded his denomination to provide leadership in movements to reform moral, social, political, and industrial conditions and to establish hospitals, homes for the aged and orphaned, and shelters for the homeless and abused. He argued, however, that "the main business of the church" was to convert individuals, place them in Christian fellowship, and equip them for serving others.

• Curtis's personal papers are at the Drew University Library Archives. Curtis provides a summary of his theology in "What I Believe," *Christian Advocate* 89 (19 Feb. 1914): 256–57. He also published *Elective Course of Lectures in Systematic Theology* (1901); *Personal Submission to Jesus Christ: Its Supreme Importance in the Christian Life and Theology* (1910); and *The Mountain and Other Nature Sketches* (1920). The best sources of information about Curtis's life, career, theology, and influence are Lynn Harold Hough, "Making Theology Live," *Methodist Review* 78 (Sept. 1918): 686–95; John Alfred Faulkner, "Dr. Olin A. Curtis," *Christian Advocate* 93 (17 Jan. 1918): 83; James Richard Joy, ed., *The Teachers of Drew, 1867–1942* (1942); and William P. Tolley, ed., *Alumni Record; Drew Theological Seminary, 1867–1925* (1926). For an analysis of his theological position, see Thomas Langford, *Wesleyan Theology: A Sourcebook* (1984), and Robert E. Chiles, *Theological Transition in American Methodism, 1790–1935* (1965). An obituary is in the *Christian Advocate* 93 (17 Jan. 1918): 68.

GARY SCOTT SMITH

CURTIS, Samuel Ryan (3 Feb. 1805–26 Dec. 1866), soldier and engineer, was born near Champlain, New York, the son of Zarah Curtis and Phalley Yale, farmers. In 1809 the family moved to Licking County, Ohio. Curtis obtained an appointment to the U.S. Military Academy and graduated in 1831. Later that year he married Belinda Buckingham; the couple had six children. Curtis served briefly with the Seventh Infantry at Fort Gibson, Indian Territory (present-day Oklahoma), but resigned his commission in 1832 and returned to Ohio. During the next decade he worked as an engineer on the National Road and was the chief engineer of the Muskingum River improvement project. He also studied law and was admitted to the Ohio bar in 1841. Curtis was active in the Ohio militia and was named adjutant general of the state when the Mexican War began, but he resigned in order to command the Third Ohio Infantry in the field. Much to his disappointment, he saw no action in Mexico but served as military governor of Matamoras, Camargo, Monterrey, and Saltillo.

After the war Curtis moved to Keokuk, Iowa. He was the chief engineer of the Des Moines River improvement project but was released when the project encountered financial difficulties. He drew up a plan to build a canal around the Mississippi River rapids at Keokuk, but the project was not undertaken until after his death. Frustrated at his lack of success in Iowa, Curtis worked for several years as chief engineer of the city of St. Louis. He constructed sewage and drainage systems and erected a dam that kept the Mississippi River flowing along the St. Louis waterfront. In 1853 he returned to Keokuk, opened a law office, and entered politics as a member of the fledgling Republican party. Reserved and undemonstrative, Curtis was not a natural politician, but he was widely respected for his integrity. He was elected mayor of Keokuk in 1856. Later that year he was elected to Congress from the First District of Iowa. In Congress Curtis served on the Committee on Military Affairs and actively promoted a transcontinental railroad, a project that he believed to be of the utmost national importance. Reelected in 1858 and 1860, he took part in the so-called Peace Convention in Washington in February 1861, which failed to solve the secession crisis. He loyally supported the Abraham Lincoln administration from the time of the inauguration in March.

When fighting erupted at Fort Sumter, Curtis hurried back to Iowa and helped to raise troops. He was elected colonel of the Second Iowa Infantry, the state's first three-year regiment. At the urging of Winfield Scott, the commanding general of the army, Curtis was commissioned a brigadier general of volunteers in May. He returned to Washington to attend a special session of Congress but resigned his seat in July because he felt he could be of more use as a soldier. His first assignment was in St. Louis, where he supervised military activities in the city and was instrumental in the removal of John C. Frémont from command of the Department of the Missouri. On 25 December 1861, the new department commander, Henry W. Halleck, placed Curtis in charge of the District of Southwest Missouri and directed him to drive Sterling Price's Confederates out of the state. Curtis and his small Army of the Southwest carried out a difficult but successful winter campaign atop the Ozark Plateau and pushed Price into northwestern Arkansas. There the Confederates, now led by Earl Van Dorn, were decisively defeated on 7–8 March at Pea Ridge. Two weeks later Curtis was promoted to major general of volunteers. During the next four months Curtis marched across Arkansas to Helena, 750 miles from his starting point in Rolla. Curtis demonstrated a high degree of tactical and administrative skill during the campaign.

In September 1862 Curtis returned to St. Louis and succeeded Halleck as commander of the Department of the Missouri. It was the high point of his military career. Unfortunately, Curtis failed to develop an effective means of suppressing the brutal guerrilla war raging in his department, and his increasingly radical political views embroiled him in difficulties with the more conservative governor of Missouri, H. R. Gamble. Unable to remove an elected governor, Lincoln instead removed Curtis in May 1863 and reassigned him to the Department of Kansas at the beginning of 1864. Though it seemed that he was now out of the war, Curtis unexpectedly made a final contribution to Union victory on 21–25 October 1864, when a scratch force under his command ended Price's Raid in a series of battles around Westport, Missouri, and Mine Creek, Kansas. Curtis personally pursued the fleeing Confederates all the way back to northwestern Arkansas. Despite his military accomplishments, Curtis was removed from the Department of Kansas in January 1865 and reassigned to the Department of the Northwest the following month. In September Curtis was one of six commissioners appointed to deal with the Sioux, Crow, Mandans, Gros Ventres, and other tribes along the upper Missouri River. It was his last military assignment; he was discharged from the army in April 1866.

During the war Curtis continued to press for a transcontinental railroad, and, in September 1862, he presided over the organizational meeting in Chicago of what would become the Union Pacific Railroad. Shortly after the close of the war, President Andrew Johnson appointed him to a three-man commission to examine newly laid sections of Union Pacific track on the Great Plains. Curtis had little time to enjoy being a part of the grand undertaking that he had advocated for so many years. He died suddenly near Council Bluffs, Iowa, while returning from an inspection trip in Nebraska.

• Personal papers are at the State Historical Society of Iowa, Des Moines; the Illinois State Historical Library, Springfield; Yale University; and the Huntington Library, San Marino, Calif. The only modern biography is Ruth Gallaher, "Samuel Ryan Curtis," *Iowa Journal of History and Politics* 25 (1927): 331–58, but Addison A. Stuart, *Iowa Colonels and Regiments* (1865), includes some useful information. Curtis is the central figure in William L. Shea and Earl J. Hess, *Pea Ridge: Civil War Campaign in the West* (1992). The Keokuk *Gate City*, 27 Dec. 1866, contains a detailed obituary.

WILLIAM L. SHEA

CURTISS, Glenn Hammond (21 May 1878–23 July 1930), aeronautical inventor and manufacturer, was born in Hammondsport, New York, the son of Frank R. Curtiss, the owner of a harness shop, and Lua Andrews. After the death of his father in 1883, Curtiss was raised by his mother and his strong-willed grandmother Ruth Curtiss in the bucolic Finger Lake region of western New York. After graduating from the eighth grade in 1892, Curtiss secured a job stenciling numbers on the backing of photographic film for the Eastman Dry Plant and Film Company (later Eastman Kodak Company) of Rochester. The next year he purchased a bicycle and found employment as a messenger for Western Union.

Bicycles became the center of Curtiss's life. He often cycled the seventy miles to Hammondsport to participate in bicycle races, and he acquired a reputation for speed and daring. On one of his weekend trips, Curtiss met Lena Pearl Neff, and they were married in 1898. The union produced two children, one of whom died in infancy.

Curtiss settled in Hammondsport after his marriage, working as a photographer for Saylor's Studio. Bicycles, however, remained his passion. In 1900 he opened a bicycle repair shop. Enamored with speed, he soon turned to motorcycles and designed a machine with a lightweight, high-power engine. The G. H. Curtiss Manufacturing Company, financed by local investors, began producing the Hercules motorcycle in 1902.

Curtiss became one of the best-known motorcycle racers of the day. Dubbed the "hell-rider" by sportswriters, he set world records for the mile (56⅖ seconds in 1903) and the ten-mile (8 minutes, 54⅖ seconds in 1904). In January 1907 he used a specially designed motorcycle with an eight-cylinder engine to establish a one-mile record of 136.3 miles per hour, the fastest speed then ever traveled by a human being.

Curtiss's lightweight, high-power engines attracted the attention of aeronautical experimenters, leading to a small sideline business for his company. In July 1904 Thomas Scott Baldwin used a Curtiss two-cylinder engine to power the *California Arrow*, the first successful dirigible to fly in the United States. Curtiss himself test flew a later version of the *Arrow* in July 1907, marking his first trip aloft.

Alexander Graham Bell, the famous inventor, also was impressed with the Curtiss engines. In July 1907, at Bell's invitation, Curtiss joined the Aerial Experiment Association (AEA) to work on the development of a man-carrying motorized kite and other aeronautical vehicles. Although Bell's kite proved a failure, the AEA's airplanes significantly advanced the new technology of powered flight. The AEA's *Red Wing* first flew (318′11″) on 12 March 1908, and two months later the improved *White Wing* took to the air. The *White Wing* employed Bell-conceived ailerons for lateral control, a system that was superior to the wing-warping used by Orville and Wilbur Wright. Curtiss made his first airplane flight in the *White Wing* on 21 May 1908, his thirtieth birthday.

Curtiss became an enthusiastic pilot. On 4 July 1908 he flew the AEA's *June Bug* more than one mile, easily winning the *Scientific American* trophy for the first public flight of more than a kilometer. The next year, after the dissolution of the AEA, Curtiss gained worldwide acclaim when he used an aircraft of his own design—known both as the *Gold Bug* and the *Golden Flier*—to capture the Gordon Bennett Trophy at the first international air meet, held in Rheims, France. Returning to the United States, Curtiss next competed for the $10,000 prize offered by the *New York World* for the first flight between Albany, New York, and New York City. On 29 May 1910 he successfully covered the 150 miles in two hours and fifty-one minutes, making two stops en route.

Curtiss's business acumen failed to keep pace with his growing piloting skills. In March 1909 he committed all his assets to a partnership with promoter Augustus M. Herring. In December 1910, however, the Herring-Curtiss Company went bankrupt, leaving a legacy of acrimonious legal complications that would last for years. Curtiss immediately formed the Curtiss Aeroplane Company, a business with $1,000 in initial working capital, and set out to rebuild his economic fortunes.

Although Curtiss became a noted exhibition flier, his interests soon shifted to the development of an airplane that could land on water. During the winter of 1910–1911 he established an aviation camp in San Diego, where he worked on a hydroplane and gave free flying lessons to military pilots. On 26 January 1911 he demonstrated a waterborne version of the basic Curtiss pusher biplane, and the next month he added a retractable wheeled landing gear to the pontoons. Impressed with the new amphibian, the U.S. Navy ordered its first aircraft, designating as A-1 the Curtiss *Triad*.

Curtiss next worked with navy pilots on the design of a flying boat. Unlike his earlier models, which were basically land planes with pontoons, his flying boat was a true seaplane that landed in the water on a hull. While landing was no problem, Curtiss discovered that suction held the hull on the water, preventing the airplane from taking off. His attempts to change the shape of the hull proved unavailing. He finally solved the problem by attaching pieces of wood to the hull, creating a shallow step. This design feature, which would become standard on flying boats, enabled the hull to break the suction and become airborne. The Curtiss "aeroboat" proved an immediate success, generating orders from both military and civilian customers.

Curtiss's growing manufacturing business led to a bitter patent battle with the Wright brothers. Holding a patent on their wing-warping control system, the Wrights sought an injunction against Curtiss. Curtiss, in turn, claimed that the aileron system did not infringe on the Wright patent. Although the Wrights ultimately prevailed in 1913, Curtiss paid no penalty, and a cross-licensing agreement permitted all manufacturers to continue production during the First World War.

On 13 January 1916 a Wall Street syndicate arranged for the formation of the Curtiss Aeroplane & Motor Company, capitalized at $9 million. Curtiss, who received $2.3 million in cash and $4.5 million in stock, became president of the new company. The larger financial base permitted rapid expansion as wartime contracts brought increased business. Employing 18,000 workers, the company's plants in the state of New York produced more than 10,000 aircraft in 1917–1918. The most widely used models were the JN-4 "Jenny" trainer (designed by D. Douglas Thomas) and the HS-1L coastal patrol flying boat.

Curtiss's efforts to develop a large flying boat culminated in 1919. He had long been interested in the possibility of a transatlantic flight. In 1914 he designed and built the *America*, a twin-engine flying boat that was to be used by Lieutenant John Cyril Porte of the Royal Navy for a planned ocean crossing. The outbreak of war in Europe, however, brought an end to the project.

In 1917 the success of the German U-boat campaign in the Atlantic led the U.S. Navy to contract with Curtiss for an experimental long-range patrol flying boat. The NC-1 first flew in October 1918. A modified version, powered by four 400-horsepower Liberty-12 engines, successfully flew six months later. Although too late for wartime purposes, the navy decided to use three of the large NC seaplanes for a transatlantic flight. One, the NC-4, became the first aircraft to cross the Atlantic when it flew from Newfoundland to Portugal (with stops) in May 1919. In many ways the triumph of the NC-4 represented a fitting climax to Curtiss's long and distinguished aeronautical career.

The Curtiss Aeroplane & Motor Company underwent major financial reorganization in 1920. Although retained as an adviser, Curtiss did not play a major role in the restructured company. Curtiss moved to southern Florida, where he became a real estate developer during the 1920s. He also invented and manufactured a streamlined trailer, called an "Aero-Car." A practicing Methodist since boyhood, he developed an interest in Christian Science. He died in Buffalo, New York, after suffering a pulmonary embolism while recovering from an operation for appendicitis.

Curtiss stands in the forefront of American aeronautical pioneers, second only to the Wright brothers in historical significance. A highly skilled pilot and flight instructor, he designed and built engines and aircraft that substantially advanced the new technology of aviation. Not a particularly reflective man, the taciturn and unpretentious Curtiss seemed most at ease when chatting with mechanics on a shop floor or discussing flight techniques with pilots. His innovative mind constantly sought practical solutions to the problems of flight. Whether designing a system of more efficient crankcase drainage for large engines or perfecting the flying boat, Curtiss demonstrated a talent for innovation that had few equals.

• The Curtiss papers are at the National Air and Space Museum in Washington, D.C. C. R. Roseberry, *Glenn Curtiss: Pioneer of Flight* (1972), is the best biography, while Louis S. Casey, *Curtiss: The Hammondsport Era, 1907–1915* (1981), contains useful information on the prewar period. An obituary is in the *New York Times*, 24 July 1930.

WILLIAM M. LEARY

CURTIZ, Michael (24 Dec. 1888–11 Apr. 1962), film director, was born Mihaly Kertész in Budapest, Hungary, the son of Ignatz Kertész, an architect, and Aranka (maiden name unknown), an opera singer. He graduated in 1906 from Markoczy School and spent the next four years with a traveling circus. He then entered the Royal Academy of Theater and Art in Budapest. Following graduation Curtiz directed Hungary's first feature film, *Today and Tomorrow* (1912). He studied at Denmark's prominent Nordisk studios in 1913. At the outbreak of World War I he was drafted into the Austro-Hungarian artillery and served on the Eastern Front. He was wounded twice and then served in Turkey with a film unit that prepared propaganda. In 1915 he married Lucy Doraine (original name Ilonka Kovács Perényi), who appeared in many of the movies that he made between 1912 and 1923. They had one daughter.

In 1917 Curtiz became manager of Phoenix Films in Hungary. In 1919, when Hungary's communist regime nationalized the film industry, he was appointed to the council that made the production decisions.

When the regime collapsed after a few months, he was able to leave Hungary. He went to Vienna and worked there between 1919 and 1926 as a film director on both Austrian and German films, using the name Michael Courtice. He also freelanced in the British, French, Italian, and Swedish film industries. In addition, throughout this period he also produced sixty plays, one of which he directed, and thirty-two films. In 1923 he and his wife divorced. A year later one of his films, *Moon of Israel* (1924), attracted the attention of a Warner Bros. studio executive, who persuaded him to come to California. He arrived in Hollywood as part of the stream of European directors lured by American studios. Curtiz soon discovered the autocratic nature of an industry in which survival depended on the large quantity of profit-making films that one turned out at nearly inhuman speed. Over the course of the next two decades Curtiz gained a reputation as a ruthless director who combined fast production work with superb craftsmanship. He was assigned at first to low-budget "B" movies. In spite of the advent of sound in cinema, his first four films were silent. In 1929 he was allowed to use partial dialogue in *Noah's Ark*, a film with a World War I love affair theme that became a box-office success. That same year he married Bess Meredyth, a screenwriter; they had no children.

Curtiz began to get better assignments. His first important American movie, *Mammy* (1930), starring Al Jolson, was shot in two-tone Technicolor. In 1933 he directed *The Mystery of the Wax Museum*, starring Glenda Farrell, Fay Wray, and Lionel Atwill; it was the first color horror movie on record and was a big moneymaker. By that time Curtiz had made twenty-five movies for Warner Bros. He threw himself completely into moviemaking, turning out film after film. The Curtiz stamp became identified with the Warner Bros. style in the 1930s and 1940s. During those years he shaped and chiseled into stardom many of the studio's foremost players. With an unerring eye for young talent, he spotted promising actors who had small parts in some of his films and developed them into top box-office draws.

Curtiz directed star swashbuckler Errol Flynn in twelve movies. Many of these were box-office record-breakers, most notably *Captain Blood* (1935), *Charge of the Light Brigade* (1936), *The Adventures of Robin Hood* (1938), and *Santa Fe Trail* (1940). Curtiz directed Bette Davis in six films, one of which, *The Private Lives of Elizabeth and Essex* (1939), costarred Flynn. Curtiz directed James Cagney in four films, including *Angels with Dirty Faces* (1938). In 1942 he directed Cagney in *Yankee Doodle Dandy*, the life story of George M. Cohan. It was Warner Bros.' most profitable World War II film, and it won Cagney an Academy Award as best actor. Curtiz led Joan Crawford to an Academy Award as best actress for her performance in *Mildred Pierce* (1945).

In 1942 Curtiz was handed a script about refugees from Nazi-occupied Europe who found a temporary haven in Casablanca. He was by now one of the most outstanding Hollywood directors. *Casablanca* (1943), starring Humphrey Bogart and Ingrid Bergman, had great box-office success. It received four Academy Awards, one of which went to Curtiz as best director. It was his second Academy Award, having received one in 1939 for *Sons of Liberty*, a short film.

During the twenty-seven years that Curtiz worked at Warner Bros., he directed some of that studio's most important films. His versatility of genres was outstanding. During the 1930s he directed Paul Muni in *Black Fury* (1935), a movie about strikebreakers, and the Lane sisters (Lola, Priscilla, and Rosemary) in four low-key family dramas; he also directed three Perry Mason mysteries. During the 1940s he directed two Doris Day musicals and made the successful saga *The Sea Wolf* (1941), based on the novel by Jack London and starring Edward G. Robinson in one of his most important roles. In 1943, at the request of President Franklin D. Roosevelt, Jack Warner agreed to produce a film on his lot that would show Stalin's communist regime in a more palatable light to the American people, who were questioning the wisdom of the United States' wartime alliance with the Soviet Union. Warner assigned Curtiz, who had become an American citizen in 1937, to direct *Mission to Moscow* (1943). (Curtiz's loyalty, however, was never questioned by the House Un-American Activities Committee.) He also directed the Irving Berlin musical film *This Is the Army* (1943), one of World War II's most popular films. Other 1940s films included *Night and Day* (1946), a biographical picture about songwriter Cole Porter, and an attractive, well-received version of the Broadway hit *Life with Father* (1947). All in all, Curtiz directed more than 100 films for Warner Bros., averaging three to four per year.

In 1954 Curtiz left Warner Bros. and began a career as a freelance director. Between 1954 and 1962 he made fifteen films, the first being *The Egyptian* (1954), which he did for 20th Century–Fox; it became one of the studio's biggest moneymakers. That same year he also directed *White Christmas* (1954) for Paramount, with music by Irving Berlin. It became one of Bing Crosby's most important movies. Curtiz's last picture was *The Comancheros* (1961), a western film starring John Wayne. Shortly after completing the film, Curtiz died at his Hollywood home.

In his lifetime Curtiz was one of the most powerful men in the Hollywood film industry and surely one of the best known. A superb technician, his films exuded energy and had tremendous impact on their audiences. He left his stamp on one of the biggest studios in the industry that he epitomized. A perfectionist by nature, he worked in all genres and certainly was among the most prolific American directors.

The 1990s witnessed an awakening of interest in Curtiz's achievements. A University of California at Los Angeles Film Series in 1990 included a Curtiz retrospective festival. In 1991 the Directors Guild of America launched its "Masters' Series" with a tribute to Curtiz and three-day retrospective screenings of his most important works. The New York Museum of Modern Art presented a Curtiz retrospective from 27 November 1992 through 23 January 1993. Other retrospective screenings have been held with increasing frequency by colleges, universities, museums, and art theaters throughout the country.

• Michael Curtiz never wrote his autobiography, but he did publish two articles, "Mr. Curtiz Will Tell You . . . ," *PIC* 20, no. 4 (Apr. 1947): 77–78, 108, and "An Independent Reward," *Independent Film Journal: Yearbook and Buyer Guide* (1947), pp. 96, 150. A steady stream of books on Curtiz have been published. The most important of these are Sidney Rosenzweig, *Casablanca and Other Major Films of Michael Curtiz* (1982); Roy Kinnard and R. J. Vitone, *The American Films of Michael Curtiz* (1986); and James C. Robertson, *The Casablanca Man: The Cinema of Michael Curtiz* (1993). The following articles about Curtiz are recommended: George Frazier, "The Machine with a Rage," *True*, Oct. 1947, pp. 60–61, 136–38; Sidney Sokolsky, "The Like of Mike," *Liberty*, Jan. 1948, p. 28; "Michael Curtiz," *Classic Images* 91 (1983): 17–19; Dick O'Donell, "The Man Who Taught Errol Flynn to Swashbuckle," *Movie Collectors World* (1988): 2; and Nova Sayre, "Curtiz: A Man of All Genres," *New York Times*, 29 Nov. 1992. See also John Wakeman, ed., *World Film Directors*, vol. 1 (1987), pp. 72–181. Works that contain sections or otherwise important references include István Nemeskürty, *Word and Image: History of the Hungarian Cinema* (1968); Kingsley Canham, *The Hollywood Professionals*, vol. 1, *Michael Curtiz, Raoul Walsh, Henry Hathaway* (1973); and William Meyer, *Warner Brothers Directors: The Hard Boiled, the Comic and the Weepers* (1978). Obituaries are in the *Los Angeles Times* and the *New York Times*, 12 Apr. 1962, and *Variety*, 18 Apr. 1962.

SHOSHANA KLEBANOFF

CURWOOD, James Oliver (12 June 1878–13 Aug. 1927), novelist, was born in Owosso, Michigan, the son of James Moran Curwood, a native of London and a cobbler, and Abigail Griffin. Supposedly, Curwood's great-uncle was the novelist Captain Frederick Marryat, and his mother's great-great-grandmother was a Mohawk Indian princess. At age six, he moved with his parents to a forty-acre farm near Vermilion, Ohio, their home for the next eight years. Curwood was given his first gun when he was eight. He began writing adventure yarns at nine. He was expelled from school in Owosso for truancy and indifference when he was sixteen, after which he toured southern states by bicycle, selling proprietary medicines. After passing an entrance examination, he attended the University of Michigan from 1898 to 1900. Later in 1900 he married Cora Leon Johnson, an art student at Ann Arbor, and became a reporter for the *Detroit News-Tribune*. While advancing to assistant editor and editor, he published short stories and articles in the *American Boy, Cosmopolitan, Frank Leslie's Popular Monthly, Munsey's, Outing, Outlook*, and *Woman's Home Companion*, and edited *Dollars and Sense*, a bankers' publication.

Curwood established his permanent residence in Owosso in 1907 and decided to become a full-time author when his first two novels, *The Courage of Captain Plum* and *The Wolf Hunters: A Tale of Adventure in the Wilderness*, were accepted for publication in 1908. He and his first wife often argued violently and were divorced in 1908; they had two children. Curwood married Ethel May Greenwood, a schoolteacher, a year after his divorce. The couple had one incorrigible child, who died when the airplane he was piloting crashed in 1930.

Curwood took numerous hunting, hiking, boating, and camping trips, mostly into Alaska and the northwestern reaches of Canada. He wrote thirty-three books published between 1908 and 1931; of these, thirty-one were novels, usually set in those remote regions. The Canadian government paid him $1,800 in 1908 to spend a year exploring and writing about unsettled areas of the Northwest in order to attract tourists and vacationers. In the process, he began to amass a huge set of big-game photographs, most of which he took himself. During 1910–1913 he wrote about thirty movie scenarios; most had original plots and many were filmed. (He eventually wrote about 200 scenarios.) In 1917–1918 he was accredited as a war correspondent but never got to Europe. By this time, several of his novels had been translated into as many as seven languages. Frequently discontented with his first publishers—Bobbs Merrill, then Harper, and then Doubleday—Curwood signed through his editor-friend Ray Long with the Cosmopolitan Book Corporation in 1919, after which sales of his books improved greatly. Also in 1919 Curwood and his wife went on location far north of Edmonton, Alberta, to oversee the filming of his *Back to God's Country*, a spectacular 1919 movie success. In 1922 he built a castle-like town studio in Owosso, patterned after a Norman gatehouse or château, with thick walls and spires at three of its corners. He was appointed to the Michigan State Conservation Commission in 1926, having become active in wildlife conservation in the early 1920s, and worked hard but abrasively for wildlife and forest conservation causes and waterway cleaning.

It was as the author of novels set in Canada and Hudson's Bay, often featuring members of the Royal Canadian Mounted Police and occasionally making heroes of animals (somewhat in the manner of Jack London), that Curwood gained his most enduring fame. His fifth novel, written during his honeymoon with his second wife in the wilds of Canada, was *Philip Steele of the Royal Northwest Mounted Police* (1911); it was especially popular. His ninth novel, *Kazan* (1914), features a magnificent animal that is one-quarter wolf and three-quarters husky. Its popular sequel was *Baree, Son of Kazan* (1917).

Curwood's work explores interrelated themes, at times repetitively. *Kazan* dramatizes a dog's contrary impulses: loyalty to his master and that man's delightful wife, murderous hatred of all other human beings, and love of the wilderness and Gray Wolf, his lost, blind mate. *God's Country—and the Woman* (1915) contains four essays on Curwood's pantheistic religion. In one essay, Curwood explains how during a hunting trip he wounded a grizzly bear, was threatened by the enormous beast, and was then miraculously forgiven by it. This brotherly act made him aware that human beings are not the crown of all natural life.

The River's End: A New Story of God's Country (1919) tells how a Mountie pursues a murderer who happens to resemble him. Dying of a frosted lung, the officer bequeaths his identity to the man, who falls in love with the dead man's sister once she comes from England to find her long-lost brother after years of separation. Not surprisingly, the pair fall in love, and the Hollywood ending is both predictable and pleasant. Curwood said that traveling 3,000 miles on the Saskatchewan River provided material for that novel. *The Valley of Silent Men: A Story of the Three River Country* (1920) has a somewhat similar plot. When a Mountie believes he is dying, he confesses to a murder that an innocent man is condemned to die for, only then to be freed by a mystery woman. The two escape on a scow but are separated on the Athabasca River. Thinking that she has drowned, the hero makes his way to her home in the valley of the title and finds her—and happiness—there.

Curwood displays old-fashioned, outmoded novelistic virtues in his work. His heroes are tall, strong, handsome, and moral in their own way. His heroines are bright, beautiful, and virtuous. His natural settings are rugged, painterly, and inspiring. Enormous royalties from his novels and short stories, along with movie rights, enabled Curwood to enjoy the best of two worlds. He relished escaping into primitive country and also enjoyed his comforts back in Owosso. He optimistically published "I Shall Live to Be 100" (*Hearst's Magazine*, June 1926), but in the spring of 1927 he was bitten by a virulent snake or spider. The wound was ineffectively treated, and he died of blood infection and kidney failure in Owosso. He left an estate valued at nearly $1 million, most of which he bequeathed to his wife and children. Willed by Curwood to his home town, "Curwood Castle" is now a museum.

• Most of Curwood's scant extant correspondence is in libraries at Columbia University and Southern Illinois University at Carbondale. See also his autobiographies *The Glory of Living: The Autobiography of an Adventurous Boy Who Grew into a Writer and a Lover of Life* (1928), full of sales and royalty figures, mock-modest self-praise, and espousals of optimistic aspects of all major religions, and *Son of the Forests: An Autobiography*, completed by Dorothea Brant (1939). The *Encyclopedia of Frontier and Western Fiction*, ed. Jon Tuska and Vicki Piekarski (1983), names more than seventy movies made from 1914 to 1953 out of plots or at least characters created by Curwood. Ray Long, "James Oliver Curwood and His Far North," *Bookman* 52 (Feb. 1921): 492–95, describes his brand of love of the North Country and his writing habits. In *The Men Who Make Our Novels* (1924), Charles C. Baldwin criticizes Curwood's books as poor mixtures of propaganda, topography, and politics, with ridiculous plots featuring manly, selfless heroes and beautiful heroines. H. D. Swiggett, *James Oliver Curwood* (1943), is a useful but uncritical biography. Judith A. Eldridge, *James Oliver Curwood: God's Country and the Man* (1993), is gossipy and full of facts, too often trivial. William Cowan's "Cree Vocabulary in the Works of James Oliver Curwood," in *Papers of the Twenty-third Algonquian Conference*, ed. Cowan (1992), suggests that

Curwood had a rough but probably adequate knowledge of Cree. Obituaries are in the *Detroit Free Press* and the *New York Times*, both 15 Aug. 1927.

ROBERT L. GALE

CUSHING, Caleb (17 Jan. 1800–2 Jan. 1879), lawyer and politician, was born in Salisbury, Massachusetts, the son of John Newmarch Cushing, a shipmaster and merchant, and Lydia Dow. In 1802 the family moved to Newburyport, where Caleb's mother died when he was ten. At Harvard he developed a lifelong interest in science, mathematics, and world literature. After graduating in 1817, a law career seemed appropriate for someone with literary ambitions, a love of public speaking, and extensive family contacts.

Cushing entered Harvard Law School and apprenticed with Ebenezer Moseley of Newburyport. Meanwhile he wrote poetry and published travel narratives. He also became a mathematics tutor, but rambunctious teenagers soured him on a teaching career. His translation of Robert James Pothier's *On Maritime Contracts* (1821) reflected Cushing's lifelong effort to broaden American law beyond its Anglo-Saxon roots. He wrote articles critical of slavery and the death penalty. The need to prove himself a worthy successor to the 1776 generation fueled his self-perception as a leader, while fascination with classical history also encouraged wider ambitions.

Cushing became involved in town affairs, served in the militia, and joined the Bunker Hill Monument Association, in fear that weakened community ties presaged social upheavals. A favorable review of Daniel Webster's *Plymouth Discourse* (1821) expressed Cushing's solidifying political loyalties at a time when parties in Massachusetts were extremely fluid. Cushing became one of Webster's leading supporters, business partner, and part-time banker. In 1824 Cushing was elected to the Massachusetts General Court. That same year he married Caroline Wilde, who encouraged her husband's ambitions and occasionally was credited with doing his writing; the couple did not have children.

Cushing's 1826 memorial address on John Adams (1735–1826) and Thomas Jefferson, his *The History of the Present State of the Town of Newburyport* (1826), and his *Summary of the Practical Principles of Political Economy* (1826) called for a partnership between business and government to dampen potentially explosive property inequalities. The emergence of a new order at odds with its roots, he sensed, required broader vision. In 1826 Cushing ran unsuccessfully for the U.S. House of Representatives as a National Republican. That same year he was elected again to the General Court and was also elected as selectman and moderator of the Newburyport town meeting.

In 1829 Cushing and his wife traveled in Europe; both published accounts of their impressions. His *Reminiscences of Spain* (1833) was informed by two of his favorite themes: the advantages of utilitarianism and democracy, and the happy state of American

womanhood because their femininity was expressed in the private sphere.

However, Cushing craved the public sphere, as his *Review, Historical and Political, of the Late Revolution in France* (1833) implied. European upheavals occurred, he argued, when lower orders lacked guidance. Ever willing to be one of those guides, in 1832 Cushing again ran for Congress, as a National Republican, but was defeated. That summer, amid a cholera epidemic, his wife died. Returning to Boston exhausted and depressed, in 1833 he ran once more for Congress, this time against anti-Masonic opposition, and lost again.

Political calculations, party needs, and advice from friends muted Cushing's antislavery pronouncements. In the spring of 1834 he joined Edward Everett in furthering Webster's presidential ambitions by helping to assemble a new coalition that would compose the local Whig party.

Cushing finally won a congressional seat in 1834 as a Whig and held it for four consecutive terms, serving as chairman of the House Committee on Foreign Affairs during his second term. While presenting constituents' petitions against the annexation of Texas, his Manifest Destiny statements and aggressive anglophobia left room for political maneuvering. (Cushing's opponents charged him with being on both sides of most issues.) In 1840 his campaign biography of William Henry Harrison attempted to rescue the Whigs from dead-end political issues and to transform Harrison into the archetypal man for all seasons. Upon Harrison's death, Cushing threw his support to Vice President John Tyler (1790–1862), whose accession, Cushing explained, provided the opportunity to revitalize Whig party machinery and elect Webster president. As Tyler began to oppose Whig policies, Cushing was required to defend his support of the administration. In his pamphlet *To My Constituents* (1841), he denied that he had betrayed New England interests. Cushing insisted he was still a Whig and called on all Whigs not bent on political suicide to rally around Tyler and Webster.

Cushing's reward was nomination for secretary of the treasury, but he was refused senatorial confirmation in March 1843. Instead he accepted a challenging mission to China. The long journey, during which he sent detailed reports to the State Department, ended in Macao, where Cushing negotiated the Treaty of Wanghia (1844), the first bilateral agreement between the United States and China. It defined "extraterritoriality" and declared the opium trade illegal.

Cushing returned to the United States via Mexico, compiling an influential report on the state of that country and calling for the annexation of Texas. Foreign policy issues, Whig animosity, and abolitionist hostilities edged Cushing ever closer to the Democrats as he resumed his legal career in Newburyport in 1845. He also wrote and lectured extensively. After the outbreak of the Mexican War in 1846, he equipped a Massachusetts Volunteer Regiment, whose officers elected him colonel. President James K. Polk then made him a brigadier general. While in Mexico, Cushing accepted the Democratic party's nomination for the Massachusetts governorship in 1847.

Cushing lost the gubernatorial race and returned to Newburyport to practice law and to recoup shaky finances. In 1848 Cushing again headed the state Democratic ticket and lost. The presidential victory of General Zachary Taylor and the death of Cushing's father provoked a mild depression, but his political fortunes brightened when Webster became secretary of state. Cushing, though a Democrat, retained his loyalty to Webster and vigorously supported the 1850 Compromise. At the same time he opposed a Democratic–Free Soiler alliance, which he regarded as suicidal to the Democratic party and dangerous to the Union. Reelected in 1850, and heading the "Indomitables," Cushing tried to block the abolitionist Charles Sumner's election to the U.S. Senate in the Massachusetts General Court and urged reconciliation between Whigs and Democrats for the sake of the Union.

While in the legislature, he secured a city charter for Newburyport in 1851 and served as that city's first mayor. In 1852 he served for a few months on the Massachusetts Supreme Judicial Court. Awarded an honorary doctor of laws degree by Harvard that summer, Cushing helped engineer Franklin Pierce's election to the White House, and his political future looked bright.

Cushing became attorney general of the United States, a close adviser to the president, and one of the administration's official spokesmen. He tried to consolidate the Democratic party by driving out Free Soilers objectionable to prosouthern voters. Cushing enforced the Fugitive Slave Law, and in 1854 he helped get the Kansas-Nebraska Act passed. He argued that Congress lacked power to exclude slavery, an acceptable labor system, from the territories. Cushing also represented Young America in the Pierce administration, touting American imperialism as a positive force. American nationality was expansive and inclusive for all, Cushing argued, except blacks, who were an inferior race.

In 1857, back in Newburyport after James Buchanan's election, Cushing involved himself in the Know Nothing controversy, attacking nativism and its restrictive vision of American nationality. He also criticized Republicans for their sectionalism and naiveté, arguing that slavery was not a moral issue and that no law could change black inferiority. Reelected to the General Court, Cushing fought unsuccessfully to repeal Massachusetts's Personal Liberty Acts, denounced John Brown's (1800–1859) raid, and warned northern do-gooders to curb their extremism lest the South secede. In 1859 he saw the North, not the South, as the aggressor bent on civil war.

When the Democratic National Convention met at Charleston, South Carolina, in April 1860, Cushing was elected permanent president. Privately he felt that only a strongman who forcibly suppressed the fratricidal rage of raving ideologues could save the Union. The new stalemate in Baltimore in June 1860 ended

when Cushing and the "Bolters" reassembled and approved a platform making the federal government responsible for protecting slavery in the territories. They nominated John C. Breckinridge of Kentucky for the presidency. Opponents hung Cushing's effigy in a Newburyport street, while others maintained that he had everything except convictions. Undaunted, Cushing argued that the Union could be saved only by a nationwide repeal of all acts nullifying the Fugitive Slave Law. At Buchanan's behest in December 1860, Cushing vainly urged Governor Francis W. Pickens to delay proclamation of South Carolina's secession ordinance. On 12 April Cushing was in Washington advising Secretary of State William H. Seward on legal matters, but when the guns sounded he returned to Newburyport, opting for war and the Union.

The former Whig and Democrat was on the way to becoming a Republican. In 1864 he voted for Abraham Lincoln and managed a spectacular comeback. In 1865 President Andrew Johnson appointed Cushing one of the commissioners to revise the statute laws of the United States. Cushing became a legal resident of Virginia and a fixture on the Washington social circuit. Sumner proved a welcoming host, and at his suggestion Cushing was appointed special minister to Colombia.

Cushing filled various posts under President Ulysses S. Grant, the most important as American counsel in Geneva in the Alabama Claims controversy, which Cushing summarized in *The Treaty of Washington* (1873). In 1872 he voted for Grant over Horace Greeley and interrupted an extensive national and international law practice to become minister to Spain. Grant submitted Cushing's name to fill a Supreme Court vacancy, but reports that reviewed Cushing's torturous political career ruined his confirmation chances. In 1874 he sailed for Spain, where among other achievements he negotiated an agreement on the *Virginius* affair. Back in the United States in the autumn of 1876, he voted for Rutherford B. Hayes, then returned to Madrid to complete a formal extradition treaty. He resigned his post in 1877 and moved back to Newburyport, where he died.

• The largest depository of Caleb Cushing manuscripts is the Library of Congress. The Essex Institute Collection in Salem, Mass., holds additional Cushing family correspondence. Cushing's legal decisions are listed in U.S. Attorney General, *Official Opinions of the Attorneys General* (12 vols., 1852–1870). Many of his speeches, judicial judgments, and legal opinions were published separately during Cushing's lifetime. His State Department reports are partly reprinted in Margaret Diamond Benetz, ed., *The Cushing Reports, 1843–1844* (1976). The standard biography is Claude M. Fuess, *The Life of Caleb Cushing* (2 vols., 1923). His career during the Pierce administration is examined in M. C. Hodgson, *Caleb Cushing, Attorney General of the United States 1853–1857* (1955). The most detailed obituaries are in the *Proceedings of the Bench and Bar of the Supreme Court of the United States in Memory of Caleb Cushing* (1879), and *A Memorial of Caleb Cushing from the City of Newburyport* (1879).

LILIAN HANDLIN

CUSHING, Frank Hamilton (22 July 1857–10 Apr. 1900), anthropologist, was born in North East, Pennsylvania, the son of Thomas Cushing, a physician, and Sarah Harding Crittenden. In 1860 the family moved to a farm outside Barre Center, New York, where, beginning apparently with the impression made by an arrowhead tossed to him by one of the field hands when he was about eight, Cushing developed an intense interest in the Indians who had once inhabited the area. He spent much of his boyhood roaming the countryside in search of Indian relics and dwelling sites and attempting to discover, through his own efforts at reproducing them, how the craft objects that he found were originally made. Largely self-trained, he became well versed in the anthropological literature of the day, most importantly that of Edward Tylor and Lewis Henry Morgan. His first published work, "Antiquities of Orleans County, New York," appeared before he was eighteen in the *Annual Report of the Board of Regents of the Smithsonian Institution, 1874* (1875). After one term at Cornell University in 1875, he was appointed in 1876 to the Smithsonian Institution as a staff member, first in the National Museum, then in the Bureau of Ethnology.

A member of the first Bureau of Ethnology expedition to the Southwest in 1879, Cushing is generally credited with having laid the foundations for scientific study of the ethnology and archaeology of the area. Settling in Zuni, New Mexico, he became the first anthropologist to conduct fieldwork by actually living with the subjects of investigation and joining in their daily activities. Inventor of the method of participant observation, if not the term, he remained at the pueblo from 1879 to 1884, residing during most of that time with the Zuni governor and his family. He learned the Zuni language, adopted Zuni dress, and was accepted into the tribe, serving frequently as its spokesman and advocate and eventually winning admission into the prestigious Priesthood of the Bow and appointment as "First War Chief." He also gained international fame when he brought a group of Zuni headmen east in the spring of 1882 for a series of public appearances in Washington and Boston. During this six-month interlude in his fieldwork, he married Emily Tennison Magill, who subsequently returned with him to Zuni. They did not have children.

In 1887 Cushing became director of the Hemenway Southwestern Archaeological Expedition, an ambitious effort to track the origins of the Pueblo peoples and cultures by examining ruins along the migration routes suggested in Zuni myth and folklore and the first undertaking of its kind in the Southwest. The principal focus of the expedition for over a year was a mound near Tempe, Arizona, under which was discovered the remains of the largest pre-Spanish community known to have existed in southern Arizona. The main collection of objects unearthed there and in other nearby settlements of the people now known as Hohokam is housed in the Peabody Museum of Harvard University. A decade later, in the Florida Keys, Cushing discovered the remains of another American Indian people until then unknown, whose elaborate settlements had been constructed over the water on piles of seashells. In the course of his underwater excavations, he found thousands of artifacts, now displayed at the National Museum of the Smithsonian and the Museum of the University of Pennsylvania. Although he issued a lengthy "preliminary" report in each case, recurrent illness and other difficulties prevented Cushing from completing the full monographic works needed to guarantee that these two spectacular ventures achieved the professional impact they deserved.

Cushing's best-known writings centered on the Zuni: *My Adventures in Zuni* (1882–1883; repr. 1941), *Zuni Breadstuff* (1884–1885; repr. 1920), *Zuni Folk Tales* (1901), and others, including "*Zuni Fetishes*" (1883; repr. 1966), and "A Study of Pueblo Pottery as Illustrative of Zuni Cultural Growth" (*Fourth Annual Report of the Bureau of Ethnology, 1882–1883* [1886]). For his exposition of the sevenfold Zuni "mytho-sociologic" organization in "Outlines of Zuni Creation Myths" (*Thirteenth Annual Report of the Bureau of Ethnology* 1891–1892 [1896]), a major inspiration and source for Émile Durkheim and Marcel Mauss in their study "De quelques formes primitives de classification" (*Année Sociologique* 6 [1903]: 1–72), Claude Lévi-Strauss accorded Cushing "a seat on Morgan's right as one of the great forerunners of social structure studies" (p. 290). More recently, Cushing also has been cited as the originator of the modern use of the term *culture* in the plural and of the concept of cultural patterns made famous by Ruth Benedict (Mark, pp. 110–14). Less well recognized is the importance of Cushing's contribution to the work of his contemporary Lucien Lévy-Bruhl (particularly in his *Les fonctions mentales dans les sociétiés inférieures* [1910]) and, by way of Lévy-Bruhl, to the conceptions of such later writers as T. S. Eliot, Owen Barfield, and Ernst Cassirer regarding the nature of "primitive" consciousness and thought processes and the ways in which they differ from the modern "dissociated sensibility."

Characteristic of all of Cushing's work, from his boyhood efforts to learn about a long-dead people by becoming an artisan of their lost art to his efforts to learn about living American Indians by immersing himself in one of their communities, was the approach that he described in a late unpublished note: "the method of ethnologic and archaeologic study by means of actual experience and experimentation, [whereby the researcher is] endeavoring always to place himself as much as possible in their position, not only physically but intellectually and morally as well, [to] gain insight into their inner life and institutions" (Southwest Museum).

What is called "modern" anthropology is commonly thought to have originated with Bronislaw Malinowski, who wrote in *Argonauts of the Western Pacific* (1922) that he had striven in his fieldwork to "grasp the native's point of view, his relation to life, to realize his vision of the world." When Cushing died (in Washington, D.C., of complications resulting from choking on a fishbone), he was not yet forty-three and far short of having fulfilled his promise. A controversial figure, he was legendary among his peers for his skills of observation and craftsmanship and for his reputed ability to "think like an Indian"; but he was criticized, particularly by later practitioners, for insufficiently disciplined subjectivity and for failure to make the most of his unparalleled research opportunities in full monographic reports. Cushing continues to command attention for what he did accomplish, in several still classic works on the Zunis and in the model he embodied, a generation ahead of Malinowski, of the modern anthropological approach.

• The main collections of Cushing's papers are held in the Southwest Museum in Los Angeles and the National Anthropological Archives of the Smithsonian Institution. Papers relating to the Hemenway Southwestern Archaeological Expedition are held in the Heye Foundation Museum of the American Indian in New York City and in the Peabody Museum at Harvard University. Papers relating to the Florida Gulf Coast excavations may be found in the University of Pennsylvania Library and the American Philosophical Society Library in Philadelphia. Works by Cushing not named in the text include "Preliminary Notes on the Origin, Working Hypothesis, and Primary Researches of the Hemenway Southwestern Archaeological Expedition," *Congrès international des américanistes, Berlin, 1888* (1890): 151–94; "Manual Concepts: A Study of the Influence of Hand-Usage on Culture Growth," *American Anthropologist* 5 (1892): 289–317; "Primitive Copper Working: An Experimental Study," *American Anthropologist* 7 (1894): 93–117; "The Arrow," *American Anthropologist* 8 (1895): 307–49; and "Exploration of Ancient Key Dwellers' Remains on the Gulf Coast of Florida," *Proceedings of the American Philosophical Society* 35 (1896): 329–448. See also Jesse Green, *Zuni: Selected Writings of Frank Hamilton Cushing* (1979) and *Cushing in Zuni: The Correspondence and Journals of Frank Hamilton Cushing, 1879–1884* (1990), both of which contain bibliographies of Cushing's publications, works concerning Cushing, and other related works. A list of Cushing's unpublished papers may be found in Raymond S. Brandes, "Frank Hamilton Cushing: Pioneer Americanist" (Ph.D. diss., Univ. of Arizona, 1965). Also see Claude Lévi-Strauss, *Structural Anthropology* (1963), and Joan Mark, "Frank Hamilton Cushing," in Mark, *Four Anthropologists: An American Science in Its Early Years* (1980), pp. 96–130. Obituaries are in *Scientific American*, 21 Apr. 1900, and *American Anthropologist*, n.s., 2 (1900): 354–79.

JESSE GREEN

CUSHING, Harvey Williams (8 Apr. 1869–7 Oct. 1939), neurosurgeon, medical historian, and bibliophile, was born in Cleveland, Ohio, in the Western Reserve of Connecticut, the son of Henry Kirke Cushing, a physician, and Betsey Maria Williams. In addition to his father, Cushing's paternal grandfather, great grandfather, and great-great grandfather were all physicians in general practice. Cushing's childhood was a happy and full one with strong parental role models. He found opportunities at home to consort, through books, with the world of ideas, and to explore history. His early education was in the public schools of Cleveland and from his mother, who taught him

French and introduced him to general literature and poetry. In 1887 Cushing entered Yale University, where he spent four happy years, achieving election to Scroll and Key (a matter of considerable importance to him) and securing the short-stop position on the Yale freshman baseball team and, later, membership on the varsity nine.

Cushing graduated from Yale in 1891 and went on to the Harvard Medical School, from which he received an M.D. cum laude in 1895. Cushing's drive, brilliance, and gift of originality became apparent at Harvard, where, during his student years, he and classmate Amory Codman developed a system for recording the pulse and respiratory rates of the anesthetized patient as a guide to the surgeon and anesthetist. Introduced in 1895 when Cushing was a fourth-year student, these "ether charts," as they were called, were the forerunner of modern operating room records. After graduation Cushing spent sixteen months in training at the Massachusetts General Hospital, where he was instrumental in purchasing an X-ray tube for the hospital within a year of the 1895 announcement of German physicist Wilhelm Konrad Roentgen's discovery of X-rays.

The following year Cushing moved to Baltimore to train as a surgeon under William Stewart Halsted, chairman of the Department of Surgery at Johns Hopkins Hospital. Cushing brought the X-ray tube with him to Baltimore, where he performed the hospital's first X-rays and published two of the earliest case reports involving the use of X-rays in clinical work (*American Journal of Medical Science* [1898]). He trained with Halsted for four years, first as assistant resident, and then as resident surgeon. He became in the process a highly accomplished general surgeon and a central figure in the Johns Hopkins department. His publications to this point included a number of papers on surgical treatment of the complications of typhoid fever; these brought him wide recognition and an invitation to join the Department of Surgery at Western Reserve University in Cleveland, which he declined.

In 1900, at the age of thirty, Cushing committed himself to an academic surgical career, and, with the encouragement of his father and especially of William Osler and William Henry Welch, major figures in the Johns Hopkins Medical Institutions, he spent fourteen months in Europe visiting most of the great clinics in England, Switzerland, Germany, and Italy. On this trip, demonstrating a clear talent for the experimental investigation of surgical problems, Cushing produced a brilliant series of studies on the effects of increased intracranial pressure on blood pressure and on blood flow to the brain (*Mittheilungen aus den Grenzgebieten der Medizin und Chirurgie* [1902]). At Pavia he found, at the Hospital of St. Matthew, the first blood pressure apparatus with an inflatable armlet. He brought a model of this back to Baltimore and helped to introduce clinical measurements of blood pressure into American operating rooms and clinics (*Boston Medical and Surgical Journal* [1903]). In addition to scientific and clinical work, his European trip introduced him to many of the great men in medicine at the time, including Theodor Kocher and Hugo Kronecker, both of the University of Berne, and W. H. Erb of Heidelberg. His interests in the history of medicine and in medical bibliophily also began to emerge and would be nurtured under the continuing stimulation of Osler. At the end of the trip he spent a month in England working with the physiologist Charles Sherrington on problems having to do with the localization of various functions of the brain. On his return to Baltimore, Cushing was appointed to the surgical faculty at Johns Hopkins. In 1902 he married Katherine Crowell, a Cleveland woman he had known from childhood; they had five children.

Although Cushing began a highly accomplished general surgical career at Johns Hopkins, his interest in surgical treatment of diseases of the central nervous system appeared early. Around the turn of the century he focused especially on the treatment of trigeminal neuralgia (tic douloureux) an intractable and extremely painful facial disorder; his operation, which consisted of extirpation of the ganglion of the fifth cranial nerve under direct vision, represented an important early advance (*Journal of the American Medical Association* [1905]). He then developed an increasing interest in the surgery of brain tumors and in refinements of operative technique. From 1908 to 1912 he turned his attention more and more to problems of pituitary disease and tumors of the cerebellum. By 1905 he had begun to define neurological surgery as a special field ("The Special Field of Neurological Surgery," *Cleveland Medical Journal* 4 [1905]: 1–25) and to write extensively on the surgical treatment of brain tumors. In so doing he succeeded in making brain surgery a specialty recognized by a large and influential group of academic surgeons, and he began to attract students who sought to learn his techniques and procedures. Around 1908 his interest turned increasingly to surgery of the pituitary gland, especially pituitary tumors. In 1912 he published a major monograph, *The Pituitary Body and Its Disorders*, which served to link clinical syndromes with abnormal endocrine physiology and helped to establish the newly emerging field of endocrinology.

The great work of Cushing's life was unquestionably his leading role in the development of neurosurgery as a field of separate and special surgical interest. Although occasional operations on the central nervous system had previously been performed, Cushing's development of surgical techniques, preoperative evaluation, and meticulous postoperative care enabled the field to advance as rapidly as it did in the first quarter of this century. He taught the importance of detailed clinical examination and of correlating observed abnormalities with anatomy and physiology. He applied a central lesson he had learned from Halsted, namely the importance of handling tissues gently and of controlling intraoperative bleeding, a major problem in neurosurgical procedures. He devised in 1904 the head tourniquet to control bleeding from the scalp and was instrumental in supplanting this technique by the

injection into the skin of epinephrine, a blood vessel constrictor. Around 1910 he popularized the use of the small silver clip for application to blood vessels that could not be tied off and the use of suction to deal with gross hemorrhage, especially in deep cavities. He was the first to establish the value in neurological surgery of employing high-frequency currents that used circuitry developed by W. T. Bovie, a physicist attached to the Harvard Cancer Commission. Bovie had developed two separate high-frequency circuits, one designed to cut tissue without bleeding, and the other to coagulate and thereby stop bleeding from vessels that had been opened. The Bovie technique became a standard in neurological surgery and permitted the resection of tumors that would not previously have been operable. Cushing's careful study of the patients who came under his care and his categorization of brain tumors, together with the technical advances he introduced, formed a solid foundation for neurosurgical therapy.

Cushing's sixteen years at Johns Hopkins were characterized by wide dissemination in the medical literature of his investigations, technical advances, and therapeutic results. In 1912 he accepted the Moseley Professorship of Surgery at the Harvard Medical School and became surgeon in chief at the newly opened Peter Bent Brigham Hospital in Boston, where he spent the remainder of his active surgical career. With U.S. entry into World War I, Cushing organized a Harvard medical unit, which served with the Ambulance Americaine for two months. Two years later he returned to France, this time with Base Hospital No. 5, a Harvard unit that he, in large part, had organized and about which he anonymously published a history in 1919. In addition, he kept an extraordinary series of war journals containing a detailed daily record of his experiences; these extended to some nine volumes of 1,000 pages each. A distillation of these journals, *From a Surgeon's Journal*, was published in 1936. He retired from Harvard in 1933, twenty years to the day after his arrival, and moved to Yale, where he had accepted a chair in neurology. He spent his last years in continued scholarly activity, including work on *Meningiomas, Their Classification, Regional Behaviour, Life History, and Surgical End Results* (1938), his great monograph on meningiomas, a common type of brain tumor, and on his brain tumor registry, *Intracranial Tumours* (1932), which categorized brain tumors and correlated their clinical manifestations and courses with tumor pathology. In the meningioma monograph Cushing and his longtime co-worker, Louise Eisenhardt, introduced the term "meningioma" and separated these from other intracranial tumors by describing their usual sites of origin and the more common regional syndromes presented by them. A personal series of 313 patients with meningioma was described in clinical as well as pathologic detail. This monumental work laid the basis for the surgical treatment of this common tumor.

Beyond his extraordinary surgical career, Cushing was an avid and sophisticated medical bibliophile and historian. Over the years Cushing's historical and bibliophilic interests were wide-ranging, but came to focus especially on the sixteenth-century anatomist Vesalius, whose works he assembled into one of the great collections of Vesaliana.

During the course of his career Cushing emerged as a major figure in American medicine. He battled the antivivisectionists, attempted to promote the emergence of a national health insurance plan, and tried from 1917 to 1919 to organize a national institute for neurologic diseases, well in advance of the development of such a unit at the National Institutes of Health in 1950. At various times he served as president of the Society of Clinical Surgery, the American Neurological Association, the American Surgical Association, and the Association for Study of Internal Secretions. In 1925 he published his famous *Life of Sir William Osler*, for which he received a Pulitzer Prize in biography the following year. His numerous additional honors included twenty-two honorary degrees and honorary membership or fellowship in numerous domestic and foreign societies. At one time or another he gave most of the distinguished international lectureships in surgery, including the Cavendish Lecture at the West London Medical-Chirurgical Society (1922), the Cameron Prize Lecture at the University of Edinburgh (1924), and the Harvey Lecture at the New York Academy of Medicine (1910 and 1933). He was the Lister Prize medalist of the Royal College of Surgeons of England in 1930 and a fellow of the American Academy of Arts and Sciences, a member of the National Academy of Sciences, and an honorary fellow of the New York Academy of Medicine. He was made a Companion of the Bath in 1919, was awarded the U.S. Distinguished Service Medal in 1926, and was made an Officer of the Légion d'Honneur in 1927. He died in New Haven.

• Cushing's personal papers and journals are at the Yale Medical School, to which he also bequeathed his extraordinary library, including the great collection of Vesaliana. Together with the libraries of his friends Arnold Klebs and John Fulton, this bequest formed the basis of a major medical collection, which is housed with Cushing's desk, chair, and other memorabilia. The most comprehensive biographical treatment is John Fulton, *Cushing: A Biography* (1946). His relationship with his mentor, William Osler, is considered in Jeremiah A. Barondess, "Osler and Cushing: The Evolution of a Friendship," *Transactions and Studies of the College of Physicians of Philadelphia* 7 (1984): 79–112. Obituaries are in the *British Medical Journal* 2 (14 Oct. 1939): 787; the *Lancet* 2 (14 Oct. 1939): 856; the *Journal of the American Medical Association* 113 (14 Oct. 1939): 1505–6; and *Nature* 144 (28 Oct. 1939): 736.

JEREMIAH A. BARONDESS

CUSHING, John Perkins (22 Apr. 1787–12 Apr. 1862), merchant, was born near Boston, Massachusetts, the son of Robert Cushing and Ann Maynard Perkins. In 1792 his mother took Cushing and his older sister Nancy to North Carolina to join her husband. But when she died in March 1793 of smallpox, his father abandoned the children. Thomas Perkins, his uncle,

brought the children to live with him in Brookline, Massachusetts. When they landed from a coaster, they reportedly "looked like wild Indians"; Perkins was so embarrassed by their appearance that he pulled down the blinds in the coach that brought them from the wharf.

In 1798 Cushing joined the firm of his uncles, James and Thomas Handasyd Perkins, as an office boy and clerk. The Perkinses had organized a series of firms beginning in 1786; this one—the first in which they had no other partners—began in 1792 and was already successfully pursuing mercantile ventures to the West Indies, to Europe, and to the Pacific Northwest Coast and China. By 1803 the Perkinses were among the leading Americans in the China trade—they had been active there from 1791—and were probably the dominant traders in the important commerce in sea otter skins from the North American Pacific Coast destined for China. But with no permanent representative in China, they found it increasingly difficult both to trade to full advantage—a ship had to sell its entire cargo, even in a down market, before taking on a return cargo—and to respond effectively to opportunities that emerged during the near five-month lag for a letter to move between Canton and Boston. Thus, they resolved to establish a permanent agent in Canton. In July 1803 Ephraim Bumstead, a trusted former apprentice in the Perkins firm who had taken at least one Perkins ship to China a few years earlier, sailed out of Boston on the large (447-ton), three-masted *Patterson*. Cushing sailed with Bumstead to serve as clerk in the new Canton office.

On 1 January 1804 Bumstead and Cushing arrived in Canton; Bumstead opened the firm E. Bumstead & Co. with the very substantial capital of $26,500 and held another $47,500 from other New England merchants to finance trade ventures. But by fall 1805 Bumstead was too ill to conduct the business; he died en route to Boston. Cushing, still a teenager, was thus thrust into managing the Perkinses' China interest. In Boston Thomas Perkins was clearly worried: he had not received a single letter from Cushing since he embarked for China. Perkins wrote a colleague that Cushing would "require the counsels of Experience" to handle affairs in Canton, and to Cushing himself, "should you be so silent on the subject of business . . . We shall have much reason for pain and mortification." His worries only increased when a shipment of tea arrived "in bad order, the chests . . . much broken." But on 6 May Cushing's first letter arrived; on 7 May the *Hazard* arrived from Canton with more letters and tea whose loading Cushing had directly supervised—the chests were in excellent order. Perkins acknowledged that the cargo and letters gave clear "proof of attention and activity."

In 1806, in recognition of his effective work, Cushing became the principal in a new Canton house, Perkins & Co., with his uncles Thomas and James as partners. For the next twenty-two years, with the exception of one brief trip home in 1807, Cushing devoted himself with single-minded attention to business in

Canton (in part, perhaps, because China forbid foreign merchants to be accompanied by families). The business first focused entirely on importing specie and otter skins and exporting tea, silks, and cotton textiles (nankeens); but after 1815 it began to include opium among its imports.

Cushing came to be the most respected—and probably the wealthiest—foreign merchant resident in Canton. He was particularly close to the dominant native merchant, Houqua, and he himself came to be called "Ku-shing." He also served as the American consul for Canton.

By 1827 Cushing had decided to close his house and return to Boston. He spent the following winter winding up many of his ventures and instructing young Thomas Forbes, who had arrived in August to take over responsibility for representing the Perkinses' interests in China. Cushing, in spite of months of work together, left Forbes with remarkably long, detailed instructions on winding up final details, closing with this advice: "I need not again remind you of the advantages that are derived in business concerns by pursuing on all occasions and with all persons with whom you have transactions an upright and honorable conduct."

The *Milo*, with Cushing aboard, docked at Boston's Central Wharf on 17 September 1828. Cushing returned, a friend noted, "*very* rich" but in poor health, "impaired," he himself explained, "by too much devotion to business in a climate not favorable to 'length of days.'" He also did not know what he wanted to do. Thomas Perkins tried to interest Cushing in putting up a third of the capital for a million-dollar partnership with Thomas Perkins, Jr., and Samuel Cabot, a partnership that would confine itself to the China trade. Cushing declined, writing Forbes in China that Cabot was "not a popular man" and the junior Perkins would "not be a desirable associate in business." By Christmas, a friend commented that Cushing had developed a clear "disinclination for business in this country." In part this attitude may have been the result of a wide number of failures among well-known Boston houses, but Cushing also told the senior Perkins that it was "impossible" for him to conduct business in Boston, it "being totally different from what I have been accustomed to." And Cushing simply did not have the desire to continue to focus on business: "I cannot by being a member of the House here feel the independence that I wish to after 25 years of fagging." He preferred to confine himself to specific ventures "when there is a prospect of doing anything to advantage."

Cushing did participate the next year—1829—in a venture that sent three ships from Europe to China, carrying iron, English cloths, and opium. He also persuaded the Barings and the Hopes to send out two ships to bring back tea cargoes. Cushing and Perkins had joined one of the ships to go to Europe themselves. While there, Cushing learned that Thomas Forbes had died in Macao; he immediately booked passage to Canton, leaving London 15 April 1830. He

declared to his good friend William Sturgis that "not caring much about being amongst the good people of this hemisphere" and "not caring a pin about Europe," he was eager to return to Canton. He arrived there in August 1830 and stayed until March 1831. He did not want to leave "as I feel better satisfied here than I ever expect to anywhere else." But leave he did, "with a heavy heart," to bring back in the *Bashaw* a particularly rich cargo. When he arrived back in Boston in August, Perkins declared that their China trade had "terminated famously."

From 1831 on Cushing rapidly and systematically withdrew from direct participation in any business. He acquired a private schooner, the sixty-foot *Sylph*, which in 1832 he raced against the schooner *Wave*, owned by John C. Stevens of Hoboken, New Jersey, on a course from Vineyard Haven on Martha's Vineyard to Tarpaulin Cove; it was America's first known yacht race. On 5 June 1833 he married "the very pretty and amiable" Mary Louise Gardiner, daughter of Rev. John Sylvester J. Gardiner, rector of Trinity Church, Boston. They had no children. Soon thereafter they bought an impressive estate, "Belmont," in what was then Watertown (now the separate Boston suburb of Belmont, named for his estate). He filled it with Chinese servants and eastern furnishings, built a first-rate library, with standing orders in London to acquire the latest books and best periodicals. He imported a piano from Europe and had a French manufacturer send rolls for a "self-performing organ" (music box). He developed first-class gardens, importing European and Chinese fruit trees, shrubs, and flowers and adding Chinese livestock—hogs and cattle ("beautiful animals" even if they produced little milk)—to an array of goats, fowl, geese, and peacocks. Cushing declared, "I have become quite a farmer & find it affords me both occupation & amusement."

Cushing's withdrawal from business actually began when he first returned from Canton in 1828. He had then asked his friend William Sturgis, an old China trader who had settled in Boston in 1810 and established the mercantile house of Bryant, Sturgis & Co., to manage $50,000 of his funds. By 1830 Sturgis held $150,000; Cushing characterized this his "'nest egg' and apart from my business concerns." By 1835 Cushing seemed barely to handle money himself; Bryant & Sturgis paid his private bills, debts, and charitable subscriptions as well as handling all his investments and the reinvestment of proceeds. Even while Cushing lived in style, spending an average of $50,000 a year, Sturgis—in what was perhaps the earliest American example of an investment trust—managed to increase Cushing's net wealth nearly fourfold, from about $640,000 when he returned from China to more than $2.4 million at the time of his death at his estate.

Sturgis's management strategy was to shift investment out of trading activities, which were of declining importance before the Opium Wars of 1840–1842 disordered what trade remained, and into domestic American industrial, financial, and infrastructure ventures. The Cushing-Sturgis relationship displayed a number of critical processes in American economic and business development: the rise and decline of mercantile activities, particularly in the Far East; the increasing importance of industrial activity, particularly in New England, and of canals and then railroads; the emerging separation of ownership from management and the associated rise of investment management and investment banking; and the general process of economic specialization that is the hallmark of a growing, evolving, increasingly complex economy.

• Papers relating to Cushing are in several depositories: Cushing's diary is at the Boston Athenaneum; the Cushing papers and the Bryant & Sturgis Papers are at Baker Library, Harvard University. The T. H. Perkins Papers are at the Massachusetts Historical Society. Substantial material about his activities is in N. S. B. Gras and Henrietta Larson, *Casebook in American Business History* (1939), and in Carl Seaburg and Stanley Paterson, *Merchant Prince of Boston: Colonel T. H. Perkins, 1764–1854* (1971). An obituary is in the *Boston Evening Transcript*, 14 Apr. 1862.

FRED CARSTENSEN

CUSHING, Richard James (23 Aug. 1895–2 Nov. 1970), Roman Catholic archbishop of Boston, was born in South Boston, Massachusetts, the third child of Patrick Cushing, a mechanic, and Mary Dahill. After schooling at Boston College and Saint John's Seminary, Brighton, he was ordained to the priesthood in 1921. His first assignment was to the Society for the Propagation of the Faith, an agency that raised money for foreign missions. The appointment, followed by his promotion to director of the society in 1928, led to a lifelong interest in missionary work. American Catholics were by this time significant supporters of church endeavors in Latin America, Africa, and Asia, contributing money, priests, and nuns. Cushing, a capable fundraiser, built the effort in Boston into one of the most active in the country. This interest was enduring: he often spoke of renouncing his titles and going to the missions himself, and in 1958 he formed the Society of Saint James the Apostle, devoted to sending priests from the United States to Latin America.

Cushing was known in Boston for his forceful, outgoing personality. While most previous American Catholic leaders had been formal and remote, he cultivated an easy, "common-touch" persona. He seemed more at home with ordinary believers, young and old, than with the leaders of society. His unusual speaking voice, characterized by its nasal twang and dramatic climaxes, became familiar through weekly radio broadcasts and his pioneering work in televising Catholic ceremonies. His off-the-cuff remarks and deliberately democratic style marked him as the popular favorite when he was made successively auxiliary bishop of Boston (1939), administrator of the archdiocese (Apr. 1944), and finally archbishop of Boston (Nov. 1944), a post he held until 1970. He was elevated to the rank of cardinal by Pope John XXIII in 1958.

As archbishop, Cushing presided over an impressive institutional expansion of the local church. The period immediately after the Second World War saw rapid population growth—Catholics came to number three of every five people in Massachusetts—and a concurrent shift away from the city to the suburban ring surrounding Boston. Cushing built hundreds of churches, schools, and hospitals, and he increased the number of parishes by more than one-quarter to 410. Typifying mid-twentieth-century American Catholicism—suburban, middle class, better educated, increasingly removed from its immigrant origins, and possessed of a firmer sense of self-confidence—Cushing promoted a distinctly lay version of Catholicism. He formed a wide range of associations for the laity, organized according to occupational groupings, and these encouraged a more active, less hierarchical style for the church.

Cushing took an active interest in interfaith cooperation. In Boston as elsewhere, joint efforts among denominations had formerly been rare, with each group keeping to itself and looking on the others with suspicion. Cushing helped reverse this trend and won praise for improving Catholic-Jewish relations in particular. Though he took no especially active role during the deliberations of the Second Vatican Council (1962–1965), he did exert some influence on the text of the decree on Catholic relations with non-Christians ("*Nostra Aetate*," Oct. 1965), specifically in changing the earlier church tradition that had blamed Jews for the death of Jesus.

Cushing's ecumenical path was not always smooth. In the early 1950s he was seriously embarrassed by the activities of Father Leonard Feeney, S.J., Catholic chaplain at Harvard University, who gained notoriety for inflexible preaching that there was no salvation outside the Catholic church and that all non-Catholics were damned. After some early reluctance to move against the strident Feeney, who was dismissed from the Jesuit order, Cushing presided over his excommunication from the church. The archbishop's awkward handling of this very public case has been blamed for the fourteen-year delay between his installation as archbishop and his elevation to the cardinalate.

Cushing was notable for his willingness to involve himself in secular politics. In 1948 he led a sophisticated election campaign to defeat a referendum question that would have liberalized the state's birth control laws. (When a similar measure was introduced in the state legislature in 1966, he signaled his intention not to oppose it, and the bill was readily approved.) Throughout the 1950s he was a vigorous Cold Warrior, writing extensively on the threat of communism and, like most Catholic bishops, supporting Senator Joseph R. McCarthy. He was also a backer of Robert Welch and the John Birch Society, which was headquartered in the Boston suburbs.

Cushing's most visible political connection was with the Kennedy family. He joined Joseph P. Kennedy and Rose Kennedy in supporting programs for mentally retarded children, and he made much of his friendship with their son, John F. Kennedy. He presided at the future president's wedding in 1953, and he played a behind-the-scenes role in resolving the so-called Catholic issue during the presidential campaign of 1960. After delivering the invocation at the inauguration in 1961 (the first ever by a Catholic clergyman), he remained a close supporter of the administration: in 1962, for example, at the request of Attorney General Robert F. Kennedy, he helped raise more than $1 million for the ransom of prisoners taken during the Bay of Pigs invasion. Cushing presided at the funeral of President Kennedy in 1963, and in 1968 he made headlines by publicly endorsing the marriage of Jacqueline Kennedy to Greek shipping magnate Aristotle Onassis, a controversial marriage for Catholics because Onassis had been divorced.

Steadily deteriorating health, aggravated by medication and alcohol, clouded Cushing's last years with administrative turmoil. He could raise money faster than could most other churchmen, but he could spend it even faster and more uncontrollably. The absence of effective internal management led to a near-total loss of confidence in him on the part of the business community, and at his retirement as archbishop in September 1970 the archdiocesan debt approached $80 million. Cushing nevertheless remained a folk hero. When he died just two months after his resignation, his tenure was remembered as a kind of golden age for Boston's Catholics.

• Cushing's extensive personal and official papers, once thought to have been largely destroyed, are now preserved in the Archives of the Archdiocese of Boston. There is no complete, serious biography of Cushing, and there may never be. His personality and public image were so well developed that separating myth from reality is especially problematic in his case. Four uncritical biographies written by journalists, all repeating the same stories from the oral tradition and compiled without extensive access either to him or to his papers, appeared during his lifetime: M. C. Devine, *The World's Cardinal* (1964); Joseph Dever, *Cushing of Boston: A Candid Portrait* (1965); John H. Fenton, *Salt of the Earth: An Informal Portrait of Richard Cardinal Cushing* (1965); and John Henry Cutler, *Cardinal Cushing of Boston* (1970). Obituaries are in the *Boston Evening Globe*, 2 Nov. 1970, and the *New York Times*, 3 Nov. 1970.

JAMES M. O'TOOLE

CUSHING, Thomas (24 Mar. 1725–28 Feb. 1788), merchant and politician, was born in Boston, Massachusetts, the son of Thomas Cushing, a prominent merchant and officeholder, and Mary Bromfield. Thomas graduated from Harvard in the class of 1744 and received a master's degree in 1747. That same year he married Deborah Fletcher, with whom he had two children. Although established as a merchant specializing in the importation of woolens, his business dwindled as his interest in local politics increased. After serving in a number of minor Boston offices, he was appointed a justice of the peace in 1760. The next year he began a fourteen-year stint in the Massachusetts General Court as a member of the Popular party, opposing the royal governor's Court party. In 1766, when Governor Francis Bernard negatived James

Otis, Jr., as Speaker, the house chose Cushing instead. He was annually reelected to this position until 1774.

As resistance to British restrictions mounted during the 1760s, Cushing favored moderation. He was reluctant to oppose the Sugar Act but in 1767 condemned the Townshend duties, largely because they discouraged commerce. He did support the nonimportation movement until 1770 but retreated when he feared it might lead to independence. The more radical Whigs such as Samuel Adams and John Hancock distrusted him; John Adams labeled him "silent and sly" (Shipton, vol. 11, p. 382). An unenthusiastic member of the Committee of Correspondence from 1773, he became more vocal after Parliament passed the Boston Port Act the next year. As a Massachusetts delegate to the First and Second Continental Congresses, Cushing remained cautious, insisting on the continued use of economic boycotts and urging the adoption of a colonial union under Great Britain. Because of his continued opposition to independence, he was replaced by the radicals in December 1775. Afterward he served briefly as agent for the Continental navy.

Returning to Massachusetts politics, Cushing was still influential enough to simultaneously hold the offices of judge of probate, chief justice of the Court of Common Pleas for Suffolk County, and justice of the Superior Court. He was a founder of the American Academy of Arts and Sciences in Boston in 1780 and supported it faithfully, as he did his alma mater, Harvard. At the state constitutional convention in 1780, he joined Samuel Adams in arguing unsuccessfully for an all-powerful single legislature, yet he was elected lieutenant governor under the new constitution in alliance with John Hancock, who became governor. They were annually reelected until 1785 when "King" Hancock unexpectedly resigned early that year, pleading ill health. Hancock thus escaped accountability for the problems of a depression and near-empty state coffers. His enemies, led by Sam Adams, James Bowdoin, and James Warren, condemned his extravagant lifestyle and raised the Tea Assembly, an innocent social club patronized by the Hancock faction, to a colossal symbol of the decline of public virtue. Because Hancock still suffered from "political gout," he refused to stand for election in 1785; Cushing ran for the governorship with his blessing. Bowdoin, leading the Reform party, narrowly won the election, but the General Court elected the innocuous Cushing to the lieutenant governorship. Both were reelected in 1786, but Bowdoin, hurt by his zeal in repressing Shays's Rebellion, was defeated by Hancock the following year. Cushing survived, again in alliance with Hancock, and remained lieutenant governor until his death, of "lung fever," in Boston. Never a showy individual but a principled, sometimes infuriating, conservative, he retained the affection of the voters of Massachusetts for more than forty years.

• Many of Thomas Cushing's papers were destroyed by the British during the siege of Boston; most of the rest disappeared after his death. Some of his correspondence is preserved in the DeBerdt Letter Book, Library of Congress, which is partly reproduced in *Massachusetts Colonial Publications* 13 (1910–1911) and *Massachusetts Historical Society Collections*, ser. 4, vol. 4 (1858). His speeches appear in the state *Journals of the House of Representatives*, in the *Journals of the Provincial Congress of Massachusetts*, and in the *Journals of the Continental Congress*. The best complete biographical sketch is Clifford Shipton, *Sibley's Harvard Graduates*, vol. 11 (1960), pp. 377–95.

GORDON E. KERSHAW

CUSHING, William (1 Mar. 1732–13 Sept. 1810), senior associate justice of the U.S. Supreme Court, was born at Scituate, Plymouth County, Massachusetts, the son of John Cushing and Mary Cotton. His father was a lawyer who became a justice of the colonial Superior Court of Judicature. William was educated at Harvard College (A.B., 1751) and taught for a year as a preceptor at the Roxbury Grammar School. He then entered a law office apprenticeship with Jeremiah Gridley in Boston.

Admitted to practice in February 1755, Cushing advanced to the rank of barrister at law in 1762. Until 1759 he practiced in his home county, mainly in the Plymouth Court of Common Pleas. Enjoying only moderate success, he moved to Pownalborough (now Dresden), the county seat of newly formed Lincoln County in the district of Maine, where he was appointed probate judge shortly after his arrival and served from 1759 to 1764. Appointed the local attorney for the Kennebec Proprietors (1760–1771), Cushing soon added other real estate speculators and companies to his clientele; he specialized in litigating land titles contested by squatters. Cushing's success was limited by jury hostility to absentee landlords and claimants, and his clients frequently sent Boston counsel to assist him in the trial of these cases. These professional associations brought him into contact with many of the future leaders of the American Revolution in Massachusetts, including John Adams and James Bowdoin.

Cushing's father conditioned his retirement from the colonial Superior Court of Judicature on Lieutenant Governor Thomas Hutchinson's agreement to appoint William to succeed him. After some hesitation Hutchinson appointed William to the post on 16 February 1772. Almost immediately after he joined the court a dispute developed between the lieutenant governor and the legislature as to whether the judges would accept their salaries from the legislature or from the Crown. The debate over the judges' salaries presented important questions concerning judicial independence of the Crown as well as the proper role of the general court (legislature) in funding the court system.

The issue quickly polarized the legal profession and the court between protagonists of Crown prerogatives and advocates of colonial legislative power. Chief Justice Peter Oliver announced his intention to accept Crown payment; Justice Edmund Trowbridge favored a legislative grant. Cushing delayed announcing his decision until the last moment, when he accepted a legislative salary on 5 February 1774. This endeared

him to the patriot cause and marked the beginning of his involvement in the campaign for independence. In the same year he married Hannah Phillips. They had no children. Neither marriage nor his election of a legislative salary grant deterred Cushing from his official duties. He continued to ride the 1,500-mile court circuit until February 1775, maintaining a vestige of the royal authority he had sworn to uphold.

After independence, the Massachusetts Provincial Congress appointed John Adams chief justice of the new Superior Court of Judicature; William Cushing became first associate justice on 28 October 1775. Adams's continual absences from the Continental Congress gave Cushing frequent opportunities to preside, and when Adams resigned Cushing was appointed chief justice.

As a delegate to the convention that met on 1 September 1779 to draft a constitution for Massachusetts, Cushing did not take a prominent role in the proceedings. Indeed they seemed to have bored him. He perhaps later regretted his inattention, for Cushing and his fellow justices subsequently labored to explain the constitution to the people through grand jury charges. Cushing's biographer, John D. Cushing, observed that in this task he exhibited "the same literal conservatism that marked his entire judicial career" and that his explanations contrasted unfavorably with the "clear, incisive approach of his colleagues."

After ratification of the constitution in 1780, Cushing was appointed chief justice of the Supreme Judicial Court, the successor to the provincial Superior Court of Judicature. In addition to his judicial duties Cushing served on a committee appointed to revise and digest state law. He accepted responsibility for recasting the statutes on religion and maritime law. He wrote an important new statute on marriage and divorce, which substituted judicial divorce on limited grounds for the cumbersome and expensive procedure of legislative divorce (Feb. 1785).

Beginning in April 1782 the Supreme Court on circuit confronted public unrest in rural areas prompted by harsh debt collection practices. By 1786 widespread violence erupted in Daniel Shays's rebellion. Chief Justice Cushing and his colleagues continued to hold court in the troubled areas, supported by militia troops assigned to protect them. Cushing presided over a series of treason trials (8 Apr.–9 May 1787) after the defeat and dispersal of Shays's supporters, of whom thirteen were sentenced to death but later pardoned. The disturbances helped convince Cushing of the need for a stronger federal government.

Cushing's legal opinion in the Quock Walker Case (*Commonwealth v. Jennison* [1783]) traditionally has been identified as the decision that abolished slavery in Massachusetts. Cushing's biographer has pointed out that it was in the earlier trial of a related case (*Caldwell v. Jennison* [Sept. 1781]) that Cushing's colleague, Associate Justice Nathaniel Peasley Sargent, first enunciated the doctrine that slavery had, in effect, been abolished by the ratification of the 1780 state constitution because the document assumed that all men were created free and equal. Cushing's 1783 opinion followed this reasoning, but being a charge to the jury it did not provide for any immediate end of slavery in the state.

After serving as vice president and presiding officer of the Massachusetts convention called to ratify the proposed Federal Constitution, Cushing received President George Washington's nomination to the Supreme Court. He was confirmed by the Senate on 27 September 1789 and became the senior associate justice of the new Supreme Court of the United States.

Though he served for twenty-two years on the Supreme Court, Cushing wrote only nineteen opinions and made only a nominal contribution to its case law. His opinions in admiralty and prize cases were significant, building on the expertise he had acquired as a judge in the New England circuits, where such cases predominated. Otherwise his opinions were distinguished by a tendency to reduce complicated cases to single issues. In *Calder v. Bull* (1798) he resolved complex property questions by announcing the simple rule that the ex post facto clause of the Federal Constitution applied to civil, and not criminal, cases.

Perhaps Cushing's most noted opinion was delivered in 1793. In *Chisholm v. Georgia* Cushing agreed with the majority of his colleagues that the state of Georgia might be sued in the Supreme Court for a debt owed to a South Carolina man. Cushing's opinion carefully reviewed the Federal Constitution's grant of judicial power to the Supreme Court and concluded that a state's sovereign immunity did not remove the case from the Court's jurisdiction. This decision aroused widespread opposition and probably contributed to Cushing's defeat by Samuel Adams in the Massachusetts gubernatorial race the next year. The Eleventh Amendment (1798) subsequently provided that thereafter no state might be sued in the Supreme Court by a citizen of another state. Although Cushing's *Chisholm* opinion supported the ultranationalist position set forth by Chief Justice John Jay, it did not contain as sweeping a rejection of state sovereign immunity, preferring to view the Supreme Court's jurisdiction over states as necessary for an effective federal system.

Cushing's other major constitutional law opinion was delivered in *Ware v. Hylton* (1796), in which the Supreme Court voided Virginia statutes that hindered collection of prewar debts owed to British merchants and thus violated the 1783 peace treaty. Treaties, like the Constitution itself, could not be superseded by individual states' laws. Not only did the state's action violate the customary law of nations, Cushing reasoned, but it also breached express treaty provisions and defied traditional principles of equity and justice. He concluded, "It can hardly be considered as an odious thing, to inforce the payment of an honest debt according to the true intent and meaning of the parties contracting."

After John Rutledge's nomination for chief justice was rejected by the Senate, that body confirmed President Washington's nomination of Cushing to be chief justice (26 Jan. 1796). He held the commission for a week and then returned it to the president, declining the appointment for reasons of health. Some authorities, notably Henry Flanders in his *Lives and Times of the Chief Justices*, have suggested that even though he had not acted under the chief justice's commission Cushing should be included among the chief justices of the United States.

Despite ill health Cushing could not afford financially to retire and persisted in office until his death at Scituate fourteen years later. Measured by the achievements of his contemporaries, his eventful life seems to have had but slight impact on the course of history. By 1796, when he declined leadership of the Supreme Court, his health and age (sixty-four) were already significant factors limiting his work on the Court. His position as senior associate justice at the beginning of the Marshall era made him more prominent in the Supreme Court's formal activities, but the frailties of old age caused serious backlogs in the work of his assigned circuit courts. Ironically Cushing was succeeded by Joseph Story, one of the most active and vigorous among Supreme Court justices.

• The best coverage of Cushing's career is John D. Cushing, "A Revolutionary Conservative: The Public Life of William Cushing, 1732–1810" (Ph.D. diss., Clark Univ., 1959). Also useful is Arthur P. Rugg, "William Cushing," *Yale Law Journal* 30 (1920–1921): 128, and Henry Flanders, *The Lives and Times of the Chief Justices of the Supreme Court of the United States*, vol. 2 (1881), pp. 11–51. Herbert A. Johnson's entry on Cushing in *The Justices of the United States Supreme Court 1789–1969: Their Lives and Major Opinions*, ed. Leon Friedman and Fred L. Israel (1969), is an extended biographical sketch with selected opinions by Cushing. Three specialized articles are F. William O'Brien, "Justice William Cushing and the Treaty-Making Power," *Vanderbilt Law Review* 10 (1957): 351–67; O'Brien, "Justice Cushing's Undelivered Speech on the Federal Constitution," *William and Mary Quarterly*, 3d ser., 15 (1958): 74; and John D. Cushing, "The Cushing Court and the Abolition of Slavery in Massachusetts," *American Journal of Legal History* 5 (1961): 118–44. The documents relating to Cushing's Supreme Court appointments are printed, with a biographical sketch, in Maeva Marcus and James R. Perry, eds., *The Documentary History of the Supreme Court of the United States, 1789–1800*, vol. 1, pt. 1 (1985), pp. 24–30, 101–4.

HERBERT A. JOHNSON

CUSHING, William Barker (4 Nov. 1842–17 Dec. 1874), naval officer, was born in Delafield, Wisconsin, the son of Milton Buckingham Cushing, a physician, and Mary Barker Smith. Having moved his family to Chicago in 1844 because of his poor health, Milton Cushing died of pneumonia three years later. His widow and her four sons then settled in Fredonia, New York, where Mary Cushing established a school.

William Cushing graduated from the Fredonia Academy in 1856 then spent the next year in Washington, D.C., as a page in the U.S. House of Representatives. In 1857 he received an appointment to the U.S. Naval Academy. His propensity to mischief-making at the expense of his professors along with a mediocre academic performance resulted in his dismissal from the academy in his senior year. Only weeks before his class was to graduate, Cushing's examination included the evaluation: "General conduct: bad. Aptitude for Naval Service: not good. Not recommended for continuance at the Academy." He was permitted to resign on 23 March 1861.

Dismayed at his dismissal and determined to redeem himself, Cushing was successful in securing appointment as acting master's mate. He was ordered to the *Minnesota* of the North Atlantic Blockading Squadron. As prize master aboard two captured blockade runners, Cushing was responsible for bringing those vessels safely to port. In August 1861 the *Minnesota* participated in the joint army-navy expedition that captured the two Confederate forts at Hatteras Inlet, North Carolina. Shortly thereafter, Cushing resigned from the service following a disagreement with his commanding officer.

Cushing was not to remain inactive. His ability and resourcefulness had impressed Navy Secretary Gideon Welles, and Cushing was reinstated on 19 October 1861 as acting midshipman, his warrant to date from 1 June. Serving aboard the *Cambridge* of the North Atlantic Squadron, Cushing saw action against the Confederate ironclad *Virginia* (*Merrimack*) off Hampton Roads, Virginia (8 Mar. 1862), receiving a minor wound. After again serving aboard the *Minnesota*, Cushing was promoted to lieutenant, 16 July 1862, and became executive officer of the sidewheel steamer *Commodore Perry*. In October of that year, in an operation against Franklin, Virginia, the *Commodore Perry* grounded while descending the Blackwater River and was in imminent danger of being captured. Coolly, Cushing and several of his sailors managed to repulse the attacking Confederates, thus saving their ship from capture.

Recognized for his bravery, Cushing was given his own ship to command, the 100-ton iron steamer *Ellis*, in October 1862. He captured one blockade runner and destroyed a major Confederate saltworks at New Topsail Inlet, on the North Carolina coast, and captured two small schooners at Jacksonville. Not long afterward, when the *Ellis* grounded, Cushing and six volunteers held back a Confederate attack and then set the *Ellis* on fire to prevent its capture. Cushing requested a court of inquiry after the incident, but instead the Navy department praised him: "We don't care for the loss of a vessel when it fought as gallantly as that." After briefly commanding the *Commodore Barney* and the *Shokoken*, Cushing was assigned command of the far superior *Monticello* (5 Sept. 1863), blockading the mouth of the Cape Fear River.

Cushing's exploits gained him a reputation for daring and successful raids behind enemy lines. In February 1864 he led twenty volunteers at night aboard two small boats, hoping to find and capture Confederate general Louis Hébert at Smithville, North Carolina, on the Cape Fear River. Although it turned out that Hébert was absent, the raiders nevertheless succeeded in capturing a Confederate officer of lesser rank. A similar night raid near Wilmington in June resulted in the capture of a mounted Confederate courier. Cush-

ing's reputation was by now above reproach. His superiors, including Secretary Welles, could count on the brash young officer for the most difficult and dangerous missions.

In October 1864 Cushing was given an assignment that many considered suicidal: the capture or destruction of the powerful Confederate ironclad *Albemarle* at Plymouth, North Carolina. Cushing himself remarked, "Another stripe or a coffin!" On the night of 27 October, Cushing and fifteen volunteers moved up the Roanoke River aboard a launch equipped with an improvised spar torpedo designed by Cushing. They broke through a raft of protective logs and exploded the torpedo under the *Albemarle*'s hull despite considerable small arms fire from the Confederates. Receiving only a minor wound, Cushing swam downstream, evaded search parties, and succeeded in reaching the safety of the Federal fleet. Only one other raider escaped death or capture. For his heroic achievement, Cushing—at only twenty-one—was promoted to lieutenant commander and received the Thanks of Congress at the request of President Abraham Lincoln.

By November 1864 Cushing was again off Wilmington, commanding the *Malvern*, flagship of the squadron. During the joint army-navy assault on Fort Fisher, 15 January 1865, Cushing, now commanding the *Monticello*, led a company of sailors and marines in a charge over the parapet. Although Cushing's force was repulsed with heavy losses, it served as a diversion for the army attack, thereby contributing to the Federal victory. Cushing continued to be active after the fall of Fort Fisher, finding and removing enemy torpedoes, occupying coastal towns, and capturing two blockade runners. Cushing's idea of using a mock monitor as a ruse resulted in panicking the Confederates into abandoning Fort Anderson. The city of Wilmington surrendered soon afterward.

From 1865 to 1867 Cushing commanded the *Lancaster* of the Pacific Squadron, then he commanded the *Maumee* of the Asiatic Squadron, 1868–1869. In 1870 he married Katherine Louise Forbes; they had two children. Promoted to commander on 31 January 1872, Cushing was assigned ordnance duty at the Boston Navy Yard. Still chafing at being inactive despite his failing health, he was finally assigned command of the *Wyoming* in 1873. Maintaining his reputation as an officer of bold action, Cushing landed at Santiago, Cuba, and demanded that the governor put an immediate stop to the execution of the crew of the *Virginius*. The American steamer *Virginius*, flying the American flag, had been used by Cuban rebels to transport men and supplies to Cuba. After its capture by the Spaniards, fifty-three passengers and crew were executed, including eight Americans. Cushing's threat of reprisal prompted the governor to stop the executions.

Cushing's brilliant career ended tragically with his complete physical and mental collapse. He died in Washington, D.C., after being taken from his home there to the Government Hospital for the Insane. Recalling Cushing after his death, Welles observed, "The very audacity of many of his suggestions startled and astounded those to whom they were communicated, but when accepted and accomplished, they extorted admiration."

• Collections of Cushing's papers are at the State Historical Society of Wisconsin, the National Archives, and the Library of Congress. Two biographies of Cushing are E. M. H. Edwards, *Commander William Barker Cushing of the United States Navy* (1898), and Ralph J. Roske and Charles Van Doren, *Lincoln's Commando; The Biography of Commander W. B. Cushing* (1957). Discussions of his career include Daniel Ammen, "The Career of Commander William B. Cushing," *United Service* 2 (June 1880): 692–97; Gershom Bradford, "Cushing in *Shokokon*," *American Neptune* 18, Apr. 1958, pp. 142–48; and Glenn Howell, "Picnic with Cushing," *United Naval Institute Proceedings* 62 (Aug. 1936): 1098–1104. Other sources of information on Cushing are Clarence E. N. Macartney, *Mr. Lincoln's Admirals* (1956); Albert F. Blaisdell and Francis K. Ball, *Heroic Deeds of American Sailors* (1915); Theron W. Haight, *Three Wisconsin Cushings* (1910); and J. R. Soley, *The Blockade and the Cruisers* (1883). An obituary is in the *Washington Evening Star*, 18 Dec. 1874.

NORMAN C. DELANEY

CUSHMAN, Charlotte Saunders (23 July 1816–18 Feb. 1876), actress, was born in Boston, Massachusetts, the daughter of Elkanah Cushman, a merchant shipper, and Mary Eliza Babbit. Due to her father's ill health and financial collapse in 1829, Charlotte was obliged to quit school at age thirteen. Between chores in her mother's boardinghouse, however, she often accompanied her uncle, Augustus Babbit, to the Tremont Theatre. Though her puritanical parents strongly opposed such pleasures, Charlotte later referred to those evenings watching top English and American actors perform as her real, true education.

Her education continued in 1829 when she joined the Second Church (Unitarian), where Ralph Waldo Emerson preached his gospel of self-reliance: "The good man reveres himself, reveres his conscience, and would rather suffer any calamity than lower himself in his own esteem." As a member of the church choir, she also learned that with proper training her contralto voice might be her best hope for financial independence.

By 1835, the signing lessons that she had paid for herself resulted in her Boston operatic debut as the Countess Almaviva in Mozart's *Marriage of Figaro*. The next day the *Boston Atlas* declared that Cushman had held the stage with "grace and dignity."

Through her singing teacher, she obtained an apprentice position at the St. Charles Theatre in New Orleans. On 1 December 1835, however, her nervous debut there as the Countess Almaviva ended in a fiasco. The next morning, the *Bee*'s newspaper critic declared that, given her incredibly shrill top tones, he would as soon "hear a peacock attempting the carols of a nightingale" as listen to Cushman's "squalling caricature of singing."

Throughout the spring of 1836, as Cushman attempted other operatic roles, the *Bee* critic did give her one hope. If she confined herself to straight acting parts, she might perform "with success." With that thought in mind, she sought the advice of a fellow performer. "You're a born actress," James Barton told her, "go on the stage." Under his guidance, her acting debut on 23 April 1836 as Lady Macbeth—clutching a pair of daggers, her eyes blazing with obsessed ambition, her chin set firmly to her bloody task—set off a frenzy of cheers.

Two weeks later, when the New Orleans theater season ended, she sailed north to brave the stricter judgments of New York. Borrowing money to buy her costumes, she opened at the Bowery Theatre as Lady Macbeth, transfixing her audience "with the horror of her infernal purpose." Her triumph, however, was short-lived. Nine days later flames roared through the Bowery Theatre, destroying all her costumes. Her contract was cancelled.

Unbowed, Cushman found a better chance to prove her abilities when she played Romeo at New York's National Theatre in 1837. "With a little more fire in the impassioned scenes," the *New York Courier* would have found her "faultless."

Within weeks she appeared in a role well suited to her broad range of talents. As Meg Merrilies in Sir Walter Scott's *Guy Mannering*, costumed in rags and clutching a staff in her bony fingers, she was a bent, hollow-eyed crone. Madly screeching or crooning a weird lullaby, she electrified the audience. At the curtain, the actor who had played opposite her rushed to her. "When I turned and saw you," he cried, "a cold chill ran all over me."

As a "walking lady" she was back in New York at the Park Theatre in the fall of 1837, playing chambermaids, old women, tragic queens, comic ladies, and young men. With her "histrionic advantages," the *New Yorker* critic predicted, Cushman could well become "a general favorite." He sincerely doubted, however, that any audience would praise her appearance. Plain-faced in the extreme—her jaw too prominent, her mouth too wide, her nose too flat—Cushman's future success, in his opinion, must depend on the rich voice and the keen intelligence that shone within her tall, boyish appearance.

At the Park she proved her worth so effectively that she was soon playing Cordelia to the King Lear of America's reigning male star, Edwin Forrest. From there she progressed to star parts in her own right: Lady Macbeth, Nancy Sykes in *Oliver Twist*, and Romeo.

After three years at the Park, as her confidence strengthened, she asked a veteran English actor what chance she might have in London, the pinnacle of the theater arts. William Chapman's reply was direct: with her "extraordinary gifts," she must go to London and let her talents be known.

Toward realizing that dream, she signed on as "leading lady" at the National Theatre in Philadelphia in August 1842. That position brought her acclaim—her name carried high on the daily playbills—and much more than the $20 per week she had received at the Park. It also brought her an even more taxing routine: in an average week, she played five or six different roles. On 1 September, she was Ellen Rivers in *The Patriarch*; on the second she was Gabrielle in *Tom Noddy's Secret*; three nights later she was Nancy in *Oliver Twist*; on the seventh she was Beatrice in *Much Ado about Nothing*; and on the eighth she played Smike in *Nicholas Nickleby*.

Though that year-long routine often left her exhausted, it gave her a chance to play opposite stars whose famous names shed luster upon her own. William Macready, London's reigning tragedian, wrote in his journal, "The Miss Cushman who acted Lady Macbeth interested me much. She has to learn her art, but she showed mind and sympathy with me" (23 Oct. 1843). By the next morning, Cushman was again voicing her great, secret dream. "I mean to go to England as soon as I can. Macready says I ought to act on an English stage and I will."

That day came on 26 October 1844 when she set sail from New York. Safely arrived in London, she mailed letters of application to the major theater managers and then accepted the most attractive offer—from J. M. Maddox at the Princess Theatre. For her London debut on 14 February 1845, she chose *Fazio*, by Henry Milman. Throughout the early scenes in the play, the other actors seemed wholly indifferent to her as Bianca; the small audience sat cold and silent. The story unfolded to reveal Fazio's illicit affair with Aldabella and his embezzlement of another man's money. When Bianca cried out in anger, "Fazio, thou hast seen Aldabella!" Cushman sensed a sudden excitement out front. Fazio was forced to stand trial for all his misdeeds. Bianca pled passionately for his life, and hearing the sentence of death, she threw herself at his feet and implored his forgiveness. A storm of applause burst from the audience.

Next morning a knock on her door brought all the London papers and a grateful note from Maddox: her success had been "splendid." To the *Herald*, she had proved herself "a great artist." To the *Sun*, she was "the greatest of actresses." Not since the debut of Edmund Kean in 1814, it continued, had there been such a debut on "the boards of an English theatre."

After her run at the Princess, Cushman's tour through the provinces brought further acclaim. Only in Edinburgh did she encounter surprise. Her Romeo, while "splendidly acted," left many in her audience strangely disturbed: how could an honorable actress display herself so questionably, playing a man?

In spite of such doubts, by August 1849 Cushman's English career had brought her financial and artistic acclaim and a devoted circle of society friends, among them Jane and Thomas Carlyle. On that note, she sailed for the United States, savoring the chance to enjoy the fruits of her English victory. At home in Boston, when she entered a theater box to watch James H. Hackett as Falstaff, she had hardly taken her seat when a buzz began filtering through the audience. Faces turned up and peered at her, and happy shouts broke out when the theatergoers recognized her: "Three cheers for Charlotte Cushman! Hurray for our Charlotte!"

That initial appearance in 1849 touched off a regal progress through Boston, New York, Philadelphia, Washington, D.C., and New Orleans. As "one of America's intellectual jewels" (*Spirit of the Times*), she had come home to great crowds of admirers, who flocked now to see her as Queen Katherine in Shakespeare's *Henry VIII*, a role in which London critics had compared her favorably to the great Sarah Siddons. That homecoming also brought her a host of new friends: Henry W. Longfellow, James Russell Lowell, Julia Ward Howe, and Fanny Kemble.

By 1852, rich and content from her labors, Cushman returned to London, the better to enjoy her wealth in a social routine that included friendships with many of London's intellectual and artistic elite. From there she moved to Rome and opened a lavish house on the Via Gregoriana that she made a social center for expatriate English and Americans, including Robert and Elizabeth Barrett Browning, Nathaniel Hawthorne and his wife, William Wetmore Story and his wife, and Cushman's American protégées, the young sculptors Harriet Hosmer and Emma Stebbins.

By 1854, however, she was restless for work. Back in London, the *Illustrated London News* spoke for the crowds that flocked to her nightly performances. "We welcome most heartily this reappearance of Miss Cushman, with powers evidently not diminished, but, as it strikes us, increased."

Lengthy "retirements" followed by eager returns to the stage—performing with top stars like Forrest, Macready, and Edwin Booth—in the United States and England spelled the remaining routine of her acting career. Although eager for rest in Rome and later in her "Villa Cushman" in Newport, Rhode Island, she soon yearned for the stage. After each "irrevocable retirement," her passion for her work would bring her back again.

But by 1874, Cusham had played out her energies. When she opened a brief run at Edwin Booth's Theatre in New York, the papers were happy to note no decline in "her awe-inspiring presence." Her final farewell in New York took place at Booth's on the night of 7 November 1874, when, after her sleepwalking scene in *Macbeth*, the curtain slowly descended, and the cheering audience leaped to their feet.

Joining her at the footlights, William Cullen Bryant read her a long testimonial. "You have taken a queenly rank in your profession. You have interpreted through the eye and ear to the sympathies of vast assemblages of men and women the words of the greatest dramatic writers." With that, Bryant settled a laurel wreath on her head, a symbol, he said, "of the regal state in your profession to which you have risen and so illustriously hold."

Fighting back tears, Cushman opened her arms and bowed low. Facing the audience, she delivered her life's manifesto. "I found life sadly real and intensely earnest, and in ignorance of other ways to study, I resolved to take therefrom my text and my watchword. To be thoroughly *in earnest*, intensely in earnest in all my thoughts and in my actions, whether in my profession or out of it, became my one single idea. And I honestly believe therein lies the secret of my success in life."

In private, Cushman had long entertained a personal conviction no less intense. Traditional society might think as it pleased, but for the abiding ties of the heart she had always, from her earliest friendship with Rosalie Sully, the daughter of Philadelphia painter Thomas Sully, enjoyed romantic attachments with kindred spirits of her own sex. Edinburgh could chide her for playing Romeo and Hamlet, but she would calmly reply that in such "breeches parts" she felt completely at ease. As her career steadily progressed, she enjoyed similar friendships with the English actress Matilda Hays and the American sculptor Emma Stebbins. When breast cancer and pneumonia at last overcame her, she was in Boston in the supportive care of Stebbins, her special companion for twenty years.

After her burial in Mount Auburn Cemetery in Cambridge, the nation's major newspapers summed up her life. According to the *New York Tribune*, "The greatness of Charlotte Cushman was that of an exceptional because grand and striking personality." To the *New York Times*, her fame would be "as enduring as any conqueror's." According to *Scribner's* magazine, Cushman's art had surpassed that of her most eminent contemporaries, George Eliot, George Sand, and Elizabeth Barrett Browning. "They do not stand as high in their respective professions as she stands on the stage."

Through her art and her shrewd investments, she left an estate worth nearly a million dollars. On 21 May 1925, a bust of Charlotte Cushman was unveiled at New York's Hall of Fame for Great Americans. She was the first native-born actress to triumph both in the United States and in Great Britain, and she was at that time the only actress accorded such acclaim.

• Major collections of Charlotte Cushman primary sources (letters, playbills, playscripts, scrapbooks of clippings, costumes, photographs, etc.) can be found at the Manuscripts Division of the Library of Congress, the Harvard University Theatre Collection, the Yale University Theatre Collection, and the Folger Shakespeare Library in Washington, D.C. Less extensive collections are available at the New York Public Library, the Boston Public Library, Radcliffe College Library in Cambridge, the Players Club in New York, and the library of the University of Texas in Austin. The major published treatments of Cushman are Emma Stebbins, *Charlotte Cushman: Her Letters and Memories of Her Life* (1878); Clara Erskine Clement, *Charlotte Cushman* (1882); W. T. Price, *A Life of Charlotte Cushman* (1894); Cornelia Carr, *Harriet Hosmer: Letters and Memories* (1912); Joseph Leach, *Bright Particular Star: The Life and Times of Charlotte Cushman* (1970); and Dolly Sherwood, *Harriet Hosmer: American Sculptor 1830–1908* (1991). Obituaries are in the *New York Times*, the *New York Herald*, and the *Boston Advertiser*.

JOSEPH LEACH

CUSHMAN, Joseph Augustine (31 Jan. 1881–16 Apr. 1949), geologist, was born in Bridgewater, Massachusetts, the son of Darius Cushman, a shoe store owner and cobbler, and Jane Frances Fuller. Cushman learned at a young age a love of nature and the impor-

tance of careful observation from his elderly father, who died shortly after Cushman finished high school. Cushman then attended Bridgewater Normal School while working to help support the family.

In 1901 Cushman obtained a scholarship to Harvard University, where he began a lifelong friendship with his advisor, the invertebrate paleontologist Robert Tracy Jackson and changed his major from cryptogamic botany (dealing with spore-producing plants such as fungi, algae, ferns, and mosses) to micropaleontology. He graduated magna cum laude in 1903. While curator of the Boston Society of Natural History, Cushman studied under Jackson toward his doctorate, which he received from Harvard in 1909.

During the summers of 1904 and 1905 Cushman had worked at the U.S. Fish Commission at the Woods Hole Biological Laboratory. There he met Mary Jane Rathbun, who, "more than any other person" (quoted in Schmitt [1950], p. 29) spurred his interest in describing and classifying foraminifera—one-celled marine animals, each characterized by a "test" or hard outer covering, found in marine sediments in both ancient and modern seas; the foraminiferal record spans 500 million years. Rathbun arranged through her brother, Richard Rathbun, the associate director of the Smithsonian in charge of the U.S. National Museum, to supply Cushman with samples of recent foraminifera from dredgings collected by the U.S. Fish Commission Steamer *Albatross*. Work with these samples set the foundation and pattern for his life's work. Cushman's bachelor's thesis, "Developmental Stages in the Lagenidae," and his doctoral dissertation, "The Phylogeny of the Miliolidae," each dealt with development and relationships within a family of foraminifera.

Cushman married Alice Edna Wilson in 1903; they had three children. Alice was diagnosed with tuberculosis in 1909, and the family was moved from Cambridge to Sharon, a small town south of Boston. Almost two years after his wife's death in 1912, he married in 1913 Frieda Gerlach Billings, who subsequently devoted her energies to maintaining a gracious and beautiful home where Cushman's hundreds of students and visitors were welcomed as guests.

In 1912 Cushman began work with the U.S. Geological Survey, which he continued until 1921 and again from 1926 until his death. Cushman outlined the first economic use of foraminifera in a brief report included in USGS Professional Paper 90-H (31 Dec. 1914) by L. W. Stephenson. Through his keen powers of observation, description, and artistic illustration, Cushman classified and cataloged exactingly foraminifera (from water supply wells in South Carolina), with distinctions finer than anyone else had been able to establish, into family, genus, species, and geologic age. He was consequently able to demonstrate that certain forms of these animals are characteristic of certain geologic ages and no others. Using the foraminifera as index fossils with a very narrow stratigraphic range, Cushman was able to use drill hole borings to correlate subsurface oil bearing and adjacent strata with an accuracy previously unapproachable.

Cushman was then asked to do more detailed studies of foraminifera for the oil industry, and in late 1922 he became a consulting geologist for the Marland Oil Company. His work almost immediately led to fewer and fewer "dry holes" being drilled, and foraminifera suddenly jumped from obscurity into the limelight of the oil exploration industry.

After a planned three-week field trip to Mexico for Marland Oil stretched to three months, Cushman returned to Sharon in March 1923, with a check for $20,000 and plans to build a laboratory behind his home. Construction began the following Monday, and Cushman began work as director of the Cushman Laboratory for Foraminiferal Research on 20 August 1923. He continued confidential work for the oil industry, using the larger part of his fees to pay for and equip his laboratory, until the end of 1925, when he terminated further commercial work. This left him free to teach at his laboratory in Sharon, conduct research, and once again publish his findings.

In 1926 Cushman offered to accept graduate students from Harvard, Radcliffe College, and Massachusetts Institute of Technology to his laboratory in Sharon, and Harvard appointed him lecturer in micropaleontology. He was quiet and unassuming, "yet friendly and most generous when once he recognized the spark of genuine interest in his students" (Todd [1950], p. 16). For twenty-three years he taught interested students at his Sharon laboratory at only a minimal charge for supplies, and his many students provided him a never-failing source of inspiration and pleasure. Harvard University, which appointed Cushman lecturer in micropaleontology in 1926 and research associate in micropaleontology in 1939, specified that no salary could be offered.

In April 1925 Cushman began the quarterly publication *Contributions from the Cushman Laboratory for Foraminiferal Research*. Twenty-five volumes (100 issues) were published, containing 332 papers, the majority by Cushman alone or jointly with one or more of his many co-workers. After his death, publication was continued by the Cushman Foundation for Foraminiferal Research as *Contributions from the Cushman Foundation for Foraminiferal Research* from 1950 through 1970, and then as the *Journal of Foraminiferal Research* from 1971.

Almost from the start Cushman believed that foraminifera could be grouped into many distinct species, just like other more complex organisms. This was a significant break with the prevailing view of the time—that the different shapes and structures of foraminifera represented only a broad range of variation within this "plastic group of animals" and that any definition of species limits was only an artificial construct. His work with the oil industry forced Cushman to split further and further the species for stratigraphic purposes. Often criticized for oversplitting by those who regarded the smaller foraminifera as "too long-ranged for stratigraphic zonation," Cushman attributed his commercial success to being able to recognize and catalog distinctions that had been overlooked by other researchers.

Although self-assured, Cushman approached his work with caution. In October 1926 Charles Schuchert, one of the most eminent and highly respected paleontologists of the time, wrote to Cushman, "I have long thought that you are afflicted with too much caution—caution is a very good quality, but too much of it places the owners into the rear guard and that is where you do not belong. Move to the front, young man, for that is where you should be" (quoted in Cifelli and Richardson, p. 65).

With this encouragement, in February 1927 Cushman published "An Outline of a Re-Classification of the Foraminifera," in which he reorganized and expanded the previous ten-family classification to forty-five families. In 1928, at his own expense and with private gifts given for the purpose, he published his classification as a textbook, *Foraminifera: Their Classification and Economic Use*. This he designated "Special Publication No. 1" of a new series, *Special Publications of the Cushman Laboratory for Foraminiferal Research*. Both the *Contributions* and the *Special Publications* became self-supporting after a few years. His new classification became widely accepted and was gradually expanded, with only minor changes through four revisions, to fifty families in 1948.

In 1927 and again in 1932 Cushman visited the museums of Europe to study their "type specimens" of foraminifera and also collected additional samples from the classic European type localities for his own specialized studies. Marshaling all these resources and his experience, Cushman brought order to a field that had been quite chaotic due to poor species definition, a limited focus on classification, and the prevailing assumption that differences between specimens were mainly random variations.

Cushman served as director of the Museum of the Boston Society of Natural History (1913–1925); as member of the Society of Economic Paleontologists and Mineralogists (president, 1930–1931), Paleontological Society (president, 1938), Geological Society of America (vice president, 1938), National Research Council (chairman of Committee on Micropaleontology, 1930–1946); and as editor of the *Journal of Paleontology* (1927–1930). He was elected Honorary Fellow of the Royal Microscopical Society (1938) and received the Hayden Memorial Geological Award and Gold Medal from the Philadelphia Academy of Natural Sciences (1945). He died in his home in Sharon, Massachusetts, after a seven-year battle with cancer.

Cushman loved and excelled in pure science and basic research long before an application was found for his work, as a student at Harvard, as a paid investigator at Woods Hole, as museum curator, and as a specialist in foraminifera with the U.S. Geological Survey. After the value of his specialty to petroleum exploration was established, he chose to return to basic research as a guide and teacher of others rather than to reap the riches and submit to the restrictions of a commercial career. Through his work with the Smithsonian Institution, the U.S. Geological Survey, and the oil companies, Cushman gained unprecedented knowledge of the varieties and distributions of foraminifera, on which he published a career total of 554 articles. His lifetime collection of more than a half million foram specimens, including 13,000 type specimens, together with the extensive library and card catalog dealing with them, were willed to the Smithsonian. Cushman's work and documented classification types became the basis for almost all future identification of foraminifera.

• The Cushman Collection at the National Museum of Natural History in Washington, D.C., contains virtually all Cushman papers and memorabilia still in existence. The files of Ruth Todd, his notable assistant and successor who moved with the Cushman Collection to the museum after his death, are particularly well organized and complete. A memorial volume, published as the Apr. 1950 edition of *Contributions from the Cushman Laboratory for Foraminiferal Research*, contains his complete bibliography along with eight articles by co-workers and colleagues (including Ruth Todd, Waldo L. Schmitt, and Kirtley F. Mather) on various facets of his life and work. Richard Cifelli and Susan L. Richardson, *A History of the Classification of Foraminifera (1836–1933)* (1990), contains a wealth of material on classification as well as the philosophies and people—especially Cushman—who made the classifications. An obituary is Lloyd G. Henbest, "Joseph Augustine Cushman and the Contemporary Epoch in Micropaleontology," *Proceedings Volume of the Geological Society of America* (July 1952): 95–102.

DAVID W. HILL

CUSHMAN, Robert (c. 1579–1625), an organizer and promoter of Plymouth Plantation in New England, was born in Canterbury, England. Little is known about his early life. He was a woolcomber by trade but evidently had some education and private means. It is known that in 1606 he intervened to protect an ill-treated apprentice in Canterbury. That year he married Sarah Reder, with whom he had one child. In 1609 he moved to Leiden, Holland, where he joined John Robinson's Separatist congregation. In 1617, a year after Sarah's death, he married Mary, the widow of Thomas Singleton. In that same year, he was appointed one of the Pilgrims' agents to make arrangements for their migration across the Atlantic.

In England almost continuously from 1617 to 1620, Cushman worked with other agents—John Carver, William Brewster (1567–1644), and Christopher Martin—to obtain a land patent, raise funds, assemble provisions, and recruit additional passengers for the initial voyage. Although the contract he negotiated with the merchant adventurers headed by Thomas Weston was criticized by the Leiden congregation for insufficiently safeguarding the settlers' economic interests, it provided the essential means for getting to, and getting started in, America.

Cushman sailed from Southampton in July 1620 with Mary and his son, Thomas, on the *Speedwell*, accompanying the *Mayflower*. When the *Speedwell* put back for repairs, he and his family stayed ashore. He made a single visit to Plymouth colony in November-December 1621, arriving with Thomas on the *Fortune*. During his brief stay he exhorted the colonists to work for the welfare of the whole community in a sermon that is regarded as the first preached in New England and the oldest extant preached in England's American colonies. Returning to England on the *Fortune* with a cargo of clapboard and furs, he evidently took with him the account of the Pilgrims' first year written principally by Edward Winslow (1595–1655) and published as *Mourt's Relation* (1622). The *Fortune* was seized en route by a French privateer, and the passengers and crew were detained for two weeks in France.

In England, Cushman promoted the plantation and dealt with the merchant adventurers on its behalf. In the preface to his published sermon he compared Plymouth's meadows and "sweet springs" to his native soil of Kent. His *Reasons and Considerations Touching the Lawfulness of Removing Out of England into the Parts of America* (appended to *Mourt's Relation*) advertized the colony as a promising place for "honest, godly, and industrious men" and as a model of good relations with the Indians. In 1622, with Winslow, he obtained a patent for land at Cape Ann, with fishing and hunting rights, an acquisition vital to the plantation's economic development. Upon Cushman's death, William Bradford (1590–1657) called him the Pilgrims' "right-hand man" in England.

Cushman's tract *The Cry of a Stone* (1642) written no earlier than 1618 and published under the name of Robert Coachman, shows that the writer was a moderate Separatist who, while attacking the Church of England, condoned attendance at its ministers' sermons. The tract defends lay preaching and presents a strong argument for separation from the established church. In all his writings, Cushman's characteristically active and plain-spoken prose makes liberal use of direct address, earthy metaphors, and dramatic tropes. Cushman's son, who remained in New England in 1621, became a leader in Plymouth's civil and church affairs.

• The principal source is Bradford's *Of Plymouth Plantation* (2 vols., 1912); see also the edition of S. E. Morison (1967), with several Cushman letters. Cushman's *A Sermon Preached at Plimmoth in New-England December 9. 1621* (1622), dated 12 December by Morison, has been several times reprinted as *The Sin and Danger of Self-Love*. Alexander Young, ed., *Chronicles of the Pilgrim Fathers* (1841), reprints *A Sermon* and *Reasons*, but compare these versions with the original texts. An accurate modern edition of *Mourt's Relation* is *A Journal of the Pilgrims at Plymouth*, ed. Dwight B. Heath (1963). A prefatory letter to *Mourt's Relation*, signed R. G. and attributed to Cushman, is discussed in Henry Martyn Dexter, ed., *Mourt's Relation . . .* (1865), pp. xxxvi–xxxvii. For Cushman's religious views see Stephen Foster, "The Faith of a Separatist Layman: The Authorship, Context, and Significance of *The Cry of a Stone*," *William and Mary Quarterly*, 3d ser., 34 (1977): 375–403.

MICHAEL MCGIFFERT

CUSTER, Elizabeth Clift Bacon (8 Apr. 1842–2 Apr. 1933), author, was born in Monroe, Michigan, the daughter of Daniel Stanton Bacon, a circuit court judge, and Eleanor Sophia Page. Her mother died of dysentery when Libbie (as she was called) was twelve. From an early age she developed a gift for literary expression and started a diary when she was ten. She graduated from the Young Ladies Seminary and Collegiate Institute in Monroe in June 1862.

The story of Elizabeth Bacon's love for George Armstrong Custer is legendary. Since he lived for a time in Monroe, they may have been childhood acquaintances. At any rate, during a party at Boyd's Institute in November 1862, while Custer was home on leave, Bacon fell in love with the flamboyant "boy general with the golden locks." They were married in a military ceremony at Monroe in February 1864. They had no children. By that time, George Custer was a brigadier general of cavalry, and during the remainder of the war Elizabeth Custer followed her husband wherever she could. She was at Richmond when Lee surrendered at Appomattox on 9 April 1865 and was afterward given the table on which the Confederate surrender terms were written by General Philip Sheridan.

Elizabeth Custer was a model army wife, enduring the hardships and sometimes crude conditions of military camps. The intimate correspondence between husband and wife reflected their warm and trusting relationship. In 1865 she accompanied Custer's regiment to Texas, and after his appointment as lieutenant colonel of the Seventh Cavalry she followed him to Fort Leavenworth, Kansas. One reason for Custer's subsequent court-martial, which resulted in a year's suspension from his command, was his absence without leave; he had left to visit his wife at Fort Leavenworth.

Following a brief tour of duty in the Department of the South, the Seventh Cavalry was transferred to the Dakota Territory in 1873. The Custers set up housekeeping at Fort Abraham Lincoln near Bismarck, and there, in the summer of 1876, she received the news of her husband's death in the battle of the Little Bighorn.

Elizabeth Custer never remarried. She contributed her share to the controversy concerning her late husband's career, however, mainly over whether he was a martyred western hero or a vain, blundering glory seeker. She lectured widely, fiercely defending his hero image against his detractors. To further protect George Custer's memory, she published three books. *Boots and Saddles* (1885) deals with the period just before the battle of the Little Bighorn, while *Tenting on the Plains* (1887) and *Following the Guidon* (1890) further describe their marriage and experiences in the Civil War and subsequent Indian campaigns. By 1926 she believed prematurely that the confusion surrounding "Custer's Last Stand" had finally been settled. She added that "perhaps it was necessary in the scheme of things" for the dispute to have risen, "for the public clamor that rose after the battle resulted in better equipment for soldiers everywhere, and very soon the Indian warfare came to its end." The false rumor that General Custer's body had not been mutilated because of Indian respect for his bravery was allegedly generat-ed by veterans out of respect for her feelings, but she outlived anyone who might ultimately have revealed the facts. In addition, she became involved in the woman suffrage movement and other feminist causes. She spent her later years in Bronxville, New York, and also maintained an apartment on Park Avenue in New York City, where she died.

• Letters and manuscripts of George A. and Elizabeth Bacon Custer are housed at Custer Battlefield National Monument, Detroit Public Library, Lincoln Memorial University, Monroe County (Mich.) Historical Museum, New-York Historical Society, United States Military Academy, and Yale University Library. Elizabeth Custer's obituary is in the *New York Times*, 5 Apr. 1933. See also John M. Carroll, *Custer in Texas* (1975); Lawrence A. Frost, *General Custer's Libbie* (1976); Jay Monaghan, *Custer* (1959); and Edgar I. Stewart, *Custer's Luck* (1955).

H. ALLEN ANDERSON

CUSTER, George Armstrong (5 Dec. 1839–25 June 1876), Civil War general and Indian fighter, was born in New Rumley, Ohio, the son of Emanuel Custer and Maria Ward, farmers. Reared in the rough-and-tumble environment of a large, rural family, "Autie" was a strapping, energetic youth who enjoyed hunting, fishing, and practical jokes and valued romantic novels over academic studies. From his family he acquired a strong affinity for Methodism and the Democratic party. Custer was educated at Stebbins Academy in Monroe, Michigan, where he lived part time with a half sister, and at McNeely Normal School in Hopedale, Ohio, and then taught briefly at two country schools in Ohio before winning, at age seventeen, an appointment to the U.S. Military Academy at West Point. Entering in June 1857, he graduated four years later, at the outbreak of the Civil War. His academic and conduct record at West Point was as dismal as his record in the combat arts was outstanding. Graduating at the foot of his class of thirty-four, he was commissioned second lieutenant in the Second U.S. Cavalry in time to take part in the first battle of Manassas.

Custer found his calling in the Civil War. Two years of staff duty, including a tour as aide to General George B. McClellan (1826–1885), established his military skill, both as a staff officer and in combat. So impressed was General Alfred Pleasanton, commander of the Cavalry Corps of the Army of the Potomac, that he recommended Custer for promotion. In June 1863 Captain Custer was appointed brigadier general of volunteers and given command of the Michigan Cavalry Brigade. At twenty-three, he was the youngest general in the Union army. Almost instantly General Custer made a dazzling name for himself. On the third day of Gettysburg the Michigan Brigade played a key role in turning back General J. E. B. Stuart's Confederate cavalry, which threatened the Union rear at the very moment of Pickett's charge on the Union center. Thereafter Custer's successes accumulated one after another. He became known throughout the army for smashing cavalry charges, for heedless bravery, for tactical brilliance more instinctive than cerebral, for heavy casualties, and, with long yellow hair and gold-bedecked black uniform, for personal flamboyance. Newspapers made him a household name. Throughout his life an incurable romantic, Custer took special pleasure in the opposite sex. In 1863 he married Elizabeth Clift Bacon. Although the marriage has come down to posterity as one of history's most idyllic, it went through periods of stress, almost certainly including infidelity on his part. There were no children.

When Ulysses S. Grant began his campaign against Richmond in the spring of 1864, General Philip H. Sheridan took command of the Cavalry Corps. In the battle of the Wilderness and the cavalry's raid on Richmond, Sheridan came to admire Custer's qualities, while Custer formed a lifelong loyalty to Sheridan. For the rest of his career, Custer benefited from Sheridan's patronage. Sheridan's campaigns in the autumn of 1864 to rid the Shenandoah Valley of Confederate forces catapulted Custer to military stardom. At Winchester and Cedar Creek, he led cavalry charges that triggered the collapse of the Confederate lines. Winchester earned him command of the Third Cavalry Division, and Cedar Creek brought him a brevet of major general, which allowed him to don two stars at the age of twenty-four. At Waynesboro, in advance of Sheridan's army, he seized the initiative and launched an attack that all but destroyed General Jubal Early's army. In the final campaigns of the war, Custer continued to add to his renown. At Dinwiddie Court House and Five Forks, and in the pursuit of Robert E. Lee's army from Petersburg to Appomattox, Custer and the Third Division won a string of victories and finally, at Appomattox Station, blocked the further retreat of the Confederate army. On the morning of 9 April 1865 the white towel signifying Lee's wish to meet with Grant was borne to General Custer. Sheridan bought the table on which the surrender was signed and presented it to Libbie Custer.

Had Custer been killed at Appomattox, he would be remembered as a great cavalry general, second only to Sheridan among Union horsemen. His tactical moves were nearly always correct and instantly executed. None excelled him in personal courage or individual battlefield combat. His casualty rates, however, gave him a reputation for recklessness, while his youth, his promotion from captain to general, his ostentation, and his heroic public image aroused jealousy and ridicule. After a brief tour in Louisiana and Texas, Custer was mustered out of the volunteer army and reverted to his regular rank of captain. With the expansion of the regular army in 1866, however, he won the lieutenant colonelcy of one of the new regiments, the Seventh Cavalry. With Sheridan's help, he was brevetted major general in the regular army. Thus, as with most other high-ranking officers who remained in active service, "General" Custer served in the actual rank of lieutenant colonel.

As an Indian fighter on the Great Plains, Custer made a new name for himself, one that eclipsed even his image as the "Boy General" of the Civil War. He began his new career inauspiciously with a clumsy performance in General Winfield S. Hancock's campaign of 1867 against the Cheyennes in Kansas, which culminated in a court-martial. Found guilty of a series of charges stemming from misconduct in the field, Custer was suspended from rank and pay for one year. On application of General Sheridan, however, he returned before completing the sentence and quickly scored a notable victory over Black Kettle's Cheyennes at the battle of the Washita in November 1868. Although immediately controversial because of the killing of women and children, the Washita established Custer's reputation as an Indian fighter. Assigned to the northern Plains in 1873, he took part in the Yellowstone Expedition, which guarded surveyors of the Northern Pacific Railroad. Two more victories, now against the Sioux, added luster to his name. In 1874 Custer led the Seventh in an exploration of the Black Hills of Dakota. Miners with the column found gold, and the ensuing gold rush laid the groundwork for the final chapter of his life.

By 1875 Custer was widely admired as the nation's foremost Indian fighter. He boasted a solid record, but the fame came as much from newspaper attention and from his own writings. He published a series of magazine articles and then consolidated them into an autobiography, which reached a large audience. Custer's final campaign, ending in the battle of the Little Bighorn on 25 June 1876, earned him immortality and a place in the national folklore. The disaster, low point for the army in the Great Sioux War of 1876, occurred when the Seventh Cavalry attacked a large Sioux and Cheyenne encampment on Montana's Little Bighorn River. Five companies under Custer's immediate command, more than two hundred officers and troopers, were wiped out by nearly two thousand warriors defending their families. The remaining seven companies of the regiment, under Major Marcus A. Reno and Captain Frederick W. Benteen, successfully defended an entrenched hilltop for two days until reinforcements arrived.

At once the subject of bitter controversy, "Custer's Last Stand" has been vigorously debated ever since. Custer has been charged with recklessness, Reno with cowardice, and their superiors with faulty strategy. Defenders ensure that the arguments will endure forever, as will the image of the doomed but heroic figure of Custer facing death on a hilltop. In large part, however, the soldiers lost because the Indians won—although in victory lay the seeds of their ultimate defeat.

• Custer's letters and other papers exist in the Marguerite Merington Collection at the New York Public Library and the Yale University Library, as well as in the Elizabeth B. Custer Collection at the Little Bighorn Battlefield National Monument, Mont. Among many biographies are Robert M. Utley, *Cavalier in Buckskin: George Armstrong Custer and the Western Military Frontier* (1988), and Jay Monaghan, *Custer: The Life of General George Armstrong Custer* (1959). The Civil War years are treated in Gregory J. W. Urwin, *Custer Victorious: The Civil War Battles of General George Armstrong Custer* (1983). Custer's autobiography is *My Life on the Plains; or,*

Personal Experiences with Indians (1874). Three autobiographical volumes by Custer's widow added greatly to the Custer legend: *Boots and Saddles; or, Life in Dakota with General Custer* (1885); *Tenting on the Plains; or, General Custer in Kansas and Texas* (1887); and *Following the Guidon* (1890). For the legend, consult Bruce A. Rosenberg, *Custer and the Epic of Defeat* (1974). For the Sioux campaign of 1876 and the battle of the Little Bighorn, see John S. Gray, *Centennial Campaign: The Sioux War of 1876* (1976), and *Custer's Last Campaign: Mitch Boyer and the Little Bighorn Reconstructed* (1991).

ROBERT M. UTLEY

CUSTIS, George Washington Parke (30 Apr. 1781–10 Oct. 1857), playwright, was born in Mount Airy, Maryland, the son of John Parke Custis, a wealthy landowner, and Eleanor Calvert. His father, the son of Martha Washington from her first marriage, died when George was very young, and the boy was brought up in one of the most famous homes in the nation, Mount Vernon. He studied the classics at Princeton (but received no degree) and was commissioned (but never served) in the U.S. Army in 1799 with the rank of colonel. In 1804 Custis married Mary Lee Fitzhugh and lived with her on his own estate in Arlington, Virginia. Here, while he managed his 8,000 acres and 300 slaves, Custis devoted himself to literary pursuits, which included writing a column for the *National Intelligencer*, often on the subject of his famous grandfather, George Washington. His "Conversations with Lafayette" was published after that hero's visit to the United States in 1824. He became particularly adept at writing and delivering eloquent speeches, notably on the death of federalist General Lingan, killed in the Baltimore riots in the early days of the War of 1812, and on the overthrow of Napoleon. Perhaps it was this gift for oratory that led Custis to write for the theater.

His first play, *The Indian Prophecy*, exploited his intimate knowledge of Washington. Billed as "a national drama in two acts," it was produced in 1827 and published the next year. The plot revolves around an incident that had occurred during Braddock's defeat at the battle of the Monongahela in 1755. In the engagement, a group of Native Americans fighting for the French had made repeated attempts to kill the young Colonel Washington, shooting two horses out from under him. Then, according to Custis's *Recollections* (p. 67), "the famed Indian commander, pointing to Washington, cried to his warriors: 'Fire at him no more; see ye not that the Great Spirit protects that Chief; he cannot die in battle.'" This dramatic incident provided the exciting climax to an otherwise pedestrian theater piece. Originally written for Washington's birthday, production was delayed until an equally patriotic occasion, 4 July 1827, when *The Indian Prophecy* opened at the Chestnut Street Theatre in Philadelphia. Only a handful of performances followed, at Baltimore and Washington, D.C., but this relatively unsuccessful debut did not deter Custis from writing at least eight more plays. He joined a small group of emerging American dramatists who answered a call by James Kirke Paulding to create a "national" drama that "showed an understanding of America and dramatized American ideas, events and idiosyncracies through American characters" (Meserve, *Heralds*, p. 164).

Custis's next play, *The Eighth of January; or, Hurrah for the Boys of the West*, was produced at the Park Theatre in New York on 8 January 1828, the anniversary of Andrew Jackson's victory at the battle of New Orleans, to celebrate that success in the field and Jackson's triumphant bid for the presidency. This play, an occasional piece, was not as well received as two others written at the same time on the same subject. In October of the same year Custis created another theatrical celebration of America, a "new national drama" called *The Railroad*, written to commemorate the Baltimore & Ohio line, completed only months before. The play, which opened at the Baltimore Theatre, revealed Custis's proclivity for scenic spectacle, an essential aspect of antebellum drama. Some of the painted scenery displayed a view of Baltimore, Fort McHenry with ships passing, and "a Distant View of a Rail Road in full Operation."

In his next play Custis returned to the popular subject of the American Indian and scored his one real theatrical success. *Pocahontas; or, The Settlers of Virginia*, opened on 16 January 1830 at the Walnut Street Theatre in Philadelphia. *Pocahontas* was a major achievement, running for a remarkable twelve performances, not consecutively but in repertory with other pieces, as was usual during that time. One of the performances was given on 22 February, his grandfather's birthday, to capitalize on the Custis-Washington connection. The play featured a combination of ingredients calculated for success on the early nineteenth-century American stage: popular characterization (the Native American as Noble Savage); fine dramatic suspense (historical chronology dispensed with in order to place the most dramatic scene, the rescue of John Smith, at the climax); and panoramic scenery (a view of the James River with ships at anchor, on one side of the stage a hut of mats and reeds, on the other rocks and cliffs with Indians watching the activity on the river).

Pocahontas marked the apex of Custis's theatrical career. He wrote two other plays on the Native American theme, *The Pawnee Chief*, which was presented at least once, on 22 February 1832, and *Monongahela*, which he worked on in 1836. There is no record of performance for the latter play nor evidence that Custis ever completed it. In 1833 the manager of the Baltimore Theatre requested a piece to commemorate the famous War of 1812 battle for Baltimore, and Custis responded with *Northpoint; or, Baltimore Defended*, which he wrote in nine hours. Another Custis drama, *The Launch of the Columbia; or, America's Blue Jackets Forever*, was commissioned to commemorate the launch of a new ship from the Washington shipyard. This play opened on his grandfather's birthday, 22 February 1836, at the Washington Theatre and was interesting primarily for its use of scenic spectacle and its patriotic appeal.

Custis's last drama, *Montgomerie; or, The Orphan of a Wreck*, was the only theater piece he wrote that was not concerned with an American theme. The subject of this "dramatic romance" was the Montgomerie clan, the setting fourteenth-century Scotland. The only recorded performance took place at Washington on 11 April 1836. Perhaps because so few of his plays had succeeded, perhaps because the care of his estates had begun to demand most of his time, George Washington Parke Custis wrote no more for the theater. The last twenty years of his life were spent at Arlington, Virginia, where he continued to write for the *National Intelligencer*, to tend his land, and to raise a daughter, Mary, who married Robert E. Lee. Custis died in Arlington.

Although Custis devoted only a comparatively brief portion of his life to playwriting he called himself "above all a writer" (Meserve, *Emerging*, pp. 249–50). He is one of that handful of Americans whom Walter Meserve dubbed "heralds of promise" for later American drama, "whose plays were being performed and who had written more than one produced play" (*Heralds*, p. 14). His most significant contribution lay in the genre of the American-Indian play, of which *Pocahontas* was one of the most effective examples. Although his plays retain only a historical interest, they represent an important part of the foundation on which American drama stands.

• Custis's *Recollections and Private Memoirs of Washington* (1859) contains biographical information in the front matter and throughout the text. Critical assessments of his plays can be found in J. N. Ireland, *Records of the New York Stage* (1866–1867); Arthur Hobson Quinn, *History of the American Drama from the Beginning to the Civil War* (1923); Murray H. Nelligan, "American Nationalism on the Stage: The Plays of George Washington Parke Custis," *Virginia Magazine of History and Biography* 58 (July 1950): 299–324; and Richard Moody, *America Takes the Stage: Romanticism in American Drama and Theatre, 1750–1900* (1955). For a recent and comprehensive examination of Custis's work see Walter J. Meserve, *An Emerging Entertainment: The Drama of the American People to 1828* (1977) and *Heralds of Promise: The Drama of the American People during the Age of Jackson, 1829–1849* (1986). *The Indian Prophecy* and *Pocahontas* can be read in *Three Centuries of Drama: American* (microcard), and *Pocahontas* is anthologized in Quinn, *Representative American Plays* (1917). An obituary is in the *New York Times*, 15 Oct. 1857.

JACK HRKACH

CUTHBERT, Marion Vera (15 Mar. 1896–5 May 1989), educator, administrator, writer, and activist, was born in St. Paul, Minnesota, the daughter of Thomas Cornelius Cuthbert and Victoria Means. She attended grammar and secondary school in her hometown and studied at the University of Minnesota before transferring to Boston University, where she completed her B.A. in 1920.

Following her graduation, Cuthbert moved to Florence, Alabama, and became an English teacher and assistant principal at Burrell Normal School. In 1925 she became its principal, leading both students and faculty in bold new perspectives on gender equality and interracial harmony.

In 1927 Cuthbert left Burrell to become one of the earliest deans of Talladega College in Talladega, Alabama. In her essay, "The Dean of Women at Work," published in the *Journal of the National Association of College Women* (Apr. 1928), she articulated her belief that covert sexism in the administration of black colleges limited their effectiveness. While dean, Cuthbert strengthened her academic credentials by completing a master's degree in psychology at Columbia University in 1931, after taking a sabbatical from Talladega during the 1930–1931 academic year to focus on her studies.

Following three years of administrative service, Cuthbert left Talladega College in 1932 to begin a twelve-year affiliation with the Young Women's Christian Association as one of the first blacks hired in the leadership division of the national office in New York City. In this capacity she was responsible for staff development and education, particularly among black employees. One of her early professional contributions was the creation of the YWCA Summer Training Institutes, which began at Oberlin College in 1938 as four-week training sessions designed to enhance the effectiveness of the YWCA and public agencies in general. She also traveled abroad to conduct similar workshops on interracial relations, volunteer education, student development, and administration. Cuthbert's influence as an executive at the YWCA's National Negro Leadership Conference held at West Virginia State College (20–23 June 1942) led to a motion to endorse a "national human relations conference, interracial in character, with common problems emphasized rather than differences." This endorsement reflected her commitment to interracial work and to promoting conferences that precluded separate black constituencies, an issue for many national organizations during that era.

Cuthbert completed her Ph.D. at Columbia University in 1942 and resumed her academic career in 1944 by joining Brooklyn College's Department of Personnel Services. Two years later she became the first black faculty member in the College's Department of Sociology and Anthropology. In addition to her academic work, Cuthbert retained her affiliation with the YWCA and rose to prominence in a wide range of national and international groups. She was a member of the board of directors and a vice president of the National Association for the Advancement of Colored people (NAACP), and she served as a counselor for the United Board of Christian Colleges in China and as an adviser to several other local and national organizations, including the Federal Council of Churches and the United Council of Church Women. She held memberships in the American Association of University Women, the American Association of University Professors, Pi Lambda Theta, Alpha Kappa Theta, and the American Sociology Society. She was also a fellow of the National Council on Religion in Higher Education.

Cuthbert's written work, published throughout her career, reflects her commitment to education, interracial harmony, and the well-being of African Americans. She frequently published articles in the *Woman's Press*—the YWCA's official publication from 1918 to 1953—and the *YWCA Magazine*, and she collaborated on numerous pamphlets and conference proceedings. She also authored four books, including *Juliette Derricotte* (1933), a short biography of a black YWCA activist; *We Sing America* (1936), a children's book highlighting the achievements of African Americans; *April Grasses* (1936), a collection of poetry; and *Songs of Creation* (1949), a book of inspirational verse. Perhaps her most significant published scholarly contribution was her doctoral dissertation, *Education and Marginality: A Study of the Negro Woman College Graduate* (1942), a work that affirms the reality of black women's oppression, especially in relation to that of black men and white women, and documents the impact of college education on their personal, social, and professional lives.

In 1961 Cuthbert retired from Brooklyn College as an associate professor and moved to Plainfield, New Hampshire, where she continued to use her gifts as an educator and administrator to serve the community. She spoke widely to various groups on social issues and literary concerns and remained active with the YWCA as an honorary national board member and a participant in international training projects. She held membership in the Plain-Meri Homemakers Group, the College Club of Windsor, and the Mothers and Daughters Club, and she attended the Plainfield Community Baptist Church. Additionally, she served as Plainfield Library Trustee and incorporator of the Sullivan County Mental Health Association.

Cuthbert never married. In 1968 she moved several times for health-related reasons between Concord, New Hampshire, Windsor, Vermont, and Claremont, New Hampshire, where she died. Her ashes were scattered from the top of Mount Ascutney in Vermont, symbolizing how much of the land and its people she had touched by her activism in the fields of education and race relations.

• Cuthbert's personal papers, which include data on the YWCA Summer Training Institutes and YWCA annual reports (1932–1980), are located in the Spelman College Archives in Atlanta, Ga. Other information on Cuthbert can be found in the Records Files Collection of the YWCA National Board Archives in New York City; in the Mugar Memorial Library at Boston University; in the Brooklyn College Archives; and in the Talladega College Archives. See also Lorraine Elena Roses and Ruth Elizabeth Randolf, *Harlem Renaissance and Beyond* (1990), and Jessie Carney Smith, ed., *Notable Black American Women* (1992).

MARILYN BUTTON

CUTLER, Elliott Carr (30 July 1888–16 Aug. 1947), surgeon and medical educator, was born in Bangor, Maine, the son of George Chalmers Cutler, a lumber merchant, and Mary Franklin Wilson. Cutler attended both Harvard College and Harvard Medical School, receiving his medical degree in 1913. He traveled to Heidelberg. where he studied pathology for one summer. Cutler then served as surgical intern at the newly opened Peter Bent Brigham Hospital, where he assisted surgeon Harvey Cushing. In 1915 Cutler joined the Harvard Unit of the American Ambulance Hospital in Paris, and upon his return he was named resident surgeon at the Massachusetts General Hospital. In 1916 Cutler declined William S. Halsted's invitation to run the Hunterian Laboratory at Johns Hopkins, opting to study immunity at the Rockefeller Institute for Medical Research in order to benefit "from the stern discipline of a meticulous laboratory worker," Simon Flexner ("The Education of the Surgeon," p. 467). America's entry into the First World War Prompted Cutler's return to France as a captain in the Army Medical Corps assigned to the Harvard Unit, Base Hospital Number 5.

After the war, Cutler returned to Boston, joining Cushing's staff at the Brigham Hospital as resident surgeon. In the spring of 1919 he married Caroline Pollard Parker, who had also worked at Base Hospital Number 5 in France. The couple had five children.

From 1921 to 1923 Cutler directed the laboratory of surgical research and was an associate in the Department of Surgery at Harvard Medical School. He left Harvard in 1924 to become professor of surgery at Western Reserve Medical School and director of surgery at the Lakeside Hospital in Cleveland, where he continued his laboratory work. He returned to Boston in 1932 when he succeeded Cushing as Moseley Professor of Surgery at Harvard Medical School and surgeon in chief at Peter Bent Brigham Hospital. The last fifteen years of his life were primarily devoted to surgical practice, teaching, and research at Harvard. At the outbreak of the Second World War, the governor of Massachusetts appointed Cutler medical director of the state committee on public safety. In 1942 he was again called into active service in the Army Medical Corps. During the war he served as chief surgical consultant and later as chief of the professional services division in the office of the surgeon general, European theater of operations. As chief surgical consultant, he played an active role in obtaining blood from the United States for use in treating wounded soldiers. In 1945 he was appointed brigadier general and received a second Distinguished Service Medal, as well as the Legion of Merit and the Order of the British Empire.

Cutler introduced several new techniques into cardiac surgery, a field then in its infancy. In 1923 he performed the first successful surgical operation for mitral valve stenosis. The possibility of surgical treatment for patients with constricted or diseased heart valves had been actively pursued for two decades by surgeons, who had attempted to approximate the condition in laboratory animals. Two years of research on animals at the Harvard surgical research laboratory emboldened Cutler and cardiologist Samuel A. Levine to attempt a surgical intervention in a young female patient with mitral valve stenosis. The surgery, hailed as a milestone by the *British Medical Journal*, proved to have a mortality rate of 90 percent; abandoned by Cutler in 1928, surgical repair for mitral valve stenosis was not reattempted until 1945. Cutler's other surgical innovations included the development of surgical instruments and techniques for treatment of pulmonary embolism and pericarditis and the development of surgical methods to treat patients with congestive heart failure, including the surgical removal of normal thyroid glands for relief of angina pectoris. In addition to more than two hundred scientific papers, he published in 1939, with Robert Zollinger, the *Atlas of Surgical Operations*. (In 1993 Zollinger and Robert Zollinger, Jr., published the seventh edition of the *Atlas*.)

As an animal experimenter and director of a surgical research laboratory, Cutler, like other researchers of his era, encountered criticism from American antivivisectionists concerned about the welfare of animals, especially dogs, used in research. In his laboratories, Cutler gave humane treatment of research animals high priority. In 1926 he became actively involved in organized medicine's defense of animal experimentation when he succeeded Harvard colleague Walter Bradford Cannon as chair of the American Medical Association's Committee for the Protection of Medical Research. For twelve years, until he reentered military service in 1942, Cutler monitored professional and popular reports of animal experimentation in an effort to forestall legislative restrictions on animal experimentation. In order to demonstrate humane conditions in research laboratories, Cutler arranged in 1938 for a photographer from *Life* magazine to photograph experimental surgical procedures on anesthetized dogs at Harvard, surgery that allowed students to "perform their first operation on man as surgeons and not as butchers."

In addition to his activities in defense of animal experimentation, Cutler held leadership positions in a number of medical societies, including the presidencies of the American Surgical Association (1947) and the Society for Clinical Surgery (1941–1946). He was one of the founders of the American Board of Surgery and served on the editorial boards of several major medical and surgical journals. The recipient of a number of honorary degrees, he was named an honorary fellow of the Royal College of Surgeons in 1943 and awarded the Henry Jacob Bigelow Medal by the Boston Surgical Society in 1947. Cutler died from prostate cancer in Brookline, Massachusetts. In 1965 Harvard Medical School established a professorship of surgery in his name.

• The Francis A. Countway Library of Medicine at Harvard holds a large collection of Cutler's office files from the years 1921 to 1942, which encompasses his teaching, hospital work, research, publications, and activities in defense of animal experimentation. In addition to the *Atlas*, Cutler's major works include "Cardiotomy and Valvulotomy for Mitral Stenosis," *Boston Medical and Surgical Journal* 188 (1923): 1023–27, with S. A. Levine; and "The Surgical Treatment of Mitral Stenosis: Experimental and Clinical Studies," *Archives of Surgery* 9 (1924): 691–821, with Levine and Claude S. Beck. For Cutler's role in efforts to upgrade surgical training, see his remarks delivered at his acceptance of the Bigelow Medal, "The Education of the Surgeon," *New England Journal of Medicine* 237 (1947): 466–70, and Peter D. Olch, "Evarts A. Graham, the American College of Surgeons, and the American Board of Surgery," *Journal of the History of Medicine* 27 (1972): 247–61.

For biographical information, see Frederick P. Ross, "Master Surgeon, Teacher, Soldier and Friend: Elliott Carr Cutler, MD (1888–1947)," *American Journal of Surgery* 137 (1979): 428–32. Cutler's role as a surgical innovator is discussed in Judith P. Swazey and Renee C. Fox, "The Clinical Moratorium: A Case Study of Mitral Valve Surgery," in *Experimentation with Human Subjects*, ed. Paul A. Freund (1970). Useful obituaries can be found in *Surgery* 23 (1948): 863–66; *New England Journal of Medicine* 237 (1947): 681; *Journal of the American Medical Association* 135 (1947): 47; and the *New York Times*, 17 Aug. and 24 Aug. 1947.

SUSAN E. LEDERER

CUTLER, Hannah Tracy (25 Dec. 1815–11 Feb. 1896), women's rights leader and physician, was born Hannah Maria Conant in Becket, Berkshire County, Massachusetts, the daughter of John Conant and Orpha Johnson. As a young girl Hannah desired an education but was deterred by a lack of learning facilities for females and by a father who regarded her interest in education as "folly." Her formal schooling was limited to the study of rhetoric, philosophy, and instruction in Latin by a family doctor. When the family moved to Rochester, Ohio, Hannah studied on her own. She wanted to attend Oberlin College and told her father that she would pay her own admission, but he denied her the chance. In 1834 she married John Martin Tracy, a theological student, with whom she had three children.

After their marriage Tracy's husband took up the study of law and lectured on abolition. She had found a receptive partner who was willing to share his knowledge with her, and they discussed at length such legal issues as married women's property rights. She began to realize that the laws meant to protect women were actually oppressing them. She became so knowledgeable that neighbors came to ask her opinion regarding their problems. In 1844, while aiding slaves on the Underground Railroad, her husband was attacked by an anti-abolitionist mob and died shortly thereafter.

Tracy and her children returned home to live in a cabin on her parents' land. She earned money by writing for local newspapers and drew inspiration from her mother as they shared thoughts on the plight of women and the injustices of slavery. Their exchanges on reform led to the formation of a Woman's Temperance Society in Rochester. After Tracy published *Woman as She Was, Is, and Should Be* (1846), in 1847 she enrolled at Oberlin College to prepare to teach and ran a boardinghouse as a means of income. Membership in a women's debating club helped hone her skills as a lecturer.

In 1848 Tracy took a position as matron at the Ohio Deaf and Dumb Asylum at Columbus, where she received a salary of $200 a year. She was distressed to learn that a male officer with a similar position was paid a salary of $500 a year. When she mentioned the discrepancy to the superintendent, he told her not to speak to the trustees or anyone else about it. Eventually the trustees learned about the inequity and Tracy's salary was increased. Two years later she became a principal in the female division of Columbus High School and supplemented her income by writing for local papers. Her series, "Letters to Housekeepers," appeared in the *Ohio Cultivator* along with her column of advice to farm girls written under the pen name Aunt Patience.

At college and in teaching Tracy met such other women's rights activists as Lucy Stone and Frances Gage, who held similar views to her own. In the next few years her activism intensified. She was secretary to the women's rights convention in Akron, Ohio, in 1851, and when the World's Peace Congress met in London in 1851, she was one of two women delegates from Oberlin. She was also hired as a correspondent by the *Ohio Statesman* to send articles from the London Exposition. During the trip she attended a temperance conference and was asked to address a question. In response she offered a speech on women's rights. She captivated the audience and was invited to speak on dress reform at other gatherings. In all, she gave twelve lectures that attracted large audiences. Her speeches addressed not only dress reform but slavery and the inequities faced by women. In England she also began to fully realize the benefits that suffrage could afford women.

After her return to the United States Tracy addressed a crowd of ten thousand people in Pittsburgh on women's rights, black rights, and dress reform. In 1852 she became the president of the Ohio Woman's Rights Association that was formed at the third women's rights convention in Ohio. In that year she married widower Colonel Samuel Cutler, and they moved to Dwight, Illinois, where they farmed for a living. She returned to Cincinnati, Ohio, to lecture at the 1855 national convention for women's rights. On the podium she called for marriages to be "complete and perfect union[s], conferring equal rights on both parties."

During the years before the Civil War Cutler had advocated legislation to give women rights of property ownership and disposition. In 1859 she campaigned in New York State, and in 1860 she canvassed with Gage in Illinois in a drive to pass a more complete married women's property bill. The following winter the bill that she drafted separating a woman's property from her husband's was passed. Shortly thereafter she left for Ohio to join women's rights advocates in appearing before a joint House-Senate committee to fight for a married woman's right to her husband's estate and the guardianship of her children.

In 1868, at the age of fifty-three, Cutler attended the Women's Medical College, a recently opened homeopathic school in Cleveland, Ohio. In 1869 she graduated with an M.D. and became a professor at the college. She attended the founding meeting of the American Woman Suffrage Association in 1870. In that year she and her husband, who had taken ill, resettled in Illinois. After her husband died in 1873, she returned to Ohio to continue her fight for suffrage. Eventually she settled in Cobden, Illinois, where she established a medical practice. In 1883 she traveled through New England with Lucy Stone to win support for a woman suffrage association in Vermont. In 1886 she published *Phillipia, or A Woman's Question* and *The Fortunes of Michael Doyle, or Home Rule for Ireland*. She continued to attend Woman's Christian Temperance Union conventions and other reform gatherings and occasionally lectured. She died in Ocean Springs, Mississippi, where she had gone to stay with her daughter.

A woman of versatility and drive, Cutler's activism was tempered by the traditional responsibilities of being a mother and homemaker. A needlecrafter, weaver, and spinner, she also tended to the garden and won awards for the syrups she made. Always thirsting for an education, she enrolled in medical school in mid-life. Her activism focused on issues of temperance, slavery, dress reform. Throughout her life she continued to speak out against and attempted to rectify the injustices to women and blacks.

• Hannah Tracy Cutler's autobiography is in the *Woman's Journal*, 19 Sept.–17 Oct. 1896. See also Elizabeth Cady Stanton et al., *History of Woman Suffrage*, vol. 1–4 (1881–1902); Una Stannard, *Mrs. Man* (1977); Blanche Glassman Hersh, *The Slavery of Sex: Feminist-Abolitionists in America* (1978); Steven M. Buechler, *The Transformation of the Woman Suffrage Movement: The Case of Illinois, 1850–1920* (1986); and Carol Lasser and Marlene Deahl Merrill, eds., *Friends and Sisters: Letters between Lucy Stone and Antoinette Brown Blackwell, 1846–93* (1987).

MARILYN ELIZABETH PERRY

CUTLER, Lizzie Petit (1831?–16 Jan. 1902), writer, was born in Milton, Virginia. While the names of her parents are unknown, her ancestry consisted of farmers on her paternal side and descendants of Jean Jacques Marie Réné de Motteville Bernard on her mother's side. She was orphaned at the age of four and raised by a grandmother and an aunt. She received an eclectic education through the writers she encountered while living with her aunt at "Brook Farm," the utopian community founded by George Ripley in West Roxbury, Massachusetts, before studying with a Dr. White, the head of a ladies' seminary in Charlottesville, Virginia.

Cutler began writing at an early age, and in 1855 she published her first book, *Light and Darkness; or, The Shadow of Fate: A Story of Fashionable Life*. Originally published anonymously, *Light and Darkness* was popular in the United States and abroad. Although the novel went through several editions in England and was translated into French, it received mixed reviews at home. One reviewer described it as "a story of high-wrought passion, with considerable power of expression, but showing more familiarity with the approved models of fictitious composition than individual invention or constructive power" (*Harper's New Monthly*

Magazine, June 1855, p. 694). Another reviewer found her style "remarkably spirited" but suggested that "the novel had far better never been published" (*Southern Literary Messenger*, Oct. 1855, p. 639). This criticism appears to stem not so much from the "story of guilty love" as it did from the author's attempt to sway the reader's sympathies in favor of the guilty characters. But if one turns to the preface of the text, the author states that her intention is "to give to each his proper share of the blame, making not one the wholly sinning, nor the other the wholly sinned against." This type of portrayal, however, was criticized, as the *Southern Literary Messenger* reviewer warns that "no display of literary and dramatic skill, can atone for the palliation of vice or the inculcation of spurious morality" (p. 639). Cutler's endeavor, however, was not to appease the morals of her readers. In the conclusion of *Light and Darkness*, the narrator observes that "we must thank the painter for the resemblance of his portrait to life rather than because it corresponds with our own taste." Cutler's goal was not to provide a moral lesson but to present real life.

In 1856 Cutler published her second novel, *Household Mysteries: A Romance of Southern Society*. Although the novel was widely distributed, it too incurred the wrath of the *Southern Literary Messenger*. According to the review, "It is by no means so vicious in sentiment as that elaborate apology for sin and suicide [*Light and Darkness*], the tone of it is in our judgment highly objectionable" (Sept. 1856, p. 239). Once again, the reviewer did not discount her talent but her choice of content. Cutler is described as a writer with "very considerable dramatic power and no lack of inventive faculty. . . . but her genius has been misdirected."

Cutler had been publishing with the Appletons, but she took her next manuscript to the Harpers, who rejected it. She then took the manuscript to the Appletons, who also rejected it. She did, however, publish *The Stars of the Crowd; or, Men and Women of the Day* in 1858, which was presumably the manuscript she initially had difficulty publishing.

Although Cutler published three novels, financial difficulties led her to the stage. She began giving public readings, which were well received. In the *New York Tribune* Cutler was described as "agreeable in voice, winning in manners, charming in personal appearance" (Forrest, p. 429). Despite her success, her stage career was short lived. Shortly after her debut, Cutler took to her bed for several months to recuperate from injuries suffered from an accident in which her gown caught on fire. It was during her recovery that she was courted by Peter G. Cutler, a New York attorney. The couple wed in 1858, and Lizzie Petit retired from the writing scene. The couple had no children. Cutler's husband died in 1870 at which time she returned to writing but without success. Cutler died in Richmond, Virginia.

Although Cutler's novels were popular, she was considered a minor writer. Cutler's writing, like that of many women of the period, was dismissed as insig-

nificant scribbling. However, in recent years feminist critics have taken a new look at sentimental and domestic fiction. Although critics of the time questioned her choice of subject matter, her writing was described as promising. As for her choice of subject matter, the fact that her novels were widely read suggests that the content did indeed appeal to a number of readers.

• Brief biographical sketches of Cutler are in Mary Forrest, *Women of the South Distinguished in Literature* (1861), and Ida Raymond [Mary T. Tardy], *Southland Writers: Biographical and Critical Sketches of the Living Female Writers of the South*, vol. 2 (1870). An obituary is in the *Richmond Times*, 17 Jan. 1902.

VENETRIA K. PATTON

CUTLER, Manasseh (13 May 1742–28 July 1823), preacher, botanist, and land promoter, was born in Killingly, Connecticut, the son of Hezekiah Cutler and Susanna Clark, prosperous farmers. After preparatory study with Killingly pastor Aaron Brown, Cutler matriculated at Yale College (A.B., 1765; A.M., 1768; LL.D., 1789). He married Mary Balch, daughter of Rev. Thomas Balch of Dedham, Massachusetts, in 1766; they had four children. During a brief residence on Martha's Vineyard (1766–1768), he completed his training for the ministry under his father-in-law's direction before being licensed to preach in 1770 and ordained at the Congregational church in Ipswich Hamlet (after 1793, Hamilton), where he remained until his death. In 1782 Cutler opened a boarding school that catered to the sons of leading Essex County families.

Cutler was an enthusiastic patriot during the revolutionary war, serving as chaplain to American forces in Massachusetts in 1776–1777 and 1778. After studying medicine with parishioner Dr. Elisha Whitney, Cutler took a prominent role in caring for smallpox victims in nearby Wenham during the 1779 epidemic. Cutler's scientific work began with the study of smallpox and later included experiments in electricity and astronomical observations. An inveterate collector and classifier, Cutler took advantage of his extensive travels throughout New England to undertake the first systematic compendium of New England flora (350 species) on Linnean lines. Although he never completed his projected study, his "Account of Some of the Vegetable Productions, Naturally Growing in This Part of America," printed in the first volume of the *Memoirs of the American Academy of Arts and Sciences* (1785), gained him wide recognition. Cutler was elected to the American Philosophical Society (1784), the American Academy of Arts and Sciences (1791), and numerous other learned societies. He corresponded with leading scientists on both sides of the Atlantic. When he visited Philadelphia in 1787 he met Benjamin Franklin (1706–1790), Benjamin Rush, and the naturalist William Bartram, who showed him his famous botanical garden.

Cutler's major contribution to the history of the new nation was to join forces with other prominent New Englanders in the Ohio Company of Associates, established in March 1786 to promote the settlement of the

Northwest Territory. Cutler, Rufus Putnam, and Samuel Holden Parsons were elected company directors in March 1787; in July Cutler traveled to New York where he consulted with congressmen on the provisions of the territorial government Ordinance of 13 July 1787 and arranged for the Associates' purchase of 1.5 million acres of Ohio land (formally completed on 27 Oct.). It is likely that Article VI of the Ordinance, outlawing the transportation of slaves to the territory, was included in the final draft at Cutler's behest. Congress thus created the optimal conditions for the movement of New Englanders into the region. Cutler's commentary on Geographer to the United States Thomas Hutchins's map of the region, published in late 1787 as a promotional pamphlet, helped mobilize public interest in the new venture. The company's expedition to the new settlement of Marietta, at the juncture of the Ohio and Muskingum rivers, set out from Cutler's home in Ipswich in December.

Cutler made his only visit to the Territory in 1788, reaching Marietta on 19 August after traveling 750 miles in twenty-nine days. His famous sermon delivered at Campus Martius on 24 August set forth Cutler's grand vision of the westward course of Christianity, commerce, and civilization. The cosmopolitanism of Cutler and his associates was characterized by a fascination with Indian antiquities and a determination to create a compact, stable, and prosperous community on the New England model. After returning to Massachusetts in 1789, Cutler never returned to the Ohio country despite the pleas of his friends in Marietta but retained a lively interest in his investment and in the settlement's development under the territorial government of Governor Arthur St. Clair and as part of the new state of Ohio (1803). In 1795 Cutler declined President George Washington's offer to become a territorial judge, one of the most powerful positions in the St. Clair administration.

Cutler's public career climaxed with service in the Massachusetts General Court (1800) and as Federalist congressman in the seventh and eighth congresses (1801–1805). A party regular in most divisions, Cutler did not take a conspicuous role in debates and maintained cordial relations with political opponents. After declining renomination to Congress due to ill health, Cutler returned to his parish in Ipswich where he survived his wife Mary by nearly eight years. Described in his later years as tall and portly, Cutler's boundless curiosity remained undiminished. He continued to preach and sustained his extensive personal and scientific correspondence until his death in Hamilton, Massachusetts.

• Cutler's papers may be consulted at Northwestern University Library. The key documents, including Cutler's promotional pamphlet, *An Explanation of the Map . . . of the Federal Lands* (1787) and his sermon at Campus Martius, have been published in William Parker Cutler and Julia Perkins Cutler, *Life Journals and Correspondence of Rev. Manasseh Cutler, LL.D.* (2 vols., 1888; repr. 1987). For other primary sources, see Archer B. Hulbert, *The Records of the Original Proceedings of the Ohio Company*, (2 vols., 1917). There is no modern bi-

ography. Cutler's scientific career is discussed in John C. Greene, *American Science in the Age of Jefferson* (1984), and his activities in the Ohio country are described in numerous sources, including Andrew R. L. Cayton, "'A Quiet Independence': The Western Vision of the Ohio Company," *Ohio History* 90 (Winter 1981): 5–32, and *Frontier Republic: Ideology and Politics in the Ohio Country, 1780–1825* (1986); and Louis W. Potts, "Manasseh Cutler, Lobbyist," *Ohio History* 96 (Summer-Autumn 1987): 101–23.

PETER S. ONUF

CUTLER, Robert (12 June 1895–8 May 1974), President Dwight D. Eisenhower's special assistant for national security affairs, was born in Brookline, Massachusetts, the son of George Chalmers Cutler, a lumber merchant, and Mary Franklin Wilson. Cutler spent almost two decades in Washington but, in the words of one observer, never overcame his love affair with Boston. He was a member of a Massachusetts family dating back to 1636 and received both his undergraduate degree (1916) and his law degree (1922) from Harvard, interrupting his education from 1917 to 1919 to serve with the U.S. Army in France and Germany during World War I. He practiced law in Boston from 1922 to 1940 and then served as corporation council of that city from 1940 to 1942. Following his service in Washington during World War II, he returned to his native city to serve as a director and then president of Old Colony Trust Company from 1946 to 1953.

It was World War II that brought Cutler to his second career in public service. Entering the Army Specialist Corps created by Secretary of War Henry Stimson in 1942 to take advantage of the special skills of civilians, he concentrated on directing the army's procurement service. He later moved to Stimson's office, where he formulated and managed a difficult plan arranging for soldiers to vote. More important, he came to know the men who would later form the nucleus for his ever-expanding network of colleagues involved in U.S. national security policy. He emerged from the war a brigadier general.

In 1948 Secretary of Defense James Forrestal asked Cutler to help General Eisenhower present the defense appropriation bill to Congress. Their paths crossed again when Eisenhower became president of Columbia University and established the American Assembly as an organization to study the foreign and domestic problems facing this country. An enthusiastic Cutler volunteered to raise the funds for the American Assembly meeting in Boston in 1950.

The following January Cutler signed the statement of the Committee on the Present Danger, which was issued just as General Eisenhower was returning to Europe as Supreme Commander of the North Atlantic Treaty Organization (NATO) forces. Noting the grave peril that now faced the United States and Europe, the statement stressed the need for national support for Eisenhower's mission, support for NATO, and support for the military strength and the national commitment necessary to combat the ambitions of the Soviet Union (USSR).

By then Cutler was exhibiting the admiration for and loyalty to Eisenhower that marked his White House career as well as his personal relationship with the general. He joined the individuals who were promoting Eisenhower for President committees and went to the Republican National Convention of 1952, during which he worked against the nomination of Senator Robert Taft. Throughout the 1952 presidential campaign, Cutler was the leading fundraiser for Eisenhower in the Boston area. On the campaign trail he did a variety of chores, from speech writing to acting as "personal secretary" to the candidate. He and Eisenhower also discussed and formulated a plan to restructure the national security process in the Executive Office of the President.

President Eisenhower appointed Cutler to the post of special assistant for national security affairs with the mandate to restructure the National Security Council (NSC). Cutler's position was clearly a managerial one, as he had virtually no experience in the formulation of national security policy. However, during the administration of Harry Truman, Cutler spent three months as a deputy to the director of the Psychological Strategy Board (PSB), Gordon Gray, where he participated in meetings of the NSC senior staff. So little was accomplished in those meetings that he probably was as convinced as Eisenhower that the reorganization was overdue. With Cutler as the presidential assistant in charge of the national security process, the Planning Board was established to write policy papers, the NSC met once a week with the president in attendance as chairman to discuss these papers and other important issues, and the Operations Coordinating Board (OCB) was established to replace the PSB and ensure that the policies were both implemented and coordinated. In spite of this elaborate structure, the NSC had a very small staff in the White House, relying instead on staffs provided by the departments and agencies represented on the council. Cutler and his assistants organized, managed, and chaired the meetings of the Planning Board and its subcommittees and attended meetings of the council and the OCB.

Cutler, who was known as "Bobby" all his life, was both a proper Bostonian and an entertaining storyteller who never hesitated to embellish his usually unprintable stories for the benefit of listeners. A bachelor, he was a workaholic who often forced his staff to work as hard and long as he did, but he was described by friends as a charming and generous man. Reflecting his earlier efforts as an author, perhaps, as well as his flair for the theatrical, he always had a verse or performance ready for the various holidays and birthdays celebrated in the White House. Bobby was known to be a favorite of Mamie Eisenhower, the president's wife.

Cutler was not an expert in national security policy but was rather the coordinator of presentations to the NSC. He rarely, if ever, expressed an opinion on policy but was content to leave policy making to Eisenhower and his secretary of state, John Foster Dulles. He excelled as a facilitator and a networker. The major criticism of his work in the White House came from those who thought that Cutler did not allow for flexibility in the NSC because he was too tied to the NSC paper process. Critics argued that, overburdened by policy papers perpetually being drafted and rewritten, the NSC became irrelevant by the end of the Eisenhower administration. Although Eisenhower often spoke of eliminating this dependency on the papers, he never did so.

Cutler left the NSC in 1955 to return to Boston and private business, but he remained available as a consultant until his return as national security assistant from January 1957 to June 1958. In February 1960 Eisenhower appointed Cutler to the position of U.S. executive director of the Inter-American Development Bank. He resigned on 15 July 1962 and returned to Boston, where he died.

• The many Cutler memorandums in the Dwight D. Eisenhower Presidential Library, Abilene, Kans., are illuminating. Cutler wrote two novels as a young man, *Louisburg Square* (1917) and *The Speckled Bird* (1923). His autobiography, *No Time for Rest*, was published in 1966. Some information on the private man can be found in A. Leviero, "'Untouchable, Unreachable and Unquotable,'" *New York Times Magazine*, 30 Jan. 1955, and [unsigned] "Puritan—Up to a Point," *New York Times*, 24 May 1957. Monographs on the Eisenhower administration discuss Cutler's work with the NSC.

ANNA KASTEN NELSON

CUTLER, Timothy (31 May 1684–17 Aug. 1765), clergyman and educator, was born in Charlestown, Massachusetts, the son of Major John Cutler, an anchorsmith and member of the General Court, and Martha Wiswall. Although his parents were well-to-do Jacobite sympathizers, Cutler was baptized as a Congregationalist, took his A.B. at Harvard College in 1701, and was admitted to membership in the Charlestown Congregational parish in 1705. It is not clear when he decided to enter the Congregational ministry, and since he was marked as a young man "of an high, lofty, & despotic mien," he did not promise to be overly popular as a minister among provincial New Englanders. On the other hand, that same "lofty" superiority gave him a valuable credential in the eyes of an emerging New England merchant class that was anxious to match the social allure of Church of England missions with examples of an equally elite Congregational ministry. To that end, Cutler was called in 1709 to the Congregational parish of Stratford, Connecticut, where a Church of England mission (under the auspices of the Society for the Propagation of the Gospel) had established a small but threatening presence in the Connecticut colony. He was ordained there on 11 January 1710. One year later, he married Elizabeth Andrew; they had eight children.

It was probably through his father-in-law, Samuel Andrew, that Cutler came to the attention of the trustees of the Collegiate School, in New Haven, Connecticut, because Andrew had been serving as the college's figurehead rector since 1707. The years of Andrew's service were full of strife and division for the college, but in 1718 a major gift from Elihu Yale and action by the Connecticut General Assembly permanently fixed the school with a new name, Yale College, and led to an invitation on 11 March 1719 for Cutler to become the new rector. Although the trustees did not confirm his appointment until September, Cutler was already at work in New Haven before the end of March. He brought with him a reputation as "an excellent Linguist" and "a good Logician, Geographer, & Rhetorician," and an attitude that ensured Yale could withstand Anglican criticism of its homespun origins.

It was whispered that Cutler was introducing the Yale students to new things, including the new Cartesian logic in the form of William Brattle's *Compendium Logicae* and its stress on the powers of human reason to achieve certainty. Although Cutler had performed his duties as parish minister in Stratford without exception and was invited to deliver the Connecticut election sermon in May 1719, he had come under the influence of a circle of clerical friends, most notably Samuel Johnson, a Yale tutor, who were increasingly troubled about the theological integrity of Congregational ordinations and were thus tempted to defect to the Church of England. By 1722 Yale was rumored to be full of "Arminian books," and Cutler himself was said to be on the verge of apostasy to Anglicanism. On 13 September 1722, following the Yale commencement, the college trustees confronted Cutler as well as two of the college tutors and four local ministers (including Samuel Johnson); all admitted that they had developed varying degrees of doubt about the validity of Congregational ordination. Cutler, moreover, informed the trustees "that he had for many years been of this persuasion" and had left his ministry in Stratford for Yale precisely on this account. The shocked trustees suspended Cutler from his duties. On 16 October, when the trustees met again to consider action, with Governor Gurdon Saltonstall presiding, no amount of persuasion or bluster could move Johnson or Cutler. Cutler was formally dismissed from his post the next day, and together with Johnson and Daniel Brown, he took ship for England on 5 November 1722, his passage paid for by Anglican well-wishers in Boston. He was reordained at St. Martin's-in-the-Fields in London on 31 March 1723 by Bishop Thomas Green of Norwich, acting for the bishop of London as ordinary for the American colonies.

With an eye to setting a convert to make more converts, Cutler was licensed by the bishop of London to undertake mission work in Massachusetts, and Cutler returned to New England in 1723 with a commission from the Society for the Propagation of the Gospel to organize Christ Church (the "Old North Church") in Boston's North End. Christ Church was Anglicanism's second outpost in Boston (after the pioneer parish, King's Chapel, which was dedicated in 1689), and its presence was an ongoing irritant to Boston Congregationalists. Cutler made matters no easier by turning all his polish and elegance into a victory for Anglicanism and a vessel of scorn for Congregationalism. He

condemned Congregational principles from his pulpit, petitioned the bishop of London for a resident Anglican bishop in America, and demanded a seat on the Harvard Board of Overseers by right as a "teaching elder" of a Boston church. But Cutler soon became an irritant to his Anglican colleagues at King's Chapel, too. Seeking the highest ground he could find from which to attack his old allegiance, Cutler began preaching a version of Anglicanism so high church in its praise of bishops and sacraments that letters soon began flying to the bishop of London from other Boston Anglicans, prophesying that Cutler would next be abandoning Anglicanism in favor of Roman Catholicism. And when the itinerant evangelical, George Whitefield, a follower of John Wesley, visited Boston as part of his American Preaching tour of 1739–1741, Cutler publicly quarreled with him by insisting that "the Church of England was the only true Apostolic Church." He might have been even unhappier with the Great Awakening that followed Whitefield had it not been for his confidence that the evangelical excesses of the awakening would drive disenchanted Congregationalists into the arms of the Church of England.

These turmoils notwithstanding, Cutler became the unofficial dean of New England's Anglican clergy in the 1750s. But the "haughty, stiff and morose" spirit that Jonathan Edwards found in Cutler crippled his capacity for effective leadership as well as the growth of Christ Church, which he was never able to wean from subsidies from England. He represented a major shift in New England's cultural elite toward Anglicization and the assimilation of English intellectual and cultural norms, but his frustrating career also illustrated how badly detached those elites had become from the larger context of colonial society. He suffered a stroke in April 1756, and from 1759 onward the church relied on an assistant, James Greaton, to carry on most of the parish duties until Cutler's death in Boston six years later.

• The bulk of Cutler's letters, papers, and reports are in the Archives of the Society for the Propagation of the Gospel in London and in smaller collections at the Massachusetts Historical Society (Bright Family Papers) and the Ohio Historical Society (Winthrop Sargent Papers). A number of these were published in William Stevens Perry, *Historical Collections Relating to the American Colonial Church*, vol. 3 (1870), and in John Nichols, *Illustrations of the Literary History of the Eighteenth Century*, vol. 4 (1822). His election sermon, *The Firm Union of a People Represented* (1717), and a later sermon before the Connecticut General Assembly, *The Depth of the Divine Thoughts* (1720), were already indicative of his restlessness with New England Congregationalism. Cutler's career at Yale and his involvement in the "Great Apostasy" of 1722 are treated in Richard Warch, *School of the Prophets: Yale College, 1701–1740* (1973), and Joseph Ellis, *The New England Mind in Transition: Samuel Johnson of Connecticut, 1696–1772* (1973). Cutler's life as an Anglican missionary is discussed in Perry, *The History of the American Episcopal Church, 1587–1883*, vol. 1 (1885); Carl Bridenbaugh, *Mitre and Sceptre: Transatlantic Faiths, Ideas, Personalities, and Politics, 1689–1775* (1962); and John F. Woolverton, *Colonial Anglicanism in North America* (1984). Brief biographical treatments of Cutler appear in Clifford K. Shipton, ed., *Sibley's Harvard Graduates: Biographical Sketches of those who attended Harvard College*, vol. 5 (1927), and William Butler Sprague, *Annals of the American Pulpit*, vol. 5 (1859). A death notice is in the *Boston News-Letter*, 22 Aug. 1756.

ALLEN C. GUELZO

CUTT, John (1625–5 Apr. 1681), merchant and colonial administrator, was born in England, the son of Richard Cutt, a Welsh merchant who moved his family to Bristol in Gloucestershire and then sat as a member of Oliver Cromwell's Parliament in 1654. His mother's name is unknown. Almost nothing is known of his early years in England, but like nearly all members of his generation he was certainly influenced by the struggle between King Charles and his Parliaments and the English Civil War (1642–1645).

Sometime prior to 1646 Cutt and his two younger brothers, Richard and Robert Cutt, emigrated from England to the mouth of the Piscataqua River in present-day New Hampshire. Drawn by the rich New England fisheries, John and Richard Cutt remained in that area for the rest of their lives, while Robert Cutt went to the West Indies. John Cutt settled at Portsmouth and became a wealthy and respected merchant of that seaport town.

During the crisis of the English Civil War and Cromwell's period as lord protector, the four towns of present-day New Hampshire (Portsmouth, Exeter, Hampton, and Dover) were integrated into the Massachusetts Bay Colony as part of Norfolk County. Cutt was one of the leading men of Portsmouth who supported this move, and during the 1650s he went to Boston to represent the town in the Massachusetts Assembly. In 1662 he married Hannah Starr; the couple had five children.

Cutt's business continued to grow during the 1660s and 1670s. He succeeded in the fishing business, then turned to the acquisition of land, and by the 1670s he owned some 350 acres in the general Portsmouth area. He acquired a liquor license by 1671, and he expanded into the lumber trade, receiving a grant to build a sawmill. In this expansion of his fortunes, Cutt was by no means unique. He was one of the most prominent members of a small merchant oligarchy that developed in the Piscataqua River area during the twenty years prior to King Philip's War. The Cutts, Waldrons, and Vaughans were the three most well-known families in the area, and they tended to dominate the local political scene. Cutt held the position of "townsman" or selectman in 1659–1662, 1665–1666, 1669–1670, 1675, and 1677–1678. Richard Cutt was a townsman in 1652, 1657–1659, 1661, and 1665–1666.

The end of the Cromwellian period and the accession of King Charles II to the throne of England in 1660 slowly brought a change to the transatlantic political climate. The Cutt brothers and their fellow oligarchs in Portsmouth were greatly resented by the grandson of Captain John Mason, Robert Tufton Mason, who claimed that he had an ancestral, proprietal right to the lands between the Merrimack and Piscata-

qua rivers. Mason's claims might have come to naught except for the fact that King Charles II was already irritated by the independent attitude of the Massachusetts Bay Colony. Upon examination of the claim, the king ruled in 1679 that the four towns were to be separated from Massachusetts and set up as a royal province. Thus, the royal province of New Hampshire came into being, and the king appointed Cutt to be the first president of the council of the province.

Edward Randolph delivered the "Cutt Commission," as it has been called, to the leaders in Portsmouth on 1 January 1680. At first the oligarchical leaders wanted to decline any participation in the new government, since they felt it would favor the proprietal claim of Mason. Seeing the hopelessness of resisting the king's commission, however, Cutt and the other appointees took their oaths on 21 January. Cutt, as the king's executor, stood at the top of the government, a nine-member governor's council stood in the middle, and a New Hampshire Assembly, elected by the voters of the province, made up the bottom tier.

Cutt and his councilors proceeded to proclaim a set of general laws and liberties. They worked against Randolph, collector of customs for New England, and fined Randolph's deputy collector in Portsmouth £10 sterling for acting in a "high and presumptuous manner" (Clark, p. 59). Cutt's actions were daring, since King Charles II had expressly indicated his determination to enforce the Navigation Acts of the 1660s.

Cutt was advanced in age when he became president of the province, and he fell ill in the spring of 1681. Accordingly, the council and assembly of the province declared 17 March 1681 as a day of public fasting and prayer because of the "sundry tokens of divine displeasure evident to us, both in the present dangerous sickness. . . . as also in respect of that awful portentous blazing star" (Belknap, p. 459). Cutt died in Portsmouth. His first wife had died, and he had married a second time, to Ursula (last name unknown).

Cutt was thoroughly a man of his generation. Raised in prosperous circumstances in England, he may well have gone to the New World to escape the tumult of the English Civil War. He prospered to such an extent that it was logical for him to become the king's representative in New Hampshire. Less well known than the other first governors in New England (William Bradford, John Winthrop, Roger Williams, and Thomas Hooker), nevertheless Cutt played an important albeit short role in the early government of New Hampshire. The decision to resist the claim of the Mason family was a courageous one, whether it was his individual daring or the collective willpower of Cutt and his council. Influenced by the English merchants' challenge to the authority of King Charles I on matters such as ship money, Cutt led a small group of oligarchs in resistance to King Charles II.

• Prominent sources on Cutt are Charles E. Clark, *The Eastern Frontier: The Settlement of Northern New England, 1610–1763* (1970); Jere R. Daniell, *Colonial New Hampshire: A*

History (1981); Jeremy Belknap, *The History of New-Hampshire* (1831); and *Collections of the New Hampshire Historical Society*, from 1680 to 1692 (1866).

SAMUEL WILLARD CROMPTON

CUTTER, Ammi Ruhamah (4 Mar. 1735–8 Dec. 1820), physician, was born in North Yarmouth, Maine, the son of Ammi Ruhamah Cutter, a Congregationalist minister, and Dorothy Bradbury. His father died of smallpox during the siege of Louisbourg in 1746. His mother, determined that he should attend Harvard College as his father and grandfather had done, in 1748 sent him to Cambridge, Massachusetts, where during the following year he was prepared for college by the Reverend Nathaniel Appleton. At Harvard, Cutter developed a close friendship with John Wentworth, nephew of New Hampshire governor Benning Wentworth. After Cutter's graduation in 1752 Wentworth urged him to settle in Portsmouth, and Wentworth may have also helped secure Cutter an apprenticeship with Clement Jackson, a leading physician there. While with Jackson, Cutter wrote a treatise, presumably from the medical point of view, for which Harvard conferred a master's degree on him in 1755.

That year Cutter joined New Hampshire's expedition to Crown Point as a surgeon. New Hampshire troops joined those of other colonies to counter the belligerent advances of French and allied Indian forces determined to halt white settlement on the frontier. After three years at Fort Edward in Nathaniel Meserve's regiment, he was detailed to the Ranger unit under Major Robert Rogers to take part in a siege of Louisbourg, where, like his father, he contracted smallpox. He recovered, however, and in August 1758 returned to Portsmouth, where he immediately established a medical practice. Later that year Cutter married Hannah Treadwell, whose father provided them with a house lot. The couple had ten children.

Cutter was described often by his contemporaries as having an even temper, moral energy, intelligence, benevolence, dignified manners, tenacious memory, felicity of language, and native humor—traits that must have contributed to his success. In conjunction with his medical practice he set up a shop selling wines, brandy, saltpeter, figs, spices, currants, linseed oil, paint, fresh medicine, and other goods.

Cutter received extensive land grants in New Hampshire, first in 1759 from the Masonian Proprietors, a wealthy and influential group of Portsmouth businessmen who owned the vacant property that was left from the original Crown grant to John Mason in 1630. His second grant came in 1770 from the New Hampshire legislature, bringing the total area of his holdings to 3,796 acres. Much of the latter lay within the town of Wolfeboro, where his grants made him second only to John Wentworth, the royal governor, in the size of his landholdings. This unusual largess of grants can be attributed in part to Cutter's influential personality and medical practice, but his twenty-year friendship with Wentworth cannot be discounted as an important factor in the making of the grants. Cutter

sometimes traveled with Wentworth, in 1771 accompanying him to the first commencement of Dartmouth College.

Among his other enterprises, Cutter in 1774 earned £300 from the New Hampshire legislature for surveying a road from Conway to the Connecticut River. With Dr. Joshua Brackett, also of Portsmouth, he opened a smallpox hospital in 1776 on Henzell's Island in Portsmouth harbor, but they closed it almost immediately in response to public fear that the facility might spread the disease.

Cutter's active involvement in government commenced in 1773, when the governor commissioned Cutter a justice of the peace. In 1774 the governor asked Cutter to serve on the Executive Council, which advised the governor, but Cutter declined because of his medical practice and "the present unhappy Controversy subsisting between the Parent state and the Colonies." He did, however, serve as a "Portsmouth Associate" to guard Wentworth and the royal stores from January to July 1775. When he joined in a request that the British warship *Scarborough* release provision ships being detained in Portsmouth harbor in the spring of 1775, he signaled his break with Wentworth's political views. However, Wentworth, after he fled to the *Scarborough* in August 1775, requested that Cutter come to confer with him. Cutter's visit, apparently principally a conversation between friends, was reportedly Wentworth's final contact with the citizens of New Hampshire in New Hampshire territory.

In 1776 Cutter signed the Association Test, which was suggested by the Continental Congress and promulgated by the New Hampshire Provincial Congress, thereby declaring support for the American cause against British arms and thus formally identifying himself as a rebel. On 11 April 1777 the Continental Congress appointed him "physician general of the hospital in the eastern department," in effect making him head of the medical department of the northern army under George Washington and in command of the hospital at Fishkill, New York. In 1778 he resigned, ostensibly owing to a need to be with his large family but probably also because of political infighting among military medical personnel.

Cutter served in the New Hampshire state constitutional convention in 1781. Though inclined to the Federalist position, he took little interest in politics. He served as an overseer of the poor in Portsmouth, as a town assessor, and as one of the committee that welcomed President Washington there in October 1789. He favored establishment of a public bath house, led the movement to incorporate the first bank in New Hampshire, and became a fellow in the New Hampshire Friendly Society. He was a charter member of the New Hampshire Medical Society in 1791 and served as its president from 1799 to 1812, a longer term than anyone before or since.

Cutter signed a number of petitions to the legislature: requesting that hogs be banned from Portsmouth streets (n.d.); remonstrating against plays and theatrical performances (1773); seeking prosecution of Tories in Portsmouth (1777); pleading for tax relief for Portsmouth (1779); urging maintenance of a bridge at Newmarket (1785); favoring a lottery to fund construction of Portsmouth public buildings (1790); supporting a public library for the town (1796); requesting construction of a bridge from Portsmouth to Rye (1797); asking permission to build an aqueduct to bring water to Portsmouth (1797); and complaining against Woodbury Langdon for failure to collect taxes in Tuftonborough (1797). Harvard University awarded Cutter an honorary M.D. in 1792. In 1794, as he neared the age of sixty, he brought his third son, William, into partnership to take over his practice. He was active in caring for patients during an outbreak of yellow fever in 1798, but he slowly retired thereafter. When he died in Portsmouth, Cutter was the last surviving member of his Harvard class.

Through his skills as a physician Cutter contributed to the health and welfare of his town and state. As an interested and active citizen he twice used those skills in military service and promoted what he considered to be the best interests of his adopted town and state. His alma mater, his state, and his neighbors rewarded his efforts with degrees, land, and a comfortable living. Through his contributions to the military phase of the Revolution, the constitutional structure of state government, and the development of the medical society and the physical health of his fellow citizens, Cutter exerted a quiet but significant and lasting influence on the development of New Hampshire.

• Few of Cutter's papers remain, but small collections of correspondence are housed at the New Hampshire Historical Society in Concord, the Portsmouth Atheneum, and the Portsmouth Public Library. Petitions and Portsmouth Town Records are on file at the New Hampshire State Archives in Concord. His journal of military experience during the French and Indian War, 1756–1758, was in the possession of his grandson, William Richard Cutter, when the latter published it as part of *A History of the Cutter Family of New England* (1871); the book is the best source for Cutter's personal life. Primary references are in Nathaniel Bouton et al., eds., *New Hampshire Provincial and State Papers* (40 vols., 1867–1940), particularly vols. 7, 8, and 20–22. Other biographical treatments are in James Thacher, *American Medical Biography*, vol. 1 (1828), and Clifford K. Shipton, *Biographical Sketches of Those Who Attended Harvard College*, vol. 13 (17 vols., 1873–1975).

FRANK C. MEVERS

CUTTER, Charles Ammi (14 Mar. 1837–6 Sept. 1903), librarian, was born in Boston, Massachusetts, the son of Caleb Champney Cutter and Hannah Biglow. He spent his boyhood in Charlestown and then in Cambridge, Massachusetts, with his grandfather and his three aunts. After attending the Hopkins Grammar School, he entered Harvard at the age of fourteen and then graduated third in a class of eighty-two in 1855. After one semester at the Lawrence Scientific School studying mathematics, Cutter entered Harvard Divinity School (1858–1859), where he was a student librarian. With another classmate, he wrote a new catalog for the collection and completely rearranged the books

on the shelves. He was attracted to librarianship and after a brief period as an unordained Unitarian minister and as a tutor, in 1860 he became a cataloging assistant to Ezra Abbott in the Harvard Library, where he attained a reputation as an expert cataloger and administrator.

Cutter married Sarah Fayerweather Appleton in 1863; they had three sons. To support his growing family, he indexed scholarly works for publication, assisted Joseph Sabin on his *Dictionary of Books Relating to America* (Bibliotheca Americana), cataloged at the Boston Public Library, and wrote articles and book reviews.

In December 1868 Cutter was elected librarian of the Boston Athenaeum, the most famous of American proprietary libraries, and turned it into a preeminent example of library progress. He earned the confidence of the Athenaeum's trustees and the admiration of the new profession of librarianship. Here he produced his monumental *Catalogue of the Library of the Boston Athenaeum, 1807–1871* (5 vols., 1874–1882; repr. 1970), which fellow librarian Justin Winsor called "the best catalogue extant." Cutter published the rationale and the methodology in the U.S. Bureau of Education's "Special Report" on *Public Libraries in the United States of America, Their History, Conditions and Management*. Part one contained his essay on library catalogs, and part two carried his *Rules for a Printed Dictionary Catalogue* (1875). These two documents quickly influenced nineteenth-century cataloging procedures. In 1882 Cutter prepared an explanation for getting books from the Athenaeum with its "new way of marking books."

With these publications, Cutter achieved considerable prominence in the library profession, and he had a major role in the organization of the American Library Association (ALA) with Melvil Dewey and others. He participated in most ALA annual conferences, helped to establish the *Library Journal* in September 1876, to which he contributed articles and reviews and edited from 1881 until 1893, and supported various ALA projects. He became one of the association's most active committee workers. On ALA's cataloging committee, Cutter prepared subject headings for use in dictionary catalogs and developed his own shelf classification system influenced by Dewey's book classification system. Cutter circulated his own preliminary schedules and the first copies of his "Author Tables," later reissued as the "Cutter Numbers," and still used for arranging books alphabetically by author.

From 1891 to 1903, Cutter remodeled his Boston Athenaeum classification and produced his two-volume *Expansive Classification*, which was considered "the most logical and scholarly of modern bibliographic schemes." It was his best but not his most important work. More popular were his cataloging rules and his alphabetic tables, which were the basis for the author name-marks once common in American libraries.

At the Athenaeum, Cutter finished his dictionary catalog and began to classify the collections, a project that dragged on for ten years, generating criticism from Athenaeum members. After much internal discord, Cutter resigned his post in April 1893 and then went to Europe where he purchased books for the new Forbes Library in Northampton, Massachusetts. In August 1894 he became the first librarian at the Forbes, which he called "a new type of public library, which, speaking broadly, will lend everything to anybody in any desired quantity for any desired time." He cultivated younger readers by lending pictures and musical scores along with books, built up the book collection to nearly 90,000 volumes, and started a branch library program. However, administrative funds were severely limited, and Cutter was unable to hire highly trained assistants, and so cataloging and classification remained rudimentary. Still, he promoted his classification scheme tirelessly as a successor to Dewey's Decimal Classification, but the work remained unfinished at his death.

Cutter participated in many professional activities, especially on the state and the local level. In 1891 he helped found the Massachusetts Library Club and in 1898 he served as first president of the new Western Massachusetts Library Club. In 1897 he went to Europe to the Second International Library Conference and to meetings of the Institut Internationale de Bibliographie to promote his expansive classification. He lectured at library schools, addressed local library groups, and between 1901 and 1903 participated in revising the ALA's catalog code. Cutter nearly died from pneumonia in the spring of 1903, prematurely returned to work, took sick again, and then died suddenly in Walpole, New Hampshire, while traveling with his wife.

Cutter was a systematizer of library ideals and an important figure in librarianship whose contributions included the organization of library materials, his most lasting achievement; the formatting of a dictionary catalog that has influenced library bibliographical arrangement; and the development of subject access and classification that became the basis for subsequent catalog subject headings and heavily influenced the Library of Congress classification system. Physically, the bespectacled Cutter was slightly built and looked like the "typical scholarly New Englander," but his relentless determination and rigorous personal standards made him imposing and authoritative to his colleagues. Friends considered him a humorous and delightful companion, an ardent lover of nature, keenly interested in the arts, and an outdoor sportsman. As an author, his books on cataloging principles and practices were analytic, scholarly, and knowledgeable and he contributed to the *Nation* for thirty-five years.

• Cutter's personal papers were destroyed, but Columbia University Library has papers relating to his professional work in the Melvil Dewey Papers and in the Mabel Winchell correspondence. Also see the Richard R. Bowker Papers in the New York Public Library and in the Manuscript Division, Library of Congress; and scattered collections in the Houghton Library, the University Archives at Harvard University, the Boston Athenaeum, the Forbes Library, North-ampton, Mass., and the American Library Association Archives at the University of Illinois, Champaign.

Short publications treating Cutter include "As It Was in the Beginning," *Public Libraries* 29 (May 1924): 236–40; Benjamin Cutter, *A History of the Cutter Family of New England* (1871); William P. Cutter, *Charles Ammi Cutter* (1931); William E. Foster, "Charles Ammi Cutter: A Memorial Sketch," *Library Journal* 28 (Oct. 1903): 697–703; Samuel S. Green, "Biographical Sketches of Librarians and Bibliographers, III: Charles Ammi Cutter, 1837–1903," *Bulletin of Bibliography* 8 (July 1914): 59–60; Green, *The Public Library Movement in the United States, 1853–1893* (1913); S. R. Gunjal, "Charles Ammi Cutter and His Contribution to Librarianship," *Herald of Library Science* 15 (July–Oct. 1976): 302–8; Francis L. Miska, ed., *Charles Ammi Cutter: Library Systematizer* (1977), which contains a biography, a selection of his writings, and a complete bibliography; Miska, "Charles Ammi Cutter: Nineteenth Century Systematizer of Libraries" (Ph.D. diss., Univ. of Chicago, 1974); Miska, "The Making of the 1876 Special Report on Public Libraries," *Journal of Library History* 8 (Jan. 1973): 30–40; Miska, *The Subject in the Dictionary Catalog from Cutter to the Present* (1983); and Thorvald Solberg, "Some Memories of Charles Ammi Cutter," *Library Journal* (Nov. 1903): 769–70. Obituaries are in *Library Journal*, Dec. 1904); the *Nation*, 17 Sept. 1903, and the *Springfield Daily Republican*, 8 Sept. 1903.

MARTIN J. MANNING

CUTTING, Bronson Murray (23 June 1888–6 May 1935), U.S. senator, was born at "Westbrook," the family estate, in Oakdale, Long Island, New York, the son of William Bayard Cutting, a director of several railroads, and Olivia Murray. Both his father and his uncle Robert Fulton Cutting were active in philanthropic and civic affairs in New York City. Cutting was educated at Groton, where he was an outstanding student, and at Harvard. Owing to illness, he was unable to graduate as a member of the class of 1910. Tuberculosis, which had claimed the life of his brother, William Bayard, led him to Sante Fe, New Mexico. As his health improved, Cutting became interested in public affairs just as New Mexico, after a long territorial period, entered the Union in January 1912. In this same year, Cutting purchased the *Santa Fe New Mexican*, the oldest newspaper in the territory, and added a Spanish edition, *El Nueva Mexicano*. He quickly became active in the state Progressive party, endorsing Theodore Roosevelt, a family friend, for president in 1912 and 1916. His newspaper, championing progressive principles by challenging corruption and calling for honesty and efficiency in public life, soon became involved in a battle involving freedom of the press. The case attracted national attention, and a compromise was finally reached while Cutting was in military service during World War I.

Working as a captain in military intelligence in London, Cutting served as a liaison officer with British and other Allied intelligence services. Returning to New Mexico, Cutting helped found and organize the American legion, both nationwide and in New Mexico, and played a prominent role in its affairs. In 1922, after the legion endorsed and helped reelect a Democratic senator, Andrieus A. Jones, Cutting was chosen to chair the Board of Commissioners of the New Mexico State Penitentiary. He soon left the board, however, and played no further political role until Republican governor Richard C. Dillon appointed him in December 1927 to fill the unexpired term of the recently deceased Senator Jones. The next year Cutting was elected in his own right by the largest plurality in the history of the young state, thanks particularly to the support of Hispanic voters, whose concerns had aroused his interest even before he worked closely with Hispanic veterans in the American Legion.

In the Senate, Cutting usually found himself in accord with the views of progressive Republicans, establishing close friendships with Robert M. La Follette, Jr., and Hiram Johnson. In 1930, during the debate on the Hawley-Smoot Tariff, he successfully challenged a provision in the measure that would have allowed Customs Bureau officials to determine what books, paintings, and other art objects could enter the country. He played a prominent role in calling for Philippine independence, cosponsoring a measure that President Herbert Hoover vetoed and that, under different sponsorship, Franklin D. Roosevelt signed.

While Cutting had endorsed Hoover for the presidency in 1928, he soon became disillusioned with him. The administration's decision to reduce disabled veterans' pensions and its lack of a meaningful program to cope with the depression crisis by emphasizing consumption rather than production led Cutting to endorse Franklin D. Roosevelt, a family friend, in the 1932 presidential campaign. While Cutting voted for most New Deal measures during the first Hundred Days, he quickly became disillusioned with Roosevelt for the same reasons he had opposed Hoover. Cutting suggested a modification of the banking system through public control of credit, hoping to give a broad segment of the consuming public better access to credit, but to no avail. According to Cutting, among early New Deal programs only the Agricultural Adjustment Administration and the short-lived Civil Works Administration were meaningful, because they put purchasing power into the hands of consumers. Recovery, more than reform, was his primary concern.

In 1934 Cutting was the only prominent Republican in New Mexico to win reelection, and his opponent, capitalizing on the Democratic sweep and with the encouragement of the administration, challenged Cutting's victory. Forced to devote much of his time to preparing his defense, Cutting was unable to participate actively in legislative affairs. Returning to Washington, D.C., to be on hand for a Senate vote on a measure affecting veterans' affairs, Cutting was killed when the plane in which he was traveling crashed near Kirksville, Missouri.

Cutting's estate, which was largely inherited, was valued at more than $3 million. His will provided specific bequests totaling almost $1.5 million to 134 beneficiaries, many of whom were Hispanic friends and associates in New Mexico. A bachelor who, because of concerns about his health, decided against marriage,

Cutting maintained close friendships with his family and school friends, members of the arts community, and associates on the *New Mexican*. He was fluent in Spanish and German. Several Hispanic veterans were among his closest friends, as were a handful of others who shared his passion for classical music. He was a good listener, respectful of views other than his own, and concerned about the plight of people oppressed by circumstances over which they had little control.

• Bronson Murray Cutting Papers are stored in 112 containers in the Manuscript Division of the Library of Congress. Cutting's complete correspondence with Ezra Pound is available in the Pound papers in the Beinecke Library at Yale University. The La Follette Family Papers, notably those of Robert M. La Follette, Jr., are housed in the Library of Congress and contain some items unavailable in Cutting's papers. Information about his school days at Groton can be found in diaries written by Theodore Roosevelt, Jr., and George Biddle, which are available in their papers in the Library of Congress. Two presidential libraries, those of Franklin Roosevelt and Herbert Hoover, contain collections yielding information about Cutting and his involvement in political affairs. At Hyde Park the New Mexico folders in the Democratic National Committee Files and the President's Office Files focus on the political scene. The President's Personal File contains a Bronson Cutting folder. At West Branch the New Mexico folders in the Republican National Committee File, the New Mexico material in the state's file, and items in the 1928 Campaign File contain much information about Cutting.

Collections housed at the University of New Mexico; at the Henry E. Huntington Library, San Marino, Calif., and in state repositories also contain Cutting material. In Albuquerque the papers of Miguel Antonio Otero, Richard Dillon, and Dennis Chavez, among others, contain significant information pertaining to Cutting. In San Marino, Calif., the Mary Austin Papers contain significant material delineating causes in which both she and Cutting were interested. In Santa Fe, at the State Records and Archives Center, the Francis Wilson Papers, chiefly his legal files, help define Wilson's association with Cutting. The papers of the various governors with whom Cutting had contact contain chiefly perfunctory items. At the Museum of New Mexico the papers of E. Dana Johnson and Edgar Lee Hewett contain information about Cutting unavailable elsewhere. See also Richard Lowitt, *Bronson Cutting: Progressive Politician* (1992). An obituary is in the *New York Times*, 7 May 1935.

RICHARD LOWITT

CUTTS, Samuel (8 Dec. 1726–29 May 1801), merchant and revolutionary activist, was born probably in Kittery, Maine, the son of Major Richard Cutt, a merchant, and Eunice Curtis. The fourth of ten children, he was of the first generation to change the spelling of the family name from Cutt to Cutts. His great-grandfather was Robert Cutt, who with two brothers had come, in the 1640s to the Piscataqua River region of northern New England where they soon became one of the dominant mercantile and landholding families. One of Robert's brothers, John Cutt, served as the first "president" when the province of New Hampshire was created in 1679.

Samuel Cutts learned the mercantile business in the countinghouse of Nathaniel Sparhawk, a prominent merchant of Kittery, to whom his father apprenticed him. Not much is known of his early business career except that he apparently worked for his father, who sent him on business errands to Boston and elsewhere where "he was thrown," according to a family historian, "among the foremost men of his day" (Howard, p. 519). It was during this phase of his life that he, his siblings, and his cousins changed the spelling of the family name to Cutts after a relative met a British officer by that name (during the siege of Louisbourg in 1745) and discovered their relationship.

In 1762 Cutts married Anna Holyoke, daughter of Harvard president Edward Holyoke; the couple had nine children. After their wedding, Cutts built a large house in Portsmouth directly across Market Street from his own wharf. He settled into the life of a prosperous trader, ship owner, and head of family.

His peaceful life was soon disrupted by the disputes over the new British commercial policies, which he actively opposed, as did the majority of Portsmouth merchants who were outside the orbit of the governing Wentworth family. He was an early and conspicuous member of a local Sons of Liberty organization formed during the Stamp Act crisis, and in 1768 defied the opposition of Governor John Wentworth by joining in the sponsorship of a New Hampshire petition for repeal of the Townshend duties. Cutts was the principal owner of the brig *Resolution*, the first of two Portsmouth vessels seized at dockside by the local customs collector George Meserve in 1769. Cutts's ship was condemned in admiralty court for importing undeclared molasses, the other for false registration.

Cutts served as a Portsmouth selectman from 1771 to 1775, and in 1774 he was elected as part of an avowedly radical (and entirely mercantile) delegation from Portsmouth to the province assembly. He was elected again in 1775 to what proved to be New Hampshire's last assembly under royal government. From his position as assemblyman in 1774 and 1775, he moved quite naturally into the various agencies of revolutionary government into which the royal regime dissolved, including the Committee of Correspondence (1774 and 1775) and the Fourth and Fifth Provincial Congresses (1775 and 1776). During the Fourth Congress, Cutts was a member of the Committee of Supplies. The Fifth Congress (the last) adopted a temporary constitution for the new state government, under which Cutts served as first justice of the Court of Common Pleas for Rockingham County and in the first House of Representatives. In that body, he chaired the committee that drafted New Hampshire's declaration of independence from Britain in June 1776.

In his capacity as chairman of Portsmouth's Committee of Ways and Means, the local ad hoc revolutionary governing committee, Cutts became the focus of the most dramatic episode of the Revolution to take place on New Hampshire soil. Acting on false rumor and an exaggerated construction of an order from Lord Dartmouth to the colonial governors that had been made public in Rhode Island, radical leaders in Boston dispatched Paul Revere to warn of troops on the way to guard the government stores at Fort William

and Mary in Portsmouth Harbor. Cutts convened his committee, which on the following day raised a mob of 400 men and boys who raided the fort, bloodlessly overcame the garrison of six men, and stole 100 barrels of gunpowder. On the night of the fifteenth another mob raised outside of Portsmouth stole the fort's sixteen cannon, about sixty muskets, and some other stores. This episode set in motion a chain of events that eventuated in August 1775 in the decision of the powerless Governor Wentworth to sail from New Hampshire in a British warship, leaving New Hampshire patriots to improvise a government.

The Revolution was unkind to Cutts's commercial fortunes, as it was to many Portsmouth merchants. "I was particularly unfortunate during the war," he wrote to his British agent after it was over, "by losing all my navigation, and not being concerned in privateering (which I could not make consonant to my own feelings) I was left at the peace without any trading stock" (Daniell, p. 138). Cutts nevertheless was able to continue his mercantile career, apparently with some success. In 1791 he wrote from Portsmouth to the Boston merchant William Smith, with whom he had just concluded a business deal, requesting advice on the importation of brandy and wines, since he had a "considerable sum to lay out" in Bordeaux, to which he was about to dispatch a ship.

As a leading player in the Piscataqua-based import-export trade both before and after the war, Cutts would have made his mark as an accomplished member of a conspicuous family even without the events of the American Revolution that overshadowed his mercantile career and shaped his reputation in successive generations.

• Genealogical and biographical information is covered conveniently in Cecil Hampden Cutts Howard, comp., *Genealogy of the Cutts Family in America* (1892), which is usefully supplemented by Joseph B. Walker, *New Hampshire's Five Provincial Congresses July 21, 1774–January 5, 1776* (1905). The letter to William Smith is in the Smith-Carter Family Papers, Massachusetts Historical Society. The two most scholarly treatments of New Hampshire in the Revolution are Richard Francis Upton, *Revolutionary New Hampshire* (1936, repr. 1971), and Jere R. Daniell, *Experiment in Republicanism: New Hampshire Politics and the American Revolution, 1741–1794* (1970). Both books, especially Daniell's, treat Cutts's various revolutionary roles.

CHARLES E. CLARK

CUYLER, Kiki (30 Aug. 1899–11 Feb. 1950), baseball player, was born Hazen Shirley Cuyler in Harrisville, Michigan, the son of George Cuyler, a coastguardsman and probate judge, and Anna (maiden name unknown). Cuyler early exhibited his athletic skills, playing baseball, basketball, and football and running track while in high school. He attended the U.S. Military Academy at West Point but resigned after only three months, and went to work in the Buick top building factory in Flint, Michigan. Probably hired by

Buick primarily to play baseball, Cuyler pitched and played the outfield. In 1919 he married Bertha Kelly, and the couple would have two sons.

Cuyler attracted the attention of organized teams at about the same time that Buick was closing the plant and eliminating the team. He then signed with Bay City, Michigan, of the Class B Michigan-Ontario League, playing part of the 1920 season with that club. The next year Cuyler played 116 games for Bay City, hitting .317. His pitching career ended when his team's management recognized his exceptional speed and poise in the outfield. The Pittsburgh Pirates of the National League bought his contract and assigned him to Charleston, South Carolina, of the South Atlantic (Sally) League for 1922 and promoted him to Nashville, Tennessee, of the Southern Association for 1923. With the latter team he led the league in six categories and batted .340. As a result he was voted the league's most valuable player that season. These records demanded promotion, and the Pirates called him up for the 1924 season.

Cuyler had played a handful of games for Pittsburgh from 1921 through 1923 and had been sent back to the minor leagues for experience, but in 1924 he became a major league fixture. Few rookies have made so quick an impression in the major leagues. In that first full season he played 117 games, hitting .354, driving in 85 runs, and stealing 32 bases. In 1925 he played the entire season with Pittsburgh, hitting .357, fourth best in the league, and leading the league in triples with 26 and runs scored with 144. That year he finished second to Rogers Hornsby in the balloting for the league's most valuable player. Now a regular, Cuyler settled in with the strong Pirate outfield, probably the fastest outfield in baseball during that era.

Probably while still in the minor leagues, Cuyler acquired the nickname "Kiki" as teammates hollered "Cuy" when they let the speedier Cuyler enter their territory to catch more difficult fly balls. Newspapermen expanded the name to "Kiki." In four full seasons with the Pirates he never hit less than .300 and was always among league leaders in many hitting and base stealing categories. Pittsburgh fans predicted he would become another Ty Cobb, but even Cobb could not throw as well as Cuyler. In 1925 the Pirates won the National League pennant for the first time since 1909; Cuyler was the star of the series as Pittsburgh defeated the Washington Senators, four games to three.

Cuyler's skills did not save him from a major humiliation, however. In 1927 the Pirates again won the National League pennant and played against the New York Yankees in the World Series. But Cuyler played only 85 games during the regular season and never left the bench during the World Series. The problem was a personality clash between Cuyler and his new manager, Donie Bush, who took over the leadership of the Pirates in 1927. Late that summer Bush and Cuyler had a serious disagreement, possibly about where Cuyler would bat in the order. Several versions of the story have been told, but Bush declared he would never use Cuyler again and kept his promise even when his team was being badly defeated by the Yankees, four games to none. Fans clamoring "We want Cuyler" had no effect on Bush.

Pittsburgh traded Cuyler to the Chicago Cubs that winter, and from 1928 through part of 1935 he maintained his spectacular level of play. The Cubs won the pennant in 1929, when Cuyler hit .360, and again in 1932. His speed and grace in the outfield made him a Wrigley Field favorite; during the team's spring training at Catalina Island the popular Cuyler regularly won the team's dancing contest. Hampered by leg injuries, he was released by the Cubs in 1935. From 1935 to 1937 he was with the Cincinnati Reds, and he finished his playing career in 1938 with the Brooklyn Dodgers. During his 18 seasons his batting average was a substantial .321. During the 1940s he coached in the major leagues and managed in the minors. His last season in the major leagues was 1949, when he coached for the Boston Red Sox. The following winter Cuyler, a zealous outdoorsman, suffered a heart attack while ice fishing and died on the way to the hospital in Ann Arbor, Michigan.

Leg injuries and his quarrels with the Pirates' management kept Cuyler from being one of the greatest outfielders of all time, but he always remained most popular with Pirates and Cubs fans. He was elected to the National Baseball Hall of Fame in 1968.

• The National Baseball Library in Cooperstown, N.Y., has a clipping file on Cuyler. A thorough article on his life is Martin Appel and Burt Goldblatt, *Baseball's Best: The Hall of Fame Gallery* (1977). Some different, if sketchier material is in Lowell Breidenbaugh, *Cooperstown* (1983), and Gene Karst, *Who's Who in Professional Baseball* (1973). A replica of Cuyler's plaque is in *National Baseball Hall of Fame* (1976). Much statistical information is in John Thorn and Pete Palmer, eds., *Total Baseball*, 3d ed. (1993). An obituary is in the *New York Times*, 12 Feb. 1950.

THOMAS L. KARNES

CUYLER, Theodore Ledyard (10 Jan. 1822–26 Feb. 1909), Presbyterian clergyman and writer, was born in Aurora, New York, the son of Benjamin Ledyard Cuyler, a lawyer, and Louisa Frances Morrell. His father died when Cuyler was a child, and he was brought up by his deeply religious mother, whose great wish was to have her son become a minister. After attending Hill Top School in Mendham, New Jersey, he entered the College of New Jersey (now Princeton University) at the age of sixteen. He graduated in 1841 and spent the following year abroad. In London he met Charles Dickens and Thomas Carlyle, and while in the Lake District he visited Wordsworth. These meetings are glowingly recalled in Cuyler's warm, somewhat ingenuous autobiography, *Recollections of a Long Life* (1902). Visiting Glasgow, he attended a temperance meeting where he was invited to speak—his first public address. After his return home, Cuyler considered beginning a career as either a lawyer or a minister but remained undecided until an experience as a speaker at a prayer meeting. Thanked for his inspiring message, he decided that "if ten minutes' talk to-day helped a few souls, why not preach all the time?" (*Recollections of a Long Life*, p. 62). Accordingly, he entered Princeton Theological Seminary and received his degree in 1846. Two years later he was ordained by the Presbytery of West Jersey while serving as a supply minister in Burlington. Between 1849 and 1853 he was pastor of the Third Church in Trenton. There he met Annie E. Mathiot; they were married in 1853 and had five children, three of whom died in their youth. In November 1853 Cuyler was appointed pastor of the Market Street Dutch Reformed Church in New York City, where he established a reputation for preaching and making converts and for his work on behalf of the poor—visiting the notorious Five Points slums, for example, in an effort to arouse public support of mission work.

After seven years in Manhattan, Cuyler was invited by the congregation of Park Presbyterian Church in Brooklyn to become its pastor. The congregation was building a new church in the Clinton Hill–Fort Greene area; completed in 1862, the church was renamed the Lafayette Avenue Presbyterian Church. Cuyler was installed in April 1860. In the course of the next thirty years he became celebrated throughout the country for the eloquence of his sermons, both from his own pulpit and as a guest preacher. His earnest evangelical addresses were delivered with great forcefulness, enlivened with striking images. Priding himself on never sparing his own lungs or his listeners' ears, he referred to preaching the Gospels as "spiritual gunnery" (*Recollections*, pp. 71–72), but at the same time he acknowledged to his congregants that "if I have given sermons to you, I have got sermons from you" (*A Thirty Years' Pastorate*, p. 34). Thanks to his efforts the congregation's membership grew from 140 to 2,330 by 1890, when it ranked as the third largest Presbyterian church in the nation and one of the most active. Mission work was expanded with the establishment of chapels in other Brooklyn neighborhoods; youth work flourished with Cuyler's organization of a Young Men's Christian Association group, a well-attended Young People's Association, and Sunday schools. As for pastoral work, Cuyler declared it "has always been my passion. It has been my rule to know everybody in this congregation, if possible, and seldom have I allowed a day to pass without a visit to some of your homes" (*A Thirty Years' Pastorate*, p. 34).

In the spring of 1890, Cuyler announced his resignation and preached his last regular sermon at Lafayette Avenue on Easter Day. As pastor emeritus, however, he remained busy serving as a guest preacher, being involved in philanthropy, and continuing to write. In the course of his career he published some twenty-two books, a number of them with the support of the American Tract Society, and wrote over 4,000 articles for the religious press, beginning in 1847 as a contributor to the *New York Observer*. It is reported that Abraham Lincoln, whom Cuyler met in Chicago in 1860, told the minister: "I have kept up with you nearly every week in the *New York Independent*" (*Recollections*, p. 142). And Cuyler boasted that he had made it a rule to contribute at least one article a week to such journals.

Many of these contributions dealt with the drinking problem. In 1865 he had been one of the founders of the National Temperance Society and later served as its president. For the most part, his books—some of them very popular—consisted of informal, down-to-earth homilies, such as *365 Stray Leaves from under the Catalpa* (1899) (the title a reference to the tree under his study window), which contains brief inspirational passages, with lines from favorite hymns, for each day of the year. *The Empty Crib: A Memorial of Little Georgie, with Words of Consolation for Bereaved Parents* (1869) was written after the death of one of his sons; other consoling thoughts are expressed in *God's Light on Dark Clouds* (1882), occasioned by his younger daughter's death. There are two collections of his sermons: *Stirring the Eagle's Nest, and Other Practical Discourses* (1892) and *A Model Christian* (1903). Another of his more popular works is *From the Nile to Norway and Homeward* (1882), a travel account.

He and that other famous Brooklyn minister Henry Ward Beecher were on friendly terms and often shared speakers' platforms; both contributed to the memorial volume *Our Martyr President, Abraham Lincoln: Voices from the Pulpit of New York and Brooklyn* (1865). Of Beecher's often controversial behavior, Cuyler would only comment: "Sometimes he sinned against good taste" (*Recollections*, p. 214). Cuyler, too, had at one point aroused controversy. In 1872 he invited the eminent Quaker leader Sarah Smiley to preach to his congregation. The Presbytery of Brooklyn, questioning his action, advised that "women should not be permitted to address a promiscuous [i.e., mixed] assemblage in any of our churches." Debate over the issue raised, as Cuyler put it, "wide and rather sensational interest" (*Recollections*, p. 250). In the end, the Presbytery withheld formal censure, but Cuyler felt obliged to note that he would never approve the ordination of women, indeed, that any woman "who neglects her nursery or her housekeeping duties . . . for any outside work in the parish does both them and herself serious injury" (*Recollections*, p. 290).

Despite Cuyler's renown, he maintained great personal modesty, wishing, for example, to be remembered only as "the Founder of the Lafayette Avenue Church." Although he had allowed a small neighborhood park, Cuyler Gore, to be named for him, he refused to have his statue placed there, noting that the money involved might better be spent on public needs. He died in Brooklyn, New York, and was buried, as he wished, in Brooklyn's famous Green-Wood Cemetery.

• The Lafayette Avenue Presbyterian Church owns copies of Cuyler's writings and some of his papers and correspondence, most of which, however, are in the possession of his descendants. His autobiography, *Recollections of a Long Life* (1902), remains the primary source of information about his career and the intellectual and social milieu that formed the background to his work. Sidelights on his work and community standing are provided in two commemorative volumes, both published by his church. The first, *Lafayette Avenue Church: Its History and Commemorative Services, 1860–1885* (1885), contains the programs celebrating the twenty-fifth anniversary of his settlement as pastor and reprints his sermons, his own historical sketch of the church, addresses given in his honor by visiting speakers, and the letters of congratulation received from his many distinguished friends. The second work, *A Thirty Years' Pastorate, with Some Accounts of the Pulpit, the Preacher, and the People, as Compiled from the Proceedings Connected with the Resignation of Rev. Theodore Ledyard Cuyler, D.D., Late Pastor of Lafayette Avenue Presbyterian Church*, was published in 1890 at the request of his congregation. A compilation of articles in the *Brooklyn Eagle* was published by the newspaper as *Theodore L. Cuyler Memorial*, Eagle Library series, no. 150 (July 1909). The volume reprints an *Eagle* editorial of 27 Feb. 1909; a sermon devoted to his life and work, delivered by the Reverend Dr. C. B. McAfee at Lafayette Avenue on 7 Mar. 1909; and Cuyler's first tract for the National Temperance Society, "A Shot at the Decanter," written in 1865. Marianne Moore mentions Cuyler and his church, and describes its setting, in her essay "Brooklyn from Clinton Hill," reprinted in *A Marianne Moore Reader* (1965): 182–92. Obituaries and related tributes are in the *New York Times*, 27 and 28 Feb. 1909.

ELEANOR F. WEDGE

CVETIC, Matthew C. (4 Mar. 1909–26 July 1962), anti-Communist and Federal Bureau of Investigation (FBI) "confidential informant," was born in Pittsburgh, Pennsylvania, the son of Frank Cvetic and Barbara (maiden name unknown), who had emigrated from a Slovenian village in 1890. His father, after some travail, earned a comfortable living as a small businessman; his ventures included renting out a former hotel and running gas stations. Cvetic graduated from St. Mary's parochial school, spent two years at St. Vincent's College Preparatory School, and in 1927 completed a two-year course of study at Curry Business College in Pittsburgh. During the early 1930s he rounded out his education with mail-order courses in penology from the Seattle-based International School of Criminology.

Between 1927 and 1937 Cvetic worked for various Pittsburgh companies as a clerk and salesman, compiled statistics for a U.S. Department of Justice crime survey at Pennsylvania's Western Penitentiary, operated one of his father's gas stations, and found employment on various Work Projects Administration (WPA) projects. In December 1937 he became a placement interviewer at the Pennsylvania State Employment Service (later part of the U.S. Employment Service). In 1929 Cvetic married Marie Dolores Barsh; they had twin sons. The couple divorced in 1946. Cvetic was a womanizer, and his wife was forced to take legal action to obtain support for herself and the children, whom Cvetic neglected during their formative years.

In the early 1940s (probably 1941), while still employed as an interviewer by the U.S. Employment Service, Cvetic became a "confidential informant" for the FBI to report on Communist activities in the western Pennsylvania area. Who initiated the relationship between Cvetic and the bureau remains unclear, as does much of the Cvetic story, which became increasingly distorted over the years because of the selective memories of all involved, including various Communist functionaries. Cvetic's memoir, *The Big Decision*, which he had privately printed in 1959, is very unreliable, and the files released by the FBI contain lacunae.

Cvetic succeeded in ingratiating himself with various Communist groups, and in 1943, to further his undercover activities, he joined the Communist party. The FBI files bear out his claims that over the next seven years he supplied the bureau with "over 30,000 pages of exhibits, letters, press-releases, pamphlets and other propaganda publications" as well as "the names of about 1000 Communist Party members."

Despite his subsequent claims of being an important Communist functionary, Cvetic remained a lower-echelon member of the party. An anti-Communist supervisor apparently forced his resignation from the U.S. Employment Service in 1945, and during the next two years Cvetic continued his FBI work as an employee of two Communist-controlled organizations, the American Committee for Yugoslav Relief and the American Slav Congress. In 1948 he put in some time at various "front groups," including the Progressive party, which nominated Henry Wallace for president that year. Thereafter Cvetic claimed he earned his livelihood as an independent insurance agent, but by all accounts he mainly lived off his bureau expense money, which by the end of 1949 reached the, at that time, considerable sum of $85 a week, tax-free.

Cvetic later claimed that "patriotism" led him to serve the FBI, but as time went on he demanded more and more expense money. Initially the bureau considered him a valuable source, especially on Communist activities in the Slav community. But his demands for more money; his alcoholism; his fits of depression; and his indiscretions, such as confiding in various people, especially women friends, about his efforts for the FBI, resulted in the bureau's decision to terminate him as an informant. That decision only became known a generation later when the author discovered it in FBI files.

In February 1950 Cvetic surfaced as a witness before the House Un-American Activities Committee (HUAC). He had made a deal with a Pittsburgh lawyer and a William Randolph Hearst newspaperman, who arranged his appearance. Cvetic agreed to share any income resulting from his revelations at a time when money could be earned from them. Testifying for six days on the "Communist presence in Western Pennsylvania," as HUAC described it, he named more than 290 men and women, described in detail allegedly "subversive activities" of various Communist leaders, and focused on "Communist infiltration of labor unions in the Pittsburgh area, especially in the United Electrical Workers."

Cvetic was neither the first nor the last FBI informant who testified in court or before congressional committees about the "Communist menace" in the red scare atmosphere of the late 1940s and early 1950s, but to the dismay of FBI head J. Edgar Hoover, who was deeply unhappy about Cvetic's claims to have been an "FBI counterspy," he garnered an enormous amount of publicity. Cvetic's managers, with whom he shortly broke, sold his story to the *Saturday Evening Post*, which ran a somewhat fanciful three-part series. That series served as the basis for a 1951 Warner Bros. film, *I Was a Communist for the F.B.I.*, a highly exaggerated, crude, propagandistic version of the Cvetic story that included romance, shootouts, and unbelievable villainy. The movie, which received an Academy Award nomination for best documentary, in turn led to a 1952–1953 radio series starring Dana Andrews that dramatized Cvetic's supposed "undercover activities."

Into the mid-1950s Cvetic earned a comfortable living on the lecture trails warning of the Communist menace and as a "professional witness" before congressional committees, at deportation hearings, and in court proceedings. His most notable court appearances were in the Pennsylvania sedition trials of Communist leader Steve Nelson and the unusual decertification of the professionally successful but Communist-controlled International Workers Order by the New York State Insurance Department. In 1954 he narrowly lost a primary election to become a Republican candidate for a central Pittsburgh congressional district.

Cvetic underwent shock treatment in early 1955. He was formally "disproved" by the Department of Justice as a witness after a U.S. Court of Appeals in June 1955 found his testimony "evasive" and "conflicting." Those who had used him as a witness were aware of his problems but ignored them until the courts finally put an end to his career. He moved to California and became involved with radical right groups. He was working as a recruiter for the John Birch Society when he suffered a fatal heart attack while taking a driving exam in Los Angeles.

Cvetic, according to one biographer, "lived a deceitful, generally unattractive life marred by womanizing, alcoholism, and emotional instability." Notwithstanding his many drawbacks, various government agencies made use of his services. Unlike many other professional anti-Communists, he is still remembered because of the continued televising of *I Was a Communist for the F.B.I.* No matter how far removed from reality, the film gives him life.

• Considerable material on Cvetic is in the papers of Hyman Schlesinger, a radical Pittsburgh attorney who gathered this material while defending himself against Cvetic's charges, in the United Electrical Workers Archive, University of Pittsburgh. Cvetic told his story to Peter Martin, "I Posed as a Communist for the FBI," *Saturday Evening Post*, 15, 22, 29 July 1950, which is propagandistic. A comprehensive overview, drawing heavily on FBI files, is Daniel J. Leab, "Anti-Communism, the FBI, and Matt Cvetic: The Ups and Downs of a Professional Informer," *Pennsylvania Magazine of History and Biography* 115 (Oct. 1991): 535–81. Obituaries are in the *New York Times* and the *Los Angeles Herald Examiner*, both 27 July 1962.

DANIEL J. LEAB

CZOLGOSZ, Leon F. (1873–29 Oct. 1901), assassin of President William McKinley, was born in Detroit, Michigan, the son of Paul Czolgosz, a menial laborer. His mother's name is unknown. His parents emigrated from southern Poland to the United States just prior to Leon's birth. As a boy Czolgosz shined shoes and sold newspapers. In 1880 the family moved to Rogers City in northern Michigan, but after five months they settled in the Polish community in Posen. Czolgosz intermittently attended public and Catholic parochial schools, and developed a lifelong interest in reading: chiefly Polish magazines. In 1885 his mother died in childbirth. That year the family moved to Alpena, near Detroit, and in 1889 to Natrona, a predominantly Polish community near Pittsburgh. There Leon worked in the searing heat of a glass factory, earning seventy-five cents a day. In 1892 the family moved to Cleveland, where he found a job tending machinery at the Newberg Wire Mills. He was a steady and quiet worker who managed to save $400, which he contributed to a family fund to buy a farm. On one occasion the wire spool snapped, slashing and scarring his face.

The depression of 1893 forced many firms to cut wages, including the Newberg Wire Mills, and its workers went on strike. Czolgosz joined them and was fired, but the following year he successfully applied for a job at the plant using the alias Fred C. Nieman. The strike and its aftermath affected him profoundly. Formerly a devout Catholic who read the Bible regularly, Czolgosz abandoned religion and was increasingly drawn to radical groups, first to a Polish Socialist club that met in a room above the small saloon his father bought in 1895. Czolgosz joined the organization though seldom took part in its discussions.

In early 1898 Czolgosz experienced some sort of health-related or emotional crisis. He seemed tired and depressed and complained of stomach and lung problems. In August he quit the wire mill and moved to the family farm near Cleveland. Mostly he lounged in his room and read newspapers, especially the Anarchist *Free Society*. He was especially fascinated by an account of Gaetano Bresci, an Anarchist from Paterson, New Jersey, who in 1900 shot and killed King Humbert I of Italy. Czolgosz kept the article by his bed.

In the spring of 1901 Czolgosz asked his family to return the money he had put up for the farm so that he could seek work in the West. They initially balked but eventually advanced him seventy dollars, which financed his subsequent travels. On 5 May he went to Cleveland and was moved by a speech by Anarchist Emma Goldman. Introducing himself as Fred Nieman, Czolgosz also approached Emil Schilling, treasurer of the Liberty Club, the Anarchist group that published *Free Society*. Schilling and other Anarchist officials were put off by Czolgosz's ignorance of Anarchist doctrine and his incautious queries, such as when he asked whether the group was "plotting something like Bresci." In late July Czolgosz took advantage of low excursion rates to travel to Buffalo, site of the Pan-American Exposition. He took a room in a boarding-house in West Seneca, outside of Buffalo, probably in the hope of finding work. McKinley's decision to visit the exposition was not made public until August.

About this time, too, the officers of the Liberty Club learned that Czolgosz had not given them his real name, and they assumed the worst: the 1 September issue of *Free Society* warned readers that a probable government spy, "well dressed, of medium height, rather narrow shouldered, blond, and about twenty-five years of age," had recently attempted to infiltrate the organization. The article may have driven Czolgosz to take desperate action to prove his loyalty. Early in September he bought a 32-caliber Iver Johnson revolver.

On 5 September Czolgosz attended the exposition. It was "President's Day" and Czolgosz was infuriated: "I thought it wasn't right for any one man to get so much ceremony," he said later. The next day Czolgosz returned to the exposition, concealed his revolver in a handkerchief, and took a place in line at the Temple of Music. When his turn came to shake hands with the president, Czolgosz pushed McKinley's arm away, thrust the revolver forward, and fired two shots through the handkerchief. McKinley stiffened and then slumped into the arms of his aides. Soldiers and Secret Service men knocked Czolgosz down and beat him. "Be easy with him, boys!" McKinley called out. After lengthy and ineffective surgery, he died eight days later.

Before the end of the month, Czolgosz was put on trial for murder. When medical experts sought to determine his sanity, he flatly admitted his culpability: "I fully understood what I was doing when I shot the President." He took no part in the trial other than to utter the word "guilty," a plea the judge could not accept. Czolgosz's court-appointed lawyers called no witnesses, and the trial lasted only eight hours. The jury deliberated thirty-four minutes before pronouncing him guilty. He was sentenced to death by electrocution. There was no appeal. On the morning of 29 October, as he was being strapped into the electric chair, Czolgosz's explanation of his actions was terse: "I killed the President because he was the enemy of the good people—the good working people. I am not sorry for my crime." He died in the Auburn penitentiary.

Czolgosz's act provoked a crackdown by federal and state law enforcement agencies on Anarchists and Socialists; prompted Congress to amend immigration laws to exclude Anarchists and other radicals; and forced the Secret Service to tighten security for the president and other key federal officials. Although most radicals distanced themselves from Czolgosz, Emma Goldman called him an idealist who hoped for a better world.

In 1902 psychiatrist Walter Channing argued that Czolgosz had been insane. He cited Czolgosz's shyness, his preference for solitary pursuits such as reading, and his avoidance of women. Nineteen years later L. Vernon Briggs expanded on Channing's analysis and claimed that Czolgosz suffered from "dementia praecox," or paranoid schizophrenia. But Czolgosz's act, though unreasonable, was not wholly irrational. McKinley's administration was in fact beholden to powerful business interests whose excesses came at the expense of poor people and helped precipitate Progressive reforms. Assassination, moreover, was consistent with the violent political doctrines of the Russian Anarchist Mikhail Bakunin. Yet it is difficult to discern a rational purpose in Czolgosz's action if only because his political beliefs were confused. Though he endorsed violence and anarchy, his favorite book was a Polish translation of Edward Bellamy's *Looking Backward* (1888), which evoked a genteel Socialist utopia, and Czolgosz had joined and sympathized with many Socialist organizations, whose goals were antithetical to those of the Anarchists.

Neither pathological nor exclusively political, Czolgosz's act was essentially that of an awkward and dull-witted young man who rarely attracted much notice, except for one day when, energized in some complex way by radical rhetoric, he set forth on a path that fatefully intersected with that of the president.

• Newspaper accounts and other materials on the assassination can be found at the Buffalo and Erie County Public Library, the Buffalo and Erie County Historical Association, and also the Courthouse Archives of Erie County, N.Y. (*People v. Leon F. Czolgosz* [1901], repr. in *American State Trials*, ed. John D. Lawson [1923]). The major biography is A. Wesley Johns, *The Man Who Shot McKinley* (1970). For the official report positing Czolgosz's sanity, see Joseph Fowler et al., "Official Report of the Experts for the People in the Case of the *People v. Leon F. Czolgosz*" (1901), repr. in *American State Trials*. On the posthumous claim that he was insane, see Walter Channing, "The Mental State of Czolgosz, the Assassin of President McKinley," *American Journal of Insanity* 59 (Oct. 1902); and L. Vernon Briggs, *The Manner of Man That Kills* (1921). See also Robert J. Donovan, *The Assassins* (1952), and Sidney Fine, "Anarchism and the Assassination of McKinley," *American Historical Review* 60, no. 4 (July 1955).

MARK C. CARNES

D

D'ABBADIE, Bernard-Anselme (1689–8 Oct. 1720), fourth baron of Saint-Castin and French officer, was born at Pentagoet on Penobscot Bay along the Maine coast, the son of Jean-Vincent D'abbadie de Saint-Castin and Pidianske (Marie-Mathilde), daughter of the Abenaki leader Madokawando. The D'abbadies had been a minor noble family in southwestern France for three centuries when, in 1654, Louis XIV awarded Bernard-Anselme's grandfather the title of baron of Saint-Castin. Bernard-Anselme's father had come to America in 1665 as a thirteen-year-old ensign in the French army and had developed friendships with the American Indian inhabitants near his station at Pentagoet. He was eventually adopted as their kinsman, married Pidianske in a Catholic ceremony in 1684, and emerged as a major Abenaki leader by the 1690s. Jean-Vincent's dual status as a French baron and son-in-law of Madokawando as well as the success of Abenaki military operations enhanced his influence among the Abenakis and his prestige among both French and British colonial officials. Jean-Vincent journeyed to France in 1701 to confront a variety of longstanding legal suits and to settle personal affairs, and he died there in 1707.

Bernard-Anselme was raised among his Abenaki relatives at Pentagoet. Nothing is known about the first fifteen years of his life during the period of his father's greatest fame. The earliest available record of him, in 1704, indicates that he was a pupil at the Petite Séminaire of Quebec, but how long he resided there is uncertain. Since he was the eldest son of a noble, it would seem likely that his father would have sent him off to school at an early age to prepare him for his inheritance. This assumption would seem to be supported by Bernard-Anselme's apparent concern during his lifetime over his French heritage, position, and title as well as his obligations as a French officer, as contrasted with his younger brothers' disregard for those issues.

Most Abenakis chose to remain neutral when the Anglo-French conflict known in New England as Queen Anne's War commenced in Europe in 1701. Anglo-Abenaki peace and trade were preserved for the first two years despite a series of Indian raids from French Canada, a Massachusetts militia raid on Pentagoet, and other isolated incidents. In August and October 1703 two separate Franco-Indian expeditions of approximately 500 men each devastated coastal towns and forts in southwestern Maine, prompting a Massachusetts declaration of war against all the Abenakis. The threat of attack by militia expeditions or scalp bounty parties forced most Abenakis to migrate to Canada for safety, but they continued to be reluctant to take an active role in the warfare. In 1704 a frustrated Governor Jacques-François de Brouillan of New France requested that D'abbadie, a fifteen-year-old student, revenge the attack on his father's home at Pentagoet and lead the Abenaki war effort until his father's return from France. D'abbadie accepted this challenge, but during the next three years his efforts to promote Abenaki raids against the New England frontier had very limited effect. In June and again in August 1707, at the age of eighteen, D'abbadie played a leading role in the successful defense of Port Royal, where he was wounded several times while defeating a force over seven times greater than his own. For these exploits he received a commission as an ensign in the French army.

D'abbadie was recuperating from his wounds at Port Royal when he learned that his father had died in France. He assumed the title of the fourth baron of Saint-Castin, and in 1707 he married Marie-Charlotte Damours de Chauffours, a member of a leading family at Port Royal. They had three children. The D'abbadies' connections with Acadian society was augmented two months later when two of D'abbadie's sisters married into highly respected families there. D'abbadie made frequent visits to Pentagoet but resided primarily at Port Royal, where his family and his sisters' families had their residences. In 1708 he was given command of all the Indians in Acadia, but during 1709 and 1710 he took time away from these responsibilities to become a very successful privateer. During one of his privateering cruises in October 1710, the English captured Port Royal. Upon his return, D'abbadie declined several English enticements to switch allegiances but agreed to convey various documents to Governor Philippe de Rigaud de Vaudreuil at Quebec. Vaudreuil appointed D'abbadie commander of Acadia with instructions to promote Indian attacks on New England and to maintain Acadian loyalty to France. In 1711 D'abbadie was promoted to lieutenant, but during the next two years Abenaki participation in frontier raids was limited. He may have been more successful in achieving the second goal, since English fears about Acadian loyalty would ultimately prompt their deportation.

The Anglo-French war concluded on 16 April 1713 with the Treaty of Utrecht, which conveyed Acadia to the English. Deprived of his home, D'abbadie spent the winter of 1713–1714 with his Abenaki relatives along the Penobscot River, attempting unsuccessfully to convince them to migrate to Cape Breton Island as French officials desired. D'abbadie had been concerned since his father's death about the unresolved legal disputes that still clouded his lands and title, so in late 1714 he and his wife journeyed to France. After several years the original suits were successfully defeated, but in the process a new legal dispute emerged between D'abbadie and his lawyer. In the midst of this second court battle, D'abbadie died in Pau in southwestern France.

• French primary sources are in the Public Archives of Canada and Reuben G. Thwaites, ed., *The Jesuit Relations and Allied Documents, 1610–1792* (1896–1902). English sources have been published in James P. Baxter, *Documentary History of the State of Maine* (24 vols., 1889–1916), and *Collections of the Massachusetts Historical Society* (1792–1871). Recent works on Franco-English-Abenaki relations during this period include Alvin Morrison, "Dawnland Decisions: Seventeenth-Century Wabanaki Leaders and Their Responses to the Differential Contact Stimuli in the Overlap Area of New France and New England" (Ph.D. diss., State Univ. of New York, 1974); Kenneth M. Morrison, *The Embattled Northeast: The Elusive Ideal of Alliance in Abenaki-Euramerican Relations* (1984); John G. Reid, *Acadia, Maine, and New Scotland: Marginal Colonies in the Seventeenth Century* (1981); and P.-André Sévigny, *Les Abénaquis: Habitat et migrations* (1976). The Saint-Castin family has been the focus of several works, including Pierre Daviault, *Le baron de Saint-Castin, chef abénaquis* (1939); Robert Le Blant, *Une figure légendaire de l'histoire acadienne: le baron de Saint-Castin* (1934); Gorham Munson, "St. Castin: a Legend Revisited," *Dalhousie Review* 45 (1965–1966): 338–60; Paul Chasse, "The D'abbadie de Saint-Castin and the Abenakis of Maine in the Seventeenth Century," *Proceedings of the French Colonial Historical Society* 10 (1984): 59–73; and John E. Godfrey, "Castin the Younger," *Maine Historical Society Collections* 7 (1876): 73–92.

DAVID L. GHERE

DABNEY, Charles William (19 June 1855–15 June 1945), educator, college president, and agrichemist, was born in Hampden-Sydney, Virginia, the son of Robert Louis Dabney, a Presbyterian theologian, and Margaretta Lavinia Morrison. His mother and father were both from prominent southern families, and his father served as chaplain to Thomas "Stonewall" Jackson during the Civil War. The third of six sons, Dabney grew up in a household that prized education and strict moral behavior.

Dabney was educated in the schools around his home and attended Hampden-Sydney College, graduating with a B.A. in 1873. Stating that he wished to be a teacher, he received a horse as a graduation present, along with his father's advice to "Go out and make yourself a school," a reference to finding a position in one of the "subscription schools" which sprang up in Virginia in the years following the Civil War. After a year of teaching, Dabney entered the University of Virginia to study the natural sciences. He earned a B.A. from that institution in 1877, and he taught at Emory and Henry College the following year before moving to Germany and continuing his studies at the University of Göttingen, where he received a Ph.D. in chemistry in 1880.

Returning to America, Dabney accepted a position as director and state chemist of the North Carolina Agricultural Experiment Station, studying the nature of soils and fertilizers and their effects on various crops. He married Mary Chilton Brent in 1881; they had

three daughters together. In 1884 he helped found the Association of Official Agricultural Chemists out of his strong interest in the benefits that industrial education could bring to the South. This interest led to his appointment as president of the University of Tennessee in 1887.

When he arrived in Knoxville, he found a university with little funding, few academic standards, and very few students. At that time the University of Tennessee was a slipshod institution functioning somewhat in the manner of a military academy. Under Dabney's leadership, however, it became a coeducational university with an enrollment that grew to nearly eight times what it was when he began. Believing that he had a strong mandate from the state, Dabney replaced many unproductive faculty members, created a school of mechanical arts, and developed new programs leading to degrees in agriculture; civil, mechanical, mining, and electrical engineering; and chemistry and metallurgy. He also opened a teacher training school and a law department.

From 1894 to 1897, Dabney took a leave from the University of Tennessee to serve as assistant secretary of agriculture under Grover Cleveland. His enthusiasm for agricultural and industrial education continued in this new position. Not only was he able to thwart a movement aimed at discontinuing federal funding for land-grant colleges, but he also reorganized divisions of the department into dairy, soil chemistry, and agrostology. By the time he returned to the University of Tennessee, Dabney was even more strongly convinced that the hope of the South lay in scientific and industrial progress, all accomplished through a proper pyramid system of education from the primary through the collegiate levels. Joining the Conference for Education in the South, a northern philanthropic organization, he helped create the Southern Education Board in 1901 as a subdivision fostering universal education in the southern states. In 1902 Dabney carried his aims further when he created a summer school training program for teachers at the University of Tennessee.

In 1904 Dabney was offered the presidency of the University of Cincinnati, a small municipal institution holding many of the same disadvantages and problems he had initially found in Tennessee. In the process of considering the position, Dabney requested a meeting with George Barnsdale Cox, the powerful local political boss. He disarmed Cox by stating that he understood the nature of the university's problems and could not take the job without assurance that both he and the university would be exempt from Cox's patronage and political machinations. Having received that assurance, as well as a pledge of support for bond and tax issues, Dabney accepted the position.

What he found at the university was disheartening. Although the University of Cincinnati had aspired to become a true urban university by combining various local colleges and providing service and leadership to the city, the intervening years from its charter in 1870 had been a period of academic warfare between benefactors, faculty, the board of directors, and Dabney's immediate predecessor, Howard Ayers. Ayers had been hired to improve the academic standards of the school, but he was not given the authority to carry it out and had left under acrimonious circumstances. Dabney insisted on authority and was granted it. He reorganized the administrative structure, sitting on committees and having decisions deferred to him.

During his tenure he created the College of Engineering (1904), Teacher's College (1905), the Graduate School (1906), and evening courses for degree programs. He also assisted in reorganizing the Miami Medical College and the Ohio Medical College to bring them under the university's wing, and he combined the University of Cincinnati's School of Law with the Cincinnati College law program. Dabney oversaw the inclusion of a school of nursing, and he worked to build a new city hospital that would rely on university training and research. His most notable achievement was his unqualified support of Herman Schneider, dean of the college of engineering, whose educational ideas led to the creation of cooperative education in 1906.

Dabney retired from the University of Cincinnati in 1920 at the mandatory age of sixty-five. He then formed his own firm of geologists and engineers in Houston, Texas. When his wife died in 1925, he relinquished that business.

In 1937 Dabney completed his monumental work, *Universal Education in the South*, a study of the history and condition of the South's public schools. The two-volume work received high praise from educators and journalists. Many of his thoughts in this work grew out of his exposure to his father's ideas that following the Civil War the South had been held down by the industries and politicians of the North, and that the only way to bring the South into an equal position with the rest of the nation was through systematic education regardless of race or financial means.

The financing of schools was important to Dabney. He firmly believed that tax dollars should support education and that a university serves as the "brain" of the body politic and civic. An integral part of his thinking was that urban universities were the natural and necessary institutions to render service and education and to bridge the gaps between urban and rural society in the twentieth century. Dabney died in Asheville, North Carolina, while traveling.

• Most of Charles Dabney's papers are housed in the Southern Historical Collection at the University of North Carolina, Chapel Hill. A lengthy unpublished memoir is located at Hampden-Sydney College Library, with copies at the University of Virginia's Alderman Library and the Archives & Rare Books Department of the University of Cincinnati. Also at the latter institution is a substantial biographical file, Dabney imprints, and materials generated while he was president. The University of Tennessee holds records on his presidency there. Some of Dabney's important writings on education include *The Meaning of the Solid South* (1909); *Freedom in the University* (1908); and *The Municipal University* (1914). For a detailed list of Dabney's speeches and publi-

cations, see Kevin Grace, *A Bibliography of the University of Cincinnati* (1995). Biographical information on Dabney and discussions of his ideas on education are available in James R. Montgomery, *The Volunteer State Forges Its University: The University of Tennessee, 1887–1919* (1966); Stanley J. Folmsbee, *Tennessee Establishes a State University: First Years of the University of Tennessee* (1961); Reginald C. McGrane, *The University of Cincinnati: A Success Story in Urban Higher Education* (1963); Kevin Grace and Greg Hand, *The University of Cincinnati* (1995); Gene D. Lewis and Zane L. Miller, "Charles W. Dabney and the Urban University: An Institution in Search of a Mission, 1904–1914" in *The Cincinnati Historical Society Bulletin*, 38, no. 5 (1980): 150–79; and F. S. K. Forary, "Higher Education at the Expense of Cities," *Ohio Illustrated Magazine*, 4, no. 5 (1908): 386–89. Obituaries are in the *New York Times* and the *Cincinnati Enquirer*, both 16 June 1945.

KEVIN GRACE

DABNEY, Richard (1787–Nov. 1825), poet, critic, and translator, was born in Louisa County, Virginia, the son of Samuel Dabney, a planter of modest means, and Jane Meriwether, aunt of the explorer Meriwether Lewis. Richard did not attend college, but at sixteen he took eagerly to languages at a Latin and Greek school and before he was twenty was invited to become an assistant Latin and Greek teacher at a Richmond academy. It is not known where Dabney learned Italian and French. His precocious assimilation of literature in four languages is remarkable in light of his scant formal education.

On 26 December 1811, Dabney was seriously burned in the disastrous fire of the Richmond Theatre. When opium was prescribed for his pain, he formed a lifelong addiction to the drug and to alcohol as well. In 1812 at Richmond, he published a small volume entitled *Poems, Original and Translated*. When it was ignored by the public, Dabney attempted to suppress it. With undefined views toward a literary career, he then moved to Philadelphia where he worked for the publisher Mathew Carey, who published in 1815 an improved edition of *Poems, Original and Translated*. Dabney is said to have written a large portion of one of Carey's editions of *The Olive Branch; or, Faults on Both Sides, Federal and Democratic* (1814), a book attempting to reconcile the opposing claims about maritime and territorial rights between England and the United States that led to the War of 1812.

The second edition of *Poems, Original and Translated* fared no better than its predecessor. The revised volume contains more than thirty translations of minor Greek, Latin, and Italian poems (and one French poem), a short essay on critical theory, and Dabney's original poems, which comprise about half of the volume. His poems show the influence of older Romantic writers and are concerned with love, nature, beauty, and death. He favors a simple vocabulary, traditional iambics, repetition and refrain, and regular rhyme schemes. Richard Beale Davis contends that although Dabney's poetry is more learned than creative, a few of his poems are "not unworthy of comparison" to Poe. These lines from Dabney are said to anticipate imagery in Poe's "To Helen":

But drive the alluring charms away,
That round thy form seductive play;
Quench the soft brilliance of thy eyes,
And stain thy cheeks' luxuriant dies;
Obscure thy neck, divinely fair,
And spoil the hyacinths of thy hair.

Most of his poems are less striking and are weighed down by a brooding, despondent tone and heavy classical allusion, as in the elaborate poem entitled "Illustrations of Simple Moral Emotions," a series of twelve poems centering on a "moral emotion," such as dissatisfaction, preceded by a learned quotation. Davis rightly admires the first poem of this series, but Jay B. Hubbell concludes that except for "Invocazione," which anticipates an idea in one of Emerson's poems, Dabney must be regarded as a better scholar than a poet.

Dabney called his poems "Gnomique" and "the moral miniature painting of poetry," which he explains in "Preliminary Remarks." The essay contributes little to understanding his poetry, though it gives evidence of Dabney's wide reading of the classics. Whether Dabney is quoting Archibald Alison's *Essays on the Nature and Principles of Taste*, or Boileau's rules of the sonnet, or making reference to such esoteric figures as Metastasio, Rolli, or Manfredi, his volume is heavy with learned quotation. Davis says that Dabney's critical theories on unified effect remind us of Poe, but *Poems* nevertheless fails to flower as poetry or criticism. Despite the apparent neglect of his publications, Dabney's work appears to have been well known enough for many readers in 1818 to believe he wrote the famous classical poem *Rhododaphne* by Thomas Love Peacock. The mistake was apparently caused by Mathew Carey, who "pirated" (Felton, p. 139) an edition of the English poem and attributed it to Dabney. Dabney repeatedly disavowed authorship of the poem.

Dabney's last years were spent at the family home in Louisa County, where he once more took up teaching and where he lived, unmarried, participating in the social life of the neighborhood. He continued his reading and study, but it is not known if he wrote again. His early death was evidently brought on by the long-term effects of the burns he suffered in the Richmond Theatre fire and by his addiction to drugs and alcohol. The obituary in the *Richmond Enquirer*, 25 November 1825, referred to his poetry but emphasized his thirst for knowledge, his scholarship, and the intellectual stimulation he provided others. Among acquaintances he was regarded as cynical, warmly affectionate, and stoical in the face of his defeats. If Dabney's work anticipated Poe and Emerson in slight ways, he must still be regarded as a minor poet, translator, and critic who attained modest success against vast odds but who did not realize his early promise.

• The revised edition of Dabney's *Poems, Original and Translated* is listed in Ralph R. Shaw and Richard H. Shoemaker, *An Index to American Bibliography: A Preliminary Checklist, 1801 to 1819* (1815), with items 34504 and 34504–34505

available on microcard. The earliest biographical source is the entry in Evert A. and George L. Duyckinck, eds., *Cyclopedia of American Literature*, vol. 1 (1856), written thirty years after the poet's death by Lucian Minor of Louisa County, Virginia; some of Minor's views are challenged by Armistead Churchill Gordon, Jr., in *Dictionary of American Biography*, vol. 5 (1930); another general account is Stanley J. Kunitz and Howard Haycraft, eds., *American Authors, 1600–1900* (1938), pp. 200–201; the most complete recent literary estimates are Jay B. Hubbell, *The South in American Literature, 1607–1900* (1954), pp. 296–98, and Richard Beale Davis, *Intellectual Life in Jefferson's Virginia, 1790–1830* (1964), pp. 337–39; the charge of pirating Peacock's poem was made in Felix Felton, *Thomas Love Peacock* (1973).

WILLIAM R. OSBORNE

DABNEY, Robert Lewis (5 Mar. 1820–3 Jan. 1898), Presbyterian minister, educator, and author, was born in Louisa County, Virginia, the son of Charles Dabney and Elizabeth Price, farmers. When his father died in 1833, young Dabney assumed much responsibility for oversight of the farm. He attended Hampden-Sydney College for three sessions in 1836 and 1837, then returned again to manage the farming enterprise and to construct an attendant stone mill, all the while also teaching in one of the local schools he had attended as a child. In 1842 Dabney graduated from the University of Virginia with an M.A., and he later credited the liberal arts education from that institution as being formative for his theology.

Dabney studied for the ministry at Union Theological Seminary in Hampden-Sydney, Virginia, where he learned especially from Francis R. Sampson, a Bible scholar. Upon ordination in 1846, Dabney served as a Presbyterian missionary in rural Virginia and then as pastor of the Tinkling Springs Church in Augusta County from 1846 until 1853. While there he married, in 1848, Lavinia Morrison; they had six children, all sons.

Invited in 1853 to become a member of the faculty at Union Seminary in Virginia, he served first as professor of ecclesiastical history and polity and later as professor of systematic theology. From 1858 until 1874 Dabney likewise served as copastor of the Presbyterian church in Hampden-Sydney. As the sentiment for secession grew in Virginia, Dabney opposed it, and his reputation as an eloquent preacher and a provocative writer grew during his first decade of ministry. He taught a warm, disciplined Calvinism, deeply influenced by the systematic theology of Francois Turretin and by exegesis of Scripture. His was a temperate voice among "Old School" Presbyterians, open to the power of revivals and insights from other parts of the Christian religion. In 1860 he was invited to teach theology at Princeton Theological Seminary in New Jersey and later that year was invited to become minister of New York's Fifth Avenue Presbyterian Church. Dabney chose to remain in the South, and he continued service at Union until 1883.

When the Civil War began, Dabney volunteered as a chaplain in the Confederate army, and in 1862 he became a chief of staff for Thomas J. "Stonewall" Jackson. Dabney respected Jackson and helped nurture the reputation of the cavalry officer by writing *The Life and Campaigns of Lieut.-Gen. Thomas J. Jackson (Stonewall Jackson)* (1866).

After the defeat of the South, Dabney also wrote *A Defense of Virginia and through Her of the South* (1867), arguing that the slave society was a moral one and beneficial to human endeavor. Romanticizing the spirit of southern culture, Dabney schemed for several years to relocate major portions of that culture elsewhere. He especially supported Presbyterian immigrants in Brazil as well as Protestant missions there. He increasingly idolized "the lost cause" in lectures and writings, such as *The New South* (1883). In one typical article in 1866, Dabney insisted that the "law of love does not require the injured Christian to approve or countenance the evil character manifested in the wrong done him."

Scholars of the period have called Dabney "the most influential theologian of his time in the South." His *Sacred Rhetoric* (1870) and *Syllabus and Notes of the Course of Systematic and Polemical Theology* (1871) influenced the theology and the tone of the Presbyterian Church in the United States, the "southern Presbyterian" denomination. Its conservative character and its interest in learning and in missions came in part from the influence of Dabney. Elected moderator of the general assembly in 1870, he became the titular head of the denomination for a year.

In 1883 the promise of a healthier climate in the Southwest attracted Dabney to the new University of Texas. He served there for ten years as professor of philosophy, and his presence and writings helped establish the fame of that institution. While in Austin, Dabney helped start what later became the Austin Presbyterian Theological Seminary. His two works of 1897, *Practical Philosophy* and *The Atonement*, provide a good look at the Calvinism and the Scottish common sense philosophy that flavored Dabney's thinking and teaching during that period. In the former, he struggled with the application of the Christian gospel to life situations. In the latter, he tried to restate classic Calvinism softly and in a way appealing to Americans. Both assumed assent to Christian facts and beliefs lay at the heart of religious growth in Christ.

Dabney grew blind in the final years of his life, and biographers point to his increasing alienation from mainstream American life during that time as well. In the 1880s he fought against James Woodrow of Columbia Seminary when Woodrow was accused of teaching evolution to those studying for Presbyterian ministry. He opposed the women who sought to organize their own circles, or small groups, and presbyterials, or regional gatherings, for mission. He declaimed against the ordination of black men as Presbyterian ministers, lest they might have some authority over white Christians. He kept alive and attractive to many southerners the vision of a romantic society that bore little resemblance to the antebellum era in the South. Dabney died in Victoria, Texas.

• The Union Theological Seminary Library Archives include a collection of Dabney papers. Thomas Cary Johnson, *Life and Letters of Robt. Lewis Dabney* (1903), is a full but uncritical biography. W. H. Dabney, *The Dabneys of Virginia* (1888), is also hagiographic. Ernest Trice Thompson, *Presbyterians in the South*, vols. 1 and 2 (1963, 1973), gives a full context of Dabney's ministry and theology. Frank B. Lewis, "Robert Lewis Dabney: Southern Presbyterian Apologist" (Ph.D. diss., Duke Univ., 1946); David H. Overy, "Robert Lewis Dabney: Apostle of the Old South" (Ph.D. diss., Univ. of Wisconsin, 1967); and Douglas F. Kelly, "Robert Lewis Dabney," in *Reformed Theology in America*, ed. David F. Wells (1985), supplement knowledge of his theology and his social commentary.

LOUIS WEEKS

DABNEY, Virginius (8 Feb. 1901–28 Dec. 1995), journalist and historian, was born in University (now Charlottesville), Virginia, the son of Richard Heath Dabney, a history professor, and Lily Heth Davis. Schooled at home until the age of thirteen, he then attended the prestigious Episcopal High School in Alexandria, Virginia. He earned a B.A. in 1902 and an M.A. in 1921 from the University of Virginia, taught French at Episcopal High School (1921–1922), and then began a long and accomplished career in journalism in Richmond, Virginia. He married Douglas Harrison Chelf in 1923; they had three children, and their marriage lasted until her death in 1994.

Dabney became one of the South's leading newspaper journalists. He worked as a reporter for the *Richmond News Leader* from 1922 to 1928. Then he moved to the *Richmond Times-Dispatch*, where he served as a member of the editorial staff (1928–1934), chief editorial writer (1934–1936), and editor (1936–1969). During his forty-seven years as a journalist he also authored three books—*Liberalism in the South* (1932), *Below the Potomac: A Book about the New South* (1942), and *Dry Messiah: The Life of Bishop Cannon* (1949)—and published essays in such national periodicals as the *New Republic*, the *Nation*, the *Saturday Evening Post*, and *Life*.

Through his newspaper editorials and other writings during the 1930s and early 1940s, Dabney became nationally known as a southern liberal. He applauded the New Deal, and his stance on various questions of civil rights placed him outside the regional mainstream. He long called for repeal of the poll tax as a condition of voting rights. In 1937 he supported enactment of a federal antilynching law. In 1942 he advocated a retrial in the first-degree murder conviction, by an all-white jury, of Odell Waller, a black sharecropper, for killing his white landlord. And in 1943 he surprised Virginians of all political stripes by calling for the desegregation of streetcars and buses in the Old Dominion. When Dabney received the Pulitzer Prize for editorial writing for 1947, observers inferred that his writings on such matters as the poll tax and Jim Crow transportation had earned him the recognition, though his editorials on those matters had appeared some years earlier.

Despite Dabney's racial liberalism on some matters, there were distinct limits to his enthusiasm for change on the racial front. He feared potential violence by white southerners in the face of change, and he himself favored greater equality of opportunity for African Americans in a more genuinely "separate but equal" world. The New South that he envisioned would retain segregation in all schools and keep the ban on interracial marriages, but Klan-type violence would end, as would restrictions against the participation of educated black southerners in politics. One writer has aptly characterized Dabney as a "genteel segregationist" (Egerton, p. 616).

As Dabney held his position but the world around him moved, the New South liberal appeared increasingly conservative. This seemed particularly evident in a January 1943 essay in the *Atlantic Monthly*, "Nearer and Nearer the Precipice," where Dabney warned of racial conflict if "Negro agitators" persisted in calls for substantial immediate change. Black spokesmen chided Dabney for his apparent change in direction. P. B. Young, editor of a black Virginia newspaper, the *Norfolk Journal and Guide*, expressed his disappointment, and the poet Langston Hughes wrote that "Mr. Dabney's article as a whole implies that Negroes, segregated, Jim-crowed, and lynched as we are, should still not seek to disturb the status quo of racial oppression" (quoted in Sosna, p. 132).

Dabney continued to twist in the wind on race. It was in response to the negative reception accorded "Nearer and Nearer the Precipice" that he issued his call in November 1943 for desegregated public transportation, a move designed to demonstrate to African Americans that liberal white southerners would reliably continue to promote racial amelioration. Suddenly, the black press praised Dabney, as did the NAACP and northern liberals. Four years later, however, Dabney resigned from the interracial Southern Regional Council when it condemned segregation, and he opposed the recommendations, reported in 1947, of President Truman's Committee on Civil Rights. Continuing to find himself caught in the middle, he lamented the Supreme Court's school desegregation decisions in *Brown v. Board of Education* (1954 and 1955) yet found Virginia's Massive Resistance, the willingness to close public schools rather than desegregate them, deeply troubling too.

As Dabney explained toward the end of his life, "Later on I believed in more or less the same things that I believed in the 30s, but they were not liberal any more" (quoted in Dunford, p. 294). The essayist and novelist Tom Wolfe nonetheless observes in his introduction to *Virginius Dabney's Virginia* (p. xiv) that, having attempted to navigate through the strife in state and nation over racial matters between the 1930s and the 1960s, Dabney took "pride in the fact that Virginia made the transition from apartheid to full political equality and participation without violence and without even any terrible bitterness."

"Continuing to scribble," as he said (*Across the Years*, p. ix), after retiring from newspaper work, Dabney became a prolific amateur historian. *Virginia: The New Dominion* (1971) and *Richmond: The Story of a City* (1976) each summarized his own observations and the researches of academic historians about his home state and city. He also published his autobiography. Then, in *The Jefferson Scandals: A Rebuttal* (1981), he challenged the notion (central to two recent publications about Thomas Jefferson) that Jefferson had maintained a sexual relationship with his slave Sally Hemings and had fathered her children. In *Mr. Jefferson's University: A History* (1981) and *Virginia Commonwealth University: A Sesquicentennial History* (1987), he chronicled the histories of two of Virginia's largest universities, the oldest, which he had attended and where his father taught for forty-nine years, and a new one, which Dabney served as a trustee for a decade. Yet another book was *Pistols and Pointed Pens: The Dueling Editors of Old Virginia* (1987). Charles F. Bryan, Jr., director of the Virginia Historical Society, concluded: "Vee Dabney will be remembered as a force in Virginia history. He was part of an old tradition of gentleman scholars, people not formally trained in history, yet who produced thorough and well-written interpretations of the past" (*Richmond Times-Dispatch*, 29 Dec. 1995).

When Dabney died in Richmond, an editorial in the *Times-Dispatch* (29 Dec. 1995) called him "a torchbearer—that was V Dabney, lighting the way"—and explained: "As an iconoclastic newspaper editor, author, and historian, he sought to illuminate the path his beloved state and region could follow out of the thickets of constricting traditions."

• The Virginius Dabney Papers are in the Alderman Library, University of Virginia. He told his own story in *Across the Years: Memories of a Virginian* (1978), and an anthology of his work is *Virginius Dabney's Virginia: Writings about the Old Dominion* (1986). Evaluations of Dabney appear in Morton Sosna, *In Search of the Silent South: Southern Liberals and the Race Issue* (1977); John T. Kneebone, *Southern Liberal Journalists and the Issue of Race, 1920–1944* (1985); John Egerton, *Speak Now against the Day: The Generation before the Civil Rights Movement in the South* (1994); and Earle Dunford, *Richmond Times-Dispatch: The Story of a Newspaper* (1995). Obituaries are in the *Richmond Times-Dispatch* and the *New York Times*, 29 Dec. 1995, and the *Washington Post*, 30 Dec. 1995.

PETER WALLENSTEIN

DABNEY, Wendell Phillips (4 Nov. 1865–5 June 1952), journalist, political leader, and publisher, was born in Richmond, Virginia, the son of John Dabney, a caterer, and Elizabeth Foster. Dabney attended elementary and secondary school in Richmond. His childhood was characterized by rigorous inculcation of John Dabney's religious and political views. His father, who had taught himself to read and write, instilled in his children the importance of religion as a vehicle for lessening racial oppression. John Dabney also passed on to his children his perception that Republicans helped African Americans and Democrats did not.

As a young student, Dabney's daily routine consisted of selling newspapers in the afternoon, doing homework in the evening, and playing the guitar with his older brother at night. During the summer months, he waited on tables at a local restaurant. As a server, Dabney developed a dislike for all white Americans. He believed that most white Americans did not look upon African Americans as human beings unless they were servants.

During his senior year at Richmond High School, Dabney led a student protest against the plan to hold the commencement ceremony for African-American students at a local church and the white students' graduation exercise in the school's theater. After several days of protest and discussion, it was decided that the African-American graduation ceremony also would be held at the high school.

In 1883 Dabney entered the preparatory department at Oberlin College. While at Oberlin, he was first violinist at the Oberlin Opera House and was accepted in the Cademian Literary Society. This experience, combined with his victory at Richmond High School, brought Dabney much needed dignity and self-respect. He gradually moved away from his earlier philosophy about white Americans. More specifically, Dabney began to believe that, despite the racial attitudes of white Americans, if given an equal opportunity black Americans could succeed.

In 1884, at the age of twenty, Dabney finished his first year at Oberlin. He returned to Richmond and obtained a job waiting tables. However, Dabney found the job too demoralizing and soon quit. In September, Dabney became a teacher at a Louisa County, Virginia, elementary school. Along with his teaching duties, Dabney taught guitar courses.

In 1890 Dabney left Richmond and opened a music school in Boston for both amateur and professional musicians. In 1893 he worked with Frederick Douglass on an exhibition for the Chicago World's Fair.

In 1894 Dabney moved to Cincinnati to oversee the business affairs of the Dumas Hotel, which his mother had inherited from her aunt Serena Webb. The Dumas Hotel, built in the early 1840s, was at one time Ohio's only African American–owned hotel. It also had been a secret station for the Underground Railroad. As a way to keep the Dumas from going bankrupt, Dabney converted one part of the hotel into a gymnasium and used the other part as a convention and meeting hall. While in Cincinnati, Dabney decided to stay, and in August 1897 he married Nellie Foster Jackson. Their only child together died in 1898, but Dabney adopted Jackson's two sons.

To generate additional income to support his family, Dabney taught music courses for upper-class white Cincinnatians. He also wrote several songs that were published by the George Jaberg and Wurlitzer Music companies.

Dabney's passion for politics forced him to end his career in music. In 1895 he became Cincinnati's first African-American license clerk. From 1898 to 1923 Dabney served as assistant, then head paymaster in the Department of Treasury in Cincinnati. These two positions enabled him to save money and start his own daily newspaper.

On 13 February 1907 Dabney established *The Union*. The newspaper's motto was "For no people can become great without being united, for in union there is strength." Until its final issue in 1952 *The Union* shaped the political and social opinions of the city's African-American community on issues such as segregated schools and mayoral elections.

Dabney was the first president of the Cincinnati branch of the National Association for the Advancement of Colored People, established in 1915. This organization staged several demonstrations against political injustice, racial violence, and segregated housing.

Dabney's major research and writing interests focused on the experiences of African Americans in Cincinnati. He claimed that, despite the harshness of political oppression and racial violence, African-American Cincinnatians had developed a vibrant and stable community. He also noted that urbanization had both a negative and positive impact on the development of the city's local African-American community. His book, *Cincinnati Colored Citizens* (1926), explores these issues in great detail. Dabney wrote several other books and articles that focus on race relations, discrimination, segregation, and urbanization on a broad scale. His most important works include *The Wolf and the Lamb* (1923), *Maggie L. Walker: The Woman and Her Work* (1927), *Chisum's Pilgrimage and Others* (1927), and "Slave Risings and Race Riots," which appeared in *A Negro Anthology*, ed. Nancy Cunard (1934).

On 4 November 1949 Dabney was given a celebrity dinner and birthday party in honor of his great achievements and to recognize his eighty-fourth birthday. More than 400 people attended the event. In January 1950 Dabney was honored by the National Convention of Negro Publishers as a pioneer and leader in the field of African-American journalism. Dabney died in Cincinnati.

• The few existing Dabney papers are at the Cincinnati Historical Society, which also has several issues of *The Union* (1923–1952). The most complete assessment of his life is Gail E. Berry, "W. P. Dabney: Leader of the Negro Protest" (master's thesis, Univ. of Cincinnati, 1965). See also Joseph T. Beaver, *I Want You to Know Wendell Phillips Dabney* (1958). An obituary is in the *Cincinnati Post*, 5 June 1952.

ERIC R. JACKSON

DACHÉ, Lilly (1892?–31 Dec. 1989), hat and fashion designer and entrepreneur, was born in Bègles, France. Because of her unconventional red hair, skinny figure, and preference for using her left hand, Daché's parents (names unknown) considered her both plain and clumsy, and in later years she attributed her desire to create beauty to an early need to feel attractive and thereby loved. Even as a child Daché decorated her hair with cherries and flower garlands and cut up her mother's clothes to make hats of her own design. Daché began her millinery training with her aunt, a dressmaker in Bordeaux, but talent and ambition soon led to a four-year apprenticeship with Caroline Reboux in Paris. She later worked for both Suzanne Talbot and Georgette, also noted Parisian milliners.

Daché arrived in New York City in 1924 determined to make her fortune. As she stood amid the skyscrapers, crowds, and traffic with just $13 of borrowed money in reserve, she thrilled to the jazz-age city's "surge of life." She immediately found work in a small hat store, the Bonnet Shop, then switched briefly to a sales position at R. H. Macy's but left because of conflicts with the floorwalker. Returning to her original job, Daché soon convinced a co-worker that they should purchase the business and become partners. Beginning with no capital or stock, Daché built up her trade, bought out her partner, hired employees, and began laying the foundation for her fashion empire. After convincing patrons that each hat had to be custommade, she would take a $2 deposit for materials on each $12.50 hat, then rush downtown, select fabrics and trimmings, and work until midnight completing hats to be sold the next morning. In the general frivolity of the Roaring Twenties, demand for Daché's unique, custommade hats soared, and her shop attracted long lines of clients, including celebrities such as Ziegfeld Follies star Marion Davies. Daché worked virtually round-the-clock—asking dates to wait (or deliver hats) while she finished up in the store; reportedly she once even sold the hat off her head for $50. Profits were plowed back into the business, which expanded to new and better locations.

In 1931 Daché married Jean Despres, a Frenchman who was then a sales manager for and later an executive vice president of Coty Inc.; four years later they purchased a country estate in Pound Ridge, New York, where they spent weekends gardening and entertaining. In 1937 Daché erected her own ultramodern, nine-story building at 78 East Fifty-sixth Street, with lower floors devoted to showrooms and workrooms and the top, two-story penthouse reserved for living. As she explained in her autobiography, "This building of chromium and pink satin and mirrors, of leopard skins and gold, is a sort of showcase for myself as well as for my hats. . . . I must live up to my legend."

By the early 1940s Daché was America's premier milliner. A profile in the *New Yorker* (4 Apr. 1942) characterized her as "restless, inquisitive, optimistic, impatient, and independent" as well as "highly perfumed" and temperamental. In 1943 she won the Coty American Fashion Critics' Award. Her self-promotional autobiography, *Talking through My Hats*, appeared in 1946. In addition to the elegant New York salon where she employed 150 milliners, Daché maintained shops in Chicago and Miami, sold wholesale designs to more than forty stores across the country, and did more than a half million dollars in business each year, selling hats priced from $35 to $500. Faithful clients included a virtual "Who's Who" of the rich and famous, particularly Hollywood stars. Daché designed hats in every style: elaborate fruited turbans for Car-

men Miranda, slouchy fedoras for Joan Crawford, sophisticated scarf-wrapped wimples for Marlene Dietrich. She was best known for her almost sculptural method of molding hats individually on each customer's head.

Even during her heyday in the 1940s and early 1950s, however, Daché was well aware that the hat was waning in popularity, especially among younger women, and she won a 1940 American Design Award for her so-called "half-hat." Essentially an elaborately decorated headband, it was later credited with attracting a new set of customers to the millinery trade, teenage girls who previously had been going hatless. Daché also introduced two mass-produced lines with styles meant to appeal to young women: "Mlle Lilly" and "Dachettes."

Her growing awareness that hats were losing their place as a vital fashion accessory, combined with her inherent ambition and energy, inspired Daché to branch out into other areas of fashion and beauty. By the mid-1950s she had completely revamped her salon and was designing, in addition to her own line of hats, dresses, accessories, jewelry, lingerie, furs, perfume, and cosmetics, plus men's shirts and ties. In 1954 she formed and became president of General Beauty Products Corporation, made up of Lucien Delong Perfumes, Marie Earle Cosmetics, and Lilly Daché Hair Products. She also published *Lilly Daché's Glamour Book* (1956) in which she spelled out her theories of fashion and beauty for a mass audience. In the late 1950s she employed talented new assistants, including hairdresser Kenneth Battell and designer Halston. In the years that followed, however, as her protégés became better known, her own renown began to fade, along with the popularity of the hats that had made her name. After her husband retired in 1969, Daché closed her salon and rented out her signature building. Eventually Daché and Despres divided their time between Delray Beach, Florida, and the Paris suburb of Meudon. She died in a nursing home in Louvecienne, France.

In the 1930s, 1940s, and 1950s, when hats were symbolic of female fashion, Lilly Daché's name was synonymous with women's hats. To the public at large she was famous as both a fashion leader and a rags-to-riches American success story. Within the fashion industry she was known for innovative methods, designs, and materials. She created thousands of flattering, stylish, unique hats—up to 9,000 in a single year—for her loyal customers. But despite her international reputation, when hats eventually lost their place as an essential element of the well-dressed woman's wardrobe, the name of Lilly Daché was no longer a household word.

• A small selection of Daché's sketches and photographs of her hats are housed in the Special Collections of the Fashion Institute of Technology in New York. The major, if not completely reliable, source for her life story is her autobiography, *Talking through My Hats* (1946); a shorter version is included in *Lilly Daché's Glamour Book* (1956.) An amusing profile by

Margaret Case Harriman, "Hats Will Be Worn," *New Yorker*, 4 Apr. 1942, pp. 20–24, reports on rumors regarding her place of birth. The Daché building is pictured and described in detail in "New York: Milliner Builds Multi-Story Establishment," *Architectural Record*, Mar. 1938, pp. 52–56. Daché's retirement was documented in a *New York Times* interview by Bernadine Morris, "The Everlasting Lilly Daché," 14 Oct. 1967. An interview with Daché in retirement, also by Morris, appears in *The Fashion Makers* (1978). Daché's contribution to the postwar millinery scene in New York City is covered extensively in Gretchen Fenston, "Millinery from 1945 to 1995: Industry in Crisis or (Fashion) Business as Usual?" (master's thesis, SUNY Fashion Institute of Technology, 1995.) An obituary is in the *New York Times*, 2 Jan. 1990.

SUSAN INGALLS LEWIS

DACOSTA, John Chalmers (16 Nov. 1863–15 May 1933), professor of surgery, was born in Washington, D.C., the son of George T. DaCosta and Margaretta Beasley. His father was president of the Camden & Atlantic Railroad; his mother taught him much of the history of Elizabethan England by the time he was eight. At the age of nine he was accidentally struck in the right eye, which led to a unilateral loss of sight. He graduated from the University of Pennsylvania in 1882 and from Jefferson Medical College in 1885. After residency training in Old Blockley (Philadelphia General) Hospital, he became assistant physician to the insane department of that institution and in 1887 to the Pennsylvania Hospital for the Insane. These experiences laid the groundwork for his lifelong interest in neurology.

In 1887 he became an assistant demonstrator of anatomy in Jefferson Medical College, where he decided to pursue a surgical career despite his visual handicap. While conducting a private practice he worked in the surgical outpatient department, gave anesthesia, and served as office assistant to Professor W. W. Keen. His spare time was spent collaborating on John Marie Keating's *New Pronouncing Dictionary of Medicine* (1892) and preparing his *A Manual of Modern Surgery, General and Operative*, which was published in 1894 and went through ten editions. In 1895 he

married Mary Roberts Brick; they had no children, and she outlived him by eighteen years.

DaCosta was appointed Jefferson Medical College's first Samuel D. Gross Professor of Surgery in 1910, a position he held for the next twenty-three years. His greatest fame lay in his uncanny diagnostic skill and in his weekly surgical teaching clinics, held in the hospital amphitheater. He impressed students, colleagues, and visitors with his foundation in anatomy, his knowledge of surgery, his anecdotes of medical history, his aphorisms, and his quotations from classic literature. He was at his best before large audiences.

In 1922 DaCosta was stricken with rheumatoid arthritis, which forced him to abandon surgery and teach from a wheelchair. He continued to give speeches, to write articles that voiced strong opinions, and to edit *Modern Surgery*. His many awards ranged from a diamond-studded badge designating him a deputy fire chief for his many years of service to members of the Philadelphia Fire Department to the establishment of a department of experimental medicine in his honor by the Jefferson Alumni Association.

DaCosta held membership in more than twenty professional organizations and was highly respected during his surgical heyday for his anatomical knowledge and sound judgment. His most enduring contribution in surgery was as a teacher. He died in his library in Philadelphia.

• The papers of John Chalmers DaCosta are in the archives of Thomas Jefferson University. In addition to many editions of *Modern Surgery*, DaCosta also published *Selections from the Papers and Speeches of John Chalmers DaCosta, M.D., LL.D.* (1931). After his death, F. E. Keller edited two additional books written by DaCosta, *Poems of John Chalmers DaCosta* (1942) and *The Trials and Triumphs of the Surgeon* (1944). Additional biographical material can be found in T. A. Shallow, "Memoir of John Chalmers DaCosta," *Transactions and Studies of the College of Physicians of Philadelphia*, 4th ser. (1933): lxx–lxxvi; and in F. B. Wagner, "John Chalmers DaCosta, M.D.," *Transactions and Studies of the College of Physicians of Philadelphia*, 5th ser. 9, no. 4 (1987): 209–26.

FREDERICK B. WAGNER, JR.